W9-CRZ-979

IN SIX VOLUMES, CAREFULLY REVISED AND CORRECTED

MATTHEW HENRY'S COMMENTARY

ON THE WHOLE BIBLE

WHEREIN EACH CHAPTER IS SUMMED UP IN ITS CONTENTS: THE SACRED TEXT INSERTED AT LARGE IN DISTINCT PARAGRAPHS; EACH PARAGRAPH REDUCED TO ITS PROPER HEADS: THE SENSE GIVEN, AND LARGELY ILLUSTRATED

WITH

PRACTICAL REMARKS AND OBSERVATIONS

VOL. V.—MATTHEW TO JOHN

World Bible Publishers
Iowa Falls, Iowa

"Printed in the United States of America"

PREFACE.

The one half of our undertaking upon the New Testament* is now, by the assistance of divine grace, finished, and presented to the reader, who, it is hoped, the Lord working with it, may hereby be somewhat helped in understanding and improving the sacred history of Christ and his apostles, and in making it, as it certainly is, the best exposition of our creed, in which these inspired writers are summed up, as is intimated by that evangelist who calls his gospel *A Declaration of those things which are most surely believed among us*, Luke i. 1. And, as there is no part of scripture in the belief of which it concerns us more to be established, so there is none with which the generality of Christians are more conversant, or which they speak of more frequently. It is therefore our duty, by constant pains in meditation and prayer, to come to an intimate acquaintance with the true intent and meaning of these narratives, what our concern is in them, and what we are to build upon them and draw from them ; that we may not rest in such a knowledge of them as that which we had when in our childhood we were taught to read English out of the translation and Greek out of the originals of these books. We ought to know them as the physician does his dispensatory, the lawyer his books of reports, and the sailor his chart and compass ; that is, to know how to make use of them in that to which we apply ourselves as our business in this world, which is to serve God here and enjoy him hereafter, and both in Christ the Mediator.

The great designs of the Christian institutes (of which these books are the fountains and foundations) were, to reduce the children of men to the fear and love of God, as the commanding active principle of their observance of him, and obedience to him,—to show them the way of their reconciliation to him and acceptance with him, and to bring them under obligations to Jesus Christ as Mediator, and thereby to engage them to all instances of devotion towards God and justice and charity towards all men, in conformity to the example of Christ, in obedience to his law, and in pursuance of his great intentions. What therefore I have endeavoured here has been with this view, to make these writings serviceable to the faith, holiness, and comfort of good Christians.

Now that these writings, thus made use of to serve these great and noble designs, may have their due influence upon us, it concerns us to be well established in our belief of their divine origin. And here we have to do with two sorts of people. Some embrace the Old Testament, but set that up in opposition to the New, pleading that, if that be right, this is wrong ; and these are the Jews. Others, though they live in a Christian nation, and by baptism wear the Christian name, yet, under pretence of freedom of thought, despise Christianity, and consequently reject the New Testament, and therefore the Old of course. I confess it is strange that any now who receive the Old Testament should reject the New, since, besides all the particular proofs of the divine authority of the New Testament, there is such an admirable harmony between it and the Old. It agrees with the Old in all the main intentions of it, refers to it, builds upon it, shows the accomplishment of its types and prophecies, and thereby is the perfection and crown of it. Nay, if it be not true, the Old Testament must be false, and all the glorious promises which shine so brightly in it, and the performance of which was limited within certain periods of time, must be a great delusion, which we are sure they are not, and therefore must embrace the New Testament to support the reputation of the Old.

Those things in the Old Testament which the New Testament lays aside are the peculiarity of the Jewish nation and the observances of the ceremonial law, both which certainly were of divine appointment ; and yet the New Testament does not at all clash with the Old ; for,

1. They were always designed to be laid aside in the fulness of time. No other is to be expected than that the morning-star should disappear when the sun rises ; and the latter parts of the Old Testament often speak of the laying aside of those things, and of the calling in of the Gentiles.

2. They were very honourably laid aside, and rather exchanged for that which was more noble and excellent, more divine and heavenly. The Jewish church was swallowed up in the Christian,

* It may be proper to apprise the reader that the volume to which this preface was originally prefixed included the Acts of the Apostles, which in the present edition will commence the second volume, in order to secure a more equal division of the New Testament—the commentary on the remaining books being less extended than the author contemplated.—Ed.

the Mosaic ritual in evangelical institutions. So that the New Testament is no more the undoing of the Old than the sending of a youth to the university is the undoing of his education in the grammar-school.

3. Providence soon determined this controversy (which is the only thing that seemed a controversy between the Old Testament and the New) by the destruction of Jerusalem, the desolations of the temple, the dissolution of the temple-service, and the total dispersion of all the remains of the Jewish nation, with a judicial defeat of all the attempts to incorporate it again, now for above 1600 years; and this according to the express predictions of Christ, a little before his death. And, as Christ would not have the doctrine of his being the Messiah much insisted on till the great conclusive proof of it was given by his resurrection from the dead, so the repeal of the ceremonial law, as to the Jews, was not much insisted on, but their keeping up the observation of it was connived at, till the great conclusive proof of its repeal was given by the destruction of Jerusalem, which made the observation of it for ever impracticable. And the manifest tokens of divine wrath which the Jews, considered as a people, even notwithstanding the prosperity of particular persons among them, continue under to this day, is a proof, not only of the truth of Christ's predictions concerning them, but that they lie under a greater guilt than that of idolatry (for which they lay under a desolation of 70 years), and this can be no other than crucifying Christ, and rejecting his gospel.

Thus evident it is that, in our expounding of the New Testament, we are not undoing what we did in expounding the Old; so far from it that we may appeal to the law and the prophets for the confirmation of the great truth which the gospels are written to prove—That our Lord Jesus is the Messiah promised to the fathers, who should come, and we are to look for no other. For though his appearing did not answer the expectation of the carnal Jews, who looked for a Messiah in external pomp and power, yet it exactly answered all the types, prophecies, and promises, of the Old Testament, which all had their accomplishment in him; and even his ignominious sufferings, which are the greatest stumbling-block to the Jews, were foretold concerning the Messiah; so that if he had not submitted to them we had failed in our proof; so far it is from being weakened by them. Bishop Kidder's *Demonstration of the Christian's Messiah* has abundantly made out this truth, and answered the cavils (for such they are, rather than arguments) of the Jews against it, above any in our language.

But we live in an age when Christianity and the New Testament are more virulently and daringly attacked by some within their own bowels than by those upon their borders. Never were Moses and his writings so arraigned and ridiculed by any Jews, or Mahomet and his Alcoran by any Mussulmans, as Christ and his gospel by men that are baptized and called Christians; and this, not under colour of any other divine revelation, but in contempt and defiance of all divine revelation; and not by way of complaint that they meet with that which shocks their faith, and which, through their own weakness, they cannot get over, and therefore desire to be instructed in, and helped in the understanding of, and the reconciling of them to the truth which they have received, but by way of resolute opposition, as if they looked upon it as their enemy, and were resolved by all means possible to be the ruin of it, though they cannot say what evil it has done to the world or to them. If the pretence of it has transported many in the church of Rome into such corruptions of worship and cruelties of government as are indeed the scandal of human nature, yet, instead of being thereby prejudiced against pure Christianity, they should the rather appear more vigorously in defence of it, when they see so excellent an institution as this is in itself so basely abused and misrepresented. They pretend to a liberty of thought in their opposition to Christianity, and would be distinguished by the name of free-thinkers. I will not here go about to produce the arguments which, to all that are not wilfully ignorant and prejudiced against the truth, are sufficient to prove the divine origin and authority of the doctrine of Christ. The learned find much satisfaction in reading the apologies of the ancients for the Christian religion, when it was struggling with the polytheism and idolatry of the Gentiles. Justin Martyr and Tertullian, Lactantius and Minutius Felix, wrote admirably in defence of Christianity, when it was further sealed by the blood of the martyrs. But its patrons and advocates in the present day have another sort of enemies to deal with. The antiquity of the pagan theology, its universal prevalence, the edicts of princes, and the traditions and usages of the country, are not now objected to Christianity; but I know not what imaginary freedom of thought, and an unheard-of privilege of human nature, are assumed, not to be bound by any divine revelation whatsoever. Now it is easy to make out,

1. That those who would be thought thus to maintain a liberty of thinking as one of the privileges of human nature, and in defence of which they will take up arms against God himself, do not themselves think freely, nor give others leave to do so. In some of them a resolute indulgence of themselves in those vicious courses which they know the gospel if they admit it will make very uneasy to them, and a secret enmity to a holy heavenly mind and life, forbid them all free thought; for so strong a prejudice have their lusts and passions laid them under against the laws of Christ that they find themselves under a necessity of opposing the truths of Christ, upon which these laws are founded. *Perit judicium, quando res transit in affectum—The judgment is overcome, when the decision is referred to the affections.* Right or wrong, Christ's bonds must be broken, and his cords cast from them; and therefore, how evident soever the premises be, the conclusion must be denied, if it tend to fasten these bands and cords upon them; and where is the freedom of thought then? *While they promise themselves liberty, they themselves are the servants of corruption; for of whom a man is overcome of the same is he brought into bondage.* In others of

them, a reigning pride and affectation of singularity, and a spirit of contradiction, those lusts of the mind, which are as impetuous and imperious as any of the lusts of the flesh and of the world, forbid a freedom of thinking, and enslave the soul in all its enquiries after religion. Those can no more think freely who resolve they will think by themselves than those can who resolve to think with their neighbours. Nor will they give others liberty to think freely; for it is not by reason and argument that they go about to convince us, but by jest and banter, and exposing Christianity and its serious professors to contempt. Now, considering how natural it is to most men to be jealous for their reputation, this is as great an imposition as can possibly be; and the unthinking are as much kept from free-thinking by the fear of being ridiculed in the club of those who set up for oracles in reason as by the fear of being cursed, excommunicated, and anathematized, by the counsel of those who set up for oracles in religion. And where is the free-thinking then?

2. That those who will allow themselves a true liberty of thinking, and will think seriously, cannot but embrace all Christ's sayings, as *faithful*, and well *worthy of all acceptation.* Let the corrupt bias of the carnal heart towards the world, and the flesh, and self (the most presumptuous idol of the three) be taken away, and let the doctrine of Christ be proposed first in its true colours, as Christ and his apostles have given it to us, and in its true light, with all its proper evidence, intrinsic and extrinsic; and then let the capable soul freely use its rational powers and faculties, and by the operation of the Spirit of grace, who alone works faith in all that believe, even the high thought, when once it becomes a free thought, freed from the bondage of sin and corruption, will, by a pleasing and happy power, be captivated, and brought into obedience to Christ; and, when he thus makes it free, it will be *free indeed.* Let any one who will give himself leave to think impartially, and be at the pains to think closely, read Mr. Baxter's *Reasons for the Christian Religion*, and he will find both that it goes to the bottom, and lays the foundation deep and firm, and also that it brings forth the top-stone in a believer's consent to God in Christ, to the satisfaction of any that are truly concerned about their souls and another world. The proofs of the truths of the gospel have been excellently well methodized, and enforced likewise, by bishop Stillingfleet, in his *Origines Sacræ;* by Grotius, in his book of the *Truth of the Christian Religion;* by Dr. Whitby, in his General Preface to his *Commentary on the New Testament;* and of late by Mr. Ditton, very argumentatively, in his discourse concerning *the Resurrection of Jesus Christ;* and many others have herein done worthily. And I will not believe any man who rejects the New Testament and the Christian religion to have thought freely upon the subject, unless he has, with humility, seriousness, and prayer to God for direction, deliberately read these or the like books, which, it is certain, were written both with liberty and clearness of thought.

For my own part, if my thoughts were worth any one's notice, I do declare I have thought of this great concern with all the liberty that a reasonable soul can pretend to, or desire; and the result is that the more I think, and the more freely I think, the more fully I am satisfied that the Christian religion is the true religion, and that which, if I submit my soul sincerely to it, I may venture my soul confidently upon. For when I think freely,

1. I cannot but think that the God who made man a reasonable creature by his power has a right to rule him by his law, and to oblige him to keep his inferior faculties of appetite and passion, together with the capacities of thought and speech, in due subjection to the superior powers of reason and conscience. And, when I look into my own heart, I cannot but think that it was this which my Maker designed in the order and frame of my soul, and that herein he intended to support his own dominion in me.

2. I cannot but think that my happiness is bound up in the favour of God, and that his favour will, or will not, be towards me, according as I do, or do not, comply with the laws and ends of my creation,—that I am accountable to this God, and that from him my judgment proceeds, not only for this world, but for my everlasting state.

3. I cannot but think that my nature is very unlike what the nature of man was as it came out of the Creator's hands,—that it is degenerated from its primitive purity and rectitude. I find in myself a natural aversion to my duty, and to spiritual and divine exercises, and a propensity to that which is evil, such an inclination towards the world and the flesh as amounts to a propensity to backslide from the living God.

4. I cannot but think that I am therefore, by nature, thrown out of the favour of God; for though I think he is a gracious and merciful God, yet I think he is also a just and holy God, and that I am become, by sin, both odious to his holiness and obnoxious to his justice. I should not think freely, but very partially, if I should think otherwise. I think I am guilty before God, have sinned, and come short of glorifying him, and of being glorified with him.

5. I cannot but think that, without some special discovery of God's will concerning me, and good-will to me, I cannot possibly recover his favour, be reconciled to him, or be so far restored to my primitive rectitude as to be capable of serving my Creator, and answering the ends of my creation, and becoming fit for another world; for the bounties of Providence to me, in common with the inferior creatures, cannot serve either as assurances that God is reconciled to me or means to reconcile me to God.

6. I cannot but think that the way of salvation, both from the guilt and from the power of sin, by Jesus Christ, and his mediation between God and man, as it is revealed by the New Testament, is admirably well fitted to all the exigencies of my case, to restore me both to the favour of God and to the government and enjoyment of myself. Here I see a proper method for the removing of the guilt of sin (that I may not die by the sentence of the law) by the all-sufficient merit and

righteousness of the Son of God in our nature, and for the breaking of the power of sin (that I may not die by my own disease) by the all-sufficient influence and operation of the Spirit of God upon our nature. Every malady has herein its remedy, every grievance is hereby redressed, and in such a way as advances the honour of all the divine attributes and is suited and accommodated to human nature.

7. I cannot but think that what I find in myself of natural religion does evidently bear testimony to the Christian religion; for all that truth which is discovered to me by the light of nature is confirmed, and more clearly discovered, by the gospel; the very same thing which the light of nature gives me a confused sight of (like the sight of men as trees walking) the New Testament gives me a clear and distinct sight of. All that good which is pressed upon me by the law of nature is more fully discovered to me, and I find myself much more strongly bound to it by the gospel of Christ, the engagements it lays upon me to my duty, and the encouragements and assistances it gives me in my duty. And this is further confirming to me that there, just there, where natural light leaves me at a loss, and unsatisfied—tells me that hitherto it can carry me, but no further—the gospel takes me up, helps me out, and gives me all the satisfaction I can desire, and that is especially in the great business of the satisfying of God's justice for the sin of man. My own conscience asks, *Wherewith shall I come before the Lord, and bow myself before the most high God? Will he be pleased with thousands of rams?* But I am still at a loss; I cannot frame a righteousness from any thing I am, or have, in myself, or from any thing I can do for God or present to God, wherein I dare appear before him; but the gospel comes, and tells me that Jesus Christ has *made his soul an offering for sin*, and God has declared himself well-pleased with all believers in him; and this makes me easy.

8. I cannot but think that the proofs by which God has attested the truth of the gospel are the most proper that could be given in a case of this nature—that the power and authority of the Redeemer in the kingdom of grace should be exemplified to the world, not by the highest degree of the pomp and authority of the kings of the earth, as the Jews expected, but by the evidences of his dominion in the kingdom of nature, which is a much greater dignity and authority than any of the kings of the earth ever pretended to, and is no less than divine. And his miracles being generally wrought upon men, not only upon their bodies, as they were mostly when Christ was here upon earth, but, which is more, upon their minds, as they were mostly after the pouring out of the Spirit in the gift of tongues and other supernatural endowments, were the most proper confirmations possible of the truth of the gospel, which was designed for the making of men holy and happy.

9. I cannot but think that the methods taken for the propagation of this gospel, and the wonderful success of those methods, which are purely spiritual and heavenly, and destitute of all secular advantages and supports, plainly show that it was of God, for God was with it; and it could never have spread as it did, in the face of so much opposition, if it had not been accompanied with a power from on high. And the preservation of Christianity in the world to this day, notwithstanding the difficulties it has struggled with, is to me a standing miracle for the proof of it.

10. I cannot but think that the gospel of Christ has had some influence upon my soul, has had such a command over me, and been such a comfort to me, as is a demonstration to myself, though it cannot be so to another, that it is of God. I have tasted in it *that the Lord is gracious;* and the most subtle disputant cannot convince one who has tasted honey that it is not sweet.

And now I appeal to him who knows the thoughts and intents of the heart that in all this I think freely (if it be possible for a man to know that he does so), and not under the power of any bias. Whether we have reason to think that those who, without any colour of reason, not only usurp, but monopolize, the character of free-thinkers, do so, let those judge who easily observe that they do not speak sincerely, but industriously dissemble their notions; and one instance I cannot but notice of their unfair dealing with their readers—that when, for the diminishing of the authority of the New Testament, they urge the various readings of the original, and quote an acknowledgment of Mr. Gregory of Christ-church, in his preface to his Works, *That no profane author whatsoever, &c.*, and yet suppress what immediately follows, as the sense of that learned man upon it, *That this is an invincible reason for the scriptures' part, &c.*

We then receive the books of the New Testament as our oracles; for it is evident that that excellent notion of Dr. Henry More's is true, that "they have a direct tendency to take us off from the animal life, and to bring us to the divine life."

But while we are thus maintaining the divine origin and authority of the New Testament, as it has been received through all the ages of the church, we find our cause not only attacked by the enemies we speak of, but in effect betrayed by one who makes our New Testament almost double to what it really is,* adding to it the *Constitutions of the Apostles*, collected by *Clement*, together with the *Apostolical Canons*, and making those to be of equal authority with the writings of the evangelists, and preferable to the Epistles. By enlarging the lines of defence thus, without either cause or precedent, he gives great advantage to the invaders. Those *Constitutions of the Apostles* have many things in them very good, and may be of use, as other human compositions; but to pretend that they were composed, as they profess to be, by the twelve apostles in concert at Jerusalem, *I Peter saying this, I Andrew saying that*, &c., is the greatest imposition that can be practised upon the credulity of the simple.

1. It is certain there were a great many spurious writings which, in the early days of the church, went under the names of the apostles and apostolical men; so that it has always been complained of as impossible to find out any thing but the canon of scripture that could with any assurance be attributed to them. Baronius himself acknowledges it, *Cum apostolorum nomine tam facta quam dicta reperiantur esse supposititia; nec sic quid de illis à veris sincerisque scriptoribus narratum sit integrum & incorruptum remanserit, in desperationem planè quandam animum dejiciunt posse unquam assequi quod verum certumque subsistat—Since so many of the acts and sayings ascribed to the apostles are found to be spurious, and even the narrations of faithful writers respecting them are not free from corruption, we must despair of ever being able to arrive at any absolute certainty about them.*—Ad An. Christ. 44, sect. 42, &c. There were Acts under the names of Andrew the apostle, Philip, Peter, Thomas; a Gospel under the name of Thaddeus, another of Barnabas, another of Bartholomew; a book concerning the infancy of our Saviour, another concerning his nativity, and many the like, which were all rejected as forgeries.

2. These *Constitutions* and *Canons*, among the rest, were condemned in the primitive church as apocryphal, and therefore justly rejected; because, though otherwise good, they pretended to be what really they were not, dictated by the twelve apostles themselves, as received from Christ. If Jesus Christ gave them such instructions, and they gave them in such a solemn manner to the church, as is pretended, it is unaccountable that there is not the least notice taken of any such thing done or designed in the *Gospels*, the *Acts*, or any of the *Epistles*.

Those who have judged the most favourably of these *Canons* and *Constitutions* have concluded that they were compiled by some officious persons under the name of *Clement*, towards the end of the second century, above 150 years after Christ's ascension, out of the common practice of the churches; that is, that which the compilers were most acquainted with, or had respect for; when at the same time we have reason to think that the far greater number of Christian churches which by that time were planted had Constitutions of their own, which, if they had had the happiness to be transmitted to posterity, would have recommended themselves as well as these, or better. But, as the legislators of old put a reputation upon their laws by pretending to have received them from some deity or other, so church-governors studied to gain reputation to their sees by placing some apostolical man or other at the head of their catalogue of bishops (*see bishop Stillingfleet's Irenicum, p.* 302), and reputation to their Canons and Constitutions by fathering them upon the apostles. But how can it be imagined that the apostles should be all together at Jerusalem, to compose this book of *Canons* with so much solemnity, when we know that their commission was to go into all the world, and to preach the gospel to every creature? Accordingly, Eusebius tells us that Thomas went into Parthia, Andrew into Scythia, John into the lesser Asia; and we have reason to think that after their dispersion they never came together again, any more than the planters of the nations did after the Most High had separated the sons of Adam.

I think that any one who will compare these *Constitutions* with the writings which we are sure were given by inspiration of God will easily discern a vast difference in the style and spirit. *What is the chaff to the wheat?* "Where are ministers, in the style of the true apostles, called priests, high priests? Where do we find in the apostolical age, that age of suffering, of the placing of the bishop in his *throne?* Or of readers, singers, and porters, in the church?"*

I fear the collector and compiler of those *Constitutions*, under the name of *Clement*, was conscious to himself of dishonesty in it, in that he would not have them published before all, because of the mysteries contained in them; nor were they known or published till the middle of the fourth century, when the forgery could not be so well disproved. I cannot see any mysteries in them, that they should be concealed, if they had been genuine; but I am sure that Christ bids his apostles publish the mysteries of the kingdom of God upon the house-tops. And St. Paul, though there are mysteries in his epistles much more sublime than any of these *Constitutions*, charges that they should be read to all the holy brethren. Nay, these *Constitutions* are so wholly in a manner taken up either with moral precepts, or rules of practice in the church, that if they had been what they pretend they had been most fit to be published before all. And though the *Apocalypse* is so full of mysteries, yet a blessing is pronounced upon the readers and hearers of that prophecy. We must therefore conclude that, whenever they were written, by declining the light they owned themselves to be apocryphal, that is, hidden or concealed; that they durst not mingle themselves with what was given by divine inspiration; to allude to what is said of the ministers (*Acts* v. 13), *Of the rest durst no man join himself to* the apostles, *for the people magnified them.* So that even by their own confession they were not delivered to the churches with the other writings, when the New-Testament canon was solemnly sealed up with that dreadful sentence passed on those that *add unto these things.*

And as we have thus had attempts made of late upon the purity and sufficiency of our New Testament, by additions to it, so we have likewise had from another quarter a great contempt put upon it by the papal power. The occasion was this:—One Father Quesnel, a French papist, but a Jansenist, nearly thirty years ago, published *the New Testament* in French, in several small volumes, *with Moral Reflections* on every verse, to render the reading of it more profitable, and meditation upon it more easy. It was much esteemed in France, for the sake of the piety and devotion which appeared in it, and it had several impressions. The Jesuits were much disgusted, and solicited the pope for the condemnation of it, though the author of it was a papist, and many things in it countenanced popishsuperstition. After much struggling about it in the court of

* Edit. Joan. Clerici, p. 245.

Rome a bull was at length obtained, at the request of the French king, from the present pope Clement XI. bearing date September 8, 1713, by which the said book, with what title or in what language soever it is printed, is prohibited and condemned; both the New Testament itself, because in many things varying from the vulgar Latin, and the Annotations, as containing divers propositions (above a hundred are enumerated) scandalous and pernicious, injurious to the church and its customs, impious, blasphemous, savouring of heresy. And the propositions are such as these—" That the grace of our Lord Jesus Christ is the effectual principle of all manner of good, is necessary for every good action; for without it nothing is done, nay nothing can be done"—" That it is a sovereign grace, and is an operation of the almighty hand of God"—" That, when God accompanies his word with the internal power of his grace, it operates in the soul the obedience which it demands"—" That faith is the first grace, and the fountain of all others"—" That it is in vain for us to call God our Father, if we do not cry to him with a spirit of love" —" That there is no God, nor religion, where there is no charity"—" That the catholic church comprehends the angels and all the elect and just men of the earth of all ages"—" That it has the Word incarnate for its head, and all the saints for its members"—That it is profitable and necessary at all times, in all places, and for all sorts of persons, to know the holy Scriptures"—" That the holy obscurity of the word of God is no reason for the laity not reading it"—" That the Lord's day ought to be sanctified by reading books of piety, especially the holy scriptures"—And " that to forbid Christians from reading the scriptures is to prohibit the use of light to the children of light." Many such positions as these, which the spirit of every good Christian cannot but relish as true and good, are condemned by the pope's bull as impious and blasphemous. And this bull, though strenuously opposed by a great number of the bishops in France, who were well affected to the notions of father Quesnel, was yet received and confirmed by the French king's letters patent, bearing date at Versailles, February 14, 1714, which forbid all manner of persons, upon pain of exemplary punishment, so much as to keep any of those books in their houses; and adjudge any that should hereafter write in defence of the propositions condemned by the pope as disturbers of the peace. It was registered the day following, February 15, by the Parliament of Paris, but with divers provisos and limitations.

By this it appears that popery is still the same thing that ever it was, an enemy to the knowledge of the scriptures, and to the honour of divine grace. What reason have we to bless God that we have liberty to read the scriptures, and have helps to understand and improve them, which we are concerned diligently to make a good use of, that we may not provoke God to give us up into the hands of those powers that would use us in like manner!

I am willing to hope that those to whom the reading of the *Exposition of the Old Testament* was pleasant will find this yet more pleasant; for this is that part of scripture which does most plainly testify of Christ, and in which that *gospel grace which appears unto all men, bringing salvation*, shines most clearly. This is the New-Testament milk for babes, the rest is strong meat for strong men. By these, therefore, let us be nourished and strengthened that we may be pressing on towards perfection; and that, having laid the foundation in the history of our blessed Saviour's life, death, and resurrection, and the first preaching of his gospel, we may build upon it by an acquaintance with the mysteries of godliness, to which we shall be further introduced in the Epistles.

I desire I may be read with a candid, and not a critical, eye. I pretend not to gratify the curious; the summit of my ambition is to assist those who are truly serious, in searching the scriptures daily. I am sure the work is designed, and hope it is calculated, to promote piety towards God and charity towards our brethren, and that there is not only something in it which may edify, but nothing which may justly offend any good Christian.

If any receive spiritual benefit by my poor endeavours, it will be a comfort to me, but let God have all the glory, and that free grace of his which has employed one that is utterly unworthy of such an honour, and enabled one thus far to go on in it who is utterly insufficient for such a service.

Having obtained help of God, I continue hitherto in it, and humbly depend upon the same good hand of my God to carry me on in that which remains, to gird my loins with needful strength and to make my way perfect; and for this I humbly desire the prayers of my friends. One volume more, I hope, will include what is yet to be done; and I will both go about it, and go on with it, as God shall enable me, with all convenient speed; but it is that part of the scripture which, of all others, requires the most care and pains in expounding it. But I trust that *as the day so shall the strength be.*

M. H.

1721.

AN

EXPOSITION,

WITH PRACTICAL OBSERVATIONS,

OF THE GOSPEL ACCORDING TO

ST. MATTHEW.

WE have now before us, I. *The New Testament of our Lord and Saviour Jesus Christ;* so this second part of the holy Bible is entitled: The *new covenant;* so it might as well be rendered; the word signifies both. But, when it is (as here) spoken of as Christ's act and deed, it is most properly rendered a *testament,* for he is the testator, and it becomes of force *by his death* (Heb. ix. 16, 17); nor is there, as in covenants, a previous treaty between the parties, but what is granted, though an estate upon condition, is owing to the will, the free-will, the good-will, of the Testator. All the grace contained in this book is owing to Jesus Christ as our Lord and Saviour; and, unless we consent to him as our Lord, we cannot expect any benefit by him as our Saviour. This is called a *new* testament, to distinguish it from that which was given by Moses, and was now antiquated; and to signify that it should be always new, and should never wax old, and grow out of date. These books contain, not only a full discovery of that grace *which has appeared to all men, bringing salvation,* but a legal instrument by which it is conveyed to, and settled upon, all believers. How carefully do we preserve, and with what attention and pleasure do we read, the last will and testament of a friend, who has therein left us a fair estate, and, with it, high expressions of his love to us! How precious then should this testament of our blessed Saviour be to us, which secures to us all his unsearchable riches! It is *his* testament; for though, as is usual, it was written by others (we have nothing upon record that was of Christ's own writing), yet he dictated it; and the night before he died, in the institution of his supper, he signed, sealed, and published it, in the presence of twelve witnesses. For, though these books were not written for some years after, for the benefit of posterity, *in perpetuam rei memoriam—as a perpetual memorial,* yet the New Testament of our Lord Jesus was settled, confirmed, and declared, from the time of his death, as a nuncupative will, with which these records exactly agree. The things which St. Luke wrote were *things which were most surely believed,* and therefore well known, before he wrote them; but, when they were written, the oral tradition was superseded and set aside, and these writings were the repository of that New Testament. This is intimated by the title which is prefixed to many Greek Copies, Τῆς καινῆς Διαθήκης Ἅπαντα—*The whole of the New Testament,* or *all the things of it.* In it is declared *the whole counsel of God* concerning our salvation, Acts xx. 27. As *the law of the Lord is perfect,* so is the gospel of Christ, and nothing is to be added to it. We have it all, and are to look for no more.

II. We have before us *The Four Gospels. Gospel* signifies *good news,* or *glad tidings;* and this history of Christ's coming *into the world to save sinners* is, without doubt, the best news that ever came from heaven to earth; the angel gave it this title (Luke ii. 10), Ἐυαγγελίζομαι ὑμῖν—*I bring you good tidings; I bring the gospel to you.* And the prophet foretold it, Isa. lii. 7; lxi. 1. It is there foretold that in the days of the Messiah *good tidings* should be preached. *Gospel* is an old Saxon word; it is *God's spell* or *word;* and God is so called because he is good, *Deus optimus—God most excellent,* and therefore it may be a good spell, or word. If we take *spell* in its more proper signification for a *charm (carmen),* and take that in a good sense, for what is moving and affecting, which is apt *lenire dolorem—to calm the spirits,* or to raise them in admiration or love, as that which is very amiable we call *charming,* it is applicable to the gospel; for in it the charmer *charmeth wisely,* though to *deaf adders,* Ps. lviii. 4, 5. Nor (one would think) can any charms be so powerful as those of the beauty and love of our Redeemer. The whole New Testament is the gospel. St. Paul calls it *his* gospel, because he was one of the preachers of it. Oh that we may each of us make it ours by our cordial acceptance of it and subjection to it! But the four books which contain the history of the Redeemer we commonly call *the four gospels*, and the inspired penmen of them *evangelists*, or *gospel-writers;* not, however, very properly, because that title belongs to a particular order of ministers, that were assistants to the apostles (Eph. iv. 11): *He gave some apostles, and some evangelists.* It was requisite that the doctrine of Christ should be interwoven with, and founded upon, the narrative of his birth, life, miracles, death, and resurrection; for then it appears in its clearest and strongest light. As in nature, so in grace, the most happy discoveries are those which take rise from the certain representations of matters of fact. Natural history is the best philosophy; and so is the sacred history, both of the Old and New Testament, the most proper and grateful vehicle of sacred truth. These four gospels were early and constantly received by the primitive church, and read in Christian assemblies, as appears by the writings of Justin Martyr and Irenæus, who lived little more than a hundred years after the ascension of Christ; they declared that neither more nor fewer than four were received by the church. A Harmony of these four evangelists was compiled by Tatian about that time, which he called, Τὸ διὰ τεσσάρων—*The Gospel out of the four.* In the third and fourth centuries there were gospels forged by divers sects, and published, one under the name of St. Peter, another of St. Thomas, another of St. Philip, &c. But they were never owned by the church, nor was any credit given to them, as the learned Dr. Whitby shows. And he gives this good reason why we should adhere to these written records, because, whatever the pretences of tradition may be, it is not sufficient to preserve things with any certainty, as appears by experience. For, whereas Christ said and did many memorable things, which *were not written* (John xx. 30; xxi. 25), tradition has not preserved any one of them to us, but all is lost except what was written; that therefore is what we must abide by; and blessed be God that we have it to abide by; it is the sure word of history.

III. We have before us *the Gospel according to St. Matthew.* The penman was by birth a Jew, by calling a publican, till Christ commanded his attendance, and then he left *the receipt of custom,* to follow him, and was one of those that accompanied him *all the time that the Lord Jesus went in and out, beginning from the baptism of John unto the day that he was taken up,* Acts i. 21, 22. He was therefore a competent witness of what he has here recorded. He is said to have written this history about eight years after Christ's ascension. Many of the ancients say that he wrote it in the Hebrew or Syriac language; but the tradition is sufficiently disproved by Dr. Whitby. Doubtless, it was written in Greek, as the other parts of the New Testament were; not in that language which was peculiar to the Jews, whose church and state were near a period, but in that which was common to the world, and in which the knowledge of Christ would be most effectually transmitted to the nations of the earth; yet it is probable that there might be an edition of it in Hebrew, published by St. Matthew himself, at the same time that he wrote it in Greek; the former for the Jews, the latter for the Gentiles, when he left Judea, to preach among the Gentiles. Let us bless God that we have it, and have it in a language we understand.

CHAP. I.

This evangelist begins with the account of Christ's parentage and birth, the ancestors from whom he descended, and the manner of his entry into the world, to make it appear that he was indeed the Messiah promised, for it was foretold that he should be the son of David, and should be born of a virgin; and that he was so is here plainly shown; for here is, I. His pedigree from Abraham in forty-two generations, three fourteens, ver. 1—17. II. An account of the circumstances of his birth, so far as was requisite to show that he was born of a virgin, ver. 18—25. Thus methodically is the life of our blessed Saviour written, as lives should be written, for the clearer proposing of the example of them.

THE book of the generation of
Jesus Christ, the son of David,
the son of Abraham. 2 Abraham
begat Isaac; and Isaac begat Jacob;
and Jacob begat Judas and his brethren; 3 And Judas begat Phares
and Zara of Thamar; and Phares
begat Esrom; and Esrom begat Aram;
4 And Aram begat Aminadab; and
Aminadab begat Naasson; and Naasson begat Salmon; 5 And Salmon
begat Booz of Rachab; and Booz
begat Obed of Ruth; and Obed begat
Jesse; 6 And Jesse begat David the
king; and David the king begat Solomon of her *that had been the wife* of
Urias; 7 And Solomon begat Roboam; and Roboam begat Abia; and
Abia begat Asa; 8 and Asa begat
Josaphat; and Josaphat begat Joram;
and Joram begat Ozias; 9 And Ozias
begat Joatham; and Joatham begat
Achaz; and Achaz begat Ezekias;
10 And Ezekias begat Manasses;
and Manasses begat Amon; and Amon
begat Josias; 11 And Josias begat
Jechonias and his brethren, about the
time they were carried away to Baby-

lon; 12 And after they were brought
to Babylon, Jechonias begat Salathiel;
and Salathiel begat Zorobabel; 13
And Zorobabel begat Abiud; and
Abiud begat Eliakim; and Eliakim
begat Azor; 14 And Azor begat Sadoc; and Sadoc begat Achim; and
Achim begat Eliud; 15 And Eliud
begat Eleazar; and Eleazar begat
Matthan; and Matthan begat Jacob;
16 And Jacob begat Joseph the husband of Mary, of whom was born
Jesus, who is called Christ. 17 So
all the generations from Abraham to
David *are* fourteen generations; and
from David until the carrying away
into Babylon *are* fourteen generations; and from the carrying away
into Babylon unto Christ *are* fourteen
generations.

Concerning this genealogy of our Saviour, observe,

I. The title of it. It is *the book* (or the account, as the Hebrew word *sepher, a book,* sometimes signifies) *of the generation of Jesus Christ,* of his ancestors according to the flesh; or, It is the narrative of his birth. It is Βίβλος Γενέσεως—*a book of Genesis.* The Old Testament begins with the book of the generation of the world, and it is its glory that it does so; but the glory of the New Testament *herein* excelleth, that it begins with *the book of the generation of* him that made the world. As God, *his outgoings were of old, from everlasting* (Mic. v. 2), and none can declare that generation; but, as man, he was *sent forth in the fulness of time, born of a woman,* and it is that generation which is here declared.

II. The principal intention of it. It is not an endless or needless genealogy; it is not a vain-glorious one, as those of great men commonly are. *Stemmata, quid faciunt?—Of what avail are ancient pedigrees?* It is like a pedigree given in evidence, to prove a title, and make out a claim; the design is to prove that our Lord Jesus is *the son of David,* and *the son of Abraham,* and therefore of that nation and family out of which the Messiah was to arise. Abraham and David were, in their day, the great trustees of the promise relating to the Messiah. *The promise* of the *blessing was made to Abraham and his seed,* of the *dominion to David and his seed;* and they who would have an interest in Christ, as *the son of Abraham, in whom all the families of the earth are to be blessed,* must be faithful, loyal subjects to him as *the son of David,* by whom *all the families of the earth* are to be ruled. It was promised to Abraham that Christ should descend from him (Gen. xii. 3; xxii. 18), and to David that he should descend from him (2 Sam. vii. 12; Ps. lxxxix. 3, &c.; cxxxii. 11); and therefore, unless it can be proved that Jesus is a *son of David,* and a *son of Abraham,* we cannot admit him to be the Messiah. Now this is here proved from the authentic records of the heralds' offices. The Jews were very exact in preserving their pedigrees, and there was a providence in it, for the clearing up of the descent of the Messiah from the fathers; and since his coming that nation is so dispersed and confounded that it is a question whether any person in the world can legally prove himself to be a *son of Abraham;* however, it is certain that none can prove himself to be either a son of Aaron or a *son of David,* so that the priestly and kingly office must either be given up, as lost for ever, or be lodged in the hands of our Lord Jesus. Christ is here first called *the son of David,* because under that title he was commonly spoken of, and expected, among the Jews. They who owned him to be *the Christ,* called him *the son of David,* ch. xv. 22; xx. 31; xxi. 15. This, therefore, the evangelist undertakes to make out, that he is not only a *son of David,* but that *son of David* on whose *shoulders the government was to be;* not only *a son of Abraham,* but that *son of Abraham* who was to be *the father of many nations.*

In calling Christ *the son of David,* and *the son of Abraham,* he shows that God is faithful to his promise, and will make good every word that he has spoken; and this, 1. Though the performance be long deferred. When God promised Abraham a son, who should be the great blessing of the world, perhaps he expected it should be his immediate son; but it proved to be one at the distance of forty-two generations, and about 2000 years: so long before can God foretel what shall be done, and so long after, sometimes, does God fulfil what has been promised. Note, Delays of promised mercies, though they exercise our patience, do not weaken God's promise. 2. Though it begin to be despaired of. This *son of David,* and *son of Abraham,* who was to be the glory of his Father's house, was born when the seed of Abraham was a despised people, recently become tributary to the Roman yoke, and when the house of David was buried in obscurity; for Christ was to be *a root out of a dry ground.* Note, God's time for the performance of his promises is when it labours under the greatest improbabilities.

III. The particular series of it, drawn in the direct line from Abraham downward, according to the genealogies recorded in the beginning of the books of Chronicles (as far as those go), and which here we see the use of.

Some particulars we may observe in this genealogy.

1. Among the ancestors of Christ who had brethren, generally he descended from

a younger brother; such Abraham himself was, and Jacob, and Judah, and David, and Nathan, and Rhesa; to show that the pre-eminence of Christ came not, as that of earthly princes, from the primogeniture of his ancestors, but from the will of God, who, according to the method of his providence, *exalteth them of low degree,* and puts *more abundant honour upon that part which lacked.*

2. Among the sons of Jacob, besides Judah, from whom Shiloh came, notice is here taken of *his brethren: Judas and his brethren.* No mention is made of Ishmael the son of Abraham, or of Esau the son of Isaac, because they were shut out of the church; whereas all the children of Jacob were taken in, and, though not fathers of Christ, were yet patriarchs of the church (Acts vii. 8), and therefore are mentioned in this genealogy, for the encouragement of the *twelve tribes that were scattered abroad,* intimating to them that they have an interest in Christ, and stand in relation to him as well as Judah.

3. Phares and Zara, the twin-sons of Judah, are likewise both named, though Phares only was Christ's ancestor, for the same reason that the brethren of Judah are taken notice of; and some think because the birth of Phares and Zara had something of allegory in it. Zara put out his hand first, as the first-born, but, drawing it in, Phares got the birth-right. The Jewish church, like Zara, reached first at the birthright, but, through unbelief, withdrawing the hand, the Gentile church, like Phares, broke forth and went away with the birthright; and thus *blindness is in part happened unto Israel, till the fulness of the Gentiles be come in,* and then Zara shall be born—*all Israel shall be saved,* Rom. xi. 25, 26.

4. There are four women, and but four, named in this genealogy; two of them were originally *strangers to the commonwealth of Israel,* Rachab a Canaanitess, and a harlot besides, and Ruth the Moabitess; for *in Jesus Christ there is neither Greek nor Jew;* those that are *strangers and foreigners* are welcome, in Christ, to *the citizenship of the saints.* The other two were adulteresses, Tamar and Bathsheba; which was a further mark of humiliation put upon our Lord Jesus, that not only he descended from such, but that his descent from them is particularly remarked in his genealogy, and no veil drawn over it. He took upon him *the likeness of sinful flesh* (Rom. viii. 3), and takes even great sinners, upon their repentance, into the nearest relation to himself. Note, We ought not to upbraid people with the scandals of their ancestors; it is what they cannot help, and has been the lot of the best, even of our Master himself. *David's begetting Solomon of her that had been the wife of Urias* is taken notice of (says Dr. Whitby) to show that that crime of David, being repented of, was so far from hindering the promise made to him, that it pleased God by this very woman to fulfil it.

5. Though divers kings are here named, yet none is expressly called a king but David (*v.* 6), *David the king;* because with him the covenant of royalty was made, and to him the promise of the kingdom of the Messiah was given, who is therefore said to inherit *the throne of his father David,* Luke i. 32.

6. In the pedigree of the kings of Judah, between Joram and Ozias (*v.* 8), there are three left out, namely, Ahaziah, Joash, and Amaziah; and therefore when it is said, *Joram begat Ozias,* it is meant, according to the usage of the Hebrew tongue, that Ozias was lineally descended from him, as it is said to Hezekiah that *the sons which he should beget should be carried to Babylon,* whereas they were removed several generations from him. It was not through mistake or forgetfulness that these three were omitted, but, probably, they were omitted in the genealogical tables that the evangelist consulted, which yet were admitted as authentic. Some give this reason for it:—It being Matthew's design, for the sake of memory, to reduce the number of Christ's ancestors to three fourteens, it was requisite that in this period three should be left out, and none more fit than they who were the immediate progeny of cursed Athaliah, who introduced the idolatry of Ahab into the house of David, for which this brand is set upon the family and the iniquity thus visited *to the third and fourth generation.* Two of these three were apostates; and such God commonly sets a mark of his displeasure upon in this world: they all three had their heads brought to the grave with blood.

7. Some observe what a mixture there was of good and bad in the succession of these kings; as for instance (*v.* 7, 8), wicked *Roboam begat* wicked *Abia;* wicked *Abia begat* good *Asa;* good *Asa begat* good *Josaphat;* good *Josaphat begat* wicked *Joram.* Grace does not run in the blood, neither does reigning sin. God's grace is his own, and he gives or withholds it as he pleases.

8. The captivity in Babylon is mentioned as a remarkable period in this line, *v.* 11, 12. All things considered, it was a wonder that the Jews were not lost in that captivity, as other nations have been; but this intimates the reason why the streams of that people were kept to run pure through that dead sea, because from them, as *concerning the flesh, Christ* was to *come. Destroy it not, for a blessing is in it,* even that blessing of blessings, Christ himself, Isa. lxv. 8, 9. It was with an eye to him that they were restored, and the desolations of the sanctuary were looked upon with favour *for the Lord's sake,* Dan. ix. 17.

9. *Josias* is said to *beget Jechonias and his brethren* (*v.* 11); by Jechonias here is meant Jehoiakim, who was the first-born of Josias; but, when it is said (*v.* 12) that *Jechonias begat Salathiel,* that Jechonias was the son of that Jehoiakim who was carried into

Babylon, and there begat *Salathiel* (as Dr. Whitby shows), and, when Jechonias is said to have been written *childless* (Jer. xxii. 30), it is explained thus: *No man of his seed shall prosper*. *Salathiel* is here said to *beget Zorobabel,* whereas Salathiel begat Pedaiah, and he begat Zorobabel (1 Chron. iii. 19): but, as before, the grandson is often called the son; Pedaiah, it is likely, died in his father's lifetime, and so his son Zorobabel was called the *son of Salathiel*.

10. The line is brought down, not to Mary the mother of our Lord, but to *Joseph the husband of Mary* (*v.* 16); for the Jews always reckoned their genealogies by the males: yet Mary was of the same tribe and family with Joseph, so that, both by his mother and by his supposed father, he was of the house of David; yet his interest in that dignity is derived by Joseph, to whom really according to the flesh he had no relation, to show that the kingdom of the Messiah is not founded in a natural descent from David.

11. The centre in whom all these lines meet is *Jesus, who is called Christ, v.* 16. This is he that was so importunately desired, so impatiently expected, and to whom the patriarchs had an eye when they were so desirous of children, that they might have the honour of coming into the sacred line. Blessed be God, we are not now in such a dark and cloudy state of expectation as they were then in, but see clearly what these prophets and kings saw as through a glass darkly. And we may have, if it be not our own fault, a greater honour than that of which they were so ambitious: for they who do the will of God are in a more honourable relation to Christ than those who were akin to him according to the flesh, *ch.* xii. 50. *Jesus* is called *Christ*, that is, the *Anointed*, the same with the *Hebrew* name *Messiah*. He is called *Messiah the Prince* (Dan. ix. 25), and often God's *Anointed* (Ps. ii. 2). Under this character he was expected: *Art thou the Christ*—the *anointed one?* David, the king, was anointed (1 Sam. xvi. 13); so was Aaron, the priest (Lev. viii. 12), and Elisha, the prophet (1 Kings xix. 16), and Isaiah, the prophet (Isa. lxi. 1). Christ, being appointed to, and qualified for, all these offices, is therefore called the *Anointed—anointed with the oil of gladness above his fellows;* and from this name of his, which is as ointment poured forth, all his followers are called *Christians,* for they also have *received the anointing*.

Lastly. The general summary of all this genealogy we have, *v.* 17, where it is summed up in three fourteens, signalized by remarkable periods. In the first fourteen, we have the family of David rising, and looking forth as the morning; in the second, we have it flourishing in its meridian lustre; in the third, we have it declining and growing less and less, dwindling into the family of a poor carpenter, and then Christ *shines forth* out of it, the *glory of his people Israel*.

18 Now the birth of Jesus Christ
was on this wise: When as his mother Mary was espoused to Joseph,
before they came together, she was
found with child of the Holy Ghost.
19 Then Joseph her husband, being
a just *man*, and not willing to make
her a public example, was minded to
put her away privily. 20 But while
he thought on these things, behold,
the angel of the Lord appeared unto
him in a dream, saying, Joseph, thou
son of David, fear not to take unto
thee Mary thy wife; for that which
is conceived in her is of the Holy
Ghost. 21 And she shall bring forth
a son, and thou shalt call his name
JESUS: for he shall save his people
from their sins. 22 Now all this was
done, that it might be fulfilled which
was spoken of the Lord by the prophet, saying, 23 Behold, a virgin
shall be with child, and shall bring
forth a son, and they shall call his name
Emmanuel; which being interpreted
is, God with us. 24 Then Joseph,
being raised from sleep, did as the
angel of the Lord had bidden him,
and took unto him his wife: 25 And
knew her not till she had brought
forth her first-born son: and he called
his name JESUS.

The mystery of Christ's incarnation is to be adored, not pried into. If we *know not the way of the Spirit* in the formation of common persons, nor *how the bones are formed in the womb of* any one *that is with child* (Eccles. xi. 5), much less do we know how the blessed Jesus was formed in the womb of the blessed virgin. When David admires how he himself was *made in secret*, and *curiously wrought* (Ps. cxxxix. 13—16), perhaps he speaks in spirit of Christ's incarnation. Some circumstances attending the birth of Christ we find here which are not in Luke, though it is more largely recorded there. Here we have,

I. Mary's espousals to Joseph. Mary, the mother of our Lord, *was espoused to Joseph*, not completely married, but contracted; a purpose of marriage solemnly declared in words *de futuro—that regarded the future*, and a promise of it made if God permit. We read of a man who *has betrothed a wife and has not taken her*, Deut. xx. 7. Christ was born of a virgin, but a betrothed virgin, 1. To put respect upon the marriage state, and to recommend it as *honourable among all*, against that doctrine of devils which *forbids to marry*, and places perfection in the single state. Who more highly favoured than Mary was in her espousals? 2. To save the credit of the blessed virgin, which otherwise would have been exposed. It was fit that her conception should be protected by a marriage, and so justified in the eye of the world. One of the ancients says, It was better it should be asked, Is not this the *son of a carpenter?* than, Is not this the *son of a harlot?* 3. That the blessed virgin might have one to be the guide of her youth, the companion of her solitude and travels, a partner in her cares, and a help meet for her. Some think that Joseph was now a widower, and that those who are called the *brethren of Christ* (*ch.* xiii. 55), were Joseph's children by a former wife. This is the conjecture of many of the ancients. Joseph was a *just man*, she a *virtuous woman*. Those who are *believers* should not be *unequally yoked with unbelievers:* but let those who are religious choose to marry with those who are so, as they expect the comfort of the relation, and God's blessing upon them in it. We may also learn, from this example, that it is good to enter into the married state with deliberation, and not hastily—to preface the nuptials with a contract. It is better to *take* time to consider before than to *find* time to repent after.

II. Her pregnancy of the promised seed; *before they came together*, she *was found with child*, which really was *of the Holy Ghost.* The marriage was deferred so long after the contract that she appeared to be *with child* before the time came for the solemnizing of the marriage, though she was contracted before she conceived. Probably, it was after her return from her cousin Elizabeth, with whom she continued *three months* (Luke i. 56), that she was perceived by Joseph to be with child, and did not herself deny it. Note, Those in whom Christ is formed will show it: it will be *found to be* a work of God which he will own. Now we may well imagine, what a perplexity this might justly occasion to the blessed virgin. She herself knew the divine original of this conception; but how could she prove it? She would be *dealt with as a harlot.* Note, After great and high advancements, lest we should be puffed up with them, we must expect something or other to humble us, some reproach, *as a thorn in the flesh*, nay, as *a sword in the bones.* Never was any daughter of Eve so dignified as the Virgin Mary was, and yet in danger of falling under the imputation of one of the worst of crimes; yet we do not find that she tormented herself about it; but, being conscious of her own innocence, she kept her mind calm and easy, and committed her cause to *him that judgeth righteously.* Note, Those who take care to keep a good conscience may cheerfully trust God with the keeping of their good names, and have reason to hope that he will clear up, not only their integrity, but their honour, as the sun at noon day.

III. Joseph's perplexity, and his care what to do in this case. We may well imagine what a great trouble and disappointment it was to him to find one he had such an opinion of, and value for, come under the suspicion of such a heinous crime. *Is this Mary?* He began to think, "How may we be deceived in those we think best of! How may we be disappointed in what we expect most from!" He is loth to believe so ill a thing of one whom he believed to be so good a woman; and yet the matter, as it is too bad to be excused, is also too plain to be denied. What a struggle does this occasion in his breast between that jealousy which is the rage of man, and is cruel as the grave, on the one hand, and that affection which he has for Mary on the other!

Observe, 1. The extremity which he studied to avoid. He was *not willing to make her a public example.* He might have done so; for, by the law, a *betrothed virgin*, if she played the harlot, was to be stoned to death, Deut. xxii. 23, 24. But he *was not willing* to take the advantage of the law against her; if she be guilty, yet it is not known, nor shall it be known from him. How different was the spirit which Joseph displayed from that of Judah, who in a similar case hastily passed that severe sentence, *Bring her forth and let her be burnt!* Gen. xxxviii. 24. How good is it to *think on things*, as Joseph did here! Were there more of deliberation in our censures and judgments, there would be more of mercy and moderation in them. Bringing her to punishment is here called *making her a public example;* which shows what is the end to be aimed at in punishment—the giving of warning to others: it is *in terrorem—that all about may hear and fear. Smite the scorner*, and the simple will beware.

Some persons of a rigorous temper would blame Joseph for his clemency: but it is here spoken of to his praise; because *he was a just man*, therefore he was not willing to expose her. He was a *religious, good man;* and therefore inclined to be merciful as God is, and to *forgive* as one that was *forgiven.* In the case of a betrothed damsel, if she were defiled in the field, the law charitably supposed that she *cried out* (Deut. xxii. 26), and she was not to be punished. Some charitable construction or other Joseph will put upon this matter; and herein he is a *just man*, tender of the good name of one who never before had done any thing to blemish it. Note, It becomes us, in many cases, to be gentle towards those that come under suspicion of having offended, to hope the best concerning them, and make the best of that which at first appears bad, in hopes that it may prove better. *Summum jus summa injuria—The rigour of the law is* (sometimes) *the height of injustice.* That court of conscience which moderates the rigour of the law we call a *court of equity.* Those who are found faulty were perhaps *overtaken in the fault*, and are therefore to be *restored with the spirit of meekness;* and threatening, even when just, must be moderated.

2. The expedient he found out for avoiding this extremity. He was *minded to put her away privily*, that is, to give a bill of divorce into her hand before two witnesses, and so to hush up the matter among themselves. Being a *just man*, that is, a strict observer of the law, he would not proceed to marry her, but resolved to *put her away;* and yet, in tenderness for her, determined to do it as privately as possible. Note, The necessary censures of those who have offended ought to be managed without noise. The *words of the wise are heard in quiet.* Christ himself *shall not strive nor cry.* Christian love and Christian prudence will *hide a multitude of sins*, and great ones, as far as may be done without having fellowship with them.

IV. Joseph's discharge from this perplexity by an express sent from heaven, *v.* 20, 21. *While he thought on these things* and knew not what to determine, God graciously directed him what to do, and made him easy. Note, Those who would have direction from God must *think on things* themselves, and consult with themselves. It is the *thoughtful*, not the *unthinking*, whom God will guide. When he was at a loss, and had carried the matter as far as he could in his own thoughts, then God came in with advice. Note, God's time to come in with instruction to his people is when they are *nonplussed* and at a stand. God's comforts most delight the soul *in the multitude* of its perplexed *thoughts.* The message was sent to Joseph by an *angel of the Lord*, probably the same angel that brought to Mary the tidings of the conception—the angel Gabriel. Now the intercourse with heaven, by angels, with which the patriarchs had been dignified, but which had been long disused, begins to be revived; for, when the *First-begotten* is to be *brought into the world*, the angels are ordered to attend his motions. How far God may now, in an invisible way, make use of the ministration of angels, for extricating his people out of their straits, we cannot say; but this we are sure of, they are all *ministering spirits* for their good. This angel appeared to Joseph *in a dream* when he was asleep, as God sometimes spoke unto the fathers. When we are most quiet and composed we are in the best frame to receive the notices of the divine will. The Spirit moves on the calm waters. This dream, no doubt, carried its own evidence along with it that it was of God, and not the production of a vain fancy. Now,

1. Joseph is here *directed* to proceed in his intended marriage. The angel calls him, *Joseph, thou son of David;* he puts him in mind of his relation to David, that he might be prepared to receive this surprising intelligence of his relation to the Messiah, who, every one knew, was to be a descendant from David. Sometimes, when great honours devolve upon those who have small estates, they care not for accepting them, but are willing to drop them; it was therefore requisite to put this poor carpenter in mind of his high birth: "Value thyself. Joseph, thou art that *son of David* through whom the line of the Messiah is to be drawn." We may thus say to every true believer, "Fear not, thou son of Abraham, thou child of God; forget not the dignity of thy birth, thy new birth." *Fear not to take Mary for thy wife;* so it may be read. Joseph, suspecting she was with child by whoredom, was afraid of *taking her*, lest he should bring upon himself either guilt or reproach. No, saith God, *Fear not;* the matter is not so. Perhaps Mary had told him that she was with child by the Holy Ghost, and he might have heard what Elizabeth said to her (Luke i. 43), when she called her the *mother of her Lord;* and, if so, he was afraid of presumption in marrying one so much above him. But, from whatever cause his fears arose, they were all silenced with this word, *Fear not to take unto thee Mary thy wife.* Note, It is a great mercy to be delivered from our fears, and to have our doubts resolved, so as to proceed in our affairs with satisfaction.

2. He is here *informed* concerning that *holy thing* with which his espoused wife was now pregnant. That which is conceived in her is of a divine original. He is so far from being in danger of sharing in an impurity by marrying her, that he will thereby share in the highest dignity he is capable of. Two things he is told,

(1.) That she had conceived *by the power of the Holy Ghost;* not by the power of nature. The Holy Spirit, who produced the world, now produced the Saviour of the world, and *prepared him a body*, as was promised him, when he said, *Lo, I come*, Heb. x. 5. Hence he is said to be *made of a woman* (Gal. iv. 4), and yet to be that second *Adam* that is the *Lord from heaven*, 1 Cor. xv. 47. He is the *Son of God*, and yet so far partakes of the substance of his mother as to be called *the fruit of her womb*, Luke i. 42. It was requisite that his conception should be otherwise than by ordinary *generation*, that so, though he partook of the human nature, yet he might escape the corruption and pollution of it, and not be *conceived* and *shapen* in iniquity. Histories tell us of some who vainly pretended to have conceived by a divine power, as the mother of Alexander; but none ever really did so, except the mother of our Lord. His name in this, as in other things, is *Wonderful.* We do not read that the virgin Mary did herself proclaim the honour done to her; but she hid it in her heart, and therefore God sent an angel to attest it. Those who seek not their own glory shall have the honour that comes from God; it is reserved for the humble.

(2.) That she should bring forth *the Saviour*

of the world (*v.* 21). *She shall bring forth a Son;* what he shall be is intimated,

[1] In the name that should be given to her Son: *Thou shalt call his name Jesus, a Saviour.* Jesus is the same name with Joshua, the termination only being changed, for the sake of conforming it to the Greek. Joshua is called *Jesus* (Acts vii. 45; Heb. iv. 8), from the Seventy. There were two of that name under the Old Testament, who were both illustrious types of Christ, Joshua who was Israel's captain at their first settlement in Canaan, and Joshua who was their high priest at their second settlement after the captivity, Zech. vi. 11, 12. Christ is our Joshua; both the *Captain of our salvation*, and the *High Priest of our profession*, and, in both, our Saviour—a Joshua who comes in the stead of Moses, and does that for us which *the law could not do, in that it was weak.* Joshua had been called *Hosea*, but Moses prefixed the first syllable of the name *Jehovah*, and so made it *Jehoshua* (Numb. xiii. 16), to intimate that the Messiah, who was to bear that name, should be *Jehovah;* he is therefore *able to save to the uttermost*, neither is there *salvation in any other.*

[2.] In the reason of that name: *For he shall save his people from their sins*; not the nation of the Jews only (he came to *his own*, and they *received him not)*, but all who were given him by *the Father's choice*, and all who have given themselves to him by *their own.* He is a king who *protects* his subjects, and, as the judges of Israel of old, *works salvation* for them. Note, Those whom Christ saves he saves *from their sins;* from the guilt of sin by the *merit of his death*, from the dominion of sin by the *Spirit of his grace.* In saving them from sin, he saves them from wrath and the curse, and all misery here and hereafter. Christ came to save his people, not *in their sins*, but *from* their sins; to purchase for them, not a liberty *to sin*, but a liberty *from sins, to redeem them from all iniquity* (Tit. ii. 14); and so to redeem them *from among men* (Rev. xiv. 4) to himself, who is *separate from sinners.* So that those who leave their sins, and give up themselves to Christ as *his people*, are interested in the Saviour, and the great salvation which he has *wrought out*, Rom. xi. 26.

V. The fulfilling of the scripture in all this. This evangelist, writing among the Jews, more frequently observes this than any other of the evangelists. Here the Old Testament prophecies had their accomplishment in our Lord Jesus, by which it appears that this was he that should come, and we are to look for no other; for this was he *to whom all the prophets bore witness.* Now the scripture that was fulfilled in the birth of Christ was that promise of a sign which God gave to king Ahaz (Isa. vii. 14), *Behold a virgin shall conceive;* where the prophet, encouraging the people of God to hope for the promised deliverance from Sennacherib's invasion, directs them to look forward to the Messiah, who was to come of the people of the Jews, and the house of David; whence it was easy to infer, that though that people and that house were afflicted, yet neither the one nor the other could be abandoned to ruin, so long as God had such an honour, such a blessing, in reserve for them. The deliverances which God wrought for the Old-Testament church were types and figures of the great salvation by Christ; and, if God will do the greater, he will not fail to do the less.

The prophecy here quoted is justly ushered in with a *Behold*, which commands both attention and admiration; for we have here the mystery of godliness, which is, without controversy, great, that *God was manifested in the flesh.*

1. The sign given is that the Messiah shall be *born of a virgin. A virgin shall conceive*, and, by her, he shall be manifested *in the flesh.* The word *Almah* signifies a *virgin* in the strictest sense, such as Mary professes herself to be (Luke i. 34), *I know not a man;* nor had it been any such wonderful sign as it was intended for, if it had been otherwise. It was intimated from the beginning that the Messiah should be born of a virgin, when it was said that he should be the *seed of the woman;* so the seed of the woman as not to be the seed of any man. Christ was born of a virgin not only because his birth was to be *supernatural*, and altogether extraordinary, but because it was to be *spotless*, and pure, and without any stain of sin. Christ would be born, not of an *empress* or *queen*, for he appeared not in outward pomp or splendour, but of a virgin, to teach us spiritual purity, to die to all the delights of sense, and so to *keep ourselves unspotted* from the world and the flesh that we may be presented *chaste virgins to Christ.*

2. The truth proved by this sign is, that he is the Son of God, and the Mediator between God and man: for *they shall call his name Immanuel;* that is, he shall be *Immanuel*; as when it is said, *He shall be called*, it is meant, he shall *be, the Lord our righteousness. Immanuel* signifies *God with us;* a mysterious name, but very precious; God *incarnate* among us, and so God *reconcilable* to us, at peace with us, and taking us into covenant and communion with himself. The people of the Jews had *God with them*, in types and shadows, dwelling between the cherubim; but never so as when the *Word was made flesh*—that was the blessed *Shechinah.* What a happy step is hereby taken toward the settling of a peace and correspondence between God and man, that the two natures are thus brought together in the person of the Mediator! by this he became an unexceptionable referee, a days-man, fit to *lay his hand upon them both*, since he partakes of the nature of both. Behold, in this, the deepest mystery, and the richest mercy, that

ever was. By the light of *nature,* we see God as a God *above us;* by the light of the *law,* we see him as a God *against us;* but by the light of the gospel, we see him as *Immanuel,* God *with us,* in our own nature, and (which is more) in our interest. Herein the Redeemer *commended his love.* With Christ's name, *Immanuel,* we may compare the name given to the gospel church (Ezek. xlviii. 35). *Jehovah Shammah—The Lord is there;* the Lord of hosts is with us.

Nor is it improper to say that the prophecy which foretold that he should be called *Immanuel* was fulfilled, in the design and intention of it, when he was called *Jesus;* for if he had not been *Immanuel—God with us,* he could not have been *Jesus—a Saviour;* and herein consists the salvation he wrought out, in the *bringing of God and man together;* this was what he designed, to bring *God* to be *with us,* which is our great happiness, and to bring *us* to *be with God,* which is our great duty.

VI. Joseph's obedience to the divine precept (*v.* 24). *Being raised from sleep* by the impression which the dream made upon him, *he did as the angel of the Lord had bidden him,* though it was contrary to his former sentiments and intentions; *he took unto him his wife;* he did it speedily, without delay, and cheerfully, without dispute; he was not disobedient to the heavenly vision. Extraordinary direction like this we are not now to expect; but God has still ways of making known his mind in doubtful cases, by hints of providence, debates of conscience, and advice of faithful friends; by each of these, applying the general rules of the written word, we should, therefore, in all the steps of our life, particularly the great turns of it, such as this of Joseph's, take direction from God, and we shall find it safe and comfortable to do as he bids us.

VII. The accomplishment of the divine promise (*v.* 25). *She brought forth her first-born* son. The circumstances of it are more largely related, Luke ii. 1, &c. Note, That which is *conceived of the Holy Ghost* never proves *abortive,* but will certainly be *brought forth* in its season. What is *of the will of the flesh,* and *of the will of man,* often miscarries; but, if Christ be *formed* in the soul, God himself has begun the good work which he will perform; what is *conceived* in grace will no doubt be *brought forth* in glory.

It is here further observed, 1. That Joseph, though he solemnized the marriage with Mary, his espoused wife, kept at a distance from her while she was with child of this Holy thing; he *knew her not till she had brought him forth.* Much has been said concerning the perpetual virginity of the mother of our Lord: Jerome was very angry with Helvidius for denying it. It is certain that it cannot be proved from scripture. Dr. *Whitby* inclines to think that when it is said, *Joseph knew her not till she had brought forth her first-born,* it is intimated that, afterward, the reason ceasing, he lived with her, according to the law, Exod. xxi. 10. 2. That Christ was the *first-born;* and so he might be called though his mother had not any other children after him, according to the language of scripture. Nor is it without a mystery that Christ is called her *first-born,* for he is the *first-born of every creature,* that is, the Heir of all things; and he is the *first-born among many brethren,* that in all things he may have the pre-eminence. 3. That *Joseph called his name Jesus,* according to the direction given him. God having *appointed* him to be the Saviour, which was intimated in his giving him the name *Jesus,* we must *accept* of him to be our Saviour, and, in concurrence with that appointment, we must call him *Jesus, our Saviour.*

CHAP. II.

In this chapter, we have the history of our Saviour's infancy, where we find how early he began to suffer, and that in him the word of righteousness was fulfilled, before he himself began to fulfil all righteousness. Here is, I. The wise men's solicitous enquiry after Christ, ver. 1—8. II. Their devout attendance on him, when they found out where he was, ver. 9—12. III. Christ's flight into Egypt, to avoid the cruelty of Herod, ver. 13—15. IV. The barbarous murder of the infants of Bethlehem, ver. 16—18. V. Christ's return out of Egypt into the land of Israel again, ver. 19—23.

NOW when Jesus was born in Bethlehem of Judea, in the days of Herod the king, behold, there came wise men from the east to Jerusalem,
2 Saying, Where is he that is born King of the Jews? for we have seen his star in the east, and are come to worship him.
3 When Herod the king had heard *these things,* he was troubled, and all Jerusalem with him.
4 And when he had gathered all the chief priests and scribes of the people together, he demanded of them where Christ should be born.
5 And they said unto him, In Bethlehem of Judea; for thus it is written by the prophet,
6 And thou Bethlehem, *in* the land of Juda, art not the least among the princes of Juda: for out of thee shall come a Governor, that shall rule my people Israel.
7 Then Herod, when he had privily called the wise men, enquired of them diligently what time the star appeared.
8 And he sent them to Bethlehem; and said, Go and search diligently for the young child; and when ye have found *him,* bring me word again, that I may come and worship him also.

It was a *mark of humiliation* put upon the Lord Jesus that, though he was the *Desire of all nations,* yet his coming into the world was little observed and taken notice of, his birth was obscure and unregarded: herein he emptied himself, and made himself of no reputation. If the Son of God must be brought into the world, one might justly expect that he should be received with all the ceremony possible, that crowns and sceptres should immediately have been laid at his feet, and that the high and mighty princes of the world should have been his humble servants; such a Messiah as this the Jews expected, but we see none of all this; he *came into the world*, and the *world knew him not;* nay, he *came to his own,* and *his own received him not;* for having undertaken to make satisfaction to his Father for the wrong done him *in his honour* by the sin of man, he did it by denying himself in, and despoiling himself of, the honours undoubtedly due to an incarnate Deity; yet, as afterward, so in his birth, some rays of glory darted forth in the midst of the greatest instances of his abasement. Though *there was the hiding of his power*, yet he had *horns coming out of his hand* (Hab. iii. 4) enough to condemn the world, and the Jews especially, for their stupidity.

The first who took notice of Christ after his birth were the shepherds (Luke ii. 15, &c.), who saw and heard glorious things concerning him, and *made them known abroad,* to the amazement of all that heard them, *v.* 17, 18. After that, Simeon and Anna spoke of him, by the Spirit, to all that were disposed to heed what they said, Luke ii. 38. Now, one would think, these hints should have been taken by the men of Judah and the *inhabitants of Jerusalem,* and they should with both arms have embraced the long-looked-for Messiah; but, for aught that appears, he continued nearly two years after at Bethlehem, and no further notice was taken of him till these wise men came. Note, Nothing will awaken those that are resolved to be regardless. Oh the amazing stupidity of these Jews! And no less that of many who are called Christians! Observe,

I. When this enquiry was made concerning Christ. It was *in the days of Herod the king.* This Herod was an Edomite, made king of Judea by Augustus and Antonius, the then chief rulers of the Roman state, a man made up of falsehood and cruelty; yet he was complimented with the title of *Herod the Great.* Christ was born in the 35th year of his reign, and notice is taken of this, to show that the *sceptre* had now *departed from Judah,* and *the lawgiver from between his feet;* and therefore now was the time for Shiloh to come, and *to him shall the gathering of the people be:* witness these wise men, Gen. xlix. 10.

II. Who and what these *wise men* were; they are here called Μάγοι—*Magicians.* Some take it in a good sense; the *Magi* among the *Persians* were their philosophers and their priests; nor would they admit any one for their king who had not first been enrolled among the *Magi;* others think they dealt in unlawful arts; the word is used of Simon, the sorcerer (Acts viii. 9, 11), and of Elymas, the sorcerer (Acts xiii. 6), nor does the scripture use it in any other sense; and then it was an early instance and presage of Christ's victory over the devil, when those who had been so much his devotees became the early adorers even of the infant Jesus; so soon were trophies of his victory over the powers of darkness erected. Well, whatever sort of wise men they were before, now they began to be *wise men* indeed when they set themselves to enquire after Christ.

This we are sure of, 1. That they were Gentiles, and not belonging to the commonwealth of Israel. The Jews regarded not Christ, but these Gentiles enquired him out. Note, Many times those who are nearest to the means, are furthest from the end. See *ch.* viii. 11, 12. The respect paid to Christ by these Gentiles was a happy presage and specimen of what would follow when those who were *afar off* should be *made nigh by Christ.* 2. That they were *scholars.* They dealt in arts, curious arts; good scholars should be good Christians, and *then* they complete their *learning* when they *learn Christ.* 3. That they were *men of the east,* who were noted for their *soothsaying,* Isa. ii. 6. Arabia is called the land of *the east* (Gen. xxv. 6), and the *Arabians* are called *men of the east,* Judg. vi. 3. The presents they brought were the products of that country; the Arabians had done homage to David and Solomon as types of Christ. Jethro and Job were of that country. More than this we have not to say of them. The traditions of the Romish church are frivolous, that they were in number three (though one of the ancients says that they were fourteen), that they were kings, and that they lie buried in Colen, thence called the *three kings of Colen;* we covet not to be wise above what is written.

III. What induced them to make this enquiry. They, in their country, which was in the *east,* had seen an *extraordinary star,* such as they had not seen before; which they took to be an indication of an extraordinary person born in the land of *Judea,* over which land this star was seen to hover, in the nature of a comet, or a meteor rather, in the lower regions of the air; this differed so much from any thing that was common that they concluded it to signify something uncommon. Note, Extraordinary appearances of God in the creatures should put us upon enquiring after his mind and will therein; Christ foretold *signs in the heavens.* The birth of Christ was notified to the Jewish shepherds by *an angel,* to the Gentile philosophers by a *star:* to both God spoke in their own language, and in the way they were best acquainted with. Some think that the light which the shepherds saw shining round about them, the night after Christ was born, was the very same which to the wise men, who lived at such a distance, appeared as a star; but this we cannot easily admit, because the same star which they had seen in the *east* they saw a great while after, leading them to the house where Christ lay; it was a candle set up on purpose to guide them to Christ. The idolaters worshipped the stars as the *host of heaven*, especially the *eastern* nations, whence the planets have the names of their idol-gods; we read of a particular *star* they had in veneration, Amos v. 26. Thus the stars that had been misused came to be put to the right use, to lead men to Christ; the gods of the heathen became his servants. Some think this star put them in mind of Balaam's prophecy, that a star should come out of Jacob, pointing at a *sceptre*, that shall *rise out of Israel*; see Numb. xxiv. 17. Balaam came from the *mountains of the east*, and was one of their *wise men*. Others impute their enquiry to the general expectation entertained at that time, in those *eastern* parts, of some great prince to appear. Tacitus, in his history (*lib.* v.), takes notice of it; *Pluribus persuasio inerat, antiquis sacerdotum literis contineri, eo ipso tempore fore, ut valesceret oriens, profectique Judæa rerum potirentur—A persuasion existed in the minds of many that some ancient writings of the priests contained a prediction that about that time an eastern power would prevail, and that persons proceeding from Judea would obtain dominion. Suetonius* also, in the life of *Vespasian*, speaks of it; so that this extraordinary phenomenon was construed as pointing to *that king*; and we may suppose a divine impression made upon their minds, enabling them to interpret this star as a signal given by Heaven of the birth of Christ.

IV. How they prosecuted this enquiry. *They came from the* east to Jerusalem, in further quest of this prince. Whither should they come to enquire for the king of the Jews, but to Jerusalem, the mother-city, *whither the tribes go up, the tribes of the Lord?* They might have said, "If such a prince be born, we shall hear of him shortly in our own country, and it will be time enough then to pay our homage to him." But so impatient were they to be better acquainted with him, that they took a long journey on purpose to enquire after him. Note, Those who truly desire to know Christ, and find him, will not regard pains or perils in seeking after him. *Then shall we know, if we follow on to know the Lord.*

Their question is, *Where is he that is born king of the* Jews? They do not ask, *whether there were such a one born?* (they are sure of that, and speak of it with assurance, so strongly was it set home upon their hearts); but, *Where is he born?* Note, Those who know *something* of Christ cannot but covet to *know more* of him. They call Christ the *King of the Jews*, for so the Messiah was expected to be: and he is Protector and Ruler of all the spiritual Israel, he is *born a King*.

To this question they doubted not but to have a ready answer, and to find all Jerusalem worshipping at the feet of this new king; but they come from door to door with this question, and no man can give them any information. Note, There is more gross ignorance in the world, and in the church too, than we are aware of. Many that we think should direct us to Christ are themselves strangers to him. They ask, as the spouse of the daughters of Jerusalem, *Saw ye him whom my soul loveth?* But they are never the wiser. However, like the spouse, they pursue the enquiry, *Where is he that is born king of the Jews?* Are they asked, "Why do ye make this enquiry?" It is because they have *seen his star in the east.* Are they asked, "What business have ye with him? What have the men of the *east* to do with the *King of the Jews?*" They have their answer ready, *We are come to worship him.* They conclude he will, in process of time, be *their king*, and therefore they will betimes ingratiate themselves with him and with those about him. Note, Those in whose hearts the day-star is risen, to give them any thing of the knowledge of Christ, must make it their business to worship him. Have we seen Christ's star? Let us study to give him honour.

V. How this enquiry was treated at Jerusalem. News of it at last came to court; and *when Herod heard it he was troubled, v.* 3. He could not be a stranger to the prophecies of the *Old Testament*, concerning the Messiah and his kingdom, and the times fixed for his appearing by Daniel's weeks; but, having himself reigned so long and so successfully, he began to hope that those promises would for ever fail, and that his kingdom would be established and perpetuated in spite of them. What a damp therefore must it needs be upon him, to hear talk of this King being born, now, when the time fixed for his appearing had come! Note, Carnal wicked hearts dread nothing so much as the fulfilling of the scriptures.

But though Herod, an Edomite, was troubled, one would have thought Jerusalem should rejoice greatly to hear that her King comes; yet, it seems, *all Jerusalem*, except the few there that *waited for the consolation of Israel, were troubled with* Herod, and were apprehensive of I know not what ill consequences of the birth of this new king, that it would involve them in war, or restrain their lusts; they, for their parts, desired no king but Herod; no, not the Messiah himself. Note, The slavery of sin is foolishly preferred by many to the glorious liberty of the children of God, only because they apprehend some present difficulties attending that necessary revolution of the government in the soul. Herod and Jerusalem were thus troubled, from a mistaken notion that the kingdom of the Messiah would clash and interfere with the secular powers; whereas the star that proclaimed him king plainly intimated that his kingdom was heavenly, and not of this lower world. Note, The reason why the kings of the earth, and the people, oppose the kingdom of Christ, is because they do not know it, but err concerning it.

VI. What assistance they met with in this enquiry from the scribes and the priests, *v.* 4—6. Nobody can pretend to tell where the King of the Jews is, but Herod enquires where it was expected *he should be born.* The persons he consults are, the chief priests, who were teachers by office; and the scribes, who made it their business to study the law; their *lips must keep knowledge,* but then the people must *enquire the law at their mouth,* Mal. ii. 7. It was generally known that Christ should be *born at Bethlehem* (John vii. 42); but Herod would have counsel's opinion upon it, and therefore applies himself to the proper persons; and, that he might be the better satisfied, he has them altogether, *all the chief priests, and all the scribes;* and *demands of them* what was the place, according to the scriptures of the Old Testament, *where Christ should be born?* Many a good question is put with an ill design, so was this by Herod.

The priests and scribes need not take any long time to give an answer to this query; nor do they differ in their opinion, but all agree that the Messiah must be *born in Bethlehem, the city of David,* here called *Bethlehem of Judea,* to distinguish it from another city of the same name in the land of Zebulun, Josh. xix. 15. *Bethlehem* signifies *the house of bread;* the fittest place for him to be born in who is the true manna, *the bread which came down from heaven,* which was *given for the life of the world.* The proof they produce is taken from Mic. v. 2, where it is foretold that though *Bethlehem be little among the thousands of Judah* (so it is in *Micah),* no very populous place, yet it shall be found *not the least among the princes of Judah* (so it is here); for Bethlehem's honour lay not, as that of other cities, in the multitude of the people, but in the magnificence of the princes it produced. Though, upon some accounts, Bethlehem was little, yet herein it had the pre-eminence above all the cities of Israel, that *the Lord shall count, when he writes up the people, that this man,* even *the man Christ Jesus, was born there,* Ps. lxxxvii. 6. *Out of thee shall come a Governor,* the *King of the Jews.* Note, Christ will be a *Saviour* to those only who are willing to take him for their *Governor.* Bethlehem was the *city of David,* and David the glory of Bethlehem; there, therefore, must David's son and successor be born. There was a famous well at *Bethlehem,* by the gate, which David longed to drink of (2 Sam. xxiii. 15); in Christ we have not only bread enough and to spare, but may come and take also *of the water of life freely.* Observe here how Jews and Gentiles compare notes about Jesus Christ. The Gentiles know the time of his birth by a star; the Jews know the place of it by the scriptures; and so they are capable of informing one another. Note, It would contribute much to the increase of knowledge, if we did thus mutually communicate what we know. Men grow rich by bartering and exchanging; so, if we have knowledge to communicate to others, they will be ready to communicate to us; thus many shall discourse, shall *run to and fro, and knowledge shall be increased.*

VII. The bloody project and design of Herod, occasioned by this enquiry, *v.* 7, 8. Herod was now an old man, and had reigned thirty-five years; this king was but newly born, and not likely to enterprise any thing considerable for many years; yet Herod is jealous of him. Crowned heads cannot endure to think of successors, much less of rivals; and therefore nothing less than the blood of this infant king will satisfy him; and he will not give himself liberty to think that, if this new-born child should be indeed the Messiah, in opposing him, or making any attempts upon him, he would *be found fighting against God,* than which nothing is more vain, nothing more dangerous. Passion has got the mastery of reason and conscience.

Now, 1. See how cunningly he laid the project (*v.* 7, 8). *He privily called the wise men,* to talk with them about this matter. He would not openly own his fears and jealousies; it would be his disgrace to let the wise men know them, and dangerous to let the people know them. Sinners are often tormented with secret fears, which they keep to themselves. Herod learns of the wise men the *time when the star appeared,* that he might take his measures accordingly; and then employs them to enquire further, and bids them bring him an account. All this might look suspicious, if he had not covered it with a show of religion: *that I may come and worship him also.* Note, The greatest wickedness often conceals itself under a mask of piety. Absalom cloaks his rebellious project with a vow.

2. See how strangely he was befooled and infatuated in this, that he trusted it with the wise men, and did not choose some other managers, that would have been true to his interests. It was but seven miles from Jerusalem; how easily might he have sent spies to watch the wise men, who might have been as soon there to destroy the child as they to worship him! Note, God can hide from the eyes of the church's enemies those methods by which they might easily destroy the church; when he intends to *lead princes away spoiled,* his way is to *make the judges fools.*

9 When they had heard the king,
they departed: and, lo, the star,
which they saw in the east, went before them, till it came and stood over
where the young child was. 10 When
they saw the star, they rejoiced with
exceeding great joy. 11 And when

they were come into the house, they saw the young child with Mary his mother, and fell down, and worshipped him: and when they had opened their treasures, they presented unto him gifts; gold, and frankincense, and myrrh.
12 And being warned of God in a dream that they should not return to Herod, they departed into their own country another way.

We have here the wise men's humble attendance upon this new-born *King of the Jews,* and the honours they paid him. From Jerusalem they went to Bethlehem, resolving to *seek till they should find;* but it is very strange that they went alone; that not one person of the court, church, or city, should accompany them, if not in conscience, yet in civility to them, or touched with a curiosity to see this young prince. As *the queen of the south,* so *the wise men of the east,* will *rise up in judgment against* the men of that generation, and of this too, *and will condemn them;* for they *came from a far country,* to worship Christ; while the Jews, his kinsmen, would not stir a step, would not go to the next town to bid him welcome. It might have been a discouragement to these wise men to find him whom they sought thus neglected at home. Are we come so far to honour *the King of the Jews,* and do the Jews themselves put such a slight upon him and us? Yet they persist in their resolution. Note, We must continue our attendance upon Christ, though we be alone in it; whatever others do, we must *serve the Lord;* if they will not go to heaven with us, yet we must not go to hell with them. Now,

I. See how they found out Christ by the same star that they had seen in their own country, *v.* 9, 10. Observe, 1. How graciously God directed them. By the first appearance of the star they were given to understand where they might enquire for this King, and then it disappeared, and they were left to take the usual methods for such an enquiry. Note, Extraordinary helps are not to be expected where ordinary means are to be had. Well, they had traced the matter as far as they could; they were upon their journey to Bethlehem, but that is a populous town, where shall they find him when they come thither? Here they were at a loss, at their wit's end, but not at their faith's end; they believed that God, who had brought them thither by his word, would not leave them there; nor did he; for, behold, *the star which they saw in the east went before them.* Note, If we go on as far as we can in the way of our duty, God will direct and enable us to do that which of ourselves we cannot do; *Up, and be doing, and the Lord will be with thee. Vigilantibus, non dormientibus, succurrit lex—The law affords its aid, not to the idle, but to the active.* The star had left them a great while, yet now returns. They who follow God in the dark shall find that light is sown, is reserved, for them. Israel was led by a pillar of fire to *the promised land,* the wise men by a star to *the promised Seed,* who is himself *the bright and morning Star,* Rev. xxii. 16. God would rather *create a new thing* than leave those at a loss who diligently and faithfully sought him. This star was the token of God's presence with them; for he is light, and goes before his people as their Guide. Note, If we by faith eye God in all our ways, we may see ourselves under his conduct; he *guides with his eye* (Ps. xxxii. 8), and saith to them, *This is the way, walk in it:* and there is a day-star that arises in the hearts of those that enquire after Christ, 2 Pet i. 19. 2. Observe how joyfully they followed God's direction (*v.* 10). *When they saw the star, they rejoiced with exceeding great joy.* Now they saw they were not deceived, and had not taken this long journey in vain. *When the desire cometh, it is a tree of life.* Now they were sure that God was with them, and the tokens of his presence and favour cannot but fill with joy unspeakable the souls of those that know how to value them. Now they could laugh at the Jews in Jerusalem, who, probably, had laughed at them as coming on a fool's errand. The watchmen can give the spouse no tidings of her beloved; yet it *is but a little that she passes from them, and she finds him,* Cant. iii. 3, 4. We cannot expect too little from man, nor too much from God. What a transport of joy these wise men were in upon this sight of the star; none know so well as those who, after a long and melancholy night of temptation and desertion, under the power of a *Spirit of bondage,* at length *receive the spirit of adoption, witnessing with their spirits that they are the children of God;* this is light out of darkness; it is life from the dead. Now they had reason to hope for a sight of *the Lord's Christ* speedily, of *the Sun of righteousness,* for they see *the Morning Star.* Note, We should be glad of every thing that will show us the way to Christ. This star was sent to meet the wise men, and to conduct them into the presence chamber of the King; by this master of the ceremonies they were introduced, to have their audience. Now God fulfils his promise of meeting those that are disposed to *rejoice and work righteousness* (Isa. lxiv. 5), and they fulfil his precept. *Let the hearts of those rejoice that seek the Lord,* Ps. cv. 3 Note, God is pleased sometimes to favour young converts with such tokens of his love as are very encouraging to them, in reference to the difficulties they meet with at their setting out in the ways of God.

II. See how they made their address to him when they had found him, *v.* 11. We may well imagine their expectations were raised to find this royal babe, though slighted by the nation, yet honourably attended at home; and what a disappointment it was to them when they found a cottage was his palace, and his own poor mother all the retinue he had! Is this *the Saviour of the world?* Is this *the King of the Jews,* nay, and *the Prince of the kings of the earth?* Yes, this is he, who, *though he was rich,* yet, *for our sakes, became* thus *poor.* However, these wise men were so wise as to see through this veil, and in this despised babe to discern *the glory as of the Only-begotten of the Father;* they did not think themselves balked or baffled in their enquiry; but, as having found the King they sought, they presented themselves first, and then their gifts, to him.

1. They presented themselves to him: *they fell down, and worshipped him.* We do not read that they gave such honour to Herod, though he was in the height of his royal grandeur; but to this babe they gave this honour, not only as to a king (then they would have done the same to Herod), but as to a God. Note, All that have found Christ fall down before him; they adore him, and submit themselves to him. *He is thy Lord, and worship thou him.* It will be the wisdom of the wisest of men, and by this it will appear they know Christ, and understand themselves and their true interests, if they be the humble, faithful worshippers of the Lord Jesus.

2. *They presented their gifts to him.* In the eastern nations, when they did homage to their kings, they made them presents; thus the subjection of the kings of Sheba to Christ is spoken of (Ps. lxxii. 10), *They shall bring presents, and offer gifts.* See Isa. lx. 6. Note, With ourselves, we must give up all that we have to Jesus Christ; and if we be sincere in the surrender of ourselves to him, we shall not be unwilling to part with what is dearest to us, and most valuable, to him and for him; nor are our gifts accepted, unless we first present ourselves to him living sacrifices. *God had respect to Abel, and* then *to his offering.* The gifts they presented were, *gold, frankincense, and myrrh,* money, and money's-worth. Providence sent this for a seasonable relief to Joseph and Mary in their present poor condition. These were the products of their own country; what God favours us with, we must honour him with. Some think there was a significancy in their gifts; they offered him *gold,* as a king, paying him tribute, *to Cæsar, the things that are Cæsar's; frankincense,* as God, for they honoured God with the smoke of incense; and *myrrh,* as a Man that should die, for *myrrh* was used in embalming dead bodies.

III. See how they left him when they had made their address to him, *v.* 12. Herod appointed them to *bring him word* what discoveries they had made, and, it is probable, they would have done so, if they had not been countermanded, not suspecting their being thus made his tools in a wicked design. Those that mean honestly and well themselves are easily made to believe that others do so too, and cannot think the world is so bad as really it is; but *the Lord knows how to deliver the godly out of temptation.* We do not find that the wise men promised to come back to Herod, and, if they had, it must have been with the usual proviso, *If God permit;* God did not permit them, and prevented the mischief Herod designed to the Child Jesus, and the trouble it would have been to the wise men to have been made involuntarily accessory to it. They were *warned of God,* χρηματισθέντες—*oraculo vel responso accepto—by an oracular intimation.* Some think it intimates that they asked counsel of God, and that this was the answer. Note, Those that act cautiously, and are afraid of sin and snares, if they apply themselves to God for direction, may expect to be led in the right way. They were *warned not to return to Herod,* nor to Jerusalem; those were unworthy to have reports brought them concerning Christ, that might have seen with their own eyes, and would not. *They departed into their own country another way,* to bring the tidings to their countrymen; but it is strange that we never hear any more of them, and that they or theirs did not afterwards attend *him* in the temple, whom they had worshipped in the cradle. However, the direction they had from God in their return would be a further confirmation of their faith in this Child, as *the Lord from heaven.*

13 And when they were departed,
behold, the angel of the Lord appeareth to Joseph in a dream, saying,
Arise, and take the young child and
his mother, and flee into Egypt, and
be thou there until I bring thee word.
for Herod will seek the young child,
to destroy him. 14 When he arose,
he took the young child and his mother by night, and departed into
Egypt: 15 And was there until the
death of Herod, that it might be fulfilled which was spoken of the Lord
by the prophet, saying, Out of Egypt
have I called my son.

We have here Christ's flight into Egypt to avoid the cruelty of Herod, and this was the effect of the wise men's enquiry after him; for, before that, the obscurity he lay in was his protection. It was but little respect (compared with what should have been) that was paid to Christ in his infancy: yet even that, instead of honouring him among his people, did but expose him.

Now here observe, I. The command given to Joseph concerning it, *v.* 13. Joseph knew neither the danger the child was in, nor how to escape it; but God, by *an angel,* tells him both *in a dream,* as before he directed him in like manner what to do, *ch.* i. 20. Joseph, before his alliance to Christ, had not been wont to converse with angels as now. Note, Those that are spiritually related to Christ by faith have that communion and correspondence with Heaven which before they were strangers to.

1. Joseph is here told what their danger was: *Herod will seek the young child to destroy him.* Note, God is acquainted with all the cruel projects and purposes of the enemies of his church. *I know thy rage against me,* saith God to Sennacherib, Isa. xxxvii. 28. How early was the blessed Jesus involved in trouble! Usually, even those whose riper years are attended with toils and perils have a peaceable and quiet infancy; but it was not so with the blessed Jesus: his life and sufferings began together; he was born *a man striven with,* as Jeremiah was (Jer. xv. 10), who was *sanctified from the womb,* Jer. i. 5. Both Christ the head, and the church his body, agree in saying, *Many a time have they afflicted me, from my youth up.* Pharaoh's cruelty fastens upon the Hebrews' children, and a great red dragon stands ready to *devour the man-child as soon as it should be born,* Rev. xii. 4.

2. He is directed what to do, to escape the danger; *Take the young child, and flee into Egypt.* Thus early must Christ give an example to his own rule (*ch.* x. 23): *When they persecute you in one city, flee to another.* He that came to die for us, when *his hour was not yet come,* fled for his own safety. Self-preservation, being a branch of the law of nature, is eminently a part of the law of God. *Flee;* but why *into Egypt?* Egypt was infamous for idolatry, tyranny, and enmity to the people of God; it had been a house of bondage to Israel, and particularly cruel to the infants of Israel; in Egypt, as much as in Ramah, *Rachel had been weeping for her children;* yet that is appointed to be a place of refuge to the holy child Jesus. Note, God, when he pleases, can make the worst of places serve the best of purposes; for *the earth is the Lord's,* he makes what use he pleases of it: sometimes the earth *helps the woman,* Rev. xii. 16. God, who made Moab a shelter to his outcasts, makes Egypt a refuge for his Son. This may be considered,

(1.) As a trial of the faith of Joseph and Mary. They might be tempted to think, "If this child be the Son of God, as we are told he is, has he no other way to secure himself from a man that is a worm, than by such a mean and inglorious retreat as this? Cannot he summon legions of angels to be his life-guard, or cherubim with flaming swords to keep this *tree of life?* Cannot he strike Herod dead, or wither the hand that is stretched out against him, and so save us the trouble of this remove?" They had been lately told that he should be *the glory of his people Israel;* and is the land of Israel so soon become too hot for him? But we find not that they made any such objections; their faith, being tried, was found firm, and they believe *this is the Son of God,* though they see no miracle wrought for his preservation; but they are put to the use of ordinary means. Joseph had great honour put upon him in being the husband of the blessed virgin; but that honour has trouble attending it, as all honours have in this world; Joseph must *take the young child,* and carry him *into Egypt*; and now it appeared how well God had provided for *the young child and his mother,* in appointing Joseph to stand in so near a relation to them; now the gold which the wise men brought would stand them in stead to bear their charges. God foresees his people's distresses, and provides against them beforehand. God intimates the continuance of his care and guidance, when he saith, *Be thou there until I bring thee word,* so that he must expect to hear from God again, and not stir without fresh orders. Thus God will keep his people still in a dependence upon him.

(2.) As an instance of the humiliation of our Lord Jesus. As there was no room for him in the inn at Bethlehem, so there was no quiet room for him in the land of Judea. Thus was he banished from the earthly Canaan, that we, who for sin were banished from the heavenly Canaan, might not be for ever expelled. If we and our infants be at any time in straits, let us remember the straits Christ in his infancy was brought into, and be reconciled to them.

(3.) As a token of God's displeasure against the Jews, who took so little notice of him; justly does he leave those who had slighted him. We have also here an earnest of his favour to the Gentiles, to whom the apostles were to bring the gospel when the Jews rejected it. If Egypt entertain Christ when he is forced out of Judea, it will not be long ere it be said, *Blessed be Egypt my people,* Isa. xix. 25.

II. Joseph's obedience to this command, *v.* 14. The journey would be inconvenient and perilous both to the young child and to his mother; they were but poorly provided for it, and were likely to meet with cold entertainment in Egypt: yet Joseph *was not disobedient to the heavenly vision,* made no objection, nor was dilatory in his obedience. As soon as he had received his orders, he immediately *arose,* and went away *by night,* the same night, as it should seem, that he received the orders. Note, Those that would make *sure* work of their obedience must make *quick* work of it. Now Joseph went out, as his father Abraham did, with an implicit dependence upon God, *not knowing whither he went,* Heb. xi. 8. Joseph and his wife, having little, had little to take care of in this remove. An abundance encumbers a necessary flight. If rich people have the advantage of the poor while they possess what they have, the poor have the advantage of the rich when they are called to part with it.

Joseph took the young child and his mother. Some observe, that *the young child* is put first, as the principal person, and Mary is called, not *the wife of Joseph,* but, which was her greater dignity, *the mother of the young child.* This was not the first Joseph that was driven from Canaan to Egypt for a shelter from the anger of his brethren; this Joseph ought to be welcome there for the sake of that.

If we may credit tradition, at their entrance into Egypt, happening to go into a temple, all the images of their gods were overthrown by an invisible power, and fell, like Dagon before the ark, according to that prophecy, *The Lord shall come into Egypt, and the idols of Egypt shall be moved at his presence,* Isa. xix. 1. They continued in Egypt till the death of Herod, which, some think, was seven years, others think, not so many months. There they were at a distance from the temple and the service of it, and in the midst of idolaters; but God sent them thither, and will *have mercy, and not sacrifice.* Though they were far from the temple of the Lord, they had with them the Lord of the temple. A forced absence from God's ordinances, and a forced presence with wicked people, may be the lot, are not the sin, yet cannot but be the grief, of good people.

III. The fulfilling of the scripture in all this—that scripture (Hos. xi. 1), *Out of Egypt have I called my son.* Of all the evangelists, Matthew takes most notice of the fulfilling of the scripture in what concerned Christ, because his gospel was first published among the Jews, with whom that would add much strength and lustre to it. Now this word of the prophet undoubtedly referred to the deliverance of Israel out of Egypt, in which God owned them for his son, his first-born (Exod. iv. 22); but it is here applied, by way of analogy, to Christ, the Head of the church. Note, The scripture has many accomplishments, so full and copious is it, and so well ordered in all things. God is every day fulfilling the scripture. Scripture is not of private interpretation: we must give it its full latitude. "*When Israel was a child, then I loved him;* and, though *I loved him,* I suffered him to be a great while in Egypt; but, because *I loved him,* in due time I called him out of Egypt." They that read this must, in their thoughts, not only look back, but look forward; *that which has been shall be again* (Eccl. i. 9); and the manner of expression intimates this; for it is not said, I called *him,* but I called *my son,* out of Egypt. Note, It is no new thing for God's sons to be in Egypt, in a strange land, in a house of bondage; but they shall be fetched out. They may be hid in Egypt, but they shall not be left there. All the elect of God, being by nature children of wrath, are born in a spiritual Egypt, and in conversion are effectually called out. It might be objected against Christ that he had been in Egypt. Must *the Sun of righteousness* arise out of that land of darkness! But this shows that to be no such strange thing; Israel was brought out of Egypt, to be advanced to the highest honours; and this is but doing the the same thing again.

16 Then Herod, when he saw that he was mocked of the wise men, was exceeding wroth, and sent forth, and slew all the children that were in Bethlehem, and in all the coasts thereof, from two years old and under, according to the time which he had diligently enquired of the wise men.
17 Then was fulfilled that which was spoken by Jeremy the prophet, saying,
18 In Rama was there a voice heard, lamentation, and weeping, and great mourning, Rachel weeping *for* her children, and would not be comforted, because they are not.

Here is, I. Herod's resentment of the departure of the wise men. He waited long for their return; he hopes, though they be slow, they will be sure, and he shall crush this rival at his first appearing; but he hears, upon enquiry, that they are gone off another way, which increases his jealousy, and makes him suspect they are in the interest of this new King, which made him *exceeding wroth;* and he is the more desperate and outrageous for his being disappointed. Note, Inveterate corruption swells the higher for the obstructions it meets with in a sinful pursuit.

II. His politic contrivance, notwithstanding this, to take off him that is *born King of the Jews.* If he could not reach him by a particular execution, he doubted not but to involve him in a general stroke, which, like the sword of war, should *devour one as well as another.* This would be sure work; and thus those that would destroy *their own* iniquity must be sure to destroy *all* their iniquities. Herod was an Edomite, enmity to Israel was bred in the bone with him. Doeg was an Edomite, who, for David's sake, *slew all the priests of the Lord.* It was strange that Herod could find any so inhuman as to be employed in such a bloody and barbarous piece of work; but wicked hands never want wicked tools to work with. Little children have always been taken under the special protection, not only of human laws, but of human nature; yet these are sacrificed to the rage of this tyrant, under whom, as under Nero, innocence is the least security. Herod was, throughout his reign, a bloody man; it was not long before, that he destroyed the whole Sanhedrim, or bench of judges; but blood to the blood-thirsty is like drink to those in a dropsy; *Quo plus sunt potæ, plus sitiuntur aquæ—The more they drink, the more thirsty they become.* Herod was now about seventy years old, so that an infant, at this time *under two years old,* was not likely ever to give him any disturbance. Nor was he a man over fond of his own children, or of their preferment, having formerly slain two of his own sons, Alexander and Aristobulus, and his son Antipater after this, but five days before he himself died; so that it was purely to gratify his own brutish lusts of pride and cruelty that he did this. All is fish that comes to his net.

Observe, What large measures he took, 1. As to time; He *slew all from two years old and under.* It is probable that the blessed Jesus was at this time not a year old; yet Herod took in all the infants *under two years old,* that he might be sure not to miss of his prey. He cares not how many heads fall, which he allows to be innocent, provided that escape not which he supposes to be guilty. 2. As to place; He kills all the male children, not only *in Bethlehem,* but *in all the coasts thereof,* in all the villages of that city. This was being *overmuch wicked,* Eccl. vii. 17. Note, An unbridled wrath, armed with an unlawful power, often transports men to the most absurd and unreasonable instances of cruelty. It was no unrighteous thing for God to permit this; every life is forfeited to his justice as soon as it commences; that sin which entered by one man's disobedience, introduced death with it; and we are not to suppose any thing more than that common guilt, we are not to suppose that these children *were sinners above all that were in Israel,* because they suffered such things. *God's judgments are a great deep.* The diseases and deaths of little children are proofs of original sin. But we must look upon this murder of the infants under another character: it was their martyrdom. How early did persecution commence against Christ and his kingdom! *Think ye that he came to send peace on the earth?* No, *but a sword,* such a sword as this, *ch.* x. 34, 35. A passive testimony was hereby given to the Lord Jesus. As when he was in the womb, he was witnessed to by a child's leaping in the womb for joy at his approach, so now, at *two years old,* he had contemporary witnesses to him of the same age. They shed their blood for him, who afterwards shed his for them. These were the infantry of *the noble army of martyrs.* If these infants were thus baptized with blood, though it were their own, into the church triumphant, it could not be said but that, with what they got in heaven, they were abundantly recompensed for what they lost on earth. *Out of the mouths of these babes and sucklings God did perfect praise;* otherwise, *it is not good to the Almighty that he should thus afflict.*

The tradition of the Greek church (and we have it in the Æthiopic missal) is, that the number of the children slain was 14,000: but that is very absurd. I believe, if the births of the male children in the weekly bills were computed, there would not be found so many *under two years old,* in one of the most populous cities in the world, much less in Bethlehem, a small town, that was not near a fortieth part of it. But it is an instance of the vanity of tradition. It is strange that Josephus does not relate this story; but he wrote long after St. Matthew, and it is probable that he *therefore* would not relate it, because he would not so far countenance the Christian history; for he was a zealous Jew; but, to be sure, if it had not been true and well attested, he would have contested it. Macrobius, a heathen writer, tells us, that when Augustus Cæsar heard that Herod, among the children he ordered to be slain *under two years old,* slew his own son, he passed this jest upon him, That it was better to be Herod's swine than his son. The usage of the country forbade him to kill a swine, but nothing could restrain him from killing his son. Some think that he had a young child at nurse in Bethlehem; others think that, through mistake, two events are confounded—the murder of the infants, and the murder of his son Antipater. But for the church of Rome to put the Holy Innocents, as they call them, into their calendar, and observe a day in memory of them, while they have so often, by their barbarous massacres, justified, and even out-done Herod, is but to do as their predecessors did, who built the tombs of the prophets, while they themselves filled up the same measure.

Some observe another design of Providence in the murder of the infants. By all the prophecies of the Old Testament it appears that Bethlehem was the place, and this the time, of the Messiah's nativity; now all the children of Bethlehem, born at this time, being murdered, and Jesus only escaping, none but Jesus could pretend to be the Messiah. Herod now thought he had baffled all the Old Testament prophecies, had defeated the indications of the star, and the devotions of the wise men, by ridding the country of this new King; having burnt the hive, he concludes he had killed the master bee; but God in heaven *laughs at* him, *and has* him *in derision.* Whatever crafty cruel devices are in men's hearts, *the counsel of the Lord shall stand.*

III. The fulfilling of the scripture in this (*v.* 17, 18); *Then was fulfilled* that prophecy (Jer. xxxi. 15), *A voice was heard in Ramah.* See and adore the fulness of the scripture! That prediction was accomplished in Jeremiah's time, when Nebuzaradan, after he had destroyed Jerusalem, brought all his prisoners to Ramah (Jer. xl. 1), and there disposed of them as he pleased, for the sword, or for captivity. Then was the cry *in Ramah heard* to Bethlehem (for those two cities, the one in Judah's lot, and the other in Benjamin's, were not far asunder); but now the prophecy is again fulfilled in the great sorrow that was for the death of these infants. The scripture was fulfilled,

1. In the place of this mourning. The noise of it was heard from Bethlehem to Ramah; for Herod's cruelty extended itself to *all the coasts of Bethlehem,* even into the lot of Benjamin, among the children of Rachel. Some think the country about Bethlehem was called *Rachel,* because there she died, and was buried. Rachel's sepulchre was hard by Bethlehem, Gen. xxxv. 16, 19. Compare 1 Sam. x. 2. Rachel had her heart much set upon children: the son she died in travail of she called *Benoni---the son of her sorrow.* These mothers were like Rachel, lived near Rachel's grave, and many of them descended from Rachel; and therefore their lamentations are elegantly represented by *Rachel's weeping.*

2. In the degree of this mourning. It was *lamentation and weeping, and great mourning;* all little enough to express the sense they had of this aggravated calamity. There was a great cry in Egypt when the first-born were slain, and so there was here when the youngest was slain; for whom we naturally have a particular tenderness. Here was a representation of this world we live in. We hear in it *lamentation, and weeping, and mourning,* and see *the tears of the oppressed,* some upon one account, and some upon another. Our way lies through a *vale of tears.* This sorrow was so great, that they *would not be comforted.* They hardened themselves in it, and took a pleasure in their grief. Blessed be God, there is no occasion of grief in this world, no, not that which is supplied by sin itself, that will justify us in refusing to *be comforted!* They *would not be comforted, because they are not,* that is, *they are not* in the land of the living, *are not* as they were, in their mothers' embraces. If, indeed, *they were not,* there might be some excuse for sorrowing as though we had no hope; but we know they are not lost, but gone before; if we forget that *they are,* we lose the best ground of our comfort, 1 Thess. iv. 13. Some make this great grief of the Bethlehemites to be a judgment upon them for their contempt of Christ. They that would not rejoice for the birth of the Son of God, are justly made to weep for the death of their own sons; for they only *wondered* at the tidings the shepherds brought them, but did not *welcome* them.

The quoting of this prophecy might serve to obviate an objection which some would make against Christ, upon this sad providence. "Can the Messiah, who is to be the Consolation of Israel, be introduced with all this lamentation?" Yes, for so it was foretold, and the scripture must be accomplished. And besides, if we look further into this prophecy, we shall find that *the bitter weeping* in Ramah was but a prologue to the greatest joy, for it follows, *Thy work shall be rewarded, and there is hope in thy end.* The worse things are, the sooner they will mend. Unto them a child was born, sufficient to repair their losses.

19 But when Herod was dead, behold, an angel of the Lord appeareth in a dream to Joseph in Egypt,
20 Saying, Arise, and take the young child and his mother, and go into the land of Israel: for they are dead which sought the young child's life.
21 And he arose, and took the young child and his mother, and came into the land of Israel.
22 But when he heard that Archelaus did reign in Judea in the room of his father Herod, he was afraid to go thither: notwithstanding, being warned of God in a dream, he turned aside into the parts of Galilee:
23 And he came and dwelt in a city called Nazareth: that it might be fulfilled which was spoken by the prophets, He shall be called a Nazarene.

We have here Christ's return out of Egypt into the *land of Israel* again. Egypt may serve to sojourn in, or take shelter in, for a while, but not to abide in. Christ was *sent to the lost sheep of the house of Israel,* and therefore to them he must return. Observe,

I. What it was that made way for his return—the death of Herod, which happened not long after the murder of the infants; some think not above three months. Such quick work did divine vengeance make! Note, Herods must die; proud tyrants, that were the terror of the mighty, and the oppressors of the godly, *in the land of the living,* their day must come to fall, and down to the pit they must go. *Who art thou then, that thou shouldest be afraid of a man that shall die?* (Isa. li. 12, 13) especially considering that at death, not only their envy and hatred are perished (Eccl. ix. 6), and they cease from troubling (Job iii. 17), but they are punished. Of all sins, the guilt of innocent blood fills the measure soonest. It is a dreadful account which Josephus gives of the death of this same Herod (Antiq. Jud. lib. xvii. cap. vi. vii.), that he was seized with a disease which burned him inwardly with an inexpressible torture; that he was insatiably greedy of meat; had the colic, and gout, and dropsy; such an intolerable stench attended his disease, that none could come near him: and so passionate and impatient was he, that he was a torment to himself, and a terror to all that attended him: his innate cruelty, being thus exasperated, made him more barbarous than ever; having ordered his own son to be put to death, he imprisoned many of the nobility and gentry, and ordered that as soon as he was dead they should be killed; but that execution was prevented. See what kind of men have been the enemies and persecutors of Christ and his followers! Few have opposed Christianity but such as have first divested themselves of humanity, as Nero and Domitian.

II. The orders given from heaven concerning their return, and Joseph's obedience to those orders, v. 19—21. God had sent Joseph into Egypt, and there he staid till the same that brought him thither ordered him thence. Note, In all our removes, it is good to see our way plain, and God going before us; we should not move either one way or the other without order. These orders were sent him by an angel. Note, Our intercourse with God, if it be kept up on our part, shall be kept up on his, wherever we are. No place can exclude God's gracious visits. Angels come to Joseph in Egypt, to Ezekiel in Babylon, and to John in Patmos. Now, 1. The angel informs him of the death of Herod and his accomplices: *They are dead, which sought the young Child's life.* They are dead, but the young Child lives. Persecuted saints sometimes live to tread upon the graves of their persecutors. Thus did the church's King weather the storm, and many a one has the church in like manner weathered. *They are dead,* to wit, Herod and his son Antipater, who, though there were mutual jealousies between them, yet, probably, concurred in seeking the destruction of this new King. If Herod first kill Antipater, and then die himself, the coasts are cleared, and *the Lord is known by the judgments which he executes,* when one wicked instrument is the ruin of another. 2. He directs him what to do. He must *go* and return *to the land of Israel;* and he did so without delay; not pleading the tolerably good settlement he had in Egypt, or the inconveniences of the journey, especially if, as is supposed, it was in the beginning of winter that Herod died. God's people follow his direction whithersoever he leads them, wherever he lodges them. Did we but look upon the world as our Egypt, the place of our bondage and banishment, and heaven only as our Canaan, our home, our rest, we should as readily *arise,* and depart thither, when we are called for, as Joseph did out of Egypt.

III. The further direction he had from God, which way to steer, and where to fix in the land of Israel, v. 22, 23. God could have given him these instructions with the former, but God reveals his mind to his people by degrees, to keep them still waiting on him, and expecting to hear further from him. These orders Joseph received *in a dream,* probably, as those before, by the ministration of an angel. God could have signified his will to Joseph by the Child Jesus, but we do not find that in those removes he either takes notice, or gives notice, of any thing that occurred; surely it was because *in all things it behoved him to be made like his brethren;* being *a Child,* he *spake as a child,* and did *as a child,* and drew a veil over his infinite knowledge and power; as a child he *increased in wisdom.*

Now the direction given this holy, royal family, is, 1. That it might not settle in Judea, v. 22. Joseph might think that Jesus, being *born in Bethlehem,* must be brought up there; yet he is prudently *afraid* for *the young Child,* because *he hears that Archelaus reigns in* Herod's stead, not over all the kingdom as his father did, but only over Judea, the other provinces being put into other hands. See what a succession of enemies there is to fight against Christ and his church! If one drop off, another presently appears, to keep up the old enmity. But for this reason Joseph must not take the young Child into Judea. Note, God will not thrust his children into the mouth of danger, but when it is for his own glory and their trial; for *precious in the sight of the Lord are the* life and the death *of his saints; precious is their blood* to him.

2. That it must settle in Galilee, *v.* 22. There Philip now ruled, who was a mild, quiet, man. Note, The providence of God commonly so orders it, that his people shall not want a quiet retreat from the storm and from the tempest; when one climate becomes hot and scorching, another shall be kept more cool and temperate. Galilee lay far north; Samaria lay between it and Judea; thither they were sent, to Nazareth, a city upon a hill, in the centre of the lot of Zebulun; there the mother of our Lord lived, when she conceived that *holy thing;* and, probably, Joseph lived there too, Luke i. 26, 27. Thither they were sent, and there they were well known, and were among their relations; the most proper place for them to be in. There they continued, and from thence our Saviour was called *Jesus of Nazareth,* which was to *the Jews a stumbling-block,* for, *Can any good thing come* out of *Nazareth?*

In this is said to be fulfilled what was *spoken by the prophets, He shall be called a Nazarene.* which may be looked upon, (1.) As a name of honour and dignity, though primarily it signifies no more than *a man of Nazareth;* there is an allusion or mystery in it, speaking Christ to be, [1.] The *Man, the Branch,* spoken of, Isaiah xi. 1. The word there is *Netzar,* which signifies either a *branch,* or *the city of Nazareth;* in being denominated from that *city,* he is declared to be that Branch. [2.] It speaks him to be the *great Nazarite;* of whom the legal Nazarites were a type and figure (especially Samson, Judg. xiii. 5), and Joseph, who is called a *Nazarite among his brethren* (Gen. xlix. 26), and to whom that which was prescribed concerning the Nazarites, has reference, Numb. vi. 2, &c. Not that Christ was, *strictly, a Nazarite,* for he drank wine, and touched dead bodies; but he was *emi-*

nently so, both as he was singularly holy, and as he was by a solemn designation and dedication set apart to the honour of God in the work of our redemption, as Samson was to save Israel. And it is a name we have all reason to rejoice in, and to know him by. Or, (2.) As a name of reproach and contempt. To be called a *Nazarene,* was to be called a *despicable man,* a man from whom no good was to be expected, and to whom no respect was to be paid. The devil first fastened this name upon Christ, to render him mean, and prejudice people against him, and it stuck as a nickname to him and his followers. Now this was not particularly foretold by any one prophet, but, in general, it was *spoken by the prophets,* that he should be *despised and rejected of men* (Isa. liii. 2, 3), a *Worm, and no man* (Ps. xxii. 6, 7), that he should be an *Alien to his brethren,* Ps. lxix. 7, 8. Let no name of reproach for religion's sake seem hard to us, when our Master was himself called a *Nazarene.*

CHAP. III.

At the story of this chapter, concerning the baptism of John, begins the gospel (Mark i. 1); what went before is but preface or introduction; this is "the beginning of the gospel of Jesus Christ." And Peter observes the same date, Acts i. 22, beginning from the baptism of John, for then Christ began first to appear in him, and then to appear to him, and by him to the world. Here is, I. The glorious rising of the morning-star—John the Baptist, ver. 1. 1. The doctrine he preached, ver. 2. 2. The fulfilling of the scripture in him, ver. 3. 3. His manner of life, ver. 4. 4. The resort of multitudes to him, and their submission to his baptism, ver. 5, 6. 5. His sermon that he preached to the Pharisees and Sadducees, wherein he endeavours to bring them to repentance (ver. 7—10), and so to bring them to Christ, ver. 11, 12. II. The more glorious shining forth of the Sun of righteousness, immediately after: where we have, 1. The honour done by him to the baptism of John, ver. 13—15. 2. The honour done to him by the descent of the Spirit upon him, and a voice from heaven, ver. 16, 17.

IN those days came John the Baptist, preaching in the wilderness of
Judea, 2 And saying, Repent ye:
for the kingdom of heaven is at hand.
3 For this is he that was spoken of
by the prophet Esaias, saying, The
voice of one crying in the wilderness,
Prepare ye the way of the Lord, make
his paths straight. 4 And the same
John had his raiment of camel's hair,
and a leathern girdle about his loins:
and his meat was locusts and wild
honey. 5 Then went out to him Jerusalem, and all Judea, and all the region
round about Jordan, 6 And were
baptized of him in Jordan, confessing
their sins.

We have here an account of the preaching and baptism of John, which were the dawning of the gospel-day. Observe,

I. The time when he appeared. *In those days* (*v.* 1), or, *after those days,* long after what was recorded in the foregoing chapter, which left the child Jesus in his infancy. *In those days,* in the time appointed of the Father for the beginning of the gospel, when the *fulness of time* was come, which was often thus spoken of in the *Old Testament, In those days.* Now the last of Daniel's weeks began, or rather, the latter half of the last week, when the Messiah was to *confirm the covenant with many,* Dan. ix. 27. Christ's appearances are all in their season. Glorious things were spoken both of John and Jesus, at and before their births, which would have given occasion to expect some extraordinary appearances of a divine presence and power with them when they were very young; but it is quite otherwise. Except Christ's disputing with the doctors at twelve years old, nothing appears remarkable concerning either of them, till they were about thirty years old. Nothing is recorded of their childhood and youth, but the greatest part of their life is *tempus ἄδηλον—wrapt up in darkness and obscurity:* these children differ little in outward appearance from other children, as the heir, while he is under age, differs nothing from a servant, though he be *lord of all.* And this was to show, 1. That even when God is acting as the God of Israel, the *Saviour,* yet *verily he is a God that hideth himself* (Isa. xlv. 15). *The Lord is in this place and I knew it not,* Gen. xxviii. 16. Our beloved stands behind the wall long before he *looks forth at the windows,* Cant. ii. 9. 2. That our faith must principally have an eye to Christ in his office and undertaking, for there is the *display* of his power; but in his person is the *hiding* of his power. All this while, Christ was God-man; yet we are not told what he said or did, till he appeared as a prophet; and then, *Hear ye him.* 3. That young men, though well qualified, should not be forward to put forth themselves in public service, but be humble, and modest, and self-diffident, *swift to hear, and slow to speak.*

Matthew says nothing of the conception and birth of John the Baptist, which is largely related by St. Luke, but finds him at full age, as if dropt from the clouds to preach in the wilderness. For above three hundred years the church had been without prophets; those lights had been long put out, that *he* might be the more desired, who was to be the great prophet. After Malachi there was no prophet, nor any pretender to prophecy, till John the Baptist, to whom therefore the prophet Malachi points more directly than any of the Old Testament prophets had done (Mal. iii. 1); *I send my messenger.*

II. The place where he appeared first. *In the wilderness of Judea.* It was not an uninhabited desert, but a part of the country not so thickly peopled, nor so much enclosed into fields and vineyards, as other parts were; it was such a wilderness as had six cities and their villages in it, which are named, Josh. xv. 61, 62. In these cities and villages John preached, for thereabouts he had hitherto lived, being born hard by, in Hebron; the scenes of his action began there, where he had long spent his time in contemplation;

and even when he showed himself to Israel, he showed how well he loved retirement, as far as would consist with his business. The *word of the Lord* found John here in a *wilderness.* Note, No place is so remote as to shut us out from the visits of divine grace; nay, commonly the sweetest intercourse the saints have with Heaven, is when they are withdrawn furthest from the noise of this world. It was in this *wilderness* of Judah that David penned the 63d Psalm, which speaks so much of the sweet communion he then had with God, Hos. ii. 14. In a wilderness the law was given; and as the *Old Testament,* so the *New Testament Israel* was first found in a desert land, and there God *led him about and instructed him,* Deut. xxxii. 10. John Baptist was a priest of the order of Aaron, yet we find him preaching in a *wilderness,* and never officiating in the *temple;* but Christ, who was not a son of Aaron, is yet often found in the temple, and sitting there as one having authority; so it was foretold, Mal. iii. 1. *The Lord whom ye seek shall suddenly come to his temple;* not the *messenger* that was to prepare his way. This intimated that the priesthood of Christ was to thrust out that of Aaron, and drive it into a wilderness.

The beginning of the gospel in a wilderness, speaks comfort to the deserts of the Gentile world. Now must the prophecies be fulfilled, *I will plant in the wilderness the cedar,* Isa. xli. 18, 19. The wilderness shall be *a fruitful field,* Isa. xxxii. 15. And the *desert shall rejoice,* Isa. xxxv. 1, 2. The Septuagint reads, *the deserts of Jordan,* the very wilderness in which John preached. In the Romish church there are those who call themselves *hermits,* and pretend to follow John; but when they say of Christ, *Behold, he is in the desert, go not forth, ch.* xxiv. 26. There was a seducer that led his followers *into the wilderness,* Acts xxi. 38.

III. His preaching. This he made his business. He came, not fighting, nor disputing, but *preaching* (v. 1); for by the foolishness of preaching, Christ's kingdom must be set up.

1. The doctrine he preached was that of repentance (*v.* 2); *Repent ye.* He preached this in *Judea,* among those that were called *Jews,* and made a profession of religion; for even they needed repentance. He preached it, not in Jerusalem, but in the wilderness of Judea, among the plain country people; for even those who think themselves most out of the way of temptation, and furthest from the vanities and vices of the town, cannot wash their hands in innocency, but must do it in repentance. John Baptist's business was to call men to *repent* of their sins; Μετανοεῖτε—*Bethink yourselves;* "Admit a second *thought,* to correct the errors of the first—an *afterthought.* Consider your ways, *change your minds;* you have thought amiss; *think again,* and *think aright.*" Note, True penitents have *other thoughts* of God and Christ, and sin and holiness, and this world and the other, than they have had, and stand otherwise affected toward them. The change of the *mind* produces a change of the *way.* Those who are truly sorry for what they have done amiss, will be careful to do so no more. This repentance is a necessary duty, in obedience to the command of God (Acts xvii. 30); and a necessary preparative and qualification for the comforts of the gospel of Christ. If the heart of man had continued upright and unstained, divine consolations might have been received without this painful operation preceding; but, being sinful, it must be first pained before it can be laid at ease, must *labour* before it can be at rest. The sore must be searched, or it cannot be cured. *I wound* and *I heal.*

2. The argument he used to enforce this call was, *For the kingdom of heaven is at hand.* The prophets of the *Old Testament* called people to *repent,* for the obtaining and securing of temporal national mercies, and for the preventing and removing of temporal national judgments: but now, though the duty pressed is the same, the reason is new, and purely evangelical. Men are now considered in their personal capacity, and not so much as then in a social and political one. Now repent, for the *kingdom of heaven is at hand;* the gospel dispensation of the covenant of grace, the opening of the kingdom of heaven to all believers, by the death and resurrection of Jesus Christ. It is a *kingdom* of which Christ is the Sovereign, and we must be the willing, loyal subjects of it. It is a kingdom of *heaven,* not of this world, a spiritual kingdom: its original from heaven, its tendency to heaven. John preached this as *at hand;* then it was at the door; to us it is come, by the pouring out of the Spirit, and the full exhibition of the riches of gospel-grace. Now, (1.) This is a great *inducement* to us *to repent.* There is nothing like the consideration of divine grace to break the heart, both *for sin* and *from sin.* That is evangelical repentance, that flows from a sight of Christ, from a sense of his love, and the hopes of pardon and forgiveness through him. Kindness is conquering; abused kindness, humbling and melting. What a wretch was I to sin against such grace, against the law and love of such a kingdom! (2.) It is a *great encouragement* to us *to repent;* "Repent, for your sins shall be pardoned upon your repentance. Return to God in a way of duty, and he will, through Christ, return to you in a way of mercy." The proclamation of pardon discovers, and fetches in, the malefactor who before fled and absconded. Thus are we drawn to it with the cords of a man, and the bands of love.

IV. The *prophecy* that was fulfilled in him, *v.* 3. This is he that was spoken of in the beginning of that part of the prophecy of Esaias, which is mostly evangelical, and which points at gospel-times and gospel-grace; see Isa. xl. 3, 4. John is here spoken of,

1. As the *voice of one crying in the wilderness.* John owned it himself (John i. 23); *I am the voice,* and that is all, God is the Speaker, who makes known his mind by John, as a man does by his voice. The word of God must be received as such (1 Thes. ii. 13); what else is Paul, and what is Apollos, but the voice! John is called the *voice, φωνὴ βοῶντος—the voice of one crying* aloud, which is startling and awakening. Christ is called *the Word,* which, being distinct and articulate, is more instructive. John as the *voice,* roused men, and then Christ, as the *Word,* taught them; as we find, Rev. xiv. 2. The voice of many waters, and of a great thunder, made way for the melodious voice of *harpers* and the *new song, v.* 3. Some observe that, as Samson's mother must drink no *strong drink,* yet he was designed to be a *strong man,* so John Baptist's father was struck dumb, and yet he was designed to be the *voice of one crying.* When the crier's voice is begotten of a dumb father, it shows the *excellency of the power to be of God, and not of man.*

2. As one whose business it was to *prepare the way of the Lord, and to make his paths straight;* so it was said of him before he was born, that he should *make ready a people prepared for the Lord* (Luke i. 17), as Christ's harbinger and forerunner: he was such a one as intimated the nature of Christ's kingdom, for he came not in the gaudy dress of a herald at arms, but in the homely one of a hermit. Officers are sent before great men to clear the way; so John prepares the way of the Lord. (1.) He himself did so among the men of that generation. In the Jewish church and nation, at that time, all was out of course; there was a great decay of piety, the vitals of religion were corrupted and eaten out by the traditions and injunctions of the elders. The *Scribes* and *Pharisees,* that is, the greatest hypocrites in the world, had the key of knowledge, and the key of government, at their girdle. The people were, generally, extremely proud of their privileges, confident of justification by their own righteousness, insensible of sin; and, though now under the most *humbling* providences, being lately made a province of the Roman Empire, yet they were *unhumbled;* they were much in the same temper as they were in Malachi's time, insolent and haughty, and ready to contradict the word of God: now John was sent to level these mountains, to take down their high opinion of themselves, and to show them their sins, that the doctrine of Christ might be the more acceptable and effectual. (2.) His doctrine of repentance and humiliation is still as necessary as it was then to prepare the way of the Lord. Note, There is a great deal to be done, to make way for Christ into a soul, to *bow the heart* for the reception of the Son of David (2 Sam. xix. 14); and nothing is more needful, in order to this, than the discovery of sin, and a conviction of the insufficiency of our own righteousness. That which lets will let, until it be taken out of the way; prejudices must be removed, high thoughts brought down, and captivated to the obedience of Christ. Gates of brass must be broken, and bars of iron cut asunder, ere the everlasting doors be opened for the King of glory to come in. The way of sin and Satan is a *crooked way;* to prepare a way for Christ, the paths must be *made straight,* Heb. xii. 13.

V. The garb in which he appeared, the figure he made, and the manner of his life, *v.* 4. They, who expected the Messiah as a temporal prince, would think that his forerunner must come in great pomp and splendour, that his equipage should be very magnificent and gay; but it proves quite contrary; he shall be *great in the sight of the Lord,* but mean in the eye of the world; and, as Christ himself, having *no form or comeliness;* to intimate betimes, that the glory of Christ's kingdom was to be spiritual, and the subjects of it such as ordinarily were either *found* by *it,* or *made* by it, poor and despised, who derived their honours, pleasures, and riches, from another world.

1. His *dress* was *plain.* This same John had *his raiment of camel's hair, and a leathern girdle about his loins;* he did not go in *long clothing,* as the *scribes,* or *soft clothing,* as the courtiers, but in the clothing of a country husbandman; for he lived in a country place, and suited his *habit* to his *habitation.* Note, It is good for us to accommodate ourselves to the place and condition which God, in his providence, has put us in. John appeared in this dress, (1.) To show that, like Jacob, he was a *plain man,* and mortified to this world, and the delights and gaieties of it. *Behold an Israelite indeed!* Those that are *lowly in heart* should show it by a holy negligence and indifference in their attire; and not make the putting on of apparel their adorning, nor value others by their attire. (2.) To show that he was a *prophet,* for prophets wore *rough garments,* as mortified men (Zech. xiii. 4); and, especially, to show that he was the Elias promised; for particular notice is taken of Elias, that he was a *hairy man* (which, some think, is meant of the hairy garments he wore), and that *he was girt with a girdle of leather about his loins,* 2 Kings i. 8. John Baptist appears no way inferior to him in mortification; this therefore is *that* Elias *that was to come.* (3.) To show that he was a man of resolution; his girdle was not *fine,* such as were then commonly worn, but it was *strong,* it was a *leathern girdle;* and blessed is that servant, whom his Lord, when he comes, finds with *his loins girt,* Luke xii. 35; 1 Pet. i. 13.

2. His *diet* was *plain;* his *meat* was *locusts*

and *wild honey;* not as if he never ate any thing else; but these he frequently fed upon, and made many meals of them, when he retired into solitary places, and continued long there for contemplation. *Locusts* were a sort of flying insect, very good for food, and allowed as clean (Lev. xi. 22); they required little dressing, and were light, and easy of digestion, whence it is reckoned among the infirmities of old age, that the *grasshopper,* or *locust,* is then *a burden* to the stomach, Eccl. xii. 5. *Wild honey* was that which *Canaan* flowed with, 1 Sam. xiv. 26. Either it was gathered immediately, as it fell in the dew, or rather, as it was found in the hollows of trees and rocks, where bees built, that were not, like those in hives, under the care and inspection of men. This intimates that he ate *sparingly,* a little served his turn; a man would be long ere he filled his belly with locusts and wild honey: *John Baptist* came *neither eating nor drinking (ch.* xi. 18)—not with the curiosity, formality, and familiarity that other people do. He was so entirely taken up with spiritual things, that he could seldom find time for a set meal. Now, (1.) This agreed with the doctrine he preached of *repentance,* and *fruits meet for repentance.* Note, Those whose business it is to call others to mourn for sin, and to mortify it, ought themselves to live a serious life, a life of self-denial, mortification, and contempt of the world. John Baptist thus showed the deep sense he had of the badness of the time and place he lived in, which made the preaching of repentance needful; every day was a *fast-day* with him. (2.) This agreed with his office as Christ's *forerunner;* by this practice he showed that he knew what the *kingdom of heaven* was, and had experienced the powers of it. Note, Those that are acquainted with divine and spiritual pleasures, cannot but look upon all the delights and ornaments of sense with a holy indifference; they know better things. By giving others this example he made way for Christ. Note, A conviction of the vanity of the world, and every thing in it, is the best preparative for the entertainment of the kingdom of heaven in the heart. *Blessed are the poor in spirit.*

VI. The people who attended upon him, and flocked after him (*v.* 5); *Then went out to him Jerusalem, and all Judea.* Great multitudes came to him from the city, and from all parts of the country; some of all sorts, men and women, young and old, rich and poor, Pharisees and publicans; they *went out to him,* as soon as they heard of his preaching the *kingdom of heaven,* that they might hear what they heard so much of. Now, 1. This was a great *honour* put upon John, that so many attended him, and with so much respect. Note, Frequently those have most real honour done them, who least court the shadow of it. Those who live a mortified life, who are humble and self-denying, and dead to the world, command respect; and men have a secret value and reverence for them, more than one would imagine. 2. This gave John a great opportunity of doing good, and was an evidence that God was with him. Now people begin to crowd and *press into the kingdom of heaven* (Luke xvi. 16); and a blessed sight it was, to see the *dew of the youth* dropping *from the womb* of the gospel-morning (Ps. cx. 3), to see the net cast where there were so many fish. 3. This was an evidence, that it was now a time of great expectation; it was generally thought that the *kingdom of God* would presently *appear* (Luke xix. 11), and therefore, when John showed himself to Israel, lived and preached at this rate, so very different from the Scribes and Pharisees, they were ready to say of him, that he was *the Christ* (Luke iii. 15); and this occasioned such a confluence of people about him. 4. Those who would have the benefit of John's ministry must *go out* to him in the wilderness, sharing in his reproach. Note, They who truly desire the sincere milk of the word, if it be not brought to them, will seek out for it: and they who would learn the doctrine of repentance must *go out* from the hurry of this world, and be still. 5. It appears by the issue, that of the many who came to John's Baptism, there were but few that adhered to it; witness the cold reception Christ had in Judea, and about Jerusalem. Note, There may be a multitude of forward hearers, where there are but a few true believers. Curiosity, and affectation of novelty and variety, may bring many to attend upon good preaching, and to be affected with it for a while, who yet are never subject to the power of it, Ezek. xxxiii. 31, 32.

VII. The rite, or ceremony, by which he admitted disciples, *v.* 6. Those who received his doctrine, and submitted to his discipline, were *baptized of him in Jordan,* thereby professing their repentance, and their belief that the kingdom of the Messiah was at hand. 1. They testified their repentance by *confessing their sins;* a general confession, it is probable, they made to John that they were *sinners,* that they were polluted by sin, and needed cleansing; but to God they made a confession of particular sins, for he is the party offended. The Jews had been taught to *justify* themselves; but John teaches them to *accuse* themselves, and not to rest, as they used to do, in the general confession of sin made for all Israel, once a year, upon the day of atonement; but to make a particular acknowledgment, every one, of *the plague of his own heart.* Note, A penitent confession of sin is required in order to peace and pardon; and those only are ready to receive Jesus Christ as their Righteousness, who are brought with sorrow and shame to own their guilt, 1 John i. 9. 2. The benefits of the *kingdom of heaven,* now *at hand,* were thereupon sealed to them by baptism. He washed them with water, in token of this—that from all their iniquities God would *cleanse them.* It was usual with the Jews to baptize those whom they admitted proselytes to their religion, especially those who were only *Proselytes of the gate*, and were not circumcised, as the *Proselytes of righteousness* were. Some think it was likewise a custom for persons of eminent religion, who set up for leaders, by baptism to admit pupils and disciples. Christ's question concerning John's Baptism, Was it *from heaven*, or *of men?* implied, that there were baptisms of men, who pretended not to a divine mission; with this usage John complied, but *his* was from heaven, and was distinguished from all others by this character, It was *the baptism of repentance*, Acts xix. 4. All Israel were baptized unto Moses, 1 Cor. x. 2. The *ceremonial law* consisted in *divers washings or baptisms* (Heb. ix. 10); but John's baptism refers to the remedial law, the law of repentance and faith. He is said to baptize them in Jordan, that river which was famous for Israel's passage through it, and Naaman's cure; yet it is probable that John did not baptize in that river at first, but that afterward, when the people who came to his baptism were numerous, he removed to Jordan. By baptism he obliged them to live a holy life, according to the profession they took upon themselves. Note, Confession of sin must always be accompanied with holy resolutions, in the strength of divine grace, not to return to it again.

7 But when he saw many of the
Pharisees and Sadducees come to his
baptism, he said unto them, O generation of vipers, who hath warned
you to flee from the wrath to come?
8 Bring forth therefore fruits meet
for repentance: 9 And think not to
say within yourselves, We have Abraham to *our* father: for I say unto
you, that God is able of these stones
to raise up children unto Abraham.
10 And now also the axe is laid unto
the root of the trees: therefore every
tree which bringeth not forth good
fruit is hewn down, and cast into the
fire. 11 I indeed baptize you with
water unto repentance: but he that
cometh after me is mightier than I,
whose shoes I am not worthy to
bear: he shall baptize you with the
Holy Ghost, and *with* fire. 12 Whose
fan *is* in his hand, and he will
throughly purge his floor, and gather
his wheat into the garner; but he
will burn up the chaff with unquenchable fire.

The doctrine John preached was that of repentance, in consideration of the *kingdom of heaven* being *at hand;* now here we have the use of that doctrine. Application is the life of preaching, so it was of John's preaching.

Observe, 1. To whom he applied it; to the Pharisees and Sadducees that came to his baptism, *v.* 7. To others he thought it enough to say, *Repent, for the kingdom of heaven is at hand;* but when he saw these Pharisees and Sadducees come about him, he found it necessary to explain himself, and deal more closely. These were two of the three noted sects among the Jews at that time, the third was that of the Essenes, whom we never read of in the gospels, for they affected retirement, and declined busying themselves in public affairs. The Pharisees were zealots for the ceremonies, for the power of the church, and the traditions of the elders; the Sadducees ran into the other extreme, and were little better than deists, denying the existence of spirits and a future state. It was strange that they came to John's baptism, but their curiosity brought them to be hearers; and some of them, it is probable, submitted to be baptized, but it is certain that the generality of them did not; for Christ says (Luke vii. 29, 30), that *when the publicans justified God, and were baptized of John, the Pharisees and lawyers rejected the counsel of God against themselves, being not baptized of him.* Note, Many come to ordinances, who come not under the power of them. Now to them John here addresses himself with all faithfulness, and what he said to them, he said to the multitude (Luke iii. 7), for they were all concerned in what he said. 2. What the application was. It is plain and home, and directed to their consciences; he speaks as one that came not to preach *before* them, but to preach *to* them. Though his education was private, he was not bashful when he appeared in public, nor did he fear the face of man, for he was full of the Holy Ghost, and of power.

I. Here is a word of conviction and awakening. He begins harshly, calls them not Rabbi, gives them not the titles, much less the applauses, they had been used to. 1. The *title* he gives them is, *O generation of vipers.* Christ gave them the same title; *ch.* xii. 34; xxiii. 33. They were as *vipers;* though specious, yet venomous and poisonous, and full of malice and enmity to every thing that was good; they were a *viperous brood,* the seed and offspring of such as had been of the same spirit; it was bred in the bone with them. They gloried in it, that they were the seed of Abraham; but John showed them that they were the serpent's seed (compare Gen. iii. 15); of their father the Devil, John viii. 44. They were a *viperous gang,* they were all alike; though enemies to one another, yet confederate in mischief. Note, A wicked generation is a *generation of vipers,* and they ought to be told so; it becomes the ministers of Christ to be bold in showing sinners their true character. 2. The *alarm* he gives them is, *Who has warned you to flee from the wrath to come?* This intimates that they were in danger of the wrath to come; and that their case was so nearly desperate, and their hearts so hardened in sin (the Pharisees by their parade of religion, and the Sadducees by their arguments against religion), that it was next to a miracle to effect any thing hopeful among them. "What brings you hither? Who thought of seeing you here? What fright have you been put into, that you enquire after the kingdom of heaven?" Note, (1.) There is a *wrath to come;* besides present wrath, the vials of which are poured out now, there is future wrath, the stores of which are treasured up for hereafter. (2.) It is the great concern of every one of us to flee from this wrath. (3.) It is wonderful mercy that we are fairly warned to flee from this wrath; think—*Who has warned us?* God has warned us, who delights not in our ruin; he warns by the written word, by ministers, by conscience. (4.) These warnings sometimes startle those who seemed to have been very much hardened in their security and good opinion of themselves.

II. Here is a word of *exhortation* and *direction* (*v.* 8); "*Bring forth therefore fruits meet for repentance. Therefore,* because you are *warned to flee from the wrath to come,* let the terrors of the Lord persuade you to a holy life." Or, "*Therefore,* because you profess repentance, and attend upon the doctrine and baptism of repentance, evidence that you are true penitents." Repentance is seated in the heart. There it is as a root; but in vain do we pretend to have it there, if we do not *bring forth the fruits* of it in a universal reformation, forsaking all sin, and cleaving to that which is good; these are fruits, ἄξιους τῆς μετάνοιας—*worthy of repentance.* Note, Those are not worthy the name of penitents, or their privileges, who say they are sorry for their sins, and yet persist in them. They that profess repentance, as all that are baptized do, must be and act as becomes penitents, and never do any thing unbecoming a penitent sinner. It becomes penitents to be humble and low in their own eyes, to be thankful for the least mercy, patient under the greatest affliction, to be watchful against all appearances of sin, and approaches towards it, to abound in every duty, and to be charitable in judging others.

III. Here is a word of caution, not to trust to their external privileges, so as with them to shift off these calls to repentance (*v.* 9); *Think not to say within yourselves, We have Abraham to our father.* Note, There is a great deal which carnal hearts are apt to say within themselves, to put by the convincing, commanding power of the word of God, which ministers should labour to meet with and anticipate; vain thoughts which lodge within those who are called to *wash their hearts,* Jer. iv. 14. Μὴ δόξητε—"*Pretend not, presume not,* to say within yourselves; be not of the opinion that this will save you; harbour not such a conceit. *Please not yourselves* with saying this" (so some read it); "rock not yourselves asleep with this, nor flatter yourselves into a fool's paradise." Note, God takes notice of what we say *within* ourselves, which we dare not speak out, and is acquainted with all the false rests of the soul, and the fallacies with which it deludes itself, but which it will not discover, lest it should be undeceived. Many hide the lie that ruins them, in *their right hand,* and roll it *under their tongue,* because they are ashamed to own it; they keep in the Devil's interest, by keeping the Devil's counsel. Now John shows them,

1. What their pretence was; "*We have Abraham to our father;* we are not sinners of the Gentiles; it is fit indeed that *they* should be called to repent; but we are Jews, a holy nation, a peculiar people, what is this to us?" Note, The word does us no good, when we will not take it as spoken to us, and belonging to us. "Think not that because you are the seed of Abraham, therefore," (1.) "You *need not repent,* you have nothing to repent of; your relation to Abraham, and your interest in the covenant made with him, denominate you so holy, that there is no occasion for you to change your mind or way." (2.) "That therefore you shall *fare well enough,* though you do not *repent.* Think not that this will bring you off in the judgment, and secure you from the wrath to come; that God will connive at your impenitence, because you are Abraham's seed." Note, It is vain presumption to think that our having good relations will save us, though we be not good ourselves. What though we be descended from pious ancestors; have been blessed with a religious education; have our lot cast in families where the fear of God is uppermost; and have good friends to advise us, and pray for us; what will all this avail us, if we do not repent, and live a life of repentance? We have Abraham to our father, and therefore are entitled to the privileges of the covenant made with him; being his seed, we are *sons of the church, the temple of the Lord,* Jer. vii. 4. Note, Multitudes, by resting in the honours and advantages of their visible church-membership, take up short of heaven.

2. How foolish and groundless this pretence was; they thought that being the seed of Abraham, they were the only people God had in the world, and therefore that, if they were cut off, he would be at a loss for a church; but John shows them the folly of this conceit; *I say unto you* (whatever you say within yourselves), that *God is able of these stones to raise up children unto Abraham.* He was now baptizing in Jordan at Bethabara (John i. 28), *the house of passage,* where the children of *Israel passed over;* and there were the twelve stones, one for each tribe,

which Joshua set up for a memorial, Josh. iv. 20. It is not unlikely that he pointed to those stones, which God could raise to be, more than in representation, the *twelve tribes of Israel*. Or perhaps he refers to Isa. li. 1, where Abraham is called *the rock out of which they were hewn*. That God who raised Isaac out of such a rock, can, if there be occasion, do as much again, for with him *nothing is impossible*. Some think he pointed to those *heathen soldiers* that were present, telling the Jews that God would raise up a church for himself among the Gentiles, and entail the blessing of Abraham upon them. Thus when our first parents fell, God could have left them to perish, and out of stones have raised up another Adam and another Eve. Or, take it thus, "Stones themselves shall be owned as Abraham's seed, rather than such hard, dry, barren sinners as you are." Note, As it is lowering to the confidence of the sinners in Zion, so it is encouraging to the hopes of the sons of Zion, that, whatever comes of the present generation, God will never want a church in the world; if the Jews fall off, the Gentiles shall be grafted in, *ch.* xxi. 43; Rom. xi. 12, &c.

IV. Here is a word of terror to the careless and secure Pharisees and Sadducees, and other Jews, that knew not the signs of the times, nor the day of their visitation, *v.* 10. "Now look about you, now that *the kingdom of God is at hand*, and be made sensible."

1. "How strict and short your trial is; *Now the axe* is carried before you, now it is *laid to the root of the tree*, now you are upon *your good behaviour*, and are to be so but a *while;* now you are marked for ruin, and cannot avoid it but by a speedy and sincere repentance. Now you must expect that God will make quicker work with you by his judgments than he did formerly, and that they will *begin at the house of God:* where God allows more means, he allows less time." *Behold, I come quickly*. Now they were put upon their last trial; now or never.

2. "How sore and severe your doom will be, if you do not improve this." It is now declared with the axe at the root, to show that God is in earnest in the declaration, that *every tree*, however *high* in gifts and honours, however *green* in external professions and performances, if it *bring not forth good fruit*, the fruits meet for repentance, is *hewn down*, disowned as a tree in God's vineyard, unworthy to have room there, and is *cast into the fire* of God's wrath—the fittest place for barren trees: what else are they good for? If not fit for fruit, they are fit for fuel. Probably this refers to the destruction of Jerusalem by the Romans, which was not, as other judgments had been, like the lopping off of the branches, or cutting down of the body of the tree, leaving the root to bud again, but it would be the total, final, and irrecoverable extirpation of that people, in which all those should perish that continued impenitent. Now God would make a full end, wrath was coming on them to the utmost.

V. A word of instruction concerning Jesus Christ, in whom all John's preaching centred. Christ's ministers preach, not themselves, but him. Here is,

1. The dignity and pre-eminence of Christ above John. See how meanly he speaks of himself, that he might magnify Christ (*v.* 11); "*I indeed baptize you with water*, that is the utmost I can do." Note, Sacraments derive not their efficacy from those who administer them; they can only apply the sign; it is Christ's prerogative to give the thing signified, 1 Cor. iii. 6; 2 Kings iv. 31. But *he that comes after me is mightier than I*. Though John had much power, for he came in the *spirit and power of Elias*, Christ had more; though John was truly great, great in the sight of the Lord (not a greater was born of woman), yet he thinks himself unworthy to be in the meanest place of attendance upon Christ, *whose shoes I am not worthy to bear*. He sees, (1.) How mighty Christ is, in comparison with him. Note, It is a great comfort to faithful ministers, to think that Jesus Christ is mightier than they, can do that *for* them, and that *by* them, which they cannot do; his strength is perfected in their weakness. (2.) How mean he is in comparison with Christ, not worthy to carry his shoes after him! Note, Those whom God puts honour upon, are thereby made very humble and low in their own eyes; willing to be abased, so that Christ may be magnified; to be any thing, to be nothing, so that Christ may be all.

2. The design and intention of Christ's appearing, which they were now speedily to expect. When it was prophesied that John should be sent as Christ's forerunner (Mal. iii. 1, 2), it immediately follows, *The Lord, whom ye seek, shall suddenly come*, and shall *sit as a refiner*, *v.* 3. And after the coming of Elijah, *the day comes that shall burn as an oven* (Mal. iv. 1), to which the Baptist seems here to refer. Christ will come to make a distinction,

(1.) By the powerful working of his grace; *He shall baptize you*, that is, some of you, *with the Holy Ghost and with fire*. Note, [1.] It is Christ's prerogative to baptize *with the Holy Ghost*. This he did in the extraordinary gifts of the Spirit conferred upon the apostles, to which Christ himself applies these words of John, Acts i. 5. This he does in the graces and comforts of the Spirit given to them that ask him, Luke xi. 13; John vii. 38, 39; See Acts xi. 16. [2.] They who are baptized with the Holy Ghost are baptized as *with fire;* the seven spirits of God appear as *seven lamps of fire*, Rev. iv. 5. Is fire enlightening? So the Spirit is a Spirit of illumination. Is it warming? And do not their hearts burn within them? Is it consuming? And does not the Spirit of judgment, as a *Spirit of burning*, consume the dross of their corruptions? Does fire make all it seizes like itself? And does it move upwards? So does the Spirit make the soul holy like itself, and its tendency is heaven-ward. Christ says *I am come to send fire,* Luke xii. 49.

(2.) By the final determinations of his judgment (*v.* 12); *Whose fan is in his hand.* His ability to distinguish, as the eternal wisdom of the Father, who sees all by a true light, and his authority to distinguish, as the Person to whom all judgment is committed, is the *fan* that is *in his hand,* Jer. xv. 7. Now he sits as a Refiner. Observe here, [1.] The visible church is Christ's floor; *O my threshing, and the corn of my floor,* Isa. xxi. 10. The temple, a type of the church, was built upon a threshing-floor. [2.] In this floor there is a mixture of wheat and chaff. True believers are as wheat, substantial, useful, and valuable; hypocrites are as chaff, light, and empty, useless and worthless, and carried about with every wind; these are now mixed, good and bad, under the same external profession; and in the same visible communion. [3.] There is a day coming when the floor shall be purged, and the wheat and chaff shall be separated. Something of this kind is often done in this world, when God calls his people out of Babylon, Rev. xviii. 4. But it is the day of the last judgment that will be the great winnowing, distinguishing day, which will infallibly determine concerning doctrines and works (1 Cor. iii. 13), and concerning persons (*ch.* xxv. 32, 33), when saints and sinners shall be parted for ever. [4.] Heaven is the garner into which Jesus Christ will shortly gather all his wheat, and not a grain of it shall be lost: he will gather them as the ripe fruits were gathered in. Death's scythe is made use of to gather them to their people. In heaven the saints are brought together, and no longer scattered; they are safe, and no longer exposed; separated from corrupt neighbours without, and corrupt affections within, and there is no chaff among them. They are not only gathered into *the barn* (*ch.* xiii. 30), but into *the garner,* where they are thoroughly purified. [5.] Hell is the *unquenchable fire,* which will burn up the chaff, which will certainly be the portion and punishment, and everlasting destruction, of hypocrites and unbelievers. So that here are life and death, good and evil, set before us; according as we now are in the *field,* we shall be then in the *floor.*

13 Then cometh Jesus from Galilee
to Jordan unto John, to be baptized
of him. 14 But John forbad him,
saying, I have need to be baptized of
thee, and comest thou to me? 15 And
Jesus answering said unto him, Suffer
it to be so now: for thus it becometh
us to fulfil all righteousness. Then
he suffered him. 16 And Jesus, when
he was baptized, went up straightway
out of the water; and, lo, the heavens
were opened unto him, and he saw the
Spirit of God descending like a dove,
and lighting upon him: 17 And, lo,
a voice from heaven, saying, This is
my beloved Son, in whom I am well
pleased.

Our Lord Jesus, from his childhood till now, when he was almost thirty years of age, had lain hid in Galilee, as it were, buried alive; but now, after a long and dark night, behold, *the Sun of righteousness* rises in glory. *The fulness of time was come* that Christ should enter upon his prophetical office; and he chooses to do it, not at Jerusalem (though it is probable that he went thither at the three yearly feasts, as others did), but there *where John was baptizing;* for to him resorted those who *waited for the consolation of Israel,* to whom alone he would be welcome. John the Baptist was six months older than our Saviour, and it is supposed that he began to preach and baptize about six months before Christ appeared; so long he was employed in preparing his way, *in the region round about Jordan;* and more was done towards it in these six months than had been done in several ages before. Christ's coming from Galilee *to Jordan, to be baptized,* teaches us not to shrink from pain and toil, that we may have an opportunity of drawing nigh to God in an ordinance. We should be willing to go far, rather than come short of communion with God. They who will find must seek.

Now in this story of Christ's baptism we may observe,

I. How hardly John was persuaded to admit of it, *v.* 14, 15. It was an instance of Christ's great humility, that he would offer himself *to be baptized of John;* that he *who knew no sin* would submit to the baptism of repentance. Note, As soon as ever Christ began to preach, he preached humility, preached it by his example, preached it to all, especially to young ministers. Christ was designed for the highest honours, yet in his first step he thus abases himself. Note, Those who would rise high must begin low. *Before honour is humility.* It was a great piece of respect done to John, for Christ thus to come to him; and it was a return for the service he did him, in giving notice of his approach. Note, Those that honour God he will honour. Now here we have,

1. The objection that John made against baptizing Jesus, *v.* 14. *John forbade him,* as Peter did, when Christ went about to wash his feet, John xiii. 6, 8. Note, Christ's gracious condescensions are so surprising, as to appear at first incredible to the strongest believers; so deep and mysterious, that even they who know his mind well cannot soon find out the meaning of them, but, *by reason*

of darkness, start objections against the will of Christ. John's modesty thinks this an honour too great for him to receive, and he expresses himself to Christ, just as his mother had done to Christ's mother (Luke i. 43); *Whence is this to me, that the mother of my Lord should come to me?* John had now obtained a great name, and was universally respected: yet see how humble he is still! Note, God has further honours in reserve for those whose spirits continue low when their reputation rises.

(1.) John thinks it necessary that he should be baptized of Christ; *I have need to be baptized of thee* with the baptism of the Holy Ghost, as of fire, for that was Christ's baptism, *v.* 11. [1.] Though *John was filled with the Holy Ghost from the womb* (Luke i. 15), yet he acknowledges he had need to be baptized with that baptism. Note, They who have much of the Spirit of God, yet, while here, in this imperfect state, see that they have need of more, and need to apply themselves to Christ for more. [2.] *John has need to be baptized,* though he was the *greatest that ever was born of woman;* yet, being born of a woman, he is polluted, as others of Adam's seed are, and owns he has need of cleansing. Note, The purest souls are most sensible of their own remaining impurity, and seek most earnestly for spiritual washing. [3.] He has *need to be baptized of* Christ, who can do that for us, which no one else can, and which must be done for us, or we are undone. Note, The best and holiest of men *have need of* Christ, and the better they are, the more they see of that need. [4.] This was said before the multitude, who had a great veneration for John, and were ready to embrace him for the Messiah; yet he publicly owns that he had *need to be baptized of* Christ. Note, It is no disparagement to the greatest of men, to confess that they are undone without Christ and his grace. [5.] John was Christ's forerunner, and yet owns that he had *need to be baptized of* him. Note, Even they who were before Christ in time depended on him, received from him, and had an eye to him. [6.] While John was dealing with others about their souls, observe how feelingly he speaks of the case of his own soul, *I have need to be baptized of thee.* Note, Ministers, who preach to others, and baptize others, are concerned to look to it that they preach to themselves, and be themselves baptized with the Holy Ghost. Take heed to thyself first; *save thyself,* 1 Tim. iv. 16.

(2.) He therefore thinks it very preposterous and absurd, that Christ should be baptized by him; *Comest thou to me?* Does the holy Jesus, that is separated from sinners, come to be baptized by a sinner, as a sinner, and among sinners? How can this be? Or what account can we give of it? Note, Christ's coming to us may well be wondered at.

2. The overruling of this objection (*v.* 15); *Jesus said, Suffer it to be so now.* Christ accepted his humility, but not his refusal; he will have the thing done; and it is fit that Christ should take his own method, though we do not understand it, nor can give a reason for it. See,

(1.) How Christ insists upon it; It must *be so now.* He does not deny that *John had need to be baptized of* him, yet he will now be *baptized of John.* Ἄφὲς ἄρτι—*Let it be yet so; suffer it to be so now.* Note, Every thing is beautiful in its season. But why *now?* Why yet? [1.] Christ is *now* in a state of humiliation: he has emptied himself, and *made himself of no reputation.* He is not only *found in fashion as a man,* but is *made in the likeness of sinful flesh,* and therefore now let him be *baptized of John;* as if he needed to be washed, though perfectly pure; and thus he *was made sin for us,* though he *knew no sin.* [2.] John's baptism is now in reputation, it is that by which God is now doing his work; that is the present dispensation, and therefore Jesus will now be baptized with water; but his baptizing with the Holy Ghost is reserved for hereafter, *many days hence,* Acts i. 5. John's baptism has *now* its day, and therefore honour must *now* be put upon that, and they who attend upon it must be encouraged. Note, They who are of greatest attainments in gifts and graces, should yet, in their place, bear their testimony to instituted ordinances, by a humble and diligent attendance on them, that they may give a good example to others. What we see God owns, and while we see he does so, we must own. John was now increasing, and therefore it must be thus yet; shortly he will decrease, and then it will be otherwise. [3.] It must *be so now,* because now is the time for Christ's appearing in public, and this will be a fair opportunity for it, See John i. 31—34. Thus he must be made manifest to Israel, and be signalized by wonders from heaven, in that act of his own, which was most condescending and self-abasing.

(2.) The reason he gives for it; *Thus it becomes us to fulfil all righteousness.* Note, [1.] There was a propriety in every thing that Christ did for us; it was all graceful (Heb. ii. 10; vii. 26); and we must study to do not only that which behoves us, but that which becomes us; not only that which is indispensably necessary, but that which is *lovely, and of good report.* [2.] Our Lord Jesus looked upon it as a thing well becoming him, *to fulfil all righteousness,* that is (as Dr. Whitby explains it), to own every divine institution, and to show his readiness to comply with all God's righteous precepts. *Thus it becomes* him to justify God, and approve his wisdom, in sending John to prepare his way by the baptism of repentance. *Thus it becomes us* to countenance and encourage every thing that is good, by pattern as well as precept. Christ often mentioned John and his baptism with honour, which that he might do the better, he was himself baptized. Thus Jesus began *first to do, and then to teach;* and his ministers must take the same method. Thus *Christ filled up the righteousness of the ceremonial law,* which consisted in divers washings; thus he recommended the gospel-ordinance of baptism to his church, put honour upon it, and showed what virtue he designed to put into it. It became Christ to submit to John's washing with water, because it was a divine appointment; but it became him to oppose the Pharisees' washing with water, because it was a human invention and imposition; and he justified his disciples in refusing to comply with it.

With the will of Christ, and this reason for it, John was entirely satisfied, and *then he suffered him.* The same modesty which made him at first decline the honour Christ offered him, now made him do the service Christ enjoined him. Note, No pretence of humility must make us decline our duty.

II. How solemnly Heaven was pleased to grace the baptism of Christ with a special display of glory (*v.* 16, 17); *Jesus when he was baptized, went up straightway out of the water.* Others that were baptized staid to *confess their sins* (*v.* 6); but Christ, having no sins to confess, *went up* immediately *out of the water;* so we read it, but not right: for it is ἀπὸ τοῦ ὕδατος—*from the water;* from the brink of the river, to which he went down to be washed with water, that is, to have his head or face washed (John xiii. 9); for here is no mention of the putting off, or putting on, of his clothes, which circumstance would not have been omitted, if he had been baptized naked. *He went up straightway,* as one that entered upon his work with the utmost cheerfulness and resolution; he would lose no time. *How was he straitened till it was accomplished!*

Now, when he was coming *up out of the water,* and all the company had their eye upon him,

1. *Lo! the heavens were opened unto him,* so as to discover something above and beyond the starry firmament, at least, to him. This was, (1.) To encourage him to go on in his undertaking, with the prospect of the glory and *joy that were set before him.* Heaven is opened to receive him, when he has finished the work he is now entering upon. (2.) To encourage us to receive him, and submit to him. Note, In and through Jesus Christ, the heavens are opened to the children of men. Sin shut up heaven, put a stop to all friendly intercourse between God and man; but now Christ *has opened the kingdom of heaven to all believers.* Divine light and love are darted down upon the children of men, and *we have boldness to enter into the holiest.* We have receipts of mercy from God, we make returns of duty to God, and all by Jesus Christ, who is the ladder that has its foot on earth and its top in heaven, by whom alone it is that we have any comfortable correspondence with God, or any hope of getting to heaven at last. *The heavens were opened* when Christ was baptized, to teach us, that when we duly attend on God's ordinances, we may expect communion with him, and communications from him.

2. *He saw the Spirit of God descending like a dove,* or *as a dove, and* coming or *lighting upon him.* Christ saw it (Mark i. 10), and John saw it (John i. 33, 34), and it is probable that all the standers-by saw it; for this was intended to be his public inauguration. Observe,

(1.) *The Spirit of God descended, and lighted on him.* In the beginning of the old world, *the Spirit of God moved upon the face of the waters* (Gen i. 2), *hovered* as a bird upon the nest. So here, in the beginning of this new world, Christ, as God, needed not to receive the Holy Ghost, but it was foretold that *the Spirit of the Lord should rest upon him* (Isa. xi. 2; lxi. 1), and here he did so; for, [1.] He was to be a Prophet; and prophets always spoke by the Spirit of God, who came upon them. Christ was to execute the prophetic office, not by his divine nature (says Dr. Whitby), but by the afflatus of the Holy Spirit. [2.] He was to be the Head of the church; and *the Spirit descended upon him,* by him to be derived to all believers, in his gifts, graces, and comforts. *The ointment on the head ran down to the skirts;* Christ *received gifts for men,* that he might give *gifts to men.*

(2.) He *descended on him like a dove;* whether it was a real, living dove, or, as was usual in visions, the representation or similitude of a dove, is uncertain. If there must be a bodily shape (Luke iii. 22), it must not be that of a man, for the being seen *in fashion as a man* was peculiar to the second person: none therefore was more fit than the shape of one of the fowls of heaven (heaven being now opened), and of all fowl none was so significant as the dove. [1.] The Spirit of Christ is a dove-like spirit; not like *a silly dove, without heart* (Hos. vii. 11), but like an innocent dove, without gall. *The Spirit descended,* not in the shape of an eagle, which is, though a royal bird, yet a bird of prey, but *in the shape of a dove,* than which no creature is more harmless and inoffensive. Such was the Spirit of Christ: *He shall not strive, nor cry;* such must Christians be, *harmless as doves.* The dove is remarkable for her eyes; we find that both the eyes of Christ (Cant. v. 12), and the eyes of the church (Cant. i. 15; iv. 1), are compared to *doves' eyes,* for they have the same spirit. The dove mourns much (Isa. xxxviii. 14). Christ wept oft; and penitent souls are compared to *doves of the valleys.* [2.] The dove was the only fowl that was offered in sacrifice (Lev. i. 14); and Christ by the Spirit, *the eternal Spirit, offered himself without spot to God.* [3.] The tidings of the decrease of Noah's flood were brought by a dove, with an olive-leaf in her mouth; fitly therefore are the glad tidings of peace with God brought by the Spirit as *a dove.* It speaks God's *good will towards men;* that his thoughts towards us are *thoughts of good, and not of evil.* By *the voice of the turtle heard in our land* (Cant. ii. 12), the Chaldee paraphrase understands, *the voice of the Holy Spirit.* That God is in Christ reconciling the world unto himself, is a joyful message, which comes to us upon the wing, *the wings of a dove.*

3. To explain and complete this solemnity, *there came a voice from heaven,* which, we have reason to think, was heard by all that were present. The Holy Spirit manifested himself in the likeness of a *dove,* but God the Father by *a voice;* for when the law was given they *saw no manner of similitude, only they heard a voice* (Deut. iv. 12); and so this gospel came, and gospel indeed it is, the best news that ever came from heaven to earth; for it speaks plainly and fully God's favour to Christ, and us in him.

(1.) See here how God owns our Lord Jesus; *This is my beloved Son.* Observe, [1.] The relation he stood in to him; He *is my Son.* Jesus Christ is the Son of God, *by eternal generation,* as he was *begotten of the Father before all worlds* (Col. i. 15; Heb. i. 3); and by supernatural conception; he was *therefore* called *the Son of God,* because he *was conceived by the power of the Holy Ghost* (Luke i. 35); yet this is not all; he is the Son of God by special designation to the work and office of the world's Redeemer. He was sanctified and sealed, and sent upon that errand, *brought up with* the Father for it (Prov. viii. 30), appointed to it; *I will make him my First-born,* Ps. lxxxix. 27. [2.] The affection the Father had for him; He *is my beloved Son;* his dear Son, *the Son of his love* (Col. i. 13); he had lain in his bosom from all eternity (John i. 18), had been *always his delight* (Prov. viii. 30), but particularly as Mediator, and in undertaking the work of man's salvation, he was his *beloved Son.* He is *my Elect, in whom my soul delights.* See Isa. xlii. 1. Because he consented to the covenant of redemption, and delighted to do that *will of God, therefore the Father loved him.* John x. 17; iii. 35. *Behold,* then, *behold,* and wonder, *what manner of love the Father has bestowed upon us,* that he should deliver up him that was the Son of his love, to suffer and die for those that were the generation of his wrath; nay, and that he *therefore* loved him, *because he laid down his life for the sheep!* Now know we that he loved us, *seeing he has not withheld his Son, his only Son, his Isaac whom he loved,* but *gave him to be a sacrifice for our sin.*

(2.) See here how ready he is to own us in him: He *is my beloved Son,* not only *with* whom, but *in* whom, I am well pleased. He is pleased with all that are in him, and are united to him by faith. Hitherto God had been displeased with the children of men, but now his anger is turned away, and he has made us *accepted in the Beloved,* Eph. i. 6. Let all the world take notice, that this is the Peace-maker, the Days-man, who has laid his hand upon us both, and that *there is no coming to God* as a Father, *but by him* as Mediator, John xiv. 6. *In him our spiritual sacrifices are acceptable,* for he is the Altar that *sanctifies every gift,* 1 Pet. ii. 5. Out of Christ, God *is a consuming Fire,* but, in Christ, a reconciled Father. This is the sum of the whole gospel; it *is a faithful saying, and worthy of all acceptation, that* God has declared, *by a voice from heaven,* that Jesus Christ is his *beloved Son, in whom he is well pleased,* with which we must by faith cheerfully concur, and say, that he *is our beloved* Saviour, *in whom we are well pleased.*

CHAP. IV.

John Baptist said concerning Christ, He must increase, but I must decrease; and so it proved. For, after John had baptized Christ, and borne his testimony to him, we hear little more of his ministry; he had done what he came to do, and thenceforward there is as much talk of Jesus as ever there had been of John. As the rising Sun advances, the morning star disappears. Concerning Jesus Christ we have in this chapter, I. The temptation he underwent, the triple assault the tempter made upon him, and the repulse he gave to each assault, ver. 1—11. II. The teaching work he undertook, the places he preached in (ver. 12—16), and the subject he preached on, ver. 17. III. His calling of disciples, Peter and Andrew, James and John, ver. 18—22. IV. His curing diseases (ver. 23, 24), and the great resort of the people to him, both to be taught and to be healed.

THEN was Jesus led up of the
Spirit into the wilderness, to be
tempted of the devil. 2 And when
he had fasted forty days and forty
nights, he was afterwards an hungred. 3 And when the tempter
came to him, he said, If thou be
the Son of God, command that
these stones be made bread. 4 But
he answered and said, It is written,
Man shall not live by bread alone, but
by every word that proceedeth out of
the mouth of God. 5 Then the devil
taketh him up into the holy city, and
setteth him on a pinnacle of the temple, 6 And saith unto him, If thou
be the Son of God, cast thyself down;
for it is written, He shall give his
angels charge concerning thee: and
in *their* hands they shall bear thee up,
lest at any time thou dash thy foot
against a stone. 7 Jesus said unto
him, It is written again, Thou shalt
not tempt the Lord thy God. 8
Again, the devil taketh him up into
an exceeding high mountain, and
showeth him all the kingdoms of the
world, and the glory of them; 9 And
saith unto him, All these things will

I give thee, if thou wilt fall down and worship me. 10 Then saith Jesus unto him, Get thee hence, Satan: for it is written, Thou shalt worship the Lord thy God, and him only shalt thou serve. 11 Then the devil leaveth him, and, behold, angels came and ministered unto him.

We have here the story of a famous duel, fought hand to hand, between Michael and the dragon, the Seed of the woman and the seed of the serpent, nay, the serpent himself; in which the seed of the woman suffers, being *tempted,* and so has his heel bruised; but the serpent is quite baffled in his temptations, and so has his head broken; and our Lord Jesus comes off a Conqueror, and so secures not only comfort, but conquest at last, to all his faithful followers. Concerning Christ's temptation, observe,

I. The time when it happened: *Then;* there is an emphasis laid upon that. Immediately after *the heavens were opened* to him, and *the Spirit descended on him,* and he was declared to be the Son of God, and the Saviour of the world, the next news we hear of him is, he is *tempted;* for *then* he is best able to grapple with the temptation. Note, 1. Great privileges, and special tokens of divine favour, will not secure us from being *tempted.* Nay, 2. After great honours put upon us, we must expect something that is humbling; as Paul had a messenger of Satan sent to buffet him, after he had been in the third heavens. 3. God usually prepares his people for temptation before he calls them to it; he *gives strength according to the day,* and, before a sharp trial, gives more than ordinary comfort. 4. The assurance of our sonship is the best preparative for temptation. If the good Spirit witness to our adoption, that will furnish us with an answer to all the suggestions of the evil spirit, designed either to debauch or disquiet us.

Then, when he was newly come from a solemn ordinance, when he was baptized, *then* he was *tempted.* Note, After we have been admitted into communion with God, we must expect to be set upon by Satan. The enriched soul must double its guard. *When thou hast eaten and art full, then beware. Then,* when he began to show himself publicly to Israel, *then* he was *tempted,* so as he never had been while he lived in privacy. Note, The Devil has a particular spite at useful persons, who are not only good, but given to do good, especially at their first setting out. It is the advice of the Son of Sirach (Ecclesiasticus ii. 1), *My son, if thou come to serve the Lord, prepare thyself for temptation.* Let young ministers know what to expect, and arm accordingly.

II. The place where it was; *in the wilderness;* probably in the great wilderness of *Sinai,* where Moses and Elijah *fasted forty days,* for no part of *the wilderness* of Judea was so abandoned to wild beasts as this is said to have been, Mark i. 13. When Christ was baptized, he did not go to Jerusalem, there to publish the glories that had been put upon him, but retired into a wilderness. After communion with God, it is good to be private awhile, lest we lose what we have received, in the crowd and hurry of worldly business. Christ withdrew into the wilderness, 1. To gain advantage to himself. Retirement gives an opportunity for meditation and communion with God; even they who are called to the most active life must yet have their contemplative hours, and must find time to be alone with God. Those are not fit to speak of the things of God in public to others, who have not first conversed with those things in secret by themselves. When Christ would appear as *a Teacher come from God,* it shall not be said of him, "He is newly come from travelling, he has been abroad, and has seen the world;" but, "He is newly come out of a desert, he has been alone conversing with God and his own heart." 2. To give advantage to the tempter, that he might have a readier access to him than he could have had in company. Note, Though solitude is a friend to a good heart, yet Satan knows how to improve it against us. *Woe to him that is alone.* Those who, under pretence of sanctity and devotion, retire into dens and deserts, find that they are not out of the reach of their spiritual enemies, and that there they want the benefit of the communion of saints. Christ retired, (1.) That Satan might have leave to do his worst. To make his victory the more illustrious, he gave the enemy sun and wind on his side, and yet baffled him. He might give the Devil advantage, for *the prince of this world had nothing in* him; but he has in us, and therefore we must pray not to be *led into temptation,* and must keep out of harm's way. (2.) That he might have an opportunity to do his best himself, that he might be exalted in his own strength; for so it was written, *I have trod the wine-press alone,* and of the people there was none with me. Christ entered the lists without a second.

III. The preparatives for it, which were two.

1. He was directed to the combat; he did not wilfully thrust himself upon it, but he *was led up of the Spirit to be tempted of the Devil.* The Spirit that *descended upon him like a dove* made him meek, and yet made him bold. Note, Our care must be, not to enter into temptation; but if God, by his providence, order us into circumstances of temptation for our trial, we must not think it strange, but double our guard. *Be strong in the Lord, resist steadfast in the faith,* and all shall be well. If we presume upon our own strength, and tempt the devil to tempt us, we provoke God to leave us to ourselves; but, whithersoever God leads us, we may

hope he will go along with us, and bring us off *more than conquerors.*

Christ *was led to be tempted of the Devil,* and of him only. Others are tempted, *when they are drawn aside of their own lust and enticed* (Jam. i. 14); the Devil takes hold of that handle, and ploughs with that heifer: but our Lord Jesus had no corrupt nature, and therefore he was led securely, without any fear or trembling, as a champion into the field, *to be tempted* purely by *the Devil.*

Now Christ's temptation is, (1.) An instance of his own condescension and humiliation. Temptations are *fiery darts, thorns in the flesh, buffetings, siftings, wrestlings, combats,* all which denote hardship and suffering; *therefore* Christ submitted to them, because he would humble himself, *in all things to be made like unto his brethren;* thus he *gave his back to the smiters.* (2.) An occasion of Satan's confusion. There is no conquest without a combat. Christ was tempted, that he might overcome the tempter. Satan tempted the first Adam, and triumphed over him; but he shall not always triumph, the second Adam shall overcome him and *lead captivity captive.* (3.) Matter of comfort to all the saints. In the temptation of Christ it appears, that our enemy is subtle, spiteful, and very daring in his temptations; but it appears withal, that he is not invincible. Though he is *a strong man armed,* yet the Captain of our salvation is *stronger than he.* It is some comfort to us to think that Christ suffered, being *tempted;* for thus it appears that temptations, if not yielded to, are not sins, they are afflictions only, and such as may be the lot of those with whom God is well-pleased. And we have a High Priest who knows, by experience, what it is to be *tempted,* and who therefore is the more tenderly touched with *the feeling of our infirmities* in an hour of temptation, Heb. ii. 18; iv. 15. But it is much more a comfort to think that Christ conquered, being *tempted,* and conquered for us; not only that the enemy we grapple with is a conquered, baffled, disarmed enemy, but that we are interested in Christ's victory over him, and through him are *more than conquerors.*

2. He was dieted for the combat, as wrestlers, who are *temperate in all things* (1 Cor. ix. 25.); but Christ beyond any other, for he *fasted forty days and forty nights,* in compliance with the type and example of Moses the great lawgiver, and of Elias, the great reformer, of the Old Testament. John Baptist came as Elias, in those things that were moral, but not in such things as were miraculous (John x. 41); that honour was reserved for Christ. Christ needed not to fast for mortification (he had no corrupt desires to be subdued); yet he *fasted,* (1.) That herein he might humble himself, and might seem as one abandoned, *whom no man seeketh after.* (2.) That he might give Satan both occasion and advantage against him; and so make his victory over him the more illustrious. (3.) That he might sanctify and recommend fasting to us, when God in his providence calls to it, or when we are reduced to straits, and are destitute of daily food, or when it is requisite for the keeping under of the body, or the quickening of prayer, those excellent preparatives for temptation. If good people are brought low, if they want friends and succours, this may comfort them, that their Master himself was in like manner exercised. A man may want bread, and yet be a favourite of heaven, and under the conduct of the Spirit. The reference which the Papists make of their lent-fast to this fasting of Christ *forty days,* is a piece of foppery and superstition which the law of our land witnesses against, Stat. 5 Eliz. chap. v. sect. 39, 40. *When he fasted forty days he was* never hungry; converse with heaven was instead of meat and drink to him, but *he was afterwards an hungred,* to show that he was really and truly Man; and he took upon him our natural infirmities, that he might atone for us. Man fell by eating, and that way we often sin, and therefore Christ *was an hungred.*

IV. The temptations themselves. That which Satan aimed at, in all his temptations, was, to bring him to *sin against God,* and so to render him for ever incapable of being a Sacrifice for the sin of others. Now, whatever the colours were, that which he aimed at was, to bring him, 1. To despair of his Father's goodness. 2. To presume upon his Father's power. 3. To alienate his Father's honour, by giving it to Satan. In the two former, that which he tempted him *to,* seemed innocent, and therein appeared the subtlety of the tempter; in the last, that which he tempted him *with,* seemed desirable. The two former are artful temptations, which there was need of great wisdom to discern; the last was a strong temptation, which there was need of great resolution to resist; yet he was baffled in them all.

1. He tempted him to despair of his Father's goodness, and to distrust his Father's care concerning him.

(1.) See how the temptation was managed (*v.* 3); *The tempter came to him.* Note, The Devil is *the tempter,* and therefore he is *Satan—an adversary;* for those are our worst enemies, that entice us to sin, and are Satan's agents, are doing his work, and carrying on his designs. He is called emphatically *the tempter,* because he was so to our first parents, and still is so, and all other tempters are set on work by him. *The tempter came to* Christ in a visible appearance, not terrible and affrighting, as afterward in his agony in the garden; no, if ever the Devil *transformed himself into an angel of light,* he did so now, and pretended to be a good genius, a guardian angel.

Observe the subtlety of *the tempter,* in joining this first temptation with what went before, to make it the stronger. [1.] Christ began to be hungry, and therefore the motion seemed very proper, to turn *stones* into *bread* for his necessary support. Note, It is one of the wiles of Satan to take advantage of our outward condition, in that to plant the battery of his temptations. He is an adversary no less watchful than spiteful; and the more ingenious he is to take advantage against us, the more industrious we must be to give him none. When he began to be hungry, and that in a *wilderness,* where there was nothing to be had, then the Devil assaulted him. Note, Want and poverty are a great temptation to discontent and unbelief, and the use of unlawful means for our relief, under pretence that necessity has no law; and it is excused with this that hunger will break through stone walls, which yet is no excuse, for the law of God ought to be stronger to us than stone walls. Agur prays against poverty, not because it is an affliction and reproach, but because it is a temptation; *lest I be poor, and steal.* Those therefore who are reduced to straits, have need to double their guard; it is better to starve to death, than live and thrive by sin. [2.] Christ was lately declared to be *the Son of God,* and here the Devil tempts him to doubt of that; *If thou be the Son of God.* Had not the Devil known that the Son of God was to come into the world, he would not have said this; and had he not suspected that this was he, he would not have said it to him, nor durst he have said it if Christ had not now drawn a veil over his glory, and if the Devil had not now put on an impudent face.

First, "Thou hast now an occasion to question whether *thou be the Son of God* or no; for can it be, that *the Son of God,* who is *Heir of all things,* should be reduced to such straits? If God were thy Father, he would not see thee starve, for *all the beasts of the forest are his,* Ps. l. 10, 12. It is true there *was a voice from heaven, This is my beloved Son,* but surely it was delusion, and thou wast imposed upon by it; for either God is not thy Father, or he is a very unkind one." Note, 1. The great thing Satan aims at, in tempting good people, is to overthrow their relation to God as a Father, and so to cut off their dependence on him, their duty to him, and their communion with him. The good Spirit, as the Comforter of the brethren, witnesses that they are the *children of God;* the evil spirit, as the accuser of the brethren, does all he can to shake that testimony. 2. Outward afflictions, wants and burdens, are the great arguments Satan uses to make the people of God question their sonship; as if afflictions could not consist with, when really they proceed from, God's fatherly love. They know how to answer this temptation, who can say with holy Job, *Though he slay me, though he* starve me, *yet will I trust in him,* and love him as a Friend, even when he seems to come forth against me as an Enemy. 3. The Devil aims to shake our faith in the word of God, and bring us to question the truth of that. Thus he began with our first parents; *Yea, has God said* so and so? Surely he has not. So here, *Has God said* that thou art his *beloved Son?* Surely he did not say so; or if he did it is not true. We then *give place to the Devil,* when we question the truth of any word that God has spoken; for his business, as the father of lies, is to oppose the true sayings of God. 4. The Devil carries on his designs very much by possessing people with hard thoughts of God, as if he were unkind, or unfaithful, and had forsaken or forgotten those who have ventured their all with him. He endeavoured to beget in our first parents a notion that God forbade them the tree of knowledge, because he grudged them the benefit of it; and so here he insinuates to our Saviour, that his Father had cast him off, and left him to shift for himself. But see how unreasonable this suggestion was, and how easily answered. If Christ seemed to be a mere Man now, because he was hungry, why was he not confessed to be more than a Man, even the *Son of God,* when for *forty days he fasted,* and was not hungry?

Secondly, "Thou hast now an opportunity to show that thou art *the Son of God. If thou* art *the Son of God,* prove it by this, *command that these stones*" (a heap of which, probably, lay now before him) "*be made bread, v.* 3. John Baptist said but the other day, that God *can out of stones raise up children to Abraham,* a divine power therefore can, no doubt, out of stones, make bread for those children; if therefore thou hast that power, exert it now in a time of need for thyself." He does not say, *Pray to thy Father* that he would turn them into *bread;* but *command* it to be done; thy Father hath forsaken thee, set up for thyself, and be not beholden to him. The Devil is for nothing that is humbling, but every thing that is assuming; and gains his point, if he can but bring men off from their dependence upon God, and possess them with an opinion of their self-sufficiency.

(2.) See how this temptation was resisted and overcome.

[1.] Christ refused to comply with it. He would not *command these stones to be made bread;* not because he could not; his power, which soon after this turned *water into wine,* could have turned *stones* into *bread;* but he would not. And why would he not? At first view, the thing appears justifiable enough, and the truth is, the more plausible a temptation is, and the greater appearance there is of good in it, the more dangerous it is. This matter would bear a dispute, but Christ was soon aware of the snake in the grass, and would not do any thing, *First,* That looked like questioning the truth of the voice he heard from heaven, or putting that upon a new trial which was already settled. *Secondly,* That looked like distrusting his

Father's care of him, or limiting him to one particular way of providing for him. *Thirdly,* That looked like setting up for himself, and being his own carver; or, *Fourthly,* That looked like gratifying Satan, by doing a thing at his motion. Some would have said, To give the Devil his due, this was good counsel; but for those who *wait upon God,* to consult *him,* is more than his due; it is like enquiring of the god Ekron, when there is a God in Israel.

[2.] He was ready to reply to it (*v.* 4); *He answered and said, It is written.* This is observable, that Christ answered and baffled all the temptations of Satan with, *It is written.* He is himself the eternal Word, and could have produced the mind of God without having recourse to the writings of Moses; but he put honour upon the scripture, and, to set us an example, he appealed to what was written in the law; and he says this to Satan, taking it for granted that he knew well enough what was written. It is possible that those who are the Devil's children may yet know very well what is written in God's book; *The devils believe and tremble.* This method we must take when at any time we are tempted to sin; resist and repel the temptation with, *It is written.* The word of God is *the sword of the Spirit,* the only offensive weapon in all the Christian armoury (Eph. vi. 17); and we may say of it as David of Goliath's sword, *None is like that* in our spiritual conflicts.

This answer, as all the rest, is taken out of the book of *Deuteronomy,* which signifies *the second law,* and in which there is very little ceremonial; the Levitical sacrifices and purifications could not drive away Satan, though of divine institution, much less holy water and the sign of the cross, which are of human invention; but moral precepts and evangelical promises, mixed with faith, these are *mighty, through God,* for the vanquishing of Satan. This is here quoted from Deut. viii. 3, where the reason given why God fed the Israelites with manna is, because he would teach them that *man shall not live by bread alone.* This Christ applies to his own case. Israel was God's son, whom he *called out of Egypt* (Hos. xi. 1), so was Christ (*ch.* ii. 15); Israel was then in a wilderness, Christ was so now, perhaps the same wilderness. Now, *First,* The Devil would have him question his sonship, because he was in straits; no, says he, Israel was God's son, and a son he was very tender of and whose manners he bore (Acts xiii. 18); and yet he brought them into straits; and it follows there (Deut. viii. 5), *As a man chasteneth his son, so the Lord thy God chasteneth thee.* Christ, *being a Son,* thus *learns obedience. Secondly,* The Devil would have him distrust his Father's love and care. "No," says he, "that would be to do as Israel did, who, when they were in want, said, *Is the Lord among us?* and, *Can he furnish a table in the wilderness? Can he give bread?*" *Thirdly,* The Devil would have him, as soon as he began to be hungry, immediately look out for supply; whereas God, for wise and holy ends, suffered Israel to hunger before he fed them; to humble them, and prove them. God will have his children, when they want, not only to wait on him, but to wait for him. *Fourthly,* The Devil would have him to supply himself with bread. "No," says Christ, "what need is there of that? It is a point long since settled, and incontestably proved, that man may live without bread, as Israel in the wilderness lived forty years upon manna." It is true, God in his providence ordinarily maintains men by *bread out of the earth* (Job xxviii. 5); but he can, if he please, make use of other means to keep men alive; *any word proceeding out of the mouth of God,* any thing that God shall order and appoint for that end, will be as good a livelihood for man as bread, and will maintain him as well. As we may *have bread,* and yet not be nourished, if God deny his blessing (Hag. i. 6, 9; Mic. vi. 14; for though bread is *the staff of life,* it is God's blessing that is *the staff of bread),* so we may *want bread,* and yet be nourished some other way. God sustained Moses and Elias without bread, and Christ himself just now for forty days; he sustained Israel with bread from heaven, angels' food; Elijah with bread sent miraculously by ravens, and another time with the widow's meal miraculously multiplied; therefore Christ need not turn stones into bread, but trust God to keep him alive some other way now that he is hungry, as he had done forty days before he hungred. Note, As in our greatest abundance we must not think to live *without* God, so in our greatest straits we must learn to live *upon* God; and when *the fig-tree does not blossom,* and *the field yields no meat,* when all ordinary means of succour and support are cut off, yet then we must *rejoice in the Lord;* then we must not think to command what we will, though contrary to his command, but must humbly pray for what he thinks fit to give us, and be thankful for the bread of our allowance, though it be a short allowance. Let us learn of Christ here to be at God's finding, rather than at our own; and not to take any irregular courses for our supply, when our wants are ever so pressing (Ps. xxxvii. 3). *Jehovah-jireh;* some way or other *the Lord will provide.* It is better to live poorly upon the fruits of God's goodness, than live plentifully upon the products of our own sin.

2. He tempted him to presume upon his Father's power and protection. See what a restless unwearied adversary the Devil is! If he fail in one assault, he tries another.

Now in this second attempt we may observe,

(1.) What the temptation was, and how it was managed. In general, finding Christ so confident of his Father's care of him, in point of nourishment, he endeavours to draw him to presume upon that care in point of safety. Note, We are in danger of missing our way, both on the right hand and on the left, and therefore must take heed, lest, when we avoid one extreme, we be brought by the artifices of Satan, to run into another; lest, by overcoming our prodigality, we fall into covetousness. Nor are any extremes more dangerous than those of despair and presumption, especially in the affairs of our souls. Some who have obtained a persuasion that Christ is able and willing to save them *from* their sins, are then tempted to presume that he will save them *in* their sins. Thus when people begin to be zealous in religion, Satan hurries them into bigotry and intemperate heats.

Now in this temptation we may observe,

[1.] How he made way for it. He took Christ, not by force and against his will, but moved him to go, and went along with him, to Jerusalem. Whether Christ went upon the ground, and so went up the stairs to the top of the temple, or whether he went in the air, is uncertain; but so it was, that he was *set upon a pinnacle*, or spire; *upon the fane* (so some), *upon the battlements* (so others), *upon the wing* (so the word is), *of the temple*. Now observe, *First*, How submissive Christ was, in suffering himself to be hurried thus, that he might let Satan do his worst and yet conquer him. The patience of Christ here, as afterward in his sufferings and death, is more wonderful than the power of Satan or his instruments; for neither he nor they could have any power against Christ but *what was given them from above*. How comfortable is it, that Christ, who let loose this power of Satan against himself, does not in like manner let it loose against us, but restrains it, for he *knows our frame! Secondly*, How subtle the Devil was, in the choice of the place for his temptations. Intending to solicit Christ to an ostentation of his own power, and a vain-glorious presumption upon God's providence, he fixes him on a public place in Jerusalem, a populous city, and *the joy of the whole earth;* in the temple, one of the wonders of the world, continually gazed upon with admiration by some one or other. There he might make himself remarkable, and be taken notice of by every body, and prove himself the Son of God; not, as he was urged in the former temptation, in the obscurities of a wilderness, but before multitudes, upon the most eminent stage of action.

Observe, 1. That Jerusalem is here called the *holy city;* for so it was in name and profession, and there was in it a *holy seed*, that was the *substance thereof*. Note, There is no city on earth so holy as to exempt and secure us from the Devil and his temptations. The first *Adam* was tempted in the *holy garden*, the second in the *holy city*. Let us not, therefore, in any place, be off our watch. Nay, the *holy city* is the place where he does, with the greatest advantage and success, tempt men to pride and presumption; but, blessed be God, into the Jerusalem above, that holy city, no unclean thing shall enter; there we shall be for ever out of temptation. 2. That he *set him upon a pinnacle of the temple*, which (as Josephus describes it, Antiq. lib. xv. cap. 14) was so very high, that it would make a man's head giddy to look down to the bottom. Note, Pinnacles of the temple are places of temptation; I mean, (1.) High places are so; they are slippery places; advancement in the world makes a man a fair mark for Satan to shoot his fiery darts at. God casts down, that he may raise up; the Devil raises up, that he may cast down: therefore they who would take heed of *falling*, must take heed of *climbing*. (2.) High places *in the church* are, in a special manner, dangerous. They who excel in gifts, who are in eminent stations, and have gained great reputation, have need to keep humble; for Satan will be sure to aim at them, to puff them up with pride, that they may *fall into the condemnation of the Devil*. Those that *stand high* are concerned to *stand fast*.

[2.] How he moved it; "*If thou be the Son of God*, now show thyself to the world, and prove thyself to be so; *cast thyself down*, and then," *First*, "Thou wilt be admired, as *under the special protection of heaven*. When they see thee receive no hurt by a fall from such a precipice, they will say" (as the barbarous people did of Paul) "that thou art a God." Tradition says, that *Simon Magus* by this very thing attempted to prove himself a god, but that his pretensions were disproved, for he fell down, and was miserably bruised. "Nay," *Secondly*, "Thou wilt be received, as coming *with a special commission from heaven*. All Jerusalem will see and acknowledge, not only that thou art more than a man, but that thou art that *Messenger*, that *Angel of the covenant*, that should *suddenly come to the temple* (Mal. iii. 1), and from thence descend into the streets of the holy city; and thus the work of convincing the Jews will be cut short, and soon done."

Observe, The Devil said, *Cast thyself down*. The Devil could not cast him down, though a little thing would have done it, from the top of a spire. Note, The power of Satan is a limited power; *hitherto he shall come, and no further*. Yet, if the Devil *had cast him down*, he had not gained his point; that had been his suffering only, not his sin. Note, Whatever real mischief is done us, it is of *our own doing;* the Devil can but persuade, he cannot compel; he can but say, *Cast thyself down;* he cannot cast us down. Every man is tempted, when he is drawn away of his own lust, and not forced, but enticed. Therefore let us not *hurt ourselves*, and then, blessed be God, no one else can hurt us, Prov. ix. 12.

[3.] How he backed this motion with a scripture; *For it is written, He shall give his angels charge concerning thee.* But *is Saul also among the prophets?* Is Satan so well versed in scripture, as to be able to quote it so readily? It seems, he is. Note, It is possible for a man to have his head full of scripture-notions, and his mouth full of scripture-expressions, while his heart is full of reigning enmity to God and all goodness. The knowledge which the devils have of the scripture, increases both their mischievousness and their torment. Never did the devil speak with more vexation to himself, than when he said to Christ, *I know thee who thou art.* The devil would persuade Christ to *throw himself down,* hoping that he would be his own murderer, and that there would be an end of him and his undertaking, which he looked upon with a jealous eye; to encourage him to do it, he tells him, that there was no danger, that the good angels would protect him, for so was the promise (Ps. xci. 11), *He shall give his angels charge over thee.* In this quotation,

First, There was *something right.* It is true, there is such a promise of the ministration of the angels, for the protection of the saints. The devil knows it by experience; for he finds his attempts against them fruitless, and he frets and rages at it, as he did at the hedge about Job, which he speaks of so sensibly, Job i. 10. He was also right in applying it to Christ, for to him all the promises of the protection of the saints primarily and eminently belong, and to them, in and through him. That promise, that *not a bone of theirs shall be broken* (Ps. xxxiv. 20), was fulfilled in Christ, John xix. 36. The angels guard the saints for Christ's sake, Rev. vii. 5, 11.

Secondly, There was a great deal *wrong in it;* and perhaps the devil had a particular spite against this promise, and perverted it, because it often stood in his way, and baffled his mischievous designs against the saints. See here, 1. How he *misquoted* it; and that was *bad.* The promise is, They shall *keep thee;* but how? *In all thy ways;* not otherwise; if we go *out of our way,* out of the way of our duty, we forfeit the promise, and put ourselves out of God's protection. Now this word made against the tempter, and therefore he industriously left it out. If Christ had *cast himself down,* he had been *out of his way,* for he had no call so to expose himself. It is good for us upon all occasions to consult the scriptures themselves, and not to take things upon trust, that we may not be imposed upon by those that maim and mangle the word of God; we must do as the noble *Bereans,* who searched the scriptures daily. 2. How he *misapplied* it; and that was *worse.* Scripture is abused when it is pressed to patronize sin; and when men thus wrest it to their own temptation, they do it to *their own destruction,* 2 Pet. iii. 16. This promise is firm, and stands good; but the devil made an ill use of it, when he used it as an encouragement to presume upon the divine care. Note, It is no new thing for the *grace of God* to be *turned into wantonness;* and for men to take encouragement in sin from the discoveries of God's good will to sinners. But *shall we continue in sin, that grace may abound?* throw ourselves down, that the angels may bear us up? God forbid.

(2.) How Christ overcame this temptation; he resisted and overcame it, as he did the former, with, *It is written.* The devil's *abusing* of scripture did not prevent Christ from using it, but he presently urges, Deut. vi. 16, *Thou shalt not tempt the Lord thy God.* The meaning of this is not, Therefore thou must not tempt me; but, Therefore *I must not tempt* my Father. In the place whence it is quoted, it is in the plural number, *You shall not tempt;* here it is singular, *Thou shalt not.* Note, We are *then* likely to get good by the word of God, when we hear and receive general promises as speaking to us in particular. Satan said, *It is written;* Christ says, *It is written;* not that one scripture contradicts another. God is one, and his word one, and he in one mind, but that is a promise, this is a precept, and therefore that is to be explained and applied by this; for scripture is the best interpreter of scripture; and they who prophesy, who expound scripture, must do it according to the proportion of faith (Rom. xii. 6), consistently with practical godliness.

If Christ should *cast himself down,* it would be the tempting of God, [1.] As it would be *requiring a further confirmation* of that which was so well confirmed. Christ was abundantly satisfied that God was already his Father, and took care of him, and gave his angels a charge concerning him; and therefore to put it upon a new experiment, would be to tempt him, as the Pharisees tempted Christ; when they had so many signs on earth, they demanded a *sign from heaven.* This is limiting the *Holy One of Israel.* [2.] As it would be *requiring a special preservation* of him, in doing that which he had no call to. If we expect that because God has promised not to forsake us, therefore he should follow us out of the way of our duty; that because he has promised to supply our wants, therefore he should humour us, and please our fancies; that because he has promised to keep us, we may wilfully thrust ourselves into danger, and may expect the desired end, without using the appointed means; this is presumption, this is tempting God. And it is an aggravation of the sin, that he is the Lord our God; it is an abuse of the privilege we enjoy, in having him for our God; he has thereby encouraged us to trust him, but we are very ungrateful, if therefore we tempt him; it is contrary to our duty to him as our God. This is to affront him whom we ought to honour. Note, We must never promise ourselves any more than God has promised us.

3. He tempted him to the most *black and*

horrid idolatry, with the proffer of the *kingdoms of the world, and the glory of them.* And here we may observe,

(1.) How the devil made this push at our Saviour, *v.* 8, 9. The worst temptation was reserved for the last. Note, Sometimes the saint's last encounter is with the sons of *Anak,* and the parting blow is the sorest; therefore, whatever temptation we have been assaulted by, still we must prepare for worse; must be armed for all attacks, with the armour of righteousness on the right hand and on the left.

In this temptation, we may observe,

[1.] What he *showed him—all the kingdoms of the world.* In order to this, he took him to an *exceeding high mountain;* in hopes of prevailing, as Balak with Balaam, he changed his ground. The pinnacle of the temple is not high enough; the prince of the power of the air must have him further up into his territories. Some think this high mountain was on the other side of Jordan, because there we find Christ next after the temptation, John i. 28, 29. Perhaps it was *mount Pisgah,* whence Moses, in communion with God, had all the kingdoms of Canaan shown him. Hither the blessed Jesus was carried for the advantage of a prospect; as if the devil could show him more of the world than he knew already, who made and governed it. Thence he might discover some of the kingdoms situate about Judea, though not *the glory of them;* but there was doubtless a juggle and a delusion of Satan's in it; it is probable that that which he showed him, was but a landscape, an airy representation in a cloud, such as that great deceiver could easily frame and put together; setting forth, in proper and lively colours, the glories and the splendid appearances of princes; their robes and crowns, their retinue, equipage, and life-guards; the pomps of thrones, and courts, and stately palaces, the sumptuous buildings in cities, the gardens and fields about the country-seats, with the various instances of their wealth, pleasure, and gaiety; so as might be most likely to strike the fancy, and excite the admiration and affection. Such was this show, and his taking him up into a high mountain, was but to *humour the thing,* and to colour the delusion; in which yet the blessed Jesus did not suffer himself to be imposed upon, but saw through the cheat, only he permitted Satan to take his own way, that his victory over him might be the more illustrious. Hence observe, concerning *Satan's temptations,* that, *First,* They often *come in at the eye,* which is blinded to the things it should see, and dazzled with the vanities it should be turned from. The first sin began in the eye, Gen iii. 6. We have therefore need to make a covenant with our eyes, and to pray that God would *turn them away from beholding vanity. Secondly,* That temptations commonly take rise from the world, and the things of it. The *lust of the flesh,* and of *the eye,* with the *pride of life,* are the topics from which the devil fetches most of his arguments. *Thirdly,* That it is a *great cheat* which the devil puts upon poor souls, in his temptations. He deceives, and so destroys; he imposes upon men with shadows and false colours; shows the world and the glory of it, and hides from men's eyes the sin and sorrow and death which stain the pride of all this glory, the cares and calamities which attend great possessions, and the thorns which crowns themselves are lined with. *Fourthly,* That the *glory of the world* is the most *charming* temptation to the *unthinking* and *unwary,* and that by which men are most imposed upon. *Laban's* sons grudge *Jacob all this glory;* the *pride of life* is the most dangerous snare.

[2.] What he *said to him* (*v.* 9); *All these things will I give thee, if thou wilt fall down and worship me.* See,

First, How *vain the promise* was. *All these things will I give thee.* He seems to take it for granted, that in the former temptations he had in part gained his point, and proved that Christ was not the *Son of God,* because he had not given him those evidences of it which he demanded; so that here he looks upon him as a mere man. "Come," says he, "it seems that the God whose Son thou thinkest thyself to be deserts thee, and starves thee—a sign that he is not thy Father; but if thou wilt be ruled by me, I will provide better for thee than so; own me for thy father, and ask my blessing, and *all this will I give thee.*" Note, Satan makes an easy prey of men, when he can persuade them to think themselves abandoned of God. The fallacy of this promise lies in that, *All this will I give thee.* And what was *all that?* It was but a map, a picture, a mere phantasm, that had nothing in it real or solid, and this he would give him; a goodly prize! Yet such are Satan's proffers. Note, Multitudes lose the sight of that which is, by setting their eyes on that which is not. The devil's baits are all a sham; they are shows and shadows with which he deceives them, or rather they deceive themselves. The *nations of the earth* had been, long before, promised to the Messiah; if he be *the Son of God,* they belong to him; Satan pretends now to be a good angel, probably one of those that were set over kingdoms, and to have received a commission to deliver possession to him according to promise. Note, We must take heed of receiving even that which God hath promised, out of the devil's hand; we do so when we precipitate the performance, by catching at it in a sinful way.

Secondly, How *vile* the *condition* was; *If thou wilt fall down, and worship me.* Note, The devil is fond of being worshipped. All the worship which the heathen performed to their gods, was directed to the devil (Deut. xxxii. 17), who is therefore called the *god of this world,* 2 Cor. iv. 4; 1 Cor. x. 20. And fain would he draw Christ into his interests, and persuade him, now that he set up for a Teacher, to preach up the Gentile idolatry, and to introduce it again among the Jews, and then the nations of the earth would soon flock in to him. What temptation could be more hideous, more black? Note, The best of saints may be tempted to the worst of sins, especially when they are under the power of melancholy; as, for instance, to atheism, blasphemy, murder, self-murder, and what not. This is their affliction, but while there is no consent to it, nor approbation of it, it is not their sin; Christ was tempted to worship Satan.

(2.) See how Christ warded off the thrust, baffled the assault, and came off a conqueror. He rejected the proposal,

[1.] With *abhorrence* and *detestation; Get thee hence, Satan.* The two former temptations had something of colour, which would admit of a consideration, but this was so gross as not to bear a parley; it appears abominable at the first sight, and therefore is immediately rejected. If the best friend we have in the world should suggest such a thing as this to us, *Go, serve other gods,* he must not be heard with patience, Deut. xiii. 6, 8. Some temptations have their wickedness written in their forehead, they are open before-hand; they are not to be disputed with, but rejected; "*Get thee hence, Satan.* Away with it, I cannot bear the thought of it!" While Satan tempted Christ to do himself a mischief, by casting himself down, though he yielded not, yet he heard it; but now that the temptation flies in the face of God, he cannot bear it; *Get thee hence, Satan.* Note, It is a just indignation, which rises at the proposal of any thing that reflects on the honour of God, and strikes at his crown. Nay, whatever is an abominable thing, which we are sure the Lord hates, we must thus abominate it; far be it from us that we should have any thing to do with it. Note, It is good to be *peremptory* in resisting temptation, and to *stop our ears* to Satan's charms.

[2.] With an argument fetched from scripture. Note, In order to the strengthening of our resolutions against sin, it is good to see what a great deal of reason there is for those resolutions. The argument is very suitable, and exactly to the purpose, taken from Deut. vi. 13, and x. 20. *Thou shalt worship the Lord thy God, and him only shalt thou serve.* Christ does not dispute whether he were an angel of light, as he pretended, or not; but though he were, yet he must not be worshipped, because that is an honour due to God only. Note, It is good to make our answers to temptation as full and as brief as may be, so as not to leave room for objections. Our Saviour has recourse to the fundamental law in this case, which is indispensable, and universally obligatory. Note, Religious worship is due to God only, and must not be given to any creature; it is a flower of the crown which cannot be alienated, a branch of God's glory which he will not give to another, and which he would not give to his own Son, by obliging all men to *honour the Son, even as they honour the Father,* if he had not been God, *equal to him,* and *one with him.* Christ quotes this law concerning religious worship, and quotes it with application to himself; *First,* To show that in his estate of humiliation he was himself *made under this law:* though, as God, he was worshipped, yet, as Man, he did worship God, both publicly and privately. He obliges us to no more than what he was first pleased to oblige himself to. Thus it became him to fulfil all righteousness. *Secondly,* To show that the law of religious worship is of eternal obligation: though he abrogated and altered many institutions of worship, yet this fundamental law of nature—That God only is to be worshipped, he came to ratify, and confirm, and enforce upon us.

V. We have here the end and issue of this combat, *v.* 11. Though the children of God may be exercised with many and great temptations, yet God will not suffer them to be tempted above the strength which either they have, or he will put into them, 1 Cor. x. 13. It is but for a season that they are in heaviness, through manifold temptations.

Now the issue was glorious, and much to Christ's honour: for,

1. The devil was baffled, and quitted the field; *Then the devil leaveth him,* forced to do so by the power that went along with that word of command, *Get thee hence, Satan.* He made a shameful and inglorious retreat, and came off with disgrace; and the more daring his attempts had been, the more mortifying was the foil that was given him. *Magnis tamen excidit ausis—The attempt, however, in which he failed, was daring.* Then, when he had done his worst, had tempted him with *all the kingdoms of the world, and the glory of them,* and found that he was not influenced by that bait, that he could not prevail with that temptation with which he had overthrown so many thousands of the children of men, then he leaves him; then he gives him over as more than a man. Since this did not move him, he despairs of moving him, and begins to conclude, that he is the *Son of God,* and that it is in vain to tempt him any further. Note, If we resist the devil, he will flee from us; he will yield, if we keep our ground; as when *Naomi* saw that *Ruth was steadfastly resolved, she left off speaking to her.* When the devil left our Saviour, he owned himself fairly beaten; his head was broken by the attempt he made to *bruise Christ's heel.* He left him because he had *nothing in him,* nothing to take hold of; he saw it was to no purpose, and so gave over. Note, The devil, though he is an enemy to all the saints, is a conquered enemy. The Captain of our salvation has defeated

and disarmed him; we have nothing to do but to *pursue the victory.*

2. The holy angels came and attended upon our victorious Redeemer; *Behold, angels came and ministered unto him.* They came in a visible appearance, as the devil had done in the temptation. While the devil was making his assaults upon our Saviour, the angels stood at a distance, and their immediate attendance and ministration were suspended, that it might appear that he vanquished Satan in his own strength, and that his victory might be the more illustrious; and that afterward, when *Michael* makes use of *his angels* in fighting with the *dragon and his angels,* it might appear, that it is not because he *needs them,* or could not do his work without them, but because he is pleased to honour them so far as to employ them. One angel might have served to bring him food, but here are many attending him, to testify their respect to him, and their readiness to receive his commands. Behold this! It is worth taking notice of; (1.) That as there is a world of wicked, malicious spirits that fight against Christ and his church, and all particular believers, so there is a world of holy, blessed spirits engaged and employed for them. In reference to our *war with devils,* we may take abundance of comfort from our *communion with angels.* (2.) That Christ's victories are the angels' triumphs. The angels came to congratulate Christ on his success, to rejoice with him, and to give him the glory due to his name; for that was sung with a loud voice in heaven, when the great dragon was cast out (Rev. xii. 9, 10), *Now is come salvation and strength.* (3.) That the angels ministered to the Lord Jesus, not only food, but whatever else he wanted after this great fatigue. See how the instances of Christ's condescension and humiliation were balanced with tokens of his glory. As when he was *crucified in weakness,* yet he *lived by the power of God;* so when in weakness he was tempted, was hungry and weary, yet by his divine power he commanded the ministration of angels. Thus the Son of man did eat angels' food, and, like Elias, is fed by an angel in the wilderness, 1 Kings xix. 4, 7. Note, Though God may suffer his people to be brought into wants and straits, yet he will take effectual care for their supply, and will rather send angels to feed them, than see them perish. *Trust in the Lord, and verily thou shalt be fed,* Ps. xxxvii. 3.

Christ was thus succoured after the temptation, [1.] For his encouragement to go on in his undertaking, that he might see the powers of heaven siding with him, when he saw the powers of hell set against him. [2.] For our encouragement to trust in him; for as he knew, by experience, what it was to *suffer, being tempted,* and how hard that was, so he knew what it was to be succoured, being tempted, and how comfortable that was; and therefore we may expect, not only that he will sympathize with his tempted people, but that he will come in with seasonable relief to them; as our great Melchizedec, who met Abraham when he returned from the battle, and as the angels here ministered to him.

Lastly, Christ, having been thus signalized and made great in the invisible world by the voice of the Father, the descent of the Spirit, his victory over devils, and his dominion over angels, was doubtless qualified to appear in the visible world as the Mediator between God and man; for *consider how great this man was!*

12 Now when Jesus had heard that John was cast into prison, he departed into Galilee: 13 And leaving Nazareth, he came and dwelt in Capernaum, which is upon the sea coast, in the borders of Zabulon and Nephthalim: 14 That it might be fulfilled which was spoken by Esaias the prophet, saying, 15 The land of Zabulon, and the land of Nephthalim, *by* the way of the sea, beyond Jordan, Galilee of the Gentiles; 16 The people which sat in darkness saw great light: and to them which sat in the region and shadow of death light is sprung up. 17 From that time Jesus began to preach, and to say, Repent: for the kingdom of heaven is at hand.

We have here an account of Christ's preaching in the synagogues of Galilee, for he came into the world to be a Preacher; the great salvation which he wrought out, he himself began to publish (Heb. ii. 3) to show how much his heart *was* upon it, and ours *should* be.

Several passages in the other gospels, especially in that of St. John, are supposed, in the order of the story of Christ's life, to intervene between his temptation and his preaching in Galilee. His first appearance after his temptation, was when John Baptist pointed to him, saying, *Behold the Lamb of God,* John i. 29. After that, he went up to Jerusalem, to the passover (John ii.), discoursed with Nicodemus (John iii.), with the woman of Samaria (John iv.), and then returned into Galilee, and preached there. But Matthew, having had his residence in Galilee, begins his story of Christ's public ministry with his preaching there, which here we have an account of. Observe,

I. The time; *When Jesus had heard that John was cast into prison,* then he *went into Galilee, v.* 12. Note, The cry of the saints' sufferings comes up into the ears of the Lord Jesus. If John be cast into prison, Jesus hears it, takes cognizance of it, and steers his course accordingly: *he remembers the bonds* and afflictions that abide his people. Observe, 1. Christ did *not* go into the country, *till he heard of* John's imprisonment; for he must have time given him to *prepare the way of the Lord,* before the Lord himself appear. Providence wisely ordered it, that John should be *eclipsed* before Christ *shone forth;* otherwise the minds of people would have been distracted between the two; one would have said, *I am of John,* and another, *I am of Jesus.* John must be Christ's harbinger, but not his rival. The moon and stars are lost when the sun rises. John had done his work by the baptism of repentance, and then he was laid aside. The witnesses were slain when they had finished their testimony, and not before, Rev. xi. 7. 2. He *did* go into the country as soon as he heard of John's imprisonment; not only to provide for his own safety, knowing that the Pharisees in Judea were as much enemies to him as Herod was to John, but to supply the want of John Baptist, and to build upon the good foundation he had laid. Note, God will not leave himself without witness, nor his church without guides; when he removes one useful instrument, he can raise up another, for he has the residue of the Spirit, and he will do it, if he has work to do. *Moses my servant is dead,* John is cast into prison; now, therefore, Joshua, arise; Jesus, arise.

II The place where he preached; in Galilee, a remote part of the country, that lay furthest from Jerusalem, and was there looked upon with contempt, as rude and boorish. The inhabitants of that country were reckoned stout men, fit for soldiers, but not polite men, or fit for scholars. Thither Christ went, there he set up the standard of his gospel; and in this, as in other things, he humbled himself. Observe,

1. The particular city he chose for his residence; not Nazareth, where he had been bred up; no, he left Nazareth; particular notice is taken of that, *v.* 13. And with good reason did he leave Nazareth; for the men of that city *thrust him out* from among them, Luke iv. 29. He made them his first, and a very fair, offer of his service, but they rejected him and his doctrine, and were filled with indignation at him and it; and therefore he left Nazareth, and shook off the dust of his feet for a testimony against those there, who would not have him to teach them. Nazareth was the first place that refused Christ, and was therefore refused by him. Note, It is just with God, to take the gospel and the means of grace from those that slight them, and thrust them away. Christ will not stay long where he is not welcome. Unhappy Nazareth! *If thou hadst known* in this thy day the things that belong to thy peace, how well had it been for thee! *But now they are hid from thine eyes.*

But he *came and dwelt in Capernaum,* which was a city of Galilee, but many miles distant from Nazareth, a great city and of much resort. It is said here to be *on the sea coast,* not the *great sea,* but the sea of Tiberias, an inland water, called also *the lake of Gennesaret.* Close by the falling of Jordan into this sea stood Capernaum, in the tribe of Naphtali, but bordering upon Zebulun; hither Christ came, and here he dwelt. Some think that his father Joseph had a habitation here, others that he took a house or lodgings at least; and some think it more than probable, that he dwelt in the house of Simon Peter; however, here he fixed not constantly, for he went about doing good; but this was for some time his head quarters: what little rest he had, was here; here he had a place, though not a place of his own, to lay his head on. And at Capernaum, it should seem, he was welcome, and met with better entertainment than he had at Nazareth. Note, If some reject Christ, yet others will receive him, and bid him welcome. Capernaum is glad of Nazareth's leavings. If Christ's own countrymen be not gathered, yet he will be glorious. "And thou, Capernaum, hast now a day of it; thou art now lifted up to heaven; be wise for thyself, and know the time of thy visitation."

2. The prophecy that was fulfilled in this, *v.* 14—16. It is quoted from Isa. ix. 1, 2, but with some variation. The prophet in that place is foretelling a greater darkness of affliction to befal the contemners of Immanuel, than befel the countries there mentioned, either in their first captivity under Benhadad, which was but light (1 Kings xv. 20), or in their second captivity under the Assyrian, which was much heavier, 2 Kings xv. 29. The punishment of the Jewish nation for rejecting the gospel should be sorer than either (see Isa. viii. 21, 22); for those captivated places had some reviving in their bondage, and saw a great light again, *ch.* ix. 2. This is Isaiah's sense; but the Scripture has many fulfillings; and the evangelist here takes only the latter clause, which speaks of the return of the light of liberty and prosperity to those countries that had been in the darkness of captivity, and applies it to the appearing of the gospel among them.

The places are spoken of, *v.* 15. *The land of Zebulun is* rightly said to be *by the sea coast,* for *Zebulun* was a *haven of ships,* and *rejoiced* in her *going out,* Gen. xlix. 13; Deut. xxxiii. 18. Of Naphtali, it had been said, that he should *give goodly words* (Gen. xlix. 21), and should be *satisfied with favour* (Deut. xxxiii. 23), for from him began the gospel; goodly words indeed, and such as bring to a soul God's satisfying favour. The country beyond Jordan is mentioned likewise, for there we sometimes find Christ preaching, and Galilee of the Gentiles, the upper Galilee to which the Gentiles resorted for traffic, and where they were mingled with the Jews; which intimates a kindness in reserve for the poor Gentiles. When Christ came to Capernaum, the gospel came to all those places round about; such diffusive influences did the Sun of righteousness cast

Now, concerning the inhabitants of these places, observe, (1.) The posture they were in before the gospel came among them (*v.* 16); they were *in darkness.* Note, Those that are without Christ, are in the dark, nay, they are darkness itself; as the darkness that was upon the *face of the deep.* Nay, they were *in the region and shadow of death;* which denotes not only *great darkness,* as the grave is a *land of darkness,* but *great danger.* A man that is desperately sick, and not likely to recover, is in the *valley of the shadow of death,* though not quite dead; so the poor people were on the borders of damnation, though not yet damned—dead in law. And, which is worst of all, they were *sitting* in this condition. Sitting is a continuing posture; where we sit, we mean to stay; they were in the dark, and likely to be so, despairing to find the way out. And it is a contented posture; they were in the dark, and they loved darkness, they chose it rather than light; they were willingly ignorant. Their condition was sad; it is still the condition of many great and mighty nations, which are to be thought of, and prayed for, with pity. But *their* condition is more sad, who sit in darkness in the midst of gospel-light. He that is in the dark because it is night, may be sure that the sun will shortly arise; but he that is in the dark because he is blind, will not so soon have his eyes opened. We have the light, but what will that avail us, if we be not light in the Lord? (2.) The privilege they enjoyed, when Christ and his gospel came among them; it was as great a reviving as ever light was to a benighted traveller. Note, When the gospel comes, light comes; when it comes to any place, when it comes to any soul, it makes day there, John iii. 19; Luke i. 78, 79. Light is discovering, it is directing; so is the gospel.

It is a *great* light; denoting the clearness and evidence of gospel-revelations; not like the light of a candle, but the light of the sun when he goes forth in his strength. *Great* in comparison with the light of the law, the shadows of which were now done away. It is a *great light,* for it discovers great things and of vast consequence; it will last long, and spread far. And it is a *growing light,* intimated in that word, It is *sprung up.* It was but *spring of day* with them; now the day dawned, which afterward *shone more and more.* The gospel-kingdom, like a grain of mustard-seed or the morning light, was small in its beginnings, gradual in its growth, but great in its perfection.

Observe, The light *sprang up to them;* they did not go to seek it, but were prevented with the blessings of this goodness. It came upon them ere they were aware, at the time appointed, by the disposal of him who *commandeth the morning,* and *causes the day-spring to know its place, that it may take hold of the ends of the earth,* Job xxxviii. 12, 13.

III. The text he preached upon (*v.* 17): *From that time,* that is, from the time of his coming into Galilee, into the land of Zebulun and Naphtali, from that time, he began to preach. He had been preaching, before this, in Judea, and had made and baptized many disciples (John iv. 1); but his preaching was not so public and constant as now it began to be. The work of the ministry is so great and awful, that it is fit to be entered upon by steps and gradual advances.

The subject which Christ dwelt upon now in his preaching (and it was indeed the sum and substance of all his preaching), was the very same that John had preached upon (*ch.* iii. 2); *Repent, for the kingdom of heaven is at hand;* for the gospel is the same for substance under various dispensations; the commands the same, and the reasons to enforce them the same; an *angel from heaven* dares not preach any other gospel (Gal. i. 8), and will preach this, for it is the *everlasting gospel. Fear God, and,* by repentance, *give honour to him,* Rev. xiv. 6, 7. Christ put a great respect upon John's ministry, when he preached to the same purport that John had preached before him. By this he showed that John was his messenger and ambassador; for when he brought the errand himself, it was the same that he had sent by him. Thus did God confirm the word of his messenger, Isa. xliv. 26. The Son came on the same errand that the servants came on (*ch.* xxi. 37), to *seek fruit,* fruits meet for repentance. Christ had lain in the bosom of the Father, and could have preached sublime notions of divine and heavenly things, that should have alarmed and amused the learned world, but he pitches upon this old, plain text, *Repent, for the kingdom of heaven is at hand.* [1.] This he preached *first* upon; he began with this. Ministers must not be ambitious of broaching new opinions, framing new schemes, or coining new expressions, but must content themselves with plain, practical things, with the word that is *nigh us,* even *in our mouth,* and *in our heart.* We need not go up to heaven, nor down to the deep, for matter or language in our preaching. As John prepared Christ's way, so Christ prepared his own, and made way for the further discoveries he designed, with the doctrine of repentance. *If any man* will do this part of *his will, he shall know* more of *his doctrine,* John vii. 17. [2.] This he preached *often* upon; wherever he went, this was his subject, and neither he nor his followers ever reckoned it worn threadbare, as those would have done, that have *itching ears,* and are fond of novelty and variety more than that which is truly edifying. Note, That which has been preached and heard before, may yet very profitably be preached and heard again; but then it should be preached and heard better, and with new affections; what Paul had said before, he said again, *weeping*, Phil. iii. 1, 18. [3.] This he preached as gospel; "Repent, review your ways, and return to yourselves." Note, The doctrine of repentance is right gospel-doctrine. Not only the austere Baptist, who was looked upon as a melancholy, morose man, but the sweet and gracious Jesus, whose lips dropped as a honey-comb, preached repentance; for it is an unspeakable privilege that room is left for repentance. [4.] The reason is still the same; The *kingdom of heaven is at hand;* for it was not reckoned to be fully come, till the pouring out of the Spirit after Christ's ascension. John had preached the kingdom of heaven at hand above a year before this; but now that it was so much nearer, the argument was so much the stronger; now is the *salvation nearer*, Rom. xiii. 11. We should be so much the more quickened to our duty, *as we see the day approaching*, Heb. x. 25.

18 And Jesus, walking by the sea
of Galilee, saw two brethren, Simon
called Peter, and Andrew his brother,
casting a net into the sea: for they
were fishers. 19 And he saith unto
them, Follow me, and I will make
you fishers of men. 20 And they
straightway left *their* nets, and followed him. 21 And going on from
thence, he saw other two brethren,
James *the son* of Zebedee, and John
his brother, in a ship with Zebedee
their father, mending their nets: and
he called them. 22 And they immediately left the ship and their
father, and followed him.

When Christ began to preach, he began to *gather disciples*, who should now be the *hearers*, and hereafter the *preachers*, of his doctrine, who should now be witnesses *of* his miracles, and hereafter *concerning* them. Now, in these verses, we have an account of the first disciples that he called into fellowship with himself.

And this was an instance, 1. Of *effectual calling* to Christ. In all his preaching he gave a common call to all the country, but in this he gave a special and particular call to those that were given him by the Father. Let us see and admire the power of Christ's grace, own his word to be the rod of his strength, and wait upon him for those powerful influences which are necessary to the efficacy of the gospel call—those distinguishing influences. All the country was *called*, but these were *called out*, were *redeemed from among them*. Christ was so manifested to them, as he was not manifested unto the world. 2. It was an instance of *ordination*, and appointment to the work of the ministry. When Christ, as a Teacher, set up his great school, one of his first works was to appoint ushers, or under masters, to be employed in the work of instruction. Now he began to give gifts unto men, to put the treasure into earthen vessels. It was an early instance of his care for his church.

Now we may observe here,

I. *Where* they were called—by the *sea of Galilee*, where Jesus was walking, Capernaum being situated near that sea. Concerning this sea of Tiberias, the Jews have a saying, That of all the seven seas that God made, he made choice of none but this sea of Gennesaret; which is very applicable to Christ's choice of it, to honour it, as he often did, with his presence and miracles. Here, on the banks of the sea, Christ was walking for contemplation, as Isaac in the field; hither he went to call disciples; not to Herod's court (for few mighty or noble are called), not to Jerusalem, among the chief priests and the elders, but to the sea of Galilee; surely Christ sees not as man sees. Not but that the same power which effectually called Peter and Andrew, would have wrought upon Annas and Caiaphas, for with God nothing is impossible; but, as in other things, so in his converse and attendance, he would humble himself, and show that God has *chosen the poor of this world*. Galilee was a remote part of the nation, the inhabitants were less cultivated and refined, their very language was broad and uncouth to the curious, their *speech betrayed them*. They who were picked up at the sea of Galilee, had not the advantages and improvements, no, not of the more polished Galileans; yet thither Christ went, to call his apostles that were to be the prime ministers of state in his kingdom, for he *chooses the foolish things of the world, to confound the wise*.

II. *Who* they were. We have an account of the call of two pair of brothers in these verses—Peter and Andrew, James and John; the two former, and, probably, the two latter also, had had acquaintance with Christ before (John i. 40, 41), but were not till now called into a close and constant attendance upon him. Note, Christ brings poor souls by degrees into fellowship with himself. They had been disciples of John, and so were the better disposed to follow Christ. Note, Those who have submitted to the discipline of repentance, shall be welcome to the joys of faith. We may observe concerning them,

1. That they were *brothers*. Note, It is a blessed thing, when they who are *kinsmen according to the flesh* (as the apostle speaks, Rom. ix. 3), are brought together into a spiritual alliance to Jesus Christ. It is the honour and comfort of a house, when those that are of the *same* family, are of *God's* family.

2. That they were *fishers*. Being fishers, (1.) They were *poor men:* if they had had estates, or any considerable stock in trade, they would not have made fishing their trade,

however they might have made it their recreation. Note, Christ does not despise the poor, and therefore we must not; the poor are evangelized, and the Fountain of honour sometimes gives more abundant honour to that part which most lacked. (2.) They were *unlearned men,* not bred up to books or literature as Moses was, who was conversant with all the learning of the Egyptians. Note, Christ sometimes chooses to endow those with the gifts of grace who have least to show of the gifts of nature. Yet this will not justify the bold intrusion of ignorant and unqualified men into the work of the ministry: extraordinary gifts of knowledge and utterance are not now to be expected, but requisite abilities must be obtained in an ordinary way, and without a competent measure of these, none are to be admitted to that service. (3.) They were *men of business,* who had been bred up to labour. Note, Diligence in an honest calling is pleasing to Christ, and no hindrance to a holy life. Moses was called from keeping sheep, and David from following the ewes, to eminent employments. Idle people lie more open to the temptations of Satan than to the calls of God. (4.) They were men that were accustomed to *hardships* and hazards; the fisher's trade, more than any other, is laborious and perilous; fishermen must be often wet and cold; they must watch, and wait, and toil, and be often in *peril by waters.* Note, Those who have learned to bear hardships, and to run hazards, are best prepared for the fellowship and discipleship of Jesus Christ. Good soldiers of Christ must endure hardness.

III. *What they were doing.* Peter and Andrew were then using their nets, they were fishing; and James and John were *mending their nets,* which was an instance of their industry and good husbandry. They did not go to their father for money to buy new nets, but took pains to mend their old ones. It is commendable to make what we have go as far, and last as long, as may be. James and John were *with their father Zebedee,* ready to assist him, and make his business easy to him. Note, It is a happy and hopeful presage, to see children careful of their parents, and dutiful to them. Observe, 1. They were *all* employed, all very busy, and none idle. Note, When Christ comes, it is good to be found doing. "Am I in Christ?" is a very needful question for us to ask ourselves; and, next to that, "Am I in my calling?" 2. They were *differently* employed; two of them were fishing, and two of them *mending their nets.* Note, Ministers should be always employed, either in teaching or studying; they may always find themselves something to do, if it be not their own fault; and *mending their nets,* is, in its season, as necessary work as fishing.

IV. *What the call was* (*v.* 19); *Follow me, and I will make you fishers of men.* They had followed Christ before, as ordinary disciples (John i. 37), but so they might follow Christ, and follow their calling too; therefore they were called to a more close and constant attendance, and must leave their calling. Note, Even they who have been called to follow Christ, have need to be called to follow on, and to follow nearer, especially when they are designed for the work of the ministry. Observe,

1. What Christ intended them for; *I will make you fishers of men;* this alludes to their former calling. Let them not be proud of the new honour designed them, they are still but fishers; let them not be afraid of the new work cut out for them, for they have been used to fishing, and fishers they are still. It was usual with Christ to speak of spiritual and heavenly things under such allusions, and in such expressions, as took rise from common things that offered themselves to his view. David was called from feeding sheep to feed God's Israel; and when he is a king, is a shepherd. Note, (1.) Ministers are *fishers of men,* not to destroy them, but to save them, by bringing them into another element. They must fish, not for wrath, wealth, honour, and preferment, to gain them to themselves, but for souls, to gain them to Christ. *They watch for your souls* (Heb. xiii. 17), *and seek not yours, but you,* 2 Cor. xii. 14, 16. (2.) It is Jesus Christ that makes them so; *I will make you fishers of men.* It is he that qualifies men for this work, calls them to it, authorizes them in it, and gives them success in it; gives them commission to fish for souls, and wisdom to win them. Those ministers are likely to have comfort in their work, who are thus made by Jesus Christ.

2. What they must do in order to this; *Follow me.* They must separate themselves to a diligent attendance on him, and set themselves to a humble imitation of him; must follow him as their Leader. Note, (1.) Those whom Christ employs in any service for him, must first be fitted and qualified for it. (2.) Those who would *preach Christ,* must first *learn* Christ, and learn of him. How can we expect to bring others to the knowledge of Christ, if we do not know him well ourselves? (3.) Those who would get an acquaintance with Christ, must be diligent and constant in their attendance on him. The apostles were prepared for their work, by *accompanying Christ all the time that he went in and out among them,* Acts i. 21. There is no learning comparable to that which is got by following Christ. Joshua, by ministering to Moses, is fitted to be his successor. (4.) Those who are to fish for men, must therein follow Christ, and do it as he did, with diligence, faithfulness, and tenderness. Christ is the great pattern for preachers, and they ought to be *workers together with him.*

V. What was the *success* of this call. Peter and Andrew *straightway left their nets* (*v.* 20); and James and John *immediately left the ship and their father* (*v.* 22); *and they* all *followed him.* Note, Those who would follow Christ aright, must *leave all* to follow him. Every Christian must leave all in affection, sit lose to all, must *hate father and mother* (Luke xiv. 26), must love them less than Christ, must be ready to part with his interest in them rather than with his interest in Jesus Christ; but those who are devoted to the work of the ministry are, in a special manner, concerned to disentangle themselves from all the affairs of this life, that they may give themselves wholly to that work which requires the whole man. Now,

1. This instance of the power of the Lord Jesus gives us good encouragement to depend upon the sufficiency of his grace. How strong and effectual is his word! *He speaks, and it is done.* The same power goes along with this word of Christ, *Follow me,* that went along with that word, *Lazarus, come forth;* a power *to make willing,* Ps. cx. 3.

2. This instance of the pliableness of the disciples, gives us a good example of obedience to the command of Christ. Note, It is the good property of all Christ's faithful servants to come when they are called, and to follow their Master wherever he leads them. They objected not their present employments, their engagements to their families, the difficulties of the service they were called to, or their own unfitness for it; but, being called, they obeyed, and, like Abraham, *went out not knowing whither they went,* but knowing very well whom they followed. James and John *left their father:* it is not said what became of him; their mother Salome was a constant follower of Christ; no doubt, their father Zebedee was a believer, but the call to follow Christ fastened on the young ones. Youth is the learning age, and the labouring age. The priests ministered in the prime of their life.

23 And Jesus went about all Galilee, teaching in their synagogues, and
preaching the gospel of the kingdom,
and healing all manner of sickness and
all manner of disease among the people. 24 And his fame went throughout all Syria: and they brought unto
him all sick people that were taken
with divers diseases and torments,
and those which were possessed with
devils, and those which were lunatic,
and those that had the palsy: and he
healed them. 25 And there followed
him great multitudes of people from
Galilee, and *from* Decapolis, and *from*
Jerusalem, and *from* Judea, and *from*
beyond Jordan.

See here, I. What an industrious preacher Christ was; He *went about all Galilee, teaching in their synagogues, and preaching the gospel of the kingdom.* Observe, 1. *What* Christ preached—*the gospel of the kingdom. The kingdom of heaven,* that is, of grace and glory, is emphatically *the kingdom, the kingdom* that was now to come; that kingdom which shall survive, as it doth surpass, all the kingdoms of the earth. *The gospel* is the charter of that kingdom, containing the King's coronation oath, by which he has graciously obliged himself to pardon, protect, and save the subjects of that kingdom; it contains also their oath of allegiance, by which they oblige themselves to observe his statutes and seek his honour; this is *the gospel of the kingdom;* this Christ was himself the Preacher of, that our faith in it might be confirmed. 2. *Where* he preached—*in the synagogues;* not there only, but there chiefly, because those were *the places of concourse,* where *wisdom* was to *lift up her voice* (Prov. i. 21); because they were *places of concourse* for religious worship, and there, it was to be hoped, the minds of the people would be prepared to receive *the gospel;* and there the scriptures of the Old Testament were read, the exposition of which would easily introduce *the gospel of the kingdom.* 3. *What pains he took* in preaching; He *went about all Galilee, teaching.* He might have issued out a proclamation to summon all to come to him; but, to show his humility, and the condescensions of his grace, he goes to them; for he *waits to be gracious,* and comes *to seek and save.* Josephus says, There were above two hundred cities and towns in Galilee, and all, or most of them, Christ visited. He *went about doing good.* Never was there such an itinerant preacher, such an indefatigable one, as Christ was; he went from town to town, to beseech poor sinners to be reconciled to God. This is an example to ministers, to lay themselves out to do good, and to *be instant,* and constant, in *season, and out of season,* to preach the word.

II. What a powerful physician Christ was; he *went about* not only *teaching,* but *healing,* and both with his word, that he might magnify that above all his name. *He sent his word, and healed them.* Now observe,

1. What diseases he cured—all without exception. He *healed all manner of sickness, and all manner of disease.* There are diseases which are called *the reproach of physicians,* being obstinate to all the methods they can prescribe; but even those were the glory of this Physician, for *he healed them* all, however inveterate. His word was the true *panpharmacon—all-heal.*

Three general words are here used to intimate this; he healed every sickness, Νόσον, as blindness, lameness, fever, dropsy; every *disease,* or languishing, Μαλακιαν, as fluxes and consumptions; and all *torments,* Βασανους, as gout, stone, convulsions, and such like torturing distempers; whether the disease was acute or chronical; whether it was a racking or a wasting disease; none was too bad, none too hard, for Christ to heal with a word's speaking.

Three particular diseases are specified; *the palsy,* which is the greatest weakness of the body; *lunacy,* which is the greatest malady of the mind, and *possession of the Devil,* which is the greatest misery and calamity of both, yet Christ healed all: for he is the sovereign Physician both of soul and body, and has command of all diseases.

2. What patients he had. A physician who was so easy of access, so sure of success, who cured immediately, without either a painful suspense and expectation, or such painful remedies as are worse than the disease; who cured gratis, and took no fees, could not but have abundance of patients. See here, what flocking there was to him from all parts; great multitudes of people came, not only *from Galilee* and the country about, but even *from Jerusalem* and *from Judea,* which lay a great way off; for *his fame went throughout all Syria,* not only among all the people of the Jews, but among the neighbouring nations, which, by the report that now spread far and near concerning him, would be prepared to receive his gospel, when afterwards it should be brought them. *This* is given as the reason why such multitudes came to him, because his fame had spread so widely. Note, What we hear of Christ from others, should invite us to him. The queen of Sheba was induced, by the fame of Solomon, to pay him a visit. The voice of fame is "Come, and see." Christ both *taught and healed.* They who came for cures, met with instruction concerning *the things that belonged to their peace.* It is well if any thing will bring people to Christ; and they who come to him will find more in him than they expected. These Syrians, like Naaman the Syrian, coming to be healed of their diseases, many of them became converts, 2 Kings v. 15, 17. They sought health for the body, and obtained the salvation of the soul; like Saul, who sought the asses, and found the kingdom. Yet it appeared, by the issue, that many of those who rejoiced in Christ as a Healer, forgot him as a Teacher.

Now concerning the cures which Christ wrought, let us, once for all, observe the *miracle,* the *mercy,* and the *mystery,* of them.

(1.) The *miracle* of them. They were wrought in such a manner, as plainly spake them to be the immediate products of a divine and supernatural power, and they were God's seal to his commission. Nature could not do these things, it was the God of nature; the cures were many, of diseases incurable by the art of the physician, of persons that were strangers, of all ages and conditions; the cures were wrought openly, before many witnesses, in mixed companies of persons that would have denied the matter of fact, if they could have had any colour for so doing; no cure ever failed, or was afterwards called in question; they were wrought speedily, and not (as cures by natural causes) gradually; they were perfect cures, and wrought with a word's speaking; all which proves him *a Teacher come from God,* for, otherwise, none could have done the works that he did, John iii. 2. He appeals to these as credentials, *ch.* xi. 4, 5; John v. 36. It was expected that the Messiah should work miracles (John vii. 31); miracles of this nature (Isa. xxxv. 5, 6); and we have this indisputable proof of his being the Messiah; never was there any man that did thus; and therefore his healing and his preaching generally went together, for the former confirmed the latter; thus here he *began to* do *and to* teach, Acts i. 1.

(2.) The *mercy* of them. The miracles that Moses wrought, to prove his mission, were most of them plagues and judgments, to intimate the terror of that dispensation, though from God; but the miracles that Christ wrought, were most of them cures, and all of them (except the cursing of the barren fig-tree) blessings and favours; for the gospel dispensation is founded, and built up in love, and grace, and sweetness; and the management is such as tends not to affright but to allure us to obedience. Christ designed by his cures to win upon people, and to ingratiate himself and his doctrine into their minds, and so to draw them with the bands of love, Hos. xi. 4. The miracle of them proved his doctrine *a faithful saying,* and convinced men's judgments; the mercy of them proved it *worthy of all acceptation,* and wrought upon their affections. They were not only *great* works, but *good works,* that he *showed them from* his *Father* (John x. 32); and this goodness was intended to *lead men to repentance* (Rom. ii. 4), as also to show that kindness, and beneficence, and doing good to all, to the utmost of our power and opportunity, are essential branches of that holy religion which Christ came into the world to establish.

(3.) The *mystery* of them. Christ, by curing *bodily diseases,* intended to show, that his great errand into the world was to cure *spiritual maladies.* He is the *Sun of righteousness,* that *arises with* this *healing under his wings.* As the Converter of sinners, he is the *Physician of souls,* and has taught us to call him so, *ch.* ix. 12, 13. Sin is the *sickness, disease,* and *torment* of the soul; Christ *came to take away sin,* and so to heal these. And the particular stories of the cures Christ wrought, may not only be applied spiritually, by way of allusion and illustration, but, I believe, are very much intended to reveal to us spiritual things, and to set before us the way and method of Christ's dealing with souls, in their conversion and sanctification; and those cures are recorded, that were most significant and instructive this way; and they are therefore so to be explained and improved, to the honour and praise of that glorious Redeemer, *who forgiveth all our iniquities, and* so *healeth all our diseases.*

CHAP. V.

This chapter, and the two that follow it, are a sermon; a famous sermon; the sermon upon the mount. It is the longest and fullest continued discourse of our Saviour that we have upon record in all the gospels. It is a practical discourse; there is not much of the credenda of Christianity in it—the things to be believed, but it is wholly taken up with the agenda—the things to be done; these Christ began with in his preaching; for if any man will do his will, he shall know of the doctrine, whether it be of God. The circumstances of the sermon being accounted for (ver. 1, 2), the sermon itself follows, the scope of which is, not to fill our heads with notions, but to guide and regulate our practice. I. He proposes blessedness as the end, and gives us the character of those who are entitled to blessedness (very different from the sentiments of a vain world), in eight beatitudes, which may justly be called paradoxes, ver. 3—12. II. He prescribes duty as the way, and gives us standing rules of that duty. He directs his disciples, 1. To understand what they are—the salt of the earth, and the lights of the world, ver. 13—16. 2. To understand what they have to do—they are to be governed by the moral law. Here is, (1.) A general ratification of the law, and a recommendation of it to us, as our rule, ver. 17—20. (2.) A particular rectification of divers mistakes; or, rather, a reformation of divers wilful, gross corruptions, which the scribes and Pharisees had introduced in their exposition of the law; and an authentic explication of divers branches which most needed to be explained and vindicated, ver. 20. Particularly, here is an explication, [1.] Of the sixth commandment, which forbids murder, ver. 21—26. [2.] Of the seventh commandment, against adultery, ver. 27—32. [3.] Of the third commandment, ver. 33—37. [4.] Of the law of retaliation, ver. 38—42. [5.] Of the law of brotherly love, ver. 43—48. And the scope of the whole is, to show that the law is spiritual.

AND seeing the multitudes, he went up into a mountain; and when he was set, his disciples came unto him: 2 And he opened his mouth, and taught them, saying.

We have here a general account of this sermon.

I. *The Preacher* was our Lord Jesus, the Prince of preachers, the great Prophet of his church, who *came into the world,* to be *the Light of the world.* The prophets and John had *done virtuously* in preaching, *but* Christ *excelled them all.* He is the eternal Wisdom, *that lay in the bosom of the Father, before all worlds,* and perfectly knew his will (John i. 18); and he is the eternal Word, by whom he *has in these last days spoken to us.* The many miraculous cures wrought by Christ in Galilee, which we read of in the close of the foregoing chapter, were intended to make way for this sermon, and to dispose people to receive instructions from one in whom there appeared so much of a divine power and goodness; and, probably, this sermon was the summary, or rehearsal, of what he had preached up and down in the synagogues of Galilee. His text was, *Repent, for the kingdom of heaven is at hand.* This is a sermon on the former part of that text, showing what it is to *repent;* it is to reform, both in judgment and practice; and he here tells us wherein, in answer to that question (Mal. iii. 7), *Wherein shall we return?* He afterward preached upon the latter part of the text, when, in divers parables, he showed what the kingdom of heaven is like, *ch.* xiii.

II. *The place* was a mountain in Galilee. As in other things, so in this, our Lord Jesus was but ill accommodated; he had no convenient place to preach in, any more than *to lay his head* on. While the scribes and Pharisees had Moses' chair to sit in, with all possible ease, honour, and state, and there corrupted the law; our Lord Jesus, the great Teacher of truth, is driven out to the desert, and finds no better a pulpit than *a mountain* can afford; and not one of the *holy mountains* neither, not one of *the mountains of Zion,* but a common *mountain;* by which Christ would intimate that there is no such distinguishing holiness of places now, under the gospel, as there was under the law; but that it is *the will of God that men should pray* and preach *every where,* any where, provided it be decent and convenient. Christ preached this sermon, which was an exposition of the law, upon a mountain, because upon *a mountain* the law was given; and this was also a solemn promulgation of the Christian law. But observe the difference: when *the law was given,* the Lord *came down* upon the *mountain;* now the Lord *went up:* then, he spoke *in thunder and lightning;* now, *in a still small voice:* then the people were ordered to keep their distance; now they are invited to draw near: a blessed change! If God's grace and goodness are (as certainly they are) his glory, then the glory of the gospel is the glory that excels, for *grace and truth came by Jesus Christ,* 2 Cor. iii. 7; Heb. xii. 18, &c. It was foretold of Zebulun and Issachar, two of the tribes of Galilee (Deut. xxxiii. 19), that *they shall call the people to the mountain;* to this *mountain* we are called, to learn *to offer the sacrifices of righteousness.* Now was this *the mountain of the Lord,* where he *taught us his ways,* Isa. ii. 2, 3. Mic. iv. 1, 2.

III. *The auditors* were *his disciples,* who *came unto him;* came at his call, as appears by comparing Mark iii. 13, Luke vi. 13. To them he directed his speech, because they followed him for love and learning, while others attended him only for cures. *He taught them,* because they were willing to be *taught (the meek will he teach his way);* because they would *understand* what he taught, which to others was foolishness; and because they were to teach others; and it was therefore requisite that they should have a clear and distinct knowledge of these things themselves. The duties prescribed in this sermon were to be conscientiously performed by all those that would *enter into that kingdom of heaven* which they were sent to set up, with hope to have the benefit of it. But though this discourse was directed to the disciples, it was in the hearing of *the multitude;* for it is said (*ch.* vii. 28), *The people were astonished.* No bounds were set about *this mountain,* to keep the people off, as were about *mount Sinai* (Exod. xix. 12); for, through Christ, we have access to God, not only to speak to him, but to hear from him. Nay, he had an eye to *the multitude,* in preaching this sermon. When the fame of his miracles had brought a vast crowd together, he took the opportunity of so great a confluence of people, to instruct them. Note, It is an encouragement to a faithful minister to cast the net of the gospel where there are a great many fishes, in hope that some will be caught. The sight of a *multitude* puts life into a preacher, which yet must arise from a desire of their profit, not his own praise.

IV. *The solemnity* of his sermon is intimated in that word, *when he was set.* Christ preached many times occasionally, and by interlocutory discourses; but this was a set sermon, *καθίσαντος αὐτοῦ,* when he had placed himself so as to be best heard. He sat down as a Judge or Lawgiver. It intimates with what sedateness and composure of mind the things of God should be spoken and heard. *He sat,* that *the scriptures might be fulfilled* (Mal. iii. 3), *He shall sit as a refiner,* to purge away the dross, the corrupt doctrines of the sons of Levi. *He sat* as *in the throne, judging right* (Ps. ix. 4); for *the word he spoke shall judge us.* That phrase, *He opened his mouth,* is only a Hebrew periphrasis of speaking, as Job iii. 1. Yet some think it intimates the solemnity of this discourse; the congregation being large, he raised his voice, and spoke louder than usual. He had spoken long *by his servants the prophets,* and *opened their mouths* (Ezek. iii. 27; xxiv. 27; xxxiii. 22); but now *he opened his* own, and spoke with freedom, *as one having authority.* One of the ancients has this remark upon it; Christ *taught* much without *opening his mouth,* that is, by his holy and exemplary life; nay, he *taught,* when, being *led as a lamb to the slaughter, he opened not his mouth,* but now *he opened his mouth, and taught,* that *the scriptures might be fulfilled,* Prov. viii. 1, 2, 6. *Doth not wisdom cry—cry on the top of high places?* And *the opening of her lips shall be right things. He taught them,* according to the promise (Isa. liv. 13), *All thy children shall be taught of the Lord;* for this purpose he had *the tongue of the learned* (Isa. l. 4), and *the Spirit of the Lord,* Isa. lxi. 1. *He taught them,* what was the evil they should abhor, and what the good they should abide and abound in; for Christianity is not a matter of speculation, but is designed to regulate the temper of our minds and the tenour of our conversations; gospel-time is a time of reformation (Heb. ix. 10); and by the gospel we must be reformed, must be made good, must be made better. *The truth, as it is in Jesus,* is *the truth which is accordingto godliness,* Tit. i. 1.

3 Blessed *are* the poor in spirit;
for theirs is the kingdom of heaven.
4 Blessed *are* they that mourn; for
they shall be comforted. 5 Blessed
are the meek: for they shall inherit
the earth. 6 Blessed *are* they which
do hunger and thirst after righteousness; for they shall be filled. 7
Blessed *are* the merciful: for they
shall obtain mercy. 8 Blessed *are*
the pure in heart; for they shall see
God. 9 Blessed *are* the peace-
makers: for they shall be called the
children of God. 10 Blessed *are*
they which are persecuted for righteousness' sake: for theirs is the kingdom of heaven. 11 Blessed are ye,
when *men* shall revile you, and persecute *you,* and shall say all manner
of evil against you falsely, for my
sake. 12 Rejoice, and be exceeding
glad: for great *is* your reward in
heaven: for so persecuted they the
prophets which were before you.

Christ begins his sermon with blessings, for *he came into the world to bless us* (Acts iii. 26), as *the great High Priest of our profession;* as *the blessed Melchizedec;* as He *in whom all the families of the earth should be blessed,* Gen. xii. 3. He came not only to purchase blessings for us, but to pour out and pronounce blessings on us; and here he does it *as one having authority,* as one that can *command the blessing, even life for evermore,* and that is the blessing here again and again promised to the good; his pronouncing them happy makes them so; for those whom he blesses, are blessed indeed. The Old Testament ended with a curse (Mal. iv. 6), the gospel begins with a blessing; for *hereunto are we called, that we should inherit the blessing.* Each of the blessings Christ here pronounces has a double intention: 1. To show who they are that are to be accounted truly happy, and what their characters are. 2. What that is wherein true happiness consists, in the promises made to persons of certain characters, the performance of which will make them happy. Now,

1. This is designed to rectify the ruinous mistakes of a blind and carnal world. Blessedness is the thing which men pretend to pursue; *Who will make us to see good?* Ps. iv. 6. But most mistake the end, and form a wrong notion of happiness; and then no wonder that they miss the way; they choose their own delusions, and court a shadow. The general opinion is, *Blessed are they* that are rich, and great, and honourable in the world; that spend their days in mirth, and their years in pleasure; that eat the fat, and drink the sweet, and carry all before them with a high hand, and have every sheaf bowing to their sheaf; *happy the people that is in such a case;* and their designs, aims, and purposes are accordingly; they *bless the covetous* (Ps. x. 3); they *will be rich.* Now our Lord Jesus comes to correct this fundamental error, to advance a new hypothesis, and to give us quite another notion of blessedness and blessed people, which, however paradoxical it may appear to those who are prejudiced, yet is in itself, and appears to be to all who are savingly enlightened, a rule

and doctrine of eternal truth and certainty, by which we must shortly be judged. If this, therefore, be the beginning of Christ's doctrine, the beginning of a Christian's practice must be to take his measures of happiness from those maxims, and to direct his pursuits accordingly.

2. It is designed to remove the discouragements of the weak and poor who receive the gospel, by assuring them that his gospel did not make those only happy that were eminent in gifts, graces, comforts, and usefulness; but that even *the least in the kingdom of heaven,* whose heart was upright with God, was happy in the honours and privileges of that kingdom.

3. It is designed to invite souls to Christ, and to make way for his law into their hearts. Christ's pronouncing these blessings, not at the end of his sermon, to dismiss the people, but at the beginning of it, to prepare them for what he had further to say to them, may remind us of mount Gerizim and mount Ebal, on which the blessings and cursings of the law were read, Deut. xxvii. 12, &c. *There* the curses are expressed, and the blessings only implied; *here* the blessings are expressed, and the curses implied: in both, *life and death are set before us;* but the law appeared more as a ministration of death, to deter us from sin; the gospel as a dispensation of life, to allure us to Christ, in whom alone all good is to be had. And those who had seen the gracious cures wrought by his hand (*ch.* iv. 23, 24), and now heard *the gracious words proceeding out of his mouth,* would say that he was all of a piece, made up of love and sweetness.

4. It is designed to settle and sum up the articles of agreement between God and man. The scope of the divine revelation is to let us know what God expects from us, and what we may then expect from him; and no where is this more fully set forth in a few words than here, nor with a more exact reference to each other; and this is that gospel which we are required to believe; for what is faith but a conformity to these characters, and a dependence upon these promises? The way to happiness is here opened, and made a *highway* (Isa. xxxv. 8); and this coming from the mouth of Jesus Christ, it is intimated that from him, and by him, we are to receive both the seed and the fruit, both the grace required, and the glory promised. Nothing passes between God and fallen man, but through his hand. Some of the wiser heathen had notions of blessedness different from the rest of mankind, and looking toward this of our Saviour. Seneca, undertaking to describe a blessed man, makes it out, that it is only an honest, good man that is to be so called: *De vita beata,* cap. iv. *Cui nullum bonum malumque sit, nisi bonus malusque animus—Quem nec extollant fortuita, nec frangant — Cui vera voluptas erit voluptatum contemptio—Cui unum bonum honestas, unum malum turpitudo.—In whose estimation nothing is good or evil, but a good or evil heart—Whom no occurrences elate or deject—Whose true pleasure consists in a contempt of pleasure—To whom the only good is virtue, and the only evil vice.*

Our Saviour here gives us eight characters of blessed people; which represent to us the principal graces of a Christian. On each of them a present blessing is pronounced; *Blessed are* they; and to each a future blessedness is promised, which is variously expressed, so as to suit the nature of the grace or duty recommended.

Do we ask then who are happy? It is answered,

I. *The poor in spirit* are happy, *v.* 3. There is a poor-spiritedness that is so far from making men blessed that it is a sin and a snare—cowardice and base fear, and a willing subjection to the lusts of men. But this poverty of spirit is a gracious disposition of soul, by which we are emptied of self, in order to our being filled with Jesus Christ. To be *poor in spirit* is, 1. To be contentedly poor, willing to be empty of worldly wealth, if God orders that to be our lot; to bring our mind to our condition, when it is a low condition. Many are poor in the world, but high in spirit, poor and proud, murmuring and complaining, and blaming their lot, but we must accommodate ourselves to our poverty, must *know how to be abased,* Phil. iv. 12. Acknowledging the wisdom of God in appointing us to poverty, we must be easy in it, patiently bear the inconveniences of it, be thankful for what we have, and make the best of that which is. It is to sit loose to all worldly wealth, and not set our hearts upon it, but cheerfully to bear losses and disappointments which may befal us in the most prosperous state. It is not, in pride or pretence, to make ourselves poor, by throwing away what God has given us, especially as those in the church of Rome, who vow poverty, and yet engross the wealth of nations; but if we be rich in the world we must be *poor in spirit,* that is, we must condescend to the poor and sympathize with them, as being touched with the feeling of their infirmities; we must expect and prepare for poverty; must not inordinately fear or shun it, but must bid it welcome, especially when it comes upon us for keeping a good conscience, Heb. x. 34. Job was *poor in spirit,* when he blessed God in *taking away,* as well as giving. 2. It is to be humble and lowly in our own eyes. To be *poor in spirit,* is to think meanly of ourselves, of what we are, and have, and do; the poor are often taken in the Old Testament for the humble and self-denying, as opposed to those that are at ease, and the proud; it is to be as little children in our opinion of ourselves, weak, foolish, and insignificant, *ch.* xviii. 4; xix. 14. Laodicea was *poor in spirituals,* wretchedly and miserably poor, and yet *rich in spirit,* so well increased with goods, as to *have need of nothing,* Rev. iii. 17. On the other hand, Paul was rich in *spirituals,* excelling most in gifts and graces, and yet *poor in spirit, the least of the apostles,* less than the least of all saints, and *nothing* in his own account. It is to look with a holy contempt upon ourselves, to value others and undervalue ourselves in comparison of them. It is to be willing to make ourselves cheap, and mean, and little, to do good; to *become all things to all men.* It is to acknowledge that God is great, and we are mean; that he is holy and we are sinful; that he is all and we are nothing, less than nothing, worse than nothing; and to humble ourselves before him, and under his mighty hand. 3. It is to come off from all confidence in our own righteousness and strength, that we may depend only upon the merit of Christ for our justification, and the spirit and grace of Christ for our sanctification. That *broken and contrite spirit* with which the publican cried for mercy to a poor sinner, is this poverty of spirit. We must call ourselves poor, because always in want of God's grace, always begging at God's door, always hanging on in his house.

Now, (1.) This poverty in spirit is put first among the Christian graces. The philosophers did not reckon humility among their moral virtues, but Christ puts it first. Self-denial is the first lesson to be learned in his school, and poverty of spirit entitled to the first beatitude. The foundation of all other graces is laid in humility. Those who would build high must begin low; and it is an excellent preparative for the entrance of gospel-grace into the soul; it fits the soil to receive the seed. Those *who are weary and heavy laden,* are *the poor in spirit,* and they shall find rest with Christ.

(2.) They are *blessed.* Now they are so, in this world. God looks graciously upon them. They are his little ones, and have their angels. To them he gives more grace; they live the most comfortable lives, and are easy to themselves and all about them, and nothing comes amiss to them; while high spirits are always uneasy.

(3.) *Theirs is the kingdom of heaven.* The kingdom of *grace* is composed of such; they only are fit to be members of Christ's church, which is called *the congregation of the poor* (Ps. lxxiv. 19); the kingdom of *glory* is prepared for them. Those who thus humble themselves, and comply with God when he humbles them, shall be thus exalted. The great, high spirits go away with the glory of *the kingdoms of the earth;* but the humble, mild, and yielding souls obtain the glory of *the kingdom of heaven.* We are ready to think concerning those who are rich, and do good with their riches, that, no doubt, *theirs is the kingdom of heaven;* for they can thus lay up in store a good security *for the time to come;* but what shall the poor do, who have not wherewithal to do good? Why, the same happiness is promised to those who are contentedly poor, as to those who are usefully rich. If I am not able to *spend* cheerfully for his sake, if I can but *want* cheerfully for his sake, even that shall be recompensed. And do not we serve a good master then?

II. *They that mourn* are happy (*v.* 4); *Blessed are they that mourn.* This is another strange blessing, and fitly follows the former. The poor are accustomed to mourn, the graciously poor mourn graciously. We are apt to think, Blessed are the *merry;* but Christ, who was himself a great mourner, says, Blessed are the *mourners.* There is a sinful mourning, which is an enemy to blessedness—*the sorrow of the world;* despairing melancholy upon a spiritual account, and disconsolate grief upon a temporal account. There is a natural mourning, which may prove a friend to blessedness, by the grace of God working with it, and sanctifying the afflictions to us, for which we mourn. But there is a gracious mourning, which qualifies for blessedness, an habitual seriousness, the mind mortified to mirth, and an actual sorrow. 1. A penitential mourning for our own sins; this is *godly sorrow,* a sorrow according to God; sorrow for sin, with an eye to Christ, Zech. xii. 10. Those are God's mourners, who live a life of repentance, who lament the corruption of their nature, and their many actual transgressions, and God's withdrawings from them; and who, out of regard to God's honour, mourn also for the sins of others, and *sigh and cry for their abominations,* Ezek. ix. 4. 2. A sympathizing mourning for the afflictions of others; the mourning of those who *weep with them that weep,* are sorrowful *for the solemn assemblies, for the desolations of Zion* (Zeph. iii. 18; Ps. cxxxvii. 1), especially who look with compassion on perishing souls, and *weep over* them, as Christ *over Jerusalem.*

Now these gracious mourners, (1.) *Are blessed.* As in vain and sinful *laughter the heart is sorrowful,* so in gracious mourning *the heart* has a serious joy, a secret satisfaction, which *a stranger does not intermeddle with.* They are *blessed,* for they are like the Lord Jesus, who *was a man of sorrows,* and of whom we never read that he laughed, but often that he wept. They are armed against the many temptations that attend vain mirth, and are prepared for the comforts of a sealed pardon and a settled peace. (2.) *They shall be comforted.* Though perhaps they are not immediately comforted, yet plentiful provision is made for their comfort; light is sown for them; and in heaven, it is certain, *they shall be comforted,* as Lazarus, Luke xvi. 25. Note, The happiness of heaven consists in being perfectly and eternally comforted, and in the *wiping away of all tears from their eyes.* It is *the joy of our Lord; a fulness of joy and pleasures for evermore;* which will be doubly sweet to those who have been prepared for them by this *godly sorrow.* Heaven will be heaven indeed to those who go mourning thither; it will be a harvest of joy, the return of a seed-time of tears (Ps. cxxvi. 5, 6); a mountain of joy, to which our way lies through a vale of tears. See Isa. lxvi. 10.

III. *The meek* are happy (*v.* 5); *Blessed are the meek.* The meek are those who quietly submit themselves to God, to his word and to his rod, who follow his directions, and comply with his designs, and are *gentle towards all men* (Tit. iii. 2); who can bear provocation without being inflamed by it; are either silent, or return a soft answer; and who can show their displeasure when there is occasion for it, without being transported into any indecencies; who can be cool when others are hot; and in their patience keep possession of their own souls, when they can scarcely keep possession of any thing else. *They* are the meek, who are rarely and hardly provoked, but quickly and easily pacified; and who would rather forgive twenty injuries than revenge one, having the rule of their own spirits.

These meek ones are here represented as happy, even in this world. 1. They are *blessed,* for they are like the blessed Jesus, in that wherein particularly they are to learn of him, *ch.* xi. 29. They are like the blessed God himself, who is Lord of his anger, and in whom fury is not. They are *blessed,* for they have the most comfortable, undisturbed enjoyment of themselves, their friends, their God; they are fit for any relation, any condition, any company; fit to live, and fit to die. 2. *They shall inherit the earth;* it is quoted from Ps. xxxvii. 11, and it is almost the only express temporal promise in all the New Testament. Not that they shall always have much of *the earth,* much less that they shall be put off with that only; but this branch of godliness has, in a special manner, *the promise of the life that now is.* Meekness, however ridiculed and run down, has a real tendency to promote our health, wealth, comfort, and safety, even in this world. *The meek* and quiet are observed to live the most easy lives, compared with the froward and turbulent. Or, *They shall inherit the land* (so it may be read), *the land of Canaan,* a type of heaven. So that all the blessedness of heaven above, and all the blessings of earth beneath, are the portion of the meek.

IV. *They that hunger and thirst after righteousness* are happy, *v.* 6. Some understand this as a further instance of outward poverty, and a low condition in this world, which not only exposes men to injury and wrong, but makes it in vain for them to seek to have justice done them; they *hunger and thirst after* it, but such is the power on the side of their oppressors, that they cannot have it; they desire only that which is just and equal, but it is denied them by those that *neither fear God nor regard man.* This is a melancholy case! Yet, *blessed are they,* if they suffer these hardships for and with a good conscience; let them hope in God, who will see justice done, right take place, and will deliver the poor from their oppressors, Ps. ciii. 6. Those who contentedly bear oppression, and quietly refer themselves to God to plead their cause, shall in due time be satisfied, abundantly satisfied, in the wisdom and kindness which shall be manifested in his appearances for them. But it is certainly to be understood spiritually, of such a desire as, being terminated on such an object, is gracious, and the work of God's grace in the soul, and qualifies for the gifts of the divine favour. 1. *Righteousness* is here put for all spiritual blessings. See Ps. xxiv. 5; *ch.* vi. 33. They are purchased for us by *the righteousness of Christ;* conveyed and secured by the imputation of that righteousness to us; and confirmed by the faithfulness of God. To have Christ *made of God to us righteousness,* and to be *made the righteousness of God in him;* to have *the whole man renewed in righteousness,* so as to become *a new man,* and to bear the image of God; to have an interest in Christ and the promises—this is *righteousness.* 2. These we must *hunger and thirst after.* We must truly and really desire them, as one who is hungry and thirsty desires meat and drink, who cannot be satisfied with any thing but meat and drink, and will be satisfied with them, though other things be wanting. Our desires of spiritual blessings must be earnest and importunate; "*Give me these, or else I die;* every thing else is dross and chaff, unsatisfying; give me these, and I have enough, though I had nothing else." *Hunger and thirst* are appetites that return frequently, and call for fresh satisfactions; so these holy desires rest not in any thing attained, but are carried out toward renewed pardons, and daily fresh supplies of grace. The quickened soul calls for constant meals of righteousness, grace to do the work of every day in its day, as duly as the living body calls for food. Those who *hunger and thirst* will labour for supplies; so we must not only desire spiritual blessings, but take pains for them in the use of the appointed means. Dr. Hammond, in his practical Catechism, distinguishes between *hunger and thirst. Hunger* is a desire of food to sustain, such is *sanctifying righteousness. Thirst* is the desire of drink to refresh, such is justifying *righteousness,* and the sense of our pardon.

Those who thus *hunger and thirst* after spiritual blessings, *are blessed* in those desires, and *shall be filled* with those blessings. (1.) They are *blessed* in those desires. Though all desires of grace are not grace (feigned, faint desires are not), yet such a desire as this is; it is an *evidence* of something *good,* and an *earnest* of something *better.* It is a desire of God's own raising, and he will not forsake the work of his own hands. Something or other the soul will be *hungering* and *thirsting* after; therefore *they* are blessed who fasten upon the right object, which is satisfying, and not deceiving; and do not *pant after the dust of the earth,* Amos ii. 7; Isa. lv. 2. (2.) They *shall be filled* with those blessings. God will give them what they desire to their complete satisfaction. It is God only who can *fill a soul,* whose grace and favour are adequate to its just desires; and he will fill those with *grace for grace,* who, in a sense of their own emptiness, have recourse to his fulness. He *fills the hungry* (Luke i. 53), *satiates* them, Jer. xxxi. 25. The happiness of heaven will certainly fill the soul; their righteousness shall be complete, the favour of God and his image, both in their full perfection.

V. The *merciful* are happy, *v.* 7. This, like the rest, is a paradox; for the merciful are not taken to be the wisest, nor are likely to be the richest; yet Christ pronounces them *blessed.* Those are the *merciful,* who are piously and charitably inclined to pity, help, and succour persons in misery. A man may be truly *merciful,* who has not wherewithal to be bountiful or liberal; and then God accepts the willing mind. We must not only bear our own afflictions patiently, but we must, by Christian sympathy, partake of the afflictions of our brethren; pity must be shown (Job vi. 14), and *bowels of mercy put on* (Col. iii. 12); and, being put on, they must put forth themselves in contributing all we can for the assistance of those who are any way in misery. We must have compassion on the souls of others, and help them; pity the ignorant, and instruct them; the careless, and warn them; those who are in a state of sin, and snatch them as *brands out of the burning.* We must have compassion on those who are melancholy and in sorrow, and comfort them (Job xvi. 5); on those whom we have advantage against, and not be rigorous and severe with them; on those who are in want, and supply them; which if we refuse to do, whatever we pretend, we *shut up the bowels of our compassion,* James ii. 15, 16; 1 John iii. 17. *Draw out thy soul* by *dealing thy bread* to the hungry, Isa. lviii. 7, 10. Nay, a *good man is merciful to his beast.*

Now, as to the merciful, 1. They are *blessed;* so it was said in the Old Testament; *Blessed is he that considers the poor,* Ps. xli. 1. Herein they resemble God, whose goodness is his glory; in being *merciful as he is merciful,* we are, in our measure, *perfect as he is perfect.* It is an evidence of love to God; it will be a satisfaction to ourselves, to be any way instrumental for the benefit of others. One of the purest and most refined delights in this world, is that of *doing good.* In this word, *Blessed are the merciful,* is included that saying of Christ, which otherwise we find not in the gospels, *It is more blessed to give than to receive,* Acts xx. 35. 2. *They shall obtain mercy;* mercy *with men,* when they need it; *he that watereth, shall be watered also himself* (we know not how soon we may stand in need of kindness, and therefore should be kind); but especially mercy *with God,* for *with the merciful he will show himself merciful,* Ps. xviii. 25. The most *merciful* and charitable cannot pretend to *merit,* but must fly to mercy. The merciful shall find with God *sparing* mercy *(ch.* vi. 14), *supplying* mercy (Prov. xix. 17), *sustaining* mercy (Ps. xli. 2), mercy in that day (2 Tim. i. 18); nay, they shall *inherit the kingdom prepared for them (ch.* xxv. 34, 35); whereas *they* shall have *judgment without mercy* (which can be nothing short of *hell-fire)* who have *shown no mercy.*

VI. The *pure in heart* are happy (*v.* 8); *Blessed are the pure in heart, for they shall see God.* This is the most comprehensive of all the beatitudes; here holiness and happiness are fully described and put together.

1. Here is the most *comprehensive character* of the blessed; they are the *pure in heart.* Note, True religion consists in heart-purity. Those who are inwardly pure, show themselves to be under the power of *pure and undefiled* religion. True Christianity lies in the heart, in the *purity of the heart;* the *washing* of that *from wickedness,* Jer. iv. 14. We must lift up to God, not only clean hands, but a pure heart, Ps. xxiv. 4, 5; 1 Tim. i. 5. The heart must be *pure,* in opposition to *mixture*—an honest heart that aims well; and pure, in opposition to *pollution* and *defilement;* as wine *unmixed,* as water *unmuddied.* The heart must be kept *pure* from *fleshly lusts,* all unchaste thoughts and desires; and from *worldly lusts;* covetousness is called *filthy lucre;* from all filthiness of flesh and spirit, all that which comes *out of the heart,* and *defiles the man.* The heart must be *purified by faith,* and entire for God; must be presented and preserved a chaste virgin to Christ. *Create in me such a clean heart, O God!*

2. Here is the most *comprehensive comfort* of the blessed; They shall see God. Note, (1.) It is the perfection of the soul's happiness to *see God; seeing him,* as we may by faith in our present state, is a *heaven upon earth;* and seeing him as we shall in the future state, is the *heaven of heaven.* To see him *as he is,* face to face, and no longer through a glass darkly; to see him as ours, and to see him and enjoy him; to see him and be like him, and be satisfied with that likeness (Ps. xvii. 15); and to see him for ever, and never lose the sight of him; this is heaven's happiness. (2.) The happiness of seeing God is promised to those, and those only, who are *pure in heart.* None but the *pure* are capable of *seeing* God, nor would it be a felicity to the impure. What pleasure could an unsanctified soul take in the vision of a holy God? As *he* cannot endure to look upon their iniquity, so *they* cannot endure to

look upon his purity; nor shall any unclean thing enter into the new Jerusalem; but all that are *pure in heart,* all that are truly sanctified, have desires wrought in them, which nothing but the sight of God will satisfy; and divine grace will not leave those desires unsatisfied.

VII. The *peace-makers* are happy, *v.* 9. The wisdom that is from above is first *pure,* and then *peaceable;* the blessed ones are *pure* toward God, and *peaceable* toward men; for with reference to both, conscience must be kept *void of offence.* The *peace-makers* are those who have, 1. *A peaceable disposition:* as, to *make a lie,* is to be given and addicted to lying, so, to *make peace,* is to have a strong and hearty affection to peace. *I am for peace,* Ps. cxx. 7. It is to love, and desire, and delight in peace; to be in it as in our element, and to study to be quiet. 2. A *peaceable conversation;* industriously, as far as we can, to preserve the peace that it be not broken, and to recover it when it is broken; to hearken to proposals of peace ourselves, and to be ready to make them to others; where distance is among brethren and neighbours, to do all we can to accommodate it, and to be *repairers of the breaches.* The *making of peace* is sometimes a *thankless office,* and it is the lot of him who parts a fray, to have *blows on both sides;* yet it is a good office, and we must be forward to it. Some think that this is intended especially as a lesson for ministers, who should do all they can to reconcile those who are at variance, and to promote Christian love among those under their charge.

Now, (1.) Such persons are *blessed;* for they have the satisfaction of *enjoying themselves,* by keeping the peace, and of being truly serviceable to others, by disposing them to peace. They are working together with Christ, who came into the world to *slay all enmities,* and to proclaim *peace on earth.* (2.) *They shall be called the children of God;* it will be an evidence to themselves that they are so; God will own them as such, and herein they will resemble him. He is the God of peace; the Son of God is the Prince of peace; the Spirit of adoption is a Spirit of peace. Since God has declared himself reconcileable to us all, he will not own those for his children who are implacable in their enmity to one another; for if the peace-makers are blessed, woe to the peace-breakers! Now by this it appears, that Christ never intended to have his religion propagated by fire and sword, or penal laws, or to acknowledge bigotry, or intemperate zeal, as the mark of his disciples. The children of this world love to fish in troubled waters, but the children of God are the peace-makers, the *quiet in the land.*

VIII. Those who are *persecuted for righteousness' sake,* are happy. This is the greatest paradox of all, and peculiar to Christianity; and therefore it is put last, and more largely insisted upon than any of the rest, *v.* 10—12. This beatitude, like Pharaoh s dream, is doubled, because hardly credited, and yet *the thing is certain;* and in the latter part there is a change of the person, "Blessed are *ye*—ye my disciples, and immediate followers. This is that which you, who excel in virtue, are more immediately concerned in; for you must reckon upon hardships and troubles more than other men." Observe here,

1. The case of suffering saints described; and it is a hard case, and a very piteous one.

(1.) They are persecuted, hunted, pursued, run down, as noxious beasts are, that are sought for to be destroyed; as if a Christian did *caput gerere lupinum—bear a wolf's head,* as an outlaw is said to do—any one that finds him may slay him; they are abandoned as the *offscouring of all things;* fined, imprisoned, banished, stripped of their estates, excluded from all places of profit and trust, scourged, racked, tortured, always delivered to death, and accounted as sheep for the slaughter. This has been the effect of the enmity of the serpent's seed against the holy seed, ever since the time *of righteous Abel.* It was so in *Old-Testament* times, as we find, Heb. xi. 35, &c. Christ has told us that it would much more be so with the Christian church, and we are not to think it strange, 1 John iii. 13. He has left us an example.

(2.) They are *reviled, and have all manner of evil said against them falsely.* Nick-names, and names of reproach, are fastened upon them, upon particular persons, and upon the generation of the righteous in the gross, to render them odious; sometimes to make them despicable, that they may be trampled upon; sometimes to make them formidable, that they may be powerfully assailed; things are laid to their charge that they knew not, Ps. xxxv. 11; Jer. xx. 18; Acts xvii. 6, 7. Those who have had no power in their hands to do them any other mischief, could yet do this; and those who have had power to *persecute,* have found it necessary to *do this too,* to justify themselves in their barbarous usage of them; they could not have baited them, if they had not dressed them in bear-skins; nor have given them the worst of treatment, if they had not first represented them as the worst of men. They will *revile you, and persecute you.* Note, *Reviling* the saints is *persecuting* them, and will be found so shortly, when *hard speeches* must be accounted for (Jude 15), and *cruel mockings,* Heb. xi. 36. They will say all *manner of evil of you falsely;* sometimes before the *seat of judgment,* as witnesses; sometimes in the *seat of the scornful,* with *hypocritical mockers at feasts;* they are the *song of the drunkards;* sometimes to their faces, as Shimei cursed David; sometimes behind their backs, as the enemies of Jeremiah did. Note, There is no evil so black and horrid, which, at one time or other, has not been said, falsely, of Christ's disciples and followers.

(3.) All this is *for righteousness' sake* (*v.* 10); *for my sake, v.* 11. If for *righteousness' sake,* then for *Christ's sake,* for he is nearly interested in the work of righteousness. Enemies to righteousness are enemies to Christ. This precludes those from this blessedness who suffer *justly,* and are evil spoken of *truly* for their real crimes; let such be ashamed and confounded, it is part of their punishment; it is not the suffering, but the cause, that makes the martyr. Those suffer *for righteousness' sake,* who suffer because they will not sin against their consciences, and who suffer for doing that which is good. Whatever pretence persecutors have, it is the power of godliness that they have an enmity to; it is really Christ and his righteousness that are maligned, hated, and persecuted; *For thy sake I have borne reproach,* Ps. lxix. 9. Rom. viii. 36.

2. The comforts of suffering saints laid down.

(1.) They *are blessed;* for they now, in their life-time, receive *their evil things* (Luke xvi. 25), and receive them upon a good account. They are *blessed,* for it is an honour to them (Acts v. 41); it is an opportunity of glorifying Christ, of doing good, and of experiencing special comforts and visits of grace and tokens of his presence, 2 Cor. i. 5; Dan. iii. 25; Rom. viii. 29.

(2.) They shall be *recompensed;* Theirs is *the kingdom of heaven.* They have at present a sure title to it, and sweet foretastes of it; and shall ere long be in possession of it. Though there be nothing in those sufferings that can, in strictness, merit of God (for the sins of the best deserve the worst), yet this is here promised as a *reward* (*v.* 12); *Great is your reward in heaven:* so great, as far to transcend the service. It is *in heaven,* future, and out of sight; but well secured, out of the reach of chance, fraud, and violence. Note, God will provide that those who lose *for* him, though it be life itself, shall not lose *by* him in the end. Heaven, at last, will be an abundant recompence for all the difficulties we meet with in our way. This is that which has borne up the suffering saints in all ages —this *joy set before them.*

(3.) "*So persecuted they the prophets that were before you, v.* 12. They were *before you* in excellency, above what you are yet arrived at; they were *before you* in time, that they might be examples to you of *suffering affliction* and *of patience,* James v. 10. They were in like manner persecuted and abused; and can you expect to go to heaven in a way by yourselves? Was not Isaiah mocked for his *line upon line? Elisha* for his *bald head?* Were not all the prophets thus treated? Therefore *marvel not* at it as a *strange* thing, *murmur not* at it as a *hard* thing; it is a comfort to see the way of suffering a beaten road, and an honour to follow such leaders. That grace which was *sufficient for them,* to carry them through their sufferings, shall not be *deficient to you.* Those who are your enemies are the seed and successors of them who of old mocked the messengers of the Lord," 2 Chron. xxxvi. 16; *ch.* xxiii. 31; Acts vii. 52.

(4.) Therefore *rejoice and be exceeding glad, v.* 12. It is not enough to be patient and content under these sufferings as under common afflictions, and not to render railing for railing; but we must rejoice, because the honour and dignity, the pleasure and advantage, of suffering for Christ, are much more considerable than the pain or shame of it. Not that we must take a *pride* in our sufferings, (that spoils all), but we must take *a pleasure* in them, as Paul (2 Cor. xii. 10); as knowing that Christ is herein *before-hand* with us, and that he will not be *behind-hand* with us, 1 Pet. iv. 12, 13.

13 Ye are the salt of the earth;
but if the salt have lost his savour,
wherewith shall it be salted? It is
thenceforth good for nothing, but to
be cast out, and to be trodden under
foot of men. 14 Ye are the light of
the world. A city that is set on a
hill cannot be hid. 15 Neither do
men light a candle, and put it under
a bushel, but on a candlestick; and
it giveth light unto all that are in the
house. 16 Let your light so shine
before men, that they may see your
good works, and glorify your Father
which is in heaven.

Christ had lately called his disciples, and told them that they should be *fishers of men;* here he tells them further what he designed them to be—*the salt of the earth,* and *lights of the world,* that they might be indeed what it was expected they should be.

I. *Ye are the salt of the earth. This* would encourage and support them under their sufferings, that, though they should be treated with contempt, yet they should really be blessings to the world, and the more so for their suffering thus. The prophets, who went before them, were the salt of the land of Canaan; but the apostles were the salt of *the whole earth,* for they must *go into all the world to preach the gospel.* It was a discouragement to them that they were so *few* and so *weak.* What could they do in so large a province as *the whole earth?* Nothing, if they were to work by force of arms and dint of sword; but, being to work silently as salt, one handful of that salt would diffuse its savour far and wide; would go a great way, and work insensibly and irresistibly as leaven, *ch.* xiii. 33. The doctrine of the gospel is as *salt;* it is penetrating, *quick,* and *powerful* (Heb. iv. 12); it reaches *the heart,* Acts ii. 37. It is cleansing, it is relishing, and preserves from putrefaction. We read of the *savour of the knowledge of Christ* (2 Cor. ii. 14); for all other learning is insipid without that. An everlasting covenant is called a *covenant of salt* (Numb. xviii. 19); and the gospel is an everlasting gospel. Salt was required in all the sacrifices (Lev. ii. 13), in Ezekiel's mystical temple, Ezek. xliii. 24. Now Christ's disciples having themselves learned the doctrine of the gospel, and being employed to teach it to others, were as salt. Note, Christians, and especially ministers, are the salt of the earth.

1. If they be such as they should be they are *as good salt*, white, and small, and broken into many grains, but very useful and necessary. Pliny says, *Sine sale, vita humana non potest degere—Without salt human life cannot be sustained.* See in this, (1.) What they are to be in themselves—seasoned with the gospel, with the salt of grace; thoughts and affections, words and actions, all seasoned with grace, Col. iv. 6. *Have salt in yourselves*, else you cannot diffuse it among others, Mark ix. 50. (2.) What they are to be to others; they must not only *be* good but *do* good, must insinuate themselves into the minds of people, not to serve any secular interest of their own, but that they may transform them into the taste and relish of the gospel. (3.) What great blessings they are to the world. Mankind, lying in ignorance and wickedness, were a vast heap of unsavoury stuff, ready to putrefy; but Christ sent forth his disciples, by their lives and doctrines, to season it with knowledge and grace, and so to render it acceptable to God, to the angels, and to all that relish divine things. (4.) How they must expect to be disposed of. They must not be laid on a heap, must not continue always together at Jerusalem, but must be scattered as salt upon the meat, here a grain and there a grain; as the Levites were dispersed in Israel, that, wherever they live, they may communicate their savour. Some have observed, that whereas it is foolishly called an ill omen to have the salt fall towards us, it is really an ill omen to have this salt fall from us.

2. If they be not, they are as *salt* that has *lost its savour*. If you, who should season others, are yourselves unsavoury, void of spiritual life, relish, and vigour; if a Christian be so, especially if a minister be so, his condition is very sad; for, (1.) He is *irrecoverable: Wherewith shall it be salted?* Salt is a remedy for *unsavoury meat*, but there is no remedy for *unsavoury salt.* Christianity will give a man a relish; but if a man can take up and continue the profession of it, and yet remain flat and foolish, and graceless and insipid, no other doctrine, no other means, can be applied, to make him savoury. If Christianity do not do it, nothing will. (2) He is *unprofitable: It is thenceforth good for nothing;* what use can it be put to, in which it will not do more hurt than good? As a man without reason, so is a Christian without grace. A wicked man is the worst of creatures; a wicked Christian is the worst of men; and a wicked minister is the worst of Christians. (3.) He is doomed to ruin and rejection; He shall be *cast out*—expelled the church and the communion of the faithful, to which he is a blot and a burden; and he shall be *trodden under foot of men.* Let God be glorified in the shame and rejection of those by whom he has been reproached, and who have made themselves fit for nothing but to be trampled upon.

II. *Ye are the light of the world, v.* 14. This also bespeaks them useful, as the former (*Sole et sale nihil utilius—Nothing more useful than the sun and salt*), but more glorious. All Christians are *light in the Lord* (Eph. v. 8), and must *shine as lights* (Phil. ii. 15), but ministers in a special manner. Christ calls himself *the Light of the world* (John viii. 12), and they are *workers together with him*, and have some of his honour put upon them. Truly *the light is sweet*, it is welcome; the light of the first day of the world was so, when it *shone out of darkness;* so is the morning light of every day; so is the gospel, and those that spread it, to all sensible people. The *world sat in darkness*, Christ raised up his disciples to shine in it; and, that they may do so, from him they borrow and derive their light.

This similitude is here explained in two things:

1. As *the lights of the world*, they are illustrious and conspicuous, and have many eyes upon them. A city that is *set on a hill cannot be hid.* The disciples of Christ, especially those who are forward and zealous in his service, become remarkable, and are taken notice of as beacons. They are for *signs* (Isa. viii. 18), *men wondered at* (Zech. iii. 8); all their neighbours have an eye upon them. Some admire them, commend them, rejoice in them, and study to imitate them; others envy them, hate them, censure them, and study to blast them. They are concerned therefore to *walk circumspectly*, because of *their observers;* they are as *spectacles to the world*, and must take heed of every thing that *looks ill*, because they are so much *looked at.* The disciples of Christ were obscure men before he called them, but the character he put upon them dignified them, and as preachers of the gospel they made a figure; and though they were reproached for it by some, they were respected for it by others, advanced to thrones, and made judges (Luke xxii. 30); for Christ will honour those that honour him.

2. As the *lights of the world*, they are intended to illuminate and give light to others (*v.* 15), and therefore, (1.) They shall be *set up* as lights. Christ having lighted these candles, they shall not be put under a bushel, not confined always, as they are now, to the cities of Galilee, or the lost sheep of the house of Israel, but they shall be sent into all the world. The churches are the candlesticks, the golden candlesticks, in which these lights are placed, that their light may be diffused;

and the gospel is so strong a light, and carries with it so much of its own evidence, that, *like a city on a hill, it cannot be hid,* it cannot but appear to be from God, to all those who do not wilfully shut their eyes against it. It will *give light to all that are in the house,* to all that will draw near to it, and come where it is. Those to whom it does not give light, must thank themselves; they will not be in the house with it; will not make a diligent and impartial enquiry into it, but are prejudiced against it. (2.) They must *shine* as lights, [1.] By their *good preaching.* The knowledge they have, they must communicate for the good of others; not put it *under a bushel,* but spread it. The talent must not be buried in a napkin, but traded with. The disciples of Christ must not muffle themselves up in privacy and obscurity, under pretence of contemplation, modesty, or self-preservation, but, *as they have received the gift,* must *minister the same,* Luke xii. 3. [2.] By their *good living.* They must be *burning and shining lights* (John v. 35); must evidence, in their whole conversation, that they are indeed the followers of Christ, James iii. 13. They must be to others for instruction, direction, quickening, and comfort, Job xxix. 11.

See here, *First, How* our light must shine —by doing such *good works* as men *may see,* and may approve of; such works as are of *good report* among them that are without, and as will therefore give them cause to think well of Christianity. We must do good works *that may be seen* to the edification of others, but not *that they may be seen* to our own ostentation; we are bid to pray in secret, and what lies between God and our souls, must be kept to ourselves; but that which is of itself open and obvious to the sight of men, we must study to make *congruous* to our profession, and praiseworthy, Phil. iv. 8. Those about us must not only *hear* our good words, but *see* our good works; that they may be convinced that religion is more than a bare name, and that we do not only make a profession of it, but abide under the power of it.

Secondly, For what *end* our light must shine—"That those who see your good works may be brought, not to glorify *you* (which was the thing the Pharisees aimed at, and it spoiled all their performances), but to *glorify your Father which is in heaven.*" Note, The glory of God is the great thing we must aim at in every thing we do in religion, 1 Pet. iv. 11. In this centre the lines of all our actions must meet. We must not only endeavour to glorify God ourselves, but we must do all we can to bring others to glorify him. The sight of our *good works* will do this, by furnishing them, 1. With *matter for praise.* "Let them see *your good works,* that they may see the power of God's grace in you, and may thank him for it, and give him the glory of it, who has given such power unto men." 2. With *motives to piety.* "Let them see your good works, that they may be convinced of the truth and excellency of the Christian religion, may be provoked by a holy emulation to imitate your good works, and so may glorify God." Note, The holy, regular, and exemplary conversation of the saints, may do much towards the conversion of sinners; those who are unacquainted with religion, may hereby be brought to know what it is. Examples teach. And those who are prejudiced against it, may hereby be brought in love with it, and thus there is a winning virtue in a godly conversation.

17 Think not that I am come to
destroy the law or the prophets: I
am not come to destroy, but to fulfil. 18. For verily I say unto you,
Till heaven and earth pass, one jot
or one tittle shall in no wise pass
from the law, till all be fulfilled. 19
Whosoever therefore shall break one
of these least commandments, and
shall teach men so, he shall be called
the least in the kingdom of heaven:
but whosoever shall do and teach
them, the same shall be called great
in the kingdom of heaven. 20 For
I say unto you, That except your
righteousness shall exceed *the righteousness* of the scribes and Pharisees,
ye shall in no case enter into the
kingdom of heaven.

Those to whom Christ preached, and for whose use he gave these instructions to his disciples, were such as in their religion had an eye, 1. To the *scriptures* of the *Old Testament* as their *rule,* and therein Christ here shows them they were in the right: 2. To the scribes and Pharisees as their *example,* and therein Christ here shows them they were in the wrong; for,

I. The rule which Christ came to establish exactly agreed with the scriptures of the *Old Testament,* here called *the law* and *the prophets.* The *prophets* were commentators upon the law, and both together made up that rule of faith and practice which Christ found upon the throne in the Jewish church, and here he keeps it on the throne.

1. He protests against the thought of cancelling and weakening the *Old Testament; Think not that I am come to destroy the law and the prophets.* (1.) "Let not the pious Jews, who have an affection for the *law and the prophets, fear* that I come to *destroy* them." Let them not be prejudiced against Christ and his doctrine, from a jealousy that this kingdom he came to set up, would derogate from the honour of the scriptures, which they had embraced as coming from God, and of which they had experienced the power and purity; no, let them be satisfied that Christ

has no ill design upon the law and the prophets. (2.) "Let not the profane Jews, who have a disaffection to the law and the prophets, and are weary of that yoke, hope that I am come to destroy them." Let not carnal libertines imagine that the Messiah is come to discharge them from the obligation of divine precepts and yet to secure to them divine promises, to make them happy and yet to give them leave to live as they list. Christ commands nothing now which was forbidden either by the law of nature or the moral law, nor forbids any thing which those laws had enjoined; it is a great mistake to think he does, and he here takes care to rectify the mistake; *I am not come to destroy.* The Saviour of souls is the *destroyer* of nothing but the *works of the devil,* of nothing that comes from God, much less of those excellent dictates which we have from Moses and the prophets. No, he came to *fulfil* them. That is, [1.] To obey the commands of the law, for he was *made under the law,* Gal. iv. 4. He in all respects yielded obedience to the law, honoured his parents, sanctified the sabbath, prayed, gave alms, and did that which never any one else did, obeyed perfectly, and never broke the law in any thing. [2.] To make good the promises of the law, and the predictions of the prophets, which did all bear witness to him. The covenant of grace is, for substance, the same now that it was then, and Christ the Mediator of it. [3.] To answer the types of the law; thus (as bishop Tillotson expresses it), he did not make *void,* but make *good,* the ceremonial law, and manifested himself to be the Substance of all those shadows. [4.] To fill up the defects of it, and so to complete and perfect it. Thus the word πληρῶσαι properly signifies. If we consider the law as a vessel that had some water in it before, he did not come to pour out the water, but to fill the vessel up to the brim; or, as a picture that is first rough-drawn, displays some outlines only of the piece intended, which are afterwards filled up; so Christ made an improvement of the law and the prophets by his additions and explications. [5.] To carry on the same design; the Christian institutes are so far from thwarting and contradicting that which was the main design of the Jewish religion, that they promote it to the highest degree. The gospel is the *time of reformation* (Heb. ix. 10), not the repeal of the law, but the amendment of it, and, consequently, its establishment.

2. He asserts the perpetuity of it; that not only he designed not the abrogation of it, but that it never should be abrogated (*v.* 18); "*Verily I say unto you,* I, the *Amen,* the faithful Witness, solemnly declare it, that *till heaven and earth pass,* when time shall be no more, and the unchangeable state of recompences shall supersede all laws, *one jot, or one tittle,* the least and most minute circumstance, *shall in no wise pass from the law till all be fulfilled;*" for what is it that God is doing in all the operations both of providence and grace, but fulfilling the scripture? Heaven and earth shall come together, and all the fulness thereof be wrapped up in ruin and confusion, rather than any word of God shall fall to the ground, or be in vain. *The word of the Lord endures for ever,* both that of the law, and that of the gospel. Observe, The care of God concerning his law extends itself even to those things that seem to be of least account in it, the iotas and the tittles; for whatever belongs to God, and bears his stamp, be it ever so little, shall be preserved. The laws of men are conscious to themselves of so much imperfection, that they allow it for a maxim, *Apices juris non sunt jura—The extreme points of law are not law,* but God will stand by and maintain every iota and tittle of his law.

3. He gives it in charge to his disciples, carefully to preserve the law, and shows them the danger of the neglect and contempt of it (*v.* 19); *Whosoever therefore shall break one of the least commandments of the law of Moses,* much more any of the greater, as the Pharisees did, who neglected the weightier matters of the law, and shall teach men so as they did, who made void the commandment of God with their traditions (*ch.* xv. 3), *he shall be called the least in the kingdom of heaven.* Though the Pharisees be cried up for such teachers as should be, they shall not be employed as teachers in Christ's kingdom; but *whosoever shall do and teach them,* as Christ's disciples would, and thereby prove themselves better friends to the *Old Testament* than the Pharisees were, they, though despised by men, shall be *called great in the kingdom of heaven.* Note, (1.) Among the commands of God there are some less than others; none absolutely little, but comparatively so. The Jews reckon the least of the commandments of the law to be that of the bird's nest (Deut. xxii. 6, 7); yet even that had a significance and an intention very great and considerable. (2.) It is a dangerous thing, in doctrine or practice, to disannul the least of God's commands; to break them, that is, to go about either to *contract the extent,* or *weaken the obligation* of them; whoever does so, will find it is at his peril. Thus to vacate any of the ten commandments, is too bold a stroke for the jealous God to pass by. It is something more than transgressing the law, it is making void the law, Ps. cxix. 126. (3.) That the further such corruptions as these spread, the worse they are. It is impudence enough to break the command, but it is a greater degree of it to teach men so. This plainly refers to those who at this time sat in Moses' seat, and by their comments corrupted and perverted the text. Opinions that tend to the destruction of serious godliness and the vitals of religion, by corrupt glosses on the scripture, are bad when they are held, but worse when they are

propagated and taught, as the word of God. He that does so, shall be called *least in the kingdom of heaven*, in the kingdom of glory; he shall never come thither, but be eternally excluded; or, rather, in the kingdom of the gospel-church. He is so far from deserving the dignity of a teacher in it, that he shall not so much as be accounted a member of it. The prophet that teaches these lies shall be the tail in that kingdom (Is. ix. 15); when truth shall appear in its own evidence, such corrupt teachers, though cried up as the Pharisees, shall be of no account with the wise and good. Nothing makes ministers more contemptible and base than corrupting the law, Mal. ii. 8, 11. Those who extenuate and encourage sin, and discountenance and put contempt upon strictness in religion and serious devotion, are the dregs of the church. But, on the other hand, Those are truly honourable, and of great account in the church of Christ, who lay out themselves by their life and doctrine to promote the purity and strictness of practical religion; who both do and teach that which is good; for those who do not as they teach, pull down with one hand what they build up with the other, and give themselves the lie, and tempt men to think that all religion is a delusion; but those who speak from experience, who live up to what they preach, are truly great; they honour God, and God will honour them (1 Sam. ii. 30), and hereafter they shall shine as the *stars in the kingdom of our Father*.

II. The righteousness which Christ came to establish by this rule, must exceed that of the scribes and Pharisees, *v.* 20. This was strange doctrine to those who looked upon the scribes and Pharisees as having arrived at the highest pitch of religion. The scribes were the most noted teachers of the law, and the Pharisees the most celebrated professors of it, and they both sat in Moses' chair (*ch.* xxiii. 2), and had such a reputation among the people, that they were looked upon as super-conformable to the law, and people did not think themselves obliged to be as good as they; it was therefore a great surprise to them, to hear that they must be better than they, or they should not go to heaven; and therefore Christ here avers it with solemnity; *I say unto you,* It is so. The scribes and Pharisees were enemies to Christ and his doctrine, and were great oppressors; and yet it must be owned, that there was something commendable in them. They were much in fasting and prayer, and giving of alms; they were punctual in observing the ceremonial appointments, and made it their business to teach others; they had such an interest in the people that they thought, if but two men went to heaven, one would be a Pharisee; and yet our Lord Jesus here tells his disciples, that the religion he came to establish, did not only exclude the badness, but excel the goodness, of the scribes and Pharisees. We must do more than they, and better than they, or we shall come short of heaven. They were *partial in the law,* and laid most stress upon the ritual part of it; but we must be *universal,* and not think it enough to give the priest his tithe, but must give God our hearts. They minded only the *outside,* but we must make conscience of *inside* godliness. They aimed at the *praise* and *applause of men,* but we must aim at *acceptance with God:* they were *proud* of what they did in religion, and trusted to it as *a righteousness;* but we, when we have done all, must *deny ourselves,* and say, We are *unprofitable servants,* and trust only to the *righteousness of Christ;* and thus we may go beyond the scribes and Pharisees.

21 Ye have heard that it was said
by them of old time, Thou shalt not
kill: and whosoever shall kill shall
be in danger of the judgment: 22
But I say unto you, That whosoever
is angry with his brother without a
cause shall be in danger of the judgment: and whosoever shall say to
his brother, Raca, shall be in danger
of the council: but whosoever shall
say, Thou fool, shall be in danger of
hell fire. 23 Therefore, if thou bring
thy gift to the altar, and there re-
memberest that thy brother hath
ought against thee; 24 Leave there
thy gift before the altar, and go
thy way; first be reconciled to thy
brother, and then come and offer thy
gift. 25 Agree with thine adversary
quickly, whiles thou art in the way
with him; lest at any time the adversary deliver thee to the judge, and
the judge deliver thee to the officer,
and thou be cast into prison. 26
Verily I say unto thee, Thou shalt
by no means come out thence, till
thou hast paid the uttermost farthing.

Christ having laid down these principles, that Moses and the prophets were still to be their rulers, but that the scribes and Pharisees were to be no longer their rulers, proceeds to expound the law in some particular instances, and to vindicate it from the corrupt glosses which those expositors had put upon it. He adds not any thing new, only limits and restrains some permissions which had been abused: and as to the precepts, shows the breadth, strictness, and spiritual nature of them, adding such explanatory statutes as made them more clear, and tended much toward the perfecting of our obedience to them. In these verses, he explains the law of the sixth commandment, according to the true intent and full extent of it.

I. Here is the *command itself* laid down (*v.* 12); *We have heard it,* and remember it; he speaks *to them who know the law,* who had Moses read to them in their synagogues every sabbath-day; you have heard that it was said *by them,* or rather as it is in the margin, *to them of old time,* to your forefathers the Jews, *Thou shalt not kill.* Note, The laws of God are not novel, upstart laws, but were delivered to them of old time; they are ancient laws, but of that nature as never to be *antiquated* nor grow *obsolete.* The moral law agrees with the law of nature, and the eternal rules and reasons of good and evil, that is, the rectitude of the eternal Mind. *Killing* is here forbidden, killing ourselves, killing any other, directly or indirectly, or being any way accessory to it. The law of God, the God of life, is a hedge of protection about our lives. It was one of the precepts of Noah, Gen. ix. 5, 6.

II. The exposition of this command which the Jewish teachers contented themselves with; their comment upon it was, *Whosoever shall kill, shall be in danger of the judgment.* This was all they had to say upon it, that wilful murderers were liable to the sword of justice, and casual ones to the judgment of the city of refuge. The courts of judgment sat in the gate of their principal cities; the judges, ordinarily, were in number twenty-three; these tried, condemned, and executed murderers; so that whoever killed, was in danger of their judgment. Now this gloss of theirs upon this commandment was faulty, for it intimated, 1. That the law of the sixth commandment was only external, and forbade no more than the act of murder, and laid no restraint upon the inward lusts, from which *wars and fightings come.* This was indeed the πρωτον ψευδος—*the fundamental error* of the Jewish teachers, that the divine law prohibited only the sinful act, not the sinful thought; they were disposed *hærere in cortice—to rest in the letter* of the law, and they never enquired into the spiritual meaning of it. Paul, while a Pharisee, did not, till, by the key of the tenth commandment, divine grace let him into the knowledge of the spiritual nature of all the rest, Rom. vii. 7, 14. 2. Another mistake of theirs was, that this law was merely *political* and *municipal,* given for them, and intended as a directory for their courts, and no more; as if they only were the people, and the wisdom of the law must die with them.

III. The exposition which Christ gave of this commandment; and we are sure that according to his exposition of it we must be judged hereafter, and therefore ought to be ruled now. *The commandment is exceeding broad,* and not to be limited by the will of the flesh, or the will of men.

1. Christ tells them that *rash anger is heart-murder* (*v.* 22); *Whosoever is angry with his brother without a cause,* breaks the sixth commandment. By our *brother* here, we are to understand any person, though ever so much our inferior, as a child, a servant, for we are all *made of one blood.* Anger is a natural passion; there are cases in which it is lawful and laudable; but it is then *sinful,* when we are angry without cause. The word is εικη, which signifies, *sine causâ, sine effectu, et sine modo—without cause, without any good effect, without moderation;* so that the anger is then sinful, (1.) When it is without any just provocation given; either for no cause, or no good cause, or no great and proportionable cause; when we are angry at children or servants for that which could not be helped, which was only a piece of forgetfulness or mistake, that we ourselves might easily have been guilty of, and for which we should not have been angry at ourselves; when we are angry upon groundless surmises, or for trivial affronts not worth speaking of. (2.) When it is without any good end aimed at, merely to show our authority, to gratify a brutish passion, to let people know our resentments, and excite ourselves to revenge, then it is in vain, it is to do hurt; whereas if we are at any time angry, it should be to awaken the offender to repentance, and prevent his doing so again; to clear ourselves (2 Cor. vii. 11), and to give warning to others. (3.) When it exceeds due bounds; when we are hardy and headstrong in our anger, violent and vehement, outrageous and mischievous, and when we seek the hurt of those we are displeased at. This is a breach of the sixth commandment, for he that is thus angry, would kill if he could and durst; he has taken the first step towards it: Cain's killing his brother began in anger; he is a murderer in the account of God, who knows his heart, whence murders proceed, *ch.* xv. 19.

2. He tells them, that giving opprobrious language to our brother is tongue-murder, calling him, *Raca,* and, *Thou fool.* When this is done with mildness and for a good end, to convince others of their vanity and folly, it is not sinful. Thus James says, *O vain man;* and Paul, *Thou fool;* and Christ himself, *O fools, and slow of heart.* But when it proceeds from anger and malice within, it is the smoke of that fire which is kindled from hell, and falls under the same character. (1.) *Raca* is a scornful word, and comes from pride, "Thou empty fellow;" it is the language of that which Solomon calls *proud wrath* (Prov. xxi. 24), which tramples upon our brother—disdains *to set him even with the dogs of our flock. This people who knoweth not the law, is cursed,* is such language, John vii. 49. (2.) *Thou fool,* is a spiteful word, and comes from hatred; looking upon him, not only as mean and not to be honoured, but as vile and not to be loved; "Thou wicked man, thou reprobate." The former speaks a man without sense, this (in

scripture language) speaks a man without grace; the more the reproach touches his spiritual condition, the worse it is; the former is a haughty taunting of our brother, this is a malicious censuring and condemning of him, as abandoned of God. Now this is a breach of the sixth commandment; malicious slanders and censures are *poison under the tongue*, that kills secretly and slowly; *bitter words* are as *arrows* that wound suddenly (Ps. lxiv. 3), or as a sword in the bones. The good name of our neighbour, which is better than life, is thereby stabbed and murdered; and it is an evidence of such an ill-will to our neighbour as would strike at his life, if it were in our power.

3. He tells them, that how light soever they made of these sins, they would certainly be reckoned for; he *that is angry with his brother shall be in danger of the judgment* and anger of God; he that calls him *Raca, shall be in danger of the council*, of being punished by the Sanhedrim for reviling an Israelite; *but whosoever saith, Thou fool*, thou profane person, thou child of hell, *shall be in danger of hell-fire*, to which he condemns his brother; so the learned Dr. Whitby. Some think, in allusion to the penalties used in the several courts of judgment among the Jews, Christ shows that the sin of rash anger exposes men to lower or higher punishments, according to the degrees of its proceeding. The Jews had three capital punishments, each worse than the other; beheading, which was inflicted by the judgment; stoning, by the council or chief Sanhedrim; and burning *in the valley of the son of Hinnom*, which was used only in extraordinary cases: it signifies, therefore, that rash anger and reproachful language are damning sins; but some are more sinful than others, and accordingly there is a greater damnation, and a sorer punishment reserved for them: Christ would thus show which sin was most sinful, by showing which it was the punishment whereof was most dreadful.

IV. From all this it is here inferred, that we ought carefully to preserve Christian love and peace with all our brethren, and that if at any time a breach happens, we should labour for a reconciliation, by confessing our fault, humbling ourselves to our brother, begging his pardon, and making restitution, or offering satisfaction for wrong done in word or deed, according as the nature of the thing is; and that we should do this quickly for two reasons:

1. Because, till this be done, we are utterly unfit for communion with God in holy ordinances, *v.* 23, 24. The case supposed is, "*That thy brother have* somewhat *against thee*, that thou hast injured and offended him, either really or in his apprehension; if thou art the party offended, there needs not this delay; if thou *have aught against thy brother*, make short work of it; no more is to be done but to forgive him (Mark xi. 25), and forgive the injury; but if the quarrel began on thy side, and the fault was either at first or afterwards thine, so *that thy brother* has a controversy with *thee, go* and *be reconciled to* him before thou *offer thy gift at the altar*, before thou approach solemnly to God in the gospel-services of prayer and praise, hearing the word or the sacraments. Note, (1.) When we are addressing ourselves to any religious exercises, it is good for us to take that occasion of serious reflection and self-examination: there are many things to be *remembered*, when we *bring our gift to the altar*, and this among the rest, whether *our brother hath aught against us;* then, if ever, we are disposed to be serious, and therefore should then call ourselves to an account. (2.) Religious exercises are not acceptable to God, if they are performed when we are in wrath; envy, malice, and uncharitableness, are sins so displeasing to God, that nothing pleases him which comes from a heart wherein they are predominant, 1 Tim. ii. 8. Prayers made in wrath are written in gall, Isa. i. 15; lviii. 4. (3.) Love or charity is so much *better than all burnt-offerings and sacrifice*, that God will have reconciliation made with an offended brother before the gift be offered; he is content to stay for the gift, rather than have it offered while we are under guilt and engaged in a quarrel. (4.) Though we are unfitted for communion with God, by a continual quarrel with a brother, yet that can be no excuse for the omission or neglect of our duty: "*Leave there thy gift before the altar*, lest otherwise, when thou hast gone away, thou be tempted not to come again." Many give this as a reason why they do not come to church or to the communion, because they are at variance with some neighbour; and whose fault is that? One sin will never excuse another, but will rather double the guilt. Want of charity cannot justify the want of piety. The difficulty is easily got over; those who have wronged us, we must forgive; and those whom we have wronged, we must make satisfaction to, or at least make a tender of it, and desire a renewal of the friendship, so that if reconciliation be not made, it may not be our fault; *and then come*, come and welcome, *come and offer thy gift*, and it shall be accepted. *Therefore* we must *not let the sun go down upon our wrath* any day, because we must go to prayer before we go to sleep; much less let the sun rise *upon our wrath* on a sabbath-day, because it is a day of prayer.

2. Because, till this be done, we lie exposed to much danger, *v.* 25, 26. It is at our peril if we do not labour after an agreement, and that quickly, upon two accounts:

(1.) Upon a temporal account. If the offence we have done to our brother, in his body, goods, or reputation, be such as will bear an action, in which he may recover considerable damages, it is our wisdom, and it is our duty to our family, to prevent that by a humble submission and a just and peaceable satisfaction; lest otherwise he recover it by law, and put us to the extremity of a prison. In such a case it is better to compound and make the best terms we can, than to stand it out; for it is in vain to contend with the law, and there is danger of our being crushed by it. Many ruin their estates by an obstinate persisting in the offences they have given, which would soon have been pacified by a little yielding at first. Solomon's advice in case of suretyship is, *Go, humble thyself,* and so secure *and deliver thyself,* Prov. vi. 1—5. It is good to agree, for the law is costly. Though we must be merciful to those we have advantage against, yet we must be just to those that have advantage against us, as far as we are able. "*Agree,* and compound *with thine adversary quickly,* lest he be exasperated by thy stubbornness, and provoked to insist upon the utmost demand, and will not make thee the abatement which at first he would have made." A prison is an uncomfortable place to those who are brought to it by their own pride and prodigality, their own wilfulness and folly.

(2.) Upon a spiritual account. "*Go,* and be *reconciled to thy brother,* be just to him, be friendly with him, because while the quarrel continues, as thou art unfit to *bring thy gift to the altar,* unfit to come to *the table of the Lord,* so thou art unfit to die: if thou persist in this sin, there is danger lest thou be suddenly snatched away by the wrath of God, whose judgment thou canst not escape nor except against; and if that iniquity be laid to thy charge, thou art undone for ever." Hell is a prison for all that live and die in malice and uncharitableness, for all that are *contentious* (Rom. ii. 8), and out of that prison there is no rescue, no redemption, no escape, to eternity.

This is very applicable to the great business of our reconciliation to God through Christ; *Agree with him quickly, whilst thou art in the way.* Note, [1.] The great God is an Adversary to all sinners, *'Αντιδικος—a law-adversary;* he has a controversy with them, an action against them. [2.] It is our concern to *agree with him,* to acquaint ourselves with him, that we may *be at peace,* Job xxii. 21; 2 Cor. v. 20. [3.] It is our wisdom to do this *quickly, while we are in the way.* While we are alive, *we are in the way;* after death, it will be too late to do it; therefore *give not sleep to thine eyes* till it be done. [4.] They who continue in a state of enmity to God, are continually exposed to the arrests of his justice, and the most dreadful instances of his wrath. Christ is the Judge, to whom impenitent sinners will be delivered; for *all judgment is committed to the Son;* he that was rejected as a Saviour, cannot be escaped as a Judge, Rev. vi. 16, 17. It is a fearful thing to be thus turned over to the Lord Jesus, when the Lamb shall become a Lion. Angels are the officers to whom Christ will deliver them (*ch.* xiii. 41, 42): devils are so too, having *the power of death* as executioners to all unbelievers, Heb. ii. 14. Hell is the prison, into which those will be cast that continue in a state of enmity to God, 2 Pet. ii. 4. [5.] Damned sinners must remain in it to eternity; they shall not *depart till they have paid the uttermost farthing,* and that will not be to the utmost ages of eternity: divine justice will be for ever in the satisfying, but never satisfied.

27 Ye have heard that it was said by them of old time, Thou shalt not commit adultery: 28 But I say unto you, That whosoever looketh on a woman to lust after her, hath committed adultery with her already in his heart. 29 And if thy right eye offend thee, pluck it out, and cast *it* from thee: for it is profitable for thee that one of thy members should perish, and not *that* thy whole body should be cast into hell. 30 And if thy right hand offend thee, cut it off, and cast *it* from thee: for it is profitable for thee that one of thy members should perish, and not *that* thy whole body should be cast into hell. 31 It hath been said, Whosoever shall put away his wife, let him give her a writing of divorcement: 32 But I say unto you, That whosoever shall put away his wife, saving for the cause of fornication, causeth her to commit adultery: and whosoever shall marry her that is divorced, committeth adultery.

We have here an exposition of the seventh commandment, given us by the same hand that made the law, and therefore was fittest to be the interpreter of it: it is the law against uncleanness, which fitly follows upon the former; *that* laid a restraint upon sinful passions, *this* upon sinful appetites, both which ought always to be under the government of reason and conscience, and if indulged, are equally pernicious.

I. The command is here laid down (*v.* 17), *Thou shalt not commit adultery;* which includes a prohibition of all other acts of uncleanness, and the desire of them: but the Pharisees, in their expositions of this command, made it to extend no further than the act of adultery, suggesting, that if the iniquity was only *regarded in the heart,* and went no further, God could not hear it, would not regard it (Ps. lxvi. 18), and therefore they thought it enough to be able to say that they were *no adulterers,* Luke xviii. 11.

II. It is here explained in the strictness of it, in three things, which would seem new and strange to those who had been always governed by the tradition of the elders, and took all for oracular that they taught.

1. We are here taught, that there is such a thing as *heart-adultery,* adulterous thoughts and dispositions, which never proceed to the act of adultery or fornication; and perhaps the defilement which these give to the soul, that is here so clearly asserted, was not only included in the seventh commandment, but was signified and intended in many of those ceremonial pollutions under the law, for which they were to *wash their clothes, and bathe their flesh in water. Whosoever looketh on a woman* (not only another man's wife, as some would have it, but any woman), *to lust after her, has committed adultery with her in his heart, v.* 28. This command forbids not only the acts of fornication and adultery, but, (1.) All appetites to them, all lusting after the forbidden object; this is the beginning of the sin, *lust conceiving* (James i. 15); it is a bad step towards the sin; and where the lust is dwelt upon and approved, and the wanton desire is rolled under the tongue as a sweet morsel, it is the commission of the sin, as far as the heart can do it; there wants nothing but a convenient opportunity for the sin itself. *Adultera mens est—The mind is debauched.* Ovid. Lust is conscience baffled or biassed: biassed, if it say nothing against the sin; baffled, if it prevail not in what it says. (2.) All approaches towards them; feeding the eye with the sight of the forbidden fruit; not only looking for that end, that I may lust; but looking till I do lust, or looking to gratify the lust, where further satisfaction cannot be obtained. The eye is both the inlet and outlet of a great deal of wickedness of this kind, witness Joseph's mistress (Gen. xxxix. 7), Samson (Judg. xvi. 1), David, 2 Sam. xi. 2. We read of *eyes full of adultery, that cannot cease from sin,* 2 Pet. ii. 14. What need have we, therefore, with holy Job, to *make a covenant with our eyes,* to make this bargain with them, that they should have the pleasure of beholding the light of the sun and the works of God, provided they would never fasten or dwell upon any thing that might occasion impure imaginations or desires; and under this penalty, that if they did, they must smart for it in penitential tears! Job xxxi. 1. What have we the covering of the eyes for, but to restrain corrupt glances, and to keep out their defiling impressions? This forbids also the using of any other of our senses to stir up lust. If ensnaring looks are forbidden fruit, much more unclean discourses, and wanton dalliances, the fuel and bellows of this hellish fire. These precepts are hedges about the law of heart-purity, *v.* 8. And if looking be lust, they who dress and deck, and expose themselves, with design to be looked at and lusted after (like Jezebel, that *painted her face and tired her head, and looked out at the window),* are no less guilty. Men sin, but devils tempt to sin.

2. That such looks and such dalliances are so very dangerous and destructive to the soul, that it is better to lose the eye and the hand that thus offend than to give way to the sin, and perish eternally in it. This lesson is here taught us, *v.* 29, 30. Corrupt nature would soon object against the prohibition of heart-adultery, that it is impossible to be governed by it; "*It is a hard saying, who can bear it?* Flesh and blood cannot but look with pleasure upon a beautiful woman; and it is impossible to forbear lusting after and dallying with such an object." Such pretences as these will scarcely be overcome by reason, and therefore must be argued against with *the terrors of the Lord,* and so they are here argued against.

(1.) It is a severe operation that is here prescribed for the preventing of these fleshly lusts. *If thy right eye offend thee,* or *cause thee to offend,* by wanton glances, or wanton gazings, upon forbidden objects; *if thy right hand offend thee,* or *cause thee to offend,* by wanton dalliances; and if it were indeed impossible, as is pretended, to govern the eye and the hand, and they have been so accustomed to these wicked practices, that they will not be withheld from them; if there were no other way to restrain them (which, blessed be God, through his grace, there is), it were better for us to *pluck out the eye,* and *cut off the hand,* though the *right eye,* and *right hand,* the more honourable and useful, than to indulge them in sin to the ruin of the soul. And if this must be submitted to, at the thought of which nature startles, much more must we resolve to *keep under the body, and to bring it into subjection;* to live a life of mortification and self-denial; to keep a constant watch over our own hearts, and to suppress the first rising of lust and corruption there; to avoid the occasions of sin, to resist the beginnings of it, and to decline the company of those who will be a snare to us, though ever so pleasing; to keep out of harm's way, and abridge ourselves in the use of lawful things, when we find them temptations to us; and to seek unto God for his grace, and depend upon that grace daily, and so to *walk in the Spirit,* as that we may not *fulfil the lusts of the flesh;* and this will be as effectual as *cutting off a right hand* or *pulling out a right eye;* and perhaps as much against the grain to flesh and blood; it is the destruction of the old man.

(2.) It is a startling argument that is made use of to enforce this prescription (*v.* 29), and it is repeated in the same words (*v.* 30), because we are loth to hear such rough things; Isa. xxx. 10. *It is profitable for thee that one of thy members should perish,* though it be an eye or a hand, which can be worst spared, *and not that thy whole body should be cast into hell.* Note, [1.] It is not unbecoming a minister of the gospel to preach of hell and damnation; nay, he *must* do it, for Christ himself did it; and we are unfaithful to our trust, if we give not warning of *the wrath to come.* [2.] There are some sins from which we need to be *saved with fear,* particularly *fleshly lusts,* which are such *natural brute beasts* as cannot be checked, but by being frightened; cannot be kept from a forbidden tree, but by *cherubim, with a flaming sword.* [3.] When we are tempted to think it hard to *deny ourselves,* and to *crucify fleshly lusts,* we ought to consider how much harder it will be to lie for ever in *the lake that burns with fire and brimstone;* those do not know or do not believe what hell is, that will rather venture their eternal ruin in those flames, than deny themselves the gratification of a base and brutish lust. [4.] In hell there will be torments for the body; the *whole body* will *be cast into hell,* and there will be torment in every part of it; so that if we have any care of our own bodies, we shall *possess them in sanctification and honour,* and *not in the lusts of uncleanness.* [5.] Even those duties that are most unpleasant to flesh and blood, are *profitable for us;* and our Master requires nothing from us but what he knows to be for our advantage.

3. That men's divorcing their wives upon dislike, or for any other cause except adultery, however tolerated and practised among the Jews, was a violation of the seventh commandment, as it opened a door to adultery, *v.* 31, 32. Here observe,

(1.) How the matter now stood with reference to divorce. *It hath been said* (he does not say as before, *It hath been said by them of old time,* because this was not a precept, as those were, though the Pharisees were willing so to understand it (*ch.* xix. 7), but only a permission), "*Whosoever shall put away his wife, let him give her a bill of divorce;* let him not think to do it by word of mouth, when he is in a passion; but let him do it deliberately, by a legal instrument in writing, attested by witnesses; if he will dissolve the matrimonial bond, let him do it solemnly." Thus the law had prevented rash and hasty divorces; and perhaps at first, when writing was not so common among the Jews, that made divorces rare things; but in process of time they became very common, and this direction how to do it, when there was just cause for it, was construed into a permission of it for any cause, *ch.* xix. 3.

(2.) How this matter was rectified and amended by our Saviour. He reduced the ordinance of marriage to its primitive institution: *They two shall be one flesh,* not to be easily separated, and therefore divorce is not to be allowed, except in case of adultery, which breaks the marriage covenant; but he that puts away his wife upon any other pretence, *causeth her to commit adultery,* and him also that shall marry her when she is thus divorced. Note, Those who lead others into temptation to sin, or leave them in it, or expose them to it, make themselves guilty of their sin, and will be accountable for it. This is one way of being *partaker with adulterers,* Ps. l. 18.

33 Again, ye have heard that it
hath been said by them of old time,
Thou shalt not forswear thyself, but
shalt perform unto the Lord thine
oaths: 34 But I say unto you,
Swear not at all: neither by heaven;
for it is God's throne: 35 Nor by
the earth; for it is his footstool:
neither by Jerusalem; for it is the
city of the great King. 36 Neither
shalt thou swear by thy head, because
thou canst not make one hair white
or black: 37 But let your communication be, Yea, yea; Nay, nay:
for whatsoever is more than these,
cometh of evil.

We have here an exposition of the third commandment, which we are the more concerned rightly to understand, because it is particularly said, that *God will not hold him guiltless,* however he may hold himself, who breaks this commandment, by *taking the name of the Lord God in vain.* Now as to this command,

I. It is agreed on all hands that it forbids perjury, forswearing, and the violation of oaths and vows, *v.* 33. This was said to them of old time, and is the true intent and meaning of the third commandment. *Thou shalt not* use, or *take up, the name of God* (as we do by an oath) *in vain,* or *unto vanity,* or *a lie.* He *hath not lift up his soul unto vanity,* is expounded in the next words, *nor sworn deceitfully,* Ps. xxiv. 4. Perjury is a sin condemned by the light of nature, as a complication of impiety toward God and injustice toward man, and as rendering a man highly obnoxious to the divine wrath, which was always judged to follow so infallibly upon that sin, that the forms of swearing were commonly turned into execrations or imprecations; as that, *God do so to me, and more also;* and with us, *So help me God;* wishing I may never have any help from God, if I swear falsely. Thus, by the consent of nations, have men cursed themselves, not doubting but that God would curse them, if they lied against the truth then, when they solemnly called God to witness to it.

It is added, from some other scriptures, *but shalt perform unto the Lord thine oaths* (Numb. xxx. 2); which may be meant, either, 1. Of those promises to which God is a party, vows made to God; these must be punctually paid (Eccl. v. 4, 5): or, 2. Of those promises made to our brethren, to which God was a Witness, he being appealed to concerning our sincerity; these must be *performed to the Lord,* with an eye to him, and for his sake: for to him, by ratifying the promise with an oath, we have made ourselves debtors; and if we break a promise so ratified, we *have not lied unto men* only, *but unto God.*

II. It is here added, that the commandment does not only forbid false swearing, but all rash, unnecessary swearing: *Swear not at all, v.* 34; Compare Jam. v. 12. Not that all swearing is sinful; so far from that, if rightly done, it is a part of religious worship, and we in it *give unto God the glory due to his name.* See Deut. vi. 13; x. 20; Isa. xlv. 23; Jer. iv. 2. We find Paul confirming what he said by such solemnities (2 Cor. i. 23), when there was a necessity for it. In swearing, we pawn the truth of something known, to confirm the truth of something doubtful or unknown; we appeal to a greater knowledge, to a higher court, and imprecate the vengeance of a righteous Judge, if we swear deceitfully.

Now the mind of Christ in this matter is,

1. That we must *not swear at all,* but when we are duly called to it, and justice or charity to our brother, or respect to the commonwealth, make it necessary for *the end of strife* (Heb. vi. 16), of which necessity the civil magistrate is ordinarily to be the judge. We may be sworn, but we must not swear; we may be adjured, and so obliged to it, but we must not thrust ourselves upon it for our own worldly advantage.

2. That we must not swear lightly and irreverently, in common discourse: it is a very great sin to make a ludicrous appeal to the glorious Majesty of heaven, which, being a sacred thing, ought always to be very serious: it is a gross profanation of God's holy name, and of one of the holy things which *the children of Israel sanctify to the Lord:* it is a sin that has no cloak, no excuse for it, and therefore a sign of a graceless heart, in which enmity to God reigns: *Thine enemies take thy name in vain.*

3. That we must in a special manner avoid promissory oaths, of which Christ more particularly speaks here, for they are oaths that are to be performed. The influence of an affirmative oath immediately ceases, when we have faithfully discovered the truth, and the whole truth; but a promissory oath binds so long, and may be so many ways broken, by the surprise as well as strength of a temptation, that it is not to be used but upon great necessity: the frequent requiring and using of oaths, is a reflection upon Christians, who should be of such acknowledged fidelity, as that their sober words should be as sacred as their solemn oaths.

4. That we must not swear by any creature. It should seem there were some, who, in civility (as they thought) to the name of God, would not make use of that in swearing, but would swear *by heaven* or *earth, &c.* This Christ forbids here (*v.* 34), and shows that there is nothing we can swear by, but it is some way or other related to God, who is the Fountain of all beings, and therefore that it is as dangerous to swear by them, as it is to swear by God himself: it is the verity of the creature that is laid at stake; now that cannot be an instrument of testimony, but as it has regard to God, who is the *summum verum—the chief Truth.* As, for instance,

(1.) *Swear not by the heaven;* "As sure as there is a heaven, this is true;" *for it is God's throne,* where he resides, and in a particular manner manifests his glory, as a Prince upon his throne: this being the inseparable dignity of the upper world, you cannot *swear by heaven,* but you swear by God himself.

(2.) *Nor by the earth, for it is his footstool.* He governs the motions of this lower world; as he rules in heaven, so he rules over the earth; and though under his feet, yet it is also under his eye and care, and stands in relation to him as his, Ps. xxiv. 1. *The earth is the Lord's;* so that in swearing by it, you swear by its Owner.

(3.) *Neither by Jerusalem,* a place for which the Jews had such a veneration, that they could not speak of any thing more sacred to *swear by;* but beside the common reference Jerusalem has to God, as part of the earth, it is in special relation to him, *for it is the city of the great King* (Ps. xlviii. 2), *the city of God* (Ps. xlvi. 4), he is therefore interested in it, and in every oath taken by it.

(4.) "*Neither shalt thou swear by thy head;* though it be near thee, and an essential part of thee, yet it is more God's than thine; for he made it, and formed all the springs and powers of it; whereas thou thyself canst not, from any natural intrinsic influence, change the colour of *one hair,* so as to make *it white or black;* so that thou canst not *swear by thy head,* but thou swearest by him who is *the Life of thy head,* and *the Lifter up of it.*" Ps. iii. 3.

5. That therefore in all our communications we must content ourselves with, *Yea, yea,* and *Nay, nay, v.* 37. In ordinary discourse, if we affirm a thing, let us only say, *Yea,* it is so; and, if need be, to evidence our assurance of a thing, we may double it, and say, *Yea, yea,* indeed it is so: *Verily, verily,* was our Saviour's *yea, yea.* So if we deny a thing, let it suffice to say, No; or if it be requisite, to repeat the denial, and say, No, no; and if our fidelity be known, that will suffice to gain us credit; and if it be questioned, to back what we say with swearing and cursing, is but to render it more suspicious. They who can *swallow* a profane oath, will not *strain at a* lie. It is a pity that this, which Christ puts in the mouths of all his disciples, should be fastened, as a name of reproach, upon a sect faulty enough other ways, when (as Dr. Hammond says) we are not only forbidden any more than *yea* and *nay,* but are in a manner directed to the use of that.

The reason is observable; *For whatsoever*

is more than these cometh of evil, though it do not amount to the iniquity of an oath. It comes εκ του Διαβολου; so an ancient copy has it: it comes *from the Devil,* the evil one; it comes from the corruption of men's nature, from passion and vehemence; from a reigning vanity in the mind, and a contempt of sacred things: it comes from that decitfulness which is in men, *All men are liars;* thereforé men use these protestations, because they are distrustful one of another, and think they cannot be believed without them. Note, Christians should, for the credit of their religion, avoid not only that which is in itself evil, but *that which cometh of evil,* and has *the appearance of* it. That may be suspected as a bad thing, which comes from a bad cause. An oath is physic, which supposes a disease.

38 Ye have heard that it hath been said, An eye for an eye, and a tooth for a tooth: 39 But I say unto you, That ye resist not evil: but whosoever shall smite thee on thy right cheek, turn to him the other also. 40 And if any man will sue thee at the law, and take away thy coat, let him have *thy* cloak also. 41 And whosoever shall compel thee to go a mile, go with him twain. 42 Give to him that asketh thee, and from him that would borrow of thee turn not thou away.

In these verses the law of retaliation is expounded, and in a manner repealed Observe,

I. What the *Old-Testament permission* was, in case of injury; and here the expression is only, *Ye have heard that it has been said;* not, as before, concerning the commands of the decalogue, *that it has been said by,* or to, *them of old time.* It was not a command, that every one should of necessity require such sàtisfaction; but they might lawfully insist upon it, if they pleased; *an eye for an eye, and a tooth for a tooth.* This we find, Exod. xxi. 24; Lev. xxiv. 20; Deut. xix. 21; in all which places it is appointed to be done by the magistrate, who *bears not the sword in vain,* but is *the minister of God, an avenger to execute wrath,* Rom. xiii. 4. It was a direction to the judges of the Jewish nation what punishment to inflict in case of maims, for terror to such as would do mischief on the one hand, and for a restraint to such as have mischief done to them on the other hand, that they may not insist on a greater punishment than is proper: it is not *a life for an eye,* nor *a limb for a tooth,* but observe a proportion; and it is intimated (Numb. xxxv. 31), that the forfeiture in this case might be redeemed with money; for when it is provided that *no ransom shall be taken for the life of a murderer,* it is supposed that for maims a pecuniary satisfaction was allowed.

But some of the Jewish teachers, who were not the most compassionate men in the world, insisted upon it as necessary that such revenge should be taken, even by private persons themselves, and that there was no room left for remission, or the acceptance of satisfaction. Even now, when they were under the government of the Roman magistrates, and consequently the judicial law fell to the ground of course, yet they were still zealous for any thing that looked harsh and severe.

Now, so far this is in force with us, as a direction to magistrates, to use the sword of justice according to the good and wholesome laws of the land, for the terror of evil-doers, and the vindication of the oppressed. That judge *neither feared God nor regarded man,* who would not *avenge* the poor widow *of her adversary,* Luke xviii. 2, 3. And it is in force as a rule to lawgivers, to provide accordingly, and wisely to apportion punishments to crimes, for the restraint of rapine and violence, and the protection of innocency.

II. What the *New-Testament precept* is. as to the complainant himself, his duty is, to *forgive the injury* as done to himself, and no further to insist upon the punishment of it than is necessary to the public good: and this precept is consonant to the meekness of Christ, and the gentleness of his yoke.

Two things Christ teaches us here:

1. We must not be revengeful (*v.* 39); *I say unto you, that ye resist not evil;*—the evil person that is injurious to you. The resisting of any ill attempt upon us, is here as generally and expressly forbidden, as *the resisting of the higher powers* is (Rom. xiii. 2); and yet this does not repeal the law of self-preservation, and the care we are to take of our families; we may *avoid evil,* and may *resist* it, so far as is necessary to our own security; but we must not *render evil for evil,* must not bear a grudge, nor avenge ourselves, nor study to be even with those that have treated us unkindly, but we must go beyond them by forgiving them, Prov. xx. 22; xxiv. 29.; xxv. 21, 22. Rom. xii. 17. The law of retaliation must be made consistent with the law of love: nor, if any have injured us, is our recompence in our own hands, but in the hands of God, to whose wrath we must give place; and sometimes in the hands of his vicegerents, where it is necessary for the preservation of the public peace; but it will not justify us in hurting our brother to say that he began, for it is the second blow that makes the quarrel; and when we were injured, we had an opportunity not to justify our injuring him, but to show ourselves the true disciples of Christ, by forgiving him.

Three things our Saviour specifies, to

show that Christians must patiently yield to those who bear hard upon them, rather than contend; and these include others.

(1.) A blow on the cheek, which is an injury to me in my body; "*Whosoever shall smite thee on thy right cheek,* which is not only a hurt, but an affront and indignity (2 Cor. xi. 20), if a man in anger or scorn thus abuse thee,"*turn to him the other cheek;*" that is, "instead of avenging that injury, prepare for another, and bear it patiently: give not the rude man as good as he brings; do not challenge him, nor enter an action against him; if it be necessary to the public peace that he be bound to his good behaviour, leave that to the magistrate; but for thy own part, it will ordinarily be the wisest course to pass it by, and take no further notice of it: there are no bones broken, no great harm done, forgive it and forget it; and if proud fools think the worse of thee, and laugh at thee for it, all wise men will value and honour thee for it, as a follower of the blessed Jesus, who, though he was the Judge of Israel, did not smite those who smote him on the cheek," Micah v. 1. Though this may perhaps, with some base spirits, expose us to the like affront another time, and so it is, in effect, to *turn the other cheek,* yet let not that disturb us, but let us trust God and his providence to protect us in the way of our duty. Perhaps, the forgiving of one injury may prevent another, when the avenging of it would but draw on another; some will be overcome by submission, who by resistance would but be the more exasperated, Prov. xxv. 22. However, our recompence is in Christ's hands, who will reward us with eternal glory for the shame we thus patiently endure; and though it be not directly inflicted, if it be quietly borne for conscience' sake, and in conformity to Christ's example, it shall be put upon the score of suffering for Christ.

(2.) The loss of a coat, which is a wrong to me in my estate (*v.* 40); *If any man will sue thee at the law, and take away thy coat.* It is a hard case. Note, It is common for legal processes to be made use of for the doing of the greatest injuries. Though judges be just and circumspect, yet it is possible for bad men who make no conscience of oaths and forgeries, by course of law to force off the coat from a man's back. *Marvel not at the matter* (Eccl. v. 8), but, in such a case, rather than go to law by way of revenge, rather than exhibit a cross bill, or stand out to the utmost, in defence of that which is thy undoubted right, *let him* even take *thy cloak also.* If the matter be small, which we may lose without any considerable damage to our families, it is good to submit to it for peace' sake. "It will not cost thee so much to buy another cloak, as it will cost thee by course of law to recover that; and therefore unless thou canst get it again by fair means, it is better to let him take it."

(3.) The going a mile by constraint, which is a wrong to me in my liberty (*v.* 41); "*Whosoever shall compel thee to go a mile,* to run of an errand for him, or to wait upon him, grudge not at it, but *go with him two miles* rather than fall out with him:" say not, "I would do it, if I were not compelled to it, but I hate to be forced;" rather say, "Therefore I will do it, for otherwise there will be a quarrel;" and it is better to serve him, than to serve thy own lusts of pride and revenge. Some give this sense of it: The Jews taught that the disciples of the wise, and the students of the law, were not to be pressed, as others might, by the king's officers, to travel upon the public service; but Christ will not have his disciples to insist upon this privilege, but to comply rather than offend the government. The sum of all is, that Christians must not be litigious; small injuries must be submitted to, and no notice taken of them; and if the injury be such as requires us to seek reparation, it must be for a good end, and without thought of revenge: though we must not invite injuries, yet we must meet them cheerfully in the way of duty, and make the best of them. If any say, Flesh and blood cannot pass by such an affront, let them remember, that *flesh and blood shall not inherit the kingdom of God.*

2. We must be charitable and beneficent (*v.* 42); must not only do no hurt to our neighbours, but labour to do them all the good we can. (1.) We must be ready to give; "*Give to him that asketh thee.* If thou hast an ability, look upon the request of the poor as giving thee an opportunity for the duty of almsgiving." When a real object of charity presents itself, we should give at the first word: *Give a portion to seven, and also to eight;* yet the affairs of our charity must be *guided with discretion* (Ps. cxii. 5), lest we give that to the idle and unworthy, which should be given to those that are necessitous, and deserve well. What God says to us, we should be ready to say to our poor brethren, *Ask, and it shall be given you.* (2.) We must be ready to lend. This is sometimes as great a piece of charity as giving; as it not only relieves the present exigence, but obliges the borrower to providence, industry, and honesty; and therefore, "*From him that would borrow of thee* something to live on, or something to trade on, *turn not thou away:* shun not those that thou knowest have such a request to make to thee, nor contrive excuses to shake them off. Be easy of access to him *that would borrow:* though he be bashful, and have not confidence to make known his case and beg the favour, yet thou knowest both his need and his desire, and therefore offer him the kindness. *Exorabor antequam rogor; honestis precibus occurram —I will be prevailed on before I am entreated; I will anticipate the becoming petition.* Seneca, *De Vitâ Beatâ.* It becomes us to be thus forward in acts of kindness, for before

we call, God hears us, and *prevents us with the blessings of his goodness.*

43 Ye have heard that it hath
been said, Thou shalt love thy neighbour, and hate thine enemy: 44 But
I say unto you, Love your enemies,
bless them that curse you, do good
to them that hate you, and pray for
them which despitefully use you and
persecute you: 45 That ye may be
the children of your Father which is
in heaven: for he maketh his sun to
rise on the evil and on the good, and
sendeth rain on the just and on the
unjust. 46 For if ye love them
which love you, what reward have
ye? Do not even the publicans the
same? 47 And if ye salute your
brethren only, what do ye more *than
others?* Do not even the publicans
so? 48 Be ye therefore perfect, even
as your Father which is in heaven is
perfect.

We have here, lastly, an exposition of that great fundamental law of the second table, *Thou shalt love thy neighbour,* which was the fulfilling of the law.

I. See here how this law was corrupted by the comments of the Jewish teachers, *v.* 43. God said, *Thou shalt love thy neighbour;* and by *neighbour* they understood those only of their own country, nation, and religion; and those only that they were pleased to look upon as their friends: yet this was not the worst; from this command, *Thou shalt love thy neighbour,* they were willing to infer what God never designed; *Thou shalt hate thine enemy;* and they looked upon whom they pleased as their enemies, thus making void the great command of God by their traditions, though there were express laws to the contrary, Exod. xxiii. 4, 5; Deut. xxiii. 7. *Thou shalt not abhor an Edomite, nor an Egyptian,* though these nations had been as much enemies to Israel as any whatsoever. It was true, God appointed them to destroy the seven devoted nations of Canaan, and not to make leagues with them; but there was a particular reason for it—to make room for Israel, and that they might not be *snares to them;* but it was very ill-natured from hence to infer, that they must hate all their enemies; yet the moral philosophy of the heathen allowed this. It is Cicero's rule, *Nemini nocere nisi prius lacessitum injuriâ—To injure no one, unless previously injured. De Offic.* See how willing corrupt passions are to fetch countenance from the word of God, and to *take occasion by the commandment* to justify themselves.

II. See how it is cleared by the command of the Lord Jesus, who teaches us another lesson: "*But I say unto you, I,* who come to be the great Peace-Maker, the general Reconciler, who loved you when you were strangers and enemies, *I say, Love your enemies,*" *v.* 44. Though men are ever so bad themselves, and carry it ever so basely towards us, yet that does not discharge us from the great debt we owe them, of love to our kind, love to our kin. We cannot but find ourselves very prone to wish the hurt, or at least very coldly to desire the good, of those *that hate* us, and have been abusive to us; but that which is at the bottom hereof is a root of bitterness, which must be plucked up, and a remnant of corrupt nature which grace must conquer. Note, It is the great duty of Christians to *love their enemies;* we cannot have complacency in one that is openly wicked and profane, nor put a confidence in one that we know to be deceitful; nor are we to love all alike; but we must pay respect to the human nature, and so far *honour all men:* we must take notice, with pleasure, of that even in our enemies which is amiable and commendable; ingenuousness, good temper, learning, moral virtue, kindness to others, profession of religion, &c., and love that, though they are our enemies. We must have a compassion for them, and a good will toward them. We are here told,

1. That we must *speak* well of them: *Bless them that curse you.* When we speak to them, we must answer their revilings with courteous and friendly words, and *not render railing for railing;* behind their backs we must commend that in them which is commendable, and when we have said all the good we can of them, not be forward to say any thing more. See 1 Pet. iii. 9. They, in whose tongues is *the law of kindness,* can give good words to those who give bad words to them.

2. That we must *do* well to them: "*Do good to them that hate you,* and that will be a better proof of love than good words. Be ready to do them all the real kindness that you can, and glad of an opportunity to do it, in their bodies, estates, names, families; and especially to do good to their souls." It was said of Archbishop Cranmer, that the way to make him a friend was to do him an ill turn; so many did he serve who had disobliged him.

3. We must *pray for them: Pray for them that despitefully use you, and persecute you.* Note, (1.) It is no new thing for the most excellent saints to be hated, and cursed, and persecuted, and despitefully used, by wicked people; Christ himself was so treated. (2.) That when at any time we meet with such usage, we have an opportunity of showing our conformity both to the precept and to the example of Christ, by praying for them who thus abuse us. If we cannot otherwise testify our love to them, yet this way we may without ostentation, and it is such a

way as surely we durst not dissemble in. We must pray that God will forgive them, that they may never fare the worse for any thing they have done against us, and that he would make them to be at peace with us; and this is one way of making them so. Plutarch, in his Laconic Apophthegms, has this of Aristo; when one commended Cleomenes's saying, who, being asked *what a good king should do*, replied, Τὸυς μὲν φίλους ἐυεργετεῖν, τὸυς δὲ ἐχθρους κακῶς ποιεῖν—*Good turns to his friends, and evil to his enemies;* he said, How much better is it τὸυς μὲν φίλους ἐυεργετεῖν, τὸυς δὲ ἐχθρους φίλους ποιεῖν—to *do good to our friends, and make friends of our enemies.* This is *heaping coals of fire on their heads.*

Two reasons are here given to enforce this command (which sounds so harsh) of *loving our enemies.* We must do it,

[1.] That we may be *like God our Father;* "that ye may be, may approve yourselves to be, *the children of your Father which is in heaven.*" Can we write after a better copy? It is a copy in which love to the worst of enemies is reconciled to, and consistent with, infinite purity and holiness. God *maketh his sun to rise,* and *sendeth rain,* on *the just and unjust, v.* 45. Note, *First, Sunshine* and *rain* are great blessings to the world, and they come from God. It is *his sun* that *shines,* and the rain is sent by him. They do not come of course, or by chance, but from God. *Secondly,* Common mercies must be valued as instances and proofs of the goodness of God, who in them shows himself a bountiful Benefactor to the world of mankind, who would be very miserable without these favours, and are utterly unworthy of the least of them. *Thirdly,* These gifts of common providence are dispensed indifferently to *good* and *evil, just* and *unjust;* so that we cannot know *love* and *hatred* by what is *before us,* but by what is *within us;* not by the shining of the sun on our heads, but by the rising of the Sun of Righteousness in our hearts. *Fourthly,* The worst of men partake of the comforts of this life in common with others, though they abuse them, and fight against God with his own weapons; which is an amazing instance of God's patience and bounty. It was but once that God forbade his sun to shine on the Egyptians, when the Israelites had *light in their dwellings;* God could make such a distinction every day. *Fifthly,* The gifts of God's bounty to wicked men that are in rebellion against him, teach us to *do good to those that hate us;* especially considering, that though there is in us a carnal mind which is enmity to God, yet we share in his bounty. *Sixthly,* Those only will be accepted as the children of God, who study to resemble him, particularly in his goodness.

[2.] That we may herein *do more than others, v.* 46, 47. *First, Publicans love their friends.* Nature inclines them to it; interest directs them to it. To do good to them who do good to us, is a common piece of humanity, which even those whom the Jews hated and despised could give as good proofs of as the best of them. The publicans were men of no good fame, yet they were grateful to such as had helped them to their places, and courteous to those they had a dependence upon; and shall we be no better than they? In doing this we serve ourselves and consult our own advantage; and what reward can we expect for that, unless a regard to God, and a sense of duty, carry us further than our natural inclination and worldly interest? *Secondly,* We must therefore love our enemies, that we may exceed them. If we must go beyond scribes and Pharisees, much more beyond publicans. Note, Christianity is something more than humanity. It is a serious question, and which we should frequently put to ourselves, "*What do we more than others? What excelling thing do we do?* We *know* more than others; we *talk* more of the things of God than others; we *profess,* and have *promised,* more than others; God has done more for us, and therefore justly expects more from us than from others; the glory of God is more concerned in us than in others; but *what do we more than others?* Wherein do we live above the rate of the children of this world? *Are we not carnal,* and do we not walk as men, below the character of Christians? In this especially we must do more than others, that while every one will render *good for good,* we must render *good for evil;* and this will speak a nobler principle, and is consonant to a higher rule, than the most of men act by. Others *salute their brethren,* they embrace those of their own party, and way, and opinion; but we must not so confine our respect, but *love our enemies,* otherwise *what reward have we?* We cannot expect the reward of Christians, if we rise no higher than the virtue of publicans." Note, Those who promise themselves a reward above others must study to *do more than others.*

Lastly, Our Saviour concludes this subject with this exhortation (*v.* 48), *Be ye therefore perfect, as your Father which is in heaven is perfect.* Which may be understood, 1. In general, including all those things wherein we must be *followers of God as dear children.* Note, It is the duty of Christians to desire, and aim at, and press towards a perfection in grace and holiness, Phil. iii. 12—14. And therein we must study to conform ourselves to the example of our heavenly Father, 1 Pet. i. 15, 16. Or, 2. In this particular before mentioned, of *doing good to our enemies;* see Luke vi. 36. It is God's perfection to *forgive injuries* and to *entertain strangers,* and to do good to the evil and unthankful, and it will be ours to be like him. We that owe *so much,* that owe *our all,* to the divine bounty, ought to copy it out as well as we can.

CHAP. VI.

Christ having, in the former chapter, armed his disciples against the corrupt doctrines and opinions of the scribes and Pharisees, especially in their expositions of the law (that was called their leaven, ch. xvi. 12), comes in this chapter to warn them against their corrupt practices, against the two sins which, though in their doctrine they did not justify, yet in their conversation they were notoriously guilty of, and so as even to recommend them to their admirers: these were hypocrisy and worldly-mindedness, sins which, of all others, the professors of religion need most to guard against, as sins that most easily beset those who have escaped the grosser pollutions that are in the world through lust, and which are therefore highly dangerous. We are here cautioned, I. Against hypocrisy; we must not be as the hypocrites are, nor do as the hypocrites do. 1. In the giving of alms, ver. 1—4. 2. In prayer, ver. 5—8. We are here taught what to pray for, and how to pray (ver. 9—13); and to forgive in prayer, ver. 14, 15. 3. In fasting, ver. 16—18. II. Against worldly-mindedness, 1. In our choice, which is the destroying sin of hypocrites, ver. 19—24. 2. In our cares, which is the disquieting sin of many good Christians, ver. 25—34.

TAKE heed that ye do not your
alms before men, to be seen of
them: otherwise ye have no reward
of your Father which is in heaven.
2 Therefore when thou doest *thine*
alms do not sound a trumpet before
thee, as the hypocrites do in the
synagogues and in the streets, that
they may have glory of men. Verily
I say unto you, They have their reward. 3 But when thou doest alms,
let not thy left hand know what thy
right hand doeth: 4 That thine
alms may be in secret: and thy
Father, which seeth in secret, himself shall reward thee openly.

As we must do better than the scribes and Pharisees in avoiding heart-sins, heart-adultery, and heart-murder, so likewise in maintaining and keeping up heart-religion, doing what we do from an inward, vital principle, that we may be approved of God, not that we may be applauded of men; that is, we must watch against hypocrisy, which was the leaven of the Pharisees, as well as against their doctrine, Luke xii. 1. *Almsgiving, prayer,* and *fasting,* are three great Christian duties—the three foundations of the law, say the Arabians: by them we do homage and service to God with our three principal interests; by *prayer* with our *souls,* by *fasting* with our *bodies,* by *alms-giving* with our *estates.* Thus we must not only *depart from evil,* but *do good,* and do it well, and so *dwell for evermore.*

Now in these verses we are cautioned against hypocrisy in giving alms. *Take heed* of it Our being bid to *take heed* of it intimates that it is sin, 1. We are in *great danger of;* it is a subtle sin; vain-glory insinuates itself into what we do ere we are aware. The disciples would be tempted to it by the power they had to do many wondrous works, and their living with some that admired them and others that despised them, both which are temptations to covet to make a fair show in the flesh. 2. It is a sin we are in *great danger by.* Take heed of hypocrisy, for if it reign in you, it will ruin you. It is the dead fly that spoils the whole box of precious ointment.

Two things are here supposed,

I. The *giving of alms* is a great duty, and a duty which all the disciples of Christ, according to their ability, must abound in. It is prescribed by the law of nature and of Moses, and great stress is laid upon it by the prophets. Divers ancient copies here for τὴν ἐλεημοσύνην—*your alms,* read τὴν δικαιοσύνην—*your righteousness,* for *alms* are *righteousness,* Ps. cxii. 9; Prov. x. 2. The Jews called the *poor's box* the *box of righteousness.* That which is given to the poor is said to be their due, Prov. iii. 27. The duty is not the less necessary and excellent for its being abused by hypocrites to serve their pride. If superstitious papists have placed a merit in works of charity, that will not be an excuse for covetous protestants that are barren in such good works. It is true, our alms-deeds do not deserve heaven; but it is as true that we cannot go to heaven without them. It is *pure religion* (Jam. i. 27), and will be the test at the great day; Christ here takes it for granted that his disciples *give alms,* nor will he own those that do not.

II. That it is such a duty as has a great reward attending it, which is lost if it be done in hypocrisy. It is sometimes rewarded in temporal things with *plenty* (Prov. xi. 24, 25; xix. 17); *security from want* (Prov. xxviii. 27; Ps. xxxvii. 21, 25); *succour in distress* (Ps. xli. 1, 2); *honour and a good* name, which follow those most that least covet them, Ps. cxii. 9. However, it shall be recompensed in the resurrection of the just (Luke xiv. 14), in *eternal riches.*

Quas dederis, solas semper habebis, opes.

The riches you impart form the only wealth you will always retain.—Martial.

This being supposed, observe now,

1. What was the *practice of the hypocrites* about this duty. They did it indeed, but not from any principle of obedience to God, or love to man, but in pride and vain-glory; not in compassion to the poor, but purely for ostentation, that they might be extolled as good men, and so might gain an interest in the esteem of the people, with which they knew how to serve their own turn, and to get a great deal more than they gave. Pursuant to this intention, they chose to give their alms *in the synagogues, and in the streets,* where there was the greatest concourse of people to observe them, who applauded their liberality because they shared in it, but were so ignorant as not to discern their abominable pride. Probably they had collections for the poor in the synagogues, and the common beggars haunted the streets and highways, and upon these public occasions they chose to give their alms. Not that it is unlawful to give alms *when men see us;* we may do it, we must do it, but not *that men may see us;* we should rather choose those objects of charity that are less observed. The hypo-

crites, if they gave alms at their own houses, *sounded a trumpet*, under pretence of calling the poor together to be served, but really to proclaim their charity, and to have that taken notice of and made the subject of discourse.

Now the doom that Christ passes upon this is very observable; *Verily I say unto you, they have their reward.* At first view this seems a promise—If they have their reward they have enough, but two words in it make it a threatening.

(1.) It is a reward, but it is *their* reward; not the reward which God promises to them that do good, but the reward which they promise themselves, and a poor reward it is; they did it to be *seen of men*, and they *are* seen of men; they *chose their own delusions* with which they cheated themselves, and they shall have what they chose. Carnal professors stipulate with God for preferment, honour, wealth, and they shall have their bellies filled with those things (Ps. xvii. 14); but let them expect no more; these are their consolation (Luke vi. 24), their good things (Luke xvi. 25), and they shall be put off with these. "*Didst thou not agree with me for a penny?* It is the bargain that thou art likely to abide by."

(2.) It is a reward, but it is a *present reward*, they *have* it; and there is none reserved for them in the future state. They now have all that they are likely to have from God; they have their reward here, and have none to hope for hereafter. Ἀπεχουσι τὸν μισθον. It signifies a *receipt in full.* What rewards the godly have in this life are but *in part of payment;* there is more behind, much more; but hypocrites have their *all* in this world, so shall their doom be; themselves have decided it. The world is but for *provision* to the saints, it is their spending-money; but it is *pay* to hypocrites, it is their portion.

2. What is the *precept of our Lord Jesus* about it, *v.* 3, 4. He that was himself such an example of humility, pressed it upon his disciples, as absolutely necessary to the acceptance of their performances. "*Let not thy left hand know what thy right hand doeth* when thou givest alms." Perhaps this alludes to the placing of the Corban, the poor man's box, or the chest into which they cast their free-will offerings, *on the right hand* of the passage into the temple; so that they put their gifts into it with the *right-hand.* Or the giving of alms with the *right hand*, intimates readiness to it and resolution in it; do it dexterously, not awkwardly nor with a sinister intention. The *right hand* may be used in helping the poor, lifting them up, writing for them, dressing their sores, and other ways besides giving to them; but, "whatever kindness thy right hand doeth to the poor, *let not thy left hand know it:* conceal it as much as possible; industriously keep it private. Do it because it is a good work, not because it will give thee a good name." *In omnibus factis, re, non teste, moveamur—In all our actions, we should be influenced by a regard to the object, not to the observer.* Cic. de Fin. It is intimated, (1.) That we must not let *others* know what we do; no, not those that stand *at our left hand*, that are very near us. Instead of acquainting them with it, keep it from them if possible; however, appear so desirous to keep it from them, as that in civility they may seem not to take notice of it, and keep it to themselves, and let it go no further. (2.) That we must not observe it too much *ourselves:* the left hand is a part of ourselves; we must not within ourselves take notice too much of the good we do, must not applaud and admire ourselves. Self-conceit and self-complacency, and an adoring of our own shadow, are branches of pride, as dangerous as vain-glory and ostentation before men. We find those had their good works remembered to their honour, who had themselves forgotten them: *When saw we thee an hungered, or athirst?*

3. What is the *promise to those who are thus sincere and humble* in their alms-giving. Let *thine alms be in secret*, and then *thy Father who seeth in secret* will observe them. Note, When we take least notice of our good deeds ourselves, God takes most notice of them. As God hears the wrongs done to us when we do not hear them (Ps. xxxviii. 14, 15), so he sees the good done by us, when we do not see it. As it is a terror to hypocrites, so it is a comfort to sincere Christians, that God *sees in secret.* But this is not all; not only the observation and praise, but the recompence is of God, *himself shall reward thee openly.* Note, They who in their alms-giving study to approve themselves to God, only turn themselves over to him as their Paymaster. The hypocrite catches at the shadow, but the upright man makes sure of the substance. Observe how emphatically it is expressed; *himself shall reward*, he will himself be the Rewarder, Heb. xi. 6. Let him alone to make it up in kind or kindness; nay, he will *himself be the Reward* (Gen. xv. 1), thine *exceeding great reward.* He will reward thee as thy Father, not as a master who gives his servant just what he earns and no more, but as a father who gives abundantly more, and without stint, to his son that serves him. Nay, he shall reward thee *openly*, if not in the present day, yet in the great day; *then shall every man have praise of God*, open praise, thou shalt be confessed *before men.* If the work be not open, the reward shall, and that is better.

5 And when thou prayest, thou shalt not be as the hypocrites *are:* for they love to pray standing in the synagogues and in the corners of the

streets, that they may be seen of men. Verily I say unto you, They have their reward. 6 But thou, when thou prayest, enter into thy closet, and when thou hast shut thy door, pray to thy Father, which is in secret; and thy Father, which seeth in secret, shall reward thee openly. 7 But when ye pray, use not vain repetitions, as the heathen *do:* for they think that they shall be heard for their much speaking. 8 Be not ye therefore like unto them: for your Father knoweth what things ye have need of, before ye ask him.

In *prayer* we have more immediately to do with God than in *giving alms,* and therefore are yet more concerned to be *sincere,* which is what we are here directed to. *When thou prayest* (*v.* 5). It is taken for granted that all the disciples of Christ *pray.* As soon as ever Paul was converted, *behold he prayeth.* You may as soon find a living man that does not breathe, as a living Christian that does not pray. *For this shall every one that is godly pray.* If prayerless, then graceless. "*Now, when thou prayest,* thou shalt not be *as the hypocrites are,* nor do as they do," *v.* 2. Note, Those who would not do as the hypocrites do in their ways and actions must not be as the hypocrites are in their frame and temper. He names nobody, but it appears by *ch.* xxiii. 13, that by the hypocrites here he means especially the scribes and Pharisees.

Now there were two great faults they were guilty of in prayer, against each of which we are here cautioned—vain-glory (*v.* 5, 6); and vain repetitions, *v.* 7, 8.

I. We must not be *proud* and *vain-glorious* in prayer, nor aim at the praise of men. And here observe,

1. What was the *way and practice of the hypocrites.* In all their exercises of devotion, it was plain, the chief thing they aimed at was to be commended by their neighbours, and thereby to make an interest for themselves. When they seemed to *soar upwards* in prayer (and if it be right, it is the soul's ascent toward God), yet even then their eye was *downwards* upon this as their *prey.* Observe,

(1.) What the *places* were which they chose for their devotion; they prayed in the *synagogues,* which were indeed proper places for public prayer, but not for personal. They pretended hereby to do honour to the place of their assemblies, but intended to do honour to themselves. They prayed in *the corners of the streets,* the broad streets (so the word signifies), which were most frequented. They withdrew thither, as if they were under a pious impulse which would not admit delay, but really it was to cause themselves to be taken notice of. There, where two streets met, they were not only within view of both, but every passenger turning close upon them would observe them, and hear what they said.

(2.) The *posture* they used in prayer; they prayed standing; this is a lawful and proper posture for prayer (Mark xi. 25, *When ye stand praying*), but kneeling being the more humble and reverent gesture, Luke xxii. 41; Acts vii. 60; Eph. iii. 14, their standing seemed to savour of pride and confidence in themselves (Luke xviii. 11), *The Pharisee stood and prayed.*

(3.) Their *pride* in choosing those public places, which is expressed in two things: [1.] They *love* to pray there. They did not love prayer for its own sake, but they loved it when it gave them an opportunity of making themselves noticed. Circumstances may be such, that our good deeds must needs be done openly, so as to fall under the observation of others, and be commended by them; but the sin and danger is when we love it, and are pleased with it, because it feeds the proud humour. [2.] It is that they may be *seen of men;* not that God might accept them, but that men might admire and applaud them; and that they might easily get the estates of widows and orphans into their hands (who would not trust such devout, praying men?) and that, when they had them, they might devour them without being suspected (*ch.* xxiii. 14); and effectually carry on their public designs to enslave the people.

(4.) The *product* of all this, *they have their reward;* they have all the recompence they must ever expect from God for their service, and a poor recompence it is. What will it avail us to have the good word of our fellow-servants, if our Master do not say, *Well done?* But if in so great a transaction as is between us and God, when we are at prayer, we can take in so poor a consideration as the praise of men is, it is just that that should be all our reward. They did it to be *seen of men,* and they are so; and much good may it do them. Note, Those that would approve themselves to God by their integrity in their religion, must have no regard to the praise of men; it is not to men that we pray, nor from them that we expect an answer; they are not to be our judges, they are dust and ashes like ourselves, and therefore we must not have our eye to them: what passes between God and our own souls must be out of sight. In our synagogue-worship, we must avoid every thing that tends to make our personal devotion remarkable, as they that caused their *voice to be heard on high,* Isa. lviii. 4. Public places are not proper for private solemn prayer.

2. What is the *will of Jesus Christ* in opposition to this. Humility and sincerity are the two great lessons that Christ teaches us; *Thou, when thou prayest,* do so and so (*v.* 6);

thou in particular by thyself, and for thyself. Personal prayer is here supposed to be the duty and practice of all Christ's disciples.

Observe, (1.) The directions here given about it.

[1.] Instead of praying in *the synagogues* and in the *corners of the streets, enter into thy closet,* into some place of privacy and retirement. Isaac went into the field (Gen. xxiv. 63), Christ to a mountain, Peter to the house-top. No place amiss in point of ceremony, if it do but answer the end. Note, Secret prayer is to be performed in retirement, that we may be unobserved, and so may avoid ostentation; undisturbed, and so may avoid distraction; unheard, and so may use the greater freedom; yet if the circumstances be such that we cannot possibly avoid being taken notice of, we must not therefore neglect the duty, lest the omission be a greater scandal than the observation of it.

[2.] Instead of doing it to be *seen of men, pray to thy Father who is in secret; to me, even to me,* Zech. vii. 5, 6. The Pharisees prayed rather to men than to God; whatever was the form of their prayer, the scope of it was to beg the applause of men, and court their favours. "Well, do thou pray to God, and let that be enough for thee. Pray to him as a Father, as thy Father, ready to hear and answer, graciously inclined to pity, help, and succour thee. Pray to thy Father *who is in secret.* Note, In secret prayer we must have an eye to God, as present in all places; he is there in thy closet when no one else is there; there especially nigh to thee in what thou *callest upon him for.* By *secret* prayer we give God the glory of his universal presence (Acts xvii. 24), and may take to ourselves the comfort of it.

(2.) The encouragements here given us to it.

[1.] Thy Father *seeth in secret;* his eye is upon thee to accept thee, when the eye of no man is upon thee to applaud thee; *under the fig-tree, I saw thee,* said Christ to Nathaniel, John i. 48. He saw Paul at prayer in such a street, at such a house, Acts ix. 11. There is not a secret, sudden breathing after God, but he observes it.

[2.] He *will reward thee openly;* they have their reward that do it openly, and thou shalt not lose thine for thy doing it in secret. It is called a *reward,* but it is *of grace,* not *of debt;* what merit can there be in begging? The reward will be open; they shall not only have it, but have it honourably: the open reward is that which hypocrites are fond of, but they have not patience to stay for it; it is that which the sincere are dead to, and they shall have it over and above. Sometimes secret prayers are rewarded openly in this world by signal answers to them, which manifests God's praying people in the consciences of their adversaries; however, at the great day there will be an open reward, when all praying people shall *appear in glory* with the great Intercessor. The Pharisees had their reward *before all the town,* and it was a *mere flash and shadow;* true Christians shall have theirs *before all the world,* angels and men, and it shall be a *weight of glory.*

II. We must not *use vain repetitions* in prayer, *v.* 7, 8. Though the life of prayer lies in *lifting up the soul and pouring out the heart,* yet there is some interest which words have in prayer, especially in joint prayer; for in that, words are necessary, and it should seem that our Saviour speaks here especially of that; for before he said, *when thou prayest,* here, when *ye pray;* and the Lord's prayer which follows is a joint prayer, and in that, he that is the mouth of others is most tempted to an ostentation of language and expression, against which we are here warned; *use not vain repetitions,* either alone or with others: the Pharisees affected this, *they made long prayers* (*ch.* xxiii. 14), all their care was to make them long. Now observe,

1. What the *fault* is that is here reproved and condemned; it is making a mere lip-labour of the duty of prayer, the service of the tongue, when it is not the service of the soul. This is expressed here by two words, Βαττολογία, Πολυλογία. (1.) *Vain repetitions*—tautology, battology, idle babbling over the same words again and again to no purpose, like *Battus, Sub illis montibus erant, erant sub montibus illis;* like that imitation of the wordiness of a fool, Eccl. x. 14, *A man cannot tell what shall be; and what shall be after him who can tell?* which is indecent and nauseous in any discourse, much more in speaking to God. It is not all repetition in prayer that is here condemned, but vain repetitions. Christ himself prayed, saying the same words (*ch.* xxvi. 44), out of a more than ordinary fervour and zeal, Luke xxii. 44. So Daniel, *ch.* ix. 18, 19. And there is a very elegant repetition of the same words, Ps. cxxxvi. It may be of use both to express our own affections, and to excite the affections of others. But the superstitious rehearsing of a tale of words, without regard to the sense of them, as the papists saying by their beads so many Ave-Marys and Paternosters; or the barren and dry going over of the same things again and again, merely to drill out the prayer to such a length, and to make a show of affection when really there is none; these are the vain repetitions here condemned. When we would fain say much, but cannot say much to the purpose; this is displeasing to God and all wise men. (2.) *Much speaking,* an affectation of prolixity in prayer, either out of pride or superstition, or an opinion that God needs either to be informed or argued with by us, or out of mere folly and impertinence, because men love to *hear themselves talk.* Not that all long prayers are forbidden; Christ prayed all night, Luke vi. 12. Solomon's was a long prayer. There is sometimes need of long prayers when our errands and our affections are extraordinary; but merely

to prolong the prayer, as if that would make it more pleasing or more prevailing with God, is that which is here condemned; it is not much *praying* that is condemned; no, we are bid to *pray always*, but much *speaking*; the danger of this error is when we only *say* our prayers, not when we *pray* them. This caution is explained by that of Solomon (Eccl. v. 2), *Let thy words be few*, considerate and well weighed; *take with you words* (Hos. xiv. 2), *choose out words* (Job ix. 14), and do not say every thing that comes uppermost.

2. What reasons are given against this.

(1.) This is the way of the heathen, *as the heathen do;* and it ill becomes Christians to worship their God as the Gentiles worship theirs. The heathen were taught by the light of nature to worship God; but becoming vain in their imaginations concerning the object of their worship, no wonder they became so concerning the manner of it, and particularly in this instance; thinking God altogether such a one as themselves, they thought he needed many words to make him understand what was said to him, or to bring him to comply with their requests; as if he were weak and ignorant, and hard to be entreated. Thus Baal's priests were hard at it from morning till almost night with their *vain repetitions; O Baal, hear us; O Baal, hear us;* and vain petitions they were; but Elijah, in a grave, composed frame, with a very concise prayer, prevailed for fire from heaven first, and then water, 1 Kings xviii. 26, 36. *Lip-labour* in prayer, though ever so well *laboured*, if that be all, is but *lost labour*.

(2.) "It need not be your way, *for your Father* in heaven *knoweth what things ye have need of before ye ask him*, and therefore there is no occasion for such abundance of words. It does not follow that therefore ye need not pray; for God requires you by prayer to own your need of him and dependence on him, and to plead his promises; but therefore you are to open your case, and pour out your hearts before him, and then leave it with him." Consider, [1.] The God we pray to is our Father by creation, by covenant; and therefore our addresses to him should be easy, natural, and unaffected; children do not use to make long speeches to their parents when they want any thing; it is enough to say, *my head, my head*. Let us come to him with the disposition of children, with love, reverence, and dependence; and then they need not say many words, that are taught by the Spirit of adoption to say that one aright, *Abba, Father*. [2.] He is a Father that knows our case and knows our wants better than we do ourselves. *He knows what things we have need of;* his eyes run to and fro through the earth, to observe the necessities of his people (2 Chron. xvi. 9), and he often gives *before we call* (Isa. lxv. 24), and *more than we ask for* (Eph. iii. 20), and if he do not give his people what they ask, it is because he knows they do not need it, and that it is not for their good; and of that he is fitter to judge for us than we for ourselves. We need not be long, nor use many words in representing our case; God knows it better than we can tell him, only he will know it *from us* (*what will ye that I should do unto you?*); and when we have told him what it is, we must refer ourselves to him, *Lord, all my desire is before thee*, Ps. xxxviii. 9. So far is God from being wrought upon by the length or language of our prayers, that the most powerful intercessions are those which are made with *groanings that cannot be uttered*, Rom. viii. 26. We are not to *pre*scribe, but *sub*scribe to God.

9 After this manner therefore pray
ye: Our Father which art in heaven,
hallowed be thy name. 10 Thy
kingdom come. Thy will be done
in earth, as *it is* in heaven. 11 Give
us this day our daily bread. 12
And forgive us our debts, as we forgive our debtors. 13 And lead us
not into temptation, but deliver us
from evil: For thine is the kingdom,
and the power, and the glory, for
ever. Amen. 14 For if ye forgive
men their trespasses, your heavenly
Father will also forgive you: 15 But
if ye forgive not men their trespasses,
neither will your Father forgive your
trespasses.

When Christ had condemned what was amiss, he directs to do better; for his are reproofs of instruction. Because we know not what to pray for as we ought, he here helps our infirmities, by putting words into our mouths; *after this manner therefore pray ye, v.* 9. So many were the corruptions that had crept into this duty of prayer among the Jews, that Christ saw it needful to give a new directory for prayer, to show his disciples what must ordinarily be the matter and method of their prayer, which he gives in words that may very well be used as a form; as the summary or contents of the several particulars of our prayers. Not that we are tied up to the use of this form only, or of this always, as if this were necessary to the consecrating of our other prayers; we are here bid to pray after this manner, with these words, or to this effect. That in Luke differs from this; we do not find it used by the apostles; we are not here taught to pray in the name of Christ, as we are afterward; we are here taught to pray that that kingdom might come which did come when the Spirit was poured out: yet, without doubt, it is very good to use it as a form, and it is a pledge of the communion of saints, it having been used by the church in all ages, at least (says Dr Whitby) from the third century. It is our

Lord's prayer, it is of his composing, of his appointing; it is very compendious, yet very comprehensive, in compassion to our infirmities in praying. The matter is choice and necessary, the method instructive, and the expression very concise. It has much in a little, and it is requisite that we acquaint ourselves with the sense and meaning of it, for it is used acceptably no further than it is used with understanding and without vain repetition.

The Lord's prayer (as indeed every prayer) is a letter sent from earth to heaven. Here is the inscription of the letter, the person to whom it is directed, *our Father;* the place where, *in heaven;* the contents of it in several errands of request; the close, *for thine is the kingdom;* the seal, *Amen;* and if you will, the date too, *this day.*

Plainly thus: there are three parts of the prayer.

I. *The preface, Our Father who art in heaven.* Before we come to our business, there must be a solemn address to him with whom our business lies; *Our Father.* Intimating, that we must pray, not only alone and for ourselves, but with and for others; for we are members one of another, and are called into fellowship with each other. We are here taught *to whom to pray,* to God only, and not to saints and angels, for they are ignorant of us, are not to have the honours we give in prayer, nor can give the favours we expect. We are taught how to address ourselves to God, and what title to give him, that which speaks him rather beneficent than magnificent, for we are to come boldly to the throne of grace.

1. We must address ourselves to him as *our Father,* and must call him so. He is a common Father to all mankind by creation, Mal. ii. 10; Acts xvii. 28. He is in a special manner a Father to the saints, by adoption and regeneration (Eph. i. 5; Gal. iv. 6); and an unspeakable privilege it is. Thus we must eye him in prayer, keep up good thoughts of him, such as are encouraging and not affrighting; nothing more pleasing to God, nor pleasant to ourselves, than to call God *Father.* Christ in prayer mostly called God *Father.* If he be our Father, he will pity us under our weaknesses and infirmities (Ps. ciii. 13), will spare us (Mal. iii. 17), will make the best of our performances, though very defective, will deny us nothing that is good for us, Luke xi. 11—13. We have access with boldness to him, as to a father, and have an *advocate with the Father,* and the Spirit of adoption. When we come repenting of our sins, we must eye God as a Father, as the prodigal did (Luke xv. 18; Jer. iii. 19); when we come begging for grace, and peace, and the inheritance and blessing of sons, it is an encouragement that we come to God, not as an unreconciled, avenging Judge, but as a loving, gracious, reconciled Father in Christ, Jer. iii. 4.

2. As our Father *in heaven:* so in heaven as to be every where else, for the heaven cannot contain him; yet so in heaven as there to manifest his glory, for it is his throne (Ps. ciii. 19), and it is to believers a throne of grace: thitherward we must direct our prayers, for Christ the Mediator is now in heaven, Heb. viii. 1. Heaven is out of sight, and a world of spirits, therefore our converse with God in prayer must be spiritual; it is on high, therefore in prayer we must be raised above the world, and lift up our hearts, Ps. v. 1. Heaven is a place of perfect purity, and we must therefore lift up pure hands, must study to sanctify his name, who is the Holy One, and dwells in that holy place, Lev. x. 3. From heaven God beholds the children of men, Ps. xxxiii. 13, 14. And we must in prayer see his eye upon us: thence he has a full and clear view of all our wants and burdens and desires, and all our infirmities. It is the firmament of his power likewise, as well as of his prospect, Ps. cl. 1. He is not only, as a Father, willing to help us, but as a heavenly Father, able to help us, able to do great things for us, more than we can ask or think; he has wherewith to supply our needs, for every good gift is from above. He is a Father, and therefore we may come to him with boldness, but a Father in heaven, and therefore we must come with reverence, Eccl. v. 2. Thus all our prayers should correspond with that which is our great aim as Christians, and that is, to be with God in heaven. God and heaven, the end of our whole conversation, must be particularly eyed in every prayer; there is the centre to which we are all tending. By prayer, we send before us thither, where we profess to be going.

II. *The petitions,* and those are six; the three first relating more immediately to God and his honour, the three last to our own concerns, both temporal and spiritual; as in the ten commandments, the four first teach us our duty toward God, and the last six our duty toward our neighbour. The method of this prayer teaches us to seek first the *kingdom of God and his righteousness,* and then to hope that *other things shall be added.*

1. *Hallowed be thy name.* It is the same word that in other places is translated *sanctified.* But here the old word *hallowed* is retained, only because people were used to it in the Lord's prayer. In these words, (1.) We give glory to God; it may be taken not as a petition, but as an adoration; as that, *the Lord be magnified,* or *glorified,* for God's holiness is the greatness and glory of all his perfections. We must begin our prayers with praising God, and it is very fit he should be first served, and that we should give glory to God, before we expect to receive mercy and grace from him. Let him have the praise of his perfections, and then let us have the benefit of them. (2.) We fix our end, and it is the right end to be aimed at, and ought to be our chief and ultimate

end in all our petitions, that God may be glorified; all our other requests must be in subordination to this, and in pursuance of it. "*Father, glorify thyself* in giving me my daily bread and pardoning my sins," &c. Since all is of him and through him, all must be to him and for him. In prayer our thoughts and affections should be carried out most to the glory of God. The Pharisees made their own name the chief end of their prayers (*v.* 5, *to be seen of men),* in opposition to which we are directed to make the name of God our chief end; let all our petitions centre in this and be regulated by it. "Do so and so for me, *for the glory of thy name,* and as far as is for the glory of it." (3.) We desire and pray that the name of God, that is, God himself, in all that whereby he has made himself known, may be sanctified and glorified both by us and others, and especially by himself. "Father, let thy name be glorified as a Father, and a Father in heaven; glorify thy goodness and thy highness, thy majesty and mercy. *Let thy name be sanctified,* for it is a holy name; no matter what becomes of our polluted names, but, Lord, *what wilt thou do to thy great name?*" When we pray that God's name may be glorified, [1.] We make a virtue of necessity; for God will *sanctify his own name,* whether we desire it or not; *I will be exalted among the heathen,* Ps. xlvi. 10. [2.] We ask for that which we are sure shall be granted; for when our Saviour prayed, *Father glorify thy name,* it was immediately answered, *I have glorified it, and will glorify it again.*

2. *Thy kingdom come.* This petition has plainly a reference to the doctrine which Christ preached at this time, which John Baptist had preached before, and which he afterwards sent his apostles out to preach—*the kingdom of heaven is at hand.* The kingdom of your Father who is in heaven, the kingdom of the Messiah, this is at hand, pray that it may come. Note, We should turn the word we hear into prayer, our hearts should echo to it; does Christ promise, *surely I come quickly?* our hearts should answer, *Even so, come.* Ministers should pray over the word: when they preach, *the kingdom of God is at hand,* they should pray, *Father, thy kingdom come.* What God has promised we must pray for; for promises are given, not to supersede, but to quicken and encourage prayer; and when the accomplishment of a promise is near and at the door, when the kingdom of heaven is at hand, we should then pray for it the more earnestly; *thy kingdom come;* as Daniel set his face to pray for the deliverance of Israel, when he understood that the time of it was at hand, Dan. ix. 2. See Luke xix. 11. It was the Jews' daily prayer to God, *Let him make his kingdom reign, let his redemption flourish, and let his Messiah come and deliver his people.* Dr. Whitby, *ex Vitringa.* "*Let thy kingdom come,* let the gospel be preached to all and embraced by all; let all be brought to subscribe to the record God has given in his word concerning his Son, and to embrace him as their Saviour and Sovereign. Let the bounds of the gospel-church be enlarged, the kingdom of the world be made Christ's kingdom, and all men become subjects to it, and live as becomes their character."

3. *Thy will be done in earth as it is in heaven.* We pray that God's kingdom being come, we and others may be brought into obedience to all the laws and ordinances of it. By this let it appear that Christ's kingdom is come, *let God's will be done;* and by this let it appear that it is come as a *kingdom of heaven,* let it introduce a *heaven upon earth.* We make Christ but a titular Prince, if we call him King, and do not do his will: having prayed that he may rule us, we pray that we may in every thing be ruled by him. Observe, (1.) The thing prayed for, *thy will be done;* "Lord, do what thou pleasest with me and mine; 1 Sam. iii. 18. I refer myself to thee, and am well satisfied that all thy counsel concerning me should be performed." In this sense Christ prayed, *not my will, but thine be done.* "Enable me to do what is pleasing to thee; give me that grace that is necessary to the right knowledge of thy will, and an acceptable obedience to it. Let thy will be done conscientiously by me and others, not our own will, the will of the flesh, or the mind, not the will of men (1 Pet. iv. 2), much less Satan's will (John viii. 44), that we may neither displease God in any thing we do *(ut nihil nostrum displiceat Deo),* nor be displeased at any thing God does" *(ut nihil Dei displiceat nobis).* (2.) The pattern of it, that it may *be done on earth,* in this place of our trial and probation (where our work must be done, or it never will be done), *as it is done in heaven,* that place of rest and joy. We pray that earth may be made more like heaven by the observance of God's will (this earth, which, through the prevalency of Satan's will, has become so near akin to hell), and that saints may be made more like the holy angels in their devotion and obedience. We are *on earth,* blessed be God, not yet *under the earth;* we pray for *the living* only, not for *the dead that have gone down into silence.*

4. *Give us this day our daily bread.* Because our natural being is necessary to our spiritual well-being in this world, therefore, after the things of God's glory, kingdom, and will, we pray for the necessary supports and comforts of this present life, which are the gifts of God, and must be asked of him, Τὸν ἄρτον ἐπιούσιον—*Bread for the day approaching,* for all the remainder of our lives. *Bread for the time to come,* or *bread for our being and subsistence,* that which is agreeable to our condition in the world (Prov. xxx. 8), *food convenient for us* and our families, according to our rank and station.

Every word here has a lesson in it: (1.) We ask for *bread;* that teaches us sobriety and temperance; we ask for *bread,* not dainties, not superfluities; that which is wholesome, though it be not nice. (2.) We ask for *our* bread; that teaches us honesty and industry: we do not ask for the bread out of other people's mouths, not *the bread of deceit* (Prov. xx. 17), not *the bread of idleness* (Prov. xxxi. 27), but the bread honestly gotten. (3.) We ask for our *daily* bread; which teaches us not to *take thought for the morrow* (*v.* 34), but constantly to depend upon divine Providence, as those that live from hand to mouth. (4.) We beg of God to *give* it us, not sell it us, nor lend it us, but *give* it. The greatest of men must be beholden to the mercy of God for their *daily bread,* (5.) We pray, "Give it to *us;* not to me only, but to others in common with me." This teaches us charity, and a compassionate concern for the poor and needy. It intimates also, that we ought to pray with our families; we and our households eat together, and therefore ought to pray together. (6.) We pray that God would give it us *this day;* which teaches us to renew the desire of our souls toward God, as the wants of our bodies are renewed; as duly as the day comes, we must pray to our heavenly Father, and reckon we could as well go a day without meat, as without prayer.

5. *And forgive us our debts, as we forgive our debtors,* This is connected with the former; *and forgive,* intimating, that unless our sins be pardoned, we can have no comfort in life, or the supports of it. *Our daily bread* does but feed us *as lambs for the slaughter,* if our sins be not pardoned. It intimates, likewise, that we must pray for daily *pardon,* as duly as we pray for daily *bread. He that is washed, needeth to wash his feet.* Here we have,

(1.) A petition; *Father in heaven forgive us our debts,* our debts to thee. Note, [1.] Our sins are our debts; there is a debt of duty, which, as creatures, we owe to our Creator; we do not pray to be discharged from that, but upon the non-payment of that there arises a debt of punishment; in default of obedience to the will of God, we become obnoxious *to the wrath of God;* and for not observing the precept of the law, we stand obliged to the penalty. A debtor is liable to process, so are we; a malefactor is a debtor to the law, so are we. [2.] Our hearts' desire and prayer to our heavenly Father every day should be, that he would *forgive us our debts;* that the obligation to punishment may be cancelled and vacated, that we may *not come into condemnation;* that we may be discharged, and have the comfort of it. In suing out the pardon of our sins, the great plea we have to rely upon is the satisfaction that was made to the justice of God for the sin of man, by the dying of the Lord Jesus our Surety, or rather Bail to the action, that undertook our discharge.

(2.) An argument to enforce this petition; *as we forgive cur debtors.* This is not a plea of merit, but a plea of grace. Note, Those that come to God for the forgiveness of their sins against him, must make conscience of forgiving those who have offended them, else they curse themselves when they say the Lord's prayer. Our duty is to *forgive our debtors;* as to debts of money, we must not be rigorous and severe in exacting them from those that cannot pay them without ruining themselves and their families; but this means debts of injury; our debtors are those that *trespass against us,* that *smite us* (*ch.* v. 39, 40), and in strictness of law, might be prosecuted for it; we must forbear, and forgive, and forget the affronts put upon us, and the wrongs done us; and this is a moral qualification for pardon and peace; it encourages to hope, that God will *forgive us;* for if there be in us this gracious disposition, it is wrought of God, and therefore is a perfection eminently and transcendently in himself; it will be an evidence to us that he has forgiven us, having wrought in us the condition of forgiveness.

6. *And lead us not into temptation, but deliver us from evil.* This petition is expressed,

(1.) Negatively: *Lead us not into temptation.* Having prayed that the guilt of sin may be removed, we pray, as is fit, that we may never return again to folly, that we may not be tempted to it. It is not as if God tempted any to sin; but, "Lord, do not let Satan loose upon us; chain up that *roaring lion,* for he is subtle and spiteful; Lord, do not leave us to ourselves (Ps. xix. 13), for we are very weak; Lord, do not *lay stumbling-blocks* and snares before us, nor put us into circumstances that may be *an occasion of falling.*" Temptations are to be prayed against, both because of the discomfort and trouble of them, and because of the danger we are in of being overcome by them, and the guilt and grief that then follow.

(2.) Positively: *But deliver us from evil;* *απὸ τοῦ πονηροῦ*—*from the evil one,* the devil, the tempter; "keep us, that either we may not be assaulted by him, or we may not be overcome by those assaults:" Or *from the evil thing,* sin, the worst of evils; an evil, an only evil; that evil thing which God hates, and which Satan tempts men to and destroys them by. "Lord, deliver us from the evil of the world, the corruption that is in the world through lust; from the evil of every condition in the world; from the evil of death; from *the sting of death, which is sin:* deliver us from ourselves, from our own evil hearts: deliver us from evil men, that they may not be a snare to us, nor we a prey to them."

III. The conclusion: *For thine is the kingdom, and the power and the glory, for ever. Amen.* Some refer this to David's doxology, 1 Chron. xxix. 11. *Thine, O Lord, is the greatness.* It is,

1. A form of plea to enforce the foregoing petitions. It is our duty to plead with God in prayer, to fill our mouth with arguments (Job xxiii. 4) not to move God, but to affect ourselves; to encourage our faith, to excite our fervency, and to evidence both. Now the best pleas in prayer are those that are taken from God himself, and from that which he has made known of himself. We must wrestle with God in his own strength, both as to the nature of our pleas and the urging of them. The plea here has special reference to the three first petitions; *Father in heaven, thy kingdom come, for thine is the kingdom; thy will be done, for thine is the power; hallowed be thy name, for thine is the glory.*" And as to our own particular errands, these are encouraging: "*Thine is the kingdom;* thou hast the government of the world, and the protection of the saints, thy willing subjects in it;" God gives and saves like a king. "*Thine is the power,* to maintain and support that kingdom, and to make good all thine engagements to thy people." *Thine is the glory,* as the end of all that which is given to, and done for, the saints, in answer to their prayers; for their *praise waiteth* for him. This is matter of comfort and holy confidence in prayer.

2. It is a form of praise and thanksgiving. The best pleading with God is praising of him; it is the way to obtain further mercy, as it qualifies us to receive it. In all our addresses to God, it is fit that praise should have a considerable share, for *praise becometh the saints;* they are to be to our God *for a name and for a praise.* It is just and equal; we praise God, and give him glory, not because he needs it—he is praised by a world of angels, but because he deserves it; and it is our duty to give him glory, in compliance with his design in revealing himself to us. Praise is the work and happiness of heaven; and all that would go to heaven hereafter, must begin their heaven now. Observe, how full this doxology is, *The kingdom, and the power, and the glory,* it is all thine. Note, It becomes us to be copious in praising God. A true saint never thinks he can speak honourably enough of God: here there should be a gracious fluency, and this *for ever.* Ascribing glory to God *for ever,* intimates an acknowledgment, that it is eternally due, and an earnest desire to be eternally doing it, with angels and saints above, Ps. lxxi. 14.

Lastly, To all this we are taught to affix our *Amen,* so be it. God's *Amen* is a grant; his *fiat* is, it shall be so: our *Amen* is only a summary desire; our *fiat* is, let it be so: it is in token of our desire and assurance to be heard, that we say *Amen. Amen* refers to every petition going before, and thus, in compassion to our infirmities, we are taught to knit up the whole in one word, and so to gather up, in the general, what we have lost and let slip in the particulars. It is good to conclude religious duties with some warmth and vigour, that we may go from them with a sweet savour upon our spirits. It was of old the practice of good people to say, *Amen,* audibly at the end of every prayer, and it is a commendable practice, provided it be done with understanding, as the apostle directs (1 Cor. xiv. 16), and uprightly, with life and liveliness, and inward impressions, answerable to that outward expression of desire and confidence.

Most of the petitions in the Lord's prayer had been commonly used by the Jews in their devotions, or words to the same effect: but that clause in the fifth petition, *As we forgive our debtors,* was perfectly new, and therefore our Saviour here shows for what reason he added it, not with any personal reflection upon the peevishness, litigiousness, and ill nature of the men of that generation, though there was cause enough for it, but only from the necessity and importance of the thing itself. God, in forgiving us, has a peculiar respect to our forgiving those that have injured us; and therefore, when we pray for pardon, we must mention our making conscience of that duty, not only to remind ourselves of it, but to bind ourselves to it. See that parable, *ch.* xviii. 23—35. Selfish nature is loth to comply with this, and therefore it is here inculcated, *v.* 14, 15.

1. In a promise. *If ye forgive, your heavenly Father will also forgive.* Not as if this were the only condition required; there must be repentance and faith, and new obedience; but as where other graces are in truth, there will be this, so this will be a good evidence of the sincerity of our other graces. He that relents toward his brother, thereby shows that he repents toward his God. Those which in the prayer are called *debts,* are here called *trespasses, debts* of injury, wrongs done us in our bodies, goods, or reputation: *trespasses* is an extenuating term for offences, *παραπτώματα—stumbles, slips, falls.* Note, It is a good evidence, and a good help of our forgiving others, to call the injuries done us by a mollifying, excusing name. Call them not *treasons,* but *trespasses;* not wilful injuries, but casual inadvertencies; *peradventure it was an oversight* (Gen. xliii. 12), therefore make the best of it. We must forgive, as we hope to be forgiven; and therefore must not only bear no malice, nor meditate revenge, but must not upbraid our brother with the injuries he has done us, nor rejoice in any hurt that befals him, but must be ready to help him and do him good, and if he repent and desire to be friends again, we must be free and familiar with him, as before.

2. In a threatening. "*But if you forgive not* those that have injured you, that is a bad sign you have not the other requisite conditions, but are altogether unqualified for pardon: and therefore *your Father,* whom you call Father, and who, as a father, offers

you his grace upon reasonable terms, will nevertheless *not forgive you.* And if other graces be sincere, and yet you be defective greatly in forgiving, you cannot expect the comfort of your pardon, but to have your spirits brought down by some affliction or other to comply with this duty." Note, Those that would find mercy with God must show mercy to their brethren; nor can we expect that he should stretch out the hands of his favour to us, unless we lift up to him *pure hands, without wrath,* 1 Tim. ii. 8. If we pray in anger, we have reason to fear God will answer in anger. It has been said, Prayers made in wrath are written in gall. What reason is it that God should forgive us the talents we are indebted to him, if we forgive not our brethren the pence they are indebted to us? Christ *came into the world* as the great Peace-Maker, not only *to reconcile us to God,* but one to another, and in this we must comply with him. It is great presumption and of dangerous consequence, for any to make a light matter of that which Christ here lays such a stress upon. Men's passions shall not frustrate God's word.

16 Moreover, when ye fast, be not, as the hypocrites, of a sad countenance: for they disfigure their faces, that they may appear unto men to fast. Verily I say unto you, They have their reward. 17 But thou, when thou fastest, anoint thine head, and wash thy face; 18 That thou appear not unto men to fast, but unto thy Father which is in secret: and thy Father, which seeth in secret, shall reward thee openly.

We are here cautioned against hypocrisy in fasting, as before in almsgiving, and in prayer.

I. It is here supposed that religious fasting is a duty required of the disciples of Christ, when God, in his providence, calls to it, and when the case of their own souls upon any account requires it; *when the bridegroom is taken away, then shall they fast, ch.* ix. 15. Fasting is here put last, because it is not so much a duty for its own sake, as a means to dispose us for other duties. Prayer comes in between almsgiving and fasting, as being the life and soul of both. Christ here speaks especially of private fasts, such as particular persons prescribe to themselves, as free-will offerings, commonly used among the pious Jews; some fasted one day, some two, every week; others seldomer, as they saw cause. On those days they did not eat till sun-set, and then very sparingly. It was not the Pharisee's fasting *twice in the week,* but his boasting of it, that Christ condemned, Luke xviii. 12. It is a laudable practice, and we have reason to lament it, that it is so generally neglected among Christians. Anna was much in fasting, Luke ii. 37. Cornelius fasted and prayed, Acts x. 30. The primitive Christians were much in it, see Acts xiii. 3; xiv. 23. Private fasting is supposed, 1 Cor. vii. 5. It is an act of self-denial, and mortification of the flesh, a holy revenge upon ourselves, and humiliation under the hand of God. The most grown Christians must hereby own, they are so far from having any thing to be proud of, that they are unworthy of their daily bread. It is a means to curb the flesh and the desires of it, and to make us more lively in religious exercises, as fulness of bread is apt to make us drowsy. Paul was *in fastings often,* and so he *kept under his body, and brought it into subjection.*

II. We are cautioned not to do this *as the hypocrites* did it, lest we lose the reward of it; and the more difficulty attends the duty, the greater loss it is to lose the reward of it.

Now, 1. The *hypocrites* pretended fasting, when there was nothing of that contrition or humiliation of soul in them, which is the life and soul of the duty. Theirs were mock-fasts, the show and shadow without the substance; they took on them to be more humbled than really they were, and so endeavoured to put a cheat upon God, than which they could not put a greater affront upon him. The fast that God has chosen, is *a day to afflict the soul, not to hang down the head like a bulrush,* nor for a man *to spread sackcloth and ashes under him;* we are quite mistaken if we call this a fast, Isa. lviii. 5. Bodily exercise, if that be all, profits little, since that is not fasting to God, even to him.

2. They proclaimed their fasting, and managed it so that all who saw them might take notice that it was a fasting-day with them. Even on these days they appeared in the streets, whereas they should have been in their closets; and they affected a downcast look, a melancholy countenance, a slow and solemn pace; and perfectly disfigured themselves, that men might see how often they fasted, and might extol them as devout, mortified men. Note, It is sad that men, who have, in some measure, mastered their pleasure, which is sensual wickedness, should be ruined by their pride, which is spiritual wickedness, and no less dangerous. Here also *they have their reward,* that praise and applause of men which they court and covet so much; *they have* it, and it is their all.

III. We are directed how to manage a private fast; we must keep it private, *v.* 17, 18. He does not tell us how often we must fast; circumstances vary, and wisdom is profitable therein to direct; the Spirit in the word has left that to the Spirit in the heart; but take this for a rule, whenever you undertake this duty, study therein to approve yourselves to God, and not to recommend yourselves to the good opinions of men; humility must evermore attend upon our humiliation. Christ does not direct to abate any thing of the reality of the fast; he does not say, "take a little meat, or a little drink, or a little cordial;" no, "let the body suffer, but lay aside the show and appearance of it; appear with thy ordinary countenance, guise, and dress; and while thou deniest thyself thy bodily refreshments, do it so as that it may not be taken notice of, no, not by those that are nearest to thee; look pleasant, *anoint thine head and wash thy face,* as thou dost on ordinary days, on purpose to conceal thy devotion; and thou shalt be no loser in the praise of it at last; for though it be not of men, it shall be of God." Fasting is the humbling of the soul (Ps. xxxv. 13), that is the inside of the duty; let that therefore be thy principal care, and as to the outside of it, covet not to let it be seen. If we be sincere in our solemn fasts, and humble, and trust God's omniscience for our witness, and his goodness for our reward, we shall find, both that he did *see in secret,* and will *reward openly.* Religious fasts, if rightly kept, will shortly be recompensed with an everlasting feast. Our acceptance with God in our private fasts should make us dead, both to the applause of men (we must not do the duty in hopes of this), and to the censures of men too (we must not decline the duty for fear of them). David's fasting was turned to his reproach, Ps. lxix. 10; and yet, *v.* 13, *As for me,* let them say what they will of me, *my prayer is unto thee in an acceptable time.*

19 Lay not up for yourselves treasures upon earth, where moth and
rust doth corrupt, and where thieves
break through and steal: 20 But
lay up for yourselves treasures in
heaven, where neither moth nor rust
doth corrupt, and where thieves do
not break through nor steal: 21 For
where your treasure is, there will
your heart be also: 22 The light
of the body is the eye: If therefore
thine eye be single, thy whole body
shall be full of light: 23 But if
thine eye be evil, thy whole body
shall be full of darkness. If therefore the light that is in thee be darkness, how great *is* that darkness!
24 No man can serve two masters:
for either he will hate the one, and
love the other; or else he will hold
to the one, and despise the other.
Ye cannot serve God and Mammon.

Worldly-mindedness is as common and as fatal a symptom of hypocrisy as any other, for by no sin can Satan have a surer and faster hold of the soul, under the cloak of a visible and passable profession of religion, than by this; and therefore Christ, having warned us against coveting *the praise of men,* proceeds next to warn us against coveting the wealth of the world; in this also we must take heed, lest we be as the hypocrites are, and do as they do: the fundamental error that they are guilty of is, that they choose the world for *their reward;* we must therefore take heed of hypocrisy and worldly-mindedness, in the choice we make of our treasure, our end, and our masters.

I. In choosing the *treasure* we *lay up.* Something or other every man has which he makes his *treasure,* his portion, which his heart is upon, to which he carries all he can get, and which he depends upon for futurity. It is *that good,* that chief good, which Solomon speaks of with such an emphasis, Eccl. ii. 3. Something the soul will have, which it looks upon as the best thing, which it has a complacency and confidence in above other things. Now Christ designs not to deprive us of our treasure, but to direct us in the choice of it; and here we have,

1. A *good caution* against making *the things that are seen,* that *are temporal,* our best things, and placing our happiness in them. *Lay not up for yourselves treasures upon earth.* Christ's disciples had left all to follow him, let them still keep in the same good mind. A *treasure* is an abundance of something that is in itself, at least in our opinion, precious and valuable, and likely to stand us in stead hereafter. Now we must *not lay up our treasures on earth,* that is, (1.) We must not count these things the best things, nor the most valuable in themselves, nor the most serviceable to us: we must not call them glory, as Laban's sons did, but see and own that they have no glory in comparison with *the glory that excelleth.* (2.) We must not covet an abundance of these things, nor be still grasping at more and more of them, and adding to them, as men do to that which is their treasure, as never knowing when we have enough. (3.) We must not confide in them for futurity, to be our security and supply in time to come; we must not say to the gold, *Thou art my hope.* (4.) We must not content ourselves with them, as all we need or desire: we must be content with a little for our passage, but not with all for our portion. These things must not be made *our consolation* (Luke vi. 24), our *good things,* Luke xvi. 25. Let us consider we are laying up, not for our *posterity* in this world, but for *ourselves* in the other world. We are put to our choice, and made in a manner our own carvers; that is ours which we *lay up for ourselves.* It concerns thee to choose wisely, for thou art choosing for thyself, and shalt have as thou choosest. If we know and consider ourselves what we are, what we are made for, how large our capacities are, and how long our continuance, and that our souls are ourselves, we shall see

it a foolish thing to *lay up* our *treasures on earth.*

2. Here is a *good reason* given why we should not look upon any thing *on earth* as our *treasure,* because it is liable to loss and decay: (1.) From corruption within. That which is treasure *upon earth moth and rust do corrupt.* If the *treasure* be laid up in fine clothes, the *moth* frets them, and they are gone and spoiled insensibly, when we thought them most securely laid up. If it be in corn or other eatables, as his was who had his barns full (Luke xii. 16, 17), *rust* (so we read it) *corrupts* that: Βρωσις—*eating,* eating by men, for *as goods are increased they are increased that eat them* (Eccl. v. 11); eating by mice or other vermin; manna itself bred worms; or it grows mouldy and musty, is struck, or smutted, or blasted; fruits soon rot. Or, if we understand it of silver and gold, they tarnish and canker; they grow less with using, and grow worse with keeping (Jam. v. 2, 3); the *rust and* the *moth* breed in the metal itself and in the garment itself. Note, Worldly riches have in themselves a principle of corruption and decay; they wither of themselves, and *make themselves wings.* (2.) From violence without. *Thieves break through and steal.* Every hand of violence will be aiming at the house where *treasure* is laid up; nor can any thing be laid up so safe, but we may be spoiled of it. *Numquam ego fortunæ credidi, etiam si videretur pacem agere; omnia illa quæ in me indulgentissime conferebat, pecuniam, honores, gloriam, eo loco posui, unde posset ea, sine metu meo, repetere—I never reposed confidence in fortune, even if she seemed propitious: whatever were the favours which her bounty bestowed, whether wealth, honours, or glory, I so disposed of them, that it was in her power to recal them without occasioning me any alarm.* Seneca. *Consol. ad Helv.* It is folly to make that our *treasure* which we may so easily be robbed of.

3. *Good counsel,* to make the joys and glories of the other world, those *things not seen* that *are eternal,* our best things, and to place our happiness in them. *Lay up for yourselves treasures in heaven.* Note, (1.) There are *treasures in heaven,* as sure as there are on this earth; and those in heaven are the only true *treasures,* the riches and glories and pleasures that are at God's right hand, which those that are sanctified truly arrive at, when they come to be sanctified perfectly. (2.) It is our wisdom to *lay up* our *treasure in* those *treasures;* to give all diligence to make sure our title to eternal life through Jesus Christ, and to depend upon that as our happiness, and look upon all things here below with a holy contempt, as not worthy to be compared with it. We must firmly believe there is such a happiness, and resolve to be content with that, and to be content with nothing short of it. If we thus make those *treasures* ours, they are laid up, and we may trust God to keep them safe for us; thither let us then refer all our designs, and extend all our desires; thither let us send before our best effects and best affections. Let us not burthen ourselves with the cash of this world, which will but load and defile us, and be liable to sink us, but lay up in store good securities. The promises are bills of exchange, by which all true believers return their *treasure* to *heaven,* payable in the future state: and thus we must make that sure that will be made sure. (3.) It is a great encouragement to us to *lay up* our *treasure in heaven,* that there it is safe; it will not decay of itself, no *moth* nor *rust* will *corrupt* it; nor can we be by force or fraud deprived of it; *thieves do not break through and steal.* It is a happiness above and beyond the changes and chances of time, *an inheritance incorruptible.*

4. A *good reason* why we should thus choose, and an evidence that we have done so (*v.* 21), *Where your treasure is,* on earth or in heaven, *there will your heart be.* We are therefore concerned to be right and wise in the choice of our *treasure,* because the temper of our minds, and consequently the tenor of our lives, will be accordingly either carnal or spiritual, earthly or heavenly. The *heart* follows the *treasure,* as the needle follows the loadstone, or the sunflower the sun. *Where the treasure is there* the value and esteem are, *there* the love and affection are (Col. iii. 2,) that way the desires and pursuits go, thitherward the aims and intents are levelled, and all is done with that in view. *Where the treasure is, there* our cares and fears are, lest we come short of it; about that we are most solicitous; *there* our hope and trust are (Prov. xviii. 10, 11); *there* our joys and delights will be (Ps. cxix. 111); and *there* our thoughts will be; *there* the *inward* thought will be, the *first* thought, the *free* thought, the *fixed* thought, the *frequent,* the *familiar* thought. The *heart* is God's due (Prov. xxiii. 26), and that he may have it, our *treasure* must be laid up with him, and then our souls will be lifted up to him.

This direction about laying up our *treasure,* may very fitly be applied to the foregoing caution, of not doing what we do in religion *to be seen of men.* Our *treasure* is our alms, prayers, and fastings, and the reward of them; if we have done these only to gain the applause of men, we have *laid up this treasure on earth,* have lodged it in the hands of men, and must never expect to hear any further of it. Now it is folly to do this, for *the praise of men* we covet so much is liable to corruption: it will soon be rusted, and moth-eaten, and tarnished; a little folly, like a dead fly, will spoil it all, Eccl. x. 1. Slander and calumny are *thieves that break through and steal* it away, and so we lose all the *treasure* of our performances; we have run in vain, and laboured in vain, because we misplaced our intentions in doing of them. Hypocritical services lay up nothing in heaven (Isa. lviii. 3); the gain of them is gone, when the soul is called for, Job xxvii. 8. But if we have prayed and fasted and given alms in truth and uprightness, with an eye to God and to his acceptance, and have approved ourselves to him therein, we have laid up that treasure *in heaven; a book of remembrance is written there* (Mal. iii. 16), and being there recorded, they shall be there rewarded, and we shall meet them again with comfort on the other side death and the grave. Hypocrites are *written in the earth* (Jer. xvii. 13), but God's faithful ones have their names *written in heaven,* Luke x. 20. Acceptance with God is *treasure in heaven,* which can neither be corrupted nor stolen. His *well done* shall stand for ever; and if we have thus laid up our *treasure* with him, with him our *hearts* will be; and where can they be better?

II. We must take heed of hypocrisy and worldly-mindedness in choosing the *end we look at.* Our concern as to this is represented by two sorts of eyes which men have, a *single eye* and an *evil eye, v.* 22, 23. The expressions here are somewhat dark because concise; we shall therefore take them in some variety of interpretation. *The light of the body is the eye,* that is plain; *the eye* is discovering and directing; the *light of the world* would avail us little without this *light of the body;* it is *the light of the eye* that *rejoiceth the heart* (Prov. xv. 30), but what is that which is here compared to *the eye* in the *body.*

1. *The eye,* that is, *the heart* (so some) if that *be single*—ἁπλοῦς—*free and bountiful* (so the word is frequently rendered, as Rom. xii. 8; 2 Cor. viii. 2, ix. 11. 13; Jam. i. 5, and we read of a *bountiful eye,* Prov. xxii. 9). If the heart be liberally affected and stand inclined to goodness and charity, it will direct the man to Christian actions, the whole conversation *will be full of light,* full of the evidences and instances of true Christianity, that *pure religion and undefiled before God and the Father* (Jam. i. 27), *full of light,* of good works, which are our *light shining before men;* but *if the heart be evil,* covetous, and hard, and envious, griping and grudging (such a temper of mind is often expressed by an *evil eye, ch.* xx. 15; Mark vii. 22; Prov. xxiii. 6, 7), *the body will be full of darkness,* the whole conversation will be heathenish and unchristian. *The instruments of the churl are* and always will be *evil,* but *the liberal deviseth liberal things,* Isa. xxxii. 5—8. *If the light that is in us,* those affections which should guide us to that which is good, *be darkness,* if these be corrupt and worldly, if there be not so much as good nature in a man, not so much as a kind disposition, *how great is* the corruption of a man, and the *darkness* in which he sits! This sense seems to agree with the context; we must *lay up treasure in heaven* by liberality in giving alms, and that not grudgingly but with cheerfulness, Luke xii. 33; 2 Cor. ix. 7. But these words in the parallel place do not come in upon any such occasion, Luke xi. 34, and therefore the coherence here does not determine that to be the sense of them.

2. *The eye,* that is, *the understanding* (so some); the practical judgment, the conscience, which is to the other faculties of the soul, as *the eye* is to the *body,* to guide and direct their motions; now *if this eye be single,* if it make a true and right judgment, and discern things that differ, especially in the great concern of *laying up the treasure* so as to choose aright in that, it will rightly guide the affections and actions, which will all be *full of the light* of grace and comfort; *but if this be evil* and corrupt, and instead of leading the inferior powers, is led, and bribed, and biassed by them, if this be erroneous and misinformed, the heart and life must needs be *full of darkness,* and the whole conversation corrupt. They that *will not understand,* are said to *walk on in darkness,* Ps. lxxxii. 5. It is sad when the spirit of a man, that should be *the candle of the Lord,* is an *ignis fatuus:* when the *leaders of the people,* the leaders of the faculties, *cause them to err,* for then *they that are led of them are destroyed,* Isa. ix. 16. An error in the practical judgment is fatal, it is that which calls *evil good and good evil* (Isa. v. 20); therefore it concerns us to understand things aright, to get our eyes anointed with eye-salve.

3. *The eye,* that is, *the aims* and *intentions;* by *the eye* we set our end before us, the mark we shoot at, the place we go to, we keep that in view, and direct our motion accordingly; in every thing we do in religion, there is something or other that we have in our *eye;* now *if our eye be single,* if we aim honestly, fix right ends, and move rightly towards them, if we aim purely and only at the glory of God, seek his honour and favour, and direct all entirely to him, then *the eye is single;* Paul's was so when he said, *To me to live is Christ;* and if we be right here, *the whole body will be full of light,* all the actions will be regular and gracious, pleasing to God and comfortable to ourselves; *but if this eye be evil,* if, instead of aiming only at the glory of God, and our acceptance with him, we look aside at the applause of men, and while we profess to honour God, contrive to honour ourselves, and seek our own things under colour of *seeking the things of Christ,* this spoils all, the whole conversation will be perverse and unsteady, and the foundations being thus out of course, there can be nothing but *confusion and every evil work* in the superstructure. Draw the lines from the circumference to any other point but the centre, and they will cross. *If the light that is in thee be* not only dim, but *darkness* itself, it is a fundamental error, and destructive to all that follows. The end specifies the action. It is of the last importance in religion, that we be right in our aims, and make *eternal things,* not *temporal,* our

scope, 2 Cor. iv. 18. The hypocrite is like the waterman, that looks one way and rows another; the true Christian like the traveller, that has his journey's end in his eye. The hypocrite soars like the kite, with his eye upon the prey below, which he is ready to come down to when he has a fair opportunity; the true Christian soars like the lark, higher and higher, forgetting the things that are beneath.

III. We must take heed of hypocrisy and worldly-mindedness in choosing the master we serve, *v.* 24. *No man can serve two masters.* Serving *two masters* is contrary to *the single eye;* for *the eye* will be to the master's hand, Ps. cxxiii. 1, 2. Our Lord Jesus here exposes the cheat which those put upon their own souls, who think to divide between God and the world, to have a *treasure on earth,* and a *treasure in heaven* too, to please God and please men too. Why not? says the hypocrite; it is good to have two strings to one's bow. They hope to make their religion serve their secular interest, and so turn to account both ways. The pretending mother was for dividing the child; the Samaritans will compound between God and idols. No, says Christ, this will not do; it is but a supposition that *gain is godliness,* 1 Tim. vi. 5. Here is,

1. A general maxim laid down; it is likely it was a proverb among the Jews, *No man can serve two masters,* much less two gods; for their commands will some time or other cross or contradict one another, and their occasions interfere. While *two masters* go together, a servant may follow them both; but when they part, you will see to which he belongs; he cannot love, and observe, and cleave to both as he should. If to the one, not to the other; either this or that must be comparatively hated and despised. This truth is plain enough in common cases.

2. The application of it to the business in hand. *Ye cannot serve God and Mammon. Mammon* is a Syriac word, that signifies gain; so that whatever in this world is, or is accounted by us to be, *gain* (Phil. iii. 7), is *mammon. Whatever is in the world, the lust of the flesh, the lust of the eye, and the pride of life,* is *mammon.* To some their belly is their *mammon,* and they serve that (Phil. iii. 19); to others their ease, their sleep, their sports and pastimes, are their *mammon* (Prov. vi. 9); to others worldly riches (James iv. 13); to others honours and preferments; the praise and applause of men was the Pharisees' *mammon;* in a word, self, the unity in which the world's trinity centres, sensual, secular self, is the *mammon* which cannot be served in conjunction with *God;* for if it be served, it is in competition with him and in contradiction to him. He does not say, We *must* not or we *should* not, but we *cannot serve God and Mammon;* we *cannot* love both (1 John ii. 15; Jam. iv. 4); or hold to both, or hold by both in observance, obedience, attendance, trust, and dependence, for they are contrary, the one to the other. *God* says, "*My son, give me thy heart.*" *Mammon* says, "No, give it me." *God* says, "*Be content with such things as ye have.*" *Mammon* says, "Grasp at all that ever thou canst. *Rem, rem, quocunque modo rem—Money, money; by fair means or by foul, money.*" *God* says, "Defraud not, never lie, be honest and just in all thy dealings." *Mammon* says, "Cheat thy own father, if thou canst gain by it." *God* says, "Be charitable." *Mammon* says, "Hold thy own: this giving undoes us all." *God* says, "*Be careful for nothing.*" *Mammon* says, "Be careful for every thing." *God* says, "*Keep holy the sabbath-day.*" *Mammon* says, "Make use of that day as well as any other for the world." Thus inconsistent are the commands of *God and Mammon,* so that we *cannot serve* both. Let us not then *halt between God and Baal, but choose ye this day whom ye will serve,* and abide by your choice.

25 Therefore I say unto you, Take
no thought for your life, what ye shall
eat, or what ye shall drink; nor yet
for your body, what ye shall put on.
Is not the life more than meat, and
the body than raiment? 26 Behold
the fowls of the air: for they sow
not, neither do they reap, nor gather
into barns; yet your heavenly Father
feedeth them. Are ye not much
better than they? 27 Which of you
by taking thought can add one cubit
unto his stature? 28 And why take
ye thought for raiment? Consider
the lilies of the field, how they grow;
they toil not, neither do they spin:
29 And yet I say unto you, That
even Solomon in all his glory was
not arrayed like one of these. 30
Wherefore, if God so clothe the grass
of the field, which to-day is, and to-
morrow is cast into the oven, *shall*
he not much more *clothe* you, O ye
of little faith? 31 Therefore take no
thought, saying, What shall we eat?
or, What shall we drink? or, Wherewithal shall we be clothed? 32 (For
after all these things do the Gentiles
seek): for your heavenly Father
knoweth that ye have need of all
these things. 33 But seek ye first
the kingdom of God, and his righteousness; and all these things shall
be added unto you. 34 Take therefore no thought for the morrow: for
the morrow shall take thought for

the things of itself. Sufficient unto the day *is* the evil thereof.

There is scarcely any one sin against which our Lord Jesus more largely and earnestly warns his disciples, or against which he arms them with more variety of arguments, than the sin of disquieting, distracting, distrustful cares about the things of this life, which are a bad sign that both the *treasure* and the heart are *on the earth;* and therefore he thus largely insists upon it. Here is,

I. The prohibition laid down. It is the counsel and command of the Lord Jesus, that we *take no thought* about the things of this world; *I say unto you.* He says it as our Lawgiver, and the Sovereign of our hearts; he says it as our Comforter, and the Helper of our joy. What is it that he says? It is this, and *he that hath ears to hear, let him hear it. Take no thought for your life, nor yet for your body* (*v.* 25). *Take no thought, saying, What shall we eat?* (*v.* 31) and again (*v.* 34), *Take no thought, μὴ μεριμνᾶτε—Be not in care.* As against hypocrisy, so against worldly cares, the caution is thrice repeated, and yet no vain repetition: *precept* must be *upon precept, and line upon line,* to the same purport, and all little enough; it is a *sin which doth so easily beset us.* It intimates how pleasing it is to Christ, and of how much concern it is to ourselves, that we should live without carefulness. It is the repeated command of the Lord Jesus to his disciples, that they should not divide and pull in pieces their own minds with care about the world. There is a *thought* concerning the things of this life, which is not only lawful, but duty, such as is commended in the virtuous woman. See Prov. xxvii. 23. The word is used concerning Paul's care of the churches, and Timothy's care for the state of souls, 2 Cor. xi. 28; Phil. ii. 20.

But the *thought* here forbidden is, 1. A disquieting, tormenting *thought,* which hurries the mind hither and thither, and hangs it in suspense; which disturbs our joy in God, and is a damp upon our hope in him; which breaks the sleep, and hinders our enjoyment of ourselves, of our friends, and of what God has given us. 2. A distrustful, unbelieving *thought.* God has promised to provide for those that are his all things need fulfor life as well as godliness, *the life that now is,* food and a covering: not dainties, but necessaries. He never said, "They shall be feasted," but, "*Verily, they shall be fed.*" Now an inordinate care for time to come, and fear of wanting those supplies, spring from a disbelief of these promises, and of the wisdom and goodness of Divine Providence; and that is the evil of it As to present sustenance, we may and must use lawful means to get it, else we tempt God; we must be diligent in our callings, and prudent in proportioning our expenses to what we have, and we must pray for *daily bread;* and if all other means fail, we may and must ask relief of those that are able to give it. He was none of the best of men that said, *To beg I am ashamed* (Luke xvi. 3); as he was, who (*v.* 21) *desired to be fed with the crumbs;* but for the future, we must *cast our care upon God,* and *take no thought,* because it looks like a jealousy of God, who knows how to give what we want when we know not how to get it. Let our souls dwell at ease in him! This gracious carelessness is the same with that sleep which God gives to his beloved, in opposition to the worldling's toil, Ps. cxxvii. 2. Observe the cautions here,

(1.) *Take no thought for your life.* Life is our greatest concern for this world; *All that a man has will he give for his life;* yet take no thought about it. [1.] Not about the *continuance* of it; refer it to God to *lengthen* or *shorten* it as he pleases; *my times are in thy hand,* and they are in a good hand. [2.] Not about the *comforts* of this life; refer it to God to embitter or sweeten it as he pleases. We must not be solicitous, no not about the necessary support of this life, *food* and *raiment;* these God has promised, and therefore we may more confidently expect; say not, *What shall we eat?* It is the language of one at a loss, and almost despairing; whereas, though many good people have the prospect of little, yet there are few but have present support.

(2.) *Take no thought for the morrow,* for the time to come. Be not solicitous for the future, how you shall live next year, or when you are old, or what you shall leave behind you. As we must not *boast of* to-morrow, so we must not *care for* to-morrow, or the events of it.

II. The reasons and arguments to enforce this prohibition. One would think the command of Christ was enough to restrain us from this foolish sin of disquieting, distrustful care, independently of the comfort of our own souls, which is so nearly concerned; but to show how much the heart of Christ is upon it, and what *pleasure he takes* in those that *hope in his mercy,* the command is backed with the most powerful arguments. If reason may but rule us, surely we shall ease ourselves of these thorns. To free us from anxious thoughts, and to expel them, Christ here suggests to us *comforting* thoughts, that we may be filled with them. It will be worth while to take pains with our own hearts, to argue them out of their disquieting cares, and to make ourselves ashamed of them. They may be weakened by right reason, but it is by an active faith only that they can be overcome. Consider then,

1. *Is not the life more than meat, and the body than raiment? v.* 25. Yes, no doubt it is; so he says who had reason to understand the true value of present things, for he made them, he supports them, and supports us by them; and the thing speaks for itself. Note, (1.) Our *life* is a greater blessing than our

livelihood. It is true, life cannot subsist without a livelihood; but the meat and raiment which are here represented as inferior to the life and body are such as are for ornament and delight; for about such we are apt to be solicitous. Meat and raiment are in order to life, and the *end* is more noble and excellent than the *means.* The daintiest food and finest raiment are from the *earth,* but life from the *breath of God.* Life is the *light of men;* meat is but the *oil* that feeds that light: so that the difference between rich and poor is very inconsiderable, since, in the greatest things, they stand on the same level, and differ only in the less. (2.) This is an encouragement to us to trust God for *food* and *raiment,* and so to ease ourselves of all perplexing cares about them. God has given us life, and given us the body; it was an act of power, it was an act of favour, it was done without our care: what cannot he do for us, who did that?—what will he not? If we take care about our souls and eternity, which are more than the body, and its life, we may leave it to God to provide for us food and raiment, which are less. God has maintained our lives hitherto; if sometimes with pulse and water, that has answered the end; he has protected us and kept us alive. He that guards us against the evils we are exposed to, will supply us with the *good things* we are in need of. If he had been pleased to kill us, to starve us, he would not so often have *given his angels a charge concerning us* to keep us.

2. *Behold the fowls of the air,* and *consider the lilies of the field.* Here is an argument taken from God's common providence toward the inferior creatures, and their dependence, according to their capacities, upon that providence. A fine pass fallen man has come to, that he must be sent to school to the *fowls of the air,* and that they must *teach him!* Job xii. 7, 8.

(1.) Look upon the *fowls,* and learn to trust God *for food* (*v.* 26), and disquiet not yourselves with thoughts *what you shall eat.*

[1.] Observe the providence of God concerning them. Look upon them, and receive instruction. There are various sorts of fowls; they are numerous, some of them ravenous, but they are all fed, and fed with food convenient for them; it is rare that any of them perish for want of food, even in winter, and there goes no little to feed them all the year round. The fowls, as they are least serviceable to man, so they are least within his care; men often feed upon them, but seldom feed them; yet they are fed, we know not how, and some of them fed best in the hardest weather; and it is *your heavenly Father that feeds them;* he *knows all the wild fowls of the mountains,* better than you know the tame ones at your own barn-door, Ps. l. 11. Not a sparrow lights to the ground, to pick up a grain of corn, but by the providence of God, which extends itself to the meanest creatures. But that which is especially observed here is, that they are fed without any care or project of their own; *they sow not, neither do they reap, nor gather into barns.* The ant indeed does, and the bee, and they are set before us as examples of prudence and industry; but the fowls of the air do not; they make no provision for the future themselves, and yet every day, as duly as the day comes, provision is made for them, and their *eyes wait on God,* that great and good Housekeeper, who *provides food for all flesh.*

[2.] Improve this for your encouragement to trust in God. *Are ye not much better than they?* Yes, certainly you are. Note, The *heirs* of heaven are much better than the *fowls* of heaven; nobler and more excellent beings, and, by faith, they soar higher; they are of a better nature and nurture, *wiser than the fowls of heaven* (Job xxxv. 11): though the children of this world, that *know not the judgment of the Lord,* are not so wise as *the stork, and the crane, and the swallow* (Jer. viii. 7), you are dearer to God, and nearer, though they fly in the open firmament of heaven. He is their Maker and Lord, their Owner and Master; but besides all this, he is your Father, and in his account *ye are of more value than many sparrows;* you are his children, his first-born; now he that feeds his birds surely will not starve his babes. They trust your Father's providence, and will not you trust it? In dependence upon that, they are careless for the morrow; and being so, they live the merriest lives of all creatures; they *sing among the branches* (Ps. civ. 12), and, to the best of their power, they praise their Creator. If we were, by faith, as unconcerned about the morrow as they are, we should sing as cheerfully as they do; for it is worldly care that mars our mirth and damps our joy, and silences our praise, as much as any thing.

(2.) Look upon the *lilies,* and learn to trust God for *raiment.* That is another part of our care, *what we shall put on;* for decency, to cover us; for defence, to keep us warm; yea, and, with many, for dignity and ornament, to make them look great and fine; and so much concerned are they for gaiety and variety in their clothing, that this care returns almost as often as that for their daily bread. Now to ease us of this care, let us *consider the lilies of the field;* not only *look upon* them (every eye does that with pleasure), but *consider* them. Note, There is a great deal of good to be learned from what we see every day, if we would but consider it, Prov. vi. 6; xxiv. 32.

[1.] Consider how *frail* the lilies are; they are the *grass of the field.* Lilies, though distinguished by their colours, are still but *grass.* Thus *all flesh is grass:* though some in the endowments of body and mind are as lilies, much admired, still they are grass; the grass of the field in nature and constitution; they stand upon the same level with others. Man's days, at best, are *as grass,* as the *flower of the grass.* 1 Pet. i. 24. This grass *to-day is,* and *to-morrow is cast into the oven;* in a little while the place that *knows us* will *know us no more.* The grave is the oven into which we shall be cast, and in which we shall be consumed as grass in the fire, Ps. xlix. 14. This intimates a reason why we should not take thought for the morrow, what we shall put on, because perhaps, by to-morrow, we may have occasion for our grave-clothes.

[2.] Consider how *free from care* the lilies are: they *toil not* as men do, to earn clothing; as servants, to earn their liveries; *neither do they spin,* as women do, to make clothing. It does not follow that we must therefore neglect, or do carelessly, the proper business of this life; it is the praise of the virtuous woman, that *she lays her hand to the spindle, makes fine linen and sells it,* Prov. xxxi. 19, 24. Idleness *tempts* God, instead of *trusting* him; but he that provides for the inferior creatures, without their labour, will much more provide for us, by blessing our labour, which he has made our duty. And if we should, through sickness, be unable to *toil* and *spin,* God can furnish us with what is necessary for us.

[3.] Consider how *fair,* how *fine* the lilies are; *how they grow;* what they *grow from.* The root of the lily or tulip, as other bulbous roots, is, in the winter, lost and buried under ground, yet, when spring returns, it appears, and starts up in a little time; hence it is promised to God's Israel, that they shall grow *as the lily,* Hos. xiv. 5. Consider what they *grow to.* Out of that obscurity in a few weeks they come to be so very gay, that even *Solomon, in all his glory, was not arrayed like one of these.* The array of Solomon was very splendid and magnificent: he that had the peculiar treasure of kings and provinces, and so studiously affected pomp and gallantry, doubtless had the richest clothing, and the best made up, that could be got; especially when he appeared in his glory on high days. And yet, let him dress himself as fine as he could, he comes far short of the beauty of the lilies, and a bed of tulips outshines him. Let us, therefore, be ambitious of the *wisdom* of Solomon, in which he was outdone by none (wisdom to do our duty in our places), rather than the *glory* of Solomon, in which he was outdone by the lilies. Knowledge and grace are the perfection of man, not beauty, much less fine clothes. Now God is here said thus to *clothe the grass of the field.* Note, All the excellences of the creature flow from God, the Fountain and spring of them. It was he that gave the horse his strength, and the lily its beauty; every creature is in itself, as well as to us, what he makes it to be.

[4.] Consider how instructive all this is to us, *v.* 30.

First, As to *fine* clothing; this teaches us not to care for it at all, not to covet it, nor to be proud of it, not to make the *putting on of apparel* our *adorning,* for after all our care in this the lilies will far outdo us; we cannot dress so fine as they do, why then should we attempt to vie with them? Their adorning will soon perish, and so will ours; they fade —*are to-day,* and *to-morrow are cast,* as other rubbish, *into the oven;* and the clothes we are proud of are wearing out, the gloss is soon gone, the colour fades, the shape goes out of fashion, or in awhile the garment itself is worn out; such is man in all his pomp (Isa. xl. 6, 7), especially rich men (Jam. i. 10); they *fade away in their ways.*

Secondly, As to *necessary* clothing; this teaches us to cast the care of it upon God—Jehovah-jireh; trust him that clothes the lilies, to provide for you what you shall *put on.* If he give such fine clothes to the grass, much more will he give fitting clothes to his own children; clothes that shall be warm upon them, not only *when he quieteth the earth with the south wind,* but when he disquiets it with the *north wind,* Job xxxvii. 17. He shall much more clothe you: for you are nobler creatures, of a more excellent being; if so he clothe the short-lived grass, much more will he clothe you that are made for immortality. Even the children of Nineveh are preferred before the gourd (Jonah iv. 10, 11), much more the sons of Zion, that are in covenant with God. Observe the title he gives them (*v.* 30), *O ye of little faith.* This may be taken, 1. As an encouragement to true faith, though it be but weak; it entitles us to the divine care, and a promise of suitable supply. Great faith shall be commended, and shall procure great things, but little faith shall not be rejected, even that shall procure food and raiment. *Sound* believers shall be provided for, though they be not *strong* believers. The babes in the family are fed and clothed, as well as those that are grown up, and with a special care and tenderness; say not, I am but a child, but a dry tree (Isaiah lvi. 3, 5), for though *poor and needy* yet *the Lord thinketh on thee.* Or, 2. It is rather a rebuke to weak faith, though it be true, *ch.* xiv. 31. It intimates what is at the bottom of all our inordinate care and thoughtfulness; it is owing to the weakness of our faith, and the remains of unbelief in us. If we had but more faith, we should have less care.

3. *Which of you,* the wisest, the strongest of you, *by taking thought, can add one cubit to his stature?* (*v.* 27) to *his age,* so some; but the measure of a cubit denotes it to be meant of the stature, and the age at longest is but a span, Ps. xxxix. 5. Let us consider, (1.) We did not arrive at the stature we are of by our own care and thought, but by the providence of God. An infant of a span long has grown up to be a man of six feet, and how was one cubit after another added to his stature? not by his own forecast or contrivance; he grew he knew not how, by the power and goodness of God. Now he that made our bodies, and made them of such a size, surely will take care to provide for them. Note, God is to be acknowledged in the increase of our bodily strength and sta-

ture, and to be trusted for all needful supplies, because he has made it to appear, that he is mindful for the body. The growing age is the thoughtless, careless age, yet we grow; and shall not he who reared us to this, provide for us now we are reared? (2.) We cannot alter the stature we are of, if we would: what a foolish and ridiculous thing would it be for a man of low stature to perplex himself, to break his sleep, and beat his brains, about it, and to be continually taking thought how he might be a cubit higher; when, after all, he knows he cannot effect it, and therefore he had better be content and take it as it is! We are not all of a size, yet the difference in stature between one and another is not material, nor of any great account; a little man is ready to wish he were as tall as such a one, but he knows it is to no purpose, and therefore does as well as he can with it. Now as we do in reference to our bodily stature, so we should do in reference to our worldly estate. [1.] We should not covet an abundance of the wealth of this world, any more than we would covet the addition of a cubit to one's stature, which is a great deal in a man's height; it is enough to grow by inches; such an addition would but make one unwieldy, and a burden to one's self. [2.] We must reconcile ourselves to our state, as we do to our stature; we must set the conveniences against the inconveniences, and so make a virtue of necessity: what cannot be remedied must be made the best of. We cannot alter the disposals of Providence, and therefore must acquiesce in them, accommodate ourselves to them, and relieve ourselves, as well as we can, against inconveniences, as Zaccheus against the inconvenience of his stature, by climbing into the tree.

4. *After all these things do the Gentiles seek, v.* 32. Thoughtfulness about the world is a *heathenish* sin, and unbecoming *Christians*. The *Gentiles* seek *these things*, because they know not *better things;* they are eager for this world, because they are strangers to a better; they seek these things with care and anxiety, because they are *without God in the world,* and understand not his providence. They fear and worship their idols, but know not how to trust them for deliverance and supply, and, therefore, are themselves full of care; but it is a shame for Christians, who build upon nobler principles, and profess a religion which teaches them not only that there is a Providence, but that there are promises made to the good of the life that now is, which teaches them a confidence in God and a contempt of the world, and gives such reasons for both; it is a shame for them to walk as Gentiles walk, and to fill their heads and hearts with these things.

5. *Your heavenly Father knows ye have need of all these things;* these necessary things, food and raiment; he knows our wants better than we do ourselves; though he be in heaven, and his children on earth, he observes what the least and poorest of them has occasion for (Rev. ii. 9), *I know thy poverty.* You think, if such a good friend did but know your wants and straits, you would soon have relief: your God knows them; and he is your Father that loves you and pities you, and is ready to help you; your heavenly Father, who has wherewithal to supply all your needs: away, therefore, with all disquieting thoughts and cares; go to thy Father; tell him, *he knows thou hast need of such and such things;* he asks you, *Children, have you any meat?* John xxi. 5. Tell him whether you have or not. Though he knows our wants, he will know them from us; and when we have opened them to him, let us cheerfully refer ourselves to his wisdom, power, and goodness, for our supply. Therefore, we should ease ourselves of the burthen of care, by casting it upon God, because it is he *that careth for us* (1 Pet. v. 7), and what needs all this ado? If he care, why should we care?

6. *Seek first the kingdom of God, and his righteousness, and all these things shall be added unto you, v.* 33. Here is a double argument against the sin of *thoughtfulness; take no thought* for your life, the life of the body; for, (1.) You have greater and better things to take thought about, the life of your soul, your eternal happiness; that is the *one thing needful* (Luke x. 42), about which you should employ your thoughts, and which is commonly neglected in those hearts wherein worldly cares have the ascendant. If we were but more careful to please God, and to work out our own salvation, we should be less solicitous to please ourselves, and work out an estate in the world. Thoughtfulness for our souls is the most effectual cure of thoughtfulness for the world. (2.) You have a surer and easier, a safer and a more compendious way to obtain the necessaries of this life, than by carking, and caring, and fretting about them; and that is, by *seeking first the kingdom of God,* and making religion your business: say not that this is the way to starve, no, it is the way to be well provided for, even in this world. Observe here,

[1.] The great duty required: it is the sum and substance of our whole duty: "*Seek first the kingdom of God;* mind religion as your great and principal concern." Our duty is to seek; to desire, pursue, and aim at these things; it is a word that has in it much of the constitution of the new covenant in favour of us; *though we have not attained,* but in many things fail and come short, sincere seeking (a careful concern and an earnest endeavour) is accepted. Now observe, *First,* The object of this seeking; *The kingdom of God, and his righteousness;* we must mind heaven as our end, and holiness as our way. "Seek the comforts of the kingdom of grace and glory as your felicity.

aim at the *kingdom of heaven;* press towards it; give diligence to make it sure; resolve not to take up short of it; seek for this glory honour, and immortality; prefer heaven and heavenly blessings far before earth and earthly delights." We make nothing of our religion, if we do not make heaven of it. And with the *happiness* of this kingdom, seek the *righteousness* of it; *God's righteousness,* the righteousness which he requires to be wrought *in* us, and wrought *by* us, such as exceeds that of the scribes and Pharisees; we must *follow peace and holiness,* Heb. xii. 14. *Secondly,* The order of it. *Seek first the kingdom of God.* Let your care for your souls and another world take place of all other cares: and let all the concerns of this life be made subordinate to those of the life to come: we must seek the things of Christ more than our own things; and if ever they come in competition, we must remember to which we are to give the preference. "Seek these things *first;* first in thy days: let the morning of youth be dedicated to God. Wisdom must be sought early; it is good beginning betimes to be religious. Seek this first every day; let waking thoughts be of God." Let this be our principle, to do that first which is most needful, and let him that is the First, have the first.

[2.] The gracious promise annexed; *all these things,* the necessary supports of life, *shall be added unto you;* shall be *given over and above;* so it is in the margin. You shall have what you seek, the *kingdom of God and his righteousness,* for never any sought *in vain,* that sought *in earnest;* and besides that, you shall have food and raiment, by way of overplus; as he that buys goods has paper and packthread given him into the bargain. *Godliness has the promise of the life that now is,* 1 Tim. iv. 8. Solomon asked wisdom, and had that and other things added to him, 2 Chron. i. 11, 12. O what a blessed change would it make in our hearts and lives, did we but firmly believe this truth, that the best way to be comfortably provided for in this world, is to be most intent upon another world! We then begin at the right end of our work, when we begin with God. If we give diligence to make sure to ourselves the kingdom of God and the righteousness thereof, as to all the things of this life, Jehovah-jireh—the Lord will provide as much of them as he sees good for us, and more we would not wish for. Have we trusted him for the *portion of our inheritance* at our end, and shall we not trust him for the *portion of our cup,* in the way to it? God's Israel were not only brought to Canaan at last, but had their charges borne through the wilderness. O that we were more thoughtful about the things that are not seen, that are eternal, and then the less thoughtful we should be, and the less thoughtful we should need to be, about the things that are seen, that are temporal! *Also regard not your stuff,* Gen. xlv. 20, 23.

7. *The morrow shall take thought for the things of itself: sufficient unto the day is the evil thereof, v.* 34. We must not perplex ourselves inordinately about future events, because every day brings along with it its own burthen of cares and grievances, as, if we look about us, and suffer not our fears to betray the succours which grace and reason offer, it brings along with it its own strength and supply too. So that we are here told,

(1.) That *thoughtfulness* for the morrow is *needless; Let the morrow take thought for the things of itself.* If wants and troubles be renewed with the day, there are aids and provisions renewed likewise; *compassions,* that are *new every morning,* Lam. iii. 22, 23. The saints have a Friend that is *their arm every morning,* and gives out fresh supplies daily (Isa. xxxiii. 2), according *as the business of every day requires* (Ezra iii. 4), and so he keeps his people in a constant dependence upon him. Let us refer it therefore to the morrow's strength, to do the morrow's work, and bear the morrow's burthen. To-morrow, and the things of it, will be provided for without us; why need we thus anxiously care for that which is so wisely cared for already? This does not forbid a prudent foresight, and preparation accordingly, but a perplexing solicitude, and a prepossession of difficulties and calamities, which may perhaps never come, or if they do, may be easily borne, and the evil of them guarded against. The meaning is, let us *mind present duty,* and then *leave events to God;* do the *work of the day in its day,* and then let *to-morrow bring its work along with it.*

(2.) That thoughtfulness for the morrow is one of those *foolish and hurtful lusts,* which those that will be rich fall into, and one of the *many sorrows,* wherewith they *pierce themselves through. Sufficient unto the day is the evil thereof.* This present day has trouble enough attending it, we need not *accumulate* burthens by *anticipating* our trouble, nor borrow perplexities from to-morrow's evils to add to those of this day. It is uncertain what to-morrow's evils may be, but whatever they be, it is time enough to take thought about them when they come. What a folly is it to take that trouble upon ourselves this day by care and fear, which belongs to another day, and will be never the lighter when it comes? Let us not pull that upon ourselves all together at once, which Providence has wisely ordered to be borne by parcels. The conclusion of this whole matter then is, that it is the will and command of the Lord Jesus, that his disciples should not be their own tormentors, nor make their passage through this world more dark and unpleasant, by their apprehension of troubles, than God has made it by the troubles themselves. By our daily prayers we may procure strength to bear us up under our daily troubles, and to arm us against the temptations that attend them, and then let none of these things move us.

CHAP. VII.

This chapter continues and concludes Christ's sermon on the mount, which is purely practical, directing us to order our conversation aright, both toward God and man; for the design of the Christian religion is to make men good, every way good. We have, I. Some rules concerning censure and reproof, ver. 1—6. II. Encouragements given us to pray to God for what we need, ver. 7—11. III. The necessity of strictness in conversation urged upon us, ver. 12—14. IV. A caution given us to take heed of false prophets, ver. 15—20. V. The conclusion of the whole sermon, showing the necessity of universal obedience to Christ's commands, without which we cannot expect to be happy, v. 21—27. VI. The impression which Christ's doctrine made upon his hearers, ver. 28, 29.

JUDGE not, that ye be not judged.
2 For with what judgment ye judge, ye shall be judged; and with what measure ye mete, it shall be measured to you again.
3 And why beholdest thou the mote that is in thy brother's eye, but considerest not the beam that is in thine own eye?
4 Or how wilt thou say to thy brother, Let me pull out the mote out of thine eye; and, behold, a beam *is* in thine own eye?
5 Thou hypocrite, first cast out the beam out of thine own eye; and then shalt thou see clearly to cast out the mote out of thy brother's eye.
6 Give not that which is holy unto the dogs, neither cast ye your pearls before swine, lest they trample them under their feet, and turn again and rend you.

Our Saviour is here directing us how to conduct ourselves in reference to the faults of others; and his expressions seem intended as a reproof to the scribes and Pharisees, who were very rigid and severe, very magisterial and supercilious, in condemning all about them, as those commonly are, that are proud and conceited in justifying themselves. We have here,

I. A caution *against judging, v.* 1, 2. There are those whose office it is to judge—magistrates and ministers. Christ, though he made not himself a Judge, yet came not to unmake them, for by him *princes decree justice;* but this is directed to private persons, to his disciples, who shall hereafter *sit on thrones judging,* but not now. Now observe,

1. The prohibition; *Judge not.* We must judge ourselves, and judge of our own acts, but we must not judge our brother, not magisterially assume such an authority over others, as we allow not them over us: since our rule is, to be *subject to one another. Be not many masters,* Jam. iii. 1. We must not sit in the judgment-seat, to make our word a law to every body. We must not judge our brother, that is, we must not *speak evil* of him, so it is explained, Jam. iv. 11. We must not *despise him,* nor *set him at nought,* Rom. xiv. 10. We must not judge rashly, nor pass such a judgment upon our brother as has no ground, but is only the product of our own jealousy and ill nature. We must not make the worst of people, nor infer such invidious things from their words and actions as they will not bear. We must not judge uncharitably, unmercifully, nor with a spirit of revenge, and a desire to do mischief. We must not judge of a man's state by a single act, nor of what he is in himself by what he is to us, because in our own cause we are apt to be partial. We must not judge the hearts of others, nor their intentions, for it is God's prerogative to try the heart, and we must not step into his throne; nor must we judge of their eternal state, nor call them *hypocrites, reprobates,* and *castaways;* that is stretching beyond our line; what have we to do, thus to judge another man's servant? Counsel him, and help him, but do not judge him.

2. The reason to enforce this prohibition. *That ye be not judged.* This intimates, (1.) That if we presume to judge others, we may expect to be ourselves judged. He who usurps the bench, shall be called to the bar; he shall be judged of men; commonly none are more censured, than those who are most censorious; every one will have a stone to throw at them; he who, like Ishmael, has his hand, his tongue, *against every man,* shall, like him, have *every man's* hand and tongue *against him* (Gen. xvi. 12); and no mercy shall be shown to the reputation of those that show no mercy to the reputation of others. Yet that is not the worst of it; they shall be judged of God; from him they shall receive the *greater condemnation,* Jam. iii. 1. Both parties must appear before him (Rom. xiv. 10), who, as he will relieve the *humble sufferer,* will also resist the *haughty scorner,* and give him enough of judging. (2.) That if we be modest and charitable in our censures of others, and decline judging them, and judge ourselves rather, *we shall not be judged of the Lord.* As God will forgive those that forgive their brethren; so he will not judge those that will not judge their brethren; the *merciful shall find mercy.* It is an evidence of humility, charity, and deference to God, and shall be owned and rewarded by him accordingly. See Rom. xiv. 10.

The judging of those that judge others is according to the law of retaliation; *With what judgment ye judge, ye shall be judged, v.* 2. The righteous God, in his judgments, often observes a rule of proportion, as in the case of Adonibezek, Judg. i. 7. See also Rev. xiii. 10; xviii. 6. Thus will he be both justified and magnified in his judgments, and all flesh will be silenced before him. *With what measure ye mete, it shall be measured to you again;* perhaps in this world, so that men may read their sin in their punishment. Let this deter us from all severity in dealing with our brother. *What then shall we do when God rises up?* Job xxxi. 14. What would become of us, if God should be as exact and severe in judging us, as we are in judging our brethren; if he should weigh us in the same balance? We may justly expect it, if we be extreme to mark what our brethren do amiss. In this, as in other things, the violent dealings of men return upon their own heads.

II. Some cautions *about reproving.* Because we must not judge others, which is a great sin, it does not therefore follow that we must not reprove others, which is a great duty, and may be a means of *saving a soul from death;* however, it will be a means of saving our souls from sharing in their guilt. Now observe here,

1. It is not every one who is fit to reprove. Those who are themselves guilty of the same faults of which they accuse others, or of worse, bring shame upon themselves, and are not likely to do good to those whom they reprove, *v.* 3—5. Here is,

(1.) A just reproof to the censorious, who quarrel with their brother for small faults, while they allow themselves in great ones; who are quick-sighted to spy *a mote* in his eye, but are not sensible of *a beam in their own;* nay, and will be very officious to *pull out the mote out of his eye,* when they are as unfit to do it as if they were themselves quite blind. Note, [1.] There are degrees in sin: some sins are comparatively but as *motes,* others as *beams;* some as a *gnat,* others as a *camel:* not that there is any sin little, for there is no little God to sin against: if it be a *mote* (or *splinter,* for so it might better be read), it is in the eye; if a *gnat,* it is in the throat; both painful and perilous, and we cannot be easy or well till they are got out. [2.] Our own sins ought to appear greater to us than the same sins in others: that which charity teaches us to call but a *splinter in our brother's eye,* true repentance and godly sorrow will teach us to call a *beam in our own;* for the sins of others must be extenuated, but our own aggravated. [3.] There are many that have *beams in their own eyes,* and yet do not consider it. They are under the guilt and dominion of very great sins, and yet are not aware of it, but justify themselves, as if they needed no repentance nor reformation; it is as strange that a man can be in such a sinful, miserable condition, and not be aware of it, as that a man should have a beam in his eye, and not consider it; but the god of this world so artfully blinds their minds, that notwithstanding, with great assurance, they say, *We see.* [4.] It is common for those who are most sinful themselves, and least sensible of it, to be most forward and free in judging and censuring others: the Pharisees, who were most haughty in justifying themselves, were most scornful in condemning others. They were severe upon Christ's disciples for *eating with unwashen hands,* which was scarcely a *mote,* while they encouraged men in a contempt of their parents, which was a *beam.* Pride and uncharitableness are commonly *beams* in the eyes of those that pretend to be critical and nice in their censures of others. Nay, many are guilty of that in secret, which they have the face to punish in others when it is discovered. *Cogita tecum, fortasse vitium de quo quereris, si te diligenter excusseris, in sinu invenies; inique publico irasceris crimini tuo—Reflect that perhaps the fault of which you complain, might, on a strict examination, be discovered in yourself; and that it would be unjust publicly to express indignation against your own crime.* Seneca, *de Beneficiis.* But, [5.] Men's being so severe upon the faults of others, while they are indulgent of their own, is a mark of hypocrisy. *Thou hypocrite, v.* 5. Whatever such a one may pretend, it is certain that he is no enemy to sin (if he were, he would be an enemy to his own sin), and therefore he is not worthy of praise; nay, it appears that he is an enemy to his brother, and therefore worthy of blame. This spiritual charity must begin at home; "*For how canst thou say,* how canst thou for shame say, to thy brother, *Let me help to reform thee,* when thou takest no care to reform thyself? Thy own heart will upbraid thee with the absurdity of it; thou wilt do it with an ill grace, and thou wilt expect every one to tell thee, that *vice corrects sin: physician, heal thyself;*" *I præ, sequar—Go you before, and I will follow.* See Rom. ii. 21. [6.] The consideration of what is amiss in ourselves, though it ought not to keep us from administering friendly reproof, ought to keep us from magisterial censuring, and to make us very candid and charitable in judging others. "Therefore *restore with the spirit of meekness, considering thyself* (Gal. vi. 1); what thou hast been, what thou art, and what thou wouldst be, if God should leave thee to thyself."

(2.) Here is a good rule for reprovers, *v.* 5. Go in the right method, *first cast the beam out of thine own eye.* Our own badness is so far from excusing us in not reproving, that our being by it rendered unfit to reprove is an aggravation of our badness; I must not say, "I have *a beam in my own eye,* and therefore I will not help my brother with the *mote out of his.*" A man's *of*fence will never be his *de*fence: but I must first reform myself, that I may thereby help to reform my brother, and may qualify myself to reprove him. Note, Those who blame others, ought to be blameless and harmless themselves. Those who are *reprovers in the gate,* reprovers by office, magistrates and ministers, are concerned to *walk circumspectly,* and to be very regular in their conversation: an *elder must have a good report,* 1 Tim. iii. 2, 7. The snuffers of the sanctuary were to be of pure gold.

2. It is not every one that is fit to be reproved; *Give not that which is holy unto the dogs, v.* 6. This may be considered, either, (1.) As a rule to the disciples in preaching the gospel; not that they must not preach it to any who were wicked and profane (Christ

himself preached to publicans and sinners), but the reference is to such as they found obstinate after the gospel was preached to them, such as blasphemed it, and persecuted the preachers of it; let them not spend much time among such, for it would be lost labour, but let them turn to others, Acts xiii. 41. So Dr. Whitby. Or, (2.) As a rule to all in giving reproof. Our zeal against sin must be guided by discretion, and we must not go about to give instructions, counsels, and rebukes, much less comforts, to hardened scorners, to whom it will certainly do no good, but who will be exasperated and enraged at us. Throw a pearl to a swine, and he will resent it, as if you threw a stone at him; *reproofs* will be called *reproaches*, as they were (Luke xi. 45; Jer. vi. 10), therefore give not to dogs and swine (unclean creatures) holy things. Note, [1.] Good counsel and reproof are a holy thing, and a pearl: they are ordinances of God, they are precious; as an *ear-ring of gold, and an ornament of fine gold,* so is the wise reprover (Prov. xxv. 12), and a wise reproof is *like an excellent oil* (Ps. cxli. 5); it is *a tree of life* (Prov. iii. 18). [2.] Among the generation of the wicked, there are some that have arrived at such a pitch of wickedness, that they are looked upon as dogs and swine; they are impudently and notoriously vile; they have so long *walked in the way of sinners,* that they have sat down *in the seat of the scornful;* they professedly hate and despise instruction, and set it at defiance, so that they are irrecoverably and irreclaimably wicked; they return with *the dog to his vomit,* and with the *sow to her wallowing in the mire.* [3.] Reproofs of instruction are ill bestowed upon such, and expose the reprover to all the contempt and mischief that may be expected from dogs and swine. One can expect no other than that they will trample the reproofs under their feet, in scorn of them, and rage against them; for they are impatient of control and contradiction; and they will turn again and rend the reprovers; rend their good names with their revilings, return them wounding words for their healing ones; rend them with persecution; Herod rent John Baptist for his faithfulness. See here what is the evidence of men's being *dogs* and *swine.* Those are to be reckoned such, who *hate reproofs* and reprovers, and fly in the face of those who, in kindness to their souls, show them their sin and danger. These sin against the remedy; who shall heal and help those that will not be healed and helped? It is plain that God has determined to destroy such. 2 Chron. xxv. 16. The rule here given is applicable to the distinguishing, sealing ordinances of the gospel; which must not be prostituted to those who are openly wicked and profane, lest holy things be thereby rendered contemptible, and unholy persons be thereby hardened. *It is not meet to take the children's bread, and cast it to the dogs.* Yet we must be very cautious whom we condemn as dogs and swine, and not do it till after trial, and upon full evidence. Many a patient is lost, by being thought to be so, who, if means had been used, might have been saved. As we must take heed of calling the *good, bad,* by judging all professors to be hypocrites; so we must take heed of calling the *bad, desperate,* by judging all the wicked to be *dogs* and *swine.* [4.] Our Lord Jesus is very tender of the safety of his people, and would not have them needlessly to expose themselves to the fury of those that will *turn again and rend* them. Let them not be *righteous over much,* so as to destroy themselves. Christ makes the law of self-preservation one of his own laws, and *precious is the blood* of his subjects to him.

7 Ask, and it shall be given you;
seek, and ye shall find; knock, and
it shall be opened unto you: 8 For
every one that asketh receiveth; and
he that seeketh findeth; and to him
that knocketh it shall be opened. 9
Or what man is there of you, whom
if his son ask bread, will he give him
a stone? 10 Or if he ask a fish, will
he give him a serpent? 11 If ye
then, being evil, know how to give
good gifts unto your children, how
much more shall your Father which
is in heaven give good things to them
that ask him?

Our Saviour, in the foregoing chapter, had spoken of prayer as a commanded duty, by which God is honoured, and which, if done aright, shall be rewarded; here he speaks of it as the appointed means of obtaining what we need, especially grace to obey the precepts he had given, some of which are so displeasing to flesh and blood.

I. Here is a precept in three words to the same purport, *Ask, Seek, Knock* (*v.* 7); that is, in one word, "Pray; pray often, pray with sincerity and seriousness; pray, and pray again; make conscience of prayer, and be constant in it; make a business of prayer, and be earnest in it. *Ask,* as a beggar asks alms." Those that would be rich in grace, must betake themselves to the poor trade of begging, and they shall find it a thriving trade. "*Ask;* represent your wants and burthens to God, and refer yourselves to him for support and supply, according to his promise. *Ask* as a traveller asks the way; to pray is to *enquire of God,* Ezek. xxxvi. 37. *Seek* as for a thing of value that we have lost, or as the merchantman that *seeks goodly pearls. Seek by prayer* Dan. ix. 3. *Knock,* as he that desires to enter into the house knocks at the door." We would be admitted to converse with God, would be taken into his love, and favour, and kingdom; sin has shut and barred the door against us; by prayer, we knock; *Lord, Lord, open to us.* Christ knocks at our door (Rev. iii. 20; Cant. v. 2); and allows us to knock at his, which is a favour we do not allow to common beggars. Seeking and knocking imply something more than asking and praying. 1. We must not only *ask* but *seek;* we must second our prayers with our endeavours; we must, in the use of the appointed means, *seek* for that which we *ask* for, else we tempt God. When the dresser of the vineyard asked for a year's respite for the barren fig-tree, he added, *I will dig about it,* Luke xiii. 7, 8. God gives knowledge and grace to those that search the scriptures, and wait at Wisdom's gates; and power against sin to those that avoid the occasions of it. 2. We must not only *ask,* but *knock;* we must come to God's door, must *ask* importunately; not only pray, but plead and wrestle with God; we must *seek* diligently; we must continue knocking; must persevere in prayer, and in the use of means; must endure to the end in the duty.

II. Here is a promise annexed: *our labour* in prayer, if indeed we do labour in it, *shall not be in vain:* where God finds a praying heart, he will be found a prayer-hearing God; *he shall give thee an answer of peace.* The precept is threefold, *ask, seek, knock;* there is *precept upon precept;* but the promise is sixfold, *line upon line,* for our encouragement; because a firm belief of the promise would make us cheerful and constant in our obedience. Now here,

1. The promise is made, and made so as exactly to answer the precept, *v.* 7. God will meet those that attend on him; *Ask, and it shall be given you;* not lent you, not sold you, but *given you;* and what is more free than gift? Whatever you pray for, according to the promise, whatever you *ask, shall be given you,* if God see it fit for you, and what would you have more? It is but *ask* and have; *ye have not, because ye ask not,* or *ask* not aright: what is not worth asking, is not worth having, and then it is worth nothing. *Seek,* and *ye shall find,* and then you do not lose your labour; God is himself *found of those that seek* him, and if we find him we have enough. "*Knock, and it shall be opened;* the door of mercy and grace shall no longer be shut against you as enemies and intruders, but opened to you as friends and children. It will be asked, *who is at the door?* If you be able to say, a friend, and have the ticket of the promise ready to produce in the hand of faith, doubt not of admission. If the door be not *opened* at the first *knock, continue instant in prayer;* it is an affront to a friend to *knock* at his door, and then go away; though he tarry, yet wait."

2. It is repeated, *v.* 8. It is to the same purport, yet with some addition. (1.) It is made to extend to all that pray aright; "Not only you my disciples shall receive wnat you pray for, but *every one that asketh, receiveth,* whether Jew or Gentile, young or old, rich or poor, high or low, master or servant, learned or unlearned, they are all alike welcome to *the throne of grace,* if they come in faith: *for God is no respecter of persons.* (2.) It is made so as to amount to a grant, in words of the present tense, which is more than a promise for the future. *Every one that asketh,* not only *shall* receive, but *receiveth;* by faith, applying and appropriating the promise, we are actually interested and invested in the good promised: so sure and inviolable are the promises of God, that they do, in effect, give present possession: an active believer enters immediately, and makes the blessings promised his own. What we have in hope, according to the promise, is as sure, and should be as sweet, as what we have in hand. *God hath spoken in his holiness,* and then *Gilead is mine, Manasseh mine* (Ps. cviii. 7, 8); it is all mine own, if I can but make it so by believing it so. Conditional grants become absolute upon the performance of the condition; so here, *he that asketh, receiveth.* Christ hereby puts his *fiat* to the petition; and he having all power, that is enough.

3. It is illustrated, by a similitude taken from earthly parents, and their innate readiness to give their children what they ask. Christ appeals to his hearers, *What man is there of you,* though never so morose and ill-humoured, *whom if his son ask bread, will he give him a stone? v.* 9, 10. Whence he infers (*v.* 11), *If ye then, being evil,* yet grant your children's requests, *much more will your heavenly Father give you the good things you ask.* Now this is of use,

(1.) To *direct* our prayers and expectations. [1.] We must come to God, as children to a *Father in heaven,* with reverence and confidence. How naturally does the child in want or distress run to the father with its complaints; *My head, my head;* thus should the new nature send us to God for supports and supplies. [2.] We must come to him for *good things,* for those he *gives to them that ask him;* which teaches us to refer ourselves to him; we know not what is good for ourselves (Eccl. vi. 12), but he knows what is good for us, we must therefore leave it with him; *Father, thy will be done.* The child is here supposed to *ask bread,* that is necessary, and *a fish,* that is wholesome; but if the child should foolishly ask for *a stone,* or *a serpent,* for unripe fruit to eat, or a sharp knife to play with, the father, though kind, is so wise as to deny him. We often ask that of God which would do us hurt if we had it; he knows this, and therefore does not give it to us. Denials in love are better than grants in anger; we should have been undone ere this if we had had all we desired; this is admirably well expressed by a heathen, Juvenal, *Sat.* 10.

Permittes ipsis expendere numinibus, quid
Conveniat nobis, rebusque sit utile nostris,
Nam pro jucundis aptissima quæque dabunt dii.
Carior est illis homo, quam sibi: nos animorum
Impulsu, et cæca, magnaque cupidine ducti,
Conjugium petimus, partumque uxoris; at illis
Notum est, qui pueri, qualisque futura sit uxor.

Entrust thy fortune to the powers above.
Leave them to manage for thee, and to grant
What their unerring wisdom sees thee want:
In goodness, as in greatness, they excel;
Ah, that we lov'd ourselves but half so well!
We, blindly by our headstrong passions led,
Seek a companion, and desire to wed;
Then wish for heirs: but to the gods alone
Our future offspring and our wives are known.

(2.) To *encourage* our prayers and expectations. We may hope that we shall not be denied and disappointed: we shall not have *a stone* for *bread,* to break our teeth (though we have a hard crust to employ our teeth), nor *a serpent* for *a fish,* to sting us; we have reason indeed to fear it, because we deserve it, but God will be better to us than the desert of our sins. The world often gives *stones for bread,* and *serpents for fish,* but God never does; nay, we shall be heard and answered, for children are by their parents. [1.] God has put into the hearts of parents a compassionate inclination to succour and supply their children, according to their need. Even those that have had little conscience of duty, yet have done it, as it were by instinct. No law was ever thought necessary to oblige parents to maintain their legitimate children, nor, in Solomon's time, their illegitimate ones. [2.] He has assumed the relation of a Father to us, and owns us for his children; that from the readiness we find in ourselves to relieve our children, we may be encouraged to apply ourselves to him for relief What love and tenderness fathers have are from him; not from nature but from the God of nature; and therefore they must needs be infinitely greater in himself. He compares his concern for his people to that of a father for his children (Ps. ciii. 13), nay, to that of a mother, which is usually more tender, Isa. lxvi. 13; xlix. 14, 15. But here it is supposed, that his love, and tenderness, and goodness, far excel that of any earthly parent; and therefore it is argued with a *much more,* and it is grounded upon this undoubted truth, that God is a better Father, infinitely better than any earthly parents are; *his thoughts are above theirs.* Our earthly fathers have taken care of us; we have taken care of our children; much more will God take care of his; for they are evil, originally so; the degenerate seed of fallen Adam; they have lost much of the good nature that belonged to humanity, and among other corruptions, have that of crossness and unkindness in them; yet they *give good things to their children,* and they *know how to give,* suitably and seasonably; *much more will* God, for he takes up when they forsake, Ps. xxvii. 10. And, *First,* God is more knowing; parents are often foolishly fond, but God is wise, infinitely so; he knows what we need, what we desire, and what is fit for us. *Secondly,* God is more kind. If all the compassions of all the tender fathers in the world were crowded into the bowels of one, yet compared *with the tender mercies of our God,* they would be but as a candle to the sun, or a drop to the ocean. God is more rich, and more ready to give to his children than the fathers of our flesh can be; for he is the Father of our spirits, an ever-loving, ever-living Father. The bowels of fathers yearn even towards undutiful children, towards prodigals, as David's toward Absalom, and will not all this serve to silence unbelief?

12 Therefore all things whatsoever
ye would that men should do to you,
do ye even so to them: for this is
the law and the prophets. 13 Enter
ye in at the strait gate: for wide *is*
the gate, and broad *is* the way, that
leadeth to destruction, and many there
be which go in thereat: 14 Because
strait *is* the gate, and narrow *is* the
way, which leadeth unto life; and
few there be that find it.

Our Lord Jesus here presses upon us that righteousness towards men which is an essential branch of true religion, and that religion towards God which is an essential branch of universal righteousness.

I. We must make righteousness our rule, and be ruled by it, *v.* 12. *Therefore,* lay this down for your principle, to do as you would be done by; therefore, that you may conform to the foregoing precepts, which are particular, that you may not judge and censure others, go by this rule in general; (you would not be censured, therefore do not censure), Or that you may have the benefit of the foregoing promises. Fitly is the law of justice subjoined to the law of prayer, for unless we be honest in our conversation, God will not hear our prayers, Isa. i. 15—17; lviii. 6, 9; Zech. vii. 9, 13. We cannot expect to receive *good things* from God, if we do not *fair* things, and that which is *honest,* and *lovely, and of good report* among men. We must not only be devout, but honest, else our devotion is but hypocrisy. Now here we have,

1. The rule of justice laid down; *Whatsoever ye would that men should do to you, do you even so to them.* Christ came to teach us, not only what we are to know and believe, but what we are to do; what we are to do, not only toward God, but toward men; not only towards our fellow-disciples, those of our party and persuasion, but towards men in general, all with whom we have to do. The golden rule of equity is, to do to others as we would they should do to us. Alexander Severus, a heathen emperor, was a great admirer of this rule, had it written upon the walls of his closet, often quoted it in giving judgment, honoured Christ, and favoured

Christians, for the sake of it. *Quod tibi, hoc alteri—do to others as you would they should do to you.* Take it negatively *(Quod tibi fieri non vis, ne alteri feceris),* or positively, it comes all to the same. We must not do to others the evil they have done to us, nor the evil which they would do to us, if it were in their power; nor may we do that which we think, if it were done to us, we could bear contentedly, but what we desire should be done to us. This is grounded upon that great commandment, *Thou shalt love thy neighbour as thyself.* As we must bear the same affection to our neighbour that we would have borne to ourselves, so we must do the same good offices. The meaning of this rule lies in three things. (1.) We must do that to our neighbour which we ourselves acknowledge to be fit and reasonable: the appeal is made to our own judgment, and the discovery of our judgment is referred to that which is our own will and expectation, when it is our own case. (2.) We must put other people upon the level with ourselves, and reckon we are as much obliged to them, as they to us. We are as much bound to the duty of justice as they, and they as much entitled to the benefit of it as we. (3.) We must, in our dealings with men, suppose ourselves in the same particular case and circumstances with those we have to do with, and deal accordingly. If I were making such a one's bargain, labouring under such a one's infirmity and affliction, how should I desire and expect to be treated? And this is a just supposition, because we know not how soon their case may really be ours: at least we may fear, lest God by his judgments should do to us as we have done to others, if we have not done as we would be done by.

2. A reason given to enforce this rule; *This is the law and the prophets.* It is the summary of that second great commandment, which is one of the two, *on which hang all the law and the prophets, ch.* xxii. 40. We have not this in so many words, either in *the law* or *the prophets,* but it is the concurring language of the whole. All that is there said concerning our duty towards our neighbour (and that is no little) may be reduced to this rule. Christ has here adopted it into this law; so that both the Old Testament and the New agree in prescribing this to us, to do as we would be done by. By this rule the law of Christ is commended, but the lives of Christians are condemned by comparing them with it. *Aut hoc non evangelium, aut hi non evangelici.—Either this is not the gospel, or these are not Christians.*

II. We must make religion our business, and be intent upon it; we must be strict and circumspect in our conversation, which is here represented to us as entering in at a *strait gate,* and walking on in a *narrow way, v.* 13, 14. Observe here,

1. The account that is given of the bad way of sin, and the good way of holiness. There are but two ways, right and wrong, good and evil; the way to heaven, and the way to hell; in the one of which we are all of us walking: no middle place hereafter, no middle way now: the distinction of the children of men into saints and sinners, godly and ungodly, will swallow up all to eternity.

Here is, (1.) An account given us of the way of sin and sinners; both what is the best, and what is the worst of it.

[1.] That which allures multitudes into it, and keeps them in it; *the gate is wide, and the way broad,* and there are many travellers in that way. *First,* "You will have abundance of liberty in that way; *the gate is wide,* and stands wide open to tempt those that go right on their way. You may go in at this gate with all your lusts about you; it gives no check to your appetites, to your passions: you may *walk in the way of your heart, and in the sight of your eyes;* that gives room enough." It is a *broad way,* for there is nothing to hedge in those that walk in it, but they wander endlessly; a *broad way,* for there are many paths in it; there is choice of sinful ways, contrary to each other, but all paths in this *broad way. Secondly,* "You will have abundance of company in that way: *many there be that go in* at this gate, and walk in this way." If we *follow the multitude,* it will be *to do evil:* if we go with the crowd, it will be the wrong way. It is natural for us to incline to go down the stream, and do as the most do; but it is too great a compliment, to be willing to be damned for company, and to go to hell with them, because they will not go to heaven with us: if many perish, we should be the more cautious.

[2.] That which should affright us all from it is, that it *leads to destruction.* Death, eternal death, is at the end of it (and the way of sin tends to it),—everlasting *destruction from the presence of the Lord.* Whether it be the high way of open profaneness, or the back way of close hypocrisy, if it be a way of sin, it will be our ruin, if we repent not.

(2.) Here is an account given us of the way of holiness.

[1.] What there is in it that frightens many from it; let us know the worst of it, that we may sit down and count the cost. Christ deals faithfully with us, and tells us,

First, That *the gate is strait.* Conversion and regeneration are *the gate,* by which we enter into this way, in which we begin a life of faith and serious godliness; out of a state of sin into a state of grace we must pass, by the new birth, John iii. 3, 5. This is a *strait gate,* hard to find, and hard to get through; like a passage between two rocks, 1 Sam. xiv. 4. There must be *a new heart, and a new spirit,* and *old things must pass away.* The bent of the soul must be changed, corrupt habits and customs broken off; what we have been doing all our days must be undone again. We must swim against the stream; much opposition must be struggled with, and broken through, from without, and from within. It is easier to set a man against all the world than against himself, and yet this must be in conversion. It is a *strait gate,* for we must stoop, or we cannot go in at it; we must become as little children; high thoughts must be brought down; nay, we must strip, must deny ourselves, put off the world, *put off the old man;* we must be willing to forsake all for our interest in Christ. *The gate is strait* to all, but to some straiter than to others; as to the rich, to some that have been long prejudiced against religion. *The gate is strait;* blessed be God, it is not shut up, nor locked against us, nor kept with a flaming sword, as it will be shortly, *ch.* xxv. 10.

Secondly, That *the way is narrow.* We are not in heaven as soon as we have got through *the strait gate,* not in Canaan as soon as we have got through the Red Sea; no, we must go through a wilderness, must travel a *narrow way,* hedged in by the divine law, which *is exceedingly broad,* and that makes *the way narrow;* self must be denied, the body kept under, corruptions mortified, that are as a *right eye* and a *right hand;* daily temptations must be resisted; duties must be done that are against our inclination. We must endure hardness, must wrestle and be in an agony, must watch in all things, and walk with care and circumspection. We must go *through much tribulation.* It is *ὁδὸς τεθλιμμένη*—*an afflicted way,* a way hedged about with thorns; blessed be God, it is not hedged up. The bodies we carry about with us, and the corruptions remaining in us, make the way of our duty difficult; but, as the understanding and will grow more and more sound, it will open and enlarge, and grow more and more pleasant.

Thirdly, The gate being so *strait and the way so narrow,* it is not strange that there are but *few that find it,* and choose it. Many pass it by, through carelessness; they will not be at the pains to find it; they are well as they are, and see no need to change their way. Others look upon it, but shun it; they like not to be so limited and restrained. Those that are going to heaven are but few, compared to those that are going to hell; a remnant, a little flock, like the grape-gleanings of the vintage; as the eight that were saved in the ark, 1 Pet. iii. 20. *In vitia alter alterum trudimus; Quomodo ad salutem revocari potest, quum nullus retrahit, et populus impellit*—*In the ways of vice men urge each other onward: how shall any one be restored to the path of safety, when impelled forwards by the multitude, without any counteracting influence?* Seneca, *Epist.* 29. This discourages many: they are loth to be singular, to be solitary; but instead of stumbling at this, say rather, If so few are going to heaven, there shall be one the more for me.

[2.] Let us see what there is in this way, which, notwithstanding this, should invite us all to it; it *leads to life,* to present comfort in the favour of God, which is the life of the soul; to eternal bliss, the hope of which, at the end of our way, should reconcile us to all the difficulties and inconveniences of the road. Life and godliness are put together (2 Pet. i. 3); *The gate is strait and the way narrow* and up-hill, but one hour in heaven will make amends for all.

2. The great concern and duty of every one of us, in consideration of all this; *Enter ye in at the strait gate.* The matter is fairly stated; life and death, good and evil, are set before us; both the ways, and both the ends: now let the matter be taken entire, and considered impartially, and then choose you this day which you will walk in; nay, the matter determines itself, and will not admit of a debate. No man, in his wits, would choose to go to the gallows, because it is a smooth, pleasant way to it, nor refuse the offer of a palace and a throne, because it is a rough, dirty way to it; yet such absurdities as these are men guilty of, in the concerns of their souls. Delay not, therefore; deliberate not any longer, but *enter ye in at the strait gate; knock* at it by sincere and constant prayers and endeavours, *and it shall be opened;* nay, a wide door shall be opened, and an effectual one. It is true, we can neither go in, nor go on, without the assistance of divine grace; but it is as true, that grace is freely offered, and shall not be wanting to those that seek it, and submit to it. Conversion is hard work, but it is needful, and, blessed be God, it is not impossible if we strive, Luke xiii. 24.

15 Beware of false prophets, which
come to you in sheep's clothing, but
inwardly they are ravening wolves.
16 Ye shall know them by their
fruits. Do men gather grapes of
thorns, or figs of thistles? 17 Even
so every good tree bringeth forth
good fruit; but a corrupt tree bringeth forth evil fruit. 18 A good tree
cannot bring forth evil fruit, neither
can a corrupt tree bring forth good
fruit. 19 Every tree that bringeth
not forth good fruit is hewn down,
and cast into the fire. 20 Wherefore
by their fruits ye shall know them.

We have here a caution against *false prophets,* to take heed that we be not deceived and imposed upon by them. *Prophets* are properly such as foretel things to come; there are some mentioned in the Old Testament, who pretended to that without warrant, and the event disproved their pretensions, as Zedekiah, 1 Kings xxii. 11, and another Zedekiah, Jer. xxix. 21. But *prophets* did also teach the people their duty, so that *false pro-*

phets here are false teachers. Christ being a Prophet and *a Teacher come from God,* and designing to send abroad teachers under him, gives warning to all to take heed of counterfeits, who, instead of healing souls with wholesome doctrine, as they pretend, would poison them.

They are false teachers and *false prophets,* 1. Who produce false commissions, who pretend to have immediate warrant and direction from God to set up for *prophets,* and to be divinely inspired, when they are not so. Though their doctrine may be true, we are to *beware* of them as *false prophets.* False apostles are those who *say they are apostles, and are not* (Rev. ii. 2); such are *false prophets.* "Take heed of those who pretend to revelation, and admit them not without sufficient proof, lest that one absurdity being admitted, a thousand follow." 2. Who preach false doctrine in those things that are essential to religion; who teach that which is contrary to *the truth as it is in Jesus,* to *the truth which is according to godliness.* The former seems to be the proper notion of *pseudopropheta,* a *false* or pretending *prophet,* but commonly the latter falls in with it; for who would hang out false colours, but with design, under pretence of them, the more successfully to attack the truth. "Well, beware of them, suspect them, try them, and when you have discovered their falsehood, avoid them, have nothing to do with them. Stand upon your guard against this temptation, which commonly attends the days of reformation, and the breakings out of divine light in more than ordinary strength and splendour. When God's work is revived, Satan and his agents are most busy. Here is,

I. A good reason for this caution, *Beware of* them, for they are *wolves in sheep's clothing, v.* 15.

1. We have need to be very cautious, because their pretences are very fair and plausible, and such as will deceive us, if we be not upon our guard. They *come in sheep's clothing,* in the habit of *prophets,* which was plain and coarse, and unwrought; they *wear a rough garment to deceive,* Zech. xiii. 4. Elijah's mantle the Septuagint calls ἡ μήλοτη—*a sheep-skin* mantle. We must take heed of being imposed upon by men's dress and garb, as by that of the scribes, who *desire to walk in long robes,* Luke xx. 46. Or it may be taken figuratively; they pretend to be sheep, and outwardly appear so innocent, harmless, meek, useful, and all that is good, as to be excelled by none; they feign themselves to be just men, and for the sake of their clothing are admitted among the sheep, which gives them an opportunity of doing them a mischief ere they are aware. They and their errors are gilded with the specious pretences of sanctity and devotion. Satan turns himself *into an angel of light,* 2 Cor. xi. 13, 14. The enemy has *horns like a lamb* (Rev. xiii. 11); *faces of men,* Rev. ix. 7, 8. Seducers in language and carriage are *soft as wool,* Rom. xvi. 18; Isa. xxx. 10.

2. Because under these pretensions their designs are very malicious and mischievous; *inwardly they are ravening wolves.* Every *hypocrite* is a *goat* in sheep's clothing; but a *false prophet* is a *wolf* in sheep's clothing; not only not a sheep, but the worst enemy the sheep has, that comes not but to tear and devour, to *scatter the sheep* (John x. 12), to drive them from God, and from one another, into crooked paths. Those that would cheat us of any truth, and possess us with error, whatever they pretend, design mischief to our souls. Paul calls them *grievous wolves,* Acts xx. 29. They raven for themselves, *serve their own belly* (Rom. xvi. 18), make a prey of you, make a gain of you. Now since it is so easy a thing, and withal so dangerous, to be cheated, *Beware of false prophets.*

II. Here is a good rule to go by in this caution; we must *prove all things* (1 Thess. v 21), *try the spirits* (1 John iv. 1), and here we have a touchstone; *ye shall know them by their fruits,* 16—20. Observe,

1. The illustration of this comparison, of the fruit's being the discovery of the tree. You cannot always distinguish them by their bark and leaves, nor by the spreading of their boughs, but *by their fruits ye shall know them.* The fruit is according to the tree. Men may, in their professions, put a force upon their nature, and contradict their inward principles, but the stream and bent of their practices will agree with them. Christ insists upon this, the agreeableness between the fruit and the tree, which is such as that, (1.) If you know what the tree is, you may know what fruit to expect. Never look to gather *grapes from thorns, nor figs from thistles;* it is not in their nature to produce such fruits. An apple may be stuck, or a bunch of grapes may hang, upon a thorn; so may a good truth, a good word or action, be found in a bad man, but you may be sure it never grew there. Note, [1.] Corrupt, vicious, unsanctified hearts are like thorns and thistles, which came in with sin, are worthless, vexing, and for the fire at last. [2.] Good works are *good fruit,* like grapes and figs, pleasing to God and profitable to men. [3.] This *good fruit* is never to be expected from bad men, any more than *a clean thing out of an unclean:* they want an influencing acceptable principle. *Out of an evil treasure* will be brought forth *evil things.* (2.) On the other hand, if you know what the fruit is, you may, by that, perceive what the tree is. *A good tree cannot bring forth evil fruit,* nay, it cannot but *bring forth good fruit;* and *a corrupt tree cannot bring forth good fruit,* nay, it cannot but *bring forth evil fruit.* But then that must be reckoned the fruit of the tree which it brings forth naturally and which is its genuine product—which it brings forth plentifully and constantly and which is its usual product. Men are known, not by particular acts, but by the course and tenour of their

conversation, and by the more frequent acts, especially those that appear to be free, and most their own, and least under the influence of external motives and inducements.

2. The application of this to the false prophets.

(1.) By way of terror and threatening (*v.* 19); *Every tree that brings not forth good fruit is hewn down.* This very saying John the Baptist had used, *ch.* iii. 10. Christ could have spoken the same sense in other words; could have altered it, or given it a new turn; but he thought it no disparagement to him to say the same that John had said before him; let not ministers be ambitious of coining new expressions, nor people's ears itch for novelties; to write and speak the same things must not be grievous, for it is safe. Here is, [1.] The description of barren trees; they are trees that do *not bring forth good fruit;* though there be fruit, if it be not *good fruit* (though that be done, which for the matter of it is good, if it be not done well, in a right manner, and for a right end), the tree is accounted barren. [2.] The doom of barren trees; *they are,* that is, certainly they shall be, *hewn down, and cast into the fire;* God will deal with them as men use to deal with dry trees that cumber the ground: he will mark them by some signal tokens of his displeasure, he will bark them by stripping them of their parts and gifts, will cut them *down* by death, *and cast* them *into the fire* of hell, a fire blown with the bellows of God's wrath, and fed with the wood of barren trees. Compare this with Ezek. xxxi. 12, 13; Dan. iv. 14; John xv. 6.

(2.) By way of trial; *By their fruits ye shall know them.*

[1.] *By the fruits* of their persons, their words and actions, and the course of their conversation. If you would know whether they be right or not, observe how they live; their works will testify for them or against them. The scribes and Pharisees sat in Moses's chair, and taught the law, but they were proud, and covetous, and false, and oppressive, and therefore Christ warned his disciples to *beware of* them and of their *leaven,* Mark xii. 38. If men pretend to be prophets and are immoral, that disproves their pretensions; those are no true friends *to the cross of Christ,* whatever they profess, *whose God is their belly,* and *who mind earthly things,* Phil. iii. 18, 19. Those are not taught nor sent of the holy God, whose lives evidence that they are led by the unclean spirit. God puts the treasure into earthen vessels, but not into such corrupt vessels: they may declare God's statutes, but what have they to do to declare them?

[2.] *By the fruits* of their doctrine; their fruits as prophets: not that this is the only way, but it is one way, of trying doctrines, *whether they be of God* or not. What do they tend to? What affections and practices will they lead those into, that embrace them? If *the doctrine be of God,* it will tend to promote serious piety, humility, charity, holiness, and love, with other Christian graces; but if, on the contrary, the doctrines these prophets preach have a manifest tendency to make people proud, worldly, and contentious, to make them loose and careless in their conversations, unjust or uncharitable, factious or disturbers of the public peace; if it indulge carnal liberty, and take people off from governing themselves and their families by the strict rules of *the narrow way,* we may conclude, that *this persuasion comes not of him that calleth us,* Gal. v. 8. *This wisdom is not from above,* James iii. 15. *Faith and a good conscience* are held together, 1 Tim. i. 19; iii. 9. Note, *Doctrines of doubtful disputation* must be tried by graces and duties of confessed certainty: those opinions come not from God that lead to sin: but if we cannot *know them by their fruits,* we must have recourse to the great touchstone, to the law, and to the testimony; do they speak according to that rule?

21 Not every one that saith unto
me, Lord, Lord, shall enter into the
kingdom of heaven; but he that
doeth the will of my Father which is
in heaven. 22 Many will say to me
in that day, Lord, Lord, have we not
prophesied in thy name? and in thy
name have cast out devils? and in
thy name done many wonderful
works? 23 And then will I profess
unto them, I never knew you: depart from me, ye that work iniquity.
24 Therefore whosoever heareth these
sayings of mine, and doeth them, I
will liken him unto a wise man, which
built his house upon a rock: 25
And the rain descended, and the
floods came, and the winds blew,
and beat upon that house; and it fell
not: for it was founded upon a rock.
26 And every one that heareth these
sayings of mine, and doeth them not,
shall be likened unto a foolish man,
which built his house upon the sand:
27 And the rain descended, and the
floods came, and the winds blew, and
beat upon that house; and it fell:
and great was the fall of it. 28 And
it came to pass, when Jesus had
ended these sayings, the people were
astonished at his doctrine: 29 For
he taught them as *one* having authority, and not as the scribes.

We have here the conclusion of this long and excellent sermon, the scope of which is to show the indispensable necessity of obedience to the commands of Christ; this is designed to clench the nail, that it might fix in a sure place: he speaks this to his disciples, that sat at his feet wherever he preached, and followed him wherever he went. Had he sought his own praise among men, he would have said, that was enough; but the religion he came to establish is in power, not in word only (1 Cor. iv. 20), and therefore something more is necessary.

I. He shows, by a plain remonstrance, that an outward profession of religion, however remarkable, will not bring us to heaven, unless there be a correspondent conversation, *v.* 21—23. All judgment is committed to our Lord Jesus; the keys are put into his hand; he has power to prescribe new terms of life and death, and to judge men according to them: now this is a solemn declaration pursuant to that power. Observe here,

1. Christ's law laid down, *v.* 21. *Not every one that saith, Lord, Lord, shall enter into the kingdom of heaven, into the kingdom of* grace and glory. It is an answer to that question, Psal. xv. 1. *Who shall sojourn in thy tabernacle?*—the church militant; *and who shall dwell in thy holy hill?*—the church triumphant. Christ here shows,

(1.) That it will not suffice to say, *Lord, Lord;* in word and tongue to own Christ for our Master, and to make addresses to him, and professions of him accordingly: in prayer to God, in discourse with men, we must call Christ, *Lord, Lord;* we *say well,* for *so he is* (John xiii. 13); but can we imagine that this is enough to bring us to heaven, that such a piece of formality as this should be so recompensed, or that he who knows and requires the heart should be so put off with shows for substance? Compliments among men are pieces of civility that are returned with compliments, but they are never paid as real services; and can they then be of any account with Christ? There may be a seeming importunity in prayer, *Lord, Lord:* but if inward *im*pressions be not answerable to outward *ex*pressions, we are but *as sounding brass and a tinkling cymbal.* This is not to take us off from saying, *Lord, Lord;* from praying, and being earnest in prayer, from professing Christ's name, and being bold in professing it, but from resting in these, in the *form of godliness,* without *the power.*

(2.) That it is necessary to our happiness that we *do the will of* Christ, which is indeed *the will of* his *Father in heaven. The will of* God, as Christ's *Father,* is his will in the gospel, for there he is made known, as *the Father of our Lord Jesus Christ:* and in him our Father. Now this is his will, that we believe in Christ, that we repent of sin, that we live a holy life, that we *love one another. This is his will, even our sanctification.* If we comply not with the will of God, we mock Christ in calling him *Lord,* as those did who put on him a gorgeous robe, and said, *Hail, King of the Jews.* Saying and doing are two things, often parted in the conversation of men: he that said, *I go, sir,* stirred never a step (*ch.* xxi. 30); but these two things *God has joined* in his command, and *let no man* that *puts* them *asunder* think to *enter into the kingdom of heaven.*

2. The hypocrite's plea against the strictness of this law, offering other things in lieu of obedience, *v.* 22. The plea is supposed to be *in that day,* that great day, when every man shall appear in his own colours; *when the secrets of all hearts shall be* manifest, and among the rest, the secret pretences with which sinners now support their vain hopes. Christ knows the strength of their cause, and it is but weakness; what they now harbour in their bosoms, they will then produce in arrest of judgment to stay the doom, but it will be in vain. They put in their plea with great importunity, *Lord, Lord;* and with great confidence, appealing to Christ concerning it; *Lord,* dost not thou know, (1.) That *we have prophesied in thy name?* Yes, it may be so; Balaam and Caiaphas were overruled to prophesy, and Saul was against his will *among the prophets,* yet that did not save them. These *prophesied in* his *name,* but he did not send them; they only made use of his name to serve a turn. Note, A man may be a preacher, may have gifts for the ministry, and an external call to it, and perhaps some success in it, and yet be a wicked man; may help others to heaven, and yet come short himself. (2.) That *in thy name we have cast out devils?* That may be too; Judas *cast out devils,* and yet was a *son of perdition.* Origen says, that in his time so prevalent was the name of Christ to *cast out devils,* that sometimes it availed when named by wicked Christians. A man might *cast devils out* of others, and yet have a devil, nay, and be a devil himself. (3.) That *in thy name we have done many wonderful works.* There may be a faith of miracles, where there is no justifying faith; none of that *faith which works by love* and obedience. Gifts of tongues and healing would recommend men to the world, but it is real holiness or sanctification that is accepted of God. Grace and love are *a more excellent way* than *removing mountains,* or *speaking with the tongues of men and of angels,* 1 Cor. xiii. 1, 2. Grace will bring a man to heaven without working miracles, but working miracles will never bring a man to heaven without grace. Observe, That which their heart was upon, in doing these works, and which they confided in, was the wonderfulness of them. Simon Magus wondered at the miracles (Acts viii. 13), and therefore would give any money for power to do the like. Observe, They had not many good works to plead: they could not pretend to have done many gracious works of piety and charity; one such would have passed better in their account than *many wonderful works,* which availed not at all, while they persisted

in disobedience. Miracles have now ceased, and with them this plea; but do not carnal hearts still encourage themselves in their groundless hopes, with the like vain supports? They think they shall go to heaven, because they have been of good repute among professors of religion, have kept fasts, and given alms, and have been preferred in the church; as if this would atone for their reigning pride, worldliness, and sensuality, and want of love to God and man. *Bethel is their confidence* (Jer. xlviii. 13), they are *haughty because of the holy mountain* (Zeph. iii. 11); and boast that they are *the temple of the Lord,* Jer. vii. 4. Let us take heed of resting in external privileges and performances, lest *we deceive ourselves,* and perish eternally, as multitudes do, *with a lie in our right hand.*

3. The rejection of this plea as frivolous. The same that is the Law-Maker (*v.* 21) is here the Judge according to that law (*v.* 23), and he will overrule the plea, will overrule it publicly; he *will profess to them* with all possible solemnity, as sentence is passed by the Judge, *I never knew you,* and therefore *depart from me, ye that work iniquity.*—Observe, (1.) Why, and upon what ground, he rejects them and their plea—because they were *workers of iniquity.* Note, It is possible for men to have a great name for piety, and yet to be *workers of iniquity;* and those that are so will *receive the greater damnation.* Secret haunts of sin, kept up under the cloak of a visible profession, will be the ruin of hypocrites. Living in known sin nullifies men's pretensions, be they ever so specious. (2.) How it is expressed; *I never knew you;* "I never owned you as my servants, no, not when you *prophesied in* my *name,* when you were in the height of your profession, and were most extolled." This intimates, that if he had ever known them, as *the Lord knows them that are his,* had ever owned them and loved them as his, he would have known them, and owned them, and *loved them, to the end;* but he *never* did *know* them, for he always knew them to be hypocrites, and rotten at heart, as he did Judas; therefore, says he, *depart from me.* Has Christ need of such guests? When he came in the flesh, he called sinners *to* him (*ch.* ix. 13), but *when he shall come again in glory,* he will drive sinners *from* him. They that would not *come to* him to be saved, must *depart from* him to be damned. To *depart from* Christ is the very hell of hell; it is the foundation of all the misery of the damned, to be cut off from all hope of benefit from Christ and his mediation. Those that go no further in Christ's service than a bare profession, he does not accept, nor will he own them in the great day. See from what a height of hope men may fall into the depth of misery! How they may go to hell, by the gates of heaven! This should be an awakening word to all Christians. If a preacher, one that *cast out devils,* and wrought miracles, be disowned of Christ for *working iniquity;* what will become of us, if we be found such? And if we *be* such, we shall certainly be found such. At God's bar, a profession of religion will not bear out any man in the practice and indulgence of sin; therefore *let every one that names the name of Christ, depart from all iniquity.*

II. He shows, by a parable, that hearing these sayings of Christ will not make us happy, if we do not make conscience of doing them; but that if we hear them and do them, we are *blessed in our deed, v.* 24—27.

1. The hearers of Christ's word are here divided into two sorts; some that hear, and do what they hear; others that hear and do not. Christ preached now to a mixed multitude, and he thus *separates them, one from the other,* as he will at the great day, when *all nations shall be gathered before him.* Christ is still speaking from heaven by his word and Spirit, speaks by ministers, by providences, and of those that hear him there are two sorts.

(1.) Some that *hear his sayings and do them:* blessed be God that there are any such, though comparatively few. To hear Christ is not barely to give him the hearing, but to obey him. Note, It highly concerns us all to do what we *hear* of the *sayings* of Christ. It is a mercy that we *hear* his *sayings: Blessed are those ears, ch.* xiii. 16, 17. But, if we practise not what we hear, we *receive* that *grace in vain.* To *do* Christ's *sayings* is conscientiously to abstain from the sins that he forbids, and to perform the duties that he requires. Our thoughts and affections, our words and actions, the temper of our minds, and the tenour of our lives, must be conformable to the gospel of Christ; that is the doing he requires. All the *sayings* of Christ, not only the laws he has enacted, but the truths he has revealed, must be done by us. *They are a light,* not only *to our eyes,* but *to our feet,* and are designed not only to *in*form our judgments, but to *re*form our hearts and lives: nor do we indeed believe them, if we do not live up to them. Observe, It is not enough to *hear* Christ's *sayings,* and understand them, *hear* them, and remember them, *hear* them, and talk of them, repeat them, dispute for them; but we must *hear, and do* them. *This do, and thou shalt live.* Those only *that hear, and do,* are *blessed* (Luke xi. 28; John xiii. 17), and are akin to Christ. *ch.* xii. 50.

(2.) There are others who *hear* Christ's *sayings and do them not;* their religion rests in bare hearing, and goes no further; like children that have the rickets, their heads swell with empty notions, and indigested opinions, but their joints are weak, and they heavy and listless; they neither can stir, nor care to stir, in any good duty; *they hear* God's *words,* as if they desired to *know his ways,* like a people *that did righteousness, but they will not do them,* Ezek. xxxiii. 30, 31; Isa. lviii. 2. Thus they deceive themselves, as Micah, who thought himself happy, because he had a Levite to be his priest, though he had not the Lord to be his God. The seed is sown, but it never comes up; they see their spots in the glass of the word, but wash them off Jam. i. 22. 24. Thus they put a cheat upon their own souls; for it is certain, if our hearing be not the means of our obedience, it will be the aggravation of our disobedience. Those who only *hear* Christ's *sayings, and do them not*, sit down in the midway to heaven, and that will never bring them to their journey's end. They are akin to Christ only by the half-blood, and our law allows not such to inherit.

2. These two sorts of hearers are here represented in their true characters, and the state of their case, under the comparison of two builders; one was *wise*, and *built upon a rock*, and his building stood in a storm; the other *foolish*, and *built upon the sand*, and his building fell.

Now, (1.) The general scope of this parable teaches us that the only way to make sure work for our souls and eternity is, to *hear and do the sayings of* the Lord Jesus, *these sayings of* his in this sermon upon the mount, which is wholly practical; some of them seem hard sayings to flesh and blood, but they must be done; and thus we *lay up in store a good foundation for the time to come* (1 Tim. vi. 19); a *good bond*, so some read it; a bond of God's making, which secures salvation upon gospel-terms, that is *a good bond;* not one of our own devising, which brings salvation to our own fancies. They make sure the *good part*, who, like Mary, when they hear the word of Christ, *sit at his feet* in subjection to it: *Speak, Lord, for thy servant heareth.*

(2.) The particular parts of it teach us divers good lessons.

[1.] That we have every one of us a house to build, and that house is our hope for heaven. It ought to be our chief and constant care, to *make our calling and election sure*, and so we make our salvation sure; to secure a title to heaven's happiness, and then to get the comfortable evidence of it; to make it sure, and sure to ourselves, *that when we fail, we* shall *be received into everlasting habitations.* Many never mind this: it is the furthest thing from their thoughts; they are building for this world, as if they were to be here always, but take no care to build for another world. All who take upon them a profession of religion, profess to enquire, what they shall *do to be saved;* how they may get to heaven at last, and may have a well-grounded hope of it in the mean time.

[2.] That there is *a rock* provided for us to build this house upon, *and that rock is Christ.* He is *laid for a foundation*, and *other foundation can no man lay*, Isa. xxviii. 16; 1 Cor. iii. 11. He *is our Hope*, 1 Tim. 1. Christ in us is so; we must ground our hopes of heaven upon the fulness of Christ's merit, for the pardon of sin, the power of his Spirit, for the sanctification of our nature, and the prevalency of his intercession, for the conveyance of all that good which he has purchased for us. There is that in him, as *he is made known*, and made over, *to us in the gospel*, whch is sufficient to redress all our grievances, and to answer all the necessities of our case, so that he is *a Saviour to the uttermost.* The church is *built upon this Rock*, and so is every believer. He is strong and immovable as a *rock;* we may venture our all upon him, and shall not be made *ashamed of our hope.*

[3.] That there is a remnant, who by hearing and doing the *sayings of* Christ, build their hopes *upon* this *Rock;* and it is their wisdom. Christ is our only *Way to the Father*, and the obedience of faith is our only *way to* Christ: for *to them that obey him*, and to *them* only, he *becomes the Author of eternal salvation.* Those *build upon* Christ, who, having sincerely consented to him, as their Prince and Saviour, make it their constant care to conform to all the rules of his holy religion, and therein depend entirely upon him for assistance from God, and acceptance with him, *and count* every *thing but loss and dung that they may win Christ*, and be found in him. Building *upon a rock* requires care and pains: they that would make their *calling and election sure*, must *give diligence.* They are wise builders who *begin to build* so as they may be *able to finish* (Luke xiv. 30), and therefore lay a firm foundation.

[4.] That there are many who profess that they hope to go to heaven, but despise this *Rock*, and build their hopes *upon the sand;* which is done without much pains, but it is their folly. Every thing besides Christ is sand. Some build their hopes upon their worldly prosperity, as if that were a sure token of God's favour, Hos. xii. 8. Others upon their external profession of religion, the privileges they enjoy, and the performances they go through, in that profession, and the reputation they have got by it. They are called Christians, were baptized, go to church, hear Christ's word, say their prayers, and do nobody any harm, and, if they perish, God help a great many! This is the light of their own fire, which they walk in; this is that, upon which, with a great deal of assurance, they venture; but it is all sand, too weak to bear such a fabric as our hopes of heaven.

[5.] That there is a storm coming, that will try what our hopes are bottomed on; *will try every man's work* (1 Cor. iii. 13); *will discover the foundation*, Hab. iii. 13. *Rain, and floods, and wind, will beat upon the house;* the trial is sometimes in this world; *when tribulation and persecution arise because of the word*, then it will be seen, who only heard the word, and who heard and practised it; then when we have occasion to use our hopes, it will be tried whether they were right, and well-grounded, or not. However, when death and judgment come, then the storm comes, and it will undoubtedly come, how calm soever things may be with us now. Then every thing else will fail us but these hopes, and then, if ever, they will be turned into everlasting fruition.

[6.] That those hopes which are built upon Christ the Rock will stand, and will stand the builder in stead when the storm comes; they will be his preservation, both from desertion, and from prevailing disquiet. His profession will not wither; his comforts will not fail; they will be his strength and song, *as an anchor of the soul, sure and steadfast.* When he comes to the last encounter, those hopes will take off the terror of death and the grave; will carry him cheerfully through that dark valley; will be approved by the Judge; will stand the test of the great day; and will be crowned with endless glory, 2 Cor. i. 12; 2 Tim. iv. 7, 8. *Blessed is that servant, whom his Lord, when he comes, finds so doing,* so hoping.

[7.] That those hopes which foolish builders ground upon any thing but Christ, will certainly fail them on a stormy day; will yield them no true comfort and satisfaction in trouble, in the hour of death, and in the day of judgment; will be no fence against temptations to apostacy, in a time of persecution. *When God takes away the soul, where is the hope of the hypocrite?* Job xxvii. 8. It is as *the spider's web,* and as *the giving up of the ghost.* He shall *lean upon his house, but it shall not stand,* Job viii. 14, 15. It fell in the storm, when the builder had most need of it, and expected it would be a shelter to him. It fell when it was too late to build another: *when a wicked man dies, his expectation perishes;* then, when he thought it would have been turned into fruition, *it fell, and great was the fall of it.* It was a great disappointment to the builder; the shame and loss were great. The higher men's hopes have been raised, the lower they fall. It is the sorest ruin of all that attends formal professors; witness Capernaum's doom.

III. In the two last verses, we are told what impressions Christ's discourse made upon the auditory. It was an excellent sermon; and it is probable that he said more than is here recorded; and doubtless the delivery of it from the mouth of him, into whose lips grace was poured, did mightily set it off. Now, 1. *They were astonished at his doctrine;* it is to be feared that few of them were brought by it to follow him: but for the present, they were filled with wonder. Note, It is possible for people to admire good preaching, and yet to remain in ignorance and unbelief; to be astonished, and yet not sanctified. 2. The reason was because he taught them *as one having authority, and not as the scribes.* The scribes pretended to as much authority as any teachers whatsoever, and were supported by all the external advantages that could be obtained, but their preaching was mean, and flat, and jejune: they spake as those that were not themselves masters of what they preached: the word did not come from them with any life or force; they delivered it as a school-boy says his lesson; but Christ delivered his discourse, as a judge gives his charge. He did indeed, *dominari in conscionibus—deliver his discourses with a tone of authority;* his lessons were laws; his word a word of command. Christ, upon the mountain, showed more true authority, than the scribes in Moses's seat. Thus when Christ teaches by his Spirit in the soul, he teaches with authority. He says, *Let there be light, and there is light.*

CHAP. VIII.

The evangelist having, in the foregoing chapters, given us a specimen of our Lord's preaching, proceeds now to give some instances of the miracles he wrought, which prove him a Teacher come from God, and the great Healer of a diseased world. In this chapter we have, I. Christ's cleansing of a leper, ver. 1—4. II. His curing a palsy and fever, ver. 5—18. III. His communing with two that were disposed to follow him, ver. 19—22. IV. His controlling the tempest, ver. 23—27. V. His casting out devils, ver. 28—34.

WHEN he was come down from
the mountain, great multitudes followed him. 2 And, behold,
there came a leper and worshipped
him, saying, Lord, if thou wilt, thou
canst make me clean. 3 And Jesus
put forth *his* hand, and touched him,
saying, I will; be thou clean. And
immediately his leprosy was cleansed.
4 And Jesus saith unto him, See
thou tell no man; but go thy way,
show thyself to the priest, and offer
the gift that Moses commanded, for a
testimony unto them.

The first verse refers to the close of the foregoing sermon: the people that heard him were *astonished at his doctrine;* and the effect was, that *when he came down from the mountain, great multitudes followed him;* though he was so strict a Lawgiver, and so faithful a Reprover, they diligently attended him, and were loth to disperse, and go from him. Note, They to whom Christ has manifested himself, cannot but desire to be better acquainted with him. They who know much of Christ should covet to know more; and *then shall we know, if we* thus *follow on to know the Lord.* It is pleasing to see people so well affected to Christ, as to think they can never hear enough of him; so well affected to the best things, as thus to flock after good preaching, and to *follow the Lamb* whithersoever he goes. Now was Jacob's prophecy concerning the Messiah fulfilled, that *unto him shall the gathering of the people be;* yet they who gathered to him did not cleave to him. They who followed him closely and constantly were but few, compared with the multitudes that were but followers at large.

In these verses we have an account of Christ's *cleansing a leper.* It should seem, by comparing Mark i. 40, and Luke v. 12, that this passage, though placed, by St. Matthew, after the sermon on the mount, because he would give account of his doctrine first, and then of his miracles, happened some time before; but that is not at all material. This is fitly recorded with the first of Christ's miracles, 1. Because the leprosy was looked upon, among the Jews, as a particular mark of God's displeasure: hence we find Miriam, Gehazi, and Uzziah, smitten with leprosy for some one particular sin; and therefore Christ, to show that he came to turn away the wrath of God, by taking away sin, began with the cure of a leper. 2. Because this disease, as it was supposed to come immediately from the hand of God, so also it was supposed to be removed immediately by his hand, and therefore it was not attempted to be cured by physicians, but was put under the inspection of the priests, the Lord's ministers, who waited to see what God would do. And its being in a garment, or in the walls of a house, was altogether supernatural: and it should seem to be a disease of a quite different nature from what we now call the leprosy. The king of Israel said, *Am I God*, that I am sent to, to *recover a man of a leprosy?* 2 Kings v. 7. Christ proved himself God, by recovering many from the leprosy, and authorizing his disciples, in his name, to do so too (*ch.* x. 8), and it is put among the proofs of his being the Messiah, *ch.* xi. 5. He also showed himself to be the Saviour of his people from their sins; for though every disease is both the fruit of sin, and a figure of it, as the disorder of the soul, yet the leprosy was in a special manner so; for it contracted such a pollution, and obliged to such a separation from holy things, as no other disease did; and therefore in the laws concerning it (Lev. xiii. and xiv), it is treated, not as a sickness, but as an uncleanness; the priest was to pronounce the party clean or unclean, according to the indications: but the honour of making the lepers clean was reserved for Christ, who was to do it as the *High Priest of our profession;* he comes to do that which the *law could not do, in that it was weak through the flesh*, Rom. viii. 3. The law discovered sin (for by the law is the knowledge of sin), and pronounced sinners unclean; it shut them up (Gal. iii. 23), as the priest did the leper, but could go no further; it could not *make the comers thereunto perfect.* But Christ takes away sin; cleanses us from it, and so *perfecteth for ever them that are sanctified.* Now here we have,

I. The leper's address to Christ. If this happened, as it is here placed, after the sermon on the mount, we may suppose that the leper, though shut out by his disease from the cities of Israel, yet got within hearing of Christ's sermon, and was encouraged by it to make his application to him; for he that taught *as one having authority*, could heal so; and therefore he *came and worshipped him*, as one clothed with a divine power. His address is, *Lord, if thou wilt, thou canst make me clean.* The cleansing of him may be considered,

1. As a temporal mercy; a mercy to the body, delivering it from a disease, which, though it did not threaten life, embittered it. And so it directs us, not only to apply ourselves to Christ, who has power over bodily diseases, for the cure of them, but it also teaches us in what manner to apply ourselves to him; with an assurance of his power, believing that he is as able to cure diseases now, as he was when on earth, but with a submission to his will; *Lord, if thou wilt, thou canst.* As to temporal mercies, we cannot be so sure of God's *will* to bestow them, as we may of his *power*, for his *power* in them is unlimited, but his *promise* of them is limited by a regard to his glory and our good: when we cannot be sure of his will, we may be sure of his wisdom and mercy, to which we may cheerfully refer ourselves; *Thy will be done:* and this makes the expectation easy, and the event, when it comes, comfortable.

2. As a typical mercy. Sin is the leprosy of the soul; it shuts us out from communion with God, to which that we may be restored, it is necessary that we be cleansed from this leprosy, and this ought to be our great concern. Now observe, It is our comfort when we apply ourselves to Christ, as the great Physician, that if he will, he can make us clean; and we should, with an humble, believing boldness, go to him and tell him so. That is, (1.) We must rest ourselves upon his power; we must be confident of this, that Christ *can* make us clean. No guilt is so great but that there is a sufficiency in his righteousness to atone for it; no corruption so strong, but there is a sufficiency in his grace to subdue it. God would not appoint a physician to his hospital that is not *par negotio—every way qualified for the undertaking.* (2.) We must recommend ourselves to his pity; we cannot demand it as a debt, but we must humbly request it as a favour; "*Lord, if thou wilt.* I throw myself at thy feet, and if I perish, I will perish there."

II. Christ's answer to this address, which was very kind, *v.* 3.

1. *He put forth his hand and touched him.* The leprosy was a noisome, loathsome disease, yet Christ touched him; for he did not disdain to converse with publicans and sinners, to do them good. There was a ceremonial pollution contracted by the touch of a leper; but Christ would show, that when he conversed with sinners, he was in no danger of being infected by them, for the prince of this world had nothing in him. If we touch pitch, we are defiled; but Christ was *separate from sinners*, even when he lived among them.

2. He said, *I will, be thou clean.* He did not say, as Elisha to Naaman, *Go, wash in*

Jordan; did not put him upon a tedious, troublesome, chargeable course of physic, but spake the word and healed him. (1.) Here is a word of kindness, *I will;* I am as willing to help thee, as thou art to be helped. Note, They who by faith apply themselves to Christ for mercy and grace, may be sure that he is willing, freely willing, to give them the mercy and grace they come to him for. Christ is a Physician, that does not need to be sought for, he is always in the way; does not need to be urged, while we are yet speaking, he hears; does not need to be feed, he heals freely, not for price nor reward. He has given all possible demonstration, that he is as willing as he is able to save sinners. (2.) A word of power, *Be thou clean.* Both a power of authority, and a power of energy, are exerted in this word. Christ heals by a word of command to us; *Be thou clean;* "Be willing to be clean, and use the means; cleanse thyself from all filthiness;" but there goes along with this a word of command concerning us, a word that does the work; *I will that thou be clean.* Such a word as this is necessary to the cure, and effectual for it; and the Almighty grace which speaks it, shall not be wanting to those who truly desire it.

III. The happy change hereby wrought: *Immediately his leprosy was cleansed.* Nature works gradually, but the God of nature works immediately; he speaks, it is done; and yet he works effectually; he *commands, and it stands fast.* One of the first miracles Moses wrought, was curing himself of a leprosy (Exod. iv. 7), for the priests under the law offered sacrifices first for their own sin; but one of Christ's first miracles was curing another of leprosy, for he had no sin of his own to atone for.

IV. The after-directions Christ gave him. It is fit that they who are cured by Christ should ever after be ruled by him.

1. *See thou tell no man;* "Tell no man till thou hast shown thyself to the priest, and he has pronounced thee clean; and so thou hast a legal proof, both that thou wast before a leper, and art now thoroughly cleansed." Christ would have his miracles to appear in their full light and evidence, and not to be published till they could appear so. Note, They that preach the truths of Christ should be able to prove them; to defend what they preach, and *convince gainsayers.* "*Tell no man, till thou hast showed thyself to the priest,* lest if he hear who cured thee, he should out of spite deny to give thee a certificate of the cure, and so keep thee under confinement." Such were the priests in Christ's time, that they who had any thing to do with them had need to have been as wise as serpents.

2. *Go show thyself to the priest,* according to the law, Lev. xiv. 2. Christ took care to have the law observed, lest he should give offence, and to show that he will have order kept up, and good discipline and respect paid to those that are in office. It may be of use to those that are cleansed of their spiritual leprosy, to have recourse to Christ's ministers, and to open their case to them, that they may assist them in their enquiries into their spiritual state, and advise, and comfort, and pray for them.

3. *Offer the gift that Moses commanded,* in token of thankfulness to God, and recompence to the priest for his pains; and this *for a testimony unto them;* either, (1.) Which *Moses commanded for a testimony:* the ceremonial laws were testimonies of God's authority over them, care of them, and of that grace which should afterwards be revealed. Or, (2.) "Do thou offer it for a testimony, and let the priest know who cleansed thee, and how; and it shall be a testimony, that there is one among them who does that which the high priest cannot do. Let it remain upon record as a witness of my power, and a testimony for me *to* them, if they will use it and improve it; but *against* them, if they will not:" for so Christ's word and works are testimonies.

5 And when Jesus was entered
into Capernaum, there came unto
him a centurion, beseeching him, 6
And saying, Lord, my servant lieth
at home sick of the palsy, grievously
tormented. 7 And Jesus saith unto
him, I will come and heal him. 8
The centurion answered and said,
Lord, I am not worthy that thou
shouldest come under my roof: but
speak the word only, and my servant
shall be healed. 9 For I am a man
under authority, having soldiers under me: and I say to this *man*, Go,
and he goeth; and to another, Come,
and he cometh; and to my servant,
Do this, and he doeth *it*. 10 When
Jesus heard *it*, he marvelled, and
said to them that followed, Verily I
say unto you, I have not found so
great faith, no, not in Israel. 11 And
I say unto you, That many shall come
from the east and west, and shall sit
down with Abraham, and Isaac, and
Jacob, in the kingdom of heaven.
12 But the children of the kingdom
shall be cast out into outer darkness:
there shall be weeping and gnashing
of teeth. 13 And Jesus said unto
the centurion, Go thy way; and as
thou hast believed, *so* be it done unto
thee. And his servant was healed in
the self-same hour.

We have here an account of Christ's curing

the centurion's servant of a palsy. This was done at Capernaum, where Christ now dwelt, *ch.* iv. 13. Christ went about doing good, and came home to do good too; every place he came to was the better for him.

The persons Christ had now to do with were,

1. A *centurion;* he was a supplicant, a Gentile, a Roman, an officer of the army; probably commander-in-chief of that part of the Roman army which was quartered at Capernaum, and kept garrison there. (1.) Though he was a soldier (and a little piety commonly goes a great way with men of that profession), yet he was a godly man; he was eminently so. Note, God has his remnant among all sorts of people. No man's calling or place in the world will be an excuse for his unbelief and impiety; none shall say in the great day, I had been religious, if I had not been a soldier; for such there are among the *ransomed of the Lord.* And sometimes where grace conquers the unlikely, it is more than a conqueror; this soldier that was good, was very good. (2.) Though he was a Roman soldier, and his very dwelling among the Jews was a badge of their subjection to the Roman yoke, yet Christ, who was *King of the Jews,* favoured him; and therein has taught us to do good to our enemies, and not needlessly to interest ourselves in national enmities. (3.) Though he was a Gentile, yet Christ countenanced him. It is true, he went not to any of the Gentile towns (it was the land of Caanan that was Immanuel's land, Isa. viii. 8), yet he received addresses from Gentiles; now good old Simeon's word began to be fulfilled, that he should be *a light to lighten the Gentiles,* as well as *the glory of his people Israel.* Matthew, in annexing this cure to that of the leper, who was a Jew, intimates this; the leprous Jews Christ touched and cured, for he preached personally to them; but the paralytic Gentiles he cured at a distance; for to them he did not go in person, but *sent his word and healed them;* yet in them he was more magnified.

2. *The centurion's servant;* he was the patient. In this also it appears, that there is no respect of persons with God; for *in Christ Jesus,* as there is *neither circumcision nor uncircumcision,* so there is *neither bond nor free.* He is as ready to heal the poorest servant, as the richest master; for himself *took upon him the form of a servant,* to show his regard to the meanest.

Now in the story of the cure of this servant, we may observe an intercourse or interchanging of graces, very remarkable between Christ and the centurion. See here,

I. The grace of the centurion working towards Christ. Can any good thing come out of a Roman soldier? any thing tolerable, much less any thing laudable? Come and see, and you will find abundance of good coming out of this centurion that was eminent and exemplary. Observe,

1. His affectionate address to Jesus Christ, which speaks,

(1.) A pious regard to our great Master, as one able and willing to succour and relieve poor petitioners. He came to him *beseeching him,* not as Naaman the Syrian (a centurion too) came to Elisha, demanding a cure, taking state, and standing upon points of honour; but with cap in hand as a humble suitor. By this it seems that he saw more in Christ than appeared at first view; saw that which commanded respect, though to those who looked no further, his visage was marred more than any man's. The officers of the army, being comptrollers of the town, no doubt made a great figure, yet he lays by the thoughts of his post of honour, when he addresses himself to Christ, and comes *beseeching him.* Note, the greatest of men must turn beggars, when they have to do with Christ. He owns Christ's sovereignty, in calling him Lord, and referring the case to him, and to his will, and wisdom, by a modest remonstrance, without any formal and express petition. He knew he had to do with a wise and gracious Physician, to whom the opening of the malady was equivalent to the most earnest request. A humble confession of our spiritual wants and diseases shall not fail of an answer of peace. Pour out thy complaint, and mercy shall be poured out.

(2.) A charitable regard to his poor servant. We read of many that came to Christ for their children, but this is the only instance of one that came to him for a servant: *Lord, my servant lieth at home sick.* Note, it is the duty of masters to concern themselves for their servants, when they are in affliction. The palsy disabled the servant for his work, and made him as troublesome and tedious as any distemper could, yet he did not turn him away when he was sick (as that Amalekite did his servants, 1 Sam. xxx. 13), did not send him to his friends, nor let him lie by neglected, but sought out the best relief he could for him; the servant could not have done more for the master, than the master did here for the servant. The centurion's servants were very dutiful to him (*v.* 9), and here we see what made them so; he was very kind to them, and that made them the more cheerfully obedient to him. As we must not despise the *cause of our servants, when they contend with us* (Job xxxi. 13, 15), so we must not despise their case when God contends with them; for we are made in the same mould, by the same hand, and stand upon the same level with them before God, and must not set them *with the dogs of our flock.* The centurion applies not to witches or wizards for his servant, but to Christ. The palsy is a disease in which the physician's skill commonly fails; it was therefore a great evidence of his faith in the power of Christ, to come to him for a cure, which was above the power of natural means to effect. Observe,

How pathetically he represents his servant's case as very sad; he is *sick of the palsy,* a disease which commonly makes the patient senseless of pain, but this person was *grievously tormented;* being young, nature was strong to struggle with the stroke, which made it painful. (It was not *paralysis simplex,* but *scorbutica*). We should thus concern ourselves for the souls of our children, and servants, that are spiritually sick of the palsy, the dead-palsy, the dumb palsy; senseless of spiritual evils, inactive in that which is spiritually good; and bring them to Christ by faith and prayer, bring them to the means of healing and health.

2. Observe his great humility and self-abasement. After Christ had intimated his readiness to come and heal his servant (*v.* 7), he expressed himself with the more humbleness of mind. Note, Humble souls are made more humble, by Christ's gracious condescensions to them. Observe what was the language of his humility; *Lord, I am not worthy that thou shouldst come under my roof* (*v.* 8), which speaks mean thoughts of himself, and high thoughts of our Lord Jesus. He does not say, "My servant is not worthy that thou shouldst come into his chamber, because it is in the garret;" But *I am not worthy that thou shouldst come into my house.* The centurion was a great man, yet he owned his unworthiness before God. Note, Humility very well becomes persons of quality. Christ now made but a mean figure in the world yet the centurion, looking upon him as prophet, *yea, more than a prophet,* paid him this respect. Note, We should have a value and veneration for what we see of God, even in those who, in outward condition, are every way our inferiors. The centurion came to Christ with a petition, and therefore expressed himself thus humbly. Note, In all our approaches to Christ, and to God through Christ, it becomes us to abase ourselves, and to lie low in the sense of our own unworthiness, as mean creatures and as vile sinners, to do any thing for God, to receive any good from him, or to have any thing to do with him.

3. Observe his great faith. The more humility the more faith; the more diffident we are of ourselves, the stronger will be our confidence in Jesus Christ. He had an assurance of faith not only that Christ could cure his servant, but,

(1.) That he could cure him at a distance. There needed not any physical contact, as in natural operations, nor any application to the part affected; but the cure, he believed, might be wrought, without bringing the physician and patient together. We read afterwards of those, who brought the *man sick of the palsy to Christ,* through much difficulty, and set him before him; and Christ commended their faith for a *working* faith. This centurion did not bring his man *sick of the palsy,* and Christ commended his faith for a *trusting* faith: true faith is accepted of Christ, though variously appearing: Christ puts the best construction upon the different methods of religion that people take, and thereby has taught us to do so too. This centurion believed, and it is undoubtedly true, that the power of Christ knows no limits, and therefore nearness and distance are alike to him. Distance of place cannot obstruct either the knowing or working of him that *fills all places. Am I a God at hand, says the Lord, and not a God afar off?* Jer xxiii. 23.

(2.) That he could cure him with a *word,* not send him a medicine, much less a charm; but *speak the word only,* and I do not question but *my servant shall be healed.* Herein he owns him to have a divine power, an authority to command all the creatures and powers of nature, which enables him to do whatsoever he pleases in the kingdom of nature; as at first he raised that kingdom by an almighty word, when he said, *Let there be light.* With men, saying and doing are two things; but not so with Christ, who is therefore the *Arm of the Lord,* because he is the *eternal Word.* His saying, *Be ye warmed and filled* (Jam. ii. 16), and healed, warms, and fills and heals.

The centurion's faith in the power of Christ he here illustrates by the dominion he had, as a centurion, over his soldiers, as a master over his servants; he says to one, *Go, and he goes, &c.* They were all at his beck and command, so as that he could by them execute things at a distance; his word was a law to them—*dictum factum;* well-disciplined soldiers know that the commands of their officers are not to be disputed, but obeyed. Thus could Christ speak, and it is done; such a power had he over all bodily diseases. The centurion had this command over his soldiers, though he was himself a *man under authority;* not a commander-in-chief, but a subaltern officer; much more had Christ this power, who is the supreme and sovereign Lord of all. The centurion's servants were very obsequious, would go and come at every the least intimation of their master's mind. Now, [1.] Such servants we all should be to God: we must go and come at his bidding, according to the directions of his word, and the disposals of his providence; run where he sends us, return when he remands us, and do what he appoints. *What saith my Lord unto his servant?* When his will crosses our own, his must take place, and our own be set aside. [2.] Such servants bodily diseases are to Christ. They seize us when he sends them; they leave us when he calls them back; they have that effect upon us, upon our bodies, upon our souls, that he orders. It is a matter of comfort to all that belong to Christ, for whose good his power is exerted and engaged, that every disease has his commission, executes his command, is under his control, and is made to serve the intentions of his grace. They need not fear sickness, nor what it can do, who see it in the hand of so good a Friend.

II. Here is the grace of Christ appearing towards this centurion; for to the gracious he will show himself gracious.

1. He complies with his address at the first word. He did but tell him his servant's case, and was going on to beg a cure, when Christ prevented him, with this good word, and comfortable word, *I will come and heal him* (*v.* 7); not *I will come and see him*—that had evinced him a kind Saviour; but, *I will come and heal him*—that shows him a mighty, an almighty Saviour; it was a great word, but no more than he could make good; for he has *healing under his wings;* his coming is healing. They who wrought miracles by a derived power, did not speak thus positively, as Christ did, who wrought them by his own power, as one that had authority. When a minister is sent for to a sick friend, he can but say, *I will come and pray for him;* but Christ says, *I will come and heal him:* it is well that Christ can do more for us than our ministers can. The centurion desired he would heal his servant; he says, *I will come and heal him;* thus expressing more favour than he did either ask or think of. Note, Christ often outdoes the expectations of poor supplicants. See an instance of Christ's humility, that he would make a visit to a poor soldier. He would not go down to see a nobleman's sick child, who insisted upon his coming down (John iv. 47—49), but he proffers to go down to see a sick servant; thus does he regard *the low estate* of his people, and give *more abundant honour to that part which lacked.* Christ's humility, in being willing to come, gave an example to him, and occasioned his humility, in owning himself unworthy to have him come. Note, Christ's gracious condescensions to us, should make us the more humble and self-abasing before him.

2. He commends his faith, and takes occasion from it to speak a kind word of the poor Gentiles, *v.* 10—12. See what great things a strong but self-denying faith can obtain from Jesus Christ, even of general and public concern.

(1.) As to the centurion himself; he not only approved him and accepted him (that honour have all true believers), but he admired him and applauded him: that honour great believers have, as Job; there is *none like unto him in the earth.*

[1.] Christ admired him, not for his greatness, but for his graces. *When Jesus heard it, he marvelled;* not as if it were to him new and surprising, he knew the centurion's faith, for he wrought it; but it was great and excellent, rare and uncommon, and Christ spoke of it as wonderful, to teach us what to admire; not worldly pomp and decorations, but the beauty of holiness, and the ornaments which are *in the sight of God of great price.* Note, The wonders of grace should affect us more than the wonders of nature or providence, and spiritual attainments more than any achievements in this world. Of those that are *rich in faith,* not of those that are *rich in gold and silver,* we should say that they have *gotten all this glory,* Gen. xxxi. 1. But whatever there is admirable in the faith of any, it must redound to the glory of Christ, who will shortly be himself *admired in all them that believe,* as having done in and for them *marvellous things.*

[2.] He *applauded* him in what he said to *them that followed.* All believers shall be, *in the other world,* but some believers are, *in this world,* confessed and acknowledged by Christ before men, in his eminent appearances for them and with them. *Verily, I have not found so great faith, no, not in Israel.* Now this speaks, *First, Honour to the centurion;* who, though not a son of Abraham's loins, was an heir of Abraham's faith, and Christ found it so. Note, The thing that Christ seeks is *faith,* and wherever it is, he finds it, though but *as a grain of mustard-seed.* He had not found *so great faith,* all things considered, and in proportion to the means; as the poor widow is said to *cast in more than they all,* Luke xxi. 3. Though the centurion was a Gentile, yet he was thus commended. Note, We must be so far from grudging, that we must be forward, to give those their due praise, that are not within our denomination or pale. *Secondly,* It speaks *shame to Israel,* to whom pertained *the adoption, the glory, the covenants,* and all the assistances and encouragements of faith. Note, When *the Son of man comes,* he *finds* little *faith,* and, therefore, he finds so little *fruit.* Note, the attainments of some, who have had but little helps for their souls, will aggravate the sin and ruin of many, that have had great plenty of the means of grace, and have not made a good improvement of them. Christ said this *to those that followed* him, if by any means he might provoke them to a holy emulation, as Paul speaks, Rom. xi. 14. They were Abraham's seed; in jealousy for that honour, let them not suffer themselves to be outstripped by a Gentile, especially in that grace for which Abraham was eminent.

(2.) As to others. Christ takes occasion from hence to make a comparison between Jews and Gentiles, and tells them two things, which could not but be very surprising to them who had been taught that *salvation was of the Jews.*

[1.] That *a great many of the Gentiles should be saved, v.* 11. The faith of the centurion was but a specimen of the conversion of the Gentiles, and a preface to their adoption into the church. This was a topic our Lord Jesus touched often upon; he speaks it with assurance; *I say unto you,* "I that know all men; and he could not say any thing more pleasing to himself, or more displeasing to the Jews; an intimation of this kind enraged the Nazarenes against him, Luke

iv. 27. Christ gives us here an *idea, First,* of the *persons* that shall be *saved;* many *from the east and the west:* he had said (*ch.* vii. 14), *Few there be that find the way to life;* and yet here *many shall come.* Few at one time, and in one place; yet, when they come altogether, they will be a great many. We now see but here and there one brought to grace; but we shall shortly see the Captain of our salvation *bringing many sons to glory,* Heb. ii. 10. He will come with *ten thousands of his saints* (Jude 14), with such a company as *no man can number* (Rev. vii. 9); *with nations of them that are saved,* Rev. xxi. 24. They shall come *from the east* and *from the west;* places far distant from each other; and yet they shall all meet at the right hand of Christ, the Centre of their unity. Note, God has his remnant in all places; *from the rising of the sun, to the going down of the same,* Mal. i. 11. The elect will be gathered from the four winds, *ch.* xxiv. 31. They are *sown in the earth,* some scattered in every corner of the field. The Gentile world lay *from east to west,* and they are especially meant here; though they were *strangers to the covenant of promise* now, and had been long, yet who knows what *hidden ones* God had among them then? As in Elijah's time in Israel (1 Kings xix. 14), soon after which they flocked into the church in great multitudes, Isa. lx. 3, 4. Note, When we come to heaven, as we shall miss a great many there, that we thought had been going thither, so we shall meet a great many there, that we did not expect. *Secondly,* Christ gives us an idea of the *salvation itself.* They shall come, shall come together, shall come together to Christ, 2 Thess. ii. 1. 1. They shall be admitted *into the kingdom of grace* on earth, into the covenant of grace made with Abraham, Isaac, and Jacob; they shall be *blessed with faithful Abraham,* whose blessing comes upon the Gentiles, Gal. iii. 14. This makes Zaccheus a son of Abraham, Luke xix. 9. 2. They shall be admitted into the *kingdom of glory in heaven.* They shall come cheerfully, flying *as doves to their windows;* they shall sit down to rest from their labours, as having done their day's work; sitting denotes *continuance:* while we *stand,* we are *going;* where we *sit,* we mean to *stay;* heaven is a *remaining* rest, it is a *continuing* city; they shall *sit down,* as upon a throne (Rev. iii. 21); as *at a table;* that is the metaphor here; they shall sit down to be *feasted;* which denotes both *fulness* of *communication,* and *freedom* and familiarity of communion, Luke xxii. 30. They shall *sit down with Abraham.* They who in this world were ever so far distant from each other in time, place, or outward condition, shall all meet together in heaven; ancients and moderns, Jews and Gentiles, rich and poor. The rich man in hell *sees* Abraham, but Lazarus *sits down with him,* leaning on his breast. Note, Holy society is a part of the felicity of heaven; and they on whom the ends of the world are come, and who are most obscure, shall share in glory with the renowned patriarchs.

[2.] That a great many of the Jews should perish, v. 12. Observe,

First, A strange sentence passed; *The children of the kingdom shall be cast out;* the Jews that persist in unbelief, though they were by birth *children of the kingdom,* yet shall be cut off from being members of the visible church: *the kingdom of God,* of which they boasted that they were *the children,* shall be taken from them, and they shall become *not a people,* not *obtaining mercy,* Rom. xi. 20; ix. 31. In the great day it will not avail men to have been *children of the kingdom,* either as Jews or as Christians; for men will then be judged, not by what they were *called,* but by what they *were. If children* indeed, *then heirs;* but many are children in profession, in the family, but not of it, that will come short of the inheritance. Being born of professing parents denominates us *children of the kingdom;* but if we rest in that, and have nothing else to show for heaven but that, we shall be *cast out.*

Secondly, A strange punishment for *the workers of iniquity* described; *They shall be cast into outer darkness,* the darkness of those that are without, of the Gentiles that were out of the church; into that the Jews were cast, and into worse; they were blinded, and hardened, and filled with terrors, as the apostle shows, Rom. xi. 8—10. A people so unchurched and given up to spiritual judgments, are in *utter darkness* already: but it looks further, to the state of damned sinners in hell, to which the other is a dismal preface. *They shall be cast out* from God, and all true comfort, and *cast into darkness.* In hell there is fire, but no light; it is *utter darkness;* darkness in extremity; the highest degree of darkness, without any remainder, or mixture, or hope, of light; not the least gleam or glimpse of it; it is darkness that results from their being shut out of heaven, the land of light; they who are *without,* are in *the regions of darkness;* yet that is not the worst of it, *there shall be weeping and gnashing of teeth.* 1. In hell there will be great grief, floods of tears shed to no purpose; anguish of spirit preying eternally upon the vitals, in the sense of the wrath of God, is the torment of the damned. 2. Great indignation: damned sinners will *gnash their teeth* for spite and vexation, *full of the fury of the Lord;* seeing with envy the happiness of others, and reflecting with horror upon the former possibility of their own being happy, which is now past.

3. He cures his servant. He not only commends his application to him, but grants him that for which he applied, which was a real answer, *v.* 13. Observe,

(1.) What Christ said to him: he said that which made the cure as great a favour to him as it was to his servant, and much greater;

As thou hast believed, so be it done to thee. The servant got a cure of his disease, but the master got the confirmation and approbation of his faith. Note, Christ often gives encouraging answers to his praying people, when they are interceding for others. It is kindness to us, to be heard for others. God turned the captivity of Job, when he prayed for his friends, Job xlii. 10. It was a great honour which Christ put upon this centurion, when he gave him a blank, as it were; *Be it done as thou believest.* What could he have more? Yet what was said to him is said to us all, *Believe, and ye shall receive; only believe.* See here the power of Christ, and the power of faith. As Christ can *do* what he will, so an active believer may *have* what he will from Christ; the oil of grace multiplies, and stays not till the vessels of faith fail.

(2.) What was the effect of this saying: the prayer of faith was a prevailing prayer, it ever was so, and ever will be so; it appears, by the suddenness of the cure, that it was *miraculous:* and by its coincidence with Christ's saying, that the miracle was *his; he spake, and it was done;* and this was a proof of his omnipotence, that he has a long arm. It is the observation of a learned physician, that the diseases Christ cured were chiefly such as were the most difficult to be cured by any natural means, and particularly the palsy. *Omnis paralysis, præsertim vetusta, aut incurabilis est, aut difficilis curatu, etiam pueris: atque soleo ego dicere, morbos omnes qui Christo curandi fuerunt propositi, difficillimos suâ naturâ curatu esse—Every kind of palsy, especially of long continuance, is either incurable, or is found to yield with the utmost difficulty to medical skill, even in young subjects; so that I have frequently remarked, that all the diseases which were referred to Christ for cure appear to have been of the most obstinate and hopeless kind.* Mercurialis *De Morbis Puerorum,* lib. 2. cap. 5.

14 And when Jesus was come
into Peter's house, he saw his wife's
mother laid, and sick of a fever. 15
And he touched her hand, and the
fever left her: and she arose, and
ministered unto them. 16 When the
even was come, they brought unto
him many that were possessed with
devils: and he cast out the spirits
with *his* word, and healed all that
were sick: 17 That it might be fulfilled which was spoken by Esaias the
prophet, saying, Himself took our
infirmities, and bare *our* sicknesses.

They who pretend to be critical in the Harmony of the evangelists, place this passage, and all that follows to the end of *ch.* ix. before the sermon on the mount, according to the order which Mark and Luke observe in placing it. Dr. Lightfoot places only this passage before the sermon on the mount, and *v.* 18, &c. after. Here we have,

I. A particular account of the cure of *Peter's wife's mother,* who was ill *of a fever;* in which observe,

1. The *case,* which was nothing extraordinary; fevers are the most common distempers; but, the patient being a near relation of Peter's, it is recorded as an instance of Christ's peculiar care of, and kindness to, the families of his disciples. Here we find, (1.) That Peter had a *wife,* and yet *was called to be an apostle of Christ;* and Christ countenanced the marriage state, by being thus kind to his *wife's* relations. The church of Rome, therefore, which forbids ministers to marry, goes contrary to that apostle from whom they pretend to derive an infallibility. (2.) That Peter had a *house,* though Christ had not, *v.* 20. Thus was the disciple better provided for than his Lord. (3.) That he had a house at Capernaum, though he was originally of Bethsaida; it is probable, he removed to Capernaum, when Christ removed thither, and made that his principal residence. Note, It is worth while to change our quarters, that we may be near to Christ, and have opportunities of converse with him. When the ark removes, Israel must remove and go after it. (4.) That he had his *wife's mother* with him in his family, which is an example to yoke-fellows to be kind to one another's relations as their own. Probably, this good woman was old, and yet was respected and taken care of, as old people ought to be, with all possible tenderness. (5.) That she lay ill *of a fever.* Neither the strength of youth, nor the weakness and coldness of age, will be a fence against diseases of this kind. The palsy was a chronical disease, the fever an acute disease, but both were brought to Christ.

2. The *cure, v.* 15. (1.) How it was *effected; He touched her hand;* not to know the disease, as the physicians do, by the pulse, but to heal it. This was an intimation of his kindness and tenderness; he is *himself touched with the feeling of our infirmities;* it likewise shows the way of spiritual healing, by the exerting of the power of Christ with his word, and the application of Christ to ourselves. The scripture *speaks the word,* the Spirit gives the touch, touches the heart, touches the hand. (2.) How it was *evidenced:* this showed that the *fever left her, she arose, and ministered to them.* By this it appears, [1.] That the mercy was perfected. They that recover from fevers by the power of nature are commonly weak and feeble, and unfit for business a great while after; to show therefore that this cure was above the power of nature, she was immediately so well as to go about the business of the house. [2.] That the mercy was sanctified; and the mercies that are so are indeed perfected. Though she was thus dignified by a peculiar favour, yet she does not assume importance,

but is as ready to wait at table, if there be occasion, as any servant. They must be humble whom Christ has honoured; being thus delivered, she studies what she shall render. It is very fit that they whom Christ hath healed should minister unto him, as his humble servants, all their days.

II. Here is a general account of the many cures that Christ wrought. This cure of Peter's mother-in-law brought him abundance of patients. "He healed such a one; why not me? Such a one's friend, why not mine?" Now we are here told,

1. What he did, *v.* 16. (1.) *He cast out devils; cast out the* evil *spirits with his word.* There may be much of Satan's agency, by the divine permission, in those diseases of which natural causes may be assigned, as in Job's boils, especially in the diseases of the mind; but, about the time of Christ's being in the world, there seems to have been more than ordinary letting loose of the devil, to possess and vex the bodies of people; he came, *having great wrath, for he knew that his time was short;* and God wisely ordered it so, that Christ might have the fairer and more frequent opportunities of showing his power over Satan, and the purpose and design of his coming into the world, which was to disarm and dispossess Satan, to break his power, and to destroy his works; and his success was as glorious as his design was gracious. (2.) *He healed all that were sick;* all without exception, though the patient was ever so mean, and the case ever so bad.

2. How the scripture was herein fulfilled, *v.* 17. The accomplishment of the Old-Testament prophecies was the great thing Christ had in his eye, and the great proof of his being the Messiah: among other things, it was written of him (Isa. liii. 4), *Surely he hath borne our griefs, and carried our sorrows*: it is referred to, 1 Pet. ii. 24, and there it is construed, *he hath borne our sins;* here it is referred to, and is construed, *he hath borne our sicknesses;* our sins make our sicknesses our griefs; Christ bore away sin by the merit of his death, and bore away sickness by the miracles of his life; nay, though those miracles are ceased, we may say, that *he bore our sicknesses* then, *when he bore our sins in his own body upon the tree;* for sin is both the cause and the sting of sickness. Many are the diseases and calamities to which we are liable in the body: and there is more, in this one line of the gospels, to support and comfort us under them, than in all the writings of the philosophers—that Jesus Christ *bore our sicknesses, and carried our sorrows;* he bore them before us; though he was never sick, yet he was hungry, and thirsty, and weary, and troubled in spirit, sorrowful and very heavy; he bore them for us in his *passion,* and bears them with us in *compassion,* being *touched with the feeling of our infirmities:* and thus he bears them off from us, and makes them sit light, if it be not our own fault. Observe how emphatically it is expressed here: *Himself took our infirmities, and bare our sicknesses;* he was both able and willing to interpose in that matter, and concerned to deal with *our infirmities and sicknesses,* as our Physician; that part of the calamity of the human nature was his particular care, which he evidenced by his great readiness to cure diseases; and he is no less powerful, no less tender now, for we are sure that never were any the worse for going to heaven.

18 Now when Jesus saw great
multitudes about him, he gave commandment to depart unto the other
side. 19 And a certain scribe came,
and said unto him, Master, I will
follow thee whithersoever thou goest.
20 And Jesus saith unto him, The
foxes have holes, and the birds of the
air *have* nests; but the Son of man
hath not where to lay *his* head. 21
And another of his disciples said
unto him, Lord, suffer me first to go
and bury my father. 22 But Jesus
said unto him, Follow me; and let
the dead bury their dead.

Here is, I. Christ's removing to *the other side of the sea of Tiberias,* and his ordering his disciples, whose boats attended him, to get their transport-vessels ready, in order to it, *v.* 18. The influences of this Sun of righteousness were not to be confined to one place, but diffused all the country over; he must go about to do good; the necessities of souls called to him, *Come over, and help us* (Acts xvi. 9); he removed *when he saw great multitudes about him.* Though by this it appeared that they were desirous to have him there, he knew there were others as desirous to have him with them, and they must have their share of him: his being acceptable and useful in one place was no objection against, but a reason for, his going to another. Thus he would try the multitudes that were *about him,* whether their zeal would carry them to follow him, and attend on him, when his preaching was removed to some distance. Many would be glad of such helps, if they could have them at next door, who will not be at the pains to follow them to *the other side;* and thus Christ shook off those who were less zealous, and the perfect were made manifest.

II. Christ's communication with two, who, upon his remove to *the other side,* were loth to stay behind, and had a mind to follow him, not as others, who were his followers at large, but to come into close discipleship, which the most were shy of; for it carried such a face of strictness as they could not like, nor be well reconciled to; but here is an account of two who seemed desirous to come into communion, and yet were not right; which is here given as a specimen of the hindrances by which many are kept from closing with Christ, and cleaving to him; and a warning to us, to set out in following Christ, so as that we may not come short; to lay such a foundation, as that our building may stand.

We have here Christ's managing of two different tempers, one quick and eager, the other dull and heavy; and his instructions are adapted to each of them, and designed for our use.

1. Here is one that was *too hasty in promising;* and he was *a certain scribe* (*v.* 19), a scholar, a learned man, one of those that studied and expounded the law; generally we find them in the gospels to be men of no good character; usually coupled with the Pharisees, as enemies to Christ and his doctrine. *Where is the scribe?* 1 Cor. i. 20. He is very seldom following Christ; yet here was one that bid pretty fair for discipleship, a *Saul among the prophets.* Now observe,

(1.) How he expressed his forwardness; *Master, I will follow thee, whithersoever thou goest.* I know not how any man could have spoken better. His profession of a self-dedication to Christ is, [1.] Very ready, and seems to be *ex mero motu—from his unbiassed inclination:* he is not called to it by Christ, nor urged by any of the disciples, but, of his own accord, he proffers himself to be a close follower of Christ; he is not a pressed man, but a volunteer. [2.] Very resolute; he seems to be at a point in this matter; he does not say, "I have a mind to *follow thee;*" but, "I am determined, *I will* do it." [3.] It was unlimited and without reserve; "*I will follow thee whithersoever thou goest;* not only to *the other side* of the country, but if it were to the utmost regions of the world." Now we should think ourselves sure of such a man as this; and yet it appears, by Christ's answer, that his resolution was rash, his ends low and carnal: either he did not consider at all, or not that which was to be considered; he saw the miracles Christ wrought, and hoped he would set up a temporal kingdom, and he wished to apply betimes for a share in it. Note, There are many resolutions for religion, produced by some sudden pangs of conviction, and taken up without due consideration, that prove abortive, and come to nothing: soon ripe, soon rotten.

(2.) How Christ tried his forwardness, whether it were sincere or not, *v.* 20. He let him know that this *Son of man,* whom he is so eager to follow, *has not where to lay his head, v.* 20. Now from this account of Christ's deep poverty, we observe,

[1.] That it is strange in itself, that the Son of God, when he came into the world, should put himself into such a very low condition, as to want the convenience of a certain resting-place, which the meanest of the creatures have. If he would *take our nature upon him,* one would think, he should have taken it in its best estate and circumstances: no, he takes it in its worst. See here, *First,* How well provided for the inferior creatures are: *The foxes have holes;* though they are not only not useful, but hurtful, to man, yet God provides holes for them in which they are earthed: man endeavours to destroy them, but thus they are sheltered; their holes are their castles. *The birds of the air,* though they take no care for themselves, yet are taken care of, and *have nests* (Ps. civ. 17); *nests* in the field; some of them *nests* in the house; in God's courts, Ps. lxxxiv. 3. *Secondly,* How poorly the Lord Jesus was provided for. It may encourage us to trust God for necessaries, that the beasts and birds have such good provision; and may comfort us, if we want necessaries, that our Master did so before us. Note, Our Lord Jesus, when he was here in the world, submitted to the disgraces and distresses of extreme poverty; *for our sakes he became poor,* very poor. He had not a settlement, had not a place of repose, not a house of his own, to put his head in, not a pillow of his own, to lay his head on. He and his disciples lived upon the charity of well-disposed people, that *ministered to him of their substance,* Luke viii. 2. Christ submitted to this, not only that he might in all respects humble himself, and fulfil the scriptures, which spake of him as *poor and needy,* but that he might show us the vanity of worldly wealth, and teach us to look upon it with a holy contempt; that he might purchase better things for us, and so *make us rich,* 2 Cor. viii. 9.

[2.] It is strange that such a declaration should be made on this occasion. When a scribe offered to follow Christ, one would think he would have encouraged him, and said, *Come, and I will take care of thee;* one scribe might be capable of doing him more credit and service than twelve fishermen: but Christ saw his heart, and answered to the thoughts of that, and therein teaches us all how to come to Christ. *First,* The scribe's resolve seems to have been sudden; and Christ would have us, when we take upon us a profession of religion, to *sit down and count the cost* (Luke xiv. 28), to do it intelligently, and with consideration, and choose the way of godliness, not because we know no other, but because we know no better. It is no advantage to religion, to take men by surprise, ere they are aware. They that take up a profession *in a pang,* will throw it off again *in a fret;* let them, therefore, *take time,* and they will have *done the sooner:* let him that will follow Christ know the worst of it, and expect to lie hard, and fare hard. *Secondly,* His resolve seems to have been from a worldly, covetous principle. He saw what abundance of cures Christ wrought, and concluded that he had large fees, and would get an estate quickly, and therefore he would follow him in hopes of growing rich with him; but Christ rectifies his mistake, and tells him, he was so far from growing rich, that he had not a place to *lay his head on;* and that if he follow him, he cannot expect to fare better than he fared. Note, Christ will accept none for his followers that aim at worldly advantages in following him, or design to make any thing but heaven of their religion. We have reason to think that this scribe, hereupon, *went away sorrowful*, being disappointed in a bargain which he thought would turn to account; he is not for following Christ, unless he can *get by him.*

2. Here is another that was too *slow in performing.* Delay in execution is as bad, on the one hand, as precipitancy in resolution is on the other hand; when we have taken time to consider, and then have determined, let it never be said, we left that to be done to-morrow, which we could do to-day. This candidate for the ministry was one of Christ's disciples already (*v.* 21), a follower of him at large. Clemens Alexandrinus tells us, from an ancient tradition, that this was Philip; he seems to be better qualified and disposed than the former; because not so confident and presumptuous: a bold, eager, over-forward temper is not the most promising in religion; sometimes the last are first, and the first last. Now observe here,

(1.) The excuse that this disciple made, to defer an immediate attendance on Christ (*v.* 21); "*Lord, suffer me first to go and bury my father.* Before I come to be a close and constant follower of thee, let me be allowed to perform this last office of respect to my father; and in the mean time, let it suffice to be a hearer of thee now and then, when I can spare time." His father (some think) was now sick, or dying, or dead; others think, he was only aged, and not likely in a course of nature, to continue long; and he desired leave to attend upon him in his sickness, at his death, and to his grave, and then he would be at Christ's service. This seemed a reasonable request, and yet it was not right. He had not the zeal he should have had for the work, and therefore pleaded this, because it seemed a plausible plea. Note, An unwilling mind never wants an excuse. The meaning of *Non vacat* is, *Non placet—The want of leisure is the want of inclination.* We will suppose it to come from a true filial affection and respect for his father, yet still the preference should have been given to Christ. Note, Many are hindered *from* and *in* the way of serious godliness, by an over-concern for their families and relations; these lawful things undo us all, and our duty to God is neglected, and postponed, under colour of discharging our debts to the world; here therefore we have need to double our guard.

(2.) Christ's disallowing of this excuse (*v.* 22); *Jesus said to him, Follow me;* and, no doubt, power accompanied this word to him, as to others, and he did *follow Christ*, and cleaved to him, as Ruth to Naomi, when the scribe, in the verses before, like Orpah, took leave of him. That said, *I will follow thee;* to this Christ said, *Follow me;* comparing them together, it is intimated that we are brought to Christ by the force of his call to us, not of our promises to him; it is *not of him that willeth, nor of him that runneth, but of God that showeth mercy;* he calls whom he will, Rom. ix. 16. And further, Note, Though chosen vessels may make excuses, and delay their compliance with divine calls a great while, yet Christ will at length answer their excuses, conquer their unwillingness, and bring them to his feet; when Christ calls, he will overcome, and make the call effectual, 1 Sam. iii. 10. His excuse is laid aside as insufficient; *Let the dead bury their dead.* It is a proverbial expression; "Let one dead man bury another: rather let them lie unburied, than that the service of Christ should be neglected. *Let the dead* spiritually *bury the dead* corporally; let worldly offices be left to worldly people; do not thou encumber thyself with them. Burying the dead, and especially a dead father, is a good work, but it is not thy work at this time: it may be done as well by others, that are not called and qualified, as thou art, to be employed for Christ; thou hast something else to do, and must not defer that." Note, Piety to God must be preferred before piety to parents, though that is a great and needful part of our religion. The Nazarites, under the law, were not to mourn for their own parents, because they were *holy to the Lord* (Numb. vi. 6—8); nor was the high priest to *defile himself for the dead*, no, not for *his own father*, Lev. xxi. 11, 12. And Christ requires of those who would follow him, that they *hate father and mother* (Luke xiv. 26); love them less than God; we must comparatively neglect and disesteem our nearest relations, when they come in competition with Christ, and either our doing for him, or our suffering for him.

23 And when he was entered into
a ship, his disciples followed him.
24 And, behold, there arose a great
tempest in the sea, insomuch that
the ship was covered with the waves:
but he was asleep. 25 And his
disciples came to *him*, and awoke
him, saying, Lord, save us: we perish.
26 And he saith unto them,
Why are ye fearful, O ye of little
faith? Then he arose, and rebuked
the winds and the sea; and there was
a great calm. 27 But the men marvelled,
saying, What manner of man
is this, that even the winds and the
sea obey him!

Christ had given sailing orders to his disciples (*v.* 18), that they should *depart to the other side of the sea of Tiberias*, into the country of Gadara, in the tribe of Gad, which lay east of Jordan; thither he would go to rescue a poor creature that was possessed *with a legion of devils,* though he foresaw how he should be affronted there. Now, 1. He chose to go by water. It had not been much about, if he had gone by land; but he chose to cross the lake, that he might have occasion to manifest himself the God *of the sea* as well as of *the dry land,* and to show that *all power is his, both in heaven and in earth.* It is a comfort to those *who go down to the sea in ships,* and are often in perils there, to reflect that they have a Saviour to trust in, and pray to, who knows what it is to be at sea, and to be in storms there. But observe, when he went to sea, he had no yacht or pleasure-boat to attend him, but made use of his disciples' fishing-boats; so poorly was he accommodated in all respects. 2. *His disciples followed him;* the twelve kept close to him, when others staid behind upon the *terra firma,* where there was sure footing. Note, They, and they only, will be found the true disciples of Christ, that are willing to go to sea with him, to follow him into dangers and difficulties. Many would be content to go the land-way to heaven, that will rather stand still, or go back, than venture upon a dangerous sea; but those that would rest with Christ hereafter must follow him now wherever he leads them, into a ship or into a prison, as well as into a palace. Now observe here,

I. The peril and perplexity of the disciples in this voyage; and in this appeared the truth of what Christ had just now said, that those who follow him must count upon difficulties, *v.* 20.

1. *There arose a very great storm, v.* 24. Christ could have prevented this storm, and have ordered them a pleasant passage, but that would not have been so much for his glory and the confirmation of their faith as their deliverance was: this storm was *for their sakes,* as John xi. 4. One would have expected, that having Christ with them, they should have had a very favourable gale, but it is quite otherwise; for Christ would show that they who are passing with him over the ocean of this world to the other side, must expect storms by the way. The church is *tossed with tempests* (Isa. liv. 11); it is only the upper region that enjoys a perpetual calm, this lower one is ever and anon disturbed and disturbing.

2. Jesus Christ *was asleep in this storm.* We never read of Christ's sleeping but at this time; he was in watchings often, and continued all night in prayer to God: this was a sleep, not of security, like Jonah's in a storm, but of holy serenity, and dependence upon his Father: he slept to show that he was really and truly man, and subject to the sinless infirmities of our nature: his work made him weary and sleepy, and he had no guilt, no fear within, to disturb his repose. Those that can lay their heads upon the pillow of a clear conscience, may sleep quietly and sweetly in a storm (Ps. iv. 8), as Peter, Acts xii. 6. He slept at this time, to try the faith of his disciples, whether they could trust him when he seemed to slight them. He slept not so much with a desire to be refreshed, as with a design to be awaked.

3. The poor disciples, though used to the sea, were in a great fright, and in their fear *came to* their Master, *v.* 25. Whither else should they go? It was well they had him so near them. They *awoke him* with their prayers; *Lord, save us, we perish.* Note, They who would learn to pray must go to sea. Imminent and sensible dangers will drive people to him who alone can help in time of need. Their prayer has life in it, *Lord, save us, we perish.* (1.) Their petition is, *Lord, save us.* They believed he *could* save them; they begged he *would.* Christ's errand into the world was *to save,* but those only *shall be saved that call on the name of the Lord,* Acts ii. 21. They who by faith are interested in the eternal salvation wrought out by Christ, may with a humble confidence apply themselves to him for temporal deliverances. Observe, They call him, *Lord,* and then pray, *Save us.* Note, Christ will save none but those that are willing to take him for their Lord; for he is a Prince and a Saviour. (2.) Their plea is, *We perish;* which was, [1.] The language of their fear; they looked upon their case as desperate, and gave up all for lost; they had received a sentence of death within themselves, and this they plead, "*We perish,* if thou dost not save us; look upon us therefore with pity." [2.] It was the language of their fervency; they pray as men in earnest, that beg for their lives; it becomes us thus to strive and wrestle in prayer; *therefore* Christ slept, that he might draw out this importunity.

II. The power and grace of Jesus Christ put forth for their succour: then the Lord Jesus awaked, as one refreshed, Ps. lxxviii. 65. Christ may sleep when his church is in a storm, but he will not outsleep himself: the time, the set time to favour his distressed church, will come, Ps. cii. 13.

1. He rebuked the disciples (*v.* 26); *Why are ye fearful, O ye of little faith?* He does not chide them for disturbing him with their prayers, but for disturbing themselves with their fears. Christ reproved them first, and then delivered them; this is his method, to prepare us for a mercy, and then to give it us. Observe, (1.) His dislike of their fears; "*Why are ye fearful?* Ye, my disciples? Let the sinners in Zion be afraid, let heathen mariners tremble in a storm, but you shall not be so. Enquire into the reasons of your fear, and weigh them." (2.) His discovery of the cause and spring of their fears; *O ye of little faith.* Many that have true faith are weak in it, and it does but little. Note, [1.] Christ's disciples are apt to be disquieted with fears in a stormy day, to torment themselves with jealousies that things are bad

with them, and dismal conclusions that they will be worse. [2.] The prevalence of our inordinate fears in a stormy day is owing to the weakness of our faith, which would be as an anchor to the soul, and would ply the oar of prayer. By faith we might see through the storm to the quiet shore, and encourage ourselves with hope that we shall weather our point. [3.] The fearfulness of Christ's disciples in a storm, and their unbelief, the cause of it, are very displeasing to the Lord Jesus, for they reflect dishonour upon him, and create disturbance to themselves.

2. *He rebukes the wind;* the former he did as the God of *grace*, and the Sovereign of the heart, who can do what he pleases *in* us; this he did as the God of *nature*, the Sovereign of the world, who can do what he pleases *for* us. It is the same *power that stills the noise of the sea*, and the tumult of fear, Ps. lxv. 7. See, (1.) How *easily* this was done, with a word's speaking. Moses commanded the waters with a rod; Joshua, with the ark of the covenant; Elisha, with the prophet's mantle; but Christ with a word. See his absolute dominion over all the creatures, which bespeaks both his honour, and the happiness of those that have him on their side. (2.) How *effectually* it was done? *There was a great calm*, all of a sudden. Ordinarily, after a storm, there is such a fret of the waters, that it is a good while ere they can settle; but if Christ speak the word, not only the storm ceases, but all the effects of it, all the remains of it. Great storms of doubt, and fear in the soul, under the power of the spirit of bondage, sometimes end in a wonderful calm, created and spoken by the Spirit of adoption.

3. This excited their astonishment (*v.* 27); *The men marvelled.* They had been long acquainted with the sea, and never saw a storm so immediately turned into a perfect calm, in all their lives. It has all the marks and signatures of a miracle upon it; *it is the Lord's doing, and is marvellous in their eyes.* Observe, (1.) Their admiration of Christ; *What manner of man is this!* Note, Christ is a Nonsuch; every thing in him is admirable: none so wise, so mighty, so amiable, as he. (2.) The reason of it; *Even the winds and the sea obey him.* Upon this account, Christ is to be admired, that he has a commanding power even over *winds and seas.* Others pretended to cure diseases, but he only undertook to command *the winds.* We know not the way of *the wind* (John iii. 8), much less can we control it; but he that *bringeth forth the wind out of his treasury* (Ps. cxxxv. 7), when it is out, gathers it into his fists, Prov. xxx. 4. He that can do this, can do any thing, can do enough to encourage our confidence and comfort in him, in the most stormy day, within or without, Isa. xxvi. 4. The Lord *sits upon the floods,* and is *mightier than the noise of many waters.* Christ, by commanding *the seas,* showed himself to be the same that *made the world, when, at his rebuke, the waters fled* (Ps. civ. 7, 8), as now, *at his rebuke,* they fell.

28 And when he was come to the other side, into the country of the Gergesenes, there met him two possessed with devils, coming out of the tombs, exceeding fierce, so that no
man might pass by that way. 29
And, behold, they cried out, saying, What have we to do with thee, Jesus, thou Son of God? art thou come hither to torment us before the time?
30 And there was a good way off from them an herd of many swine
feeding. 31 So the devils besought him, saying, If thou cast us out, suffer us to go away into the herd
of swine. 32 And he said unto them, Go. And when they were come out, they went into the herd of swine: and, behold, the whole herd of swine ran violently down a steep place into the sea, and perished
in the waters. 33 And they that kept them fled, and went their ways into the city, and told every thing, and what was befallen to the pos-
sessed of the devils. 34 And, behold, the whole city came out to meet Jesus: and when they saw *him*, they besought him that he would depart out of their coasts.

We have here the story of Christ's casting the devils out of two men that were possessed. The scope of this chapter is to show the divine power of Christ, by the instances of his dominion over bodily diseases, which to us are irresistible; over winds and waves, which to us are yet more uncontrollable; and lastly, over devils, which to us are most formidable of all. Christ has not only all *power in heaven and earth* and all deep places, but has the keys of hell too. *Principalities and powers were made subject to him,* even while he was in his estate of humiliation, as an earnest of what should be at his entrance into his glory (Eph. i. 21); he spoiled them, Col. ii. 15. It was observed in general (*v.* 16), that Christ *cast out the spirits with his word;* here we have a particular instance of it, which have some circumstances more remarkable than the rest. This miracle was wrought in the country of the Gergesenes; some think, they were the remains of the old Girgashites, Deut. vii. 1. Though Christ was sent chiefly *to the lost sheep of the house of Israel,* yet some sallies he made among the borderers, as here, to gain this victory over Satan, which was a specimen of the conquest of his legions in the Gentile world.

Now, besides the general instance which this gives us of Christ's power over Satan, and his design against him to disarm and dispossess him, we have here especially discovered to us the way and manner of evil spirits in their enmity to man. Observe, concerning this legion of devils, What work they made where they *were,* and where they *went.*

I. What work they made where they *were;* which appears in the miserable condition of these two that were possessed by them; and some think, these two were man and wife, because the other Evangelists speak but of one.

1. They dwelt among *the tombs;* thence they came when they met Christ. The devil having *the power of death,* not as judge, but as executioner, he delighted to converse among the trophies of his victory, the dead bodies of men; but there, where he thought himself in the greatest triumph and elevation, as afterwards in Golgotha, the place of a skull, did Christ conquer and subdue him. Conversing among the graves increased the melancholy and frenzy of the poor possessed creatures, and so strengthened the hold he had of them by their bodily distemper, and also made them more formidable to other people, who generally startle at any thing that stirs among *the tombs.*

2. They were *exceeding fierce;* not only ungovernable themselves, but mischievous to others, frightening many, having hurt some; *so that no man durst pass that way.* Note, The devil bears malice to mankind, and shows it by making men spiteful and malicious one to another. Mutual enmities, where there should be mutual endearments and assistances, are effects and evidences of Satan's enmity to the whole race; he makes one man a wolf, a bear, a devil, to another—*Homo homini lupus.* Where Satan rules in a man spiritually, by those lusts that war in the members, pride, envy, malice, revenge, they make him as unfit for human society, as unworthy of it, and as much an enemy to the comfort of it, as these poor possessed creatures were.

3. They bid defiance to Jesus Christ, and disclaimed all interest in him, *v.* 29. It is an instance of the power of God over the devils, that, notwithstanding the mischief they studied to do *by* and *to* these poor creatures, yet they could not keep them from meeting Jesus Christ, who ordered the matter so as to meet them. It was his overpowering hand that dragged these unclean spirits into his presence, which they dreaded more than any thing else: his chains could hold them, when the chains that men made for them could not. But being brought before him, they protested against his jurisdiction, and broke out into a rage, *What have we to do with thee, Jesus, thou Son of God?* Here is,

(1.) *One* word that the devil spoke like a *saint;* he addressed himself to Christ as *Jesus the Son of God;* a *good* word, and at this time, when it was a truth but in the proving, it was a *great* word too, what flesh and blood did not reveal to Peter, *ch.* xvi. 17. Even the devils know, and believe, and confess Christ to be the *Son of God,* and yet they are devils still, which makes their enmity to Christ so much the more wicked, and indeed a perfect torment to themselves; for how can it be otherwise, to oppose one they know to be the *Son of God?* Note, It is not knowledge, but love, that distinguishes saints from devils. He is the first-born of hell, that knows Christ and yet hates him, and will not be subject to him and his law. We may remember that not long since the devil made a doubt whether Christ were *the Son of God* or not, and would have persuaded him to question it (*ch.* iv. 33), but now he readily owns it. Note, Though God's children may be much disquieted in an hour of temptation, by Satan's questioning their relation to God as a Father, yet the Spirit of adoption shall at length clear it up to them so much to their satisfaction, as to set it even above the devil's contradiction.

(2.) *Two* words that he said like a *devil,* like himself.

[1.] A word of defiance; *What have we to do with thee?* Now, *First,* It is true that the devils have nothing to do with Christ as a Saviour, *for he took not on him the nature of the angels* that fell, nor did he lay hold on them (Heb. ii. 16); they are in no relation to him, they neither have, nor hope for, any benefit by him. O the depth of this mystery of divine love, that fallen man hath so much *to do with Christ,* when fallen angels have nothing *to do with* him! Surely here was torment enough before the time, to be forced to own the excellency *that is in Christ,* and yet that he has no interest in him. Note, It is possible for men to call Jesus *the Son of God,* and yet have nothing to do with him. *Secondly,* It is as true, that the devils desire not to have any thing *to do with Christ* as a Ruler; they hate him, they are filled with enmity against him, they stand in opposition to him, and are in open rebellion against his crown and dignity. See whose language they speak, that will have nothing *to do with the* gospel of Christ, with his laws and ordinances, that throw off his yoke, that *break his bands in sunder,* and *will not have him to reign over them;* that say *to the Almighty* Jesus, *Depart from us: they are of their father the devil, they do his lusts,* and speak his language. *Thirdly,* But it is not true, that the devils have nothing *to do with Christ* as a Judge, for they have, and they know it. These devils could not say, *What hast thou to do with us?* could not deny that the Son of God is the Judge of devils; to his judgment they are bound over in chains of darkness, which they would fain shake off, and shake off the thought of.

[2.] A word of dread and deprecation; "*Art thou come hither to torment us*—to cast us out from these men, and to restrain us from doing the hurt we would do?" Note, To be turned out, and tied up, from doing mischief, is a torment to the devil, all whose comfort and satisfaction are man's misery and destruction. Should not we then count it our heaven to be doing well, and reckon that our torment, whether within or without, that hinders us from well-doing? Now must we be tormented by thee *before the time*; Note, *First*, There is a time in which devils will be more tormented than they are, and they know it. The great assize at the last day is the time fixed for their complete torture, in that Tophet which is ordained of old *for the king, for the prince of the devils, and his angels* (Isa. xxx. 33; Matt. xxv. 41); *for the judgment of that day* they are *reserved*, 2 Pet. ii. 4. Those malignant spirits that are, by the divine permission, prisoners *at large*, walking to and fro through the earth (Job i. 7), are even now in a chain; hitherto shall their power reach, and no further; they will then be made *close* prisoners: they have now some ease; they will then be in torment without ease. This they here take for granted, and ask not never to be tormented (despair of relief is the misery of their case), but they beg that they may not be tormented *before the time;* for though they knew not when the day of judgment should be, they knew it should not be yet. *Secondly*, The devils have *a certain fearful looking for of that judgment and fiery indignation*, upon every approach of Christ, and every check that is given to their power and rage. The very sight of Christ and his word of command to come out of the man, made them thus apprehensive of their torment. Thus *the devils believe, and tremble*, Jam. ii. 19. It is their own enmity to God and man that puts them upon the rack, and *torments them before the time*. The most desperate sinners, whose damnation is sealed, yet cannot quite harden their hearts against the surprise of fearfulness, *when they see the day approaching*.

II. Let us now see what work they made where they *went*, when they were turned out of the men possessed, and that was into *a herd of swine*, which *was a good way off*, *v*. 30. These Gergesenes, though living on the other side Jordan, were Jews. What had they to do with *swine*, which by the law were unclean, and not to be eaten nor touched? Probably, lying in the outskirts of the land, there were many Gentiles among them, to whom this *herd of swine* belonged: or they kept them to be sold, or bartered, to the Romans, with whom they had now great dealings, and who were admirers of *swine's* flesh. Now observe,

1. How the devils seized the *swine*. Though they were *a good way off*, and, one would think, out of danger, yet the devils had an eye upon them, to do them a mischief: for they *go up and down, seeking to devour*, seeking an opportunity; and they seek not long but they find. Now here,

(1.) They *asked* leave to enter *into the swine* (*v*. 31); *they besought him*, with all earnestness, *If thou cast us out, suffer us to go away into the herd of swine*. Hereby, [1.] They discover their own inclination to do mischief, and what a pleasure it is to them; those, therefore, are their children, and resemble them, *whose sleep departeth from them, except they cause some to fall*, Prov. iv. 16. "Let us go *into the herd of swine*, any where rather than into the place of torment, any where to do mischief." If they might not be suffered to hurt men in their bodies, they would hurt them in their goods, and in that too they intend hurt to their souls, by making Christ a burthen to them: such malicious devices hath that old subtle serpent! [2.] They own Christ's power over them; that, without his sufferance and permission, they could not so much as hurt a *swine*. This is comfortable to all the Lord's people, that, though the devil's power be very great, yet it is limited, and not equal to his malice (what would become of us, if it were?) especially that it is under the control of our Lord Jesus, our most faithful, powerful friend and Saviour; that Satan and his instruments can go no further than he is pleased to permit; *here shall their proud waves be stayed*.

(2.) They *had* leave. Christ said unto them, *Go* (*v*. 32), as God did to Satan, when he desired leave to afflict Job. Note, God does often, for wise and holy ends, permit the efforts of Satan's rage, and suffer him to do the mischief he would, and even by it serve his own purposes. The devils are not only Christ's captives, but his vassals; his dominion over them appears in the harm they do, as well as in the hindrance of them from doing more. Thus even their wrath is made to praise Christ, and the remainder of it he does and will restrain. Christ permitted this, [1.] For the conviction of the Sadducees that were then among the Jews, who denied the existence of spirits, and would not own that there were such beings, because they could not see them. Now Christ would, by this, bring it as near as might be to an ocular demonstration of the being, multitude, power, and malice, of evil spirits, that, if they were not hereby convinced, they might be left inexcusable in their infidelity. We see not the wind, but it would be absurd to deny it, when we see trees and houses blown down by it. [2.] For the punishment of the Gadarenes, who perhaps, though Jews, took a liberty to eat *swine's* flesh, contrary to the law: however, their keeping *swine* bordered upon evil; and Christ would also show what a hellish crew they were delivered from, which, if he had permitted it, would soon have choked them, as they did their *swine*. The devils, in obedience to Christ's command, came out of the men, and having permission, *when they were come out, immediately they went into the herd of swine.* See what an industrious enemy Satan is, and how expeditious; he will lose no time in doing mischief. Observe,

2. *Whither they hurried them,* when they had seized them. They were not bid to *save their lives,* and, therefore, they were made to *run violently down a steep place into the sea,* where they all perished, to the number of about *two thousand,* Mark v. 13. Note, The possession which the devil gets is for destruction. Thus the devil hurries people to sin, hurries them to that which they have resolved against, and which they know will be shame and grief to them: with what a force doth the evil spirit *work in the children of disobedience,* when by so many foolish and hurtful lusts they are brought to act in direct contradiction, not only to religion, but to right reason, and their interest in this world! Thus, likewise, he hurries them to ruin, for he is Apollyon and Abaddon, the great destroyer. By his lusts which men do, they are *drowned in destruction and perdition.* This is Satan's will, to *swallow up* and to *devour;* miserable then is the condition of those that are led *captive by him at his will.* They are hurried into a worse lake than this, a lake that *burns with fire and brimstone.* Observe,

3. *What effect this had upon the owners.* The report of it was soon brought them by the swine-herds, who seemed to be more concerned for the loss of the swine than any thing else, for they went not to tell *what was befallen to the possessed of the devils,* till the swine were lost, *v.* 33. Christ went not *into the city,* but the news of his being there did, by which he was willing to feel how their pulse beat, and what influence it had upon them, and then act accordingly.

Now, (1.) Their curiosity brought them out to see Jesus. The *whole city came out to meet him,* that they might be able to say, they had seen a man who did such wonderful works. Thus many go out, in profession, to meet Christ for company, that have no real affection for him, nor desire to know him.

(2.) Their covetousness made them *willing to be rid of him.* Instead of inviting him into their city, or bringing their sick to him to be healed, they desired him *to depart out of their coasts,* as if they had borrowed the words of the devils, *What have we to do with thee, Jesus thou Son of God?* And now the devils had what they aimed at in drowning the swine; *they* did it, and then made the people believe that *Christ* had done it, and so prejudiced them against him. He seduced our first parents, by possessing them with hard thoughts of God, and kept the Gadarenes from Christ, by suggesting that he came into their country to destroy their cattle, and that he would do more hurt than good; for though he had cured two men, yet he had drowned two thousand swine. Thus the devil sows tares in God's field, does mischief in the Christian church, and then lays the blame upon Christianity, and incenses men against that. They besought him that he would depart, lest like Moses in Egypt, he should proceed to some other plague. Note, There are a great many who prefer their swine before their Saviour, and so come short of Christ, and salvation by him. They desire Christ to depart out of their hearts, and will not suffer his word to have a place in them, because he and his word will be the destruction of their brutish lusts — those swine which they give up themselves to feed. And justly will Christ forsake those that thus are weary of him, and say to them hereafter, *Depart, ye cursed,* who now say to the Almighty, *Depart from us.*

CHAP IX.

We have in this chapter remarkable instances of the power and pity of the Lord Jesus, sufficient to convince us that he is both able to save to the uttermost all that come to God by him, and as willing as he is able. His power and pity appear here in the good offices he did, I. To the bodies of people, in curing the palsy (ver. 2—8); raising to life the ruler's daughter, and healing the bloody issue (ver. 18—26); giving sight to two blind men (ver. 27—31); casting the devil out of one possessed (ver. 32—34); and healing all manner of sickness, ver. 35. II. To the souls of people; in forgiving sins (ver. 2); calling Matthew, and conversing freely with publicans and sinners (ver. 9—13); considering the frame of his disciples, with reference to the duty of fasting (ver. 14—17); preaching the gospel, and, in compassion to the multitude, providing preachers for them (v. 35—38). Thus did he prove himself to be, as undoubtedly he is, the skilful, faithful Physician, both of soul and body, who has sufficient remedies for all the maladies of both: for which we must, therefore, apply ourselves to him, and glorify him both with our bodies and with our spirits, which are his, in return to him for his kindness to both.

AND he entered into a ship, and passed over, and came into
his own city. 2 And, behold, they
brought to him a man sick of the palsy, lying on a bed: and Jesus seeing their faith said unto the sick of the palsy, Son, be of good cheer; thy sins be forgiven thee. 3 And,
behold, certain of the scribes said within themselves, This *man* blasphemeth. 4 And Jesus knowing
their thoughts said, Wherefore think ye evil in your hearts? 5 For
whether is easier, to say, *Thy* sins be forgiven thee; or to say, Arise, and walk? 6 But that ye may know
that the Son of man hath power on earth to forgive sins (then saith he to the sick of the palsy), Arise, take up thy bed, and go unto thine
house. 7 And he arose, and departed
to his house. 8 But when the multitudes saw *it,* they marvelled, and glorified God, which had given such power unto men.

The first words of this chapter oblige us to look back to the close of that which precedes it, where we find the Gadarenes so resenting the loss of their swine, that they were disgusted with Christ's company, and besought him to *depart out of their coasts.* Now here it follows, *He entered into a ship, and passed over.* They bid him begone, and he took them at their word, and we never read that he came into their coasts again. Now here observe, 1. His justice—that he left them. Note, Christ will not tarry long where he is not welcome. In righteous judgment, he forsakes those places and persons that are weary of him, but abides with those that covet and court his stay. *If the unbeliever will depart* from Christ, *let him depart;* it is at his peril, 1 Cor. vii. 15. 2. His patience—that he did not leave some destroying judgment behind him, to punish them, as they deserved, for their contempt and contumacy. How easily, how justly, might he have sent them after their swine, who were already so much under the devil's power. The provocation, indeed, was very great: but he put it up, and passed it by; and, without any angry resentments or upbraidings, he *entered into a ship, and passed over.* This was the day of his patience; he came not to *destroy men's lives,* but to save them; not to kill, but to cure. Spiritual judgments agree more with the constitution of gospel times; yet some observe, that in those bloody wars which the Romans made upon the Jews, which began not many years after this, they first besieged the town of Gadara, where these Gadarenes dwelt. Note, Those that drive Christ from them, draw all miseries upon them. Woe unto us, if God depart from us.

He came *into his own city, Capernaum,* the principal place of his residence at present (Mark ii. 1), and therefore called *his own city.* He had himself testified, that a prophet is least honoured in *his own country* and *city,* yet thither he came; for he *sought not his own honour;* but, being in a state of humiliation, he was content to be despised of the people. At Capernaum all the circumstances recorded in this chapter happened, and are, therefore, put together here, though, in the harmony of the evangelists, other events intervened. When the Gadarenes desired Christ to depart, they of Capernaum received him. If Christ be affronted by some, there are others in whom he will be glorious; if one will not, another will.

Now the first occurrence, after Christ's return to Capernaum, as recorded in these verses, was the cure of the man sick of the palsy. In which we may observe,

I. The *faith of his friends* in bringing him to Christ. His distemper was such, that he could not come to Christ himself, but as he was carried. Note, Even the halt and the lame may be brought to Christ, and they shall not be rejected by him. If we do as well as we can, he will accept of us. Christ had an eye to their faith. Little children cannot go to Christ themselves, but he will have an eye to the faith of those that bring them, and it shall not be in vain. *Jesus saw their faith,* the faith of the paralytic himself, as well as of them that brought him; Jesus saw the habit of faith, though his distemper, perhaps, impaired his intellect, and obstructed the actings of it. Now their faith was, 1. A strong faith; they firmly believed that Jesus Christ both could and would heal him; else they would not have brought the sick man to him so publicly, and through so much difficulty. 2. A humble faith; though the sick man was unable to stir a step, they would not ask Christ to make him a visit, but brought him to attend on Christ. It is fitter that we should wait on Christ, than he on us. 3. An active faith; in the belief of Christ's power and goodness, they brought the sick man to him, *lying on a bed,* which could not be done without a deal of pains. Note, a strong faith regards no obstacles in pressing after Christ.

II. The *favour of Christ,* in what he said to him; *Son, be of good cheer, thy sins be forgiven thee.* This was a sovereign cordial to a sick man, and was enough to *make all his bed in his sickness;* and to make it easy to him. We read not of any thing said to Christ; probably the poor sick man could not speak for himself, and they that brought him chose rather to speak by actions than words; they set him before Christ; that was enough. Note, It is not in vain to present ourselves and our friends to Christ, as the objects of his pity. Misery cries as well as sin, and mercy is no less quick of hearing than justice. Here is, in what Christ said, 1. A kind compellation; *Son.* Note, Exhortations and consolations to the afflicted speak to them as to sons, for afflictions are fatherly discipline, Heb. xii. 5. 2. A gracious encouragement; "*Be of good cheer. Have a good heart on it;* cheer up thy spirits." Probably the poor man, when let down among them all in his bed, was put out of countenance, was afraid of a rebuke for being brought in so rudely: but Christ does not stand upon ceremony; he bids him *be of good cheer;* all would be well, he should not be laid before Christ in vain. Christ bids him *be of good cheer;* and then cures him. He would have those to whom he deals his gifts, to be cheerful in seeking him, and in trusting in him; to be of good courage. 3. A good reason for that encouragement; *Thy sins are forgiven thee.* Now this may be considered, (1.) as an introduction to the cure of his bodily distemper; "Thy sins are *pardoned,* and therefore thou shalt be healed." Note, As sin is the cause of sickness, so the remission of sin is the comfort of recovery from sickness; not but that sin may be pardoned, and yet the sickness not removed; not but that the sickness may be removed, and yet the sin not pardoned: but if we have the comfort of our reconciliation to God, with the comfort of our recovery from sickness, this makes it a mercy indeed to us, as to Hezekiah, Isa. xxxviii. 17. Or, (2.) As a reason of the command to *be of good cheer,* whether he were cured of his disease or not; "Though I should not heal thee, wilt thou not say thou hast not sought in vain, if I assure thee that *thy sins are pardoned;* and wilt thou not look upon that as a sufficient ground of comfort, though thou shouldst continue *sick of the palsy?*" Note, They who, through grace, have some evidence of the forgiveness of their sins, have reason to be of good cheer, whatever outward troubles or afflictions they are under; see Isa. xxxiii. 24.

III. The *cavil of the scribes* at that which Christ said (*v.* 3); They *said within themselves,* in their hearts, *among themselves,* in their secret whisperings, *This man blasphemeth.* See how the greatest instance of heaven's power and grace is branded with the blackest note of hell's enmity; Christ's pardoning sin is termed blasphemy; nor had it been less, if he had not had commission from God for it. They, therefore, are guilty of blasphemy, that have no such commission, and yet pretend to pardon sin.

IV. The conviction which Christ gave them of the unreasonableness of this cavil, before he proceeded.

1. He *charged them with it.* Though they did but say it within themselves, he *knew their thoughts.* Note, Our Lord Jesus has the perfect knowledge of all that we say within ourselves. Thoughts are secret and sudden, yet naked and open before Christ, the eternal Word (Heb. iv. 12, 13), and he *understands them afar off,* Ps. cxxxix. 2. He could say to them (which no mere man could), *Wherefore think ye evil in your hearts?* Note, There is a great deal of evil in sinful thoughts, which is very offensive to the Lord Jesus. He being the Sovereign of the heart, sinful thoughts invade his right, and disturb his possession; therefore he takes notice of them, and is much displeased with them. In them lies the *root of bitterness,* Gen. vi. 5. The sins that begin and end in the heart, and go no further, are as dangerous as any other.

2. He *argued them out of it, v.* 5, 6. Where observe,

(1.) How he *asserts* his authority in the *kingdom of grace.* He undertakes to make out, that the *Son of man,* the Mediator, has *power on earth to forgive sins;* for *therefore* the Father has *committed all judgment to the Son,* and has given him this authority, *because he is the Son of man,* John v. 22, 27. If he has *power to give eternal life,* as he certainly has (John xvii. 2), he must have power to forgive sin; for guilt is a bar that must be removed, or we can never get to heaven. What an encouragement is this to poor sinners to repent, that the power of pardoning sin is put into the hands of the *Son of man,* who is bone of our bone! And if he had this *power on earth,* much more now that he is exalted to the Father's right hand, to give *repentance and remission of sins,* and so to be both *a Prince and a Saviour,* Acts v. 31.

(2.) How he *proves* it, by his power in the kingdom of nature; his power to cure diseases. Is it not as easy to say, *Thy sins are forgiven thee,* as to say, *Arise and walk?* He that can cure the disease, whether *declaratively* as a Prophet, or *authoritatively* as God, can, in like manner, forgive the sin. Now, [1.] This is a general argument to prove that Christ had a divine mission. His miracles, especially his miraculous cures, confirm what he said of himself, that he was the Son of God; the *power* that appeared in his cures proved him *sent of God;* and the *pity* that appeared in them proved him sent of God *to heal and save.* The God of truth would not set his seal to a lie. [2.] It had a particular cogency in this case. The palsy was but a symptom of the disease of sin; now he made it to appear, that he could effectually cure the original disease, by the immediate removal of that symptom; so close a connection was there between the sin and the sickness. He that had power to remove the punishment, no doubt, had power to remit the sin. The scribes stood much upon a legal righteousness, and placed their confidence in that, and made no great matter of the *forgiveness of sin,* the doctrine upon which Christ hereby designed to put honour, and to show that his great errand to the world was, to *save his people from their sins.*

V. The immediate cure of the sick man. Christ turned from disputing with them, and spake healing to him. The most necessary arguings must not divert us from doing the good that our *hand finds to do.* He saith to *the sick of the palsy, Arise, take up thy bed, and go to thine house;* and a healing, quickening, strengthening power accompanied this word (*v.* 7): *he arose and departed to his house.* Now, 1. Christ bid him *take up his bed,* to show that he was *perfectly cured,* and that not only he had no more occasion to be *carried* upon his bed, but that he had strength to *carry it.* 2. He sent him to *his house,* to be a blessing to his family, where he had been so long a burthen; and did not take him along with him for a show, which those would do in such a case who seek the honour that comes from men.

VI. The impression which this made upon the multitude (*v.* 8); they *marvelled,* and *glorified God.* Note, All our wonder should help to enlarge our hearts in *glorifying God,* who alone does marvellous things. They glorified God for what he had done for this poor man. Note, Others' mercies should be our praises, and we should give him thanks for them, for we are members one of another. Though few of this multitude were so convinced, as to be brought to believe in Christ, and to follow him, yet they admired him, not as God, or the Son of God, but as a *man* to whom God *had given such power.* Note,

God must be glorified in all the power that is *given to men* to do good. For all power is originally his; it is in him, as the Fountain, in men, as the cisterns.

9 And as Jesus passed forth from
thence, he saw a man, named Matthew, sitting at the receipt of custom:
and he saith unto him, Follow me.
And he arose, and followed him.
10 And it came to pass, as Jesus
sat at meat in the house, behold,
many publicans and sinners came
and sat down with him and his
disciples. 11 And when the Pharisees saw *it*, they said unto his disciples, Why eateth your Master with
publicans and sinners? 12 But when
Jesus heard *that*, he said unto them,
They that be whole need not a physician, but they that are sick. 13
But go ye and learn what *that* meaneth, I will have mercy, and not sacrifice: for I am not come to call the
righteous, but sinners to repentance.

In these verses we have an account of the grace and favour of Christ to poor publicans, particularly to Matthew. What he did to the bodies of people was to make way for a kind design upon their souls. Now observe here,

I. The call of Matthew, the penman of this gospel. Mark and Luke call him Levi; it was ordinary for the same person to have two names: perhaps Matthew was the name he was most known by as a publican, and, therefore, in his humility, he called himself by that name, rather than by the more honourable name of Levi. Some think Christ gave him the name of Matthew when he called him to be an apostle; as Simon, he surnamed Peter. Matthew signifies, *the gift of God.* Ministers are God's gifts to the church; their ministry, and their ability for it, are God's gifts to them. Now observe,

1. The posture that Christ's call found Matthew in. He was *sitting at the receipt of custom,* for he was a publican, Luke v. 27. He was a custom-house officer at the port of Capernaum, or an exciseman, or collector of the land-tax. Now, (1.) He was in his calling, as the rest of them whom Christ called, *ch.* iv. 18. Note, As Satan chooses to come, with his temptations, to those that are idle, so Christ chooses to come, with his calls, to those that are employed. But, (2.) It was a calling of ill fame among serious people; because it was attended with so much corruption and temptation, and there were so few in that business that were honest men. Matthew himself owns what he was before his conversion, as does St. Paul (1 Tim. i. 13), that the grace of Christ in calling him might be the more magnified, and to show, that God has his remnant among all sorts of people. None can justify themselves in their unbelief, by their calling in the world; for there is no *sinful* calling, but some have been saved *out of it,* and no *lawful calling,* but some have been saved *in it.*

2. The preventing power of this call. We find not that Matthew looked after Christ, or had any inclination to follow him, though some of his kindred were already disciples of Christ, but Christ prevented him with the blessings of his goodness. He is found of those that seek him not. Christ *spoke first;* we have not chosen him, but he hath chosen us. He said, *Follow me;* and the same divine, almighty power accompanied this word to convert Matthew, which attended that word (*v.* 6), *Arise and walk,* to cure the man sick of the palsy. Note, A saving change is wrought in the soul by Christ as the *Author,* and his word as the *means.* His gospel is the *power of God unto salvation,* Rom. i. 16. The call was effectual, for he came at the call; *he arose, and* followed him immediately; neither denied, nor deferred his obedience. The power of divine grace soon answers and overcomes all objections. Neither his commission for his place, nor his gains by it, could detain him, when Christ called him. *He conferred not with flesh and blood,* Gal i. 15, 16. He quitted his post, and his hopes of preferment in that way; and, though we find the disciples that were fishers occasionally fishing again afterwards, we never find Matthew at the receipt of custom again.

II. Christ's converse with publicans and sinners upon this occasions; Christ called Matthew, to introduce himself into an acquaintance with the people of that profession. *Jesus sat at meat in the house, v.* 10. The other evangelists tell us, that Matthew made a *great feast,* which the poor fishermen, when they were called, were not able to do. But when he comes to speak of this himself, he neither tells us that it was his own house, nor that it was a feast, but only that he *sat at meat in the house;* preserving the remembrance of Christ's favours to the publicans, rather than of the respect he had paid to Christ. Note, It well becomes us to speak sparingly of our own good deeds.

Now observe, 1. When Matthew invited Christ, he invited his disciples to *come along with him.* Note, They that welcome Christ, must welcome all that are his, for his sake, and let them have a room in their hearts. 2. He invited many publicans and sinners to *meet him.* This was the chief thing Matthew aimed at in this treat, that he might have an opportunity of bringing his old associates acquainted with Christ. He knew by experience what their temptations were, and pitied them; knew by experience what the grace of Christ could do, and would not despair concerning them. Note, They who are effectually brought to Christ themselves, cannot but be desirous that others also may be brought to him, and ambitious of contributing something towards it. True grace will not contentedly eat its morsels alone, but will invite others. When by the conversion of Matthew the fraternity was broken, presently his house was filled with publicans, and surely some of them will *follow him,* as he *followed Christ.* Thus did Andrew and Philip, John i. 41, 45; iv. 29. See Judges xiv. 9.

III. The displeasure of the Pharisees at this, *v.* 11. They cavilled at it; *why eateth your Master with publicans and sinners?* Here observe, 1. That Christ was quarrelled with. It was not the least of his sufferings, that he *endured the contradiction of sinners against himself.* None was more quarrelled with by men, than he that came to take up the great quarrel between God and man. Thus he denied himself the honour due to an incarnate Deity, which was to be justified in what he spake, and to have all he said readily subscribed to: for though he never spoke or did any thing amiss, every thing he said and did was found fault with. Thus he taught us to expect and prepare for reproach, and to bear it patiently. 2. They that quarrelled with him were the Pharisees; a proud generation of men, conceited of themselves, and censorious of others; of the same temper with those in the prophet's time, who said, *Stand by thyself, come not near me; I am holier than thou:* they were very strict in avoiding *sinners,* but not in avoiding *sin;* none greater zealots than they for the *form* of godliness, nor greater enemies to the *power* of it. They were for keeping up the traditions of the elders to a nicety, and so propagating the same spirit that they were themselves governed by. 3. They brought their cavil, not to Christ himself; they had not the courage to face him with it, but to his disciples. The disciples were in the same company, but the quarrel is with the Master: for they would not have done it, if he had not; and they thought it worse in him who was a prophet, than in them; his dignity, they thought, should set him at a greater distance from such company than others. Being offended at the Master, they quarrel with the disciples. Note, It concerns Christians to be able to vindicate and justify Christ, and his doctrines and laws, and to be *ready always to give an answer to those that ask them a reason of the hope that is in them,* 1 Pet. iii. 15. While he is an Advocate for us in heaven, let us be advocates for him on earth, and make his reproach our own. 4. The complaint was his *eating with publicans and sinners:* to be intimate with wicked people is against the law of God (Ps. cxix. 115; i. 1); and perhaps by accusing Christ of this to his disciples, they hoped to tempt them from him, to put them out of conceit with him, and so to bring them over to themselves to be their disciples, who kept better company; for they *compassed sea and land to make proselytes.* To be intimate with publicans was against the *tradition of the elders,* and, therefore, they looked upon it as a heinous thing. They were angry with Christ for this, (1.) Because they *wished ill to him,* and sought occasion to misrepresent him. Note, It is an easy and very common thing to put the worst constructions upon the best words and actions. (2.) Because they *wished no good to* publicans and sinners, but envied Christ's favour to them, and were grieved to see them brought to repentance Note, It may justly be suspected, that they have not the grace of God themselves, who grudge others a share in that grace, who are not pleased with it.

IV. The defence that Christ made for himself and his disciples, in justification of their converse with publicans and sinners. The disciples, it should seem, being yet weak, had to seek for an answer to the Pharisees' cavil, and, therefore, bring it to Christ, and he heard it (*v.* 12), or perhaps overheard them whispering it to his disciples. Let him alone to vindicate himself and to plead his own cause, to answer for himself and for us too. Two things he urges in his defence,

1. The necessity and exigence of the case of the publicans, which called aloud for his help, and therefore justified him in conversing with them for their good. It was the extreme necessity of poor, lost sinners, that brought Christ from the pure regions above, to these impure ones; and the same was it, that brought him into this company which was thought impure. Now,

(1.) He proves the necessity of the case of the publicans: *they that be whole need not a physician, but they that are sick.* The publicans are sick, and they need one to help and heal them, which the Pharisees think they do not. Note,

[1]. Sin is the sickness of the soul; sinners are spiritually sick. Original corruptions are the diseases of the soul, actual transgressions are its wounds, or the eruptions of the disease. It is deforming, weakening, disquieting, wasting, killing, but, blessed be God, not incurable. [2.] Jesus Christ is the great Physician of souls. His curing of bodily diseases signified this, that he arose with *healing under his wings.* He is a skilful, faithful, compassionate Physician, and it is his office and business to heal the sick. Wise and good men should be as physicians to all about them; Christ was so. *Hunc affectum versus omnes habet sapiens, quem versus ægros suos medicus—A wise man cherishes towards all around him the feelings of a physician for his patient.* Seneca *De Const.* [3.] Sin-sick souls have need of this Physician, for their disease is dangerous; nature will not help itself; no man can help us; such need have we of Christ, that we are undone, eternally undone, without him. Sensible sinners see their need, and apply themselves to him ac-

cordingly. [4.] There are multitudes who fancy themselves to be sound and whole, who think they have *no need of Christ*, but that they can shift for themselves well enough without him, as Laodicea, Rev. iii. 17. Thus the Pharisees desired not the knowledge of Christ's word and ways, not because they had no need of him, but because they thought they had none. See John ix. 40, 41.

(2.) He proves, that their necessity did sufficiently justify his conduct, in conversing familiarly with them, and that he ought not to be blamed for it; for that necessity made it *an act of charity*, which ought always to be preferred before the formalities of a religious profession, in which *bene*ficence and *muni*ficence are far better than *magni*ficence, as much as substance is better than shows or shadows. Those duties, which are of moral and natural obligation, are to take place even of those divine laws which are positive and ritual, much more of those impositions of men, and traditions of the elders, which make God's law stricter than he has made it. This he proves (*v.* 13) by a passage quoted out of Hos. vi. 6, *I will have mercy and not sacrifice.* That morose separation from the society of publicans, which the Pharisees enjoined, was *less than sacrifice;* but Christ's conversing with them was more than an act of common mercy, and therefore to be preferred before it. If to do well ourselves is better than sacrifice, as Samuel shows (1 Sam. xv. 22, 23), much more to do good to others. Christ's conversing with sinners is here called mercy: to promote the conversion of souls is the greatest act of mercy imaginable; it is *saving a soul from death*, Jam. v. 20. Observe how Christ quotes this, *Go ye and learn what that meaneth.* Note, It is not enough to be acquainted with the letter of scripture, but we must learn to understand the meaning of it. And they have best learned the meaning of the scriptures, that have learned how to apply them as a reproof to their own faults, and a rule for their own practice. This scripture which Christ quoted, served not only to vindicate him, but, [1.] To show wherein true religion consists; not in external observances: not *in meats and drinks* and shows of sanctity, not in little particular opinions and doubtful disputations, but in doing all the good we can to the bodies and souls of others; in righteousness and peace; in *visiting the fatherless and widows.* [2.] To condemn the Pharisaical hypocrisy of those who place religion in rituals, more than in morals, *ch.* xxiii. 23. They espouse those forms of godliness which may be made consistent with, and perhaps subservient to, their pride, covetousness, ambition, and malice, while they hate that power of it which is mortifying to those lusts.

2. He urges the nature and end of his own commission. He must keep to his orders, and prosecute that for which he was appointed to be the great Teacher; now, says he, "*I am not come to call the righteous, but sinners to repentance*, and therefore must converse with publicans." Observe, (1.) What his errand was; it was to *call to repentance.* This was his first text (*ch.* iv. 17), and it was the tendency of all his sermons. Note, The gospel call is a call to repentance; a call to us to change our mind and to change our way. (2.) With whom his errand lay; not with *the righteous*, but with *sinners.* That is, [1.] If the children of men had not been *sinners*, there had been no occasion for Christ's coming among them. He is the Saviour, not of man as *man*, but of man as *fallen* Had the first Adam continued in his original *righteousness*, we had not needed a second Adam. [2.] Therefore his *greatest business* lies with the *greatest sinners;* the more dangerous the sick man's case is, the more occasion there is for the physician's help. Christ came into the world to *save sinners*, but especially *the chief* (1 Tim. i. 15); to call not those so much, who, though sinners, are comparatively righteous, but the worst of sinners. [3.] The more sensible any sinners are of their sinfulness, the more welcome will Christ and his gospel be to them; and every one chooses to go where his company is desired, not to those who would rather have his room. Christ came not with an expectation of succeeding among *the righteous*, those who conceit themselves so, and therefore will sooner be sick of their Saviour, than sick of their sins, but among the convinced humble *sinners;* to them Christ will come, for to them he will be welcome.

14 Then came to him the disciples
of John, saying, Why do we and the
Pharisees fast oft, but thy disciples
fast not? 15 And Jesus said unto
them, Can the children of the bride-
chamber mourn, as long as the bridegroom is with them? but the days
will come, when the bridegroom shall
be taken from them, and then shall
they fast. 16 No man putteth a
piece of new cloth unto an old garment; for that which is put in to
fill it up taketh from the garment,
and the rent is made worse. 17
Neither do men put new wine into
old bottles: else the bottles break,
and the wine runneth out, and the
bottles perish: but they put new
wine into new bottles, and both are
preserved.

The objections which were made against Christ and his disciples gave occasion to some of the most profitable of his discourses; thus are the interests of truth often served, even by the opposition it meets with from gainsayers, and thus the wisdom of Christ brings good out of evil. This is the third instance of it in this chapter; his discourse of his power to forgive sin, and his readiness to receive sinners, was occasioned by the cavils of the scribes and Parisees; so here, from a reflection upon the conduct of his family, arose a discourse concerning his tenderness for it. Observe,

I. The objection which the disciples of John made against Christ's disciples, for not fasting so often as they did; which they are charged with, as another instance of the looseness of their profession, besides that of eating with publicans and sinners; and it is therefore suggested to them, that they should change that profession for another more strict. It appears by the other evangelists (Mark ii. 18 and Luke v. 33) that the disciples of the Pharisees joined with them, and we have reason to suspect that they instigated them, making use of John's disciples as their spokesmen, because they, being more in favour with Christ and his disciples, could do it more plausibly. Note, It is no new thing for bad men to set good men together by the ears: if the people of God differ in their sentiments, designing men will take that occasion to sow discord, and to incense them one against another, and alienate them one from another, and so make an easy prey of them. If the disciples of John and of Jesus clash, we have reason to suspect the Pharisees have been at work underhand, blowing the coals. Now the complaint is, *Why do we and the Pharisees fast often, but thy disciples fast not?* It is pity the duties of religion, which ought to be the confirmations of holy love, should be made the occasions of strife and contention; but they often are so, as here; where we may observe,

1. How they boasted of their own fasting. *We and the Pharisees fast often.* Fasting has in all ages of the church been consecrated, upon special occasions, to the service of religion; the Pharisees were much in it; many of them kept two fast-days in a week, and yet the generality of them were hypocrites and bad men. Note, False and formal professors often excel others in outward acts of devotion, and even of mortification. The disciples of John *fasted often,* partly in compliance with their master's practice, for he came *neither eating nor drinking* (*ch.* xi. 18); and people are apt to imitate their leaders, though not always from the same inward principle; partly in compliance with their master's doctrine of repentance. Note, The severer part of religion is often most *minded* by those that are yet under the discipline of the Spirit, as a *Spirit of bondage,* whereas, though these are good in their place, we must pass through them to that life of delight in God and dependence on him, to which these should lead. Now they come to Christ to tell him that they *fasted often,* at least they thought it often. Note, *Most men will proclaim every one his own goodness,* Prov. xx. 6. There is a proneness in professors to brag of their own performances in religion, especially if there be any thing extraordinary in them; nay, and not only to boast of them before men, but to plead them before God, and confide in them as a righteousness.

2. How they blamed Christ's disciples for not fasting so often as they did. *Thy disciples fast not.* They could not but know, that Christ had instructed his disciples to keep their fasts private, and to manage themselves so as that they might not *appear unto men to fast;* and, therefore, it was very uncharitable in them to conclude they did *not fast,* because they did not proclaim their fasts. Note, We must not judge of people's religion by that which falls under the eye and observation of the world. But suppose it was so, that Christ's disciples did not *fast* so often or so long as they did, why truly, they would therefore have it thought, that they had more religion in them than Christ's disciples had. Note, It is common for vain professors to make themselves a standard in religion, by which to try and measure persons and things, as if all who differed from them were so far in the wrong; as if all that did less than they, did too little, and all that did more than they, did too much, which is a plain evidence of their want of humility and charity.

3. How they brought this complaint to Christ. Note, If Christ's disciples, either by omission or commission, give offence, Christ himself will be sure to hear of it, and be reflected upon for it. *O, Jesus, are these thy Christians?* Therefore, as we tender the honour of Christ, we are concerned to conduct ourselves well. Observe, The quarrel with Christ was brought to the disciples (*v.* 11), the quarrel with the disciples was brought to Christ (*v.* 14), this is the way of sowing discord and killing love, to set people against ministers, ministers against people, and one friend against another.

II. The apology which Christ made for his disciples in this matter. Christ might have upbraided John's disciples with the former part of their question, *Why do ye fast often?* "Nay, you know best why you do it; but the truth is, many abound in external instances of devotion, that scarcely do themselves know why and wherefore." But he only vindicates the practice of his disciples; when they had nothing to say for themselves, he had something ready to say for them. Note, As it is wisdom's honour to be justified of all her children, so it is her children's happiness to be all justified of wisdom. What we do according to the precept and pattern of Christ, he will be sure to bear us out in, and we may with confidence leave it to him to clear up our integrity.

But thou shalt answer, Lord, for me.

Herbert.

Two things Christ pleads in defence of their *not fasting*.

1. That it was not a season proper for that duty (*v.* 15): *Can the children of the bride-chamber mourn, as long as the bridegroom is with them?* Observe, Christ's answer is so framed, as that it might sufficiently justify the practice of his own disciples, and yet not condemn the institution of John, or the practice of his disciples. When the Pharisees fomented this dispute, they hoped Christ would cast blame, either on his own disciples, or on John's, but he did neither. Note, When at any time we are unjustly censured, our care must be only to clear ourselves, not to recriminate, or throw dirt upon others; and such a variety may there be of circumstances, as may justify us in our practice, without condemning those that practise otherwise.

Now his argument is taken from the common usage of joy and rejoicing during the continuance of marriage solemnities; when all instances of melancholy and sorrow are looked upon as improper and absurd, as it was at Samson's wedding, Judges xiv. 17. Now, (1.) The disciples of Christ were the *children of the bride-chamber*, invited to the wedding-feast, and welcome there; the disciples of the Pharisees were not so, but *children of the bond-woman* (Gal. iv. 25, 31), continuing under a dispensation of darkness and terror. Note, The faithful followers of Christ, who have the Spirit of adoption, have a continual feast, while they who have the spirit of bondage and fear, cannot rejoice for joy, as other people, Hos. ix. 1. (2.) The disciples of Christ had *the bridegroom with them*, which the disciples of John had not; their master was now cast into prison, and lay there in continual danger of his life, and therefore it was seasonable for them to *fast often*. Such a day would come upon the disciples of Christ, when the bridegroom should be taken from them, when they should be deprived of his bodily presence, and *then should they fast*. The thoughts of parting grieved them when he was going, John xvi. 6. Tribulation and affliction befel them when he was gone, and gave them occasion of *mourning* and *praying*, that is, of religious fasting. Note, [1.] Jesus Christ is the Bridegroom of his Church, and his disciples are the *children of the bride-chamber*. Christ speaks of himself to John's disciples under this similitude, because that John had used it, when he called himself a friend of the bridegroom, John iii. 29. And if they would by this hint call to mind what their master then said, they would answer themselves. [2.] The condition of those who are the children of the bride-chamber is liable to many changes and alterations in this world; they sing of mercy and judgment. [3.] It is merry or melancholy with the children of the bride-chamber, according as they have more or less of the bridegroom's presence. When he is with them, the candle of God shines upon their head, and all is well; but when he is withdrawn, though but for a small moment, *they are troubled*, and walk heavily; the presence and nearness of the sun makes day and summer, his absence and distance, night and winter. Christ is all in all to the church's joy. [4.] Every duty is to be done in its proper season. See Eccles. vii. 14; Jam. v. 13. There is a time to mourn and a time to laugh, to each of which we should accommodate ourselves, and bring forth fruit in due season. In fasts, regard is to be had to the methods of God's grace towards us; when he *mourns to us*, we must *lament;* and also to the dispensations of his providence concerning us; there are times when *the Lord God calls to weeping and mourning;* regard is likewise to be had to any special work before us, *ch.* xvii. 21; Acts xiii. 2.

2. That they had not strength sufficient for that duty. This is set forth in two similitudes, one of putting *new cloth into an old garment*, which does but pull the old to pieces (*v.* 16); the other of putting *new wine into old bottles*, which does but burst the bottles, *v.* 17. Christ's disciples were not able to bear these severe exercises so well as those of John and of the Pharisees, which the learned Dr. Whitby gives this reason for: There were among the Jews not only sects of the Pharisees and Essenes, who led an austere life, but also *schools of the prophets*, who frequently lived in mountains and deserts, and were many of them Nazarites; they had also private academies to train men up in a strict discipline; and possibly from these many of John's disciples might come, and many of the Pharisees; whereas Christ's disciples, being taken immediately from their callings, had not been used to such religious austerities, and were unfit for them, and would by them be rather unfitted for their other work. Note, (1.) Some duties of religion are harder and more difficult than others, like *new cloth* and *new wine*, which require most intenseness of mind, and are most displeasing to flesh and blood; such are religious fasting and the duties that attend it. (2.) The best of Christ's disciples pass through a state of infancy; all the trees in Christ's garden are not of a growth, nor all his scholars in the same form; there are *babes in Christ* and grown men. (3.) In the enjoining of religious exercises, the weakness and infirmity of young Christians ought to be considered: as the food provided for them must be such as is proper for their age (1 Cor. iii. 2; Heb. v. 12), so must the work be that is cut out for them. Christ would not speak to his disciples that which they could not then bear, John xvi. 12. Young beginners in religion must not be put upon the hardest duties at first, lest they be discouraged. Such as was God's care of his Israel, when he brought them out of Egypt, not to lead

them by the way of the Philistines (Exod. xiii. 17, 18), and such as was Jacob's care of his children and cattle, not to overdrive them (Gen. xxxiii. 13), such is Christ's care of the little ones of his family, and the lambs of his flock: he gently leads them. For want of this care, many times, *the bottles break*, and *the wine is spilled;* the profession of many miscarries and comes to nothing, through indiscretion at first. Note, There may be *over*-doing even in *well*-doing, a being *righteous over-much;* and such an *over*-doing as may prove an *un*doing through the subtlety of Satan.

18 While he spake these things
unto them, behold, there came a certain ruler and worshipped him, saying, My daughter is even now dead:
but come and lay thy hand upon her,
and she shall live. 19 And Jesus
arose and followed him, and *so did*
his disciples. 20 And, behold, a
woman, which was diseased with an
issue of blood twelve years, came
behind *him,* and touched the hem of
his garment: 21 For she said within
herself, If I may but touch his garment, I shall be whole. 22 But
Jesus turned him about; and when
he saw her, he said, Daughter, be of
good comfort; thy faith hath made
thee whole. And the woman was
made whole from that hour. 23 And
when Jesus came into the ruler's
house, and saw the minstrels and the
people making a noise, 24 He said
unto them, Give place: for the maid
is not dead, but sleepeth. And they
laughed him to scorn. 25 But when
the people were put forth, he went
in, and took her by the hand, and the
maid arose. 26 And the fame hereof
went abroad into all that land.

We have here two passages of history put together; that of the raising of Jairus's daughter to life, and that of the curing of the woman that had *the bloody issue,* as he was going to Jairus's house, which is introduced in a parenthesis, in the midst of the other; for Christ's miracles were thick sown, and interwoven; *the work of him that sent* him was his daily work. He was called to do these good works from speaking the things foregoing, in answer to the cavils of the Pharisees, *v.* 18: *While he spake these things;* and we may suppose it a pleasing interruption given to that unpleasant work of disputation, which, though sometimes needful, a good man will gladly leave, to go about a work of devotion or charity. Here is,

I. The ruler's address to Christ, *v.* 18. *A certain ruler*, a ruler of the synagogue, *came and worshipped him. Have any of the rulers believed on him?* Yes, here was one, a church ruler, whose faith condemned the unbelief of the rest of the rulers. This ruler had a little daughter, of twelve years old, just dead, and this breach made upon his family comforts was the occasion of his coming to Christ. Note, In trouble we should visit God: the death of our relations should drive us to Christ, who is our life; it is well if any thing will do it. When affliction is in our families, we must not sit down astonished, but, as Job, *fall down and worship.* Now observe,

1. His humility in this address to Christ. He came with his errand to Christ himself, and did not send his servant. Note, It is no disparagement to the greatest rulers, personally to attend on the Lord Jesus. He *worshipped him,* bowed the knee to him, and gave him all imaginable respect. Note, They that would receive mercy from Christ must give honour to Christ.

2. His faith in this address; "*My daughter is even now dead,* and though any other physician would now come too late (nothing more absurd than *post mortem medicina—medicine after death),* yet Christ comes not too late; he is a Physician after death, for he is *the resurrection and the life;* " *O come* then, *and lay thy hand upon her, and she shall live.*" This was quite above the power of nature *(a privatione ad habitum non datur regressus—life once lost cannot be restored),* yet within the power of Christ, who has *life in himself, and quickeneth whom he will.* Now Christ works in an ordinary way, *by* nature and not *against* it, and, therefore, we cannot in faith bring him such a request as this; while there is life, there is hope, and room for prayer; but when our friends are dead, the case is determined; *we shall go to them, but they shall not return to us.* But while Christ was here upon earth working miracles, such a confidence as this was not only allowable but very commendable.

II. The readiness of Christ to comply with his address, *v.* 19. *Jesus* immediately *arose,* left his company, *and followed him;* he was not only willing to grant him what he desired, in raising his daughter to life, but to gratify him so far as to come to his house to do it. Surely *he never said to the seed of Jacob, Seek ye me in vain.* He denied to go along with the nobleman, who said, *Sir, come down ere my child die* (John iv. 48—50), yet he went along with the ruler of the synagogue, who said, *Sir, come down, and my child shall live.* The variety of methods which Christ took in working his miracles is perhaps to be attributed to the different frame and temper of mind which they were in who applied to him, which he *who searcheth the heart* perfectly knew, and accommodated himself to. He knows what is in man, and what course to take with him. And observe, when *Jesus followed him, so did his disciples,* whom he had chosen for his constant companions; it was not for state, or that he might come with observation, that he took his attendants with him, but that they might be the witnesses of his miracles, who were hereafter to be the preachers of his doctrine.

III. The healing of the poor woman's bloody issue. I call her a poor woman, not only because her case was piteous, but because, though she had had something in the world, she had *spent it all upon physicians,* for the cure of her distemper, and was never the better; which was a double aggravation of the misery of her condition, that she had been full, but was now empty; and that she had impoverished herself for the recovery of her health, and yet had not her health neither. This *woman was diseased with a constant issue of blood twelve years* (*v.* 20); a disease, which was not only weakening and wasting, and under which the body must needs languish; but which also rendered her ceremonially unclean, and shut her *out from the courts of the Lord's house;* but it did not cut her off from approaching to Christ. She applied herself to Christ, and received mercy from him, by the way, as he followed the ruler, whose daughter was dead, to whom it would be a great encouragement, and a help to keep up his faith in the power of Christ. So graciously does Christ consider the frame, and consult the case, of weak believers. Observe,

1. The woman's great faith in Christ, and in his power. Her disease was of such a nature, that her modesty would not suffer her to speak openly to Christ for a cure, as others did, but by a peculiar impulse of the Spirit of faith, she believed him to have such an overflowing fulness of healing virtue, that the very *touch of his garment* would be her cure. This, perhaps, had something of fancy mixed with faith; for she had no precedent for this way of application to Christ, unless, as some think, she had an eye to the raising of the dead man by the touch of Elisha's bones, 2 Kings xiii. 21. But what *weakness of understanding* there was in it, Christ was pleased to overlook, and to accept the sincerity and strength of her faith; for he *eateth the honey-comb with the honey,* Cant. iv. 11. She believed she should be healed if she did but *touch the* very *hem of his garment,* the very extremity of it. Note, There is virtue in every thing that belongs to Christ. The holy oil with which the high priest was anointed, *ran down to the skirts of his garments,* Ps. cxxxiii. 2. Such a fulness of grace is there in Christ, that *from it we may all receive,* John i. 16.

2. Christ's great favour to this woman. He did not suspend (as he might have done) his healing influences, but suffered this bashful patient to steal a cure unknown to any one else, though she could not think to do it unknown to him. And now she was well content to be gone, for she had what she came for, but Christ was not willing to let her go so; he will not only have his power magnified in her cure, but his grace magnified in her comfort and commendation: the triumphs of her faith must be to her praise and honour. He *turned about* to see for her (*v.* 22), and soon discovered her. Note, It is great encouragement to humble Christians, that they who hide themselves from men are known to Christ, who sees in secret their applications to heaven when most private. Now here,

(1.) He *puts gladness into her heart,* by that word, *Daughter, be of good comfort.* She feared being chidden for coming clandestinely, but she is encouraged. [1.] He calls her *daughter,* for he spoke to her with the tenderness of a father, as he did *to the man sick of the palsy* (*v.* 2), whom he called *son.* Note, Christ has comforts ready for *the daughters of Zion,* that are of a sorrowful spirit, as Hannah was, 1 Sam. i. 15. Believing women are Christ's *daughters,* and he will own them as such. [2.] He bids her *be of good comfort:* she has reason to be so, if Christ own her for a *daughter.* Note, The saints' consolation is founded in their adoption. His bidding her *be comforted,* brought comfort with it, as his saying, *Be ye whole,* brought health with it. Note, It is the will of Christ that his people should be comforted, and it is his prerogative to command comfort to troubled spirits. He *creates the fruit of the lips, peace,* Isa. lvii. 19.

(2.) He puts honour upon her faith. That grace of all others gives most honour to Christ, and therefore he puts most honour upon it; *Thy faith has made thee whole.* Thus *by faith she obtained a good report.* And as of all graces Christ puts the greatest honour upon faith, so of all believers he puts the greatest honour upon those that are most humble; as here on this woman, who had more faith than she thought she had. She had reason to *be of good comfort,* not only because she was *made whole,* but because her *faith had made her whole;* that is, [1.] She was spiritually healed; that cure was wrought in her which is the proper fruit and effect of faith, the pardon of sin and the work of grace. Note, We may then be abundantly comforted in our temporal mercies when they are accompanied with those spiritual blessings that resemble them; our food and raiment will be comfortable, when by faith we are fed with *the bread of life,* and *clothed with the righteousness of Jesus Christ;* our rest and sleep will be comfortable, when by faith we repose in God, and dwell at ease in him; our health and prosperity will be comfortable, when by faith our souls prosper, and are in health. See Isa. xxxviii. 16, 17. [2.] Her bodily cure was the fruit of faith, of her faith, and that made it a happy, comfortable cure indeed. They out of whom the devils were cast, were helped by Christ's sovereign power; some by the faith of others (as *v.* 2); but it is *thy faith that has made thee whole.* Note, Temporal mercies are then comforts indeed to us, when they are received by faith. If, when in pursuit of mercy, we prayed for it in faith, with an eye to the promise, and in dependence upon that, if we desired it for the sake of God's glory, and with a resignation to God's will, and have our hearts enlarged by it in faith, love, and obedience, we may then say, it was received by faith.

IV. The posture in which he found the ruler's house, *v.* 23.—He *saw the people and the minstrels,* or musicians, *making a noise.* The house was in a hurry: such work does death make, when it comes into a family; and, perhaps, the necessary cares that arise at such a time, when our dead is to be decently buried out of our sight, give some useful diversion to that grief which is apt to prevail and play the tyrant. The people in the neighbourhood came together to condole on account of the loss, to comfort the parents, to prepare for, and attend on, the funeral, which the Jews were not wont to defer long. The musicians were among them, according to the custom of the Gentiles, with their doleful, melancholy tunes, to increase the grief, and stir up the lamentations of those that attended on this occasion; as (they say) is usual among the Irish, with their Ahone, Ahone. Thus they indulged a passion that is apt enough of itself to grow intemperate, and affected to *sorrow as those that had no hope.* See how religion provides cordials, where irreligion administers corrosives. Heathenism aggravates that grief which Christianity studies to assuage. Or perhaps these musicians endeavoured on the other hand to divert the grief and exhilarate the family; but, *as vinegar upon nitre, so is he that sings songs to a heavy heart.* Observe, The parents, who were immediately touched with the affliction, were silent, while *the people and minstrels,* whose lamentations were forced, made such a noise. Note, The loudest grief is not always the greatest; rivers are most noisy where they run shallow. *Ille dolet vere, qui sine teste dolet—That grief is most sincere, which shuns observation.* But notice is taken of this, to show that the girl was really dead, in the undoubted apprehension of all about her.

V. The rebuke that Christ gave to this hurry and noise, *v.* 24. He said, *Give place.* Note, Sometimes, when *the sorrow of the world* prevails, it is difficult for Christ and his comforts to enter. They that harden themselves in sorrow, and, like Rachel, *refuse to be comforted,* should think they hear Christ saying to their disquieting thoughts, *Give place:* "Make room for him who is *the Consolation of Israel,* and brings with him *strong consolations,* strong enough to overcome the confusion and tyranny of these worldly griefs, if he may but be admitted into the soul." He gives a good reason why they should not thus disquiet themselves and one another; *The maid is not dead but sleepeth.* 1. This was eminently true of this maid, that was immediately to be raised to life; she was really dead, but not so to Christ, who knew within himself what he would do, and could do, and who had determined to make her death but as a sleep. There is little more difference between sleep and death, but in continuance; whatever other difference there is, it is but a dream. This death must be but of short continuance, and therefore is but a sleep, like one night's rest. He that quickens the dead, may well call the things which be not as though they were, Rom. iv. 17. 2. It is in a sense true of all that die, chiefly of them *that die in the Lord.* Note, (1.) Death is a sleep. All nations and languages, for the softening of that which is so dreadful, and withal so unavoidable, and the reconciling of themselves to it, have agreed to call it so. It is said, even of the wicked kings, that they *slept with their fathers;* and of those that shall arise to everlasting contempt, that they *sleep in the dust,* Dan. xii. 2. It is not the sleep of the soul; its activity ceases not; but the sleep of the body, which lies down in the grave, still and silent, regardless and disregarded, wrapt up in darkness and obscurity. Sleep is a short death, and death a long sleep. But *the death of the righteous* is in a special manner to be looked upon as a sleep, Isa. lvii. 2. They sleep in Jesus (1 Thess. iv. 14); they not only rest from the toils and labours of the day, but *rest in hope* of a joyful waking again in the morning of the resurrection, when they shall wake refreshed, wake to a new life, wake to be richly dressed and crowned, and *wake to sleep no more.* (2.) The consideration of this should moderate our grief at the death of our dear relations: "say not, They *are* lost; no, they are but *gone before:* say not, They are *slain;* no, they are but *fallen asleep;* and the apostle speaks of it as an absurd thing to imagine that *they that are fallen asleep in Christ are perished* (1 Cor. xv. 18); *give place,* therefore, to those comforts which the covenant of grace ministers, fetched from the future *state, and the glory to be revealed.*"

Now could it be thought that such a comfortable word as this, from the mouth of our Lord Jesus, should be ridiculed as it was? *They laughed him to scorn.* These people lived in Capernaum, knew Christ's character, that he never spake a rash or foolish word; they knew how many mighty works he had done; so that if they did not understand what he meant by this, they might at least have been silent in expectation of the issue. Note, The words and works of Christ which cannot be understood, yet are not therefore to be despised. We must adore the mystery of divine sayings, even when they seem to contradict what we think ourselves most confident of. Yet even this tended to the confirmation of the miracle: for it seems she was so apparently dead, that it was thought a very ridiculous thing to say otherwise.

VI. The raising of the damsel to life by the power of Christ, *v.* 25. *The people were put forth.* Note, Scorners that laugh at what they see and hear that is above their capacity, are not proper witnesses of the wonderful works of Christ, the glory of which lies not in pomp, but in power. The widow's son at Nain, and Lazarus, were raised from the dead openly, but this damsel privately; for Capernaum, that had slighted the lesser miracles of restoring health, was unworthy to see the greater, of restoring life; these *pearls were not* to be *cast before* those that would *trample them under their feet.*

Christ went in and *took her by the hand,* as it were to awake her, and to help her up, prosecuting his own metaphor of her being asleep. The high priest, that typified Christ, was not to come near the dead (Lev. xxi. 10, 11), but Christ *touched the dead.* The Levitical priesthood leaves the dead in their uncleanness, and therefore keeps at a distance from them, because it cannot remedy them; but Christ, having power to raise the dead, is above the infection, and therefore is not shy of touching them. He *took her by the hand, and the maid arose.* So easily, so effectually was the miracle wrought; not by prayer, as Elijah did (1 Kings xvii. 21), and Elisha (2 Kings iv. 33), but by a touch. They did it as servants, he as a Son, as a God, *to whom belong the issues from death.* Note, Jesus Christ is the Lord of souls, he commands them forth, and commands them back, when and as he pleases. Dead souls are not raised to spiritual life, unless Christ *take them by the hand:* it is done in the *day of his power.* He helps us up, or we lie still.

VII. The general notice that was taken of this miracle, though it was wrought privately; *v.* 26. *the fame thereof went abroad into all that land:* it was the common subject of discourse. Note, Christ's works are more talked of than considered and improved. And doubtless, they that heard only the report of Christ's miracles, were accountable for that as well as they that were eye-witnesses of them. Though we at this distance have not seen Christ's miracles, yet having an authentic history of them, we are bound, upon the credit of that, to receive his doctrine; and blessed *are they that have not seen, and yet have believed,* John xx. 29.

27 And when Jesus departed thence,
two blind men followed him, crying,
and saying, *Thou* son of David, have
mercy on us. 28 And when he was
come into the house, the blind men
came to him: and Jesus saith unto
them, Believe ye that I am able to
do this? They said unto him, Yea,
Lord. 29 Then touched he their
eyes, saying, According to your faith
be it unto you. 30 And their eyes
were opened: and Jesus straitly
charged them saying, See *that* no man
know *it.* 31 But they, when they
were departed, spread abroad his fame
in all that country. 32 As they
went out, behold, they brought to
him a dumb man possessed with a
devil. 33 And when the devil was
cast out, the dumb spake: and the
multitudes marvelled, saying, It was
never so seen in Israel. 34 But the
Pharisees said, He casteth out devils
through the prince of the devils.

In these verses we have an account of two more miracles wrought together by our Saviour.

I. The giving of sight to two blind men, *v.* 27—31. Christ is the Fountain of light as well as life; and as, by raising the dead, he showed himself to be the same that at first *breathed into man the breath of life,* so, by giving sight to the blind, he showed himself to be the same that at first *commanded the light to shine out of darkness.* Observe,

1. The importunate address of the blind men to Christ. He was returning from the ruler's house to his own lodgings, and these *blind men followed him,* as beggars do, with their incessant cries, *v.* 27. He that cured diseases so easily, so effectually, and, withal, at so cheap a rate, shall have patients enough. As for other things, so he is famed for an Oculist. Observe,

(1.) The title which these blind men gave to Christ; *Thou Son of David, have mercy on us.* The promise made to David, that of his loins the Messiah should come, was well known, and the Messiah was therefore commonly called *the Son of David.* At this time there was a general expectation of his appearing; these blind men know, and own, and proclaim it in the streets of Capernaum, that he is come, and that this is he; which aggravates the folly and sin of the chief priests and Pharisees who denied and opposed him. They could not see him and his miracles, but *faith comes by hearing.* Note, They who, by the providence of God, are deprived of bodily sight, may yet, by the grace of God, have *the eyes of their understanding so enlightened,* as to discern those great things of God, *which are hid from the wise and prudent.*

(2.) Their petition, *Have mercy on us.* It was foretold that the *Son of David* should be *merciful* (Ps. lxxii. 12, 13), and in him *shines the tender mercy of our God,* Luke i. 78. Note, Whatever our necessities and burthens are, we need no more for supply and support, than a share in the *mercy of our Lord Jesus.* Whether he heal us or no, if he *have mercy on us,* we have enough; as to the particular instances and methods of mercy, we may safely and wisely refer ourselves to the wisdom of Christ. They did not each of them say for himself, *Have mercy on me,* but both for one another, *Have mercy on us.* Note, It becomes those that are under the same affliction, to concur in the same prayers for relief. Fellow-sufferers should be joint-petitioners. In Christ there is enough for all.

(3.) Their importunity in this request; they *followed him, crying.* It seems, he did not take notice of them at first, for he would try their faith, which he knew to be strong; would quicken their prayers, and make his cures the more valued, when they did not always come at the first word; and would teach us to *continue instant in prayer, always to pray, and not to faint:* and, though the answer do not come presently, yet to wait for it, and to follow providence, even in those steps and outgoings of it which seem to neglect or contradict our prayers. Christ would not heal them publicly in the streets, for this was a cure he would have kept private (*v.* 30), but *when he came into the house,* they *followed him* thither, and *came to him.* Note, Christ's doors are always open to believing and importunate petitioners; it seemed rude in them to rush into the house after him, when he desired to retire; but, such is the tenderness of our Lord Jesus, that they were not more bold than welcome.

2. The confession of faith, which Christ drew from them upon this occasion. When they came to him for mercy, he asked them, *Believe ye that I am able to do this?* Note, Faith is the great condition of Christ's favours. They who would receive the *mercy* of Christ, must firmly believe the *power* of Christ. What we would have him do for us, we must be fully assured that he is *able to do.* They followed Christ, and followed him crying, but the great question is, *Do ye believe?* Nature may work fervency, but it is only grace that can work faith; spiritual blessings are obtained only by faith. They had intimated their faith in the office of Christ as *Son of David,* and in his mercy; but Christ demands likewise a profession of faith in his power. *Believe ye that I am able?* Note, Christ will have the glory of his power ascribed to him, by all those who hope to have the benefit of it. *Believe ye that I am able to do this;* to bestow this favour; to give sight to the blind, as well as to cure the palsy and raise the dead? Note, It is good to be particular in the exercise of faith, to apply the general assurances of God's power and good will, and the general promises, to our particular exigencies. *All shall work for good,* and if all, then this. "*Believe ye that I am able,* not only to prevail with God for it, as a prophet, but *that I am able to do it* by my own power?" This will amount to their belief of his being not only *the Son of David,* but *the Son of God;* for it is God's prerogative to *open the eyes of the blind* (Ps. cxlvi. 8); he makes *the seeing eye,* Exod. iv. 11. Job *was eyes to the blind* (Job xxix. 15); was to them instead of eyes, but he could not *give* eyes to the blind. Still it is put to us, *Believe we that Christ is able to do for us,* by the power of his merit and intercession in heaven, of his Spirit and grace in the heart, and of his providence and dominion in the world? To believe the power of Christ is not only to assure ourselves of it, but to commit ourselves to it, and encourage ourselves in it.

To this question they give an immediate answer, without hesitation: they said, *Yea, Lord.* Though he had kept them in suspense awhile, and had not helped them at first, they honestly imputed that to his wisdom, not to his weakness, and were still confident of his ability. Note, The treasures of mercy that are laid up in the power of Christ, are *laid out and wrought for those that trust in him,* Ps. xxxi. 19.

3. The cure that Christ wrought on them; *he touched their eyes, v.* 29. This he did to encourage their faith, which, by his delay, he had tried, and to show that he gives sight to blind souls by the operations of his grace accompanying the word, *anointing the eyes with eye-salve:* and he put the cure upon their faith, *According to your faith be it unto you.* When they begged for a cure, he enquired into their faith (*v.* 28), *Believe ye that I am able?* He did not enquire into their wealth, whether they were able to pay him for a cure; nor into their reputation, should he get credit by curing them; but into their faith; and now they had professed their faith he referred the matter to that: "I know you do believe, and the power you believe in shall be exerted for you; *According to your faith be it unto you.*" This speaks, (1.) His knowledge of the sincerity of their faith, and his acceptance and approbation of it. Note, It is a great comfort to true believers, that Jesus Christ knows their faith, and is well pleased with it. Though it be weak, though others do not discern it, though they themselves are ready to question it, it is known to him. (2.) His insisting upon their faith as necessary; "If you believe, take what you come for." Note, They who apply themselves to Jesus Christ, shall be dealt with *according to their faith;* not according to their *fancies,* nor according to their *profession,* but *according to their faith;* that is, unbelievers cannot expect to find any favour with God, but true believers may be sure to find all that favour which is offered in the gospel; and our comforts ebb or flow, according as our faith is stronger or weaker; we are not straitened in Christ, let us not then be straitened in ourselves.

4. The charge he gave them to keep it private (*v.* 30), *See that no man know it.* He gave them this charge, (1.) To set us an example of that humility and lowliness of

mind, which he would have us to learn of him. Note, In the good we do, we must not seek our own praise, but only the glory of God. It must be more our care and endeavour to be useful, than to be known and observed to be so, Prov. xx. 6; xxv. 27. Thus Christ seconded the rule he had given, *Let not thy left hand know what thy right hand doeth.* (2.) Some think that Christ, in keeping it private, showed his displeasure against the people of Capernaum, who had seen so many miracles, and yet believed not. Note, The silencing of those who should proclaim the works of Christ is a judgment to any place or people: and it is just in Christ to deny the means of conviction to those that are obstinate in their infidelity; and to shroud the light from those that shut their eyes against it. (3.) He did it in discretion, for his own preservation; because the more he was proclaimed, the more jealous would the rulers of the Jews be of his growing interest among the people. (4.) Dr. Whitby gives another reason, which is very considerable, why Christ sometimes concealed his miracles, and afterwards forbid the publishing of his transfiguration; because he would not indulge that pernicious conceit which obtained among the Jews, that their Messiah should be a temporal prince, and so give occasion to the people to attempt the setting up of his kingdom, by tumults and seditions, as they offered to do, John vi. 15. But when, after his resurrection (which was the full proof of his mission), his spiritual kingdom was set up, then that danger was over, and they must be published to all nations. And he observes, that the miracles which Christ wrought among the Gentiles and the Gadarenes, were ordered to be published, because with them there was not that danger.

But honour is like the shadow, which, as it flees from those that follow it, so it follows those that flee from it (*v.* 31); *They spread abroad his fame.* This was more an act of zeal, than of prudence; and though it may be excused as honestly meant for the honour of Christ, yet it cannot be justified, being done against a particular charge. Whenever we profess to direct our intention to the glory of God, we must see to it that the action be according to the will of God.

II. The healing of a *dumb man,* that was *possessed with a devil.* And here observe,

1. His case, which was very sad. He was under the power of the devil in this particular instance, that he was disabled from speaking, *v.* 32. See the calamitous state of this world, and how various the afflictions of the afflicted are! We have no sooner dismissed *two blind men,* but we meet with a *dumb man.* How thankful should we be to God for our sight and speech! See the malice of Satan against mankind, and in how many ways he shows it. This man's dumbness was the effect of his being *possessed with a devil;* but it was better he should be unable to say any thing, than be forced to say, as those demoniacs did (*ch.* viii. 29), *What have we to do with thee?* Of the two, better a dumb devil than a blaspheming one. When the devil gets possession of a soul, it is made silent as to any thing that is good; dumb in prayers and praises, which the devil is a sworn enemy to. This poor creature *they brought to Christ,* who entertained not only those that came of themselves in their own faith, but those that were *brought to him* by their friends in the faith of others. Though *the just shall live* eternally *by his faith,* yet temporal mercies may be bestowed on us with an eye to their faith who are intercessors on our behalf. They brought him in just as *the blind man went out.* See how unwearied Christ was in doing good; how closely one good work followed another! Treasures of mercy, wondrous mercy, are hid in him; which may be continually communicated, but can never be exhausted.

2. His cure, which was very sudden (*v.* 33), *When the devil was cast out, the dumb spake.* Note, Christ's cures strike at the root, and remove the effect by taking away the cause; they open the lips, by breaking Satan's power in the soul. In sanctification he heals the waters by casting salt into the spring. When Christ, by his grace, *casts the devil out* of a soul, presently *the dumb speaks.* When Paul was converted, *behold, he prays;* then *the dumb spake.*

3. The consequences of this cure.

(1.) *The multitudes marvelled;* and well they might; though *few believed, many wondered.* The admiration of the common people is sooner raised than any other affection. It was foretold, that the new song, the New-Testament song, should be sung for *marvellous works,* Ps. xcviii. 1. They said, *It was never so seen in Israel,* and therefore never so seen any where; for no people experienced such wonders of mercy as Israel did. There had been those in Israel that were famous for working miracles, but Christ excelled them all. The miracles Moses wrought had reference to Israel as a people, but Christ's were brought home to particular persons

(2.) *The Pharisees* blasphemed, *v.* 34. When they could not gainsay the convincing evidence of these miracles, they fathered them upon the devil, as if they had been wrought by compact and collusion: *he casteth out devils* (say they) by *the prince of the devils*—a suggestion horrid beyond expression; we shall hear more of it afterwards, and Christ's answer to it (*ch.* xii. 25); only observe here, how *evil men and seducers wax worse and worse* (2 Tim. iii. 13), and it is both their sin and their punishment. Their quarrels with Christ for taking upon him to *forgive sin* (*v.* 3), for *conversing with publicans and sinners* (*v.* 11), for *not fasting* (*v.* 14), though spiteful enough, yet had some colour of piety, purity, and devotion in them; but this (which they are left to, to punish them for those) breathes nothing but malice and falsehood, and hellish enmity in the highest degree; it is diabolism all over, and was therefore justly pronounced unpardonable. Because the people marvelled, they must say something to diminish the miracle, and this was all they could say.

35 And Jesus went about all the cities and villages, teaching in their synagogues, and preaching the gospel of the kingdom, and healing every sickness and every disease among the people. 36 But when he saw the multitudes, he was moved with compassion on them, because they fainted, and were scattered abroad, as sheep having no shepherd. 37 Then saith he unto his disciples, The harvest truly *is* plenteous, but the labourers *are* few; 38 Pray ye therefore the Lord of the harvest, that he will send forth labourers into his harvest.

Here is, I. A conclusion of the foregoing account of Christ's preaching and miracles (*v.* 35); *He went about all the cities teaching and healing.* This is the same we had before, iv. 23. There it ushers in the more particular record of Christ's preaching (*ch.* v. vi. and vii.) and of his cures (*ch.* viii and ix), and here it is elegantly repeated in the close of these instances, as the *quod erat demonstrandum—the point to be proved;* as if the evangelist should say, "Now I hope I have made it out, by an induction of particulars, that Christ preached and healed; for you have had the heads of his sermons, and some few instances of his cures, which were wrought to confirm his doctrine: and *these were written that you might believe.*" Some think that this was a second perambulation in Galilee, like the former; he visited again those whom he had before preached to. Though the Pharisees cavilled at him and opposed him, he went on with his work; he *preached the gospel of the kingdom.* He told them of a kingdom of grace and glory, now to be set up under the government of a Mediator: this was gospel indeed, *good news, glad tidings of great joy.*

Observe how Christ in his preaching had respect,

1. To the private towns. He visited not only the great and wealthy cities, but the poor, obscure villages; there he preached, there he healed. The souls of those that are meanest in the world are as precious to Christ, and should be to us, as the souls of those that make the greatest figure. *Rich and poor meet together* in him, citizens and boors: his *righteous acts towards the inhabitants of his villages* must be *rehearsed,* Judg. v. 11.

2. To the public worship. He taught *in their synagogues,* (1.) That he might bear a testimony to solemn assemblies, even then when there were corruptions in them. We *must not forsake the assembling of ourselves together, as the manner of some is.* (2.) That he might have an opportunity of preaching there, where people were gathered together, with an expectation to hear. Thus, even where the gospel church was founded, and Christian meetings erected, the apostles often *preached in the synagogues of the Jews.* It is the wisdom of the prudent, to make the best of that which is.

II. A preface, or introduction, to the account in the following chapter, of his sending forth his apostles. *He* took notice of *the multitude* (*v.* 36); not only of the crowds that *followed him,* but of the vast numbers of people with whom (as he passed along) he observed the country to be replenished; he noticed what nests of souls the towns and cities were, and how thick of inhabitants; what abundance of people there were in every synagogue, and what places of concourse the openings of the gates were: so very populous was that nation now grown; and it was the effect of God's blessing on Abraham. Seeing this,

1. He pitied them, and was concerned for them (*v.* 36); *He was moved with compassion on them;* not upon a temporal account, as he pitied the blind, and lame, and sick; but upon a spiritual account; he was concerned to see them ignorant and careless, and ready to perish for lack of vision. Note, Jesus Christ is a very compassionate friend to precious souls; here his bowels do in a special manner yearn. It was pity to souls that brought him from heaven to earth, and there to the cross. Misery is the object of mercy; and the miseries of sinful, self-destroying souls, are the greatest miseries: Christ pities those most that pity themselves least; so should we. The most Christian compassion is compassion to souls; it is most Christ-like.

See what moved this pity. (1.) *They fainted;* they were destitute, vexed, wearied. *They strayed,* so some; were loosed one from another; *The staff of bands was broken,* Zech. xi. 14. They wanted help for their souls, and had none at hand that was good for any thing. The scribes and Pharisees filled them with vain notions, burthened them with the traditions of the elders, deluded them into many mistakes, while they were not instructed in their duty, nor acquainted with the extent and spiritual nature of the divine law; therefore *they fainted;* for what spiritual health, and life, and vigour can there be in those souls, that are fed with husks and ashes, instead of *the bread of life?* Precious souls *faint* when duty is to be done, temptations to be resisted, afflictions to be borne, being not nourished up with the word of truth. (2.) *They were scattered abroad, as sheep having no shepherd.* That expression is borrowed from 1 Kings xxii. 17, and it sets forth the sad condition of those that are destitute of faithful guides to go before them in the things of God. No creature is more apt to go astray than a sheep, and when gone astray more helpless, shiftless, and exposed, or more unapt to find the way home again: sinful souls *are as lost sheep;* they need the care of shepherds to bring them back. The teachers the Jews then had pretended to be *shepherds,* yet Christ says they had no *shepherds,* for they were worse than none; idle shepherds that led them away, instead of leading them back, and fleeced the flock, instead of feeding it: such shepherds as were described, Jer. xxiii. 1, &c. Ezek. xxxiv. 2, &c. Note, The case of those people is very pitiable, who either have no ministers at all, or those that are as bad as none; that seek their own things, not *the things of Christ* and souls.

2. He excited his disciples to pray for them. His pity put him upon devising means for the good of these people. It appears (Luke vi. 12, 13) that upon this occasion, before he sent out his apostles, he did himself spend a great deal of time in prayer. Note, Those we pity we should pray for. Having spoken to God for them he turns to his disciples, and tells them,

(1.) How the case stood; *The harvest truly is plenteous, but the labourers are few.* People desired good preaching, but there were few good preachers. There was a great deal of work to be done, and a great deal of good likely to be done, but there wanted hands to do it. [1.] It was an encouragement, that *the harvest* was so *plenteous.* It was not strange, that there were multitudes that needed instruction, but it was what does not often happen, that they who needed it, desired it, and were forward to receive it. They that were ill taught were desirous to be better taught; people's expectations were raised, and there was such a moving of affections, as promised well. Note, It is a blessed thing, to see people in love with good preaching. The valleys are then covered over with corn, and there are hopes it may be well gathered in. That is a gale of opportunity, that calls for a double care and diligence in the improvement of it; a harvest-day should be a busy day. [2.] It was a pity when it was so that *the labourers* should be so *few;* that the corn should shed and spoil, and rot upon the ground for want of reapers; loiterers many, but *labourers* very *few.* Note, It is ill with the church, when good work stands still, or goes slowly on, for want of good workmen; when it is so, the *labourers* that there are have need to be very busy.

(2.) What was their duty in this case (*v.* 38); *Pray ye therefore the Lord of the harvest.* Note, The melancholy aspect of the times, and the deplorable state of precious souls, should much excite and quicken prayer When things look discouraging, we should pray more, and then we should complain and fear less. And we should adapt our prayers to the present exigences of the church; such an understanding we ought to have of the times, as to know, not only what Israel ought to do, but what Israel ought to pray for. Note, [1.] God is *the Lord of the harvest; my Father is the Husbandman,* John xv. 1. It is *the vineyard of the Lord of hosts,* Isa. v. 7. It is for him and to him, and to his service and honour, that *the harvest* is gathered in. *Ye are God's husbandry* (1 Cor. iii. 9); *his threshing, and the corn of his floor,* Isa. xxi. 10. He orders every thing concerning *the harvest* as he pleases; when and where *the labourers* shall work, and how long; and it is very comfortable to those who wish well to *the harvest-work,* that God himself presides in it, who will be sure to order all for the best. [2.] Ministers are and should be *labourers* in God's *harvest;* the ministry is a *work* and must be attended to accordingly; it is *harvest-work,* which is needful work; work that requires every thing to be done in its season, and diligence to do it thoroughly; but it is pleasant work; they *reap in joy,* and the joy of the preachers of the gospel is likened to the *joy of harvest* (Isa. ix. 2, 3); and *he that reapeth receiveth wages; the hire of the labourers* that reap down God's field, shall not be *kept back,* as theirs was, Jam. v. 4. [3.] It is God's work to *send forth labourers;* Christ makes ministers (Eph. iv. 11); the office is of his appointing, the qualifications of his working, the call of his giving. They will not be owned nor paid as *labourers,* that run without their errand, unqualified, uncalled. *How shall they preach except they be sent?* [4.] All that love Christ and souls, should show it by their earnest prayers to God, especially when *the harvest is plenteous, that he would send forth* more skilful, faithful, wise, and industrious *labourers into his harvest;* that he would raise up such as he will own in the conversion of sinners and the edification of saints; would give them a spirit for the work, call them to it, and succeed them in it; *that he would* give them *wisdom to win souls; that he would thrust forth labourers,* so some; intimating unwillingness to go forth, because of their own weakness and the people's badness, and opposition from men, that endeavour to thrust them out of *the harvest;* but we should pray that all contradiction from within and from without, may be conquered and got over. Christ puts his friends upon praying this, just before he sends apostles forth to labour in *the harvest.* Note, It is a good sign God is about to bestow some special mercy upon a people, when he stirs up those that have an interest at the throne of grace, to pray for it, Ps. x. 17. Further observe, that Christ said this to his disciples, who were to be employed as *labourers.* They must pray, First, That God *would send them forth. Here am I, send me,* Isa. vi. 8. Note, Commissions, given in answer to prayer, are most likely to be successful; Paul is a chosen vessel, for *behold he prays,* Acts ix. 11, 15. Secondly, That he would send others forth. Note, Not the people only, but those who are themselves ministers, should pray for the increase of ministers. Though self-interest makes those that seek their own things desirous to be placed alone (the fewer ministers the more preferments), yet those that *seek the things of Christ,* desire more workmen, that more work may be done, though they be eclipsed by it.

CHAP. X.

This chapter is an ordination sermon, which our Lord Jesus preached, when he advanced his twelve disciples to the degree and dignity of apostles. In the close of the foregoing chapter, he had stirred up them and others to pray that God would send forth labourers, and here we have an immediate answer to that prayer: while they are yet speaking he hears and performs. What we pray for, according to Christ's direction, shall be given. Now here we have, I. The general commission that was given them, ver. 1. II. The names of the persons to whom this commission was given, ver. 2—4. III. The instructions that were given them, which are very full and particular; 1. Concerning the services they were to do; their preaching; their working miracles; to whom they must apply themselves; how they must behave themselves; and in what method they must proceed, ver. 5—15. 2. Concerning the sufferings they were to undergo. They are told what they should suffer, and from whom; counsels are given them what course to take when persecuted, and encouragements to bear up cheerfully under their sufferings, ver. 16—42. These things, though primarily intended for direction to the apostles, are of use to all Christ's ministers, with whom, by his word, Christ is, and will be always to the end of the world.

AND when he had called unto *him*
his twelve disciples, he gave
them power *against* unclean spirits,
to cast them out, and to heal all manner of sickness and all manner of
disease. 2 Now the names of the
twelve apostles are these: The first,
Simon, who is called Peter, and Andrew his brother: James *the son* of
Zebedee, and John his brother; 3
Philip, and Bartholomew; Thomas,
and Matthew the publican; James
the son of Alpheus, and Lebbeus,
whose surname was Thaddeus; 4
Simon the Canaanite; and Judas
Iscariot, who also betrayed him.

Here we are told, I. Who they were that Christ ordained to be his apostles or ambassadors; they were his disciples, *v.* 1. He had called them some time before to be disciples, his immediate followers and constant attendants, and he then told them that they should be made fishers of men, which promise he now performed. Note, Christ commonly confers honours and graces by degrees; the light of both, like that of the morning, *shines more and more.* All this while Christ had kept these twelve,

1. In a state of probation. Though he knows what is in man, though he knew from the first what was in them (John vi. 70), yet he took this method to give an example to his church. Note, The ministry being a great trust, it is fit that men should be tried for a time, before they are entrusted with it. Let them *first be proved,* 1 Tim. iii. 10. Therefore, hands must not be laid suddenly on any man, but let him first be observed as a candidate and probationer, a proposant (that is the term the French churches use), because some men's sins go before, others follow, 1 Tim. v. 22.

2. In a state of preparation. All this while he had been fitting them for this great work. Note, Those whom Christ intends for, and calls to, any work, he first prepares and qualifies, in some measure, for it. He prepared them, (1.) By *taking them to be with him.* Note, The best preparative for the work of the ministry, is an acquaintance and communion with Jesus Christ. They that would *serve Christ,* must first be *with him* (John xii. 26). Paul had Christ revealed, not only *to him,* but *in him,* before he went to preach him among the Gentiles, Gal. i. 16. By the lively acts of faith, and the frequent exercise of prayer and meditation, that fellowship with Christ must be maintained and kept up, which is a requisite qualification for the work of the ministry. (2.) By *teaching them;* they were with him as scholars or pupils, and he taught them privately, besides the benefit they derived from his public preaching; he opened the scriptures to them, and opened their understandings to understand the scriptures: to them it was given to *know the mysteries of the kingdom of heaven,* and to them they were *made plain.* Note, They that design to be teachers must first be learners; they must receive, that they may give; they must be *able to teach others,* 2 Tim. ii. 2. Gospel truths must be first committed to them, before they be commissioned to be gospel ministers. To give men *authority* to teach others, that have not an *ability,* is but a mockery to God and the church; it is *sending a message by the hand of a fool,* Prov. xxvi. 6. Christ *taught his disciples* before he sent them forth (*ch.* v. 2), and afterwards, when he enlarged their commission, he gave them more ample instructions, Acts i. 3.

II. What the commission was that he gave them.

1. He *called them to him, v.* 1. He had called them to come *after* him before; now he calls them to come *to* him, admits them to a greater familiarity, and will not have them to keep at such a distance as they had hitherto observed. They that *humble themselves* shall thus be *exalted.* The priests under the law were said to *draw near* and *approach* unto God, nearer than the people; the same may be said of gospel ministers; they are called to draw near to Christ, which, as it is an honour, so should strike an awe upon them, remembering that Christ will be sanctified in those that *come nigh unto him.* It is observable, that when the disciples were to be *instructed,* they *came unto* him of their

own accord, *ch.* v. 1. But now they were to be *ordained,* he *called them.* Note, It well becomes the disciples of Christ to be more forward to learn than to teach. In the sense of our own ignorance, we must seek opportunities to be taught; and in the same sense we must *wait for a call,* a clear call, ere we take upon us to *teach others;* for *no man ought to take this honour to himself.*

2. He *gave them power, ἐξουσίαν, authority* in his name, to command men to obedience, and for the confirmation of that authority, to command devils too into a subjection. Note, All rightful authority is derived from Jesus Christ. All power is given to him without limitation, and the subordinate powers that be are ordained of him. Some of his honour he put on his ministers, as Moses put some of his on Joshua. Note, It is an undeniable proof of the fulness of power which Christ used as Mediator, that he could impart his power to those he employed, and enable them to work the same miracles that he wrought in his name. He gave them *power over unclean spirits,* and over *all manner of sickness.* Note, The design of the gospel was to *conquer the devil* and to *cure the world.* These preachers were sent out destitute of all external advantages to recommend them; they had no wealth, nor learning, nor titles of honour, and they made a very mean figure; it was therefore requisite that they should have some extraordinary power to advance them above the scribes.

(1.) He gave them power *against unclean spirits, to cast them out.* Note, The power that is committed to the ministers of Christ, is directly levelled against the devil and his kingdom. The devil, as an *unclean spirit,* is working both in doctrinal errors (Rev. xvi. 13), and in practical debauchery (2 Pet. ii. 10); and in both these, ministers have a charge against him. Christ gave them power to cast him out of the bodies of people; but that was to signify the destruction of his *spiritual kingdom,* and all the works of the devil; for which purpose the *Son of God* was *manifested.*

(2.) He gave them power to *heal all manner of sickness.* He authorized them to work miracles for the confirmation of their doctrine, to prove that it was of God; and they were to work useful miracles for the illustration of it, to prove that it is not only faithful, but well *worthy of all acceptation;* that the design of the gospel is to heal and save. Moses's miracles were many of them for destruction; those Mahomet pretended to, were for ostentation; but the miracles Christ wrought, and appointed his apostles to work, were all for edification, and evince him to be, not only the great Teacher and Ruler, but the great Redeemer, of the world. Observe what an emphasis is laid upon the extent of their power to *all manner of sickness,* and *all manner of disease,* without the exception even of those that are reckoned incurable, and the reproach of physicians. Note, In the grace of the gospel there is a salve for every sore, a remedy for every malady. There is no spiritual disease so malignant, so inveterate, but there is a sufficiency of power in Christ for the cure of it. Let none therefore say there is no hope, or that the breach is wide as the sea, that cannot be healed.

III. The number and names of those that were commissioned; they are made apostles, that is, messengers. An angel, and an apostle, both signify the same thing—one *sent on an errand,* an ambassador. All faithful ministers are sent of Christ, but they that were first, and immediately, sent by him, are eminently called *apostles,* the prime ministers of state in his kingdom. Yet this was but the infancy of their office; it was when Christ *ascended on high* that he *gave some apostles,* Eph. iv. 11. Christ himself is called an apostle (Heb. iii. 1), for he was *sent by the Father,* and so sent them, John xx. 21. The prophets were called God's messengers.

1. Their number was twelve, referring to the number of the tribes of Israel, and the sons of Jacob that were the patriarchs of those tribes. The gospel church must be the Israel of God; the Jews must be first invited into it; the apostles must be spiritual fathers, to beget a seed to Christ. Israel after the flesh is to be rejected for their infidelity; these twelve, therefore, are appointed to be the fathers of another Israel. These twelve, by their doctrine, were to judge the twelve tribes of Israel, Luke xxii. 30. These were the twelve stars that made up the church's crown (Rev. xii. 1): the twelve foundations of the new Jerusalem (Rev. xxi. 12, 14), typified by the twelve precious stones in Aaron's breast-plate, the twelve loaves on the table of show-bread, the twelve wells of water at Elim. This was that famous jury (and to make it a grand jury, Paul was added to it) that was impanelled to enquire between the King of kings, and the body of mankind; and, in this chapter, they have their charge given them, by him to whom *all judgment was committed.*

2. Their names are here left upon record, and it is their honour; yet in this they had more reason to rejoice, that their names were *written in heaven* (Luke x. 20), while the high and mighty names of the great ones of the earth are *buried in the dust.* Observe,

(1.) There are some of these twelve apostles, of whom we know no more, from the scripture, than their names; as Bartholomew, and Simon the Canaanite; and yet they were faithful servants to Christ and his church. Note, all the good ministers of Christ are not alike famous, nor their actions alike celebrated.

(2.) They are named by couples; for at first they were sent forth *two and two,* because *two are better than one;* they would be serviceable to each other, and the more serviceable jointly to Christ and souls; what one forgot the other would remember, and *out of the mouth of two witnesses every word would be established.* Three couple of them were brethren; Peter and Andrew, James and John, and the other James and Lebbeus. Note, Friendship and fellowship ought to be kept up among relations, and to be made serviceable to religion. It is an excellent thing, when brethren by nature are brethren by grace, and those two bonds strengthen each other.

(3.) Peter is named first, because he was first called; or because he was the most forward man among them, and upon all occasions made himself the mouth of the rest, and because he was to be the apostle of the circumcision; but that gave him no power over the rest of the apostles, nor is there the least mark of any supremacy that was given to him, or ever claimed by him, in this sacred college.

(4.) Matthew, the penman of this gospel, is here joined with Thomas (*v.* 3), but in two things there is a variation from the accounts of Mark and Luke, Mark iii. 18; Luke vi. 15. There, Matthew is put first; in that order it appears he was ordained before Thomas; but here, in his own catalogue, Thomas is put first. Note, It well becomes the disciples of Christ in honour to prefer one another. There, he is only called Matthew, here Matthew the publican, the toll-gatherer or collector of the customs, who was called from that infamous employment to be an apostle. Note, It is good for those who are advanced to honour with Christ, to look *unto the rock whence they were hewn;* often to remember what they were before Christ called them, that thereby they may be kept humble, and divine grace may be the more glorified. Matthew the apostle was Matthew the publican.

(5.) Simon is called the Canaanite, or rather the Canite, from Cana of Galilee, where probably he was born; or Simon the Zealot, which some make to be the signification of Καναν́ιτης.

(6.) Judas Iscariot is always named last, and with that black brand upon his name, *who also betrayed him;* which intimates that from the first, Christ knew what a wretch he was, that he had a devil, and would prove a traitor; yet Christ took him among the apostles, that it might not be a surprise and discouragement to his church, if, at any time, the vilest scandals should break out in the best societies. Such spots there have been in our feasts of charity; tares among the wheat, wolves among the sheep; but there is a day of discovery and separation coming, when hypocrites shall be unmasked and discarded. Neither the apostleship, nor the rest of the apostles, were ever the worse for Judas's being one of the twelve, while his wickedness was concealed and did not break out.

5 These twelve Jesus sent forth,
and commanded them, saying, Go
not into the way of the Gentiles, and
into *any* city of the Samaritans enter
ye not: 6 But go rather to the lost
sheep of the house of Israel. 7 And,
as ye go, preach, saying, The kingdom of heaven is at hand. 8 Heal
the sick, cleanse the lepers, raise the
dead, cast out devils: freely ye have
received, freely give. 9 Provide
neither gold, nor silver, nor brass, in
your purses, 10 Nor scrip for *your*
journey, neither two coats, neither
shoes, nor yet staves: for the workman is worthy of his meat. 11 And
into whatsoever city or town ye shall
enter, enquire who in it is worthy;
and there abide till ye go thence.
12 And when ye come into an house,
salute it. 13 And if the house be
worthy, let your peace come upon it:
but if it be not worthy, let your
peace return to you. 14 And whosoever shall not receive you, nor hear
your words, when ye depart out of
that house or city, shake off the dust
of your feet. 15 Verily I say unto
you, It shall be more tolerable for
the land of Sodom and Gomorrah in
the day of judgment, than for that
city.

We have here the instructions that Christ gave to his disciples, when he gave them their commission. Whether this charge was given them in a continued discourse, or the several articles of it hinted to them at several times, is not material; in this he *commanded them.* Jacob's blessing his sons, is called his *commanding* them, and with these commands Christ commanded a blessing. Observe,

I. The people to whom he sent them. These ambassadors are directed what places to go to.

1. Not to the Gentiles nor the Samaritans. They must not *go into the way of the Gentiles,* nor into any road out of the land of Israel, whatever temptations they might have. The Gentiles must not have the gospel brought them, till the Jews have first refused it. As to the Samaritans, who were the posterity of that mongrel people that the king of Assyria planted about Samaria, their country lay between Judea and Galilee, so that they could not avoid *going into the way* of the Samaritans, but they must *not enter into any of their cities.* Christ had declined manifesting himself to the Gentiles or Sama-

ritans, and therefore the apostles must not preach to them. If the gospel be hid from any place, Christ thereby hides himself from that place. This restraint was upon them only in their first mission, afterwards they were appointed to go *into all the world,* and teach *all nations.*

2. But *to the lost sheep of the house of Israel.* To them Christ appropriated his own ministry (*ch.* xv. 24), for he was a *minister of the circumcision* (Rom. xv. 8): and, therefore, to them the apostles, who were but his attendants and agents, must be confined. The first offer of salvation must be made to the Jews, Acts iii. 26. Note, Christ had a particular and very tender concern for the *house of Israel;* they were *beloved for the fathers' sakes,* Rom. xi. 28. He looked with compassion upon them as *lost sheep,* whom he, as a shepherd, was to gather out of the by-paths of sin and error, into which they were gone astray, and in which, if not brought back, they would wander endlessly; see Jer. ii. 6. The Gentiles also had been as lost sheep, 1 Pet. ii. 25. Christ gives this description of those to whom they were sent, to quicken them to diligence in their work, they were sent to the house of Israel (of which number they themselves lately were), whom they could not but pity, and be desirous to help.

II. The preaching work which he appointed them. He did not send them forth without an errand; no, *As ye go, preach, v.* 7. They were to be itinerant preachers: wherever they come they must proclaim the beginning of the gospel, saying, *The kingdom of heaven is at hand.* Not that they must say nothing else, but this must be their text; on this subject they must enlarge: let people know, that the kingdom of the Messiah, who is the Lord from heaven, is now to be set up according to the scriptures; from whence it follows, that men must *repent* of their sins and forsake them, that they might be admitted to the privileges of that kingdom. It is said (Mark vi. 12), *they went out, and preached that men should repent;* which was the proper use and application of this doctrine, concerning the approach of the *kingdom of heaven.* They must, therefore, expect to hear more of this long-looked-for Messiah shortly, and must be ready to receive his doctrine, to believe in him, and to submit to his yoke. The preaching of this was like the morning light, to give notice of the approach of the rising sun. How unlike was this to the preaching of Jonah, which proclaimed ruin at hand! Jonah iii. 4. This proclaims salvation at hand, *nigh them that fear God; mercy and truth meet together* (Ps. lxxxv. 9, 10), that is, *the kingdom of heaven at hand:* not so much the personal presence of the king; that must not be doated upon; but a spiritual kingdom which is to be set up, when his bodily presence is removed, in the hearts of men.

Now this was the same that John the Baptist and Christ had preached before. Note, People need to have good truths pressed again and again upon them, and if they be preached and heard with new affections, they are as if they were fresh to us. Christ, in the gospel, is *the same yesterday, to-day, and for ever,* Heb. xiii. 8. Afterwards, indeed, when the Spirit was poured out, and the Christian church was formed, this *kingdom of heaven came,* which was now spoken of as *at hand;* but the *kingdom of heaven* must still be the subject of our preaching: now it is come, we must tell people it is come to them, and must lay before them the precepts and privileges of it; and there is a kingdom of glory yet to come, which we must speak of as at hand, and quicken people to diligence from the consideration of that.

III. The power he gave them to work miracles for the confirmation of their doctrine, *v.* 8. When he sent them to preach the same doctrine that he had preached, he empowered them to confirm it, by the same divine seals, which could never be set to a lie. This is not necessary now the kingdom of God is come; to call for miracles now is to lay again the foundation when the building is reared. The point being settled, and the doctrine of Christ sufficiently attested, by the miracles which Christ and his apostles wrought, it is tempting God to ask for more signs. They are directed here,

1. To use their power in doing good: not "Go and remove mountains," or "fetch fire from heaven," but, *Heal the sick, cleanse the lepers.* They are sent abroad as public blessings, to intimate to the world, that love and goodness were the spirit and genius of that gospel which they came to preach, and of that kingdom which they were employed to set up. By this it would appear, that they were the servants of that God who is good and does good, and whose mercy is *over all his works;* and that the intention of the doctrine they preached, was to heal sick souls, and to *raise* those that were *dead in sin;* and therefore, perhaps, that of *raising the dead* is mentioned; for though we read not of their raising any to life before the *resurrection of Christ,* yet they were instrumental to raise many to *spiritual life.*

2. In *doing good freely; Freely ye have received, freely give.* Those that had power to heal all diseases, had an opportunity to enrich themselves; who would not purchase such easy certain cures at any rate? Therefore they are cautioned not to make a gain of the power they had to work miracles: they must cure *gratis,* further to exemplify the nature and complexion of the gospel kingdom, which is made up, not only of grace, but of free grace. *Gratia gratis data* (Rom. iii. 24), *freely by his grace.* Buy medicines *without money, and without price,* Isa. lv. 1. And the reason is, because *freely you have received.* Their power to heal the sick cost them no

thing, and, therefore, they must not make any secular advantage to themselves of it. Simon Magus would not have offered money for the gifts of the Holy Ghost, if he had not hoped to get money by them; Acts viii. 18. Note, The consideration of Christ's freeness in doing good to us, should make us free in doing good to others.

IV. The provision that must be made for them in this expedition; it is a thing to be considered in sending an ambassador, who must bear the charge of the embassy. As to that,

1. They must make no provision for it themselves, *v.* 9, 10. *Provide neither gold nor silver.* As, on the one hand, they shall not raise estates by their work, so, on the other hand, they shall not spend what little they have of their own upon it. This was confined to the present mission, and Christ would teach them, (1.) To act *under the conduct of human prudence.* They were now to make but a short excursion, and were soon to return to their Master, and to their head-quarters again, and, therefore, why should they burthen themselves with that which they would have no occasion for? (2.) To act in *dependence upon Divine Providence.* They must be taught to live, without *taking thought for life, ch.* vi. 25, &c. Note, They who go upon Christ's errand, have, of all people, most reason to trust him for *food convenient.* Doubtless he will not be wanting to those that are working for him. Those whom he employs, as they are taken under special protection, so they are entitled to special provisions. Christ's hired servants shall have *bread enough and to spare;* while we abide faithful to God and our duty, and are in care to do our work well, we may cast all our other care upon God; Jehovah-jireh, let the Lord provide for us and ours as he thinks fit.

2. They might expect that those to whom they were sent would *provide for them* what was necessary, *v.* 10. The *workman is worthy of his meat.* They must not expect to be fed by miracles, as Elijah was: but they might depend upon God to incline the hearts of those they went among, to be kind to them, and provide for them. Though they who *serve at the altar* may not expect to grow rich by the altar, yet they may expect to live, and to live comfortably upon it, 1 Cor. ix. 13, 14. It is fit they should have their maintenance from their work. Ministers are, and must be, workmen, labourers, and they that are so are *worthy of their meat,* so as not to be forced to any other labour for the earning of it. Christ would have his disciples, as not to distrust their God, so not to distrust their countrymen, so far as to doubt of a comfortable subsistence among them. If you preach to them, and endeavour to do good among them, surely they will give you meat and drink enough for your necessities: and if they do, never desire dainties; God will pay you your wages hereafter, and it will be running on in the mean time.

V. The proceedings they were to observe in dealing with any place, *v.* 11—15. They went abroad they knew not whither, uninvited, unexpected, knowing none, and known of none; the land of their nativity was to them a strange land; what rule must they go by? what course must they take? Christ would not send them out without full instructions, and here they are.

1. They are here directed how to conduct themselves toward those that were *strangers to them;* How to do,

(1.) In *strange towns and cities:* when you come to a town, *enquire who* in it *is worthy.* [1.] It is supposed that there were some such in every place, as were better disposed than others to receive the gospel, and the preachers of it; though it was a time of general corruption and apostasy. Note, In the worst of times and places, we may charitably hope that there are some who distinguish themselves, and are better than their neighbours; some who swim against the stream, and are as wheat among the chaff. There were saints in Nero's household. Enquire who is worthy, who there are that have some fear of God before their eyes, and have made a good improvement of the light and knowledge they have. The best are far from meriting the favour of a gospel offer; but some would be more likely than others to give the apostles and their message a favourable entertainment, and would not trample these pearls under their feet. Note, Previous dispositions to that which is good, are both directions and encouragements to ministers, in dealing with people. There is most hope of the word being profitable to those who are already so well inclined, as that it is acceptable to them; and there is here and there one such. [2.] They must enquire out such; not enquire for the best inns; public houses were no proper places for them that neither took money with them (*v.* 9), nor expected to receive any (*v.* 8); but they must look out for accommodations in private houses, with those that would entertain them well, and expect no other recompence for it but a prophet's reward, an apostle's reward, their praying and preaching. Note, They that entertain the gospel, must neither grudge the expense of it, nor promise themselves to get by it in this world. They must enquire, not who is rich, but who is worthy; not who is the best gentleman, but who is the best man. Note, Christ's disciples, wherever they come, should ask for the good people of the place, and be acquainted with them; when we took God for our God, we took his people for our people, and like will rejoice in its like. Paul in all his travels found out the brethren, if there were any, Acts xxviii. 14. It is implied, that if they did enquire who was worthy, they might discover them. They that were better than their neighbours would be taken notice of, and any one could tell them, there lives an honest, sober, good man; for this is a character which, like the ointment of the right hand, betrays itself, and fills the house with its odours. Every body knew where the seer's house was, 1 Sam. ix. 18. [3.] In the house of those they found worthy, they must continue; which intimates that they were to make so short a stay at each town, that they needed not change their lodging, but whatever house providence brought them to at first, there they must continue till they left that town. They are justly suspected, as having no good design, that are often changing their quarters. Note, It becomes the disciples of Christ to make the best of that which is, to abide by it, and not be for shifting upon every dislike or inconvenience.

(2.) In strange houses. When they had found the house of one they thought worthy, they must at their entrance salute it. "In those common civilities, be beforehand with people, in token of your humility. Think it not a disparagement, to invite yourselves into a house, nor stand upon the *punctilio* of being invited. Salute the family, [1.] To draw on further discourse, and so to introduce your message." (From matters of common conversation, we may insensibly pass into that communication which is good to the use of edifying.) [2.] "To try whether you are welcome or not; you will take notice whether the salutation be received with shyness and coldness, or with a ready return. He that will not receive your salutation kindly, will not receive your message kindly; for he that is unskilful and unfaithful in a little, will also be in much, Luke xvi. 10. [3.] To insinuate yourselves into their good opinion. *Salute the family,* that they may see that though you are serious, you are not morose." Note, Religion teaches us to be courteous and civil, and obliging to all with whom we have to do. Though the apostles went out backed with the authority of the Son of God himself, yet their instructions were, when they came into a house, not to *command it,* but to *salute* it; for *love's sake rather to beseech,* is the evangelical way, Philemon 8, 9. Souls are first drawn to Christ with the *cords of a man,* and kept to him by the *bands of love,* Hos. xi. 4 When Peter made the first offer of the gospel to Cornelius, a Gentile, Peter was first saluted; see Acts x. 25, for the Gentiles courted that which the Jews were courted to.

When they had saluted the family after a godly sort, they must, by the return, judge concerning the family, and proceed accordingly. Note, The eye of God is upon us, to observe what entertainment we give to good people and good ministers; if *the house be worthy, let your peace come* and rest *upon it; if not, let it return to you, v.* 13. It seems then, that after they had enquired for the *most worthy* (*v.* 11), it was possible they might light upon those that were unworthy. Note, Though it is wisdom to hearken to, yet it is folly to rely upon, common report and opinion; we ought to use a judgment of discretion, and to see with our own eyes. *The wisdom of the prudent is* himself to *understand his* own *way.* Now this rule is intended,

First, For satisfaction to the apostles. The common salutation was, *Peace be unto you;* this, as they used it, was turned into gospel; it was the *peace of God,* the peace of the kingdom of heaven, that they wished. Now lest they should make a scruple of pronouncing this blessing upon all promiscuously, because many were utterly unworthy of it, this is to clear them of that scruple; Christ tells them that this gospel prayer (for so it was now become) should be put up for all, as the gospel proffer was made to all indefinitely, and that they should leave it to God who knows the heart, and every man's true character, to determine the issue of it. If the house be worthy, it will reap the benefit of your blessing; if not, there is no harm done, you will not lose the benefit of it; *it shall return to you,* as David's prayers for his ungrateful enemies did, Ps. xxxv. 13. Note, It becomes us to judge charitably *of all,* to pray heartily *for all,* and to conduct ourselves courteously *to all,* for that is our part, and then to leave it with God to determine what effect it shall have upon them, for that is his part.

Secondly, For direction to them. "If, upon your salutation, it appear that they are indeed worthy, let them have more of your company, and so *let your peace come upon them;* preach the gospel to them, peace by Jesus Christ; but if otherwise, if they carry it rudely to you, and shut their doors against you, *let your peace,* as much as in you lies, *return to you.* Retract what you have said, and turn your backs upon them; by slighting this, they have made themselves unworthy of the rest of your favours, and cut themselves short of them." Note, Great blessings are often lost by a neglect seemingly small and inconsiderable, when men are in their probation and upon their behaviour. Thus Esau lost his birthright (Gen. xxv. 34), and Saul his kingdom, 1 Sam. xiii. 13, 14.

2. They are here directed how to carry it towards those that were refusers of them. The case is put (*v.* 14) of those that *would not receive them, nor hear their words.* The apostles might think, that now they had such a doctrine to preach, and such a power to work miracles for the confirmation of it, no doubt but they should be universally entertained and made welcome: they are, therefore, told before, that there would be those that would slight them, and put contempt on them and their message. Note, The best and most powerful preachers of the gospel must expect to meet with some, that will not

so much as give them the hearing, nor show them any token of respect. Many turn *a deaf ear*, even to the *joyful sound*, and will not *hearken to the voice of the charmers, charm they never so wisely*. Observe, "They will not *receive you*, and they will not *hear your words*." Note, Contempt of the gospel, and contempt of gospel ministers, commonly go together, and they will either of them be construed into a contempt of Christ, and will be reckoned for accordingly.

Now in this case we have here,

(1.) The directions given to the apostles what to do. They must *depart out of that house or city*. Note, The gospel will not tarry long with those that put it away from them. At their departure they must *shake off the dust of their feet*, [1.] In detestation of their wickedness; it was so abominable, that it did even pollute the ground they went upon, which must therefore be *shaken off* as a filthy thing. The apostles must have no fellowship nor communion with them; must not so much as carry away the dust of their city with them. *The work of them that turn aside* shall *not cleave to me*, Ps. ci. 3. The prophet was not to *eat or drink* in *Bethel*, 1 Kings xiii. 9. [2.] As a denunciation of wrath against them. It was to signify, that they were base and vile as dust, and that God would *shake them off*. The dust of the apostles' feet, which they left behind them, would witness against them, and be brought in as evidence, that the gospel had been preached to them, Mark vi. 11. Compare Jam. v. 3. See this practised, Acts xiii. 51, xviii. 6. Note, They who *despise* God and his gospel shall be *lightly esteemed*.

(2.) The *doom passed* upon such *wilful recusants, v.* 15. It shall be *more tolerable, in the day of judgment, for the land of* Sodom, as wicked a place as it was. Note, [1.] There is a day of judgment coming, when all those that refused the gospel will certainly be called to account for it; however they now make a jest of it. They that would not hear the doctrine that would save them, shall be made to hear the sentence that will ruin them. Their judgment is respited till *that day*. [2.] There are different degrees of punishment in that day. All the pains of hell will be *intolerable;* but some will be more so than others. Some sinners sink deeper into hell than others, and are beaten with more stripes. [3.] The condemnation of those that reject the gospel, will in that day be severer and heavier than that of Sodom and Gomorrah. Sodom is said to suffer the vengeance of eternal fire, Jude 7. But that *vengeance* will come with an aggravation upon those that despise the great salvation. Sodom and Gomorrah were exceedingly wicked (Gen. xiii. 13), and that which filled up the measure of their iniquity was, that they *received not* the angels that were sent to them, but abused them (Gen. xix. 4, 5), and *hearkened not to their words, v.* 14. And yet it will be more tolerable for them than for those who receive not Christ's ministers and hearken not to their words. God's wrath against them will be more flaming, and their own reflections upon themselves more cutting. *Son, remember!* will sound most dreadfully in the ears of such as had a fair offer made them of *eternal life*, and chose death rather. The iniquity of Israel, when God sent them his servants the prophets, is represented as, upon that account, more heinous than the iniquity of Sodom (Ezek. xvi. 48, 49), much more now he sent them his Son, the great Prophet.

16 Behold, I send you forth as
sheep in the midst of wolves: be ye
therefore wise as serpents, and harmless as doves. 17 But beware of
men: for they will deliver you up to
the councils, and they will scourge
you in their synagogues; 18 And
ye shall be brought before governors
and kings for my sake, for a testimony against them and the Gentiles.
19 But when they deliver you up,
take no thought how or what ye shall
speak; for it shall be given you in
that same hour what ye shall speak.
20 For it is not ye that speak, but
the Spirit of your Father which speaketh in you. 21 And the brother shall
deliver up the brother to death, and
the father the child: and the children
shall rise up against *their* parents,
and cause them to be put to death.
22 And ye shall be hated of all *men*
for my name's sake; but he that endureth to the end shall be saved.
23 But when they persecute you in
this city, flee ye into another: for
verily I say unto you, Ye shall not
have gone over the cities of Israel
till the Son of man be come. 24 The
disciple is not above *his* master, nor
the servant above his lord. 25 It is
enough for the disciple that he be as
his master, and the servant as his
lord. If they have called the master
of the house Beelzebub, how much
more *shall they call* them of his
household? 26 Fear not them therefore; for there is nothing covered
that shall not be revealed; and hid,
that shall not be known. 27 What
I tell you in darkness, *that* speak ye
in light: and what ye hear in the
ear, *that* preach ye upon the house-

tops. 28 And fear not them which
kill the body, but are not able to kill
the soul: but rather fear him which
is able to destroy both soul and body
in hell. 29 Are not two sparrows
sold for a farthing? and one of them
shall not fall on the ground without
your Father. 30 But the very hairs of
your head are all numbered. 31 Fear
ye not therefore; ye are of more value
than many sparrows. 32 Whosoever
therefore shall confess me before men,
him will I confess also before my
Father which is in heaven. 33 But
whosoever shall deny me before men,
him will I also deny before my Father
which is in heaven. 34 Think not
that I am come to send peace on
earth: I came not to send peace, but
a sword. 35 For I am come to set
a man at variance against his father,
and the daughter against her mother,
and the daughter-in-law against her
mother-in-law. 36 And a man's foes
shall be they of his own household.
37 He that loveth father or mother
more than me is not worthy of me:
and he that loveth son or daughter
more than me is not worthy of me.
38 And he that taketh not his cross,
and followeth after me, is not worthy
of me. 39 He that findeth his life
shall lose it: and he that loseth his
life for my sake shall find it. 40 He
that receiveth you, receiveth me;
and he that receiveth me, receiveth
him that sent me. 41 He that receiveth a prophet, in the name of a
prophet, shall receive a prophet's reward; and he that receiveth a righteous man, in the name of a righteous
man, shall receive a righteous man's
reward. 42 And whosoever shall give
to drink unto one of these little ones
a cup of cold *water* only in the name
of a disciple, verily I say unto you,
he shall in no wise lose his reward.

All these verses relate to the sufferings of Christ's ministers in their work, which they are here taught to expect, and prepare for; they are directed also how to bear them, and how to go on with their work in the midst of them. This part of the sermon looks further than to their present mission; for we find not that they met with any great hardships or persecutions while Christ was with them, nor were they well able to bear them; but they are here forewarned of the troubles they should meet with, when, after Christ's resurrection, their commission should be *enlarged*, and the kingdom of heaven, which was now *at hand*, should be actually set up; they dreamed of nothing then, but outward pomp and power; but Christ tells them, they must expect greater sufferings than they were yet called to; that they should then be made prisoners, when they expected to be made princes. It is good to be told what troubles we may hereafter meet with, that we may provide accordingly, and may not boast, as if we had put off the harness, when we are yet but girding it on.

We have here intermixed, I. Predictions of trouble: and, II. Prescriptions of counsel and comfort, with reference to it.

I. We have here predictions of trouble: which the disciples should meet with in their work: Christ foresaw *their* sufferings as well as his own, and yet will have them go on, as he went on himself; and he foretold them, not only that the troubles might not be a surprise to them, and so a shock to their faith, but that, being the accomplishment of a prediction, they might be a confirmation to their faith.

He tells them what they should suffer, and from whom.

1. *What they should suffer:* hard things to be sure; for, *Behold, I send you forth as sheep in the midst of wolves, v.* 16. And what may a flock of poor, helpless, unguarded sheep expect, in the midst of a herd of ravenous wolves, but to be worried and torn? Note, Wicked men are like wolves, in whose nature it is to devour and destroy. God's people, and especially his ministers, are like sheep among them, of a contrary nature and disposition, exposed to them, and commonly an easy prey to them. It looked unkind in Christ to expose them to so much danger, who had left all to follow him; but he knew that the glory reserved for his sheep, when in the great day they shall be set on his right hand, would be a recompence sufficient for sufferings as well as services. They are as *sheep among wolves*, that is frightful; but Christ sends them forth, that is comfortable; for he that sends them forth will protect them, and bear them out. But that they might know the worst, he tells them particularly what they must expect.

(1.) They must expect to be hated, *v.* 22. *Ye shall be hated for my name's sake:* that is the root of all the rest, and a bitter root it is. Note, Those whom Christ loves, the world hates; as whom the court blesses the country curses. *If the world hated Christ without a cause* (John xv. 25), no marvel if it hated those that bore his image and served his interests. We hate what is nauseous, and they *are counted as the offscouring of all things*, 1 Cor. iv. 13. We hate what is noxious, and they are counted *the troublers of the land*

1 Kings xviii. 17), and the tormentors of their neighbours, Rev. xi. 10. It is grievous to be *hated,* and to be the object of so much ill-will, but it is *for thy name's sake;* which, as it speaks the true reason of the hatred, whatever is pretended, so it speaks comfort to them who are thus hated; it is for a good cause, and they have a good friend that shares with them in it, and takes it to himself.

(2.) They must expect to be apprehended and arraigned as malefactors. Their restless malice is resistless malice, and they will not only attempt, but will prevail, to *deliver you up to the councils* (*v.* 17, 18), to the bench of aldermen or justices, that take care of the public peace. Note, A deal of mischief is often done to good men, under colour of law and justice. In *the place of judgment there is wickedness,* persecuting wickedness, Eccl. iii. 16. They must look for trouble, not only from inferior magistrates in the councils, but from governors and kings, the supreme magistrates. To be brought before them, under such black representations as were commonly made of Christ's disciples, was dreadful and dangerous; for *the wrath of a king is as the roaring of a lion.* We find this often fulfilled in the *acts of the apostles.*

(3.) They must expect to be put to death (*v.* 21); *They shall deliver them to death,* to death in state, with pomp and solemnity, when it shows itself most as *the king of terrors.* The malice of the enemies rages so high as to inflict this; it is *the blood of the saints* that they thirst after: the faith and patience of the saints stand so firm as to expect this; *Neither count I my life dear to myself:* the wisdom of Christ permits it, knowing how to make the blood of the martyrs *the seal of the truth,* and *the seed of the church.* By this noble army's not loving *their lives to the death,* Satan has been vanquished, and the kingdom of Christ and its interests greatly advanced, Rev. xi. 11. They were put to death as criminals, so the enemies meant it, but really as sacrifices (Phil. ii. 17; 2 Tim. iv. 6); as burnt offerings, sacrifices of acknowledgment to the honour of God, and in his truth and cause.

(4.) They must expect, in the midst of these sufferings, to be branded with the most odious and ignominious names and characters that could be. Persecutors would be ashamed in this world, if they did not first dress up those in bear-skins whom they thus bait, and represent them in such colours as may serve to justify such cruelties. The blackest of all the ill characters they give them is here stated; they call them Beelzebub, the name of the prince of the devils, *v.* 25. They represent them as ringleaders of the interest of the kingdom of darkness, and since every one thinks he hates the devil, thus they endeavour to make them odious to all mankind. See, and be amazed to see, how this world is imposed upon: [1.] Satan's sworn enemies are represented as his friends; the apostles, who pulled down the devil's kingdom, were called devils. Thus *men laid to their charge,* not only *things which they knew not,* but *things which they* abhorred, and were directly contrary to, and the reverse of. [2.] Satan's sworn servants would be thought to be his enemies, and they never more effectually do his work, than when they pretend to be fighting against him. Many times they who themselves are nearest akin to the devil, are most apt to father others upon him; and those that paint him on others' clothes have him reigning in their own hearts. It is well there is a day coming, when (as it follows here, *v.* 26) that which is hid will be brought to light.

(5.) These sufferings are here represented by a sword and division, *v.* 34, 35. *Think not that I am come to send peace,* temporal peace and outward prosperity; they thought Christ came to give all his followers wealth and power in the world; "no," says Christ, "I did not come with a view to give them *peace; peace* in heaven they may be sure of, but not *peace* on earth." Christ came to give us *peace* with God, *peace* in our consciences, *peace* with our brethren, but *in the world ye shall have tribulation.* Note, They mistake the design of the gospel, who think their profession of it will secure them from, for it will certainly expose them to, trouble in this world. If all the world would receive Christ, there would then follow a universal *peace,* but while there are and will be so many that reject him (and those not only *the children of this world,* but *the seed of the serpent*), the children of God, that are called out of the world, must expect to feel the fruits of their enmity.

[1.] Look not for *peace, but a sword.* Christ came to give *the sword of the word,* with which his disciples fight against the world, and *conquering* work this sword has made (Rev. vi. 4; xix. 21), and *the sword of persecution,* with which the world fights against the disciples, being *cut to the heart* with *the sword of the word* (Acts vii. 54), and tormented by the testimony of Christ's witnesses (Rev. xi. 10), and *cruel* work this sword made. Christ sent that gospel, which gives occasion for the drawing of this sword, and so may be said to send this sword; he orders his church into a suffering state for the trial and praise of his people's graces, and *the filling up of the measure of their* enemies' sins.

[2.] Look not for *peace,* but division (*v.* 35), *I am come to set men at variance.* This effect of the preaching of the gospel is not the fault of the gospel, but of those who do not receive it. When some *believe the things that are spoken, and others believe them not,* the faith of those that believe condemns those that believe not, and, therefore, they have an enmity against them that believe. Note, the most violent and implacable feuds have ever been those that have arisen from difference in religion; no enmity like that of the persecutors, no resolution like that of the persecuted. Thus Christ tells his disciples what they should suffer, and these were hard sayings; if they could bear these, they could bear any thing. Note, Christ has dealt fairly and faithfully with us, in telling us the worst we can meet with in his service; and he would have us deal so with ourselves, in sitting down and counting the cost.

2. They are here told from whom, and by whom, they should suffer these hard things. Surely hell itself must be let loose, and devils, those desperate and despairing spirits, that *have no part nor lot in* the great salvation, must become incarnate, ere such spiteful enemies could be found to a doctrine, the substance of which was *good will toward men,* and *the reconciling of the world to God;* no, would you think it? all this mischief arises to the preachers of the gospel, from those to whom they came to preach salvation. Thus *the blood-thirsty hate the upright, but the just seek his soul* (Prov. xxix. 10), and therefore heaven is so much opposed on earth, because earth is so much under the power of hell, Eph. ii. 2.

These hard things Christ's disciples must suffer,

(1.) From men (*v.* 17). "*Beware of men;* you will have need to stand upon your guard, even against those who are of the same nature with you"—such is the depravity and degeneracy of that nature *(homo homini lupus,—man is a wolf to man),* crafty and politic as men, but cruel and barbarous as beasts, and wholly divested of the thing called humanity. Note, Persecuting rage and enmity turn men into brutes, into devils. Paul at Ephesus fought with beasts in the shape of men, 1 Cor. xv. 32. It is a sad pass that the world is come to, when the best friends it has, have need to *beware of men.* It aggravates the troubles of Christ's suffering servants, that they arise from those who *are bone of their bone,* made of the same blood. Persecutors are, in this respect, worse than beasts, that they prey upon those of their own kind; *Sævis inter se convenit ursis—Even savage bears agree among themselves.* It is very grievous to have *men rise up against us* (Ps. cxxiv.), from whom we might expect protection and sympathy; *men,* and no more: mere *men; men,* and not saints; *natural men* (1 Cor. ii. 14); *men of this world,* Ps. xvii. 14. Saints are more than *men,* and are *redeemed from among men,* and therefore are *hated by them.* The nature of man, if it be not sanctified, is the worst nature in the world next to that of devils. *They are men,* and therefore subordinate, dependent, dying creatures; *they are men,* but *they are but men* (Ps. ix. 20), and *who art thou, that thou shouldst be afraid of a man that shall die?* Isa. li. 12. *Beware of the men,* so Dr. Hammond; those you are acquainted with, the men of the Jewish sanhedrim, which disallowed Christ, 1 Pet. ii. 4.

(2.) From professing men, men that *have a form of godliness,* and make a show of religion. *They will scourge you in their synagogues,* their places of meeting for the worship of God, and for the exercise of their church-discipline: so that they looked upon the scourging of Christ's ministers to be a branch of their religion. Paul was *five times scourged in the synagogues,* 2 Cor. xi. 24. The Jews, under colour of zeal for Moses, were the most bitter persecutors of Christ and Christianity, and placed those outrages to the score of their religion. Note, Christ's disciples have suffered much from conscientious persecutors, that *scourge them in their synagogues,* cast them out and kill them, and *think they do God good service* (John xvi. 2), and say, *Let the Lord be glorified,* Isa. lxvi. 5; Zech. xi. 4, 5. But the synagogue will be so far from consecrating the persecution, that the persecution, doubtless, profanes and desecrates the synagogue.

(3.) From great men, and men in authority. The Jews did not only scourge them, which was the utmost their remaining power extended to, but when they could go no further themselves, they delivered them up to the Roman powers, as they did Christ, John xviii. 30. *Ye shall be brought before governors and kings* (*v.* 18), who, having more power, are in a capacity of doing the more mischief. *Governors and kings* receive their power from Christ (Prov. viii. 15), and should be his servants, and his church's protectors and nursing-fathers, but they often use their power against him, and are rebels to Christ, and oppressors of his church. *The kings of the earth* set themselves against his kingdom, Ps. ii. 1, 2; Acts iv. 25, 26. Note, It has often been the lot of good men to have great men for their enemies.

(4.) From all men (*v.* 22). *Ye shall be hated of all men,* of all wicked men, and these are the generality of men, *for the whole world lies in wickedness.* So few are there that love, and own, and countenance Christ's righteous cause, that we may say, the friends of it are *hated of all men;* they *are all gone astray,* and, therefore, *eat up my people,* Ps. xiv. 3. As far as the apostasy from God goes, so far the enmity against the saints goes; sometimes it appears more general than at other times, but there is something of this poison lurking in the hearts of all *the children of disobedience. The world hates you,* for it *wonders after the beast,* Rev. xiii. 3. *Every man is a liar,* and therefore a hater of truth.

(5.) From those of their own kindred. *The brother shall deliver up the brother to death, v.* 21. *A man shall be,* upon this account, *at variance with his own father;* nay, and those of the weaker and tenderer sex too shall become persecutors and persecuted; *the persecuting daughter will be against the believing mother,* where natural affection and filial duty, one would think, should prevent or soon extinguish the quarrel; and then, no marvel *if the daughter-in-law be against the mother-in-law;* where, too often, the coldness of love seeks occasion of contention, *v.* 35. In general, *a man's foes shall be they of his own household* (*v.* 36). They who should be his friends will be incensed against him for embracing Christianity, and especially for adhering to it when it comes to be persecuted, and will join with his persecutors against him. Note, The strongest bonds of relative love and duty have often been broken through, by an enmity against Christ and his doctrine. Such has been the power of prejudice against the true religion, and zeal for a false one, that all other regards, the most natural and sacred, the most engaging and endearing, have been sacrificed to these Molochs. They who *rage against the Lord, and his anointed ones, break* even *these bonds in sunder, and cast away* even *these cords from them,* Ps. ii. 2, 3. Christ's spouse suffers hard things from the anger of *her own mother's children,* Cant. i. 6. Sufferings from such are more grievous; nothing cuts more than this, *It was thou, a man, mine equal* (Ps. lv. 12, 13); and the enmity of such is commonly most implacable; *a brother offended is harder to be won than a strong city,* Prov. xviii. 19. The martyrologies, both ancient and modern, are full of instances of this. Upon the whole matter, it appears, that *all that will live godly in Christ Jesus, must suffer persecution; and through* many *tribulations we must* expect to *enter into the kingdom of God.*

II. With these predictions of trouble, we have here prescriptions of counsels and comforts for a time of trial. He sends them out exposed to danger indeed, and expecting it, but well armed with instructions and encouragements, sufficient to bear them up, and bear them out, in all these trials. Let us gather up what he says,

1. By way of counsel and direction in several things.

(1.) *Be ye wise as serpents, v.* 16. "You may be so" (so some take it, only as a permission); "you may be as wary as you please, provided you be harmless as doves." But it is rather to be taken as a precept, recommending to us that wisdom of the prudent, which is to understand his way, as useful at all times, but especially in suffering times. "*Therefore,* because you are exposed, as sheep among wolves; *be ye wise as serpents;* not wise as foxes, whose cunning is to deceive others; but as *serpents,* whose policy is only to defend themselves, and to shift for their own safety." The disciples of Christ are hated and persecuted as *serpents,* and their ruin is sought, and, therefore, they need the *serpent's* wisdom. Note, It is the will of Christ that his people and ministers, being so much exposed to troubles in this world, as they usually are, should not needlessly expose themselves, but use all fair and lawful means for their own preservation. Christ gave us an example of this wisdom, *ch.* xxi. 24, 25; xxii 17, 18, 19; John viii. 6, 7; besides the many escapes he made out of the hands of his enemies, till his hour was come. See an instance of Paul's wisdom, Acts xxiii. 6, 7. In the cause of Christ we must sit loose to life and all its comforts, but must not be prodigal of them. It is the wisdom of the *serpent* to secure his head, that that may not be broken, to *stop his ear to the voice of the charmer* (Ps. lviii. 4, 5), and *to take shelter in the clefts of the rocks;* and herein we may *be wise as serpents.* We must *be wise,* not to pull trouble upon our own heads; *wise* to keep silence in an evil time, and not to give offence, if we can help it.

(2) *Be ye harmless as doves.* "Be mild, and meek, and dispassionate; not only do nobody any hurt, but bear nobody any ill will; be without gall, *as doves* are; this must always go along with the former." They are *sent forth among wolves,* therefore must *be as wise as serpents,* but they are *sent forth as sheep,* therefore must *be harmless as doves.* We must *be wise,* not to wrong ourselves, but rather so than wrong any one else; must use the harmlessness of the *dove* to bear twenty injuries, rather than the subtlety of the *serpent* to offer or to return one. Note, It must be the continual care of all Christ's disciples, to be innocent and inoffensive in word and deed, especially in consideration of the enemies they are in the midst of. We have need of a *dove-like* spirit, when we are beset with birds of prey, that we may neither provoke them nor be provoked by them: David coveted *the wings of a dove,* on which to fly away and be at rest, rather than the wings of a hawk. *The Spirit descended on Christ as a dove,* and all believers partake of *the Spirit of Christ, a dove-like* spirit, made for love, not for war.

(3.) *Beware of men, v.* 17. "Be always upon your guard, and avoid dangerous company; take heed what you say and do, and presume not too far upon any man's fidelity; be jealous of the most plausible pretensions; *trust not in a friend,* no, not *in the wife of thy bosom,*" Micah vii. 5. Note, It becomes those who are gracious to be cautious, for we are taught to *cease from man.* Such a wretched world do we live in, that we know not whom to trust. Ever since our Master was betrayed with a kiss, by one of his own disciples, we have need to *beware of men, of false brethren.*

(4.) *Take no thought how or what ye shall speak, v.* 19. "When you are brought before magistrates, conduct yourselves decently, but afflict not yourselves with care how you shall come off. A prudent thought there must be, but not an anxious, perplexing, disquieting thought; let this *care be cast upon God,* as well as that—*what you shall eat and what you shall drink.* Do not study to make fine speeches, *ad captandam benevolentiam*——*to ingratiate yourselves;* affect not quaint expressions, flourishes of wit, and laboured periods, which only serve to gild a bad cause;

the gold of a good one needs it not. It argues a diffidence of your cause, to be solicitous in this matter, as if it were not sufficient to speak for itself. You know upon what grounds you go, and then *verbaque prævisam rem non invita sequentur—suitable expressions will readily occur.*" Never any spoke better before governors and kings than those three champions, who took *no thought before, what they should speak: O Nebuchadnezzar, we are not careful to answer thee in this matter,* Dan. iii. 16. See Ps. cxix. 46. Note, The disciples of Christ must be more thoughtful how to *do* well than how to *speak* well; how to *keep* their integrity than how to *vindicate* it. *Non magna loquimur, sed vivimus—Our lives, not boasting words,* form the best apology.

(5.) *When they persecute you in this city, flee to another, v.* 23. "Thus reject them who reject you and your doctrine, and try whether others will not receive you and it. Thus shift for your own safety." Note, In case of imminent peril, the disciples of Christ may and must secure themselves by flight, when God, in his providence, opens to *them a door of escape.* He that flies may fight again. It is no inglorious thing for Christ's soldiers to quit their ground, provided they do not quit their colours: they may go out of the way of *danger,* though they must not go out of the way of *duty.* Observe Christ's care of his disciples, in providing places of retreat and shelter for them; ordering it so, that persecution rages not in all places at the same time; but *when one city* is made too hot for them, *another* is reserved for a cooler shade, and *a little sanctuary;* a favour to be used and not to be slighted; yet always with this proviso, that no sinful, unlawful means be used to make the escape; for then it is not a door of God's opening. We have many examples to this rule in the history both of Christ and his apostles, in the application of all which to particular cases *wisdom* and integrity are *profitable to direct.*

(6.) *Fear them not* (*v.* 26), because *they can but kill the body* (*v.* 28). Note, it is the duty and interest of Christ's disciples, not to fear the greatest of their adversaries. They who truly fear God, need not fear man; and they who are afraid of the least sin, need not be afraid of the greatest trouble. *The fear of man brings a snare,* a perplexing snare, that disturbs our peace; an entangling snare, by which we are drawn into sin; and, therefore, it must be carefully watched, and striven, and prayed against. Be the times never so difficult, enemies never so outrageous, and events never so threatening, yet need we not fear, *yet will we not fear, though the earth be removed,* while we have so good a God, so good a cause, and so *good a hope through grace.*

Yes, this is soon said; but when it comes to the trial, racks and tortures, dungeons and galleys, axes and gibbets, fire and faggot, are terrible things, enough to make the stoutest heart to tremble, and to start back, especially when it is plain, that they may be avoided by a few declining steps; and therefore, to fortify us against this temptation, we have here,

[1.] A good reason against this fear, taken from the limited power of the enemies; they *kill the body,* that is the utmost their rage can extend to; hitherto they can go, if God permit them, but no further; *they are not able to kill the soul,* nor to do it any hurt, and the soul is the man. By this it appears, that the soul does not (as some dream) fall asleep at death, nor is deprived of thought and perception; for then the killing of the body would be the killing of the soul too. The soul is killed when it is separated from God and his love, which is its life, and is made a vessel of his wrath; now this is out of the reach of their power. *Tribulation, distress, and persecution* may separate us from all the world, but cannot part between us and God, cannot make us either not to love him, or not to be loved by him, Rom. viii. 35, 37. If, therefore, we were more concerned about our souls, as our jewels, we should be less afraid of men, whose power cannot rob us of them; they can but *kill the body,* which would quickly die of itself, *not the soul,* which will enjoy itself and its God in spite of them. They can but crush the cabinet: a heathen set the tyrant at defiance with this, *Tunde capsam Anaxarchi, Anaxarchum non lædis—you may abuse the case of Anaxarchus, you cannot injure Anaxarchus himself.* The pearl of price is untouched. Seneca undertakes to make it out, that you cannot hurt a wise and good man, because death itself is no real evil to him. *Si maximum illud ultra quod nihil habent iratæ leges, aut sævissimi domini minantur, in quo imperium suum fortuna consumit, æquo placidoque animo accipimus, et scimus mortem malum non esse ob hoc, ne injuriam quidem—If with calmness and composure we meet that last extremity, beyond which injured laws and merciless tyrants have nothing to inflict, and in which fortune terminates her dominion, we know that death is not an evil, because it does not occasion the slightest injury.* Seneca *De Constantiâ.*

[2.] A good remedy against it, and that is, to fear God. *Fear him who is able to destroy both soul and body in hell.* Note, First, *Hell* is the destruction both of *soul and body;* not of the *being* of either, but the *well*-being of both; it is the ruin of the whole man; if the soul be lost, the body is lost too. They sinned together; the body was the soul's tempter to sin, and its tool in sin, and they must eternally suffer together. Secondly, This destruction comes from the power of God: he *is able to destroy;* it is a destruction from his *glorious power* (2 Thess. i. 9); *he will* in it *make his power known;* not only his authority to sentence, but his ability to execute the sentence, Rom. ix. 22. Thirdly, God *is therefore to be feared,* even by the best saints in this world. *Knowing the terrors of the Lord, we persuade men to stand in awe of him. If according to his fear so is his wrath,* then *according to his wrath so* should *his fear* be, especially because *none knows the power of his anger,* Ps. xc. 11. When Adam, in innocency, was awed by a threatening, let none of Christ's disciples think that they need not the restraint of a holy fear. *Happy is the man that fears always.* The *God of Abraham,* who was then dead, is called the *Fear of Isaac,* who was yet alive, Gen. xxxi. 42, 53. Fourthly, The fear of God, and of his power reigning in the soul, will be a sovereign antidote against the fear of man. It is better to fall under the frowns of all the world, than under God's frowns, and therefore, as it is most right in itself, so it is most safe for us, *to obey God rather than men,* Acts iv. 19. They who *are afraid of a man that shall die, forget the Lord their Maker,* Isa. li. 12, 13; Neh. iv. 14.

(7.) *What I tell you in darkness, that speak ye in light* (*v.* 27); "whatever hazards you run, go on with your work, publishing and proclaiming the everlasting gospel to all the world; that is your business, mind that. The design of the enemies is not merely to destroy *you,* but to suppress *that,* and, therefore, whatever be the consequence, publish *that.*" *What I tell you, that speak ye.* Note, That which the apostles have delivered to us is the same that *they received from Jesus Christ,* Heb. ii. 3. They spake what he told them—*that, all that,* and *nothing but that.* Those ambassadors received their instructions in private, *in darkness,* in the ear, in corners, in parables. *Many things Christ spake openly, and nothing in secret* varying from what he preached in public, John xviii. 20. But the particular instructions which he gave his disciples after his resurrection, concerning *the things pertaining to the kingdom of God,* were whispered in the ear (Acts i. 3), for then *he never showed himself openly.* But they must deliver their embassy publicly, *in the light,* and *upon the house-tops;* for the doctrine of the gospel is what all are concerned in (Prov. i. 20, 21; viii. 2, 3), therefore *he that hath ears to hear, let him hear.* The first indication of the reception of the Gentiles into the church, was *upon a house-top,* Acts x. 9. Note, There is no part of Christ's gospel that needs, upon any account, to be concealed; *the whole counsel of God must be revealed,* Acts xx. 27. In never so mixed a multitude let it be plainly and fully delivered.

2. By way of comfort and encouragement. Here is very much said to that purpose, and all little enough, considering the many hardships they were to grapple with, throughout the course of their ministry, and their present weakness, which was such, as that, without some powerful support, they could scarcely bear even the prospect of such usage; Christ therefore shows them why they should be of good cheer.

(1.) Here is one word peculiar to their present mission, *v.* 23. *Ye shall not have gone over the cities of Israel, till the Son of man be come.* They were to preach that *the kingdom of the Son of man,* the Messiah, was *at hand;* they were to pray, *Thy kingdom come:* now they should *not have gone over all the cities of Israel,* thus praying and thus preaching, before that kingdom should come, in the exaltation of Christ, and the pouring out of the Spirit. It was a comfort, [1.] That what they said should be made good: they said *the Son of man* is coming, and *behold, he comes.* Christ *will confirm the word of his messengers,* Isa. xliv. 26. [2.] That it should be made good quickly. Note, It is matter of comfort to Christ's labourers, that their working time will be short, and soon over; the hireling has his day; the work and warfare will in a little time be accomplished. [3.] That then they should be advanced to a higher station. *When the Son of man comes, they shall be endued with greater power from on high;* now they were sent forth as agents and envoys, but in a little time their commission should be enlarged, and they should be sent forth as plenipotentiaries into all the world.

(2.) Here are many words that relate to their work in general, and the troubles they were to meet with in it; and *they are good words and comfortable words.*

[1.] That their sufferings were *for a testimony against them and the Gentiles, v.* 18. When the Jewish consistories transfer you to the Roman governors, that they may have you put to death, your being hurried thus from one judgment-seat to another, will help to make your testimony the more public, and will give you an opportunity of bringing the gospel to the Gentiles, as well as to the Jews; nay, you will testify to them, and against them, by the very troubles you undergo. Note, God's people, and especially God's ministers, are his witnesses (Isa. xliii. 10), not only in their *doing* work, but in their *suffering* work. Hence they are called martyrs—*witnesses* for Christ, that his truths are of undoubted certainty and value; and, being witnesses for him, they are witnesses against those who oppose him and his gospel. The sufferings of the martyrs, as they witness to the truth of the gospel they profess, so they are testimonies of the enmity of their persecutors, and both ways they are a testimony against them, and will be produced in evidence in the great day, when *the saints shall judge the world;* and the reason of the sentence will be, *Inasmuch as ye did it unto these, ye did it unto me.* Now if their sufferings be a testimony, how cheerfully should they be borne! for the testimony is not finished till those come, Rev. xi. 7. If they be Christ's witnesses, they shall be sure to have their charges borne.

[2.] That upon all occasions they should have God's special presence with them, and the immediate assistance of his Holy Spirit, particularly when they should be called out to bear their testimony *before governors and kings; it shall be given you* (said Christ) *in that same hour what ye shall speak.* Christ's disciples were chosen *from among the foolish of the world,* unlearned and ignorant men, and, therefore, might justly distrust their own abilities, especially when they were called before great men. When Moses was sent to Pharaoh, he complained, *I am not eloquent,* Exod. iv. 10. When Jeremiah was set over the kingdoms, he objected, *I am but a child,* Jer. i. 6, 10. Now, in answer to this suggestion, First, they are here promised that *it should be given them,* not some time before, but *in that same hour, what they should speak.* They shall speak *extempore,* and yet shall speak as much to the purpose, as if it had been never so well studied. Note, When God calls us out to speak for him, we may depend upon him to teach us what to say; even then, when we labour under the greatest disadvantages and discouragements. Secondly, They are here assured, that the blessed Spirit should draw up their plea for them. *It is not ye that speak, but the Spirit of your Father, which speaketh in you, v.* 20. They were not left to themselves upon such an occasion, but God undertook for them; his Spirit of wisdom spoke *in* them, as sometimes his providence wonderfully spoke *for* them, and by both together they were manifested in the consciences even of their persecutors. God gave them an ability, not only to speak to the purpose, but what they did say, to say it with holy zeal. The same Spirit that assisted them in the pulpit, assisted them at the bar. They cannot but come off well, who have such an advocate; to whom God says, as he did to Moses (Exod. iv. 12), *Go, and I will be with thy mouth, and with thy heart.*

[3.] That *he that endures to the end shall be saved, v.* 22. Here it is very comfortable to consider, First, that there will be an *end* of these troubles; they may last long, but will not last always. Christ comforted himself with this, and so may his followers; *The things concerning me have an end,* Luke xxii. 37. *Dabit Deus his quoque finem—These also will God bring to a termination.* Note, A believing prospect of the period of our troubles, will be of great use to support us under them. *The weary will be at rest, when the wicked cease from troubling,* Job iii. 17. God will give an expected *end,* Jer. xxix. 11. The troubles may seem tedious, *like the days of a hireling,* but, blessed be God, they are not everlasting. Secondly, That while they continue, they may be *endured;* as they are not *eternal,* so they are not *intolerable;* they may be borne, and borne *to the end,* because the sufferers shall be borne up under them, in everlasting arms: *The strength shall be according to the day,* 1 Cor. x. 13. Thirdly, Salvation will be the eternal recompence of all those *that endure to the end.* The weather stormy, and the way foul, but the pleasure of home will make amends for all. A believing regard to the crown of glory has been in all ages the cordial and support of suffering saints, 2 Cor. iv. 16, 17, 18; Heb. x. 34. This is not only an encouragement to us to *endure,* but an engagement to *endure to the end.* They who *endure but awhile, and in time of temptation fall away,* have run in vain, and lose all that they have attained; but they who persevere, are sure of the prize, and they only. *Be faithful unto death,* and then thou shalt have *the crown of life.*

[4.] That whatever hard usage the disciples of Christ meet with, it is no more than what their Master met with before (*v.* 24, 25). *The disciple is not above his master.* We find this given them as a reason, why they should not hesitate to perform the meanest duties, no, not washing one another's feet. John xiii. 16. Here it is given as a reason, why they should not stumble at the hardest sufferings. They are reminded of this saying, John xv. 20. It is a proverbial expression, *The servant is not better than his master,* and, therefore, let him not expect to fare *better.* Note, First, Jesus Christ is our *Master,* our teaching *Master,* and we are his disciples, to learn of him; our ruling *Master,* and we are his servants to obey him: He is *Master* of the house, *οικοδεσπότης,* has a despotic power in the church, which is his family. Secondly, Jesus Christ our Lord and Master met with very hard usage from the world; they called him Beelzebub, the god of flies, the name of the chief of the devils, with whom they said he was in league. It is hard to say which is here more to be wondered at, the wickedness of men who thus abused Christ, or the patience of Christ, who suffered himself to be thus abused; that he who was the God of glory should be stigmatized as the god of flies; the King of Israel, as the god of Ekron; the Prince of light and life, as the prince of the powers of death and darkness; that Satan's greatest Enemy and Destroyer should be run down as his confederate, and yet *endure such contradiction of sinners.* Thirdly, The consideration of the ill treatment which Christ met with in the world, should engage us to expect and prepare for the like, and to bear it patiently. Let us not think it strange, if they who hated him hate his followers, for his sake; nor think it hard if they who are shortly to be made *like him in glory,* be now made *like him in sufferings.* Christ began in the *bitter cup,* let us be willing to pledge him; his bearing the cross made it easy for us.

[5.] That *there is nothing covered that shall not be revealed, v.* 26. We understand this, First, Of the revealing of the gospel to all the world. "Do you *publish* it (*v.* 27), for it shall be published. The truths which are now, as mysteries, hid from the children of men, shall all be made known, to all nations, in their own language," Acts ii. 11. The *ends of the earth must see this salvation.*

Note, It is a great encouragement to those who are doing Christ's work, that it is a work which shall certainly be done. It is a plough which God will speed. Or, Secondly, Of the clearing up of the innocency of Christ's suffering servants, that are called Beelzebub; their true character is now invidiously disguised with false colours, but however their innocency and excellency are now *covered,* they *shall be revealed:* sometimes it is in a great measure done in this world, when the righteousness of the saints is made, by subsequent events, to *shine forth as the light:* however it will be done at the great day, when their glory shall be manifested to all the world, angels and men, to whom they are now *made spectacles,* 1 Cor. iv. 9. All their reproach shall be rolled away, and their graces and services, that are now *covered, shall be revealed,* 1 Cor. iv. 5. Note, It is matter of comfort to the people of God, under all the calumnies and censures of men, that there will be a resurrection of *names* as well as of *bodies,* at the last day, when *the righteous shall shine forth as the sun.* Let Christ's ministers faithfully reveal his truths, and then leave it to him, in due time, to reveal their integrity.

[6.] That the providence of God is in a special manner conversant about the saints, in their suffering, *v.* 29—31. It is good to have recourse to our first principles, and particularly to the doctrine of God's universal providence, extending itself to all the creatures, and all their actions, even the smallest and most minute. The light of nature teaches us this, and it is comfortable to all men, but especially to all good men, who can in faith call this God their Father, and for whom he has a tender concern. See here,

First, The general extent of providence to all the creatures, even the least, and least considerable, to the *sparrows, v.* 29. These little animals are of so small account, that one of them is not valued; there must go two to be worth *a farthing* (nay, you shall have five for a halfpenny, Luke xii. 6), and yet they are not shut out of the divine care; *One of them shall not fall to the ground without your Father:* That is, 1. They do not not light on *the ground* for food, to pick up a grain of corn, but *your* heavenly *Father,* by his providence, laid it ready for them. In the parallel place, Luke xii. 6, it is thus expressed, *Not one of them is forgotten before God,* forgotten to be provided for; *he feedeth them, ch.* vi. 26. Now he that feeds the sparrows, will not starve the saints. 2. They do *not fall to the ground* by death, either a natural or a violent death, without the notice of God: though they are so small a part of the creation, yet even their death comes within the notice of the divine providence; much more does the death of his disciples. Observe, The birds that soar above, when they die, *fall to the ground;* death brings the highest to the earth. Some think that Christ here alludes to the *two sparrows* that were used in cleansing the leper (Lev. xiv. 4—6); the two birds in the margin are called *sparrows;* of these one was killed, and so *fell to the ground,* the other was let go. Now it seemed a casual thing which of the two was killed; the persons employed took which they pleased, but God's providence designed, and determined which. Now this God, who has such an eye to the sparrows, because they are his creatures, much more will have an eye to you, who are his children. If a sparrow die not *without your Father,* surely a man does not,—a Christian,—a minister,—my friend, my child. A bird falls not into the fowler's net, nor by the fowler's shot, and so comes not to be sold in the market, but according to the direction of providence; your enemies, like subtle fowlers, *lay snares for* you, and *privily shoot at* you, but they cannot take you, they cannot hit you, unless God give them leave. Therefore be not afraid of death, for your enemies have no power against you, but what is *given them from above.* God can break their bows and snares (Ps. xxxviii. 12—15; lxiv. 4, 7), and make our souls to *escape as a bird* (Ps. cxxiv. 7); *Fear ye not, therefore, v.* 31. Note, There is enough in the doctrine of God's providence to silence all the fears of God's people: *Ye are of more value than many sparrows.* All men are so, for the other creatures were made for man, and *put under his feet* (Ps. viii. 6—8); much more the disciples of Jesus Christ, who are the excellent ones of the earth, however contemned, as if not worth one sparrow.

Secondly, The particular cognizance which providence takes of the disciples of Christ, especially in their sufferings (*v.* 30), *But the very hairs of your head are all numbered.* This is a proverbial expression, denoting the account which God takes and keeps of all the concernments of his people, even of those that are most minute, and least regarded. This is not to be made a matter of curious enquiry, but of encouragement to live in a continual dependence upon God's providential care, which extends itself to all occurrences, yet without disparagement to the infinite glory, or disturbance to the infinite rest, of the Eternal Mind. If God numbers their hairs, much more does he number their heads, and take care of their lives, their comforts, their souls. It intimates, that God takes more care of them, than they do of themselves. They who are solicitous to number their money, and goods, and cattle, yet were never careful to number their hairs, which fall and are lost, and they never miss them: but God *numbers the hairs of* his people, and *not a hair of their head shall perish* (Luke xxi. 18); not the least hurt shall be done them, but upon a valuable consideration: so precious to God are his saints, and their lives and deaths!

[7.] That he will shortly, in the day of

triumph, own those who now own him, in the day of trial, when those who deny him shall be for ever disowned and rejected by him, *v.* 32, 33. Note, First, It is our duty, and if we do it, it will hereafter be our unspeakable honour and happiness, to *confess Christ before men.* 1. It is our duty, not only to believe in Christ, but to profess that faith, in suffering for him, when we are called to it, as well as in serving him. We must never be ashamed of our relation to Christ, our attendance on him, and our expectations from him: hereby the sincerity of our faith is evidenced, his name glorified, and others edified. 2. However this may expose us to reproach and trouble now, we shall be abundantly recompensed for that, *in the resurrection of the just,* when it will be our unspeakable honour and happiness to hear Christ say (what would we more?) "*Him will I confess,* though a poor worthless worm of the earth; this is one of mine, one of my friends and favourites, who loved me and was beloved by me; the purchase of my blood, the workmanship of my Spirit; *I will confess him before my Father,* when it will do him the most service; I will speak a good word for him, when he appears before *my Father* to receive his doom; I will present him, will represent him to *my Father.*" Those who honour Christ he will thus honour. They honour him *before men;* that is a *poor* thing: he will honour them *before* his *Father;* that is a *great* thing. Secondly, It is a dangerous thing for any to deny and disown *Christ before men;* for they who do so will be disowned by him *in the great day,* when they have most need of him: he will not own them for his servants who would not own him for their Master: *I tell you, I know you not, ch.* vii. 23. In the first ages of Christianity, when for a man to *confess Christ* was to venture all that was dear to him in this world, it was more a trial of sincerity, than it was afterwards, when it had secular advantages attending it.

[8.] That the foundation of their discipleship was laid in such a temper and disposition, as would make sufferings very light and easy to them; and it was upon the condition of a preparedness for suffering, that Christ took them to be his followers, *v.* 37—39. He told them at first, that they were *not worthy of* him, if they were not willing to part with all for him. Men hesitate not at those difficulties which necessarily attend their profession, and which they counted upon, when they undertook that profession; and they will either cheerfully submit to those fatigues and troubles, or disclaim the privileges and advantages of their profession. Now, in the Christian profession, they are reckoned unworthy the dignity and felicity of it, that put not such a value upon their interest in Christ, as to prefer that before any other interests. They cannot expect the gains of a bargain, who will not come up to the terms of it. Now thus the terms are settled; if religion be worth *any* thing, it is worth *every* thing: and, therefore, all who believe the truth of it, will soon come up to the price of it; and they who make it their business and bliss, will make every thing else to yield to it. They who like not Christ on these terms, may leave him at their peril. Note, It is very encouraging to think, that whatever we leave, or lose, or suffer for Christ, we do not make a hard bargain for ourselves. Whatever we part with for this pearl of price, we may comfort ourselves with this persuasion, that it is well worth what we give for it. The terms are, that we must prefer Christ.

First, Before our nearest and dearest relations; *father or mother, son or daughter.* Between these relations, because there is little room left for envy, there is commonly more room for love, and, therefore, these are instanced, as relations which are most likely to affect us. Children must love their parents, and parents must love their children; but if they love them better than Christ, they are unworthy of him. As we must not be *deterred* from Christ by the hatred of our relations which he spoke of (*v.* 21, 35, 36), so we must not be *drawn* from him, by their love. Christians must be as Levi, who *said to his father, I have not seen him,* Deut. xxxiii. 9.

Secondly, Before our ease and safety. We must *take up our cross* and *follow him,* else we are *not worthy* of him. Here observe, 1. They who would *follow Christ,* must expect *their cross* and *take it up.* 2. In taking *up the cross,* we must *follow Christ's* example, and bear it as he did. 3. It is a great encouragement to us, when we meet with crosses, that in bearing them we *follow Christ,* who has showed us the way; and that if we follow him faithfully, he will lead us through sufferings like him, to glory with him.

Thirdly, Before life itself, *v.* 39. *He that findeth his life shall lose it;* he that thinks he has found it when he has saved it, and kept it, by denying Christ, *shall lose it* in an eternal death; but *he that loseth his life for Christ's sake,* that will part with it rather than deny Christ, *shall find it,* to his unspeakable advantage, an eternal life. They are best prepared for the life to come, that sit most loose to this present life.

[9.] That Christ himself would so heartily espouse their cause, as to show himself a friend to all their friends, and to repay all the kindnesses that should at any time be bestowed upon them, *v.* 40—42. *He that receiveth you, receiveth me.*

First, It is here implied, that though the generality would reject them, yet they should meet with some who would receive and entertain them, would bid the message welcome to their hearts, and the messengers to their houses, for the sake of it. Why was the gospel market made, but that if some will not, others will. In the worst of times there is a remnant according to the election of grace. Christ's ministers shall not *labour in vain.*

Secondly, Jesus Christ takes what is done to his faithful ministers, whether in kindness or in unkindness, as done to himself, and reckons himself *treated* as they are *treated. He that receiveth you, receiveth me.* Honour or contempt put upon an ambassador reflects honour or contempt upon the prince that sends him, and ministers are *ambassadors for Christ.* See how Christ may still be entertained by those who would testify their respects to him; his people and ministers we have always with us; and he is *with them always,* even to the end of the world. Nay, the honour rises higher, *He that receiveth me, receiveth him that sent me.* Not only Christ takes it as done to himself, but through Christ God does so too. By entertaining Christ's ministers, they entertain not *angels unawares,* but Christ, nay, and God himself, and *unawares* too, as appears, *ch.* xxv. 37. *When saw we thee an hungered?*

Thirdly, That though the kindness done to Christ's disciples be never so small, yet if there be occasion for it, and ability to do no more, it shall be accepted, though it be *but a cup of cold water given to one of these little ones, v.* 42. They are *little ones,* poor and weak, and often stand in need of refreshment, and glad of the least. The extremity may be such, that a *cup of cold water* may be a great favour. Note, Kindnesses shown to Christ's disciples are valued in Christ's books, not according to the cost of the gift, but according to the love and affection of the giver. On that score the widow's mite not only passed current, but was stamped high, Luke xxi. 3, 4. Thus they who are truly rich in graces may be rich in good works, though poor in the world.

Fourthly, That kindness to Christ's disciples which he will accept, must be done with an eye to Christ, and for his sake. A prophet must be received *in the name of a prophet,* and a *righteous man* in the name of a *righteous man,* and one of those *little ones* in *the name of a disciple;* not because they are learned, or witty, nor because they are our relations or neighbours, but because they are righteous, and so bear Christ's image; because they are prophets and disciples, and so are sent on Christ's errand. It is a believing regard to Christ that puts an acceptable value upon the kindnesses done to his ministers. Christ does not interest himself in the matter, unless we first interest him in it. *Ut tibi debeam aliquid pro eo quod præstas, debes non tantum mihi præstare, sed tanquam mihi—If you wish me to feel an obligation to you for any service you render, you must not only perform the service, but you must convince me that you do it for my sake.* Seneca.

Fifthly, That kindnesses shown to Christ's people and ministers, shall not only be accepted, but richly and suitably rewarded. There is a great deal to be gotten, by doing good offices to Christ's disciples. If it be done to the Lord, he will repay them again with interest; for he is *not unrighteous to forget any labour of love,* Heb. vi. 10. 1. They shall *receive a reward,* and in no wise *lose it.* He does not say, that they *deserve* a reward; we cannot merit any thing as wages, from the hand of God; but they shall *receive a reward* from the free gift of God; and they shall *in no wise lose it,* as good services often do among men; because they who should reward them are either false or forgetful. The reward may be deferred, the full reward will be deferred, till the resurrection of the just; but it shall in no wise be *lost,* nor shall they be any *losers* by the delay. 2. This is a *prophet's reward,* and a *righteous man's.* That is, either, (1.) The reward that God gives to prophets and righteous men; the blessings conferred upon them shall distil upon their friends. Or, (2.) The reward he gives by prophets and righteous men; in answer to their prayers (Gen. xx. 7), *He is a prophet, and he shall pray for thee,* that is a prophet's reward; and by their ministry; when he gives the instructions and comforts of the word, to those who are kind to the preachers of the word, then he sends a *prophet's reward.* Prophets' rewards are spiritual blessings in heavenly things, and if we know how to value them, we shall reckon them good payment.

CHAP. XI.

In this chapter we have, I. The constant and unwearied diligence of our Lord Jesus in his great work of preaching the gospel, ver. 1. II. His discourse with the disciples of John concerning his being the Messiah, 2—6. III. The honourable testimony that Christ bore to John Baptist, ver. 7—15. IV. The sad account he gives of that generation in general, and of some particular places with reference to the success, both of John's ministry and of his own, 16—24. V. His thanksgiving to his Father for the wise and gracious method he had taken in revealing the great mysteries of the gospel, ver. 25, 26. VI. His gracious call and invitation of poor sinners to come to him, and to be ruled, and taught, and saved by him, ver. 27—30. No where have we more of the terror of gospel woes for warning to us, or of the sweetness of gospel grace for encouragement to us, than in this chapter, which sets before us life and death, the blessing and the curse.

AND it came to pass, when Jesus
had made an end of command-
ing his twelve disciples, he departed
thence, to teach and to preach in their
cities. 2 Now when John had heard
in the prison the works of Christ, he
sent two of his disciples, 3 And said
unto him, Art thou he that should
come, or do we look for another? 4
Jesus answered and said unto them,
Go and show John again those things
which ye do hear and see: 5 The
blind receive their sight, and the lame
walk, the lepers are cleansed, and the
deaf hear, the dead are raised up, and
the poor have the gospel preached to

them. 6 And blessed is *he*, whosoever shall not be offended in me.

The first verse of this chapter some join to the foregoing chapter, and make it (not unfitly) the close of that.

1. The ordination sermon which Christ preached to his disciples in the foregoing chapter is here called his commanding them. Note, Christ's commissions imply commands. Their preaching of the gospel was not only permitted them, but it was enjoined them. It was not a thing respecting which they were left at their liberty, but *necessity was laid upon them,* 1 Cor. ix. 16. The promises he made them are included in these commands, for the covenant of grace is a *word which he hath commanded,* Ps. cv. 8. He *made an end of commanding,* ἐτέλεσεν διατάσσων. Note, The instructions Christ gives are full instructions. He goes through with his work.

2. When Christ had said what he had to say to his disciples, he *departed thence.* It should seem they were very loth to leave their Master, till *he departed* and separated himself from them; as the nurse withdraws the hand, that the child may learn to go by itself. Christ would now teach them how to live, and how to work, without his bodily presence. It was *expedient for them,* that Christ should thus go away for awhile, that they might be prepared for his long departure, and that, by the help of the Spirit, their own hands might be *sufficient for them* (Deut. xxxiii. 7), and they might not be always children. We have little account of what they did now pursuant to their commission. They went abroad, no doubt; probably into Judea (for in Galilee the gospel had been mostly preached hitherto), publishing the doctrine of Christ, and working miracles in his name: but still in a more immediate dependence upon him, and not being long from him; and thus they were trained up, by degrees, for their great work.

3. Christ departed, *to teach and preach* in the cities whither he sent his disciples before him to *work miracles* (*ch.* x. 1—8), and so to raise people's expectations, and to make way for his entertainment. Thus was the *way of the Lord prepared;* John prepared it by bringing people to *repentance,* but he did *no miracles.* The disciples go further, they *work miracles* for confirmation. Note, Repentance and faith prepare people for the blessings of the kingdom of heaven, which Christ gives. Observe, When Christ empowered them to *work miracles,* he employed himself in *teaching* and *preaching,* as if that were the more honourable of the two. That was but in order to do this. Healing the sick was the *saving of bodies,* but preaching the gospel was to the *saving of souls.* Christ had directed his disciples to preach (*ch.* x. 7), yet he did not leave off preaching himself. He set them to work, not for his own ease, but for the ease of the country, and was not the less busy for employing them. How unlike are they to Christ, who yoke others only that they may themselves be idle! Note, the increase and multitude of labourers in the Lord's work should be made not an excuse for our negligence, but an encouragement to our diligence. The more busy others are, the more busy we should be, and all little enough, so much work is there to be done. Observe, He went to preach *in their cities,* which were populous places; he cast the net of the gospel where there were most fish to be enclosed. Wisdom cries in *the cities* (Prov. i. 21), *at the entry of the city* (Prov. viii. 3), in *the cities of the Jews,* even of them who made light of him, who notwithstanding had the first offer.

What he preached we are not told, but it was probably to the same purpose with his sermon on the mount. But here is next recorded a message which John Baptist sent to Christ, and his return to it, *v.* 2—6. We heard before that Jesus heard of John's sufferings, *ch.* iv. 12. Now we are told that John, in prison, hears of Christ's doings. He *heard in the prison the works of Christ;* and no doubt he was glad to hear of them, for he was a true friend of the Bridegroom, John iii. 29. Note, When one useful instrument is laid aside, God knows how to raise up many others in the stead of it. The work went on, though John was in prison, and it added no affliction, but a great deal of consolation, to his bonds. Nothing more comfortable to God's people in distress, than to *hear of the works of Christ;* especially to experience them in their own souls. This turns a prison into a palace. Some way or other Christ will convey the notices of his love to those that are in trouble for conscience' sake. John could not see the works of Christ, but he heard of them with pleasure. And blessed are they who *have not seen,* but only heard, and yet *have believed.*

Now John Baptist, hearing of Christ's works, sent two of his disciples to him; and what passed between them and him we have here an account of. Here is,

I. The question they had to propose to him: *Art thou he that should come, or do we look for another?* This was a serious and important question; *Art thou the Messiah promised, or not? Art thou the Christ? Tell us.* 1. It is taken for granted that the Messiah should come. It was one of the names by which he was known to the Old-Testament saints, *he that cometh or shall come,* Ps. cxviii. 26. He is now come, but there is another coming of his which we still expect. 2. They intimate, that if this be not *he,* they would *look for another.* Note, We must not be weary of looking for him that is to come, nor ever say, we will no more expect him till we come to enjoy him. Though he tarry, wait for him, for he that shall come will come, though not in our time. 3 They intimate likewise, that if they be convinced that this is he, they will not be sceptics, they will be satisfied, and will look *for no other*. 4. They therefore ask, *Art thou he?* John had said for his part, *I am not the Christ*, John i. 20. Now, (1.) Some think that John sent this question for his own satisfaction. It is true he had borne a noble testimony to Christ; he had declared him to be the *Son of God* (John i. 34), the Lamb of God (*v.* 29), and he that *should baptize with the Holy Ghost* (*v.* 33), and *sent of God* (John iii. 34), which were great things. But he desired to be further and more fully assured, that he was the Messiah that had been so long promised and expected. Note, In matters relating to Christ and our salvation by him, it is good to be sure. Christ appeared not in that external pomp and power in which it was expected he should appear; his own disciples stumbled at this, and perhaps John did so; Christ saw something of this at the bottom of this enquiry, when he said, *blessed is he who shall not be offended in me*. Note, It is hard, even for good men, to bear up against vulgar errors. (2.) John's doubt might arise from his own présent circumstances. He was a prisoner, and might be tempted to think, if Jesus be indeed the Messiah, whence is it that I, his friend and forerunner, am brought into this trouble, and am left to be so long in it, and he never looks after me, never visits me, nor sends to me, enquires not after me, does nothing either to sweeten my imprisonment or hasten my enlargement? Doubtless there was a good reason why our Lord Jesus did not go to John in prison, lest there should seem to have been a compact between them: but John construed it into a neglect, and it was perhaps a shock to his faith in Christ. Note, [1.] Where there is true faith, yet there may be a mixture of unbelief. The best are not always alike strong. [2.] Troubles for Christ, especially when they continue long unrelieved, are such trials of faith as sometimes prove too hard to be borne up against. [3.] The remaining unbelief of good men may sometimes, in an hour of temptation, strike at the root, and call in question the most fundamental truths which were thought to be well settled. *Will the Lord cast off for ever?* But we will hope that John's faith did not fail in this matter, only he desired to have it strengthened and confirmed. Note, The best saints have need of the best helps they can get for the strengthening of their faith, and the arming of themselves against temptations to infidelity. Abraham believed, and yet desired a sign (Gen. xv. 6, 8), so did Gideon, Judg. vi. 36, 37. But, (3.) Others think that John sent his disciples to Christ with this question, not so much for his own satisfaction as for theirs. Observe, Though he was a prisoner they adhered to him, attended on him, and were ready to receive instructions from him; they loved him, and would not leave him. Now, [1.] They were weak in knowledge, and wavering in their faith, and needed instruction and confirmation; and in this matter they were somewhat prejudiced; being jealous *for their* master, they were jealous *of our* Master; they were loth to acknowledge Jesus to be the Messiah, because he eclipsed John, and are loth to believe their own master when they think he speaks against himself and them. Good men are apt to have their judgments biassed by their interest. Now John would have their mistakes rectified, and wished them to be as well satisfied as he himself was. Note, The strong ought to consider the infirmities of the weak, and to do what they can to help them: and such as we cannot help ourselves we should send to those that can. *When thou art converted, strengthen thy brethren.* [2.] John was all along industrious to turn over his disciples to Christ, as from the grammar-school to the academy. Perhaps he foresaw his death approaching, and therefore would bring his disciples to be better acquainted with Christ, under whose guardianship he must leave them. Note, Ministers' business is to direct every body to Christ. And those who would know the certainty of the doctrine of Christ, must apply themselves to him, who is come to give an understanding. They who would grow in grace must be inquisitive.

II. Here is Christ's answer to this question, *v.* 4—6. It was not so direct and express, as when he said, *I that speak unto thee am he;* but it was a real answer, an answer in fact. Christ will have us to spell out the convincing evidences of gospel truths, and to take pains in digging for knowledge.

1. He points them to what they heard and saw, which they must tell John, that he might from thence take occasion the more fully to instruct and convince them out of their own mouths. Go and tell him *what you hear and see.* Note, Our senses may and ought to be appealed to in those things that are their proper objects. Therefore the popish doctrine of the real presence agrees not with the truth *as it is in Jesus;* for Christ refers us to the things we *hear and see. Go and tell John,*

(1.) *What you see* of the *power of Christ's miracles;* you see how, by the word of Jesus, *the blind receive their sight,* the *lame walk, &c.* Christ's miracles were done openly, and in the view of all; for they feared not the strongest and most impartial scrutiny. *Veritas non quærit angulos—Truth seeks not concealment.* They are to be considered, [1.] As the *acts of a divine power.* None but the God of nature could thus overrule and outdo the power of nature. It is particularly spoken of as God's prerogative to *open the eyes of the blind,* Psal. cxlvi. 8. Miracles are therefore the broad seal of heaven, and the doctrine they are affixed to must be of God, for his power will never contradict his truth; nor can it be imagined that he should set his seal to a lie; however *lying wonders* may be vouched for in proof of *false doctrines, true miracles* evince a divine commission; such Christ's were, and they leave no room to doubt that he was sent of God, and that his doctrine was his that *sent him.* [2.] As the *accomplishment of a divine prediction.* It was foretold (Isa. xxxv. 5, 6), that our God should come, and that then *the eyes of the blind should be opened.* Now if the works of Christ agree with the words of the prophet, as it is plain they do, then no doubt but this is our God whom we have waited for, who shall *come with a recompence;* this is he who is so much wanted.

(2.) Tell him *what you hear* of the *preaching of his gospel,* which accompanies his miracles. Faith, though confirmed by seeing, comes by hearing. Tell him, [1.] That *the poor preach the gospel;* so some read it. It proves Christ's divine mission, that those whom he employed in founding his kingdom were poor men, destitute of all secular advantages, who, therefore, could never have carried their point, if they had not been carried on by a divine power. [2.] That *the poor have the gospel preached to them.* Christ's auditory is made up of such as the scribes and Pharisees despised, and looked upon with contempt, and the *rabbies* would not instruct, because they were not able to pay them. The *Old-Testament* prophets were sent mostly to kings and princes, but Christ preached to the *congregations of the poor.* It was foretold that the *poor of the flock* should *wait upon him,* Zech. xi. 11. Note, Christ's gracious condescensions and compassions to *the poor,* are an evidence that it was he that should bring to the world the tender mercies of our God. It was foretold that the *Son of David* should be the *poor man's King,* Ps. lxxii. 2, 4, 12, 13. Or we may understand it, not so much of the *poor of the world,* as the *poor in spirit,* and so that scripture is fulfilled, Isa. lxi. 1, *He hath anointed me to preach glad tidings to the meek.* Note, It is a proof of Christ's divine mission that his doctrine is gospel indeed; good news to those who are truly humbled in sorrow for their sins, and truly humble in the denial of self; to them it is accommodated, for whom God always declared he had mercy in store. [3.] That the *poor receive the gospel,* and are wrought upon by it, they are evangelized, they receive and entertain the gospel, are leavened by it, and delivered into it as into a mould. Note, The wonderful efficacy of the gospel is a proof of its divine original. The poor are *wrought upon* by it. The prophets complained of *the poor,* that they *knew not the way of the Lord,* Jer. v. 4. They could do no good upon them; but the gospel of Christ made its way into their untutored minds.

2. He pronounces a *blessing* on those that *were not offended in him, v.* 6. So clear are these evidences of Christ's mission, that they who are not wilfully prejudiced against him, and scandalized in him (so the word is), cannot but receive his doctrine, and so be *blessed in him.* Note, (1.) There are many things in Christ which they who are ignorant and unthinking are apt to be offended at, some circumstances for the sake of which they reject the substance of his gospel. The meanness of his appearance, his education at Nazareth, the poverty of his life, the despicableness of his followers, the slights which the great men put upon him, the strictness of his doctrine, the contradiction it gives to flesh and blood, and the sufferings that attend the profession of his name; these are things that keep many from him, who otherwise cannot but see much of God in him. Thus he is set *for the fall of many,* even in Israel (Luke ii. 34), a *Rock of offence,* 1 Pet. ii. 8. (2.) They are happy who get over these offences. *Blessed are they.* The expression intimates, that it is a difficult thing to conquer these prejudices, and a dangerous thing not to conquer them; but as to those, who, notwithstanding this opposition, do believe in Christ, their faith will be found so much the more, to *praise, and honour, and glory.*

7 And, as they departed, Jesus
began to say unto the multitudes concerning John, What went ye out into
the wilderness to see? A reed shaken
with the wind? 8 But what went
ye out for to see? A man clothed in
soft raiment? behold, they that wear
soft *clothing* are in kings' houses. 9
But what went ye out for to see? a
prophet? yea, I say unto you, and
more than a prophet. 10 For this is
he of whom it is written, Behold, I
send my messenger before thy face,
which shall prepare thy way before
thee. 11 Verily I say unto you, Among
them that are born of women there
hath not risen a greater than John
the Baptist: notwithstanding, he that
is least in the kingdom of heaven is
greater than he. 12 And from the
days of John the Baptist until now
the kingdom of heaven suffereth violence, and the violent take it by force.
13 For all the prophets and the law
prophesied until John. 14 And if ye
will receive *it,* this is Elias, which was
for to come. 15 He that hath ears
to hear, let him hear.

We have here the high encomium which our Lord Jesus gave of John the Baptist; not only to revive his honour, but to revive his work. Some of Christ's disciples might perhaps take occasion from the question John sent, to reflect upon him, as weak and wavering, and inconsistent with himself, to prevent which Christ gives him this character. Note, It is our duty to consult the reputation of our brethren, and not only to remove, but to obviate and prevent, jealousies and ill thoughts of them; and we must take all occasions, especially such as discover any thing of infirmity, to speak well of those who are praiseworthy, and to give them that *fruit of their hands.* John the Baptist, when he was upon the stage, and Christ in privacy and retirement, bore testimony to Christ; and now that Christ appeared publicly, and John was under a cloud, he bore testimony to John. Note, They who have a confirmed interest themselves, should improve it for the helping of the credit and reputation of others, whose character claims it, but whose temper or present circumstances put them out of the way of it. This is giving honour to whom honour is due. John had abased himself to honour Christ (John iii. 29, 30, *ch.* iii. 11), had made himself nothing, that Christ might be All, and now Christ dignifies him with this character. Note, They who humble themselves shall be exalted, and those that honour Christ he will honour; those that confess him before men, he will confess, and sometimes *before men* too, even in this world. John had now *finished his testimony,* and now Christ commends him. Note, Christ reserves honour for his servants when they *have done their work,* John xii. 26.

Now concerning this commendation of John, observe.

I. That Christ spoke thus honourably of John, not in the hearing of John's disciples, but *as they departed,* just after they were gone, Luke vii. 24. He would not so much as seem to flatter John, nor have these praises of him reported to him. Note, Though we must be forward to give to all their due praise for their encouragement, yet we must avoid every thing that looks like flattery, or may be in danger of puffing them up. They who in other things are mortified to the world, yet cannot well bear their own praise. Pride is a corrupt humour, which we must not feed either in others or in ourselves.

II. That what Christ said concerning John, was intended not only for his praise, but for the people's profit, to revive the remembrance of John's ministry, which had been well attended, but which was now (as other such things used to be) strangely forgotten: they did for a season, and but *for a season, rejoice in his light,* John v. 35. "Now, consider, *what went ye out into the wilderness to see?* Put this question to yourselves." 1. John preached *in the wilderness,* and thither people flocked in crowds to him, though in a *remote* place, and an *inconvenient* one. If teachers be removed into corners, it is better to go after them than to be without them. Now if his preaching was worth taking so much pains to hear it, surely it was worth taking some care to recollect it. The greater the difficulties we have broken through to hear the word, the more we are concerned to profit by it. 2. They went out to him to see him; rather to feed their eyes with the unusual appearance of his person, than to feed their souls with his wholesome instructions; rather for curiosity than for conscience. Note, Many that attend on the word come rather to see and be seen, than to learn and be taught, to have something to talk of, than to be made wise to salvation. Christ puts it to them, *what went ye out to see?* Note, They who attend on the word will be called to an account, what their intentions and what their improvements were. We think when the sermon is done, the care is over; no, then the greatest of the care begins. It will shortly be asked, "What business had you such a time at such an ordinance? *What brought you thither?* Was it custom or company, or was it a desire to honour God and get good? *What have you brought thence?* What knowledge, and grace, and comfort? *What went you to see?*" Note, When we go to read and hear the word, we should see that we aim right in what we do.

III. Let us see what the commendation of John was. They know not what answer to make to Christ's question; well, says Christ, "I will tell you what a man John the Baptist was."

1. "He was a firm, resolute man, and not *a reed shaken with the wind; you* have been so in your thoughts of him, but *he* was not so. He was not wavering in his principles, nor uneven in his conversation; but was remarkable for his steadiness and constant consistency with himself." They who are *weak* as reeds will be *shaken* as reeds; but John was *strong in spirit,* Eph. iv. 14. When the wind of popular applause on the one hand blew fresh and fair, when the storm of Herod's rage on the other hand grew fierce and blustering, John was still the same, the same in all weathers. The testimony he had borne to Christ was not the testimony of *a reed,* of a man who was of one mind to-day, and of another to-morrow; it was not a weather-cock testimony; no, his constancy in it is intimated (John i. 20); he *confessed and denied not, but confessed,* and stood to it afterwards, John iii. 28. And therefore this question sent by his disciples was not to be construed into any suspicion of the truth of what he had formerly said: therefore the people flocked to him, because he was not as a reed. Note, There is nothing lost in the long run by an unshaken resolution to go on with our work, neither courting the smiles, nor fearing the frowns of men.

2. He was a *self-denying* man, and *mortified* to this world. "Was he a man *clothed in soft raiment?* If so, you would not have gone *into the wilderness* to see him, but to the *court.* You went to see one that had *his*

raiment of camel's hair, and a *leathern girdle about his loins;* his mien and habit showed that he was dead to all the pomps of the world and the pleasures of sense; his clothing agreed with the *wilderness* he lived in, and the doctrine he preached there, that of repentance. Now you cannot think that he who was such a stranger to the pleasures of a court, should be brought to change his mind by the terrors of a prison, and now to question whether Jesus be the Messiah or not?" Note, they who have lived a life of mortification, are least likely to be driven off from their religion by persecution. He was not a man clothed in *soft raiment;* such *there are,* but they are *in kings' houses.* Note, It becomes people in all their appearances to be consistent with their character and their situation. They who are preachers must not affect to look like courtiers; nor must they whose lot is cast in common dwellings, be ambitious of the soft clothing which they wear who are in kings' houses. Prudence teaches us to be *of a piece.* John appeared rough and unpleasant, yet they flocked after him. Note, The remembrance of our former zeal in attending on the word of God, should quicken us to, and in, our present work: let it not be said that we have done and suffered so many things *in vain,* have *run in vain* and *laboured in vain.*

3. His greatest commendation of all was his office and ministry, which was more his honour than any personal endowments or qualifications could be; and therefore this is most enlarged upon in a full encomium.

(1.) He was *a prophet,* yea, and *more than a prophet* (*v.* 9); so he said of him who was the great Prophet, to whom all the prophets bear witness. John said of himself, he was not *that prophet,* that great prophet, the Messiah himself; and now Christ (a very competent Judge) says of him, that he was *more than a prophet.* He owned himself inferior to Christ, and Christ owned him superior to all other prophets. Observe, The forerunner of Christ was not a king, but a prophet, lest it should seem that the kingdom of the Messiah had been laid in earthly power; but his immediate forerunner was, as such, a *transcendent* prophet, more than an *Old-Testament prophet;* they all *did virtuously,* but John excelled them all; they *saw Christ's day* at a distance, and their vision was yet for a great while to come; but John saw the day dawn, he saw the sun rise, and told the people of the Messiah, as one that stood among them. They spake of Christ, but he pointed to him; they said, *A virgin shall conceive:* he said, *Behold the Lamb of God!*

(2.) He was the same that was predicted to be Christ's forerunner (*v.* 10); *This is he of whom it is written.* He was prophesied of by the other prophets, and therefore was greater than they. Malachi prophesied concerning John, *Behold, I send my messenger before thy face.* Herein some of Christ's honour was put upon him, that the *Old-Testament* prophets spake and wrote of him; and this honour have all the saints, that their *names* are *written in the Lamb's book of life.* It was great preferment to John above all the prophets, that he was Christ's harbinger. He was a *messenger* sent on a great errand; a messenger, *one among a thousand,* deriving his honour from him whose messenger he was: he is *my messenger* sent *of God,* and sent before the *Son of God.* His business was to *prepare Christ's way,* to dispose people to receive the Saviour, by discovering to them their sin and misery, and their need of a Saviour. This he had said of himself (John i. 23) and now Christ said it of him; intending hereby not only to put an honour upon John's ministry, but to revive people's regard to it, as making way for the Messiah. Note, Much of the beauty of God's dispensations lies in their mutual connection and coherence, and the reference they have one to another. That which advanced John above the *Old-Testament* prophets was, that he went immediately before Christ. Note, The nearer any are to Christ, the more truly honourable they are.

(3.) There *was not a greater born of women* than John the Baptist, *v.* 11. Christ knew how to value persons according to the degrees of their worth, and he prefers John before all that went before him, before all that were *born of women* by ordinary generation. Of all that God had raised up and called to any service in his church, John is the most eminent, even beyond Moses himself; for he began to preach the gospel doctrine of remission of sins to those who are truly penitent; and he had more signal revelations from heaven than any of them had; for he *saw heaven opened,* and the *Holy Ghost descend.* He also had great success in his ministry; almost the whole nation flocked to him: none rose on so great a design, or came on so noble an errand, as John did, or had such claims to a welcome reception. Many had been born of women that made a great figure in the world, but Christ prefers John before them. Note, Greatness is not to be measured by appearances and outward splendour, but they are the greatest men who are the greatest saints, and the greatest blessings, who are, as John was, *great in the sight of the Lord,* Luke i. 15.

Yet this high encomium of John has a surprising limitation, *notwithstanding, he that is least in the kingdom of heaven is greater than he.* [1.] In the kingdom *of glory.* John was a *great* and *good* man, but he was yet in a state of infirmity and imperfection, and therefore came short of glorified saints, and the *spirits of just men made perfect.* Note, First, There are degrees of glory in heaven, some that are less than others there; though every vessel is alike full, all are not alike large and capacious. Secondly, The least saint in heaven is *greater*, and knows more, and loves more, and does more in praising God, and receives more from him, than the greatest in this world. The saints on earth are excellent ones (Ps. xvi. 3), but those in heaven are much more excellent; the best in this world are *lower than the angels* (Ps. viii. 5), the least there are *equal with the angels*, which should make us long for that blessed state, where the *weak shall be as David*, Zech. xii. 8. [2.] By the *kingdom of heaven* here, is rather to be understood the *kingdom of grace*, the gospel dispensation in the perfection of its power and purity; and ὁ *μικρότερος*—*he that is less* in that is *greater than John*. Some understand it of Christ himself, who was younger than John, and, in the opinion of some, less than John, who always spoke diminishingly of himself; *I am a worm, and no man*, yet greater than John; so it agrees with what John the Baptist said (John i. 15), *He that cometh after me is preferred before me*. But it is rather to be understood of the apostles and ministers of the *New Testament*, the evangelical prophets; and the comparison between them and John is not with respect to their personal sanctity, but to their office; John preached Christ coming, but they preached Christ not only come, but *crucified* and *glorified*. John came to the dawning of the gospel-day, and therein excelled the foregoing prophets, but he was taken off before the noon of that day, before the rending of the veil, before Christ's death and resurrection, and the pouring out of the Spirit; so that the least of the apostles and evangelists, having greater discoveries made to them, and being employed in a greater embassy, is *greater than John*. John did no miracles; the apostles wrought many. The ground of this preference is laid in the preference of the *New*-Testament dispensation to that of the *Old* Testament. Ministers of the New Testament therefore excel, because their minstration does so, 2 Cor. iii. 6, &c. John was a *maximum quod sic*—*the greatest of his order;* he went to the utmost that the dispensation he was under would allow; but *minimum maximi est majus maximo minimi*—*the least of the highest order is superior to the first of the lowest;* a dwarf upon a mountain sees further than a giant in the valley. Note, All the true greatness of men is derived from, and denominated by, the gracious manifestation of Christ to them. The best men are no better than he is pleased to make them. What reason have we to be thankful that our lot is cast in the days of the *kingdom of heaven*, under such advantages of light and love! And the greater the advantages, the greater will the account be, if we *receive the grace of God in vain*.

(4.) The great commendation of John the Baptist was, that God owned his ministry, and made it wonderfully successful for the breaking of the ice, and the preparing of people for the *kingdom of heaven*. *From the days of* the first appearing of *John the Baptist*, until now (which was not much above two years), a great deal of good was done; so quick was the motion when it came near to Christ the Centre; *The kingdom of heaven suffereth violence*—Βιάζεται—*vim patitur*, like the violence of an army taking a city by storm, or of a crowd bursting into a house, so the *violent take it by force*. The meaning of this we have in the parallel place, Luke xvi. 16. Since that time *the kingdom of God is preached, and every man presseth into it*. Multitudes are wrought upon by the ministry of John, and become his disciples. And it is,

[1.] An *improbable* multitude. Those strove for a place in this kingdom, that one would think had no right nor title to it, and so seemed to be intruders, and to make a *tortuous* entry, as our law calls it, a wrongful and forcible one. When the *children of the kingdom* are excluded out of it, and many come into it *from the east and the west*, then it *suffers violence*. Compare this with *ch.* xxi. 31, 32. The publicans and harlots believed John, whom the scribes and Pharisees rejected, and so went into the kingdom of God before them, *took it over their heads*, while they trifled. Note, It is no breach of good manners to go to heaven before our betters: and it is a great commendation of the gospel from the days of its infancy, that it has brought many to holiness that were very unlikely.

[2.] An *importunate* multitude. This violence denotes a strength, and vigour, and earnestness of desire and endeavour, in those who followed John's ministry, else they would not have come so far to attend upon it. It shows us also, what fervency and zeal are required of all those who design to make heaven of their religion. Note, They who would *enter into the kingdom of heaven* must *strive to enter;* that kingdom suffers a holy violence; self must be denied, the bent and bias, the frame and temper, of the mind must be altered; there are hard services to be done, and hard sufferings to be undergone, a force to be put upon the corrupt nature; we must run, and wrestle, and fight, and be *in an agony*, and all little enough to win such a prize, and to get over such opposition from without and from within. *The violent take it by force*. They who will have an interest in the great salvation are carried out towards it with a strong desire, will have it *upon any terms*, and not think them hard, nor quit their hold without a blessing, Gen. xxxii. 26. They who will make their calling and election sure must give diligence. The kingdom of heaven was never intended to indulge the ease of triflers, but to be the rest of them that labour. It is a blessed sight; Oh that we could see a greater number, not with an *angry* contention thrusting others out of the kingdom of heaven, but with a *holy* contention thrusting themselves into it!

(5.) The ministry of John was the *beginning of the gospel*, as it is reckoned, Mark i. 1; Acts i. 22. This is shown here in two things:

[1.] In John the Old Testament dispensation began to die, *v.* 13. So long that ministration continued in full force and virtue, but then it began to decline. Though the obligation of the law of Moses was not removed till Christ's death, yet the discoveries of the Old Testament began to be superseded by the more clear manifestation of the *kingdom of heaven* as *at hand.* Because the *light of the gospel* (as that of nature) was to precede and make way for its *law*, therefore the prophecies of the Old Testament came to an end *(finis perficiens*, not *interficiens—an end of completion, not of duration)*, before the precepts of it; so that when Christ says, *all the prophets and the law prophesied until John*, he shows us, First, How the light of the Old Testament was set up; it was set up in *the law and the prophets*, who spoke, though darkly, of Christ and his kingdom. Observe, The *law* is said to prophesy, as well as the *prophets*, concerning him that was to come. Christ *began at Moses* (Luke xxiv. 27); Christ was foretold by the dumb signs of the Mosaic work, as well as by the more articulate voices of the prophets, and was exhibited, not only in the verbal predictions, but in the personal and real types. Blessed be God that we have both the New-Testament doctrine to explain the Old-Testament prophecies, and the Old-Testament prophecies to confirm and illustrate the New-Testament doctrine (Heb. i. 1); like the two cherubim, they look at each other. The law was given by Moses long ago, and there had been no prophets for three hundred years before John, and yet they are both said to *prophecy until John*, because the law was still observed, and Moses and the prophets still read. Note, The scripture is teaching to this day, though the penmen of it are gone. Moses and the prophets are dead; the apostles and evangelists are dead (Zech. i. 5), but the *word of the Lord endures for ever* (1 Pet. i. 25); the *scripture* is *speaking expressly*, though the writers are silent in the dust. Secondly, How this light was *laid aside:* when he says, they *prophesied until John*, he intimates, that their glory was eclipsed by the glory which excelled; their predictions superseded by John's testimony, *Behold the Lamb of God!* Even before the sun rises, the morning light makes candles to shine dim. Their prophecies of a Christ to come became out of date, when John said, *He is come.*

[2.] In him the New-Testament day began to dawn; for (*v.* 14) *This is Elias, that was for to come.* John was as the loop that coupled the two Testaments; as Noah was *Fibula utriusque mundi—the link connecting both worlds*, so was he *utriusque Testamenti —the link connecting both Testaments.* The concluding prophecy of the Old Testament was, *Behold, I will send you Elijah*, Mal. iv. 5, 6. Those words prophesied until John, and then, being turned into a history, they ceased to prophesy. First, Christ speaks of it as a great truth, that John the Baptist is the Elias of the New Testament; not Elias *in propriâ personâ—in his own person*, as the carnal Jews expected; he denied that (John i. 21), but one that should come in the spirit and power of Elias (Luke i. 17), like him in temper and conversation, that should press repentance with terrors, and especially as it is in the prophecy, that should *turn the hearts of the fathers to the children.* Secondly, He speaks of it as a truth, which would not be easily apprehended by those whose expectations fastened upon the temporal kingdom of the Messiah, and introductions to it agreeable. Christ suspects the welcome of it, *if ye will receive it.* Not but that it was true, whether they would receive it or not, but he upbraids them with their prejudices, that they were backward to receive the greatest truths that were opposed to their sentiments, though never so favourable to their interests. Or, "If *you will receive him*, or if you will receive the ministry of John as that of the promised Elias, he will be an Elias to you, to turn you and prepare you for the Lord." Note, Gospel truths are as they are received, a savour of life or death. Christ is a Saviour, and John an Elias, to those who will receive the truth concerning them.

Lastly, Our Lord Jesus closes this discourse with a solemn demand of attention (*v.* 15): *He that hath ears to hear, let him hear;* which intimates, that those things were dark and hard to be understood, and therefore needed attention, but of great concern and consequence, and therefore well deserved it. "Let all people take notice of this, if John be the Elias prophesied of, then certainly here is a great revolution on foot, the Messiah's kingdom is at the door, and the world will shortly be surprised into a happy change. These are things which require your serious consideration, and therefore you are all concerned to hearken to what I say." Note, The things of God are of great and common concern: every one that has *ears to hear* any thing, is concerned to hear this. It intimates, that God requires no more from us but the right use and improvement of the faculties he has already given us. He requires those to hear that have ears, those to use their reason that have reason. Therefore people are ignorant, not because they want power, but because they want will; therefore they do not hear, because, like the deaf adder, they *stop their ears.*

16 But whereunto shall I liken this
generation? It is like unto children
sitting in the markets, and calling unto
their fellows, 17 And saying, We have
piped unto you, and ye have not

danced; we have mourned unto you,
and ye have not lamented. 18 For
John came neither eating nor drinking; and they say, He hath a devil.
19 The Son of man came eating and
drinking, and they say, Behold a man
gluttonous, and a winebibber, a friend
of publicans and sinners. But wisdom is justified of her children. 20
Then began he to upbraid the cities
wherein most of his mighty works
were done, because they repented not:
21 Woe unto thee, Chorazin! woe
unto thee, Bethsaida! for if the mighty
works which were done in you had
been done in Tyre and Sidon, they
would have repented long ago in sackcloth and ashes. 22 But I say unto
you, It shall be more tolerable for Tyre
and Sidon at the day of judgment,
than for you. 23 And thou, Capernaum, which art exalted unto heaven,
shall be brought down to hell: for if
the mighty works which have been
done in thee had been done in Sodom,
it would have remained until this day.
24 But I say unto you, That it shall
be more tolerable for the land of Sodom in the day of judgment than for
thee.

Christ was going on in the praise of John the Baptist and his ministry, but here stops on a sudden, and turns that to the reproach of those who enjoyed both that, and the ministry of Christ and his apostles too, in vain. As to that generation, we may observe to whom he *compares them* (*v.* 16—19), and as to the particular places he instances in, we may observe with whom he *compares them, v.* 20—24.

I. As to that *generation,* the body of the Jewish people at that time. There were many indeed that pressed into the kingdom of heaven; but the generality continued in unbelief and obstinacy. John was a great and good man, but the generation in which his lot was cast was as barren and unprofitable as could be, and unworthy of him. Note, The badness of the places where good ministers live serves for a foil to their beauty. It was Noah's praise that he was *righteous in his generation.* Having commended John, he condemns those who had him among them, and did not profit by his ministry. Note, The more praise-worthy the minister is, the more blame-worthy the people are, if they slight him, and so it will be found in the day of account.

This our Lord Jesus here sets forth in a parable, yet speaks as if he were at a loss to find out a similitude proper to represent this, *Whereunto shall I liken this generation?* Note, There is not a greater absurdity than that which they are guilty of who have good preaching among them, and are never the better for it. It is hard to say *what they are like.* The similitude is taken from some common custom among the Jewish children at their play, who, as is usual with children, imitated the fashions of grown people at their marriages and funerals, *rejoicing* and *lamenting;* but being all a jest, it made no impression; no more did the ministry either of John the Baptist or of Christ upon that generation. He especially reflects on the scribes and Pharisees, who had a proud conceit of themselves; therefore to humble them he compares them to children, and their behaviour to children's play.

The parable will be best explained by opening it and the illustration of it together in these five observations.

Note, 1. The God of heaven uses a variety of proper means and methods for the conversion and salvation of poor souls; he would *have all men to be saved,* and therefore leaves no stone unturned in order to it. The great thing he aims at, is the *melting* of our *wills* into a compliance with the will of God, and in order to this the affecting of us with the discoveries he has made of himself. Having various affections to be wrought upon, he uses various ways of working upon them, which though differing one from another, all tend to the same thing, and God is in them all carrying on the same design. In the parable, this is called his *piping* to us, and his *mourning* to us; he hath *piped to us* in the precious promises of the gospel, proper to work upon hope, and mourned to us in the dreadful threatenings of the law, proper to work upon fear, that he might frighten us out of our sins and allure us to himself. He has *piped to us* in gracious and merciful providences, *mourned to us* in calamitous, afflicting providences, and has set the one over against the other. He has taught his ministers to *change their voice* (Gal. iv. 20); sometimes to speak in thunder from *mount Sinai,* sometimes in a still small voice from *mount Sion.*

In the explanation of the parable is set forth the different temper of John's ministry and of Christ's, who were the two great lights of that generation.

(1.) On the one hand, John came *mourning to them, neither eating nor drinkiug;* not conversing familiarly with people, nor ordinarily eating in company, but alone, in his cell in the wilderness, where *his meat was locusts and wild honey.* Now this, one would think, should work upon them; for such an austere, mortified life as this, was very agreeable to the doctrine he preached: and that minister is most likely to do good, whose conversation is according to his doctrine;

and yet the preaching even of such a minister is not always effectual.

(2.) On the other hand, *the Son of man came eating and drinking*, and so he *piped unto them.* Christ conversed familiarly with all sorts of people, not affecting any peculiar strictness or austerity; he was affable and easy of access, not shy of any company, was often at feasts, both with Pharisees and publicans, to try if this would win upon those who were not wrought upon by John's reservedness: those who were not awed by John's frowns, would be allured by Christ's smiles; from whom St. Paul learned to become *all things to all men,* 1 Cor. ix. 22. Now our Lord Jesus, by his freedom, did not at all condemn John, any more than John did condemn him, though their deportment was so very different. Note, Though we are never so clear in the goodness of our own practice, yet we must not judge of others by it. There may be a *great diversity of operations,* where *it is the same God that worketh all in all* (1 Cor. xii. 6), and this *various manifestation of the Spirit is given to every man to profit withal, v.* 7. Observe especially, that God's ministers are variously gifted: the ability and genius of some lie one way, of others, another way: some are Boanerges —*sons of thunder;* others, Barnabases—*sons of consolation;* yet *all these worketh that one and the self-same Spirit* (1 Cor. xii. 11), and therefore we ought not to condemn either, but to praise both, and praise God for both, who thus tries various ways of dealing with persons of various tempers, that sinners may be either made pliable or left inexcusable, so that, whatever the issue is, God will be glorified.

Note, 2. The various methods which God takes for the conversion of sinners, are with many fruitless and ineffectual: "*Ye have not danced, ye have not lamented;* you have not been suitably affected either with the one or with the other." Particular means have, as in medicine, their particular intentions, which must be answered, particular impressions, which must be submitted to, in order to the success of the great and general design; now if people will be neither bound by laws, nor invited by promises, nor frightened by threatenings, will neither be awakened by the *greatest* things, nor allured by the *sweetest* things, nor startled by the most *terrible* things, nor be made sensible by the *plainest* things; if they will hearken to the voice neither of scripture, nor reason, nor experience, nor providence, nor conscience, nor interest, what more can be done? *The bellows are burned, the lead is consumed, the founder melteth in vain; reprobate silver shall men call them,* Jer. vi. 29. Ministers' labour is bestowed in vain (Isa. xlix. 4), and, which is a much greater loss, *the grace of God received in vain,* 2 Cor. vi. 1. Note, It is some comfort to faithful ministers, when they see little success of their labours, that it is no new thing for the best preachers and the best preaching in the world to come short of the desired end. *Who has believed our report?* If from *the blood of the slain,* from *the fat of the mighty,* the bow of those great commanders, Christ and John, returned so often empty (2 Sam. i. 22), no marvel if ours do so, and we prophesy to so little purpose upon dry bones.

Note, 3. That commonly those persons who do not profit by the means of grace, are perverse, and reflect upon the ministers by whom they enjoy those means; and because they do not get good themselves, they do all the hurt they can to others, by raising and propagating prejudices against the word, and the faithful preachers of it. Those who will not comply with God, and walk after him, confront him, and walk contrary to him. So *this generation* did; because they were resolved not to believe Christ and John, and to own them, as they ought to have done, for the best of men, they set themselves to abuse them, and to represent them as the worst. (1.) As for John the Baptist, they say, *He has a devil.* They imputed his strictness and reservedness to melancholy, and some kind or degree of a possession of Satan. "Why should we heed him? he is a poor hypochondriacal man, full of fancies, and under the power of a crazed imagination." (2.) As for Jesus Christ, they imputed his free and obliging conversation to the more vicious habit of luxury and flesh-pleasing: *Behold a gluttonous man and a wine-bibber.* No reflection could be more foul and invidious; it is the charge against the rebellious son (Deut. xxi. 20), *He is a glutton and a drunkard;* yet none could be more false and unjust; for Christ *pleased not himself* (Rom. xv. 3), nor did ever any man live such a life of self-denial, mortification, and contempt of the world, as Christ lived: he that was *undefiled, and separate from sinners,* is here represented as in league with them, and polluted by them. Note, The most unspotted innocency, and the most unparalleled excellency, will not always be a fence *against the reproach of tongues:* nay, a man's best gifts and best actions, which are both well intended and well calculated for edification, may be made the matter of his reproach. The best of our actions may become the worst of our accusations, as David's fasting, Ps. lxix. 10. It was true in some sense, that Christ was *a Friend to publicans and sinners,* the best Friend they ever had, for he *came into the world to save sinners,* great sinners, even the chief; so he said very feelingly, who had been himself not a *publican and sinner,* but a Pharisee and sinner; but this is, and will be to eternity, Christ's praise, and they forfeited the benefit of it who thus turned it to his reproach.

Note, 4. That the cause of this great unfruitfulness and perverseness of people under the means of grace, is that they are *like children sitting in the markets;* they are foolish as children, froward as children, mindless and playful as children; would they but *show themselves men* in understanding, there would be some hopes of them. *The market-place they sit in* is to some a place of idleness (*ch.* xx. 3); to others a place of worldly business (James iv. 13); to all a place of noise or diversion; so that if you ask the reason why people get so little good by the means of grace, you will find it is because they are slothful and trifling, and do not love to take pains; or because their heads, and hands, and hearts are full of the world, the cares of which *choke the word,* and choke their souls at last (Ezek. xxxiii. 31; Amos viii. 5); and they study to divert their own thoughts from every thing that is serious. Thus *in the markets* they are, and there they *sit;* in these things their hearts rest, and by them they resolve to abide.

Note, 5. Though the means of grace be thus slighted and abused by many, by the most, yet there is a remnant that through grace do improve them, and answer the designs of them, to the glory of God, and the good of their own souls. *But wisdom is justified of her children.* Christ is *Wisdom;* in him *are hid treasures of wisdom;* the saints are the *children God has given* him, Heb. ii. 13. The gospel is *wisdom,* it is *the wisdom from above:* true believers are begotten again by it, and born from above too: they are wise *children,* wise for themselves, and their true interests; not *like the foolish children that sat in the markets.* These *children of wisdom justify wisdom;* they comply with the designs of Christ's grace, answer the intentions of it, and are suitably affected with, and impressed by, the various methods it takes, and so evidence the wisdom of Christ in taking these methods. This is explained, Luke vii. 29. *The publicans justified God, being baptized with the baptism of John,* and afterwards embracing the gospel of Christ. Note, The success of the means of grace justifies the wisdom of God in the choice of these means, against those who charge him with folly therein. The cure of every patient, that observes the physician's orders, justifies the wisdom of the physician: and therefore Paul is *not ashamed of the gospel of Christ,* because, whatever it is to others, *to them that believe it is the power of God unto salvation,* Rom. i. 16. When *the cross of Christ,* which to others is *foolishness* and *a stumbling-block,* is *to them that are called the wisdom of God and the power of God* (1 Cor. i. 23, 24), so that they make the knowledge of that the summit of their ambition (1 Cor. ii. 2), and the efficacy of that the crown of their glorying (Gal. vi. 14), here is *wisdom justified of her children. Wisdom's children* are *wisdom's* witnesses in the world (Isa. xliii. 10), and shall be produced as witnesses in that day, when *wisdom,* that is now *justified* by *the saints,* shall *be glorified in the saints,* and *admired in all them that believe,* 2 Thess. i. 10. If the unbelief of some reproach Christ by giving him the lie, the faith of others shall honour him by setting to its seal that he is true, and that *he also is wise,* 1 Cor. i. 25. Whether we do it or not, it will be done; not only God's equity, but his *wisdom, will be justified when he speaks, when he judges.*

Well, this is the account Christ gives of that *generation,* and that *generation is not passed away,* but remains in a succession of the like; for as it was then, it has been since and is still; *some believe the things which are spoken, and some believe not,* Acts xxviii. 24.

II. As to the particular *places* in which Christ was most conversant. What he said in general of that *generation,* he applied in particular to those *places,* to affect them. *Then began he to upbraid them, v.* 20. He began to preach to them long before (*ch.* iv. 17), but he did not *begin to upbraid* till now. Note, Rough and unpleasing methods must not be taken, till gentler means have first been used. Christ is not apt *to upbraid; he gives liberally, and upbraideth not,* till sinners by their obstinacy extort it from him. *Wisdom* first invites, but when her invitations are slighted, then she *upbraids,* Prov. i. 20, 24. Those do not go in Christ's method, who begin with upbraidings. Now observe,

1. The sin charged upon them; not any against the moral law, then an appeal would have lain to the gospel, which would have relieved, but a sin against the gospel, the remedial law, and that is impenitency: this was it he upbraided them with, or reproached them for, as the most shameful, ungrateful thing that could be, that *they repented not.* Note, Wilful impenitency is the great damning sin of multitudes that enjoy the gospel, and which (more than any other) sinners will be upbraided with to eternity. The great doctrine that both John the Baptist, and Christ, and the apostles preached, was repentance; the great thing designed, both in the *piping* and in the *mourning,* was to prevail with people to change their minds and ways, to leave their sins and turn to God; and this they would not be brought to. He does not say, because they *believed* not (for some kind of faith many of them had) that Christ was a *Teacher come from God;* but because *they repented not:* their faith did not prevail to the transforming of their hearts, and the reforming of their lives. Christ reproved them for their other sins, that he might *lead them to repentance;* but when *they repented not, He upbraided them* with that, as their refusal *to be healed: He upbraided them* with it, that they might upbraid themselves, and might at length see the folly of it, as that which alone makes the sad case a desperate one, and the wound incurable.

2. The aggravation of the sin; they were *the cities in which most of his mighty works*

were done; for thereabouts his principal residence had been for some time. Note, Some places enjoy the means of grace in greater plenty, power, and purity, than other places. God is a free agent, and acts so in all his disposals, both as the God of nature and as the God of grace, common and distinguishing grace. By Christ's *mighty works* they should have been prevailed with, not only to receive his doctrine, but to obey his law; the curing of bodily diseases should have been the healing of their souls, but it had not that effect. Note, The stronger inducements we have to repent, the more heinous is the impenitency and the severer will the reckoning be, for Christ keeps account of the *mighty works done* among us, and of the gracious works done for us too, by which also we should be *led to repentance,* Rom. ii. 4.

(1.) Chorazin and Bethsaida are here instanced (*v.* 21, 22), they have each of them their woe: *Woe unto thee, Chorazin, woe unto thee, Bethsaida.* Christ came *into the world to bless us;* but if that blessing be slighted, he has woes in reserve, and his woes are of all others the most terrible. These two cities were situate upon *the sea of Galilee,* the former on the east side, and the latter on the west, rich and populous places; Bethsaida was lately advanced to a city by Philip the tetrarch; out of it Christ took at least three of his apostles: thus highly were these places favoured! Yet because they *knew not the day of their visitation,* they fell under these woes, which stuck so close to them, that soon after this they decayed, and dwindled into mean, obscure villages. So fatally does sin ruin cities, and so certainly does the word of Christ take place!

Now Chorazin and Bethsaida are here compared with Tyre and Sidon, two maritime cities we read much of in the Old Testament, that had been brought to ruin, but began to flourish again; these cities bordered upon Galilee, but were in a very ill name among the Jews for idolatry and other wickedness. Christ sometimes went *into the coasts of Tyre and Sidon (ch.* xv. 21), but never thither; the Jews would have taken it very heinously if he had; therefore Christ, to convince and humble them, here shows,

[1.] That Tyre and Sidon would not have been so bad as Chorazin and Bethsaida. If they had had the same word preached, and the same miracles wrought among them, *they would have repented,* and that *long ago,* as Nineveh did, in *sackloth and ashes.* Christ, who knows the hearts of all, knew that if he had gone and lived among them, and preached among them, he should have done more good there than where he was; yet he continued where he was for some time, to encourage his ministers to do so, though they see not the success they desire. Note, Among the children of disobedience, some are more easily wrought upon than others; and it is a great aggravation of the impenitency of those who plentifully enjoy the means of grace, not only that there are many who sit under the same means that are wrought upon, but that there are many more that would have been wrought upon, if they had enjoyed the same means. See Ezek. iii. 6, 7 Our repentance is slow and delayed, but theirs would have been speedy; they would have repented long ago. Ours has been slight and superficial; theirs would have been deep and serious, in *sackcloth and ashes.* Yet we must observe, with an awful adoration of the divine sovereignty, that the Tyrians and Sidonians will justly perish in their sin, though, if they had had the means of grace, they would have repented; for God is a *debtor to no man.*

[2.] That therefore Tyre and Sidon shall not be so miserable as Chorazin and Bethsaida, but it shall be *more tolerable* for them in the *day of judgment, v.* 22. Note, First, At the *day of judgment* the everlasting state of the children of men will, by an unerring and unalterable doom, be determined; happiness or misery, and the several degrees of each. Therefore it is called the *eternal judgment* (Heb. vi. 2), because decisive of the eternal state. Secondly, In that judgment, all the means of grace that were enjoyed in the state of probation will certainly come into the account, and it will be enquired, not only how bad we were, but how much better we might have been, had it not been our own fault, Isa. v. 3, 4. Thirdly, Though the damnation of all that perish will be intolerable, yet the damnation of those who had the fullest and clearest discoveries made them of the power and grace of Christ, and yet repented not, will be of all others the most intolerable. The gospel light and sound open the faculties, and enlarge the capacities of all that see and hear it, either to receive the riches of *divine grace,* or (if that grace be slighted) to take in the more plentiful effusions of *divine wrath.* If self-reproach be the torture of hell, it must needs be hell indeed to those who had such a fair opportunity of getting to heaven. *Son, remember that.*

(2.) Capernaum is here condemned with an emphasis (*v.* 23), "*And thou, Capernaum,* hold up thy hand, and hear thy doom." Capernaum, above all the cities of Israel, was dignified with Christ's most usual residence; it was like Shiloh of old, the place which he chose, to put his name there, and it fared with it as with Shiloh. Jer. vii. 12, 14. Christ's miracles here were *daily bread,* and therefore, as the manna of old, were despised and called light bread. Many a sweet and comfortable lecture of grace Christ had read them to little purpose, and therefore here he reads them a dreadful lecture of wrath: those who will not hear the former shall be made to feel the latter.

We have here Capernaum's doom,

[1.] Put absolutely; Thou *which art exalted to heaven shalt be brought down to hell.*

Note, First, Those who enjoy the gospel in power and purity, are thereby *exalted to heaven;* they have therein a great honour for the present, and a great advantage for eternity; they are lifted up toward *heaven;* but if, notwithstanding, they still *cleave to the earth,* they may thank themselves that they are not lifted up *into heaven.* Secondly, Gospel advantages and advancements abused will sink sinners so much lower into hell. Our external privileges will be so far from saving us, that if our hearts and lives be not agreeable to them, they will but inflame the reckoning: the higher the precipice is, the more fatal is the fall from it: Let us *not therefore be high-minded, but fear;* not slothful, but diligent. See Job xx. 6, 7.

[2.] We have it here put in comparison with the doom of Sodom—a place more remarkable, both for sin and ruin, than perhaps any other; and yet Christ here tells us,

First, That Capernaum's means would have saved Sodom. If these miracles had been done among the Sodomites, as bad as they were, they would have repented, and *their city would have remained unto this day* a monument of sparing mercy, as now it is of destroying justice, Jude 7. Note, Upon true repentance through Christ, even the greatest sin shall be pardoned and the greatest ruin prevented, that of Sodom not excepted. Angels were sent to Sodom, and yet it remained not; but if Christ had been sent thither, it *would have remained;* how well is it for us, then, that the world to come is *put in subjection to Christ,* and *not to angels!* Heb. ii. 5. Lot would not have *seemed as one that mocked,* if he had wrought miracles.

Secondly, That Sodom's ruin will therefore be less at the great day than Capernaum's. Sodom will have many things to answer for, but not the sin of neglecting Christ, as Capernaum will. If the gospel prove *a savour of death,* a killing savour, it is doubly so; it is *of death unto death,* so great a death (2 Cor. ii. 16); Christ had said the same of all other places that receive not his ministers nor bid his gospel welcome (*ch.* x. 15); *It shall be more tolerable for the land of Sodom than for that city.* We that have now the written word in our hands, the gospel preached, and the gospel ordinances administered to us, and live under the dispensation of the Spirit, have advantages not inferior to those of Chorazin, and Bethsaida, and Capernaum, and the account in the great day will be accordingly. It has therefore been justly said, that the professors of this age, whether they go to heaven or hell, will be the greatest debtors in either of these places; if to heaven, the greatest debtors to divine mercy for those rich means that brought them thither; if to hell, the greatest debtors to divine justice, for those rich means that would have kept them from thence.

25 At that time Jesus answered and
said, I thank thee, O Father, Lord of
heaven and earth, because thou hast
hid these things from the wise and
prudent, and hast revealed them unto
babes. 26 Even so, Father: for so
it seemed good in thy sight. 27 All
things are delivered unto me of my
Father; and no man knoweth the Son
but the Father: neither knoweth any
man the Father, save the Son, and *he*
to whomsoever the Son will reveal
him. 28 Come unto me all *ye* that
labour and are heavy laden, and I will
give you rest. 29 Take my yoke
upon you, and learn of me; for I
am meek and lowly in heart: and ye
shall find rest unto your souls. 30 For
my yoke *is* easy, and my burden is
light.

In these verses we have Christ looking up to heaven, with thanksgiving to his Father for the sovereignty and security of the covenant of redemption; and looking around him upon this earth, with an offer to all the children of men, to whom these presents shall come, of the privileges and benefits of the covenant of grace.

I. Christ here returns thanks to God for his favour to those *babes* who had the mysteries of he gospel *revealed to them* (*v.* 25, 26). *Jesus answered and said.* It is called an answer, though no other words are before recorded but his own, because it is so comfortable a reply to the melancholy considerations preceding, and is aptly set in the balance against them. The sin and ruin of those woeful cities, no doubt, was a grief to the Lord Jesus; he could not but *weep over* them, as he did *over Jerusalem* (Luke xix. 41); with this thought therefore he refreshes himself; and to make it the more refreshing, he puts it into a thanksgiving; that for all this, *there is a remnant,* though but *babes,* to whom the things of the gospel are *revealed. Though Israel be not gathered, yet shall he be glorious.* Note, We may take great encouragement in looking upward to God, when round about us we see nothing but what is discouraging. It is sad to see how regardless most men are of their own happiness, but it is comfortable to think that the wise and faithful God will, however, effectually secure the interests of his own glory. *Jesus answered and said, I thank thee.* Note, Thanksgiving is a proper answer to dark and disquieting thoughts, and may be an effectual means to silence them. Songs of praise are sovereign cordials to drooping souls, and will help to cure melancholy When we have no other answer ready to the suggestions of grief and fear, we may have recourse to this, *I thank thee, O Father;* let us bless God that it is not worse with us than it is.

Now in this thanksgiving of Christ, we may observe,

1. The titles he gives to God; *O Father, Lord of heaven and earth.* Note, (1.) In all our approaches to God, by praise as well as by prayer, it is good for us to eye him as a Father, and to fasten on that relation, not only when we ask for the mercies we want, but when we give thanks for the mercies we have received. Mercies are then doubly sweet, and powerful to enlarge the heart in praise, when they are received as tokens of a Father's love, and gifts of a Father's hand; *Giving thanks to the Father,* Col. i. 12. It becomes children to be grateful, and to say, *Thank you, father,* as readily as, *Pray, father.* (2.) When we come to God as a Father, we must withal remember, that he is *Lord of heaven and earth;* which obliges us to come to him with reverence, as to the sovereign Lord of all, and yet with confidence, as one able to do for us whatever we need or can desire; to defend us from all evil and to supply us with all good. Christ, in Melchizedec, had long since *blessed God* as the Possessor, or *Lord of heaven and earth;* and in all our thanksgivings for mercies in the stream, we must give him the glory of the all-sufficiency that is in the fountain.

2. The thing he gives thanks for: *Because thou hast hid these things from the wise and prudent, and yet revealed them to babes. These things;* he does not say what things, but means the great things of the gospel, *the things that belong to our peace,* Luke xix. 42. He spoke thus emphatically of them, *these things,* because they were things that filled him, and should fill us: all other things are as nothing to *these things.*

Note (1.) The great things of the everlasting gospel have been and are hid from many that were *wise and prudent,* that were eminent for learning and worldly policy; some of the greatest scholars and the greatest statesmen have been the greatest strangers to gospel mysteries. *The world by wisdom knew not God,* 1 Cor. i. 21. Nay, there is an opposition given to the gospel, by a *science falsely so called,* 1 Tim. vi. 20. Those who are most expert in things sensible and secular, are commonly least experienced in spiritual things. Men may dive deeply into the mysteries of nature and into the mysteries of state, and yet be ignorant of, and mistake about, the mysteries of *the kingdom of heaven,* for want of an experience of the power of them.

(2.) While *the wise and prudent men* of the world are in the dark about gospel mysteries, even the *babes in Christ* have the sanctifying saving knowledge of them: *Thou hast revealed them unto babes.* Such the disciples of Christ were; men of mean birth and education; no scholars, no artists, no politicians, unlearned and ignorant men, Acts iv. 13. Thus are the secrets of wisdom, which are double to that which is (Job xi. 6), made known *to babes and sucklings,* that *out of their mouth strength* might be *ordained* (Ps. viii. 2), and God's *praise* thereby *perfected.* The learned men of the world were not made choice of to be the preachers of the gospel, but *the foolish things of the world* (1 Cor. ii. 6, 8, 10).

(3.) This difference between *the prudent* and the *babes* is of God's own making. [1.] It is he that has *hid these things from the wise and prudent;* he gave them parts, and learning, and much of human understanding above others, and they were proud of that, and rested in it, and looked no further; and therefore God justly denies them the Spirit of wisdom and revelation, and then, though they hear the sound of the gospel tidings, they are to them as a *strange thing.* God is not the Author of their ignorance and error, but he leaves them to themselves, and their sin becomes their punishment, and the Lord is righteous in it. See John xii. 39, 40; Rom. xi. 7, 8; Acts xxviii. 26, 27. Had they honoured God with the wisdom and prudence they had, he would have given them the knowledge of these better things; but because they served their lusts with them, he has *hid their hearts from this understanding.* [2.] It is he that has *revealed them unto babes.* Things revealed belong to our children (Deut. xxix. 29), and to them he *gives an understanding* to receive these things, and the impressions of them. Thus *he resists the proud,* and *gives grace to the humble,* Jam. iv. 6.

(4.) This dispensation must be resolved into the divine sovereignty. Christ himself referred it to that; *Even so, Father, for so it seemed good in thy sight.* Christ here subscribes to the will of his Father in this matter; *Even so.* Let God take what way he pleases to glorify himself, and make use of what instruments he pleases for the carrying on of his own work; his grace is his own, and he may give or withhold it as he pleases. We can give no reason why Peter, a fisherman, should be made an apostle, and not Nicodemus, a Pharisee, and a ruler of the Jews, though he also believed in Christ; but *so it seemed good in God's sight.* Christ said this in the hearing of his disciples, to show them that it was not for any merit of their own that they were thus dignified and distinguished, but purely from God's good pleasure; he made them to differ.

(5.) This way of dispensing divine grace is to be acknowledged by us, as it was by our Lord Jesus, with all thankfulness. We must thank God, [1.] That *these things are revealed;* the mystery hid from ages and generations is manifested; that they are *revealed,* not to a few, but to be published to all the world. [2.] That they are *revealed to babes;* that the meek and humble are beautified with this salvation; and this honour put upon those whom the world pours contempt upon. [3.] It magnifies the mercy to them, that *these things* are *hid from the wise and prudent:* distinguishing favours are most obliging. As Job adored *the name of the Lord* in *taking away* as well as in *giving,* so may we in *hiding these things from the wise and prudent,* as well as in *revealing them unto babes;* not as it is their misery, but as it is a method by which self is abased, proud thoughts brought down, all flesh silenced, and divine power and wisdom made to shine the more bright. See 1 Cor. i. 27, 31.

II. Christ here makes a gracious offer of the benefits of the gospel to all, and these are the things which are *revealed to babes, v.* 25, &c. Observe here,

1. The solemn preface which ushers in this call or invitation, both to command our attention to it, and to encourage our compliance with it. That we *might have strong consolation,* in flying for refuge to this *hope set before us,* Christ prefixes his authority, produces his credentials; we shall see he is empowered to make this offer.

Two things he here lays before us, *v.* 27.

(1.) His commission from the Father: *All things are delivered unto me of my Father.* Christ, as God, is equal in power and glory with the Father; but as Mediator he receives his power and glory from the Father; has *all judgment committed to him.* He is authorized to settle a new covenant between God and man, and to offer peace and happiness to the apostate world, upon such terms as he should think fit: he was sanctified and sealed to be the sole Plenipotentiary, to concert and establish this great affair. In order to this, he has *all power* both *in heaven and in earth* (*ch.* xxviii. 18); power over all flesh (John xvii. 2); authority to execute judgment, John v. 22, 27. This encourages us to come to Christ, that he is commissioned to receive us, and to give us what we come for, and has *all things delivered to him* for that purpose, by him who is *Lord of all.* All powers, all treasures are in his hand. Observe, The Father has delivered his all into the hands of the Lord Jesus; let us but deliver our all into his hand and the work is done; God has made him the great Referee, the blessed Daysman, to lay his hand upon us both; that which we have to do is to agree to the reference, to submit to the arbitration of the Lord Jesus, for the taking up of this unhappy controversy, and to enter into bonds to stand to his award.

(2.) His intimacy with the Father: *No man knoweth the Son but the Father, Neither knoweth any man the Father save the Son.* This gives us a further satisfaction, and an abundant one. Ambassadors use to have not only their commissions, which they produce, but their instructions, which they reserve to themselves, to be made use of as there is occasion in their negociations our Lord Jesus had both, not only authority, but ability, for his undertaking. In transacting the great business of our redemption, the Father and the Son are the parties principally concerned; *the counsel of peace is between them,* Zech. vi. 13. It must therefore be a great encouragement to us to be assured, that they understood one another very well in this affair; that the Father knew the Son, and the Son knew the Father, and both perfectly (a mutual consciousness we may call it, between the Father and the Son), so that there could be no mistake in the settling of this matter; as often there is among men, to the overthrow of contracts, and the breaking of the measures taken, through their misunderstanding one another. The Son had *lain in the bosom of the Father* from eternity; he was *à secretioribus—of the cabinet-council,* John 1. 18. He was *by him, as one brought up with him* (Prov. viii. 30), so that *none knows the Father save the Son,* he adds, *and he to whom the Son will reveal him.* Note, [1.] The happiness of men lies in an acquaintance with God; it *is life eternal,* it is the perfection of rational beings. [2.] Those who would have an acquaintance with God, must apply themselves to Jesus Christ; for the light of the knowledge of the glory of God shines in the face of Christ, 2 Cor. iv. 6. We are obliged to Christ for all the revelation we have of God the Father's will and love, ever since Adam sinned; there is no comfortable intercourse between a holy God and sinful man, but in and by a Mediator, John xiv. 6.

2. Here is the offer itself that is made to us, and an invitation to accept of it. After so solemn a preface, we may well expect something very great; and it is *a faithful saying,* and well *worthy of all acceptation; words whereby we may be saved.* We are here invited to Christ as our Priest, Prince, and Prophet, to be saved, and, in order to that, to be ruled and taught by him.

(1.) We must come to Jesus Christ as our Rest, and repose ourselves in him (*v.* 28), *Come unto me all ye that labour.* Observe, [1.] The character of the persons invited; *all that labour, and are heavy laden.* This is a word in season to him that is weary, Isa. l. 4. Those who complain of the burthen of the ceremonial law, which was an intolerable yoke, and was made much more so by the tradition of the elders (Luke xi. 46), let them come to Christ, and they shall be made easy; he came to free his church from this yoke, to cancel the imposition of those carnal ordinances, and to introduce a purer and more spiritual way of worship; but it is rather to be understood of the burthen of sin, both the guilt and the power of it. Note, All those, and those only, are invited to rest in Christ, that are sensible of sin as a burthen, and groan under it; that are not only convinced of the evil of sin, of their own sin, but are contrite in soul for it; that are really sick of their sins, weary of the service of the world and of the flesh; that see their state sad and dangerous by reason of sin, and are in pain and fear about it, as Ephraim (Jer. xxxi. 18—20), the prodigal (Luke xv. 17), the publican (Luke xviii. 13), Peter's hearers (Acts ii. 37), Paul (Acts ix. 4, 6, 9), the jailor (Acts xvi. 29, 30). This is a necessary preparative for pardon and peace. The Comforter must first convince (John xvi. 8); I have torn and then will heal.

[2.] The invitation itself: *Come unto me.* That glorious display of Christ's greatness which we had (*v.* 27), as Lord of all, might frighten us from him, but see here how he holds out *the golden sceptre,* that we may touch the top of it and may live. Note, It is the duty and interest of weary *and heavy laden* sinners to *come to Jesus Christ.* Renouncing all those things which stand in opposition to him, or in competition with him, we must accept of him, as our Physician and Advocate, and give up ourselves to his conduct and government; freely willing to be saved by him, in his own way, and upon his own terms. *Come* and *cast that burden upon* him, under which thou art *heavy laden.* This is the gospel call, *The Spirit saith, Come;* and *the bride saith, Come; Let him that is athirst come; Whoever will, let him come.*

[3.] The blessing promised to those that do come: *I will give you rest.* Christ is our Noah, whose name signifies *rest,* for *this same shall give us rest.* Gen. v. 29; viii. 9. Truly *rest is good* (Gen. xlix. 15), especially to those *that labour and are heavy laden,* Eccl. v. 12. Note, Jesus Christ will give assured rest to those weary souls, that by a lively faith come to him for it; *rest* from the terror of sin, in a well-grounded peace of conscience; *rest* from the power of sin, in a regular order of the soul, and its due government of itself; a *rest* in God, and a complacency of soul, in his love. Ps. xi. 6, 7. This is that *rest which remains for the people of God* (Heb. iv. 9), begun in grace, and perfected in glory.

(2.) We must come to Jesus Christ as our Ruler, and submit ourselves to him (*v.* 29). *Take my yoke upon you.* This must go along with the former, for Christ is exalted to be both a *Prince and a Saviour,* a *Priest upon his throne.* The *rest* he promises is a release from the drudgery of sin, not from the service of God, but an obligation to the duty we owe to him. Note, Christ has a *yoke* for our necks, as well as a *crown* for our heads, and this *yoke* he expects we should *take upon* us and draw in. To call those who are weary *and heavy laden,* to *take a yoke upon* them, looks like adding *affliction to the afflicted;* but the pertinency of it lies in the word *my:* "You are under a *yoke* which makes you weary: shake that off and try mine, which will make you easy." Servants are said to be *under the yoke* (1 Tim. vi. 1), and subjects, 1 Kings xii. 10. To take Christ's *yoke upon* us, is to put ourselves into the relation to servants and subjects to him, and then of conduct ourselves accordingly, in a conscientious obedience to all his commands, and a cheerful submission to all his disposals: it is to *obey the gospel of Christ, to yield ourselves to the Lord:* it is Christ's *yoke;* the *yoke* he has appointed; a *yoke* he has himself drawn in before us, for *he learned obedience,* and which he does by his Spirit draw in with us, for *he helpeth our infirmities,* Rom. viii. 26. A *yoke* speaks some hardship, but if the beast must draw, the *yoke* helps him. Christ's commands are all in our favour: we must take this *yoke upon* us to draw in it. We are yoked to work, and therefore must be diligent; we are yoked to submit, and therefore must be humble and patient: we are yoked together with our fellow-servants, and therefore must keep up the communion of saints: and *the words of the wise are as goads,* to those who are thus yoked.

Now this is the hardest part of our lesson, and therefore it is qualified (*v.* 30). *My yoke is easy and my burden is light;* you need not be afraid of it.

[1.] The *yoke* of Christ's commands is an *easy yoke;* it is χρηστὸς, not only *easy,* but gracious, so the word signifies; it is sweet and pleasant; there is nothing in it to gall the yielding neck, nothing to hurt us, but, on the contrary, much to refresh us. It is a *yoke* that is lined with love. Such is the nature of all Christ's commands, so reasonable in themselves, so profitable to us, and all summed up in one word, and that a sweet word, love. So powerful are the assistances he gives us, so suitable the encouragements, and so strong the consolations, that are to be found in the way of duty, that we may truly say, it is a *yoke* of pleasantness. It is easy to the new nature, very *easy to him that understandeth,* Prov. xiv. 6. It may be a little hard at first, but it is easy afterwards; the love of God and the hope of heaven will make it *easy.*

[2.] The *burden* of Christ's cross is a *light burden,* very *light:* afflictions from Christ, which befal us as men; afflictions for Christ, which befal us as Christians; the latter are especially meant. This *burden* in itself is *not joyous, but grievous;* yet as it is Christ's, it is *light.* Paul knew as much of it as any man, and he calls it a *light affliction,* 2 Cor. iv. 17. God's presence (Isa. xliii. 2), Christ's sympathy (Isa. lxiii. 9, Dan. iii. 25), and especially the Spirit's aids and comforts (2 Cor. i. 5), make suffering for Christ *light* and *easy.* As afflictions abound, and are prolonged, consolations abound, and are prolonged too. Let this therefore reconcile us to the difficulties, and help us over the discouragements, we may meet with, both in doing work and suffering work; though we may lose *for* Christ, we shall not lose *by him.*

(3.) We must come to Jesus Christ as our Teacher, and set ourselves to learn of him, *v.* 29. Christ has erected a great school, and has invited us to be his scholars. We must enter ourselves, associate with his scholars, and daily attend the instructions he gives by his word and Spirit. We must converse much with what he said, and have it ready to use upon all occasions; we must conform to what he did, and follow his steps, 1 Pet. ii. 21. Some make the following words, *for I am meek and lowly in heart,* to be the particular lesson we are required to learn from the example of Christ. We must learn of him to be *meek* and *lowly,* and must mortify our pride and passion, which render us so unlike to him. We must so *learn of Christ* as to *learn Christ* (Eph. iv. 20), for he is both Teacher and Lesson, Guide and Way, and All in All.

Two reasons are given why we must *learn of Christ.*

[1.] *I am meek and lowly in heart,* and therefore fit to teach you.

First, He is *meek,* and can have *compassion on the ignorant,* whom others would be in a passion with. Many able teachers are hot and hasty, which is a great discouragement to those who are dull and slow; but Christ knows how to bear with such, and to open their understandings. His carriage towards his twelve disciples was a specimen of this; he was mild and gentle with them, and made the best of them; though they were heedless and forgetful, he was not extreme to mark their follies. Secondly, *He is lowly in heart.* He condescends to teach poor scholars, to teach novices; he chose disciples, not from the court, nor the schools, but from the seaside. He teaches the first principles, such things as are milk for babes; he stoops to the meanest capacities; he taught Ephraim to go, Hos. xi. 3. Who teaches like him? It is an encouragement to us to put ourselves to school to such a Teacher. This humility and meekness, as it qualifies him to be a Teacher, so it will be the best qualification of those who are to be taught by him; *for the meek will he guide in judgment,* Ps. xxv. 9.

[2.] *You shall find rest to your souls.* This promise is borrowed from Jer. vi. 16, for Christ delighted to express himself in the language of the prophets, to show the harmony between the two Testaments. Note, First, Rest for the soul is the most desirable rest; to have the soul to *dwell at ease.* Secondly, The only way, and a sure way to find *rest for our souls* is, to sit at Christ's feet and hear his word. The way of duty is the way of rest. The *understanding* finds *rest* in the *knowledge of* God and Jesus Christ, and is there abundantly satisfied, finding *that* wisdom in the gospel which has been sought for in vain throughout the whole creation, Job xxviii. 12. The truths Christ teaches are such as we may venture our souls upon. The affections find rest in the love of God and Jesus Christ, and meet with that in them which gives them an abundant satisfaction; quietness and assurance for ever. And those satisfactions will be perfected and perpetuated in heaven, where we shall see and enjoy God immediately, shall see him as he is, and enjoy him as he is ours. This rest is to be had with Christ for all those who learn of him.

Well, this is the sum and substance of the gospel call and offer: we are here told, in a few words, what the Lord Jesus requires of us, and it agrees with what God said of him once and again. *This is my beloved Son, in whom I am well pleased, hear ye him.*

CHAP. XII.

In this chapter, we have, I. Christ's clearing of the law of the fourth commandment concerning the sabbath-day, and vindicating it from some superstitious notions advanced by the Jewish teachers; showing that works of necessity and mercy are to be done on that day, ver. 1—13. II. The prudence, humility, and self-denial of our Lord Jesus in working his miracles, ver. 14—21. III. Christ's answer to the blasphemous cavils and calumnies of the scribes and Pharisees, who imputed his casting out devils to a compact with the devil, ver. 22—37. IV. Christ's reply to a tempting demand of the scribes and Pharisees, challenging him to show them a sign from heaven, ver. 38—45. V. Christ's judgment about his kindred and relations, ver. 46—50.

AT that time Jesus went on the
the sabbath day through the
corn; and his disciples were an hungred, and began to pluck the ears of
corn, and to eat. 2 But when the
Pharisees saw *it,* they said unto him,
Behold, thy disciples do that which
is not lawful to do upon the sabbath
day. 3 But he said unto them, Have
ye not read what David did when he
was an hungred, and they that were
with him; 4 How he entered into the
house of God, and did eat the show-
bread, which was not lawful for him
to eat, neither for them which were with
him, but only for the priests? 5 Or
have ye not read in the law, how that
on the sabbath days the priests in the
temple profane the sabbath, and are
blameless? 6 But I say unto you,
That in this place is *one* greater than
the temple. 7 But if ye had known
what *this* meaneth, I will have mercy,
and not sacrifice, ye would not have
condemned the guiltless. 8 For the
Son of man is Lord even of the sabbath day. 9 And when he was departed thence, he went into their
synagogue: 10 And, behold, there was
a man which had *his* hand withered.
And they asked him, saying, Is it
lawful to heal on the sabbath days?
that they might accuse him. 11 And
he said unto them, What man shall
there be among you that shall have
one sheep, and if it fall into a pit on
the sabbath day, will he not lay hold

on it, and lift *it* out? 12 How much then is a man better than a sheep? Wherefore it is lawful to do well on the sabbath days. 13 Then saith he to the man, Stretch forth thine hand. And he stretched *it* forth; and it was restored whole, like as the other.

The Jewish teachers had corrupted many of the commandments, by interpreting them more loosely than they were intended; a mistake which Christ discovered and rectified (*ch.* v.) in his sermon on the mount: but concerning the fourth commandment, they had erred in the other extreme, and interpreted it too strictly. Note, It is common for men of corrupt minds, by their zeal in rituals, and the external services of religion, to think to atone for the looseness of their morals. But they are cursed who *add to,* as well as they who *take from, the words of this book,* Rev. xxii. 16, 19; Prov. xxx. 6.

Now that which our Lord Jesus here lays down is, that the works of necessity and mercy are lawful on the sabbath day, which the Jews in many instances were taught to make a scruple of. Christ's industrious explanation of the fourth commandment, intimates its perpetual obligation to the religious observation of *one day in seven,* as a *holy sabbath.* He would not expound a law that was immediately to expire, but doubtless intended hereby to settle a point which would be of use to his church in all ages; and so it is to teach us, that our Christian sabbath, though under the direction of the fourth commandment, is not under the injunctions of the Jewish elders.

It is usual to settle the meaning of a law by judgments given upon cases that happen in fact, and in like manner is the meaning of this law settled. Here are two passages of story put together for this purpose, happening at some distance of time from each other, and of a different nature, but both answering this intention.

I. Christ, by justifying his disciples in plucking the ears of corn on the sabbath-day, shows that *works of necessity* are *lawful* on that day. Now here observe,

1. What it was that the disciples did. They were following their Master one sabbath day through a corn-field; it is likely they were going to the synagogue (*v.* 9), for it becomes not Christ's disciples to take *idle walks* on that day, and *they were hungry;* let it be no disparagement to our Master's house-keeping. But we will suppose they were so intent upon the sabbath work, that they forgot to eat bread; had spent so much time in their morning worship, that they had no time for their morning meal, but came out fasting, because they would not come late to the synagogue. Providence ordered it that they *went through the corn,* and there they were supplied. Note, God has many ways of bringing suitable provision to his people when they need it, and will take particular care of them when they are going to the synagogue, as of old for them that went up to Jerusalem to worship (Ps. lxxxiv. 6, 7), for whose use the rain filled the pools: while we are in the way of duty, *Jehovah-jireh,* let God alone to provide for us. Being in the corn-fields, they began to *pluck the ears of corn;* the law of God allowed this (Deut. xxiii. 25), to teach people to be neighbourly, and not to insist upon property in a small matter, whereby another may be benefited. This was but slender provision for Christ and his disciples, but it was the best they had, and they were content with it. The famous Mr. Ball, of Whitmore, used to say he had two dishes of meat to his sabbath dinner, a dish of hot milk, and a dish of cold, and he had enough and enough.

2. What was the offence that the Pharisees took at this. It was but a dry breakfast, yet the Pharisees would not let them eat that in quietness. They did not quarrel with them for taking another man's corn (they were no great zealots for justice), but for doing it *on the sabbath day;* for plucking and rubbing the ears of corn on that day was expressly forbidden by the tradition of the elders, for this reason, because it was *a kind of reaping.*

Note, It is no new thing for the most harmless and innocent actions of Christ's disciples to be evil spoken of, and reflected upon as unlawful, especially by those who are zealous for their own inventions and impositions. The Pharisees complained of them to their Master for doing that which it was not *lawful to do.* Note, Those are no friends to Christ and his disciples, who make that to be unlawful which God has not made to be so.

3. What was Christ's answer to this cavil of the Pharisees. The disciples could say little for themselves, especially because those who quarrelled with them seemed to have the strictness of the sabbath sanctification on their side; and it is safest to err on that hand: but Christ came to free his followers, not only from the corruptions of the Pharisees, but from their unscriptural impositions, and therefore has something to say for them, and justifies what they did, though it was a transgression of the canon.

(1.) He justifies them by precedents, which were allowed to be good by the Pharisees themselves.

[1.] He urges an ancient instance of David, who in a case of necessity did that which otherwise he ought not to have done (*v.* 3, 4); "*Have ye not read* the story (1 Sam. xxi. 6) of David's eating the show-bread, which by the law was appropriated to the priest? (Lev. xxiv. 5—9). *It is most holy to Aaron and his sons;* and (Exod. xxix. 33) *a stranger shall not eat of it;* yet the priest gave it to David and his men; for though the exception of a case of necessity was not expressed, yet it was implied in that and all other ritual institutions. That which bore out David in eating the show-bread was not his dignity (Uzziah, that invaded the priest's office in the pride of his heart, though a king, was struck with a leprosy for it, 2 Chron. xxvi. 16, &c.), but his hunger. The greatest shall not have their lusts indulged, but the meanest shall have their wants considered. Hunger is a natural desire which cannot be mortified, but must be gratified, and cannot be put off with any thing but meat; therefore we say, It will *break through stone walls.* Now the *Lord is for the body,* and allowed his own appointment to be dispensed with in a case of distress; much more might the tradition of the elders be dispensed with. Note, That may be done in a case of necessity which may not be done at another time; there are laws which necessity has not, but it is a law to itself. *Men do not despise,* but pity, *a thief that steals to satisfy his soul when he is hungry,* Prov. vi. 30.

[2.] He urges a daily instance of the priests, which they likewise *read in the law,* and according to which was the constant usage, *v.* 5. *The priests in the temple* did a great deal of servile work on the sabbath day; killing, flaying, burning the sacrificed beasts, which in a common case would *have been profaning the sabbath;* and yet it was never reckoned any transgression of the fourth commandment, because the temple-service required and justified it. This intimates, that those labours are lawful on the sabbath day which are necessary, not only to the *support of life,* but to the *service of the day;* as tolling a bell to call the congregation together, travelling to church, and the like. Sabbath rest is to promote, not to hinder, sabbath worship.

(2.) He justifies them by arguments, three cogent ones.

[1.] *In this place is one greater than the temple, v.* 6. If the temple-service would justify what the priests did in their ministration, the service of Christ would much more justify the disciples in what they did in their attendance upon him. The Jews had an extreme veneration for the temple: it *sanctified the gold;* Stephen was accused for *blaspheming that holy place* (Acts vi. 13); but Christ, in a corn-field, was *greater than the temple,* for in him dwelt not the *presence of God* symbolically, but *all the fulness of the Godhead bodily.* Note, If whatever we do, we do it *in the name of Christ,* and *as unto him,* it shall be graciously accepted of God, however it may be censured and cavilled at by men.

[2.] *God will have mercy and not sacrifice, v.* 7. Ceremonial duties must give way to moral, and the natural, royal law of love and self-preservation must take place of ritual observances. This is quoted from Hos. vi. 6. It was used before, *ch.* ix. 13, in vindication of mercy to the souls of men; here, of mercy to their bodies. The rest of the sabbath was ordained for man's good, in favour of the body, Deut. v. 14. Now no law must be construed so as to contradict its own end. *If you had known what this means,* had known what it is to be of a merciful disposition, you would have been sorry that they were forced to do this to satisfy their hunger, and would *not have condemned the guiltless.* Note, *First,* Ignorance is the cause of our rash and uncharitable censures of our brethren. *Secondly,* It is not enough for us to know the scriptures, but we must labour to *know the meaning* of them. *Let him that readeth understand. Thirdly,* Ignorance of the meaning of the scripture is especially shameful in those who take upon them to teach others.

[3.] *The Son of man is Lord even of the sabbath day, v.* 8. That law, as all the rest, is put into the hand of Christ, to be altered, enforced, or dispensed with, as he sees good. It was by *the Son* that God *made the world,* and by him he instituted the sabbath in innocency; by him he gave the ten commandments at mount Sinai, and as Mediator he is entrusted with the institution of ordinances, and to make what changes he thought fit; and particularly, as being *Lord of the sabbath,* he was authorized to make such an alteration of that day, as that it should become the Lord's day, the Lord Christ's day. And if Christ be the *Lord of the sabbath,* it is fit the day and all the work of it should be dedicated to him. By virtue of this power Christ here enacts, that works of necessity, if they be really such, and not a pretended and self-created necessity, are lawful on the sabbath day; and this explication of the law plainly shows that it was to be perpetual. *Exceptio firmat regulam—The exception confirms the rule.*

Christ having thus silenced the Pharisees, and got clear of them (*v.* 9), *departed,* and *went into their synagogue,* the synagogue of these Pharisees, in which they presided, and toward which he was going, when they picked this quarrel with him. Note, *First,* We must take heed lest any thing that occurs in our way to holy ordinances unfit us for, or divert us from, our due attendance on them. Let us proceed in the way of our duty, notwithstanding the artifices of Satan, who endeavours, by the *perverse disputings of men of corrupt minds,* and many other ways, to ruffle and discompose us. *Secondly,* We must not, for the sake of private feuds and personal piques, draw back from public worship. Though the Pharisees had thus maliciously cavilled at Christ, yet he *went into their synagogue.* Satan gains this point, if, by sowing discord among brethren, he prevail to drive them, or any of them, from the synagogue, and the communion of the faithful.

II. Christ, by *healing the man that had the withered hand on the sabbath day,* shows that works of mercy are lawful and proper to be done on that day. The work of necessity was done by the disciples, and justified by him; the work of mercy was done by himself; the works of mercy were his works of necessity; it was his *meat and drink* to *do good. I must preach,* says he, Luke iv. 43. This cure is recorded for the sake of the time when it was wrought, on the sabbath.

Here is, 1. The affliction that this poor man was in; his hand was withered so that he was utterly disabled to get his living by *working with his hands.* St. Jerome says, that the gospel of Matthew in Hebrew, used by the Nazarenes and Ebionites, adds this circumstance to this story of the man with the withered hand, that he was *Cæmentarius —a bricklayer,* and applied himself to Christ thus; "Lord, I am a bricklayer, and *have got my living by my labour (manibus victum quæritans);* I beseech thee, O Jesus, restore me the use of my hand, *that I may not be obliged to beg my bread" (ne turpiter mendicem cibos.)* Hieron. *in loc.* This poor man was in the synagogue. Note, Those who can do but little, or have but little to do for the world, must do so much the more for their souls; as the rich, the aged, and the infirm.

2. A spiteful question which the Pharisees put to Christ upon the sight of this man. *They asked him, saying, Is it lawful to heal?* We read not here of any address this poor man made to Christ for a cure, but they observed Christ began to take notice of him, and knew it was usual for him to be *found of those that sought him not,* and therefore with their badness they anticipated his goodness, and started this case as a stumbling-block in the way of doing good; *Is it lawful to heal on the sabbath-day?* Whether it was lawful for *physicians to heal* on that day or not, which was the thing disputed in their books, one would think it past dispute, that it is lawful for *prophets to heal,* for him to heal who discovered a divine power and goodness in all he did of this kind, and manifested himself to be *sent of God.* Did ever any ask, whether it is lawful for God to heal, to send his word and heal? It is true, Christ was now *made under the law,* by a voluntary submission to it, but he was never made under the precepts of the elders. *Is it lawful to heal?* To enquire into the lawfulness and unlawfulness of actions is very good, and we cannot apply ourselves to any with such enquiries more fitly than to Christ; but they asked here, not that they might be instructed by him, but *that they might accuse him.* If he should say that it was lawful to heal on the sabbath day, they would accuse him of a contradiction to the fourth commandment; to so great a degree of superstition had the Pharisees brought the sabbath rest, that, unless in peril of life, they allowed not any medicinal operations on the sabbath day. If he should say that it was not lawful, they would accuse him of partiality, having lately justified his disciples in plucking the ears of corn on that day.

3. Christ's answer to this question, by way of appeal to themselves, and their own opinion and practice, *v.* 11, 12. In case a *sheep* (though but one, of which the loss would not be very great) should fall into a pit on the sabbath day, *would they not lift it out?* No doubt they might do it, the fourth commandment allows it; they must do it, for a *merciful man regardeth the life of his beast,* and for their parts they would do it, rather than lose a sheep; does Christ take care for sheep? Yes, he does; he preserves and provides for both man and beast. But here he says it for our sakes (1 Cor. ix. 9, 10), and hence argues, *How much then is a man better than a sheep?* Sheep are not only harmless but useful creatures, and are prized and tended accordingly; yet a man is here preferred far before them. Note, Man, in respect of his being, is a great deal better, and more valuable, than the best of the brute creatures: man is a reasonable creature, capable of knowing, loving, and glorifying God, and therefore is better than a sheep. The sacrifice of a sheep could therefore not atone for the sin of a soul. They do not consider this, who are more solicitous for the education, preservation, and supply of their horses and dogs than of God's poor, or perhaps their own household.

Hence Christ infers a truth, which, even at first sight, appears very reasonable and good-natured; that *it is lawful to do well on the sabbath days;* they had asked, *Is it lawful to heal?* Christ proves it is lawful to *do well,* and let any one judge whether healing, as Christ healed, was not *doing well.* Note, There are more ways of *doing well* upon sabbath days, than by the duties of God's immediate worship; attending the sick, relieving the poor, helping those who are fallen into sudden distress, and call for speedy relief; this is *doing good:* and this must be done from a principle of love and charity, with humility and self-denial, and a heavenly frame of spirit, and this is *doing well,* and it *shall be accepted,* Gen. iv. 7.

4. Christ's curing of the man, notwithstanding the offence which he foresaw the Pharisees would take at it, *v.* 13. Though they could not answer Christ's arguments, they were resolved to persist in their prejudice and enmity; but Christ went on with his work notwithstanding. Note, Duty is not to be left undone, nor opportunities of doing good neglected, for fear of giving offence. Now the manner of the cure is observable; he said to the man, "*Stretch forth thy hand,* exert thyself as well as thou canst;" and he did so, *and it was restored whole.* This, as other cures Christ wrought, had a spiritual significancy. (1.) By nature our hands are withered, we are utterly unable of ourselves to doing any thing that is good. (2.) It is Christ only, by the power of his grace, that cures us; he heals the withered hand by putting life into the dead

soul, works in us both to will and to do. (3.) In order to our cure, he commands us to *stretch forth our hands,* to improve our natural powers, and do as well as we can; to stretch them out in prayer to God, to stretch them out to lay hold on Christ by faith, to stretch them out in holy endeavours. Now this man could not stretch forth his withered hand of himself, any more than the impotent man could arise and carry his bed, or Lazarus come forth out of his grave; yet Christ bid him do it. God's commands to us to do the duty which of ourselves we are not able to do are no more absurd or unjust, than this command to the man with the withered hand, *to stretch it forth;* for with the command, there is a promise of grace which is given by the word. *Turn ye at my reproof, and I will pour out my Spirit,* Prov. i. 23. Those who perish are as inexcusable as this man would have been, if he had not attempted to stretch forth his hand, and so had not been healed. But those who are saved have no more to boast of than this man had of contributing to his own cure, by stretching forth his hand, but are as much indebted to the power and grace of Christ as he was.

14 Then the Pharisees went out,
and held a council against him, how
they might destroy him. 15 But
when Jesus knew *it*, he withdrew
himself from thence: and great multitudes followed him, and he healed
them all; 16 And charged them that
they should not make him known:
17 That it might be fulfilled which
was spoken by Esaias the prophet,
saying, 18 Behold my servant, whom
I have chosen; my beloved, in whom
my soul is well-pleased: I will put
my spirit upon him, and he shall shew
judgment to the Gentiles. 19 He
shall not strive, nor cry; neither shall
any man hear his voice in the streets.
20 A bruised reed shall he not break,
and smoking flax shall he not quench,
till he send forth judgment unto victory. 21 And in his name shall the
Gentiles trust.

As in the midst of Christ's greatest humiliations, there were proofs of his dignity, so in the midst of his greatest honours, he gave proofs of his humility; and when the mighty works he did gave him an opportunity of making a figure, yet he made it appear that *he emptied himself*, and *made himself of no reputation.* Here we have,

I. The cursed malice of the Pharisees against Christ (*v.* 14); being enraged at the convincing evidence of his miracles, they *went out, and held a council against him, how they might destroy him.* That which vexed them was, not only that by his miracles his honour eclipsed theirs, but that the doctrine he preached was directly opposite to their pride, and hypocrisy, and worldly interest; but they pretended to be displeased at his breaking the sabbath day, which was by the law a capital crime, Exod. xxxv. 2. Note, It is no new thing to see the vilest practices cloaked with the most specious pretences. Observe their policy; they took counsel about it, considered with themselves which way to do it effectually; they took counsel together in a close cabal about it, that they might both animate and assist one another. Observe their cruelty; they took counsel, not to imprison or banish him, but to destroy him, to be the death of him who came *that we might have life.* What an indignity was hereby put upon our Lord Jesus, to run him down as an outlaw *(qui caput gerit lupinum—carries a wolf's head)*, and the plague of his country, who was the greatest blessing of it, the Glory of his people Israel!

II. Christ's absconding upon this occasion, and the privacy he chose, to decline, not his work, but his danger; because *his hour was not yet come* (*v.* 15), *he withdrew himself from thence.* He could have secured himself by miracle, but chose to do it in the ordinary way of flight and retirement; because in this, as in other things, he would submit to the sinless infirmities of our nature. Herein he humbled himself, that he was driven to the common shift of those who are most helpless; thus also he would give an example to his own rule, *When they persecute you in one city, flee to another.* Christ had said and done enough to convince those Pharisees, if reason or miracles would have done it; but instead of yielding to the conviction, they were hardened and enraged, and therefore he left them as incurable, Jer. li. 9.

Christ did not retire for his own ease, nor seek an excuse to leave off his work; no, his retirements were filled up with business, and he was even then doing good, when he was forced to flee for the same. Thus he gave an example to his ministers, to do what they can, when they cannot do what they would, and to continue teaching, even when they are removed into corners. When the Pharisees, the great dons and doctors of the nation, drove Christ from them, and forced him to withdraw himself, yet the common people crowded after him; *great multitudes followed him* and found him out. This some would turn to his reproach, and call him the ringleader of the mob; but it was really his honour, that all who were unbiassed and unprejudiced, and not blinded by the pomp of the world, were so hearty, so zealous for him, that they would follow him whithersoever he went, and whatever hazards they ran with him; as it was also the honour of his grace, that the poor were evangelized; that when they received him, he received them and healed them all. Christ came into the world to be a Physican-general, as the sun to the lower world, *with healing under his wings.* Though the Pharisees persecuted Christ for doing good, yet he went on in it, and did not let the people fare the worse for the wickedness of their rulers. Note, though some are unkind to us, we must not on that account be unkind to others.

Christ studied to reconcile usefulness and privacy; he *healed them all,* and yet (*v.* 16), *charged them that they should not make him known;* which may be looked upon, 1. As an act of prudence; it was not so much the miracles themselves, as the public discourse concerning them, that enraged the Pharisees (*v.* 23, 24); therefore Christ, though he would not omit doing good, yet would do it with as little noise as possible, to avoid offence to them and peril to himself. Note, Wise and good men, though they covet to do good, yet are far from coveting to have it talked of when it is done; because it is God's acceptance, not men's applause, that they aim at. And in suffering times, though we must boldly go on in the way of duty, yet we must contrive the circumstances of it so as not to exasperate, more than is necessary, those who seek occasion against us; *Be ye wise as serpents, ch.* x. 16. 2. It may be looked upon as an act of righteous judgment upon the Pharisees, who were unworthy to hear of any more of his miracles, having made so light of those they had seen. By shutting their eyes against the light, they had forfeited the benefit of it. 3. As an act of humility and self-denial. Though Christ's intention in his miracles was to prove himself the Messiah, and so to bring men to believe on him, in order to which it was requisite that they should be known, yet sometimes he charged the people to conceal them, to set us an example of humility, and to teach us not to proclaim our own goodness or usefulness, or to desire to have it proclaimed. Christ would have his disciples to be the reverse of those who did all their works *to be seen of men.*

III. The fulfilling of the scriptures in all this, *v.* 17. Christ retired into privacy and obscurity, that though he was eclipsed, the word of God might be fulfilled, and so illustrated and glorified, which was the thing his heart was upon. The scripture here said to be fulfilled is Isa. xlii. 1—4, which is quoted at large, *v.* 18—21. The scope of it is to show how mild and quiet, and yet how successful, our Lord Jesus should be in his undertaking; instances of both which we have in the foregoing passages. Observe here,

1. The pleasure of the Father in Christ (*v.* 18); *Behold, my Servant whom I have chosen, my Beloved in whom my soul is well pleased.* Hence we may learn,

(1.) That our Saviour was God's Servant in the great work of our redemption. He therein submitted himself to the Father's will (Heb. x. 7), and set himself to serve the design of his grace and the interests of his glory, in repairing the breaches that had been made by man's apostasy. As a *Servant,* he had a great work appointed him, and a great trust reposed in him. This was a part of his humiliation, that though he *thought it not robbery to be equal with God,* yet that in the work of our salvation he took upon him the form of a servant, received a law, and came into bonds. *Though he were a son, yet learned he this obedience,* Heb. v. 8. The motto of this Prince is, *Ich dien—I serve.*

(2.) That Jesus Christ was chosen of God, as the only fit and proper person for the management of the great work of our redemption. He is *my Servant whom I have chosen,* as *par negotio—equal to the undertaking.* None but he was able to do the Redeemer's work, or fit to wear the Redeemer's crown. He was *one chosen out of the people* (Ps. lxxxix. 19), chosen by Infinite Wisdom to that post of service and honour, for which neither man nor angel was qualified; none but Christ, that he might in all things have the pre-eminence. Christ did not thrust himself upon this work, but was duly chosen into it; Christ was so God's Chosen as to be the Head of election, and of all other the Elect, for we are *chosen in him,* Eph. i. 4.

(3.) That Jesus Christ is God's Beloved, his beloved Son; as God, he lay from eternity in his bosom (John i. 18); he was *daily his delight,* Prov. viii. 30. Between the Father and the Son there was before all time an eternal and inconceivable intercourse and interchanging of love, and thus *the Lord possessed him in the beginning of his way,* Prov. viii. 22. As Mediator, the Father loved him; then when it pleased the Lord to bruise him, and he submitted to it, *therefore did the Father love him,* John x. 17.

(4.) That Jesus Christ is one in whom the Father is well pleased, in whom his soul is pleased; which denotes the highest complacency imaginable. God declared, by a voice from heaven, that he was his beloved Son in whom he is well pleased; well pleased *in him,* because he was the ready and cheerful Undertaker of that work of wonder which God's heart was so much upon, and he is well pleased with us in him; for he has *made us accepted in the Beloved,* Eph. i. 6. All the interest which fallen man has or can have in God is grounded upon and owing to God's *well-pleasedness* in Jesus Christ; for there is *no coming to the Father but by him,* John xiv. 6.

2. The promise of the Father to him in two things.

(1.) That he should be every way well qualified for his undertaking; *I will put my Spirit upon him,* as a Spirit of *wisdom and counsel,* Isa. xi. 2, 3. Those whom God calls to any service, he will be sure to fit and qualify for it; and by that it will appear that he called them to it, as Moses, Exod. iv. 12. Christ, as God, was equal in power and glory with the Father; as Mediator, he received from the Father power and glory, and received that he might give: and all that the Father gave him, to qualify him for his undertaking, was summed up in this, he *put his Spirit upon him:* this was that *oil of gladness* with which he was *anointed above his fellows,* Heb. i. 9. He received the Spirit, not by measure, but *without measure,* John iii. 34. Note, Whoever they be that God has chosen, and in whom he is well pleased, he will be sure to *put his Spirit upon them.* Wherever he confers his love, he confers somewhat of his likeness.

(2.) That he should be abundantly successful in his undertaking. Those whom God sends he will certainly own. It was long since secured by promise to our Lord Jesus, that the *good pleasure of the Lord should prosper in his hand,* Isa. liii. 10. And here we have an account of that prospering good pleasure.

[1.] He shall *show judgment to the Gentiles.* Christ in his own person preached to those who bordered upon the heathen nations (see Mark iii. 6—8), and by his apostle showed his gospel, called here his *judgment,* to the Gentile world. The way and method of salvation, the *judgment* which is *committed to the Son,* is not only wrought out by him as our great High Priest, but showed and published by him as our great Prophet. The gospel, as it is a rule of practice and conversation, which has a direct tendency to the reforming and bettering of men's hearts and lives, shall be showed to the Gentiles. God's judgments had been the Jews' peculiar (Psal. cxlvii. 19), but it was often foretold, by the Old-Testament prophets, that they should be *showed to the Gentiles,* which therefore ought not to have been such a surprise as it was to the unbelieving Jews, much less a vexation.

[2.] *In his name shall the Gentiles trust, v.* 21. He shall so show judgment to them, that they shall heed and observe what he shows them, and be influenced by it to depend upon him, to devote themselves to him, and conform to that judgment. Note, The great design of the gospel, is to bring people to trust in the name of Jesus Christ; his name Jesus, a Saviour, that precious name whereby he is called, and which is as ointment poured forth; *The Lord our Righteousness.* The evangelist here follows the Septuagint (or perhaps the latter editions of the Septuagint follow the evangelist); the Hebrew (Isa. xlii. 4) is, *The isles shall wait for his law.* The isles of the Gentiles are spoken of (Gen. x. 5), as peopled by the sons of Japhet, of whom it was said (Gen. ix. 27), *God shall persuade Japhet to dwell in the tents of Shem;* which was now to be fulfilled, when *the isles* (says the prophet), *the Gentiles* (says the evangelist), *shall wait for his law,* and *trust in his name:* compare these together, and observe, that they, and they only, can with confidence *trust in Christ's name,* that *wait for his law* with a resolution to be ruled by it. Observe also, that the law we wait for is the law of faith, the law of trusting in his name. This is now his great commandment, that we *believe in Christ,* 1 John iii. 23.

3. The prediction concerning him, and his mild and quiet management of his undertaking, *v.* 19, 20. It is chiefly for the sake of this that it is here quoted, upon occasion of Christ's affected privacy and concealment.

(1.) That he should carry on his undertaking without noise or ostentation. *He shall not strive, or make an outcry.* Christ and his kingdom *come not with observation,* Luke xvii. 20, 21. When the First-begotten was brought into the world, it was not with state and ceremony; he made no public entry, had no harbingers to proclaim him King. He *was in the world and the world knew him not.* Those were mistaken who fed themselves with hopes of a pompous Saviour. *His voice was not heard in the streets;* "Lo, here is Christ;" or, "Lo, he is there:" he spake in a still small voice, which was alluring to all, but terrifying to none; he did not affect to make a noise, but came down silently like the dew. What he spake and did was with the greatest possible humility and self-denial. His kingdom was spiritual, and therefore not to be advanced by force or violence, or by high pretensions. No, *the kingdom of God is not in word, but in power.*

(2.) That he should carry on his undertaking without severity and rigour (*v.* 20). *A bruised reed shall he not break.* Some understand this of his patience in bearing with the wicked; he could as easily have broken these Pharisees as a bruised reed, and have quenched them as soon as smoking flax; but he will not do it till the judgment-day, when all his enemies shall be made his footstool. Others rather understand it of his power and grace in bearing up the weak. In general, the design of his gospel is to establish such a method of salvation as encourages sincerity, though there be much infirmity; it does not insist upon a sinless obedience, but accepts an upright, willing mind. As to particular persons, that follow Christ in meekness, and in fear, and in much trembling, observe, [1.] How their case is here described—they are like *a bruised reed,* and *smoking flax.* Young beginners in religion are weak as a bruised reed, and their weakness offensive like smoking flax; some little life they have, but it is like that of a bruised reed; some little heat, but like that of smoking flax. Christ's disciples were as yet but weak, and many are so that have a place in his family. The grace and goodness in them are as a bruised reed, the corruption and badness in them are as smoking flax, as the wick of a candle when it is put out and is yet smoking. [2] What is the compassion of our Lord Jesus toward them?

He will not discourage them, much less reject them or cast them off; the reed that is bruised shall not be broken and trodden down, but shall be supported, and made as strong as a cedar or flourishing palm-tree. The candle newly lighted, though it only smokes and does not flame, shall not be blown out, but blown up. The *day of small things* is the day of *precious* things, and therefore he will not despise it, but make it *the day of great things*, Zech. iv. 10. Note, Our Lord Jesus deals very tenderly with those who have true grace, though they be weak in it, Isa. xl. 11; Heb. v. 2. He remembers not only that we are dust, but that we are flesh. [3.] The good issue and success of this, intimated in that, *till he send forth judgment unto victory*. That judgment which he showed to the Gentiles shall be victorious, he will go on conquering and to conquer, Rev. vi. 2. Both the preaching of the gospel in the world, and the power of the gospel in the heart, shall prevail. Grace shall get the upper hand of corruption, and shall at length be perfected in glory. Christ's judgment will be brought forth to victory, for when he judges he will overcome. He shall *bring forth judgment unto truth;* so it is, Isa. xlii. 3. Truth and victory are much the same, for *great is the truth, and will prevail.*

22 Then was brought unto him
one possessed with a devil, blind and
dumb: and he healed him, insomuch
that the blind and dumb both spake
and saw. 23 And all the people were
amazed, and said, Is not this the son
of David? 24 But when the Pharisees
heard *it*, they said, This *fellow* doth
not cast out devils, but by Beelzebub
the prince of the devils. 25 And
Jesus knew their thoughts, and said
unto them, Every kingdom divided
against itself is brought to desolation;
and every city or house divided against
itself shall not stand: 26 And if
Satan cast out Satan, he is divided
against himself; how shall then his
kingdom stand? 27 And if I by
Beelzebub cast out devils, by whom
do your children cast *them* out?
therefore they shall be your judges.
28 But if I cast out devils by the
Spirit of God, then the kingdom of
God is come unto you. 29 Or else
how can one enter into a strong man's
house, and spoil his goods, except he
first bind the strong man? and then
he will spoil his house. 30 He that
is not with me, is against me; and
he that gathereth not with me scattereth abroad. 31 Wherefore I say
unto you, All manner of sin and
blasphemy shall be forgiven unto
men: but the blasphemy *against* the
Holy Ghost shall not be forgiven
unto men. 32 And whosoever speaketh a word against the Son of man,
it shall be forgiven him: but whosoever speaketh against the Holy Ghost,
it shall not be forgiven him, neither
in this world, neither in the *world*
to come. 33 Either make the tree
good, and his fruit good; or else
make the tree corrupt, and his fruit
corrupt: for the tree is known by *his*
fruit. 34 O generation of vipers, how
can ye, being evil, speak good things?
for out of the abundance of the heart
the mouth speaketh. 35 A good
man out of the good treasure of the
heart bringeth forth good things:
and an evil man out of the evil treasure bringeth forth evil things. 36
But I say unto you, That every idle
word that men shall speak, they shall
give account thereof in the day of
judgment. 37 For by thy words thou
shalt be justified, and by thy words
thou shalt be condemned.

In these verses we have,

I. Christ's glorious conquest of Satan, in the gracious cure of one who, by the divine permission, was under his power, and in his possession, *v.* 22. Here observe,

1. The man's case was very sad; he was *possessed with a devil.* More cases of this kind occurred in Christ's time than usual, that Christ's power might be the more magnified, and his purpose the more manifested, in opposing and dispossessing Satan; and that it might the more evidently appear, that he *came to destroy the works of the devil.* This poor man that was possessed was blind and dumb; a miserable case! he could neither see to help himself, nor speak to others to help him. A soul under Satan's power, and led captive by him, is blind in the things of God, and dumb at the throne of grace; sees nothing, and says nothing to the purpose. Satan blinds the eye of faith, and seals up the lips of prayer.

2. His cure was very strange, and the more so, because sudden; *he healed him.* Note, The conquering and dispossessing of Satan is the healing of souls. And the cause being removed, immediately the effect ceased; the *blind and dumb both spake and saw.* Note, Christ's mercy is directly opposite to Satan's malice; his favours, to the

devil's mischiefs. When Satan's power is broken in the soul, the eyes are opened to see God's glory, and the lips opened to speak his praise.

II. The conviction which this gave to the people, to *all the people: they were amazed.* Christ had wrought divers miracles of this kind before; but his works are not the less wonderful, nor the less to be wondered at, for their being often repeated. They inferred from it, "*Is not this the Son of David?* The Messiah promised, that was to spring from the loins of David? Is not this he that should come? We may take this, 1. As an *enquiring* question; they asked, *Is not this the Son of David?* But they did not stay for an answer: the impressions were cogent, but they were transient. It was a good question that they started; but, it should seem, it was soon lost, and was not prosecuted. Such convictions as these should be brought to a head, and then they are likely to be brought to the heart. Or, 2. as an *affirming* question; *Is not this the Son of David?* "Yes, certainly it is, it can be no other; such miracles as these plainly evince that the kingdom of the Messiah is now setting up." And they were the people, the vulgar sort of the spectators, that drew this inference from Christ's miracles. Atheists will say, "That was because they were less prying than the Pharisees;" no, the matter of fact was obvious, and required not much search: but it was because they were less prejudiced and biassed by worldly interest. So plain and easy was the way made to this great truth of Christ being the Messiah and Saviour of the world, that the common people could not miss it; the *wayfaring men, though fools, could not err therein.* See Isa. xxxv. 8. It was found of them that sought it. It is an instance of the condescensions of divine grace, that the things that were *hid from the wise and prudent* were *revealed unto babes.* The world by wisdom knew not God, and by the foolish things the wise were confounded.

III. The blasphemous cavil of the Pharisees, *v.* 24. The Pharisees were a sort of men that pretended to more knowledge in, and zeal for, the divine law, than other people; yet they were the most inveterate enemies to Christ and his doctrine. They were proud of the reputation they had among the people; *that* fed their pride, supported their power, and filled their purses; and when they heard the people say, *Is not this the Son of David?* they were extremely irritated, more at that than at the miracle itself; this made them jealous of our Lord Jesus, and apprehensive, that as *his* interest in the people's esteem increased, *theirs* must of course be eclipsed and diminished; therefore they envied him, as Saul did his father David, because of what the women sang of him, 1 Sam. xviii. 7, 8. Note, Those who bind up their happiness in the praise and applause of men, expose themselves to a perpetual uneasiness upon every favourable word that they hear said of any other. The shadow of honour followed Christ, who fled from it, and fled from the Pharisees, who were eager in the pursuit of it. They said, "*This fellow does not cast out devils, but by Beelzebub the prince of the devils,* and therefore is not the Son of David." Observe,

1. How scornfully they speak of Christ, *this fellow;* as if that precious name of his, which is *as ointment poured forth,* were not worthy to be taken into their lips. It is an instance of their pride and superciliousness, and their diabolical envy, that the more people magnified Christ, the more industrious they were to vilify him. It is a bad thing to speak of good men with disdain because they are poor.

2. How blasphemously they speak of his miracles; they could not deny the matter of fact; it was as plain as the sun, that devils were cast out by the word of Christ; nor could they deny that it was an extraordinary thing, and supernatural. Being thus forced to grant the premises, they had no other way to avoid the conclusion, that *this is the Son of David,* than by suggesting that *Christ cast out devils by Beelzebub;* that there was a compact between Christ and the devil; pursuant to that, the devil was not cast out, but did voluntarily retire, and give back by consent and with design: or as if, by an agreement with the ruling devil, he had power to cast out the inferior devils. No surmise could be more palpably false and vile than this; that he, who is Truth itself, should be in combination with the father of lies, to cheat the world. This was the last refuge, or subterfuge rather, of an obstinate infidelity, that was resolved to stand it out against the clearest conviction. Observe, Among the devils there is a prince, the ringleader of the apostasy from God and rebellion against him; but this prince is Beelzebub—the god of a fly, or a dunghill god. How art thou fallen, O Lucifer! from an angel of light, to be a lord of flies! Yet this is the prince of the devils too, the chief of the gang of infernal spirits.

IV. Christ's reply to this base insinuation, *v.* 25—30. *Jesus knew their thoughts.* Note, Jesus Christ knows what we are thinking at any time, knows what is in man; he *understands our thoughts afar off.* It should seem that the Pharisees could not for shame speak it out, but kept it in their minds; they could not expect to satisfy the people with it; they therefore reserved it for the silencing of the convictions of their own consciences. Note, Many are kept off from their duty by that which they are ashamed to own, but which they cannot hide from Jesus Christ: yet it is probable that the Pharisees had whispered what they thought among themselves, to help to harden one another; but Christ's reply is said to be to their thoughts, because he knew with what mind, and from what principle, they said it; that they did not say it in their haste, but that it was the product of a rooted malignity.

Christ's reply to this imputation is copious and cogent, that *every mouth may be stopped* with sense and reason, before it be stopped with fire and brimstone. Here are three arguments by which he demonstrates the unreasonableness of this suggestion.

1. It would be very strange, and highly improbable, that Satan should be cast out by such a compact, because then Satan's *kingdom would be divided against itself;* which, considering his subtlety, is not a thing to be imagined, *v.* 25, 26.

(1.) Here is a known rule laid down, that in all societies a common ruin is the consequence of mutual quarrels: *Every kingdom divided against itself is brought to desolation;* and every family too: *Quæ enim domus tam stabilis est, quæ tam firma civitas, quæ non odiis atque dissidiis funditùs everti possit?—For what family is so strong, what community so firm, as not to be overturned by enmity and dissension?* Cic. *Læl.* 7. Divisions commonly end in desolations; if we clash, we break; if we divide one from another, we become an easy prey to a common enemy; much more *if we bite and devour one another,* shall *we be consumed one of another,* Gal. v. 15. Churches and nations have known this by sad experience.

(2.) The application of it to the case in hand (*v.* 26), *If Satan cast out Satan;* if the prince of the devils should be at variance with the inferior devils, the whole kingdom and interest would soon be broken; nay, if Satan should come into a compact with Christ, it must be to his own ruin; for the manifest design and tendency of Christ's preaching and miracles was to overthrow the kingdom of Satan, as a kingdom of darkness, wickedness, and enmity to God; and to set up, upon the ruins of it, a kingdom of light, holiness, and love. *The works of the devil,* as a rebel against God, and a tyrant over the souls of men, were destroyed by Christ; and therefore it was the most absurd thing imaginable, to think that Beelzebub should at all countenance such a design, or come into it: if he should fall in with Christ, *how should then his kingdom stand?* He would himself contribute to the overthrow of it. Note, The devil has a kingdom, a common interest, in opposition to God and Christ, which, to the utmost of his power, he will make to stand, and he will never come into Christ's interests; he must be conquered and broken by Christ, and therefore cannot submit and bend to him. *What concord or communion can there be between light and darkness, Christ and Belial, Christ and Beelzebub?* Christ will destroy the devil's kingdom, but he needs not do it by any such little arts and projects as that of a secret compact with Beelzebub; no, this victory must be obtained by nobler methods. Let the prince of the devils muster up all his forces, let him make use of all his powers and politics, and keep his interests in the closest confederacy, yet Christ will be too hard for his united force, and his kingdom shall not stand.

2. It was not at all strange, or improbable, that devils should be cast out by the Spirit of God; for,

(1.) *How* otherwise *do your children cast them out?* There were those among the Jews who, by invocation of the name of the most high God, or the God of Abraham, Isaac, and Jacob, did sometimes cast out devils. Josephus speaks of some in his time that did it; we read of *Jewish exorcists* (Acts xix. 13), and of some that *in Christ's name cast out devils,* though they did not follow him (Mark ix. 38), or were not faithful to him, *ch.* vii. 22 These the Pharisees condemned not, but imputed what they did to the Spirit of God, and valued themselves and their nation upon it. It was therefore merely from spite and envy to Christ, that they would own that others cast out devils by the Spirit of God, but suggest that he did it by compact with Beelzebub. Note, It is the way of malicious people, especially the malicious persecutors of Christ and Christianity, to condemn the same thing in those they hate, which they approve of and applaud in those they have a kindness for: the judgments of envy are made, not by things, but persons; not by reason, but prejudice. But those were very unfit to sit in Moses's seat, who knew faces, and knew nothing else in judgment: *Therefore they shall be your judges;* "This contradicting of yourselves will rise up in judgment against you at the last great day, and will condemn you." Note, In the last judgment, not only every sin, but every aggravation of it, will be brought into the account, and some of our notions that were right and good will be brought in evidence against us, to convict us of partiality.

(2.) This casting out of devils was a certain token and indication of the approach and appearance of the kingdom of God (*v.* 28); "But if it be indeed that *I cast out devils by the Spirit of God,* as certainly I do, then you must conclude, that though you are unwilling to receive it, yet the kingdom of the Messiah is now about to be set up among you." Other miracles that Christ wrought proved him *sent of God,* but this proved him sent of God to destroy the devil's kingdom and his works. Now that great promise was evidently fulfilled, that *the seed of the woman should break the serpent's head,* Gen. iii. 15. "Therefore that glorious dispensation of the kingdom of God, which has been long expected, is now commenced; slight it at your peril." Note, [1.] The destruction of the devil's power is wrought by the Spirit of God; that Spirit who works to the obedience of faith, overthrows the interest of that spirit who *works in the children of* unbelief and *disobedience.* [2.] The casting out of devils is a certain introduction to the kingdom of God. If the devil's interest in a soul be not only checked by custom or external restraints, but sunk and broken by the Spirit of God, as a Sanctifier, no doubt but *the kingdom of God is come* to that soul, the kingdom of grace, a blessed earnest of the kingdom of the glory.

3. The comparing of Christ's miracles, particularly this of casting out devils, with his doctrine, and the design and tendency of his holy religion, evidenced that he was so far from being in league with Satan, that he was at open enmity and hostility against him (*v.* 29); *How can one enter into a strong man's house, and plunder his goods,* and carry them away, *except he first bind the strong man? And then he* may do what he pleases with his goods. The world, that sat in darkness, and lay in wickedness, was in Satan's possession, and under his power, as a house in the possession and under the power of a strong man; so is every unregenerate soul; there Satan resides, there he rules. Now, (1.) The design of Christ's gospel was to spoil the devil's house, which, as a strong man, he kept in the world; *to turn the people from darkness to light,* from sin to holiness, from this world to a better, *from the power of Satan unto God* (Acts xxvi. 18); to alter the property of souls. (2.) Pursuant to this design, he bound the strong man, when he cast out unclean spirits by his word: thus he wrested the *sword* out of the devil's hand, that he might wrest the *sceptre* out of it. The doctrine of Christ teaches us how to construe his miracles, and when he showed how easily and effectually he could cast the devil out of people's bodies, he encouraged all believers to hope that, whatever power Satan might usurp and exercise in the souls of men, Christ by his grace would break it: he will spoil him, for it appears that he can bind him. When nations were turned *from the service of idols to serve the living God,* when some of the worst of sinners were sanctified and justified, and became the best of saints, then Christ spoiled the devil's house, and will spoil it more and more.

4. It is here intimated, that this holy war, which Christ was carrying on with vigour against the devil and his kingdom, was such as would not admit of a neutrality (*v.* 30), *He that is not with me is against me.* In the little differences that may arise between the disciples of Christ among themselves, we are taught to lessen the matters in variance, and to seek peace, by accounting those who *are not against us, to be with us* (Luke ix. 50); but in the great quarrel between Christ and the devil, no peace is to be sought, nor any such favourable construction to be made of any indifference in the matter; he that is not hearty *for* Christ, will be reckoned with as really *against* him: he that is cold in the cause, is looked upon as an enemy. When the dispute is between God and Baal, there is no halting between two (1 Kings xviii. 21), there is no trimming between Christ and Belial; for the kingdom of Christ, as it is eternally opposite to, so it will be eternally victorious over, the devil's kingdom; and therefore in this cause there is no sitting still with *Gilead beyond Jordan, or Asher on the sea-shore* (Judg. v. 16, 17), we must be entirely, faithfully, and immovably, on Christ's side: it is the *right* side, and will at last be the *rising* side. See Exod. xxxii. 26.

The latter clause is to the same purport: *He that gathereth not with me scattereth.* Note, (1.) Christ's errand into the world was to gather, to gather in his harvest, to gather in those whom the Father had given him, John xi. 52; Eph. i. 10. (2.) Christ expects and requires from those who are with him, that they gather with him; that they not only gather to him themselves, but do all they can in their places to gather others to him, and so to strengthen his interest. (3.) Those who will not appear, and act, as furtherers of Christ's kingdom, will be looked upon, and dealt with, as hinderers of it; if we *gather not with Christ, we scatter;* it is not enough, not to do hurt, but we must do good. Thus is the breach widened between Christ and Satan, to show that there was no such compact between them as the Pharisees whispered.

V. Here is a discourse of Christ's upon this occasion, concerning tongue-sins; *Wherefore I say unto you.* He seems to turn from the Pharisees to the people, from disputing to instructing; and from the sin of the Pharisees he warns the people concerning three sorts of tongue-sins; for others' harms are admonitions to us.

1. Blasphemous words against the Holy Ghost are the worst kind of tongue-sins, and unpardonable, *v.* 31, 32.

(1.) Here is a gracious assurance of the pardon of all sin upon gospel terms: this Christ says to us, and it is a comfortable saying, that the greatness of sin shall be no bar to our acceptance with God, if we truly repent and believe the gospel: *All manner of sin and blasphemy shall be forgiven unto men.* Though the sin has been *as scarlet and crimson* (Isa. i. 18), though ever so heinous in its nature, ever so much aggravated by its circumstances, and ever so often repeated, though it *reach up to the heavens,* yet *with the Lord there is mercy, that reacheth beyond the heavens;* mercy will be extended even to blasphemy, a sin immediately touching God's name and honour. Paul obtained mercy, who had *been a blasphemer,* 1 Tim. i. 13. Well may we say, *Who is a God like unto thee, pardoning iniquity?* Micah vii. 18. Even *words spoken against the Son of man shall be forgiven;* as theirs were who reviled him at his death, many of whom repented and found mercy. Christ herein has set an example to all the sons of men, to be ready to forgive words spoken against them: *I, as a deaf man, heard not.* Observe, *They shall be forgiven unto men,* not to devils; this is love to the whole world of mankind, above the world of fallen angels, that all sin is pardonable to them.

(2.) Here is an exception of *the blasphemy against the Holy Ghost,* which is here declared to be the only unpardonable sin. See here,

[1.] What this sin is; it is *speaking against the Holy Ghost.* See what malignity there is in tongue-sins, when the only unpardonable sin is so. *But Jesus knew their thoughts, v.* 25. It is not all speaking against the person or essence of the Holy Ghost, or some of his more private operations, or merely the resisting of his internal working in the sinner himself, that is here meant; for *who then should be saved?* It is adjudged in our law, that an act of indemnity shall always be construed in favour of that grace and clemency which is the intention of the act; and therefore the exceptions in the act are not to be extended further than needs must. The gospel is an act of indemnity; none are excepted by name, nor any by description, but those only *that blaspheme the Holy Ghost;* which therefore must be construed in the narrowest sense: all presuming sinners are effectually cut off by the conditions of the indemnity, faith and repentance; and therefore the other exceptions must not be stretched far: and this blasphemy is excepted, not for any defect of mercy in God or merit in Christ, but because it inevitably leaves the sinner in infidelity and impenitency. We have reason to think that none are guilty of this sin, who believe that Christ is *the Son of God,* and sincerely desire to have part in his merit and mercy: and those who fear they have committed this sin, give a good sign that they have not. The learned Dr. Whitby very well observes, that Christ speaks not of what was now said or done, but of what should be (Mark iii. 28; Luke xii. 10); *Whosoever shall blaspheme.* As for those who blasphemed Christ when he was here upon earth, and called him a Winebibber, a Deceiver, a Blasphemer, and the like, they had some colour of excuse, because of the meanness of his appearance, and the prejudices of the nation against him; and the proof of his divine mission was not perfected till after his ascension; and therefore, upon their repentance, they shall be pardoned: and it is hoped that they may be convinced by the pouring out of the Spirit, as many of them were, who had been his betrayers and murderers. But if, when the Holy Ghost is given, in his inward gifts of revelation, speaking with tongues, and the like, such as were the distributions of the Spirit among the apostles, if they continue to blaspheme the Spirit likewise, as an evil spirit, there is no hope of them, that they will ever be brought to believe in Christ; for, *First,* Those gifts of the Holy Ghost in the apostles were the last proof that God designed to make use of for the confirming of the gospel, and were still kept in reserve, when other methods preceded. *Secondly,* This was the most powerful evidence, and more apt to convince than miracles themselves. *Thirdly,* Those therefore who blaspheme this dispensation of the Spirit, cannot possibly be brought to believe in Christ; those who shall impute them to a collusion with Satan, as the Pharisees did the miracles, what can convince them? This is such a strong hold of infidelity as a man can never be beaten out of, and is therefore unpardonable, because hereby repentance is hid from the sinner's eyes.

[2.] What the sentence is that is passed upon it; *It shall not be forgiven, neither in this world, nor in the world to come.* As in the then present state of the Jewish church, there was no sacrifice of expiation for *the soul that sinned presumptuously;* so neither under the dispensation of gospel grace, which is often in scripture called *the world to come,* shall there be any pardon to *such as tread underfoot the blood of the covenant, and do despite to the Spirit of grace:* there is no cure for a sin so directly against the remedy. It was a rule in our old law, No sanctuary for sacrilege. Or, *It shall be forgiven neither now,* in the sinner's own conscience, *nor in the great day,* when the pardon shall be published. Or, this is a sin that exposes the sinner both to temporal and eternal punishment, both to present wrath and *the wrath to come.*

2. Christ speaks here concerning other wicked words, the products of corruption reigning in the heart, and breaking out thence, *v.* 33—35. It was said (*v.* 25) that *Jesus knew their thoughts,* and here he spoke with an eye to them, showing that it was not strange that they should speak so ill, when their hearts were so full of enmity and malice; which yet they often endeavoured to cloak and cover, by feigning themselves just men. Our Lord Jesus therefore points to the springs and heals them; let the heart be sanctified and it will appear in our words.

(1.) The heart is the *root,* the language is the *fruit* (*v.* 33); if the nature of the tree be good, it will bring forth fruit accordingly. Where grace is the reigning principle in the heart, the language will be the language of Canaan; and, on the contrary, whatever lust reigns in the heart it will break out; diseased lungs make an offensive breath: men's language discovers what country they are of, so likewise *what manner of spirit they are of:* "*Either make the tree good, and then the fruit will be good;* get pure hearts and then you will have pure lips and pure lives; or else *the tree will be corrupt, and the fruit* accordingly. You may make a crab-stock to become a good tree, by grafting into it a shoot from a good tree, and then the fruit will be good; but if the tree be still the same, plant it where you will, and water it how you will, the fruit will be still corrupt." Note, Unless the heart be *trans*formed, the life will never be thoroughly *re*formed. These Pharisees were shy of speaking out their wicked thoughts of Jesus Christ; but Christ here intimates, how vain it was for them to seek to hide that root of bitterness in them, that bore this gall and wormwood, when they never sought to mortify it. Note, It should be more our care to be good really, than to seem good outwardly.

(2.) The heart is the *fountain*, the words are the streams (*v.* 34); *Out of the abundance of the heart the mouth speaks,* as the streams are the overflowings of the spring. A wicked heart is said to *send forth wickedness, as a fountain casts forth her waters,* Jer. vi. 7. *A troubled fountain, and a corrupt spring,* such as Solomon speaks of (Prov. xxv. 26), must needs *send forth muddy and unpleasant streams.* Evil words are the natural, genuine product of an evil heart. Nothing but the salt of grace, cast into the spring, will heal the waters, *season the speech,* and purify the *corrupt communication.* This they wanted, they were evil; *and how can ye, being evil, speak good things?* They were *a generation of vipers;* John Baptist had called them so (*ch.* iii. 7), and they were still the same; for *can the Ethiopian change his skin?* The people looked upon the Pharisees as a generation of saints, but Christ calls them *a generation of vipers, the seed of the serpent,* that had an enmity to Christ and his gospel. Now what could be expected from *a generation of vipers,* but that which is poisonous and malignant? Can the viper be otherwise than venomous? Note, Bad things may be expected from bad people, as said the proverb of the ancients, *Wickedness proceedeth from the wicked,* 1 Sam. xxiv. 13. *The vile person will speak villany,* Isa. xxxii. 6. Those who are themselves evil, have neither skill nor will to speak good things, as they should be spoken. Christ would have his disciples know what sort of men they were to live among, that they might know what to look for. They are as Ezekiel *among scorpions* (Ezek. ii. 6), and must not think it strange if they be stung and bitten.

(3.) The heart is the *treasury*, the words are the things brought out of that treasury (*v.* 35); and from hence men's characters may be drawn, and may be judged of.

[1.] It is the character of a *good man,* that he has a *good treasure in his heart,* and from thence *brings forth good things,* as there is occasion. Graces, comforts, experiences, good knowledge, good affections, good resolutions, these are a *good treasure in the heart;* the word of God hidden there, the law of God written there, divine truths dwelling and ruling there, are a treasure there, valuable and suitable, kept safe and kept secret, as the stores of the good householder, but ready for use upon all occasions. *A good man,* thus furnished, will *bring forth,* as Joseph out of his stores; will be speaking and doing that which is good, for God's glory, and the edification of others. See Prov. x. 11, 13, 14, 20, 21, 31, 32. This is *bringing forth good things.* Some pretend to good expenses that have not a *good treasure*—such will soon be bankrupts: some pretend to have a good treasure within, but give no proof of it: they hope they have it in them, and thank God, whatever their words and actions are, they have good hearts; but *faith without works is dead:* and some have a *good treasure* of wisdom and knowledge, but they are not communicative, they do not *bring forth* out of it: they have a talent, but know not how to trade with it. The complete Christian in *this* bears the image of God, that he both *is good, and does good.*

[2.] It is the character of *an evil man,* that he has an *evil treasure in his heart,* and out of it *bringeth forth evil things.* Lusts and corruptions dwelling and reigning in the heart are an evil treasure, out of which the sinner brings forth bad words and actions, to the dishonour of God, and the hurt of others. See Gen. vi. 5, 12; Matth. xv. 18—20; Jam. i. 15. But *treasures of wickedness* (Prov. x. 2) will be *treasures of wrath.*

3. Christ speaks here concerning *idle words,* and shows what evil there is in them (*v.* 36, 37); much more is there in such wicked words as the Pharisees spoke. It concerns us to think much of the day of judgment, that *that* may be a check upon our tongues; and let us consider,

(1.) How particular the account will be of tongue-sins in that day: even *for every idle word,* or discourse, *that men speak, they shall give account.* This intimates, [1.] That God takes notice of every word we say, even that which we ourselves do not notice. See Psalm cxxxix. 4. *Not a word in my tongue but thou knowest it:* though spoken without regard or design, God takes cognizance of it. [2.] That vain, idle, impertinent talk is displeasing to God, which tends not to any good purpose, is not good to any use of edifying; it is the product of a vain and trifling heart. These *idle words* are the same with that *foolish talking and jesting* which is forbidden, Eph. v. 4. This is that sin which is seldom wanting in *the multitude of words, unprofitable talk,* Job xv. 3. [3.] We must shortly account for these idle words; they will be produced in evidence against us, to prove us unprofitable servants, that have not improved the faculties of reason and speech, which are part of the talents we are entrusted with. If we repent not of our idle words, and our account for them be not balanced by the blood of Christ, we are undone.

(2.) How strict the judgment will be upon that account (*v.* 37); *By thy words thou shalt be justified or condemned;* a common rule in men's judgments, and here applied to God's. Note, The constant tenour of our discourse, according as it is gracious or not gracious, will be an evidence for us, or against us, at the great day. Those who seemed to be religious, but bridled not their tongue, will then be found to have put a cheat upon themselves with a vain religion, Jam. i. 26. Some think that Christ here refers to that of Eliphaz (Job xv. 6), *Thine own mouth condemneth thee, and not I;* or, rather, to that of Solomon (Prov. xviii. 21), *Death and life are in the power of the tongue.*

38 Then certain of the scribes and
of the Pharisees answered, saying,
Master, we would see a sign from
thee. 39 But he answered and said
unto them, An evil and adulterous
generation seeketh after a sign; and
there shall no sign be given to it, but
the sign of the prophet Jonas: 40
For as Jonas was three days and
three nights in the whale's belly; so
shall the Son of man be three days
and three nights in the heart of the
earth. 41 The men of Nineveh shall
rise in judgment with this generation,
and shall condemn it: because they
repented at the preaching of Jonas;
and, behold, a greater than Jonas *is*
here. 42 The queen of the south
shall rise up in judgment with this
generation, and shall condemn it: for
she came from the uttermost parts of
the earth to hear the wisdom of Solomon; and, behold, a greater than
Solomon *is* here. 43 When the unclean spirit is gone out of a man, he
walketh through dry places, seeking
rest, and findeth none. 44 Then he
saith, I will return into my house from
whence I came out; and when he is
come, he findeth *it* empty, swept, and
garnished. 45 Then goeth he, and
taketh with himself seven other spirits
more wicked than himself, and they
enter in and dwell there: and the last
state of that man is worse than the
first. Even so shall it be also unto
this wicked generation.

It is probable that these Pharisees with whom Christ is here in discourse were not the same that cavilled at him (*v.* 24), and would not credit the signs he gave; but another set of them, who saw that there was no reason to discredit them, but would not content themselves with the signs he gave, nor admit the evidence of them, unless he would give them such further proof as they should demand. Here is,

I. Their address to him, *v.* 38. They compliment him with the title of *Master*, pretending respect for him, when they intended to abuse him; all are not indeed Christ's servants, who call him *Master*. Their request is, *We would see a sign from thee.* It was highly reasonable that they should see a sign, that he should by miracles prove his divine mission: see Exod. iv. 8, 9. He came to take down a model of religion that was set up by miracles, and therefore it was requisite he should produce the same credentials; but it was highly unreasonable to demand a sign now, when he had given so many signs already, that did abundantly prove him *sent of God.* Note, It is natural to proud men to *pre*scribe to God, and then to make that an excuse for not *sub*scribing to him; but a man's *of*fence will never be his *de*fence.

II. His answer to this address, this insolent demand.

1. He condemns the demand, as the language of *an evil and adulterous generation, v.* 39. He fastens the charge, not only on *the scribes and Pharisees,* but the whole nation of the Jews; they were all like their leaders, a seed and succession of evil-doers: they were an evil generation indeed, that not only hardened themselves against the conviction of Christ's miracles, but set themselves to abuse him, and put contempt on his miracles. They were *an adulterous generation,* (1.) As an adulterous brood; so miserably degenerated from the faith and obedience of their ancestors, that Abraham and Israel acknowledged them not. See Isa. lvii. 3. Or, (2.) As an adulterous wife; they departed from that God, to whom by covenant they had been espoused: they were not guilty of the whoredom of idolatry, as they had been before the captivity, but they were guilty of infidelity, and all iniquity, and that is whoredom too: they did not look after gods of their own making, but they looked for signs of their own devising; and that was adultery.

2. He refuses to give them any other sign than he has already given them, but *that of the prophet Jonas.* Note, Though Christ is always ready to hear and answer holy desires and prayers, yet he will not gratify corrupt lusts and humours. Those who *ask amiss, ask, and have not.* Signs were granted to those who desired them for the confirmation of their faith, as to Abraham and Gideon; but were denied to those who demanded them for the excuse of their unbelief.

Justly might Christ have said, They shall never see another miracle: but see his wonderful goodness; (1.) They shall have the same signs still repeated, for their further benefit, and more abundant conviction. (2.) They shall have one sign of a different kind from all these, and that is, *the resurrection of Christ from the dead by his own power,* called here *the sign of the prophet Jonas;* this was yet reserved for their conviction, and was intended to be the great proof of Christ's being the Messiah; for by that he was *declared to be the Son of God with power,* Rom. i. 4. That was such a sign as surpassed all the rest, completed and crowned them. "*If they will not believe* the former signs, they will believe this (Exod. iv. 9), and if this will not convince them, nothing will." And yet the unbelief of the Jews found out an evasion to shift off that too, by saying, *His disciples came and stole him away;* for none are so incurably blind as those who are resolved they will not see.

Now this sign of the prophet Jonas he further explains here; (*v.* 40.) *As Jonas was three days and three nights in the whale's belly,* and then came out again safe and well, thus Christ shall be so long in the grave, and then shall rise again. [1.] The grave was to Christ as the belly of the fish was to Jonah; thither he was thrown, as a Ransom for lives ready to be lost in a storm; there he lay, as *in the belly of hell* (Jonah ii. 2), and seemed to be cast out of God's sight. [2.] He continued in the grave just as long as Jonah continued in the fish's belly, *three days and three nights;* not three whole days and nights: it is probable, Jonah did not lie so long in the whale's belly, but part of three natural days (νυχθήμεραι, the Greeks called them); he was buried in the afternoon of the sixth day of the week, and rose again in the morning of the first day; it is a manner of speech very usual; see 1 Kings xx. 29; Esth. iv. 16; v. 1; Luke ii. 21. So long Jonah was a prisoner for his own sins, so long Christ was a Prisoner for ours. [3.] As Jonah in the whale's belly comforted himfelf with an assurance that yet he should look again *toward God's holy temple* (Jonah ii. 4), so Christ when he lay in the grave, is expressly said to *rest in hope,* as one assured he should *not see corruption,* Acts ii. 26, 27. [4.] As Jonah on the third day was discharged from his prison, and came to the land of the living again, from *the congregation of the dead* (for dead things are said to be *formed from under the waters,* Job xxvi. 5), so Christ on the third day should return to life, and rise out of his grave to send abroad the gospel to the Gentiles.

3. Christ takes this occasion to represent the sad character and condition of that generation in which he lived, a generation that would not be reformed, and therefore could not but be ruined; and he gives them their character, as it would stand in the day of judgment, under the full discoveries and final sentences of that day. Persons and things now appear under false colours; characters and conditions are here changeable: if therefore we would make a right estimate, we must take our measures from the last judgment; things are really, what they are eternally.

Now Christ represents the people of the Jews,

(1.) As a generation that would be condemned by *the men of Nineveh,* whose *repenting at the preaching of Jonas* would *rise up in judgment* against them, *v.* 41. Christ's resurrection will be the sign of the prophet Jonas to them: but it will not have so happy an effect upon them, as that of Jonas had upon the Ninevites, for they were by it brought to such a repentance as prevented their ruin; but the Jews will be hardened in an unbelief that shall hasten their ruin; and in the day of judgment, the repentance of the Ninevites will be mentioned as an aggravation of the sin, and consequently the condemnation of those to whom Christ preached then, and of those to whom Christ is preached now; for this reason, because Christ is greater than Jonah. [1] Jonah was but a man, subject to like passions, to like sinful passions, as we are; but Christ is the Son of God. [2.] Jonah was a stranger in Nineveh, he came among the strangers that were prejudiced against his country; but Christ came to his own, when he preached to the Jews, and much more when he is preached among professing Christions, that are called by his name. [3] Jonah preached but one short sermon, and that with no great solemnity, but as he passed along the streets; Christ renews his calls, sat and taught, taught in the synagogues. [4.] Jonah preached nothing but wrath and ruin within forty days, gave no instructions, directions, or encouragements, to repent: but Christ, besides the warning given us of our danger, has shown wherein we must repent, and assured us of acceptance upon our repentance, because *the kingdom of heaven is at hand.* [5.] Jonah wrought no miracle to confirm his doctrine, showed no good will to the Ninevites; but Christ wrought abundance of miracles, and all miracles of mercy: yet the Ninevites *repented at the preaching of Jonas,* but the Jews were not wrought upon by Christ's preaching. Note, the goodness of some, who have less helps and advantages for their souls, will aggravate the badness of those who have much greater. Those who by the twilight discover *the things that belong to their peace,* will shame those who grope at noon-day.

(2.) As a generation that would be condemned by the queen of the south, the queen of Sheba, *v.* 42. The Ninevites would shame them for not repenting, the queen of Sheba for not believing in Christ. She came from a far country to hear the wisdom of Solomon; yet people will not be persuaded to come and hear the wisdom of Christ, though he is in every thing greater than Solomon. [1.] The queen of Sheba had no invitation to come to Solomon, nor any promise of being welcome; but we are invited to Christ, to sit at his feet and hear his word. [2.] Solomon was but a wise man, but Christ is wisdom itself, *in whom are hid all the treasures of wisdom.* [3.] The queen of Sheba had many difficulties to break through; she was a woman, unfit for travel, the journey long and perilous; she was a queen, and what would become of her own country in her absence? We have no such cares to hinder us. [4.] She could not be sure that it would be worth her while to go so far on this errand; fame uses to flatter men, and perhaps she might have in her own country or court wise men sufficient to instruct her; yet, having heard of Solomon's fame, she would see him; but we come not to Christ upon such uncertainties. [5.] *She came from the uttermost parts of the earth*, but we have Christ among us, and his word nigh us: *Behold he stands at the door, and knocks.* [6.] It should seem the wisdom the queen of Sheba came for was only philosophy and politics; but the wisdom that is to be had with Christ is wisdom to salvation. [7.] She could only *hear* Solomon's wisdom; he could not *give* her wisdom: but Christ will give wisdom to those who come to him; nay, he will himself be *made of God to them Wisdom;* so that, upon all these accounts, if we do not hear the wisdom of Christ, the forwardness of the queen of Sheba to come and hear the wisdom of Solomon will rise up in judgment against us and condemn us; for Jesus Christ is greater than Solomon.

(3.) As a generation that were resolved to continue in the possession, and under the power, of Satan, notwithstanding all the methods that were used to dispossess him and rescue them. They are compared to one out of whom the devil is gone, but returns with double force, *v.* 43—45. The devil is here called *the unclean spirit*, for he has lost all his purity, and delights in and promotes all manner of impurity among men. Now,

[1.] The parable represents his possessing men's bodies: Christ having lately cast out a devil, and they having said *he had a devil*, gave occasion to show how much they were under the power of Satan. This is a further proof that Christ did not cast out devils by compact with the devil, for then he would soon have returned again; but Christ's ejectment of him was final, and such as barred a re-entry: we find him charging the evil spirit to *go out, and enter no more*, Mark ix. 25. Probably the devil was wont sometimes thus to sport with those he had possession of; he would go out, and then return again with more fury; hence the lucid intervals of those in that condition were commonly followed with the more violent fits. When the devil is gone out, he is uneasy, for *he sleeps not except he have done mischief* (Prov. iv. 16); *he walks in dry places*, like one that is very melancholy; he *seeks rest but finds none*, till he returns again. When Christ cast the legion out of the man, they begged leave to enter into the swine, where they went not long in dry places, but into the lake presently.

[2.] The application of the parable makes it to represent the case of the body of the Jewish church and nation: *So shall it be with this wicked generation*, that now resist, and will finally reject, the gospel of Christ. The devil, who by the labours of Christ and his disciples had been cast out of many of the Jews, sought for rest among the heathen, from whose persons and temples the Christians would every where expel him: so Dr. Whitby: or finding no where else in the heathen world such pleasant, desirable habitations, to his satisfaction, as here in the heart of the Jews: so Dr. Hammond: he shall therefore enter again into them, for Christ had not found admission among them, and they, by their prodigious wickedness and obstinate unbelief, were still more ready than ever to receive him; and then he shall take a durable possession here, and the state of this people is likely to be more desperately damnable (so Dr. Hammond) than it was before Christ came among them, or would have been if Satan had never been cast out.

The body of that nation is here represented, *First*, As an apostate people. After the captivity in Babylon, they began to reform, left their idols, and appeared with some face of religion; but they soon corrupted themselves again: though they never relapsed into idolatry, they fell into all manner of impiety and profaneness, grew worse and worse, and added to all the rest of their wickedness a wilful contempt of, and opposition to, Christ and his gospel. *Secondly*, As a people marked for ruin. A new commission was passing the seals against that hypocritical nation, the people of God's wrath (like that, Isa. x. 6), and their destruction by the Romans was likely to be greater than any other, as their sins had been more flagrant: then it was *that wrath came upon them to the uttermost*, 1 Thess. ii. 15, 16. Let this be a warning to all nations and churches, to take heed of leaving their first love, of letting fall a good work of reformation begun among them, and returning to that wickedness which they seemed to have forsaken; *for the last state of such will be worse than the first.*

46 While he yet talked to the
people, behold, *his* mother and his
brethren stood without, desiring to
speak with him. 47 Then one said
unto him, Behold, thy mother and
thy brethren stand without, desiring
to speak with thee. 48 But he answered and said unto him that told
him, Who is my mother? and
who are my brethren? 49 And he
stretched forth his hand towards his
disciples, and said, Behold my mother
and my brethren! 50 For whosoever
shall do the will of my Father which
is in heaven, the same is my brother,
and sister, and mother.

Many excellent, useful sayings came from the mouth of our Lord Jesus upon particular occasions; even his digressions were instructive, as well as his set discourses: as here,

Observe, I. How Christ was interrupted

in his preaching by *his mother and his brethren,* that *stood without, desiring to speak with him* (*v.* 46, 47); which desire of theirs was conveyed to him through the crowd. It is needless to enquire which of his brethren they were that came along with his mother (perhaps they were those *who did not believe in him,* John vii. 5); or what their business was; perhaps it was only designed to oblige him to break off, for fear he should fatigue himself, or to caution him to take heed of giving offence by his discourse to the Pharisees, and of involving himself in a difficulty; as if they could teach *him* wisdom.

1. He was as yet talking to the people. Note, Christ's preaching was talking; it was plain, easy, and familiar, and suited to their capacity and case. What Christ had delivered had been cavilled at, and yet he went on. Note, The opposition we meet with in our work, must not drive us from it. He left off talking with the Pharisees, for he saw he could do no good with them; but continued to talk to the common people, who, not having such a conceit of their knowledge as the Pharisees had, were willing to learn.

2. His mother and brethren stood without, desiring to speak with him, when they should have been standing within, desiring to hear him. They had the advantage of his daily converse in private, and therefore were less mindful to attend upon his public preaching. Note, Frequently those who are nearest to the means of knowledge and grace, are most negligent. Familiarity and easiness of access breed some degree of contempt. We are apt to neglect *that* this day, which we think we may have any day, forgetting that it is only the present time we can be sure of; to-morrow is none of ours. There is too much truth in that common proverb, "The nearer the church, the further from God;" it is pity it should be so.

3. They not only would not hear him themselves, but they interrupted others that *heard him gladly.* The devil was a sworn enemy to our Saviour's preaching. He had sought to baffle his discourse by the unreasonable cavils of the scribes and Pharisees, and when he could not gain his point that way, he endeavoured to break it off by the unseasonable visits of relations. Note, We often meet with hindrances and obstructions in our work, by our friends that are about us, and are taken off by civil respects from our spiritual concerns. Those who really wish well to us and to our work, may sometimes, by their indiscretion, prove our back-friends, and impediments to us in our duty; as *Peter* was offensive to Christ, with his, "*Master, spare thyself,*" when he thought himself very officious. The mother of our Lord desired to speak with him; it seemed she had not then learned to command her Son, as the iniquity and idolatry of the church of Rome has since pretended to teach her: nor was she so free from fault and folly as they would make her. It was Christ's prerogative, and not his mother's, to do every thing wisely, and well, and in its season. Christ once said to his mother, *How is it that ye sought me? Wist ye not, that I must be about my Father's business?* And it was then said, she *laid up that saying in her heart* (Luke ii. 49); but if she had remembered it now, she would not have given him this interruption when he was about his Father's business. Note, There is many a good truth that we thought was well laid up when we heard it, which yet is out of the way when we have occasion to use it.

II. How he resented this interruption, *v.* 48—50.

1. He would not hearken to it; he was so intent upon his work, that no natural or civil respects should take him off from it. *Who is my mother and who are my brethren?* Not that natural affection is to be put off, or that, under pretence of religion, we may be disrespectful to parents, or unkind to other relations; but *every thing is beautiful in its season,* and the less duty must stand by, while the greater is done. When our regard to our relations comes in competition with the service of God, and the improving of an opportunity to *do good,* in such a case, we must *say to our Father, I have not seen him,* as Levi did, Deut. xxxiii. 9. The nearest relations must be comparatively hated, that is, we must love them less than Christ (Luke xiv. 26), and our duty to God must have the preference. This Christ has here given us an example of; *the zeal of God's house* did so far *eat him up,* that it made him not only forget himself, but forget his dearest relations. And we must not take it ill of our friends, nor put it upon the score of their wickedness, if they prefer the pleasing of God before the pleasing of us; but we must readily forgive those neglects which may be easily imputed to a pious zeal for God's glory and others' good. Nay, we must deny ourselves and our own satisfaction, rather than do that which may any way divert our friends from, or distract them in, their duty to God.

2. He took that occasion to prefer his disciples, who were his spiritual kindred, before his natural relations as such: which was a good reason why he would not leave preaching to speak with his brethren. He would rather be profiting his disciples, than pleasing his relations. Observe,

(1.) The description of Christ's disciples. They are such as *do the will of his Father;* not only hear it, and know it, and talk of it, but *do it;* for doing the will of God is the best preparative for discipleship (John vii. 17), and the best proof of it (*ch.* vii. 21); *that* denominates us his disciples indeed. Christ does not say, "Whosoever shall do my will," for he came not to seek or do his own will distinct from his Father's: his will and his Father's are the same; but he refers us to his Father's will, because now in his present state and work he referred himself to it, John vi. 38.

(2.) The dignity of Christ's disciples: *The same is my brother, and sister, and mother.* His disciples, that had left all to follow him, and embraced his doctrine, were dearer to him than any that were akin to him according to the flesh. They had preferred Christ before their relations); they *left their father* (*ch.* iv. 22; x. 37); and now to make them amends, and to show that there was no love lost, he preferred them before his relations. Did not they hereby receive, in point of honour, *a hundred fold? ch.* xix. 29. It was very endearing and very encouraging for Christ to say, *Behold my mother and my brethren;* yet it was not *their* privilege alone, *this honour have all the saints.* Note, All obedient believers are near akin to Jesus Christ. They wear his name, bear his image, have his nature, are of his family. He loves them, converses freely with them as his relations. He bids them welcome to his table, takes care of them, provides for them, sees that they want nothing that is fit for them: when he died he left them rich legacies, now he is in heaven he keeps up a correspondence with them, and will have them all with him at last, and will in nothing fail to *do the kinsman's part* (Ruth iii. 13), nor will ever be ashamed of his poor relations, but will confess them before men, before the angels, and before his Father.

CHAP. XIII.

In this chapter, we have, I. The favour which Christ did to his countrymen in preaching the kingdom of heaven to them, ver. 1—2. He preached to them in parables, and here gives the reason why he chose that way of instructing, ver. 10—17. And the evangelist gives another reason, ver. 34, 35. There are eight parables recorded in this chapter, which are designed to represent the kingdom of heaven, the method of planting the gospel kingdom in the world, and of its growth and success. The great truths and laws of that kingdom are in other scriptures laid down plainly, and without parables: but some circumstances of its beginning and progress are here laid open in parables. 1. Here is one parable to show what are the great hindrances of people's profiting by the word of the gospel, and in how many it comes short of its end, through their own folly, and that is the parable of the four sorts of ground, delivered ver. 3—9, and expounded ver. 18—23. 2. Here are two parables intended to show that there would be a mixture of good and bad in the gospel church, which would continue till the great separation between them in the judgment-day: the parable of the tares put forth (ver. 24—30), and expounded at the request of the disciples (ver. 36—43); and that of the net cast into the sea, ver. 47—50. 3. Here are two parables intended to show that the gospel church should be very small at first, but that in process of time it should become a considerable body: that of the grain of mustard-seed (ver. 31, 32), and that of the leaven, ver. 33. 4. Here are two parables intended to show that those who expect salvation by the gospel must be willing to venture all, and quit all, in the prospect of it, and that they shall be no losers by the bargain; that of the treasure hid in the field (ver. 44), and that of the pearl of great price, ver. 45, 46. 5. Here is one parable intended for direction to the disciples, to make use of the instructions he had given them for the benefit of others; and that is the parable of the good householder, ver. 51, 52. II. The contempt which his countrymen put upon him on account of the meanness of his parentage, ver. 53—58.

THE same day went Jesus out of
the house, and sat by the sea
side. 2 And great multitudes were
gathered together unto him, so that
he went into a ship, and sat; and the
whole multitude stood on the shore.
3 And he spake many things unto
them in parables, saying, Behold, a
sower went forth to sow; 4 And
when he sowed, some *seeds* fell by
the way side, and the fowls came and
devoured them up. 5 Some fell upon
stony places, where they had not much
earth: and forthwith they sprung
up, because they had no deepness of
earth: 6 And when the sun was up,
they were scorched; and because they
had no root, they withered away.
7 And some fell among thorns; and
the thorns sprung up, and choked
them. 8 But other fell into good
ground, and brought forth fruit, some
an hundredfold, some sixtyfold, some
thirtyfold. 9 Who hath ears to hear,
let him hear. 10 And the disciples
came, and said unto him, Why speakest thou unto them in parables? 11
He answered and said unto them,
Because it is given unto you to know
the mysteries of the kingdom of heaven, but to them it is not given. 12
For whosoever hath, to him shall be
given, and he shall have more abundance: but whosoever hath not, from
him shall be taken away even that he
hath. 13 Therefore speak I to them
in parables: because they seeing see
not; and hearing they hear not;
neither do they understand. 14 And
in them is fulfilled the prophecy of
Esaias, which saith, By hearing ye shall
hear, and shall not understand; and
seeing ye shall see, and shall not perceive: 15 For this people's heart is
waxed gross, and *their* ears are dull
of hearing, and their eyes they have
closed; lest at any time they should
see with *their* eyes, and hear with *their*
ears, and should understand with *their*
heart, and should be converted, and
I should heal them. 16 But blessed
are your eyes, for they see: and your
ears, for they hear. 17 For verily I
say unto you, That many prophets and
righteous *men* have desired to see
those things which ye see, and have
not seen *them;* and to hear *those
things* which ye hear, and have not
heard *them.* 18 Hear ye therefore
the parable of the sower. 19 When
any one heareth the word of the kingdom, and understandeth *it* not, then
cometh the wicked *one,* and catcheth

away that which was sown in his heart. This is he which received seed by the way side. 20 But he that received the seed into stony places, the same is he that heareth the word, and anon with joy receiveth it; 21 Yet hath he not root in himself, but dureth for a while: for when tribulation or persecution ariseth because of the word, by and by he is offended. 22 He also that received seed among the thorns is he that heareth the word; and the care of this world, and the deceitfulness of riches, choke the word, and he becometh unfruitful. 23 But he that received seed into the good ground is he that heareth the word, and understandeth *it;* which also beareth fruit, and bringeth forth, some an hundredfold, some sixty, some thirty.

We have here Christ preaching, and may observe,

1. *When* Christ preached this sermon; it was the same day that he preached the sermon in the foregoing chapter: so unwearied was he in doing good, and working the works of him that sent him. Note, Christ was for preaching both ends of the day, and has by his example recommended that practice to his church; we must *in the morning sow our seed, and in the evening not withhold our hand,* Eccl. xi. 6. An afternoon sermon well heard, will be so far from driving out the morning sermon, that it will rather clench it, and fasten the nail in a sure place. Though Christ had been in the morning opposed and cavilled at by his enemies, disturbed and interrupted by his friends, yet he went on with his work; and in the latter part of the day, we do not find that he met with such discouragements. Those who with courage and zeal break through difficulties in God's service, will perhaps find them not so apt to recur as they fear. Resist them, and they will flee.

2. *To whom* he preached; there were *great multitudes gathered together to him,* and they were the auditors; we do not find that any of the scribes or Pharisees were present. They were willing to hear him when he preached in the synagogue (*ch.* xii. 9, 14), but they thought it below them to hear a sermon by the sea-side, though Christ himself was the preacher: and truly he had better have their room than their company, for now they were absent, he went on quietly and without contradiction. Note, Sometimes there is most of the *power* of religion where there is least of the *pomp* of it: *the poor receive the gospel.* When Christ went to the *sea-side, multitudes* were presently *gathered together to him.* Where the king is, there is the court; where Christ is, there is the church, though it be by the sea-side. Note, Those who would get good by the word, must be willing to follow it in all its removes; when the ark shifts, shift after it. The Pharisees had been labouring, by base calumnies and suggestions, to drive the people off from following Christ, but they still flocked after him as much as ever. Note, Christ will be glorified in spite of all opposition; he will be followed.

3. *Where* he preached this sermon.

(1.) His meeting-place was the sea-side. He went out of the house (because there was no room for the auditory) into the open air. It was pity but such a Preacher should have had the most spacious, sumptuous, and convenient place to preach in, that could be devised, like one of the Roman theatres; but he was now in his state of humiliation, and in this, as in other things, he denied himself the honours due to him; as he had not a house of his own to live in, so he had not a chapel of his own to preach in. By this he teaches us in the external circumstances of worship not to covet that which is stately, but to make the best of the conveniences which God in his providence allots to us. When Christ was born, he was crowded into the stable, and now to the sea-side, upon the strand, where all persons might come to him with freedom. He that was truth itself sought no corners (no *adyta*), as the pagan mysteries did. *Wisdom crieth without,* Prov. i. 20; John xiii. 20.

(2.) His pulpit was a ship; not like Ezra's pulpit, that was *made for the purpose* (Neh. viii. 4); but converted to this use for want of a better. No place amiss for such a Preacher, whose presence dignified and consecrated any place: let not those who preach Christ be ashamed, though they have mean and inconvenient places to preach in. Some observe, that the people stood upon dry ground and firm ground, while the Preacher was upon the water in more hazard. Ministers are most exposed to trouble. Here was a true rostrum, a ship pulpit.

4. *What* and *how* he preached. (1.) *He spake many things unto them.* Many more it is likely than are here recorded, but all excellent and necessary things, things that belong to our peace, things pertaining to the kingdom of heaven: they were not trifles, but things of everlasting consequence, that Christ spoke of. It concerns us to give a more earnest heed, when Christ has so many things to say to us, that we miss not any of them. (2.) What he spake was in parables. a parable sometimes signifies any wise. weighty saying that is instructive; but here in the gospels it generally signifies a continued similitude or comparison, by which spiritual or heavenly things were described in language borrowed from the things of this life. It was a way of teaching used very

much, not only by the Jewish rabbin, but by the Arabians, and the other wise men of the east; and it was found very profitable, and the more so from its being pleasant. Our Saviour used it much, and in it condescended to the capacities of people, and lisped to them in their own language. God had long *used similitudes by his servants the prophets* (Hos. xii 10), and to little purpose; now he uses similitudes by his Son; surely they will reverence him who speaks from heaven, and of heavenly things, and yet clothes them with expressions borrowed from things earthly. See John iii. 12. So descending in a cloud. Now,

I. We have here the general reason why Christ taught in parables. The disciples were a little surprised at it, for hitherto, in his preaching, he had not much used them, and therefore they ask, *Why speakest thou to them in parables?* Because they were truly desirous that the people might hear with understanding. They do not say, Why speakest thou to *us?* (they knew how to get the parables explained) but to *them.* Note, We ought to be concerned for the edification of others, as well as for our own, by the word preached; and if ourselves be *strong,* yet to *bear the infirmities of the weak.*

To this question Christ answers largely, *v.* 11—17, where he tells them, that *therefore* he preached by parables, because thereby the things of God were made more plain and easy to them who were willing to be taught, and at the same time more difficult and obscure to those who were willingly ignorant; and thus the gospel would be *a savour of life* to some, and *of death* to others. A parable, like the pillar of cloud and fire, turns a dark side towards Egyptians, which confounds them, but a light side towards Israelites, which comforts them, and so answers a double intention. The same light directs the eyes of some, but dazzles the eyes of others. Now,

1. This reason is laid down (*v.* 11): *Because it is given unto you to know the mysteries of the kingdom of heaven, but to them it is not given.* That is, (1.) The disciples had knowledge, but the people had not. You know already something of these mysteries, and need not in this familiar way to be instructed; but the people are ignorant, are yet but babes, and must be taught as such by plain similitudes, being yet incapable of receiving instruction in any other way: for though they have eyes, they know not how to use them; so some. Or, (2.) The disciples were well inclined to the knowledge of gospel mysteries, and would search into the parables, and by them would be led into a more intimate acquaintance with those mysteries; but the carnal hearers that rested in bare hearing, and would not be at the pains to look further, nor to ask the meaning of the parables, would be never the wiser, and so would justly suffer for their remissness. A parable is a shell that keeps good fruit *for* the diligent, but keeps it *from* the slothful. Note, There are mysteries in the kingdom of heaven, and *without controversy, great is the mystery of godliness:* Christ's incarnation, satisfaction, intercession, our justification and sanctification by union with Christ, and indeed the whole work of redemption, from first to last, are *mysteries,* which could never have been discovered but by divine revelation (1 Cor. xv. 51), were at this time discovered but in part to the disciples, and will never be fully discovered till the veil shall be rent; but the mysteriousness of gospel truth should not discourage us from, but quicken us in, our enquiries after it and searches into it. [1.] It is graciously given to the disciples of Christ to be acquainted with these mysteries. Knowledge is the first gift of God, and it is a distinguishing gift (Prov. ii. 6); it was given to the apostles, because they were Christ's constant followers and attendants. Note, The nearer we draw to Christ, and the more we converse with him, the better acquainted we shall be with gospel mysteries. [2.] It is given to all true believers, who have an experimental knowledge of the gospel mysteries, and that is without doubt the best knowledge: a principle of grace in the heart, is that which makes men of quick understanding in *the fear of the Lord,* and in the faith of Christ, and so in the meaning of parables; and for want of that, Nicodemus, a master in Israel, talked of the *new birth* as a blind man of colours. [3.] There are those to *whom this knowledge is not given,* and a man can *receive nothing unless it be given him from above* (John iii. 27); and be it remembered that God is debtor to no man; his grace is his own; he gives or withholds it at pleasure (Rom. xi. 35); the difference must be resolved into God's sovereignty, as before, *ch.* xi. 25, 26.

2. This reason is further illustrated by the rule God observes in dispensing his gifts; he bestows them on those who improve them, but takes them away from those who bury them. It is a rule among men, that they will rather entrust their money with those who have increased their estates by their industry, than with those who have diminished them by their slothfulness.

(1.) Here is a promise to him that has, that has true grace, pursuant to the election of grace, that has, and uses what he has; he shall have more abundance: God's favours are earnests of further favours; where he lays the foundation, he will build upon it. Christ's disciples used the knowledge they now had, and they had more abundance at the pouring out of the Spirit, Acts ii. They who have the *truth* of grace, shall have the *increase* of grace, even to an abundance in glory, Prov. iv. 18. *Joseph—he will add,* Gen. xxx. 24.

(2.) Here is a threatening to him that has

not, that has no desire of grace, that makes no right use of the gifts and graces he has: has no root, no solid principle; that has, but uses not what he has; from him shall be *taken away* that which he has or seems to have. His leaves shall wither, his gifts decay; the means of grace he has, and makes no use of, shall be taken from him; God will *call in* his talents out of their hands that are likely to become bankrupts quickly.

3. This reason is particularly explained, with reference to the two sorts of people Christ had to do with.

(1.) Some were willingly ignorant; and such were amused by the parables (*v.* 13); *because they seeing, see not.* They had shut their eyes against the clear light of Christ's plainer preaching, and therefore were now left in the dark. Seeing Christ's person, they see not his glory, see no difference between him and another man; seeing his miracles, and hearing his preaching, they see not, they hear not with any concern or application; they understand neither. Note, [1.] There are many that see the gospel light, and hear the gospel sound, but it never reaches their hearts, nor has it any place in them. [2.] It is just with God to take away the light from those who shut their eyes against it; that such as will be ignorant, may be so; and God's dealing thus with them magnifies his distinguishing grace to his disciples.

Now in this the scripture would be fulfilled, *v.* 14, 15. It is quoted from Isa. vi. 9, 10. The evangelical prophet that spoke most plainly of gospel grace, foretold the contempt of it, and the consequences of that contempt. It is referred to no less than six times in the New Testament, which intimates, that in gospel times spiritual judgments would be most common, which make least noise, but are most dreadful. That which was spoken of the sinners in Isaiah's time was fulfilled in those in Christ's time, and it is still fulfilling every day; for while the wicked heart of man keeps up the same sin, the righteous hand of God inflicts the same punishment. Here is,

First. A description of sinners' wilful blindness and hardness, which is their sin. *This people's heart is waxed gross;* it is *fattened,* so the word is; which denotes both sensuality and senselessness (Ps. cxix. 70); secure under the word and rod of God, and scornful as Jeshurun, that *waxed fat and kicked,* Deut. xxxii. 15. And when the heart is thus heavy, no wonder that the ears are dull of hearing; the whispers of the Spirit they hear not at all; the loud calls of the word, though the word be nigh them, they regard not, nor are at all affected by them: *they stop their ears,* Ps. lviii. 4, 5. And because they are resolved to be ignorant, they shut both the learning senses; for their eyes also they have closed, resolved that they would not see light come into the world, when the Sun of Righteousness arose, but they shut their windows, because they *loved darkness rather than light,* John iii. 19; 2 Pet. iii. 5.

Secondly, A description of that judicial blindness, which is the just punishment of this. "*By hearing, ye shall hear, and shall not understand;* what means of grace you have, shall be to no purpose to you; though, in mercy to others, they are continued, yet, in judgment to you, the blessing upon them is denied." The saddest condition a man can be in on this side hell, is to sit under the most lively ordinances with a dead, stupid, untouched heart. To hear God's word, and see his providences, and yet not to understand and perceive his will, either in the one or in the other, is the greatest sin and the greatest judgment that can be. Observe, It is God's work to *give an understanding heart,* and he often, in a way of righteous judgment, denies it to those to whom he has given the hearing ear, and the seeing eye, in vain. Thus does God choose sinners' delusions (Isa. lxvi. 4), and bind them over to the greatest ruin, by giving them up to their own hearts' lusts (Ps. lxxxi. 11, 12); *let them alone* (Hos. iv. 17); *my Spirit shall not always strive,* Gen. vi. 3.

Thirdly, The woeful effect and consequence of this; *Lest at any time they should see.* They will not see because they will not turn; and God says that they shall not see, because they shall not turn: *Lest they should be converted, and I should heal them.*

Note, 1. That seeing, hearing, and understanding, are necessary to conversion; for God, in working grace, deals with men as men, as rational agents; he draws with the cords of a man, changes the heart by opening the eyes, and turns *from the power of Satan unto God,* by turning first *from darkness to light,* Acts xxvi. 18. 2. All those who are truly converted to God, shall certainly be healed by him. "If they be converted I shall heal them, I shall save them:" so that if sinners perish, it is not to be imputed to God, but to themselves; they foolishly expected to be healed, without being converted. 3. It is just with God to deny his grace to those who have long and often refused the proposals of it, and resisted the power of it. Pharaoh, for a good while, hardened his own heart (Exod. viii. 15, 32), and afterwards God hardened it, *ch.* ix. 12; x. 20. Let us therefore fear, lest by sinning against the divine grace, we sin it away.

(2.) Others were effectually called to be the disciples of Christ, and were truly desirous to be taught of him; and they were instructed, and made to improve greatly in knowledge, by these parables, especially when they were expounded; and by them the things of God were made more plain and easy, more intelligible and familiar, and more apt to be remembered (*v.* 16, 17). *Your eyes see, your ears hear.* They saw the glory of

God in Christ's person; they heard the mind of God in Christ's doctrine; they saw much, and were desirous to see more, and thereby were prepared to receive further instruction; they had opportunity for it, by being constant attendants on Christ, and they should have it from day to day, and grace with it. Now this Christ speaks of,

[1.] As a blessing; "*Blessed are your eyes for they see, and your ears for they hear;* it is your happiness, and it is a happiness for which you are indebted to the peculiar favour and blessing of God." It is a promised blessing, that in the days of the Messiah *the eyes of them that see shall not be dim,* Isa. xxxii. 3. The eyes of the meanest believer that knows experimentally the grace of Christ, are more blessed than those of the greatest scholars, the greatest masters in experimental philosophy, that are strangers to God; who, like the other gods they serve, *have eyes, and see not. Blessed are your eyes.* Note, True blessedness is entailed upon the right understanding and due improvement of the mysteries of the kingdom of God. The hearing ear and the seeing eye are God's work in those who are sanctified; they are the work of his grace (Prov. xx. 12), and they are a blessed work, which shall be fulfilled with power, when those who *now see through a glass darkly, shall see face to face.* It was to illustrate this blessedness that Christ said so much of the misery of those who are left in ignorance; *they have eyes and see not;* but *blessed are your eyes.* Note, The knowledge of Christ is a distinguishing favour to those who have it, and upon that account it lays under the greater obligations; see John xiv. 22. The apostles were to teach others, and therefore were themselves blessed with the clearest discoveries of divine truth. *The watchmen shall see eye to eye,* Isa. lii. 8.

[2.] As a transcendent blessing, desired by, but not granted to, many prophets and righteous men, *v.* 17. The Old-Testament saints, who had some glimpses, some glimmerings of gospel light, coveted earnestly further discoveries. They had the types, shadows, and prophecies, of those things, but longed to see the Substance, that glorious end of those things which they could not steadfastly look unto; that glorious inside of those things which they could not look into. They desired to see the great Salvation, the Consolation of Israel, but did not see it, because the fulness of time was not yet come. Note, *First,* Those who know something of Christ, cannot but covet to know more. *Secondly,* The discoveries of divine grace are made, even to prophets and righteous men, but according to the dispensation they are under. Though they were the favourites of Heaven, with whom God's secret was, yet they have not seen the things which they desired to see, because God had determined not to bring them to light yet; and his favours shall not anticipate his counsels. There was then, as there is still, a *glory to be revealed;* something in reserve, *that they without us should not be made perfect,* Heb. xi. 40. *Thirdly,* For the exciting of our thankfulness, and the quickening of our diligence, it is good for us to consider what means we enjoy, and what discoveries are made to us, now under the gospel, above what they had, and enjoyed, who lived under the Old-Testament dispensation, especially in the revelation of the atonement for sin; see what are the advantages of the New Testament above the Old (2 Cor. iii. 7, &c. Heb. xii. 18); and see that our improvements be proportionable to our advantages.

II. We have, in these verses, one of the parables which our Saviour put forth; it is that of the *sower and the seed;* both the parable itself, and the explanation of it. Christ's parables are borrowed from common, ordinary things, not from any philosophical notions or speculations, or the unusual phenomena of nature, though applicable enough to the matter in hand, but from the most obvious things, that are of every day's observation, and come within the reach of the meanest capacity; many of them are fetched from the husbandman's calling, as this of the sower, and that of the tares. Christ chose to do thus, 1. That spiritual things might hereby be made more plain, and, by familiar similitudes, might be made the more easy to slide into our understandings. 2. That common actions might hereby be spiritualized, and we might take occasion from those things which fall so often under our view, to meditate with delight on the things of God; and thus, when our hands are busiest about the world, we may not only notwithstanding that, but even with the help of that, be led to have our hearts in heaven. Thus the word of God shall talk with us, talk familiarly with us, Prov. vi. 22.

The parable of the sower is plain enough, *v.* 3—9. The exposition of it we have from Christ himself, who knew best what was his own meaning. The disciples, when they asked, *Why speakest thou unto them in parables?* (*v.* 10) intimated a desire to have the parable explained for the sake of the people; nor was it any disparagement to their own knowledge to desire it for themselves. Our Lord Jesus kindly took the hint, and gave the sense, and caused them to understand the parable, directing his discourse to the disciples, but in the hearing of the multitude, for we have not the account of his dismissing them till *v.* 36. "*Hear ye therefore the parable of the sower* (*v.* 18); you have heard it, but let us go over it again." Note, It is of good use, and would contribute much to our understanding the word and profiting by it, to hear over again what we have heard (Phil. iii. 1); "You have heard it, but hear the interpretation of it." Note, *Then* only we hear the word aright, and to good purpose, when we understand what we hear; it is no hearing at all, if it be not with understanding, Neh. viii. 2. It is God's grace indeed that gives the understanding, but it is our duty to give our minds to understand.

Let us therefore compare the parable and the exposition.

(1.) The seed sown is the word of God, here called *the word of the kingdom* (*v.* 19): the kingdom of heaven, that is the kingdom; the kingdoms of the world, compared with that, are not to be called kingdoms. The gospel comes *from* that kingdom, and conducts *to* that kingdom; the word of the gospel is the word of the kingdom; it is the word of the King, and where that is, *there is power;* it is a law, by which we must be ruled and governed. This word is the seed sown, which seems a dead, dry thing, but all the product is virtually in it. It is *incorruptible seed* (1 Pet. i. 23); it is the gospel that *brings forth fruit* in souls, Col. i. 5, 6.

(2.) The sower that scatters the seed is our Lord Jesus Christ, either by himself, or by his ministers; see *v.* 37. The people are God's husbandry, his tillage, so the word is; and ministers are *labourers together with God*, 1 Cor. iii. 9. Preaching to a multitude is sowing the corn; we know not where it must light; only see that it be good, that it be clean, and be sure to give it seed enough. The sowing of the word is the sowing of a people for God's field, the *corn of his floor*, Isa. xxi. 10.

(3.) The ground in which this seed is sown is the hearts of the children of men, which are differently qualified and disposed, and accordingly the success of the word is different. Note, Man's heart is like soil, capable of improvement, of bearing good fruit; it is pity it should lie fallow, or be like the field of the slothful, Prov. xxiv. 30. The soul is the proper place for the word of God to dwell, and work, and rule in; its operation is upon conscience, it is to light that candle of the Lord. Now according as we are, so the word is to us: *Recipitur ad modum recipientis—The reception depends upon the receiver.* As it is with the earth; some sort of ground, take ever so much pains with it, and throw ever so good seed into it, yet it brings forth no fruit to any purpose; while the good soil brings forth plentifully: so it is with the hearts of men, whose different characters are here represented by four sorts of ground, of which *three* are bad, and but *one* good. Note, The number of fruitless hearers is very great, even of those who heard Christ himself. *Who has believed our report?* It is a melancholy prospect which this parable gives us of the congregations of those who hear the gospel preached, that scarcely one in four brings forth fruit to perfection. Many are called with the common call, but in few is the eternal choice evidenced by the efficacy of that call, *ch.* xx. 16.

Now observe the characters of these four sorts of ground.

[1.] The highway ground, *v.* 4—19. They had pathways through their corn-fields (*ch.* xii. 1), and the seed that fell on them never entered, and so the birds picked it up. The place where Christ's hearers now stood represented the characters of most of them, the sand on the sea-shore, which was to the seed like the highway ground.

Observe, *First,* What kind of hearers are compared to *the highway ground;* such as *hear the word and understand it not;* and it is their own fault that they do not. They take no heed to it, take no hold of it; they do not come with any design to get good, as the highway was never intended to be sown. They *come before God as his people come, and sit before him as his people sit;* but it is merely for fashion-sake, to see and be seen; they mind not what is said, it comes in at one ear and goes out at the other, and makes no impression.

Secondly, How they come to be unprofitable hearers. The *wicked one,* that is, the devil, *cometh and catcheth away that which was sown.*—Such mindless, careless, trifling hearers are an easy prey to Satan; who, as he is the great murderer of souls, so he is the great thief of sermons, and will be sure to rob us of the word, if we take not care to keep it: as the birds pick up the seed that falls on the ground that is neither ploughed before nor harrowed after. If we break not up the fallow ground, by preparing our hearts for the word, and humbling them to it, and engaging our own attention; and if we cover not the seed afterwards, by meditation and prayer; if we give not a *more earnest heed to the things which we have heard,* we are as the highway ground. Note, The devil is a sworn enemy to our profiting by the word of God; and none do more befriend his design than heedless hearers, who are thinking of something else, when they should be thinking of the things that belong to their peace.

[2.] The *stony ground. Some fell upon stony places* (*v.* 5, 6), which represents the case of hearers that go further than the former, who receive some good impressions of the word, but they are not lasting, *v.* 20, 21. Note, It is possible we may be a great deal better than some others, and yet not be so good as we should be; may go beyond our neighbours, and yet come short of heaven. Now observe, concerning these hearers that are represented by the stony ground,

First, How far they went. 1. They *hear the word;* they turn neither their backs upon it, nor a deaf ear to it. Note, Hearing the word, though ever so frequently, ever so gravely, if we rest in that, will never bring us to heaven. 2. They are *quick in hearing,* swift to hear, *he anon receiveth it,* εὐθὺς, he is ready to receive it, *forthwith it sprung up* (*v.* 5), it sooner appeared above ground than that which was sown in the good soil. Note, Hypocrites often get the start of true Christians in the shows of profession, and are often too hot to hold. He *receiveth it straightway*, without trying it; swallows it without chewing, and then there can never be a good digestion. Those are most likely to *hold fast that which is good*, that *prove all things*, 1 Thess. v. 21. 3. They receive it with joy. Note, There are many that are very glad to hear a good sermon, that yet do not profit by it; they may be pleased with the word, and yet not changed and ruled by it; the heart may melt under the word, and yet not be melted down by the word, much less into it, as into a mould. Many *taste the good word of God* (Heb. vi. 5), and say they find sweetness in it, but some beloved lust is *rolled under the tongue*, which it would not agree with, and so they spit it out again. 4. They *endure for awhile*, like a violent motion, which continues as long as the impression of the force remains, but ceases when that has spent itself. Note, Many endure for awhile, that do not endure to the end, and so come short of the happiness which is promised to them only that persevere (*ch.* x. 22); they did run well, but something hindered them, Gal. v. 7.

Secondly, How they fell away, so that no fruit was brought to perfection; no more than the corn, that having no depth of earth from which to draw moisture, is scorched and withered by the heat of the sun. And the reason is,

1. They have *no root in themselves*, no settled, fixed principles in their judgments, no firm resolution in their wills, nor any rooted habits in their affections: nothing firm that will be either the sap or the strength of their profession. Note, (1.) It is possible there may be the green blade of a profession, where yet there is not the root of grace; hardness prevails in the heart, and what there is of soil and softness is only in the surface; inwardly they are no more affected than a stone; they have no root, they are not by faith united to Christ who is our Root; they derive not from him, they depend not on him. (2.) Where there is not a principle, though there be a profession, we cannot expect perseverance. Those who have no root will endure but awhile. A ship without ballast, though she may at first out-sail the laden vessel, yet will certainly fail in stress of weather, and never make her port.

2. Times of trial come, and then they come to nothing. *When tribulation and persecution arise because of the word, he is offended;* it is a stumbling-block in his way which he cannot get over, and so he flies off, and this is all his profession comes to. Note, (1.) After a fair gale of opportunity usually follows a storm of persecution, to try who have received the word in sincerity, and who have not. When the word of Christ's kingdom comes to be the word of Christ's patience (Rev. iii. 10), then is the trial, who keeps it, and who does not, Rev. i. 9. It is wisdom to prepare for such a day. (2.) When trying times come, those who have no root are soon offended; they first quarrel with their profession, and then quit it; first find fault with it, and then throw it off. Hence we read of *the offence of the cross*, Gal. v. 11. Observe, Persecution is represented in the parable by *the scorching sun* (*v.* 6); the same sun which warms and cherishes that which was well rooted, withers and burns up that which wanted root. As the word of Christ, so the cross of Christ, is to some *a savour of life unto life*, to others *a savour of death unto death:* the same tribulation which drives some to apostasy and ruin, works for others *a far more exceeding and eternal weight of glory.* Trials which shake some, confirm others, Phil. i. 12. Observe how soon they fall away, by and by; as soon rotten as they were ripe; a profession taken up without consideration is commonly let fall without it: "Lightly come, lightly go."

[3.] The thorny ground, *Some fell among thorns* (which are a good guard to the corn when they are in the hedge, but a bad inmate when they are in the field); *and the thorns sprung up*, which intimates that they did not appear, or but little, when the corn was sown, but afterwards they proved choking to it, *v.* 7. This went further than the former, for it had root; and it represents the condition of those who do not quite cast off their profession, and yet come short of any saving benefit by it; the good they gain by the word, being insensibly overcome and overborne by the things of this world. Prosperity destroys the word in the heart, as much as persecution does; and more dangerously, because more silently: the stones spoiled the root, the thorns spoil the fruit.

Now what are these choking thorns?

First, The cares of this world. Care for another world would quicken the springing of this seed, but care for this world chokes it. Worldly cares are fitly compared to thorns, for they came in with sin, and are a fruit of the curse; they are good in their place to stop a gap, but a man must be well armed that deals much in them (2 Sam. xxiii 6, 7); they are entangling, vexing, scratching, and *their end is to be burned*, Heb. vi. 8. These thorns choke the good seed. Note, Worldly cares are great hindrances to our profiting by the word of God, and our proficiency in religion. They eat up that vigour of soul which should be spent in divine things; divert us from duty, distract us in duty, and do us most mischief of all afterwards; quenching the sparks of good affections, and bursting the cords of good resolutions; those who *are careful and cumbered about many things*, commonly neglect *the one thing needful.*

Secondly, The deceitfulness of riches. Those who, by their care and industry, have raised estates, and so the danger that arises from care seems to be over, and they *continue hearers of the word*, yet are still in a snare (Jer. v. 4, 5); it is *hard for them to enter into the kingdom of heaven:* they are apt to promise themselves that in riches which is not in them; to rely upon them, and to take an inordinate complacency in them; and this chokes the word as much as care did. Observe, It it is not so much riches, as *the deceitfulness of riches,* that does the mischief: now they cannot be said to be deceitful to us unless we put our confidence in them, and raise our expectations from them, and then it is that they choke the good seed.

[4.] The good ground (*v.* 18); *Others fell into good ground,* and it is pity but that good seed should always meet with good soil, and then there is no loss; such are *good hearers of the word, v.* 23. Note, Though there are many that *receive the grace of God,* and the word of his grace, *in vain,* yet God has a remnant by whom it is received to good purpose; for God's *word shall not return empty,* Isa. lv. 10, 11.

Now that which distinguished this good ground from the rest, was, in one word, fruitfulness. By *this* true Christians are distinguished from hypocrites, that they *bring forth the fruits of righteousness; so shall ye be my disciples,* John xv. 8. He does not say that this good ground has no stones in it, or no thorns; but there were none that prevailed to hinder its fruitfulness. Saints, in this world, are not perfectly free from the remains of sin; but happily freed from the reign of it.

The hearers represented by the good ground are,

First, Intelligent hearers; they *hear the word and understand it;* they understand not only the sense and meaning of the word, but their own concern in it; they understand it as a man of business understands his business. God in his word deals with men as men, in a rational way, and gains possession of the will and affections by opening the understanding: whereas Satan, who is *a thief and a robber, comes not in by* that *door, but climbeth up another way.*

Secondly, Fruitful hearers, which is an evidence of their good understanding: which *also beareth fruit.* Fruit is to every seed its own body, a substantial product in the heart and life, agreeable to the seed of the word received. We *then* bear fruit, when we practise according to the word; when the temper of our minds and the tenour of our lives are conformable to the gospel we have received, and we do as we are taught.

Thirdly, Not all alike fruitful; *some a hundred-fold, some sixty, some thirty.* Note, Among fruitful Christians, some are more fruitful than others: where there is true grace, yet there are degrees of it; some are of greater attainments in knowledge and holiness than others; all Christ's scholars are not in the same form. We should aim at the highest degree, to bring *forth a hundred-fold,* as Isaac's ground did (Gen. xxvi. 12), *abounding in the work of the Lord,* John xv. 8. But if the ground be good, and the fruit right, the heart honest, and the life of a piece with it, those who bring forth but thirty-fold shall be graciously accepted of God, and it will be fruit abounding to their account, for *we are under grace, and not under the law.*

Lastly, He closes the parable with a solemn call to attention (*v.* 9), *Who hath ears to hear, let him hear.* Note, The sense of hearing cannot be better employed than in hearing the word of God. Some are for hearing sweet melody, their ears are only *the daughters of music* (Eccl. xii. 4): there is no melody like that of the word of God: others are for hearing *new things* (Acts xvii. 21) no news like that.

24 Another parable put he forth
unto them, saying, The kingdom of
heaven is likened unto a man which
sowed good seed in his field: 25 But
while men slept, his enemy came and
sowed tares among the wheat, and
went his way. 26 But when the
blade was sprung up, and brought
forth fruit, then appeared the tares
also. 27 So the servants of the
householder came and said unto him,
Sir, didst not thou sow good seed in
thy field? from whence then hath it
tares? 28 He said unto them, An
enemy hath done this. The servants
said unto him, Wilt thou then that
we go and gather them up? 29 But
he said, Nay; lest while ye gather up
the tares, ye root up also the wheat
with them. 30 Let both grow together until the harvest: and in the time
of harvest I will say to the reapers,
Gather ye together first the tares, and
bind them in bundles to burn them:
but gather the wheat into my barn.
31 Another parable put he forth unto
them, saying, The kingdom of heaven
is like to a grain of mustard seed,
which a man took and sowed in his
field: 32 Which indeed is the least
of all seeds: but when it is grown, it
is the greatest among herbs, and becometh a tree, so that the birds of the
air come and lodge in the branches
thereof. 33 Another parable spake
he unto them; The kingdom of heaven is like unto leaven, which a woman
took, and hid in three measures of
meal, till the whole was leavened.
34 All these things spake Jesus unto
the multitude in parables; and with-

out a parable spake he not unto them:
35 That it might be fulfilled which
was spoken by the prophet, saying, I
will open my mouth in parables; I
will utter things which have been kept
secret from the foundation of the
world. 36 Then Jesus sent the multitude away, and went into the house:
and his disciples came unto him, saying, Declare unto us the parable of
the tares of the field. 37 He answered and said unto them, He that
soweth the good seed is the Son of
man; 38 The field is the world; the
good seed are the children of the kingdom; but the tares are the children
of the wicked *one*; 39 The enemy
that sowed them is the devil; the
harvest is the end of the world; and
the reapers are the angels. 40 As
therefore the tares are gathered and
burned in the fire; so shall it be in
the end of this world. 41 The Son
of man shall send forth his angels,
and they shall gather out of his kingdom all things that offend, and them
which do iniquity; 42 And shall cast
them into a furnace of fire: there shall
be wailing and gnashing of teeth. 43
Then shall the righteous shine forth
as the sun, in the kingdom of their
Father. Who hath ears to hear, let
him hear.

In these verses, we have, I. Another reason given why Christ preached by parables, *v.* 34, 35. *All these things he spoke in parables,* because the time was not yet come for the more clear and plain discoveries of the mysteries of the kingdom. Christ, to keep the people attending and expecting, preached in *parables, and without a parable spake he not unto them;* namely, at this time and in this sermon. Note, Christ tries all ways and methods to do good to the souls of men, and to make impressions upon them; if men will not be instructed and influenced by plain preaching, he will try them with parables; and the reason here given is, *That the scripture might be fulfilled.* The passage here quoted for it, is part of the preface to that historical Psalm, lxxviii. 2, *I will open my mouth in a parable.* What the Psalmist David, or Asaph, says there of his narrative, is accommodated to Christ's sermons; and that great precedent would serve to vindicate this way of preaching from the offence which some took at it. Here is, 1. The matter of Christ's preaching; he preached *things which had been kept secret from the foundation of the world.* The mystery of the gospel had been *hid in God,* in his councils and decrees, *from the beginning of the world.* Eph. iii. 9. Compare Rom. xvi. 25; 1 Cor. ii. 7; Col. i. 26. If we delight in the records of ancient things, and in the revelation of secret things, how welcome should the gospel be to us, which has in it such antiquity and such mystery! It was *from the foundation of the world* wrapt up in types and shadows, which are *now done away;* and those secret things are now become such things revealed *as belong to us and to our children,* Deut. xxix. 29. 2. The manner of Christ's preaching; he preached by parables; wise sayings, but figurative, and which help to engage attention and a diligent search. Solomon's sententious dictates, which are full of similitudes, are called *proverbs,* or *parables;* it is the same word; but in this, as in other things, *Behold a greater than Solomon is here, in whom are hid treasures of wisdom.*

II. The parable of the *tares,* and the exposition of it; they must be taken together, for the exposition explains the parable and the parable illustrates the exposition.

Observe, 1. The disciples' request to their Master to have this parable expounded to them (*v.* 36); *Jesus sent the multitude away;* and it is to be feared many of them went away no wiser than they came; they had heard a sound of words, and that was all. It is sad to think how many go away from sermons with the word of grace in their ears, but not the work of grace in their hearts. Christ *went into the house,* not so much for his own repose, as for particular converse with his disciples, whose instruction he chiefly intended in all his preaching. He was ready to do good in all places; the disciples laid hold on the opportunity, and *they came to him.* Note, Those who would be wise for every thing else, must be wise to discern and improve their opportunities, especially of converse with Christ, of converse with him alone, in secret meditation and prayer. It is very good, when we return from the solemn assembly, to talk over what we have heard there, and by familiar discourse to help one another to understand and remember it, and to be affected with it; for we lose the benefit of many a sermon by vain and unprofitable discourse after it. See Luke xxiv. 32; Deut. vi. 6, 7. It is especially good, if it may be, to ask of the ministers of the word the meaning of the word, for *their lips should keep knowledge,* Mal. ii. 7. Private conference would contribute much to our profiting by public preaching. Nathan's *Thou art the man,* was that which touched David to the heart.

The disciples' request to their Master was, *Declare unto us the parable of the tares.* This implied an acknowledgment of their ignorance, which they were not ashamed to make. It is probable they apprehended the general scope of the parable, but they desired to understand it more particularly, and to be assured that they took it right. Note, Those are rightly disposed for Christ's teaching, that are sensible of their ignorance, and sincerely desirous to be taught. He will *teach the humble* (Ps. xxv. 8, 9), but *will for this be enquired of. If any man lack* instruction, *let him ask it of God.* Christ had expounded the foregoing parable unasked, but for the exposition of this they ask him. Note, The mercies we have received must be improved, both for direction what to pray for, and for our encouragement in prayer. The first light and the first grace are given in a preventing way, further degrees of both which must be daily prayed for.

2. The exposition Christ gave of the parable, in answer to their request; so ready is Christ to answer such desires of his disciples. Now the drift of the parable is, to represent to us the present and future state of the kingdom of heaven, the gospel church: Christ's care of it, the devil's enmity against it, the mixture that there is in it of good and bad in this world, and the separation between them in the other world. Note, The visible church is the kingdom of heaven; though there be many hypocrites in it, Christ rules in it as a King; and there is a remnant in it, that are the subjects and heirs of heaven, from whom, as the better part, it is denominated: the church is *the kingdom of heaven* upon earth.

Let us go over the particulars of the exposition of the parable.

(1.) *He that sows the good seed is the Son of man.* Jesus Christ is the Lord of the field, *the Lord of the harvest*, the Sower of good seed. When *he ascended on high, he gave gifts to* the world; not only good ministers, but other good men. Note, Whatever good seed there is in the world, it all comes from the hand of Christ, and is of his sowing: truths preached, graces planted, souls sanctified, are good seed, and all owing to Christ. Ministers are instruments in Christ's hand to sow good seed; are employed by him and under him, and the success of their labours depends purely upon his blessing; so that it may well be said, It is Christ, and no other, that sows the good seed; he *is the Son of man*, one of us, that his terror might not make us afraid; *the Son of man*, the Mediator, and that has authority.

(2.) *The field is the world;* the world of mankind, a large field, capable of bringing forth good fruit; the more is it to be lamented that it brings forth so much bad fruit: the world here is the visible church, scattered all the world over, not confined to one nation. Observe, In the parable it is called *his field; the world* is Christ's *field*, for *all things are delivered unto him of the Father:* whatever power and interest the devil has in the world, it is usurped and unjust; when Christ comes to take possession, he comes whose right it is; it is his field, and because it is his he took care to sow it with good seed.

(3.) *The good seed are the children of the kingdom*, true saints. They are, [1.] The *children of the kingdom;* not in profession only, as the Jews were (*ch.* viii. 12), but in sincerity; Jews inwardly, Israelites indeed, incorporated in faith and obedience to Jesus Christ the great King of the church. [2.] They are the good seed, precious as seed, Ps. cxxvi. 6. The seed is the substance of the field; so the holy seed, Isa. vi. 13. The seed is scattered, so are the saints; dispersed, here one and there another, though in some places thicker sown than in others. The seed is that from which fruit is expected; what fruit of honour and service God has from this world he has from the saints, whom he has *sown unto himself in the earth*, Hos. ii. 23.

(4.) *The tares are the children of the wicked one.* Here is the character of sinners, hypocrites, and all profane and wicked people. [1.] They are the children of the devil, as a wicked one. Though they do not own his name, yet they bear his image, do his lusts, and from him they have their education; he rules over them, he works in them, Eph. ii. 2; John viii. 44. [2.] They are tares in the field of this world; they do no good, they do hurt; unprofitable in themselves, and hurtful to *the good seed*, both by temptation and persecution: they are weeds in the garden, have the same rain, and sunshine, and soil, with the good plants, but are good for nothing: the *tares are among the wheat.* Note, God has so ordered it, that good and bad should be mixed together in this world, that the good may be exercised, the bad left inexcusable, and a difference made between earth and heaven.

(5.) *The enemy that sowed the tares is the devil;* a sworn enemy to Christ and all that is good, to the glory of the good God, and the comfort and happiness of all good men. He is an enemy to the field of the world, which he endeavours to make his own, by sowing his tares in it. Ever since he became a wicked spirit himself, he has been industrious to promote wickedness, and has made it his business, aiming therein to counterwork Christ.

Now concerning the sowing of the tares, observe in the parable,

[1.] That they were sown *while men slept.* Magistrates slept, who by their power, ministers slept, who by their preaching, should have prevented this mischief. Note, Satan watches all opportunities, and lays hold of all advantages, to propagate vice and profaneness. The prejudice he does to particular persons is when reason and conscience sleep, when they are off their guard; we have therefore need to *be sober, and vigilant.* It was in the night, for that is the sleeping time. Note, Satan rules in *the darkness of this world;* that gives him an opportunity to sow tares, Ps. civ. 20. It was *while men slept;* and there is no remedy but men must have some sleeping time. Note, It is as impossible for us to prevent hypocrites being in the church, as it is for the husbandman, when he is asleep, to hinder an enemy from spoiling his field.

[2.] The enemy, when he had sown the tares, *went his way* (*v.* 25), that it might not be known who did it. Note, When Satan is doing the greatest mischief, he studies most to conceal himself; for his design is in danger of being spoiled if he be seen in it; and therefore, when he comes to sow tares, he *transforms himself into an angel of light,* 2 Cor. xi. 13, 14. He *went his way,* as if he had done no harm; *such is the way of the adulterous woman,* Prov. xxx. 20. Observe, Such is the proneness of fallen man to sin, that if the enemy sow the tares, he may even go his way, they will spring up of themselves and do hurt; whereas, when good seed is sown, it must be tended, watered, and fenced, or it will come to nothing.

[3.] The tares appeared not till *the blade sprung up, and brought forth fruit, v.* 26. There is a great deal of secret wickedness in the hearts of men, which is long hid under the cloak of a plausible profession, but breaks out at last. As the good seed, so the tares, lie a great while under the clods, and at first springing up, it is hard to distinguish them; but when a trying time comes, when fruit is to be brought forth, when good is to be done that has difficulty and hazard attending it, then you will return and discern between the sincere and the hypocrite: then you may say, This is wheat, and that is tares.

[4.] The servants, when they were aware of it, complained to their master (*v.* 27); *Sir, didst thou not sow good seed in thy field?* No doubt he did; whatever is amiss in the church, we are sure it is not of Christ: considering the seed which Christ sows, we may well ask, with wonder, *Whence* should *these tares come?* Note, The rise of errors, the breaking out of scandals, and the growth of profaneness, are matter of great grief to all the servants of Christ; especially to his faithful ministers, who are directed to complain of it to him whose the field is. It is sad to see such tares, such weeds, in the garden of the Lord; to see the good soil wasted, the good seed choked, and such a reflection cast on the name and honour of Christ, as if his field were no better than *the field of the slothful, all grown over with thorns.*

[5.] The Master was soon aware whence it was (*v.* 28); *An enemy has done this.* He does not lay the blame upon the servants; they could not help it, but had done what was in their power to prevent it. Note, The ministers of Christ, that are faithful and diligent, shall not be judged of Christ, and therefore should not be reproached by men, for the mixture of bad with good, hypocrites with the sincere, in the field of the church. *It must needs be that such offences will come;* and they shall not be laid to our charge, if we do our duty, though it have not the desired success. Though they sleep, if they do not love sleep; though tares be sown, if they do not sow them nor water them, nor allow of them, the blame shall not lie at their door.

[6.] The servants were very forward to have these tares rooted up. "*Wilt thou that we go* and do it presently?" Note, The over-hasty and inconsiderate zeal of Christ's servants, before they have consulted with their Master, is sometimes ready, with the hazard of the church, to root out all that they presume to be tares: *Lord, wilt thou that we call for fire from heaven?*

[7.] The Master very wisely prevented this (*v.* 29); *Nay, lest while ye gather up the tares, ye root up also the wheat with them.* Note, It is not possible for any man infallibly to distinguish between tares and wheat, but he may be mistaken; and therefore such is the wisdom and grace of Christ, that he will rather permit the tares, than any way endanger the wheat. It is certain, scandalous offenders are to be censured, and we are to withdraw from them; those who are openly *the children of the wicked one,* are not to be admitted to special ordinances; yet it is possible there may be a discipline, either so mistaken in its rules, or so over-nice in the application of them, as may prove vexatious to many that are truly godly and conscientious. Great caution and moderation must be used in inflicting and continuing church censures, lest the wheat be trodden down, if not plucked up. The *wisdom from above,* as it *is pure,* so it is *peaceable,* and those who oppose themselves must not be cut off, but instructed, and *with meekness,* 2 Tim. ii. 25. The tares, if continued under the means of grace, may become good corn; therefore have patience with them.

(6.) *The harvest is the end of the world, v.* 39. This world will have an end; though it continue long, it will not continue always; time will shortly be swallowed up in eternity. At the end of the world, there will be a great harvest-day, a day of judgment; at harvest all is ripe and ready to be cut down: both good and bad are ripe at the great-day, Rev. vi. 11. It is *the harvest of the earth,* Rev. xiv. 15. At harvest the reapers cut down all before them; not a field, not a corner, is left behind; so at the great day all must be judged (Rev. xx. 12, 13); God has *set a harvest* (Hos. vi. 11), and it shall not fail, Gen. viii. 22. At harvest every man reaps as he sowed; every man's ground, and seed, and skill, and industry, will be manifested: see Gal. vi. 7, 8. Then they who *sowed precious seed, will come again with rejoicing* (Ps. cxxvi. 5, 6), with *the joy of harvest* (Isa. ix. 3); when *the sluggard, who would not plough by reason of cold, shall beg, and have nothing* (Prov. xx. 4); shall cry, *Lord, Lord,* but in vain; when the harvest of those who sowed to the flesh, shall *be a day of grief, and of desperate sorrow,* Isa. xvii. 11.

(7.) *The reapers are the angels:* they shall be employed, in the great day, in executing Christ's righteous sentences, both of approbation and condemnation, as ministers of his justice, *ch.* xxv. 31. The angels are skilful, strong, and swift, obedient servants to Christ, holy enemies to the wicked, and faithful friends to all the saints, and therefore fit to be thus employed. *He that reapeth receiveth wages,* and the angels will not be unpaid for their attendance; for *he that soweth, and he that reapeth, shall rejoice together* (John iv. 36); that *is joy in heaven in the presence of the angels of God.*

(8.) Hell-torments are the *fire,* into which the *tares* shall then be cast, and in which they shall be burned. At the great day a distinction will be made, and with it a vast difference; it will be a notable day indeed.

[1.] The tares will then be gathered out: *The reapers* (whose primary work it is to gather in the corn) shall be charged first to *gather out the tares.* Note, Though good and bad are together in this world undistinguished, yet at the great day they shall be parted; no tares shall then be among the wheat; no sinners among the saints: then you shall plainly discern *between the righteous and the wicked,* which here sometimes it is hard to do, Mal. iii. 18; iv. 1. Christ will not bear always, Ps. l. 1, &c. They shall *gather out of his kingdom all wicked things that offend, and all wicked persons that do iniquity*: *when he begins, he will make a full end.* All those corrupt doctrines, worships, and practices, which have offended, have been scandals to the church, and stumbling-blocks to men's consciences, shall be condemned by the righteous Judge in that day, and consumed by *the brightness of his coming;* all *the wood, hay, and stubble* (1 Cor. iii. 12); and then *woe to them that do iniquity, that make a trade of it,* and persist in it; not only those in the last age of Christ's kingdom upon earth, but those in every age. Perhaps here is an allusion to Zeph. i. 3, *I will consume the stumbling-blocks with the wicked.*

[2.] They will then be *bound in bundles, v.* 30. Sinners of the same sort will be bundled together in the great day: a bundle of atheists, a bundle of epicures, a bundle of persecutors, and a great bundle of hypocrites. Those who have been associates in sin, will be so in shame and sorrow; and it will be an aggravation of their misery, as the society of glorified saints will add to their bliss. Let us pray, as David, *Lord, gather not my soul with sinners* (Ps. xxvi. 9), but let it be bound in *the bundle of life, with the Lord our God,* 1 Sam. xxv. 29.

[3.] They will *be cast into a furnace of fire;* such will be the end of wicked, mischievous people, that are in the church as *tares in the field;* they are fit for nothing but fire; to it they shall go, it is the fittest place for them. Note, Hell is a furnace of fire, kindled by the wrath of God, and kept burning by the bundles of tares cast into it, who will be ever in the consuming, but never consumed. But he slides out of the metaphor into a description of those torments that are designed to be set forth by it: *There shall be weeping, and gnashing of teeth;* comfortless sorrow, and an incurable indignation at God, themselves, and one another, will be the endless torture of damned souls. Let us therefore, *knowing these terrors of the Lord,* be persuaded not to do iniquity.

(9.) Heaven is the *barn* into which all God's wheat shall be gathered in that harvest-day. *But gather the wheat into my barn:* so it is in the parable, *v.* 30. Note, [1.] In the field of this world good people are the wheat, the most precious grain, and the valuable part of the field. [2.] This wheat shall shortly be gathered, gathered from among the tares and weeds: all *gathered together in a general assembly,* all the Old-Testament saints, all the New-Testament saints, not one missing. *Gather my saints together unto me,* Ps. l. 5. [3.] All God's wheat shall be lodged together in God's barn: particular souls are housed at death as a shock of corn (Job v. 26), but the general in-gathering will be at the end of time: God's wheat will then be put together, and no longer scattered; there will be sheaves of corn, as well as bundles of tares: they will then be secured, and no longer exposed to wind and weather, sin and sorrow: no longer afar off, and at a great distance, in the field, but near, in the barn. Nay, heaven is a *garner* (*ch.* iii. 12), in which the wheat will not only be separated from the tares of ill companions, but sifted from the chaff of their own corruptions.

In the explanation of the parable, this is gloriously represented (*v.* 43); *Then shall the righteous shine forth as the sun in the kingdom of their Father. First,* It is their present honour, that God is their Father. *Now are we the sons of God* (1 John iii. 2); *our Father in heaven* is King there. Christ, when he went to heaven, went to his *Father, and our Father,* John xx. 17. It is our *Father's house,* nay, it is *our Father's* palace, his throne, Rev. iii. 21. *Secondly,* The honour in reserve for them is, that they *shall shine forth as the sun in that kingdom.* Here they are obscure and hidden (Col. iii. 3), their beauty is eclipsed by their poverty, and the meanness of their outward condition; their own weaknesses and infirmities, and the reproach and disgrace cast upon them, cloud them; but then they shall shine forth as the sun from behind a dark cloud; at death they shall shine forth to themselves; at the great day they will shine forth publicly before all the world, *their bodies will be made like Christ's glorious body:* they shall shine by reflection, with a light borrowed from the

Fountain of light; their sanctification will be perfected, and their justification published; God will own them for his children, and will produce the record of all their services and sufferings for his name: they shall shine as the sun, the most glorious of all visible beings. The glory of the saints is in the Old Testament compared to that of the firmament and the stars, but here to that of the sun; *for life and immortality are brought to* a much clearer *light by the gospel,* than under the law. Those who shine as lights in this world, that God may be glorified, shall shine as the sun in the other world, that *they* may be glorified. Our Saviour concludes, as before, with a demand of attention; *Who hath ears to hear, let him hear.* These are things which it is our happiness to hear of, and our duty to hearken to.

III. Here is the parable of the *grain of mustard-seed, v.* 31, 32. The scope of this parable is to show, that the beginnings of the gospel *would be small, but that its latter end would greatly increase.* In this way the gospel church, *the kingdom of God among us,* would be *set up in the world;* in this way the work of grace in the heart, *the kingdom of God within us,* would be carried on in particular persons.

Now concerning the work of the gospel, observe,

1. That it is commonly very weak and small at first, *like a grain of mustard-seed, which is one of the least of all seeds.* The kingdom of the Messiah, which was now in the setting up, made but a small figure; Christ and the apostles, compared with the grandees of the world, appeared *like a grain of mustard-seed, the weak things of the world.* In particular places, the first breaking out of the gospel light is but as *the dawning of the day;* and in particular souls, it is at first *the day of small things,* like a bruised reed. Young converts are like *lambs* that must be *carried in his arms,* Isa. xl. 11. There is a little faith, but there is much lacking in it (1 Thess. iii. 10), and the *groanings* such as *cannot be uttered,* they are so small; a principle of spiritual life, and some motion, but scarcely discernible.

2. That yet it is growing and coming on. Christ's kingdom strangely got ground; great accessions were made to it; nations were born at once, in spite of all the oppositions it met with from hell and earth. In the soul where grace is true it will grow really, though perhaps insensibly. *A grain of mustard-seed* is small, but however it is seed, and has in it a disposition to grow. Grace will be getting ground, shining more and more, Prov. iv. 18. Gracious habits confirmed, actings quickened, and knowledge more clear, faith more confirmed, love more inflamed; here is the seed growing.

3. That it will at last come to a great degree of strength and usefulness; *when it is grown to* some maturity, *it becomes a tree,* much larger in those countries than in ours. The church, like *the vine brought out of Egypt,* has taken root, and *filled the earth,* Ps. lxxx. 9—11. The church is like a great tree, in which the fowls of the air do lodge; God's people have recourse to it for food and rest, shade and shelter. In particular persons, the principle of grace, if true, will persevere and be perfected at last: growing grace will be strong grace, and will bring much to pass. Grown Christians must covet to be useful to others, as the mustard-seed when grown is to the birds; that those who dwell near or under their shadow may be the better for them, Hos. xiv. 7.

IV. Here is the parable of the *leaven, v.* 33. The scope of this is much the same with that of the foregoing parable, to show that the gospel should prevail and be successful by degrees, but silently and insensibly; the preaching of the gospel is like leaven, and works like leaven in the hearts of those who receive it.

1. *A woman took* this *leaven;* it was her work. Ministers are employed in leavening places, in leavening souls, with the gospel. *The woman is the weaker vessel,* and we have this treasure in such vessels.

2. The leaven was *hid in three measures of meal.* The heart is, as the meal, soft and pliable; it is the tender heart that is likely to profit by the word: leaven among corn unground does not work, nor does the gospel in souls unhumbled and unbroken for sin: the law grinds the heart, and then the gospel leavens it. It is *three measures of meal,* a great quantity, for *a little leaven leaveneth the whole lump.* The meal must be kneaded, before it receive the leaven; our hearts, as they must be broken, so they must be moistened, and pains taken with them to prepare them for the word, that they may receive the impressions of it. The leaven must be *hid in the heart* (Ps. cxix. 11), not so much for secrecy (for it will show itself) as for safety; our inward thought must be upon it, we must lay it up, as Mary laid up the sayings of Christ, Luke ii. 51. When the woman hides the leaven in the meal, it is with an intention that it should communicate its taste and relish to it; so we must treasure up the word in our souls, that we may be sanctified by it, John xvii. 17.

3. The leaven thus hid in the dough, works there, it ferments; *the word is quick and powerful,* Heb. iv. 12. The leaven works speedily, so does the word, and yet gradually. What a sudden change did Elijah's mantle make upon Elisha! 1 Kings xix. 20. It works silently and insensibly (Mark iv. 26), yet strongly and irresistibly: it does its work without noise, for so is *the way of the Spirit,* but does it without fail. Hide but the leaven in the dough, and all the world cannot hinder it from communicating its taste and relish to it, and yet none sees how it is done, but by degrees *the whole is leavened.*

(1.) Thus it was in the world. The apostles, by their preaching, hid a handful of leaven in the great mass of mankind, and it had a strange effect; it put the world into a ferment, and in a sense turned it *upside down* (Acts xvii. 6), and by degrees made a wonderful change in the taste and relish of it: the savour of the gospel was *manifested in every place*, 2 Cor. ii. 14; Rom. xv. 19. It was thus effectual, not by outward force, and therefore not by any such force resistible and conquerable, but by *the Spirit of the Lord of hosts, who works, and none can hinder*.

(2.) Thus it is in the heart. When the gospel comes into the soul, [1.] It works a change, not in the substance; the dough is the same, but in the quality; it makes us to savour otherwise than we have done, and other things to savour with us otherwise than they used to do, Rom. viii. 5. [2.] It works a universal change; it diffuses itself into all the powers and faculties of the soul, and alters the property even of the members of the body, Rom. vi. 13. [3.] This change is such as makes the soul to partake of the nature of the word, as the dough does of the leaven. We are delivered into it as into a mould (Rom. vi. 17), changed into the same image (2 Cor. iii. 18), like the impression of the seal upon the wax. The gospel savours of God, and Christ, and free grace, and another world, and these things now relish with the soul. It is a word of faith and repentance, holiness and love, and these are wrought in the soul by it. This savour is communicated insensibly, for *our life is hid;* but inseparably, for grace is a *good part that shall never be taken away* from those who have it. When the dough is leavened, then to the oven with it; trials and afflictions commonly attend this change; but thus saints are fitted to be bread for our Master's table.

44 Again, the kingdom of heaven
is like unto treasure hid in a field;
the which when a man hath found, he
hideth, and for joy thereof goeth and
selleth all that he hath, and buyeth
that field. 45 Again, the kingdom
of heaven is like unto a merchant man,
seeking goodly pearls: 46 Who, when
he had found one pearl of great price,
went and sold all that he had, and
bought it. 47 Again, the kingdom
of heaven is like unto a net, that was
cast into the sea, and gathered of
every kind: 48 Which, when it was
full, they drew to shore, and sat down,
and gathered the good into vessels,
but cast the bad away. 49 So shall
it be at the end of the world: the
angels shall come forth, and sever
the wicked from among the just, 50
And shall cast them into the furnace
of fire: there shall be wailing and
gnashing of teeth. 51 Jesus saith
unto them, Have ye understood all
these things? They say unto him,
Yea, Lord. 52 Then said he unto
them, Therefore every scribe *which is*
instructed unto the kingdom of heaven, is like unto a man *that is* an
householder, which bringeth forth out
of his treasure *things* new and old.

We have four short parables in these verses.

I. That of the *treasure hid in the field.* Hitherto he had compared *the kingdom of heaven* to small things, because its beginning was small; but, lest any should thence take occasion to think meanly of it, in this parable and the next he represents it as of great value in itself, and of great advantage to those who embrace it, and are willing to come up to its terms; it is here likened *to a treasure hid in the field*, which, if we will, we may make our own.

1. Jesus Christ is the true Treasure; in him there is an abundance of all that which is rich and useful, and will be a portion for us: *all fulness* (Col. i. 19; John i. 16): *treasures of wisdom and knowledge* (Col. ii. 3), of righteousness, grace, and peace; these are laid up for us in Christ; and, if we have an interest in him, it is all our own.

2. The gospel is the field in which this treasure is hid: it is hid in the word of the gospel, both the Old-Testament and the New-Testament gospel. In gospel ordinances it is hid as the milk in the breast, the marrow in the bone, the manna in the dew, the water in the well (Isa. xii. 3), *the honey in the honey-comb.* It is hid, not *in a garden enclosed*, or *a spring shut up*, but *in a field*, an open field; *whoever will, let him come, and search the scriptures;* let him dig in *this field* (Prov. ii. 4); and whatever royal mines we find, they are all our own, if we take the right course.

3. It is a great thing to discover the treasure hid in this field, and the unspeakable value of it. The reason why so many slight the gospel, and will not be at the expense, and run the hazard, of entertaining it, is because they look only upon the surface of the field, and judge by that, and so see no excellency in the Christian institutes above those of the philosophers; nay, the richest mines are often in grounds that appear most barren; and therefore they will not so much as bid for the field, much less come up to the price. *What is thy beloved more than another beloved?* What is the Bible more than other good books? The gospel of Christ more than Plato's philosophy, or Confucius's morals? but those who have *searched the scriptures*, so as in them to find Christ and *eternal life* (John v. 39), have discovered such a trea-

sure in this field as makes it infinitely more valuable.

4. Those who discern this treasure in the field, and value it aright, will never be easy till they have made it their own upon any terms. He that has found this treasure, hides it, which denotes a holy jealousy, *lest we come short* (Heb. iv. 1), *looking diligently* (Heb. xii. 15), lest Satan come between us and it. He rejoices in it, though as yet the bargain be not made; he is glad there is such a bargain to be had, and that he is in a fair way to have an interest in Christ; that the matter is in treaty: their *hearts* may *rejoice*, who are yet *but seeking the Lord*, Ps. cv. 3. He resolves to *buy this field:* they who embrace gospel offers, upon gospel terms, buy this field; they make it their own, for the sake of the unseen treasure in it. It is Christ in the gospel that we are to have an eye to; we need not go up to heaven, but Christ in the word is nigh us. And so intent he is upon it, *that he sells all to buy this field:* they who would have saving benefit by Christ, must be willing to part with all, that they may make it sure to themselves; must *count every thing but loss, that they may win Christ, and be found in him.*

II. That of *the pearl of price* (*v.* 45, 46), which is to the same purport with the former, of the treasure. *The dream is thus doubled, for the thing is certain.*

Note, 1. All the children of men are busy, *seeking goodly pearls:* one would be rich, another would be honourable, another would be learned; but the most are imposed upon, and take up with counterfeits for pearls.

2. Jesus Christ is a *Pearl of great price*, a Jewel of inestimable value, which will make those who have it rich, truly rich, rich toward God; in having him, we have enough to make us happy here and for ever.

3. A true Christian is a spiritual *merchant*, that seeks and finds this pearl of price; that does not take up with any thing short of an interest in Christ, and, as one that is resolved to be spiritually rich, trades high: *He went and bought that pearl;* did not only bid for it, but purchased it. What will it avail us to know Christ, if we do not know him as ours, *made to us wisdom?* 1 Cor. i. 30.

4. Those who would have a saving interest in Christ, must be willing to part with all for him, leave all to follow him. Whatever stands in opposition to Christ, or in competition with him for our love and service, we must cheerfully quit it, though ever so dear to us. A man may buy gold too dear, but not this pearl of price.

III. That of the *net cast into the sea, v.* 47—49.

1. Here is the parable itself. Where note, (1.) The world is a vast sea, and the children of men *are things creeping innumerable, both small and great*, in that sea, Ps. civ. 25. Men in their natural state are *like the fishes of the sea* that have no ruler over them, Hab. i. 14. (2.) The preaching of the gospel is the casting of a net into this sea, to catch something out of it, for his glory who has the sovereignty of the sea. Ministers are *fishers of men*, employed in casting and drawing this net; and *then* they speed, when at Christ's word they let down the net; otherwise, they *toil and catch nothing.* (3.) This net gathers of every kind, as large drag-nets do. In the visible church there is a deal of trash and rubbish, dirt and weeds and vermin, as well as fish. (4.) There is a time coming when this net will be full, and drawn to the shore; a set time when the gospel shall have fulfilled that for which it was sent, and we are sure it shall not return void, Is. lv. 10, 11. The net is now filling; sometimes it fills faster than at other times, but still it fills, and will be drawn to shore, when the *mystery of God shall be finished.* (5.) When the net is full and drawn to the shore, there shall be a separation between the good and bad that were gathered in it. Hypocrites and true Christians shall then be parted; the good shall be gathered into vessels, as valuable, and therefore to be carefully kept, but the bad shall be cast away, as vile and unprofitable; and miserable is the condition of those who are cast away in that day. While the net is in the sea, it is not known what is in it, the fishermen themselves cannot distinguish; but they carefully draw it, and all that is in it, to the shore, for the sake of the good that is in it. Such is God's care for the visible church, and such should ministers' concern be for those under their charge, though they are mixed.

2. Here is the explanation of the latter part of the parable, the former is obvious and plain enough: we see gathered in the visible church, *some of every kind:* but the latter part refers to that which is yet to come, and is therefore more particularly explained, *v.* 49, 50. *So shall it be at the end of the world;* then, and not till then, will the dividing, discovering day be. We must not look for the net full of all good fish; the vessels will be so, but in the net they are mixed. See here, (1.) The distinguishing of the wicked from the righteous. The angels of heaven shall come forth to do that which the angels of the churches could never do; they shall *sever the wicked from among the just;* and we need not ask how they will distinguish them when they have both their commission and their instructions from him that knows all men, and particularly knows them that are *his*, and them that are *not*, and we may be sure there shall be no mistake or blunder either way. (2.) The doom of the wicked when they are thus severed. They shall be *cast into the furnace.* Note, Everlasting misery and sorrow will certainly be the portion of those who live among sanctified ones, but themselves die unsanctified. This is the same with what we had before, *v.* 42. Note, Christ himself preached often of hell-torments, as the ever-

lasting punishment of hypocrites; and it is good for us to be often reminded of this awakening, quickening truth.

IV. Here is the parable of the *good householder*, which is intended to rivet all the rest.

1. The occasion of it was the good proficiency which the disciples had made in learning, and their profiting by this sermon in particular. (1.) He asked them, *Have ye understood all these things?* Intimating, that if they had not, he was ready to explain what they did not understand. Note, It is the will of Christ, that all those who read and hear the word should understand it; for otherwise how should they get good by it? It is therefore good for us, when we have read or heard the word, to examine ourselves, or to be examined, whether we have understood it or not. It is no disparagement to the disciples of Christ to be catechised. Christ invites us to seek to him for instruction, and ministers should proffer their service to those who have any good question to ask concerning what they have heard. (2.) They answered him, *Yea, Lord:* and we have reason to believe they said true, because, when they did not understand, they asked for an explication, *v.* 36. And the exposition of that parable was a key to the rest. Note, The right understanding of one good sermon, will very much help us to understand another; for good truths mutually explain and illustrate one another; and *knowledge is easy to him that understandeth.*

2. The scope of the parable itself was to give his approbation and commendation of their proficiency. Note, Christ is ready to encourage willing learners in his school, though they are but weak; and to say, *Well done, well said.*

(1.) He commends them as *scribes instructed unto the kingdom of heaven.* They were now learning that they might teach, and the teachers among the Jews were the scribes. Ezra, who *prepared his heart to teach in Israel,* is called *a ready scribe,* Ezra vii. 6, 10. Now a skilful, faithful minister of the gospel is a scribe too; but for distinction, he is called a scribe *instructed unto the kingdom of heaven,* well versed in the things of the gospel, and well able to teach those things. Note, [1.] Those who are to instruct others, have need to be well instructed themselves. If the priest's lips must keep knowledge, his head must first have knowledge. [2.] The instruction of a gospel minister must be in the *kingdom of heaven,* that is it about which his business lies. A man may be a great philosopher and politician, and yet if not instructed to the kingdom of heaven, he will make but a bad minister.

(2.) He compares them to a good householder, who *brings forth out of his treasure things new and old;* fruits of last year's growth and this year's gathering, abundance and variety, for the entertainment of his friends, Cant. vii. 13. See here, [1.] What should be a minister's furniture, *a treasure of things new and old.* Those who have so many and various occasions, have need to stock themselves well in their gathering days with truths new and old, out of the Old Testament and out of the New; with ancient and modern improvements, *that the man of God may be thoroughly furnished,* 2 Tim. iii. 16, 17. Old experiences, and new observations, all have their use; and we must not content ourselves with old discoveries, but must be adding new. Live and learn. [2.] What use he should make of this furniture; he should *bring forth:* laying up is in order to laying out, for the benefit of others. *Sic vos non vobis—You are to lay up, but not for yourselves.* Many are full, but they have no vent (Job xxxii. 19); have a talent, but they bury it; such are unprofitable servants; Christ himself received that he might give; so must we, and we shall have more. In bringing forth, things new and old do best together; old truths, but new methods and expressions, especially new affections.

53 And it came to pass, *that* when
Jesus had finished these parables, he
departed thence. 54 And when he
was come into his own country, he
taught them in their synagogue, insomuch that they were astonished, and
said, Whence hath this *man* this wisdom, and *these* mighty works? 55
Is not this the carpenter's son? is
not his mother called Mary? and his
brethren, James, and Joses, and Simon,
and Judas? 56 And his sisters, are
they not all with us? Whence then
hath this *man* all these things? 57
And they were offended in him. But
Jesus said unto them, A prophet is
not without honour, save in his own
country, and in his own house. 58
And he did not many mighty works
there, because of their unbelief.

We have here Christ in his own country. He went about doing good, yet left not any place till he had finished his testimony there at that time. His own countrymen had rejected him once, yet he came to them again. Note, Christ does not take refusers at their first word, but repeats his offers to those who have often repulsed them. In this, as in other things, Christ was like his brethren; he had a natural affection to his own country; *Patriam quisque amat, non quia pulchram, sed quia suam—Every one loves his country, not because it is beautiful, but because it is his own.* Seneca. His treatment this time was much the same as before, scornful and spiteful. Observe,

I. How they expressed their contempt of him. When he *taught them in their syna-*

gogue, they were astonished; not that they were taken with his preaching, or admired his doctrine in itself, but only that it should be his; looking upon him as unlikely to be such a teacher. Two things they upbraided him with.

1. His want of academical education. They owned that he had wisdom, and did mighty works; but the question was, Whence he had them: for they knew that he was not brought up at the feet of their rabbin: he had never been at the university, nor taken his degree, nor was called of men, *Rabbi, Rabbi.* Note, Mean and prejudiced spirits are apt to judge of men by their education, and to enquire more into their rise than into their reasons. "*Whence has this man these mighty works?* Did he come honestly by them? Has he not been studying the black art?" Thus they turned that against him which was really for him; for if they had not been wilfully blind, they must have concluded him to be divinely assisted and commissioned, who without the help of education gave such proofs of extraordinary wisdom and power.

2. The meanness and poverty of his relations, *v.* 55, 56.

(1.) They upbraid him with his father. *Is not this the carpenter's son?* Yes, it is true he was reputed so: and what harm in that? No disparagement to him to be the son of an honest tradesman. They remember not (though they might have known it) that this carpenter was *of the house of David* (Luke i. 27), *a son of David* (*ch.* i. 20); though a carpenter, yet a person of honour. Those who are willing to pick quarrels will overlook that which is worthy and deserving, and fasten upon that only which seems mean. Some sordid spirits regard no branch, no not the Branch from the stem of Jesse (Isa. xi. 1), if it be not the top branch.

(2.) They upbraid him with his mother; and what quarrel have they with her? Why, truly, *his mother is called Mary,* and that was a very common name, and they all knew her, and knew her to be an ordinary person; she *was called Mary,* not *Queen Mary,* nor *Lady Mary,* nor so much as *Mistress Mary,* but plain *Mary;* and this is turned to his reproach, as if men had nothing to be valued by but foreign extraction, noble birth, or splendid titles; poor things to measure worth by.

(3.) They upbraid him with his brethren, whose names they knew, and had them ready enough to serve this turn; James, and Joses, and Simon, and Judas, good men but poor men, and therefore despised; and Christ for their sakes. These brethren, it is probable, were Joseph's children by a former wife; or whatever their relation was to him, they seem to have been brought up with him in the same family. And therefore of the calling of three of these, who were of the twelve, to that honour (James, Simon, and Jude, the same with Thaddeus), we read not particularly, because they needed not such an express call into acquaintance with Christ who had been the companions of his youth.

(4.) His sisters too are all with us; they should therefore have loved him and respected him the more, because he was one of themselves, but therefore they despised him. They were *offended in him:* they stumbled at these stumbling-stones, for he was set for *a sign that should be spoken against,* Luke ii. 34; Isa. viii. 14.

II. See how he resented this contempt, *v.* 57, 58.

1. It did not trouble his heart. It appears he was not much concerned at it; he *despised the shame,* Heb. xii. 2. Instead of aggravating the affront, or expressing an offence at it, or returning such an answer to their foolish suggestions as they deserved, he mildly imputes it to the common humour of the children of men, to undervalue excellences that are cheap, and common, and home-bred. It is usually so. *A prophet is not without honour, save in his own country.* Note, (1.) Prophets should have honour paid them, and commonly have; men of God are great men, and men of honour, and challenge respect. It is strange indeed if prophets have not honour. (2.) Notwithstanding this, they are commonly least regarded and reverenced in their own country, nay, and sometimes are most envied. Familiarity breeds contempt.

2. It did for the present (to speak with reverence), in effect, tie his hands: *He did not many mighty works there, because of their unbelief.* Note, Unbelief is the great obstruction to Christ's favours. *All things are* in general *possible to God* (*ch.* xix. 26), but then it is *to him that believes* as to the particulars, Mark ix. 23. The gospel is *the power of God unto salvation,* but then it is to *every one that believes,* Rom. i. 16. So that if mighty works be not wrought in us, it is not for want of power or grace in Christ, but for want of faith in us. *By grace ye are saved,* and that is a mighty work, but it is *through faith,* Eph. ii. 8.

CHAP. XIV.

John the Baptist had said concerning Christ, He must increase, but I must decrease, John iii. 30. The morning-star is here disappearing, and the Sun of righteousness rising to its meridian lustre. Here is, I. The martyrdom of John; his imprisonment for his faithfulness to Herod (ver. 1—5), and the beheading of him to please Herodias, ver. 6—12. II. The miracles of Christ. 1. His feeding five thousand men that came to him to be taught, with five loaves and two fishes, ver. 13—21. 2. Christ's walking on the waves to his disciples in a storm, ver. 22—23. 3. His healing the sick with the touch of the hem of his garment, ver. 34—36. Thus he went forth, thus he went on, conquering and to conquer, or rather, curing and to cure.

AT that time Herod the tetrarch
heard of the fame of Jesus, 2
And said unto his servants, This is
John the Baptist: he is risen from
the dead; and therefore mighty works
do show forth themselves in him. 3
For Herod had laid hold on John,
and bound him, and put *him* in pri-

son for Herodias' sake, his brother
Philip's wife. 4 For John said unto
him, It is not lawful for thee to have
her. 5 And when he would have put
him to death, he feared the multitude,
because they counted him as a prophet.
6 But when Herod's birthday was kept, the daughter of Herodias danced before them, and pleased
Herod. 7 Whereupon he promised
with an oath to give her whatsoever
she would ask. 8 And she, being
before instructed of her mother, said,
Give me here John Baptist's head in
a charger. 9 And the king was sorry:
nevertheless, for the oath's sake, and
them which sat with him at meat, he
commanded *it* to be given *her*. 10
And he sent, and beheaded John in
the prison. 11 And his head was
brought in a charger, and given to the
damsel: and she brought *it* to her
mother. 12 And his disciples came,
and took up the body, and buried it,
and went and told Jesus.

We have here the story of John's martyrdom. Observe,

I. The occasion of relating this story here, *v.* 1, 2. Here is,

1. The account brought to Herod of the miracles which Christ wrought. Herod the tetrarch or chief governor of Galilee *heard of the fame of Jesus.* At that time, when his countrymen slighted him, upon the account of his meanness and obscurity, he began to be famous at court. Note, God will honour those that are despised for his sake. And the gospel, like the sea, gets in one place what it loses in another. Christ had now been preaching and working miracles above two years; yet, it should seem, Herod had not heard of him till now, and now only heard the fame of him. Note, It is the unhappiness of the great ones of the world, that they are most out of the way of hearing the best things (1 Cor. ii. 8). *Which none of the princes of this world knew,* 1 Cor. i. 26. Christ's disciples were now sent abroad to preach, and to work miracles in his name, and this spread the fame of him more than ever; which was an indication of the spreading of the gospel by their means after his ascension.

2. The construction he puts upon this (*v.* 2); *He said to his servants* that told him of the fame of Jesus, as sure as we are here, *this is John the Baptist; he is risen from the dead.* Either the leaven of Herod was not Sadducism, *for the Sadducees say, There is no resurrection* (Acts xxiii. 8); or else Herod's guilty conscience (as is usual with atheists) did at this time get the mastery of his opinion, and now he concludes, whether there be a general resurrection or no, that *John Baptist is certainly risen,* and therefore *mighty works do show forth themselves in him.* John, while he lived, *did no miracle* (John x. 41); but Herod concludes, that, being risen from the dead, he is clothed with a greater power than he had while he was living. And he very well calls the miracles he supposed him to work, not *his mighty works,* but *mighty works showing forth themselves in him.* Observe here concerning Herod,

(1.) How he was disappointed in what he intended by beheading John. He thought if he could get that troublesome fellow out of the way, he might go on in his sins, undisturbed and uncontrolled; yet no sooner is that effected, than he hears of Jesus and his disciples preaching the same pure doctrine that John preached; and, which is more, even the disciples confirming it by miracles in their Master's name. Note, Ministers may be silenced, and imprisoned, and banished, and slain, but the word of God cannot be run down. The prophets *live not for ever, but the word takes hold,* Zech. i. 5, 6. See 2 Tim. ii. 9. Sometimes God raises up many faithful ministers out of the ashes of one. This *hope* there is of God's trees, *though they be cut down,* Job xiv. 7—9.

(2.) How he was filled with causeless fears, merely from the guilt of his own conscience. Thus *blood cries,* not only *from the earth* on which it was shed, but from the heart of him that shed it, and makes him *Magor-missabib —A terror round about,* a terror to himself. A guilty conscience suggests every thing that is frightful, and, like a whirlpool, gathers all to itself that comes near it. Thus *the wicked flee when none pursue* (Prov. xxviii. 1); are in *great fear, where no fear is,* Ps. xiv. 5. Herod, by a little enquiry, might have found out that this Jesus was in being long before John Baptist's death, and therefore could not be *Johannes redivivus—John restored to life;* and so he might have undeceived himself; but God justly left him to this infatuation.

(3.) How, notwithstanding this, he was hardened in his wickedness; for though he was convinced that John was a prophet, and one owned of God, yet he does not express the least remorse or sorrow for his sin in putting him to death. The devils believe and tremble, but they never believe and repent. Note, There may be the terror of strong convictions, where there is not the truth of a saving conversion.

II. The story itself of the imprisonment and martyrdom of John. These extraordinary sufferings of him who was the first preacher of the gospel, plainly show that bonds and afflictions will abide the professors of it. As the first Old-Testament saint, so the first New-Testament minister, died a martyr. And if Christ's forerunner was thus treated, let not his followers expect to be caressed by the world. Observe here,

1. John's faithfulness in reproving Herod, *v.* 3, 4. Herod was one of John's hearers (Mark vi. 20), and therefore John might be the more bold with him. Note, Ministers, who are reprovers by office, are especially obliged to reprove those that are under their charge, and *not to suffer sin upon them;* they have the fairest opportunity of dealing with them, and with them may expect the most favourable acceptance.

The particular sin he reproved him for was, marrying his brother Philip's wife, not his widow (that had not been so criminal), but his wife. Philip was now living, and Herod inveigled his wife from him, and kept her for his own. Here was a complication of wickedness, adultery, incest, besides the wrong done to Philip, who had had a child by this woman; and it was an aggravation of the wrong, that he was his brother, his half-brother, by the father, but not by the mother. See Ps. l. 20. For this sin John reproved him; not by tacit and oblique allusions, but in plain terms, *It is not lawful for thee to have her.* He charges it upon him as a sin; not, It is not honourable, or, It is not safe, but, It is not *lawful;* the *sinfulness* of sin, as it is the *transgression of the law,* is the worst thing in it. This was Herod's own iniquity, his beloved sin, and therefore John Baptist tells him of this particularly. Note, (1.) That which by the law of God is unlawful to other people, is by the same law unlawful to princes and the greatest of men. They who rule over men must not forget that they are themselves but men, and subject to God. "*It is not lawful for thee,* any more than for the meanest subject thou hast, to debauch another man's wife." There is no prerogative, no, not for the greatest and most arbitrary kings, to break the laws of God. (2.) If princes and great men break the law of God, it is very fit they should be told of it by proper persons, and in a proper manner. As they are not above the commands of God's word, so they are not above the reproofs of his ministers. *It is not fit* indeed, *to say to a king, Thou art Belial* (Job xxxiv. 18), any more than to call a brother *Raca,* or, *Thou fool:* it is not fit, while they keep within the sphere of their own authority, to arraign them. But it is fit that, by those whose office it is, they should be told what is unlawful, and told with application, *Thou art the man;* for it follows there (*v.* 19), that God (whose agents and ambassadors faithful ministers are) *accepteth not the persons of princes, nor regardeth the rich more than the poor.*

2. The imprisonment of John for his faithfulness, *v.* 3. *Herod laid hold on John* when he was going on to preach and baptize, put an end to his work, *bound him, and put him in prison;* partly to gratify his own revenge, and partly to please Herodias, who of the two seemed to be most incensed against him; it was *for her sake* that he did it. Note, (1.) Faithful reproofs, if they do not profit, usually provoke; if they do not do good, they are resented as affronts, and they that will not bow to the reproof, will fly in the face of the reprover and hate him, as Ahab hated Micaiah, 1 Kings xxii. 8. See Prov. ix. 8; xv. 10, 12. *Veritas odium parit—Truth produces hatred.* (2.) It is no new thing for God's ministers to suffer ill for doing well. Troubles abide those most that are most diligent and faithful in doing their duty, Acts xx. 20, 23. It was so with the Old-Testament prophets. See 2 Chron. xvi. 10; xxiv. 20, 21. Perhaps some of John's friends would blame him as indiscreet in reproving Herod, and tell him he had better be silent than provoke Herod, whose character he knew very well, thus to deprive him of his liberty; but away with that discretion that would hinder men from doing their duty as magistrates, ministers, or Christian friends; I believe John's own heart did not reproach him for it, but this testimony of his conscience for him made his bonds easy, that he suffered for well-doing, and not as a *busy-body in other men's matters,* 1 Pet. iv. 15.

3 The restraint that Herod lay under from further venting of his rage against John, *v.* 5.

(1.) He would have put him to death. Perhaps that was not intended at first when he imprisoned him, but his revenge by degrees boiled up to that height. Note, The way of sin, especially the sin of persecution, is down-hill; and when once a respect to Christ's ministers is cast off and broken through in one instance, that is at length done, which the man would sooner have thought himself a dog than to have been guilty of, 2 Kings viii. 13.

(2.) That which hindered him was his *fear of the multitude, because they counted John as a prophet.* It was not because he feared God (if the fear of God had been before his eyes he would not have imprisoned him), nor because he feared John, though formerly he had had a reverence for him (his lusts had overcome that), but because he feared the people; he was afraid for himself, his own safety, and the safety of his government, his abuse of which he knew had already rendered him odious to the people, whose resentments being so far heated already would be apt, upon such a provocation as the putting of a prophet to death, to break out into a flame. Note, [1.] Tyrants have their fears. Those who are, and affect to be, *the terror of the mighty,* are many times the greatest terror of all to themselves; and when they are most ambitious to be feared by the people, are most afraid of them. [2.] Wicked men are restrained from the most wicked practices, merely by their secular interest, and not by any regard to God. A concern for their ease, credit, wealth, and safety, being their reigning principle, as it keeps them from many duties, so it keeps them from many sins, which otherwise they would not be restrained from; and this is one means by which sinners are kept from being overmuch wicked, Eccl. vii. 17. The danger of sin that appears to sense, or to fancy only, influences men more than that which appears to faith. Herod feared that the putting of John to death might raise a mutiny among the people, which it did not; but he never feared it might raise a mutiny in his own conscience, which it did, *v.* 2. Men fear being hanged for that which they do not fear being damned for.

4. The contrivance of bringing John to his death. Long he lay in prison; and, against the liberty of the subject (which, blessed be God, is secured to us of this nation by law), might neither be tried nor bailed. It is computed that he lay a year and a half a close prisoner, which was about as much time as he had spent in his public ministry, from his first entrance into it. Now here we have an account of his release, not by any other discharge than death, the period of all a good man's troubles, that brings the prisoners to rest together, so that *they hear not the voice of the oppressor*, Job iii. 18.

Herodias laid the plot; her implacable revenge thirsted after John's blood, and would be satisfied with nothing less. Cross the carnal appetites, and they turn into the most barbarous passions; it was a woman, a whore, and the mother of harlots, that was *drunk with the blood of the saints*, Rev. xvii. 5, 6. Herodias contrived how to bring about the murder of John so artificially as to save Herod's credit, and so to pacify the people. A sorry excuse is better than none But I am apt to think, that if the truth were known, Herod was himself in the plot; and with all his pretences of surprise and sorrow, was privy to the contrivance, and knew before what would be asked. And his pretending his oath, and respect to his guests, was all but sham and grimace. But if he were trepanned into it ere he was aware, yet because it was the thing he might have prevented, and would not, he is justly found guilty of the whole contrivance. Though Jezebel bring Naboth to his end, yet if Ahab take possession, *he hath killed.* So, though Herodias contrive the beheading of John, yet, if Herod consent to it, and take pleasure in it, he is not only an accessary, but a principal murderer. Well, the scene being laid behind the curtain, let us see how it was acted upon the stage, and in what method. Here we have,

(1.) The humouring of Herod by the damsel's dancing upon a birth-day. It seems, Herod's birth-day was kept with some solemnity; in honour of the day, there must needs be, as usual, a ball at court; and, to grace the solemnity, the daughter of Herodias danced before them; who being the queen's daughter, it was more than she ordinarily condescended to do. Note, Times of carnal mirth and jollity are convenient times for carrying on bad designs against God's people. When the king was *made sick with bottles of wine, he stretched out his hand with scorners* (Hos. vii. 5), for it is part of the *sport of a fool* to do mischief, Prov. x. 23. The Philistines, when their heart was merry, called for Samson to abuse him. The Parisian massacre was at a wedding. This young lady's dancing pleased Herod. We are not told who danced with her, but none pleased Herod like her dancing. Note, A vain and graceless heart is apt to be greatly in love with the lusts of the flesh and of the eye, and when it is so, it is entering into further temptation; for by that Satan gets and keeps possession. See Prov. xxiii. 31—33. Herod was now in a mirthful mood, and nothing was more agreeable to him than that which fed his vanity.

(2.) The rash and foolish promise which Herod made to this wanton girl, to give her whatsoever she would ask: and this promise confirmed with an oath, *v.* 7. It was a very extravagant obligation which Herod here entered into, and no way becoming a prudent man that is afraid of being *snared in the words of his mouth* (Prov. vi. 2), much less a good man that fears an oath, Eccl. ix. 2. To put this blank into her hand, and enable her to draw upon him at pleasure, was too great a recompense for such a sorry piece of merit; and, I am apt to think, Herod would not have been guilty of such an absurdity, if he had not been instructed of Herodias, as well as the damsel. Note, Promissory oaths are ensnaring things, and, when made rashly, are the products of inward corruption, and the occasion of many temptations. Therefore, swear not so at all, lest thou have occasion to say, *It was an error*, Eccl. v. 6.

(3.) The bloody demand the young lady made of John the Baptist's head, *v.* 8. She was before instructed of her mother. Note, the case of those children is very sad, whose parents are *their counsellors to do wickedly*, as Ahaziah's (2 Chron. xxii. 3); who instruct them and encourage them in sin, and set them bad examples; for the corrupt nature will sooner be quickened by bad instructions than restrained and mortified by good ones. Children ought not to *obey their parents* against *the Lord*, but if they command them to sin, must say, as Levi did to *father and mother*, they *have not seen them.*

Herod having given her her commission, and Herodias her instructions, she requires John the Baptist's head in a charger. Perhaps Herodias feared lest Herod should grow weary of her (as lust useth to nauseate and be cloyed), and then would make John Baptist's reproof a pretence to dismiss her; to prevent which she contrives to harden Herod in it by engaging him in the murder of John. John must be beheaded then; that is the death by which he must glorify God; and because it was *his* who died first after the beginning of the gospel, though the martyrs died various kinds of deaths, and not so easy and honourable as this, yet this is put for all the rest, Rev. xx. 4, where we read of *the souls of those that were beheaded for the witness of Jesus.* Yet this is not enough, the thing must be humoured too, and not only a revenge, but a fancy must be gratified; it must be *given her here in a charger,* served up in blood, as a dish of meat at the feast, or sauce to all the other dishes; it is reserved for the third course, to come up with the rarities. He must have no trial, no public hearing, no forms of law or justice must add solemnity to his death; but he is tried, condemned, and executed, in a breath. It was well for him he was so mortified to the world that death could be no surprise to him, though ever so sudden. It must be given her, and she will reckon it a recompence for her dancing, and desire no more.

(4.) Herod's grant of this demand (*v.* 9); *The king was sorry,* at least took on him to be so, but, *for the oath's sake, he commanded it to be given her.* Here is,

[1.] A pretended concern for John. *The king was sorry.* Note, Many a man sins with regret, that never has any true regret for his sin; is sorry to sin, yet is utterly a stranger to godly sorrow; sins with reluctancy, and yet goes on to sin. Dr. Hammond suggests, that one reason of Herod's sorrow was, because it was his birth-day festival, and it would be an ill omen to shed blood on that day, which, as other days of joy, used to be graced with acts of clemency; *Natalem colimus, tacete lites—We are celebrating the birth-day, let there be no contentions.*

[2.] Here is a pretended conscience of his oath, with a specious show of honour and honesty; he must needs do something, for the oath's sake. Note, it is a great mistake to think that a wicked oath will justify a wicked action. It was implied so necessarily, that it needed not be expressed, that he would do any thing for her that was lawful and honest; and when she demanded what was otherwise, he ought to have declared, and he might have done it honourably, that the oath was null and void, and the obligation of it ceased. No man can lay himself under an obligation to sin, because God has already so strongly obliged every man against sin.

[3.] Here is a real baseness in compliance with wicked companions. Herod yielded, not so much for the sake of the oath, but because it was public, and in compliment to *them that sat at meat with him;* he granted the demand that he might not seem, before them, to have broken his engagement. Note, A point of honour goes much further with many than a point of conscience. Those who sat at meat with him, probably, were as well pleased with the damsel's dancing as he, and therefore would have her by all means to be gratified in a frolic, and perhaps were as willing as she to see John the Baptist's head off. However, none of them had the honesty to interpose, as they ought to have done, for the preventing of it, as Jehoiakim's princes did, Jer. xxxvi. 25. If some of the common people had been here, they would have rescued this Jonathan, as 1 Sam. xiv. 45.

[4.] Here is a real malice to John at the bottom of this concession, or else he might have found out evasions enough to have got clear of his promise. Note, Though a wicked mind never wants an excuse, yet the truth of the matter is, that *every man is tempted when he is drawn aside of his own lust, and enticed,* Jam. i. 14. Perhaps Herod presently reflecting upon the extravagance of his promise, on which she might ground a demand of some vast sum of money, which he loved a great deal better than John the Baptist, was glad to get clear of it so easily; and therefore immediately issues out a warrant for the beheading of John the Baptist, it should seem not in writing, but only by word of mouth; so little account is made of that precious life; *he commanded it to be given her.*

(5.) The execution of John, pursuant to this grant (*v.* 10); *He sent and beheaded John in the prison.* It is probable the prison was very near, at the gate of the palace; and thither an officer was sent to cut off the head of this great man. He must be beheaded with expedition, to gratify Herodias, who was in a longing condition till it was done. It was done in the night, for it was at supper-time, after supper, it is likely. It was done in the prison, not at the usual place of execution, for fear of an uproar. A great deal of innocent blood, of martyr's blood, has thus been huddled up in corners, which, when God comes to make inquisition for blood, the earth shall disclose, and shall no more cover, Isa. xxvi. 21; Ps. ix. 12.

Thus was that voice silenced, that burning and shining light extinguished; thus did that prophet, that Elias, of the New Testament, fall a sacrifice to the resentments of an imperious, whorish woman. Thus did he, who was great in the sight of the Lord, *die as a fool dieth, his hands were bound, and his feet put into fetters; and as a man falleth before wicked men,* so he fell, a true martyr to all intents and purposes: dying, though not for the profession of his faith, yet for the performance of his duty. However, though his work was soon done, *it was done and his testimony finished,* for till then none of God's witnesses are slain. And God brought this good out of it, that hereby his disciples, who while he lived, though in prison, kept close to him, now after his death heartily closed with Jesus Christ.

5. The disposal of the poor remains of this blessed saint and martyr. The head and body being separated,

(1.) The damsel brought the head in triumph to her mother, as a trophy of the victories of her malice and revenge, *v.* 11.

Jerome ad Rufin, relates, that when Herodias had John the Baptist's head brought her, she gave herself the barbarous diversion of pricking the tongue with a needle, as Fulvia did Tully's. Note, Bloody minds are pleased with bloody sights, which those of tender spirits shrink and tremble at. Sometimes the insatiable rage of bloody persecutors has fallen upon the dead bodies of the saints, and made sport with them, Ps. lxxix. 2. When the witnesses are slain, they that *dwell on the earth rejoice over them, and make merry*, Rev. xi. 10; Ps. xiv. 4, 5.

(2.) The disciples *buried the body*, and brought the news in tears to our Lord Jesus. The disciples of John had fasted often while their master was in prison, their *bridegroom was taken away from them*, and they prayed earnestly for his deliverance, as the church did for Peter's, Acts xii. 5. They had free access to him in prison, which was a comfort to them, but they wished to see him at liberty, that he might preach to others; but now on a sudden all their hopes are dashed. Disciples weep and lament, when the world rejoices. Let us see what they did.

[1.] *They buried the body*. Note, There is a respect owing to the servants of Christ, not only while they live, but in their bodies and memories when they are dead. Concerning the first two New-Testament martyrs, it is particularly taken notice of, that they were decently buried, John the Baptist by his disciples, and Stephen by devout men (Acts viii. 2); yet there was no enshrining of their bones or other relics, a piece of superstition which sprung up long after, when the enemy had sowed tares. That over-doing, in respect to the bodies of the saints, is undoing; though they are not to be vilified, yet they are not to be deified.

[2.] *They went and told Jesus;* not so much that he might shift for his own safety (no doubt he heard it from others, the country rang of it), as that they might receive comfort from him, and be taken in among his disciples. Note, *First*, When any thing ails us at any time, it is our duty and privilege to make Christ acquainted with it. It will be a relief to our burthened spirits to unbosom ourselves to a friend we may be free with. Such a relation dead or unkind, such a comfort lost or embittered, go and tell Jesus, who knows already, but will know from us, the trouble of *our souls in adversity*. *Secondly*, We must take heed, lest our religion and the profession of it die with our ministers; when John was dead, they did not return every man to his own, but resolved to abide by it still. When the shepherds are smitten, the sheep need not be scattered while they have the great Shepherd of the sheep to go to, who is still the same, Heb. xiii. 8, 20. The removal of ministers should bring us nearer to Christ, into a more immediate communion with him. *Thirdly*, Comforts otherwise highly valuable, are sometimes *therefore* taken from us, because they come between us and Christ, and are apt to carry away that love and esteem which are due to him only: John had long since directed his disciples to Christ, and turned them over to him, but they could not leave their old master while he lived; therefore he is removed that they may go to Jesus, whom they had sometimes emulated and envied for John's sake. It is better to be drawn to Christ by want and loss, than not to come to him at all. If our masters be taken from our head, this is our comfort, we have a Master in heaven, who himself is our Head.

Josephus mentions this story of the death of John the Baptist (*Antiquit.* lib. 18, cap. 7), and adds, that a fatal destruction of Herod's army in his war with Aretas, king of Petrea (whose daughter was Herod's wife, whom he put away to make room for Herodias), was generally considered by the Jews to be a just judgment upon him, for putting John the Baptist to death. Herod having, at the instigation of Herodias, disobliged the emperor, was deprived of his government, and they were both banished to Lyons in France; which, says Josephus, was his just punishment for hearkening to her solicitations. And, lastly, it is storied of this daughter of Herodias, that going over the ice in winter, the ice broke, and she slipt in up to her neck, which was cut through by the sharpness of the ice. God requiring her head (says Dr. Whitby) for that of the Baptist; which, if true, was a remarkable providence.

13 When Jesus heard *of it*, he departed thence by ship into a desert
place apart: and when the people had
heard *thereof*, they followed him on
foot out of the cities. 14 And Jesus
went forth, and saw a great multitude,
and was moved with compassion toward them, and he healed their sick.
15 And when it was evening his disciples came to him, saying, This is a
desert place, and the time is now past;
send the multitude away, that they
may go into the villages, and buy
themselves victuals. 16 But Jesus
said unto them, They need not depart; give ye them to eat. 17 And
they say unto him, We have here but
five loaves, and two fishes. 18 He
said, Bring them hither to me. 19
And he commanded the multitude to
sit down on the grass, and took the
five loaves, and the two fishes, and
looking up to heaven, he blessed, and
brake, and gave the loaves to *his*
disciples, and the disciples to the multitude. 20 And they did all eat, and

were filled: and they took up of the fragments that remained twelve baskets full. 21 And they that had eaten were about five thousand men, beside women and children.

This passage of story, concerning Christ's feeding *five thousand men with five loaves and two fishes,* is recorded by all the four Evangelists, which very few, if any, of Christ's miracles are: this intimates that there is something in it worthy of special remark. Observe,

I. The great resort of people to Christ, when he was retired *into a desert place, v.* 13. He withdrew into privacy when he heard, not of John's death, but of the thoughts Herod had concerning him, that he was *John the Baptist risen from the dead,* and therefore so feared by Herod as to be hated; he departed further off, to get out of Herod's jurisdiction. Note, In times of peril, when God opens a door of escape, it is lawful to flee for our own preservation, unless we have some special call to expose ourselves. Christ's *hour was not yet come,* and therefore he would not thrust himself upon suffering. He could have secured himself by divine power, but because his life was intended for an example, he did it by human prudence; *he departed by ship.* But *a city on a hill cannot be hid; when the people heard it, they followed him on foot* from all parts. Such an interest Christ had in the affections of the multitude, that his withdrawing from them did but draw them after him with so much the more eagerness. Here, as often, *the scripture was fulfilled,* that *unto him shall the gathering of the people be.* It should seem, there was more crowding to Christ after John's martyrdom than before. Sometimes *the sufferings of the saints* are made to further the gospel (Phil. i. 12), and "the blood of the martyrs is the seed of the church." Now John's testimony was finished, it was recollected, and more improved than ever. Note, 1. When Christ and his word withdraw from us, it is best for us (whatever flesh and blood may object to the contrary) to follow it, preferring opportunities for our souls before any secular advantages whatsoever. *When the ark removes, ye shall remove, and go after it,* Josh. iii. 3. 2. *Those that truly desire the sincere milk of the word,* will not stick at the difficulties they may meet with in their attendance on it. The presence of Christ and his gospel makes a desert place not only tolerable, but desirable; it makes the wilderness an Eden, Isa. li. 3; xli. 19, 20.

II. The tender compassion of our Lord Jesus towards those who thus followed him, *v.* 14. 1. He went forth, and appeared publicly among them. Though he retired for his own security, and his own repose, yet he went forth from his retirement, when he saw people desirous to hear him, as one willing both to toil himself, and to expose himself, for the good of souls; for *even Christ pleased not himself.* 2. *When he saw the multitude, he had compassion on them.* Note, The sight of a great multitude may justly move compassion. To see a great multitude, and to think how many precious, immortal souls here are, the greatest part of which, we have reason to fear, are neglected and ready to perish, would grieve one to the heart. None like Christ for pity to souls; *his compassions fail not.* 3. He did not only pity them, but he helped them; many of them were *sick, and he, in compassion to them, healed them;* for he came into the world to be the great Healer. After awhile, they were all hungry, *and he, in compassion to them, fed them.* Note, In all the favours Christ shows to us, he is *moved with compassion,* Isa. lxiii. 9.

III. The motion which the disciples made for the dismissing of the congregation, and Christ's setting aside the motion. 1. The *evening* drawing on, the disciples moved it to Christ to send the multitude away; they thought there was a good day's work done, and it was time to disperse. Note, Christ's disciples are often more careful to show their discretion, than to show their zeal; and their abundant consideration, rather than their abundant affection in the things of God. 2. Christ would not dismiss them hungry as they were, nor detain them longer without meat, nor put them upon the trouble and charge of buying meat for themselves, but orders his disciples to provide for them. Christ all along expressed more tenderness toward the people than his disciples did; for what are the compassions of the most merciful men, compared with *the tender mercies of God in Christ?* See how loth Christ is to part with those who are resolved to cleave to him! *They need not depart.* Note, Those who have Christ have enough, and need not depart to seek a happiness and livelihood in the creature; they that have made sure of *the one thing needful,* need not be *cumbered about much serving:* nor will Christ put his willing followers upon a needless expense, but will make their attendance cheap to them.

But if they be hungry, they have need to depart, for that is a necessity which has no law, therefore *give you them to eat.* Note, *The Lord is for the body;* it is *the work of his hands,* it is part of his purchase; he was himself clothed with a body, that he might encourage us to depend upon him for the supply of our bodily wants. But he takes a particular care of the body, when it is employed to serve the soul in his more immediate service. If we *seek first the kingdom of God,* and make that our chief care, we may depend upon God to *add other things to* us, as far as he sees fit, and may *cast all care* of them *upon him.* These followed Christ but for a trial, in a present fit of zeal, and yet Christ took this care of them; much more will he provide for those who follow him fully.

IV. The slender provision that was made for this great multitude; and here we must compare the number of invited guests with the bill of fare.

1. The number of the guests was *five thousand of men, besides women and children;* and it is probable the women and children might be as many as the men, if not more. This was a vast auditory that Christ preached to, and we have reason to think an attentive auditory; and yet, it should seem, far the greater part, notwithstanding all this seeming zeal and forwardness, came to nothing; they went off and followed him no more; *for many are called, but few chosen.* We would rather perceive the acceptableness of the word by the conversion, than by the crowds, of its hearers; though that also is a good sight and a good sign.

2. The bill of fare was very disproportionable to the number of the guests, but *five loaves and two fishes.* This provision the disciples carried about with them for the use of the family, now they *were retired into the desert.* Christ could have fed them by miracle, but to set us an example of providing for those of our own households, he will have their own camp victualled in an ordinary way. Here is neither plenty, nor variety, nor dainty; a dish of fish was no rarity to them that were fishermen, but it was food convenient for the twelve; two fishes for their supper, and bread to serve them perhaps for a day or two: here was no wine or strong drink; fair water from the rivers in the desert was the best they had to drink with their meat; and yet out of this Christ will have the multitude fed. Note, Those who have but a little, yet when the necessity is urgent, must relieve others out of that little, and that is the way to make it more. *Can God furnish a table in the wilderness?* Yes, he can, when he pleases, a plentiful table.

V. The liberal distribution of this provision among the multitude (*v.* 18, 19); *Bring them hither to me.* Note, The way to have our creature-comforts, comforts indeed to us, is to bring them to Christ; for every thing is sanctified by his word, and by prayer to him: that is likely to prosper and do well with us, which we put into the hands of our Lord Jesus, that he may dispose of it as he pleases, and that we may take it back from his hand, and then it will be doubly sweet to us. What we give in charity, we should bring to Christ first, that he may graciously accept it from us, and graciously bless it to those to whom it is given; this is *doing it as unto the Lord.*

Now at this miraculous meal we may observe,

1. The seating of the guests (*v.* 19); *He commanded them to sit down;* which intimates, that while he was preaching to them, they were standing, which is a posture of reverence, and readiness for motion. But what shall we do for chairs for them all? Let them *sit down on the grass.* When Ahasuerus would *show the riches of his glorious kingdom, and the honour of his excellent majesty, in a royal feast for the great men of all his provinces,* the beds or couches they sat on *were of gold and silver, upon a pavement of red, and blue, and white, and black marble,* Esther i. 6. Our Lord Jesus did now show, in a divine feast, the riches of a more glorious kingdom than that, and the honour of a more excellent majesty, even a dominion over nature itself; but here is not so much as a cloth spread, no plates or napkins laid, no knives or forks, nor so much as a bench to sit down on; but, as if Christ intended indeed to reduce the world to the plainness and simplicity, and so to the innocency and happiness, of Adam in paradise, *he commanded them to sit down on the grass.* By doing every thing thus, without any pomp or splendour, he plainly showed *that his kingdom was not of this world,* nor *cometh with observation.*

2. The craving of a blessing. He did not appoint one of his disciples to be his chaplain, but he himself *looked up to heaven, and blessed, and gave thanks;* he praised God for the provision they had, and prayed to God to bless it to them. His craving a blessing, was commanding a blessing; for as he preached, so he prayed, *like one having authority;* and in this prayer and thanksgiving, we may suppose, he had special reference to the multiplying of this food; but herein he has taught us that good duty of craving a blessing and giving thanks at our meals: God's good creatures must be *received with thanksgiving,* 1 Tim. iv. 4. Samuel *blessed* the feast, 1 Sam. ix. 13; Acts ii. 46, 47; xxvii. 34, 35. This is *eating and drinking to the glory of God* (1 Cor. x. 31); *giving God thanks* (Rom. xiv. 6); *eating before God,* as Moses, and his father-in-law, Exod. xviii. 12, 15. When Christ *blessed, he looked up to heaven,* to teach us, in prayer, to eye God as a *Father in heaven;* and when we receive our creature-comforts to look thitherward, as taking them from God's hand, and depending on him for a blessing.

3. The carving of the meat. The Master of the feast was himself head-carver, for *he brake, and gave the loaves to the disciples, and the disciples to the multitude.* Christ intended hereby to put honour upon his disciples, that they might be respected *as workers together with him;* as also to signify in what way the spiritual food of the word should be dispensed to the world; from Christ, as the original Author, by his ministers. What Christ designed for *the churches he signified to his servant John* (Rev. i. 1, 4); *they delivered all that,* and that only, *which they received from the Lord,* 1 Cor. xi. 23. Ministers can never fill the people's hearts, unless Christ first fill their hands: and what he has given to the disciples, they must give to the multitude; for they are *stewards, to give to every one his portion of meat, ch.* xxiv. 45. And,

blessed be God, be the multitude ever so great, there is enough for all, enough for each.

4. The increase of the meat. This is taken notice of only in the effect, not in the cause or manner of it; here is no mention of any word that Christ spoke, by which the food was multiplied; the purposes and intentions of his mind and will shall take effect, though they be not spoken out: but this is observable, that the meat was multiplied, not in the heap at first, but in the distribution of it. As the widow's oil increased in the pouring out, so here the bread in the breaking. Thus grace grows by being acted, and, while other things perish in the using, spiritual gifts increase in the using. God ministers seed to the sower, and multiplies not the seed hoarded up, but *the seed sown,* 2 Cor. ix. 10. Thus *there is that scattereth, and yet increaseth;* that scattereth, and so increaseth.

VI. The plentiful satisfaction of all the guests with this provision. Though the disproportion was so great, yet there was enough and to spare.

1. There was enough: *They did all eat, and were filled.* Note, Those whom Christ feeds, he fills; so runs the promise (Ps. xxxvii. 19), *They shall be satisfied.* As there was enough for all, *they did all eat,* so there was enough for each, *they were filled;* though there was but a little, there was enough, and that is as good as a feast. Note, The blessing of God can make a little go a great way; as, if God blasts what we have, *we eat, and have not enough,* Hag. i. 6.

2. There was to spare; *They took up of the fragments that remained, twelve baskets full,* one basket for each apostle: thus what they gave they had again, and a great deal more with it; and they were so far from being nice, that they could make this broken meat serve another time, and be thankful. This was to manifest and magnify the miracle, and to show that the provision Christ makes for those who are his is not bare and scanty, but rich and plenteous; *bread enough, and to spare* (Luke xv. 17), an overflowing fulness. Elisha's multiplying the loaves was somewhat like this, but far short of it; and then it was said, *They shall eat and leave,* 2 Kings iv. 43.

It is the same divine power, though exerted in an ordinary way, which multiplies *the seed sown in the ground* every year, and makes *the earth yield her increase;* so that what was brought out by handfuls, is brought home in sheaves. *This is the Lord's doing;* it is *by Christ* that all natural things consist, and *by the word of his power* that they are upheld.

22 And straightway Jesus constrained his disciples to get into a
ship, and to go before him unto the
other side, while he sent the multitudes away. 23 And when he had
sent the multitudes away, he went up
into a mountain apart to pray: and
when the evening was come, he was
there alone. 24 But the ship was
now in the midst of the sea, tossed
with waves; for the wind was contrary. 25 And in the fourth watch
of the night Jesus went unto them,
walking on the sea. 26 And when
the disciples saw him walking on the
sea, they were troubled, saying, It is
a spirit; and they cried out for fear.
27 But straightway Jesus spake unto
them, saying, Be of good cheer; it is
I; be not afraid. 28 And Peter answered him and said, Lord, if it be
thou, bid me come unto thee on the
water. 29 And he said, Come. And
when Peter was come down out of
the ship, he walked on the water, to
go to Jesus. 30 But when he saw
the wind boisterous, he was afraid;
and beginning to sink, he cried, saying, Lord, save me. 31 And immediately Jesus stretched forth *his* hand,
and caught him, and said unto him,
O thou of little faith, wherefore didst
thou doubt? 32 And when they were
come into the ship, the wind ceased.
33 Then they that were in the ship
came and worshipped him, saying, Of
a truth thou art the Son of God.

We have here the story of another miracle which Christ wrought for the relief of his friends and followers, his *walking upon the water to his disciples.* In the foregoing miracle he acted as the Lord of nature, improving its powers for the supply of those who were in want; in this, he acted as the Lord of nature, correcting and controlling its powers for the succour of those who were in danger and distress. Observe,

I. Christ's dismissing of his disciples and *the multitude,* after he had fed them miraculously. He *constrained his disciples to get into a ship, and to go before him unto the other side, v.* 22. St. John gives a particular reason for the hasty breaking up of this assembly, because the people were so affected with the miracle of the loaves, that they were about *to take him by force, and make him a King* (John vi. 15); to avoid which, he immediately scattered the people, sent away the disciples, lest they should join with them, and he himself withdrew, John vi. 15.

When they had *sat down to eat and drink, they* did not *rise up to play,* but each went to his business.

1. Christ sent the people away. It intimates somewhat of solemnity in the dismissing of them; he sent them away with a blessing, with some parting words of caution, counsel, and comfort, which might abide with them.

2. He *constrained the disciples to go into a ship* first, for till they were gone the people would not stir. The disciples were loth to go, and would not have gone, if he had not *constrained* them. They were loth to go to sea without him. *If thy presence go not with us, carry us not up hence.* Exod. xxxiii. 15. They were loth to leave him alone, without any attendance, or any ship to wait for him; but they did it in pure obedience.

II. Christ's retirement hereupon (*v.* 23); *He went up into a mountain apart to pray.* Observe here,

1. That he was alone; *he went apart into a solitary place, and was there all alone.* Though he had so much work to do with others, yet he chose sometimes to be alone, to set us an example. Those are not Christ's followers that do not care for being alone; that cannot enjoy themselves in solitude, when they have none else to converse with, none else to enjoy, but God and their own hearts.

2. That he was alone at prayer; that was his business in this solitude, to pray. Though Christ, as God, was Lord of all, and was prayed to, yet Christ, as Man, had *the form of a servant*, of a beggar, and prayed. Christ has herein set before us an example of secret prayer, and the performance of it secretly, according to the rule he gave, *ch.* vi. 6. Perhaps in this mountain there was some private oratory or convenience, provided for such an occasion; it was usual among the Jews to have such. Observe, When the disciples went to sea, their Master went to prayer; when Peter was to be *sifted as wheat, Christ prayed for him.*

3. That he was long alone; *there he was when the evening was come,* and, for aught that appears, there he was till towards morning, *the fourth watch of the night. The night* came on, and it was a stormy, tempestuous night, yet he continued *instant in prayer.* Note, It is good, at least sometimes, upon special occasions, and when we find our hearts enlarged, to continue long in secret prayer, and to take full scope in *pouring out our hearts before the Lord.* We must not *restrain prayer*, Job xv. 4.

III. The condition that the poor disciples were in at this time: *Their ship was now in the midst of the sea, tossed with waves, v.* 24. We may observe here,

1. That they were got into the midst of the sea when the storm rose. We may have fair weather at the beginning of our voyage, and yet meet with storms before we arrive at the port we are bound for. Therefore *let not him that girdeth on the harness boast as he that puts it off,* but after a long calm expect some storm or other.

2. The disciples were now where Christ sent them, and yet met with this storm. Had they been flying from their Master, and their work, as Jonah was, when he was arrested by the storm, it had been a dreadful one indeed; but they had a special command from their Master to go to sea at this time, and were going about their work. Note, It is no new thing for Christ's disciples to meet with storms in the way of their duty, and to be sent to sea then when their Master foresees a storm; but let them not take it unkindly; what he does they *know not now, but they shall know hereafter,* that Christ designs hereby to manifest himself with the more wonderful grace to them and for them.

3. It was a great discouragement to them now that they had not Christ with them, as they had formerly when they were in a storm; though he was then asleep indeed, yet he was soon awaked (*ch.* viii. 24), but now he was not with them at all. Thus Christ used his disciples first to less difficulties, and then to greater, and so trains them up by degrees to live *by faith, and not by sense.*

4. Though *the wind was contrary,* and they were tossed with waves, yet being ordered by their Master *to the other side,* they did not tack about and come back again, but made the best of their way forward. Note, Though troubles and difficulties may disturb us in our duty, they must not drive us from it; but through the midst of them we must press forwards.

IV. Christ's approach to them in this condition (*v.* 25); and in this we have an instance,

1. Of his goodness, that he went unto them, as one that took cognizance of their case, and was under a concern about them, as a father about his children. Note, The extremity of the church and people of God is Christ's opportunity to visit them and appear for them: but he came not till *the fourth watch,* toward three o'clock in the morning, for then the fourth watch began. It was *in the morning-watch* that the Lord appeared for Israel in the Red sea (Exod. xiv. 24), so was this. *He that keepeth Israel neither slumbers nor sleeps,* but, when there is occasion, *walks in darkness* for their succour; helps, and that right early.

2. Of his power, that he *went unto them, walking on the sea.* This is a great instance of Christ's sovereign dominion over all the creatures; they are all under his feet, and at his command; they forget their natures, and change the qualities that we call essential. We need not enquire how this was done, whether by condensing the surface of the water (when God pleases, *the depths are congealed in the heart of the sea,* Exod. xv. 8), or by suspending the gravitation of his body, which was transfigured as he pleased; it is sufficient that it proves his divine power, for it is God's prerogative to *tread upon the waves of the sea* (Job ix. 8), as it is *to ride*

upon the wings of the wind. He *that made the waters of the sea a wall for the redeemed of the Lord* (Isa. li. 10), here makes them a walk for the Redeemer himself, who, as Lord of all, appears with one foot on the sea and the other on dry land, Rev. x. 2. The same power that made iron to swim (2 Kings vi. 6), did this. *What ailed thee, O thou sea?* Ps. cxiv. 5. *It was at the presence of the Lord. Thy way, O God, is in the sea,* Ps. lxxvii. 19. Note, Christ can take what way he pleases to save his people.

V. Here is an account of what passed between Christ and his distressed friends upon his approach.

1. Between him and all the disciples. We are here told,

(1.) How their fears were raised (*v.* 26); *When they saw him walking on the sea, they were troubled, saying, It is a spirit; φάντασμα ἐστι—It is an apparition;* so it might much better be rendered. It seems, the existence and appearance of spirits were generally believed in by all except the Sadducees, whose doctrine Christ had warned his disciples against; yet, doubtless, many supposed apparitions have been merely the creatures of men's own fear and fancy. These disciples said, *It is a spirit;* when they should have said, *It is the Lord;* it can be no other. Note, [1.] Even the appearances and approaches of deliverance are sometimes the occasions of trouble and perplexity to God's people, who are sometimes most frightened when they are least hurt; nay, when they are most favoured, as the Virgin Mary, Luke i. 29; Exod. iii. 6, 7. The comforts of *the Spirit of adoption* are introduced by the terrors of *the spirit of bondage,* Rom. viii. 15. [2.] The appearance of a spirit, or the fancy of it, cannot but be frightful, and strike a terror upon us, because of the distance of the world of spirits from us, the just quarrel good spirits have with us, and the inveterate enmity evil spirits have against us: see Job iv. 14, 15. The more acquaintance we have with God, the Father of spirits, and the more careful we are to keep ourselves in his love, the better able we shall be to deal with those fears. [3.] The perplexing, disquieting fears of good people, arise from their mistakes and misapprehensions concerning Christ, his person, offices, and undertaking; the more clearly and fully we know his name, with the more assurance we shall trust in him, Ps. ix. 10. [4.] A little thing frightens us in a storm. When *without are fightings,* no marvel that *within are fears.* Perhaps the disciples fancied it was some evil spirit that raised the storm. Note, Most of our danger from outward troubles arises from the occasion they give for inward trouble.

(2.) How these fears were silenced, *v.* 27. He straightway relieved them, by showing them their mistake; when they were wrestling *with the waves,* he delayed his succour for some time; but he hastened his succour against their fright, as much the more dangerous; he straightway laid that storm with his word, *Be of good cheer; it is I; be not afraid.*

[1.] He rectified their mistake, by making himself known to them, as Joseph to his brethren; *It is I.* He does not name himself, as he did to Paul, *I am Jesus;* for Paul as yet knew him not: but to these disciples it was enough to say, *It is I;* they *knew his voice, as his sheep* (John x. 4), as Mary Magdalene, John xx. 16. They need not ask, *Who art thou, Lord? Art thou for us or for our adversaries?* They could say with the spouse, *It is the voice of my beloved,* Cant. ii. 8; v. 2. True believers know it by a good token. It was enough to make them easy, to understand who it was they saw. Note, A right knowledge opens the door to true comfort, especially the knowledge of Christ.

[2.] He encouraged them against their fright; *It is I,* and therefore, *First, Be of good cheer; θαρσεῖτε—"Be courageous;* pluck up your spirits, and be courageous." If Christ's disciples be not cheerful in a storm, it is their own fault, he would have them so. *Secondly, Be not afraid;* 1. "Be not afraid of me, now that you know it is I; surely you will not fear, for you know I mean you no hurt." Note, Christ will not be a terror to those to whom he manifests himself; when they come to understand him aright, the terror will be over. 2. "*Be not afraid* of the tempest, of the winds and waves, though noisy and very threatening; fear them not, while I am so near you. I am he that concerns himself for you, and will not stand by and see you perish." Note, Nothing needs be a terror to those that have Christ near them, and know he is theirs; no, not death itself.

2. Between him and Peter, *v.* 28—31, where observe,

(1.) Peter's courage, and Christ's countenancing that.

[1.] It was very bold in Peter, that he would venture to come to Christ *upon the water* (*v.* 28); *Lord, if it be thou, bid me come unto thee.* Courage was Peter's master grace; and that made him so forward above the rest to express his love to Christ, though others perhaps loved him as well.

First, It is an instance of Peter's affection to Christ, that he desired to come to him. When he sees Christ, whom, doubtless, during the storm, he had many a time wished for, he is impatient to be with him. He does not say, *Bid me walk on the waters,* as desiring it for the miracle sake; but, *Bid me come to thee,* as desiring it for Christ's sake; "Let me come to thee, no matter how." Note, True love will break through fire and water, if duly called to it, to come to Christ. Christ was coming to them, to succour and deliver them. *Lord,* said Peter, *bid me come to thee.* Note, When Christ is coming towards us in a way of mercy, we must go forth to meet him in a way of duty; and herein we must be willing and bold to venture with him and venture for him. Those that would have benefit by Christ as a Saviour, must thus by faith come to him. Christ had been now, for some time, absent, and hereby it appears why he absented himself; it was to endear himself so much the more to his disciples at his return, to make it highly seasonable and doubly acceptable. Note, When, for a small moment, Christ has forsaken his people, his returns are welcome, and most affectionately embraced; when gracious souls, after long seeking, find their Beloved at last, they *hold him, and will not let him go,* Cant. iii. 4.

Secondly, It is an instance of Peter's caution and due observance of the will of Christ, that he would not come without a warrant. Not, "If it be thou, I will come;" but *If it be thou, bid me come.* Note, The boldest spirits must wait for a call to hazardous enterprizes, and we must not rashly and presumptuously thrust ourselves upon them. Our will to services and sufferings is interpreted, not willingness, but wilfulness, if it have not a regard to the will of Christ, and be not regulated by his call and command. Such extraordinary warrants as this to Peter we are not now to expect, but must have recourse to the general rules of the word, in the application of which to particular cases, with the help of providential hints, *wisdom is profitable to direct.*

Thirdly, It is an instance of Peter's faith and resolution, that he ventured upon the water when Christ bid him. To quit the safety of the ship, and throw himself into the jaws of death, to despise the threatening waves he so lately dreaded, argued a very strong dependence upon the power and word of Christ. What difficulty or danger could stand before such a faith and such a zeal?

[2.] It was very kind and condescending in Christ, that he was pleased to own him in it, *v.* 29. He might have condemned the proposal as foolish and rash; nay, and as proud and assuming; "Shall Peter pretend to do as his Master does?" But Christ knew that it came from a sincere and zealous affection to him, and graciously accepted of it. Note, Christ is well pleased with the expressions of his people's love, though mixed with manifold infirmities, and makes the best of them.

First, He bid him *come.* When the Pharisees asked a sign, they had not only a repulse, but a reproof, for it, because they did it with a design to tempt Christ; when Peter asked a sign, he had it, because he did it with a resolution to trust Christ. The gospel call is, "*Come, come,* to Christ; venture all in his hand, and commit the keeping of your souls to him; venture through a stormy sea, a troublesome world, to Jesus Christ."

Secondly, He bore him out when he did come; *Peter walked upon the water.* The communion of true believers with Christ is represented by their being *quickened with him, raised up with him, made to sit with him* (Eph. ii. 5, 6), and being *crucified with him,* Gal. ii. 20. Now, methinks, it is represented in this story by their *walking with him on the water.* Through the strength of Christ we are borne up above the world, enabled to trample upon it, kept from sinking into it, from being overwhelmed by it, obtain a victory over it (1 John v. 4), by faith in Christ's victory (John xvi. 33), and with him are *crucified to it,* Gal. vi. 14. See blessed Paul walking upon the water with Jesus, and *more than a conqueror through him,* and treading upon all the threatening waves, as *not able to separate him from the love of Christ,* Rom. viii. 35, &c. Thus the sea of the world is become like a sea of glass, congealed so as to bear; and they that have gotten the victory, stand upon it and sing, Rev. xv. 2, 3.

He walked upon the water, not for diversion or ostentation, but to go to Jesus; and in that he was thus wonderfully borne up. Note, When *our souls are following hard after God,* then it is that his *right hand upholds us;* it was David's experience, Ps. lxiii. 8. Special supports are promised, and are to be expected, only in spiritual pursuits. When God bears his Israel upon eagles' wings, it is *to bring them to himself* (Exod. xix. 4); nor can we ever come to Jesus, unless we be upheld by his power; it is in his own strength that we wrestle with him, that we reach after him, that we *press forward toward the mark,* being *kept by the power of God,* which power we must depend upon, as Peter when he *walked upon the water:* and there is no danger of sinking while *underneath are the everlasting arms.*

(2.) Here is Peter's cowardice, and Christ's reproving him and succouring him. Christ bid him come, not only that he might walk upon the water, and so know Christ's power, but that he might sink, and so know his own weakness; for as he would encourage his faith, so he would check his confidence, and make him ashamed of it. Observe then,

[1.] Peter's great fear (*v.* 30); *He was afraid.* The strongest faith and the greatest courage have a mixture of fear. Those that can say, *Lord, I believe;* must say, *Lord, help my unbelief.* Nothing but *perfect love* will quite *cast out fear.* Good men often fail in those graces which they are most eminent for, and which they have then in exercise; to show that they have not yet attained. Peter was very stout at first, but afterwards his heart failed him. The lengthening out of a trial discovers the weakness of faith.

Here is, *First,* The cause of this fear; *He saw the wind boisterous.* While Peter kept his eye fixed upon Christ, and upon his word and power, he *walked upon the water* well enough; but when he took notice withal of the danger he was in, and observed how *the floods lift up their waves*, then he feared. Note, Looking at difficulties with an eye of sense more than at precepts and promises with an eye of faith is at the bottom of all our inordinate fears, both as to public and personal concerns. Abraham was strong in faith, because he *considered not his own body* (Rom. iv. 19); he minded not the discouraging improbabilities which the promise lay under, but kept his eye on God's power; and so, *against hope, believed in hope, v.* 18. Peter, *when he saw the wind boisterous*, should have remembered what he had seen (*ch.* viii. 27), when the winds and the sea obeyed Christ; but *therefore* we *fear continually every day*, because *we forget the Lord our Maker*, Isa. li. 12, 13.

Secondly, The effect of this fear; *He began to sink.* While faith kept up, he kept above water: but when faith staggered, *he began to sink.* Note, The sinking of our spirits is owing to the weakness of our faith; we are upheld (but it is as we are saved) *through faith* (1 Pet. i. 5); and therefore, when our *souls are cast down and disquieted*, the sovereign remedy is, *to hope in God*, Ps. xliii. 5. It is probable that Peter, being bred a fisherman, could swim very well (John xxi. 7); and perhaps he trusted in part to that, when he cast himself into the sea; if he could not walk, he could swim; but Christ let him begin to sink, to show him that it *was Christ's right hand and his holy arm*, not any skill of his own, that was his security. It was Christ's great mercy to him, that, upon the failing of his faith, he did not leave him to sink outright, to sink to the *bottom as a stone* (Exod. xv. 5), but gave him time to cry, *Lord, save me.* Such is the care of Christ concerning true believers; though weak, they do but begin to sink! A man is never sunk, never undone, till he is in hell. Peter *walked* as he *believed;* to him, as to others, the rule held good, *According to your faith be it unto you.*

Thirdly, The remedy he had recourse to in this distress, the old, tried, approved remedy, and that was prayer: he cried, *Lord, save me.* Observe, 1. The manner of his praying; it is fervent and importunate; *He cried.* Note, When faith is weak, prayer should be strong. Our Lord Jesus has taught us in the day of our fear to *offer up strong cries*, Heb. v. 7. Sense of danger will make us cry, sense of duty and dependence on God should make us cry to him. 2. The matter of his prayer was pertinent and to the purpose; *He cried, Lord, save me.* Christ is the great Saviour, he came to save; those that would be saved, must not only *come* to him, but *cry* to him for salvation; but we are never brought to this, till we find ourselves sinking; sense of need will drive us to him.

[2.] Christ's great favour to Peter, in this fright. Though there was a mixture of presumption with Peter's faith in his first adventure, and of unbelief with his faith in his after-fainting, yet Christ did not cast him off; for,

First, He saved him; *he answered him with the saving strength of his right hand* (Ps. xx. 6), for immediately *he stretched forth his hand, and caught him.* Note, Christ's time to save is, when we sink (Ps. xviii. 4—7): he helps at a dead lift. Christ's hand is still stretched out to all believers, to keep them from sinking. Those whom he hath once apprehended as his own, and hath snatched as *brands out of the burning*, he will catch out of the water too. Though he may seem to have left his hold, he doth but seem to do so, for they shall *never perish, neither shall any man pluck them out of his hand*, John x. 28. Never fear, he will hold his own. Our deliverance from our own fears, which else would overwhelm us, is owing to the hand of his power and grace, Ps. xxxiv. 4

Secondly, He rebuked him; for as many as he loves and saves, he reproves and chides; *O thou of little faith, wherefore didst thou doubt?* Note, 1. Faith may be true, and yet weak; at first, like a grain of mustard-seed. Peter had faith enough to bring him upon the water, yet, because not enough to carry him through, Christ tells him he had but *little.* 2. Our discouraging doubts and fears are all owing to the weakness of our faith: *therefore* we *doubt*, because we are but *of little faith.* It is the business of faith to resolve doubts, the doubts of sense, in a stormy day, so as even then to keep the head above water. Could we but believe more, we should doubt less. 3. The weakness of our faith, and the prevalence of our doubts, are very displeasing to our Lord Jesus. It is true, he doth not cast off weak believers, but it is as true, that he is not pleased with weak faith, no, not in those that are nearest to him. *Wherefore didst thou doubt?* What reason was there for it? Note, Our doubts and fears would soon vanish before a strict enquiry into the cause of them; for, all things considered, there is no good reason why Christ's disciples should be of a doubtful mind, no, not in a stormy day, because he is ready to them, *a very present Help.*

VI. The *ceasing of the storm, v.* 32. When Christ was come into the ship, they were presently at the shore. Christ *walked upon the water* till he came to the ship, and then went into that, when he could as easily have walked to the shore; but when ordinary means are to be had, miracles are not to be expected. Though Christ needs not instruments for the doing of his work, he is pleased to use them. Observe, when Christ came into the ship, Peter came in with him. Companions with Christ in his patience, shall be companions in his kingdom, Rev. i. 9. Those that walk with him shall reign with him; those that are exposed, and that suffer with him, shall triumph with him.

When they were come into the ship, immediately the storm ceased, for it had done its work, its trying work. He that has *gathered the winds into his fists, and bound the waters in a garment*, is the same that *ascended and descended;* and *his word* even *stormy winds fulfil*, Ps. cxlviii. 8. When Christ comes into a soul, he makes winds and storms to cease there, and commands peace. Welcome Christ, and *the noise of her waves will soon be quelled.* The way to be still is, to know that he is God, that he is the *Lord with us.*

VII. The adoration paid to Christ hereupon (*v.* 33); *They that were in the ship came and worshipped him, and said, Of a truth, thou art the Son of God.* Two good uses they made of this distress, and this deliverance.

1. It was a confirmation of their faith in Christ, and abundantly convinced them that *the fulness of the Godhead dwelt in him;* for none but the world's Creator could multiply the loaves, none but its Governor could tread upon the waters of the sea; they therefore yield to the evidence, and make confession of their faith; *Thou truly art the Son of God.* They knew before that he was the Son of God, but now they know it better. Faith, after a conflict with unbelief, is sometimes the more active, and gets to greater degrees of strength by being exercised. Now they *know it of a truth.* Note, It is good for us to know more and more of *the certainty of those things wherein we have been instructed*, Luke i. 4. Faith *then* grows, when it arrives at a full assurance, when it sees clearly, and saith, *Of a truth.*

2. They took occasion from it to *give him the glory due unto his name.* They not only owned that great truth, but were suitably affected by it; *they worshipped Christ.* Note, When Christ manifests his glory for us, we ought to return it to him (Ps. l. 15); *I will deliver thee, and thou shalt glorify me.* Their worship and adoration of Christ were thus expressed, *Of a truth thou art the Son of God.* Note, The matter of our creed may and must be made the matter of our praise. Faith is the proper principle of worship, and worship the genuine product of faith. *He that comes to God must believe;* and he that *believes* in God, will *come*, Heb. xi. 6.

34 And when they were gone over, they came into the land of Gennesaret.
35 And when the men of that place had knowledge of him, they sent out into all that country round about, and brought unto him all that were diseased;
36 And besought him that they might only touch the hem of his garment: and as many as touched were made perfectly whole.

We have here an account of miracles by wholesale, which Christ wrought on the other side of the water, in the land of Gennesaret. Whithersoever Christ went, he was doing good. Gennesaret was a tract of land that lay between Bethsaida and Capernaum, and either gave the name to, or took the name from, this sea, which is called (Luke v. 1) *The lake of Gennesaret;* it signifies the valley of branches. Observe here,

I. The forwardness and faith of *the men of that place.* These were more noble than the Gergesenes, their neighbours, who were borderers upon the same lake. Those *besought Christ to depart* from them, they had no occasion for him; these besought him to help them, they had need of him. Christ reckons it the greatest honour we can do him, to make use of him. Now here we are told,

1. How *the men of that place* were brought to Christ; they *had knowledge of him.* It is probable that his miraculous passage over the sea, which they that were in the ship would industriously spread the report of, might help to make way for his entertainment in those parts; and perhaps it was one thing Christ intended in it, for he has great reaches in what he does. This they had knowledge of, and of the other miracles Christ had wrought, and therefore they flocked to him. Note, They that know Christ's name, will make their application to him: if Christ were better known, he would not be neglected as he is; he is trusted as far as he is known.

They *had knowledge of him*, that is, of his being among them, and that he would be but awhile among them. Note, The discerning of the day of our opportunities is a good step toward the improvement of it. This was *the condemnation of the world*, that Christ *was in the world, and the world knew him not* (John i. 10); Jerusalem knew him not (Luke xix. 42), but there were some who, when he was among them, *had knowledge of him.* It is better to know that there *is* a prophet among us than that there *has been* one, Ezek. ii. 5.

2. How they brought others to Christ, by giving notice to their neighbours of Christ's being come into those parts; *They sent out into all that country.* Note, those that have got the knowledge of Christ themselves, should do all they can to bring others acquainted with him too. We must not eat these spiritual morsels alone; there is in Christ enough for us all, so that there is nothing got by monopolizing. When we have opportunities of getting good to our souls, we should bring as many as we can to share with us. More than we think of would close with opportunities, if they were but called upon and invited to them. *They sent into their own country*, because it was their own, and they desired the welfare of it. Note, We can no better testify our love to our country than by promoting and propagating the knowledge of Christ in it. Neighbourhood is an advantage of doing good which must be improved. Those that are near to us, we should contrive to do something for, at least by our example, to bring them near to Christ.

3. What their business was with Christ;

not only, perhaps not chiefly, if at all, to be taught, but to have their sick healed; *They brought unto him all that were diseased.* If love to Christ and his doctrine will not bring them to him, yet self-love would. Did we but rightly seek our own things, the things of our own peace and welfare, we should seek the things of Christ. We should do him honour, and please him, by deriving grace and righteousness from him. Note, Christ is the proper Person to bring the diseased to; whither should they go but to the Physician, to *the Sun of Righteousness, that hath healing under his wings?*

4. How they made their application to him; *They besought him that they might only touch the hem of his garment, v.* 36. They applied themselves to him, (1.) With great importunity; they besought him. Well may we beseech to be healed, when God by his ministers beseecheth us that we will be healed. Note, The greatest favours and blessings are to be obtained from Christ by entreaty; *Ask, and it shall be given.* (2.) With great humility; they came to him as those that were sensible of their distance, humbly beseeching him to help them; and their desiring to touch the hem of his garment, intimates that they thought themselves unworthy that he should take any particular notice of them, that he should so much as speak to their case, much less touch them for their cure; but they will look upon it as a great favour, if he will give them leave to *touch the hem of his garment.* The eastern nations show respect to their princes, by kissing their sleeve or skirt. (3.) With great assurance of the all-sufficiency of his power, not doubting but that they should be healed, even by touching the hem of his garment; that they should receive abundant communications from him by the smallest token or symbol of communion with him. They did not expect the formality of striking his hand over the place or persons diseased, as Naaman did (2 Kings v. 11); but they were sure that there was in him such an overflowing fulness of healing virtue, that *they* could not fail of a cure, who were but admitted near him. It was in this country and neighbourhood that the woman with the bloody issue was cured by *touching the hem of his garment,* and was commended for her faith (*ch.* ix. 20—22); and thence, probably, they took occasion to ask this. Note, The experiences of others in their attendance upon Christ may be of use both to direct and to encourage us in our attendance on him. It is good using those means and methods which others before us have sped well in the use of.

II. The fruit and success of this their application to Christ. It was not in vain that these seed of Jacob sought him, for as *many as touched, were made perfectly whole.* Note, 1. Christ's cures are perfect cures. Those that he heals, he heals perfectly. He doth not do his work by halves. Though spiritual healing be not perfected at first, yet, doubtless, *he that has begun the good work will perform it,* Phil. i. 6. 2. There is abundance of healing virtue in Christ for all that apply themselves to him, be they ever so many. That *precious ointment* which was poured on his head, *ran down to the skirts of his garment,* Ps. cxxxiii. 2. The least of Christ's institutions, like the hem of his garment, is replenished with the overflowing fulness of his grace, and he is able to *save to the uttermost.* 3. The healing virtue that is in Christ, is put forth for the benefit of those that by a true and lively faith touch him. Christ is in heaven, but his word is nigh us, and he himself in that word. When we mix faith with the word, apply it to ourselves, depend upon it, and submit to its influences and commands, then we touch the hem of Christ's garment. It is but thus touching, and we are made whole. On such easy terms are spiritual cures offered by him, that he may truly be said to heal *freely;* so that if our souls die of their wounds, it is not owing to our Physician, it is not for want of skill or will in him; but it is purely owing to ourselves. He *could* have healed us, he *would* have healed us, but we *would not be healed;* so that our blood will lie upon our own heads.

CHAP. XV.

In this chapter, we have our Lord Jesus, as the great Prophet teaching, as the great Physician healing, and as the great Shepherd of the sheep feeding; as the Father of spirits instructing them: as the Conqueror of Satan dispossessing him; and as concerned for the bodies of his people, providing for them. Here is, I. Christ's discourse with the scribes and Pharisees about human traditions and injunctions, ver. 1—9. II. His discourse with the multitude, and with his disciples, concerning the things that defile a man, ver. 10—20. III. His casting of the devil out of the woman of Canaan's daughter, ver. 21—28. IV. His healing of all that were brought to him, ver. 29—31. V. His feeding of four thousand men, with seven loaves and a few little fishes, ver. 32—39.

THEN came to Jesus scribes and
Pharisees, which were of Jerusalem, saying, 2 Why do thy disciples transgress the tradition of the
elders? for they wash not their hands
when they eat bread. 3 But he answered and said unto them, Why do
ye also transgress the commandment
of God by your tradition? 4 For God
commanded, saying, Honour thy father and mother: and, He that curseth
father or mother, let him die the death,
5 But ye say, Whosoever shall say
to *his* father or *his* mother, *It is* a
gift, by whatsoever thou mightest be
profited by me, 6 And honour not
his father or his mother, *he shall be*
free. Thus have ye made the commandment of God of none effect by
your tradition. 7 *Ye* hypocrites!
well did Esaias prophecy of you,
saying, 8 This people draweth nigh

unto me with their mouth, and honoureth me with *their* lips; but their heart is far from me. 9 But in vain they do worship me, teaching *for* doctrines the commandments of men.

Evil manners, we say, beget good laws. The intemperate heat of the Jewish teachers for the support of their hierarchy, occasioned many excellent discourses of our Saviour's for the settling of the truth, as here.

I. Here is the cavil of the scribes and Pharisees at Christ's disciples, for *eating with unwashen hands.* The scribes and Pharisees were the great men of the Jewish church, men whose gain was godliness, great enemies to the gospel of Christ, but colouring their opposition with a pretence of zeal for the law of Moses, when really nothing was intended but the support of their own tyranny over the consciences of men. They were men of learning and men of business. These scribes and Pharisees here introduced were of Jerusalem, the holy city, the head city, whither *the tribes went up,* and where *were set the thrones of judgment;* they should therefore have been better than others, but they were worse. Note, External privileges, if they be not duly improved, commonly swell men up the more with pride and malignity. Jerusalem, which should have been a pure spring, was now become a poisoned sink. *How is the faithful city become a harlot!*

Now if these great men be the accusers, pray what is the accusation? What articles do they exhibit against the disciples of Christ? Why, truly, the thing laid to their charge, is, nonconformity to the canons of their church (*v.* 2); *Why do thy disciples transgress the tradition of the elders?* This charge they make good in a particular instance; *They wash not their hands when they eat bread.* A very high misdemeanor! It was a sign that Christ's disciples conducted themselves inoffensively, when this was the worst thing they could charge them with.

Observe, 1. What was the *tradition of the elders*—That people should often wash their hands, and always at meat. This they placed a great deal of religion in, supposing that the meat they touched with unwashen hands would be defiling to them. The Pharisees practised this themselves, and with a great deal of strictness imposed it upon others, not under civil penalties, but as matter of conscience, and making it a sin against God if they did not do it. Rabbi Joses determined, "that to eat with unwashen hands is as great a sin as adultery." And Rabbi Akiba being kept a close prisoner, having water sent him both to wash his hands with, and to drink with his meat, the greatest part being accidentally shed, he washed his hands with the remainder, though he left himself none to drink, saying he would rather die than transgress the tradition of the elders. Nay, they would not eat meat with one that did not wash before meat. This mighty zeal in so small a matter would appear very strange, if we did not still see it incident to church-oppressors, not only to be fond of practising their own inventions, but to be furious in pressing their own impositions.

2. What was the transgression of this tradition or injunction by the disciples; it seems, they did not wash their hands when they ate bread, which was the more offensive to the Pharisees, because they were men who in other things were strict and conscientious. The custom was innocent enough, and had a decency in its civil use. We read of the water for purifying at the marriage where Christ was present (John ii. 6), though Christ turned it into wine, and so put an end to that use of it. But when it came to be practised and imposed as a religious rite and ceremony, and such a stress laid upon it, the disciples, though weak in knowledge, yet were so well taught as not to comply with it, or observe it; no not when the scribes and Pharisees had their eye upon them. They had already learned St. Paul's lesson, *All things are lawful for me;* no doubt, it is lawful to wash before meat; but I will not be brought under the power of any; especially not of those who *said to their souls, Bow down, that we may go over.* 1 Cor. vi. 12.

3. What was the complaint of the scribes and Pharisees against them. They quarrel with Christ about it, supposing that he allowed them in it, as he did, no doubt, by his own example; "*Why do thy disciples transgress* the canons of the church? And why dost thou suffer them to do it?" It was well that the complaint was made to Christ; for the disciples themselves, though they knew their duty in this case, were perhaps not so well able to give a reason for what they did as were to be wished.

II. Here is Christ's answer to this cavil, and his justification of the disciples in that which was charged upon them as a transgression. Note, While we stand fast in the liberty wherewith Christ has made us free, he will be sure to bear us out in it.

Two ways Christ replies upon them;

1. By way of recrimination, *v.* 3—6. They were spying motes in the eyes of his disciples, but Christ shows them a beam in their own. But that which he charges upon them is not barely a recrimination, for it will be no vindication of ourselves to condemn our reprovers; but it is such a censure of their tradition (and the authority of that was what they built their charge upon) as makes not only a non-compliance lawful, but an opposition a duty. That human authority must never be submitted to, which sets up in competition with divine authority.

(1.) The charge in general is, *You transgress the commandment of God by your tradition.* They called it the *tradition of the elders,* laying stress upon the antiquity of the usage, and the authority of them that imposed it, as the church of Rome does upon fathers and councils; but Christ calls it *their* tradition. Note, Illegal impositions will be laid to the charge of those who support and maintain them, and keep them up, as well as of those who first invented and enjoined them; Mic. vi. 16. *You transgress the commandment of God.* Note, Those who are most zealous of their own impositions, are commonly most careless of God's commands; which is a good reason why Christ's disciples should stand upon their guard against such impositions, lest, though at first they seem only to infringe the liberty of Christians, they come at length to confront the authority of Christ. Though the Pharisees, in this command of washing before meat, did not entrench upon any command of God; yet, because in other instances they did, he justifies his disciples' disobedience to this.

(2.) The proof of this charge is in a particular instance, that of their transgressing the fifth commandment.

[1.] Let us see what the command of God is (*v.* 4), what the precept, and what the sanction of the law is.

The precept is, *Honour thy father and thy mother;* this is enjoined by the common Father of mankind, and by paying respect to them whom Providence has made the instruments of our being, we give honour to him who is the Author of it, who has thereby, as to us, put some of his image upon them. The whole of children's duty to their parents is included in this of honouring them, which is the spring and foundation of all the rest, *If I be a father, where is my honour?* Our Saviour here supposes it to mean the duty of children's maintaining their parents, and ministering to their wants, if there be occasion, and being every way serviceable to their comfort. *Honour widows,* that is, maintain them, 1 Tim. v. 3.

The sanction of this law in the fifth commandment, is, a promise, *that thy days may be long;* but our Saviour waives that, lest any should thence infer it to be only a thing commendable and profitable, and insists upon the penalty annexed to the breach of this commandment in another scripture, which denotes the duty to be highly and indispensably necessary; *He that curseth father or mother, let him die the death:* this law we have, Exod. xxi. 17. The sin of cursing parents is here opposed to the duty of honouring them. Those who speak ill of their parents, or wish ill to them, who mock at them, or give them taunting and opprobrious language, break this law. If to call a brother *Raca* be so penal, what is it to call a father so? By our Saviour's application of this law, it appears, that denying service or relief to parents is included in cursing them. Though the language be respectful enough, and nothing abusive in it, yet what will that avail, if the deeds be not agreeable? it is but like him that said, *I go, Sir, and went not, ch.* xxi. 30.

[2.] Let us see what was the contradiction which the tradition of the elders gave to this command. It was not direct and downright, but implicit; their casuists gave them such rules as furnished them with an easy evasion from the obligation of this command, *v.* 5, 6. You hear what God saith, *but ye say* so and so. Note, That which men say, even great men, and learned men, and men in authority, must be examined by that which God saith; and if it be found either contrary or inconsistent, it may and must be rejected, Acts iv. 19. Observe,

First, What their tradition was; That a man could not in any case bestow his worldly estate better than to give it to the priests, and devote it to the service of the temple: and that when any thing was so devoted, it was not only unlawful to alienate it, but all other obligations, though ever so just and sacred, were thereby superseded, and a man was thereby discharged from them. And this proceeded partly from their ceremoniousness, and the superstitious regard they had to the temple, and partly from their covetousness, and love of money: for what was given to the temple they were gainers by. The former was, in pretence, the latter was, in truth, at the bottom of this tradition.

Secondly, How they allowed the application of this to the case of children. When their parents' necessities called for their assistance, they pleaded, that all they could spare from themselves and their children, they had devoted to the treasury of the temple; *It is a gift, by whatsoever thou mightest be profited by me,* and therefore their parents must expect nothing from them; suggesting withal, that the spiritual advantage of what was so devoted, would redound to the parents, who must live upon that air. This, they taught, was a good and valid plea, and many undutiful, unnatural children made use of it, and they justified them in it, and said, *He shall be free;* so we supply the sense. Some go further, and supply it thus, "*He doth well, his days shall be long in the land,* and he shall be looked upon as having duly observed the fifth commandment." The pretence of religion would make his refusal to provide for his parents not only passable but plausible. But the absurdity and impiety of this tradition were very evident: for revealed religion was intended to improve, not to overthrow, natural religion; one of the fundamental laws of which is this of honouring our parents; and had they known what that meant, *I will have justice, and mercy, and not sacrifice,* they had not thus made the most arbitrary rituals destructive of the most necessary morals. This was *making the command of God of no effect.* Note, Whatever leads to, or countenances, disobedience, does, in effect, make void the command; and they that take upon them to dispense with God's law, do, in Christ's account, repeal and disannul it. To break the law is bad, but to *teach men so,* as the scribes and Pharisees did, is much worse, *ch.* v. 19. To what purpose is the command given, if it be not obeyed? The rule is, as to us, of none effect, if we be not ruled by it. *It is time for thee, Lord, to work;* high time for the great Reformer, the great Refiner, to appear; for they have *made void thy law* (Ps. cxix. 126); not only sinned *against* the commandment, but, as far as in them lay, sinned *away* the commandment. But, thanks be to God, in spite of them and all their traditions, the command stands in full force, power, and virtue.

2. The other part of Christ's answer is by way of reprehension; and that which he here charges them with, is hypocrisy; *Ye hypocrites, v.* 7. Note, It is the prerogative of him who searcheth the heart, and knows what is in man, to pronounce who are hypocrites. The eye of man can perceive open profaneness, but it is only the eye of Christ that can discern hypocrisy, Luke xvi. 15. And as it is a sin which his eye discovers, so it is a sin which of all others his soul hates.

Now Christ fetches his reproof from Isa. xxix. 13. *Well did Esaias prophesy of you.* Isaiah spoke it of the men of that generation to which he prophesied, yet Christ applies it to these scribes and Pharisees. Note, The reproofs of sin and sinners, which we find in scripture, were designed to reach the like persons and practices to the end of the world; for they are not of private interpretation, 2 Pet. i. 20. The sinners of the latter days are prophesied of, 1 Tim. iv. 1; 2 Tim. iii. 1; 2 Pet. iii. 3. Threatenings directed against others, belong to us, if we be guilty of the same sins. Isaiah prophesied not of them only, but of all other hypocrites, against whom that word of his is still levelled, and stands in force. The prophecies of scripture are every day in the fulfilling.

This prophecy exactly deciphers a hypocritical nation, Isa. ix. 17; x. 6. Here is,

(1.) The description of hypocrites, in two things.

[1.] In their own performances of religious worship, *v.* 8, when they *draw nigh to God with their mouth, and honour him with their lips, their heart is far from him.* Observe,

First, How far a hypocrite goes; he draws nigh to God, and honours him; he is, in profession, a worshipper of God. The *Pharisee went up to the temple, to pray;* he does not stand at that distance which those are at, who *live without God in the world,* but has a name among the people near unto him. They honour him; that is, they take on them to honour God, they join with those that do so. Some honour God has even from the services of hypocrites, as they help to keep up the face and form of godliness in the world, whence God fetches honour to himself, though they intend it not to him. When God's enemies submit themselves but feignedly, when *they lie unto him,* so the word is (Ps. lxvi. 3), it redounds to his honour, and he *gets himself a name.*

Secondly, Where he rests and takes up; this is done but with his mouth and with his lips. It is piety but from the teeth outwards; he shows much love, and that is all, there is in his heart no true love; *they make their voices to be heard* (Isa. lviii. 4), mention the name of the Lord, Isa. xlviii 1. Hypocrites are those that only make a lip-labour of religion and religious worship. In word and tongue, the worst hypocrites may do as well as the best saints, and speak as fair with Jacob's voice.

Thirdly, What that is wherein he comes short; it is in the main matter; *Their heart is far from me,* habitually alienated and estranged (Eph. iv. 18), actually wandering and dwelling upon something else; no serious thoughts of God, no pious affections toward him, no concern about the soul and eternity, no thoughts agreeable to the service. God is *near in their mouth, but far from their reins,* Jer. xii. 2; Ezek. xxxiii. 31. The heart, with the *fool's eyes, is in the ends of the earth.* It is a silly dove that is without heart, and so it is a *silly duty,* Hos. vii. 11. A hypocrite says one thing, but thinks another. The great thing that God looks at and requires is the heart (Prov. xxiii. 26); if that be far from him, it is not a reasonable service and therefore not an acceptable one; it is the sacrifice of fools, Eccl. v. 1.

[2.] In their prescriptions to others. This is an instance of their hypocrisy, that *they teach for doctrines the commandments of men.* The Jews then, as the papists since, paid the same respect to oral tradition that they did to the word of God, receiving it *pari pietatis affectu ac reverentiâ—with the same pious affection and reverence.* Conc. Trident. *Sess.* 4. *Decr.* 1. When men's inventions are tacked to God's institutions, and imposed accordingly, this is hypocrisy, a mere human religion. The commandments of men are properly conversant about the things of men, but God will have his own work done by his own rules, and accepts not that which he did not himself appoint. That only comes *to* him, that comes *from* him.

(2.) The doom of hypocrites; it is put in a little compass; *In vain do they worship me.* Their worship does not attain the end for which it was appointed; it will neither please God, nor profit themselves. If it be not *in spirit,* it is not *in truth,* and so it is all nothing. That man who only *seems* to be religious, but is not so, his *religion is vain* (James i. 26); and if our religion be a vain oblation, a vain religion, *how great is that vanity!* How sad is it to live in an age of prayers and sermons, and sabbaths and sacraments, *in vain,* to *beat the air in* all these; it is so, if the heart be not with God in them. Lip-labour is lost labour, Isa. i. 11. Hypocrites sow the wind and reap the whirlwind; they trust in vanity, and vanity will be their recompence.

Thus Christ justified his disciples in their disobedience to the traditions of the elders; and this the scribes and Pharisees got by their cavilling. We read not of any reply they made; if they were not satisfied, yet they were silenced, and could not resist the power wherewith Christ spake.

10 And he called the multitude,
and said unto them, Hear, and understand: 11 Not that which goeth
into the mouth defileth a man; but
that which cometh out of the mouth,
this defileth a man. 12 Then came
his disciples, and said unto him,
Knowest thou that the Pharisees were
offended, after they heard this saying?
13 But he answered and said, Every
plant, which my heavenly Father hath
not planted, shall be rooted up. 14
Let them alone: they be blind leaders
of the blind. And if the blind lead
the blind, both shall fall into the ditch.
15 Then answered Peter and said
unto him, Declare unto us this parable. 16 And Jesus said, Are ye also
yet without understanding? 17 Do
not ye yet understand, that whatsoever entereth in at the mouth goeth
into the belly, and is cast out into the
draught? 18 But those things which
proceed out of the mouth come forth
from the heart; and they defile the
man. 19 For out of the heart proceed evil thoughts, murders, adulteries, fornications, thefts, false witness, blasphemies: 20 These are *the
things* which defile a man: but to
eat with unwashen hands defileth not
a man.

Christ having proved that the disciples, in eating with unwashen hands, were not to be blamed, as transgressing the traditions and injunctions of the elders, comes here to show that they were not to be blamed, as having done any thing that was in itself evil. In the former part of his discourse he overturned the authority of the law, and in this the reason of it. Observe,

I. The solemn introduction to this discourse (*v.* 10); *He called the multitude.* They were withdrawn while Christ discoursed with the scribes and Pharisees; probably those proud men ordered them to withdraw, as not willing to talk with Christ in their hearing; Christ must favour them at their pleasure with a discourse in private. But Christ had a regard to the multitude; he soon despatched the scribes and Pharisees, and then turned them off, and invited the mob, the multitude, to be his hearers: thus the poor are evangelized; and the foolish things of the world, and things that are despised, hath Christ chosen. The humble Jesus embraced those whom the proud Pharisees looked upon with disdain, and to them he designed it for a mortification. He turns from them as wilful and unteachable, and turns to the multitude, who, though weak, were humble, and willing to be taught. To them he said, *Hear and understand.* Note, What we hear from the mouth of Christ, we must give all diligence to understand. Not only scholars, but even the multitude, the ordinary people, must apply their minds to understand the words of Christ. He *therefore* calls upon them to understand, because the lesson he was now about to teach them, was contrary to the notions which they had sucked in with their milk from their teachers; and overturned many of the customs and usages which they were wedded to, and laid stress upon. Note, There is need of a great attention of mind and clearness of understanding to free men from those corrupt principles and practices which they have been bred up in and long accustomed to; for in that case the understanding is commonly bribed and biassed by prejudice.

II. The truth itself laid down (*v.* 11), in two propositions, which were opposite to the vulgar errors of that time, and were therefore surprising.

1. *Not that which goes into the mouth defileth the man.* It is not the kind or quality of our food, nor the condition of our hands, that affects the soul with any moral pollution or defilement. *The kingdom of God is not meat and drink,* Rom. xiv. 17. That defiles the man, by which guilt is contracted before God, and the man is rendered offensive to him, and disfitted for communion with him; now what we eat, if we do not eat unreasonably and immoderately, does not this; for *to the pure all things are pure,* Tit. i. 15. The Pharisees carried the ceremonial pollutions, by eating such and such meats, much further than the law intended, and burthened it with additions of their own, which our Saviour witnesses against; intending hereby to pave the way to a repeal of the ceremonial law in that matter. He was now beginning to teach his followers to *call nothing common or unclean;* and if Peter, when he was bid to *kill and eat,* had remembered this word, he would not have said, *Not so, Lord,* Acts x. 13—15, 28.

2. *But that which comes out of the mouth, this defiles a man.* We are polluted, not by the meat we eat with unwashen hands, but by the words we speak from an unsanctified heart; [illegible] it is that *the mouth causeth the*

flesh to sin, Eccl. v. 6. Christ, in a former discourse, had laid a great stress upon our *words* (*ch.* xii. 36, 37); and that was intended for reproof and warning to those that cavilled at him; this here is intended for reproof and warning to those that cavilled at the disciples, and censured them. It is not the disciples that defile themselves with what they eat, but the Pharisees that defile themselves with what they speak spitefully and censoriously of them. Note, Those who charge guilt upon others for transgressing the commandments of men, many times bring greater guilt upon themselves, by transgressing the law of God against rash judging. Those most defile themselves, who are most forward to censure the defilements of others.

III. The offence that was taken at this truth and the account brought to Christ of that offence (*v.* 12); "*The disciples said unto him, Knowest thou that the Pharisees were offended,* and didst thou not foresee that they would be so, *at this saying,* and would think the worse of thee and of thy doctrine for it, and be the more enraged at thee?"

1. It was not strange that the Pharisees should be offended at this plain truth, for they were men made up of error and enmity, mistake and malice. Sore eyes cannot bear clear light; and nothing is more provoking to proud imposers than the undeceiving of those whom they have first blindfolded, and then enslaved. It should seem that the Pharisees, who were strict observers of the traditions, were more offended than the scribes, who were the teachers of them; and perhaps they were as much galled with the latter part of Christ's doctrine, which taught a strictness in the government of our tongue, as with the former part, which taught an indifference about washing our hands; great contenders for the formalities of religion, being commonly as great contemners of the substantials of it.

2. The disciples thought it strange that their Master should say that which he knew would give so much offence; he did not use to do so: surely, think they, if he had considered how provoking it would be, he would not have said it. But he knew what he said, and to whom he said it, and what would be the effect of it; and would teach us, that though in indifferent things we must be tender of giving offence, yet we must not, for fear of that, evade any truth or duty. Truth must be owned, and duty done; and if any be offended, it is his own fault; it is scandal, not given, but taken.

Perhaps the disciples themselves stumbled at the word Christ said, which they thought bold, and scarcely reconcileable with the difference that was put by the law of God between *clean* and *unclean* meats; and therefore objected this to Christ, that they might themselves be better informed. They seem likewise to have a concern upon them for the Pharisees, though they had quarrelled with them; which teaches us to forgive, and seek the good, especially the spiritual good, of our enemies, persecutors, and slanderers. They would not have the Pharisees go away displeased at any thing Christ had said; and therefore, though they do not desire him to retract it, they hope he will explain, correct, and modify it. Weak hearers are sometimes more solicitous than they should be not to have wicked hearers offended. But if we please men with the concealment of truth, and the indulgence of their errors and corruptions, we are not the servants of Christ

IV. The doom passed upon the Pharisees and their corrupt traditions; which comes in as a reason why Christ cared not though he offended them, and therefore why the disciples should not care; because they were a generation of men that hated to be reformed, and were marked out for destruction. Two things Christ here foretels concerning them.

1. The rooting out of them and their traditions (*v.* 13); *Every plant which my heavenly Father hath not planted, shall be rooted up.* Not only the corrupt opinions and superstitious practices of the Pharisees, but their sect, and way, and constitution, were plants not of God's planting. The rules of their profession were no institutions of his, but owed their origin to pride and formality. The people of the Jews were planted *a noble vine;* but now that they are become the degenerate plant of a strange vine, God disowned them, as not of his planting. Note, (1.) In the visible church, it is no strange thing to find plants that our heavenly Father has not planted. It is implied, that whatever is good in the church is of God's planting, Isa. xli. 19. But let the husbandman be ever so careful, his ground will cast forth weeds of itself, more or less, and there is an enemy busy sowing tares. What is corrupt, though of God's permitting, is not of his planting; he sows nothing but *good seed in his field.* Let us not therefore be deceived, as if all must needs be right that we find in the church, and all those persons and things our Father's plants that we find in our Father's garden. *Believe not every spirit, but try the spirits;* see Jer. xix. 5; xxiii. 31, 32. (2.) Those that are of the spirit of the Pharisees, proud, formal, and imposing, what figure soever they make, and of what denomination soever they be, God will not own them as of his planting. *By their fruit you shall know them.* (3.) Those plants that are not of God's planting, shall not be of his protecting, but shall undoubtedly be rooted up. What is not of God shall not stand, Acts v. 38. What things are unscriptural, will wither and die of themselves, or be justly exploded by the churches; however in the great day these tares that offend will be bundled for the fire. What is become of the Pharisees and their traditions? They are long since

abandoned; but the gospel of truth is great, and will remain. It cannot be rooted up.

2. The ruin of them; and their followers, who had their persons and principles in admiration, *v.* 14. Where,

(1.) Christ bids his disciples *let them alone.* "Have no converse with them or concern for them; neither court their favour, nor dread their displeasure; care not though they be offended, they will take their course, and let them take the issue of it. They are wedded to their own fancies, and will have every thing their own way; let them alone. Seek not to please a generation of men that please not God (1 Thess. ii. 15), and will be pleased with nothing less than an absolute dominion over your consciences. They are *joined to idols,* as Ephraim (Hos. iv. 17), the idols of their own fancy; *let them alone, let them be filthy still,*" Rev. xxii. 11. The case of those sinners is sad indeed, whom Christ orders his ministers to let alone.

(2.) He gives them two reasons for it. *Let them alone;* for,

[1.] They are proud and ignorant; two bad qualities that often meet, and render a man incurable in his folly, Prov. xxvi. 12. *They are blind leaders of the blind.* They are grossly ignorant in the things of God, and strangers to the spiritual nature of the divine law; and yet so proud, that they think they see better and further than any, and therefore undertake to be leaders of others, to show others the way to heaven, when they themselves know not one step of the way; and, accordingly, they prescribe to all, and proscribe those who will not follow them. Though they were blind, if they had owned it, and come to Christ for eye-salve, they might have seen, but they disdained the intimation of such a thing (John ix. 40); *Are we blind also?* They were confident that *they themselves were guides of the blind* (Rom. ii. 19, 20), were appointed to be so, and fit to be so; that every thing they said was an oracle and a law; "Therefore *let them alone,* their case is desperate; do not meddle with them; you may soon provoke them, but never convince them." How miserable was the case of the Jewish Church now when their leaders were blind, so self-conceitedly foolish, as to be peremptory in their conduct, while the people were so sottishly foolish as to follow them with an implicit faith and obedience, and *willingly walk after the commandment,* Hos. v. 11. Now the prophecy was fulfilled, Isa. xxix. 10, 14. And it is easy to imagine *what will be in the end hereof,* when *the prophets prophesy falsely, and the priests bear rule by their means, and the people love to have it so,* Jer. v. 31.

[2.] They are posting to destruction, and will shortly be plunged into it; *Both shall fall into the ditch.* This must needs be the end of it, if both be so blind, and yet both so bold, venturing forward, and yet not aware of danger. Both will be involved in the general desolation coming upon the Jews, and both drowned in eternal destruction and perdition. The blind leaders and the blind followers will perish together. We find (Rev. xxii. 15), that hell is the portion of those that *make a lie,* and of those that *love* it when it is made. *The deceived and the deceiver* are obnoxious to the judgment of God, Job xii. 16. Note, *First,* Those that by their cunning craftiness draw others to sin and error, shall not, with all their craft and cunning, escape ruin themselves. If *both fall together into the ditch,* the blind leaders will fall undermost, and have the worst of it; see Jer. xiv. 15, 16. *The prophets shall be consumed first,* and then the *people to whom they prophesy,* Jer. xx. 6; xxviii. 15, 16. *Secondly,* The sin and ruin of the deceivers will be no security to those that are deceived by them. Though the leaders of this people *cause them to err,* yet they that are *led of them are destroyed* (Isa. ix. 16), because they shut their eyes against the light which would have rectified their mistake. Seneca, complaining of most people's being led by common opinion and practice *(Unusquisque mavult credere quam judicare—Things are taken upon trust, and never examined),* concludes, *Inde ista tanta coacervatio aliorum super alios ruentium—Hence crowds fall upon crowds, in vast confusion.* De Vitâ Beatâ. The falling of both together will aggravate the fall of both; for they that have thus mutually increased each other's sin, will mutually exasperate each other's ruin.

V. Instruction given to the disciples concerning the truth Christ had laid down, *v.* 10. Though Christ rejects the wilfully ignorant who care not to be taught, he can have compassion on the ignorant who are willing to learn, Heb. v. 2. If the Pharisees, who made void the law, be offended, let them be offended: but this *great peace have they who love the law,* that *nothing shall offend them,* but, some way or other, the offence shall be taken off, Ps. cxix. 165.

Here is, 1. Their desire to be better instructed in this matter (*v.* 15); in this request as in many others, Peter was their speaker; the rest, it is probable, putting him on to speak, or intimating their concurrence; *Declare unto us this parable.* What Christ said was plain, but, because it agreed not with the notions they had imbibed, though they would not contradict it, yet they call it a parable, and cannot understand it. Note, (1.) Weak understandings are apt to turn plain truths into parables, and to seek for a knot in a bulrush. The disciples often did so, as John xvi. 17. Even the grasshopper is a burthen to a weak stomach, and babes in understanding cannot bear and digest strong meat. (2.) Where a weak head doubts concerning any word of Christ, an upright heart and a willing mind will seek for instruction. The Pharisees were offended, but kept it to themselves; hating to be *re*formed, they hated to be *in*formed; but the disciples, though offended, sought for satisfaction, imputing the offence, not to the doctrine delivered, but to the shallowness of their own capacity.

2. The reproof Christ gave them for their weakness and ignorance (*v.* 16); *Are ye also yet without understanding?* As many as Christ loves and teaches, he thus rebukes. Note, They are very ignorant indeed, who understand not that moral pollutions are abundantly worse and more dangerous than ceremonial ones. Two things aggravate their dulness and darkness.

(1.) That they were the disciples of Christ; "Are *ye* also without understanding? Ye whom I have admitted into so great a degree of familiarity with me, are ye so unskilful in the word of righteousness?" Note, The ignorance and mistakes of those that profess religion, and enjoy the privileges of church-membership, are justly a grief to the Lord Jesus. "No wonder that the Pharisees understand not this doctrine, who know nothing of the Messiah's kingdom: but ye that have heard of it, and embraced it yourselves, and preached it to others, are ye also such strangers to the spirit and genius of it?"

(2.) That they had been a great while Christ's scholars; "Are ye *yet* so, after ye have been so long under my teaching?" Had they been but of yesterday in Christ's school, it had been another matter, but to have been for so many months Christ's constant hearers, and yet to be without understanding, was a great reproach to them. Note, Christ expects from us some proportion of knowledge, and grace, and wisdom, according to the time and means we have had. See John xiv. 9; Heb. v. 12; 2 Tim. iii. 7, 8.

3. The explication Christ gave them of this doctrine of pollutions. Though he chid them for their dulness, he did not cast them off, but pitied them, and taught them, as Luke xxiv. 25—27. He here shows us,

(1.) What little danger we are in of pollution from that which *entereth in at the mouth, v.* 17. An inordinate appetite, intemperance, and excess in eating, come out of the heart, and are defiling; but meat in itself is not so, as the Pharisees supposed. What there is of dregs and defilement in our meat, nature (or rather the God of nature) has provided a way to clear us of it; *it goes in at the belly, and is cast out into the draught,* and nothing remains to us but pure nourishment. So *fearfully* and *wonderfully are we made* and preserved, and our souls held in life. The expulsive faculty is as necessary in the body as any other, for the discharge of that which is superfluous, or noxious; so happily is nature enabled to help itself, and shift for its own good: by this means nothing defiles; if we eat with unwashen hands, and so any thing unclean mix with our food, nature will separate it, and cast it out, and it will be no defilement to us. It may be a piece of cleanliness, but it is no point of conscience, to wash before meat; and we go upon a great mistake if we place religion in it. It is not the practice itself, but the opinion it is built upon, that Christ condemns, as if meat commended us to God (1 Cor. viii. 8); whereas Christianity stands not in such observances.

(2.) What great danger we are in of pollution from that which *proceeds out of the mouth* (*v.* 18), out of the abundance of the heart: compare *ch.* xii. 34. There is no defilement in the products of God's bounty; the defilement arises from the products of our corruption. Now here we have,

[1.] The corrupt fountain of that which proceeds out of the mouth; it comes from the heart; that is the spring and source of all sin, Jer. viii. 7. It is the heart that is so desperately wicked (Jer. xvii. 9); for there is no sin in word or deed, which was not first in the heart. There is the root of bitterness, which *bears gall and wormwood.* It is the inward part of a sinner, that is very wickedness, Ps. v. 9. All evil speakings come forth from the heart, and are defiling; from the corrupt heart comes the corrupt communication.

[2.] Some of the corrupt streams which flow from this fountain, specified; though they do not all *come out of the mouth,* yet they all come out of the man, and are the fruits of that wickedness which is in the heart, and is wrought there, Ps. lviii. 2.

First, Evil thoughts, sins against all the commandments. Therefore David puts vain thoughts in opposition to the whole law, Ps. cxix. 113. These are the first-born of the corrupt nature, the beginning of its strength, and do most resemble it. These, as the son and heir, *abide in the house, and lodge within us.* There is a great deal of sin that begins and ends in the heart, and goes no further. Carnal fancies and imaginations are evil thoughts, wickedness in the contrivance (Διαλογισμοὶ πονηροί), wicked plots, purposes, and devices of mischief to others, Mic. ii. 1.

Secondly, Murders, sins against the sixth commandment; these come from a malice in the heart against our brother's life, or a contempt of it. Hence he *that hates his brother,* is said to be a *murderer;* he is so at God's bar, 1 John iii. 15. *War is in the heart,* Ps. lv. 21; James iv. 1.

Thirdly, Adulteries and *fornications,* sins against the seventh commandment; these come from the wanton, unclean, carnal heart; and the lust that reigns there, is conceived there, and brings forth these sins, James i. 15. There is adultery in the heart first, and then in the act, *ch.* v. 28.

Fourthly, Thefts, sins against the eighth commandment; cheats, wrongs, rapines, and all injurious contracts; the fountain of all these is in the heart, that is it that is *exercised in these covetous practices* (2 Pet. ii. 14), that is set upon riches, Ps. lxii. 10. *Achan coveted, and then took*, Joshua vii. 20, 21.

Fifthly, False witness, against the ninth commandment; this comes from a complication of falsehood and covetousness, or falsehood and malice in the heart. If truth, holiness, and love, which God *requires in the inward parts*, reigned as they ought, there would be no false witness bearing, Ps. lxiv. 6; Jer. ix. 8.

Sixthly, Blasphemies, speaking evil of God, against the third commandment; speaking evil of our neighbour, against the ninth commandment; these come from a contempt and disesteem of both in the heart; thence *the blasphemy against the Holy Ghost* proceeds (*ch*. xii. 31, 32); these are the overflowing of the gall within.

Now *these are the things which defile a man*, *v*. 20. Note, Sin is defiling to the soul, renders it unlovely and abominable in the eyes of the pure and holy God; unfit for communion with him, and for the enjoyment of him in the new Jerusalem, into which nothing shall enter that defileth or worketh iniquity. The mind and conscience are defiled by sin, and that makes every thing else so, Tit. i. 15. This defilement by sin was signified by the ceremonial pollutions which the Jewish doctors added to, but understood not. See Heb. ix. 13, 14; 1 John i. 7.

These therefore are the things we must carefully avoid, and all approaches toward them, and not lay stress upon the washing of the hands. Christ doth not yet repeal the law of the distinction of meats (that was not done till Acts x.), but the tradition of the elders, which was tacked to that law; and therefore he concludes, *To eat with unwashen hands* (which was the matter now in question), *this defileth not a man*. If he wash, he is not the better before God; if he wash not, he is not the worse.

21 Then Jesus went thence, and
departed into the coasts of Tyre and
Sidon. 22 And, behold, a woman of
Canaan came out of the same coasts,
and cried unto him, saying, Have
mercy on me, O Lord, *thou* son of David;
my daughter is grievously vexed
with a devil. 23 But he answered
her not a word. And his disciples
came and besought him, saying, Send
her away; for she crieth after us. 24
But he answered and said, I am not
sent but unto the lost sheep of the
house of Israel. 25 Then came she
and worshipped him, saying, Lord,
help me. 26 But he answered and
said, It is not meet to take the children's
bread, and to cast *it* to dogs.
27 And she said, Truth, Lord: yet
the dogs eat of the crumbs which fall
from their masters' table. 28 Then
Jesus answered and said unto her, O
woman, great *is* thy faith: be it unto
thee even as thou wilt. And her
daughter was made whole from that
very hour.

We have here that famous story of Christ's *casting the devil out of the woman of Canaan's daughter*; it has something in it singular and very surprising, and which looks favourably upon the poor Gentiles, and is an earnest of that mercy which Christ had in store for them. Here is a gleam of that *light* which was *to lighten the Gentiles*, Luke ii. 32. Christ *came to his own, and his own received him not*; but many of them quarrelled with him, and were offended in him; and observe what follows, *v*. 21.

I. *Jesus went thence*. Note, Justly is the light taken from those that either play by it, or rebel against it. When Christ and his disciples could not be quiet among them, he left them, and so left an example to his own rule (*ch*. x. 14), *Shake off the dust of your feet*. Though Christ endure long, he will not always *endure, the contradiction of sinners against himself*. He had said (*v*. 14), *Let them alone*, and he did so. Note, Wilful prejudices against the gospel, and cavils at it, often provoke Christ to withdraw, and *to remove the candlestick out of its place*. Acts xiii. 46, 51.

II. When he went thence, he *departed into the coasts of Tyre and Sidon*; not to those cities (they were excluded from any share in *Christ's mighty works*, *ch*. xi. 21, 22), but into that part of the land of Israel which lay that way: thither he went, as Elias *to Sarepta, a city of Sidon* (Luke iv. 26); thither he went to look after this poor woman, whom he had mercy in reserve for. While he went about doing good, he was never out of his way. The dark corners of the country, which lay most remote, shall have their share of his benign influences; and as now *the ends of the land*, so afterward *the ends of the earth, shall see his salvation*, Isa. xlix. 6. Here it was that this miracle was wrought, in the story of which we may observe,

1. The address of the woman of Canaan to Christ, *v*. 22. She was a Gentile, *a stranger to the commonwealth of Israel*; probably one of the posterity of those accursed nations that were devoted by that word, *Cursed be Canaan*. Note, The doom of political bodies doth not always reach every individual member of them. God will have his remnant out of all nations, chosen vessels in all coasts, even the most unlikely: she came out of the same coasts. If Christ had not now made a visit to these coasts, though the mercy was worth travelling far for, it is probable that she had never come to him. Note, It is often an excitement to a dormant faith and zeal, to have

opportunities of acquaintance with Christ brought to our doors, to have the word nigh us.

Her address was very importunate, she *cried* to Christ, as one in earnest; cried, as being at some distance from him, not daring to approach too near, being a Canaanite, lest she should give offence. In her address,

(1.) She relates her misery; *My daughter is grievously vexed with a devil, κακῶς δαιμονίζεται—She is ill-bewitched,* or *possessed.* There were degrees of that misery, and this was the worst sort. It was a common case at that time, and very calamitous. Note, The vexations of children are the trouble of parents, and nothing should be more so than their being under the power of Satan. Tender parents very sensibly feel the miseries of those that are pieces of themselves. "Though vexed with the devil, yet she is my daughter still." The greatest afflictions of our relations do not dissolve our obligations to them, and therefore ought not to alienate our affections from them. It was the distress and trouble of her family, that now brought her to Christ; she came to him, not for teaching, but for healing; yet, because she came in faith, he did not reject her. Though it is need that drives us to Christ, yet we shall not therefore be driven from him. It was the affliction of her daughter, that gave her this occasion of applying to Christ. It is good to make the afflictions of others our own, in sense and sympathy, that we may make them our own, in improvement and advantage.

(2.) She requests for mercy; *Have mercy on me, O Lord, thou Son of David.* In calling him *Lord, the Son of David,* she owns him to be the Messiah: that is the great thing which faith should fasten upon, and fetch comfort from. From the Lord we may expect acts of power: he can command deliverances; from the Son of David we may expect all the mercy and grace which were foretold concerning him. Though a Gentile, she owns *the promise made to the fathers* of the Jews, and the honour of the house of David. The Gentiles must receive Christianity, not only as an improvement of natural religion, but as the perfection of the Jewish religion, with an eye to the Old Testament.

Her petition is, *Have mercy on me.* She does not limit Christ to this or that particular instance of mercy, but mercy, mercy is the thing she begs: she pleads not merit, but depends upon mercy; *Have mercy upon me.* Mercies to the children are mercies to the parents; favours to ours are favours to us, and are so to be accounted. Note, It is the duty of parents to pray for their children, and to be earnest in prayer for them, especially for their souls; "I have a son, a daughter, grievously vexed with a proud will, an unclean devil, a malicious devil, led captive by him at his will; *Lord, help them.*" This is a case more deplorable than that of a bodily possession. Bring them to Christ by faith and prayer, who alone is able to heal them. Parents should look upon it as a great mercy to themselves, to have Satan's power broken in the souls of their children.

2. The discouragement she met with in this address; in all the story of Christ's ministry we do not meet with the like. He was wont to countenance and encourage all that came to him, and either *to answer before they called,* or *to hear while they were yet speaking;* but here was one otherwise treated: and what could be the reason of it? (1.) Some think that Christ showed himself backward to gratify this poor woman, because he would not give offence to the Jews, by being as free and as forward in his favour to the Gentiles as to them. He had bid his disciples *not go into the way of the Gentiles* (*ch.* x. 5), and therefore would not himself seem so inclinable to them as to others, but rather more shy. Or rather, (2.) Christ treated her thus, to try her; he knows what is in the heart, knew the strength of her faith, and how well able she was, by his grace, to break through such discouragements; he *therefore* met her with them, *that the trial of her faith might be found unto praise, and honour, and glory,* 1 Pet. i. 6, 7. This was like God's tempting Abraham (Gen. xxii. 1), like the angel's wrestling with Jacob, only to put him upon wrestling, Gen. xxxii. 24. Many of the methods of Christ's providence, and especially of his grace, in dealing with his people, which are dark and perplexing, may be explained with the key of this story, which is for that end left upon record, to teach us that there may be love in Christ's heart while there are frowns in his face, and to encourage us, therefore, *though he slay us, yet to trust in him.*

Observe the particular discouragements given her:

[1.] When she cried after him, *he answered her not a word, v.* 23. His ear was wont to be always open and attentive to the cries of poor supplicants, and his lips, which dropped as the honeycomb, always ready to give an answer of peace; but to this poor woman he turned a deaf ear, and she could get neither an alms nor an answer. It was a wonder that she did not fly off in a fret, and say, "Is this he that is so famed for clemency and tenderness? Have so many been heard and answered by him, as they talk, and must I be the first rejected suitor? Why so distant to me, if it be true that he hath stooped to so many?" But Christ knew what he did, and *therefore* did not answer, that she might be the more earnest in prayer. He heard her, and was pleased with her, and *strengthened her with strength in her soul* to prosecute her request (Ps. cxxxviii. 3; Job xxiii. 6), though he did not immediately give her the answer she expected. By seeming to draw away the desired mercy from her, he drew her on to be so much the more importunate for it. Note, Every accepted prayer is not immediately an answered prayer. Sometimes God seems not to regard his people's prayers, like a man asleep or astonished (Ps. xliv. 23; Jer. xiv. 9; Ps. xxii. 1, 2); nay, to be angry at them (Ps. lxxx. 4; Lam. iii. 8, 44); but it is to prove, and so to *improve,* their faith, and to make his after-appearances for them the more glorious to himself, and the more welcome to them; for *the vision, at the end, shall speak, and shall not lie,* Heb. ii. 3. See Job xxxv. 14.

[2.] When the disciples spake a good word for her, he gave a reason why he refused her, which was yet more discouraging.

First, It was some little relief, that the disciples interposed on her behalf; they said, *Send her away, for she crieth after us.* It is desirable to have an interest in the prayers of good people, and we should be desirous of it. But the disciples, though wishing she might have what she came for, yet therein consulted rather their own ease than the poor woman's satisfaction; "*Send her away* with a cure, *for she cries,* and is in good earnest; *she cries after us,* and is troublesome to us, and shames us." Continued importunity may be uneasy to men, even to good men; but Christ loves to be cried after.

Secondly, Christ's answer to the disciples quite dashed her expectations; "*I am not sent, but to the lost sheep of the house of Israel;* you know I am not, she is none of them, and would you have me go beyond my commission?" Importunity seldom conquers the settled reason of a wise man; and those refusals are most silencing, which are so backed. He doth not only not answer her, but he argues against her, and stops her mouth with a reason. It is true, she is a *lost sheep,* and hath as much need of his care as any, but she is not *of the house of Israel,* to whom he was first sent (Acts iii. 26), and therefore not immediately interested in it, and entitled to it. Christ was *a Minister of the circumcision* (Rom. xv. 8); and though he was intended for *a Light to the Gentiles,* yet *the fulness of time* for that *was* not now *come, the veil was* not yet *rent,* nor *the partition-wall taken down.* Christ's personal ministry was *to be the glory of his people Israel;* "If I am sent to them, what have I to do with those that are none of them." Note, It is a great trial, when we have occasion given us to question whether we be of those to whom Christ was sent. But, blessed be God, no room is left for that doubt; the distinction between Jew and Gentile is taken away; we are sure that he *gave his life a ransom for many,* and if for many, why not for me?

Thirdly, When she continued her importunity, he insisted upon the unfitness of the thing, and gave her not only a repulse, but a seeming reproach too (*v.* 26); *It is not meet to take the children's bread and to cast it to dogs.* This seems to cut her off from all hope, and might have driven her to despair, if she had not had a very strong faith indeed. Gospel grace and miraculous cures (the appurtenances of it), were children's bread; they belonged to them *to whom pertained the adoption* (Rom. ix. 4), and lay not upon the same level with that rain from heaven, and those fruitful seasons, which God gave to the nations whom he suffered *to walk in their own ways* (Acts xiv. 16, 17); no, these were peculiar favours, appropriated to the peculiar people, the garden enclosed. Christ preached to the Samaritans (John iv. 41), but we read not of any cures he wrought among them; *that salvation was of the Jews:* it is not meet therefore to alienate these. The Gentiles were looked upon by the Jews with great contempt, were called and counted *dogs;* and, in comparison with the house of Israel, who were so dignified and privileged, Christ here seems to allow it, and therefore thinks it not meet that the Gentiles should share in the favours bestowed on the Jews. But see how the tables are turned; after the bringing of the Gentiles into the church, the Jewish zealots for the law are called *dogs,* Phil. iii. 2.

Now this Christ urgeth against this woman of Canaan; "How can she expect to eat of the children's bread, who is not of the family?" Note, 1. Those whom Christ intends most signally to honour, he first humbles and lays low in a sense of their own meanness and unworthiness. We must first see ourselves to be as dogs, *less than the least of all God's mercies,* before we are fit to be dignified and privileged with them. 2. Christ delights to exercise great faith with great trials, and sometimes reserves the sharpest for the last, that, *being tried, we may come forth like gold.* This general rule is applicable to other cases for direction, though here used only for trial. Special ordinances and church-privileges are children's bread, and must not be prostituted to the grossly ignorant and profane. Common charity must be extended to all, but spiritual dignities are appropriated to the household of faith; and therefore promiscuous admission to them, without distinction, wastes the children's bread, and is the *giving of that which is holy to the dogs, ch.* vii. 6. *Procul hinc, procul inde, profani—Off, ye profane.*

3. Here is the strength of her faith and resolution, in breaking through all these discouragements. Many a one, thus tried, would either have sunk into silence, or broken out into passion. "Here is cold comfort," might she have said, "for a poor distressed creature; as good for me to have staid at home, as come hither to be taunted at and abused at this rate; not only to have a piteous case slighted, but to be called a *dog!*" A proud, unhumbled heart would not have borne it. The reputation of the house of Israel was not now so great in the world, but that this slight put upon the Gentiles was capable of being retorted, had the poor woman been so minded. It might

have occasioned a reflection upon Christ, and might have been a blemish upon his reputation, as well as a shock to the good opinion she had entertained of him; for we are apt to judge of persons as we ourselves find them; and think that they are what they are to us. "*Is this the Son of David?*" (might she have said): "Is this he that has such a reputation for kindness, tenderness, and compassion? I am sure I have no reason to give him that character, for I was never treated so roughly in my life; he might have done as much for me as for others; or, if not, he needed not to have *set me with the dogs of his flock.* I am not a dog, I am a woman, and an honest woman, and a woman in misery; and I am sure it is not meet to call me *dog.*" No, here is not a word of this. Note, A humble, believing soul, that truly loves Christ, takes every thing in good part that he saith and doeth, and puts the best construction upon it.

She breaks through all these discouragements,

(1.) With a holy earnestness of desire in prosecuting her petition. This appeared upon the former repulse (*v.* 25); *Then came she, and worshipped him, saying, Lord, help me.* [1.] She continued to pray. What Christ said, silenced the disciples; you hear no more of them; they took the answer, but the woman did not. Note, The more sensibly we feel the burthen, the more resolutely we should pray for the removal of it. *And it is the will of God that we should continue instant in prayer, should always pray, and not faint.* [2.] She improved in prayer. Instead of blaming Christ, or charging him with unkindness, she seems rather to suspect herself, and lay the fault upon herself. She fears lest, in her first address, she had not been humble and reverent enough, and therefore now *she came, and worshipped him,* and paid him more respect than she had done; or she fears that she had not been earnest enough, and therefore now she cries, *Lord, help me.* Note, When the answers of prayer are deferred, God is thereby teaching us to pray more, and pray better. It is then time to enquire wherein we have come short in our former prayers, that what has been amiss may be amended for the future. Disappointments in the success of prayer, must be excitements to the duty of prayer. Christ, in his agony, *prayed more earnestly.* [3.] She waives the question, whether she was of those to whom Christ was sent or no; she will not argue that with him, though perhaps she might have claimed some kindred to the house of Israel; but, "Whether an Israelite or no, I come to the Son of David for mercy, and *I will not let him go, except he bless me.*" Many weak Christians perplex themselves with questions and doubts about their election, whether they are of the house of Israel or no; such had better mind their errand to God, and continue instant in prayer for mercy and grace; throw themselves by faith at the feet of Christ, and say, *If I perish, I will perish here;* and then that matter will by degrees clear itself. If we cannot *reason* down our unbelief, let us *pray* it down. A fervent, affectionate *Lord, help me,* will help us over many of the discouragements which are sometimes ready to bear us down and overwhelm us. [4.] Her prayer is very short, but comprehensive and fervent, *Lord, help me.* Take this, *First,* As lamenting her case; "If the Messiah be sent only to the house of Israel, the *Lord help me,* what will become of me and mine." Note, It is not in vain for broken hearts to bemoan themselves; God looks upon them then, Jer. xxxi. 18. Or, *Secondly,* As begging grace to assist her in this hour of temptation. She found it hard to keep up her faith when it was thus frowned upon, and therefore prays, "*Lord, help me;* Lord, strengthen my faith now; *Lord, let thy right hand uphold me,* while my soul is *following hard after thee,*" Ps. lxiii. 8. Or, *Thirdly,* As enforcing her original request, "*Lord, help me;* Lord, give me what I come for." She believed that Christ could and would help her, though she was not of the house of Israel; else she would have dropt her petition. Still she keeps up good thoughts of Christ, and will not quit her hold. *Lord, help me,* is a good prayer, if well put up; and it is pity that it should be turned into a byword, and that we should take God's name in vain in it.

(2.) With a holy skilfulness of faith, suggesting a very surprising plea. Christ had placed the Jews with the children, *as olive-plants round about* God's *table,* and had put the Gentiles with the dogs, under the table; and she doth not deny the aptness of the similitude. Note, There is nothing got by contradicting any word of Christ, though it bear ever so hard upon us. But this poor woman, since she cannot object against it, resolves to make the best of it (*v.* 27); *Truth, Lord; yet the dogs eat of the crumbs.* Now, here,

[1.] Her acknowledgment was very humble: *Truth, Lord.* Note, You cannot speak so meanly and slightly of a humble believer, but he is ready to speak as meanly and slightly of himself. Some that seem to dispraise and disparage themselves, will yet take it as an affront if others do so too; but one that is humbled aright, will subscribe to the most abasing challenges, and not call them abusing ones. "*Truth, Lord;* I cannot deny it; I am a dog, and have no right to the children's bread." David, *Thou hast done foolishly, very foolishly; Truth, Lord.* Asaph, Thou *hast been as a beast before God; Truth, Lord.* Agur, Thou art *more brutish than any man; Truth, Lord.* Paul, Thou hast been *the chief of sinners, art less than the least of saints, not meet to be called an apostle; Truth, Lord.*

[2.] Her improvement of this into a plea

was very ingenious; *Yet the dogs eat of the crumbs.* It was by a singular acumen, and spiritual quickness and sagacity, that she discerned matter of argument in that which looked like a slight. Note, A lively, active faith will make that to be for us, which seems to be against us; will fetch *meat out of the eater, and sweetness out of the strong.* Unbelief is apt to mistake recruits for enemies, and to draw dismal conclusions even from comfortable premises (Judges xiii. 22, 23); but faith can find encouragement even in that which is discouraging, and get nearer to God by taking hold on that hand which is stretched out to push it away. So good a thing it is to be of *quick understanding in the fear of the Lord,* Isa. xi. 3.

Her plea is, *Yet the dogs eat of the crumbs.* It is true, the full and regular provision is intended for the children only, but the small, casual, neglected crumbs are allowed to the dogs, and are not grudged them; that is to the dogs under the table, that attend there expecting them. We poor Gentiles cannot expect the stated ministry and miracles of the Son of David, that belongs to the Jews; but they begin now to be weary of their meat, and to play with it, they find fault with it, and crumble it away; surely then some of the broken meat may fall to a poor Gentile; "I beg a cure by the by, which is but as a crumb, though of the same precious bread, yet but a small inconsiderable piece, compared with the loaves which they have." Note, When we are ready to surfeit on the children's bread, we should remember how many there are, that would be glad of the crumbs. Our broken meat in spiritual privileges, would be a feast to many a soul; Acts xiii. 42. Observe here,

First, Her humility and necessity made her glad of crumbs. Those who are conscious to themselves that they deserve nothing, will be thankful for any thing; and *then* we are prepared for the greatest of God's mercies, when we see ourselves less than the least of them. The least of Christ is precious to a believer, and the very crumbs of the bread of life.

Secondly, Her faith encouraged her to expect these crumbs. Why should it not be at Christ's table as at a great man's, where the dogs are fed as sure as the children? Observe, She calls it their *master's* table; if she were a dog, she was *his* dog, and it cannot be ill with us, if we stand but in the meanest relation to Christ; "Though unworthy to be called children, yet *make me as one of thy hired servants:* nay, rather let me be set with the dogs than turned out of the house; for *in my Father's house there is not only bread enough, but to spare,* Luke xv. 17—19. It is good lying in God's house, though we lie at the threshold there.

4. The happy issue and success of all this. She came off with credit and comfort from this struggle; and, though a Canaanite, approved herself a true daughter of Israel, who, *like a prince, had power with God, and prevailed.* Hitherto Christ hid his face from her, but now *gathers her with everlasting kindness, v.* 28. *Then Jesus said, O woman, great is thy faith.* This was like Joseph's making himself known to his brethren, *I am Joseph;* so here, in effect, *I am Jesus.* Now he begins to speak like himself, and to put on his own countenance. *He will not contend for ever.*

(1.) He commended her faith. *O woman, great is thy faith.* Observe, [1.] It is her faith that he commends. There were several other graces that shone bright in her conduct of this affair—wisdom, humility, meekness, patience, perseverance in prayer; but these were the product of her faith, and therefore Christ fastens upon that as most commendable; because of all graces faith honours Christ most, therefore of all graces Christ honours faith most. [2.] It is the greatness of her faith. Note, *First,* Though the faith of all the saints is alike precious, yet it is not in all alike strong; all believers are not of the same size and stature. *Secondly,* The greatness of faith consists much in a resolute adherence to Jesus Christ as an all-sufficient Saviour, even in the face of discouragements; to love him, and trust him, as a Friend, even then when he seems to come forth against us as an Enemy. This is *great faith! Thirdly,* Though weak faith, if true, shall not be rejected, yet great faith shall be commended, and shall appear greatly well-pleasing to Christ; for in them that thus believe he is most admired. Thus Christ commended the faith of the centurion, and he was a Gentile too, he had a strong faith in the power of Christ, this woman in the good-will of Christ; both were acceptable.

(2.) He cured her daughter; "*Be it unto thee even as thou wilt*: I can deny thee nothing, take what thou camest for." Note, Great believers may have what they will for the asking. When our will conforms to the will of Christ's precept, his will concurs with the will of our desire. Those that will deny Christ nothing, shall find that he will deny them nothing at last, though for a time he seems to hide his face from them. "Thou wouldst have thy sins pardoned, thy corruptions mortified, thy nature sanctified; *be it unto thee even as thou wilt.* And what canst thou desire more?" When we come, as this poor woman did, to pray against Satan and his kingdom, we concur with the intercession of Christ, and it shall be accordingly. Though Satan may *sift* Peter, and *buffet* Paul, yet, through Christ's prayer and the sufficiency of his grace, *we shall be more than conquerors,* Luke xxii. 31, 32; 2 Cor. xii. 7—9; Rom xvi. 20.

The event was answerable to the word of Christ; *Her daughter was made whole from that very hour;* from thenceforward was never vexed with the devil any more; the mother's faith prevailed for the daughter's cure. Though the patient was at a distance, that was no hindrance to the efficacy of Christ's word. *He spake, and it was done.*

29 And Jesus departed from
thence, and came nigh unto the sea
of Galilee; and went up into a mountain, and sat down there. 30 And
great multitudes came unto him,
having with them *those that were*
lame, blind, dumb, maimed, and many
others, and cast them down at Jesus'
feet; and he healed them: 31 Insomuch that the multitude wondered,
when they saw the dumb to speak,
the maimed to be whole, the lame to
walk, and the blind to see: and they
glorified the God of Israel. 32 Then
Jesus called his disciples *unto him,*
and said, I have compassion on the
multitude, because they continue with
me now three days, and have nothing
to eat: and I will not send them away
fasting, lest they faint in the way.
33 And his disciples say unto him,
Whence should we have so much
bread in the wilderness, as to fill so
great a multitude? 34 And Jesus
saith unto them, How many loaves
have ye? And they said, Seven, and
a few little fishes. 35 And he commanded the multitude to sit down on
the ground. 36 And he took the
seven loaves and the fishes, and gave
thanks, and brake *them,* and gave to
his disciples, and the disciples to the
multitude. 37 And they did all eat,
and were filled: and they took up of
the broken *meat* that was left seven
baskets full. 38 And they that did
eat were four thousand men, beside
women and children. 39 And he
sent away the multitude, and took
ship, and came into the coasts of
Magdala.

Here is, I. A general account of Christ's cures, his curing by wholesale. The tokens of Christ's power and goodness are neither scarce nor scanty; for there is in him an overflowing fulness. Now observe,

1. The place where these cures were wrought; it was *near the sea of Galilee,* a part of the country Christ was much conversant with. We read not of any thing he did in the coasts of Tyre and Sidon, but the casting of the devil out of the woman of Canaan's daughter, as if he took that journey on purpose, with that in prospect. Let not ministers grudge their pains to do good, though but to few. He that knows the worth of souls, would go a great way to help to save one from death and Satan's power.

But *Jesus departed thence.* Having let fall that crumb under the table, he here returns to make a full feast for the children. We may do that occasionally for one, which we may not make a constant practice of. Christ steps into the coast of Tyre and Sidon, but he *sits down by the sea of Galilee* (*v.* 29), sits down not on a stately throne, or tribunal of judgment, but on a mountain: so mean and homely were his most solemn appearances in the days of his flesh! He *sat down on a mountain,* that all might see him, and have free access to him; for he is an open Saviour. He sat down there, as one tired with his journey, and willing to have a little rest; or rather, as one waiting to be gracious. He sat, expecting patients, as Abraham at his tent-door, ready to entertain strangers. He settled himself to this good work.

2. The multitudes and maladies that were healed by him (*v.* 30); *Great multitudes came to him;* that the scripture might be fulfilled, *Unto him shall the gathering of the people be,* Gen. xlix. 10. If Christ's ministers could cure bodily diseases as Christ did, there would be more flocking to them than there is; we are soon sensible of bodily pain and sickness, but few are concerned about their souls and their spiritual diseases.

Now, (1.) Such was the goodness of Christ, that he admitted all sorts of people; the poor as well as the rich are welcome to Christ, and with him there is room enough for all comers. He never complained of crowds or throngs of seekers, or looked with contempt upon the vulgar, the *herd,* as they are called; for the souls of peasants are as precious with him as the souls of princes.

(2.) Such was the power of Christ, that he healed all sorts of diseases; those that came to him, brought their sick relations and friends along with them, and *cast them down at Jesus' feet, v.* 30. We read not of any thing they said to him, but they laid them down before him as objects of pity, to be looked upon by him. Their calamities spake more for them than the tongue of the most eloquent orator could. *David showed before God his trouble,* that was enough, he then left it with him, Ps. cxlii. 2. Whatever our case is, the only way to find ease and relief, is, to lay it at Christ's feet, to spread it before him, and refer it to his cognizance, and then submit it to him, and refer it to his disposal. Those that would have spiritual healing from Christ, must lay themselves at his feet, to be ruled and ordered as he pleaseth.

Here were *lame, blind, dumb, maimed, and many others,* brought to Christ. See what work sin has made! It has turned the world into an hospital: what various diseases are human bodies subject to! See what work the Saviour makes! He conquers those hosts of enemies to mankind. Here were such diseases as a flame of fancy could contribute neither to the cause of nor to the cure of; as lying not in the humours, but in the members of the body; and yet these were subject to the commands of Christ. *He sent his word, and healed them.* Note, All diseases are at the command of Christ, to go and come as he bids them. This is an instance of Christ's power, which may comfort us in all our weaknesses; and of his pity, which may comfort us in all our miseries.

3. The influence that this had upon the people, *v.* 31.

(1.) They *wondered,* and well they might. Christ's works should be our wonder. *It is the Lord's doing, and it is marvellous,* Ps. cxviii. 23. The spiritual cures that Christ works are wonderful. When blind souls are made to see by faith, *the dumb to speak* in prayer, *the lame to walk* in holy obedience, it is to be wondered at. *Sing unto the Lord a new song, for* thus *he has done marvellous things.*

(2.) *They glorified the God of Israel,* whom the Pharisees, when they saw these things, blasphemed. Miracles, which are the matter of our wonder, must be the matter of our praise; and mercies, which are the matter of our rejoicing, must be the matter of our thanksgiving. Those that were healed, glorified God; if he heal our diseases, all that is within us must bless his holy name; and if we have been graciously preserved from blindness, and lameness, and dumbness, we have as much reason to bless God as if we had been cured of them; nay, and the standers-by glorified God. Note, God must be acknowledged with praise and thankfulness in the mercies of others as in our own. *They glorified* him as *the God of Israel,* his church's God, a God in covenant with his people, who hath sent the Messiah promised; and this is he. See Luke i. 68. *Blessed be the Lord God of Israel.* This was done by the power of the God of Israel, and no other could do it.

II. Here is a particular account of his feeding *four thousand men* with *seven loaves, and a few little fishes,* as he had lately fed *five thousand with five loaves.* The guests indeed were now not quite so many as then, and the provision a little more; which does not intimate that Christ's arm was shortened, but that he wrought his miracles as the occasion required, and not for ostentation, and therefore he suited them to the occasion: both then and now he took as many as were to be fed, and made use of all that was at hand to feed them with. When once the utmost powers of nature are exceeded, we must say, *This is the finger of God;* and it is neither here nor there how far they are outdone; so that this is no less a miracle than the former.

Here is, 1. Christ's pity (*v.* 32); *I have compassion on the multitude.* He tells his disciples this, both to try and to excite their compassion. When he was about to work this miracle, he called them to him, and made them acquainted with his purpose, and discoursed with them about it; not because he needed their advice, but because he would give an instance of his condescending love to them. He called them not *servants,* for *the servant knows not what his Lord doeth,* but treated them as his friends and counsellors. *Shall I hide from Abraham the thing that I do?* Gen. xviii. 17. In what he said to them, Observe,

(1.) The case of the multitude; *They continue with me now three days, and have nothing to eat.* This is an instance of their zeal, and the strength of their affection to Christ and his word, that they not only left their callings, to attend upon him on week-days, but underwent a deal of hardship, to continue with him; they wanted their natural rest, and, for aught that appeared, lay like soldiers in the field; they wanted necessary food, and had scarcely enough to keep life and soul together. In those hotter countries they could better bear long fasting than we can in these colder climates: but though it could not but be grievous to the body, and might endanger their health, yet *the zeal of God's house thus ate them up,* and they esteemed the words of Christ more than their necessary food. We think three hours too much to attend upon public ordinances; but these people staid together three days, and yet snuffed not at it, nor said, *Behold, what a weariness is it!* Observe, With what tenderness Christ spoke of it; *I have compassion on them.* It had become them to have compassion on him, who took so much pains with them for three days together, and was so indefatigable in teaching and healing; so much virtue had gone out of him, and yet for aught that appears he was fasting too: but he prevented them with his compassion. Note, Our Lord Jesus keeps an account how long his followers continue their attendance on him, and takes notice of the difficulty they sustain in it (Rev. ii. 2); *I know thy works, and thy labour, and thy patience:* and it shall *in no wise lose its reward.*

Now the exigence the people were reduced to serves to magnify. [1.] The mercy of their supply: he fed them when they were hungry; and then food was doubly welcome. He treated them as he did Israel of old; *he suffered them to hunger, and then fed them* (Deut. viii. 3); for that is *sweet to the hungry soul,* which *the full soul loathes.* [2.] The miracle of their supply: having been so long fasting, their appetites were the more craving. If two hungry meals make the third a glutton, what would three hungry days do? And yet *they did all eat and were filled.* Note, There are mercy and grace enough with Christ, to give the most earnest and enlarged desire an abundant satisfaction; *Open thy mouth wide, and I will fill it. He replenisheth even the hungry soul.*

(2.) The care of our master concerning them; *I will not send them away fasting, lest they should faint by the way;* which would be a discredit to Christ and his family, and a discouragement both to them and to others. Note, It is the unhappiness of our present state, that when our souls are in some measure elevated and enlarged, our bodies cannot keep pace with them in good duties. The weakness of the flesh is a great grievance to the willingness of the spirit. It will not be so in heaven, where the body shall be made spiritual, where *they rest not, day and night, from praising God,* and yet faint not; where *they hunger no more, nor thirst any more,* Rev. vii. 16.

Here is, 2. Christ's power. His pity of their wants sets his power on work for their supply. Now observe,

(1.) How his power was distrusted by his disciples (*v.* 33); *whence should we have so much bread in the wilderness?* A proper question, one would think, like that of Moses (Numb. xi. 22). *Shall the flocks and the herds be slain to suffice them?* But it was here an improper question, considering not only the general assurance the disciples had of the power of Christ, but the particular experience they lately had of a seasonable and sufficient provision by miracle in a like case; they had been not only the witnesses, but the ministers, of the former miracle; the multiplied bread went through their hands; so that it was an instance of great weakness for them to ask, *Whence shall we have bread?* Could they be at a loss, while they had their Master with them? Note, Forgetting former experiences leaves us under present doubts.

Christ knew how slender the provision was, but he would know it from them (*v.* 34); *How many loaves have ye?* Before he would work, he would have it seen how little he had to work on, that his power might shine the brighter. What they had, they had for themselves, and it was little enough for their own family; but Christ would have them bestow it all upon the multitude, and trust Providence for more. Note, it becomes Christ's disciples to be generous, their Master was so: what we have, we should be free of, as there is occasion; *given to hospitality;* not like Nabal (1 Sam. xxv. 11), but like Elisha, 2 Kings iv. 42. Niggardliness to-day, out of thoughtfulness for to-morrow, is a complication of corrupt affection that ought to be mortified. If we be prudently kind and charitable with what we have, we may piously hope that God will send more. *Jehovah-jireh, The Lord will provide.* The disciples asked, *Whence should we have bread?* Christ asked, *How many loaves have ye?* Note, When we cannot have what we would, we must make the best of what we have, and do good with it as far as it will go; we must not think so much of our wants as of our havings. Christ herein went according to the rule he gave to Martha, not to be *troubled about many things, nor cumbered about much serving.* Nature is content with little, grace with less, but lust with nothing.

(2.) How his power was discovered to the multitude, in the plentiful provision he made for them; the manner of which is much the same as before, *ch.* xiv. 18, &c. Observe here,

[1.] The provision that was at hand; *seven loaves, and a few little fishes:* the fish not proportionable to the bread, for bread is the staff of life. It is probable that the fish was such as they had themselves taken; for they were fishers, and were now near the sea. Note, It is comfortable to *eat the labour of our hands* (Ps. cxxviii. 2), and to enjoy that which is any way the product of our own industry, Prov. xii. 27. And what we have got by God's blessing on our labour we should be free of; for *therefore* we must labour, *that we may have to give,* Eph. iv. 28.

[2.] The putting of the people in a posture to receive it (*v.* 35); *He commanded the multitude to sit down on the ground.* They saw but very little provision, yet they must sit down, in faith that they should have a meal's meat out of it. They who would have spiritual food from Christ, must sit down at his feet, to hear his word, and expect it to come in an unseen way.

[3.] The distributing of the provision among them. He first *gave thanks—ἐυχαριστήσας.* The word used in the former miracle was ἐυλόγησε—*he blessed.* It comes all to one; giving thanks to God is a proper way of craving a blessing from God. And when we come to ask and receive further mercy, we ought to give thanks for the mercies we have received. He then *broke the loaves* (for it was in the breaking that the bread multiplied) *and gave to his disciples, and they to the multitude.* Though the disciples had distrusted Christ's power, yet he made use of them now as before; he is not provoked, as he might be, by the weakness and infirmities of his ministers, to lay them aside; but still he gives to them, and they to his people, of the word of life.

[4.] The plenty there was among them (*v.* 37). *They did all eat, and were filled.* Note, Those whom Christ feeds, he fills. While we labour for the world, we labour for that which satisfieth not (Isa. lv. 2); but those that duly wait on Christ shall be *abundantly satisfied with the goodness of his house,* Ps. lxv. 4. Christ thus fed people once and again, to intimate that though he was called Jesus of Nazareth, yet he was *of Bethlehem, the house of bread;* or rather, that he was himself *the Bread of life.*

To show that they had all enough, there was a great deal left—*seven baskets full of broken meat;* not so much as there was before, because they did not gather after so many eaters, but enough to show that with Christ *there is bread enough, and to spare;* supplies of grace for more than seek it, and for those that seek more.

[5.] The account taken of the guests; not that they might pay their share (here was no reckoning to be discharged, they were fed gratis), but that they might be witnesses to the power and goodness of Christ, and that this might be some resemblance of that universal providence that *gives food to all flesh*, Ps. cxxxvi. 25. Here were four thousand men fed; but what were they to that great family which is provided for by the divine care every day? God is a great House-keeper, on whom *the eyes of all the creatures wait, and he giveth them their food in due season*, Ps. civ. 27;—cxlv. 15.

[6.] The dismission of the multitude, and Christ's departure to another place (*v.* 39). He *sent away* the people. Though he had fed them twice, they must not expect miracles to be their daily bread. Let them now go home to their callings, and to their own tables. And he himself departed by ship to another place; for, being the *Light of the world*, he must be still *in motion*, and *go about to do good.*

CHAP. XVI.

None of Christ's miracles are recorded in this chapter, but four of his discourses. Here is, I. A conference with the Pharisees, who challenged him to show them a sign from heaven, ver. 1—4. II. Another with his disciples about the leaven of the Pharisees, ver. 5—12. III. Another with them concerning himself, as the Christ, and concerning his church built upon him, ver. 13—20. IV. Another concerning his sufferings for them, and theirs for him, ver. 21—28. And all these are written for our learning.

THE Pharisees also with the Sadducees came, and tempting desired him that he would show them a sign from heaven. 2 He answered and said unto them, When it is evening, ye say, *It will be* fair weather: for the sky is red. 3 And in the morning, *It will be* foul weather to day; for the sky is red and lowring. O *ye* hypocrites! ye can discern the face of the sky; but can ye not *discern* the signs of the times? 4 A wicked and adulterous generation seeketh after a sign; and there shall no sign be given unto it, but the sign of the prophet Jonas. And he left them, and departed.

We have here Christ's discourse with the Pharisees and Sadducees, men at variance among themselves, as appears Acts xxiii. 7, 8, and yet unanimous in their opposition to Christ; because his doctrine did equally overthrow the errors and heresies of the Sadducees, who denied the existence of spirits and a future state; and the pride, tyranny, and hypocrisy of the Pharisees, who were the great imposers of the traditions of the elders. Christ and Christianity meet with opposition on all hands. Observe,

I. Their demand, and the design of it.

1. The demand was of a sign from heaven; this they desired him to show them; pretending they were very willing to be satisfied and convinced, when really they were far from being so, but sought excuses from an obstinate infidelity. That which they pretended to desire was,

(1.) Some other sign than what they had yet had. They had great plenty of signs; every miracle Christ wrought was a sign, for *no man could do what he did unless God were with him.* But this will not serve, they must have a sign of their own choosing; they despised those signs which relieved the necessity of the sick and sorrowful, and insisted upon some sign which would gratify the curiosity of the proud. It is fit that the proofs of divine revelation should be chosen by the wisdom of God, not by the follies and fancies of men. The evidence that is given is sufficient to satisfy an unprejudiced understanding, but was not intended to please a vain humour. And it is an instance of the deceitfulness of the heart, to think that we should be wrought upon by the means and advantages which we have not, while we slight those which we have. *If we hear not Moses and the prophets*, neither would we be wrought upon *though one rose from the dead.*

(2.) It must be a sign from heaven. They would have such miracles to prove his commission, as were wrought at the giving of the law upon mount Sinai: thunder, and lightning, and the voice of words, were the sign from heaven they required. Whereas the sensible signs and terrible ones were not agreeable to the spiritual and comfortable dispensation of the gospel. Now the word comes more nigh us (Rom. x. 8), and therefore the miracles do so, and do not oblige us to keep such a distance as these did, Heb. xii. 18.

2. The design was to tempt him; not to be taught by him, but to ensnare him. If he should show them a sign from heaven, they would attribute it to a confederacy with the *prince of the power of the air;* if he should not, as they supposed he would not, they would have that to say for themselves, *why they did not believe on him.* They now tempted Christ as Israel did, 1 Cor. x. 9. And observe their perverseness; *then,* when they had signs from heaven, they tempted Christ, saying, *Can he furnish a table in the wilderness?* Now that he had furnished a table in the wilderness, they tempted him, saying, *Can he give us a sign from heaven?*

II. Christ's reply to this demand; lest they should be *wise in their own conceit,* he *answered these fools according to their folly,* Prov. xxvi. 5. In his answer,

1. He condemns their overlooking of the signs they had, *v.* 2, 3. They were seeking for the signs of the kingdom of God, when

it was already among them. *The Lord was in this place,* and they *knew it not.* Thus their unbelieving ancestors, when miracles were their daily bread, asked, *Is the Lord among us, or is he not?*

To expose this, he observes to them,

(1.) Their skilfulness and sagacity in other things, particularly in natural prognostications of the weather; "You know that a red sky over-night is a presage of fair weather, and a red sky in the morning of foul weather. There are common rules drawn from observation and experience, by which it is easy to foretel very probably what weather it will be. When second causes have begun to work, we may easily guess at their issue, so uniform is nature in its motions, and so consistent with itself. We *know not the balancing of the clouds* (Job xxxvii. 16), but we may spell something from the faces of them. This gives no countenance at all to the wild and ridiculous predictions of *the astrologers, the star-gazers, and the monthly prognosticators* (Isa. xlvii. 13) concerning the weather long before, with which weak and foolish people are imposed upon; we are sure, in general, that *seed-time and harvest, cold and heat, summer and winter, shall not cease.* But as to the particulars, till, by the weather-glasses, or otherwise, we perceive the immediate signs and harbingers of the change of weather, it is not for us to know, no, not *that* concerning the times and seasons. Let it suffice, that it shall be what weather pleases God; and that which pleases God, should not displease us.

(2.) Their sottishness and stupidity in the concerns of their souls; *Can ye not discern the signs of the times?*

[1.] "Do you not see that the Messiah is come?" The sceptre was departed from Judah, Daniel's weeks were just expiring, and yet they regarded not. The miracles Christ wrought, and the gathering of the people to him, were plain indications that the *kingdom of heaven was at hand,* that this was *the day of their visitation.* Note, *First,* There are signs of the times, by which wise and upright men are enabled to make moral prognostications, and so far to understand the motions and methods of Providence, as from thence to take their measures, and to know what Israel ought to do, as the men of Issachar, as the physician from some certain symptoms finds a crisis formed. *Secondly,* There are many who are skilful enough in other things, and yet cannot or will not discern the day of their opportunities, are not aware of the wind when it is fair for them, and so let slip the gale. See Jer. viii. 7; Isa. i. 3. *Thirdly,* It is great hypocrisy, when we slight the signs of God's ordaining, to seek for signs of our owr prescribing.

[2.] "Do not you foresee your own ruin coming for rejecting him? You will not entertain the gospel of peace, and can you not evidently discern that hereby you pull an inevitable destruction upon your own heads?" Note, It is the undoing of multitudes, that they are not aware what will be the end of their refusing Christ.

2. He refuses to give them any other sign (*v.* 4), as he had done before in the same words, *ch.* xii. 39. Those that persist in the same iniquities, must expect to meet with the same reproofs. Here, as there, (1.) He calls them *an adulterous generation;* because, while they professed themselves of the true church and spouse of God, they treacherously departed from him, and brake their covenants with him. The Pharisees were *a generation pure in their own eyes,* having the way of the adulterous woman, that thinks she has done no wickedness, Prov. xxx. 20. (2.) He refuses to gratify their desire. Christ will not be prescribed to; *we ask, and have not, because we ask amiss.* (3.) He refers them to the sign of the prophet Jonas, which should yet be given them; his resurrection from the dead, and his preaching by his apostles to the Gentiles; these were reserved for the last and highest evidences of his divine mission. Note, Though the fancies of proud men shall not be humoured, yet the faith of the humble shall be supported, and the unbelief of them that perish left for ever inexcusable, and *every mouth shall be stopped.*

This discourse broke off abruptly; *he left them and departed.* Christ will not tarry long with those that tempt him, but justly withdraws from those that are disposed to quarrel with him. He left them as irreclaimable; *Let them alone.* He left them to themselves, left them in the hand of their own counsels; *so he gave them up to their own hearts' lust.*

5 And when his disciples were come
to the other side, they had forgotten
to take bread. 6 Then Jesus said
unto them, Take heed, and beware of
the leaven of the Pharisees and of
the Sadducees. 7 And they reasoned
among themselves, saying, *It is* because we have taken no bread. 8
Which when Jesus perceived, he said
unto them, O ye of little faith, why
reason ye among yourselves, because
ye have brought no bread? 9 Do ye
not yet understand, neither remember
the five loaves of the five thousand,
and how many baskets ye took up?
10 Neither the seven loaves of the
four thousand, and how many baskets
ye took up? 11 How is it that ye
do not understand that I spake *it* not
to you concerning bread, that ye
should beware of the leaven of the
Pharisees and of the Sadducees? 12

Then understood they how that he bade *them* not beware of the leaven of bread, but of the doctrine of the Pharisees and of the Sadducees.

We have here Christ's discourse with his disciples concerning bread, in which, as in many other discourses, he speaks to them of spiritual things under a similitude, and they misunderstand him of carnal things. The occasion of it was, their forgetting to victual their ship, and to take along with them provisions for their family on the other side the water; usually they carried bread along with them, because they were sometimes in desert places; and when they were not, yet they would not be burthensome. But now they forgot; we will hope it was because their minds and memories were filled with better things. Note, Christ's disciples are often such as have no great forecast for the world.

I. Here is the caution Christ gave them, to *beware of the leaven of the Pharisees.* He had now been discoursing with the Pharisees and Sadducees, and saw them to be men of such a spirit, that it was necessary to caution his disciples to have nothing to do with them. Disciples are in most danger from hypocrites; against those that are openly vicious they stand upon their guard, but against Pharisees, who are great pretenders to devotion, and Sadducees, who pretend to a free and impartial search after truth, they commonly lie unguarded: and therefore the caution is doubled, *Take heed, and beware.*

The corrupt principles and practices of the Pharisees and Sadducees are compared to leaven; they were souring, and swelling, and spreading, like leaven; they fermented wherever they came.

II. Their mistake concerning this caution, *v.* 7. They thought Christ hereby upbraided them with their improvidence and forgetfulness, that they were so busy attending to his discourse with the Pharisees, that *therefore* they forgot their private concerns. Or, because having no bread of their own with them, they must be beholden to their friends for supply, he would not have them to ask it of the Pharisees and Sadducees, nor to receive of *their* alms, because he would not so far countenance them; or, for fear, lest, under pretence of feeding them, they should do them a mischief. Or, they took it for a caution, not to be familiar with the Pharisees and Sadducees, not to eat with them (Prov. xxiii. 6), whereas the danger was not in their bread (Christ himself did eat with them, Luke vii. 36; xi. 37; xiv. 1), but in their principles.

III. The reproof Christ gave them for this.

1. He reproves their distrust of his ability and readiness to supply them in this strait (*v.* 8); "*O ye of little faith,* why are ye in such perplexity because ye have *taken no bread,* that ye can mind nothing else, that ye think your Master is as full of it as you, and apply every thing he saith to that?" He does not chide them for their little forecast, as they expected he would. Note, Parents and masters must not be angry at the forgetfulness of their children and servants, more than is necessary to make them take more heed another time; we are all apt to be forgetful of our duty. This should serve to excuse a fault, *Peradventure it was an oversight.* See how easily Christ forgave his disciples' carelessness, though it was in such a material point as taking bread; and do likewise. But that which he chides them for is their little faith.

(1.) He would have them to depend upon him for supply, though it were in a wilderness, and not to disquiet themselves with anxious thoughts about it. Note, Though Christ's disciples be brought into wants and straits, through their own carelessness and incogitancy, yet he encourages them to trust in him for relief. We must not therefore use this as an excuse for our want of charity to those who are really poor, that they should have minded their own affairs better, and then they would not have been in need. It may be so, but they must not therefore be left to starve when they are in need.

(2.) He is displeased at their solicitude in this matter. The weakness and shiftlessness of good people in their worldly affairs is that for which men are apt to condemn them; but it is not such an offence to Christ as their inordinate care and anxiety about those things. We must endeavour to keep the mean between the extremes of carelessness and carefulness; but of the two, the excess of thoughtfulness about the world worst becomes Christ's disciples. "*O ye of little faith,* why are ye disquieted for want of bread?" Note, To distrust Christ, and to disturb ourselves when we are in straits and difficulties, is an evidence of the weakness of our faith, which, if it were in exercise as it should be, would ease us of the burthen of care, by casting it on the Lord, who *careth for us.*

(3.) The aggravation of their distrust was the experience they had so lately had of the power and goodness of Christ in providing for them, *v.* 9, 10. Though they had no bread with them, they had him with them who could provide bread for them. If they had not the cistern, they had the Fountain. *Do ye not yet understand, neither remember?* Note, Christ's disciples are often to be blamed for the shallowness of their understandings, and the slipperiness of their memories. "Have ye forgot those repeated instances of merciful and miraculous supplies; five thousand fed with five loaves, and four thousand with seven loaves, and yet they had enough and to spare? Remember *how many baskets ye took up.*" These baskets were intended for memorials, by which to keep the mercy in remembrance, as the pot of manna which was preserved in the ark,

Exod. xvi. 32. The fragments of those meals would be a feast now; and he that could furnish them with such an overplus then, surely could furnish them with what was necessary now. That meat for their bodies was intended to be meat for their faith (Ps. lxxiv. 14), which therefore they should have lived upon, now that they had forgotten to take bread. Note, We are *therefore* perplexed with present cares and distrusts, because we do not duly remember our former experiences of divine power and goodness.

2. He reproves their misunderstanding of the caution he gave them (*v.* 11); *How is it that you do not understand?* Note, Christ's disciples may well be ashamed of the slowness and dulness of their apprehensions in divine things; especially when they have long enjoyed the means of grace; *I spake it not unto you concerning bread.* He took it ill, (1.) That they should think him as thoughtful about bread as they were; whereas his *meat and drink were to do his Father's will.* (2.) That they should be so little acquainted with his way of preaching, as to take that literally which he spoke by way of parable; and should thus make themselves like the multitude, who, when Christ spoke to them in parables, seeing, saw not, and hearing, heard not, *ch.* xiii. 13.

IV. The rectifying of the mistake by this reproof (*v.* 12); *Then understood they* what he meant. Note, Christ *therefore* shows us our folly and weakness, that we may stir up ourselves to take things right. He did not tell them expressly what he meant, but repeated what he had said, that they should beware of the leaven; and so obliged them, by comparing this with his other discourses, to arrive at the sense of it in their own thoughts. Thus Christ teaches by the Spirit of wisdom in the heart, opening the understanding to the Spirit of revelation in the word. And those truths are most precious, which we have thus digged for, and have found out after some mistakes. Though Christ did not tell them plainly, yet now they were aware that by the leaven of the Pharisees and Sadducees, he meant their doctrine and way, which were corrupt and vicious, but, as they managed them, very apt to insinuate themselves into the minds of men like leaven, and to *eat like a canker.* They were leading men, and were had in reputation, which made the danger of infection by their errors the greater. In our age, we may reckon atheism and deism to be the leaven of the Sadducees, and popery to be the leaven of the Pharisees, against both which it concerns all Christians to stand upon their guard.

13 When Jesus came into the coasts
of Cæsarea Philippi, he asked his disciples, saying, Whom do men say that
I the Son of man am? 14 And they
said, Some *say that thou art* John
the Baptist: some, Elias; and others,
Jeremias, or one of the prophets. 15
He saith unto them, But whom say
ye that I am? 16 And Simon Peter
answered and said, Thou art the
Christ, the Son of the living God.
17 And Jesus answered and said unto
him, Blessed art thou, Simon Bar-
jona: for flesh and blood hath not revealed *it* unto thee, but my Father
which is in heaven. 18 And I say
unto thee, That thou art Peter, and
upon this rock I will build my church,
and the gates of hell shall not prevail
against it. 19 And I will give unto thee
the keys of the kingdom of heaven:
and whatsoever thou shalt bind on
earth shall be bound in heaven: and
whatsoever thou shalt loose on earth
shall be loosed in heaven. 20 Then
charged he his disciples that they
should tell no man that he was Jesus
the Christ.

We have here a private conference which Christ had with his disciples concerning himself. It was in the coasts of Cesarea Philippi, the utmost borders of the land of Canaan northward; there in that remote corner, perhaps, there was less flocking after him than in other places, which gave him leisure for this private conversation with his disciples. Note, When ministers are abridged in their public work, they should endeavour to do the more in their own families.

Christ is here catechising his disciples.

I. He enquires what the opinions of others were concerning him; *Who do men say that I, the Son of man, am?*

1. He calls himself the *Son of man;* which may be taken either, (1.) As a title common to him with others. He was called, and justly, *the Son of God,* for so he was (Luke i. 35); but he called himself the Son of man; for he is really and truly "Man, made of a woman." In courts of honour, it is a rule to distinguish men by their highest titles; but Christ, having now emptied himself, though he was the Son of God, will be known by the style and title of the Son of man. Ezekiel was often so called to *keep* him humble; Christ called himself so, to show that he *was* humble. Or, (2.) As a title peculiar to him as Mediator. He is made known, in Daniel's vision, as the *Son of man,* Dan. vii. 13. I am the Messiah, that Son of man that was promised. But,

2. He enquires what people's sentiments were concerning him: "*Who do men say that I am? The Son of man?*" (So I think it might better be read). "Do they own me for the Messiah? He asks not, "Who do the *scribes* and *Pharisees* say that I am?"

They were prejudiced against him, and said that he was a deceiver and in league with Satan; but, "Who do *men* say that I am?" He referred to the common people, whom the Pharisees despised. Christ asked this question, not as one that knew not; for if he knows what men think, much more what they say; nor as one desirous to hear his own praises, but to make the disciples solicitous concerning the success of their preaching, by showing that he himself was so. The common people conversed more familiarly with the disciples than they did with their Master, and therefore from them he might better know what they said. Christ had not plainly said who he was, but left people to infer it from his works, John x. 24, 25. Now he would know what inferences the people drew from *them,* and from the miracles which his apostles wrought in his name.

3. To this question the disciples gave him an answer (*v.* 14), *Some say, thou art John the Baptist, &c.* There were some that said, he was the *Son of David* (*ch.* xii. 23), and the great Prophet, John vi. 14. The disciples, however, do not mention that opinion, but only such opinions as were wide of the truth, which they had gathered up from their countrymen. Observe,

(1.) They are different opinions; some say one thing, and others another. Truth is one; but those who vary from that commonly vary one from another. Thus Christ came eventually to send division, Luke xii. 51. Being so noted a Person, every one would be ready to pass his verdict upon him, and, "Many men, many minds;" those that were not willing to own him to be the Christ, wandered in endless mazes, and followed the chase of every uncertain guess and wild hypothesis.

(2.) They are honourable opinions, and bespeak the respect they had for him, according to the best of their judgment. These were not the sentiments of his enemies, but the sober thoughts of those that followed him with love and wonder. Note, It is possible for men to have good thoughts of Christ, and yet not right ones, a high opinion of him, and yet not high enough.

(3.) They all suppose him to be *one risen from the dead;* which perhaps arose from a confused notion they had of the resurrection of the Messiah, before his public preaching, as of Jonas. Or their notions arose from an excessive value for antiquity; as if it were not possible for an excellent man to be produced in their own age, but it must be one of the ancients returned to life again.

(4.) They are all false opinions, built upon mistakes, and wilful mistakes. Christ's doctrines and miracles bespoke him to be an extraordinary Person; but because of the meanness of his appearance, so different from what they expected, they would not own him to be the Messiah, but will grant him to be any thing rather than that.

[1.] *Some say, thou art John the Baptist.* Herod said so (*ch.* xiv. 2), and those about him would be apt to say as he said. This notion might be strengthened by an opinion they had, that those who died as martyrs, should rise again before others; which some think the second of the seven sons refers to, in his answer to Antiochus, 2 Macc. vii. 9, *The King of the world shall raise us up, who have died for his laws, unto everlasting life.*

[2.] *Some Elias;* taking occasion, no doubt, from the prophecy of Malachi (*ch.* iv. 5), *Behold, I will send you Elijah.* And the rather, because Elijah (as Christ) did many miracles, and was himself, in his translation, the greatest miracle of all.

[3.] *Others Jeremias:* they fasten upon him, either because he was the weeping prophet, and Christ was often in tears; or because God had *set him over the kingdoms and nations* (Jer. i. 10), which they thought agreed with their notion of the Messiah.

[4.] *Or, one of the prophets.* This shows what an honourable idea they entertained of the prophets; and yet they were *the children of them that persecuted and slew them, ch.* xxiii. 29. Rather than they would allow Jesus of Nazareth, one of their own country, to be such an extraordinary Person as his works bespoke him to be, they would say, "It was not he, but *one of the old prophets.*"

II. He enquires what *their* thoughts were concerning him; "*But who say ye that I am? v.* 15. Ye tell me what other people say of me; can ye say better?" 1. The disciples had themselves been better taught than others; had, by their intimacy with Christ, greater advantages of getting knowledge than others had. Note, It is justly expected that those who enjoy greater plenty of the means of knowledge and grace than others, should have a more clear and distinct knowledge of the things of God than others. Those who have more acquaintance with Christ than others, should have truer sentiments concerning him, and be able to give a better account of him than others. 2. The disciples were trained up to teach others, and therefore it was highly requisite that they should understand the truth themselves: "Ye that are to preach the gospel of the kingdom, what are your notions of him that sent you?" Note, Ministers must be examined before they be sent forth, especially what their sentiments are of Christ, and who they say that he is; for how can they be owned as ministers of Christ, that are either ignorant or erroneous concerning Christ? This is a question we should every one of us be frequently putting to ourselves, "*Who* do we say, *what* kind of one do we say, that *the Lord Jesus is?* Is he precious to us? Is he in our eyes the chief of ten thousand? Is he the Beloved of our souls?" It is well or ill with us, according as our thoughts are right or wrong concerning Jesus Christ.

Well, this is the question; now let us observe,

(1.) Peter's answer to this question, *v.* 16. To the former question concerning the opinion others had of Christ, several of the disciples answered, according as they had heard people talk; but to this Peter answers in the name of all the rest, they all consenting to it, and concurring in it. Peter's temper led him to be forward in speaking upon all such occasions, and sometimes he spoke well, sometimes amiss; in all companies there are found some warm, bold men, to whom a precedency of speech falls of course; Peter was such a one: yet we find other of the apostles sometimes speaking as the mouth of the rest; as *John* (Mark ix. 38), *Thomas, Philip,* and *Jude,* John xiv. 5, 8, 22. So that this is far from being a proof of such primacy and superiority of Peter above the rest of the apostles, as the church of Rome ascribes to him. They will needs advance him to be a judge, when the utmost they can make of him, is, that he was but foreman of the jury, to speak for the rest, and that only *pro hâc vice—for this once;* not the perpetual dictator or speaker of the house, only chairman upon this occasion.

Peter's answer is short, but it is full, and true, and to the purpose; *Thou art the Christ, the Son of the living God.* Here is a confession of the Christian faith, addressed to Christ, and so made an act of devotion. Here is a confession of the true God as the living God, in opposition to dumb and dead idols, and of *Jesus Christ, whom he hath sent,* whom to know is *life eternal.* This is the conclusion of the whole matter.

[1.] The people called him *a Prophet, that Prophet* (John vi. 14); but the disciples own him to be the Christ, the anointed One; the great Prophet, Priest, and King of the church; the true Messiah promised to the fathers, and depended on by them as *He that shall come.* It was a great thing to believe this concerning one whose outward appearance was so contrary to the general idea the Jews had of the Messiah.

[2.] He called himself the *Son of Man;* but they owned him to be *the Son of the living God.* The *people's* notion of him was, that he was the ghost of a dead man, Elias or Jeremias; but *they* know and believe him to be *the Son of the living God,* who has life in himself, and has given to his Son to have life in himself, and to be the *Life of the world.* If he be *the Son of the living God,* he is of the same nature with him: and though his divine nature was now veiled with the cloud of flesh, yet there were those who looked through it, and *saw his glory, the glory as of the Only-Begotten of the Father, full of grace and truth.* Now can we with an assurance of faith subscribe to this confession? Let us then, with a fervency of affection and adoration, go to Christ, and tell him so; Lord Jesus, *thou art the Christ, the Son of the living God.*

(2.) Christ's approbation of his answer (*v.* 17—19); in which Peter is replied to, both as a believer and as an apostle.

[1.] As a believer, *v.* 17. Christ shows himself well pleased with Peter's confession, that it was so clear and express, without *ifs* or *ands,* as we say. Note, The proficiency of Christ's disciples in knowledge and grace is very acceptable to him; and Christ shows him whence he received the knowledge of this truth. At the first discovery of this truth in the dawning of the gospel day, it was a mighty thing to believe it; *all men had not this knowledge,* had not this faith. But,

First, Peter had the happiness of it; *Blessed art thou, Simon Bar-jona.* He reminds him of his rise and original, the meanness of his parentage, the obscurity of his extraction; he was *Bar-jonas—The son of a dove;* so some. Let him remember *the rock out of which he was hewn,* that he may see he was not born to this dignity, but preferred to it by the divine favour; it was free grace that made him to differ. Those that have received the Spirit must remember who is their Father, 1 Sam. x. 12. Having reminded him of this, he makes him sensible of his great happiness as a believer; *Blessed art thou.* Note, True believers are truly blessed, and those are blessed indeed whom Christ pronounces blessed; his saying they are so, makes them so. "Peter, thou art a happy man, who thus *knowest the joyful sound,*" Ps. lxxxix. 15. *Blessed are your eyes, ch.* xiii. 16. All happiness attends the right knowledge of Christ.

Secondly, God must have the glory of it; "*For flesh and blood have not revealed it to thee.* Thou hadst this neither by the invention of thy own wit and reason, nor by the instruction and information of others; this light sprang neither from nature nor from education, but from my Father who is in heaven." Note, 1. The Christian religion is a revealed religion, has its rise in heaven; it is a religion from above, given by inspiration of God, not the learning of philosophers, nor the politics of statesmen. 2. Saving faith is the gift of God, and, wherever it is, is wrought by him, as the Father of our Lord Jesus Christ, for his sake, and upon the score of his mediation, Phil. i. 29. *Therefore* thou art blessed, because *my Father has revealed it to thee.* Note, The revealing of Christ to us and in us is a distinguishing token of God's good will, and a firm foundation of true happiness; and blessed are they that are thus highly favoured.

Perhaps Christ discerned something of pride and vain-glory in Peter's confession; a subtle sin, and which is apt to mingle itself even with our good duties. It is hard for good men to compare themselves with others, and not to have too great a conceit of themselves; to prevent which, we should consider that our preference to others is no achievement of our own, but the free gift of God's grace to us, and not to others; so that we have nothing to boast of, Ps. cxv. 1; 1 Cor. iv. 7.

[2.] Christ replies to him as an apostle or minister, *v.* 18, 19. Peter, in the name of the church, had confessed Christ, and to him therefore the promise intended for the church is directed. Note, There is nothing lost by being forward to confess Christ; for those who thus honour him, he will honour.

Upon occasion of this great confession made of Christ, which is the church's homage and allegiance, he signed and published this royal, this divine charter, by which that body politic is incorporated. Such is the communion between Christ and the church, the Bridegroom and the spouse. God had a church in the world from the beginning, and it was built upon the rock of the promised Seed, Gen. iii. 15. But now, that promised Seed being come, it was requisite that the church should have a new charter, as Christian, and standing in relation to a Christ already come. Now here we have that charter; and a thousand pities it is, that this word, which is the great support of the kingdom of Christ, should be wrested and pressed into the service of antichrist. But the devil has employed his subtlety to pervert it, as he did that promise, Ps. xci. 11, which he perverted to his own purpose, *ch.* iv. 6, and perhaps both that scripture and this he thus perverted because they stood in his way, and therefore he owed them a spite.

Now the purport of this charter is,

First, To establish the being of the church; *I say also unto thee.* It is Christ that makes the grant, he who is the church's Head, and Ruler, to whom all judgment is committed, and from whom all power is derived; he who makes it pursuant to the authority received from the Father, and his undertaking for the salvation of the elect. The grant is put into Peter's hand; "I say it to *thee.*" The Old Testament promises relating to the church were given immediately to particular persons, eminent for faith and holiness, as to Abraham and David; which yet gave no supremacy to them, much less to any of their successors; so the New-Testament charter is here delivered to Peter as an agent, but to the use and behoof of the church in all ages, according to the purposes therein specified and contained. Now it is here promised,

1. That Christ would build his church upon a rock. This body politic is incorporated by the style and title of *Christ's church.* It is a number of the children of men called out of the world, and set apart from it, and dedicated to Christ. It is not *thy* church, but *mine.* Peter remembered this, when he cautioned ministers *not to lord it over God's heritage.* The church is Christ's peculiar, appropriated to him. The world is God's, and they that dwell therein; but the church is a chosen remnant, that stands in relation to God through Christ as Mediator. It bears his image and superscription.

(1.) The Builder and Maker of the church is Christ himself; *I will build it.* The church is a temple which Christ is the Builder of, Zech. vi. 11—13. Herein Solomon was a type of Christ, and Cyrus, Isa. xliv. 28. The materials and workmanship are his. By the working of his Spirit with the preaching of his word he adds souls to his church, and so builds it up with living stones, 1 Pet. ii. 5. *Ye are God's building;* and building is a progressive work; the church in this world is but *in fieri—in the forming,* like a house in the building. It is a comfort to all those who wish well to the church, that Christ, who has divine wisdom and power, undertakes to build it.

(2.) The foundation on which it is built is, *this Rock.* Let the architect do his part ever so well, if the foundation be rotten, the building will not stand; let us therefore see what the foundation is, and it must be meant of Christ, for *other foundation can no man lay.* See Isa. xxviii. 16.

[1.] The church is built upon a *rock;* a firm, strong, and lasting foundation, which time will not waste, nor will it sink under the weight of the building. Christ would not build his house upon the sand, for he knew that storms would arise. A rock is high, Ps. lxi. 2. Christ's church does not stand upon a level with this world; a rock is large, and extends far, so does the church's foundation; and the more large, the more firm; those are not the church's friends that narrow its foundation.

[2.] It is built upon *this* rock; thou art *Peter,* which signifies *a stone* or *rock;* Christ gave him that name when he first called him (John i. 42), and here he confirms it; "Peter, thou dost answer thy name, thou art a solid, substantial disciple, fixed and stayed, and one that there is some hold of. Peter is thy name, and strength and stability are with thee. Thou art not shaken with the waves of men's fluctuating opinions concerning me, but established in the present truth," 2 Pet. i. 12. From the mention of this significant name, occasion is taken for this metaphor of *building upon a rock.*

First, Some by this rock understand Peter himself as an apostle, the chief, though not the prince, of the twelve, senior among them, but not superior over them. The church is built upon the foundation of the apostles, Eph. ii. 20. The first stones of that building were laid in and by their ministry; hence their names are said to be *written in the foundations* of the new Jerusalem, Rev. xxi. 14. Now Peter being that apostle by whose hand the first stones of the church were laid, both in Jewish converts (Acts ii.), and in the Gentile converts (Acts x.), he might in some sense be said to be the rock on which it was built. *Cephas* was one that seemed to be a pillar, Gal. ii. 9. But it sounds very harsh, to call a man that only lays the first stone of a building, which is a transient act, the foundation on which it is built, which is an abiding thing. Yet if it were so, this would not serve to support the pretensions of the Bishop of Rome; for Peter had no such headship as he claims, much less could derive it to his successors, least of all to the Bishops of Rome, who, whether they are so in place or no, is a question, but that they are not so in the truth of Christianity, is past all question.

Secondly, Others, by this *rock,* understand *Christ;* "*Thou art Peter,* thou hast the name of a *stone,* but *upon this rock,* pointing to himself, *I will build my church.*" Perhaps he laid his hand on his breast, as when he said, *Destroy this temple* (John ii. 19), when he *spoke of the temple of his body.* Then he took occasion from the temple, where he was, so to speak of himself, and gave occasion to some to misunderstand him of that; so here he took occasion from Peter, to speak of himself as the Rock, and gave occasion to some to misunderstand him of Peter. But this must be explained by those many scriptures which speak of Christ as the only Foundation of the church; see 1 Cor. iii. 11; 1 Pet. ii. 6. Christ is both its Founder and its Foundation; he draws souls, and draws them to himself; to him they are united, and on him they rest and have a constant dependence.

Thirdly, Others by this *rock* understand this confession which Peter made of Christ, and this comes all to one with understanding it of Christ himself. It was a good confession which Peter witnessed, *Thou art the Christ, the Son of the living God;* the rest concurred with him in it. "Now," saith Christ, "this is that great truth *upon which I will build my church.*" 1. Take away this truth itself, and the universal church falls to the ground. If Christ be not the Son of God, Christianity is a cheat, and the church is a mere chimera; *our preaching is vain, your faith is vain, and you are yet in your sins,* 1 Cor. xv. 14—17. If Jesus be not the Christ, those that own him are not of the church, but deceivers and deceived. 2. Take away the faith and confession of this truth from any particular church, and it ceases to be a part of Christ's church, and relapses to the state and character of infidelity. This is *articulus stantis et cadentis ecclesiæ—that article, with the admission or the denial of which the church either rises or falls;* "the main hinge on which the door of salvation turns;" those who let go this, do not hold the foundation; and though they may call themselves Christians, they give themselves the lie; for the church is a sacred society, incorporated upon the certainty and assurance of this great truth; and great it is, and has prevailed.

2. Christ here promises to preserve and secure his church, when it is built; *The gates of hell shall not prevail against it;* neither against this truth, nor against the church which is built upon it.

(1.) This implies that the church has enemies that fight against it, and endeavour its ruin and overthrow, here represented by *the gates of hell, that is,* the city of hell; (which is directly opposite to this heavenly city, this *city of the living God*), the devil's interest among the children of men. The gates of hell are the powers and policies of the devil's kingdom, the dragon's head and horns, by which he *makes war with the Lamb;* all that comes out of hell-gates, as being hatched and contrived there. These fight against the church by opposing gospel truths, corrupting gospel ordinances, persecuting good ministers and good Christians; drawing or driving, persuading by craft or forcing by cruelty, to that which is inconsistent with the purity of religion; this is the design of the gates of hell, to root out the name of Christianity (Ps. lxxxiii. 4), *to devour the man-child* (Rev. xii. 9), to raze this city to the ground.

(2.) This assures us that the enemies of the church shall not gain their point. While the world stands, Christ will have a church in it, in which his truths and ordinances shall be owned and kept up, in spite of all the opposition of the powers of darkness; *They shall not prevail against it,* Ps. cxxix. 1, 2. This gives no security to any particular church, or church-governors, that they shall never err, never apostatize or be destroyed; but that somewhere or other the Christian religion shall have a being, though not always in the same degree of purity and splendour, yet so as that the entail of it shall never be quite cut off. The *woman lives, though in a wilderness* (Rev. xii. 14), *cast down but not destroyed* (2 Cor. iv. 9), *as dying, and behold we live,* 2 Cor. vi. 9. Corruptions grieving, persecutions grievous, but neither fatal. The church may be foiled in particular encounters, but in the main battle it shall come off *more than a conqueror.* Particular believers are *kept by the power of God, through faith, unto salvation,* 1 Pet. i. 5.

Secondly, The other part of this charter is, to settle the order and government of the church, *v.* 19. When a city or society is incorporated, officers are appointed and empowered to act for the common good. A city without government is a chaos. Now this constituting of the government of the church, is here expressed by the delivering of the keys, and, with them, a power to bind and loose. This is not to be understood of any peculiar power that Peter was invested with, as if he were sole door-keeper of the kingdom of heaven, and had that key of David which belongs only to the Son of David; no, this invests all the apostles and their successors with a ministerial power to guide and govern the church of Christ, as it exists in particular congregations or churches, according to the rules of the gospel. *Claves regni cœlorum in*

B. Petro apostolo cuncti suscepimus sacerdotes—All we that are priests, received, in the person of the blessed apostle Peter, the keys of the kingdom of heaven; so Ambrose *De Dignit. Sacerd.* Only the keys were first put into Peter's hand, because he was the first *that opened the door of faith to the Gentiles,* Acts x. 28. As the king, in giving a charter to a corporation, empowers the magistrates to hold courts in his name, to try matters of fact, and determine therein according to law, confirming what is so done regularly as if done in any of the superior courts; so Christ, having incorporated his church, hath appointed the office of the ministry for the keeping up of order and government, and to see that his laws be duly served; *I will give thee the keys.* He doth not say, "I *have* given them," or "I *do* now;" but "I *will* do it," meaning after his resurrection; *when he ascended on high, he gave those gifts,* Ephes. iv. 8; then this power was actually given, not to Peter only, but to all the rest, *ch.* xxviii. 19, 20; John xx. 21. He doth not say, The keys *shall* be given, but, *I will give* them; for ministers derive their authority from Christ, and all their power is to be used in his name, 1 Cor. v. 4.

Now, 1. The power here delegated is a spiritual power; it is a power *pertaining to the kingdom of heaven,* that is, to the church, that part of it which is militant here on earth, to the gospel dispensation; that is it about which the apostolical and ministerial power is wholly conversant. It is not any civil, secular power that is hereby conveyed, Christ's *kingdom is not of this world;* their instructions afterward were *in things pertaining to the kingdom God,* Acts i. 3.

2. It is the *power* of the keys that is given, alluding to the custom of investing men with authority in such a place, by delivering to them the keys of the place. Or as the master of the house gives the keys to the steward, the keys of the stores where the provisions are kept, that he may give to every one in the house *his portion of meat in due season* (Luke xii. 42), and deny it as there is occasion, according to the rules of the family. Ministers are *stewards,* 1 Cor. iv. 1; Tit. i. 7. Eliakim, who had *the key* of the house of David, *was over the household,* Isa. xxii. 22.

3. It is a power to *bind and loose,* that is (following the metaphor of the keys), to shut and open. Joseph, who was lord of Pharaoh's house, and steward of the stores, had power *to bind his princes, and to teach his senators wisdom,* Ps. cv. 21, 22. When the stores and treasures of the house are shut up from any, they are bound, *interdico tibi aquâ et igne—I forbid thee the use of fire and water;* when they are opened to them again, they are loosed from that bond, are discharged from the censure, and restored to their liberty.

4. It is a power which Christ has promised to own the due administration of; he will ratify the sentences of his stewards with his own approbation; *It shall be bound in heaven, and loosed in heaven:* not that Christ hath hereby obliged himself to confirm all church-censures, right or wrong; but such as are duly passed according to the word, *clave non errante—the key turning the right way,* such are sealed in heaven; that is, the word of the gospel, in the mouth of faithful ministers, is to be looked upon, not as the word of man, but as the word of God, and to be received accordingly, 1 Thes. ii. 13; John xii. 20.

Now *the keys of the kingdom of heaven are,*

(1.) The key of *doctrine,* called the key of *knowledge.* "Your business shall be to explain to the world the will of God, both as to truth and duty; and for this you shall have your commissions, credentials, and full instructions to bind and loose:" these, in the common speech of the Jews, at that time, signified to prohibit and permit; to teach or declare a thing to be unlawful was *to bind;* to be lawful, was to *loose.* Now the apostles had an extraordinary power of this kind; some things forbidden by the law of Moses were now to be allowed, as the eating of such and such meats; some things allowed there were now to be forbidden, as divorce; and the apostles were empowered to declare this to the world, and men might take it upon their words. When Peter was first taught himself, and then taught others, *to call nothing common or unclean,* this power was exercised. There is also an ordinary power hereby conveyed to all ministers, to preach the gospel as appointed officers; to tell people, in God's name, and according to the scriptures, *what is good, and what the Lord requires of them:* and they who *declare the whole counsel of God,* use these keys well, Acts xx. 27.

Some make the giving of the keys to allude to the custom of the Jews in creating a doctor of the law, which was to put into his hand the keys of the chest where the book of the law was kept, denoting his being authorized to take and read it; and *the binding and loosing,* to allude to the fashion about their books, which were in rolls; they shut them by binding them up with a string, which they untied when they opened them. Christ gives his apostles power to shut or open the book of the gospel to people, as the case required. See the exercise of this power, Acts xiii. 46; xviii. 6. When ministers preach pardon and peace to the penitent, wrath and the curse to the impenitent, in Christ's name, they act then pursuant to this authority of binding and loosing.

(2.) The key of *discipline,* which is but the application of the former to particular persons, upon a right estimate of their characters and actions. It is not legislative power that is hereby conferred, but judicial; the judge doth not make the law, but only declares what is law, and upon an impartial enquiry into the merits of the cause, gives sentence accordingly. Such is *the power of the keys,* wherever it is lodged, with reference to church-membership and the privileges thereof. [1.] Christ's ministers have a power to admit into the church; "*Go, disciple all nations, baptizing them;* those who profess faith in Christ, and obedience to him, admit them and their seed members of the church by baptism." Ministers are to let in to *the wedding-feast those that are bidden;* and to keep out such as are apparently unfit for so holy a communion. [2.] They have a power to expel and cast out such as have forfeited their church-membership, that is binding; refusing to unbelievers the application of gospel promises and the seals of them; and declaring to such as appear to be *in the gall of bitterness and bond of iniquity,* that *they have no part or lot in the matter,* as Peter did to Simon Magus, though he had been baptized; and this is a binding over to the judgment of God. [3.] They have a power to restore and to receive in again, upon their repentance, such as had been thrown out; to loose those whom they had bound; declaring to them, that, if their repentance be sincere, the promise of pardon belongs to them. The apostles had a miraculous gift of *discerning spirits;* yet even *they* went by the rule of outward appearances (as Acts viii. 21; 1 Cor. v. 1; 2 Cor. ii. 7; 1 Tim. i. 20), which ministers may still make a judgment upon, if they be skilful and faithful.

Lastly, Here is the charge which Christ gave his disciples, to keep this private for the present (*v.* 20); *They must tell no man that he was Jesus the Christ.* What they had professed to him, they must not yet publish to the world, for several reasons; 1. Because this was the time of preparation for his kingdom: the great thing now preached, was, that *the kingdom of heaven was at hand;* and therefore those things were now to be insisted on, which were proper to make way for Christ; as the doctrine of repentance; not this great truth, in and with which *the kingdom of heaven* was to be actually set up. Every thing is beautiful in its season, and it is good advice, *Prepare thy work, and afterwards build,* Prov. xxiv. 27. 2. Christ would have his Messiahship proved by his works, and would rather *they* should testify of him than that his *disciples* should, because their testimony was but as his own, which he insisted not on. See John v. 31, 34. He was so secure of the demonstration of his miracles, that he waived other witnesses, John x. 25, 38. 3. If they had known *that he was Jesus the Christ, they would not have crucified the Lord of glory,* 1 Cor. ii. 8. 4. Christ would not have the apostles preach this, till they had the most convincing evidence ready to allege in confirmation of it. Great truths may suffer damage by being asserted before they can be sufficiently proved. Now the great proof of Jesus being the Christ was his resurrection: by that *he was declared to be the Son of God, with power;* and therefore the divine wisdom would not have this truth preached, till that could be alleged for proof of it. 5. It was requisite that the preachers of so great a truth should be furnished with greater measures of the Spirit than the apostles as yet had; therefore the open asserting of it was adjourned till the Spirit should be poured out upon them. But when Christ was glorified and the Spirit poured out, we find Peter proclaiming upon the house-tops what was here spoken in a corner (Acts ii. 36), *That God hath made this same Jesus both Lord and Christ;* for, as there is a time to keep silence, so there is a time to speak.

21 From that time forth began
Jesus to show unto his disciples, how
that he must go unto Jerusalem, and
suffer many things of the elders and
chief priests and scribes, and be killed,
and be raised again the third day.
22 Then Peter took him, and began
to rebuke him, saying, Be it far from
thee, Lord: this shall not be unto
thee. 23 But he turned, and said
unto Peter, Get thee behind me,
Satan: thou art an offence unto me:
for thou savourest not the things that
be of God, but those that be of men.

We have here Christ's discourse with his disciples concerning his own sufferings; in which observe,

I. Christ's foretelling of his sufferings. Now he *began* to do it, and from this time he frequently spake of them. Some hints he had already given of his sufferings, as when he said, *Destroy this temple:* when he spake of *the Son of man being lifted up,* and of *eating his flesh, and drinking his blood:* but now he *began* to show it, to speak plainly and expressly of it. Hitherto he had not touched upon this, because the disciples were weak, and could not well bear the notice of a thing so very strange, and so very melancholy; but now that they were more ripe in knowledge, and strong in faith, he began to tell them this. Note, Christ reveals his mind to his people gradually, and lets in light as they can bear it, and are fit to receive it.

From that time, when they had made that full confession of Christ, that he was the Son of God, then he began to show them this. When he found them knowing in one truth, he taught them another; *for to him that has, shall be given.* Let them first be established in the principles of the doctrine of Christ, and then go on to perfection, Heb. vi. 1. If they had not been well grounded in the belief of Christ's being the Son of God, it would have been a great shaking to their faith. All truths are not to be spoken to all persons at all times, but such as are proper and suitable to their present state. Now observe,

1. What he foretold concerning his sufferings, the particulars and circumstances of them, and all surprising.

(1.) The place where he should suffer. He must go to Jerusalem, the head city, the holy city, and suffer there. Though he lived most of his time in Galilee, he must die at Jerusalem; there all the sacrifices were offered, there therefore *he* must die, *who is the great sacrifice.*

(2.) The persons by whom he should suffer; *the elders, and chief priests, and scribes;* these made up the great sanhedrim, which sat at Jerusalem, and was had in veneration by the people. Those that should have been most forward in owning and admiring Christ, were the most bitter in persecuting him. It was strange that men of knowledge in the scripture, who professed to expect the Messiah's coming, and pretended to have something sacred in their character, should use him thus barbarously when he did come. It was the Roman power that condemned and crucified Christ, but he lays it at the door of *the chief priests and scribes,* who were the first movers.

(3.) What he should suffer; *he must suffer many things, and be killed.* His enemies' insatiable malice, and his own invincible patience, appear in the variety and multiplicity of his sufferings (he suffered many things) and in the extremity of them; nothing less than his death would satisfy them, he must be killed. The suffering of many things, if not unto death, is more tolerable; for while there is life, there is hope; and death, without such prefaces, would be less terrible; but *he must* first *suffer many things, and* then *be killed.*

(4.) What should be the happy issue of all his sufferings; he shall *be raised again the third day.* As the prophets, so Christ himself, when he testified beforehand his sufferings, testified withal the glory that should follow, 1 Pet. i. 11. His rising again the third day proved him to be the Son of God, notwithstanding his sufferings; and therefore he mentions that, to keep up their faith. When he spoke of the cross and the shame, he spoke in the same breath of *the joy set before him,* in the prospect of which *he endured the cross, and despised the shame.* Thus we must look upon Christ's suffering for us, trace in it the way to his glory; and thus we must look upon our suffering for Christ, look through it to the recompence of reward. *If we suffer with him, we shall reign with him.*

2. Why he foretold his sufferings. (1.) To show that they were the product of an eternal counsel and consent; were agreed upon between the Father and the Son from eternity; *Thus it behoved Christ to suffer.* The matter was settled in *the determinate counsel and foreknowledge,* in pursuance of his own voluntary susception and undertaking for our salvation; his sufferings were no surprise to him, did not come upon him as a snare, but he had a distinct and certain foresight of them, which greatly magnifies his love, John xviii. 4. (2.) To rectify the mistakes which his disciples had imbibed concerning the external pomp and power of his kingdom. Believing him to be the Messiah, they counted upon nothing but dignity and authority in the world; but here Christ reads them another lesson, tells them of the cross and sufferings; nay, that the chief priests and the elders, whom, it is likely, they expected to be the supports of the Messiah's kingdom, should be its great enemies and persecutors; this would give them quite another idea of that kingdom which they themselves had preached the approach of; and it was requisite that this mistake should be rectified Those that follow Christ must be dealt plainly with, and warned not to expect great things in this world. (3.) It was to prepare them for the share, at least, of sorrow and fear, which they must have in his sufferings. When he suffered many things, the disciples could not but suffer some; if their Master be killed, they will be seized with terror; let them know it before, that they may provide accordingly, and, being fore-*warned,* may be fore-*armed.*

II. The offence which Peter took at this he said, *Be it far from thee, Lord:* probabl he spake the sense of the rest of the disciples, as before, for he was chief speaker. *He took him, and began to rebuke him.* Perhaps Peter was a little elevated with the great things Christ had now said unto him, which made him more bold with Christ than did become him; so hard is it to keep the spirit low and humble in the midst of great advancements!

1. It did not become Peter to contradict his Master, or take upon him to advise him; he might have wished, *that, if it were possible, this cup might pass away,* without saying so peremptorily, *This shall not be,* when Christ had said, *It must be. Shall any teach God knowledge? He that reproveth God, let him answer it.* Note, When God's dispensations are either intricate or cross to us, it becomes us silently to acquiesce in, and not to prescribe to, the divine will; God knows what he has to do, without our teaching. Unless we know the mind of the Lord, it is not for us to be his counsellors, Rom. xi. 34.

2. It savoured much of fleshly wisdom, for him to appear so warmly against suffering, and to startle thus at the offence of the cross. It is the corrupt part of us, that is thus solicitous to sleep in a whole skin. We are apt to look upon sufferings as they relate to this present life, to which they are uneasy; but there are other rules to measure them by, which, if duly observed, will enable us cheerfully to bear them, Rom. viii. 18. See how passionately Peter speaks: "*Be it far from*

thee, Lord. God forbid, that thou shouldst suffer and be killed; we cannot bear the thoughts of it." *Master, spare thyself:* so it might be read; ἵλεώς σοι, κύριε—"*Be merciful to thyself,* and then no one else can be cruel to thee; pity thyself, and then *this shall not be to thee.*" He would have Christ to dread suffering as much as he did; but we mistake, if we measure Christ's love and patience by our own. He intimates, likewise, the improbability of the thing, humanly speaking; "*This shall not be unto thee.* It is impossible that one who hath so great an interest in the people as thou hast, should be crushed by the elders, who fear the people: this can never be; we that have followed thee, will fight for thee, if occasion be; and there are thousands that will stand by us."

III. Christ's displeasure against Peter for this suggestion of his, *v.* 23. We do not read of any thing said or done by any of his disciples, at any time, that he resented so much as this, though they often offended.

Observe, 1. How he expressed his displeasure: He turned upon Peter, and (we may suppose) with a frown said, *Get thee behind me, Satan.* He did not so much as take time to deliberate upon it, but gave an immediate reply to the temptation, which was such as made it to appear how ill he took it. Just now, he had said, *Blessed art thou, Simon,* and had even laid him in his bosom; but here, *Get thee behind me, Satan;* and there was cause for both. Note, A good man may by a surprise of temptation soon grow very unlike himself. He answered him as he did Satan himself, *ch.* iv. 10. Note, (1.) It is the subtlety of Satan, to send temptations to us by the unsuspected hands of our best and dearest friends. Thus he assaulted Adam by Eve, Job by his wife, and here Christ by his beloved Peter. It concerns us therefore not to be ignorant of his devices, but to stand against his wiles and depths, by standing always upon our guard against sin, whoever moves us to it. Even the kindnesses of our friends are often abused by Satan, and made use of as temptations to us. (2.) Those who have their spiritual senses exercised, will be aware of the voice of Satan, even in a friend, a disciple, a minister, that dissuades them from their duty. We must not regard who speaks, so much as what is spoken; we should learn to know the devil's voice when he speaks in a saint as well as when he speaks in a serpent. Whoever takes us off from that which is good, and would have us afraid of doing too much for God, speaks Satan's language. (3.) We must be free and faithful in reproving the dearest friend we have, that saith or doth amiss, though it may be under colour of kindness to us. We must not compliment, but rebuke, mistaken courtesies. *Faithful are the wounds of a friend.* Such smitings must be accounted kindnesses, Ps. cxli. 5. (4.) Whatever appears to be a temptation to sin, must be resisted with abhorrence, and not parleyed with.

2. What was the ground of this displeasure; why did Christ thus resent a motion that seemed not only harmless, but kind? Two reasons are given:

(1.) *Thou art an offence to me*—Σκάνδαλον μοῦ εἶ—*Thou art my hindrance* (so it may be read); "thou standest in my way." Christ was hastening on in the work of our salvation, and his heart was so much upon it, that he took it ill to be hindered, or tempted to start back from the hardest and most discouraging part of his undertaking. So strongly was he engaged for our redemption, that they who but indirectly endeavoured to divert him from it, touched him in a very tender and sensible part. Peter was not so sharply reproved for disowning and denying his Master in his sufferings as he was for dissuading him from them; though that was the defect, this the excess, of kindness. It argues a very great firmness and resolution of mind in any business, when it is *an offence* to be dissuaded, and a man will not endure to hear any thing to the contrary; like that of Ruth, *Entreat me not to leave thee.* Note, Our Lord Jesus preferred our salvation before his own ease and safety; for *even Christ pleased not himself* (Rom. xv. 3); he came into the world, not to spare himself, as Peter advised, but to spend himself.

See why he called Peter *Satan,* when he suggested this to him; because, whatever stood in the way of our salvation, he looked upon as coming from the devil, who is a sworn enemy to it. The same Satan that afterward entered into Judas, maliciously to destroy him in his undertaking, here prompted Peter plausibly to divert him from it. Thus *he changes himself into an angel of light.*

Thou art an offence to me. Note, [1.] Those that engage in any great and good work must expect to meet with hindrance and opposition from friends and foes, from within and from without. [2.] Those that obstruct our progress in any duty must be looked upon as an offence to us. *Then* we do the will of God, as Christ did, *whose meat and drink it was to do it,* when it is a trouble to us to be solicited from our duty. Those that hinder us from doing or suffering for God, when we are called to it, whatever they are in other things in that they are *Satans, adversaries* to us.

(2.) *Thou savourest not the things that are of God, but those that are of men.* Note, [1.] *The things that are of God,* that is, the concerns of his will and glory, often clash and interfere with *the things that are of men,* that is, with our own wealth, pleasure, and reputation. While we mind Christian duty as our way and work, and the divine favour as our end and portion, we *savour the things of God;* but if these be minded, the flesh must be denied, hazards must be run and hardships borne; and here is the trial which of the two we savour. [2.] Those that inordinately fear, and industriously decline suffering for Christ, when they are called to it, savour more of the things of man than of the things of God; they relish those things more themselves, and make it appear to others that they do so.

24 Then said Jesus unto his disciples,
If any *man* will come after me, let
him deny himself, and take up his
cross, and follow me. 25 For whosoever will save his life shall lose it:
and whosoever will lose his life for
my sake shall find it. 26 For what
is a man profited, if he shall gain the
whole world, and lose his own soul?
or what shall a man give in exchange
for his soul? 27 For the Son of man
shall come in the glory of his Father
with his angels; and then he shall
reward every man according to his
works. 28 Verily I say unto you,
There be some standing here, which
shall not taste of death, till they see
the Son of man coming in his kingdom.

Christ, having shown his disciples that *he* must suffer, and that he was ready and willing to suffer, here shows them that *they* must suffer too, and must be ready and willing. It is a weighty discourse that we have in these verses.

I. Here is the law of discipleship laid down, and the terms fixed, upon which we may have the honour and benefit of it, *v.* 24. He said this to his disciples, not only that they might instruct others concerning it, but that by this rule they might examine their own sincerity. Observe,

1. What it is to be a disciple of Christ; it is to come after him. When Christ called his disciples, this was the word of command, *Follow me.* A true disciple of Christ is one that doth follow him in duty, and shall follow him to glory. He is one that comes after Christ, not one that prescribes to him, as Peter now undertook to do, forgetting his place. A disciple of Christ comes after him, as the sheep after the shepherd, the servant after his master, the soldiers after their captain; he is one that aims at the same end that Christ aimed at, the glory of God, and the glory of heaven: and one that walks in the same way that he walked in, is led by his Spirit, treads in his steps, submits to his conduct, and *follows the Lamb, whithersoever he goes,* Rev. xiv. 4.

2. What are the great things required of those that will be Christ's disciples; *If any man will come,* εἰ τις θέλει—*If any man be willing* to come. It denotes a deliberate choice, and cheerfulness and resolution in that choice. Many are disciples more by chance or the will of others than by any act of their own will; but Christ will have his people volunteers, Ps. cx. 3. It is as if Christ had said, "If any of the people that are not my disciples, be steadfastly minded to come to me, and if you that are, be in like manner minded to adhere to me, it is upon these terms, these and no other; you must *follow me* in sufferings as well as in other things, and therefore when you sit down to count the cost, reckon upon it."

Now what are these terms?

(1.) *Let him deny himself.* Peter had advised Christ to spare himself, and would be ready, in the like case, to take the advice; but Christ tells them all, they must be so far from *sparing* themselves, that they must *deny* themselves. Herein they must come after Christ, for his birth, and life, and death, were all a continued act of self-denial, a self-emptying, Phil. ii. 7, 8. If self-denial be a hard lesson, and against the grain to flesh and blood, it is no more than what our Master learned and practised before us and for us, both for our redemption and for our instruction; and *the servant is not above his lord.* Note, All the disciples and followers of Jesus Christ must deny themselves. It is the fundamental law of admission into Christ's school, and the first and great lesson to be learned in this school, to deny ourselves; it is both the *strait* gate, and the *narrow* way; it is necessary in order to our learning all the other good lessons that are there taught. We must deny ourselves absolutely, we must not admire our own shadow, nor gratify our own humour; we must not lean to our own understanding, nor seek our own things, nor be our own end. We must deny ourselves comparatively; we must deny ourselves for Christ, and his will and glory, and the service of his interest in the world; we must deny ourselves for our brethren, and for their good; and we must deny ourselves for ourselves, deny the appetites of the body for the benefit of the soul.

(2.) *Let him take up his cross.* The cross is here put for all sufferings, as men or Christians; providential afflictions, persecutions for righteousness' sake, every trouble that befals us, either for doing well or for not doing ill. The troubles of Christians are fitly called *crosses,* in allusion to the death of the cross, which Christ was obedient to; and it should reconcile us to troubles, and take off the terror of them, that they are what we bear in common with Christ, and such as he hath borne before us. Note, [1.] Every disciple of Christ hath his cross, and must count upon it; as each hath his special duty to be done, so each hath his special trouble to be borne, and every one feels most from his own burthen. Crosses are the common lot of God's children, but of this common lot each hath his particular share. That is our cross which Infinite Wisdom has appointed for us, and a Sovereign Providence has laid on us, as fittest for us. It is good for us to call the cross we are under *our own,* and entertain it accordingly. We are apt to think we could bear such a one's cross better than our own; but that is best which is, and we ought to make the best of it. [2.] Every disciple of Christ must take up that which the wise God hath made his cross. It is an allusion to the Roman custom of compelling those that were condemned to be crucified, to carry their cross: when Simon carried Christ's cross after him, this phrase was illustrated. *First,* It is supposed that the cross lies in our way, and is prepared for us. We must not make crosses to ourselves, but must accommodate ourselves to those which God has made for us. Our rule is, not to go a step out of the way of duty, either to meet a cross, or to miss one. We must not by our rashness and indiscretion pull crosses down upon our own heads, but must take them up when they are laid in our way. We must so manage an affliction, that it may not be a stumbling-block or hindrance to us in any service we have to do for God. We must take it up out of our way, by getting over *the offence of the cross; None of these things move me;* and we must then go on with it in our way, though it lie heavy. *Secondly,* That which we have to do, is, not only to bear the cross (that a stock, or a stone, or a stick may do), not only to be silent under it, but we must *take up* the cross, must improve it to some good advantage. We should not say, "This is an evil, and I must bear it, because I cannot help it;" but, "This is an evil, and I will bear it, because it shall work for my good." When we *rejoice in our afflictions, and glory in them,* then we take up the cross. This fitly follows upon denying ourselves; for he that will not deny himself the pleasures of sin, and the advantages of this world for Christ, when it comes to the push, will never have the heart to take up his cross. "He that cannot take up the resolution to live a saint, has a demonstration within himself, that he is never likely to die a martyr;" so Archbishop Tillotson.

(2.) *Let him follow me,* in this particular of taking up the cross. Suffering saints must look unto Jesus, and take from him both direction and encouragement in suffering. Do we bear the cross? We therein follow Christ, who bears it *before* us, bears it *for* us, and so bears it *from* us. He bore the heavy end of the cross, the end that had the curse upon it, that was a heavy end, and so made the other light and easy for us. Or, we may take it in general, we must follow Christ in all instances of holiness and obedience. Note, The disciples of Christ must study to imitate their Master, and conform themselves in every thing to his example, and continue in well-doing, whatever crosses lie in their way. To do well and to suffer ill, is to follow Christ. *If any man will come after me, let him follow me;* that seems to be *idem per idem—the same thing over again.* What is the difference? Surely it is this, "*If any man will come after me,* in profession, and so have the name and credit of a disciple, *let him follow me in truth,* and so do the work and duty of a disciple." Or thus, "*If any man will set out after me,* in good beginnings, *let him* continue to *follow me* with all perseverance." That is *following the Lord fully,* as Caleb did. Those that come after Christ, must follow after him.

II. Here are arguments to persuade us to submit to these laws, and come up to these terms. Self-denial, and patient suffering, are hard lessons, which will never be learned if we consult with flesh and blood; let us therefore consult with our Lord Jesus, and see what advice he gives us; and here he gives us,

1. Some considerations proper to engage us to these duties of self-denial and suffering for Christ. Consider,

(1.) The weight of that eternity which depends upon our present choice (*v.* 25); *Whosoever will save his life,* by denying Christ, *shall lose it: and whosoever* is content to *lose his life,* for owning Christ, *shall find it.* Here are *life and death, good and evil, the blessing and the curse, set before us.* Observe,

[1.] The misery that attends the most plausible apostasy. *Whosoever will save his life* in this world, if it be by sin, he *shall lose it* in another; he that forsakes Christ, to preserve a temporal life and avoid a temporal death, will certainly come short of eternal life, and will be hurt of the second death, and eternally held by it. There cannot be a fairer pretence for apostasy and iniquity than saving the life by it, so cogent is the law of self-preservation; and yet even that is folly, for it will prove in the end self-destruction; the life saved is but for a moment, the death shunned is but as a sleep; but the life lost is everlasting, and the death run upon is the depth and complement of all misery, and an endless separation from all good. Now, let any rational man consider of it, take advice and speak his mind, whether there is any thing got, at long run, by apostasy, though a man save his estate, preferment, or life, by it.

[2.] The advantage that attends the most perilous and expensive constancy; *Whosoever will lose his life for Christ's sake* in this world, *shall find it* in a better, infinitely to his advantage. Note, *First,* Many a life is lost, for Christ's sake, in doing his work, by labouring fervently for his name; in suffering work, by choosing rather to die than to deny him or his truths and ways. Christ's holy religion is handed down to us, sealed with the blood of thousands, that have *not known their own souls,* but have *despised their lives* (as Job speaks in another case), though very valuable ones, when they have stood in competition with their duty and *the testimony of Jesus,* Rev. xx. 4. *Secondly,* Though many have been losers for Christ, even of life itself, yet never any one was, or will be, a loser by him in the end. The loss of other comforts, for Christ, may possibly be made up in this world (Mark x. 30); the loss of life cannot, but it shall be made up in the other world, in an eternal life; the believing prospect of which hath been the great support of suffering saints in all ages. An assurance of the life they should find, in lieu of the life they hazarded, hath enabled them to triumph over death in all its terrors; to go smiling to a scaffold, and stand singing at a stake, and to call the utmost instances of their enemies' rage but *a light affliction.*

[3.] The worth of the soul which lies at stake, and the worthlessness of the world in comparison of it (*v.* 26). *What is a man profited, if he gain the whole world and lose his own soul? τὴν ψυχὴν αυτοῦ*; the same word which is translated *his life* (*v.* 25), for the *soul* is the *life,* Gen. ii. 7. This alludes to that common principle, that, whatever a man gets, if he lose his life, it will do him no good, he cannot enjoy his gains. But it looks higher, and speaks of the soul as immortal, and a loss of it beyond death, which cannot be compensated by the gain of the whole world. Note, *First,* Every man has a soul of his own. The soul is the spiritual and immortal part of man, which thinks and reasons, has a power of reflection and prospect, which actuates the body now, and will shortly act in a separation from the body. Our souls are our own not in respect of dominion and property (for we are not our *own, All souls are mine,* saith God), but in respect of nearness and concern; our souls are our own, for they are ourselves. *Secondly,* It is possible for the soul to be lost, and there is danger of it. The soul is lost when it is eternally separated from all the good to all the evil that a soul is capable of; when it dies as far as a soul can die; when it is separated from the favour of God, and sunk under his wrath and curse. A man is never undone till he is in hell. *Thirdly,* If the soul be lost, it is of the sinner's own losing. The *man loses his own soul,* for he does that which is certainly destroying to it, and neglects that which alone would be saving, Hos. xiii. 9. The sinner dies because he will die; *his blood is on his own head. Fourthly,* One soul is worth more than all the world; our own souls are of greater value to us than all the wealth, honour, and pleasures of this present time, if we had them. Here is *the whole world* set in the scale against *one soul,* and *Tekel* written upon it; it is weighed in the balance, and found too light to weigh it down. This is Christ's judgment upon the matter, and he is a competent Judge; he had reason to know the price of *souls,* for he redeemed them; nor would he under-rate the world, for he made it. *Fifthly,* The winning of the world is often the losing of the soul. Many a one has ruined his eternal interests by his preposterous and inordinate care to secure and advance his temporal ones. It is *the love of the world,* and the eager pursuit of it, *that drowns men in destruction and perdition. Sixthly,* The loss of the soul is so great a loss, that the gain of the whole world will not countervail it, or make it up. He that loses his soul, though it be to gain the world, makes a very bad bargain for himself, and will sit down at last an unspeakable loser. When he comes to balance the account, and to compare profit and loss, he will find that, instead of the advantage he promised himself, he is ruined to all intents and purposes, is irreparably broken.

What shall a man give in exchange for his soul? Note, If once the soul be lost, it is lost for ever. There is no ἀνταλλάγμα—*counter-price,* that can be paid, or will be accepted. It is a loss that can never be repaired, never be retrieved. If, after that great price which Christ laid down to redeem our souls, and to restore us to the possession of them, they be so neglected for the world, that they come to be lost, that new mortgage will never be taken off; there remains no more sacrifice for sins, nor price for souls, but the equity of redemption is eternally precluded. Therefore it is good to be wise in time, and do well for ourselves.

2. Here are some considerations proper to encourage us in self-denial and suffering for Christ.

(1.) The assurance we have of Christ's glory, at his second coming to judge the world, *v.* 27. If we look to the end of all these things, the period of the world, and the posture of souls then, we shall thence form a very different idea of the present state of things. If we see things as they *will* appear then, we shall see them as they *should* appear now.

The great encouragement to steadfastness in religion is taken from the second coming of Christ, considering it,

[1.] As his honour; *The Son of man shall come in the glory of his Father, with his angels.* To look upon Christ in his state of humiliation, so abased, so abused, *a reproach of men, and despised of the people,* would discourage his followers from taking any pains, or running any hazards for him; but with an eye of faith to see the Captain of our salvation coming in his glory, in all the pomp and power of the upper world, will animate us, and make us think nothing too much to do, or too hard to suffer, for him. *The Son of man shall come.* He here gives himself the title of his humble state (he is the *Son of man*), to show that he is not ashamed to own it. His first coming was in the meanness of his children, who being partakers of flesh, he took part of the same; but his second coming will be in the glory of his Father. At his first coming, he was attended with poor disciples; at his second coming, he will be attended with glorious angels; and *if we suffer with him, we shall be glorified with him,* 2 Tim. ii. 12.

[2.] As our concern; *Then he shall reward*

every man according to his works. Observe, *First,* Jesus Christ will come as a Judge, to dispense rewards and punishments, infinitely exceeding the greatest that any earthly potentate has the dispensing of. The terror of men's tribunal (*ch.* x. 18) will be taken off by a believing prospect of the glory of Christ's tribunal. *Secondly,* Men will then be rewarded, not according to their gains in this world, but according to their works, according to what they were and did. In that day, the treachery of backsliders will be punished with eternal destruction, and the constancy of faithful souls recompensed with a crown of life. *Thirdly,* The best preparative for that day is to *deny ourselves, and take up our cross, and follow Christ;* for so we shall make the Judge our Friend, and these things will then pass well in the account. *Fourthly,* The rewarding of men according to their works is deferred till that day. Here good and evil seem to be dispensed promiscuously; we see not apostasy punished with immediate strokes, nor fidelity encouraged with immediate smiles, from heaven; but in that day all will be set to rights. Therefore *judge nothing before the time,* 2 Tim. iv. 6—8.

(2.) The near approach of his kingdom in this world, *v.* 28. It was so near, that there were some attending him who should live to see it. As Simeon was assured that he should not see death till he had seen the Lord's Christ come in the flesh; so some here are assured that they shall not taste death (death is a sensible thing, its terrors are seen, its bitterness is tasted) till they had seen the Lord's Christ coming in his kingdom. At the end of time, he shall come in his Father's glory; but now, in the fulness of time, he was to come in his own kingdom, his mediatorial kingdom. Some little specimen was given of his glory a few days after this, in his transfiguration (*ch.* xvii. 1); then he tried his robes. But this points at Christ's coming by the pouring out of his Spirit, the planting of the gospel church, the destruction of Jerusalem, and the taking away of the place and nation of the Jews, who were the most bitter enemies to Christianity. Here was *the Son of man coming in his kingdom.* Many then present lived to see it, particularly John, who lived till after the destruction of Jerusalem, and saw Christianity planted in the world. Let *this* encourage the followers of Christ to suffer for him, [1.] That their undertaking shall be succeeded; the apostles were employed in setting up Christ's kingdom; let them know, for their comfort, that whatever opposition they meet with, yet they shall carry their point, shall *see of the travail of their soul.* Note, It is a great encouragement to suffering saints to be assured, not only of the safety, but of the advancement of Christ's kingdom among men; not only *notwithstanding* their sufferings, but *by* their sufferings. A believing prospect of the success of the kingdom of grace, as well as of our share in the kingdom of glory, may carry us cheerfully through our sufferings. [2.] That their cause shall be pleaded; their deaths shall be revenged, and their persecutors reckoned with. [3.] That this shall be done shortly, in the present age. Note, The nearer the church's deliverances are, the more cheerful should we be in our sufferings for Christ. *Behold the Judge standeth before the door.* It is spoken as a favour to those that should survive the present cloudy time, that they should see better days. Note, It is desirable to share with the church in her joys, Dan. xii. 12. Observe, Christ saith, *Some* shall live to see those glorious days, not *all;* some shall enter into the promised land, but others shall fall in the wilderness. He does not tell them *who* shall live to see this kingdom, lest if they had known, they should have put off the thoughts of dying, but *some* of them shall; *Behold, the Lord is at hand. The Judge standeth before the door; be patient, therefore, brethren.*

CHAP. XVII.

In this chapter we have, I. Christ in his pomp and glory transfigured, ver. 1—13. II. Christ in his power and grace, casting the devil out of a child, ver. 14—21. And, III. Christ in his poverty and great humiliation, 1. Foretelling his own sufferings ver. 22, 23. 2. Paying tribute, ver. 24—27. So that here is Christ, the Brightness of his Father's glory, by himself purging our sins, paying our debts, and destroying for us him that had the power of death, that is, the devil. Thus were the several indications of Christ's gracious intentions admirably interwoven.

AND after six days Jesus taketh
Peter, James, and John his brother, and bringeth them up into an
high mountain apart, 2 And was
transfigured before them: and his
face did shine as the sun, and his
raiment was white as the light. 3
And, behold, there appeared unto
them Moses and Elias talking with
him. 4 Then answered Peter, and
said unto Jesus, Lord, it is good for
us to be here: if thou wilt, let us
make here three tabernacles; one for
thee, and one for Moses, and one for
Elias. 5 While he yet spake, behold,
a bright cloud overshadowed them:
and behold a voice out of the cloud,
which said, This is my beloved Son,
in whom I am well pleased; hear ye
him. And when the disciples heard
it, they fell on their face, and were
sore afraid. 7 And Jesus came and
touched them, and said, Arise, and be
not afraid. 8 And when they had
lifted up their eyes, they saw no man,
save Jesus only. 9 And as they
came down from the mountain, Jesus
charged them, saying, Tell the vision
to no man, until the Son of man be

risen again from the dead. 10 And
his disciples asked him, saying, Why
then say the scribes that Elias must
first come? 11 And Jesus answered
and said unto them, Elias truly shall
first come, and restore all things. 12
But I say unto you, that Elias is come
already, and they knew him not, but
have done unto him whatsoever they
listed. Likewise shall also the Son
of man suffer of them. 13 Then
the disciples understood that he spake
unto them of John the Baptist.

We have here the story of Christ's transfiguration; he had said that the *Son of man should* shortly *come in his kingdom,* with which promise all the three evangelists industriously connect this story; as if Christ's transfiguration were intended for a specimen and an earnest of the kingdom of Christ, and of that light and love of his, which therein appears to his select and sanctified ones. Peter speaks of this as *the power and coming of our Lord Jesus* (2 Pet. i. 16); because it was an emanation of his power, and a previous notice of his coming, which was fitly introduced by such prefaces.

When Christ was here in his humiliation, though his state, in the main, was a state of abasement and afflictions, there were some glimpses of his glory intermixed, that he himself might be the more encouraged in his sufferings, and others the less offended. His birth, his baptism, his temptation, and his death, were the most remarkable instances of his humiliation; and these were each of them attended with some signal points of glory, and the smiles of heaven. But the series of his public ministry being a continued humiliation, here, just in the midst of that, comes in this discovery of his glory. As, now that he is in heaven, he has his condescensions, so, when he was on earth, he had his advancements.

Now concerning Christ's transfiguration, observe,

I. The circumstances of it, which are here noted, *v.* 1.

1. The time; *six days* after he had the solemn conference with his disciples, *ch.* xvi. 21. St. Luke saith, *It was about eight days after,* six whole days intervening, and this the eighth day, that day seven-night. Nothing is recorded to be said or done by our Lord Jesus for six days before his transfiguration; thus, before some great appearances, *there was silence in heaven for the space of half an hour,* Rev. viii. 1. *Then* when Christ seems to be doing nothing for his church, expect, ere long, something more than ordinary.

2. The place; it was *on the top of a high mountain apart.* Christ chose a mountain, (1.) As a secret place. He went apart; for though a city upon a hill can hardly be hid, two or three persons upon a hill can hardly be found; therefore their private oratories were commonly on mountains. Christ chose a retired place to be transfigured in, because his appearing publicly in his glory was not agreeable to his present state; and thus he would show his humility, and teach us that privacy much befriends our communion with God. Those that would maintain intercourse with Heaven, must frequently withdraw from the converse and business of this world; and they will find themselves never less alone than when alone, for the Father is with them. (2.) Though a sublime place, elevated above things below. Note, Those that would have a transforming fellowship with God, must not only retire, but ascend; lift up their hearts, and *seek things above.* The call is, *Come up hither,* Rev. iv. 1.

3. The witnesses of it. He took with him Peter and James and John. (1.) He took three, a competent number to testify what they should see; for *out of the mouth of two or three witnesses shall every word be established.* Christ makes his appearances certain enough, but not too common; *not to all the people, but to witnesses* (Acts x. 41), that they might be blessed, who have not seen, and yet have believed. (2.) He took these three because they were the chief of his disciples, the first three of the worthies of the Son of David; probably they excelled in gifts and graces; they were Christ's favourites, singled out to be the witnesses of his retirements. They were present when he raised the damsel to life, Mark v. 37. They were afterward to be the witnesses of his agony, and this was to prepare them for that. Note, A sight of Christ's glory, while we are here in this world, is a good preparative for our sufferings with him, as these are preparatives for the sight of his glory in the other world. Paul, who had abundance of trouble, had abundance of revelations.

II. The manner of it (*v.* 2); *He was transfigured before them.* The substance of his body remained the same, but the accidents and appearances of it were greatly altered; he was not turned into a spirit, but his body, which had appeared in weakness and dishonour, now appeared in power and glory. *He was transfigured, μεταμορφώθη—he was metamorphosed.* The profane poets amused and abused the world with idle extravagant stories of metamorphoses, especially the metamorphoses of their gods, such as were disparaging and diminishing to them, equally false and ridiculous; to these some think Peter has an eye, when, being about to mention this transfiguration of Christ, he saith, *We have not followed cunningly devised fables when we made it known unto you,* 2 Pet. i. 16. Christ was both God and man; but, in the days of his flesh, he took on him the *form of a servant—μορφὴν δούλου,* Phil. ii. 7. He drew a veil over the glory of his godhead; but now, in his transfiguration, he put by that veil, appeared ἐν μορφῇ θεοῦ—in the form of God (Phil. ii. 6), and gave his disciples a glimpse of his glory, which could not but change his form.

The great truth which we declare, is, that *God is Light* (1 John i. 5), *dwells in light* (1 Tim. vi. 16), *covers himself with light*, Ps. civ. 2. And therefore when Christ would appear in the *form of God*, he appeared *in light*, the most glorious of all visible beings, the first-born of the creation, and most nearly resembling the eternal Parent. Christ is *the Light;* while he was in the world, he *shined in darkness*, and therefore *the world knew him not* (John i. 5, 10); but, at this time, that Light shined out of the darkness.

Now his transfiguration appeared in two things:

1. *His face did shine as the sun.* The face is the principal part of the body, by which we are known; therefore such a brightness was put on Christ's face, that face which afterward *he hid not from shame and spitting.* It shone as the sun when he goes forth in his strength, so clear, so bright; for he is the Sun of righteousness, the Light of the world. The face of Moses shone but as the moon, with a borrowed reflected light, but Christ's shone as the sun, with an innate inherent light, which was the more sensibly glorious, because it suddenly broke out, as it were, from behind a black cloud.

2. *His raiment was white as the light.* All his body was altered, as his face was; so that beams of light, darting from every part through his clothes, made them white and glittering. The shining of the face of Moses was so weak, that it could easily be concealed by a thin veil; but such was the glory of Christ's body, that his clothes were enlightened by it.

III. The companions of it. He will come, at last, *with ten thousands of his saints;* and, as a specimen of that, there now *appeared unto them Moses and Elias talking with him*, *v.* 3. Observe, 1. There were glorified saints attending him, that, when there were *three to bear record on earth*, Peter, James, and John, there might be some to bear record from heaven too. Thus here was a lively resemblance of Christ's kingdom, which is made up of saints in heaven and saints on earth, and to which belong *the spirits of just men made perfect.* We see here, that they who are fallen asleep in Christ are not perished, but exist in a separate state, and shall be forthcoming when there is occasion. 2. These two were Moses and Elias, men very eminent in their day. They had both fasted forty days and forty nights, as Christ did, and wrought other miracles, and were both remarkable at their going out of the world as well as in their living in the world. Elias was carried to heaven in a fiery chariot, and died not. The body of Moses was never found, possibly it was preserved from corruption, and reserved for this appearance. The Jews had great respect for the memory of Moses and Elias, and therefore they came to witness of him, they came to carry tidings concerning him to the upper world. In them the law and the prophets honoured Christ, and bore testimony to him. Moses and Elias appeared to the disciples; they saw them, and heard them talk, and, either by their discourse or by information from Christ, they knew them to be Moses and Elias; glorified saints shall know one another in heaven. They talked with Christ. Note, Christ has communion with the blessed, and will be no stranger to any of the members of that glorified corporation. Christ was now to be sealed in his prophetic office, and therefore these two great prophets were fittest to attend him, as transferring all their honour and interest to him; for *in these last days God speaks to us by his Son*, Heb. i. 1.

IV. The great pleasure and satisfaction that the disciples took in the sight of Christ's glory. Peter, as usual, spoke for the rest; *Lord, it is good for us to be here.* Peter here expresses,

1. The delight they had in this converse; *Lord, it is good to be here.* Though upon a high mountain, which we may suppose rough and unpleasant, bleak and cold, yet *it is good to be here.* He speaks the sense of his fellow-disciples; It is good not only for *me*, but for *us.* He did not covet to monopolize this favour, but gladly takes them in. He saith this to Christ. Pious and devout affections love to pour out themselves before the Lord Jesus. The soul that loves Christ, and loves to be with him, loves to go and tell him so; *Lord, it is good for us to be here.* This intimates a thankful acknowledgment of his kindness in admitting them to this favour. Note, Communion with Christ is the delight of Christians. All the disciples of the Lord Jesus reckon it is good for them to be with him in the holy mount. It is good to be here where Christ is, and whither he brings us along with him by his appointment; it is good to be here, retired and alone with Christ; to be here, where we may behold the beauty of the Lord Jesus, Ps. xxvii. 4. It is pleasant to hear Christ compare notes with Moses and the prophets, to see how all the institutions of the law, and all the predictions of the prophets, pointed at Christ, and were fulfilled in him.

2. The desire they had of the continuance of it; *Let us make here three tabernacles.* There was in this, as in many other of Peter's sayings, a mixture of weakness and of goodwill, more zeal than discretion.

(1.) Here was a zeal for this converse with heavenly things, a laudable complacency in the sight they had of Christ's glory. Note, Those that by faith *behold the beauty of the Lord* in his house, cannot but desire to *dwell there all the days of their life.* It is good having a nail in God's holy place (Ezra ix. 8), a constant abode; to be in holy ordinances as a man at home, not as a wayfaring man. Peter thought this mountain was a fine spot of ground to build upon, and he was for making tabernacles there; as Moses in the wilderness made a tabernacle for the Shechinah, or divine glory.

It argued great respect for his Master and the heavenly guests, with some commendable forgetfulness of himself and his fellow-disciples, that he would have tabernacles for Christ, and Moses, and Elias, but none for himself. He would be content to lie in the open air, on the cold ground, in such good company; if his Master have but where to lay his head, no matter whether he himself has or no.

(2.) Yet in this zeal he betrayed a great deal of weakness and ignorance. What need had Moses and Elias of tabernacles? They belonged to that blessed world, *where they hunger no more, nor doth the sun light upon them.* Christ had lately foretold his sufferings, and bidden his disciples expect the like; Peter forgets this, or, to prevent it, will needs be building tabernacles in the mount of glory, out of the way of trouble. Still he harps upon, *Master, spare thyself,* though he had been so lately checked for it. Note, There is a proneness in good men to expect the crown without the cross. Peter was for laying hold of this as the prize, though he had not yet fought his fight, nor finished his course, as those other disciples, *ch.* xx. 21. We are out in our aim, if we look for a heaven here upon earth. It is not for strangers and pilgrims (such as we are in our best circumstances in this world), to talk of building, or to expect a continuing city.

Yet it is some excuse for the incongruity of Peter's proposal, not only that *he knew not what he said* (Luke ix. 33), but also that he submitted the proposal to the wisdom of Christ; *If thou wilt, let us make tabernacles.* Note, Whatever tabernacles we propose to make to ourselves in this world, we must always remember to ask Christ's leave.

Now to this which Peter said, there was no reply made; the disappearing of the glory would soon answer it. They that promise themselves great things on this earth will soon be undeceived by their own experience.

V. The glorious testimony which God the Father gave to our Lord Jesus, in which *he received from him honour and glory* (2 Pet. i. 17), when *there came this voice from the excellent glory.* This was like proclaiming the titles of honour or the royal style of a prince, when, at his coronation, he appears in his robes of state; and be it known, to the comfort of mankind, the royal style of Christ is taken from his mediation. Thus, in vision, he appeared with a rainbow, the seal of the covenant, about his throne (Rev. iv. 3); for it is his glory to be our Redeemer.

Now concerning this testimony from heaven to Christ, observe.

1. How it came, and in what manner it was introduced.

(1.) There was a cloud. We find often in the Old Testament, that a cloud was the visible token of God's presence; he came down upon mount Sinai in a cloud (Exod. xix. 9), and so to Moses, Exod. xxxiv. 5; Numb. xi. 25. He took possession of the tabernacle in a cloud, and afterwards of the temple; where Christ was in his glory, the temple was, and there God showed himself present. We know not the balancing of the clouds, but we know that much of the intercourse and communication between heaven and earth is maintained by them. By the clouds vapours *as*cend, and rains *de*scend; therefore God is said to make *the clouds his chariots;* so he did here when he descended upon this mount.

(2.) It was a bright cloud. Under the law it was commonly a thick and dark cloud that God made the token of his presence; he came down upon mount Sinai in a thick cloud (Exod. xix. 16), and said he would *dwell in thick darkness;* see 1 Kings viii. 12. But *we are now come, not to the mount that was covered with blackness and darkness* (Heb. xii. 18), but to the mount that is crowned with a bright cloud. Both the Old-Testament and the New-Testament dispensation had tokens of God's presence; but that was a dispensation of darkness, and terror, and bondage, this of light, love, and liberty.

(3.) It overshadowed them. This cloud was intended to break the force of that great light which otherwise would have overcome the disciples, and have been intolerable; it was like the veil which Moses put upon his face when it shone. God, in manifesting himself to his people, considers their frame. This cloud was to their eyes as parables to their understandings, to convey spiritual things by things sensible, as they were able to bear them.

(4.) *There came a voice out of the cloud,* and it was the voice of God, who now, as of old, *spake in the cloudy pillar,* Ps. xcix. 7. Here was no thunder, or lightning, or voice of a trumpet, as there was when the law was given by Moses, but only a voice, a still small voice, and that not ushered in with a strong wind, or an earthquake, or fire, as when God spake to Elias, 1 Kings xix. 11, 12. Moses then and Elias were witnesses, that *in these last days God hath spoken to us by his Son,* in another way than he spoke formerly to them. This voice came from the excellent glory (2 Pet. i. 17), the glory which excelleth, in comparison of which the former had no glory; though the excellent glory was clouded, yet thence came a voice, for *faith comes by hearing.*

2. What this testimony from heaven was; *This is my beloved Son, hear ye him.* Here we have,

(1.) The great gospel mystery revealed; *This is my beloved Son, in whom I am well pleased.* This was the very same that was spoken from heaven at his baptism (*ch.* iii.17); and it was the best news that ever came from heaven to earth since man sinned. It is to the same purport with that great doctrine (2 Cor. v. 19), *That God was in Christ, reconciling the world unto himself.* Moses and Elias were great men, and favourites of Heaven, yet they were but servants, and servants that God was not always well pleased in; for Moses spoke unadvisedly, and Elias was a man subject to passions; but Christ is *a Son,* and in him God was always well pleased. Moses and Elias were sometimes instruments of reconciliation between God and Israel; Moses was a great intercessor, and Elias a great reformer; but in Christ God is reconciling the world; his intercession is more prevalent than that of Moses, and his reformation more effectual than that of Elias.

This repetition of the same voice that came from heaven at his baptism was no vain repetition; but, like the doubling of Pharaoh's dream, was to show the thing was established. What God hath thus spoken once, yea twice, no doubt he will stand to, and he expects we should take notice of it. It was spoken at his baptism, because then he was entering upon his temptation, and his public ministry; and now it was repeated, because he was entering upon his sufferings, which are to be dated from hence; for now, and not before, he began to foretel them, and immediately after his transfiguration it is said (Luke ix. 51), that *the time was come that he should be received up;* this therefore was then repeated, to arm him against the terror, and his disciples against the offence, of the cross. When sufferings begin to abound, consolations are given in more abundantly, 2 Cor. i. 5.

(2.) The great gospel duty required, and it is the condition of our benefit by Christ; *Hear ye him.* God is well pleased with none in Christ but those that hear him. It is not enough to give him the hearing (what will that avail us?) but we must hear him and believe him, as the great Prophet and Teacher; hear him, and be ruled by him, as the great Prince and Lawgiver; hear him, and heed him. Whoever would know the mind of God, must hearken to Jesus Christ; for by him God has in these last days spoken to us. This voice from heaven has made all the sayings of Christ as authentic as if they had been thus spoken out of a cloud. God does here, as it were, turn us over to Christ for all the revelations of his mind; and it refers to that prediction concerning *the Prophet God would raise up like unto Moses* (Deut. xviii. 18); *him shall ye hear.*

Christ now appeared in glory; and the more we see of Christ's glory, the more cause we shall see to hearken to him: but the disciples were gazing on that glory of his which they saw; they are therefore bid not to look at him, but to hear him. Their sight of his glory was soon intercepted by the cloud, but their business was to hear him. We walk *by faith,* which *comes by hearing,* not *by sight,* 2 Cor. v. 7.

Moses and Elias were now with him; the law and the prophets; hitherto it was said, *Hear them,* Luke xvi. 29. The disciples were ready to equal them with Christ, when they must have tabernacles for them as well as for him. They had been talking with Christ, and probably the disciples were very desirous to know what they said, and to hear something more from them; No, saith God, *hear him,* and that is enough; him, and not Moses and Elias, who were present, and whose silence gave consent to this voice; they had nothing to say to the contrary; whatever interest they had in the world as prophets, they were willing to see it all transferred to Christ, that in *all things he might have the pre-eminence.* Be not troubled that Moses and Elias make so short a stay with you; hear Christ, and you will not want them.

VI. The fright which the disciples were put into by this voice, and the encouragement Christ gave them.

1. The disciples *fell on their faces, and were sore afraid.* The greatness of the light, and the surprise of it, might have a natural influence upon them, to dispirit them. But that was not all, ever since man sinned, and heard God's voice in the garden, extraordinary appearances of God have ever been terrible to man, who, knowing he has no reason to expect any good, has been afraid to hear any thing immediately from God. Note, even then when *fair weather* comes *out of the secret place,* yet *with God* is *terrible majesty,* Job xxxvii. 22. See what dreadful work *the voice of the Lord makes,* Ps. xxix. 4. It is well for us that God speaks to us by men like ourselves, whose terror shall not make us afraid.

2. Christ graciously raised them up with abundance of tenderness. Note, The glories and advancements of our Lord Jesus do not at all lessen his regard to, and concern for, his people that are compassed about with infirmity. It is comfortable to think, that now, in his exalted state, he has a compassion for, and condescends to, the meanest true believer. Observe here, (1.) What he did; *he came, and touched them.* His approaches banished their fears; and when they apprehended that they were apprehended of Christ, there needed no more to make them easy. Christ laid his right hand upon John in a like case, and upon Daniel, Rev. i. 17; Dan. viii. 18; x. 18. Christ's touches were often healing, and here they were strengthening and comforting. (2.) What he said; *Arise, and be not afraid.* Note, Though a fear of reverence in our converse with Heaven is pleasing to Christ, yet a fear of amazement is not so, but must be striven against. Christ said, *Arise.* Note, It is Christ by his word, and the power of

his grace going along with it, that raises up good men from their dejections, and silences their fears; and none but Christ can do it; *Arise, be not afraid.* Note, causeless fears would soon vanish, if we would not yield to them, and lie down under them, but get up, and do what we can against them. Considering what they had seen and heard, they had more reason to rejoice than to fear, and yet, it seems, they needed this caution. Note, Through the infirmity of the flesh, we often frighten ourselves with that wherewith we should encourage ourselves. Observe, After they had an express command from heaven to hear Christ, the first word they had from him was, *Be not afraid,* hear that. Note, Christ's errand into the world was to give comfort to good people, that, being delivered out of the hands of their enemies, they might *serve God without fear,* Luke i. 74, 75.

VII. The disappearing of the vision (*v.* 8); *They* lift up themselves, and then *lift up their eyes,* and *saw no man, save Jesus only.* Moses and Elias were gone, the rays of Christ's glory were laid aside, or veiled again. They hoped this had been the day of Christ's entrance into his kingdom, and his public appearance in that external splendour which they dreamed of; but see how they are disappointed. Note, It is not wisdom to raise our expectations high in this world, for the most valuable of our glories and joys here are vanishing, even those of near communion with God are so, not a continual feast, but a running banquet. If sometimes we are favoured with special manifestations of divine grace, glimpses and pledges of future glory, yet they are withdrawn presently; two heavens are too much for those to expect that never deserve one. Now *they saw no man, save Jesus only.* Note, Christ will tarry with us when Moses and Elias are gone. The *prophets do not live for ever* (Zech. i. 5), and we see the period of our ministers' conversation; but *Jesus Christ is the same yesterday, to-day, and for ever,* Heb. xiii. 7, 8.

VIII. The discourse between Christ and his disciples as they came down from the mountain, *v.* 9—13.

Observe, 1. *They came down from the mountain.* Note, We must come down from the holy mountains, where we have communion with God, and complacency in that communion, and of which we are saying, *It is good to be here;* even there we have no continuing city. Blessed be God, there is a mountain of glory and joy before us, whence we shall never come down. But observe, When the disciples came down, Jesus came with them. Note, When we return to the world again after an ordinance, it must be our care to take Christ with us, and then it may be our comfort that he is with us.

2. As they came down, they talked of Christ. Note, When we are returning from holy ordinances, it is good to entertain ourselves and one another with discourse suitable to the work we have been about. That communication which is good to the use of edifying is then in a special manner seasonable; as, on the contrary, that which is corrupt, is worse then than at another time.

Here is, (1.) The charge that Christ gave the disciples to keep the vision very private for the present (*v.* 9); *Tell it to no man till the Son of man is risen.* If they had proclaimed it, the credibility of it would have been shocked by his sufferings, which were now hastening on. But let the publication of it be adjourned till after his resurrection, and then that and his subsequent glory will be a great confirmation of it. Note, Christ observed a method in the manifestation of himself; he would have his works put together, mutually to explain and illustrate each other, that they might appear in their full strength and convincing evidence. Every thing is beautiful in its season. Christ's resurrection was properly the beginning of the gospel state and kingdom, to which all before was but preparatory and by way of preface; and therefore, though this was transacted before, it must not be produced as evidence till then (and then it appears to have been much insisted on by 2 Pet. i. 16—18), when the religion it was designed for the confirmation of was brought to its full consistence and maturity. Christ's time is the best and fittest for the manifesting of himself and must be attended to by us.

(2.) An objection which the disciples made against something Christ had said (*v.* 10); "*Why then say the scribes that Elias must first come?* If Elias make so short a stay, and is gone so suddenly, and we must say nothing of him; why have we been taught out of the law to expect his public appearance in the world immediately before the setting up of the Messiah's kingdom? Must the coming of Elias be a secret, which every body looks for?" Or thus; "If the resurrection of the Messiah, and with it the beginning of his kingdom, be at hand, what becomes of that glorious preface and introduction to it, which we expect in the coming of Elias?" The scribes, who were the public expositors of the law, said this according to the scripture (Mal. iv. 5); *Behold I send you Elijah the prophet.* The disciples spoke the common language of the Jews, who made that the saying of the scribes which was the saying of the scripture; whereas of that which ministers speak to us according to the word of God, we should say, "*God* speaks it to us, not the *ministers;*" for we must not receive it *as the word of men,* 1 Thess. ii. 13.. Observe, When the disciples could not reconcile what Christ said with what they had heard out of the Old Testament, they desired him to explain it to them. Note, When we are puzzled with scripture difficulties, we must apply ourselves to Christ by prayer for his Spirit to open our understandings and to lead us into all truth.

(3.) The solving of this objection. *Ask, and it shall be given;* ask instruction, and it shall be given.

[1.] Christ allows the prediction (*v.* 11); "*Elias truly shall first come, and restore all things;* so far you are in the right." Christ did not come to alter or invalidate any thing foretold in the Old Testament. Note, Corrupt and mistaken glosses may be sufficiently rejected and exploded, without diminishing or derogating from the authority or dignity of the sacred text. New-Testament prophecies are true and good, and are to be received and improved, though some hot foolish men may have misinterpreted them and drawn wrong inferences from them. He shall come, and restore all things; not restore them to their former state (John Baptist went not about to do that), but he shall accomplish all things (so it may be read), all things that were written of him, all the predictions of the coming of Elias. John Baptist came to restore things spiritually, to revive the decays of religion, to *turn the hearts of the fathers to the children;* which means the same with this, *he shall restore all things.* John preached repentance, and that restores all things.

[2.] He asserts the accomplishment. The scribes say true, that *Elias shall come; but I say unto you,* what the scribes could not say, that *Elias is come, v.* 12. Note, God's promises are often fulfilled, and men perceive it not, but enquire, *Where is the promise?* when it is already performed. *Elias is come, and they knew him not;* they knew him not to be the Elias promised, the forerunner of the Messiah. The scribes busied themselves in criticising upon the scripture, but understood not by the signs of the times the fulfilling of the scripture. Note, It is easier to explain the word of God than to apply it and make a right use of it. But it is no wonder that the morning star was not observed, when he who is the Sun itself, was *in the world, and the world knew him not.*

Because they knew him not, *they have done to him whatsoever they listed;* if they had known, they would not have crucified Christ, or beheaded John. 1 Cor. ii. 8. They ridiculed John, persecuted him, and at last put him to death; which was Herod's doing, but is here charged upon the whole generation of unbelieving Jews, and particularly the scribes, who, though they could not prosecute John themselves, were pleased with what Herod did. He adds, *Likewise also shall the Son of man suffer of them.* Marvel not that Elias should be abused and killed by those who pretended, with a great deal of reverence, to expect him, when the Messias himself will be in like manner treated. Note, The sufferings of Christ took off the strangeness of all other sufferings (John xv. 18); when they had imbrued their hands in the blood of John Baptist, they were ready to do the like to Christ. Note, As men deal with Christ's servants, so they would deal with him himself; and they that are drunk with the blood of the martyrs still cry, *Give, give,* Acts xii. 1—3.

(4.) The disciples' satisfaction in Christ's reply to their objection (*v.* 13); *They understood that he spake unto them of John the Baptist.* He did not name John, but gives them such a description of him as would put them in mind of what he had said to them formerly concerning him; *This is Elias.* This is a profitable way of teaching; it engages the learners' own thoughts, and makes them, if not their own teachers, yet their own remembrancers; and thus knowledge becomes easy to him that understands. When we diligently use the means of knowledge, how strangely are mists scattered and mistakes rectified!

14 And when they were come to
the multitude, there came to him a
certain man, kneeling down to him,
and saying, 15 Lord, have mercy on
my son: for he is lunatic, and sore
vexed: for ofttimes he falleth into
the fire, and oft into the water. 16
And I brought him to thy disciples,
and they could not cure him. 17
Then Jesus answered and said, O
faithless and perverse generation, how
long shall I be with you? how long
shall I suffer you? bring him hither
to me. 18 And Jesus rebuked the
devil; and he departed out of him:
and the child was cured from that
very hour. 19 Then came the disciples to Jesus apart, and said, Why
could not we cast him out? 20 And
Jesus said unto them, Because of
your unbelief: for verily I say unto
you, If ye have faith as a grain o
mustard seed, ye shall say unto this
mountain, Remove hence to yonder
place; and it shall remove; and nothing shall be impossible unto you.
21 Howbeit this kind goeth not out
but by prayer and fasting.

We have here the miraculous cure of a child that was lunatic and vexed with a devil. Observe,

I. A melancholy representation of the case of this child, made to Christ by the afflicted father. This was immediately upon his coming down from the mountain where he was transfigured. Note, Christ's glories do not make him unmindful of us and of our wants and miseries. Christ, when he came down from the mount, where he had conversation with Moses and Elias, did not take state upon him, but was as easy of access, as ready to poor beggars, and as familiar with the multitude, as ever he used to be. This poor man's address was very importunate; he came kneeling to Christ. Note, Sense of misery will bring people to their knees. Those who see their need of Christ will be earnest, will be in good earnest, in their applications to him; and he delights to be thus wrestled with.

Two things the father of the child complains of.

1. The distress of his child (*v.* 15); *Lord, have mercy on my son.* The affliction of the children cannot but affect the tender parents, for they are pieces of themselves. And the case of afflicted children should be presented to God by faithful and fervent prayer. This child's distemper, probably, disabled him to pray for himself. Note, Parents are doubly concerned to pray for their children, not only that are weak and cannot, but much more that are wicked and will not, pray for themselves. Now, (1.) The nature of this child's disease was very sad; *He was lunatic and sore vexed.* A lunatic is properly one whose distemper lies in the brain, and returns with the change of the moon. The devil, by the divine permission, either caused this distemper, or at least concurred with it, to heighten and aggravate it. The child had the falling-sickness, and the hand of Satan was in it; by it he tormented then, and made it much more grievous than ordinarily it is. Those whom Satan got possession of, he afflicted by those diseases of the body which do most affect the mind; for it is the soul that he aims to do mischief to. The father, in his complaint, saith, *He is lunatic,* taking notice of the effect; but Christ, in the cure, rebuked the devil, and so struck at the cause. Thus he doth in spiritual cures. (2.) The effects of the disease were very deplorable; *He oft falls into the fire, and into the water.* If the force of the disease made him to fall, the malice of the devil made him to fall into the fire or water; so mischievous is he where he gains possession and power in any soul. He *seeks to devour,* 1 Pet. v. 8.

2. The disappointment of his expectation from the disciples (*v.* 16); *I brought him to thy disciples, and they could not cure him.* Christ gave his disciples power to cast out devils (*ch.* x. 1, 8), and therein they were successful (Luke x. 17); yet at this time they failed in the operation, though there were nine of them together, and before a great multitude. Christ permitted this, (1.) To keep them humble, and to show their dependence upon him, that without him they could do nothing. (2.) To glorify himself and his own power. It is for the honour of Christ to come in with help at a dead-lift, when other helpers cannot help. Elisha's staff in Gehazi's hand will not raise the child: he must come himself. Note, There are some special favours which Christ reserves the bestowment of to himself; and sometimes he keeps the cistern empty, that he may bring us to himself, the Fountain. But the failures of instruments shall not hinder the operations of his grace, which will work, if not *by* them, yet *without* them.

II. The rebukes that Christ gave to the people first, and then to the devil.

1. He chid those about him (*v.* 17); *O faithless and perverse generation!* This is not spoken to the disciples, but to the people, and perhaps especially to the scribes, who are mentioned in Mark ix. 14, and who, as it should seem, insulted over the disciples, because they had now met with a case that was too hard for them. Christ himself could not do many mighty works among a people in whom unbelief reigned. It was here owing to the faithlessness of this generation, that they could not obtain those blessings from God, which otherwise they might have had; as it was owing to the weakness of the disciples' faith, that they could not do those works for God, which otherwise they might have done. They were faithless and perverse. Note, Those that are faithless will be perverse; and perverseness is sin in its worst colours. Faith is compliance with God, unbelief is opposition and contradiction to God. Israel of old was perverse, because faithless (Ps. xcv. 9), froward, for in them is no faith, Deut. xxxii. 20.

Two things he upbraids them with. (1.) His presence with them so long; "*How long shall I be with you?* Will you always need my bodily presence, and never come to such maturity as to be fit to be left, the people to the conduct of the disciples, and the disciples to the conduct of the Spirit and of their commission? Must the child be always carried, and will it never learn to go alone?" (2.) His patience with them so long; *How long shall I suffer you?* Note, [1.] The faithlessness and perverseness of those who enjoy the means of grace are a great grief to the Lord Jesus. Thus did he suffer the manners of Israel of old, Acts xiii. 18. [2.] The longer Christ has borne with a perverse and faithless people, the more he is displeased with their perverseness and unbelief; and he is God, and not man, else he would not suffer so long, nor bear so much, as he doth.

2. He cured the child, and set him to-rights again. He called, *Bring him hither to me.* Though the people were perverse, and Christ was provoked, yet care was taken of the child. Note, Though Christ may be angry, he is never unkind, nor doth he, in the greatest of his displeasure, shut up the bowels of his compassion from the miserable; *Bring him to me.* Note, When all other helps and succours fail, we are welcome to Christ, and may be confident in him and in his power and goodness.

See here an emblem of Christ's undertaking as our Redeemer.

(1.) He breaks the power of Satan (*v.* 18); *Jesus rebuked the devil,* as one having authority, who could back with force his word of command. Note, Christ's victories over Satan are obtained by the power of his word, the sword that comes out of his mouth, Rev. xix. 21. Satan cannot stand before the rebukes of Christ, though his possession has been ever so long. It is comfortable to those who are wrestling with principalities and powers, that Christ hath spoiled them, Colos. ii. 15. The lion of the tribe of Judah will be too hard for the roaring lion that seeks to devour.

(2.) He redresses the grievances of the children of men; *The child was cured from that very hour.* It was an immediate cure, and a perfect one. This is an encouragement to parents to bring their children to Christ, whose souls are under Satan's power; he is able to heal them, and as willing as he is able. Not only bring them to Christ by prayer, but bring them to the word of Christ, the ordinary means by which Satan's strongholds are demolished in the soul. Christ's rebukes, brought home to the heart, will ruin Satan's power there.

III. Christ's discourse with his disciples hereupon.

1. They ask the reason why they could not cast out the devil at this time (*v.* 19); *They came to Jesus apart.* Note, Ministers, who are to deal for Christ in public, have need to keep up a private communion with him, that they may in secret, where no eye sees, bewail their weakness and straitness, their follies and infirmities, in their public performances, and enquire into the cause of them. We should make use of the liberty of access we have to Jesus apart, where we may be free and particular with him. Such questions as the disciples put to Christ, we should put to ourselves, in communing with our own hearts upon our beds; Why were we so dull and careless at such a time? Why came we so much short in such a duty? That which is amiss may, when found out, be amended.

2. Christ gives them two reasons why they failed.

(1.) It was *because of their unbelief*, *v.* 20. When he spake to the father of the child and to the people, he charged it upon their unbelief; when he spake to his disciples, he charged it upon theirs; for the truth was, there were faults on both sides; but we are more concerned to hear of our own faults than of other people's, and to impute what is amiss to ourselves than to others. When the preaching of the word seems not to be so successful as sometimes it has been, the people are apt to lay all the fault upon the ministers, and the ministers upon the people; whereas, it is more becoming for each to own his own faultiness, and to say, "It is owing to me." Ministers, in reproving, must learn thus to give to each his portion of the word; and to take people off from judging others, by teaching all to judge themselves; *It is because of your unbelief.* Though they had faith, yet that faith was weak and ineffectual. Note, [1.] As far as faith falls short of its due strength, vigour, and activity, it may truly be said, "There is unbelief." Many are chargeable with unbelief, who yet are not to be called *unbelievers.* [2.] It is because of our unbelief, that we bring so little to pass in religion, and so often miscarry, and come short, in that which is good.

Our Lord Jesus takes this occasion to show them the power of faith, that they might not be defective in that, another time, as they were now; *If ye have faith as a grain of mustard-seed,* ye shall do wonders, *v.* 20. Some make the comparison to refer to the quality of the mustard-seed, which is, when bruised, sharp and penetrating; "If you have an active growing faith, not dead, flat, or insipid, you will not be baffled thus." But it rather refers to the quantity; "If you had but a grain of true faith, though so little that it were like that which is the least of all seeds, you would do wonders." Faith in general is a firm assent to, a compliance with, and a confidence in, all divine revelation. The faith here required, is that which had for its object that particular revelation by which Christ gave his disciples power to work miracles in his name, for the confirmation of the doctrine they preached. It was a faith in this revelation that they were defective in; either doubting the validity of their commission, or fearing that it expired with their first mission, and was not to continue when they were returning to their Master; or that it was some way or other forfeited or withdrawn. Perhaps their Master's absence with the three chief of his disciples, with a charge to the rest not to follow them, might occasion some doubts concerning their power, or rather the power of the Lord with them, to do this; however, there were not, at present, such a strong actual dependence upon, and confidence in, the promise of Christ's presence with them, as there should have been. It is good for us to be diffident of ourselves and of our own strength; but it is displeasing to Christ, when we distrust any power derived from him or granted by him.

If ye have ever so little of this faith in sincerity, if ye truly rely upon the powers committed to you, *ye shall say to this mountain, Remove.* This is a proverbial expression, denoting that which follows, and no more, *Nothing shall be impossible to you.* They had a full commission, among other things, to cast out devils without exception; but, this devil being more than ordinarily malicious and inveterate, they distrusted the power they had received, and so failed. To convince them of this, Christ shows them what they might have done. Note, An active faith can remove mountains, not of itself, but in the virtue of a divine power engaged by a divine promise, both which faith fastens upon.

(2.) Because there was something in the kind of the malady, which rendered the cure more than ordinarily difficult (*v.* 21); "*This kind goes not out but by prayer and fasting.* This possession, which works by a falling-sickness, or this kind of devils that are thus furious, is not cast out ordinarily but by great acts of devotion, and therein ye were defective." Note, [1.] Though the adversaries we wrestle with, be all principalities and powers, yet some are stronger than others, and their power more hardly broken. [2.] The extraordinary power of Satan must not discourage our faith, but quicken us to a greater intenseness in the acting of it, and more earnestness in praying to God for the increase of it; so some understand it here; "This kind of faith (which removeth mountains) doth not proceed, is not obtained, from God, nor is it carried up to its full growth, nor drawn out into act and exercise, but by earnest prayer." [3.] Fasting and prayer are proper means for the bringing down of Satan's power against us, and the fetching in of divine power to our assistance. Fasting is of use to put an edge upon prayer; it is an evidence and instance of humiliation which is necessary in prayer, and is a means of mortifying some corrupt habits, and of disposing the body to serve the soul in prayer. When the devil's interest in the soul is confirmed by the temper and constitution of the body, fasting must be joined with prayer, to keep under the body.

22 And while they abode in Galilee, Jesus said unto them, The Son of man shall be betrayed into the hands of men: 23 And they shall kill him, and the third day he shall be raised again. And they were exceeding sorry.

Christ here foretels his own sufferings; he began to do it before (*ch.* xvi. 21); and, finding that it was to his disciples a hard saying, he saw it necessary to repeat it. There are some things which *God speaketh once, yea twice, and yet man perceiveth it not.* Observe here,

1. What he foretold concerning himself—that he should be betrayed and killed. He perfectly knew, before, all things that should come to him, and yet undertook the work of our redemption, which greatly commends his love; nay, his clear foresight of them was a kind of ante-passion, had not his love to man made all easy to him.

(1.) He tells them that he should *be betrayed into the hands of men.* He *shall be delivered up* (so it might be read and understood of his Father's delivering him up *by his determined counsel and fore-knowledge,* Acts ii. 23; Rom. viii. 32); but as we render it, it refers to Judas's betraying him into the hands of the priests, and their betraying him into the hands of the Romans. He was *betrayed into the hands of men;* men to whom he was allied by nature, and from whom therefore he might expect pity and tenderness; men whom he had undertaken to save, and from whom therefore he might expect honour and gratitude; yet these are his persecutors and murderers.

(2.) That *they should kill him;* nothing less than that would satisfy their rage; it was his blood, his precious blood, that they thirsted after. *This is the heir, come, let us kill him.* Nothing less would satisfy God's justice, and answer his undertaking; if he be a Sacrifice of atonement, he must be killed; without blood no remission.

(3.) That *he shall be raised again the third day.* Still, when he spoke of his death, he gave a hint of his resurrection, *the joy set before him,* in the prospect of which *he endured the cross, and despised the shame.* This was an encouragement, not only to him, but to his disciples; for if he rise the third day, his absence from them will not be long, and his return to them will be glorious.

2. How the disciples received this; *They were exceedingly sorry.* Herein appeared their love to their Master's person, but with all their ignorance and mistake concerning his undertaking. Peter indeed durst not say any thing against it, as he had done before (*ch.* xvi. 22), having then been severely chidden for it; but he, and the rest of them, greatly lamented it, as it would be their own loss, their Master's grief, and the sin and ruin of them that did it.

24 And when they were come to Capernaum, they that received tribute *money* came to Peter, and said, Doth not your master pay tribute? 25 He saith, Yes. And when he was come into the house, Jesus prevented him, saying, What thinkest thou, Simon? of whom do the kings of the earth take custom or tribute? of their own children, or of strangers? 26 Peter saith unto him, Of strangers. Jesus saith unto him, Then are the children free. 27 Notwithstanding, lest we should offend them, go thou to the sea, and cast an hook, and take up the fish that first cometh up; and when thou hast opened his mouth, thou shalt find a piece of money: that take, and give unto them for me and thee.

We have here an account of Christ's paying tribute.

I. Observe how it was demanded, *v.* 24. Christ was now at Capernaum, his head quarters, where he mostly resided; he did not keep from thence, to decline being called upon for his dues, but the rather came thither, to be ready to pay them.

1. The tribute demanded was not any civil payment to the Roman powers, that was strictly exacted by the publicans, but the church-duties, the half shekel, about fifteen pence, which were required from every person for the service of the temple, and the defraying of the expenses of the worship there; it is called *a ransom for the soul,* Exod. xxx. 12, &c. This was not so strictly exacted now as sometimes it had been, especially not in Galilee.

2. The demand was very modest; the collectors stood in such awe of Christ, because of his mighty works, that they durst not speak to him about it, but applied themselves to Peter, whose house was in Capernaum, and probably in his house Christ lodged; he therefore was fittest to be spoken to as the housekeeper, and they presumed he knew his Master's mind. Their question is, *Doth not your master pay tribute?* Some think that they sought an occasion against him, designing, if he refused, to represent him as disaffected to the temple-service, and his followers as lawless people, that would pay *neither toll, tribute, nor custom,* Ezra. iv. 13. It should rather seem, they asked this with respect, intimating, that if he had any privilege to exempt him from this payment, they would not insist upon it.

Peter presently passed his word for his Master; "*Yes,* certainly; my *Master pays tribute;* it is his principle and practice; you need not fear moving it to him." (1.) *He was made under the law* (Gal. iv. 4); therefore under this law he was paid for at forty days old (Luke ii. 22), and now he paid for himself, as one who, in his state of humiliation, *had taken upon him the form of a servant,* Phil. ii. 7, 8. (2.) *He was made sin for us,* and was *sent forth in the likeness of sinful flesh,* Rom. viii. 3. Now this tax paid to the temple is called *an atonement for the soul,* Exod. xxx. 15. Christ, that in every thing he might *appear in the likeness of sinners,* paid it though he had no sin to atone for. (3.) *Thus it became him to fulfil all righteousness, ch.* iii. 15. He did this to set us an example, [1.] Of *rendering to all their due, tribute to whom tribute is due,* Rom. xiii. 7. The kingdom of Christ not being of this world, the favourites and officers of it are so far from having a power granted them, as such, to tax other people's purses, that theirs are made liable to the powers that are. [2.] Of contributing to the support of the public worship of God in the places where we are. If we reap spiritual things, it is fit that we should return carnal things. The temple was now made a den of thieves, and the temple-worship a pretence for the opposition which the chief priests gave to Christ and his doctrine; and yet Christ paid this tribute. Note, Church-duties, legally imposed, are to be paid, notwithstanding church-corruptions. We must take care not to use *our liberty as a cloak of covetousness or maliciousness,* 1 Pet. ii. 16. If Christ pay tribute, who can pretend an exemption?

II. How it was disputed (*v.* 25), not with the collectors themselves, lest they should be irritated, but with Peter, that he might be satisfied in the reason why Christ paid tribute, and might not mistake about it. He brought the collectors into the house; but Christ anticipated him, to give him a proof of his omniscience, and that no thought can be withholden from him. The disciples of Christ are never attacked without his knowledge.

Now, 1. He appeals to the way of the kings of the earth, which is, to take tribute of strangers, of the subjects of their kingdom, or foreigners that deal with them, but not of their own children that are of their families; there is such a community of goods between parents and children, and a joint-interest in what they have, that it would be absurd for the parents to levy taxes upon the children, or demand any thing from them; it is like one hand taxing the other.

2. He applies this to himself; *Then are the children free.* Christ is the Son of God, and Heir of all things; the temple is his temple (Mal. iii. 1), his Father's house (John ii. 16), in it *he is faithful as a Son in his own house* (Heb. iii. 6), and therefore not obliged to pay this tax for the service of the temple. Thus Christ asserts his right, lest his paying this tribute should be misimproved to the weakening of his title as the Son of God, and the King of Israel, and should have looked like a disowning of it himself. These immunities of the children are to be extended no further than our Lord Jesus himself. God's children are freed by grace and adoption from the slavery of sin and Satan, but not from their subjection to civil magistrates in civil things; here the law of Christ is express; *Let every soul* (sanctified souls not excepted) *be subject to the higher powers. Render to Cæsar the things that are Cæsar's.*

III. How it was paid, notwithstanding, *v.* 27.

1. For what reason Christ waived his privilege, and paid this tribute, though he was entitled to an exemption—*Lest we should offend them.* Few knew, as Peter did, that he was *the Son of God;* and it would have been a diminution to the honour of that great truth, which was yet a secret, to advance it now, to serve such a purpose as this. Therefore Christ drops that argument, and considers, that if he should refuse this payment, it would increase people's prejudice against him and his doctrine, and alienate their affections from him, and therefore he resolves to pay it. Note, Christian prudence and humility teach us, in many cases, to recede from our right, rather than give offence by insisting upon it. We must never decline our duty for fear of giving offence (Christ's preaching and miracles offended them, yet he went on with them (*ch.* xv. 12, 13), better

offend men than God); but we must sometimes deny ourselves in that which is our secular interest, rather than give offence; as Paul, 1 Cor. viii. 13; Rom. xiv. 13.

2. What course he took for the payment of this tax; he furnished himself with money for it out of the mouth of a fish (*v.* 27), wherein appears,

(1.) The poverty of Christ; he had not fifteen pence at command to pay his tax with, though he cured so many that were diseased; it seems, he did all gratis; *for our sakes he became poor,* 2 Cor. viii. 9. In his ordinary expenses, he lived upon alms (Luke viii. 3), and in extraordinary ones, he lived upon miracles. He did not order Judas to pay this out of the bag which he carried; that was for subsistence, and he would not order that for his particular use, which was intended for the benefit of the community.

(2.) The power of Christ, in fetching money out of a fish's mouth for this purpose. Whether his omnipotence put it there, or his omniscience knew that it was there, it comes all to one; it was an evidence of his divinity, and that he is Lord of hosts. Those creatures that are most remote from man are at the command of Christ, even the fishes of the sea are under his feet (Ps. viii. 5); and to evidence his dominion in this lower world, and to accommodate himself to his present state of humiliation, he chose to take it out of a fish's mouth, when he could have taken it out of an angel's hand. Now observe,

[1.] Peter must catch the fish by angling. Even in miracles he would use means to encourage industry and endeavour. Peter has something to do, and it is in the way of his own calling too; to teach us diligence in the employment we are called *to,* and called *in.* Do we expect that Christ should give to us? Let us be ready to work for him.

[2.] The fish came up, with money in the mouth of it, which represents to us the reward of obedience in obedience. What work we do at Christ's command brings its own pay along with it: *In* keeping God's commands, as well as *after* keeping them, *there is great reward,* Ps. xix. 11. Peter was made a fisher of men, and those that he caught thus, came up; where the heart is opened to entertain Christ's word, the hand is open to encourage his ministers.

[3.] The piece of money was just enough to pay the tax for Christ and Peter. Thou shalt find *a stater,* the value of a Jewish shekel, which would pay the poll-tax for two, for it was half a shekel, Exod. xxx. 13. Christ could as easily have commanded a bag of money as a piece of money; but he would teach us not to covet superfluities, but, having enough for our present occasions, therewith to be content, and not to distrust God, though we live but from hand to mouth. Christ made the fish his cash-keeper; and why may not we make God's providence our storehouse and treasury? If we have a competency for to-day, *let to-morrow take thought for the things of itself.* Christ paid for himself and Peter, because it is probable that here *he* only was assessed, and of him it was at this time demanded; perhaps the rest had paid already, or were to pay elsewhere. The Papists make a great mystery of Christ's paying for Peter, as if this made him the head and representative of the whole church; whereas the payment of tribute for him was rather a sign of subjection than of superiority. His pretended successors pay no tribute, but exact it. Peter fished for this money, and therefore part of it went for his use. Those that are *workers together with Christ* in winning souls shall be sharers with him in his glory, and shall shine with him. *Give it for thee and me.* What Christ paid for himself was looked upon as a debt; what he paid for Peter was a courtesy to him. Note, it is a desirable thing, if God so please, to have wherewithal of this world's goods, not only to be just, but to be kind; not only to be charitable to the poor, but obliging to our friends. What is a great estate good for, but that it enables a man to do so much the more good?

Lastly, Observe, The evangelist records here the orders Christ gave to Peter, the warrant; the effect is not particularly mentioned, but taken for granted, and justly; for, with Christ, saying and doing are the same thing.

CHAP. XVIII.

The gospels are, in short, a record of what Jesus began both to do and to teach. In the foregoing chapter, we had an account of his doings, in this, of his teachings; probably, not all at the same time, in a continued discourse, but at several times, upon divers occasions, here put together, as near akin. We have here, I. Instructions concerning humility, ver. 1—6. II. Concerning offences in general (ver. 7), particularly offences given, 1. By us to ourselves, ver. 8, 9. 2. By us to others, ver. 10—14. 3. By others to us; which are of two sorts, (1.) Scandalous sins, which are to be reproved, ver. 15—20. (2.) Personal wrongs, which are to be forgiven, ver. 21—35. See how practical Christ's preaching was; he could have revealed mysteries, but he pressed plain duties, especially those that are most displeasing to flesh and blood.

AT the same time came the disciples unto Jesus, saying, Who is
the greatest in the kingdom of heaven?
2 And Jesus called a little child unto
him, and set him in the midst of them.
3 And said, Verily I say unto you,
Except ye be converted, and become
as little children, ye shall not enter
into the kingdom of heaven. 4 Whosoever therefore shall humble himself
as this little child, the same is greatest
in the kingdom of heaven. 5 And
whoso shall receive one such little
child in my name receiveth me. 6
But whoso shall offend one of these
little ones which believe in me, it were
better for him that a millstone were
hanged about his neck, and *that* he
were drowned in the depth of the sea.

As there never was a greater pattern of humility, so there never was a greater preacher of it, than Christ; he took all occasions to command it, to commend it, to his disciples and followers.

I. The occasion of this discourse concerning humility was an unbecoming contest among the disciples for precedency; they *came to him, saying,* among themselves (for they were ashamed to ask him, Mark ix. 34), *Who is the greatest in the kingdom of heaven?* They mean not, *who* by character (then the question had been good, that they might know what graces and duties to excel in), but *who* by name. They had heard much, and preached much, of the kingdom of heaven, the kingdom of the Messiah, his church in this world; but as yet they were so far from having any clear notion of it, that they dreamt of a temporal kingdom, and the external pomp and power of it. Christ had lately foretold his sufferings, and the glory that should follow, that he should rise again, from whence they expected his kingdom would commence; and now they thought it was time to put in for their places in it; it is good, in such cases, to speak early. Upon other discourses of Christ to that purport, debates of this kind arose (*ch.* xx. 19, 20; Luke xxii. 22, 24); he spoke many words of his sufferings, but only one of his glory; yet they fasten upon that, and overlook the other; and, instead of asking how they might have strength and grace to suffer with him, they ask him, "Who shall be highest in reigning with him." Note, Many love to hear and speak of privileges and glory, who are willing to pass by the thoughts of work and trouble. They look so much at the crown, that they forget the yoke and the cross. So the disciples here did, when they asked, *Who is the greatest in the kingdom of heaven?*

1. They suppose that all who have a place in that kingdom are great, for it is a kingdom of priests. Note, Those are truly great who are truly good; and they will appear so at last, when Christ shall own them as his, though ever so mean and poor in the world.

2. They suppose that there are degrees in this greatness. All the saints are honourable, but not all alike so; *one star differs from another star in glory.* All David's officers were not worthies, nor all his worthies of the first three.

3. They suppose it must be some of them, that must be prime ministers of state. To whom should King Jesus delight to do honour, but to them who had left all for him, and were now his companions in patience and tribulation?

4. They strive who it should be, each having some pretence or other to it. Peter was always the chief speaker, and already had the keys given him; he expects to be lord-chancellor, or lord-chamberlain of the household, and so to be the greatest. Judas had the bag, and therefore he expects to be lord-treasurer, which, though now he come last, he hopes, will then denominate him the greatest. Simon and Jude are nearly related to Christ, and they hope to take place of all the great officers of state, as princes of the blood. John is the beloved disciple, the favourite of the Prince, and therefore hopes to be the greatest. Andrew was first called, and why should not he be first preferred? Note, We are very apt to amuse and humour ourselves with foolish fancies of things that will never be.

II. The discourse itself, which is a just rebuke to the question, *Who shall be greatest?* We have abundant reason to think, that if Christ ever intended that Peter and his successors at Rome should be heads of the church, and his chief vicars on earth, having so fair an occasion given him, he would now have let his disciples know it; but so far is he from this, that his answer disallows and condemns the thing itself. Christ will not lodge such an authority or supremacy any where in his church; whoever pretend to it are usurpers; instead of settling any of the disciples in this dignity, he warns them all not to put in for it.

Christ here teacheth them to be humble,

1. By a sign (*v.* 2); *He called a little child to him, and set him in the midst of them.* Christ often taught by signs or sensible representations (comparisons to the eye), as the prophets of old. Note, Humility is a lesson so hardly learned, that we have need by all ways and means to be taught it. When we look upon a little child, we should be put in mind of the use Christ made of this child. Sensible things must be improved to spiritual purposes. *He set him in the midst of them;* not that they might play with him, but that they might learn by him. Grown men, and great men, should not disdain the company of little children, or think it below them to take notice of them. They may either speak to them, and give instruction to them; or look upon them, and receive instruction from them. Christ himself, when a child, was *in the midst of the doctors,* Luke ii. 46.

2. By a sermon upon this sign; in which he shows them and us,

(1.) The necessity of humility, *v.* 3. His preface is solemn, and commands both attention and assent; *Verily I say unto you, I, the Amen, the faithful Witness,* say it, *Except ye be converted, and become as little children, ye shall not enter into the kingdom of heaven.* Here observe,

[1.] What it is that he requires and insists upon.

First, "You must be converted, you must be of another mind, and in another frame and temper, must have other thoughts, both of yourselves and of the kingdom of heaven, before you be fit for a place in it. The pride, ambition, and affectation of honour and dominion, which appear in you, must be repented of, mortified, and reformed, and you must come to yourselves." Note, Besides the first conversion of a soul from a state of nature to a state of grace, there are after-conversions from particular paths of backsliding, which are equally necessary to salvation. Every step out of the way by sin, must be a step into it again by repentance. When Peter repented of his denying his Master, he was converted. *Secondly,* You must *become as little children.* Note, Converting grace makes us like little children, not foolish as children (1 Cor. xiv. 20), nor fickle (Eph. iv. 14), nor playful (*ch.* xi. 16); but, *as children,* we must *desire the sincere milk of the word* (1 Pet. ii. 2); as children, we must be careful for nothing, but leave it to our heavenly Father to care for us (*ch.* vi. 31); we must, as children, be harmless and inoffensive, and void of malice (1 Cor. xiv. 20), governable, and under command (Gal. iv. 2); and (which is here chiefly intended) we must be humble as little children, who do not take state upon them, nor stand upon the punctilios of honour; the child of a gentleman will play with the child of a beggar (Rom. xii. 16), the child in rags, if it have the breast, is well enough pleased, and envies not the gaiety of the child in silk; little children have no great aims at great places, or projects to raise themselves in the world; they *exercise not themselves in things too high for them;* and we should in like manner *behave, and quiet ourselves,* Ps. cxxxi. 1, 2. As children are little in body and low in stature, so we must be little and low in spirit, and in our thoughts of ourselves. This is a temper which leads to other good dispositions; the age of childhood is the learning age.

[2.] What stress he lays upon this; Without this, *you shall not enter into the kingdom of heaven.* Note, Disciples of Christ have need to be kept in awe by threatenings, that they may fear *lest they seem to come short,* Heb. iv. 1. The disciples, when they put that question (*v.* 1), thought themselves sure of the kingdom of heaven; but Christ awakens them to be jealous of themselves. They were ambitious of being *greatest in the kingdom of heaven;* Christ tells them, that, except they came to a better temper, they should never come thither. Note, Many that set up for great ones in the church, prove not only little, but nothing, and are found to *have no part or lot in the matter.* Our Lord designs here to show the great danger of pride and ambition; whatever profession men make, if they allow themselves in this sin, they will be rejected both from God's tabernacle and from his holy hill. Pride threw the angels that sinned out of heaven, and will keep us out, if we be not converted from it. They that are lifted up with pride, *fall into the condemnation of the devil;* to prevent this, we must become as little children, and, in order to that, *must be born again, must put on the new man,* must be like *the holy child Jesus;* so he is called, even after his ascension, Acts iv. 27.

(2.) He shows the honour and advancement that attend humility (*v.* 4), thus furnishing a direct but surprising answer to their question. He that humbles himself as a little child, though he may fear that hereby he will render himself contemptible, as men of timid minds, who thereby throw themselves out of the way of preferment, yet *the same is greatest in the kingdom of heaven.* Note, The humblest Christians are the best Christians, and most like to Christ, and highest in his favour; are best disposed for the communications of divine grace, and fittest to serve God in this world, and enjoy him in another. They are great, for God overlooks heaven and earth, to look on such; and certainly those are to be most respected and honoured in the church that are most humble and self-denying; for, though they least seek it, they best deserve it.

(3.) The special care Christ takes for those that are humble; he espouses their cause, protects them, interests himself in their concerns, and will see that they are not wronged, without being righted.

Those that thus humble themselves will be afraid,

[1.] That nobody will receive them; but (*v.* 5), *Whoso shall receive one such little child in my name, receiveth me.* Whatever kindnesses are done to such, Christ takes as done to himself. Whoso entertains a meek and humble Christian, keeps him in countenance, will not let him lose by his modesty, takes him into his love and friendship, and society and care, and studies to do him a kindness; and doth this in Christ's name, for his sake, because he bears the image of Christ, serves Christ, and because Christ has received him; this shall be accepted and recompensed as an acceptable piece of respect to Christ. Observe, Though it be but one such little child that is received in Christ's name, it shall be accepted. Note, The tender regard Christ has to his church extends itself to every particular member, even the meanest; not only to the whole family, but to every child of the family; the less they are in themselves, to whom we show kindness, the more there is of good will in it to Christ; the less it is for their sakes, the more it is for his; and he takes it accordingly. If Christ were personally among us, we think we should never do enough to welcome him; *the poor, the poor in spirit, we have always with us,* and they are his receivers. See *ch.* xxv. 35—40.

[2.] They will be afraid that every body will abuse them; the basest men delight to trample upon the humble; *Vexat censura columbas—Censure pounces on doves.* This objection he obviates (*v.* 6), where he warns all people, as they will answer it at their utmost peril, not to offer any injury to one of Christ's little ones. This word makes a wall of fire about them; he that touches them, touches the apple of God's eye.

Observe, *First,* The crime supposed; *offending one of these little ones that believe in Christ.* Their believing in Christ, though they be little ones, unites them to him, and interests him in their cause, so that, as they partake of the benefit of his sufferings, he also partakes in the wrong of theirs. Even the little ones that believe have the same privileges with the great ones, for they have all obtained like precious faith. There are those that offend these little ones, by drawing them to sin (1 Cor. viii. 10, 11), grieving and vexing their righteous souls, discouraging them, taking occasion from their mildness to make a prey of them in their persons, families, goods, or good name. Thus the best men have often met with the worst treatment in this world.

Secondly, The punishment of this crime; intimated in that word, *Better for him that he were drowned in the depth of the sea.* The sin is so heinous, and the ruin proportionably so great, that he had better undergo the sorest punishments inflicted on the worst of malefactors, which can only kill the body. Note, 1. Hell is worse than the depth of the sea; for it is a bottomless pit, and it is a burning lake. The depth of the sea is only killing, but hell is tormenting. We meet with one that had comfort in the depth of the sea, it was Jonah (*ch.* ii. 2, 4, 9); but never any had the least grain or glimpse of comfort in hell, nor will have to eternity. 2. The irresistible irrevocable doom of the great Judge will sink sooner and surer, and bind faster, than *a mill-stone hanged about the neck.* It fixes a great gulf, which can never be broken through, Luke xvi. 26. Offending Christ's little ones, though by omission, is assigned as the reason of that dreadful sentence, *Go ye cursed,* which will at last be the doom of proud persecutors.

7 Woe unto the world because of
offences! for it must needs be that
offences come; but woe to that man
by whom the offence cometh! 8
Wherefore if thy hand or thy foot
offend thee, cut them off, and cast
them from thee: it is better for thee
to enter into life halt or maimed, rather than having two hands or two
feet to be cast into everlasting fire.
9 And if thine eye offend thee, pluck
it out, and cast *it* from thee: it is
better for thee to enter into life with
one eye, rather than having two eyes
to be cast into hell fire. 10 Take
heed that ye despise not one of these
little ones; for I say unto you, That
in heaven their angels do always behold the face of my Father which is
in heaven. 11 For the Son of man
is come to save that which was lost.
12 How think ye? if a man have an
hundred sheep, and one of them be
gone astray, doth he not leave the
ninety and nine, and goeth into the
mountains, and seeketh that which is
gone astray? 13 And if so be that
he find it, verily I say unto you, he
rejoiceth more of that *sheep*, than of
the ninety and nine which went not
astray. 14 Even so it is not the
will of your Father which is in heaven, that one of these little ones should
perish.

Our Saviour here speaks of offences, or scandals,

I. In general, *v.* 7. Having mentioned the offending of little ones, he takes occasion to speak more generally of offences. That is an offence, 1. Which occasions guilt, which by enticement or affrightment tends to draw men from that which is good to that which is evil. 2. Which occasions grief, which *makes the heart of the righteous sad.* Now, concerning offences, Christ here tells them,

(1.) That they were certain things; *It must needs be, that offences come.* When we are sure there is danger, we should be the better armed. Not that Christ's word necessitates any man to offend, but it is a prediction upon a view of the causes; considering the subtlety and malice of Satan, the weakness and depravity of men's hearts, and the foolishness that is found there, it is morally impossible but that there should be offences; and God has determined to permit them for wise and holy ends, that both *they which are perfect, and they which are not, may be made manifest.* See 1 Cor. xi. 19; Dan. xi. 35. Being told, before, that there will be seducers, tempters, persecutors, and many bad examples, let us stand upon our guard, *ch.* xxiv. 24; Acts xx. 29, 30.

(2.) That they would be woeful things, and the consequence of them fatal. Here is a double woe annexed to offences:

[1.] A woe to the careless and unguarded, to whom the offence is given; *Woe to the world because of offences.* The obstructions and oppositions given to faith and holiness in all places are the bane and plague of mankind, and the ruin of thousands. This present world is an evil world, it is so full of offences, of sins, and snares, and sorrows; a dangerous road we travel, full of stumbling-blocks, precipices, and false guides. Woe to the world. As for those whom God hath chosen and called out of the world, and delivered from it, they are preserved by the power of God from the prejudice of these offences, are helped over all these stones of stumbling. *They that love God's law have great peace, and nothing shall offend them,* Ps. cxix. 165.

[2.] A woe to the wicked, who wilfully give the offence; *But woe to that man by whom the offence comes.* Though it must needs be, that the offence will come, that will be no excuse for the offenders. Note, Though God makes the sins of sinners to serve his purposes, that will not secure them from his wrath; and the guilt will be laid at the door of those who give the offence, though they also fall under a woe who take it. Note, They who any way hinder the salvation of others, will find their own condemnation the more intolerable, like *Jeroboam, who sinned, and made Israel to sin.* This woe is the moral of that judicial law (Exod. xxi. 33, 34—xxii. 6), that he who opened the pit, and kindled the fire, was accountable for all the damage that ensued. The antichristian generation, by whom came the great offence, will fall under this woe, for their delusion of sinners (2 Thess. ii. 11, 12), and their persecutions of saints (Rev. xvii. 1, 2, 6), for the righteous God will reckon with those who ruin the eternal interests of precious souls, and the temporal interests of precious saints; for *precious in the sight of the Lord is* the blood of souls and *the blood of saints;* and men will be reckoned with, not only for their doings, but for the fruit of their doings, the mischief done by them.

II. In particular, Christ here speaks of offences given,

1. By us to ourselves, which is expressed by our hand or foot offending us; in such a case, it must be *cut off, v.* 8, 9. This Christ had said before (*ch.* v. 29, 30), where it especially refers to seventh-commandment sins; here it is taken more generally. Note, Those hard sayings of Christ, which are displeasing to flesh and blood, need to be repeated to us again and again, and all little enough. Now observe,

(1.) What it is that is here enjoined. We must part with an *eye,* or a *hand,* or a *foot,* that is, that, whatever it is, which is dear to us, when it proves unavoidably an occasion of sin to us. Note, [1.] Many prevailing temptations to sin arise from within ourselves; our own eyes and hands offend us; if there were never a devil to tempt us, we should be drawn away of our own lust: nay, those things which in themselves are good, and may be used as instruments of good, even those, through the corruptions of our hearts, prove snares to us, incline us to sin, and hinder us in duty. [2.] In such a case, we must, as far as lawfully we may, part with that which we cannot keep without being entangled in sin by it. *First,* It is certain, the inward lust must be mortified, though it be dear to us as an eye, or a hand. *The flesh, with its affections and lusts, must be mortified,* Gal. v. 24. *The body of sin must be destroyed;* corrupt inclinations and appetites must be checked and crossed; the beloved lust, that has been rolled under the tongue as a sweet morsel, must be abandoned with abhorrence. *Secondly,* The outward occasions of sin must be avoided, though we thereby put as great a violence upon ourselves as it would be to cut off a hand, or pluck out an eye. When Abraham quitted his native country, for fear of being ensnared in the idolatry of it, and when Moses quitted Pharaoh's court, for fear of being entangled in the sinful pleasures of it, there was a right hand cut off. We must think nothing too dear to part with, for the keeping of a good conscience.

(2.) Upon what inducement this is required; *It is better for thee to enter into life maimed, than, having two hands, to be cast into hell.* The argument is taken from the future state, from heaven and hell; thence are fetched the most cogent dissuasives from sin. The argument is the same with that of the apostle, Rom. viii. 13. [1.] *If we live after the flesh, we shall die;* having two eyes, no breaches made upon the body of sin, inbred corruption like Adonijah never displeased, we shall *be cast into hell-fire.* [2.] *If we through the Spirit mortify the deeds of the body, we shall live;* that is meant by our *entering into life maimed,* that is, the body of sin maimed; and it is but maimed at the best, while we are in this world. If the right hand of the old man be cut off, and its right eye plucked out, its chief policies blasted and powers broken, it is well; but there is still an eye and a hand remaining, with which it will struggle. They that are Christ's have nailed the flesh to the cross, but it is not yet dead; its life is prolonged, but its *dominion taken away* (Dan. vii. 12), and the deadly wound given it, that shall not be healed.

1. Concerning offences given by us to others, especially Christ's little ones, which we are here charged to take heed of, pursuant to what he had said, *v.* 6. Observe,

(1.) The caution itself; *Take heed that ye despise not one of these little ones.* This is spoken to the disciples. As Christ will be displeased with the enemies of his church, if they wrong any of the members of it, even the least, so he will be displeased with the great ones of the church, if they despise the little ones of it. "You that are striving who shall be greatest, take heed lest in this contest you despise the little ones." We may understand it literally of little children; of them Christ was speaking, *v.* 2, 4. The infant seed of the faithful belong to the family of Christ, and are not to be despised. Or, figuratively; true but weak believers are these little ones, who in their outward condition, or the frame of their spirits, are like little children, the lambs of Christ's flock.

[1.] We must not despise them, not think meanly of them, as lambs despised, Job xii. 5. We must not make a jest of their infirmities, not look upon them with contempt, not conduct ourselves scornfully or disdainfully toward them, as if we cared not what became of them; we must not say, "Though they be offended, and grieved, and stumble, what is that to us?" Nor should we make a slight matter of doing that which will entangle and perplex them. This despising of the little ones is what we are largely cautioned against, Rom. xiv. 3, 10, 15, 20, 21. We must not impose upon the consciences of others, nor bring them into subjection to our humours, as they do who say to men's souls, *Bow down, that we may go over*. There is a respect owing to the conscience of every man who appears to be conscientious.

[2.] We must take heed that we do not despise them; we must be afraid of the sin, and be very cautious what we say and do, lest we should through inadvertency give offence to Christ's little ones, lest we put contempt upon them, without being aware of it. There were those that hated them, and cast them out, and yet said, *Let the Lord be glorified*. And we must be afraid of the punishment; "Take heed of despising them, for it is at your peril if you do."

(2.) The reasons to enforce the caution. We must not look upon these little ones as contemptible, because really they are considerable. Let not earth despise those whom heaven respects; let not *those* be looked upon by us with disdain, whom God has put honour upon, and looks upon with respect, as his favourites. To prove that the little ones which believe in Christ are worthy to be respected, consider,

[1.] The ministration of the good angels about them; *In heaven their angels always behold the face of my Father*. This Christ saith to us, and we may take it upon *his* word, who came from heaven to let us know what is done there by the world of angels. Two things he lets us know concerning them,

First, That they are the little ones' angels. God's angels are theirs; for all his is ours, if we be Christ's. 1 Cor. iii. 22. They are theirs; for they have a charge concerning them to minister for their good (Heb. i. 14), to pitch their tents about them, and bear them up in their arms. Some have imagined that every particular saint has a guardian angel; but why should we suppose this, when we are sure that every particular saint, when there is occasion, has a guard of angels? This is particularly applied here to the little ones, because they are most despised and most exposed. They have but little that they can call their own, but they can look by faith on the heavenly hosts, and call them theirs. While the great ones of the world have honourable men for their retinue and guards, the little ones of the church are attended with glorious angels; which bespeaks not only their dignity, but the danger those run themselves upon, who despise and abuse them. It is bad being enemies to those who are so guarded; and it is good having God for our God, for then we have his angels for our angels.

Secondly, That *they always behold the face of the Father in heaven*. This bespeaks, 1. The angels' continual felicity and honour. The happiness of heaven consists in the vision of God, seeing him face to face as he is, beholding his beauty; this the angels have without interruption; when they are ministering to us on earth, yet even then by contemplation they behold the face of God, for they are *full of eyes within*. Gabriel, when speaking to Zecharias, yet stands in the presence of God, Rev. iv. 8; Luke i. 19. The expression intimates, as some think, the special dignity and honour of the little ones' angels; the prime ministers of state are said to *see the king's face* (Esth. i. 14), as if the strongest angels had the charge of the weakest saints. 2. It bespeaks their continual readiness to minister to the saints. They behold the face of God, expecting to receive orders from him what to do for the good of the saints. *As the eyes of the servant are to the hand of his master*, ready to go or come upon the least beck, so the eyes of the angels are upon the face of God, waiting for the intimations of his will, which those winged messengers fly swiftly to fulfil; they *go and return like a flash of lightning*, Ezek. i. 14. If we would behold the face of God in glory hereafter, as the angels do (Luke xx. 36), we must behold the face of God now, in readiness to our duty, as they do, Acts ix. 6.

[2.] The gracious design of Christ concerning them (*v.* 11); *For the Son of man is come to save that which was lost*. This is a reason, *First*, Why the little ones' angels have such a charge concerning them, and attend upon them; it is in pursuance of Christ's design to save them. Note, The ministration of angels is founded in the mediation of Christ; through him angels are reconciled to us; and, when they celebrated God's goodwill toward men, to it they annexed their own. *Secondly*, Why they are not to be despised; because Christ came to save them, to save them that are lost, the little ones that are lost in their own eyes (Isa. lxvi. 3), that are at a loss within themselves. Or rather, the children of men. Note, 1. Our souls by nature are lost souls; as a traveller is lost, that is out of his way, as a convicted prisoner is lost. God lost the service of fallen man, lost the honour he should have had from him. 2. Christ's errand into the world was to *save that which was lost*, to reduce us to our allegiance, restore us to our work, reinstate us in our privileges, and so to put us into the right way that leads to our great end; to save those that are spiritually lost from being eternally so. 3. This is a good reason why the least and weakest believers should not be despised or offended. If Christ put such a value upon them, let us not undervalue them. If he denied himself so much for their salvation, surely we should deny ourselves for their edification and consolation. See this argument urged, Rom. xiv. 15; 1 Cor. viii. 11, 12. Nay, if Christ came into the world to save souls, and his heart is so much upon that work, he will reckon severely with those that obstruct and hinder it, by obstructing the progress of those that are setting their faces heavenward, and so thwart his great design.

[3.] The tender regard which our heavenly Father has to these little ones, and his concern for their welfare. This is illustrated by a comparison, *v.* 12—14. Observe the gradation of the argument; the angels of God are their servants, the Son of God is their Saviour, and, to complete their honour, God himself is their Friend. *None shall pluck them out of my Father's hand,* John x. 28.

Here is, *First,* The comparison, *v.* 12, 13. The owner that had lost one sheep out of a hundred, does not slight it, but diligently enquires after it, is greatly pleased when he has found it, and has in that a sensible and affecting joy, more than in the ninety and nine that wandered not. The fear he was in of losing that one, and the surprise of finding it, add to the joy. Now this is applicable, 1. To the state of fallen man in general; he is strayed like a lost sheep, the angels that stood were as the ninety-nine that never went astray; wandering man is sought upon the mountains, which Christ, in great fatigue, traversed in pursuit of him, and he is found; which is matter of joy. Greater joy there is in heaven for returning sinners than for remaining angels. 2. To particular believers, who are offended and put out of their way by the stumbling-blocks that are laid in their way, or the wiles of those who seduce them out of the way. Now though but one of a hundred should hereby be driven off, as sheep easily are, yet that one shall be looked after with a great deal of care, the return of it welcomed with a great deal of pleasure; and therefore the wrong done to it, no doubt, will be reckoned for with a great deal of displeasure. If there be joy in heaven for the finding of one of these little ones, there is wrath in heaven for the offending of them. Note, God is graciously concerned, not only for his flock in general, but for every lamb, or sheep, that belongs to it. Though they are many, yet out of those many he can easily miss one, for he is a *great* Shepherd, but not so easily lose it, for he is a *good* Shepherd, and takes a more particular cognizance of his flock than ever any did; for he *calls his own sheep by name,* John x. 3. See a full exposition of this parable, Ezek. xxxiv. 2, 10, 16, 19.

Secondly, The application of this comparison (*v.* 14); *It is not the will of your Father, that one of these little ones should perish.* More is implied than is expressed. It is not his will that any should perish, but, 1. It is his will, that these little ones should be saved; it is the will of his design and delight: he has designed it, and set his heart upon it, and he will effect it; it is the will of his precept, that all should do what they can to further it, and nothing to hinder it. 2. This care extends itself to every particular member of the flock, even the meanest. We think if but *one* or *two* be offended and ensnared, it is no great matter, we need not mind it; but God's thoughts of love and tenderness are above ours. 3. It is intimated that those who do any thing by which any of these little ones are brought into danger of perishing, contradict the will of God, and highly provoke him; and though they cannot prevail in it, yet they will be reckoned with for it by him, who, in his saints, as in other things, is jealous of his honour, and will not bear to have it trampled on. See Isa. iii. 15, *What mean ye, that ye beat my people?* Ps. lxxvi. 8, 9.

Observe, Christ called God, *v.* 19, *my Father which is in heaven;* he calls him, *v.* 14, *your Father which is in heaven;* intimating that he is not ashamed to call his poor disciples *brethren;* for have not he and they one Father? *I ascend to my Father and your Father* (John xx. 17); therefore ours because his. This intimates likewise the ground of the safety of his little ones; that God is their Father, and is therefore inclined to succour them. A father takes care of all his children, but is particularly tender of the little ones, Gen. xxxiii. 13. He is their Father in heaven, a place of prospect, and therefore he sees all the indignities offered them; and a place of power, therefore he is able to avenge them. This comforts offended little ones, that their Witness is in heaven (Job xvi. 19), their Judge is there, Ps. lxviii. 5.

15 Moreover if thy brother shall
trespass against thee, go and tell him
his fault between thee and him alone:
if he shall hear thee, thou hast gained
thy brother. 16 But if he will not
hear *thee, then* take with thee one or
two more, that in the mouth of two
or three witnesses every word may be
established. 17 And if he shall neglect to hear them, tell *it* unto the
church: but if he neglect to hear the
church, let him be unto thee as an
heathen man and a publican. 18
Verily I say unto you, Whatsoever
ye shall bind on earth shall be bound
in heaven: and whatsoever ye shall
loose on earth shall be loosed in heaven. 19 Again I say unto you, That
if two of you shall agree on earth as
touching any thing that they shall ask,
it shall be done for them of my Father
which is in heaven. 20 For where
two or three are gathered together in
my name, there am I in the midst of
them.

Christ, having cautioned his disciples not

to give offence, comes next to direct them what they must do in case of offences given them; which may be understood either of personal injuries, and then these directions are intended for the preserving of the peace of the church; or of public scandals, and then they are intended for the preserving of the purity and beauty of the church. Let us consider it both ways.

I. Let us apply it to the quarrels that happen, upon any account, among Christians. If thy brother trespass against thee, by grieving thy soul (1 Cor. viii. 12), by affronting thee, or putting contempt or abuse upon thee; if he blemish thy good name by false reports or tale-bearing; if he encroach on thy rights, or be any way injurious to thee in thy estate; if he be guilty of any of those trespasses that are specified, Lev. vi. 2, 3; if he transgress the laws of justice, charity, or relative duties; these are trespasses against us, and often happen among Christ's disciples, and sometimes, for want of prudence, are of very mischievous consequence. Now observe what is the rule prescribed in this case,

1. *Go, and tell him his fault between thee and him alone.* Let this be compared with, and explained by, Lev. xix. 17, *Thou shalt not hate thy brother in thy heart;* that is, "If thou hast conceived a displeasure at thy brother for any injury he hath done thee, do not suffer thy resentments to ripen into a secret malice (like a wound, which is most dangerous when it bleeds inwardly), but give vent to them in a mild and grave admonition, let them so spend themselves, and they will expire the sooner; do not go and rail against him behind his back, but *thou shalt in any ways reprove him.* If he has indeed done thee a considerable wrong, endeavour to make him sensible of it, but let the rebuke be private, between thee and him alone; if thou wouldest convince him, do not expose him, for that will but exasperate him, and make the reproof look like a revenge." This agrees with Prov. xxv. 8, 9, "*Go not forth hastily to strive,* but *debate thy cause with thy neighbour himself,* argue it calmly and amicably; and *if he shall hear thee,* well and good, *thou hast gained thy brother,* there is an end of the controversy, and it is a happy end; let no more be said of it, but let the falling out of friends be the renewing of friendship."

2. "*If he will not hear thee,* if he will not own himself in a fault, nor come to an agreement, yet do not despair, but try what he will say to it, if thou take *one or two more,* not only to be witnesses of what passes, but to reason the case further with him; he will be the more likely to hearken to them because they are disinterested; and if reason will rule him, the word of reason in the mouth of two or three witnesses will be better spoken to him" *(Plus vident oculi quam oculus—Many eyes see more than one),* "and more regarded by him, and perhaps it will influence him to acknowledge his error, and to say, *I repent.*"

3. "If *he shall neglect to hear them,* and will not refer the matter to their arbitration, then *tell it to the church,* to the ministers, elders, or other officers, or the most considerable persons in the congregation you belong to, make them the referees to accommodate the matter, and do not presently appeal to the magistrate, or fetch a writ for him." This is fully explained by the apostle (1 Cor. vi.), where he reproves those that went to law before the unjust, and not before the saints (*v.* 1), and would have the saints to judge those small matters (*v.* 2) that pertain to this life, *v.* 3. If you ask, "Who is *the church* that must be told?" the apostle directs there (*v.* 5), *Is there not a wise man among you?* Those of the church that are presumed to be most capable of determining such matters; and he speaks ironically, when he says (*v.* 4), "*Set them to judge who are least esteemed in the church;* those, if there be no better, those, rather than suffer an irreconcileable breach between two church members." This rule was then in a special manner requisite, when the civil government was in the hands of such as were not only aliens, but enemies.

4. "If he will not *hear the church,* will not stand to their award, but persists in the wrong he has done thee, and proceeds to do thee further wrong, *let him be to thee as a heathen man, and a publican;* take the benefit of the law against him, but let that always be the last remedy; appeal not to the courts of justice till thou hast first tried all other means to compromise the matter in variance. Or thou mayest, if thou wilt, break off thy friendship and familiarity with him; though thou must by no means study revenge, yet thou mayest choose whether thou wilt have any dealings with him, at least, in such a way as may give him an opportunity of doing the like again. Thou wouldest have healed him, wouldest have preserved his friendship, but he would not, and so has forfeited it." If a man cheat and abuse me once, it is his fault; if twice, it is my own.

II. Let us apply it to scandalous sins, which are an offence to the little ones, of bad example to those that are weak and pliable, and of great grief to those that are weak and timorous. Christ, having taught us to indulge the weakness of our brethren, here cautions us not to indulge their wickedness under pretence of that. Christ, designing to erect a church for himself in the world, here took care for the preservation, 1. Of its purity, that it might have an expulsive faculty, a power to cleanse and clear itself, like a fountain of living waters, which is necessary as long as the net of the gospel brings up both good fish and bad. 2. Of its peace and order, that every member may know his place and duty, and the purity of it may be preserved in a regular way and not tumultuously. Now let us see,

(1.) What is the case supposed? *If thy*

brother trespass against thee. [1.] "The offender is a brother, one that is in Christian communion, that is baptized, that hears the word, and prays with thee, with whom thou joinest in the worship of God, statedly or occasionally." Note, Church discipline is for church members. *Them that are without God judges,* 1 Cor. v. 12, 13. When any trespass is done against us, it is good to remember that the trespasser is a brother, which furnishes us with a qualifying consideration. [2.] "The offence is a trespass against thee; if thy brother sin against thee (so the word is), if he do any thing which is offensive to thee as a Christian." Note, A gross sin against God is a trespass against his people, who have a true concern for his honour. Christ and believers have twisted interests; what is done against them Christ takes as done against himself, and what is done against him they cannot but take as done against themselves. *The reproaches of them that reproached thee are fallen upon me,* Ps. lxix. 9.

(2.) What is to be done in this case. We have here,

[1.] The rules prescribed, *v.* 15—17. Proceed in this method:

First, "*Go and tell him his fault between thee and him alone.* Do not stay till he comes to thee, but go to him, as the physician visits the patient, and the shepherd goes after the lost sheep." Note, We should think no pains too much to take for the recovering of a sinner to repentance. "*Tell him his fault,* remind him of what he has done, and of the evil of it, *show him his abominations.*" Note, People are loth to see their faults, and have need to be told of them. Though the fact is plain, and the fault too, yet they must be put together with application. Great sins often amuse conscience, and for the present stupify and silence it; and there is need of help to awaken it. David's own heart smote him, when he had cut off Saul's skirt, and when he had numbered the people; but (which is very strange) we do not find that it smote him in the matter of Uriah, till Nathan told him, *Thou art the man.*

"*Tell him his fault,* ἔλεγξον ἀυτὸν—*argue the case with him*" (so the word signifies); "and do it with reason and argument, not with passion." Where the fault is plain and great, the person proper for us to deal with, and we have an opportunity for it, and there is no apparent danger of doing more hurt than good, we must with meekness and faithfulness tell people of what is amiss in them. Christian reproof is an ordinance of Christ for the bringing of sinners to repentance, and must be managed as an ordinance. "Let the reproof be private, between thee and him alone; that it may appear you seek not his reproach, but his repentance." Note, It is a good rule, which should ordinarily be observed among Christians, not to speak of our brethren's faults to others, till we have first spoken of them to themselves; this would make less reproaching and more reproving; that is, less sin committed, and more duty done. It will be likely to work upon an offender, when he sees his reprover concerned not only for his salvation, in telling him his fault, but for his reputation in telling him of it privately.

"*If he shall hear thee*"—that is, "heed thee—if he be wrought upon by the reproof, it is well, *thou hast gained thy brother;* thou hast helped to save him from sin and ruin, and it will be thy credit and comfort," James v. 19, 20. Note, The converting of a soul is the winning of that soul (Prov. xi. 30); and we should covet it, and labour after it, as gain to us; and, if the loss of a soul be a great loss, the gain of a soul is sure no small gain.

Secondly, If that doth not prevail, *then take with thee one or two more, v.* 16. Note, We must not be weary of well-doing, though we see not presently the good success of it. "If he will not hear thee, yet do not give him up as in a desperate case; say not, It will be to no purpose to deal with him any further; but go on in the use of other means; even those that harden their necks must be often reproved, and those that oppose themselves instructed in meekness." In work of this kind we must *travail in birth again* (Gal. iv. 19); and it is after many pains and throes that the child is born.

"*Take with thee one or two more;* 1. To assist thee; they may speak some pertinent convincing word which thou didst not think of, and may manage the matter with more prudence than thou didst." Note, Christians should see their need of help in doing good, and pray in the aid one of another; as in other things, so in giving reproofs, that the duty may be done, and may be done well. 2. "To affect him; he will be the more likely to be humbled for his fault, when he sees it witnessed against by *two or three.*" Deut. xix. 15. Note, Those should think it high time to repent and reform, who see their misconduct become a general offence and scandal. Though in such a world as this it is rare to find one good whom *all men speak well of,* yet it is more rare to find one good whom *all men speak ill of.* 3. "To be witnesses of his conduct, in case the matter should afterward be brought before the church." None should come under the censure of the church as obstinate and contumacious, till it be very well proved that they are so.

Thirdly, If he neglect to hear them, and will not be humbled, *then tell it to the church, v.* 17. There are some stubborn spirits to whom the likeliest means of conviction prove ineffectual; yet such must not be given over as incurable, but let the matter be made more public, and further help called in. Note, 1. Private admonitions must always go before public censures; if gentler methods will do the work, those that are more rough and severe must not be used, Tit. iii. 10. Those that will be reasoned out of their sins, need not be shamed out of them. Let God's work be done effectually, but with as little noise as may be; his kingdom comes with power, but not with observation. But, 2. Where private admonition does not prevail, there public censure must take place. The church must receive the complaints of the offended, and rebuke the sins of the offenders, and judge between them, after an impartial enquiry made into the merits of the cause.

Tell it to the church. It is a thousand pities that this appointment of Christ, which was designed to end differences, and remove offences, should itself be so much a matter of debate, and occasion differences and offences, through the corruption of men's hearts. What church must be told—is the great question. The civil magistrate, say some; The Jewish sanhedrim then in being, say others; but by what follows, *v.* 18, it is plain that he means a Christian church, which, though not yet formed, was now in the embryo. "*Tell it to the church,* that particular church in the communion of which the offender lives; make the matter known to those of that congregation who are by consent appointed to receive informations of that kind. Tell it to the guides and governors of the church, the minister or ministers, the elders or deacons, or (if such the constitution of the society be) tell it to the representatives or heads of the congregation, or to all the members of it; let them examine the matter and, if they find the complaint frivolous and groundless, let them rebuke the complainant; if they find it just, let them rebuke the offender, and call him to repentance, and this will be likely to put an edge and an efficacy upon the reproof, because given," 1. "With greater solemnity," and, 2. "With greater authority." It is an awful thing to receive a reproof from a church, from a minister, a reprover by office; and therefore it is the more regarded by such as pay any deference to an institution of Christ and his ambassadors.

Fourthly, "*If he neglect to hear the church,* if he slight the admonition, and will neither be ashamed of his faults, nor amend them, *let him be unto thee as a heathen man and a publican;* let him be cast out of the communion of the church, secluded from special ordinances, degraded from the dignity of a church member, let him be put under disgrace, and let the members of the society be warned to withdraw from him, that he may be ashamed of his sin, and they may not be infected by it, or made chargeable with it." Those who put contempt on the orders and rules of a society, and bring reproach upon it, forfeit the honours and privileges of it, and are justly laid aside till they repent and submit, and reconcile themselves to it again. Christ has appointed this method for the vindicating of the church's honour, the preserving of its purity, and the conviction and reformation of those that are scandalous. But observe, he doth not say, "Let him be to thee as a devil or damned spirit, as one whose case is desperate," but "as a heathen and a publican, as one in a capacity of being restored and received in again. Count him not as an enemy, but admonish him as a brother." The directions given to the church of Corinth concerning the incestuous person, agree with the rules here; he must be *taken away from among them* (1 Cor. v. 2), must be *delivered to Satan;* for if he be cast out of Christ's kingdom, he is looked upon as belonging to Satan's kingdom; they must not keep company with him, *v.* 11, 13. But when by this he is humbled and reclaimed, he must be welcomed into communion again, and all shall be well.

[2.] Here is a warrant signed for the ratification of all the church's proceedings according to these rules, *v.* 18. What was said before to Peter is here said to all the disciples, and in them to all the faithful office-bearers in the church, to the world's end. While ministers preach the word of Christ faithfully, and in their government of the church strictly adhere to his laws *(clave non errante—the key not turning the wrong way),* they may be assured that he will own them, and stand by them, and will ratify what they say and do, so that it shall be taken as said and done by himself. He will own them,

First, In their sentence of suspension; *Whatsoever ye shall bind on earth shall be bound in heaven.* If the censures of the church duly follow the institution of Christ, his judgments will follow the censures of the church, his spiritual judgments, which are the sorest of all other, such as the rejected Jews fell under (Rom. xi. 8), a *spirit of slumber;* for Christ will not suffer his own ordinances to be trampled upon, but will say *amen* to the righteous sentences which the church passes on obstinate offenders. How light soever proud scorners may make of the censures of the church, let them know that they are confirmed in the court of heaven; and it is in vain for them to appeal to that court, for judgment is there already given against them. They that are shut out from the *congregation of the righteous* now shall not *stand in it* in the great day, Ps. i. 5. Christ will not own those as his, nor receive them to himself, whom the church has duly delivered to Satan; but, if through error or envy the censures of the church be unjust, Christ will graciously find those who are so cast out, John ix. 34, 35.

Secondly, In their sentence of absolution; *Whatsoever ye shall loose on earth shall be loosed in heaven.* Note, 1. No church censures bind so fast, but that, upon the sinner's repentance and reformation, they may and must be loosed again. Sufficient is the punishment which has attained its end, and the offender must then be forgiven and comforted. 2 Cor. ii. 6. There is no unpassable gulf fixed but that between hell and heaven. 2. Those who, upon their repentance, are received by the church into communion again may take the comfort of their absolution in heaven, if their hearts be upright with God As suspension is for the terror of the obstinate, so absolution is for the encouragement of the penitent. St. Paul speaks in the person of Christ, when he saith, *To whom ye forgive any thing, I forgive also,* 2 Cor. ii. 10.

Now it is a great honour which Christ here puts upon the church, that he will condescend not only to take cognizance of their sentences, but to confirm them; and in the following verses we have two things laid down as the ground of this.

(1.) God's readiness to answer the church's prayers (*v.* 19); *If two of you shall agree* harmoniously, *touching any thing that they shall ask, it shall be done for them.* Apply this,

[1.] In general, to all the requests of the faithful praying seed of Jacob; they shall not *seek God's face in vain.* Many promises we have in scripture of a gracious answer to the prayers of faith, but this gives a particular encouragement to joint-prayer; "the requests which two of you agree in, much more which many agree in." No law of heaven limits the number of petitioners. Note, Christ has been pleased to put an honour upon, and to allow a special efficacy in, the joint-prayers of the faithful, and the common supplications they make to God. If they join in the same prayer, if they meet by appointment to come together to the throne of grace on some special errand, or, though at a distance, agree in some particular matter of prayer, they shall speed well. Besides the general regard God has to the prayers of the saints, he is particularly pleased with their union and communion in those prayers. See 2 Chron. v. 13; Acts iv. 31.

[2.] In particular, to those requests that are put up to God about binding and loosing; to which this promise seems more especially to refer. Observe, *First,* That the power of church discipline is not here lodged in the hand of a single person, but two, at least, are supposed to be concerned in it. When the incestuous Corinthian was to be cast out, the church was gathered together (1 Cor. v. 4), and it was a punishment inflicted of many, 2 Cor. ii. 6. In an affair of such importance, *two are better than one, and in the multitude of counsellors there is safety. Secondly,* It is good to see those who have the management of church discipline, agreeing in it. Heats and animosities, among those whose work it is to remove offences, will be the greatest offence of all. *Thirdly,* Prayer must evermore go along with church discipline. Pass no sentence, which you cannot in faith ask God to confirm. The binding and loosing spoken of (*ch.* xvi. 19) was done by preaching, this by praying. Thus the whole power of gospel ministers is resolved into the word and prayer, to which they must wholly give themselves. He doth not say, "If you shall agree to sentence and decree a thing, it shall be done" (as if ministers were judges and lords); but, "If you agree to ask it of God, from him you shall obtain it." Prayer must go along with all our endeavours for the conversion of sinners; see Jas. v. 16. *Fourthly,* The unanimous petitions of the church of God, for the ratification of their just censures, shall be heard in heaven, and obtain an answer; "*It shall be done,* it shall be bound and loosed in heaven; God will set his fiat to the appeals and applications you make to him." If Christ (who here speaks as one having authority) say, "It shall be done," we may be assured that it is done, though we see not the effect in the way that we look for it. God doth especially own and accept us, when we are praying for those that have offended him and us. *The Lord turned the captivity of Job,* not when he prayed for himself, but when he prayed for his friends who had trespassed against him.

(2.) The presence of Christ in the assemblies of Christians, *v.* 20. Every believer has the presence of Christ with him; but the promise here refers to the meetings where two or three are gathered in his name, not only for discipline, but for religious worship, or any act of Christian communion. Assemblies of Christians for holy purposes are hereby appointed, directed, and encouraged.

[1.] They are hereby appointed; the church of Christ in the world exists most visibly in religious assemblies; it is the will of Christ that these should be set up, and kept up, for the honour of God, the edification of men, and the preserving of a face of religion upon the world. When God intends special answers to prayer, he calls for a solemn assembly, Joel ii. 15, 16. If there be no liberty and opportunity for large and numerous assemblies, yet then it is the will of God that two or three should gather together, to show their good-will to the great congregation. Note, When we cannot do what we would in religion, we must do as we can, and God will accept us.

[2.] They are hereby directed to gather together in Christ's name. In the exercise of church discipline, they must *come together in the name of Christ,* 1 Cor v. 4. That name gives to what they do an authority on earth, and an acceptableness in heaven. In meeting for worship, we must have an eye to Christ; must come together by virtue of his warrant and appointment, in token of our relation to him, professing faith in him, and in communion with all that in every place call upon him. When we come together, to worship God in a dependence upon the Spirit and grace of Christ as Mediator for assistance, and upon his merit and righteousness as Mediator for acceptance, having an actual regard to him as our Way to the Father, and our Advocate with the Father, then we are met together in his name.

[3.] They are hereby encouraged with an assurance of the presence of Christ; *There am I in the midst of them.* By his common presence he is in all places, as God; but this is a promise of his special presence. Where his saints are, his sanctuary is, and there he will dwell; it is his rest (Ps. cxxxii. 14), it is his walk (Rev. ii. 1); he is in the midst of them, to quicken and strengthen them, to refresh and comfort them, as the sun in the midst of the universe. He is in the midst of them, that is, in their hearts; it is a spiritual presence, the presence of Christ's Spirit with their spirits, that is here intended. *There am I,* not only *I will be* there, but *I am there;* as if he came first, is ready before them, they shall find him there; he repeated this promise at parting (*ch.* xxviii. 20), *Lo, I am with you always.* Note, The presence of Christ in the assemblies of Christians is promised, and may in faith be prayed for and depended on; *There am I.* This is equivalent to the Shechinah, or special presence of God in the tabernacle and temple of old, Exod. xl. 34; 2 Chron. v. 14.

Though but two or three are met together, Christ is among them; this is an encouragement to the meeting of a few, when it is either, *First,* Of choice. Besides the secret worship performed by particular persons, and the public services of the whole congregation, there may be occasion sometimes for two or three to come together, either for mutual assistance in conference or joint assistance in prayer, not in contempt of public worship, but in concurrence with it; there Christ will be present. Or, *Secondly,* By constraint; when there are not more than two or three to come together, or, if there be, they dare not, *for fear of the Jews,* yet Christ will be *in the midst of them,* for it is not the multitude, but the faith and sincere devotion, of the worshippers, that invites the presence of Christ; and though there be but two or three, the smallest number that can be, yet, if Christ make one among them, who is the principal one, their meeting is as honourable and comfortable as if they were two or three thousand.

21 Then came Peter to him, and
said, Lord, how oft shall my brother
sin against me, and I forgive him?
till seven times? 22 Jesus saith unto
him, I say not unto thee, Until seven
times: but, Until seventy times seven.
23 Therefore is the kingdom of heaven likened unto a certain king, which
would take account of his servants.
24 And when he had begun to reckon,
one was brought unto him, which
owed him ten thousand talents. 25
But forasmuch as he had not to
pay, his lord commanded him to be
sold, and his wife, and children, and
all that he had, and payment to be
made. 26 The servant therefore fell
down, and worshipped him, saying,
Lord, have patience with me, and I
will pay thee all. 27 Then the lord of
that servant was moved with compassion, and loosed him, and forgave
him the debt. 28 But the same
servant went out, and found one of his
fellowservants, which owed him an
hundred pence: and he laid hands
on him, and took *him* by the throat,
saying, Pay me that thou owest. 29
And his fellowservant fell down at his
feet, and besought him, saying, Have
patience with me, and I will pay thee
all. 30 And he would not: but went
and cast him into prison, till he should
pay the debt. 31 So when his fellowservants saw what was done, they
were very sorry, and came and told
unto their lord all that was done. 32
Then his lord, after that he had called
him, said unto him, O thou wicked
servant, I forgave thee all that
debt, because thou desiredst me: 33
Shouldest not thou also have had
compassion on thy fellowservant, even
as I had pity on thee? 34 And his
lord was wroth, and delivered him to
the tormentors, till he should pay all
that was due unto him. 35 So likewise shall my heavenly Father do also
unto you, if ye from your hearts forgive not every one his brother their
trespasses.

This part of the discourse concerning offences is certainly to be understood of personal wrongs, which it is in our power to forgive. Now observe,

I. Peter's question concerning this matter (*v.* 21); *Lord, how oft shall my brother trespass against me, and I forgive him?* Will it suffice to do it *seven times?*

1. He takes it for granted that he must forgive; Christ had before taught his disciples this lesson (*ch.* vi. 14, 15), and Peter has not forgotten it. He knows that he must not only not bear a grudge against his brother, or meditate revenge, but be as good a friend as ever, and forget the injury.

2. He thinks it a great matter to forgive till seven times; he means not *seven times a day,* as Christ said (Luke xvii. 4), but seven times in his life; supposing that if a man had any way abused him seven times, though he were ever so desirous to be reconciled, he

might then abandon his society, and have no more to do with him. Perhaps Peter had an eye to Prov. xxiv. 16. *A just man falleth seven times;* or to the mention of *three transgressions,* and *four,* which God would no more pass by, Amos ii. 1. Note, There is a proneness in our corrupt nature to stint ourselves in that which is good, and to be afraid of doing too much in religion, particularly of forgiving too much, though we have so much forgiven us.

II. Christ's direct answer to Peter's question; *I say not unto thee, Until seven times* (he never intended to set up any such bounds), but, *Until seventy times seven;* a certain number for an indefinite one, but a great one. Note, It does not look well for us to keep count of the offences done against us by our brethren. There is something of ill-nature in scoring up the injuries we forgive, as if we would allow ourselves to be revenged when the measure is full. God keeps an account (Deut. xxxii. 34), because he is the Judge, and vengeance is his; but we must not, lest we be found stepping into his throne. It is necessary to the preservation of peace, both within and without, to pass by injuries, without reckoning how often; to forgive, and forget. God multiplies his pardons, and so should we, Ps. lxxviii. 38, 40. It intimates that we should make it our constant practice to forgive injuries, and should accustom ourselves to it till it becomes habitual.

III. A further discourse of our Saviour's, by way of parable, to show the necessity of forgiving the injuries that are done to us. Parables are of use, not only for the explaining of Christian doctrines, but for the pressing of Christian duties; for they make and leave an impression. The parable is a comment upon the fifth petition of the Lord's prayer, *Forgive us our trespasses, as we forgive them that trespass against us.* Those, and those only, may expect to be forgiven of God, who forgive their brethren. The parable represents the *kingdom of heaven,* that is, the church, and the administration of the gospel dispensation in it. The church is God's family, it is his court; there he dwells, there he rules. God is our master; his servants we are, at least in profession and obligation. In general, the parable intimates how much provocation God has from his family on earth, and how untoward his servants are.

There are three things in the parable.

1. The master's wonderful clemency to his servant who was indebted to him; he forgave him ten thousand talents, out of pure compassion to him, *v.* 23—27. Where observe,

(1.) Every sin we commit is a debt to God; not like a debt to an equal, contracted by buying or borrowing, but to a superior; like a debt to a prince when a recognizance is forfeited, or a penalty incurred by a breach of the law or a breach of the peace; like the debt of a servant to his master, by withholding his service, wasting his lord's goods, breaking his indentures, and incurring the penalty. We are all debtors; we owe satisfaction, and are liable to the process of the law.

(2.) There is an account kept of these debts, and we must shortly be reckoned with for them. This king *would take account of his servants.* God now reckons with us by our own consciences; conscience is an auditor for God in the soul, to call us to account, and to account with us. One of the first questions that an awakened Christian asks, is, *How much owest thou unto my Lord?* And unless it be bribed, it will tell the truth, and not write fifty for a hundred. There is another day of reckoning coming, when these accounts will be called over, and either passed or disallowed, and nothing but the blood of Christ will balance the account.

(3.) The debt of sin is a very great debt; and some are more in debt, by reason of sin, than others. When he *began to reckon,* one of the first defaulters appeared to owe *ten thousand talents.* There is no evading the enquiries of divine justice; your sin will be sure to find you out. The debt was ten thousand talents, a vast sum, amounting by computation to one million eight hundred and seventy-five thousand pounds sterling; a king's ransom or a kingdom's subsidy, more likely than a servant's debt; see what our sins are, [1.] For the heinousness of their nature; they are talents, the greatest denomination that ever was used in the account of money or weight. Every sin is the load of a talent, *a talent of lead, this is wickedness,* Zech. v. 7, 8. The trusts committed to us, as stewards of the grace of God, are each of them a talent (*ch.* xxv. 15), a talent of gold, and for every one of them buried, much more for every one of them wasted, we are a talent in debt, and this raises the account. [2.] For the vastness of their number; they are ten thousand, a myriad, more than *the hairs on our head,* Ps. xl. 12. Who can understand *the number of his errors, or tell how oft he offends?* Ps. xix. 12.

(4.) The debt of sin is so great, that we are not able to pay it; *He had not to pay.* Sinners are insolvent debtors; the scripture, *which concludeth all under sin,* is a statute of bankruptcy against us all. Silver and gold would not pay our debt, Ps. xlix. 6, 7. Sacrifice and offering would not do it; our good works are but God's work in us, and cannot make satisfaction; we are without strength, and cannot help ourselves.

(5.) If God should deal with us in strict justice; we should be condemned as insolvent debtors, and God might exact the debt by glorifying himself in our utter ruin. Justice demands satisfaction, *Currat lex—Let the sentence of the law be executed.* The servant had contracted this debt by his wastefulness and wilfulness, and therefore might justly be left to lie by it. *His lord commanded him to be sold,* as a bond-slave into the galleys, sold to grind in the prison-house; *his wife and children to be sold, and all that he had, and payment to be made.* See here what every sin deserves; this is *the wages of sin.* [1.] To be sold. Those that *sell themselves to work wickedness,* must be sold, to make satisfaction. Captives to sin are captives to wrath. He that is sold for a bond-slave is deprived of all his comforts, and has nothing left him but his life, that he may be sensible of his miseries; which is the case of damned sinners. [2.] Thus he would have *payment to be made,* that is, something done towards it; though it is impossible that the sale of one so worthless should amount to the payment of so great a debt. By the damnation of sinners divine justice will be to eternity in the satisfying, but never satisfied.

(6.) Convinced sinners cannot but humble themselves before God, and pray for mercy. *The servant,* under this charge, and this doom, *fell down* at the feet of his royal master, *and worshipped him;* or, as some copies read it, *he besought him;* his address was very submissive and very importunate; *Have patience with me, and I will pay thee all, v.* 26. The servant knew before that he was so much in debt, and yet was under no concern about it, till he was called to an account. Sinners are commonly careless about the pardon of their sins, till they come under the arrests of some awakening word, some startling providence, or approaching death, and then, *Wherewith shall I come before the Lord?* Mic. vi. 6. How easily, how quickly, can God bring the proudest sinner to his feet; Ahab to his sackcloth, Manasseh to his prayers, Pharaoh to his confessions, Judas to his restitution, Simon Magus to his supplication, Belshazzar and Felix to their tremblings. The stoutest heart will fail, when God sets the sins in order before it. This servant doth not deny the debt, nor seek evasions, nor go about to abscond.

But, [1.] He begs time; *Have patience with me.* Patience and forbearance are a great favour, but it is folly to think that these alone will save us; reprieves are not pardons. Many are borne with, who are not thereby *brought to repentance* (Rom. ii. 4), and then their being borne with does them no kindness.

[2.] He promises payment; *Have patience* awhile, *and I will pay thee all.* Note, It is the folly of many who are under convictions of sin, to imagine that they can make God satisfaction for the wrong they have done him; as those who, like a compounding bankrupt, would discharge the debt, by giving their *first-born for their transgressions* (Mic. vi. 7), who *go about to establish their own righteousness,* Rom. x. 3. He that *had nothing to pay* with (*v.* 25) fancied he could pay *all.* See how close pride sticks, even to awakened sinners; they are convinced, but not humbled.

(7.) The God of infinite mercy is very ready, out of pure compassion, to forgive the sins of those that humble themselves before him (*v.* 27); *The lord of that servant,* when he might justly have ruined him, mercifully released him; and, since he could not be satisfied by the payment of the debt, he would be glorified by the pardon of it. The servant's prayer was, *Have patience with me;* the master's grant is a discharge in full. Note, [1.] The pardon of sin is owing to the mercy of God, to his tender mercy (Luke i. 77, 78); *He was moved with compassion.* God's reasons of mercy are fetched from within himself; he has mercy *because he will have mercy.* God looked with pity on mankind in general, because miserable, and sent his Son to be a Surety for them; he looks with pity on particular penitents, because sensible of their misery (their hearts broken and contrite), and accepts them in the Beloved. [2.] There is forgiveness with God for the greatest sins, if they be repented of. Though the debt was vastly great, he *forgave it all, v.* 32. Though our sins be very numerous and very heinous, yet, upon gospel terms, they may be pardoned. [3.] The forgiving of the debt is the loosing of the debtor; *He loosed him.* The obligation is cancelled, the judgment vacated; we never walk at liberty till our sins are forgiven. But observe, Though he discharged him from the penalty as a debtor, he did not discharge him from his duty as a servant. The pardon of sin doth not slacken, but strengthen, our obligations to obedience; and we must reckon it a favour that God is pleased to continue such wasteful servants as we have been in such a gainful service as his is, and should therefore *deliver us, that we might serve him,* Luke i. 74. *I am thy servant, for thou hast loosed my bonds.*

2. The servant's unreasonable severity toward his fellow-servant, notwithstanding his lord's clemency toward him, *v.* 28—30. This represents the sin of those who, though they are not unjust in demanding that which is not their own, yet are rigorous and unmerciful in demanding that which is their own, to the utmost of right, which sometimes proves a real wrong. *Summum jus summa injuria—Push a claim to an extremity, and it becomes a wrong.* To exact satisfaction for debts of injury, which tends neither to reparation nor to the public good, but purely for revenge, though the law may allow it, *in terrorem—in order to strike terror,* and for the hardness of men's hearts, yet savours not of a Christian spirit. To sue for money-debts, when the debtor cannot possibly pay them, and so let him perish in prison, argues a greater love of money, and a less love of our neighbour, than we ought to have, Neh. v. 7.

See here, (1.) How small the debt was, how very small, compared with the *ten thousand talents* which his lord forgave him; *He owed him a hundred pence,* about three pounds and half a crown of our money.

Note, Offences done to men are nothing to those which are committed against God. Dishonours done to a man like ourselves are but as *pence, motes, gnats;* but dishonours done to God are as *talents, beams, camels.* Not that *therefore* we may make light of wronging our neighbour, for that is also a sin against God; but *therefore* we should make light of our neighbour's wronging us, and not aggravate it, or study revenge. David was unconcerned at the indignities done to him; *I, as a deaf man, heard not;* but laid much to heart the sins committed against God; for them, *rivers of tears ran down his eyes.*

(2.) How severe the demand was; *He laid hands on him, and took him by the throat.* Proud and angry men think, if the matter of their demand be just, that will bear them out, though the manner of it be ever so cruel and unmerciful; but it will not hold. What needed all this violence? The debt might have been demanded without taking the debtor by the throat; without sending for a writ, or setting the bailiff upon him. How lordly is this man's carriage, and yet how base and servile is his spirit! If he had been himself going to prison for his debt to his lord, his occasions would have been so pressing, that he might have had some pretence for going to this extremity in requiring his own; but frequently pride and malice prevail more to make men severe than the most urgent necessity would do.

(3.) How submissive the debtor was; *His fellow servant,* though his equal, yet knowing how much he lay at his mercy, *fell down at his feet,* and humbled himself to him for this trifling debt, as much as he did to his lord for that great debt; for *the borrower is servant to the lender,* Prov. xxii. 7. Note, Those who cannot pay their debts ought to be very respectful to their creditors, and not only give them good words, but do them all the good offices they possibly can: they must not be angry at those who claim their own, nor speak ill of them for it, no, not though they do it in a rigorous manner, but in that case leave it to God to plead their cause. The poor man's request is, *Have patience with me;* he honestly confesses the debt, and puts not his creditor to the charge of proving it, only begs time. Note, Forbearance, though it be no acquittance, is sometimes a piece of needful and laudable charity. As we must not be hard, so we must not be hasty, in our demands, but think how long God bears with us.

(4.) How implacable and furious the creditor was (*v.* 30); *He would not have patience with him,* would not hearken to his fair promise, but without mercy *cast him into prison.* How insolently did he trample upon one as good as himself, that submitted to him! How cruelly did he use one that had done him no harm, and though it would be no advantage to himself! In this, as in a glass, unmerciful creditors may see their own faces, who take pleasure in nothing more than to swallow up and destroy (2 Sam. xx. 19), and glory in having their poor debtors' bones.

(5.) How much concerned the rest of the servants were; *They were very sorry* (*v.* 31), sorry for the creditor's cruelty, and for the debtor's calamity. Note, The sins and sufferings of our fellow-servants should be matter of grief and trouble to us. It is sad that any of our brethren should either make themselves beasts of prey, by cruelty and barbarity; or be made beasts of slavery, by the inhuman usage of those who have power over them. To see a fellow-servant, either raging like a bear or trampled on like a worm, cannot but occasion great regret to all that have any jealousy for the honour either of their nature or of their religion. See with what eye Solomon looked both upon *the tears of the oppressed,* and *the power of the oppressors,* Eccl. iv. 1.

(6.) How notice of it was brought to the master; *They came, and told their lord.* They durst not reprove their fellow-servant for it, he was so unreasonable and outrageous (*let a bear robbed of her whelps meet a man, rather than such a fool in his folly*); but they went to their lord, and besought him to appear for the oppressed against the oppressor. Note, That which gives us occasion for sorrow, should give us occasion for prayer. Let our complaints both of the wickedness of the wicked and of the afflictions of the afflicted, be brought to God, and left with him.

3. The master's just resentment of the cruelty his servant was guilty of. If the servants took it so ill, much more would the master, whose compassions are infinitely above ours. Now observe here,

(1.) How he reproved his servant's cruelty (*v.* 32, 33); *O thou wicked servant.* Note, Unmercifulness is wickedness, it is great wickedness. [1.] He upbraids him with the mercy he had found with his master; *I forgave thee all that debt.* Those that will use God's favours, shall never be upbraided with them, but those that abuse them, may expect it, *ch.* xi. 20. Consider, It was *all that debt,* that great debt. Note, The greatness of sin magnifies the riches of pardoning mercy: we should think *how much has been forgiven us,* Luke vii. 47. [2.] He thence shows him the obligation he was under to be merciful to his fellow-servant; *Shouldst not thou also have had compassion on thy fellow-servant, even as I had pity on thee?* Note, It is justly expected, that such as have received mercy, should show mercy. *Dat ille veniam facile, cui venia est opus—He who needs forgiveness, easily bestows it.* Senec. Agamemn. He shows him, *First,* That he should have been more compassionate to the distress of his fellow servant, because he had himself experienced the same distress. What we have had the feeling of ourselves, we can the better have the fellow feeling of with our brethren. The *Israelites knew the heart of a stranger, for they were strangers;* and this servant should have better known the heart of an arrested debtor, than to have been thus hard upon such a one. *Secondly,* That he should have been more conformable to the example of his master's tenderness, having himself experienced it, so much to his advantage. Note, The comfortable sense of pardoning mercy tends much to the disposing of our hearts to forgive our brethren. It was in the close of the day of atonement that the jubilee trumpet sounded *a release of debts* (Lev. xxv. 9); for we must have compassion on our brethren, as God has on us.

(2.) How he revoked his pardon and cancelled the acquittance, so that the judgment against him revived (*v.* 34); *He delivered him to the tormentors, till he should pay all that was due unto him.* Though the wickedness was very great, his lord laid upon him no other punishment than the payment of his own debt. Note, Those that will not come up to the terms of the gospel need be no more miserable than to be left open to the law, and to let that have its course against them. See how the punishment answers the sin; he that would not forgive shall not be forgiven; *He delivered him to the tormentors;* the utmost he could do to his fellow servant was but to cast him into prison, but he was himself delivered to the tormentors. Note, The power of God's wrath to ruin us, goes far beyond the utmost extent of any creature's strength and wrath. The reproaches and terrors of his own conscience would be his tormentors, for that is a worm that dies not; devils, the executioners of God's wrath, that are sinners' tempters now, will be their tormentors for ever. He was sent to Bridewell till he should pay all. Note, Our debts to God are never compounded; either all is forgiven or all is exacted; glorified saints in heaven are pardoned all, through Christ's complete satisfaction; damned sinners in hell are paying all, that is, are punished for all. The offence done to God by sin is in point of honour, which cannot be compounded for without such a diminution as the case will by no means admit, and therefore, some way or other, by the sinner or by his surety, it must be satisfied.

Lastly, Here is the application of the whole parable (*v.* 35); *So likewise shall my heavenly Father do also unto you.* The title Christ here gives to God was made use of, *v.* 19, in a comfortable promise; *It shall be done for them of my Father which is in heaven;* here it is made use of in a terrible threatening. If God's governing be fatherly, it follows thence, that it is righteous, but it does not therefore follow that it is not rigorous, or that under his government we must not be kept in awe by the fear of the divine wrath. When we pray to God as *our Father in heaven,* we are taught to ask for *the forgiveness of sins, as we forgive our debtors.* Observe here,

1. The duty of forgiving; we must *from our hearts* forgive. Note, We do not forgive our offending brother aright, nor acceptably, if we do not forgive from the heart; for that is it that God looks at. No malice must be harboured there, nor ill will to any person, one or another; no projects of revenge must be hatched there, nor desires of it, as there are in many who outwardly appear peaceable and reconciled. Yet this is not enough; we must from the heart desire and seek the welfare even of those that have offended us.

2. The danger of not forgiving; *So shall your heavenly Father do.* (1.) This is not intended to teach us that God reverses his pardons to any, but that he denies them to those that are unqualified for them, according to the tenour of the gospel; though having seemed to be humbled, like Ahab, they thought themselves, and others thought them, in a pardoned state, and they made bold with the comfort of it. Intimations enough we have in scripture of the forfeiture of pardons, for caution to the presumptuous; and yet we have security enough of the continuance of them, for comfort to those that are sincere, but timorous; that the one may fear, and the other may hope. Those that do not *forgive their brother's trespasses,* did never truly repent of their own, nor ever truly believe the gospel; and therefore that which is *taken away* is only what *they seemed to have,* Luke viii. 18. (2.) This is intended to teach us, that *they shall have judgment without mercy, that have showed no mercy,* Jam. ii. 13. It is indispensably necessary to pardon and peace, that we not only *do justly,* but *love mercy.* It is an essential part of that religion which is *pure and undefiled before God and the Father,* of that *wisdom from above,* which *is gentle, and easy to be entreated.* Look how *they* will answer it another day, who, though they bear the Christian name, persist in the most rigorous and unmerciful treatment of their brethren, as if the strictest laws of Christ might be dispensed with for the gratifying of their unbridled passions; and so they curse themselves every time they say the Lord's prayer.

CHAP. XIX.

In this chapter, we have, I. Christ changing his quarters, leaving Galilee, and coming into the coasts of Judea, ver. 1, 2. II. His dispute with the Pharisees about divorce, and his discourse with his disciples upon occasion of it, ver. 3—12. III. The kind entertainment he gave to some little children which were brought to him, ver. 13—15. IV. An account of what passed between Christ and a hopeful young gentleman that applied himself to him, ver. 16—22. V. His discourse with his disciples upon that occasion, concerning the difficulty of the salvation of those that have much in the world, and the certain recompence of those that leave all for Christ, ver. 23—30.

AND it came to pass, *that* when Jesus had finished these sayings, he departed from Galilee, and came into the coasts of Judea, beyond Jordan; 2 And great multitudes followed him; and he healed them there.

We have here an account of Christ's removal. Observe,

1. He left Galilee. There he had been brought up, and had spent the greatest part of his life in that remote despicable part of the country; it was only upon occasion of the feasts, that he *came up to Jerusalem, and manifested himself there;* and, we may suppose, that, having no constant residence there when he did come, his preaching and miracles were the more observable and acceptable. But it was an instance of his humiliation, and in this, as in other things, he appeared in a mean state, that he would go under the character of a Galilean, a north-countryman, the least polite and refined part of the nation. Most of Christ's sermons hitherto had been preached, and most of his miracles wrought, in Galilee; but now, having *finished these sayings, he departed from Galilee,* and it was his final farewell; for (unless his *passing through the midst of Samaria and Galilee,* Luke xvii. 11, was after this, which yet was but a visit *in transitu—as he passed through the country*) he never came to Galilee again till after his resurrection, which makes this transition very remarkable. Christ did not take his leave of Galilee till he had done his work there, and then he departed thence. Note, As Christ's faithful ministers are not taken out of the world, so they are not removed from any place, till they have finished their testimony in that place, Rev. xi. 7. This is very comfortable to those that follow not their own humours, but God's providence, in their removals, that their sayings shall be finished before they depart. And who would desire to continue any where longer than he has work to do for God there?

2. *He came into the coasts of Judea, beyond Jordan,* that *they* might have their day of visitation as well as Galilee, for they also belonged *to the lost sheep of the house of Israel.* But still Christ kept to those parts of Canaan that lay towards other nations; Galilee is called *Galilee of the Gentiles;* and the Syrians dwelt beyond Jordan. Thus Christ intimated, that, while he kept within the confines of the Jewish nation, he had his eye upon the Gentiles, and his gospel was aiming and coming toward them.

3. *Great multitudes followed him.* Where Shiloh is, there will *the gathering of the people be.* The *redeemed of the Lord* are such as *follow the Lamb whithersoever he goes,* Rev. xiv. 4. When Christ departs, it is best for us to follow him. It was a piece of respect to Christ, and yet it was a continual trouble, to be thus crowded after, wherever he went; but he sought not his own ease, nor, considering how mean and contemptible this mob was (as some would call them), his own honour much, in the eye of the world; he *went about doing good;* for so it follows, *he healed them there.* This shows what they followed him for, to have their sick healed; and they found him as able and ready to help here, as he had been in Galilee; for, wherever this *Sun of righteousness arose,* it was *with healing under his wings. He healed them there,* because he would not have them follow him to Jerusalem, lest it should give offence. *He shall not strive, nor cry.*

3 The Pharisees also came unto
him, tempting him, and saying unto
him, Is it lawful for a man to put
away his wife for every cause? 4
And he answered and said unto them,
Have ye not read, that he which made
them at the beginning made them male
and female. 5 And said, For this
cause shall a man leave father and
mother, and shall cleave to his wife:
and they twain shall be one flesh? 6
Wherefore they are no more twain,
but one flesh. What therefore God
hath joined together, let not man put
asunder. 7 They say unto him, Why
did Moses then command to give a
writing of divorcement, and to put
her away? 8 He saith unto them,
Moses because of the hardness of
your hearts suffered you to put away
your wives: but from the beginning
it was not so. 9 And I say unto you,
Whosoever shall put away his wife,
except *it be* for fornication, and shall
marry another, committeth adultery:
and whoso marrieth her which is put
away doth commit adultery. 10 His
disciples say unto him, If the case of
the man be so with *his* wife, it is not
good to marry. 11 But he said unto
them, All *men* cannot receive this
saying, save *they* to whom it is given.
12 For there are some eunuchs, which
were so born from *their* mother's
womb: and there are some eunuchs,
which were made eunuchs of men:
and there be eunuchs, which have
made themselves eunuchs for the kingdom of heaven's sake. He that is able
to receive *it,* let him receive *it.*

We have here the law of Christ in the case of divorce, occasioned, as some other declarations of his will, by a dispute with *the Pharisees.* So patiently did he endure the contradiction of sinners, that he turned it into instructions to his own disciples! Observe here,

I. The case proposed by the Pharisees (*v.* 3); *Is it lawful for a man to put away his wife?* This they asked, tempting him, not desiring to be taught by him. Some time ago, he had, in Galilee, declared his mind in this matter, against that which was the common practice (*ch.* v. 31, 32); and if he would, in like manner, declare himself now against divorce, they would make use of it for the prejudicing and incensing of the people of this country against him, who would look with a jealous eye upon one that attempted to cut them short in a liberty they were fond of. They hoped he would lose himself in the affections of the people as much by this as by any of his precepts. Or, the temptation might be designed thus: If he should say that divorces were not lawful, they would reflect upon him as an enemy to the law of Moses, which allowed them; if he should say that they were, they would represent his doctrine as not having that perfection in it which was expected in the doctrine of the Messiah; since, though divorces were tolerated, they were looked upon by the stricter sort of people as not of good report. Some think, that, though the law of Moses did permit divorce, yet, in assigning the just causes for it, there was a controversy between the Pharisees among themselves, and they desired to know what Christ said to it. Matrimonial cases have been numerous, and sometimes intricate and perplexed; made so not by the law of God, but by the lusts and follies of men; and often in these cases people resolve, before they ask, what they will do.

Their question is, *Whether a man may put away his wife for every cause.* That it might be done for some cause, even for that of fornication, was granted; but may it be done, as now it commonly was done, by the looser sort of people, for every cause; for any cause that a man shall think fit to assign, though ever so frivolous; upon every dislike or displeasure? The toleration, in this case, permitted it, *in case she found no favour in his eyes, because he hath found some uncleanness in her*, Deut. xxiv. 1. This they interpreted so largely as to make any disgust, though causeless, the ground of a divorce.

II. Christ's answer to this question; though it was proposed to tempt him, yet, being a case of conscience, and a weighty one, he gave a full answer to it, not a direct one, but an effectual one; laying down such principles as undeniably prove that such arbitrary divorces as were then in use, which made the matrimonial bond so very precarious, were by no means lawful. Christ himself would not give the rule without a reason, nor lay down his judgment without scripture proof to support it. Now his argument is this; "If husband and wife are by the will and appointment of God joined together in the strictest and closest union, then they are not to be lightly, and upon every occasion, separated; if the knot be sacred, it cannot be easily untied." Now, to prove that there is such a union between man and wife, he urges three things.

1. The creation of Adam and Eve, concerning which he appeals to their own knowledge of the scriptures; *Have ye not read?* It is some advantage in arguing, to deal with those that own, and have read, the scriptures; *Ye have read* (but have not considered) *that he which made them at the beginning, made them male and female,* Gen. i. 27; v. 2. Note, It will be of great use to us often to think of our creation, how and by whom, what and for what, we were created. *He made them male and female,* one female for one male; so that Adam could not divorce his wife, and take another, for there was no other to take. It likewise intimated an inseparable union between them; Eve was a rib out of Adam's side, so that he could not put her away, but he must put away a piece of himself, and contradict the manifest indications of her creation. Christ hints briefly at this, but, in appealing to what they had read, he refers them to the original record, where it is observable, that, though the rest of the living creatures were made male and female, yet it is not said so concerning any of them, but only concerning mankind; because between man and woman the conjunction is rational, and intended for nobler purposes than merely the pleasing of sense and the preserving of a seed; and it is therefore more close and firm than that between male and female among the brutes, who were not capable of being such help-meets for one another as Adam and Eve were. Hence the manner of expression is somewhat singular (Gen. i. 27), *In the image of God created he him, male and female created he them; him* and *them* are used promiscuously; being one by creation before they were two, when they became one again by marriage-covenant, that oneness could not but be closer and indissoluble.

2. The fundamental law of marriage, which is, that *a man shall leave father and mother, and shall cleave to his wife, v.* 5. The relation between husband and wife is nearer than that between parents and children; now, if the filial relation may not easily be violated, much less may the marriage union be broken. May a child desert his parents, or may a parent abandon his children, for any cause, for every cause? No, by no means. Much less may a husband put away his wife, betwixt whom, though not by nature, yet by divine appointment, the relation is nearer, and the bond of union stronger, than between parents and children; for that is in a great measure superseded by marriage, when a man must leave his parents, to cleave to his wife. See here the power of a divine institution, that the result of it is a union stronger than that which results from the highest obligations of nature.

3. The nature of the marriage contract;

it is a union of persons; *They twain shall be one flesh,* so that (*v.* 6) *they are no more twain, but one flesh.* A man's children are pieces of himself, but his wife is himself. As the conjugal union is closer than that between parents and children, so it is in a manner equivalent to that between one member and another in the natural body. As this is a reason why husbands should love their wives, so it is a reason why they should not put away their wives; for *no man ever yet hated his own flesh,* or cut it off, *but nourishes and cherishes it,* and does all he can to preserve it. They two shall be one, therefore there must be but one wife, for God made but one Eve for one Adam, Mal. ii. 15.

From hence he infers, *What God hath joined together, let not man put asunder.* Note (1.) Husband and wife are of God's joining together; *συνέζευξεν—he hath yoked them together,* so the word is, and it is very significant. God himself instituted the relation between husband and wife in the state of innocence. Marriage and the sabbath are the most ancient of divine ordinances. Though marriage be not peculiar to the church, but common to the world, yet, being stamped with a divine institution, and here ratified by our Lord Jesus, it ought to be managed *after a godly sort, and sanctified by the word of God, and prayer.* A conscientious regard to God in this ordinance would have a good influence upon the duty, and consequently upon the comfort, of the relation. (2.) Husband and wife, being joined together by the ordinance of God, are not to be put asunder by any ordinance of man. Let not man put them asunder; not the husband himself, nor any one for him; not the magistrate, God never gave him authority to do it. The God of Israel hath said, that *he hateth putting away,* Mal. ii. 16. It is a general rule that man must not go about to *put asunder what God hath joined together.*

III. An objection started by the Pharisees against this; an objection not destitute of colour and plausibility (*v.* 7); "*Why did Moses command to give a writing of divorcement,* in case a man did put away his wife?" He urged scripture reason against divorce; they allege scripture authority for it. Note, The seeming contradictions that are in the word of God are great stumbling-blocks to men of corrupt minds. It is true, *Moses was faithful to him that appointed him,* and commanded nothing but *what he received from the Lord;* but as to the thing itself, what they call a *command* was only an *allowance* (Deut. xxiv. 1), and designed rather to restrain the exorbitances of it than to give countenance to the thing itself. The Jewish doctors themselves observe such limitations in that law, that it could not be done without great deliberation. A particular reason must be assigned, the bill of divorce must be written, and, as a judicial act, must have all the solemnities of a deed, executed and enrolled. It must be given into the hands of the wife herself, and (which would oblige men, if they had any consideration in them, to consider) they were expressly forbidden ever to come together again.

IV. Christ's answer to this objection, in which,

1. He rectifies their mistake concerning the law of Moses; they called it a *command,* Christ calls it but a *permission,* a *toleration.* Carnal hearts will take an ell if but an inch be given them. The law of Moses, in this case, was a political law, which God gave, as the Governor of that people; and it was for reasons of state, that divorces were tolerated. The strictness of the marriage union being the result, not of a natural, but of a positive law, the wisdom of God dispensed with divorces in some cases, without any impeachment of his holiness.

But Christ tells them there was a reason for this toleration, not at all for their credit; *It was because of the hardness of your hearts,* that you were permitted to *put away your wives.* Moses complained of the people of Israel in his time, that *their hearts were hardened* (Deut. ix. 6; xxxi. 27), hardened against God; this is here meant of their being hardened against their relations; they were generally violent and outrageous, which way soever they took, both in their appetites and in their passions; and therefore if they had not been allowed to put away their wives, when they had conceived a dislike of them, they would have used them cruelly, would have beaten and abused them, and perhaps have murdered them. Note, There is not a greater piece of hard-heartedness in the world, than for a man to be harsh and severe with his own wife. The Jews, it seems, were infamous for this, and therefore were allowed to put them away; better divorce them than do worse, than that *the altar of the Lord should be covered with tears,* Mal. ii. 13. A little compliance, to humour a madman, or a man in a frenzy, may prevent a greater mischief. Positive laws may be dispensed with for the preservation of the law of nature, for God *will have mercy and not sacrifice*; but then those are hard-hearted wretches, who have made it necessary; and none can wish to have the liberty of divorce, without virtually owning the hardness of their hearts. Observe, He saith, It is for the hardness of *your* hearts, not only theirs who lived then, but all their seed. Note, God not only sees, but foresees, the hardness of men's hearts; he suited both the ordinances and providences of the Old Testament to the temper of that people, both in terror. Further observe, The law of Moses considered the hardness of men's hearts, but the gospel of Christ cures it; and his grace *takes away the heart of stone, and gives a heart of flesh.* By the law was the knowledge of sin, but by the gospel was the conquest of it.

2. He reduces them to the original institution; *But from the beginning it was not so.* Note, Corruptions that are crept into any ordinance of God must be purged out by having recourse to the primitive institution. If the copy be vicious, it must be examined and corrected by the original. Thus, when St. Paul would redress the grievances in the church of Corinth about the Lord's supper, he appealed to the appointment (1 Cor. xi. 23), So and so *I received from the Lord.* Truth was from the beginning; we must therefore enquire for *the good old way* (Jer. vi. 16), and must reform, not by later patterns, but by ancient rules.

3. He settles the point by an express law; *I say unto you* (*v.* 9); and it agrees with what he said before (*ch.* v. 32); there it was said in preaching, here in dispute, but it is the same, for Christ is constant to himself. Now, in both these places,

(1.) He allows divorce, in case of adultery; the reason of the law against divorce being this, *They two shall be one flesh.* If the wife play the harlot, and make herself one flesh with an adulterer, the reason of the law ceases, and so does the law. By the law of Moses adultery was punished with death, Deut. xxii. 22. Now our Saviour mitigates the rigour of that, and appoints divorce to be the penalty. Dr. Whitby understands this, not of adultery, but (because our Saviour uses the word *πορνεία—fornication)* of uncleanness committed before marriage, but discovered afterward; because, if it were committed after, it was a capital crime, and there needed no divorce.

(2.) He disallows it in all other cases; *Whosoever puts away his wife, except for fornication, and marries another, commits adultery.* This is a direct answer to their query, that it is not lawful. In this, as in other things, gospel times are *times of reformation,* Heb. ix. 10. The law of Christ tends to reinstate man in his primitive integrity; the law of love, conjugal love, is no new commandment, but was from the beginning. If we consider what mischiefs to families and states, what confusions and disorders, would follow upon arbitrary divorces, we shall see how much this law of Christ is for our own benefit, and what a friend Christianity is to our secular interests.

The law of Moses allowing divorce for the hardness of men's hearts, and the law of Christ forbidding it, intimate, that Christians being under a dispensation of love and liberty, tenderness of heart may justly be expected among them, that they will not be hard-hearted, like Jews, *for God has called us to peace.* There will be no occasion for divorces, if we *forbear one another, and forgive one another, in love,* as those that are, and hope to be, forgiven, and have found God not forward *to put us away,* Isa. l. 1. No need of divorces, if *husbands love their wines, and wives be obedient to their husbands,* and they live together as heirs of the grace of life: and these are the laws of Christ, such as we find not in all the law of Moses.

V. Here is a suggestion of the disciples against this law of Christ (*v.* 10); *If the case of the man be so with his wife, it is better not to marry.* It seems, the disciples themselves were loth to give up the liberty of divorce, thinking it a good expedient for preserving comfort in the married state; and therefore, like sullen children, if they have not what they would have, they will throw away what they have. If they may not be allowed to put away their wives when they please, they will have no wives at all; though, from the beginning, when no divorce was allowed, God said, *It is not good for man to be alone, and blessed them,* pronounced them blessed who were thus strictly joined together; yet, unless they may have a liberty of divorce, they think it is good for a man not to marry. Note, 1. Corrupt nature is impatient of restraint, and would fain break Christ's bonds in sunder, and have a liberty for its own lusts. 2. It is a foolish, peevish thing for men to abandon the comforts of this life, because of the crosses that are commonly woven in with them, as if we must needs go out of the world, because we have not every thing to our mind in the world; or must enter into no useful calling or condition, because it is made our duty to abide in it. No, whatever our condition is, we must bring our minds to it, be thankful for its comforts, submissive to its crosses, and, as God has done, *set the one over against the other,* and make the best of that which is, Eccl. vii. 14. If the yoke of marriage may not be thrown off at pleasure, it does not follow that *therefore* we must not come under it; but *therefore,* when we do come under it, we must resolve to comport with it, by love, and meekness, and patience, which will make divorce the most unnecessary undesirable thing that can be.

VI. Christ's answer to this suggestion (*v.* 11, 12), in which,

1. He allows it good for some not to marry; *He that is able to receive it, let him receive it.* Christ allowed what the disciples said, *It is good not to marry;* not as an objection against the prohibition of divorce, as they intended it, but as giving them a rule (perhaps no less unpleasing to them), that they who have the gift of continence, and are not under any necessity of marrying, do best if they continue single (1 Cor vii. 1); for they that are unmarried have opportunity, if they have but a heart, to care more *for the things of the Lord, how they may please the Lord* (1 Cor. vii. 32—34), being less encumbered with the cares of this life, and having a greater vacancy of thought and time to mind better things. The increase of grace is better than the increase of the family, and fellowship

with the Father and with his Son Jesus Christ is to be preferred before any other fellowship.

2. He disallows it, as utterly mischievous, to forbid marriage, because *all men cannot receive this saying;* indeed few can, and therefore the crosses of the married state must be borne, rather than that men should run themselves into temptation, to avoid them; *better marry than burn.*

Christ here speaks of a twofold unaptness to marriage.

(1.) That which is a calamity by the providence of God; such as those labour under who are born eunuchs, or made so by men, who, being incapable of answering one great end of marriage, ought not to marry. But to that calamity let them oppose the opportunity that there is in the single state of serving God better, to balance it.

(2.) That which is a virtue by the grace of God; such is theirs who *have made themselves eunuchs for the kingdom of heaven's sake.* This is meant of an unaptness for marriage, not in body (which some, through mistake of this scripture, have foolishly and wickedly brought upon themselves), but in mind. Those have thus made themselves eunuchs who have attained a holy indifference to all the delights of the married state, have a fixed resolution, in the strength of God's grace, wholly to abstain from them; and by fasting, and other instances of mortification, have subdued all desires toward them. These are they that *can receive* this saying; and yet these are not to bind themselves by a vow that they will never marry, only that, in the mind they are now in, they purpose not to marry.

Now, [1.] This affection to the single state must be given of God; for none can receive it, *save they to whom it is given.* Note, Continence is a special gift of God to some, and not to others; and when a man, in the single state, finds by experience that he has this gift, he may determine with himself, and (as the apostle speaks, 1 Cor. vii. 37), stand steadfast in his heart, having no necessity, but having power over his own will, that he will keep himself so. But men, in this case, must take heed lest they boast of a false gift, Prov. xxv. 14.

[2.] The single state must be chosen for the kingdom of heaven's sake; in those who resolve never to marry, only that they may save charges, or may gratify a morose selfish humour, or have a greater liberty to serve other lusts and pleasures, it is so far from being a virtue, that it is an ill-natured vice; but when it is for religion's sake, not as in itself a meritorious act (which the papists make it), but only as a means to keep our minds more entire for, and more intent upon, the services of religion, and that, having no families to provide for, we may do the more works of charity, then it is approved and accepted of God. Note That condition is best for us, and to be chosen and stuck to accordingly, which is best for our souls, and tends most to the preparing of us for, and the preserving of us to, the kingdom of heaven.

13 Then were there brought unto him little children, that he should put *his* hands on them, and pray: and the disciples rebuked them.
14 But Jesus said, Suffer little children, and forbid them not, to come unto me: for of such is the kingdom of heaven.
15 And he laid *his* hands on them, and departed thence.

We have here the welcome which Christ gave to some little children that were brought to him. Observe,

I. The faith of those that brought them. How many they were, that were brought, we are not told; but they were so little as to be taken up in arms, a year old, it may be, or two at most. The account here given of it, is, that *there were brought unto him little children, that he should put his hands on them, and pray, v.* 13. Probably they were their parents, guardians, or nurses, that brought them; and herein, 1. They testified their respect to Christ, and the value they had for his favour and blessing. Note, Those who glorify Christ by coming to him themselves, should further glorify him by bringing all they have, or have influence upon, to him likewise. Thus give him the honour of his unsearchable riches of grace, his overflowing, never-failing, fulness. We cannot better honour Christ than by making use of him. 2. They did a kindness to their children, not doubting but they would fare the better, in this world and the other, for the blessing and prayers of the Lord Jesus, whom they looked upon at least as an extraordinary person, as a prophet, if not as a priest and king; and the blessings of such were valued and desired. Others brought their children to Christ, to be healed when they were sick; but these children were under no present malady, only they desired a blessing for them. Note, It is a good thing when we come to Christ ourselves, and bring our children to him, before we are driven to him (as we say) by woe-need; not only to visit him when we are in trouble, but to address ourselves to him in a sense of our general dependence on him, and of the benefit we expect by him, this is pleasing to him.

They desired that he would put his hands on them, and pray. Imposition of hands was a ceremony used especially in paternal blessings; Jacob used it when he blessed and adopted the sons of Joseph, Gen. xlviii. 14. It intimates something of love and familiarity mixed with power and authority, and bespeaks an efficacy in the blessing. Whom Christ prays for in heaven, he *puts his hand upon* by his Spirit. Note, (1.) Little children may be brought to Christ as needing, and being capable of receiving, blessings from him, and having an interest in his intercession. (2.) Therefore they should be brought to him. We cannot do better for our children than to commit them to the Lord Jesus, to be wrought upon, and prayed for, by him. We can but beg a blessing for them, it is Christ only that can command the blessing.

II. The fault of the disciples in rebuking them. They discountenanced the address as vain and frivolous, and reproved them that made it as impertinent and troublesome. Either they thought it below their Master to take notice of little children, except any thing in particular ailed them; or, they thought he had toil enough with his other work, and would not have him diverted from it; or, they thought if such an address as this were encouraged, all the country would bring their children to him, and they should never see an end of it. Note, It is well for us, that Christ has more love and tenderness in him than the best of his disciples have. And let us learn of him not to discountenance any willing well-meaning souls in their enquiries after Christ, though they are but weak. If *he* do not break the bruised reed, *we* should not. Those that seek unto Christ, must not think it strange if they meet with opposition and rebuke, even from good men, who think they know the mind of Christ better than they do.

III. The favour of our Lord Jesus. See how he carried it here.

1. He rebuked the disciples (*v.* 14); *Suffer little children, and forbid them not;* and he rectifies the mistake they went upon, *Of such is the kingdom of heaven.* Note, (1.) The children of believing parents belong to the kingdom of heaven, and are members of the visible church. Of such, not only of such in *disposition and affection* (that might have served for a reason why doves or lambs should be brought to him), but of such, *in age,* is the kingdom of heaven; to them pertain the privileges of visible church-membership, as among the Jews of old. *The promise is to you, and to your children. I will be a God to thee and thy seed.* (2.) That for this reason they are welcome to Christ, who is ready to entertain those who, when they cannot come themselves, are brought to him. And this, [1.] In respect to the little children themselves, whom he has upon all occasions expressed a concern for; and who, having participated in the malignant influences of the first Adam's sin, must needs share in the riches of the second Adam's grace, else what would become of the apostle's parallel, 1 Cor. xv. 22; Rom. v. 14, 15, &c.? Those who are given to Christ, as part of his purchase, he will in no wise cast out. [2.] With an eye to the faith of the parents who brought them, and presented them as living sacrifices. Parents are trustees of their children's wills, are empowered by nature to transact for their benefit; and therefore Christ accepts their dedication of them as their act and deed, and will own these dedicated things in the day he makes up his jewels. [3.] Therefore he takes it ill of those who forbid them, and exclude those whom he has received: who cast them out from the inheritance of the Lord, and say, *Ye have no part in the Lord* (see Josh. xxii. 27); and who forbid water, that they should be baptized, who, if that promise be fulfilled (Isa. xliv. 3), *have received the Holy Ghost as well as we,* for aught we know.

2. *He received the little children,* and did as he was desired; *he laid his hands on them,* that is, *he blessed them.* The strongest believer lives not so much by apprehending Christ as by being apprehended of him (Phil. iii. 12), not so much by knowing God as by being known of him (Gal. iv. 9); and this the least child is capable of. If they cannot stretch out their hands to Christ, yet he can lay his hands on them, and so make them his own, and own them for his own.

Methinks it has something observable in it, that, when he had done this, he departed thence, *v.* 15. As if he reckoned he had done enough there, when he had thus asserted the rights of the lambs of his flock, and made this provision for a succession of subjects in his kingdom.

16 And, behold, one came and
said unto him, Good Master, what
good thing shall I do, that I may have
eternal life? 17 And he said unto
him, Why callest thou me good?
there is none good but one, *that is,*
God: but if thou wilt enter into life,
keep the commandments. 18 He
saith unto him, Which? Jesus said,
Thou shalt do no murder, Thou shalt
not commit adultery, Thou shalt not
steal, Thou shalt not bear false witness,
19 Honour thy father and *thy*
mother: and, Thou shalt love thy
neighbour as thyself. 20 The young
man saith unto him, All these things
have I kept from my youth up: what
lack I yet? 21 Jesus said unto him,
If thou wilt be perfect, go *and* sell
that thou hast, and give to the poor,
and thou shalt have treasure in heaven:
and come *and* follow me. 22
But when the young man heard that
saying, he went away sorrowful: for
he had great possessions.

Here is an account of what passed between Christ and a hopeful young gentleman that addressed himself to him upon a serious errand; he is said to be a *young man* (*v.* 20);

and I called him a *gentleman,* not only because he had great possessions, but because he was a ruler (Luke xviii. 18), a magistrate, a justice of peace in his country; it is probable that he had abilities beyond his years, else his youth would have debarred him from the magistracy.

Now concerning this young gentleman, we are told how fair he bid for heaven and came short.

I. How fair he bid for heaven, and how kindly and tenderly Christ treated him, in favour to good beginnings. Here is,

1. The gentleman's serious address to Jesus Christ (*v.* 16); *Good Master, what good thing shall I do, that I may have eternal life?* Not a better question could be asked, nor more gravely.

(1.) He gives Christ an honourable title, *Good Master*—Διδάσκαλε ἀγαθὲ. It signifies not a ruling, but a teaching Master. His calling him *Master,* bespeaks his submissiveness, and willingness to be taught;, and *good Master,* his affection and peculiar respect to the Teacher, like that of Nicodemus, *Thou art a Teacher come from God.* We read not of any that addressed themselves to Christ more respectfully than that Master in Israel and this ruler. It is a good thing when men's quality and dignity increase their civility and courtesy. It was gentleman-like to give this title of respect to Christ, notwithstanding the present meanness of his appearance. It was not usual among the Jews to accost their teachers with the title of *good;* and therefore this bespeaks the uncommon respect he had for Christ. Note, Jesus Christ is a good Master, the best of teachers; none teaches like him; he is distinguished for his goodness, for *he can have compassion on the ignorant; he is meek and lowly in heart.*

(2.) He comes to him upon an errand of importance (none could be more so), and he came not to tempt him, but sincerely desiring to be taught by him. His question is, *What good thing shall I do, that I may have eternal life?* By this it appears, [1.] That he had a firm belief of eternal life; he was no Sadducee. He was convinced that there is a happiness prepared for those in the other world, who are prepared for it in this world. [2.] That he was concerned to make it sure to himself that he should live eternally, and was desirous of that life more than of any of the delights of this life. It was a rare thing for one of his age and quality to appear so much in care about another world. The rich are apt to think it below them to make such an enquiry as this; and young people think it time enough yet; but here was a young man, and a rich man, solicitous about his soul and eternity. [3.] That he was sensible something must be done, some good thing, for the attainment of this happiness. It is *by patient continuance in well-doing* that *we seek for immortality,* Rom. ii. 7. We must be doing, and doing that which is good. The blood of Christ is the only purchase of eternal life (he merited it for us), but obedience to Christ is the appointed way to it, Heb. v. 9. [4.] That he was, or at least thought himself, willing to do what was to be done for the obtaining of this eternal life. Those that know what it is to have eternal life, and what it is to come short of it, will be glad to accept of it upon any terms. Such a holy violence does the kingdom of heaven suffer. Note, While there are many that say, *Who will show us any good?* our great enquiry should be, *What shall we do, that we may have eternal life?* What shall we do, to be for ever happy, happy in another world? For this world has not that in it that will make us happy.

2. The encouragement that Jesus Christ gave to this address. It is not his manner to send any away without an answer, that come to him on such an errand, for nothing pleases him more, *v.* 17. In his answer,

(1.) He tenderly assists his faith; for, doubtless, he did not mean it for a reproof, when he said, *Why callest thou me good?* But he would seem to find that faith in what he said, when he called him *good Master,* which the gentleman perhaps was not conscious to himself of; he intended no more than to own and honour him as a good man, but Christ would lead him to own and honour him as a good God; for *there is none good but one, that is God.* Note, As Christ is graciously ready to make the best that he can of what is said or done amiss; so he is ready to make the most that can be of what is well said and well done. His constructions are often better than our intentions; as in that, "*I was hungry, and you gave me meat,* though you little thought it was to me." Christ will have this young man either know him to be God, or not call him *good;* to teach us to transfer to God all the praise that is at any time given to us. Do any call us *good?* Let us tell them all goodness is from God, and therefore not to us, but to him give glory. All crowns must lie before his throne. Note, God only is good, and there is none essentially, originally, and unchangeably, good, but God only. His goodness is of and from himself, and all the goodness in the creature is from him; he is the Fountain of goodness, and whatever the streams are, *all the springs are in him,* Jam. i. 17. He is the great Pattern and Sample of goodness; by him all goodness is to be measured; that is good which is like him, and agreeable to his mind. We in our language call him *God,* because he is good. In this, as in other things, our Lord Jesus was *the Brightness of his glory* (and his goodness is his glory), and *the express image of his person,* and therefore fitly called *good Master.*

(2.) He plainly directs his practice, in answer to his question. He started that thought of his being good, and therefore God, but did not stay upon it, lest he should seem to divert from, and so to drop, the main question, as many do in needless disputes and strifes of words. Now Christ's answer is, in short, this, *If thou wilt enter into life, keep the commandments.*

[1.] The end proposed is, entering into life. The young man, in his question, spoke of eternal life. Christ, in his answer, speaks of *life;* to teach us, that eternal life is the only true life. The words concerning that are the words of *this life,* Acts v. 20. The present life scarcely deserves the name of life, for *in the midst of life we are in death.* Or into *life,* that spiritual life which is the beginning and earnest of eternal life. He desired to know how he might *have* eternal life ; Christ tells him how he might *enter into it:* we *have* it by the merit of Christ, a mystery which was not as yet fully revealed, and therefore Christ waives that; but the way of *entering into it,* is, by obedience, and Christ directs us in that. By the former we *make* our title, by this, as by our evidence, we *prove* it; it is *by adding to faith virtue,* that an *entrance* (the word here used) is *ministered to us into the everlasting kingdom,* 2 Pet. i. 5, 11. Christ, who is our Life, is the Way to the Father, and to the vision and fruition of him; he is the only Way, but duty, and the obedience of faith, are the way to Christ. There is an entrance into life hereafter, at death, at the great day, a complete entrance, and those only shall then enter into life, that do their duty; it is the diligent faithful servant that shall then *enter into the joy of his Lord,* and that joy will be his eternal life. There is an entrance into life now; *we who have believed, do enter into rest,* Heb. 4. 3. We have peace, and comfort, and joy, in the believing prospect of the glory to be revealed, and to this also sincere obedience is indispensably necessary.

[2.] The way prescribed is, keeping the commandments. Note, Keeping the commandments of God, according as they are revealed and made known to us, is the only way to life and salvation; and sincerity herein is accepted through Christ as our gospel perfection, provision being made of pardon, upon repentance, wherein we come short. Through Christ we are delivered from the condemning power of the law, but the commanding power of it is lodged in the hand of the Mediator, and under that, in that hand, we still are *under the law to Christ* (1 Cor. ix. 21), under it as a rule, though not as a covenant. *Keeping the commandments* includes *faith in Jesus Christ,* for that is the great commandment (1 John iii. 23), and it was one of the laws of Moses, that, when the great Prophet should be raised up, they should hear him. Observe, In order to our happiness here and for ever, it is not enough for us to *know* the commandments of God, but we must *keep* them, keep in them as our way, keep to them as our rule, keep them as our treasure, and with care, as the apple of our eye.

[3.] At his further instance and request, he mentions some particular commandments which he must keep (*v.* 18, 19); *The young man saith unto him, Which?* Note, Those that would do the commandments of God, must seek them diligently, and enquire after them, what they are. Ezra set himself to seek the law, and to *do it,* Ezra vii. 10. "There were many commandments in the law of Moses; good Master, let me know which those are, the keeping of which is necessary to salvation."

In answer to this, Christ specifies several, especially the commandments of the second table. *First,* That which concerns our own and our neighbour's life; *Thou shalt do no murder. Secondly,* Our own and our neighbour's chastity, which should be as dear to us as life itself; *Thou shalt not commit adultery. Thirdly,* Our own and our neighbour's wealth and outward estate, as hedged about by the law of property; *Thou shalt not steal. Fourthly,* That which concerns truth, and our own and our neighbour's good name; *Thou shalt not bear false witness,* neither *for thyself,* nor *against thy neighbour;* for so it is here left at large. *Fifthly,* That which concerns the duties of particular relations; *Honour thy father and mother. Sixthly,* That comprehensive law of love, which is the spring and summary of all these duties, whence they all flow, on which they are all founded, and in which they are all fulfilled; *Thou shalt love thy neighbour as thyself* (Gal. v. 14; Rom. xiii. 9), that *royal* law, Jas. ii. 8. Some think this comes in here, not as the sum of the second table, but as the particular import of the tenth commandment; *Thou shalt not covet,* which in Mark is, *Defraud not;* intimating that it is not lawful for me to design advantage or gain to myself by the diminution or loss of another; for that is to covet, and to love myself better than my neighbour, whom I ought to love as myself, and to treat as I would myself be treated.

Our Saviour here specifies second-table duties only; not as if the first were of less account, but, 1. Because they that now sat in Moses's seat, either wholly neglected, or greatly corrupted, these precepts in their preaching. While they pressed the tithing of *mint, anise, and cummin,—judgment, and mercy, and faith,* the summary of second-table duties, were overlooked, *ch.* xxiii. 23. Their preaching ran out all in rituals and nothing in morals; and therefore Christ pressed that most, which they least insisted on. As one truth, so one duty, must not jostle out another, but each must know its place, and be kept in it; but equity requires that that be helped up, which is most in danger of being thrust out. That is the present truth which we are called to bear our testimony to, not only which is opposed, but which is neglected. 2. Because he would teach him, and us all, that moral honesty is a necessary branch of true Christianity, and to be minded accordingly. Though a mere moral man comes short of being a complete Christian, yet an immoral man is certainly no true Christian; for the grace of God teaches us to live soberly and righteously, as well as godly. Nay, though first-table duties have in them more of the essence of religion, yet second-table duties have in them more of the evidence of it. Our light *burns* in love to God, but it *shines* in love to our neighbour.

II. See here how he came short, though he bid thus fair, and wherein he failed; he failed by two things.

1. By pride, and a vain conceit of his own merit and strength; this is the ruin of thousands, who keep themselves miserable by fancying themselves happy. When Christ told him what commandments he must keep, he answered very scornfully, *All these things have I kept from my youth up*, *v.* 20.

Now, (1.) According as he understood the law, as prohibiting only the outward acts of sin, I am apt to think that he said true, and Christ knew it, for he did not contradict him; nay, it is said in Mark, *He loved him;* so far was very good and pleasing to Christ. St. Paul reckons it a privilege, not contemptible in itself, though it was dross in comparison with Christ, that he was, *as touching the righteousness that is in the law, blameless*, Phil. iii. 6. His observance of these commands was universal; *All these have I kept:* it was early and constant; *from my youth up*. Note, A man may be free from gross sin, and yet come short of grace and glory. His hands may be clean from external pollutions, and yet he may perish eternally in his heart-wickedness. What shall we think then of those who do not attain to this; whose fraud and injustice, drunkenness and uncleanness, witness against them, that all these they have broken from their youth up, though they have named the name of Christ? Well, it is sad to come short of those that come short of heaven.

It was commendable also, that he desired to know further what his duty was; *What lack I yet?* He was convinced that he wanted something to fill up his works before God, and was therefore desirous to know it, because, if he was not mistaken in himself, he was willing to do it. Having not yet attained, he thus seemed to press forward. And he applied himself to Christ, whose doctrine was supposed to improve and perfect the Mosaic institution. He desired to know what were the peculiar precepts of his religion, that he might have all that was in them to polish and accomplish him. Who could bid fairer?

But, (2.) Even in this that he said, he discovered his ignorance and folly. [1.] Taking the law in its spiritual sense, as Christ expounded it, no doubt, in many things he had offended against all these commands. Had he been acquainted with the extent and spiritual meaning of the law, instead of saying, *All these have I kept; what lack I yet?* he would have said, with shame and sorrow, "All these have I broken, what shall I do to get my sins pardoned?" [2.] Take it how you will, what he said savoured of pride and vain-glory, and had in it too much of that boasting which is excluded by the law of faith (Rom. iii. 27), and which excludes from justification, Luke xviii. 11, 14. He valued himself too much, as the Pharisees did, upon the plausibleness of his profession before men, and was proud of that, which spoiled the acceptableness of it. That word, *What lack I yet?* perhaps was not so much a desire of further instruction as a demand of the praise of his present fancied perfection, and a challenge to Christ himself to show him any one instance wherein he was deficient.

2. He came short by an inordinate love of the world, and his enjoyments in it. This was the fatal rock on which he split. Observe,

(1.) How he was tried in this matter (*v.* 21); *Jesus said unto him, If thou wilt be perfect, go and sell that thou hast.* Christ waived the matter of his boasted obedience to the law, and let that drop, because this would be a more effectual way of discovering him than a dispute of the extent of the law. "Come," saith Christ, "if thou wilt be perfect, if thou wilt approve thyself sincere in thine obedience" (for sincerity is our gospel perfection), "if thou wilt come up to that which Christ has added to the law of Moses, if thou wilt be perfect, if thou wilt *enter into life*, and so be perfectly happy;" for that which Christ here prescribes, is not a thing of supererogation, or a perfection we may be saved without; but, in the main scope and intendment of it, it is our necessary and indispensable duty. What Christ said to him, he thus far said to us all, that, if we would approve ourselves Christians indeed, and would be found at last the heirs of eternal life, we must do these two things:

[1.] We must practically prefer the heavenly treasures before all the wealth and riches in this world. That glory must have the pre-eminence in our judgment and esteem before this glory. No thanks to us to prefer heaven before hell, the worst man in the world would be glad of that Jerusalem for a refuge when he can stay no longer here, and to have it in reserve; but to make it our choice, and to prefer it before this earth—that is to be a Christian indeed. Now, as an evidence of this, *First*, We must dispose of what we have in this world, for the honour of God, and in his service: "*Sell that thou hast, and give to the poor.* If the occasions of charity be very pressing, sell thy possessions that thou mayest have to give to them that need; as the first Christians did, with an eye to this precept, Acts iv. 34. Sell what thou canst spare for pious uses, all thy superfluities; if thou canst not otherwise do good with it, sell it. Sit loose to it, be willing to part with it for the honour of God, and the relief of the poor." A gracious contempt of the world, and compassion of the poor and afflicted ones in it, are in all a necessary condition of salvation; and in those that have wherewithal, giving of alms is as necessary an evidence of that contempt of the world, and compassion to our brethren; by this the trial will be at the great day, *ch.* xxv. 35. Though many that call themselves Christians, do not act as if they believed it; it is certain, that, when we embrace Christ, we must let go the world, for we cannot serve God and mammon. Christ knew that covetousness was the sin that did most easily beset this young man, that, though what he had he had got honestly, yet he could not cheerfully part with it, and by this he discovered his insincerity. This command was like the call to Abraham, *Get thee out of thy country, to a land that I will show thee.* As God tries believers by their strongest graces, so hypocrites by their strongest corruptions. *Secondly,* We must depend upon what we hope for in the other world as an abundant recompence for all we have left, or lost, or laid out, for God in this world; *Thou shalt have treasure in heaven.* We must, in the way of chargeable duty, trust God for a happiness out of sight, which will make us rich amends for all our expenses in God's service. The precept sounded hard and harsh; "Sell that thou hast, and give it away;" and the objection against it would soon arise, that "Charity begins at home;" therefore Christ immediately annexes this assurance of a treasure in heaven. Note, Christ's promises make his precepts easy, and his yoke not only tolerable, but pleasant, and sweet, and very comfortable; yet this promise was as much a trial of this young man's faith as the precept was of his charity, and contempt of the world.

[2.] We must devote ourselves entirely to the conduct and government of our Lord Jesus; *Come, and follow me.* It seems here to be meant of a close and constant attendance upon his person, such as the selling of what he had in the world was as necessary to as it was to the other disciples to quit their callings; but of us it is required that we follow Christ, that we duly attend upon his ordinances, strictly conform to his pattern, and cheerfully submit to his disposals, and by upright and universal obedience observe his statutes, and keep his laws, and all this from a principle of love to him, and dependence on him, and with a holy contempt of every thing else in comparison of him, and much more in competition with him. This is to *follow Christ fully.* To sell all, and give to the poor, will not serve, unless we come, and follow Christ. If I give all my goods to feed the poor, and have not love, it profits me nothing. Well, on these terms, and on no lower, is salvation to be had; and they are very easy and reasonable terms, and will appear so to those who are brought to be glad of it upon any terms.

(2.) See how he was discovered. This touched him in a tender part (*v.* 22); *When he heard that saying, he went away sorrowful, for he had great possessions.*

[1.] He was a rich man, and loved his riches, and therefore went away. He did not like eternal life upon these terms. Note, *First,* Those who have much in the world are in the greatest temptation to love it, and to set their hearts upon it. Such is the bewitching nature of worldly wealth, that those who want it least desire it most; when riches increase, then is the danger of setting the heart upon them, Ps. lxii. 10. If he had had but two mites in all the world, and had been commanded to give them to the poor, or but one handful of meal in the barrel, and a little oil in the cruse, and had been bidden to make a cake of that for a poor prophet, the trial, one would think, had been much greater, and yet those trials have been overcome (Luke xxi. 4, and 1 Kings xvii. 14); which shows that the love of the world draws stronger than the most pressing necessities. *Secondly,* The reigning love of this world keeps many from Christ, who seem to have some good desires toward him. A great estate, as to those who are got above it, is a great furtherance, so to those who are entangled in the love of it, it is a great hindrance, in the way to heaven.

Yet something of honesty there was in it, that, when he did not like the terms, he went away, and would not pretend to that, which he could not find in his heart to come up to the strictness of; better so than do as Demas did, who, *having known the way of righteousness,* afterward turned aside, out of love to this present world, to the greater scandal of his profession; since he could not be a complete Christian, he would not be a hypocrite.

[2.] Yet he was a thinking man, and well-inclined, and therefore *went away sorrowful.* He had a leaning toward Christ, and was loth to part with him. Note, Many a one is ruined by the sin he commits with reluctance; leaves Christ sorrowfully, and yet is never truly sorry for leaving him, for, if he were, he would return to him. Thus this man's wealth was *vexation of spirit* to him, then when it was his temptation. What then would the sorrow be afterward, when his possessions would be gone, and all hopes of eternal life gone too?

23 Then said Jesus unto his disciples, Verily I say unto you, That a
rich man shall hardly enter into the
kingdom of heaven. 24 And again
I say unto you, It is easier for a camel
to go through the eye of a needle,
than for a rich man to enter into the
kingdom of God. 25 When his disciples heard *it,* they were exceedingly
amazed, saying, Who then can be
saved? 26 But Jesus beheld *them,*

and said unto them, With men this
is impossible; but with God all things
are possible. 27 Then answered
Peter and said unto him, Behold,
we have forsaken all, and followed
thee; what shall we have therefore?
28 And Jesus said unto them, Verily
I say unto you, That ye which have
followed me, in the regeneration when
the Son of man shall sit in the throne
of his glory, ye also shall sit upon
twelve thrones, judging the twelve
tribes of Israel. 29 And every one
that hath forsaken houses, or brethren,
or sisters, or father, or mother, or
wife, or children, or lands, for my
name's sake, shall receive an hundred-
fold, and shall inherit everlasting life.
30 But many *that are* first shall be
last; and the last *shall be* first.

We have here Christ's discourse with his disciples upon occasion of the rich man's breaking with Christ.

I. Christ took occasion from thence to show the difficulty of the salvation of rich people, *v.* 23—26.

1. That it is a very hard thing for a rich man to get to heaven, such a rich man as this here. Note, From the harms and falls of others it is good for us to infer that which will be of caution to us.

Now, (1.) This is vehemently asserted by our Saviour, *v.* 23, 24. He said this to his disciples, who were poor, and had but little in the world, to reconcile them to their condition with this, that the less they had of worldly wealth, the less hindrance they had in the way to heaven. Note, It should be a satisfaction to them who are in a low condition, that they are not exposed to the temptations of a high and prosperous condition: if they live more hardy in this world than the rich, yet, if withal they get more easily to a better world, they have no reason to complain. This saying is ratified, *v.* 23. *Verily I say unto you.* He that has reason to know what the way to heaven is, for he has laid it open, he tells us that this is one of the greatest difficulties in that way. It is repeated, *v.* 24. *Again I say unto you.* Thus he speaks once, yea, twice that which man is loth to perceive and more loth to believe.

[1.] He saith that it is a hard thing for a rich man to be a good Christian, and to be saved; to enter into the kingdom of heaven, either here or hereafter. The way to heaven is to all a narrow way, and the gate that leads into it, a strait gate; but it is particularly so to rich people. More duties are expected from them than from others, which they can hardly do; and more sins do easily beset them, which they can hardly avoid. Rich people have great temptations to resist, and such as are very insinuating; it is hard not to be charmed with a smiling world; very hard, when we are filled with these hid treasures, not to take up with them for a portion. Rich people have a great account to make up for their estates, their interest, their time, and their opportunities of doing and getting good, above others. It must be a great measure of divine grace that will enable a man to break through these difficulties.

[2.] He saith that the conversion and salvation of a rich man is so extremely difficult, that *it is easier for a camel to go through the eye of a needle, v.* 24. This is a proverbial expression, denoting a difficulty altogether unconquerable by the art and power of man; nothing less than the almighty grace of God will enable a rich man to get over this difficulty. The difficulty of the salvation of apostates (Heb. vi. 4), and of old sinners (Jer. xiii. 23), is thus represented as an impossibility. The salvation of any is so very difficult (even *the righteous scarcely are saved*), that, where there is a peculiar difficulty, it is fitly set forth thus. It is very rare for a man to be rich, and not to set his heart upon his riches; and it is utterly impossible for a man that sets his heart upon his riches, to get to heaven; for *if any man love the world, the love of the Father is not in him,* 1 John ii. 15; James iv. 4. *First,* The way to heaven is very fitly compared to a *needle's eye,* which is hard to hit and hard to get through. *Secondly,* A rich man is fitly compared to a *camel,* a beast of burthen, for he has riches, as a camel has his load, he carries it, but it is another's, he has it from others, spends it for others, and must shortly leave it to others; it is a burthen, for *men load themselves with thick clay,* Hab. ii. 6. A camel is a large creature, but unwieldy.

(2.) This truth is very much wondered at, and scarcely credited by the disciples (*v.* 25); *They were exceedingly amazed, saying, Who then can be saved?* Many surprising truths Christ told them, which they were astonished at, and knew not what to make of; this was one, but their weakness was the cause of their wonder. It was not in contradiction to Christ, but for awakening to themselves, that they said, *Who then can be saved?* Note, Considering the many difficulties that are in the way of salvation, it is really strange that any are saved. When we think how good God is, it may seem a wonder that so *few* are his; but when we think how bad man is, it is more a wonder that so *many* are, and Christ will be eternally admired in them. *Who then can be saved?* Since so many are rich, and have great possessions, and so many more would be rich, and are well affected to great possessions; who can be saved? If riches are a hindrance to rich people, are not pride and luxury incident to those that are not rich, and as dangerous to them? and who then can get to heaven? This is a good reason why rich people should strive against the stream.

2. That, though it be hard, yet it is not impossible, for the rich to be saved (*v.* 26); *Jesus beheld them,* turned and looked wistfully upon his disciples, to shame them out of their fond conceit of the advantages rich people had in spiritual things. He beheld them as men that had got over this difficulty, and were in a fair way for heaven, and the more so because poor in this world; *and he said unto them, with men this is impossible, but with God all things are possible.* This is a great truth in general, that God is able to do that which quite exceeds all created power; that nothing is too hard for God, Gen. xviii. 14; Numb. xi. 23. When men are at a loss, God is not, for his power is infinite and irresistible; but this truth is here applied, (1.) To the salvation of any. *Who can be saved?* say the disciples. None, saith Christ, by any created power. *With men this is impossible:* the wisdom of man would soon be nonplussed in contriving, and the power of man baffled in effecting, the salvation of a soul. No creature can work the change that is necessary to the salvation of a soul, either in itself or in any one else. With men it is impossible that so strong a stream should be turned, so hard a heart softened, so stubborn a will bowed. It is a creation, it is a resurrection, and with men this is impossible; it can never be done by philosophy, medicine, or politics; but *with God all things are possible.* Note, The beginning, progress, and perfection, of the work of salvation, depend entirely upon the almighty power of God, to which all things are possible. Faith is wrought by that power (Eph. i. 19), and is kept by it, 1 Pet. i. 5. Job's experience of God's convincing, humbling grace, made him acknowledge more than any thing else, *I know that thou canst do every thing,* Job xlii. 2. (2.) To the salvation of rich people especially; it is impossible with men that such should be saved, but with God even this is possible; not that rich people should be saved *in* their worldliness, but that they should be saved *from* it. Note, The sanctification and salvation of such as are surrounded with the temptations of this world are not to be despaired of; it is possible; it may be brought about by the all-sufficiency of the divine grace; and when such are brought to heaven, they will be there everlasting monuments of the power of God. I am willing to think that in this word of Christ there is an intimation of mercy Christ had yet in store for this young gentleman, who was now gone away sorrowful; it was not impossible to God yet to recover him, and bring him to a better mind.

II. Peter took occasion from hence to enquire what *they* should get by it, who had come up to these terms, upon which this young man broke with Christ, and had left all to follow him, *v.* 27, *&c.* We have here the disciples' expectations from Christ, and his promises to them.

1. We have their expectations from Christ; Peter, in the name of the rest, signifies that they depended upon him for something considerable in lieu of what they had left for him; *Behold, we have forsaken all, and have followed thee; what shall we have therefore?* Christ had promised the young man, that, if he would sell all, and come and follow him, he should *have treasure in heaven;* now Peter desires to know,

(1.) Whether they had sufficiently come up to those terms: they had not sold all (for they had many of them wives and families to provide for), but they had *forsaken all;* they had not given it to the poor, but they had renounced it as far as it might be any way a hindrance to them in serving Christ. Note, When we hear what are the characters of those that shall be saved, it concerns us to enquire whether we, through grace, answer those characters. Now Peter hopes that, as to the main scope and intendment of the condition, they had come up to it, for God had wrought in them a holy contempt of the world and the things that are seen, in comparison with Christ and the things that are not seen; and how this must be evidenced, no certain rule can be given, but according as we are called.

Lord, saith Peter, *we have forsaken all.* Alas! it was but a poor *all* that they had forsaken; one of them had indeed quitted a place in the custom-house, but Peter and the most of them had only left a few boats and nets, and the appurtenances of a poor fishing-trade; and yet observe how Peter there speaks of it, as if it had been some mighty thing; *Behold, we have forsaken all.* Note, We are too apt to make the most of our services and sufferings, our expenses and losses, for Christ, and to think we have made him much our debtor. However, Christ does not upbraid them with this; though it was but little that they had forsaken, yet it was their *all,* like the widow's two mites, and was as dear to them as if it had been more, and therefore Christ took it kindly that they left it to follow him; for he accepts *according to what a man hath.*

(2.) Whether therefore they might expect *that treasure* which the young man shall have if he will sell all. "Lord," saith Peter, "shall *we* have it, who have left all?" All people are for what they can get; and Christ's followers are allowed to consult their own true interest, and to ask, *What shall we have?* Christ *looked at the joy set before him,* and Moses *at the recompence of reward.* For this end it is set before us, that *by a patient continuance in well-doing* we may seek for it. Christ encourages us to ask what we shall gain by leaving all to follow him; that we may see he doth not call us to our prejudice, but unspeakably to our advantage. As it is the language of an obediential faith to ask, "What shall we *do?*" with an eye to the precepts; so it is of a hoping, trusting faith, to ask, "What shall we *have?*" with an eye to the promises. But observe, The disciples had long since left all to engage themselves in the service of Christ, and yet never till now asked, *What shall we have?* Though there was no visible prospect of advantage by it, they were so well assured of his goodness, that they knew they should not lose by him at last, and therefore referred themselves to him, in what way he would make up their losses to them; minded their work, and asked not what should be their wages. Note, It honours Christ, to trust him and serve him, and not to bargain with him. Now that this young man was gone from Christ to his possessions, it was time for them to think which they should take to, what they should trust to. When we see what others keep by their hypocrisy and apostasy, it is proper for us to consider what we hope, through grace, to gain, not *for*, but *by*, our sincerity and constancy, and then we shall see more reason to pity them than to envy them.

2. We have here Christ's promises to them, and to all others that tread in the steps of their faith and obedience. What there was either of vain-glory or of vain hopes in that which Peter said, Christ overlooks, and is not extreme to mark it, but takes this occasion to give the bond of a *promise*,

(1.) To his immediate followers, *v.* 28. They had signalized their respect to him, as the first that followed him, and to them he promises not only *treasure*, but *honour*, in heaven; and here they have a grant or patent for it from him who is the fountain of honour in that kingdom; *Ye which have followed me in the regeneration shall sit upon twelve thrones.* Observe,

[1.] The *preamble* to the patent, or the *consideration* of the grant, which, as usual, is a recital of their services; "You have followed me in the regeneration, and therefore this will I do for you." The time of Christ's appearing in this world was a time of regeneration, of reformation (Heb. ix. 10), when old things began to pass away, and all things to look new. The disciples had followed Christ when the church was yet in the embryo state, when the gospel temple was but in the framing, when they had more of the work and service of apostles than of the dignity and power that belonged to their office. Now they followed Christ with constant fatigue, when few did; and therefore on them he will put particular marks of honour. Note, Christ hath special favour for those who begin early with him, who trust him further than they can see him, as they did who *followed him in the regeneration.* Observe, Peter spoke of their forsaking *all*, to follow him, Christ only speaks of their *following* him, which was the main matter.

[2.] The *date* of their honour, which fixes the time when it should commence; not immediately from the day of the date of *these presents*, no, they must continue a while in obscurity, as they were. But *when the Son of man shall sit in the throne of his glory;* and to this some refer that, *in the regeneration;* "You who now have followed me, shall, in the regeneration, be thus dignified." Christ's second coming will be a regeneration, when there shall be *new heavens, and a new earth, and the restitution of all things.* All that partake of the regeneration in grace (John iii. 3) shall partake of the regeneration in glory; for as grace is the first resurrection (Rev. xx. 6), so glory is the second regeneration.

Now their honour being adjourned till the Son of man's sitting in the throne of his glory, intimates, *First,* That they must stay for their advancement till then. Note, As long as our Master's glory is delayed, it is fit that ours should be so too, and that we should wait for it with an earnest expectation, as of a *hope not seen.* Rom. viii. 19. We must live, and work, and suffer, in faith, and hope, and patience, which therefore must be tried by these delays. *Secondly,* That they must share with Christ in his advancement; their honour must be a communion with him in his honour. They, having suffered with a suffering Jesus, must reign with a reigning Jesus, for both here and hereafter Christ will be *all in all;* we must *be where he is* (John xii. 26), must *appear with him* (Col. iii. 4); and this will be an abundant recompence not only for our loss, but for the delay; and when our Lord comes, we shall receive not only *our own*, but our own *with usury.* The longest voyages make the richest returns.

[3.] The honour itself hereby granted; *Ye also shall sit upon twelve thrones, judging the twelve tribes of Israel.* It is hard to determine the particular sense of this promise, and whether it was not to have many accomplishments, which I see no harm in admitting. *First,* When Christ is ascended to the right hand of the Father, and sits on the throne of his glory, then the apostles shall receive power by the Holy Ghost (Acts i. 8); shall be so much advanced above themselves as they are now, that they shall think themselves upon thrones, in promoting the gospel; they shall deliver it with authority, as a judge from the bench; they shall then have their commission enlarged, and shall publish the laws of Christ, by which the church, God's spiritual Israel (Gal. vi. 16), shall be governed, and *Israel according to the flesh,* that continues in infidelity, with all others that do likewise, shall be condemned. The honour and power given them, may be explained by Jer. i. 10, *See, I have set thee over the nations;* and Ezek. xx. 4, *Wilt thou judge them?* and Dna. vii. 18, *The saints shall take the kingdom;* and Rev.

xii. 1, where the doctrine of Christ is called *a crown of twelve stars. Secondly,* When Christ appears for the destruction of Jerusalem (*ch.* xxiv. 31), then shall he send the apostles to judge the Jewish nation, because in that destruction their predictions, according to the word of Christ, would be accomplished. *Thirdly,* Some think it has reference to the conversion of the Jews, which is yet to come, at the latter end of the world, after the fall of antichrist; so Dr. Whitby; and that "it respects the apostles' government of *the twelve tribes of Israel,* not by a resurrection of their persons, but by a reviviscence of that Spirit which resided in them, and of that purity and knowledge which they delivered to the world, and, chiefly, by admission of their gospel to be the standard of their faith, and the direction of their lives." *Fourthly,* It is certainly to have its full accomplishment at the second coming of Jesus Christ, when *the saints* in general *shall judge the world,* and the twelve apostles especially, as assessors with Christ, *in the judgment of the great day,* when all the world shall receive their final doom, and they shall ratify and applaud the sentence. But the *tribes* of Israel are named, partly because the number of the apostles was designedly the same with the number of the tribes; partly because the apostles were Jews, befriended them most, but were most spitefully persecuted by them; and it intimates that the saints will judge their acquaintance and kindred according to the flesh, and will, in the great day, judge those they had a kindness for; will judge their persecutors, who in this world judged them.

But the general intendment of this promise is, to show the glory and dignity reserved for the saints in heaven, which will be an abundant recompence for the disgrace they suffered here in Christ's cause. There are higher degrees of glory for those that have done and suffered most. The apostles in this world were hurried and tossed, there they shall sit down at rest and ease; here *bonds, and afflictions, and deaths, did abide them,* but there they *shall sit on thrones of glory;* here they were dragged to the bar, there they shall be advanced to the bench; here the twelve tribes of Israel trampled upon them, there they shall tremble before them. And will not this be recompence enough to make up all their losses and expenses for Christ? Luke xxii. 29.

[4.] The ratification of this grant; it is firm, it is inviolably immutably sure; for Christ hath said, "*Verily I say unto you, I the Amen, the faithful Witness,* who am empowered to make this grant, I have said it, and it cannot be disannulled."

(2.) Here is a promise to all others that should in like manner leave all to follow Christ. It was not peculiar to the apostles, to be thus preferred, but *this honour have all his saints.* Christ will take care they shall none of them lose by him (*v.* 29); *Every one that has forsaken* any thing for Christ, *shall receive.*

[1.] Losses for Christ are here supposed. Christ had told them that his disciples must deny themselves in all that is done to them in this world; now here he specifies particulars; for it is good to count upon the worst. If they have not forsaken all, as the apostles did, yet they have forsaken a great deal, houses suppose, and have turned themselves out, to wander in deserts; or dear relations, that would not go with them, to follow Christ; these are particularly mentioned, as hardest for a tender gracious spirit to part with; *brethren, or sisters, or father, or mother, or wife, or children;* and *lands* are added in the close, the profits of which were the support of the family.

Now, *First,* the loss of these things is supposed to be *for Christ's name's sake;* else he doth not oblige himself to make it up. Many forsake brethren, and wife, and children, in humour and passion, as *the bird that wanders from her nest;* that is a sinful desertion But if we forsake them *for Christ's sake,* because we cannot keep them and keep a good conscience, we must either quit them, or quit our interest in Christ; if we do not quit our concern for them, or our duty to them, but our comfort in them, and will do it rather than deny Christ, and this with an eye to him, and to his will and glory, this is that which shall be thus recompensed. It is not the suffering, but the cause, that makes both the martyr and the confessor.

Secondly, It is supposed to be a great loss; and yet Christ undertakes to make it up, for he is able to do it, be it ever so great. See the barbarity of the persecutors, that they stripped innocent people of all they had, for no other crime than their adherence to Christ! See the patience of the persecuted; and the strength of their love to Christ, which was such as all these waters could not quench!

[2.] A recompence of these losses is here secured. Thousands have dealt with Christ, and have trusted him far; but never any one lost by him, never any one but was an unspeakable gainer by him, when the account came to be balanced. Christ here gives his word for it, that he will not only indemnify his suffering servants, and save them harmless, but will abundantly reward them. Let them make a schedule of their losses for Christ, and they shall be sure to receive,

First, A hundred-fold in this life; sometimes in *kind,* in the things themselves which they have parted with. God will raise up for his suffering servants more friends, that will be so to them for Christ's sake, than they have left that were so for their own sakes. The apostles, wherever they came, met with those that were kind to them, and entertained them, and opened their hearts and doors to them. However, they *shall receive a hundred-fold,* in *kindness,* in those things that are abundantly better and more valuable. Their graces shall increase, their comforts abound, they shall have tokens of God's love, more free communion with him, more full communications from him, clearer foresights, and sweeter foretastes, of *the glory to be revealed;* and then they may truly say, they have received a hundred times more comfort in God and Christ than they could have had in *wife, or children.*

Secondly, Eternal life at last. The former is reward enough, if there were no more; cent. per cent. is great profit; what then is a hundred to one? But this comes in over and above, as it were, into the bargain. The *life* here promised includes in it all the comforts of life in the highest degree, and all *eternal.* Now if we could but mix faith with the promise, and trust Christ for the performance of it, surely we should think nothing too much to do, nothing too hard to suffer, nothing too dear to part with, for him.

Our Saviour, in the last verse, obviates a mistake of some, as if pre-eminence in glory went by precedence in time, rather than the measure and degree of grace. No; *Many that are first, shall be last, and the last, first, v.* 30. God will cross hands; will *reveal that to babes,* which he *hid from the wise and prudent;* will reject unbelieving Jews and receive believing Gentiles. The heavenly inheritance is not given as earthly inheritances commonly are, by seniority of age, and priority of birth, but according to God's pleasure. This is the text of another sermon, which we shall meet with in the next chapter,

CHAP. XX.

We have four things in this chapter; I. The parable of the labourers in the vineyard, ver. 1—16. II. A prediction of Christ's approaching sufferings, ver. 17—19. III. The petition of two of the disciples, by their mother, reproved, ver. 20—28. IV. The petition of the two blind men granted, and their eyes opened, ver. 29—34.

FOR the kingdom of heaven is like
unto a man *that is* an householder, which went out early in the
morning to hire labourers into his
vineyard. 2 And when he had agreed
with the labourers for a penny a day,
he sent them into his vineyard. 3
And he went out about the third hour,
and saw others standing idle in the
marketplace. 4 And said unto them;
Go ye also into the vineyard, and
whatsoever is right I will give you.
And they went their way. 5 Again
he went out about the sixth and ninth
hour, and did likewise. 6 And about
the eleventh hour he went out, and
found others standing idle, and saith
unto them, Why stand ye here all the
day idle? 7 They say unto him,
Because no man hath hired us. He
saith unto them, Go ye also into the
vineyard; and whatsoever is right,
that shall ye receive. 8 So when
even was come, the lord of the vineyard saith unto his steward, Call the
labourers, and give them *their* hire,
beginning from the last unto the first.
9 And when they came that *were
hired* about the eleventh hour, they
received every man a penny. 10 But
when the first came, they supposed
that they should have received more;
and they likewise received every man
a penny. 11 And when they had
received *it,* they murmured against
the goodman of the house. 12 Saying, These last have wrought *but* one
hour, and thou hast made them equal
unto us, which have borne the burden
and heat of the day. 13 But he answered one of them, and said, Friend,
I do thee no wrong: didst not thou
agree with me for a penny? 14 Take
that thine *is,* and go thy way: I will
give unto this last, even as unto thee.
15 Is it not lawful for me to do what
I will with mine own? Is thine eye
evil, because I am good? 16 So the
last shall be first, and the first last:
for many be called, but few chosen.

This parable of the labourers in the vineyard is intended,

I. To represent to us *the kingdom of heaven* (*v* 1), that is, the way and method of the gospel dispensation. The laws of that kingdom are not wrapt up in parables, but plainly set down, as in the sermon upon the mount; but the mysteries of that kingdom are delivered in parables, in sacraments, as here and *ch.* xiii. The duties of Christianity are more necessary to be known than the notions of it; and yet the notions of it are more necessary to be illustrated than the duties of it; which is that which parables are designed for.

II. In particular, to represent to us that concerning the kingdom of heaven, which he had said in the close of the foregoing chapter, that *many that are first shall be last, and the last, first;* with which this parable is connected; that truth, having in it a seeming contradiction, needed further explication.

Nothing was more a mystery in the gospel dispensation than the rejection of the Jews and the calling in of the Gentiles; so the apostle speaks of it (Eph. iii. 3—6); that the Gentiles should be fellow-heirs: nor was any thing more provoking to the Jews than the intimation of it. Now this seems to be the principal scope of this parable, to show that the Jews should be first called into the vineyard, and many of them should come at the call; but, at length, the gospel should be preached to the Gentiles, and they should receive it, and be admitted to equal privileges and advantages with the Jews; should be *fellow-citizens with the saints,* which the Jews, even those of them that believed, would be very much disgusted at, but without reason.

But the parable may be applied more generally, and shows us, 1. That God is debtor to no man; a great truth, which the contents in our Bible give as the scope of this parable. 2. That many who begin last, and promise little in religion, sometimes, by the blessing of God, arrive at greater attainments in knowledge, grace, and usefulness, than others whose entrance was more early, and who promised fairer. Though Cushi gets the start of Ahimaaz, yet Ahimaaz, choosing *the way of the plain,* outruns Cushi. John is swifter of foot, and comes *first to the sepulchre:* but Peter has more courage, and goes *first into it.* Thus *many that are last, shall be first.* Some make it a caution to the disciples, who had boasted of their timely and zealous embracing of Christ; they had left all, to follow him; but let them look to it, that they keep up their zeal; let them press forward and persevere; else their good beginnings will avail them little; they that seemed to be *first,* would be *last.* Sometimes those that are converted later in their lives, outstrip those that are converted earlier. Paul was *as one born out of due time, yet came not behind the chiefest of the apostles,* and outdid those that were in Christ before him. Something of affinity there is between this parable and that of the prodigal son, where he that returned from his wandering, was as dear to his father as he was, that never went astray; *first and last alike.* 3. That *the recompence of reward* will be given to the saints, not according to the time of their conversion, but according to the preparations for it by grace in this world; not according to the seniority (as Gen. xliii. 33), but *according to the measure of the stature of the fulness of Christ.* Christ had promised the apostles, who followed him *in the regeneration,* at the beginning of the gospel dispensation, great glory (*ch.* xix. 38); but he now tells them that those who are in like manner faithful to him, even in the latter end of the world, shall have the same reward, shall *sit with Christ on his throne,* as well as the apostles, Rev. ii. 26—iii. 21. Sufferers for Christ in the latter days, shall have the same reward with the martyrs and confessors of the primitive times, though they are more celebrated; and faithful ministers now, the same with the first fathers.

We have two things in the parable; the *agreement* with the labourers, and the *account* with them.

(1.) Here is the agreement made with the labourers (*v.* 1—7); and here it will be asked, as usual,

[1.] Who hires them? *A man that is a householder.* God is the great Householder, *whose we are, and whom we serve;* as a householder, he has work that he will have to be done, and servants that he will have to be doing; he has a great family in heaven and earth, which is named from Jesus Christ (Eph. iii. 15), which he is Owner and Ruler of. God hires labourers, not because he needs them or their services (for, *if we be righteous, what do we unto him?),* but as some charitable generous householders keep poor men to work, in kindness to them, to save them from idleness and poverty, and pay them for working for themselves.

[2.] Whence they are hired? Out of *the market-place,* where, till they are hired into God's service, they *stand idle* (*v.* 3), *all the day idle* (*v.* 6). Note, *First,* The soul of man stands ready to be hired into some service or other; it was (as all the creatures were) created to work, and is either a *servant to iniquity,* or a *servant to righteousness,* Rom. vi. 19. The devil, by his temptations, is *hiring labourers* into his field, to *feed swine* God, by his gospel, is *hiring labourers into his vineyard, to dress it, and keep it,* paradise-work. We are put to our choice; for hired we must be (Josh. xxiv. 15); *Choose ye this day whom ye will serve. Secondly,* Till we are hired into the service of God, we are standing all the day idle; a sinful state, though a state of drudgery to Satan, may really be called *a state of idleness;* sinners are doing nothing, nothing to the purpose, nothing of the great work they were sent into the world about, nothing that will pass well in the account. *Thirdly,* The gospel call is given to those that *stand idle in the market-place.* The market-place is *a place of concourse,* and there *Wisdom cries* (Prov. i. 20, 21); it is a place of sport, there the *children are playing* (*ch.* xi. 16); and the gospel calls us from vanity to seriousness; it is a place of business, of noise and hurry; and from that we are called to retire. "Come, come from this market-place."

[3.] What are they hired to do? To labour in his vineyard. Note, *First,* The church is God's vineyard; it is of his planting, watering, and fencing; and the fruits of it must be to his honour and praise. *Secondly,* We are all called upon to be labourers in this vineyard. The work of religion is vineyard-work, pruning, dressing, digging, watering, fencing, weeding. We have each of us our own vineyard to keep, our own soul; and it is God's, and to be kept and dressed for him. In this work we must not be slothful, not loiterers, but *labourers,* working, and *working out our own salvation.* Work for God will not admit of trifling. A man may go idle to hell; but he that will go to heaven, must be busy.

[4.] What shall be their wages? He promises, *First, A penny, v.* 2. The Roman penny was, in our money, of the value of sevenpence-halfpenny, a day's wages for a day's work, and the wages sufficient for a day's maintenance. This doth not prove that the reward of our obedience to God is *of works*, or *of debt* (no, it is *of grace, free grace*, Rom. iv. 4), or that there is any proportion between our services and heaven's glories; no, when we have done all, *we are unprofitable servants;* but it is to signify that there is a reward set before us, and a sufficient one. *Secondly, Whatsoever is right*, *v.* 4—7. Note, God will be sure not to be behind-hand with any for the service they do him: never any lost by working for God. The crown set before us is *a crown of righteousness, which the righteous Judge shall give.*

[5.] For what term are they hired? For *a day*. It is but a day's work that is here done. The time of life is the day, in which *we must work the works of him that sent us* into the world. It is a short time; the reward is for eternity, the work is but for *a day;* man is said *to accomplish, as a hireling, his day*, Job xiv. 6. This should quicken us to expedition and diligence in our work, that we have but a little time to work in, and *the night* is hastening on, *when no man can work;* and if our great work be undone when our day is done, we are undone for ever. It should also encourage us in reference to the hardships and difficulties of our work, that it is but for *a day;* the approaching *shadow, which the servant earnestly desireth*, will bring with it both rest, and *the reward of our work*, Job vii. 2. Hold out, faith, and patience, yet a little while.

[6.] Notice is taken of the several hours of the day, at which the labourers were hired. The apostles were sent forth at *the first and third hour* of the gospel day; they had a first and a second mission, while Christ was on earth, and their business was to call in the Jews; after Christ's ascension, about *the sixth and ninth hour*, they went out again on the same errand, *preaching the gospel to the Jews only, to them in Judea first*, and afterward to them of the dispersion; but, at length, as it were *about the eleventh hour*, they called the Gentiles to the same work and privilege with the Jews, and told them that in Christ Jesus there should be *no difference* made *between Jew and Greek.*

But this may be, and commonly is, applied to the several ages of life, in which souls are converted to Christ. The common call is promiscuous, to come and work in the vineyard; but the effectual call is particular, and it is *then* effectual when we come at the call.

First, Some are effectually called, and begin to work in the vineyard when they are very young; are sent in early in the morning, whose tender years are seasoned with grace, and the remembrance of their Creator. John the Baptist was *sanctified from the womb*, and therefore *great* (Luke i. 15); Timothy *from a child* (2 Tim. iii. 15); Obadiah *feared the Lord from his youth.* Those that have such a journey to go, had need set out betimes, the sooner the better.

Secondly, Others are savingly wrought upon in middle age; *Go work in the vineyard, at the third, sixth, or ninth hour.* The power of divine grace is magnified in the conversion of some, when they are in the midst of their pleasures and worldly pursuits, as Paul. God has work for all ages; no time amiss to turn to God; none can say, "It is all in good time;" for, whatever hour of the day it is with us, the time past of our life may suffice that we have served sin; *Go ye also into the vineyard.* God turns away none that are willing to be hired, for *yet there is room.*

Thirdly, Others are hired into the vineyard in old age, at *the eleventh hour*, when *the day of life is far spent*, and there is but *one hour* of the twelve remaining. None are hired at the twelfth hour; when life is done, opportunity is done; but "while there is life, there is hope." 1. There is hope *for* old sinners; for if, in sincerity, they turn to God, they shall doubtless be accepted; true repentance is never too late. And, 2. There is hope *of* old sinners, that they may be brought to true repentance; nothing is too hard for Almighty grace to do, it *can change the Ethiopian's skin, and the leopard's spots;* can set those to work, who have contracted a habit of idleness. Nicodemus may *be born again when he is old*, and *the old man may be put off, which is corrupt.*

Yet let none, upon this presumption, put off their repentance till they are old. These were *sent into the vineyard*, it is true, *at the eleventh hour;* but nobody had hired them, or offered to hire them, before. The Gentiles came in *at the eleventh hour*, but it was because the gospel had not been before preached to them. Those that have had gospel offers made them *at the third, or sixth hour*, and have resisted and refused them, will not have that to say for themselves at the eleventh hour, that these had; *No man has hired us;* nor can they be sure that any man will hire them at the ninth or eleventh hour; and therefore not to discourage any, but to awaken all, be it remembered, that *now is the accepted time; if we will hear his voice*, it must be *to-day.*

(2.) Here is the account with the labourers. Observe,

[1.] When the account was taken; *when the evening was come*, then, as usual, the day-labourers were called and paid. Note, Evening time is the reckoning time; the particular account must be given up in the evening of our life; for after death cometh the judgment. Faithful labourers shall receive their reward when they die; it is deferred till then, that they may wait with patience for it, but no longer; for God will observe his own rule, *The hire of the labourers shall not abide with thee all night, until the morning.* See Deut. xxiv. 15. When Paul, that faithful labourer, departs, he is with Christ presently.

The payment shall not be wholly deferred till *the morning of the resurrection;* but then, in the evening of the world, will be the general account, when *every one shall receive according to the things done in the body.* When time ends, and with it the world of work and opportunity, then the state of retribution commences; then call the labourers, and give them their hire. Ministers call them into the vineyard, to do their work; death calls them out of the vineyard, to receive their penny: and those to whom the call into the vineyard is effectual, the call out of it will be joyful. Observe, They did not come for their pay till they were called; we must with patience wait God's time for our rest and recompence; go by our master's clock. *The last trumpet, at the great day, shall call the labourers,* 1 Thess. iv. 16. *Then shalt thou call,* saith the good and faithful servant, *and I will answer.* In calling the labourers, they must begin from the last, and so to the first. Let not those that come in at the eleventh hour, be put behind the rest, but, lest they should be discouraged, call them first. *At the great day,* though *the dead in Christ shall rise first,* yet *they which are alive and remain, on whom the ends of the world* (the eleventh hour of its day) *comes, shall be caught up together with them in the clouds;* no preference shall be given to seniority, but every man *shall stand in his own lot at the end of the days.*

[2.] What the account was; and in that observe,

First, The general pay (*v.* 9, 10); *They received every man a penny.* Note, *All that by patient continuance in well-doing, seek for glory, honour, and immortality,* shall undoubtedly *obtain eternal life* (Rom. ii. 7), not as *wages* for the value of their work, but as the *gift* of God. Though there be degrees of glory in heaven, yet it will be to all a complete happiness. They that come from the east and west, and so come in late, that are picked up out of *the highways and the hedges, shall sit down with Abraham, Isaac, and Jacob,* at the same feast, *ch.* vii. 11. In heaven, every vessel will be full, brimful, though every vessel is not alike large and capacious. In the distribution of future joys, as it was in the gathering of the manna, he that shall gather much, will have nothing over, and he that shall gather little, will have no lack, Exod. xvi. 18. Those whom Christ fed miraculously, though of different sizes, *men, women, and children, did all eat, and were filled.*

The giving of a whole day's wages to those that had not done the tenth part of a day's work, is designed to show that God distributes his rewards by *grace* and *sovereignty,* and not of *debt.* The best of the labourers, and those that begin soonest, having so many empty spaces in their time, and their works not being filled up before God, may truly be said to labour in the vineyard scarcely one hour of their twelve; but because *we are under grace,* and *not under the law,* even such defective services, done in sincerity, shall not only be accepted, but by free grace richly rewarded. Compare Luke xvii. 7, 8, with Luke xii. 37.

Secondly, The particular pleading with those that were offended with this distribution in gavel-kind. The circumstances of this serve to adorn the parable; but the general scope is plain, that *the last shall be first.* We have here,

1. The offence taken (*v.* 11, 12); *They murmured at the good man of the house;* not that there is, or can be, any discontent or murmuring in heaven, for that is both guilt and grief, and in heaven there is neither; but there may be, and often are, discontent and murmuring concerning heaven and heavenly things, while they are in prospect and promise in this world. This signifies the jealousy which the Jews were provoked to by the admission of the Gentiles into the kingdom of heaven. As the elder brother, in the parable of the prodigal, repined at the reception of his younger brother, and complained of his father's generosity to him; so these labourers quarrelled with their master, and found fault, not because they had not enough, so much as because others were made *equal* with them. They boast, as the prodigal's elder brother did, of their good services; *We have borne the burthen and heat of the day;* that was the most they could make of it. Sinners are said to *labour in the very fire* (Hab. ii. 13), whereas God's servants, at the worst, do but labour in the sun; not in the heat of the iron furnace, but only in the heat of the day. Now *these last have worked but one hour,* and that too in the cool of the day; and yet *thou hast made them equal with us.* The Gentiles, who are newly called in, have as much of the privileges of the kingdom of the Messiah as the Jews have, who have so long been labouring in the vineyard of the Old-Testament church, under the yoke of the ceremonial law, in expectation of that kingdom. Note, There is a great proneness in us to think that we have too little, and others too much, of the tokens of God's favour; and that we do too much, and others too little, in the work of God. Very apt we all are to undervalue the deserts of others, and to overvalue our own. Perhaps, Christ here gives an intimation to Peter, not to boast too much, as he seemed to do, of his having *left all to follow Christ;* as if, because he and the rest of them had borne the burthen and heat of the day thus, they must have a heaven by themselves. It is hard for those that do or suffer more than ordinary for God, not to be elevated too much with the thought of it, and to expect to merit by it. Blessed Paul guarded against this, when, though *the chief of the apostles,* he owned himself to be *nothing,* to be *less than the least of all saints.*

2. The offence removed. Three things the master of the house urges, in answer to this ill-natured surmise.

(1.) That the complainant had no reason at all to say he had any wrong done to him, *v.* 13, 14. Here he asserts his own justice; *Friend, I do thee no wrong.* He calls him *friend*; for in reasoning with others we should use soft words and hard arguments; if our inferiors are peevish and provoking, yet we should not thereby be put into a passion, but speak calmly to them. [1.] It is incontestably true, that God can do no wrong. This is the prerogative of the King of kings. *Is there unrighteousness with God?* The apostle startles at the thought of it; *God forbid!* Rom. iii. 5, 6. His word should silence all our murmurings, that, whatever God does to us, or withholds from us, he does us no wrong. [2.] If God gives that grace to others, which he denies to us, it is kindness to them, but no injustice to us; and bounty to another, while it is no injustice to us, we ought not to find fault with. Because it is free grace, that is given to those that have it, boasting is for ever excluded; and because it is free grace, that is withheld from those that have it not, murmuring is for ever excluded. Thus *shall every mouth be stopped, and all flesh be silent before God.*

To convince the murmurer that he did no wrong, he refers him to the bargain: "*Didst not thou agree with me for a penny?* And if thou hast what thou didst agree for, thou hast no reason to cry out of wrong; thou shalt have what we agreed for." Though God is a debtor to none, yet he is graciously pleased to make himself a debtor by his own promise, for the benefit of which, through Christ, believers agree with him, and he will stand to his part of the agreement. Note, It is good for us often to consider what it was that we agreed with God for. *First,* Carnal worldlings agree with God for their penny in this world; they choose *their portion in this life* (Ps. xvii. 14); in these things they are willing to *have their reward* (*ch.* vi. 2, 5), *their consolation* (Luke vi. 24), *their good things* (Luke xvi. 25); and with these they shall be put off, shall be cut off from spiritual and eternal blessings; and herein God does them no wrong; they have what they chose, the penny they agreed for; *so shall their doom be, themselves have decided it;* it is conclusive against them. *Secondly,* Obedient believers agree with God for their penny in the other world, and they must remember that they have so agreed. Didst not thou agree to take God's word for it? Thou didst; and wilt thou go and agree with the world? Didst not thou agree to take up with heaven as thy portion, thy all, and to take up with nothing short of it? And wilt thou seek for a happiness in the creature, or think from thence to make up the deficiencies of thy happiness in God?

He therefore, 1. Ties him to his bargain (*v.* 14); *Take that thine is, and go thy way.* If we understand it of that which is ours by debt or absolute propriety, it would be a dreadful word; we are all undone, if we be put off with that only which we can call our *own.* The highest creature must go away into nothing, if he must go away with that only which is his own: but if we understand it of that which is ours by *gift,* the free gift of God, it teaches us *to be content with such things as we have.* Instead of repining that we have no more, let us take what we have, and be thankful. If God be better in any respect to others than to us, yet we have no reason to complain while he is so much better to us than we deserve, in giving us our penny, though we are unprofitable servants. 2. He tells him that those he envied should fare as well as he did; "*I will give unto this last, even as unto thee;* I am resolved I will." Note, The unchangeableness of God's purposes in dispensing his gifts should silence our murmurings. If he will do it, it is not for us to gainsay; for *he is in one mind, and who can turn him? Neither giveth he an account of any of his matters;* nor is it fit he should.

(2.) He had no reason to quarrel with the master; for what he gave was absolutely his own, *v.* 15. As before he asserted his justice, so here his sovereignty; *Is it not lawful for me to do what I will with my own?* Note, [1.] God is the Owner of all good; his propriety in it is absolute, sovereign, and unlimited. [2.] He may therefore give or withhold his blessings, as he pleases. What we have, is not our *own,* and therefore *it is not lawful for us to do what we will with* it; but what God has, is his own; and this will justify him, *First,* In all the disposals of his providence; when God takes from us that which was dear to us, and which we could ill spare, we must silence our discontents with this; *May he not do what he will with his own? Abstulit, sed et dedit—He hath taken away; but he originally gave.* It is not for such depending creatures as we are to quarrel with our Sovereign. *Secondly,* In all the dispensations of his grace, God gives or withholds the means of grace, and the Spirit of grace, as he pleases. Not but that there is a counsel in every will of God, and what seems to us to be done arbitrarily, will appear at length to have been done wisely, and for holy ends. But this is enough to silence all murmurers and objectors, that God is sovereign Lord of all, and *may do what he will with his own.* We are in his hand, as clay in the hands of a potter; and it is not for us to prescribe to him, or strive with him.

(3.) He had no reason to envy his fellow servant, or to grudge at him; or to be angry that he came into the vineyard no sooner; for he was not sooner called; he had no reason to be angry that the master had given him wages for the whole day, when he had idled away the greatest part of it; for, *Is thine eye evil, because I am good?* See here, [1.] The nature of envy; It is an evil eye. The eye is often both the inlet and the outlet of this sin. *Saul saw that David prospered, and he eyed him,* 1 Sam. xviii. 9, 15. It is an evil eye, which is displeased at the good of others, and desires their hurt. What can have more evil in it? It is grief to ourselves, anger to God, and ill-will to our neighbours; and it is a sin that has neither pleasure, profit, nor honour, in it; *it is an evil, an only evil.*

[2.] The aggravation of it; "It is because I am good." Envy is unlikeness to God, who is good, and doeth good, and delighteth in doing good; nay, it is an opposition and contradiction to God; it is a dislike of his proceedings, and a displeasure at what he does, and is pleased with. It is a direct violation of both the two great commandments at once; both that of love to God, in whose will we should acquiesce, and love to our neighbour, in whose welfare we should rejoice. Thus man's badness takes occasion from God's goodness to be more exceedingly sinful.

Lastly, Here is the application of the parable (*v.* 16), in that observation which occasioned it (*ch.* xix. 30); *So the first shall be last, and the last first.* There were many that followed Christ now in the regeneration, when the gospel kingdom was first set up, and these Jewish converts seemed to have got the start of others; but Christ, to obviate and silence their boasting, here tells them,

1. That they might possibly be outstripped by their successors in profession, and, though they were before others in profession, might be found inferior to them in knowledge, grace, and holiness. The Gentile church, which was as yet unborn, the Gentile world, which as yet stood *idle in the market-place,* would produce greater numbers of eminent, useful Christians, than were found among the Jews. More and more excellent shall be *the children of the desolate than those of the married wife,* Isa. liv. 1. Who knows but that the church, in its old age, may be more fat and flourishing than ever, to show that the Lord is upright? Though primitive Christianity had more of the purity and power of that holy religion than is to be found in the degenerate age wherein we live, yet what *labourers* may be *sent into the vineyard in the eleventh hour of the* church's *day,* in the Philadelphian period, and what plentiful effusions of the Spirit may then be, above what has been yet, who can tell?

2. That they had reason to fear, lest they themselves should be found hypocrites at last; for *many are called but few chosen.* This is applied to the Jews (*ch.* xxii. 14); it was so then, it is too true still; many are called with a common call, that are not chosen with a saving choice. All that are chosen from eternity, are effectually called, *in the fulness of time* (Rom. viii. 30), so that in making our effectual calling sure we *make sure our election* (2 Pet. i. 10); but it is not so as to the outward call; *many are called,* and yet refuse (Prov. i. 24), nay, as they are called *to* God, so they go *from* him (Hos. xi. 2, 7), by which it appears that they were not chosen, for *the election will obtain,* Rom. xi. 7. Note, There are but few *chosen* Christians, in comparison with the many that are only *called* Christians; it therefore highly concerns us to build our hope for heaven upon the rock of an eternal choice, and not upon the sand of an external call; and we should fear lest we be found but seeming Christians, and so should really come short; nay, lest we be found blemished Christians, and so should *seem to come short,* Heb. iv. 1.

17 And Jesus going up to Jerusalem took the twelve disciples apart
in the way, and said unto them, 18
Behold, we go up to Jerusalem; and
the Son of man shall be betrayed unto
the chief priests and unto the scribes,
and they shall condemn him to death,
19 And shall deliver him to the Gentiles to mock, and to scourge, and to
crucify *him:* and the third day he
shall rise again.

This is the third time that Christ gave his disciples notice of his approaching sufferings; he was now going up to Jerusalem to celebrate the passover, and to offer up himself the great Passover; both must be done at Jerusalem: there *the passover must be kept* (Deut. xii. 5), and there a prophet must perish, because there the great Sanhedrim sat, who were judges in that case, Luke xiii. 33. Observe,

I. The privacy of this prediction; *He took the twelve disciples apart in the way.* This was one of those things which were told to them in *darkness,* but which they were afterward to *speak in the light, ch.* x. 27. His secret was with them, as his friends, and this particularly. It was a hard saying, and, if any could bear it, they could. They would be more immediately exposed to peril with him, and therefore it was requisite that they should know of it, that, being fore-warned, they might be fore-armed. It was not fit to be spoken publicly as yet, 1. Because many that were cool toward him, would hereby have been driven to turn their backs upon him; the scandal of the cross would have frightened them from following him any longer. 2. Because many that were hot for him, would hereby be driven to take up arms in his defence, and it might have occasioned *an uproar among the people* (*ch.* xxvi. 5), which would have been laid to his charge, if he had told them of it publicly before: and, besides that such methods are utterly disagreeable to the genius of his kingdom, which is not of this world, he never countenanced any thing which had a tendency to prevent his sufferings. This discourse was not in the synagogue, or in the house, but *in the way,* as they travelled along; which teaches us, in our walks or travels with our friends, to keep up such discourse as *is good, and to the use of edifying.* See Deut. xvi. 7.

II. The prediction itself, *v.* 18, 19. Observe,

1. It is but a repetition of what he had once and again said before, *ch.* xvi. 21; xvii. 22, 23. This intimates that he not only saw clearly what troubles lay before him, but that his heart was upon his suffering-work; it filled him, not with fear, then he would have studied to avoid it, and could have done it, but with desire and expectation; he spoke thus frequently of his sufferings, because through them he was to enter into his glory. Note, It is good for us to be often thinking and speaking of our death, and of the sufferings which, it is likely, we may meet with betwixt this and the grave; and thus, by making them more familiar, they would become less formidable. This is one way of dying daily, and of taking up our cross daily, to be daily speaking of the cross, and of dying; which would come neither the sooner nor the surer, but much the better, for our thoughts and discourses of them.

2. He is more particular here in foretelling his sufferings than any time before. He had said (*ch.* xvi. 21), that he *should suffer many things, and be killed;* and (*ch.* xvii. 22), that he should *be betrayed into the hands of men, and they should kill him;* but here he adds, that he shall be *condemned, and delivered to the Gentiles,* that *they shall mock him, and scourge him, and crucify him.* These are frightful things, and the certain foresight of them was enough to damp an ordinary resolution, yet (as was foretold concerning him, Isa. xlii. 4) *he did not fail, nor was discouraged;* but the more clearly he foresaw his sufferings, the more cheerfully he went forth to meet them. He foretels by whom he should suffer, by *the chief priests and the scribes;* so he had said before, but here he adds, *They shall deliver him to the Gentiles,* that he might be the better understood; for the chief priests and scribes had no power to put him to death, nor was crucifying a manner of death in use among the Jews. Christ suffered from the malice both of Jews and Gentiles, because he was to suffer for the salvation both of Jews and Gentiles; both had a hand in his death, because he was to reconcile both by his cross, Eph. ii. 16.

3. Here, as before, he annexes the mention of his resurrection and his glory to that of his death and sufferings; *The third day he shall rise again.* He still brings this in, (1.) To encourage himself in his sufferings, and to carry him cheerfully through them. *He endured the cross for the joy set before him;* he foresaw he should rise again, and rise quickly, the third day. He shall be straightway glorified, John xiii. 32. The reward is not only sure, but very near. (2.) To encourage his disciples, and comfort them, who would be overwhelmed and greatly terrified by his sufferings. (3.) To direct us, under all *the sufferings of this present time,* to keep up a believing prospect of *the glory to be revealed,* to look at *the things that are not seen, that are eternal,* which will enable us to call the present afflictions light, and but for a moment.

20 Then came to him the mother
of Zebedee's children with her sons,
worshipping *him,* and desiring a certain thing of him.
21 And he said
unto her, What wilt thou? She saith
unto him, Grant that these my two
sons may sit, the one on thy right
hand, and the other on the left, in thy
kingdom.
22 But Jesus answered
and said, Ye know not what ye ask.
Are ye able to drink of the cup that
I shall drink of, and to be baptized
with the baptism that I am baptized
with? They say unto him, We are
able.
23 And he saith unto them,
Ye shall drink indeed of my cup, and
be baptized with the baptism that I
am baptized with: but to sit on my
right hand, and on my left, is not
mine to give, but *it shall be given to
them* for whom it is prepared of my
Father.
24 And when the ten heard
it, they were moved with indignation
against the two brethren.
25 But
Jesus called them *unto him,* and said,
Ye know that the princes of the Gentiles exercise dominion over them,
and they that are great exercise authority upon them.
26 But it shall
not be so among you: but whosoever
will be great among you, let him be
your minister;
27 And whosoever
will be chief among you, let him be
your servant:
28 Even as the Son of
man came not to be ministered unto,
but to minister, and to give his life a
ransom for many.

Here is, first, the request of the two disciples to Christ, and the rectifying of the mistake upon which that was grounded, *v.* 20—23. The sons of Zebedee were James and John, two of the first three of Christ's disciples; Peter and they were his favourites; John was the disciple whom Jesus loved; yet none were so often reproved as they; whom Christ loves best he reproves most, Rev. iii. 19.

I. Here is the ambitious address they

made to Christ—that they might sit, the one on his right hand, and the other on his left, in his kingdom, *v.* 20, 21. It was a great degree of faith, that they were confident of his kingdom, though now he appeared in meanness; but a great degree of ignorance, that they still expected a temporal kingdom, with worldly pomp and power, when Christ had so often told them of sufferings and self-denial. In this they expected to be grandees. They ask not for employment in this kingdom, but for honour only; and no place would serve them in this imaginary kingdom, but the highest, next to Christ, and above every body else. It is probable that the last word in Christ's foregoing discourse gave occasion to this request, that *the third day he should rise again.* They concluded that his resurrection would be his entrance upon his kingdom, and therefore were resolved to put in betimes for the best place; nor would they lose it for want of speaking early. What Christ said to comfort them, they thus abused, and were puffed up with. Some cannot bear comforts, but they turn them to a wrong purpose; as sweetmeats in a foul stomach produce bile. Now observe,

1. There was policy in the management of this address, that they put their mother on to present it, that it might be looked upon as her request, and not theirs. Though proud people think well of themselves, they would not be thought to do so, and therefore affect nothing more than *a show of humility* (Col. ii. 18), and others must be put on to court that honour for them, which they are ashamed to court for themselves. The mother of James and John was Salome, as appears by comparing *ch.* xxvii. 61, with Mark xv. 40. Some think she was daughter of Cleophas or Alpheus, and sister or cousin german to Mary the mother of our Lord. She was one of those women that attended Christ, and ministered to him; and they thought she had such an interest in him, that he could deny her nothing, and therefore they made her their advocate. Thus when Adonijah had an unreasonable request to make to Solomon, he put Bathsheba on to speak for him. It was their mother's weakness thus to become the tool of their ambition, which she should have given a check to. Those that are wise and good, would not be seen in an ill-favoured thing. In gracious requests, we should learn this wisdom, to desire the prayers of those that have an interest at the throne of grace; we should beg of our praying friends to pray for us, and reckon it a real kindness.

It was likewise policy to ask first for a general grant, that he would do a *certain* thing for them, not in faith, but in presumption, upon that general promise; *Ask, and it shall be given you;* in which is implied this qualification of our request, that it be according to the revealed will of God, otherwise we *ask and have not,* if we ask to *consume it upon our lusts,* Jam. iv. 3.

2. There was pride at the bottom of it, a proud conceit of their own merit, a proud contempt of their brethren, and a proud desire of honour and preferment; pride is a sin that most easily besets us, and which it is hard to get clear of. It is a holy ambition to strive to excel others in grace and holiness; but it is a sinful ambition to covet to exceed others in pomp and grandeur. *Seekest thou great things for thyself,* when thou hast just now heard of thy Master's being mocked, and scourged, and crucified? For shame! *Seek them not,* Jer. xlv. 5.

II. Christ's answer to this address (*v.* 22, 23), directed not to the mother, but to the sons that set her on. Though others be our mouth in prayer, the answer will be given to us according as we stand affected. Christ's answer is very mild; they were overtaken in the fault of ambition, but Christ *restored them with the spirit of meekness.* Observe,

1. How he reproved the ignorance and error of their petition; *Ye know not what ye ask.* (1.) They were much in the dark concerning the kingdom they had their eye upon; they dreamed of a temporal kingdom, whereas Christ's kingdom is not of this world. They knew not what it was to sit on his right hand, and on his left; they talked of it as blind men do of colours. Our apprehensions of that glory which is yet to be revealed, are like the apprehensions which a child has of the preferments of grown men. If at length, through grace, we arrive at perfection, we shall then put away such childish fancies: when we come to see face to face, we shall know what we enjoy; but now, alas, we know not what we ask; we can but ask for the good as it lies in the promise, Tit. i. 2. What it will be in the performance, eye has not seen, nor ear heard. (2.) They were much in the dark concerning the way to that kingdom. *They* know not what they ask, who ask for the end, but overlook the means, and so put asunder what God has joined together. The disciples thought, when they had left what little *all* they had for Christ, and had gone about the country awhile preaching the gospel of the kingdom, all their service and sufferings were over, and it was now time to ask, *What shall we have?* As if nothing were now to be looked for but crowns and garlands; whereas there were far greater hardships and difficulties before them than they had yet met with. They imagined their warfare was accomplished when it was scarcely begun, and they had yet but run with the footmen. They dream of being in Canaan presently, and consider not what they shall do in the swellings of Jordan. Note, [1.] We are all apt, when we are but *girding on the harness, to boast* as though we *had put it off.* [2.] We know not what we ask, when we ask for the glory of wearing the crown, and

ask not for grace to bear the cross in our way to it.

2. How he repressed the vanity and ambition of their request. They were pleasing themselves with the fancy of sitting on his right hand, and on his left, in great state; now, to check this, he leads them to the thoughts of their sufferings, and leaves them in the dark about their glory.

(1.) He leads them to the thoughts of their sufferings, which they were not so mindful of as they ought to have been. They looked so earnestly upon the crown, the prize, that they were ready to plunge headlong and unprepared into the foul way that led to it; and therefore he thinks it necessary to put them in mind of the hardships that were before them, that they might be no surprise or terror to them.

Observe, [1.] How fairly he puts the matter to them, concerning these difficulties (*v.* 22); "You would stand candidates for the first post of honour in the kingdom; but *are you able to drink of the cup that I shall drink of?* You talk of what great things you must have when you have done your work; but are you able to hold out to the end of it? Put the matter seriously to yourselves. These same two disciples once knew not what manner of spirit they were of, when they were disturbed with anger, Luke ix. 55; and now they were not aware what was amiss in their spirits when they were lifted up with ambition. Christ sees that pride in us which we discern not in ourselves.

Note, *First,* That to suffer for Christ is *to drink of a cup,* and *to be baptized with a baptism.* In this description of sufferings, 1. It is true, that affliction doth abound. It is supposed to be a bitter cup, that is drunk of, wormwood and gall, those waters of a full cup, that are wrung out to God's people (Ps. lxxiii. 10); a cup of trembling indeed, but not of fire and brimstone, the portion of the cup of wicked men, Ps. xi. 6. It is supposed to be a baptism, a washing with the waters of affliction; some are dipped in them, the waters compass them about even to the soul (Jonah ii. 5); others have but a sprinkling of them; both are baptisms, some are overwhelmed in them, as in a deluge, others ill wet, as in a sharp shower. But, 2. Even in this, *consolation doth more abound.* It is but a cup, not an ocean; it is but a draught, bitter perhaps, but we shall see the bottom of it; it is a cup in the hand of a Father (John xviii. 11); and it is full of mixture, Ps. lxxv. 8. It is but a baptism; if dipped, that is the worst of it, not drowned; perplexed, but not in despair. Baptism is an ordinance by which we join ourselves to the Lord in covenant and communion; and so is suffering for Christ, Ezek. xx. 37; Isa. xlviii. 10. Baptism is "an outward and visible sign of an inward and spiritual grace;" and so is suffering for Christ, for *unto us it is given,* Phil. i. 29.

Secondly, It is to drink of the same cup that Christ drank of, and to be baptized with the same baptism that he was baptised with. Christ is beforehand with us in suffering, and in that as in other things left us an example. 1. It bespeaks the condescension of a suffering Christ, that he would drink of such a cup (John xviii. 11), nay, and such a brook (Ps. cx. 7), and drink so deep, and yet so cheerfully; that he would be baptized with such a baptism, and was so forward to it, Luke xii. 50. It was much that he would be baptized with water as a common sinner, much more with blood as an uncommon malefactor. But in all this he was made *in the likeness of sinful flesh,* and *was made sin for us.* 2. It bespeaks the consolation of suffering Christians, that they do but pledge Christ in the bitter cup, are *partakers of his sufferings,* and *fill up that which is behind* of them; we must therefore arm ourselves with the same mind, and *go to him without the camp.*

Thirdly, It is good for us to be often putting it to ourselves, whether we are able to drink of this cup, and to be baptized with this baptism. We must expect suffering, and not look upon it as a hard thing to suffer well and as becomes us. Are we able to suffer cheerfully, and in the worst of times still to hold fast our integrity? What can we afford to part with for Christ? How far will we give him credit? Could I find in my heart to drink of a bitter cup, and to be baptized with a bloody baptism, rather than let go my hold of Christ? The truth is, Religion, if it be worth any thing, is worth every thing; but it is worth little, if it be not worth suffering for. Now let us sit down, and count the cost of dying for Christ rather than denying him, and ask, Can we take him upon these terms?

[2.] See how boldly they engage for themselves; they said, *We are able,* in hopes of sitting on his right hand, and on his left; but at the same time they fondly hoped that they should never be tried. As before they knew not what they asked, so now they knew not what they answered. *We are able;* they would have done well to put in, "*Lord, by thy strength,* and *in thy grace, we are able,* otherwise we are not." But the same that was Peter's temptation, to be confident of his own sufficiency, and presume upon his own strength, was here the temptation of James and John; and it is a sin we are all prone to. They knew not what Christ's cup was, nor what his baptism, and therefore they were thus bold in promising for themselves. But those are commonly most confident, that are least acquainted with the cross.

[3.] See how plainly and positively their sufferings are here foretold (*v.* 23); *Ye shall drink of my cup.* Sufferings foreseen will be the more easily borne, especially if looked upon under a right notion, as drinking of his cup, and being baptized with his baptism Christ began in suffering for us, and expects we should pledge him in suffering for him. Christ will have us know the worst, that we may make the best of our way to heaven; *Ye shall drink;* that is, ye shall suffer. James drank the bloody cup first of all the apostles, Acts xii. 2. John, though at last he died in his bed, if we may credit the ecclesiastical historians, yet often drank of this bitter cup, as when he was banished into the isle of Patmos (Rev. i. 9), and when (as they say) at Ephesus he was put into a caldron of boiling oil, but was miraculously preserved. He was, as the rest of the apostles, in deaths often. He took the cup, offered himself to the baptism, and it was accepted.

(2.) He leaves them in the dark about the degrees of their glory. To carry them cheerfully through their sufferings, it was enough to be assured that they should have *a place in his kingdom*. The lowest seat in heaven is an abundant recompence for the greatest sufferings on earth. But as to the preferments there, it was not fit there should be any intimation given for whom they were intended; for the infirmity of their present state could not bear such a discovery with any evenness; "*To sit on my right hand and on my left is not mine to give,* and therefore it is not for you to ask it or to know it; *but it shall be given to them for whom it is prepared of my Father.*" Note, [1.] It is very probable that there are degrees of glory in heaven; for our Saviour seems to allow that there are some that shall sit on his right hand and on his left, in the highest places. [2.] As the future glory itself, so the degrees of it, are purposed and prepared in the eternal counsel of God; as the common salvation, so the more peculiar honours, are appointed, the whole affair is long since settled, and there is a certain measure of the stature, both in grace and glory, Eph. iv. 13. [3.] Christ, in dispensing the fruits of his own purchase, goes exactly by the measures of his Father's purpose; *It is not mine to give, save to them* (so it may be read) *for whom it is prepared.* Christ has the sole power of giving eternal life, but then it is *to as many as were given him,* John xvii. 2. *It is not mine to give,* that is, to *promise* now; that matter is already settled and concerted, and the Father and Son understand one another perfectly well in this matter. "It is not mine to give to those that seek and are ambitious of it, but to those that by great humility and self-denial are prepared for it."

III. Here are the reproof and instruction which Christ gave to the other ten disciples for their displeasure at the request of James and John. He had much to bear with in them all, they were so weak in knowledge and grace, yet he bore their manners.

1. The fret that the ten disciples were in (*v.* 24). *They were moved with indignation against the two brethren;* not because they were desirous to be preferred, which was their sin, and for which Christ was displeased with them, but because they were desirous to be preferred *before them,* which was a reflection upon them. Many seem to have indignation at sin; but it is not because it is sin, but because it touches them. They will inform against a man that swears; but it is only if he swear at them, and affront them, not because he dishonours God. These disciples were angry at their brethren's ambition, though they themselves, nay *because* they themselves, were as ambitious. Note, It is common for people to be angry at those sins in others which they allow of and indulge in themselves. Those that are proud and covetous themselves do not care to see others so. Nothing makes more mischief among brethren, or is the cause of more indignation and contention, than ambition, and desire of greatness. We never find Christ's disciples quarrelling, but something of this was at the bottom of it.

2. The check that Christ gave them, which was very gentle, rather by way of instruction what they should be, than by way of reprehension for what they were. He had reproved this very sin before (*ch.* xviii. 3), and told them they must be humble as little children; yet they relapsed into it, and yet he reproved them for it thus mildly.

He called them unto him, which intimates great tenderness and familiarity. He did not, in anger, bid them get out of his presence, but called them, in love, to come into his presence: for *therefore* he is fit to teach, and we are invited to learn of him, because *he is meek and lowly in heart.* What he had to say concerned both the two disciples and the ten, and therefore he will have them all together. And he tells them, that, whereas they were asking which of them should have dominion in a temporal kingdom, there was really no such dominion reserved for any of them. For,

(1.) They must not be *like the princes of the Gentiles.* Christ's disciples must not be like Gentiles, no not like princes of the Gentiles. Principality doth no more become ministers than Gentilism doth Christians.

Observe, [1.] What is the way of the princes of the Gentiles (*v.* 25); to *exercise dominion and authority* over their subjects, and (if they can but win the upper hand with a strong hand) over one another too. That which bears them up in it is, that they are great, and great men think they may do any thing. Dominion and authority are the great things which the princes of the Gentiles pursue, and pride themselves in; they would bear sway, would carry all before them, have every body truckle to them, and every sheaf bow to theirs. They would have it cried before them, *Bow the knee;* like Nebuchadnezzar, who slew, and kept alive, at pleasure.

[2.] What is the will of Christ concerning his apostles and ministers, in this matter.

First, "*It shall not be so among you.* The

constitution of the spiritual kingdom is quite different from this. You are to teach the subjects of this kingdom, to instruct and beseech them, to counsel and comfort them, to take pains with them, and suffer with them, not to exercise dominion or authority over them; you are not to *lord it over God's heritage* (1 Pet. v. 3), but to labour in it." This forbids not only tyranny, and abuse of power, but the claim or use of any such secular authority as the princes of the Gentiles lawfully exercise. So hard is it for vain men, even good men, to have such authority, and not to be puffed up with it, and do more hurt than good with it, that our Lord Jesus saw fit wholly to banish it out of his church. Paul himself disowns dominion over the faith of any, 2 Cor. i. 24. The pomp and grandeur of the princes of the Gentiles ill become Christ's disciples. Now, if there were no such power and honour intended to be in the church, it was nonsense for them to be striving who should have it. *They knew not what they asked.*

Secondly, How then shall it be among the disciples of Christ? Something of greatness among them Christ himself had intimated, and here he explains it; "*He that will be great among you,* that *will be chief,* that would really be so, and would be found to be so at last, *let him be your minister, your servant,*" *v.* 26, 27. Here observe, 1. That it is the duty of Christ's disciples to serve one another, for mutual edification. This includes both humility and usefulness. The followers of Christ must be ready to stoop to the meanest offices of love for the good one of another, must *submit one to another* (1 Pet. v. 5; Eph. v. 21), and *edify one another* (Rom. xiv. 19), *please one another* for good, Rom. xv. 2. The great apostle made himself every one's servant; see 1 Cor. ix. 19. 2. It is the dignity of Christ's disciples faithfully to discharge this duty. The way to be great and chief is to be humble and serviceable. Those are to be best accounted of, and most respected, in the church, and will be so by all that understand things aright; not those that are dignified with high and mighty names, like the names of the great ones of the earth, that appear in pomp, and assume to themselves a power proportionable, but those that are most humble and self-denying, and lay out themselves most to do good, though to the diminishing of themselves. These honour God most, and those he will honour. As he must become a fool that would be wise, so he must become a servant that would be chief. St. Paul was a great example of this; he *laboured more abundantly than they all,* made himself (as some would call it) a drudge to his work; and is not he chief? Do we not by consent call him the *great* apostle, though he called himself *less than the least?* And perhaps our Lord Jesus had an eye to him, when he said, There were *last* that should be *first;* for Paul was *one born out of due time* (1 Cor. xv. 8); not only the youngest child of the family of the apostles, but a posthumous one, yet he became greatest. And perhaps he it was for whom the first post of honour in Christ's kingdom was reserved and prepared of his Father, not for James who sought it; and therefore just before Paul began to be famous as an apostle, Providence ordered it so that James was cut off (Acts xii. 2), that in the college of the twelve Paul might be substituted in his room.

(2.) They must be like the Master himself; and it is very fit that they should, that, while they were in the world, they should be as he was when he was in the world; for to both the present state is a state of humiliation, the crown and glory were reserved for both in the future state. Let them consider that the *Son of man came not to be ministered to, but to minister, and to give his life a ransom for many, v.* 28. Our Lord Jesus here sets himself before his disciples as a pattern of those two things before recommended, humility, and usefulness.

[1.] Never was there such an example of humility and condescension as there was in the life of Christ, who came not to be *ministered unto, but to minister.* When the Son of God came into the world, his Ambassador to the children of men, one would think he should have been ministered to, should have appeared in an equipage agreeable to his person and character; but he did not so; he made no figure, had no pompous train of state-servants to attend him, nor was he clad in robes of honour, for he took upon him the *form of a servant.* He was indeed ministered to as a poor man, which was a part of his humiliation; there were those that *ministered to him of their substance* (Luke viii. 2, 3); but he was never ministered to as a great man; he never took state upon him, was not waited on at table; he once washed his disciples' feet, but we never read that they washed his feet. He came to minister help to all that were in distress; he made himself a servant to the sick and diseased; was as ready to their requests as ever any servant was at the beck of his master, and took as much pains to serve them; he attended continually to this very thing, and denied himself both food and rest to attend to it.

[2.] Never was there such an example of beneficence and usefulness as there was in the death of Christ, who *gave his life a ransom for many.* He lived as a servant, and went about doing good; but he died as a sacrifice, and in that he did the greatest good of all. He came into the world on purpose to give his life a ransom; it was first in his intention. The aspiring princes of the Gentiles make the lives of many a ransom for their own honour, and perhaps a sacrifice to their own humour. Christ doth not do so; his subjects' blood is precious to him, and he is not prodigal of it (Ps. lxxii. 14); but on the contrary, he gives his honour and life too a ransom for his subjects. Note, *First*, Jesus Christ laid down his life for a ransom. Our lives were forfeited into the hands of divine justice by sin. Christ, by parting with his life, made atonement for sin, and so rescued ours; *he was made sin, and a curse for us*, and died, not only *for our good, but in our stead*, Acts xx. 28; 1 Pet. i. 18, 19. *Secondly*, It was a ransom for many, sufficient for all, effectual for many; and, if for many, then, saith the poor doubting soul, "Why not for me?" It was for many, that by him many may be made righteous. These many were his seed, for which his soul travailed (Isa. liii. 10, 11); for many, so they will be when they come all together, though now they appear but a little flock.

Now this is a good reason why we should not strive for precedency, because the cross is our banner, and our Master's death is our life. It is a good reason why we should study to do good, and, in consideration of the love of Christ in dying for us, not hesitate *to lay down our lives for the brethren*, 1 John iii. 16. Ministers should be more forward than others to serve and suffer for the good of souls, as blessed Paul was, Acts xx. 24; Phil. ii. 17. The nearer we are all concerned in, and the more we are advantaged by, the humility and humiliation of Christ, the more ready and careful we should be to imitate it.

29 And as they departed from Jericho, a great multitude followed him.
30 And, behold, two blind men sitting
by the way side, when they heard
that Jesus passed by, cried out, saying, Have mercy on us, O Lord, *thou*
son of David. 31 And the multitude
rebuked them, because they should
hold their peace: but they cried the
more, saying, Have mercy on us, O
Lord, *thou* son of David. 32 And
Jesus stood still, and called them, and
said, What will ye that I shall do unto
you? 33 They say unto him, Lord,
that our eyes may be opened. 34
So Jesus had compassion *on them*,
and touched their eyes: and immediately their eyes received sight, and
they followed him.

We have here an account of the cure of two poor blind beggars; in which we may observe,

I. Their address to Christ, *v.* 29, 30. And in this,

1. The circumstances of it are observable. It was as Christ and his disciples departed from Jericho; of that devoted place, which was rebuilt under a curse, Christ took his leave with this blessing, for he received gifts even for the rebellious. It was in the presence of *a great multitude that followed him;* Christ had a numerous, though not a pompous, attendance, and did good to them, though he did not take state to himself. This multitude that followed Christ was a mixed multitude. Some followed him for loaves, and some for love, some for curiosity, and some in expectation of his temporal reign, which the disciples themselves dreamed of, very few with desire to be taught their duty; yet, for the sake of those few, he confirmed his doctrine by miracles wrought in the presence of great multitudes; who, if they were not convinced by them, would be the more inexcusable. Two blind men concurred in their request; for joint-prayer is pleasing to Christ, *ch.* xviii. 19. These joint-sufferers were joint-suitors; being companions in the same tribulation, they were partners in the same supplication. Note, It is good for those that are labouring under the same calamity, or infirmity of body or mind, to join together in the same prayer to God for relief, that they may quicken one another's fervency, and encourage one another's faith. There is mercy enough in Christ for all the petitioners. These blind men were *sitting by the way-side*, as blind beggars used to do. Note, Those that would receive mercy from Christ, must place themselves there where his out-goings are; where he manifests himself to those that seek him. It is good thus to way-lay Christ, to be in his road.

They heard that Jesus passed by. Though they were blind, they were not deaf. Seeing and hearing are the learning senses. It is a great calamity to want either; but the defect of one may be, and often is, made up in the acuteness of the other; and therefore it has been observed by some as an instance of the goodness of Providence, that none were ever known to be born both blind and deaf; but that, one way or other, all are in a capacity of receiving knowledge. These blind men had heard of Christ by the hearing of the ear, but they desired that their eyes might see him. *When they heard that Jesus passed by*, they asked no further questions, who were with him, or whether he was in haste, but immediately *cried out*. Note, It is good to improve the present opportunity, to make the best of the price now in the hand, because, if once let slip, it may never return; these blind men did so, and did wisely; for we do not find that Christ ever came to Jericho again. *Now is the accepted time.*

2. The address itself is more observable; *Have mercy on us, O Lord, thou Son of David*, repeated again, *v.* 31. Four things are recommended to us for an example in this address; for, though the eye of the body was dark, the eye of the mind was enlightened concerning truth, duty, and interest.

(1.) Here is an example of importunity in prayer. They cried out as men in earnest; men in want are earnest, of course. Cold desires do but beg denials. Those that would prevail in prayer, must stir up themselves to take hold on God in the duty. When they were discountenanced in it, they cried the more. The stream of fervency, if it be stopped, will rise and swell the higher. This is wrestling with God in prayer, and makes us the fitter to receive mercy; for the more it is striven for, the more it will be prized and thankfully acknowledged.

(2.) Of humility in prayer; in that word, *Have mercy on us,* not specifying the favour, or prescribing what, much less pleading merit, but casting themselves upon, and referring themselves cheerfully to, the Mediator's mercy, in what way he pleases; "Only have mercy." They ask not for silver and gold, though they were poor, but mercy, mercy. This is that which our hearts must be upon, when we come to *the throne of grace, that we may find mercy,* Heb. iv. 16; Ps. cxxx. 7.

(3.) Of faith in prayer; in the title they gave to Christ, which was in the nature of a plea; *O Lord, thou Son of David;* they confess that *Jesus Christ is Lord,* and therefore had authority to command deliverance for them. Surely it was by the Holy Ghost that they called Christ *Lord,* 1 Cor. xii. 3. Thus they take their encouragement in prayer from his power, as in calling him the Son of David they take encouragement from his goodness, as Messiah, of whom so many kind and tender things had been foretold, particularly his compassion to the poor and needy, Ps. lxxii. 12, 13. It is of excellent use, in prayer, to eye Christ in the grace and glory of his Messiahship; to remember that he is the Son of David, whose office it is to help, and save, and to plead it with him.

(4.) Of perseverance in prayer, notwithstanding discouragement. *The multitude rebuked them,* as noisy, clamorous, and impertinent, and bid them *hold their peace,* and not disturb the Master, who perhaps at first himself seemed not to regard them. In following Christ with our prayers, we must expect to meet with hindrances and manifold discouragements from within and from without, something or other that bids us hold our peace. Such rebukes are permitted, that faith and fervency, patience and perseverance, may be tried. These poor blind men were rebuked by the multitude that followed Christ. Note, the sincere and serious beggars at Christ's door commonly meet with the worst rebukes from those that follow him but in pretence and hypocrisy. But they would not be beaten off so; when they were in pursuit of such a mercy, it was no time to compliment, or to practise a timid delicacy; no, *they cried the more.* Note, *Men ought always to pray, and not to faint;* to *pray with all perseverance* (Luke xviii. 1); to continue in prayer with resolution, and not to yield to opposition.

II. The answer of Christ to this address of theirs. The multitude rebuked them; but Christ encouraged them. It were sad for us, if the Master were not more kind and tender than the multitude; but he loves to countenance those with special favour, that are under frowns, and rebukes, and contempts from men. He will not suffer his humble supplicants to be run down, and put out of countenance.

1. *He stood still, and called them,* v. 32. He was now going up to Jerusalem, and was straitened till his work there was accomplished; and yet he stood still to cure these blind men. Note, When we are ever so much in haste about any business, yet we should be willing to stand still to do good. *He called them,* not because he could not cure them at a distance, but because he would do it in the most obliging and instructive way, and would countenance weak but willing patients and petitioners. Christ not only enjoins us to pray, but invites us; holds out the golden sceptre to us, and bids us come touch the top of it.

2. He enquired further into their case; *What will ye that I shall do unto you?* This implies, (1.) A very fair offer; "Here I am; let me know what you would have, and you shall have it." What would we more? He is able to do for us, and as willing as he is able; *Ask, and it shall be given you.* (2.) A condition annexed to this offer, which is a very easy and reasonable one—that they should tell him what they would have him do for them. One would think this a strange question, any one might tell what they would have. Christ knew well enough; but he would know it from them, whether they begged only for an alms, as from a common person, or for a cure, as from the Messiah. Note, It is the will of God that we should in every thing make our requests known to him by prayer and supplication; not to inform or move him, but to qualify ourselves for the mercy. The waterman in the boat, who with his hook takes hold of the shore, does not thereby pull the shore to the boat, but the boat to the shore. So in prayer we do not draw the mercy to ourselves, but ourselves to the mercy.

They soon made known their request to him, such a one as they never made to any one else; *Lord, that our eyes may be opened.* The wants and burthens of the body we are soon sensible of, and can readily relate; *Ubi dolor, ubi digitus—The finger promptly points to the seat of pain.* O that we were but as apprehensive of our spiritual maladies, and could as feelingly complain of them, especially our spiritual blindness! Lord, that the eyes of our mind may be opened! Many are spiritually blind, and yet say they see, John ix. 41. Were we but sensible of our darkness, we should soon apply ourselves to him, who alone has the eye-salve, with this request, *Lord, that our eyes may be opened.*

3. He cured them; when he encouraged them to seek him, he did not say, *Seek in vain.* What he did was an instance,

(1.) Of his pity; *He had compassion on them.* Misery is the object of mercy. They that are poor and blind are *wretched and miserable* (Rev. iii. 17), and the objects of compassion. It was the tender mercy of our God, that gave light and sight to them that sat in darkness, Luke i. 78, 79. We cannot help those that are under such calamities, as Christ did; but we may and must pity them, as Christ did, and draw out our soul to them.

(2.) Of his power; *He that formed the eye, can he not heal it?* Yes, he can, he did, he did it easily, he touched their eyes; he did it effectually, *Immediately their eyes received sight.* Thus he not only proved that he was sent of God, but showed on what errand he was sent—to give sight to those that are spiritually blind, *to turn them from darkness to light.*

Lastly, These blind men, when they had received sight, *followed him.* Note, None follow Christ blindfold. He first by his grace opens men's eyes, and so draws their hearts after him. They followed Christ, as his disciples, to learn of him, and as his witnesses, eye-witnesses, to bear their testimony to him and to his power and goodness. The best evidence of spiritual illumination is a constant inseparable adherence to Jesus Christ as our Lord and Leader.

CHAP. XXI.

The death and resurrection of Jesus Christ are the two main hinges upon which the door of salvation turns. He came into the world on purpose to give his life a ransom; so he had lately said, ch. 20, 28. And therefore the history of his sufferings, even unto death, and his rising again, is more particularly recorded by all the evangelists than any other part of his story; and to that this evangelist now hastens apace. For at this chapter begins that which is called the passion-week. He had said to his disciples more than once, Behold, we go up to Jerusalem, and there the Son of man must be betrayed. A great deal of good work he did by the way, and now at length he is come up to Jerusalem; and here we have, I. The public entry which he made into Jerusalem, upon the first day of the passion-week, ver. 1—11. II. The authority he exercised there, in cleansing the temple, and driving out of it the buyers and sellers, ver. 12—16. III. The emblem he gave of the state of the Jewish church, in cursing the barren fig-tree, and his discourse with his disciples thereupon, ver. 17—22. IV. His justifying his own authority, by appealing to the baptism of John, ver. 23—27. V. His shaming the infidelity and obstinacy of the chief priests and elders, with the repentance of the publicans, illustrated by the parable of the two sons, ver. 29—32. VI. His reading the doom of the Jewish church for its unfruitfulness, in the parable of the vineyard let out to unthankful husbandmen, ver. 33—46.

AND when they drew nigh unto
Jerusalem, and were come to
Bethphage, unto the mount of Olives,
then sent Jesus two disciples, 2 Saying unto them, Go into the village
over against you, and straightway ye
shall find an ass tied, and a colt with
her: loose *them*, and bring *them* unto
me. 3 And if any *man* say ought
unto you, ye shall say, The Lord hath
need of them; and straightway he
will send them. 4 All this was done,
that it might be fulfilled which was
spoken by the prophet, saying, 5 Tell
ye the daughter of Zion, Behold, thy
King cometh unto thee, meek, and
sitting upon an ass, and a colt the
foal of an ass. 6 And the disciples
went, and did as Jesus commanded
them, 7 And brought the ass, and
the colt, and put on them their clothes,
and they set *him* thereon. 8 And a
very great multitude spread their garments in the way; others cut down
branches from the trees, and strewed
them in the way. 9 And the multitudes that went before, and that followed, cried, saying, Hosanna to the
son of David: Blessed *is* he that
cometh in the name of the Lord;
Hosanna in the highest. 10 And
when he was come into Jerusalem,
all the city was moved, saying, Who
is this? 11 And the multitude said,
This is Jesus the prophet of Nazareth
of Galilee.

All the four evangelists take notice of this passage of Christ's *riding in triumph into Jerusalem,* five days before his death. The passover was on the fourteenth day of the month, and this was the tenth; on which day the law appointed that the paschal lamb should be taken up (Exod. xii. 3), and set apart for that service; on that day therefore Christ our Passover, who was to be sacrificed for us, was publicly showed. So that this was the prelude to his passion. He had lodged at Bethany, a village not far from Jerusalem, for some time; at a supper there the night before Mary had *anointed his feet,* John xii. 3. But, as is usual with ambassadors, he deferred his public entry till some time after his arrival. Our Lord Jesus travelled much, and his custom was to travel on foot from Galilee to Jerusalem, some scores of miles, which was both humbling and toilsome; many a dirty weary step he had when *he went about doing good.* How ill does it become Christians to be inordinately solicitous about their own ease and state, when their Master had so little of either! Yet once in his life he rode in triumph; and it was now when he went into Jerusalem, to suffer and die, as if that were the pleasure and preferment he courted; and then he thought himself begin to look great.

Now here we have,

I. The provision that was made for this solemnity; and it was very poor and ordinary, and such as bespoke his *kingdom* to be *not of this world.* Here were no heralds at arms provided, no trumpet sounded before him, no chariots of state, no liveries; such things as these were not agreeable to his present state of humiliation, but will be far outdone at his second coming, to which his magnificent appearance is reserved, when the last trumpet shall sound, the glorious angels shall be his heralds and attendants, and the clouds his chariots. But in this public appearance,

1. The preparation was sudden and off-hand. For his glory in the other world, and ours with him, preparation was made before the foundation of the world, for that was the glory his heart was upon; his glory in this world he was dead to, and therefore, though he had it in prospect, did not forecast for it, but took what came next. They were come to Bethphage, which was the suburb of Jerusalem, and was accounted (say the Jewish doctors) in all things, as Jerusalem, a long scattering street that lay toward the mount of Olives; when he entered upon that, *he sent two of his disciples,* some think Peter and John, to fetch him an ass, for he had none ready for him.

2. It was very mean. He sent only for an ass and her colt, *v.* 2. Asses were much used in that country for travel; horses were kept only by great men, and for war. Christ could have summoned a cherub to carry him (Ps. xviii. 10); but though *by his name Jah,* which speaks him God, *he rides upon the heavens,* yet now by his name Jesus, *Immanuel, God with us,* in his state of humiliation, he *rides upon an ass.* Yet some think that he had herein an eye to the custom in Israel for the judges to ride upon white asses (Judg. v. 10), and their sons on ass-colts, Judg. xii. 14. And Christ would thus enter, not as a Conqueror, but as the Judge of Israel, *who for judgment came into this world.*

3. It was not his own, but borrowed. Though he had not a house of his own, yet, one would think, like some wayfaring men that live upon their friends, he might have had an ass of his own, to carry him about; but for our sakes he became in all respects poor, 2 Cor. viii. 9. It is commonly said, "They that live on borrowing, live on sorrowing;" in this therefore, as in other things, Christ *was a man of sorrows*—that he had nothing of this world's goods but what was given him or lent him.

The disciples who were sent to borrow this ass are directed to say, *The Lord has need of him.* Those that are in need, must not be ashamed to own their need, nor say, as the unjust steward, *To beg I am ashamed,* Luke xvi. 3. On the other hand, none ought to impose upon the kindness of their friends, by going to beg or borrow when they have not need. In the borrowing of this ass,

(1.) We have an instance of Christ's knowledge. Though the thing was altogether contingent, yet Christ could tell his disciples where they should find an ass tied, and a colt with her. His omniscience extends itself to the meanest of his creatures; asses and their colts, and their being bound or loosed. *Doth God take care for oxen?* (1 Cor. ix. 9.) No doubt he doth, and would not see Balaam's ass abused. He knows all the creatures, so as to make them serve his own purpose.

(2.) We have an instance of his power over the spirits of men. The hearts of the meanest subjects, as well as of kings, *are in the hand of the Lord.* Christ asserts his right to use the ass, in bidding them bring it to him; the fulness of the earth is the Lord Christ's; but he foresees some hindrance which the disciples might meet with in this service; they must not take them *clam et secreto—privily,* but in the sight of the owner, much less *vi et armis—with force and arms,* but with the consent of the owner, which he undertakes they shall have; *If any man say aught to you, ye shall say, The Lord hath need of him.* Note, What Christ sets us to do, he will bear us out in the doing of, and furnish us with answers to the objections we may be assaulted with, and make them prevalent; as here, *Straightway he will send them.* Christ, in commanding the ass into his service, showed that he is Lord of hosts; and, in inclining the owner to send him without further security, showed that he is the *God of the spirits of all flesh,* and can bow men's hearts.

(3.) We have an example of justice and honesty, in not using the ass, though for so small a piece of service as riding the length of a street or two, without the owner's consent. As some read the latter clause, it gives us a further rule of justice; "*You shall say the Lord hath need of them, and he*" (that is, *the Lord)* "*will presently send them back,* and take care that they be safely delivered to the owner, as soon as he has done with them." Note, What we borrow we must restore in due time and in good order; for *the wicked borrows and pays not again.* Care must be taken of borrowed goods, that they be not damaged. *Alas, Master, for it was borrowed!*

II. The prediction that was fulfilled in this, *v.* 4, 5. Our Lord Jesus, in all that he did and suffered, had very much his eye upon this, *That the scriptures might be fulfilled.* As the prophets looked forward to him (to him they all bare witness), so he looked upon them, that all things which were written of the Messiah, might be punctually accomplished in him. This particularly which was written of him, Zech. ix. 9, where it ushers in a large prediction of the kingdom of the Messiah, *Tell ye the daughter of Sion, Behold, thy King cometh,* must be accomplished. Now observe here,

1. How the coming of Christ is foretold; *Tell ye the daughter of Sion,* the church, the holy mountain, *Behold, thy King cometh unto thee.* Note, (1.) Jesus Christ is the church's King, one of our brethren like unto us, according to the law of the kingdom, Deut. xvii. 15. He is appointed King over the church, Ps. ii. 6. He is accepted King by the church; the daughter of Sion swears allegiance to him, Hos. i. 11. (2.) Christ, the King of his church, came to his church, even in this lower world; he comes to thee, to rule thee, to rule in thee, to rule for thee; he

is *Head over all things to the church. He came to Sion* (Rom. xi. 26), that out of Sion the law might go forth; for the church and its interests were all in all with the Redeemer. (3.) Notice was given to the church beforehand of the coming of her King; *Tell the daughter of Sion.* Note, Christ will have his coming looked for, and waited for, and his subjects big with expectation of it; *Tell the daughters of Sion,* that they may *go forth, and behold king Solomon,* Cant. iii. 11. Notices of Christ's coming are usually ushered in with a *Behold!* A note commanding both attention and admiration; *Behold thy King cometh;* behold, and wonder at him, behold, and welcome him. Here is a royal progress truly admirable. Pilate, like Caiaphas, said he knew not what, in that great word (John xix. 14), *Behold your King.*

2. How his coming is described. When a king comes, something great and magnificent is expected, especially when he comes to take possession of his kingdom. The King, the Lord of hosts, was seen *upon a throne, high and lifted up* (Isa. vi. 1); but there is nothing of that here; *Behold, he cometh to thee, meek, and sitting upon an ass.* When Christ would appear in his glory, it is in his meekness, not in his majesty.

(1.) His temper is very mild. He comes not in wrath to take vengeance, but in mercy to work salvation. He is meek to suffer the greatest injuries and indignities for Sion's cause, meek to bear with the follies and unkindness of Sion's own children. He is easy of access, easy to be entreated. He is meek not only as a Teacher, but as a Ruler; he rules by love. His government is mild and gentle, and his laws not written in the blood of his subjects, but in his own. His yoke is easy.

(2.) As an evidence of this, his appearance is very mean, sitting upon an ass, a creature made not for state, but service, not for battles, but for burthens; slow in its motions, but sure, and safe, and constant. The foretelling of this so long before, and the care taken that it should be exactly fulfilled, intimate it to have a peculiar significancy, for the encouragement of poor souls to apply themselves to Christ. Sion's King comes riding, not on a prancing horse, which the timorous petitioner dares not come near, or a running horse, which the slow-footed petitioner cannot keep pace with, but on a quiet ass, that the poorest of his subjects may not be discouraged in their access to him. Mention is made in the prophecy of *a colt, the foal of an ass;* and *therefore* Christ sent for the colt with the ass, that the scripture might be fulfilled.

III. The procession itself, which was answerable to the preparation, both being destitute of worldly pomp, and yet both accompanied with a spiritual power.

Observe, 1. His equipage; *The disciples did as Jesus commanded them* (*v.* 6); they went to fetch the ass and the colt, not doubting but to find them, and to find the owner willing to lend them. Note, Christ's commands must not be disputed, but obeyed; and those that sincerely obey them, shall not be balked or baffled in it; *They brought the ass and the colt.* The meanness and contemptibleness of the beast Christ rode on, might have been made up with the richness of the trappings; but those were, like all the rest, such as came next to hand; they had not so much as a saddle for the ass, but the disciples threw some of their clothes upon it, and that must serve for want of better accommodations. Note, We ought not to be nice or curious, or to affect exactness, in outward conveniences. A holy indifference or neglect well becomes us in these things: it will evidence that our heart is not upon them, and that we have learned the apostle's rule (Rom. xii. 16, margin), *to be content with mean things.* Any thing will serve travellers; and there is a beauty in some sort of carelessness, a noble negligence; yet the disciples furnished him with the best they had, and did not object the spoiling of their clothes when *the Lord had need of them.* Note, We must not think the clothes on our backs too dear to part with for the service of Christ, for the clothing of his poor destitute and afflicted members. *I was naked, and you clothed me, ch.* xxv. 36. Christ stripped himself for us.

2. His retinue; there was nothing in this stately or magnificent. Sion's King comes to Sion, and the daughter of Sion was told of his coming long before; yet he is not attended by the gentlemen of the country, nor met by the magistrates of the city in their formalities as one might have expected; he should have had the keys of the city presented to him, and should have been conducted with all possible convenience to *the thrones of judgment, the thrones of the house of David;* but here is nothing of all this; yet he has his attendants, *a very great multitude;* they were only the common people, the mob (the *rabble* we should have been apt to call them), that graced the solemnity of Christ's triumph, and none but such. The chief priests and the elders afterward herded themselves with the multitude that abused him upon the cross; but we find none of them here joining with the multitude that did him honour. Ye see here your calling, brethren, *not many mighty, or noble,* attend on Christ, but *the foolish things of this world, and base things, which are despised,* 1 Cor. i. 26, 28. Note, Christ is honoured by the multitude, more than by the magnificence, of his followers; for he values men by their souls, not by their preferments, names, or titles of honour.

Now, concerning this great multitude, we are here told,

(1.) What they did; according to the best of their capacity, they studied to do honour to Christ. [1.] *They spread their garments in the way,* that he might ride upon them. When Jehu was proclaimed king, the captains put their garments under him, in token of their subjection to him. Note, Those that take Christ for their King must lay their all under his feet; the clothes, in token of the heart; for when Christ comes, though not when any one else comes, it must be *said to the soul, Bow down, that he may go over.* Some think that these garments were spread, not upon the ground, but on the hedges or walls, to adorn the roads; as, to beautify a cavalcade, the balconies are hung with tapestry. This was but a poor piece of state, yet Christ accepted their good-will; and we are hereby taught to contrive how to make Christ welcome, Christ and his grace, Christ and his gospel, into our hearts and houses. How shall we express our respects to Christ? What honour and what dignity shall be done to him? [2.] *Others cut down branches from the trees, and strewed them in the way,* as they used to do at the feast of tabernacles, in token of liberty, victory, and joy; for the mystery of that feast is particularly spoken of as belonging to gospel times, Zech. xiv. 16.

(2.) What they said; *They that went before, and they that followed,* were in the same tune; both those that gave notice of his coming, and those that attended him with their applauses, *cried, saying, Hosanna to the Son of David, v.* 9. When they carried branches about at the feast of tabernacles, they were wont to cry *Hosanna,* and from thence to call their bundles of branches their *hosannas. Hosanna* signifies, *Save now, we beseech thee*; referring to Ps. cxviii. 25, 26, where the Messiah is prophesied of as the *Head-stone of the corner,* though *the builders refused him;* and all his loyal subjects are brought in triumphing with him, and attending him with hearty good wishes to the prosperity of all his enterprises. *Hosanna to the Son of David* is, "This we do in honour of the Son of David."

The hosannas with which Christ was attended bespeak two things:

[1.] Their welcoming his kingdom. *Hosanna* bespeaks the same with, *Blessed is he that cometh in the name of the Lord.* It was foretold concerning this Son of David, that *all nations shall call him blessed* (Ps. lxxii. 17); these here began, and all true believers in all ages concur in it, and call him blessed; it is the genuine language of faith. Note, *First,* Jesus Christ *comes in the name of the Lord;* he is sanctified, and sent into the world, as Mediator; *him hath God the Father sealed. Secondly,* The coming of Christ in the name of the Lord, is *worthy of all acceptation;* and we all ought to say, *Blessed is he that cometh;* to praise him, and be pleased in him. Let his coming in the name of the Lord be mentioned with strong affections, to our comfort, and joyful acclamations, to his glory. Well may we say, *Blessed is he;* for it is in him that we are blessed. Well may we follow *him* with our blessings, who meets us with his.

[2.] Their wishing well to his kingdom; intimated in their *Hosanna;* earnestly desiring that prosperity and success may attend it, and that it may be a victorious kingdom; "*Send now prosperity* to that kingdom." If they understood it of a temporal kingdom, and had their hearts carried out thus toward that, it was their mistake, which a little time would rectify; however, their good-will was accepted. Note, It is our duty earnestly to desire and pray for the prosperity and success of Christ's kingdom in the world. Thus *prayer must be made for him continually* (Ps. lxxii. 15), that all happiness may attend his interest in the world, and that, though he may ride on an ass, yet in his majesty he may *ride prosperously, because of* that *meekness,* Ps. xlv. 4. This we mean when we pray, *Thy kingdom come.* They add, *Hosanna in the highest:* Let prosperity in the highest degree attend him, let him have a name above every name, a throne above every throne; or, Let us praise him in the best manner with exalted affections; or, Let our prayers for his church ascend to heaven, to the highest heavens, and fetch in peace and salvation from thence. See Ps. xx. 6. *The Lord saveth his Anointed, and will hear from his* high, his *holy heaven.*

3. We have here his entertainment in Jerusalem (*v.* 10); *When he was come into Jerusalem, all the city was moved;* every one took notice of him, some were moved with wonder at the novelty of the thing, others with laughter at the meanness of it; some perhaps were moved with joy, *who waited for the Consolation of Israel;* others, of the Pharisaical class, were moved with envy and indignation. So various are the motions in the minds of men upon the approach of Christ's kingdom!

Upon this commotion we are further told,

(1.) What the citizens said; *Who is this?* [1.] They were, it seems, ignorant concerning Christ. Though he was *the Glory of his people Israel,* yet *Israel knew him not;* though he had distinguished himself by the many miracles he wrought among them, yet *the daughters of Jerusalem* knew him not *from another beloved,* Cant. v. 9. The Holy One unknown in the holy city! In places where the clearest light shines, and the greatest profession of religion is made, there is more ignorance than we are aware of. [2.] Yet they were inquisitive concerning him. Who is this that is thus cried up, and comes with so much observation? *Who is this King of glory,* that demands admission into our hearts? Ps. xxiv. 8; Isa. lxiii. 1.

(2.) How the multitude answered them; *This is Jesus, v.* 11. The multitude were better acquainted with Christ than the great ones. *Vox populi—The voice of the people,* is sometimes *vox Dei—the voice of God.* Now, in the account they give of him, [1.] They were right in calling him *the Prophet, that great Prophet.* Hitherto he had been known as a Prophet, teaching and working miracles; now they attend him as a King; Christ's priestly office was, of all the three, last discovered. [2.] Yet they missed it, in saying he was *of Nazareth;* and it helped to confirm some in their prejudices against him. Note, Some that are willing to honour Christ, and bear their testimony to him, yet labour under mistakes concerning him, which would be rectified if they would take pains to inform themselves.

12 And Jesus went into the temple of God, and cast out all them that sold and bought in the temple, and overthrew the tables of the money-changers, and the seats of them that sold doves,
13 And said unto them,
It is written, My house shall be called the house of prayer; but ye have made it a den of thieves.
14 And the blind and the lame came to him in the temple; and he healed them.
15 And when the chief priests and scribes saw the wonderful things that he did, and the children crying in the temple, and saying, Hosanna to the son of David; they were sore displeased,
16 And said unto him, Hearest thou what these say? And Jesus saith unto them, Yea; have ye never read, Out of the mouth of babes and sucklings thou hast perfected praise?
17 And he left them, and went out of the city into Bethany; and he lodged there.

When Christ came into Jerusalem, he did not go up to the court or the palace, though he came in as a King, but *into the temple*; for his kingdom is spiritual, and *not of this world;* it is in holy things that he rules, in the temple of God that he exercises authority. Now, what did he do there?

I. Thence he drove the buyers and sellers. Abuses must first be purged out, and the plants not of God's planting be plucked up, before that which is right can be established. The great Redeemer appears as a great Reformer, that turns away ungodliness, Rom. xi. 26. Here we are told,

1. What he did (*v.* 12); *He cast out all them that sold and bought;* he had done this once before (John ii. 14, 15), but there was occasion to do it again. Note, Buyers and sellers driven out of the temple, will return and nestle there again, if there be not a continual care and oversight to prevent it, and if the blow be not followed, and often repeated.

(1.) The abuse was, buying and selling, and changing money, in the temple. Note, Lawful things, ill timed and ill placed, may become sinful things. That which was decent enough in another place, and not only lawful, but laudable, on another day, *defiles the sanctuary,* and *profanes the sabbath.* This buying and selling, and changing money, though secular employments, yet had the pretence of being *in ordine ad spiritualia—for spiritual purposes.* They sold beasts for sacrifice, for the convenience of those that could more easily bring their money with them than their beast; and they changed money for those that wanted the half shekel, which was their yearly poll, or redemption-money; or, upon the bills of return; so that this might pass for the outward business of the house of God; and yet Christ will not allow of it. Note, Great corruptions and abuses come into the church by the practices of those whose *gain is godliness,* that is, who make worldly gain the end of their godliness, and counterfeit godliness their way to worldly gain (1 Tim. vi. 5); *from such withdraw thyself.*

(2.) The purging out of this abuse. Christ *cast them out that sold.* He did it before *with a scourge of small cords* (John ii. 15); now he did it with a look, with a frown, with a word of command. Some reckon this none of the least of Christ's miracles, that he should himself thus clear the temple, and not be opposed in it by them who by this craft got their living, and were backed in it by the priests and elders. It is an instance of his power over the spirits of men, and the hold he has of them by their own consciences. This was the only act of regal authority and coercive power that Christ did in the days of his flesh; he began with it, John ii. and here ended with it. Tradition says, that his face shone, and beams of light darted from his blessed eyes, which astonished these market-people, and compelled them to yield to his command; if so, the scripture was fulfilled, Prov. xx. 8, *A King that sitteth in the throne of judgment scattereth away all evil with his eyes. He overthrew the tables of the money-changers;* he did not take the money to himself, but scattered it, threw it to the ground, the fittest place for it. The Jews, in Esther's time, *on the spoil laid not their hand,* Esther ix. 10.

2. What he said, to justify himself, and to convict them (*v.* 13); *It is written.* Note, In the reformation of the church, the eye must be upon the scripture, and that must be adhered to as the rule, the pattern in the mount; and we must go no further than we can justify ourselves with, *It is written.* Reformation is *then* right, when corrupted ordinances are reduced to their primitive institution.

(1.) He shows, from a scripture prophecy, what the temple should be, and was designed to be; *My house shall be called the house of prayer;* which is quoted from Isa. lvi. 7. Note, All the ceremonial institutions were intended to be subservient to moral duties; the house of sacrifices was to be a house of prayer, for that was the substance and soul of all those services; the temple was in a special manner sanctified to be a house of prayer, for it was not only the place of that worship, but the medium of it, so that the prayers made in or toward that house had a particular promise of acceptance (2 Chron. vi. 21), as it was a type of Christ; therefore Daniel looked that way in prayer; and in this sense no house or place is now, or can be, a house of prayer, for Christ is our Temple; yet in some sense the appointed places of our religious assemblies may be so called, as *places where prayer is wont to be made*, Acts xvi. 13.

(2.) He shows, from a scripture reproof, how they had abused the temple, and perverted the intention of it; *Ye have made it a den of thieves.* This is quoted from Jer. vii. 11, *Is this house become a den of robbers in your eyes?* When dissembled piety is made the cloak and cover of iniquity, it may be said that *the house of prayer* is become *a den of thieves,* in which they lurk, and shelter themselves. Markets are too often dens of thieves, so many are the corrupt and cheating practices in buying and selling; but markets in the temple are certainly so, for they rob God of his honour, the worst of thieves, Mal. iii. 8. The priests lived, and lived plentifully, upon the altar; but, not content with that, they found other ways and means to squeeze money out of the people; and therefore Christ here calls them *thieves,* for they exacted that which did not belong to them.

II. There, in the temple, *he healed the blind and the lame, v.* 14. When he had driven the buyers and sellers out of the temple, he invited the blind and lame into it; for *he fills the hungry with good things, but the rich he sends empty away.* Christ, in the temple, by his word there preached, and in answer to the prayers there made, heals those that are spiritually blind and lame. It is good coming to the temple, when Christ is there, who, as he shows himself jealous for the honour of his temple, in expelling those who profane it, so he shows himself gracious to those who humbly seek him. *The blind and the lame* were debarred David's palace (2 Sam. v. 8), but were admitted into God's house; for the state and honour of his temple lie not in those things wherein the magnificence of princes' palaces is supposed to consist; from them blind and lame must keep their distance, but from God's temple only the wicked and profane. The temple was profaned and abused when it was made a market-place, but it was graced and honoured when it was made an hospital; to be doing good in God's house, is more honourable, and better becomes it, than to be getting money there. Christ's healing was a real answer to that question, *Who is this?* His works testified of him more than the *hosannas;* and his healing in the temple was the fulfilling of the promise, that *the glory of the latter house should be greater than the glory of the former.*

There also he silenced the offence which the chief priests and scribes took at the acclamations with which he was attended, *v.* 15, 16. They that should have been most forward to give him honour, were his worst enemies.

1. They were inwardly vexed at the wonderful things that he did; they could not deny them to be true miracles, and therefore were cut to the heart with indignation at them, as Acts iv. 16; v. 33. The works that Christ did, recommended themselves to every man's conscience. If they had any sense, they could not but own the miracle of them; and if any good nature, could not but be in love with the mercy of them: yet, because they were resolved to oppose him, for these they envied him, and bore him a grudge.

2. They openly quarrelled at the children's hosannas; they thought that hereby an honour was given him, which did not belong to him, and that it looked like ostentation. Proud men cannot bear that honour should be done to any but to themselves, and are uneasy at nothing more than at the just praises of deserving men. Thus Saul envied David the women's songs; and "Who can stand before envy?" When Christ is most honoured, his enemies are most displeased.

Just now we had Christ preferring the blind and the lame before the buyers and sellers; now here we have him (*v.* 16), taking part with the children against priests and scribes.

Observe, (1.) The children were in the temple, perhaps playing there; no wonder, when the rulers make it a *market-place,* that the children make it a place of pastime; but we are willing to hope that many of them were worshipping there. Note, It is good to bring children betimes to the house of prayer, *for of such is the kingdom of heaven.* Let children be taught to keep up the form of godliness, it will help to lead them to the power of it. Christ has a tenderness for the lambs of his flock.

(2.) They were there *crying Hosanna to the Son of David.* This they learned from those that were grown up. Little children say and do as they hear others say, and see others do; so easily do they imitate; and therefore great care must be taken to set them good examples, and no bad ones. *Maxima debetur puero reverentia—Our intercourse with the young should be conducted with the most scrupulous care.* Children will learn of those that are with them, either to curse and swear, or to pray and praise. The Jews did betimes teach their children to carry branches at the feast of tabernacles, and to cry *Hosanna;* but God taught them here to apply it to Christ. Note, *Hosanna to the Son of David* well becomes the mouths of little children, who should learn young the language of Canaan.

(3.) Our Lord Jesus not only allowed it, but was very well pleased with it, and quoted a scripture which was fulfilled in it (Ps. viii. 2), or, at least, may be accommodated to it; *Out of the mouth of babes and sucklings thou hast perfected praise;* which, some think, refers to the children's joining in the acclamations of the people, and the women's songs with which David was honoured when he returned from the slaughter of the Philistine, and therefore is very fitly applied here to the hosannas with which the Son of David was saluted, now that he was entering upon his conflict with Satan, that Goliath. Note, [1.] Christ is so far from being ashamed of the services of little children, that he takes particular notice of them (and children love to be taken notice of), and is well pleased with them. If God may be honoured by babes and sucklings, who are made to hope at the best, much more by children who are grown up to maturity and some capacity. [2.] Praise is perfected out of the mouth of such; it has a peculiar tendency to the honour and glory of God for little children to join in his praises; the praise would be accounted defective and imperfect, if they had not their share in it; which is an encouragement for children to be good betimes, and to parents to teach them to be so; the labour neither of the one nor of the other shall be in vain. In the psalm it is, *Thou hast ordained strength.* Note, God *perfecteth praise,* by *ordaining strength out of the mouths of babes and sucklings.* When great things are brought about by weak and unlikely instruments, God is thereby much honoured, for his *strength is perfected in weakness,* and the infirmities of the babes and sucklings serve for a foil to the divine power. That which follows in the psalm, *That thou mightest still the enemy and the avenger,* was very applicable to the priests and scribes; but Christ did not apply it to them, but left it to them to apply it.

Lastly, Christ, having thus silenced them, forsook them, *v.* 17. *He left them,* in prudence, lest they should now have seized him before his hour was come; in justice, because they had forfeited the favour of his presence. By repining at Christ's praises we drive him from us. *He left them* as incorrigible, and he *went out of the city to Bethany,* which was a more quiet retired place; not so much that he might *sleep* undisturbed as that he might *pray* undisturbed. *Bethany was but two little miles from Jerusalem;* thither he went on foot, to show that, when he rode, it was only to *fulfil the scripture.* He was not lifted up with the hosannas of the people; but, as having forgot them, soon returned to his mean and toilsome way of travelling.

18 Now in the morning as he returned into the city, he hungered.
19 And when he saw a fig tree in the
way, he came to it, and found nothing
thereon, but leaves only, and said
unto it, Let no fruit grow on thee
henceforth for ever. And presently
the fig tree withered away. 20 And
when the disciples saw *it,* they marvelled, saying, How soon is the fig
tree withered away! 21 Jesus answered and said unto them, Verily I
say unto you, If ye have faith, and
doubt not, ye shall not only do this
which is done to the fig tree, but also
if ye shall say unto this mountain, Be
thou removed, and be thou cast into
the sea; it shall be done. 22 And
all things, whatsoever ye shall ask in
prayer, believing, ye shall receive.

Observe,

I. Christ *returned in the morning to Jerusalem, v.* 18. Some think that he went out of the city over-night, because none of his friends there durst entertain him, for fear of the great men; yet, having work to do there, he returned. Note, We must never be driven off from our duty either by the malice of our foes, or the unkindness of our friends. Though he knew that in this city *bonds and afflictions did abide him, yet none of these things moved* him. Paul followed him when he *went bound in the spirit to Jerusalem,* Acts xxx. 22.

II. *As he went, he hungered.* He was a Man, and submitted to the infirmities of nature; he was an active Man, and was so intent upon his work, that he neglected his food, and came out, fasting; for *the zeal of God's house* did even *eat him up,* and his *meat and drink was to do his Father's will.* He was a poor Man, and had no present supply; he was a Man that pleased not himself, for he would willingly have taken up with green raw figs for his breakfast, when it was fit that he should have had something warm.

Christ *therefore* hungered, that he might have occasion to work this miracle, in cursing and so withering the barren fig-tree, and therein might give us an instance of his justice and his power, and both instructive.

1. See his *justice, v.* 19. He went to it, expecting fruit, because it had leaves; but, finding none, he sentenced it to a perpetual barrenness. The miracle had its significance, as well as others of his miracles. All Christ's miracles hitherto were wrought for the good of men, and proved the power of his grace and blessing (the sending the devils into the herd of swine was but a permission); all he did was for the benefit and comfort of his friends, none for the terror or punishment of his enemies; but now, at last, to show that *all judgment is committed to him,* and that *he*

is able not only *to save, but to destroy,* he would give a specimen of the power of his wrath and curse; yet this not on any man, woman, or child, because *the great day of his wrath is not yet come,* but on an inanimate tree; that is set forth for an example; *Come, learn a parable of the fig-tree, ch.* xxiv. 32. The scope of it is the same with *the parable of the fig-tree,* Luke xiii. 6.

(1.) This cursing of the barren fig-tree, represents the state of hypocrites in general; and so it teaches us, [1.] That the fruit of fig-trees may justly be expected from those that have the leaves. Christ looks for the power of religion from those that make profession of it; the favour of it from those that have the show of it; grapes from the vineyard that is planted in a fruitful hill: he hungers after it, his soul *desires the first ripe fruits.* [2.] Christ's just expectations from flourishing professors are often frustrated and disappointed; he comes to many, seeking fruit, and finds leaves only, and he discovers it. Many have a name to live, and are not alive indeed; dote on the form of godliness, and yet deny the power of it. [3.] The sin of barrenness is justly punished with the curse and plague of barrenness; *Let no fruit grow on thee henceforward for ever.* As one of the chiefest blessings, and which was the first, is, *Be fruitful;* so one of the saddest curses is, *Be no more fruitful.* Thus the sin of hypocrites is made their punishment; they *would* not do good, and therefore they *shall* do none; he that is fruitless, let him be fruitless still, and lose his honour and comfort. [4.] A false and hypocritical profession commonly withers in this world, and it is the effect of Christ's curse; the fig-tree that had no fruit, soon lost its leaves. Hypocrites may look plausible for a time, but, having no principle, *no root in themselves,* their profession will soon come to nothing; the gifts wither, common graces decay, the credit of the profession declines and sinks, and the falseness and folly of the pretender are manifested to all men.

(2.) It represents the state of the nation and people of the Jews in particular; they were a fig-tree planted in Christ's way, as a church. Now observe, [1.] The disappointment they gave to our Lord Jesus. He came among them, expecting to find some fruit, something that would be pleasing to him; he hungered after it; not that he *desired a gift,* he needed it not, *but fruit that might abound to a good account.* But his expectations were frustrated; he found nothing but leaves; they called *Abraham their father, but did not do the works of Abraham;* they professed themselves expectants of the promised Messiah, but, when he came, they did not receive and entertain him. [2.] The doom he passed upon them, *that never any fruit should grow upon them,* or be gathered from them, as a church or as a people, *from henceforward for ever.* Never any good came from them (except the particular persons among them that believed), after they rejected Christ; they became worse and worse; blindness and hardness happened to them, and grew upon them, till they were unchurched, unpeopled, and undone, and their place and nation rooted up; their beauty was defaced, their privileges and ornaments, their temple, and priesthood, and sacrifices, and festivals, and all the glories of their church and state, fell like leaves in autumn. How soon did their fig-tree wither away, after they said, *His blood be on us, and on our children!* And the Lord was righteous in it.

2. See the *power* of Christ; the former is wrapped up in the figure, but this more fully discoursed of; Christ intending thereby to direct his disciples in the use of their powers.

(1.) The disciples admired the effect of Christ's curse (*v.* 20); *They marvelled;* no power could do it but his, *who spake, and it was done.* They marvelled at the suddenness of the thing; *How soon is the fig-tree withered away!* There was no visible cause of the fig-tree's withering, but it was a secret blast, a worm at the root; it was not only the leaves of it that withered, but the body of the tree; it withered away in an instant, and became like a dry stick. Gospel curses are, upon this account, the most dreadful—that they work insensibly and silently, by a fire not blown, but effectually.

(2.) Christ empowered them by faith to do the like (*v.* 21, 22); as he said (John xiv. 12), *Greater works than these shall ye do.*

Observe, [1.] The description of this wonder-working faith; *If ye have faith, and doubt not.* Note, Doubting of the power and promise of God is the great thing that spoils the efficacy and success of faith. "If you have faith, and dispute not" (so some read it), "dispute not with yourselves, dispute not with the promise of God; if you *stagger npt at the promise*" (Rom. iv. 20); for, as far as we do so, our faith is deficient; as certain as the promise is, so confident our faith should be.

[2.] The power and prevalence of it expressed figuratively; *If ye shall say to this mountain,* meaning the mount of Olives, *Be thou removed, it shall be done.* There might be a particular reason for his saying so of this mountain, for there was a prophecy, that *the mount of Olives, which is before Jerusalem, should cleave in the midst, and then remove,* Zech. xiv. 4. Whatever was the intent of that word, the same must be the expectation of faith, how impossible soever it might appear to sense. But this is a proverbial expression; intimating that we are to believe that nothing is impossible with God, and therefore that what he has promised shall certainly be performed, though to us it seem impossible. It was among the Jews a usual commendation of their learned Rabbin, that they were removers of mountains, that is, could solve the greatest difficulties; now this may be done by faith acted on the word of God, which will bring great and strange things to pass.

[3.] The way and means of exercising this faith, and of doing that which is to be done by it; *All things whatsoever ye shall ask in prayer, believing, ye shall receive.* Faith is the soul, prayer is the body; both together make a complete man for any service. Faith, if it be right, will excite prayer; and prayer is not right, if it do not spring from faith. This is the condition of our receiving—we must *ask in prayer, believing.* The requests of prayer shall not be denied; the expectations of faith shall not be frustrated. We have many promises to this purport from the mouth of our Lord Jesus, and all to encourage faith, the principal grace, and prayer, the principal duty, of a Christian. It is but ask and have, believe and receive; and what would we more? Observe, How comprehensive the promise is—*all things whatsoever ye shall ask;* this is like all and every the premises in a conveyance. *All things,* in general; *whatsoever,* brings it to particulars; though generals include particulars, yet such is the folly of our unbelief, that, though we think we assent to promises in the general, yet we fly off when it comes to particulars, and therefore, *that we might have strong consolation,* it is thus copiously expressed, *All things whatsoever.*

23 And when he was come into the temple, the chief priests and the elders of the people came unto him as he was teaching, and said, By what authority doest thou these things? and who gave thee this authority?
24 And Jesus answered and said unto them, I also will ask you one thing, which if ye tell me, I in like wise will tell you by what authority I do these things.
25 The baptism of John, whence was it? from heaven, or of men? And they reasoned with themselves, saying, If we shall say, From heaven; he will say unto us, Why did ye not then believe him?
26 But if we shall say, Of men; we fear the people; for all hold John as a prophet.
27 And they answered Jesus, and said, We cannot tell. And he said unto them, Neither tell I you by what authority I do these things.

Our Lord Jesus (like St. Paul after him) preached his gospel *with much contention;* his first appearance was in a dispute with *the doctors in the temple, when he was twelve years old;* and here, just before he died, we have him engaged in controversy. In this sense, he was like Jeremiah, *a man of contention; not striving, but striven with.* The great contenders with him, were, *the chief priests and the elders,* the judges of two distinct courts: the chief priests presided in the ecclesiastical court, in all matters of the Lord, as they are called; the elders of the people were judges of the civil courts, in temporal matters. See an idea of both, 2 Chron. xix. 5, 8, 11. These joined to attack Christ, thinking they should find or make him obnoxious either to the one or to the other. See how woefully degenerate that generation was, when the governors both in church and state, who should have been the great promoters of the Messiah's kingdom, were the great opposers of it! Here we have them disturbing him when he was preaching, *v.* 23. They would neither receive his instructions themselves, nor let others receive them. Observe,

I. As soon as he came into Jerusalem, he went to the temple, though he had been affronted there the day before, was there in the midst of enemies and in the mouth of danger; yet thither he went, for there he had a fairer opportunity of doing good to souls than any where else in Jerusalem. Though he came hungry to the city, and was disappointed of a breakfast at the barren fig-tree, yet, for aught that appears, he went straight to the temple, as one that *esteemed the words of God's mouth,* the preaching of them, *more than his necessary food.*

II. In the temple he was teaching; he had called it *a house of prayer* (*v.* 13), and here we have him preaching there. Note, In the solemn assemblies of Christians, praying and preaching must go together, and neither must encroach upon, or jostle out, the other. To make up communion with God, we must not only speak to him in prayer, but hear what he has to say to us by his word; ministers must *give themselves both to the word and to prayer,* Acts vi. 4. Now that Christ *taught in the temple,* that scripture was fulfilled (Isa. ii. 3), *Let us go up to the house of the Lord, and he will teach us his ways.* The priests of old often taught there *the good knowledge of the Lord;* but they never had such a teacher as this.

III. When Christ was teaching the people, the priests and elders came upon him, and challenged him to produce his orders; the hand of Satan was in this, to hinder him in his work. Note, It cannot but be a trouble to a faithful minister, to be taken off, or diverted from, plain and practical preaching, by an unavoidable necessity of engaging in controversies; yet good was brought out of this evil, for hereby occasion was given to Christ to dispel the objections that were advanced against him, to the greater satisfaction of his followers; and, while his adversaries thought by their power to have silenced him, he by his wisdom silenced them.

Now, in this dispute with them, we may observe,

1. How he was assaulted by their insolent

demand; *By what authority doest thou these things, and who gave thee this authority?* Had they duly considered his miracles, and the power by which he wrought them, they needed not to have asked this question; but they must have something to say for the shelter of an obstinate infidelity. "Thou ridest in triumph into Jerusalem, receivest the hosannas of the people, controllest in the temple, drivest out such as had license to be there, from the rulers of the temple, and paid them rent; thou art here preaching a new doctrine; whence hadst thou a commission to do all this? Was it from Cæsar, or from the high priest, or from God? Produce thy warrant, thy credentials. Dost not thou take too much upon thee?" Note, It is good for all that take upon them to act with authority, to put this question to themselves, "Who gave us that authority?" For, unless a man be clear in his own conscience concerning that, he cannot act with any comfort or hope of success. They who run before their warrant, run without their blessing, Jer. xxiii. 21, 22.

Christ had often said it, and proved it beyond contradiction, and Nicodemus, a master in Israël, had owned it, that he was *a teacher sent of God* (John iii. 2); yet, at this time of day, when that point had been so fully cleared and settled, they come to him with this question. (1.) In the ostentation of their own power, as chief priests and elders, which they thought authorized them to call him to an account in this manner. How haughtily do they ask, *Who gave thee this authority?* Intimating that he could have no authority, because he had none from them, 1 Kings xxii. 24; Jer. xx. 1. Note, It is common for the greatest abusers of their power to be the most rigorous assertors of it, and to take a pride and pleasure in any thing that looks like the exercise of it. (2.) It was to ensnare and entangle him. Should he refuse to answer this question, they would enter judgment against him upon *Nihil dicit—He says nothing;* would condemn him as standing mute; and would insinuate to the people, that his silence was a tacit confessing of himself to be a usurper: should he plead an authority from God, they would, as formerly, demand a sign from heaven, or make his *de*fence his *of*fence, and accuse him of blasphemy for it.

2. How he answered this demand with another, which would help them to answer it themselves (*v.* 24, 25); *I also will ask you one thing.* He declined giving them a direct answer, lest they should take advantage against him; but answers them with a question. Those that are *as sheep in the midst of wolves,* have need to *be wise as serpents: the heart of the wise studieth to answer.* We must *give a reason of the hope that is in us,* not only *with meekness, but with fear* (1 Pet. iii. 15), with prudent caution, lest truth be damaged, or ourselves endangered.

Now this question is concerning John's baptism, here put for his whole ministry, preaching as well as baptizing; "Was this *from heaven, or of men?* One of the two it must be; either what he did was of his own head, or he was sent of God to do it." Gamaliel's argument turned upon this hinge (Acts v. 38, 39); either *this counsel is of men or of God.* Though that which is manifestly bad cannot be of God, yet that which is seemingly good may be of men, nay of Satan, when *he transforms himself into an angel of light.* This question was not at all shuffling, to evade theirs; but,

(1.) If they answered this question, it would answer theirs: should they say, against their consciences, that John's baptism was of men, yet it would be easy to answer, *John did no miracle* (John x. 41), Christ did many; but should they say, as they could not but own, that John's baptism was from heaven (which was supposed in the questions sent him, John i. 21, *Art thou Elias, or that prophet?)* then their demand was answered, for he bare testimony to Christ. Note, Truths appear in the clearest light when they are taken in their due order; the resolving of the *previous* question will be a key to the *main* question.

(2.) If they refused to answer it, that would be a good reason why he should not offer proofs of his authority to men that were obstinately prejudiced against the strongest conviction; it was but to cast pearls before swine. Thus *he taketh the wise in their own craftiness* (1 Cor. iii. 19); and those that would not be convinced of the plainest truths, shall be convicted of the vilest malice, against John first, then against Christ, and in both against God.

3. How they were hereby baffled and run aground; they knew the truth, but would not own it, and so were taken in the snare they laid for our Lord Jesus. Observe,

(1.) How *they reasoned with themselves,* not concerning the merits of the cause, what proofs there were of the divine original of John's baptism; no, their care was, how to make their part good against Christ. Two things they considered and consulted, in this reasoning with themselves—their credit, and their safety; the same things which *they* principally aim at, who *seek their own things.*

[1.] They consider their own credit, which they would endanger if they should own John's baptism to be of God; for then Christ would ask them, before all the people, *Why did ye not believe him?* And to acknowledge that a doctrine is from God, and yet not to receive and entertain it, is the greatest absurdity and iniquity that a man can be charged with. Many that will not be kept by the fear of sin from neglecting and opposing that which they know to be true and good are kept by the fear of shame from owning that to be true and good which they neglect and oppose. Thus they *reject the counsel of*

God against themselves, in not submitting to John's baptism, and are left without excuse.

[2.] They consider their own safety, that they would expose themselves to the resentments of the people, if they should say that John's baptism was of men; *We fear the people, for all hold John as a prophet.* It seems, then, *First,* That the people had truer sentiments of John than the chief priests and the elders had, or, at least, were more free and faithful in declaring their sentiments. This people, of whom they said in their pride that they *knew not the law, and were cursed* (John vii. 49), it seems, knew the gospel, and were blessed. *Secondly,* That the chief priests and elders stood in awe of the common people, which is an evidence that things were in disorder among them, and that mutual jealousies were at a great height; that the government was become obnoxious to the hatred and scorn of the people, and the scripture was fulfilled, *I have made you contemptible and base,* Mal. ii. 8, 9. If they had kept their integrity, and done their duty, they had kept up their authority, and needed not to fear the people. We find sometimes that the people feared them, and it served them for a reason why they did not confess Christ, John ix. 22, xii. 42. Note, Those could not but fear the people, who studied only how to make the people fear them. *Thirdly,* That it is usually the temper even of common people, to be zealous for the honour of that which they account sacred and divine. If they *account John as a prophet,* they will not endure that it should be said, *His baptism was of men;* hence the hottest contests have been about holy things. *Fourthly,* That the chief priests and elders were kept from an open denial of the truth, even against the conviction of their own minds, not by the fear of God, but purely by the fear of the people; as the *fear of man* may *bring* good people into *a snare* (Prov. xxix. 25), so sometimes it may keep bad people from being *overmuch wicked, lest they should die before their time,* Eccl. vii. 17. Many bad people would be much worse than they are, if they durst.

(2.) How they replied to our Saviour, and so dropped the question. They fairly confessed *We cannot tell;* that is, "We will not;" ὀυκ ὄι δαμεν—*We never knew.* The more shame for them, while they pretended to be leaders of the people, and by their office were obliged to take cognizance of such things; when they would not confess their knowledge, they were constrained to confess their ignorance. And observe, by the way, when they said, *We cannot tell,* they told a lie, for they knew that John's baptism was of God. Note, There are many who are more afraid of the *shame* of lying than of the *sin,* and therefore scruple not to speak that which they know to be false concerning their own thoughts and apprehensions, their affections and intentions, or their remembering or forgetting of things, because in those things they know nobody can disprove them.

Thus Christ avoided the snare they laid for him, and justified himself in refusing to gratify them; *Neither tell I you by what authority I do these things.* If they be so wicked and base as either not to believe, or not to confess, that the baptism of John was from heaven (though it obliged to repentance, that great duty, and sealed the kingdom of God at hand, that great promise), they were not fit to be discoursed with concerning Christ's authority; for men of such a disposition could not be convinced of the truth, nay, they could not but be provoked by it, and therefore *he that is thus ignorant, let him be ignorant still.* Note, Those that imprison the truths they know, in unrighteousness (either by not professing them, or by not practising according to them), are justly denied the further truths they enquire after, Rom. i. 18, 19. Take away the talent from him that buried it; those that *will not* see, *shall not* see.

28 But what think ye? A *certain*
man had two sons; and he came to
the first, and said, Son, go work to
day in my vineyard. 29 He answered
and said, I will not: but afterward
he repented, and went. 30 And he
came to the second, and said likewise.
And he answered and said, I *go,* sir:
and went not. 31 Whether of them
twain did the will of *his* father? They
say unto him, The first. Jesus saith
unto them, Verily I say unto you,
That the publicans and the harlots go
into the kingdom of God before you.
32 For John came unto you in the
way of righteousness, and ye believed
him not: but the publicans and the
harlots believed him: and ye, when
ye had seen *it,* repented not afterward, that ye might believe him.

As Christ instructed his disciples by parables, which made the instructions the more easy, so sometimes he convinced his adversaries by parables, which bring reproofs more close, and make men, or ever they are aware, to reprove themselves. Thus Nathan convinced David by a parable (2 Sam. xii. 1), and the woman of Tekoa surprised him in like manner, 2 Sam. xiv. 2. Reproving parables are appeals to the offenders themselves, and judge them out of their own mouths. This Christ designs here, as appears by the first words (*v.* 28), *But what think you?*

In these verses, we have the parable of the *two sons* sent to work in the vineyard, the scope of which is to show that they who knew not John's baptism to be of God, were shamed even by the publicans and harlots, who knew it, and owned it. Here is,

I. The parable itself, which represents two sorts of persons; some that prove better than they promise, represented by the first of those sons; others that promise better than they prove, represented by the second.

1. They had both one and the same father, which signifies that God is a common Father to all mankind. There are favours which all alike receive from him, and obligations which all alike lie under to him; *Have we not all one Father?* Yes, and yet there is a vast difference between men's characters.

2. They had both the same command given them; *Son, go work to-day in my vineyard.* Parents should not breed up their children in idleness; nothing is more pleasing, and yet nothing more pernicious, to youth than that. Lam. iii. 27. God sets his children to work, though they are all heirs. This command is given to every one of us. Note, (1.) The work of religion, which we are called to engage in, is vineyard work, creditable, profitable, and pleasant. By the sin of Adam we were turned out to work upon the common, and to eat the herb of the field; but by the grace of our Lord Jesus we are called to work again in the vineyard. (2.) The gospel call to work in the vineyard, requires present obedience; *Son, go work* to-day, while it is called to-day, because *the night comes when no man can work.* We were not sent into the world to be idle, nor had we daylight given us to play by; and therefore, if ever we mean to do any thing for God and our souls, why not now? Why not to-day? (3.) The exhortation to go *work to-day in the vineyard,* speaketh unto us *as unto children* (Heb. xii. 5); *Son, go work.* It is the command of a Father, which carries with it both authority and affection, a Father that pities his children, and considers their frame, and will not overtask them (Ps. ciii. 13, 14), a Father that is very tender of *his Son that serves him,* Mal iii. 17. If we work in our Father's vineyard, we work for ourselves.

3. Their conduct was very different.

(1.) One of the sons did better than he said, proved better than he promised. His answer was bad, but his actions were good.

[1.] Here is the untoward answer that he gave to his father; he said, flat and plain, *I will not.* See to what a degree of impudence the corrupt nature of man rises, to say, *I will not,* to the command of a Father; such a command of such a Father; they are impudent children and stiff-hearted. Those that will not bend, surely they cannot blush; if they had any degree of modesty left them, they could not say, *We will not.* Jer. ii. 25. Excuses are bad, but downright denials are worse; yet such peremptory refusals do the calls of the gospel often meet with. *First,* Some love their ease, and will not work; they would live in the world, as leviathan in the waters, to play therein (Ps. civ. 26); they do not love working. *Secondly,* Their hearts are so much upon their own fields, that they are not for working in God's vineyard. They love the business of the world better than the business of their religion. Thus some by the delights of sense, and others by the employments of the world, are kept from doing that great work which they were sent into the world about, and so *stand all the day idle.*

[2.] Here is the happy change of his mind, and of his way, upon second thoughts; *Afterward he repented, and went.* Note, There are many who in the beginning are wicked and wilful, and very unpromising, who afterward repent and mend, and come to something. Some that God hath chosen, are suffered for a great while to run to a great excess of riot; *Such were some of you,* 1 Cor. vi. 11. These are set forth for *patterns of long-suffering,* 1 Tim. i. 16. *Afterward he repented.* Repentance is *μετανοία — an after-wit:* and *μεταμελεία—an after-care.* Better late than never. Observe, When he repented, he went; that was the *fruit meet for repentance.* The only evidence of our repentance for our former resistance, is, immediately to comply, and set to work; and then what is past, shall be pardoned, and all shall be well. See what a kind Father God is; he resents not the affront of our refusals, as justly he might. He that told his father to his face, that he *would not* do as he bid him, deserved to be turned out of doors, and disinherited; but our God *waits to be gracious,* and, notwithstanding our former follies, if we repent and mend, will favourably accept of us; blessed be God, we are under a covenant that leaves room for such a repentance.

(2.) The other son said better than he did, promised better than he proved; his answer was good but his actions bad. To him the father *said likewise, v.* 30. The gospel call, though very different, is, in effect, the same to all, and is carried on with an even tenour. We have all the same commands, engagements, encouragements, though to some they are a savour of life unto life, to others of death unto death. Observe,

[1.] How fairly this other son promised; *He said, I go, sir.* He gives his father a title of respect, *sir.* Note, It becomes children to speak respectfully to their parents. It is one branch of that honour which the fifth commandment requires. He professes a ready obedience, *I go;* not, "I will go by and by," but, "Ready, sir, you may depend upon it, I go just now." This answer we should give from the heart heartily to all the calls and commands of the word of God. See Jer. iii. 22; Ps. xxvii. 8.

[2.] How he failed in the performance; *He went not.* Note, There are many that give good words, and make fair promises, in religion, and those from some good motions for the present, that rest there, and go no further, and so come to nothing. Saying and doing are two things; and many there are that say, and do not; it is particularly charged upon the Pharisees, *ch.* xxiii. 3. Many with their mouth show much love, but their heart goes another way. They had a good mind to be religious, but they met with something to be done, that was too hard, or something to be parted with, that was too dear, and so their purposes are to no purpose. Buds and blossoms are not fruit.

II. A general appeal upon the parable; *Whether of them twain did the will of his father? v.* 31. They both had their faults, one was rude, and the other was false; such variety of exercises parents sometimes have in the different humours of their children, and they have need of a great deal of wisdom and grace to know what is the best way of managing them. But the question is, Which was the better of the two, and the less faulty? And it was soon resolved; the first, because his actions were better than his words, and his latter end than his beginning. This they had learned from the common sense of mankind, who would much rather deal with one that will be better than his word, than with one that will be false to his word. And, in the intention of it, they had learned from the account God gives of the rule of his judgment (Ezek. xviii. 21—24), that if *the sinner turn from his wickedness,* he shall be pardoned; and *if the righteous man turn from his righteousness,* he shall be rejected. The tenour of the whole scripture gives us to understand that those are accepted as doing their Father's will, who, wherein they have missed it, are sorry for it, and do better.

III. A particular application of it to the matter in hand, *v.* 31, 32. The primary scope of the parable is, to show how the publicans and harlots, who never talked of the Messiah and his kingdom, yet entertained the doctrine, and submitted to the discipline, of John the Baptist, his forerunner, when the priests and elders, who were big with expectations of the Messiah, and seemed very ready to go into his measures, slighted John the Baptist, and ran counter to the designs of his mission. But it has a further reach; the Gentiles were *sometimes disobedient,* had been long so, children of disobedience, like the elder son (Tit. iii. 3, 4); yet, when the gospel was preached to them, they became obedient to the faith; whereas the Jews who said, *I go, sir,* promised fair (Exod. xxiv. 7; Josh. xxiv. 24); yet went not; they did but flatter God with their mouth, Ps. lxxviii. 36.

In Christ's application of this parable, observe,

1. How he proves that John's baptism was *from heaven, and not of men.* "If you *cannot* tell," saith Christ, "you *might* tell,"

(1.) By the scope of his ministry; *John came unto you in the way of righteousness.* Would you know whether John had his commission from heaven, remember the rule of trial, *By their fruits ye shall know them;* the fruits of their doctrines, the fruits of their doings. Observe but their way, and you may trace out both their rise and their tendency. Now it was evident that John came *in the way of righteousness.* In his ministry, he taught people to repent, and to work the works of righteousness. In his conversation, he was a great example of strictness, and seriousness, and contempt of the world, denying himself, and doing good to every body else. Christ *therefore* submitted to the baptism of John, because it *became him to fulfil all righteousness.* Now, if John thus came in the way of righteousness, could they be ignorant that his baptism was from heaven, or make any doubt of it?

(2.) By the success of his ministry; *The publicans and the harlots believed him;* he did abundance of good among the worst sort of people. St. Paul proves his apostleship by the seals of his ministry, 1 Cor. ix. 2. If God had not sent John the Baptist, he would not have crowned his labours with such wonderful success, nor have made him so instrumental as he was for the conversion of souls. If publicans and harlots believe his report, surely the arm of the Lord is with him. The people's profiting is the minister's best testimonial.

2. How he reproves them for their contempt of John's baptism, which yet, for fear of the people, they were not willing to own. To shame them for it, he sets before them the faith, repentance, and obedience, of the publicans and harlots, which aggravated their unbelief and impenitence. As he shows, *ch.* xi. 21, that the less likely would have repented, so here that the less likely did repent.

(1.) The publicans and harlots were like the first son in the parable, from whom little of religion was expected. They promised little good, and those that knew them promised themselves little good from them. Their disposition was generally rude, and their conversation profligate and debauched; and yet many of them were wrought upon by the ministry of John, who came in the spirit and power of Elias. See Luke vii. 29. These fitly represented the Gentile world; for, as Dr. Whitby observes, the Jews generally ranked the publicans with the heathen; nay, and the heathen were represented by the Jews as harlots, and born of harlots, John viii. 41.

(2.) The scribes and Pharisees, the chief priests and elders, and indeed the Jewish nation in general, were like the other son that gave good words; they made a specious profession of religion, and yet, when the kingdom of the Messiah was brought among them by the baptism of John, they slighted it, they turned their back upon it, nay they *lifted up the heel against it.* A hypocrite is more hardly convinced and converted than a gross sinner; the form of godliness, if that be rested in, becomes one of Satan's strongholds, by which he opposes the power of godliness. It was an aggravation of their unbelief, [1.] That John was such an excellent person, that he came, and came to them, in *the way of righteousness.* The better the means are, the greater will the account be, if not improved. [2.] That, when they saw the publicans and harlots go before them into the kingdom of heaven, they did not afterward repent and believe; were not thereby provoked to a holy emulation, Rom. xi. 14. Shall publicans and harlots go away with grace and glory; and shall not we put in for a share? Shall our inferiors be more holy and more happy than we? They had not the wit and grace that Esau had, who was moved to take other measures than he had done, by the example of his younger brother, Gen. xxviii. 6. These proud priests, that set up for leaders, scorned to follow, though it were into the kingdom of heaven, especially to follow publicans; through the pride of their countenance, they would not seek after God, after Christ, Ps. x. 4.

33 Hear another parable: There was a certain householder, which planted a vineyard, and hedged it round about, and digged a winepress in it, and built a tower, and let it out to husbandmen, and went into a far country: 34 And when the time of the fruit drew near, he sent his servants to the husbandmen, that they might receive the fruits of it. 35 And the husbandmen took his servants, and beat one, and killed another, and stoned another. 36 Again, he sent other servants more than the first: and they did unto them likewise. 37 But last of all he sent unto them his son, saying, They will reverence my son. 38 But when the husbandmen saw the son, they said among themselves, This is the heir; come, let us kill him, and let us seize on his inheritance. 39 And they caught him, and cast *him* out of the vineyard, and slew *him.* 40 When the lord therefore of the vineyard cometh, what will he do unto those husbandmen? 41 They say unto him, He will miserably destroy those wicked men, and will let out *his* vineyard unto other husbandmen, which shall render him the fruits in their seasons. 42 Jesus saith unto them, Did ye never read in the scriptures, The stone which the builders rejected, the same is become the head of the corner: this is the Lord's doing, and it is marvellous in our eyes? 43 Therefore say I unto you, The kingdom of God shall be taken from you, and given to a nation bringing forth the fruits thereof. 45 And whosoever shall fall on this stone shall be broken: but on whomsoever it shall fall, it will grind him to powder. 45 And when the chief priests and Pharisees had heard his parables, they perceived that he spake of them. 46 But when they sought to lay hands on him, they feared the multitude, because they took him for a prophet.

This parable plainly sets forth the sin and ruin of the Jewish nation; they and their leaders are the husbandmen here; and what is spoken for conviction to them, is spoken for caution to all that enjoy the privileges of the visible church, not to be high-minded, but fear.

I. We have here the privileges of the Jewish church, represented by the letting out of a vineyard to the husbandmen; they were as tenants holding by, from, and under, God the great Householder. Observe,

1. How God established a church for himself in the world. The kingdom of God upon earth is here compared to a vineyard, furnished with all things requisite to an advantageous management and improvement of it. (1.) He planted this vineyard. The church is *the planting of the Lord,* Isa. lxi. 3. The forming of a church is a work by itself, like the planting of a vineyard, which requires a great deal of cost and care. It is *the vineyard which his right hand has planted* (Ps. lxxx. 15), planted with the *choicest vine* (Isa. v. 2), *a noble vine,* Jer. ii. 21. The earth of itself produces thorns and briars; but vines must be planted. The being of a church is owing to God's distinguishing favour, and his manifesting himself to some, and not to others. (2.) He hedged it round about. Note, God's church in the world is taken under his special protection. It is *a hedge round about,* like that about Job on every side (Job i. 10), a wall of fire, Zech. ii. 5. Wherever God has a church, it is, and will always be, his peculiar care. The covenant of circumcision and the ceremonial law were a hedge or a wall of partition about the Jewish church, which is taken down by Christ; who yet has appointed a gospel order and discipline to be the hedge of his church. He will not have his vineyard to lie in common, that those who are without, may thrust in at pleasure; not to lie at large, that those who are within, may lash out at pleasure; but care is taken to set bounds about this holy mountain. (3.) He *digged a wine-press and built a tower.* The altar of

burnt-offerings was the wine-press, to which all the offerings were brought. God instituted ordinances in his church, for the due oversight of it, and for the promoting of its fruitfulness. What could have been done more to make it every way convenient?

2. How he entrusted these visible church-privileges with the nation and people of the Jews, especially their chief priests and elders; he let it out to them as husbandmen, not because he had need of them as landlords have of their tenants, but because he would try them, and be honoured by them. When in Judah God was known, and his name was great, when they were taken to be to God *for a people, and for a name, and for a praise* (Jer. xiii. 11), when he *revealed his word unto Jacob* (Ps. cxlvii. 19), when the *covenant of life and peace* was made with Levi (Mal. ii. 4, 5), then this vineyard was let out. See an abstract of the lease, Cant. viii. 11, 12. The Lord of the vineyard was to have *a thousand pieces of silver* (compare Isa. vii. 13); the main profit was to be his, but the keepers were to have two hundred, a competent and comfortable encouragement. And then he *went into a far country*. When God had in a visible appearance settled the Jewish church at mount Sinai, he did in a manner withdraw; they had no more such open vision, but were left to the written word. Or, they imagined that he was gone into a far country, as Israel, when they made the calf, fancied that Moses was gone. They put far from them the evil day.

II. God's expectation of rent from these husbandmen, *v.* 34. It was a reasonable expectation; for *who plants a vineyard, and eats not of the fruit thereof?* Note, From those that enjoy church-privileges, both ministers and people, God looks for fruit accordingly. 1. His expectations were not hasty; he did not demand a fore-rent, though he had been at such expense upon it; but staid *till the time of the fruit drew near*, as it did now that John preached the *kingdom of heaven is at hand*. God waits to be gracious, that he may give us time. 2. They were not high; he did not require them to come at their peril, upon penalty of forfeiting their lease if they ran behind-hand; but he sent his *servants to them*, to remind them of their duty, and of the rent-day, and to help them in gathering in the fruit, and making return of it. These servants were the prophets of the Old Testament, who were sent, and sometimes directly, to the people of the Jews, to reprove and instruct them. 3. They were not hard; it was only to *receive the fruits*. He did not demand more than they could make of it, but some fruit of that which he himself planted—an observance of the laws and statutes he gave them. What could have been done more reasonable? Israel was an empty vine, nay it was become the degenerate plant of a strange vine, and brought forth wild grapes.

III. The husbandmen's baseness in abusing the messengers that were sent to them.

1. When he sent them his servants, they abused them, though they represented the master himself, and spoke in his name. Note, The calls and reproofs of the word, if they do not engage, will but exasperate. See here what hath all along been the lot of God's faithful messengers, more or less; (1.) To suffer; *so persecuted they the prophets*, who were hated with a cruel hatred. They not only despised and reproached them, but treated them as the worst of malefactors—they beat them, and killed them, and stoned them. They beat Jeremiah, killed Isaiah, stoned Zechariah the son of Jehoiada in the temple. If they that *live godly in Christ Jesus* themselves shall *suffer persecution*, much more they that press others to it. This was God's old quarrel with the Jews, misusing his prophets, 2 Chron. xxxvi. 16. (2.) It has been their lot to suffer from their Master's own tenants; they were the husbandmen that treated them thus, the chief priests and elders that *sat in Moses's chair*, that professed religion and relation to God; these were the most bitter enemies of the Lord's prophets, that cast them out, and killed them, and said, *Let the Lord be glorified*, Isa. lxvi. 5. See Jer. xx. 1, 2; xxvi. 11.

Now see, [1.] How God persevered in his goodness to them. He sent other servants, more than the first; though the first sped not, but were abused. He had sent them John the Baptist, and him they had beheaded; and yet he sent them his disciples, to prepare his way. O the riches of the patience and forbearance of God, in keeping up in his church a despised, persecuted ministry! [2.] How they persisted in their wickedness. They *did unto them likewise*. One sin makes way for another of the same kind. They that are drunk with the blood of the saints, add drunkenness to thirst, and still cry, Give, give.

2. At length, he sent them his Son; we have seen God's goodness in sending, and their badness in abusing, the servants; but in the latter instance both these exceed themselves.

(1.) Never did grace appear more gracious than in *sending the Son*. This was done *last of all*. Note, All the prophets were harbingers and forerunners to Christ. He was sent last; for if nothing else would work upon them, surely this would; it was therefore reserved for the *ratio ultima—the last expedient*. *Surely they will reverence my Son*, and therefore I will send him. Note, It might reasonably be expected that the Son of God, when he came to his own, should be reverenced; and reverence to Christ would be a powerful and effectual principle of fruitfulness and obedience, to the glory of God; if they will but reverence the Son, the point is gained. *Surely they will reverence my Son*, for he comes with more authority than the servants could; judgment is committed to him, that *all men should honour him.* There is greater danger in refusing him than in despising Moses's law.

(2.) Never did sin appear more sinful than in the abusing of him, which was now to be done in two or three days. Observe,

[1.] How it was plotted (*v.* 38); *When they saw the Son:* when he came, whom the people owned and followed as the Messiah, who would either have the rent paid, or distrain for it; this touched their copyhold, and they were resolved to make one bold push for it, and to preserve their wealth and grandeur by taking *him* out of the way, who was the only hindrance of it, and rival with them. *This is the heir, come, let us kill him.* Pilate and Herod, the princes of this world, *knew not;* for *if they had known, they would not have crucified the Lord of glory,* 1 Cor. ii. 8. But the *chief priests and elders* knew that *this was the heir,* at least, some of them; and therefore *Come, let us kill him.* Many are killed for what they have. The chief thing they envied him, and for which they hated and feared him, was his interest in the people, and their hosannas, which, if he was taken off, they hope to engross securely to themselves. They pretended that he must die, to save the people from the Romans (John xi. 50); but really he must die, to save their hypocrisy and tyranny from that reformation which the expected kingdom of the Messiah would certainly bring along with it. He drives the buyers and sellers out of the temple; and therefore *let us kill him;* and then, as if the premises must of course go to the occupant, *let us seize on his inheritance.* They thought, if they could but get rid of this Jesus, they should carry all before them in the church without control, might impose what traditions, and force the people to what submissions, they pleased. Thus they *take counsel against the Lord and his Anointed;* but he that *sits in heaven,* laughs to see them *outshot in their own bow;* for, while they thought to kill him, and so to seize on his inheritance, he went by his cross to his crown, and they were broken in pieces with a rod of iron, and their inheritance seized, Ps. ii. 2, 3, 6, 9.

[2.] How this plot was executed, *v.* 39. While they were so set upon killing him, in pursuance of their design to secure their own pomp and power, and while he was so set upon dying, in pursuance of his design to subdue Satan, and save his chosen, no wonder if they soon *caught him, and slew him,* when his hour was come. Though the Roman power condemned him, yet it is still charged upon the chief priests and elders; for they were not only the prosecutors, but the principal agents, and had *the greater sin. Ye have taken,* Acts ii. 23. Nay, looking upon him to be as unworthy to live, as they were unwilling he should, *they cast him out of the vineyard,* out of the holy church, which they supposed themselves to have the key of, and out of the holy city, for he was crucified *without the gate,* Heb. xiii. 12. As if *He* had been the shame and reproach, who was the greatest glory, of his people Israel. Thus they who persecuted the servants, persecuted the Son; as men treat God's ministers, they would treat Christ himself, if he were with them.

IV. Here is their doom read out of their own mouths, *v.* 40, 41. He puts it to them, *When the Lord of the vineyard cometh, what will he do unto these husbandmen?* He puts it to themselves, for their stronger conviction, that *knowing the judgment of God* against them which do such things, they might be the more inexcusable. Note, God's proceedings are so unexceptionable, that there needs but an appeal to sinners themselves concerning the equity of them. God will be *justified when he speaks.* They could readily answer, *He will miserably destroy those wicked men.* Note, Many can easily prognosticate the dismal consequences of other people's sins, that see not what will be the end of their own.

1. Our Saviour, in his question, supposes that *the lord of the vineyard will come,* and reckon with them. God is the Lord of the vineyard; the property is his, and he will make *them* know it, who now *lord it over his heritage,* as if it were all their own. The Lord of the vineyard will come. Persecutors say in their hearts, He *delays his coming,* he *doth not see,* he *will not require;* but they shall find, though he bear long with them, he will not bear always. It is comfort to abused saints and ministers, that *the Lord is at hand,* the *Judge stands before the door.* When he comes, what will he do to carnal professors? What will he do to cruel persecutors? They must be called to account, they have their day now; but he *sees that his day is coming.*

2. They, in their answer, suppose that it will be a terrible reckoning; the crime appearing so very black, you may be sure,

(1.) That he will *miserably destroy those wicked men;* it is destruction that is their doom. Κακѳς κακῶς ἀπολέσει—*Malos male perdet.* Let men never expect to do ill, and fare well. This was fulfilled upon the Jews, in that miserable destruction which was brought upon them by the Romans, and was completed about forty years after this; an unparalleled ruin, attended with all the most dismal aggravating circumstances. It will be fulfilled upon all that tread in the steps of their wickedness; hell is everlasting destruction, and it will be the most miserable destruction to them of all others, that have enjoyed the greatest share of church privileges, and have not improved them. The hottest place in hell will be the portion of hypocrites and persecutors.

(2.) That he will *let out his vineyard to other husbandmen.* Note, God will have a church in the world, notwithstanding the unworthiness and opposition of many that abuse the privileges of it. The unbelief and frowardness of man shall not make the word of God of no effect. If one will not, another will. The Jews' leavings were the Gentiles' feast. Persecutors may destroy the ministers, but cannot destroy the church. The Jews imagined that no doubt *they were the people*, and wisdom and holiness must *die with them;* and if they were cut off, what would God do for a church in the world? But when God makes use of any to bear up his name, it is not because he needs them, nor is he at all beholden to them. If we were made a desolation and an astonishment, God could build a flourishing church upon our ruins; for he is never at a loss what to do for his great name, whatever becomes of us, and of our place and nation.

V. The further illustration and application of this by Christ himself, telling them, in effect, that they had rightly judged.

1. He illustrates it by referring to a scripture fulfilled in this (*v.* 42); *Did ye never read in the scriptures?* Yes, no doubt, they had often read and sung it, but had not considered it. We lose the benefit of what we read for want of meditation. The scripture he quotes is Ps. cxviii. 22, 23, the same context out of which the children fetched their hosannas. The same word yields matter of praise and comfort to Christ's friends and followers, which speaks conviction and terror to his enemies. Such a two-edged sword is the word of God. That scripture, the *Stone which the builders refused is become the headstone of the corner*, illustrates the preceding parable, especially that part of it which refers to Christ.

(1.) The builders' rejecting of the stone is the same with the husbandmen's abusing of the son that was sent to them. The chief priests and the elders were the builders, had the oversight of the Jewish church, which was God's building: and they would not allow Christ a place in their building, would not admit his doctrine or laws into their constitution; they threw him aside as a despised broken vessel, a stone that would serve only for a stepping-stone, to be trampled upon.

(2.) The advancing of this stone to be the head of the corner is the same with *letting out the vineyard to other husbandmen.* He who was rejected by the Jews was embraced by the Gentiles; and to that church where there is no difference of circumcision or uncircumcision, *Christ is all, and in all.* His authority over the gospel church, and influence upon it, his ruling it as the Head, and uniting it as the Corner-stone, are the great tokens of his exhaltation. Thus, in spite of the malice of the priests and elders, he *divided a portion with the great,* and received *his kingdom,* though they would not have him to reign over them.

(3.) The hand of God was in all this; *This is the Lord's doing.* Even the rejecting of him by the Jewish builders was by the determinate counsel and foreknowledge of God; he permitted and overruled it; much more was his advancement to the Head of the corner; his right hand and his holy arm brought it about; it was God himself that *highly exalted him,* and gave him *a name above every name; and it is marvellous in our eyes.* The wickedness of the Jews that rejected him is marvellous; that men should be so prejudiced against their own interest! See Isa. xxix. 9, 10, 14. The honour done him by the Gentile world, notwithstanding the abuses done him by his own people, is marvellous; that he whom men despised and abhorred, should be adored by kings! Isa. xlix. 7. But *it is the Lord's doing.*

2. He applies it to them, and application is the life of preaching.

(1.) He applies the sentence which they had passed (*v.* 41), and turns it upon themselves; not the former part of it, concerning the miserable destruction of the husbandmen (he could not bear to speak of that), but the latter part, of *letting out the vineyard to others;* because though it looked black upon the Jews, it spoke good to the Gentiles. Know then,

[1.] That the Jews shall be unchurched; *The kingdom of God shall be taken from you.* This turning out of the husbandmen speaks the same doom with that of dismantling the vineyard, and laying it common, Isa. v. 5. To the Jews had long pertained *the adoption and the glory* (Rom. ix. 4); to them were committed the *oracles of God* (Rom. iii. 2), and the sacred trust of revealed religion, and bearing up of God's name in the world (Ps. lxxvi. 1, 2); but now it shall be so no longer. They were not only unfruitful in the use of their privileges, but, under pretence of them, opposed the gospel of Christ, and so forfeited them, and it was not long ere the forfeiture was taken. Note, It is a righteous thing with God to remove church privileges from those that not only sin against them, but sin with them, Rev. ii. 4, 5. The kingdom of God was taken from the Jews, not only by the temporal judgments that befel them, but by the spiritual judgments they lay under, their blindness of mind, hardness of heart, and indignation at the gospel, Rom. xi. 8—10; 1 Thess. ii. 15.

[2.] That the Gentiles shall be taken in. God needs not ask us leave whether he shall have a church in the world; though his vine be plucked up in one place, he will find another to plant it in. He will give it ἔθνει—*to the Gentile world,* that will *bring forth the fruit of it.* They who had been not a people, and had not obtained mercy, became favourites of Heaven. This is the mystery which blessed Paul was so much affected with (Rom. xi. 30, 33), and which the Jews were so much affronted by, Acts xxii. 21, 22. At the first planting of Israel in Canaan, the *fall of the Gentiles was the riches of Israel* (Ps. cxxxv. 10, 11), so, at their extirpation, the fall of Israel was the riches of the Gentiles, Rom. xi. 12. It shall go to *a nation bringing forth the fruits thereof.* Note, Christ knows beforehand who will bring forth gospel fruits in the use of gospel means; because our fruitfulness is all the work of his own hands, and *known unto God are all his works.* They shall bring forth the fruits better than the Jews had done; God has had more glory from the New-Testament church than from that of the Old Testament; for, when he changes, it shall not be to his loss.

(2.) He applies the scripture which he had quoted (*v.* 42), to their terror, *v.* 44. This *Stone,* which the *builders refused, is set for the fall of many in Israel;* and we have here the doom of two sorts of people, for whose fall it proves that Christ is set.

[1.] Some, through ignorance, stumble at Christ in his estate of humiliation; when this Stone lies on the earth, where the builders threw it, they, through their blindness and carelessness, fall on it, fall over it, and *they shall be broken.* The offence they take at Christ, will not hurt him, any more than he that stumbles, hurts the stone he stumbles at; but it will hurt themselves; they will fall, and be broken, and snared, Isa. viii. 14; 1 Pet. ii. 7, 8. The unbelief of sinners will be their ruin.

[2.] Others, through malice, oppose Christ, and bid defiance to him in his estate of exaltation, when this Stone is advanced to the head of the corner; and on them *it shall fall,* for they pull it on their own heads, as the Jews did by that challenge, *His blood be upon us and upon our children,* and *it will grind them to powder.* The former seems to bespeak the sin and ruin of all unbelievers; this is the greater sin, and sorer ruin, of persecutors, that *kick against the pricks,* and persist in it. Christ's kingdom will be a burthensome stone to all those that attempt to overthrow it, or heave it out of its place; see Zech. xii. 3. This Stone cut out of the mountain without hands, will break in pieces all opposing power, Dan. ii. 34, 35. Some make this an allusion to the manner of stoning to death among the Jews. The malefactors were first thrown down violently from a high scaffold upon a great stone, which would much bruise them; but then they threw another great stone upon them, which would crush them to pieces: one way or other, Christ will utterly destroy all those that fight against him. If they be so stout-hearted, that they are not destroyed by falling on this stone, yet it shall fall on them, and so destroy them. He will *strike through kings,* he will *fill the places with dead bodies,* Ps. cx. 5, 6. None ever hardened his heart against God and prospered.

Lastly, The entertainment which this discourse of Christ met with among the chief priests and elders, that heard his parables.

1. *They perceived that he spake of them* (*v.* 45), and that in what they said (*v.* 41) they had but read their own doom. Note, A guilty conscience needs no accuser, and sometimes will save a minister the labour of saying, *Thou art the man. Mutato nomine, de te fabula narratur—Change but the name, the tale is told of thee.* So quick and powerful is the word of God, and such a discerner of the thoughts and intents of the heart, that it is easy for bad men (if conscience be not quite seared) to perceive that it speaks of them.

2. *They sought to lay hands on him.* Note, When those who hear the reproofs of the word, perceive that it speaks of them, if it do not do them a great deal of good, it will certainly do them a great deal of hurt. If they be not pricked to the heart with conviction and contrition, as they were Acts ii. 37, they will be cut to the heart with rage and indignation, as they were Acts v. 33.

3. They durst not do it, *for fear of the multitude, who took him for a prophet,* though not for the Messiah; this served to keep the Pharisees in awe. The fear of the people restrained them from speaking ill of John (*v.* 26), and here from doing ill to Christ. Note, God has many ways of restraining the remainders of wrath, as he has of making that which breaks out redound to his praise, Ps. lxxvi. 10.

CHAP. XXII.

This chapter is a continuation of Christ's discourses in the temple, two or three days before he died. His discourses then are largely recorded, as being of special weight and consequence. In this chapter, we have, I. Instruction given, by the parable of the marriage-supper, concerning the rejection of the Jews, and the calling of the Gentiles (ver. 1—10), and, by the doom of the guest that had not the wedding-garment, the danger of hypocrisy in the profession of Christianity, ver. 11—14. II. Disputes with the Pharisees, Sadducees, and scribes, who opposed Christ, 1. Concerning paying tribute to Cæsar, ver. 15—22. 2. Concerning the resurrection of the dead, and the future state, ver. 23—33. 3. Concerning the great commandment of the law, ver. 34—40. 4. Concerning the relation of the Messiah to David, ver. 41—46.

AND Jesus answered and spake
unto them again by parables,
and said, 2 The kingdom of heaven
is like unto a certain king, which made
a marriage for his son, 3 And sent
forth his servants to call them that
were bidden to the wedding: and they
would not come. 4 Again, he sent
forth other servants, saying, Tell them
which are bidden, Behold, I have prepared my dinner: my oxen and *my*
fatlings *are* killed, and all things *are*
ready: come unto the marriage. 5
But they made light of *it,* and went
their ways, one to his farm, another
to his merchandise: 6 And the remnant took his servants, and entreated
them spitefully, and slew *them.* 7
But when the king heard *thereof,* he
was wroth: and he sent forth his
armies, and destroyed those murderers, and burned up their city. 8

Then saith he to his servants, The
wedding is ready, but they which were
bidden were not worthy. 9 Go ye
therefore into the highways, and as
many as ye shall find, bid to the marriage. 10 So those servants went out
into the highways, and gathered together all as many as they found, both
bad and good: and the wedding was
furnished with guests. 11 And when
the king came in to see the guests, he
saw there a man which had not on a
wedding garment: 12 And he saith
unto him, Friend, how camest thou in
hither not having a wedding garment?
and he was speechless. 13 Then
said the king to his servants, Bind
him hand and foot, and take him
away, and cast *him* into outer darkness; there shall be weeping and
gnashing of teeth. 14 For many are
called, but few *are* chosen.

We have here the parable of the guests invited to *the wedding-feast.* In this it is said (*v.* 1), *Jesus answered,* not to what his opposers *said* (for they were put to silence), but to what they *thought,* when they were wishing for an opportunity to *lay hands on him, ch.* xxi. 46. Note, Christ knows how to answer men's thoughts, for he is a Discerner of them. Or, He *answered,* that is, he continued his discourse to the same purport; for this parable represents the gospel offer, and the entertainment it meets with, as the former, but under another similitude. The parable of the vineyard represents the sin of the rulers that persecuted the prophets; it shows also the sin of the people, who generally neglected the message, while their great ones were persecuting the messengers.

I. Gospel preparations are here represented by a feast which a king made *at the marriage of his son;* such is *the kingdom of heaven,* such the provision made for precious souls, in and by the new covenant. The *King* is God, *a great King, King of kings.* Now,

1. Here is *a marriage made for his son.* Christ is the Bridegroom, the church is the bride; the gospel-day is *the day of his espousals,* Cant. iii. 11. Behold by faith *the church of the first-born, that are written in heaven,* and were given to Christ by him whose they were; and in them you see *the bride, the Lamb's wife,* Rev. xxi. 9. The gospel covenant is a marriage covenant betwixt Christ and believers, and it is a marriage of God's making. This branch of the similitude is only mentioned, and not prosecuted here.

2. Here is *a dinner prepared for this marriage, v.* 4. All the privileges of church-membership, and all the blessings of the new covenant, pardon of sin, the favour of God, peace of conscience, the promises of the gospel, and all the riches contained in them, access to the throne of grace, the comforts of the Spirit, and a well-grounded hope of eternal life. These are the preparations for this feast, a heaven upon earth now, and a heaven in heaven shortly. God has prepared it in his counsel, in his covenant. It is a dinner, denoting present privileges in the midst of our day, beside the supper at night in glory.

(1.) It is *a feast.* Gospel preparations were prophesied of as *a feast* (Isa. xxv. 6), *a feast of fat things,* and were typified by the many festivals of the ceremonial law (1 Cor. v. 8); *Let us keep the feast.* A *feast is a good day* (Esth. viii. 17); so is the gospel; it is a continual feast. *Oxen and fatlings are killed* for this feast; no niceties, but substantial food; enough, and enough of the best. The day of a feast is *a day of slaughter,* or sacrifice, Jam. v. 5. Gospel preparations are all founded in the death of Christ, his sacrifice of himself. A feast was made for love, it is a reconciliation feast, a token of God's good-will toward men. It was made *for laughter* (Eccl. x. 19), it is a rejoicing feast. It was made for fulness; the design of the gospel was to fill every *hungry soul with good things.* It was made for fellowship, to maintain an intercourse between heaven and earth. We are sent for *to the banquet of wine, that we may tell what is our petition, and what is our request.*

(2.) It is a *wedding feast.* Wedding feasts are usually rich, free, and joyful. The first miracle Christ wrought, was, to make plentiful provision for a wedding feast (John ii. 7); and surely then he will not be wanting in provision for his own wedding feast, when *the marriage of the Lamb is come, and the bride hath made herself ready,* a victorious triumphant feast, Rev. xix. 7, 17, 18.

(3.) It is a *royal wedding feast;* it is *the feast of a king* (1 Sam. xxv. 36), at the marriage, not of a servant, but of a son; and then, if ever, he will, like Ahasuerus, show *the riches of his glorious kingdom,* Esth. i. 4. The provision made for believers in the covenant of grace, is not such as worthless worms, like us, had any reason to expect, but such as it becomes *the King of glory* to give. He gives like himself; for he gives himself to be to them *El shaddai—a God that is enough,* a feast indeed for a soul.

II. Gospel calls and offers are represented by an invitation to this feast. Those that make a feast will have guests to grace the feast with. God's guests are the children of men. *Lord, what is man,* that he should be thus dignified! *The guests* that were first invited were the Jews; wherever the gospel is preached, this invitation is given; ministers are the *servants* that are sent to invite, Prov. ix. 4, 5.

Now, 1. The guests *are called, bidden* to the wedding. All that are within hearing of the joyful sound of the gospel, to them is the word of this invitation sent. The servants that bring the invitation do not set down their names in a paper; there is no occasion for that, since none are excluded but those that exclude themselves. *Those that are bidden to the dinner are bidden to the wedding;* for all that partake of gospel privileges are to give a due and respectful attendance on the Lord Jesus, as the faithful friends and humble servants of the Bridegroom. They are *bidden to the wedding,* that they may *go forth to meet the bridegroom;* for it is the Father's will that *all men should honour the Son.*

2. The guests are called upon; for in the gospel there are not only gracious proposals made, but gracious persuasives. *We persuade men, we beseech them in Christ's stead,* 2 Cor. v. 11, 20. See how much Christ's heart is set upon the happiness of poor souls! He not only provides for them, in consideration of their want, but sends to them, in consideration of their weakness and forgetfulness. When the invited guests were slack in coming, the king *sent forth other servants, v.* 4. When the prophets of the Old Testament prevailed not, nor John the Baptist, nor Christ himself, who told them the entertainment was almost ready *(the kingdom of God was at hand),* the apostles and ministers of the gospel were sent after Christ's resurrection, to tell them it was come, it was quite ready; and to persuade them to accept the offer. One would think it had been enough to give men an intimation that they had leave to come, and should be welcome; that, during the solemnity of the wedding, the king kept open house; but, because *the natural man discerns not,* and therefore desires not, *the things of the Spirit of God,* we are pressed to accept the call by the most powerful inducements, *drawn with the cords of a man, and all the bonds of love.* If the repetition of the call will move us, *Behold, the Spirit saith, Come; and the bride saith, Come; let him that heareth say, Come; let him that is athirst come,* Rev. xxii. 17. If the reason of the call will work upon us, *Behold, the dinner is prepared, the oxen and fatlings are killed, and all things are ready;* the Father is ready to accept of us, the Son to intercede for us, the Spirit to sanctify us; pardon is ready, peace is ready, comfort is ready; the promises are ready, as *wells of living water* for supply; ordinances are ready, as golden pipes for conveyance; angels are ready to attend us, creatures are ready to be in league with us, providences are ready to work for our good, and heaven, at last, is ready to receive us; it is *a kingdom prepared, ready to be revealed in the last time.* Is all this ready; and shall we be unready? Is all this preparation made for us; and is there any room to doubt of our welcome, if we come in a right manner? Come, therefore, O *come to the marriage; we beseech you, receive not* all this *grace of God in vain,* 2 Cor. vi. 1.

III. The cold treatment which the gospel of Christ often meets with among the children of men, represented by the cold treatment that this message met with and the hot treatment that the messengers met with, in both which the king himself and the royal bridegroom are affronted. This reflects primarily upon the Jews, who rejected the counsel of God against themselves; but it looks further, to the contempt that would, by many in all ages, be put upon, and the opposition that would be given to, the gospel of Christ.

1. The message was basely slighted (*v* 3); *They would not come.* Note, The reason why sinners come not to Christ and salvation by him is, not because they *cannot,* but because *they will not* (John v. 40); *Ye will not come to me.* This will aggravate the misery of sinners, that they might have had happiness for the coming for, but it was their own act and deed to refuse it. *I would, and ye would not.* But this was not all (*v.* 5); *they made light of it;* they thought it not worth coming for; thought the messengers made more ado than needs; let them magnify the preparations ever so much, they could feast as well at home. Note, Making light of Christ, and of the great salvation wrought out by him, is the damning sin of the world. Ἀμελήσαντες—*They were careless.* Note, Multitudes perish eternally through mere carelessness, who have not any direct aversion, but a prevailing indifference, to the matters of their souls, and an unconcernedness about them.

And the reason why *they made light of the marriage feast* was, because they had other things that they minded more, and had more mind to; *they went their ways, one to his farm, and another to his merchandise.* Note, The business and profit of worldly employments prove to many a great hindrance in closing with Christ: none turn their back on the feast, but with some plausible excuse or other, Luke xiv. 18. The country people have their farms to look after, about which there is always something or other to do; the town's people must tend their shops, and be constant upon the exchange; they must *buy, and sell, and get gain.* It is true, that both farmers and merchants must be diligent in their business, but not so as to keep them from making religion their main business. *Licitis perimus omnes—These lawful things undo us,* when they are unlawfully managed, when we are so *careful and troubled about many things* as to neglect the *one thing needful.* Observe, Both the city and the country have their temptations, the merchandise in the one, and the farms in the other; so that, whatever we have of the world in our hands, our care must be to keep it out of our hearts, lest it come between us and Christ.

2. The messengers were basely abused; *The remnant,* or the rest of them, that is, those who did not go to the *farms,* or *merchandise,* were neither husbandmen nor trades-

men, but ecclesiastics, *the scribes, and Pharisees, and chief priests;* these were the persecutors, these *took the servants, and treated them spitefully, and slew them.* This, in the parable, is unaccountable, never any could be so rude and barbarous as this, to servants that came to invite them to a feast; but, in the application of the parable, it was matter of fact; they whose *feet* should have been *beautiful,* because they brought *the glad tidings of the solemn feasts* (Nahum i. 15), were *treated as the offscouring of all things,* 1 Cor. iv. 13. The prophets and John the Baptist had been thus abused already, and the apostles and ministers of Christ must count upon the same. The Jews were, either directly or indirectly, agents in most of the persecutions of the first preachers of the gospel; witness the history of *the Acts,* that is, the sufferings *of the apostles.*

IV. The utter ruin that was coming upon the Jewish church and nation is here represented by the revenge which the king, in wrath, took on these insolent recusants (*v.* 7); *He was wroth.* The Jews, who had been the people of God's love and blessing, by rejecting the gospel became the generation of his wrath and curse. *Wrath came upon them to the uttermost,* 1 Thess. ii. 16. Now observe here,

1. What was the crying sin that brought the ruin; it was their being *murderers.* He does not say, he destroyed those *despisers of his call,* but *those murderers of his servants;* as if God were more jealous for the lives of his ministers than for the honour of his gospel; he that *toucheth them, toucheth the apple of his eye.* Note, Persecution of Christ's faithful ministers fills the measure of guilt more than any thing. *Filling Jerusalem with innocent blood* was that sin of Manasseh which *the Lord would not pardon,* 2 Kings xxiv. 4.

2. What was the ruin itself, that was coming; *He sent forth his armies.* The Roman armies were his armies, of his raising, of his sending against the people of his wrath; and he *gave them a charge to tread them down,* Isa. x. 6. God is the Lord of men's hosts, and makes what use he pleases of them, to serve his own purposes, though they *mean not so, neither doth their heart think so,* Isa. x. 7. See Mic. iv. 11, 12. *His armies destroyed those murderers, and burnt up their city.* This points out very plainly the destruction of the Jews, and the burning of Jerusalem, by the Romans, forty years after this. No age ever saw a greater desolation than that, nor more of the direful effects of fire and sword. Though Jerusalem had been a *holy city, the city that God had chosen, to put his name there, beautiful for situation, the joy of the whole earth;* yet that city being now *become a harlot, righteousness being no longer lodged in it, but murderers, the worst of murderers* (as the prophet speaks, Isa. i. 21), judgment came upon it, and ruin without remedy; and it is set forth for an example to all that should oppose Christ and his gospel. It was the Lord's doing, to avenge the quarrel of his covenant.

V. The replenishing of the church again, by the bringing in of the Gentiles, is here represented by the furnishing of the feast with guests *out of the high-ways, v.* 8—10.

Here is, 1. The complaint of the master of the feast concerning those that were first bidden (*v.* 8), *The wedding is ready,* the covenant of grace ready to be sealed, a church ready to be founded; *but they which were bidden,* that is, the Jews, *to whom pertained the covenant and the promises,* by which they were of old invited to the *feast of fat things,* they *were not worthy,* they were utterly unworthy, and, by their contempt of Christ, had forfeited all the privileges they were invited to. Note, It is not owing to God, that sinners perish, but to themselves. Thus, when Israel of old was within sight of Canaan, the land of promise was ready, the milk and honey ready, but their unbelief and murmuring, and contempt of that pleasant land, shut them out, and their carcases were left to perish in the wilderness; and *these things happened to them for ensamples.* See 1 Cor. x. 11; Heb. iii. 16—iv. 1.

2. The commission he gave to the servants, to invite other guests. The inhabitants of the *city* (*v.* 7) had refused; *Go into the high-ways* then; into *the way of the Gentiles,* which at first they were to decline, *ch.* x. 5. Thus by the fall of the Jews salvation is come to the Gentiles, Rom. xi. 11, 12; Eph. iii. 8. Note, Christ will have a *kingdom in the world,* though many reject the grace, and resist the power, of that kingdom. *Though Israel be not gathered, he will be glorious.* The offer of Christ and salvation to the Gentiles was, (1.) Unlooked for and unexpected; such a surprise as it would be to wayfaring men upon the road to be met with an invitation to a wedding feast. The Jews had notice of the gospel, long before, and expected the Messiah and his kingdom; but to the Gentiles it was all new, what they had never heard of before (Acts xvii. 19, 20), and, consequently, what they could not conceive of as belonging to them. See Isa. lxv. 1, 2. (2.) It was universal and undistinguishing; *Go, and bid as many as you find.* The highways are public places, and there *Wisdom cries,* Prov. i. 20. "Ask them that go by the way, ask any body (Job xxi. 29), high and low, rich and poor, bond and free, young and old, Jew and Gentile; tell them all, that they shall be welcome to gospel-privileges upon gospel-terms; whoever will, let him come, without exception."

3. The success of this second invitation; if some will not come, others will (*v.* 10); *They gathered together all, as many as they found.* The servants obeyed their orders. Jonah was sent *into the high-ways,* but was so tender of the honour of his country, that he avoided the errand; but Christ's apostles,

though Jews, preferred the service of Christ before their respect to their nation; and St. Paul, though sorrowing for the Jews, yet magnifies his office as the apostle of the Gentiles. *They gathered together all.* The design of the gospel is, (1.) To gather souls together; not the nation of the Jews only, but *all the children of God* who were *scattered abroad* (John xi. 52), *the other sheep that were not of that fold,* John x. 16. They were gathered into one body, one family, one corporation. (2.) To gather them together to the wedding-feast, to pay their respect to Christ, and to partake of the privileges of the new covenant. Where the dole is, there will the poor be gathered together.

Now the guests that were gathered were, [1.] A multitude, *all, as many as they found;* so many, that the guest-chamber was filled. The sealed ones of the Jews were numbered, but those of other nations *were without number, a very great multitude,* Rev. vii. 9. See Isa. lx. 4, 8. [2.] A mixed multitude, *both bad and good;* some that before their conversion were sober and well-inclined, as the devout Greeks (Acts xvii. 4), and Cornelius; others that had run to an excess of riot, as the Corinthians (1 Cor. vi. 11); *Such were some of you;* or, some that after their conversion proved bad, that *turned not to the Lord with all their heart,* but feignedly; others that were upright and sincere, and proved of the right class. Ministers, in casting the net of the gospel, enclose *both good* fish *and bad; but the Lord knows them that are his.*

VI. The case of hypocrites, who are *in* the church, but not *of* it, who have a name to live, but are not alive indeed, is represented by *the guest that had not on a wedding garment;* one of the bad that were gathered in. Those come short of salvation by Christ, not only who refuse to take upon them the profession of religion, but who are not sound at heart in that profession. Concerning this hypocrite observe,

1. His discovery, how he was found out, *v.* 11.

(1.) *The king came in to see the guests,* to bid those welcome who came prepared, and to turn those out who came otherwise. Note, The God of heaven takes particular notice of those who profess religion, and have a place and a name in the visible church. Our Lord Jesus *walks among the golden candlesticks,* and therefore *knows their works.* See Rev. ii. 1, 2; Cant. vii. 12. Let this be a warning to us against hypocrisy, that disguises will shortly be stripped off, and every man will appear in his own colours; and an encouragement to us in our sincerity, that God is a witness to it.

Observe, This hypocrite was never discovered to be without *a wedding garment,* till *the king himself came in to see the guests.* Note, It is God's prerogative to know who are sound at heart in their profession, and who are not. We may be deceived in men, either one way or other; but He cannot. The day of judgment will be the great discovering day, when all the guests will be presented to the King: then *he will separate between the precious and the vile* (*ch.* xxv. 32), *the secrets of all hearts will then be made manifest,* and we shall infallibly discern *between the righteous and the wicked,* which now it is not easy to do. It concerns all the guests, to prepare for the scrutiny, and to consider how they will pass the piercing eye of the heart-searching God.

(2.) As soon as he came in, he presently espied the hypocrite; *He saw there a man which had not on a wedding garment;* though but one, he soon had his eye upon him; there is no hope of being hid in a crowd from the arrests of divine justice; he had not on a wedding garment; he was not dressed as became a nuptial solemnity; he had not his best clothes on. Note, Many come to the wedding feast without a wedding garment. If the gospel be the wedding feast, then the wedding garment is a frame of heart, and a course of life agreeable to the gospel and our profession of it, *worthy of the vocation wherewith we are called* (Eph. iv. 1), *as becomes the gospel of Christ,* Phil. i. 27. *The righteousness of saints,* their real holiness and sanctification, and Christ, *made Righteousness to them, is the clean linen,* Rev. xix. 8. This man was not naked, or in rags; some raiment he had, but not a wedding garment. Those, and those only, who *put on the Lord Jesus,* that have a Christian temper of mind, and are adorned with Christian graces, who live by faith in Christ, and to whom he is all in all, have the wedding garment.

2. His trial (*v.* 12); and here we may observe,

(1.) How he was arraigned (*v.* 12); *Friend, how camest thou in hither, not having a wedding garment?* A startling question to one that was priding himself in the place he securely possessed at the feast. *Friend!* That was a cutting word; a seeming friend, a pretended friend, a friend in profession, under manifold ties and obligations to be a friend. Note, There are many in the church who are false friends to Jesus Christ, who say that they love him, while their hearts are not with him. *How camest thou in hither?* He does not chide the servants for letting him in (the wedding garment is an inward thing, ministers must go according to that which falls within their cognizance); but he checks his presumption in crowding in, when he knew that his heart was not upright; "How durst thou claim a share in gospel benefits, when thou hadst no regard to gospel rules? *What hast thou to do to declare my statutes?*" Ps. l. 16, 17. Such are spots in the feast, dishonour the bridegroom, affront the company, and disgrace themselves; and therefore, *How camest thou in hither?* Note, The day is coming, when hypocrites will be called to an account for all their presumptuous intrusion into gospel ordinances, and usurpation of gospel privileges. *Who hath required this at your hand?* Isa. i. 12. Despised sabbaths and abused sacraments must be reckoned for, and judgment taken out upon an action of waste against all those who *received the grace of God in vain.* "How camest thou to the Lord's table, at such a time, unhumbled and unsanctified? What brought thee to sit before God's prophets, as his people do, when thy heart went after thy covetousness? *How camest thou in?* Not by the door, but *some other way, as a thief and a robber.* It was a tortuous entry, a possession without colour of a title." Note, It is good for those that have a place in the church, often to put it to themselves, "How came I in hither? Have I a wedding-garment?" If we would thus *judge ourselves, we should not be judged.*

(2.) How he was convicted; *he was speechless: ἐφιμώθη—he was muzzled* (so the word is used, 1 Cor. ix. 9); the man stood mute, upon his arraignment, being convicted and condemned by his own conscience. They who live within the church, and die without Christ, will not have one word to say for themselves in the judgment of the great day, they will be without excuse; should they plead, *We have eaten and drunk in thy presence,* as they do, Luke xiii. 26, that is to plead guilty; for the crime they are charged with, is thrusting themselves into the presence of Christ, and to his table, before they were called. They who never heard a word of this wedding feast will have more to say for themselves; their sin will be more excusable, and their condemnation more tolerable, than theirs who came to the feast without the wedding garment, and so sin against the clearest light and dearest love.

3. His sentence (*v.* 13); *Bind him hand and foot,* &c.

(1.) He is ordered to be pinioned, as condemned malefactors are, to be manacled and shackled. Those that will not work and walk as they should, may expect to be bound hand and foot. There is a binding in this world by the servants, the ministers, whose suspending of persons that walk disorderly, to the scandal of religion, is called binding of them, *ch.* xviii. 18. "Bind them up from partaking of special ordinances, and the peculiar privileges of their church-membership; bind them over to the righteous judgment of God." *In the day of judgment,* hypocrites will be bound; *the angels shall bind up these tares in bundles for the fire, ch.* xiii. 41. Damned sinners are bound hand and foot by an irreversible sentence; this signifies the same with the fixing of the great gulf; they can neither resist nor outrun their punishment.

(2.) He is ordered to be carried off from the wedding feast; *Take him away.* When the wickedness of hypocrites appears, they are to be taken away from the communion of the faithful, to be cut off as withered branches. This bespeaks the punishment of loss in the other world; they shall be taken away from the king, from the kingdom, from the wedding feast, *Depart from me, ye cursed.* It will aggravate their misery, that (like the unbelieving lord, 2 Kings vii. 2), *they shall see all this plenty with their eyes, but shall not taste of it.* Note, Those that walk unworthy of their Christianity, forfeit all the happiness they presumptuously laid claim to, and complimented themselves with a groundless expectation of.

(3.) He is ordered into a doleful dungeon; *Cast him into utter darkness.* Our Saviour here insensibly slides out of this parable into that which it intimates—the damnation of hypocrites in the other world. Hell is utter darkness, it is darkness out of heaven, the land of light; or it is extreme darkness, darkness to the last degree, without the least ray or spark of light, or hope of it, like that of Egypt; *darkness which might be felt; the blackness of darkness, as darkness itself,* Job x. 22. Note, Hypocrites go by the light of the gospel itself down to utter darkness; and hell will be hell indeed to such, a condemnation more intolerable; *there shall be weeping, and gnashing of teeth.* This our Saviour often uses as part of the description of hell-torments, which are hereby represented, not so much by the misery itself, as by the resentment sinners will have of it; there shall be *weeping,* an expression of great sorrow and anguish; not a gush of tears, which gives present ease, but constant weeping, which is constant torment; and the *gnashing of teeth* is an expression of the greatest rage and indignation; they will be *like a wild bull in a net, full of the fury of the Lord,* Isa. li. 20; viii. 21, 22. Let us therefore hear and fear.

Lastly, The parable is concluded with that remarkable saying which we had before (*ch.* xx. 16), *Many are called, but few are chosen, v.* 14. Of the many that are called to the wedding feast, if you set aside all those as unchosen that make light of it, and avowedly prefer other things before it; if then you set aside all that make a profession of religion, but the temper of whose spirits and the tenour of whose conversation are a constant contradiction to it; if you set aside all the profane, and all the hypocritical, you will find that they are few, very few, that are chosen; many called to the wedding feast, but few chosen to the wedding garment, that is, to *salvation, by sanctification of the Spirit.* This *is the strait gate, and narrow way,* which *few find.*

15 Then went the Pharisees, and took counsel how them might entangle him in *his* talk. 16 And they sent out unto him their disciples with the Herodians, saying, Master, we know that thou art true, and teachest

the way of God in truth, neither carest thou for any *man:* for thou regardest not the person of men. 17
Tell us therefore, What thinkest thou? Is it lawful to give tribute unto Cæsar,
or not? 18 But Jesus perceived their wickedness, and said, Why tempt ye
me, *ye* hypocrites? 19 Show me the
tribute money. And they brought
unto him a penny. 20 And he saith
unto them, Whose *is* this image and
superscription? 21 They say unto
him, Cæsar's. Then saith he unto them, Render therefore unto Cæsar the things which are Cæsar's; and unto
God the things that are God's. 22
When they had heard *these words,* they marvelled, and left him, and went their way.

It was not the least grievous of the sufferings of Christ, that *he endured the contradiction of sinners against himself*, and had snares laid for him by those that sought how to take him off with some pretence. In these verses, we have him attacked by the Pharisees and Herodians with a question about paying tribute to Cæsar. Observe,

I. What the design was, which they proposed to themselves; *They took counsel to entangle him in his talk.* Hitherto, his rencounters had been mostly with the chief priests and the elders, men in authority, who trusted more to their power than to their policy, and examined him concerning his commission (*ch.* xxi. 23); but now he is set upon from another quarter; the Pharisees will try whether they can deal with him by their learning in the law, and in casuistical divinity, and they have a *tentamen novum—a new trial* for him. Note, It is in vain for the best and wisest of men to think that, by their ingenuity, or interest, or industry, or even by their innocence and integrity, they can escape the hatred and ill will of bad men, or screen themselves from *the strife of tongues.* See how unwearied the enemies of Christ and his kingdom are in their opposition!

1. *They took counsel.* It was foretold concerning him, that *the rulers* would *take counsel against him* (Ps. ii. 2); and *so persecuted they the prophets. Come, and let us devise devices against Jeremiah.* See Jer. xviii. 18; xx. 10. Note, The more there is of contrivance and consultation about sin, the worse it is. There is a particular *woe to them that devise iniquity,* Mic. ii. 1. The more there is of the wicked wit in the contrivance of a sin, the more there is of the wicked will in the commission of it.

2. That which they aimed at was *to entangle him in his talk.* They saw him free and bold in speaking his mind, and hoped by that, if they could bring him to some nice and tender point, to get an advantage against him. It has been the old practice of Satan's agents and emissaries, to make a man an offender for a word, a word misplaced, or mistaken, or misunderstood; a word, though innocently designed, yet perverted by strained inuendos: thus they lay a snare for him that *reproveth in the gate* (Isa. xxix. 21), and represent the greatest teachers as the greatest troublers of Israel: thus *the wicked plotteth against the just,* Ps. xxxvii. 12, 13.

There are two ways by which the enemies of Christ might be revenged on him, and be rid of him; either by law or by force. By law they could not do it, unless they could make him obnoxious to the civil government; for *it was not lawful for them to put any man to death* (John xviii. 31); and the Roman powers were not apt to concern themselves about *questions of words, and names, and their law,* Acts xviii. 15. By force they could not do it, unless they could make him obnoxious to the people, who were always the hands, whoever were the heads, in such acts of violence, which they call the beating of the rebels; but the people took Christ for a Prophet, and therefore his enemies could not raise the mob against him. Now (as the old serpent was from the beginning *more subtle than any beast of the field),* the design was, to bring him into such a dilemma, that he must make himself liable to the displeasure either of the Jewish multitude, or of the Roman magistrates; let him take which side of the question he will, he shall run himself into a premunire; and so they will gain their point, and make his own tongue to fall upon him.

II. The question which they put to him pursuant to this design, *v.* 16, 17. Having devised this iniquity in secret, in a close cabal, behind the curtain, when they went abroad without loss of time they practised it. Observe,

1. The persons they employed; they did not go themselves, lest the design should be suspected and Christ should stand the more upon his guard; but they sent their disciples, who would look less like tempters, and more like learners. Note, Wicked men will never want wicked instruments to be employed in carrying on their wicked counsels. Pharisees have their disciples at their beck, who will go on any errand for them, and say as they say; and they have this in their eye, when they are so industrious to make proselytes.

With them they sent the Herodians, a party among the Jews, who were for a cheerful and entire subjection to the Roman emperor, and to Herod his deputy; and who made it their business to reconcile people to that government, and pressed all to pay their tribute. Some think that they were the collectors of the land tax, as the publicans were of the customs, and that they went with the Pharisees to Christ, with this blind upon their plot, that while the Herodians demanded the tax, and the Pharisees denied it, they were both willing to refer it to Christ, as a proper Judge to decide the quarrel. Herod being obliged, by the charter of the sovereignty, to take care of the tribute, these Herodians, by assisting him in that, helped to endear him to his great friends at Rome. The Pharisees, on the other hand, were zealous for the liberty of the Jews, and did what they could to make them impatient of the Roman yoke. Now, if he should countenance the paying of tribute, the Pharisees would incense the people against him; if he should discountenance or disallow it, the Herodians would incense the government against him. Note, It is common for those that oppose one another, to continue in an opposition to Christ and his kingdom. Samson's foxes looked several ways, but met in one firebrand. See Ps. lxxxiii. 3, 5, 7, 8. If they are unanimous in opposing, should not we be so in maintaining, the interests of the gospel?

2. The preface, with which they were plausibly to introduce the question; it was highly complimentary to our Saviour (*v.* 16); *Master, we know that thou art true, and teachest the way of God in truth.* Note, It is a common thing for the most spiteful projects to be covered with the most specious pretences. Had they come to Christ with the most serious enquiry, and the most sincere intention, they could not have expressed themselves better. Here is *hatred covered with deceit*, and a *wicked heart with burning lips* (Prov. xxvi. 23); as Judas, who kissed, and betrayed, as Joab, who kissed, and killed.

Now, (1.) What they said of Christ was right, and whether they knew it or no, blessed be God, we know it.

[1.] That Jesus Christ was a faithful Teacher; *Thou art true, and teachest the way of God in truth.* For himself, *he is true, the Amen, the faithful Witness;* he is the Truth itself. As for his doctrine, the matter of his teaching was the way of God, the way that God requires us to walk in, the way of duty, that leads to happiness; that is the way of God. The manner of it was in truth; he showed people *the right way, the way in which they should go.* He was a skilful Teacher, and knew the way of God; and a faithful Teacher, that would be sure to let us know it. See Prov. viii. 6—9. This is the character of a good teacher, to preach the truth, the whole truth, and nothing but the truth, and not to suppress, pervert, or stretch, any truth, for favour or affection, hatred or good will, either out of a desire to please, or a fear to offend, any man.

[2.] That he was a bold Reprover. In preaching, he *cared not for any;* he valued no man's frowns or smiles, he did not court, he did not dread, either the great or the many, for he *regarded not the person of man.* In his evangelical judgment, he did not know faces; that *Lion of the tribe of Judah, turned not away for any* (Prov. xxx. 30), turned not a step from the truth, nor from his work, for fear of the most formidable. He *reproved with equity* (Isa. xi. 4), and never with partiality.

(2.) Though what they said was true for the matter of it, yet there was nothing but flattery and treachery in the intention of it. They called him *Master,* when they were contriving to treat him as the worst of malefactors; they pretended respect for him, when they intended mischief against him; and they affronted his wisdom as Man, much more his omniscience as God, of which he had so often given undeniable proofs, when they imagined that they could impose upon him with these pretences, and that he could not see through them. It is the grossest atheism, that is the greatest folly in the world, to think to put a cheat upon Christ, who searches the heart, Rev. ii. 23. Those that mock God do but deceive themselves, Gal. vi. 7.

3. The proposal of the case; *What thinkest thou?* As if they had said, "Many men are of many minds in this matter; it is a case which relates to practice, and occurs daily; let us have thy thoughts freely in the matter, *Is it lawful to give tribute to Cæsar, or not?*" This implies a further question; Has Cæsar a right to demand it? The nation of the Jews was lately, about a hundred years before this, conquered by the Roman sword, and so, as other nations, made subject to the Roman yoke, and became a province of the empire; accordingly, toll, tribute, and custom, were demanded from them, and sometimes poll-money. By this it appeared that *the sceptre was departed from Judah* (Gen. xlix. 10); and therefore, if they had understood the signs of the times, they must have concluded that *Shiloh was come,* and either that this was he, or they must find out another more likely to be so.

Now the question was, Whether it was lawful to pay these taxes voluntarily, or, Whether they should not insist upon the ancient liberty of their nation, and rather suffer themselves to be distrained upon? The ground of the doubt was, that they *were Abraham's seed,* and should not by consent be *in bondage to any man,* John viii. 33. God had given them a law, that they should not *set a stranger over them.* Did not that imply, that they were not to yield any willing subjection to any prince, state, or potentate, that was not of their own nation and religion? This was an old mistake, arising from that *pride and* that *haughty spirit* which bring *destruction and a fall.* Jeremiah, in his time, though he spoke in God's name, could not possibly beat them off it, nor persuade them to submit to the king of Babylon; and their obstinacy in that matter was then their ruin (Jer. xxvii. 12, 13): and now again they stumbled at the same stone; and it was the very thing which, in a few years after, brought final destruction upon them by the Romans. They quite mistook the sense both of the precept and of the privilege, and, under colour of God's word, contended with his providence, when they should have kissed the rod, and accepted the punishment of their iniquity.

However, by this question they hoped to entangle Christ, and, which way soever he resolved it, to expose him to the fury either of the jealous Jews, or of the jealous Romans; they were ready to triumph, as Pharaoh did over Israel, that *the wilderness had shut him in*, and his doctrine would be concluded either injurious to the rights of the church, or hurtful to kings and provinces.

III. The breaking of this snare by the wisdom of the Lord Jesus.

1. He discovered it (*v.* 18); *He perceived their wickedness;* for, *surely in vain is the net spread in the sight of any bird*, Prov. i. 17. A temptation perceived is half conquered, for our greatest danger lies from snakes under the green grass; *and he said, Why tempt ye me, ye hypocrites?* Note, Whatever vizard the hypocrite puts on, our Lord Jesus sees through it; he perceives all the wickedness that is in the hearts of pretenders, and can easily convict them of it, and set it in order before them. He cannot be imposed upon, as we often are, by flatteries and fair pretences. He that searches the heart can call hypocrites by their own name, as Ahijah did the wife of Jeroboam (1 Kings xiv. 6), *Why feignest thou thyself to be another? Why tempt ye me, ye hypocrites?* Note, Hypocrites tempt Jesus Christ; they try his knowledge, whether he can discover them through their disguises; they try his holiness and truth, whether he will allow of them in his church; but if they that of old *tempted Christ*, when he was but darkly revealed, *were destroyed of serpents, of how much sorer punishment shall they be thought worthy* who tempt him now in the midst of gospel light and love! Those that presume to tempt Christ will certainly find him too hard for them, and that he is of more piercing eyes than not to see, and more pure eyes than not to hate, the disguised wickedness of hypocrites, that dig deep to hide their counsel from him.

2. He evaded it; his convicting them of hypocrisy might have served for an answer (such captious malicious questions deserve a reproof, not a reply): but our Lord Jesus gave a full answer to their question, and introduced it by an argument sufficient to support it, so as to lay down a rule for his church in this matter, and yet to avoid giving offence, and to break the snare.

(1.) He forced them, ere they were aware, to confess Cæsar's authority over them, *v.* 19, 20. In dealing with those that are captious, it is good to give our reasons, and, if possible, reasons of confessed cogency, before we give our resolutions. Thus the evidence of truth may silence gainsayers by surprise, while they only stood upon their guard against the truth itself, not against the reason of it; *Show me the tribute-money.* He had none of his own to convince them by; it should seem, he had not so much as one piece of money about him, for for our sakes he emptied himself, and became poor; he despised the wealth of this world, and thereby taught us not to over-value it: silver and gold he had none; why then should we covet to load ourselves with the thick clay? The Romans demanded their tribute in their own money, which was current among the Jews at that time: that therefore is called the *tribute-money;* he does not name what piece, but the *tribute-money*, to show that he did not mind things of that nature, nor concern himself about them; his heart was upon better things, the kingdom of God and the riches and righteousness thereof, and ours should be so too. They presently *brought him a penny*, a Roman penny in silver, in value about sevenpence half-penny of our money, the most common piece then in use: it was stamped with the emperor's image and superscription, which was the warrant of the public faith for the value of the pieces so stamped; a method agreed on by most nations, for the more easy circulation of money with satisfaction. The coining of money has always been looked upon as a branch of the prerogative, a flower of the crown, a royalty belonging to the sovereign powers; and the admitting of that as the good and lawful money of a country is an implicit submission to those powers, and an owning of them in money matters. How happy is our constitution, and how happy we, who live in a nation where, though the image and superscription be the sovereign's, the property is the subject's, under the protection of the laws, and what we have we can call our own!

Christ asked them, *Whose image is this?* They owned it to be Cæsar's, and thereby convicted those of falsehood who said, *We were never in bondage to any;* and confirmed what afterward they said, *We have no king but Cæsar.* It is a rule in the Jewish Talmud, that "he is the king of the country whose coin is current in the country." Some think that the superscription upon this coin was a memorandum of the conquest of Judea by the Romans, *anno post captam Judæam—the year after that event;* and that they admitted that too.

(2.) From thence he inferred the lawfulness of paying tribute to Cæsar (*v.* 21); *Render therefore to Cæsar the things that are Cæsar's;* not, "*Give* it him" (as they expressed it, *v.* 17), but, "*Render* it; Return," or "Restore it; if Cæsar fill the purses, let Cæsar command them. It is too late now to dispute paying tribute to Cæsar; for you are become a province of the empire, and, when once a relation is admitted, the duty of it must be performed. *Render to all their due,* and particularly *tribute to whom tribute is due.*" Now by this answer,

[1.] No offence was given. It was much to the honour of Christ and his doctrine, that he did not interpose as a Judge or a

Divider in matters of this nature, but left them as he found them, for *his kingdom is not of this world;* and in this he hath given an example to his ministers, who deal in sacred things, not to meddle with disputes about things secular, not to wade far into controversies relating to them, but to leave that to those whose proper business it is. Ministers that would mind their business, and please their master, must not *entangle themselves in the affairs of this life:* they forfeit the guidance of God's Spirit, and the convoy of his providence. when they thus go out of their way. Christ discusses not the emperor's title, but enjoins a peaceable subjection to *the powers that be.* The government therefore had no reason to take offence at his determination, but to thank him, for it would strengthen Cæsar's interest with the people, who held him for a Prophet; and yet such was the impudence of his prosecutors, that, though he had expressly charged them to *render to Cæsar the things that are Cæsar's,* they laid the direct contrary in his indictment, that he *forbade to give tribute to Cæsar,* Luke xxiii. 2. As to the people, the Pharisees could not accuse him to them, because they themselves had, before they were aware, yielded the premises, and then it was too late to evade the conclusion. Note, Though truth seeks not a fraudulent concealment, yet it sometimes needs a prudent management, to prevent the offence which may be taken at it.

[2.] His adversaries were reproved. *First,* Some of them would have had him make it unlawful to give tribute to Cæsar, that they might have a pretence to save their money. Thus many excuse themselves from that which they must do, by arguing whether they may do it or no. *Secondly,* They all withheld from God his dues, and are reproved for that: while they were vainly contending about their civil liberties, they had lost the life and power of religion, and needed to be put in mind of their duty to God, with that to Cæsar.

[3.] His disciples were instructed, and standing rules left to the church.

First, That the Christian religion is no enemy to civil government, but a friend to it. Christ's kingdom doth not clash or interfere with the kingdoms of the earth, in any thing that pertains to their jurisdiction. By Christ kings reign.

Secondly, It is the duty of subjects to render to magistrates that which, according to the laws of their country, is their due. The higher powers, being entrusted with the public welfare, the protection of the subject, and the conservation of the peace, are entitled, in consideration thereof, to a just proportion of the public wealth, and the revenue of the nation. *For this cause pay we tribute,* because *they attend continually to this very thing* (Rom. xiii. 6); and it is doubtless a greater sin to cheat the government than to cheat a private person. Though it is the constitution that determines what is Cæsar's, yet, when that is determined, Christ bids us render it to him; my coat is my coat, by the law of man; but he is a thief, by the law of God, that takes it from me.

Thirdly, When we render to Cæsar the things that are Cæsar's, we must remember withal to render to God the things that are God's. If our purses be Cæsar's, our consciences are God's; he hath said, *My son, give me thy heart:* he must have the innermost and uppermost place there; we must render to God that which is his due, out of our time and out of our estates; from them he must have his share as well as Cæsar his; and if Cæsar's commands interfere with God's *we must obey God rather than men.*

Lastly, Observe how they were nonplussed by this answer; they *marvelled, and left him, and went their way, v.* 22. They admired his sagacity in discovering and evading a snare which they thought so craftily laid. Christ is, and will be, the Wonder, not only of his beloved friends, but of his baffled enemies. One would think they should have marvelled and followed him, marvelled and submitted to him; no, they marvelled and left him. Note, There are many in whose eyes Christ is marvellous, and yet not precious. They admire his wisdom, but will not be guided by it, his power, but will not submit to it. *They went their way,* as persons ashamed, and made an inglorious retreat. The stratagem being defeated, they quitted the field. Note, There is nothing got by contending with Christ.

23 The same day came to him the
Sadducees, which say that there is no
resurrection, and asked him, 24 Saying, Master, Moses said, If a man
die, having no children, his brother
shall marry his wife, and raise up seed
unto his brother. 25 Now there
were with us seven brethren: and
the first, when he had married a wife,
deceased, and, having no issue, left his
wife unto his brother: 26 Likewise
the second also, and the third, unto
the seventh. 27 And last of all the
woman died also. 28 Therefore in
the resurrection whose wife shall she
be of the seven? for they all had her.
29 Jesus answered and said unto
them, Ye do err, not knowing the
scriptures, nor the power of God.
30 For in the resurrection they neither marry, nor are given in marriage,
but are as the angels of God in heaven. 31 But as touching the resurrection of the dead, have ye not read
that which was spoken unto you by

God, saying, 32 I am the God of Abraham, and the God of Isaac, and the God of Jacob? God is not the God of the dead, but of the living.
33 And when the multitude heard *this*, they were astonished at his doctrine.

We have here Christ's dispute with the Sadducees concerning the resurrection; it was the same day on which he was attacked by the Pharisees about paying tribute. Satan was now more busy than ever to ruffle and disturb him; it was *an hour of temptation*, Rev. iii. 10. The truth as it is in Jesus will still meet with contradiction, in some branch or other of it. Observe here,

I. The opposition which the Sadducees made to a very great truth of religion; they say, *There is no resurrection*, as there are some fools who say, *There is no God*. These heretics were called *Sadducees* from one Sadoc, a disciple of Antigonus Sochæus, who flourished about two hundred and eighty-four years before our Saviour's birth. They lie under heavy censures among the writers of their own nation, as men of base and debauched conversations, which their principles led them to. They were the fewest in number of all the sects among the Jews, but generally persons of some rank. As the Pharisees and Essenes seemed to follow Plato and Pythagoras, so the Sadducees were much of the genius of the Epicureans; they denied the resurrection, they said, There is no future state, no life after this; that, when the body dies, the soul is annihilated, and dies with it; that there is no state of rewards or punishments in the other world; no judgment to come in heaven or hell. They maintained, that, except God, there is no spirit (Acts xxiii. 8), nothing but matter and motion. They would not own the divine inspiration of the prophets, nor any revelation from heaven, but what God himself spoke upon mount Sinai. Now the doctrine of Christ carried that great truth of the resurrection and a future state much further than it had yet been revealed, and therefore the Sadducees in a particular manner set themselves against it. The Pharisees and Sadducees were contrary to each other, and yet confederates against Christ. Christ's gospel hath always suffered between superstitious ceremonious hypocrites and bigots on the one hand, and profane deists and infidels on the other. The former abusing, the latter despising, the *form* of godliness, but both denying the *power* of it.

II. The objection they made against the truth, which was taken from a supposed case of a woman that had seven husbands successively; now they take it for granted, that, if there be a resurrection, it must be a return to such a state as this we are now in, and to the same circumstances, like the imaginary Platonic year; and if so, it is an invincible absurdity for this woman in the future state to have seven husbands, or else an insuperable difficulty which of them should have her, he whom she had first, or he whom she had last, or he whom she loved best, or he whom she lived longest with.

1. They suggest the law of Moses in this matter (*v.* 24), that the next of kin should marry the widow of him that died childless (Deut. xxv. 5); we have it practised Ruth iv. 5. It was a political law, founded in the particular constitution of the Jewish commonwealth, to preserve the distinction of families and inheritances, of both which there was special care taken in that government.

2. They put a case upon this statute, which, whether it were a *case in fact* or only a *moot case*, is not at all material; if it had not really occurred, yet possibly it might. It was of seven brothers, who married the same woman, *v.* 25—27. Now this ease supposes,

(1.) The desolations that death sometimes makes in families when it comes with commission; how it often sweeps away a whole fraternity in a little time: seldom (as the case is put) according to seniority (the land of darkness is without any order), but *heaps upon heaps;* it diminishes families that had multiplied greatly, Ps. cvii. 38, 39. When there were seven brothers grown up to man's estate, there was a family very likely to be built up; and yet this numerous family leaves *neither son nor nephew, nor any remaining in their dwellings*, Job xviii. 19. Well may we say then, *Except the Lord build the house, they labour in vain that build it*. Let none be sure of the advancement and perpetuity of their names and families, unless they could *make a covenant* of peace *with death*, or be at an *agreement with the grave*.

(2.) The obedience of these seven brothers to the law, though they had a power of refusal under the penalty of a reproach, Deut. xxv. 7. Note, Discouraging providences should not keep us from doing our duty; because we must be governed by the rule, not by the event. The seventh, who ventured last to marry the widow many a one would say) was a *bold* man. I would say, if he did it purely in obedience to God, he was a *good* man, and one that made conscience of his duty.

But, *last of all, the woman died also*. Note, Survivorship is but a reprieve; they that live long, and bury their relations and neighbours one after another, do not thereby acquire an immortality; no, their day will come to fall. Death's bitter cup goes round, and, sooner or later, we must all pledge in it, Jer. xxv. 26.

3. They propose a doubt upon this case (*v.* 28); "*In the resurrection, whose wife shall she be of the seven?* You cannot tell whose; and therefore we must conclude *there is no resurrection.*" The Pharisees, who professed to believe a resurrection, had very gross and carnal notions concerning it, and concerning

the future state; expecting to find there, as the Turks in their paradise, the delights and pleasures of the animal life, which perhaps drove the Sadducees to deny the thing itself; for nothing gives greater advantage to atheism and infidelity than the carnality of those that make religion, either in its professions or in its prospects, a servant to their sensual appetites and secular interests; while those that are erroneous deny the truth, those that are superstitious betray it to them. Now they, in this objection, went upon the Pharisees' hypothesis. Note, It is not strange that carnal minds have very false notions of spiritual and eternal things. The natural man receiveth not these things, *for they are foolishness to him*, 1 Cor. ii. 14. Let truth be set in a clear light, and then it appears in its full strength.

III. Christ's answer to this objection; by reproving their ignorance, and rectifying their mistake, he shows the objection to be fallacious and unconcluding.

1. He reproves their ignorance (*v.* 29); *Ye do err.* Note, Those do greatly err, in the judgment of Christ, who deny the resurrection and a future state. Here Christ reproves with the meekness of wisdom, and is not so sharp upon them (whatever was the reason) as sometimes he was upon the chief priests and elders; *Ye do err, not knowing.* Note, Ignorance is the cause of error; those that are in the dark, miss their way. The patrons of error do *therefore* resist the light, and do what they can to take away the key of knowledge; *Ye do err* in this matter, *not knowing.* Note, Ignorance is the cause of error about the resurrection and the future state. *What* it is in its particular instances, the wisest and best know not; it doth not yet appear what we shall be, it is a glory that is to be revealed: when we speak of the state of separate souls, the resurrection of the body, and of eternal happiness and misery, we are soon at a loss; we cannot order our speech, by reason of darkness, but that it *is* is a thing about which we are not left in the dark; blessed be God, we are not; and those who deny it are guilty of a willing and affected ignorance. It seems, there were some Sadducees, some such monsters, among professing Christians, *some among you, that say, There is no resurrection of the dead* (1 Cor. xv. 12) and some that did in effect deny it, by turning it into an allegory, saying, The *resurrection is past already.* Now observe,

(1.) *They know not the power of God;* which would lead men to infer that there *may be* a resurrection and a future state. Note, The ignorance, disbelief, or weak belief, of God's power, is at the bottom of many errors, particularly theirs who deny the resurrection. When we are told of the soul's existence and agency in a state of separation from the body, and especially that a dead body, which has lain many ages in the grave, and is turned into common and undistinguished dust, that this shall be raised the same body that it was, and live, move, and act, again; we are ready to say, *How can these things be?* Nature allows it for a maxim, *A privatione ad habitum non datur regressus—The habits attaching to a state of existence vanish irrecoverably with the state itself.* If a man die, shall he live again? And vain men, because they cannot comprehend the *way* of it, question the *truth* of it; whereas, if we firmly believe in God the Father Almighty, that nothing is impossible with God, all these difficulties vanish. This therefore we must fasten upon, in the first place, that God is omnipotent, and can do what he will; and then no room is left for doubting but that he will do what he has promised; and, if so, *why should it be thought a thing incredible with you that God should raise the dead?* Acts xxvi. 8. His power far exceeds the power of nature.

(2.) *They know not the scriptures,* which decidedly affirm that there shall be a resurrection and a future state. The power of God, determined and engaged by his promise, is the foundation for faith to build upon. Now the scriptures speak plainly, that the soul is immortal, and there is another life after this; it is the scope both of the law and of the prophets, *that there shall be a resurrection of the dead, both of the just and of the unjust,* Acts xxiv. 14, 15. Job knew it (Job xix. 26), Ezekiel foresaw it (Ezek. xxxvii.), and Daniel plainly foretold it, Dan. xii. 2. Christ rose again *according to the scriptures* (1 Cor. xv. 3); and so shall we. Those therefore who deny it, either have not conversed with the Scriptures, or do not believe them, or do not take the true sense and meaning of them. Note, Ignorance of the scripture is the rise of abundance of mischief.

2. He rectifies their mistake, and (*v.* 30) corrects those gross ideas which they had of the resurrection and a future state, and fixes these doctrines upon a true and lasting basis. Concerning that state, observe,

(1.) It is not like the state we are now in upon earth; *They neither marry, nor are given in marriage.* In our present state marriage is necessary; it was instituted in innocency; whatever intermission or neglect there has been of other institutions, this was never laid aside, nor will be till the end of time. In the old world, they were *marrying, and giving in marriage;* the Jews in Babylon, when cut off from other ordinances, yet were bid to *take them wives,* Jer. xxix. 6. All civilized nations have had a sense of the obligation of the marriage covenant; and it is requisite for the gratifying of the desires, and recruiting the deficiencies, of the human nature. But, in the resurrection, there is no occasion for marriage; whether in glorified bodies there will be any distinction of sexes some too curiously dispute (the ancients are divided in their opinions about it); but, whether there will be a distinction or no, it is certain that there will be no conjunction; where God will be *all in all,* there needs no other *meet-help;* the body will be *spiritual,* and there will be in it no carnal desires to be gratified: when the mystical body is completed, there will be no further occasion to *seek a godly seed,* which was one end of the institution of marriage, Mal. ii. 15. In heaven there will be no decay of the individuals, and therefore no eating and drinking; no decay of the species, and therefore no marrying; *where there shall be no more deaths* (Rev. xxi. 4), there need be no more births. The married state is a composition of joys and cares; those that enter upon it are taught to look upon it as subject to changes, *richer and poorer, sickness and health;* and therefore it is fit for this mixed, changing world; but as in hell, where there is no joy, the voice of the bridegroom and the voice of the bride shall be heard no more at all, so in heaven, where there is all joy, and no care or pain or trouble, there will be no marrying. The joys of that state are pure and spiritual, and arise from the marriage of all of them to the Lamb, not of any of them to one another.

(2.) It is like the state angels are now in, in heaven; *They are as the angels of God in heaven;* they *are* so, that is, undoubtedly they shall be so. They are so already in Christ their Head, who has made them *sit with him in heavenly places,* Eph. ii. 6. The spirits of just men already made perfect are of the same corporation with the innumerable company of angels, Heb. xii. 22, 23. Man in his creation was *made a little lower than the angels* (Ps. viii. 5); but in his complete redemption and renovation will be as the angels; pure and spiritual as the angels, knowing and loving as those blessed seraphim, ever praising God like them and with them. The bodies of the saints shall be raised incorruptible and glorious, like the uncompounded vehicles of those pure and holy spirits (1 Cor xv. 42, &c.), swift and strong, like them. We should *therefore* desire and endeavour to do the will of God now as the angels do it in heaven, because we hope shortly to be like the angels who always behold our Father's face. He saith nothing of the state of the wicked in the resurrection; but, by consequence, they shall be like the devils, whose lusts they have done.

IV. Christ's argument to confirm this great truth of the resurrection and a future state; the matters being of great concern, he did not think it enough (as in some other disputes) to discover the fallacy and sophistry of the objections, but backed the truth with a solid argument; for Christ *brings forth judgment to truth* as well as victory, and enables his followers to give a reason of the hope that is in them. Now observe,

1. Whence he fetched his argument—from the scripture; that is the great magazine or armoury whence we may be furnished with spiritual weapons, offensive and defensive. *It is written* is Goliath's sword. *Have ye not read that which was spoken to you by God?* Note, (1.) What the scripture speaks God speaks. (2.) What was spoken to Moses was spoken to us; it was spoken and *written for our learning.* (3.) It concerns us to read and hear what God hath spoken, because it is spoken to us. It was spoken to you Jews in the first place, for to them were committed the oracles of God. The argument is fetched from the books of Moses, because the Sadducees received *them* only, as some think, or, at least, them chiefly, for canonical scriptures; Christ therefore fetched his proof from the most indisputable fountain. The latter prophets have more express proofs of a future state than the law of Moses has; for though the law of Moses supposes the immortality of the soul and a future state, as principles of what is called natural religion, yet no express revelation of it is made by the law of Moses; because so much of that law was peculiar to that people, and was therefore guarded as municipal laws used to be with temporal promises and threatenings, and the more express revelation of a future state was reserved for the latter days; but our Saviour finds a very solid argument for the resurrection even in the writings of Moses. Much scripture treasure lies under ground, that must be digged for.

2. What his argument was (*v* 32); *I am the God of Abraham.* This was not an express proof, *totidem verbis—in so many words;* and yet it was really a conclusive argument. Consequences from scripture, if rightly deduced, must be received as scripture; for it was written for those that have the use of reason.

Now the drift of the argument is to prove,

(1.) That there is a future state, another life after this, in which the righteous shall be truly and constantly happy. This is proved from what God said; *I am the God of Abraham.*

[1.] For God to be any one's God supposes some very extraordinary privilege and happiness; unless we know fully what God is, we could not comprehend the riches of that word, *I will be to thee a God,* that is, a Benefactor like myself. The God *of* Israel is a God *to* Israel (1 Chron. xvii. 24), a spiritual Benefactor; for he is the Father of spirits, and blesseth with spiritual blessings: it is to be an all-sufficient Benefactor, a God that is enough, a complete Good, and an eternal Benefactor; for he is himself an everlasting God, and will be to those that are in covenant with him an everlasting Good. This great word God had often said to Abraham, Isaac, and Jacob; and it was intended as a recompence for their singular faith and obedience, in quitting their country at God's call. The Jews had a profound veneration for those three patriarchs, and would extend the promise God made them to the uttermost.

[2.] It is manifest that these good men had no such extraordinary happiness, in *this* life, as might look any thing like the accomplishment of so great a word as that. They were strangers in the land of promise, wandering, pinched with famine; they had not a foot of ground of their own but a burying-place, which directed them to look for something beyond this life. In present enjoyments they came far short of their neighbours that were strangers to this covenant. What was there in this world to distinguish them and the heirs of their faith from other people, any whit proportionable to the dignity and distinction of this covenant? If no happiness had been reserved for these great and good men on the other side death, that melancholy word of poor Jacob's, when he was old (Gen. xlvii. 9), *Few and evil have the days of the years of my life been*, would have been an eternal reproach to the wisdom, goodness, and faithfulness, of that God who had so often called himself *the God of Jacob*.

[3.] Therefore there must certainly be a future state, in which, as God will ever live to be eternally rewarding, so Abraham, Isaac, and Jacob, will ever live to be eternally rewarded. That of the apostle (Heb. xi. 16), is a key to this argument, where, when he had been speaking of the faith and obedience of the patriarchs in the land of their pilgrimage, he adds, *Wherefore God is not ashamed to be called their God;* because *he has provided for them a city*, a heavenly city; implying, that if he had not provided so well for them in the other world, considering how they sped in this, he would have been ashamed to have called himself *their God;* but now he is not, having done that for them which answers it in its true intent and full extent.

(2.) That the soul is immortal, and the body shall rise again, to be united; if the former point be gained, these will follow; but they are likewise proved by considering the time when God spoke this; it was to Moses at the bush, long after Abraham, Isaac, and Jacob, were dead and buried; and yet God saith, not, "*I was*," or "*have been*," but, *I am the God of Abraham*. Now *God is not* *God of the dead, but of the living*. He is a living God, and communicates vital influences to those to whom he is a God. If, when Abraham died, there had been an end of him, there had been an end likewise of God's relation to him as his God; but at that time, when God spoke to Moses, he was the God of Abraham, and therefore Abraham must be then alive; which proves the immortality of the soul in a state of bliss; and that, by consequence, infers the resurrection of the body; for there is such an inclination in the human soul to its body, as would make a final and eternal separation inconsistent with the bliss of those that have God for *their God*. The Sadducees' notion was, that the union between body and soul is so close, that, when the body dies, the soul dies with it. Now, upon the same hypothesis, if the soul lives, as it certainly does, the body must some time or other live with it. And besides, the Lord is for the body, it is an essential part of the man; there is a covenant with the dust, which will be remembered, otherwise *the man* would not be happy. The charge which the dying patriarchs gave concerning their bones, and that *in faith*, was an evidence that they had some expectation of the resurrection of their bodies. But this doctrine was reserved for a more full revelation after the resurrection of Christ, who *was the first-fruits of them that slept*.

Lastly, We have the issue of this dispute. The Sadducees were *put to silence* (*v.* 34), and so put to shame. They thought by their subtlety to put Christ to shame, when they were preparing shame for themselves. But the multitude *were astonished at his doctrine*, *v.* 33. 1. Because it was new to them. See to what a sad pass the exposition of scripture was come among them, when people were astonished at it as a miracle to hear the fundamental promise applied to this great truth; they had sorry scribes, or this had been no news to them. 2. Because it had something in it very good and great. Truth often shows the brighter, and is the more admired, for its being opposed. Observe, Many gainsayers are silenced, and many hearers astonished, without being savingly converted; yet even in the silence and astonishment of unsanctified souls God magnifies his law, magnifies his gospel, and makes both honourable.

34 But when the Pharisees had
heard that he had put the Sadducees
to silence, they were gathered together.
35 Then one of them, *which*
was a lawyer, asked *him a question*,
tempting him, and saying, 36 Master,
which *is* the great commandment
in the law? 37 Jesus said unto him,
Thou shalt love the Lord thy God
with all thy heart, and with all thy
soul, and with all thy mind. 38 This
is the first and great commandment.
39 And the second *is* like unto it,
Thou shalt love thy neighbour as
thyself. 40 On these two commandments
hang all the law and the prophets.

Here is a discourse which Christ had with a Pharisee-lawyer, about the great commandment of the law. Observe,

I. The combination of the Pharisees against Christ, *v.* 34. They heard *that he had put the Sadducees to silence*, had stopped their mouths, though their understandings were not opened; and they were *gathered together*, not to return him the thanks of their party, as they ought to have done, for his effectually asserting and confirming of the truth against the Sadducees, the common enemies of their religion, but to *tempt him,* in hopes to get the reputation of puzzling him who had puzzled the Sadducees. They were more vexed that Christ was honoured, than pleased that the Sadducees were silenced; being more concerned for their own tyranny and traditions, which Christ opposed, than for the doctrine of the resurrection and a future state, which the Sadducees opposed. Note, It is an instance of Pharisaical envy and malice, to be displeased at the maintaining of a confessed truth, when it is done by those we do not like; to sacrifice a public good to private piques and prejudices. Blessed Paul was otherwise minded, Phil. i. 18.

II. The lawyer's question, which he put to Christ. The lawyers were students in, and teachers of, the law of Moses, as the scribes were; but some think that in *this* they differed, that they dealt more in practical questions than the scribes; they studied and professed casuistical divinity. This lawyer *asked him a question, tempting him;* not with any design to ensnare him, as appears by St. Mark's relation of the story, where we find that this was he to whom Christ said, *Thou art not far from the kingdom of God,* Mark xii. 34, but only to see what he would say, and to draw on discourse with him, to satisfy his own and his friends' curiosity.

1. The question was, *Master, which is the greatest commandment of the law?* A needless question, when all the things of God's law are great things (Hos. viii. 12), and the wisdom from above is without partiality, partiality in the law (Mal. ii. 9), and hath respect to them all. Yet it is true, there are some commands that are the principles of the oracles of God, more extensive and inclusive than others. Our Saviour speaks of the *weightier matters of the law, ch.* xxiii. 23.

2. The design was to try him, or tempt him; to try, not so much his knowledge as his judgment. It was a question disputed among the critics in the law. Some would have the law of circumcision to be the great commandment, others the law of the sabbath, others the law of sacrifices, according as they severally stood affected, and spent their zeal; now they would try what Christ said to this question, hoping to incense the people against him, if he should not answer according to the vulgar opinion; and if he should magnify one commandment, they would reflect on him as vilifying the rest. The question was harmless enough; and it appears by comparing Luke x. 27, 28, that it was an adjudged point among the lawyers, that the *love of God* and our *neighbour* is the great commandment, and the sum of all the rest, and Christ had there approved it; so that the putting of it to him here seems rather a scornful design to catechise him as a child, than a spiteful design to dispute with him as an adversary.

III. Christ's answer to this question; it is well for us that such a question was asked him, that we might have his answer. It is no disparagement to great men to answer plain questions. Now Christ recommends to us those as the great commandments, not which are so exclusive of others, but which are *therefore* great because inclusive of others. Observe,

1. Which these great commandments are (*v.* 37—39); not the judicial laws, those could not be the greatest now that the people of the Jews, to whom they pertained, were so little; not the ceremonial laws, those could not be the greatest, now that they were waxen old, and were ready to vanish away; nor any particular moral precept; but the love of God and our neighbour, which are the spring and foundation of all the rest, which (these being supposed) will follow of course.

(1.) All the law is fulfilled in one word, and that is, *love.* See Rom. xiii. 10. All obedience begins in the affections, and nothing in religion is done right, that is not done there first. Love is the leading affection, which gives law, and gives ground, to the rest; and therefore that, as the main fort, is to be first secured and garrisoned for God. Man is a creature cut out for love; thus therefore is the law written in the heart, that it is a *law of love.* Love is a short and sweet word; and, if that be *the fulfilling of the law,* surely the yoke of the command is very easy. Love is the rest and satisfaction of the soul; if we walk in this good old way, we shall find rest.

(2.) The *love of God* is the first and great commandment of all, and the summary of all the commands of the first table. The proper act of love being complacency, good is the proper object of it. Now God, being good infinitely, originally, and eternally, is to be loved in the first place, and nothing loved beside him, but what is loved for him. *Love* is the first and great thing that God demands from us, and therefore the first and great thing that we should devote to him.

Now here we are directed,

[1.] To love God as ours; *Thou shalt love the Lord thy God* as thine. The first commandment is, *Thou shalt have no other God;* which implies that we must have him for our God, and that will engage our love to him. Those that made the sun and moon their gods, loved them, Jer. viii. 2; Judges xviii. 24. To love God as ours is to love him because he is ours, our Creator, Owner, and Ruler, and to conduct ourselves to him as ours, with obedience to him, and dependence on him. We must love God as reconciled to us, and made ours by covenant; that is the foundation of this, *Thy God.*

[2.] To love him *with all our heart, and soul, and mind.* Some make these to signify one and the same thing, to love him with all our powers; others distinguish them; the heart, soul, and mind, are the will, affections, and understanding; or the vital, sensitive, and intellectual, faculties. Our love of God must be a sincere love, and not in word and tongue only, as theirs is who say they love him, but their hearts are not with him. It must be a strong love, we must love him in the most intense degree; as we must *praise* him, so we must *love* him, with *all that is within us,* Ps. ciii. 1. It must be a singular and superlative love, we must love him more than any thing else; this way the stream of our affections must entirely run. The heart must be united to love God, in opposition to a divided heart. All our love is too little to bestow upon him, and therefore all the powers of the soul must be engaged for him, and carried out toward him. *This is the first and great commandment;* for obedience to this is the spring of obedience to all the rest; which is *then* only acceptable, when it flows from love.

(3.) *To love our neighbour as ourselves* is the *second* great commandment (*v.* 39); *It is like unto that first;* it is inclusive of all the precepts of the second table, as that is of the first. It is *like* it, for it is founded upon it, and flows from it; and a right love to our brother, whom we have seen, is both an instance and an evidence of our *love to God, whom we have not seen,* 1 John iv. 20.

[1.] It is implied, that we do, and should, love ourselves. There is a self-love which is corrupt, and the root of the greatest sins, and it must be put off and mortified: but there is a self-love which is natural, and the rule of the greatest duty, and it must be preserved and sanctified. We must love ourselves, that is, we must have a due regard to the dignity of our own natures, and a due concern for the welfare of our own souls and bodies.

[2.] It is prescribed, that we *love our neighbour as ourselves.* We must honour and esteem all men, and must wrong and injure none; must have a good will to all, and good wishes for all, and, as we have opportunity, must do good to all. We must love our neighbour as ourselves, as truly and sincerely as we love ourselves, and in the same instances; nay, in many cases we must deny ourselves for the good of our neighbour, and must make ourselves servants to the true welfare of others, and be willing to *spend and be spent for them,* to *lay down our lives for the brethren.*

2. Observe what the weight and greatness of these commandments is (*v.* 40); *On these two commandments hang all the law and the prophets;* that is, This is the sum and substance of all those precepts relating to practical religion which were written in men's hearts by nature, revived by Moses, and backed and enforced by the preaching and writing of the prophets. All hang upon the law of love; take away this, and all falls to the ground, and comes to nothing. Rituals and ceremonials must give way to these, as must all spiritual gifts, for love is the more excellent way. This is the spirit of the law, which animates it, the cement of the law, which joins it; it is the root and spring of all other duties, the compendium of the whole Bible, not only of the law and the prophets, but of the gospel too, only supposing this love to be the fruit of faith, and that we love God in Christ, and our neighbour for his sake. All hangs on these two commandments, as the effect doth both on its efficient and on its final cause; for *the fulfilling of the law is love* (Rom. xiii. 10), and *the end of the law is love,* 1 Tim. i. 5. The law of love is the nail, is the *nail in the sure place, fastened by the masters of assemblies* (Eccl. xii. 11), on which is hung all *the glory of the law and the prophets* (Isa. xxii. 24), a nail that shall never be drawn; for on this nail all the glory of the new Jerusalem shall eternally hang. *Love never faileth.* Into these two great commandments therefore let our hearts be delivered as into a mould; in the defence and evidence of these let us spend our zeal, and not in notions, names, and strifes of words, as if those were the mighty things on which the law and the prophets hung, and to them the love of God and our neighbour must be sacrificed; but to the commanding power of these let every thing else be made to bow.

41 While the Pharisees were gathered together, Jesus asked them,
42 Saying, What think ye of Christ? whose son is he? They say unto him, *The son* of David.
43 He saith unto them, How then doth David in spirit call him Lord, saying,
44 The LORD said unto my Lord, Sit thou on my right hand, till I make thine enemies thy footstool?
45 If David then call him Lord, how is he his son?
46 And no man was able to answer him a word, neither durst any *man* from that day forth ask him any more *questions.*

Many questions the Pharisees had asked Christ, by which, though they thought to pose him, they did but *ex*pose themselves; but now let him ask them a question; and he will do it when they are gathered together, *v.* 41. He did not take some one of them apart from the rest, *(ne Hercules contra duos—Hercules himself may be overmatched),* but, to shame them the more, he took them all together, when they were in confederacy and consulting against him, and yet puzzled them. Note, God delights to baffle his enemies when they most strengthen themselves; he gives them all the advantages they can wish for, and yet conquers them. *Associate yourselves, and you shall be broken in pieces,* Isa. iii. 9, 10. Now here,

I. Christ proposes a question to them, which they could easily answer; it was a question in their own catechism; "*What think ye of Christ? Whose Son is he?* Whose Son do you expect the Messiah to be, who was promised to the fathers?" This they could easily answer, *The Son of David.* It was the common periphrasis of the Messiah; they called him *the Son of David.* So the scribes, who expounded the scripture, had taught them, from Ps. lxxxix. 35, 36, *I will not lie unto David; his seed shall endure for ever* (Isa. ix. 7), *upon the throne of David.* And Isa. xi. 1, *A rod out of the stem of Jesse.* The covenant of royalty made with David was a figure of the covenant of redemption made with Christ, who, as David, was made King *with an oath,* and was first humbled and then advanced. If Christ was the Son of David, he was really and truly Man. Israel said, *We have ten parts in David;* and Judah said, *He is our bone and our flesh;* what part have we then in the Son of David, who took our nature upon him?

What think ye of Christ? They had put questions to him, one after another, out of the law; but he comes and puts a question to them upon the promise. Many are so full of the law, that they forget Christ, as if their duties would save them without his merit and grace. It concerns each of us seriously to ask ourselves, What think we of Christ? Some think not of him at all, he is not in all, not in any, of their thoughts; some think meanly, and some think hardly, of him; but *to them that believe he is precious;* and *how precious then are the thoughts of him!* While *the daughters of Jerusalem* think no more of Christ than of *another beloved,* the spouse thinks of him as *the Chief of ten thousands.*

II. He starts a difficulty upon their answer, which they could not so easily solve, *v.* 43—45. Many can so readily affirm the truth, that they think they have knowledge enough to be proud of, who, when they are called to confirm the truth, and to vindicate and defend it, show they have ignorance enough to be ashamed of. The objection Christ raised was, *If Christ be David's son, how then doth David, in spirit, call him Lord?* He did not hereby design to ensnare them, as they did him, but to instruct them in a truth they were loth to believe—that the expected Messiah is God.

1. It is easy to see that David calls Christ *Lord,* and this in spirit being divinely inspired, and actuated therein by a spirit of prophecy; for it was *the Spirit of the Lord that spoke by him,* 2 Sam. xxiii. 1, 2. David was one of those *holy men that spoke as* they were *moved by the Holy Ghost,* especially in calling Christ *Lord;* for it was then, as it is still (1 Cor. xii. 3), that *no man can say that Jesus is the Lord, but by the Holy Ghost.* Now, to prove that David, in spirit, called Christ *Lord,* he quotes Ps. cx. 1, which psalm the scribes themselves understood of Christ; of him, it is certain, the prophet there speaks, of him and of no other man; and it is a prophetical summary of the doctrine of Christ, it describes him executing the offices of a Prophet, Priest, and King, both in his humiliation and also in his exaltation.

Christ quotes the whole verse, which shows the Redeemer in his exaltation; (1.) *Sitting at the right hand of God.* His sitting denotes both rest and rule; his sitting at God's right hand denotes superlative honour and sovereign power. See in what great words this is expressed (Heb. viii. 1); *He is set on the right hand of the throne of the Majesty.* See Phil. ii. 9; Eph. i. 20. He did not take this honour to himself, but was entitled to it by covenant with his Father, and invested in it by commission from him, and here is that commission. (2.) Subduing his enemies. There he shall sit, till they be all made either his friends or his footstool. *The carnal mind,* wherever it is, *is enmity to Christ;* and that is subdued in the *conversion of the willing people that are called to his foot* (as the expression is, Isa. xli. 2), and in the confusion of his impenitent adversaries, who shall be brought under his foot, as the kings of Canaan were under the feet of Joshua.

But that which this verse is quoted for is, that David calls the Messiah *his Lord; the Lord,* Jehovah, *said unto my Lord.* This intimates to us, that in expounding scripture we must take notice of, and improve, not only that which is the main scope and sense of a verse, but of the words and phrases, by which the Spirit chooses to express that sense, which have often a very useful and instructive significance. Here is a good note from that word, *My Lord.*

2. It is not so easy for those who believe not the Godhead of the Messiah, to clear this from an absurdity, if Christ be David's son. It is incongruous for the father to speak of his son, the predecessor of his successor, as his *Lord.* If David call him *Lord,* that is laid down (*v.* 45) as the *magis notum—the more evident truth;* for whatever is said of Christ's humanity and humiliation must be construed and understood in consistency with the truth of his divine nature and dominion. We must hold this fast, that he is David's Lord, and by that explain his being David's son. The seeming differences of scripture, as here, may not only be accommodated, but contribute to the beauty and harmony of the whole. *Amicæ scripturarum lites, utinam et nostræ—The differences observable in the scriptures are of a friendly kind; would to God that our differences were of the same kind!*

III. We have here the success of this gentle trial which Christ made of the Pharisees' knowledge, in two things.

1. It puzzled them (*v.* 46); *No man was able to answer him a word.* Either it was their ignorance that they did not know, or their impiety that they would not own, the Messiah to be God; which truth was the only key to unlock this difficulty. What

those Rabbies could not then answer, blessed be God, the plainest Christian that is led into the understanding of the gospel of Christ, can now account for; that Christ, as God, was David's *Lord;* and Christ, as Man, was David's *son.* This he did not now himself explain, but reserved it till the proof of it was completed by his resurrection; but we have it fully explained by him in his glory (Rev. xxii. 16); *I am the root and the offspring of David.* Christ, as God, was David's *Root;* Christ, as Man, was David's *Offspring.* If we hold not fast this truth, that Jesus Christ is over all God blessed for ever, we run ourselves into inextricable difficulties. And well might David, his remote ancestor, call him *Lord,* when Mary, his immediate mother, after she had conceived him, *called him, Lord and God, her Saviour,* Luke i. 46, 47.

2. It silenced them, and all others that sought occasion against him; *Neither durst any man, from that day forth, ask him any more* such captious, tempting, ensnaring *questions.* Note, God will glorify himself in the silencing of many whom he will not glorify himself in the salvation of. Many are convinced, that are not converted, by the word. Had these been converted, they would have asked him more questions, especially that great question, *What must we do to be saved?* But since they could not gain their point, they would have no more to do with him. But, thus all that strive with their Master shall be convinced, as these Pharisees and lawyers here were, of the inequality of the match.

CHAP. XXIII.

In the foregoing chapter, we had our Saviour's discourses with the scribes and Pharisees; here we have his discourse concerning them, or rather against them. I. He allows their office, ver. 2, 3. II. He warns his disciples not to imitate their hypocrisy and pride, ver. 4—12. III. He exhibits a charge against them for divers high crimes and misdemeanors, corrupting the law, opposing the gospel, and treacherous dealing both with God and man; and to each article he prefixes a woe, ver. 13—33. IV. He passes sentence upon Jerusalem, and fortels the ruin of the city and temple, especially for the sin of persecution, ver. 34—39.

THEN spake Jesus to the multitude, and to his disciples, 2
Saying, The scribes and the Pharisees
sit in Moses' seat: 3 All therefore
whatsoever they bid you observe,
that observe and do; but do not ye
after their works: for they say, and
do not. 4 For they bind heavy burdens and grievous to be borne, and
lay *them* on men's shoulders; but
they *themselves* will not move them
with one of their fingers. 5 But all
their works they do for to be seen of
men: they make broad their philac-
teries, and enlarge the borders of their
garments, 6 And love the uppermost
rooms at feasts, and the chief seats
in the synagogues, 7 And greetings
in the markets, and to be called of
men, Rabbi, Rabbi. 8 But be not ye
called Rabbi: for one is your Master,
even Christ; and all ye are brethren.
9 And call no *man* your father upon
the earth: for one is your Father,
which is in heaven. 10 Neither be
ye called masters: for one is your
Master, *even* Christ. 11 But he that
is greatest among you shall be your
servant. 12 And whosoever shall
exalt himself shall be abased; and
he that shall humble himself shall be
exalted.

We find not Christ, in all his preaching, so severe upon any sort of people as upon these *scribes and Pharisees;* for the truth is, nothing is more directly opposite to the spirit of the gospel than the temper and practice of that generation of men, who were made up of pride, worldliness, and tyranny, under a cloak and pretence of religion; yet these were the idols and darlings of the people, who thought, if but two men went to heaven, one would be a Pharisee. Now Christ directs his discourse here *to the multitude, and to his disciples* (*v.* 1), to rectify their mistakes concerning these scribes and Pharisees, by painting them out in their true colours, and so to take off the prejudice which some of the multitude had conceived against Christ and his doctrine, because it was opposed by those men of their church, that called themselves the people's guides. Note, It is good to know the true characters of men, that we may not be imposed upon by great and mighty names, titles, and pretensions to power. People must be told of *the wolves* (Acts xx. 29, 30), *the dogs* (Phil. iii. 2), *the deceitful workers* (2 Cor. xi. 13), that they may know where to stand upon their guard. And not only the mixed multitude, but even the disciples, need these cautions; for good men are apt to have their eyes dazzled with worldly pomp.

Now, in this discourse,

I. Christ allows their office as expositors of the law; *The scribes and Pharisees* (that is, the whole Sanhedrim, who sat at the helm of church government, who were all called *scribes,* and were some of them Pharisees), they *sit in Moses' seat* (*v.* 2), as public teachers and interpreters of the law; and, the law of Moses being the municipal law of their state, they were as judges, or a bench of justices; teaching and judging seem to be equivalent, comparing 2 Chron. xvii. 7, 9, with 2 Chron. xix. 5, 6, 8. They were not the itinerant judges that rode the circuit, but the standing bench, that determined on appeals, special verdicts, or writs of error by the law; they sat in Moses's seat, not as he was Mediator between God and Israel, but only as he was chief justice, Exod. xviii. 26.

Or, we may apply it, not to the Sanhedrim, but to the other Pharisees and scribes, that expounded the law, and taught the people how to apply it to particular cases. *The pulpit of wood*, such as was made for Ezra, *that ready scribe in the law of God* (Neh. viii. 4), is here called *Moses's seat*, because Moses had those in every city (so the expression is, Acts xv. 21), who in those pulpits preached him; this was their office, and it was just and honourable; it was requisite that there should be some at whose mouth the people might *enquire the law*, Mal. ii. 7. Note, 1. Many a good place is filled with bad men; it is no new thing for the vilest men to be exalted even to *Moses's seat* (Ps. xii. 8); and, when it is so, the men are not so much honoured by the seat as the seat is dishonoured by the men. Now they that sat in Moses's seat were so wretchedly degenerated, that it was time for the great Prophet to arise, like unto Moses, to erect another seat. 2. Good and useful offices and powers are not *therefore* to be condemned and abolished, because they fall sometimes into the hands of bad men, who abuse them. We must not *therefore* pull down Moses's seat, because scribes and Pharisees have got possession of it; rather than so, *let both grow together until the harvest, ch.* xiii. 30.

Hence he infers (*v.* 3), "*Whatsoever they bid you observe, that observe and do.* As far as they *sit in Moses's seat*, that is, read and preach the law that was given by Moses" (which, as yet, continued in full force, power, and virtue), "and judge according to that law, so far you must hearken to them, as remembrancers to you of the written word." The scribes and Pharisees made it their business to study the scripture, and were well acquainted with the language, history, and customs of it, and its style and phraseology. Now Christ would have the people to make use of the helps they gave them for the understanding of the scripture, and do accordingly. As long as their comments did illustrate the text and not pervert it; did make plain, and not *make void, the commandment of God;* so far they must be observed and obeyed, but with caution and a judgment of discretion. Note, We must not think the worse of good truths for their being preached by bad ministers; nor of good laws for their being executed by bad magistrates. Though it is most desirable to have our food brought by angels, yet, if God send it to us by ravens, if it be good and wholesome, we must take it, and thank God for it. Our Lord Jesus premiseth this, to prevent the cavil which some would be apt to make at his following discourse; as if, by condemning the scribes and Pharisees, he designed to bring the law of Moses into contempt, and to draw people off from it; whereas he *came not to destroy, but to fulfil.* Note, It is wisdom to obviate the exceptions which may be taken at just reproofs, especially when there is occasion to distinguish between officers and their offices, *that the ministry be not blamed* when the ministers are.

II. He condemns the men. He had ordered the multitude to do as they taught; but here he annexeth a caution not to do as they did, to beware of their leaven; *Do not ye after their works.* Their traditions were their works, were their idols, the works of their fancy. Or, "Do not according to their example." Doctrines and practices are spirits that must be tried, and, where there is occasion, must be carefully separated and distinguished; and as we must not swallow corrupt doctrines for the sake of any laudable practices of those that teach them, so we must not imitate any bad examples for the sake of the plausible doctrines of those that set them. The scribes and Pharisees boasted as much of the goodness of their works as of the orthodoxy of their teaching, and hoped to be justified by them; it was the plea they put in (Luke xviii. 11, 12); and yet these things, which they valued themselves so much upon, were an abomination in the sight of God.

Our Saviour here, and in the following verses, specifies divers particulars of their works, wherein we must not imitate them. In general, they are charged with hypocrisy, dissimulation, or double-dealing in religion; a crime which cannot be enquired of at men's bar, because we can only judge according to outward appearance; but God, who searcheth the heart, can convict of hypocrisy; and nothing is more displeasing to him, for he desireth truth.

Four things are in these verses charged upon them.

1. Their saying and doing were two things. Their practice was no way agreeable either to their preaching or to their profession; for *they say, and do not;* they teach out of the law that which is good, but their conversation gives them the lie; and they seem to have found another way to heaven for themselves than what they show to others. See this illustrated and charged home upon them, Rom. ii. 17—24. Those are of all sinners most inexcusable that allow themselves in the sins they condemn in others, or in worse. This doth especially touch wicked ministers, who will be sure to have their portion appointed them with hypocrites (*ch.* xxiv. 51); for what greater hypocrisy can there be, than to press that upon others, to be believed and done, which they themselves disbelieve and disobey; pulling down in their practice what they build up in their preaching; when in the pulpit, preaching so well that it is a pity they should ever come out; but, when out of the pulpit, living so ill that it is a pity they should ever come in; like bells, that call others to church, but hang out of it themselves; or Mercurial posts, that point the way to others, but stand still themselves? Such will *be judged out of their own mouths.*

It is applicable to all others that say, and do not; that make a plausible profession of religion, but do not live up to that profession; that make fair promises, but do not perform their promises; are full of good discourse, and can lay down the law to all about them, but are empty of good works; great talkers, but little doers; *the voice is Jacob's voice, but the hands are the hands of Esau. Vox et præterea nihil—mere sound.* They speak fair, *I go, sir;* but there is no trusting them, for *there are seven abominations in their heart.*

2. They were very severe in imposing upon others those things which they were not themselves willing to submit to the burthen of (*v.* 4); *They bind heavy burthens, and grievous to be borne;* not only insisting upon the minute circumstances of the law, which is called *a yoke* (Acts xv. 10), and pressing the observation of them with more strictness and severity than God himself did (whereas the maxim of the lawyers is, *Apices juris non sunt jura—Mere points of law are not law),* but by adding to his words, and imposing their own inventions and traditions, under the highest penalties. They loved to show their authority and to exercise their domineering faculty, lording it over God's heritage, and saying to men's souls, *Bow down, that we may go over;* witness their many additions to the law of the fourth commandment, by which they made the sabbath a burthen on men's shoulders, which was designed to be the joy of their hearts. Thus with force and cruelty did those shepherds *rule the flock,* as of old, Ezek. xxxiv. 4.

But see their hypocrisy; *They themselves will not move them with one of their fingers.* (1.) They would not exercise themselves in those things which they imposed upon others; they pressed upon the people a strictness in religion which they themselves would not be bound by; but secretly transgressed their own traditions, which they publicly enforced. They indulged their pride in giving law to others; but consulted their ease in their own practice. Thus it has been said, to the reproach of the popish priests, that they fast with wine and sweetmeats, while they force the people to fast with bread and water; and decline the penances they enjoin the laity. (2.) They would not ease the people in these things, nor put a finger to lighten their burthen, when they saw it pinched them. They could find out loose constructions to put upon God's law, and could dispense with that, but would not bate an ace of their own impositions, nor dispense with a failure in the least punctilio of them. They allowed no chancery to relieve the extremity of their common law. How contrary to this was the practice of Christ's apostles, who would allow to others that use of Christian liberty which, for the peace and edification of the church, they would deny themselves in! They would lay no other burthen than necessary things, and those easy, Acts xv. 28. How carefully doth Paul spare those to whom he writes! 1 Cor. vii. 28; ix. 12.

3. They were all for show, and nothing for substance, in religion (*v.* 5); *All their works they do, to be seen of men.* We must do such good works, that they who see them may glorify God; but we must not proclaim our good works, with design that others may see them, and glorify us; which our Saviour here chargeth upon the Pharisees in general, as he had done before in the particular instances of prayer and giving of alms. All their end was to be praised of men, and therefore all their endeavour was to be seen of men, to *make a fair show in the flesh.* In those duties of religion which fall under the eye of men, none were so constant and abundant as they; but in what lies between God and their souls, in the retirement of their closets, and the recesses of their hearts, they desire to be excused. The *form* of godliness will get them a name to live, which is all they aim at, and therefore they trouble not themselves with the *power* of it, which is essential to a life indeed. He that does all to be seen does nothing to the purpose.

He specifies two things which they did to be seen of men.

(1.) *They made broad their phylacteries.* Those were little scrolls of paper or parchment, wherein were written, with great niceness, these four paragraphs of the law, Exod. xiii. 2—11; xiii. 11—16; Deut. vi. 4—9; xi. 13—21. These were sewn up in leather, and worn upon their foreheads and left arms. It was a tradition of the elders, which had reference to Exod. xiii. 9, and Prov. vii. 3, where the expressions seem to be figurative, intimating no more than that we should bear the things of God in our minds as carefully as if we had them bound between our eyes. Now the Pharisees made broad these phylacteries, that they might be thought more holy, and strict, and zealous for the law, than others. It is a gracious ambition to covet to be really more holy than others, but it is a proud ambition to covet to appear so. It is good to excel in real piety, but not to exceed in outward shows; for overdoing is justly suspected of design, Prov. xxvii. 14. It is the guise of hypocrisy to make more ado than needs in external services, more than is needful either to prove, or to *im*prove, the good affections and dispositions of the soul.

(2.) *They enlarged the borders of their garments.* God appointed the Jews to make borders or fringes upon their garments (Numb. xv. 38), to distinguish them from other nations, and to be a memorandum to them of their being a peculiar people; but the Pharisees were not content to have these borders like other people's, which might serve God's design in appointing them; but they must be larger than ordinary, to answer their design of making themselves to be taken notice of; as if they were more religious than others. But those who thus enlarge their phylacteries, and the borders of their garments, while their hearts are straitened, and destitute of the love of God and their neighbour, though they may now deceive others, will in the end deceive themselves.

4. They much affected pre-eminence and superiority, and prided themselves extremely in it. Pride was the darling reigning sin of the Pharisees, *the sin that did most easily beset them,* and which our Lord Jesus takes all occasions to witness against.

(1.) He describes their pride, *v.* 6, 7. They courted, and coveted,

[1.] Places of honour and respect. In all public appearances, as *at feasts, and in the synagogues,* they expected, and had, to their hearts' delight, *the uppermost rooms, and the chief seats.* They took place of all others, and precedency was adjudged to them, as persons of the greatest note and merit; and it is easy to imagine what a complacency they took in it; *they loved to have the preeminence,* 3 John 9. It is not possessing the uppermost rooms, nor sitting in the chief seats, that is condemned (somebody must sit uppermost), but *loving* them; for men to value such a little piece of ceremony as sitting highest, going first, taking the wall, or the better hand, and to value themselves upon it, to seek it, and to feel resentment if they have it not; what is that but making an idol of ourselves, and then falling down and worshipping it—the worst kind of idolatry! It is bad any where, but especially in the synagogues. *There* to seek honour to ourselves, where we appear in order to give glory to God, and to humble ourselves before him, is indeed to mock God instead of serving him. David would willingly lie at the threshold in God's house; so far was he from coveting *the chief seat* there, Ps. lxxxiv. 10. It savours much of pride and hypocrisy, when people do not care for going to church, unless they can look fine and make a figure there.

[2.] Titles of honour and respect. They *loved greetings in the markets,* loved to have people put off their hats to them, and show them respect when they met them in the streets. O how it pleased them, and fed their vain humour, *digito monstrari et dicier, Hic est—to be pointed out, and to have it said, This is he,* to have way made for them in the crowd of market people; "Stand off, here is a Pharisee coming!" and to be complimented with the high and pompous title of *Rabbi, Rabbi!* This was meat and drink and dainties to them; and they took as great a satisfaction in it as Nebuchadnezzar did in his palace, when he said, *Is not this great Babylon that I have built?* The *greetings* would not have done them half so much good, if they had not been in the markets, where every body might see how much they were respected, and how high they stood in the opinion of the people. It was but a little before Christ's time, that the Jewish teachers, the masters of Israel, had assumed the title of *Rabbi, Rab,* or *Rabban,* which signifies *great or much;* and was construed as *Doctor,* or *My lord.* And they laid such a stress upon it, that they gave it for a maxim that "he who salutes his teacher, and does not call him Rabbi, provokes the divine Majesty to depart from Israel;" so much religion did they place in that which was but a piece of good manners! For him that is taught in the word to give respect to him that teaches is commendable enough in him that gives it; but for him that teaches to love it, and demand it, and affect it, to be puffed up with it, and to be displeased if it be omitted, is sinful and abominable; and, instead of teaching, he has need to learn the first lesson in the school of Christ, which is humility.

(2.) He cautions his disciples against being herein like them; herein they must not do after their works; "But be not ye called so, for ye shall not be of such a spirit," *v.* 8, &c.

Here is, [1.] A prohibition of pride. They are here forbidden,

First, To challenge titles of honour and dominion to themselves, *v.* 8—10. It is repeated twice; *Be not called Rabbi, neither be ye called Master* or *Guide:* not that it is unlawful to give civil respect to *those that are over us in the Lord,* nay, it is an instance of the honour and esteem which it is our duty to show them; but, 1. Christ's ministers must not affect the name of *Rabbi* or *Master,* by way of distinction from other people; it is not agreeable to the simplicity of the gospel, for them to covet or accept the honour which they have that are in kings' palaces. 2. They must not assume the authority and dominion implied in those names; they must not be magisterial, nor domineer over their brethren, or over God's heritage, as if they had dominion over the faith of Christians: what they received of the Lord, all must receive from them; but in other things they must not make their opinions and wills a rule and standard to all other people, to be admitted with an implicit obedience. The reasons for this prohibition are,

(1.) *One is your Master, even Christ, v.* 8, and again, *v.* 10. Note, [1.] Christ is our Master, our Teacher, our Guide. Mr. George Herbert, when he named the name of *Christ,* usually added, *My Master.* [2.] Christ only is our Master, ministers are but ushers in the school. Christ only is the Master, the great Prophet, whom we must hear, and be ruled and overruled by; whose word must be an oracle and a law to us; *Verily I say unto you,* must be enough to us. And if he only be our Master, then for his ministers to set up for dictators, and to pretend to a supremacy and an infallibility, is a daring usurpation of that honour of Christ which he will not give to another.

(2.) *All ye are brethren.* Ministers are

brethren not only to one another, but to the people; and therefore it ill becomes them to be masters, when there are none for them to master it over but their brethren; yea, and we are all younger brethren, otherwise the eldest might claim an *excellency of dignity and power*, Gen. xlix. 3. But, to preclude that, Christ himself is *the first-born among many brethren*, Rom. viii. 29. Ye are brethren, as ye are all disciples of the same Master. School-fellows are brethren, and, as such, should help one another in getting their lesson; but it will by no means be allowed that one of the scholars step into the master's seat, and give law to the school. If we are all brethren, we must not be *many masters.* Jam. iii. 1.

Secondly, They are forbidden to ascribe such titles to others (*v.* 9); "*Call no man your father upon the earth;* constitute no man the father of your religion, that is, the founder, author, director, and governor, of it." The fathers of our flesh must be called *fathers,* and as such we must *give them reverence;* but God only must be allowed as *the Father of our spirits,* Heb. xii. 9. Our religion must not be derived from, or made to depend upon, any man. We are born again to the spiritual and divine life, *not of corruptible seed, but by the word of God; not of the will of the flesh, or the will of man, but of God.* Now the will of man, not being the rise of our religion, must not be the rule of it. We must not *jurare in verba magistri—swear to the dictates of any creature,* not the wisest or best, nor pin our faith on any man's sleeve, because we know not whither he will carry it. St. Paul calls himself *a Father* to those whose conversion he had been an instrument of (1 Cor. iv. 15; Phil. 10); but he pretends to no dominion over them, and uses that title to denote, not authority, but affection: therefore he calls them not his *obliged,* but his *beloved,* sons, 1 Cor. iv. 14.

The reason given is, *One is your Father, who is in heaven.* God is our Father, and is All in all in our religion. He is the Fountain of it, and its Founder; the Life of it, and its Lord; from whom alone, as the Original, our spiritual life is derived, and on whom it depends. He is *the Father of* all *lights* (Jam. i. 17), that *one Father, from whom are all things, and we in him,* Eph. iv. 6. Christ having taught us to say, *Our Father, who art in heaven;* let us *call no man Father upon earth;* no man, because *man is a worm, and the son of man is a worm,* hewn out of the same rock with us; especially not upon earth, for man upon earth is a sinful worm; *there is not a just man upon earth, that doeth good, and sinneth not,* and therefore no one is fit to be called *Father.*

[2.] Here is a precept of humility and mutual subjection (*v.* 11); *He that is greatest among you shall be your servant;* not only call himself so (we know of one who styles himself *Servus servorum Dei—Servant of the servants of God,* but acts as Rabbi, and father, and master, and *Dominus Deus noster—The Lord our God,* and what not), but he shall be so. Take it as a promise; "*He* shall be accounted greatest, and stand highest in the favour of God, that is most submissive and serviceable:" or as a precept; "He that is advanced to any place of dignity, trust, and honour, in the church, *let him be your servant*" (some copies read ἔστω for ἔσται), "let him not think that his patent of honour is a writ of ease; no; *he that is greatest* is not a lord, but a minister." St. Paul, who knew his privilege as well as duty, though *free from all, yet made himself servant unto all* (1 Cor. ix. 19); and our Master frequently pressed it upon his disciples to be humble and self-denying, mild and condescending, and to abound in all offices of Christian love, though mean, and to the meanest; and of this he hath set us an example.

[3.] Here is a good reason for all this, *v.* 12. Consider,

First, The punishment intended for the proud; *Whosoever shall exalt himself shall be abased.* If God give them repentance, they will be abased in their own eyes, and will abhor themselves for it; if they repent not, sooner or later they will be abased before the world. Nebuchadnezzar, in the height of his pride, was turned to be a fellow-commoner with the beasts; Herod, to be a feast for the worms; and Babylon, that sat as a queen, to be the scorn of nations. God made the proud and aspiring priests contemptible and base (Mal. ii. 9), and the lying prophet to be *the tail,* Isa. ix. 15. But if proud men have not marks of humiliation set upon them in this world, there is a day coming, when they shall *rise to everlasting shame and contempt* (Dan. xii. 2); *so plentifully will he reward the proud doer!* Ps. xxxi. 23.

Secondly, The preferment intended for the humble; *He that shall humble himself shall be exalted.* Humility is that *ornament which is in the sight of God of great price.* In this world the humble have the honour of being accepted with the holy God, and respected by all wise and good men; of being qualified for, and often called out to, the most honourable services; for honour is like the shadow, which flees from those that pursue it, and grasp at it, but follows those that flee from it. However, in the other world, they that have humbled themselves in contrition for their sin, in compliance with their God, and in condescension to their brethren, shall be exalted to inherit the throne of glory; shall be not only owned, but crowned, before angels and men.

13 But woe unto you, scribes and
Pharisees, hypocrites! for ye shut up
the kingdom of heaven against men:
for ye neither go in *yourselves,* neither
suffer ye them that are entering to go

in. 14 Woe unto you, scribes and
Pharisees, hypocrites! for ye devour
widows' houses, and for a pretence
make long prayer: therefore ye shall
receive the greater damnation. 15
Woe unto you, scribes and Pharisees,
hypocrites! for ye compass sea and
land to make one proselyte, and when
he is made, ye make him twofold more
the child of hell than yourselves. 16
Woe unto you, *ye* blind guides, which
say, Whosoever shall swear by the
temple, it is nothing; but whosoever
shall swear by the gold of the temple,
he is a debtor! 17 *Ye* fools and
blind: for whether is greater, the gold,
or the temple that sanctifieth the gold?
18 And, Whosoever shall swear by
the altar, it is nothing; but whosoever
sweareth by the gift that is upon it,
he is guilty. 19 *Ye* fools and blind:
for whether *is* greater, the gift, or the
altar that sanctifieth the gift? 20
Whoso therefore shall swear by the
altar, sweareth by it, and by all things
thereon. 21 And whoso shall swear
by the temple, sweareth by it, and by
him that dwelleth therein. 22 And
he that shall swear by heaven, sweareth
by the throne of God, and by him that
sitteth thereon. 23 Woe unto you,
scribes and Pharisees, hypocrites! for
ye pay tithe of mint, and anise, and
cummin, and have omitted the weightier *matters* of the law, judgment,
mercy, and faith: these ought ye to
have done, and not to leave the other
undone. 24 *Ye* blind guides, which
strain at a gnat, and swallow a camel.
25 Woe unto you, scribes and Pharisees, hypocrites! for ye make clean
the outside of the cup and of the
platter, but within they are full of extortion and excess. 26 *Thou* blind
Pharisee, cleanse first that *which is*
within the cup and platter, that the
outside of them may be clean also.
27 Woe unto you, scribes and Pharisees, hypocrites! for ye are like unto
whited sepulchres, which indeed appear beautiful outward, but are within
full of dead *men's* bones, and of all
uncleanness. 28 Even so ye also
outwardly appear righteous unto men,
but within ye are full of hypocrisy
and iniquity. 29 Woe unto you,
scribes and Pharisees, hypocrites!
because ye build the tombs of the
prophets, and garnish the sepulchres
of the righteous, 30 And say, If we
had been in the days of our fathers,
we would not have been partakers
with them in the blood of the prophets. 31 Wherefore ye be witnesses
unto yourselves, that ye are the children of them which killed the prophets.
32 Fill ye up then the measure of
your fathers. 33 *Ye* serpents, *ye*
generation of vipers, how can ye escape the damnation of hell?

In these verses we have eight woes levelled directly against the scribes and Pharisees by our Lord Jesus Christ, like so many claps of thunder, or flashes of lightning, from mount Sinai. *Three* woes are made to look very dreadful (Rev. viii. 13; ix. 12); but here are *eight* woes, in opposition to the eight beatitudes, Matt. v. 3. The gospel has its woes as well as the law, and gospel curses are of all curses the heaviest. These woes are the more remarkable, not only because of the authority, but because of the meekness and gentleness, of him that denounced them. He came to bless, and loved to bless; but, if his wrath be kindled, there is surely cause for it: and who shall entreat for him that the great Intercessor pleads against? A woe from Christ is a remediless woe.

This is here the burthen of the song, and it is a heavy burthen; *Woe unto you, scribes and Pharisees, hypocrites.* Note, 1. The scribes and Pharisees were hypocrites; that is it in which all the rest of their bad characters are summed up; it was the leaven which gave the relish to all they said and did. A hypocrite is a stage-player in religion (that is the primary signification of the word); he personates or acts the part of one that he neither is nor may be, or perhaps that he neither is nor would be. 2. That hypocrites are in a woeful state and condition. *Woe to hypocrites*; so *he* said whose saying that their case is miserable makes it so: while they live, their religion is vain; when they die, their ruin is great.

Now each of these woes against the scribes and Pharisees has a reason annexed to it, containing a separate crime charged upon them, proving their hypocrisy, and justifying the judgment of Christ upon them; for his woes, his curses, are never causeless.

I. They were sworn enemies to the gospel of Christ, and consequently to the salvation of the souls of men (*v.* 13); *They shut up the kingdom of heaven against men,* that is, they did all they could to keep people from believing in Christ, and so entering into his kingdom. Christ came to *open the kingdom of heaven,* that is, to lay open for us *a new and living way* into it, to bring men to be subjects of that kingdom. Now the scribes and Pharisees, who sat in Moses's seat, and pretended to the key of knowledge, ought to have contributed their assistance herein, by opening those scriptures of the Old Testament which pointed at the Messiah and his kingdom, in their true and proper sense; they that undertook to expound Moses and the prophets should have showed the people how they testified of Christ; that Daniel's weeks were expiring, *the sceptre was departed from Judah,* and therefore now was the time for the Messiah's appearing. Thus they might have facilitated that great work, and have helped thousands to heaven; but, instead of this, they shut up the kingdom of heaven; they made it their business to press the ceremonial law, which was now in the vanishing, to suppress the prophecies, which were now in the accomplishing, and to beget and nourish up in the minds of the people prejudices against Christ and his doctrine.

1. They would not go in themselves; *Have any of the rulers,* or *of the Pharisees, believed on him?* John vii. 48. No; they were too proud to stoop to his meanness, too formal to be reconciled to his plainness; they did not like a religion which insisted so much on humility, self-denial, contempt of the world, and spiritual worship. Repentance was the door of admission into this kingdom, and nothing could be more disagreeable to the Pharisees, who justified and admired themselves, than to repent, that is, to accuse and abase and abhor themselves; therefore they *went not in themselves;* but that was not all.

2. They would not *suffer them that were entering to go in.* It is bad to keep away from Christ ourselves, but it is worse to keep others from him; yet that is commonly the way of hypocrites: they do not love that any should go beyond them in religion, or be better than they. Their not going in themselves was a hindrance to many; for, they having so great an interest in the people, multitudes rejected the gospel only because their leaders did; but, besides that, they opposed both Christ's entertaining of sinners (Luke vii. 39), and sinners' entertaining of Christ; they perverted his doctrine, confronted his miracles, quarrelled with his disciples, and represented him, and his institutes and economy, to the people in the most disingenuous, disadvantageous manner imaginable; they thundered out their excommunications against those that confessed him, and used all their wit and power to serve their malice against him; and thus they *shut up the kingdom of heaven,* so that *they who would enter* into it must *suffer violence* (*ch.* xi. 12), and *press into it* (Luke xvi. 16), through a crowd of scribes and Pharisees, and all the obstructions and difficulties they could contrive to lay in their way. How well is it for us that our salvation is not entrusted in the hands of any man or company of men in the world! if it were, we should be undone. They that shut out of the church would shut out of heaven if they could; but the malice of men cannot *make the promise of God* to his chosen *of no effect;* blessed be God, it cannot.

II. They made religion and the form of godliness a cloak and stalking-horse to their covetous practices and desires, *v.* 14. Observe here,

1. What their wicked practices were; they *devoured widows' houses,* either by quartering themselves and their attendants upon them for entertainment, which must be of the best for men of their figure; or by insinuating themselves into their affections, and so getting to be the trustees of their estates, which they could make an easy prey of; for who could presume to call such as they were to an account? The thing they aimed at was to enrich themselves; and, this being their chief and highest end, all considerations of justice and equity were laid aside, and even widows' houses were sacrificed to this. Widows are of the weaker sex in its weakest state, easily imposed upon; and therefore they fastened on them, to make a prey of. They devoured those whom, by the law of God, they were particularly obliged to protect, patronise, and relieve. There is a woe in the Old Testament to those that *made widows their prey* (Isa. x. 1, 2); and Christ here seconded it with his woe. God is the judge of the widows; they are his peculiar care, he *establisheth their border* (Prov. xv. 25), and *espouseth their cause* (Exod. xxii. 22, 23); yet these were they whose houses the Pharisees devoured by wholesale; so greedy were they to get *their bellies filled with the treasures of wickedness!* Their devouring denotes not only covetousness, but cruelty in their oppression, described Mic. iii. 3, *They eat the flesh, and flay off the skin.* And doubtless they did all this under colour of law; for they did it so artfully that it passed uncensured, and did not at all lessen the people's veneration for them.

2. What was the cloak with which they covered this wicked practice; *For a pretence they made long prayers;* very long indeed, if it be true which some of the Jewish writers tell us, that they spent three hours at a time in the formalities of meditation and prayer, and did it thrice every day, which is more than an upright soul, that makes a conscience of being inward with God in the duty, dares pretend ordinarily to do; but to the Pharisees it was easy enough, who never made a business of the duty, and always made a trade of the outside of it. By this craft they got their wealth, and maintained their grandeur. It is not probable that these long prayers were extemporary, for then (as Mr. Baxter observes) the Pharisees had much more the gift of prayer than Christ's disciples had;

but rather that they were stated forms of words in use among them, which they said over by tale, as the papists drop their beads. Christ doth not here condemn long prayers, as in themselves hypocritical; nay if there were not a great appearance of good in them, they would not have been used for a pretence; and the cloak must be very thick which was used to cover such wicked practices. Christ himself *continued all night in prayer to God,* and we are commanded to *pray without ceasing* too soon; where there are many sins to be confessed, and many wants to pray for the supply of, and many mercies to give thanks for, there is occasion for long prayers. But the Pharisees' long prayers were made up of vain repetitions, and (which was the end of them) they were for a *pretence;* by them they got the reputation of pious devout men, that loved prayer, and were the favourites of Heaven; and by this means people were made to believe it was not possible that such men as they should cheat them; and, therefore, happy the widow that could get a Pharisee for her trustee, and guardian to her children! Thus, while they seemed to soar heaven-ward, upon the wings of prayer, their eye, like the kite's, was all the while upon their prey on the earth, some widow's house or other that lay convenient for them. Thus circumcision was the cloak of the Shechemites' covetousness (Gen. xxxiv. 22, 23), the payment of a vow in Hebron the cover of Absalom's rebellion (2 Sam. xv. 7), a fast in Jezreel must patronise Naboth's murder, and the extirpation of Baal is the footstool of Jehu's ambition. Popish priests, under pretence of long prayers for the dead, masses and dirges, and I know not what, enrich themselves by devouring the houses of the widows and fatherless. Note, It is no new thing for the show and form of godliness to be made a cloak to the greatest enormities. But dissembled piety, however it passeth now, will be reckoned for as double iniquity, *in the day when God shall judge the secrets of men.*

3. The doom passed upon them for this; *Therefore ye shall receive the greater damnation.* Note, (1.) There are degrees of damnation; there are some whose sin is more inexcusable, *and whose ruin will therefore be more intolerable.* (2.) The pretences of religion, with which hypocrites disguise or excuse their sin now, will aggravate their condemnation shortly. Such is the deceitfulness of sin, that the very thing by which sinners hope to expiate and atone for their sins will come against them, and make their sins more exceedingly sinful. But it is sad for the criminal, when his *de*fence proves his *of*fence, and his plea *(We have prophesied in thy name, and in thy name* made long prayers) heightens the charge against him.

III. While they were such enemies to the conversion of souls to Christianity, they were very industrious in the perversion of them to their faction. They shut up the kingdom of heaven against those that would turn to Christ, but at the same time *compassed sea and land to make proselytes* to themselves, *v.* 15. Observe here,

1. Their commendable industry in making proselytes to the Jewish religion, not only proselytes of *the gate,* who obliged themselves to no more than the observance of the seven precepts of the sons of Noah, but proselytes of *righteousness,* who addicted themselves wholly to all the rites of the Jewish religion, for that was the game they flew at; for this, for one such, though but one, they compass sea and land, had many a cunning reach, and laid many a plot, rode and run, and sent and wrote, and laboured unweariedly. And what did they aim at? Not the glory of God, and the good of souls; but that they might have the credit of making them proselytes, and the advantage of making a prey of them when they were made. Note, (1.) The making of proselytes, if it be to the truth and serious godliness, and be done with a good design, is a good work, well worthy of the utmost care and pains. Such is the value of souls, that nothing must be thought too much to do, to save a soul from death. The industry of the Pharisees herein may show the negligence of many who would be thought to act from better principles, but will be at no pains or cost to propagate the gospel. (2.) To make a proselyte, sea and land must be compassed; all ways and means must be tried; first one way, and then another, must be tried, all little enough; but all well paid, if the point be gained. (3.) Carnal hearts seldom shrink from the pains necessary to carry on their carnal purposes; when a proselyte is to be made to serve a turn for themselves, they will compass sea and land to make him, rather than be disappointed.

2. Their cursed impiety in abusing their proselytes when they were made; "Ye make him the disciple of a Pharisee presently, and he sucks in all a Pharisee's notions; and so *ye make him twofold more the child of hell than yourselves.*" Note, (1.) Hypocrites, while they fancy themselves heirs of heaven, are, in the judgment of Christ, the children of hell. The rise of their hypocrisy is from hell, for the devil is the father of lies; and the tendency of their hypocrisy is toward hell, that is the country they belong to, the inheritance they are heirs to; they are called *children of hell,* because of their rooted enmity to the kingdom of heaven, which was the principle and genius of Pharisaism. (2.) Though all that maliciously oppose the gospel are children of hell, yet some are twofold more so than others, more furious and bigoted and malignant. (3.) Perverted proselytes are commonly the greatest bigots; the scholars outdid their masters, [1.] In fondness of ceremony; the Pharisees themselves saw the folly of their own impositions, and in

their hearts smiled at the obsequiousness of those that conformed to them; but their proselytes were eager for them. Note, Weak heads commonly admire those shows and ceremonies which wise men (however for public ends they countenance them) cannot but think meanly of. [2.] In fury against Christianity; the proselytes readily imbibed the principles which their crafty leaders were not wanting to possess them with, and so became extremely hot against the truth. The most bitter enemies the apostles met with in all places were the Hellenist Jews, who were mostly proselytes, Acts xiii. 45; xiv. 2—19; xvii. 5; xviii. 6. Paul, a disciple of the Pharisees, was *exceedingly mad against the Christians* (Acts xxvi. 11), when his master, Gamaliel, seems to have been more moderate.

IV. Their seeking their own worldly gain and honour more than God's glory put them upon coining false and unwarrantable distinctions, with which they led the people into dangerous mistakes, particularly in the matter of oaths; which, as an evidence of a universal sense of religion, have been by all nations accounted sacred (*v.* 16); *Ye blind guides.* Note, 1. It is sad to think how many are under the guidance of such as are themselves blind, who undertake to show others that way which they are themselves willingly ignorant of. *His watchmen are blind* (Isa. lvi. 10); and too often the people love to have it so, and say to the seers, *See not.* But the case is bad, when the leaders of the people *cause them to err,* Isa. ix. 16. 2. Though the condition of those whose guides are blind is very sad, yet that of the blind guides themselves is yet more woeful. Christ denounces a woe to the blind guides that have the blood of so many souls to answer for.

Now, to prove their blindness, he specifies the matter of swearing, and shows what corrupt casuists they were.

(1.) He lays down the doctrine they taught.

[1.] They allowed swearing by creatures, provided they were consecrated to the service of God, and stood in any special relation to him. They allowed swearing by the temple and the altar, though they were the work of men's hands, intended to be the servants of God's honour, not sharers in it. An oath is an appeal to God, to his omniscience and justice; and to make this appeal to any creature is to put that creature in the place of God. See Deut. vi. 13.

[2.] They distinguished between an oath by *the temple* and an oath by the *gold of the temple;* an oath by *the altar* and an oath by *the gift upon the altar;* making the latter binding, but not the former. Here was a double wickedness; *First,* That there were some oaths which they dispensed with, and made light of, and reckoned a man was not bound by to assert the truth, or perform a promise. They ought not to have sworn by the temple or the altar; but, when they had so sworn, they were taken in the words of their mouth. That doctrine cannot be of the God of truth which gives countenance to the breach of faith in any case whatsoever. Oaths are edge-tools and are not to be jested with. *Secondly,* That they preferred the gold before the temple, and the gift before the altar, to encourage people to bring gifts to the altar, and gold to the treasures of the temple, which they hoped to be gainers by. Those who had made gold their hope, and whose eyes were blinded by gifts in secret, were great friends to the Corban; and, gain being their godliness, by a thousand artifices they made religion truckle to their worldly interests. Corrupt church-guides make things to be sin or no sin as it serves their purposes, and lay a much greater stress on that which concerns their own gain than on that which is for God's glory and the good of souls.

(2.) He shows the folly and absurdity of this distinction (*v.* 17—19); *Ye fools, and blind.* It was in the way of a necessary reproof, not an angry reproach, that Christ called them *fools.* Let it suffice us from the word of wisdom to show the folly of sinful opinions and practices: but, for the fastening of the character upon particular persons, leave that to Christ, who knows what is in man, and has forbidden us to say, *Thou fool.*

To convict them of folly, he appeals to themselves, *Whether is greater, the gold* (the golden vessels and ornaments, or the gold in the treasury), *or the temple that sanctifies the gold; the gift, or the altar that sanctifies the gift?* Any one will own, *Propter quod aliquid est tale, id est magis tale—That, on account of which any thing is qualified in a particular way, must itself be much more qualified in the same way.* They that sware by the gold of the temple had an eye to it as holy; but what was it that made it holy but the holiness of the temple, to the service of which it was appropriated? And therefore the temple cannot be less holy than the gold, but must be more so; for the less is blessed and sanctified of the better, Heb. vii. 7. The temple and altar were dedicated to God fixedly, the gold and gift but secondarily. Christ is our altar (Heb. xiii. 10), our temple (John ii. 21); for it is he that sanctifies all our gifts, and puts an acceptableness in them, 1 Pet. ii. 5. Those that put their own works into the place of Christ's righteousness in justification are guilty of the Pharisees' absurdity, who preferred the gift before the altar. Every true Christian is a living temple; and by virtue thereof common things are sanctified to him; *unto the pure all things are pure* (Tit. i. 15), and *the unbelieving husband is sanctified by the* believing *wife,* 1 Cor. vii. 14.

(3.) He rectifies the mistake (*v.* 20—22), by reducing all the oaths they had invented to the true intent of an oath, which is, By the name of the Lord: so that though an oath by the temple, or the altar, or heaven, be formally bad, yet it is binding. *Quod fieri non debuit, factum valet—Engagements which ought not to have been made, are yet, when made, binding.* A man shall never take advantage of his own fault.

[1.] He that swears by the altar, let him not think to shake off the obligation of it by saying, "The altar is but wood, and stone, and brass;" for his oath shall be construed most strongly against himself; because he was culpable, and so as that the obligation of it may be preserved, *ut res potius valeat quam pereat—the obligation being hereby strengthened rather than destroyed.* And therefore an oath by the altar shall be interpreted by it and by all things thereon; for the appurtenances pass with the principal. And, the things thereon being offered up to God, to swear by it and them was, in effect, to call God himself to witness: for it was the altar of God; and he that went to that, went to God, Ps. xliii. 4; xxvi. 6.

[2.] He that swears by the temple, if he understand what he does, cannot but apprehend that the ground of such a respect to it, is, not because it is a fine house, but because it is the house of God, dedicated to his service, the place which he has chosen to put his name there; and therefore he swears *by it, and by him that dwells therein;* there he was pleased in a peculiar manner to manifest himself, and give tokens of his presence; so that whoso swears by it, swears by him who had said, *This is my rest, here will I dwell.* Good Christians are God's temples, and the Spirit of God dwells in them (1 Cor. iii. 16; vi. 19), and God takes what is done to them as done to himself; he that grieves a gracious soul, grieves it and the Spirit that dwells in it. Eph. iv. 30.

[3.] If a man swears by heaven, he sins (*ch.* v. 34); yet he shall not therefore be discharged from the obligation of his oath; no, God will make him know that the heaven he swears by, is his throne (Isa. lxvi. 1); and he that swears by the throne, appeals to him that sits upon it; who, as he resents the affront done to him in the form of the oath, so he will certainly revenge the greater affront done to him by the violation of it. Christ will not countenance the evasion of a solemn oath, though ever so plausible.

V. They were very strict and precise in the smaller matters of the law, but as careless and loose in the weightier matters, *v.* 23, 24. They were *partial in the law* (Mal. ii. 9), would pick and choose their duty, according as they were interested or stood affected. Sincere obedience is universal, and he that from a right principle obeys any of God's precepts, will have respect to them all, Ps. cxix. 6. But hypocrites, who act in religion for themselves, and not for God, will do no more in religion than they can serve a turn by for themselves. The partiality of the scribes and Pharisees appears here, in two instances.

1. They observed smaller duties, but omitted greater; they were very exact in paying tithes, till it came to *mint, anise,* and *cummin,* their exactness in tithing of which would not cost them much, but would be cried up, and they should buy reputation cheap. The Pharisee boasted of this, *I give tithes of all that I possess,* Luke xviii. 12. But it is probable that they had ends of their own to serve, and would find their own account in it; for the priests and Levites, to whom the tithes were paid, were in their interests, and knew how to return their kindness. Paying tithes was their duty, and what the law required; Christ tells them they ought not to leave it undone. Note, All ought in their places to contribute to the support and maintenance of a standing ministry: withholding tithes is called *robbing God,* Mal. iii. 8—10. They that *are taught in the word,* and do not *communicate to them that teach them,* that love a cheap gospel, come short of the Pharisees.

But that which Christ here condemns them for, is, that they *omitted the weightier matters of the law, judgment, mercy, and faith;* and their niceness in paying tithes, was, if not to atone before God, yet at least to excuse and palliate to men the omission of those. All the things of God's law are weighty, but those are most weighty, which are most expressive of inward holiness in the heart; the instances of self-denial, contempt of the world, and resignation to God, in which lies the life of religion. Judgment and mercy toward men, and faith toward God, are the weightier matters of the law, the *good things* which the *Lord our God requires* (Mic. vi. 8); to do justly, and love mercy, and humble ourselves by faith to walk with God. This is the obedience which is better than sacrifice or tithe; judgment is preferred before sacrifice, Isa. i. 11. To be just to the priests in their tithe, and yet to cheat and defraud every body else, is but to mock God, and deceive ourselves. Mercy also is preferred before sacrifice, Hos. vi. 6. To feed those who *made themselves fat with the offerings of the Lord,* and at the same time to shut up the bowels of compassion from a brother or a sister that is naked, and destitute of daily food, to pay tithe-mint to the priest, and to deny a crumb to Lazarus, is to lie open to that judgment without mercy, which is awarded to those who pretended to judgment, and showed no mercy; nor will judgment and mercy serve without faith in divine revelation; for God will be honoured in his truths as well as in his laws.

2. They avoided lesser sins, but committed greater (*v.* 24); *Ye blind guides;* so he had called them before (*v.* 16), for their corrupt teaching; here he calls them so for their corrupt living, for their example was leading as well as their doctrine; and in this also they were blind and partial; they *strained at a gnat, and swallowed a camel.* In their doctrine they strained at gnats, warned people against every the least violation of the tradition of the elders. In their practice they

strained at gnats, heaved at them, with a seeming dread, as if they had a great abhorrence of sin, and were afraid of it in the least instance; but they made no difficulty of those sins which, in comparison with them, were as a camel to a gnat; when they devoured widows' houses, they did indeed *swallow a camel;* when they gave Judas the price of innocent blood, and yet scrupled to put the returned money into the treasury (*ch.* xxvii. 6); when they would not go into the judgment-hall, for fear of being defiled, and yet would stand at the door, and cry out against the holy Jesus (John xviii. 28); when they quarrelled with the disciples for eating with unwashen hands, and yet, for the filling of the Corban, taught people to break the fifth commandment, they strained at gnats, or lesser things, and yet swallowed camels. It is not the scrupling of a little sin that Christ here reproves; if it be a sin, though but a gnat, it must be strained at, but the doing of that, and then swallowing a camel. In the smaller matters of the law to be superstitious, and to be profane in the greater, is the hypocrisy here condemned.

VI. They were all for the outside, and not at all for the inside, of religion. They were more desirous and solicitous to appear pious to men than to approve themselves so toward God. This is illustrated by two similitudes.

1. They are compared to a vessel that is clean washed on the outside, but all dirt within, *v.* 25, 26. The Pharisees placed religion in that which at best was but a point of decency—the *washing of cups,* Mark vii. 4. They were in care to eat their meat in clean cups and platters, but made no conscience of getting their meat by extortion, and using it to excess. Now what a foolish thing would it be for a man to wash only the outside of a cup, which is to be looked at, and to leave the inside dirty, which is to be used; so they do who only avoid scandalous sins, that would spoil their reputation with men, but allow themselves in heart-wickedness, which renders them odious to the pure and holy God. In reference to this, observe,

(1.) The practice of the Pharisees; they made clean the outside. In those things which fell under the observation of their neighbours, they seemed very exact, and carried on their wicked intrigues with so much artifice, that their wickedness was not suspected; people generally took them for very good men. But within, in the recesses of their hearts and the close retirements of their lives, they were *full of extortion and excess;* of *violence and incontinence* (so Dr. Hammond); that is, of injustice and intemperance. While they would seem to be godly, they were neither sober nor righteous. Their *inward part was very wickedness* (Ps. v. 9); and that we are really, which we are inwardly.

(2.) The rule Christ gives, in opposition to this practice, *v.* 26. It is addressed to the blind Pharisees. They thought themselves the *seers of the land,* but (John ix. 39) Christ calls them *blind.* Note, those are blind, in Christ's account, who (how quick-sighted soever they are in other things) are strangers, and no enemies, to the wickedness of their own hearts; who see not, and hate not, the secret sin that lodgeth there. Self-ignorance is the most shameful and hurtful ignorance, Rev. iii 17. The rule is, *Cleanse first that which is within.* Note, the principal care of every one of us should be to wash our hearts from wickedness, Jer. iv. 14. The main business of a Christian lies within, to get cleansed from the *filthiness of the spirit.* Corrupt affections and inclinations, the secret lusts that lurk in the soul, unseen and unobserved, these must first be mortified and subdued. Those sins must be conscientiously abstained from, which the eye of God only is a witness to, who searcheth the heart.

Observe the method prescribed; *Cleanse first that which is within;* not that *only,* but that *first;* because, if due care be taken concerning that, the outside will be clean also. External motives and inducements may keep the outside clean, while the inside is filthy; but if renewing, sanctifying grace make clean the inside, that will have an influence upon the outside, for the commanding principle is within. If the heart be well kept, all is well, for *out of it are the issues of life;* the eruptions will vanish of course. If the heart and spirit be made new, there will be a newness of life; here therefore we must begin with ourselves; first cleanse that which is within; we then make sure work, when this is our first work.

2. They are compared to *whited sepulchres, v.* 27, 28.

(1.) They were fair without, like sepulchres, *which appear beautiful outward.* Some make it to refer to the custom of the Jews to whiten graves, only for the notifying of them, especially if they were in unusual places, that people might avoid them, because of the ceremonial pollution contracted by the touch of a grave, Numb. xix. 16. And it was part of the charge of the overseers of the highways, to repair that whitening when it was decayed. Sepulchres were thus made remarkable, 2 Kings xxiii. 16, 17. The formality of hypocrites, by which they study to recommend themselves to the world, doth but make all wise and good men the more careful to avoid them, for fear of being defiled by them. *Beware of the scribes,* Luke xx. 46. It rather alludes to the custom of whitening the sepulchres of eminent persons, for the beautifying of them. It is said here (*v.* 29), that they *garnished the sepulchres of the righteous;* as it is usual with us to erect monuments upon the graves of great persons, and to strew flowers on the graves of dear friends. Now the righteousness of the scribes and Pharisees was like the ornaments of a grave, or the dressing up of a dead body, only for show. The top of their ambition was to *appear righteous before men,* and to be applauded and had in admiration by them. But,

(2.) They were *foul* within, like sepulchres, *full of dead men's bones, and all uncleanness:* so vile are our bodies, when the soul has deserted them! Thus were they full of hypocrisy and iniquity. Hypocrisy is the worst iniquity of all other. Note, It is possible for those that have their hearts full of sin, to have their lives free from blame, and to appear very good. But what will it avail us, to have the good word of our fellow-servants, if our Master doth not say, *Well done?* When all other graves are opened, these whited sepulchres will be looked into, and the dead men's bones, and all the uncleanness, shall be *brought out,* and be *spread before all the host of heaven,* Jer. viii. 1, 2. For it is the day when God shall judge, not the shows, but the secrets, of men. And it will then be small comfort to them who shall have their portion with hypocrites, to remember how creditably and plausibly they went to hell, applauded by all their neighbours.

VII. They pretended a deal of kindness for the memory of the prophets that were dead and gone, while they hated and persecuted those that were present with them. This is put last, because it was the blackest part of their character. God is jealous for his honour in his laws and ordinances, and resents it if they be profaned and abused; but he has often expressed an equal jealousy for his honour in his prophets and ministers, and resents it worse if they be wronged and persecuted: and therefore, when our Lord Jesus comes to this head, he speaks more fully than upon any of the other (*v.* 29—37); for he that toucheth his ministers, *toucheth his Anointed,* and toucheth the *apple of his eye.* Observe here,

1. The respect which the scribes and Pharisees pretended for the prophets that were gone, *v.* 29, 30. This was the varnish, and that in which they outwardly appeared righteous.

(1.) They honoured the relics of the prophets, they built their tombs, and garnished their sepulchres. It seems, the places of their burial were known, David's sepulchre was with them, Acts ii. 29. There was a title upon the sepulchre of *the man of God* (2 Kings xxiii. 17), and Josiah thought it respect enough not to *move his bones, v.* 18. But they would do more, rebuild and beautify them. Now consider this, [1.] As an instance of honour done to deceased prophets, who, while they lived, were counted as the off-scouring of all things, and had all manner of evil spoken against them falsely. Note, God can extort, even from bad men, an acknowledgment of the honour of piety and holiness. Them that honour God he will honour, and sometimes with those from whom contempt is expected, 2 Sam. vi. 22. *The memory of the just is blessed,* when the names of those that hated and persecuted them shall be covered with shame. The honour of constancy and resolution in the way of duty will be a lasting honour; and those that are manifest to God, will be manifest in the consciences of those about them. [2.] As an instance of the hypocrisy of the scribes and Pharisees, who paid their respect to them. Note, Carnal people can easily honour the memories of faithful ministers that are dead and gone, because they do not reprove them, nor disturb them, in their sins. Dead prophets are *seers that see not,* and those they can bear well enough; they do not torment them, as the living witnesses do, that bear their testimony *viva voce—with a living voice,* Rev. xi. 10. They can pay respect to the writings of the dead prophets, which tell them what they *should be;* but not the reproofs of the living prophets, which tell them what they *are. Sit divus, modo non sit vivus—Let there be saints; but let them not be living here.* The extravagant respect which the church of Rome pays to the memory of saints departed, especially the martyrs, dedicating days and places to their names, enshrining their relics, praying to them, and offering to their images, while they make themselves drunk with the blood of the saints of their own day, is a manifest proof that they not only *suc*ceed, but *ex*ceed, the scribes and Pharisees in a counterfeit hypocritical religion, which builds the prophets' tombs, but hates the prophets' doctrine.

(2.) They protested against the murder of them (*v.* 30); *If we had been in the days of our fathers, we would not have been partakers with them.* They would never have consented to the silencing of Amos, and the imprisonment of Micaiah, to the putting of Hanani in the stocks, and Jeremiah in the dungeon, to the stoning of Zechariah, the mocking of all the messengers of the Lord, and the abuses put upon his prophets; no, not they, they would sooner have lost their right hands than have done any such thing. *What, is thy servant a dog?* And yet they were at this time plotting to murder Christ, *to whom all the prophets bore witness.* They think, if they had lived in the days of the prophets, they would have heard them gladly and obeyed; and yet they rebelled against the light that Christ brought into the world. But it is certain, a Herod and an Herodias to John the Baptist, would have been an Ahab and a Jezebel to Elijah. Note, The deceitfulness of sinners' hearts appears very much in this, that, while they go down the stream of the sins of their own day, they fancy they should have swum against the stream of the sins of the former days; that, if they had had other people's opportunities, they should have improved them more faithfully; if they had been in other people's temptations, they should have resisted them more vigorously; when yet they improve not the opportunities they have, nor resist the temptations they are in. We are sometimes thinking, if we had lived when Christ was upon earth, how constantly we would have followed him; we would not have despised and rejected him, as they then did; and yet Christ in his Spirit, in his word, in his ministers, is still no better treated.

2. Their enmity and opposition to Christ and his gospel, notwithstanding, and the ruin they were bringing upon themselves and upon that generation thereby, *v.* 31—33. Observe here,

(1.) The indictment proved; *Ye are witnesses against yourselves.* Note, Sinners cannot hope to escape the judgment of Christ for want of proof against them, when it is easy to find them witnesses against themselves; and their very pleas will not only be overruled, but turned to their conviction, and *their own tongues* shall be made to *fall upon them,* Ps. lxiv. 8.

[1.] By their own confession, it was the great wickedness of their forefathers, to kill the prophets; so that they knew the fault of it, and yet were themselves guilty of the same fact. Note, They who condemn sin in others, and yet allow the same or worse in themselves, are of all others most inexcusable, Rom. i. 32.—ii. 1. They knew they ought not to have been partakers with persecutors, and yet were the followers of them. Such self-contradictions now will amount to self-condemnations in the great day. Christ puts another construction upon their building of the tombs of the prophets than what they intended; as if by beautifying their graves they justified their murderers (Luke xi. 48), for they persisted in the sin.

[2.] By their own confession, these notorious persecutors were their ancestors; *Ye are the children of them.* They meant no more than that they were their children by blood and nature; but Christ turns it upon them, that they were so by spirit and disposition; *You are of those fathers, and their lusts you will do.* They are, as you say, *your fathers,* and you *patrizare—take after your fathers;* it is the sin that runs in the blood among you. *As your fathers did, so do ye,* Acts vii. 51. They came of a persecuting race, were *a seed of evil doers* (Isa. i. 4), *risen up in their fathers' stead,* Numb. xxxii. 14. Malice, envy, and cruelty, were bred in the bone with them, and they had formerly espoused it for a principle, to *do as their fathers did,* Jer. xliv. 17. And it is observable here (*v.* 30) how careful they are to mention the relation; "They were *our* fathers, that killed the prophets, and they were men in honour and power, whose sons and successors we are." If they had detested the wickedness of their ancestors, as they ought to have done, they would not have been so fond to call them *their fathers;* for it is no credit to be akin to persecutors, though they have ever so much dignity and dominion.

(2.) The sentence passed upon them. Christ here proceeds,

[1.] To give them up to sin as irreclaimable (*v.* 32); *Fill ye up then the measure of your fathers.* If Ephraim be joined to idols, and hate to be reformed, *let him alone. He that is filthy, let him be filthy still.* Christ knew they were now contriving his death, and in a few days would accomplish it; "Well," saith he, "go on with your plot, take your course, walk in the way of your heart and in the sight of your eyes, and see what will come of it. *What thou doest, do quickly.* You will but fill up the measure of guilt, which will then overflow in a deluge of wrath." Note, *First,* There is a measure of sin to be filled up, before utter ruin comes upon persons and families, churches and nations. God will bear long, but the time will come when he can *no longer forbear,* Jer. xliv. 22. We read of the measure of the Amorites that was to be filled (Gen. xv. 16), of the *harvest* of the earth *being ripe for the sickle* (Rev. xiv. 15—19), and of sinners *making an end to deal treacherously,* arriving at a full stature in treachery, Isa. xxxiii. 1. *Secondly,* Children fill up the measure of their fathers' sins when they are gone, if they persist in the same or the like. That national guilt which brings national ruin is made up of the sin of many in several ages, and in the successions of societies there is a score going on; for God justly visits the iniquity of the fathers upon the children that tread in the steps of it. *Thirdly,* Persecuting Christ, and his people and ministers, is a sin that fills the measure of a nation's guilt sooner than any other. This was it that brought wrath without remedy upon the fathers (2 Chron. xxxvi. 16), and wrath to the utmost upon the children too, 1 Thess. ii. 16. This was that fourth transgression, of which, when added to the other three, the Lord *would not turn away the punishment,* Amos i. 3, 6, 9, 11, 13. *Fourthly,* It is just with God to give those up to their own heart's lusts, who obstinately persist in the gratification of them. Those who will run headlong to ruin, let the reins be laid on their neck, and it is the saddest condition a man can be in on this side hell.

[2.] He proceeds to give them up to ruin as irrecoverable, to a personal ruin in the other world (*v.* 33); *Ye serpents, ye generation of vipers, how can ye escape the damnation of hell?* These are strange words to come from the mouth of Christ, into whose lips grace was poured. But he can and will speak terror, and in these words he explains and sums up the *eight* woes he had denounced against the scribes and Pharisees.

Here is, *First,* Their description; *Ye serpents.* Doth Christ call names? Yes, but this doth not warrant us to do so. He infallibly knew what was in man, and knew them to be subtle as serpents, cleaving to the earth, feeding on dust; they had a specious outside, but were within malignant, had poison under their tongues, the seed of the old serpent. They were a *generation of vipers;*

they and those that went before them, they and those that joined with them, were a generation of envenomed, enraged, spiteful adversaries to Christ and his gospel. They loved to be called of men, *Rabbi, rabbi,* but Christ calls them *serpents* and *vipers;* for he gives men their true characters, and delights to put contempt upon the proud.

Secondly, Their doom. He represents their condition as very sad, and in a manner desperate; *How can ye escape the damnation of hell?* Christ himself preached hell and damnation, for which his ministers have often been reproached by those that care not to hear of it. Note, 1. The damnation of hell will be the fearful end of all impenitent sinners. This doom coming from Christ, was more terrible than coming from all the prophets and ministers that ever were, for he is the Judge, into whose hands the keys of hell and death are put, and his saying they were damned, made them so. 2. There is a way of escaping this damnation, this is implied here; some are *delivered from the wrath to come.* 3. Of all sinners, those who are of the spirit of the scribes and Pharisees, are least likely to escape this damnation; for repentance and faith are necessary to that escape; and how will *they* be brought to these, who are so conceited of themselves, and so prejudiced against Christ and his gospel, as they were? How could *they* be healed and saved, who could not bear to have their wound searched, nor the balm of Gilead applied to it? Publicans and harlots, who were sensible of their disease and applied themselves to the Physician, were more likely to escape the damnation of hell than those who, though they were in the high road to it, were confident they were in the way to heaven.

34 Wherefore, behold, I send unto
you prophets, and wise men, and
scribes: and *some* of them ye shall
kill and crucify; and *some* of them
shall ye scourge in your synagogues,
and persecute *them* from city to city:
35 That upon you may come all the
righteous blood shed upon the earth,
from the blood of righteous Abel unto
the blood of Zacharias son of Barachias, whom ye slew between the
temple and the altar. 36 Verily I
say unto you, All these things shall
come upon this generation. 37 O
Jerusalem, Jerusalem, *thou* that killest
the prophets, and stonest them which
are sent unto thee, how often would
I have gathered thy children together,
even as a hen gathereth her chickens
under *her* wings, and ye would not!
38 Behold, your house is left unto
you desolate. 39 For I say unto
you, Ye shall not see me henceforth,
till ye shall say, Blessed *is* he that
cometh in the name of the Lord.

We have left the blind leaders fallen into the ditch, under Christ's sentence, into the damnation of hell; let us see what will become of the blind followers, of the body of the Jewish church, and particularly Jerusalem.

I. Jesus Christ designs yet to try them with the means of grace; *I send unto you prophets, and wise men, and scribes.* The connection is strange; "*You are a generation of vipers,* not likely to *escape the damnation of hell;*" one would think it should follow, "Therefore you shall never have a prophet sent to you any more;" but no, "*Therefore I will send unto you prophets,* to see if you will yet at length be wrought upon, or else to leave you inexcusable, and to justify God in your ruin." It is therefore ushered in with a note of admiration, behold! Observe,

1. It is Christ that sends them; *I send.* By this he avows himself to be God, having power to gift and commission prophets. It is an act of kingly office; he sends them as ambassadors to treat with us about the concerns of our souls. After his resurrection, he made this word good, when he said, *So send I you,* John xx. 21. Though now he appeared mean, yet he was entrusted with this great authority.

2. He sends them to the Jews first; "I send them to *you.*" They began at Jerusalem; and, wherever they went, they observed this rule, to make the first tender of gospel grace *to the Jews,* Acts xiii. 46.

3. Those he sends are called *prophets, wise men,* and *scribes,* Old-Testament names for New-Testament officers; to show that the ministers sent to them now should not be inferior to the prophets of the Old Testament, to Solomon the wise, or Ezra the scribe. The extraordinary ministers, who in the first ages were divinely inspired, were as the prophets commissioned immediately from heaven; the ordinary settled ministers, who were then, and continue in the church still, and will do to the end of time, are as the wise men and scribes, to guide and instruct the people in the things of God. Or, we may take the apostles and evangelists for the prophets and wise men, and the pastors and teachers for the scribes, *instructed to the kingdom of heaven* (*ch.* xiii. 52); for the office of a scribe was honourable till the men dishonoured it.

II. He foresees and foretels the ill usage that his messengers would meet with among them; "*Some of them ye shall kill and crucify,* and yet I will send them." Christ knows beforehand how ill his servants will be treated, and yet sends them, and appoints them their measure of sufferings; yet he loves them never the less for his thus exposing them, for he designs to glorify himself by their sufferings, and them after them; he will counterbalance them, though not prevent them. Observe,

1. The cruelty of these persecutors; *Ye shall kill and crucify them.* It is no less than the blood, the life-blood, that they thirst after; their lust is not satisfied with any thing short of their destruction, Exod. xv. 9. They killed the two James's, crucified Simon the son of Cleophas, and scourged Peter and John; thus did the members partake of the sufferings of the Head, he was killed and crucified, and so were they. Christians must expect to resist unto blood.

2. Their unwearied industry; *Ye shall persecute them from city to city.* As the apostles went from city to city, to preach the gospel, the Jews dodged them, and haunted them, and stirred up persecution against them, Acts xiv. 19; xvii. 13. They that *did not believe in Judea* were more bitter enemies to the gospel than any other unbelievers, Rom. xv. 31.

3. The pretence of religion in this; they scourged them in their synagogues, their places of worship, where they kept their ecclesiastical courts; so that they did it as a piece of service to the church; cast them out, and said, *Let the Lord be glorified,* Isa. lxvi. 5; John xvi. 2.

III. He imputes the sin of their fathers to them, because they imitated it; *That upon you may come all the righteous blood shed upon the earth, v.* 35, 36. Though God bear long with a persecuting generation, he will not bear always; and patience abused, turns into the greatest wrath. The longer sinners have been heaping up treasures of wickedness, the deeper and fuller will the treasures of wrath be; and the breaking of them up will be like breaking up the fountains of the great deep.

Observe, 1. The extent of this imputation; it takes in *all the righteous blood shed upon the earth,* that is, the blood shed for righteousness' sake, which has all been laid up in God's treasury, and not a drop of it lost, for *it is precious,* Ps. lxxii.14. He dates the account *from the blood of righteous Abel,* thence this *æra martyrum—age of martyrs*—commences; he is called *righteous* Abel, for he obtained witness from heaven, that he was *righteous, God testifying of his gifts.* How early did martyrdom come into the world! The first that died, died for his religion, and, *being dead, he yet speaketh.* His blood not only cried against Cain, but continues to cry against all that walk in the way of Cain, and hate and persecute their brother, *because their works are righteous.* He extends it *to the blood of Zacharias, the son of Barachias* (*v.* 36), not Zecharias the prophet (as some would have it), though he was *the son of Barachias* (Zech. i. 1), nor Zecharias the father of John Baptist, as others say; but, as is most probable, *Zechariah the son of Jehoiada,* who was *slain in the court of the Lord's house,* 2 Chron. xxiv. 20, 21. His father is called *Barachias,* which signifies much the same with Jehoiada; and it was usual among the Jews for the same person to have two names; *whom ye slew,* ye of this nation, though not of this generation. This is specified, because the requiring of that is particularly spoken of (2 Chron. xxiv. 22), as that of Abel's is. The Jews imagined that the captivity had sufficiently atoned for that guilt; but Christ lets them know that it was not yet fully accounted for, but remained upon the score. And some think that this is mentioned with a prophetical hint, for there was one Zecharias, the son of Baruch, whom Josephus speaks of (*De Bello Judaico, lib.* 5, *cap.* 1), who was a just and good man, who was killed in the temple a little before it was destroyed by the Romans. Archbishop Tillotson thinks that Christ both alludes to the history of the former Zecharias in *Chronicles,* and foretels the death of this latter in Josephus. Though the latter was not yet slain, yet, before this destruction comes, it would be true that they had slain him; so that all shall be put together from first to last.

2. The effect of it; *All these things shall come;* all the guilt of this blood, all the punishment of it, it shall *all come upon this generation.* The misery and ruin that are coming upon them, shall be so very great, that, though, considering the evil of their own sins, it was less than even those deserved; yet, comparing it with other judgments, it will seem to be a general reckoning for all the wickedness of their ancestors, especially their persecutions, to all which God declared this ruin to have special reference and relation. The destruction shall be so dreadful, as if God had once for all arraigned them for all the righteous blood shed in the world. It shall *come upon this generation;* which intimates, that it shall come quickly; some here shall live to see it. Note, The sorer and nearer the punishment of sin is, the louder is the call to repentance and reformation.

IV. He laments the wickedness of Jerusalem, and justly upbraids them with the many kind offers he had made them, *v.* 37. See with what concern he speaks of that city; *O Jerusalem, Jerusalem!* The repetition is emphatical, and bespeaks abundance of commiseration. A day or two before Christ had wept over Jerusalem, now he sighed and groaned over it. Jerusalem, *the vision of peace* (so it signifies), must now be the seat of war and confusion. Jerusalem, that had been *the joy of the whole earth,* must now be *a hissing, and an astonishment, and a by-word:* Jerusalem, that has been *a city compact together,* shall now be shattered and ruined by its own intestine broils. Jerusalem, *the place that God has chosen to put his name there,* shall now be abandoned to the spoil and the robbers, Lam. i. 1, iv. 1. But wherefore will the Lord do all this to Jerusalem? Why? *Jerusalem hath grievously sinned,* Lam. i. 8.

1. She persecuted God's messengers; *Thou that killest the prophets, and stonest them that*

are sent unto thee. This sin is especially charged upon Jerusalem; because there the Sanhedrim, or great council, sat, who took cognizance of church matters, and therefore a prophet could not perish but in Jerusalem, Luke xiii. 33. It is true, they had not now a power to put any man to death, but they killed the prophets in popular tumults, mobbed them, as Stephen, and put the Roman powers on to kill them. At Jerusalem, where the gospel was first preached, it was first persecuted (Acts viii. 1), and that place was the head-quarters of the persecutors; thence warrants were issued out to other cities, and thither the saints were brought bound, Acts ix. 2. *Thou stonest them:* that was a capital punishment, in use only among the Jews. By the law, false prophets and seducers were to *be stoned* (Deut. xiii. 10), under colour of which law, they put the true prophets to death. Note, It has often been the artifice of Satan, to turn that artillery against the church, which was originally planted in the defence of it. Brand the true prophets as seducers, and the true professors of religion as heretics and schismatics, and then it will be easy to persecute them. There was abundance of other wickedness in Jerusalem; but this was the sin that made the loudest cry, and which God had an eye to more than any other, in bringing that ruin upon them, as 2 Kings xxiv. 4; 2 Chron. xxxvi. 16. Observe, Christ speaks in the present tense; *Thou killest, and stonest;* for all they had done, and all they would do, was present to Christ's notice.

2. She refused and rejected Christ, and gospel offers. The former was a sin *without* remedy, this *against* the remedy. Here is, (1.) The wonderful grace and favour of Jesus Christ toward them; *How often would I have gathered thy children together, as a hen gathers her chickens under her wings!* Thus kind and condescending are the offers of gospel grace, even to Jerusalem's children, bad as she is, the inhabitants, the little ones not excepted. [1.] The favour proposed was the gathering of them. Christ's design is to gather poor souls, gather them in from their wanderings, gather them home to himself, as the Centre of unity; for *to him must the gathering of the people be.* He would have taken the whole body of the Jewish nation into the church, and so gathered them all (as the Jews used to speak of proselytes) *under the wings of the Divine Majesty.* It is here illustrated by a humble similitude; *as a hen* clucks *her chickens together.* Christ would have gathered them, *First,* With such a tenderness of affection as the hen does, which has, by instinct, a peculiar concern for her young ones. Christ's gathering of souls, comes from his love, Jer. xxxi. 3. *Secondly,* For the same end. *The hen gathered her chickens under her wings,* for protection and safety, and for warmth and comfort; poor souls have in Christ both refuge and refreshment. The chickens naturally run to the hen for shelter, when they are threatened by the birds of prey; perhaps Christ refers to that promise (Ps. xci. 4), *He shall cover thee with his feathers.* There is *healing under Christ's wings* (Mal. iv. 2); that is more than the hen has for her chickens.

[2.] The forwardness of Christ to confer this favour. His offers are, *First,* Very free; *I would have done it.* Jesus Christ is truly willing to receive and save poor souls that come to him. He desires not their ruin, he delights in their repentance. *Secondly,* Very frequent; *How often!* Christ often came up to Jerusalem, preached, and wrought miracles there; and the meaning of all this, was, he would have gathered them. He keeps account how often his calls have been repeated. As often as we have heard the sound of the gospel, as often as we have felt the strivings of the Spirit, so often Christ would have gathered us.

[3.] Their wilful refusal of this grace and favour; *Ye would not.* How emphatically is their obstinacy opposed to Christ's mercy! I would, and *ye would not.* He was willing to save them, but they were not willing to be saved by him. Note, It is wholly owing to the wicked wills of sinners, that they are not gathered under the wings of the Lord Jesus. They did not like the terms upon which Christ proposed to gather them; they loved their sins, and yet trusted to their righteousness; they would not submit either to the grace of Christ or to his government, and so the bargain broke off.

V. He reads Jerusalem's doom (*v.* 38, 39); *Therefore behold your house is left unto you desolate.* Both the city and the temple, God's house and their own, all shall be laid waste. But it is especially meant of the temple, which they boasted of, and trusted to; that holy mountain because of which they were so haughty. Note, they that will not be gathered by the love and grace of Christ shall be consumed and scattered by his wrath; *I would, and you would not. Israel would none of me, so I gave them up,* Ps. lxxxi. 11, 12.

1. Their house shall be *deserted; It is left unto you.* Christ was now departing from the temple, and never came into it again, but by this word abandoned it to ruin. They doated on it, would have it to themselves; Christ must have no room or interest there. "Well," saith Christ, "it is left to you; take it, and make your best of it; I will never have any thing more to do with it." They had made it *a house of merchandise, and a den of thieves,* and so it is left to them. Not long after this, the voice was heard in the temple, "Let us depart hence." When Christ went, *Ichabod, the glory departed.* Their city also was left to them, destitute of God's presence and grace; he was no longer *a wall of fire about them,* nor *the glory in the midst of them.*

2. It shall be *desolate; It is left unto you desolate;* it is left ἔρημος — *a wilderness.*

(1.) It was immediately, when Christ left it, in the eyes of all that understood themselves, a very dismal melancholy place. Christ's departure makes the best furnished, best replenished place a wilderness, though it be the temple, the chief place of concourse; for what comfort can there be where Christ is not? Though there may be a crowd of other contentments, yet, if Christ's special spiritual presence be withdrawn, that soul, that place, is *become a wilderness, a land of darkness, as darkness itself.* This comes of men's rejecting Christ, and driving him away from them. (2.) It was, not long after, destroyed and ruined, and *not one stone left upon another.* The lot of Jerusalem's enemies will now become Jerusalem's lot, *to be made of a city a heap, of a defenced city a ruin* (Isa. xxv. 2), *a lofty city laid low, even to the ground,* Isa. xxvi. 5. The temple, that holy and beautiful house, became desolate. When God goes out, all enemies break in.

Lastly, Here is the final farewell that Christ took of them and their temple; *Ye shall not see me henceforth, till ye shall say, Blessed is he that cometh.* This bespeaks,

1. His departure from them. The time was at hand, when *he should leave the world, to go to his Father,* and be seen no more. *After his resurrection, he was seen only by a few chosen witnesses,* and they saw him not long, but he soon removed to the invisible world, and there will be *till the time of the restitution of all things,* when his welcome at his first coming will be repeated with loud acclamations; *Blessed is he that cometh in the name of the Lord.* Christ will not be seen again till he *come in the clouds, and every eye shall see him* (Rev. i. 7); and then, even they, who, when time was, rejected and pierced him, will be glad to come in among his adorers; then every knee shall bow to him, even those that had bowed to Baal; and even the workers of iniquity will then cry, *Lord, Lord,* and will own, when his wrath is kindled, that *blessed are all they that put their trust in him.* Would we have our lot in that day with those that say, *Blessed is he that cometh?* let us be with them now, with them that truly worship, and truly welcome, Jesus Christ.

2. Their continued blindness and obstinacy; *Ye shall not see me,* that is, not see me to be the Messiah (for otherwise they did see him upon the cross), not see the light of the truth concerning me, nor *the things that belong to your peace, till ye shall say, Blessed is he that cometh.* They will never be convinced, till Christ's second coming convince them, when it will be too late to make an interest in him, and nothing will remain *but a fearful looking for of judgment.* Note, (1.) Wilful blindness is often punished with judicial blindness. If they *will* not see, they *shall* not see. With this word he concludes his public preaching. *After his resurrection,* which was *the sign of the prophet Jonas,* they should have no other sign given them, till they should *see the sign of the Son of man, ch.* xxiv. 30. (2.) When *the Lord comes with ten thousand of his saints,* he will convince all, and will force acknowledgments from the proudest of his enemies, of his being the Messiah, and even *they shall be found liars to him.* They that would not now come at his call, shall then be forced to depart with his curse. The chief priests and scribes were displeased with the children for crying *hosanna* to Christ; but the day is coming, when proud persecutors would gladly be found in the condition of the meanest and poorest they now trample upon. They who now reproach and ridicule the hosannas of the saints will be of another mind shortly; it were therefore better to be of that mind now. Some make this to refer to the conversion of the Jews to the faith of Christ; then they shall see him, and own him, and *say, Blessed is he that cometh;* but it seems rather to look further, for the complete manifestation of Christ, and conviction of sinners, are reserved to be the glory of the last day.

CHAP. XXIV.

Christ's preaching was mostly practical; but, in this chapter, we have a prophetical discourse, a prediction of things to come; such however as had a practical tendency, and was intended, not to gratify the curiosity of his disciples, but to guide their consciences and conversations, and it is therefore concluded with a practical application. The church has always had particular prophecies, besides general promises, both for direction and for encouragement to believers; but it is observable, Christ preached this prophetical sermon in the close of his ministry, as the Apocalypse is the last book of the New Testament, and the prophetical books of the Old Testament are placed last, to intimate to us, that we must be well grounded in plain truths and duties, and those must first be well digested, before we dive into those things that are dark and difficult; many run themselves into confusion by beginning their Bible at the wrong end. Now, in this chapter, we have, I. The occasion of this discourse, ver. 1—3. II. The discourse itself, in which we have, 1. The prophecy of divers events, especially referring to the destruction of Jerusalem, and the utter ruin of the Jewish church and nation, which were now hastening on, and were completed about forty years after; the prefaces to that destruction, the concomitants and consequences of it; yet looking further, to Christ's coming at the end of time, and the consummation of all things, of which that was a type and figure, ver. 4—31. 2. The practical application of this prophecy for the awakening and quickening of his disciples to prepare for these great and awful things, ver. 32—51.

AND Jesus went out, and departed
from the temple: and his disciples came to *him* for to show him the
buildings of the temple. 2 And Jesus
said unto them, See ye not all these
things? verily I say unto you, There
shall not be left here one stone upon
another, that shall not be thrown
down. 3 And as he sat upon the
mount of Olives, the disciples came
unto him privately, saying, Tell us,
when shall these things be? and what
shall be the sign of thy coming, and
of the end of the world?

Here is,

I. Christ's quitting *the temple,* and his public work there. He had said, in the close of the foregoing chapter, *Your house is left unto you desolate;* and here he made his words good; *He went out, and departed from the temple.* The manner of expression is observable; he not only went out of the temple, but departed from it, took his final farewell of it; he departed from it, never to return to it any more; and then immediately follows a prediction of its ruin. Note, That house is left desolate indeed, which Christ leaves. *Woe unto them when I depart,* Hos. ix. 12; Jer. vi. 8. It was now time to groan out their *Ichabod, The glory is departed, their defence is departed.* Three days after this, the veil of the temple was rent; when Christ left it, all became *common and unclean;* but Christ departed not till they drove him away; did not reject them, till they first rejected him.

II. His private discourse with his disciples; he left the temple, but he did not leave the twelve, who were the seed of the gospel church, which the casting off of the Jews was the enriching of. When he left the temple, his disciples left it too, and came to him. Note, It is good being where Christ is, and leaving that which he leaves. They came to him, to be instructed in private, when his public preaching was over; for *the secret of the Lord is with them that fear him.* He had spoken of the destruction of the Jewish church to the multitude in parables, which here, as usual, he explains to his disciples. Observe,

1. *His disciples came to him, to show him the buildings of the temple.* It was a stately and beautiful structure, one of the wonders of the world; no cost was spared, no art left untried, to make it sumptuous. Though it came short of Solomon's temple, and *its beginning was small,* yet *its latter end did greatly increase.* It was richly furnished with gifts and offerings, to which there were continual additions made. They showed Christ these things, and desired him to take notice of them, either,

(1.) As being greatly pleased with them themselves, and expecting he should be so too. They had lived mostly in Galilee, at a distance from the temple, had seldom seen it, and therefore were the more struck with admiration at it, and thought he should admire as much as they did *all this glory* (Gen. xxxi. 1); and they would have him divert himself (after his preaching, and from his sorrow which they saw him perhaps almost overwhelmed with) with looking about him. Note, Even good men are apt to be too much enamoured with outward pomp and gaiety, and to overvalue it, even in the things of God; whereas we should be, as Christ was, dead to it, and look upon it with contempt. The temple was indeed glorious, but, [1.] Its glory was sullied and stained with the sin of the priests and people; that wicked doctrine of the Pharisees, which preferred the gold before the temple that sanctified it, was enough to deface the beauty of all the ornaments of the temple. [2.] Its glory was eclipsed and outdone by the presence of Christ in it, who was *the glory of this latter house* (Hag. ii. 9), so that the buildings had no glory, in comparison with that glory which excelled.

Or, (2.) As grieving that this house should be left desolate; they showed him the buildings, as if they would move him to reverse the sentence; "Lord, let not this holy and beautiful house, where our fathers praised thee, be made a desolation." They forgot how many providences, concerning Solomon's temple, had manifested how little God cared for that outward glory which they had so much admired, when the people were wicked, 2 Chron. vii. 21. *This house, which is high,* sin will bring low. Christ had lately looked upon *the precious souls, and wept for them,* Luke xix. 41. The disciples look upon the pompous buildings, and are ready to weep for them. In this, as in other things, *his thoughts are not like ours.* It was weakness, and meanness of spirit, in the disciples, to be so fond of fine buildings; it was a childish thing. *Animo magno nihil magnum—To a great mind nothing is great.* Seneca.

2. Christ, hereupon, foretels the utter ruin and destruction that were coming upon this place, *v.* 2. Note, A believing foresight of the defacing of all worldly glory will help to take us off from admiring it, and overvaluing it. The most beautiful body will be shortly worms' meat, and the most beautiful building a ruinous heap. And shall we then set our eyes upon that which so soon is not, and look upon that with so much admiration which ere long we shall certainly look upon with so much contempt? *See ye not all these things?* They would have Christ look upon them, and be as much in love with them as they were; he would have them look upon them, and be as dead to them as he was. There is such a sight of these things as will do us good; so to see them as to see through them and see to the end of them.

Christ, instead of reversing the decree, ratifies it; *Verily, I say unto you, there shall not be left one stone upon another.*

(1.) He speaks of it as a certain ruin; "*I say unto you. I,* that know what I say, and know how to make good what I say; take my word for it, it shall be so; *I, the Amen, the true Witness, say it to you.*" All judgment being committed to the Son, the threatenings, as well as the promises, are all *yea, and amen, in him.* Heb. vi. 17, 18.

(2.) He speaks of it as an utter ruin. The temple shall not only be stripped, and plundered, and defaced, but utterly demolished and laid waste; *Not one stone shall be left upon another.* Notice is taken, in the *building* of the second temple, of the *laying of one stone upon another* (Hag. ii. 15); and here, in the *ruin,* of *not leaving one stone upon another.* History tells us, that this was fulfilled in the latter; for though Titus, when he took the city, did all he could to preserve the temple, yet he could not restrain the enraged soldiers from destroying it utterly; and it was done to that degree, that Turnus Rufus ploughed up the ground on which it had stood: thus that scripture was fulfilled (Mic. iii. 12), *Zion shall, for your sake, be ploughed as a field.* And afterward, in Julian the Apostate's time, when the Jews were encouraged by him to rebuild their temple, in opposition to the Christian religion, what remained of the ruins was quite pulled down, to level the ground for a new foundation; but the attempt was defeated by the miraculous eruption of fire out of the ground, which destroyed the foundation they laid, and frightened away the builders. Now this prediction of the final and irreparable ruin of the temple includes a prediction of the period of the Levitical priesthood and the ceremonial law.

3. The disciples, not disputing either the truth or the equity of this sentence, nor doubting of the accomplishment of it, enquire more particularly of the time when it should come to pass, and the signs of its approach, *v.* 3. Observe,

(1.) Where they made this enquiry; privately, *as he sat upon the mount of Olives;* probably, he was returning to Bethany, and there sat down by the way, to rest him; the mount of Olives directly faced the temple, and from thence he might have a full prospect of it at some distance; there he sat as a Judge upon the bench, the temple and city being before him as at the bar, and thus he passed sentence on them. We read (Ezek. xi. 23) of the removing of the glory of the Lord from the temple to the mountain; so Christ, the great Shechinah, here removes to this mountain.

(2.) What the enquiry itself was; *When shall these things be; and what shall be the sign of thy coming, and of the end of the world?* Here are three questions.

[1.] Some think, these questions do all point at one and the same thing—the destruction of the temple, and the period of the Jewish church and nation, which Christ had himself spoken of as his coming (*ch.* xvi. 28), and which would be the consummation of the age (for so it may be read), the finishing of that dispensation. Or, they thought the destruction of the temple must needs be the end of the world. If that house be laid waste, the world cannot stand; for the Rabbin used to say that the house of the sanctuary was one of the seven things for the sake of which the world was made; and they think, if so, the world will not survive the temple.

[2.] Others think their question, *When shall these things be?* refers to the destruction of Jerusalem, and the other two to the end of the world; or Christ's coming may refer to his setting up his gospel kingdom, and the end of the world to the day of judgment. I rather incline to think that their question looked no further than the event Christ now foretold; but it appears by other passages, that they had very confused thoughts of future events; so that perhaps it is not possible to put any certain construction upon this question of theirs.

But Christ, in his answer, though he does not expressly rectify the mistakes of his disciples (that must be done by the pouring out of the Spirit), yet looks further than their question, and instructs his church, not only concerning the great events of that age, the destruction of Jerusalem, but concerning his second coming at the end of time, which here he insensibly slides into a discourse of, and of that it is plain he speaks in the next chapter, which is a continuation of this sermon.

4 And Jesus answered and said
unto them, Take heed that no man
deceive you. 5 For many shall come
in my name, saying, I am Christ; and
shall deceive many. 6 And ye shall
hear of wars and rumours of wars:
see that ye be not troubled: for all
these things must come to pass, but
the end is not yet. 7 For nation
shall rise against nation, and kingdom
against kingdom: and there shall be
famines, and pestilences, and earthquakes, in divers places. 8 All these
are the beginning of sorrows. 9 Then
shall they deliver you up to be afflicted,
and shall kill you: and ye shall be
hated of all nations for my name's
sake. 10 And then shall many be
offended, and shall betray one another,
and shall hate one another. 11 And
many false prophets shall rise, and
shall deceive many. 12 And because
iniquity shall abound, the love of many
shall wax cold. 13 But he that shall
endure unto the end, the same shall
be saved. 14 And this gospel of the
kingdom shall be preached in all the
world for a witness unto all nations;
and then shall the end come. 15
When ye therefore shall see the abomination of desolation, spoken of by
Daniel the prophet, stand in the holy
place (whoso readeth let him understand); 16 Then let them which be in
Judæa flee into the mountains: 17
Let him which is on the housetop
not come down to take any thing out
of his house: 18 Neither let him
which is in the field return back to
take his clothes. 19 And woe unto
them that are with child, and to them

that give suck in those days! 20 But
pray ye that your flight be not in the
winter, neither on the sabbath day:
21 For then shall be great tribulation,
such as was not since the beginning
of the world to this time, no, nor ever
shall be. 22 And except those days
should be shortened, there should no
flesh be saved: but for the elect's
sake those days shall be shortened.
23 Then if any man shall say unto
you, Lo, here *is* Christ, or there; believe *it* not. 24 For there shall arise
false Christs, and false prophets, and
shall show great signs and wonders;
insomuch that, if *it were* possible,
they shall deceive the very elect. 25
Behold, I have told you before. 26
Wherefore if they shall say unto you,
Behold, he is in the desert; go not
forth: behold, *he is* in the secret
chambers; believe *it* not. 27 For as
the lightning cometh out of the east,
and shineth even unto the west; so
shall also the coming of the Son of
man be. 28 For wheresoever the
carcase is, there will the eagles be
gathered together. 29 Immediately
after the tribulation of those days
shall the sun be darkened, and the
moon shall not give her light, and the
stars shall fall from heaven, and the
powers of the heavens shall be shaken:
30 And then shall appear the sign of
the Son of man in heaven: and then
shall all the tribes of the earth mourn,
and they shall see the Son of man
coming in the clouds of heaven with
power and great glory. 31 And he
shall send his angels with a great
sound of a trumpet, and they shall
gather together his elect from the four
winds, from one end of heaven to the
other.

The disciples had asked concerning the times, *When shall these things be?* Christ gives them no answer to that, after what number of days and years his prediction should be accomplished, for *it is not for us to know the times* (Acts i. 7); but they had asked, *What shall be the sign?* That question he answers fully, for we are concerned to *understand the signs of the times, ch.* xvi. 3. Now the prophecy primarily respects the events near at hand—the destruction of Jerusalem, the period of the Jewish church and state, the calling of the Gentiles, and the setting up of Christ's kingdom in the world; but as the prophecies of the Old Testament, which have an immediate reference to the affairs of the Jews and the revolutions of their state, under the figure of them do certainly look further, to the gospel church and the kingdom of the Messiah, and are so expounded in the New Testament, and such expressions are found in those predictions as are peculiar thereto and not applicable otherwise; so this prophecy, under the type of Jerusalem's destruction, looks as far forward as the general judgment; and, as is usual in prophecies, some passages are most applicable to the type, and others to the antitype; and toward the close, as usual, it points more particularly to the latter. It is observable, that what Christ here saith to his disciples tends more to engage their caution than to satisfy their curiosity; more to prepare them for the events that should happen than to give them a distinct idea of the events themselves. This is that good understanding of the times which we should all covet, thence to infer what Israel ought to do: and so this prophecy is of standing lasting use to the church, and will be so to the end of time; for *the thing that hath been, is that which shall be* (Eccl. i. 5, 6, 7, 9), and the series, connection, and presages, of events, are much the same still that they were then; so that upon the prophecy of this chapter, pointing at that event, moral prognostications may be made, and such constructions of the signs of the times as the wise man's heart will know how to improve.

I. Christ here foretels the going forth of deceivers; he begins with a caution, *Take heed that no man deceive you.* They expected to be told when these things should be, to be let into that secret; but this caution is a check to their curiosity, "*What is that to you?* Mind you your duty, follow me, and be not seduced from following me." Those that are most inquisitive concerning the secret things which belong not to them are most easily imposed upon by seducers, 2 Thess. ii. 3. The disciples, when they heard that the Jews, their most inveterate enemies, should be destroyed, might be in danger of falling into security; "Nay," saith Christ, "you are more exposed other ways." Seducers are more dangerous enemies to the church than persecutors.

Three times in this discourse he mentions the appearing of *false prophets,* which was, 1. A presage of Jerusalem's ruin. Justly were they who killed the true prophets, left to be ensnared by false prophets; and they who crucified the true Messiah, left to be deceived and broken by false Christs and pretended Messiahs. The appearing of these was the occasion of dividing that people into parties and factions, which made their ruin the more easy and speedy; and the sin of the many that were led aside by them, helped to fill the measure. 2. It was a trial to the disciples of Christ, and therefore agreeable to their state of probation, *that they which are perfect, may be made manifest.*

Now concerning these deceivers, observe here,

(1.) The pretences they should come under. Satan acts most mischievously, when he appears as an angel of light: the colour of the greatest good is often the cover of the greatest evil.

[1.] There should appear *false prophets* (*v.* 11—24); the deceivers would pretend to divine inspiration, an immediate mission, and a spirit of prophecy, when it was all a lie. Such there had been formerly (Jer. xxiii. 16; Ezek. xiii. 6), as was foretold, Deut. xiii. 3. Some think, the seducers here pointed to were such as had been settled teachers in the church, and had gained reputation as such, but afterward betrayed the truth they had taught, and revolted to error; and from such the danger is the greater, because least suspected. One false traitor in the garrison may do more mischief than a thousand avowed enemies without.

[2.] There should appear *false Christs, coming in Christ's name* (*v.* 5), assuming to themselves the name peculiar to him, and saying, *I am Christ, pseudo-christs, v.* 24. There was at that time a general expectation of the appearing of the Messias; they spoke of him; as *he that should come;* but when he did come, the body of the nation rejected him; which those who were ambitious of making themselves a name, took advantage of, and set up for Christs. Josephus speaks of several such impostors between this and the destruction of Jerusalem; one Theudas, that was defeated by Cospius Fadus; another by Felix, another by Festus. Dosetheus said he was the Christ foretold by Moses. *Origen adversus Celsum.* See Acts v. 36, 37. Simon Magus pretended to be *the great power of God,* Acts viii. 10. In after-ages there have been such pretenders; one about a hundred years after Christ, that called himself *Bar-cochobas—The son of a star,* but proved *Bar-cosba—The son of a lie.* About fifty years ago Sabbati-Levi set up for a Messiah in the Turkish empire, and was greatly caressed by the Jews; but in a short time *his folly was made manifest.* See Sir Paul Rycaut's *History.* The popish religion doth, in effect, set up a false Christ; the Pope comes, in Christ's name, as his vicar, but invades and usurps all his offices, and so is a rival with him, and, as such, an enemy to him, a deceiver, and an antichrist.

[3.] These false Christs and false prophets would have their agents and emissaries busy in all places to draw people in to them, *v.* 23. *Then* when public troubles are great and threatening, and people will be catching at any thing that looks like deliverance, then Satan will take the advantage of imposing on them; then they will say, *Lo, here is a Christ, or there* is one; but do not mind them: the true Christ did not strive, nor cry; nor was it said of him, *Lo, here! or Lo, there!* (Luke xvii. 21), therefore if any man say so concerning him, look upon it as a temptation. The hermits, who place religion in a monastical life, say, *He is in the desert;* the priests, who make the consecrated wafer to be Christ, say, "He is ἐν τοῖς ταμείοις—*in the cupboards, in the secret chambers:* lo, he is in this shrine, in that image." Thus some appropriate Christ's spiritual presence to one party or persuasion, as if they had the monopoly of Christ and Christianity; and the kingdom of Christ must stand and fall, must live and die, with them; "Lo, he is in this church, in that council:" whereas Christ is All in all, not here or there, but meets his people with a blessing *in every place where he records his name.*

(2.) The proof they should offer for the making good of these pretences; *They shall show great signs and wonders* (*v.* 24), not true miracles, those are a divine seal, and with those the doctrine of Christ stands confirmed; and therefore if any offer to draw us from that by signs and wonders, we must have recourse to that rule given of old (Deut. xiii. 1—3), *If the sign or wonder come to pass,* yet follow not him that would draw you *to serve other gods,* or believe in other Christs, *for the Lord your God proveth you.* But these were *lying wonders* (2 Thess. ii. 9), wrought by Satan (God permitting him), who is *the prince of the power of the air.* It is not said, *They shall work miracles,* but, *They shall show great signs;* they are but a show; either they impose upon men's credulity by false narratives, or deceive their senses by tricks of legerdemain, or arts of divination, as the magicians of Egypt by their enchantments.

(3.) The success they should have in these attempts,

[1.] *They shall deceive many* (*v.* 5), and again, *v.* 11. Note, The devil and his instruments may prevail far in deceiving poor souls; few find the strait gate, but many are drawn into the broad way; many will be imposed upon by their signs and wonders, and many drawn in by the hopes of deliverance from their oppressions. Note, Neither miracles nor multitudes are certain signs of a true church; for *all the world wonders after the beast,* Rev. xiii. 3.

[2.] *They shall deceive, if it were possible, the very elect, v.* 24. This bespeaks, *First,* The strength of the delusion; it is such as many shall be carried away by (so strong shall the stream be), even those that were thought to stand fast. Men's knowledge, gifts, learning, eminent station, and long profession, will not secure them; but, notwithstanding these, many will be deceived; nothing but the almighty grace of God, pursuant to his eternal purpose, will be a protection. *Secondly,* The safety of the elect in the midst of this danger, which is taken for granted in that parenthesis, *If it were pos-*

sible, plainly implying that it is not possible, for they are *kept by the power of God*, that *the purpose of God, according to the election, may stand.* It is possible for those that have been enlightened to fall away (Heb. vi. 4, 5, 6), but not for those that were elected. If God's chosen ones should be deceived, God's choice would be defeated, which is not to be imagined, *for whom he did predestinate, he called, justified, and glorified,* Rom. viii. 30. They were given to Christ; and of all that were given to him, he will lose none, John x. 28. Grotius will have this to be meant of the great difficulty of drawing the primitive Christians from their religion, and quotes it as used proverbially by Galen; when he would express a thing very difficult and morally impossible, he saith, "You may sooner draw away a Christian from Christ."

(4.) The repeated cautions which our Saviour gives to his disciples to stand upon their guard against them; *therefore* he gave them warning, that they might watch (*v.* 25); *Behold, I have told you before.* He that is told before where he will be assaulted, may save himself, as the king of Israel did, 2 Kings vi. 9, 10. Note, Christ's warnings are designed to engage our watchfulness; and though the elect shall be preserved from delusion, yet they shall be preserved by the use of appointed means, and a due regard to the cautions of the word; we are kept through faith, faith in Christ's word, which he has told us before.

[1.] We must not believe those who say, *Lo, here is Christ;* or, *Lo, he is there, v.* 23. We believe that the true Christ is at the right hand of God, and that his spiritual presence is *where two or three are gathered together in his name;* believe not those therefore who would draw you off from a Christ in heaven, by telling you he is any where on earth; or draw you off from the catholic church on earth, by telling you he is here, or he is there; believe it not. Note, There is not a greater enemy to true faith than vain credulity. The simple believeth every word, and runs after every cry. Μέμνησο ἀπιστεῖν—*Beware of believing.*

[2.] We must not go forth after those that say, *He is in the desert,* or, *He is in the secret chambers, v.* 26. We must not hearken to every empiric and pretender, nor follow every one that puts up the finger to point us to a new Christ, and a new gospel; "Go not forth, for if you do, you are in danger of being taken by them; therefore keep out of harm's way, *be not carried about with every wind;* many a man's vain curiosity to go forth hath led him into a fatal apostasy; your strength at such a time is to sit still, to have the heart established with grace."

II. He foretels wars and great commotions among the nations, *v.* 6, 7. When Christ was born, there was a universal peace in the empire, the temple of Janus was shut; but *think not that Christ came to send,* or continue such a *peace* (Luke xii. 51); no, his city and his wall are to be built even in troublesome times, and even wars shall forward his work. From the time that the Jews rejected Christ, and he *left their house desolate, the sword did never depart from their house, the sword of the Lord* was never quiet, because he had given it a charge against a hypocritical nation and the people of his wrath, and by it brought ruin upon them.

Here is, 1. A prediction of the event of the day; You will now shortly *hear of wars, and rumours of wars.* When wars are, they will be heard; for *every battle of the warrior is with confused noise,* Isa. ix. 5 See how terrible it is (Jer. iv. 19), *Thou hast heard, O my soul, the alarm of war!* Even the quiet in the land, and the least inquisitive after new things, cannot but hear the rumours of war. See what comes of refusing the gospel! Those that will not hear the messengers of peace, shall be made to hear the messengers of war. God has a sword ready to avenge the quarrel of his covenant, his new covenant. *Nation shall rise up against nation,* that is, one part or province of the Jewish nation against another, one city against another (2 Chron. xv. 5, 6); and in the same province and city one party or faction shall rise up against another, so that they shall be devoured by, and dashed in pieces against one another, Isa. ix. 19—21.

2. A prescription of the duty of the day; *See that ye be not troubled.* Is it possible to hear such sad news, and not be troubled? Yet, where the heart is fixed, trusting in God, it is kept in peace, and is not afraid, no not of the evil tidings of wars, and rumours of wars; no not the noise of *Arm, arm. Be not troubled;* Μὴ θροεῖθε—*Be not put into confusion or commotion;* not put into throes, as a woman with child by a fright; *see that ye be not* ὁρᾶτε. Note, There is need of constant care and watchfulness to keep trouble from the heart when there are wars abroad; and it is against the mind of Christ, that his people should have troubled hearts even in troublous times.

We must not be troubled, for two reasons.

(1.) Because we are bid to expect this: the Jews must be punished, ruin must be brought upon them; by this the justice of God and the honour of the Redeemer must be asserted; and therefore *all those things must come to pass;* the word is gone out of God's mouth, and it shall be accomplished in its season. Note, The consideration of the unchangeableness of the divine counsels, which govern all events, should compose and quiet our spirits, whatever happens. God is but performing the thing that is appointed for us, and our inordinate trouble is an interpretative quarrel with that appointment. Let us therefore acquiesce, because *these things must come to pass;* not only *necessitate decreti—as the product of the divine counsel,* but *necessitate medii—as a means in order to a further end.* The old house must be taken down (though it cannot be done without noise, and dust, and danger), ere the new fabric can be erected: the things that are shaken (and ill shaken they were) *must be removed, that the things which cannot be shaken may remain,* Heb. xii. 27.

(2.) Because we are still to expect worse; *The end is not yet;* the end of time is not, and, while time lasts, we must expect trouble, and that the end of one affliction will be but the beginning of another; or, "The end of these troubles is not yet; there must be more judgments than one made use of to bring down the Jewish power; more vials of wrath must yet be poured out; there is but one woe past, more woes are yet to come, more arrows are yet to be spent upon them out of God's quiver; therefore be not troubled, do not give way to fear and trouble, sink not under the present burthen, but rather gather in all the strength and spirit you have, to encounter what is yet before you. Be not troubled to hear of wars and rumours of wars; for then what will become of you when the famines and pestilences come?" If it be to us a vexation but to *understand the report* (Isa. xxviii. 19), what will it be to feel the stroke when it *toucheth the bone and the flesh?* If running with the footmen weary us, how shall we contend with horses? And if we be frightened at a little brook in our way, *what shall we do in the swellings of Jordan?* Jer. xii. 5.

III. He foretels other judgments more immediately sent of God—*famines, pestilences, and earthquakes.* Famine is often the effect of war, and pestilence of famine. These were the three judgments which David was to choose one out of; and he was in a great strait, for he knew not which was the worst: but what dreadful desolations will they make, when they all pour in together upon a people! Beside war (and that is enough), there shall be,

1. *Famine,* signified by the *black horse* under the *third seal,* Rev. vi. 5, 6. We read of a famine in Judea, not long after Christ's time, which was very impoverishing (Acts xi. 28); but the sorest famine was in Jerusalem during the siege. See Lam. iv. 9, 10.

2. *Pestilences,* signified by the *pale horse, and death upon him,* and *the grave at his heels,* under the *fourth seal,* Rev. vi. 7, 8. This destroys without distinction, and in a little time lays heaps upon heaps.

3. *Earthquakes in divers places,* or from place to place, pursuing those that flee from them, as they did from the earthquake *in the days of Uzziah,* Zech. xiv. 5. Great desolations have sometimes been made by earthquakes, of late and formerly; they have been the death of many, and the terror of more. In the apocalyptic visions, it is observable, that earthquakes bode good, and no evil, to the church, Rev. vi. 12. Compare Rev. vi. 15; xi. 12, 13, 19; xvi. 17—19. When God *shakes terribly the earth* (Isa. ii. 21), it is to *shake the wicked out of it* (Job xxxviii. 13), and to introduce *the desire of all nations,* Hag. ii. 6, 7. But here they are spoken of as dreadful judgments, and yet but *the beginning of sorrows, ὠδίνων—of travailing pains,* quick, violent, yet tedious too. Note, When God judgeth, he will overcome; *when he begins* in wrath, *he will make* a full *end,* 1 Sam. iii. 12. When we look forward to the eternity of misery that is before the obstinate refusers of Christ and his gospel, we may truly say, concerning the greatest temporal judgments, "They are but the beginning of sorrows; bad as things are with them, there are worse behind."

IV. He foretels the persecution of his own people and ministers, and a general apostasy and decay in religion thereupon, *v.* 9, 10, 12. Observe,

1. The *cross* itself foretold, *v.* 9. Note, Of all future events we are as much concerned, though commonly as little desirous, to know of our own sufferings as of any thing else. *Then,* when famines and pestilences prevail, then they shall impute them to the Christians, and make that a pretence for persecuting them; *Christianos ad leones—Away with Christians to the lions.* Christ had told his disciples, when he first sent them out, what hard things they should suffer; but they had hitherto experienced little of it, and therefore he reminds them again, that the less they had suffered, the more there was behind to be filled up, Col. i. 24.

(1.) They shall be *afflicted* with bonds and imprisonments, *cruel mockings and scourgings,* as blessed Paul (2 Cor. xi. 23—25); not killed outright, but *killed all the day long, in deaths often,* killed so as to feel themselves die, *made a spectacle to the world,* 1 Cor. iv. 9, 11.

(2.) They shall be *killed;* so cruel are the church's enemies, that nothing less will satisfy them than the blood of the saints, which they thirst after, suck, and shed, like water.

(3.) They shall be *hated of all nations for Christ's name's sake,* as he had told them before, *ch.* x. 22. The world was generally leavened with enmity and malignity to Christians: the Jews, though spiteful to the Heathen, were never persecuted by them as the Christians were; they were hated by the Jews that were dispersed among the nations, were the common butt of the world's malice. What shall we think of this world, when the best men had the worst usage in it? It is the cause that makes the martyr, and comforts him; it was for Christ's sake that they were thus hated; their professing and preaching his name incensed the nations so much against them; the devil, finding a fatal shock thereby given to his kingdom, and that his time was likely to be short, *came down, having great wrath.*

2. *The offence of the cross, v.* 10—12. Satan thus carries on his interest by force of arms, though Christ, at length, will bring

glory to himself out of the sufferings of his people and ministers. Three ill effects of persecution are here foretold.

(1.) The *apostasy* of some. When the profession of Christianity begins to cost men dear, *then shall many be offended,* shall first fall out with, and then fall off from, their profession; they will begin to pick quarrels with their religion, sit loose to it, grow weary of it, and at length revolt from it. Note, [1.] It is no new thing (though it is a strange thing) for those that have known the way of righteousness, to turn aside out of it. Paul often complains of deserters, who began well, but something hindered them. They were with us, but went out from us, because never truly of us, 1 John ii. 19. We are told of it before. [2.] Suffering times are shaking times; and those fall in the storm, that stood in fair weather, like the *stony ground hearers, ch.* xiii. 21. Many will follow Christ in the sunshine, who will shift for themselves, and leave him to do so too, in the cloudy dark day. They like their religion while they can have it cheap, and sleep with it in a whole skin; but, if their profession cost them any thing, they quit it presently.

(2.) The *malignity* of others. When persecution is in fashion, envy, enmity, and malice, are strangely diffused into the minds of men by contagion: and charity, tenderness, and moderation, are looked upon as singularities, which make a man like a speckled bird. Then *they shall betray one another,* that is, "Those that have treacherously deserted their religion, shall hate and betray those who adhere to it, for whom they have pretended friendship." Apostates have commonly been the most bitter and violent persecutors. Note, Persecuting times are discovering times. Wolves in sheep's clothing will then throw off their disguise, and appear wolves: they shall *betray one another, and hate one another.* The times must needs be perilous, when treachery and hatred, two of the worst things that can be, because directly contrary to two of the best (truth and love), shall have the ascendant. This seems to refer to the barbarous treatment which the several contending factions among the Jews gave to one another; and justly were they who ate up God's people as they ate bread, left thus to bite and devour one another till they were *consumed one of another;* or, it may refer to the mischiefs done to Christ's disciples by those that were nearest to them, as *ch.* x. 21. *The brother shall deliver up the brother to death.*

(3.) The general *declining* and *cooling* of most, *v.* 12. In seducing times, when false prophets arise, in persecuting times, when the saints are hated, expect these two things,

[1.] The *abounding* of iniquity; though the world always lies in wickedness, yet there are some times in which it may be said, that *iniquity doth* in a special manner abound; as when it is more extensive than ordinary, as in the old world, when *all flesh had corrupted their way;* and when it is more *excessive* than ordinary, when *violence is risen up to a rod of wickedness* (Ezek. vii. 11), so that hell seems to be broke loose in blasphemies against God, and enmities to the saints.

[2.] The *abating* of love; this is the consequence of the former; *Because iniquity shall abound, the love of many shall wax cold.* Understand it in general of true serious godliness, which is all summed up in *love;* it is too common for professors of religion to grow cool in their profession, when the wicked are hot in their wickedness; as the church of Ephesus in bad times *left her first love,* Rev. ii. 2—4. Or, it may be understood more particularly of brotherly love. When iniquity abounds, seducing iniquity, persecuting iniquity, this grace commonly waxes cold. Christians begin to be shy and suspicious one of another, affections are alienated, distances created, parties made, and so love comes to nothing. The devil is the accuser of the brethren, not only to their enemies, which makes persecuting iniquity abound, but one to another, which makes the love of many to wax cold.

This gives a melancholy prospect of the times, that there shall be such a great decay of love; but, *First,* It is of the love of *many,* not of *all.* In the worst of times, God has his remnant that hold fast their integrity, and retain their zeal, as in Elijah's days, when he thought himself left alone. *Secondly,* This love is grown cold, but not dead; it abates, but is not quite cast off. There is life in the root, which will show itself when the winter is past. The new nature may *wax cold,* but shall not *wax old,* for then it would decay and vanish away.

3. Comfort administered in reference to this offence of the cross, for the support of the Lord's people under it (*v.* 13); *He that endures to the end, shall be saved.* (1.) It is comfortable to those who wish well to the cause of Christ in general, that, though many are offended, yet some shall endure to the end. When we see so many drawing back, we are ready to fear that the cause of Christ will sink for want of supporters, and his name be left and forgotten for want of some to make profession of it; but even at this time there is *a remnant according to the election of grace,* Rom. xi. 5. It is spoken of the same time that this prophecy has reference to; a remnant who are not of *them that draw back unto perdition,* but believe and persevere *to the saving of the soul;* they endure to the end, to the end of their lives, to the end of their present state of probation, or to the end of these suffering trying times, to the last encounter, though they should be called to resist unto blood. (2.) It is comfortable to those who do thus endure to the end, and suffer for their constancy, that they shall be saved. Perseverance wins the crown, through free grace, and shall wear it. *They*

shall be saved: perhaps they may be delivered out of their troubles, and comfortably survive them in this world; but it is eternal salvation that is here intended. They that endure to the end of their days, shall then receive the end of their faith and hope, *even the salvation of their souls,* 1 Pet. i. 9; Rom. ii. 7; Rev. iii. 20. The crown of glory will make amends for all; and a believing regard to that will enable us to choose rather to die at a stake with the persecuted, than to live in a palace with the persecutors.

V. He foretels the preaching of the gospel in all the world (*v.* 14); *This gospel shall be preached, and then shall the end come.* Observe here, 1. It is called *the gospel of the kingdom,* because it reveals the kingdom of grace, which leads to the kingdom of glory; sets up Christ's kingdom in this world; and secures ours in the other world. 2. This gospel, sooner or later, is to be preached in all the world, to every creature, and all nations are to be discipled by it; for in it Christ is to be *Salvation to the ends of the earth;* for this end the gift of tongues was *the first-fruits of the Spirit.* 3. The gospel is preached *for a witness to all nations,* that is, a faithful declaration of the mind and will of God concerning the duty which God requires from man, and the recompence which man may expect from God. It is a *record* (1 John v. 11), it is a *witness,* for those who believe, that they shall be saved, and against those who persist in unbelief, that they shall be damned. See Mark xvi. 16. But how does this come in here?

(1.) It is intimated that the gospel should be, if not heard, yet at least heard of, throughout the then known world, before the destruction of Jerusalem; that the Old-Testament church should not be quite dissolved till the New Testament was pretty well settled, had got considerable footing, and began to make some figure. Better is the face of a corrupt degenerate church than none at all. Within forty years after Christ's death, the *sound* of the gospel was *gone forth to the ends of the earth,* Rom. x. 18. St. Paul *fully preached the gospel from Jerusalem, and round about unto Illyricum;* and the other apostles were not idle. The persecuting of the saints at Jerusalem helped to disperse them, so that they *went every where, preaching the word,* Acts viii. 1—4. And when the tidings of the Redeemer are sent over all parts of the world, then shall come the end of the Jewish state. Thus, that which they thought to prevent, by putting Christ to death, they thereby procured; all men *believed on him, and the Romans came, and took away their place and nation,* John xi. 48. Paul speaks of the gospel being *come to all the world, and preached to every creature,* Col. i. 6—23.

(2.) It is likewise intimated that even in times of temptation, trouble, and persecution, the gospel of the kingdom shall be preached and propagated, and shall force its way through the greatest opposition. Though the enemies of the church grow very *hot,* and many of her friends very *cool,* yet the gospel shall be preached. And even *then,* when many fall by the sword and by flame, and many do wickedly, and are corrupted by flatteries, yet then the people that do know their God, shall be strengthened to do the greatest exploits of all, in instructing many; see Dan. xi. 32, 33; and see an instance, Phil. i. 12—14.

(3.) That which seems chiefly intended here, is, that the end of the world shall be *then,* and not till then, when the gospel has done its work in the world. The gospel shall be preached, and that work carried on, when you are dead; so that all nations, first or last, shall have either the enjoyment, or the refusal, of the gospel; and *then cometh the end,* when the kingdom *shall be delivered up to God, even the Father;* when the mystery of God shall be finished, the mystical body completed, and the nations either converted and saved, or convicted and silenced, by the gospel; *then shall the end come,* of which he had said before (*v.* 6, 7), *not yet,* not till those intermediate counsels be fulfilled. The world shall stand as long as any of God's chosen ones remain uncalled; but, when they are all gathered in, it will be set on fire immediately.

VI. He foretels more particularly the ruin that was coming upon the people of the Jews, their city, temple, and nation, *v.* 15, &c. Here he comes more closely to answer their questions concerning the desolation of the temple; and what he said here, would be of use to his disciples, both for their conduct and for their comfort, in reference to that great event; he describes the several steps of that calamity, such as are usual in war.

1. The Romans *setting up the abomination of desolation in the holy place, v.* 15. Now, (1.) Some understand by this an image, or statue, set up in the temple by some of the Roman governors, which was very offensive to the Jews, provoked them to rebel, and so brought the desolation upon them. The image of Jupiter Olympius, which Antiochus caused to be set upon the altar of God, is called Βδέλυγμα ἐρημώσεως—*The abomination of desolation,* the very word here used by the historian, 1 Mac. i. 54. Since the captivity in Babylon, nothing was, nor could be, more distasteful to the Jews than an image in the holy place, as appeared by the mighty opposition they made when Caligula offered to set up his statue there, which had been of fatal consequence, if it had not been prevented, and the matter accommodated, by the conduct of Petronius; but Herod did set up an eagle over the temple-gate; and, some say, the statue of Titus was set up in the temple. (2.) Others choose to expound it by the parallel place (Luke xxi. 20), *when ye shall see Jerusalem compassed with armies.* Jerusalem was the holy city, Canaan the holy land, the Mount Moriah, which lay about Jerusalem,

for its nearness to the temple was, they thought, in a particular manner holy ground; on the country lying round about Jerusalem the Roman army was encamped, that was the abomination that made desolate. The land of an enemy is said to be *the land which thou abhorrest* (Isa. vii. 16); so an enemy's army to a weak but wilful people may well be called *the abomination.* Now this is said to be *spoken of by Daniel, the prophet,* who spoke more plainly of the Messiah and his kingdom than any of the Old-Testament prophets did. He speaks of an abomination making desolate, which should be set up by Antiochus (Dan. xi. 31; xii. 11); but this that our Saviour refers to, we have in the message that the angel brought him (Dan. ix. 27), of what should come at the end of seventy weeks, long after the former; *for the overspreading of abominations,* or, as the margin reads it, *with the abominable armies* (which comes home to the prophecy here), *he shall make it desolate.* Armies of idolaters may well be called *abominable armies;* and some think, the tumults, insurrections, and abominable factions and seditions, in the city and temple, may at least be taken in as part of the abomination making desolate. Christ refers them to that prophecy of Daniel, that they might see how the ruin of their city and temple was spoken of in the Old Testament, which would both confirm his prediction, and take off the odium of it. They might likewise from thence gather the time of it—soon after the cutting off of Messiah the prince; the sin that procured it—their rejecting him, and the certainty of it—*it is a desolation determined.* As Christ by his precepts confirmed the law, so by his predictions he confirmed the prophecies of the Old Testament, and it will be of good use to compare both together.

Reference being here had to a prophecy, which is commonly dark and obscure, Christ inserts this memorandum, "*Whoso readeth, let him understand;* whoso readeth the prophecy of Daniel, let him understand that it is to have its accomplishment now shortly in the desolations of Jerusalem." Note, Those that read the scriptures, should labour to understand the scriptures, else their reading is to little purpose; we cannot use that which we do not understand. See John v. 39; Acts viii. 30. The angel that delivered this prophecy to Daniel, stirred him up to *know and understand,* Dan. ix. 25. And we must not despair of understanding even dark prophecies; the great New-Testament prophecy is called a *revelation,* not a *secret.* Now *things revealed belong to us,* and therefore must be humbly and diligently searched into. Or, *Let him understand,* not only the scriptures which speak of those things, but by the scriptures let him *understand the times,* 1 Chron. xii. 32. Let him observe, and take notice; so some read it; let him be assured, that, notwithstanding the vain hopes with which the deluded people feed themselves, the abominable armies will make desolate.

2. The means of preservation which thinking men should betake themselves to (*v.* 16, 20); *Then let them which are in Judea, flee.* Then conclude there is no other way to help yourselves than by flying for the same. We may take this,

(1.) As a prediction of the ruin itself; that it should be irresistible; that it would be impossible for the stoutest hearts to make head against it, or contend with it, but they must have recourse to the last shift, getting out of the way. It bespeaks that which Jeremiah so much insisted upon, but in vain, when Jerusalem was besieged by the Chaldeans, that it would be to no purpose to resist, but that it was their wisdom to yield and capitulate; so Christ here, to show how fruitless it would be to stand it out, bids every one make the best of his way.

(2.) We may take it as a direction to the followers of Christ what to do, not to *say, A confederacy* with those who fought and warred against the Romans for the preservation of their city and nation, only that they might consume the wealth of both upon their lusts (for to this very affair, the struggles of the Jews against the Roman power, some years before their final overthrow, the apostle refers, Jam. iv. 1—3); but let them acquiesce in the decree that was gone forth, and with all speed quit the city and country, as they would quit a falling house or a sinking ship, as Lot quitted Sodom, and Israel the tents of Dathan and Abiram; he shows them,

[1.] Whither they must flee—from Judea *to the mountains;* not the mountains round about Jerusalem, but those in the remote corners of the land, which would be some shelter to them, not so much by their strength as by their secrecy. Israel is said to be *scattered upon the mountains* (2 Chron. xviii. 16); and see Heb. xi. 38. It would be safer among the lions' dens, and the mountains of the leopards, than among the seditious Jews or the enraged Romans. Note, In times of imminent peril and danger, it is not only lawful, but our duty, to seek our own preservation by all good and honest means; and if God opens a door of escape, we ought to make our escape, otherwise we do not trust God but tempt him. There may be a time when even *those that are in Judea,* where God is known, and his name is great, must *flee to the mountains;* and while we only go out of the way of danger, not out of the way of duty, we may trust God to provide *a dwelling for his outcasts,* Isa. xvi. 4, 5. In times of public calamity, when it is manifest that we cannot be serviceable at home and may be safe abroad, Providence calls us to make our escape. He that flees, may fight again.

[2.] What haste they must make, *v.* 17, 18. The life will be in danger, in imminent danger, the scourge will slay suddenly; and therefore he *that is on the house-top,* when the alarm comes, let him not *come down into the house,* to look after his effects there, but go the nearest way down, to make his escape; and so he that shall be *in the field,* will find it his wisest course to run immediately, and not return to fetch his clothes or the wealth of his house, for two reasons, *First,* Because the time which would be taken up in packing up his things, would delay his flight. Note, When death is at the door, delays are dangerous; it was the charge to Lot, *Look not behind thee.* Those that are convinced of the misery of a sinful state, and the ruin that attends them in that state, and, consequently, of the necessity of their fleeing to Christ, must take heed, lest, after all these convictions, they perish eternally by delays. *Secondly,* Because the carrying of his clothes, and his other movables and valuables with him, would but burthen him, and clog his flight. The Syrians, in their flight, *cast away their garments,* 2 Kings vii. 15. At such a time, we must be thankful *if our lives be given us for a prey,* though we can save nothing, Jer. xlv. 4, 5. *For the life is more than meat, ch.* vi. 25. Those who carried off least, were safest in their flight. *Cantabit vacuus coram latrone viator—The pennyless traveller can lose nothing by robbers.* It was to his own disciples that Christ recommended this forgetfulness of their house and clothes, who had a habitation in heaven, treasure there, and durable clothing, which the enemy could not plunder them of. *Omnia mea mecum porto—I have all my property with me,* said Bias the philosopher in his flight, empty-handed. He that has grace in his heart carries his all along with him, when stripped of all.

Now those to whom Christ said this immediately, did not live to see this dismal day, none of all the twelve but John only; they needed not to be hidden in the mountains (Christ hid them in heaven), but they left the direction to their successors in profession, who pursued it, and it was of use to them; for when the Christians in Jerusalem and Judea saw the ruin coming on, they all retired to a town called *Pella,* on the other side Jordan, where they were safe; so that of the many thousands that perished in the destruction of Jerusalem, there was not so much as one Christian. See *Euseb. Eccl. Hist.* lib. 3, cap. 5. Thus *the prudent man foresees the evil, and hides himself,* Prov. xxii. 3; Heb. xi. 7. This warning was not kept private. St. Matthew's gospel was published long before that destruction, so that others might have taken the advantage of it; but their perishing through their unbelief of this, was a figure of their eternal perishing through their unbelief of the warnings Christ gave concerning the wrath to come.

[3.] Whom it would go hard with at that time (*v.* 19); *Woe to them that are with child, and to them that give suck.* To this same event that saying of Christ at his death refers (Luke xxiii. 29), They shall say, *Blessed are the wombs that never bare, and the paps that never gave suck.* Happy are they that have no children to see the murder of; but most unhappy they whose wombs are then bearing, their paps then giving suck: they of all others will be in the most melancholy circumstances. *First,* To them the famine would be most grievous, when they should see the *tongue of the sucking child cleaving to the roof of his mouth for thirst,* and themselves by the calamity made more cruel than the sea monsters, Lam. iv. 3. 4. *Secondly,* To them the sword would be most terrible, when in the hand of worse than brutal rage. It is a direful midwifery, when the women with child come to be ripped up by the enraged conqueror (2 Kings xv. 16; Hos. xiii. 16; Amos. i. 13), or the children *brought forth to the murderer,* Hos. ix. 13. *Thirdly,* To them also the flight would be most afflictive; the women with child cannot make haste, or go far; the sucking child cannot be left behind, or, if it should, *can a woman forget it, that she should not have compassion on it?* If it be carried along, it retards the mother's flight, and so exposes her life, and is in danger of Mephibosheth's fate, who was lamed by a fall he got in his nurse's flight. 2 Sam. iv. 4.

[4.] What they should pray against at that time—*that your flight be not in the winter, nor on the sabbath day, v.* 20. Observe, in general, it becomes Christ's disciples, in times of public trouble and calamity, to be much in prayer; that is a salve for every sore, never out of season, but in a special manner seasonable when we are distressed on every side. There is no remedy but you must flee, the decree is gone forth, so that God will not be entreated to take away his wrath, no, not if *Noah, Daniel, and Job, stood before him. Let it suffice thee, speak no more of that matter,* but labour to make the best of that which is; and when you cannot in faith pray that you may not be forced to flee, yet pray that the circumstances of it may be graciously ordered, that, though the cup may not pass from you, yet the extremity of the judgment may be prevented. Note, God has the disposing of the circumstances of events, which sometimes make a great alteration one way or other; and therefore in those our eyes must be ever toward him. Christ's bidding them pray for this favour, intimates his purpose of granting it to them; and in a general calamity we must not overlook a circumstantial kindness, but see and own wherein it might have been worse. Christ still bids his disciples to pray for themselves and their friends, that, whenever they were forced to flee, it might be in the most convenient time. Note, When trouble is in prospect, at a great distance, it is good to lay in a stock of prayers beforehand; they must pray, *First, That their flight,* if it were the will of God, *might not be in the winter,* when the days are short, the weather cold, the ways dirty, and therefore travelling very uncomfortable, especially for whole families. Paul hastens Timothy to come to him before winter, 2 Tim. iv. 21. Note, Though the ease of the body is not to be *mainly* consulted, it ought to be *duly* considered; though we must take what God sends, and when he sends it, yet we may pray against bodily inconveniences, and are encouraged to do so, in that *the Lord is for the body. Secondly,* That it might not be *on the sabbath day;* not on the Jewish sabbath, because travelling then would give offence to them who were angry with the disciples for plucking the ears of corn on that day; not on the Christian sabbath, because being forced to travel on that day would be a grief to themselves. This intimates Christ's design, that a weekly sabbath should be observed in his church after the preaching of the gospel to all the world. We read not of any of the ordinances of the Jewish church, which were purely ceremonial, that Christ ever expressed any care about, because they were all to vanish; but for the sabbath he often showed a concern. It intimates likewise that the sabbath is ordinarily to be observed as a day of rest from travel and worldly labour; but that, according to his own explication of the fourth commandment, works of necessity were lawful on the sabbath day, as this of fleeing from an enemy to save our lives: had it not been lawful, he would have said, "Whatever becomes of you, do not flee on the sabbath day, but abide by it, though you die by it." For we must not commit the least sin, to escape the greatest trouble. But it intimates, likewise, that it is very uneasy and uncomfortable to a good man, to be taken off by any work of necessity from the solemn service and worship of God on the sabbath day. We should pray that we may have quiet undisturbed sabbaths, and may have no other work than sabbath work to do on sabbath days; that we may attend upon the Lord without distraction. It was desirable, that, if they must flee, they might have the benefit and comfort of one sabbath more to help to bear their charges. To flee in the winter is uncomfortable to the body; but to flee on the sabbath day is so to the soul, and the more so when it remembers former sabbaths, as Ps. xlii. 4.

3. The greatness of the troubles which should immediately ensue (*v.* 21); *Then shall be great tribulation;* then when the measure of iniquity is full; then when the servants of God are sealed and secured, then come the troubles; nothing can be done against Sodom till Lot is entered into Zoar, and then look for fire and brimstone immediately. *There shall be great tribulation.* Great, indeed, when within the city plague and famine raged, and (worse than either) faction and division, so that every man's sword was against his fellow; then and there it was that the hands of the pitiful women flayed their own children. Without the city was the Roman army ready to swallow them up, with a particular rage against them, not only as Jews, but as rebellious Jews. War was the only one of the three sore judgments that David excepted against; but that was it by which the Jews were ruined; and there were famine and pestilence in extremity besides. Josephus's *History of the Wars of the Jews,* has in it more tragical passages than perhaps any history whatsoever.

(1.) It was a desolation unparalleled, such as *was not since the beginning of the world, nor ever shall be.* Many a city and kingdom has been made desolate, but never any with a desolation like this. Let not daring sinners think that God has done his worst, he can heat the furnace seven times and yet seven times hotter, and will, when he sees greater and still greater abominations. The Romans, when they destroyed Jerusalem, were degenerated from the honour and virtue of their ancestors, which had made even their victories easy to the vanquished. And the wilfulness and obstinacy of the Jews themselves contributed much to the increase of the tribulation. No wonder that the ruin of Jerusalem was an unparalleled ruin, when the sin of Jerusalem was an unparalleled sin — even their crucifying Christ. The nearer any people are to God in profession and privileges, the greater and heavier will his judgments be upon them, if they abuse those privileges, and be false to that profession, Amos iii. 2.

(2.) It was a desolation which, if it should continue long, would be intolerable, so that *no flesh should be saved, v.* 22. So triumphantly would death ride, in so many dismal shapes, and with such attendants, that there would be no escaping, but, first or last, all would be cut off. He that escaped one sword, would fall by another, Isa. xxiv. 17, 18. The computation which Josephus makes of those that were slain in several places, amounts to above two millions. *No flesh shall be saved;* he doth not say, "No *soul* shall be saved," for the destruction of the flesh may be for *the saving of the spirit in the day of the Lord Jesus;* but temporal lives will be sacrificed so profusely, that one would think, if it last awhile, it would make a full end.

But here is one word of comfort in the midst of all this terror—that *for the elects' sake these days shall be shortened,* not made shorter than what God had determined (for *that which is determined, shall be poured upon the desolate,* Dan. ix. 27), but shorter than what he might have decreed, if he had dealt with them according to their sins; shorter than what the enemy designed, who would have cut all off, if God who made use of them to serve his own purpose, had not set bounds to their wrath; shorter than one who judged by human probabilities would have imagined Note, [1.] In times of common calamity God manifests his favour to the elect remnant; his jewels, which he will then make up; his peculiar treasure, which he will secure when the lumber is abandoned to the spoiler. [2.] The shortening of calamities is a kindness God often grants for the elects' sake. Instead of complaining that our afflictions last so long, if we consider our defects, we shall see reason to be thankful that they do not last always; when it is bad with us, it becomes us to say, "Blessed be God that it is no worse; blessed be God that it is not hell, endless and remediless misery." It was a lamenting church that said, *It is of the Lord's mercies that we are not consumed;* and it is for the sake of the elect, lest their spirit should fail before them, if he should contend for ever, and lest they should be tempted to put forth, if not their heart, yet their hand, to iniquity.

And now comes in the repeated caution, which was opened before, to take heed of being ensnared by false Christs, and false prophets (*v.* 23, &c.), who would promise them deliverance, as the lying prophets in Jeremiah's time (Jer. xiv. 13; xxiii. 16, 17; xxvii. 16; xxviii. 2), but would delude them. Times of great trouble are times of great temptation, and therefore we have need to double our guard then. If they shall say, *Here is a Christ, or there is one,* that shall deliver us from the Romans, do not heed them, it is all but talk; such a deliverance is not to be expected, and therefore not such a deliverer.

VII. He foretels the sudden spreading of the gospel in the world, about the time of these great events (*v.* 27, 28); *As the lightning comes out of the east, so shall the coming of the Son of man be.* It comes in here as an antidote against the poison of those seducers, that said, *Lo, here is Christ,* or, *Lo, he is there;* compare Luke xvii. 23, 24. Hearken not to them, for the coming of the Son of man will be as the lightning.

1. It seems primarily to be meant of his coming to set up his spiritual kingdom in the world; where the gospel came in its light and power, there the Son of man came, and in a way quite contrary to the fashion of the seducers and false Christs, who came creeping *in the desert,* or the *secret chambers* (2 Tim. iii. 6); whereas Christ comes not with such a *spirit of fear,* but *of power, and of love, and of a sound mind.* The gospel would be remarkable for two things.

(1.) Its swift spreading; it shall fly as the lightning; so shall the gospel be preached and propagated. The gospel is light (John iii. 19); and it is not in this as the lightning, that it is a sudden flash, and away, for it is sun-light, and day-light; but it is as lightning in these respects:

[1.] It is light from heaven, as the lightning. It is God, and not man, that sends the lightnings, and summons them, that they may go, and say, *Here we are,* Job xxxviii. 35. It is God that directs it (Job xxxvii. 3); to man it is one of nature's miracles, above his power to effect, and one of nature's mysteries, above his skill to account for: but it is from above; *his lightnings enlightened the world,* Ps. xcvii. 4.

[2.] It is visible and conspicuous as the lightning. The seducers carried on their depths of Satan in the desert and the secret chambers, shunning the light; heretics were called *lucifugæ—light-shunners.* But truth seeks no corners, however it may sometimes be forced into them, as the *woman in the wilderness,* though *clothed with the sun,* Rev. xii. 1, 6. Christ preached his gospel openly (John xviii. 20), and his apostles on *the house-top* (*ch.* x. 27), not *in a corner,* Acts xxvi. 26. See Ps. xcviii. 2.

[3.] It was sudden and surprising to the world as the lightning; the Jews indeed had predictions of it, but to the Gentiles it was altogether unlooked for, and came upon them with unaccountable energy, or ever they were aware. It was *light out of darkness, ch.* iv. 16; 2 Cor. iv. 6. We read of the discomfiting of armies by lightning, 2 Sam. xxii. 15; Ps. cxliv. 6. The powers of darkness were dispersed and vanquished by the gospel lightning.

[4.] It spread far and wide, and that quickly and irresistibly, like the lightning, which comes, suppose, out of the east (Christ is said to ascend *from the east,* Rev. vii. 2; Isa. xli. 2), and lighteneth to the west. The propagating of Christianity to so many distant countries, of divers languages, by such unlikely instruments, destitute of all secular advantages, and in the face of so much opposition, and this in so short a time, was one of the greatest miracles that was every wrought for the confirmation of it; here was Christ upon his white horse, denoting speed as well as strength, and *going on conquering and to conquer,* Rev. vi. 2. Gospel light rose with the sun, and went with the same, so that the beams of it reached to the ends of the earth, Rom. x. 18. Compare with Ps. xix. 3, 4. Though it was fought against, it could never be cooped up in a desert, or in a secret place, as the seducers were; but by this, according to Gamaliel's rule, proved itself to be *of God,* that it *could not be overthrown,* Acts v. 38, 39. Christ speaks of *shining into the west,* because it spread most effectually into those countries which lay west from Jerusalem, as Mr. Herbert observes in his *Church-militant.* How soon did the gospel lightning reach this island of Great Britain! Tertullian, who wrote in the second century, takes notice of it, *Britannorum inaccessa Romanis loca, Christo tamen subdita—The fastnesses of Britain, though inaccessible to the Romans, were occupied by Jesus Christ.* This was the Lord's doing.

(2.) Another thing remarkable concerning the gospel, was, its strange success in those places to which it was spread; it gathered in multitudes, not by external compulsion, but as it were by such a natural instinct and inclination, as brings the birds of prey to their prey; for *wheresoever the carcase is, there will the eagles be gathered together* (*v.* 28), where Christ is preached, souls will be gathered in to him. The *lifting up of Christ from the earth,* that is, the preaching of Christ crucified, which, one would think, should drive all men from him, will *draw all men to him* (John xii. 32), according to Jacob's prophecy, that *to him shall the gathering of the people be,* Gen. xlix. 10. See Isa. lx. 8. The eagles will be where the carcase is, for it is food for them, it is a feast for them; *where the slain are, there is she,* Job xxxix. 30. Eagles are said to have a strange sagacity and quickness of scent to find out the prey, and they fly swiftly to it, Job ix. 26. So those whose spirits God shall stir up, will be effectually drawn to Jesus Christ, to feed upon him; whither should the eagle go but to the prey? Whither should the soul go but to Jesus Christ, who *has the words of eternal life?* The eagles will distinguish what is proper for them from that which is not; so those who have spiritual senses exercised, will know the voice of the good Shepherd from that of a thief and a robber. Saints will be where the true Christ is, not the false Christs. This is applicable to the desires that are wrought in every gracious soul after Christ, and communion with him. Where he is in his ordinances, there will his servants choose to be. A living principle of grace is a kind of natural instinct in all the saints, drawing them to Christ to live upon him.

2. Some understand these verses of the coming of the Son of man *to destroy Jerusalem,* Mal. iii. 1, 2, 5. So much was there of an extraordinary display of divine power and justice in that event, that it is called *the coming of Christ.*

Now here are two things intimated concerning it.

(1.) That to the most it would be as unexpected as a flash of lightning, which indeed gives warning of the clap of thunder which follows, but is itself surprising. The seducers say, *Lo, here is Christ* to deliver us; or there is one, a creature of their own fancies; but ere they are aware, the wrath of the Lamb, the true Christ, will arrest them, and they shall not escape.

(2.) That it might be as justly expected as that the eagle should fly to the carcases; though they put far from them the evil day, yet the desolation will come as certainly as the birds of prey to a dead carcase, that lies exposed in the open field. [1.] The Jews were so corrupt and degenerate, so vile and vicious, that they were become a carcase, obnoxious to the righteous judgment of God; they were also so factious and seditious, and every way so provoking to the Romans, that they had made themselves obnoxious to their resentments, and an inviting prey to them. [2.] The Romans were as an eagle, and the ensign of their armies was an eagle. The army of the Chaldeans is said *to fly as the eagle that hasteth to eat,* Hab. i. 8. The ruin of the New-Testament Babylon is represented by a call to the birds of prey to come and feast upon the slain, Rev. xix. 17, 18. Notorious malefactors have their eyes eaten out by *the young eagles* (Prov. xxx. 17); the Jews were hung up in chains, Jer. vii. 33; xvi. 4. [3.] The Jews can no more preserve themselves from the Romans than the carcase can secure itself from the eagles. [4.] The destruction shall find out the Jews wherever they are, as the eagle scents the prey. Note, When a people do by their sin make themselves carcases, putrid and loathsome, nothing can be expected but that God should send eagles among them, to devour and destroy them.

3. It is very applicable to the day of judgment, the coming of our Lord Jesus Christ in that day, and *our gathering together unto him,* 2 Thess. ii. 1. Now see here,

(1.) How he shall come; *as the lightning.* The time was now at hand, when he should *depart out of the world, to go to the Father.* Therefore those that enquire after Christ must not go into the desert or the secret places, nor listen to every one that will put up the finger to invite them to a sight of Christ; but let them look upward, for the heavens must contain him, and thence *we look for the Saviour* (Phil. iii. 20); he shall *come in the clouds,* as the lightning doth, and *every eye shall see him,* as they say it is natural for all living creatures to turn their faces towards the lightning, Rev. i. 7. Christ will appear to all the world, from one end of heaven to the other; nor shall any thing be hid from the light and heat of that day.

(2.) How the saints shall be gathered to him; as the eagles are to the carcase by natural instinct, and with the greatest swiftness and alacrity imaginable. Saints, when they shall be fetched to glory, will be carried as on eagles' wings (Exod. xix. 4), as on angels' wings. *They shall mount up with wings, like eagles,* and like them renew their youth.

VIII. He foretels his second coming at the *end of time, v.* 29—31. *The sun shall be darkened,* &c.

1. Some think this is to be understood only of the destruction of Jerusalem and the Jewish nation; the darkening of the sun, moon, and stars, denotes the eclipse of the glory of that state, its convulsions, and the general confusion that attended that desolation. Great slaughter and devastation are in the Old Testament thus set forth (as Isa. xiii. 10; xxxiv. 4; Ezek. xxxii. 7; Joel ii. 31); or by the sun, moon, and stars, may be meant the temple, Jerusalem, and the cities of Judah, which should all come to ruin. The *sign of the Son of man* (*v.* 30) means a signal appearance of the power and justice of the Lord Jesus in it, avenging his own blood on them that imprecated the guilt of it upon themselves and their children; and the gathering *of his elect* (*v.* 31) signifies the delivering of a remnant from this sin and ruin.

2. It seems rather to refer to Christ's second coming. The destruction of the particular enemies of the church was typical of the com-

plete conquest of them all; and therefore what will be done really at the great day, may be applied metaphorically to those destructions: but still we must attend to the principal scope of them; and while we are all agreed to expect Christ's second coming, what need is there to put such strained constructions as some do, upon these verses, which speak of it so clearly, and so agreeably to other scriptures, especially when Christ is here answering an enquiry concerning his coming at the end of the world, which Christ was never shy of speaking of to his disciples?

The only objection against this, is, that it is said to be *immediately after the tribulation of those days;* but as to that, (1.) It is usual in the prophetical style to speak of things great and certain as near and just at hand, only to express the greatness and certainty of them. Enoch spoke of Christ's second coming as within ken, *Behold, the Lord cometh,* Jude 14. (2.) *A thousand years are* in God's sight *but as one day,* 2 Pet. iii. 8. It is there urged, with reference to this very thing, and so it might be said to be immediately after. The tribulation of those days includes not only the destruction of Jerusalem, but all the other tribulations which the church must pass through; not only its share in the calamities of the nations, but the tribulations peculiar to itself; while the nations are torn with wars, and the church with schisms, delusions, and persecutions, we cannot say that the tribulation of those days is over; the whole state of the church on earth is militant, we must count upon that; but when the church's tribulation is over, her warfare accomplished, and what is behind of the sufferings of Christ filled up, then look for the end.

Now concerning Christ's second coming, it is here foretold,

[1.] That there shall be then a great and amazing change of the creatures, and particularly the *heavenly bodies* (*v.* 29). *The sun shall be darkened, and the moon shall not give her light.* The moon shines with a borrowed light, and therefore if the sun, from whom she borrows her light, is turned into darkness, she must fail of course, and become bankrupt. *The stars shall fall;* they shall lose their light, and disappear, and be as if they were fallen; and *the powers of heaven shall be shaken.* This intimates,

First, That there shall be a great change, in order to the making of all things new. Then shall be *the restitution of all things,* when the heavens shall not be cast away as a rag, but *changed as a vesture,* to be worn in a better fashion, Ps. cii. 26. They shall *pass away with a great noise,* that there may be *new heavens,* 2 Pet. iii. 10—13.

Secondly, It shall be a visible change, and such as all the world must take notice of; for such the darkening of the sun and moon cannot but be: and it would be an amazing change; for the heavenly bodies are not so liable to alteration as the creatures of this lower world are. The days of heaven, and the continuance of the sun and moon, are used to express that which is lasting and unchangeable (as Ps. lxxxix. 29; xxxvi. 37); yet they shall thus be shaken.

Thirdly, It shall be a universal change. If the sun be turned into darkness, and the powers of heaven be shaken, the earth cannot but be turned into a dungeon, and its foundation made to tremble. *Howl, fir trees, if the cedars be shaken.* When the stars of heaven drop, no marvel if the *everlasting mountains melt,* and the *perpetual hills bow.* Nature shall sustain a general shock and convulsion, which yet shall be no hindrance to the joy and rejoicing of heaven and earth *before the Lord, when he cometh to judge the world* (Ps. xcvi. 11, 13); they shall as it were *glory in the tribulation.*

Fourthly, The darkening of the sun, moon, and stars, which were *made to rule over the day, and over the night* (which is the first dominion we find of any creature, Gen. i. 16—18), signifies the *putting down of all rule, authority, and power* (even that which seems of the greatest antiquity and usefulness), *that the kingdom may be delivered up to God, even the Father,* and he may be *All in all,* 1 Cor. xv. 24, 28. The sun was darkened at the death of Christ, for then was in one sense *the judgment of this world* (John xii. 31), an indication what would be at the general judgment.

Fifthly, The glorious appearance of our Lord Jesus, who will then show himself as the *Brightness of his Father's glory, and the express Image of his person,* will darken the sun and moon, as a candle is darkened in the beams of the noon-day sun; they will have no glory, *by reason of the glory that excelleth,* 2 Cor. iii. 10. Then *the sun shall be ashamed, and the moon confounded,* when God shall appear, Isa. xxiv. 23.

Sixthly, The sun and moon shall be then darkened, because there will be no more occasion for them. To sinners, that choose their portion in this life, all comfort will be eternally denied; as they shall not have a drop of water, so not a ray of light. Now God causeth his sun to rise on the earth, but then *Interdico tibi sole et luna—I forbid thee the light of the sun and the moon.* Darkness must be their portion. To the saints that had their treasure above, such light of joy and comfort will be given as shall supersede that of the sun and moon, and render it useless. What need is there of vessels of light, when we come to *the Fountain and Father of light?* See Isa. lx. 19; Rev. xxii. 5.

[2.] That *then shall appear the sign of the Son of man in heaven* (*v.* 30), the Son of man himself, as it follows here, *They shall see the Son of man coming in the clouds.* At his first coming, he was *set for a Sign that should be spoken against* (Luke ii. 34), but at his second coming, a sign that should be admired. Ezekiel was *a son of man set for a sign,* Ezek. xii. 6. Some make this a prediction of the harbingers and forerunners of his coming, giving notice of his approach; *a light shining before him, and the fire devouring* (Ps. l. 3; 1 Kings xix. 11, 12), *the beams coming out of his hand, where had long been the hiding of his power,* Hab. iii. 4. It is a groundless conceit of some of the ancients, that this sign of the Son of man, will be the sign of the cross displayed as a banner. It will certainly be such a clear convincing sign as will dash infidelity quite out of countenance, and fill their faces with shame, who said, *Where is the promise of his coming?*

[3.] That *then all the tribes of the earth shall mourn, v.* 30. See Rev. i. 7. *All the kindreds of the earth shall then wail because of him;* some of all the tribes and kindreds of the earth shall mourn; for the greater part will tremble at his approach, while the chosen remnant, one of a family and two of a tribe, shall lift up their heads with joy, knowing that their redemption draws nigh, and their Redeemer. Note, Sooner or later, all sinners will be mourners; penitent sinners look to Christ, and mourn after a godly sort; and they who sow in those tears, shall shortly reap in joy; impenitent sinners *shall look unto him whom they have pierced,* and, though they laugh now, shall mourn and weep after a devilish sort, in endless horror and despair.

[4.] That *then they shall see the Son of man coming in the clouds of heaven, with power and great glory.* Note, *First,* The judgment of the great day will be committed to the Son of man, both in pursuance and in recompence of his great undertaking for us as Mediator, John v. 22, 27. *Secondly,* The Son of man will at that day come in the clouds of heaven. Much of the sensible intercourse between heaven and earth is by the clouds; they are betwixt them, as it were, the *medium participationis—the medium of participation,* drawn by heaven from the earth, distilled by heaven upon the earth. Christ went to heaven in a cloud, and *will in like manner come again,* Acts i. 9, 11. *Behold, he cometh in the clouds,* Rev. i. 7. A cloud will be the Judge's chariot (Ps. civ. 3), his robe (Rev. x. 1), his pavilion (Ps. xviii. 11), his throne, Rev. xiv. 14. When the world was destroyed by water, the judgment came in the clouds of heaven, for the windows of heaven were opened; so shall it be when it shall be destroyed by fire. Christ went before Israel in a cloud, which had a bright side and a dark side; so will the cloud have in which Christ will come at the great day, it will bring both comfort and terror. *Thirdly,* He will *come with power and great glory:* his first coming was in weakness and great meanness (2 Cor. xiii. 4); but his second coming will be with power and glory, agreeable both to the dignity of his person and to the purposes of his coming. *Fourthly,* He will be seen with bodily eyes in his coming: *therefore* the Son of man will be the Judge, that he may be seen, that sinners thereby may be the more confounded, who shall see him as Balaam did, *but not nigh* (Numb. xxiv. 17), see him, but not as theirs. It added to the torment of that damned sinner, that *he saw Abraham afar off.* "Is this he whom we have slighted, and rejected, and rebelled against; whom we have crucified to ourselves afresh; who might have been our Saviour, but is our Judge, and will be our enemy for ever?" *The Desire of all nations* will then be their dread.

[5.] That *he shall send his angels with a great sound of a trumpet, v.* 31. Note, *First,* The angels shall be attendants upon Christ at his second coming; they are called *his* angels, which proves him to be God, and Lord of the angels; they shall be obliged to wait upon him. *Secondly,* These attendants shall be employed by him as officers of the court in the judgment of that day; they are now ministering spirits sent forth by him (Heb. i. 14), and will be so then. *Thirdly,* Their ministration will be ushered in with a great sound of a trumpet, to awaken and alarm a sleeping world. This trumpet is spoken of, 1 Cor. xv. 52, and 1 Thess. iv. 16. At the giving of the law on mount Sinai, the sound of the trumpet was remarkably terrible (Exod. xix. 13, 16); but much more will it be so in the great day. By the law, trumpets were to be sounded for the calling of assemblies (Numb. x. 2), in praising God (Ps. lxxxi. 3), in offering sacrifices (Numb. x. 10), and in proclaiming the year of jubilee, Lev. xxv. 9. Very fitly therefore shall there be the sound of a trumpet at the last day, when the general assembly shall be called, when the praises of God shall be gloriously celebrated, when sinners shall fall as sacrifices to divine justice, and when the saints shall enter upon their eternal jubilee.

[6.] That *they shall gather together his elect from the four winds.* Note, At the second coming of Jesus Christ, there will be a general meeting of all the saints. *First,* The *elect* only will be gathered, the chosen remnant, who are but few in comparison with the many that are only *called.* This is the foundation of the saints' eternal happiness, that they are God's elect. The gifts of love to eternity follow the thoughts of love from eternity; and *the Lord knows them that are his. Secondly,* The angels shall be employed to bring them together, as Christ's servants, and as the saints' friends; we have the commission given them, Ps. l. 5. *Gather my saints together unto me;* nay, it will be said to them, *Habetis fratres—These are your brethren;* for the elect will then *be equal to the angels,* Luke xx. 36. *Thirdly,* They *shall be gathered from one end of heaven to the other;* the elect of God are scattered abroad (John xi. 52), there are some in all places, in all nations (Rev. vii. 9); but when that great gathering day comes, there shall not one of them be missing; distance of place shall keep none out of heaven, if distance of affection do not. *Undique ad cœlos tantundem est viæ—Heaven is equally accessible from every place.* See *ch.* viii. 11; Isa. xliii. 6; xlix. 12.

32 Now learn a parable of the fig
tree; When his branch is yet tender, and putteth forth leaves, ye know
that summer *is* nigh: 33 So likewise
ye, when ye shall see all these things,
know that it is near, *even* at the doors.
34 Verily I say unto you, This gene
ration shall not pass, till all these
things be fulfilled. 35 Heaven and
earth shall pass away, but my words
shall not pass away. 36 But of that
day and hour knoweth no *man*, no,
not the angels of heaven, but my Father only. 37 But as the days of Noe
were, so shall also the coming of the
Son of man be. 38 For as in the
days that were before the flood they
were eating and drinking, marrying
and giving in marriage, until the day
that Noe entered into the ark, 39
And knew not until the flood came,
and took them all away; so shall also
the coming of the Son of man be. 40
Then shall two be in the field; the
one shall be taken, and the other left.
41 Two *women shall be* grinding at
the mill; the one shall be taken, and
the other left. 42 Watch therefore:
for ye know not what hour your Lord
doth come. 43 But know this, that
if the goodman of the house had
known in what watch the thief would
come, he would have watched, and
would not have suffered his house to
be broken up. 44 Therefore be ye
also ready: for in such an hour as ye
think not the Son of man cometh.
45 Who then is a faithful and wise
servant, whom his lord hath made
ruler over his household, to give them
meat in due season? 46 Blessed *is*
that servant, whom his lord when he
cometh shall find so doing. 47 Verily
I say unto you, That he shall make
him ruler over all his goods. 48 But
and if that evil servant shall say in
his heart, My lord delayeth his coming; 49 And shall begin to smite *his*
fellowservants, and to eat and drink
with the drunken; 50 The lord of
that servant shall come in a day when
he looketh not for *him*, and in an
hour that he is not aware of, 51 And
shall cut him asunder, and appoint
him his portion with the hypocrites:
there shall be weeping and gnashing
of teeth.

We have here the practical application of the foregoing prediction; in general, we must expect and prepare for the events here foretold.

I. We must expect them; "*Now learn a parable of the fig-tree, v.* 32, 33. Now learn what use to make of the things you have heard; so observe and understand the signs of the times, and compare them with the predictions of the word, as from thence to foresee what is at the door, that you may provide accordingly." The parable of the fig-tree is no more than this, that its budding and blossoming are a presage of summer; for as the *stork* in the heaven, so the trees of the field, *know their appointed time.* The beginning of the working of second causes assures us of the progress and perfection of it. Thus when God begins to fulfil prophecies, he will make an end. There is a certain series in the works of providence, as there is in the works of nature. The signs of the times are compared with the prognostics of *the face of the sky* (*ch.* xvi. 3), so here with those of *the face of the earth;* when that is renewed, we foresee that summer is coming, not immediately, but at some distance; after *the branch grows tender,* we expect the March winds, and the April showers, before the summer comes; however, we are sure it is coming; "so likewise ye, when the gospel day shall dawn, count upon it, that through this variety of events which I have told you of, the perfect day will come. *The things revealed must shortly come to pass* (Rev. i. 1); they must come in their own order, in the order appointed for them. *Know that it is near.*" He does not here say what, but it is that which the hearts of his disciples are upon, and which they are inquisitive after, and long for; *the kingdom of God is near,* so it is expressed in the parallel place, Luke xxi. 31. Note, When the trees of righteousness begin to bud and blossom, when God's people promise faithfulness, it is a happy presage of good times. In them God begins his work, first prepares their heart, and then he will go on with it; for, *as for God, his work is perfect;* and he will *revive it in the midst of their years.*

Now touching the events foretold here, which we are to expect,

1. Christ here assures us of the certainty of them (*v.* 35); *Heaven and earth shall pass away;* they continue this day indeed, according to God's ordinance, but they shall not continue for ever (Ps. cii. 25, 26; 2 Pet. iii. 10); *but my words shall not pass away.* Note, The word of Christ is more sure and

lasting than heaven and earth. *Hath he spoken? And shall he not do it?* We may build with more assurance upon the word of Christ than we can upon the pillars of heaven, or the strong foundations of the earth; for, when they shall be made to tremble and totter, and shall be no more, the word of Christ shall remain, and be in full force, power, and virtue. See 1 Pet. i. 24, 25. *It is easier for heaven and earth to pass,* than the word of Christ; so it is expressed, Luke xvi. 17. Compare Isa. liv. 10. The accomplishment of these prophecies might seem to be delayed, and intervening events might seem to disagree with them, but do not think that therefore the word of Christ is fallen to the ground, for that shall never pass away: though it be not fulfilled, either in the time or in the way that we have prescribed; yet, in God's time, which is the best time, and in God's way, which is the best way, it shall certainly be fulfilled. Every word of Christ is very pure, and therefore very sure.

2. He here instructs us as to the time of them, *v.* 34, 36. As to this, it is well observed by the learned Grotius, that there is a manifest distinction made between the *ταῦτα* (*v.* 34), and the *ἐκείνη* (*v.* 36), *these things,* and *that day and hour;* which will help to clear this prophecy.

(1.) As to *these things,* the wars, seductions, and persecutions, here foretold, and especially the ruin of the Jewish nation; "*This generation shall not pass away, till all these things be fulfilled* (*v.* 34); there are those now alive, that shall see Jerusalem destroyed, and the Jewish church brought to an end." Because it might seem strange, he backs it with a solemn asseveration; "*Verily, I say unto you.* You may take my word for it, these things are at the door." Christ often speaks of the nearness of that desolation, the more to affect people, and quicken them to prepare for it. Note, There may be greater trials and troubles yet before us, in our own day, than we are aware of. They that are old, know not what sons of Anak may be reserved for their last encounters.

(2.) But as to *that day and hour* which will put a period to time, *that knoweth no man, v.* 36. Therefore take heed of confounding these two, as *they* did, who, from the words of Christ and the apostles' letters, inferred that *the day of Christ was at hand,* 2 Thess. ii. 2. No, it was not; *this generation,* and many another, *shall pass,* before *that day and hour* come. Note, [1.] There is a certain day and hour fixed for the judgment to come; it is called *the day of the Lord,* because so unalterably fixed. None of God's judgments are adjourned *sine die—without the appointment of a certain day.* [2.] That day and hour are a great secret.

Prudens futuri temporis exitum
Caliginosa nocte premit Deus.

But Heaven has wisely hid from human sight
The dark decrees of future fate,
And sown their seeds in depth of night.—HORACE.

No man knows it; not the wisest by their sagacity, not the best by any divine discovery. We all know that there shall be such a day; but none knows when it shall be, no, not the angels; though their capacities for knowledge are great, and their opportunities of knowing this advantageous (they dwell at the fountain-head of light), and though they are to be employed in the solemnity of that day, yet they are not told when it shall be: none *knows but my Father only.* This is one of those *secret things* which *belong to the Lord our God.* The uncertainty of the time of Christ's coming, is, to those who are watchful, *a savour of life unto life,* and makes them more watchful; but to those who are careless, it is *a savour of death unto death,* and makes them more careless.

II. To this end we must expect these events, that we may prepare for them; and here we have a caution against security and sensuality, which will make it a dismal day indeed to us, *v.* 37—41. In these verses we have such an idea given us of the judgment day, as may serve to startle and awaken us, that we may not sleep as others do.

It will be a surprising day, and a separating day.

1. It will be a surprising day, as the deluge was to the old world, *v.* 37—39. That which he here intends to describe, is, the posture of the world at the coming of the Son of man; besides his first coming, to save, he has other comings to judge. He saith (John ix. 39), *For judgment I am come;* and for judgment he will come; for all judgment is committed to him, both that of the word, and that of the sword.

Now this here is applicable,

(1.) To *temporal judgments,* particularly that which was now hastening upon the nation and people of the Jews; though they had fair warning given them of it, and there were many prodigies that were presages of it, yet it found them secure, crying, *Peace and safety,* 1 Thess. v. 3. The siege was laid to Jerusalem by Titus Vespasian, when they were met at the passover in the midst of their mirth; like the men of Laish, they dwelt careless when the ruin arrested them, Judg. xviii. 7, 27. The destruction of Babylon, both that in the Old Testament and that in the New, comes when she saith, *I shall be a lady for ever,* Isa. xlvii. 7—9; Rev. xviii. 7. Therefore the plagues come in a moment, in one day. Note, Men's unbelief shall not make God's threatenings of no effect.

(2.) To *the eternal judgment;* so the judgment of the great day is called, Heb. vi. 2. Though notice has been given of it from Enoch, yet, when it comes, it will be unlooked for by the most of men; the latter days, which are nearest to that day, will produce scoffers, that say, *Where is the promise of his coming?* 2 Pet. iii. 3, 4; Luke xviii. 8. Thus it will be when the world that now is shall be destroyed by fire; for thus it was when the old world, being overflowed by water, perished, 2 Pet. iii. 6, 7. Now Christ here shows what were the temper and posture of the old world when the deluge came.

[1.] They were sensual and worldly; *they were eating and drinking, marrying and giving in marriage.* It is not said, They were killing and stealing, and whoring and swearing (these were indeed the horrid crimes of some of the worst of them; *the earth was full of violence);* but they were all of them, except Noah, over head and ears in the world, and regardless of the word of God, and this ruined them. Note, Universal neglect of religion is a more dangerous symptom to any people than particular instances here and there of daring irreligion. *Eating and drinking* are necessary to the preservation of man's life; *marrying and giving in marriage* are necessary to the preservation of mankind; but, *Licitus perimus omnes—These lawful things undo us,* unlawfully managed. *First,* They were unreasonable in it, inordinate and entire in the pursuit of the delights of sense, and the gains of the world; they were wholly taken up with these things, ἦσαν τρώγοντες—*they were eating;* they were in these things as in their element, as if they had their being for no other end than *to eat and drink,* Isa. lvi. 12. *Secondly,* They were unreasonable in it; they were entire and intent upon the world and the flesh, when the destruction was at the door, which they had had such fair warning of. They were eating and drinking, when they should have been repenting and praying; when God, by the ministry of Noah, called to *weeping and mourning, then joy and gladness.* This was to them, as it was to Israel afterwards, the unpardonable sin (Isa. xxii. 12, 14), especially, because it was in defiance of those warnings by which they should have been awakened. "*Let us eat and drink, for to-morrow we die;* if it must be a short life, let it be a merry one." The apostle James speaks of this as the general practice of the wealthy Jews before the destruction of Jerusalem; when they should have been *weeping for the miseries that were coming upon them, they were living in pleasure, and nourishing their hearts as in a day of slaughter,* Jam. v. 1, 5.

[2.] They were secure and careless; *they knew not, until the flood came, v.* 39. *Knew not!* Surely they could not but know. Did not God, by Noah, give them fair warning of it? Did he not call them to repentance, while his long-suffering waited? 1 Pet. iii. 19, 20. But they knew not, that is, they believed not; they might have known, but would not know. Note, What we know of *the things that belong to our everlasting peace,* if we do not mix faith with it, and improve it, is all one as if we did not know it at all. Their *not knowing* is joined with their *eating, and drinking, and marrying;* for, *First, Therefore* they were sensual, because they were secure. Note, the reason why people are so eager in the pursuit, and so entangled in the pleasures of this world, is, because they do not know, and believe, and consider, the eternity which they are upon the brink of. Did we know aright that all these things must shortly be dissolved, and we must certainly survive them, we should not set our eyes and hearts so much upon them as we do. *Secondly, Therefore* they were secure, because they were sensual; *therefore* they knew not that the flood was coming, because they were eating and drinking; were so taken up with things seen and present, that they had neither time nor heart to mind the things not seen as yet, which they were warned of. Note, As security bolsters men up in their brutal sensuality; so sensuality rocks them asleep in their carnal security. *They knew not, until the flood came.* 1. The flood did come, though they would not foresee it. Note, Those that will not know by faith, shall be made to know by feeling, *the wrath of God revealed from heaven against their ungodliness and unrighteousness.* The evil day is never the further off for men's putting it far off from them. 2. They did not know it till it was too late to prevent it, as they might have done if they had known it in time, which made it so much the more grievous. Judgments are most terrible and amazing to the secure, and those that have made a jest of them.

The application of this, concerning the old world, we have in these words; *So shall the coming of the Son of man be;* that is, (1.) In such a posture shall he find people, eating and drinking, and not expecting him. Note, Security and sensuality are likely to be the epidemical diseases of the latter days. All *slumber and sleep, and at midnight the bridegroom comes.* All are off their watch, and at their ease. (2.) With such a power, and for such a purpose, will he come upon them. As the flood took away the sinners of the old world, irresistibly and irrecoverably; so shall secure sinners, that mocked at Christ and his coming, be taken away by *the wrath of the Lamb, when the great day of his wrath comes,* which will be like the coming of the deluge, a destruction which there is no fleeing from.

2. It will be a separating day (*v.* 40, 41); *Then shall two be in the field.* Two ways this may be applied.

(1.) We may apply it to the success of the gospel, especially at the first preaching of it; it divided the world; *some believed the things which were spoken,* and were taken to Christ; *others believed not,* and were left to perish in their unbelief. Those of the same age, place, capacity, employment, and condition, in the world, *grinding in the same mill,* those of the same family, nay, those that were joined in the same bond of marriage, were, one effectually called, the other passed by, and left in the gall of bitterness. This is that division, that separating fire, which Christ *came to send,* Luke xii. 49, 51. *This* renders free grace the more obliging, that it is distinguishing; *to us, and not to the world* (John xiv. 22), nay to us, and not to those in the same field, the same mill, the same house.

When ruin came upon Jerusalem, a distinction was made by Divine Providence, according to that which had been before made by divine grace; for all the Christians among them were saved from perishing in that calamity, by the special care of Heaven. If two were at work in the field together, and one of them was a Christian, he was taken into a place of shelter, and had his life given him for a prey, while the other was left to the sword of the enemy. Nay, if but two women were grinding at the mill, if one of them belonged to Christ, though but a woman, a poor woman, a servant, she was taken to a place of safety, and the other abandoned. Thus *the meek of the earth are hid in the day of the Lord's anger* (Zeph. ii. 3), either in heaven, or *under* heaven. Note, Distinguishing preservations, in times of general destruction, are special tokens of God's favour, and ought so to be acknowledged. If we are safe when thousands fall on our right hand and our left, are not consumed when others are consumed round about us, so that we are as brands plucked out of the fire, we have reason to say, *It is of the Lord's mercies,* and it is a great mercy.

(2.) We may apply it to the second coming of Jesus Christ, and the separation which will be made in that day. He had said before (*v.* 31), that the elect will be *gathered together.* Here he tells us, that, in order to that, they will be distinguished from those who were nearest to them in this world; the choice and chosen ones taken to glory, the other left to perish eternally. Those who sleep in the dust of the earth, two in the same grave, their ashes mixed, shall yet arise, one to be taken to everlasting life, the other left *to shame and everlasting contempt,* Dan. xii. 2. Here it is applied to them who shall be found alive. Christ will come unlooked for, will find people busy at their usual occupations, *in the field, at the mill;* and then, according as they are vessels of mercy prepared for glory, or vessels of wrath prepared for ruin, accordingly it will be with them; the one taken *to meet the Lord and his angels in the air, to be for ever with him and them;* the other left to the devil and his angels, who, when Christ has gathered out his own, will sweep up the residue. This will aggravate the condemnation of sinners that others shall be taken from the midst of them to glory, and they left behind. And it speaks abundance of comfort to the Lord's people. [1.] Are they mean and despised in the world, as the man-servant in the field, or the maid at the mill (Exod. xi. 5)? Yet they shall not be forgotten or overlooked in that day. The poor in the world, if rich in faith, are *heirs of the kingdom.* [2.] Are they dispersed in distant and unlikely places, where one would not expect to find the heirs of glory, *in the field, at the mill?* Yet the angels will find them there (hidden as Saul among the stuff, when they are to be enthroned), and fetch them thence; and well may they be said to be *changed,* for a very great change it will be, to go to heaven from ploughing and grinding. [3.] Are they weak, and unable of themselves to move heavenward? They shall be taken, or *laid hold of,* as Lot was taken out of Sodom by a gracious violence, Gen. xix. 16. Those whom Christ has once apprehended and laid hold on, he will never lose his hold of. [4.] Are they intermixed with others, linked with them in the same habitations, societies, employments? Let not that discourage any true Christian; God knows how to separate between the precious and the vile, the gold and dross in the same lump, the wheat and chaff in the same floor.

III. Here is a general exhortation to us, *to watch, and be ready* against that day comes, enforced by divers weighty considerations, *v.* 42, &c. Observe,

1. The duty required; *Watch, and be ready, v.* 42, 44.

(1.) *Watch therefore, v.* 42. Note, It is the great duty and interest of all the disciples of Christ to watch, to be awake and keep awake, that they may mind their business. As a sinful state or way is compared to *sleep,* senseless and inactive (1 Thess. v. 6), so a gracious state or way is compared to *watching* and *waking.* We must watch for our Lord's coming, to us in particular at our death, *after which is the judgment,* that is *the great day* with us, the end of our time; and his coming at the end of all time to judge the world, the *great day* with all mankind. To watch implies not only to believe that our Lord will come, but to desire that he would come, to be often thinking of his coming, and always looking for it as sure and near, and the time of it uncertain. To watch for Christ's coming, is to maintain that grac ous temper and disposition of mind which we should be willing that our Lord, when he comes, should find us in. To watch is to be aware of the first notices of his approach, that we may immediately attend his motions, and address ourselves to the duty of meeting him. Watching is supposed to be in the night, which is sleeping time; while we are in this world, it is *night* with us, and we must take pains to keep ourselves awake.

(2.) *Be ye also ready.* We wake in vain, if we do not get ready. It is not enough to *look* for such things; but we must therefore *give diligence,* 2 Pet. iii. 11, 14. We have then our Lord to attend upon, and we must have our lamps ready trimmed; a cause to be tried, and we must have our plea ready drawn and signed by our Advocate; a reckoning to make up, and we must have our accounts ready stated and balanced; there is an inheritance which we then hope to enter upon, and we must have ourselves ready, made meet to partake of it, Col. i. 12.

2. The reasons to induce us to this watchfulness and diligent preparation for that day; which are two.

(1.) Because the time of our Lord's coming is very uncertain. This is the reason immediately annexed to the double exhortation (*v.* 42, 44); and it is illustrated by a comparison, *v.* 43. Let us consider then,

[1.] That *we know not what hour he will come, v.* 42. We know not *the day of our death,* Gen. xxvii. 2. We may know that we have but *a little time to live* (*The time of my departure is at hand,* 2 Tim. iv. 6); but we cannot know that we have a long time to live, for our souls are continually in our hands; nor can we know how little a time we have to live, for it may prove less than we expect; much less do we know the time fixed for the general judgment. Concerning both we are kept at uncertainty, that we may, every day, expect that which may come any day; may never boast of a year's continuance (James iv. 13), no, nor of to-morrow's return, as if it were ours, Prov. xxvii. 1; Luke xii. 20.

[2.] That he may *come at such an hour as we think not, v.* 44. Though there be such uncertainty in the time, there is none in the thing itself: though we know not *when* he will come, we are sure he *will* come. His parting word was, *Surely I come quickly:* his saying, "I come *surely,*" obliges us to expect him: his saying "I come *quickly,*" obliges us to be always expecting him; for it keeps us in a state of expectancy. *In such an hour as you think not,* that is, such an hour as they who are unready and unprepared, think not (*v.* 50); nay, such an hour as the most lively expectants perhaps thought least likely. The bridegroom came when the wise were slumbering. It is agreeable to our present state, that we should be under the influence of a constant and general expectation, rather than that of particular presages and prognostications, which we are sometimes tempted vainly to desire and wish for.

[3.] That the children of this world are thus wise in their generation, that, when they know of a danger approaching, they will keep awake, and stand on their guard against it. This he shows in a particular instance, *v.* 43. If the master of a house had notice that a thief would come such a night, and such a watch of the night (for they divided the night into four watches, allowing three hours to each), and would make an attempt upon his house, though it were the midnight-watch, when he was most sleepy, yet he would be up, and listen to every noise in every corner, and be ready to give him a warm reception. Now, though we know not *just when* our Lord will come, yet, knowing that he *will* come, and come quickly, and without any other warning than what he hath given in his word, it concerns us to watch always. Note, *First,* We have every one of us a house to keep, which lies exposed, in which all we are worth is laid up: that house is our own souls, which we must *keep with all diligence. Secondly,* The day of the Lord comes *by surprise, as a thief in the night.* Christ chooses to come when he is least expected, that the triumphs of his enemies may be turned into the greater shame, and the fears of his friends into the greater joy. *Thirdly,* If Christ, when he comes, finds us asleep and unready, our house will be broken up, and we shall lose all we are worth, not as by a thief unjustly, but as by a just and legal process; death and judgment will seize upon all we have, to our irreparable damage and utter undoing. Therefore be ready, *be ye also ready;* as ready at all times as the good man of the house would be at the hour when he expected the thief: we must put on the armour of God, that we may not only stand in that evil day, but, as more than conquerors, may divide the spoil.

(2.) Because the issue of our Lord's coming will be very happy and comfortable to those that shall be found ready, but very dismal and dreadful to those that shall not, *v.* 45, &c. This is represented by the different state of good and bad servants, when their lord comes to reckon with them. It is likely to be well or ill with us to eternity, according as we are found ready or unready at that day; for Christ comes *to render to every man according to his works.* Now this parable, with which the chapter closes, is applicable to all Christians, who are in profession and obligation God's servants; but it seems especially intended as a warning to ministers; for the servant spoken of is a *steward.* Now observe what Christ here saith,

[1.] Concerning the *good servant;* he shows here what he is—*a ruler of the household;* what, being so, he should be—*faithful* and *wise;* and what, if he be so, he shall be eternally—*blessed.* Here are good instructions and encouragements to the ministers of Christ.

First, We have here his place and office. He is one *whom his Lord has made ruler over his household, to give them meat in due season.* Note, 1. The church of Christ is his household, or family, standing in relation to him as the Father and Master of it. It is *the household of God,* a family named from Christ, Eph. iii. 15. 2. Gospel ministers are appointed *rulers* in this household; not as princes (Christ has entered a caveat against that), but as stewards, or other subordinate officers; not as lords, but as guides; not to prescribe new ways, but to show and lead in the ways that Christ has appointed: that is the signification of the ἡγούμενοι, which we translate, *having rule over you* (Heb. xiii. 17); as *overseers,* not to cut out new work, but to direct in, and quicken to, the work which Christ has ordered; that is the signification of ἐπίσκοποι—*bishops.* They are rulers by Christ; what power they have is derived from him, and none may take it from them, or abridge it to them; he is one whom *the Lord has made ruler;* Christ has the *making* of ministers. They are rulers *under* Christ, and act in subordination to him; and rulers *for* Christ, for the advancement of his kingdom. 3. The work of gospel ministers is to give to Christ's household their meat in due season, as stewards, and therefore they have the keys delivered to them. (1.) Their work is *to give*, not take to themselves (Ezek. xxxiv. 8), but give to the family what the Master has bought, to *dispense* what Christ has *purchased*. And to ministers it is said, that *it is more blessed to give than to receive*, Acts xx. 35. (2.) It is to give *meat;* not to give *law* (that is Christ's work), but to deliver those doctrines to the church which, if duly digested, will be nourishment to souls. They must give, not the poison of false doctrines, not the stones of hard and unprofitable doctrines, but the meat that is *sound* and *wholesome*. (3.) It must be given *in due season*, *ἐν καιρῷ—while there is time for it;* when eternity comes, it will be too late; we must *work while it is day:* or *in time*, that is, whenever any opportunity offers itself; or in the stated time, time after time, according as the duty of every day requires.

Secondly, His right discharge of this office. The good servant, if thus preferred, will be a good *steward;* for,

1. He is *faithful;* stewards must be so, 1 Cor. iv. 2. He that is *trusted*, must be trusty; and the greater the trust is, the more is expected from them. It is a great good thing that is committed to *ministers* (2 Tim. i. 14); and they must be faithful, as Moses was, Heb. iii. 2. Christ counts those ministers, and those only, that are *faithful*, 1 Tim. i. 12. A faithful minister of Jesus Christ is one that sincerely designs his master's honour, not his own; delivers *the whole counsel of God*, not his own fancies and conceits; follows Christ's institutions and adheres to them; regards the meanest, reproves the greatest, and doth not respect persons.

2. He is wise to understand his duty and the proper season of it; and in guiding of the flock there is need, not only of the integrity of the heart, but the skilfulness of the hands. Honesty may suffice for a good *servant*, but wisdom is necessary to a *good steward;* for it is profitable to direct.

3. He is doing; *so doing* as his office requires. The ministry is a good work, and they whose office it is, have always something to do; they must not indulge themselves in ease, nor leave the work undone, or carelessly turn it off to others, but be doing, and doing to the purpose—*so doing*, giving meat to the household, minding their own business, and not meddling with that which is foreign; *so doing* as the Master has appointed, as the office imports, and as the case of the family requires; not *talking*, but *doing*. It was the motto Mr. Perkins used, *Minister verbi es—You are a minister of the word.* Not only *Age—Be doing;* but *Hoc age—Be* so *doing*.

4. He is *found doing* when his Master comes; which intimates, (1.) Constancy at his work. At what hour soever his Master comes, he is found busy at the work of the day. Ministers should not leave empty spaces in their time, lest their Lord should come in one of those empty spaces. As with a good God the end of one mercy is the beginning of another, so with a good man, a good minister, the end of one duty is the beginning of another. When Calvin was persuaded to remit his ministerial labours, he answered, with some resentment, "What, would you have my Master find me idle?" (2.) Perseverance in his work till the Lord come. *Hold fast till then*, Rev. ii. 25. *Continue in these things*, 1 Tim. iv. 16; vi. 14. Endure to the end.

Thirdly, The recompence of reward intended him for this, in three things.

1. He shall be taken notice of. This is intimated in these words, Who then is that *faithful and wise servant?* Which supposes that there are but few who answer this character; such an interpreter is *one of a thousand*, such a faithful and wise *steward*. Those who thus distinguish themselves now by humility, diligence, and sincerity in their work, Christ will in the great day both dignify and distinguish by the glory conferred on them.

2. He shall be blessed? *Blessed is that servant;* and Christ's pronouncing him blessed makes him so. All the dead that die in the Lord are blessed, Rev. xiv. 13. But there is a peculiar blessedness secured to them that approve themselves faithful stewards, and are found so doing. Next to the honour of those who die in the field of battle, suffering for Christ as the martyrs, is the honour of those that die in the field of service, ploughing, and sowing, and reaping, for Christ.

3. He shall be preferred (*v.* 47); *He shall make him ruler over all his goods.* The allusion is to the way of great men, who, if the stewards of their house conduct themselves well in that place, commonly prefer them to be the managers of their estates; thus Joseph was preferred in the house of Potiphar, Gen. xxxix. 4, 6. But the greatest honour which the kindest master ever did to his most tried servants in this world, is nothing to that weight of glory which the Lord Jesus will confer upon his faithful watchful servants in the world to come. What is here said by a similitude, is the same that is said more plainly, John xii. 26, *Him will my Father honour.* And God's servants, when thus preferred; shall be perfect in wisdom and holiness to bear that weight of glory, so that there is no danger from these servants when they reign.

[2.] Concerning the *evil* servant. Here we have,

First, His description given (*v.* 48, 49); where we have the wretch drawn in his own colours. The vilest of creatures is a wicked man, the vilest of men is a wicked Christian, and the vilest of them a wicked minister. *Corruptio optimi est pessima—What is best, when corrupted, becomes the worst.* Wickedness in the prophets of Jerusalem is a *horrible* thing indeed, Jer. xxiii. 14. Here is,

1. The cause of his wickedness; and that is, a practical disbelief of Christ's second coming; He hath *said in his heart, My Lord delays his coming;* and therefore he begins to think he will never come, but has quite forsaken his church. Observe, (1.) Christ knows what *they* say in their hearts, who with their lips cry, *Lord, Lord,* as this servant here. (2.) The delay of Christ's coming, though it is a gracious instance of his patience, is greatly abused by wicked people, whose hearts are thereby hardened in their wicked ways. When Christ's coming is looked upon as doubtful, or a thing at an immense distance, the hearts of *men are fully set to do evil,* Eccl. viii. 11. See Ezek. xii. 27. They that walk by sense, are ready to say of the unseen Jesus, as the people did of Moses when he tarried in the mount upon their errand, *We wot not what is become of him,* and therefore *up, make us gods,* the world a god, the belly a god, any thing but him that should be.

2. The particulars of his wickedness; and they are sins of the first magnitude; he is a slave to his passions and his appetites.

(1.) Persecution is here charged upon him. He begins to *smite his fellow servants.* Note, [1.] Even the stewards of the house are to look upon all the servants of the house as their fellow servants, and therefore are forbidden to *lord it over them.* If the angel call himself *fellow servant* to John (Rev. xix. 10), no marvel if John have learned to call himself *brother* to the Christians of the churches of Asia, Rev. i. 9. [2.] It is no new thing to see evil servants smiting their fellow servants; both private Christians and faithful ministers. He smites them, either because they reprove him, or because they will not bow, and do him reverence; will not say as he saith, and do as he doeth, against their consciences: he smites them with the tongue, as they smote the prophet, Jer. xviii. 18. And if he get power into his hand, or can press those into his service that have, as the ten horns upon the head of the beast, it goes further. Pashur the priest smote Jeremiah, and put him in the stocks,. Jer. xx. 2. The revolters have often been of all others most *profound to make slaughter,* Hos. v. 2. The steward, when he smites his fellow servants, does it under colour of his Master's authority, and in his name; he says, *Let the Lord be glorified* (Isa. lxvi. 5); but he shall know that he could not put a greater affront upon his Master.

(2.) Profaneness and immorality; *He begins to eat and drink with the drunken.* [1.] He associates with the worst of sinners, has fellowship with them, is intimate with them; he walks in their counsel, stands in their way, sits in their seat, and sings their songs. The drunken are the merry and jovial company, and those he is for, and thus he hardens them in their wickedness. [2.] He does like them; *eats, and drinks, and is drunken;* so it is in Luke. This is an inlet to all manner of sin. Drunkenness is a leading wickedness; they who are slaves to that, are never masters of themselves in any thing else. The persecutors of God's people have commonly been the most vicious and immoral men. Persecuting consciences, whatever the pretensions be, are commonly the most profligate and debauched consciences. What will not *they* be drunk with, that will be *drunk with the blood of the saints?* Well, this is the description of a wicked minister, who yet may have the common gifts of learning and utterance above others; and, as hath been said of some, may preach so well in the pulpit, that it is a pity he should ever come out, and yet live so ill out of the pulpit, that it is a pity he should ever come in.

Secondly, His doom read, *v.* 50, 51. The coat and character of wicked ministers will not only not secure them from condemnation, but will greatly aggravate it. They can plead no exemption from Christ's jurisdiction, whatever they pretend to, in the church of Rome, from that of the civil magistrate; there is no benefit of clergy at Christ's bar. Observe,

1. The surprise that will accompany his doom (*v.* 50); *The Lord of that servant will come.* Note, (1.) Our putting off the thoughts of Christ's coming will not put off his coming. Whatever fancy he deludes himself with, his Lord will come. The unbelief of man shall not make that great promise, or threatening (call it which you will), of no effect. (2.) The coming of Christ will be a most dreadful surprise to secure and careless sinners, especially to wicked ministers; *He shall come in a day when he looketh not for him.* Note, Those that have slighted the warnings of the word, and silenced those of their own consciences concerning the judgment to come, cannot expect any other warnings; these will be adjudged sufficient legal notice given, whether taken or no; and no unfairness can be charged on Christ, if he come suddenly, without giving other notice. Behold, he has told us before.

2. The severity of his doom, *v.* 51. It is not more severe than righteous, but it is a doom that carries in it utter ruin, wrapt up in two dreadful words, *death* and *damnation.*

(1.) Death. His Lord shall *cut him asunder, δικοτομήσει ἀυτὸν,* "he shall cut him off from the land of the living," from the congregation of the righteous, shall separate him unto evil; which is the definition of a *curse* (Deut. xxix. 21), shall cut him down, as a tree that cumbers the ground; perhaps it alludes to the sentence often used in the law, *That soul shall be cut off from his people;* denoting an utter extirpation. Death cuts off a good man, as a choice imp is cut off to be grafted in a better stock; but it cuts off a wicked man, as a withered branch is cut off for the fire—cuts him off from this world, which he set his heart so much upon, and was, as it were, one with. Or, as we read it, *shall cut him asunder,* that is, part body and soul, send the body to the grave to be a prey for worms, and the soul to hell to be a prey for devils, and there is the sinner cut asunder. The soul and body of a godly man at death part fairly, the one cheerfully lifted up to God, the other left to the dust; but the soul and body of a wicked man at death are cut asunder, torn asunder, for to them death is the *king of terrors,* Job xviii. 14. The wicked servant divided himself between God and the world, Christ and Belial, his profession and his lusts, justly therefore will he thus be divided.

(2.) Damnation. He *shall appoint him his portion with the hypocrites,* and a miserable portion it will be, for *there shall be weeping.* Note, [1.] There is a place and state of everlasting misery in the other world, where there is nothing but *weeping and gnashing of teeth;* which speaks the soul's tribulation and anguish under God's indignation and wrath. [2.] The divine sentence will appoint this place and state as the portion of those who by their own sin were fitted for it. Even he of whom he said, that he was *his* Lord, shall thus appoint him his portion. He that is now *the Saviour,* will then be *the Judge,* and the everlasting state of the children of men will be as he appoints. They that choose the world for their portion in this life, will have hell for their portion in the other life. *This is the portion of a wicked man from God,* Job xx. 29. [3.] Hell is the proper place of hypocrites. This wicked servant has *his portion with the hypocrites.* They are, as it were, the freeholders, other sinners are but as inmates with them, and have but a portion of their misery. When Christ would express the most severe punishment in the other world, he calls it *the portion of hypocrites.* If there be any place in hell hotter than other, as it is likely there is, it will be the allotment of those that have the form, but hate the power of godliness. [4.] Wicked ministers will have their portion in the other world with the worst of sinners, even with the hypocrites, and justly, for they are the worst of hypocrites. The blood of Christ, which they have by their profaneness trampled under their feet, and the blood of souls, which they have by their unfaithfulness brought upon their heads, will bear hard upon them in that *place of torment. Son, remember,* will be as cutting a word to a minister if he perish as to any other sinner whatsoever. Let them therefore who preach to others, fear, lest they themselves should be cast-aways.

CHAP. XXV.

This chapter continues and concludes our Saviour's discourse, which began in the foregoing chapter, concerning his second coming and the end of the world. This was his farewell sermon of caution, as that, John xiv. 15, 16, was of comfort to his disciples; and they had need of both in a world of so much temptation and trouble as this is. The application of that discourse, was, Watch therefore, and be ye also ready. Now, in prosecution of these serious awakening cautions, in this chapter we have three parables, the scope of which is the same—to quicken us all with the utmost care and diligence to get ready for Christ's second coming, which, in all his farewells to his church, mention was made of, as in that before he died (John xiv. 2), in that at his ascension (Acts i. 11), and in that at the shutting up of the canon of the scriptures, Rev. xxii. 20. Now it concerns us to prepare for Christ's coming; I. That we may then be ready to attend upon him; and this is shown in the parable of the ten virgins, ver. 1—13. II. That we may then be ready to give up our account to him; and this is shown in the parable of the three servants, ver. 14—30. III. That we may then be ready to receive from him our final sentence, and that it may be to eternal life; and this is shown in a more plain description of the process of the last judgment, ver. 31—46. These are things of awful consideration, because of everlasting concern to every one of us.

THEN shall the kingdom of heaven be likened unto ten virgins,
which took their lamps, and went
forth to meet the bridegroom. 2 And
five of them were wise, and five *were*
foolish. 3 They that *were* foolish
took their lamps, and took no oil with
them: 4 But the wise took oil in their
vessels with their lamps. 5 While
the bridegroom tarried, they all slumbered and slept. 6 And at midnight
there was a cry made, Behold, the
bridegroom cometh; go ye out to meet
him. 7 Then all those virgins arose,
and trimmed their lamps. 8 And the
foolish said unto the wise, Give us of
your oil; for our lamps are gone out.
9 But the wise answered, saying, *Not
so;* lest there be not enough for us
and you: but go ye rather to them
that sell, and buy for yourselves. 10
And while they went to buy, the
bridegroom came; and they that were
ready went in with him to the marriage: and the door was shut. 11
Afterward came also the other virgins,
saying, Lord, Lord, open to us. 12
But he answered and said, Verily I
say unto you, I know you not. 13
Watch therefore, for ye know neither
the day nor the hour wherein the Son
of man cometh.

Here,

I. That in general which is to be illustrated is, *the kingdom of heaven,* the state of things under the gospel, the external kingdom of Christ, and the administration and success of it. Some of Christ's parables had shown us what it is like now in the present reception of it, as *ch.* xiii. This tells us what it shall be like, when the mystery of God shall be finished, and that kingdom delivered up to the Father. The administration of Christ's government, towards the ready and the unready in the great day, may be illustrated by this similitude; or the kingdom is put for the subjects of the kingdom. The professors of Christianity shall then be likened to these ten virgins, and shall be thus distinguished.

II. That by which it is illustrated, is, a marriage solemnity. It was a custom sometimes used among the Jews on that occasion, that the bridegroom came, attended with his friends, late in the night, to the house of the bride, where she expected him, attended with her bride-maids; who, upon notice given of the bridegroom's approach, were to go out with lamps in their hands, to light him into the house with ceremony and formality, in order to the celebrating of the nuptials with great mirth. And some think that on these occasions they had usually *ten virgins;* for the Jews never held a synagogue, circumcised, kept the passover, or contracted marriage, but ten persons at least were present. Boaz, when he married Ruth, had *ten witnesses,* Ruth iv. 2. Now in this parable,

1. The *Bridegroom* is our Lord Jesus Christ; he is so represented in the 45th Psalm, Solomon's Song, and often in the New Testament. It bespeaks his singular and superlative love to, and his faithful and inviolable covenant with, his spouse the church. Believers are now betrothed to Christ (Hos. ii. 19); but the solemnizing of the marriage is reserved for the great day, when the bride, the Lamb's wife, will have made herself completely ready, Rev. xix. 7, 9.

2. The virgins are the professors of religion, members of the church; but here represented as *her companions* (Ps. xlv. 14), as elsewhere her *children* (Isa. liv. 1), her *ornaments,* Isa. xlix. 18. They that follow the Lamb, are said to be *virgins* (Rev. xiv. 4); this denotes their beauty and purity; they are to be presented as chaste *virgins to Christ,* 2 Cor. xi. 2. The bridegroom is a king; so these virgins are *maids of honour,* virgins *without number* (Cant. vi. 8), yet here said to be *ten.*

3. The office of these virgins is to meet the bridegroom, which is as much their happiness as their duty. They come to wait *upon* the bridegroom when he appears, and in the mean time to wait *for* him. See here the nature of Christianity. As Christians, we profess ourselves to be, (1.) Attendants upon Christ, to do him honour, as the glorious Bridegroom, to be to him for a name and a praise, especially then when he shall come to be glorified in his saints. We must follow him as honorary servants do their masters, John xii. 26. Hold up the name, and hold forth the praise of the exalted Jesus; this is our business. (2.) Expectants of Christ, and of his second coming. As Christians, we profess, not only to believe and look for, but to love and long for, the appearing of Christ, and to act in our whole conversation with a regard to it. The second coming of Christ is the centre in which all the lines of our religion meet, and to which the whole of the divine life hath a constant reference and tendency.

4. Their chief concern is to have lights in their hands, when they attend the bridegroom, thus to do him honour and do him service. Note, Christians are children of light. The gospel is light, and they who receive it must not only be enlightened by it themselves, but must *shine as lights,* must *hold it forth,* Phil. ii. 15, 16. This in general.

Now concerning these ten virgins, we may observe,

(1.) Their different character, with the proof and evidence of it.

[1.] Their character was, that *five were wise, and five foolish* (*v.* 2); and *wisdom excelleth folly, as far as light excelleth darkness;* so saith Solomon, a competent judge, Eccl. ii. 13. Note, Those of the same profession and denomination among men, may yet be of characters vastly different in the sight of God. Sincere Christians are the *wise* virgins, and hypocrites the *foolish ones,* as in another parable they are represented by wise and foolish builders. Note, Those are wise or foolish indeed, that are so in the affairs of their souls. True religion is true wisdom; sin is folly, but especially the sin of hypocrisy, for those are the greatest fools, that are *wise in their own conceit,* and those the worst of sinners, that *feign themselves just men.* Some observe from the equal number of the wise and foolish, what a charitable decorum (it is Archbishop Tillotson's expression) Christ observes, as if he would hope that the number of true believers was nearly equal to that of hypocrites, or, at least, would teach us to hope the best concerning those that profess religion, and to think of them with a bias to the charitable side. Though, in judging of ourselves, we ought to remember that the gate is strait, and few find it; yet, in judging of others, we ought to remember that the Captain of our salvation brings many sons to glory.

[2.] The evidence of this character was in the very thing which they were to attend to; by that they are judged of.

First, It was the folly of the foolish virgins, that they *took their lamps, and took no oil with them, v.* 3. They had just oil enough to make their lamps burn for the present, to make a show with, as if they intended to meet the bridegroom; but no cruse or bottle of oil with them for a recruit if the bridegroom tarried; thus hypocrites,

1. They have no principle within. They have a lamp of profession in their hands, but have not in their hearts that stock of sound knowledge, rooted dispositions, and settled resolutions, which is necessary to carry them through the services and trials of the present state. They act under the influence of external inducements, but are void of spiritual life; like a tradesman, that sets up without a stock, or the seed on the stony ground, that wanted root.

2. They have no prospect of, nor make provision for, what is to come. They took

lamps for a present show, but not oil for after use. This incogitancy is the ruin of many professors; all their care is to recommend themselves to their neighbours, whom they now converse with, not to approve themselves to Christ, whom they must hereafter appear before; as if any thing will serve, provided it will but serve for the present. Tell them of things not seen as yet, and you are like Lot to his sons-in-law, as one that mocked. They do not provide for hereafter, as the ant does, nor *lay up for the time to come,* 1 Tim. vi. 19.

Secondly, It was the wisdom of the wise virgins, that *they took oil in their vessels with their lamps, v.* 4. They had a good principle within, which would maintain and keep up their profession. 1. The heart is the vessel, which it is our wisdom to get furnished; for, out of a good treasure there, good things must be brought; but if that root be rottenness, the blossom will be dust. 2. Grace is the *oil* which we must have in this *vessel;* in the tabernacle there was constant provision made of *oil for the light,* Exod. xxxv. 14. Our light must shine before men in good works, but this cannot be, or not long, unless there be a fixed active principle in the heart, of faith in Christ, and love to God and our brethren, from which we must act in every thing we do in religion, with an eye to what is before us. They that took oil in their vessels, did it upon supposition that perhaps the bridegroom might tarry. Note, In looking forward it is good to prepare for the worst, to lay in for a long siege. But remember that this oil which keeps the lamps burning, is derived to the candlestick from Jesus Christ, the great and good *Olive,* by the *golden pipes* of the ordinances, as it is represented in that vision (Zech. iv. 2, 3, 12), which is explained John i. 16, *Of his fulness have all we received, and grace for grace.*

(2.) Their common fault, during the bridegroom's delay; *They all slumbered and slept, v.* 5. Observe here,

[1.] The bridegroom tarried, that is, he did not come out so soon as they expected. What we look for as certain, we are apt to think is very near; many in the apostles' times imagined that the *day of the Lord was at hand,* but it is not so. Christ, as to us, *seems* to tarry, and yet really *does not,* Hab. ii. 3. There is good reason for the Bridegroom's tarrying; there are many intermediate counsels and purposes to be accomplished, the elect must all be called in, God's patience must be manifested, and the saints' patience tried, the harvest of the earth must be ripened, and so must the harvest of heaven too. But though Christ tarry past *our* time, he will not tarry past the *due* time.

[2.] While he tarried, those that waited for him, grew careless, and forgot what they were attending; *They all slumbered and slept;* as if they had given over looking for him; for *when the Son of man cometh,* he will *not find faith,* Luke xviii. 8. Those that inferred the suddenness of it from its certainty, when that answered not their expectation, were apt from the delay to infer its uncertainty. The wise virgins slumbered, and the foolish slept; so some distinguish it; however, they were both faulty. The wise virgins kept their lamps burning, but did not keep themselves awake. Note, Too many good Christians, when they have been long in profession, grow remiss in their preparations for Christ's second coming; they intermit their care, abate their zeal, their graces are not lively, nor their works found perfect before God; and though all *love* be not lost, yet the *first* love is left. If it was hard to the disciples to watch with Christ *an hour,* much more to watch with him *an age. I sleep,* saith the spouse, *but my heart wakes.* Observe, *First,* They slumbered, and then they slept. Note, One degree of carelessness and remissness makes way for another. Those that allow themselves in slumbering, will scarcely keep themselves from sleeping; therefore dread the beginning of spiritual decays; *Venienti occurrite morbo—Attend to the first symptoms of disease.* The ancients generally understood the virgins' slumbering and sleeping of their dying; they all died, wise and foolish (Ps. xlix. 10), before judgment-day. So Ferus, *Antequam veniat sponsus omnibus obdormiscendum est,* hoc est, *moriendum—Before the Bridegroom come, all must sleep, that is, die.* So Calvin. But I think it is rather to be taken as we have opened it.

(3.) The surprising summons given them, to attend the bridegroom (*v.* 6); *At midnight there was a cry made, Behold, the bridegroom cometh.* Note, [1.] Though Christ tarry long, he will come at last; though he seem slow, he is sure. In his first coming, he was thought long by those that waited for the consolation of Israel; yet in the *fulness of time* he came; so his second coming, though long deferred, is not forgotten; his enemies shall find, to their cost, that forbearance is no acquittance; and his friends shall find, to their comfort, that *the vision is for an appointed time, and at the end it shall speak, and not lie.* The year of the redeemed is fixed, and it will come. [2.] Christ's coming will be at our midnight, when we least look for him, and are most disposed to take our rest. His coming for the relief and comfort of his people, often is when the good intended seems to be at the greatest distance; and his coming to reckon with his enemies, is when they put the evil day furthest from them. It was at midnight that the first-born of Egypt were destroyed, and Israel delivered, Exod. xii. 29. Death often comes when it is least expected; the soul is *required this night,* Luke xii. 20. Christ will come when he pleases, to show his sovereignty, and will not let us know when, to teach us our duty. [3.] When Christ comes, we must *go forth to meet him.* As Christians we are bound to attend all the motions of the Lord Jesus, and meet him in all his out-goings. When he comes to us at death, we must go forth out of the body, out of the world, to meet him with affections and workings of soul suitable to the discoveries we then expect him to make of himself. *Go ye forth to meet him,* is a call to those who are habitually prepared, to be actually ready. [4.] The notice given of Christ's approach, and the call to meet him, will be awakening; *There was a cry made.* His first coming was not with any observation at all, nor did they say, *Lo, here is Christ,* or *Lo, he is there; he was in the world, and the world knew him not;* but his second coming will be with the observation of all the world; *Every eye shall see him.* There will be a cry from heaven, for he shall *descend with a shout, Arise, ye dead, and come to judgment;* and a cry from the earth too, a *cry to rocks and mountains,* Rev. vi. 16.

(4.) The address they all made to answer this summons (*v.* 7); *They all arose, and trimmed their lamps,* snuffed them and supplied them with oil, and went about with all expedition to put themselves in a posture to receive the bridegroom. Now, [1.] This, in the wise virgins, bespeaks an actual preparation for the Bridegroom's coming. Note, even those that are best prepared for death, have, upon the immediate arrests of it, work to do, to get themselves actually ready, that they may be *found in peace* (2 Pet. iii. 14), *found doing* (*ch.* xxiv. 46), and not *found naked,* 2 Cor. v. 3. It will be a day of search and enquiry; and it concerns us to think how we shall then be found. When we see the day approaching, we must address ourselves to our dying work with all seriousness, renewing our repentance for sin, our consent to the covenant, our farewells to the world; and our souls must be carried out toward God in suitable breathings. [2.] In the foolish virgins, it denotes a vain confidence, and conceit of the goodness of their state, and their readiness for another world. Note, Even counterfeit graces will serve a man to make a show of when he comes to die, as well as they have done all his life long; the hypocrite's hopes blaze when they are just expiring, like a lightening before death.

(5.) The distress which the foolish virgins were in, for want of *oil, v.* 8, 9. This bespeaks, [1.] The apprehensions which some hypocrites have of the misery of their state, even on this side death, when God opens their eyes to see their folly, and themselves perishing *with a lie in their right hand.* Or, however, [2.] The real misery of their state on the other side death, and in the judgment; how far their fair, but false, profession of religion will be from availing them any thing in the great day; see what comes of it.

First, Their lamps are gone out. The lamps of hypocrites often go out in this life; when they who have begun in the spirit, end in the flesh, and the hypocrisy breaks out in an open apostasy, 2 Pet. ii. 20. The profession withers, and the credit of it is lost; the hopes fail, and the comfort of them is gone; how often is *the candle of the wicked* thus *put out?* Job xxi. 17. Yet many a hypocrite keeps up his credit, and the comfort of his profession, such as it is, to the last; but what is it when *God taketh away his soul?* Job xxvii. 8. If his candle be not put out *before* him, it is put out *with him,* Job xviii. 5, 6. He shall *lie down in sorrow,* Isa. l. 11. The gains of a hypocritical profession will not follow a man to judgment, *ch.* vii. 22, 23. The lamps are gone out, when the hypocrite's hope proves *like the spider's web* (Job viii 11, &c.), and like the *giving up of the ghost* (Job xi. 20), like Absalom's mule that left him in the oak.

Secondly, They wanted oil to supply them when they were going out. Note, Those that take up short of true grace, will certainly find the want of it one time or other. An external profession well humoured may carry a man far, but it will not carry him through; it may light him along this world, but the damps of the valley of the shadow of death will put it out.

Thirdly, They would gladly be beholden to the wise virgins for a supply out of their vessels; *Give us of your oil.* Note, The day is coming, when carnal hypocrites would gladly be found in the condition of true Christians. Those who now hate the strictness of religion, will, at death and judgment, wish for the solid comforts of it. Those who care not to live the life, yet would die the death, of the righteous. The day is coming when those who now look with contempt upon humble contrite saints, would gladly get an interest in them, and would value those as their best friends and benefactors, whom now they *set with the dogs of their flock. Give us of your oil;* that is, "Speak a good word for us;" so some; but there is no occasion for vouchers in the great day, the Judge knows what is every man's true character. But is it not well that they are brought to say, *Give us of your oil?* It is so; but, 1. This request was extorted by sensible necessity. Note, Those will see their need of grace hereafter, when it should save them, who will not see their need of grace now, when it should sanctify and rule them. (2.) It comes too late. God would have given them oil, had they asked in time; but there is no buying when the market is over, no bidding when the inch of candle is dropped.

Fourthly, They were denied a share in their companions' oil. It is a sad presage of a repulse with God, when they were thus repulsed by good people. *The wise answered, Not so;* that peremptory denial is not in the original, but supplied by the translators: these wise virgins would rather give a reason without a positive refusal, than (as many do) give a positive refusal without a reason. They were well inclined to help their neighbours in distress; but, We must not, we cannot, we dare not, do it, *lest there be not enough for us and you;* charity begins at home; but *go, and buy for yourselves.* Note, 1. Those that would be saved, must have grace of their own. Though we have benefit by the communion of saints, and the faith and prayers of others may now redound to our advantage, yet our own sanctification is indispensably necessary to our own salvation. The just shall live by his faith. Every man shall give account of himself, and therefore let every man *prove his own work;* for he cannot get another to muster for him in that day. 2. Those that have most grace, have none to spare; all we have, is little enough for ourselves to appear before God in. The best have need to borrow from Christ, but they have none to lend to any of their neighbours. The church of Rome, which dreams of works of supererogation and the imputation of the righteousness of saints, forgets that it was the wisdom of the wise virgins to understand that they had but oil enough for themselves, and none for others. But observe, These wise virgins do not upbraid the foolish with their neglect, nor boast of their own forecast, nor torment them with suggestions tending to despair, but give them the best advice the case will bear, *Go ye rather to them that sell.* Note, Those that deal foolishly in the affairs of their souls, are to be pitied, and not insulted over; for who made thee to differ? When ministers attend such as have been mindless of God and their souls all their days, but are under death-bed convictions; and, because true repentance is never too late, direct them to repent, and turn to God, and close with Christ; yet, because late repentance is seldom true, they do but as these wise virgins did by the foolish, even make the best of bad. They can but tell them what is to be done, if it be not too late; but whether the door may not be shut before it is done, is an unspeakable hazard. It is good advice now, if it be taken in time, *Go to them that sell, and buy for yourselves.* Note, Those that would have grace, must have recourse to, and attend upon, the means of grace. See Isa. lv. 1.

(6.) The coming of the bridegroom, and the issue of all this different character of the wise and foolish virgins. See what came of it.

[1.] *While they went out to buy, the bridegroom came.* Note, With regard to those that put off their great work to the last, it is a thousand to one, that they have not time to do it then. Getting grace is a work of time, and cannot be done in a hurry. While the poor awakened soul addresses itself, upon a sick bed, to repentance and prayer, in awful confusion, it scarcely knows which end to begin at, or what to do first; and presently death comes, judgment comes, and the work is undone, and the poor sinner undone for ever. This comes of having oil to buy when we should burn it, and grace to get when we should use it.

The bridegroom came. Note, Our Lord Jesus will come to his people, at the great day, as a Bridegroom; will come in pomp and rich attire, attended with his friends: now that the Bridegroom is taken away from us, *we fast* (*ch.* ix. 15), but then will be an everlasting feast. Then the Bridegroom will fetch home his bride, to be *where he is* (John xvii. 24), and will *rejoice over his bride,* Isa. lxii. 5.

[2.] *They that were ready, went in with him to the marriage.* Note, *First,* To be eternally glorified is to go in with Christ to the marriage, to be in his immediate presence, and in the most intimate fellowship and communion with him in a state of eternal rest, joy, and plenty. *Secondly,* Those, and those only, shall go to heaven hereafter, that are made ready for heaven here, that are *wrought to the self-same thing,* 2 Cor. v. 5. *Thirdly,* The suddenness of death, and of Christ's coming to us then, will be no obstruction to our happiness, if we have been habitually prepared.

[3.] *The door was shut,* as is usual when all the company is come, that are to be admitted. The door was shut, *First,* To secure those that were within; that, being now made *pillars in the house of our God, they may go no more out,* Rev. iii. 12. Adam was put into paradise, but the door was left open and so he went out again; but when glorified saints are put into the heavenly paradise, they are shut in. *Secondly,* To exclude those that were out. The state of saints and sinners will then be unalterably fixed, and those that are shut out then, will be shut out for ever. Now the gate is strait, yet it is open; but then it will be shut and bolted, and *a great gulf fixed.* This was like the shutting of the door of the ark when Noah was in; as he was thereby preserved, so all the rest were finally abandoned.

[4.] The foolish virgins came when it was *too late* (*v.* 11); *Afterward came also the other virgins.* Note, *First,* There are many that will seek admission into heaven when it is too late; as profane Esau, who *afterward would have inherited the blessing.* God and religion will be glorified by those late solicitations, though sinners will not be saved by them; it is for the honour of *Lord, Lord,* that is, of fervent and importunate prayer, that those who slight it now, will flee to it shortly, and it will not be called whining and canting then. *Secondly,* The vain confidence of hypocrites will carry them very far in their expectations of happiness. They go to heaven-gate, and demand entrance, and yet are shut out; lifted up to heaven in a fond conceit of the goodness of their state, and yet thrust down to hell.

[5.] They were *rejected,* as Esau was (*v.* 12); *I know you not.* Note, We are all concerned to *seek the Lord while he may be found;* for there is a time coming when he will not be found. Time was, when, *Lord, Lord, open to us,* would have sped well, by virtue of that promise, *Knock, and it shall be opened to you;* but now it comes too late. The sentence is solemnly bound on with, *Verily I say unto you,* which amounts to no less than *swearing in his wrath, that they shall never enter into his rest.* It bespeaks him resolved, and them silenced by it.

Lastly, Here is a practical inference drawn from this parable (*v.* 13); *Watch therefore.* We had it before (*ch.* xxiv. 42), and here it is repeated as the most needful caution. Note, 1. Our great duty is to watch, to attend to the business of our souls with the utmost diligence and circumspection. Be awake, and be wakeful. 2. It is a good reason for our watching, that the time of our Lord's coming is very uncertain; *we know neither the day nor the hour.* Therefore every day and every hour we must be ready, and not off our watch any day in the year, or any hour in the day. Be thou *in the fear of the Lord* every day and *all the day long.*

14 For *the kingdom of heaven is*
as a man travelling into a far country,
who called his own servants, and delivered unto them his goods. 15 And
unto one he gave five talents, to another two, and to another one; to every
man according to his several ability;
and straightway took his journey. 16
Then he that had received the five
talents went and traded with the same,
and made *them* other five talents. 17
And likewise he that *had received*
two, he also gained other two. 18
But he that had received one went
and digged in the earth, and hid his
lord's money. 19 After a long time
the lord of those servants cometh,
and reckoneth with them. 20 And
so he that had received five talents
came and brought other five talents,
saying, Lord, thou deliveredst unto me
five talents: behold, I have gained
beside them five talents more. 21 His
lord said unto him, Well done, *thou*
good and faithful servant: thou hast
been faithful over a few things, I will
make thee ruler over many things:
enter thou into the joy of thy lord.
22 He also that had received two
talents came and said, Lord, thou deliveredst unto me two talents: behold,
I have gained two other talents beside
them. 23 His lord said unto him,
Well done, good and faithful servant;
thou hast been faithful over a few
things, I will make thee ruler over
many things: enter thou into the joy
of thy lord. 24 Then he which had
received the one talent came and said,
Lord, I knew thee that thou art an
hard man, reaping where thou hast
not sown, and gathering where thou
hast not strewed: 25 And I was
afraid, and went and hid thy talent in
the earth: lo, *there* thou hast *that is*
thine. 26 His lord answered and
said unto him, *Thou* wicked and slothful servant, thou knewest that I reap
where I sowed not, and gather where
I have not strewed: 27 Thou oughtest
therefore to have put my money to
the exchangers, and *then* at my coming
I should have received mine own with
usury. 28 Take therefore the talent
from him, and give *it* unto him which
hath ten talents. 29 For unto every
one that hath shall be given, and he
shall have abundance: but from him
that hath not shall be taken away even
that which he hath. 30 And cast ye
the unprofitable servant into outer
darkness: there shall be weeping and
gnashing of teeth.

We have here the parable of the *talents* committed to three servants; this implies that we are in a state of work and business, as the former implies that we are in a state of expectancy. *That* showed the necessity of habitual preparation, *this* of actual diligence in our present work and service. In *that* we were stirred up to do well for our own souls; in *this* to lay out ourselves for the glory of God and the good of others.

In this parable, 1. The *Master* is Christ, who is the absolute Owner and Proprietor of all persons and things, and in a special manner of his church; into his hands all things are delivered. 2. The *servants* are Christians, his own servants, so they are called; born in his house, bought with his money, devoted to his praise, and employed in his work. It is probable that *ministers* are especially intended here, who are more immediately attending on him, and sent by him. St. Paul often calls himself a *servant of Jesus Christ.* See 2 Tim. ii. 24.

We have three things, in general, in this parable.

I. The trust committed to these servants; Their master *delivered to them his goods:* having appointed them to work (for Christ keeps no servants to be idle), he left them something to work upon. Note, 1. Christ's servants have and receive their all from him; for they are of themselves worth nothing, nor have any thing they can call their own but sin. 2. Our receiving from Christ is in order to our working for him. Our privileges are intended to find us with business. The *manifestation of the Spirit* is given to every man to *profit withal.* 3. Whatever we receive to be made use of for Christ, still the property is vested in him; we are but tenants upon his land, *stewards of his manifold grace,* 1 Pet. iv. 10. Now observe here,

(1.) On what occasion this trust was committed to these servants; The master was *travelling into a far country.* This is explained, Eph. iv. 8. *When he ascended on high, he gave gifts unto men.* Note, [1.] When Christ went to heaven, he was as a man *travelling into a far country;* that is, he went with a purpose to be away a great while. [2.] When he went, he took care to furnish his church with all things necessary for it during his personal absence. For, and in consideration of, his departure, he committed to his church truths, laws, promises, and powers; these were the παρακαταθήκη—*the great depositum* (as it is called, 1 Tim. vi. 20; 2 Tim. i. 14), the *good thing* that is committed to us; and he sent his Spirit to enable his servants to teach and profess those truths, to press and observe those laws, to improve and apply those promises, and to exercise and employ those powers, ordinary or extraordinary. Thus Christ, at his ascension, left his goods to his church.

(2.) In what proportion this trust was committed. [1.] He gave *talents;* a talent of silver is computed to be in our money three hundred and fifty-three pounds eleven shillings and ten pence halfpenny; so the learned Bishop Cumberland. Note, Christ's gifts are rich and valuable, the purchases of his blood inestimable, and none of them mean. [2.] He gave to some more, to others less; to one *five* talents, to another *two,* to another *one;* to every one according to his several ability. When Divine Providence has made a difference in men's ability, as to mind, body, estate, relation, and interest, divine grace dispenses spiritual gifts accordingly, but still the ability itself is from him. Observe, *First,* Every one had some one talent at least, and that is not a despicable stock for a poor servant to begin with. A *soul* of our own is the *one* talent we are every one of us entrusted with, and it will find us with work. *Hoc nempe ab homine exigitur, ut prosit hominibus; si fieri potest, multis; si minus, paucis; si minus, proximis; si minus, sibi: nam cum se utilem cæteris efficit, commune agit negotium. Et si quis bene de se meretur, hoc ipso aliis prodest quod aliis profuturum parat—It is the duty of a man to render himself beneficial to those around him; to a great number if possible; but if this is denied him, to a few; to his intimate connections; or, at least, to himself. He that is useful to others, may be reckoned a common good. And whoever entitles himself to his own approbation, is serviceable to others, as forming himself to those habits which will result in their favour.* Seneca de Otio Sapient. *Secondly,* All had not alike, for they had not all alike abilities and opportunities. God is a free Agent, *dividing to every man severally as he will;* some are cut out for service in one kind, others in another, as the members of the natural body. When the householder had thus settled his affairs, he *straightway took his journey.* Our Lord Jesus, when he had given commandments to his apostles, as one in haste to be gone, went to heaven.

II. The different management and improvement of this trust, which we have an account of, *v.* 16—18.

1. Two of the servants did well.

(1.) They were diligent and faithful; *They went, and traded;* they put the money they were entrusted with, to the use for which it was intended—laid it out in goods, and made returns of it; as soon as ever their master was gone, they immediately applied themselves to their business. Those that have so much work to do, as every Christian has, need to set about it quickly, and lose no time. *They went, and traded.* Note, A true Christian is a spiritual tradesman. Trades are called *mysteries,* and *without controversy great is the mystery of godliness;* it is a manufacture trade; there is something to be done by us upon our own hearts, and for the good of others. It is a merchant-trade; things of less value to us are parted with for things of greater value; *wisdom's merchandize,* Prov. iii. 15; Matt. xiii. 45. A tradesman is one who, having made his trade his choice, and taken pains to learn it, makes it his business to follow it, lays out all he has for the advancement of it, makes all other affairs bend to it, and lives upon the gain of it. Thus does a true Christian act in the work of religion; we have no stock of our *own* to trade with, but trade as factors with our master's stock. The endowments of the mind—reason, wit, learning, must be used in subserviency to religion; the enjoyments of the world—estate, credit, interest, power, preferment, must be improved for the honour of Christ. The ordinances of the gospel, and our opportunities of attending them, bibles, ministers, sabbaths, sacraments, must be improved for the end for which they were instituted, and communion with God kept up by them, and the gifts and graces of the Spirit must be exercised; and this is trading with our talents.

(2.) They were successful; they doubled their stock, and in a little time made *cent. per cent.* of it: he that had *five talents,* soon made them *other five.* Trading with our talents is not always successful with others, but, however, it shall be so to ourselves, Isa. xlix. 4. Note, The hand of the diligent makes rich in graces, and comforts, and treasures of good works. There is a great deal to be got by industry in religion.

Observe, The returns were in proportion

to the receivings. [1.] From those to whom God hath given five talents, he expects the improvement of five, and to reap plentifully where he sows plentifully. The greater gifts any have, the more pains they ought to take, as those must that have a large stock to manage. [2.] From those to whom he has given but two talents, he expects only the improvement of two, which may encourage those who are placed in a lower and narrower sphere of usefulness; if they lay out themselves to do good according to the best of their capacity and opportunity, they shall be accepted, though they do not so much good as others.

2. The third did ill (*v.* 18); *He that had received one talent, went, and hid his lord's money.* Though the parable represents but one in three unfaithful, yet in a history that answers this *parable,* we find the disproportion quite the other way, when *ten lepers were cleansed, nine* of the *ten* hid the talent, and *only one returned to give thanks,* Luke xvii. 17, 18. The unfaithful servant was he that had but *one* talent: doubtless there are many that have five talents, and bury them all; great abilities, great advantages, and yet do no good with them: but Christ would hint to us, (1.) That if he that had but one talent, be reckoned with thus for burying that one, much more will they be accounted offenders, tnat have more, that have many, and bury them. If he that was but of small capacity, was cast into outer darkness because he did not improve what he had as he might have done, *of how much sorer punishment, suppose ye, shall he be thought worthy, that tramples underfoot the greatest advantages?* (2.) That those who have least to do for God, frequently do least of what they have to do. Some make it an excuse for their laziness, that they have not the opportunities of serving God that others have; and because they have not wherewithal to do what they say they would, they will not do what we are sure they can, and so sit down and do nothing; it is really an aggravation of their sloth, that when they have but one talent to take care about, they neglect that one.

He digged in the earth, and hid the talent, for fear it should be stolen; he did not mispend or misemploy it, did not embezzle it or squander it away, but he *hid it.* Money is like manure (so my Lord Bacon used to say), good for nothing in the heap, but it must be spread; yet it is an evil which we have often seen under the sun, *treasure heaped together* (Jam. v. 3; Eccl. vi. 1, 2), which does good to nobody; and so it is in spiritual gifts; many have them, and make no use of them for the end for which they were given them. Those that have estates, and do not lay them out in works of piety and charity; that have power and interest, and do not with it promote religion in the places where they live; ministers that have capacities and opportunities of doing good, but do not stir up the gift that is in them, are those slothful servants that seek their own things more than Christ's.

He hid his *lord's* money; had it been his *own,* he might have done as he pleased; but, whatever abilities and advantages we have, they are not our *own,* we are but stewards of them, and must give account to our Lord, whose goods they are. It was an aggravation of his slothfulness, that his fellow-servants were busy and successful in trading, and their zeal should have provoked his. Are others active, and shall we be idle?

III. The account of this improvement, *v.* 19. 1. The account is deferred; it is not *till after a long time* that they are reckoned with; not that the master neglects his affairs, or that God is *slack concerning his promise* (2 Pet. iii. 9); no, he is *ready to judge* (1 Pet. iv. 5); but every thing must be done in its time and order. 2. Yet the day of account comes at last; *The lord of those servants reckoneth with them.* Note, The stewards of the manifold grace of God must shortly *give account of their stewardship.* We must all be reckoned with—what good we have got to our own souls, and what good we have done to others by the advantages we have enjoyed. See Rom. xiv. 10, 11. Now here is,

(1.) The good account of the faithful servants; and here observe,

[1.] The servants *giving up the account* (*v.* 20, 22); "*Lord, thou deliveredst to me five talents,* and to me *two;* behold, *I have gained five talents,* and I *two* talents *more.*"

First, Christ's faithful servants acknowledge with thankfulness his vouchsafements to them; *Lord, thou deliveredst to me* such and such things. Note, 1. It is good to keep a particular account of our receivings from God, to remember what we have received, that we may know what is expected from us, and may render according to the benefit. 2. We must never look upon our improvements but with a general mention of God's favour to us, of the honour he has put upon us, in entrusting us with his goods, and of that grace which is the spring and fountain of all the good that is in us or is done by us. For the truth is, the more we do for God, the more we are indebted to him for making use of us, and enabling us, for his service.

Secondly, They produce, as an evidence of their faithfulness, what they have gained. Note, God's good stewards have something to show for their diligence; *Show me thy faith by thy works.* He that is a good man, *let him show it,* Jam. iii. 13. If we be careful in our spiritual trade, it will soon be seen by us, and *our works will follow us,* Rev. xiv. 13. Not that the saints will in the great day make mention of their own good deeds; no, Christ will do that for them (*v.* 35); but it intimates that they who faithfully improve their talents, *shall have boldness in the day of Christ,* 1 John ii. 28.—iv. 17. And it is observable that he who had but *two* talents, gave up his account as cheerfully as he who had *five;* for our comfort, in the day of account, will be according to our faithfulness, not according to our usefulness; our sincerity, not our success; according to the uprightness of our hearts, not according to the degree of our opportunities.

[2.] The master's acceptance and approbation of their account, *v.* 21, 23.

First, He commended them; *Well done, good and faithful servant.* Note, The diligence and integrity of those who approve themselves the good and faithful servants of Jesus Christ, will certainly be *found to praise, and honour, and glory, at his appearing,* 1 Pet. i. 7. Those that own and honour God now, he will own and honour shortly. 1. Their persons will be accepted; *Thou good and faithful servant.* He that knows the integrity of his servants now, will witness to it in the great day; and they that are found faithful, shall be called so. Perhaps they were censured by men, as *righteous overmuch;* but Christ will give them their just characters, of *good and faithful.* 2. Their performances will be accepted; *Well done.* Christ will call those, and those only, *good servants,* that have done well; for it is *by patient continuance in well-doing* that we seek for this glory and honour; and if we seek, we shall find; if we do that which is good, and do it well, we shall have *praise of the same.* Some masters are so morose, that they will not commend their servants, though they do their work ever so well; it is thought enough not to chide: but Christ will commend his servants that do well; whether their praise be of men or no, it is of him; and if we have the good word of our Master, the matter is not great what our fellow-servants say of us; if he saith, *Well done,* we are happy, and it should then be a small thing to us to be judged of men's judgment; as, on the contrary, not he who commendeth himself, or whom his neighbours commend, is approved, but whom the Lord commends.

Secondly, He rewards them. The faithful servants of Christ shall not be put off with bare commendation; no, all their work and labour of love shall be rewarded.

Now this reward is here expressed two ways.

1. In one expression agreeable to the parable; *Thou hast been faithful over a few things, I will make thee ruler over many things.* It is usual in the courts of princes, and families of great men, to advance those to higher offices, that have been faithful in lower. Note, Christ is a master that will prefer his servants who acquit themselves well. Christ has honour in store for those that honour him—*a crown* (2 Tim. iv. 8), *a throne* (Rev. iii. 21), *a kingdom, ch.* xxv. 34. Here they are beggars; in heaven they shall be rulers. The upright shall have dominion: Christ's servants are all princes.

Observe the disproportion between the work and the reward; there are but few things in which the saints are serviceable to the glory of God, but there are many things wherein they shall be glorified with God. What charge we receive from God, what work we do for God in this world, is but little, very little, compared with *the joy set before us.* Put together all our services, all our sufferings, all our improvements, all the good we do to others, all we get to ourselves, and they are but a few things, next to nothing, not worthy to be compared, not fit to be named the same day with the glory to be revealed.

2. In another expression, which slips out of the parable into the thing signified by it; *Enter thou into the joy of thy Lord.* Note, (1.) The state of the blessed is a state of joy, not only because all tears shall then be wiped away, but all the springs of comfort shall be opened to them, and the fountains of joy broken up. Where there are the vision and fruition of God, a perfection of holiness, and the society of the blessed, there cannot but be a fulness of joy. (2.) This joy is the *joy of their Lord;* the joy which he himself has purchased and provided for them; the joy of the redeemed, bought with the sorrow of the Redeemer. It is the joy which he himself is in the possession of, and which he had his eye upon when he *endured the cross, and despised the shame,* Heb. xii. 2. It is the joy of which he himself is the fountain and centre. It is the joy of our Lord, for it is *joy in the Lord,* who is our exceeding joy. Abraham was not willing that the *steward of his house,* though *faithful,* should be *his heir* (Gen. xv. 3); but Christ admits his faithful stewards into his own joy, to be joint-heirs with him. (3.) Glorified saints shall enter into this joy, shall have a full and complete possession of it, as the heir when he comes of age enters upon his estate, or as they that were ready, *went* in to the marriage feast. Here the joy of our Lord enters into the saints, in the earnest of the Spirit; shortly they shall enter into it, shall be in it to eternity, as in their element.

(2.) The bad account of the slothful servant. Observe,

[1.] His apology for himself, *v.* 24, 25. Though he had received but *one* talent, for that one he is called to account. The smallness of our receiving will not excuse us from a reckoning. None shall be called to an account for more than they have received; but for what we have, we must all account.

Observe, *First,* What he confides in. He comes to the account with a deal of assurance, relying on the plea he had to put in, that he was able to say, "*Lo, there thou hast that is thine;* if I have not made it more, as the others have done, yet this I can say, I have not made it less." This, he thinks, may serve to bring him off, if not with praise, yet with safety.

Note, Many a one goes very securely to judgment, presuming upon the validity of a plea that will be overruled as vain and frivolous. Slothful professors, that are afraid of doing too much for God, yet hope to come off as well as those that take so much pains in religion. Thus *the sluggard is wiser in his own conceit than seven men that can render a reason,* Prov. xxvi. 16. This servant thought that his account would pass well enough, because he could say, *There thou hast that is thine.* "Lord, I was no spendthrift of my estate, no prodigal of my time, no profaner of my sabbaths, no opposer of good ministers and good preaching; Lord, I never ridiculed my bible, nor set my wits to work to banter religion, nor abused my power to persecute any good man; I never drowned my parts, nor wasted God's good creatures in drunkenness and gluttony, nor ever to my knowledge did I injury to any body." Many that are called Christians, build great hopes for heaven upon their being able to make such an account; yet all this amounts to no more than *there thou hast that is thine;* as if no more were required, or could be expected.

Secondly, What he confesses. He owns the burying of his talent; *I hid thy talent in the earth.* He speaks as if that were no great fault; nay, as if he deserved praise for his prudence in putting it in a safe place, and running no hazards with it. Note, It is common for people to make a very light matter of that which will be their condemnation in the great day. Or, if he was conscious to himself that it was his fault, it intimates how easily slothful servants will be convicted in the judgment; there will need no great search for proof, for *their own tongues shall fall upon them.*

Thirdly, What he makes his excuse; *I knew that thou wert a hard man, and I was afraid.* Good thoughts of God would beget love, and that love would make us diligent and faithful; but hard thoughts of God beget fear, and that fear makes us slothful and unfaithful. His excuse bespeaks,

1. The sentiments of an enemy; *I knew thee, that thou art a hard man.* This was like that wicked saying of the house of Israel, *The way of the Lord is not equal,* Ezek. xviii. 25. Thus his *de*fence is his *of*fence. *The foolishness of man perverteth his way,* and then, as if that would mend the matter, *his heart fretteth against the Lord.* This is covering the transgression, as Adam, who implicitly laid the fault on God himself; *The woman which thou gavest me.* Note, Carnal hearts are apt to conceive false and wicked opinions concerning God, and with them to harden themselves in their evil ways. Observe how confidently he speaks; *I knew thee to be so.* How could he know him to be so? *What iniquity have we or our fathers found in him?* Jer. ii. 5. Wherein has he wearied us with his work, or deceived us in his wages? Mic. vi. 3. Has he *been a wilderness to us, or a land of darkness?* Thus long God has governed the world, and may ask with more reason than Samuel himself could, *Whom have I defrauded? or whom have I oppressed?* Does not all the world know the contrary, that he is so far from being a hard master, that *the earth is full of his goodness,* so far from reaping where he sowed not, that he sows a great deal where he reaps nothing? For he *causes the sun to shine, and his rain to fall, upon the evil and unthankful, and fills their hearts with food and gladness* who say to the Almighty, *Depart from us.* This suggestion bespeaks the common reproach which wicked people cast upon God, as if all the blame of their sin and ruin lay at his door, for denying them his grace; whereas it is certain that never any who faithfully improved the common grace they had, perished for want of special grace; nor can any show what could in reason have been done more for an unfruitful vineyard than God has done in it. God does not demand brick, and deny straw; no, whatever is required in the covenant, is promised in the covenant; so that if we perish, it is owing to ourselves.

2. The spirit of a slave; *I was afraid.* This ill affection toward God arose from his false notions of him; and nothing is more unworthy of God, nor more hinders our duty to him, than slavish fear. This has bondage and torment, and is directly opposite to that entire love which the great commandment requires. Note, Hard thoughts of God drive us from, and cramp us in his service. Those who think it impossible to please him, and in vain to serve him, will do nothing to purpose in religion.

[2.] His Lord's answer to this apology. His plea will stand him in no stead, it is overruled, nay, it is made to turn against him, and he is struck speechless with it; for here we have his conviction and his condemnation.

First, His conviction, *v.* 26, 27. Two things he is convicted of.

1. Slothfulness; *Thou wicked and slothful servant.* Note, Slothful servants are wicked servants, and will be reckoned with as such by their master, for he that is *slothful in his work,* and neglects the good that God has commanded, *is brother to him that is a great waster,* by doing the evil that God has forbidden, Prov. xviii. 9. He that is careless in God's work, is near akin to him that is busy in the devil's work. *Satis est mali nihil fecisse boni—To do no good is to incur very serious blame.* Omissions are sins, and must come into judgment; slothfulness makes way for wickedness; all become *filthy,* for *there is none that doeth good,* Ps. xiv. 3. When the house is empty, the unclean spirit takes possession. Those that are idle in the affairs of their souls, are not only idle, but something worse, 1 Tim. v. 13. When men sleep, the enemy sows tares.

2. Self-contradiction (*v.* 26, 27); *Thou knewest that I reap where I sowed not: thou oughtest therefore to have put my money to the exchangers.* Note, The hard thoughts which

sinners have of God, though false and unjust, will be so far from justifying their wickedness and slothfulness, that they will rather aggravate and add to their guilt. Three ways this may be taken; (1.) "Suppose I had been so hard a master, shouldest not thou therefore have been the more diligent and careful to please me, if not for *love*, yet for *fear*, and for that reason oughtest not thou to have minded thy work?" If our God be a consuming fire, in consideration of that let us study how to serve him. Or thus, (2.) "If thou didst think me to be a hard master, and therefore durst not trade with the money thyself, for fear of losing by it, and being made to stand to the loss, yet thou mightest have put it into the hands of the exchangers, or goldsmiths, mightest have brought it into the bank, and then at my coming, if I could not have had the greater improvement, by trade and merchandize (as of the other talents), yet I might have had the less improvement, of bare interest, and should have received *my own with usury;*" which, it seems, was a common practice at that time, and not disallowed by our Saviour. Note, If we could not, or durst not, do what we would, yet that excuse will not serve, when it will be made to appear that we did not do what we could and durst. If we could not find in our hearts to venture upon more difficult and hazardous services, yet will that justify us in shrinking from those that were more safe and easy? Something is better than nothing; if we fail of showing our courage in bold enterprises, yet we must not fail to testify our goodwill in honest endeavours; and our Master *will not despise the day of small things.* Or thus, (3.) "Suppose I did reap *where I sowed not*, yet that is nothing to thee, for I had sowed upon thee, and the talent was my money which thou wast entrusted with, not only to keep, but to improve." Note, In the day of account, wicked and slothful servants will be left quite without excuse; frivolous pleas will be overruled, and every mouth will be stopped; and those who now stand so much upon their own justification will not have one word to say for themselves.

Secondly, His condemnation. The slothful servant is sentenced,

1. To be deprived of his talent (*v.* 28, 29); *Take therefore the talent from him.* The talents were first disposed of by the Master, as an absolute Owner, but this was now disposed of by him as a Judge; he takes it from the unfaithful servant, to punish him, and gives it to him that was eminently faithful, to reward him. And the meaning of this part of the parable we have in the reason of the sentence (*v.* 29), *To every one that hath shall be given.* This may be applied, (1.) To the blessings of this life—worldly wealth and possessions. These we are entrusted with, to be used for the glory of God, and the good of those about us. Now *he that hath* these things, and useth them for these ends, he *shall have abundance;* perhaps abundance of the things themselves, at least, abundance of comfort in them, and of better things; but *from him that hath not*, that is, that hath these things as if he had them not, had not power to eat of them, or to do good with them *(Avaro deest, tam quod habet, quam quod non habet—The miser may be considered as destitute of what he has, as well as of what he has not)*, they *shall be taken away.* Solomon explains this, Prov. xi. 24. *There is that scattereth, and yet increaseth; and there is that withholdeth more than is meet, and it tendeth to poverty.* Giving to the poor is trading with what we have, and the returns will be rich; it will multiply the meal in the barrel, and the oil in the cruse: but those that are sordid, and niggardly, and uncharitable, will find that those riches which are so got, *perish by evil travail*, Eccl. v. 13, 14. Sometimes Providence strangely transfers estates from those that do no good with them to those that do; they are *gathered for him that will pity the poor*, Prov. xxviii. 8. See Prov. xiii. 22; Job xxvii. 16, 17; Eccl. ii. 26. (2.) We may apply it to the means of grace. They who are diligent in improving the opportunities they have, God will enlarge them, will *set before them an open door* (Rev. iii. 8); but they who know not the day of their visitation, shall have the things that belong to their peace hid from their eyes. For proof of this, *go see what God did to Shiloh*, Jer. vii. 12. (3.) We may apply it to the common gifts of the Spirit. He that hath these, and doeth good with them, shall have abundance; these gifts improve by exercise, and brighten by being used; the more we do, the more we may do, in religion; but those who stir not up the gift that is in them, who do not exert themselves according to their capacity, their gifts rust, and decay, and go out like a neglected fire. From him that hath not a living principle of grace in his soul, shall be taken away the common gifts which he hath, as the lamps of the foolish virgins went out for want of oil, *v.* 8. Thus the arm of the *idle shepherd*, which he had sluggishly folded up in his bosom, comes to be dried up, and his right eye, which he had carelessly or wilfully shut, becomes utterly darkened, as it is threatened, Zech. xi. 17.

2. He is sentenced to be *cast into outer darkness*, *v.* 30. Here,

(1.) His character is that of an *unprofitable servant.* Note, Slothful servants will be reckoned with as unprofitable servants, who do nothing to the purpose of their coming into the world, nothing to answer the end of their birth or baptism, who are no way serviceable to the glory of God, the good of others, or the salvation of their own souls. A slothful servant is a withered member in the body, a barren tree in the vineyard, an idle drone in the hive, he is good for nothing. In one sense, we are all *unprofitable servants* (Luke xvii. 10); we cannot *profit God*, Job

xxii. 2. But to others, and to ourselves, it is required that we be profitable; if we be not, Christ will not own us as his servants: it is not enough not to do hurt, but we must do good, must bring forth fruit, and though thereby God is not profited, yet he is glorified, John xv. 8.

(2.) His doom is, to be *cast into outer darkness.* Here, as in what was said to the faithful servants, our Saviour slides insensibly out of the parable into the thing intended by it, and it serves as a key to the whole; for, *outer darkness, where there is weeping and gnashing of teeth,* is, in Christ's discourses, the common periphrasis of the miseries of the damned in hell. Their state is, [1.] Very dismal; it is outer darkness. Darkness is uncomfortable and frightful: it was one of the plagues of Egypt. In hell there are *chains of darkness,* 2 Pet. ii. 4. In the dark *no man can work,* a fit punishment for a slothful servant. It is *outer* darkness, *out* from the light of heaven, *out* from the joy of their Lord, into which the faithful servants were admitted; *out* from the feast. Compare *ch.* viii. 12; xxii. 13. [2.] Very doleful; there is weeping, which bespeaks great sorrow, and gnashing of teeth, which bespeaks great vexation and indignation. This will be the portion of the slothful servant.

31 When the Son of man shall
come in his glory, and all the holy
angels with him, then shall he sit upon
the throne of his glory: 32 And before
him shall be gathered all nations; and
he shall separate them one from another, as a shepherd divideth *his* sheep
from the goats: 33 And he shall set
the sheep on his right hand, but the
goats on the left. 34 Then shall the
King say unto them on his right hand,
Come, ye blessed of my Father, inherit the kingdom prepared for you
from the foundation of the world: 35
For I was an hungred, and ye gave
me meat: I was thirsty, and ye gave
me drink: I was a stranger, and ye
took me in: 36 Naked, and ye clothed
me: I was sick, and ye visited me:
I was in prison, and ye came unto me.
37 Then shall the righteous answer
him, saying, Lord, when saw we thee
an hungred, and fed *thee?* or thirsty,
and gave *thee* drink? 38 When saw
we thee a stranger, and took *thee* in?
or naked, and clothed *thee?* 39 Or
when saw we thee sick, or in prison,
and came unto thee? 40 And the
King shall answer and say unto them,
Verily I say unto you, Inasmuch as
ye have done *it* unto one of the least of
these my brethren, ye have done *it* unto
me. 41 Then shall he say also unto
them on the left hand, Depart from
me, ye cursed, into everlasting fire,
prepared for the devil and his angels:
42 For I was an hungred, and ye gave
me no meat: I was thirsty and ye
gave me no drink: 43 I was a stranger,
and ye took me not in: naked, and ye
clothed me not: sick, and in prison,
and ye visited me not. 44 Then
shall they also answer him, saying,
Lord, when saw we thee an hungred,
or athirst, or a stranger, or naked, or
sick, or in prison, and did not minister
unto thee? 45 Then shall he answer
them, saying, Verily I say unto you,
Inasmuch as ye did *it* not to one of
the least of these, ye did *it* not to me.
46 And these shall go away into everlasting punishment: but the righteous
into life eternal.

We have here a description of the process of the last judgment in the great day. There are some passages in it that are parabolical; as the separating between the sheep and the goats, and the dialogues between the judge and the persons judged: but there is no thread of similitude carried through the discourse, and therefore it is rather to be called a draught or delineation of the final judgment, than a parable; it is, as it were, the explanation of the former parables. And here we have,

I. The placing of the judge upon the judgment-seat (*v.* 31); *When the Son of man shall come.* Observe here,

1. That there is a judgment to come, in which every man shall be sentenced to a state of everlasting happiness, or misery, in the world of recompence or retribution, according to what he did in this world of trial and probation, which is to be judged of by the rule of the everlasting gospel.

2. The administration of the judgment of the great day is committed to the Son of man; for by him God will judge the world (Acts xvii. 31), and to him all judgment is committed, and therefore the judgment of that day, which is the centre of all. Here, as elsewhere, when the last judgment is spoken of, Christ is called *the son of man,* because he is to judge the sons of men (and, being himself of the same nature, he is the more unexceptionable); and because his wonderful condescension to take upon him our nature, and to become the son of man, will be recompensed by his exaltation in that day, and an honour put upon the human nature.

3. Christ's appearing to judge the world will be splendid and glorious. Agrippa and

Bernice came to the judgment-seat with *great pomp* (Acts xxv. 23); but that was (as the original word is) *great fancy*. Christ will come to the judgment-seat in real glory: the Sun of righteousness shall then shine in his meridian lustre, and the Prince of the kings of the earth shall show the riches of his glorious kingdom, and the honours of his excellent majesty; and all the world shall see what the saints only do now believe—that he is the brightness of his Father's glory. He shall come not only in the glory of his Father, but in his own glory, as mediator: his first coming was under a black cloud of obscurity; his second will be in a bright cloud of glory. The assurance Christ gave his disciples of his future glory, might help to take off the offence of the cross, and his approaching disgrace and suffering.

4. When Christ comes in his glory to judge the world, he will bring all his holy angels with him. This glorious person will have a glorious retinue, his holy myriads, who will be not only his attendants, but ministers of his justice; they shall come with him both for state and service. They must come to call the court (1 Thess. iv. 16), to gather the elect (*ch.* xxiv. 31), to bundle the tares (*ch.* xiii. 40), to be witnesses of the saints' glory (Luke xii. 8), and of sinners' misery, Rev. xiv. 10.

5. He will then sit upon the throne of his glory. He is *now* set down with the Father upon his throne; and it is a throne of grace, to which we may come boldly; it is a throne of government, the throne of his father David; he is a priest upon that throne: but *then* he will sit upon the throne of glory, the throne of jugment. See Dan. vii. 9, 10. Solomon's throne, though there was not its like in any kingdom, was but a dunghill to it. Christ, in the days of his flesh, was arraigned as a prisoner at the bar; but at his second coming, he will sit as a judge upon the bench.

II. The appearing of all the children of men before him (*v.* 32); *Before him shall be gathered all nations.* Note, The judgment of the great day will be a general judgment. All must be summoned before Christ's tribunal; all of every age of the world, from the beginning to the end of time; all of every place on earth, even from the remotest corners of the world, most obscure, and distant from each other; all nations, all those nations of men that are made of one blood, to dwell on all the face of the earth.

III. The distinction that will then be made between the precious and the vile; *He shall separate them one from another,* as the tares and wheat are separated at the harvest, the good fish and the bad at the shore, the corn and chaff in the floor. Wicked and godly here dwell together in the same kingdoms, cities, churches, families, and are not certainly distinguishable one from another; such are the infirmities of saints, such the hypocrisies of sinners, and one event to both: but in that day they will be separated, and parted for ever; *Then shall ye return, and discern between the righteous and the wicked,* Mal. iii. 18. They cannot separate themselves one from another in this world (1 Cor. v. 10), nor can any one else separate them (*ch.* xiii. 29); but the Lord knows them that are his, and he can separate them. This separation will be so exact, that the most inconsiderable saints shall not be lost in the crowd of sinners, nor the most plausible sinner hid in the crowd of saints (Ps. i. 5), but every one shall go to his own place. This is compared to a shepherd's dividing between the sheep and the goats; it is taken from Ezek. xxxiv. 17, *Behold, I judge between cattle and cattle.* Note, 1. Jesus Christ is the great Shepherd; he now feeds his flock like a shepherd, and will shortly distinguish between those that are his, and those that are not, as Laban divided his sheep from Jacob's, and set three days' journey between them, Gen. xxx. 35, 36. 2. The godly are like sheep—innocent, mild, patient, useful: the wicked are like goats, a baser kind of animal, unsavoury and unruly. The sheep and goats are here feeding all day in the same pasture, but will be coted at night in different folds. Being thus divided, he will set the *sheep on his right hand,* and the *goats on his left, v.* 33. Christ puts honour upon the godly, as we show respect to those we set on our right hand; but the wicked shall rise to everlasting shame, Dan. xii. 2. It is not said that he shall put the rich on his right hand, and the poor on his left; the learned and noble on his right hand, and the unlearned and despised on his left; but the godly on his right hand, and the wicked on his left. All other divisions and subdivisions will then be abolished; but the great distinction of men into saints and sinners, sanctified and unsanctified, will remain for ever, and men's eternal state will be determined by it. The wicked took up with left-handed blessings, riches and honour, and so shall their doom be.

IV. The process of the judgment concerning each of these.

1. Concerning the godly, on the right hand. Their cause must be first despatched, that they may be assessors with Christ in the judgment of the wicked, whose misery will be aggravated by their seeing Abraham, and Isaac, and Jacob, admitted into the kingdom of heaven, Luke xiii. 28. Observe here,

(1.) The *glory* conferred upon them; the sentence by which they shall be not only acquitted, but preferred and rewarded (*v.* 34); *The king shall say unto them.* He that was the Shepherd (which bespeaks the care and tenderness wherewith he will make this disquisition), is here the King, which bespeaks the authority wherewith he will then pronounce the sentence: where the word of this King is, there is power. Here are two things in this sentence:

[1.] The acknowledging of the saints to

be the blessed of the Lord; *Come, ye blessed of my Father. First,* He pronounces them *blessed;* and his saying they are blessed, makes them so. The law curses them for their many discontinuances; but Christ having redeemed them from the curse of the law, and purchased a blessing for them, commands a blessing on them. *Secondly, Blessed of his Father;* reproached and cursed by the world, but blessed of God. As the Spirit glorifies the Son (John xvi. 14), so the Son glorifies the Father by referring the salvation of the saints to him as the First Cause; all our blessings in heavenly things flow to us from God, as the Father of our Lord Jesus Christ, Eph. i. 3. *Thirdly,* He calls them *to come:* this *come* is, in effect, "*Welcome,* ten thousand welcomes, to the blessings of my Father; come to me, come to be for ever with me; you that followed me bearing the cross, now come along with me wearing the crown. The blessed of my Father are the beloved of my soul, that have been too long at a distance from me; come, now, come into my bosom, come into my arms, come into my dearest embraces!" O with what joy will this fill the hearts of the saints in that day! We now come boldly to the throne of grace, but we shall then come boldly to the throne of glory; and this word holds out the golden sceptre, with an assurance that our requests shall be granted to more than the half of the kingdom. Now the Spirit saith, *Come,* in the word; and the bride saith, *Come,* in prayer; and the result hereof is a sweet communion: but the perfection of bliss will be, when *the King shall say, Come.*

[2.] The admission of the saints into the blessedness and kingdom of the Father; *Inherit the kingdom prepared for you.*

First, The happiness they shall be possessed of is very rich; we are told what it is by him who had reason to know it, having purchased it for them, and possessed it himself.

1. It is a *kingdom;* which is reckoned the most valuable possession on earth, and includes the greatest wealth and honour. Those that inherit kingdoms, wear all the glories of the crown, enjoy all the pleasures of the court, and command the peculiar treasures of the provinces; yet this is but a faint resemblance of the felicities of the saints in heaven. They that here are beggars, prisoners, accounted as the off-scouring of all things, shall then inherit a kingdom, Ps. cxiii. 7; Rev. ii. 26, 27.

2. It is a kingdom *prepared:* the happiness must needs be great, for it is the product of the divine counsels. Note, There is great preparation made for the entertainment of the saints in the kingdom of glory. The Father designed it for them in his thoughts of love, and provided it for them in the greatness of his wisdom and power. The Son purchased it for them, and is entered as the fore-runner to prepare a place, John xiv. 2. And the blessed Spirit, in preparing them for the kingdom, in effect, is preparing it for them.

3. It is prepared *for them.* This bespeaks, (1.) The suitableness of this happiness; it is in all points adapted to the nature of a soul, and to the new nature of a sanctified soul. (2.) Their property and interest in it. It is prepared on purpose for them; not only for such as you, but for you, you by name, you personally and particularly, who were chosen to salvation through sanctification.

4. It is prepared *from the foundation of the world.* This happiness was designed for the saints, and they for it, before time began, from all eternity, Eph. i. 4. The end, which is last in execution, is first in intention. Infinite Wisdom had an eye to the eternal glorification of the saints, from the first founding of the creation; *All things are for your sakes,* 2 Cor. iv. 15. Or, it denotes the preparation of the place of this happiness, which is to be the seat and habitation of the blessed, in the very beginning of the work of creation, Gen. i. 1. There in the heaven of heavens the morning stars were singing together, when the foundations of the earth were fastened, Job xxxviii. 4—7.

Secondly, The tenure by which they shall hold and possess it is very good, they shall come and *inherit it.* What we come to by inheritance, is not got by any procurement of our own, but purely, as the lawyers express it, *by the act of God.* It is God that makes heirs, heirs of heaven. We come to an inheritance by virtue of our sonship, our adoption; *if children, then heirs.* A title by inheritance is the sweetest and surest title; it alludes to possessions in the land of Canaan, which passed by inheritance, and would not be alienated longer than to the year of Jubilee. Thus is the heavenly inheritance indefeasible, and unalienable. Saints, in this world, are as heirs under age, tutored and governed till the time appointed of the Father (Gal. iv. 1, 2); and then they shall be put in full possession of that which now through grace they have a title to; *Come,* and inherit it.

(2.) The ground of this (*v.* 35, 36), *For I was an hungered, and ye gave me meat.* We cannot hence infer that any good works of ours merit the happiness of heaven, by any intrinsic worth or excellency in them: our goodness extends not unto God; but it is plain that Jesus Christ will judge the world by the same rule by which he governs it, and therefore will reward those that have been obedient to that law; and mention will be made of their obedience, not as their title, but as their evidence of an interest in Christ, and his purchase. This happiness will be adjudged to obedient believers, not upon a *quantum meruit—an estimate of merit,* which supposes a proportion between the work and the reward, but upon the promise of God purchased by Jesus Christ, and the benefit of it secured under certain provisos and limitations; and it is the purchase and promise that give the title, the obedience is only the qualification of the person designed. An estate made by deed or will upon condition, when the condition is performed according to the true intent of the donor or testator, becomes absolute; and then, though the title be built purely upon the deed or will, yet the performing of the condition must be given in evidence: and so it comes in here; for Christ is the Author of eternal salvation to those only that obey him, and who patiently continue in well doing.

Now the good works here mentioned are such as we commonly call works of charity to the poor: not but that many will be found on the right hand who never were in a capacity to feed the hungry, or clothe the naked, but were themselves fed and clothed by the charity of others; but one instance of sincere obedience is put for all the rest, and it teaches us this in general, that faith working by love is all in all in Christianity; *Show me thy faith by thy works:* and nothing will abound to a good account hereafter, but the fruits of righteousness in a good conversation now. The good works here described imply three things, which must be found in all that are saved.

[1.] Self-denial, and contempt of the world; reckoning the things of the world no further good things, than as we are enabled to do good with them: and those who have not wherewithal to do good, must show the same disposition, by being contentedly and cheerfully poor. Those are fit for heaven that are mortified to the earth.

[2.] Love to our brethren; which is the second great commandment, the fulfilling of the law, and an excellent preparative for the world of everlasting love. We must give proof of this love by our readiness to do good, and to communicate; good wishes are but mockeries without good works, Jam. ii. 15, 16; 1 John iii. 17. Those that have not to give, must show the same disposition some other way.

[3.] A believing regard to Jesus Christ. That which is here rewarded is the relieving of the poor for Christ's sake, out of love to him, and with an eye to him. *This* puts an excellency upon the good work, when in it we serve the Lord Christ, which those may do that work for their own living, as well as those that help to keep others alive. See Eph. vi. 5—7. Those good works shall then be accepted which are done in the name of the Lord Jesus, Col. iii. 17.

I was hungry, that is, my disciples and followers were so, either by the persecutions of enemies for well-doing, or by the common dispensations of Providence; for in these things there is one event to the righteous and wicked: and *you gave them meat.* Note, *First,* Providence so variously orders and disposes of the circumstances of his people in this world, as that while some are in a condition to give relief, others need it. It is no new thing for those that are feasted with the dainties of heaven to be hungry and thirsty, and to want daily food; for those that are at home in God, to be strangers in a strange land; for those that have put on Christ, to want clothes to keep them warm; for those that have healthful souls, to have sickly bodies; and for those to be in prison, that Christ has made free. *Secondly,* Works of charity and beneficence, according as our ability is, are necessary to salvation; and there will be more stress laid upon them in the judgment of the great day, than is commonly imagined; these must be the proofs of our love, and of our professed subjection to the gospel of Christ, 2 Cor. ix. 13. But they that show no mercy, shall have judgment without mercy.

Now this reason is modestly excepted against by the righteous, but is explained by the Judge himself.

1. It is questioned by the righteous, *v.* 37—39. Not as if they were loth to inherit the kingdom, or were ashamed of their good deeds, or had not the testimony of their own consciences concerning them: but, (1.) The expressions are parabolical, designed to introduce and impress these great truths, that Christ has a mighty regard to works of charity, and is especially pleased with kindnesses done to his people for his sake. Or, (2.) They bespeak the humble admiration which glorified saints will be filled with, to find such poor and worthless services, as theirs are, so highly celebrated, and richly rewarded: *Lord, when saw we thee an hungered, and fed thee?* Note, Gracious souls are apt to think meanly of their own good deeds; especially as unworthy to be compared with the glory that shall be revealed. Far from this is the temper of those who said, *Wherefore have we fasted, and thou seest not?* Isa. lviii. 3. Saints in heaven will wonder what brought them thither, and that God should so regard them and their services. It even put Nathanael to the blush, to hear Christ's encomium of him: *Whence knowest thou me?* John i. 47, 48. See Eph. iii. 20. "*When saw we thee an hungered?* We have seen the poor in distress many a time; but when saw we thee?" Note, Christ is more among us than we think he is; surely the Lord is in this place, by his word, his ordinances, his ministers, his Spirit, yea, and his poor, and we know it not: *When thou wert under the fig-tree, I saw thee,* John i. 48.

2. It is explained by the Judge himself (*v.* 40); *Inasmuch as ye have done it to these my brethren,* to the least, to one of the least of them, *ye have done it unto me.* The good works of the saints, when they are produced in the great day, (1.) Shall all be remembered; and not the least, not one of the least, overlooked, no not a cup of cold water. (2.) They shall be interpreted most to their advantage, and the best construction that can be put upon them. As Christ makes the best of their infirmities, so he makes the most of their services.

We see what recompences Christ has for those that feed the hungry, and clothe the naked; but what will become of the godly poor, that had not wherewithal to do so? Must they be shut out? No, [1.] Christ will own them, even the least of them, as his brethren; he will not be ashamed, nor think it any disparagement to him, *to call them brethren,* Heb. ii. 11. In the height of his glory, he will not disown his poor relations; Lazarus is there laid in his bosom, as a friend, as a brother. Thus he will confess them, *ch.* x. 32. [2.] He will take the kindness done to them, as done to himself; *Ye have done it unto me;* which shows a respect to the poor that were relieved, as well as to the rich that did relieve them. Note, Christ espouses his people's cause, and interests himself in their interests, and reckons himself received, and loved, and owned in them. If Christ himself were among us in poverty, how readily would we relieve him? In prison, how frequently would we visit him? We are ready to envy the honour they had, who ministered to him of their substance, Luke viii. 3. Wherever poor saints and poor ministers are, there Christ is ready to receive our kindnesses in them, and they shall be put to his account.

2. Here is the process concerning the wicked, those on the left hand. And in that we have,

(1.) The sentence passed upon them, *v.* 41. It was a disgrace to be set on the left hand; but that is not the worst of it, he shall say to them, *Depart from me, ye cursed.* Every word has terror in it, like that of the trumpet at mount Sinai, waxing louder and louder, every accent more and more doleful, and exclusive of comfort.

[1.] To be so near to Christ was some satisfaction, though under his frowns; but that will not be allowed, *Depart from me.* In this world they were often called to come to Christ, to come for life and rest, but they turned a deaf ear to his calls; justly therefore are they bid to depart from Christ, that would not come to him. "Depart from me the Fountain of all good, from me the Saviour, and therefore from all hope of salvation; I will never have any thing more to say to you, or do with you." Here they said to the Almighty, *Depart from us;* then he will *choose their delusions,* and say to them, *Depart from me.* Note, It is the hell of hell to depart from Christ.

[2.] If they must depart, and depart from Christ, might they not be dismissed with a blessing, with one kind and compassionate word at least? No, *Depart, ye cursed.* They that would not come to Christ, to inherit a blessing, must depart from him under the burthen of a curse, that curse of the law on every one that breaks it, Gal. iii. 10. *As they loved cursing, so it shall come unto them.* But observe, The righteous are called *the blessed of my Father;* for their blessedness is owing purely to the grace of God and his blessing, but the wicked are called only *ye cursed,* for their damnation is of themselves. Hath God sold them? No, they have sold themselves, have laid themselves under the curse, Isa. l. 1.

[3.] If they must depart, and depart with a curse, may they not go into some place of ease and rest? Will it not be misery enough for them to bewail their loss? No, there is a punishment of sense as well as loss; they must depart into *fire,* into torment as grievous as that of fire is to the body, and much more. This fire is the wrath of the eternal God fastening upon the guilty souls and consciences of sinners that have made themselves fuel for it. Our God is a consuming fire, and sinners fall immediately into his hands, Heb. x. 31; Rom. ii. 8, 9.

[4.] If into fire, may it not be some light or gentle fire? No, it is *prepared* fire; it is a torment *ordained of old,* Isa. xxx. 33. The damnation of sinners is often spoken of as an act of the divine power; *he is able to cast into hell.* In the vessels of wrath he makes his power known; it is a *destruction from the presence of the Lord, and from the glory of his power.* In it shall be seen what a provoked God can do to make a provoking creature miserable.

[5.] If into fire, prepared fire, O let it be but of short continuance, let them but pass *through* fire; no, the fire of God's wrath will be an *everlasting* fire; a fire, that, fastening and preying upon immortal souls, can never go out for want of fuel; and, being kindled and kept burning by the wrath of an immortal God, can never go out for want of being blown and stirred up; and, the streams of mercy and grace being for ever excluded, there is nothing to extinguish it. If a drop of water be denied to cool the tongue, buckets of water will never be granted to quench this flame.

[6.] If they must be doomed to such a state of endless misery, yet may they not have some good company there? No, none but *the devil and his angels,* their sworn enemies, that helped to bring them to this misery, and will triumph over them in it. They served the devil while they lived, and therefore are justly sentenced to be where he is, as those that served Christ, are taken to be with him where he is. It is terrible to lie in a house haunted with devils; what will it be then to be companions with them for ever? Observe here, *First,* Christ intimates that there is one that is the prince of the devils, the ring-leader of the rebellion, and that the rest are his angels, his messengers, by whose agency he supports his kingdom. Christ and his angels will in that day triumph over the dragon and his, Rev. xii. 7, 8. *Secondly,* The fire is said to be prepared, not primarily for the wicked, as the kingdom is prepared for the righteous; but it was originally intended for *the devil and his angels.* If sinners make themselves associates with Satan by indulging their lusts, they may thank themselves if they become sharers in that misery which was prepared for him and his associates. Calvin notes upon this, that *therefore* the torment of the damned is said to be *prepared for the devil and his angels,* to cut off all hope of escaping it; the devil and his angels are already made prisoners in that pit, and can worms of the earth think to escape?

(2.) The reason of this sentence assigned. God's judgments are all just, and he will be justified in them. He is Judge himself, and therefore *the heavens shall declare his righteousness.*

Now, [1.] All that is charged upon them, on which the sentence is grounded, is, omission; as, before, the servant was condemned, not for wasting his talent, but for burying it; so here, he doth not say, "I was hungry and thirsty, for you took my meat and drink from me; I was a stranger, for you banished me; naked, for you stripped me; in prison, for you laid me there:" but, "When I was in these distresses, you were so selfish, so taken up with your own ease and pleasure, made so much of your labour, and were so loth to part with your money, that you did not *minister* as you might have done to my relief and succour. You were like those epicures that were at ease in Zion, and were not *grieved for the affliction of Joseph,*" Amos vi. 4—6. Note, Omissions are the ruin of thousands.

[2.] It is the omission of works of charity to the poor. They are not sentenced for omitting their sacrifices and burnt-offerings (they abounded in these, Ps. l. 8), but for omitting the weightier matters of the law, *judgment, mercy, and faith.* The Ammonites and Moabites were excluded the sanctuary, because they *met not Israel with bread and water,* Deut. xxiii. 3, 4. Note, Uncharitableness to the poor is a damning sin. If we will not be brought to works of charity by the hope of reward, let us be influenced by fear of punishment; for *they shall have judgment without mercy, that have showed no mercy.* Observe, He doth not say, "I was sick, and you did not cure me; in prison, and you did not release me" (perhaps that was more than they could do); but, "You *visited me not,* which you might have done." Note, Sinners will be condemned, at the great day, for the omission of that good which it was in the power of their hand to do. But if the doom of the uncharitable be so dreadful, how much more intolerable will the doom of the cruel be, the doom of persecutors! Now this reason of the sentence is,

First, Objected against by the prisoners (*v.* 44); *Lord, when saw we thee an hungered, or athirst?* Condemned sinners, though they have no plea that will bear them out, will yet in vain offer at excuses. Now, 1. The manner of their pleading bespeaks their present precipitation. They cut it short, as men in haste; *when saw we thee hungry, or thirsty, or naked?* They care not to repeat the charge, as conscious to themselves of their own guilt, and unable to bear the terrors of the judgment. Nor will they have time allowed them to insist upon such frivolous pleas; for it is all (as we say) but "trifling with the court." 2. The matter of their plea bespeaks their former inconsideration of that which they might have known, but would not till now that it was too late. They that had slighted and persecuted poor Christians, would not own that they had slighted and persecuted Christ: no, they never intended any affront to him, nor expected that so great a matter would have been made of it. They imagined it was only a company of poor, weak, silly, and contemptible people, who made more ado than needed about religion, that they put those slights upon; but they who do so, will be made to know, either in the day of their conversion, as Paul, or of their condemnation, as these here, that it was *Jesus whom they persecuted.* And, if they say, *Behold, we knew it not: doth not he that pondereth the heart consider it?* Prov. xxiv. 11, 12.

Secondly, Justified by the Judge, who will convince all the ungodly of the hard speeches spoken against him in those that are his, Jude 15. He goes by this rule (*v.* 45); *Inasmuch as ye did it not to one of the least of these, ye did it not to me.* Note, What is done against the faithful disciples and followers of Christ, even the least of them, he takes as done against himself. He is reproached and persecuted in them, for they are reproached and persecuted for his sake, and *in all their afflictions he is afflicted.* He that touches them, touches him in a part no less tender than the apple of his eye.

Lastly, Here is the execution of both these sentences, *v.* 46. Execution is the life of the law, and Christ will take care that that be done according to the sentence.

1. *The wicked shall go away into everlasting punishment.* Sentence will then be executed speedily, and no reprieve granted, nor any time allowed to move in arrest of judgment. The execution of the wicked is first mentioned; for first the tares are gathered and burned. Note, (1.) The punishment of the wicked in the future state will be an everlasting punishment, for that state is an unalterable state. It can neither be thought that sinners should change their own natures, nor that God should give his grace to change them, when in this world the day of grace was misspent, the Spirit of grace resisted, and the means of grace abused and baffled. (2.) The wicked shall be made to *go* away into that punishment; not that they will go voluntarily, no, they are *driven* from light into darkness; but it bespeaks an irresistible conviction of guilt, and a final despair of mercy.

2. *The righteous shall go away into life eternal;* that is, they shall *inherit the kingdom, v.* 34. Note, (1.) Heaven is life, it is all

happiness. The life of the soul results from its union with God by the mediation of Jesus Christ, as that of the body from its union with the soul by the animal spirits. The heavenly life consists in the vision and fruition of God, in a perfect conformity to him, and an immediate uninterrupted communion with him. (2.) It is *eternal* life. There is no death to put a period to the life itself, nor old age to put a period to the comfort of it, or any sorrow to embitter it. Thus life and death, good and evil, the blessing and the curse, are set before us, that we may choose our way; and so shall our end be. Even the heathen had some notion of these different states of good and bad in the other world. Cicero in his *Tusculan Questions*, lib. 1, brings in Socrates thus speaking, *Duæ sunt viæ, duplicesque cursus è corpore exeuntium: nam qui se vitiis humanis contaminarunt, et libidinibus se tradiderunt, iis devium quoddam iter est, seclusum à consilio deorum; qui autem se integros castosque servarunt, quibusque fuerit minima cum corporibus contagio, suntque in corporibus humanis vitam imitati deorum, iis ad illos a quibus sunt profecti facile patet reditus—Two paths open before those who depart out of the body. Such as have contaminated themselves with human vices, and yielded to their lusts, occupy a path that conducts them far from the assembly and council of the gods; but the upright and chaste, such as have been least defiled by the flesh, and have imitated, while in the body, the gods, these find it easy to return to the sublime beings from whom they came.*

CHAP. XXVI.

The narrative of the death and sufferings of Christ is more particularly and fully recorded by all the four evangelists than any part of his history; for what should we determine, and desire to know, but Christ, and him crucified? And this chapter begins that memorable narrative. The year of the redeemed was now come, the seventy weeks determined were now accomplished, when transgression must be finished, reconciliation made, and an everlasting righteousness brought in, by the cutting off of Messiah the Prince, Dan. ix. 24, 26. That awful scene is here introduced, to be read with reverence and holy fear. In this chapter, we have, I. The preliminaries, or prefaces, to Christ's sufferings. 1. The previous notice given by him to his disciples, ver. 1, 2. 2. The rulers' conspiracy against him, ver. 3—5. 3. The anointing of his head at a supper in Bethany, ver. 6—13. 4. Judas's bargain with the priests to betray him, ver. 14—16. 5. Christ eating the passover with his disciples, ver. 17—25. 6. His instituting the Lord's supper, and his discourse with his disciples after it, ver. 26—35. II. His entrance upon them, and some of the particulars of them. 1. His agony in the garden, ver. 36—46. 2. The seizing of him by the officers, with Judas's help, ver. 47—56. 3. His arraignment before the chief priest, and his condemnation in his court, ver. 57—68. 4. Peter's denying him, ver. 69—75.

AND it came to pass, when Jesus had finished all these sayings, he said unto his disciples, 2 Ye know that after two days is *the feast of* the passover, and the Son of man is betrayed to be crucified. 3 Then assembled together the chief priests, and the scribes, and the elders of the people, unto the palace of the high priest, who was called Caiaphas, 4 And consulted that they might take Jesus by subtlety, and kill *him*. 5 But they said, Not on the feast *day*, lest there be an uproar among the people.

Here is, 1. The notice Christ gave his disciples of the near approach of his sufferings, *v.* 1, 2. While his enemies were preparing trouble for him, he was preparing himself and his followers for it. He had often told them of his sufferings at a distance, now he speaks of them as at the door; *after two days.* Note, After many former notices of trouble we still have need of fresh ones. Observe,

(1.) The *time* when he gave this alarm; *when he had finished all these sayings.* [1.] Not till he had finished all he had to say. Note, Christ's witnesses die not till they have finished their testimony. When Christ had gone through his undertaking as a prophet, he entered upon the execution of his office as a priest. [2.] After he had finished these sayings, which go immediately before; he had bid his disciples to expect sad times, bonds and afflictions, and then tells them, *The Son of man is betrayed;* to intimate that they should fare no worse than he should, and that his sufferings should take the sting out of theirs. Note, Thoughts of a suffering Christ are great supports to a suffering Christian, suffering with him and for him.

(2.) The thing itself he gave them notice of; *The Son of man is betrayed.* The thing was not only so sure, but so near, that it was as good as done. Note, It is good to make sufferings that are yet to come, as present to us. He *is* betrayed, for Judas was then contriving and designing to betray him.

2. The plot of the chief priests, and scribes, and elders of the people, against the life of our Lord Jesus, *v.* 3—5. Many consultations had been held against the life of Christ; but this plot was laid deeper than any yet, for the grandees were all engaged in it. The chief priests, who presided in ecclesiastical affairs; the elders, who were judges in civil matters, and the scribes, who, as doctors of the law, were directors to both—these composed the sanhedrim, or great council that governed the nation, and these were confederate against Christ. Observe, (1.) The *place* where they met; *in the palace of the high priest,* who was the centre of their unity in this wicked project. (2.) The plot itself; to *take Jesus by subtlety, and kill him;* nothing less than his blood, his life-blood, would serve their turn. So cruel and bloody have been the designs of Christ's and his church's enemies. (3.) The policy of the plotters; *Not on the feast-day.* Why not? Was it in regard to the holiness of the time, or because they would not be disturbed in the religious services of the day? No, but *lest there should be an uproar among the people.* They knew Christ had a great interest in the common people, of whom there was a great concourse on the feast-day, and they would be in dan-

ger of taking up arms against their rulers, if they should offer to lay violent hands on Christ, whom all held for a prophet. They were awed, not by the fear of God, but by the fear of the people; all their concern was for their own safety, not God's honour. They would have it done at the feast; for it was a tradition of the Jews, that malefactors should be put to death at one of the three feasts, especially rebels and impostors, that *all Israel might see and fear;* but *not on the feast-day.*

6 Now when Jesus was in Bethany,
in the house of Simon the leper, 7
There came unto him a woman having
an alabaster box of very precious ointment, and poured it on his head, as
he sat *at meat.* 8 But when his disciples saw *it,* they had indignation,
saying, To what purpose *is* this waste?
9 For this ointment might have been
sold for much, and given to the poor.
10 When Jesus understood *it,* he said
unto them, Why trouble ye the woman?
for she hath wrought a good work
upon me. 11 For ye have the poor
always with you; but me ye have not
always. 12 For in that she hath
poured this ointment on my body, she
did *it* for my burial. 13 Verily I say
unto you, Wheresoever this gospel
shall be preached in the whole world,
there shall also this, that this woman
hath done, be told for a memorial of
her.

In this passage of story, we have,

I. The singular kindness of a good woman to our Lord Jesus in anointing his head, *v.* 6, 7. It was *in Bethany,* a village hard by Jerusalem, and *in the house of Simon the leper.* Probably, he was one who had been miraculously cleansed from his leprosy by our Lord Jesus, and he would express his gratitude to Christ by entertaining him; nor did Christ disdain to converse with him, to come in to him, and sup with him. Though he was cleansed, yet he was called *Simon the leper.* Those who are guilty of scandalous sins, will find that, though the sin be pardoned, the reproach will cleave to them, and will hardly be wiped away. The woman that did this, is supposed to have been Mary, the sister of Martha and Lazarus. And Dr. Lightfoot thinks it was the same that was called *Mary Magdalene.* She had a *box of ointment very precious,* which she *poured upon the head* of Christ as he sat at meat. This, among us, would be a strange sort of compliment. But it was then accounted the highest piece of respect; for the smell was very grateful, and the ointment itself refreshing to the head. David had his *head anointed,* Ps. xxiii. 5; Luke vii. 46. Now this may be looked upon,

1. As an act of faith in our Lord Jesus, the Christ, the Messiah, the anointed. To signify that she believed in him as God's anointed, whom he had set king, she anointed him, and made him her king. They shall *appoint themselves one head,* Hos. i. 11. This is *kissing the Son.*

2. As an act of love and respect to him. Some think that this was she who *loved much* at first, and *washed Christ's feet with her tears* (Luke vii. 38, 47); and that she had not left her first love, but was now as affectionate in the devotions of a grown Christian as she was in those of a young beginner. Note, Where there is true love in the heart to Jesus Christ, nothing will be thought too good, no, nor good enough, to bestow upon him.

II. The offence which the disciples took at this. They *had indignation* (*v.* 8, 9), were vexed to see this ointment thus spent, which they thought might have been better bestowed.

1. See how they expressed their offence at it. They said, *To what purpose is this waste?* Now this bespeaks,

(1.) Want of tenderness toward this good woman, in interpreting her over-kindness (suppose it was so) to be wastefulness. Charity teaches us to put the best construction upon every thing that it will bear, especially upon the words and actions of those that are *zealously affected in doing a good thing,* though we may think them not altogether so discreet in it as they might be. It is true, there may be over-doing in well-doing; but thence we must learn to be cautious ourselves, lest we run into extremes, but not to be censorious of others; because that which we may impute to the want of prudence, God may accept as an instance of abundant love. We must not say, Those do too much in religion, that do more than we do, but rather aim to do as much as they.

(2.) Want of respect to their Master. The best we can make of it, is, that they knew their Master was perfectly dead to all the delights of sense; he that was so much *grieved for the affliction of Joseph,* cared not for being *anointed with the chief ointments,* Amos. vi. 6. And therefore they thought such pleasures ill bestowed upon one who took so little pleasure in them. But supposing that, it did not become them to call it *waste,* when they perceived that he admitted and accepted it as a token of his friend's love. Note, We must take heed of thinking any thing waste, which is bestowed upon the Lord Jesus, either by others or by ourselves. We must not think that time waste, that is spent in the service of Christ, or that money waste, which is laid out in any work of piety; for, though it seem to be cast upon the waters, to be thrown down the river, we shall *find it again,* to advantage, *after many days,* Eccl. xi. 1.

2. See how they excused their offence at it, and what pretence they made for it; *This*

ointment might have been sold for much, and given to the poor. Note, It is no new thing for bad affections to shelter themselves under specious covers; for people to shift off works of piety under colour of works of charity.

III. The reproof Christ gave to his disciples for the offence at this good woman (*v.* 10, 11); *Why trouble ye the woman?* Note, It is a great trouble to good people to have their good works censured and misconstrued; and it is a thing that Jesus Christ takes very ill. He here took part with a good, honest, zealous, well-meaning woman, against all his disciples, though they seemed to have so much reason on their side; so heartily does he espouse the cause of the *offended little ones, ch.* xviii. 10.

Observe his reason; *You have the poor always with you.* Note,

1. There are some opportunities of doing and getting good which are constant, and which we must give constant attendance to the improvement of. Bibles we have always with us, sabbaths always with us, and so *the poor we have always with us.* Note, Those who have a heart to do good, never need complain for want of opportunity. The poor never ceased even out of the land of Israel, Deut. xv. 11. We cannot but see some in this world, who call for our charitable assistance, who are as God's receivers, some poor members of Christ, to whom he will have kindness shown as to himself.

2. There are other opportunities of doing and getting good, which come but seldom, which are short and uncertain, and require more peculiar diligence in the improvement of them, and which ought to be preferred before the other; "*Me ye have not always,* therefore use me while ye have me." Note, (1.) Christ's constant *bodily* presence was not to be expected here in this world; it was expedient that he should go away; his *real* presence in the eucharist is a fond and groundless conceit, and contradicts what he here said, *Me ye have not always.* (2.) Sometimes special works of piety and devotion should take place of common works of charity. The poor must not rob Christ; we must do good to all, but *especially to the household of faith.*

IV. Christ's approbation and commendation of the kindness of this good woman. The more his servants and their services are cavilled at by men, the more he manifests his acceptance of them. He calls it a *good work* (*v.* 10), and says more in praise of it than could have been imagined; particularly,

1. That the meaning of it was mystical (*v.* 12); *She did it for my burial.* (1.) Some think that she *intended* it so, and that the woman better understood Christ's frequent predictions of his death and sufferings than the apostles did; for which they were recompensed with the honour of being the first witnesses of his resurrection. (2.) However, Christ interpreted it so; and he is always willing to make the best, to make the most of his people's well-meant words and actions. This was as it were the embalming of his body; because the doing of that after his death would be prevented by his resurrection, it was therefore done before; for it was fit that it should be done some time, to show that he was still the Messiah, even when he seemed to be triumphed over by death. The disciples thought the ointment wasted, which was poured upon his head. "But," saith he, "if so much ointment were poured upon a dead body, according to the custom of your country, you would not grudge it, or think it waste. Now this is, in effect, so; the body she anoints is as good as dead, and her kindness is very seasonable for that purpose; therefore rather than call it waste, put it upon that score."

2. That the memorial of it should be honourable (*v.* 13); *This shall be told for a memorial.* This act of faith and love was so remarkable, that the preachers of Christ crucified, and the inspired writers of the history of his passion, could not choose but take notice of this passage, proclaim the notice of it, and perpetuate the memorial of it. And being once enrolled in these records, it was *graven as with an iron pen and lead in the rock for ever,* and could not possibly be forgotten. None of all the trumpets of fame sound so loud and so long as the everlasting gospel. Note, (1.) The story of the death of Christ, though a tragical one, is gospel, glad-tidings, because he died for us. (2.) The gospel was to be preached in the whole world; not in Judea only, but in every nation, to every creature. Let the disciples take notice of this, for their encouragement, that their sound should go to the ends of the earth. (3.) Though the honour of Christ is principally designed in the gospel, yet the honour of his saints and servants is not altogether overlooked. The memorial of this woman was to be preserved, not by dedicating a church to her, or keeping an annual feast in honour of her, or preserving a piece of her broken box for a sacred relic; but by mentioning her faith and piety in the preaching of the gospel, for example to others, Heb. vi. 12. Hereby honour redounds to Christ himself, who in this world, as well as in that to come, will be *glorified in his saints, and admired in all them that believe.*

14 Then one of the twelve, called
Judas Iscariot, went unto the chief
priests, 15 And said *unto them,* What
will ye give me, and I will deliver him
unto you? And they covenanted with
him for thirty pieces of silver. 16
And from that time he sought opportunity to betray him.

Immediately after an instance of the greatest kindness done to Christ, follows an instance of the greatest unkindness; such mixture is there of good and bad among the followers of Christ; he hath some faithful friends, and some false and feigned ones. What could be more base than this agreement which Judas here made with the chief priests, to betray Christ to them?

I. The traitor was Judas Iscariot; he is said to be *one of the twelve,* as an aggravation of his villany. When the *number of the disciples was multiplied* (Acts vi. 1), no marvel if there were some among them that were a shame and trouble to them; but when there were but twelve, and one of them was *a devil,* surely we must never expect any society perfectly pure on this side heaven. The twelve were Christ's chosen friends, that had the privilege of his special favour; they were his constant followers, that had the benefit of his most intimate converse, that upon all accounts had reason to love him and be true to him; and yet one of them betrayed him. Note, No bonds of duty or gratitude will hold those that have a devil, Mark v. 3, 4.

II. Here is the proffer which he made to the chief priests; he *went to them, and said, What will ye give me? v.* 15. They did not send for him, nor make the proposal to him; they could not have thought that one of Christ's own disciples should be false to him. Note, There are those, even among Christ's followers, that are worse than any one can imagine them to be, and want nothing but opportunity to show it.

Observe, 1. What Judas promised; "*I will deliver him unto you;* I will let you know where he is, and undertake to bring you to him, at such a convenient time and place that you may seize him without noise, or danger of an uproar." In their conspiracy against Christ, this was it they were at a loss about, *v.* 4, 5. They durst not meddle with him in public, and knew not where to find him in private. Here the matter rested, and the difficulty was insuperable; till Judas came, and offered them his service. Note, Those that give up themselves to be led by the devil, find him readier than they imagine to help them at a dead lift, as Judas did the chief priests. Though the rulers, by their power and interest, could kill him when they had him in their hands, yet none but a disciple could betray him. Note, The greater profession men make of religion, and the more they are employed in the study and service of it, the greater opportunity they have of doing mischief, if their hearts be not right with God. If Judas had not been an apostle, he could not have been a traitor; if men had not known the way of righteousness, they could not have abused it.

I will deliver him unto you. He did not offer himself, nor did they tamper with him, to be a witness against Christ, though they wanted evidence, *v.* 59. And if there had been any thing to be alleged against him, which had but the colour of proof that he was an impostor, Judas was the likeliest person to have attested it; but this is an evidence of the innocency of our Lord Jesus, that his own disciple, who knew so well his doctrine and manner of life, and was false to him, could not charge him with any thing criminal, though it would have served to justify his treachery.

2. What he asked in consideration of this undertaking; *What will ye give me?* This was the only thing that made Judas betray his Master; he hoped to get money by it: his Master had not given him any provocation, though he knew from the first that he *had a devil;* yet, for aught that appears, he showed the same kindness to him that he did to the rest, and put no mark of disgrace upon him that might disoblige him; he had placed him in a post that pleased him, had made him purse-bearer, and though he had embezzled the common stock (for he is called *a thief,* John xii. 6), yet we do not find he was in any danger of being called to account for it; nor does it appear that he had any suspicion that the gospel was a cheat: no, it was not the hatred of his Master, nor any quarrel with him, but purely the love of money; that, and nothing else, made Judas a traitor.

What will ye give me? Why, what did he want? Neither bread to eat, nor raiment to put on; neither necessaries nor conveniences. Was not he welcome, wherever his Master was? Did he not fare as he fared? Had he not been but just now nobly entertained at a supper in Bethany, in the house of Simon the leper, and a little before at another, where no less a person than Martha herself waited at table? And yet this covetous wretch could not be content, but comes basely cringing to the priests with, *What will ye give me?* Note, It is not the *lack* of money, but the *love* of money, that is the root of all evil, and particularly of apostasy from Christ; witness Demas, 2 Tim. iv. 10. Satan tempted our Saviour with this bait, *All these things will I give thee* (*ch.* iv. 9); but Judas offered himself to be tempted with it; he asks, *What will ye give me?* as if his Master was a commodity that stuck on his hands.

III. Here is the bargain which the chief priests made with him; *they covenanted with him for thirty pieces of silver;* thirty shekels, which in our money is about three pounds eight shillings, so some; three pounds fifteen shillings, so others. It should seem, Judas referred himself to them, and was willing to take what they were willing to give; he catches at the first offer, lest the next should be worse. Judas had not been wont to trade high, and therefore a little money went a great way with him. By the law (Exod. xxi. 32), thirty pieces of silver was the price of a slave—a goodly price, at which Christ was valued! Zech. xi. 13. No wonder that Zion's sons, though comparable to fine gold, are esteemed as earthen pitchers, when Zion's King himself was thus undervalued. They *covenanted with him; ἔστησαν—appenderunt—they paid it down,* so some; gave him his wages in hand, to secure him and to encourage him.

IV. Here is the industry of Judas, in pursuance of his bargain (*v.* 16); *he sought opportunity to betray him,* his head was still working to find out how he might do it effectually. Note, 1. It is a very wicked thing to seek opportunity to sin, and to devise mischief; for it argues the heart fully set in men to do evil, and a malice prepense. 2. Those that are *in,* think they must *on,* though the matter be ever so bad. After he had made that wicked bargain, he had time to repent, and to revoke it; but now by his covenant the devil has one hank more upon him than he had, and tells him that he must be true to his word, though ever so false to his Master, as Herod must behead John *for his oath's sake.*

17 Now the first *day* of the *feast*
of unleavened bread the disciples came
to Jesus, saying unto him, Where
wilt thou that we prepare for thee to
eat the passover? 18 And he said,
Go into the city to such a man, and
say unto him, The Master saith, My
time is at hand; I will keep the passover at thy house with my disciples.
19 And the disciples did as Jesus
had appointed them; and they made
ready the passover. 20 Now when
the even was come, he sat down with
the twelve. 21 And as they did eat,
he said, Verily I say unto you, that
one of you shall betray me. 22 And
they were exceeding sorrowful, and
began every one of them to say unto
him, Lord, is it I? 23 And he answered and said, He that dippeth *his*
hand with me in the dish, the same
shall betray me. 24 The Son of man
goeth as it is written of him: but woe
unto that man by whom the Son of
man is betrayed! it had been good
for that man if he had not been born.
25 Then Judas, which betrayed him,
answered and said, Master, is it I?
He said unto him, Thou hast said.

We have here an account of Christ's keeping the passover. Being made under the law, he submitted to all the ordinances of it, and to this among the rest; it was kept in remembrance of Israel's deliverance out of Egypt, the birth-day of that people; it was a tradition of the Jews, that in the days of the Messiah they should be redeemed on the very day of their coming out of Egypt; and it was exactly fulfilled, for Christ died the day after the passover, in which day they began their march.

I. The time when Christ ate the passover, was the usual time appointed by God, and observed by the Jews (*v.* 17); *the first day of the feast of unleavened bread,* which that year happened on the fifth day of the week, which is our Thursday. Some have advanced a suggestion, that our Lord Jesus celebrated the passover at this time of day sooner than other people did; but the learned Dr. Whitby has largely disproved it.

II. The place where, was particularly appointed by himself to the disciples, upon their enquiry (*v.* 17): they asked, *Where wilt thou that we prepare the passover?* Perhaps Judas was one of those that asked this question (where he would eat the passover), that he might know the better how to lay his train; but the rest of the disciples asked it as usual, that they might do their duty.

1. They took it for granted that their Master would eat the passover, though he was at this time persecuted by the chief priests, and his life sought; they knew that he would not be put by his duty, either by frightenings without or fears within. Those do not follow Christ's example who make it an excuse for their not attending on the Lord's supper, our gospel passover, that they have many troubles and many enemies, are full of care and fear; for, if so, they have the more need of that ordinance, to help to silence their fears, and comfort them under their troubles, to help them in forgiving their enemies, and casting all their cares on God.

2. They knew very well that there must be preparation made for it, and that it was their business, as his servants, to make preparation; *Where wilt thou that we prepare?* Note, Before solemn ordinances there must be solemn preparation.

3. They knew that he had no house of his own wherein to eat the passover; in this, as in other things, *for our sakes he became poor.* Among all Zion's palaces there was none for Zion's King; but his kingdom was not of this world. See John i. 11.

4. They would not pitch upon a place without direction from him, and from him they had direction; he sent them to *such a man* (*v.* 18), who probably was a friend and follower of his, and to his house he invited himself and his disciples.

(1.) Tell him, *My time is at hand;* he means the time of his death, elsewhere called *his hour* (John viii. 20; xiii. 1); the time, the hour, fixed in the counsel of God, which his heart was upon, and which he had so often spoken of. He knew when it was at hand, and was busy accordingly; we *know not our time* (Eccl. ix. 12), and therefore must never be off our watch; *our time is always ready* (John vii. 6), and therefore we must be always ready. Observe, Because his *time was at hand,* he would *keep the passover.* Note, The consideration of the near approach of death should quicken us to a diligent improvement of all our opportunities for our souls. Is our time at hand, and an eternity just before us? *Let us then keep the feast with the unleavened bread of sincerity.* Observe, When our Lord Jesus invited himself to this good man's house, he sent him this intelligence, that his time was at hand. Note, Christ's secret is with them that entertain him in their hearts. Compare John xiv. 21 with Rev. iii. 20.

(2.) Tell him, *I will keep the passover at thy house.* This was an instance of his authority, as *the Master,* which it is likely this man acknowledged; he did not beg, but command, the use of his house for this purpose. Thus, when Christ by his Spirit comes into the heart, he demands admission, as one whose own the heart is and cannot be denied, and he gains admission as one who has all power in the heart and cannot be resisted; if he saith, "I will keep a feast in such a soul," he will do it; for he works, and none can hinder; his people shall be willing, for he makes them so. *I will keep the passover with my disciples.* Note, Wherever Christ is welcome, he expects that his disciples should be welcome too. When we take God for our God, we take his people for our people.

III. The preparation was made by the disciples (*v.* 19); *They did as Jesus had appointed.* Note, Those who would have Christ's presence with them in the gospel passover, must strictly observe his instructions, and do as he directs; *They made ready the passover;* they got the lamb killed in the court of the temple, got it roasted, the bitter herbs provided, bread and wine, the cloth laid, and every thing set in readiness for such a sacred solemn feast.

IV. They ate the passover according to the law (*v.* 20); *He sat down,* in the usual table-gesture, not lying on one side, for it was not easy to eat, nor possible to drink, in that posture, but sitting upright, though perhaps sitting low. It is the same word that is used for his posture at other meals, *ch.* ix. 10; Luke vii. 37; *ch.* xxvi. 7. It was only the first passover in Egypt, as most think, that was eaten with *their loins girded, shoes on their feet, and staff in their hand,* though all that might be in a sitting posture. His sitting down, denotes the composedness of his mind, when he addressed himself to this solemnity; *He sat down with the twelve,* Judas not excepted. By the law, they were to *take a lamb for a household* (Exod. xii. 3, 4), which were to be not less than ten, nor more than twenty; Christ's disciples were his household. Note, They whom God has charged with families, must have their houses with them in serving the Lord.

V. We have here Christ's discourse with his disciples at the passover-supper. The usual subject of discourse at that ordinance, was the deliverance of Israel out of Egypt (Exod. xii. 26, 27); but the great Passover is now ready to be offered, and the discourse of that swallows up all talk of the other, Jer. xvi. 14, 15. Here is,

1. The general notice Christ gives his disciples of the treachery that should be among them (*v.* 21); *One of you shall betray me.* Observe, (1.) Christ knew it. We know not what troubles will befal us, nor whence they will arise: but Christ knew all his, which, as it proves his omniscience, so it magnifies his love, that he knew all things that should befal him, and yet did not draw back. He foresaw the treachery and baseness of a disciple of his own, and yet went on; took care of those that were given him, though he knew there was a Judas among them; would pay the price of our redemption, though he foresaw some would *deny the Lord that bought them;* and shed his blood, though he knew it would be *trodden under foot as an unholy thing.* (2.) When there was occasion, he let those about him know it. He had often told them that the Son of man should be betrayed; now he tells them that one of them should do it, that when they saw it, they might not only be the less surprised, but have their faith in him confirmed, John xiii. 19; xiv. 29.

2. The disciples' feelings on this occasion, *v.* 22. How did they take it?

(1.) *They were exceeding sorrowful.* [1.] It troubled them much to hear that their Master should be betrayed. When Peter was first told of it, he said, *Be it far from thee;* and therefore it must needs be a great trouble to him and the rest of them, to hear that it was very *near* to him. [2.] It troubled them more to hear that one of them should do it. It would be a reproach to the fraternity, for an apostle to prove a traitor, and this grieved them; gracious souls grieve for the sins of others, especially of those that have made a more than ordinary profession of religion, 2 Cor. xi 29. [3.] It troubled them most of all, that they were left at uncertainty which of them it was, and each of them was afraid for himself, lest, as Hazael speaks (2 Kings viii. 13), he was the *dog* that should *do this great thing.* Those that know the strength and subtlety of the tempter, and their own weakness and folly, cannot but be in pain for themselves, when they hear that *the love of many will wax cold.*

(2.) *They began every one of them to say, Lord, is it I?*

[1.] They were not apt to suspect Judas. Though he was *a thief,* yet, it seems, he had carried it so plausibly, that those who were intimate with him, were not jealous of him: none of them so much as looked upon him, much less said, *Lord, is it Judas?* Note, It is possible for a hypocrite to go through the world, not only undiscovered, but unsuspected; like bad money so ingeniously counterfeited that nobody questions it.

[2.] They were apt to suspect themselves; *Lord, is it I?* Though they were not conscious to themselves of any inclination that way (no such thought had ever entered into their mind), yet they feared the worst, and asked Him who knows us better than we know ourselves, *Lord, is it I?* Note, It well becomes the disciples of Christ always to be jealous over themselves with a godly jealousy, especially in trying times. We know not how strongly we may be tempted, nor how far God may leave us to ourselves, and therefore have reason, *not to be high-minded, but fear.* It is observable that our Lord Jesus, just before he instituted the Lord's supper, put his disciples upon this trial and suspicion of themselves, to teach us to examine and *judge ourselves, and so to eat of that bread, and drink of that cup.*

3. Further information given them concerning this matter (*v.* 23, 24), where Christ tells them, (1.) That the traitor was a familiar friend; *He that dippeth his hand with me in the dish,* that is, One of you that are now with me at the table. He mentions this, to make the treachery appear the more exceeding sinful. Note, External communion with Christ in holy ordinances is a great aggravation of our falseness to him. It is base ingratitude to dip with Christ in the dish, and yet betray him. (2.) That this was according to the scripture, which would take off the offence at it. Was Christ betrayed by a disciple? So it was written (Ps. lxi. 9); *He that did eat bread with me, hath lifted up his heel against me.* The more we see of the fulfilling of the scripture in our troubles, the better we may bear them. (3.) That it would prove a very dear bargain to the traitor; *Woe to that man by whom the Son of man is betrayed.* This he said, not only to awaken the conscience of Judas, and bring him to repent, and revoke his bargain, but for warning to all others to take heed of sinning like Judas; though God can serve his own purposes by the sins of men, that doth not make the sinner's condition the less woeful; *It had been good for that man, if he had not been born.* Note, The ruin that attends those who betray Christ, is so great, that it were more eligible by far not to be at all than to be thus miserable.

4. The conviction of Judas, *v.* 25. (1.) He asked, *Is it I?* to avoid coming under the suspicion of guilt by his silence. He knew very well that it was he, and yet wished to appear a stranger to such a plot. Note, Many whose consciences condemn them are very industrious to justify themselves before men, and put a good face on it, with, *Lord, is it I?* He could not but know that Christ knew, and yet trusted so much to his courtesy, because he had hitherto concealed it, that he had the impudence to challenge him to tell: or, perhaps, he was so much under the power of infidelity, that he imagined Christ did not know it, as those who said, *The Lord shall not see* (Ps. xciv. 7), and asked, *Can he judge through the dark clouds?* (2.) Christ soon answered this question; *Thou hast said,* that is, It is as thou hast said. This is not spoken out so plainly as Nathan's, *Thou art the man;* but it was enough to convict him, and, if his heart had not been wretchedly hardened, to have broken the neck of his plot, when he saw it discovered to his Master, and discovered by him. Note, They who are contriving to betray Christ, will, some time or other, betray themselves, and *their own tongues will fall upon them.*

26 And as they were eating, Jesus
took bread, and blessed *it,* and brake
it, and gave *it* to the disciples, and
said, Take, eat; this is my body. 27
And he took the cup, and gave thanks,
and gave *it* to them, saying, Drink ye
all of it; 28 For this is my blood of
the new testament, which is shed for
many for the remission of sins. 29
But I say unto you, I will not drink
henceforth of this fruit of the vine,
until that day when I drink it new
with you in my Father's kingdom.
30 And when they had sung an
hymn, they went out into the mount
of Olives.

We have here the institution of the great gospel ordinance of the Lord's supper, which was received of the Lord. Observe,

I. The time when it was instituted—*as they were eating.* At the latter end of the passover-supper, before the table was drawn, because, as a feast upon a sacrifice, it was to come in the room of that ordinance. Christ is to us the Passover-sacrifice by which atonement is made (1 Cor. v. 7); *Christ our Passover is sacrificed for us.* This ordinance is to us the passover-supper, by which application is made, and commemoration celebrated, of a much greater deliverance than that of Israel out of Egypt. All the legal sacrifices of propitiation being summed up in the death of Christ, and so abolished, all the legal feasts of rejoicing were summed up in this sacrament, and so abolished.

II. The institution itself. A sacrament must be instituted; it is no part of moral worship, nor is it dictated by natural light, but has both its being and significancy from the institution, from a divine institution; it is his prerogative who established the covenant, to appoint the seals of it. Hence the apostle (1 Cor. xi. 23, &c.), in that discourse of his concerning this ordinance, all along calls Jesus Christ *the Lord,* because, as *Lord,* as Lord of the covenant, Lord of the church, he appointed this ordinance. In which,

1. The body of Christ is signified and represented by bread; he had said formerly (John vi. 35), *I am the bread of life,* upon which metaphor this sacrament is built; as the life of the body is supported by bread, which is therefore put for all bodily nourish-

ment (*ch.* iv. 4; vi. 11), so the life of the soul is supported and maintained by Christ's mediation.

(1.) *He took bread, τὸν ἄρτον—the loaf;* some loaf that lay ready at hand, fit for the purpose; it was, probably, unleavened bread; but, that circumstance not being taken notice of, we are not to bind ourselves to that, as some of the Greek churches do. His taking the bread was a solemn action, and was, probably, done in such a manner as to be observed by them that sat with him, that they might expect something more than ordinary to be done with it. Thus was the Lord Jesus set apart in the counsels of divine love for the working out of our redemption.

(2.) *He blessed it;* set it apart for this use by prayer and thanksgiving. We do not find any set form of words used by him upon this occasion; but what he said, no doubt, was accommodated to the business in hand, that new testament which by this ordinance was to be sealed and ratified. This was like God's *blessing the seventh day* (Gen. ii. 3), by which it was separated to God's honour, and made to all that duly observe it, a blessed day: Christ could command the blessing, and we, in his name, are emboldened to beg the blessing.

(3.) *He brake it;* which denotes, [1.] The breaking of Christ's body for us, that it might be fitted for our use; *He was bruised for our iniquities,* as *bread-corn is bruised* (Isa. xxviii. 28); though *a bone of him was not broken* (for all his breaking did not weaken him), yet his flesh was *broken with breach upon breach,* and his wounds were multiplied (Job ix. 17; xvi. 14), and that pained him. God complains that he is broken with the *whorish heart* of sinners (Ezek. vi. 9); his law broken, our covenants with him broken; now justice requires *breach for breach* (Lev. xxiv. 20), and Christ was broken, to satisfy that demand. [2.] The breaking of Christ's body to us, as the father of the family breaks the bread to the children. The breaking of Christ to us, is to facilitate the application; every thing is made ready for us by the grants of God's word and the operations of his grace.

(4.) *He gave it to his disciples,* as the Master of the family, and the Master of this feast; it is not said, He gave it *to the apostles,* though they were so, and had been often called so before this, but *to the disciples,* because all the disciples of Christ have a right to this ordinance; and those shall have the benefit of it who are his disciples indeed; yet he gave it to them as he did the multiplied loaves, by them to be handed to all his other followers.

(5.) *He said, Take, eat; this is my body,* *v.* 26. He here tells them,

[1.] What they should do with it; "*Take, eat;* accept of Christ as he is offered to you, receive the atonement, approve of it, consent to it, come up to the terms on which the benefit of it is proposed to you; submit to his grace and to his government." Believing on Christ is expressed by *receiving him* (John i. 12), and *feeding upon him,* John vi. 57, 58. Meat looked upon, or the dish ever so well garnished, will not nourish us; it must be fed upon: so must the doctrine of Christ.

[2.] What they should have with it; *This is my body,* not οὗτος—*this bread,* but τοῦτο—*this eating and drinking.* Believing carries all the efficacy of Christ's death to our souls. *This is my body,* spiritually and sacramentally; this signifies and represents my body. He employs sacramental language, like that, Exod. xii. 11. *It is the Lord's passover.* Upon a carnal and much-mistaken sense of these words, the church of Rome builds the monstrous doctrine of Transubstantiation, which makes the bread to be changed into the substance of Christ's body, only the accidents of bread remaining; which affronts Christ, destroys the nature of a sacrament, and gives the lie to our senses. We partake of the sun, not by having the bulk and body of the sun put into our hands, but the beams of it darted down upon us; so we partake of Christ by partaking of his grace, and the blessed fruits of the breaking of his body.

2. The blood of Christ is signified and represented by the wine; to make it a complete feast, here is not only bread to strengthen, but wine to *make glad the heart* (*v.* 27, 28); *He took the cup,* the grace-cup, which was set ready to be drank, after thanks returned, according to the custom of the Jews at the passover; this Christ took, and made the sacramental-cup, and so altered the property. It was intended for a *cup of blessing* (so the Jews called it), and therefore St. Paul studiously distinguished between the cup of blessing which *we* bless, and that which *they* bless. *He gave thanks,* to teach us, not only in every ordinance, but in every part of the ordinance, to have our eyes up to God.

This cup he gave to the disciples,

(1.) With a command; *Drink ye all of it.* Thus he welcomes his guests to his table, obliges them all to drink of his cup. Why should he so expressly command them all to drink, and to see that none let it pass them, and press that more expressly in this than in the other part of the ordinance? Surely it was because he foresaw how in after-ages this ordinance would be dismembered by the prohibition of the cup to the laity, with an express *non obstante—notwithstanding* to the command.

(2.) With an explication; *For this is my blood of the New Testament.* Therefore drink it with appetite, delight, because it is so rich a cordial. Hitherto the blood of Christ had been represented by the blood of beasts, real blood: but, after it was actually shed, it was represented by the blood of grapes, metaphorical blood; so wine is called in an Old-Testament prophecy of Christ, Gen. xlix. 10, 11.

Now observe what Christ saith of his blood represented in the sacrament.

[1.] *It is my blood of the New Testament.*

The Old Testament was confirmed by the *blood of bulls and goats* (Heb. ix. 19, 20; Exod. xxiv. 8); but the New Testament with the blood of Christ, which is here distinguished from that; *It is my blood of the New Testament.* The covenant God is pleased to make with us, and all the benefits and privileges of it, are owing to the merits of Christ's death.

[2.] *It is shed;* it was not shed till next day, but it was now upon the point of being shed, it is as good as done. "Before you come to repeat this ordinance yourselves, it will be shed." He was *now ready to be offered,* and his blood to be poured out, as the blood of the sacrifices which made atonement.

[3.] *It is shed for many.* Christ came to confirm *a covenant with many* (Dan. ix. 27), and the intent of his death agreed. The blood of the Old Testament was shed for a few: it confirmed a covenant, which (saith Moses) the Lord has *made with you,* Exod. xxiv. 8. The atonement was made only *for the children of Israel* (Lev. xvi. 34): but Jesus Christ is a propitiation *for the sins of the whole world,* 1 John ii. 2.

[4.] *It is shed for the remission of sins,* that is, to purchase remission of sins for us. The redemption which we have through his blood, is *the remission of sins,* Eph. i. 7. The new covenant which is procured and ratified by the blood of Christ, is a charter of pardon, an act of indemnity, in order to a reconciliation between God and man; for sin was the only thing that made the quarrel, and *without shedding of blood is no remission,* Heb. ix. 22. The pardon of sin is that great blessing which is, in the Lord's supper, conferred upon all true believers; it is the foundation of all other blessings, and the spring of everlasting comfort, *ch.* ix. 2, 3. A farewell is now bidden to the fruit of the vine, *v.* 29. Christ and his disciples had now feasted together with a deal of comfort, in both an Old Testament and a New Testament festival, *fibula utriusque Testamenti—the connecting tie of both Testaments.* How amiable were these tabernacles! How good to be here! Never such a heaven upon earth as was at this table; but it was not intended for a perpetuity; he now told them (John xvi. 16), that *yet a little while and they should not see him: and again a little while and they should see him,* which explains this here.

First, He takes leave of such communion; *I will not drink henceforth of this fruit of the vine,* that is, now that I am no more in the world (John xvii. 11); I have had enough of it, and am glad to think of leaving it, glad to think that this is the last meal. *Farewell this fruit of the vine,* this passover-cup, this sacramental wine. Dying saints take their leave of sacraments, and the other ordinances of communion which they enjoy in this world, with comfort, for the joy and glory they enter into supersede them all; when the sun rises, farewell the candles.

Secondly, He assures them of a happy meeting again at last. It is a long, but not an everlasting, farewell; *until that day when I drink it new with you.* 1. Some understand it of the interviews he had with them after his resurrection, which was the first step of his exaltation *into the kingdom of his Father;* and though during those forty days he did not converse with them so constantly as he had done, yet he *did eat and drink with them* (Acts x. 41), which, as it confirmed their faith, so doubtless it greatly comforted their hearts, for they were overjoyed at it, Luke xxiv. 41. 2. Others understand it of the joys and glories of the future state, which the saints shall partake of in everlasting communion with the Lord Jesus, represented here by the pleasures of *a banquet of wine.* That will be the kingdom of his Father, for unto him shall the kingdom be then delivered up; *the wine of consolation* (Jer. xvi. 7) will there be always new, never flat or sour, as wine with long keeping; never nauseous or unpleasant, as wine to those that have drank much; but ever fresh. Christ will himself partake of those pleasures; it was *the joy set before him,* which he had in his eye, and all his faithful friends and followers shall partake with him.

Lastly, Here is the close of the solemnity with a hymn (*v.* 30); *They sang a hymn* or psalm; whether the psalms which the Jews usually sang at the close of the passover-supper, which they called *the great hallel,* that is, Ps. cxiii. and the five that follow it, or whether some new hymn more closely adapted to the occasion, is uncertain; I rather think the former; had it been new, John would not have omitted to record it. Note, 1. Singing of psalms is a gospel-ordinance. Christ's removing the hymn from the close of the passover to the close of the Lord's supper, plainly intimates that he intended that ordinance should continue in his church, that, as it had not its birth with the ceremonial law, so it should not die with it. 2. It is very proper after the Lord's supper, as an expression of our joy in God through Jesus Christ, and a thankful acknowledgment of that great love wherewith God has loved us in him. 3. It is not unseasonable, no, not in times of sorrow and suffering; the disciples were in sorrow, and Christ was entering upon his sufferings, and yet they could sing a hymn together. Our spiritual joy should not be interrupted by outward afflictions.

When this was done, they *went out into the mount of Olives.* He would not stay in the house to be apprehended, lest he should bring the master of the house into trouble; nor would he stay in the city, lest it should occasion an uproar; but he retired into the adjacent country, the mount of Olives, the same mount that David in his distress went *up the ascent of, weeping,* 2 Sam. xv. 30. They had the benefit of moon-light for this walk, for the passover was always at the full moon. Note, After we have received the Lord's supper, it is good for us to retire for prayer and meditation, and to be alone with God.

31 Then saith Jesus unto them,
All ye shall be offended because of
me this night: for it is written, I will
smite the shepherd, and the sheep of
the flock shall be scattered abroad.
32 But after I am risen again, I will
go before you into Galilee. 33 Peter
answered and said unto him, Though
all *men* shall be offended because of
thee, *yet* will I never be offended. 34
Jesus said unto him, Verily I say unto
thee, That this night, before the cock
crow, thou shalt deny me thrice. 35
Peter said unto him, Though I should
die with thee, yet will I not deny thee.
Likewise also said all the disciples.

We have here Christ's discourse with his disciples upon the way, as they were going to the mount of Olives. Observe,

I. A prediction of the trial which both he and his disciples were now to go through. He here foretels,

1. A dismal scattering storm just arising, *v.* 31.

(1.) That they should *all be offended because of Christ that very night;* that is, they would all be so frightened with the sufferings, that they would not have the courage to cleave to him in them, but would all basely desert him; *Because of me this night, ἐν ἐμοὶ ἐν τῇ νυκτὶ ταύτῃ—because of me, even because of this night;* so it might be read; that is, because of what happens to me this night. Note, [1.] Offences will come among the disciples of Christ in an hour of trial and temptation; it cannot be but they should, for they are weak; Satan is busy; God permits offences; even they whose hearts are upright may sometimes be overtaken with an offence. [2.] There are some temptations and offences, the effects of which are general and universal among Christ's disciples; *All you shall be offended.* Christ had lately discovered to them the treachery of Judas; but let not the rest be secure; though there will be but one traitor, they will be all deserters. This he saith, to alarm them all, that they might all watch. [3.] We have need to prepare for sudden trials, which may come to extremity in a very little time. Christ and his disciples had eaten their supper well together in peace and quietness; yet that very night proved such a night of offence. How soon may a storm arise! We know not what a day, or a night, may bring forth, nor what great event may be in the teeming womb of a little time, Prov. xxvii. 1. [4.] The cross of Christ is the great stumbling-block to many that pass for his disciples; both the cross he bore for us (1 Cor. i. 23), and that which we are called out to bear for him, *ch.* xvi. 24.

(2.) That herein the scripture would be fulfilled; *I will smite the Shepherd.* It is quoted from Zech. xiii. 7. [1.] Here is the smiting of the Shepherd in the sufferings of Christ. God awakens the sword of his wrath against the Son of his love, and he is smitten. [2.] The scattering of the sheep, thereupon, in the flight of the disciples. When Christ fell into the hands of his enemies, his disciples ran, one one way and another another; it was each one's care to shift for himself, and happy he that could get furthest from the cross.

2. He gives them the prospect of a comfortable gathering together again after this storm (*v.* 32); "*After I am risen again, I will go before you.* Though you will forsake me, I will not forsake you; though you fall, I will take care you shall not fall finally: we shall have a meeting again in Galilee, *I will go before you,* as the shepherd before the sheep." Some make the last words of that prophecy (Zech. xiii. 7), a promise equivalent to this here; *and I will bring my hand again to the little ones.* There is no bringing them back but by bringing his hand to them. Note, The captain of our salvation knows how to rally his troops, when, through their cowardice, they have been put into disorder.

II. The presumption of Peter, that he should keep his integrity, whatever happened (*v.* 33); *Though all men be offended, yet will I never be offended.* Peter had a great stock of confidence, and was upon all occasions forward to speak, especially to speak for himself; sometimes it did him a kindness, but at other times it betrayed him, as it did here. Where observe,

1. How he bound himself with a promise, that he would never be offended in Christ; not only not this night, but at no time. If this promise had been made in a humble dependence upon the grace of Christ, it had been an excellent word. Before the Lord's supper, Christ's discourse led his disciples to *examine* themselves with, *Lord, is it I?* For that is our preparatory duty; after the ordinance, his discourse leads them to an *engaging* of themselves to close walking, for that is the subsequent duty.

2. How he fancied himself better armed against temptation than any one else, and this was his weakness and folly; *Though all men shall be offended yet will not I.* This was worse than Hazael's, *What! is thy servant a dog?* For he supposed the thing to be so bad, that no man would do it. But Peter supposes it possible that *some,* nay that *all,* might be offended, and yet he escape better than any. Note, It argues a great degree of self-conceit and self-confidence, to think ourselves either safe from the temptations, or free from the corruptions, that are common to men. We should rather say, If it be possible that others may be offended, there is dan-

ger that I may be so. But it is common for those who think too well of themselves, easily to admit suspicions of others. See Gal. vi. 1.

III. The particular warning Christ gave Peter of what he would do, *v.* 34. He imagined that in the hour of temptation he should come off better than any of them, and Christ tells him that he should come off worse. The warning is introduced with a solemn asseveration; "*Verily, I say unto thee;* take my word for it, who know thee better than thou knowest thyself." He tells him,

1. That he should deny him. Peter promised that he would not be so much as offended in him, not desert him; but Christ tells him that he will go further, he will disown him. He said, "Though all men, yet not I;" and he did it sooner than any.

2. How quickly he should do it; *this night,* before to-morrow, nay, *before cock-crowing.* Satan's temptations are compared to *darts* (Eph. vi. 16), which wound ere we are aware; *suddenly doth he shoot.* As we know not how near we may be to trouble, so we know not how near we may be to sin; if God leave us to ourselves, we are always in danger.

3. How often he should do it; *thrice.* He thought that he should never once do such a thing; but Christ tells him that he would do it again and again; for, when once our feet begin to slip, it is hard to recover our standing again. *The beginnings of sin are as the letting forth of water.*

IV. Peter's repeated assurances of his fidelity (*v.* 35); *Though I should die with thee.* He supposed the temptation strong, when he said, *Though all men do it, yet will not I.* But here he supposeth it stronger, when he puts it to the peril of life; *Though I should die with thee.* He knew what he *should* do—rather die with Christ than deny him, it was the condition of discipleship (Luke xiv. 26); and he thought what he *would* do—never be false to his Master whatever it cost him; yet, it proved, he was. It is easy to talk boldly and carelessly of death at a distance; "I will rather die than do such a thing:" but it is not so soon done as said, when it comes to the setting-to, and death shows itself in its own colours.

What Peter said the rest subscribed to; *likewise also said all the disciples.* Note, 1. There is a proneness in good men to be over-confident of their own strength and stability. We are ready to think ourselves able to grapple with the strongest temptations, to go through the hardest and most hazardous services, and to bear the greatest afflictions for Christ; but it is because we do not know ourselves. 2. Those often fall soonest and foulest that are most confident of themselves. Those are least safe that are most secure. Satan is most active to seduce such; they are most off their guard, and God leaves them to themselves, to humble them. See 1 Cor. x. 12.

36 Then cometh Jesus with them
unto a place called Gethsemane, and
saith unto the disciples, Sit ye here,
while I go and pray yonder. 37 And
he took with him Peter and the two
sons of Zebedee, and began to be
sorrowful and very heavy. 38 Then
saith he unto them, My soul is exceeding
sorrowful, even unto death: tarry
ye here, and watch with me. 39 And
he went a little farther, and fell on
his face, and prayed, saying, O my
Father, if it be possible, let this cup
pass from me: nevertheless not as I
will, but as thou *wilt.* 40 And he
cometh unto the disciples, and findeth
them asleep, and saith unto Peter,
What, could ye not watch with me
one hour? 41 Watch and pray, that
ye enter not into temptation: the spirit
indeed *is* willing, but the flesh *is* weak.
42 He went away again the second
time, and prayed, saying, O my Father,
if this cup may not pass away
from me, except I drink it, thy will be
done. 43 And he came and found
them asleep again: for their eyes were
heavy. 44 And he left them, and
went away again, and prayed the third
time, saying the same words. 45
Then cometh he to his disciples, and
saith unto them, Sleep on now, and
take *your* rest: behold, the hour is
at hand, and the Son of man is betrayed
into the hands of sinners. 46
Rise, let us be going: behold he is at
hand that doth betray me.

Hitherto, we have seen the preparatives for Christ's sufferings; now, we enter upon the bloody scene. In these verses we have the story of his agony in the garden. This was the beginning of sorrows to our Lord Jesus. Now the *sword of the Lord* began to awake against *the man that was his Fellow; and how should it be quiet when the Lord had given it a charge?* The clouds had been gathering a good while, and looked black. He had said, some days before, *Now is my soul troubled,* John xii. 27. But now the storm began in good earnest. He put himself into this agony, before his enemies gave him any trouble, to show that he was a Free-will offering; that his life was not forced from him, but he *laid it down of himself.* John x. 18. Observe,

I. The place where he underwent this mighty agony; it was *in a place called Gethsemane.* The name signifies, *torculus olei—an olive-mill,* a press for olives, like a wine-press, where they *trod the olives,* Mic. vi. 15. And this was the proper place for such a thing, at the foot of the mount of Olives. There our Lord Jesus began his passion; there it pleased the Lord to bruise him, and crush him, that fresh oil might flow to all believers from him, that we might partake of the root and fatness of that *good Olive.* There he trod the wine-press of his Father's wrath, and trod it alone.

II. The company he had with him, when he was in this agony.

1. He took all the twelve disciples with him to the garden, except Judas, who was at this time otherwise employed. Though it was late in the night, near bed-time, yet they kept with him, and took this walk by moonlight with him, as Elisha, who, when he was told that his master should shortly be taken from his head, declared that he *would not leave him,* though he *led him about;* so these follow the Lamb, wheresoever he goes.

2. He took only Peter, and James, and John, with him into that corner of the garden where he suffered his agony. He left the rest at some distance, perhaps at the garden door, with this charge, *Sit ye here, while I go and pray yonder;* like that of Abraham to his *young men* (Gen. xxii. 5), *Abide ye here, and I will go yonder and worship.* (1.) Christ went to pray alone, though he had lately prayed with his disciples, John xvii. 1. Note, Our prayers with our families must not excuse us from our secret devotions. (2.) He ordered them to sit here. Note, We must take heed of giving any disturbance or interruption to those who retire for secret communion with God. He took these three with him, because they had been the witnesses of his glory in his transfiguration (*ch.* xvii. 1, 2), and that would prepare them to be the witnesses of his agony. Note, Those are best prepared to suffer with Christ, that have by faith beheld his glory, and have conversed with the glorified saints upon the holy mount. *If we suffer with Christ, we shall reign with him;* and if we hope to reign with him, why should we not expect to suffer with him?

III. The agony itself that he was in; *He began to be sorrowful, and very heavy.* It is called an agony (Luke xxii. 44), a conflict. It was not any bodily pain or torment that he was in, nothing occurred to hurt him; but, whatever it was, it was from within; he troubled himself, John xi. 33. The words here used are very emphatical; he began λυπεῖσθαι καὶ ἀδημονεῖν—*to be sorrowful, and in a consternation.* The latter word signifies such a sorrow as makes a man neither fit for company nor desirous of it. He had like a weight of lead upon his spirits. Physicians use a word near akin to it, to signify the disorder a man is in in a fit of an ague, or beginning of a fever. Now was fulfilled, Ps. xxii. 14, *I am poured out like water, my heart is like wax, it is melted;* and all those passages in the Psalms where David complains of the sorrows of his soul, Ps. xviii. 4, 5; xlii. 7; lv. 4, 5; lxix. 1—3; lxxxviii. 3; cxvi. 3, and Jonah's complaint, *ch.* ii. 4, 5.

But what was the cause of all this? What was it that put him into this agony? *Why art thou cast down,* blessed Jesus, and *why disquieted?* Certainly, it was nothing of despair or distrust of his Father, much less any conflict or struggle with him. As the Father loved him because he laid down his life for the sheep, so he was entirely subject to his Father's will in it. But,

1. He engaged in an encounter with the powers of darkness; so he intimates (Luke xxii. 53); *This is your hour, and the power of darkness:* and he spoke of it just before (John xiv. 30, 31); "*The prince of this world cometh.* I see him rallying his forces, and preparing for a general assault; but *he has nothing in me,* no garrisons in his interest, none that secretly hold correspondence with him; and therefore his attempts, though fierce, will be fruitless: but *as the Father gave me commandment, so I do;* however it be, I must have a struggle with him, the field must be fairly fought; and therefore *arise, let us go hence,* let us hasten to the field of battle, and meet the enemy." Now is the close engagement in single combat between Michael and the dragon, hand to hand; *now is the judgment of this world;* the great cause is now to be determined, and the decisive battle fought, in which the *prince of this world* will certainly be beaten and *cast out,* John xii. 31. Christ, when he works salvation, is described like a champion taking the field, Isa. lix. 16—18. Now the serpent makes his fiercest onset on the seed of the woman, and directs his sting, the sting of death, to his very heart; *animamque in vulnere ponit—and the wound is mortal.*

2. He was now *bearing the iniquities* which the Father laid upon him, and, by his sorrow and amazement, he accommodated himself to his undertaking. The sufferings he was entering upon were for our sins; they were all made to meet upon him, and he knew it. As we are obliged to be sorry for our particular sins, so was he grieved for the sins of us all. So Bishop Pearson, p. 191. Now, *in the valley of Jehoshaphat,* where Christ now was, God *gathered all nations,* and *pleaded with them in his* Son, Joel iii. 2, 12. He knew the malignity of the sins that were laid upon him, how provoking to God, how ruining to man; and these being all set in order before him, and charged upon him, he was *sorrowful and very heavy.* Now it was that *iniquities took hold on him;* so that he was *not able to look up,* as was foretold concerning him, Ps. xl. 7, 12.

3. He had a full and clear prospect of all the sufferings that were before him. He foresaw the treachery of Judas, the unkindness of Peter, the malice of the Jews, and their base ingratitude. He knew that he should now in a few hours be scourged, spit

upon, crowned with thorns, nailed to the cross; death in its most dreadful appearances, death in pomp, attended with all its terrors, looked him in the face; and this made him sorrowful, especially because it was the wages of our sin, which he had undertaken to satisfy for. It is true, the martyrs that have suffered for Christ, have entertained the greatest torments, and the most terrible deaths, without any such sorrow and consternation; have called their prisons their delectable orchards, and a bed of flames a bed of roses: but then, (1.) Christ was now denied the supports and comforts which they had; that is, he denied them to himself, and *his soul refused to be comforted*, not in passion, but in justice to his undertaking. Their cheerfulness under the cross was owing to the divine favour, which, for the present, was suspended from the Lord Jesus. (2.) His sufferings were of another nature from theirs. St. Paul, when he is to be offered upon the sacrifice and service of the saints' faith, can *joy and rejoice with them all;* but to be offered a sacrifice, to make atonement for sin, is quite a different case. On the saints' cross there is a blessing pronounced, which enables them to rejoice under it (*ch.* v. 10, 12); but to Christ's cross there was a curse annexed, which made him sorrowful and very heavy under it. And his sorrow under the cross was the foundation of their joy under it.

IV. His complaint of this agony. Finding himself under the arrests of his passion, he goes to his disciples (*v.* 38), and,

1. He acquaints them with his condition; *My soul is exceedingly sorrowful, even unto death.* It gives some little ease to a troubled spirit, to have a friend ready to unbosom itself to, and give vent to its sorrows. Christ here tells them, (1.) What was the seat of his sorrow; it was his soul that was now in an agony. This proves that Christ had a true human soul; for he suffered, not only in his body, but in his soul. We had sinned both against our own bodies, and against our souls; both had been used in sin, and both had been wronged by it; and therefore Christ suffered in soul as well as in body. (2.) What was the degree of his sorrow. He was *exceedingly sorrowful, περίλυποσ—compassed about with sorrow on all hands.* It was sorrow in the highest degree, even unto death; it was a killing sorrow, such sorrow as no mortal man could bear and live. He was ready to die for grief; they were sorrows of death. (3.) The duration of it; it will continue even unto death. "My soul will be sorrowful as long as it is in this body; I see no outlet but death." He now *began* to be sorrowful, and never ceased to be so till he said, *It is finished;* that grief is now finished, which began in the garden. It was prophesied of Christ, that he should be *a Man of sorrows* (Isa. liii. 3); he was so all along, we never read that he laughed; but all his sorrows hitherto were nothing to this

2. He bespeaks their company and attendance; *Tarry ye here, and watch with me.* Surely he was destitute indeed of help, when he entreated theirs, who, he knew, would be but miserable comforters; but he would hereby teach us the benefit of the communion of saints. It is good to have, and therefore good to seek, the assistance of our brethren, when at any time we are in an agony; *for two are better than one.* What he said to them, he saith to all, *Watch,* Mark xiii. 37. Not only watch for him, in expectation of his future coming, but watch with him, in application to our present work.

V. What passed between him and his Father when he was in this agony; *Being in an agony, he prayed.* Prayer is never out of season, but it is especially seasonable in an agony.

Observe, 1. The place where he prayed; *He went a little further,* withdrew from them, that the scripture might be fulfilled, *I have trod the wine-press alone;* he retired for prayer; a troubled soul finds most ease when it is alone with God, who understands the broken language of sighs and groans. Calvin's devout remark upon this is worth transcribing, *Utile est seorsim orare, tunc enim magis familiariter sese denudat fidelis animus, et simplicius sua vota, gemitus, curas, pavores, spes, et gaudia in Dei sinum exonerat—It is useful to pray apart; for then the faithful soul develops itself more familiarly, and with greater simplicity pours forth its petitions, groans, cares, fears, hopes, and joys, into the bosom of God.* Christ has hereby taught us that secret prayer must be made secretly. Yet some think that even the disciples whom he left at the garden door, overheard him; for it is said (Heb. v. 7), they were *strong cries.*

2. His posture in prayer; *He fell on his face;* his lying prostrate denotes, (1.) The agony he was in, and the extremity of his sorrow. Job, in great grief, *fell on the ground;* and great anguish is expressed by *rolling in the dust,* Mic. i. 10. (2.) His humility in prayer. This posture was an expression of his, *ἐνλαβεία—his reverential fear* (spoken of Heb. v. 7), with which he offered up these prayers: and it was *in the days of his flesh,* in his estate of humiliation, to which hereby he accommodated himself.

3. The prayer itself; wherein we may observe three things.

(1.) The title he gives to God; *O my Father.* Thick as the cloud was, he could see God as a Father through it. Note, In all our addresses to God we should eye him as a Father, as our Father; and it is in a special manner comfortable to do so, when we are in an agony. It is a pleasing string to harp upon at such a time, *My Father;* whither should the child go, when any thing grieves him, but to his father?

(2.) Thefavour he begs; *If it be possible, let this cup pass from me.* He calls his sufferings a *cup;* not a river, not a sea, but a cup, which we shall soon see the bottom of. When we are under troubles, we should make the best, the least, of them, and not aggravate them. His sufferings might be called a *cup*, because allotted him, as at feasts a cup was set to every mess. He begs that this cup might *pass from him*, that is, that he might avoid the sufferings now at hand; or, at least, that they might be shortened. This intimates no more than that he was really and truly Man, and as a Man he could not but be averse to pain and suffering. This is the first and simple act of man's will—to start back from that which is sensibly grievous to us, and to desire the prevention and removal of it. The law of self-preservation is impressed upon the innocent nature of man, and rules there till overruled by some other law; therefore Christ admitted and expressed a reluctance to suffer, to show that he was *taken from among men* (Heb. v. 1), was touched with *the feeling of our infirmities* (Heb. iv. 15), and *tempted as we are; yet without sin.* Note, A prayer of faith against an affliction, may very well consist with the patience of hope under affliction. When David had said, *I was dumb, I opened not my mouth, because thou didst it;* his very next words were, *Remove thy stroke away from me*, Ps. xxxix. 9, 10. But observe the proviso; *If it be possible.* If God may be glorified, man saved, and the ends of his undertaking answered, without his drinking of this bitter cup, he desires to be excused; otherwise not. What we cannot do with the securing of our great end, we must reckon to be in effect impossible; Christ did so. *Id possumus quod jure possumus—We can do that which we can do lawfully.* We *can* do nothing, not only we *may* do nothing, against the truth.

(3.) His entire submission to, and acquiescence in, the will of God; *Nevertheless, not as I will, but as thou wilt.* Not that the human will of Christ was adverse or averse to the divine will; it was only, in its first act, diverse from it; to which, in the second act of the will, which compares and chooses, he freely submits himself. Note, [1.] Our Lord Jesus, though he had a quick sense of the extreme bitterness of the sufferings he was to undergo, yet was freely willing to submit to them for our redemption and salvation, and *offered himself, and gave himself, for us.* [2.] The reason of Christ's submission to his sufferings, was, his Father's will; *as thou wilt, v.* 39. He grounds his own willingness upon the Father's will, and resolves the matter wholly into that; *therefore* he did what he did, and did it with delight, because it was the will of God, Ps. xl. 8. This he had often referred to, as that which put him upon, and carried him through, his whole undertaking; *This is the Father's will,* John vi. 39, 40. This he sought (John v. 30); it was his *meat and drink* to do it, John iv. 34. [3.] In conformity to this example of Christ, we must drink of the bitter cup which God puts into our hands, be it ever so bitter; though nature struggle, grace must submit. We then are disposed as Christ was, when our wills are in every thing melted into the will of God, though ever so displeasing to flesh and blood; *The will of the Lord be done,* Acts xxi. 14.

4. The repetition of the prayer; *He went away again the second time, and prayed* (*v.* 42), and again the third time (*v.* 44), and all to the same purport; only, as it is related here, he did not, in the second and third prayer, expressly ask that the cup might pass from him, as he had done in the first. Note, Though we may pray to God to prevent and remove an affliction, yet our chief errand, and that which we should most insist upon, must be, that he will give us grace to bear it well. It should be more our care to get our troubles sanctified, and our hearts satisfied under them, than to get them taken away. *He prayed, saying, Thy will be done.* Note, Prayer is the offering up, not only of our desires, but of our resignations, to God. It amounts to an acceptable prayer, when at any time we are in distress, to refer ourselves to God, and to commit our way and work to him; *Thy will be done.* The third time he *said the same words, τὸν ἀυτὸν λόγον—the same word*, that is, the same matter or argument; he spoke to the same purport. We have reason to think that this was not all he said, for it should seem by *v.* 40 that he continued *an hour* in his agony and prayer; but, whatever more he said, it was to this effect, deprecating his approaching sufferings, and yet resigning himself to God's will in them, in the expressions of which we may be sure he was not straitened.

But what answer had he to this prayer? Certainly it was not made in vain; he that heard him *always*, did not deny him *now.* It is true, the cup did not pass from him, for he withdrew that petition, and did not insist upon it (if he had, for aught I know, the cup had passed away); but he had an answer to his prayer; for, (1.) *He was strengthened with strength in his soul,* in the day when he cried (Ps. cxxxviii. 3); and that was a real answer, Luke xxii. 43. (2.) He was delivered from that which he feared, which was, lest by impatience and distrust he should offend his Father, and so disable himself to go on with his undertaking, Heb. v. 7. In answer to his prayer, God provided that he should not fail or be discouraged.

VI. What passed between him and his three disciples at this time; and here we may observe,

1. The fault they were guilty of; that when he was in his agony, sorrowful and heavy, sweating and wrestling and praying, they were so little concerned, that they could not keep awake; he comes, and *finds them asleep, v.* 40. The strangeness of the thing should have roused their spirits to *turn aside now, and see this great sight—the bush burning, and yet not consumed;* much more should

their love to their Master, and their care concerning him, have obliged them to a more close and vigilant attendance on him; yet they were so dull, that they could not keep their eyes open. What had become of us, if Christ had been now as sleepy as his disciples were? It is well for us that our salvation is in the hand of one who *neither slumbers nor sleeps.* Christ engaged them to watch with him, as if he expected some succour from them, and yet they slept; surely it was the unkindest thing that could be. When David wept at this mount of Olives, all his followers wept with him (2 Sam. xv. 30); but when the Son of David was here in tears, his followers were asleep. His enemies, who watched for him, were wakeful enough (Mark xiv. 43); but his disciples, who should have watched with him, were asleep. Lord, what is man! What are the best of men, when God leaves them to themselves! Note, Carelessness and carnal security, especially when Christ is in his agony, are great faults in any, but especially in those who profess to be nearest in relation to him. The church of Christ, which is his body, is often in an agony, fightings without and fears within; and shall we be asleep then, like Gallio, that *cared for none of these things;* or those (Amos vi. 6) that *lay at ease, and were not grieved for the affliction of Joseph?*

2. Christ's favour to them, notwithstanding. Persons in sorrow are too apt to be cross and peevish with those about them, and to lay it grievously to heart, if they but seem to neglect them; but Christ in his agony is as meek as ever, and carries it as patiently toward his followers as toward his Father, and is not apt to take things ill.

When Christ's disciples put this slight upon him,

(1.) *He came to them,* as if he expected to receive some comfort from them; and if they had put him in mind of what they had heard from him concerning his resurrection and glory perhaps it might have been some help to him; but, instead of that, they added grief to his sorrow; and yet he came to them, more careful for them than they were for themselves; when he was most engaged, yet he came to look after them; for those that were given him, were upon his heart, living and dying.

(2.) He gave them a gentle reproof, for as many as he loves he rebukes; he directed it to Peter, who used to *speak* for them; let him now *hear* for them. The reproof was very melting; *What! could ye not watch with me one hour?* He speaks as one amazed to see them so stupid; every word, when closely considered, shows the aggravated nature of the case. Consider, [1.] Who *they* were; "Could not *ye* watch—ye, my disciples and followers? No wonder if others neglect me, if *the earth sit still, and be at rest* (Zech. i. 11); but from you I expected better things." [2.] Who *he* was; "Watch with *me.* If one of yourselves were ill and in an agony, it would be very unkind not to watch with him; but it is undutiful not to watch with your Master, who has long watched over you for good, has led you, and fed you, and taught you, borne you, and borne with you; do ye thus requite him?" He awoke out of his sleep, to help them when they were in distress (*ch.* viii. 36); and could not they keep awake, at least to show their good-will to him, especially considering that he was now suffering *for them,* in an agony *for them? Jam tua res agitur—I am suffering in your cause.* [3.] How small a thing it was that he expected from them—only to *watch with him.* If he had bid them do some great thing, had bid them be in an agony with him, or die with him, they thought they could have done it; and yet they could not do it, when he only desired them to *watch with him,* 2 Kings v. 13. [4.] How short a time it was that he expected it—but *one hour;* they were not set upon the guard whole nights, as the prophet was (Isa. xxi. 8), only *one hour.* Sometimes he *continued all night in prayer to God,* but did not then expect that his disciples should watch with him; only now, when he had but one hour to spend in prayer.

(3.) He gave them good counsel; *Watch and pray, that ye enter not into temptation, v.* 41. [1.] There was an hour of temptation drawing on, and very near; the troubles of Christ were temptations to his followers to disbelieve and distrust him, to deny and desert him, and renounce all relation to him. [2.] There was danger of their entering into the temptation, as into a snare or trap; of their entering into a parley with it, or a good opinion of it, of their being influenced by it, and inclining to comply with it; which is the first step toward being overcome by it. [3.] He therefore exhorts them to watch and pray; *Watch with me, and pray with me.* While they were sleeping, they lost the benefit of joining in Christ's prayer. "Watch *yourselves,* and pray *yourselves.* Watch and pray against this present temptation to drowsiness and security; *pray* that you may *watch;* beg of God by his grace to keep you awake, now that there is occasion." When we are drowsy in the worship of God, we should pray, as a good Christian once did, "The Lord deliver me from this sleepy devil!" *Lord, quicken thou me in thy way.* Or, "Watch and pray against the further temptation you may be assaulted with; *watch and pray* lest this sin prove the inlet of many more." Note, When we find ourselves entering into temptation, we have need to watch and pray.

(4.) He kindly excused for them; *The spirit indeed is willing, but the flesh is weak.* We do not read of one word they had to say for themselves (the sense of their own weakness stopped their mouth); but then he had a tender word to say on their behalf, for it is his office to be an Advocate; in this he sets us an example of that love *which covers a multitude of sins.* He considered their frame, and did not chide them, for he remembered that they were but flesh; *and the flesh is weak, though the spirit be willing,* Ps. lxxviii. 38, 39. Note, [1.] Christ's disciples, as long as they are here in this world, have bodies as well as souls, and a principle of remaining corruption as well as of reigning grace, like Jacob and Esau in the same womb, *Canaanites* and *Israelites* in the same land, Gal. v. 17, 24. [2.] It is the unhappiness and burthen of Christ's disciples, that their bodies cannot keep pace with their souls in works of piety and devotion, but are many a time a cloud and clog to them; that, when the spirit is free and disposed to that which is good, the flesh is averse and indisposed. This St. Paul laments (Rom. vii. 25); *With my mind I serve the law of God, but with my flesh the law of sin.* Our impotency in the service of God is the great iniquity and infidelity of our nature, and it arises from these sad remainders of corruption, which are the constant grief and burthen of God's people. [3.] Yet it is our comfort, that our Master graciously considers this, and accepts the willingness of the spirit, and pities and pardons the weakness and infirmity of the flesh; for *we are under grace, and not under the law.*

(5.) Though they continued dull and sleepy, he did not any further rebuke them for it; for, though we daily offend, yet he will not always chide. [1.] When he came to them the second time, we do not find that he said any thing to them (*v.* 43); *he findeth them asleep again.* One would have thought that he had said enough to them to keep them awake; but it is hard to recover from a spirit of slumber. Carnal security, when once it prevails, is not easily shaken off. *Their eyes were heavy,* which intimates that they strove against it as much as they could, but were overcome by it, like the spouse; *I sleep, but my heart waketh* (Cant. v. 2); and therefore their Master looked upon them with compassion. [2.] When he came the third time, he left them to be alarmed with the approaching danger (*v.* 45, 46); *Sleep on now, and take your rest.* This is spoken ironically; "Now sleep if you can, sleep if you dare; I would not disturb you if Judas and his band of men would not." See here how Christ deals with those that suffer themselves to be overcome by security, and will not be awakened out of it. *First,* Sometimes he gives them up to the power of it; *Sleep on now.* He that will sleep, let him sleep still. The curse of spiritual slumber is the just punishment of the sin of it, Rom. xi. 8; Hos. iv. 17. *Secondly,* Many times he sends some startling judgment, to awaken those that would not be wrought upon by the word; and those who will not be alarmed by reasons and arguments, had better be alarmed by swords and spears than left to perish in their security. Let those that would not believe, be made to feel.

As to the disciples here, 1. Their Master gave them notice of the near approach of his enemies, who, it is likely, were now within sight or hearing, for they came with candles and torches, and, it is likely, made a great noise; *The Son of man is betrayed into the hands of sinners.* And again, *He is at hand that doth betray me.* Note, Christ's sufferings were no surprise to him; he knew what, and when, he was to suffer. By this time the extremity of his agony was pretty well over, or, at least, diverted; while with an undaunted courage he addresses himself to the next encounter, as a champion to the combat. 2. He called them to rise, and be going: not, "Rise, and let us flee from the danger;" but, "Rise, and let us go meet it;" before he had prayed, he feared his sufferings, but now he had got over his fears. But, 3. He intimates to them their folly, in sleeping away the time which they should have spent in preparation; now the event found them unready, and was a terror to them.

47 And while he yet spake, lo,
Judas, one of the twelve, came, and
with him a great multitude with swords
and staves, from the chief priests and
elders of the people. 48 Now he
that betrayed him gave them a sign,
saying, Whomsoever I shall kiss, that
same is he: hold him fast. 49 And
forthwith he came to Jesus, and said,
Hail, master; and kissed him. 50
And Jesus said unto him, Friend,
wherefore art thou come? Then came
they, and laid hands on Jesus, and
took him. 51 And, behold, one of
them which were with Jesus stretched
out *his* hand, and drew his sword, and
struck a servant of the high priest's,
and smote off his ear. 52 Then said
Jesus unto him, Put up again thy
sword into his place: for all they that
take the sword shall perish with the
sword. 53 Thinkest thou that I cannot now pray to my Father, and he
shall presently give me more than
twelve legions of angels? 54 But
how then shall the scriptures be fulfilled, that thus it must be? 55 In
that same hour said Jesus to the multitudes, Are ye come out as against a
thief with swords and staves for to
take me? I sat daily with you teaching in the temple, and ye laid no hold
on me. 56 But all this was done,
that the scriptures of the prophets

might be fulfilled. Then all the disciples forsook him, and fled.

We are here told how the blessed Jesus was seized, and taken into custody; this followed immediately upon his agony, *while he yet spake;* for from the beginning to the close of his passion he had not the least intermission or breathing-time, but *deep called unto deep.* His trouble hitherto was raised within himself; but now the scene is changed, now the Philistines are upon thee, thou blessed Samson; *the Breath of our nostrils, the Anointed of the Lord is taken in their pits,* Lam. iv. 20.

Now concerning the apprehension of the Lord Jesus, observe,

I. Who the persons were, that were employed in it. 1. Here was *Judas, one of the twelve,* at the head of this infamous guard: *he was guide to them that took Jesus* (Acts i. 16); without his help they could not have found him in this retirement. Behold, and wonder; the first that appears with his enemies, is one of his own disciples, who an hour or two ago was eating bread with him! 2. Here was *with him a great multitude;* that the scripture might be fulfilled, *Lord, how are they increased that trouble me!* Ps. iii. 1. This multitude was made up partly of a detachment out of the guards, that were posted in the tower of Antonia by the Roman governor; these were Gentiles, *sinners,* as Christ calls them, *v.* 45. The rest were the servants and officers of the High Priest, and they were Jews; they that were at variance with each other, agreed against Christ.

II. How they were armed for this enterprise.

1. What weapons they were armed with; They came *with swords and staves.* The Roman soldiers, no doubt, had swords; the servants of the priests, those of them that had not swords, brought staves or clubs. *Furor arma ministrat—Their rage supplied their arms.* They were not regular troops, but a tumultuous rabble. But wherefore is this ado? If they had been ten times as many, they could not have taken him had he not yielded; and, his hour being come for him to give up himself, all this force was needless. When a butcher goes into the field to take out a lamb for the slaughter, does he raise the militia, and come armed? No, he needs not; yet is there all this force used to seize the Lamb of God.

2. What warrant they were armed with; *They came from the chief priests, and elders of the people;* this armed multitude was sent by them upon this errand. He was taken up by a warrant from the great sanhedrim, as a person obnoxious to them. Pilate, the Roman governor, gave them no warrant to search for him, he had no jealousy of him; but they were men who pretended to religion, and presided in the affairs of the church, that were active in this prosecution, and were the most spiteful enemies Christ had. It was a sign that he was supported by a divine power, for by all earthly powers he was not only deserted, but opposed; Pilate upbraided him with it; *Thine own nation and the chief priests delivered thee to me,* John xviii. 35.

III. The manner how it was done, and what passed at that time.

1. How Judas betrayed him; he did his business effectually, and his resolution in this wickedness may shame us who fail in that which is good. Observe,

(1.) The instructions he gave to the soldiers (*v.* 48); *He gave them a sign;* as commander of the party in this action, he gives the word or signal. He *gave them a sign,* lest by mistake they should seize one of the disciples instead of him, the disciples having so lately said, in Judas's hearing, that they would be willing to die for him. What abundance of caution was here, not to miss him—*That same is he;* and when they had him in their hands, not to lose him—*Hold him fast;* for he had sometimes escaped from those who thought to secure him; as Luke iv. 30. Though the Jews, who frequented the temple, could not but know him, yet the Roman soldiers perhaps had never seen him, and the sign was to direct them; and Judas by his kiss intended not only to distinguish him, but to detain him, while they came behind him, and laid hands on him.

(2.) The dissembling compliment he gave his Master. He came close up to Jesus; surely now, if ever, his wicked heart will relent; surely when he comes to look him in the face, he will either be awed by its majesty, or charmed by its beauty. Dares he to come into his very sight and presence, to betray him? Peter denied Christ, but when *the Lord turned and looked* upon him, he relented presently; but Judas comes up to his Master's face, and betrays him. *Me mihi (perfide) prodis? me mihi prodis?—Perfidious man, betrayest thou me to thyself?* He said, *Hail, Master; and kissed him.* It should seem, our Lord Jesus had been wont to admit his disciples to such a degree of familiarity with him, as to give them his cheek to kiss after they had been any while absent, which Judas villanously used to facilitate this treason. A kiss is a token of allegiance and friendship, Ps. ii. 12. But Judas, when he broke all the laws of love and duty, profaned this sacred sign to serve his purpose. Note, There are many that betray Christ with *a kiss,* and *Hail, Master;* who, under pretence of doing him honour, betray and undermine the interests of his kingdom. *Mel in ore, fel in corde—Honey in the mouth, gall in the heart.* Καταφιλεῖν οὐκ ἐστι φιλεῖν *To embrace is one thing, to love is another. Philo Judæus.* Joab's kiss and Judas's were much alike.

(3.) The entertainment his Master gave him, *v.* 50.

[1.] He calls him *friend.* If he had called him *villain,* and *traitor, raca, thou fool,* and *child of the devil,* he had not *mis*-called him;

but he would teach us under the greatest provocation to forbear bitterness and evil-speaking, and to show all meekness. *Friend,* for a friend he had been, and should have been, and seemed to be. Thus he upbraids him, as Abraham, when he called the rich man in hell, *son.* He calls him *friend,* because he furthered his sufferings, and so *befriended* him; whereas, he called Peter *Satan* for attempting to hinder them.

[2.] He asks him, "*Wherefore art thou come?* Is it peace, Judas? Explain thyself; if thou come as an enemy, what means this kiss? If as a friend, what mean these swords and staves? *Wherefore art thou come?* What harm have I done thee? Wherein have I wearied thee? ἐφ' ᾧ πάρει—*Wherefore art thou present?* Why hadst thou not so much shame left thee, as to keep out of sight, which thou mightest have done, and yet have given the officers notice where I was?" This was an instance of great impudence, for him to be so forward and barefaced in this wicked transaction. But it is usual for apostates from religion to be the most bitter enemies to it; witness Julian. Thus Judas did his part.

2. How the officers and soldiers secured him; *Then came they, and laid hands on Jesus, and took him;* they made him their prisoner. *How were they not afraid to stretch forth their hands against the Lord's Anointed?* We may well imagine what rude and cruel hands they were, which this barbarous multitude laid on Christ; and now, it is probable, they handled him the more roughly for their being so often disappointed when they sought to lay hands on him. They could not have taken him, if he had not surrendered himself, and been *delivered by the determinate counsel and foreknowledge of God,* Acts ii. 23. He who said concerning his anointed servants, *Touch them not,* and *do them no harm* (Ps. cv. 14, 15), *spared not his anointed Son, but delivered him up for us all;* and again, *gave his strength into captivity, his glory into the enemies' hands,* Ps. lxxviii. 61. See what was the complaint of Job (*ch.* xvi. 11), *God hath delivered me to the ungodly,* and apply that and other passages in that book of Job as a type of Christ.

Our Lord Jesus was made a prisoner, because he would in all things be treated as a malefactor, punished for our crime, and as a surety under arrest for our debt. The yoke of our transgressions was bound by the Father's hand upon the neck of the Lord Jesus, Lam. i. 14. He became a prisoner, that he might set us at liberty; for he said, *If ye seek me, let these go their way* (John xviii. 8); and those are free indeed, whom he makes so.

3. How Peter fought for Christ, and was checked for his pains. It is here only said to be *one of them that were with Jesus in the garden;* but John xviii. 10, we are told that it was Peter who signalized himself upon this occasion. Observe,

(1.) Peter's rashness (*v.* 51); He *drew his sword.* They had but two swords among them all (Luke xxii. 38), and one of them, it seems, fell to Peter's share; and now he thought it was time to draw it, and he laid about him as if he would have done some great matter; but all the execution he did was the cutting off an ear from a servant of the High Priest; designing, it is likely, to cleave him down the head, because he saw him more forward than the rest in laying hands on Christ, he missed his blow. But if he would be striking, in my mind he should rather have aimed at Judas, and have marked him for a rogue. Peter had talked much of what he would do for his Master, he would *lay down his life for him;* yea, that he would; and now he would be as good as his word, and venture his life to rescue his Master: and thus far was commendable, that he had a great *zeal* for Christ, and his honour and safety; but it was not *according to knowledge,* nor guided by discretion; for [1.] He did it without warrant; some of the disciples asked indeed, *Shall we smite with the sword?* (Luke xxii. 49) But Peter struck before they had an answer We must see not only our cause good, but our call clear, before we draw the sword; we must show by what authority we do it, and who gave us that authority. [2.] He indiscreetly exposed himself and his fellow-disciples to the rage of the multitude; for what could they with two swords do against a band of men?

(2.) The rebuke which our Lord Jesus gave him (*v.* 52); *Put up again thy sword into its place.* He does not command the officers and soldiers to put up their swords that were drawn against him, he left them to the judgment of God, who judges them that are without; but he commands Peter to put up his sword, does not chide him indeed for what he had done, because done out of good will, but stops the progress of his arms, and provides that it should not be drawn into a precedent. Christ's errand into the world was to make peace. Note, *The weapons of our warfare are not carnal, but spiritual;* and Christ's ministers, though they are his soldiers, do not *war after the flesh,* 2 Cor. x. 3, 4. Not that the law of Christ overthrows either the law of nature or the law of nations, as far as those warrant subjects to stand up in defence of their civil rights and liberties, and their religion, when it is incorporated with them; but it provides for the preservation of public peace and order, by forbidding private persons, *qua tales—as such,* to resist the powers that are; nay, we have a general precept that we *resist not evil* (*ch.* v. 39), nor will Christ have his ministers propagate his religion by force of arms, *Religio cogi non potest; et defendenda non occidendo, sed moriendo—Religion cannot be forced; and it should be defended, not by killing, but by dying.* Lactantii Institut. As Christ forbade his disciples the sword of justice (*ch.* xx. 25, 26), so here the sword of war. Christ bade Peter put up his sword, and never bade him draw it again; yet that which Peter is here blamed for is his doing it unseasonably; the hour was come for Christ to suffer and die, he knew Peter knew it, the *sword of the Lord was drawn against him* (Zech. xiii. 7), and for Peter to draw his sword for him, was like, *Master, spare thyself.*

Three reasons Christ gives to Peter for this rebuke:

[1.] His drawing the sword would be dangerous to himself and to his fellow-disciples; *They that take the sword, shall perish with the sword;* they that use violence, fall by violence; and men hasten and increase their own troubles by blustering bloody methods of self-defence. They that take the sword before it is given them, that use it without warrant or call, expose themselves to the sword of war, or public justice. Had it not been for the special care and providence of the Lord Jesus, Peter and the rest of them had, for aught I know, been cut in pieces immediately. Grotius gives another, and a probable sense of this blow, making those that take the sword to be, not Peter, but the officers and soldiers that come with swords *to take Christ;* They shall *perish with the sword.* "Peter, thou needest not draw thy sword to punish them. God will certainly, shortly, and severely, reckon with them." They took the Roman sword to seize Christ with, and by the Roman sword, not long after, they and their place and nation were destroyed. *Therefore* we must not *avenge ourselves,* because *God will repay* (Rom. xii. 19); and therefore we must suffer with faith and patience, because persecutors will be paid in their own coin. See Rev. xiii. 10.

[2.] It was needless for him to draw his sword in defence of his Master, who, if he pleased, could summon into his service all the hosts of heaven (*v.* 53); "*Thinkest thou that I cannot now pray to my Father, and he shall send* from heaven effectual succours? Peter, if I would put by these sufferings, I could easily do it without thy hand or thy sword." Note, God has no need of us, of our services, much less of our sins, to bring about his purposes; and it argues our distrust and disbelief of the power of Christ, when we go out of the way of our duty to serve his interests. God can do his work without us; if we look into the heavens, and see how he is attended there, we may easily infer, that, *though we be righteous,* he is not beholden to us, Job xxxv. 5, 7. Though Christ was crucified through weakness, it was a voluntary weakness; he submitted to death, not because he could not, but because he would not contend with it. This takes off the offence of the cross, and proves Christ crucified the power of God; even now in the depth of his sufferings he could call in the aid of legions of angels. *Now, ἄρτι—yet;* "Though the business is so far gone, I could yet with a word speaking turn the scale." Christ here lets us know,

First, What a great interest he had in his Father; *I can pray to my Father, and he will send me help from the sanctuary.* I can *παρακαλέσαι—demand of my Father these succours.* Christ prayed *as one having authority.* Note, It is a great comfort to God's people, when they are surrounded with enemies on all hands, that they have a way open heavenward; if they can do nothing else, they can pray to him that can do every thing. And they who are much in prayer at other times, have most comfort in praying when troublesome times come. Observe, Christ saith, not only that God could send him such a number of angels, but that, if he insisted upon it, he would do it. Though he had undertaken the work of our redemption, yet, if he had desired to be released, it should seem by this that the Father would not have held him to it. He might yet have gone out free from the service, but he loved it, and would not; so that it was only with the cords of his own love that he was bound to the altar.

Secondly, What a great interest he had in the heavenly hosts; *He shall presently give me more than twelve legions of angels,* amounting to above seventy-two thousand. Observe here, 1. There is an *innumerable company of angels,* Heb. xii. 22. A detachment of more than twelve legions might be spared for our service, and yet there would be no miss of them about the throne. See Dan. vii. 10. They are marshalled in exact order, like the well-disciplined legions; not a confused multitude, but regular troops; all know their post, and observe the word of command. 2. This innumerable company of angels are all at the disposal of our heavenly Father, and do his pleasure, Ps. ciii. 20, 21. 3. These angelic hosts were ready to come in to the assistance of our Lord Jesus in his sufferings, if he had needed or desired it. See Heb. i. 6, 14. They would have been to him as they were to Elisha, *chariots of fire, and horses of fire,* not only to secure him, but to consume those that set upon him. 4. Our heavenly Father is to be eyed and acknowledged in all the services of the heavenly hosts; *He shall give them me:* therefore angels are not to be prayed to, but the Lord of the angels, Ps. xci. 11. 5. It is matter of comfort to all that wish well to the kingdom of Christ, that there is a world of angels always at the service of the Lord Jesus, that can do wonders. He that has the armies of heaven at his beck, can do what he pleases among the *inhabitants of the earth;* He shall *presently* give them me. See how ready his Father was to hear his prayer, and how ready the angels were to observe his orders; they are willing servants, winged messengers, they *fly swiftly.* This is very encouraging to those that have the honour of Christ, and the welfare of his church, much at heart. Think they that they have more care and concern for Christ and his church, than God and the holy angels have?

[3.] It was no time to make any defence at all, or to offer to put by the stroke; *For how then shall the scriptures be fulfilled, that thus it must be? v.* 54. It was written, that Christ should be *led as a lamb to the slaughter,* Isa. liii. 7. Should he summon the angels to his assistance, he would not be led to the slaughter at all; should he permit his disciples to fight, he would not be led as a lamb quietly and without resistance; therefore he and his disciples must yield to the accomplishment of the predictions. Note, In all difficult cases, the word of God must be conclusive against our own counsels, and nothing must be done, nothing attempted, against the fulfilling of the scripture. If the easing of our pains, the breaking of our bonds, the saving of our lives, will not consist with the fulfilling of the scripture, we ought to say, "Let God's word and will take place, let his law be magnified and made honourable, whatever becomes of us." Thus Christ checked Peter, when he set up for his champion, and captain of his life-guard.

4. We are next told how Christ argued the case with them that came to take him (*v.* 55); though he did not resist them, yet he did reason with them. Note, It will consist with Christian patience under our sufferings, calmly to expostulate with our enemies and persecutors, as David with Saul, 1 Sam. xxiv. 14; xxvi. 18. *Are ye come out,* (1.) With rage and enmity, *as against a thief,* as if I were an enemy to the public safety, and deservedly suffered this? Thieves draw upon themselves the common odium; every one will lend a hand to stop a thief: and thus they fell upon Christ as the offscouring of all things. If he had been the plague of his country, he could not have been prosecuted with more heat and violence. (2.) With all this power and force, as against the worst of thieves, that dare the law, bid defiance to public justice, and add rebellion to their sin? You are come out as against a thief, with swords and staves, as if there were danger of resistance; whereas ye have *killed the just One, and he doth not resist you,* Jam. v. 6. If he had not been willing to suffer, it was folly to *come with swords and staves, for they could not conquer him;* had he been minded to resist, he would have esteemed their iron as straw, and their swords and staves would have been as briars before a consuming fire; but, being willing to suffer, it was folly to come thus armed, for he would not contend with them.

He further expostulates with them, by reminding them how he had behaved himself hitherto toward them, and they toward him. [1.] Of his public appearance; *I sat daily with you in the temple teaching.* And, [2.] Of their public connivance; *Ye laid no hold on me.* How comes then this change? They were very unreasonable, in treating him as they did. *First,* He had given them no occasion to look upon him as a thief, for he had taught in the temple. And such were the matter, and such the manner of his teaching, that he was manifested in the consciences of all that heard him, not to be a bad man. Such gracious words as came from his mouth, were not the words of a thief, nor of one that had a devil. *Secondly,* Nor had he given them occasion to look upon him as one that absconded, or fled from justice, that they should come in the night to seize him; if they had any thing to say to him, they might find him every day in the temple, ready to answer all challenges, all charges, and there they might do as they pleased with him; for the chief priests had the custody of the temple, and the command of the guards about it; but to come upon him thus clandestinely, in the place of his retirement, was base and cowardly. Thus the greatest hero may be villanously assassinated in a corner, by one that in open field would tremble to look him in the face.

But all this was done (so it follows, *v.* 56) *that the scriptures of the prophets might be fulfilled.* It is hard to say, whether these are the words of the sacred historian, as a comment upon this story, and a direction to the Christian reader to compare it with the scriptures of the Old Testament, which pointed at it; or, whether they are the words of Christ himself, as a reason why, though he could not but resent this base treatment, he yet submitted to it, that the scriptures of the prophets might be fulfilled, to which he had just now referred himself, *v.* 54. Note, The scriptures are in the fulfilling every day; and all those scriptures which speak of the Messiah, had their full accomplishment in our Lord Jesus.

5. How he was, in the midst of this distress, shamefully deserted by his disciples; *They all forsook him, and fled, v.* 56.

(1.) This was their sin; and it was a great sin for them who had left all to follow him, now to leave him for they knew not what. There was unkindness in it, considering the relation they stood in to him, the favours they had received from him, and the melancholy circumstances he was now in. There was unfaithfulness in it, for they had solemnly promised to adhere to him, and never to forsake him. He had indented for their safe conduct (John xviii. 8); yet they could not rely upon that, but shifted for themselves by an inglorious flight. What folly was this, for fear of death to flee from him whom they themselves knew and had acknowledged to be the *Fountain of life?* John vi. 67, 68. *Lord, what is man!*

(2.) It was a part of Christ's suffering, it added affliction to his bonds, to be thus deserted, as it did to Job (*ch.* xix. 13), *He hath put my brethren far from me;* and to David (Ps. xxxviii. 11), *Lovers and friends stand aloof from my sore.* They should have staid with him, to minister to him, to countenance him, and, if need were, to be witnesses for him at his trial; but they treacherously deserted him, as, at St. Paul's *first answer, no man stood with him.* But there was a mystery in this. [1.] Christ, as a sacrifice for sins, stood thus abandoned. The deer that by the keeper's arrow is marked out to be hunted and run down, is immediately deserted by the whole herd. In this he was made a curse for us, being left as one separated to evil. [2.] Christ, as the Saviour of souls, stood thus alone; as he needed not, so he had not the assistance of any other in working out our salvation; he bore all, and did all himself. He *trod the wine-press alone,* and when there was *none to uphold,* then *his own arm wrought salvation,* Isa. lxiii. 3, 5. So *the Lord alone did lead his Israel,* and they *stand still, and only see this great salvation,* Deut. xxxii. 12.

57 And they that had laid hold on
Jesus led *him* away to Caiaphas the
high priest, where the scribes and the
elders were assembled. 58 But Peter
followed him afar off unto the high
priest's palace, and went in, and sat
with the servants, to see the end.
59 Now the chief priests, and elders,
and all the council, sought false
witness against Jesus, to put him to
death; 60 But found none: yea,
though many false witnesses came,
yet found they none. At the last
came two false witnesses, 61 And
said, This *fellow* said, I am able to
destroy the temple of God, and to
build it in three days. 62 And the
high priest arose, and said unto him,
Answerest thou nothing? what *is it*
which these witness against thee? 63
But Jesus held his peace. And the
high priest answered and said unto
him, I adjure thee by the living God,
that thou tell us whether thou be the
Christ, the Son of God. 64 Jesus
saith unto him, Thou hast said: nevertheless I say unto you, Hereafter
shall ye see the Son of man sitting
on the right hand of power, and coming in the clouds of heaven. 65 Then
the high priest rent his clothes, saying, He hath spoken blasphemy; what
further need have we of witnesses?
behold, now ye have heard his blasphemy. 66 What think ye? They
answered and said, He is guilty of
death. 67 Then did they spit in his
face, and buffeted him; and others
smote *him* with the palms of their
hands, 68 Saying, Prophesy unto us,
thou Christ, Who is he that smote thee?

We have here the arraignment of our Lord Jesus in the ecclesiastical court, before the great sanhedrim. Observe,

I. The sitting of the court; the scribes and the elders were assembled, though it was in the dead time of the night, when other people were fast asleep in their beds; yet, to gratify their malice against Christ, they denied themselves that natural rest, and sat up all night, to be ready to fall upon the prey which Judas and his men, they hoped, would *seize.*

See, 1. Who they were, that were assembled; the *scribes,* the principal teachers, and *elders,* the principal rulers, of the Jewish church: these were the most bitter enemies to Christ our great teacher and ruler, on whom therefore they had a jealous eye, as one that eclipsed them; perhaps some of these scribes and elders were not so malicious at Christ as some others of them were; yet, in concurrence with the rest, they made themselves guilty. Now the scripture was fulfilled (Ps. xxii. 16); *The assembly of the wicked have enclosed me.* Jeremiah complains of an assembly of treacherous men; and David of his enemies *gathering themselves together against him,* Ps. xxxv. 15.

2. Where they were assembled; *in the palace of Caiaphas the High Priest;* there they assembled two days before, to lay the plot (*v.* 3), and there they now convened again, to prosecute it. The *High Priest* was *Ab-beth-din—the father of the house of judgment,* but he is now the patron of wickedness; his house should have been the sanctuary of oppressed innocency, but it is become the throne of iniquity; and no wonder, when even God's house of prayer was made a den of thieves.

II. The setting of the prisoner to the bar; they that had *laid hold on Jesus, led him away,* hurried him, no doubt, with violence, led him as a trophy of their victory, led him as a victim to the altar; he was brought into Jerusalem through that which was called the *sheep-gate,* for that was the way into town from the mount of Olives; and it was so called because the sheep appointed for sacrifice were brought that way to the temple; very fitly therefore is Christ led that way, who is the Lamb of God, that takes away the sin of the world. Christ was led first to the High Priest, for by the law all sacrifices were to be first *presented to the priest, and delivered into his hand,* Lev. xvii. 5.

III. The cowardice and faint-heartedness of Peter (*v.* 58); *But Peter followed afar off.* This comes in here, with an eye to the following story of his denying him. He forsook him as the rest did, when he was seized, and what is here said of his following him is easily reconcilable with his forsaking him; such following was no better than forsaking him; for,

1. He followed him, but it was *afar off.* Some sparks of love and concern for his Master there were in his breast, and therefore he followed him; but fear and concern for his own safety prevailed, and therefore he

followed afar off. Note, It looks ill, and bodes worse, when those that are willing to be Christ's disciples, are not willing to be known to be so. Here began Peter's denying him; for to follow him afar off, is by little and little to go back from him. There is danger in drawing back, nay, in looking back.

2. He followed him, but he *went in, and sat with the servants.* He should have gone up to the court, and attended on his Master, and appeared for him; but he went in where there was a good fire, and sat with the servants, not to silence their reproaches, but to screen himself. It was presumption in Peter thus to thrust himself into temptation; he that does so, throws himself out of God's protection. Christ had told Peter that he could not follow him now, and had particularly warned him of his danger *this night;* and yet he would venture into the midst of this wicked crew. It helped David to walk in his integrity, that he *hated the congregation of evil doers, and would not sit with the wicked.*

3. He followed him, but it was only *to see the end,* led more by his curiosity than by his conscience; he attended as an idle spectator rather than as a disciple, a person concerned. He should have gone in, to do Christ some service, or to get some wisdom and grace to himself, by observing Christ's behaviour under his sufferings: but he went in, only to look about him; it is not unlikely that Peter went in, expecting that Christ would have made his escape miraculously out of the hands of his persecutors; that, having so lately struck them down, who came to seize him, he would now have struck them dead, who sat to judge him; and this he had a mind to see: if so, it was folly for him to think of seeing any other end than what Christ had foretold, that he should be put to death. Note, It is more our concern to prepare for the end, whatever it may be, than curiously to enquire what the end will be. The event is God's, but the duty is ours.

IV. The trial of our Lord Jesus in this court.

1. They examined witnesses against him, though they were resolved, right or wrong, to condemn him; yet, to put the better colour upon it, they would produce evidence against him. The crimes properly cognizable in their court, were, false doctrine and blasphemy; these they endeavoured to prove upon him. And observe here,

(1.) Their search for proof; *They sought false witness against him;* they had seized him, bound him, abused him, and after all have to seek for something to lay to his charge, and can show no cause for his commitment. They tried if any of them could allege seemingly from their own knowledge any thing against him; and suggested one calumny and then another, which, if true, might touch his life. Thus *evil men dig up mischief,* Prov. xvi. 27. Here they trod in the steps of their predecessors, who *devised devices against Jeremiah,* Jer. xviii. 18; xx. 10. They made proclamation, that, if any one could give information against the prisoner at the bar, they were ready to receive it, and presently many bore false witness against him (*v.* 60); for if *a ruler hearken to lies, all his servants are wicked,* and will carry false stories to him, Prov. xxix. 12. This is an evil often seen under the sun, Eccl. x. 5. If Naboth must be taken off, there are sons of Belial to swear against him.

(2.) Their success in this search; in several attempts they were baffled, they sought false testimonies among themselves, others came in to help them, and yet they found none; they could make nothing of it, could not take the evidence together, or give it any colour of truth or consistency with itself, no, not they themselves being judges. The matters alleged were such palpable lies, as carried their own confutation along with them. This redounded much to the honour of Christ now, when they were loading him with disgrace.

But at last they met with *two* witnesses, who, it seems, agreed in their evidence, and therefore were hearkened to, in hopes that now the point was gained. The words they swore against him, were, that he should say, *I am able to destroy the temple of God, and to build it in three days, v.* 61. Now by this they designed to accuse him, [1.] As an enemy to the temple, and one that sought for the destruction of it, which they could not bear to hear of; for they valued themselves by *the temple of the Lord* (Jer. vii. 4), and, when they abandoned other idols, made a perfect idol of that. Stephen was accused for *speaking against this holy place,* Acts vi. 13, 14. [2.] As one that dealt in witchcraft, or some such unlawful arts, by the help of which he could rear such a building in three days: they had often suggested that he was in league with Beelzebub. Now, as to this, *First,* The words were mis-recited; he said, *Destroy ye this temple* (John ii. 19), plainly intimating that he spoke of a temple which his enemies would seek to destroy; they come, and swear that he said, *I am able to destroy* this temple, as if the design against it were his. He said, *In three days I will raise it up—ἐγερῶ ἀυτὸν,* a word properly used of a living temple; *I will raise it to life.* They come, and swear that he said, *I am able, οικοδομῆσαι—to build it;* which is properly used of a house temple. *Secondly,* The words were misunderstood; *he spoke of the temple of his body* (John ii. 21), and perhaps when he said, *this temple,* pointed to, or laid his hand upon, his own body; but they swore that he said the *temple of God,* meaning this holy place. Note, There have been, and still are, such as *wrest* the sayings of Christ *to their own destruction,* 2 Pet. iii. 16. *Thirdly,* Make the worst they could of it, it was no capital crime, even by their own law; if it had been, no question but he had been prosecuted for it, when he spoke the words in a public discourse some years ago; nay, the words were capable of a laudable construction, and such as bespoke a kindness for the temple; if it were destroyed, he would exert himself to the utmost to rebuild it. But any thing that looked criminal, would serve to give colour to their malicious prosecution. Now the scriptures were fulfilled, which said, *False witnesses are risen up against me* (Ps. xxvii. 12); and see Ps. xxxv. 11. *Though I have redeemed them, yet they have spoken lies against me,* Hos. vii. 13. We stand justly accused, the law *accuseth us,* Deut. xxvii. 26; John v. 45. Satan and our own consciences accuse us, 1 John iii. 20. The creatures cry out against us. Now, to discharge us from all these just accusations, our Lord Jesus submitted to this, to be unjustly and falsely accused, that in the virtue of his sufferings we may be enabled to triumph over all challenges; *Who shall lay any thing to the charge of God's elect?* Rom viii. 33, 34. He was accused, that he might not be condemned; and if at any time we suffer thus, have all manner of evil, not only said, but *sworn, against us falsely,* let us remember that we cannot expect to fare better than our Master.

(3.) Christ's silence under all these accusations, to the amazement of the court, *v.* 62. The High Priest, the judge of the court, arose in some heat, and said, "*Answerest thou nothing?* Come, you the prisoner at the bar; you hear what is sworn against you, what have you now to say for yourself? What defence can you make? Or what pleas have you to offer in answer to this charge?" *But Jesus held his peace* (*v.* 63), not as one sullen, or as one self-condemned, or as one astonished and in confusion; not because he wanted something to say, or knew not how to say it, but that the scripture might be fulfilled (Isa. liii. 7); *As the sheep is dumb before the shearer,* and before the butcher, *so he opened not his mouth;* and that he might be the Son of David, who, when his enemies spoke mischievous things against him, was *as a deaf man that heard not,* Ps. xxxviii. 12—14. He was silent, because *his hour was come;* he would not deny the charge, because he was willing to submit to the sentence; otherwise, he could as easily have put them to silence and shame now, as he had done many a time before. If God had entered into judgment with us, we had been *speechless* (*ch.* xxii. 12), not able to *answer for one of a thousand,* Job ix. 3. Therefore, when Christ was *made sin for us,* he was silent, and left it to his blood to speak, Heb. xii. 24. He stood mute at this bar, that we might have something to say at God's bar.

Well, this way will not do; *aliâ aggrediendum est viâ—recourse must be had to some other expedient.*

2. They examined our Lord Jesus himself upon an oath like that *ex officio;* and, since they could not accuse him, they will try, contrary to the law of equity, to make him accuse himself.

(1.) Here is the interrogatory put to him by the High Priest.

Observe, [1.] The question itself; *Whether thou be the Christ, the Son of God?* That is, Whether thou pretend to be so? For they will by no means admit it into consideration, whether he be really so or no; though the Messiah was to *be the Consolation of Israel,* and glorious things were spoken concerning him in the Old Testament, yet so strangely besotted were they with a jealousy of any thing that threatened their exorbitant power and grandeur, that they would never enter into the examination of the matter, whether Jesus was the Messiah or no; never once put the case, suppose he should be so; they only wished him to confess that he called himself so, that they might on that indict him as a deceiver. What will not pride and malice carry men to?

[2.] The solemnity of the proposal of it; *I adjure thee by the living God, that thou tell us.* Not that he had any regard to the living God, but took his name in vain; only thus he hoped to gain his point with our Lord Jesus; "If thou hast any value for the blessed name of God, and reverence for his Majesty, tell us this." If he should refuse to answer when he was thus adjured, they would charge him with contempt of the blessed name of God. Thus the persecutors of good men often take advantage against them by their consciences, as Daniel's enemies did against him in the matter of his God.

(2.) Christ's answer to this interrogatory (*v.* 64), in which,

[1.] He owns himself to be *the Christ the Son of God. Thou hast said;* that is, "It is as thou hast said;" for in St. Mark it is, *I am.* Hitherto, he seldom professed himself expressly to be the Christ, the Son of God; the tenour of his doctrine bespoke it, and his miracles proved it: but now he would not omit to make a confession of it, *First,* Because that would have looked like a disowning of that truth which he came into the world to bear witness to. *Secondly,* It would have looked like declining his sufferings, when he knew the acknowledgment of this would give his enemies all the advantage they desired against him. He thus confessed himself, for example and encouragement to his followers, when they are called to it, to *confess him before men,* whatever hazards they run by it. And according to this pattern the martyrs readily confessed themselves Christians, though they knew they must die for it, as the martyrs at Thebais, *Euseb. Hist.* l. 8, c. 9. That Christ answered out of a regard to the adjuration which Caiaphas had profanely used by the *living God,* I cannot think, any more than that he had any regard to the like adjuration in the devil's mouth, Mark v. 7.

[2.] He refers himself, for the proof of this, to his second coming, and indeed to his whole estate of exaltation. It is probable that they looked upon him with a scornful disdainful smile, when he said, *I am;*" "A likely fellow," thought they, "to be the Messiah, who is expected to come in so much pomp and power;" and to that this *nevertheless* refers. "Though now you see me in this low and abject state, and think it a ridiculous thing for me to call myself the Messiah, *nevertheless* the day is coming when I shall appear otherwise." *Hereafter, ἀπ' ἄρτι—à modo—shortly;* for his exaltation began in a few days; now shortly his kingdom began to be set up; and *hereafter ye shall see the Son of man sitting on the right hand of power, to judge the world;* of which his coming shortly to judge and destroy the Jewish nation would be a type and earnest. Note, The terrors of the judgment-day will be a sensible conviction to the most obstinate infidelity, not in order to conversion (that will be then too late), but in order to an eternal confusion. Observe, *First,* Whom they should see; *the Son of man.* Having owned himself the Son of God, even now in his estate of humiliation, he speaks of himself as the Son of man, even in his estate of exaltation; for he had these two distinct natures in one person. The incarnation of Christ has made him Son of God and Son of man; for he is *Immanuel,* God with us. *Secondly,* In what posture they should see him; 1. *Sitting on the right hand of power,* according to the prophecy of the Messiah (Ps. cx. 1); *Sit thou at my right hand;* which denotes both the dignity and the dominion he is exalted to. Though now he stood at the bar, they should shortly see him sit on the throne. 2. *Coming in the clouds of heaven;* this refers to another prophecy concerning the *Son of man* (Dan. vii. 13, 14), which is applied to Christ (Luke i. 33), when he came to destroy Jerusalem; so terrible was the judgment, and so sensible the indications of the wrath of the Lamb in it, that it might be called *a visible appearance of Christ;* but doubtless it has reference to the general judgment; to this day he appeals, and summons them to an appearance, then and there to answer for what they are now doing. He had spoken of this day to his disciples, awhile ago, for their comfort, and had bid them *lift up their heads* for joy in the prospect of it, Luke xxi. 27, 28. Now he speaks of it to his enemies, for their terror; for nothing is more comfortable to the righteous, nor more terrible to the wicked, than Christ's judging the world at the last day.

V. His conviction upon this trial; *The High Priest rent his clothes,* according to the custom of the Jews, when they heard or saw any thing done or said, which they looked upon to be a reproach to God; as Isa. xxxvi. 22; xxxvii. 1; Acts xiv. 14. Caiaphas would be thought extremely tender of the glory of God *(Come, see his zeal for the Lord of hosts);* but, while he pretended an abhorrence of blasphemy, he was himself the greatest blasphemer; he now forgot the law which forbade the High Priest in any case to rend his clothes, unless we will suppose this an excepted case.

Observe, 1. The crime he was found guilty of; *blasphemy. He hath spoken blasphemy;* that is, he hath spoken reproachfully of the living God; that is the notion we have of blasphemy; because we by sin had reproached the Lord, therefore Christ, when *he was made Sin for us,* was condemned as a blasphemer for the truth he told them.

2. The evidence upon which they found him guilty; *Ye have heard the blasphemy;* why should we trouble ourselves to examine *witnesses* any further? He owned the fact, that he did profess himself the *Son of God;* and then they made blasphemy of it, and convicted him upon his confession. The High Priest triumphs in the success of the snare he had laid; "Now I think I have done his business for him." *Aha, so would we have it.* Thus was he *judged out of his own mouth* at their bar, because we were liable to be so judged at God's bar. There is no need of witnesses against us; our own consciences are against us instead of a thousand witnesses.

VI. His sentence passed, upon this conviction, *v.* 66.

Here is, 1. Caiaphas's appeal to the bench; *What think ye?* See his base hypocrisy and partiality; when he had already prejudged the cause, and pronounced him a blasphemer, then, as if he were willing to be advised, he asks the judgment of his brethren; but hide malice ever so cunningly under the robe of justice, some way or other it will break out. If he would have dealt fairly, he should have collected the votes of the bench *seriatim—in order,* and begun with the junior, and delivered his own opinion last; but he knew that by the authority of his place he could sway the rest, and therefore declares his judgment, and presumes they are all of his mind; he takes the crime, with regard to Christ, *pro confesso—as a crime confessed;* and the judgment, with regard to the court, *pro concesso—as a judgment agreed to.*

2. Their concurrence with him; they said, *He is guilty of death;* perhaps they did not all concur: it is certain that Joseph of Arimathea, if he was present, dissented (Luke xxiii. 51); so did Nicodemus, and, it is likely, others with them; however, the majority carried it that way; but, perhaps, this being an extraordinary council, or cabal rather, none had notice to be present but such as they knew would concur, and so it might be voted *nemine contradicente — unanimously.* The judgment was, "*He is guilty of death;* by the law he deserves to die." Though they had not power now to put any man to death, yet by such a judgment as this they made a man an *outlaw* among his people *(qui caput gerit lupinum—he carries a wolf's head;* so our old law describes an outlaw), and so exposed him to the fury either of a popular tumult, as Stephen was, or to be clamoured

against before the governor, as Christ was. Thus was the Lord of life condemned to die, that through him there may be *no condemnation to us.*

VII. The abuses and indignities done to him after sentence passed (*v.* 67, 68); *Then,* when he was found guilty, they *spat in his face.* Because they had not power to put him to death, and could not be sure that they should prevail with the governor to be their executioner, they would do him all the mischief they could, now that they had him in their hands. Condemned prisoners are taken under the special protection of the law, which they are to make satisfaction to, and by all civilized nations have been treated with tenderness; sufficient is this punishment. But when they had passed sentence upon our Lord Jesus, he was treated as if hell had broken loose upon him, as if he were not only *worthy of death,* but as if that were too good for him, and he were unworthy of the compassion shown to the worst malefactors. Thus *he was made a curse for us.* But who were they that were thus barbarous? It should seem, the very same that had passed sentence upon him. *They said, He is guilty of death, and then did they spit in his face.* The priests began, and then no wonder if the servants, who would do any thing to make sport to themselves, and curry favour with their wicked masters, carried on the humour. See how they abused him.

1. *They spat in his face.* Thus the scripture was fulfilled (Isa. l. 6), *He hid not his face from shame and spitting.* Job complained of this indignity done to him, and herein was a type of Christ (Job xxx. 10); *They spare not to spit in my face.* It is an expression of the greatest contempt and indignation possible; looking upon him as more despicable than the very ground they spit upon. When Miriam was under the leprosy, it was looked upon as a disgrace to her, like that of *her father spitting in her face,* Num. xii. 14. He that refused to raise up seed to his brother, was to undergo this dishonour, Deut. xxv. 9. Yet Christ, when he was repairing the decays of the great family of mankind, submitted to it. That face which was *fairer than the children of men,* which was *white and ruddy,* and which angels reverence, was thus filthily abused by the basest and vilest of the children of men. Thus was confusion poured upon his face, that ours might not be filled with everlasting shame and contempt. They who now profane his blessed name, abuse his word, and hate his image in his sanctified ones; what do they better than spit in his face? They would do that, if it were in their reach.

2. *They buffeted him, and smote him with the palms of their hands.* This added pain to the shame, for both came in with sin. Now the scripture was fulfilled (Isa. l. 6), *I gave my cheeks to them that plucked off the hair; and* (Lam. iii. 30), *He giveth his cheek to him that smiteth him; he is filled with reproach,* and yet *keepeth silence* (*v.* 28); and (Mic. v. 1), *They shall smite the Judge of Israel with a rod upon the cheek;* here the margin reads it, *They smote him with rods;* for so ἐρράπισαν signifies, and this he submitted to.

3. They challenged him to tell who struck him, having first blindfolded him; *Prophesy unto us, thou Christ, who is he that smote thee?* (1.) They made sport of him, as the Philistines did with Samson; it is grievous to those that are in misery, for people to make merry *about* them, but much more to make merry *with* them and their misery. Here was an instance of the greatest depravity and degeneracy of the human nature that could be, to show that there was need of a religion that should recover men to humanity. (2.) They made sport with his prophetical office. They had heard him called a *prophet,* and that he was famed for wonderful discoveries; this they upbraided him with, and pretended to make a trial of; as if the divine omniscience must stoop to a piece of children's play. *They* put a like affront upon Christ, who profanely jest with the scripture, and make themselves merry with holy things; like Belshazzar's revels in the temple bowls.

69 Now Peter sat without in the
palace: and a damsel came unto him,
saying, Thou also wast with Jesus of
Galilee. 70 But he denied before
them all, saying, I know not what thou
sayest. 71 And when he was gone
out into the porch, another *maid* saw
him, and said unto them that were
there, This *fellow* was also with Jesus
of Nazareth. 72 And again he denied with an oath, I do not know the
man. 73 And after a while came unto
him they that stood by, and said to
Peter, Surely thou also art *one* of
them; for thy speech bewrayeth thee.
74 Then began he to curse and to
swear, *saying,* I know not the man.
And immediately the cock crew. 75
And Peter remembered the word of
Jesus, which said unto him, Before
the cock crow, thou shalt deny me
thrice. And he went out, and wept
bitterly.

We have here the story of Peter's denying his Master, and it comes in as a part of Christ's sufferings. Our Lord Jesus was now in the High Priest's hall, not to be tried, but baited rather; and then it would have been some comfort to him to see his friends near him. But we do not find any friend he had about the court, save Peter only, and it would have been better if he had been at a distance. Observe how he fell, and how he got up again by repentance.

I. His sin, which is here impartially related, to the honour of the penmen of scripture, who dealt faithfully. Observe,

1. The immediate occasion of Peter's sin. He sat without in the palace, among the servants of the High Priest. Note, Bad company is to many an occasion of sin; and those who needlessly thrust themselves into it, go upon the devil's ground, venture into his crowds, and may expect either to be tempted and ensnared, as Peter was, or to be ridiculed and abused, as his Master was; they scarcely can come out of such company, without guilt or grief, or both. He that would keep God's commandments and his own covenant, must say to evil-doers, *Depart from me*, Ps. cxix. 115. Peter spoke from his own experience, when he warned his new converts to *save themselves from that untoward generation;* for he had like to have ruined himself by but going once among them.

2. The temptation to it. He was challenged as a retainer to Jesus of Galilee. First one maid, and then another, and then the rest of the servants, charged it upon him; *Thou also wert with Jesus of Galilee, v.* 69. And again, *This fellow was with Jesus of Nazareth, v.* 71. And again (*v.* 73), *Thou also art one of them, for thy speech betrayeth thee* to be a Galilean; whose dialect and pronunciation differed from that of the other Jews. Happy he whose speech betrays him to be a disciple of Christ, by the holiness and seriousness of whose discourse it appears that he has been with Jesus! Observe how scornfully they speak of Christ—Jesus *of Galilee*, and *of Nazareth,* upbraiding him with the country he was of: and how disdainfully they speak of Peter—*This fellow;* as if they thought it a reproach to them to have such a man in their company, and he was well enough served for coming among them; yet they had nothing to accuse him of, but that he was with Jesus, which, they thought, was enough to render him both a scandalous and a suspected person.

3. The sin itself. When he was charged as one of Christ's disciples, he denied it, was ashamed and afraid to own himself so, and would have all about him to believe that he had no knowledge of him, nor any kindness or concern for him.

(1.) Upon the first mention of it, he said, *I know not what thou sayest.* This was a shuffling answer; he pretended that he did not understand the charge, that he knew not whom she meant by *Jesus of Galilee,* or what she meant by being *with* him; so making strange of that which his heart was now as full of as it could be. [1.] It is a fault thus to misrepresent our own apprehensions, thoughts, and affections, to serve a turn; to pretend that we do not understand, or did not think of, or remember, that which yet we do apprehend, and did think of, and remember; this is a species of lying which we are more prone to than any other, because in this a man is not easily disproved; for *who knows the spirit of a man, save himself?* But God knows it, and we must be restrained from this wickedness by a fear of him, Prov. xxiv. 12. [2.] It is yet a greater fault to be shy of Christ, to dissemble our knowledge of him, and to shift off a confession of him, when we are called to it; it is, in effect, to *deny* him.

(2.) Upon the next attack, he said, flat and plain, *I know not the man,* and backed it with an oath, *v.* 72. This was, in effect, to say, I will not own him, I am no Christian; for Christianity is the knowledge of Christ. Why, Peter? Canst thou look upon yonder Prisoner at the bar, and say thou dost not know him? Didst not thou quit all to follow him? And hast thou not been the man of his counsel? Hast thou not known him better than any one else? Didst thou not confess him to be the Christ, the Son of the Blessed? Hast thou forgotten all the kind and tender looks thou hast had from him, and all the intimate fellowship thou hast had with him? Canst thou look him in the face, and say that thou dost not know him?

(3.) Upon the third assault, *he began to curse and to swear, saying, I know not the man, v.* 74. This was worst of all, for the way of sin is down-hill. He cursed and swore, [1.] To back what he said, and to gain credit to it, that they might not any more call it in question; he did not only *say* it, but *swear* it; and yet what he said, was false. Note, We have reason to suspect the truth of that which is backed with rash oaths and imprecations. None but the devil's sayings need the devil's proofs. He that will not be restrained by the third commandment from mocking his God, will not be kept by the ninth from deceiving his brother. [2.] He designed it to be an evidence for him, that he was none of Christ's disciples, for this was none of their language. Cursing and swearing suffice to prove a man no disciple of Christ; for it is the language of his enemies thus to *take his name in vain.*

This is written for warning to us, that we sin not after the similitude of Peter's transgression; that we never, either directly or indirectly, deny Christ the Lord that bought us, by rejecting his offers, resisting his Spirit, dissembling our knowledge of him, and being ashamed of him and his words, or afraid of suffering for him and with his suffering people.

4. The aggravations of this sin, which it may be of use to take notice of, that we may observe the like transgressions in our own sins. Consider, (1.) Who he was: an apostle, one of the first three, that had been upon all occasions the most forward to speak to the honour of Christ. The greater profession we make of religion, the greater is our sin if in any thing we walk unworthily. (2.) What fair warning his Master had given him of his danger; if he had regarded this as he ought to have done, he would not have run himself

into the temptation. (3.) How solemnly he had promised to adhere to Christ in this night of trial; he had said again and again, "*I will never deny thee;* no, I will die with thee first;" yet he broke these bonds in sunder, and his word was yea and nay. (4.) How soon he fell into this sin after the Lord's supper. There to receive such an inestimable pledge of redeeming love, and yet the same night, before morning, to disown his Redeemer, was indeed *turning aside quickly.* (5.) How weak comparatively the temptation was; it was not the judge, nor any of the officers of the court, that charged him with being a disciple of Jesus, but a silly maid or two, that probably designed him no hurt, nor would have done him any if he had owned it. This was but *running with the footmen,* Jer. xii. 5. (6.) How often he repeated it; even after the cock had crowed once he continued in the temptation, and a second and third time relapsed into the sin. Is this Peter? *How art thou fallen!*

Thus was his sin aggravated; but on the other hand there is this to extenuate it, that, what he said he said *in his haste,* Ps. cxvi. 11. He fell into the sin by surprise, not as Judas, with design; his heart was against it; he spoke very ill, but it was unadvisedly, and before he was aware.

II. Peter's repentance for this sin, *v.* 75. The former is written for our admonition, that we may not sin; but, if at any time we be overtaken, this is written for our imitation, that we may make haste to repent. Now observe,

1. What it was, that brought Peter to repentance.

(1.) *The cock crew* (*v.* 74); a common contingency; but, Christ having mentioned the crowing of *the cock* in the warning he gave him, that made it a means of bringing him to himself. The word of Christ can put a significancy upon whatever sign he shall please to choose, and by virtue of that word he can make it very beneficial to the souls of his people. The crowing of a cock is to Peter instead of a John Baptist, the voice of one calling to repentance. Conscience should be to us as the crowing of the cock, to put us in mind of what we had forgotten. When *David's heart smote him* the cock crew. Where there is a living principle of grace in the soul, though for the present overpowered by temptation, a little hint will serve, only for a memorandum, when God sets in with it, to recover it from a by-path. Here was the crowing of a cock made a happy occasion of the conversion of a soul. Christ comes sometimes in mercy *at cock-crowing.*

(2.) *He remembered the words of the Lord;* this was it that brought him to himself, and melted him into tears of godly sorrow; a sense of his ingratitude to Christ, and the slight regard he had had to the gracious warning Christ had given him. Note, A serious reflection upon the words of the Lord Jesus will be a powerful inducement to repentance, and will help to break the heart for sin. Nothing grieves a penitent more than that he has sinned against the grace of the Lord Jesus and the tokens of his love.

2. How his repentance was expressed; *He went out, and wept bitterly.*

(1.) His sorrow was secret; he went out, out of the High Priest's hall, vexed at himself that ever he came into it, now that he found what a snare he was in, and got out of it as fast as he could. He went out into the porch before (*v.* 71); and if he had gone quite off then, his second and third denial had been prevented; but then he came in again, now he went out and came in no more. He went out to some place of solitude and retirement, where he might *bemoan* himself, *like the doves of the valleys,* Ezek. vii. 16; Jer. ix. 1, 2. He went out, that he might not be disturbed in his devotions on this sad occasion. We may *then* be most free in our communion with God, when we are most free from the converse and business of this world. In mourning for sin, we find *the families apart, and their wives apart,* Zech. xii. 11, 12.

(2.) His sorrow was serious; *He wept bitterly.* Sorrow for sin must not be slight, but great and deep, like that for an only son. Those that have sinned sweetly, must weep bitterly; for, sooner or later, sin will be bitterness. This deep sorrow is requisite, not to satisfy divine justice (a sea of tears would not do that), but to evidence that there is a real change of mind, which is the essence of repentance, to make the pardon the more welcome, and sin for the future the more loathsome. Peter, who wept so bitterly for denying Christ, never denied him again, but *confessed* him often and openly, and in the mouth of danger; so far from ever saying, *I know not the man,* that he made all the house of *Israel know assuredly that this same Jesus was Lord and Christ.* True repentance for any sin will be best evidenced by our abounding in the contrary grace and duty; that is a sign of our weeping, not only bitterly, but sincerely. Some of the ancients say, that as long as Peter lived, he never heard a cock crow but it set him a weeping. Those that have truly sorrowed for sin, will sorrow upon every remembrance of it; yet not so as to hinder, but rather to increase, their joy in God and in his mercy and grace.

CHAP. XXVII.

It is a very affecting story which is recorded in this chapter concerning the sufferings and death of our Lord Jesus. Considering the thing itself, there cannot be a more tragical story told us; common humanity would melt the heart, to find an innocent and excellent person thus misused. But considering the design and fruit of Christ's sufferings, it is gospel, it is good news, that Jesus Christ was thus delivered for our offences; and there is nothing we have more reason to glory in than the cross of Christ. In this chapter, observe, I. How he was prosecuted. 1. The delivering of him to Pilate, ver. 1, 2. 2. The despair of Judas, ver. 3—10. The arraignment and trial of Christ before Pilate, ver. 11—14. 4. The clamours of the people against him, ver. 15—25. 5. Sentence passed, and the warrant signed for his execution, ver. 26. II. How he was executed. 1. He was barbarously used, ver. 27—30. 2. Led to the place of execution, ver. 31—33. 3. There he had all possible indignities done him, and reproaches cast upon him, ver. 34—44. 4. Heaven frowned upon him, ver. 45—49. 5. Many remarkable things attended his death. ver. 50—56. He was buried and a watch set on his grave, ver. 57—66.

WHEN the morning was come,
all the chief priests and elders
of the people took counsel against
Jesus to put him to death: 2 And
when they had bound him, they led
him away, and delivered him to Pontius Pilate the governor. 3 Then
Judas, which had betrayed him, when
he saw that he was condemned, repented himself, and brought again
the thirty pieces of silver to the chief
priests and elders, 4 Saying, I have
sinned in that I have betrayed the
innocent blood. And they said, What
is that to us? see thou *to that.* 5
And he cast down the pieces of silver
in the temple, and departed, and went
and hanged himself. 6 And the chief
priests took the silver pieces, and said,
It is not lawful for to put them into
the treasury, because it is the price of
blood. 7 And they took counsel, and
bought with them the potter's field,
to bury strangers in. 8 Wherefore
that field was called, The field of blood,
unto this day. 9 Then was fulfilled
that which was spoken by Jeremy the
prophet, saying, And they took the
thirty pieces of silver, the price of him
that was valued, whom they of the
children of Israel did value; 10 And
gave them for the potter's field, as the
Lord appointed me.

We left Christ in the hands of the chief priests and elders, condemned to die, but they could only show their teeth; about two years before this the Romans had taken from the Jews the power of capital punishment; they could put no man to death, and therefore early in the morning another council is held, to consider what is to be done. And here we are told what was done in that morning-council, after they had been for two or three hours consulting with their pillows.

I. Christ is delivered up to Pilate, that he might execute the sentence they had passed upon him. Judea having been almost one hundred years before this conquered by Pompey, had ever since been tributary to Rome, and was lately made part of the province of Syria, and subject to the government of the president of Syria, under whom there were several *procurators,* who chiefly attended the business of the *revenues,* but sometimes, as Pilate particularly, had the whole power of the president lodged in them. This was a plain evidence that *the sceptre was departed from Judah,* and that therefore now *the Shiloh must come,* according to Jacob's prophecy, Gen. xlix. 10. Pilate is characterized by the Roman writers of that time, as a man of a rough and haughty spirit, wilful and implacable, and extremely covetous and oppressive; the Jews had a great enmity to his person, and were weary of his government, and yet they made use of him as the tool of their malice against Christ.

1. They *bound* Jesus. He was bound when he was first seized; but either they took off these bonds when he was before the council, or now they added to them. Having found him guilty, they tied his hands behind him, as they usually do with convicted criminals. He was already bound with the bonds of love to man, and of his own undertaking, else he had soon broken these bonds, as Samson did his. We were fettered with the *bond of iniquity,* held in the cords of our sins (Prov. v. 22); but God had bound the *yoke of our transgressions* upon the neck of the Lord Jesus (Lam. 1. 14), that we might be loosed by his bonds, as we are *healed by his stripes.*

2. *They led him away* in a sort of triumph, led him *as a lamb to the slaughter; so was he taken from prison and from judgment,* Isa. liii. 7, 8. It was nearly a mile from Caiaphas's house to Pilate's. All that way they led him through the streets of Jerusalem, when in the morning they began to fill, to make him a spectacle to the world.

3. They *delivered him to Pontius Pilate;* according to that which Christ had often said, that he should be *delivered to the Gentiles.* Both Jews and Gentiles were obnoxious to the judgment of God, and *concluded under sin,* and Christ was to be the Saviour both of Jews and Gentiles; and therefore Christ was brought into the judgment both of Jews and Gentiles, and both had a hand in his death. See how these corrupt church-rulers abused the civil magistrate, making use of him to execute their unrighteous decrees, and *inflict the grievance which they had prescribed,* Isa. x. 1. Thus have the kings of the earth been wretchedly imposed upon by the papal powers, and condemned to the drudgery of extirpating with the sword of war, as well as that of justice, those whom they have marked for heretics, right or wrong, to the great prejudice of their own interests.

II. The money which they had paid to Judas for betraying Christ, is by him delivered back to them, and Judas, in despair, hangs himself. The chief priests and elders supported themselves with *this,* in prosecuting Christ, that his own disciple betrayed him to them; but now, in the midst of the prosecution, that string failed them, and even *he* is made to them a *witness* of Christ's innocency and a monument of God's justice; which served, 1. For glory to Christ in the midst of his sufferings, and a specimen of his victory over Satan who had entered into Judas. 2. For warning to his persecutors, and to leave them the more inexcusable. If their heart had not been fully set in them to do this evil, what Judas said and did, one would think, should have stopped the prosecution.

(1.) See here how Judas *repented:* not like Peter, who repented, believed, and was pardoned: no, he repented, despaired, and was ruined. Now observe here,

[1.] What induced him to repent. It was *when he saw that he was condemned.* Judas, it is probable, expected that either Christ would have made his escape out of their hands, or would so have pleaded his own cause at their bar as to have come off, and then Christ would have had the honour, the Jews the shame, and he the money, and no harm done. This he had no reason to expect, because he had so often heard his Master say that he must be *crucified;* yet it is probable that he did expect it, and when the event did not answer his vain fancy, then he fell into this horror, when he saw the stream strong against Christ, and him yielding to it. Note, Those who measure actions by the consequences of them rather than by the divine law, will find themselves mistaken in their measures. The way of sin is down-hill; and if we cannot easily stop ourselves, much less can we stop others whom we have set a going in a sinful way. He *repented himself;* that is, he was filled with grief, anguish, and indignation, at himself, when reflecting upon what he had done. When he was tempted to betray his Master, the thirty pieces of silver looked very fine and glittering, like the *wine, when it is red, and gives its colour in the cup.* But when the thing was done, and the money paid, the silver was become dross, it *bit like a serpent, and stung like an adder.* Now his conscience flew in his face; "What have I done! What a fool, what a wretch, am I, to sell my Master, and all my comfort and happiness in him, for such a trifle! All these abuses and indignities done him are chargeable upon me; it is owing to me, that he is bound and condemned, spit upon and buffeted. I little thought it would have come to this, when I made that wicked bargain; so foolish was I, and ignorant, and so like a beast." Now he curses the bag he carried, the money he coveted, the priests he dealt with, and the day that he was born. The remembrance of his Master's goodness to him, which he had so basely requited, the bowels of mercy he had spurned at, and the fair warnings he had slighted, steeled his convictions, and made them the more piercing. Now he found his Master's words true; *It were better for that man, that he had never been born.* Note, Sin will soon change its taste. Though it be *rolled under the tongue* as a *sweet morsel,* in the bowels it will be turned into the *gall of asps* (Job xx. 12—14), like John's book, Rev. x. 9.

[2.] What were the indications of his repentance.

First, He made restitution; *He brought again the thirty pieces of silver to the chief priests,* when they were all together publicly. Now the money burned in his conscience, and he was as sick of it as ever he had been fond of it. Note, That which is ill gotten, will never do good to those that get it, Jer. xiii. 10; Job xx. 15. If he had repented, and brought the money back before he had betrayed Christ, he might have done it with comfort, then he had *agreed while yet in the way;* but now it was too late, now he cannot do it without horror, wishing ten thousand times he had never meddled with it. See Jam. v. iii. He brought it again. Note, what is unjustly gotten, must not be kept; for that is a continuance in the sin by which it was got, and such an avowing of it as is not consistent with repentance. He brought it to those from whom he had it, to let them know that he repented his bargain. Note, Those who have served and hardened others in their sin, when God gives them repentance, should let them know it whose sins they have been partakers in, that it may be a means to bring them to repentance.

Secondly, He made confession (*v.* 4); *I have sinned, in that I have betrayed innocent blood.* 1. To the *honour of Christ,* he pronounces his blood *innocent.* If he had been guilty of any sinful practices, Judas, as his disciple, would certainly have known it, and, as his betrayer, would certainly have discovered it; but he, freely and without being urged to it, pronounces him innocent, to the face of those who had pronounced him *guilty.* 2. To *his own shame,* he confesses that he had sinned, in betraying this blood. He does not lay the blame on any one else; does not say, "You have sinned, in hiring me to do it;" but takes it all to himself; "I have sinned, in doing it." Thus far Judas went toward his repentance, yet it was *not to salvation.* He confessed, but not to God, did not go to him, and say, *I have sinned, Father, against heaven.* He confessed the betraying of innocent blood, but did not confess that wicked love of money, which was the root of this evil. There are those who betray Christ, and yet justify themselves in it, and so come short of Judas.

(2.) See here how the chief priests and elders entertained Judas's penitential confession; they said, *What is that to us? See thou to that.* He made them his confessors, and that was the *absolution* they gave him; more like the priests of devils than like the priests of the holy living God.

[1.] See here how carelessly they speak of the betraying of Christ. Judas had told them that the blood of Christ was innocent blood; and they said, *What is that to us?* Was it nothing to them that they had thirsted after this blood, and hired Judas to betray it, and had now condemned it to be shed unjustly? Is this nothing to them? Does it give no check to the violence of their prosecution, no warning to take heed what they do to this just man? Thus do fools make a mock at sin, as if no harm were done, no hazard run, by the commission of the greatest wickedness. Thus light do many make of Christ crucified; what is it to them, that he suffered such things?

[2.] See here how carelessly they speak of the sin of Judas; he said, *I have sinned,* and they said, "*What is that to us?* What are we concerned in thy sin, that thou tellest us of it?" Note, It is folly for us to think that the sins of others are nothing to us, especially those sins that we are any way accessary to, or partakers in. Is it nothing to us, that God is dishonoured, souls wounded, Satan gratified and his interests served, and that we have aided and abetted it? If the elders of Jezreel, to please Jezebel, murder Naboth, is that nothing to Ahab? Yes, *he has killed,* for he has *taken possession,* 1 Kings xxi. 19. The guilt of sin is not so easily transferred as some people think it is. If there were guilt in the matter, they tell Judas that he must *look to it,* he must *bear it. First,* Because he had betrayed him to them. His was indeed *the greater sin* (John xix. 11); but it did not therefore follow, that theirs was no sin. It is a common instance of the deceitfulness of our hearts, to extenuate our own sin by the aggravation of other people's sins. But the judgment of God is according to truth, not according to comparison. *Secondly,* Because he knew and believed him to be innocent. "If he be innocent, see thou to it, that is more than we know; we have adjudged him *guilty,* and therefore may justly prosecute him as such." Wicked practices are buoyed up by wicked principles, and particularly by this, That sin is sin only to those that think it to be so; that it is no harm to persecute a good man, if we take him to be a bad man; but those who thus think to mock God, will but deceive and destroy themselves.

[3.] See how carelessly they speak of the conviction, terror, and remorse, that Judas was under. They were glad to make use of him in the sin, and were then very fond of him; none more welcome to them than Judas, when he said, *What will ye give me, and I will betray him to you?* They did not say, *What is that to us?* But now that his sin had put him into a fright, now they slighted him, had nothing to say to him, but turned him over to his own terrors; why did he come to trouble them with his melancholy fancies? They had something else to do than to heed him. But why so shy? *First,* Perhaps they were in some fear lest the sparks of his conviction, brought too near, should kindle a fire in their own consciences, and lest his moans, listened to, should give an alarm to their own convictions. Note, Obstinate sinners stand upon their guard against convictions; and those that are resolvedly impenitent, look with disdain upon the penitent. *Secondly,* However, they were in no concern to succour Judas; when they had brought him into the snare, they not only left him, but laughed at him. Note, Sinners, under convictions, will find their old companions in sin but miserable comforters. It is usual for those that love the treason, to hate the traitor.

(3.) Here is the utter despair that Judas was hereby driven into. If the chief priests had promised him to stay the prosecution, it would have been some comfort to him; but, seeing no hopes of that, he grew desperate, *v.* 5.

[1.] *He cast down the pieces of silver in the temple.* The chief priests would not take the money, for fear of taking thereby the whole guilt to themselves, which they were willing that Judas should bear the load of; Judas would not keep it, it was too hot for him to hold, he therefore threw it down in the temple, that, whether they would or no, it might fall into the hands of the chief priests. See what a *drug* money was, when the guilt of *sin* was tacked to it, or was thought to be so.

[2.] *He went, and hanged himself. First, He retired*—*ἀνεχώρησε*; he withdrew into some solitary place, like the possessed man that was drawn by the devil into the wilderness, Luke viii. 29. Woe to him that is in despair, and is alone. If Judas had gone to Christ, or to some of the disciples, perhaps he might have had relief, bad as the case was; but, missing of it with the chief priests, he abandoned himself to despair: and the same devil that with the help of the priests drew him to the sin, with their help drove him to despair. *Secondly,* He became his own executioner; *He hanged himself;* he was *suffocated* with grief, so Dr. Hammond: but Dr. Whitby is clear that our translation is right. Judas had a *sight* and *sense* of sin, but no apprehension of the mercy of God in Christ, and so *he pined away in his iniquity.* His sin, we may suppose, was not in its own nature unpardonable: there were some of those saved, that had been Christ's betrayers and murderers; but he concluded, as Cain, that his iniquity was greater than could be forgiven, and would rather throw himself on the devil's mercy than God's. And some have said, that Judas sinned more in *despairing* of the mercy of God, than in *betraying* his Master's blood. Now the terrors of the Almighty set themselves in array against him. All the curses written in God's book now *came into his bowels like water, and like oil into his bones,* as was foretold concerning him (Ps. cix. 18, 19), and drove him to this desperate shift, for the escaping of a *hell* within him, to leap into *that* before him, which was but the perfection and perpetuity of this horror and despair. He throws himself into the fire, to avoid the flame; but miserable is the case when a man must go to hell for ease.

Now, in this story, 1. We have an instance of the wretched end of those into whom Satan enters, and particularly those that are given up to the love of money. This is the destruction in which many are drowned by it, 1 Tim. vi. 9, 10. Remember what became of the swine into which, and of the traitor into whom, *the devil entered;* and *give not place to the devil.* 2. We have an instance of the wrath of God revealed from heaven against the ungodliness and unrighteousness of men, Rom. i. 18. As in the story of Peter we behold the goodness of God, and the triumphs of Christ's grace in the conversion of some sinners; so in the story of Judas we behold the severity of God, and the triumphs of Christ's power and justice in the confusion of other sinners. When Judas, into whom Satan entered, was thus *hung up,* Christ made an open show of the principalities and powers he undertook the *spoiling of,* Col. ii. 15. 3. We have an instance of the direful effects of despair; it often ends in self-murder. *Sorrow,* even that for sin, if not *according to God, worketh death* (2 Cor. vii. 10), the worst kind of death; for *a wounded spirit, who can bear?* Let us think as bad as we can of sin, provided we do not think it unpardonable; let us despair of help in ourselves, but not of help in God. He that thinks to ease his conscience by destroying his life, doth, in effect, dare God Almighty to do his worst. And self-murder, though prescribed by some of the heathen moralists, is certainly a remedy worse than the disease, how bad soever the disease may be. Let us watch against the beginnings of melancholy, and pray, Lord, *lead us not into temptation.*

(4.) The disposal of the money which Judas brought back, *v.* 6—10. It was laid out in the purchase of a field, called *the potter's field;* because some potter had owned it, or occupied it, or lived near it, or because broken potters' vessels were thrown into it. And this field was to be a burying-place for strangers, that is, proselytes to the Jewish religion, who were of other nations, and, coming to Jerusalem to worship, happened to die there. [1.] It looks like an instance of their humanity, that they took care for the *burying of strangers;* and it intimates that they themselves allowed (as St. Paul saith, Acts xxiv. 15), *that there shall be a resurrection of the dead, both of the just and of the unjust;* for we *therefore* take care of the dead body, not only because it has been the habitation of a rational soul, but because it must be so again. But, [2.] It was no instance of their humility that they would bury strangers in a place by themselves, as if they were not worthy to be laid in their burying-places; strangers must keep their distance, alive and dead, and that principle must go down to the grave, *Stand by thyself, come not near me, I am holier than thou,* Isa. lxv. 5. The sons of Heth were better affected towards Abraham, though a stranger among them, when they offered him the choicest of their own sepulchres, Gen. xxiii. 6. But *the sons of the stranger, that have joined themselves to the Lord,* though buried by themselves, shall rise with all that are *dead in Christ.*

This buying of the potter's field did not take place on the day that Christ died (they were then too busy to mind any thing else but hunting him down); but it took place not long after; for Peter speaks of it soon after Christ's ascension; yet it is here recorded.

First, To show the hypocrisy of the chief priests and elders. They were maliciously persecuting the blessed Jesus, and now,

1. They scruple to put that money into the treasury, or *corban,* of the temple, with which they had hired the traitor. Though perhaps they had taken it out of the treasury, pretending it was for the public good, and though they were great sticklers for the *corban,* and laboured to draw all the wealth of the nation into it, yet they would not put that money into it, which was the price of blood. The hire of a traitor they thought parallel to the hire of a whore, and the price of a malefactor (such a one they made Christ to be) equivalent to the price of a dog, neither of which was to be *brought into the house of the Lord,* Deut. xxiii. 18. They would thus save their credit with the people, by possessing them with an opinion of their great reverence for the temple. Thus they that *swallowed a camel, strained at a gnat.*

2. They think to *atone* for what they had done, by this public good act of providing a burying-place for strangers, though not at their own charge. Thus in times of ignorance people were made to believe that building churches and endowing monasteries would make amends for immoralities.

Secondly, To signify the favour intended by the blood of Christ to *strangers,* and sinners of the Gentiles. Through the price of his blood, a resting place is provided for them after death. Thus many of the ancients apply this passage. The *grave* is the potter's field, where the bodies are thrown as despised broken vessels; but Christ by his blood *purchased* it for those who by confessing themselves *strangers* on earth seek the better country; he has altered the property of it (as a purchaser doth), so that now death is ours, the grave is ours, a bed of rest for us. The Germans, in their language, call burying-places *God's fields;* for in them God *sows* his people as a *corn of wheat,* John xii. 24. See Hos. ii. 23; Isa. xxvi. 19.

Thirdly, To perpetuate the infamy of those that bought and sold the blood of Christ. This field was commonly called *Aceldama—the field of blood;* not by the chief priests, they hoped in this burying-place to bury the remembrance of their own crime; but by the people; who took notice of Judas's acknowledgment that he had betrayed the innocent blood, though the chief priests made nothing of it. They fastened this name upon the field *in perpetuam rei memoriam—for a perpetual memorial.* Note, Divine Providence has many ways of entailing disgrace upon the wicked practices even of great men, who, though they seek to cover their shame, are *put to a perpetual reproach.*

Fourthly, That we may see how the scripture was fulfilled (*v.* 9, 10); *Then was fulfilled that which was spoken by Jeremy the prophet.* The words quoted are found in the prophecy of Zechariah, *ch.* xi. 12. How they are here said to be spoken by Jeremy is a difficult question; but the credit of Christ's doctrine does not depend upon it; for that proves itself perfectly divine, though there should appear something human as to small circumstances in the penmen of it. The Syriac version, which is ancient, reads only, *It was spoken by the prophet,* not naming any, whence some have thought that *Jeremy* was added by some scribe; some think that the whole volume of the prophets, being in one book, and the prophecy of Jeremiah put first, it might not be improper, *currente calamo—for a transcriber* to quote any passage out of that volume, under his name. The Jews used to say, *The spirit of Jeremiah was in Zechariah,* and so they were as one prophet. Some suggest that it was *spoken* by Jeremiah, but written by Zechariah; or that Jeremiah wrote the ninth, tenth, and eleventh chapters of Zechariah. Now this passage in the prophet is a representation of the great contempt of God, that was found among the Jews, and the poor returns they made to him for rich receivings from him. But here that is really acted, which was there but figuratively expressed. The sum of money is the same—*thirty pieces of silver;* this they *weighed for his price,* at this rate they valued him; a goodly price; and this was *cast to the potter in the house of the Lord;* which was here literally accomplished. Note, We should better understand the events of Providence, if we were better acquainted even with the language and expressions of scripture; for even those also are sometimes written upon the dispensations of Providence so plainly, that *he who runs may read them.* What David spoke figuratively (Ps. xlii. 7), Jonah made a literal application of; *All thy waves and thy billows are gone over me,* Jonah iii. 3.

The giving of the price of him that was valued, not for him, but for the *potter's field,* bespeaks, 1. The high value that ought to be put upon Christ. The price was given, not for him; no, when it was given for him, it was soon brought back again with disdain, as infinitely below his worth; he cannot be *valued with the gold of Ophir,* nor this unspeakable Gift *bought with money.* 2. The low value that was put upon him. *They of the children of Israel* did strangely undervalue him, when his price did but reach to buy a potter's field, a pitiful sorry spot of ground, not worth looking upon. It added to the reproach of his being bought and sold, that it was at so low a rate. *Cast it to the potter,* so it is in Zechariah; a contemptible petty chapman, not the merchant that deals in things of value. And observe, *They of the children of Israel* thus *undervalued him;* they who were his own people, that should have known better what estimate to put upon him, they to whom he was first sent, whose glory he was, and whom he had valued so highly, and bought so dear. He gave kings' ransoms for them, and the richest countries (so *precious were they in his sight,* Isa. xliii. 3, 4), Egypt, and Ethiopia, and Seba; but they gave a slave's ransom for him (see Exod. xxi. 32), and valued him but at the rate of a potter's field; so was that blood trodden under foot, which bought the kingdom of heaven for us. But all this was *as the Lord appointed;* so the prophetic vision was, which typified this event, and so the event itself, as the other instances of Christ's sufferings, was *by the determinate counsel and foreknowledge of God.*

11 And Jesus stood before the governor: and the governor asked him,
saying, Art thou the King of the Jews?
And Jesus said unto him, Thou sayest.
12 And when he was accused of the
chief priests and elders, he answered
nothing. 13 Then said Pilate unto
him, Hearest thou not how many
things they witness against thee? 14
And he answered him to never a word;
insomuch that the governor marvelled
greatly. 15 Now at *that* feast the
governor was wont to release unto
the people a prisoner, whom they
would. 16 And they had then a notable prisoner, called Barabbas. 17
Therefore when they were gathered
together, Pilate said unto them, Whom
will ye that I release unto you?
Barabbas, or Jesus which is called
Christ? 18 For he knew that for
envy they had delivered him. 19
When he was set down on the judgment seat, his wife sent unto him,
saying, Have thou nothing to do with
that just man: for I have suffered
many things this day in a dream because of him. 20 But the chief priests
and elders persuaded the multitude
that they should ask Barabbas, and
destroy Jesus. 21 The governor answered and said unto them, Whether
of the twain will ye that I release
unto you? They said, Barabbas. 22
Pilate saith unto them, What shall I
do then with Jesus which is called
Christ? *They* all say unto him let him
be crucified. 23 And the governor
said, Why, what evil hath he done?
But they cried out the more, saying,
Let him be crucified. 24 When

Pilate saw that he could prevail nothing, but *that* rather a tumult was made, he took water, and washed *his* hands before the multitude, saying, I am innocent of the blood of this just person: see ye *to it.* 25 Then answered all the people, and said, His blood *be* on us, and on our children.

We have here an account of what passed in Pilate's judgment-hall, when the blessed Jesus was brought thither betimes in the morning. Though it was no court-day, Pilate immediately took his case before him. We have here,

I. The trial Christ had before Pilate.

1. His arraignment; *Jesus stood before the governor,* as the prisoner before the judge. We could not stand before God because of our sins, nor lift up our face in his presence, if Christ had not been thus made sin for us. He was arraigned that we might be discharged. Some think that this bespeaks his courage and boldness; he stood *undaunted,* unmoved by all their rage. He thus stood in this judgment, that we might stand in God's judgment. He stood for a *spectacle,* as Naboth, when he was arraigned, was *set on high among the people.*

2. His indictment; *Art thou the king of the Jews?* The Jews were now not only under the government, but under the very jealous inspection, of the Roman powers, which they were themselves to the highest degree disaffected to, and yet now pretended a concern for, to serve this turn; accusing Jesus as an Enemy to Cæsar (Luke xxiii. 2), which they could produce no other proof of, than that he himself had newly owned he was *the Christ.* Now they thought that whoever was the Christ, must be the *king of the Jews,* and must deliver them from the Roman power, and restore to them a temporal dominion, and enable them to trample upon all their neighbours. According to this chimera of their own, they accused our Lord Jesus, as making himself king of the Jews, in opposition to the Roman yoke; whereas, though he said that he was the Christ, he meant not such a Christ as this. Note, Many oppose Christ's holy religion, upon a mistake of the nature of it; they dress it up in false colours, and then fight against it. They assuring the governor that, if he made himself Christ, he made himself king of the Jews, the governor takes it for granted, that he goes about to pervert the nation, and subvert the government. *Art thou a king?* It was plain that he was not so *de facto—actually;* "But dost thou lay any claim to the government, or pretend a right to rule the Jews?" Note, It has often been the hard fate of Christ's holy religion, unjustly to fall under the suspicions of the civil powers, as if it were hurtful to kings and provinces, whereas it tends mightily to the benefit of both.

3. His plea; *Jesus said unto him,* "*Thou sayest.* It is as thou sayest, though not as thou meanest; I am a king, but not such a king as thou dost suspect me to be." Thus before Pilate he witnessed a good confession, and was not ashamed to own himself a king, though it looked ridiculous, nor afraid, though at this time it was dangerous.

4. The evidence (*v.* 12); He was *accused of the chief priests.* Pilate found *no fault in him;* whatever was said, nothing was proved, and therefore what was wanting in matter they made up in noise and violence, and followed him with repeated accusations, the same as they had given in before; but by the repetition they thought to force a belief from the governor. They had learned, not only *calumniari—to calumniate,* but *fortiter calumniari—to calumniate stoutly.* The best men have often been accused of the worst crimes.

5. The prisoner's silence as to the prosecutors' accusations; *He answered nothing,* (1.) Because there was no occasion; nothing was alleged but what carried its own confutation along with it. (2.) He was now taken up with the great concern that lay between him and his Father, to whom he was offering up himself a Sacrifice, to answer the demands of his justice, which he was so intent upon, that he minded not what they said against him. (3.) His hour was come, and he submitted to his Father's will; *Not as I will, but as thou wilt.* He knew what his Father's will was, and therefore silently *committed himself to him that judgeth righteously. We* must not thus by our silence throw away our lives, because we are not lords of our lives, as Christ was of his; nor can we know, as he did, when our hour is come. But hence we must learn, *not to render railing for railing,* 1 Pet. ii. 23.

Now, [1.] Pilate pressed him to make some reply (*v.* 13); *Hearest thou not how many things they witness against thee?* What these things were, may be gathered from Luke xxiii. 3, 5, and John xix. 7. Pilate, having no malice at all against him, was desirous he should clear himself, urges him to it, and believes he could do it; *Hearest thou not?* Yes, he did hear; and still he hears all that is witnessed unjustly against his truths and ways; but he keeps silence, because it is the day of his patience, and doth not answer, as he will shortly, Ps. l. 3. [2.] He wondered at his silence; which was not interpreted so much into a contempt of the court, as a contempt of himself. And therefore Pilate is not said to be angry at it, but to have *marvelled greatly* at it, as a thing very unusual. He believed him to be innocent, and had heard perhaps that *never man spake like him;* and therefore he thought it strange that he had not one word to say for himself. We have,

II. The outrage and violence of the people, in pressing the governor to crucify Christ. The chief priests had a great interest in the people, they called them *Rabbi, Rabbi,* made idols of them, and oracles of all they said; and they made use of this to incense them against him, and by the power of the mob gained the point which they could not otherwise carry. Now here are two instances of their outrage.

1. Their preferring Barabbas before him, and choosing to have him released rather than Jesus.

(1.) It seems it was grown into a custom with the Roman governors, for the humouring of the Jews, to grace the feast of the passover with the release of a prisoner, *v.* 15. This, they thought, did honour to the feast, and was agreeable to the commemoration of their deliverance; but it was an invention of their own, and no divine institution; though some think that it was ancient, and kept up by the Jewish princes, before they became a province of the empire. However, it was a bad custom, an obstruction to justice, and an encouragement to wickedness. But our gospel-passover is celebrated with the release of prisoners, by him who hath *power on earth to forgive sins.*

(2.) The prisoner put in competition with our Lord Jesus was Barabbas; he is here called a *notable* prisoner (*v.* 16); either because by birth and breeding he was of some note and quality, or because he had signalized himself by something remarkable in his crimes; whether he was so *notable* as to recommend himself the more to the favours of the people, and so the more likely to be interceded for, or whether so *notable* as to make himself more liable to their rage, is uncertain. Some think the latter, and therefore Pilate mentioned him, as taking it for granted that they would have desired any one's release rather than his. *Treason, murder,* and *felony,* are the three most enormous crimes that are usually punished by the sword of justice; and Barabbas was guilty of all three, Luke xxiii. 19; John xviii. 40. A *notable prisoner* indeed, whose crimes were so complicated.

(3.) The proposal was made by Pilate the governor (*v.* 17); *Whom will ye that I release unto you?* It is probable that the judge had the nomination of two, one of which the people were to *choose.* Pilate proposed to them to have Jesus *released;* he was convinced of his innocency, and that the prosecution was malicious; yet had not the courage to acquit him, as he ought to have done, by his own power, but would have him released by the people's election, and so he hoped to satisfy both his own *conscience,* and the *people* too; whereas, finding no fault in him, he ought not to have *put him upon the country,* or brought him *into peril of his life.* But such little tricks and artifices as these, to trim the matter, and to keep in with conscience and the world too, are the common practice of those that seek more to please men than God. *What shall I do then,* saith Pilate, *with Jesus, who is called Christ?* He puts the people in mind of this, that this *Jesus,* whose release he proposed, was looked upon by some among them as the Messiah, and had given pregnant proofs of his being so; "Do not *reject* one of whom your nation has professed such an expectation."

The reason why Pilate *laboured* thus to get Jesus *discharged* was because he knew that *for envy the chief priests had delivered him up* (*v.* 18); that it was not his *guilt,* but his goodness, that they were provoked at; and for this reason he *hoped* to bring him off by the people's act, and that they would be for his release. When David was *envied* by Saul, he was the *darling of the people;* and any one that heard the *hosannas* with which Christ was but a few days ago brought into Jerusalem, would have thought that he had been so, and that Pilate might safely have referred this matter to the commonalty, especially when so notorious a rogue was set up as a rival with him for their favours. But it proved otherwise.

(4.) While Pilate was thus labouring the matter, he was confirmed in his unwillingness to condemn Jesus, by a message sent him from his wife (*v.* 19), by way of caution; *Have thou nothing to do with that just man* (together with the reason), *for I have suffered many things this day in a dream because of him.* Probably, this message was delivered to Pilate publicly, in the hearing of all that were present, for it was intended to be a warning not to him only, but to the prosecutors. Observe,

[1.] The special providence of God, in sending this dream to Pilate's wife; it is not likely that she had heard any thing, before, concerning Christ, at least not so as to occasion her dreaming of him, but it was immediately from God: perhaps she was one of the *devout and honourable women,* and had some sense of religion; yet God revealed himself by dreams to some that had not, as to Nebuchadnezzar. She *suffered many things* in this dream; whether she dreamed of the cruel usage of an innocent person, or of the judgments that would fall upon those that had any hand in his death, or both, it seems that it was a frightful dream, and her thoughts *troubled her,* as Dan. ii. 1; iv. 5. Note, The Father of spirits has many ways of access to the spirits of men, and can *seal their instruction in a dream, or vision of the night,* Job xxxiii. 15, 16. Yet to those who have the written word, God more ordinarily speaks by conscience on a waking bed, than by dreams, when *deep sleep falls upon men.*

[2.] The tenderness and care of Pilate's wife, in sending this caution, thereupon, to her husband; *Have nothing to do with that just man. First,* This was an honourable testimony to our Lord Jesus, witnessing for him that he was a *just man,* even then when he was persecuted as the worst of malefactors: when his friends were afraid to appear in defence of him, God made even those that were strangers and enemies, to speak in his favour; when Peter denied him, Judas confessed him; when the chief priests pronounced him guilty of death, Pilate declared he *found no fault* in him; when the women that loved him stood afar off, Pilate's wife, who knew little of him, showed a concern for him. Note, God will not leave himself without witnesses to the truth and equity of his cause, even when it seems to be most spitefully run down by its enemies, and most shamefully deserted by its friends. *Secondly,* It was a fair warning to Pilate; *Have nothing to do with him.* Note, God has many ways of giving checks to sinners in their sinful pursuits, and it is a great mercy to have such checks from Providence, from faithful friends, and from our own consciences; it is also our great duty to hearken to them. *O do not this abominable thing which the Lord hates,* is what we may hear said to us, when we are entering into temptation, if we will but regard it. Pilate's lady sent him this warning, out of the love she had to him; she feared not a rebuke from him for meddling with that which belonged not to her; but, let him take it how he would, she would give him the caution. Note, It is an instance of true love to our friends and relations, to do what we can to keep them from sin; and the nearer any are to us, and the greater affection we have for them, the more solicitous we should be not to suffer sin to come or lie upon them, Lev. xix. 17. The best friendship is friendship to the soul. We are not told how Pilate turned this off, probably with a jest; but by his proceeding against the just man it appears that he did not regard it. Thus faithful admonitions are made light of, when they are given as warnings against sin, but will not be so easily made light of, when they shall be reflected upon as aggravations of sin.

(5.) The chief priests and the elders were busy, all this while, to influence the people in favour of Barabbas, *v.* 20. They *persuaded the multitude,* both by themselves and their emissaries, whom they sent abroad among them, *that they should ask Barabbas, and destroy Jesus;* suggesting that this Jesus was a deceiver, in league with Satan, an enemy to their church and temple; that, if he were let alone, the Romans would come, and take away their place and nation; that Barabbas, though a bad man, yet, having not the interest that Jesus had, could not do so much mischief. Thus they managed the mob, who otherwise were well affected to Jesus, and, if they had not been so much at the beck of their priests, would never have done such a preposterous thing as to prefer Barabbas before Jesus. Here, [1] We cannot but look upon these wicked priests with indignation; by the law, in *matters of controversy between blood and blood,* the people were to be guided by the priests, and to do as they informed them, Deut. xvii. 8, 9. This great power put into their hands they wretchedly abused, and the leaders of the people caused them to err. [2.] We cannot but look upon the deluded people with pity; *I have compassion on the multitude,* to see them hurried thus violently to so great wickedness, to see them thus priest-ridden, and falling in the ditch with their *blind leaders.*

(6.) Being thus over-ruled by the priests, at length they made their choice, *v.* 21. *Whether of the twain* (saith Pilate) *will ye that I release unto you?* He hoped that he had gained his point, to have Jesus released. But, to his great surprise, they said *Barabbas;* as if his *crimes* were *less,* and therefore he less *deserved to die;* or as if his *merits* were *greater,* and therefore he better *deserved to live.* The cry for Barabbas was so universal, one and all, that there was no colour to demand a poll between the candidates. *Be astonished, O heavens, at this, and, thou earth, be horribly afraid!* Were ever men that pretended to reason or religion, guilty of such prodigious madness, such horrid wickedness! This was it that Peter charged so home upon them (Acts iii. 14); *Ye desired a murderer to be granted to you;* yet multitudes who choose the world, rather than God, for their ruler and portion, thus *choose their own delusions.*

2. Their pressing earnestly to have Jesus crucified, *v.* 22, 23. Pilate, being amazed at their choice of Barabbas, was willing to hope that it was rather from a fondness for him than from an enmity to Jesus; and therefore he puts it to them, "*What shall I do then with Jesus?* Shall I release him likewise, for the greater honour of your feast, or will you leave it to me? No, *they all said, Let him be crucified.* That death they desired he might die, because it was looked upon as the most scandalous and ignominious; and they hoped thereby to make his followers ashamed to own him, and their relation to him. It was absurd for them to prescribe to the judge what sentence he should pass; but their malice and rage made them forget all rules of order and decency, and turned a court of justice into a *riotous, tumultuous,* and *seditious assembly.* Now was truth fallen in the street, and equity could not enter; where one *looked for judgment, behold, oppression,* the worst kind of oppression; for righteousness, behold, a cry, the worst cry that ever was, *Crucify, crucify* the Lord of glory. Though they that cried thus, perhaps, were not the same persons that the other day cried *Hosanna,* yet see what a change was made upon the mind of the populace in a little time: when he *rode in triumph* into Jerusalem, so *general* were the *acclamations of praise,* that one would have thought he had *no enemies;* but now when he was *led in triumph* to Pilate's judgment-seat, so *general* were the *outcries* of enmity, that one would think he had *no friends.* Such revolutions are there in this changeable world, through which our way to heaven lies, as our Master's did, *by honour*

and dishonour, by evil report, and good report, counter-changed (2 Cor. vi. 8); that we may not be lifted up by honour, as if, when we were applauded and caressed, we had *made our nest among the stars,* and should *die in that nest;* nor yet be dejected or discouraged by dishonour, as if, when we were despised and trampled upon, we were trodden to the lowest hell, from which there is *no redemption. Vides tu istos qui te laudant; omnes aut sunt hostes, aut (quod in æquo est) esse possunt—You observe those who applaud you; either they are all your enemies, or, which is equivalent, they may become so.* Seneca de Vita Beat.

Now, as to this demand, we are further told,

(1.) How Pilate objected against it; *Why, what evil hath he done?* A proper question to ask before we censure any in common discourse, much more for a judge to ask before he pass a sentence of death. Note, It is much for the honour of the Lord Jesus, that, though he suffered as an evil-doer, yet neither his judge nor his prosecutors could find that he had done any evil. Had he done any evil *against God?* No, he *always did those things that pleased him.* Had he done any evil against the *civil government?* No, as he did himself, so he taught others, to *render to Cæsar the things that were Cæsar's.* Had he done any evil against the *public peace?* No, he did not *strive or cry,* nor did his kingdom *come with observation.* Had he done any evil to particular persons? *Whose ox had he taken, or whom had he defrauded?* No, so far from that, that he *went about doing good.* This repeated assertion of his unspotted innocency, plainly intimates that he died to satisfy for the sins of others; for if it had not been for our transgressions that he was thus wounded, and for our offences that he was delivered up, and that upon his own voluntary undertaking to atone for them, I see not how these extraordinary sufferings of a person that had never thought, said, or done, any thing amiss, could be reconciled with the justice and equity of that providence that governs the world, and at least *permitted* this to be done in it.

(2.) How they *insisted* upon it; *They cried out the more, Let him be crucified.* They do not go about to show any evil he had done, but, right or wrong, he must be *crucified.* Quitting all pretensions to the proof of the premises, they resolve to hold the conclusion, and what was wanting in evidence to make up in clamour; this unjust judge was wearied by importunity into an unjust sentence, as he in the parable into a just one (Luke xviii. 4, 5), and the cause carried purely by noise.

III. Here is the *devolving* of the *guilt* of Christ's blood upon the *people* and *priests.*

1. Pilate endeavours to transfer it from himself, *v.* 24.

(1.) He sees it *to no purpose to contend.* What he said, [1.] Would do no good; *he could prevail nothing;* he could not convince them what an unjust unreasonable thing it was for him to condemn a man whom he believed innocent, and whom they could not prove guilty. See how strong the stream of lust and rage sometimes is; neither authority nor reason will prevail to give check to it. Nay, [2.] It was more likely to *do hurt;* he saw that rather a *tumult was made.* This rude and brutish people fell to high words, and began to threaten Pilate what they would do if he did not gratify them; and how great a matter might this fire kindle, especially when the priests, those great incendiaries, blew the coals! Now this turbulent tumultuous temper of the Jews, by which Pilate was awed to condemn Christ against his conscience, contributed more than any thing to the ruin of that nation not long after; for their frequent insurrections provoked the Romans to destroy them, though they had reduced them, and their inveterate quarrels among themselves made them an easy prey to the common enemy. Thus their sin was their ruin.

Observe how easily we may be mistaken in the inclination of the common people; the priests were apprehensive that their endeavours to *seize* Christ would have caused an uproar, especially *on the feast day;* but it proved that Pilate's endeavour to *save* him, caused an uproar, and that on the feast day; so uncertain are the sentiments of the crowd.

(2.) This puts him into a *great strait,* betwixt the peace of his own mind, and the peace of the city; he is loth to condemn an innocent man, and yet loth to *disoblige* the people, and raise a devil that would not be soon laid. Had he steadily and resolutely adhered to the sacred laws of justice, as a judge ought to do, he had not been in any perplexity; the matter was plain and past dispute, that a man in whom was found *no fault,* ought not to be crucified, upon any pretence whatsoever, nor must an unjust thing be done, to gratify any man or company of men in the world; the cause is soon decided; *Let justice be done, though heaven and earth come together—Fiat justitia, ruat cœlum.* If *wickedness proceed from the wicked,* though they be priests, yet *my hand shall not be upon him.*

(3.) Pilate thinks to trim the matter, and to pacify both the people and his own conscience too, by *doing it,* and yet *disowning* it, *acting* the thing, and yet *acquitting* himself from it at the same time. Such absurdities and self-contradictions do *they* run upon, whose convictions are *strong,* but their corruptions *stronger. Happy is he* (saith the apostle, Rom. xiv. 22) *that condemneth not himself in that thing which he alloweth;* or, which is all one, that *allows* not himself in that thing which he *condemns.*

Now Pilate endeavours to clear himself from the guilt,

[1.] By a *sign;* He *took water, and washed his hands before the multitude;* not as if he thought thereby to cleanse himself from any guilt contracted before God, but to acquit himself before the people, from so much as contracting any guilt in this matter; as if he had said, "If it be done, bear witness that it is none of my doing." He *borrowed* the ceremony from that law which appointed it to be used for the clearing of the country from the guilt of an undiscovered murder (Deut. xxi. 6, 7); and he used it the more to affect the people with the conviction he was under of the prisoner's innocency; and, probably, such was the noise of the rabble, that, if he had not used some such surprising sign, in the view of them all, he could not have been heard.

[2.] By a *saying;* in which, *First,* He *clears* himself; *I am innocent of the blood of this just person.* What nonsense was this, to condemn him, and yet protest that he was innocent of his blood! For men to protest against a thing, and yet to practise it, is only to proclaim that they sin against their consciences. Though Pilate professed his innocency, God charges him with guilt, Acts iv. 27. Some think to justify themselves, by pleading that their *hands* were not in the sin; but David kills by the sword of the children of Ammon, and Ahab by the elders of Jezreel. Pilate here thinks to justify himself, by pleading that his *heart* was not in the action; but this is an averment which will never be admitted. *Protestatio non valet contra factum—In vain does he protest against the deed which at the same time he perpetrates. Secondly,* He casts it upon the priests and people; "*See ye to it;*" if it must be done, I cannot help it, do you answer it before God and the world." Note, Sin is a brat that nobody is willing to own; and many deceive themselves with this, that they shall bear no blame if they can but find any to lay the blame upon; but it is not so easy a thing to transfer the guilt of sin as many think it is. The condition of him that is infected with the plague is not the less dangerous, either for his catching the infection from others, or his communicating the infection to others; we may be *tempted* to sin, but cannot be *forced.* The priests threw it upon Judas; *See thou to it;* and now Pilate throws it upon them; *See ye to it; for with what measure ye mete, it shall be measured to you.*

2. The priests and people *consented* to take the guilt *upon themselves;* they all said, "*His blood be on us, and on our children;* we are so well assured that there is neither sin nor danger in putting him to death, that we are willing to run the hazard of it;" as if the guilt would do no harm to them or theirs. They saw that it was the dread of guilt that made Pilate hesitate, and that he was getting over this difficulty by a fancy of transferring it; to prevent the return of his hesitation, and to confirm him in that fancy, they, in the heat of their rage, agreed to it, rather than lose the prey they had in their hands, and cried, *His blood be upon us.* Now,

(1.) By this they designed to indemnify Pilate, that is, to make him think himself indemnified, by becoming bound to divine justice, to save him harmless. But those that are themselves bankrupts and beggars will never be admitted security for others, nor taken as a bail for them. None could bear the sin of others, except him that had none of his own to answer for; it is a bold undertaking, and too big for any creature, to become bound for a sinner to Almighty God.

(2.) But they did really imprecate wrath and vengeance upon themselves and their posterity. What a desperate word was this, and how little did they think what was the direful import of it, or to what an abyss of misery it would bring them and theirs! Christ had lately told them, that upon them would come *all the righteous blood shed upon the earth,* from that of the righteous Abel; but as if that were too little, they here imprecate upon themselves the guilt of that blood which was more precious than all the rest, and the guilt of which would lie heavier. O the daring presumption of wilful sinners, that *run upon God, upon his neck,* and defy his justice! Job xv. 25, 26. Observe,

[1.] How *cruel* they were in their *imprecation.* They imprecated the punishment of this sin, not only upon themselves, but upon *their children* too, even those that were yet unborn, without so much as limiting the entail of the curse, as God himself had been pleased to limit it, to the *third and fourth generation.* It was madness to pull it upon themselves, but the height of barbarity to entail it on their posterity. Surely they were like the ostrich; they were *hardened against their young ones,* as though they were not *theirs.* What a dreadful conveyance was this of guilt and wrath to them and their heirs for ever, and this delivered by *joint consent, nemine contradicente—unanimously,* as their own *act and deed;* which certainly amounted to a forfeiture and defeasance of that ancient charter, *I will be a God to thee, and to thy seed.* Their entailing the curse of the Messiah's blood upon their nation, cut off the entail of the blessings of that blood from *their* families, that, according to another promise made to Abraham, in him *all the families of the earth* might be blessed. See what enemies wicked men are to their own children and families; those that damn their own souls, care not how many they take to hell with them.

[2.] How righteous God was, in his retribution according to this imprecation; they said, *His blood be on us, and on our children;* and God said *Amen* to it, so shall thy doom be; as they *loved cursing,* so it came upon them. The wretched remains of that abandoned people feel it to this day; from the time they imprecated this blood upon them, they were followed with one judgment after another, till they were quite laid waste, and made an astonishment, a hissing, and a byword; yet on some of them, and some of theirs, this blood came, not to *condemn* them, but to *save* them; divine mercy, upon their repenting and believing, cut off this entail, and then *the promise* was again *to them, and to their children.* God is better to us and ours than we are.

26 Then released he Barabbas unto
them: and when he had scourged
Jesus, he delivered *him* to be crucified.
27 Then the soldiers of the governor
took Jesus into the common hall, and
gathered unto him the whole band *of*
soldiers. 28 And they stripped him,
and put on him a scarlet robe. 29
And when they had platted a crown
of thorns, they put *it* upon his head,
and a reed in his right hand: and
they bowed the knee before him, and
mocked him, saying, Hail, king of the
Jews! 30 And they spit upon him,
and took the reed, and smote him on
the head. 31 And after that they
had mocked him, they took the robe
off from him, and put his own raiment
on him, and led him away to crucify
him. 32 And as they came out, they
found a man of Cyrene, Simon by
name: him they compelled to bear
his cross.

In these verses we have the *preparatives* for, and *prefaces* to, the crucifixion of our Lord Jesus. Here is,

I. The sentence passed, and the warrant signed for his execution; and this *immediately,* the same hour.

1. Barabbas was released, that notorious criminal: if he had not been put in competition with Christ for the favour of the people, it is probable that he had died for his crimes; but that proved the means of his escape; to intimate that Christ was condemned for this purpose, that sinners, even the chief of sinners, might be *released;* he was *delivered up,* that we might be delivered; whereas the *common instance* of divine Providence, is, that *the wicked is a ransom for the righteous, and the transgressor for the upright,* Prov. xxi. 18; xi. 18. In this *unparalleled instance* of divine grace, the *upright* is a *ransom for the transgressors,* the just for the unjust.

2. Jesus was *scourged;* this was an ignominious cruel punishment, especially as it was inflicted by the Romans, who were not under the moderation of the Jewish law, which forbade scourgings, above forty stripes; this punishment was most unreasonably inflicted on one that was sentenced to die: the *rods* were not to introduce the axes, but to supersede them. Thus the scripture was fulfilled, *The ploughers ploughed upon my back* (Ps. cxxix. 3), *I gave my back to the smiters* (Isa. l. 6), and, *By his stripes we are healed,* Isa. liii. 5. He was *chastised with whips,* that we might not be for ever *chastised with scorpions.*

3. He was then *delivered to be crucified;* though his chastisement was in order to our peace, yet there is no peace made but by the *blood of his cross* (Col. i. 20); therefore the scourging is not enough, he must be *crucified;* a kind of death used only among the Romans; the manner of it is such, that it seems to be the result of wit and cruelty in combination, each putting forth itself to the utmost, to make death in the highest degree terrible and miserable. A cross was set up in the ground, to which the hands and feet were nailed, on which nails the weight of the body hung, till it died of the pain. This was the death to which Christ was condemned, that he might answer the type of the brazen serpent lifted up upon a pole. It was a bloody death, a painful, shameful, cursed death; it was so miserable a death, that merciful princes appointed those who were condemned to it by the law, to be strangled first, and then nailed to the cross; so Julius Cæsar did by some pirates, *Sueton. lib.* 1. Constantine, the first Christian emperor, by an edict abolished the use of that punishment among the Romans, *Sozomen, Hist. lib.* 1. *ch.* 8. *Ne salutare signum subserviret ad perniciem—That the symbol of salvation might not be subservient to the victim's destruction.*

II. The barbarous treatment which the soldiers gave him, while things were getting ready for his execution. When he was condemned, he ought to have had some time allowed him to prepare for death. There was a law made by the Roman senate, in Tiberius's time, perhaps upon complaint of this and the like precipitation, that the execution of criminals should be deferred at least *ten days* after sentence. *Sueton in Tiber. cap.* 25. But there were scarcely allowed so many minutes to our Lord Jesus; nor had he any breathing-time during those minutes; it was a *crisis,* and there were no *lucid intervals* allowed him; *deep called unto deep,* and the storm continued without any intermission.

When he was *delivered* to be *crucified,* that was enough; they that *kill the body,* yield that there is no more that they *can do,* but Christ's enemies will *do more,* and, if it be possible, wrap up a thousand deaths in one. Though Pilate pronounced him innocent, yet his soldiers, his guards, set themselves to abuse him, being swayed more by the fury of the people *against him,* than by their master's testimony *for him;* the Jewish *rabble* infected the Roman soldiery, or perhaps it was not so much in spite to him, as to make *sport* for themselves, that they thus abused him. They understood that he *pretended to a crown; to taunt* him with that gave them some diversion, and an opportunity to make themselves and one another merry. Note, It is an argument of a base, servile, sordid spirit, to insult over those that are in misery, and to make the calamities of any matter of sport and merriment.

Observe, 1. *Where* this was done—in the *common hall.* The *governor's house,* which should have been a shelter to the wronged and abused, is made the theatre of this barbarity. I wonder that the governor, who was so desirous to acquit himself from the blood of this just person, would suffer this to be done in *his* house. Perhaps he did not order it to be done, but he *connived* at it; and those in authority will be accountable, not only for the wickedness which they *do,* or *appoint,* but for that which they do not restrain, when it is in the power of their hands. Masters of families should not suffer their houses to be places of abuse to any, nor their servants to make sport with the sins, or miseries, or religion, of others.

2. *Who* were concerned in it. They gathered the *whole band,* the soldiers that were to attend the execution, would have the whole regiment (at least five hundred, some think twelve or thirteen hundred) to share in the diversion. If Christ was thus made a *spectacle,* let none of his followers think it strange to be so used, 1 Cor. iv. 9; Heb. x. 33.

3. What particular indignities were done him.

(1.) They *stripped him, v.* 28. The shame of nakedness came in with sin (Gen. iii. 7); and therefore Christ, when he came to satisfy for sin, and take it away, was *made naked,* and submitted to *that shame,* that he might prepare for us *white raiment, to cover us,* Rev. iii. 18.

(2.) They *put on him a scarlet robe,* some old red cloak, such as the Roman soldiers wore, in imitation of the *scarlet robes* which kings and emperors wore; thus upbraiding him with his being called *a King.* This *sham* of majesty they put upon him in his dress, when nothing but meanness and misery appeared in his countenance, only to expose him to the spectators, as the more *ridiculous;* yet there was something of *mystery* in it; this was he that was *red in his apparel* (Isa. lxiii. 1, 2), that *washed his garments in wine* (Gen. xlix. 11); therefore he was dressed in a *scarlet robe.* Our sins were as *scarlet and crimson.* Christ being clad in a *scarlet robe,* signified his bearing our sins, to his shame, in his own body upon the tree; that we might wash our robes, and make them white, in the blood of the Lamb.

(3.) They *platted a crown of thorns, and put it upon his head, v.* 29. This was to carry on the humour of making him a *mock-king;* yet, had they intended it only for a *reproach,* they might have *platted a crown of straw,* or *rushes,* but they designed it to be painful to him, and to be *literally,* what crowns are said to be figuratively, lined with thorns; he that invented this abuse, it is likely, valued himself upon the wit of it; but there was a mystery in it. [1.] Thorns came in with sin, and were part of the curse that was the product of sin, Gen. iii. 18. Therefore Christ, being made a *curse for us,* and dying to remove the curse from us, felt the pain and smart of those thorns, nay, and *binds them as a crown* to him (Job xxxi. 36); for his sufferings for us were *his glory.* [2.] Now he answered to the type of Abraham's ram that was *caught in the thicket,* and so offered up instead of Isaac, Gen. xxii. 13. [3.] Thorns signify afflictions, 2 Chron. xxxiii. 11. These Christ put into a *crown;* so much did he alter the property of them to them that are his, giving them cause to *glory in tribulation,* and making it to work for them a weight of glory. [4.] Christ was crowned with thorns, to show that *his kingdom was not of this world,* nor the glory of it worldly glory, but is attended here with bonds and afflictions, while the glory of it is *to be revealed.* [5.] It was the custom of some heathen nations, to bring their sacrifices to the altars, crowned with garlands; these thorns were the garlands with which this great Sacrifice was crowned. [6.] These thorns, it is likely, fetched blood from his blessed head, which trickled down his face, *like the precious ointment* (typifying the blood of Christ with which he consecrated himself) *upon the head, which ran down upon the beard, even Aaron's beard,* Ps. cxxxiii. 2. Thus, when he came to espouse to himself his love, his dove, his undefiled church, his *head was filled with dew,* and his *locks with the drops of the night,* Cant. v. 2.

(4.) They *put a reed in his right hand;* this was intended for a *mock-sceptre,* another of the *insignia* of the majesty they jeered him with; as if this were a sceptre good enough for such a King, as was like *a reed shaken with the wind* (*ch.* xi. 7); like sceptre, like kingdom, both weak and wavering, and withering and worthless; but they were quite mistaken, for his throne is *for ever and ever,* and the *sceptre of his kingdom is a right sceptre,* Ps. xlv. 6.

(5.) *They bowed the knee before him, and mocked him, saying, Hail, King of the Jews!* Having made him a sham King, they thus make a jest of doing homage to him, thus ridiculing his pretensions to sovereignty, as Joseph's brethren (Gen. xxxvii. 8); *Shalt thou indeed reign over us?* But as they were afterward compelled to do obeisance to him, and enrich his dreams, so these here bowed the knee, in scorn to him who was, soon after this, exalted to the right hand of God, that *at his name every knee might bow,* or break before him; it is ill jesting with that which, sooner or later, will come in earnest.

(6.) They *spit upon him;* thus he had been abused in the High Priest's hall, *ch.* xxvi. 67. In doing homage, the subject kissed the sovereign, in token of his allegiance; thus Samuel kissed Saul, and we are bid to *kiss the Son:* but they, in this mock-homage, instead of kissing him, spit in his face; that blessed face which outshines the sun, and before which the angels cover theirs, was thus polluted. It is strange that the sons of men should ever do such a piece of *villany,* and that the Son of God should ever *suffer* such a piece of *ignominy.*

(7.) They *took the reed, and smote him on the head.* That which they had made the *mock-ensign* of his royalty, they now make the real instrument of *their* cruelty, and *his pain.* They smote him, it is probable, upon the *crown of thorns,* and so struck them into his head, that they might wound it the deeper, which made the more sport for them, to whom his pain was the greatest pleasure. Thus was he *despised and rejected of men; a man of sorrows, and acquainted with grief.* All this misery and shame he underwent, that he might purchase for us everlasting life, and joy, and glory.

III. The conveying of him to the place of execution. After they had mocked and abused him, as long as they thought fit, they then *took the robe off from him;* to signify their divesting him of all the kingly authority they had invested him with, by putting it on him; and they put his own raiment on him, because that was to fall to the soldiers' share, that were employed in the execution. They took off the robe, but no mention is made of their taking off the *crown of thorns,* whence it is commonly supposed (though there is no certainty of it) that he was crucified with that on his head; for as he is a Priest upon his throne, so he was a King upon his cross. Christ was led to be crucified in *his own raiment,* because he himself was to *bear our sins in his own body upon the tree.* And here,

1. They *led him away* to be *crucified;* he was led *as a lamb to the slaughter,* as a sacrifice to the altar. We may well imagine how they hurried him on, and dragged him along, with all the speed possible, lest any thing should intervene to prevent the glutting of their cruel rage with his precious blood. It is probable that they now loaded him with taunts and reproaches, and treated him as the off-scouring of all things. They led him away *out of the city;* for Christ, that he might sanctify the people with his own blood, *suffered without the gate* (Heb. xiii. 12), as if he that was the glory of them that *waited for redemption* in Jerusalem was not worthy to live among them. To this he himself had an eye, when in the parable he speaks of his being *cast out of the vineyard, ch.* xxi. 39.

2. They compelled Simon of Cyrene *to bear his cross, v.* 32. It seems, at first he *carried the cross* himself, as Isaac carried the wood for the burnt-offering, which was to burn him. And this was intended, as other things, both for pain and shame to him. But after a while they *took the cross* off from him, either, (1.) In compassion to him, because they saw it was too great a load for him. We can hardly think that they had any consideration of that, yet it teaches us that God *considers the frame* of his people, and will not *suffer them to be tempted above what they are able;* he gives them some breathing-time, but they must expect that the cross will return, and the lucid intervals only give them space to prepare for the next fit. But, (2.) Perhaps it was because he could not, with the cross on his back, go forward so fast as they would have him. Or, (3.) They were afraid, lest he should faint away under the load of his cross, and die, and so prevent what their malice further intended to do against him: thus even the *tender mercies of the wicked* (which seem to be so) *are* really *cruel.* Taking the cross off from him, they *compelled* one Simon of Cyrene to bear it, pressing him to the service by the authority of the governor or the priests. It was a reproach, and none would do it but by compulsion. Some think that this Simon was a disciple of Christ, at least a well-wisher to him, and that they knew it, and therefore put this upon him. Note, All that will approve themselves disciples indeed, must follow Christ, *bearing his cross* (*ch.* xvi. 24), *bearing his reproach,* Heb. xiii. 13. We must know the *fellowship of his sufferings for us,* and patiently submit to all the sufferings for him we are called out to; for those only shall *reign with him,* that *suffer with him;* shall sit with him in his kingdom, that drink of *his cup,* and are baptized with *his baptism.*

33 And when they were come unto
a place called Golgotha, that is to say,
a place of a skull, 34 They gave
him vinegar to drink mingled with
gall: and when he had tasted *thereof,*
he would not drink. 35 And they
crucified him, and parted his garments, casting lots: that it might
be fulfilled which was spoken by the
prophet, They parted my garments
among them, and upon my vesture
did they cast lots. 36 And sitting
down they watched him there; 37
And set up over his head his accusation written, THIS IS JESUS
THE KING OF THE JEWS. 38
Then were there two thieves crucified
with him, one on the right hand, and
another on the left. 39 And they
that passed by reviled him, wagging
their heads, 40 And saying, Thou
that destroyest the temple, and buildest
it in three days, save thyself. If thou
be the Son of God, come down from
the cross. 41 Likewise also the chief
priests mocking *him,* with the scribes
and elders, said, 42 He saved others;
himself he cannot save. If he be the
King of Israel, let him now come
down from the cross, and we will believe him. 43 He trusted in God;
let him deliver him now, if he will
have him: for he said, I am the Son
of God. 44 The thieves also, which

were crucified with him, cast the same
in his teeth. 45 Now from the sixth
hour there was darkness over all the
land unto the ninth hour. 46 And
about the ninth hour Jesus cried with
a loud voice, saying, Eli, Eli, lama
sabachthani? that is to say, My God,
my God, why hast thou forsaken me?
47 Some of them that stood there,
when they heard *that*, said, This *man*
calleth for Elias. 48 And straightway
one of them ran, and took a sponge, and
filled *it* with vinegar, and put *it* on a
reed, and gave him to drink. 49 The
rest said, Let be, let us see whether
Elias will come to save him.

We have here the crucifixion of our Lord Jesus.

I. The place where our Lord Jesus was put to death.

1. They came to a place called *Golgotha*, near adjoining to Jerusalem, probably the common place of execution. If he had had a house of his own in Jerusalem, probably, for his greater disgrace, they would have crucified him before his own door. But now in the same place where criminals were sacrificed to the justice of the government, was our Lord Jesus sacrificed to the justice of God. Some think that it was called *the place of a skull*, because it was the common charnel-house, where the bones and skulls of dead men were laid together out of the way, lest people should touch them, and be defiled thereby. Here lay the trophies of death's victory over multitudes of the children of men; and when by dying Christ would destroy death, he added this circumstance of honour to his victory, that he triumphed over death upon his own dunghill.

2. There they *crucified* him (*v.* 35), nailed his hands and feet to the cross, and then reared it up, and him hanging on it; for so the manner of the Romans was to crucify. Let our hearts be touched with the feeling of that exquisite pain which our blessed Saviour now endured, and let us look upon him who was thus pierced, and mourn. Was ever sorrow like unto his sorrow? And when we behold what manner of death he died, let us in that behold with *what manner of love* he *loved us*.

II. The barbarous and abusive treatment they gave him, in which their wit and malice vied which should excel. As if death, so great a death, were not bad enough, they contrived to add to the bitterness and terror of it.

1. By the drink they provided for him before he was nailed to the cross, *v.* 34. It was usual to have a cup of spiced wine for those to drink of, that were to be put to death, according to Solomon's direction (Prov. xxxi. 6, 7), *Give strong drink to him that is ready to perish;* but with that cup which Christ was to drink of, they mingled *vinegar and gall*, to make it sour and bitter. This signified, (1.) The *sin of man*, which is a *root of bitterness, bearing gall and wormwood*, Deut. xxix. 18. The sinner perhaps rolls it under his tongue as a sweet morsel, but to God it is *grapes of gall*, Deut. xxxii. 32. It was so to the Lord Jesus, when he bare our sins, and sooner or later it will be so to the sinner himself, *bitterness at the latter end, more bitter than death*, Eccl. vii. 26. (2.) It signified the *wrath of God*, that cup which his Father *put into his hand*, a bitter cup indeed, like the *bitter water which caused the curse*, Num. v. 18. This drink they offered him, as was literally foretold, Ps. lxix. 21. And, [1.] He *tasted thereof*, and so had the *worst* of it, took the bitter taste into his mouth; he let no bitter cup go by him untasted, when he was making atonement for all our sinful tasting of forbidden fruit; now he was *tasting* death in its full bitterness. [2.] He *would not drink it*, because he would not have the *best of it;* would have nothing like an opiate to lessen his sense of pain, for he would die so as to *feel himself die*, because he had so much *work* to *do*, as our High Priest, in his suffering work.

2. By the dividing of his garments, *v.* 35. When they nailed him to the cross, they *stripped* him of his garments, at least his *upper garments;* for by sin we were made naked, to our shame, and thus he purchased for us white raiment to cover us. If we be at any time stripped of our comforts for Christ, let us bear it patiently; he was stripped for us. Enemies may strip us of our *clothes*, but cannot strip us of our *best comforts;* cannot take from us the *garments of praise*. The clothes of those that are executed are the executioner's fee: four soldiers were employed in crucifying Christ, and they must each of them have a share: his upper garment, if it were divided, would be of no use to any of them, and therefore they agreed to *cast lots* for it. (1.) Some think that the garment was so fine and rich, that it was worth contending for; but that agreed not with the poverty Christ appeared in. (2.) Perhaps they had heard of those that had been cured by touching the hem of his garment, and they thought it valuable for some magic virtue in it. Or, (3.) They hoped to get money of his friends for such a sacred relic. Or, (4.) Because, in derision, they would seem to put a value upon it, as royal clothing. Or, (5.) It was for diversion; to pass away the time while they waited for his death, they would play a game at dice for the clothes; but, whatever they designed, the word of God is herein accomplished. In that famous *psalm*, the first words of which Christ made use of upon the cross, it was said, *They parted my garments among them, and cast lots upon my vesture*, Ps. xxii. 18. This was never true of David, but looks *primarily*

at Christ, of whom David, in spirit, spoke. Then is the offence of this part of the cross ceased; for it appears to have been by the *determinate counsel and foreknowledge of God.* Christ stripped himself of his glories, to divide them among us.

They now *sat down, and watched him, v.* 36. The chief priests were careful, no doubt, in setting this guard, lest the people, whom they still stood in awe of, should rise, and rescue him. But Providence so ordered it, that those who were appointed to *watch* him, thereby became unexceptionable witnesses for him; having the opportunity to see and hear that which extorted from them that noble confession (*v.* 54), *Truly this was the Son of God.*

3. By the *title* set up over his head, *v.* 37. It was usual for the vindicating of public justice, and putting the greater shame upon malefactors that were executed, not only by a crier to proclaim before them, but by a writing also over their heads to notify what was the crime for which they suffered; so they set up over Christ's head his accusation written, to give public notice of the charge against him; *This is Jesus the King of the Jews.* This they designed for his reproach, but God so overruled it, that even his accusation redounded to his honour. For, (1.) Here was no crime alleged against him. It is not said that he was a pretended Saviour, or a usurping King, though they would have it thought so (John xix. 21); but, *This is Jesus, a Saviour;* surely that was no crime; and, *This is the King of the Jews;* nor was that a crime; for they expected that the Messiah should be so: so that, his enemies themselves being judges, he *did no evil.* Nay, (2.) Here was a very glorious truth asserted concerning him—that he is *Jesus the King of the Jews*, that King whom the Jews expected and ought to have submitted to; so that his accusation amounts to this, That he was the true Messiah and Saviour of the world; as Balaam, when he was sent for to curse Israel, blessed them all together, and that three times (Num. xxiv. 10), so Pilate, instead of accusing Christ as a Criminal, proclaimed him a *King*, and that *three times,* in three inscriptions. Thus God makes men to serve *his* purposes, quite beyond *their own.*

4. By his companions with him in suffering, *v.* 38. There were *two thieves crucified with him* at the same time, in the same place, under the same guard; two highway-men, or robbers upon the road, as the word properly signifies. It is probable that this was appointed to be *execution-day;* and therefore they hurried the prosecution of Christ in the morning, that they might have him ready to be executed with the other criminals. Some think that Pilate ordered it thus, that this piece of necessary justice, in executing these thieves, might atone for his injustice in condemning Christ; others, that the Jews contrived it, to add to the ignominy of the sufferings of our Lord Jesus: however it was, the scripture was fulfilled in it (Isa. liii. 12), *He was numbered with the transgressors.*

(1.) It was a reproach to him, that he was *crucified with them.* Though, while he lived, he was *separate from sinners,* yet *in their deaths they were not divided,* but he was made to partake with the vilest malefactors in their plagues, as if he had been a partaker with them in their sins; for he was made sin for us, and took upon him the *likeness of sinful flesh.* He was, at his death, numbered among the transgressors, and had his lot with the wicked, that we, at our death, might be *numbered among the saints,* and have our *lot among the chosen.*

(2.) It was an additional reproach, that he was crucified *in the midst, between them,* as if he had been the worst of the three, the principal malefactor; for among *three* the *middle* is the place for the chief. Every circumstance was contrived to his dishonour, as if the great Saviour were of all others the *greatest sinner.* It was also intended to ruffle and discompose him, in his last moments, with the shrieks, and groans, and blasphemies, of these malefactors, who, it is likely, made a hideous outcry when they were nailed to the cross; but thus would Christ affect himself with the miseries of sinners, when he was suffering for their salvation. Some of Christ's apostles were afterwards crucified, as Peter, and Andrew, but none of them were crucified *with him,* lest it should have looked as if they had been joint undertakers with him, in satisfying for man's sin, and joint purchasers of life and glory; therefore he was crucified between two malefactors, who could not be supposed to contribute any thing to the merit of his death; for he himself bare our sins *in his own body.*

5. By the blasphemies and revilings with which they loaded him when he was hanging upon the cross; though we read not that they cast any reflections on the thieves that were crucified with him. One would have thought that, when they had nailed him to the cross, they had done their worst, and malice itself had been exhausted: indeed if a criminal be put into the pillory, or carted, because it is a punishment less than death, it is usually attended with such expressions of abuse; but a dying man, though an infamous man, should be treated with compassion. It is an insatiable revenge indeed which will not be satisfied with death, *so great a death.* But, to complete the humiliation of the Lord Jesus, and to show that, when he was dying, he was *bearing iniquity,* he was then *loaded with reproach,* and, for aught that appears, not one of his friends, who the other day cried *Hosanna* to him, durst be seen to show him any respect.

(1.) The common *people, that passed by, reviled him.* His extreme misery and exemplary patience under it, did not mollify them, or make them to relent; but they who by their outcries brought him to this, now think to justify themselves in it by their reproaches, as if they *did well* to *condemn* him. They *reviled* him; *εβλασφήμουν—they blasphemed* him; and *blasphemy* it was, in the strictest sense, speaking evil of him who *thought it not robbery to be equal with God.* Observe here,

[1.] The persons that reviled him; *they that passed by,* the travellers that went along the road, and it was a great *road,* leading from Jerusalem to Gibeon; they were possessed with prejudices against him by the reports and clamours of the High Priest's creatures. It is a hard thing, and requires more application and resolution than is ordinarily met with, to keep up a good opinion of persons and things that are *every where* run down, and spoken against. Every one is apt to say as the most say, and to throw a stone at that which is put into an ill name. *Turba Remi sequitur fortunam semper et odit damnatos—The Roman rabble fluctuate with a man's fluctuating fortunes, and fail not to depress those that are sinking.* Juvenal.

[2.] The gesture they used, in contempt of him—*wagging their heads;* which signifies their triumph in his fall, and their insulting over him, Isa. xxxvii. 22; Jer. xviii. 16; Lam. ii. 15. The language of it was, *Aha, so would we have it,* Ps. xxxv. 25. Thus they insulted over him that was the Saviour of their country, as the Philistines did over Samson the destroyer of their country. This very gesture was prophesied of (Ps. xxii. 7); *They shake the head at me.* And Ps. cix. 25.

[3.] The taunts and jeers they uttered. These are here recorded.

First, They upbraided him with his *destroying of the temple.* Though the judges themselves were sensible that what he had said of that was misrepresented (as appears Mark xiv. 59), yet they industriously spread it among the people, to bring an *odium* upon him, that he had a design to destroy the temple; than which nothing would more *incense* the people against him. And this was not the only time that the enemies of Christ had laboured to *make others believe* that of religion and the people of God, which they themselves have known to be *false,* and the charge *unjust* "*Thou that destroyest the temple,* that vast and strong fabric, try thy strength now in plucking up that *cross,* and drawing those *nails,* and so *save thyself;* if thou hast the power thou hast boasted of, this is a proper time to exert it, and give proof of it; for it is supposed that every man will do his utmost to *save himself.*" This made the cross of Christ such a *stumbling-block* to the Jews, that they looked upon it to be inconsistent with the *power* of the Messiah; he was *crucified in weakness* (2 Cor. xiii. 4), so it seemed to them; but indeed Christ crucified is the *Power of God.*

Secondly, They upbraided him with his saying that he was *the Son of God;* If thou be so, say they, *come down from the cross.* Now they take the devil's words out of his mouth, with which he tempted him in the wilderness (*ch.* iv. 3, 6), and renew the same assault; *If thou be the Son of God.* They think that now, or never, he must prove himself to be the *Son of God;* forgetting that he had proved it by the miracles he wrought, particularly his raising of the dead; and unwilling to wait for the complete proof of it by his own resurrection, to which he had so often referred himself and them; which, if they had observed it, would have anticipated the offence of the cross. This comes of judging things by the present aspect of them, without a due remembrance of what is *past,* and a patient expectation of *what may further be produced.*

(2.) The *chief priests and scribes,* the church rulers, and the *elders,* the state rulers, they mocked him, *v.* 41. They did not think it enough to invite the rabble to do it, but gave Christ the dishonour, and themselves the diversion, of reproaching him in their own proper persons. They should have been in the temple at their devotion, for it was the first day of the feast of unleavened bread, when there was to be a *holy convocation* (Lev. xxiii. 7); but they were here at the place of execution, spitting their venom at the Lord Jesus. How much below the grandeur and gravity of their character was this! Could any thing tend more to make them *contemptible and base before the people?* One would have thought, that, though they neither feared God nor regarded man, yet common prudence should have taught them who had so great a hand in Christ's death, to keep as much as might be behind the curtain, and to play least in sight; but nothing is so mean as that malice may stick at it. Did they disparage themselves thus, to do despite to Christ, and shall we be afraid of disparaging ourselves, by joining with the multitude to *do him honour,* and not rather say, *If this be to be vile, I will be yet more vile?*

Two things the priests and elders upbraided him with.

[1.] That he could not *save himself, v.* 42. He had been before abused in his prophetical and kingly office, and now in his priestly office as a Saviour. *First,* They take it for granted that he *could not* save himself, and therefore had not the power he pretended to, when really he *would not* save himself, because he would die to *save us.* They should have argued, "He *saved others,* therefore he *could* save himself, and if he do not, it is for some good reason." But, *Secondly,* They would insinuate, that, because he did not now save himself, therefore all his pretence to save others was but sham and delusion, and was never really done; though the truth of his miracles was demonstrated beyond contradiction. *Thirdly,* They upbraid him with being *the King of Israel.* They dreamed of the external pomp and power of the Messiah, and therefore thought *the cross* altogether disagreeable to the King of Israel, and inconsistent with that character. Many people would like the *King of Israel* well enough, if he would but *come down from the cross,* if they could have his kingdom without the tribulation through which they must *enter into* it. But the matter is settled; if no cross, then no Christ, no crown. Those that would reign with him, must be willing to suffer with him, for Christ and his cross are *nailed together* in this world. *Fourthly,* They challenged him to *come down from the cross.* And what had become of us then, and the work of our redemption and salvation? If he had been provoked by these scoffs to *come down from the cross,* and so to have left his undertaking *unfinished,* we had been for ever *undone.* But his unchangeable love and resolution set him above, and fortified him against, this temptation, so that he did not *fail,* nor was *discouraged. Fifthly,* They promised that, if he would *come down from the cross, they would believe him.* Let him give them that proof of his being the Messiah, and they will own him to be so. When they had formerly demanded a sign, he told them that the sign he would give them, should be not his *coming down from the cross,* but, which was a greater instance of his power, his *coming up from the grave,* which they had not patience to wait two or three days for. If he had *come down from the cross,* they might with as much reason have said that the soldiers had juggled in nailing him to it, as they said, when he was raised from the dead, that the *disciples came by night, and stole him away.* But to promise ourselves that we would believe, if we had such and such means and motives of faith as we ourselves would prescribe, when we do not improve what God has appointed, is not only a gross instance of the deceitfulness of our hearts, but the sorry *refuge,* or *subterfuge* rather, of an obstinate destroying infidelity.

[2.] That God, *his Father,* would *not save him* (*v.* 43); *He trusted in God,* that is, he pretended to do so; for he said, *I am the Son of God.* Those who call God *Father,* and themselves *his children,* thereby profess to put a confidence in him, Ps. ix. 10. Now they suggest, that he did but deceive himself and others, when he made himself so much the *darling of heaven;* for, if he had been the Son of God (as *Job's* friends argued concerning him), he would not have been *abandoned to* all this misery, much less *abandoned in* it. This was a *sword in his bones,* as David complains of the like (Ps. xlii. 10); and it was a *two-edged* sword, for it was intended, *First,* To *vilify* him, and to make the standers-by think him a deceiver and an impostor; as if his saying, that he was the *Son of God,* were now effectually *disproved. Secondly,* To *terrify* him, and drive him to distrust and despair of his Father's power and love; which some think, was the thing *he feared, religiously feared,* prayed against, and was *delivered from,* Heb. v. 7. David complained more of the endeavours of his persecutors to *shake his faith,* and drive him from his hope in God, than of their attempts to *shake his throne,* and drive him from his kingdom; their saying, There is *no help for him in God* (Ps. iii. 2), and, *God has forsaken him,* Ps. lxxi. 11. In this, as in other things, he was a type of Christ. Nay, these very words David, in that famous prophecy of Christ, mentions, as spoken by *his enemies* (Ps. xxii. 8); He *trusted on the Lord that he would deliver him.* Surely these priests and scribes had forgotten their psalter, or they would not have used the same words, so exactly to answer the type and prophecy: but the *scriptures must be fulfilled.*

(3.) To complete the reproach, the *thieves also that were crucified with him* were not only not reviled as he was, as if they had been saints compared with him, but, though fellow-sufferers with him, joined in with his prosecutors, and *cast the same in his teeth;* that is, one of them did, who said, *If thou be the Christ, save thyself and us,* Luke xxiii. 39. One would think that of all people this thief had *least cause,* and should have had *least mind,* to banter Christ. Partners in suffering, though for different causes, usually commiserate one another; and few, whatever they have done before, will breathe their last in revilings. But, it seems, the greatest mortifications of the body, and the most humbling rebukes of Providence, will not of themselves mortify the corruptions of the soul, nor suppress the wickedness of the wicked, without the grace of God.

Well, thus our Lord Jesus having undertaken to satisfy the justice of God for the wrong done him in his honour by sin, he did it by suffering *in his honour;* not only by divesting himself of that which was due to him as the Son of God, but by submitting to the utmost indignity that could be done to the worst of men; because he was made sin for us, he was thus made a curse for us, to make reproach easy to us, if at any time we suffer it, and have all manner of evil said against us falsely, for righteousness' sake.

III. We have here the frowns of heaven, which our Lord Jesus was under, in the midst of all these injuries and indignities from men. Concerning which, observe,

1. How this was signified—by an extraordinary and miraculous eclipse of the sun, which continued for *three hours, v.* 45. There was darkness ἐπὶ πᾶσαν τὴν γῆν—*over all the earth;* so most interpreters understand it, though our translation confines it to *that land.* Some of the ancients appealed to the annals of the nation concerning this extraordinary eclipse at the death of Christ, as a thing well known, and which gave notice to those parts of the world of something great then in doing; as the sun's going back in Hezekiah's time did. It is reported that Dionysius, at Heliopolis in Egypt, took notice of this darkness, and said, *Aut Deus naturæ patitur, aut mundi machina dissolvitur*—

Either the God of nature is suffering, or the machine of the world is tumbling into ruin. An extraordinary light gave intelligence of the birth of Christ (*ch.* ii. 2), and therefore it was proper that an extraordinary darkness should notify his death, for he is the *Light of the world.* The indignities done to our Lord Jesus, made the *heavens astonished,* and *horribly afraid,* and even put them into disorder and confusion; such wickedness as this the sun never saw before, and therefore withdrew, and would not see this. This surprising, amazing, darkness was designed to stop the mouths of those blasphemers, who were reviling Christ as he hung on the cross; and it should seem that, for the present, it struck such a terror upon them, that though their hearts were not changed, yet they were silent, and stood doubting what this should mean, till after *three hours* the darkness *scattered,* and then (as appears by *v.* 47), like Pharaoh when the plague was over, they hardened their hearts. But that which was principally intended in this darkness, was, (1.) Christ's present *conflict* with the *powers of darkness.* Now the prince of this world, and his forces, the *rulers of the darkness of this world,* were to be cast out, to be spoiled and vanquished; and to make his victory the more illustrious, he fights them on their own ground; gives them all the advantage they could have against him by this darkness, lets them take the *wind* and *sun,* and yet baffles them, and so becomes more than a conqueror. (2.) His present want of heavenly comforts. This darkness signified that dark cloud which the human soul of our Lord Jesus was now under. God makes his sun to shine upon the just and upon the unjust; but even the light of the sun was withheld from our Saviour, when he was *made sin for us. A pleasant thing it is for the eyes to behold the sun;* but because now his soul was exceeding sorrowful, and the cup of divine displeasure was filled to him without mixture, even the light of the sun was suspended. When earth denied him a drop of cold water, heaven denied him a beam of light; having to deliver us from *utter darkness,* he did himself, in the depth of his sufferings, walk in darkness, and had no light, Isa. l. 10. During the *three hours* that this darkness continued, we do not find that he said *one word,* but passed this time in a silent retirement into his own soul, which was now in agony, wrestling with the powers of darkness, and taking in the impressions of his Father's displeasure, not against himself, but the sin of man, which he was now *making his soul an offering for.* Never were there three such hours since the day that God created man upon the earth, never such a dark and awful scene; the *crisis* of that great affair of man's redemption and salvation.

2. How he complained of it (*v.* 46); *About the ninth hour,* when it began to clear up, after a long and silent conflict. *Jesus cried, Eli, Eli, lama sabachthani?* The words are related in the Syriac tongue, in which they were spoken, because worthy of double remark, and for the sake of the perverse construction which his enemies put upon them, in putting *Elias* for *Eli.* Now observe here,

(1.) Whence he borrowed this complaint—from Ps. xxii. 1. It is not probable (as some have thought) that he repeated the whole psalm; yet hereby he intimated that the whole was to be applied to him, and that David, in spirit, there spoke of his humiliation and exaltation. This, and that other word, *Into thy hands I commit my spirit,* he fetched from David's psalms (though he could have expressed himself in his own words), to teach us of what use the word of God is to us, to direct us in prayer, and to recommend to us the use of scripture-expressions in prayer, which will *help our infirmities.*

(2.) How he uttered it—*with a loud voice;* which bespeaks the extremity of his pain and anguish, the strength of nature remaining in him, and the great earnestness of his spirit in this expostulation. Now the scripture was fulfilled (Joel iii. 15, 16); *The sun and the moon shall be darkened. The Lord shall also roar out of Zion, and utter his voice from Jerusalem.* David often speaks of his *crying aloud* in prayer, Ps. lv. 17.

(3.) What the complaint was—*My God, My God, why hast thou forsaken me?* A strange complaint to come from the mouth of our Lord Jesus, who, we are sure, was *God's elect, in whom his soul delighted* (Isa. xlii. 1), and one in whom he was always *well pleased.* The Father now loved him, nay, he knew that *therefore he loved him, because he laid down his life for the sheep;* what, and yet forsaken of him, and in the midst of his sufferings too! Surely never sorrow was like unto that sorrow which extorted such a complaint as this from one who, being perfectly free from sin, could never be a terror to himself; but the heart knows its own bitterness. No wonder that such a complaint as this made the earth to quake, and rent the rocks; for it is enough to make both the *ears of every one that hears it to tingle,* and ought to be spoken of with great reverence.

Note, [1.] That our Lord Jesus was, in his sufferings, for a time, *forsaken by his Father.* So he saith himself, who we are sure was under no mistake concerning his own case. Not that the union between the divine and human nature was in the least weakened or shocked; no, he was *now by the eternal Spirit offering himself:* nor as if there were any abatement of his Father's love to him, or his to his Father; we are sure that there was upon his mind no horror of God, or despair of his favour, nor any thing of the torments of hell; but his Father forsook him; that is, *First,* He delivered him up into the hands of his enemies, and did not appear to deliver him out of their hands. He let loose the powers of darkness against him, and suffered them to do their worst, worse than against Job. Now was that scripture fulfilled (Job xvi. 11), *God hath turned me over into the hands of the wicked;* and no angel is sent from heaven to deliver him, no friend on earth raised up to appear for him. *Secondly,* He withdrew from him the present comfortable sense of his complacency in him. When *his soul* was first *troubled,* he had a *voice from heaven* to comfort him (John xii. 27, 28); when he was in his agony in the garden, there appeared an angel from heaven strengthening him; but now he had neither the one nor the other. God hid his face from him, and for awhile withdrew his rod and staff in the darksome valley. God *forsook* him, not as he forsook Saul, leaving him to an endless despair, but as sometimes he forsook David, leaving him to a present despondency. *Thirdly,* He let out upon his soul an afflicting sense of his wrath against man for sin. Christ was made *Sin* for us, a *Curse* for us; and therefore, though God loved him as a Son, he frowned upon him as a Surety. These impressions he was pleased to *admit,* and to *waive* that *resistance* of them which he *could have made;* because he would accommodate himself to this part of his undertaking, as he had done to all the rest, when it was in his power to have avoided it.

[2.] That Christ's being *forsaken* of his Father was the most grievous of his sufferings, and that which he complained most of. Here he laid the most doleful accents; he did not say, "Why am I scourged? And why spit upon? And why nailed to the cross?" Nor did he say to his disciples, when they turned their back upon him, *Why have ye forsaken me?* But when his Father stood at a distance, he cried out thus; for this was it that *put wormwood and gall* into the affliction and misery. This brought the *waters into the soul,* Ps. lxix. 1—3.

[3.] That our Lord Jesus, even when he was thus forsaken of his Father, kept hold of him as his God, notwithstanding; *My God, my God;* though forsaking me, yet *mine.* Christ was God's *servant* in carrying on the work of redemption, to him he was to make satisfaction, and by him to be carried through and crowned, and upon that account he calls him *his God;* for he was now *doing his will.* See Isa. xlix. 5—9. This supported him, and bore him up, that even in the depth of his sufferings God was his God, and this he resolves to keep fast hold of.

(4.) See how his enemies impiously bantered and ridiculed this complaint (*v.* 47); *They said, This man calleth for Elias.* Some think that this was the ignorant mistake of the Roman soldiers, who had heard talk of Elias, and of the Jews' expectation of the coming of Elias, but knew not the signification of *Eli, Eli,* and so made this blundering comment upon these words of Christ, perhaps not hearing the latter part of what he said, for the noise of the people. Note, Many of the reproaches cast upon the word of God and the people of God, take rise from gross mistakes. Divine truths are often corrupted by ignorance of the language and style of the scripture. Those that hear by the halves, pervert what they hear. But others think that it was the wilful mistake of some of the Jews, who knew very well what he said, but were disposed to abuse him, and make themselves and their companions merry, and to misrepresent him as one who, being forsaken of God, was driven to trust in creatures; perhaps hinting also, that he who had pretended to be himself the Messiah, would now be glad to be beholden to Elias, who was expected to be only the harbinger and forerunner of the Messiah. Note, It is no new thing for the most pious devotions of the best men to be ridiculed and abused by profane scoffers; nor are we to think it strange if what is well said in praying and preaching be misconstrued, and turned to our reproach; Christ's words were so, though he spoke as never man spoke.

IV. The cold comfort which his enemies ministered to him in this agony, which was like all the rest.

1. Some *gave him vinegar to drink* (*v.* 48); instead of some cordial-water to revive and refresh him under this heavy burthen, they tantalized him with that which did not only add to the reproach they were loading him with, but did too sensibly represent that cup of trembling which his Father had *put into his hand. One of them ran* to fetch it, seeming to be officious to him, but really glad of an opportunity to abuse and affront him, and afraid lest any one should take it out of his hands.

2. Others, with the same purpose of disturbing and abusing him, refer him to Elias (*v.* 49); "*Let be, let us see whether Elias will come to save him.* Come, let him alone, his case is desperate, neither heaven nor earth can help him; let us do nothing either to hasten his death, or to retard it; he has appealed to Elias, and *to Elias let him go.*"

50 Jesus, when he had cried again
with a loud voice, yielded up the
ghost. 51 And, behold, the veil of
the temple was rent in twain from the
top to the bottom; and the earth did
quake, and the rocks rent; 52 And
the graves were opened; and many
bodies of the saints which slept arose,
53 And came out of the graves after
his resurrection, and went into the
holy city, and appeared unto many.
54 Now when the centurion, and they
that were with him, watching Jesus,
saw the earthquake, and those things
that were done, they feared greatly,
saying, Truly this was the Son of God.
55 And many women were there be-

holding afar off, which followed Jesus
from Galilee, ministering unto him: 56
Among which was Mary Magdalene,
and Mary the mother of James and
Joses, and the mother of Zebedee's
children.

We have here, at length, an account of the death of Christ, and several remarkable passages that attended it.

I. The *manner* how he breathed his last (*v.* 50); between the third and the sixth hour, that is, between nine and twelve o'clock, as we reckon, he was nailed to the cross, and soon after the ninth hour, that is, between three and four o'clock in the afternoon, he *died.* That was the time of the offering of the evening sacrifice, and the time when the paschal lamb was killed; and Christ our Passover was sacrificed for us and offered himself in the evening of the world a sacrifice to God of a sweet-smelling savour. It was at that time of the day, that the angel Gabriel delivered to Daniel that glorious prediction of the Messiah, Dan. ix. 21, 24, &c. And some think that from that very time when the angel spoke it, to this time when Christ died, was just seventy weeks, that is, four hundred and ninety years to a day, to an hour; as the departure of *Israel* out of Egypt was at the end of the four hundred and thirty years, *even the self-same day,* Exod. xii. 41.

Two things are here noted concerning the manner of Christ's dying.

1. That he *cried with a loud voice,* as before, *v.* 46. Now,

(1.) This was a sign, that, after all his pains and fatigues, his life was *whole* in him, and nature *strong.* The voice of dying men is one of the first things that fails; with a panting breath and a faltering tongue, a few broken words are hardly spoken, and more hardly heard. But Christ, just before he expired, spoke like a man *in his full strength,* to show that his life was not forced from him, but was freely *delivered* by him into his Father's hands, as *his own act and deed.* He that had strength to cry thus when he died, could have got loose from the arrest he was under, and have bid defiance to the powers of death; but to show that *by the eternal Spirit he offered himself,* being the Priest as well as the Sacrifice, he *cried with a loud voice.*

(2.) It was significant. This *loud voice* shows that he attacked our spiritual enemies with an undaunted courage, and such a bravery of resolution as bespeaks him hearty in the cause and daring in the encounter. He was now *spoiling principalities and powers,* and in this loud voice he did, as it were, *shout for mastery,* as one *mighty to save,* Isa. lxiii. 1. Compare with this, Isa. xlii. 13, 14. He now bowed himself with all his might, as Samson did, when he said, *Let me die with the Philistines,* Judg. xvi. 30. *Animamque in vulnere ponit—And lays down his life.* His crying with a loud voice when he died, signified that his death should be published and proclaimed to all the world; all mankind being concerned in it, and obliged to take notice of it. Christ's loud cry was like a trumpet blown over the sacrifices.

2. That then he *yielded up the ghost.* This is the usual periphrasis of dying; to show that the Son of God upon the cross did truly and properly die by the violence of the pain he was put to. His *soul* was separated from his *body,* and so his body was left really and truly dead. It was certain that he *did die,* for it was requisite that he should die; *thus it was written,* both in the *close rolls* of the *divine counsels,* and in the *letters patent* of the *divine predictions,* and therefore thus *it behoved him to suffer.* Death being the penalty for the breach of the first covenant *(Thou shalt surely die),* the Mediator of the new covenant must make atonement *by means of death,* otherwise no remission, Heb. ix. 15. He had undertaken to make his soul an *offering for sin;* and he did it, when he *yielded up the ghost,* and voluntarily resigned it.

II. The miracles that attended his death. So many miracles being wrought *by him* in his life, we might well expect some to be wrought concerning him at his death, for his name was called *Wonderful.* Had he been fetched away as Elijah in a *fiery chariot,* that had itself been miracle enough; but, being sent for away by an ignominous cross, it was requisite that his humiliation should be attended with some signal emanations of the divine glory.

1. *Behold, the veil of the temple was rent in twain.* This relation is ushered in with *Behold;* "Turn aside, and see this great sight, and be astonished at it." Just as our Lord Jesus expired, at the time of the offering of the evening-sacrifice, and upon a solemn day, when the priests were officiating in the temple, and might themselves be eye-witnesses of it, *the veil of the temple was rent* by an invisible power; that veil which parted between the *holy place* and the *most holy.* They had condemned him for saying, *I will destroy this temple,* understanding it literally; now by this specimen of his power he let them know that, if he had pleased, he could have made his words good. In this, as in others of Christ's miracles, there was a mystery.

(1.) It was in correspondence with the temple of Christ's body, which was now in the dissolving. This was the true temple, in which dwelt *the fulness of the Godhead;* when Christ *cried with a loud voice, and gave up the ghost,* and so dissolved that temple, the literal temple did, as it were, echo to that cry, and answer the stroke, by *rending its veil.* Note, Death is the rending of the veil of flesh which interposes between us and the holy of holies; the death of Christ was so, the death of true Christians is so.

(2.) It signified the revealing and unfolding of the mysteries of the Old Testament. The veil of the temple was for concealment, as was that on the face of Moses, therefore it was called the *veil of the covering;* for it was highly penal for any person to see the furniture of the most holy place, except the High-Priest, and he but once a year, with great ceremony and through a cloud of smoke; all which signified the darkness of that dispensation, 2 Cor. iii. 13. But now, at the death of Christ, all was laid open, the mysteries were unveiled, so that now he that runs may read the meaning of them. Now we see that the mercy-seat signified *Christ* the great *Propitiation;* the pot of *manna* signified Christ the Bread of life. Thus *we all with open face behold, as in a glass* (which helps the sight, as the veil hindered it), *the glory of the Lord. Our eyes see the salvation.*

(3.) It signified the uniting of Jew and Gentile, by the removing of the partition wall between them, which was the ceremonial law, by which the Jews were distinguished from all other people (as a *garden enclosed)*, were brought near to God, while others were made to *keep their distance.* Christ, in his death, repealed the ceremonial law, cancelled that *hand-writing of ordinances,* took it out of the way, nailed it to his cross, and so *broke down the middle wall of partition;* and by abolishing those institutions *abolished the enmity,* and *made in himself of twain one new man* (as two rooms are made one, and that large and lightsome, by taking down the partition), so *making peace,* Eph. ii. 14—16. Christ died, to rend all dividing veils, and to make all his one, John xvii. 21.

(4.) It signified the consecrating and laying open of *a new and living way* to God. The veil kept people off from drawing near to the most holy place, where the *Shechinah* was. But the rending of it signified that Christ by his death opened a way to God, [1.] *For himself.* This was the great *day of atonement,* when our Lord Jesus, as the great *High-Priest,* not *by the blood of goats and calves, but by his own blood, entered once for all into the holy place;* in token of which the veil was rent, Heb. ix. 7, *&c.* Having offered his sacrifice in the outer court, the blood of it was now to be sprinkled upon the mercy-seat within the veil; wherefore *lift up your heads, O ye gates,* and *be ye lift up, ye everlasting doors; for the King of glory,* the Priest of glory, *shall come in.* Now was he caused to draw near, and made to approach, Jer. xxx. 21. Though he did not personally ascend into the holy place not made with hands till above forty days after, yet he immediately acquired a right to enter, and had a virtual admission. [2.] *For us in him:* so the apostle applies it, Heb. x. 19, 20. We have *boldness to enter into the holiest, by that new and living way which he has consecrated for us through the veil.* He died, to *bring us to God,* and, in order thereunto, to rend that veil of guilt and wrath which interposed between us and him, to take away the *cherubim* and *flaming sword,* and to open the way to *the tree of life.* We have free access through Christ to the throne of grace, or mercy-seat, now, and to the throne of glory hereafter, Heb. iv. 16; vi. 20. The rending of the veil signified (as that ancient hymn excellently expresses it), that, *when Christ had overcome the sharpness of death, he opened the kingdom of heaven to all believers.* Nothing can obstruct or discourage our access to heaven, for the veil is rent; *a door is opened in heaven,* Rev. iv. 1.

2. The *earth did quake;* not only mount Calvary, where Christ was crucified, but the *whole land,* and the adjacent countries. This earthquake signified two things.

(1.) The *horrible* wickedness of *Christ's crucifiers.* The earth, by trembling under such a load, bore its testimony to the innocency of him that was persecuted, and against the impiety of those that persecuted him. Never did the whole creation, before, groan under such a burthen as the Son of God crucified, and the guilty wretches that crucified him. The earth *quaked,* as if it *feared to open its mouth* to *receive* the blood of Christ, so much more precious than that of Abel, which it had received, and was *cursed* for it (Gen. iv. 11, 12); and as if it *fain would open its mouth,* to swallow up those rebels that put him to death, as it had swallowed up Dathan and Abiram for a much less crime. When the prophet would express God's great displeasure against the wickedness of the wicked, he asks, *Shall not the land tremble for this?* Amos viii. 8.

(2.) The *glorious* achievements of *Christ's cross.* This *earthquake* signified the mighty shock, nay, the fatal blow, now given to the devil's kingdom. So vigorous was the assault Christ now made upon the infernal powers, that (as of old, *when he went out of Seir, when he marched through the field of Edom)* the *earth trembled,* Judg. v. 4; Ps. lxviii. 7, 8. God shakes all nations, when the Desire of all nations is to come; and there is a *yet once more,* which perhaps refers to this shaking, Hag. ii. 6, 21.

3. The *rocks rent;* the hardest and firmest part of the earth was made to feel this mighty shock. Christ had said, that if the children should cease to cry *Hosanna, the stones would immediately cry out;* and now, in effect, they did so, proclaiming the glory of the suffering Jesus, and themselves more sensible of the wrong done him than the hard-hearted Jews were, who yet will shortly be glad to find a *hole in the rocks, and a cleft in the ragged rocks,* to hide them from the face of him that sitteth on the throne. See Rev. vi. 16; Isa. ii. 21. But when God's *fury is poured out like fire, the rocks are thrown down by him,* Nah. i. 6. Jesus Christ is *the Rock;* and the rending of *these* rocks, signified the rending of *that* rock, (1.) That in the clefts of it we may be *hid,* as Moses in the cleft of the rock at Horeb, that there we may *behold the*

glory of the Lord, as he did, Exod. xxxiii. 22. Christ's dove is said to be *hid in the clefts of the rock* (Cant. ii. 14), that is, as some make the allusion, sheltered in the wounds of our Lord Jesus, the Rock rent. (2.) That from the cleft of it rivers of living water may flow, and follow us in this wilderness, as from the rock which Moses *smote* (Exod. xvii. 6), and which God clave (Ps. lxxviii. 15); and *that rock was Christ,* 1 Cor. x. 4. When we celebrate the memorial of Christ's death, our hard and rocky hearts must be *rent*—the heart, and not the garments. That heart is harder than a rock, that will not *yield,* that will not *melt,* where Jesus Christ is *evidently set forth crucified.*

4. The *graves were opened.* This matter is not related so fully as our curiosity would wish; for the scripture was not intended to gratify that; it should seem, the same earthquake that rent the rocks, *opened the graves,* and many bodies of *saints which slept, arose.* Death to the saints is but the *sleep* of the body, and the *grave* the bed it *sleeps in;* they awoke by the power of the Lord Jesus, and (*v.* 53) came *out of the graves after his resurrection, and went into Jerusalem, the holy city, and appeared unto many.* Now here,

(1.) We may raise many enquiries concerning it, which we cannot resolve: as, [1.] *Who* these *saints* were, that *did arise.* Some think, the *ancient patriarchs,* that were in such care to be buried in the land of Canaan, perhaps in the believing foresight of the advantage of this early resurrection. Christ had lately proved the doctrine of the resurrection from the instance of the patriarchs (*ch.* xxii. 32), and here was a speedy confirmation of his argument. Others think, these that arose were *modern saints,* such as had seen Christ in the flesh, but died before him; as his father Joseph, Zecharias, Simeon, John Baptist, and others, that had been known to the disciples, while they lived, and therefore were the fitter to be witnesses to them in an *apparition* after. What if we should suppose that they were the *martyrs,* who in the Old-Testament times had sealed the truths of God with their blood, that were thus *dignified* and *distinguished?* Christ particularly points at them as his forerunners, *ch.* xxiii. 35. And we find (Rev. xx. 4. 5), that those who were *beheaded for the testimony of Jesus,* arose *before the rest of the dead.* Sufferers with Christ shall *first* reign with him. [2.] It is uncertain whether (as some think) they arose to life, now at the death of Christ, and disposed of themselves elsewhere, but did not *go into the city* till after his resurrection; or whether (as others think), though *their sepulchres* (which the *Pharisees* had *built* and *garnished* (*ch.* xxiii. 29), and so made remarkable, were shattered now by the earthquake (so little did God regard that hypocritical respect), yet they did not *revive* and *rise* till after the resurrection; only, for brevity-sake, it is mentioned here, upon the mention of the *opening of the graves,* which seems more probable. [3.] Some think that they arose only to bear witness of Christ's resurrection to those to whom they appeared, and, having finished their testimony, retired to their graves again. But it is more agreeable, both to Christ's honour and theirs, to *suppose,* though we cannot *prove,* that they arose as Christ did, to *die no more,* and therefore ascended with him to glory. Surely on them who did partake of his first resurrection, a *second* death had no power. [4.] To whom they appeared (not *to all the people* it is certain, but to *many*), whether enemies or friends, in what manner they appeared, how often, what they said and did, and how they disappeared, are secret things which belong not to us; we must not covet to be *wise above what is written.* The relating of this matter so briefly, is a plain intimation to us, that we must not look that way for a confirmation of our faith; we have a more sure word of prophecy. See Luke xvi. 31.

(2.) Yet we may learn many good lessons from it. [1.] That even those who lived and died before the death and resurrection of Christ, had saving benefit thereby, as well as those who have lived since; for he *was* the same *yesterday* that he is *to-day,* and will be *for ever,* Heb. xiii. 8. [2.] That Jesus Christ, by dying, conquered, disarmed, and disabled, death. These saints that arose, were the present trophies of the victory of Christ's cross over the powers of *death,* which he thus *made a show of openly.* Having by death destroyed him that had the power of death, he thus *led captivity captive,* and gloried in these *re-taken prizes,* in them fulfilling that scripture, *I will ransom them from the power of the grave.* [3.] That, in virtue of Christ's resurrection, the bodies of all the saints shall, in the fulness of time, *rise again.* This was an earnest of the general resurrection at the last day, when *all that are in the graves shall hear the voice of the Son of God.* And perhaps Jerusalem is *therefore* called here the *holy city,* because the saints, at the general resurrection, shall enter into the *new Jerusalem;* which will be indeed what the other was in name and type only, the *holy city,* Rev. xxi. 2. [4.] That all the saints do, by the influence of Christ's death, and in conformity to it, rise from the *death of sin* to the *life of righteousness.* They are *raised up with him* to a divine and spiritual life; they go *into the holy city,* become *citizens* of it, have their conversation in it, and *appear to many,* as persons not of this world.

III. The conviction of his enemies that were employed in the execution (*v.* 54), which some make no less than another miracle, all things considered. Observe,

1. The persons convinced; *the centurion, and they that were with him watching Jesus;* a captain and his company, that were set on the guard on this occasion. (1.) They were *soldiers,* whose profession is commonly harden-

ing, and whose breasts are commonly not so susceptible as some others of the impressions either of fear or pity. But there is no spirit too big, too bold, for the power of Christ to break and humble. (2.) They were *Romans, Gentiles,* who knew not the scriptures which were now fulfilled; yet they only were convinced. A sad presage of the *blindness* that should *happen to Israel,* when the gospel should be sent to the Gentiles, to open their eyes. Here were the Gentiles *softened,* and the Jews *hardened.* (3.) They were the persecutors of Christ, and those that but just before had reviled him, as appears Luke xxiii. 36. How soon can God, by the power he has over men's consciences, alter their language, and fetch confessions of his truths, to his own glory, out of the mouths of those that have *breathed* nothing but *threatenings, and slaughter,* and blasphemies!

2. The means of their conviction; they perceived *the earthquake,* which frightened them, and saw the other *things that were done.* These were designed to assert the honour of Christ in his sufferings, and had their end on these soldiers, whatever they had on others. Note, The dreadful appearances of God in his providence sometimes work strangely for the conviction and awakening of sinners.

3. The expressions of this conviction, in two things.

(1.) The *terror* that was *struck* upon them; they *feared greatly;* feared lest they should have been buried in the darkness, or swallowed up in the earthquake. Note, God can easily frighten the most daring of his adversaries, and make them know themselves to be but men. Guilt puts men into fear. He that, when iniquity abounds, doth not *fear always,* with a fear of *caution,* when judgments are abroad, cannot but *fear greatly,* with a fear of *amazement;* whereas there are those who will not fear, *though the earth be removed,* Ps. xlvi. 1, 2.

(2.) The *testimony* that was *extorted* from them; they said, *Truly this was the Son of God;* a noble confession; Peter was blessed for it, *ch.* xvi. 16, 17. It was the great matter now in dispute, the point upon which he and his enemies had *joined issue, ch.* xxvi. 63, 64. His disciples believed it, but at this time durst not confess it; our Saviour himself was tempted to question it, when he said, *Why hast thou forsaken me?* The Jews, now that he was dying upon the cross, looked upon it as plainly determined against him, that he was not the Son of God, because he did not come down from the cross. And yet now this centurion and the soldiers make this voluntary confession of the Christian faith, *Truly this was the Son of God.* The best of his disciples could not have said more at any time, and at this time they had not faith and courage enough to say thus much. Note, God can maintain and assert the honour of a truth then when it seems to be crushed, and run down; for *great is the truth, and will prevail.*

IV. The attendance of his friends, that were witnesses of his death, *v.* 55, 56. Observe,

1. Who they were; *many women who followed him from Galilee.* Not his apostles (only elsewhere we find John by the cross, John xix. 26), their hearts failed them, they durst not appear, for fear of coming under the same condemnation. But here were a company of women, some would have called them *silly* women, that *boldly* stuck to Christ, when the rest of his disciples had basely deserted him. Note, Even those of the weaker sex are often, by the grace of God, made strong in faith, that Christ's strength may be made perfect in weakness. There have been women martyrs, famous for courage and resolution in Christ's cause. Now of these women it is said, (1.) That they had *followed Jesus from Galilee,* out of the great love they had to him, and a desire to hear him preach; otherwise, the males only were obliged to come up, to worship at the feast. Now having followed him such a long journey as from Galilee to Jerusalem, eighty or a hundred miles, they resolved not to forsake him now. Note, Our former services and sufferings for Christ should be an argument with us, faithfully to persevere to the end in our attendance on him. Have we followed him *so far* and so long, done so much, and laid out so much for him, and shall we forsake him now? Gal. iii. 3, 4. (2.) That they *ministered to him* of their substance, for his necessary subsistence. How gladly would they have ministered to him now, if they might have been admitted! But, being forbidden that, they resolved to *follow him.* Note, When we are restrained from doing what we *would,* we must do what we can, in the service of Christ. Now that he is *in heaven,* though he is out of the reach of our *ministration,* he is not out of the reach of our *believing views.* (3.) Some of them are particularly named; for God will *honour* those that *honour* Christ. They were such as we have several times met with *before,* and it was their praise, that we meet with them *to the last.*

2. What they did; they were *beholding afar off.*

(1.) They stood *afar off.* Whether their own fear or their enemies' fury kept them at a distance, is not certain; however, it was an aggravation of the sufferings of Christ, that his *lovers and friends stood aloof from his sore,* Ps. xxxviii. 11; Job xix. 13. Perhaps they might have come nearer, if they would; but good people, when they are in sufferings, must not think it strange, if some of their best friends be shy of them. When Paul's danger was imminent, *no man stood by him,* 2 Tim. iv. 16. If we be thus looked strangely upon, remember, our Master was so before us.

(2.) They were there *beholding,* in which they showed a concern and kindness for Christ; when they were debarred from doing any other office of love to him, they looked a look of love toward him. [1.] It was a *sorrowful* look; they looked unto him who was now pierced, and *mourned;* and no doubt, were *in bitterness* for him. We may well imagine how it cut them to the heart, to see him in this torment; and what floods of tears it fetched from their eyes. Let us with an eye of faith behold Christ and him crucified, and be affected with that great love wherewith he loved us. But, [2.] It was no more than a look; they beheld him, but they could not *help him.* Note, When Christ was in his sufferings, the best of his friends were but spectators and lookers on, even the *angelic guards stood trembling by,* saith Mr. Norris, for he *trod the wine-press alone,* and of the people there was none with him; so *his own arm wrought salvation.*

57 When the even was come, there
came a rich man of Arimathæa, named
Joseph, who also himself was Jesus'
disciple: 58 He went to Pilate, and
begged the body of Jesus. Then
Pilate commanded the body to be
delivered. 59 And when Joseph had
taken the body, he wrapped it in a
clean linen cloth, 60 And laid it in
his own new tomb, which he had
hewn out in the rock: and he rolled
a great stone to the door of the sepulchre, and departed. 61 And there
was Mary Magdalene, and the other
Mary, sitting over against the sepulchre. 62 Now the next day, that
followed the day of the preparation,
the chief priests and Pharisees came
together unto Pilate, 63 Saying, Sir,
we remember that that deceiver said,
while he was yet alive, After three
days I will rise again. 64 Command
therefore that the sepulchre be made
sure until the third day, lest his disciples come by night, and steal him
away, and say unto the people, He is
risen from the dead: so the last error
shall be worse than the first. 65
Pilate said unto them, Ye have a
watch: go your way, make *it* as sure
as ye can. 66 So they went, and
made the sepulchre sure, sealing the
stone, and setting a watch.

We have here an account of Christ's *burial,* and the manner and circumstances of it, concerning which observe, 1. The *kindness* and *good will* of his friends that *laid him in the grave.* 2. The *malice* and *ill will* of his enemies that were very solicitous to keep him there.

I. His friends gave him a *decent burial.* Observe,

1. In general, that Jesus Christ was *buried;* when his precious soul was gone to paradise, his blessed body was deposited in the chambers of the grave, that he might answer the type of Jonas, and fulfil the prophecy of Isaias; he *made his grave with the wicked.* Thus in all things he must be made *like unto his brethren,* sin only excepted, and, like us, unto dust *he must return.* He was buried, to make his death the more certain, and his resurrection the more illustrious. Pilate would not deliver his body to be buried, till he was well assured that he was really dead; while the witnesses lay *unburied,* there were some hopes concerning them, Rev. xi. 8. But Christ, the great Witness, is as one *free among the dead, like the slain that lie in the grave.* He was *buried,* that he might take off the terror of the grave, and make it easy to us, might warm and perfume that cold noisome bed for us, and that we might be *buried with him.*

2. The particular circumstances of his burial here related.

(1.) The time *when* he was buried; *when the evening was come;* the same evening that he died, before sun-set, as is usual in burying malefactors. It was not deferred till the next day, because it was *the sabbath;* for burying the dead is not proper work either for a day of rest or for a day of rejoicing, as the sabbath is.

(2.) The person that took care of the funeral was Joseph of Arimathea. The apostles had all fled, and none of them appeared to show this respect to their Master, which the disciples of John *showed* to him after he was beheaded, who *took up his body, and buried it, ch.* xiv. 12. The women that followed him durst not move in it; then did God stir up this good man to do it; for what work God has to do, he will find out instruments to do it. Joseph was a fit man, for, [1.] He had wherewithal to do it, being a *rich man.* Most of Christ's disciples were poor men, such were most fit to go about the country to preach the gospel; but here was one that was a *rich man,* ready to be employed in a piece of service which required *a man of estate.* Note, Worldly wealth, though it is to many an objection in religion's way, yet, in some services to be done for Christ, it is an advantage and an opportunity, and it is well for those who have it, if withal they have a heart to use it for God's glory. [2.] He was well affected to our Lord Jesus, for he was himself *his disciple,* believed in him, though he did not openly profess it. Note, Christ has more secret disciples than we are aware of; seven thousand in Israel, Rom. xi. 4.

(3.) The grant of the dead body procured from Pilate, *v.* 58. Joseph *went to* Pilate, the proper person to be applied to on this occasion, who had the disposal of the body; for in things wherein the power of the magistrate is concerned, due regard must be had to that power, and nothing done to break in upon it. What we do that is good, must be done peaceably, and not tumultuously. Pilate was willing to give the body to one that would inter it decently, that he might do something towards atoning for the guilt his conscience charged him with in condemning an innocent person. In Joseph's petition, and Pilate's ready grant of it, *honour* was done to Christ, and a testimony borne to his *integrity*.

(4.) The dressing of the body in its grave-clothes (*v.* 59); though he was an honourable counsellor, yet he himself *took the body*, as it should seem, into his own arms, from the infamous and accursed tree (Acts xiii. 29); for where there is true love to Christ, no service will be thought too mean to stoop to for him. Having taken it, he wrapped it in a *clean linen cloth;* for burying in linen was then the common usage, which Joseph complied with. Note, Care is to be taken of the dead bodies of good men, for there is a glory intended for them at the resurrection, which we must hereby testify our belief of, and wind up the dead body as designed for a better place. This common act of humanity, if done after a *godly sort,* may be made an acceptable piece of Christianity.

(5.) The depositing of it in the sepulchre, *v.* 60. Here there was nothing of that pomp and solemnity with which the grandees of the world are *brought to the grave, and laid in the tomb,* Job xxi. 32. A private funeral did best befit him whose kingdom came not with observation.

[1.] He was laid in a *borrowed* tomb, in Joseph's burying place; as he had not a house of his own, wherein to *lay his head* while he lived, so he had not a grave of his own, wherein to *lay his body* when he was dead, which was an instance of his poverty; yet in this there might be somewhat of a mystery. The grave is the peculiar heritage of a *sinner,* Job xxiv. 19. There is nothing we can truly call our own but our sins and our graves; he *returneth to his earth,* Psalm cxlvi. 4. When we go to the grave, we go to our own place; but our Lord Jesus, who had no sin of his own, had no grave of his own; dying under imputed sin, it was fit that he should be buried in a *borrowed* grave; the Jews designed that he should have *made his grave with the wicked,* should have been buried with the thieves with whom he was crucified, but God over-ruled it, so as that he should make it *with the rich in his death,* Isa. liii. 9.

[2.] He was laid in a *new tomb,* which Joseph, it is likely, designed *for himself;* it would, however, be *never the worse* for *his* lying in it, who was to rise so quickly, but a *great deal the better* for *his* lying in it, who has altered the property of the grave, and made it *anew* indeed, by turning it into a *bed of rest,* nay into a *bed of spices,* for all the saints.

[3.] In a tomb that was *hewn out of a rock;* the ground about Jerusalem was generally rocky. Shebna had his sepulchre hewn out thereabouts *in a rock,* Isa. xxii. 16. Providence ordered it that Christ's sepulchre should be in a solid entire rock, that no room might be left to suspect his disciples had access to it by some underground passage, or broke through the back wall of it, to steal the body; for there was no access to it but by the door, which was watched.

[4.] A *great stone was rolled to the door of his sepulchre;* this also was according to the custom of the Jews in burying their dead, as appears by the description of the grave of Lazarus (John xi. 38), signifying that those who are dead, are *separated* and *cut off from all the living;* if the grave were his prison, now was the prison-door locked and bolted. The rolling of the stone to the grave's mouth, was with them as filling up the grave is with us, it completed the funeral. Having thus in silence and sorrow deposited the precious body of our Lord Jesus in the grave, the house *appointed for all living,* they *departed* without any further ceremony. It is the most melancholy circumstance in the funerals of our Christian friends, when we have laid their bodies in the dark and silent grave, to go home, and leave them behind; but alas, it is not we that *go home,* and *leave them behind,* no, it is they that are gone to the better home, and have left us behind.

(6.) The company that attended the funeral; and that was very *small* and *mean.* Here were none of the relations in mourning, to follow the corpse, no formalities to grace the solemnity, but some good women that were true mourners—*Mary Magdalene, and the other Mary, v.* 56. These, as they had attended him *to the cross,* so they followed him to *the grave;* as if they composed themselves to sorrow, they *sat over against the sepulchre,* not so much to fill their eyes with the sight of what was done, as to empty them in rivers of tears. Note, True love to Christ will carry us through, to the utmost, in following him. Death itself cannot quench that divine fire, Cant. viii. 6, 7.

II. His enemies did what they could to prevent his resurrection; what they did herein was *the next day that followed the day of the preparation, v.* 62. That was the seventh day of the week, the Jewish *sabbath,* yet not expressly called so, but described by this periphrasis, because it was now shortly to give way to the Christian sabbath, which began the day after. Now, 1. All that day, Christ lay dead in the grave; having for six days laboured and done all his work, on the seventh day he *rested,* and was *refreshed.* 2. On that day, the *chief priests and Pharisees,* when they should have been at their devotions, asking pardon for the sins of the week past, were dealing with Pilate about securing the sepulchre, and so *adding rebellion to their sin.* They that had so often quarrelled with

Christ for works of the greatest mercy on that day, were themselves busied in a work of the greatest malice. Observe here,

(1.) Their address to *Pilate;* they were vexed that the body was given to one that would bury it decently; but, since it must be so, they desire a guard may be set on the sepulchre.

[1.] Their petition sets forth, that *that deceiver* (so they call him who is truth itself) *had said, After three days I will rise again.* He had said so, and his disciples *remembered* those very words for the confirmation of their faith, but his persecutors remember them for the provocation of their rage and malice. Thus the same word of Christ to the one was a savour of life unto life, to the other of death unto death. See how they compliment Pilate with the title of *Sir,* while they reproach Christ with the title of *Deceiver.* Thus the most malicious slanderers of *good men* are commonly the most sordid flatterers of *great men.*

[2.] It further sets forth their jealousy; *lest his disciples come by night, and steal him away, and say, He is risen.*

First, That which *really* they were afraid of, was, his *resurrection;* that which is most Christ's honour and his people's joy, is most the terror of his enemies. That which exasperated Joseph's brethren against him, was the presage of his rise, and of his having dominion over them (Gen. xxxvii. 8); and all they aimed at, in what they did against him, was, to prevent that. Come, say they, let us *slay him,* and see *what will become of his dreams.* So the chief priests and Pharisees laboured to defeat the predictions of Christ's resurrection, saying, as David's enemies of him (Ps. xli. 8), *Now that he lieth, he shall rise up no more;* if he should rise, that would break all their measures. Note, Christ's enemies, even when they have gained their point, are still in fear of losing it again. Perhaps the priests were surprised at the respect shown to Christ's dead body by Joseph and Nicodemus, two honourable counsellors, and looked upon it as an ill presage; nor can they forget his raising Lazarus from *the dead,* which so confounded them.

Secondly, That which they took on them to be afraid of, was, lest *his disciples should come by night, and steal him away,* which was a very improbable thing; for, 1. They had not the courage to own him while he lived, when they might have done him and themselves real service; and it was not likely that his death should put courage into such cowards. 2. What could they promise themselves by stealing away his body, and making people believe he was risen; when, if he should not rise, and so prove himself a deceiver, his disciples, who had left all for him in this world, in dependence upon a recompence in the other world, would of all others suffer most by the imposture, and would have had reason to throw the first stone at his name? What good would it do them, to carry on a cheat upon themselves, to steal away his body, and say, *He is risen;* when, if he were not risen, their faith was vain, and they were *of all men the most miserable?* The chief priests apprehend that if the doctrine of Christ's resurrection be once preached and believed, the *last error will be worse than the first;* a proverbial expression, intimating no more than this, that we shall all be routed, all undone. They think it was *their error,* that they had so long connived at his preaching and miracles, which *error* they thought they had *rectified* by putting him to death; but if people should be persuaded of his resurrection, that would *spoil all* again, his interest would revive with him, and theirs must needs sink, who had so barbarously murdered him. Note, Those that oppose Christ and his kingdom, will see not only their attempts baffled, but themselves miserably *plunged* and *embarrassed,* their errors each worse than other, and the last worst of all, Ps. ii. 4, 5.

[3.] In consideration hereof, they humbly move to have a guard set upon the sepulchre till the third day; *Command that the sepulchre be made sure.* Pilate must still be their drudge, his civil and military power must both be engaged to serve their malice; one would think that death's prisoners needed no other guard, and that the grave were *security* enough to itself; but what will not those fear, who are conscious to themselves both of *guilt* and *impotency,* in opposing the Lord and his anointed?

(2.) Pilate's answer to this address (*v.* 65); *Ye have a watch, make it sure, as sure as you can.* He was ready to gratify Christ's friends, in allowing them the body, and his enemies, in setting a guard upon it, being desirous to please all sides, while perhaps he laughed in his sleeve at both for making such ado, *pro* and *con,* about the dead body of a man, looking upon the hopes of one side and the fears of the other to be alike ridiculous. *Ye have a watch;* he means the constant guard that was kept in the tower of Antonia, out of which he allows them to detach as many as they pleased for that purpose, but, as if ashamed to be himself seen in such a thing, he leaves the management of it wholly to them. Methinks that word, *Make it as sure as you can,* looks like a banter, either, [1.] Of their *fears;* "Be sure to set a strong guard upon the dead man;" or rather, [2.] Of their *hopes;* "Do your worst, try your wit and strength to the utmost; but if he be of God, he will rise, in spite of you and all your guards." I am apt to think, that by this time Pilate had had some talk with the centurion, his own officer, of whom he would be apt to enquire how that *just man* died, whom he had condemned with such reluctance; and that he gave him such an account of those things as made him conclude that *truly he was the Son of God;* and Pilate would give more credit to him than to a thousand of those spiteful priests that called him a *Deceiver;* and if so, no marvel that he tacitly derides their project, in thinking to secure the sepulchre upon him who had so lately rent the rocks, and made the earth to quake. Tertullian, speaking of Pilate, saith, *Ipse jam pro suâ conscientiâ Christianus—In his conscience he was a Christian;* and it is possible that he might be under such convictions at this time, upon the centurion's report, and yet never be thoroughly persuaded, any more than Agrippa or Felix was, to be a Christian.

(3.) The wonderful care they took, hereupon, to secure the sepulchre (*v.* 66); *They sealed the stone;* probably with the great seal of their *sanhedrim,* whereby they interposed their authority, for who durst break the public seal? But not trusting too much to that, withal they *set a watch,* to keep *his disciples* from coming to *steal him away,* and, if possible, to hinder *him* from coming out of the grave. So they intended, but God brought this good out of it, that they who were set to *oppose* his resurrection, thereby had an opportunity to observe it, and did so, and told the chief priests what they observed, who were thereby rendered the more inexcusable. Here was all the power of earth and hell combined to keep Christ a prisoner, but all in vain, when his hour was come; death, and all those sons and heirs of death, could then no longer hold him, no longer have dominion over him. To guard the sepulchre against the poor weak disciples, was folly, because *needless;* but to think to guard it against the power of God was folly, because *fruitless* and to no purpose; and yet they thought they had *dealt wisely.*

CHAP. XXVIII.

In the foregoing chapters, we saw the Captain of our salvation engaged with the powers of darkness, attacked by them, and vigorously attacking them; victory seemed to hover between the combatants; nay, at length, it inclined to the enemies' side, and our Champion fell before them; behold, God has delivered his strength into captivity, and his glory into the enemies' hand. Christ in the grave is like the ark in Dagon's temple; the powers of darkness seemed to ride masters, but then the Lord awaked as one out of sleep, and like a mighty man that shouteth by reason of wine, Ps. lxxviii. 61, 65. The Prince of our peace is in this chapter rallying again, coming out of the grave, a Conqueror, yea, more than a conqueror, leading captivity captive; though the ark be a prisoner, Dagon falls before it, and it proves that none is able to stand before the holy Lord God. Now the resurrection of Christ being one of the main foundations of our religion, it is requisite that we should have infallible proofs of it; four of which proofs we have in this chapter, which are but a few of many, for Luke and John give a larger account of the proofs of Christ's resurrection than Matthew and Mark do. Here is, I. The testimony of the angel to Christ's resurrection, ver. 1—8. II. His appearance himself to the women, ver. 9, 10. III. The confession of the adversaries that were upon the guard, ver. 11—15. IV. Christ's appearance to the disciples in Galilee, and the commission he gave them, ver. 16—20.

IN the end of the sabbath, as it began to dawn toward the first *day*
of the week, came Mary Magdalene
and the other Mary to see the sepulchre. 2 And, behold, there was a
great earthquake: for the angel of
the Lord descended from heaven, and
came and rolled back the stone from
the door, and sat upon it. 3 His
countenance was like lightning, and
his raiment white as snow: 4 And
for fear of him the keepers did shake,
and became as dead *men.* 5 And the
angel answered and said unto the
women, Fear not ye: for I know that
ye seek Jesus, which was crucified.
6 He is not here: for he is risen, as
he said. Come, see the place where
the Lord lay. 7 And go quickly, and
tell his disciples that he is risen from
the dead; and, behold, he goeth before you into Galilee; there shall ye
see him: lo, I have told you. 8 And
they departed quickly from the sepulchre with fear and great joy; and did
run to bring his disciples word. 9
And as they went to tell his disciples,
behold, Jesus met them, saying, All
hail. And they came and held him
by the feet, and worshipped him. 10
Then said Jesus unto them, Be not
afraid: go tell my brethren that they
go into Galilee, and there shall they
see me.

For the proof of Christ's resurrection, we have here the testimony of *the angel,* and of *Christ* himself, concerning his resurrection. Now we may think that it would have been better, if the matter had been so ordered, that a competent number of witnesses should have been present, and have seen the stone rolled away by the angel, and the dead body reviving, as people saw Lazarus come out of the grave, and then the matter had been past dispute; but let us not prescribe to Infinite Wisdom, which ordered that the witnesses of his resurrection should see him *risen,* but not see him *rise.* His incarnation was a mystery; so was this *second incarnation* (if we may so call it), this *new making* of the body of Christ, for his exalted state; it was therefore *made in secret. Blessed are they that have not seen, and yet have believed.* Christ gave such proofs of his resurrection as were *corroborated* by the scriptures, and by the *word* which he had *spoken* (Luke xxiv. 6, 7—44; Mark xvi. 7); for here we must *walk by faith, not by sight.* We have here,

I. The *coming* of the *good women* to the *sepulchre.*

Observe, 1. *When* they came; *in the end of the sabbath, as it began to dawn toward the first day of the week, v.* 1. This fixes the time of Christ's resurrection.

(1.) He arose the *third day* after his death; that was the time which he had often prefixed, and he kept within it. He was buried in the evening of the sixth day of the week, and arose in the morning of the first day of the following week, so that he lay in the grave about thirty-six or thirty-eight hours. He lay so long, to show that he was really and truly dead; and no longer, that he might not *see corruption.* He arose the third day, to answer the type of the prophet Jonas (*ch.* xii. 40), and to accomplish that prediction (Hos. vi. 2), *The third day he will raise us up, and we shall live in his sight.*

(2.) He arose *after the Jewish sabbath,* and it was the passover-sabbath; all that day he lay in the grave, to signify the abolishing of the Jewish feasts and the other parts of the ceremonial law, and that his people must be dead to such observances, and take no more notice of them than he did when he *lay in the grave.* Christ on *the sixth day finished* his work; he said, *It is finished;* on the seventh day he rested, and then on the first day of the next week did as it were begin a new world, and enter upon new work. Let no man therefore judge us now in respect of *the new moons,* or of the *Jewish sabbaths,* which were indeed a shadow of good things to come, but the *substance* is *of Christ.* We may further observe, that the time of the saints' lying in the grave, is a sabbath to them (such as the Jewish sabbath was, which consisted chiefly in bodily rest), for there they *rest from their labours* (Job iii. 17); and it is owing to Christ.

(3.) He arose upon the *first day of the week;* on the first day of the first week God *commanded the light to shine out of darkness;* on this day therefore did he who was to be the Light of the world, shine out of the darkness of the grave; and the seventh-day sabbath being buried with Christ, it arose again in the first-day sabbath, called the *Lord's day* (Rev. i. 10), and no other day of the week is from henceforward mentioned in all the New Testament than this, and this often, as the day which Christians religiously observed in solemn assemblies, to the honour of Christ, John xx. 19, 26; Acts xx. 7; 1 Cor. xvi. 2. If the deliverance of Israel out of the land of the north superseded the remembrance of that out of Egypt (Jer. xxiii. 7, 8), much more doth our redemption by Christ eclipse the glory of God's former works. The sabbath was instituted in remembrance of the *perfecting* of the work of creation, Gen ii. 1. Man by his revolt made a breach upon that *perfect* work, which was never perfectly repaired till Christ arose from the dead, and the *heavens and the earth were* again *finished,* and the disordered *hosts of them* modelled anew, and the day on which this was done was justly *blessed and sanctified,* and the seventh day from that. He who on that day arose from the dead, is the same by whom, and for whom, all things were at first created, and now anew created.

(4.) He arose *as it began to dawn* toward that day; as soon as it could be said that the *third day* was come, the time prefixed for his resurrection, he *arose;* after his withdrawings from his people, he returns with all convenient *speed,* and *cuts the work* as *short in righteousness* as may be. He had said to his disciples, that though within a little while they *should not see him,* yet again *a little while,* and they *should see him,* and accordingly he made it as little a while as possible, Isa. liv. 7, 8. Christ arose *when the day began* to *dawn,* because then the day-spring from on high did again visit us, Luke i. 78. His passion began in the night; when he hung on the cross the sun was darkened; he was laid in the grave in the dusk of the evening; but he arose from the grave when the sun was near rising, for he is the *bright and morning Star* (Rev. xxii. 16), the *true Light.* Those who address themselves early in the morning to the religious services of the Christian sabbath, that they may take the day before them, therein follow this example of Christ, and that of David, *Early will I seek thee.*

2. Who they were, that came to the sepulchre; *Mary Magdalene and the other Mary,* the same that attended the funeral, and *sat over against the sepulchre,* as before they *sat over against the cross;* still they studied to express their love to Christ; still they were enquiring after him. Then shall we *know,* if we thus *follow on to know.* No mention is made of the Virgin Mary being with them; it is probable that the *beloved disciple,* who had taken her to his own home, hindered her from *going to the grave to weep there.* Their attendance on Christ not only *to* the grave, but *in* the grave, represents his like care for those that are his, when they have *made their bed in the darkness.* As Christ in the grave was beloved of the *saints,* so the saints in the grave are beloved of Christ; for death and the grave cannot slacken that bond of love which is between them.

3. What they *came to do:* the other evangelists say that they came to anoint the body; Matthew saith that they came to *see the sepulchre,* whether it was as they left it; hearing perhaps, but not being sure, that the chief priests had set a guard upon it. They went, to show their good-will in another visit to the dear remains of their beloved Master, and perhaps not without some thoughts of his resurrection, for they could not have quite forgotten all he had said of it. Note, Visits to the grave are of great use to Christians, and will help to make it familiar to them, and to take off the terror of it, especially visits to the grave of our Lord Jesus, where we may see sin buried out of sight, the pattern of our sanctification, and the great proof of redeeming love shining illustriously even in that *land of darkness.*

II. The appearance of an angel of the Lord to them, *v.* 2—4. We have here an account of the manner of the resurrection of Christ, as far as it was fit that we should know.

1. There was a *great earthquake.* When he died, the earth that *received him,* shook for fear; now that he arose, the earth that *resigned him,* leaped for joy in his exaltation

This earthquake did as it were *loose* the bond of death, and *shake off* the fetters of the grave, and introduce the *Desire of all nations,* Hag. ii. 6, 7. It was the *signal* of Christ's victory; notice was hereby given of it, that, when the *heavens rejoiced,* the *earth* also might be *glad.* It was a *specimen* of the *shake* that will be given to the earth at the general resurrection, when mountains and islands shall be removed, that the earth may no longer *cover her slain.* There was a *noise and a shaking* in the valley, when the *bones were to come together, bone to his bone,* Ezek. xxxvii. 7. The kingdom of Christ, which was now to be set up, made the earth to quake, and *terribly shook it.* Those who are sanctified, and thereby raised to a spiritual life, while it is in the doing find an earthquake in their own bosoms, as Paul, who *trembled* and was *astonished.*

2. The *angel of the Lord descended from heaven.* The angels frequently attended our Lord Jesus, at his birth, in his temptation, in his agony; but upon the cross we find no angel attending him: when his Father *forsook him,* the angels withdrew from him; but now that he is resuming the glory he had before the foundation of the world, now, behold, the *angels of God worship him.*

3. He came, and rolled back the stone from the door, and sat upon it. Our Lord Jesus could have *rolled back the stone* himself by his own power, but he chose to have it done by an angel, to signify that having undertaken to make satisfaction for our sin, imputed to him, and being under arrest pursuant to that imputation, he did not *break prison,* but had a fair and *legal discharge,* obtained from heaven; he did not break prison, but an officer was sent on purpose to *roll away the stone,* and so to open the prison door, which would never have been done, if he had not made a *full satisfaction.* But being delivered for our offences, to complete the deliverance, he was *raised again for our justification;* he died to pay our debt, and rose again to take out our acquittance. The *stone* of our sins was *rolled* to the door of the grave of our Lord Jesus (and we find the rolling of a great stone to signify the *contracting of guilt,* 1 Sam. xiv. 33); but to demonstrate that divine justice was satisfied, an angel was commissioned to roll back the stone; not that the angel *raised him from the dead,* any more than those that *took away the stone* from Lazarus's grave raised him, but thus he intimated the consent of Heaven to his release, and the joy of Heaven in it. The enemies of Christ had sealed the stone, resolving, like Babylon, not to *open the house of his prisoners; shall the prey be taken from the mighty?* For this was *their hour;* but all the powers of death and darkness are under the control of the God of light and life. An angel from heaven has power to *break the seal,* though it were the *great seal of Israel,* and is able to *roll away the stone,* though ever so great. Thus the *captives of the mighty are taken away.* The angel's *sitting* upon the *stone,* when he had *rolled it away,* is very observable, and bespeaks a secure triumph over all the obstructions of Christ's resurrection. There he sat, defying all the powers of hell to roll the stone to the grave again. Christ erects his seat of rest and seat of judgment upon the opposition of his enemies; *the Lord sitteth upon the floods.* The angel sat as a guard to the grave, having frightened away the enemies' *black* guard; he sat, expecting the women, and ready to give them an account of his resurrection.

4. That his *countenance was like lightning, and his raiment white as snow, v.* 3. This was a visible representation, by that which we call *splendid* and *illustrious,* of the *glories* of the invisible world, which know no *difference of colours.* His look upon the keepers was like *flashes of lightning; he cast forth lightning, and scattered them,* Ps. cxliv. 6. The *whiteness* of his raiment was an emblem not only of purity, but of joy and triumph. When Christ died, the court of heaven *went into deep mourning,* signified by the *darkening of the sun;* but when he arose, they again put on the *garments of praise.* The glory of this angel represented the glory of Christ, to which he was now risen, for it is the same description that was given of him in his transfiguration (*ch.* xvii. 2); but when he conversed with his disciples after his resurrection, he drew a veil over it, and it bespoke the glory of the saints in their resurrection, when they shall be *as the angels of God in heaven.*

5. That *for fear of him the keepers did shake, and became as dead men, v.* 4. They were *soldiers,* that thought themselves hardened against fear, yet the very sight of an angel struck them with terror. Thus *when* the Son of *God arose to judgment, the stout-hearted were spoiled,* Ps. lxxvi. 5, 9. Note, The resurrection of Christ, as it is the joy of his friends, so it is the terror and confusion of his enemies. *They did shake;* the word ἐσείσθησαν is the same with that which was used for the earthquake, *v.* 2, σείσμος. When the *earth* shook, these *children of the earth,* that had their portion in it, *shook too;* whereas, those that have their happiness in things above, *though the earth be removed, yet are without fear.* The keepers became *as dead men,* when he whom they kept guard upon became alive, and they whom they kept guard against revived with him. It struck a terror upon them, to see themselves baffled in that which was their business here. They were posted here, to *keep a dead man in his grave*—as easy a piece of service surely as was ever assigned them, and yet it proves too hard for them. They were told that they must expect to be assaulted by a company of feeble faint-hearted disciples, who for fear of them would soon *shake* and become as *dead men,* but are amazed when they find themselves attacked by a *mighty angel,* whom they dare not look in

the face. Thus doth God *frustrate* his enemies by *frightening them,* Ps. ix. 20.

III. The message which this angel delivered to the women, *v.* 5—7.

1. He *encourages them against their fears, v.* 5. To come near to graves and tombs, especially in silence and solitude, has something in it *frightful,* much more was it so to those women, to find an angel at the sepulchre; but he soon makes them easy with the word, *Fear not ye.* The keepers shook, and became as dead men, but, *Fear not ye.* Let the sinners in Zion be afraid, for there is cause for it; but, *Fear not, Abraham,* nor any of the faithful seed of Abraham; why should the daughters of Sarah, that *do well,* be afraid *with any amazement?* 1 Pet. iii. 6. "*Fear not ye.* Let not the news I have to tell you, be any surprise to you, for you were told before that your Master would rise; let it be no terror to you, for his resurrection will be your consolation; fear not any hurt, that I will do you, nor any evil tidings I have to tell you. *Fear not ye, for I know that ye seek Jesus.* I know you are friends to the cause. I do not come to frighten you, but to encourage you." Note, Those that *seek Jesus,* have no reason to be *afraid;* for, if they seek him diligently they shall *find him,* and shall find him their *bountiful Rewarder.* All our believing enquiries after the Lord Jesus are observed, and taken notice of, in heaven; *I know that ye seek Jesus;* and shall certainly be answered, as these were, *with good words, and comfortable words. Ye seek Jesus that was crucified.* He mentions his being crucified, the more to commend their love to him; "You seek him still, though *he was crucified;* you retain your kindness for him notwithstanding." Note, True believers love and seek Christ, not only *though* he was crucified, but *because* he was so.

2. He *assures them of the resurrection of Christ;* and there was enough in that to silence their fears (*v.* 6); He *is not here, for he is risen.* To be told *He is not here,* would have been no welcome news to those who sought him, if it had not been added, *He is risen.* Note, It is matter of comfort to those who seek Christ, and miss of finding him where they expected, that *he is risen:* if we find him not in sensible comfort, yet *he is risen.* We must not hearken to those who say, *Lo, here is Christ, or, Lo, he is there,* for he is not *here,* he is not *there,* he is *risen.* In all our enquiries after Christ, we must remember that he is *risen;* and we must seek him as one *risen.* (1.) Not with any *gross carnal* thoughts of him. There were those that *knew Christ after the flesh;* but now henceforth know we him so no more, 2 Cor. v. 16. It is true, he had a body; but it is now a *glorified body.* They that make pictures and images of Christ, forget that *he is not here, he is risen;* our communion with him must be spiritual, by faith in his word, Rom. x. 6—9. (2.) We must seek him with great *reverence* and *humility,* and an awful regard to his glory, for *he is risen.* God has *highly exalted him,* and *given him a name above every name,* and therefore every knee and every soul must *bow before him.* (3.) We must seek him with a *heavenly mind;* when we are ready to make this world our home, and to say, *It is good to be here,* let us remember our Lord Jesus *is not here, he is risen,* and therefore let not our *hearts* be *here,* but let them *rise too,* and *seek the things that are above,* Col. iii. 1—3; Phil. iii. 20.

Two things the angel refers these women to, for the confirmation of their faith, touching Christ's resurrection.

[1.] To his *word* now *fulfilled,* which they might *remember; He is risen, as he said.* This he vouches as the proper object of faith; "He said that he *would rise,* and you know that he is the *Truth* itself, and therefore have reason to expect that he *should rise;* why should you be backward to *believe* that which he told you would be?" Let us never think that strange, of which the word of Christ has raised our expectations, whether the *sufferings of this present time,* or the *glory* that is *to be revealed.* If we remember what Christ hath said *to us,* we shall be the less surprised at what he does *with us.* This angel, when he said. *He is not here, he is risen,* makes it to appear that he preaches no other gospel than what they had already received, for he refers himself to the word of Christ as sufficient to bear him out; *He is risen, as he said.*

[2.] To his *grave* now *empty,* which they might *look into;* "*Come, see the place where the Lord lay.* Compare what you have *heard,* with what you *see,* and, putting both together, you will *believe.* You see that *he is not here,* and, remembering what he said, you may be satisfied that *he is risen;* come, *see the place,* and you will see that he is not there, you will see that he could not be stolen thence, and therefore must conclude that he is risen." Note, It may be of use to affect us, and may have a good influence upon us, to come, and with an eye of faith *see the place where the Lord lay.* See the marks he has there left of his love in condescending so low for us; see how *easy* he has made that *bed,* and how *lightsome,* for us, by lying in it himself; when we look into the grave, where we expect we must lie, to take off the terror of it, let us look into the grave where the Lord lay; the place where *our Lord* lay, so the Syriac. The angels own him for *their* Lord, as well as *we;* for the *whole family,* both in heaven and earth, is *named from him.*

3. He *directs them* to go *carry the tidings* of it to his disciples (*v.* 7); Go *quickly, and tell his disciples.* It is probable that they were for entertaining themselves with the sight of the sepulchre and discourse with the angels. It was good to be here, but they have other work appointed them; *this is a day of good tidings,* and though they have the *premier seisin* of the comfort, the *first taste* of it, yet

they must not have the *monopoly* of it, must not hold their peace, any more than those lepers, 2 Kings vii. 9. They must go *tell the disciples.* Note, Public usefulness to others must be preferred before the pleasure of secret communion with God ourselves: for *it is more blessed to give than to receive.* Observe,

(1.) The *disciples* of Christ must first be *told the news;* not, Go, tell the *chief priests* and the *Pharisees,* that they may be *confounded;* but, Tell the disciples, that they may be *comforted.* God anticipates the joy of his friends more than the *shame* of his enemies, though the perfection of both is reserved for hereafter. *Tell his disciples;* it may be they will believe your report, however tell them, [1.] That they may encourage themselves under their present sorrows and dispersions. It was a dismal time with them, between grief and fear; what a cordial would this be to them now, to hear, *their Master is risen!* [2.] That they may enquire further into it themselves. This alarm was sent them, to awaken them from that strange stupidity which had seized them, and to raise their expectations. This was to set them on seeking him, and to prepare them for his appearance to them. General hints excite to closer searches. They shall now hear of him, but shall very shortly see him. Christ discovers himself *gradually.*

(2.) The *women* are sent to tell it to them, and so are made, as it were, the *apostles of the apostles.* This was an honour put upon them, and a recompence for their constant affectionate adherence to him, at the cross, and in the grave, and a rebuke to the disciples who forsook him. Still God chooses the weak things of the world, to confound the mighty, and puts the treasure, not only into *earthen* vessels, but here into the *weaker* vessels; as *the woman, being deceived* by the suggestions of an evil angel, *was first in the transgression* (1 Tim. ii. 14), so these women, being duly informed by the instructions of a good angel, were first in the belief of the redemption from transgression by Christ's resurrection, that that reproach of their sex might be rolled away, by putting this in the balance against it, which is their perpetual praise.

(3.) They were bid to *go quickly* upon this errand. Why, what haste was there? Would not the news keep cold, and be welcome to them at any time? Yes, but they were now overwhelmed with grief, and Christ would have this cordial hastened to them; when Daniel was humbling himself before God for sin, the angel Gabriel was caused to fly *swiftly* with a message of comfort, Dan. ix. 21. We must always be ready and forward; [1.] To obey the commands of God, Ps. cxix. 60. [2.] To do good to our brethren, and to carry comfort to them, as those that felt from their afflictions; *Say not, Go, and come again, and to-morrow I will give;* but now quickly.

(4.) They were directed to appoint the disciples to *meet him in Galilee.* There were other appearances of Christ to them before that in *Galilee,* which were sudden and surprising; but he would have one to be solemn and public, and gave them notice of it before. Now this general rendezvous was appointed in Galilee, eighty or a hundred miles from Jerusalem; [1.] *In kindness* to those of his disciples that remained in Galilee, and *did not* (perhaps they *could not*) come up to Jerusalem; into that country therefore he would go, to manifest himself to his friends there. *I know thy works, and where thou dwellest.* Christ knows where his disciples dwell, and will visit there. Note, The exaltation of Christ doth not make him forget the the meaner and poorer sort of his disciples, but even to them that are at a distance from the plenty of the means of grace he will graciously *manifest himself.* [2.] In consideration of the weakness of his disciples that were now at Jerusalem, who as yet were *afraid of the Jews,* and durst not appear publicly, and therefore this meeting was adjourned to Galilee. Christ knows our fears, and considers our frame, and made his appointment where there was least danger of disturbance.

Lastly, The angel solemnly affirms upon his word the truth of what he had related to them; "*Lo, I have told you,* you may be assured of it, and depend upon it; *I* have told you, who dare not tell a lie. *The word spoken by angels was stedfast,* Heb. ii. 2. God had been wont formerly to make known his mind to his people by the ministration of angels, as at the giving of the law; but as he intended in gospel times to lay aside that way of communication (for *unto the angels hath he not put in subjection the world to come,* nor appointed them to be the preachers of the gospel), this angel was *now* sent to certify the resurrection of Christ to the disciples, and so leave it in their hands to be published to the world, 2 Cor. iv. 7. In saying, *Lo, I have told you,* he doth, as it were, discharge himself from the blame of their unbelief, if they should not receive this record, and throw it upon them; "*I have done my errand,* I have faithfully delivered my message, now look you to it, believe it at your peril; whether you will hear or whether you will forbear, *I have told you.*" Note, Those messengers from God, that discharge their trust faithfully, may take the comfort of that, whatever the success be, Acts xx. 26, 27.

IV. The women's *departure* from the *sepulchre,* to bring notice to the disciples, *v.* 8. And observe,

1. What frame and temper of spirit they were in; They *departed with fear and great joy;* a strange mixture, fear and joy at the same time, in the same soul. To hear that Christ was risen, was matter of joy; but to be led into his grave, and to see an angel, and talk with him about it, could not but cause fear. It was good news, but they were *afraid* that it was too *good* to be true. But

observe, it is said of their *joy*, It was *great* joy; it is not said so of their fear. Note, (1.) Holy fear has joy attending it. They that serve the Lord with *reverence*, serve him with *gladness*. (2.) Spiritual joy is mixed with trembling, Ps. ii. 11. It is only perfect love and joy that will cast out all fear.

2. What haste they made; *They did run*. The fear and joy together quickened their pace, and added wings to their motion; the angel bid them *go quickly*, and they *ran*. Those that are sent on God's errand must not loiter, or lose time; where the *heart* is *enlarged* with the glad tidings of the gospel, the feet will *run the way of God's commandments*.

3. What errand they went upon; They ran, to *bring his disciples word*. Not doubting but it would be joyful news to them, they ran, to comfort them with the same comforts wherewith they themselves were comforted of God. Note, The disciples of Christ should be forward to communicate to each other their experiences of sweet communion with heaven; should tell others what God has *done for their souls*, and spoken to them. Joy in Christ Jesus, like the ointment of the right hand, will betray itself, and fill all places within the lines of its communication with its odours. When Samson found honey, he brought it to his parents.

V. Christ's appearing to the women, to confirm the testimony of the angel, *v.* 9, 10. These zealous good women not only heard the first tidings of him, but had the first sight of him, after his resurrection. The angel directed those that would see him, to go to Galilee, but before that time came, even *here also*, they *looked after him* that lives, and sees them. Note, Jesus Christ is often better than his word, but never worse; often anticipates, but never frustrates, the believing expectations of his people.

Here is, 1. Christ's surprising appearance to the women; *As they went to tell his disciples, behold, Jesus met them*. Note, God's gracious visits usually meet us in the way of duty, and to those who use what they have for others' benefit, more shall be given. This interview with Christ was unexpected, *or ever they were aware*, Cant. vi. 12. Note, Christ is nearer to his people than they imagine. They needed not *descend into the deep*, to fetch Christ thence; he *was not there, he was risen;* nor *go up to heaven*, for he *was not yet ascended:* but Christ was *nigh them*, and still in *the word is nigh us*.

2. The salutation wherewith he accosted them; *All hail*—χαίρετε. We use the old *English form of salutation*, wishing *all health* to those we meet; for so *All hail* signifies, and is expressive of the Greek form of salutation here used, answering to that of the Hebrew, *Peace be unto you*. And it bespeaks, (1.) The good-will of Christ to us and our happiness, even since he entered upon his state of exaltation. Though he is advanced, he wishes us as well as ever, and is as much concerned for our comfort. (2.) The freedom and holy familiarity which he used in his fellowship with his disciples; for he called them *friends*. But the Greek word signifies, *Rejoice ye*. They were affected both with *fear* and *joy;* what he said to them tended to encourage their joy (*v.* 9), *Rejoice ye*, and to silence their fear (*v.* 10), *Be not afraid*. Note, It is the will of Christ that his people should be a cheerful joyful people, and his resurrection furnishes them with abundant matter for joy.

3. The affectionate respect they paid him; *They came, and held him by the feet, and worshipped him*. Thus they expressed, (1.) The *reverence* and *honour* they had *for* him; they threw themselves at his feet, put themselves into a posture of adoration, and *worshipped him* with humility and godly fear, as the Son of God, and now exalted. (2.) The *love* and *affection* they had *to* him; they *held him, and would not let him go*, Cant. iii. 4. How *beautiful* were the *feet of the Lord Jesus* to them! Isa. lii. 7. (3.) The *transport of joy* they were in, now that they had this further assurance of his resurrection; they welcomed it with both arms. Thus we must embrace Jesus Christ offered us in the gospel, with *reverence* cast ourselves at his feet, by faith *take hold* of him, and with love and joy lay him near our hearts.

4. The encouraging words Christ said to them, *v.* 10. We do not find that they said any thing to him, their affectionate embraces and adorations spoke plainly enough; and what he said to them was no more than what the angel had said (*v.* 5, 7); for he will *confirm the word of his messengers* (Isa. xliv. 26); and his way of *comforting* his people, is, by his Spirit to speak over again to their hearts the same that they had heard before from *his angels*, the ministers. Now observe here,

(1.) How he rebukes their fear; *Be not afraid*. They must not fear being imposed upon by these repeated notices of his resurrection, nor fear any hurt from the appearance of one from the dead; for the news, though strange, was both *true* and *good*. Note, Christ arose from the dead, to silence his people's fears, and there is enough in that to silence them.

(2.) How he repeats their message; "*Go, tell my brethren*, that they must prepare for a journey into Galilee, and there *they shall see me*." If there be any communion between our souls and Christ, it is he that *appoints the meeting*, and he will observe the appointment. Jerusalem had forfeited the honour of Christ's presence, it was a *tumultuous* city, therefore he adjourns the meeting to Galilee. *Come, my beloved, let us go forth*, Cant. vii. 11. But that which is especially observable here, is, that he calls his disciples *his brethren*. Go, tell *my brethren*, not only those of them that were akin to him, but all the rest, for they are all his brethren (*ch.* xii. 50), but he never called them so till after his resurrection, here and John xx. 17. Being by the resurrection himself declared to be the *Son of God with power,* all the children of God were thereby declared to be *his brethren.* Being the *First-begotten from the dead,* he is become the *First-born among many brethren,* even of all that are planted together in the likeness of his resurrection. Christ did not now converse so constantly and familiarly with his disciples as he had done before his death; but, lest they should think him grown strange to them, he gives them this endearing title, *Go to my brethren,* that the scripture might be fulfilled, which, speaking of his entrance upon his exalted state, saith, *I will declare thy name unto my brethren.* They had shamefully *deserted* him in his sufferings; but, to show that he could forgive and forget, and to teach us to do so, he not only continues his purpose to *meet* them, but calls them *brethren.* Being all *his brethren,* they were *brethren* one to another, and must love as brethren. His owning them for his brethren put a great honour upon them, but withal gave them an example of humility in the midst of that honour.

11 Now when they were going, behold, some of the watch came into the city, and showed unto the chief priests all the things that were done.
12 And when they were assembled with the elders, and had taken counsel, they gave large money unto the soldiers,
13 Saying, Say ye, His disciples came by night, and stole him *away* while we slept.
14 And if this come to the governor's ears, we will persuade him, and secure you.
15 So they took the money, and did as they were taught: and this saying is commonly reported among the Jews until this day.

For the further proof of the resurrection of Christ, we have here the confession of the adversaries that were upon the guard; and there are two things which strengthen this testimony—that they were *eye-witnesses,* and did themselves see the glory of the resurrection, which none else did—and that they were *enemies,* set there to oppose and obstruct his resurrection. Now observe here,

I. How this testimony was *given in* to the chief priests (*v.* 11); *when* the women *were going* to bring that news to the disciples, which would *fill their hearts with joy,* the soldiers went to bring the same news to the chief priests, which would *fill their faces with shame. Some of the watch,* probably those of them that commanded in chief, *came into the city,* and brought to those who employed them, the report of their disappointment. *They showed to the chief priests all the things that were done;* told them of the earthpuake, the descent of the angel, the rolling of the stone away, and the coming of the body of Jesus alive out of the grave. Thus the *sign* of the prophet Jonas was brought to the chief priests with the most clear and incontestable evidence that could be; and so the utmost means of conviction were afforded them; we may well imagine what a mortification it was to them, and that, like the enemies of the Jews, they were *much cast down in their own eyes,* Neh. vi. 16. It might justly have been expected that they should now have believed in Christ, and repented their putting him to death; but they were obstinate in their infidelity, and therefore sealed up under it.

II. How it was baffled and stifled by them. They called an assembly, and considered what was to be done. For their own parts, they were resolved not to believe that Jesus was risen; but their care was, to keep others from believing, and themselves from being quite ashamed from their disbelief of it. They had put him to death, and there was no way of standing to what they had done, but by confronting the evidence of his resurrection. Thus they who have sold themselves to work wickedness, find that one sin draws on another, and that they have plunged themselves into a wretched necessity of *adding iniquity to iniquity,* which is part of the curse of Christ's persecutors, Ps. lxix. 27.

The result of their debate was, that those soldiers must by all means be bribed off, and hired not to tell tales.

1. They *put money into their hands;* and what wickedness is it which men will not be brought to by the love of money? They *gave large money,* probably a great deal more than they gave to Judas, unto *the soldiers.* These chief priests loved their money as well as most people did, and were as loth to part with it; and yet, to carry on a malicious design against the gospel of Christ, they were very prodigal of it; they gave the soldiers, it is likely, as much as they asked, and they knew how to improve their advantages. Here was *large money* given for the advancing of that which they knew to be a lie, yet many grudge a little money for the advancement of that which they know to be the truth, though they have a promise of being reimbursed in the resurrection of the just. Let us never starve a good cause, when we see a bad one so liberally supported.

2. They *put a lie into their mouths* (*v.* 13); *Say ye, His disciples came by night, and stole him away while we slept;* a sorry shift is better than none, but this is a sorry one indeed. (1.) The sham was *ridiculous,* and carried along with it its own confutation. If *they slept,* how could they know any thing of the matter, or say who came? If *any one* or them was awake to *observe it,* no doubt, he would awake them all to *oppose it;* for that was the only thing they had in charge. It was altogether improbable that a company of poor, weak, cowardly, dispirited men should

expose themselves for so inconsiderable an achievement as the rescue of the dead body. Why were not the houses where they lodged diligently searched, and other means used to discover the dead body; but this was so thin a lie as one might easily see through. But had it been ever so plausible, (2.) It was a wicked thing for these priests and elders to hire those soldiers to tell a deliberate lie (if it had been in a matter of ever so small importance), against their consciences. Those know not what they do, who draw others to commit one wilful sin; for that may debauch conscience, and be an inlet to many. But, (3.) Considering this as intended to overthrow the great doctrine of Christ's resurrection, this was a sin against the last remedy, and was, in effect, a blasphemy *against the Holy Ghost*, imputing *that* to the roguery of the disciples, which was done by *the power of the Holy Ghost.*

But lest the soldiers should object the penalty they incurred by the Roman law for *sleeping upon the guard*, which was very severe (Acts xii. 19), they promised to interpose with the governor; "*We will persuade him, and secure you.* We will use our own interest in him, to get him not to take notice of it;" and they had lately found how easily they could manage him. If really these soldiers had slept, and so suffered the disciples to steal him away, as they would have the world believe, the priests and elders would certainly have been the forwardest to solicit the governor to punish them for their treachery; so that *their* care for the soldiers' safety plainly gives the lie to the story. They undertook to *secure* them from the sword of Pilate's justice, but could not secure them from the sword of God's justice, which hangs over the head of those that love and make a lie. *They* promise more than they can perform who undertake to save a man harmless in the commission of a wilful sin.

Well, thus was the plot laid; now what success had it?

[1.] Those that were *willing to deceive*, took the money, and did as they were taught. They cared as little for Christ and his religion as the chief priests and elders did; and men that have no religion at all, can be very well pleased to see Christianity run down, and lend a hand to it, if need be, to serve a turn. They *took the money;* that was it they aimed at, and nothing else. Note, Money is a bait for the blackest temptation; mercenary tongues will sell the truth for it.

The great argument to prove Christ to be the Son of God, is, his resurrection, and none could have more convincing proofs of the truth of that than these soldiers had; they saw the angel descend from heaven, saw the stone rolled away, saw the body of Christ come out of the grave, unless the consternation they felt hindered them; and yet they were so far from being convinced by it themselves, that they were hired to belie him, and to hinder others from believing in him. Note, The most sensible evidence will not convince men, without the concurring operation of the Holy Spirit.

[2.] Those that were willing to be deceived, not only credited, but propagated, the story; This *saying is commonly reported among the Jews until this day.* The sham took well enough, and answered the end. The Jews, who persisted in their infidelity, when they were pressed with the argument of Christ's resurrection, had this still ready to reply, *His disciples came, and stole him away.* To this purport was the solemn narrative, which (as Justin Martyr relates in his dialogue with Typho the Jew) the great sanhedrim sent to all the Jews of the dispersion concerning this affair, exciting them to a vigorous resistance of Christianity—that, *when they had crucified, and buried him, the disciples came by night, and stole him out of the sepulchre,* designing thereby not only to overthrow the truth of Christ's resurrection, but to render his disciples odious to the world, as the greatest villains in nature. When once a lie is raised, none knows how far it will spread, nor how long it will last, nor what mischief it will do. Some give another sense of this passage, *This saying is commonly reported,* that is, "Notwithstanding the artifice of the chief priests, thus to impose upon the people, the collusion that was between them and the soldiers, and the money that was given to support the cheat, were commonly *reported* and whispered among the Jews;" for one way or other *truth will out.*

16 Then the eleven disciples went
away into Galilee, into a mountain
where Jesus had appointed them. 17
And when they saw him, they worshipped him: but some doubted. 18
And Jesus came and spake unto them,
saying, All power is given unto me in
heaven and in earth. 19 Go ye therefore, and teach all nations, baptizing
them in the name of the Father, and
of the Son, and of the Holy Ghost:
20 Teaching them to observe all
things whatsoever I have commanded
you: and, lo, I am with you alway,
even unto the end of the world. Amen.

This evangelist passes over several other appearances of Christ, recorded by Luke and John, and hastens to this, which was of all other the most solemn, as being promised and appointed again and again before his death, and after his resurrection. Observe,

I. How the disciples attended his appearance, according to the appointment (*v.* 16); *They went into Galilee,* a long journey to go for one sight of Christ, but it was worth while. They had seen him several times at

Jerusalem, and yet they went into Galilee, to see him there.

1. Because he appointed them to do so. Though it seemed a needless thing to go into Galilee, to see him whom they might see at Jerusalem, especially when they must so soon come back again to Jerusalem, before his ascension, yet they had learned to obey Christ's commands and not object against them. Note, Those who would maintain communion with Christ, must attend him there where he has appointed. Those who have met him in one ordinance, must attend him in another; those who have seen him at Jerusalem, must go to Galilee.

2. Because that was to be a public and general meeting. They had seen him themselves, and conversed with him in private, but that should not excuse their attendance in a solemn assembly, where many were to be gathered together to see him. Note, Our communion with God in secret must not supersede our attendance on public worship, as we have opportunity; for *God loves the gates of Zion,* and so must we. The place was a *mountain in Galilee,* probably the same mountain on which he was transfigured. There they met, for privacy, and perhaps to signify the exalted state into which he was entered, and his advances toward the upper world.

II. How they were affected with the appearance of Christ to them, *v.* 17. Now was the time that he was *seen of above five hundred brethren at once,* 1 Cor. xv. 6. Some think that they saw him, at first, at some distance, above in the air, ἐφθη επανω—*He was seen above, of five hundred brethren* (so they read it); which gave occasion to some to doubt, till he *came nearer* (*v.* 18), and then they were satisfied. We are told,

1. That they *worshipped him;* many of them did so, nay, it should seem, they all did that, they gave divine honour to him, which was signified by some outward expressions of adoration. Note, All that see the Lord Jesus with an eye of faith are obliged to *worship him.*

2. But *some doubted,* some of those that were then present. Note, Even among those that *worship* there are some that *doubt.* The faith of those that are sincere, may yet be very weak and wavering. They *doubted,* εδίσταασαν—*they hung in suspense,* as the scales of the balance, when it is hard to say which preponderates. These doubts were afterward removed, and their faith grew up to a full assurance, and it tended much to the honour of Christ, that the disciples *doubted* before they *believed;* so that they cannot be said to be credulous, and willing to be imposed upon; for they first *questioned,* and *proved all things,* and then *held fast* that which was *true,* and which they found to be so.

III. What Jesus Christ said to them (*v.* 18—20); *Jesus came, and spoke unto them.* Though there were those that doubted, yet, he did not therefore reject them; for he will not *break the bruised reed.* He did not stand at a distance, but *came near,* and gave them such convincing proofs of his resurrection, as turned the wavering scale, and made their faith to triumph over their doubts. *He came, and spoke* familiarly *to them,* as one friend speaks to another, that they might be fully satisfied in the commission he was about to give them. He that *drew near* to God, to speak for us to him, *draws near* to us, to speak from him to us. Christ now delivered to his apostles the great charter of his kingdom in the world, was sending them out as his ambassadors, and here gives them their credentials.

In opening this great charter, we may observe two things.

1. The commission which our Lord Jesus received himself from the Father. Being about to *authorize* his apostles, if any ask by what authority he doeth it, and who gave him that authority, here he tells us, *All power is given unto me in heaven and in earth;* a very great word, and which none but he could say. Hereby he asserts his universal dominion as Mediator, which is the great foundation of the Christian religion. He has *all power.* Observe, (1.) *Whence* he hath this power. He did not assume it, or usurp it, but it was *given* him, he was legally entitled to it, and invested in it, by a grant from him who is the Fountain of all being, and consequently of all power. God *set him King* (Ps. ii. 6), inaugurated and enthroned him, Luke i. 32. As God, equal with the Father, all power was originally and essentially *his;* but as Mediator, as God-man, *all power* was *given him;* partly in *recompence* of his work (because he humbled himself, therefore God thus *exalted him),* and partly in *pursuance* of his design; he had this *power* given him *over all flesh,* that he might *give eternal life to as many as were given him* (John xvii. 2), for the more effectual carrying on and completing our salvation. This power he was now more signally invested in, upon his resurrection, Acts xiii. 33. He had power before, *power to forgive sins* (*ch.* ix. 6); but now *all power* is given him. He is now going to *receive for himself a kingdom* (Luke xix. 12), to sit down *at the right hand,* Ps. cx. 1. Having purchased it, nothing remains but to take possession; it is *his own* for ever. (2.) *Where* he has this power; in *heaven and earth,* comprehending the universe. Christ is the sole universal Monarch, he is *Lord of all,* Acts x: 36. He has all *power in heaven.* He has power of dominion over the angels, they are all his humble servants, Eph. i. 20, 21. He has power of intercession with his Father, in the virtue of his satisfaction and atonement; he intercedes, not as a suppliant, but as a demandant; *Father, I will.* He has *all power on earth* too; having prevailed with God, by the sacrifice of atonement, he prevails with men, and deals with them as

one having authority, by the ministry of reconciliation. He is indeed, in all causes and over all persons, supreme Moderator and Governor. *By him kings reign.* All souls are his, and to him *every* heart and *knee must bow,* and *every tongue confess* him to be the *Lord.* This our Lord Jesus tells them, not only to satisfy them of the authority he had to commission them, and to bring them out in the execution of their commission, but to take off the offence of the cross; they had no reason to be ashamed of *Christ crucified,* when they saw him *thus glorified.*

2. The commission he gives to those whom he sent forth; *Go ye therefore.* This commission is given, (1.) To the *apostles* primarily, the chief ministers of state in Christ's kingdom, the architects that laid the foundation of the church. Now those that had followed Christ in the regeneration, were *set on thrones* (Luke xxii. 30); *Go ye.* It is not only a word of command, like that, *Son, go work,* but a word of encouragement, *Go,* and *fear not, have I not sent you?* Go, and make a business of this work. They must not *take state,* and issue out summons to the nations to attend upon them; but they must go, and bring the gospel to their doors, *Go ye.* They had doted on Christ's *bodily presence,* and hung upon *that,* and built all their joys and hopes upon *that;* but now Christ discharges them from further attendance on his person, and sends them abroad about other work. *As an eagle stirs up her nest, flutters over her young,* to excite them to fly (Deut. xxxii. 11), so Christ stirs up his disciples, to disperse themselves over all the world. (2.) It is given to their successors, the ministers of the gospel, whose business it is to transmit the gospel from age to age, to the end of the world in time, as it was theirs to transmit it from nation to nation, to the end of the world in place, and no less necessary. The Old-Testament promise of a gospel ministry is made to a succession (Isa. lix. 21); and this must be so understood, otherwise how could Christ be with them always to the *consummation of the world?* Christ, at his ascension, gave not only apostles and prophets, but *pastors and teachers,* Eph. iv. 11. Now observe,

[1.] How far his commission is extended; to *all nations.* Go, and disciple *all nations.* Not that they must go all together into every place, but by consent disperse themselves in such manner as might best *diffuse* the light of the gospel. Now this plainly signifies it to be the will of Christ, *First,* That the covenant of peculiarity, made with the Jews, should now be cancelled and disannulled. This word broke down the middle wall of partition, which had so long excluded the Gentiles from a visible church-state; and whereas the apostles, when first sent out, were forbidden to go into the way of the Gentiles, now they were sent to *all nations. Secondly,* That salvation by Christ should be offered to all, and none excluded that did not by their unbelief and impenitence exclude themselves. The salvation they were to preach is a *common salvation;* whoever will, let him come, and take the benefit of the *act of indemnity;* for there is no difference of Jew or Greek in Christ Jesus. *Thirdly,* That Christianity should be twisted in with national constitutions, that the kingdoms of the world should become Christ's kingdoms, and their kings the church's nursing-fathers.

[2.] What is the principal intention of this commision; to *disciple* all nations. Μαθητεύσατε—"*Admit them disciples;* do your utmost to make the nations Christian nations;" not, "Go to the nations, and denounce the judgments of God against them, as Jonah against Nineveh, and as the other Old-Testament prophets" (though they had reason enough to expect it for their wickedness), "but go, and *disciple them.*" Christ the Mediator is setting up a kingdom in the world, bring the nations to be his subjects; setting up a school, bring the nations to be his scholars; raising an army for the carrying on of the war against the powers of darkness, enlist the nations of the earth under his banner. The work which the apostles had to do, was, to set up the Christian religion in all places, and it was honourable work; the achievements of the mighty heroes of the world were nothing to it. They conquered the nations for themselves, and made them miserable; the apostles conquered them for Christ, and made them happy.

[3.] Their instructions for executing this commission.

First, They must *admit disciples* by the *sacred rite of baptism;* "Go into all nations, preach the gospel to them, work miracles among them, and persuade them to come in themselves, and bring their children with them, into the church of Christ, and then admit them and theirs into the church, by washing them with water;" either dipping them in the water, or pouring or sprinkling water upon them, which seems the more proper, because the thing is most frequently expressed so, as Isa. xliv. 3, *I will pour my Spirit on thy seed.* And, Tit. iii. 5, 6, *Which he shed on us abundantly.* And, Ezek. xxxvi. 25, *I will sprinkle clean water upon you.* And, Isa. lii. 15, *So shall he sprinkle many nations;* which seems a prophecy of this commission to *baptize the nations.*

Secondly, This baptism must be administered *in the name of the Father, and of the Son, and of the Holy Ghost.* That is, 1. *By authority from heaven,* and not *of man;* for his ministers act by authority from the three persons in the Godhead, who all concur, as to our *creation,* so to our *redemption;* they have their commission under the great seal of heaven, which puts an honour upon the ordinance, though to a carnal eye, like him that instituted it, it has *no form or comeliness.*

2. *Calling upon the name* of the Father, Son, and Holy Ghost. Every thing is sanctified by prayer, and particularly the waters of baptism. The prayer of faith obtains the presence of God with the ordinance, which is its lustre and beauty, its life and efficacy. But, 3. It is *into the name* (εις το ονομα) of *Father, Son, and Holy Ghost;* this was intended as the *summary* of the first principles of the Christian religion, and of the new covenant, and according to it the ancient creeds were drawn up. By our being baptized, we solemnly profess, (1.) Our *assent* to the scripture-revelation concerning *God, the Father, Son, and Holy Ghost.* We confess our belief that there is a God, that there is but *one God,* that in the Godhead there is a *Father* that *begets,* a *Son* that is *begotten,* and a Holy *Spirit* of both. We are baptized, not into the *names,* but into the *name,* of Father, Son, and Spirit, which plainly intimates that *these three are one,* and *their name one.* The distinct mentioning of the *three persons* in the Trinity, both in the *Christian baptism* here, and in the *Christian blessing* (2 Cor. xiii. 14), as it is a full proof of the doctrine of the Trinity, so it has done much towards preserving it pure and entire through all ages of the church; for nothing is more great and awful in *Christian assemblies* than these two. (2.) Our *consent* to a covenant-relation to God, *the Father, Son, and Holy Ghost.* Baptism is a *sacrament,* that is, it is *an oath; super sacramentum dicere,* is *to say upon oath.* It is an oath of *abjuration,* by which we renounce the world and the flesh, as rivals with God for the throne in our hearts; and an oath of *allegiance,* by which we resign and give up *ourselves* to God, to be *his,* our own selves, our whole selves, *body, soul, and spirit,* to be governed by his will, and made happy in his favour; *we become his men,* so the form of homage in our law runs. Therefore *baptism* is applied to *the person,* as *livery* and *seisin* is given of the premises, because it is the person that is *dedicated* to God. [1.] It is into the name of *the Father,* believing him to be the *Father of our Lord Jesus Christ* (for that is principally intended here), by *eternal generation,* and *our Father,* as our Creator, Preserver, and Benefactor, to whom therefore we resign ourselves, as our absolute *owner* and *proprietor,* to actuate us, and dispose of us; as our supreme *rector* and *governor,* to rule us, as free agents, by his law; and as our *chief good,* and *highest* end. [2.] It is into the name of *the Son,* the *Lord Jesus Christ,* the *Son of God,* and *correlate* to the Father. Baptism was in a particular manner administered *in the name of the Lord Jesus,* Acts viii. 16; xix. 5. In baptism we *assent,* as Peter did, *Thou art Christ, the Son of the living God* (*ch.* xvi. 16), and *consent,* as Thomas did, *My Lord, and my God,* John xx. 28. We take Christ to be our Prophet, Priest, and King, and give up ourselves to be taught, and saved, and ruled, by him. [3.] It is into the name of *the Holy Ghost.* Believing the Godhead of the Holy Spirit, and his agency in carrying on our redemption, we give up ourselves to his conduct and operation, as our sanctifier, teacher, guide, and comforter.

Thirdly, Those that are thus baptized, and enrolled among the disciples of Christ, must be taught (*v.* 20); *Teaching them to observe all things, whatsoever I have commanded you.* This denotes two things.

1. The duty of *disciples,* of all *baptized Christians;* they must observe all things whatsoever Christ has commanded, and, in order to that, must submit to the teaching of those whom he sends. Our admission into the visible church is in order to something further; when Christ hath *discipled* us, he hath not *done with us;* he *enlists* soldiers that he may *train them* up for his service.

All that are baptized, are thereby obliged, (1.) To make the command of Christ their rule. There is a *law of faith,* and we are said to be *under the law to Christ;* we are by baptism *bound,* and must *obey.* (2.) To *observe* what Christ has commanded. Due *obedience* to the commands of Christ requires a diligent observation; we are in danger of missing, if we take not *good heed:* and in all our obedience, we must have an eye to the command, and do what we do as unto the Lord. (3.) To observe *all things,* that he has commanded, without exception; all the *moral* duties, and all the *instituted* ordinances. Our obedience to the laws of Christ is not *sincere,* if it be not universal; we must *stand complete in his whole will.* (4.) To confine themselves to the commands of Christ, and as not to *diminish* from them, so not to *add* to them. (5.) To learn their duty according to the law of Christ, from those whom he has appointed to be teachers in his school, for *therefore* we were entered into his school.

2. The duty of the apostles of Christ, and his ministers; and that is, to *teach* the commands of Christ, to expound them to his disciples, to press upon them the necessity of obedience, and to assist them in applying the general commands of Christ to particular cases. They must teach *them,* not their own inventions, but the institutions of Christ; to them they must religiously adhere, and in the knowledge of *them* Christians must be *trained up.* A *standing* ministry is hereby *settled* in the church, for the *edifying* of the body of Christ, *till we all come to the perfect man,* Eph. iv. 11—13. The heirs of heaven, till they come to age, must be *under tutors and governors.*

3. Here is the assurance he gives them of his spiritual presence with them in the execution of this commission; *And lo, I am with you always, even unto the end of the world.* This exceeding great and precious promise is ushered in with a *behold,* to strengthen their faith, and engage their observation of it. "Take notice of this; it is what you may assure yourselves of and venture upon. Observe,

(1.) The favour promised them; *I am with*

you. Not, *I will be* with you, but *I am—ἐγὼ εἰμι.* As God sent Moses, so Christ sent his apostles, by this name, *I am;* for he is God, to whom past, present, and to come, are the same. See Rev. i. 8. He was now about to leave them; his bodily presence was now to be removed from them, and this grieved them; but he assures them of his *spiritual* presence, which was more expedient for them than his bodily presence could be; *I am with you;* that is, "My Spirit is with you, the Comforter shall *abide with you,* John xvi. 7. I am *with you,* and not *against you:* with you to take your part, to be on your side, and to *hold* with you, as Michael our prince is said to do, Dan. x. 21. I am *with you,* and not *absent from you,* not at a distance; I am a very *present help,*" Ps. xlvi. 1. Christ was now sending them to set up his kingdom in the world, which was a great undertaking. And then doth he seasonably promise them his presence with them, [1.] To *carry them* on through the difficulties they were likely to meet with. "I am with you, to *bear you up,* to plead your cause; with you in all your services, in all your sufferings, to bring you through them with comfort and honour. *When you go through the fire or water, I will be with you.* In the pulpit, in the prison, *lo, I am with you.*" [2.] To *succeed* this great undertaking; "Lo, *I am with you,* to make your ministry effectual for the discipling of the nations, for the *pulling down* of the strong holds of Satan, and the setting up of stronger for the Lord Jesus." It was an unlikely thing that they should unhinge national constitutions in religion, and turn the stream of so long a usage; that they should *establish* a doctrine so directly contrary to the genius of the age, and persuade people to become the disciples of a *crucified* Jesus; but *lo, I am with you,* and therefore you shall *gain your point.*

(2.) The continuance of the favour, *always, even unto the end of the world.*

[1.] They shall have his *constant* presence; *always, πάσας τὰς ἡμέρας—all days,* every day. "I will be with you on sabbath days and week days, fair days and foul days, winter days and summer days." There is no day, no hour of the day, in which our Lord Jesus is not present with his churches and with his ministers; if there were, that day, that hour, they were undone. Since his resurrection he had appeared to them *now and then,* once a week it may be, and scarcely that. But he assures them that they shall have his spiritual presence continued to them without intermission. Wherever we are the word of Christ is nigh us, even *in our mouth,* and the Spirit of Christ nigh us, even *in our hearts.* The *God of Israel,* the *Saviour,* is sometimes *a God that hideth himself* (Isa. xlv. 15), but never a God that absenteth himself; sometimes *in the dark,* but never *at a distance.*

[2.] They shall have his perpetual presence, even to *the end of the world.* There is a world before us, that will never have an end, but this is hastening towards its period; and even till then the Christian religion shall, in one part of the world or other, be *kept up,* and the presence of Christ continued with his ministers. I am with you *to the end of the world,* not with your persons, they died quickly, but, *First,* With *you and your writings.* There is a divine power going along with the scriptures of the New Testament, not only preserving them in being, but producing strange effects by them, which will continue to the end of time. *Secondly,* With you and *your successors;* with you and all the ministers of the gospel in the several ages of the church; with all to whom this commission extends, with all who, being duly called and sent, thus *baptize* and thus *teach.* When the *end of the world* is come, and the kingdom delivered up to God, even the Father, there will then be no further need of ministers and their ministration; but till then they shall continue, and the great intentions of the institution shall be answered. This is an encouraging word to all the faithful ministers of Christ, that what was said to the apostles, was said to them all, *I will never leave thee, nor forsake thee.*

Two solemn farewells we find our Lord Jesus giving to his church, and his parting word at both of them is very encouraging; one was here, when he closed up his personal converse with them, and then his parting word was, "*Lo, I am with you always;* I leave you, and yet still I am with you;" the other was, when he closed up the canon of the scripture by the pen of his beloved disciple, and then his parting word was, "*Surely, I come quickly.* I leave you for awhile, but I will be with you again shortly," Rev. xxii. 20. By this it appears that he did not part in anger, but in love, and that it is his will we should keep up both our communion with him and our expectation of him.

There is one word more remaining, which must not be overlooked, and that is *Amen;* which is not a cipher, intended only for a concluding word, like *finis* at the end of a book, but it has its significancy. 1. It bespeaks Christ's confirmation of this promise, *Lo, I am with you.* It is his *Amen,* in whom all the promises are *Yea and Amen.* "*Verily* I am, and will be, with you; I the Amen, the faithful Witness, do assure you of it." Or, 2. It bespeaks the church's concurrence with it, in their desire, and prayer, and expectation. It is the evangelist's *Amen—So be it,* blessed Lord. Our *Amen* to Christ's promises turns them into prayers. Hath Christ promised to be present with his ministers, present in his word, present in the assemblies of his people, though but two or three are gathered together in his name, and this *always, even to the end of the world?* Let us heartily say *Amen* to it; believe that it *shall be so,* and pray that it *may be so:* Lord, *Remember this word unto thy servants, upon which thou hast caused us to hope.*

AN

EXPOSITION,

WITH PRACTICAL OBSERVATIONS,

OF THE GOSPEL ACCORDING TO

ST. MARK.

We have heard the evidence given in by the first witness to the doctrine and miracles of our Lord Jesus; and now here is another witness produced, who calls for our attention. The second *living creature* saith, *Come, and see*, Rev. vi. 3. Now let us enquire a little,

I. Concerning *this witness*. His name is *Mark*. *Marcus* was a Roman name, and a very common one, and yet we have no reason to think, but that he was by birth a Jew; but as Saul, when he went among the nations, took the Roman name of *Paul*, so he of *Mark*, his Jewish name perhaps being *Mardocai*; so Grotius. We read of John whose surname was *Mark*, sister's son to Barnabas, whom Paul was displeased with (Acts xv. 37, 38), but afterward had a great kindness for, and not only ordered the churches to receive him (Col. iv. 10), but sent for him to be his assistant, with this encomium, *He is profitable to me for the ministry* (2 Tim. iv. 11); and he reckons him among his fellow-labourers, Philem. 24. We read of Marcus whom Peter calls his *son*, he having been an instrument of his conversion (1 Pet. v. 13); whether that was the same with the other, and, if not, which of them was the penman of this gospel, is altogether uncertain. It is a tradition very current among the ancients, that St. Mark wrote this gospel under the direction of St. Peter, and that it was confirmed by his authority; so Hieron. Catal. Script. Eccles. *Marcus discipulus et interpres Petri, juxta quod Petrum referentem audierat, legatus Roma à fratribus, breve scripsit evangelium—Mark, the disciple and interpreter of Peter, being sent from Rome by the brethren, wrote a concise gospel*; and Tertullian saith (Adv. Marcion. lib. 4, cap. 5), *Marcus quod edidit, Petri affirmetur, cujus interpres Marcus—Mark, the interpreter of Peter, delivered in writing the things which had been preached by Peter*. But as Dr. Whitby very well suggests, Why should we have recourse to the authority of Peter for the support of this gospel, or say with St. Jerome that Peter approved of it and recommended it by his authority to the church to be read, when, though it is true Mark was no apostle, yet we have all the reason in the world to think that both he and Luke were of the number of the seventy disciples, who *companied with the apostles all along* (Acts i. 21), who had a commission like that of the apostles (Luke x. 19, compared with Mark xvi. 18), and who, it is highly probable, received the Holy Ghost when they did (Acts i. 15; ii. 1—4), so that it is no diminution at all to the validity or value of this gospel, that Mark was not one of the twelve, as Matthew and John were? St. Jerome saith that, after the writing of this gospel, he went into Egypt, and was the first that preached the gospel at Alexandria, where he founded a church, to which he was a great example of holy living. *Constituit ecclesiam tantâ doctrinâ et vitæ continentiâ, ut omnes sectatores Christi ad exemplum sui cogeret—He so adorned, by his doctrine and his life, the church which he founded, that his example influenced all the followers of Christ.*

II. Concerning *this testimony*. Mark's gospel, 1. Is but short, much shorter than Matthew's, not giving so full an account of Christ's sermons as that did, but insisting chiefly on his miracles. 2. It is very much a repetition of what we had in Matthew; many remarkable circumstances being added to the stories there related, but not many new matters. When many witnesses are called to prove the same fact, upon which a judgment is to be given, it is not thought *tedious*, but highly *necessary*, that they should each of them relate it in their own words, again and again, that by the agreement of the testimony the thing may be established; and therefore we must not think this book of scripture needless, for it is written not only to confirm our belief that *Jesus is the Christ the Son of God*, but to put us in mind of things which we have read in the foregoing gospel, that we may *give the more earnest heed to them*, lest at any time we let them slip; and even *pure minds* have need to be *thus stirred up by way of remembrance*. It was fit that such great things as these should be spoken and written, once, yea twice, because man is so *unapt* to *perceive* them, and so *apt* to *forget* them. There is no ground for the tradition, that this gospel was written first in Latin, though it was written at Rome; it was written in Greek, as was St. Paul's epistle to the Romans, the Greek being the more universal language.

CHAP. I

Mark's narrative does not take rise so early as those of Matthew and Luke do, from the birth of our Saviour, but from John's baptism, from which he soon passes to Christ's public ministry. Accordingly, in this chapter, we have, I. The office of John Baptist illustrated by the prophecy of him (ver. 1—3), and by the history of him, ver. 4—8. II. Christ's baptism, and his being owned from heaven, ver. 9—11. III. His temptation, ver. 12, 13. IV. His preaching, ver. 14, 15, 21, 22, 38, 39. V. His calling disciples, ver. 16—20. VI. His praying, ver. 35. VII. His working miracles. 1. His rebuking an unclean spirit, ver. 23—28. 2. His curing Peter's mother-in-law, who was ill of a fever, ver. 29—31. 3. His healing all that came to him, ver. 32, 34. 4. His cleansing a leper, ver. 40—45.

THE beginning of the gospel of
Jesus Christ, the Son of God;
2 As it is written in the prophets,
Behold, I send my messenger before
thy face, which shall prepare thy way
before thee. 3 The voice of one crying in the wilderness, Prepare ye the
way of the Lord, make his paths
straight. 4 John did baptize in the
wilderness, and preach the baptism
of repentance for the remission of
sins. 5 And there went out unto
him all the land of Judæa, and they
of Jerusalem, and were all baptized
of him in the river of Jordan, confessing their sins. 6 And John was
clothed with camel's hair, and with a
girdle of a skin about his loins; and
he did eat locusts and wild honey;
7 And preached, saying, There cometh
one mightier than I after me, the
latchet of whose shoes I am not
worthy to stoop down and unloose.
8 I indeed have baptized you with
water: but he shall baptize you with
the Holy Ghost.

We may observe here,

I. What the New Testament is—the *divine* testament, to which we *adhere* above all that is *human;* the new testament, which we *advance* above that which was old. It is *the gospel of Jesus Christ the Son of God, v.* 1. 1. It is *gospel;* it is God's word, and is *faithful* and *true;* see Rev. xix. 9; xxi. 5; xxii. 6. It is a *good word,* and well *worthy of all acceptation;* it brings us glad tidings. 2. It is the *gospel of Jesus Christ,* the *anointed Saviour,* the Messiah promised and expected. The foregoing gospel began with the *generation of Jesus Christ*—that was but preliminary, this comes immediately to the business—*the gospel of Christ.* It is called *his,* not only because he is the *Author* of it, and it comes *from him,* but because he is the *Subject of it,* and it treats wholly *concerning him.* 3. This Jesus is the *Son of God.* That truth is the foundation on which the gospel is built, and which it is written to demonstrate; for if Jesus be not *the Son of God,* our *faith is vain.*

II. What the *reference* of the New Testament is to the Old, and its *coherence* with it. The gospel of Jesus Christ *begins,* and so we shall find it *goes on,* just *as it is written in the prophets* (*v.* 2); for it *saith no other things than those which the prophets and Moses said should come* (Acts xxvi. 22), which was most proper and powerful for the conviction of the Jews, who believed the Old-Testament prophets to be sent of God and ought to have *evidenced* that they did so by welcoming the accomplishment of their prophecies in its season; but it is of use to us all, for the confirmation of our faith both in the Old Testament and in the New, for the exact harmony that there is between both shows that they both have the same divine original.

Quotations are here borrowed from two prophecies—that of Isaiah, which was the *longest,* and that of Malachi, which was the *latest* (and there were above three hundred years between them), both of whom spoke to the same purport concerning *the beginning of the gospel of Jesus Christ,* in the ministry of John.

1. Malachi, in whom we had the Old-Testament *farewell,* spoke very plainly (*ch.* iii. 1) concerning John Baptist, who was to give the New-Testament *welcome. Behold, I send my messenger before thy face, v.* 2. Christ himself had taken notice of this, and applied it to John (Matt. xi. 10), who was God's *messenger,* sent to *prepare Christ's way.*

2. Isaiah, the most evangelical of all the prophets, *begins* the evangelical part of his prophecy with this, which points to the *beginning of the gospel of Christ* (Isa. xl. 3); *The voice of him that crieth in the wilderness, v.* 3. Matthew had taken notice of this, and applied it to John, *ch.* iii. 3. But from these two put together here, we may observe, (1.) That Christ, in his gospel, *comes among us,* bringing with him a treasure of grace, and a sceptre of government. (2.) Such is the corruption of the world, that there is something to do to *make room* for him, and to remove that which gives not only *obstruction,* but *opposition* to his progress. (3.) When God sent his Son into the world, he *took care,* and when he sends him into the heart, he *takes care,* effectual care, to *prepare his way before him;* for the designs of his grace shall not be *frustrated;* nor may any expect the comforts of that grace, but such as, by conviction of sin and humiliation for it, are *prepared* for those comforts, and disposed to receive them. (4.) When the *paths* that were *crooked,* are *made straight* (the mistakes of the judgment rectified, and the *crooked ways* of the affections), then way is made for Christ's comforts. (5.) It is in a *wilderness,* for such this world is, that *Christ's way* is prepared, and theirs that follow him, like that which Israel passed through to Canaan. (6.) The messengers of conviction and terror, that come to prepare Christ's way, are *God's messengers,* whom he sends and will own, and must be *received* as such. (7.) They that are sent to *prepare the way of the Lord,* in such a vast howling wilderness as this is, have need to

cry aloud, and not spare, and to *lift up their voice like a trumpet.*

III. What the *beginning* of the New Testament was. The gospel began in John Baptist; for *the law and the prophets were, until John,* the only divine revelation, but then the *kingdom of God began to be preached,* Luke xvi. 16. Peter begins *from the baptism of John,* Acts i. 22. The gospel did not begin *so soon* as the *birth* of Christ, for he took time to *increase in wisdom and stature,* not so late as his entering upon his public ministry, but half a year before, when John began to preach the same doctrine that Christ afterward preached. His baptism was the dawning of the *gospel day;* for,

1. In John's way of *living* there was the beginning of a *gospel spirit;* for it bespoke great self-denial, mortification of the flesh, a holy contempt of the world, and nonconformity to it, which may truly be called the *beginning of the gospel of Christ* in any soul, *v.* 6. He was *clothed with camels' hair,* not with soft raiment; was girt, not with a golden, but with a *leathern girdle;* and, in contempt of dainties and delicate things, his meat was *locusts and wild honey.* Note, The more we sit loose to the body, and live above the world, the better we are prepared for Jesus Christ.

2. In John's *preaching* and *baptizing* there was the *beginning* of the *gospel doctrines and ordinances,* and the first fruits of them. (1.) He preached the *remission of sins,* which is the great gospel privilege; showed people their *need* of it, that they were *undone* without it, and that it might be obtained. (2.) He preached *repentance,* in order to it; he told people that there must be a renovation of their hearts and a reformation of their lives, that they must forsake their sins and turn to God, and upon those terms and no other, their sins should be forgiven. *Repentance for the remission of sins,* was what the apostles were commissioned to *preach to all nations,* Luke xxiv. 47. (3.) He preached Christ, and directed his hearers to *expect him* speedily to appear, and to *expect great things* from him. The preaching of Christ is pure gospel, and that was John Baptist's preaching, *v.* 7, 8. Like a true gospel minister, he preaches, [1.] The great *pre-eminence* Christ is *advanced to;* so high, so great, is Christ, that John, though one of the greatest that was born of women, thinks himself unworthy to be employed in the meanest office about him, even to *stoop down,* and *untie his shoes.* Thus industrious is he to give honour to him, and to bring others to do so too. [2.] The great *power* Christ is *invested with;* He *comes after me* in time, but he is *mightier than I,* mightier than the mighty ones of the earth, for he is able to *baptize with the Holy Ghost;* he can *give* the Spirit of God, and by him *govern* the spirits of men. [3.] The great *promise* Christ makes in his gospel to those who have *repented,* and have had their sins forgiven them; They shall be *baptized with* the Holy Ghost, shall be *purified* by his graces, and *refreshed* by his comforts. And, *lastly,* All those who received his doctrine, and submitted to his institution, he *baptized with water,* as the manner of the Jews was to admit proselytes, in token of their *cleansing themselves* by repentance and reformation (which were the duties required), and of God's *cleansing them* both by remission and by sanctification, which were the blessings promised. Now this was afterward to be advanced into a gospel ordinance, which John's using it was a preface to.

3. In the success of John's preaching, and the disciples he admitted by baptism, there was the *beginning of a gospel church.* He baptized *in the wilderness,* and declined going into the cities; but *there went out unto him all the land of Judea, and they of Jerusalem,* inhabitants both of city and country, families of them, and *were all baptized of him.* They entered themselves his disciples, and bound themselves to his discipline; in token of which, they *confessed their sins;* he admitted them his disciples, in token of which, he *baptized* them. Here were the stamina of the gospel church, the *dew of its youth* from *the womb of the morning,* Ps. cx. 3. Many of these afterward became followers of Christ, and preachers of his gospel, and this grain of mustard-seed became a *tree.*

9 And it came to pass in those
days, that Jesus came from Nazareth
of Galilee, and was baptized of John
in Jordan. 10 And straightway
coming up out of the water, he saw
the heavens opened, and the Spirit
like a dove descending upon him: 11
And there came a voice from heaven,
saying, Thou art my beloved Son, in
whom I am well pleased. 12 And
immediately the spirit driveth him
into the wilderness. 13 And he was
there in the wilderness forty days,
tempted of Satan; and was with the
wild beasts; and the angels ministered
unto him.

We have here a brief account of Christ's baptism and temptation, which were largely related Matt. iii. and iv.

I. His *baptism,* which was his first public apppearance, after he had long lived obscurely *in Nazareth.* O how much *hidden worth* is there, which in this world is either lost in the dust of contempt and *cannot* be known, or wrapped up in the veil of humility and *will not* be known! But sooner or later it *shall be* known, as Christ's was.

1. See how *humbly* he *owned* God, by coming to be *baptized of John;* and thus *it became him to fulfil all righteousness.* Thus he *took upon him the likeness of sinful flesh,* that, though he was perfectly pure and unspotted,

yet he was *washed* as if he had been *polluted;* and thus *for our sakes he sanctified himself, that we also might be sanctified,* and be baptized with him, John xvii. 19.

2. See how *honourably* God owned him, when he submitted to John's *baptism.* Those who *justify God,* as *they* are said to do, who were *baptized with the baptism* of John, he will *glorify,* Luke vii. 29, 30.

(1.) He *saw the heavens opened;* thus he was owned to be the Lord from heaven, and had a glimpse of the glory and joy that were *set before him,* and *secured* to him, as the recompence of his undertaking. Matthew saith, *The heavens were opened to him.* Mark saith, *He saw them opened.* Many have the heavens opened to receive them, but they do not see it; Christ had not only a clear foresight of his sufferings, but of his glory too.

(2.) He *saw the Spirit like a dove descending upon him.* Note, *Then* we may see heaven opened to us, when we perceive the Spirit *descending* and working upon us. God's good work in us is the surest evidence of his good will towards us, and his preparations for us. Justin Martyr says, that *when Christ was baptized, a fire was kindled in Jordan:* and it is an ancient tradition, that *a great light shone round the place;* for the Spirit brings both *light* and *heat.*

(3.) He heard a voice which was intended for his encouragement to proceed in his undertaking, and therefore it is here expressed as directed *to him, Thou art my beloved Son.* God lets him know, [1.] That he *loved him* never the *less* for that *low* and *mean* estate to which he had now *humbled himself;* "Though thus emptied and made of no reputation, yet he is my *beloved Son* still." [2.] That he *loved him* much the *more* for that *glorious* and *kind* undertaking in which he had now *engaged himself.* God is *well pleased* in him, as referee of all matters in controversy between him and man; and so well pleased in him, as to be well pleased *with us* in him.

II. His *temptation.* The *good Spirit* that descended upon him, *led him into the wilderness, v.* 12. Paul mentions it as a proof that he had his doctrine from God, and not from man—that, as soon as he was called, he *went not to Jerusalem,* but *went into Arabia,* Gal. i. 17. Retirement from the world is an opportunity of more free converse with God, and therefore must sometimes be chosen, for a while, even by those that are called to the greatest business. Mark observes this circumstance of his being *in the wilderness*—that he was *with the wild beasts.* It was an instance of his Father's care of him, that he was preserved from being torn in pieces by the wild beasts, which encouraged him the more that his Father would provide for him when he was hungry. Special protections are earnests of seasonable supplies. It was likewise an intimation to him of the inhumanity of the men of that generation, whom he was to live among—no better than *wild beasts* in the *wilderness,* nay abundantly worse. In that wilderness,

1. The *evil spirits* were *busy with him;* he *was tempted of Satan;* not by any inward injections (the prince of this world had *nothing in him* to fasten upon), but by outward solicitations. Solicitude often gives advantages to the tempter, therefore *two are better than one.* Christ himself was tempted, not only to teach us, that *it is no sin to be tempted,* but to direct us whither to go for succour when we are tempted, even to him that *suffered,* being *tempted;* that he might experimentally sympathize with us when we are *tempted.*

2. The *good spirits* were *busy about him;* the *angels ministered to him,* supplied him with what he needed, and dutifully attended him. Note, The ministration of the good angels about us, is matter of great comfort in reference to the malicious designs of the evil angels against us; but much more doth it befriend us, to have the indwelling of the spirit in our hearts, which they that have, are so *born of God,* that, as far as they are so, *the evil one toucheth them not,* much less shall he *triumph* over them.

14 Now after that John was put
in prison, Jesus came into Galilee,
preaching the gospel of the kingdom
of God, 15 And saying, The time is
fulfilled, and the kingdom of God is
at hand: repent ye, and believe the
gospel. 16 Now as he walked by the
sea of Galilee, he saw Simon and
Andrew his brother casting a net into
the sea: for they were fishers. 17
And Jesus said unto them, Come ye
after me, and I will make you to become fishers of men. 18 And straightway they forsook their nets, and followed him. 19 And when he had
gone a little further thence, he saw
James the *son* of Zebedee, and John
his brother, who also were in the ship
mending their nets. 20 And straightway he called them: and they left
their father Zebedee in the ship with
the hired servants, and went after him.
21 And they went into Capernaum;
and straightway on the sabbath day
he entered into the synagogue, and
taught. 22 And they were astonished
at his doctrine: for he taught them
as one that had authority, and not as
the scribes.

Here is, I. A general account of Christ's preaching in Galilee. John gives an account of his preaching in Judea, before this (*ch.* ii. and iii.), which the other evangelists had omitted, who chiefly relate what occurred in

Galilee, because that was least known at Jerusalem. Observe,

1. When Jesus began to preach in Galilee; *After that John was put in prison.* When he had *finished* his testimony, then Jesus *began* his. Note, The silencing of Christ's ministers shall not be the suppressing of Christ's gospel; if some be laid aside, others shall be raised up, perhaps mightier than they, to carry on the same work.

2. What he preached; *The gospel of the kingdom of God.* Christ came to set up the kingdom of God among men, that they might be brought into *subjection to it,* and might obtain *salvation in it;* and he set it up by the preaching of his gospel, and a power going along with it.

Observe, (1.) The great *truths* Christ preached; *The time is fulfilled, and the kingdom of God is at hand.* This refers to the Old Testament, in which the kingdom of the Messiah was promised, and the time fixed for the introducing of it. They were not so well versed in those prophecies, nor did they so well observe the signs of the times, as to understand it themselves, and therefore Christ gives them notice of it; "The time prefixed is now *at hand;* glorious discoveries of divine light, life, and love, are now to be made; a new dispensation far more spiritual and heavenly than that which you have hitherto been under, is now to commence." Note, God keeps time; when *the time is fulfilled,* the *kingdom of God is at hand,* for the vision is *for an appointed time,* which will be punctually observed, though it tarry past our time.

(2.) The great *duties* inferred from thence. Christ gave them to *understand the times,* that they might know *what Israel ought to do;* they fondly expected the Messiah to appear in external pomp and power, not only to free the Jewish nation from the Roman yoke, but to make it have dominion over all its neighbours, and therefore thought, when that *kingdom of God* was *at hand,* they must prepare for war, and for victory and preferment, and great things in the world; but Christ tells them, in the prospect of that kingdom approaching, they must *repent, and believe the gospel.* They had broken the *moral law,* and could not be saved by a *covenant of innocency,* for both Jew and Gentile are concluded *under guilt.* They must therefore take the benefit of a *covenant of grace,* must submit to a *remedial law,* and this is it —*repentance towards God, and faith towards our Lord Jesus Christ.* They had not made use of the prescribed preservatives, and therefore must have recourse to the prescribed restoratives. By repentance we must lament and forsake our sins, and by faith we must receive the forgiveness of them. By repentance we must give glory to our Creator whom we have offended; by faith we must give glory to our Redeemer who came to *save us from our sins.* Both these must go together: we must not think either that reforming our lives will save us without trusting in the righteousness and grace of Christ, or that trusting in Christ will save us without the reformation of our hearts and lives. Christ hath joined these two together, and let no man think to put them asunder. They will mutually assist and befriend each other. Repentance will quicken faith, and faith will make repentance evangelical; and the sincerity of both together must be evidenced by a diligent conscientious obedience to all God's commandments. Thus the preaching of the gospel began, and thus it continues; still the call is, Repent, and believe, and live a *life of repentance* and a *life of faith.*

II. Christ appearing as a teacher, here is next his *calling of disciples, v.* 16—20. Observe, 1. Christ will have followers. If he set up a school, he will have scholars; if he set up his standard, he will have soldiers; if he preach, he will have hearers. He has taken an effectual course to secure this; for *all that the Father has given him, shall,* without fail, *come to him.* 2. The instruments Christ chose to employ in setting up his kingdom, were the *weak* and *foolish things of the world;* not called from the great sanhedrim, or the schools of the rabbin, but picked up from among the tarpaulins *by the sea-side, that the excellency of the power* might appear to be wholly *of God,* and not at all *of them.* 3. Though Christ needs not the help of man, yet he is pleased to make use of it in setting up his kingdom, that he might deal with us not in a formidable but in a familiar way, and that in his kingdom the *nobles and governors may be of ourselves,* Jer. xxx. 21. 4. Christ puts honour upon those who, though mean in the world, are *diligent in their business,* and *loving to one another;* so those were, whom Christ called. He found them *employed,* and employed *together. Industry* and and unity are *good* and *pleasant,* and there the Lord Jesus commands the blessing, even this blessing, *Follow me.* 5. The business of ministers is to *fish for souls,* and *win them to Christ.* The children of men, in their natural condition, are lost, wander endlessly in the great ocean of this world, and are carried down the stream of its course and way; they are unprofitable. Like leviathan in the waters, they *play therein;* and often, like the fishes of the sea, they devour one another. Ministers, in preaching the gospel, *cast the net* into the waters, Matt. xiii. 47. Some are enclosed and brought to shore, but far the greater number escape. *Fishermen* take great pains, and expose themselves to great perils, so do *ministers;* and they have need of wisdom. If many a draught brings home nothing, yet they must go on. 6. Those whom Christ calls, must *leave all,* to follow him; and by his grace he inclines them to do so. *Not that we must needs go out of the world* immediately, but we must sit loose to the world, and forsake every thing that is inconsistent with our duty to Christ, and that cannot be kept without prejudice to our souls. Mark takes notice of James and John, that they left not only *their father* (which we had in Matthew), but *the hired servants,* whom perhaps they loved as their own brethren, being their *fellow-labourers* and pleasant comrades; not only relations, but companions, must be left for Christ, and old acquaintance. Perhaps it is an intimation of their care for their father; they did not leave him without assistance, they left the *hired servants* with him. Grotius thinks it is mentioned as an evidence that their calling was gainful to them, for it was worth while to keep servants in pay, to help them in it, and their *hands* would be much *missed,* and yet they *left it.*

III. Here is a particular account of his preaching in Capernaum, one of the *cities* of Galilee; for though John Baptist chose to preach *in a wilderness,* and did *well,* and did *good,* yet it doth not therefore follow, that Jesus must do so too; the inclinations and opportunities of ministers may very much differ, and yet both be in the *way of their duty,* and both useful. Observe, 1. When Christ *came into Capernaum,* he *straightway* applied himself to his work there, and took the *first* opportunity of preaching the gospel. Those will think themselves concerned not to *lose time,* who consider what a deal of work they have to do, and what a little time to do it in. 2. Christ religiously observed the sabbath day, though not by tying himself up to the tradition of the elders, in all the niceties of the *sabbath-rest,* yet (which was far better) by applying himself to, and abounding in, the *sabbath-work,* in order to which the sabbath-rest was instituted. 3. Sabbaths are to be sanctified in *religious assemblies,* if we have opportunity; it is a *holy day,* and must be honoured with a *holy convocation;* this was the *good old way,* Acts xiii. 27; xv. 21. On the sabbath-day, τοῖς σαββασιν—*on the sabbath-days;* every sabbath-day, as duly as it returned, he *went into the synagogue.* 4. In *religious assemblies* on sabbath-days, the gospel is to be preached, and those to be *taught,* who are willing to learn the *truth as it is in Jesus.* 5. Christ was a non-such preacher; he did not preach *as the scribes,* who expounded the law of Moses by rote, as a school-boy says his lesson, but were neither *acquainted* with it (Paul himself, when a Pharisee, was ignorant of the law), nor *affected* with it; it came not *from the heart,* and therefore came not *with authority.* But Christ taught *as one that had authority,* as one that knew the mind of God, and was commissioned to declare it. 6. There is much in the doctrine of Christ, that is *astonishing;* the more we hear it, the more cause we shall see to *admire it.*

23 And there was in their synagogue a man with an unclean spirit;
and he cried out, 24 Saying, Let *us*
alone; what have we to do with thee,
thou Jesus of Nazareth? art thou
come to destroy us? I know thee
who thou art, the Holy One of God.
25 And Jesus rebuked him, saying,
Hold thy peace, and come out of him.
26 And when the unclean spirit had
torn him, and cried with a loud voice,
he came out of him. 27 And they
were all amazed, insomuch that they
questioned among themselves, saying,
What thing is this? what new doctrine
is this? for with authority commandeth
he even the unclean spirits, and they
do obey him. 28 And immediately
his fame spread abroad throughout all
the region round about Galilee.

As soon as Christ began to preach, he began to work miracles for the confirmation of his doctrine; and they were such as intimated the design and tendency of his doctrine, which were to conquer Satan, and cure sick souls.

In these verses, we have,

I. Christ's *casting the devil* out of a man that was possessed, in the synagogue at Capernaum. This passage was not related in Matthew, but is afterward in Luke iv. 33. *There was in the synagogue a man with an unclean spirit,* εν πνεύματι ἀκαθάρτω—*in an unclean spirit;* for the spirit had the man in his possession, and led him captive at his will. So the whole world is said to lie ἐν τῷ πονερῷ—*in the wicked one.* And some have thought it more proper to say, The *body* is *in the soul,* because it is governed by it, than the soul *in the body.* He was *in the unclean* spirit, as a man is said to be *in a fever,* or in a frenzy, quite overcome by it. Observe, The devil is here called *an unclean spirit,* because he has lost all the purity of his nature, because he acts in direct opposition to the *Holy* Spirit of God, and because with his suggestions he pollutes the spirits of men. This man *was in the synagogue;* he did not come either to be taught or to be healed, but, as some think, to confront Christ and oppose him, and hinder people from believing on him. Now here we have,

1. The rage which the unclean spirit expressed at Christ; *He cried out,* as one in an agony, at the presence of Christ, and afraid of being dislodged; thus the *devils believe and tremble,* have a horror of Christ, but no hope in him, nor reverence for him. We are told what he said, *v.* 24, where he doth not go about to *capitulate* with him, or *make terms* (so far was he from being in league or compact with him), but speaks as one that knew his doom. (1.) He calls him *Jesus of Nazareth;* for aught that appears, he was the first that called him so, and he did it with design to possess the minds of the people with *low thoughts* of him, because no good

thing was expected out of Nazareth; and with *prejudices* against him as a Deceiver, because every body knew the Messiah must be of Bethlehem. (2.) Yet a confession is extorted from him—that he is *the holy One of God,* as was from the damsel that had the spirit of divination concerning the apostles—that they were the *servants of the most high God,* Acts xvi. 16, 17. Those who have only a *notion* of Christ—that he is the *holy One of God,* and have no faith in him, or love to him, go no further than the devil doth. (3.) He in effect acknowledgeth that Christ was too hard for him, and that he could not stand before the power of Christ; "*Let us alone;* for if thou take us to task, we are undone, thou canst *destroy us.*" This is the misery of those wicked spirits, that they persist in their rebellion, and yet know it will end in their destruction. (4.) He desires to have *nothing to do* with Jesus Christ; for he *despairs* of being *saved* by him, and *dreads* being *destroyed* by him. "*What have we to do with thee?* If thou wilt let us alone, we will let thee alone." See whose language they speak, that *say to the Almighty, Depart from us.* This, being an *unclean spirit,* therefore hated and dreaded Christ, because he knew him to be a *holy One;* for the *carnal mind is enmity against God,* especially against *his holiness.*

2. The victory which Jesus Christ obtained over the unclean spirit; *for this purpose was the Son of God manifested, that he might destroy the works of the devil,* and so he makes it to appear; nor will he be turned back from prosecuting this war, either by his flatteries or by his menaces. It is in vain for Satan to beg and pray, *Let us alone;* his power must be broken, and the poor man must be relieved; and therefore, (1.) Jesus *commands.* As he taught, so he healed, *with authority.* Jesus *rebuked him;* he chid him and threatened him, imposed silence upon him; *Hold thy peace; φιμώθητι—be muzzled.* Christ has a muzzle for that unclean spirit when he *fawns* as well as when he *barks;* such acknowledgments of him as this was, Christ *disdains,* so far is he from *accepting* them. Some confess Christ to be the *holy One of God,* that under the cloak of that profession they may carry on malicious mischievous designs; but their confession is doubly an abomination to the Lord Jesus, as it sues in his name for a license to sin, and shall therefore be put to silence and shame. But this is not all, he must not only *hold his peace,* but he must *come out of the man;* this was it he dreaded—his being restrained from doing further mischief. But, (2.) The unclean spirit *yields,* for there is no remedy (*v.* 26); He *tore him,* put him into a *strong convulsion;* that one could have thought he had been pulled in pieces; when he would not *touch* Christ, in fury at him he grievously disturbed this poor creature. Thus, when Christ by his grace delivers poor souls out of the hands of Satan, it is not without a grievous toss and tumult in the soul; for that spiteful enemy will *disquiet* those whom he cannot *destroy.* He *cried with a loud voice,* to frighten the spectators, and make himself seem terrible, as if he would have it thought that though he was conquered, he was but just conquered, and that he hoped to rally again, and recover his ground.

II. The impression which this miracle made upon the minds of the people, *v.* 27, 28.

1. It astonished them that saw it; *They were all amazed.* It was evident, beyond contradiction, that the man was possessed—witness the tearing of him, and the *loud voice* with which the *spirit cried;* it was evident that he was *forced out* by the authority of Christ; this was surprising to them, and put them upon considering with themselves, and enquiring of one another, "*What is this new doctrine?* For it must certainly be of God, which is thus confirmed. *He* hath certainly an authority to command us, who hath ability to *command even the unclean spirits,* and they cannot resist him, but are forced *to obey him.*" The Jewish exorcists pretended by charm or invocation to drive away evil spirits; but this was quite another thing, *with authority he commands them.* Surely it is our interest to make *him* our Friend, who has the control of infernal spirits.

2. It raised his reputation among all that heard it; *Immediately his fame spread abroad into the whole adjacent region of Galilee,* which was a third part of the land of Canaan. The story was presently got into every one's mouth, and people wrote it to their friends all the country over, together with the remark made upon it, *What new doctrine is this?* So that it was universally concluded, that he was a *Teacher come from God,* and under that character he shone more bright than if he had appeared in all the external pomp and power which the Jews expected their Messiah to *appear* in; and thus he *prepared his own way,* now that John, who was his harbinger, was clapped up; and the fame of this miracle spread the further, because as yet the Pharisees, who *envied* his fame, and laboured to *eclipse* it, had not advanced their blasphemous suggestion, that he *cast out devils* by compact with the *prince of the devils.*

29 And forthwith, when they were
come out of the synagogue, they
entered into the house of Simon and
Andrew, with James and John. 30
But Simon's wife's mother lay sick of
a fever, and anon they tell him of her.
31 And he came and took her by the
hand, and lifted her up; and immediately the fever left her, and she
ministered unto them. 32 And at
even, when the sun did set, they
brought unto him all that were diseased, and them that were possessed

with devils. 33 And all the city was
gathered together at the door. 34
And he healed many that were sick
of divers diseases, and cast out many
devils; and suffered not the devils to
speak, because they knew him. 35
And in the morning, rising up a great
while before day, he went out, and
departed into a solitary place, and
there prayed. 36 And Simon and
they that were with him followed
after him. 37 And when they had
found him, they said unto him, All
men seek for thee. 38 And he said
unto them, Let us go into the next
towns, that I may preach there also:
for therefore came I forth. 39 And
he preached in their synagogues
throughout all Galilee, and cast out
devils.

In these verses, we have,

I. A particular account of one miracle that Christ wrought, in the cure of Peter's wife's mother, who was ill of a fever. This passage we had before, in Matthew. Observe,

1. When Christ had done that which *spread his fame* throughout all parts, he did not then sit still, as some think that they may *lie in bed* when their *name is up.* No, he continued to *do good,* for that was it he aimed at, and not his own honour. Nay, those who are in reputation, had need be busy and careful to keep it up.

2. When he *came out of the synagogue,* where he had taught and healed with a divine authority, yet he conversed familiarly with the poor fishermen that attended him, and did not think it below him. Let the same mind, the same lowly mind, be in us, that was in him.

3. He went into Peter's house, probably invited thither to such entertainment as a poor fisherman could give him, and he accepted of it. The apostles left all for Christ; so far as that what they had should not hinder them from him, yet not so, but that they might use it for him.

4. He cured his mother-in-law, who was sick. Wherever Christ comes, he comes to do good, and will be sure to pay richly for his entertainment. Observe, How complete the cure was; when *the fever left her,* it did not, as usual, leave her *weak,* but the same hand that *healed* her, *strengthened* her, so that she was able to *minister* to them; the cure is in order to that, to fit for action, that we may minister to Christ, and to those that are *his* for his sake.

II. A general account of many cures he wrought—diseases healed, devils expelled. It was on the *evening of the sabbath,* when the *sun did set,* or *was set;* perhaps many scrupled bringing their sick to him, till the sabbath was over, but their weakness therein was no prejudice to them in applying to Christ. Though he proved it *lawful to heal on the sabbath days,* yet, if any stumbled at it, they were welcome at another time. Now observe,

1. How *numerous* the patients were; *All the city was gathered at the door,* as beggars for a dole. That *one cure* in the synagogue occasioned this crowding after him. Others speeding well with Christ should quicken us in our enquiries after him. Now the *Sun of righteousness rises with healing under his wings;* to him shall the *gathering of the people be.* Observe, How Christ was flocked after in a *private house,* as well as in the *synagogue;* wherever he is, there let his servants, his patients, be. And in the *evening of the sabbath,* when the public worship is over, we must continue our attendance upon Jesus Christ; he healed, as Paul preached, publicly, and from house to house.

2. How *powerful* the Physician was; he *healed all* that were brought to him, though ever so many. Nor was it some one particular disease, that Christ set up for the cure of, but he healed those that were *sick of divers* diseases, for his word was a *panpharmacon—a salve for every sore.* And that miracle particularly which he wrought in the synagogue, he *repeated in the house* at night; for he *cast out many devils,* and *suffered not the devils to speak,* for he made them *know who he was,* and that silenced them. Or, He *suffered them not to say that they knew him* (so it may be read); he would not permit any more of them to say, as they did (*v.* 24), *I know thee, who thou art.*

III. His *retirement* to his *private devotion* (*v.* 35); *He prayed,* prayed alone; to set us an example of secret prayer. Though as God he was *prayed to,* as man he *prayed.* Though he was glorifying God, and doing good, in his public work, yet he found time to be alone with his Father; and thus *it became him to fulfil all righteousness.* Now observe,

1. The time *when* Christ prayed. (1.) It was *in the morning,* the morning after the *sabbath day.* Note, When a sabbath day is over and past, we must not think that we may intermit our devotion till the next sabbath: no, though we go not *to the synagogue,* we must go to the *throne of grace,* every day in the week; and the morning after the sabbath particularly, that we may preserve the good impressions of the day. This *morning* was the morning of the *first day of the week,* which afterward he sanctified, and made remarkable, by another sort of *rising early.* (2.) It was early, *a great while before day.* When others were asleep in their beds, he was *praying,* as a genuine Son of David, who seeks God *early,* and *directs his prayer in the morning;* nay, and *at midnight will rise to give thanks.* It has been said, *The morning is a friend to the Muses—Aurora Musis amica;* and it is no less so to the *Graces.* When our spirits are most fresh and lively, then we

should take time for *devout* exercises. He that is the *first* and *best,* ought to have the *first* and *best.*

2. The place *where* he prayed; He *departed into a solitary place,* either out of town, or some remote garden or out-building. Though he was in no danger of distraction, or of temptation to vain-glory, yet he retired, to set us an example to his own rule, *When thou prayest enter into thy closet.* Secret prayer must be made secretly. Those that have the most business in public, and of the best kind, must sometimes be *alone with God;* must retire into *solitude,* there to converse with God, and keep up communion with him.

IV. His *return* to his *public* work. The disciples thought they were *up early,* but found their Master was up *before them,* and they enquired which way he went, *followed him* to his *solitary place,* and there *found him* at prayer, *v.* 36, 37. They told him that he was much wanted, that there were a great many patients waiting for him; *All men seek for thee.* They were proud that their Master was become so popular already, and would have him appear *in public,* yet more in that place, because it was *their own city;* and we are apt to be partial to the places we know and are interested in. "No," saith Christ, "Capernaum must not have the monopoly of the Messiah's preaching and miracles. *Let us go into the next towns,* the *villages* that lie about here, *that I may preach there also,* and work miracles there, *for therefore came I forth,* not to be constantly resident in one place, but to *go about doing good.*" Even the *inhabitants of the villages in Israel* shall *rehearse the righteous acts of the Lord,* Judg. v. 11. Observe, Christ had still an eye to the end *wherefore he came forth,* and closely pursued that; nor will he be drawn by importunity, or the persuasions of his friends, to decline from that; for (*v.* 39) he *preached in their synagogues throughout all Galilee,* and, to illustrate and confirm his doctrine, *he cast out devils.* Note, Christ's doctrine is Satan's destruction.

40 And there came a leper to him,
beseeching him, and kneeling down to
him, and saying unto him, If thou
wilt, thou canst make me clean. 41
And Jesus, moved with compassion,
put forth *his* hand, and touched him,
and saith unto him, I will; be thou
clean. 42 And as soon as he had
spoken, immediately the leprosy departed from him, and he was cleansed.
43 And he straitly charged him, and
forthwith sent him away; 44 And
saith unto him, See thou say nothing
to any man: but go thy way, show
thyself to the priest, and offer for thy
cleansing those things which Moses
commanded, for a testimony unto
them. 45 But he went out, and began
to publish *it* much, and to blaze
abroad the matter, insomuch that
Jesus could no more openly enter
into the city, but was without in desert places: and they came to him
from every quarter.

We have here the story of Christ's *cleansing* a *leper,* which we had before, Matt. viii 2—4. It teaches us,

1. *How to apply ourselves to Christ;* come as this leper did, (1.) With great *humility;* this leper came *beseeching him, and kneeling down to him* (*v.* 40); whether giving divine honour to him as God, or rather a less degree of respect as a *great Prophet,* it teaches us that those who would receive grace and mercy from Christ, must ascribe honour and glory to Christ, and approach to him with humility and reverence. (2.) With a firm belief of *his power; Thou canst make me clean.* Though Christ's outward appearance was but *mean,* yet he had this faith in his power, which implies his belief that he was *sent of God.* He believes it with application, not only in general, *Thou canst do every thing* (as John xi. 22), but, *Thou canst make me clean.* Note, What we believe of the power of Christ we must bring home to our particular case; *Thou canst do this for me.* (3.) With submission to the will of Christ; *Lord, if thou wilt.* Not as if he had any doubt of Christ's readiness in general to help the distressed, but, with the modesty that became a poor petitioner, he refers his own particular case to him.

2. *What to expect from Christ;* that according to our faith it shall be to us. His address is not in the form of prayer, yet Christ answered it as a request. Note, Affectionate professions of faith in Christ, and resignations to him, are the most prevailing petitions for mercy from him, and shall speed accordingly. (1.) Christ was *moved with compassion.* This is added here, in Mark, to show that Christ's power is employed by his pity for the relief of poor souls; that his reasons are fetched from within himself, and we have nothing in us to recommend us to his favour, but our *misery* makes us the objects of his *mercy.* And what he does for us he does with all possible tenderness. (2.) He *put forth his hand, and touched him.* He *exerted* his power, and directed it to *this* creature. In healing souls, Christ *toucheth them,* 1 Sam. x. 26. When the queen toucheth for the evil, she saith, *I touch, God heals;* but Christ *toucheth and healeth too.* (3.) He said, *I will, be thou clean.* Christ's power was put forth in and by a *word,* to signify in what way Christ would ordinarily work spiritual cures; *He sends his word and heals,* Ps. cvii. 20; John xv. 3; xvii. 17. The poor leper put an *if* upon the will of Christ; *If thou wilt;* but that *doubt* is soon put *out of doubt; I will.*

Christ most readily *wills* favours to those that most readily *refer themselves* to his will. He was confident of Christ's *power;* Thou *canst make me clean;* and Christ will show how much his power is drawn out into act by the faith of his people, and therefore speaks the word as one having authority, *Be thou clean.* And power accompanied this word, and the cure was perfect in an instant; *Immediately his leprosy* vanished, and there remained no more sign of it, *v.* 42.

3. *What to do when we have received mercy from Christ.* We must with his favours receive his commands. When Christ had cured him, *he strictly charged him;* the word here is very significant, ἐμβριμησάμενος—*graviter interminatus—prohibiting with threats.* I am apt to think that this refers not to the directions he gave him to conceal it (*v.* 44), for those are mentioned by themselves; but that this was such a charge as he gave to the impotent man whom he cured, John v. 14, *Sin no more, lest a worse thing come unto thee;* for the *leprosy* was ordinarily the punishment of some particular sinners, as in Miriam's, Gehazi's, and Uzziah's, case; now, when Christ healed him, he *warned* him, he *threatened* him with the fatal consequence of it if he should *return to sin* again. He also appointed him, (1.) To *show himself to the priest,* that the priest by his own judgment of this leper might be a witness for Christ, that he was the Messiah, Matt. xi. 5. (2.) Till he had done that, not to *say any thing* of it *to any man*: this is an instance of the *humility* of Christ and his self-denial, that he did not seek his own honour, *did not strive or cry,* Is. xlii. 2. And it is an example to us, not to *seek our own glory,* Prov. xxv. 27. He must not *proclaim* it, because that would much increase the crowd that followed Christ, which he thought was too great already; not as if he were unwilling to *do good to all,* to as many as came; but he would do it with as little *noise* as might be, would have no offence given to the government, no disturbance of the public peace, not any thing done that looked like ostentation, or an affecting of popular applause. What to think of the leper's *publishing* it, and *blazing it abroad,* I know not; the concealment of the good characters and good works of good men better become *them* than *their friends;* nor are we always bound by the modest commands of humble men. The leper ought to have observed his orders; yet, no doubt, it was with a good design that he *proclaimed* the cure, and it had no other ill effect than that it increased the multitudes which followed Christ, to that degree, that he *could no more openly enter into the city;* not upon the account of persecution (there was no danger of that yet,) but because the crowd was so great, that the streets would not hold them, which obliged him to go into *desert places,* to a *mountain* (*ch.* iii. 13), to the *sea-side, ch.* iv. 1. This shows how *expedient* it was for us, that Christ should *go away,* and *send the Comforter,* for his bodily presence could be but in one place at a time; and those that *came to him from every quarter,* could not get *near him;* but by his spiritual presence he is with his people wherever they are, and comes to them to *every quarter.*

CHAP. II.

In this chapter, we have, I. Christ's healing a man that was sick of a palsy, ver. 1—12. II. His calling of Matthew from the receipt of custom, and his eating, upon that occasion, with publicans and sinners, and justifying himself in so doing, ver. 13—17. III. His justifying his disciples in not fasting so much as those of the Pharisees did, ver. 18—22. IV. His justifying them in plucking the ears of corn on the sabbath day, ver. 23—28. All which passages we had before, Matt. ix. and xii.

AND again he entered into Capernaum after *some* days; and it
was noised that he was in the house.
2 And straightway many were gathered together, insomuch that there
was no room to receive *them,* no, not
so much as about the door: and he
preached the word unto them. 3
And they come unto him, bringing
one sick of the palsy, which was borne
of four. 4 And when they could not
come nigh unto him for the press,
they uncovered the roof where he
was: and when they had broken *it*
up, they let down the bed wherein the
sick of the palsy lay. 5 When Jesus
saw their faith, he said unto the sick
of the palsy, Son, thy sins be forgiven
thee. 6 But there were certain of
the scribes sitting there, and reasoning
in their hearts, 7 Why doth this
man thus speak blasphemies? who
can forgive sins but God only? 8
And immediately when Jesus perceived in his spirit that they so reasoned within themselves, he said unto
them, Why reason ye these things in
your hearts? 9 Whether is it easier
to say to the sick of the palsy, *Thy*
sins be forgiven thee; or to say, Arise,
and take up thy bed, and walk? 10
But that ye may know that the Son
of man hath power on earth to forgive
sins (he saith unto the sick of the
palsy), 11 I say unto thee, Arise, and
take up thy bed, and go thy way into
thine house. 12 And immediately
he arose, took up the bed, and went
forth before them all; insomuch that
they were all amazed, and glorified
God, saying, We never saw it on this
fashion.

Christ, having been for some time preaching about in the country, here returns to

Capernaum his head-quarters, and makes his appearance there, in hopes that by this time the talk and crowd would be somewhat abated. Now observe,

I. The great resort there was to him. Though he was *in the house,* either Peter's house, or some lodgings of his own which he had taken, yet people came to him as soon as it was *noised* that he was in town; they did not stay till he appeared in the synagogue, which they might be sure he would do on the *sabbath day,* but *straightway many were gathered together to him.* Where the king is, there is the court; where Shiloh is, there *shall the gathering of the people be.* In improving opportunities for our souls, we must take care not to *lose time.* One invited another (Come, let us go see Jesus), so that his house could not contain his visitants. *There was no room to receive them,* they were so numerous, *no not so much as about the door.* A blessed sight, to see people thus flying like a cloud to Christ's house, though it was but a poor one, and *as the doves to their windows!*

II. The good entertainment Christ gave them, the best his house would afford, and better than any other could; he *preached the word unto them, v.* 2. Many of them perhaps came only for cures, and many perhaps only for curiosity, to get a sight of him; but when he had them together he *preached to them.* Though the synagogue-door was open to him at proper times, he thought it not at all amiss to preach in a house, on a week day; though some might reckon it both an improper place and an improper time. *Blessed are ye that sow beside all waters,* Isa. xxxii. 20.

III. The presenting of a poor cripple to him, to be helped by him. The patient was one *sick of the palsy,* it should seem not as that, Matt. viii. 6, *grievously tormented,* but perfectly disabled, so that he was *borne of four,* was carried upon *a bed,* as if he had been upon *a bier,* by four persons. It was his misery, that he needed to be so carried, and bespeaks the calamitous state of human life; it was their charity, who did so carry him, and bespeaks the compassion that it is justly expected should be in the children of men toward their fellow-creatures in distress, because we know not how soon the distress may be *our own.* These kind relations or neighbours thought, if they could but carry this poor man once to Christ, they should not need to carry him any more; and therefore made hard shift to get him to him; and when they could not otherwise get to him, they *uncovered the roof where he was, v.* 4. I see no necessity to conclude that Christ was preaching in an *upper room,* though in such the Jews that had stately houses, had their oratories; for then to what purpose should the crowd stand *before the door,* as wisdom's clients used to do? Prov. viii. 34. But I rather conjecture that the house he was in, was so little and mean (agreeable to his present state), that it had no *upper room,* but the *ground-floor* was open to the roof: and these petitioners for the poor paralytic, resolving not to be disappointed, when they could not get through the crowd at the door, got their friend by some means or other to the roof of the house, took off some of the tiles, and so let him down upon his bed with cords into the house where Christ was preaching. This bespoke both their *faith* and their *fervency* in this address to Christ. Hereby it appeared that they were in earnest, and would not go away, nor *let Christ go without a blessing.* Gen. xxxii. 26.

IV. The kind word Christ said to this poor patient; *He saw their faith;* perhaps not so much his, for his distemper hindered him from the exercise of faith, but *theirs* that brought him. In curing the centurion's servant, Christ took notice of it as an instance of *his faith,* that he did not bring him to Christ, but believed he could cure him at a distance; here he commended *their faith,* because they did bring their friend through so much difficulty. Note, True faith and strong faith may work variously, conquering sometimes the objections of reason, sometimes those of sense; but, however manifested, it shall be accepted and approved by Jesus Christ. Christ said, *Son, thy sins be forgiven thee.* The *compellation* is very *tender—Son;* intimating a fatherly *care* of him and *concern* for him. Christ owns true believers as his sons: *a son,* and yet sick of the palsy. Herein God *deals with you as with sons.* The *cordial* is very rich; *Thy sins are forgiven thee.* Note, 1. Sin is the procuring cause of all our pains and sicknesses. The word of Christ was to take his thoughts off from the disease, which was the effect, and to lead them to the sin, the cause, that he might be more concerned about that, to get that pardoned. 2. God doth *then* graciously take away the sting and malignity of sickness, when he forgives sin; recovery from sickness is *then* a mercy indeed, when way is made for it by the pardon of sin. See Isa. xxxviii. 17; Ps. ciii. 3. The way to remove the effect, is, to take away the cause. Pardon of sin strikes at the root of all diseases, and either cures them, or alters their property.

V. The cavil of the scribes at that which Christ said, and a demonstration of the unreasonableness of their cavil. They were expositors of the law, and their doctrine was *true*—that it is blasphemy for any creature to undertake the pardon of sin, and that it is God's prerogative, Isa. xliii. 25. But, as is usual with such teachers, their application was *false,* and was the effect of their ignorance and enmity to Christ. It is *true, None can forgive sins but God only;* but it is false that therefore Christ cannot, who had abundantly proved himself to have a divine power. But Christ *perceived in his spirit that they so reasoned within themselves;* this proves him to be God, and therefore confirmed what was to be proved, that he had authority to *forgive sins;* for he *searched* the heart, and knew *what was in man,* Rev. ii. 23. God's royalties are inseparable, and he that could *know thoughts,* could *forgive sins.* This magnifies the grace of Christ, in *pardoning sin,* that he knew men's thoughts, and therefore knows more than any other can know, both of the sinfulness of their sins and the particulars of them, and yet is ready to pardon. Now he proves his power to *forgive sin,* by demonstrating his power to cure the *man sick of the palsy, v.* 9—11. He would not have pretended to do *the one,* if he could not have done *the other; that ye may know that the Son of man,* the Messiah, *has power on earth to forgive sin,* that I have that power, *Thou that art* sick of the palsy, *arise, take up thy bed.* Now, 1. This was a *suitable* argument in itself. He could not have cured the disease, which was the effect, if he could not have taken away the sin, which was the cause. And besides, his curing diseases was a figure of his pardoning sin, for sin is the disease of the soul; when it is pardoned, it is healed. He that could by a word accomplish the sign, could doubtless perform the thing signified, 2. It was suited to them. These carnal scribes would be more affected with such a suitable effect of a pardon as the cure of the disease, and be sooner convinced by it, than by any other more spiritual consequences; therefore it was proper enough to appeal, whether it is easier to say, *Thy sins are forgiven thee,* or to say, *Arise, and walk?* The removing of the punishment as such, was the remitting of the sin; he that could go so far in the cure, no doubt could perfect it. See Isa. xxxiii. 24.

VI. The cure of the sick man, and the impression it made upon the people, *v.* 12. He not only *arose* out of his bed, perfectly well, but, to show that he had perfect strength restored to him, *he took up his bed,* because it lay in the way, *and went forth before them all;* and *they were all amazed,* as well they might, and *glorified God,* as indeed they ought; saying, "*We never saw it on this fashion;* never were such wonders as these done before in our time." Note, Christ's works were without precedent. When we see what he does in healing souls, we must own that we *never saw the like.*

13 And he went forth again by the
sea side; and all the multitude resorted unto him, and he taught them.
14 And as he passed by, he saw Levi
the *son* of Alphæus sitting at the receipt of custom, and said unto him,
Follow me. And he arose and followed him. 15 And it came to pass,
that, as Jesus sat at meat in his house,
many publicans and sinners sat also
together with Jesus and his disciples:
for there were many, and they followed him. 16 And when the scribes
and Pharisees saw him eat with publicans and sinners, they said unto his
disciples, How is it that he eateth
and drinketh with publicans and sinners? 17 When Jesus heard *it*, he
saith unto them, They that are whole
have no need of the physician, but
they that are sick: I came not to call
the righteous, but sinners to repentance.

Here is,

I. Christ preaching by the *sea-side* (*v.* 13), whither he went *for room,* because he found, upon second trial, no house or street large enough to contain his auditory; but upon the strand there might come as many as would. It should seem by this, that our Lord Jesus had a strong voice, and could and did speak loud; for *wisdom crieth without* in the *places of concourse.* Wherever he goes, though it be to the sea-side, *multitudes resort to him.* Wherever the doctrine of Christ is faithfully preached, though it be driven into corners or into deserts, we must follow it.

II. His calling Levi; the same with Matthew, who had a place in the custom-house at Capernaum, from which he was denominated a *publican;* his place fixed him by the water-side, and thither Christ went to meet with him, and to give him an effectual call. This Levi is here said to be *the son of Alpheus* or *Cleophas,* husband to that Mary who was sister or near kinswoman to the virgin Mary and if so, he was own brother to James the less, and Jude, and Simon the Canaanite, so that there were four brothers of them apostles, It is probable that Matthew was but a loose extravagant young man, or else, being a Jew, he would never have been a publican. However, Christ called him to *follow him.* Paul, though a Pharisee, had been one of the chief of sinners, and yet was called to be an apostle. With God, through Christ, there is mercy to pardon the greatest sins, and grace to sanctify the greatest sinners. Matthew, that had been a publican, became an evangelist, the *first* that put pen to paper, and the *fullest* in writing the life of Christ. Great sin and scandal before conversion, are no bar to great gifts, graces, and advancements, after; nay, God may be the more glorified. Christ prevented him with this call; in bodily cures, ordinarily, he was *sought unto,* but in these spiritual cures, he was *found of them that sought him not.* For this is the great evil and peril of the disease of sin, that those who are under it, desire not to be *made whole.*

III. His familiar converse with *publicans and sinners,* ver. 15. We are here told, 1. That Christ *sat at meat in Levi's house,* who invited *him and his disciples* to the farewell-feast he made to his friends, when he left all to attend on Christ: such a feast he made, as Elisha did (1 Kings xix. 21), to show, not only with what cheerfulness in himself, but with what thankfulness to God, he quitted all, in compliance with Christ's call. Fitly did he make the *day of his espousals* to Christ a festival day. This was also to testify his respect to Christ, and the grateful sense he had of his kindness, in snatching him from the receipt of custom as a brand out of the burning. 2. That *many publicans and sinners* sat with Christ in Levi's house (for *there were many* belonging to that custom-house); and *they followed him.* They followed Levi; so some understand it, supposing that, like Zaccheus, he was *chief among the publicans,* and was *rich;* and for that reason, the inferior sort of them attended him for what they could get. I rather take it, that they *followed Jesus* because of the report they had heard of him. They did not *for conscience-sake* leave all to follow him, but *for curiosity-sake* they came to Levi's feast, to see him; whatever brought them thither, they were sitting with *Jesus and his disciples.* The publicans are here and elsewhere ranked with *sinners,* the worst of *sinners.* (1.) Because commonly they *were such;* so general were the corruptions in the execution of that office, oppressing, exacting, and taking bribes or fees to extortion, and *accusing falsely,* Luke iii. 13, 14. A faithful fair-dealing publican was so rare, even at Rome, that one Sabinus, who kept a clean reputation in that office, was, after his death, honoured with this inscription, Καλῶς τελωνήσαντι—*Here lies an honest publican.* (2.) Because the Jews had a particular antipathy to them and their office, as an affront to the liberty of their nation and a badge of their slavery, and therefore put them into an ill name, and thought it scandalous to be seen in their company. Such as these our blessed Lord was pleased to converse with, when he appeared *in the likeness of sinful flesh.*

IV. The *offence* which the scribes and Pharisees took at this, *v.* 16. They would not come to hear him preach, which they might have been convinced and edified by; but they would come themselves to *see him* sit with publicans and sinners, which they would be provoked by. They endeavoured to put the disciples out of conceit with their Master, as a man not of such sanctity and severe morals as became his character; and therefore put the question to them. *How is it, that he eateth and drinketh with publicans and sinners?* Note, It is no new thing for that which is both well-*done,* and well-*designed,* to be misrepresented, and turned to the reproach of the wisest and best of men.

V. Christ's justification of himself in it, *v.* 17. He stood to what he did, and would not withdraw, though the Pharisees were offended, as Peter afterwards did, Gal. ii. 12. Note, Those are too tender of their own *good name,* who, to preserve it with some nice people, will decline a *good work.* Christ would not do so. They thought the publicans were to be *hated.* "No," saith Christ, "they are to be *pitied,* they are *sick* and *need a physician;* they are sinners, and need a Saviour." They thought Christ's character should separate him from them; "No," saith Christ, "my commission directs me to them; *I came not to call the righteous, but sinners to repentance.* If the world had been *righteous,* there had been no occasion for my coming, either to *preach* repentance, or to *purchase* remission. It is to a *sinful world* that I am sent, and therefore my business lies most with those that are the greatest sinners in it." Or thus; "*I am not come to call the righteous,* the proud Pharisees that think themselves righteous, that ask, *Wherein shall we return?* (Mal. iii. 7), Of what shall we repent? But poor publicans, that own themselves to be sinners, and are glad to be invited and encouraged to repent." It is good dealing with those that there is hope of; now there is *more hope of a fool* than of one that is *wise in his own conceit,* Prov. xxvi. 12.

18 And the disciples of John and
of the Pharisees used to fast: and
they come and say unto him, Why do
the disciples of John and of the Pharisees fast, but thy disciples fast not?
19 And Jesus said unto them, Can
the children of the bridechamber fast,
while the bridegroom is with them?
as long as they have the bridegroom
with them, they cannot fast. 20 But
the days will come, when the bridegroom shall be taken away from them,
and then shall they fast in those days.
21 No man also seweth a piece of
new cloth on an old garment: else
the new piece that filled it up taketh
away from the old, and the rent is
made worse. 22 And no man putteth
new wine into old bottles: else the
new wine doth burst the bottles, and
the wine is spilled, and the bottles
will be marred: but new wine must
be put into new bottles. 23 And it
came to pass, that he went through
the corn fields on the sabbath day;
and his disciples began, as they went,
to pluck the ears of corn. 24 And
the Pharisees said unto him, Behold,
why do they on the sabbath day that
which is not lawful? 25 And he
said unto them, Have ye never read
what David did, when he had need,
and was an hungred, he, and they that
were with him? 26 How he went
into the house of God in the days of
Abiathar the high priest, and did eat
the showbread, which is not lawful to

eat but for the priests, and gave also to them which were with him? 27
And he said unto them, The sabbath was made for man, and not man for the sabbath: 28 Therefore the Son of man is Lord also of the sabbath.

Christ had been put to *justify* himself in conversing with *publicans and sinners:* here he is put to justify his disciples; and in what they do according to his will he will justify them, and bear them out.

I. He justifies them in their *not fasting,* which was turned to their reproach by the Pharisees. Why do the Pharisees and the disciples of John fast? They *used to fast,* the Pharisees fasted *twice in the week* (Luke xviii. 12), and probably the disciples of John did so too; and, it should seem, this very day, when Christ and his disciples were feasting in Levi's house, was their *fast-day,* for the word is *νηστεύουσι—they do fast,* or *are fasting,* which aggravated the offence. Thus apt are strict professors to make their own practice a standard, and to censure and condemn all that do not fully come up to it. They invidiously suggest that if Christ went among sinners to do them *good,* as he had pleaded, yet the disciples went to indulge their appetites, for they never knew what it was to fast, or to deny themselves. Note, Ill-will always suspects the worst.

Two things Christ pleads in excuse of his disciples *not fasting.*

1. That these were *easy days* with them, and fasting was not so *seasonable* now as it would be hereafter, *v.* 19, 20. There is a time for all things. Those that enter into the married state, must expect care and *trouble in the flesh,* and yet, during the nuptial solemnity, they are merry, and think it becomes them to be so; it was very absurd for Samson's bride to *weep before* him, *during the days that the feast lasted,* Judg. xiv. 17. Christ and his disciples were but newly married, the bridegroom was *yet with them,* the nuptials were yet in the celebrating (Matthew's particularly); when the bridegroom should be removed from them to the far country, about his business, then would be a proper time to sit as a widow, in solitude and fasting.

2. That these were *early days* with them, and they were not so able for the severe exercises of religion as hereafter they would be. The Pharisees had long accustomed themselves to such austerities; and John Baptist himself came neither eating nor drinking. His disciples from the first inured themselves to hardships, and thus found it easier to bear strict and frequent fasting, but it was not so with Christ's disciples; their Master came *eating and drinking,* and had not bred them up to the difficult services of religion as yet, for it was all in good time. To put them upon such frequent fasting at first, would be a discouragement to them, and perhaps drive them off from following Christ; it would be of as ill consequence as *putting new wine into old casks,* or sewing *new cloth* to that which is worn thin and threadbare, *v.* 21, 22. Note, God graciously *considers the frame* of young Christians, that are *weak* and *tender,* and so must we; nor must we expect more than the *work of the day in its day,* and that day according to the strength, because it is not in our hands to give strength according to the day. Many contract an antipathy to some kind of food, otherwise good, by being surfeited with it when they are young; so, many entertain prejudices against the exercises of devotion by being burthened with them, and *made to serve with an offering,* at their setting out. Weak Christians must take heed of *overtasking* themselves, and of making the yoke of Christ otherwise than as it is, easy, and sweet, and pleasant.

II. He justifies them in *plucking the ears of corn on the sabbath day,* which, I will warrant you, a disciple of the Pharisees would not dare to have done; for it was contrary to an express tradition of their elders. In this instance, as in that before, they reflect upon the discipline of Christ's school, as if it were not so strict as that of theirs: so common it is for those who deny the *power of godliness,* to be jealous for the *form,* and censorious of those who affect not *their* form.

Observe, 1. What a poor breakfast Christ's disciples had on a sabbath-day morning, when they were going to church (*v.* 23); they *plucked the ears of corn,* and that was the best they had. They were so intent upon spiritual dainties, that they forgot even their *necessary food;* and the word of Christ was to them instead of that; and their zeal for it even *ate them up.* The Jews made it a piece of religion, to eat dainty food on sabbath days, but the disciples were content with any thing.

2. How even this was *grudged them* by the Pharisees, upon supposition that it was not lawful to *pluck the ears of corn* on the sabbath day, that that was as much a servile work as *reaping* (*v.* 24); *Why do they on the sabbath day that which is not lawful?* Note, If Christ's disciples do that which is unlawful, Christ will be reflected upon, and upbraided with it, as he was here, and dishonour will redound to his name. It is observable, that when the Pharisees thought Christ did amiss, they told the disciples (*v.* 16); and now when they thought the disciples did amiss, they spoke to Christ, as make-bates, that did what they could to sow discord between Christ and his disciples, and make a breach in the family.

3. How Christ defended them in what they did.

(1.) By example. They had a good precedent for it in David's eating the *show-bread,* when he was hungry, and there was no other bread to be had (*v.* 25, 26); *Have ye never read?* Note, Many of our mistakes would be rectified, and our unjust censures of others corrected, if we would but recollect what *we have read* in the scripture; appeals to that are most convincing. "You have read that David, the man after God's own heart, *when he was hungry*, made no difficulty of eating *the show-bread*, which by the law none might eat of but the priests and their families." Note, Ritual observances must give way to moral obligations; and that may be done in a case of necessity, which otherwise may not be done. This, it is said, David did in the days of *Abiathar the High-Priest;* or *just before* the days of Abiathar, who immediately succeeded Abimelech his father in the pontificate, and, it is probable, was at that time his father's deputy, or assistant, in the office; and he it was that escaped the massacre, and brought the ephod to David.

(2.) By argument. To reconcile them to the disciples' *plucking the ears of corn*, let them consider,

[1.] Whom the sabbath was *made for* (*v.* 27); *it was made for man, and not man for the sabbath.* This we had not in Matthew. The sabbath is a sacred and divine institution; but we must receive and embrace it as a privilege and a benefit, not as a task and a drudgery. *First,* God never designed it to be an *imposition* upon us, and therefore we must not make it so to ourselves. *Man was not made for the sabbath,* for he was made a day before the sabbath was instituted. Man was made *for God,* and for his honour and service, and he must rather die than deny him; but he was not *made for the sabbath,* so as to be tied up by the law of it, from that which is necessary to the support of his life. *Secondly,* God did design it to be an *advantage* to us, and so we must make it, and improve it. He made it *for man.* 1. He had *some* regard to our *bodies* in the institution, that they might rest, and not be tired out with the constant business of this world (Deut. v. 14); *that thy man-servant and thy maid-servant may rest.* Now he that intended the *sabbath-rest* for the *repose* of our bodies, certainly never intended it should restrain us, in a case of necessity, from fetching in the necessary *supports* of the body; it must be construed so as not to contradict itself—for *edification,* and not for *destruction.* 2. He had *much more* regard to our *souls.* The *sabbath* was made a day of rest, only in order to its being a day of holy work, a day of communion with God, a day of praise and thanksgiving; and the rest from worldly business is *therefore* necessary, that we may closely apply ourselves to this work, and spend the whole time in it, in public and in private; but then time is allowed us for that which is necessary to the fitting of our bodies for the service of our souls in God's service, and the enabling of them to *keep pace* with them in that work. See here, (1.) What a *good Master* we serve, all whose institutions are for our own benefit, and if we be so wise as to observe them, we are *wise for ourselves;* it is not he, but we, that are gainers by our service. (2.) What we should aim at in our *sabbath work,* even the good of our own souls. If the sabbath was made for man, we should then ask ourselves at night, "What am I the better for this sabbath day?" (3.) What care we ought to take not to make those exercises of religion burthens to ourselves or others, which God ordained to be blessings; neither adding to the command by unreasonable strictness, nor indulging those corruptions which are adverse to the command, for thereby we make those devout exercises a penance to ourselves, which otherwise would be a pleasure.

[2.] Whom the sabbath was *made by* (*v.* 28); "*The Son of man is Lord also of the sabbath;* and therefore he will not see the kind intentions of the institution of it frustrated by your impositions." Note, The sabbath days are *days of the Son of man;* he is the Lord of the day, and to his honour it must be observed; by him God made the worlds, and so it was by him that the sabbath was first instituted; by him God gave the law at mount Sinai, and so the *fourth* commandment was *his law;* and that little alteration that was shortly to be made, by the shifting of it one day forward to the first day of the week, was to be in remembrance of *his* resurrection, and therefore the Christian sabbath was to be called *the Lord's day* (Rev. i. 10), the Lord Christ's day; and the *Son of man,* Christ, as Mediator, is always to be looked upon as Lord of the sabbath. This argument he largely insists upon in his own justification, when he was charged with having broken the sabbath, John v. 16.

CHAP. III.

In this chapter, we have, I. Christ's healing a man that had a withered hand, on the sabbath day, and the combination of his enemies against him for it, ver. 1—6. II. The universal resort of people to him from all parts, to be healed, and the relief they all found with him, ver. 7—12. III. His ordaining his twelve apostles to be attendants on him, and the preachers of his gospel, ver. 13—21. IV. His answer to the blasphemous cavils of the scribes, who imputed his power to cast out devils to a confederacy with the prince of the devils, ver. 22—30. V. His owning his disciples for his nearest and dearest relations, ver. 31—35.

AND he entered again into the
synagogue; and there was a man
there which had a withered hand. 2
And they watched him, whether he
would heal him on the sabbath-day;
that they might accuse him. 3 And
he saith unto the man which had the
withered hand, Stand forth. 4 And
he saith unto them, Is it lawful to do
good on the sabbath days, or to do
evil? to save life, or to kill? But
they held their peace. 5 And when
he had looked round about on them

with anger, being grieved for the hardness of their hearts, he saith unto the
man, Stretch forth thine hand. And
he stretched *it* out: and his hand was
restored whole as the other. 6 And
the Pharisees went forth, and straightway took counsel with the Herodians
against him, how they might destroy
him: 7 But Jesus withdrew himself
with his disciples to the sea: and a
great multitude from Galilee followed
him, and from Judæa, 8 And from
Jerusalem, and from Idumæa, and
from beyond Jordan; and they about
Tyre and Sidon, a great multitude,
when they had heard what great things
he did, came unto him. 9 And he
spake to his disciples, that a small
ship should wait on him because of
the multitude, lest they should throng
him. 10 For he had healed many;
insomuch that they pressed upon him
for to touch him, as many as had
plagues. 11 And unclean spirits, when
they saw him, fell down before him,
and cried, saying, Thou art the Son
of God. 12 And he straitly charged
them that they should not make him
known.

Here, as before, we have our Lord Jesus busy at work *in the synagogue* first, and then by *the sea side;* to teach us that his presence should not be confined either to the one or to the other, but, wherever any are gathered together in his name, whether *in the synagogue* or any where else, there is he in the midst of them. *In every place where he records his name*, he will meet his people, and *bless them;* it is his will that men *pray every where.* Now here we have some account of what he did.

I. When he *entered again into the synagogue*, he improved the opportunity he had there, of doing good, and having, no doubt, preached a sermon there, he wrought a miracle for the confirmation of it, or at least for the confirmation of this truth—that *it is lawful to do good on the sabbath day.* We had the narrative, Matt. xii. 9.

1. The patient's case was piteous; he had a *withered hand*, by which he was disabled to work for his living; and those that are so, are the most proper objects of charity; let those be helped that cannot help themselves.

2. The spectators were very unkind, both to the patient and to the Physician; instead of interceding for a poor neighbour, they did what they could to hinder his cure: for they intimated that if Christ cured him now on the sabbath day, they would accuse him as a *Sabbath breaker.* It had been very unreasonable, if they should have opposed a physician or surgeon in helping any poor body in misery, by ordinary methods; but much more absurd was it to oppose him that cured without any labour, but by a word's speaking.

3. Christ dealt very fairly with the spectators, and dealt with them *first,* if possible to *prevent* the offence.

(1.) He laboured to convince their judgment. He bade the man *stand forth* (*v.* 3), that by the sight of him they might be moved with compassion toward him, and might not, for shame, account his cure a crime. And then he appeals to their own consciences; though the thing *speaks itself*, yet *he* is pleased to *speak* it; "*Is it lawful to do good on the sabbath days,* as I design to do, *or to do evil,* as you design to do? Whether is better, to *save life* or to *kill?*" What fairer question could be put? And yet, because they saw it would turn against them, *they held their peace.* Note, Those are obstinate indeed in their infidelity, who, when they can say nothing *against* a truth, will say nothing *to it;* and, when they cannot *resist*, yet will not *yield.*

(2.) When they rebelled against the light, he *lamented their stubbornness* (*v.* 5); *He looked round about on them with anger, being grieved for the hardness of their hearts.* The *sin* he had an eye to, was, the *hardness of their hearts*, their insensibleness of the evidence of his miracles, and their inflexible resolution to persist in unbelief. We hear what is said amiss, and see what is done amiss; but Christ looks at the *root of bitterness* in the heart, the blindness and hardness of *that.* Observe, [1.] How he was *provoked* by the sin; he looked *round upon them;* for they were so many, and had so placed themselves, that they surrounded him: and he looked *with anger;* his anger, it is probable, appeared in his countenance; his anger was, like God's, without the least *perturbation* to himself, but not without great *provocation* from us. Note, The sin of sinners is very displeasing to Jesus Christ; and the way to be angry, and not to sin, is to be angry, as Christ was, at nothing but sin. Let hard-hearted sinners tremble to think of the anger with which he will *look round* upon them shortly, when the *great day of his wrath comes.* [2.] How he *pitied* the sinners; he was *grieved for the hardness of their hearts;* as God was grieved forty years for the hardness of the hearts of their fathers in the wilderness. Note, It is a great grief to our Lord Jesus, to see sinners bent upon their own ruin, and obstinately set against the methods of their conviction and recovery, for he would not that any should perish. This is a good reason why the hardness of our own hearts and of the hearts of others, should be a grief to us.

4. Christ dealt very kindly with the patient; he bade him *stretch forth his hand,* and it was immediately *restored.* Now, (1.) Christ

has hereby taught us to go on with resolution in the way of our duty, how violent soever the opposition is, that we meet with in it. We must deny ourselves sometimes in our ease, pleasure, and convenience, rather than give offence even to those who causelessly take it; but we must not deny ourselves the satisfaction of serving God, and doing good, though offence may unjustly be taken at it. None could be more tender of giving offence than Christ; yet, rather than send this poor man away uncured, he would venture offending all the scribes and Pharisees that compassed him about. (2.) He hath hereby given us a *specimen* of the cures wrought by his grace upon *poor souls;* our hands are spiritually *withered,* the powers of our souls weakened by sin, and disabled for that which is good. The great healing day is the *sabbath,* and the healing place the *synagogue;* the healing power is that of Christ. The gospel command is like this recorded here; and the command is rational and just; though our hands are withered, and we cannot of ourselves *stretch them forth,* we must attempt it, must, as well as we can, *lift them up* to God in prayer, *lay hold* on Christ and eternal life, and employ them in good works; and if we do our endeavour, power goes along with the word of Christ, he effects the cure. Though our hands be *withered,* yet, if we will not offer to *stretch them out,* it is our own fault that we are not healed; but if we do, and are healed, Christ and his power and grace must have all the glory.

5. The enemies of Christ dealt very barbarously with him. Such a work of *mercy* should have engaged their love *to him,* and such a work of *wonder* their faith *in him.* But, instead of that, the Pharisees, who pretended to be oracles in the church, and the Herodians, who pretended to be the supporters of the state, though of opposite interests one to another, *took counsel together against him, how they might destroy him.* Note, They that suffer for doing good, do but suffer as their Master did.

II. When he withdrew *to the sea,* he did good there. While his enemies sought to *destroy him,* he quitted the place; to teach us in troublous times to shift for our own safety; but see here,

1. How he was followed into his retirement. When some had such an enmity to him, that they drove him out of their country, others had such a value for him, that they followed him wherever he went; and the enmity of their leaders to Christ did not cool their respect to him. *Great multitudes* followed him from all parts of the nation; as far north, as *from Galilee;* as far south, as from Judea and Jerusalem; nay, and from Idumea; as far east, as from beyond Jordan; and west, as from about Tyre and Sidon, *v.* 7, 8. Observe, (1.) What induced them to follow him; it was the report they heard of the *great things he did* for all that applied themselves to him; some wished *to see* one that had done such *great things,* and others hoped he would do great things *for them.* Note, The consideration of the *great things* Christ has done, should engage us to *come to him.* (2.) What they followed him for (*v.* 10); They *pressed upon him, to touch him, as many as had plagues.* Diseases are here called *plagues, μάστιγας—corrections, chastisements;* so they are designed to be, to make us *smart* for our sins, that thereby we may be made *sorry* for them, and may be warned not to return to them. Those that were under these *scourgings* came to Jesus; this is the errand on which sickness is sent, to quicken us to enquire after Christ, and apply ourselves to him as our Physician. They *pressed upon him,* each striving which should get *nearest to* him, and which should be *first served.* They *fell down before him* (so Dr. Hammond), as petitioners for his favour; they desired leave but to *touch him,* having faith to be healed, not only by *his* touching *them,* but by *their* touching him; which no doubt they had many instances of. (3.) What provision he made to be ready to attend them (*v.* 9); He *spoke to his disciples,* who were fishermen, and had fisher-boats at command, that a *small ship should* constantly *wait on him,* to carry him from place to place on the same coast; that, when he had despatched the necessary business he had to do in one place, he might easily remove to another, where his presence was requisite, without pressing through the crowds of people that followed him for curiosity. Wise men, as much as they can, decline a crowd.

2. What abundance of good he did in his retirement. He did not withdraw to be idle, nor did he send back those who rudely crowded after him when he withdrew, but took it kindly, and gave them what they came for; for he never said to any that sought him diligently, *Seek ye me in vain.* (1.) Diseases were effectually cured; He *healed many;* divers sorts of patients, ill of divers sorts of diseases; though numerous, though various, he *healed them.* (2.) *Devils* were effectually *conquered;* those whom unclean spirits had got possession of, *when they saw him,* trembled at his presence, and they also *fell down before him,* not to supplicate his favour, but to deprecate his wrath, and by their own terrors were compelled to own that *he was the Son of God, v.* 11. It is sad that this great truth should be denied by any of the children of men, who may have the benefit of it, when a confession of it has so often been extorted from devils, who are excluded from having benefit by it. (3.) Christ sought not applause to himself in doing those great things, for *he strictly charged* those for whom he did them, *that they should not make him known* (*v.* 12); that they should not be *industrious* to spread the notice of his cures, as it were by advertisements in the newspapers, but let them leave *his own works to praise*

him, and let the report of them *diffuse itself,* and make its own way. Let not those that are cured, be forward to divulge it, lest it should feed their pride who are so *highly favoured;* but let the *standers-by* carry away the intelligence of it. When we do that which is *praiseworthy,* and yet covet not to be *praised of men* for it, then *the same mind is in us,* which was *in Christ Jesus.*

13 And he goeth up into a mountain, and calleth *unto him* whom he
would: and they came unto him. 14
And he ordained twelve, that they
should be with him, and that he might
send them forth to preach, 15 And
to have power to heal sicknesses, and
to cast out devils: 16 And Simon he
surnamed Peter; 17 And James the
son of Zebedee, and John the brother
of James; and he surnamed them
Boanerges, which is, The sons of thunder: 18 And Andrew, and Philip,
and Bartholomew, and Matthew, and
Thomas, and James the *son* of Alphæus, and Thaddæus, and Simon the
Canaanite, 19 And Judas Iscariot,
which also betrayed him: and they
went into a house. 20 And the
multitude cometh together again, so
that they could not so much as eat
bread. 21 And when his friends
heard *of it,* they went out to lay hold
on him: for they said, He is beside
himself.

In these verses, we have,

I. The choice Christ made of the *twelve apostles* to be his constant followers and attendants, and to be sent abroad as there was occasion, to preach the gospel. Observe,

1. The introduction to this *call* or *promotion* of disciples; He *goes up into a mountain,* and his errand thither was *to pray.* Ministers must be set apart with solemn prayer for the pouring out of the Spirit upon them; though Christ had authority to confer the gifts of the Holy Ghost, yet, to set us an example, he prayed for them.

2. The rule he went by in his choice, and that was his own good pleasure; *He called unto him whom he would.* Not such as we should have thought *fittest to be called, looking upon the countenance, and the height of the stature;* but such as he *thought fit* to call, and determined to *make fit* for the service to which he called them: *even so,* blessed Jesus, *because it seemed good in thine eyes.* Christ calls *whom he will;* for he is a free Agent, and his grace is his own.

3. The efficacy of the call; He *called them* to separate themselves from the crowd, and stand by him, and they *came unto him.* Christ calls those who were *given him* (John xvii. 6); and *all that the Father gave him, shall come to him,* John vi. 37. Those whom it was his *will* to call, he made *willing to come;* his *people shall be willing in the day of his power.* Perhaps they came to him readily enough, because they were in expectation of *reigning with him* in temporal pomp and power; but when afterward they were *undeceived* in that matter, yet they had such a prospect given them of better things, that they would not say they were *deceived* in their Master, nor repented their leaving all to be with him.

4. The end and intention of this call; He *ordained them* (probably by the imposition of hands, which was a ceremony used among the Jews), *that they should be with him* constantly, to be witnesses of *his doctrine, manner of life, and patience,* that they might *fully know it,* and be able to give an account of it; and especially that they might attest the truth of his miracles; they must be *with him,* to receive instructions *from him,* that they might be qualified to give instructions *to others.* It would *require time* to fit them for that which he designed them for; for they must be *sent forth to preach;* not to preach till they were *sent,* and not to be *sent* till by a long and intimate acquaintance with Christ they were fitted. Note, Christ's ministers must be much *with him.*

5. The power he gave them to work miracles; and hereby he put a very great honour upon them, beyond that of the great men of the earth. He ordained them to *heal sicknesses and to cast out devils.* This showed that the power which Christ had to work these miracles was an *original* power; that he had it not *as a Servant,* but *as a Son in his own house,* in that he could confer it upon others, and invest them with it: they have a rule in the law, *Deputatus non potest deputare—He that is only deputed himself, cannot depute another;* but our Lord Jesus had *life in himself,* and the Spirit without measure; for he could give this power even to the *weak* and *foolish things* of the world.

6. Their number and names; He *ordained twelve,* according to the number of the twelve tribes of Israel. They are here named not just in the same order as they were in Matthew, nor by couples, as they were there; but as there, so here, Peter is put first and Judas last. Here Matthew is put before Thomas, probably being called in that order; but in that catalogue which Matthew himself drew up, he puts himself after Thomas; so far was he from insisting upon the precedency of his consecration. But that which Mark only takes notice of in this list of the apostles, is, that Christ called James and John *Boanerges,* which is, *The sons of thunder;* perhaps they were remarkable for a loud commanding voice, they were thundering preachers; or, rather, it denotes the zeal and fervency of their spirits, which would make them active

for God above their brethren. These two (saith Dr. Hammond) were to be special eminent ministers of the gospel, which is called *a voice shaking the earth*, Heb. xii. 26. Yet John, one of those *sons of thunder*, was full of love and tenderness, as appears by his epistles, and was the beloved disciple.

7. Their retirement with their Master, and close adherence to him; *They went into a house.* Now that this jury was impanelled, they *stood together, to hearken to their evidence.* They went together into the house, to settle the orders of their infant college; and now, it is likely, the bag was given to Judas, which pleased him, and made him easy.

II. The continual crowds that attended Christ's motions (*v.* 20); The *multitude cometh together again*, unsent for, and unseasonably pressing upon him, some with one errand and some with another; so that he and his disciples could not get time *so much as to eat bread*, much less for a set and full meal. Yet he did not shut his doors against the petitioners, but bade them welcome, and gave to each of them *an answer of peace.* Note, They whose hearts are enlarged in the work of God, can easily bear with great inconveniences to themselves, in the prosecution of it, and will rather lose a meal's meat at any time than slip an opportunity of doing good. It is happy when zealous *hearers* and zealous *preachers* thus *meet*, and encourage one another. Now the *kingdom of God was preached*, and men pressed into it, Luke xvi. 16. This was a gale of opportunity worth improving; and the disciples might well afford to adjourn their meals, to lay hold on it. It is good striking while the iron is hot.

III. The care of his relations concerning him (*v.* 21); *When his friends* in Capernaum heard how he was followed, and what pains he took, they *went out, to lay hold on him*, and fetch him home, for they said, *He is beside himself.* 1. Some understand it of an absurd preposterous care, which had more in it of reproach to him than of respect; and so we must take it as we read it, *He is beside himself;* either they suspected it themselves, or it was suggested to them, and they gave credit to the suggestion, that he was *gone distracted*, and therefore his friends ought to bind him, and put him in a dark room, to bring him to his right mind again. His kindred, many of them, had mean thoughts of him (John vii. 5), and were willing to hearken to this ill construction which some put upon his great zeal, and to conclude him crazed in his intellects, and under that pretence to take him off from his work. The prophets were called *mad fellows*, 2 Kings ix. 11. 2. Others understand it of a *well-meaning* care; and then they read ἐξέστη—"*He fainteth*, he has no time to *eat bread*, and therefore his strength will fail him; he will be stifled with the crowd of people, and will have his spirits quite exhausted with constant speaking, and the virtue that *goes out of him* in his miracles; and therefore let us use a friendly violence with him, and get him a little *breathing-time.*" In his preaching-work, as well as his suffering-work, he was attacked with, *Master, spare thyself.* Note, They who go on with vigour and zeal in the work of God, must expect to meet with hindrances, both from the groundless disaffection of their enemies, and the mistaken affections of their friends, and they have need to stand upon their guard against both.

22 And the scribes which came
down from Jerusalem said, He hath
Beelzebub, and by the prince of the
devils casteth he out devils. 23 And
he called them *unto him*, and said
unto them in parables, How can Satan
cast out Satan? 24 And if a kingdom
be divided against itself, that kingdom
cannot stand. 25 And if a house be
divided against itself, that house cannot stand.
26 And if Satan rise up
against himself, and be divided, he
cannot stand, but hath an end. 27
No man can enter into a strong man's
house, and spoil his goods, except he
will first bind the strong man; and
then he will spoil his house. 28 Verily
I say unto you, All sins shall be forgiven
unto the sons of men, and blasphemies
wherewith soever they shall
blaspheme: 29 But he that shall
blaspheme against the Holy Ghost
hath never forgiveness, but is in danger
of eternal damnation: 30 Because
they said, He hath an unclean spirit.

I. Here is, The impudent impious brand which the scribes fastened upon Christ's casting out devils, that they might evade and invalidate the conviction of it, and have a poor excuse for not yielding to it. These *scribes came down from Jerusalem*, *v.* 22. It should seem they came this long journey on purpose to hinder the progress of the doctrine of Christ; such pains did they take to do mischief; and, coming from Jerusalem, where were the most polite and learned scribes, and where they had opportunity of *consulting* together *against the Lord and his Anointed*, they were in the greater capacity to do mischief; the reputation of scribes from Jerusalem would have an influence not only upon the *country people*, but upon the *country scribes;* they had never thought of this base suggestion concerning Christ's miracles till the *scribes from* Jerusalem put it into their heads. They could not deny but that he cast out devils, which plainly bespoke him sent of God; but they insinuated that *he had Beelzebub* on his side, was in league with him, and by *the prince of the devils cast out devils.* There is a trick in the case; Satan is not *cast out,* he only *goes out* by consent. There was nothing in the manner of Christ's *casting out devils,* that gave any cause to suspect this; he did it *as one having authority;* but so they will have it, who resolve not to believe him.

II. The rational answer which Christ gave to this objection, demonstrating the absurdity of it.

1. Satan is so *subtle,* that he will never voluntarily quit his possession; *If Satan cast out Satan, his kingdom is divided against itself,* and it *cannot stand, v.* 23—26. He *called them to him,* as one desirous they should be convinced; he treated them with all the freedom, friendliness, and familiarity that could be; he vouchsafed to reason the case with them, *that every mouth may be stopped.* It was plain that the doctrine of Christ *made war* upon the devil's kingdom, and had a direct tendency to break his power, and crush his interest in the souls of men; and it was as plain that the casting of him out of the bodies of people confirmed that doctrine, and gave it the setting on; and therefore it cannot be imagined that he should come into such a design; every one knows that Satan is no *fool,* nor will act so directly against his own interest.

2. Christ is so *wise,* that, being engaged in war with him, he will attack his forces wherever he meets them, whether in the bodies or souls of people, *v.* 27. It is plain, Christ's design is to *enter into the strong man's house,* to take possession of the interest he has in the world, and to *spoil his goods,* and convert them to his own service; and therefore it is natural to suppose that he will thus *bind the strong man,* will forbid him to *speak* when he would, and to *stay* where he would, and thus show that he has gained a victory over him.

III. The awful warning Christ gave them to take heed how they spoke such dangerous words as these; however they might make light of them, as only conjectures, and the language of *free-thinking,* if they persisted in it, it would be of fatal consequence to them; it would be found a sin against the last remedy, and consequently *unpardonable;* for what could be imagined possible to bring *them* to repentance for their sin in blaspheming Christ, who would set aside such a *strong* conviction with such a *weak* evasion? It is true, the gospel *promiseth,* because Christ hath *purchased,* forgiveness for the greatest sins and sinners, *v.* 28. Many of those who reviled Christ on the cross (which was a *blaspheming of the Son of man,* aggravated to the highest degree), found mercy, and Christ himself prayed, *Father, forgive them;* but this was *blaspheming the Holy Ghost,* for it was by the Holy Spirit that he *cast out* devils, and they said, It was *by the unclean spirit, v.* 30. By this method they would outface the conviction of all the gifts of the Holy Ghost after Christ's ascension, and defeat them all, after which there remained no more proof, and therefore they should *never have forgiveness,* but were *liable to eternal damnation.* They were in imminent danger of that everlasting punishment, from which there was *no redemption,* and in which there was no *intermission,* no *remission.*

31 There came then his brethren
and his mother, and, standing without,
sent unto him, calling him. 32 And
the multitude sat about him, and
they said unto him, Behold, thy mother and thy brethren without seek
for thee. 33 And he answered them,
saying, Who is my mother, or my
brethren? 34 And he looked round
about on them which sat about him,
and said, Behold my mother and my
brethren! 35 For whosoever shall do
the will of God, the same is my brother, and my sister, and mother.

Here is, 1. The *disrespect* which Christ's *kindred, according to the flesh,* showed to him, when he was preaching (and they knew very well that he was then in his element); they not only *stood without,* having no desire to come in, and hear him, but they sent in a message to *call him out to them* (*v.* 31, 32), as if he must leave his work, to hearken to their *impertinences;* it is probable that they had *no business with him,* only sent for him on purpose to oblige him to *break off,* lest he should *kill himself.* He knew how far his strength would go, and preferred the salvation of souls before his own life, and soon after made it to appear with a witness; it was therefore an *idle thing* for them, under pretence of his sparing himself, to interrupt him; and it was worse, if really they had business with him, when they knew he preferred his business, as a Saviour, so much before any other business.

2. The *respect* which Christ showed to his spiritual kindred upon this occasion. Now, as at other times, he put a *comparative neglect* upon his mother, which seemed purposely designed to obviate and prevent the extravagant respect which men in aftertimes would be apt to pay her. *Our* respect ought to be guided and governed by Christ's; now the virgin Mary, or Christ's mother, is not equalled with, but postponed to, ordinary believers, on whom Christ here puts a *superlative* honour. He looked upon those that *sat about* him, and pronounced those of them that not only heard, but did, the will of God, to be to him as *his brother, and sister, and mother;* as much esteemed, loved, and cared for, as his nearest relations, *v.* 33—35. This is a good reason why we should *honour those that fear the Lord,* and choose them for our people; why we should be not hearers of the word only, but doers of the work, that we may share with the saints in this honour,

Surely it is good to be akin to those who are thus nearly allied to Christ, and to have fellowship with those that have fellowship with Christ; and woe to those that hate and persecute Christ's kindred, that are *his bone and his flesh,* every one *resembling the children of a king* (see Judg. viii. 18, 19); for he will with jealousy plead their cause, and avenge their blood.

CHAP. IV.

In this chapter, we have, I. The parable of the seed, and the four sorts of ground (ver 1—9), with the exposition of it (ver. 10—20), and the application of it, ver. 21—25. II. The parable of the seed growing gradually, but insensibly, ver. 26—29. III. The parable of the grain of mustard-seed, and a general account of Christ's parables, ver. 30—34. IV. The miracle of Christ's sudden stilling a storm at sea, ver. 35—41.

AND he began again to teach by the
sea side: and there was gathered
unto him a great multitude, so that
he entered into a ship, and sat in the
sea; and the whole multitude was by
the sea on the land. 2 And he taught
them many things by parables, and
said unto them in his doctrine, 3
Hearken; Behold, there went out a
sower to sow: 4 And it came to pass,
as he sowed, some fell by the way
side, and the fowls of the air came and
devoured it up. 5 And some fell on
stony ground, where it had not much
earth; and immediately it sprang up,
because it had no depth of earth: 6
But when the sun was up, it was
scorched; and because it had no root,
it withered away. 7 And some fell
among thorns, and the thorns grew up,
and choked it, and it yielded no fruit.
8 And other fell on good ground, and
did yield fruit that sprang up and increased;
and brought forth, some
thirty, and some sixty, and some a
hundred. 9 And he said unto them,
He that hath ears to hear, let him
hear. 10 And when he was alone,
they that were about him with the
twelve asked of him the parable. 11
And he said unto them, Unto you it
is given to know the mystery of the
kingdom of God: but unto them that
are without, all *these* things are done
in parables: 12 That seeing they may
see, and not perceive; and hearing
they may hear, and not understand;
lest at any time they should be converted,
and *their* sins should be forgiven
them. 13 And he said unto
them, Know ye not this parable? and
how then will ye know all parables?
14 The sower soweth the word. 15
And these are they by the way side,
where the word is sown; but when
they have heard, Satan cometh immediately,
and taketh away the word
that was sown in their hearts. 16
And these are they likewise which are
sown on stony ground; who, when
they have heard the word, immediately
receive it with gladness; 17
And have no root in themselves, and
so endure but for a time: afterwards,
when affliction or persecution ariseth
for the word's sake, immediately they
are offended. 18 And these are they
which are sown among thorns; such
as hear the word, 19 And the cares
of this world, and the deceitfulness of
riches, and the lusts of other things
entering in, choke the word, and it
becometh unfruitful. 20 And these
are they which are sown on good
ground; such as hear the word, and
receive *it,* and bring forth fruit, some
thirtyfold, some sixty, and some a
hundred.

The foregoing chapter began with Christ's *entering into the synagogue* (*v.* 1); this chapter begins with Christ's *teaching again by the sea side.* Thus he changed his method, that if possible all might be reached and wrought upon. To gratify the nice and more genteel sort of people that had seats, *chief seats, in the synagogue,* and did not care for hearing a sermon any where else, he did not preach always by the *sea side,* but, having liberty, went often *into the synagogue,* and taught there; yet, to gratify the poor, the mob, that could not get room in the synagogue, he did not always preach there, but *began again to teach by the sea side,* where they could come *within hearing.* Thus are we *debtors both to the wise and to the unwise,* Rom. i. 14.

Here seems to be a new convenience found out, which had not been used before, though he had before preached by the sea side (*ch.* ii. 13), and that was—his standing *in a ship,* while his hearers *stood upon the land;* and that inland sea of Tiberias having no tide, there was no ebbing and flowing of the waters to disturb them. Methinks Christ's carrying his doctrine into a ship, and preaching it thence, was a presage of his sending the gospel to the *isles of the Gentiles,* and the shipping off of the kingdom of God (that rich cargo) from the Jewish nation, to be sent to a people that would bring forth more of the fruits of it. Now observe here,

I. The *way of teaching* that Christ used with the *multitude* (*v.* 2); He *taught them many things,* but it was *by parables* or similitudes, which would *tempt them to hear;* for people love to be spoken to in their own language, and careless hearers will catch at a plain comparison borrowed from common things, and will retain and repeat that, when they have *lost,* or perhaps never *took,* the truth which it was designed to explain and illustrate: but unless they would take pains to search into it, it would but amuse them; *seeing they would see, and not perceive* (*v.* 12); and so, while it gratified their curiosity, it was the punishment of their stupidity; they wilfully shut their eyes against the light, and therefore justly did Christ put it into the dark lantern of a parable, which had a bright side toward those who applied it to themselves, and were willing to be guided by it; but to those who were only *willing for a season to play with it,* it only gave a flash of light now and then, but sent them away in the dark. It is just with God to say of those that *will not see,* that they *shall not see,* and to hide from their eyes, who only look about them with a great deal of carelessness, and never look before them with any concern upon the things that belong to their peace.

II. The way of *expounding* that he used with his *disciples; When he was alone* by himself, not only the *twelve,* but others that were *about him with the twelve,* took the opportunity to *ask him* the meaning of the parables, *v.* 10. They found it good to be *about Christ;* the nearer him the better; good to be *with the twelve,* to be conversant with those that are intimate with him. And he told them what a distinguishing favour it was to them, that they were made acquainted with the *mystery of the kingdom of God, v.* 11. *The secret of the Lord was with them.* That *instructed* them, which others were only *amused* with, and they were made to increase in knowledge by every parable, and understood more of the way and method in which Christ designed to set up his kingdom in the world, while others were dismissed, never the wiser. Note, Those who know the *mystery* of the *kingdom of heaven,* must acknowledge that it is *given to them;* they receive both the light and the sight from Jesus Christ, who, after his resurrection, both *opened the scriptures,* and *opened the understanding,* Luke xxiv. 27,45.

In particular, we have here,

1. The parable of the sower, as we had it, Matt. xiii. 3, &c. He begins (*v.* 3), with, *Hearken,* and concludes (*v.* 9) with, *He that hath ears to hear, let him hear.* Note, The words of Christ demand attention, and those who speak from him, may command it, and should stir it up; even that which as yet we do not *thoroughly* understand, or not *rightly,* we must carefully attend to, believing it to be both intelligible and weighty, that at length we may understand it; we shall find more in Christ's sayings than at first there seemed to be.

2. The exposition of it to the disciples. Here is a question Christ put to them before he expounded it, which we had not in Matthew (*v.* 13); "*Know ye not this parable?* Know ye not the meaning of it? *How then will ye know all parables?*" (1.) "If ye know not this, which is so plain, how will ye understand other parables, which will be more dark and obscure? If ye are gravelled and run aground with this, which bespeaks so plainly the different success of the word preached upon those that hear it, which ye yourselves may see easily, how will ye understand the parables which hereafter will speak of the rejection of the Jews, and the calling of the Gentiles, which is a thing ye have no idea of?" Note, This should quicken us both to prayer and pains that we may get knowledge, that there are a great many things which we are concerned to know; and if we understand not the plain truths of the gospel, how shall we master those that are more difficult? *Vita brevis, ars longa—Life is short, art is long. If we have run with the footmen, and they have wearied us,* and run us down, then *how shall we contend with horses?* Jer. xii. 5. (2.) "If ye know not this, which is intended for your direction in hearing the word, that ye may profit by it; how shall ye profit by what ye are further to hear? This parable is to teach you to be attentive to the word, and affected with it, that you may *understand* it. If ye receive not this, ye will not know how to use the key by which ye must be let into all the rest." If we understand not the rules we are to observe in order to our profiting by the word, how shall we profit by any other rule? Observe, Before Christ expounds the parable, [1.] He shows them how sad *their* case was, who were not let into the meaning of the doctrine of Christ; *To you it is given, but not to them.* Note, It will help us to put a value upon the privileges we enjoy as disciples of Christ, to consider the deplorable state of those who want such privileges, especially that they are out of the ordinary way of conversion; *lest they should be converted, and their sins should be forgiven them, v.* 12. Those only who are *converted,* have *their sins forgiven them:* and it is the misery of *unconverted* souls, that they lie under *unpardoned* guilt. [2.] He shows them what a shame it was, that they needed such particular explanations of the word they heard, and did not apprehend it at first. Those that would improve in knowledge, must be made sensible of their ignorance.

Having thus prepared them for it, he gives them the interpretation of the parable of the sower, as we had it before in Matthew. Let us only observe here,

First, That in the great field of the church, the word of God is dispensed to all promiscuously; *The sower soweth the word* (*v.* 14), sows it at a venture, *beside all waters,* upon all sorts of ground (Isa. xxxii. 20), not knowing where it will light, or what fruit it will bring forth. He *scatters* it, in order to the *increase* of it. Christ was awhile *sowing* himself, when he went about teaching and preaching; now he sends his ministers, and sows by their hand. Ministers are sowers; they have need of the skill and discretion of the husbandman (Isa. xxviii. 24—26); they must not observe winds and clouds (Eccl. xi. 4, 6), and must look up to God, who *gives seed to the sower*, 2 Cor. ix. 10.

Secondly, That of the many that hear the word of the gospel, and read it, and are conversant with it, there are, comparatively, but few that receive it, so as to bring forth the fruits of it; here is but one in four, that comes to good. It is sad to think, how much of the precious seed of the word of God is lost, and *sown in vain;* but there is a day coming when *lost sermons* must be accounted for. Many that have heard Christ himself *preach in their streets*, will hereafter be bidden to depart from him; those therefore who place all their religion in hearing, as if that alone would save them, do but deceive themselves, and build their hope upon the sand, Jam. i. 22.

Thirdly, Many are much affected with the word for the present, who yet receive no abiding benefit by it. The motions of soul they have, answerable to what they hear, are but a mere flash, like the crackling of thorns under a pot. We read of hypocrites, that they *delight to know God's ways* (Isa. lviii. 2); of Herod, that he heard John gladly (*ch.* vi. 20); of others, that they *rejoiced in his light* (John v. 35); of those to whom Ezekiel was a *lovely song* (Ezek. xxxiii. 32); and those represented here by the stony ground, received the word *with gladness*, and yet came to nothing.

Fourthly, The reason why the word doth not leave commanding, abiding, impressions upon the minds of the people, is, because their hearts are not duly disposed and prepared to receive it; the fault is in themselves, not in the word; some are careless forgetful hearers, and these get *no good at all* by the word; it comes in at one ear, and goes out at the other; others have their convictions overpowered by their corruptions, and they lose the good impressions the word has made upon them, so that they get no *abiding* good by it.

Fifthly, The devil is very busy about loose, careless hearers, as the fowls of the air go about the seed that lies above ground; when the heart, like the *highway*, is unploughed, unhumbled, when it *lies common*, to be trodden on by every passenger, as theirs that are great company-keepers, then the devil is *like the fowls;* he comes swiftly, and carries away the word ere we are aware. When therefore these fowls come down upon the sacrifices, we should take care, as *Abram* did, to *drive them away* (Gen. xv. 11); that, though we cannot keep them from hovering over our heads, we may not let them nestle in our hearts.

Sixthly, Many that are not openly *scandalized*, so as to throw off their profession, as they on the stony ground did, yet have the efficacy of it secretly *choked* and stifled, so that it comes to nothing; they continue in a barren, hypocritical profession, which brings nothing to pass, and so go down as certainly, though more plausibly, to hell.

Seventhly, Impressions that are not *deep*, will not be *durable*, but will wear off in suffering, trying times; like footsteps on the sand of the sea, which are gone the next high tide of persecution; when *that* iniquity doth abound, the love of many to the ways of God waxeth cold; many that keep their profession in fair days, lose it in a storm; and do as those that go to sea only for pleasure, come back again when the wind arises. It is the ruin of hypocrites, that they *have no root;* they do not act from a living fixed principle; they do not mind *heart-work*, and without that religion is nothing; for he is the Christian, that is *one inwardly*.

Eighthly, Many are hindered from profiting by the word of God, by their abundance of the world. Many a good lesson of humility, charity, self-denial, and heavenly-mindedness, is choked and lost by that prevailing complacency in the world, which *they* are apt to have, on whom it smiles. Thus many professors, that otherwise might have come to something, prove like Pharaoh's *lean kine* and *thin ears*.

Ninthly, Those that are not encumbered with the cares of the world, and the deceitfulness of riches, may yet lose the benefit of their profession by the *lusts of other things;* this is added here in Mark; *by the desires which are about other things* (so Dr. Hammond), an inordinate appetite toward those things that are pleasing to sense or to the fancy. Those that have but little of the world, may yet be ruined by an indulgence of the body.

Tenthly, Fruit is the thing that God expects and requires from those that enjoy the gospel: fruit according to the *seed;* a temper of mind, and a course of life, agreeable to the gospel; Christian graces daily exercised, Christian duties duly performed. This is *fruit*, and it will abound to our account.

Lastly, No good fruit is to be expected but from good seed. If the seed be sown on *good ground*, if the heart be humble, and holy, and heavenly, there will be *good fruit*, and it will *abound* sometimes even to a *hundred fold*, such a crop as Isaac reaped, Gen. xxvi. 12.

21 And he said unto them, Is a
candle brought to be put under a
bushel, or under a bed? and not to be
set on a candlestick? 22 For there
is nothing hid, which shall not be
manifested; neither was any thing
kept secret, but that it should come
abroad. 23 If any man have ears to

hear, let him hear. 24 And he said
unto them, Take heed what ye hear:
with what measure ye mete, it shall
be measured to you: and unto you
that hear shall more be given. 25
For he that hath, to him shall be
given: and he that hath not, from
him shall be taken even that which
he hath. 26 And he said, So is the
kingdom of God, as if a man should
cast seed into the ground; 27 And
should sleep, and rise night and day,
and the seed should spring and grow
up, he knoweth not how. 28 For
the earth bringeth forth fruit of herself; first the blade, then the ear,
after that the full corn in the ear. 29
But when the fruit is brought forth,
immediately he putteth in the sickle,
because the harvest is come. 30 And
he said, Whereunto shall we liken the
kingdom of God? or with what comparison shall we compare it? 31 *It
is* like a grain of mustard seed, which,
when it is sown in the earth, is less
than all the seeds that be in the earth:
32 But when it is sown, it groweth
up, and becometh greater than all
herbs, and shooteth out great branches;
so that the fowls of the air may lodge
under the shadow of it. 33 And with
many such parables spake he the word
unto them, as they were able to hear
it. 34 But without a parable spake
he not unto them: and when they
were alone, he expounded all things
to his disciples.

The lessons which our Saviour designs to teach us here by parables and figurative expressions are these:—

I. That those who *are good* ought to consider the obligations they are under to *do good;* that is, as in the parable before, to *bring forth fruit.* God expects a grateful return of his gifts to us, and a useful improvement of his gifts in us; for (*v.* 21), *Is a candle brought to be put under a bushel, or under a bed?* No, but that it may be *set on a candlestick.* The apostles were ordained, to receive the gospel, not for themselves only, but for the good of others, to communicate it to them. All Christians, as they have *received the gift,* must *minister the same.* Note, 1. Gifts and graces make a man *as a candle;* the *candle of the Lord* (Prov. xx. 27), lighted by the Father of lights; the most eminent are but candles, poor lights, compared with the *Sun of righteousness.* A candle gives light but a *little way,* and but a *little while,* and is easily blown out, and continually burning down and wasting. 2. Many who are *lighted* as candles, put themselves *under a bed, or under a bushel:* they do not *manifest* grace themselves, nor *minister* grace to others; they have estates, and do no good with them; have their limbs and senses, wit and learning perhaps, but nobody is the better for them; they have spiritual gifts, but do not use them; like a taper in an urn, they burn to themselves. 3. Those who are lighted as candles, should set themselves *on a candlestick;* that is, should improve all opportunities of doing good, as those that were made for the glory of God, and the service of the communities they are members of; we are not born for ourselves.

The reason given for this, is, because *there is nothing hid, which shall not be manifested,* which *should not* be made manifest (so it might better be read), *v.* 22. There is no treasure of gifts and graces lodged in any but with design to be communicated; nor was the gospel made a *secret* to the apostles, to be concealed, but that it should *come abroad,* and be divulged to all the world. Though Christ expounded the parables to his disciples privately, yet it was with design to make them the more publicly useful; they were *taught,* that they might teach; and it is a general rule, that *the ministration of the Spirit is given to every man to profit withal,* not himself only, but others also.

II. It concerns those who hear the word of the gospel, to *mark* what they hear, and to *make a good use* of it, because their *weal* or *woe* depends upon it; what he had said before he saith again, *If any man have ears to hear, let him hear, v.* 23. Let him give the gospel of Christ a fair hearing; but that is not enough, it is added (*v.* 24), *Take heed what ye hear,* and give a due regard to that which ye do hear; *Consider what ye* hear, so Dr. Hammond reads it. Note, What we hear, doth us no good, unless we consider it; those especially that are to teach others must themselves be very observant of the things of God; must take notice of the message they are to deliver, that they may be exact. We must likewise *take heed what we hear,* by *proving* all things, that we may *hold fast that which is good.* We must be *cautious,* and stand upon our guard, lest we be imposed upon. To enforce this caution, consider,

1. As we deal with God, God will deal with us, so Dr. Hammond explains these words, "*With what measure ye mete, it shall be measured to you.* If ye be faithful servants to him, he will be a faithful Master to you: *with the upright he will show himself upright.*"

2. As we improve the talents we are entrusted with, we shall increase them; if we make use of the knowledge we have, for the glory of God and the benefit of others, it shall sensibly grow, as stock in trade doth by being turned; *Unto you that hear, shall more be given; to you that have, it shall be given, v.*

25. If the disciples *deliver* that to the church, which they have *received of the Lord,* they shall be *led* more into the *secret of the Lord.* Gifts and graces multiply by being exercised; and God has promised to bless the *hand of the diligent.*

3. If we do not *use,* we *lose,* what we have; *From him that hath not,* that doeth no good with what he hath, and so hath it in vain, is as if he had it not, *shall be taken even that which he hath.* Burying a talent is the betraying of a trust, and amounts to a forfeiture; and gifts and graces *rust* for want of *wearing.*

III. The good seed of the gospel sown in the world, and sown in the heart, doth by degrees produce wonderful effects, but without noise (*v.* 26, &c.); *So is the kingdom of God;* so is the gospel, when it is sown, and received, as seed in good ground.

1. It will *come up;* though it seem lost and buried under the clods, it will find or make its way through them. The seed *cast into the ground will spring.* Let but the word of Christ have the place it ought to have in a soul, and it will show itself, as the *wisdom from above* doth in a *good conversation.* After a field is sown with corn, how soon is the surface of it altered! How gay and pleasant doth it look, when it is covered with green!

2. The husbandman cannot describe how it comes up; it is one of the mysteries of nature; It *springs and grows up, he knows not how, v.* 27. He sees it has grown, but he cannot tell in what manner it grew, or what was the cause and method of its growth. Thus we know not how the Spirit by the word makes a change in the heart, any more than we can account for the blowing of the wind, which we hear the sound of, but cannot tell whence it comes, or whither it goes. Without controversy, great is the mystery of godliness; how *God manifested in the flesh* came to be *believed on in the world,* 1 Tim. iii. 16.

3. The husbandman, when he hath sown the seed, doth nothing toward the springing of it up; *He sleeps, and rises, night and day;* goes to sleep *at night,* gets up *in the morning,* and perhaps never so much as thinks of the corn he hath sown, or ever looks upon it, but follows his pleasures or other business, and yet *the earth brings forth fruit of itself,* according to the ordinary course of nature, and by the concurring power of the God of nature. Thus the *word of grace,* when it is received in faith, is in the heart a *work of grace,* and the preachers contribute nothing to it. The Spirit of God is carrying it on when *they sleep,* and can do no business (Job xxxiii. 15, 16), or when they rise to go about other business. The prophets do not *live for ever;* but the word which they preached, is doing its work, when they are in their graves, Zech. i. 5, 6. The dew by which the seed is brought up *tarrieth not for man, nor waiteth for the sons of men,* Mic. v. 7.

4. It grows gradually; *first the blade, then the ear, after that the full corn in the ear, v.* 28. When it is sprung up, it will go forward; nature will have its course, and so will grace. Christ's interest, both in the world and in the heart, is, and will be, a *growing* interest; and though *the beginning be small, the latter end will greatly increase.* Though thou sowest not that body that shall be, but *bare grain,* yet God *will give to every seed its own body;* though at first it is but a tender *blade,* which the frost may nip, or the foot may crush, yet it will increase to *the ear,* to the *full corn in the ear. Natura nil facit per saltum—Nature does nothing abruptly.* God carries on his work insensibly and without noise, but insuperably and without fail.

5. It comes to perfection at last (*v.* 29); *When the fruit is brought forth,* that is, when it is *ripe,* and ready to be *delivered* into the owner's hand; then he *puts in the sickle.* This intimates, (1.) That Christ *now accepts* the services which are done to him by an honest heart from a good principle; from the fruit of the gospel taking place and working in the soul, Christ *gathers in* a harvest of honour to himself. See John iv. 35. (2.) That he will reward them in eternal life. When those that receive the gospel aright, have finished their course, the harvest comes, when they shall be gathered as *wheat into God's barn* (Matt. xiii. 30), as a shock of corn *in his season.*

IV. The work of grace is small in its beginnings, but comes to be great and considerable at last (*v.* 30—32); "*Whereunto shall I liken the kingdom of God,* as now to be set up by the Messiah? How shall I make you to understand the designed method of it?" Christ speaks as one considering and consulting with himself, how to illustrate it with an apt similitude; *With what comparison shall we compare it?* Shall we fetch it from the motions of the sun, or the revolutions of the moon? No, the comparison is borrowed from this earth, it is *like a grain of mustard-seed;* he had compared it before to *seed sown,* here to *that seed,* intending thereby to show,

1. That the beginnings of the *gospel kingdom* would be very small, like that which is *one of the least of all seeds.* When a Christian church was *sown in the earth* for God, it was all contained in one room, and the *number of the names* was but one hundred and twenty (Acts i. 15), as the children of Israel, when they went down into Egypt, were but seventy souls. The work of grace in the soul, is, at first, but the *day of small things;* a *cloud* no *bigger than a man's hand.* Never were there such great things undertaken by such an inconsiderable handful, as that of the discipling of the nations by the ministry of the apostles; nor a work that was to end in such great glory, as the work of grace raised from such weak and unlikely beginnings. *Who hath begotten me these?*

2. That the perfection of it will be very great; *When it grows up, it becomes greater than all herbs.* The gospel kingdom in the

world, shall increase and spread to the remotest nations of the earth, and shall continue to the latest ages of time. The *church* hath *shot out great branches,* strong ones, spreading far, and fruitful. The *work of grace* in the soul has mighty products, now while it is in its growth; but what will it be, when it is perfected in heaven? The difference between a *grain of mustard seed* and a *great tree,* is nothing to that between a *young convert* on earth and a *glorified saint* in heaven. See John xii. 24.

After the parables thus specified the historian concludes with this general account of Christ's preaching—that *with many such parables he spoke the word unto them* (*v.* 33); probably designing to refer us to the larger account of the parables of this kind, which we had before, Matt. xiii. He spoke in parables, *as they were able to hear them;* he fetched his comparisons from those things that were familiar to them, and level to their capacity, and delivered them in plain expressions, in condescension to their capacity; though he did not let them into the *mystery* of the parables, yet his manner of expression was easy, and such as they might hereafter recollect to their edification. But, for the present, *without a parable spoke he not unto them, v.* 34. The glory of the Lord was covered with a cloud, and God speaks to us in the language of the *sons of men,* that, though not *at first,* yet *by degrees,* we may understand his meaning; the disciples themselves understood those sayings of Christ afterward, which at first they did not rightly take the sense of. But these parables *he expounded to them, when they were alone.* We cannot but wish we had had that exposition, as we had of the parable of the sower; but it was not so needful; because, when the church should be enlarged, that would *expound* these parables to us, without any more ado.

35 And the same day, when the
even was come, he saith unto them,
Let us pass over unto the other side.
36 And when they had sent away
the multitude, they took him even as
he was in the ship. And there were
also with him other little ships. 37
And there arose a great storm of wind,
and the waves beat into the ship, so
that it was now full. 38 And he was
in the hinder part of the ship, asleep
on a pillow: and they awake him,
and say unto him, Master, carest thou
not that we perish? 39 And he
arose, and rebuked the wind, and said
unto the sea, Peace, be still. And
the wind ceased, and there was a great
calm. 40 And he said unto them,
Why are ye so fearful? how is it that
ye have no faith? 41 And they
feared exceedingly, and said one to
another, What manner of man is this,
that even the wind and the sea obey
him?

This miracle which Christ wrought for the relief of his disciples, in stilling the storm, we had before (Matt. viii. 23, &c.); but it is here more fully related. Observe,

1. It was *the same day* that he had preached out of a ship, *when the even was come, v.* 35. When he had been *labouring in the word and doctrine* all day, instead of *re*posing himself, he *ex*poseth himself, to teach us not to think of a constant remaining rest till we come to heaven. The end of a toil may perhaps be but the beginning of a toss. But observe, the ship that Christ made his pulpit is taken under his special protection, and, though in danger, cannot sink. What is used for Christ, he will take particular care of.

2. He himself proposed putting to sea at night, because he would lose no time; *Let us pass over to the other side;* for we shall find, in the next chapter, he has work to do there. Christ went about doing good, and no difficulties in his way should hinder him; thus industrious we should be in serving him, and our generation according to his will.

3. They did not put to sea, till *they had sent away the multitude,* that is, had given to each of them that which they came for, and answered all their requests; for he sent none home complaining that they had attended him *in vain.* Or, They sent them away *with a solemn blessing;* for Christ came into the world, not only to pronounce, but to *command,* and to *give,* the blessing.

4. They took him *even as he was,* that is, in the same dress that he was in when he preached, without any cloak to throw over him, which he ought to have had, to keep him *warm,* when he went to sea at night, especially after preaching. We must not hence infer that we may be careless of our health, but we may learn hence not to be over nice and solicitous about the body.

5. The storm was so great, that the ship was *full of water* (*v.* 37), not by springing a leak, but perhaps partly with the shower, for the word here used signifies a *tempest of wind with rain;* however, the ship being little, the waves beat into it so that *it was full.* Note, It is no new thing for that ship to be greatly hurried and endangered, in which Christ and his disciples, Christ and his name and gospel, are embarked.

6. There were *with him other little ships,* which, no doubt, shared in the distress and danger. Probably, these *little ships* carried those who were desirous to go along with Christ, for the benefit of his preaching and miracles on the other side. The *multitude went away* when he put to sea, but some there were, that would venture upon the

water with him. Those follow the Lamb aright, that follow him *wherever he goes.* And those that hope for a happiness in Christ, must be willing to take their lot with him, and run the same risks that he runs. One may boldly and cheerfully put to sea in Christ's company, yea though we foresee a storm.

7. Christ was asleep in this storm; and here we are told that it was *in the hinder part of the ship,* the pilot's place: he lay at the helm, to intimate that, as Mr. George Herbert expresses it,

> When winds and waves assault my keel,
> He doth preserve it, he doth steer,
> Ev'n when the boat seems most to reel.
> Storms are the triumph of his art;
> Though he may close his eyes, yet not his heart.

He had a *pillow* there, such a one as a fisherman's ship would furnish him with. And he *slept,* to try the faith of his disciples and to stir up prayer: upon the trial, their faith appeared *weak,* and their prayers *strong.* Note, Sometimes when the church is in a storm, Christ seems as if he were asleep, unconcerned in the troubles of his people, and regardless of their prayers, and doth not presently appear for their relief. *Verily he is a God that hideth himself,* Isa. xlv. 15. But as, when he tarries, he doth not tarry (Hab. ii. 3), so when he sleeps he doth not sleep; the keeper of Israel doth not so much as slumber (Ps. cxxi. 3, 4); he slept, but his heart was awake, as the spouse, Cant. v. 2.

8. His disciples encouraged themselves with their having his presence, and thought it the best way to improve that, and appeal to that, and ply the oar of prayer rather than their other oars. Their confidence lay in this, that they had their Master with them; and the ship that has Christ in it, though it may be *tossed,* cannot *sink;* the bush that has God in it, though it may *burn,* shall not *consume.* Cæsar encouraged the master of the ship, that had him on board, with this, *Cæsarem vehis, et fortunam Cæsaris—Thou hast Cæsar on board, and Cæsar's fortune.* They *awoke Christ.* Had not the necessity of the case called for it, they would not have *stirred up* or *awoke* their Master, *till he had pleased* (Cant. ii. 7); but they knew he would *forgive them this wrong.* When Christ seems as if he slept in a storm, he is awaked by the prayers of his people; when we know not what to do, our eye must be to him (2 Chron. xx. 12); we may be at our wits' end, but not at our faith's end, while we have such a Saviour to go to. Their address to Christ is here expressed very emphatically; *Master, carest thou not that we perish?* I confess this sounds somewhat harsh, rather like chiding him for sleeping than begging him to awake. I know no excuse for it, but the great familiarity which he was pleased to admit them into, and the freedom he allowed them; and the present distress they were in, which put them into such a fright, that they knew not what they said. *They* do Christ a deal of wrong, who suspect him to be *careless* of his people in distress. The matter is not so; he is not willing that any should perish, much less any of his little ones, Matt. xviii. 14.

9. The word of command with which Christ rebuked the storm, we have here, and had not in Matthew, *v.* 39. He says, *Peace, be still—Σιώπα, πεφίμωσο—be silent, be dumb.* Let not the wind any longer roar, nor the sea rage. Thus he *stills the noise of the sea, the noise of her waves;* a particular emphasis is laid upon the noisiness of them, Ps. lxv. 7, and xciii. 3, 4. The noise is threatening and terrifying; let us hear no more of it. This is, (1.) A word of command to us; when our wicked hearts are *like the troubled sea which cannot rest* (Isa. lvii. 20); when our passions are up, and are unruly, let us think we hear the law of Christ, saying, *Be silent, be dumb.* Think not confusedly, speak not unadvisedly; but *be still.* (2.) A word of comfort to us, that, be the storm of trouble ever so loud, ever so strong, Jesus Christ can lay it with a word's speaking. When without are fightings, and within are fears, and the spirits are in a tumult, Christ can *create the fruit of the lips, peace.* If he say, *Peace, be still,* there is a *great calm* presently. It is spoken of as God's prerogative to command the seas, Jer. xxxi. 35. By this therefore Christ proves himself to be God. He that made the seas, can make them *quiet.*

10. The reproof Christ gave them for their fears, is here carried further than in Matthew. There it is, *Why are ye fearful?* Here, *Why are ye so fearful?* Though there may be cause for some fear, yet not for fear to such a degree as this. There it is, *O ye of little faith.* Here it is, *How is it that ye have no faith?* Not that the disciples were without faith. No, they believed that *Jesus is the Christ, the Son of God;* but at this time their fears prevailed so that they seemed to *have no faith* at all. It was out of the way, when they had occasion for it, and so it was as if they had not had it. "*How is it, that in this matter ye have no faith,* that ye think I would not come in with seasonable and effectual relief?" Those may suspect their faith, who can entertain such a thought as that Christ *careth not* though his *people perish,* and Christ justly takes it ill.

Lastly, The impression this miracle made upon the disciples, is here differently expressed. In Matthew it is said, *The men marvelled;* here it is said, *They feared greatly.* They *feared a great fear;* so the original reads it. Now their fear was rectified by their faith. When they feared the winds and the seas, it was for want of the reverence they ought to have had for Christ. But now that they saw a demonstration of his power over them, they feared *them* less, and *him* more. They *feared* lest they had offended Christ by their unbelieving fears; and therefore studied now to give him honour. They had *feared* the power and wrath of the Creator in the storm, and that fear had torment and amazement in it; but now they feared the power and grace of the Redeemer in the calm; they *feared the Lord and his goodness,* and it had pleasure and satisfaction in it, and by it they gave glory to Christ, as Jonah's mariners, who, when the *sea ceased from her raging, feared the Lord exceedingly, and offered a sacrifice unto the Lord,* Jon. i. 16. This sacrifice they offered to the honour of Christ; they said, *What manner of man is this?* Surely more than a man, *for even the winds and the seas obey him.*

CHAP. V.

In this chapter, we have, I. Christ's casting the legion of devils out of the man possessed, and suffering them to enter into the swine, ver. 1—20. II. Christ's healing the woman with the bloody issue, in the way as he was going to raise Jairus's daughter to life, ver. 21—43. These three miracles we had the story of before (Matt. viii. 28, &c. and Matt. ix. 18, &c.) but more fully related here.

AND they came over unto the
other side of the sea, into the
country of the Gadarenes. 2 And
when he was come out of the ship.
immediately there met him out of the
tombs a man with an unclean spirit,
3 Who had *his* dwelling among the
tombs; and no man could bind him,
no, not with chains: 4 Because that
he had been often bound with fetters
and chains, and the chains had been
plucked asunder by him, and the
fetters broken in pieces: neither could
any *man* tame him. 5 And always,
night and day, he was in the mountains,
and in the tombs, crying, and
cutting himself with stones. 6 But
when he saw Jesus afar off, he ran
and worshipped him, 7 And cried
with a loud voice, and said, What
have I to do with thee, Jesus, *thou*
Son of the most high God? I adjure
thee by God, that thou torment me
not. 8 For he said unto him, Come
out of the man, *thou* unclean spirit.
9 And he asked him, What *is* thy
name? And he answered, saying,
My name *is* Legion: for we are many.
10 And he besought him much that
he would not send them away out
of the country. 11 Now there was
there nigh unto the mountains a great
herd of swine feeding. 12 And all
the devils besought him, saying, Send
us into the swine, that we may enter
into them. 13 And forthwith Jesus
gave them leave. And the unclean
spirits went out, and entered into the
swine: and the herd ran violently
down a steep place into the sea (they
were about two thousand): and were
choked in the sea. 14 And they that
fed the swine fled, and told *it* in the
city, and in the country. And they
went out to see what it was that was
done. 15 And they come to Jesus,
and see him that was possessed with
the devil, and had the legion, sitting,
and clothed, and in his right mind:
and they were afraid. 16 And they
that saw *it* told them how it befel to
him that was possessed with the devil,
and *also* concerning the swine. 17
And they began to pray him to depart
out of their coasts. 18 And when he
was come into the ship, he that had
been possessed with the devil prayed
him that he might be with him. 19
Howbeit Jesus suffered him not, but
saith unto him, Go home to thy
friends, and tell them how great things
the Lord hath done for thee, and hath
had compassion on thee. 20 And he
departed, and began to publish in
Decapolis how great things Jesus had
done for him: and all *men* did marvel.

We have here an instance of Christ's dispossessing the strong man armed, and disposing of him as he pleased, to make it appear that he was *stronger than he.* This he did when he was come *to the other side,* whither he went through a storm; his business there was to rescue this poor creature out of the hands of Satan, and when he had done that, he returned. Thus he came from heaven to earth, and returned, in a storm, to redeem a remnant of mankind out of the hands of the devil, though but a *little remnant,* and did not think his pains *ill bestowed.*

In Matthew, they were said to be *two* possessed with devils; here it is said to be a *man* possessed with an unclean spirit. If there were *two,* there was one, and Mark doth not say that there was *but one;* so that this difference cannot give us any just offence; it is probable that one of them was much more remarkable than the other, and said what was said. Now observe here,

I. The miserable condition that this poor creature was in; he was under the power of an *unclean spirit,* the devil got possession of him, and the effect of it was not, as in many, a silent melancholy, but a raging frenzy; he was raving mad; his condition seems to have been worse than any of the possessed, that were Christ's patients.

1. He had *his dwelling among the tombs,* among the graves of dead people. Their tombs were out of the cities, in *desolate places* (Job iii. 14); which gave the devil great advantage: for *woe to him that is alone.* Perhaps

the devil drove him to *the tombs,* to make people fancy that the souls of the dead were turned into dæmons, and did what mischief was done, so to excuse themselves from it. The touch of a grave was polluting, Num. xix. 16. The *unclean spirit* drives people into that company that is *defiling,* and so keeps possession of them. Christ, by rescuing souls out of Satan's power, *saves the living from among the dead.*

2. He was very strong and ungovernable; *No man could bind him,* as it is requisite both for their own good, and for the safety of others, that those who are distracted should be. Not only cords would not hold him, but *chains* and *fetters of iron* would not, *v.* 3, 4. Very deplorable is the case of such as *need to be* thus *bound,* and of all miserable people in this world they are most to be pitied; but his case was worst of all, in whom the devil was so strong, that he could not be *bound.* This sets forth the sad condition of those souls in which the devil has dominion; those *children of disobedience,* in whom that unclean spirit works. Some notoriously wilful sinners are like this madman; all are herein *like the horse and the mule,* that they need to be *held in with bit and bridle;* but some are like the *wild ass,* that will not be so held. The commands and curses of the law are as *chains* and *fetters,* to restrain sinners from their wicked courses; but they *break those bands in sunder,* and it is an evidence of the power of the devil in them.

3. He was a terror and torment to himself and to all about him, *v.* 5. The devil is a *cruel* master to those that are *led captive* by him, a perfect tyrant; this wretched creature was *night and day in the mountains and in the tombs, crying, and cutting himself with stones,* either bemoaning his own deplorable case, or in a rage and indignation against heaven. Men in frenzies often wound and destroy themselves; what is a man, when reason is *de*throned and Satan *en*throned? The worshippers of Baal in their fury *cut themselves,* like this madman in his. The voice of God is, *Do thyself no harm;* the voice of Satan is, *Do thyself all the harm thou canst;* yet God's word is despised, and Satan's regarded. Perhaps his *cutting himself with stones* was only cutting his feet with the sharp stones he ran barefoot upon.

II. His application to Christ (*v.* 6); *When he saw Jesus afar off,* coming ashore, he *ran, and worshipped him.* He usually *ran upon* others with *rage,* but he *ran to* Christ with *reverence.* That was done by an invisible hand of Christ, which could not be done with chains and fetters; his fury was all on a sudden curbed. Even the devil, in this poor creature, was forced to tremble before Christ, and bow to him: or, rather, the poor man came, and *worshipped Christ,* in a sense of the need he had of his help, the power of Satan in and over him being, for this instant, suspended.

III. The word of command Christ gave to the unclean spirit, to quit his possession (*v.* 8); *Come out of him, thou unclean spirit.* He made the man desirous to be relieved, when he enabled him to *run, and worship him,* and then put forth his power for his relief. If Christ *work in us* heartily to pray for a deliverance from Satan, he will work for us that deliverance. Here is an instance of the power and authority with which Christ *commanded the unclean spirits, and they obeyed him, ch.* i. 27. He said, *Come out of the man.* The design of Christ's gospel is to *expel* unclean spirits out of the souls of people; "*Come out of the man, thou unclean spirit,* that the Holy Spirit may enter, may take possession of the heart, and have dominion in it."

IV. The dread which the devil had of Christ. The *man ran,* and *worshipped Christ;* but it was the devil in the man, that *cried with a loud voice* (making use of the poor man's tongue), *What have I to do with thee? v.* 7. Just as that other unclean spirit, *ch.* i. 24. 1. He calls God the *most high God,* above all other gods. By the name *Elion—the Most High,* God was *known* among the Phœnicians, and the other nations that bordered upon Israel; and by that name the devil calls him. 2. He owns Jesus to be the *Son of God.* Note, It is no strange thing to hear the best words drop from the worst mouths. There is such a way of saying this as none can attain to but *by the Holy Ghost* (1 Cor. xii. 3); yet it may be said, after a sort, by the *unclean spirit.* There is no judging of men by their loose sayings; but by their fruits ye shall know them. Piety from the teeth outward is an easy thing. The most fair-spoken hypocrite cannot say better than to call Jesus the Son of God, and yet that the devil did. 3. He disowns any design against Christ; "*What have I to do with thee?* I have no need of thee, I pretend to none; I desire to have nothing to do with thee; I *cannot stand* before thee, and *would not* fall." 4. He deprecates his wrath; I *adjure thee,* that is, "I earnestly beseech thee, by all that is sacred, I beg of thee for God's sake, by whose permission I have got possession of this man, that, though thou drive me out hence, yet that thou *torment me not,* that thou do not restrain me from doing mischief somewhere else; though I know I am *sentenced,* yet let me not be *sent* to the chains of darkness, or hindered from going to and fro, to *devour.*"

V. The account Christ took from this unclean spirit of his name. This we had not in Matthew. Christ asked him, *What is thy name?* Not but that Christ could call all the *fallen* stars, as well as the *morning* stars, by their names; but he demands this, that the standers by might be affected with the vast numbers and power of those malignant infernal spirits, as they had reason to be, when the answer was, *My name is Legion, for we are many;* a *legion* of soldiers among the

Romans consisted, some say, of six thousand men, others of twelve thousand and five hundred; but the number of a legion with them, like that of a regiment with us, was not always the same. Now this intimates that the devils, the infernal powers, are, 1. *Military* powers; a legion is a number of soldiers in arms. The devils war against God and his glory, Christ and his gospel, men and their holiness and happiness. They are such as we are to *resist* and *wrestle against*, Eph. vi. 12. 2. That they are *numerous;* he *owns,* or rather he *boasts—We are many;* as if he hoped to be *too many* for Christ himself to deal with. What multitudes of apostate spirits were there, and all enemies to God and man; when here were a legion posted to keep garrison in one poor wretched creature against Christ! Many there are that rise up against us. 3. That they are *unanimous;* they are *many* devils, and yet but *one legion* engaged in the same wicked cause; and therefore that cavil of the Pharisees, which supposed Satan to cast out Satan, and to be divided against himself, was altogether groundless. It was not *one* of this legion that betrayed the rest, for they all said, as one man, *What have I to do with thee?* 4. That they are very *powerful;* Who can stand before a *legion?* We are not a match for our spiritual enemies, in our own strength; but *in the Lord, and in the power of his might,* we shall be able to *stand against them,* though there are legions of them. 5. That there is *order* among them, as there is in a *legion;* there are *principalities, and powers, and rulers of the darkness of this world,* which supposes that there are those of a lower rank; the *devil* and his angels; the *dragon* and his; the prince of the devils and his subjects: which makes those enemies the more formidable.

VI. The request of this legion, that Christ would suffer them to go into a herd of swine that was *feeding nigh unto the mountains* (*v.* 11), those mountains which the demoniacs haunted, *v.* 5. Their request was, 1. That he *would not send them away out of the country* (*v.* 10); not only that he would not *commit* them, or *confine* them, to their infernal prison, and so *torment them before the time;* but that he would not *banish* them *that country,* as justly he might, because in this poor man they had been such a terror to it, and done so much mischief. They seem to have had a particular affection for *that country;* or, rather, a particular spite to it; and to have liberty to walk *to and fro through* the rest of *the earth,* will not serve (Job i. 7), unless the *range of those mountains* be allowed them for their pasture, Job xxxix. 8. But why would they abide in *that country?* Grotius saith, Because in *that country* there were many *apostate Jews,* who had thrown themselves out of the covenant of God, and had thereby given Satan power over them. And some suggest, that, having by experience got the knowledge of the dispositions and manners of the people of that country, they could the more effectually do them mischief by their temptations. 2. That he would suffer them to *enter into the swine,* by destroying which they hoped to do more mischief to the souls of all the people in the country, than they could by entering into the body of any particular person, which therefore they did not ask leave to do, for they knew Christ would not grant it.

VII. The permission Christ gave them to enter into the swine, and the immediate destruction of the swine thereby; *He gave them leave* (*v.* 13), he did not forbid or restrain them, he let them do as they had a mind. Thus he would let the Gadarenes see what powerful spiteful enemies devils are, that they might thereby be induced to make him their Friend, who alone was able to control and conquer them, and had made it appear that he was so. Immediately the *unclean spirits entered into the swine,* which by the law were unclean creatures, and naturally love to *wallow in the mire,* the fittest place for them. Those that, like the swine, delight in *the mire* of sensual lusts, are fit habitations for Satan, and are, like Babylon, the *hold of every foul spirit,* and a *cage of every unclean and hateful bird* (Rev. xviii. 2), as pure souls are habitations of the Holy Spirit. The consequence of the devils entering into the swine, was, that they all *ran mad* presently, and ran headlong into the adjoining sea, where they were all drowned, to the number of *two thousand.* The man they possessed did only *cut himself,* for God had said, *He is in your hands, only save his life.* But thereby it appeared, that, if he had not been so restrained, the poor man would have *drowned himself.* See how much we are indebted to the providence of God, and the ministration of good angels, for our preservation from malignant spirits.

VIII. The report of all this dispersed through the country immediately. They that *fed the swine,* hastened to the owners, to give an account of their charge, *v.* 14. This drew the people together, to see what was done: and, 1. When they saw how wonderfully the poor man was cured, they hence conceived a *veneration for Christ, v.* 15. They saw him that was *possessed with the devil,* and knew him well enough, by the same token that they had many a time been frightened at the sight of him; and were now as much surprised to see him *sitting clothed and in his right mind;* when Satan was cast out, he came to himself, and was his own man presently. Note, Those who are grave and sober, and live by rule and with consideration, thereby make it appear that by the power of Christ the devil's power is broken in their souls. The sight of this *made them afraid;* it astonished them, and forced them to own the power of Christ, and that he is *worthy to be feared.* But, 2. When they found that their swine were lost, they thence conceived a *dislike of Christ,* and wished to have rather his room than his company; they prayed him to *depart out of their coasts*, for they think not any good he can do them sufficient to make them amends for the loss of so many swine, fat swine, it may be, and ready for the market. Now the devils had what they would have; for by no handle do these evil spirits more effectually manage sinful souls than by that of the love of the world. They were afraid of some further punishment, if Christ should tarry among them, whereas, if they would but part with their sins, he had life and happiness for them; but, being loth to quit either their sins or their swine, they chose rather to abandon their Saviour. Thus *they* do, who, rather than let go a base lust, will throw away their interest in Christ, and their expectations from him. They should rather have argued, "If he has such a power as this over devils and all creatures, it is good having him our Friend; if the devils have leave to tarry *in our country* (*v.* 10), let us entreat *him* to tarry in it too, who alone can control them." But, instead of this, they wished him further off. Such strange misconstructions do carnal hearts make of the just judgments of God; instead of being by them driven to him as they ought, they set him at so much the greater distance; though he hath said, *Provoke me not, and I will do you no hurt*, Jer. xxv. 6.

IX. An account of the conduct of the poor man after his deliverance. 1. He *desired that he might go along with Christ* (*v.* 18), perhaps for fear lest the evil spirit should again seize him; or, rather, that he might receive instruction from him, being unwilling to stay among those heathenish people that desired him to depart. Those that are freed from the evil spirit, cannot but covet acquaintance and fellowship with Christ. 2. Christ *would not suffer him* to go with him, lest it should savour of ostentation, and to let him know that he could both protect and instruct him at a distance. And besides, he had other work for him to do; he must go home to his friends, and tell them what *great things the Lord had done for him*, the Lord Jesus had done; that Christ might be honoured, and his neighbours and friends might be edified, and invited to believe in Christ. He must take particular notice rather of Christ's *pity* than of his *power*, for that is it which especially he glories in; he must tell them what *compassion* the Lord had had on him in his misery. 3. The man, in a transport of joy, proclaimed, all the country over, what *great things Jesus had done for him*, *v.* 20. This is a debt we owe both to Christ and to our brethren, that he may be glorified and they edified. And see what was the effect of it; *All men did marvel*, but few went any further. Many that cannot but wonder at the works of Christ, yet do not, as they ought, *wonder after him*.

21 And when Jesus was passed over
again by ship unto the other side, much
people gathered unto him: and he was
nigh unto the sea. 22 And, behold,
there cometh one of the rulers of the
synagogue, Jairus by name; and when
he saw him, he fell at his feet, 23
And besought him greatly, saying,
My little daughter lieth at the point
of death: *I pray thee*, come and lay
thy hands on her, that she may be
healed; and she shall live. 24 And
Jesus went with him; and much people
followed him, and thronged him. 25
And a certain woman, which had an
issue of blood twelve years, 26 And
had suffered many things of many
physicians, and had spent all that she
had, and was nothing bettered, but
rather grew worse, 27 When she
had heard of Jesus, came in the press
behind, and touched his garment. 28
For she said, If I may touch but
his clothes, I shall be whole. 29 And
straightway the fountain of her blood
was dried up; and she felt in *her*
body that she was healed of that
plague. 30 And Jesus, immediately
knowing in himself that virtue had
gone out of him, turned him about
in the press, and said, Who touched
my clothes? 31 And his disciples
said unto him, Thou seest the multitude thronging thee, and sayest thou,
Who touched me? 32 And he looked
round about to see her that had done
this thing. 33 But the woman fearing and trembling, knowing what was
done in her, came and fell down before him, and told him all the truth.
34 And he said unto her, Daughter,
thy faith hath made thee whole; go
in peace, and be whole of thy plague.

The Gadarenes having desired Christ to leave their country, he did not stay to trouble them long, but presently went by water, as he came, back *to the other side* (*v.* 21), and there *much people gathered to him*. Note, If there be some that reject Christ, yet there are others that receive him, and bid him welcome. A despised gospel will *cross the water*, and go where it will have better entertainment. Now among the many that applied themselves to him,

I. Here is one, that comes *openly* to *beg* a cure for a sick child; and it is no less a person than one of the *rulers of the synagogue*, one that presided in the synagogue-worship or, as some think, one of the judges of the consistory court, which was in every city, consisting of *twenty-three.* He was not named in Matthew, he is here, *Jairus,* or *Jair,* Judg. x. 3. He addressed himself to Christ, though a ruler, with great humility and reverence; *When he saw him, he fell at his feet,* giving honour to him as one really greater than he appeared to be; and with great importunity, he *besought him greatly,* as one in earnest, as one that not only valued the mercy he came for, but that knew he could obtain it no where else. The case is this, He has a *little daughter,* about twelve years old, the darling of the family, and she *lies a dying;* but he believes that if Christ will but come, and *lay his hands upon her,* she will return even from the gates of the grave. He said, at first, when he came, *She lies a dying* (so Mark); but afterward, upon fresh information sent him, he saith, *She is even now dead* (so Matthew); but he still prosecutes his suit; see Luke viii. 42—49. Christ readily agreed, and went with him, *v.* 24.

II. Here is another, that comes *clandestinely* to *steal* a cure (if I may so say) for herself; and she got the relief she came for. This cure was wrought by *the way,* as he was going to raise the ruler's daughter, and was followed by a crowd. See how Christ improved his time, and lost none of the precious moments of it. Many of his discourses, and some of his miracles, are dated *by the way-side;* we should be doing good, not only when we *sit in the house,* but when we *walk by the way,* Deut. vi. 7. Now observe,

1. The piteous case of this poor woman. She had a constant *issue of blood* upon her, for *twelve years,* which had thrown her, no doubt, into great weakness, had embittered the comfort of her life, and threatened to be her death in a little time. She had had the best advice of physicians, that she could get, and had made use of the many medicines and methods they prescribed: as long as she had any thing to give them, they had kept her in hopes that they could cure her; but now that she had spent all she had among them, they gave her up as incurable. See here, (1.) That skin for skin, and all that a man has, will he give for life and health; she spent all she had upon physicians. (2.) It is ill with those patients whose physicians are their worst disease; who *suffer* by their physicians, instead of being relieved by them. (3.) Those that are not *bettered* by medicines, commonly *grow worse,* and the disease gets the more ground. (4.) It is usual with people not to apply themselves to Christ, till they have tried in vain all other helpers, and find them, as certainly they will, *physicians of no value.* And he will be found a *sure refuge,* even to those who make him their *last refuge.*

2. The strong faith that she had in the power of Christ to heal her; she said within herself, though it doth not appear that she was encouraged by any preceding instance to say it, *If I may but touch his clothes, I shall be whole, v.* 28. She believed that he cured, not as a prophet, by virtue *derived* from God, but as the Son of God, by a virtue *inherent* in himself. Her case was such as she could not in modesty tell him publicly, as others did their grievances, and therefore a private cure was what she wished for, and her faith was suited to her case.

3. The wonderful effect produced by it; *She came in the* crowd *behind* him, and with much ado got to *touch his garment,* and immediately she felt the cure wrought, *v.* 29. The flux of blood was *dried up,* and she felt herself perfectly well all over her, as well as ever she was in her life, in an instant; by this it appears that the cure was altogether miraculous; for those that in such cases are cured by natural means, recover their strength slowly and gradually, and not *per saltum—all at once;* but *as for God, his work is perfect.* Note, Those whom Christ heals of the disease of sin, that bloody issue, cannot but experience in themselves a universal change for the better.

4. Christ's enquiry after his concealed patient, and the encouragement he gave her, upon the discovery of her; Christ *knew in himself that virtue had gone out of him, v.* 30. He knew it not by any deficiency of spirits, through the exhausting of this virtue, but rather by an agility of spirits, in the exerting of it, and the innate and inseparable pleasure he had in doing good. And being desirous to see his patient, he asked, not in displeasure, as one affronted, but in tenderness, as one concerned, *Who touched my clothes?* The disciples, not without a show of rudeness and indecency, almost ridiculed his question (*v.* 31); *The multitudes throng thee, and sayest thou, Who touched me?* As if it had been an improper question. Christ passed by the affront, and *looks around* to *see her that had done this thing;* not that he might *blame* her for her presumption, but that he might *commend* and *encourage* her faith, and by his own act and deed might *warrant* and *confirm* the cure, and *ratify* to her that which she had *surreptitiously* obtained. He needed not that any should inform him, for he had presently his eye upon her. Note, As secret acts of sin, so secret acts of faith, are known to the Lord Jesus, and are under his eye. If believers derive virtue from Christ ever so closely, he knows it, and is pleased with it. The poor woman, hereupon, presented herself to the Lord Jesus (*v.* 33), *fearing and trembling,* not knowing how he would take it. Note, Christ's patients are often trembling, when they have reason to be triumphing. She might have come boldly, *knowing what was done in her;* yet, *knowing that,* she *fears* and *trembles.* It was a *surprise,* and was not yet, as it should have been, a *pleasing* surprise. However, she *fell down before him.* Note, There is nothing better for those that fear and tremble, than to throw them-

selves at the feet of the Lord Jesus; to humble themselves before him, and refer themselves to him. And she *told him all the truth.* Note, We must not be ashamed to own the secret transactions between Christ and our souls; but, when called to it, mention, to his praise, and the encouragement of others, what he has done for our souls, and the experience we have had of *healing virtue* derived from him. And the consideration of this, that nothing can be hid from Christ, should engage us to confess all to him. See what an encouraging word he gave her (*v.* 34); *Daughter, thy faith hath made thee whole.* Note, Christ puts honour upon faith, because faith gives honour to Christ. But see how *what is done by faith* on earth is ratified in heaven; Christ saith, *Be whole of thy disease.* Note, If our faith sets the seal of its *amen* to the power and promise of God, saying, "So it is, and so let it be to me;" God's grace will set the seal of its *amen* to the prayers and hopes of faith, saying, "So be it, and so it shall be, to thee." And therefore, "*Go in peace;* be well satisfied that thy cure is honestly come by, is effectually wrought, and take the comfort of it." Note, They that by faith are healed of their spiritual diseases, have reason to *go in peace.*

35 While he yet spake, there came
from the ruler of the synagogue's
house certain which said, Thy daughter
is dead: why troublest thou the Master any further? 36 As soon as Jesus
heard the word that was spoken, he
saith unto the ruler of the synagogue,
Be not afraid, only believe. 37 And
he suffered no man to follow him,
save Peter, and James, and John the
brother of James. 38 And he cometh
to the house of the ruler of the synagogue, and seeth the tumult, and them
that wept and wailed greatly. 39
And when he was come in, he saith
unto them, Why make ye this ado,
and weep? the damsel is not dead,
but sleepeth. 40 And they laughed
him to scorn. But when he had put
them all out, he taketh the father and
the mother of the damsel, and them
that were with him, and entereth in
where the damsel was lying. 41 And
he took the damsel by the hand, and
said unto her, Talitha cumi; which is,
being interpreted, Damsel, I say unto
thee, arise. 42 And straightway the
damsel arose, and walked; for she
was *of the age* of twelve years. And
they were astonished with a great
astonishment. 43 And he charged
them straitly that no man should know
it; and commanded that something
should be given her to eat.

Diseases and deaths came into the world by the sin and disobedience of the first Adam; but by the grace of the second Adam both are conquered. Christ, having healed an incurable disease, here goes on to triumph over death, as in the beginning of the chapter he had triumphed over an outrageous devil.

I. The melancholy news is brought to Jairus, that his *daughter is dead,* and therefore, if Christ be as other physicians, he comes too late. While there is life, there is hope, and room for the use of means; but when life is gone, it is past recal; *Why troublest thou the Master any further? v.* 35. Ordinarily, the proper thought in this case, is, "The matter is determined, the will of God is done, and I submit, I acquiesce; *The Lord gave, and the Lord hath taken away. While the child was alive, I fasted and wept; for I said, Who can tell but God will yet be gracious to me,* and *the child shall live?* But *now that it is dead, wherefore should I weep? I shall go to it, but it shall not return to me.*" With such words we should *quiet ourselves* at such a time, that our souls may be *as a child that is weaned from his mother:* but here the case was extraordinary; the death of the child doth not, as usually, put an end to the narrative.

II. Christ encourageth the afflicted father yet to hope that his application to Christ on the behalf of his child should not be in vain. Christ had staid to work a cure by the way, but he shall be no sufferer by that, nor loser by the gain of others; *Be not afraid, only believe.* We may suppose Jairus at a pause, whether he should ask Christ to go on or no; but have we not as much occasion for the grace of God, and his consolations, and consequently of the prayers of our ministers and Christian friends, when death is in the house, as when sickness is? Christ therefore soon determines this matter; "*Be not afraid* that my coming will be to no purpose, only believe that I will make it turn to a good account." Note, 1. We must not despair concerning our relations that are dead, nor *sorrow* for them *as those that have no hope.* See what is said to Rachel, who *refused to be comforted concerning her children,* upon the presumption that they *were not; Refrain thy voice from weeping, and thine eyes from tears; for there is hope in thine end, that thy children shall come again,* Jer. xxxi. 16, 17. Therefore fear not, faint not. 2. Faith is the only remedy against disquieting grief and fear at such a time: let that silence them, *Only believe.* Keep up a confidence in Christ, and a dependence upon him, and he will do what is for the best. Believe the resurrection, and then be not afraid.

III. He went with a select company to the house where the dead child was. He had, by the crowd that attended him, given advantage to the poor woman he last healed, and, having done that, now he shook off the crowd, and *suffered no man to follow him* (to *follow with him,* so the word is), but his three bosom-disciples, Peter, and James, and John; a competent number to be witnesses of the miracle, but not such a number as that his taking them with him might look like vainglory.

IV. He raised the dead child to life; the circumstances of the narrative here are much the same as we had them in Matthew; only here we may observe,

1. That the child was extremely well beloved, for the relations and neighbours *wept and wailed greatly.* It is very afflictive when that which is come forth like a flower is so *soon cut down,* and withereth before it is grown up; when that grieves us, of which we said, *This same shall comfort us.*

2. That it was evident beyond dispute, that the child was really and truly dead. Their *laughing* Christ to *scorn,* for saying, *She is not dead, but sleepeth,* though highly reprehensible, serves for the proof of this.

3. That Christ put those out as unworthy to be witnesses of the miracle, who were noisy in their sorrow, and were so ignorant in the things of God, as not to understand him when he spoke of death as a *sleep,* or so scornful, as to ridicule him for it.

4. That he took the parents of the child to be witnesses of the miracle, because in it he had an eye to *their faith,* and designed it for *their* comfort, who were the *true,* for they were the *silent* mourners.

5. That Christ raised the child to life by a word of power, which is recorded here, and recorded in Syriac, the language in which Christ spoke, for the greater certainty of the thing; *Talitha, cumi; Damsel, I say unto thee, Arise.* Dr. Lightfoot saith, It was customary with the Jews, when they gave physic to one that was *sick,* to say, *Arise from thy disease;* meaning, *We wish* thou mayest arise: but to one that was *dead,* Christ said, *Arise from the dead;* meaning, *I command* that thou arise; nay, there is more in it—the dead have not power to arise, therefore power goes along with this word, to make it effectual. *Da quod jubes, et jube quod vis—Give what thou commandest, and command what thou wilt.* Christ works while he commands, and works by the command, and therefore may command what he pleaseth, even the dead to arise. Such is the gospel call to those that are by nature dead in trespasses and sins, and can no more rise from that death by their own power, than this child could; and yet that word, *Awake, and arise from the dead,* is neither vain, nor in vain, when it follows immediately, *Christ shall give thee light,* Eph. v. 14. It is by the word of Christ that spiritual life is given, *I said unto thee, Live,* Ezek. xvi. 6.

6. That the damsel, as soon as life returned, *arose, and walked, v.* 42. Spiritual life will appear by our *rising* from the bed of sloth and carelessness, and our *walking* in a religious conversation, our walking *up and down* in Christ's name and strength; even from those that are *of the age of twelve years,* it may be expected that they should walk as those whom Christ has *raised to life,* otherwise than in the native *vanity of their minds.*

7. That all who saw it, and heard of it, admired the miracle, and him that wrought it; *They were astonished with a great astonishment.* They could not but acknowledge that there was something in it extraordinary and very great, and yet they knew not what to make of it, or to infer from it. Their wonder should have worked forward to a lively faith, but it rested in a *stupor* or *astonishment.*

8. That Christ endeavoured to conceal it; *He charged them straitly, that no man should know it.* It was sufficiently known to a competent number, but he would not have it as yet *proclaimed* any further; because his own resurrection was to be the great instance of his power over death, and therefore the divulging of other instances must be reserved till that great proof was given: let one part of the evidence be kept private, till the other part, on which the main stress lies, be made ready.

9. That Christ took care something should be *given her to eat.* By this it appeared that she was raised not only to life, but to a good state of health, that she had an appetite to her meat; even the new-born babes in Christ's house desire the sincere milk, 1 Pet. ii. 1, 2. And it is observable, that, as Christ, when at first he had made man, presently provided food for him, and food out of the earth of which he was made (Gen. i. 29), so now when he had given a new life, he took care that something should be given to eat; for if he has given *life,* he may be trusted to give *livelihood,* because *the life is more than meat,* Matt. vi. 25. Where Christ hath given *spiritual life,* he will provide food for the support and nourishment of it unto life eternal, for he will *never forsake,* or be wanting to, the *work of his own hands.*

CHAP. VI.

A great variety of observable passages we have, in this chapter, concerning our Lord Jesus, the substance of all which we had before in Matthew, but divers circumstances we have, which we did not there meet with. Here is, I. Christ contemned by his countrymen, because he was one of them, and they knew, or thought they knew, his original, ver. 1—6. II. The just power he gave his apostles over unclean spirits, and an account given of their negociation, ver. 7—13. III. A strange notion which Herod and others had of Christ, upon which occasion we have the story of the martyrdom of John Baptist, ver. 14—29. IV. Christ's retirement into a desert place with his disciples; the crowds that followed him thither to receive instruction from him; and his feeding five thousand of them with five loaves and two fishes, ver. 30—44. V. Christ's walking upon the sea to his disciples, and the abundance of cures he wrought on the other side of the water, ver. 45—56.

AND he went out from thence,
and came into his own country;
and his disciples follow him. 2
And when the sabbath day was come,
he began to teach in the synagogue:

and many hearing *him* were astonished,
saying, From whence hath this *man*
these things? and what wisdom *is*
this which is given unto him, that even
such mighty works are wrought by
his hands? 3 Is not this the carpenter,
the son of Mary, the brother of James,
and Joses, and of Juda, and Simon?
and are not his sisters here with us?
And they were offended at him. 4
But Jesus said unto them, A prophet
is not without honour, but in his own
country, and among his own kin, and
in his own house. 5 And he could
there do no mighty work, save that
he laid his hands upon a few sick folk,
and healed *them.* 6 And he marvelled because of their unbelief. And
he went round about the villages,
teaching.

Here, I. Christ makes a visit to *his own country,* the place not of his birth, but of his education; that was *Nazareth;* where his relations were. He had been in danger of his life among them (Luke iv. 29), and yet he came among them again; so strangely doth he wait to be gracious, and seek the salvation of his enemies. Whither he went, though it was into danger, *his disciples followed him* (*v.* 1); for they had left all, to follow him whithersoever he went.

II. There he *preached* in their *synagogue,* on the *sabbath day, v.* 2. It seems, there was not such flocking to him there as in other places, so that he had no opportunity of preaching till they came together on the sabbath day; and then he expounded a portion of scripture with great clearness. In religious assemblies, on sabbath days, the word of God is to be preached according to Christ's example. We *give glory* to God by receiving instruction from him.

III. They could not but own that which was very honourable concerning him. 1. That he spoke with great *wisdom,* and that this wisdom was *given to him,* for they knew he had no learned education. 2. That he did *mighty works,* did them with his own hands, for the confirming of the doctrine he taught. They acknowledged the two great proofs of the divine original of his gospel—the *divine wisdom* that appeared in the contrivance of it, and the *divine power* that was exerted for the ratifying and recommending of it; and yet, though they could not deny the premises, they would not admit the conclusion.

IV. They studied to disparage him, and to raise prejudices in the minds of people against him, notwithstanding. All this *wisdom,* and all these *mighty works,* shall be of no account, because he had a home-education, had never travelled, nor been at any university, or bred up at the feet of any of their doctors (*v.* 3); *Is not this the Carpenter?* In Matthew, they upbraid him with being the carpenter's son, his supposed father Joseph being of that trade. But, it seems, they could say further, *Is not this the Carpenter?* our Lord Jesus, it is probable, employing himself in that business with his father, before he entered upon his public ministry, at least, sometimes in journey-work. 1. He would thus *humble himself,* and make himself of no reputation, as one that had taken upon him the form of a servant, and came to minister. Thus low did our Redeemer stoop, when he came to redeem us out of our low estate. 2. He would thus teach us to *abhor idleness,* and to find *ourselves something to do* in this world; and rather to take up with mean and laborious employments, and such as no more is to be got by than a bare livelihood, than indulge ourselves in sloth. Nothing is more pernicious for young people than to get a *habit of sauntering.* The Jews had a good rule for this—that their young men who were designed for scholars, were yet bred up to some trade, as Paul was a tent-maker, that they might have some business to fill up their time with, and, if need were, to get their bread with. 3. He would thus put an honour upon despised mechanics, and encourage those who eat the labour of their hands, though great men look upon them with contempt.

Another thing they upbraided him with, was, the meanness of his relations; "*He is the son of Mary;* his *brethren* and *sisters* are here *with us;* we know his family and kindred;" and therefore, though they were *astonished* at his doctrine (*v.* 2), yet they were *offended* at his person (*v.* 3), were prejudiced against him, and looked upon him with contempt; and for that reason would not receive his doctrine, though ever so well recommended. May we think that if they had not known his pedigree, but he had dropped among them from the clouds, without father, without mother, and without descent, they would have entertained him with any more respect? Truly, no; for in Judea, where this was not known, that was made an objection against him (John ix. 29); *As for this fellow, we know not from whence he is.* Obstinate unbelief will never want excuses.

V. Let us see how Christ bore this contempt. 1. He partly *excused it,* as a common thing, and what might be expected, though not reasonably or justly (*v.* 4); *A prophet is not despised any where but in his own country.* Some exceptions there may be to this rule; doubtless many have got over this prejudice, but ordinarily it holds good, that ministers are seldom so acceptable and successful in their own country as among strangers; *familiarity* in the younger years breeds a contempt, the advancement of one that was an inferior begets *envy,* and men will hardly set those among the guides of their souls whose fathers they were ready to set with the dogs of their flock; in such a case therefore it must not be thought hard, it is common treatment, it was Christ's, and *wisdom is profitable to direct* to other soil.

2. He did *some good* among them, notwithstanding the slights they put upon him, for he is kind even to the evil and unthankful; *He laid his hands upon a few sick folks, and healed them.* Note, It is generous, and becoming the followers of Christ, to content themselves with the pleasure and satisfaction of doing good, though they be unjustly denied the praise of it.

3. Yet he *could there do* no such mighty works, at least not so many, as in other places, because of the unbelief that prevailed among the people, by reason of the prejudices which their leaders instilled into them against Christ, *v.* 5. It is a strange expression, as if unbelief tied the hands of omnipotence itself; he *would have done* as many miracles there as he had done elsewhere, but he could not, because people would not make application to him, nor sue for his favours; he could have wrought them, but they forfeited the honour of having them wrought for them. Note, By unbelief and contempt of Christ men stop the current of his favours to them, and put a bar in their own door.

4. He *marvelled because of their unbelief*, *v.* 6. We never find Christ wondering but at the *faith* of the Gentiles that were strangers, as the *centurion* (Matt. viii. 10), and the woman of Samaria, and at the unbelief of Jews that were his own countrymen. Note, The unbelief of those that enjoy the means of grace, is a most amazing thing.

5. He *went round about the villages, teaching.* If we cannot do good where we would, we must do it where we can, and be glad if we may have any opportunity, though but in the villages, of serving Christ and souls. Sometimes the gospel of Christ finds better entertainment in the country villages, where there is less wealth, and pomp, and mirth, and subtlety, than in the populous cities.

7 And he called *unto him* the twelve,
and began to send them forth by two
and two; and gave them power over
unclean spirits; 8 And commanded
them that they should take nothing
for *their* journey, save a staff only;
no scrip, no bread, no money in *their*
purse: 9 But *be* shod with sandals;
and not put on two coats. 10 And
he said unto them, In what place
soever ye enter into a house, there
abide till ye depart from that place.
11 And whosoever shall not receive
you, nor hear you, when ye depart
thence, shake off the dust under your
feet for a testimony against them.
Verily I say unto you, It shall be
more tolerable for Sodom and Go-
morrha in the day of judgment, than
for that city. 12 And they went out,
and preached that men should repent.
13 And they cast out many devils,
and anointed with oil many that were
sick, and healed *them*.

Here is, I. The commission given to the twelve apostles, to preach and work miracles; it is the same which we had more largely, Matt. x. Mark doth not name them here, as Matthew doth, because he had named them before, when they were first called into fellowship with him, *ch.* iii. 16—19. Hitherto they had been conversant with Christ, and had set at his feet, had heard his doctrine, and seen his miracles; and now he determines to make some use of them; they had *received*, that they might *give*, had *learned*, that they might *teach;* and therefore now he *began to send them forth.* They must not always be studying in the academy, to get knowledge, but they must preach in the country, to do good with the knowledge they have got. Though they were not as yet so well accomplished as they were to be, yet, according to their present ability and capacity, they must be set to work, and make further improvements afterward. Now observe here,

1. That Christ sent them forth *by two and two;* this Mark takes notice of. They went two and two to a place, that out of the mouth of two witnesses every word might be established; and that they might be company for one another when they were among strangers, and might strengthen the hands, and encourage the hearts, one of another; might help one another if any thing should be amiss, and keep one another in countenance. Every common soldier has his comrade; and it is an approved maxim, *Two are better than one.* Christ would thus teach his ministers to associate, and both lend and borrow help.

2. That he *gave them power over unclean spirits.* He commissioned them to attack the devil's kingdom, and empowered them, as a specimen of their breaking his interest in the souls of men by their doctrine, to cast him out of the bodies of those that were possessed. Dr. Lightfoot suggests, that they cured diseases, and cast out devils, by the Spirit, but preached that only which they had learned from the mouth of Christ.

3. That he *commanded them* not to take provisions along with them, neither *victuals* nor *money*, that they might appear, wherever they came, to be poor men, men not of this world, and therefore might with the better grace call people off from it to another world. When afterward he bid them *take purse and scrip* (Luke xxii. 36), that did not intimate (as Dr. Lightfoot observes) that his care of them was abated from what it had been; but

that they should meet with worse times and worse entertainment than they met with at their first mission. In Matthew and Luke they are forbidden to *take staves* with them, that is, fighting staves; but here in Mark they are bid to take nothing save a *staff only*, that is, a walking staff, such as pilgrims carried. They must not put on *shoes*, but *sandals* only, which were only the soles of shoes tied under their feet, or like pumps, or slippers; they must go in the readiest plainest dress they could, and must not so much as have *two coats;* for their stay abroad would be short, they must return before winter, and what they wanted, those they preached to would cheerfully accommodate them with.

4. He directed them, whatever city they came to, to make that house their head-quarters, which happened to be their first quarters (*v.* 10); "*There abide, till ye depart from that place.* And since ye know ye come on an errand sufficient to make you welcome, have such charity for your friends that first invited you, as to believe they do not think you burthensome."

5. He pronounces a very heavy doom upon those that rejected the gospel they preached (*v.* 11); "*Whosoever shall not receive you,* or will not so much as *hear you, depart thence* (if one will not, another will), and *shake off the dust under your feet, for a testimony against* them. Let them know that they have had a fair offer of life and happiness made them, witness that dust; but that, since they have refused it, they cannot expect ever to have another; let them take up with their own dust, for so shall their doom be." That dust, like the dust of Egypt (Exod. ix. 9), shall turn into a plague to them; and their condemnation in the great day, will be more intolerable than *that of Sodom:* for the angels were sent to Sodom, and were abused there; yet that would not bring on so great a guilt and so great a ruin as the contempt and abuse of the apostles of Christ, who bring with them the offers of gospel grace.

II. The apostles' conduct in pursuance of their commission. Though they were conscious to themselves of great weakness, and expected no secular advantage by it, yet, in obedience to their Master's order, and in dependence upon his strength, they *went out* as Abraham, not knowing whither they went. Observe here,

1. The doctrine they preached; *They preached that men should repent* (*v.* 12); that they should change their minds, and reform their lives, in consideration of the near approach of the kingdom of the Messiah. Note, The great design of gospel preachers, and the great tendency of gospel preaching, should be, to bring people to repentance, to a *new heart* and a *new way*. They did not amuse people with curious speculations, but told them that they must repent of their sins, and turn to God.

2. The miracles they wrought. The power Christ gave them *over unclean spirits,* was not ineffectual, nor did they receive it in vain, but used it, for they *cast out many devils* (*v.* 13); and they *anointed with oil many that were sick, and healed them.* Some think this oil was used *medicinally*, according to the custom of the Jews; but I rather think it was used as a *sign of miraculous* healing, by the appointment of Christ, though not mentioned; and it was afterward used by those *elders of the church,* to whom *by the Spirit* was given the *gift of healing,* Jam. v. 14. It is certain here, and therefore probable there, that *anointing the sick with oil,* is appropriated to that extraordinary power which has long ceased, and therefore that sign must cease with it.

14 And king Herod heard *of him;*
(for his name was spread abroad:)
and he said, That John the Baptist
was risen from the dead, and therefore mighty works do show forth themselves in him. 15 Others said, That
it is Elias. And others said, That it
is a prophet, or as one of the prophets.
16 But when Herod heard *thereof,*
he said, It is John, whom I beheaded:
he is risen from the dead. 17 For
Herod himself had sent forth and laid
hold upon John, and bound him in
prison for Herodias' sake, his brother
Philip's wife: for he had married her.
18 For John had said unto Herod,
It is not lawful for thee to have thy
brother's wife. 19 Therefore Herodias had a quarrel against him, and
would have killed him; but she could
not: 20 For Herod feared John,
knowing that he was a just man and
a holy, and observed him; and when
he heard him, he did many things,
and heard him gladly. 21 And when
a convenient day was come, that Herod
on his birthday made a supper to his
lords, high captains, and chief *estates*
of Galilee; 22 And when the daughter
of the said Herodias came in, and
danced, and pleased Herod and them
that sat with him, the king said unto
the damsel, Ask of me whatsoever
thou wilt, and I will give *it* thee. 23
And he sware unto her, Whatsoever
thou shalt ask of me, I will give *it*
thee, unto the half of my kingdom.
24 And she went forth, and said unto
her mother, What shall I ask? And
she said, The head of John the Bap-

tist. 25 And she came in straightway
with haste unto the king, and asked,
saying, I will that thou give me by
and by in a charger the head of John
the Baptist. 26 And the king was
exceeding sorry; *yet* for his oath's
sake, and for their sakes which sat
with him, he would not reject her.
27 And immediately the king sent an
executioner, and commanded his head
to be brought: and he went and beheaded him in the prison, 28 And
brought his head in a charger, and
gave it to the damsel: and the damsel
gave it to her mother. 29 And when
his disciples heard *of it*, they came
and took up his corpse, and laid it in
a tomb.

Here is, I. The wild notions that the people had concerning our Lord Jesus, *v.* 15. His own countrymen could believe nothing great concerning him, because they knew his poor kindred; but others that were not under the power of that prejudice against him, were yet willing to believe any thing rather than the truth—that he was the Son of God, and the true Messias: they said, He is Elias, whom they expected; or, *He is a prophet,* one of the Old-Testament prophets raised to life, and returned to this world; or *as one of the prophets,* a prophet now newly raised up, equal to those under the Old Testament.

II. The opinion of Herod concerning him. He heard of *his name* and fame, of what he said and what he did; and he said, "It is certainly John Baptist, *v.* 14. As sure as we are here, *It is John, whom I beheaded, v.* 16. He is *risen from the dead;* and though while he was with us *he did no miracle*, yet, having removed for awhile to another world, he is come again with greater power, and *now mighty works do show forth themselves in him.*"

Note, 1. Where there is an *idle faith,* there is commonly a *working fancy.* The people said, It is a prophet risen from the dead; Herod said, It is *John Baptist risen from the dead.* It seems by this, that the *rising of a prophet from the dead,* to do *mighty works,* was a thing expected, and was thought neither impossible nor improbable, and it was now readily suspected when it was *not true;* but afterward, when *it was true* concerning Christ, and a truth undeniably evidenced, yet then it was obstinately gainsaid and denied. Those who most wilfully disbelieve the truth, are commonly most credulous of errors and fancies.

2. They who fight against the cause of God, will find themselves baffled, even when they think themselves conquerors; they cannot gain their point, for the word of the Lord endures for ever. They who rejoiced when the witnesses were slain, fretted as much, when in three or four days they *rose again* in their successors, Rev. xi. 10, 11. The impenitent unreformed sinner, that escapeth the sword of Jehu, shall Elisha slay.

3. A guilty conscience needs no accuser or tormentor but itself. Herod charges himself with the murder of John, which perhaps no one else dare charge him with; *I beheaded him;* and the terror of it made him imagine that Christ was John risen. He feared John while he lived, and now, when he thought he had got clear of him, fears him ten times worse when he is dead. One might as well be haunted with ghosts and furies, as with the horrors of an accusing conscience; those therefore who would keep an undisturbed peace, must keep an undefiled conscience, Acts xxiv. 16.

4. There may be the terrors of strong conviction, where there is not the truth of a saving conversion. This Herod, who had this notion concerning Christ, afterward sought to kill him (Luke xiii. 31), and did set him at nought (Luke xxiii. 11); so that he will not be persuaded, though it be *by one risen from the dead;* no, not by a John the Baptist risen from the dead.

III. A narrative of Herod's putting John Baptist to death, which is brought in upon this occasion, as it was in Matthew. And here we may observe,

1. The great value and veneration which Herod had some time had for John Baptist, which is related only by this evangelist, *v.* 20. Here we see what a great way a man may go toward grace and glory, and yet come short of both, and perish eternally.

(1.) He *feared John, knowing that he was a just man, and a holy.* It is possible that a man may have a great reverence for good men, and especially for good ministers, yea, and for that in them that is good, and yet himself be a bad man. Observe, [1.] John was a *just man, and a holy;* to make a complete good man, both justice and holiness are necessary; holiness toward God, and justice toward men. John was mortified to this world, and so was a good friend both to justice and holiness. [2.] Herod knew this, not only by common fame, but by personal acquaintance with him. Those that have but little justice and holiness themselves, may yet discern it with respect in others. And, [3.] He therefore *feared* him, he honoured him. Holiness and justice command veneration, and many that are not good themselves, have respect for those that are.

(2.) He *observed* him; he sheltered him from the malice of his enemies (so some understand it); or, rather, he had a regard to his exemplary conversation, and took notice of that in him that was praiseworthy, and commended it in the hearing of those about him; he made it appear that he observed what John said and did.

(3.) He *heard him* preach; which was great condescension, considering how mean John's appearance was. To hear Christ himself preach in our streets will be but a poor plea in the great day, Luke xiii. 26.

(4.) He *did many of those things* which John in his preaching taught him. He was not only a *hearer of the word,* but in part a *doer of the work.* Some sins which John in his preaching reproved, he forsook, and some duties he bound himself to; but it will not suffice to do *many* things, unless we have *respect to all* the commandments.

(5.) He *heard him gladly.* He did not hear him with terror as Felix heard Paul, but heard him with pleasure. There is a flashy joy, which a hypocrite may have in hearing the word; Ezekiel was to his hearers as a *lovely song* (Ezek. xxxiii. 32); and the *stony ground received the word with joy,* Luke viii. 13.

2. John's faithfulness to Herod, in telling him of his faults. Herod had married his brother Philip's wife, *v.* 17. All the country, no doubt, cried shame on him for it, and reproached him for it; but John *reproved* him, told him plainly, *It is not lawful for thee to have thy brother's wife.* This was Herod's own iniquity, which he could not leave, when he did many things that John taught him; and therefore John tells him of this particularly. Though he were a king, he would not spare him, any more than Elijah did Ahab, when he said, *Hast thou killed and also taken possession?* Though John had an interest in him, and he might fear this plain-dealing would destroy his interest, yet he reproved him; for *faithful are the wounds of a friend* (Prov. xxvii. 6); and though there are some swine that will *turn again, and rend* those that *cast pearls* before them, yet, ordinarily, *he that rebuketh a man* (if the person reproved has any thing of the understanding of a man), *afterwards shall find more favour than he that flattereth with his tongue,* Prov. xxviii. 23. Though it was dangerous to offend Herod, and much more to offend Herodias, yet John would run the hazard rather than be wanting in his duty. Note, Those ministers that would be found faithful in the work of God, must not be afraid of the face of man. If we seek to please men, further than is for their spiritual good, we are not the servants of Christ.

3. The malice which Herodias bore to John for this (*v.* 19); She *had a quarrel with him, and would have killed him;* but when she could not obtain that, she got him committed to prison, *v.* 17. Herod respected him, till he touched him in his Herodias. Many that pretend to honour prophesying, are for smooth things only, and love good preaching, if it keep far enough from their beloved sin; but if that be touched, they cannot bear it. No marvel if the world hate those who testify of it that its works are evil. But it is better that sinners persecute ministers now for their faithfulness, than curse them eternally for their unfaithfulness.

4. The plot laid to take off John's head. I am apt to think that Herod was himself in the plot, notwithstanding his pretences to be displeased and surprised, and that the thing was concerted between him and Herodias; for it is said to be *when a convenient day was come* (*v.* 21), fit for such a purpose. (1.) There must be a ball at court, upon the king's birth-day, and a supper prepared for *his lords, high captains, and chief estates of Galilee.* (2.) To grace the solemnity, the daughter of Herodias must *dance* publicly, and Herod must take on him to be wonderfully charmed with her dancing; and if he be, they that *sit with him* cannot but, in compliment to him, be so too. (3.) The king hereupon must make her an extravagant promise, to give her *whatever she would ask,* even to the *half of the kingdom;* and yet, that, if rightly understood, would not have reached the end designed, for John Baptist's head was worth more than his *whole kingdom.* This promise is bound with an oath, that no room might be left to fly off from it; *He sware unto her, Whatsoever thou shalt ask, I will give.* I can scarcely think he would have made such an unlimited promise, but that he knew what she would ask. (4.) She, being instructed by Herodias her mother, asked the *head of John Baptist;* and she must have it brought her *in a charger,* as a pretty thing for her to play with (*v.* 24, 25); and there must be no delay, no time lost, she must have it *by and by.* (5.) Herod granted it, and the execution was done immediately while the company were together, which we can scarcely think the king would have done, if he had not determined the matter before. But he takes on him, [1.] To be very backward to it, and that he would not for all the world have done it, if he had not been surprised into such a promise; The *king was exceeding sorry,* that is, he seemed to be so, he said he was so, he looked as if he had been so; but it was all sham and grimace, he was really pleased that he had found a pretence to get John out of the way. *Qui nescit dissimulare, nescit regnare—The man who cannot dissemble, knows not how to reign.* And yet he was not without sorrow for it; he could not do it but with great regret and reluctancy; natural conscience will not suffer men to sin easily; the very commission of it is vexatious; what then will the reflection upon it be? [2.] He takes on him to be very sensible of the obligation of his oath; whereas if the damsel had asked but a fourth part of his kingdom, I doubt not but he would have found out a way to evade his oath. The promise was rashly made, and could not bind him to do an unrighteous thing. Sinful oaths must be repented of, and therefore not performed; for repentance is the undoing of what we have done amiss, as far as is in our power. When Theodosius the emperor was urged by a suitor with a *promise,* he answered, *I said it,* but did not *promise* it if it be unjust. If we may suppose that Herod knew nothing of the design when he made that rash promise, it is probable that he was hurried into

the doing of it by those about him, only to carry on the humour; for he did it *for their sakes who sat with him,* whose company he was proud of, and therefore would do any thing to gratify them. Thus do princes make themselves slaves to those whose respect they covet, and both value and secure themselves by. None of Herod's subjects stood in more awe of him than he did of *his lords, high captains, and chief estates.* The king sent an *executioner,* a soldier of his guard. Bloody tyrants have executioners ready to obey their most cruel and unrighteous decrees. Thus Saul has a *Doeg* at hand, to *fall upon the priests of the Lord,* when his own footmen declined it.

5. The effect of this is, (1.) That Herod's wicked court is *all in triumph,* because this prophet tormented them; the head is made a present of *to the damsel,* and by her to her *mother, v.* 28. (2.) That John Baptist's sacred college is *all in tears;* the disciples of John little thought of this; but, when they *heard of it,* they came, and took up the neglected *corpse,* and *laid it in a tomb;* where Herod, if he had pleased, might have found it, when he frightened himself with the fancy that John Baptist was *risen from the dead.*

30 And the apostles gathered themselves together unto Jesus, and told
him all things, both what they had
done, and what they had taught. 31
And he said unto them, Come ye
yourselves apart into a desert place,
and rest awhile: for there were many
coming and going, and they had no
leisure so much as to eat. 32 And
they departed into a desert place by
ship privately. 33 And the people
saw them departing, and many knew
him, and ran afoot thither out of all
cities, and outwent them, and came
together unto him. 34 And Jesus,
when he came out, saw much people,
and was moved with compassion toward them, because they were as
sheep not having a shepherd: and he
began to teach them many things.
35 And when the day was now far
spent, his disciples came unto him,
and said, This is a desert place, and
now the time *is* far passed: 36 Send
them away, that they may go into the
country round about, and into the
villages, and buy themselves bread:
for they have nothing to eat. 37 He
answered and said unto them, Give
ye them to eat. And they say unto
him, Shall we go and buy two hundred
pennyworth of bread, and give them
to eat? 38 He saith unto them,
How many loaves have ye? go and
see. And when they knew, they say,
Five, and two fishes. 39 And he
commanded them to make all sit down
by companies upon the green grass.
40 And they sat down in ranks, by
hundreds, and by fifties. 41 And
when he had taken the five loaves and
the two fishes, he looked up to heaven, and blessed, and brake the loaves,
and gave *them* to his disciples to set
before them; and the two fishes divided he among them all. 42 And
they did all eat, and were filled. 43
And they took up twelve baskets full
of the fragments, and of the fishes.
44 And they that did eat of the loaves
were about five thousand men.

In these verses, we have,

I. The return to Christ of the apostles whom he had sent forth (*v.* 7), to preach, and work miracles. They had dispersed themselves into several quarters of the country for some time, but when they had made good their several appointments, by consent they *gathered themselves together,* to compare notes, and came to Jesus, the centre of their unity, to give him an account of what they had done pursuant to their commission: as the servant that was sent to invite to the feast, and had received answers from the guests, came, and *showed his Lord all those things,* so did the apostles here; they *told him all things,* both *what they had done, and what they had taught.* Ministers are accountable both for what they *do,* and for what they *teach;* and must both watch over their own souls, and watch for the souls of others, as those that must *give account,* Heb. xiii. 17. Let them not either *do* any thing, or *teach* any thing, but what they are willing should be related and repeated to the Lord Jesus. It is a comfort to faithful ministers, when they can appeal to Christ concerning their doctrine and manner of life, both which perhaps have been misrepresented by men; and he gives them leave to be free with him, and to lay open their case before him, to *tell him all things,* what treatment they have met with, what success, and what disappointment.

II. The tender care Christ took for their repose, after the fatigue they had (*v.* 31); *He said unto them,* perceiving them to be almost spent, and out of breath, *Come ye yourselves apart into a desert place, and rest awhile.* It should seem that John's disciples came to Christ with the mournful tidings of their master's death, much about the same time that his own disciples came to him with the report of their negociation. Note, Christ takes cognizance of the *frights* of some, and the *toils* of others, of his disciples, and provides suitable relief for both, rest for those that are tired, and refuge for those that are terrified. With what kindness and compassion doth Christ say to them, *Come, and rest!* Note, The most active servants of Christ cannot be always upon the stretch of business, but have bodies that require some relaxation, some breathing-time; we shall not be able to serve God without ceasing, day and night, till we come to heaven, where they *never rest* from praising him, Rev. iv. 8. And the Lord is for the body, considers its frame, and not only allows it time for rest, but puts it in mind of resting. *Come, my people, enter thou into thy chambers. Return to thy rest.* And those that work diligently and faithfully, may cheerfully retire to rest. *The sleep of the labouring man is sweet.* But observe, 1. Christ calls them to come *themselves apart;* for, if they had any body with them, they would have something to say, or something to do, for their good; if they must *rest,* they must be *alone.* 2. He invites them not to some pleasant country-seat, where there were fine buildings and fine gardens, but *into a desert place,* where the accommodations were very poor, and which was fitted by nature only, and not by art, for quietness and rest. But it was of a piece with all the other circumstances he was in; no wonder that he who had but a ship for his preaching place, had but a desert for his resting place. 3. He calls them only to rest *awhile;* they must not expect to rest *long,* only to *get breath,* and then to go to work again. There is no *remaining rest* for the people of God till they come to heaven. 4. The reason given for this, is, not so much because they had been in *constant work,* but because they now were in a *constant hurry;* so that they had not their work in any order; *for there were many coming and going, and they had no leisure so much as to eat.* Let but proper time be set, and kept for every thing, and a great deal of work may be done with a great deal of ease; but if people be continually coming and going, and no rule or method be observed, a little work will not be done without a deal of trouble. 5. They withdrew, accordingly, *by ship;* not crossing the water, but making a coasting voyage to the desert of Bethsaida, *v.* 32. Going *by water* was much less toilsome than going *by land* would have been. They went away *privately,* that they might be by themselves. The most public persons cannot but wish to be private sometimes.

III. The diligence of the people to follow him. It was rude to do so, when he and his disciples were desirous, for such good reason, to *retire;* and yet they are not blamed for it, nor bid to go back, but bid welcome. Note, A failure in good manners will easily be excused in those who follow Christ, if it be but made up in a fulness of good affections. They followed him of their own accord, without being called upon. Here is no time set, no meeting appointed, no bell tolled; yet they thus fly like a cloud, and as the doves to their windows. They followed him *out of the cities,* quitted their houses and shops, their callings and affairs, to hear him preach. They followed him *afoot,* though he was gone by sea, and so, to try them, seemed to put a slight upon them, and to endeavour to shake them off; yet they stuck to him. They *ran* afoot, and made such haste, that they *out-went* the disciples, and *came together* to him with an appetite to the word of God. Nay they followed him, though it was into a *desert place,* despicable and inconvenient. The presence of Christ will turn a wilderness into a paradise.

IV. The entertainment Christ gave them (*v.* 34); *When he saw much people,* instead of being moved with displeasure, because they disturbed him when he desired to be private, as many a man, many a good man, would have been, he was *moved with compassion toward them,* and looked upon them with concern, because *they* were *as sheep having no shepherd,* they seemed to be well-inclined, and manageable as sheep, and willing to be taught, but they had *no shepherd,* none to lead and guide them in the right way, none to feed them with good doctrine: and therefore, in compassion to them, he not only *healed their sick,* as it is in Matthew, but he *taught them many things,* and we may be sure that they were all true and good, and fit for them to learn.

V. The provision he made for them all; all his hearers he generously made his guests, and treated them at a *splendid* entertainment: so it might truly be called, because a *miraculous* one.

1. The disciples moved that they should be *sent home.* When *the day was now far spent,* and night drew on, they said, *This is a desert place,* and *much time is now past; send them away to buy bread, v.* 35, 36. This the disciples suggested to Christ; but we do not find that the multitude themselves did. They did not say, *Send us away* (though they could not but be hungry), for they *esteemed the words of Christ's mouth more than their necessary food,* and forgot themselves when they were hearing him; but the disciples thought it would be a kindness to them to dismiss them. Note, Willing minds will do more, and hold out longer, in that which is good, than one would expect from them.

2. Christ ordered that they should all be fed (*v.* 37); *Give ye them to eat.* Though their crowding after him and his disciples hindered them from eating (*v.* 31), yet he would not *therefore,* to be even with them, send them away fasting, but, to teach us to be kind to those who are rude to us, he ordered provision to be made for them; that bread which Christ and his disciples took with them into the desert, that they might make a quiet meal of it for themselves, he will have them to partake of. Thus was he

given to hospitality. They attended on the spiritual food of his word, and then he took care that they should not want corporal food. The way of duty, as it is the way of safety, so it is the way to supply. Let God alone to fill the pools with rain from heaven, and so to make a well even in the valley of Baca, for those that are going Zion-ward, from strength to strength, Ps. lxxxiv. 6, 7. Providence, not *tempted,* but duly *trusted,* never yet failed any of God's faithful servants, but has refreshed many with seasonable and surprising relief. It has often been seen in the *mount of the Lord, Jehovah-jireh,* that *the Lord will provide* for those that wait on him.

3. The disciples objected against it as impracticable; *Shall we go, and buy two hundred penny-worth of bread, and give them to eat?* Thus, through the weakness of their faith, instead of waiting for directions from Christ, they perplex the cause with projects of their own. It was a question, whether they had two hundred pence with them, whether the country would of a sudden afford so much bread if they had, and whether that would suffice so great a company; but thus Moses objected (Numb. xi. 22), *Shall the flocks and the herds be slain for them?* Christ would let them see their folly in forecasting for themselves, that they might put the greater value upon his provision for them.

4. Christ effected it, to universal satisfaction. They had brought with them *five loaves,* for the victualling of their ship, and *two fishes* perhaps they caught as they came along; and that is the bill of fare. This was but a little for Christ and his disciples, and yet this they must give away, as the widow her *two mites,* and as the church of Macedonia's *deep poverty abounded to the riches of their liberality.* We often find Christ entertained at other people's tables, dining with one friend, and supping with another: but here we have him supping a great many at his own charge, which shows that, when others *ministered to him of their substance,* it was not because he could not supply himself otherwise (if he was *hungry,* he needed not *tell them*); but it was a piece of humiliation, that he was pleased to submit to, nor was it agreeable to the intention of miracles, that he should work them for himself. Observe,

(1.) The provision was *ordinary.* Here were no rarities, no varieties, though Christ, if he had pleased, could have furnished his table with them; but thus he would teach us to be content with food convenient for us, and not to be desirous of dainties. If we have for necessity, it is no matter though we have not for delicacy and curiosity. God, in love, gives *meat for our hunger;* but, in wrath, gives *meat for our lusts,* Ps. lxxviii. 18. The promise to them that fear the Lord, is, that verily they shall be fed; he doth not say, They shall be *feasted.* If Christ and his disciples took up with mean things, surely we may.

(2.) The guests were *orderly;* for they *sat down by companies on the green grass* (*v.* 39), they *sat down in ranks by hundreds and by fifties* (*v.* 40), that the provision might the more easily and regularly be distributed among them; for God is the God of order, and not of confusion. Thus care was taken that every one should have enough, and none be over-looked, nor any have more than was fitting.

(3.) A blessing was craved upon the meat; *He looked up to heaven, and blessed.* Christ did not call one of his disciples to crave a blessing, but did it himself (*v.* 41); and by virtue of this blessing the bread strangely multiplied, and so did the fishes, for they did *all eat; and were filled,* though they were to the number of *five thousand, v.* 42, 44. This miracle was significant, and shows that Christ came into the world, to be the great feeder as well as the great healer; not only to restore, but to preserve and nourish, spiritual life; and in him there is enough for all that come to him, enough to fill the soul, to fill the treasures; none are sent empty away from Christ, but those that come to him full of themselves.

(4.) Care was taken of the fragments that remained, with which they filled *twelve baskets.* Though Christ had bread enough at command, he would hereby teach us, not to make waste of any of God's good creatures; remembering how many there are that do want, and that we know not but we may some time or other want such fragments as we throw away.

45 And straightway he constrained
his disciples to get into the ship, and
to go to the other side before unto
Bethsaida, while he sent away the
people. 46 And when he had
sent them away, he departed into a
mountain to pray. 47 And when even
was come, the ship was in the midst
of the sea, and he alone on the land.
48 And he saw them toiling in rowing; for the wind was contrary unto
them: and about the fourth watch of
the night he cometh unto them, walking upon the sea, and would have
passed by them. 49 But when they
saw him walking upon the sea, they
supposed it had been a spirit, and
cried out: 50 For they all saw him,
and were troubled. And immediately he talked with them, and saith
unto them, Be of good cheer: it is I;
be not afraid. 51 And he went up
unto them into the ship; and the
wind ceased: and they were sore
amazed in themselves beyond measure, and wondered. 52 For they

considered not *the miracle* of the
loaves: for their heart was hardened.
53 And when they had passed over,
they came into the land of Gennesaret and drew to the shore. 54 And
when they were come out of the ship,
straightway they knew him, 55 And
ran through that whole region round
about, and began to carry about in
beds those that were sick, where they
heard he was. 56 And whithersoever
he entered, into villages, or cities, or
country, they laid the sick in the
streets, and besought him that they
might touch if it were but the border
of his garment: and as many as
touched him were made whole.

This passage of story we had Matt. xiv. 22, &c., only what was there related concerning Peter, is omitted here. Here we have,

I. The dispersing of the assembly; Christ *constrained his disciples* to go before by ship to Bethsaida, intending to follow them, as they supposed, by land. The people were loth to scatter, so that it cost him some time and pains to send them away. For now that they had got a good supper, they were in no haste to leave him. But as long as we are here in this world, we have no continuing city, no not in communion with Christ. The everlasting feast is reserved for the future state.

II. Christ departed *into a mountain, to pray.* Observe, 1. He *prayed;* though he had so much preaching-work upon his hands, yet he was much in prayer; he prayed often, and prayed long, which is an encouragement to us to depend upon the intercession he is making for us at the right hand of the Father, that *continual* intercession. 2. He went *alone,* to pray; though he needed not to retire for the avoiding either of distraction or of ostentation, yet, to set us an example, and to encourage us in our *secret* addresses to God, he prayed *alone,* and, for want of a closet, went up into a mountain, to pray. A good man is never less alone than when alone with God.

III. The disciples were in distress at sea; *The wind was contrary* (*v.* 48), so that they *toiled in rowing,* and could not get forward. This was a specimen of the hardships they were to expect, when hereafter he should send them abroad to preach the gospel; it would be like sending them to sea at this time with the *wind in their teeth:* they must expect to toil in rowing, they must work hard to strive against so strong a stream; they must likewise expect to be tossed with waves, to be persecuted by their enemies; and by exposing them now he intended to train them up for such difficulties, that they might learn to *endure hardness.* The church is often like a ship at sea, *tossed with tempests, and not comforted* we may have Christ for us, and yet wind and tide against us; but it is a comfort to Christ's disciples in a storm, that their Master is in the heavenly mount, interceding for them.

IV. Christ made them a kind visit upon the water. He could have checked the winds, where he was, or have sent an angel to their relief; but he chose to help them in the most endearing manner possible, and therefore came to them himself.

1. He did not come till the *fourth watch of the night,* not till after three o'clock in the morning; but then he came. Note, If Christ's visits to his people be deferred long, yet at length he will come; and their extremity is his opportunity to appear for them so much the more seasonably. Though the salvation tarry, yet we must wait for it; *at the end it shall speak,* in the fourth watch of the night, *and not lie.*

2. He came, walking upon the waters. The sea was now tossed with waves, and yet Christ came, walking upon it; for though the *floods lift up their voice, the Lord on high is mightier,* Ps. xciii. 3, 4. No difficulties can obstruct Christ's gracious appearances for his people, when the set time is come. He will either find, or force, a way through the most tempestuous sea, for their deliverance, Ps. xlii. 7, 8,

3. He *would have passed by them,* that is, he set his face and steered his course, as if he would have gone further, and took no notice of them; this he did, to awaken them to call to him. Note, Providence, when it is acting designedly and directly for the succour of God's people, yet sometimes seems as if it were *giving them the go-by,* and regarded not their case. They thought that *he would,* but we may be sure that he would not, *have passed by them.*

4. They were frightened at the sight of him, supposing him to have been an apparition; *They all saw him, and were troubled* (*v.* 50), thinking it had been some dæmon, or evil genius, that haunted them, and raised this storm. We often perplex and frighten ourselves with phantasms, the creatures of our own fancy and imagination.

5. He encouraged them, and silenced their fears, by making himself known to them; *he talked* familiarly with them, saying, *Be of good cheer, it is I; be not afraid.* Note, (1.) We know not Christ till he is pleased to reveal himself to us. "*It is I;* I your Master, I your friend, I your Redeemer and Saviour. *It is I,* that came to a troublesome earth, and now to a tempestuous sea, to look after you." (2.) The knowledge of Christ, as he is in himself, and near to us, is enough to make the disciples of Christ cheerful even in a storm, and no longer fearful. *If it be so, why am I thus?* If it is Christ that is with thee, *be of good cheer, be not afraid.* Our fears are soon satisfied, if our mistakes be but rectified, especially our mistakes concerning Christ. See Gen. xxi. 19; 2 Kings vi. 15—

17. Christ's presence with us in a stormy day, is enough to make us of good cheer, though clouds and darkness be round about us. He said, *It is I.* He doth not tell them who he was (there was no occasion), they knew his voice, as the sheep know the voice of their own shepherd, John x. iv. How readily doth the spouse say, once and again, *It is the voice of my beloved!* Cant. ii. 8; v. 2. He said, ἐγώ εἰμι—*I am he;* or *I am;* it is God's name, when he comes to deliver Israel, Exod. iii. 14. So it is Christ's, now that he comes to deliver his disciples. When Christ said to those that came to apprehend him by force, *I am he,* they were struck down by it, John xviii. 6. When he saith to those that come to apprehend him by faith, *I am he,* they are raised up by it, and comforted.

6. He *went up to them into the ship,* embarked in the same bottom with them, and so made them perfectly easy. Let them but have their Master with them, and all is well. And as soon as he was come into the ship, *the wind ceased.* In the former storm that they were in, it is said, *He arose, and rebuked the winds, and said to the sea, Peace, be still* (*ch.* iv. 39); but here we read of no such formal command given, only the wind ceased all of a sudden. Note, Our Lord Jesus will be sure to do his own work always effectually, though not always alike solemnly, and with observation. Though we hear not the command given, yet, if thus the wind cease, and we have the comfort of a calm, say, It is because Christ is in the ship, and his decree is gone forth *or ever we are aware,* Cant. vi. 12. When we come with Christ to heaven, the wind ceaseth presently; there are no storms in the upper region.

7. They were more surprised and astonished at this miracle than did become them, and there was that at the bottom of their astonishment, which was really culpable; *They were sore amazed in themselves,* were in a perfect ecstasy; as if it were a new and unaccountable thing, as if Christ had never done the like before, and they had no reason to expect he should do it now; they ought to admire the power of Christ, and to be confirmed hereby in their belief of his being the Son of God: but why all this confusion about it? It was because they *considered not the miracle of the loaves;* had they given that its due weight, they would not have been so much surprised at this; for his multiplying the bread was as great an instance of his power as his walking on the water. They were strangely stupid and unthinking, and their heart was hardened, or else they would not have thought it a thing incredible that Christ should command a calm. It is for want of a right understanding of Christ's former works, that we are transported at the thought of his present works, as if there never were the like before.

V. When they came to the land of Gennesaret, which lay between Bethsaida and Capernaum, the people bid them very welcome; *The men of that place* presently *knew Jesus* (*v.* 54), and knew what mighty works he did wherever he came, what a universal Healer he was; they knew likewise that he used to stay but a little while at a place, and therefore they were concerned to improve the opportunity of this kind visit which he made them; *They ran through that whole region round about,* with all possible expedition, and *began to carry about in beds those that were sick,* and not able to go themselves; there was no danger of their getting cold when they hoped to get a cure, *v.* 55. Let him go where he would, he was crowded with patients—in the towns, in the cities, in the villages about the cities; they *laid the sick in the streets,* to be in his way, and begged leave for them to touch if it were but *the border of his garment,* as the woman with the bloody issue did, by whom, it should seem, this method of application was first brought in; *and as many as touched, were made whole.* We do not find that they were desirous to be taught by him, only to be healed. If ministers could now cure people's bodily diseases, what multitudes would attend them! But it is sad to think how much more concerned the most of men are about their bodies than about their souls.

CHAP. VII.

In this chapter we have, I. Christ's dispute with the scribes and Pharisees about eating meat with unwashen hands (ver. 1—13); and the needful instructions he gave to the people on that occasion, and further explained to his disciples, ver. 14—23. II. His curing of the woman Canaan's daughter that was possessed, ver. 24—30. III. The relief of a man that was deaf, and had an impediment in his speech, ver. 31—37.

THEN came together unto him
the Pharisees, and certain of the
scribes, which came from Jerusalem.
2 And when they saw some of his
disciples eat bread with defiled, that
is to say, with unwashen, hands, they
found fault. 3 For the Pharisees,
and all the Jews, except they wash
their hands oft, eat not, holding the
tradition of the elders. 4 And *when*
they come from the market, except
they wash, they eat not. And many
other things there be, which they have
received to hold, *as* the washing of
cups, and pots, brazen vessels, and of
tables. 5 Then the Pharisees and
scribes asked him, Why walk not thy
disciples according to the tradition of
the elders, but eat bread with unwashen hands? 6 He answered and
said unto them, Well hath Esaias prophesied of you hypocrites, as it is
written, This people honoureth me
with *their* lips, but their heart is far
from me. 7 Howbeit in vain do they

worship me, teaching *for* doctrines
the commandments of men. 8 For
laying aside the commandments of
God, ye hold the tradition of men, *as*
the washing of pots and cups: and
many other such like things ye do.
9 And he said unto them, Full well
ye reject the commandment of God,
that ye may keep your own tradition.
10 For Moses said, Honour thy father and thy mother; and, Whoso
curseth father or mother, let him die
the death: 11 But ye say, If a man
shall say to his father or mother, *It*
is Corban, that is to say, a gift, by
whatsoever thou mightest be profited
by me; *he shall be free.* 12 And ye
suffer him no more to do ought for
his father or his mother; 13 Making
the word of God of none effect through
your tradition, which ye have delivered: and many such like things do
ye. 14 And when he had called all
the people *unto him,* he said unto
them, Hearken unto me every one *of*
you, and understand: 15 There is
nothing from without a man, that
entering into him can defile him: but
the things which come out of him,
those are they that defile the man.
16 If any man have ears to hear, let
him hear. 17 And when he was entered into the house from the people,
his disciples asked him concerning the
parable. 18 And he saith unto them,
Are ye so without understanding also?
Do ye not perceive, that whatsoever
thing from without entereth into the
man, *it* cannot defile him; 19 Because
it entereth not into his heart, but
into the belly, and goeth out into the
draught, purging all meats? 20 And
he said, That which cometh out of
the man, that defileth the man. 21
For from within, out of the heart of
men, proceed evil thoughts, adulteries,
fornications, murders, 22 Thefts,
covetousness, wickedness, deceit, lasciviousness, an evil eye, blasphemy,
pride, foolishness: 23 All these evil
things come from within, and defile
the man.

One great design of Christ's coming, was, to set aside the ceremonial law which God made, and to put an end to it; to make way for which he begins with the ceremonial law which men had made, and added to the law of God's making, and discharges his disciples from the obligation of that; which here he doth fully, upon occasion of the offence which the Pharisees took at them for the violation of it. These Pharisees and scribes with whom he had this argument, are said to *come from Jerusalem* down to Galilee—fourscore or a hundred miles, to pick quarrels with our Saviour there, where they supposed him to have the greatest interest and reputation. Had they come so far to be taught by him, their zeal had been commendable; but to come so far to oppose him, and to check the progress of his gospel, was great wickedness. It should seem that the scribes and Pharisees at Jerusalem pretended not only to a pre-eminence above, but to an authority over, the country clergy, and therefore kept up their visitations and sent inquisitors among them, as they did to John when he appeared, John i. 19.

Now in this passage we may observe,

I. What the tradition of the elders was: by it all were enjoined to *wash their hands* before meat; a cleanly custom, and no harm in it; and yet as such to be over-nice in it discovers too great a care about the body, which is *of the earth;* but they placed religion in it, and would not leave it indifferent, as it was in its own nature; people were at their liberty to do it or not to do it; but they interposed their authority, and commanded all to do it upon pain of excommunication; this they kept up as a *tradition of the elders.* The Papists pretend to a zeal for the authority and antiquity of the church and its canons, and talk much of councils and fathers, when really it is nothing but a zeal for their own wealth, interest, and dominion, that governs them; and so it was with the Pharisees.

We have here an account of the practice of the Pharisees and *all the Jews, v.* 3, 4. 1. They *washed their hands oft;* they washed them, πυγμῇ; the critics find a great deal of work about that word, some making it to denote the frequency of their washing (so we render it); others think it signifies the pains they took in washing their hands; they washed with great care, they washed their hands *to their wrists* (so some); they lifted up their hands when they were wet, that the water might *run to their elbows.* 2. They particularly washed before they *ate bread;* that is, before they sat down to a solemn meal; for that was the rule; they must be sure to wash before they ate the bread on which they begged a blessing. "Whosoever eats the bread over which they recite the benediction, *Blessed be he that produceth bread,* must wash his hands before and after," or else he was thought to be defiled. 3. They took special care, when they came in *from the markets,* to wash their hands; from the *judgment-halls,* so some; it signifies any place of concourse where there were people of all sorts, and, it might be supposed, some heathen or Jews under a ceremonial pollution, by coming near to whom they thought themselves polluted; saying, *Stand by thyself, come not near me, I am holier than thou,* Isa. lxv. 5. They say, The rule of the rabbies was—That, if they washed their hands well in the morning, the first thing they did, it would serve for all day, provided they kept alone; but, if they went into company, they must not, at their return, either eat or pray till they had washed their hands; thus the elders gained a reputation among the people for sanctity, and thus they exercised and kept up an authority over their consciences. 4. They added to this the washing of *cups,* and *pots,* and *brazen vessels,* which they suspected had been made use of by heathens, or persons polluted; nay, and the very *tables* on which they ate their meat. There were many cases in which, by the law of Moses, washings were appointed; but they *added* to them, and enforced the observation of their own impositions as much as of God's institutions.

II. What the practice of Christ's disciples was; they knew what the law was, and the common usage; but they understood themselves so well that they would not be bound up by it: they ate bread with *defiled,* that is, with *unwashen, hands, v.* 2. Eating with *unwashen hands* they called eating with *defiled* hands; thus men keep up their superstitious vanities by putting every thing into an ill name that contradicts them. The disciples knew (it is probable) that the Pharisees had their eye upon them, and yet they would not humour them by a compliance with their traditions, but took their liberty as at other times, and ate bread with *unwashen* hands; and herein *their righteousness,* however it might seem to come short, did really *exceed, that of the scribes and Pharisees,* Matt. v. 20.

III. The offence which the Pharisees took at this; They *found fault* (*v.* 2); they censured them as profane, and men of a loose conversation, or rather as men that would not submit to the power of the church, to decree rites and ceremonies, and were therefore rebellious, factious, and schismatical. They brought a complaint against them to their Master, expecting that he should check them, and order them to conform; for they that are fond of their own inventions and impositions, are commonly ready to appeal to Christ, as if he should countenance them, and as if his authority must interpose for the enforcing of them, and the rebuking of those that do not comply with them. They do not ask, Why do not thy disciples *do as we do?* (Though that was what they meant, coveting to make themselves the standard.) But, Why do not they *walk according to the tradition of the elders? v.* 5. To which it was easy to answer, that, by receiving the doctrine of Christ, they had *more understanding than all their teachers,* yea *more than the ancients,* Ps. cxix. 99, 100.

IV. Christ's vindication of them; in which,

1. He argues with the Pharisees concerning the authority by which this ceremony was imposed; and *they* were the fittest to be discoursed with concerning that, who were the great sticklers for it: but this he did not speak of publicly to the multitude (as appears by his *calling the people* to him, *v.* 14) lest he should have seemed to stir them up to faction and discontent at their governors; but addressed it as a reproof to the persons concerned: for the rule is, *Suum cuique—Let every one have his own.*

(1.) He reproves them for their hypocrisy in pretending to honour God, when really they had no such design in their religious observances (*v.* 6, 7); *They honour me with their lips,* they pretend it is for the glory of God that they impose those things, to distinguish themselves from the heathen; but really *their heart is far from God,* and is governed by nothing but ambition and covetousness. They would be thought hereby to appropriate themselves as a holy people to the Lord their God, when really it is the furthest thing in their thought. They rested in the outside of all their religious exercises, and their hearts were not right with God in them, and this was worshipping God in vain; for neither was he pleased with such sham-devotions, nor were they profited by them.

(2.) He reproves them for placing religion in the inventions and injunctions of their elders and rulers; They *taught for doctrines the traditions of men.* When they should have been pressing upon people the great principles of religion, they were enforcing the canons of their church, and judged of people's being Jews or no, according as they did, or did not, conform to them, without any consideration had, whether they lived in obedience to God's laws or no. It was true, there were *divers washings* imposed by the law of Moses (Heb. ix. 10), which were intended to signify that inward purification of the heart from worldly fleshly lusts, which God requires as absolutely necessary to our communion with him; but, instead of providing the substance, they presumptuously added to the ceremony, and were very nice in *washing pots and cups;* and observe, he adds, *Many other such like things ye do, v.* 8. Note, Superstition is an endless thing. If one human invention and institution be admitted, though seemingly ever so innocent, as this of washing hands, *behold, a troop comes,* a door is opened for *many other such things.*

(3.) He reproves them for *laying aside the commandment of God,* and overlooking that, not urging that in their preaching, and in their discipline conniving at the violation of that, as if that were no longer of force, *v.* 8. Note, It is the mischief of impositions, that too often they who are zealous for them, have little zeal for the essential duties of religion, but can contentedly see them laid aside. Nay, they *rejected the commandment of God, v.* 9. *Ye do fairly disannul and abolish the commandment of God;* and even *by* your traditions *make the word of God of no effect, v.* 13. God's statutes shall not only *lie forgotten,* as antiquated obsolete laws, but they shall, in effect, *stand repealed,* that their traditions may take place. They were entrusted to expound the law, and to enforce it; and, under pretence of using that power, they violated the law, and dissolved the bonds of it; destroying the text with the comment.

This he gives them a particular instance of, and a flagrant one—God commanded children to *honour their parents,* not only by the law of Moses, but, antecedent to that, by the law of nature; and whoso *revileth,* or *speaketh evil of,* father or mother, *let him die the death, v.* 10. Hence it is easy to infer, that it is the duty of children, if their parents be poor, to relieve them, according to their ability; and if those children are worthy to die, that curse their parents, much more those that starve them. But if a man will but conform himself in all points to the tradition of the elders, they will find him out an expedient by which he may be discharged from this obligation, *v.* 11. If his parents be in want. and he has wherewithal to help them, but has no mind to do it, let him swear by the *Corban,* that is, by the *gold of the temple,* and the *gift upon the altar,* that his parents shall not be profited by him, that he will not relieve them; and, if they ask any thing of him, let him tell them this, and it is enough; as if by the obligation of this wicked vow he had discharged himself from the obligation of God's holy law; thus Dr. Hammond understands it: and it is said to be an ancient canon of the rabbin, That vows take place in things commanded by the law, as well as in things indifferent; so that, if a man make a vow which cannot be ratified without breaking a commandment, the vow must be ratified, and the commandment violated; so Dr. Whitby. Such doctrine as this the Papists teach, discharging children from all obligation to their parents by their monastic vows, and their entrance into religion, as they call it. He concludes, *And many such like things do ye.* Where will men stop, when once they have made the word of God give way to their tradition? These eager imposers of such ceremonies, at first only *made light* of God's commandments *in comparison* with their traditions, but afterward *made void* God's commandments, if they stood *in competition* with them. All this, in effect, Isaiah prophesied of them; what he said of the hypocrites of his own day, was applicable to the scribes and Pharisees, *v.* 6. Note, When we see, and complain of, the wickedness of the present times, yet we do not *enquire wisely of that matter,* if we say that all *the former days were better than these,* Eccl. vii. 10. The worst of hypocrites and evil doers have had their predecessors.

2. He instructs the people concerning the principles upon which this ceremony was grounded. It was requisite that this part of his discourse should be public, for it related to daily practice, and was designed to rectify a great mistake which the people were led into by their elders; he therefore *called the people unto him* (*v.* 14), and bid them *hear and understand.* Note, It is not enough for the common people to *hear,* but they must *understand* what they hear. When Christ would run down the tradition of the Pharisees about washing before meat, he strikes at the opinion which was the root of it. Note, Corrupt customs are best cured by rectifying corrupt notions.

Now that which he goes about to set them right in, is, what the pollution is, which we are in danger of being damaged by, *v.* 15. (1.) Not by the *meat we eat,* though it be eaten with unwashen hands; that is but from without, and goes through a man. But, (2.) It is by the breaking out of the corruption that is in our hearts; the mind and conscience are defiled, guilt is contracted, and we become odious in the sight of God by that which *comes out* of us; our wicked thoughts and affections, words and actions, these defile us, and these only. Our care must therefore be, to *wash our heart from wickedness.*

3. He gives his disciples, in private, an explication of the instructions he gave the people. They *asked* him, when they had him by himself, *concerning the parable* (*v.* 17); for to them, it seems, it was a parable. Now, in answer to their enquiry, (1.) He reproves their dulness; "*Are ye so without understanding also?* Are ye dull *also,* as dull as the people that *cannot* understand, as dull as the Pharisees that *will not?* Are ye *so* dull?" He doth not expect they should understand every thing; "But are ye so weak as not to understand *this?*" (2.) He explains this truth to them, that they might *perceive* it, and then they would *believe* it, for it carried its own evidence along with it. Some truths prove themselves, if they be but rightly explained and apprehended. If we understand the spiritual nature of God and of his law, and what it is that is offensive to him, and disfits us for communion with him, we shall soon perceive, [1.] That that which we eat and drink cannot defile us, so as to call for any religious washing; it *goes into the stomach,* and passes the several digestions and secretions that nature has appointed, and what there may be in it that is defiling is voided and gone; *meats for the belly, and the belly for meats,* but *God shall destroy both it and them.* But, [2.] It is that which *comes out from* the heart, the corrupt heart, that defiles us. As by the ceremonial law, whatsoever (almost) comes out of a man, defiles him (Lev. xv. 2; Deut. xxiii. 13), so what comes out from the *mind* of a man is that which defiles him before God, and calls for a religious washing (*v.* 21); *From within, out*

of the heart of men, which they boast of the *goodness* of, and think is the best part of them, thence that which defiles proceeds, thence comes all the mischief. As a corrupt fountain sends forth corrupt streams, so doth a corrupt heart send forth corrupt reasonings, corrupt appetites and passions, and all those wicked words and actions which are produced by them. Divers particulars are specified, as in Matthew; we had one there, which is not here, and that is, *false witness-bearing;* but *seven* are mentioned here, to be added to those we had there. *First, Covetousnesses,* for it is plural; πλεονεξίαι—*immoderate desires* of more of the wealth of the world, and the gratifications of sense, and still more, still crying, *Give, give.* Hence we read of a *heart exercised with covetous practices,* 2 Pet. ii. 14. *Secondly, Wickedness*—πονηρίαι; malice, hatred, and ill-will, a desire to do mischief, and a delight in mischief done. *Thirdly, Deceit;* which is wickedness covered and disguised, that it may be the more securely and effectually committed. *Fourthly, Lasciviousness;* that filthiness and foolish talking which the apostle condemns; the eye full of adultery, and all wanton dalliances. *Fifthly,* The *evil eye;* the envious eye, and the covetous eye, grudging others the good we give them, or do for them (Prov. xxiii. 6), or grieving at the good they do or enjoy. *Sixthly, Pride*—ὑπερηφανία; exalting ourselves in our own conceit above others, and looking down with scorn and contempt upon others. *Seventhly, Foolishness*—ἀφροσύνη; imprudence, inconsideration; some understand it especially of vainglorious boasting, which St. Paul calls *foolishness* (2 Cor. xi. 1, 19), because it is here joined with *pride;* I rather take it for that rashness in speaking and acting, which is the cause of so much evil. *Ill-thinking* is put first, as that which is the spring of all our commissions, and *unthinking* put last, as that which is the spring of all our omissions. Of all these he concludes (*v.* 23), 1. That they *come from within,* from the corrupt nature, the carnal mind, the evil treasure in the heart; justly is it said, that the *inward part is very wickedness,* it must needs be so, when all this comes from within. 2. That they *defile the man;* they render a man unfit for communion with God, they bring a stain upon the conscience; and, if not mortified and rooted out, will shut men out of the new Jerusalem, into which no *unclean thing shall enter.*

24 And from thence he arose, and
went into the borders of Tyre and
Sidon, and entered into a house,
and would have no man know *it:* but
he could not be hid. 25 For a *certain*
woman, whose young daughter had an
unclean spirit, heard of him, and came
and fell at his feet: 26 The woman
was a Greek, a Syrophenician by nation; and she besought him that he
would cast forth the devil out of her
daughter. 27 But Jesus said unto
her, Let the children first be filled:
for it is not meet to take the children's
bread, and to cast *it* unto the dogs.
28 And she answered and said unto
him, Yes, Lord: yet the dogs under
the table eat of the children's crumbs.
29 And he said unto her, For this
saying go thy way; the devil is gone
out of thy daughter. 30 And when
she was come to her house, she found
the devil gone out, and her daughter
laid upon the bed.

See here, I. How *humbly* Christ was pleased to *conceal himself.* Never man was so cried up as he was in Galilee, and therefore, to teach us, though not to decline any opportunity of doing good, yet not to be fond of popular applause, he arose from thence, and *went into the borders* of Tyre and Sidon, where he was little known; and there he entered, not into a synagogue, or place of concourse, but *into a* private *house,* and he *would have no man to know it;* because it was foretold concerning him, *He shall not strive nor cry, neither shall his voice be heard in the streets.* Not but that he was willing to preach and heal here as well as in other places, but for this he would be sought unto. Note, As there is a time to *appear,* so there is a time to *retire.* Or, he would not be known, because he was upon the borders of Tyre and Sidon, among Gentiles, to whom he would not be so forward to show himself as to the tribes of Israel, whose glory he was to be.

II. How *graciously* he was pleased to *manifest himself,* notwithstanding. Though he would not carry a harvest of miraculous cures into those parts, yet, it should seem, he came on purpose to drop a handful, to let fall this one which we have here an account of. *He could not be hid;* for, though a candle may be put under a bushel, the sun cannot. Christ was too well known to be long *incognito—hid,* any where; the oil of gladness which he was anointed with, like ointment of the right hand, would betray itself, and fill the house with its odours. Those that had only heard his fame, could not converse with him, but they would soon say, "This must be Jesus." Now observe,

1. The application made to him by a poor woman in distress and trouble. She was a Gentile, a Greek, *a stranger to the commonwealth of Israel, an alien to the covenant of promise;* she was by extraction a Syrophenician, and not in any degree proselyted to the Jewish religion; she had a *daughter,* a *young* daughter, that was possessed *with the devil.* How many and grievous are the cala-

mities that young children are subject to! Her address was, (1.) Very humble, pressing, and importunate; *She heard of him*, and *came, and fell at his feet*. Note, Those that would obtain mercy from Christ, must throw themselves at his feet; must refer themselves to him, humble themselves before him, and give up themselves to be ruled by him. Christ never put any from him, that fell at his feet, which a poor trembling soul may do, that has not boldness and confidence to throw itself into his arms. (2.) It was very particular; she tells him what she wanted. Christ gave poor supplicants leave to be thus free with him; she besought him that he would *cast forth the devil out of her daughter*, *v.* 26. Note, The greatest blessing we can ask of Christ for our children is, that he would break the power of Satan, that is, the power of sin, in their souls; and particularly, that he would cast forth the *unclean spirit*, that they may be temples of the Holy Ghost, and he may dwell in them.

2. The discouragement he gave to this address (*v.* 27); He said unto her, "*Let the children first be filled;* let the Jews have all the miracles wrought for them, that they have occasion for, who are in a particular manner God's chosen people; and let not that which was intended for them, be thrown to those who are not of God's family, and who have not that knowledge of him, and interest in him, which they have, and who are as *dogs in comparison of them*, vile and profane, and who are as *dogs to them*, snarling at them, spiteful toward them, and ready to worry them." Note, Where Christ knows the faith of poor supplicants to be strong, he sometimes delights to try it, and put it to the stretch. But his saying, *Let the children first be filled*, intimates that there was mercy in reserve for the Gentiles, and not far off; for the Jews began already to be surfeited with the gospel of Christ, and some of them had desired him to *depart out of their coasts*. The children begin to play with their meat, and their leavings, their loathings, would be a feast for the Gentiles. The apostles went by this rule, *Let the children first be filled*, let the Jews have the first offer; and if their full souls loathe this honeycomb, *Lo, we turn to the Gentiles!*

3. The turn she gave to this word of Christ, which made against her, and her improvement of it, to make for her, *v.* 28. She said, "*Yes, Lord*, I own it is true that the *children's bread* ought not to be cast to the dogs; but they were never denied the *crumbs* of that bread, nay it belongs to them, and they are allowed a place *under the table*, that they may be ready to receive them. I ask not for a *loaf*, no, nor for a *morsel*, only for a *crumb;* do not refuse me that." This she speaks, not as undervaluing the mercy, or making light of it in itself, but magnifying the abundance of miraculous cures with which she heard the Jews were feasted, in comparison with which a single cure was but as a crumb. Gentiles do not come in crowds, as the Jews do; *I come alone*. Perhaps she had heard of Christ's feeding five thousand lately at once, after which, even when they had gathered up the fragments, there could not but be some crumbs left for the dogs.

4. The grant Christ thereupon made of her request. Is she thus humble, thus earnest? For *this saying, Go thy way*, thou shalt have what thou camest for, *the devil is gone out of thy daughter*, *v.* 29. This encourages us to *pray* and not to *faint*, to continue instant in prayer, not doubting but to prevail at last; the vision at the end shall *speak, and not lie*. Christ's saying that it *was done*, did it effectually, as at other times his saying, *Let it be done;* for (*v.* 30) she *came to her house*, depending upon the word of Christ, that her daughter was healed, and so she *found it*, the *devil was gone out*. Note, Christ can conquer Satan at a distance; and it was not only when the demoniacs *saw him*, that they yielded to his power (as *ch.* iii. 11), but when they saw him not, for the Spirit of the Lord is not *bound*, nor *bounded*. She found her daughter not in any toss or agitation, but very quietly *laid on the bed*, and reposing herself; waiting for her mother's return, to rejoice with her, that she was so *finely well*.

31 And again, departing from the
coasts of Tyre and Sidon, he came
unto the sea of Galilee, through the
midst of the coasts of Decapolis. 32
And they bring unto him one that
was deaf, and had an impediment in
his speech; and they beseech him to
put his hand upon him. 33 And he
took him aside from the multitude,
and put his fingers into his ears, and
he spit, and touched his tongue; 34
And looking up to heaven, he sighed,
and saith unto him, Ephphatha, that
is, Be opened. 35 And straightway
his ears were opened, and the string
of his tongue was loosed, and he spake
plain. 36 And he charged them that
they should tell no man: but the
more he charged them, so much the
more a great deal they published *it;*
37 And were beyond measure astonished, saying, He hath done all things
well: he maketh both the deaf to
hear, and the dumb to speak.

Our Lord Jesus seldom staid long in a place, for he knew where his work lay, and attended the changes of it. When he had cured the woman of Canaan's daughter, he had done what he had to do in that place, and therefore presently left those parts, and returned *to the sea of Galilee,* whereabout his usual residence was; yet he did not come directly thither, but fetched a compass *through the midst of the coasts of Decapolis,* which lay mostly on the other side Jordan; such long walks did our Lord Jesus take, when he *went about doing good.*

Now here we have the story of a cure that Christ wrought, which is not recorded by any other of the evangelists; it is of one that was *deaf* and *dumb.*

I. His case was sad, *v.* 32. There were those that brought to him one that was *deaf;* some think, born deaf, and then he must be dumb of course; others think that by some distemper or disaster he was become deaf, or, at least, thick of hearing; and he had an *impediment in his speech.* He was *μογιλάλος*; some think that he was quite dumb; others, that he could not speak but with great difficulty to himself, and so as scarcely to be understood by those that heard him. He was *tongue-tied,* so that he was perfectly unfit for conversation, and deprived both of the pleasure and of the profit of it; he had not the satisfaction either of hearing other people talk, or of telling his own mind. Let us take occasion from hence to give thanks to God for preserving to us the sense of hearing, especially that we may be capable of hearing the word of God; and the faculty of speech, epecially that we may be capable of speaking God's praises; and let us look with compassion upon those that are deaf or dumb, and treat them with great tenderness. They that brought this poor man to Christ, besought him that he would *put his hand upon him,* as the prophets did upon those whom they *blessed* in the name of the Lord. It is not said, They besought him to *cure him,* but to *put his hand upon him,* to take cognizance of his case, and put forth his power to do to him as he pleased.

II. His cure was solemn, and some of the circumstances of it were singular.

1. Christ *took him aside from the multitude, v.* 33. Ordinarily, he wrought his miracles publicly before all the people, to show that they would bear the strictest scrutiny and inspection; but this he did privately, to show that he did not seek his own glory, and to teach us to avoid every thing that savours of ostentation. Let us learn of Christ to be humble, and to do good where no eye sees, but his that is *all eye.*

2. He used more significant actions, in the doing of this cure, than usual. (1.) He *put his fingers into his ears,* as if he would *syringe* them, and fetch out that which stopped them up. (2.) He spit upon his own finger, and then *touched his tongue,* as if he would moisten his mouth, and so loosen that with which his tongue was tied; these were no causes that could in the least contribute to his cure, but only signs of the exerting of that power which Christ had in himself to cure him, for the encouraging of his faith, and theirs that brought him. The application was all from himself, it was his own *fingers* that he put into his ears, and his own *spittle* that he put upon his tongue; for he alone heals.

3. He *looked up to heaven,* to give his Father the praise of what he did; for he sought his praise, and did his will, and, as Mediator, acted in dependence on him, and with an eye to him. Thus he signified that it was by a divine power, a power he had as the Lord from heaven, and brought with him thence, that he did this; for the *hearing ear* and the *seeing eye* the *Lord has made,* and can remake even *both of them.* He also hereby directed his patient who could *see,* though he could not *hear,* to look up to heaven for relief. Moses with his stammering tongue is directed to look that way (Exod. iv. 11); *Who hath made man's mouth? Or who maketh the dumb or deaf, or the seeing or the blind? Have not I the Lord?*

4. He sighed; not as if he found any difficulty in working this miracle, or obtaining power to do it from his Father; but thus he expressed his pity for the miseries of human life, and his sympathy with the afflicted in their afflictions, as one that was himself *touched with the feeling of their infirmities.* And as to this man, he *sighed,* not because he was loth to do him this kindness, or did it with reluctancy; but because of the many temptations which he would be exposed to, and the sins he would be in danger of, the tongue-sins, after the restoring of his speech to him, which before he was free from. He had better be *tongue-tied* still, unless he have grace to *keep his mouth as with a bridle,* Ps. xxxix. 1.

5. He said, *Ephphatha;* that is, *Be opened.* This was nothing that looked like *spell* or *charm,* such as they used, who had *familiar spirits,* who *peeped and muttered,* Isa. viii. 19. Christ speaks as one having authority, and power went along with the word. *Be opened,* served both parts of the cure; "Let the *ears* be *opened,* let the *lips* be *opened,* let him hear and speak freely, and let the restraint be taken off;" and the effect was answerable (*v.* 35); *Straightway his ears were opened, and the string of his tongue was loosed,* and all was well: and happy he who, as soon as he had his hearing and speech, had the blessed Jesus so near him, to converse with.

Now this cure was, (1.) A proof of Christ's being the Messiah; for it was foretold that by his power the *ears of the deaf should be unstopped,* and the *tongue of the dumb* should be made to *sing,* Isa. xxxv. 5, 6. (2.) It was a specimen of the operations of his gospel upon the minds of men. The great command of the gospel, and grace of Christ to poor sinners, is *Ephphatha—Be opened.* Grotius applies it thus, that the internal impediments of the mind are removed by the Spirit of Christ, as those bodily impediments were by the word of his power. He *opens the heart.*

as he did Lydia's, and thereby opens the ear to receive the word of God, and opens the mouth in prayer and praises.

6. He ordered it to be kept very private, but it was made very public. (1.) It was his humility, that he *charged them they should tell no man, v.* 36. Most men will proclaim their own goodness, or, at least, desire that others should proclaim it; but Christ, though he was himself in no danger of being puffed up with it, knowing that we are, would thus set us an example of self-denial, as in other things, so especially in praise and applause. We should take pleasure in doing good, but not in its being known. (2.) It was their zeal, that, though he charged them to say nothing of it, yet they published it, before Christ would have had it published. But they meant honestly, and therefore it is to be reckoned rather an act of indiscretion than an act of disobedience, *v.* 36. But they that told it, and they that heard it, were *beyond measure astonished, ὑπερπερισσῶς—more than above measure;* they were exceedingly affected with it, and this was said by every body, it was the common verdict, *He hath done all things well* (*v.* 37); whereas there were those that hated and persecuted him as an *evil-doer,* they are ready to witness for him, not only that he has done no evil, but that he has done a great deal of good, and has done it well, modestly and humbly, and very devoutly, and all gratis, *without money and without price,* which added much to the lustre of his good works. He *maketh both the deaf to hear, and the dumb to speak;* and that is *well,* it is well for them, it is well for their relations, to whom they had been a burthen; and therefore *they* are inexcusable who speak ill of him.

CHAP. VIII.

In this chapter, we have, I. Christ's miraculous feeding of four thousand with seven loaves and a few small fishes, ver. 1—9. II. His refusing to give the Pharisees a sign from heaven, ver. 10—13. III. His cautioning his disciples to take heed of the leaven of Pharisaism and Herodianism, ver. 14—21. IV. His giving of sight to a blind man at Bethsaida, ver. 22—26. V. Peter's confession of him, ver. 27—30. VI. The notice he gave his disciples of his own approaching sufferings (ver. 31—33), and the warning he gave them to prepare for sufferings likewise, ver. 34—38.

IN those days the multitude being
very great, and having nothing to
eat, Jesus called his disciples *unto*
him, and saith unto them, 2 I have
compassion on the multitude, because
they have now been with me three
days, and have nothing to eat: 3 And
if I send them away fasting to their
own houses, they will faint by the
way: for divers of them came from
far. 4 And his disciples answered
him, From whence can a man satisfy
these *men* with bread here in the wilderness? 5 And he asked them, How
many loaves have ye? And they said,
Seven. 6 And he commanded the
people to sit down on the ground:
and he took the seven loaves, and gave
thanks, and brake, and gave to his
disciples to set before *them;* and they
did set *them* before the people. 7
And they had a few small fishes: and
he blessed, and commanded to set
them also before *them.* 8 So they
did eat, and were filled: and they
took up of the broken *meat* that was
left seven baskets. 9 And they that
had eaten were about four thousand:
and he sent them away.

We had the story of a miracle very like this before, in this gospel (*ch.* vi. 35), and of this same miracle (Matt. xv. 32), and here is little or no addition or alteration as to the circumstances. Yet observe,

1. That our Lord Jesus was greatly followed; *The multitude was very great* (*v.* 1); notwithstanding the wicked arts of the scribes and Pharisees to blemish him, and to blast his interest, the common people, who had more honesty, and therefore more true wisdom, than their leaders, kept up their high thoughts of him. We may suppose that this multitude were generally of the meaner sort of people, with such Christ conversed, and was familiar; for thus he humbled himself, and made himself of no reputation, and thus encouraged the meanest to come to him for life and grace.

2. Those that followed him, underwent a great deal of difficulty in following him; *They were with him three days, and had nothing to eat,* that was hard service. Never let the Pharisee say, that *Christ's disciples fast not.* There were those, probably, that brought some food with them from home; but by this time it was all spent, and they had a great way home; and yet they *continued* with Christ, and did not speak of leaving him till he spoke of dismissing them. Note, True zeal makes nothing of hardships in the way of duty. They that have a full feast for their souls may be content with slender provision for their bodies. It was an old saying among the Puritans, *Brown bread and the gospel are good fare.*

3. As Christ has a *compassion* for all that are in wants and straits, so he has a special *concern* for those that are reduced to straits by their zeal and diligence in attending on him. Christ said, *I have compassion on the multitude.* Whom the proud Pharisees looked upon with disdain, the humble Jesus looked upon with pity and tenderness; and thus must we *honour all men.* But that which he chiefly considers, is, *They have been with me three days, and have nothing to eat.* Whatever losses we sustain, or hardships we go through, for Christ's sake, and in love to him, he will take care that they shall be

made up to us one way or other. *They that seek the Lord, shall not* long *want any good thing,* Ps. xxxiv. 10. Observe with what sympathy Christ saith (*v.* 3), *If I send them away fasting to their own houses, they will faint by the way,* for hunger. Christ knows and considers our frame; and he is *for the body,* if with it we glorify him, *verily we shall be fed.* He considered that *many of them came from far,* and had a great way home. When we see *multitudes* attending upon the word preached, it is comfortable to think that Christ knows whence they all come, though we do not. *I know thy works, and where thou dwellest,* Rev. ii. 13. Christ would by no means have them go home fasting, for it is not his manner to send those *empty* away from him, that in a right manner attend on him.

4. The doubts of Christians are sometimes made to work for the magnifying of the power of Christ. The disciples could not imagine whence so many men should be *satisfied with bread* here in this wilderness, *v.* 4. That therefore must needs be *wonderful,* and appear so much the more so, which the disciples looked upon as *impossible.*

5. Christ's time to act for the relief of his people, is, when things are brought to the last extremity; when they were ready to *faint,* Christ provided for them. That he might not invite them to follow him for the *loaves,* he did not supply them but when they were utterly reduced, and then he *sent them away.*

6. The bounty of Christ is inexhaustible, and, to evidence that, Christ *repeated* this miracle, to show that he is still the same for the succour and supply of his people that attend upon him. His favours are renewed, as our wants and necessities are. In the former miracle, Christ used all the bread he had, which was *five loaves,* and fed all the guests he had, which were *five thousand,* and so he did now; though he might have said, "If five loaves would feed five thousand, four may feed four thousand;" he took all the seven loaves, and fed with them the four thousand; for he would teach us to take things as they are, and accommodate ourselves to them; to use what we have, and make the best of that which is. Here it was, as in the dispensing of the manna, *He that gathered much had nothing over, and he that gathered little had no lack.*

7. In our Father's house, in our Master's house, *there is bread enough, and to spare;* there is a fulness in Christ, which he communicates to all that passes through his hands; so that from it we receive, and *grace for grace,* John i. 16. Those need not fear wanting, that have Christ to live upon.

8. It is good for those that follow Christ, *to keep together;* these followers of Christ continued in a body, *four thousand* of them together, and Christ fed them all. Christ's sheep must abide by the flock, and go forth by their footsteps, and verily they shall be fed.

10 And straightway he entered into
a ship with his disciples, and came
into the parts of Dalmanutha. 11
And the Pharisees came forth, and
began to question with him, seeking
of him a sign from heaven, tempting
him. 12 And he sighed deeply in
his spirit, and saith, Why doth this
generation seek after a sign? verily I
say unto you, There shall no sign be
given unto this generation. 13 And
he left them, and entering into the ship
again departed to the other side. 14
Now *the disciples* had forgotten to
take bread, neither had they in the
ship with them more than one loaf. 15
And he charged them, saying, Take
heed, beware of the leaven of the
Pharisees, and *of* the leaven of Herod.
16 And they reasoned among themselves, saying, *It is* because we have
no bread. 17 And when Jesus knew
it, he saith unto them, Why reason
ye, because ye have no bread? perceive ye not yet, neither understand?
have ye your heart yet hardened?
18 Having eyes, see ye not? and
having ears, hear ye not? and do ye
not remember? 19 When I brake
the five loaves among five thousand,
how many baskets full of fragments
took ye up? They say unto him,
Twelve. 20 And when the seven
among four thousand, how many
baskets full of fragments took ye up?
And they said, Seven. 21 And he
said unto them, How is it that ye do
not understand?

Still Christ is upon motion; now he visits the parts of Dalmanutha, that no corner of the land of Israel might say that they had not had his presence with them. He came thither *by ship* (*v.* 10); but, meeting with occasions of dispute there, and not with opportunities of doing good, he *entered into the ship again* (*v.* 13), and came back. In these verses, we are told,

I. How he refused to gratify the Pharisees, who challenged him to give them a *sign from heaven.* They *came forth* on purpose to *question with him;* not to propose questions to him, that they might learn of him, but to cross question with him, that they might ensnare him.

1. They demanded of him a *sign from heaven,* as if the signs he gave them on earth, which were more familiar to them, and were more capable of being examined and enquired into, were not sufficient. There was a sign

from heaven at his baptism, in the descent of the dove, and the voice (Matt. iii. 16, 17); it was public enough; and if they had attended John's baptism as they ought to have done, they might themselves have seen it. Afterward, when he was nailed to the cross, they prescribed a new sign; *Let him come down from the cross, and we will believe him;* thus obstinate infidelity will still have something to say, though ever so unreasonable. They demanded this sign, *tempting him;* not in hopes that he would give it them, that they might be satisfied, but in hopes that he would not, that they might imagine themselves to have a pretence for their infidelity.

2. He denied them their demand; He *sighed deeply in his spirit, v.* 12. He *groaned* (so some), being grieved for the *hardness of their hearts,* and the little influence that his preaching and miracles had had upon them. Note, The infidelity of those that have long enjoyed the means of conviction, is a great grief to the Lord Jesus; it troubles him, that sinners should thus stand in their own light, and put a bar in their own door. (1.) He expostulates with them upon this demand; "*Why doth this generation seek after a sign;* this generation, that is so unworthy to have the gospel brought to it, and to have any sign accompanying it; *this generation,* that so greedily swallows the traditions of the elders, without the confirmation of any sign at all; *this generation,* into which, by the calculating of the times prefixed in the Old Testament, they might easily perceive that the coming of the Messiah must fall; *this generation,* that has had such plenty of sensible and merciful signs given them in the cure of their sick? What an absurdity is it for them to desire a sign!" (2.) He refuses to answer their demand; *Verily, I say unto you, there shall no sign,* no such sign, *be given to this generation.* When God spoke to particular persons in a particular case, out of the road of his common dispensation, they were encouraged to ask a sign, as Gideon and Ahaz; but when he speaks in general to all, as in the law and gospel, sending each with their own evidence, it is presumption to prescribe other signs than what he has given. *Shall any teach God knowledge?* He denied them, and then *left them,* as men not fit to be talked with; if they will not be convinced, they shall not; leave them to their strong delusions.

II. How he warned his disciples against the leaven of the Pharisees and of Herod. Observe here,

1. What the caution was (*v.* 15); "*Take heed, beware,* lest ye partake of the *leaven of the Pharisees,* lest ye embrace the tradition of the elders, which they are so wedded to, lest ye be proud, and hypocritical, and ceremonious, like them." Matthew adds, *and of the Sadducees;* Mark adds, *and of Herod:* whence some gather, that Herod and his courtiers were generally Sadducees, that is, deists, men of no religion. Others give this sense, The Pharisees demanded a *sign from heaven;* and Herod was long *desirous* to see some miracle wrought by Christ (Luke xxiii. 8); such as he should prescribe, so that the leaven of both was the same; they were unsatisfied with the signs they had, and would have others of their own devising; "Take heed of *this leaven*" (saith Christ), "be convinced by the miracles ye have seen, and covet not to see more."

2. How they misunderstood this caution. It seems, at their putting to sea this time, they had *forgotten to take bread,* and *had not in their ship more than one loaf, v.* 14. When therefore Christ bid them *beware of the leaven of the Pharisees,* they understood it as an intimation to them, not to apply themselves to any of the Pharisees for relief, when they came to the other side, for they had lately been offended at them for eating with *unwashen hands.* They *reasoned among themselves,* what should be the meaning of this caution, and concluded, "*It is because we have no bread;* he saith this, to reproach us for being so careless as to go to sea, and go among strangers, with but one loaf of bread; he doth, in effect, tell us, we must be brought to *short allowance,* and must eat our bread by weight." They *reasoned it*—*διελογίζοντο,* they *disputed* about it; one said, "It was owing to you;" and the other said, "It was owing to you, that we are so ill provided for this voyage." Thus distrust of God makes Christ's disciples quarrel among themselves.

3. The reproof Christ gave them for their uneasiness in this matter, as it argued a disbelief of his power to supply them, notwithstanding the abundant experience they had had of it. The reproof is given with some warmth, for he knew their hearts, and knew they needed to be thus soundly chidden; "*Perceive ye not yet, neither understand,* that which you have had so many demonstrations of? *Have ye your hearts yet hardened,* so as that nothing will make any impression upon them, or bring them to compliance with your Master's designs? *Having eyes, see ye not* that which is plain before your eyes? *Having ears, hear ye not* that which you have been so often told? How strangely stupid and senseless are ye! *Do ye not remember* that which was done but the other day, *when I broke the five loaves among the five thousand,* and soon after, the *seven loaves among the four thousand?* Do ye not remember *how many baskets full ye took up* of the fragments?" Yes, they did remember, and could tell that they took up *twelve* baskets full one time, and *seven* another; "Why then," saith he, "*how is it that ye do not understand?* As if he that multiplied *five* loaves, and *seven,* could not multiply one." They seemed to suspect that that one was not matter enough to work upon, if he should have a mind to entertain his hearers a third

time: and if that was their thought, it was indeed a very senseless one, as if it were not all alike to the Lord, to save by many or few, and as easy to make one loaf to feed five thousand as five. It was therefore proper to remind them, not only of the sufficiency, but of the overplus, of the former meals; and justly were they chidden for not understanding what Christ therein designed, and what they from thence might have learned. Note, (1.) The experiences we have had of God's goodness to us in the way of duty, greatly aggravate our distrust of him, which is *therefore* very provoking to the Lord Jesus. (2.) Our *not understanding* of the true intent and meaning of God's favours to us, is equivalent to our not remembering of them. (3.) We are *therefore* overwhelmed with present cares and distrusts, because we do not *understand,* and remember, what we have known and seen of the power and goodness of our Lord Jesus. It would be a great support to us, to *consider the days of old,* and we are wanting both to God and ourselves if we do not. (4.) When we thus *forget the works of God,* and distrust him, we should chide ourselves severely for it, as Christ doth his disciples here; "Am I thus without understanding? How is it that my heart is thus hardened?"

22 And he cometh to Bethsaida;
and they bring a blind man unto him,
and besought him to touch him. 23
And he took the blind man by the
hand, and led him out of the town;
and when he had spit on his eyes,
and put his hands upon him, he asked
him if he saw aught. 24 And he
looked up, and said, I see men as trees,
walking. 25 After that he put *his*
hands again upon his eyes, and made
him look up: and he was restored,
and saw every man clearly. 26 And
he sent him away to his house, saying, Neither go into the town, nor tell
it to any in the town.

This cure is related only by this evangelist, and there is something singular in the circumstances.

I. Here is a *blind man* brought to Christ by his friends, with a desire that he would *touch him, v.* 22. Here appears the faith of those that brought him—they doubted not but that one touch of Christ's hand would recover him his sight; but the man himself showed not that earnestness for, or expectation of, a cure that other blind men did. If those that are spiritually blind, do not pray for themselves, yet let their friends and relations pray for them, that Christ would be pleased to *touch them.*

II. Here is Christ *leading* this blind man, *v.* 23. He did not bid his friends lead him, but (which bespeaks his wonderful condescension) he himself *took him by the hand, and led him,* to teach us to be as Job was, *eyes to the blind,* Job xxix. 15. Never had poor blind man such a Leader. He led him *out of the town.* Had he herein only designed privacy, he might have led him into a house, into an inner chamber, and have cured him there; but he intended hereby to upbraid Bethsaida with the *mighty works* that had *in vain* been done *in her* (Matt. xi. 21), and was telling her, in effect, she was unworthy to have any more done within her walls. Perhaps Christ took the blind man *out of the town,* that he might have a larger prospect in the *open fields,* to try his sight with, than he could have in the *close streets.*

III. Here is the cure of the blind man, by that blessed Oculist, who came into the world to *preach the recovering of sight to the blind* (Luke iv. 18), and to *give* what he *preached.* In this cure we may observe, 1. That Christ used a *sign;* he *spat on his eyes* (spat *into* them, so some), and *put his hand upon him.* He could have cured him, as he did others, with a word speaking, but thus he was pleased to assist his faith which was very weak, and to help him against his *unbelief.* And this spittle signified the *eye-salve* wherewith Christ anoints the eyes of those that are spiritually blind, Rev. iii. 18. 2. That the cure was wrought *gradually,* which was not usual in Christ's miracles. He *asked him if he saw aught, v.* 23. Let him tell what condition his sight was in, for the satisfaction of those about him. And he *looked up;* so far he *recovered his sight,* that he could open his eyes, and he said, *I see men as trees walking;* he could not distinguish men from trees, otherwise than that he could discern them to move. He had some glimmerings of sight, and betwixt him and the sky could perceive a man erect like a tree, but *could not discern the form thereof,* Job iv. 16. But, 3. It was soon completed; Christ never doeth *his work* by the halves, nor leaves it till he can say, *It is finished.* He *put his hands again upon his eyes,* to disperse the remaining darkness, and then bade him look up again, and he *saw every man clearly, v.* 25. Now Christ took this way, (1.) Because he would not *tie himself to a method,* but would show with what liberty he acted in all he did. He did not cure by *rote,* as I may say, and in a *road,* but *varied* as he thought fit. Providence gains the same end in different ways, that men may attend its motions with an *implicit faith.* (2.) Because it should be to the patient *according to his faith;* and perhaps this man's faith was at first very weak, but afterward gathered strength, and accordingly his cure was. Not that Christ always went by this rule, but thus he would sometimes put a rebuke upon those who came to him, doubting. (3.) Thus Christ would show how, and in what method, those are healed by his grace, who by nature are *spiritually blind;* at first, their knowledge is confused, they see *men as trees walking;* but, like the light of the morning, it *shines more and more to the perfect day*, and then they *see all things clearly*, Prov. iv. 18. Let us enquire then, if we *see aught* of those things which *faith* is the *substance* and *evidence* of; and if through grace we see *any thing* of them, we may hope that we shall see yet *more* and *more,* for Jesus Christ will *perfect* for ever those that are *sanctified.*

IV. The directions Christ gave the man he had cured, not to *tell it to any in the town of Bethsaida,* nor so much as to *go into the town,* where probably there were some expecting him to come back, who had seen Christ lead him out of the town, but, having been eye-witnesses of so many miracles, had not so much as the curiosity to follow him: let not those be gratified with the sight of him when he was cured, who would not show so much respect to Christ as to go a step out of the town, to see this cure wrought. Christ doth not forbid him to tell it to others, but he must not tell it to *any in the town.* Slighting Christ's favours is forfeiting them; and Christ will make those know the worth of their privileges by the want of them, that would not know them otherwise. Bethsaida, in the day of her visitation, would not know the things that belonged to her peace, and now they are *hid from her eyes.* They will not see, and therefore shall not see.

27 And Jesus went out, and his
disciples, into the towns of Cæsarea
Philippi: and by the way he asked
his disciples, saying unto them, Whom
do men say that I am? 28 And
they answered, John the Baptist: but
some *say*, Elias; and others, One of
the prophets. 29 And he saith unto
them, But whom say ye that I am?
And Peter answereth and saith unto
him, Thou art the Christ. 30 And
he charged them that they should tell
no man of him. 31 And he began
to teach them, that the Son of man
must suffer many things, and be rejected of the elders, and *of* the chief
priests, and scribes, and be killed, and
after three days rise again. 32 And
he spake that saying openly. And
Peter took him, and began to rebuke
him. 33 But when he had turned
about and looked upon his disciples,
he rebuked Peter, saying, Get thee
behind me, Satan: for thou savourest
not the things that be of God, but
the things that be of men. 34 And
when he had called the people *unto
him* with his disciples also, he said
unto them, Whosoever will come after
me, let him deny himself, and take up
his cross, and follow me. 35 For
whosoever will save his life shall lose
it; but whosoever shall lose his life
for my sake and the gospel's, the same
shall save it. 36 For what shall it
profit a man, if he shall gain the whole
world, and lose his own soul? 37 Or
what shall a man give in exchange for
his soul? 38 Whosoever therefore
shall be ashamed of me and my words
in this adulterous and sinful generation; of him also shall the Son of
man be ashamed, when he cometh in
the glory of his Father with the holy
angels.

We have read a great deal of the doctrine Christ preached, and the miracles he wrought, which were many, and strange, and well-attested, of various kinds, and wrought in several places, to the astonishment of the multitudes that were eye-witnesses of them. It is now time for us to pause a little, and to consider what these things mean; the wondrous works which Christ then forbade the publishing of, being recorded in these sacred writings, are thereby published to all the world, to us, to all ages; now what shall we think of them? Is the record of those things designed only for an amusement, or to furnish us with matter for discourse? No, certainly *these things are written, that we may believe that Jesus is the Christ the Son of God* (John xx. 31); and this discourse which Christ had with his disciples, will assist us in making the necessary reflections upon the miracles of Christ, and a right use of them. Three things we are here taught to infer from the miracles Christ wrought.

I. They *prove* that he is *the true Messiah,* the Son of God, and Saviour of the world: this the works he did witnessed concerning him; and this his disciples, who were the eye-witnesses of those works, here profess their belief of; which cannot but be a satisfaction to us in making the same inference from them.

1. Christ enquired of them what the sentiments of the people were concerning him; *Who do men say that I am? v.* 27. Note, Though it is a small thing for us to be judged of men, yet it may sometimes do us good to know what people say of us, not that we may seek our own glory, but that we may hear of our faults. Christ asked them, not that he might be informed, but that they might observe it themselves, and inform one another.

2. The account they gave him, was such as plainly intimated the *high opinion* the people had of him. Though they came short of the truth, yet they were convinced by his

miracles that he was an extraordinary person, sent from the invisible world with a divine commission. It is probable that they would have acknowledged him to be the Messiah, if they had not been possessed by their teachers with a notion that the Messiah must be a temporal Prince, appearing in external pomp and power, which the figure Christ made, would not comport with; yet (whatever the Pharisees said, whose copyhold was touched by the strictness and spirituality of his doctrine) none of the people said that he was a Deceiver, but some said that *he was John Baptist*, others *Elias*, others *one of the prophets*, *v.* 28. All agreed that he was one *risen from the dead.*

3. The account they gave him of their own sentiments concerning him, intimated their abundant satisfaction in him, and in their having left all to follow him, which now, after some time of trial, they see no reason to repent; *But whom say ye that I am?* To this they have an answer ready, *Thou art the Christ*, the Messiah often promised, and long expected, *v.* 29. To be a Christian indeed, is, sincerely to believe that Jesus is the Christ, and to act accordingly; and that he is so, plainly appears by his wondrous works. This they knew, and must shortly publish and maintain; but for the present they must keep it secret (*v.* 30), till the proof of it was completed, and they were completely qualified to maintain it, by the pouring out of the Holy Ghost; and then *let all the house of Israel know assuredly that God has made this same Jesus, whom ye crucified, both Lord and Christ*, Acts ii. 36.

II. These miracles of Christ *take off the offence of the cross*, and assure us that Christ was, in it, not conquered, but a Conqueror. Now that the disciples are convinced that Jesus is the Christ, they may bear to hear of his sufferings, which Christ now *begins* to give them notice of, *v.* 31.

1. Christ *taught* his disciples that he must *suffer many things*, Though they had got over the vulgar error of the Messiah's being a temporal Prince, so far as to believe their Master to be the Messiah, notwithstanding his present meanness, yet still they retained it, so far as to expect that he would *shortly* appear in outward pomp and grandeur, and *restore the kingdom to Israel;* and therefore, to rectify that mistake, Christ here gives them a prospect of the contrary, that he must be *rejected of the elders, and the chief priests*, and *the scribes*, who, they expected, should be brought to own and prefer him; that, instead of being crowned, *he must be killed*, he must be crucified, and *after three days he must rise again* to a heavenly life, and to be *no more in this world.* This he spoke *openly* *v.* 32), παῤῥησία. He said it freely and plainly, and did not wrap it up in ambiguous expressions. The disciples might easily understand it, if they had not been very much under the power of prejudice: or, it intimates that he spoke it cheerfully and without any terror, and would have them to hear it so: he spoke that saying *boldly*, as one that not only knew he *must* suffer and die, but was resolved he *would*, and made it his own act and deed.

2. Peter opposed it; *He took him, and began to rebuke him.* Here Peter showed more love than discretion, a zeal for Christ and his safety, but not according to knowledge. He *took him*—προσλαβόμενος ἀυτὸν. He took hold of him, as it were to stop and hinder him, took him in his arms, and embraced him (so some understand it); he fell on his neck, as impatient to hear that his dear Master should suffer such hard things; or he took him aside privately, and *began to rebuke* him. This was not the language of the least authority, but of the greatest affection, of that *jealousy* for the welfare of those we love, which is *strong as death.* Our Lord Jesus allowed his disciples to be free with him, but Peter here took too great a liberty.

3. Christ checked him for his opposition (*v.* 33); He *turned about*, as one offended, and *looked on his disciples*, to see if the rest of them were of the same mind, and concurred with Peter in this, that, if they did, they might take the reproof to themselves, which he was now about to give to Peter; and he said, *Get thee behind me, Satan.* Peter little thought to have had such a sharp rebuke for such a kind dissuasive, but perhaps expected as much commendation now for his love as he had lately had for his faith. Note, Christ sees that amiss in what we say and do, which we ourselves are not aware of, and knows what manner of spirit we are of, when we ourselves do not. (1.) Peter spoke as one that did not rightly understand, nor had duly considered, the purposes and counsels of God. When he saw such proofs as he every day saw of the *power* of Christ, he might conclude that he could not be *compelled to suffer;* the most potent enemies could not overpower him whom diseases and deaths, whom winds and waves and devils themselves, were forced to obey and yield to: and when he saw so much of the *wisdom* of Christ every day, he might conclude that he would not *choose to suffer* but for some very great and glorious purposes; and therefore he ought not thus to have contradicted him, but to have acquiesced. He looked upon his death only as a *martyrdom*, like that of the prophets, which he thought might be prevented, if either he would take a little care not to provoke the chief priests, or to keep out of the way; but he knew not that the thing was necessary for the glory of God, the destruction of Satan, and the salvation of man, that the Captain of our salvation must be *made perfect through sufferings*, and so must *bring many sons to glory.* Note, The wisdom of man is perfect folly, when it pretends to give measures to the divine counsels. The cross of Christ, the greatest instance of God's power and wisdom, was to some a stumbling-block, and to others

foolishness. (2.) Peter spoke as one that did not rightly understand, nor had duly considered, the nature of Christ's kingdom; he took it to be *temporal* and *human*, whereas it is *spiritual* and *divine*. *Thou savourest not the things that are of God, but those that are of men; ϐ φρονεῖς—thou mindest not;* so the word is rendered, Rom. viii. 5. Peter seemed to mind more the things that relate to the lower world, and the life that now is, than those which relate to the upper world, and the life to come. Minding the *things of men* more than the *things of God*, our own credit, ease, and safety, more than the *things of God*, and his glory and kingdom, is a very great sin, and the root of much sin, and very common among Christ's disciples; and it will appear in suffering times, those times of temptation, when those in whom the *things of* men have the ascendant, are in danger of falling off. *Non sapis—Thou art not wise* (so it may be read) *in the things of God*, but in the *things of men*. It is important to consider what *generation* we appear *wise in*, Luke xvi. 8. It seems policy to shun trouble, but if with that we shun duty, it is fleshly wisdom (2 Cor. i. 12), and it will be folly in the end.

III. These miracles of Christ should engage us all to *follow him*, whatever it cost us, not only as they were *confirmations* of his *mission*, but as they were *explications* of his *design*, and the tendency of that grace which he came to bring; plainly intimating that by his Spirit he would do that for our blind, deaf, lame, leprous, diseased, possessed *souls*, which he did for the *bodies* of those many who in those distresses applied themselves to him. Frequent notice had been taken of the great flocking that there was to him for help in various cases: now this is written, that we may believe that he is the great Physician of souls, and may become his patients, and submit to his *regimen;* and here he tells us upon what terms we may be admitted; and he *called all the people to him*, to hear this, who modestly stood at some distance when he was in private conversation with his disciples. This is that which all are concerned to know, and consider, if they expect Christ should heal *their souls*.

1. They must not be *indulgent* of the *ease of the body;* for (*v.* 34), "*Whosoever will come after me* for spiritual cures, as these people do for bodily cures, *let him deny himself*, and live a life of self-denial, mortification, and contempt of the world; let him not pretend to be his own physician, but renounce all confidence in himself and his own righteousness and strength, and let him *take up his cross*, conforming himself to the pattern of a crucified Jesus, and accommodating himself to the will of God in all the afflictions he lies under; and thus let him continue to *follow me;*" as many of those did, whom Christ healed. Those that will be Christ's patients must attend on him, converse with him, receive instruction and reproof from him, as those did that *followed* him, and must resolve they will never forsake him.

2. They must not be *solicitous*, no, not for *the life of the body*, when they cannot keep it without quitting Christ, *v.* 35. Are we invited by the words and works of Christ to follow him? Let us sit down, and count the cost, whether we can prefer our advantages by Christ before life itself, whether we can bear to think of losing our life *for Christ's sake and the gospel's*. When the devil is drawing away disciples and servants after him, he conceals the worst of it, tells them only of the pleasure, but nothing of the peril, of his service; *Ye shall not surely die;* but what there is of trouble and danger in the service of Christ, he tells us of it before, tells us we shall *suffer*, perhaps we shall *die*, in the cause; and represents the discouragements not *less*, but *greater*, than commonly they prove, that it may appear he *deals fairly* with us, and is not afraid that we should know the worst; because the *advantages* of his service abundantly suffice to *balance* the *discouragements*, if we will but impartially set the one over against the other. In short,

(1.) We must *not dread the loss of our lives*, provided it be *in the cause of Christ* (*v.* 35); *Whosoever will save his life*, by declining Christ, and refusing to come to him, or by disowning and denying him after he has in profession come to Christ, he shall *lose it*, shall lose the comfort of his natural life, the root and fountain of his spiritual life, and all his hopes of eternal life; such a bad bargain will he make for himself. But whosoever *shall lose his life*, shall be truly willing to lose it, shall venture it, shall lay it down when he cannot keep it without denying Christ, he shall *save it*, he shall be an unspeakable gainer; for the loss of his life shall be made up to him in a better life. It is looked upon to be some kind of recompence to those who lose their lives in the service of their prince and country, to have their memories honoured and their families provided for; but what is that to the recompence which Christ makes in eternal life to all that die for him?

(2.) We must *dread the loss of our souls*, yea, though we should *gain the whole world* by it (*v.* 36, 37); *For what shall it profit a man, if he should gain the whole world*, and all the wealth, honour, and pleasure, in it, by denying Christ, and *lose his own soul?* "True it is," said Bishop Hooper, the night before he suffered martyrdom, "that *life is sweet*, and *death is bitter*, but *eternal death is more bitter*, and *eternal life is more sweet.*" As the happiness of heaven with Christ, is enough to countervail the loss of life itself for Christ, so the gain of all the world *in sin*, is not sufficient to countervail the ruin of the soul *by sin*.

What that is that men do, to *save their lives*, and *gain the world*, he tells us (*v.* 38), and of what fatal consequence it will be to them;

Whosoever therefore shall be ashamed of me, and of my words, in this adulterous and sinful generation, of him shall the Son of man be ashamed. Something like this we had, Matt. x. 33. But it is here expressed more fully. Note, [1.] The disadvantage that the cause of Christ labours under in this world, is, that it is to be owned and professed in an *adulterous and sinful generation;* such the generation of mankind is, gone a whoring from God, in the impure embraces of the world and the flesh, lying in wickedness; some ages, some places, are more especially adulterous and sinful, as that was in which Christ lived; in such a *generation* the cause of Christ is opposed and run down, and those that own it, are exposed to reproach and contempt, and every where ridiculed and *spoken against.* [2.] There are many, who, though they cannot but own that the cause of Christ is a righteous cause, are *ashamed* of it, because of the reproach that attends the professing of it; they are *ashamed* of their relation to Christ, and *ashamed* of the credit they cannot but give to *his words;* they cannot bear to be frowned upon and despised, and therefore throw off their profession, and go down the stream of a prevailing apostasy. [3.] There is a day coming, when the cause of Christ will appear as bright and illustrious as now it appears mean and contemptible; when the Son of man comes *in the glory of his Father with his holy angels,* as the true Shechinah, the brightness of his Father's glory, and the Lord of angels. [4.] Those that are ashamed of Christ in this world where he is despised, he will be ashamed of in that world where he is eternally adored. *They* shall not share with him in his glory then, that were not willing to share with him in his disgrace now.

CHAP. IX.

In this chapter, we have, I. Christ's transfiguration upon the mount, ver. 1—13. II. His casting the devil out of a child, when the disciples could not do it, ver. 14—29. III. His prediction of his own sufferings and death, ver. 30—32. IV. The check he gave to his disciples for disputing who should be greatest (ver. 33—37); and to John for rebuking one who cast out devils in Christ's name, and did not follow with them, ver. 38—41. V. Christ's discourse with his disciples of the danger of offending one of his little ones (ver. 42), and of indulging that in ourselves, which is an offence and an occasion of sin to us (ver. 43—50), most of which passages we had before, Matt. xvii. and xviii.

AND he said unto them, Verily
I say unto you, That there be
some of them that stand here, which
shall not taste of death, till they have
seen the kingdom of God come with
power. 2 And after six days Jesus
taketh *with him* Peter, and James,
and John, and leadeth them up into
a high mountain apart by themselves:
and he was transfigured before them.
3 And his raiment became shining,
exceeding white as snow; so as no
fuller on earth can white them. 4
And there appeared unto them Elias
with Moses: and they were talking
with Jesus. 5 And Peter answered
and said to Jesus, Master, it is good
for us to be here: and let us make
three tabernacles; one for thee, and
one for Moses, and one for Elias. 6
For he wist not what to say; for they
were sore afraid. 7 And there was a
cloud that overshadowed them: and
a voice came out of the cloud, saying,
This is my beloved Son: hear him.
8 And suddenly, when they had looked
round about, they saw no man any
more, save Jesus only with themselves. 9 And as they came down
from the mountain, he charged them
that they should tell no man what
things they had seen, till the Son of
man were risen from the dead. 10
And they kept that saying with themselves, questioning one with another
what the rising from the dead should
mean. 11 And they asked him, saying, Why say the scribes that Elias
must first come? 12 And he answered and told them, Elias verily
cometh first, and restoreth all things;
and how it is written of the Son of
man, that he must suffer many things,
and be set at nought. 13 But I say
unto you, That Elias is indeed come,
and they have done unto him whatsoever they listed, as it is written of him.

Here is, I. A prediction of Christ's kingdom now near approaching, *v.*1. That which is foretold, is, 1. That the *kingdom of God* would *come,* and would come so as to be *seen:* the kingdom of the Messiah shall be set up in the world by the utter destruction of the Jewish polity, which stood in the way of it; this was the restoring of the kingdom of God among men, which had been in a manner lost by the woeful degeneracy both of Jews and Gentiles. 2. That it would come *with power,* so as to make its own way, and bear down the opposition that was given to it. It came *with power,* when vengeance was taken on the Jews for crucifying Christ, and when it conquered the idolatry of the Gentile world. 3. That it would come while some now *present were alive;* There are some *standing here, that shall not taste of death,* till they *see* it; this speaks the same with Matt. xxiv. 34, This *generation shall not pass, till all these things be fulfilled.* Those that were standing here with Christ, should see it, when the others could not discern it to be the kingdom of God, for it came not with observation.

II. A specimen of that kingdom in the

transfiguration of Christ, *six days* after Christ spoke that prediction. He had begun to give notice to his disciples of his death and sufferings; and, to prevent their offence at that, he gives them this glimpse of his glory, to show that his sufferings were voluntary, and what a virtue the dignity and glory of his person would put into them, and to prevent the *offence of the cross.*

1. It was on the top of a *high mountain,* like the converse Moses had with God, which was on the top of mount Sinai, and his prospect of Canaan from the top of mount Pisgah. Tradition saith, It was on the top of mount Tabor that Christ was transfigured; and if so, the scripture was fulfilled, *Tabor and Hermon shall rejoice in thy name,* Ps. lxxxix. 12. Dr. Lightfoot, observing that the last place where we find Christ was in the coasts of Cæsarea-Philippi, which was far from mount Tabor, rather thinks it was a high mountain which Josephus speaks of, near Cæsarea.

2. The witnesses of it were Peter, James, and John; these were the *three* that were to *bear record on earth,* answering to Moses, Elias, and the *voice from heaven,* the three that were to bear record from above. Christ did not take all the disciples with him, because the thing was to be kept very private. As there are distinguishing favours which are given to disciples and not to the world, so there are to some disciples and not to others. All the saints are a people *near to Christ,* but some lie in his bosom. James was the first of all the twelve that died for Christ, and John survived them all, to be the last eyewitness of this glory; he bore record (John i. 14); *We saw his glory:* and so did Peter, 2 Pet. i. 16—18.

3. The manner of it; *He was transfigured before them;* he appeared in another manner than he used to do. This was a change of the accidents, the substance remaining the same, and it was a miracle. But transubstantiation, the change of the substance, all the accidents remaining the same, is not a miracle, but a fraud and imposture, such a work as Christ never wrought. See what a great change human bodies are capable of, when God is pleased to put an honour upon them, as he will upon the bodies of the saints, at the resurrection. He was transfigured *before them;* the change, it is probable, was *gradual,* from glory to glory, so that the disciples, who had their eye upon him all the while, had the clearest and most certain evidence they could have, that this glorious appearance was no other than the blessed Jesus himself, and there was no illusion in it. John seems to refer to this (1 John i. 1), when he speaks of the *word of life,* as that which they had *seen with their eyes, and looked upon.* His *raiment became shining;* so that, though probably, it was sad-coloured, if not black, yet it was now *exceeding white as snow,* beyond what the fuller's art could do toward whitening it

4. His companions in this glory were Moses and Elias (*v.* 4); They appeared *talking with him,* not to *teach* him, but to *testify* to him, and to be *taught* by him; by which it appears that there are converse and intercourse between glorified saints, they have ways of talking one with another, which we understand not. Moses and Elias lived at a great distance of time one from another, but that breaks no squares in heaven, where the *first shall be last, and the last first,* that is, all one in Christ.

5. The great delight that the disciple's took in seeing this sight, and hearing this discourse, is expressed by Peter, the mouth of the rest; *He said, Master, it is good for us to be here, v.* 5. Though Christ was transfigured, and was in discourse with Moses and Elias, yet he gave Peter leave to speak to him, and to be as free with him as he used to be. Note, Our Lord Jesus, in his exaltation and glory, doth not at all abate of his condescending kindness to his people. Many, when they are in their greatness, oblige their friends to keep their distance; but even to the glorified Jesus true believers have access with boldness, and freedom of speech with him. Even in this heavenly discourse there was room for Peter to put in a word; and this is it, "*Lord, it is good to be here,* it is good *for us* to be here; here *let us make tabernacles;* let this be our rest for ever." Note, Gracious souls reckon it *good to be* in communion with Christ, good to be near him, good to be *in the mount* with him, though it be a cold and solitary place; it is good to be here retired from the world, and alone with Christ: and if it is good to be with Christ transfigured only upon a mountain with Moses and Elias, how good will it be to be with Christ glorified in heaven with all the saints! But observe, While Peter was for staying here, he forgot what need there was of the presence of Christ, and the preaching of his apostles, among the people. At this very time, the other disciples wanted them greatly, *v.* 14. Note, When it is well with us, we are apt to be mindless of others, and in the fulness of our *enjoyments* to forget the *necessities* of our brethren; it was a weakness in Peter to prefer private communion with God before public usefulness. Paul is willing to *abide in the flesh,* rather than depart to the mountain of glory (though that be far better), when he sees it needful for the church, Phil. i. 24, 25. Peter talked of making three distinct tabernacles for Moses, Elias, and Christ, which was not well-contrived; for such a perfect harmony there is between the law, the prophets, and the gospel, that one tabernacle will hold them all; they dwell together in unity. But whatever was incongruous in what he said, he may be excused, for they were all *sore afraid;* and he, for his part, *wist not what to say* (*v.* 6), not knowing what would be the end thereof.

6. The voice that came from heaven, was

an attestation of Christ's mediatorship, *v.* 7. *There was a cloud that overshadowed them,* and was a shelter to them. Peter had talked of making tabernacles for Christ and his friends; but *while he yet spoke,* see how his project was superseded; this cloud was unto them instead of tabernacles for their shelter (Isa. iv. 5); while he *spoke* of his tabernacles, God created his tabernacle *not made with hands.* Now out of this cloud (which was but a shade to *the excellent glory* Peter speaks of, whence *this voice* came) it was said, *This is my beloved Son, hear him.* God owns him, and accepts him, as his beloved Son, and is ready to accept of us in him; we must then own and accept him as our beloved Saviour, and must give up ourselves to be ruled by him.

7. The vision, being designed only to introduce this voice, when that was delivered, disappeared (*v.* 8); *Suddenly when they had looked round about,* as men amazed to see where they were, all was gone, *they saw no man any more.* Elias and Moses were vanished out of sight, and Jesus only remained with them, and he not transfigured, but as he used to be. Note, Christ doth not leave the soul, when extraordinary joys and comforts leave it. Though more sensible and ravishing communications may be withdrawn, Christ's disciples have, and shall have, his ordinary presence with them always, even to the end of the world, and that is it we must depend upon. Let us thank God for *daily bread,* and not expect a continual feast on this side heaven.

8. We have here the discourse between Christ and his disciples, as they came down from the mount.

(1.) He charged them to keep this matter very private, till he was *risen from the dead,* which would complete the proof of his divine mission, and then this must be produced with the rest of the evidence, *v.* 9. And besides, he, being now in a state of humiliation, would have nothing publicly taken notice of, that might seem disagreeable to such a state; for to that he would in every thing accommodate himself. This enjoining of silence to the disciples, would likewise be of use to them, to prevent their boasting of the intimacy they were admitted to, that they might not be *puffed up* with the *abundance of the revelations.* It is a mortification to a man, to be tied up from telling of his advancements, and may help to hide pride from him.

(2.) The disciples were at a loss what the *rising from the dead* should mean; they could not form any notion of the Messiah's dying (Luke xviii. 34), and therefore were willing to think that the *rising* he speaks of, was figurative, his rising from his present mean and low estate to the dignity and dominion they were in expectation of. But if so, here is another thing that embarrasses them (*v.* 11); *Why say the Scribes,* that before the appearing of the Messiah in his glory, according to the order settled in the prophecies of the Old Testament, *Elias must first come?* But Elias was gone, and Moses too. Now that which raised this difficulty, was, that the scribes taught them to expect the person of Elias, whereas the prophecy intended one *in the spirit and power of Elias.* Note, The misunderstanding of scripture is a great prejudice to the entertainment of truth.

(3.) Christ gave them a key to the prophecy concerning Elias (*v.* 12, 13); "It is indeed prophesied that Elias will come, and will *restore all things,* and set them to rights; and (though you will not understand it) it is also prophesied of the *Son of man,* that he must *suffer many things,* and be *set at nought,* must be a reproach of men, and despised of the people: and though the scribes do not tell you so, the *scriptures* do, and you have as much reason to expect that as the other, and should not *make so strange* of it; but as to Elias, I tell you *he is come;* and if you consider a little, you will understand whom I mean, it is one to whom they have *done whatsoever they listed;*" which was very applicable to the ill usage they had given John Baptist. Many of the ancients, and the Popish writers generally, think, that besides the coming of John Baptist in the spirit of Elias, himself in his own person is to be expected, with Enoch, before the second appearance of Christ, wherein the prophecy of Malachi will have a more full accomplishment than it had in John Baptist. But it is a groundless fancy; the true Elias, as well as the true Messiah promised, is come, and we are to look for *no other.* These words *as it is* written of him, refer not to their *doing to him whatever they listed* (that comes in in a parenthesis), but only to his coming. He is come, and hath been, and done, according as was *written of him.*

14 And when he came to *his* disciples, he saw a great multitude about
them, and the scribes questioning
with them. 15 And straightway all
the people, when they beheld him,
were greatly amazed, and running to
him saluted him. 16 And he asked
the scribes, What question ye with
them? 17 And one of the multitude
answered and said, Master, I have
brought unto thee my son, which
hath a dumb spirit; 18 And wheresoever he taketh him, he teareth him:
and he foameth, and gnasheth with
his teeth, and pineth away: and I
spake to thy disciples that they should
cast him out; and they could not.
19 He answereth him, and saith, O
faithless generation, how long shall I
be with you? how long shall I suffer

you? bring him unto me. 20 And
they brought him unto him: and
when he saw him, straightway the
spirit tare him; and he fell on the
ground, and wallowed foaming. 21
And he asked his father, How long is
it ago since this came unto him? And
he said, Of a child. 22 And ofttimes
it hath cast him into the fire, and into
the waters, to destroy him: but if thou
canst do any thing, have compassion
on us, and help us. 23 Jesus said
unto him, If thou canst believe, all
things *are* possible to him that believeth. 24 And straightway the father of the child cried out, and said
with tears, Lord, I believe; help thou
mine unbelief. 25 When Jesus saw
that the people came running together,
he rebuked the foul spirit, saying unto
him, *Thou* dumb and deaf spirit, I
charge thee, come out of him, and
enter no more into him. 26 And *the*
spirit cried, and rent him sore, and
came out of him: and he was as one
dead; insomuch that many said, He
is dead. 27 But Jesus took him by
the hand, and lifted him up; and he
arose. 28 And when he was come
into the house, his disciples asked
him privately, Why could not we cast
him out? 29 And he said unto them,
This kind can come forth by nothing,
but by prayer and fasting.

We have here the story of Christ's casting the devil out of a child, somewhat more fully related than it was Matt. xvii. 14, &c. Observe here,

I. Christ's return to his disciples, and the perplexity he found them in. He laid aside his robes of glory, and came to look after his family, and to enquire what was become of them. Christ's glory above does not make him forget the concerns of his church below, which he visits in *great humility*, *v.* 14. And he came very seasonably, when the disciples were embarrassed and run a-ground; the scribes, who were sworn enemies both to him and them, had gained an advantage against them. A child possessed with a devil was brought to them, and they could not cast out the devil, whereupon the scribes insulted over them, and reflected upon their Master, and triumphed as if the day were their own. He *found the scribes questioning with them,* in the hearing of the multitude, some of whom perhaps began to be shocked by it. Thus Moses, when he came down from the mount, found the camp of Israel in great disorder; so soon were Christ and Moses missed. Christ's return was very welcome, no doubt, to the disciples, and *un*welcome to the scribes. But particular notice is taken of its being very surprising to the people, who perhaps were ready to say, *As for this Jesus, we wot not what is become of him;* but when they *beheld him* coming to them again, they were *greatly amazed* (some copies add, *καὶ ἐξεφοβήθησαν—and they were afraid*); and *running to him* (some copies, for *προστρέχοντες*, read *προσχαίροντες—congratulating* him, or bidding him welcome), they saluted him. It is easy to give a reason why they should be glad to see him; but why were they *amazed, greatly amazed,* when they beheld him? Probably, there might remain something unusual in his countenance; as Moses's *face shone* when he came down from the mount, which made the people *afraid to come nigh him,* Exod. xxxiv. 30. So perhaps did Christ's face, in some measure; at least, instead of seeming *fatigued,* there appeared a wonderful briskness and sprightliness in his looks, which *amazed* them.

II. The case which perplexed the disciples, brought before him. He asked the scribes, who, he knew, were always *vexatious* to his disciples, and *teazing* them upon every occasion, "*What question ye with them?* What is the quarrel now?" The scribes made no answer, for they were confounded at his presence; the disciples made none, for they were comforted, and now left all to him. But the father of the child opened the case, *v.* 17, 18. 1. His child is possessed with *a dumb spirit;* he has the falling-sickness, and in his fits *is speechless;* his case is very sad, for, wheresoever the fit takes him, the spirit *tears* him, throws him into such violent convulsions as almost pull him to pieces; and, which is very grievous to himself, and frightful to those about him, *he foams* at the mouth, and *gnashes with his teeth,* as one in pain and great misery; and though the fits go off presently, yet they leave him so weak, that he *pines away,* is worn to a skeleton; his flesh is *dried* away; so the word signifies, Ps. cii. 3—5. This was a constant affliction to a tender father. 2. The disciples cannot give him any relief; "I *desired they would cast him out,* as they had done many, and they would willingly have done it, but *they could not;* and therefore thou couldest never have come in better time; *Master, I have brought him to thee.*"

III. The rebuke he gave to them all (*v.* 19); *O faithless generation, how long shall I be with you? How long shall I suffer you?* Dr. Hammond understands this as spoken to the disciples, reproving them for not exerting the power he had given them, and because they did not *fast* and *pray,* as in some cases he had directed them to do. But Dr. Whitby takes it as a rebuke to the scribes, who gloried in this disappointment that the disciples met with, and hoped to run them down with it. Them he calls a *faithless generation,* and speaks as one weary of *being with them,* and of *bearing with* them. We never hear him complaining, "How long shall I be in this low condition, and suffer that?" But, "How long shall I be among these *faithless* people, and suffer them?"

IV. The deplorable condition that the child was actually in, when he was brought to Christ, and the doleful representation which the father made of it. When the child saw Christ, he fell into a fit; *The spirit straightway tore him, boiled within him, troubled him* (so Dr. Hammond); as if the devil would set Christ at defiance, and hoped to be too hard for him too, and to keep possession in spite of him. The child *fell* on the *ground, and wallowed foaming.* We may put another construction upon it—that the devil raged, and had so much the greater wrath, because he *knew* that *his time was short,* Rev. xii. 12. Christ asked, *How long since this came to him?* And, it seems, the disease was of long standing; it came to him *of a child* (*v.* 21), which made the case the more sad, and the cure the more difficult. We are all by nature *children of disobedience,* and in such the evil spirit *works,* and has done so from our childhood; for *foolishness is bound in the heart of a child,* and nothing but the mighty grace of Christ can cast it out.

V. The pressing instances which the father of the child makes with Christ for a cure (*v.* 22); *Ofttimes it hath cast him into the fire, and into the waters, to destroy him.* Note, The devil aims at the ruin of those in whom he rules and works, and seeks *whom he may devour.* But *if thou canst do any thing, have compassion on us, and help us.* The leper was confident of Christ's power, but put an *if* upon his will (Matt. viii. 2); *If thou wilt, thou canst.* This poor man referred himself to his good-will, but put an *if* upon his power, because his disciples, who cast out devils *in his name,* had been non-plussed in this case. Thus Christ suffers in his honour by the difficulties and follies of his disciples.

VI. The answer Christ gave to his address (*v.* 23); *If thou canst believe, all things are possible to him that believeth.* Here, 1. He tacitly checks the weakness of his faith. The sufferer put it upon Christ's power, *If thou canst do any thing,* and reflected on the want of power in the disciples; but Christ turns it upon him, and puts him upon questioning his own faith, and will have him impute the disappointment to the want of that; *If thou canst believe.* 2. He graciously encourages the strength of his desire; "*All things are possible,* will appear possible, *to him that believes* the almighty power of God, to which all things are possible;" or, "That shall be done by the grace of God, for them that believe in the promise of God, which seemed utterly impossible." Note, In dealing with Christ, very much is put upon our believing, and very much promised to it. *Canst thou believe?* Darest thou believe? Art thou willing to venture thy all in the hands of Christ? To venture all thy spiritual concerns with him, and all thy temporal concerns for him? Canst thou find in thy heart to do this? If so, it is not impossible but that, though thou hast been a great sinner, thou mayest be reconciled; though thou art very mean and unworthy, thou mayest get to heaven. *If thou canst believe,* it is possible that thy hard heart may be softened, thy spiritual diseases may be cured; and that, weak as thou art, thou mayest be able to hold out to the end.

VII. The *profession of faith* which the poor man made hereupon (*v.* 24); He cried out, "*Lord, I believe;* I am fully persuaded both of thy power and of thy pity; my cure shall not be prevented by the want of faith; *Lord, I believe.*" He adds a prayer for grace to enable him more firmly to rely upon the assurances he had of the ability and willingness of Christ to save; *Help thou my unbelief.* Note, 1. Even those who through grace can say, *Lord, I believe,* have reason to complain of their unbelief; that they cannot so readily apply to themselves, and their own case, the word of Christ as they should, nor so cheerfully depend upon it. 2. Those that complain of unbelief, must look up to Christ for grace to *help* them against it, *and his grace* shall be *sufficient for them.* "*Help mine unbelief,* help me to a pardon for it, help me with power against it; help out what is wanting in my faith with thy grace, the strength of which is perfected in our weakness."

VIII. The cure of the child, and the conquest of this raging devil in the child. Christ *saw the people come running together,* expecting to see the issue of this trial of skill, and therefore kept them in suspense no longer, but *rebuked the foul spirit;* the *unclean spirit,* so it should be rendered, as in other places. Observe, 1. What the charge was which Christ gave to this unclean spirit; "*Thou dumb and deaf spirit,* that makest the poor child dumb and deaf, but shalt thyself be made to *hear* thy doom, and not be able to *say* any thing against it, *come out of him* immediately, and *enter no more into him.* Let him not only be brought out of this fit, but let his fits never return." Note, Whom Christ cures, he cures effectually. Satan may *go out himself,* and yet recover possession; but if Christ *cast* him out, he will *keep* him out. 2. How the unclean spirit took it; he grew yet more outrageous, he *cried,* and *rent him sore,* gave him such a twitch at parting, that he was *as one dead;* so loth was he to quit his hold, so exasperated at the superior power of Christ, so malicious to the child, and so desirous was he to kill him. *Many said, He is dead.* Thus the toss that a soul is in at the breaking of Satan's power in it may perhaps be frightful for the present, but opens the door to lasting comfort. 3. How the child was perfectly restored (*v.* 27); *Jesus took him by the hand, κρατήσας—took fast hold of him,* and strongly bore him up, and he arose and recovered, and all was well.

IX. The reason he gave to the disciples why they could not cast out this devil. They *enquired* of him privately *why they could not,* that wherein they were defective might be made up another time, and they might not again be thus publicly shamed; and he told them (*v.* 29), *This kind can come forth by nothing* but *prayer and fasting.* Whatever other difference there really might be, none appears between this and other kinds, but that the unclean spirit had had possession of this poor patient *from a child,* and that strengthened his interest, and confirmed his hold. When *vicious habits* are rooted by long usage, and begin to plead prescription, like chronical diseases they are *hardly cured. Can the Æthiopian change his skin?* The disciples must not think to do their work always with a like ease; some services call them to take more than ordinary pains: but Christ can do that with a word's speaking, which they must prevail for the doing of by *prayer and fasting.*

30 And they departed thence, and
passed through Galilee; and he would
not that any man should know *it.*
31 For he taught his disciples, and
said unto them, The Son of man is
delivered into the hands of men, and
they shall kill him; and after that he
is killed, he shall rise the third day.
32 But they understood not that saying, and were afraid to ask him. 33
And he came to Capernaum: and
being in the house he asked them,
What was it that ye disputed among
yourselves by the way? 34 But they
held their peace: for by the way they
had disputed among themselves, who
should be the greatest. 35 And he
sat down, and called the twelve, and
saith unto them, If any man desire
to be first, *the same* shall be last of
all, and servant of all. 36 And he
took a child, and set him in the midst
of them: and when he had taken him
in his arms, he said unto them, 37
Whosoever shall receive one of such
children in my name, receiveth me:
and whosoever shall receive me, receiveth not me, but him that sent me.
38 And John answered him, saying,
Master, we saw one casting out devils
in thy name, and he followeth not us:
and we forbad him, because he followeth not us. 39 But Jesus said,
Forbid him not: for there is no man
which shall do a miracle in my name,
that can lightly speak evil of me. 40
For he that is not against us is on
our part.

Here, I. Christ foretels his own approaching sufferings. He *passed through Galilee* with more expedition than usual, and *would not that any man should know it* (*v.* 30); because he had done many mighty and good works among them in vain, they shall not be invited to see them and have the benefit of them, as they have been. The time of his sufferings drew nigh, and therefore he was willing to be private awhile, and to converse only with his disciples, to prepare them for the approaching trial, *v.* 31. He said to them, *The Son of man is delivered* by the determinate counsel and fore-knowledge of God *into the hands of men* (*v.* 31), and *they shall kill him.* Had he been delivered into the hands of devils, and they had worried him, it had not been so strange; but that *men,* who have *reason,* and should have *love,* that they should be thus spiteful to the *Son of man,* who came to redeem and save them, is unaccountable. But still it is observable that when Christ spoke of his death, he always spoke of his resurrection, which took away the reproach of it from himself, and should have taken away the grief of it from his disciples. But they *understood not that saying, v.* 32. The words were plain enough, but they could not be reconciled to the thing, and therefore would suppose them to have some mystical meaning which they did not understand, and they were *afraid to ask him;* not because he was difficult of access, or stern to those who consulted him, but either because they were loth to know the truth, or because they expected to be chidden for their backwardness to receive it. Many remain ignorant because they are ashamed to enquire.

II. He rebukes his disciples for magnifying themselves. When he came to Capernaum, he privately asked his disciples what it was that they *disputed among themselves by the way, v.* 33. He knew very well what the dispute was, but he would know it *from them,* and would have them to confess their fault and folly in it. Note, 1. We must all expect to be called to an account by our Lord Jesus, concerning what passes while we are in the way in this state of passage and probation. 2. We must in a particular manner be called to an account about our discourses among ourselves; for by our words we must be justified or condemned. 3. As our other discourses among ourselves by the way, so especially our disputes, will be all called over again, and we shall be called to an account about them. 4 Of all disputes, Christ will be sure to reckon with his disciples for their disputes about precedency and superiority: that was the subject of the debate here, *who should be the greatest, v.* 34. Nothing could be more contrary to the two great laws of Christ's kingdom, lessons of his school, and instructions of his example, which are *humi-*

lity and *love*, than *desiring* preferment in the world, and *disputing* about it. This ill temper he took all occasions to check, both because it arose from a mistaken notion of his kingdom, as if it were of this world, and because it tended so directly to the debasing of the honour, and the corrupting of the purity, of his gospel, and, he foresaw, would be so much the bane of the church.

Now, (1.) They were willing to *cover this fault* (*v.* 34); they *held their peace.* As they would not *ask* (*v.* 32), because they were ashamed to own their ignorance, so here they would not *answer* because they were ashamed to own their pride. (2.) He was willing to *amend this fault* in them, and to bring them to a better temper; and therefore *sat down*, that he might have a solemn and full discourse with them about this matter; he *called the twelve to him*, and told them, [1.] That ambition and affectation of dignity and dominion, instead of gaining them preferment in his kingdom, would but postpone their preferment; *If any man desire* and aim *to be first*, he *shall be last;* he that exalteth himself, shall be abased, and men's *pride* shall *bring them low.* [2.] That there is no preferment to be had under him, but an opportunity for, and an obligation to, so much the more labour and condescension; *If any man desire to be first*, when he is so, he must be much the more busy and serviceable to every body. *He that desires the office of a bishop, desires a good work*, for he must, as St. Paul did, labour the more abundantly, and make himself the *servant of all.* [3.] That those who are most humble and self-denying, do most resemble Christ, and shall be most tenderly owned by him. This he taught them by a sign; *He took a child in his arms*, that had nothing of pride and ambition in it. "Look you," saith he; "*whosoever shall receive* one like this child, *receives me.* Those of a humble, meek, mild disposition are such as I will own and countenance, and encourage every body else to do so too, and will take what is done to them as done to myself; and so will my Father too, for he who thus *receiveth me, receiveth him that sent me*, and it shall be placed to his account, and repaid with interest."

III. He rebukes them for *villifying all but themselves;* while they are striving which of them should be greatest, they will not allow those who are not in communion with them to be any thing. Observe,

1. The account which John gave him, of the restraint they had laid upon one from making use of the name of Christ, because he was not of their society. Though they were ashamed to own their contests for preferment, they seem to boast of this exercise of their authority, and expected their Master would not only justify them in it, but commend them for it; and hoped he would not blame them for desiring to be great, when they would thus use their power for maintaining the honour of the sacred college. *Master*, saith John, *we saw one casting out devils in thy name, but he followeth not us*, *v.* 38. (1.) It was strange that one who was not a professed disciple and follower of Christ, should yet have power to *cast out devils*, in his name, for that seemed to be peculiar to those whom he called, *ch.* vi. 7. But some think that he was a disciple of John, who made use of the name of the Messiah, not as come, but as near at hand, not knowing that Jesus was he. It should rather seem that he made use of the name of Jesus, believing him to be the Christ, as the other apostles did. And why might not he receive that power from Christ, whose *Spirit*, like the wind, *blows where it listeth*, without such an outward call as the apostles had? And perhaps there were many more such. Christ's grace is not tied to the visible church. (2.) It was strange that one who *cast out devils* in the name of Christ, did not join himself to the apostles, and follow Christ with them, but should continue to act in *separation* from them. I know of nothing that could hinder him from following them, unless because he was loth to leave all to follow them; and if so, that was an ill principle. The thing did not look well, and therefore the disciples *forbade him* to make use of Christ's name as they did, unless he would follow him as they did. This was like the motion Joshua made concerning Eldad and Medad, that prophesied in the camp, and went not up with the rest to the door of the tabernacle; "*My lord Moses, forbid them* (Num. xi. 28); restrain them, silence them, for it is a schism." Thus apt are we to imagine that those do not follow Christ at all, who do not follow him *with us*, and that those do nothing well, who do not just as we do. But the *Lord knows them that are his*, however they are dispersed; and this instance gives us a needful caution, to take heed lest we be carried, by an excess of zeal for the unity of the church, and for that which we are sure is right and good, to oppose that which yet may tend to the enlargement of the church, and the advancement of its true interests another way.

2. The rebuke he gave to them for this (*v.* 39); *Jesus said*, "*Forbid him not*, nor any other that does likewise." This was like the check Moses gave to Joshua; *Enviest thou for my sake?* Note, That which is good, and doeth good, must not be prohibited, though there may be some defect or irregularity in the manner of doing it. *Casting out devils*, and so destroying Satan's kingdom, doing this *in Christ's name*, and so owning him to be sent of God, and giving honour to him as the Fountain of grace, preaching down sin, and preaching up Christ, are good things, very good things, which ought not to be forbidden to any, merely because they *follow not with us.* If Christ be preached, Paul therein doth, and will rejoice, though he be eclipsed by it Phil. i. 18. Two reasons

Christ gives why such should not be forbidden. (1.) Because we cannot suppose that any man who makes use of Christ's name in working miracles, should blaspheme his name, as the scribes and Pharisees did. There were those indeed that did *in Christ's name cast out devils,* and yet in other respects were *workers of iniquity;* but they did not *speak evil of Christ.* (2.) Because those that differed in communion, while they agreed to fight against Satan under the banner of Christ, ought to look upon one another as on the same side, notwithstanding that difference. *He that is not against us is on our part.* As to the great controversy between Christ and Beelzebub, he had said, *He that is not with me is against me,* Matt. xii. 30. He that will not own Christ, owns Satan. But as to those that own Christ, though not in the same circumstances, that follow him, though *not with us,* we must reckon that though these differ from us, they are not against us, and therefore are *on our part,* and we must not be any hindrance to their usefulness.

41 For whosoever shall give you a
cup of water to drink in my name,
because ye belong to Christ, verily I
say unto you, he shall not lose his
reward. 42 And whosoever shall offend one of *these* little ones that believe in me, it is better for him that
a millstone were hanged about his
neck, and he were cast into the sea.
43 And if thy hand offend thee, cut
it off: it is better for thee to enter
into life maimed, than having two
hands to go into hell, into the fire
that never shall be quenched: 44
Where their worm dieth not, and the
fire is not quenched. 45 And if thy
foot offend thee, cut it off: it is better for thee to enter halt into life,
than having two feet to be cast into
hell, into the fire that never shall be
quenched: 46 Where their worm
dieth not, and the fire is not quenched.
47 And if thine eye offend thee, pluck
it out: it is better for thee to enter
into the kingdom of God with one
eye, than having two eyes to be cast
into hell fire: 48 Where their worm
dieth not, and the fire is not quenched.
49 For every one shall be salted with
fire, and every sacrifice shall be salted
with salt. 50 Salt *is* good: but if
the salt have lost his saltness, wherewith will ye season it? Have salt in
yourselves, and have peace one with
another.

Here, I. Christ promiseth a reward to all those that are any way kind to his disciples (*v.* 41); "*Whosoever shall give you a cup of water,* when you need it, and it will be a refreshment to you, *because ye belong to Christ,* and are of his family, *he shall not lose his reward.*" Note, 1. It is the honour and happiness of Christians, that they *belong to Christ,* they have joined themselves to him, and are owned by him; they wear his livery as retainers to his family; nay, they are more nearly related, they are *members of his body.* 2. They who belong to Christ, may sometimes be reduced to such straits as to be glad of a *cup of cold water.* 3. The relieving of Christ's poor in their distresses, is a good deed, and will turn to a good account; he accepts it, and will reward it. 4. What kindness is done to Christ's poor, must be done them *for his sake,* and *because they belong to him;* for that is it that sanctifies the kindness, and puts a value upon it in the sight of God. 5. This is a reason why we must not discountenance and discourage those who are serving the interests of Christ's kingdom, though they are not in every thing of our mind and way. It comes in here as a reason why those must not be hindered, that cast out devils in Christ's name, though they did not follow him; for (as Dr. Hammond paraphrases it) "It is not only the great eminent performances which are done by you my constant attendants and disciples, that are accepted by me, but every the least degree of sincere faith and Christian performance, proportionable but to the expressing the least kindness, as giving a cup of water to a disciple of mine for being such, shall be accepted and rewarded." If Christ reckons *kindnesses to us* services to *him,* we ought to reckon *services to him* kindnesses to us, and to encourage them, though done by those that follow not with us.

II. He threatens those that *offend* his *little ones,* that wilfully are the occasion of sin or trouble to them, *v.* 42. Whosoever shall grieve any true Christians, though they be of the weakest, shall oppose their *entrance* into the ways of God, or discourage and obstruct their *progress* in those ways, shall either restrain them from doing good, or draw them in to commit sin, it were *better for him that a millstone were hanged about his neck, and he were cast into the sea:* his punishment will be very great, and the death and ruin of his soul more terrible than such a death and ruin of his body would be. See Matt. xviii. 6.

III. He warns all his followers to take heed of ruining their own souls. This charity must begin at home; if we must take heed of doing any thing to hinder others from good, and to occasion their sin, much more careful must we be to avoid every thing that will take us off from our duty, or lead us to sin; and that which doth so we must part with, though it be ever so dear to us. This we had twice in

Matthew, *ch.* v. 29, 30, and *ch.* xviii. 8, 9. It is here urged somewhat more largely and pressingly; certainly this requires our serious regard, which is so much insisted upon. Observe,

1. The case supposed, that our own *hand*, or *eye*, or *foot*, *offends us;* that the impure *corruption* we indulge is as dear to us as an eye or a hand; or that that which is to us as an eye or a hand, is become an invisible *temptation* to sin, or *occasion* of it. Suppose the beloved is become a sin, or the sin a beloved. Suppose we cannot keep that which is dear to us, but it will be a snare and a stumbling-block; suppose we must part with it, or part with Christ and a good conscience.

2. The duty prescribed in that case; *Pluck out the eye, cut off the hand and foot,* mortify the darling lust, kill it, crucify it, starve it, make no provision for it. Let the idols that have been *delectable* things, be cast away as *detestable* things; keep at a distance from that which is a temptation, though ever so pleasing. It is necessary that the part which is gangrened, should be taken off for the preservation of the whole. *Immedicabile vulnus ense recidendum est, ne pars sincera trahatur—The part that is incurably wounded must be cut off, lest the parts that are sound be corrupted.* We must put ourselves to pain, that we may not bring ourselves to ruin; self must be denied, that it may not be destroyed.

3. The necessity of doing this. The flesh must be mortified, that we may *enter into life* (*v.* 43, 45), into the kingdom of God, *v.* 47. Though, by abandoning sin, we may, for the present, feel ourselves as if we were *halt* and *maimed* (it may seem to be a force put upon ourselves, and may create us some uneasiness), yet it is for *life;* and all that men have, they will give for their lives: it is for a *kingdom*, the *kingdom of God,* which we cannot otherwise obtain; these *halts* and *maims* will be the *marks of the Lord Jesus,* will be in that kingdom *scars of honour.*

4. The danger of not doing this. The matter is brought to this issue, that either sin must die, or we must die. If we will lay this *Delilah* in our bosom, it will betray us; if we be *ruled* by sin, we shall inevitably be *ruined* by it; if we must keep our *two hands,* and *two eyes,* and *two feet,* we must with them be *cast into hell.* Our Saviour often pressed our duty upon us, from the consideration of the torments of hell, which we run ourselves into if we continue in sin. With what an emphasis of terror are those words repeated three times here, *Where their worm dieth not, and the fire is not quenched!* The words are quoted from Isa. lxvi. 24. (1.) The reflections and reproaches of the sinner's own conscience are the *worm that dieth not;* which will cleave to the damned soul as the worms do to the dead body, and prey upon it, and never leave it till it is quite devoured. *Son, remember,* will set this worm a gnawing; and how terribly will it bite with that word (Prov. v. 12, 23), *How have I hated instruction!* The soul that is food to this worm, dies not; and the worm is bred in it, and one with it, and therefore neither doth that die. Damned sinners will be to eternity accusing, condemning, and upbraiding, themselves with their own follies, which, how much soever they are now in love with them, will at the last *bite like a serpent,* and *sting like an adder.* (2.) The wrath of God fastening upon a guilty and polluted conscience, is the *fire* that is *not quenched;* for it is the wrath of the living God, the eternal God, into whose hands it is a fearful thing to fall. There are no operations of the Spirit of grace upon the souls of damned sinners, and therefore there is nothing to alter the nature of the fuel, which must remain for ever combustible; nor is there any application of the merit of Christ to them, and therefore there is nothing to appease or quench the violence of the fire. Dr. Whitby shows that the eternity of the torments of hell was not only the constant faith of the Christian church, but had been so of the Jewish church. Josephus saith, The Pharisees held that the souls of the wicked were to be *punished with perpetual punishment;* and that there was appointed for them *a perpetual prison.* And Philo saith, The punishment of the wicked is *to live for ever dying,* and to be *for ever in pains and griefs that never cease.*

The two last verses are somewhat difficult, and interpreters agree not in the sense of them; *for every one* in general, or rather every one *of them* that are cast into hell, shall be *salted with fire, and every sacrifice shall be salted with salt.* Therefore *have salt in yourselves.* [1.] It was appointed by the law of Moses, that every sacrifice should be *salted with salt,* not to *preserve* it (for it was to be immediately consumed), but because it was the food of God's table, and no flesh is eaten without salt; it was therefore particularly required in the meat-offerings, Lev. ii. 13. [2.] The nature of man, being *corrupt,* and as such being called *flesh* (Gen. vi. 3; Ps. lxxviii. 39), some way or other must be *salted,* in order to its being a sacrifice to God. The *salting* of fish (and I think of other things) they call the *curing* of it. [3.] Our chief concern is, to present ourselves *living sacrifices* to the grace of God (Rom. xii. 1), and, in order to our acceptableness, we must be *salted with salt,* our corrupt affections must be subdued and mortified, and we must have in our souls a savour of grace. Thus the *offering up* or *sacrificing* of the Gentiles is said to be *acceptable, being sanctified by the Holy Ghost,* as the sacrifices were *salted,* Rom. xv. 16. [4.] Those that have the salt of grace, must make it appear that they have it; that they *have salt in themselves,* a living principle of grace in their hearts, which works out all corrupt dispositions, and every thing in the soul that tends to *putrefaction,* and would *offend* our God, or our own consciences, as unsavoury meat doth. Our *speech* must be *always with grace sea-*

soned with this salt, that no *corrupt communication* may *proceed out of our mouth*, but we may loathe it as much as we would to put putrid meat into our mouths. [5.] As this gracious salt will keep our own consciences void of offence, so it will keep our conversation with others so, that we may not offend any of Christ's little ones, but may be *at peace one with another*. [6.] We must not only have this salt of grace, but we must always retain the relish and savour of it; for if this *salt lose its saltness*, if a Christian revolt from his Christianity, if he lose the savour of it, and be no longer under the power and influence of it, what can recover him, or *wherewith will ye season him?* This was said Matt. v. 13. [7.] Those that present not themselves *living* sacrifices to God's grace, shall be made for ever *dying* sacrifices to his justice, and since they would not give honour to him, he will get him honour upon them; they would not be *salted with the salt* of divine grace, would not admit that to subdue their corrupt affections, no, they would not submit to the operation, could not bear the corrosives that were necessary to eat out the proud flesh, it was to them like cutting off a hand, or plucking out an eye; and therefore in hell they shall be *salted with fire;* coals of fire shall be *scattered* upon them (Ezek. x. 2), as salt upon the meat, and *brimstone* (Job xviii. 15), as fire and brimstone were rained on Sodom; the pleasures they have lived *in, shall eat their flesh, as it were fire*, Jam. v. 3. The pain of mortifying the flesh now is no more to be compared with the punishment for not mortifying it, than *salting* with *burning*. And since he had said, that the *fire* of hell *shall not be quenched*, but it might be objected, that the fuel will not last always, he here intimates, that by the power of God it shall be made to last always; for those that are *cast into hell*, will find the fire to have not only the *corroding* quality of salt, but its *preserving* quality; whence it is used to signify that which is *lasting:* a covenant of *salt* is a *perpetual* covenant, and Lot's wife being turned into a *pillar of salt*, made her a remaining monument of divine vengeance. Now since this will certainly be the doom of those that do not crucify the flesh with its affections and lusts, let us, knowing this *terror of the Lord*, be *persuaded* to do it.

CHAP. X.

In this chapter, we have, I. Christ's dispute with the Pharisees concerning divorce, ver. 1—12. II. The kind entertainment he gave to the little children that were brought to him to be blessed, ver. 13—16. III. His trial of the rich man that enquired what he must do to get to heaven, ver. 17—22. IV. His discourse with his disciples, upon that occasion, concerning the peril of riches (v. 23—27), and the advantage of being impoverished for his sake, ver. 28—31. V. The repeated notice he gave his disciples of his sufferings and death approaching, ver. 32—34. VI. The counsel he gave to James and John, to think of suffering with him, rather than of reigning with him, ver. 15—45. VII. The cure of Bartimeus, a poor blind man, ver. 46—52. All which passages of story we had the substance of before, Matt. xix. and xx.

AND he arose from thence, and
cometh into the coasts of Judæa
by the farther side of Jordan: and
the people resort unto him again;
and, as he was wont, he taught them
again. 2 And the Pharisees came to
him, and asked him, Is it lawful for
a man to put away *his* wife? tempting
him. 3 And he answered and said
unto them, What did Moses command
you? 4 And they said, Moses suffered to write a bill of divorcement,
and to put *her* away. 5 And Jesus
answered and said unto them, For
the hardness of your heart he wrote
you this precept. 6 But from the
beginning of the creation God made
them male and female. 7 For this
cause shall a man leave his father and
mother, and cleave to his wife; 8
And they twain shall be one flesh:
so then they are no more twain, but
one flesh. 9 What therefore God
hath joined together, let not man put
asunder. 10 And in the house his
disciples asked him again of the same
matter. 11 And he saith unto them,
Whosoever shall put away his wife,
and marry another, committeth adultery against her. 12 And if a woman
shall put away her husband, and be
married to another, she committeth
adultery.

Our Lord Jesus was an itinerant Preacher, did not continue long in a place, for the whole land of Canaan was his parish, or diocese, and therefore he would visit every part of it, and give instructions to those in the remotest corners of it. Here we have him in the *coasts* of Judea, by the further side of Jordan eastward, as we found him, not long since, in the utmost borders westward, near Tyre and Sidon. Thus was his circuit like that of the sun, from whose light and heat nothing is hid. Now here we have him,

I. *Resorted to* by the *people*, *v.* 1. Wherever he was, they flocked after him in crowds; they came to him *again*, as they had done when he had formerly been in these parts, and, *as he was wont, he taught them again*. Note, Preaching was Christ's constant practice; it was what he was used to, and, wherever he came, he did *as he was wont*. In Matthew it is said, *He healed them;* here it is said, *He taught them:* his cures were to confirm his doctrine, and to recommend it, and his doctrine was to explain his cures, and illustrate them. His *teaching* was *healing* to poor souls. He *taught them again*. Note, Even those whom Christ hath taught, have need to be taught *again*. Such is the fulness of the Christian doctrine, that there is still more to be learned; and such our forgetfulness, that we need to be reminded of what we do know.

II. We have him *disputed with* by the Pharisees, who envied the progress of his spiritual arms, and did all they could to obstruct and oppose it; to divert him, to perplex him, and to prejudice the people against him.

Here is, 1. A question they started concerning divorce (*v.* 2); *Is it lawful for a man to put away his wife?* This was a good question, if it had been well put, and with a humble desire to know the mind of God in this matter; but they proposed it, *tempting him,* seeking an occasion against him, and an opportunity to expose him, which side soever he should take of the question. Ministers must stand upon their guard, lest, under pretence of being advised with, they be ensnared.

2. Christ's reply to them with a question (*v.* 3); *What did Moses command you?* This he asked them, to testify his respect to the law of Moses, and to show that he came not to destroy it; and to engage them to a universal impartial respect for Moses's writings and to compare one part of them with another.

3. The fair account they gave of what they found in the law of Moses, expressly concerning divorce, *v.* 4. Christ asked, *What did Moses command you?* They own that Moses only *suffered,* or *permitted,* a man to write his wife a *bill of divorce,* and to put *her away,* Deut. xxiv. 1. "If you *will* do it, you must do it *in writing,* delivered into her own hand, and so put her way, and never return to her again."

4. The answer that Christ gave to their question, in which he abides by the doctrine he had formerly laid down in this case (Matt. v. 32), *That whosoever puts away his wife, except for fornication, causeth her to commit adultery.* And to clear this he here shows,

(1.) That the reason why Moses, in his *law,* permitted divorce, was such, as that they ought not to make use of that permission; for it was only *for the hardness of their hearts* (*v.* 5), lest, if they were not permitted to divorce their wives, they should murder them; so that none must put away their wives but such as are willing to own that their hearts were so hard as to need this permission.

(2.) That the account which Moses, in this *history, gives* of the institution of marriage, affords such a reason against divorce, as amounts to a prohibition of it. So that if the question be, *What did Moses command?* (*v.* 3), it must be answered, "Though by a temporary proviso he allowed divorce to the Jews, yet by an eternal reason he forbade it to all the children of Adam and Eve, and that is it which we must abide by."

Moses tells us, [1.] That God made man *male and female, one* male, and *one* female; so that *Adam could not* put away his wife and take another, for there was no other to take, which was an intimation to all his sons, that they *must not.* [2.] When this male and this female were, by the ordinance of God, joined together in holy marriage, the law was, That a man must *leave his father and mother, and cleave to his wife* (*v.* 7); which intimates not only the nearness of the relation, but the perpetuity of it; he shall so cleave to his wife as not to be separated from her. [3.] The result of the relation is, That, though they are *two,* yet they are *one,* they are *one flesh, v.* 8. The union between them is the most intimate that can be, and, as Dr. Hammond expresses it, a sacred thing that must not be violated. [4.] God himself has *joined them together;* he has not only, as Creator, fitted them to be comforts and helps meet for each other, but he has, in wisdom and goodness, appointed them who are thus joined together, to live together in love till death parts them. Marriage is not an invention of men, but a divine institution, and therefore is to be religiously observed, and the more, because it is a figure of the mystical inseparable union between Christ and his church.

Now from all this he infers, that men ought not to *put* their wives *asunder* from them, whom God has put so near to them. The bond which God himself has tied, is not to be lightly untied. They who are for divorcing their wives for every offence, would do well to consider what would become of them, if God should in like manner deal with them. See Isa. l. 1: Jer. iii. 1.

5. Christ's discourse with his disciples, in private, about this matter, *v.* 10—12. It was an advantage to them, that they had opportunity of personal converse with Christ, not only about gospel mysteries, but about moral duties, for their further satisfaction. No more is here related of this private conference, than the law Christ laid down in this case—That it is adultery for a man to put away his wife, and marry another; it is adultery *against the wife* he puts away, it is a wrong to her, and a breach of his contract with her, *v.* 11. He adds, *If a woman shall put away her husband,* that is, elope from him, leave him by consent, and *be married to another,* she *commits adultery* (*v.* 12), and it will be no excuse at all for her to say that it was with the consent of her husband. Wisdom and grace, holiness and love, reigning in the heart, will make those commands easy which to the carnal mind may be as a heavy yoke.

13 And they brought young children to him, that he should touch
them: and *his* disciples rebuked those
that brought *them.* 14 But when
Jesus saw *it,* he was much displeased,
and said unto them, Suffer the little
children to come unto me, and forbid
them not: for of such is the kingdom
of God. 15 Verily I say unto you,

Whosoever shall not receive the kingdom of God as a little child, he shall not enter therein. 16 And he took them up in his arms, put *his* hands upon them, and blessed them.

It is looked upon as the indication of a kind and tender disposition to take notice of little children, and this was remarkable in our Lord Jesus, which is an encouragement not only to little children to apply themselves to Christ when they are very young, but to grown people, who are conscious to themselves of weakness and childishness, and of being, through manifold infirmities, helpless and useless, like little children. Here we have,

I. Little children brought to Christ, *v.* 13. Their parents, or whoever they were that had the nursing of them, brought them to him, that he should *touch them,* in token of his commanding and conferring a blessing on them. It doth not appear that they needed any bodily *cure,* nor were they capable of being *taught:* but it seems, 1. They that had the care of them were mostly concerned *about their souls,* their better part, which ought to be the principal care of all parents for their children; for that is the principal part, and it is well with them, if it be well with their souls. 2. They believed that Christ's blessing would do their souls good; and therefore to him they brought them, that he might *touch* them, knowing that he could reach their hearts, when nothing their parents could say to them, or do for them, would reach them. We may present our children to Christ, now that he is in heaven, for from thence he can reach them with his blessing, and therein we may act faith upon the fulness and extent of his grace, the kind intimations he hath always given of favour to the seed of the faithful, the tenour of the covenant with Abraham, and the promise *to us and to our children,* especially that great promise of pouring his *Spirit upon our seed,* and his *blessing* upon *our offspring,* Isa. xliv. 3.

II The *dis*couragement which the disciples gave to the bringing of children to Christ; *They rebuked them that brought them;* as if they had been sure that they knew their Master's mind in this matter, whereas he had lately cautioned them not to *despise the little ones.*

III. The *en*couragement Christ gave to it. 1. He took it very ill that his disciples should keep them off; *When he saw it, he was much displeased, v.* 14. "What do you mean? Will you hinder me from doing good, from doing good to the rising generation, to the lambs of the flock?" Christ is very angry with his own disciples, if they discountenance any in coming to him themselves, or in bringing their children to him. 2. He ordered that they should be *brought to him,* and nothing said or done to hinder them; suffer *little children,* as soon as they are capable, to *come to me,* to offer up their supplications to me, and to receive instructions from me. Little children are welcome betimes to the throne of grace with their Hosannas. 3. He owned them as members of his church, as they had been of the Jewish church. He came to set up the *kingdom of God* among men, and took this occasion to declare that that kingdom admitted *little children* to be the subjects of it, and gave them a title to the privileges of subjects. Nay, the kingdom of God is to be kept up by such: they must be taken in when they are little children, that they may be secured for hereafter, to bear up the name of Christ. 4. That there must be something of the temper and disposition of little children found in all that Christ will own and bless. We must *receive the kingdom of God as little children* (*v.* 15); that is, we must stand affected to Christ and his grace as little children do to their parents, nurses, and teachers. We must be *inquisitive,* as children, must learn as children (that is the learning age), and in learning must *believe, Oportet discentem credere—A learner must believe.* The mind of a child is white paper (*tabula rasa—a mere blank*), you may write upon it what you will; such must our minds be to the pen of the blessed Spirit. Children are under government; so must we be. *Lord, what wilt thou have me to do?* We must receive the kingdom of God as the child Samuel did, *Speak, Lord, for thy servant heareth.* Little children depend upon their parents' wisdom and care, are carried in their arms, go where they send them, and take what they provide for them; and thus must we receive the *kingdom of God,* with a humble resignation of ourselves to Jesus Christ, and an easy dependence upon him, both for strength and righteousness, for tuition, provision, and a portion. 5 He received the children, and gave them what was desired (*v.* 16); *He took them up in his arms,* in token of his affectionate concern for them; *put his hands upon them,* as was desired, and *blessed them.* See how he out-did the desires of these parents; they begged he would touch them, but he did more. (1.) He *took them in his arms.* Now the scripture was fulfilled (Isa. xl. 11), *He shall gather the lambs in his arms, and carry them in his bosom.* Time was, when Christ himself was taken up in old Simeon's arms, Luke ii. 28. And now he took up these children, not complaining of the burthen (as Moses did, when he was bid to *carry Israel,* that peevish child, *in his bosom, as a nursing father bears the sucking child,* Num. xi. 12), but pleased with it. If we in a ·at manner bring our children to Christ, he will take them up, not only in the arms of his power and providence, but in the arms of his pity and grace (as Ezek. xvi. 8); underneath them are the *everlasting arms.* (2.) He *put his hands upon them,* denoting the bestowing of his Spirit upon them (for that is the hand of the Lord), and his setting them apart for himself. (3.) He *blessed* them with the spiritual blessings he came to give. Our children are happy, if they have but the *Mediator's blessing* for their portion. It is true, we do not read that he baptized these children, baptism was not fully settled as the door of admission into the church till after Christ's resurrection; but he asserted their visible church-membership, and by another sign bestowed those blessings upon them, which are now appointed to be conveyed and conferred by baptism, the seal of the promise, which is *to us* and *to our children*.

17 And when he was gone forth
into the way, there came one running,
and kneeled to him, and asked him,
Good Master, what shall I do that I
may inherit eternal life? 18 And
Jesus said unto him, Why callest
thou me good? *there is* none good
but one, *that is*, God. 19 Thou
knowest the commandments, Do not
commit adultery, Do not kill, Do not
steal, Do not bear false witness, Defraud not, Honour thy father and
mother. 20 And he answered and
said unto him, Master, all these have
I observed from my youth. 21 Then
Jesus beholding him loved him, and
said unto him, One thing thou lackest: go thy way, sell whatsoever thou
hast, and give to the poor, and thou
shalt have treasure in heaven: and
come, take up the cross, and follow
me. 22 And he was sad at that saying, and went away grieved: for he
had great possessions. 23 And Jesus
looked round about, and saith unto
his disciples, How hardly shall they
that have riches enter into the kingdom of God! 24 And the disciples
were astonished at his words. But
Jesus answereth again, and saith unto
them, Children, how hard is it for
them that trust in riches to enter into
the kingdom of God! 25 It is easier
for a camel to go through the eye of
a needle, than for a rich man to enter
into the kingdom of God. 26 And
they were astonished out of measure,
saying among themselves, Who then
can be saved? 27 And Jesus looking
upon them saith, With men *it is* impossible, but not with God: for with
God all things are possible. 28 Then
Peter began to say unto him, Lo, we
have left all, and have followed thee.

29 And Jesus answered and said,
Verily I say unto you, There is no
man that hath left house, or brethren,
or sisters, or father, or mother, or
wife, or children, or lands, for my
sake, and the gospel's, 30 But he
shall receive an hundredfold now in
this time, houses, and brethren, and
sisters, and mothers, and children,
and lands, with persecutions; and in
the world to come eternal life. 31
But many *that are* first shall be last;
and the last first.

I. Here is a *hopeful meeting* between Christ and a *young man;* such he is said to be (Matt. xix. 20, 22), and a *ruler* (Luke xviii. 18), a person of quality. Some circumstances here are, which we had not in Matthew, which makes his address to Christ very promising.

1. He came *running* to Christ, which was an indication of his humility; he laid aside the gravity and grandeur of a ruler, when he came to Christ: thus too he manifested his earnestness and importunity; he *ran* as one *in haste*, and longing to be in conversation with Christ. He had now an opportunity of consulting this great Prophet, in the things that belonged to his peace, and he would not let slip the opportunity.

2. He came to him when he was *in the way*, in the midst of company: he did not insist upon a private conference with him by night, as Nicodemus did, though like him he was a ruler, but *when he shall find him without*, will *embrace* that opportunity of advising with him, *and not be ashamed*, Cant. viii. 1.

3. He *kneeled to him*, in token of the great value and veneration he had for him, as a teacher come from God, and his earnest desire to be taught by him. He bowed the knee to the Lord Jesus, as one that would not only *do obeisance* to him now, but would *yield obedience* to him always; he *bowed the knee*, as one that meant to *bow the soul* to him.

4. His address to him was serious and weighty; *Good Master, what shall I do, that I may inherit eternal life?* Eternal life was an article of his creed, though then denied by the Sadducees, a prevailing party: he thinks it a thing possible, that he may *inherit eternal life*, looking upon it not only as set before us, but as offered to us; he asks, What he shall do now that he may be happy for ever. Most men enquire for good to be *had* in this world (Ps. iv. 6), *any good;* he asks for *good to be done* in this world, in order to the enjoyment of the greatest good in the other world; not, Who will make us to *see good?* But, "Who will make us to *do good?*" He enquires for *happiness* in the way of *duty;* the *summum bonum—chief good* which Solomon was in quest of, was *that good for the sons of men which they should do*, Eccl. ii. 3. Now this was, (1.) A very serious question

in itself; it was about eternal things, and his own concern in those things. Note, *Then* there begins to be some hope of people, when they begin to enquire solicitously, what they shall do to get to heaven. (2.) It was proposed to a right person, one that was every way fit to answer it, being himself *the Way, the Truth,* and *the Life,* the true way to life, to eternal life; who came *from heaven* on purpose, first to *lay open for us,* and then to *lay open to us;* first to make, and then to make known, the way *to heaven.* Note, Those who would know what they shall do to be saved, must apply themselves to Christ, and enquire of him; it is peculiar to the Christian religion, both to show eternal life, and to show the way to it. (3.) It was proposed with a good design—to be instructed. We find this same question put by a lawyer, not *kneeling,* but standing up (Luke x. 25), with a bad design, to pick quarrels with him; he *tempted him, saying, Master, what shall I do?* It is not so much the good *words* as the good *intention* of them that Christ looks at.

5. Christ encouraged this address, (1.) By *assisting his faith, v.* 18. He called him *good Master;* Christ would have him mean thereby, that he looked upon him to be *God,* since there is none good but *one,* that is *God,* who is one, and his name one, Zech. xiv. 9. Our English word *God* doubtless hath affinity with *good;* as the Hebrews name God by his power, *Elohim,* the *strong God;* so we by his goodness, the *good God.* (2.) By directing his practice (*v.* 19); *Keep the commandments;* and thou *knowest* what they are. He mentions the six commandments of the second table, which prescribe our duty to our neighbour; he inverts the order, putting the seventh commandment before the sixth, to intimate that *adultery* is a sin no less heinous than *murder* itself. The fifth commandment is here put last, as that which should especially be remembered and observed, to keep us to all the rest. Instead of the tenth commandment, *Thou shalt not covet,* our Saviour here puts, *Defraud not.* Μὴ ἀποστερήσῃς—that is, saith Dr. Hammond, "Thou shalt rest contented with thy own, and not seek to increase it by the diminution of other men's." It is a rule of justice not to advance or enrich ourselves by doing wrong or injury to any other.

6. The young man bid fair for heaven, having been free from any open gross violations of the divine commands. Thus far he was able to say in some measure (*v.* 20), *Master, all these have I observed from my youth.* He thought he had, and his neighbours thought so too. Note, Ignorance of the extent and spiritual nature of the divine law, makes people think themselves in a better condition than really they are. Paul was alive *without the law.* But when he saw that to be *spiritual,* he saw himself to be *carnal,* Rom. vii. 9, 14. However, he that could say he was free from scandalous sin, went further than many in the way to eternal life. But though we *know nothing by ourselves, yet are we not thereby justified.* 1 Cor. iv. 4.

7. Christ had a kindness for him; *Jesus, beholding him, loved him, v.* 21. He was pleased to find that he had lived inoffensively, and pleased to see that he was inquisitive how to live better than so. Christ particularly *loves* to see young people, and rich people, *asking the way to heaven, with their faces thitherward.*

II. Here is a *sorrowful parting* between Christ and this young man.

1. Christ gave him a command of trial, by which it would appear whether he did in sincerity aim at eternal life, and press towards it: he seemed to have his heart much upon it, and if so, he is what he should be; but has he indeed his heart upon it? Bring him to the touchstone. (1.) Can he find in his heart to *part with his riches* for the service of Christ? He hath a good estate, and now, shortly, at the first founding of the Christian church, the necessity of the case will require that those who have *lands, sell them, and lay the money at the apostles' feet;* and how will he dispense with that? Acts iv. 34, 35. After awhile, tribulation and persecution will arise, because of the word; and he must be forced to sell his estate, or have it taken from him, and how will he like that? Let him know the worst now; if he will not come up to these terms, let him quit his pretensions; as good at first as at last. "*Sell whatsoever thou hast* over and above what is necessary for thy support;" probably, he had no family to provide for; let him therefore be a *father to the poor,* and make them his heirs. Every man, according to his ability, must relieve the poor, and be content, when there is occasion, to straiten himself to do it. Worldly wealth is given us, not only as *maintenance* to bear our charges through this world, according to our place in it, but as a *talent,* to be used and employed for the glory of our great Master in the world, who hath so ordered it, that the poor we should have always with us as his receivers. (2.) Can he find in his heart to go through the hardest costliest services he may be called to as a disciple of Christ, and depend upon him for a recompence *in heaven?* He asks Christ what he shall do more than he has done to obtain *eternal life,* and Christ puts it to him, whether he has indeed that firm belief of, and that high value for, eternal life that he seems to have. Doth he really believe there is a treasure in heaven sufficient to make up all he can leave, or lose, or lay out, for Christ? Is he willing to deal with Christ *upon trust?* Can he give him credit for all he is worth; and be willing to bear a present cross, in expectation of a future crown?

2. Upon this he flew off (*v.* 22); *He was sad at that saying;* was sorry that he could not be a follower of Christ upon any easier terms than leaving all to follow him; that he could not *lay hold* on eternal life, and *keep hold* of his temporal possessions too. But since he

could not come up to the terms of discipleship, he was so fair as not to pretend to it; *He went away grieved.* Here appeared the truth of that (Matt. vi. 24), *Ye cannot serve God and mammon;* while he held to mammon he did in effect *despise* Christ, as all those do who prefer the world before him. He bids for what he has a mind for in the market, yet goes away grieved, and leaves it, because he cannot have it at his own price. Two words to a bargain. Motions are not marriages. That which ruined this young man was, *he had great possessions:* thus the *prosperity of fools destroys them,* and those who spend their days in wealth are tempted to say to God, *Depart from us;* or to their hearts, *Depart from God.*

III. Here is Christ's discourse with his disciples. We are tempted to wish that Christ had *mollified* that saying which frightened this young gentleman from following him, and by any explanation taken off the harshness of it: but he knew all men's hearts; he would not court him to be his follower, because he was a *rich man* and a ruler; but, if he will go, let him go. Christ will keep no man against his will; and therefore we do not find that Christ called him back, but took this occasion to instruct his disciples in two things.

1. The difficulty of the salvation of those who have an abundance of this world; because there are few who have *a deal to leave,* that can be *persuaded to leave it* for Christ, or to lay it out in doing good.

(1.) Christ asserts this here; *He looked about* upon his *disciples,* because he would have them all take notice of what he said, that by it they might have their judgments rightly informed, and their mistakes rectified, concerning worldly wealth, which they were apt to over-rate; *How hardly shall they who have riches enter into the kingdom of God! v.* 23. They have many temptations to grapple with, and many difficulties to get over, which lie not in the way of poor people. But he explains himself, *v.* 24, where he calls the disciples *children,* because as such they should be *taught* by him, and *portioned* by him with better things than this young man left Christ to cleave to; and whereas he had said, *How hardly will those who have riches get to heaven;* here he tells them, that the danger arose not so much from their *having* riches as from their *trusting to them,* and placing their confidence in them, expecting protection, provision, and a portion from them; saying that *to their gold,* which they should say only to their God, *Thou art my hope,* Job xxxi. 24. They that have such a value as this for the wealth of the world, will never be brought to put a right value upon Christ and his grace. They that *have* ever so much riches, but do not *trust in them,* that see the vanity of them, and their utter insufficiency to make a soul happy, have got over the difficulty, and can easily part with them for Christ: but they that have ever so little, if they set their hearts upon that little, and place their happiness in it, it will keep them from Christ. He enforces this assertion with, *v.* 25, *It is easier for a camel to go through the eye of a needle, than for a rich man,* that *trusts in riches,* or inclines to do so, *to enter into the kingdom of God.* The disproportion here seems so great (though the more it is so the more it answers the intention), that some have laboured to bring the camel and the eye of the needle a little nearer together. [1.] Some imagine there might be some wicket-gate, or door, to Jerusalem, commonly known by the name of *the needle's eye,* for its straitness, through which a camel could not be got, unless he were unloaded, and made to kneel, as those camels, Gen. xxiv. 11. So a rich man cannot get to heaven, unless he be willing to part with the burthen of his worldly wealth, and stoop to the duties of a humble religion, and so enter in *at the strait gate.* [2.] Others suggest that the word we translate a *camel,* sometimes signifies a *cable-rope,* which, though not to be got through a needle's eye, yet is of greater affinity to it. A rich man, compared with the poor, is as a cable to a single thread, stronger, but not so pliable, and it will not go through the *needle's eye,* unless it be untwisted. So the rich man must be loosed and disentangled from his riches, and then there is some hope of him, that thread by thread he may be got through the eye of the needle, otherwise he is good for nothing but to cast anchor in the earth.

(2.) This truth was very surprising to the disciples; *They were astonished at his words, v.* 24. *They were astonished out of measure, and said among themselves, Who then can be saved?* They knew what were generally the sentiments of the Jewish teachers, who affirmed that the Spirit of God chooses to reside in rich men; nay, they knew what abundance of promises there were, in the Old Testament, of temporal good things; they knew likewise that all either are rich, or fain would be so, and that they who are rich, have so much the larger opportunities of doing good, and therefore were amazed to hear that it should be so hard for rich people to go to heaven.

(3.) Christ reconciled them to it, by referring it to the almighty power of God, to help even rich people over the difficulties that lie in the way of their salvation (*v.* 27); He *looked upon them,* to engage their attention, and said, "*With men it is impossible;* rich people cannot by their own skill or resolution get over these difficulties, but the grace of God can do it, for *with him all things are possible.*" If *the righteous scarcely are saved,* much more may we say so of the *rich;* and therefore when any get to heaven, they must give all the glory to God, who worketh in them *both to will and to do.*

2. The greatness of the salvation of those that have but a little of this world, and leave it for Christ. This he speaks of, upon occa-

sion of Peter's mentioning what he and the rest of the disciples had left to follow him; *Behold* (saith he), *we have left all to follow thee, v.* 28. "You have *done well,*" saith Christ, "and it will prove in the end that you have done well *for yourselves;* you shall be abundantly recompensed, and not only you shall be *reimbursed,* who have left but a little, but those that have ever so much, though it were so much as this young man had, that could not persuade himself to quit it for Christ; yet they shall have much more than an equivalent for it." (1.) The loss is supposed to be very great; he specifies, [1.] Worldly wealth; *houses* are here put first, and *lands* last: if a man quit his *house,* which should be for his habitation, and his *land,* which should be for his maintenance, and so make himself a beggar and an outcast. This has been the choice of suffering saints; farewell houses and lands, though ever so convenient and desirable, though the inheritance of fathers, for the house which is from heaven, and the inheritance of the saints in light, where are many mansions. [2.] Dear relations. *Father and mother, wife and children, brethren and sisters.* In these, as much as in any temporal blessing, the comfort of life is bound up; without these the world would be a wilderness; yet, when we must either forsake these or Christ, we must remember that we stand in nearer relation to Christ than we do to any creature; and therefore to keep in with him, we must be content to break with all the world, and to say to father and mother, as Levi did, *I have not known you.* The greatest trial of a good man's constancy is, when his love to Christ comes to stand in competition with a love that is lawful, nay, that is his duty. It is easy to such a one to forsake a *lust* for Christ, for he hath that within him, that rises against it; but to forsake a *father,* a *brother,* a *wife,* for Christ, that is, to forsake those whom he knows he must love, is hard. And yet he must do so, rather than deny or disown Christ. Thus great is the loss supposed to be; but it is *for Christ's sake,* that he may be honoured, and the *gospel's,* that it may be promoted and propagated. It is not the *suffering,* but the *cause,* that makes the *martyr.* And therefore, (2.) The advantage will be great. [1.] *They shall receive a hundred-fold in this time, houses, and brethren, and sisters;* not *in specie,* but that which is equivalent. He shall have abundance of comfort while he lives, sufficient to make up all his losses; his relation to Christ, his communion with the saints, and his title to eternal life, shall be to him *brethren,* and *sisters,* and *houses,* and all. God's providence gave Job double to what he had had, but suffering Christians shall have a *hundred-fold* in the comforts of the Spirit sweetening their creature comforts. But observe, It is added here in Mark, *with persecutions.* Even when they are gainers by Christ, let them still expect to be sufferers for him; and not to be out of the reach of persecution, till they come to heaven. Nay, The *persecutions* seem to come in here among *the receivings* in this present time; for unto you it is given, not only to believe in Christ, but also to *suffer for his name;* yet this is not all, [2.] They shall have *eternal life in the world to come.* If they receive a hundred-fold in this world, one would think they should not be encouraged to expect any more. Yet, as if that were a small matter, they shall have *life eternal* into the bargain; which is more than ten thousand-fold, ten thousand times told, for all their losses. But because they talked so much, and really more than became them, of *leaving all* for Christ, he tells them, though they were *first called,* that there should be disciples called after them, that should be preferred before them; as St. Paul, who was one *born out of due time,* and yet laboured more abundantly than all the rest of the apostles, 1 Cor. xv. 10. Then the *first* were *last,* and the last *first.*

32 And they were in the way going
up to Jerusalem; and Jesus went
before them: and they were amazed;
and as they followed, they were afraid.
And he took again the twelve, and
began to tell them what things should
happen unto him, 33 *Saying,* Behold, we go up to Jerusalem; and
the Son of man shall be delivered
unto the chief priests, and unto the
scribes; and they shall condemn him
to death, and shall deliver him to the
Gentiles: 34 And they shall mock
him, and shall scourge him, and shall
spit upon him, and shall kill him:
and the third day he shall rise again.
35 And James and John, the sons
of Zebedee, come unto him, saying,
Master, we would that thou shouldest
do for us whatsoever we shall desire.
36 And he said unto them, What
would ye that I should do for you?
37 They said unto him, Grant unto
us that we may sit, one on thy right
hand, and the other on thy left hand,
in thy glory. 38 But Jesus said unto
them, Ye know not what ye ask: can
ye drink of the cup that I drink of?
and be baptized with the baptism
that I am baptized with? 39 And
they said unto him, We can. And
Jesus said unto them, Ye shall indeed
drink of the cup that I drink of; and
with the baptism that I am baptized
withal shall ye be baptized: 40 But
to sit on my right hand and on my

left hand is not mine to give; but *it
shall be given to them* for whom it is
prepared. 41 And when the ten heard
it, they began to be much displeased
with James and John. 42 But Jesus
called them *to him*, and saith unto
them, Ye know that they which are accounted to rule over the Gentiles exercise lordship over them; and their
great ones exercise authority upon
them. 43 But so shall it not be
among you: but whosoever will be
great among you, shall be your minister: 44 And whosoever of you
will be the chiefest, shall be servant
of all. 45 For even the Son of man
came not to be ministered unto, but
to minister, and to give his life a ransom for many.

Here is, I. Christ's prediction of his own sufferings; this string he harped much upon, though in the ears of his disciples it sounded very harsh and unpleasing.

1. See here how bold he was; when they were going up to Jerusalem, *Jesus went before them,* as the *captain of our salvation,* that was now to be *made perfect through sufferings, v.* 32. Thus he showed himself forward to go on with his undertaking, even when he came to the hardest part of it. Now that the time was at hand, he said, *Lo, I come;* so far was he from *drawing back,* that now, more than ever, he *pressed forward. Jesus went before them, and they were amazed.* They began now to consider what imminent danger they ran themselves into, when they went to Jerusalem; how very malicious the Sanhedrim which sat there was against their Master and them; and they were ready to tremble at the thought of it. To hearten them, therefore, Christ *went before them.* "Come," saith he, "surely you will venture where your Master ventures." Note, When we see ourselves entering upon sufferings, it is encouraging to see our Master go before us. Or, *He went before them,* and *therefore* they were *amazed;* they admired to see with what cheerfulness and alacrity he went on, though he knew he was going to suffer and die. Note, Christ's courage and constancy in going on with his undertaking for our salvation, are, and will be, the wonder of all his disciples.

2. See here how timorous and faint-hearted his disciples were; *As they followed, they were afraid,* afraid for themselves, as being apprehensive of their own danger; and justly might they be *ashamed* of their being thus *afraid.* Their Master's courage should have put spirit into them.

3. See here what method he took to silence their fears. He did not go about to make the matter better than it was, nor to feed them with hopes that he might escape the storm, but told them *again* what he had often told them before, the *things that should happen to him.* He knew the worst of it, and therefore went on thus boldly, and he will let them know the worst of it. Come, *be not afraid;* for, (1.) There is no remedy, the matter is determined, and cannot be avoided. (2.) It is only the *Son of man* that shall suffer; their time of suffering was not at hand, he will now provide for their security. (3.) He *shall rise again;* the issue of his sufferings will be glorious to himself, and advantageous to all that are his, *v.* 33, 34. The method and particulars of Christ's sufferings are more largely foretold here than in any other of the predictions—that he shall first be delivered up by Judas to the *chief priests and the scribes;* that they shall condemn him to death, but, not having power to put him to death, shall *deliver him to the Gentiles,* to the Roman powers, and they shall *mock him,* and *scourge him,* and *spit upon him,* and *kill him.* Christ had a perfect foresight, not only of his own death, but of all the aggravating circumstances of it; and yet he thus went forth to meet it.

II. The check he gave to two of his disciples for their ambitious request. This story is much the same here as we had it Matt. xx. 20. Only there they are said to have made their request by their mother, here they are said to make it themselves; she introduced them, and presented their petition, and then they seconded it, and assented to it.

Note, 1. As, on the one hand, there are some that do not *use,* so, on the other hand, there are some that *abuse,* the great encouragements Christ has given us in prayer. He hath said, *Ask, and it shall be given you;* and it is a commendable faith to ask for the great things he has promised; but it was a culpable presumption in these disciples to make such a boundless demand upon their Master; *We would that thou shouldest do for us whatsoever we shall desire.* We had much better leave it to him to do for us what he sees fit, and he will do more than we can desire, Eph. iii. 20.

2. We must be cautious how we make general promises. Christ would not engage to do for them whatever they desired, but would know from them what it was they did desire; *What would ye that I should do for you?* He would have them go on with their suit, that they might be made ashamed of it.

3. Many have been led into a snare by false notions of Christ's kingdom, as if it were *of this world,* and like the kingdoms of the potentates of this world. James and John conclude, If Christ *rise again,* he must be a king, and if he be a king, his apostles must be peers, and one of these would willingly be the *Primus par regni—The first peer of the realm,* and the other next him, like Joseph in Pharaoh's court, or Daniel in Darius's.

4. Worldly honour is a glittering thing, with which the eyes of Christ's own disciples have many a time been dazzled. Whereas to *be good* should be more our care than to *look great,* or to have the pre-eminence.

5. Our weakness and short-sightedness appear as much in our prayers as in any thing. We cannot order our speech, when we speak to God, by reason of darkness, both concerning him and concerning ourselves. It is folly to *pre*scribe to God, and wisdom to *sub*scribe.

6. It is the will of Christ that we should prepare for sufferings, and leave it to him to recompense us for them. He needs not be put in mind, as Ahasuerus did, of the services of his people, nor can he forget their *work of faith and labour of love.* Our care must be, that we may have wisdom and grace to know how to suffer with him, and then we may trust him to provide in the best manner how we shall reign with him, and when, and where, and what, the degrees of our glory shall be.

III. The check he gave to the rest of the disciples, for their uneasiness at it. *They began to be much displeased,* to have *indignation about James and John, v.* 41. They were angry at them for affecting precedency, not because it did so ill become the disciples of Christ, but because each of them hoped to have it himself. When the Cynic trampled on Alexander's foot-cloth, with *Calco fastum Alexandri—Now I tread on Alexander's pride,* he was seasonably checked with *Sed majori fastu—But with greater pride of thine own.* So these discovered their own ambition, in their displeasure at the ambition of James and John; and Christ took this occasion to warn them against it, and all their successors in the ministry of the gospel, *v.* 42—44. He *called them to him* in a familiar way, to give them an example of condescension, then when he was reproving their ambition, and to teach them never to bid their disciples keep their distance. He shows them,

1. That dominion was generally *abused in the world* (*v.* 42); *They that seem to rule over the* Gentiles, that have the name and title of rulers, *they exercise lordship over them,* that is all they study and aim at, not so much to protect them, and provide for their welfare, as to *exercise authority upon them;* they *will be obeyed,* aim to be arbitrary, and to have their will in every thing. *Sic volo, sic jubeo, stat pro ratione voluntas—Thus I will, thus I command; my good pleasure is my law.* Their care is, what they shall get by their subjects to support their own pomp and grandeur, not what they shall do for them.

2. That therefore it ought not to be *admitted into the church;* "*It shall not be so among you;* those that shall be put under your charge, must be as sheep under the charge of the *shepherd,* who is to tend them and feed them, and be a servant to them, not as horses under the command of the driver, that works them and beats them, and gets his pennyworths out of them. He that affects to be great and chief, that thrusts himself into a secular dignity and dominion, *he shall be servant of all,* he shall be mean and contemptible in the eyes of all that are wise and good; *he that exalteth himself shall be abased.*" Or rather, "He that would be *truly* great and chief, he must lay out himself to do good to all, must stoop to the meanest services, and labour in the hardest services. Those not only shall be most *honoured* hereafter, but are most *honourable* now, who are most useful." To convince them of this, he sets before them his own example (*v.* 45); "The *Son of man* submits first to the greatest hardships and hazards, and then enters into his glory, and can you expect to come to it any other way; or to have more ease and honour than he has?" (1.) He takes upon him *the form of a servant,* comes not to be *ministered to,* and waited upon, but *to minister,* and wait to be gracious. (2.) He becomes *obedient to death,* and to its dominion, for he *gives his life a ransom for many;* did he die for the benefit of good people, and shall not we study to live for their benefit?

46 And they came to Jericho: and
as he went out of Jericho with his
disciples and a great number of people, blind Bartimæus, the son of Timæus, sat by the highway side begging.
47 And when he heard that it was
Jesus of Nazareth, he began to cry
out, and say, Jesus, *thou* son of David,
have mercy on me. 48 And many
charged him that he should hold
his peace: but he cried the more
a great deal, *Thou* son of David,
have mercy on me. 49 And Jesus
stood still, and commanded him to be
called. And they call the blind man,
saying unto him, Be of good comfort,
rise; he calleth thee. 50 And he,
casting away his garment, rose, and
came to Jesus. 51 And Jesus answered and said unto him, What wilt
thou that I should do unto thee? The
blind man said unto him, Lord, that
I might receive my sight. 52 And
Jesus said unto him, Go thy way;
thy faith hath made thee whole. And
immediately he received his sight, and
followed Jesus in the way.

This passage of story agrees with that, Matt. xx. 29, &c. Only that there we were told of *two* blind men; here, and Luke xviii. 35, only of *one:* but if there were *two,* there was *one.* This one is named here, being a *blind beggar that* was much talked of; he was called *Bartimeus,* that is, the *son of Timeus;* which, some think, signifies *the son of a blind man;* he was the blind son of a blind father, which made the case the worse, and the cure the more wonderful, and the more proper to typify the spiritual cures wrought by the grace of Christ, on those that not only are born blind, but are born of those that are blind.

I. This blind man sat *begging;* as they do with us. Note, Those who by the providence of God are disabled to get a livelihood by their own labour, and have not any other way of subsisting, are the most proper objects of charity; and particular care ought to be taken of them.

II. He cried out to the Lord Jesus for *mercy; Have mercy on me, O Lord, thou Son of David.* Misery is the object of mercy, his own miserable case he recommends to the compassion of the *Son of David,* of whom it was foretold, that, when he should come to save us, *the eyes of the blind should be opened,* Isa. xxxv. 5. In coming to Christ for help and healing, we should have an eye to him as the promised Messiah, the Trustee of mercy and grace.

III. Christ encouraged him to hope that he should find mercy; for he *stood still, and commanded him to be called.* We must never reckon it a hindrance to us in our way, to *stand still,* when it is to do a good work. Those about him, who had discouraged him at first, perhaps were now the persons that signified to him the gracious call of Christ; "*Be of good comfort, rise, he calls thee;* and if he calls thee, he will cure thee." Note, The gracious invitations Christ gives us to come to him, are great encouragements to our hope, that we shall speed well if we come to him, and shall have what we come for. Let the guilty, the empty, the tempted, the hungry, the naked, be of good comfort, for he *calls them* to be pardoned, to be supplied, to be succoured, to be filled, to be clothed, to have all that done for them, which their case calls for.

IV. The poor man, hereupon, made the best of his way to Christ; He *cast away his* loose upper *garment,* and came to Jesus (*v.* 50); he cast away every thing that might be in danger of throwing him down, or might any way hinder him in coming to Christ, or retard his motion. Those who would come to Jesus, must cast away the garment of their own sufficiency, must strip themselves of all conceit of that, and must free themselves from *every weight,* and the sin that, like long garments, doth *most easily beset them,* Heb. xii. 1.

V. The particular favour he begged, was, that his *eyes might be opened;* that so he might be able to work for his living, and might be no longer burthensome to others. It is a very desirable thing to be in a capacity of earning our own bread; and where God has given men their limbs and senses, it is a shame for men by their foolishness and slothfulness to make themselves, in effect, *blind* and *lame.*

VI. This favour he received; his eyes were opened (*v.* 52); and two things Mark here adds, which intimate, 1. How Christ made it a double favour to him, by putting the honour of it upon his faith; "*Thy faith hath made thee whole;* faith in Christ as the Son of David, and in his pity and power; not thy importunity, but *thy faith,* setting Christ on work, or rather Christ setting thy faith on work." Those supplies are most comfortable, that are fetched in by our faith. 2. How he made it a double favour to himself; When he had *received his sight,* he *followed Jesus by the way.* By this he made it appear that he was thoroughly cured, that he no more needed one to lead him, but could go himself; and by this he evidenced the grateful sense he had of Christ's kindness to him, that, when he had his sight, he made this use of it. It is not enough to *come to Christ* for spiritual healing, but, when we are healed, we must continue to follow him; that we may do honour to him, and receive instruction from him. Those that have spiritual eye-sight, see that beauty in Christ, that will effectually draw them to *run after him.*

CHAP. XI.

We are now come to the Passion-Week, the week in which Christ died, and the great occurrences of that week. I. Christ's riding in triumph into Jerusalem, ver. 1—11. II. His cursing the barren fig-tree, ver. 12—14. III. His driving those out of the temple that turned it into an exchange, ver. 15—19. IV. His discourse with his disciples concerning the power of faith and the efficacy of prayer, on occasion of the withering of the fig-tree he cursed, ver. 20—26. V. His reply to those who questioned his authority, ver. 27—33.

AND when they came nigh to
Jerusalem, unto Bethphage and
Bethany, at the mount of Olives, he
sendeth forth two of his disciples, 2
And saith unto them, Go your way into
the village over against you: and as
soon as ye be entered into it, ye shall
find the colt tied, whereon never man
sat; loose him, and bring *him.* 3
And if any man say unto you, Why
do ye this? say ye that the Lord hath
need of him; and straightway he will
send him hither. 4 And they went
their way, and found the colt tied by
the door without in a place where two
ways met; and they loose him. 5
And certain of them that stood there
said unto them, What do ye, loosing
the colt? 6 And they said unto them
even as Jesus had commanded: and
they let them go. 7 And they brought
the colt to Jesus, and cast their garments on him; and he sat upon him.
8 And many spread their garments

in the way: and others cut down
branches off the trees, and strewed
them in the way. 9 And they that
went before, and they that followed,
cried, saying, Hosanna; Blessed *is* he
that cometh in the name of the Lord:
10 Blessed *be* the kingdom of our father David, that cometh in the name
of the Lord: Hosanna in the highest.
11 And Jesus entered into Jerusalem,
and into the temple: and when he
had looked round about upon all
things, and now the eventide was
come, he went out unto Bethany with
the twelve.

We have here the story of the public entry Christ made into Jerusalem, four or five days before his death. And he came into town thus remarkably, 1. To show that he was not afraid of the power and malice of his enemies in Jerusalem. He did not steal into the city *incognito,* as one that durst not show his face; no, they needed not send spies to search for him, he comes in with observation. This would be an encouragement to his disciples that were timorous, and cowed at the thought of their enemies' power and rage; let them see how bravely their Master sets them all at defiance. 2. To show that he was not cast down or disquieted at the thoughts of his approaching sufferings. He came, not only publicly, but cheerfully, and with acclamations of joy. Though he was now but taking the field, and *girding on the harness,* yet, being fully assured of a complete victory, he thus triumphs as though he had put it off.

I. The *outside* of this triumph was very *mean;* he rode upon an ass's *colt,* which being an ass, looked contemptible, and made no figure; and, being but a *colt, whereon never man sat,* we may suppose, was rough and untrimmed, and not only so, but rude and ungovernable, and would disturb and disgrace the solemnity. This *colt* was borrowed too. Christ went upon the water in a *borrowed* boat, ate the passover in a *borrowed* chamber, was buried in a *borrowed* sepulchre, and here rode on a *borrowed* ass. Let not Christians scorn to be beholden one to another, and, when need is, to go a borrowing, for our Master did not. He had no rich trappings; they threw their clothes upon the colt, and so he *sat upon him, v.* 7. The persons that attended, were mean people; and all the show they could make, was, by *spreading their garments in the way,* and *strewing branches of trees in the way* (*v.* 8), as they used to do at the feast of tabernacles. All these were marks of his humiliation; even when he would be taken notice of, he would be taken notice of for his meanness; and they are instructions to us, not to *mind high things,* but to *condescend to them of low estate.* How ill doth it become Christians to *take state,* when Christ was so far from affecting it!

II. The *inside* of this triumph was very *great;* not only as it was the fulfilling of the scripture (which is not taken notice of here, as it was in Matthew), but as there were several rays of Christ's glory shining forth in the midst of all this meanness. 1. Christ showed his knowledge of things distant, and his power over the wills of men, when he sent his disciples for the colt, *v.* 1—3. By this it appears that he can *do every thing,* and *no thought can be withholden from him.* 2. He showed his dominion over the *creatures* in riding on *a colt that was never backed.* The subjection of the inferior part of the creation to man is spoken of with application to Christ (Ps. viii. 5, 6, compared with Heb. ii. 8); for to him it is owing, and to his mediation, that we have any remaining benefit by the grant God made to man, of a sovereignty in this lower world, Gen. i. 28. And perhaps Christ, in riding the ass's colt, would give a shadow of his power over the spirit of man, who is born as *the wild ass's colt,* Job xi. 12. 3. The colt was brought from a place *where two ways met* (*v.* 4), as if Christ would show that he came to direct those into the right way, who had *two ways* before them, and were in danger of taking the wrong. 4. Christ received the joyful *hosannas* of the people; that is, both the *welcome* they gave him, and their *good wishes* to the prosperity of his kingdom, *v.* 9. It was God that put it into the hearts of these people to cry *Hosanna,* who were not by art and management brought to it, as those were who afterward cried, *Crucify, crucify.* Christ reckons himself honoured by the faith and praises of the multitude, and it is God that brings people to do him this honour beyond their own intentions.

(1.) They *welcomed* his *person* (*v.* 9); *Blessed is he that cometh,* the ὁ ἐρχόμενος, *he that should come,* so often promised, so long expected; he comes *in the name of the Lord,* as God's Ambassador to the world; *Blessed be he:* let him have our applauses, and best affections; he is a *blessed* Saviour, and brings blessings to us, and blessed be he that sent him. Let him be *blessed in the name of the Lord,* and let all nations and ages call him *Blessed,* and think and speak highly and honourably of him.

(2.) They *wished well* to his *interest, v.* 10. They believed that, mean a figure as he made, he had a *kingdom,* which should shortly be set up in the world, that it was the kingdom of *their father David* (that father of his country), the kingdom promised to him and his seed for ever; a kingdom that came *in the name of the Lord,* supported by a divine authority. *Blessed be this kingdom;* let it take place, let it get ground, let it come in the power of it, and let all opposing rule, principality, and power, be put down; let it go on *conquering, and to conquer. Hosanna* to this kingdom; prosperity be to it; all happiness attend it. The proper signification of *hosanna* is that which we find, Rev. vii. 10. *Salvation to our God, that sitteth on the throne, and to the Lamb;* success to religion, both *natural* and *revealed, Hosanna in the highest.* Praises be to our God, who is in the *highest heavens* over all, God blessed for ever; or, Let him be praised by his angels, that are *in the highest* heavens, let our *hosannas* be an echo to theirs.

Christ, thus *attended,* thus *applauded,* came into the city, and went directly *to the temple.* Here was no banquet of wine prepared for his entertainment, nor the least refreshment; but he immediately applied himself to his work, for that was his *meat and drink.* He went *to the temple,* that the scripture might be fulfilled; "*The Lord whom ye seek, shall suddenly come to his temple,* without sending any immediate notice before him; he shall surprise you with a *day of visitation,* for he shall be *like a refiner's fire, and like fuller's soap,*" Mal. iii. 1—3. He came to the temple, and took a view of the present state of it, *v.* 11. He *looked round about upon all things,* but as yet said nothing. He saw many disorders there, but *kept silence,* Ps. l. 21. Though he intended to suppress them, he would not go about the doing of it all *on a sudden,* lest he should seem to have done it *rashly;* he let things be as they were for this night, intending the next morning to apply himself to the necessary reformation, and to take the day before him. We may be confident that God sees all the wickedness that is in the world, though he do not presently reckon for it, nor cast it out. Christ, having made his remarks upon what he saw in the temple, retired in the evening to a friend's house at Bethany, because there he would be more out of the noise of the town, and out of the way of being suspected, as designing to head a faction.

12 And on the morrow, when they
were come from Bethany, he was
hungry: 13 And seeing a fig tree afar
off having leaves, he came, if haply
he might find any thing thereon: and
when he came to it, he found nothing
but leaves: for the time of figs was
not *yet.* 14 And Jesus answered
and said unto it, No man eat fruit of
thee hereafter for ever. And his disciples heard *it.* 15 And they come
to Jerusalem: and Jesus went into
the temple, and began to cast out
them that sold and bought in the
temple, and overthrew the tables of
the moneychangers, and the seats of
them that sold doves; 16 And would
not suffer that any man should carry
any vessel through the temple. 17
And he taught, saying unto them, Is
it not written, My house shall be
called of all nations the house of
prayer? but ye have made it a den
of thieves. 18 And the scribes and
chief priests heard *it,* and sought how
they might destroy him: for they
feared him, because all the people
was astonished at his doctrine. 19
And when even was come, he went
out of the city. 20 And in the morning, as they passed by, they saw the
fig tree dried up from the roots. 21
And Peter calling to remembrance
saith unto him, Master, behold, the fig
tree which thou cursedst is withered
away. 22 And Jesus answering saith
unto them, Have faith in God. 23
For verily I say unto you, That whosoever shall say unto this mountain,
Be thou removed, and be thou cast
into the sea; and shall not doubt in
his heart, but shall believe that those
things which he saith shall come to
pass; he shall have whatsoever he
saith. 24 Therefore I say unto you,
What things soever ye desire, when ye
pray, believe that ye receive *them,*
and ye shall have *them.* 25 And
when ye stand praying, forgive, if ye
have aught against any: that your
Father also which is in heaven may
forgive you your trespasses. 26 But
if ye do not forgive, neither will your
Father which is in heaven forgive
your trespasses.

Here is, I. Christ's cursing the fruitless fig-tree. He had a convenient resting-place at Bethany, and therefore thither he went at resting-time; but his work lay at Jerusalem, and thither therefore he returned in the morning, at working-time; and so intent was he upon his work, that he went out from Bethany without breakfast, which, before he was gone far, he found the want of, and *was hungry* (*v.* 12), for he was subject to all the sinless infirmities of our nature. Finding himself in want of food, he went to a *fig-tree,* which he saw at some distance, and which being well *adorned* with green leaves he hoped to find *enriched* with some sort of fruit. But he *found nothing but leaves;* he hoped to find some fruit, *for* though *the time of* gathering in *figs* was near, it *was not yet;* so that it could not be pretended that it had had fruit, but that it was gathered and gone; for the season had not yet arrived. Or, He found none, for indeed *it was not a season of figs,* it was no good fig-year. But this was worse than any other fig-tree, for there was not so much as one fig to be found upon it, though it was so full of leaves. However, Christ was willing to make an example of it, not to the *trees*, but to the *men*, of that generation, and therefore cursed it with that curse which is the reverse of the first blessing, *Be fruitful;* he said unto it, *Never let any man eat fruit of thee hereafter for ever*, *v.* 14. *Sweetness and good fruit* are, in Jotham's parable, the honour of the *fig-tree* (Judg. ix. 11), and its serviceableness therein to man, preferable to the preferment of being *promoted over the trees;* now to be deprived of that, was a grievous *curse*. This was intended to be a type and figure of the doom passed upon the Jewish church, to which he came, *seeking fruit, but found none* (Luke xiii. 6, 7); and though it was not, according to the doom in the parable, immediately cut down, yet, according to this in the history, *blindness* and *hardness* befel them (Rom. xi. 8, 25), so that they were from henceforth *good for nothing*. The *disciples heard* what sentence Christ passed on this tree, and took notice of it. Woes from Christ's mouth are to be observed and kept in mind, as well as blessings.

II. His clearing the temple of the market-people that frequented it, and of those that made it a thoroughfare. We do not find that Christ met with food elsewhere, when he missed of it on the fig-tree; but the zeal of God's house so ate him up, and made him forget himself, that he came, hungry as he was, to Jerusalem, and went straight to the temple, and began to reform those abuses which the day before he had marked out; to show that when the Redeemer came to Zion, his errand was, to *turn away ungodliness from Jacob* (Rom. xi. 26), and that he came not, as he was falsely accused, to *destroy* the temple, but to purify and refine it, and reduce his church to its primitive rectitude.

1. He cast out the *buyers* and *sellers, overthrew the tables of the money-changers* (and threw the money to the ground, the fitter place for it), and threw down the *seats of them that sold doves*. This he did as one having authority, as *a Son in his own house*. The filth of the daughter of Zion is purged away, not by might, nor by power, but by *the spirit of judgment, and the spirit of burning*. And he did it without opposition; for what he did, was manifested to be right and good, even in the consciences of those that had connived at it, and countenanced it, because they got money by it. Note, It may be some encouragement to zealous reformers, that frequently the purging out of corruptions, and the correcting of abuses, prove an easier piece of work than was apprehended. Prudent attempts sometimes prove successful beyond expectation, and there are not those lions *found* in the way, that were feared to be.

2. He *would not suffer that any man should carry any vessel*, any sort of goods or wares, *through the temple*, or any of the courts of it, because it was the nearer way, and would save them the labour of going about, *v.* 16. The Jews owned that it was one of the instances of honour due to the temple, not to make the mountain of the house, or the court of the Gentiles, a road, or common passage, or to come into it with any bundle.

3. He gave a good reason for this; because it was written, *My house shall be called of all nations, The house of prayer*, *v.* 17. So it is written, Isa. lvi. 7. It shall pass among all people under that character. *It shall be the house of prayer to all nations;* it was so in the first institution of it; when Solomon dedicated it, it was with an eye to the sons of the strangers, 1 Kings viii. 41. And it was prophesied that it should be yet more so. Christ will have the temple, as a type of the gospel-church, to be, (1.) A *house of prayer*. After he had turned out the oxen and doves, which were things for sacrifice, he revived the appointment of it as a *house of prayer*, to teach us that when all sacrifices and offerings should be abolished, the spiritual sacrifices of prayer and praise should continue and remain for ever. (2.) That it should be so *to all nations*, and not to the people of the Jews only; for *whosoever shall call on the name of the Lord, shall be saved*, though not of the seed of Jacob, according to the flesh. It was therefore insufferable for them to *make it a den of thieves*, which would prejudice those nations against it, whom they should have invited to it. When Christ drove out the buyers and sellers at the beginning of his ministry, he only charged them with making the temple *a house of merchandise* (John ii. 16); but now he chargeth them with making it a *den of thieves*, because since then they had twice gone about to stone him in the temple (John viii. 59; x. 31), or because the traders there were grown notorious for cheating their customers, and imposing upon the ignorance and necessity of the country people, which is no better than downright thievery. Those that suffer vain worldly thoughts to lodge within them when they are at their devotions, turn the *house of prayer* into a *house of merchandise;* but they that make long prayers for a pretence to devour widows' houses, turn it into a *den of thieves*.

4. The scribes and the chief priests were extremely nettled at this, *v.* 18. They hated him, and hated to be reformed by him; and yet they *feared him*, lest he should next overthrow *their* seats, and expel *them*, being conscious to themselves of the profaning and abusing of their power. They found that he had a great interest, that *all the people were astonished at his doctrine*, and that every thing he said, was an oracle and a law to them; and what durst *he* not attempt, what could *he* not effect, being thus supported? They therefore sought, not how they might make their peace with him, but *how they might*

destroy him. A desperate attempt, and which, one would think, they themselves could not but fear was *fighting against God.* But they care not what they do, to support their own power and grandeur.

III. His discourse with his disciples, upon occasion of the fig-tree's withering away which he had cursed. At *even*, as usual, he *went out of the city* (*v.* 19), to Bethany; but it is probable that it was in the dark, so that they could not see the fig-tree; but the next morning, as they *passed by*, they observed the *fig-tree dried up from the roots, v.* 20. More is *included* many times in Christ's curses than is *expressed*, as appears by the effects of them. The curse was no more than that it should never bear fruit again, but the effect goes further, *it is dried up from the roots.* If it bear no fruit, it shall bear no leaves to cheat people. Now observe,

1. How the disciples were affected with it. Peter remembered Christ's words, and said, with surprise, *Master, behold, the fig-tree which thou cursedst is withered away, v.* 21. Note, Christ's curses have wonderful effects, and make those to wither presently, that flourished like the green bay-tree. *Those whom he curseth are cursed indeed.* This represented the character and state of the Jewish church; which, from henceforward, was a tree dried up from the roots; no longer fit for food, but for fuel only. The first establishment of the Levitical priesthood was ratified and confirmed by the miracle of a *dry rod*, which in *one night* budded, and blossomed, and brought forth almonds (Num. xvii. 8), a happy omen of the fruitfulness and flourishing of that priesthood. And now, by a contrary miracle, the expiration of that priesthood was signified by a flourishing tree dried up in a night; the just punishment of those priests that had abused it. And this seemed very strange to the disciples, and scarcely credible, that the Jews, who had been so long God's own, his only professing people in the world, should be thus abandoned; they could not imagine how that *fig-tree* should *so soon wither away:* but this comes of rejecting Christ, and being rejected by him.

2. The good instructions Christ gave them from it; for of *those* even this *withered* tree was *fruitful.*

(1.) Christ teacheth them from hence to *pray in faith* (*v.* 22); *Have faith in God.* They admired the power of Christ's word of command; "Why," saith Christ, "a lively active faith would put as great a power into your prayers, *v.* 23, 24. *Whosoever shall say to this mountain*, this mount of Olives, *Be removed, and be cast into the sea;* if he has but any word of God, general or particular, to build his faith upon, and if he *shall not doubt in his heart, but shall believe that those things which he saith*, according to the warrant he has from what God hath said, *shall come to pass, he shall have whatsoever he saith.*" Through the strength and power of God in Christ, the greatest difficulty shall be got over, and the thing shall be effected. And therefore (*v.* 24), "*What things soever ye desire, when ye pray believe that ye shall* receive them; nay, believe that ye *do receive them*, and he that has power to give them, saith, *Ye shall have them. I say unto you*, Ye shall, *v.* 24. *Verily* I say unto you, Ye shall," *v.* 23. Now this is to be applied, [1.] To that *faith of miracles* which the apostles and first preachers of the gospel were endued with, which did wonders in *things natural*, healing the sick, raising the dead, casting out devils; these were, in effect, the removing of mountains. The apostle speaks of a faith which would do that, and yet might be found where holy love was not, 1 Cor. xiii. 2. [2.] It may be applied to that *miracle of faith*, which all true Christians are endued with, which doeth wonders in *things spiritual. It justifies* us (Rom. v. 1), and so removes mountains of guilt, and casts them into the *depths of the sea*, never to rise up in judgment against us, Mic. vii. 19. It *purifies* the heart (Acts xv. 9), and so removes mountains of corruption, and *makes them plains* before the grace of God, Zech. iv. 7. It is by faith that the world is conquered, Satan's fiery darts are quenched, a soul is crucified with Christ, and yet lives; by faith we set the Lord always before us, and see him that is invisible, and have him present to our minds; and this is effectual to remove mountains, for at the presence of the Lord, at the presence of the God of Jacob, the mountains were not only moved, but *re*moved, Ps. cxiv. 4—7.

(2.) To this is added here that necessary qualification of the prevailing prayer, that we freely forgive those who have been any way injurious to us, and be in charity with all men (*v.* 25, 26); *When ye stand praying*, forgive. Note, Standing is no improper posture for prayer; it was generally used among the Jews; hence they called their prayers, their *standings;* when they would say how the world was *kept up* by prayer, they expressed it thus, *Stationibus stat mundus—The world is upheld by standings.* But the primitive Christians generally used the more humble and reverent gesture of kneeling, especially on fasting days, though not on Lord's days. When we are at prayer, we must remember to pray for others, particularly for our enemies, and those that have wronged us; now we cannot pray sincerely that God would do them good, if we bear malice to them, and wish them ill. If we have injured others before we pray, we must go and *be reconciled to them*, Matt. v. 23, 24. But if they have injured us, we go a nearer way to work, and must immediately from our hearts *forgive* them. [1.] Because this is a *good step* towards obtaining the *pardon* of our own sins: *Forgive*, that *your Father may forgive you;* that is, "that ye may be qualified to receive forgiveness, that he may forgive you without injury to his honour, as it would be, if he should suffer those to have such benefit by his mercy, as are so far from being conformable to the pattern of it." [2.] Because the want of this is a certain bar to the obtaining of the pardon of our sins; "*If ye do not forgive* those who have injured you, if ye hate their persons, bear them a grudge, meditate revenge, and take all occasions to speak ill of them, *neither will your Father forgive your trespasses.*" This ought to be remembered in prayer, because one great errand we have to the throne of grace, is, to pray for the pardon of our sins: and care about it ought to be our daily care, because prayer is a part of our daily work. Our Saviour often insists on this, for it was his great design to engage his disciples to love one another.

27 And they come again to Jerusalem:
and as he was walking in the temple,
there come to him the chief priests,
and the scribes, and the elders, 28 And
say unto him, By what authority doest
thou these things? and who gave
thee this authority to do these things?
29 And Jesus answered and said unto
them, I will also ask of you one question, and answer me, and I will tell
you by what authority I do these
things. 30 The baptism of John,
was *it* from heaven, or of men? answer me. 31 And they reasoned with
themselves, saying, If we shall say,
From heaven; he will say, Why then
did ye not believe him? 32 But if
we shall say, Of men; they feared
the people: for all *men* counted John,
that he was a prophet indeed. 33
And they answered and said unto
Jesus, We cannot tell. And Jesus
answering saith unto them, Neither
do I tell you *by* what authority I do
these things.

We have here Christ examined by the great Sanhedrim concerning his authority; for they claimed a power to call prophets to an account concerning their mission. They came to him when he was *walking in the temple,* not for his diversion, but *teaching* the people, first one company and then another. The Peripatetic philosophers were so called from the custom they had of *walking* when they taught. The cloisters, or piazzas, in the courts of the temple, were fitted for this purpose. The great men were vexed to see him followed and heard with attention, and therefore *came to him* with some solemnity, and did as it were arraign him at the bar with this question, *By what authority doest thou these things? v.* 28. Now observe,

I. How they designed hereby to run him aground, and embarrass him. If they could make it out before the people, that he had not a *legal mission,* that he was not duly *ordained,* though he was ever so well qualified, and preached ever so profitably and well, they would tell the people that they *ought not to hear him.* This they made the last refuge of an obstinate unbelief; because they were resolved not to receive his doctrine, they were resolved to find some flaw or other in his commission, and will conclude it invalid, if it be not produced and ratified in their court. Thus the Papists resolve their controversy with us very much into the mission of our ministers, and if they have but any pretence to overthrow that, they think they have gained their point, though we have the scripture ever so much on our side. But this is indeed a question, which all that act either as magistrates or as ministers, ought to be furnished with a good answer to, and often put to themselves, *By what authority do I these things?* For *how can men preach except they be sent?* Or how can they act with comfort, or confidence, or hope of success, except they be authorized? Jer. xxiii. 32.

II. How he effectually ran them aground, and embarrassed them, with this question, "What are your thoughts concerning *the baptism of John? Was it from heaven, or of men?* By what authority did John preach, and baptize, and gather disciples? *Answer me, v.* 30. Deal fairly and ingenuously, and give a categorical answer, one way or the other." By the resolving of *their* question into *this,* our Saviour intimates how near akin his doctrine and baptism were to John's; they had the same original, and the same design and tendency—to introduce the gospel kingdom. Christ might with the better grace put this question to *them,* because they had sent a committee of their own house to examine John, John i. 19. "Now," saith Christ, "what was the result of your enquiries concerning him?"

They knew what they *thought* of this question; they could not but think that *John Baptist* was a man sent of God. But the difficulty was, what they should *say to it* now. Men that oblige not themselves to speak *as they think* (which is a certain rule) cannot avoid perplexing themselves thus.

1. If they own the baptism of John to be *from heaven,* as really it was, they *shame themselves;* for Christ will presently turn it upon them, *Why did ye not then believe him,* and receive his baptism? They could not bear that Christ should say this, but they could bear it that their own consciences should say so, because they had an art of stifling and silencing them, and because what conscience said, though it might gall and grate them a little, would not *shame them;* and then *they* would do well enough, who looked no further than Saul's care, when he was convicted, *Honour me now before this people,* 1 Sam. xv. 30.

2. If they say, "*It is of men,* he was not sent of God, but his doctrine and baptism were inventions of his own," they *expose themselves,* the people will be ready to do them a mischief, or at least clamour upon them; for *all men counted John that he was a prophet indeed,* and therefore they could not bear that he should be reflected on. Note, There is a carnal slavish fear, which not only wicked subjects but wicked rulers likewise are liable to, which God makes use of as a means to keep the world in some order, and to suppress *violence,* that it shall not always *grow up into a rod of wickedness.* Now by this dilemma to which Christ brought them, (1.) They were confounded and baffled, and forced to make a dishonourable retreat; to pretend ignorance—*We cannot tell* (and that was mortification enough to those proud men), but really to discover the greatest malice and wilfulness. What Christ did by his wisdom, we must labour to do by our well doing—*put to silence the ignorance of foolish men,* 1 Pet. ii. 15. (2.) Christ came off with honour, and justified himself in refusing to give them an answer to their imperious demand; *Neither tell I you by what authority I do these things.* They did not deserve to be told; for it was plain that they contended not for truth, but victory; nor did *he* need to *tell them,* for the works which he did, told them plainly that he had authority from God to do what he did; since no man could do those miracles which he did unless God were with him. Let them wait but three or four days, and his resurrection shall tell them who gave him his authority, for by that he will be *declared to be the Son of God with power,* as by their rejecting of him, notwithstanding, they will be declared to be the enemies of God.

CHAP. XII.

In this chapter, we have, I. The parable of the vineyard let out to unthankful husbandmen, representing the sin and ruin of the Jewish church, ver. 1—12. II. Christ's silencing those who thought to ensnare him with a question about paying tribute to Cæsar, ver. 13—17. III. His silencing the Sadducees, who attempted to perplex the doctrine of the resurrection, ver. 18—27. IV. His conference with a scribe about the first and great command of the law, ver. 28—34. V. His puzzling the scribes with a question about Christ's being the Son of David, ver. 35—37. VI. The caution he gave the people, to take heed of the scribes, ver. 38—40. VII. His commendation of the poor widow that cast her two mites into the treasury, ver. 41—44.

AND he began to speak unto them
by parables. A *certain* man
planted a vineyard, and set a hedge
about *it*, and digged *a place for* the
winefat, and built a tower, and let it
out to husbandmen, and went into a
far country. 2 And at the season he
sent to the husbandmen a servant,
that he might receive from the husbandmen of the fruit of the vineyard.
3 And they caught *him*, and beat him,
and sent *him* away empty. 4 And
again he sent unto them another
servant; and at him they cast stones,
and wounded *him* in the head, and
sent *him* away shamefully handled.
5 And again he sent another; and
him they killed, and many others;
beating some, and killing some. 6
Having yet therefore one son, his
wellbeloved, he sent him also last
unto them, saying, They will reverence
my son. 7 But those husbandmen
said among themselves, This is the
heir; come, let us kill him, and the
inheritance shall be ours. 8 And
they took him, and killed *him*, and
cast *him* out of the vineyard. 9 What
shall therefore the lord of the vineyard do? he will come and destroy
the husbandmen, and will give the
vineyard unto others. 10 And have
ye not read this scripture; The stone
which the builders rejected is become
the head of the corner: 11 This was
the Lord's doing, and it is marvellous
in our eyes? 12 And they sought to
lay hold on him, but feared the people: for they knew that he had spoken
the parable against them: and they
left him and went their way.

Christ had formerly in parables showed how he designed to set up the gospel church; now he begins in parables to show how he would lay aside the Jewish church, which it might have been grafted into the *stock of,* but was built upon the *ruins of.* This parable we had just as we have it here, Matt. xxi. 33. We may observe here,

I. They that enjoy the privileges of the visible church, have a vineyard let out to them, which is capable of great improvement, and from the occupiers of which rent is justly expected. When God *showed his word unto Jacob, his statutes and judgments unto Israel* (Ps. cxlvii. 19), when he set up his temple among them, his priesthood, and his ordinances, then he *let out* to them the *vineyard* he had *planted;* which he *hedged,* and in which he *built a tower, v.* 1. Members of the church are God's tenants, and they have both a good Landlord and a good bargain, and may live well upon it, if it be not their own fault.

II. Those whom God lets out his vineyard to, he sends his servants to, to put them in mind of his just expectations from them, *v.* 2. He was not *hasty* in his demands, nor *high,* for he did not send for the rent till they could make it, *at the season;* nor did he put them to the trouble of making money of it, but was willing to take it *in specie.*

III. It is sad to think what base usage God's faithful ministers have met with, in all ages, from those that have enjoyed the privileges of the church, and have not brought forth fruit answerable. The Old-Testament prophets were persecuted even by those that went under the name of the Old-Testament church. They *beat them,* and *sent them empty away* (*v.* 3); that was bad: they *wounded them,* and *sent them away shamefully entreated* (*v.* 4); that was worse: nay, at length, they came to such a pitch of wickedness, that they *killed* them, *v.* 5.

IV. It was no wonder if those who abused the prophets, abused Christ himself. God did at length send them his Son, his *well-beloved;* it was therefore so much the greater kindness in him to send him; as in Jacob to send Joseph to visit his brethren, Gen. xxxvii. 14. And it might be expected that he whom their Master *loved,* they also should respect and love (*v.* 6); "*They will reverence my son,* and, in reverence to him, will pay their rent." But, instead of *reverencing* him because he was the son and heir, they *therefore* hated him, *v.* 7. Because Christ, in calling to repentance and reformation, made his demands with more authority than the prophets had done, they were the more enraged against him, and determined to put him to death, that they might engross all church power to themselves, and that all the respect and obedience of the people might be paid to them only; "*The inheritance shall be ours,* we will be lords paramount, and bear all the sway." There is an *inheritance,* which, if they had duly *reverenced the Son,* might have been theirs, a heavenly inheritance; but they slighted that, and would have their inheritance in the wealth, and pomp, and powers, of this world. So they *took him, and killed him;* they had not done it yet, but they would do it in a little time; and they *cast him out of the vineyard,* they refused to admit his gospel when he was gone; it would by no means agree with their scheme, and so they threw it out with disdain and detestation.

V. For such sinful and shameful doings nothing can be expected but a fearful doom (*v.* 9); *What shall therefore the Lord of the vineyard do?* It is easy to say what, for nothing could be done more provoking.

1. He will *come, and destroy the husbandmen,* whom he would have saved. When they only denied the fruit, he did not *distrain* upon them for the rent, nor *disseize* them and *dispossess* them for *non-payment;* but when they killed his servants, and his Son, he determined to *destroy* them; and this was fulfilled when Jerusalem was laid waste, and the Jewish nation extirpated and made a desolation.

2. He will *give the vineyard to others.* If he have not the rent from them, he will have it from another people, for God will be no loser by any. This was fulfilled in the taking in of the Gentiles, and the abundance of fruit which the *gospel brought forth in all the world,* Col. i. 6. If some from whom we expected well, prove bad, it doth not follow but that others will be better. Christ encouraged himself with this in his undertaking; *Though Israel be not gathered,* not gathered to him, but gathered against him, *yet shall I be glorious* (Isa. xlix. 5, 6), as a *Light to lighten the Gentiles.*

3. Their opposition to Christ's exaltation shall be no obstruction to it (*v.* 10, 11); *The stone which the builders rejected,* notwithstanding that, is become *the Head of the corner,* is highly advanced as the *Head-stone,* and of necessary use and influence as the *Corner-stone.* God will set Christ as *his King,* upon his *holy hill of Zion,* in spite of *their* project, who would *break his bands asunder* And all the world shall see and own this to be *the Lord's doing,* in justice to the Jews, and in compassion to the Gentiles. The exaltation of Christ *was the Lord's doing,* and it is *his doing* to exalt him in our hearts, and to set up his throne there; and if it be done, it cannot but be marvellous in our eyes.

Now what effect had this parable upon the chief priests and scribes, whose conviction was designed by it? They knew *he spoke this parable against them, v.* 12. They could not but see their own faces in the glass of it; and one would think it showed them their sin so very heinous, and their ruin so certain and great, that it should have frightened them into a compliance with Christ and his gospel, should have prevailed to bring them to repentance, at least to make them desist from their malicious purpose against him: but, instead of that, (1.) They *sought to lay hold on him,* and make him their prisoner immediately, and so to fulfil what he had just now said they would do to him, *v.* 8. (2.) Nothing restrained them from it but the awe they stood in of the people; they did not *reverence* Christ, nor had any *fear of* God before their eyes, but were afraid, if they should publicly lay hold on Christ, the mob would rise, and lay hold on them, and rescue him. (3.) They *left him, and went their way;* if they could not do hurt to him, they resolved he should not do good to them, and therefore they got out of the hearing of his powerful preaching, *lest they should be converted and healed.* Note, If men's prejudices be not conquered by the evidence of truth, they are but confirmed; and if the corruptions of the heart be not subdued by faithful reproofs, they are but enraged and exasperated. If the gospel be not a *savour of life unto life,* it will be a *savour of death unto death.*

13 And they send unto him certain
of the Pharisees and of the Herodians,
to catch him in *his* words. 14 And
when they were come, they say unto
him, Master, we know that thou art
true, and carest for no man: for thou
regardest not the person of men, but
teachest the way of God in truth: Is

it lawful to give tribute to Cæsar, or
not? 15 Shall we give, or shall we
not give? But he, knowing their
hypocrisy, said unto them, Why tempt
ye me? bring me a penny, that I may
see *it*. 16 And they brought *it*.
And he saith unto them, Whose *is*
this image and superscription? And
they said unto him, Cæsar's. 17 And
Jesus answering said unto them,
Render to Cæsar the things that are
Cæsar's, and to God the things that
are God's. And they marvelled at him.

When the enemies of Christ, who thirsted for his blood, could not find occasion against him from what he said against them, they tried to ensnare him by putting questions to him. Here we have him tempted, or *attempted* rather, with a question about the lawfulness of paying tribute to Cæsar. We had this narrative, Matt. xxii. 15.

I. The persons they employed were the *Pharisees* and the *Herodians*, men that in this matter were contrary to one another, and yet concurred against Christ, *v.* 13. The Pharisees were great sticklers for the liberty of the Jews, and, if he should say, It is lawful to give tribute to Cæsar, they would incense the common people against him, and the Herodians would, underhand, assist them in it. The Herodians were great sticklers for the Roman power, and, if he should discountenance the paying of tribute to Cæsar, they would incense the governor against him, yea, and the Pharisees, against their own principles, would join with them in it. It is no new thing for those that are at variance in other things, to join in a confederacy against Christ.

II. The pretence they made was, that they desired him to resolve them a case of conscience, which was of great importance in the present juncture; and they take on them to have a high opinion of his ability to resolve it, *v.* 14. They complimented him at a high rate, called him *Master*, owned him for a Teacher of the *way of God*, a Teacher of it *in truth*, one who taught what was good, and upon principles of truth, who would not be brought by smiles or frowns to depart a step from the rules of equity and goodness; "*Thou carest for no man*, nor *regardest the person of men*, thou art not afraid of offending either the jealous prince on one hand, or the jealous people on the other; *thou art right*, and always in the right, and dost in a right manner declare good and evil, truth and falsehood." If they spoke as they thought concerning Christ, when they said, *We know that thou art right*, their persecuting him, and putting him to death, as a deceiver, was sin against knowledge; they knew him, and yet crucified him. However, a man's testimony shall be taken most strongly against himself, and *out of their own mouths are they judged;* they knew that he taught the way of God in truth, and yet rejected the counsel of God against themselves. The professions and pretences of hypocrites will be produced in evidence against them, and they will be self-condemned. But if they did not know or believe it, they *lied unto God with their mouth, and flattered him with their tongue.*

III. The question they put was, *Is it lawful to give tribute to Cæsar, or not?* They would be thought desirous to know their duty. *As a nation that did righteousness, they ask of God the ordinances of justice*, when really they desired nothing but to know what he would say, in hopes that, which side soever he took of the question, they might take occasion from it to accuse him. Nothing is more likely to ensnare ministers, than bringing them to meddle with controversies about civil rights, and to settle land-marks between the prince and the subject, which it is fit should be done, while it is not at all fit that they should have the doing of it. They seemed to refer the determining of this matter to Christ; and he indeed was fit to determine it, for *by him kings reign, and princes decree justice;* they put the question fairly, *Shall we give, or shall we not give?* They seemed resolved to stand to his award; "If thou sayest that we must pay tribute, we will do it, though we be made beggars by it. If thou sayest that we must not, we will not, though we be made traitors for it." Many seem desirous to know their duty, who are no ways disposed to do it; as those proud men, Jer. xlii. 20.

IV. Christ determined the question, and evaded the snare, by referring them to their national concessions already made, by which they were precluded from disputing this matter, *v.* 15—17. He *knew their hypocrisy*, the malice that was in their hearts against him, while *with their mouth they showed all this love.* Hypocrisy, though ever so artfully managed, cannot be concealed from the Lord Jesus. He sees the *potsherd* that is *covered* with the *silver dross.* He knew they intended to ensnare him, and therefore contrived the matter so as to ensnare them, and to oblige them by their own words to do what they were unwilling to do, which was, to pay their taxes honestly and quietly, and yet at the same time to screen himself against their exceptions. He made them acknowledge that the current money of their nation was Roman money, had the emperor's image on one side, and his *superscription* on the reverse; and if so, 1. *Cæsar* might command their money for the public benefit, because he has the custody and conduct of the state, wherein he ought to have his charges borne; *Render to Cæsar the things that are Cæsar's.* The circulation of the money is from him as the fountain, and therefore it must return to him. As far as it is *his*, so far it must be rendered to him; and how far it is *his*, and may be commanded by him, is to be judged by the constitution of the government, according as it is, and hath settled the prerogative of the prince and the property of the subject. 2. Cæsar might not command their consciences, nor did he pretend to it; he offered not to make any alteration in their religion. "Pay your tribute, therefore, without murmuring or disputing, but be sure to *render to God the things that are God's.*" Perhaps he referred to the parable he had just now put forth, in which he had condemned them for not *rendering* the fruits to the Lord of the vineyard, *v.* 2. Many that seem careful to give to men their due, are in no care to give to God *the glory due to his name;* whereas our hearts and best affections are as much due to him as ever rent was to a landlord, or tribute to a prince. All that heard Christ, *marvelled* at the discretion of his answer, and how ingeniously he avoided the snare; but I doubt none were brought by it, as they ought to be, to render to God themselves and their devotions. Many will commend the wit of a sermon, that will not be commanded by the divine laws of a sermon.

18 Then come unto him the Sadducees, which say there is no resurrection; and they asked him, saying,
19 Master, Moses wrote unto us, If
a man's brother die, and leave *his* wife
behind him, and leave no children,
that his brother should take his wife,
and raise up seed unto his brother.
20 Now there were seven brethren:
and the first took a wife, and dying
left no seed. 21 And the second
took her, and died, neither left he any
seed: and the third likewise. 22 And
the seven had her, and left no seed:
last of all the woman died also. 23
In the resurrection therefore, when
they shall rise, whose wife shall she
be of them? for the seven had her
to wife. 24 And Jesus answering
said unto them, Do ye not therefore
err, because ye know not the scriptures, neither the power of God? 25
For when they shall rise from the dead,
they neither marry, nor are given in
marriage; but are as the angels which
are in heaven. 26 And as touching
the dead, that they rise: have ye not
read in the book of Moses, how in the
bush God spake unto him, saying, I
am the God of Abraham, and the God
of Isaac, and the God of Jacob? 27
He is not the God of the dead, but
the God of the living: ye therefore
do greatly err.

The Sadducees, who were the deists of that age, here attack our Lord Jesus, it should seem, not as the scribes, and Pharisees, and chief-priests, with any malicious design upon his person; they were not bigots and persecutors, but sceptics and infidels, and their design was upon his doctrine, to hinder the spreading of that: they denied that there was any resurrection, any world of spirits, any state of rewards and punishments on the other side of death: now those great and fundamental truths which they denied, Christ had made it his business to establish and prove, and had carried the notion of them much further than ever it was before carried; and therefore they set themselves to perplex his doctrine.

I. See here the method they take to entangle it; they quote the ancient law, by which, if a man died without issue, his brother was obliged to marry his widow, *v.* 19. They suppose a case to happen that, according to that law, seven brothers were, successively, the husbands of one woman, *v.* 20. Probably, these Sadducees, according to their wonted profaneness, intended hereby to ridicule that law, and so to bring the whole frame of the Mosaic institution into contempt, as absurd and inconvenient in the practice of it. Those who deny divine truths, commonly set themselves to disparage divine laws and ordinances. But this was only by the by; their design was to expose the doctrine of the resurrection; for they suppose that if there be a future state, it must be such a one as this, and then the doctrine, they think, is clogged either with this invincible absurdity, that a woman in that state must have seven husbands, or else with this insolvable difficulty, whose wife she must be. See with what subtlety these heretics *undermine* the truth; they do not *deny* it, nor say, *There can be* no resurrection; nay, they do not seem to doubt of it, nor say, *If there be a resurrection,* whose wife shall she be? as the devil to Christ, *If thou be the Son of God*. But, as though these beasts of the field were more subtle than the serpent himself, they pretend to own the truth, as if they were not Sadducees, no not they; who said that they denied the resurrection? They take it for granted that there is a resurrection, and would be thought to desire instruction concerning it, when really they are designing to give it a fatal stab, and think that they shall do it. Note, It is the common artifice of heretics and Sadducees to perplex and entangle the truth, which they have not the impudence to deny.

II. See here the method Christ takes to clear and establish this truth, which they attempted to darken, and give a shock to. This was a matter of moment, and therefore Christ does not pass it over lightly, but enlarges upon it, that, if they should not be reclaimed, yet others might be confirmed.

1. He charges the Sadducees with *error,* and charges that upon their *ignorance.* They

who banter the doctrine of the resurrection, as some do in our age, would be thought the only knowing men, because the only *free thinkers,* when really they are the fools in Israel, and the most *enslaved* and prejudiced thinkers in the world. *Do ye not therefore err?* Ye cannot but be sensible of it yourselves, and that the cause of your error is, (1.) Because ye do not *know the scriptures.* Not but that the Sadducees had read the scriptures, and perhaps were ready in them; yet they might be truly said not to *know the scriptures,* because they did not know the sense and meaning of them, but put false constructions upon them; or they did not receive the scriptures as the word of God, but set up their own corrupt reasonings in opposition to the scripture, and would believe nothing but what they could see. Note, A right knowledge of the scripture, as the fountain whence all revealed religion now flows, and the foundation on which it is built, is the best preservative against error. Keep the truth, the scripture-truth, and it shall keep thee. (2.) Because ye *know not the power of God.* They could not but know that God is almighty, but they would not apply that doctrine to this matter, but gave up the truth to the objections of the impossibility of it, which would all have been answered, if they had but stuck to the doctrine of God's omnipotence, to which *nothing is impossible.* This therefore which God hath spoken once, we are concerned to hear twice, to hear and believe, to hear and apply—that *power belongs to God,* Ps. lxii. 11; Rom. iv. 19—21. The same power that made soul and body, and preserved them while they were together, can preserve the body safe, and the soul active, when they are parted, and can unite them together again; for *behold, the Lord's arm is not shortened.* The power of God, seen in the return of the spring (Ps. civ. 30), in the reviving of the corn (John xii. 24), in the restoring of an abject people to their prosperity (Ezek. xxxvii. 12—14), in the raising of so many to life, miraculously, both in the Old Testament and in the New, and especially in the resurrection of Christ (Eph. i. 19, 20), are all earnests of our resurrection by the same power (Phil. iii. 21); *according to the mighty working whereby he is able to subdue all things to himself.*

2. He sets aside all the force of their objection, by setting the doctrine of the future state in a true light (*v.* 25); *When they shall rise from the dead, they neither marry, nor are given in marriage.* It is a folly to ask, *Whose wife shall she be of the seven?* For the relation between husband and wife, though instituted in the earthly paradise, will not be known in the heavenly one. Turks and infidels expect sensual pleasures in their fools' paradise, but Christians *know* better things—that *flesh and blood shall not inherit the kingdom of God* (1 Cor. xv. 50); and *expect* better things—even a full satisfaction in God's love and likeness (Ps. xvii. 15); they are *as the angels of God in heaven,* and we know that they have neither wives nor children. It is no wonder if we confound ourselves with endless absurdities, when we measure our ideas of the world of spirits by the affairs of this world of sense.

III. He builds the doctrine of the future state, and of the blessedness of the righteous in that state, upon the covenant of God with Abraham, which God was pleased to own, being after Abraham's death, *v.* 26, 27. He appeals to the scriptures; *Have ye not read in the book of Moses?* We have some advantage in dealing with those that have *read the scriptures,* though many that have read them, *wrest them,* as these Sadducees did, to *their own destruction.* Now that which he refers them to is, what God said to Moses at the bush, *I am the God of Abraham;* not only, I *was* so, but I *am* so; I am the portion and happiness of Abraham, a God all-sufficient to him. Note, It is absurd to think that God's relation to Abraham should be continued, and thus solemnly recognised, if Abraham was annihilated, or that the *living God* should be the portion and happiness of a man that is dead, and must be for ever so; and therefore you must conclude, 1. That Abraham's soul exists and acts in a state of separation from the body. 2. That therefore, some time or other, the body must rise again; for there is such an innate inclination in a human soul towards its body, as would make a total and everlasting separation inconsistent with the ease and repose, much more with the bliss and joy of those souls that have the Lord for their God. Upon the whole matter, he concludes, *Ye therefore do greatly err.* Those that deny the resurrection, greatly err, and ought to be told so.

28 And one of the scribes came,
and having heard them reasoning together, and perceiving that he had answered them well, asked him, Which
is the first commandment of all? 29
And Jesus answered him, The first of all the commandments *is,* Hear, O Israel; The Lord our God is one
Lord: 30 And thou shalt love the Lord thy God with all thy heart, and with all thy soul, and with all thy mind, and with all thy strength: this
is the first commandment. 31 And
the second *is* like, *namely* this, Thou shalt love thy neighbour as thyself. There is none other commandment
greater than these. 32 And the
scribe said unto him, Well, Master, thou hast said the truth: for there is one God; and there is none other
but he: 33 And to love him with all

the heart, and with all the understanding, and with all the soul, and
with all the strength, and to love *his*
neighbour as himself, is more than all
whole burnt offerings and sacrifices.
34 And when Jesus saw that he answered discreetly, he said unto him,
Thou art not far from the kingdom of
God. And no man after that durst
ask him *any question.*

The scribes and Pharisees were (however bad otherwise) enemies to the Sadducees; now one would have expected that, when they heard Christ argue so well against the Sadducees, they would have countenanced him, as they did Paul when he appeared against the Sadducees (Acts xxiii. 9); but it had not that effect: because he did not fall in with them in the ceremonials of religion, his agreeing with them in the essentials, gained him no manner of respect with them. Only we have here an account of *one* of them, a scribe, who had so much civility in him as to take notice of Christ's answer to the Sadducees, and to own that he had *answered well,* and much to the purpose (*v.* 28); and we have reason to hope that he did not join with the other scribes in persecuting Christ; for here we have his application to Christ for instruction, and it was such as became him; not tempting Christ, but desiring to improve his acquaintance with him.

I. He enquired, *Which is the first commandment of all? v.* 28. He doth not mean the first in *order,* but the first in *weight* and *dignity;* "Which is that command which we ought to have in a special manner an eye to, and our obedience to which will lay a foundation for our obedience to all the rest?" Not that any commandment of God is little (they are all the commands of a great God), but some are greater than others, moral precepts than rituals, and of some we may say, They are the *greatest of all.*

II. Christ gave him a direct answer to this enquiry, *v.* 29—31. Those that sincerely desire to be instructed concerning their duty, Christ will *guide in judgment,* and *teach his way.* He tells him,

1. That the great commandment of all, which is indeed inclusive of all, is, that of *loving God with all our hearts.* (1.) Where this is the commanding principle in the soul, there is a disposition to every other duty. Love is the leading affection of the soul; the love of God is the leading grace in the renewed soul. (2.) Where this is not, nothing else that is good is done, or done aright, or accepted, or done long. Loving God with all our heart, will effectually take us off from, and arm us against, all those things that are rivals with him for the throne in our souls, and will engage us to every thing by which he may be honoured, and with which he will be pleased: and no commandment will be grievous where this principle commands, and has the ascendant. Now here in, Mark, our Saviour prefixes to this command the great doctrinal truth upon which it is built (*v.* 29); *Hear, O Israel, The Lord our God is one Lord;* if we firmly believe this, it will follow, that we shall love him *with all our heart.* He is Jehovah, who has all amiable perfections in himself; he is *our God,* to whom we stand related and obliged; and therefore we ought to *love him,* to set our affections on him, let out our desire toward him, and take a delight in him; and he is *one Lord,* therefore he must be loved with our *whole heart;* he has the sole *right to us,* and therefore ought to have the sole *possession of us.* If he be one, our hearts must be one with him, and since there is no God besides, no rival must be admitted with him upon the throne.

2. That the second great commandment is, to *love our neighbour as ourselves* (*v.* 31), as truly and sincerely as we love ourselves, and in the same instances, and we must show it by *doing as we would be done by.* As we must therefore love God better than ourselves, because he is Jehovah, a being infinitely better than we are, and must love him with *all our heart,* because he is *one Lord,* and there is no other like him; so we must *love our neighbour as ourselves,* because he is of the same nature with ourselves; our hearts are fashioned alike, and my neighbour and myself are of one body, of one society, that of the world of mankind; and if a fellow-Christian, and of the same sacred society, the obligation is the stronger. *Hath not one God created us?* Mal. ii. 10. Has not one Christ redeemed us? Well might Christ say, *There is no other commandment greater than these;* for in these all the law is fulfilled, and if we make conscience of obedience to these, all other instances of obedience will follow of course.

III. The scribe consented to what Christ said, and descanted upon it, *v.* 32, 33. 1. He commends Christ's decision of this question; *Well, Master, thou hast said the truth.* Christ's assertions needed not the scribe's attestations; but this scribe, being a man in authority, thought it would put some reputation upon what Christ said, to have it commended by him; and it shall be brought in evidence against those who persecuted Christ, as a deceiver, that one of themselves, even a scribe of their own, confessed that he *said the truth,* and said it *well.* And thus must we subscribe to Christ's sayings, must set to our seal that they are true. 2. He comments upon it. Christ had quoted that great doctrine, that *the Lord our God is one Lord;* and this he not only assented to, but added, "*There is none other but he;* and therefore we must have no other God besides." This excludes all rivals with him, and secures the throne in the heart entire for him. Christ had laid down that great law, of loving God *with all our heart;* and this also he explains —that it is loving him *with the understanding,* as those that know what abundant reason we have to love him. Our love to God, as it must be an *entire,* so it must be an *intelligent,* love; we must love him with *all* the understanding, ἐξ ὅλης τῆς συνέσεως—*out of the whole understanding;* our rational powers and faculties must all be set on work to lead out the affections of our souls toward God. Christ had said, "To love God and our neighbour is the greatest commandment of all;" "Yea," saith the scribe, "it is better, it is *more than all whole-burnt-offerings and sacrifices,* more acceptable to God, and will turn to a better account to ourselves." There were those who held, that the law of *sacrifices* was the *greatest commandment* of all; but this scribe readily agreed with our Saviour in this —that the law of love to God and our neighbour is greater than that of *sacrifice,* even than that of *whole-burnt-offerings,* which were intended purely for the honour of God.

IV. Christ approved of what he said, and encouraged him to proceed in his enquiries of him, *v.* 34. 1. He owned that he understood well, as far as he went; so far, so good. *Jesus saw that he answered discreetly,* and was the more pleased with it, because he had of late met with so many even of the scribes, men of letters, that answered *indiscreetly,* as those that had *no understanding,* nor desired to have any. He answered νουνεχῶς—*as one that had a mind;* as a rational intelligent man, as one that had his wits about him; as one whose reason was not blinded, whose judgment was not biassed, and whose forethought was not fettered, by the prejudices which other scribes were so much under the power of. He answered as one that allowed himself liberty and leisure to consider, and as one that had considered. 2. He owned that he stood fair for a further advance; "*Thou art not far from the kingdom of God,* the kingdom of grace and glory; thou art in a likely way to be a Christian, a disciple of Christ. For the doctrine of Christ insists most upon these things, and is designed, and has a tendency direct, to bring thee to this." Note, There is hope of those who make a good use of the light they have, and go as far as that will carry them, that by the grace of God they will be led further, by the clearer discoveries God has to make to them. What became of this scribe we are not told, but would willingly hope that he took the hint Christ hereby gave him, and that, having been told by him, so much to his satisfaction, what was the great commandment of the law, he proceeded to enquire of him, or his apostles, what was the great commandment of the gospel too. Yet, if he did not, but took up here, and went no further, we are not to think it strange; for there are many who are *not far from the kingdom of God,* and yet never come thither. Now, one would think, this should have invited many to consult him: but it had a contrary effect; *No man, after that, durst ask him any question;* every thing he said, was spoken with such authority and majesty, that every one stood in awe of him; those that desired to *learn,* were *ashamed* to ask, and those that designed to *cavil,* were *afraid* to ask

35 And Jesus answered and said,
while he taught in the temple, How
say the scribes that Christ is the son
of David? 36 For David himself
said by the Holy Ghost, the LORD
said to my Lord, Sit thou on my right
hand, till I make thine enemies thy
footstool. 37 David therefore himself calleth him Lord; and whence
is he *then* his son? And the common
people heard him gladly. 38 And
he said unto them in his doctrine,
Beware of the scribes, which love to
go in long clothing, and *love* salutations in the marketplaces, 39 And the
chief seats in the synagogues, and the
uppermost rooms at feasts: 40 Which
devour widows' houses, and for a pretence make long prayers: these shall
receive greater damnation.

Here, I. Christ shows the people how weak and defective the scribes were in their preaching, and how unable to solve the difficulties that occurred in the scriptures of the Old Testament, which they undertook to expound. Of this he gives an instance, which is not so fully related here as it was in Matthew. Christ was *teaching in the temple:* many things he said, which were not written; but notice is taken of this, because it will stir us up to enquire *concerning Christ,* and to enquire *of him;* for none can have the right knowledge of him but *from himself;* it is not to be had from *the scribes,* for they will soon be run aground.

1. They told the people that the Messiah was to be the *Son of David* (*v.* 35), and they were in the right; he was not only to descend from his loins, but to fill his throne (Luke i. 32); *The Lord God shall give him the throne of his father David.* The scripture said it often, but the people took it as what the scribes said; whereas the truths of God should rather be quoted from our Bibles than from our ministers, for there is the original of them. *Dulcius ex ipso fonte bibuntur aquæ—The waters are sweetest when drawn immediately from their source.*

2. Yet they could not tell them how, notwithstanding that it was very proper for David, in spirit, the spirit of prophecy, to call him *his Lord,* as he doth, Ps. cx. 1. They had taught the people that concerning the Messiah, which would be for the honour of their nation—that he should be a branch of their royal family; but they had not taken

care to teach them that which was for the honour of the Messiah himself—that he should be the Son of God, and, as such, and not otherwise, *David's Lord.* Thus they *held the truth in unrighteousness,* and were *partial* in the gospel, as well as in the law, of the Old Testament. They were able to say it, and prove it—that Christ was to be David's son; but if any should object, *How then doth David himself call him Lord?* they would not know how to avoid the force of the objection. Note, Those are unworthy to sit in Moses's seat, who, though they are able to preach the truth, are not in some measure able to defend it when they have preached it, and to convince gainsayers.

Now this galled the scribes, to have their ignorance thus exposed, and, no doubt, incensed them more against Christ; but the *common people heard him gladly, v.* 37. What he preached was surprising and affecting; and though it reflected upon the scribes, it was instructive to them, and they had never heard such preaching. Probably there was something more than ordinarily commanding and charming in his voice and way of delivery, which recommended him to the affections of the common people; for we do not find that any were wrought upon to *believe* in him, and to *follow* him, but he was to them as a *lovely song of one that could play well on an instrument;* as Ezekiel was to his hearers, Ezek. xxxiii. 32. And perhaps some of these cried, *Crucify him,* as Herod heard John Baptist gladly, and yet cut off his head.

II. He cautions the people to take heed of suffering themselves to be imposed upon by the scribes, and of being infected with their pride and hypocrisy; *He said unto them in his doctrine, "Beware of the scribes* (*v.* 38); stand upon your guard, that you neither imbibe their peculiar opinions, nor the opinions of the people concerning them." The charge is long as drawn up against them in the parallel place (Matt. xxiii.); it is here contracted.

1. They affect to appear *very great;* for they go in *long clothing,* with vestures *down to their feet,* and in those they walk *about the streets,* as princes, or judges, or gentlemen of the long robe. Their going in such clothing was not sinful, but their *loving* to go in it, priding themselves in it, valuing themselves on it, commanding respect by it, saying to their long clothes, as Saul to Samuel, *Honour me now before this people,* this was a product of pride. Christ would have his disciples go with *their loins girt.*

2. They affect to appear *very good;* for they pray, they make *long prayers,* as if they were very intimate with heaven, and had a deal of business there. They took care it should be known that they prayed, that they prayed long, which, some think, intimates that they prayed not for themselves only, but for others, and therein were very particular and very large; this they did *for a pretence,* that they might seem to love prayer, not only for God's sake, whom hereby they pretended to glorify, but for their neighbour's sake, whom hereby they pretended to be serviceable to.

3. They herein aimed to *advance* themselves: they coveted applause, and were fond of it; they loved *salutations in the market-places,* and the *chief seats in the synagogues, and the uppermost rooms at feasts;* these pleased a vain fancy; to have these given them, they thought, expressed the value *they* had for them, who did know them, and gained them respect for those who did not.

4. They herein aimed to *enrich* themselves They *devoured widows' houses,* made themselves masters of their estates by some trick or other; it was to screen themselves from the suspicion of dishonesty, that they put on the mask of piety; and that they might not be thought as bad as the worst, they were studious to seem as good as the best. Let fraud and oppression be thought the worse of for their having *profaned* and *disgraced* long prayers; but let not prayers, no nor *long prayers,* be thought the worse of, if made in humility and sincerity, for their having been by some thus abused. But as iniquity, thus disguised with a show of piety, is *double* iniquity, so its doom will be doubly heavy; *These shall receive greater damnation;* greater than those that live without prayer, greater than they would have received for the wrong done to the poor widows, if it had not been thus disguised. Note, The damnation of hypocrites will be of all others the greatest damnation.

41 And Jesus sat over against the
treasury, and beheld how the people
cast money into the treasury: and
many that were rich cast in much.
42 And there came a certain poor
widow, and she threw in two mites,
which make a farthing. 43 And he
called *unto him* his disciples, and saith
unto them, Verily I say unto you,
That this poor widow hath cast more
in, than all they which have cast into
the treasury: 44 For all *they* did cast
in of their abundance; but she of her
want did cast in all that she had, *even*
all her living.

This passage of story was not in Matthew, but is here and in Luke; it is Christ's commendation of the poor widow, that cast *two mites* into the treasury, which our Saviour, busy as he was in preaching, found leisure to take notice of. Observe,

I. There was a *public fund* for charity, into which contributions were brought, and out of which distributions were made; a poor's-box, and this in *the temple;* for works of charity and works of piety very fitly go together; where God is honoured by our worship, it is proper he should be honoured by the relief of his poor; and we often find *prayers* and *alms* in conjunction, as Acts x. 2, 4. It is good to erect public receptacles of charity for the inviting and directing of private hands in giving to the poor; nay it is good for those who are of ability to have funds of their own, to *lay by as God has prospered them* (1 Cor. xvi. 2), that they may have something ready to give when an object of charity offers itself, which is before dedicated to such uses.

II. Jesus Christ had *an eye* upon it; *He sat over against the treasury, and beheld how the people cast money into it;* not grudging either that he had none to cast in, or had not the disposal of that which was cast in, but observing what was cast in. Note, Our Lord Jesus takes notice of what we contribute to pious and charitable uses; whether we give liberally or sparingly; whether cheerfully or with reluctance and ill-will: nay, he looks at the heart; he observes what principles we act upon, and what our views are, in giving alms; and whether we do it as unto the Lord, or only to be seen of men.

III. He saw *many that were rich cast in much:* and it was a good sight to see rich people charitable, to see *many* rich people so, and to see them not only cast in, but cast in *much.* Note, Those that are rich, ought to give richly; if God give abundantly to us, he expects we should give abundantly to the poor; and it is not enough for those that are rich, to say, that they give as much as others do, who perhaps have much less of the world than they have, but they must give in proportion to their estates; and if objects of charity do not present themselves, that require so much, they ought to enquire them out, and to *devise liberal things.*

IV. There was a *poor widow that cast in two mites, which make a farthing* (*v.* 42); and our Lord Jesus highly commended her; *called his disciples* to him, and bid them take notice of it (*v.* 43); told them that she could very ill spare that which she gave, she had scarcely enough for herself, it was *all her living,* all she had to live upon for that day, and perhaps a great part of what she had earned by her labour the day before; and that forasmuch as he knew she did it from a truly charitable disposition, he reckoned it more than all that put together, which the rich people threw in; for they did *cast in of their abundance, but she of her want, v.* 44. Now many would have been ready to censure this *poor widow,* and to think she did ill; why should she give to others, when she had little enough for herself? Charity begins at home; or, if she would give it, why did she not bestow it upon some poor body that she knew? What occasion was there for her bringing it to the *treasury* to be disposed of by the chief priests, who, we have reason to fear, were partial in the disposal of it? It is so rare a thing to find any that would not blame this widow, that we cannot expect to find any that will imitate her; and yet our Saviour commends her, and therefore we are sure that she did very well and wisely. If Christ saith, *Well-done,* no matter who saith otherwise; and we must hence learn, 1. That *giving alms,* is an excellent good thing, and highly pleasing to the Lord Jesus; and if we be humble and sincere in it, he will graciously accept of it, though in some circumstances there may not be all the discretion in the world. 2. Those that have but a *little,* ought to give alms out of *their little.* Those that live by their labour, from hand to mouth, must *give to those that need,* Eph. iv. 28. 3. It is very good for us to straiten and deny ourselves, that we may be able to give the more to the poor; to deny ourselves not only superfluities, but even conveniences, for the sake of charity. We should in many cases pinch ourselves, that we may supply the necessities of others; this is loving our neighbours as ourselves. 4. Public charities should be encouraged, for they bring upon a nation public blessings; and though there may be some mismanagement of them, yet that is not a good reason why we should not bring in our *quota* to them. 5. Though we can give but *a little* in charity, yet if it be according to our ability, and be given with an upright heart, it shall be accepted of Christ, who requires *according to what a man has, and not according to what he has not;* two mites shall be put upon the score, and brought to account, if given in a right manner, as if they had been two pounds. 6. It is much to the praise of charity, when we give not only *to our power,* but *beyond our power,* as the Macedonian churches, whose *deep poverty abounded to the riches of their liberality,* 2 Cor. viii. 2, 3. When we can cheerfully provide for others, out of our own necessary provision, as the widow of Sarepta for Elijah, and Christ for his five thousand guests, and trust God to provide for us some other way, *this is thank-worthy.*

CHAP. XIII.

We have here the substance of that prophetical sermon which our Lord Jesus preached, pointing at the destruction of Jerusalem, and the consummation of all things; it was one of the last of his sermons, and not ad populum—to the people, but ad clerum—to the clergy; it was private, preached only to four of his disciples, with whom his secret was. Here is, I. The occasion of his prediction—his disciples' admiring the buildings of the temple (ver. 1, 2), and their enquiry concerning the time of the desolation of them, ver. 3, 4. II. The predictions themselves, 1. Of the rise of deceivers, ver. 5, 6, 21—23. 2. Of the wars of the nations, ver. 7, 8. 3. Of the persecution of Christians, ver. 9—13. 4. Of the destruction of Jerusalem, ver. 14—20. 5. Of the end of the world, ver. 24—27. III. Some general intimations concerning the time of them, ver. 28—32 IV. Some practical inferences from all, ver. 33—37.

AND as he went out of the temple, one of his disciples saith
unto him, Master, see what manner
of stones and what buildings *are here!*
2 And Jesus answering said unto him,
Seest thou these great buildings? there
shall not be left one stone upon another, that shall not be thrown down.
3 And as he sat upon the mount of

Olives over against the temple, Peter
and James and John and Andrew
asked him privately, 4 Tell us, when
shall these things be? and what *shall*
be the sign when all these things shall
be fulfilled?

We may here see,

I. How apt many of Christ's own disciples are to idolize things that look *great*, and have been long looked upon as *sacred.* They had heard Christ complain of those who had made the temple a *den of thieves;* and yet, when he quitted it, for the wickedness that remained in it, they court him to be as much in love as they were with the stately structure and adorning of it. One of them said to him, "Look, Master, *what manner of stones, and what buildings are here, v.* 1. We never saw the like in Galilee; O do not leave this fine place."

II. How little Christ values external pomp, where there is not real purity; "*Seest thou these great buildings*" (saith Christ), "and admirest thou them? I tell thee, the time is at hand when *there shall not be left one stone upon another, that shall not be thrown down,*" *v.* 2. And the sumptuousness of the fabric shall be no security to it, no nor move any compassion in the Lord Jesus towards it. He looks with *pity* upon the ruin of precious souls, and weeps over them, for on them he has put a great value; but we do not find him look with any pity upon the ruin of a magnificent house, when he is driven out of it by sin, for that is of small value with him. With what little concern doth he say, *Not one stone shall be left on another!* Much of the strength of the temple lay in the largeness of the stones, and if these be thrown down, no footstep, no remembrance, of it will remain. While any part remained standing, there might be some hopes of the repair of it; but what hope is there, when not one stone is *left upon another?*

III. How natural it is to us to desire to know things to come, and the times of them; more inquisitive we are apt to be about that than about our duty. His disciples knew not how to *digest* this doctrine of the ruin of the temple, which they thought must be their Master's royal palace, and in which they expected their preferment, and to have the posts of honour; and therefore they were in pain till they got him alone, and got more out of him concerning this matter. As he was returning to Bethany therefore, he *sat upon the mount of Olives, over against the temple,* where he had a full view of it; and there four of them agreed to *ask him privately,* what he meant by the destroying of the temple, which they understood no more than they did the predictions of his own death, so inconsistent was it with their scheme. Probably, though these four proposed the question, yet Christ's discourse, in answer to it, was in the hearing of the rest of the disciples, yet *privately,* that is, apart from the multitude. Their enquiry is, *When shall these things be?* They will not question, at least not seem to question, whether they shall be or no (for their Master has said that they shall), but are willing to hope it is a great way off. Yet they ask not precisely the day and year (therein they were modest), but say, "Tell us *what shall be the sign, when all these things shall be fulfilled?* What presages shall there be of them, and how may we prognosticate their approach?"

5 And Jesus answering them began
to say, Take heed lest any *man* deceive you: 6 For many shall come
in my name, saying, I am *Christ;*
and shall deceive many. 7 And when
ye shall hear of wars and rumours of
wars, be ye not troubled: for *such*
things must needs be; but the end
shall not *be* yet. 8 For nation shall
rise against nation, and kingdom
against kingdom: and there shall be
earthquakes in divers places, and there
shall be famines and troubles: these
are the beginnings of sorrows. 9 But
take heed to yourselves: for they shall
deliver you up to councils; and in
the synagogues ye shall be beaten:
and ye shall be brought before rulers
and kings for my sake, for a testimony
against them. 10 And the gospel
must first be published among all nations. 11 But when they shall lead
you, and deliver you up, take no
thought beforehand what ye shall
speak, neither do ye premeditate: but
whatsoever shall be given you in that
hour, that speak ye: for it is not ye
that speak, but the Holy Ghost. 12
Now the brother shall betray the
brother to death, and the father the
son; and children shall rise up against
their parents, and shall cause them to
be put to death. 13 And ye shall
be hated of all *men* for my name's
sake: but he that shall endure unto
the end, the same shall be saved.

Our Lord Jesus, in reply to their question, sets himself, not so much to satisfy their curiosity as to direct their consciences; leaves them still in the dark concerning the *times* and *seasons,* which the father has *kept in his own power,* and which *it was not for them to know;* but gives them the cautions which were needful, with reference to the events that should now shortly come to pass.

I. They must take heed that they be not *deceived* by the *seducers* and *impostors* that should now shortly arise (*v.* 5, 6); "*Take heed lest any man deceive you,* lest, having found the *true Messiah,* you lose him again in the crowd of *pretenders,* or be inveigled to embrace others in rivalship with him. Many shall come *in my name* (not in the name of *Jesus),* but saying, *I am Christ,* and so claiming the dignities which I only am entitled to." After the Jews had rejected the true Christ, they were imposed upon, and so *ex*posed by many false Christs, but never before; those false Christs *deceived many;* Therefore *take heed lest they deceive you.* Note, When many are deceived, we should thereby be awakened to look to ourselves.

II. They must take heed that they be not *disturbed* at the noise of wars, which they should be alarmed with, *v.* 7, 8. Sin introduced *wars,* and they come *from men's lusts.* But at some times the nations are more distracted and wasted with wars than at other times; so it shall be now; Christ was born into the world when there was a general peace, but soon after he went out of the world there were general wars; *Nation shall rise against nation, and kingdom against kingdom.* And what will become of them then who are to preach the gospel to every nation? *Inter arma silent leges—Amidst the clash of arms, the voice of law is not heard.* "But *be not troubled at it.*" 1. "Let it be no *surprise* to you; you are bid to expect it, and *such things must needs be,* for God has appointed them, in order to the further accomplishment of his purposes, and by the *wars of the Jews*" (which Josephus has given us a large account of) "God will punish the *wickedness of the Jews.*" 2. "Let it be no *terror* to you, as if your interest were in danger of being overthrown, or your work obstructed by these wars; you have no concern in them, and therefore need not be apprehensive of any damage by them." Note, Those that despise the smiles of the world, and do not court and covet them, may despise the frowns of the world, and need not fear them. If we seek not to rise with them that *rise in the world,* why should we dread falling with them that fall in the world? 3. "Let it not be looked upon as an omen of the approaching period of the world, for the *end is not yet, v.* 7. Think not that these *wars* will bring the world to a period; no, there are other intermediate counsels to be fulfilled betwixt that end and the end of all things, which are designed to prepare you for the end, but not to hasten it out of due time." 4. "Let it not be looked upon as if in them God had done his worst; no, he has more arrows in his quiver, and they are *ordained against the persecutors;* be not troubled at the wars you shall hear of, for they are but *the beginnings of sorrows,* and therefore, instead of being disturbed at *them,* you ought to *prepare for worse;* for there shall also be *earthquakes in divers places,* which shall bury multitudes in the ruins of their own houses, and there *shall be famines,* by which many of the poor shall perish for want of bread, and *troubles* and commotions; so that there shall be no peace to him that *goes out* or *comes in.* The world shall be full of *troubles,* but *be not ye troubled;* without are *fightings,* within are *fears,* but *fear not ye their fear.*" Note, The disciples of Christ, if it be not their own fault, may enjoy a holy security and serenity of mind, when all about them is in the greatest disorder.

III. They must take heed that they be not *drawn away* from Christ, and from their duty to him, by the sufferings they should meet with for Christ's sake. Again, he saith, "*Take heed to yourselves, v.* 9. Though you may escape the *sword of war,* better than some of your neighbours, because you interest not yourselves in the public quarrels, yet be not secure; you will be exposed to the *sword of justice* more than others, and the parties that contend with one another, will unite against you. *Take heed* therefore lest you *deceive* yourselves with the hopes of outward prosperity, and such a temporal kingdom as you have been dreaming of, when it is *through many tribulations* that *you must enter into the kingdom of God.* Take heed lest you needlessly expose yourselves to trouble, and pull it upon your own head. *Take heed* what you say and do, for you will have many eyes upon you." Observe,

1. What the trouble is which they must expect.

(1.) They shall be *hated of all men;* trouble enough! The thoughts of *being hated* are grievous to a tender spirit, and the fruits of that hatred must needs be a constant vexation; those that are *malicious,* will be *mischievous.* It was not for any thing amiss in them, or done amiss by them, that they were *hated,* but for Christ's name's sake, because they were called by his name, called upon his name, preached his name, and wrought miracles in his name. The world hated them because he loved them.

(2.) Their own *relations* shall *betray them,* those to whom they were most nearly allied, and on whom therefore they depended for protection; "They *shall betray you,* shall inform against you, and be your prosecutors." If a father has a child that is a Christian, he shall become void of natural affection, it shall all be swallowed up in bigotry, and he shall betray his own child to the persecutors, as if he were a worshipper of other gods, Deut. xiii. 6—10.

(3.) Their *church-rulers* shall inflict *their censures* upon them; "You shall be *delivered up* to the great Sanhedrim at Jerusalem, and to the inferior courts and consistories in other cities, and shall be *beaten in the synagogues* with forty stripes at a time, as offenders against the law which was read in the synagogue." It is no new thing for the church's artillery, through the treachery of its officers, to be turned against some of its best friends.

(4.) *Governors* and *kings* shall use their power against them. Because the Jews have not power to put them to death, they shall incense the Roman powers against them, as they did Herod against James and Peter; and they shall *cause you to be put to death,* as enemies to the empire. They must resist unto blood, and still resist.

2. What they shall have to comfort themselves with, in the midst of these great and sore troubles.

(1.) That the work they were called to should be carried on and prosper, notwithstanding all this opposition which they should meet with in it (*v.* 10); "*The gospel* shall, for all this, be *published among all nations,* and before the destruction of Jerusalem the *sound* of it shall *go forth into all the earth;* not only through all the nation of the Jews, but to all the nations of the earth." It is comfort to those who suffer for the gospel, that, though they may be crushed and borne down, the gospel cannot; it shall keep its ground, and carry the day.

(2.) That their sufferings, instead of obstructing their work, should forward it; "Your being *brought before governors and kings* shall be for *a testimony of them* (so some read it, *v.* 9); it shall give you an opportunity of preaching the gospel to those before whom you are brought as criminals, to whom otherwise you could not have access." Thus St. Paul's being brought before Felix, and Festus, and Agrippa, and Nero, was a testimony to them concerning Christ and his gospel. Or, as we read it, It shall be for a testimony *against them,* against both the judges and the prosecutors, who pursue those with the utmost rage that appear, upon examination, to be not only innocent but excellent persons. The gospel is a testimony to us concerning Christ and heaven. If we receive it, it will be a testimony for us: it will justify and save us; if not, it will be a testimony *against* us in the great day.

(3.) That, when they were brought before kings and governors for Christ's sake, they should have special assistance from heaven, to plead Christ's cause and their own (*v.* 11); "*Take no thought before-hand what ye shall speak,* be not solicitous how to address yourselves to great men, so as to obtain their favour; your cause is just and glorious, and needs not to be supported by premeditated speeches and harangues; but *whatsoever shall be given you in that hour,* whatsoever shall be suggested to you, and put into your minds, and into your mouths" *(pro re natâ—on the spur of the occasion),* "that *speak ye,* and fear not the success of it, because it is *off-hand,* for *it is not ye that speak,* purely by the strength of your own wisdom, consideration, and resolution, but it is *the Holy Ghost.*" Note, Those whom Christ calls out to be advocates for him, shall be furnished with full instructions: and when we are engaged in the service of Christ, we may depend upon the aids of the Spirit of Christ.

(4.) That heaven at last would *make amends for all;* "You will meet with a great deal of hardship in your way, but have a good heart on it, your warfare will be accomplished, and your testimony finished, and *he that shall endure to the end, the same shall be saved,*" *v.* 13. Perseverance gains the crown. The salvation here promised is more than a deliverance from evil, it is an everlasting blessedness, which shall be an abundant recompence for all their services and sufferings. All this we have, Matt. x. 17, &c.

14 But when ye shall see the abomination of desolation, spoken of by
Daniel the prophet, standing where
it ought not (let him that readeth
understand), then let them that be in
Judæa flee to the mountains: 15 And
let him that is on the housetop not
go down into the house, neither enter
therein, to take any thing out of his
house: 16 And let him that is in the
field not turn back again for to take
up his garment. 17 But woe to them
that are with child, and to them that
give suck in those days! 18 And
pray ye that your flight be not in the
winter. 19 For *in* those days shall
be affliction, such as was not from the
beginning of the creation which God
created unto this time, neither shall
be. 20 And except that the Lord
had shortened those days, no flesh
should be saved: but for the elect's
sake, whom he hath chosen, he hath
shortened the days. 21 And then
if any man shall say to you, Lo, here
is Christ: or, lo, *he is* there; believe
him not: 22 For false Christs and
false prophets shall rise, and shall
show signs and wonders, to seduce,
if *it were* possible, even the elect. 23
But take ye heed: behold, I have
foretold you all things.

The Jews, in rebelling against the Romans, and in persecuting the Christians, were hastening their own ruin apace, both efficiently and meritoriously, were setting both God and man against them; see 1 Thess. ii. 15. Now here we have a prediction of that ruin which came upon them within less than forty years after this: we had it before, Matt. xxiv. 15, &c. Observe,

I. What is here foretold concerning it.

1. That the Roman *armies* should make a descent upon Judea, and invest Jerusalem, the holy city. These were the *abomination*

of *desolation,* which the Jews did *abominate,* and by which they should be made *desolate.* The country of thine enemy is called *the land which thou abhorrest,* Isa. vii. 16. *Therefore* it was an abomination, because it brought with it nothing but desolation. They had rejected Christ as an *abomination,* who would have been their *salvation;* and now God brought upon them an abomination that would be their *desolation,* thus spoken of by Daniel *the prophet* (*ch.* ix. 27), as that by which this sacrifice and offering should be made to cease. This army stood *where it ought not,* in and about the *holy city,* which the heathen ought not to have approached, nor would have been suffered to approach, if Jerusalem had not first profaned the crown of their holiness. This the church complains of, Lam. i. 10, The *heathen entered into her sanctuary, whom thou didst command that they should not enter into the congregation;* but sin made the breach, at which the glory went out, and the abomination of desolation broke in, *and stood where it ought not.* Now, let *him that readeth* this, *understand it,* and endeavour to take it right. Prophecies should not be too plain, and yet intelligible to those that search them; and they are best understood by comparing them first with one another, and at last with the event.

2. That when the Roman *army* should come into the country, there would be no safety any where but by quitting the country, and that with all possible expedition. It will be in vain to *fight,* the enemies will be too hard for them; in vain to *abscond,* the enemies will find them out; and in vain to *capitulate,* the enemies will give them no quarter; a man cannot have so much as his life given him for a prey, but by *fleeing to the mountains* out of Judea; and let him take the first alarm, and make the best of his way. If he be *on the house-top,* trying from thence to discover the motions of the enemy, and spies them coming, let him not *go down, to take any thing out of the house,* for it will occasion his losing of time, which is more precious than his best goods, and will but encumber him, and embarrass his flight. If he be in the field, and there discover the approach of the enemy, let him get away as he is, and not *turn back again, to take up his garment, v.* 16. If he can save his life, let him reckon it a good bargain, though he can save nothing else, and be thankful to God, that, though he is cut short, he is not cut of.

3. That it would go very hard at that time with poor mothers and nurses (*v.* 17); "*Woe to them that are with child,* that dare not go into strange places, that cannot shift for themselves, nor make haste as others can. And *woe to them that give suck,* that know not how either to leave the tender infants behind them, or to carry them along with them." Such is the vanity of the creature, that the time may often be, when the greatest comforts may prove the greatest burthens. It would likewise be very uncomfortable, if they should be forced to flee *in the winter* (*v.* 18), when the *weather* and *ways* were bad, when the roads would be scarcely passable, especially in those mountains to which they must flee. If there be no remedy but that trouble must come, yet we may desire and pray that, if it be God's will, the circumstances of it may be so ordered as to be a mitigation of the trouble; and when things are bad, we ought to consider they might have been worse. It is bad to be forced to flee, but it would have been worse if it had been *in the winter.*

4. That throughout all the country of the Jews, there should be such destruction and desolation made, as could not be paralleled in any history (*v.* 19); *In those days shall be affliction, such as was not from the beginning* of time; that is, *of the creation which God created,* for time and the creation are of equal date, *unto this day, neither shall be* to the end of time; such a complication of miseries, and of such continuance. The destruction of Jerusalem by the Chaldeans was very terrible, but this exceeded it. It threatened a universal slaughter of all the people of the Jews; so barbarously did they devour one another, and the Romans devour them all, that, if their wars had continued a little longer, *no flesh could have been saved,* not one Jew could have been left alive; but in the midst of wrath God remembered mercy; and, (1.) He *shortened the days;* he let fall his controversy before he had *made a full end.* As a church and nation the ruin was complete, but many particular persons had their lives given them for a prey, by the storm's subsiding when it did. 2. It was *for the elects' sake* that those days were shortened; *many* among them fared the better for the sake of the *few* among them that believed in Christ, and were faithful to him. There was a promise, that *a remnant* should be saved (Isa. x. 22), and that God would not, for his servants' sakes, *destroy them all* (Isa. lxv. 8); and these promises must be fulfilled. God's own *elect cry day and night to him,* and their prayers must be answered, Luke xviii. 7.

II. What directions are given to the disciples with reference to it.

1. They must shift for the safety of *their lives;* "When you see the country invaded, and the city invested, flatter not yourselves with thoughts that the enemy will retire, or that you may be able to make your part good with them; but, without further deliberation or delay, *let them that are in Judea, flee to the mountains, v.* 14. Meddle not with strife that *belongs not to you; let the potsherds strive with the potsherds of the earth,* but do you go out of the ship when you see it sinking, that you die not the *death of the uncircumcised* in heart."

2. They must provide for the safety of *their souls;* "*Seducers* will be busy at that time, for they love to fish in troubled waters, and therefore then you must double your guard; *then, if any man shall* say unto you, *Lo, here*

is Christ, or, *Lo, he is there,* you know he is in heaven, and will come again at the end of time, to judge the world, and therefore *believe them not;* having received *Christ,* be not drawn into the snares of any *antichrist;* for *false Christs,* and *false prophets, shall arise,*" *v.* 22. When the gospel kingdom was in the setting up, Satan mustered all his force, to oppose it, and made use of all his wiles; and God permitted it, for the trial of the sincerity of some, the discovery of the hypocrisy of others, and the confusion of those who rejected Christ, when he was offered to them. *False Christs* shall *rise,* and false prophets that shall preach them up; or such, as, though they pretend not to be Christs, set up for *prophets,* and undertake to foretel things to come, and they shall *show signs* and lying *wonders;* so early did the *mystery of iniquity* begin to *work,* 2 Thess. ii. 7. They *shall seduce, if it were possible, the very elect;* so plausible shall their pretences be, and so industrious shall they be to impose upon people, that they shall draw away many that were forward and zealous professors of religion, many that were very likely to have persevered; for nothing will be effectual to secure men but that foundation of God which stands immovably sure, *The Lord knoweth them that are his,* who shall be preserved when the faith of some is overthrown, 2 Tim. ii. 18, 19. They *shall seduce, if it were possible, the very elect;* but it is not possible to seduce them; the *election shall obtain,* whoever are *blinded,* Rom. xi. 7. But, in consideration hereof, let the disciples be cautious whom they give credit to (*v.* 23); But *take ye heed.* Christ knew that they were of the *elect,* who could not possibly be *seduced,* and yet he said to them, *Take heed.* An assurance of persevering, and cautions against apostasy, will very well consist with each other. Though Christ said to them, *Take heed,* it doth not therefore follow, that their perseverance was doubtful, for they were kept by the power of God; and though their perseverance was secured, yet it doth not therefore follow, that this caution was needless, because they must be kept in the use of proper means. God will keep them, but they must keep themselves. "*I have foretold you all things;* have foretold you of this danger, that, being *fore-warned,* you may be *fore-armed;* I have foretold *all things* which you needed to have foretold to you, and therefore take heed of hearkening to such as pretend to be prophets, and to foretel more than I have foretold." The sufficiency of the scripture is a good argument against listening to such as pretend to inspiration.

24 But in those days, after that
tribulation, the sun shall be darkened,
and the moon shall not give her light,
25 And the stars of heaven shall fall,
and the powers that are in heaven
shall be shaken. 26 And then shall
they see the Son of man coming in
the clouds with great power and glory.
27 And then shall he send his angels,
and shall gather together his elect
from the four winds, from the uttermost
part of the earth to the uttermost
part of heaven.

These verses seem to point at Christ's second coming, to judge the world; the disciples, in their question, had confounded the *destruction* of Jerusalem and the *end of the world* (Matt. xxiv. 3), which was built upon a mistake, as if the temple must needs stand as long as the world stands; this mistake Christ rectifies, and shows that the *end of the world in those days,* those other days you enquire about, the day of Christ's coming, and the day of judgment, shall be *after that tribulation,* and not coincident with it. Let those who live to see the Jewish nation destroyed, take heed of thinking that, because the Son of man doth not visibly come in the clouds *then,* he will never *so* come; no, he will come *after that.* And here he foretels,

1. The final dissolution of the present frame and fabric of the world; even of that part of it which seems least liable to change, the upper part, the purer and more refined part; *The sun shall be darkened,* and the *moon* shall no more *give her light;* for they shall be quite outshone by the glory of the Son of man, Isa. xxiv. 23. The *stars of heaven,* that from the beginning had kept their place and regular motion, shall fall as leaves in autumn; and the *powers that are in heaven,* the heavenly bodies, the fixed stars, *shall be shaken.*

2. The visible appearance of the Lord Jesus, to whom the judgment of that day shall be committed (*v.* 26); *Then shall they see the Son of man coming in the clouds.* Probably he will come over that very place where he sat when he said this; for the clouds are in the lower region of the air. He shall come with *great power and glory,* such as will be suited to the errand on which he comes. *Every eye shall then see him.*

3. The gathering together of all the elect to him (*v.* 27); He shall *send his angels,* and *gather together his elect* to him, to *meet him in the air,* 1 Thess. iv. 17. They shall be fetched from one end of the world to the other, so that none shall be missing from that *general* assembly; they shall be fetched *from the uttermost part of the earth,* most remote from the place where Christ's tribunal shall be set, and shall be brought to the *uttermost part of heaven;* so sure, so swift, so easy, shall their conveyance be, that there shall none of them miscarry, though they were to be brought from the uttermost part of the earth one way, to the uttermost part of the heaven another way. A faithful Israelite shall be carried safely, though it were from the utmost border of the land of bondage to the utmost border of the land of promise.

28 Now learn a parable of the fig
tree; When her branch is yet tender,
and putteth forth leaves, ye know that
summer is near: 29 So ye in like
manner, when ye shall see these things
come to pass, know that it is nigh,
even at the doors. 30 Verily I say
unto you, that this generation shall
not pass, till all these things be done.
31 Heaven and earth shall pass away:
but my words shall not pass away.
32 But of that day and *that* hour
knoweth no man, no, not the angels
which are in heaven, neither the Son,
but the Father. 33 Take ye heed,
watch and pray: for ye know not
when the time is. 34 *For the Son
of man is* as a man taking a far journey, who left his house, and gave
authority to his servants, and to every
man his work, and commanded the
porter to watch. 35 Watch ye therefore: for ye know not when the master of the house cometh, at even, or
at midnight, or at the cockcrowing,
or in the morning: 36 Lest coming
suddenly he find you sleeping. 37
And what I say unto you I say unto
all, Watch.

We have here the application of this prophetical sermon; *now learn* to look forward in a right manner.

I. "As to the *destruction* of Jerusalem, *expect* it to come very *shortly;* as when the *branch of the fig-tree becomes soft*, and the *leaves sprout forth*, ye expect that summer will come shortly, *v.* 28. When second causes begin to work, ye expect their effects in their proper order and time. So when *ye see these things come to pass*, when ye see the Jewish nation embroiled in wars, distracted by false Christs and prophets, and drawing upon them the displeasure of the Romans, especially when ye see them persecuting you for your Master's sake, and thereby standing to what they did when they put him to death, and repeating it, and so filling up the measure of their iniquity, then say that their *ruin is nigh, even at the door*, and provide for yourselves accordingly." The disciples themselves were indeed all of them, except John, taken away from the evil to come, but the next generation whom they were to train up, would live to see it; and by these instructions which Christ left behind him would be kept from sharing in it; "*This generation* that is now rising up, shall not all be worn off before *all these things* come to pass, which I have told you of, relating to Jerusalem, and they shall begin to take effect now shortly. And as this destruction is near and within ken, so it is sure. The decree is gone forth, it is a *consummation determined*," Dan. ix. 27. Christ doth not speak these things, merely to frighten them; no, they are the declarations of God's fixed purpose; "*Heaven and earth shall pass away*, at the end of time; but *my words shall not pass away* (*v.* 31), not one of these predictions shall fail of a punctual accomplishment."

II. "As to the *end of the world*, do not enquire when it will come, for it is not a question fit to be asked, for of *that day*, and *that hour, knoweth no man;* it is a thing at a great distance; the exact time is fixed in the counsel of God, but is not revealed by any word of God, either to *men* on earth, or to *angels in heaven;* the angels shall have timely notice to prepare to attend in that day, and it shall be published, when it comes to the children of men, with sound of trumpet; but, at present, *men* and *angels* are kept in the dark concerning the precise time of it, that they may both attend to their proper services in the present day." But it follows, *neither the Son;* but is there any thing which the Son is ignorant of? We read indeed of a book which was sealed, till the Lamb opened the seals; but did not he know what was in it, before the seals were opened? Was not he privy to the writing of it? There were those in the primitive times, who taught from this text, that there were some things that Christ, as man, was *ignorant* of; and from thence were called *Agnoetæ;* they said, "It was no more absurd to say so, than to say that his human soul suffered grief and fear;" and many of the orthodox fathers approved of this. Some would evade it, by saying that Christ spoke this in a way of prudential economy, to divert the disciples from further enquiry: but to this one of the ancients answers, *It is not fit to speak too nicely in this matter—οὐ δεῖ πάνυ ἀκριβολογεῖν*, so Leontius in Dr. Hammond, "It is certain (says Archbishop Tillotson) that Christ, as God, could not be ignorant of any thing; but the divine wisdom which dwelt in our Saviour, did communicate itself to his human soul, according to the divine pleasure, so that his human nature might sometimes not know some things; therefore Christ is said to grow in wisdom (Luke ii. 52), which he could not be said to do, if the human nature of Christ did necessarily know all things by virtue of its union with the divinity." Dr. Lightfoot explains it thus; Christ calls himself the Son, as Messiah. Now the Messiah, as such, was the Father's servant (Isa. xlii. 1), sent and deputed by him, and as such a one he refers himself often to his Father's will and command, and owns he *did nothing of himself* (John v. 19); in like manner he might be said to *know nothing of himself*. The revelation of Jesus Christ was what *God gave unto him*, Rev. i. 1. He thinks, therefore, that we are to distinguish between those excellencies and perfections of his, which resulted from the personal union between the divine and human nature, and those which flowed from the anointing of the Spirit; from the former flowed the infinite dignity of his person, and his perfect freedom from all sin; but from the latter flowed his power of working miracles, and his foreknowledge of things to come. What therefore (saith he) was to be revealed by him to his church, he was pleased to take, not from the union of the human nature with the divine, but from the revelation of the Spirit, by which he yet knew not this, but *the Father* only knows it; that is, God only, the Deity; for (as Archbishop Tillotson explains it) it is not used here *personally*, in distinction from the Son and the Holy Ghost, but as the Father is, *Fons et Principium Deitatis—The Fountain of Deity.*

III. "As to both, your duty is to *watch and pray.* Therefore the time is kept a secret, that you may be engaged to stand always upon your guard (*v.* 33); *Take ye heed* of every thing that would indispose you for your Master's coming, and would render your accounts *perplexed*, and your spirits so too; *watch* for his coming, that it may not at any time be a surprise to you, and *pray* for that grace which is necessary to qualify you for it, for *ye know not when the time is;* and you are concerned to be ready for that *every day*, which may come *any day.*" This he illustrates, in the close, by a parable.

1. Our Master is gone away, and left us something in trust, in charge, which we must give account of, *v.* 34. He is *as a man taking a far journey;* for he is gone to be away a great while, he has *left his house* on earth, and left his servants in their offices, given *authority* to some, who are to be overseers, and *work* to others, who are to be labourers. They that have *authority* given them, in that had *work* assigned them, for those that have the greatest *power* have the most *business;* and to them to whom he gave *work*, he gave some sort of *authority*, to do that work. And when he took his last leave, he *appointed the porter to watch*, to be sure to be ready to open to him at his return; and in the mean time to take care to whom he opened his gates, not to thieves and robbers, but only to his Master's friends and servants. Thus our Lord Jesus, when he *ascended on high*, left something for all his servants to do, expecting they should all do him service in his absence, and be ready to receive him at his return. *All* are appointed to work, and some authorized to rule.

2. We ought to be always upon our watch, in expectation of his return, *v.* 35—37. (1.) Our Lord *will come*, and will come as the *Master of the house*, to take account of his servants, of their work, and of the improvement they have made. (2.) We know not *when he will come;* and he has very wisely kept us at uncertainty, that we might be always ready. We know not *when he will come*, just at what precise time; the *Master of the house* perhaps will come *at even*, at nine at night; or it may be *at midnight*, or at *cock-crowing*, at three in the morning, or perhaps not till six. This is applicable to his coming to us in particular, at our death, as well as to the general judgment. Our present life is a *night*, a dark night, compared with the other life; we know not in which watch of the night our Master will come, whether in the days of youth, or middle age, or old age; but, as soon as we are born, we begin to die, and therefore, as soon as we are capable of expecting any thing, we must expect death. (3.) Our great care must be, that, whenever our Lord comes, he do not *find us sleeping*, secure in ourselves, off our guard, indulging ourselves in ease and sloth, mindless of our work and duty, and thoughtless of our Lord's coming; *ready* to say, He will not come, and *unready* to meet him. (4.) His coming will indeed be *coming suddenly;* it will be a great *surprise* and *terror* to those that are careless, and asleep, it will come upon them as a thief in the night. (5.) It is therefore the indispensable duty of all Christ's disciples, to *watch*, to be awake, and keep awake; "*What I say unto you* four (*v.* 37), I *say unto all* the twelve, or rather to *you* twelve, I say unto all my disciples and followers; what I say to you of this generation, I say to all that shall believe in me, through your word, in every age, *Watch, watch*, expect my second coming, prepare for it, that you may be found in peace, without spot, and blameless."

CHAP. XIV.

In this chapter begins the account which this evangelist gives of the death and sufferings of our Lord Jesus, which we are all concerned to be acquainted, not only with the history of, but with the mystery of. Here is, I. The plot of the chief priests and scribes against Christ, ver. 1, 2. II. The anointing of Christ's head at a supper in Bethany, two days before his death, ver. 3—9. III. The contract Judas made with the chief priests, to betray him, ver. 10, 11. IV. Christ's eating the passover with his disciples, his instituting the Lord's supper, and his discourse with his disciples, at and after supper, ver. 12—31. V. Christ's agony in the garden, ver. 32—42. VI. The betraying of him by Judas, and the apprehending of him by the chief priests' agents, ver. 43—52. VII. His arraignment before the high priest, his conviction, and the indignities done him at that bar, ver. 53—65. VIII. Peter's denying him, ver. 66—72. Most of which passages we had before, Matt. xxvi.

AFTER two days was *the feast of*
the passover, and of unleavened
bread: and the chief priests and the
scribes sought how they might take
him by craft, and put *him* to death.
2 But they said, Not on the feast *day*,
lest there be an uproar of the people.
3 And being in Bethany, in the house
of Simon the leper, as he sat at meat,
there came a woman having an alabaster box of ointment of spikenard,
very precious; and she brake the box,
and poured *it* on his head. 4 And
there were some that had indignation
within themselves, and said, Why was
this waste of the ointment made? 5

For it might have been sold for more
than three hundred pence, and have
been given to the poor. And they
murmured against her. 6 And Jesus
said, Let her alone; why trouble ye
her? she hath wrought a good work
on me. 7 For ye have the poor with
you always, and whensoever ye will
ye may do them good: but me ye
have not always. 8 She hath done
what she could: she is come aforehand to anoint my body to the burying. 9 Verily I say unto you, Wheresoever this gospel shall be preached
throughout the whole world, *this* also
that she hath done shall be spoken of
for a memorial of her. 10 And Judas
Iscariot, one of the twelve, went unto
the chief priests, to betray him unto
them. 11 And when they heard *it*,
they were glad, and promised to give
him money. And he sought how he
might conveniently betray him.

We have here instances,

I. Of the *kindness of Christ's friends,* and the provision made of respect and honour for him. Some friends he had, even in and about Jerusalem, that loved him, and never thought they could do enough for him, among whom, though Israel be not gathered, he is, and will be, glorious.

1. Here was *one friend,* that was so kind as to *invite him to sup with him;* and he was so kind as to accept the invitation, *v.* 3. Though he had a prospect of his death approaching, yet he did not abandon himself to a melancholy retirement from all company, but conversed as freely with his friends as usual.

2. Here was *another friend,* that was so kind as to *anoint his head* with very precious ointment as he *sat at meat.* This was an extraordinary piece of respect paid him by a good woman that thought nothing too good to bestow upon Christ, and to do him honour. Now the scripture was fulfilled, *When the king sitteth at his table, my spikenard sendeth forth the smell thereof,* Cant. i. 12. Let us *anoint* Christ as our *Beloved,* kiss him with a kiss of *affection;* and anoint him as our *Sovereign,* kiss him with a kiss of *allegiance.* Did he pour out his soul unto death for us, and shall we think any box of ointment too precious to pour out upon him? It is observable that she took care to pour it all out upon Christ's head; she *broke the box* (so we read it); but because it was an *alabaster box,* not easily broken, nor was it necessary that it should be broken, to get out the ointment, some read it, she *shook* the box, or *knocked it to the ground,* to loosen what was in it, that it might be got out the better; or, she *rubbed* and *scraped* out all that stuck to the sides of it. Christ must be honoured with *all we* have, and we must not think to keep back any part of the price. Do we give him the *precious ointment* of our best affections? Let him have them *all;* love him *with all the heart.*

Now, (1.) There were those that put a *worse construction* upon this than it *deserved.* They called it a *waste of the ointment, v.* 4. Because they could not have found in their hearts to put themselves to such an expense for the honouring of Christ, they thought that she was *prodigal,* who did. Note, As the *vile person* ought not to be *called liberal,* nor the *churl* said to be *bountiful* (Isa. xxxii. 5); so the *liberal* and *bountiful* ought not to be called *wasteful.* They pretended it might have been *sold,* and *given to the poor, v.* 5. But as a *common piety* to the *corban* will not excuse from a *particular charity* to a poor parent (*ch.* vii. 11), so a common charity to the poor will not excuse from a particular act of piety to the Lord Jesus. What thy hand finds to do, that is good, *do it with thy might.*

(2.) Our Lord Jesus put a *better construction* upon it than, for aught that appears, was *designed.* Probably, she intended no more, than to show the great honour she had for him, before all the company, and to complete his entertainment. But Christ makes it to be an act of *great faith,* as well as *great love* (*v.* 8); "*She is come aforehand, to anoint my body to the burying,* as if she foresaw that my resurrection would prevent her doing it afterward." This funeral rite was a kind of presage of, or prelude to, his death approaching. See how Christ's heart was filled with the thoughts of his death, how every thing was construed with a reference to that, and how familiarly he spoke of it upon all occasions. It is usual for those who are *condemned to die,* to have their coffins prepared, and other provision made for their funerals, while they are yet alive; and *so* Christ accepted *this.* Christ's death and burial were the lowest steps of his humiliation, and therefore, though he cheerfully submitted to them, yet he would have some marks of honour to attend them, which might help to take off the *offence of the cross,* and be an intimation how *precious in the sight of the Lord the death of his saints is.* Christ never rode in triumph into Jerusalem, but when he came thither to suffer; nor had ever his head anointed, but for *his burial.*

(3.) He recommended this piece of heroic piety to the applause of the church in all ages; *Wherever this gospel shall be preached, it shall be spoken of, for a memorial of her, v.* 9. Note, The honour which attends well-doing, even in this world, is sufficient to balance the reproach and contempt that are cast upon it. *The memory of the just is blessed,* and they that had *trial of cruel mockings,* yet *obtained a good report,* Heb. xi. 36, 39. Thus was this good woman repaid for her box of ointment, *Nec oleum perdidit nec operam—She lost neither her oil nor her labour.* She got by it that good name which is *better than precious ointment.* Those that *honour* Christ *he will honour.*

II. Of the *malice of Christ's enemies,* and the preparation made by them to do him mischief.

1. The chief priests, his *open enemies,* consulted how they might *put him to death, v.* 1, 2. The feast of the *passover* was now at hand, and at *that* feast he must be crucified, (1.) That his death and sufferings might be the more public, and that all *Israel,* even those *of the dispersion,* who came from all parts to the feast, might be witnesses of it, and of the wonders that attended it. (2.) That the Anti-type might answer to the type. Christ, our Passover, was sacrificed for us, and brought us out of the house of bondage, at the same time that the paschal lamb was sacrificed, and Israel's deliverance out of Egypt was *commemorated.*

Now see, [1.] How *spiteful* Christ's enemies were; they did not think it enough to banish or imprison him, for they aimed not only to *silence* him, and *stop* his progress for the future, but to be revenged on him for all the good he had done. [2.] How *subtle* they were; *Not on the feast-day,* when the people are together; they do not say, Lest they should be disturbed in their devotions, and diverted from them, but, *Lest there should be an uproar* (*v.* 2); lest they should rise, and rescue him, and *fall foul* upon those that *attempt* any thing against him. They who *desired* nothing more than the *praise* of men, dreaded nothing more than the rage and displeasure of men.

2. Judas, his *disguised enemy,* contracted with them for the betraying of him, *v.* 10, 11. He is said to be *one of the twelve* that were Christ's family, intimate with him, trained up for the service of his kingdom; and he *went to the chief priests,* to tender his service in this affair.

(1.) That which he proposed to them, was, to *betray Christ* to them, and to give them notice when and where they might find him, and seize him, without making an *uproar among the people,* which they were afraid of, if they should seize him when he appeared *in public,* in the midst of his admirers. Did he know then what help it was they wanted, and where they were run aground in their counsels? It is probable that he did not, for the debate was held in their close *cabal.* Did they know that he had a mind to serve them, and make court to him? No, they could not imagine that any of his intimates should be so base; but Satan, who was entered into Judas, knew what occasion they had for him, and could guide him to be *guide to them,* who were contriving to *take Jesus.* Note, The spirit that works in all the children of disobedience, knows how to bring them in to the assistance one of another in a wicked project, and then to harden them in it, with the fancy that Providence favours them.

(2.) That which he proposed to himself, was, to *get money* by the bargain; he had what he aimed at, when *they promised to give him money.* Covetousness was Judas's master-lust, *his own iniquity,* and that betrayed him to the sin of betraying his Master; the devil suited his temptation to *that,* and so conquered him. It is not said, They promised him *preferment* (he was not ambitious of that), but, They promised him *money.* See what need we have to double our guard against the sin that *most easily besets us.* Perhaps it was Judas's covetousness that brought him at first to *follow Christ,* having a promise that he should be cash-keeper, or purser, to the society, and he loved in his heart to be fingering money; and now that there was money to be got on the other side, he was as ready to betray him as ever he had been to follow him. Note, Where the principle of men's profession of religion is carnal and worldly, and the serving of a secular interest, the very same principle, whenever the wind turns, will be the bitter root of a vile and scandalous apostasy.

(3.) Having secured the money, he set himself to make good his bargain; he sought *how he might conveniently betray him,* how he might *seasonably deliver him up,* so as to answer the intention of those who had hired him. See what need we have to be careful that we do not ensnare ourselves in sinful engagements. If at any time we be so ensnared in the words of our mouths, we are concerned to deliver ourselves by a speedy retreat, Prov. vi. 1—5. It is a rule in our law, as well as in our religion, that an *obligation* to do an *evil thing* is *null* and *void;* it binds to repentance, not to performance. See how the way of sin is down-hill—when men are *in,* they must *on;* and what *wicked* contrivances many have in their sinful pursuits, to compass their designs *conveniently;* but such conveniences will prove mischiefs in the end.

12 And the first day of unleavened
bread, when they killed the passover,
his disciples said unto him, Where
wilt thou that we go and prepare that
thou mayest eat the passover? 13
And he sendeth forth two of his disciples, and saith unto them, Go ye
into the city, and there shall meet you
a man bearing a pitcher of water:
follow him. 14 And wheresoever he
shall go in, say ye to the goodman of
the house, The Master saith, Where
is the guest chamber, where I shall
eat the passover with my disciples?
15 And he will show you a large
upper room furnished *and* prepared:

there make ready for us. 16 And
his disciples went forth, and came
into the city, and found as he had
said unto them: and they made ready
the passover. 17 And in the evening he cometh with the twelve. 18
And as they sat and did eat, Jesus
said, Verily I say unto you, One of
you which eateth with me shall betray
me. 19 And they began to be sorrowful, and to say unto him one by
one, *Is* it I? and another *said*, *Is* it
I? 20 And he answered and said
unto them, *It is* one of the twelve,
that dippeth with me in the dish. 21
The Son of man indeed goeth, as it
is written of him: but woe to that
man by whom the Son of man is betrayed! good were it for that man if
he had never been born. 22 And as
they did eat, Jesus took bread, and
blessed, and brake *it*, and gave to
them, and said, Take, eat: this is my
body. 23 And he took the cup, and
when he had given thanks, he gave *it*
to them: and they all drank of it.
24 And he said unto them, This is
my blood of the new testament, which
is shed for many. 25 Verily I say
unto you, I will drink no more of the
fruit of the vine, until that day that I
drink it new in the kingdom of God.
26 And when they had sung a hymn,
they went out into the mount of
Olives. 27 And Jesus saith unto
them, All ye shall be offended because
of me this night; for it is written, I
will smite the shepherd, and the sheep
shall be scattered. 28 But after that
I am risen, I will go before you into
Galilee. 29 But Peter said unto him,
Although all shall be offended, yet
will not I. 30 And Jesus saith unto
him, Verily I say unto thee, That this
day, *even* in this night, before the cock
crow twice, thou shalt deny me thrice.
31 But he spake the more vehemently, If I should die with thee, I
will not deny thee in any wise. Likewise also said they all.

In these verses we have,

I. Christ's eating the passover with his disciples, the night before he died, with the joys and comforts of which ordinance he prepared himself for his approaching sorrows, the full prospect of which did not indispose him for that solemnity. Note, No apprehension of trouble, come or coming, should put us by, or put us out of frame for, our attendance on holy ordinances, as we have opportunity for it.

1. Christ ate the passover at the *usual time* when the other Jews did, as Dr. Whitby has fully made out, and not, as Dr. Hammond would have it, the night before. It was on the first day of that feast, which (taking in all the eight days of the feast) was called, *The feast of unleavened bread*, even that day when they *killed the passover*, *v.* 12.

2. He directed his disciples how to find the place where he intended to eat the passover; and hereby gave such another proof of his infallible knowledge of things distant and future (which to us seem altogether *contingent*), as he had given when he sent them for the ass on which he rode in triumph (*ch.* xi. 6); "*Go into the city* (for the *passover* must be *eaten* in Jerusalem), and *there shall meet you a man bearing a pitcher of water* (a servant sent for water to clean the rooms in his master's house); *follow him, go in* where he *goes*, enquire for his master, *the good man of the house* (*v.* 14), and desire him to show you a room." No doubt, the inhabitants of Jerusalem had rooms fitted up to be *let out*, for this occasion, to those that came out of the country to keep the passover, and one of those Christ made use of; not any friend's house, nor any house he had formerly frequented, for then he would have said, "Go to such a friend," or, "You know where we used to be, go thither and prepare." Probably he went where he was not known, that he might be *undisturbed* with his disciples. Perhaps he notified it by *a sign*, to conceal it from Judas, that he might not know till he came to the place; and by *such a sign* to intimate that he will dwell in the *clean heart*, that is, *washed* as with *pure water*. Where he designs to come, a pitcher of water must go before him; see Isa. i. 16—18.

3. He ate the passover in an *upper room furnished*, *ἐστρωμένον—laid with carpets* (so Dr. Hammond); it would seem to have been a very handsome *dining-room*. Christ was far from affecting any thing that looked stately in eating his common meals; on the contrary, he chose that which was homely, sat down on the grass: but, when he was to keep a sacred feast, in honour of that he would be at the expense of as good a room as he could get. God looks not at *outward pomp*, but he looks at the tokens and expressions of *inward reverence* for a divine institution, which, it is to be feared, those want, who, to save charges, deny themselves decencies in the worship of God.

4. He ate it *with the twelve*, who were his family, to teach those who have the charge of families, not only families of *children*, but families of *servants*, or families of *scholars*, or *pupils*, to keep up religion among them,

and worship God with them. If Christ came *with the twelve*, then Judas was with them, though he was at this time contriving to betray his Master; and it is plain by what follows (*v.* 20), that he was there: he did not absent himself, lest he should have been suspected; had his *seat* been *empty* at this feast, they would have said, as Saul of David, *He is not clean, surely he is not clean*, 1 Sam. xx. 26. Hypocrites, though they know it is at their peril, yet crowd into special ordinances, to keep up their repute, and palliate their secret wickedness. Christ did not *exclude* him from the feast, though he *knew* his wickedness, for it was not as yet become public and scandalous. Christ, designing to put the *keys of the kingdom of heaven* into the hands of men, who can judge only according to outward appearance, would hereby both direct and encourage them in their admissions to his table, to be satisfied with a justifiable profession, because they cannot discern the *root of bitterness* till it *springs up*.

II. Christ's discourse with his disciples, as they were *eating* the passover. It is probable that they had discourse, according to the custom of the feast, of the deliverance of Israel out of Egypt, and the preservation of the first-born, and were as pleasant as they used to be together on this occasion, till Christ told them that which would mix *trembling* with their *joys*.

1. They were *pleasing* themselves with the society of *their Master;* but he tells them that they must now presently lose him; *The Son of man is betrayed;* and they knew, for he had often told them, what followed—If he be *betrayed*, the next news you will hear of him, is, that he is *crucified* and *slain;* God hath determined it concerning him, and he agrees to it; *The Son of man goes, as it is written of him*, *v.* 21. It was *written* in the counsels of God, and *written* in the prophecies of the Old Testament, not one jot or tittle of either of which can *fall to the ground*.

2. They were *pleasing* themselves with the society *one of another*, but Christ casts a damp upon the joy of that, by telling them, *One of you that eateth with me shall betray me*, *v.* 18. Christ said this, if it might be, to startle the conscience of Judas, and to awaken him to repent of his wickedness, and to draw back (for it was not too late) from the brink of the pit. But for aught that appears, he who was *most concerned in* the warning, was *least concerned at* it. All the rest were affected with it. (1.) They began to be *sorrowful*. As the remembrance of our former falls into sin, so the fear of the like again, doth often much embitter the comfort of our spiritual feasts, and damp our joy. Here were the *bitter herbs*, with which this *passover-feast* was taken. (2.) They began to be *suspicious* of themselves; they said *one by one, Is it I? And another said, Is it I?* They are to be commended for their *charity*, that they were more jealous of themselves than of *one another*. It is the law of charity, to *hope the best* (1 Cor. xiii. 5—7), because we assuredly *know*, therefore we may justly *suspect*, more evil by ourselves than by our brethren. They are also to be commended for their acquiescence in what Christ said; they trusted more to *his words* than to *their own hearts;* and therefore do not say, "I am sure *it is not I*," but, "*Lord, is it I?* see if there be such a *way of wickedness in us*, such a *root of bitterness*, and discover it to us, that we may pluck up that *root*, and stop up that *way*."

Now, in answer to their enquiry, Christ saith that, [1.] Which would make them easy; "It is not *you*, nor *you;* it is this that now *dips with me in the dish*; the adversary and enemy is this wicked Judas." [2.] Which, one would think, should make Judas very *uneasy*. If he go on in his undertaking, it is upon the sword's point, for *woe to that man by whom the Son of man is betrayed;* he is undone, for ever undone; his sin will soon *find him out;* and it were *better for him that he had never been born*, had never had a being than such a miserable one as he must have. It is very probable that Judas encouraged himself in it with *this* thought, that his Master had often said he must be betrayed; "And if it must be done, surely God *will not find fault* with him that doth it, for who *hath resisted his will?*" As that objector argues, Rom. ix. 19. But Christ tells him that this will be no shelter or excuse to him; *The Son of man indeed goes, as it is written of him*, as a lamb to the slaughter; but *woe to that man by whom he is betrayed*. God's decrees to permit the sins of men, and bring glory to himself out of them, do neither necessitate their sins, nor determine to them, nor will they be any *excuse* of the sin, or *mitigation* of the punishment. Christ was delivered indeed by *the determinate counsel and fore-knowledge of God;* but, notwithstanding that, it is *with wicked hands that he is crucified and slain*, Acts ii. 23.

III. The institution of the Lord's supper.

1. It was instituted in the close of a *supper*, when they were sufficiently fed with the *paschal lamb*, to show that in the Lord's supper there is no *bodily repast* intended; to preface it with such a thing, is to revive Moses again. But it is food for *the soul* only, and therefore a very little of that which is for the body, as much as will serve for a *sign*, is enough. It was at the close of the *passover-supper*, which by this was evangelized, and then superseded and set aside. Much of the doctrine and duty of the eucharist is illustrated to us by the law of the passover (Exod. xii.); for the Old-Testament institutions, though they do not *bind us*, yet *instruct* us, by the help of a gospel-key to them. And these two ordinances lying here so near together, it may be good to compare them, and observe how much shorter and plainer the institution of the Lord's supper is, than that of the pass-

over was. Christ's yoke is easy in comparison with that of the ceremonial law, and his ordinances are more spiritual.

2. It was instituted by the *example* of Christ himself; not with the ceremony and solemnity of a law, as the ordinance of baptism was, after Christ's resurrection (Matt. xxviii. 19), with, *Be it enacted by the authority aforesaid,* by a power given to Christ *in heaven and on earth* (*v.* 18); but by the practice of our Master himself, because intended for those who are already his disciples, and taken into covenant with him: but it has the obligation of a law, and was intended to remain in full force, power, and virtue, till his second coming.

3. It was instituted with *blessing* and *giving of thanks;* the gifts of common providence are to be so received (1 Tim. iv. 4, 5), much more the gifts of special grace. He *blessed* (*v.* 22), and *gave thanks, v.* 23. At his other meals, he was wont to *bless,* and *give thanks* (*ch.* vi. 41; viii. 7) so remarkably, that he was known by it, Luke xxiv. 30, 31. And he did the same at this meal.

4. It was instituted to be a *memorial* of his *death;* and therefore he *broke* the bread, to show how it pleased the Lord to *bruise him;* and he called the *wine,* which is the blood of the grape, the *blood of the New Testament.* The death Christ died was a *bloody death,* and frequent mention is made of the *blood,* the *precious* blood, as the price of our redemption; for the blood is *the life,* and made *atonement for the soul,* Lev. xvii. 11—14. The pouring out of the blood was the most sensible indication of the *pouring out of his soul,* Isa. liii. 12. Blood has a *voice* (Gen. iv. 10); and *therefore* the blood is so often mentioned, because it was to *speak,* Heb. xii. 24. It is called the *blood of the New Testament;* for the covenant of grace became a *testament,* and of force by the death of Christ, the testator, Heb. ix. 16. It is said to be *shed for many,* to justify *many* (Isa. liii. 11), to bring *many* sons to glory, Heb. ii. 10. It was sufficient for *many,* being of infinite value; it has been of use to *many;* we read of a great multitude which no man could number, that had all *washed their robes, and made them white in the blood of the Lamb* (Rev. vii. 9—14); and still it is a *fountain opened.* How comfortable is this to poor repenting sinners, that the blood of Christ is *shed for many!* And if for *many,* why not for *me?* If for sinners, sinners of the Gentiles, the chief of sinners, then *why not for me?*

5. It was instituted to be a *ratification* of the covenant made with us in him, and a sign of the conveyance of those benefits to us, which were purchased for us by his death; and therefore he broke the bread *to them* (*v.* 22), and said, *Take, eat* of it: he gave the cup *to them,* and ordered them to *drink of it, v.* 23. Apply the doctrine of Christ crucified to yourselves, and let it be *meat* and *drink* to your souls, strengthening, nourishing, and refreshing, to you, and the support and comfort of your spiritual life.

6. It was instituted with an eye to the happiness of heaven, and to be an earnest and fore-taste of that, and thereby to put our mouths out of taste for all the pleasures and delights of sense (*v.* 25); *I will drink no more of the fruit of the vine,* as it is a bodily refreshment. I have done with it. *No one, having tasted spiritual* delights, *straightway desires* sensitive ones, for he saith, The *spiritual* is better (Luke v. 39); but *every one* that hath tasted *spiritual* delights, straightway desires *eternal* ones, for he saith, Those are *better still;* and therefore let me *drink no more of the fruit of the vine,* it is dead and flat to those that have been made to *drink* of the *river* of God's pleasures; but, Lord, hasten the day, when I shall *drink* it new and fresh *in the kingdom of God,* where it shall be for ever new, and in perfection.

7. It was closed with a *hymn, v.* 26. Though Christ was in the midst of his enemies, yet he did not, for fear of them, omit this sweet duty of singing psalms. Paul and Silas sang, when the *prisoners heard them.* This was an *evangelical song,* and gospel times are often spoken of in the Old Testament, as times of rejoicing, and praise is expressed by *singing.* This was Christ's *swan-like* song, which he sung just before he entered upon his agony; probably, that which was usually sung, Ps. cxiii. to cxviii.

IV. Christ's discourse with his disciples, as they were returning to Bethany by moonlight. When they had *sung the hymn,* presently they *went out.* It was now near bedtime, but our Lord Jesus had his heart so much upon his suffering, that he would not *come into the tabernacle of his house,* nor *go up into his bed,* nor *give sleep to his eyes,* when that work was to be done, Ps. cxxxii. 3, 4. The Iraelites were forbidden to go out of their houses the night that they ate the passover, for fear of the sword of the destroying angel, Exod. xii. 22, 23. But because Christ, the *great shepherd,* was to be *smitten,* he *went out* purposely to expose himself to the sword, as a champion; they *evaded* the destroyer, but Christ *conquered* him, and brought *destructions to a perpetual end.*

1. Christ here foretels that in his sufferings he should be *deserted* by all his disciples; "*You will all be offended because of me, this night.* I know you will (*v.* 27), and what I tell you now, is no other than what the scripture has told you before; *I will smite the shepherd,* and then *the sheep will be scattered.*" Christ knew this before, and yet welcomed them at his table; he foresees the falls and miscarriages of his disciples, and yet doth not refuse them. Nor should we be discouraged from coming to the Lord's supper, by the fear of relapsing into sin afterward; but, the greater our danger is, the more need we have to fortify ourselves by

the diligent conscientious use of holy ordinances. Christ tells them that they would be *offended in him,* would begin to question whether he were the Messiah or no, when they saw him *overpowered* by his enemies. Hitherto, they had *continued with him in his temptations;* though they had sometimes offended him, yet they had not been *offended in him,* nor turned the back upon him; but now the storm would be so great, that they would all *slip their anchors,* and be in danger of *shipwreck.* Some trials are more particular (as Rev. ii. 10, *The devil shall cast some of you into prison);* but others are more general, an *hour of temptation, which shall come upon all the world,* Rev. iii. 10. The *smiting* of the shepherd is often the *scattering* of the sheep: magistrates, ministers, masters of families, if these are, as they should be, *shepherds* to those under their charge, when any thing comes amiss to them, the whole flock suffers for it, and is endangered by it.

But Christ encourages them with a promise that they shall rally again, shall return both to their duty and to their comfort (*v.* 28); "*After I am risen,* I will *gather you in* from all the places *whither you are scattered,* Ezek. xxxiv. 12. I will *go before you into Galilee,* will see our friends, and enjoy one another there."

2. He foretels that he should be *denied* particularly by Peter. When they *went out* to go to the mount of Olives, we may suppose that they dropped Judas (he stole away from them), whereupon the rest began to think *highly* of themselves, that they *stuck* to their Master, when Judas quitted him. But Christ tells them, that though they should be kept by his grace from Judas's apostasy, yet they would have no reason to boast of their constancy. Note, Though God keeps us from being as bad as the worst, yet we may well be ashamed to think that we are not better than we are.

(1.) Peter is confident that he should not *do so ill* as the rest of the disciples (*v.* 29); *Though all should be offended,* all his brethren here present, *yet will not I.* He supposes himself not only stronger than others, but so much stronger, as to be able to receive the shock of a temptation, and bear up against it, *all alone;* to *stand,* though nobody stood *by him.* It is bred in the bone with us, to *think well* of ourselves, and *trust* to *our own hearts.*

(2.) Christ tells him that he will *do worse* than any of them. They will all *desert* him, but he will *deny* him; not once, but *thrice;* and that presently; "*This day, even this night before the cock crow twice,* thou wilt *deny* that ever thou hadst any knowledge of me, or acquaintance with me, as one ashamed and afraid to own me."

(3.) He stands to his promise; "*If I should die with thee, I will not deny thee;* I will adhere to thee, though it cost me my life:" and, no doubt, he thought as he said. Judas said nothing like this, when Christ told him he would betray him. He sinned by contrivance, Peter by surprise; he *devised the wickedness* (Mic. ii. 1), Peter was *overtaken in this fault,* Gal. vi. 1. It was ill done of Peter, to contradict his Master. If he had said, with fear and trembling, "Lord, give me grace to keep me from denying thee, lead me not into this temptation, deliver me from this evil," it might have been prevented: but they were all thus confident; they who said, *Lord, is it I?* now said, *It shall never be me.* Being acquitted from their fear of betraying Christ, they were now secure. But he that thinks he stands, must learn to take heed lest he fall; and he that *girdeth on the harness,* not boast *as though he had put it off.*

32 And they came to a place which
was named Gethsemane: and he saith
to his disciples, Sit ye here, while I
shall pray. 33 And he taketh with
him Peter and James and John, and
began to be sore amazed, and to be
very heavy; 34 And saith unto them,
My soul is exceeding sorrowful unto
death: tarry ye here, and watch.
35 And he went forward a little, and
fell on the ground, and prayed that,
if it were possible, the hour might
pass from him. 36 And he said,
Abba, Father, all things *are* possible
unto thee; take away this cup from
me: nevertheless not what I will, but
what thou wilt. 37 And he cometh,
and findeth them sleeping, and saith
unto Peter, Simon, sleepest thou?
couldest not thou watch one hour?
38 Watch ye and pray, lest ye enter
into temptation. The spirit truly
is ready, but the flesh *is* weak. 39
And again he went away, and prayed,
and spake the same words. 40 And
when he returned, he found them
asleep again (for their eyes were
heavy), neither wist they what to answer him. 41 And he cometh the
third time, and saith unto them, Sleep
on now, and take *your* rest: it is
enough, the hour is come; behold, the
Son of man is betrayed into the hands
of sinners. 42 Rise up, let us go:
lo, he that betrayeth me is at hand.

Christ is here entering upon his sufferings, and begins with those which were the sorest of all his sufferings, those in his *soul.* Here we have him in his *agony;* this melancholy story we had in Matthew; this *agony* in soul was the *wormwood and the gall* in the *affliction and misery;* and thereby it appeared that no sorrow was *forced upon him*, but that it was what he *freely* admitted.

I. He retired for prayer; *Sit ye here* (saith he to his disciples), while I go a little further, and *pray*. He had lately prayed *with them* (John xvii); and now he appoints them to withdraw while he goes to his Father upon an errand peculiar to himself. Note, Our praying with our families will not excuse our neglect of secret worship. When Jacob entered into his agony, he first *sent over all that he had*, and was *left alone*, and then *there wrestled a man with him* (Gen. xxxii. 23, 24), though he had been at prayer before (*v.* 9), it is likely, with his family.

II. Even into that retirement he took with him *Peter, and James, and John* (*v.* 33), three competent witnesses of this part of his humiliation; and though great spirits care not how few know any thing of their agonies, he was not ashamed that they should see. These three had boasted most of their ability and willingness to suffer with him; Peter here, in this chapter, and James and John (*ch* x. 39); and therefore Christ takes them to stand by, and see what a struggle he had with the *bloody baptism* and the *bitter cup*, to convince them that they knew not what they said. It is fit that they who are most confident, should be *first* tried, that they may be made sensible of their folly and weakness.

III. There he was in a tremendous agitation (*v.* 33); *He began to be sore amazed*—*ἐκθαμβεῖσθαι*, a word not used in Matthew, but very significant; it bespeaks something like that *horror of great darkness*, which *fell upon Abraham* (Gen. xv. 12), or, rather, something much worse, and more frightful. The *terrors of God set themselves in array against him*, and he allowed himself the actual and intense contemplation of them. Never was *sorrow* like unto *his* at that time; never any had such experience as he had from eternity of divine favours, and therefore never any had, or could have, such a sense as he had of divine favours. Yet there was not the least disorder or irregularity in this commotion of his spirits; his affections rose not tumultuously, but under direction, and as they were called up, for he had no corrupt nature to mix with them, as we have. If water have a sediment at the bottom, though it may be clear while it stands still, yet, when shaken, it grows muddy; so it is with our affections: but pure water in a clean glass, though ever so much stirred, continues clear; and so it was with Christ. Dr. Lightfoot thinks it very probable that the devil did now appear to our Saviour in a visible shape, in his *own shape* and *proper colour*, to terrify and affright him, and to drive him from his hope in God (which he aimed at in persecuting Job, a type of Christ, to make him *curse God, and die*), and to deter him from the further prosecution of his undertaking; whatever hindered him from that, he looked upon as coming from Satan, Matt. xvi. 23. When the devil had tempted him in the wilderness, it is said, He departed *from him for a season* (Luke iv. 13), intending another grapple with him, and in another way; finding that he could not by his flatteries *allure* him into sin, he would try by his terrors to *affright* him into it, and so *make void* his design.

IV. He made a sad complaint of this agitation. He said, *My soul is exceeding sorrowful.* 1. He was *made sin for us*, and therefore was thus *sorrowful;* he fully knew the *malignity* of the *sins* he was to *suffer for;* and having the highest degrees of love to God, who was *offended* by them, and of love to *man*, who was damaged and endangered by them, now that those were set in order before him, no marvel that *his soul* was *exceeding sorrowful.* Now he was made to *serve with our sins*, and was thus *wearied with our iniquities.* 2. He was *made a curse* for us; the curses of the law were transferred to him as our surety and representative, not as originally *bound with us*, but as *bail to the action.* And when his soul was thus exceeding sorrowful, he did, as it were, yield to them, and lie down under the load, until by his death he had satisfied for sin, and so for ever abolished the curse. He now *tasted death* (as he is said to do, Heb. ii. 9), which is not an extenuating expression, as if he did *but* taste it; no, he *drank up* even the dregs of the cup; but it is rather *aggravating;* it did not go down by wholesale, but he *tasted* all the bitterness of it. This was that *fear* which the apostle speaks of (Heb. v. 7), a natural fear of pain and death, which it is natural to human nature to startle at.

Now the consideration of Christ's sufferings in *his soul*, and his *sorrows* for us, should be of use to us,

(1.) To *embitter our sins.* Can we ever entertain a *favourable* or so much as a *slight* thought of sin, when we see what impression sin (though but imputed) made upon the Lord Jesus? Shall that *sit light* upon our souls, which sat *so heavy* upon his? Was Christ in such an agony for our sins, and shall we never be in an agony about them? How should we look upon him whom we have *pressed*, whom we have *pierced*, and *mourn*, and be *in bitterness!* It becomes us to be *exceeding sorrowful* for sin, because Christ was so, and never to *make a mock* at it. If Christ thus suffered for sin, let us *arm ourselves with the same mind.*

(2.) To *sweeten our sorrows;* if our souls be at any time *exceeding sorrowful*, through the afflictions of this present time, let us remember that our Master was so before us, and the *disciple is not greater than his Lord.* Why should we affect to *drive away* sorrow, when Christ for our sakes courted it, and submitted to it, and thereby not only took out the *sting* of it, and made it *tolerable*, but put *virtue* into it, and made it *profitable* (for *by the sadness of the countenance the heart is made better)*, nay, and put *sweetness* into it, and made it comfortable. Blessed Paul was *sorrowful*, and yet *always rejoicing*. If we be *exceeding sorrowful*, it is but *unto death;* that will be the period of all our sorrows, if Christ be *ours;* when the *eyes* are closed, all tears are *wiped away* from them.

V. He ordered his disciples to keep with him, not because he needed their help, but because he would have them to *look upon him and receive instruction;* he said to them, *Tarry ye here and watch.* He had said to the other disciples nothing but, Sit ye here (*v.* 32); but these three he bids to tarry *and watch,* as expecting more from them than from the rest.

VI. He addressed himself to God by prayer (*v.* 35); He *fell on the ground, and prayed.* It was but a little before this, that in prayer he *lifted up his eyes* (John xvii. 1); but here, being in an agony, he *fell upon his face,* accommodating himself to his present humiliation, and teaching us thus to abase ourselves before God; it becomes us to *be low*, when we come into the presence of the *Most High.* 1. As *Man*, he *deprecated* his sufferings, that, *if it were possible, the hour might pass from him* (*v.* 35); "This *short*, but *sharp* affliction, that which I am now *this hour* to enter upon, let man's salvation be, *if possible,* accomplished without it." We have his very words (*v.* 36), *Abba, Father.* The Syriac word is here retained, which Christ used, and which signifies *Father*, to intimate what an emphasis our Lord Jesus, in his *sorrows*, laid upon it, and would have us to lay. It is with an eye to this, that St. Paul retains this word, putting it into the mouths of all that have the *Spirit of adoption;* they are taught to cry, *Abba, Father,* Rom. viii. 15; Gal. iv. 6. Father, *all things are possible to thee.* Note, Even that which we cannot expect to be done for us, we ought yet to believe that God is *able to do:* and when we submit to his will, and refer ourselves to his wisdom and mercy, it must be with a believing acknowledgment of his power, that *all things are possible to him.* 2. As *Mediator*, he *acquiesced* in the will of God concerning them; "*Nevertheless, not what I will, but what thou wilt.* I know the matter is settled, and cannot be altered, *I must suffer* and die, and I bid it welcome."

VII. He roused his disciples, who were dropped asleep while he was at prayer, *v.* 37, 38. He comes to look after them, since they did not look after him; and he *finds them asleep*, so little affected were they with his sorrows, his complaints, and prayers. This carelessness of theirs was a presage of their further offence in deserting him; and it was an aggravation of it, that he had so lately commended them for *continuing with him in his temptations,* though they had not been without their faults. Was he so willing to make the best of them, and were they so indifferent in approving themselves to him? They had lately promised not to be *offended in him;* what! and yet mind him so little? He particularly upbraided Peter with his drowsiness; *Simon, sleepest thou?* Καὶ συ τέκνον;—"*What thou, my son?* Thou that didst so positively promise thou wouldest not deny me, dost thou slight me thus? From thee I expected better things. *Couldest thou not watch one hour?*" He did not require him to watch *all night* with him, only for *one hour.* It aggravates our faintness and short continuance in Christ's service, that he doth not over-task us, nor weary us with it, Isa. xliii. 23. He puts upon us *no other burthen* than to *hold fast till he comes* (Rev. ii. 24, 25); and behold, *he comes quickly*, Rev. iii. 11.

As those whom Christ *loves* he *rebukes* when they do amiss, so those whom he *rebukes* he counsels and comforts. 1. It was a very wise and faithful word of advice which Christ here gave to his disciples; *Watch and pray, lest ye enter into temptation, v.* 38. It was bad to *sleep* when Christ was in his agony, but they were entering into further temptation, and if they did not stir up themselves, and fetch in grace and strength from God by prayer, they would *do worse;* and so they did, when they all forsook him, and fled. 2. It was a very kind and tender excuse that Christ made for them; "*The spirit truly is willing;* I know it is, it is *ready*, it is *forward;* you would willingly *keep awake*, but you cannot." This may be taken as a reason for that exhortation, "*Watch and pray;* because, though *the spirit is willing*, I grant it is (you have sincerely resolved never to be *offended in me*), yet *the flesh is weak*, and if you do not *watch* and *pray*, and use the means of perseverance, you may be overcome, notwithstanding." The consideration of the *weakness* and infirmity *of our flesh* should engage and quicken us to *prayer* and *watchfulness*, when we are entering into temptation.

VIII. He *repeated* his address to his Father (*v.* 39); *He went again, and prayed,* saying, τὸν ἀυτὸν λόγον—*the same word,* or matter, or business; he spoke to the same purport, and again *the third time.* This teaches us, that *men ought always to pray, and not to faint,* Luke xviii. 1. Though the answers to our prayers do not come quickly, yet we must renew our requests, and *continue instant in prayer;* for *the vision is for an appointed time, and at the end it shall speak, and not lie,* Hab. ii. 3. Paul, when he was *buffeted by a messenger of Satan, besought the Lord thrice,* as Christ did here, before he obtained an answer of peace, 2 Cor. xii. 7, 8. A little before this, when Christ, in the *trouble of his soul,* prayed, *Father, glorify thy name,* he had an immediate answer by a voice from heaven, *I have both glorified it, and I will glorify it yet again;* but now he must come a second and a third time, for the visits of God's grace, in answer to prayer, come sooner or later, according to the pleasure of his will, that we may be kept depending.

IX. He *repeated* his visits to his disciples. Thus he gave a specimen of his continued care for his church on earth, even when it is *half asleep*, and not duly concerned for itself, while he ever lives making intercession with his Father *in heaven*. See how, as became a *Mediator*, he passes and repasses between both. He came the *second time* to his disciples, and *found them asleep again, v.* 40. See how the infirmities of Christ's disciples *return* upon them, notwithstanding their resolutions, and *overpower* them, notwitstanding their resistance; and what clogs those bodies of ours are to our souls, which should make us long for that blessed state in which they shall be no more our encumbrance This second time he spoke to them as before, but *they wist not what to answer him;* they were ashamed of their drowsiness, and had nothing to say in excuse for it. Or, They were so overpowered with it, that, like men between sleeping and waking, they knew not where they were, or what they said. But, the *third time*, they were bid to *sleep* if they would (*v.* 41); " *Sleep on now, and take your rest.* I have now no more occasion for your watching, you may sleep, if you will, for me." *It is enough;* we had not that word in Matthew. " You have had warning enough to keep awake, and would not take it; and now you shall see what little reason you have to be secure." 'Απέκει, *I discharge you* from any *further attendance;* so some understand it; " Now *the hour is come,* in which I knew you would all forsake me, even take your course;" as he said to Judas, *What thou doest, do quickly.* The *Son of man* is now *betrayed into the hands of sinners*, the chief priests and elders; those *worst* of sinners, because they made a profession of sanctity. " Come, *rise up*, do not lie dozing there. *Let us go* and meet the enemy, for *lo, he that betrayeth me is at hand*, and I must not now think of making an escape." When we see trouble at the door, we are concerned to stir up ourselves to get ready for it.

43 And immediately, while he yet
spake, cometh Judas, one of the twelve,
and with him a great multitude with
swords and staves, from the chief
priests and the scribes and the elders.
44 And he that betrayed him had
given them a token, saying, Whomsoever I shall kiss, that same is he;
take him, and lead *him* away safely.
45 And as soon as he was come, he
goeth straightway to him, and saith,
Master, master; and kissed him. 46
And they laid their hands on him, and
took him. 47 And one of them that
stood by drew a sword, and smote a
servant of the high priest, and cut off
his ear. 48 And Jesus answered and
said unto them, Are ye come out, as
against a thief, with swords and *with*
staves to take me? 49 I was daily
with you in the temple teaching, and
ye took me not: but the scriptures
must be fulfilled. 50 And they all
forsook him, and fled. 51 And there
followed him a certain young man,
having a linen cloth cast about *his*
naked *body;* and the young men laid
hold on him: 52 And he left the
linen cloth, and fled from them naked.

We have here the *seizing* of our Lord Jesus by the officers of the chief priests. This was what his enemies had long aimed at, they had often sent to *take him;* but he had escaped out of their hands, because *his hour was not come*, nor could they now have taken him, had he not freely surrendered himself. He began first to suffer *in his soul*, but afterward suffered in his body, that he might satisfy for sin, which begins in the heart, but afterward makes the members of the body *instruments of unrighteousness.*

I. Here is a band of rude miscreants employed to *take* our Lord Jesus and make him a prisoner; *a great multitude with swords and staves.* There is no wickedness so black, no villany so horrid, but there may be found among the children of men fit tools to be made use of, that will not scruple to be employed; so miserably depraved and vitiated is mankind. At the head of this rabble is Judas, *one of the twelve*, one of those that had been many years intimately conversant with our Lord Jesus, had prophesied in his name, and in his name cast out devils, and yet *betrayed* him. It is no new thing for a very fair and plausible profession to end in a shameful and fatal apostasy. *How art thou fallen, O Lucifer!*

II. Men of no less figure than the *chief priests, and the scribes,* and *the elders*, sent them, and set them on work, who pretended to expect the Messiah, and to be ready to welcome him; and yet, when he *is come*, and has given undeniable proofs that it is he that *should come*, because he doth not make court to them, nor countenance and support their pomp and grandeur, because he appears not as a temporal prince, but sets up a spiritual kingdom, and preaches repentance, reformation, and a holy life, and directs men's thoughts, and affections, and aims, to another world, they set themselves against him, and, without giving the credentials he produces an impartial examination, resolve to run him down.

III. Judas betrayed him *with a kiss;* abusing the freedom Christ used to allow his disciples of kissing his cheek at their return when they had been any time absent. He called him, *Master, Master, and kissed him;* he said, *Rabbi, Rabbi*, as if he had been now more respectful to him than ever. It is enough to put one for ever out of conceit with being called of men *Rabbi, Rabbi* (Matt. xxiii. 7), since it was with this compliment that Christ was betrayed. He bid them take him, and *lead him away safely*. Some think that he spoke this *ironically*, knowing that they could not secure him unless he pleased, that this Samson could break their bonds asunder as threads of tow, and make his escape, and then he should get the money, and Christ the honour, and no harm done; and I should think so too, but that Satan was *entered into him*, so that the worst and most malicious intention of this action is not too black to be supposed. Nay, he had often heard his Master say, that, being *betrayed*, he should be *crucified*, and had no reason to think otherwise.

IV. They arrested him, and made him their prisoner (*v.* 46); *They laid their hands on him*, rude and violent hands, and *took him* into custody; triumphing, it is likely, that they had done that which had been often before attempted in vain.

V. Peter laid about him in defence of his Master, and wounded one of the assailants, being for the present mindful of his promise, to venture his life with his Master. He was *one of them that stood by*, of them that *were with him* (so the word signifies), of *those three* disciples that were *with him* in the garden; he *drew a sword*, and aimed, it is likely, to cut off the head, but missed his blow, and only *cut off the ear*, of a servant of the high priest, *v.* 47. It is easier to *fight* for Christ, than to *die* for him; but Christ's good soldiers overcome, not by taking away other people's lives, but by laying down their own, Rev. xii. 11.

VI. Christ argues with them that had seized him, and shows them the absurdity of their proceedings against him. 1. That they came out *against him*, as against a *thief*, whereas he was *innocent* of any crime; he *taught daily in the temple*, and if he had any wicked design, there it would some time or other have been discovered; nay, these officers of the *chief priests*, being *retainers* to the temple, may be supposed to have heard his sermons there (I was *with you* in the temple); and had he not taught them excellent doctrine, even his enemies themselves being judges? Were not *all the words of his mouth in righteousness?* Was there any thing *froward or perverse in them?* Prov. viii. 8. By his fruits he was known to be a good tree; why then did they come out against him *as a thief?* 2. That they came to take him thus *privately*, whereas he was neither *ashamed* nor *afraid* to appear *publicly* in the temple. He was none of those *evil-doers* that *hate the light*, neither come *to the light*, John iii. 20. If their masters had any thing to say to him, they might meet him any day in the temple, where he was ready to answer all challenges, all charges; and there they might do as they pleased with him, for the priests had the custody of the temple, and the command of the guards about it: but to come upon him thus at midnight, and in the place of his retirement, was base and cowardly. This was to do as David's enemy, that *sat in the lurking places of the villages, to murder the innocent*, Ps. x. 8. But this was not all. 3. They came *with swords and staves*, as if he had been in arms against the government, and must have the *posse comitatus* raised to reduce him. There was no occasion for those weapons; but they made this ado, (1.) To secure themselves from the rage of some; they came armed, because they *feared the people;* but thus *were they in great fear, where no fear was*, Ps. liii. 5. (2.) To expose him to the rage of others. By coming *with swords and staves to take him*, they represented him to the people (who are apt to take impressions this way) as a dangerous turbulent man, and so endeavoured to incense them against him, and make them cry out, *Crucify him, crucify him*, having no other way to gain their point.

VII. He reconciled himself to all this injurious, ignominious treatment, by referring himself to the Old-Testament predictions of the Messiah. I am hardly used, *but* I submit, for *the scriptures must be fulfilled*, *v.* 49. 1. See here what a regard Christ had to the *scriptures;* he would bear any thing rather than that the least jot or tittle of the word of God should fall to the ground; and as he had an eye to them in his sufferings, so he has in his glory; for what is Christ doing in the government of the world, but *fulfilling the scriptures?* 2. See what use we are to make of the Old Testament; we must search for Christ, the true *treasure hid in that field:* as the history of the New Testament expounds the prophecies of the Old, so the prophecies of the Old Testament illustrate the history of the New.

VIII. All Christ's disciples, hereupon, deserted him (*v.* 50); *They all forsook him, and fled*. They were very confident that they should adhere to him; but even good men know not what they will do, till they are tried. If it was such a comfort to him as he had lately intimated, that they had hitherto *continued with him* in his lesser trials (Luke xxii. 28), we may well imagine what a grief it was to him, that they deserted him now in the greatest, when they might have done him some service—when he was abused, to protect him, and when accused, to witness for him. Let not those that suffer for Christ, think it strange, if they be thus deserted, and if all the herd shun the wounded deer; they are not better than their Master, nor can expect to be better used either by their enemies or by their friends. When St. Paul was in peril, none *stood by him*, but *all men forsook him*, 2 Tim. iv. 16.

IX. The noise disturbed the neighbourhood, and some of the neighbours were brought into danger by the riot, *v.* 51, 52. This passage of story we have not in any other of the evangelists. Here is an account of a *certain young man,* who, as it should seem, was no disciple of Christ, nor, as some have imagined, a servant of the house wherein Christ had eaten the passover, who *followed him* to see what would become of him (as the *sons of the prophets,* when they understood that Elijah was to be *taken up,* went to *view afar off,* 2 Kings ii. 7), but some young man that lived near the garden, perhaps in the house to which the garden belonged. Now observe concerning him,

1. How he was *frightened out of his bed,* to be a *spectator* of Christ's sufferings. Such a *multitude,* so armed, and coming with so much fury, and in the dead of the night, and in a quiet village, could not but produce a great stir; this alarmed our *young man,* who perhaps thought there was some tumult or rising in the city, some *uproar among the people,* and had the curiosity to go, and see what the matter was, and was in such haste to inform himself, that he could not stay to dress himself, but threw a sheet about him, as if he would appear like a walking ghost, in grave clothes, to frighten those who had frightened him, and ran among the thickest of them with this question, *What is to do here?* Being told, he had a mind to see the issue, having, no doubt, heard much of the fame of this Jesus; and therefore, when all his disciples had quitted him, he continued to *follow him,* desirous to *hear* what he would say, and *see* what he would do. Some think that his having no other garment than this *linen cloth* upon his naked body, intimates that he was one of those Jews who made a greater profession of piety than their neighbours, in token of which, among other instances of austerity and mortification of the body, they used no clothes but one linen garment, which, though contrived to be modest enough, was thin and cold. But I rather think that this was not his constant wear.

2. See how he was *frightened into his bed* again, when he was in danger of being made a *sharer* in Christ's sufferings. His own disciples had run away from him; but this young man, having no concern for him, thought he might securely attend him, especially being so far from being armed, that he was not so much as clothed; but *the young men,* the Roman soldiers, who were called to assist, *laid hold of him,* for all was fish that came to their net. Perhaps they were now vexed at themselves, that they had suffered the disciples to *run away,* and they being got out of their reach they resolved to seize the first they could *lay their hands on;* though this young man was perhaps one of the *strictest sect* of the Jewish church, yet the Roman soldiers made no conscience of abusing him upon this occasion. Finding himself in danger, he *left the linen cloth* by which they had *caught hold of him,* and *fled away naked.* This passage is recorded to show what a barbarous crew this was, that was sent to seize Christ, and what a narrow escape the disciples had of falling into their hands, out of which nothing could have kept them but their Master's care of them; *If ye seek me, let these go their way,* John xviii. 8. It also intimates that there is *no hold* of those who are led by curiosity only, and not by faith and conscience, to follow Christ.

53 And they led Jesus away to the
high priest: and with him were assembled all the chief priests and the
elders and the scribes. 54 And Peter
followed him afar off, even into the
palace of the high priest: and he sat
with the servants, and warmed himself at the fire. 55 And the chief
priests and all the council sought for
witness against Jesus to put him to
death; and found none. 56 For
many bare false witness against him,
but their witness agreed not together.
57 And there arose certain, and bare
false witness against him, saying, 58
We heard him say, I will destroy this
temple that is made with hands, and
within three days I will build another
made without hands. 59 But neither
so did their witness agree together.
60 And the high priest stood up in
the midst, and asked Jesus, saying,
Answerest thou nothing? what *is it*
which these witness against thee? 61
But he held his peace, and answered
nothing. Again the high priest asked
him, and said unto him, Art thou the
Christ, the Son of the Blessed? 62
And Jesus said, I am: and ye shall
see the Son of man sitting on the
right hand of power, and coming in
the clouds of heaven. 63 Then the
high priest rent his clothes, and saith,
What need we any further witnesses?
64 Ye have heard the blasphemy:
what think ye? And they all condemned him to be guilty of death.
65 And some began to spit on him,
and to cover his face, and to buffet
him, and to say unto him, Prophesy:
and the servants did strike him with
the palms of their hands.

We have here Christ's arraignment, trial, conviction, and condemnation, in the *ecclesiastical* court, before the great sanhedrim, of which the *high priest* was president, or judge of the court; the same Caiaphas that had lately adjudged it expedient he should be put to death, guilty or not guilty (John xi. 50), and who therefore might justly be excepted against as partial.

I. Christ is hurried away to his *house,* his *palace* it is called, such state did he live in. And there, though in the dead of the night, *all the chief priests, and elders, and scribes,* that were in the secret, were *assembled,* ready to receive the prey; so sure were they of it.

II. *Peter followed* at a distance, such a degree of cowardice was his late courage dwindled into, *v.* 54. But when he came to the high priest's palace, he *sneakingly* went, and *sat with the servants,* that he might not be suspected to belong to Christ. The high priest's fire side was no proper place, nor his servants proper company, for Peter, but it was his *entrance into a temptation.*

III. Great diligence was used to procure, for love or money, false witnesses against Christ. They had seized him as a malefactor, and now they had him they had no indictment to prefer against him, no crime to lay to his charge, but they *sought for witnesses against him;* pumped some with ensnaring questions, offered bribes to others, if they *would accuse him,* and endeavoured to frighten others, if they *would not, v.* 55, 56. The chief priests and elders were by the law entrusted with the prosecuting and punishing of *false witnesses* (Deut. xix. 16, 17); yet those were now ringleaders in a crime that tends to the overthrow of all justice. It is time to cry, *Help, Lord,* when the physicians of a land are its troublers, and those that should be the conservators of peace and equity, are the corrupters of both.

IV. He was at length charged with words spoken some years ago, which, as they were represented, seemed to threaten *the temple,* which they had made no better than an idol of (*v* 57, 58); but the witnesses to this matter did not agree (*v.* 59), for one swore that he said, *I am able to destroy the temple of God, and to build it in three days* (so it is in Matthew); the other swore that he said, *I will destroy this temple, that is made with hands,* and *within three days, I will build* not it, but *another made without hands;* now these two differ much from each other; *οὐδὲ ἴση ἦν ἡ μαρτυρία—their testimony was not sufficient,* nor equal to the charge of a capital crime; so Dr. Hammond: they did not accuse him of that upon which a *sentence of death* might be founded, no not by the utmost stretch of their law.

V. He was urged to be his own accuser (*v.* 60); The *high priest stood up* in a heat, and said, *Answerest thou nothing?* This he said under pretence of justice and fair dealing, but really with a design to ensnare him, that they might *accuse him,* Luke xi. 53, 54; xx. 20. We may well imagine with what an air of haughtiness and disdain this proud high priest brought our Lord Jesus to this question; "Come you, the prisoner at the bar, you hear what is sworn against you; what have you now to say for yourself?" Pleased to think that *he* seemed silent, who had so often silenced those that picked quarrels with him. Still Christ *answered nothing,* that he might set us an example, 1. Of *patience* under calumnies and false accusations; when we are *reviled,* let us not *revile again,* 1 Pet. ii. 23. And, 2. Of *prudence,* when a man shall be made an *offender for a word* (Isa. xxix. 21), and our *de*fence made our *of*fence; it is an evil time indeed when the prudent shall *keep silence* (lest they make bad worse), *and commit their cause to him that judgeth righteously.* But,

VI. When he was asked *whether he was the Christ,* he confessed, and denied not, that *he was, v.* 61, 62. He asked, *Art thou the Son of the Blessed?* that is, the Son of *God?* for, as Dr. Hammond observes, the Jews, when they named *God,* generally added, *blessed for ever;* and thence *the Blessed* is the title of *God,* a peculiar title, and applied to Christ, Rom. ix. 5. And for the proof of his being the *Son of God,* he binds them over to his second coming; "*Ye shall see the Son of man sitting on the right hand of power;* that *Son of man* that now appears so mean and despicable, whom you *see* and trample upon (Isa. liii. 2, 3), you shall shortly see and *tremble before.*" Now, one would think that such a word as this which our Lord Jesus seems to have spoken with a grandeur and majesty not agreeable to his present appearance (for through the thickest cloud of his humiliation some rays of glory were still darted forth), should have startled the court, and at least, in the opinion of some of them, should have amounted to a *demurrer,* or *arrest of judgment,* and that they should have stayed process till they had considered further of it; when Paul at the bar reasoned of the *judgment to come,* the judge *trembled,* and adjourned the trial, Acts xxiv. 25. But these chief priests were so miserably blinded with malice and rage, that, like the horse rushing into the battle, they *mocked at fear, and were not affrighted,* neither *believed they that it was the sound of the trumpet,* Job xxxix. 22, 24. And see Job xv. 25, 26.

VII. The high priest, upon this confession of his, convicted him as *a blasphemer* (*v.* 63); He *rent his clothes—χιτῶνας αὐτοῦ.* Some think that the word signifies his pontifical vestments, which, for the greater state, he had put on, though in the night, upon this occasion. As before, in his enmity to Christ, he said he knew not what (John xi. 51, 52), so now he did he knew not what. If Saul's rending Samuel's mantle was made to signify the rending of the kingdom from him (1 Sam. xv. 27, 28), much more did Caiaphas's rending his own clothes signify the rending of the priesthood from him, as the rending of the veil, at Christ's death, signified the throwing of all open. Christ's clothes, even when he was crucified, were kept entire, and not rent; for when the Levitical priesthood was rent in pieces and done away, *This Man, because he continues ever, has an unchangeable priesthood.*

VIII. They agreed that he was a blasphemer, and, as such, was guilty of a capital crime, *v.* 64. The question *seemed* to be put fairly, *What think ye?* But it was really *prejudged,* for the high priest had said, *Ye have heard the blasphemy;* he gave judgment first, who, as president of the court, ought to have voted last. So they *all condemned him* to be *guilty of death;* what friends he had in the great sanhedrim, did not appear, it is probable that they had not notice.

IX. They set themselves to abuse him, and, as the Philistines with Samson, to make sport with him, *v.* 65. It should seem that some of the priests themselves that had condemned him, so far forgot the dignity, as well as duty, of their place, and the gravity which became them, that they helped their servants in playing the fool with a condemned prisoner. This they made their diversion, while they *waited for the morning,* to complete their villany. That *night of observations* (as the passover-night was called) they *made a merry night of.* If they did not think it below them to abuse Christ, shall we think any thing below us, by which we may do him honour?

66 And as Peter was beneath in
the palace, there cometh one of the
maids of the high priest: 67 And
when she saw Peter warming himself,
she looked upon him, and said, And
thou also wast with Jesus of Nazareth. 68 But he denied, saying, I
know not, neither understand I what
thou sayest. And he went out into
the porch; and the cock crew. 69
And a maid saw him again, and began
to say to them that stood by, This is
one of them. 70 And he denied it
again. And a little after, they that
stood by said again to Peter, Surely
thou art *one* of them: for thou art
a Galilæan, and thy speech agreeth
thereto. 71 But he began to curse
and to swear, *saying,* I know not this
man of whom ye speak. 72 And the
second time the cock crew. And
Peter called to mind the word that
Jesus said unto him, Before the cock
crow twice, thou shalt deny me thrice.
And when he thought thereon, he
wept.

We have here the story of Peter's denying Christ.

1. It began in *keeping at a distance* from him. Peter had followed *afar off* (*v.* 54), and now was *beneath in the palace,* at the lower end of the hall. Those that are *shy* of Christ, are in a fair way to *deny* him, that are shy of attending on holy ordinances, shy of the communion of the faithful, and loth to be seen on the side of despised godliness.

2. It was occasioned by his associating with the high priest's servants, and sitting among them. They that think it dangerous to be in company with Christ's disciples, because thence they may be drawn in to *suffer for him,* will find it much more dangerous to be in company with his enemies, because there they may be drawn in to *sin against him.*

3. The temptation was, his being charged as a disciple of Christ; *Thou also wert with Jesus of Nazareth, v.* 67. *This is one of them* (*v.* 69), *for thou art a Galilean,* one may know that by thy speaking broad, *v.* 70. It doth not appear that he was *challenged* upon it, or in danger of being *prosecuted* as a criminal for it, but only *bantered* upon it, and in danger of being ridiculed as a fool for it. While the chief priests were abusing the Master, the servants were abusing the disciples. Sometimes the cause of Christ seems to fall so much on the losing side, that every body has a stone to throw at it, and even the *abjects gather themselves together against* it. When Job was on the dunghill, he was had in derision of those that were the *children of base men,* Job xxx. 8. Yet, all things considered, the temptation could not be called *formidable;* it was only a *maid* that casually cast her eye upon him, and, for aught that appears, without design of giving him any trouble, said, *Thou art one of them,* to which he needed not to have made any reply, or might have said, "And if I be, I hope that is no treason."

4. The sin was very great; he *denied Christ before men,* at a time when he ought to have confessed and owned him, and to have appeared in court a witness for him. Christ had often given notice to his disciples of his own sufferings; yet, when they came, they were to Peter as great a surprise and terror as if he had never heard of them before. He had often told them that they must *suffer* for him, must *take up their cross,* and follow him; and yet Peter is so terribly afraid of suffering, upon the very first alarm of it, that he will lie and swear, and do any thing, to avoid it. When Christ was admired and flocked after, he could readily own him; but now that he is deserted, and despised, and run down, he is ashamed of him, and will own no relation to him.

5. His repentance was very speedy. He repeated his denial thrice, and the third was worst of all, for then he *cursed* and *swore,* to confirm his denial; and that third blow, which, one would think, should have *stunned him,* and knocked him down, *startled him,* and roused him up. Then the *cock crew* the second time, which put him in mind of his Master's words, the warning he had given him, with that particular circumstance of

the *cock crowing twice;* by recollecting that, he was made sensible of his sin and the aggravations of it; and when he thought thereon, he wept. Some observe that this evangelist, who wrote, as some have thought, by St. Peter's direction, speaks as fully of Peter's sin as any of them, but more briefly of his *sorrow,* which Peter, in modesty, would not have to be magnified, and because he thought he could never sorrow enough for so great a sin. His repentance here is thus expressed, ἐπιβαλὼν ἔκλαιε, where something must be supplied. He *added to weep,* so some; making it a Hebraism; he wept, and the more he thought of it, the more he wept; he continued weeping; he *flung out,* and wept; *burst out* into tears; *threw himself down,* and wept; he *covered his face,* and wept, so some; cast his garment about his head, that he might not be seen to weep; he *cast his eyes* upon his Master, who turned, and looked upon him; so Dr. Hammond supplies it, and it is a probable conjecture. Or, as we understand it, *fixing his mind upon it,* he wept. It is not a transient thought of that which is humbling, that will suffice, but we must dwell upon it. Or, what if this word should mean his *laying a load* upon himself, throwing confusion into his own face? he did as the *publican* that smote his breast, in sorrow for sin; and this amounts to his weeping bitterly.

CHAP. XV.

What we read of the sufferings of Christ, in the foregoing chapter, was but the prologue or introduction; here we have the completing of them. We left him condemned by the chief priests; but they could only show their teeth, they could not bite. Here we have him, I. Arraigned and accused before Pilate the Roman governor, ver. 1—5. II. Cried out against by the common people, at the instigation of the priests, ver. 6—14. III. Condemned to be crucified immediately, ver. 15. IV. Bantered and abused, as a mock-king, by the Roman soldiers, ver. 16—19. V. Led out to the place of execution with all possible ignominy and disgrace, ver. 20—24. VI. Nailed to the cross between two thieves, ver. 25—28. VII Reviled and abused by all that passed by, ver. 29—32. VIII. Forsaken for a time by his father, ver. 33—36. IX. Dying, and rending the veil, ver. 37, 38. X. Attested and witnessed to by the centurion and others, ver. 39—41. XI. Buried in the sepulchre of Joseph of Arimathea, ver. 42—47.

AND straightway in the morning
the chief priests held a consultation with the elders and scribes and
the whole council, and bound Jesus,
and carried *him* away, and delivered
him to Pilate. 2 And Pilate asked
him, Art thou the King of the Jews?
And he answering said unto him,
Thou sayest *it.* 3 And the chief
priests accused him of many things:
but he answered nothing. 4 And
Pilate asked him again, saying, Answerest thou nothing? behold how
many things they witness against thee.
5 But Jesus yet answered nothing;
so that Pilate marvelled. 6 Now at
that feast he released unto them one
prisoner, whomsoever they desired.
7 And there was *one* named Barabbas,
which lay bound with them that had
made insurrection with him, who had
committed murder in the insurrection.
8 And the multitude crying aloud began to desire *him to do* as he had ever
done unto them. 9 But Pilate answered them, saying, Will ye that I
release unto you the King of the Jews?
10 For he knew that the chief priests
had delivered him for envy. 11 But
the chief priests moved the people,
that he should rather release Barabbas
unto them. 12 And Pilate answered
and said again unto them, What will
ye then that I shall do *unto him* whom
ye call the King of the Jews? 13
And they cried out again, Crucify
him. 14 Then Pilate said unto them,
Why, what evil hath he done? And
they cried out the more exceedingly,
Crucify him.

Here we have, I. A *consultation* held by the great Sanhedrim for the effectual prosecution of our Lord Jesus. They met *early in the morning* about it, and went into a grand committee, to find out *ways and means* to get him put to death; they lost no time, but followed their blow in good earnest, lest there should be an *uproar among the people.* The unwearied industry of wicked people in doing that which is evil, should shame us for our backwardness and slothfulness in that which is good. They that *war* against Christ and thy soul, are up early; *How long then wilt thou sleep, O sluggard?*

II. The delivering of him up a prisoner to Pilate; they *bound him.* He was to be the great sacrifice, and sacrifices must be bound with cords, Ps. cxviii. 27. Christ was bound, to make bonds easy to us, and enable us, as Paul and Silas, to sing in bonds. It is good for us often to *remember the bonds* of the Lord Jesus, as bound with him who was *bound for us.* They led him through the streets of Jerusalem, to expose *him* to contempt, who, while he taught in the temple, but a day or two before, was had in veneration; and we may well imagine how miserably he looked after such a night's usage as he had had; so buffeted, spit upon, and abused. Their delivering him to the Roman power was a type of the ruin of their church, which hereby they merited, and brought upon themselves; it signified that the promise, the covenant, and the oracles, of God, and the visible church state, which were the glory of Israel, and had been so long in their possession, should now be delivered up to the Gentiles. By delivering up *the king* they do, in effect, deliver up the *kingdom of God,* which is therefore, as it were, by their own consent, taken from them, and given to another nation. If they had delivered up Christ, to gratify the desires of the Romans, or to satisfy any jealousies of theirs concerning him, it had been another matter; but they voluntarily betrayed him that was *Israel's crown,* to them that were *Israel's yoke.*

III. The examining of him by Pilate upon interrogatories (*v.* 2); "*Art thou the king of the Jews?* Dost thou pretend to be so, to be that Messiah whom the Jews expect as a temporal prince?"—"Yea," saith Christ, "it is as *thou sayest,* I am that Messiah, but not such a one as they expect." He is the king that rules and protects his Israel according to the spirit, who are Jews inwardly by the circumcision of the spirit, and the king that will restrain and punish the carnal Jews, who continue in unbelief.

IV. The articles of impeachment exhibited against him, and his silence under the charge and accusation. The chief priests forgot the dignity of their place, when they turned informers, and did in person *accuse Christ of many things* (*v.* 3), and witness against him, *v.* 4. Many of the Old-Testament prophets charge the priests of their times with great wickedness, in which *well did they prophesy* of these priests; see Ezek. xxii. 26; Hos. v. 1; vi. 9; Mic. iii. 11; Zeph. iii. 4; Mal. i. 6; ii. 8. The destruction of Jerusalem by the Chaldeans is said to be for the *iniquity of the priests that shed the blood of the just,* Lam. iv. 13. Note, Wicked priests are generally the worst of men. The better any thing is, the worse it is when it is corrupted. Lay persecutors have been generally found more compassionate than ecclesiastics. These priests were very eager and noisy in their accusation; but Christ *answered nothing, v.* 3. When Pilate urged him to clear himself, and was desirous he should (*v.* 4), yet still he stood mute (*v.* 5), he *answered nothing,* which Pilate thought very strange. He gave Pilate a direct answer (*v.* 2), but would not answer the prosecutors and witnesses, because the things they alleged, were notoriously false, and he knew Pilate himself was convinced they were so. Note, As Christ *spoke* to admiration, so he *kept silence* to admiration.

V. The proposal Pilate made to the people, to have Jesus released to them, since it was the custom of the feast to grace the solemnity with the release of one prisoner. The people expected and demanded that he should do *as he had ever done to them* (*v.* 8); it was an ill usage, but they would have it kept up. Now Pilate perceived that the chief priests delivered up Jesus *for envy,* because he had got such a reputation among the people as eclipsed theirs, *v.* 10. It was easy to see, comparing the eagerness of the prosecutors with the slenderness of the proofs, that it was not his *guilt,* but his *goodness,* not any thing *mischievous* or *scandalous,* but something *meritorious* and *glorious,* that they were provoked at. And therefore, hearing how much he was the darling of the crowd, he thought that he might safely appeal from the priests to the people, and that they would be proud of rescuing him out of the priests' hands; and he proposed an expedient for their doing it without danger of an *uproar;* let them demand him to be *released,* and Pilate will readily do it, and stop the mouths of the priests with this—that the people insisted upon his release. There was indeed another prisoner, *one Barabbas,* that had an interest, and would have some votes; but he questioned not but Jesus would out-poll him.

VI. The unanimous outrageous clamours of the people to have *Christ put to death,* and particularly to have him *crucified.* It was a great surprise to Pilate, when he found the people so much under the influence of the priests, that they all agreed to desire that Barabbas might be *released, v.* 11. Pilate opposed it all he could; "*What will ye that I shall do to him whom ye call the King of the Jews?* Would not ye then have him released too?" *v.* 12. No, say they, *Crucify him.* The priests having put that in their mouths, they insist upon it; when Pilate objected, *Why, what evil has he done?* (a very material question in such a case), they did not pretend to answer it, but *cried out the more exceedingly,* as they were more and more instigated and irritated by the priests, *Crucify him, crucify him.* Now the priests, who were very busy dispersing themselves and their creatures among the mob, to keep up the cry, promised themselves that it would influence Pilate two ways to condemn him. 1. It might incline him to believe Christ *guilty,* when there was so general an out-cry against him. "Surely," might Pilate think, "he must needs be a bad man, whom all the world is weary of." He would now conclude that he had been *misinformed,* when he was told what an interest he had in the people, and that the matter was not so. But the priests had hurried on the prosecution with so much expedition, that we may suppose that they who were Christ's friends, and would have opposed this cry, were at the other end of the town, and knew nothing of the matter. Note, It has been the common artifice of Satan, to put Christ and his religion into an ill name, and so to run them down. When once this sect, as they called it, comes to be *every where spoken against,* though *without cause,* then that is looked upon as *cause enough* to condemn it. But let us *judge* of persons and things by their merits, and the standard of God's word, and not prejudge by common fame and the cry of the country. 2. It might induce him to condemn Christ, to *please* the people, and indeed for *fear* of *displeasing* them. Though he was not so *weak* as to be governed by their opinion, to believe him guilty, yet he was so *wicked* as to be swayed by their outrage, to condemn him, though he believed him innocent; induced thereunto by reasons of state, and the wisdom of this world. Our Lord Jesus dying as a *sacrifice* for the *sins of many*, he fell a sacrifice to the *rage of many*.

15 And *so* Pilate, willing to content the people, released Barabbas unto them, and delivered Jesus, when he had scourged *him*, to be crucified.
16 And the soldiers led him away into the hall, called Prætorium; and they call together the whole band.
17 And they clothed him with purple, and platted a crown of thorns, and put it about his *head*,
18 And began to salute him, Hail, King of the Jews!
19 And they smote him on the head with a reed, and did spit upon him, and bowing *their* knees worshipped him.
20 And when they had mocked him, they took off the purple from him, and put his own clothes on him, and led him out to crucify him.
21 And they compel one Simon a Cyrenian, who passed by, coming out of the country, the father of Alexander and Rufus, to bear his cross.

Here, I. Pilate, to gratify the Jews' malice, delivers Christ to be *crucified, v.* 15. *Willing to content the people,* to *do enough* for them (so the word is), and make them easy, that he might keep them quiet, he *released Barabbas unto them,* who was the scandal and plague of their nation, and *delivered Jesus* to be *crucified,* who was the glory and blessing of their nation. Though he *had scourged him* before, hoping that would *content* them, and then not designing to crucify him, yet he went on to that; for no wonder that he who could persuade himself to *chastise* one that was innocent (Luke xxiii. 16), could by degrees persuade himself to *crucify* him.

Christ was *crucified,* for that was, 1. A *bloody* death, and *without blood no remission,* Heb. ix. 22. The blood is *the life* (Gen. ix 4); it is the *vehicle* of the *animal* spirits, which *connect* the soul and body, so that the exhausting of the blood is the exhausting of the life. Christ was to lay down *his life* for us, and therefore shed *his blood.* Blood *made atonement for the soul* (Lev. xvii. 11), and therefore in every sacrifice of propitiation special order was given for the *pouring out* of the blood, and the *sprinkling* of that before the Lord. Now, that Christ might answer all these types, he *shed his blood.* 2. It was a *painful* death; the pains were exquisite and acute, for death made its assaults upon the vitals by the exterior parts, which are *quickest of sense.* Christ died, so as that he might *feel himself die,* because he was to be both the priest and the sacrifice; so that he might be *active* in dying, because he was to *make his soul an offering* for sin. Tully calls crucifixion, *Teterrimum supplicium—A most tremendous punishment:* Christ would meet death in its greatest terror, and so conquer it. 3. It was a *shameful* death, the death of slaves, and the vilest malefactors; so it was accounted among the Romans. The *cross* and the *shame* are put together. God having been injured in his honour by the sin of man, it is *in his honour* that Christ makes him *satisfaction,* not only by denying himself in, and divesting himself of, the honours due to his divine nature, for a time, but by submitting to the greatest reproach and ignominy the human nature was capable of being loaded with. Yet this was not the worst. 4. It was a *cursed* death; thus it was branded by the Jewish law (Deut. xxi. 23); *He that is hanged, is accursed of God,* is under a particular mark of God's displeasure. It was the death that Saul's sons were put to, when the guilt of their father's bloody house was to be expiated, 2 Sam. xxi. 6. Haman and his sons were *hanged,* Esth. vii. 10; ix. 13. We do not read of any of the prophets of the Old Testament that were *hanged;* but now that Christ has submitted to be *hanged upon a tree,* the reproach and curse of that kind of death are quite rolled away, so that it ought not to be any hindrance to the comfort of those who die either innocently or penitently, nor any diminution from, but rather an addition to, the glory of those who die martyrs for Christ, to be as he was, hanged upon a tree.

II. Pilate, to gratify the gay humour of the Roman soldiers, delivered him to them, to be abused and spitefully treated, while they were preparing for the execution. They called together *the whole regiment* that was then in waiting, and they went into an inner hall, where they ignominiously abused our Lord Jesus, as a king, just as in the high priest's hall his servants had ignominiously abused him as a Prophet and Saviour. 1. Do kings wear robes of purple or scarlet? They *clothed him with purple.* This abuse done to Christ in his apparel should be an intimation to Christians, not to make the putting on of apparel *their adorning,* 1 Pet. iii. 4. Shall a purple or scarlet robe be matter of pride to a Christian, which was matter of reproach and shame to Christ? 2. Do kings wear *crowns?* They *platted a crown of thorns,* and *put it on his head.* A crown of straw, or rushes, would have been banter enough; but this was pain also. He wore the crown of thorns which we had deserved, that we might wear the crown of glory which he merited. Let us be *taught* by these *thorns,* as Gideon taught the men of Succoth, to hate sin, and be uneasy under it, and to be in love with Jesus Christ, who is here a lily among thorns. If we be at any time afflicted with a *thorn in the flesh,* let it be our comfort, that our high priest is touched with the feeling of our infirmities, having himself known what *thorns in the flesh* meant. 3. Are kings attended with the acclamations of their subjects, *O king, live for ever?* That also is mimicked; they saluted him with "*Hail, King of the Jews;* such a prince, and such a people, even good enough for one another." 4. Kings have *sceptres* put into their hand, marks of dominion, as the crown is of dignity; to imitate this, they put a *reed in his right hand.* Those who despise the authority of the Lord Jesus, as not to be observed and obeyed, who regard not either the precepts of his word, or the threatenings of his wrath, do, in effect, *put a reed in his hand;* nay, and, as these here, *smite him on the head* with it, such is the indignity they do him. 5. Subjects, when they swear allegiance, were wont to *kiss* their sovereign; and this they offered to do, but, instead of that, *spit upon him.* 6. Kings used to be addressed upon the *knee;* and this also they brought into the jest, they *bowed the knee, and worshipped him;* this they did in scorn, to make themselves and one another laugh. We were by sin become liable to *everlasting shame and contempt,* to deliver us from which, our Lord Jesus submitted to this shame and contempt for us. He was thus mocked, not in *his own clothes,* but in another's, to signify that he suffered not for his own sin; the crime was ours, the shame his. Those who pretend subjection to Christ, but at the same time give themselves up to the service of the world and the flesh, do, in effect, the same that they did, who bowed the knee to him in mockery, and abused him with, *Hail, king of the Jews,* when they said, *We have no king bat Cæsar.* Those that bow the knee to Christ, but do not bow the soul, that *draw nigh to him with their mouths,* and *honour him with their lips,* but *their hearts are far from him,* put the same affront upon him that these here did.

III. The soldiers, at the hour appointed, led him away from Pilate's judgment-hall to the place of execution (*v.* 20), as a sheep to the slaughter; he was *led forth with the workers of iniquity,* though he did no sin. But lest his death, under the load of his cross, which he was to carry, should prevent the further cruelties they intended, they compelled one Simon of Cyrene to carry his cross for him. He *passed by, coming out of the country* or out of the *fields,* not thinking of any such matter. Note, We must not think it strange, if crosses come upon us suddenly, and we be surprised by them. The cross was a very troublesome unwieldy load: but he that carried it a few minutes, had the honour to have his name upon record in the book of God, though otherwise an obscure person; so that, wherever this gospel is preached, there shall this be told for a memorial of him: in like manner, though *no affliction,* no cross, *for the present, be joyous, but grievous,* yet afterward it yields a crown of glory to them that are exercised thereby.

22 And they bring him unto the
place Golgotha, which is, being interpreted, The place of a scull. 23 And
they gave him to drink wine mingled
with myrrh: but he received *it* not.
24 And when they had crucified him,
they parted his garments, casting lots
upon them, what every man should
take. 25 And it was the third hour,
and they crucified him. 26 And the
superscription of his accusation was
written over, THE KING OF THE
JEWS. 27 And with him they crucify two thieves; the one on his right
hand, and the other on his left. 28
And the scripture was fulfilled, which
saith, And he was numbered with
the transgressors. 29 And they that
passed by railed on him, wagging their
heads, and saying, Ah, thou that destroyest the temple, and buildest *it* in
three days, 30 Save thyself, and come
down from the cross. 31 Likewise
also the chief priests mocking said
among themselves with the scribes,
He saved others; himself he cannot
save. 32 Let Christ the King of
Israel descend now from the cross,
that we may see and believe. And
they that were crucified with him reviled him.

We have here the *crucifixion* of our Lord Jesus.

I. The *place where* he was crucified; it was called *Golgotha—the place of a scull:* some think, because of the heads of malefactors that were there cut off: it was the common place of execution, as Tyburn, for he was in all respects numbered with the transgressors. I know not how to give any credit to it, but divers of the ancients mention it as a current tradition, that in this place our first father Adam was buried, and they think it highly congruous that there Christ should be crucified; for as in Adam all die, so in Christ shall all be made alive. Tertullian, Origen, Chrysostom, and Epiphanius (great names), take notice of it; nay, Cyprian adds, *Creditur à piis—Many good people believe* that the blood of Christ crucified did trickle down upon the scull of Adam, who was buried in the same place. Something more credible is the tradition, that this mount Calvary was *that mountain in the land of Moriah* (and in the land of Moriah it certainly was, for so the country about Jerusalem was called), on which Isaac was to be offered; and the ram was offered instead of him; and then Abraham had an eye to *this day* of Christ, when he called the place *Jehovah-jireh—The Lord will provide,* expecting that so it would be seen in the *mount of the Lord.*

II. The *time when* he was crucified; it was the *third hour, v.* 25. He was brought before Pilate about the sixth hour (John xix. 14), according to the Roman way of reckoning, which John uses, with which ours at this day agrees, that is at six o'clock in the morning; and then, at the *third hour,* according to the Jews' way of reckoning, that is, about nine of the clock in the morning, or soon after, they nailed him to the cross. Dr. Lightfoot thinks the *third hour* is here mentioned, to intimate an aggravation of the wickedness of the priests, that they were here prosecuting Christ to the death, though it was after the *third hour,* when they ought to have been attending the service of the temple, and offering the peace-offerings; it being the first day of the *feast of unleavened bread,* when there was to be a *holy convocation.* At that very time, when they should have been, according to the duty of their place, presiding in the public devotions, were they here venting their malice against the Lord Jesus; yet these were the men that seemed so zealous for the temple, and condemned Christ for speaking against it. Note, There are many who pretend to be *for the church,* who yet care not how seldom they *go to church.*

III. The indignities that were done him, when he was nailed to the cross; as if that had not been ignominious enough, they added several things to the ignominy of it.

1. It being the custom to give *wine* to persons that were to be *put to death,* they *mingled* his with *myrrh,* which was *bitter,* and made it *nauseous;* he *tasted* it, but would not drink it; was willing to admit the bitterness of it, but not the benefit of it.

2. The garments of those that were crucified, being, as with us, the executioners' fee, the soldiers *cast lots* upon his garments (*v.* 24), threw dice (as our soldiers do upon a drum-head, for them: so making themselves merry with his misery, and sitting at their sport while he was hanging in pain.

3. They set a superscription over his head, by which they intended to reproach him, but really did him both justice and honour, *The king of the Jews, v.* 26. Here was no crime alleged, but his sovereignty owned. Perhaps Pilate meant to cast disgrace upon Christ as a baffled king, or upon the Jews, who by their importunity had forced him, against his conscience, to condemn Christ, as a people that deserved no better a king than he seemed to be: however, God intended it to be the proclaiming even of Christ upon the cross, the *king of Israel;* though Pilate know not what he wrote, any more than Caiaphas what he said, John xi. 51. Christ crucified is king of his church, his spiritual Israel; and even then when he hung on the cross, he was like a king, *conquering* his and his people's enemies, and *triumphing* over them, Col. ii. 15. Now he was writing his laws in his own blood, and preparing his favours for his subjects. Whenever we look unto Christ crucified, we must remember the inscription over his head, that he is a king, and we must give up ourselves to be his subjects, as Israelites indeed.

4. They crucified *two thieves* with him, *one on his right hand, the other on his left,* and him in the midst as the worst of the three (*v.* 27); so great a degree of dishonour did they hereby intend him. And, no doubt, it gave him *disturbance* too. Some that have been imprisoned in the common gaols, for the testimony of Jesus, have complained of the company of cursing, swearing prisoners, more than of any other of the grievances of their prison. Now, in the midst of such our Lord Jesus was *crucified:* while he lived he had, as there was occasion, *associated* with sinners, to do them good; and now when he died, he was for the same purpose joined with them, for he *came into the world,* and went out of it, to *save sinners,* even the chief. But this evangelist takes particular notice of the fulfilling of the scriptures in it, *v.* 28. In that famous prediction of Christ's sufferings (Isa. liii. 12), it was foretold that he should be numbered with the *transgressors,* because he was made *sin for us.*

5. The spectators, that is, the generality of them, instead of condoling with him in his misery, added to it by insulting over him. Surely never was such an instance of barbarous inhumanity toward the vilest malefactor: but thus the devil showed the utmost rage against him, and thus he submitted to the greatest dishonours that could be done him.

(1.) Even they that *passed by,* that were no way concerned, *railed on him, v.* 29. If their hearts were so hardened, that their compassions were not moved with such a spectacle, yet they should have thought it enough to have their curiosity gratified; but that will not serve: as if they were not only divested of all humanity, but were devils in human shape, they taunted him, and expressed themselves with the utmost detestation of him, and indignation at him, and shot thick at him their arrows, even *bitter words.* The chief priests, no doubt, put these sarcasms into their mouths, *Thou that destroyest the temple, and buildest it in three days, now,* if thou canst, *save thyself,* and *come down from the cross.* They triumph as if now that they had got him to the cross, there were no danger of his *destroying the temple;* whereas the *temple* of which *he* spoke, he was now *destroying,* and did within *three days build it up;* and the temple of which *they* spoke, he did by men, that were *his sword* and *his hand,* destroy not many years after. When secure sinners think the danger is over, it is then most ready to seize them: the day of the Lord *comes as a thief* upon those that *deny* his coming, and say, Where is the promise of it? much more upon those that *defy* his coming, and say, *Let him make speed, and hasten his work.*

(2.) Even the chief priests, who, being *taken from among men* and ordained for men, should have compassion even on those that are out of the way, should be tender of those that are suffering and dying (Heb. v. 1, 2), yet they poured vinegar instead of oil into his wounds, they *talked to the grief* of him *whom God had smitten* (Ps. lxix. 26), they *mocked him,* they said, *He saved others,* healed and helped them, but now it appears that it was not by his own power, for *himself he cannot save.* They challenged him to *come down from the cross,* if he could, *v.* 32. Let them but *see* that, and they would *believe;* whereas they would not believe, when he gave them a more convincing sign than that, when he came up from the grave. These chief priests, one would think, might now have found themselves *other work* to do: if they would not go to do their duty in *the temple,* yet they might have been employed in an office not foreign to their profession; though they would not offer any counsel or comfort to the Lord Jesus, yet they might have given some help to the thieves in their dying moments (the monks and priests in Popish countries are very officious about criminals broken upon the wheel, a death much like that of the cross); but they did not think that their business.

(3.) Even they that were crucified with him, reviled him (*v.* 32); one of them did, so wretchedly was his heart hardened even in the depth of misery, and at the door of eternity.

33 And when the sixth hour was
come, there was darkness over the
whole land until the ninth hour. 34
And at the ninth hour Jesus cried
with a loud voice, saying, Eloi, Eloi,
lama sabachthani? which is, being
interpreted, My God, my God, why
hast thou forsaken me? 35 And
some of them that stood by, when
they heard *it*, said, Behold, he calleth
Elias. 36 And one ran and filled a
sponge full of vinegar, and put *it* on
a reed, and gave him to drink, saying,
Let alone; let us see whether Elias
will come to take him down. 37 And
Jesus cried with a loud voice, and gave
up the ghost. 38 And the veil of
the temple was rent in twain from
the top to the bottom. 39 And
when the centurion, which stood over
against him, saw that he so cried out,
and gave up the ghost, he said, Truly
this man was the Son of God. 40
There were also women looking on
afar off: among whom was Mary
Magdalene, and Mary the mother of
James the less and of Joses, and Salome; 41 (Who also, when he was
in Galilee, followed him, and ministered unto him); and many other
women which came up with him unto
Jerusalem.

Here we have an account of Christ's dying, how his enemies abused him, and God honoured him at his death.

I. There was a thick *darkness* over *the whole land* (some think over the whole earth), for three hours, from noon till three of the clock. Now the scripture was fulfilled (Amos viii. 9), *I will cause the sun to go down at noon,* and I will *darken the earth in the clear day;* and Jer. xv. 9, *Her sun is gone down while it is yet day.* The Jews had often demanded of Christ a *sign from heaven;* and now they had one, but such a one as signified the blinding of their eyes. It was a sign of the darkness that was come, and coming, upon the Jewish church and nation. They were doing their utmost to extinguish the Sun of righteousness, which was now setting, and the rising again of which they would never own; and what then might be expected among them but a worse than Egyptian darkness? This intimated to them, that the things which belonged to their peace, were now *hid from their eyes,* and that the day of the Lord was at hand, which should be to them a *day of darkness and gloominess,* Joel ii. 1, 2. It was the power of darkness that they were now under, the works of darkness that they were now doing; and such as this should their doom justly be, who *loved darkness rather than light.*

II. Toward the close of this darkness, our Lord Jesus, in the agony of his soul, cried out, *My God, my God, why hast thou forsaken me? v.* 34. The darkness signified the present cloud which the human soul of Christ was under, when he was making it an *offering for sin.* Mr. Fox, in his *Acts and Monuments* (vol. iii. p. 160), tells of one Dr. Hunter, a martyr in queen Mary's time, who, being fastened to the stake, to be burnt, put up this short prayer, *Son of God, shine upon me;* and immediately the sun in the firmament shone out of a dark cloud, so full in his face, that he was forced to look another way, which was very comfortable to him. But our Lord Jesus, on the contrary, was denied the light of the sun, when he was in his sufferings, to signify the withdrawing of the light of God's countenance. And this he complained of more than any thing; he did not complain of his disciples' forsaking him, but of his Father's, 1. Because this *wounded his spirit;* and that is a thing *hard to bear*

(Prov. xviii. 14); this brought the waters into his soul, Ps. lxix. 1—3. 2. Because in this especially he was *made sin for us;* our iniquities had deserved *indignation and wrath* upon the soul (Rom. ii. 8), and therefore, Christ, being made a *sacrifice*, underwent as much of it as he was capable of; and it could not but bear hard indeed upon him who had lain *in the bosom* of the Father from eternity, and was *always his delight.* These symptoms of divine wrath, which Christ was under in his sufferings, were like that fire from heaven which had been sent sometimes, in extraordinary cases, to consume the sacrifices (as Lev. ix. 24; 2 Chron. vii. 1; 1 Kings xviii. 38); and it was always a token of God's acceptance. The fire that should have fallen upon the *sinner*, if God had not been *pacified*, fell upon the *sacrifice*, as a token that he was so; therefore it now fell upon Christ, and extorted from him this *loud* and *bitter* cry. When Paul was to be *offered* as a sacrifice for *the service of saints*, he could *joy* and *rejoice* (Phil. ii. 17); but it is another thing to be offered as a sacrifice for *the sin of sinners.* Now, at the *sixth hour*, and so to the *ninth*, the *sun* was *darkened* by an extraordinary eclipse; and if it be true, as some astronomers compute, that in the evening of this day on which Christ died there was an eclipse of the moon, that was natural and expected, in which seven digits of the moon were darkened, and it continued from five o'clock till seven, it is remarkable, and yet further significant of the darkness of the time that then was. When the *sun* shall be *darkened*, the *moon* also shall *not give her light.*

III. Christ's prayer was bantered by them that stood by (*v.* 35, 36); because he cried, *Eli, Eli*, or (as Mark has it, according to the Syriac dialect) *Eloi, Eloi*, they said, *He calls for Elias*, though they knew very well what he said, and what it signified, *My God, My God.* Thus did they represent him as *praying to saints*, either because he had abandoned God, or God had abandoned him; and hereby they would make him more and more odious to the people. One of them *filled a sponge with vinegar*, and reached it up to him upon a reed; "Let him cool his mouth with that, it is drink good enough for him," *v.* 36. This was intended for a further affront and abuse to him; and whoever it was that checked him who did it, did but add to the reproach; "*Let him alone;* he has called for Elias: *let us see whether Elias will come to take him down;* and if not, we may conclude that he also hath abandoned him."

IV. Christ did again *cry with a loud voice*, and so *gave up the ghost, v.* 37. He was now commending his soul into his Father's hand; and though God is not moved with any *bodily exercise*, yet this loud voice signified the great strength and ardency of affection wherewith he did it; to teach us, in every thing wherein we have to do with God, to put forth our utmost vigour, and to perform all the duties of religion, particularly that of *self-resignation*, with our whole heart and our whole soul; and then, though speech fails, that we cannot *cry with a loud voice*, as Christ did, yet if God be the *strength of the heart*, that will not fail. Christ was really and truly *dead*, for he *gave up the ghost;* his human soul departed to the world of spirits, and left his body a breathless clod of clay.

V. Just at that instant that Christ died upon *mount Calvary*, the veil of the *temple* was *rent in twain from the top to the bottom, v.* 38. This bespoke a great deal, 1. Of terror to the unbelieving Jews; for it was a presage of the utter destruction of their church and nation, which followed not long after; it was like the cutting asunder of the *staff of beauty* (for this veil was exceedingly splendid and glorious, Exod. xxvi. 31), and that was done at the same time when they gave for his price *thirty pieces of silver* (Zech. xi. 10, 12), to *break the covenant which he had made with that people.* Now it was time to cry, *Ichabod, The glory is departed from Israel.* Some think that the story which Josephus relates, of the temple door opening of its own accord, with that voice, *Let us depart hence*, some years before the destruction of Jerusalem, is the same with this; but that is not probable: however, this had the same signification, according to that (Hos. v. 14), *I will tear, and go away.* 2. It bespeaks a great deal of comfort to all believing Christians, for it signifies the consecrating and laying open to us of a *new and living way into the holiest* by the *blood of Jesus.*

VI. The centurion who commanded the detachment which had the oversight of the execution was convinced, and confessed that this Jesus was the *Son of God, v.* 39. One thing that satisfied him, was, that he *so cried out, and gave up the ghost:* that one who was ready to give up the ghost, should be able to cry out so, was very surprising. Of all the sad spectacles of this kind he never observed the like; and that one who had strength to cry so loud, should yet immediately give up the ghost, this also made him wonder; and he said, to the honour of Christ, and the shame of those that abused him, *Truly this man was the Son of God.* But what reason had he to say so? I answer, 1. He had reason to say that he suffered *unjustly*, and had a great deal of wrong done him. Note, He suffered for saying that he was *the Son of God;* and it was true, he did say so, so that if he suffered unjustly, as it was plain by all the circumstances of his sufferings that he did, then what he said was true, and he was indeed the *Son of God.* 2. He had reason to say that he was a *favourite of heaven*, and one for whom the almighty power was particularly engaged, seeing how Heaven did him honour at his death, and frowned upon his persecutors. "Surely," thinks he, "this must be some divine person, highly beloved of God." This he expresses by such words as denote his eternal generation as God, and his special designation to the office of Mediator, though he meant not so. Our Lord Jesus, even in the depth of his sufferings and humiliation, was the Son of God, and was declared to be so *with power*.

VII. There were some of his friends, the good women especially, that attended him (*v.* 40, 41); *There were women looking on afar off:* the *men* durst not be seen at all, the mob was so very outrageous; *Currenti cede furori—Give way to the raging torrent*, they thought, was good counsel now. The women durst not come near, but stood at a distance, overwhelmed with grief. Some of these women are here named. *Mary Magdalene* was one; she had been his patient, and owed all her comfort to his power and goodness, which rescued her out of the possession of seven devils, in gratitude for which she thought she could never do enough for him. *Mary* also was there, *the mother of James the little, Jacobus parvus*, so the word is; probably, he was so called because he was, like Zaccheus, little of stature. This Mary was the wife of Cleophas or Alpheus, sister to the virgin Mary. These women had followed Christ *from Galilee*, though they were not required to attend the feast, as the males were; but it is probable that they came, in expectation that his temporal kingdom would now shortly be set up, and big with hopes of preferment for themselves, and their relations under him. It is plain that the mother of Zebedee's children was so (Matt. xx. 21); and now to see *him* upon a cross, whom they thought to have seen upon a throne, could not but be a great disappointment to them. Note, Those that follow Christ, in expectation of great things in this world by him, and by the profession of his religion, may probably live to see themselves sadly disappointed.

42 And now when the even was
come, because it was the preparation,
that is, the day before the sabbath,
43 Joseph of Arimathæa, an honourable counsellor, which also waited for
the kingdom of God, came, and went
in boldly unto Pilate, and craved the
body of Jesus. 44 And Pilate marvelled if he were already dead: and
calling *unto him* the centurion, he
asked him whether he had been any
while dead. 45 And when he knew
it of the centurion, he gave the body
to Joseph. 46 And he bought fine
linen, and took him down, and wrapped him in the linen, and laid him in
a sepulchre which was hewn out of a
rock, and rolled a stone unto the door
of the sepulchre. 47 And Mary
Magdalene and Mary *the mother* of
Joses beheld where he was laid.

We are here attending the funeral of our Lord Jesus, a solemn, mournful funeral. O that we may by grace be planted in the likeness of it! Observe,

I. How the body of Christ was *begged*. It was, as the dead bodies of malefactors are, at the disposal of the government. Those that hurried him to the cross, designed that he should make *his grave with the wicked;* but God designed he should make it *with the rich* (Isa. liii. 9), and so he did. We are here told,

1. When the body of Christ was begged, in order to its being buried, and why such haste was made with the funeral; *The even was come*, and it was *the preparation*, that is, *the day before the sabbath*, *v.* 42. The Jews were more strict in the observation of the sabbath than of any other feast; and therefore, though this day was itself a *feast-day*, yet they observed it more religiously as the *eve* of the *sabbath;* when they prepared their houses and tables for the *splendid* and *joyful* solemnizing of the sabbath day. Note, The day before the sabbath should be a day of preparation for the sabbath, not of our houses and tables, but of our hearts, which, as much as possible, should be *freed* from the cares and business of the world, and *fixed*, and put in frame for the service and enjoyment of God. Such work is to be done, and such advantages are to be gained on the sabbath day, that it is requisite we should get ready for it a day before; nay, the whole week should be divided between the improvement of the foregoing sabbath and the preparation for the following sabbath.

2. Who it was that begged the body, and took care for the decent interment of it; it was *Joseph of Arimathea*, who is here called an *honourable counsellor* (*v.* 43), a person of character and distinction, and in an office of public trust; some think *in the state*, and that he was one of Pilate's privy council; his post rather seems to have been *in the church*, he was one of the *great Sanhedrim* of the Jews, or one of the high priest's council. He was εὐσχήμων βȣλευτὴς—*a counsellor that conducted himself in his place as did become him.* Those are truly honourable, and those only, in places of power and trust, who make conscience of their duty, and whose deportment is agreeable to their preferment. But here is a more shining character put upon him; he was one that *waited for the kingdom of God*, the kingdom of grace on earth, and of glory in heaven, the kingdom of the Messiah. Note, Those who *wait for the kingdom of God*, and hope for an interest in the privileges of it, must show it by their forwardness to own Christ's cause and interest, even then when it seems to be crushed and run down. Observe, Even among the *honourable counsellors* there were some, there was *one* at least, that waited for the kingdom of God, whose faith will condemn the unbelief of all the rest. This man God raised up for this necessary service, when none of Christ's disciples could,

or durst, undertake it, having neither purse, nor interest, nor courage, for it. *Joseph went in boldly to Pilate;* though he knew how much it would affront the chief priests, who had loaded him with so much reproach, to see any honour done him, yet he *put on courage;* perhaps at first he was a little afraid, but *τολμήσας—taking heart on it,* he determined to show this respect to the remains of the Lord Jesus, let the worst come to the worst.

3. What a surprise it was to Pilate, to hear that he was *dead* (Pilate, perhaps, expecting that he would have saved himself, and come down from the cross), especially that he was *already dead,* that one who seemed to have more than ordinary vigour, should so soon yield to death. Every circumstance of Christ's dying was marvellous; for from first to last his name was called *Wonderful.* Pilate doubted (so some understand it) whether he was yet dead or no, fearing lest he should be imposed upon, and the body should be *taken down alive,* and recovered, whereas the sentence was, as with us, to hang *till the body be dead.* He therefore called the centurion, his own officer, and asked him *whether he had been any while dead* (*v.* 44), whether it was so long since they perceived any sign of life in him, any breath or motion, that they might conclude he was dead past recal. The centurion could assure him of this, for he had particularly observed how he *gave up the ghost, v.* 39. There was a special providence in it, that Pilate should be so strict in examining this, that there might be no pretence to say that he was buried alive, and so to take away the truth of his resurrection; and so fully was this determined, that that objection was never started. Thus the truth of Christ gains confirmation, sometimes, even from its enemies.

II. How the body of Christ was *buried.* Pilate gave Joseph leave to take down the body, and do what he pleased with it. It was a wonder the chief priests were not too quick for him, and had not first begged the body of Pilate, to expose it and drag it about the streets, but that remainder of their wrath did God restrain, and gave that invaluable prize to Joseph, who knew how to value it; and the hearts of the priests were so influenced, that they did not oppose it. *Sit divus, modo non sit vivus—We care not for his being adored, provided he be not revived.*

1. Joseph bought *fine linen* to wrap the body in, though in such a case old linen that had been worn might have been thought sufficient. In paying respects to Christ it becomes us to be *generous,* and to serve him with the *best* that can be got, not with that which can be got at the best hand.

2. He *took down* the body, mangled and macerated as it was, and *wrapt it in the linen* as a treasure of great worth. Our Lord Jesus hath commanded himself to be delivered to us sacramentally in the ordinance of the Lord's supper, which we should receive in such a manner as may best express our love to him who loved us and died for us.

3. He *laid it in a sepulchre* of his own, in a private place. We sometimes find it spoken of in the story of the kings of Judah, as a slur upon the memory of the wicked kings, that they were not buried in the *sepulchres of the kings;* our Lord Jesus, though he did no evil but much good, and to him was given the throne of his father David, yet was buried in the graves of the common people, for it was not in this world, but in the other, that *his rest was glorious.* This sepulchre belonged to Joseph. Abraham when he had no other possession in the land of Canaan, yet had a burying-place, but Christ had not so much as that. This sepulchre was *hewn out of a rock,* for Christ died to make the grave a *refuge* and shelter to the saints, and being hewn out of a rock, it is a *strong* refuge. *O that thou wouldest hide me in the grave!* Christ himself is a *hiding place* to his people, that is, *as the shadow of a great rock.*

4. He *rolled a stone to the door of the sepulchre,* for so the manner of the Jews was to bury. When Daniel was put into the lions' den, a stone was laid to the mouth of it to keep him in, as here to the door of Christ's sepulchre, but neither of them could keep off the angels' visits to the prisoners.

5. Some of the good women attended the funeral, and *beheld where he was laid,* that they might come after the sabbath to anoint the dead body, because they had not time to do it now. When Moses, the mediator and lawgiver of the Jewish church, was buried, care was taken that no man should *know of his sepulchre* (Deut. xxxiv. 6), because the respects of the people towards his person were to die with him; but when our great Mediator and Lawgiver was buried, special notice was taken of his sepulchre, because he was to *rise again:* and the care taken of his body, bespeaks the care which he himself will take concerning his body the church. Even when it seems to be a dead body, and as a valley full of dry bones, it shall be preserved in order to a resurrection; as shall also the dead bodies of the saints, with whose dust there is a covenant in force which shall not be forgotten. Our meditations on Christ's burial should lead us to think of our own, and should help to make the grave familiar to us, and so to render that bed easy which we must shortly make in the darkness. Frequent thoughts of it would not only take off the dread and terror of it, but quicken us, since the *graves* are always ready for us, to get ready for the graves, Job xvii. 1.

CHAP. XVI.

In this chapter, we have a short account of the resurrection and ascension of the Lord Jesus: and the joys and triumphs which it furnishes all believers with, will be very acceptable to those who sympathised and suffered with Christ in the foregoing chapters. Here is, I. Christ's resurrection notified by an angel to the women that came to the sepulchre to anoint him, ver. 1—8. II. His appearance to Mary Magdalene, and the account she gave of it to the disciples, ver. 9—11. III. His appearance to the two disciples, going to Emmaus, and the report they made of it to their brethren, ver. 12, 13. IV. His appearance to the eleven with the commission he gave them to set up his kingdom in the world, and full instructions and credentials in order thereunto, ver. 14—18. V. His ascension into heaven, the apostles' close application to their work, and God's owning of them in it, ver. 19, 20.

AND when the sabbath was past
Mary Magdalene, and Mary the
mother of James, and Salome, had
bought sweet spices, that they might
come and anoint him. 2 And very
early in the morning the first *day* of
the week, they came unto the sepulchre at the rising of the sun. 3 And
they said among themselves, Who shall
roll us away the stone from the door
of the sepulchre? 4 And when they
looked, they saw that the stone was
rolled away: for it was very great.
5 And entering into the sepulchre,
they saw a young man sitting on the
right side, clothed in a long white garment; and they were affrighted. 6
And he saith unto them, Be not affrighted: Ye seek Jesus of Nazareth,
which was crucified: he is risen; he
is not here: behold the place where
they laid him. 7 But go your way,
tell his disciples and Peter that he
goeth before you into Galilee: there
shall ye see him, as he said unto you.
8 And they went out quickly, and
fled from the sepulchre; for they
trembled and were amazed: neither
said they any thing to any *man*; for
they were afraid.

Never was there such a *sabbath* since the sabbath was first instituted as this was, which the first words of this chapter tell us was *now past;* during all this sabbath our Lord Jesus lay in the grave. It was *to him* a sabbath of *rest*, but a *silent* sabbath; it was to his disciples a melancholy sabbath, spent in tears and fears. Never were the sabbath services in the temple such an *abomination to God*, though they had been often so, as they were now, when the chief priests, who presided in them, had their hands full of blood, the blood of Christ. Well, this sabbath is over, and the first day of the week is the first day of a new world. We have here,

I. The affectionate visit which the good women that had attended Christ, now made to his sepulchre—not a *superstitious* one, but a *pious* one. They set out from their lodgings *very early in the morning*, at break of day, or sooner; but either they had a long walk, or they met with some hindrance, so that it was *sun-rising* by the time they got to the sepulchre. They had *bought sweet spices* too, and came not only to *bedew* the dead body with their tears (for nothing could more renew their grief than this), but to *perfume* it with their *spices, v.* 1. Nicodemus had bought a very large quantity of *dry spices, myrrh* and *aloes*, which served to dry the wounds, and dry up the blood, John xix. 39. But these good women did not think that enough; they bought spices, perhaps of another kind, some perfumed oils, to *anoint him.* Note, The respect which others have showed to Christ's name, should not hinder us from showing our respect to it.

II. The care they were in about the rolling away of the stone, and the superseding of that care (*v.* 3, 4); *They said among themselves*, as they were coming along, and now drew near the sepulchre, *Who shall roll us away the stone from the door of the sepulchre? For it was very great*, more than they with their united strength could move. They should have thought of this before they came out, and then discretion would have bid them not go, unless they had those to go with them, who could do it. And there was another difficulty much greater than this, to be got over, which they knew nothing of, to wit, a guard of soldiers set to *keep* the sepulchre; who, had they come before they were frightened away, would have frightened them away. But their gracious love to Christ carried them to the sepulchre; and see how by the time they came thither, both these difficulties were removed, both the *stone* which they *knew of*, and the *guard* which they *knew not of.* They *saw that the stone was rolled away*, which was the first thing that amazed them. Note, They who are carried by a holy zeal, to seek Christ diligently, will find the difficulties that lie in their way strangely to vanish, and themselves helped over them beyond their expectation.

III. The assurance that was given them by an angel, that the Lord Jesus was risen from the dead, and had taken leave of his sepulchre, and had left him there to tell those so who came thither to enquire after him.

1. They *entered into the sepulchre*, at least, a little way in, and saw that the body of Jesus was not there where they had left it the other night. He, who by his death undertook to pay our debt, in his resurrection took out our acquittance, for it was his discharge out of prison, and it was a fair and legal discharge, by which it appeared that his satisfaction was accepted for all the purposes for which it was intended, and the matter in dispute was determined by an incontestable evidence that he was the Son of God.

2. They saw a *young man sitting on the right side* of the sepulchre. The angel appeared in the likeness of *a man*, of a *young man;* for angels, though created in the beginning, grow not *old*, but are always in the same perfection of beauty and strength; and so shall glorified saints be, when they are *as the angels.* This angel was *sitting* on *the right hand* as they went into the sepulchre, *clothed with a long white garment*, a garment down to the

feet, such as great men were arrayed with. The sight of him might justly have encouraged them, but they were *affrighted.* Thus many times that which should be matter of comfort to us, through our own mistakes and misapprehensions proves a terror to us.

3. He silences their fears by assuring them that here was cause enough for triumph, but none for trembling (*v.* 6); *He saith to them, Be not affrighted.* Note, As angels rejoice in the conversion of sinners, so they do also in the consolation of saints. Be not affrighted. for, (1.) " Ye are faithful lovers of Jesus Christ, and therefore, instead of being *confounded,* ought to be *comforted. Ye seek Jesus of Nazareth, which was crucified.*" Note, The enquiries of believing souls after Christ, have a particular regard to him as *crucified* (1 Cor. ii. 2), that they may know him, and the fellowship of his sufferings. His being *lifted up from the earth,* is that which *draws all men unto him.* Christ's cross is the ensign to which the Gentiles seek. Observe, He speaks of Jesus as one that *was crucified;* " The thing is *past,* that scene is over, ye must not dwell so much upon the sad circumstances of his crucifixion as to be unapt to believe the joyful news of his resurrection. He was *crucified in weakness,* yet that doth not hinder but that he may be raised in power, and therefore ye that seek him, be not *afraid* of *missing* of him." He *was* crucified, but he *is* glorified; and the shame of his sufferings is so far from lessening the glory of his exaltation, that that glory perfectly wipes away all the reproach of his sufferings. And therefore after his entrance upon his glory, he never drew any veil over his sufferings, nor was shy of having his cross spoken of. The angel here that proclaims his resurrection, calls him Jesus that *was crucified.* He himself owns (Rev. i. 18), *I am he that liveth, and was dead;* and he appears in the midst of the praises of the heavenly host as a *Lamb that had been slain,* Rev. v. 6. (2.) " It will therefore be good news to you, to hear that, instead of anointing him dead, you may rejoice in him living. *He is risen, he is not here,* not dead, but alive again. We cannot as yet show you *him,* but hereafter you will see him, and you may here see *the place where they laid him.* You see he is gone hence, not stolen either by his enemies or by his friends, but *risen.*"

4. He orders them to give speedy notice of this to his disciples. Thus they were made the apostles of the apostles, which was a recompence of their affection and fidelity to him, in attending him on the cross, to the grave, and in the grave. They first came, and were first served; no other of the disciples durst come near his sepulchre, or enquire after him; so little danger was there of their coming by night to *steal him away,* that none came near him but a few women, who were not able so much as to *roll away the stone.*

(1.) They must tell the *disciples,* that *he is risen.* It is a dismal time with them, their dear Master is dead, and all their hopes and joys are buried in his grave; they look upon their cause as sunk, and themselves ready to fall an easy prey into the hands of their enemies, so that there remains no more spirit in them, they are perfectly at their wits' end, and every one is contriving how to shift for himself. " O, go quickly to them," saith the angel, " tell them that *their Master is risen;* this will put some life and spirit into them, and keep them from sinking into despair." Note, [1.] Christ is not ashamed to own his poor disciples, no, not now that he is in his exalted state; his preferment doth not make him shy of them, for he took early care to have it *notified* to them. [2.] Christ is not extreme to mark what *they* do amiss, whose hearts are upright with him. The disciples had very unkindly deserted him, and yet he testified this concern for them. [3.] Seasonable comforts shall be sent to those that are lamenting after the Lord Jesus, and he will find a time to manifest himself to them.

(2.) They must be sure to tell Peter. This is particularly taken notice of by this evangelist, who is supposed to have written by Peter's direction. If it were told the disciples, it would be told Peter, for, as a token of his repentance for disowning his Master, he still associated with his disciples; yet he is particularly named: *Tell Peter,* for, [1.] It will be good news to him, more welcome to him than to any of them; for he is in sorrow for sin, and no tidings can be more welcome to true penitents than to hear of the resurrection of Christ, because he rose again for *their justification.* [2.] He will be afraid, lest the joy of this good news do not belong to him. Had the angel said only, *Go, tell his disciples,* poor Peter would have been ready to sigh, and say, " But I doubt I cannot look upon myself as one of them, for I disowned him, and deserve to be disowned by him;" to obviate that, " Go to Peter by name, and tell him, he shall be as welcome as any of the rest to *see* him in Galilee." Note, A sight of Christ will be very welcome to a true penitent, and a true penitent shall be very welcome to a sight of Christ, for there is joy in heaven concerning him.

(3.) They must appoint them all, and Peter by name, to give him the meeting in Galilee, as *he said unto you,* Matt. xxvi. 32. In their journey down into Galilee they would have time to recollect themselves, and call to mind what he had often said to them there, that he should suffer and die, and *the third day be raised again;* whereas while they were at Jerusalem, among strangers and enemies, they could not recover themselves from the fright they had been in, nor compose themselves to the due entertainment of better tidings. Note, [1.] All the meetings between Christ and his disciples are of his own appointing. [2.] Christ never forgets his appointment, but will be sure to meet his people with the promised blessing in every place where he records his name. [3.] In all meetings between Christ and his disciples, he is the most forward. *He goes before you.*

IV. The account which the women did bring of this to the disciples (*v.* 8); They *went out quickly*, and *ran from the sepulchre*, to make all the haste they could to the disciples, *trembling* and *amazed*. See how much we are enemies to ourselves and our own comfort, in not considering and mixing faith with what Christ hath said to us. Christ had often told them, that *the third day he would rise again;* had they given that its due notice and credit, they would have come to the sepulchre, expecting to have found him risen, and would have received the news of it with a joyful assurance, and not with all this terror and amazement. But, being ordered to tell the disciples, because they were to tell it to all the world, they would not tell it to any one else, they showed not any thing of it to any man that they *met by the way*, for *they were afraid*, afraid it was too good news to be true. Note, Our disquieting fears often hinder us from doing that service to Christ and to the souls of men, which if faith and the *joy of fvith* were strong, we might do.

9 Now when *Jesus* was risen early
the first *day* of the week, he appeared
first to Mary Magdalene, out of whom
he had cast seven devils. 10 *And* she
went and told them that had been
with him, as they mourned and wept.
11 And they, when they had heard that
he was alive, and had been seen of her,
believed not. 12 After that he appeared in another form unto two of
them, as they walked, and went into
the country. 13 And they went and
told *it* unto the residue: neither believed they them.

We have here a very short account of two of Christ's appearances, and the little credit which the report of them gained with the disciples.

I. He appeared to Mary Magdalene, to her first in the garden, which we have a particular narrative of, John xx. 14. It was she *out of whom he had cast seven devils;* much was forgiven her, and much was given her, and done for her, and she *loved much;* and this honour Christ did her, that she was the first that saw him after his resurrection. The closer we cleave to Christ, the sooner we may expect to see him, and the more to see of him.

Now, 1. She brings notice of what she had seen, to the disciples; not only to the *eleven*, but to the rest that followed him, *as they mourned and wept, v.* 10. Now was the time of which Christ had told them, that they should *mourn and lament*, John xvi. 20. And it was an evidence of their great love to Christ, and the deep sense they had of their loss of him. But when their *weeping* had *endured a night* or two, comfort returned, as Christ had promised them; *I will see you again, and your heart shall rejoice.* Better news cannot be brought to disciples in tears, than to tell them of Christ's resurrection. And we should study to be comforters to disciples that are mourners, by communicating to them our experiences, and what we have *seen of Christ.*

2. They could not give credit to the report she brought them. They heard that *he was alive*, and had been seen of her. The story was plausible enough, and yet *they believed not.* They would not say that she made the story herself, or designed to deceive them; but they fear that she is *imposed upon*, and that it was but a fancy that she *saw him.* Had they believed the *frequent* predictions of it from his own mouth, they would not have been now so incredulous of the report of it.

II. He appeared to two of the disciples, *as they went into the country, v.* 12. This refers, no doubt, to that which is largely related (Luke xxiv. 13, &c.), of what passed between Christ and the two disciples *going to Emmaus.* He is here said to have appeared to them in *another form*, in another dress than what he usually wore, in the form of a *traveller*, as, in the garden, in such a dress, that Mary Magdalene took him for the gardener; but that he had really his own countenance, appears by this, that *their eyes were holden, that they should not know him;* and when that restraint on *their* eyes was taken off, immediately they *knew him*, Luke xxiv. 16—31. Now,

1. These *two* witnesses gave in their *testimony* to this proof of Christ's resurrection; *They went and told it to the residue, v.* 13. Being *satisfied* themselves, they were desirous to give their brethren the *satisfaction* they had, that they might be comforted as they were.

2. This did not gain credit with all; *Neither believed they them.* They suspected that their eyes also deceived them. Now there was a wise providence in it, that the proofs of Christ's resurrection were given in thus *gradually*, and admitted thus *cautiously*, that so the assurance with which the apostles preached this doctrine afterward, when they ventured their all upon it, might be the more satisfying. We have the more reason to believe those who did themselves believe so slowly: had they swallowed it presently, they might have been thought *credulous*, and their testimony the less to be *regarded;* but their *disbelieving* at first, shows that they did not believe it afterward but upon a full conviction.

14 Afterward he appeared unto
the eleven as they sat at meat, and
upbraided them with their unbelief
and hardness of heart, because they
believed not them which had seen
him after he was risen. 15 And
he said unto them, Go ye into all
the world, and preach the gospel

to every creature. 16 He that believeth and is baptized shall be saved;
but he that believeth not shall be
damned. 17 And these signs shall
follow them that believe; In my name
shall they cast out devils; they shall
speak with new tongues; 18 They
shall take up serpents; and if they
drink any deadly thing, it shall not
hurt them; they shall lay hands on
the sick, and they shall recover.

Here is, I. The *conviction* which Christ gave his apostles of the truth of his resurrection (*v.* 14); He *appeared to them* himself, when they were all together, *as they sat at meat*, which gave him an opportunity to *eat and drink with them*, for their full satisfaction; see Acts x. 41. And still, when he appeared to them, he *upbraided them with their unbelief and hardness of heart*, for even at the general meeting in *Galilee*, *some doubted*, as we find Matt. xxviii. 17. Note, The evidences of the truth of the gospel are so full, that those who receive it not, may justly be *upbraided* with their unbelief; and it is owing not to any weakness or deficiency in the proofs, but to the *hardness of their heart*, its senselessness and stupidity. Though they had not till now seen him themselves, they are justly blamed *because they believed not them who had seen him after he was risen;* and perhaps it was owing in part to the *pride of their hearts*, that they did not; for they thought, "If indeed he be risen, *to whom should he delight to do* the *honour* of showing himself but to us?" And if he *pass them by*, and show himself to *others* first, they cannot believe it is he. Thus many disbelieve the doctrine of Christ, because they think it *below them* to give credit to such as he has chosen to be the witnesses and publishers of it. Observe, It will not suffice for an excuse of our infidelity in the great day, to say, "*We did not see him* after he was risen," for we ought to have believed the testimony of those who did see him.

II. The *commission* which he gave them to set up his kingdom among men by the preaching of his *gospel*, the glad tidings of reconciliation to God through a Mediator. Now observe,

1. *To whom* they were to preach *the gospel.* Hitherto they had been sent only to *the lost sheep of the house of Israel*, and were forbidden to go into the *way of the Gentiles*, or into any city of the Samaritans; but now their commission is enlarged, and they are authorized to *go into all the world*, into all parts of the world, the habitable world, and to *preach the gospel* of Christ to *every creature*, to the Gentiles as well as to the Jews; to every human creature that is capable of receiving it. "Inform them concerning Christ, the history of *his life*, and *death*, and *resurrection;* instruct them in the *meaning* and *intention* of these, and of the advantages which the children of men have, or may have, hereby; and invite them, without exception, to come and share in them. This is *gospel.* Let this be *preached* in all places, to all persons." These eleven men could not themselves preach it to all the world, much less to *every creature* in it; but they and the other disciples, seventy in number, with those who should afterward be added to them, must *disperse* themselves several ways, and, wherever they went, carry the gospel along with them. They must send *others* to those places whither they could not *go themselves*, and, in short, make it the business of their lives to send those glad tidings *up and down the world* with all possible fidelity and care, not as an amusement or entertainment, but as a solemn message from God to men, and an appointed means of making men happy. "Tell as many as you can, and bid them tell others; it is a message of universal concern, and *therefore* ought to *have* a universal welcome, because it *gives* a universal welcome."

2. What is the *summary of the gospel* they are to preach (*v.* 16); "Set before the world life and death, good and evil. Tell the children of men that they are all in a state of misery and danger, *condemned* by their prince, and *conquered* and *enslaved* by their enemies." This is supposed in their being *saved*, which they would not need to be if they were not *lost.* "Now go and tell them," (1.) "That if they *believe the gospel*, and give up themselves to be Christ's disciples; if they *renounce* the devil, the world, and the flesh, and be *devoted* to Christ as their prophet, priest, and king, and to God in Christ as their God in covenant, and evidence by their constant adherence to this covenant their sincerity herein, they *shall be saved* from the guilt and power of sin, it shall not *rule* them, it shall not *ruin* them. He that is a true Christian, shall be saved through Christ." *Baptism* was appointed to be the *inaugurating* rite, by which those that embraced Christ owned him; but it is here put rather for the *thing signified* than for the sign, for Simon Magus *believed* and was *baptized*, yet was not *saved*, Acts viii. 13. *Believing with the heart, and confessing with the mouth the Lord Jesus* (Rom. x. 9), seem to be much the same with this here. Or thus, We must *as*sent to gospel-truths, and *con*sent to gospel-terms. (2.) "*If they believe not*, if they receive not the record God gives concerning his Son, they cannot expect any other way of salvation, but must inevitably perish; *they shall be damned*, by the sentence of a *despised* gospel, added to that of a broken law." And even this is *gospel*, it is good news, that nothing else but unbelief shall damn men, which is a sin against the remedy. Dr. Whitby here observes, that they who hence infer "that the infant seed of believers are not capable of baptism, because they cannot believe, must

hence also infer that they cannot be saved; *faith* being here more expressly required to salvation than to baptism. And that in the latter clause baptism is omitted, because it is not simply the want of baptism, but the contemptuous neglect of it, which makes men guilty of damnation, otherwise infants might be damned for the mistakes or profaneness of their parents."

3. What power they should be endowed with, for the confirmation of the doctrine they were to preach (*v.* 17); *These signs shall follow them that believe.* Not that all who believe, shall be able to produce these signs, but some, even as many as were employed in propagating the faith, and bringing others to it; for signs are intended *for them that believe not;* see 1 Cor. xiv. 22. It added much to the glory and evidence of the gospel, that the preachers not only wrought miracles themselves, but conferred upon others a power to work miracles, which power *followed* some of them that believed, wherever they went to preach. They shall do wonders *in Christ's name,* the same name into which they were baptized, in the virtue of power derived from him, and fetched in by prayer. Sóme particular signs are mentioned; (1.) They shall *cast out devils;* this power was more common among Christians than any other, and lasted longer, as appears by the testimonies of Justin Martyr, Origen, Irenæus, Tertullian, Minutius Felix, and others, cited bý Grotius on this place. (2.) They shall *speak with new tongues,* which they had never learned, or been acquainted with; and this was both a *miracle* (a miracle *upon the mind*), for the confirming of the truth of the gospel, and a *means* of spreading the gospel among those nations that had not heard it. It saved the preachers a vast labour in learning the languages; and, no doubt, they who by *miracle* were made *masters of languages,* were *complete* masters of them and of all their native elegancies, which were proper both to *instruct* and *affect,* which would very much recommend them and their preaching. (3.) They shall *take up serpents.* This was fulfilled in Paul, who was not hurt by the *viper* that *fastened on his hand,* which was acknowledged a great miracle by the barbarous people, Acts xxviii. 5, 6. They shall be kept unhurt by that *generation of vipers* among whom they live, and by the malice of the *old serpent.* (4.) If they be compelled by their persecutors to *drink any deadly* poisonous thing, *it shall not hurt them:* of which very thing some instances are found in ecclesiastical history. (5.) They shall not only be preserved from hurt themselves, but they shall be enabled to do good to others; *They shall lay hands on the sick, and they shall recover,* as multitudes had done by their master's *healing* touch. Many of the elders of the church had this power, as appears by Jam. v. 14, where, as an instituted sign of this miraculous healing, they are said to *anoint* the sick *with oil in the name of the Lord.* With what assurance of success might they go about the executing of their commission, when they had such credentials as these to produce!

19 So then after the Lord had spoken unto them, he was received up into heaven, and sat on the right hand of God. 20 And they went forth, and preached every where, the Lord working with *them,* and confirming the word with signs following. Amen.

Here is, 1. Christ *welcomed* into the *upper world* (*v.* 19): *After the Lord had spoken* what he had to say to his disciples, he *went up into heaven,* in a cloud; which we have a particular account of (Acts i. 9), and he had not only an admission, but an abundant *entrance,* into his kingdom there; he was *received up,* received in state, with loud acclamations of the heavenly hosts; and he *sat on the right hand of God:* sitting is a posture of *rest,* for now he had finished his work, and a posture of *rule,* for now he took possession of his kingdom; he sat *at the right hand of God,* which denotes the sovereign dignity he is advanced to, and the universal agency he is entrusted with. Whatever God does concerning us, gives to us, or accepts from us, it is *by his Son.* Now he is glorified with the glory he had before the world.

2. Christ *welcomed* in this *lower world;* his being *believed on in the world,* and *received up into glory,* are put together, 1. Tim. iii. 16. (1.) We have here the apostles working diligently for him; they *went forth, and preached every where* far and near. Though the doctrine they preached, was *spiritual* and *heavenly,* and directly contrary to the *spirit* and *genius* of the world, though it met with abundance of opposition, and was utterly destitute of all secular supports and advantages, yet the preachers of it were neither *afraid* nor *ashamed;* they were so industrious in spreading the gospel, that within a few years the sound of it *went forth into the ends of the earth,* Rom. x. 18. (2.) We have here God *working* effectually *with them,* to make their labours successful, by *confirming the word with signs following,* partly by the miracles that were wrought upon the *bodies* of people, which were divine seals to the Christian doctrine, and partly by the influence it had upon the *minds* of people, through the operation of the Spirit of God, see Heb. ii. 4. These were properly *signs following* the word —the reformation of the world, the destruction of idolatry, the conversion of sinners, the comfort of saints; and these signs still follow it, and that they may do so more and more, for the honour of Christ and the good of mankind, the evangelist prays, and teaches us to say *Amen.* Father in heaven, thus let thy name be hallowed, and let thy kingdom come.

AN

EXPOSITION,

WITH PRACTICAL OBSERVATIONS,

OF THE GOSPEL ACCORDING TO

ST. LUKE.

We are now entering into the labours of another evangelist; his name *Luke*, which some take to be a contraction of *Lucilius;* born at Antioch, so St. Jerome. Some think that he was the only one of all the penmen of the scripture that was not of the seed of Israel. He was a Jewish proselyte, and, as some conjecture, converted to Christianity by the ministry of St. Paul at Antioch; and after his coming into Macedonia (Acts xvi. 10) he was his constant companion. He had employed himself in the study and practice of physic; hence, Paul calls him *Luke the beloved Physician*, Col. iv. 14. Some of the pretended ancients tell you that he was a painter, and drew a picture of the virgin Mary. But Dr. Whitby thinks that there is nothing certain to the contrary, and that therefore it is probable that he was one of the seventy disciples, and a follower of Christ when he was here upon earth; and, if so, he was a native Israelite. I see not what can be objected against this, except some uncertain traditions of the ancients, which we can build nothing upon, and against which may be opposed the testimonies of Origen and Epiphanius, who both say that he was one of the seventy disciples. He is supposed to have written this gospel when he was associated with St. Paul in his travels, and by direction from him: and some think that this is *the brother* whom Paul speaks of (2 Cor. viii. 18), *whose praise is in the gospel throughout all the churches of Christ;* as if the meaning of it were, that he was celebrated *in all the churches* for writing *this gospel;* and that St. Paul means this when he speaks sometimes of *his* gospel, as Rom. ii. 16. But there is no ground at all for this. Dr. Cave observes that his way and manner of writing are accurate and exact, his style polite and elegant, sublime and lofty, yet perspicuous; and that he expresses himself in a vein of purer Greek than is to be found in the other writers of the holy story. Thus he relates divers things more copiously than the other evangelists; and thus he especially treats of those things which relate to the priestly office of Christ. It is uncertain when, or about what time, this gospel was written. Some think that it was written in Achaia, during his travels with Paul, seventeen years (twenty-two years, say others) after Christ's ascension; others, that it was written at Rome, a little before he wrote his history of the *Acts of the Apostles* (which is a continuation of this), when he was there with Paul, while he was a prisoner, and preaching in *his own hired house*, with which the history of the Acts concludes; and then Paul saith that *only Luke was with him*, 2 Tim. iv. 11. When he was under that voluntary confinement with Paul, he had leisure to compile these two histories (and many excellent writings the church has been indebted to a prison for): if so, it was written about twenty-seven years after Christ's ascension, and about the fourth year of Nero. Jerome says, He died when he was eighty-four years of age, and was never married. Some write that he suffered martyrdom; but, if he did, where and when is uncertain. Nor indeed is there much more credit to be given to the Christian traditions concerning the writers of the New Testament than to the Jewish traditions concerning those of the Old Testament.

CHAP. I.

The narrative which this evangelist gives us (or rather God by him) of the life of Christ begins earlier than either Matthew or Mark. We have reason to thank God for them all, as we have for all the gifts and graces of Christ's ministers, which in one make up what is wanting in the other, while all put together make a harmony. In this chapter we have, I. Luke's preface to his gospel, or his epistle dedicatory to his friend Theophilus, ver. 1—4. II. The prophecy and history of the conception of John Baptist, who was Christ's forerunner, ver. 5—25. The annunciation of the virgin Mary, or the notice given to her that she should be the mother of the Messiah, ver. 26—38. IV. The interview between Mary the mother of Jesus and Elisabeth the mother of John, when they were both with child of those pregnant births, and the prophecies they both uttered upon that occasion, ver. 39—56. V. The birth and circumcision of John Baptist, six months before the birth of Christ, ver. 57—66. VI. Zacharias's song of praise, in thankfulness for the birth of John, and in prospect of the birth of Jesus, ver. 67—79. VII. A short account of John Baptist's infancy, ver. 80. And these do more than give us an entertaining narrative; they will lead us into the understanding of the mystery of godliness, God manifest in the flesh.

FORASMUCH as many have taken in hand to set forth in order a declaration of those things which are most surely believed among us, 2 Even as they delivered them unto us, which from the beginning were eyewitnesses, and ministers of the word; 3 It seemed good to me also, having had perfect understanding of all things from the very first, to write unto thee in order, most excellent Theophilus, 4 That thou mightest know the certainty of those things, wherein thou hast been instructed.

Complimental prefaces and dedications, the language of flattery and the food and fuel of pride, are justly condemned by the wise and good; but it doth not therefore follow, that such as are useful and instructive are to be run down; such is this, in which St. Luke dedicates his gospel to his friend Theophilus, not as to his *patron,* though he was a man of honour, to protect it, but as to his *pupil,* to learn it, and hold it fast. It is not certain who this Theophilus was; the name signifies a *friend of God;* some think that it does not mean any particular person, but every one that is a *lover of God;* Dr. Hammond quotes some of the ancients understanding it so: and then it teaches us, that those who are truly lovers of God, will heartily welcome the gospel of Christ, the design and tendency of which are, to bring us to God. But it is rather to be understood of some particular person, probably a magistrate; because Luke gives him here the same title of respect which St. Paul gave to Festus the governor, κράτιστε (Acts xxvi. 25), which we there translate *most noble Festus,* and here *most excellent Theophilus.* Note, Religion does not destroy civility and good manners, but teaches us, according to the usages of our country, to *give honour to them to whom honour is due.*

Now observe here, I. Why St. Luke wrote this gospel. It is certain that he was moved by the Holy Ghost, not only *to* the writing, but *in* the writing of it; but in both he was moved as a reasonable creature, and not as a mere machine; and he was made to consider,

1. That the things he wrote of were things that were *most surely believed among all Christians,* and therefore things which they ought to be instructed in, that they may know what they believe, and things which ought to be transmitted to posterity (who are as much concerned in them as we are); and, in order to that, to be committed to writing, which is the surest way of conveyance to the ages to come. He will not write about things of *doubtful disputation,* things about which Christians may safely differ from one another and hesitate within themselves; but the things which are, and ought to be, most *surely believed,* πράγματα πεπληροφορημένα—*the things which were performed* (so some), which Christ and his apostles did, and did with such circumstances as gave a full assurance that they were really done, so that they have gained an established lasting credit. Note, Though it is not the foundation of our faith, yet it is a support to it, that the articles of our creed are things that have been long *most surely believed.* The doctrine of Christ is what thousands of the wisest and best of men have *ventured their souls upon* with the greatest assurance and satisfaction.

2. That it was requisite there should be a *declaration made in order* of those things; that the history of the life of Christ should be *methodized,* and committed to writing, for the greater certainty of the conveyance. When things are *put in order,* we know the better where to *find them* for *our own* use, and how to *keep* them for the benefit of *others.*

3. That there were *many who had undertaken* to *publish* narratives of the *life of Christ,* many well-meaning people, who *designed* well, and *did* well, and what they published had *done good,* though not done by divine inspiration, nor so well done as might be, nor intended for perpetuity. Note, (1.) The labours of others in the gospel of Christ, if faithful and honest, we ought to *commend* and *encourage,* and not to *despise,* though chargeable with many deficiencies. (2.) Others' services to Christ must not be reckoned to supersede ours, but rather to quicken them.

4. That the truth of the things he had to write was *confirmed* by the *concurring testimony* of those who were competent and unexceptionable witnesses of them; what had been published in writing already, and what he was now about to publish, agreed with that which had been delivered by word of mouth, over and over, by those who from the beginning were *eye-witnesses and ministers of the word, v.* 2. Note, (1.) The apostles were *ministers of the word* of Christ, who is *the Word* (so some understand it), or of the doctrine of Christ; they, having received it themselves, ministered it to others, 1 John i. 1. They had not a gospel to make as masters, but a gospel to preach as ministers. (2.) The

ministers of the word were *eye-witnesses* of the things which they preached, and, which is also included, *ear-witnesses.* They did themselves *hear* the doctrine of Christ, and *see* his miracles, and had them not by report, at second hand; and therefore they could not but speak, with the greatest assurance, the things which they had *seen and heard,* Acts iv. 20. (3.) They were so *from the beginning* of Christ's ministry, *v.* 2. He had his disciples with him when he wrought his *first miracle,* John ii. 11. They *companied with him all the time that he went in and out among them* (Acts i. 21), so that they not only heard and saw all that which was sufficient to confirm their faith, but, if there had been any thing to shock it, they had opportunity to discover it. (4.) The *written* gospel, which we have to *this day,* exactly agrees with the gospel which was *preached* in the *first days* of the church. (5.) That he himself had a *perfect understanding* of the *things* he wrote of, *from the first, v.* 3. Some think that here is a tacit reflection upon those who had written before him, that they had not a *perfect understanding* of what they wrote, and therefore, *Here am I, send me (—facit indignatio versum—my wrath impels my pen);* or rather, without reflecting on them, he asserts his own ability for this undertaking: "It seemed good to me, having attained to the exact knowledge of all things, *ἄνωθεν—from above;*" so I think it should be rendered; for if he meant the same with *from the beginning* (*v.* 2), as our translation intimates, he would have used the same word. [1.] He had diligently *searched* into these things, had *followed* after them (so the word is), as the Old-Testament prophets are said to have *enquired* and *searched diligently,* 1 Pet. i. 10. He had not taken things so easily and superficially as others who had written before him, but made it his business to inform himself concerning particulars. [2.] He had received his intelligence, not only by tradition, as others had done, but by revelation, confirming that tradition, and securing him from any error or mistake in the recording of it. He sought it *from above* (so the word intimates), and from thence he had it; thus, like Elihu, he *fetched his knowledge* from afar. He wrote his history as Moses wrote his, of things *reported* by tradition, but *ratified* by inspiration. [3.] He could therefore say that he had a *perfect understanding* of these things. He knew them, *ἀκριβῶς—accurately,* exactly. "Now, having received this *from above,* it seemed good to me to communicate it;" for such a talent as this ought not to be buried.

II. Observe why he sent it to *Theophilus:* "I wrote unto thee these things *in order,* not that thou mayest give reputation to the work, but that thou mayest be edified by it (*v.* 4); *that thou mightest know the certainty of those things wherein thou hast been instructed.*" 1. It is implied, that he had been *instructed* in these things either before his baptism, or since, or both, according to the rule, Matt. xxviii. 19, 20. Probably, Luke had baptized him, and knew how well instructed he was; *περὶ ὧν κατηχήθης—concerning which thou hast been catechized;* so the word is; the most knowing Christians began with being catechized. Theophilus was a person of quality, perhaps of noble birth; and so much the more pains should be taken with such when they are young, to teach them the principles of the oracles of God, that they may be fortified against the temptations, and furnished for the opportunities, of a high condition in the world. 2. It was intended that he should *know the certainty of those things,* should understand them more clearly and believe them more firmly. There is a *certainty* in the gospel of Christ, there is that therein which we may build upon; and those who have been well instructed in the things of God when they were young should afterwards give diligence to *know the certainty* of those things, to know not only what we believe, but why we believe it, that we may be able to give a *reason of the hope that is in us.*

THERE was in the days of Herod,
the king of Judæa, a certain
priest named Zacharias, of the course
of Abia: and his wife *was* of the
daughters of Aaron, and her name
was Elisabeth. 6 And they were
both righteous before God, walking
in all the commandments and ordinances of the Lord blameless. 7 And
they had no child, because that Elisabeth was barren, and they both
were *now* well stricken in years. 8
And it came to pass, that while he
executed the priest's office before God
in the order of his course, 9 According to the custom of the priest's office,
his lot was to burn incense when he
went into the temple of the Lord. 10
And the whole multitude of the people were praying without at the time
of incense. 11 And there appeared
unto him an angel of the Lord standing on the right side of the altar of
incense. 12 And when Zacharias saw
him, he was troubled, and fear fell
upon him. 13 But the angel said
unto him, Fear not, Zacharias: for
thy prayer is heard; and thy wife
Elisabeth shall bear thee a son, and
thou shalt call his name John. 14
And thou shalt have joy and gladness;
and many shall rejoice at his birth.
15 For he shall be great in the sight
of the Lord, and shall drink neither

wine nor strong drink; and he shall
be filled with the Holy Ghost, even
from his mother's womb. 16 And
many of the children of Israel shall
he turn to the Lord their God. 17
And he shall go before him in the
spirit and power of Elias, to turn the
hearts of the fathers to the children,
and the disobedient to the wisdom
of the just; to make ready a people
prepared for the Lord. 18 And Zacharias said unto the angel, Whereby
shall I know this? for I am an old
man, and my wife well stricken in
years. 19 And the angel answering
said unto him, I am Gabriel, that
stand in the presence of God; and
am sent to speak unto thee, and to
show thee these glad tidings. 20 And,
behold, thou shalt be dumb, and not
able to speak, until the day that these
things shall be performed, because
thou believest not my words, which
shall be fulfilled in their season. 21
And the people waited for Zacharias,
and marvelled that he tarried so long
in the temple. 22 And when he
came out, he could not speak unto
them: and they perceived that he
had seen a vision in the temple: for
he beckoned unto them, and remained
speechless. 23 And it came to pass,
that, as soon as the days of his ministration were accomplished, he departed to his own house. 24 And
after those days his wife Elisabeth
conceived, and hid herself five months,
saying, 25 Thus hath the Lord dealt
with me in the days wherein he looked
on *me*, to take away my reproach
among men.

The two preceding evangelists had agreed to begin the gospel with the baptism of John and his ministry, which commenced about six months before our Saviour's public ministry (and now, things being near a crisis, six months was *a deal* of time, which before was but *a little*), and therefore this evangelist, designing to give a more particular account than had been given of our Saviour's conception and birth, determines to do so of John Baptist, who in both was his harbinger and forerunner, the morning-star to the Sun of righteousness. The evangelist determines thus, not only because it is commonly reckoned a satisfaction and entertainment to know something of the original extraction and early days of those who afterwards prove great men, but because in the beginning of these there were many things miraculous, and presages of what they afterwards proved. In these verses our inspired historian begins as early as the conception of John Baptist. Now observe here,

I. The account given of *his parents* (*v.* 5): They lived *in the days of Herod the king*, who was a foreigner, and a deputy for the Romans, who had lately made Judea a province of the empire. This is taken notice of to show that the sceptre was quite departed from Judah, and therefore that now was the time for Shiloh to come, according to Jacob's prophecy, Gen. xlix. 10. The family of David was now sunk, when it was to rise, and flourish again, in the Messiah. Note, None ought to despair of the reviving and flourishing of religion, even then when civil liberties are lost. Israel is enslaved, yet then comes the glory of Israel.

Now the father of John Baptist was a priest, a son of Aaron; his name *Zacharias.* No families in the world were ever so honoured of God as those of Aaron and David; with one was made the covenant of priesthood, with the other that of royalty; they had both forfeited their honour, yet the gospel again puts honour upon both in their latter days, on that of Aaron in John Baptist, on that of David in Christ, and then they were both extinguished and lost. Christ was of David's house, his forerunner of Aaron's; for his priestly agency and influence opened the way to his kingly authority and dignity. This Zacharias was *of the course of Abia.* When in David's time the family of Aaron was multiplied, he divided them into twenty-four courses, for the more regular performance of their office, that it might never be either *neglected* for want of hands or *engrossed* by a few. The eighth of those was that of *Abia* (1 Chron. xxiv. 10), who was descended from Eleazar, Aaron's eldest son; but Dr. Lightfoot suggests that many of the families of the priests were lost in the captivity, so that after their return they took in those of other families, retaining the names of the heads of the respective courses. The wife of this Zacharias was of the daughters of Aaron too, and her name was *Elisabeth,* the very same name with *Elisheba* the wife of Aaron, Exod. vi. 23. The priests (Josephus saith) were very careful to marry within their own family, that they might maintain the dignity of the priesthood and keep it without mixture.

Now that which is observed concerning Zacharias and Elisabeth is,

1. That they were a very religious couple (*v.* 6): *They were both righteous before God;* they were so in his sight whose judgment, we are sure, is *according to truth;* they were sincerely and really so. They are righteous indeed that are so *before God,* as Noah in his generation, Gen. vii. 1. They *approved* themselves *to him,* and he was graciously

pleased to accept them. It is a happy thing when those who are joined to each other in marriage are both *joined to the Lord;* and it is especially requisite that the priests, the Lord's ministers, should with their yoke-fellows be *righteous before God,* that they may be *examples to the flock,* and rejoice their hearts. *They walked in all the commandments and ordinances of the Lord, blameless.* (1.) Their being *righteous before God* was evidenced by the course and tenour of their conversations; they showed it, not by their talk, but by their *works;* by the way they walked in and the rule they walked by. (2.) They were *of a piece* with themselves; for their devotions and their conversations agreed. They walked not only in the *ordinances* of the Lord, which related to divine worship, but in the *commandments* of the Lord, which have reference to all the instances of a good conversation, and must be regarded. (3.) They were universal in their obedience; not that they never did in any thing *come short* of their duty, but it was their constant care and endeavour to *come up* to it. (4.) Herein, though they were not *sinless,* yet they were *blameless;* nobody could charge them with any open scandalous sin; they lived *honestly* and *inoffensively,* as ministers and their families are in a special manner concerned to do, that the ministry be not blamed in *their* blame.

2. That they had been long *childless, v.* 7. Children are a *heritage of the Lord.* But there are many of his heirs in a married state, that yet are denied this *heritage;* they are valuable desirable blessings; yet many there are, who are *righteous before God,* and, if they had children, would bring them up in his fear, who yet are not thus blessed, while the *men of this world* are *full of children* (Ps. xvii. 14), *and send forth their little ones like a flock,* Job xxi. 11. Elisabeth was *barren,* and they began to despair of ever having children, for they were both now *well stricken in years,* when the women that have been most fruitful *leave off bearing.* Many eminent persons were born of mothers that had been long childless, as Isaac, Jacob, Joseph, Samson, Samuel, and so here John Baptist, to make their birth the more remarkable and the blessing of it the more valuable to their parents, and to show that when God keeps his people long waiting for mercy he sometimes is pleased to recompense them for their patience by *doubling* the worth of it when it comes.

II. The appearing of an angel to his father Zacharias, as he was ministering in the temple, *v.* 8—11. Zechariah the prophet was the last of the Old Testament that was conversant with angels, and Zacharias the priest the first in the New Testament. Observe,

1. How Zacharias was employed in the service of God (*v.* 8): He *executed the priest's office, before God, in the order of his course;* it was his *week of waiting,* and he was *upon duty.* Though his family was not built up, or made to grow, yet he made conscience of doing the work of his own place and day. Though we have not *desired mercies,* yet we must keep close to *enjoined services;* and, in our diligent and constant attendance on them, we may hope that mercy and comfort will come at last. Now it fell to Zacharias's lot to burn incense morning and evening for that week of his waiting, as other services fell to other priests *by lot* likewise. The services were directed by lot, that some might not decline them and others engross them, and that, the *disposal of the lot* being *from the Lord,* they might have the satisfaction of a divine call to the work. This was not the high priest's burning incense on the day of atonement, as some have fondly imagined, who have thought by that to find out the time of our Saviour's birth; but it is plain that it was the burning of the daily incense at the *altar of incense* (*v.* 11), which was *in the temple* (*v.* 9), not in the most holy place, into which the high priest entered. The Jews say that one and the same priest burned not incense twice in all his days (there were such a multitude of them), at least never more than one week. It is very probable that this was *upon the sabbath day,* because there was a *multitude of people* attending (*v.* 10), which ordinarily was not on a week day; and thus God usually puts honour upon *his own day.* And then if Dr. Lightfoot reckon, with the help of the Jewish calenders, that this course of Abia fell on the seventeenth day of the third month, the month Sivan, answering to part of May and part of June, it is worth observing that the portions of the law and the prophets which were read this day in the synagogues were very agreeable to that which was doing in the temple; namely, the law of the Nazarites (Num. vi.), and the conception of Samson, Judg. xiii.

While Zacharias was burning incense in the temple, *the whole multitude of the people were praying without, v.* 10. Dr. Lightfoot says that there were constantly in the temple, at the hour of prayer, the priests of the course that then served, and, if it were the sabbath day, those of that course also that had been in waiting the week before, and the Levites that served under the priests, and the *men of the station,* as the Rabbin call them, who were the representatives of the people, in putting their hands upon the head of the sacrifices, and many besides, who, moved by devotion, left their employments, for that time, to be present at the service of God; and those would make up *a great multitude,* especially on sabbaths and feast-days: now these all addressed themselves to their devotions (in mental prayer, for their voice was not heard), when by the tinkling of a bell they had notice that the priest was gone in to burn incense. Now observe here, (1.) That the true Israel of God always were a *praying* people; and prayer is the great and principal piece of service by which we give honour to God, fetch in favours from him, and keep up our communion with him. (2.) That *then,* when ritual and ceremonial appointments were in full force, as this of *burning incense,* yet moral and spiritual duties were required to go along with them, and were principally looked at. David knew that when he was at a distance from the altar his prayer might be heard *without incense,* for it might be directed before God *as incense,* Ps. cxli. 2. But, when he was *compassing the altar,* the incense could not be accepted *without prayer,* any more than the shell without the kernel. (3.) That it is not enough for us to be where God is worshipped, if our hearts do not join in the worship, and go along with the minister, in all the parts of it. If he burn the incense ever so well, in the most pertinent, judicious, lively prayer, if we be not at the same time *praying* in concurrence with him, what will it avail us? (4.) All the prayers we offer up to God here in his courts are acceptable and successful only in virtue of the incense of Christ's intercession in the temple of God above. To this usage in the temple-service there seems to be an allusion (Rev. viii. 1, 3, 4), where we find that *there was silence in heaven,* as there was in the temple, *for half an hour,* while the people were *silently* lifting up their hearts to God in prayer; and that there was an *angel,* the angel of the covenant, who offered up *much incense with the prayers of all saints before the throne.* We cannot expect an interest in Christ's intercession if we do not *pray,* and pray *with our spirits,* and continue instant in prayer. Nor can we expect that the best of our prayers should gain acceptance, and bring in an answer of peace, but through the mediation of Christ, who *ever lives, making intercession.*

2. How, when he was thus employed, he was *honoured* with a messenger, a special messenger sent from heaven to him (*v.* 11): *There appeared unto him an angel of the Lord.* Some observe, that we never read of an angel appearing in the temple, with a message from God, but only this one to Zacharias, because *there* God had other ways of making known his mind, as the Urim and Thummim, and by a still small voice from between the cherubim; but the ark and the oracle were wanting in the second temple, and therefore, when an express was to be sent to a priest in the temple, an angel was to be employed in it, and thereby the gospel was to be introduced, for *that,* as the *law,* was given at first very much by *the ministry of angels,* the appearance of which we often read of in the Gospels and the Acts, though the design both of the law and of the gospel, when brought to perfection, was to settle another way of correspondence, more spiritual, between God and man. This angel stood *on the right side of the altar of incense,* the north side of it, saith Dr. Lightfoot, on Zacharias's right hand; compare this with Zech. iii. 1, where Satan stands at the *right hand* of Joshua the priest, to *resist him;* but Zacharias had a good angel standing *at his right hand,* to encourage him. Some think that this angel appeared coming *out of the most holy place,* which led him to stand at the right side of the altar.

3. What impression this made upon Zacharias (*v.* 12): *When Zacharias saw him,* it was a surprise upon him, even to a degree of terror, for he was *troubled,* and *fear fell upon him, v.* 12. Though he was *righteous before God,* and *blameless* in his conversation, yet he could not be without some apprehensions at the sight of one whose visage and surrounding lustre bespoke him more than *human.* Ever since man sinned, his mind has been unable to bear the glory of such revelations and his conscience afraid of evil tidings brought by them; even Daniel himself could not bear it, Dan. x. 8. And for this reason God chooses to speak to us by men like ourselves, whose *terror* shall *not make us afraid.*

III. The message which the angel had to deliver to him, *v.* 13. He began his message, as angels generally did, with, *Fear not.* Perhaps it had never been Zacharias's lot to *burn incense* before; and, being a very serious conscientious man, we may suppose him full of care to do it *well,* and perhaps when he saw the angel he was afraid lest he came to rebuke him for some mistake or miscarriage; "No," saith the angel, "*fear not;* I have no ill tidings to bring thee from heaven. *Fear not,* but compose thyself, that thou mayest with a sedate and even spirit receive the message I have to deliver to thee." Let us see what that is.

1. The *prayers* he has often made shall now receive an *answer of peace: Fear not, Zacharias, for thy prayer is heard.* (1.) If he means his particular prayer *for a son* to build up his family, it must be the prayers he had formerly made for that mercy, when he was likely to have children; but we may suppose, now that he and his wife were both *well stricken in years,* as they had done expecting it, so they had done praying for it: like Moses, it *sufficeth them,* and they *speak no more to God of that matter,* Deut. iii. 26. But God will now, in giving this mercy, look a great way back to the prayers that he had made long since for and with his wife, as Isaac for and with his, Gen. xxv. 21. Note, Prayers of faith are *filed* in heaven, and are not *forgotten,* though the thing prayed for is not presently *given* in. Prayers made when we were young and coming into the world may be answered when we are old and going out of the world. But, (2.) If he means the prayers he was *now making,* and offering up with his incense, we may suppose that those were according to the duty of his place, for the Israel of God and their welfare, and the performance of the promises made to them concerning the Messiah and the coming of his kingdom: "This prayer of thine is now

heard; for thy wife shall shortly conceive him that is to be the Messiah's forerunner." Some of the Jewish writers themselves say that the priest, when he burnt incense, prayed for the *salvation of the whole world;* and now that prayer shall be heard. Or, (3.) In general, "The prayers thou *now* makest, and all thy prayers, are accepted of God, and *come up for a memorial* before him" (as the angel said to Cornelius, when he visited him at prayer, Acts x. 30, 31); "and this shall be the sign that thou art accepted of God, Elisabeth shall *bear thee a son.*" Note, It is very comfortable to praying people to know that their *prayers* are *heard;* and those mercies are doubly sweet that are given in answer to prayer.

2. He shall have a son in his old age, by Elisabeth his wife, who had been long barren, that by his birth, which was *next* to miraculous, people might be prepared to receive and believe a virgin's bringing forth of a son, which was *perfectly* miraculous. He is directed what name to give his son: *Call him John,* in Hebrew *Johanan,* a name we often meet with in the Old Testament: it signifies *gracious.* The priests must *beseech God that he will be gracious* (Mal. i. 9), and must so *bless the people,* Num. vi. 25. Zacharias was now praying thus, and the angel tells him that his prayer is heard, and he shall have a son, whom, in token of an answer to his prayer, he shall call *Gracious,* or, *The Lord will be gracious,* Isa. xxx. 18, 19.

3. This son shall be the joy of his family and of all his relations, *v.* 14. He shall be another Isaac, thy laughter; and some think that is partly intended in his name, *John.* He shall be a *welcome child. Thou* for thy part *shalt have joy and gladness.* Note, Mercies that have been long *waited for,* when they *come at last,* are the more acceptable. "He shall be such a son as thou shalt have reason to rejoice in; many parents, if they could foresee what their children will prove, instead of *rejoicing* at their birth, would wish they had *never been;* but I will tell thee what thy son will be, and then thou wilt not need to *rejoice with trembling* at his birth, as the best must do, but mayest rejoice with triumph at it. Nay, and *many shall rejoice at his birth;* all the relations of the family will rejoice in it, and all its well-wishers, because it is for the honour and comfort of the family, *v.* 58. All good people will rejoice that such a religious couple as Zacharias and Elisabeth have a son, because they will give him a good education, such as, it may be hoped, will make him a public blessing to his generation. Yea, and perhaps many shall rejoice by an *unaccountable instinct,* as a presage of the joyous days the gospel will introduce.

4. This son shall be a distinguished *favourite of Heaven,* and a distinguished *blessing to the earth.* The honour of having *a son* is nothing to the honour of having *such a son.*

(1.) He shall be *great in the sight of the Lord;* those are great indeed that are so in God's sight, not those that are so in the eye of a vain and carnal world. God will *set him before his face* continually, will employ him in his work and send him on his errands; and that shall make him truly *great* and honourable. He shall be a *prophet,* yea *more than a prophet,* and upon that account as great as any that ever were *born of women,* Matt. xi. 11. He shall live very much *retired* from the world, out of men's sight, and, when he makes a public appearance, it will be very *mean;* but he shall be *much,* he shall be *great, in the sight of the Lord.*

(2.) He shall be a Nazarite, set apart to God from every thing that is *polluting;* in token of this, according to the law of Nazariteship, he *shall drink neither wine nor strong drink,*—or, rather, neither *old* wine nor *new;* for most think that the word here translated *strong drink* signifies some sort of wine, perhaps those that we call *made wines,* or any thing that is *intoxicating.* He shall be, as Samson was by the divine precept (Judg. xiii. 7), and Samuel by his mother's vow (1 Sam. i. 11), a Nazarite for life. It is spoken of as a great instance of God's favour to his people that he *raised up* of *their sons for prophets,* and their *young men for Nazarites* (Amos ii. 11), as if those that were designed for prophets were trained up under the discipline of the Nazarites; Samuel and John Baptist were; which intimates that those that would be *eminent* servants of God, and employed in *eminent* services, must learn to live a life of self-denial and mortification, must be dead to the pleasures of sense, and keep their minds from every thing that is darkening and disturbing to them.

(3.) He shall be abundantly fitted and qualified for those great and eminent services to which in due time he shall be called: *He shall be filled with the Holy Ghost, even from his mother's womb,* and as soon as it is possible he shall appear to have been so. Observe, [1.] Those that would be filled with the Holy Ghost must be sober and temperate, and very moderate in the use of wine and strong drink; for *that* is it that fits him for *this. Be not drunk with wine,* but *be filled with the Spirit,* with which that is not consistent, Eph. v. 18. [2.] It is possible that infants may be wrought upon by the *Holy Ghost,* even from their *mother's womb;* for John Baptist even then was *filled with the Holy Ghost,* who took possession of his heart betimes; and an early specimen was given of it, when he *leaped in his mother's womb for joy,* at the approach of the Saviour; and afterwards it appeared very early that he was *sanctified.* God has promised to *pour out his Spirit* upon the *seed* of believers (Isa. xliv. 3), and their first *springing up* in a dedication of themselves betimes to God is the fruit of it, *v.* 4, 5. Who then can forbid water, that they should not be baptized who for aught we know (and we can say no more of the adult, witness Simon Magus) have received the Holy Ghost as well as we, and have the *seeds of grace* sown in their hearts? Acts x. 47.

(4.) He shall be instrumental for the conversion of many souls to God, and the preparing of them to receive and entertain the gospel of Christ, *v.* 16, 17.

[1.] He shall be sent to the *children of Israel*, to the nation of the Jews, to whom the Messiah also was *first* sent, and not to the Gentiles; to the *whole* nation, and not to the family of *the priests only*, with which, though he was himself of that family, we do not find he had any particular intimacy or influence.

[2.] He shall go before *the Lord their God*, that is, before the Messiah, whom they must expect to be, not *their king*, in the sense wherein they commonly take it, a *temporal prince* to their nation, but *their Lord* and *their God*, to rule and defend, and serve them in a *spiritual* way by his influence on their hearts. Thomas knew this, when he said to Christ, *My Lord* and *my God*, better than Nathanael did, when he said, *Rabbi, thou art the king of Israel.* John shall *go before him*, a little before him, to give notice of his approach, and to prepare people to receive him.

[3.] He shall go *in the spirit and power of Elias.* That is, *First*, He shall be such a man as Elias was, and do such works as Elias did,—shall, like him, wear a hairy garment and a leathern girdle, and live retired from the world,—shall, like him, preach the necessity of repentance and reformation to a very corrupt and degenerate age,—shall, like him, be bold and zealous in reproving sin and witnessing against it even in the greatest, and be hated and persecuted for it by a Herod and his Herodias, as Elijah was by an Ahab and his Jezebel. He shall be carried on in his work, as Elijah was, by a divine *spirit* and *power*, which shall crown his ministry with wonderful success. As Elias went *before* the *writing* prophets of the Old Testament, and did as it were *usher* in that *signal* period of the Old-Testament dispensation by a little *writing* of his own (2 Chron. xxi. 12), so John Baptist went before Christ and his apostles, and introduced the gospel dispensation by preaching the substance of the gospel doctrine and duty, *Repent, with an eye to the kingdom of heaven. Secondly*, He shall be that very person who was prophesied of by Malachi under the name of Elijah (Mal. iv. 5), who should be sent *before the coming of the day of the Lord.* Behold, I *send you a prophet, even Elias*, not Elias the Tishbite (as the LXX. have corruptly read it, to favour the Jews' traditions), but a prophet *in the spirit and power of Elias*, as the angel here expounds it.

[4.] He shall *turn many of the children of Israel to the Lord their God*, shall incline their hearts to receive the Messiah, and bid him welcome, by awakening them to a sense of sin and a desire of righteousness. Whatever has a tendency to *turn us from iniquity*, as John's preaching and baptism had, will turn us to Christ as *our Lord and our God;* for those who through grace are wrought upon to shake off the yoke of sin, that is, the dominion of the world and the flesh, will soon be persuaded to take upon them the yoke of the *Lord Jesus.*

[5.] Hereby he shall *turn the hearts of the fathers to the children*, that is, of the Jews to the Gentiles; shall help to conquer the rooted prejudices which the Jews have against the Gentiles, which was done by the gospel, as far as it prevailed, and was begun to be done by John Baptist, who came *for a witness, that all through him might believe*, who baptized and taught Roman soldiers as well as Jewish Pharisees, and who cured the pride and confidence of those Jews who gloried in their having Abraham to their father, and told them that God would *out of stones raise up children unto Abraham* (Matt. iii. 9), which would tend to *cure* their enmity to the Gentiles. Dr. Lightfoot observes, It is the constant usage of the prophets to speak of the church of the Gentiles as children to the Jewish church, Isa. liv. 5, 6, 13; lx. 4, 9; lxii. 5; lxvi. 12. When the Jews that embraced the faith of Christ were brought to join in communion with the Gentiles that did so too, then the heart of the fathers was turned to the children. And he shall *turn the disobedient to the wisdom of the just*, that is, he shall introduce the gospel, by which the Gentiles, who are now *disobedient*, shall be turned, not so much to their fathers the Jews, but to the faith of Christ, here called the *wisdom of the just*, in communion with the believing Jews; or thus, He shall *turn the hearts of the fathers with the children*, that is, the hearts of old and young, shall be instrumental to bring some of every age to be *religious*, to work a great reformation in the Jewish nation, to bring them *off from* a ritual traditional religion which they had rested in, and to bring them up to *substantial serious* godliness: and the effect of this will be, that enmities will be slain and discord made to cease; and they that are at variance, being united in his baptism, will be better reconciled one to another. This agrees with the account Josephus gives of John Baptist, *Antiq. lib.* 18. *cap.* 7. "That he was a good man, and taught the Jews the exercise of virtue, in piety towards God, and righteousness towards one another, and that they should convene and knit together in baptism." And he saith, "The people flocked after him, and were exceedingly delighted in his doctrine." Thus he turned the hearts of fathers and children to God and one another, by *turning the disobedient to the wisdom of the just.* Observe, *First*, True religion is *the wisdom of just men*, in distinction from the *wisdom of this world.* It is both our wisdom and our duty to be religious; there is both equity and prudence in it. *Secondly*, It is not impossible but that those who have been unbelieving and *disobedient* may be turned to the *wisdom of the just;*

divine grace can conquer the greatest ignorance and prejudice. *Thirdly,* The great design of the gospel is to bring people *home* to God, and to bring them nearer to *one another;* and on this errand John Baptist is sent. In the mention that is *twice* made of his *turning* people, there seems to be an allusion to the name of the Tishbite, which is given to Elijah, which, some think, does not denote the country or city he was of, but has an appellative signification, and therefore they render it Elijah the *converter,* one that was much employed, and very successful, in *conversion-work.* The Elias of the New Testament is therefore said to *turn* or *convert* many to the Lord their God.

[6.] Hereby he shall *make ready a people prepared for the Lord,* shall dispose the minds of people to receive the doctrine of Christ, that thereby they may be *prepared* for the comforts of his coming. Note, *First,* All that are to be *devoted* to the Lord, and *made happy* in him, must first be *prepared* and *made ready* for him. We must be prepared by grace in this world for glory in the other, by the terrors of the law for the comforts of the gospel, by the spirit of bondage for the Spirit of adoption. *Secondly,* Nothing has a more direct tendency to prepare people for Christ than the doctrine of repentance received and submitted to. When sin is thereby made grievous, Christ will become very precious.

IV. Zacharias's unbelief of the angel's prediction, and the rebuke he was laid under for that unbelief. He heard all that the angel had to say, and should have bowed his head, and worshipped the Lord, saying, *Be it unto thy servant according to the word* which thou hast spoken; but it was not so. We are here told,

1. What his unbelief spoke, *v.* 18. He said to the angel, *Whereby shall I know this?* This was not a humble petition for the confirming of his faith, but a peevish objection against what was said to him as altogether incredible; as if he should say, "I can never be made to believe this." He could not but perceive that it was *an angel* that spoke to him; the message delivered, having reference to the Old-Testament prophecies, carried much of its own evidence along with it. There are many instances in the Old Testament of those that had children when they were old, yet he cannot believe that he shall have this child of promise: "*For I am an old man,* and my wife hath not only been all her days barren, but is now well *stricken in years,* and not likely ever to have children. "Therefore he must have *a sign* given him, or he will not believe. Though the appearance of an angel, which had been long disused in the church, was sign enough,—though he had this notice given him in the temple, the place of God's oracles, where he had reason to think no evil angel would be permitted to come,—though it was given him when he was praying, and burning incense,—and though a firm belief of that great principle of religion that God has an almighty power, and with him *nothing is impossible,* which we ought not only to *know,* but to teach others, was enough to silence all objections,—yet, considering his own body and his wife's too much, unlike a son of Abraham, he *staggered at the promise,* Rom. iv. 19, 20.

2. How his unbelief was *silenced,* and he *silenced* for it.

(1.) The angel *stops his mouth,* by *asserting* his authority. Doth he ask, *Whereby shall I know this?* Let him know it by this, *I am Gabriel, v.* 19. He puts his name to his prophecy, doth as it were sign it with his own hand, *teste meipso—take my word for it.* Angels have sometimes refused to tell their names, as to Manoah and his wife; but this angel readily saith, *I am Gabriel,* which signifies *the power of God,* or, the *mighty one of God,* intimating that the God who bade him say this was able to make it good. He also makes himself known by this name to put him in mind of the notices of the Messiah's coming sent to Daniel by the *man Gabriel,* Dan. viii. 16; ix. 21. "*I am the same* that was sent then, and am sent now in pursuance of the same intention." He is Gabriel, who *stands in the presence of God,* an immediate attendant upon the throne of God. The prime ministers of state in the Persian court are described by this, that they *saw the king's face,* Esth. i. 14. "Though I am now talking with thee here, yet *I stand in the presence of God.* I know his eye is upon me, and I dare not say any more than I have warrant to say. But I declare *I am sent to speak to thee,* sent on purpose to *show thee these glad tidings,* which, being so well worthy of all acceptation, thou oughtest to have received cheerfully."

(2.) The angel *stops his mouth* indeed, by *exerting his power:* "That thou mayest object no more, *behold thou shalt be dumb, v.* 20. If thou wilt have a sign for the support of thy faith, it shall be such a one as shall be also the punishment of thine unbelief; thou *shalt not be able to speak till the day that these things shall be performed," v.* 20. Thou shalt be both *dumb* and *deaf;* the same word signifies both, and it is plain that he lost his hearing as well as his speech, for his friends *made signs* to him (*v.* 62), as well as he to them, *v.* 22. Now, in striking him dumb, [1.] God dealt *justly* with him, because he had objected against God's word. Hence we may take occasion to admire the patience of God and his forbearance towards us, that we, who have so often spoken to his dishonour, have not been struck dumb, as Zacharias was, and as we had been if God had dealt with us according to our sins. [2.] God dealt *kindly* with him, and very tenderly and graciously. For, *First,* Thus he prevented his speaking any more such distrustful unbelieving words. If he has *thought evil,* and will not himself *lay his hands upon his mouth,* nor keep it as with a bridle, God will. It is better not to speak at all than to *speak wickedly*. *Secondly,* Thus he *confirmed* his faith; and, by his being disabled to *speak*, he is enabled to *think* the better. If by the rebukes we are under for our sin we be brought to give more credit to the word of God, we have no reason to complain of them. *Thirdly,* Thus he was kept from divulging the vision, and boasting of it, which otherwise he would have been apt to do, whereas it was designed for the present to be lodged as a secret with him. *Fourthly,* It was a great mercy that God's words should be fulfilled in their season, notwithstanding his sinful distrust. The *unbelief of man* shall not *make the promises of God of no effect,* they shall be *fulfilled in their season,* and he shall not be for ever *dumb,* but only *till the day that these things shall be performed,* and then thy *lips* shall be *opened,* that thy *mouth* may *show forth God's praise.* Thus, though God *chastens* the *iniquity* of his people *with the rod,* yet his *loving kindness* he *will not take away.*

V. The return of Zacharias to the people, and at length to his family, and the conception of this child of promise, the son of his old age.

1. The people staïd, expecting Zacharias to come out of the temple, because he was to pronounce the blessing upon them in the name of the Lord; and, though he staid beyond the usual time, yet they did not, as is too common in Christian congregations, hurry away without the blessing, but *waited* for him, marvelling that he *tarried so long in the temple,* and afraid lest something was amiss, *v.* 21.

2. When he came out, he was *speechless, v.* 22. He was now to have dismissed the congregation with a blessing, but was dumb and not able to do it, that the people may be minded to expect the Messiah, who can *command* the blessing, who *blesseth indeed,* and in whom all *the nations of the earth are blessed.* Aaron's priesthood is now shortly to be *silenced* and *set aside,* to make way for the *bringing in* of a *better hope.*

3. He made a shift to give them to understand that he had *seen a vision,* by some awful signs he made, for he *beckoned to them,* and *remained speechless, v.* 22. This represents to us the weakness and deficiency of the Levitical priesthood, in comparison with Christ's priesthood and the dispensation of the gospel. The Old Testament speaks by signs, gives us some intimations of divine and heavenly things, but *imperfect* and uncertain; it *beckons to us,* but *remains speechless.* It is the gospel that speaks to us articulately, and gives us a clear view of that which in the Old Testament was seen *through a glass darkly.*

4. He staid out the *days of his ministration;* for, his lot being to *burn incense,* he could do that, though he was *dumb* and *deaf.* When we cannot perform the service of God so well as we would, yet, if we perform it as well as we can, God will accept of us in it.

5. He then returned to his family, and his *wife conceived, v.* 23, 24. She conceived by virtue of the promise, and, being sensible of it, *she hid herself five months;* she kept house, and kept it private, and did not go abroad so much as she used to do, (1.) Lest she should do herself any prejudice, so as might occasion her miscarrying, or any hurt to the conception. (2.) Lest she should contract any ceremonial pollution which might intrench upon the Nazariteship of her child, remembering the command given to Samson's mother in a like case, and applying it to herself; she must not *touch any unclean thing* while she is with child of a Nazarite, Judg. xiii. 14. And though *five months* are mentioned, because of what follows *in the sixth month,* yet we may suppose that she did in like manner take care of herself during the whole time of her being with child. (3.) Some think it was in an excess of modesty that she *hid herself,* ashamed it should be said that one of her age should be with child. *Shall she have pleasure, being old, her lord being old also?* Gen. xviii. 12. Or, it was in token of her humility, that she might not seem to boast of the honour God had put upon her. (4.) She *hid herself* for devotion, that she might spend her time in prayer and praise. The saints are God's *hidden ones;* she gives this reason for her retirement, "*For thus hath the Lord dealt with me;* not only thus *graciously* in giving me a child, but thus *honourably* in giving me such a child as is to be a Nazarite" (for so her husband might by writing signify to her); "he hath *taken away my reproach among men.*" Fruitfulness was looked upon to be so great a blessing among the Jews, because of the promises of the increase of their nation, and the rising of the Messiah among them, that it was a great reproach to be barren; and those who were so, though ever so *blameless,* were concluded to be guilty of some great sin *unknown,* for which they were so punished. Now Elisabeth triumphs, that not only this reproach is taken away, but great glory is put upon her instead of it: *Thus hath the Lord dealt with me,* beyond any thought or expectation of mine, *in the days wherein he looked on me.* Note, In God's gracious dealings with us we ought to observe his gracious regards to us. He has *looked on us* with compassion and favour, and therefore has thus *dealt with us.*

26 And in the sixth month the
angel Gabriel was sent from God unto
a city of Galilee, named Nazareth,
27 To a virgin espoused to a man
whose name was Joseph, of the house
of David; and the virgin's name *was*
Mary. 28 And the angel came in
unto her, and said, Hail, *thou that*
art highly favoured, the Lord *is* with
thee: blessed *art* thou among women.

29 And when she saw *him*, she was
troubled at his saying, and cast in her
mind what manner of salutation this
should be. 30 And the angel said
unto her, Fear not, Mary: for thou
hast found favour with God. 31 And,
behold, thou shalt conceive in thy
womb, and bring forth a son, and
shalt call his name JESUS. 32 He
shall be great, and shall be called the
Son of the Highest: and the Lord
God shall give unto him the throne
of his father David: 33 And he shall
reign over the house of Jacob for ever;
and of his kingdom there shall be no
end. 34 Then said Mary unto the
angel, How shall this be, seeing I know
not a man? 35 And the angel answered and said unto her, The Holy
Ghost shall come upon thee, and the
power of the Highest shall overshadow thee: therefore also that holy
thing which shall be born of thee
shall be called the Son of God. 36
And, behold, thy cousin Elisabeth,
she hath also conceived a son in her
old age: and this is the sixth month
with her, who was called barren. 37
For with God nothing shall be impossible. 38 And Mary said, Behold
the handmaid of the Lord; be it unto
me according to thy word. And the
angel departed from her.

We have here notice given us of all that it was fit we should know concerning the incarnation and conception of our blessed Saviour, six months after the conception of John. The same angel, Gabriel, that was employed in making known to Zacharias God's purpose concerning *his son*, is employed in this also; for in this, the same glorious work of redemption, which was *begun* in that, is *carried on*. As bad angels are none of the redeemed, so good angels are none of the redeemers; yet they are employed by the Redeemer as his messengers, and they go cheerfully on his errands, because they are his Father's humble servants, and his children's hearty friends and well-wishers.

I. We have here an account given of the mother of our Lord, of whom he was to be born, whom, though we are not to pray to, yet we ought to praise God for.

1. Her name was *Mary*, the same name with *Miriam*, the sister of Moses and Aaron; the name signifies *exalted*, and a great elevation it was to her indeed to be thus *favoured* above all the daughters of the house of David.

2. She was a daughter of the royal family, lineally descended from David, and she herself and all her friends knew it, for she went under the title and character of the *house of David*, though she was poor and low in the world; and she was enabled by God's providence, and the care of the Jews, to preserve their genealogies, to *make it out*, and as long as the promise of the Messiah was to be fulfilled it was *worth keeping;* but for those now, who are brought low in the world, to have descended from persons of honour, is not worth mentioning.

3. She was *a virgin*, a pure unspotted one, but *espoused* to one of the same royal stock, like her, however, of low estate; so that upon both accounts there was (as it was fit there should be) an equality between them; his name was Joseph; he also was *of the house of David*, Matt. i. 20. Christ's mother was a *virgin*, because he was not to be born by ordinary generation, but miraculously; it was necessary that he should be so, that, though he must partake of the nature of man, yet not of the corruption of that nature: but he was born of a *virgin espoused*, made up to be married, and contracted, to put honour upon the married state, that that might not be brought into contempt (which was an ordinance in innocency) by the Redeemer's being born of a virgin.

4. She lived in Nazareth, a *city of Galilee*, a remote corner of the country, and in no reputation for religion or learning, but which bordered upon the heathen, and therefore was called *Galilee of the Gentiles*. Christ's having his relations resident there intimates favour in reserve for the Gentile world. And Dr. Lightfoot observes that Jonah was by birth a Galilean, and Elijah and Elisha very much conversant in Galilee, who were all famous *prophets of the Gentiles*. The angel was sent to her from Nazareth. Note, No distance or disadvantage of place shall be a prejudice to those for whom God has favours in store. The angel Gabriel carries his message as cheerfully to Mary at Nazareth in Galilee as to Zacharias in the temple at Jerusalem.

II. The *address* of the angel to her, *v.* 28. We are not told what she was doing, or how employed, when the angel came *unto her;* but he surprised her with this salutation, *Hail, thou that art highly favoured*. This was intended to raise in her, 1. A value for *herself;* and, though it is very rare that any need to have any sparks struck into their breast with such design, yet in some, who like Mary pore only on their *low estate*, there is occasion for it. 2. An expectation of great news, not from abroad, but from above. Heaven designs, no doubt, uncommon favours for one whom an angel makes court to with such respect, *Hail thou, χαῖρε—rejoice thou;* it was the usual form of salutation; it expresses an esteem of her, and good-will to her and her prosperity.

(1.) She is dignified: "Thou art *highly favoured*. God, in his choice of thee to be the mother of the Messiah, has put an honour upon thee peculiar to thyself, above that of Eve, who was the mother of *all living.*" The vulgar Latin translates this *gratiâ plena—full of grace*, and thence gathers that she had more of the inherent graces of the Spirit than ever any had; whereas it is certain that this bespeaks no other than the singular favour done her in preferring her to conceive and bear our blessed Lord, an honour which, since he was to be the *seed of the woman*, some woman must have, not for *personal merit*, but purely for the sake of *free grace*, and she is pitched upon. *Even so, Father, because it seemed good unto thee.*

(2.) She has the presence of God with her: "*The Lord is with thee*, though poor and mean, and perhaps now forecasting how to get a livelihood and maintain a family in the married state." The angel with this word raised the faith of Gideon (Judg. vi. 12): *The Lord is with thee.* Nothing is to be despaired of, not the performance of any service, not the obtaining of any favour, though ever so great, if we have *God with us.* This word might put her in mind of the Immanuel, *God with us*, which a virgin shall *conceive* and *bear* (Isa. vii. 14), and why not she?

(3.) She has the blessing of God upon her: "*Blessed art thou among women;* not only thou shalt be accounted so by men, but thou shalt be so. Thou that art so *highly favoured* in this instance mayest expect in other things to be *blessed.*" She explains this herself (*v.* 48), *All generations shall call me blessed.* Compare it with that which Deborah saith of Jael, another that was the glory of her sex (Judg. v. 24), *Blessed shall she be above women in the tent.*

III. The consternation she was in, upon this address (*v.* 29). *When she saw him*, and the glories with which he was surrounded, she was *troubled* at the sight of him, and much more *at his saying.* Had she been a proud ambitious young woman, that aimed high, and flattered herself with the expectation of great things in the world, she would have been *pleased* at his saying, would have been puffed up with it, and (as we have reason to think she was a young woman of very good sense) would have had an answer ready, signifying so much: but, instead of that, she is *confounded* at it, as not conscious to herself of any thing that either *merited* or *promised* such great things; and she *cast in her mind what manner of salutation this should be.* Was it from heaven or of men? Was it to amuse her? was it to ensnare her? was it to banter her? or was there something substantial and weighty in it? But, of all the thoughts she had as to *what manner of salutation it should be*, I believe she had not the least idea of its being ever intended or used for a prayer, as it is, and has been, for many ages, by the corrupt, degenerate, and anti-christian ages of the church, and to be ten times repeated for the Lord's prayer once; so it is in the church of Rome. But her thoughtfulness upon this occasion gives a very useful intimation to young people of her sex, when addresses are made to them, to consider and *cast in their minds* what manner of *salutations* they are, whence they come, and what their tendency is, that they may receive them accordingly, and may always *stand on their guard.*

IV. The message itself which the angel had to deliver to her. Some time the angel gives her to *pause;* but, observing that this did but increase her perplexity, he went on with his errand, *v.* 30. To what he had said she made no reply; he therefore confirms it: "*Fear not, Mary*, I have no other design than to assure thee that *thou hast found favour with God* more than thou thinkest of, as there are many who think they are more favoured of God than really they are." Note, Those that have *found favour with God* should not give way to disquieting distrustful fears. Doth God favour thee? Fear not, though the world frown upon thee. Is he for thee? No matter who is against thee.

1. Though she is a *virgin*, she shall have the honour of being a *mother:* "*Thou shalt conceive in thy womb, and bring forth a son*, and thou shalt have the naming of him; thou shalt *call his name Jesus*," *v.* 31. It was the sentence upon Eve, that, though she should have the honour to be the *mother of all living*, yet this mortification shall be an allay to that honour, that *her desire shall be to her husband*, and he *shall rule over her*, Gen. iii. 16. But Mary has the honour without the allay.

2. Though she lives in *poverty* and *obscurity*, yet she shall have the honour to be the mother of the Messiah; her son shall be named *Jesus—a Saviour*, such a one as the world *needs*, rather than such a one as the Jews *expect.*

(1.) He will be very *nearly allied* to the *upper world.* He *shall be great*, truly great, incontestably great; for he shall be called *the Son of the Highest*, the Son of God who is *the Highest;* of the same nature, as the son is of the same nature with the father; and very dear to him, as the son is to the father. He shall be *called*, and not *miscalled*, the *Son of the Highest;* for he is himself *God over all, blessed for evermore*, Rom. ix. 5. Note, Those who are the children of God, though but by adoption and regeneration, are *truly great*, and therefore are concerned to be *very good*, 1 John iii. 1, 2.

(2.) He will be very *highly preferred* in the *lower world;* for, though born under the most disadvantageous circumstances possible, and appearing in the form of a servant, yet *the Lord God shall give unto him the throne of his father David*, *v.* 32. He puts her in mind that she was *of the house of David;* and that therefore, since neither the *Salique law*, nor the right of primogeniture, took place in the entail of his throne, it was not impossible but that she might bring forth an *heir* to it, and therefore might the more easily *believe* it when she was told by an angel from heaven that she *should* do so, that after the sceptre had been long *departed* from that ancient and honourable family it should now at length return to it again, to remain in it, not by succession, but in the same hand to eternity. His people will not *give him that throne*, will not acknowledge his right to *rule them;* but the *Lord God* shall give him a right to *rule them*, and set him as *his king* upon the *holy hill of Zion.* He assures her, [1.] That his kingdom shall be *spiritual:* he shall *reign over the house of Jacob*, not *Israel according to the flesh*, for they neither came into his interests nor did they continue long a people; it must therefore be a *spiritual* kingdom, the house of Israel *according to promise*, that he must *rule over.* [2.] That it shall be eternal: he shall reign *for ever*, and *of his kingdom there shall be no end*, as there had been long since of the temporal reign of David's house, and would shortly be of the state of Israel. Other crowns endure not *to every generation*, but Christ's doth, Prov. xxvii. 24. The gospel is the *last* dispensation, we are to look for no other.

V. The further information given her, upon her enquiry concerning the birth of this prince.

1. It is a just enquiry which she makes: "*How shall this be? v.* 34. How can I now presently conceive a child" (for so the angel meant) "when I *know not a man;* must it therefore be otherwise than by ordinary generation? If so, let me know *how?*" She knew that the Messiah must be born of *a virgin;* and, if she must be his mother, she desires to know how. This was not the language of her distrust, or any doubt of what the angel said, but of a desire to be further instructed.

2. It is a satisfactory answer that is given to it, *v.* 35. (1.) She shall conceive by *the power of the Holy Ghost*, whose proper work and office it is to *sanctify*, and therefore to sanctify the virgin for this purpose. The Holy Ghost is called the *power of the Highest.* Doth she ask how this shall be? This is enough to help her over all the difficulty there appears in it; a divine power will undertake it, not the power of an angel employed in it, as in other works of wonder, but the power of *the Holy Ghost* himself.

(2.) She must *ask no questions* concerning the way and manner how it shall be wrought; for the Holy Ghost, as the *power of the Highest*, shall *overshadow* her, as the *cloud* covered the tabernacle when the glory of God took possession of it, to conceal it from those that would too curiously observe the motions of it, and pry into the mystery of it. The formation of every babe in the womb, and the entrance of the spirit of life into it, is a mystery in nature; none knows *the way of the spirit, nor how the bones are formed in the womb of her that is with child*, Eccl. xi. 5. We were *made in secret*, Ps. cxxxix. 15, 16. Much more was the formation of the child Jesus a *mystery;* without controversy, *great was the mystery of godliness, God manifest in the flesh*, 1 Tim. iii. 16. It is a *new thing created in the earth* (Jer. xxxi. 22), concerning which we must not covet to be *wise above what is written.*

(3.) The child she shall conceive is a *holy thing*, and therefore must not be conceived by *ordinary generation*, because he must not share in the common corruption and pollution of the human nature. He is spoken of emphatically, *That Holy Thing*, such as never was; and he shall be called *the Son of God*, as the Son of the Father by eternal generation, as an indication of which he shall now be formed by the Holy Ghost in the present conception. His human nature must be so produced, as it was fit that should be which was to be taken into union with the divine nature.

3. It was a further encouragement to her faith to be told that *her cousin Elisabeth*, though stricken in years, was *with child, v.* 36. Here is an age of wonders beginning, and therefore be not surprised: here is one among thy own relations truly great, though not altogether so great as this; it is usual with God to advance in working wonders. *Greater works than these shall ye do.* Though Elisabeth was, on the father's side, of the *daughters of Aaron* (*v.* 5), yet on the mother's side she might be of the house of David, for those two families often intermarried, as an earnest of the uniting of the royalty and the priesthood in the Messiah. *This is the sixth month with her that was called barren.* This intimates, as Dr. Lightfoot thinks, that all the instances in the Old Testament of those having children that had been long barren, which was above nature, were designed to prepare the world for the belief of a virgin's bearing a son, which was against nature. And therefore, even in the birth of Isaac, Abraham saw Christ's day, foresaw such a miracle in the birth of Christ. The angel assures Mary of this, to encourage her faith, and concludes with that great truth, of undoubted certainty and universal use, *For with God nothing shall be impossible* (*v.* 37), and, if nothing, then not this. Abraham therefore staggered not at the belief of the divine promise, because he was strong in his belief of the divine power, Rom. iv. 20, 21. No *word* of God must be *incredible to us*, as long as no *work* of God is *impossible to him.*

VI. Her acquiescence in the will of God concerning her, *v.* 38. She owns herself, 1. A believing subject to the divine authority: "*Behold, the handmaid of the Lord.* Lord, I am at thy service, at thy disposal, to do what thou commandest me." She objects not the danger of spoiling her marriage, and blemishing her reputation, but leaves the issue with God, and submits entirely to his will. 2. A believing expectant of the divine favour. She is not only content that it should be so, but humbly desires that it may be so: *Be it unto me according to thy word.* Such a favour as this it was not for her to slight, or be indifferent to; and for what God has *promised* he will be *sought unto;* by prayer we must put our *amen,* or *so be it,* to the promise. *Remember,* and perform *thy word unto thy servant, upon which thou hast caused me to hope.* We must, as Mary here, *guide* our desires by the word of God, and *ground* our hopes *upon* it. Be it unto me *according to thy word;* just so, and no otherwise.

Hereupon, *the angel departed from her;* having completed the errand he was sent upon, he returned, to give account of it, and receive new instructions. Converse with angels was always a transient thing, and soon over; it will be constant and permanent in the future state. It is generally supposed that just at this instant the virgin *conceived,* by the *overshadowing power* of the Holy Ghost: but, the scripture being decently silent concerning that, it doth not become us to be *inquisitive,* much less *positive.*

39 And Mary arose in those days,
and went into the hill country with
haste, into a city of Juda; 40 And
entered into the house of Zacharias,
and saluted Elisabeth. 41 And it
came to pass, that, when Elisabeth
heard the salutation of Mary, the babe
leaped in her womb; and Elisabeth
was filled with the Holy Ghost: 42
And she spake out with a loud voice,
and said, Blessed *art* thou among
women, and blessed *is* the fruit of thy
womb. 43 And whence *is* this to
me, that the mother of my Lord
should come to me? 44 For, lo, as
soon as the voice of thy salutation
sounded in mine ears, the babe leaped
in my womb for joy. 45 And blessed
is she that believed: for there shall
be a performance of those things which
were told her from the Lord. 46 And
Mary said, My soul doth magnify
the Lord, 47 And my spirit hath
rejoiced in God my Saviour. 48 For
he hath regarded the low estate of his
handmaiden: for, behold, from henceforth all generations shall call me
blessed. 49 For he that is mighty
hath done to me great things; and
holy *is* his name. 50 And his mercy
is on them that fear him from generation to generation. 51 He hath
showed strength with his arm; he
hath scattered the proud in the imagination of their hearts. 52 He hath
put down the mighty from *their* seats,
and exalted them of low degree. 53
He hath filled the hungry with good
things; and the rich he hath sent
empty away. 54 He hath holpen his
servant Israel, in remembrance of *his*
mercy; 55 As he spake to our fathers,
to Abraham, and to his seed for ever.
56 And Mary abode with her about
three months, and returned to her
own house.

We have here an interview between the two happy mothers, Elisabeth and Mary: the angel, by intimating to Mary the favour bestowed on her cousin Elisabeth (*v.* 36), gave occasion for it; and sometimes it may prove a better piece of service than we think to bring good people together, to compare notes. Here is,

I. The visit which Mary made to Elisabeth. Mary was the *younger,* and younger with child; and therefore, if they must come together, it was fittest that Mary should take the journey, not insisting on the preference which the greater dignity of her conception gave her, *v.* 39. She *arose,* and left her affairs, to attend this greater matter: *in those days, at that time* (as it is commonly explained, Jer. xxxiii. 15; l. 4), in a day or two after the angel had visited her, taking some time first, as it is supposed, for her devotion, or rather hastening away to her cousin's, where she would have more leisure, and better help, in the family of a priest. She went, μετὰ σπȣδῆς—*with care, diligence,* and *expedition;* not as young people commonly go abroad and visit their friends, to *divert* herself, but to *inform* herself: she went *to a city of Judah in the hill-country;* it is not named, but by comparing the description of it here with Josh. xxi. 10, 11, it appears to be *Hebron,* for that is there said to be *in the hill-country of Judah,* and to belong to the priests, the sons of Aaron; thither Mary hastened, though it was a long journey, some scores of miles.

1. Dr. Lightfoot offers a conjecture that she was to *conceive* our Saviour there at Hebron, and perhaps had so much intimated to her by the angel, or some other way; and therefore she made such haste thither. He thinks it probable that Shiloh, of the tribe of Judah, and the seed of David, should be *conceived* in a city of Judah and of David, as he was to be born in Bethlehem, another city which belonged to them both. In Hebron the promise was given of Isaac, circumcision was instituted. Here (saith he) Abraham had his first land, and David his first crown: here lay interred the three couple, Abraham and Sarah, Isaac and Rebecca, Jacob and Leah, and, as antiquity has held,

Adam and Eve. He therefore thinks that it suits singularly with the harmony and consent which God uses in his works that the promise should begin to take place by the conception of the Messias, even among those patriarchs to whom it was given. I see no improbability in the conjecture, but add this for the support of it, that Elisabeth said (*v.* 45), *There shall be a performance;* as if it were not performed yet, but was to be performed there.

2. It is generally supposed that she went thither for the confirming of her faith by the sign which the angel had given her, her cousin's being with child, and to rejoice with her sister-favourite. And, besides, she went thither, perhaps, that she might be more retired from company, or else might have more agreeable company than she could have in Nazareth. We may suppose that she did not acquaint any of her neighbours at Nazareth with the message she had received from heaven, yet longed to *talk over* a thing she had a thousand times *thought over,* and knew no person in the world with whom she could *freely* converse concerning it but her cousin Elisabeth, and therefore she hastened to her. Note, It is very beneficial and comfortable for those that have a good work of grace begun in their souls, and Christ in the *forming* there, to consult those who are in the same case, that they may communicate experiences one to another; and they will find that, as in water face answers to face, so doth the heart of man to man, of Christian to Christian.

II. The meeting between Mary and Elisabeth. Mary entered into the house of Zacharias; but he, being *dumb* and *deaf,* kept his chamber, it is probable, and saw no company; and therefore she *saluted Elisabeth* (*v.* 40), told her that she was come to make her a visit, to know her state, and *rejoice with her* in her joy.

Now, at their first coming together, for the confirmation of the faith of both of them, there was something very extraordinary. Mary knew that Elisabeth was with child, but it does not appear that Elisabeth had been told any thing of her cousin Mary's being designed for the mother of the Messiah; and therefore what knowledge she appears to have had of it must have come by a *revelation,* which would be a great encouragement to Mary.

1. The babe *leaped in her womb, v.* 41. It is very probable that she had been several weeks *quick* (for she was six months gone), and that she had often felt the child stir; but this was a more than ordinary motion of the child, which alarmed her to expect something very extraordinary, ἐσκίρτησε. It is the same word that is used by the LXX. (Gen. xxv. 22) for the *struggling* of Jacob and Esau in Rebecca's womb, and the mountains *skipping,* Ps. cxiv. 4. The *babe leaped* as it were to give a signal to his mother that *he* was now at hand whose forerunner he was to be, about six months in ministry, as he was in being; or, it was the effect of some strong impression made upon the mother. Now began to be fulfilled what the angel said to his father (*v.* 15), that he should be *filled with the Holy Ghost, even from his mother's womb;* and perhaps he himself had some reference to this, when he said (John iii. 29), *The friend of the Bridegroom rejoiceth greatly, because of the Bridegroom's voice,* heard, though not by him, yet by his mother.

2. Elisabeth was herself *filled with the Holy Ghost,* or a Spirit of prophecy, by which, as well as by the particular suggestions of the Holy Ghost she was filled with, she was given to understand that the Messiah was at hand, in whom prophecy should revive, and by whom the Holy Ghost should be more plentifully poured out than ever, according to the expectations of those who *waited for the consolation of Israel.* The uncommon motion of the babe in her womb was a token of the extraordinary emotion of her spirit under a divine impulse. Note, Those whom Christ graciously visits may know it by their being *filled with the Holy Ghost;* for, *if any man have not the Spirit of Christ, he is none of his.*

III. The welcome which Elisabeth, by the Spirit of prophecy, gave to Mary, the mother of our Lord; not as to a common friend making a common visit, but as to one of whom the Messiah was to be born.

1. She congratulates her on her honour, and, though perhaps she knew not of it till *just now,* she acknowledges it with the greatest assurance and satisfaction. She *spoke with a loud voice,* which does not at all intimate (as some think) that there was a floor or a wall between them, but that she was in a transport or exultation of joy, and said what she cared not who knew. She said, *Blessed art thou among women,* the same word that the angel had said (*v.* 28); for thus this will of God, concerning honouring the Son, should be done *on earth* as it is *done in heaven.* But Elisabeth adds a reason, *Therefore blessed art thou* because *blessed is the fruit of thy womb;* thence it was that she derived this excelling dignity. Elisabeth was the wife of a priest, and in years, yet she *grudges* not that her kinswoman, who was many years younger than she, and every way her inferior, should have the honour of conceiving in her virginity, and being the mother of the Messiah, whereas the honour put upon her was *much less;* she *rejoices* in it, and is well pleased, as her son was afterwards, that she who *cometh after her is preferred before her,* John i. 27. Note, While we cannot but own that we are more *favoured* of God than we deserve, let us by no means envy that others are *more highly* favoured than we are.

2. She acknowledges her condescension, in making her this visit (*v.* 43): *Whence is this to me, that the mother of my Lord should come to me?* Observe, (1.) She calls the vir-

gin Mary the *mother of her Lord* (as David, in spirit, called the Messiah Lord, *his Lord*), for she knew he was to be *Lord of all.* (2.) She not only bids her welcome to her house, though perhaps she came but in mean circumstances, but reckons this visit a great favour, which she thought herself unworthy of. *Whence is this to me?* It is in reality, and not in compliment, that she saith, "This was a greater favour than I could have expected." Note, Those that are filled with the Holy Ghost have *low thoughts* of their own merits, and high thoughts of God's favours. Her son the Baptist spoke to the same purport with this, when he said, *Comest thou to me?* Matt. iii. 14.

3. She acquaints her with the concurrence of the babe in her womb, in this welcome to her (*v.* 44): "Thou certainly bringest some extraordinary tidings, some extraordinary blessing, with thee; for *as soon as the voice of thy salutation sounded in my ears,* not only my heart *leaped for joy,* though I knew not immediately why or wherefore, but the *babe in my womb,* who was not capable of knowing it, *did so* too." He *leaped* as it were *for joy* that the Messiah, whose harbinger he was to be, would himself come so soon after him. This would serve very much to strengthen the faith of the virgin, that there were such assurances as these given to others; and it would be in part the accomplishment of what had been so often foretold, that there should be *universal joy before the Lord, when he cometh,* Ps. xcviii. 8, 9.

4. She commends her faith, and encourages it (*v.* 45): *Blessed is she that believed.* Believing souls are blessed souls, and will be found so at last; this blessedness cometh *through faith,* even the blessedness of being related to Christ, and having him *formed in the soul.* They are *blessed* who *believe* the word of God, for that word will not fail them; *there shall,* without doubt, *be a performance of those things which are told her from the Lord.* Note, The inviolable certainty of the promise is the undoubted felicity of those that build upon it and expect their all from it. The faithfulness of God is the blessedness of the faith of the saints. Those that have experienced the performance of God's promises themselves should encourage others to hope that he will be as good as his word to them also: *I will tell you what God has done for my soul.*

IV. Mary's song of praise, upon this occasion. Elisabeth's prophecy was an echo to the virgin Mary's salutation, and this song is yet a stronger *echo* to that prophecy, and shows her to be no less filled with the Holy Ghost than Elisabeth was. We may suppose the blessed virgin to come in, very much *fatigued* with her journey; yet she forgets that, and is inspired with new life, and vigour, and joy, upon the confirmation she here meets with of her faith; and since, by this sudden inspiration and transport, she finds that this was designed to be her errand hither, weary as she is, like Abraham's servant, she would *neither eat nor drink till she had told her errand.*

1. Here are the expressions of joy and praise, and God alone the object of the praise and centre of the joy. Some compare this song with that which her name-sake Miriam, the sister of Moses, sung, upon the triumphant departure of Israel out of Egypt, and their triumphant passage through the Red Sea; others think it better compared with the song of Hannah, upon the birth of Samuel, which, like this, passes from a family mercy to a public and general one. *This* begins, like *that, My heart rejoiceth in the Lord,* 1 Sam. ii. 1. Observe how Mary here speaks of God.

(1.) With great reverence of him, as *the Lord: "My soul doth magnify the Lord;* I never saw him so *great* as now I find him so *good.*" Note, Those, and those only, are *advanced* in mercy, who are thereby brought to think the more *highly* and *honourably* of God; whereas there are those whose prosperity and preferment make them say, *What is the Almighty, that we should serve him?* The more honour God has any way put upon us, the more honour we must study to give to him; and *then* only are we accepted in magnifying the Lord, when our *souls* magnify him, and *all that is within us.* Praising work must be soul work.

(2.) With great complacency in him as *her Saviour: My spirit rejoiceth in God my Saviour.* This seems to have reference to the Messiah, whom she was to be the mother of. She calls him *God her Saviour;* for the angel had told her that he should be the *Son of the Highest,* and that his name should be *Jesus, a Saviour;* this she fastened upon, with application to herself: *He is God my Saviour.* Even the mother of our Lord had need of an interest in him as her Saviour, and would have been undone without it: and she glories more in that happiness which she had in common with all believers than in being his mother, which was an honour peculiar to herself, and this agrees with the preference Christ gave to obedient believers above his mother and brethren; see Matt. xii. 50; Luke xi. 27, 28. Note, Those that have Christ for their God and Saviour have a great deal of reason to rejoice, to *rejoice in spirit,* that is rejoicing as Christ did (Luke x. 21), with spiritual joy.

2. Here are just causes assigned for this joy and praise.

(1.) Upon *her own* account, *v.* 48, 49. [1.] Her *spirit rejoiced in the Lord,* because of the *kind* things he had done for her: his *condescension* and *compassion* to her. *He has regarded the low estate of his handmaiden;* that is, he has *looked* upon her *with pity,* for so the word is commonly used. "He has chosen me to this honour, notwithstanding my great meanness, poverty, and obscurity."

Nay, the expression seems to intimate, not only (to allude to that of Gideon, Judg. vi. 15) that her *family* was poor in Judah, but that she was the *least in her father's house,* as if she were under some particular contempt and disgrace among her relations, was unjustly neglected, and the outcast of the family, and God put this honour upon her, to balance abundantly that contempt. I the rather suggest this, for we find something toward such honour as this put upon others, on the like consideration. Because God saw that Leah *was hated,* he *opened her womb,* Gen. xxix. 31. Because Hannah was provoked, and made to fret, and insulted over, by Peninnah, therefore God gave her a son, 1 Sam. i. 19. Whom men wrongfully depress and despise God doth sometimes, in compassion to them, especially if they have borne it patiently, prefer and advance; see Judg. xi. 7. So in Mary's case. And, if God *regards her low estate,* he not only thereby gives a specimen of his favour to the whole race of mankind, whom he *remembers in their low estate,* as the psalmist speaks (Ps. cxxxvi. 23), but secures a lasting honour to her (for such the honour is that God bestows, honour that fades not away): "*From henceforth all generations shall call me blessed,* shall think me a happy woman and highly advanced." All that embrace Christ and his gospel will say, *Blessed was the womb that bore him and the paps which he sucked,* Luke xi. 27. Elisabeth had once and again called her *blessed:* "But that is not all," saith she, "all generations of Gentiles as well as Jews shall call me so."

[2.] Her *soul magnifies* the Lord, because of the *wonderful* things he has done for her (*v.* 49): *He that is mighty has done to me great things.* A *great* thing indeed, that a *virgin* should *conceive.* A *great* thing indeed, that Messiah, who had been so long ago promised to the church, and so long expected by the church, should now at length be born. It is the *power of the Highest* that appears in this. She adds, *and holy is his name;* for so Hannah saith in her song, *There is none holy as the Lord,* which she explains in the next words, *for there is none beside thee,* 1 Sam. ii. 2. God is a Being *by himself,* and he manifests himself to be so, especially in the work of our redemption. He that is *mighty,* even he *whose name is holy,* has *done to me great things.* Glorious things may be expected from him that is both *mighty* and *holy;* who *can do every thing,* and *will* do every thing *well* and *for the best.*

(2.) Upon the account of *others.* The virgin Mary, as the mother of the Messiah, is become a kind of public person, wears a public character, and is therefore immediately endued with another spirit, a more public spirit than before she had, and therefore *looks abroad,* looks *about her,* looks *before her,* and takes notice of God's various dealings with the children of men (*v.* 50, &c.), as Hannah (1 Sam. ii. 3, &c.) In this she has especially an eye to the coming of the Redeemer and God's manifesting himself therein.

[1.] It is a certain truth that *God has mercy in store,* mercy in reserve, *for all that have a reverence for his majesty,* and a due regard to his sovereignty and authority. But never did this appear so as in sending his Son into the world to save us (*v.* 50): *His mercy is on them that fear him;* it has always been so; he has ever looked upon *them* with an eye of *peculiar favour* who have looked up to him with an eye of *filial fear.* But he hath manifested this *mercy,* so as never before, in sending his Son to bring in an everlasting righteousness, and work out an everlasting salvation, for them that fear him, and this *from generation to generation;* for there are gospel privileges transmitted by entail, and intended for perpetuity. Those that *fear God,* as their Creator and Judge, are encouraged to hope for *mercy in him,* through their Mediator and Advocate; and in him *mercy* is settled upon all that *fear God,* pardoning mercy, healing mercy, accepting mercy, crowning mercy, *from generation to generation,* while the world stands. In Christ he *keepeth mercy for thousands.*

[2.] It has been a common observation that God in his providence puts *contempt* upon the *haughty* and *honour* upon the *humble;* and this he has done remarkably in the whole economy of the work of man's redemption. As God had, with his *mercy* to her, shown himself *mighty* also (*v.* 48, 49), so he had, with his *mercy on them that fear him, shown strength* likewise *with his arm. First,* In the course of his providence, it is his usual method to *cross the expectations of men,* and proceed quite otherwise than they promise themselves. *Proud men* expect to carry all before them, to have their way and their will; but he *scatters them in the imagination of their hearts,* breaks their measures, blasts their projects, nay, and brings them low, and brings them down, by those very counsels with which they thought to advance and establish themselves. The *mighty* think to secure themselves by might *in their seats,* but he *puts them down,* and overturns their seats; while, on the other hand, those of *low degree,* who despaired of ever advancing themselves, and thought of no other than of being *ever low,* are wonderfully *exalted.* This observation concerning *honour* holds likewise concerning *riches;* many who were so poor that they had not bread for themselves and their families, by some surprising turn of Providence in favour of them, come to be *filled with good things;* while, on the other hand, those who were rich, and thought no other than that to-morrow should be as this day, that their mountain stood strong and should never be moved, are strangely impoverished, and *sent away empty.* Now this is the same observation that Hannah had made, and enlarged upon, in her song, with application to the case of herself and her adversary (1 Sam. ii.

4—7), which very much illustrates this here. And compare also Ps. cvii. 33—41; cxiii. 7—9; and Eccl. ix. 11. God takes a pleasure in *disappointing* their expectations who promise themselves *great things* in the world, and in *out-doing* the expectations of those who promise themselves but *a little;* as a *righteous* God, it is his glory to *abase* those who *exalt* themselves, and strike terror on the secure; and, as a *good* God, it is his glory to exalt those who humble themselves, and to speak comfort to those who fear before him. *Secondly,* This doth especially appear in the methods of gospel grace.

1. In the *spiritual honours* it dispenses. When the proud Pharisees were rejected, and Publicans and sinners went *into the kingdom of heaven* before them,—when the Jews, who *followed after the law of righteousness,* did not attain it, and the Gentiles, who never thought of it, attained to righteousness (Rom. ix. 30, 31),—when God chose not the *wise men after the flesh,* not the *mighty,* or the *noble,* to preach the gospel, and plant Christianity in the world, but the *foolish* and *weak* things of the world, and things that were despised (1 Cor. i. 26, 27)—then he *scattered the proud,* and *put down the mighty,* but *exalted them of low degree.* When the tyranny of the chief priests and elders was brought down, who had long *lorded it over God's heritage,* and hoped *always* to do so, and Christ's disciples, a company of poor despised fishermen, by the power they were clothed with, were made to *sit on thrones,* judging the twelve tribes of Israel,—when the power of the four monarchies was broken, and the kingdom of the Messiah, that *stone cut out of the mountain without hands,* is made to *fill the earth,*—then are the *proud scattered,* and those of low degree *exalted.*

2. In the *spiritual riches* it dispenses, *v.* 53. (1.) Those who see their need of Christ, and are importunately desirous of righteousness and life in him, he *fills* with *good things,* with the *best things;* he gives liberally to them, and they are *abundantly satisfied* with the blessings he gives. Those who are weary and heavy-laden shall find rest with Christ, and those who thirst are called to *come to him and drink;* for they only know how to value his gifts. *To the hungry soul every bitter thing is sweet,* manna is angels' food; and to the *thirsty* fair water *is honey out of the rock.* (2.) Those who are rich, who are not *hungry,* who, like Laodicea, think they have *need of nothing,* are full of themselves and their own righteousness, and think they have a sufficiency in themselves, those he *sends away* from his door, they are not welcome to him, he sends them *empty* away, they come *full of self,* and are sent away *empty of Christ.* He sends them to the *gods whom they served,* to their own righteousness and strength which they trusted to.

[3.] It was always expected that the Messiah should be, in a special manner, the strength and glory of his people Israel, and so he is in a peculiar manner (*v.* 54): *He hath helped his servant Israel, ἀντελάβετο.* He hath taken them by the hand, and *helped them up* that were fallen and could not help themselves. Those that were sunk under the burdens of a broken covenant of innocency are *helped up* by the blessings of a renewed covenant of grace. The sending of the Messiah, on whom *help* was *laid* for poor sinners, was the greatest kindness that could be done, the greatest help that could be provided for his people Israel, and that which magnifies it is,

First, That it is *in remembrance of his mercy,* the mercifulness of his nature, the mercy he has in store for *his servant Israel.* While this blessing was deferred, his people, who waited for it, were often ready to ask, *Has God forgotten to be gracious?* But now he made it appear that he had not forgotten, but *remembered, his mercy.* He remembered his former mercy, and repeated that to them in *spiritual* blessings which he had done formerly to them in *temporal* favours. *He remembered the days of old. Where is he that brought them up out of the sea,* out of Egypt? Isa. lxiii. 11. He will do the like again, which that was a type of.

Secondly, That it is *in performance of his promise.* It is a mercy not only designed, but declared (*v.* 55); it was *what he spoke to our fathers,* that the Seed of the woman should break the head of the serpent; that God should dwell in the tents of Shem; and particularly to Abraham, that *in his seed all the families of the earth shall be blessed,* with the best of blessings, with the blessings that are *for ever,* and to the seed that shall be for ever; that is, his *spiritual* seed, for his carnal seed were *cut off* a little after this. Note, What God hath spoken he will perform; what he hath spoken to the fathers will be performed to their seed; to their seed's seed, in blessings that shall last for ever.

Lastly, Mary's return to Nazareth (*v.* 56), after she had continued with Elisabeth about *three months,* so long as to be fully satisfied concerning herself that she was *with child,* and to be confirmed therein by her cousin Elisabeth. Some think, though her return is here mentioned before Elisabeth's being delivered, because the evangelist would finish this passage concerning Mary before he proceeded with the story of Elisabeth, yet that Mary staid till her cousin was (as we say) *down and up again;* that she might attend on her, and be with her in her lying-in, and have her own faith confirmed by the full accomplishment of the promise of God concerning Elisabeth. But most bind themselves to the order of the story as it lies, and think she returned again when Elisabeth was near her time; because she still affected retirement, and therefore would not be there when the birth of this child of promise would draw a great deal of company to the house. Those in whose hearts Christ is formed take more delight than they used to do in *sitting alone* and *keeping silence.*

57 Now Elisabeth's full time came
that she should be delivered; and she
brought forth a son. 58 And her
neighbours and her cousins heard how
the Lord had showed great mercy
upon her; and they rejoiced with her.
59 And it came to pass, that on the
eighth day they came to circumcise
the child; and they called him Zacharias, after the name of his father. 60
And his mother answered and said,
Not *so;* but he shall be called John.
61 And they said unto her, There is
none of thy kindred that is called by
this name. 62 And they made signs
to his father, how he would have him
called. 63 And he asked for a writing
table, and wrote, saying, His name is
John. And they marvelled all. 64
And his mouth was opened immediately, and his tongue *loosed,* and he
spake and praised God. 65 And fear
came on all that dwelt round about
them: and all these sayings were
noised abroad throughout all the hill
country of Judæa. 66 And all they
that heard *them* laid *them* up in their
hearts, saying, What manner of child
shall this be! and the hand of the
Lord was with him.

In these verses, we have,

I. The birth of John Baptist, *v.* 57. Though he was conceived in the womb by miracle, he continued in the womb according to the ordinary course of nature (so did our Saviour): *Elisabeth's full time came, that she should be delivered,* and then *she brought forth a son.* Promised mercies are to be expected when the *full time* for them is come, and not before.

II. The great joy that was among all the relations of the family, upon this extraordinary occasion (*v.* 58): *Her neighbours and her cousins heard of it;* for it would be in every body's mouth, as next to miraculous. Dr. Lightfoot observes that Hebron was inhabited by priests of the family of Aaron, and that those were the cousins here spoken of; but the fields and villages about, by the children of Judah, and that those were the *neighbours.* Now these here discovered, 1. A *pious* regard to God. They acknowledged that *the Lord had magnified his mercy to her,* so the word is. It was a mercy to have her reproach taken away, a mercy to have her family built up, and the more being a family of *priests,* devoted to God, and employed for him. Many things concurred to make the mercy *great*—that she had been long barren, was now old, but especially that the child should be *great in the sight of the Lord.* 2. A *friendly* regard to Elisabeth. When she rejoiced, they *rejoiced with her.* We ought to take *pleasure* in the prosperity of our neighbours and friends, and to be thankful to God for *their* comforts as for our own.

III. The dispute that was among them concerning the naming him (*v.* 59): *On the eighth day,* as God had appointed, they *came together,* to *circumcise the child;* it was here, in Hebron, that *circumcision* was first instituted; and Isaac, who, like John Baptist, was born *by promise,* was one of the first that was submitted to it, at least the chief eyed in the institution of it. They that rejoiced in the birth of the child came together to the circumcising of him. Note, The greatest comfort we can take in our children is in *giving them up to God,* and recognizing their covenant-relation to him. The baptism of our children should be more our joy than their birth.

Now it was the custom, when they circumcised their children, to *name them,* because, when *Abram* was circumcised God gave him a new name, and called him *Abraham;* and it is not unfit that they should be left *nameless* till they are by name *given up to God.* Now,

1. *Some* proposed that he should be called by his father's name, *Zacharias.* We have not any instance in scripture that the child should bear the father's name; but perhaps it was of late come into use among the Jews, as it is with us, and they intended hereby to do honour to the father, who was not likely to have another child.

2. The *mother* opposed it, and would have him called *John;* having learned, either by inspiration of the Holy Ghost (as is most probable), or by information in writing from her husband, that God appointed this to be his name (*v.* 60): *He shall be called Johanan—Gracious,* because he shall introduce the gospel of Christ, wherein God's grace shines more brightly than ever.

3. The *relations* objected against that (*v.* 61): "*There is none of thy kindred,* none of the relations of thy family, *that is called by that name;* and therefore, if he may not have his father's name, yet let him have the name of some of his kindred, who will take it as a piece of respect to have such a *child of wonders* as this named from them." Note, As those that *have friends* must *show themselves friendly,* so those that have relations must be *obliging* to them in all the usual regards that are paid to *kindred.*

4. They appealed to the *father,* and would try if they could possibly get to know his mind; for it was his office to *name the child, v.* 62. They *made signs* to him, by which it appears that he was *deaf* as well as *dumb;* nay, it should seem, *mindless* of any thing, else one would think they should at first have desired him to write down his child's name, if

he had ever yet communicated any thing by writing since he was *struck*. However, they would carry the matter as far as they could, and therefore gave him to understand what the dispute was which he only could determine; whereupon he made signs to them to give him a *table-book*, such as they then used, and with the pencil he wrote these words, *His name is John*, *v.* 63. Not, "It shall be so," or, "I would have it so," but, "It is so." The matter is determined already; the *angel* had given him that name. Observe, When Zacharias could not *speak*, he *wrote*. When ministers have their mouths stopped, that they cannot preach, yet they may be doing good as long as they have not their hands tied, that they cannot write. Many of the martyrs in prison wrote letters to their friends, which were of great use; blessed Paul himself did so. Zacharias's pitching upon the same name that Elisabeth had chosen was a great surprise to the company: *They marvelled all;* for they knew not that, though by reason of his deafness and dumbness they could not *converse together*, yet they were both guided by *one and the same Spirit:* or perhaps they *marvelled* that he wrote so distinctly and intelligently, which (the stroke he was under being somewhat like that of a palsy) he had not done before.

5. He thereupon recovered the use of his speech (*v.* 64): *His mouth was opened immediately*. The time prefixed for his being silenced was *till the day that these things shall be fulfilled* (*v.* 20); not *all the things* going before concerning John's ministry, but those which relate to his birth and name (*v.* 13). That time was now expired, whereupon the restraint was taken off, and God gave him the *opening of the mouth again,* as he did to Ezekiel, *ch.* iii. 27. Dr. Lightfoot compares this case of Zacharias with that of Moses, Exod. iv. 24—26. Moses, for distrust, is in danger of his life, as Zacharias, for the same fault, is *struck dumb;* but, upon the circumcising of his child, and recovery of his faith, there, as here, the danger is removed. Infidelity closed his mouth, and now believing opens it again; *he believes, therefore he speaks.* David lay under guilt from the conception of his child till a few days after its birth; then *the Lord takes away his sin:* upon his repentance, he shall not die. So here he shall be no longer dumb; *his mouth was opened, and he spoke, and praised God.* Note, When God opens our lips, our mouths must *show forth his praise.* As good be without our speech as not use it in *praising God;* for then our tongue is most *our glory* when it is employed for *God's glory*.

6. These things were told all the country over, to the great amazement of all that heard them, *v.* 65, 66. The sentiments of the people are not to be slighted, but taken notice of. We are here told, (1.) That *these sayings were discoursed of*, and were the common talk all about the *hill-country of Judea.* It is a pity but a narrative of them had been drawn up, and published in the world, immediately. (2.) That most people who heard of these things were put into consternation by them: *Fear came on all them that dwelt round about* there. If we have not a *good hope*, as we ought to have, built upon the gospel, we may expect that the tidings of it will fill us with *fear*. They believed and trembled, whereas they should have believed and triumphed. (3.) It raised the expectations of people concerning this child, and obliged them to have their eye upon him, to see what he would come to. They *laid up these* presages *in their hearts*, treasured them up in mind and memory, as foreseeing they should hereafter have occasion to *recollect* them. Note, What we hear, that may be of use to us, we should *treasure* up, that we may be able to bring forth, for the benefit of others, things new and old, and, when things come to perfection, may be able to look back upon the presages thereof, and to say, "It was what we might expect." They said *within* themselves, and said *among* themselves, "*What manner of child shall this be?* What will be the fruit when these are the buds, or rather when the *root* is out of such a *dry ground?*" Note, When children are born into the world, it is very uncertain what they will prove; yet sometimes there have been early indications of something great, as in the birth of Moses, Samson, Samuel, and here of John. And we have reason to think that there were some of those living at the time when John began his public ministry who could, and did, remember these things, and relate them to others, which contributed as much as any thing to the great flocking there was after him.

Lastly, It is said, *The hand of the Lord was with him;* that is, he was taken under the special protection of the Almighty, from his birth, as one designed for something great and considerable, and there were many instances of it. It appeared likewise that the Spirit was at work upon his soul very early. As soon as he began to speak or go, you might perceive something in him very extraordinary. Note, God has ways of operating upon children in their infancy, which we cannot account for. God never made a soul but he knew how to sanctify it.

67 And his father Zacharias was
filled with the Holy Ghost, and prophesied, saying, 68 Blessed *be* the
Lord God of Israel; for he hath
visited and redeemed his people, 69
And hath raised up an horn of salvation for us in the house of his servant
David; 70 As he spake by the mouth
of his holy prophets, which have been
since the world began: 71 That we
should be saved from our enemies,
and from the hand of all that hate us;

72 To perform the mercy *promised*
to our fathers, and to remember his
holy covenant; 73 The oath which he
sware to our father Abraham, 74 That
he would grant unto us, that we being
delivered out of the hand of our enemies might serve him without fear,
75 In holiness and righteousness before him, all the days of our life. 76
And thou, child, shalt be called the
prophet of the Highest: for thou shalt
go before the face of the Lord to prepare his ways; 77 To give knowledge
of salvation unto his people by the
remission of their sins, 78 Through
the tender mercy of our God; whereby
the dayspring from on high hath visited
us, 79 To give light to them that sit
in darkness and *in* the shadow of
death, to guide our feet into the way
of peace. 80 And the child grew, and
waxed strong in spirit, and was in the
deserts till the day of his showing
unto Israel.

We have here the song wherewith Zacharias *praised God* when his *mouth* was *opened;* in it he is said to *prophesy* (*v.* 67), and so he did in the strictest sense of *prophesying;* for he foretold things to come concerning the kingdom of the Messiah, to which all the prophets bear witness. Observe,

I. How he was qualified for this: *He was filled with the Holy Ghost,* was endued with more than ordinary measures and degrees of it, for this purpose; he was divinely inspired. God not only *forgave* him his unbelief and distrust (which was signified by discharging him from the punishment of it), but, as a *specimen* of the *abounding* of grace towards believers, he *filled him* with the *Holy Ghost,* and put this honour upon him, to employ him for his honour.

II. What the matter of his song was. Here is nothing said of the private concerns of his own family, the rolling away of the reproach from it and putting of a reputation upon it, by the birth of this child, though, no doubt, he found a time to give thanks to God for this, with his family; but in this song he is wholly taken up with the kingdom of the Messiah, and the public blessings to be introduced by it. He could have little pleasure in this *fruitfulness* of his *vine,* and the *hopefulness* of his *olive-plant,* if herein he had not foreseen the *good of Jerusalem, peace upon Israel,* and *blessings* on both *out of Zion,* Ps. cxxviii. 3, 5, 6. The Old-Testament prophecies are often expressed in *praises* and *new songs,* so is this beginning of New-Testament prophecy: *Blessed be the Lord God of Israel.* The *God of the whole earth shall he be called;* yet Zacharias, speaking of the work of redemption, called him the *Lord God of Israel,* because to Israel the prophecies, promises, and types, of the redemption had hitherto been given, and to them the first proffers and proposals of it were now to be made. Israel, as a chosen people, was a type of the *elect of God* out of all nations, whom God had a particular eye to, in sending the Saviour; and therefore he is therein called the *Lord God of Israel.*

Now Zacharias here blesses God,

1. For the work of *salvation* that was to be wrought out by the Messiah himself, *v.* 68—75. This it is that *fills him,* when he is *filled with the Holy Ghost,* and it is that which all who have the *Spirit of Christ* are *full of.*

(1.) In sending the Messiah, God has *made a gracious visit* to his people, whom for many ages he had seemed to neglect, and to be estranged from; he hath *visited them* as a friend, to take cognizance of their case. God is said to have *visited* his people in bondage when he *delivered* them (Exod. iii. 16; iv. 31), to have *visited* his people in famine when he *gave them bread,* Ruth i. 6. He had often sent to them by his prophets, and had still kept up a correspondence with them; but now he himself made them a *visit.*

(2.) He has *wrought out redemption* for them: *He has redeemed his people.* This was the errand on which Christ *came into the world,* to redeem those that were sold *for* sin, and sold *under* sin; even God's own people, his Israel, his son, his *first-born,* his *free-born,* need to be *redeemed,* and are undone if they be not. Christ redeems them by *price* out of the hands of God's justice, and redeems them by *power* out of the hands of Satan's tyranny, as Israel out of Egypt.

(3.) He has fulfilled the *covenant of royalty* made with the most famous *Old-Testament prince,* that is, David. Glorious things had been said of his family, that on him, as a *mighty one, help* should be *laid,* that *his horn should be exalted,* and his *seed* perpetuated, Ps. lxxxix. 19, 20, 24, 29. But that family had been long in a manner *cast off* and *abhorred,* Ps. lxxxix. 38. Now here it is gloried in, that, according to the promise, the *horn* of David should again be *made to bud;* for, Ps. cxxxii. 17, he *hath raised up a horn of salvation for us in the house of his servant David* (*v.* 69), there, where it was promised and expected to arise. David is called God's *servant,* not only as a good man, but as a king that *ruled for God;* and he was an instrument of the *salvation* of Israel, by being employed in the *government* of Israel; so Christ is the *author of eternal redemption to those* only *that obey him.* There is in Christ, and in him only, *salvation for us,* and it is a *horn of salvation;* for, [1.] It is an *honourable* salvation. It is *raised up* above all other salvations, none of which are to be compared with it: in it the glory both of the Redeemer and of the redeemed are advanced, and their *horn exalted with honour*. [2.] It is a *plentiful salvation*. It is a *cornucopia—a horn of plenty*, a *salvation* in which we are blessed with *spiritual* blessings, in *heavenly things*, abundantly. [3.] It is a *powerful salvation:* the strength of the beast is in his *horn*. He has raised up such a salvation as shall *pull down* our spiritual enemies, and *protect* us from them. In the *chariots* of this *salvation* the Redeemer shall go forth, and go on, *conquering and to conquer*.

(4.) He has fulfilled all the precious promises made to the church by the most famous *Old-Testament prophets* (*v.* 70): *As he spoke by the mouth of his holy prophets*. His doctrine of salvation by the Messiah is confirmed by an appeal to the prophets, and the greatness and importance of that salvation thereby evidenced and magnified; it is the same that they spoke of, which therefore ought to be expected and welcomed; it is what they *enquired and searched diligently after* (1 Pet. i. 10, 11), which therefore ought not to be slighted or thought meanly of. God is now *doing* that which he has long ago *spoken of;* and therefore *be silent, O all flesh, before him*, and attend to him. See, [1.] How *sacred* the prophecies of this salvation were. The prophets who delivered them were *holy prophets*, who durst not deceive and who aimed at promoting holiness among men; and it was the *holy God* himself that *spoke by* them. [2.] How *ancient* they were: ever *since the world began*. God having promised, when the world began, that the *Seed of the woman should break the serpent's head*, that promise was echoed to when Adam called his wife's name *Eve—Life*, for the sake of that Seed of hers; when Eve called her first son *Cain*, saying, *I have gotten a man from the Lord*, and another son, Seth, *settled;* when Noah was called *rest*, and foretold that God should dwell in the tents of Shem. And it was not long after the new world began in Noah that the promise was made to Abraham that in his Seed the *nations of the earth* should be *blessed*. [3.] What a wonderful *harmony* and *concert* we perceive among them. God spoke the same thing by them all, and therefore it is said to be διὰ στόματος, not by the *mouths*, but by the *mouth*, of the prophets, for they all speak of Christ as it were with *one mouth*.

Now what is this *salvation* which was prophesied of?

First, It is a *rescue* from the malice of *our enemies;* it is σωτηρίαν ἐξ ἐχθρῶν ἡμῶν—*a salvation out of our enemies*, from among them, and *out of the power of them that hate us* (*v.* 71); it is a salvation from sin, and the dominion of Satan over us, both by corruptions within and temptations without. The carnal Jews expected to be delivered from under the Roman yoke, but intimation was betimes given that it should be a redemption of another nature. He shall *save his people from their sins*, that they may not have dominion over them, Matt. i. 21.

Secondly, It is a *restoration* to the *favour of God;* it is to *perform the mercy promised to our forefathers*, *v.* 72. The Redeemer shall not only break the head of the serpent that was the author of our ruin, but he shall *reinstate* us in the *mercy of God* and *re-establish* us in *his covenant;* he shall bring us as it were into a paradise again, which was signified by the *promises* made to the patriarchs, and the *holy covenant* made with them, *the oath which he sware to our father Abraham*, *v.* 73. Observe, 1. That which was promised to the fathers, and is performed to us, is *mercy*, pure mercy; nothing in it is owing to our *merit* (we deserve wrath and the curse), but all to the *mercy* of God, which *designed* us grace and life: *ex mero motu—of his own good pleasure*, he loved us because he would love us. 2. God herein had an eye to *his covenant*, his *holy* covenant, that covenant with Abraham: I *will be a God to thee and thy seed*. This his seed had *really forfeited* by their transgressions; this he *seemed to have forgotten* in the calamities brought upon them; but he will now *remember* it, will make it appear that he remembers it, for upon that are grounded all his returns of mercy: Lev. xxvi. 42, *Then will I remember my covenant*.

Thirdly, It is a qualification for, and an encouragement to, the service of God. Thus was *the oath he sware to our Father Abraham*, That he would *give us* power and grace to *serve him*, in an acceptable manner to him and a comfortable manner to ourselves, *v.* 74, 75. Here seems to be an allusion to the deliverance of Israel out of Egypt, which, God tells Moses, was in pursuance of the covenant he made with Abraham (Exod. iii. 6—8), and that this was the design of his bringing them out of Egypt, *that they might serve God upon this mountain*, Exod. iii. 12. Note, The great design of gospel grace is not to discharge us from, but to engage us to, and encourage us in, the service of God. Under this notion Christianity was always to be looked upon, as intended to make us truly religious, to admit us into the service of God, to bind us to it, and to quicken us in it. We are *therefore* delivered from the iron yoke of sin, that our necks may be put under the sweet and easy yoke of the Lord Jesus. *The very bonds which he has loosed do bind us faster unto him*, Ps. cxvi. 16. We are hereby enabled, 1. To serve God *without fear—ἀφόβως*. We are *therefore* put into a state of *holy safety* that we might serve God with a *holy security* and *serenity of mind*, as those that are *quiet from the fears of evil*. God must be served with a *filial fear*, a reverent obedient fear, an awakening quickening fear, but not with a *slavish fear*, like that of the slothful servant, who represented him to himself as a *hard master*, and unreasonable; not with that fear that has *torment* and *amazement* in it; not with the fear of a legal spirit, a *spirit of bond-*

age, but with the boldness of an evangelical spirit, a *spirit of adoption*. 2. To serve him in *holiness and righteousness*, which includes the whole duty of man towards God and our neighbour. It is both the intention and the direct tendency of the gospel to renew upon us that image of God in which man was at first made, which consisted *in righteousness and true holiness*, Eph. iv. 24. Christ redeemed us *that we might serve God*, not in the legal services of sacrifice and offerings, but in the *spiritual services of holiness and righteousness*, Ps. l. 14. 3. To serve him, *before him*, in the duties of his *immediate* worship, wherein we present ourselves *before the Lord*, to serve him as those that have an eye always upon him, and see his eye always upon us, upon our inward man, that is serving him *before him*. 4. To serve him *all the days of our life*. The design of the gospel is to engage us to constancy and perseverance in the service of God, by showing us how much depends upon our not drawing back, and by showing us how Christ *loved us to the end*, and thereby engaged us to *love him to the end*.

2. He *blessed God* for the work of *preparation* for this salvation, which was to be done by John Baptist (*v.* 76): *Thou child*, though now but a child of eight days' old, shalt be called *the prophet of the Highest*. Jesus Christ is *the Highest*, for he is *God over all, blessed for evermore* (Rom. ix. 5), equal with the Father. John Baptist was *his prophet*, as Aaron was Moses's prophet (Exod. vii. 1); what he said was as his mouth, what he did was as his harbinger. Prophecy had now long ceased, but in John it *revived*, as it had done in Samuel, who was born of an aged mother, as John was, after a long cessation. John's business was,

(1.) To prepare people for the salvation, by preaching repentance and reformation as great gospel duties: *Thou shalt go before the face of the Lord*, and but a little before him, to *prepare his ways*, to call people to make room for him, and get ready for his entertainment. Let every thing that may obstruct his progress, or embarrass it, or hinder people from coming to him, be taken away: see Isa. xl. 3, 4. Let *valleys* be *filled*, and *hills* be brought *low*.

(2.) To give people a general idea of the salvation, that they might know, not only what to do, but what to expect; for the doctrine he preached was that the *kingdom of heaven* is at hand. There are two things in which you must know that this salvation consists:—

[1.] The *forgiveness* of what we have *done amiss*. It is salvation *by the remission of sins*, those sins which stand in the way of the salvation, and by which we are all become liable to ruin and condemnation, *v.* 77. John Baptist gave people to understand that, though their case was sad, by reason of sin, it was not desperate, for pardon might be obtained *through the tender mercy of our God* (the *bowels of mercy*, so the word is): there was nothing in us but a *piteous case* to recommend us to the divine compassion.

[2.] *Direction* to *do better* for the time to come. The gospel salvation not only encourages us to hope that the works of darkness shall be forgiven us, but sets up a clear and true light, by which we may order our steps aright. In it *the day-spring hath visited us from on high* (*v.* 78); and this also is owing to the *tender mercy of our God*. Christ is ἀνατολὴ—*the morning Light*, the *rising Sun*, Mal. iv. 2. The gospel brings *light* with it (John iii. 19), leaves us not to wander in the darkness of Pagan ignorance, or in the moon-light of the Old-Testament types or figures, but in it the day dawns; in John Baptist it began to break, but increased apace, and *shone more and more to the perfect day*. We have as much reason to welcome the gospel day who enjoy it as those have to welcome the morning who had long waited for it. *First*, The gospel is *discovering*; it shows us that which before we were utterly in the dark about (*v.* 79); it is to *give light to them that sit in darkness*, the *light of the knowledge of the glory of God in the face of Jesus Christ*; the day-spring *visited* this dark world to *lighten the Gentiles*, Acts xxvi. 18. *Secondly*, It is *reviving*; it brings light to them that sit *in the shadow of death*, as condemned prisoners in the dungeon, to bring them the tidings of a *pardon*, at least of a *reprieve* and opportunity of procuring a pardon; it proclaims the *opening of the prison* (Isa. lxi. 1), brings the *light of life*. How pleasant is that light! *Thirdly*, It is *directing*; it is to *guide our feet in the way of peace*, into that way which will bring us to peace at last. It is not only a light *to our eyes*, but a light *to our feet* (Ps. cxix. 105); it guides us into the way of making our peace with God, of keeping up a comfortable communion; that *way of peace* which as sinners we have wandered from and *have not known* (Rom. iii. 17), nor could ever have known of ourselves.

In the last verse, we have a short account of the younger years of John Baptist. Though he was the son of a priest, he did not, like Samuel, go up, when he was a child, to minister before the Lord; for he was to prepare the way for a better priesthood. But we are here told,

1. Of his *eminence* as to the *inward man*: The *child grew* in the capacities of his mind, much more than other children; so that he *waxed strong in spirit*, had a strong judgment and strong resolution. Reason and conscience (both which are the candle of the Lord) were so strong in him that he had the inferior faculties of appetite and passion in complete subjection betimes. By this it appeared that he was betimes *filled with the Holy Ghost*; for those that are strong in the Lord are *strong in spirit*.

2. Of his *obscurity* as to the *outward man*: *He was in the deserts*; not that he lived a

hermit, cut off from the society of men. No, we have reason to think that he went up to Jerusalem at the *feasts*, and frequented the synagogues on the sabbath day, but his constant residence was in some of those scattered houses that were in the wilderness of Zuph or Maon, which we read of in the story of David. There he spent most of his time, in contemplation and devotion, and had not his education in the schools, or at the feet of the rabbin. Note, Many a one is qualified for great usefulness, who yet is buried alive; and many are long so buried who are designed, and are thereby in the fitting, for so much greater usefulness at last; as John Baptist, who was *in the desert* only *till the day of his showing to Israel,* when he was in the thirtieth year of his age. Note, There is a time fixed for the *showing* of those favours to Israel which are reserved; *the vision* of them *is for an appointed time, and at the end it shall speak, and shall not lie.*

CHAP. II.

In this chapter, we have an account of the birth and infancy of our Lord Jesus: having had notice of his conception, and of the birth and infancy of his forerunner, in the former chapter. The First-begotten is here brought into the world; let us go meet him with our hosannas, blessed is he that cometh. Here is, I. The place and other circumstances of his birth, which proved him to be the true Messiah, and such a one as we needed, but not such a one as the Jews expected, ver. 1—7. II. The notifying of his birth to the shepherds in that neighbourhood by an angel, the song of praise which the angels sung upon that occasion, and the spreading of the report of it by the shepherds, ver. 8—20. III. The circumcision of Christ, and the naming of him, ver. 21. IV. The presenting of him in the temple, ver. 22—24. V. The testimonies of Simeon, and Anna the prophetess, concerning him, ver. 25—39. VI. Christ's growth and capacity, ver. 40—52. VIII. His observing the passover at twelve years old, and his disputing with the doctors in the temple, ver. 41—51. And this, with what we have met with (Matt. i. and ii.), is all we have concerning our Lord Jesus, till he entered upon his public work in the thirtieth year of his age.

AND it came to pass in those days,
that there went out a decree from
Cæsar Augustus, that all the world
should be taxed. 2 (*And* this taxing
was first made when Cyrenius was
governor of Syria.) 3 And all went
to be taxed, every one into his own
city. 4 And Joseph also went up
from Galilee, out of the city of Nazareth, into Judæa, unto the city of David, which is called Bethlehem (because
he was of the house and lineage of
David): 5 To be taxed with Mary
his espoused wife, being great with
child. 6 And so it was, that, while
they were there, the days were accomplished that she should be delivered.
7 And she brought forth her first-born
son, and wrapped him in swaddling clothes, and laid him in a manger; because there was no room for them in the inn.

The *fulness of time* was now come, when God would send forth his Son, *made of a woman,* and *made under the law;* and it was foretold that he should be born at Bethlehem. Now here we have an account of the time, place, and manner of it.

I. The time when our Lord Jesus was born. Several things may be gathered out of these verses which intimate to us that it was the *proper time.*

1. He was born at the time when the *fourth monarchy* was in its height, just when it was become, more than any of the three before it, a *universal monarchy.* He was born *in the days* of Augustus Cæsar, when the Roman empire extended itself further than ever before or since, including Parthia one way, and Britain another way; so that it was then called *Terrarum orbis imperium—The empire of the whole earth;* and here that empire is called *all the world* (*v.* 1), for there was scarcely any part of the civilized world, but what was dependent on it. Now this was the time when the Messiah was to be born, according to Daniel's prophecy (Dan. ii. 44): *In the days of these kings,* the kings of the fourth monarchy, *shall the God of heaven set up a kingdom which shall never be destroyed.*

2. He was born when Judea was become a province of the empire, and tributary to it; as appears evidently by this, that when all the Roman empire was taxed, the Jews were taxed among the rest. Jerusalem was taken by Pompey the Roman general, about sixty years before this, who granted the government of the church to Hyrcanus, but not the government of the state; by degrees it was more and more reduced, till now at length it was quite subdued; for Judea was ruled by Cyrenius the Roman governor of Syria (*v.* 2): the Roman writers call him *Sulpitius Quirinus.* Now just at this juncture, the Messiah was to be born, for so was dying Jacob's prophecy, that Shiloh should come when the *sceptre was departed from Judah,* and the *lawgiver from between his feet,* Gen. xlix. 10. This was the *first taxing* that was made in Judea, the first badge of their servitude; therefore now Shiloh must come, to set up his kingdom.

3. There is another circumstance, as to the time, implied in this general enrolment of all the subjects of the empire, which is, that there was now universal peace in the empire. The temple of Janus was now shut, which it never used to be if any wars were on foot; and now it was fit for the Prince of peace to be born, in whose days *swords should be beaten into plough-shares.*

II. The place where our Lord Jesus was born is very observable. He was born at *Bethlehem;* so it was foretold (Mic. v. 2), the scribes so understood it (Matt. ii. 5, 6), so did the common people, John vii. 42. The name of the place was significant. Bethlehem signifies *the house of bread;* a proper place for him to be born in who is the Bread of life, the Bread that *came down from heaven.* But that was not all; Bethlehem was the city of David, where he was born, and therefore there *he* must be born who was the *Son of David.* Zion was also called *the city of David* (2 Sam. v. 7), yet Christ was not born there; for Bethlehem was that city of David where he was born in meanness, to be a *shepherd;* and this our Saviour, when he humbled himself, chose for the place of his birth; not Zion, where he ruled in power and prosperity, that was to be a type of the church of Christ, *that mount Zion.* Now when the virgin Mary was with child, and near her time, Providence so ordered it that, by order from the emperor, all the subjects of the *Roman empire* were to be *taxed;* that is, they were to *give in their names* to the proper officers, and they were to be *registered* and *enrolled,* according to their families, which is the proper signification of the word here used; their being *taxed* was but secondary. It is supposed that they made profession of subjection to the Roman empire, either by some set form of words, or at least by payment of some small tribute, a penny suppose, in token of their allegiance, like a man's *atturning* tenant Thus are they vassals upon record, and may thank themselves.

According to this *decree,* the Jews (who were now nice in distinguishing their tribes and families) provided that in their enrolments particular care should be had to preserve the memory of them. Thus foolishly are they solicitous to save the *shadow,* when they had lost the *substance.*

That which Augustus designed was either to gratify his *pride* in knowing the numbers of his people, and proclaiming it to the world, or he did it in *policy,* to strengthen his interest, and make his government appear the more formidable; but Providence had another reach in it. All the world shall be at the trouble of being *enrolled,* only that Joseph and Mary may. This brought them up from Nazareth in Galilee to Bethlehem in Judea, because they were *of the stock and lineage of David* (*v.* 4, 5); and perhaps, being poor and low, they thought the royalty of their extraction rather a burden and expense to them than a matter of pride. Because it is difficult to suppose that every Jew (women as well as men) was obliged to repair to the city of which their ancestors were, and there be enrolled, now, at a time when they kept not to the bounds of their tribes, as formerly, it may be offered as a conjecture that this great exactness was used only with the *family of David,* concerning which, it is probable, the emperor gave particular orders, it having been the royal family, and still talked of as designed to be so, that he might know its number and strength. Divers ends of Providence were served by this.

1. Hereby the virgin Mary was brought, *great with child,* to Bethlehem, to be *delivered* there, according to the prediction; whereas she had designed to lie in at Nazareth. See how *man purposes and God disposes;* and how Providence orders all things for the fulfilling of the scripture, and makes use of the projects men have for serving their own purposes, quite beyond their intention, to serve his.

2. Hereby it appeared that Jesus Christ was of the *seed* of David; for what brings his mother to Bethlehem now, but because she *was of the stock and lineage of David?* This was a material thing to be proved, and required such an authentic proof as this. Justin Martyr and Tertullian, two of the earliest advocates for the Christian religion, appeal to these *rolls* or *records* of the *Roman empire,* for the proof of Christ's being born of the house of David.

3. Hereby it appeared that he was *made under the law;* for he became a subject of the Roman empire as soon as he was born, a *servant of rulers,* Isa. xlix. 7. Many suppose that, being born during the time of the taxing, he was enrolled as well as his father and mother, that it might appear how *he made himself of no reputation,* and *took upon him the form of a servant.* Instead of having kings tributaries to him, when he came into the world he was himself a tributary.

III. The circumstances of his birth, which were very mean, and under all possible marks of contempt. He was indeed a *first-born son;* but it was poor honour to be the first-born of such a poor woman as Mary was, who had no inheritance to which he might be entitled as first-born, but what was *in nativity.*

1. He was under some abasements in common with other children; he was *wrapped in swaddling clothes,* as other children are when they are new-born, as if he could be bound, or needed to be kept straight. He that makes darkness a *swaddling band for the sea* was himself wrapped in *swaddling bands,* Job xxxviii. 9. The everlasting Father became a child of time, and men said of him whose out-goings were of old from everlasting, *We know this man, whence he is,* John vii. 27. The Ancient of days became an infant of a span long.

2. He was under some abasements peculiar to himself.

(1.) He was born *at an inn.* That son of David that was the glory of his father's house had no inheritance that he could command, no not in the city of David, no nor a friend that would accommodate his mother in distress with lodgings to be brought to bed in. Christ was born *in an inn,* to intimate that he came into the world but to sojourn here for awhile, as in an inn, and to teach us to do likewise. An inn receives all comers, and so does Christ. He hangs out the banner of love for his sign, and whoever comes to him, he will in no wise cast out; only, unlike other inns, he welcomes those that come *without money and without price.* All is on free cost.

(2.) He was born *in a stable;* so some think the word signifies which we translate *a manger,* a place for cattle to stand to be fed in. Because there was *no room in the inn,* and for want of conveniences nay for want of necessaries, he was laid *in the manger,* instead of a cradle. The word which we render *swaddling clothes* some derive from a word that signifies to *rend,* or *tear,* and thence infer that he was so far from having a good suit of child-bed linen, that his very swaddles were ragged and torn. His being born in a stable and laid in a manger was an instance, [1.] Of the poverty of his parents. Had they been rich, room would have been made for them; but, being poor, they must *shift* as they *could.* [2.] Of the corruption and degeneracy of manners in that age; that a woman in reputation for virtue and honour should be used so barbarously. If there had been any common humanity among them, they would not have turned a woman in travail into a stable. [3.] It was an instance of the humiliation of our Lord Jesus. We were become by sin like an out-cast infant, helpless and forlorn; and such a one Christ was. Thus he would answer the type of Moses, the great prophet and lawgiver of the Old Testament, who was in his infancy cast out in an ark of bulrushes, as Christ *in a manger.* Christ would hereby put a contempt upon all worldly glory, and teach us to slight it. Since *his own received him not,* let us not think it strange if they *receive us not.*

8 And there were in the same
country shepherds abiding in the
field, keeping watch over their flock
by night. 9 And, lo, the angel of
the Lord came upon them, and the
glory of the Lord shone round about
them: and they were sore afraid. 10
And the angel said unto them, Fear
not: for, behold, I bring you good
tidings of great joy, which shall be to
all people. 11 For unto you is born
this day in the city of David a Saviour,
which is Christ the Lord. 12 And
this *shall be* a sign unto you; Ye shall
find the babe wrapped in swaddling
clothes, lying in a manger. 13 And
suddenly there was with the angel a
multitude of the heavenly host praising
God, and saying, 14 Glory to God
in the highest, and on earth peace,
good will toward men. 15 And it
came to pass, as the angels were gone
away from them into heaven, the
shepherds said one to another, Let
us now go even unto Bethlehem, and
see this thing which is come to pass,
which the Lord hath made known
unto us. 16 And they came with
haste, and found Mary, and Joseph,
and the babe lying in a manger. 17
And when they had seen *it,* they
made known abroad the saying which
was told them concerning the child.
18 And all they that heard *it* wondered
at those things which were told
them by the shepherds. 19 But
Mary kept all these things, and pondered
them in her heart. 20 And
the shepherds returned, glorifying and
praising God for all the things that
they had heard and seen, as it was
told unto them.

The meanest circumstances of Christ's humiliation were all along attended with some discoveries of his glory, to balance them, and take off the offence of them; for even when he humbled himself God did in some measure exalt him and give him earnests of his future exaltation. When we saw him *wrapped in swaddling clothes* and *laid in a manger,* we were tempted to say, "Surely this cannot be the *Son of God.*" But see his birth attended, as it is here, with a choir of angels, and we shall say, "Surely it can be no other than the *Son of God,* concerning whom it was said, when he was *brought into the world, Let all the angels of God worship him,*" Heb. i. 6.

We had in Matthew an account of the notice given of the arrival of this ambassador, this prince from heaven, to the wise men, who were Gentiles, by a star; here we are told of the notice given of it to the shepherds, who were Jews, by an angel: to each God chose to speak in the language they were most conversant with.

I. See here how the shepherds were employed; they were *abiding in the fields* adjoining to Bethlehem, and *keeping watch over their flocks by night, v.* 8 The angel was not sent to the chief priests or the elders (they were not prepared to receive these tidings), but to a company of poor shepherds, who were like Jacob, *plain men dwelling in tents,* not like Esau, *cunning hunters.* The patriarchs were shepherds. Moses and David particularly were called from keeping sheep to rule God's people; and by this instance God would show that he had still a favour for those of that innocent employment. Tidings were brought to Moses of the deliverance of Israel out of Egypt, when he was keeping sheep, and to these shepherds, who, it is probable, were devout pious men, the tidings were brought of a *greater salvation.* Observe, 1. They were not *sleeping* in their beds, when this news was brought them (though many had very acceptable intelligence from heaven in *slumbering upon the bed),* but *abiding in the fields,* and *watching.* Those that would hear from God must *stir up themselves.* They were broad awake, and therefore could not be deceived in what they saw and heard, so as those may be who are half asleep. 2. They were employed now, not in acts of devotion, but in the business of their calling; they were *keeping watch over their flock,* to secure them from thieves and beasts of prey, it being probably in the summer time, when they kept their cattle out all night, as we do now, and did not house them. Note, We are not out of the way of divine visits when we are sensibly employed in an honest calling, and abide with God in it.

II. How they were surprised with the appearance of an angel (*v.* 9): *Behold, an angel of the Lord came upon them,* of a sudden, ἐπέστη—*stood over them;* most probably, in the air over their heads, as coming immediately from heaven. We read it, *the angel,* as if it were the same that appeared once and again in the chapter before, *the angel Gabriel,* that was caused to fly swiftly; but that is not certain. The angel's *coming upon them* intimates that they little thought of such a thing, or expected it; for it is in a *preventing* way that gracious visits are made us from heaven, *or ever we are aware.* That they might be sure it was an angel from heaven, they saw and heard the *glory of the Lord round about them;* such as made the night as bright as day, such a glory as used to attend God's appearance, a *heavenly* glory, or an *exceedingly great glory,* such as they could not bear the dazzling lustre of. This made them *sore afraid,* put them into a great consternation, as fearing some evil tidings. While we are conscious to ourselves of so much guilt, we have reason to fear lest every express from heaven should be a messenger of wrath.

III. What the message was which the angel had to deliver to the shepherds, *v.* 10—12. 1. He gives a *supersedeas* to their *fears* "*Fear not,* for we have nothing to say to you that needs be a terror to you; you *need not* fear your enemies, and *should not* fear your friends." 2. He furnishes them with abundant matter for joy: "Behold, I *evangelize to you great joy;* I solemnly declare it, and you have reason to bid it welcome, for it shall bring *joy to all people,* and not to the people of the Jews only; that *unto you is born this day,* at this time, *a Saviour,* the Saviour that has been so long expected, *which is Christ the Lord, in the city of David,*" *v.* 11. Jesus is the Christ, the Messiah, the Anointed; he is *the Lord,* Lord of all; he is a sovereign prince; nay, he is God, for *the Lord,* in the Old Testament, answers to *Jehovah.* He is a Saviour, and he will be a Saviour to those only that accept of him for their Lord. "The Saviour *is born,* he is born *this day;* and, since it is matter of *great joy to all people,* it is not to be kept secret, you may proclaim it, may tell it to whom you please. He is born in the place where it was foretold he should be born, in the *city of David;* and he is born *to you;* to you Jews he is sent in the first place, to *bless you,* to you *shepherds,* though poor and mean in the world." This refers to Isa. ix. 6, *Unto us a child is born, unto us a son is given.* To *you* men, not to *us* angels; he took not on him the nature of angels. This is matter of *joy* indeed to all people, great joy. Long-looked for is come at last. Let heaven and earth rejoice before this Lord, *for he cometh.* 3. He gives them a sign for the confirming of their faith in this matter. "How shall we find out this child in Bethlehem, which is now full of the descendants from David?" "You will find him by this token: he is lying in a *manger,* where surely never any new-born infant was laid before." They expected to be told, "You shall find him, though a babe, dressed up in robes, and lying in the best house in the town, lying in state, with a numerous train of attendants in rich liveries." "No, you will find him wrapped in *swaddling clothes,* and *laid in a manger.* When Christ was here upon earth, he *distinguished* himself, and made himself remarkable, by nothing so much as the instances of his *humiliation.*

IV. The angels' *doxology* to God, and *congratulations* of men, upon this solemn occasion, *v.* 13, 14. The message was no sooner delivered by one angel (that was sufficient to go express) than suddenly there was with that angel *a multitude of the heavenly hosts;* sufficient, we may be sure, to make a *chorus,* that were heard by the shepherds, *praising God;* and certainly their song was not like that (Rev. xiv. 3) which *no man could learn,* for it was designed that we should all learn it. 1. Let God have the honour of this work: *Glory to God in the highest.* God's good-will to men, manifested in sending the Messiah, redounds very much to his praise; and angels in the highest heavens, though not immediately interested in it themselves, will celebrate it to his honour, Rev. v. 11, 12. *Glory to God,* whose kindness and love designed this favour, and whose wisdom contrived it in such a way as that one divine attribute should not be glorified at the expense of another, but the honour of all effectually secured and advanced. Other works of God are for his glory, but the redemption of the world is for his *glory in the highest.* 2. Let men have the joy of it: *On earth peace, good-will toward men.* God's *good-will* in sending the Messiah introduced peace in this lower world, slew the enmity that sin had raised between God and man, and resettled a peaceable correspondence. If God be at peace with us, all peace results from it: peace of conscience, peace with angels, peace between Jew and Gentile. Peace is here put for *all good,* all that good which flows to us from the incarnation of Christ. All the *good* we have, or hope, is owing to God's *good-will;* and, if we have the comfort of it, he must have the glory of it. Nor must any *peace,* any *good,* be expected in a way inconsistent with the glory of God; therefore not in any way of sin, nor in any way but by *a Mediator.* Here was the *peace proclaimed* with great solemnity; whoever will, let them come and take the benefit of it. It is on earth peace, to *men of good-will* (so some copies read it), ἐν ἀνθρώποις εὐδοκίας; to men who have a *good-will to God*, and are willing to be reconciled; or to men whom God has a *good-will to*, though vessels of his mercy. See how well affected the angels are to man, and to his welfare and happiness; how well pleased they were in the incarnation of the Son of God, though he passed by their nature; and ought not we much more to be affected with it? This is a *faithful saying*, attested by an innumerable company of angels, and well *worthy of all acceptation, That the good-will of God toward men is glory to God in the highest, and peace on the earth.*

V. The visit which the shepherds made to the new-born Saviour. 1. They consulted about it, *v.* 15. While the angels were singing their hymn, they could attend to that only; but, *when they were gone away from them into heaven* (for angels, when they appeared, never made any long stay, but returned as soon as they had despatched their business), *the shepherds said one to another, Let us go to Bethlehem.* Note, When extraordinary messages from the upper world are no more to be expected, we must set ourselves to improve the advantages we have for the confirming of our faith, and the keeping up of our communion with God in this lower world. And it is no reflection upon the testimony of angels, no nor upon a divine testimony itself, to get it corroborated by observation and experience. But observe, These shepherds do not speak doubtfully, "Let us go see whether it be so or no;" but with assurance, *Let us go see this thing which is come to pass;* for what room was left to doubt of it, when *the Lord had* thus *made it known to them?* The *word spoken by angels was stedfast* and unquestionably true. 2. They immediately made the visit, *v.* 16. They lost no time, but *came with haste* to the place, which, probably, the angel directed them to more particularly than is recorded ("Go to the stable of such an inn"); and there *they found Mary and Joseph,* and *the babe lying in the manger.* The poverty and meanness in which they found *Christ the Lord* were no shock to their faith, who themselves knew what it was to live a life of comfortable communion with God in very poor and mean circumstances. We have reason to think that the shepherds told Joseph and Mary of the vision of the angels they had seen, and the song of the angels they had heard, which was a great encouragement to them, more than if a visit had been made them by the best ladies in the town. And it is probable that Joseph and Mary told the shepherds what visions they had had concerning the child; and so, by communicating their experiences to each other, they greatly strengthened one another's faith.

VI. The care which the shepherds took to spread the report of this (*v.* 17): *When they had seen it,* though they saw nothing in the child that should induce them to believe that he was *Christ the Lord,* yet the circumstances, how mean soever they were, agreeing with the sign that the angel had given them, they were abundantly satisfied; and as the lepers argued (2 Kings vii. 9, This being *a day of good tidings,* we dare not *hold our peace),* so they made *known abroad* the whole story of what was *told them,* both by the *angels,* and by Joseph and Mary, *concerning this child,* that he was the Saviour, even *Christ the Lord,* that in him there is *peace on earth,* and that he was *conceived by the power of the Holy Ghost,* and *born of a virgin.* This they told every body, and agreed in their testimony concerning it. And now if, when he *is in the world,* the world knows him not, it is *their own fault,* for they have sufficient notice given them. What impression did it make upon people? Why truly, *All they that heard it wondered at those things which were told them by the shepherds, v.* 18. The shepherds were plain, downright, *honest men,* and they could not suspect them guilty of any design to impose upon them; what they had said therefore was likely to be true, and, if true, they could not but wonder at it, that the Messiah should be born *in a stable* and not in a palace, that angels should bring news of it to *poor shepherds* and not to the chief priests. They wondered, but never *enquired any further* about the Saviour, their duty to him, or advantages by him, but let the thing drop as a *nine days' wonder.* O the amazing stupidity of the men of that generation! Justly were the things which belonged to their peace *hid from their eyes,* when they thus wilfully *shut their eyes* against them.

VII. The use which those made of these things, who did believe them, and receive the impression of them. 1. The virgin Mary made them the matter of her *private meditation.* She said little, but *kept all these things,* and *pondered them in her heart, v.* 19. She laid the evidences together, and kept them in reserve, to be compared with the discoveries that should afterwards be made her. As she had silently left it to God to clear up her virtue, when that was suspected, so she silently leaves it to him to publish her honour, now when it was veiled; and it is satisfaction enough to find that, if no one else takes notice of the birth of her child, angels do. Note, The truths of Christ are worth keeping; and the way to keep them safe is to *ponder them.* Meditation is the best help to memory. 2. The shepherds made them the matter of their more *public praises.* If others were not affected with those things, yet they themselves were (*v.* 20): They *returned, glorifying and praising God,* in concurrence with the holy angels. If others would not regard the report they made to them, God would accept the thanksgivings they offered to him. They praised God for what *they had heard* from the angel, and for what *they had seen,* the babe *in the manger,* and just then *in the swaddling,* when they came in, as it had been spoken to them. They thanked God that they had seen Christ, though in the depth of his humiliation. As afterwards the cross of Christ, so now his *manger*, was to some *foolishness* and a *stumbling-block*, but others saw in it, and admired, and praised, the wisdom *of God* and the *power of God*.

21 And when eight days were accomplished for the circumcising of the child, his name was called JESUS, which was so named of the angel before he was conceived
in the womb. 22 And when the days of her purification according to the law of Moses were accomplished, they brought him to Jerusalem, to present *him* to the Lord; 23 (As it is written
in the law of the Lord, Every male that openeth the womb shall be called holy to the Lord); 24 And to offer a
sacrifice according to that which is said in the law of the Lord, A pair of turtledoves, or two young pigeons.

Our Lord Jesus, being *made of a woman*, was *made under the law*, Gal. iv. 4. He was not only, as the son of a daughter of Adam, made under the law of *nature*, but as the son of a daughter of Abraham he was made under the law of *Moses;* he put his neck under that yoke, though it was a heavy yoke, and a *shadow of good things to come*. Though its institutions were *beggarly elements*, and *rudiments of this world*, as the apostle calls them, Christ submitted to it, that he might with the better grace cancel it, and set it aside for us.

Now here we have two instances of his being *made under* that *law*, and submitting to it.

I. He was *circumcised* on the very day that the law appointed (*v.* 21): *When eight days were accomplished*, that day seven-night that he was born, they *circumcised* him. 1. Though it was a *painful* operation (*Surely* a *bloody husband thou hast been*, said Zipporah to Moses, *because of the circumcision*, Exod. iv. 25), yet Christ would undergo it for us; nay, *therefore* he submitted to it, to give an instance of his early obedience, his obedience unto blood. Then he shed his blood by drops, which afterwards he poured out in purple streams. 2. Though it supposed him a *stranger*, that was by that ceremony to be admitted into covenant with God, whereas he had always been his *beloved Son;* nay, though it supposed him a *sinner*, that needed to have his filthiness taken away, whereas he had no impurity or superfluity of naughtiness to be cut off, *yet* he submitted to it; nay, *therefore* he submitted to it, because he would be made in the likeness, not only of *flesh*, but of *sinful flesh*, Rom. viii. 3. 3. Though thereby he made himself a *debtor to the whole law* (Gal. v. 3), yet he submitted to it; nay, *therefore* he submitted to it, because he would take upon him the form of a servant, though he was free-born. Christ was circumcised, (1.) That he might own himself of the seed of Abraham, and of that nation *of whom, as concerning the flesh, Christ came*, and who was to *take on him the seed of Abraham*, Heb. ii. 16. (2.) That he might own himself a surety for our sins, and an undertaker for our safety. Circumcision (saith Dr. Goodwin) was our *bond*, whereby we acknowledged ourselves *debtors to the law;* and Christ, by being circumcised, did as it were set his hand to it, being *made sin for us*. The ceremonial law consisted much in sacrifices; Christ hereby obliged himself to offer, not the blood of bulls or goats, but his own blood, which none that ever were circumcised before could oblige themselves to. (3.) That he might justify, and put an honour upon, the dedication of the infant seed of the church to God, by that ordinance which is the instituted seal of the covenant, and of the righteousness which is by faith, as circumcision was (Rom. iv. 11), and baptism is. And certainly his being circumcised at eight days old doth make much more for the dedicating of the seed of the faithful by baptism in their infancy than his being baptized at thirty years old doth for the deferring of it till they are grown up. The change of the ceremony alters not the substance.

At his circumcision, according to the custom, he had his name given him; he was called *Jesus* or *Joshua*, for he was *so named of the angel* to his mother Mary *before he was conceived in the womb* (Luke i. 31), and to his supposed father Joseph after, Matt. i. 21. [1.] It was a *common name* among the Jews, as John was (Col. iv. 11), and in this he would be made *like unto his brethren*. [2.] It was the name of two eminent types of him in the Old Testament, Joshua, the successor of Moses, who was commander of Israel, and conqueror of Canaan; and Joshua, the high priest, who was therefore purposely crowned, that he might prefigure Christ as a *priest upon his throne*, Zech. vi. 11, 13. [3.] It was very significant of his undertaking. Jesus signifies a *Saviour*. He would be denominated, not from the glories of his divine nature, but from his gracious designs as Mediator; he *brings salvation*.

II. He was *presented* in the temple. This was done with an eye to the law, and at the time appointed by the law, when he was forty days old, *when the days of her purification were accomplished*, *v.* 22. Many copies, and authentic ones, read *αὐτῶν* for *αὐτῆς*, *the days of their purification*, the purification both of the mother and of the child, for so it was intended to be by the law; and our Lord Jesus, though he had no impurity to be cleansed from, yet submitted to it, as he did to circumcision, because he was made *sin for us;* and that, as by the *circumcision of Christ* we might be *circumcised*, in the virtue of our union and communion with him, with a spiritual circumcision *made without hands* (Col. ii. 11), so in the *purification* of Christ we might be *spiritually purified* from the filthiness and corruption which we brought into the world with us. Now, according to the law,

1. The child Jesus, being a first-born son, was *presented to the Lord,* in one of the courts of the temple. The law is here recited (*v.* 23): *Every male that opens the womb shall be called holy to the Lord,* because by a special writ of protection the first-born of Israel were preserved, when the first-born of the Egyptians were slain by the destroying angel; so that Christ, as first-born, was a priest by a title surer than that of Aaron's house. Christ was the *first-born* among many brethren, and was *called holy to the Lord,* so as never any other was; yet he was *presented to the Lord* as other first-born were, and no otherwise. Though he was newly come out of the bosom of the Father, yet he was *presented* to him by the hands of a priest, as if he had been a stranger, that needed one to introduce him. His being *presented to the Lord* now signified his *presenting himself* to the Lord as Mediator, when he was caused to *draw near* and *approach unto him,* Jer. xxx. 21. But, according to the law, he was *redeemed,* Num. xviii. 15. *The first-born of man shalt thou redeem,* and *five shekels* was the value, Lev. xxvii. 6; Num. xviii. 16. But probably in case of poverty the priest was allowed to take less, or perhaps nothing; for no mention is made of it here. Christ was *presented to the Lord,* not to be *brought back,* for his *ear* was *bored* to God's *door-post* to serve him for ever; and though he is not left in the temple as Samuel was, to minister there, yet like him he is given to the Lord *as long as he lives,* and ministers to him in the true temple *not made with hands.*

2. The mother brought her offering, *v.* 24. When she had presented that son of hers unto the Lord who was to be the great sacrifice, she might have been excused from offering any other; but so *it is said in the law of the Lord,* that law which was yet in force, and therefore so it must be done, she must offer *a pair of turtle-doves, or two young pigeons;* had she been of ability, she must have brought a *lamb for a burnt-offering,* and a *dove for a sin-offering;* but, being poor, and not able to reach the price of a lamb, she brings *two doves,* one for *a burnt-offering and the other for a sin-offering* (see Lev. xii. 6, 8), to teach us in every address to God, and particularly in those upon special occasions, both to give thanks to God for his mercies to us and to acknowledge with sorrow and shame our sins against him; in both we must give glory to him, nor do we ever want matter for both. Christ was not *conceived* and *born* in sin, as others are, so that there was not that occasion in his case which there is in others; yet, because he was made under the law, he complied with it. *Thus it became him to fulfil all righteousness.* Much more doth it become the best of men to join in confessions of sin; for *who can say, I have made my heart clean?*

25 And, behold, there was a man
in Jerusalem, whose name *was* Simeon;
and the same man *was* just
and devout, waiting for the consolation
of Israel: and the Holy Ghost
was upon him. 26 And it was revealed
unto him by the Holy Ghost,
that he should not see death, before
he had seen the Lord's Christ. 27
And he came by the Spirit into the
temple: and when the parents brought
in the child Jesus, to do for him after
the custom of the law, 28 Then took
he him up in his arms, and blessed
God, and said, 29 Lord, now lettest
thou thy servant depart in peace, according
to thy word: 30 For mine
eyes have seen thy salvation, 31
Which thou hast prepared before the
face of all people; 32 A light to
lighten the Gentiles, and the glory of
thy people Israel. 33 And Joseph
and his mother marvelled at those
things which were spoken of him.
34 And Simeon blessed them, and
said unto Mary his mother, Behold,
this *child* is set for the fall and rising
again of many in Israel; and for a
sign which shall be spoken against;
35 (Yea, a sword shall pierce through
thy own soul also), that the thoughts
of many hearts may be revealed. 36
And there was one Anna, a prophetess,
the daughter of Phanuel, of the tribe
of Aser: she was of a great age, and
had lived with a husband seven years
from her virginity; 37 And she *was*
a widow of about fourscore and four
years, which departed not from the
temple, but served *God* with fastings
and prayers night and day. 38 And
she coming in that instant gave thanks
likewise unto the Lord, and spake of
him to all them that looked for redemption
in Jerusalem. 39 And
when they had performed all things
according to the law of the Lord, they
returned into Galilee, to their own
city Nazareth. 40 And the child
grew, and waxed strong in spirit, filled
with wisdom: and the grace of God
was upon him.

Even when he humbles himself, still Christ has honour done him to balance the offence of it. That we might not be stumbled at the *meanness of his birth, angels* then did him honour; and now, that we may not be offended at his being presented in the temple, like other children born in sin, and without any manner of solemnity peculiar to him, but silently, and in the crowd of other children, Simeon and Anna now do him honour, by the inspiration of the Holy Ghost.

I. A very honourable testimony is borne to him by Simeon, which was both a reputation to the child and an encouragement to the parents, and might have been a happy introduction of the priests into an acquaintance with the Saviour, if those *watchmen* had not been *blind*. Now observe here,

1. The account that is given us concerning this Simeon, or Simon. He dwelt now in Jerusalem, and was eminent for his piety and communion with God. Some learned men, who have been conversant with the Jewish writers, find that there was at this time one Simeon, a man of great note in Jerusalem, the son of Hillel, and the first to whom they gave the title of *Rabban*, the highest title that they gave to their doctors, and which was never given but to seven of them. He succeeded his father Hillel, as president of the college which his father founded, and of the great Sanhedrim. The Jews say that he was endued with a *prophetical* spirit, and that he was turned out of his place because he witnessed against the common opinion of the Jews concerning the temporal kingdom of the Messiah; and they likewise observe that there is no mention of him in their Mishna, or book of traditions, which intimates that he was no patron of those fooleries. One thing objected against this conjecture is that at this time his father Hillel was living, and that he himself lived many years after this, as appears by the Jewish histories; but, as to that, he is not here said to be old; and his saying, *Now let thy servant depart* intimates that he was willing to die *now*, but does not conclude that therefore he did die quickly. St. Paul lived many years after he had spoken of his death as *near*, Acts xx. 25. Another thing objected is that the son of Simeon was Gamaliel, a Pharisee, and an enemy to Christianity; but, as to that, it is no new thing for a faithful lover of Christ to have a son a bigoted Pharisee.

The account given of him here is, (1.) That he was *just* and *devout, just* towards men and *devout* towards God; these two must always go together, and each will befriend the other, but neither will atone for the defect of the other. (2.) That he *waited for the consolation of Israel*, that is, for the coming of the Messiah, in whom alone the nation of Israel, that was now miserably harassed and oppressed, would find *consolation*. Christ is not only the author of his people's comfort, but the matter and ground of it, the *consolation of Israel*. He was long a coming, and they who believed he would come continued *waiting, desiring* his coming, and *hoping* for it with *patience;* I had almost said, with some degree of *impatience* waiting till it came. He *understood by books*, as Daniel, that the time was at hand, and therefore was now more than ever big with expectation of it. The unbelieving Jews, who still expect that which is already come, use it as an oath, or solemn protestation, *As ever I hope to see the consolation of Israel*, so and so it is. Note, The consolation of Israel is to be waited for, and it is worth waiting for, and it will be very welcome to those who have *waited* for it, and continue waiting. (3.) The *Holy Ghost* was upon him, not only as a Spirit of holiness, but as a Spirit of prophecy; he was *filled with the Holy Ghost*, and enabled to speak things above himself. (4.) He had a gracious promise made him, that before he died he should have a sight of the Messiah, *v.* 26. He was searching *what manner of time* the Spirit of Christ in the Old-Testament prophets did signify, and whether it were not now at hand; and he received *this oracle* (for so the word signifies), *that he should not see death before he had seen* the Messiah, *the Lord's Anointed*. Note, Those, and those only, can with courage *see death*, and look it in the face without terror, that have had by faith a sight of Christ.

2. The seasonable coming of Simeon into the temple, at the time when Christ was presented there, *v.* 27. Just then, when Joseph and Mary brought in the child, to be registered as it were in the church-book, among the first-born, Simeon came, by direction of *the Spirit*, into the temple. The same Spirit that had provided for the support of his hope now provided for the transport of his joy. It was whispered in his ear, "Go to the temple now, and you shall see what you have longed to see." Note, Those that would see Christ must go to his temple; for there *the Lord, whom ye seek*, shall suddenly come to *meet you*, and there you must be ready to *meet him*.

3. The abundant satisfaction wherewith he welcomed this sight: *He took him up in his arms* (*v.* 28), he *embraced* him with the greatest affection imaginable, laid him in his bosom, as near his heart as he could, which was as full of joy as it could hold. He *took him up in his arms*, to present him to the Lord (so some think), to do either the parent's part or the priest's part; for divers of the ancients say that he was himself a priest. When we receive the record which the gospel gives us of Christ with a lively faith, and the offer it makes us of Christ with love and resignation, then we *take Christ in our arms*. It was promised him that he should have a sight of Christ; but more is *performed* than was *promised:* he has him in his arms.

4. The solemn declaration he made hereupon: *He blessed God*, and said, *Lord, now let thou thy servant depart in peace, v.* 29—32.

(1.) He has a pleasant prospect *concerning himself*, and (which is a great attainment) is got quite above the love of life and fear of death; nay, he is arrived at a holy contempt of life, and desire of death: "*Lord, now let thou thy servant depart*, for mine eyes have seen the salvation I was promised a sight of before I died." Here is, [1.] An acknowledgment that God had been *as good as his word;* there has not failed one tittle of his good promises, as Solomon owns, 1 Kings viii. 56. Note, Never any that hoped in God's word were made ashamed of their hope. [2.] A thanksgiving for it. He *blessed God* that he saw that salvation in his arms which many prophets and kings desired to see, and might not. [3.] A confession of his faith, that this child in his arms was the *Saviour*, the *Salvation* itself; *thy salvation*, the salvation of thine appointing, the salvation *which thou hast prepared* with a great deal of contrivance. And, while it has been thus long *in the coming*, it hath still been *in the preparing*. [4.] It is a farewell to this world: "*Now let thy servant depart;* now mine eyes have been blessed with this sight, let them be closed, and see no more in this world." The eye is not satisfied with seeing (Eccl. i. 8), till it hath *seen Christ*, and then it is. What a poor thing doth this world look to one that hath Christ in his arms and salvation in his eye! Now adieu to all my friends and relations, all my enjoyments and employments here, even the temple itself. [5.] It is a welcome to death: *Now let thy servant depart*. Note, Death is a departure, the soul's departure out of the body, from the world of sense to the world of spirits. We must not depart till God give us our discharge, for we are his *servants* and must not quit his service till we have accomplished our time. Moses was promised that he should see Canaan, and then *die;* but he prayed that that word might be altered, Deut. iii. 24, 25. Simeon is promised that he should not *see death* till he had *seen Christ;* and he is willing to construe that beyond what was expressed, as an intimation that, when he had seen Christ, he should die: *Lord, be it so*, saith he, *now let me depart*. See here, *First*, How *comfortable* the death of a good man is; he departs *as God's servant* from the place of his toil to that of his rest. He departs *in peace*, peace with God, peace with his own conscience; in *peace* with death, well-reconciled to it, well-acquainted with it. He departs *according to God's word*, as Moses at the *word of the Lord* (Deut. xxxiv. 5): the word of precept, *Go up and die;* the word of promise, *I will come again and receive you to myself*. *Secondly*, What is the ground of this comfort? *For mine eyes have seen thy salvation*. This bespeaks more than a great complacency in the sight, like that of Jacob (Gen. xlvi. 30), *Now let me die, since I have seen thy face*. It bespeaks a believing expectation of a happy state on the other side death, through this salvation he now had a sight of, which not only takes off the terror of death, but makes it *gain*, Phil. i. 21. Note, Those that have welcomed Christ may welcome death.

(2.) He has a pleasant prospect concerning the world, and concerning the church. This salvation shall be,

[1.] A blessing to the world. It is *prepared before the face of all people*, not to be hid in a corner, but to be made known; to be a *light to lighten the Gentiles* that now sit in darkness: they shall have the knowledge of him, and of God, and another world through him. This has reference to Isa. xlix. 6, *I will give thee for a light to the Gentiles;* for Christ came to be the light of the world, not a candle in the Jewish candlestick, but the *Sun of righteousness*.

[2.] A blessing to the church: *the glory of thy people Israel*. It was an honour to the Jewish nation that the Messiah sprang out of one of their tribes, and was born, and lived, and died, among them. And of those who were Israelites indeed, of the spiritual Israel, he was indeed *the glory*, and will be so to eternity, Isa. lx. 19. They shall *glory* in him. *In the Lord shall all the seed of Israel be justified and shall glory*, Isa. xlv. 25. When Christ ordered his apostles to preach the gospel to all nations, therein he made himself a *light to lighten the Gentiles;* and when he added, *beginning at Jerusalem*, he made himself *the glory of his* people Israel.

5. The prediction concerning this child, which he delivered, with his blessing, to Joseph and Mary. They *marvelled at those things* which were still more and more fully and plainly spoken concerning this child, *v.* 33. And because they were affected with, and had their faith strengthened by, that which was said to them, here is more said to them.

(1.) Simeon shows them what reason they had to *rejoice;* for he *blessed them* (*v.* 34), he pronounced them blessed who had the honour to be related to this child, and were entrusted with the bringing him up. He *prayed* for them, that God would *bless* them, and would have others do so too. They had reason to rejoice, for this child should be, not only a comfort and honour to them, but a public blessing. He is set *for the rising again of many in Israel*, that is, for the conversion of many to God that are dead and buried in sin, and for the consolation of many in God that are sunk and lost in sorrow and despair. Those whom he is set *for the fall of* may be the same with those whom he is set for the *rising again of*. He is set εἰς πτῶσιν καὶ ἀνάστασιν—*for their fall, in order to their rising again;* to humble and abase them, and bring them off from all confidence in themselves, that they may be exalted by relying on Christ; he wounds and then heals, Paul *falls*, and rises again.

(2.) He shows them likewise what reason

they had to *rejoice with trembling*, according to the advice given of old, with reference to the Messiah's kingdom, Ps. ii. 11. Lest Joseph, and Mary especially, should be *lifted up* with the abundance of the revelations, here is a *thorn in the flesh* for them, an allay to their joy; and it is what we sometimes need.

[1.] It is true, Christ shall be a blessing to Israel; but there are those in Israel whom he is *set for the fall of*, whose corruptions will be provoked, who will be prejudiced and enraged against him, and offended, and whose sin and ruin will be aggravated by the revelation of Jesus Christ; many who will extract poison to themselves out of the balm of Gilead, and split their souls on the Rock of salvation, to whom this precious Foundation-stone will be a *stone of stumbling*. This refers to that prophecy (Isa. viii. 14, 15), He shall be *for a sanctuary* to some, and yet for a *snare* to others, 1 Pet. ii. 7, 8. Note, As it is pleasant to think how many there are to whom Christ and his gospel are a savour of life unto life, so it is sad to think how many there are to whom it is a savour of death unto death. He is set for *a sign*, to be admired by some, but by others, by many, spoken against. He had many *eyes upon him*, during the time of his public ministry, he was a *sign*, but he had many *tongues against* him, the contradiction and reproach of sinners, he was continually cavilled at and abused; and the effects of this will be that the *thoughts of many hearts will be revealed* (*v.* 35), that is, upon this occasion, men will *show themselves*, will discover, and so distinguish, themselves. The secret good affections and dispositions in the minds of some will be revealed by their embracing Christ, and closing with him; the secret corruptions and vicious dispositions of others, that otherwise would never have appeared so bad, will be revealed by their enmity to Christ and their rage against him. Men will be judged of by the thoughts of their hearts, their thoughts concerning Christ; are they for *him*, or are they for his *adversaries?* The *word of God* is a discerner of the *thoughts* and *intents of the heart*, and by it we are discovered to ourselves, and shall be judged hereafter.

[2.] It is true, Christ shall be a comfort to his mother; but be not thou too proud of it, for *a sword shall pass through thine own soul also*. He shall be a suffering Jesus; and, *First*, "Thou *shalt suffer with him*, by sympathy, more than any other of his friends, because of the nearness of thy relation, and strength of affection, to him." When he was abused, it was *a sword in her bones*. When she stood by his cross, and saw him dying, we may well think her inward grief was such that it might truly be said, *A sword pierced through her soul*, it cut her to the heart. *Secondly*, Thou shalt *suffer for him*. Many understand it as a prediction of her martyrdom; and some of the ancients say that it had its accomplishment in that. Note, In the midst of our greatest delights and advancements in this world, it is good for us to know that bonds and afflictions abide us.

II. He is taken notice of by one *Anna*, or *Ann*, a *prophetess*, that one of each sex might bear witness to him in whom both *men* and *women* are invited to believe, that they may be saved. Observe,

1. The account here given of this Anna, who she was. She was, (1.) *A prophetess;* the Spirit of prophecy now began to revive, which had ceased in Israel above three hundred years. Perhaps no more is meant than that she was one who had understanding in the scriptures above other women, and made it her business to instruct the *younger women* in the things of God. Though it was a very degenerate age of the church, yet God *left not himself without witness*. (2.) She was *the daughter of Phanuel;* her father's name (says Grotius) is mentioned, to put us in mind of Jacob's *Phanuel*, or *Penuel* (Gen. xxxii 30), that now the mystery of that should be unfolded, when in Christ we should as it were see God face to face, and our lives be preserved; and her name signifies *gracious*. (3.) She was of *the tribe of Asher*, which was in Galilee; this, some think, is taken notice of to refute those who said, *Out of Galilee ariseth no prophet*, when no sooner did prophecy revive but it appeared from Galilee. (4.) She was of *a great age*, a widow of about eighty-four years; some think she had now been eighty-four years a widow, and then she must be considerably above a hundred years old; others, rather than suppose that a woman so very old should be capable of fasting and praying as she did, suppose that she was only eighty-four years of age, and had been long a widow. Though she was a young widow, and had lived with her husband but seven years, yet she never married again, but continued a widow to her dying day, which is mentioned to her praise. (5.) She was a constant resident *in* or at least attendant *on* the temple. Some think she had lodgings in the courts of the temple, either in an alms-house, being maintained by the temple charities; or, as a prophetess, she was lodged there, as in a proper place to be consulted and advised with by those that desired to know the mind of God; others think her not *departing from the temple* means no more, than that she was constantly there at the time of divine service: when any good work was to be done, she was ready to join in it. It is most probable she had an apartment of her own among the out-buildings of the temple; and, besides her constant attendance on the public worship, abounded in private devotions, for she *served God with fastings and prayers night and day:* having no secular business to employ herself in, or being past it, she gave up herself wholly to her devotions, and not only *fasted twice in the week*, but always lived a mortified life, and spent that time in religious exercises which others

spent in eating and drinking and sleeping; she not only observed the *hours of prayer*, but prayed *night and day;* was always in a praying frame, lived a life of prayer, gave herself to prayer, was frequent in ejaculations, large in solemn prayers, and very particular in her intercessions. And in these she *served* God; that was it that put a value upon them and an excellency into them. The Pharisees *fasted often*, and made *long prayers*, but they served themselves, and their own pride and covetousness, in their fastings and prayers; but this good woman not only did that which was good, but did it from a good principle, and with a good end; she *served God*, and aimed at his honour, in *fasting and praying*. Note, [1.] Devotion is a thing we ought to be constant in; other duties are in season now and then, but we must *pray always*. [2.] It is a pleasant sight to see aged Christians abounding in acts of devotion, as those that are not *weary of well-doing*, that do not think themselves *above* these exercises, or *past* them, but that take more and more pleasure in them, and see more and more need of them, till they come to heaven. [3.] Those that are diligent and faithful in improving the light and means they have shall have further discoveries made them. Anna is now at length abundantly recompensed for her attendance so many years in the temple.

2. The testimony she bore to our Lord Jesus (*v.* 38): *She came in at that instant* when the child was presented, and Simeon discoursed concerning him; she, who was so *constant* to the temple, could not miss the opportunity.

Now, (1.) She *gave thanks likewise to the Lord*, just as Simeon, perhaps like him, wishing now to depart in peace. Note, Those to whom Christ is *made known* have reason enough to *give thanks to the Lord* for so great a favour; and we should be excited to that duty by the praises and thanksgivings of others; why should not we *give thanks likewise*, as well as they? Anna concurred with Simeon, and helped to make up the harmony. *She confessed unto the Lord* (so it may be read); she made an open profession of her faith concerning this child.

(2.) She, as a prophetess, instructed others concerning him: She *spoke of him to all them* that believed the Messiah would come, and with him *looked for redemption in Jerusalem*. Redemption was the thing wanted, waited for, and wished for; redemption *in Jerusalem*, for thence the *word of the Lord was to go forth*, Isa. ii. 3. Some there were in Jerusalem that *looked for redemption;* yet but a few, for Anna, it should seem, had acquaintance with all them that were joint-expectants with her of the Messiah; she knew where to find them, or they where to find her, and she told them all the good news, that she had seen the Lord; and it was great news, this of his birth now, as afterwards that of his resurrection. Note, Those that have an acquaintance with Christ *themselves* should do all they can to bring *others* acquainted with him.

Lastly, Here is a short account of the infancy and childhood of our Lord Jesus.

1. *Where* he spent it, *v.* 39. When the ceremony of presenting the child, and purifying the mother, was all over, they *returned into Galilee*. Luke relates no more concerning them, till they were returned into Galilee; but it appears by St. Matthew's gospel (*ch.* ii.) that from Jerusalem they returned to Bethlehem, where the wise men of the east found them, and there they continued till they were directed to flee into Egypt, to escape the malice and rage of Herod; and, returning thence when Herod was dead, they were directed to go to their old quarters in Nazareth, whence they had been perhaps some years absent. It is here called *their own city*, because there they had lived a great while, and their relations were there. He was ordered further from Jerusalem, because his kingdom and priesthood were to have no affinity with the present government of the Jewish church or state. He is sent into a place of obscurity and reproach; for in this, as in other things, he must humble himself and *make himself of no reputation*.

2. *How* he spent it, *v.* 40. In all things *it behoved him to be made like unto his brethren*, and therefore he passed through infancy and childhood as other children did, yet without sin; nay, with manifest indications of a divine nature in him. As other children, he *grew* in stature of body, and the improvement of understanding in his human soul, that his *natural* body might be a figure of his *mystical* body, which, though animated by a perfect spirit, yet *maketh increase of itself* till it comes to the *perfect man*, Eph. iv. 13, 16. But, (1.) Whereas other children are weak in understanding and resolution, he was *strong in spirit*. By the Spirit of God his human soul was endued with extraordinary vigour, and all his faculties performed their offices in an extraordinary manner. He reasoned strongly, and his judgment was penetrating. (2.) Whereas other children have *foolishness bound in their hearts*, which appears in what they say or do, he was *filled with wisdom*, not by any advantages of instruction and education, but by the operation of the Holy Ghost; every thing he said and did was wisely said, and wisely done, above his years. (3.) Whereas other children show that the corruption of nature is in them, and *the tares of sin* grow up with the *wheat of reason*, he made it appear that nothing but *the grace of God was upon him* (the wheat sprang up without tares), and that, whereas other children are by nature children of wrath, he was *greatly beloved*, and high in the favour of God; that God loved him, and cherished him, and took a particular care of him.

41 Now his parents went to Jerusalem every year at the feast of the

passover. 42 And when he was
twelve years old, they went up to
Jerusalem after the custom of the
feast. 43 And when they had fulfilled the days, as they returned, the
child Jesus tarried behind in Jerusalem;
and Joseph and his mother knew not
of it. 44 But they, supposing him
to have been in the company, went a
day's journey; and they sought him
among *their* kinsfolk and acquaintance. 45 And when they found him
not, they turned back again to Jerusalem, seeking him. 46 And it came
to pass, that after three days they found
him in the temple, sitting in the midst
of the doctors, both hearing them,
and asking them questions. 47 And
all that heard him were astonished at
his understanding and answers. 48
And when they saw him, they were
amazed: and his mother said unto
him, Son, why hast thou thus dealt
with us? behold, thy father and I
have sought thee sorrowing. 49 And
he said unto them, How is it that ye
sought me? wist ye not that I must
be about my Father's business? 50
And they understood not the saying
which he spoke unto them. 51 And
he went down with them, and came
to Nazareth, and was subject unto
them: but his mother kept all these
sayings in her heart. 52 And Jesus
increased in wisdom and stature, and
in favour with God and man.

We have here the only passage of story recorded concerning our blessed Saviour, from his infancy to the day of his showing to Israel at twenty-nine years old, and therefore we are concerned to make much of this, for it is in vain to wish we had more. Here is,

I. Christ's *going up with his parents* to Jerusalem, at the feast of the passover, *v.* 41, 42. 1. It was their constant practice to attend there, according to the law, though it was a long journey, and they were poor, and perhaps not well able, without straitening themselves, to bear the expenses of it. Note, Public ordinances must be frequented, and we must *not forsake the assembling of ourselves together, as the manner of some is.* Worldly business must give way to spiritual concerns. Joseph and Mary had a son in the house with them, that was able to teach them better than all the rabbin at Jerusalem; yet they *went up* thither, *after the custom of the feast. The Lord loves the gates of Zion more than all the dwellings of Jacob,* and so should we. We have reason to suppose that Joseph went up likewise at the feasts of *pentecost* and *tabernacles;* for all the males were to appear there *thrice a year,* but Mary only at the *passover,* which was the greatest of the three feasts, and had most gospel in it. 2. The child Jesus, at *twelve years old,* went up with them. The Jewish doctors say that at twelve years old children must begin to fast from time to time, that they may learn to fast on the day of atonement; and that at thirteen years old a child begins to be *a son of the commandment,* that is, obliged to the duties of adult church-membership, having been from his infancy, by virtue of his circumcision, *a son of the covenant.* It is not said that this was the *first time* that Jesus went up to Jerusalem to worship at the feast: probably he had done it for some years before, having spirit and wisdom above his years; and all should attend on public worship that can *hear with understanding,* Neh. viii. 2. Those children that are forward in other things should be put forward in religion. It is for the honour of Christ that children should attend on public worship, and he is pleased with their hosannas; and those children that were in their infancy dedicated to God should be called upon, when they are grown up, to come to the *gospel passover,* to the Lord's supper, that they may make it their own act and deed to join themselves to the Lord.

II. Christ's *tarrying behind his parents at Jerusalem,* unknown to them, in which he designed to give an early specimen of what he was reserved for.

1. His parents did not return till they had *fulfilled the days;* they had staid there all the seven days at the feast, though it was not absolutely necessary that they should stay longer than the two first days, after which many went home. Note, It is good to stay to the conclusion of an ordinance, as becomes those who say, *It is good to be here,* and not to hasten away, as if we were like Doeg, *detained before the Lord.*

2. The child *tarried behind in Jerusalem,* not because he was loth to go home, or shy of his parents' company, but because he had business to do there, and would let his parents know that he had a *Father in heaven,* whom he was to be *observant* of more than of *them;* and respect to *him* must not be construed disrespect *to them.* Some conjecture that he tarried behind in the temple, for it was the custom of the pious Jews, on the morning that they were to go home, to go first to the temple, to worship God; there he *staid behind,* and found entertainment there till they found him again. Or, perhaps, he staid at the house where they lodged, or some other friend's house (and such a child as he was could not but be the darling of all that knew him, and every one would court his company), and went up to the temple only at church-time; but so it was that he staid be-

hind. It is good to see young people willing to *dwell in the house of the Lord;* they are then like Christ.

3. His parents went the *first day's journey* without any suspicion that he was left behind, for they *supposed him to have been in the company, v.* 44. On these occasions, the crowd was very great, especially the first day's journey, and the roads full of people; and they concluded that he came along with some of their neighbours, and they *sought him among their kindred and acquaintance,* that were upon the road, going down. Pray did *you* see our Son? or, Did *you* see him? Like the spouse's enquiry, *Saw ye him whom my soul loveth?* This was a jewel worth seeking after. They knew that every one would be desirous of his company, and that he would be willing to do good among *his kinsfolk and acquaintance,* but among them they *found him not, v.* 45. There are many, too many, who are our kinsfolk and acquaintance, that we cannot avoid conversing with, among whom we find little or nothing of Christ. When they could not hear of him in this and the other company upon the road, yet they hoped they should meet with him at the place where they lodged that night; but *there* they could learn no tidings of him. Compare this with Job xxiii. 8, 9.

4. When they found him not at their quarters at night, they *turned back again,* next morning, *to Jerusalem, seeking him.* Note, Those that would find Christ must *seek till they find;* for he will at length be found of those that seek him, and will be found their bountiful rewarder. Those that have lost their comforts in Christ, and the evidences of their interest in him, must bethink themselves where, and when, and how, they lost them, and must *turn back again* to the place where they last had them; must *remember whence they are fallen, and repent, and do their first works,* and *return to their first love,* Rev. ii. 4, 5. Those that would recover their lost acquaintance with Christ must go to Jerusalem, the *city of our solemnities,* the place which he has *chosen to put his name there;* must attend upon him in his ordinances, in the gospel-passover, there they may hope to meet him.

5. The *third day* they found him *in the temple,* in some of the apartments belonging to the temple, where the doctors of the law kept, not their courts, but their conferences rather, or their schools for disputation; and there they found him *sitting in the midst of them* (*v.* 46), not standing as a *catechumen* to be examined or instructed by them, for he had discovered such measures of knowledge and wisdom that they admitted him to sit among them as a fellow or member of their society. This is an instance, not only that he was *filled with wisdom* (*v.* 40), but that he had both a desire to increase it and a readiness to communicate it; and herein he is an example to children and young people, who should learn of Christ to delight in the company of those they may get good by, and choose to *sit in the midst of* the doctors rather than in the midst of the players. Let them begin at *twelve years old,* and sooner, to enquire after knowledge, and to associate with those that are able to instruct them; it is a hopeful and promising presage in youth to be desirous of instruction. Many a youth at Christ's age now would have been playing with the *children in the temple,* but he was sitting with the *doctors in the temple.* (1.) He *heard* them. Those that would *learn* must be *swift to hear.* (2.) He *asked them questions;* whether, as a teacher (he had authority so to ask) or as a learner (he had humility so to ask) I know not, or whether as an associate, or joint-searcher after truth, which must be found out by mutual amicable disquisitions. (3.) He returned *answers* to them, which were very surprising and satisfactory, *v.* 47. And his wisdom and *understanding* appeared as much in the questions he asked as in the answers he gave, so that all who heard him *were astonished:* they never heard one so young, nor indeed any of their greatest doctors, talk sense at the rate that he did; like David, he had *more understanding than all his teachers,* yea, *than the ancients,* Ps. cxix. 99, 100. Now Christ showed forth some rays of his glory, which were presently drawn in again. He *gave them a taste* (says Calvin) of his divine wisdom and knowledge. Methinks this public appearance of Christ in the temple, as a teacher, was like Moses's early attempt to deliver Israel, which Stephen put this construction upon, that *he supposed his brethren would have understood,* by that, *how God by his hand would deliver them,* Acts vii. 24, 25. They might have taken the hint, and been delivered then, but *they understood not;* so they here might have had Christ (for aught I know) to enter upon his work now, but they were only *astonished,* and *understood not* the indication; and therefore, like Moses, he retires into obscurity again, and they hear no more of him for many years after.

6. His mother talked with him privately about it. When the company broke up, she took him aside, and examined him about it with a deal of tenderness and affection, *v.* 48. Joseph and Mary were both *amazed* to find him there, and to find that he had so much respect showed him as to be admitted to *sit among the doctors,* and to be taken notice of. His father knew he had only the name of a father, and therefore said nothing. But, (1.) His mother told him how ill they took it: "*Son, why hast thou thus dealt with us?* Why didst thou put us into such a fright?" They were ready to say, as Jacob of Joseph, "*A wild beast has devoured him;* or, He is fallen into the hands of some more cruel enemy, who has at length found out that he was the young child whose life Herod had sought some years ago." A thousand ima-

ginations, we may suppose, they had concerning him, each more frightful than another. "Now, why hast thou given us occasion for these fears? *Thy father and I have sought thee, sorrowing;* not only troubled that we lost thee, but vexed at ourselves that we did not take more care of thee, to bring thee along with us." Note, Those may have leave to complain of their losses that think they have lost Christ. But their *weeping* did not hinder *sowing;* they did not sorrow and sit down in despair, but sorrowed and *sought.* Note, If we would find Christ, we must seek him *sorrowing,* sorrowing that we have lost him, that we have provoked him to withdraw, and that we have sought him no sooner. They that thus seek him in sorrow shall find him, at length, with so much the greater joy. (2.) He gently reproved their inordinate solicitude about him (*v.* 49): "*How is it that you sought me?* You might have depended upon it, I would have followed you home when I had done the business I had to do here. I could not be lost in Jerusalem. Wist ye not that I *ought to* be, ἐν τοῖς τοῦ πατρός μȣ;—*in my Father's house?*" so some read it; "where else should the Son be, who *abideth in the house for ever?* I ought to be," [1.] "*Under my Father's care* and protection; and therefore you should have cast the care of me upon him, and not have burdened yourselves with it." Christ is a shaft hid in his Father's quiver, Isa. xlix. 2. He takes care of his church likewise, and therefore let us never despair of its safety. [2.] "*At my Father's work*" (so we take it): "I must be *about my Father's business,* and therefore could not go home as soon as you might. *Wist ye not?* Have you not already perceived that concerning me, that I have devoted myself to the service of religion, and therefore must employ myself in the affairs of it?" Herein he hath left us an example; for it becomes the children of God, in conformity to Christ, to attend their heavenly Father's business, and to make all other business give way to it. This word of Christ we now think we understand very well, for he hath explained it in what he hath done and said. It was his errand into the world, and his meat and drink in the world, to do his Father's will, and finish his work: and yet at that time his parents *understood not this saying, v.* 50. They did not understand what business he had to do then in the temple for his Father. They believed him to be the Messiah, that should have the throne of his father David; but they thought that should rather bring him to the royal palace than to the temple. They *understood not* his prophetical office; and he was to do much of his work in that.

Lastly, Here is their return to Nazareth. This glimpse of his glory was to be short. It was now over, and he did not urge his parents either to come and settle at Jerusalem or to settle him there (though that was the place of improvement and preferment, and where he might have the best opportunities of showing his wisdom), but very willingly retired into his obscurity at Nazareth, where for many years he was, as it were, buried alive. Doubtless, he came up to Jerusalem, to worship at the feasts, three times a year, but whether he ever went again into the temple, to dispute with the doctors there, we are not told; it is not improbable but he might. But here we are told,

1. That he was *subject to his parents.* Though once, to show that he was *more than a man,* he withdrew himself from his parents, to attend his heavenly Father's business, yet he did not, as yet, make that his constant practice, nor for many years after, but was *subject to them,* observed their orders, and went and came as they directed, and, as it should seem, worked with his father at the trade of a carpenter. Herein he hath given an example to children to be dutiful and obedient to their parents in the Lord. Being *made of a woman,* he was made under the law of the fifth commandment, to teach the *seed* of the faithful thus to approve themselves to him a faithful seed. Though his parents were poor and mean, though his father was only his *supposed* father, yet he was *subject to them;* though he was *strong in spirit,* and *filled with wisdom,* nay though he was the Son of God, yet he was subject to his parents; how then will *they* answer it who, though foolish and weak, yet are disobedient to their parents?

2. That his mother, though she did not perfectly understand her son's sayings, yet *kept them in her heart,* expecting that hereafter they would be explained to her, and she should fully understand them, and know how to make use of them. However we may neglect men's sayings because they are obscure (*Si non vis intelligi debes negligi—If it be not intelligible, it is not valuable*), yet we must not think so of God's sayings. That which at first is dark, so that we know not what to make of it, may afterwards become plain and easy; we should therefore *lay it up* for hereafter. See John ii. 22. We may find use for that another time which now we see not how to make useful to us. A *scholar* keeps those grammar rules in memory which at present he understands not the use of, because he is told that they will hereafter be of use to him; so we must do by Christ's sayings.

3. That he improved, and came on, to admiration (*v.* 52): *He increased in wisdom and stature.* In the perfections of his divine nature there could be no increase; but this is meant of his human nature, his body increased in *stature* and bulk, he grew in the growing age; and his soul increased *in wisdom,* and in all the endowments of a human soul. Though the Eternal Word was united to the human soul from his conception, yet the divinity that dwelt in him manifested itself to his humanity by degrees, *ad modum*

recipientis—in proportion to his capacity; as the faculties of his human soul grew more and more capable, the gifts it received from the divine nature were more and more communicated. And he increased in *favour with God and man,* that is, in all those graces that rendered him acceptable to God and man. Herein Christ accommodated himself to his estate of humiliation, that, as he condescended to be an infant, a child, a youth, so the image of God shone brighter in him, when he grew up to be a youth, than it did, or could, while he was an *infant* and a *child.* Note, Young people, as they grow in stature, should grow in wisdom, and then, as they grow in wisdom, they will grow in favour *with God and man.*

CHAP. III.

Nothing is related concerning our Lord Jesus from his twelfth year to his entrance on his thirtieth year. We often think it would have been a pleasure and advantage to us if we had journals, or at least annals, of occurrences concerning him; but we have as much as Infinite Wisdom thought fit to communicate to us, and, if we improve not that, neither should we have improved more if we had had it. The great intention of the evangelists was to give us an account of the gospel of Christ, which we are to believe, and by which we hope for salvation: now that began in the ministry and baptism of John, and therefore they hasten to give us an account of that. We could wish, perhaps, that Luke had wholly passed by what was related by Matthew and Mark, and had written only what was new, as he has done in his two first chapters. But it was the will of the Spirit that some things should be established out of the mouth, not only of two, but of three witnesses; and we must not reckon it a needless repetition, nor shall we do so if we renew our meditations upon these things, with suitable affections. In this chapter we have, I. The beginning of John's baptism, and the scope and intention of it, ver. 1—6. His exhortation to the multitude (ver. 7—9), and the particular instructions he gave to those who desired to be told their duty, ver. 10—14. II. The notice he gave them of the approach of the Messiah (ver. 15—18), to which is added (though it happened after what follows) the mention of his imprisonment, ver. 19—20. III. Christ coming to be baptized of John, and his entrance therein upon the execution of his prophetical office, ver. 21, 22. IV. His pedigree and genealogy recorded up to Adam, ver. 23—38.

NOW in the fifteenth year of the
reign of Tiberius Cæsar, Pontius Pilate being governor of Judæa,
and Herod being tetrarch of Galilee,
and his brother Philip tetrarch of
Ituræa and of the region of Trachonitis, and Lysanias the tetrarch of
Abilene, 2 Annas and Caiaphas being
the high priests, the word of God
came unto John the son of Zacharias
in the wilderness. 3 And he came
into all the country about Jordan,
preaching the baptism of repentance
for the remission of sins; 4 As it is
written in the book of the words of
Esaias the prophet, saying, The voice
of one crying in the wilderness, Prepare ye the way of the Lord, make
his paths straight. 5 Every valley
shall be filled, and every mountain
and hill shall be brought low; and
the crooked shall be made straight,
and the rough ways *shall be* made
smooth; 6 And all flesh shall see the
salvation of God. 7 Then said he
to the multitude that came forth to
be baptized of him, O generation of
vipers, who hath warned you to flee
from the wrath to come? 8 Bring
forth therefore fruits worthy of repentance, and begin not to say within
yourselves, We have Abraham to *our*
father: for I say unto you, That God
is able of these stones to raise up
children unto Abraham. 9 And now
also the axe is laid unto the root of
the trees: every tree therefore which
bringeth not forth good fruit is hewn
down, and cast into the fire. 10 And
the people asked him, saying, What
shall we do then? 11 He answereth
and saith unto them, He that hath
two coats, let him impart to him that
hath none; and he that hath meat,
let him do likewise. 12 Then came
also publicans to be baptized, and said
unto him, Master, what shall we do?
13 And he said unto them, Exact no
more than that which is appointed you.
14 And the soldiers likewise demanded
of him, saying, And what shall we do?
And he said unto them, Do violence
to no man, neither accuse *any* falsely;
and be content with your wages.

John's baptism introducing a new dispensation, it was requisite that we should have a particular account of it. Glorious things were said of John, what a distinguished favourite of Heaven he should be, and what a great blessing to this earth (*ch.* i. 15, 17); but we lost him in the deserts, and there he remains until *the day of his showing unto Israel, ch.* i. 80. And now at last that day dawns, and a welcome day it was to them that waited for it more than they that waited for the morning. Observe here,

I. The date of the beginning of John's baptism, when it was that he appeared; this is here taken notice of, which was not by the other evangelists, that the truth of the thing might be confirmed by the exact fixing of the time. And it is dated,

1. By the government of the heathen, which the Jews were under, to show that they were a conquered people, and therefore it was time for the Messiah to come to set up a spiritual kingdom, and an eternal one, upon the ruins of all the temporal dignity and dominion of David and Judah.

(1.) It is dated by the reign of the Roman emperor; it was in the fifteenth year of Tiberius Cæsar, the third of the twelve Cæsars, a very bad man, given to covetousness, drunkenness, and cruelty; such a man is mentioned first (saith Dr. Lightfoot), as it were, to teach us what to look for from that cruel and abominable city wherein Satan reigned in all ages and successions. The people of the Jews, after a long struggle, were of late made a province of the empire, and were under the dominion of this Tiberius; and that country which once had made so great a figure, and had many nations tributaries to it, in the reigns of David and Solomon, is now itself an inconsiderable despicable part of the Roman empire, and rather trampled upon than triumphed in.

———En quo discordia cives
Perduxit miseros———
What dire effects from civil discord flow!

The lawgiver was now departed from between Judah's feet; and, as an evidence of that, their public acts are dated by the reign of the Roman emperor, and therefore now Shiloh must come.

(2.) It is dated by the governments of the viceroys that ruled in the several parts of the Holy Land under the Roman emperor, which was another badge of their servitude, for they were all foreigners, which bespeaks a sad change with that people whose *governors* used to be *of themselves* (Jer. xxx. 21), and it was their glory. *How is the gold become dim!* [1.] Pilate is here said to be the governor, president, or procurator, of Judea. This character is given of him by some other writers, that he was a wicked man, and one that made no conscience of a lie. He reigned ill, and at last was displaced by Vitellius, president of Syria, and sent to Rome, to answer for his mal-administrations. [2.] The other three are called *tetrarchs*, some think from the countries which they had the command of, each of them being over a *fourth part* of that which had been entirely under the government of Herod the Great. Others think that they are so called from the post of honour they held in the government; they had the *fourth* place, or were *fourth-rate* governors: the emperor was the *first*, the *proconsul*, who governed a province, the *second*, a *king* the *third*, and a *tetrarch* the *fourth*. So Dr. Lightfoot.

2. By the government of the Jews among themselves, to show that they were a corrupt people, and that therefore it was time that the Messiah should come, to reform them, *v.* 2. Annas and Caiaphas were the high priests. God had appointed that there should be but one high priest at a time, but here were two, to serve some ill turn or other: one served one year and the other the other year; so some. One was the high priest, and the other the *sagan*, as the Jews called him, to officiate for him when he was disabled; or, as others say, one was high priest, and represented Aaron, and that was *Caiaphas;* Annas, the other, was *nasi*, or head of the sanhedrim, and represented Moses. But to us there is but one high priest, one Lord of all, to whom all judgment is committed.

II. The origin and tendency of John's baptism.

1. The origin of it was *from heaven The word of God came unto John, v.* 2. He received full commission and full instructions from God to do what he did. It is the same expression that is used concerning the Old-Testament prophets (Jer. i. 2); for John was a prophet, yea, more than a prophet, and in him prophecy revived, which had been long suspended. We are not told how *the word of the Lord came* to John, whether by an angel, as to his father, or by dream, or vision, or voice, but it was to his satisfaction, and ought to be to ours. John is here called *the son of Zacharias*, to refer us to what the angel said to his father, when he assured him that he should have this son. The word of the Lord came to him *in the wilderness;* for those whom God *fits* he will find out, wherever they are. As the word of the Lord is not *bound* in a *prison*, so it is not *lost* in a *wilderness*. The *word of the Lord* made its way to Ezekiel among the captives by the river of Chebar, and to John in the isle of Patmos. John was the *son of a priest*, now entering upon the thirtieth year of his age; and therefore, according to the custom of the temple, he was now to be admitted into the temple-service, where he should have attended as a candidate five years before. But God had called him to a more honourable ministry, and therefore the Holy Ghost enrols him here, since he was not enrolled in the archives of the temple: *John the son of Zacharias began his ministration such a time.*

2. The scope and design of it were to bring all the people of his country off from their sins and home to their God, *v.* 3. *He came* first *into all the country about Jordan*, the neighbourhood wherein he resided, that part of the country which Israel took possession of first, when they entered the land of promise under Joshua's conduct; there was the banner of the gospel first displayed. John resided in the most solitary part of the country; but, when the word of the Lord came to him, he quitted his deserts, and came into the inhabited country. Those that are *best pleased* in their retirements must cheerfully *exchange* them, when God calls them into places of concourse. *He came* out of the wilderness *into all the country*, with some marks of distinction, *preaching* a new *baptism;* not a sect, or party, but a *profession*, or distinguishing badge The sign, or ceremony, was such as was ordinarily used among the Jews, *washing with water*, by which proselytes were sometimes admitted, or disciples to some great master; but the meaning of it was, *repentance for the remission of sins:* that is, all that submitted to his baptism,

(1.) Were thereby obliged to *repent of their sins*, to be *sorry* for what they had done amiss, and to *do so no more*. The former they *professed*, and were concerned to be *sincere* in their professions; the latter they *promised*, and were concerned to *make good* what they promised. He bound them, not to such ceremonious observances as were imposed by the tradition of the elders, but to change their mind, and change their way, to *cast away from them all their transgressions,* and to *make them new hearts* and to live new lives. The design of the gospel, which now began, was to make men devout and pious, holy and heavenly, humble and meek, sober and chaste, just and honest, charitable and kind, and good in every relation, who had been much otherwise; and this is to *repent.*

(2.) They were thereby assured of the pardon of their sins, upon their repentance. As the baptism he administered bound them not to submit to the power of sin, so it sealed to them a gracious and pleadable discharge from the guilt of sin. *Turn yourselves from all your transgressions, so iniquity shall not be your ruin;* agreeing with the word of the Lord, by the Old-Testament prophets, Ezek. xviii. 30.

III. The fulfilling of the scriptures in the ministry of John. The other evangelists had referred us to the same text that is here referred to, that of Esaias, *ch.* xl. 3. It is *written in the book of the words of Esaias the prophet,* which he heard from God, which he spoke for God, those words of his which were *written* for the generations to come. Among them it is found that there should be *the voice of one crying in the wilderness;* and John is that voice, a clear distinct voice, a loud voice, an articulate one; he cries, *Prepare ye the way of the Lord, and make his paths straight.* John's business is to *make way* for the entertainment of the gospel in the hearts of the people, to bring them into such a frame and temper as that Christ might be welcome to them, and they welcome to Christ. Luke goes further on with the quotation than Matthew and Mark had done, and applies the following words likewise to John's ministry (*v.* 5, 6), *Every valley shall be filled.* Dr. Hammond understands this as a prediction of the desolation coming upon the people of the Jews for their infidelity: the land should be made plain by the pioneers for the Roman army, and should be laid waste by it, and there should then be a visible distinction made between the impenitent on the one side and the receivers of the gospel on the other side. But it seems rather to be meant of the immediate tendency of John's ministry, and of the gospel of Christ, of which that was the introduction. 1. The humble shall by it be *enriched* with grace: *Every valley* that lies *low* and *moist* shall be *filled* and be *exalted.* 2. The proud shall by it be humbled; the *self-confident* that stand upon *their own bottom,* and the *self-conceited* that lift up *their own top,* shall have contempt put upon them: *Every mountain and hill shall be brought low.* If they repent, they are brought to the dust; if not, to the lowest hell. 3. Sinners shall be converted to God: *The crooked ways* and the *crooked* spirits shall be *made straight;* for, though *none can make that straight which God hath made crooked* (Eccl. vii. 13), yet God by his grace can make that straight which sin hath made crooked. 4. Difficulties that were hindering and discouraging in the way to heaven shall be removed: *The rough ways shall be made smooth;* and they that love God's law shall have *great peace,* and *nothing shall offend them.* The gospel has made the way to heaven *plain* and easy to be *found, smooth* and easy to be *walked in.* 5. The great salvation shall be more fully discovered than ever, and the discovery of it shall spread further (*v.* 6): *All flesh shall see the salvation of God;* not the Jews only, but the Gentiles. All shall *see* it; they shall have it set before them and offered to them, and some of all sorts shall *see* it, enjoy it, and have the benefit of it. When way is made for the gospel into the heart, by the captivating of high thoughts and bringing them into obedience to Christ, by the levelling of the soul and the removing of all obstructions that stand in the way of Christ and his grace, then prepare to bid the salvation of God welcome.

IV. The general warnings and exhortations which he gave to those who submitted to his baptism, *v.* 7—9. In Matthew he is said to have preached these same things to *many of the Pharisees and Sadducees,* that *came to his baptism* (Matt. iii. 7—10); but here he is said to have spoken them *to the multitude, that came forth to be baptized of him, v.* 7. This was the purport of his preaching to all that came to him, and he did not alter it in compliment to the Pharisees and Sadducees, when they came, but dealt as plainly with them as with any other of his hearers. And as he did not flatter the *great,* so neither did he compliment the *many,* or make his court to them, but gave the same reproofs of sin and warnings of wrath to the *multitude* that he did to the Sadducees and Pharisees; for, if they had not the same faults, they had others as bad. Now observe here,

1. That the guilty corrupted race of mankind is become a *generation of vipers;* not only poisoned, but poisonous; hateful to God, hating one another. This magnifies the patience of God, in continuing the race of mankind upon the earth, and not destroying that *nest of vipers.* He did it once by water, and will again by fire.

2. This generation of vipers is fairly warned to *flee from the wrath to come,* which is certainly before them if they continue such; and their being a *multitude* will not be at all their security, for it will be neither *reproach* nor *loss* to God to cut them off. We are not only warned of this wrath, but are put into a way to escape it, if we look about us in time.

3. There is no way of *fleeing from the wrath to come,* but by *repentance.* They that submitted to the baptism of repentance thereby evidenced that they were *warned* to flee from the wrath to come and *took* the warning; and we by our baptism profess to have fled out of Sodom, for fear of what is coming upon it.

4. Those that profess repentance are highly

concerned to live like penitents (*v.* 8): *Bring forth therefore fruits meet for repentance,* else, notwithstanding your professions of repentance, you cannot escape *the wrath to come.*" By the fruits of repentance it will be known whether it be sincere or no. By the change of our way must be evidenced the change of our mind.

5. If we be not really holy, both in heart and life, our profession of religion and relation to God and his church will stand us in no stead at all: *Begin not* now to frame excuses from this great duty of repentance, by *saying within yourselves, We have Abraham to our father.* What will it avail us to be the children of godly parents if we be not godly, to be within the pale of the church if we be not brought into the bond of the covenant?

6. We have therefore no reason to depend upon our external privileges and professions of religion, because God has no need of us or of our services, but can effectually secure his own honour and interest without us. If we were cut off and ruined, he could raise up to himself a church out of the most unlikely,—*children to Abraham* even *out of stones.*

7. The greater professions we make of repentance, and the greater assistances and encouragements are given us to repentance, the nearer and the sorer will our destruction be if we do not *bring forth fruits meet for repentance.* Now that the gospel begins to be preached, now that the kingdom of heaven is at hand, *now* that the *axe is laid to the root of the tree,* threatenings to the wicked and impenitent are now more terrible than before, as encouragements to the penitent are now more comfortable. "Now that you are upon your behaviour, look to yourselves."

8. Barren trees will be cast into the fire at length; it is the fittest place for them: *Every tree* that doth not bring forth fruit, *good fruit,* is *hewn down,* and *cast into the fire.* If it serve not for fruit, to the honour of God's grace, let it serve for fuel, to the honour of his justice.

V. The particular instructions he gave to several sorts of persons, that enquired of him concerning their duty: the *people,* the *publicans,* and the *soldiers.* Some of the Pharisees and Sadducees came to his baptism; but we do not find them asking, *What shall we do?* They thought they knew what they had to do as well as he could tell them, or were determined to do what they pleased, whatever he told them. But the *people,* the *publicans,* and the *soldiers,* who knew that they had done amiss, and that they ought to do better, and were conscious to themselves of great ignorance and unacquaintedness with the divine law, were particularly inquisitive: *What shall we do?* Note, 1. Those that are *baptized* must be *taught,* and those that have baptized them are concerned, as they have opportunity, to teach them, Matt. xxviii. 19, 20. 2. Those that profess and promise repentance in general must evidence it by particular instances of reformation, according as their place and condition are. 3. They that would do their duty must desire to know their duty, and enquire concerning it. The first good word Paul said, when he was converted, was, *Lord, what wilt thou have me to do?* These here enquire, not, *What shall this man do?* but, What shall *we* do? What *fruits meet for repentance* shall we *bring forth?* Now John gives answer to each, according to their place and station.

(1.) He tells the *people* their duty, and that is to be charitable (*v.* 11): *He that has two coats,* and, consequently, one to spare, let him *give,* or *lend* at least, *to him that has none,* to keep him warm. Perhaps he saw among his hearers some that were overloaded with clothes, while others were ready to perish in rags, and he puts those who had superfluities upon contributing to the relief of those that had not necessaries. The gospel requires *mercy,* and not sacrifice; and the design of it is to engage us to do all the good we can *Food and raiment* are the two supports o. life; he that hath *meat* to spare, let him give to him that is destitute of *daily food,* as well as he that hath clothes to spare: what we have we are but stewards of, and must use it, accordingly, as our Master directs.

(2.) He tells the *publicans* their duty, the collectors of the emperor's revenue (*v.* 13): *Exact no more than that which is appointed you.* They must do justice between the government and the merchant, and not oppress the people in levying the taxes, nor any way make them heavier or more burdensome than the law had made them. They must not think that because it was their office to take care that the people did not defraud the prince they might therefore, by the power they had, bear hard upon the people; as those that have ever so little a branch of power are apt to abuse it: "No, keep to your *book of rates,* and reckon it enough that you collect for Cæsar the things that are Cæsar's, and do not enrich yourselves by taking more." The public revenues must be applied to the public service, and not to gratify the avarice of private persons. Observe, He does not direct the publicans to quit their places, and to go no more to the receipt of custom; the employment is in itself lawful and necessary, but let them be just and honest in it.

(3.) He tells the *soldiers* their duty, *v.* 14. Some think that these soldiers were of the Jewish nation and religion: others think that they were Romans; for it was not likely either that the Jews would serve the Romans or that the Romans would trust the Jews in their garrisons in their own nation; and then it is an early instance of Gentiles embracing the gospel and submitting to it. Military men seldom seem inclined to religion; yet these submitted even to the Baptist's strict profession, and desired to receive the *word of command* from him: *What must we do?* Those who more than other men have their lives in their hands, and are in deaths often, are concerned to enquire what they shall do that they may be *found in peace.* In answer to this enquiry, John does not bid them lay down their arms, and desert the service, but cautions them against the sins that soldiers were commonly guilty of; for this is fruit meet for repentance, to *keep ourselves from our iniquity.* [1.] They must not be injurious to *the people* among whom they were quartered, and over whom indeed they were set: "*Do violence to no man.* Your business is to keep the peace, and prevent men's doing violence to one another; but do not you *do violence* to any. *Shake no man*" (so the word signifies); "do not put people into fear; for the sword of war, as well as that of justice, is to be a terror only to evil doers, but a protection to those that do well. Be not rude in your quarters; force not money from people by frightening them. Shed not the blood of war in peace; offer no incivility either to man or woman, nor have any hand in the barbarous devastations that armies sometimes make." Nor must they *accuse any falsely* to the government, thereby to make themselves formidable, and get bribes. [2.] They must not be injurious to their *fellow-soldiers;* for some think that caution, not to *accuse falsely,* has special reference to them: "Be not forward to complain one of another to your superior officers, that you may be revenged on those whom you have a pique against, or undermine those above you, and get into their places." *Do not oppress any;* so some think the word here signifies, as used by the LXX. in several passages of the Old Testament. [3.] They must not be given to mutiny, or contend with their generals about their pay: "*Be content with your wages.* While you have what you agreed for, do not murmur that it is not more." It is discontent with what they have that makes men oppressive and injurious; they that never think they have enough themselves will not scruple at any the most irregular practices to make it more, by defrauding others. It is a rule to all servants that they *be content with their wages;* for they that indulge themselves in discontents expose themselves to many temptations, and it is wisdom to make the best of that which is.

15 And as the people were in expectation, and all men mused in their
hearts of John, whether he were the
Christ, or not; 16 John answered,
saying unto *them* all, I indeed baptize
you with water; but one mightier
than I cometh, the latchet of whose
shoes I am not worthy to unloose:
he shall baptize you with the Holy
Ghost and with fire: 17 Whose fan
is in his hand, and he will thoroughly
purge his floor, and will gather the
wheat into his garner: but the chaff
he will burn with fire unquenchable.
18 And many other things in his exhortation preached he unto the people.
19 But Herod the tetrarch, being reproved by him for Herodias his brother Philip's wife, and for all the evils
which Herod had done, 20 Added
yet this above all, that he shut up
John in prison.

We are now drawing near to the appearance of our Lord Jesus publicly; the Sun will not be long after the morning-star. We are here told,

I. How the people took occasion, from the ministry and baptism of John, to think of the Messiah, and to think of him as at the door, as now come. Thus the way of the Lord was *prepared,* and people were prepared to bid Christ welcome; for, when men's expectations are raised, that which they are in expectation of becomes doubly acceptable. Now when they observed what an excellent doctrine John Baptist preached, what a divine power went along with it, and what a tendency it had to reform the world, 1. They began presently to consider that now was the time for the Messiah to appear. The sceptre was departed from Judah, for they had no king but Cæsar; nay, and the lawgiver too was gone from between his feet, for Herod had lately slain the sanhedrim. Daniel's seventy weeks were now expiring; and therefore it was but three or four years after this that they looked that the kingdom of heaven should appear immediately, Luke xix. 11. Never did the corrupt state of the Jews more need a reformation, nor their distressed state more need a deliverance, than now. 2. Their next thought was, "Is not this he that should come?" *All* thinking *men mused,* or reasoned, *in their hearts,* concerning John, *whether he were the Christ or not.* He had indeed none of the external pomp and grandeur in which they generally expected the Messiah to appear; but his life was holy and strict, his preaching powerful and with authority, and therefore "why may we not think that he is the Messiah, and that he will shortly throw off this disguise, and appear in more glory?" Note, That which puts people upon considering, reasoning with themselves, prepares the way for Christ.

II. How John disowned all pretensions to the honour of being himself the Messiah, but confirmed them in their expectations of him that really was the Messiah, *v.* 16, 17. John's office, as a crier or herald, was to give notice that the *kingdom of God* and the King of that kingdom were *at hand;* and therefore, when he had told all manner of people severally what they must do ("You must do this, and you must do that"), he tells them one thing more which they must all do: they must expect the Messiah now shortly to appear. And this serves as an *answer* to their *musings* and debates concerning himself. Though he knew not their thoughts, yet, in declaring this, he *answered* them.

1. He declares that the utmost he could do was to *baptize* them *with water*. He had no access to *the Spirit,* nor could command *that* or work upon *that;* he could only exhort them to *repent,* and assure them of forgiveness, upon repentance; he could not work repentance in them, nor confer remission on them.

2. He consigns them, and turns them over, as it were, to Jesus Christ, for whom he was sent to *prepare the way,* and to whom he was ready to transfer all the interest he had in the affections of the people, and would have them no longer to *debate* whether John was the Messiah or no, but to look for him that was really so.

(1.) John owns the Messiah to have a greater *excellency* than he had, and that he was in all things preferable to him; he is one the *latchet of whose shoe* he does not think himself *worthy to loose;* he does not think himself worthy to be the meanest of his servants, to help him on and off with his shoes. John was *a prophet,* yea *more than a prophet,* more so than any of the Old-Testament prophets; but Christ was a prophet more than John, for it was both *by the Spirit of Christ,* and *of the grace of Christ,* that all the prophets prophesied, and John among the rest, 1 Pet. i. 10, 11. This was a great truth which John came to preach; but the manner of his expressing it bespeaks his humility, and in it he not only *does justice* to the Lord Jesus, but *does him honour* too: "He is one whom I am not worthy to approach, or draw nigh to, no not as a servant." Thus highly does it become us to speak of Christ, and thus humbly of ourselves.

(2.) He owns him to have a greater *energy* than he had: "He is *mightier than I,* and does that which I cannot do, both for the comfort of the faithful and for the terror of hypocrites and dissemblers." They thought that a wonderful power went along with John; but what was that compared with the power which Jesus would come clothed with? [1.] John can do no more than *baptize with water,* in token of this, that they ought to purify and cleanse themselves; but Christ can, and will, *baptize with the Holy Ghost;* he can give the Spirit to cleanse and purify the heart, not only as *water* washes off the *dirt* on the outside, but as *fire* purges out the *dross* that is within, and *melts down* the metal, that it may be cast into a *new mould.* [2.] John can only preach a *distinguishing* doctrine, and by word and sign *separate between the precious and the vile;* but Christ hath his *fan in his hand,* with which he can, and will, perfectly separate between the wheat and the chaff. He *will thoroughly purge his floor;* it is *his own,* and therefore he will *purge* it, and will cast out of his church the unbelieving impenitent Jews, and confirm in his church all that faithfully follow him. [3.] John can only *speak comfort* to those that receive the gospel, and like other prophets, *say to the righteous* that *it shall be well with them;* but Jesus Christ will *give them comfort.* John can only promise them that they shall be safe; but Christ will make them so: he will *gather the wheat into his garner;* good, serious, solid people he will gather now into his church on earth, which shall be made up of such, and he will shortly gather them into his church in heaven, where they shall be for ever sheltered. [4.] John can only *threaten* hypocrites, and tell the *barren trees* that they shall be *hewn down* and *cast into the fire;* but Christ can execute that threatening; those that are as *chaff,* light, and vain, and worthless, *he will burn with fire unquenchable.* John refers here to Mal. iii. 18; iv. 1, 2. *Then,* when the *floor is purged, ye shall return, and discern between the righteous and the wicked,* for *the day comes that shall burn as an oven.*

The evangelist concludes his account of John's preaching with an *et cætera* (*v.* 18): *Many other things in his exhortation preached he unto the people,* which are not recorded. *First,* John was an *affectionate* preacher. He was παρακαλῶν—*exhorting,* beseeching; he pressed things home upon his hearers, followed his doctrine close, as one in earnest. *Secondly,* He was a *practical* preacher. Much of his preaching was *exhortation,* quickening them to their duty, directing them in it, and not amusing them with matters of nice speculation. *Thirdly,* He was a *popular* preacher. Though he had scribes and Pharisees, men of polite learning, attending his ministry, and Sadducees, men of *free thought,* as they pretended, yet he addressed himself *to the people,* πρὸς τόν λαόν—*to the laity,* and accommodated himself to their capacity, as promising himself best success among them. *Fourthly,* He was an *evangelical* preacher, for so the word here used signifies, εὐηγγελίζετο—*he preached the gospel* to the people; in all his *exhortations,* he directed people to Christ, and excited and encouraged their expectations of *him.* When we press duty upon people, we must direct them to Christ, both for righteousness and strength. *Fifthly,* He was a *copious* preacher: *Many other things he preached,* πολλὰ μὲν καὶ ἕτερα—*many things, and different.* He preached a great deal, shunned not to declare the whole counsel of God; and he *varied* in his preaching, that those who were not reached, and touched, and wrought upon, by one truth, might be by another.

III. How full a stop was put to John's preaching. When he was in the midst of his usefulness, going on thus successfully, he was imprisoned by the malice of Herod (*v.* 19, 20): *Herod the tetrarch being reproved by him,* not only for living in incest with his brother Philip's wife, but for the many other *evils which Herod had done* (for those that are wicked in one instance are commonly so in many others), he could not *bear it,* but contracted an antipathy to him for his plain dealing, and *added* this wickedness to all the rest, which was indeed *above all,* that he *shut up John in prison,* put that burning and shining light under a bushel. Because he could not bear his reproofs, others should be deprived of the benefit of his instructions and counsels. Some little good he might do to those who had access to him, when he was in prison; but nothing to what he might have done if he had had liberty to go about all the country, as he had done. We cannot think of Herod's doing this without the greatest compassion and lamentation, nor of God's permitting it without admiring the depth of the divine counsels, which we cannot account for. Must he be silenced who is the *voice of one crying in the wilderness?* Must such a preacher be shut up in prison, who ought to have been set up in the courts of the temple? But thus the faith of his disciples must be tried; thus the unbelief of those who rejected him must be punished; thus he must be Christ's forerunner in suffering as well as preaching; and thus, having been for about a year and a half preparing people for Christ, he must now give way to him, and, the Sun being risen, the morning-star must of course disappear.

21 Now when all the people were
baptized, it came to pass, that Jesus
also being baptized, and praying, the
heaven was opened. 22 And the
Holy Ghost descended in a bodily
shape like a dove upon him, and a
voice came from heaven, which said,
Thou art my beloved Son; in thee I
am well pleased. 23 And Jesus himself began to be about thirty years of
age, being (as was supposed) the son
of Joseph, which was *the son* of Heli,
24 Which was *the son* of Matthat,
which was *the son* of Levi, which was
the son of Melchi, which was *the son*
of Janna, which was *the son* of Joseph,
25 Which was *the son* of Mattathias,
which was *the son* of Amos, which
was *the son* of Naum, which was *the
son* of Esli, which was *the son* of
Nagge, 26 Which was *the son* of
Maath, which was *the son* of Mattathias, which was *the son* of Semei,
which was *the son* of Joseph, which
was *the son* of Juda, 27 Which was *the
son* of Joanna, which was *the son* of
Rhesa, which was *the son* of Zorobabel, which was *the son* of Salathiel,
which was *the son* of Neri, 28 Which
was *the son* of Melchi, which was *the
son* of Addi, which was *the son* of
Cosam, which was *the son* of Elmodam,
which was *the son* of Er, 29 Which
was *the son* of Jose, which was *the
son* of Eliezer, which was *the son* of
Jorim, which was *the son* of Matthat,
which was *the son* of Levi, 30 Which
was *the son* of Simeon, which was *the
son* of Juda, which was *the son* of
Joseph, which was *the son* of Jonan,
which was *the son* of Eliakim, 31
Which was *the son* of Melea, which
was *the son* of Menan, which was *the
son* of Mattatha, which was *the son*
of Nathan, which was *the son* of
David, 32 Which was *the son* of
Jesse, which was *the son* of Obed,
which was *the son* of Booz, which was
the son of Salmon, which was *the son*
of Naasson, 33 Which was *the son* of
Aminadab, which was *the son* of Aram,
which was *the son* of Esrom, which
was *the son* of Phares, which was *the
son* of Juda, 34 Which was *the son*
of Jacob, which was *the son* of Isaac,
which was *the son* of Abraham, which
was *the son* of Thara, which was *the
son* of Nachor, 35 Which was *the son*
of Saruch, which was *the son* of Ra-
gau, which was *the son* of Phalec,
which was *the son* of Heber, which
was *the son* of Sala, 36 Which was
the son of Cainan, which was *the son*
of Arphaxad, which was *the son* of
Sem, which was *the son* of Noe, which
was *the son* of Lamech, 37 Which
was *the son* of Mathusala, which was
the son of Enoch, which was *the son*
of Jared, which was *the son* of Ma-
leleel, which was *the son* of Cainan,
38 Which was *the son* of Enos, which
was *the son* of Seth, which was *the son*
of Adam, which was *the son* of God.

The evangelist mentioned John's imprisonment before Christ's being baptized, though it was nearly a year after it, because he would finish the story of John's ministry, and then introduce that of Christ. Now here we have,

I. A short account of Christ's baptism, which had been more fully related by St. Matthew. Jesus came, to be baptized of John, and he was so, *v.* 21, 22.

1. It is here said that, *when all the people were baptized,* then *Jesus was baptized:* all that were then present. Christ would be baptized last, among the common people, and in the rear of them; thus he humbled himself, and made himself of no reputation, as

one of the least, nay, as less than the least. He saw what multitudes were hereby prepared to receive him, and then he appeared.

2. Notice is here taken of Christ's *praying* when he was *baptized*, which was not in Matthew: being baptized, and *praying*. He did not *confess sin*, as others did, for he had none to confess; but he *prayed*, as others did, for he would thus keep up communion with his Father. Note, The inward and spiritual grace of which sacraments are the outward and visible signs must be fetched in by prayer; and therefore prayer must always accompany them. We have reason to think that Christ now prayed for this manifestation of God's favour to him which immediately followed; he prayed for the discovery of his Father's favour to him, and the descent of the Spirit. What was promised to Christ, he must obtain by prayer: *Ask of me and I will give thee, &c.* Thus he would put an honour upon prayer, would tie us to it, and encourage us in it.

3. When he prayed, *the heaven was opened.* He that by his power parted the waters, to make a way through them to Canaan, now by his power parted the air, another fluid element, to open a correspondence with the heavenly Canaan. Thus was there opened to Christ, and by him to us, *a new and living way into the holiest;* sin had shut up heaven, but Christ's prayer opened it again. Prayer is an ordinance that *opens heaven: Knock, and it shall be opened unto you.*

4. *The Holy Ghost descended in a bodily shape like a dove upon him;* our Lord Jesus was now to receive greater measures of the Spirit than before, to qualify him for his prophetical office, Isa. lxi. 1. When he begins to preach, *the Spirit of the Lord is upon him.* Now this is here expressed by a sensible evidence for his encouragement in his work, and for the satisfaction of John the Baptist; for he was told before that by this sign it should be notified to him which was the Christ. Dr. Lightfoot suggests that the Holy Ghost descended in a bodily shape, that he might be revealed to be a personal substance, and not merely an operation of the Godhead: and thus (saith he) was made a full, clear, and sensible demonstration of the Trinity, at the beginning of the gospel; and very fitly is this done at Christ's baptism, who was to make the ordinance of baptism a badge of the profession of that faith in the doctrine of the Trinity, *Father, Son, and Holy Ghost.*

5. There came *a voice from heaven*, from God the Father, from the *excellent glory* (so it is expressed, 2 Pet. i. 17), *Thou art my beloved Son.* Here, and in Mark, it is expressed as spoken *to* Christ; in Matthew as spoken *of* him: *This is my beloved Son.* It comes all to one; it was intended to be a notification to John, and as such was properly expressed by, *This is my beloved Son;* and likewise an answer to his prayer, and so it is most fitly expressed by, *Thou art.* It was foretold concerning the Messiah, *I will be his Father, and he shall be my Son,* 2 Sam. vii. 14. *I will make him my First-born,* Ps. lxxxix. 27. It was also foretold that he should be God's *elect, in whom his soul delighted* (Isa. xlii. 1); and, accordingly, it is here declared, *Thou art my beloved Son, in whom I am well pleased.*

II. A long account of Christ's pedigree, which had been more briefly related by St. Matthew. Here is,

1. His age: *He now began to be about thirty years of age.* So old Joseph was when he stood before Pharaoh (Gen. xli. 46), David when he began to reign (2 Sam. v. 4), and at this age the priests were to enter upon the full execution of their office, Num. iv. 3. Dr. Lightfoot thinks that it is plain, by the manner of expression here, that he was just twenty-nine years old complete, and entering upon his thirtieth year, in the month *Tisri;* that, after this, he lived three years and a half, and died when he was thirty-two years and a half old. *Three years and a half*, the time of Christ's ministry, is a period of time very remarkable in scripture. *Three years and six months* the heavens were shut up in Elijah's time, Luke iv. 25; Jam. v. 17. This was the half week in which the Messiah was to confirm the covenant, Dan. ix. 27. This period is expressed in the prophetical writings by a time, times, and half a time (Dan. xii. 7; Rev. xii. 14); and by forty-two months, and a thousand two hundred and threescore days, Rev. xi. 2, 3. It is the time fixed for the witnesses' prophesying in sackcloth, in conformity to Christ's preaching in his humiliation just so long.

2. His pedigree, *v.* 23, &c. Matthew had given us somewhat of this. He goes no higher than Abraham, but Luke brings it as high as Adam. Matthew designed to show that Christ was the son of Abraham, in whom *all the families of the earth are blessed,* and that he was heir to the throne of David; and therefore he begins with Abraham, and brings the genealogy down to Jacob, who was the father of Joseph, an heir-male of the house of David: but Luke, designing to show that Christ was the *seed of the woman,* that should break the serpent's head, traces his pedigree upward as high as Adam, and begins it with Eli, or Heli, who was the father, not of Joseph, but of the virgin Mary. And some suggest that the supply which our translators all along insert here is not right, and that it should not be read *which,* that is, which Joseph was the son of Heli, but which *Jesus;* he was *the son of Joseph, of Eli, of Matthat,* &c., and he, that is, Jesus, was the son *of Seth, of Adam, of God, v.* 38. The difference between the two evangelists in the genealogy of Christ has been a stumbling-block to infidels that cavil at the word, but such a one as has been removed by the labours of learned men, both in the early ages of the

church and in latter times, to which we refer ourselves. Matthew draws the pedigree from Solomon, whose natural line ending in Jechonias, the legal right was transferred to Salathiel, who was of the house of Nathan, another son of David, which line Luke here pursues, and so leaves out all the kings of Judah. It is well for us that our salvation doth not depend upon our being able to solve all these difficulties, nor is the divine authority of the gospels at all weakened by them; for the evangelists are not supposed to write these genealogies either of their own knowledge or by divine inspiration, but to have copied them out of the authentic records of the genealogies among the Jews, the heralds' books, which therefore they were obliged to follow; and in them they found the pedigree of Jacob, the father of Joseph, to be as it is set down in Matthew; and the pedigree of Heli, the father of Mary, to be as it is set down here in Luke. And this is the meaning of ὡς ἐνομίζετο (*v.* 23), not, *as it was supposed,* referring only to Joseph, but *uti sancitum est lege—as it is entered into the books,* as we find it upon record; by which it appeared that Jesus was both by father and mother's side the Son of David, witness this extract out of their own records, which any one might at that time have liberty to compare with the original, and further the evangelists needed not to go; nay, had they varied from that, they had not gained their point. Its not being contradicted at that time is satisfaction enough to us now that it is a true copy, as it is further worthy of observation, that, when those records of the Jewish genealogies had continued thirty or forty years after these extracts out of them, long enough to justify the evangelists therein, they were all lost and destroyed with the Jewish state and nation; for now there was no more occasion for them.

One difficulty occurs between Abraham and Noah, which gives us some perplexity, *v.* 35, 36. Sala is said to be the *son of Cainan,* and he *the son of Arphaxad,* whereas Sala was the son of Arphaxad (Gen. x. 24; xi. 12), and there is no such man as Cainan found there. But, as to that, it is sufficient to say that the Seventy Interpreters, who, before our Saviour's time, translated the Old Testament into Greek, for reasons best known to themselves inserted that Cainan; and St. Luke, writing among the *Hellenist Jews,* was obliged to make use of that translation, and therefore to take it as he found it.

The genealogy concludes with this, *who was the son of Adam, the son of God.* (1.) Some refer it to Adam; he was in a peculiar manner the *son of God,* being, more immediately than any of his offspring, the offspring of God by creation. (2.) Others refer it to Christ, and so make the last words of this genealogy to denote his divine and human nature. He was both the *Son of Adam* and the *Son of God,* that he might be a proper Mediator between God and the sons of Adam, and might bring the sons of Adam to be, through him, the *sons of God.*

CHAP. IV.

We left Christ newly baptized, and owned by a voice from heaven and the descent of the Holy Ghost upon him. Now, in this chapter, we have, I. A further preparation of him for his public ministry by his being tempted in the wilderness, of which we had the same account before in Matthew as we have here, (ver. 1—13.) II. His entrance upon his public work in Galilee (ver. 14, 15), particularly, 1. At Nazareth, the city where he had been bred up (ver. 16—30), which we had no account of before in Matthew. 2. At Capernaum, where, having preached to admiration (ver. 31—32), he cast the devil out of a man that was possessed (ver. 33—37), cured Peter's mother-in-law of a fever (ver. 38, 39), and many others that were sick and possessed, (ver. 40, 41), and then went and did the same in other cities of Galilee, ver. 42—44.

AND Jesus being full of the Holy
Ghost returned from Jordan, and
was led by the Spirit into the wilderness, 2 Being forty days tempted of
the devil. And in those days he did
eat nothing: and when they were
ended, he afterward hungered. 3
And the devil said unto him, If thou
be the Son of God, command this
stone that it be made bread. 4 And
Jesus answered him, saying, It is
written, That man shall not live by
bread alone, but by every word of
God. 5 And the devil, taking him
up into a high mountain, showed
unto him all the kingdoms of the
world in a moment of time. 6 And
the devil said unto him, All this power
will I give thee, and the glory of them:
for that is delivered unto me; and to
whomsoever I will I give it. 7 If
thou therefore wilt worship me, all
shall be thine. 8 And Jesus answered and said unto him, Get thee
behind me, Satan: for it is written,
Thou shalt worship the Lord thy God,
and him only shalt thou serve. 9 And
he brought him to Jerusalem, and set
him on a pinnacle of the temple, and
said unto him, If thou be the Son of
God, cast thyself down from hence:
10 For it is written, He shall give
his angels charge over thee, to keep
thee: 11 And in *their* hands they
shall bear thee up, lest at any time
thou dash thy foot against a stone.
12 And Jesus answering said unto
him, It is said, Thou shalt not tempt
the Lord thy God. 13 And when
the devil had ended all the temptation,
he departed from him for a season.

The last words of the foregoing chapter, that Jesus was the *Son of Adam,* bespeak him to be the *seed of the woman;* being so, we have him here, according to the promise, *breaking the serpent's head,* baffling and foiling the devil in all his temptations, who by one temptation had baffled and foiled our first parents. Thus, in the beginning of the war, he made reprisals upon him, and conquered the conqueror.

In this story of Christ's temptation, observe,

I. How he was *prepared* and *fitted* for it. He that designed him the trial furnished him accordingly; for though we know not what exercises may be before us, nor what encounters we may be reserved for, Christ did, and was provided accordingly; and God doth for us, and we hope will provide accordingly.

1. He was *full of the Holy Ghost,* who had *descended* on him *like a dove.* He had now greater measures of the gifts, graces, and comforts, of the Holy Ghost than ever before. Note, Those are well armed against the strongest temptations that are *full of the Holy Ghost.*

2. He was newly *returned from Jordan,* where he was baptized, and owned by a voice from heaven to be the beloved Son of God; and thus he was *prepared* for this combat. Note, When we have had the most comfortable communion with God, and the clearest discoveries of his favour to us, we may expect that Satan will set upon us (the richest ship is the pirate's prize), and that God will suffer him to do so, that the power of his grace may be manifested and magnified.

3. He was *led by the Spirit into the wilderness,* by the good Spirit, who led him as a champion into the field, to fight the enemy that he was sure to conquer. His being *led into the wilderness,* (1.) *Gave* some advantage to the tempter; for there he had him alone, no friend with him, by whose prayers and advice he might be assisted in the hour of temptation. *Woe to him that is alone! He might* give Satan advantage, who knew his own strength; *we may not,* who know our own weakness. (2.) He *gained* some advantage to himself, during his forty days' fasting in the wilderness. We may suppose that he was wholly taken up in proper meditation, and in consideration of his own undertaking, and the work he had before him; that he spent all his time in immediate, intimate, converse with his Father, as Moses in the mount, without any diversion, distraction, or interruption. Of all the days of Christ's life in the flesh, these seem to come nearest to the angelic perfection and the heavenly life, and this prepared him for Satan's assaults, and hereby he was fortified against them.

4. He continued fasting (*v.* 2): *In those days he did eat nothing.* This fast was altogether miraculous, like those of Moses and Elijah, and shows him to be, like them, a prophet *sent of God.* It is probable that it was in the wilderness of Horeb, the same wilderness in which Moses and Elijah fasted. As by retiring into the *wilderness* he showed himself perfectly indifferent to the *world,* so by his *fasting* he showed himself perfectly indifferent to the *body;* and Satan cannot easily take hold of those who are thus loosened from, and dead to, the *world* and the *flesh.* The more we *keep under the body,* and bring it into subjection, the less advantage Satan has against us.

II. How he was assaulted by one temptation after another, and how he defeated the design of the tempter in every assault, and became more than a conqueror. During the *forty days,* he was *tempted of the devil* (*v.* 2), not by any inward suggestions, for the prince of this world had nothing in Christ by which to inject any such, but by outward solicitations, perhaps in the likeness of a serpent, as he tempted our first parents. But at the end of the forty days he came nearer to him, and did as it were close with him, when he perceived *that he was hungry, v.* 2. Probably, our Lord Jesus then began to look about among the trees, to see if he could find any thing that was eatable, whence the devil took occasion to make the following proposal to him.

1. He tempted him to *distrust his Father's* care of him, and to *set up for himself,* and shift for provision for himself in such a way as his Father had not appointed for him (*v.* 3): *If thou be the Son of God,* as the voice from heaven declared, *command this stone to be made bread.* (1.) "I counsel thee to do it; for God, if he be thy Father, has forgotten thee, and it will be long enough ere he sends either ravens or angels to feed thee." If we begin to think of being our own carvers, and of living by our own forecast, without depending upon divine Providence, of getting wealth *by our might and the power of our hands,* we must look upon it as a temptation of Satan's, and reject it accordingly; it is Satan's counsel to think of an independence upon God. (2.) "I *challenge* thee to do it, if thou canst; if thou dost not do it, I will say thou art *not the Son of God;* for John Baptist said lately, *God is able of stones to raise up children to Abraham,* which is the greater; thou therefore hast not the power of the *Son of God,* if thou dost not *of stones make bread* for thyself, when thou needest it, which is the less." Thus was God himself tempted in the wilderness: *Can he furnish a table? Can he give bread?* Ps. lxxviii. 19, 20.

Now, [1.] Christ yielded not to the temptation; he would not *turn* that *stone* into *bread;* no, though he was hungry; *First,* Because he would not do what Satan bade him do, for that would have looked as if there had been indeed a compact between him and the prince of the devils. Note, We must not do any thing that looks like *giving place to the devil.* Miracles were wrought for the confirming of faith, and the devil had no faith to be confirmed, and therefore he would not do it *for him.* He did his signs *in the presence of his disciples* (John xx. 30), and particularly the *beginning of his miracles,* turning water into wine, which he did, that his disciples might believe on him (John ii. 11); but here in the wilderness he had no disciples with him. *Secondly,* He wrought miracles for the ratification of his doctrine, and therefore till he began to *preach* he would not begin to work miracles. *Thirdly,* He would not work miracles *for himself* and his own supply, lest he should seem impatient of *hunger,* whereas he came not to *please himself,* but to *suffer grief,* and that grief among others; and because he would show that he *pleased not himself,* he would rather turn *water into wine,* for the credit and convenience of his friends, than *stones into bread,* for his own *necessary supply. Fourthly,* He would reserve the proof of his being the Son of God for hereafter, and would rather be upbraided by Satan with being weak, and not able to do it, than be persuaded by Satan to do that which it was not fit for him to do; thus he was upbraided by his enemies as if he could not *save himself,* and *come down from the cross,* when he could have come down, but would not, because it was not fit that he should. *Fifthly,* He would not do any thing that looked like distrust of his Father, or *acting separately* from him, or any thing disagreeable to his present state. Being in all things *made like unto his brethren,* he would, like the other children of God, live in a dependence upon the divine Providence and promise, and trust him either to send him a supply into the wilderness or to *lead him to a city of habitation* where there was a supply, as he used to do (Ps. cvii. 5—7), and in the mean time would *support* him, though he was hungry, as he had done these forty days past.

[2.] He returned a scripture-answer to it (*v.* 4): *It is written.* This is the first word recorded as spoken by Christ after his instalment in his prophetical office; and it is a quotation out of the Old Testament, to show that he came to assert and maintain the authority of the scripture as uncontrollable, even by Satan himself. And though he had the Spirit without measure, and had a doctrine of his own to preach and a religion to found, yet it agreed with Moses and the prophets, whose writings he therefore lays down as a rule to himself, and recommends to us as a reply to Satan and his temptations. The word of God is our *sword,* and faith in that word is our *shield;* we should therefore be *mighty in the scriptures,* and *go in that might,* go forth, and go on, in our spiritual warfare, know *what is written,* for it is *for our learning,* for *our use.* The text of scripture he makes use of is quoted from Deut. viii. 3: "*Man shall not live by bread alone.* I need not turn the stone into bread, for God can send *manna* for my nourishment, as he did for Israel; man can live *by every word of God,* by whatever God will appoint that he shall live by." How had Christ lived, lived comfortably, these last forty days? Not *by bread,* but by the *word of God,* by meditation upon that word, and communion with it, and with God in and by it; and in like manner he could *live yet,* though now he began to be *hungry.* God has many ways of providing for his people, without the ordinary means of subsistence; and therefore he is not at any time to be distrusted, but at all times to be depended upon, in the way of duty. If meat be wanting, God can take away the appetite, or give such degrees of patience as will enable a man even to *laugh at destruction and famine* (Job v. 22), or make *pulse and water* more nourishing than *all the portion of the king's meat* (Dan. i. 12, 13), and enable his people to *rejoice in the Lord,* when the *fig-tree doth not blossom,* Hab. iii. 17. She was an active believer who said that she had made many a meal's meat of the promises when she wanted bread.

2. He tempted him to *accept from him* the kingdom, which, as the *Son of God,* he expected to receive from *his Father,* and to *do him homage* for, *v.* 5—7. This evangelist puts this temptation second, which Matthew had put last, and which, it should seem, was really the last; but Luke was full of it, as the blackest and most violent, and therefore hastened to it. In the devil's tempting of our first parents, he presented to them the forbidden fruit, first as *good for food,* and then as *pleasant to the eyes;* and they were overpowered by both these charms. Satan here first tempted Christ to turn the stones into bread, which would be good for food, and then showed him the kingdoms of the world and the glory of them, which were *pleasant to the eyes;* but in both these he overpowered Satan, and, perhaps with an eye to that, Luke changes the order. Now observe,

(1.) How Satan *managed* this temptation, to prevail with Christ to become a tributary to him, and to receive his kingdom by delegation from him.

[1.] He gave him a prospect of *all the kingdoms of the world in a moment of time,* an airy representation of them, such as he thought most likely to strike the fancy, and seem a *real* prospect. To succeed the better, he *took him up* for this purpose *into a high mountain;* and, because we next after the temptation find Christ on the other side Jordan, some think it probable that it was to the top of Pisgah that the devil took him, whence Moses had a sight of Canaan. That it was but a phantasm that the devil here presented our Saviour with, as the prince of the power of the air, is confirmed by that circumstance which Luke here takes notice of, that it was done *in a moment of time;* whereas, if a man take a prospect of but one country, he must do it successively, must turn himself round, and take a view first of one part and then of another. Thus the devil thought to impose upon our Saviour with a fallacy—*a deceptio visus;* and, by making him believe that he could *show him all the kingdoms of* the world, would draw him into an opinion that he could *give him* all those kingdoms.

[2.] He boldly alleged that these kingdoms were *all delivered to him,* that he had power to dispose of them and all their *glory,* and to give them to *whomsoever he would, v.* 6. Some think that herein he pretended to be an angel of light, and that, as one of the angels that was set over the kingdoms, he had out-bought, or out-fought, all the rest, and so was *entrusted* with the disposal of them all, and, in God's name, would give them to him, knowing they were designed for him; but clogged with this condition, that he should *fall down and worship him,* which a good angel would have been so far from demanding that he would not have admitted it, no, not upon showing much greater things than these, as appears, Rev. xix. 10; xxii. 9. But I rather take it that he claimed this power as Satan, and as *delivered to him,* not by *the Lord,* but by the kings and people of these kingdoms, who gave their power and honour to the devil, Eph. ii. 2. Hence he is called the *god of this world,* and the *prince of this world.* It was promised to the Son of God that he should have *the heathen for his inheritance,* Ps. ii. 8.' "Why," saith the devil, "the heathen are *mine,* are my subjects and votaries; but, however, they shall be thine, I will give them *thee,* upon condition that thou *worship me* for them, and say that they are the *rewards which I have given thee,* as others have done before *thee* (Hos. ii. 12), and consent to have and *hold them by, from, and under, me.*"

[3.] He demanded of him homage and adoration: *If thou wilt worship me, all shall be thine, v.* 7. *First,* He would have him worship him himself. Perhaps he does not mean so as never to worship God, but let him worship him in conjunction with God; for the devil knows, if he can but once come in a partner, he shall soon be sole proprietor. *Secondly,* He would indent with him, that, when, according to the promise made to him, he had got possession of the kingdoms of this world, he should make no alteration of religions in them, but permit and suffer the nations, as they had done hitherto, to *sacrifice to devils* (1 Cor. x. 20); that he should still keep up *demon-worship* in the world, and then let him take all the power and glory of the kingdoms if he pleased. Let who will take the wealth and grandeur of this earth, Satan has all he would have if he can but have men's hearts, and affections, and adorations, can but *work in the children of* disobedience; for then he effectually *devours them.*

(2.) How our Lord Jesus *triumphed* over this temptation. He gave it a peremptory repulse, rejected it with abhorrence (*v.* 8): "*Get thee behind me, Satan,* I cannot bear the mention of it. What! worship the enemy of God whom I came to serve? and of man whom I came to save? No, I will never do it." Such a temptation as this was not to be *reasoned with,* but immediately refused; it was presently knocked on the head with one word, *It is written, Thou shalt worship the Lord thy God;* and not only so, but *him only,* him and *no other.* And therefore Christ will not worship Satan, nor, when he has the *kingdoms of the world delivered* to him by his Father, as he expects shortly to have, will he suffer any remains of the worship of the devil to continue in them. No, it shall be perfectly rooted out and abolished, wherever his gospel comes. He will make no composition with him. *Polytheism* and *idolatry* must go down, as Christ's kingdom gets up. Men must be *turned from the power of Satan unto God,* from the worship of devils to the worship of the only living and true God. This is the great divine law that Christ will re-establish among men, and by his holy religion reduce men to the obedience of, *That God only is to be served and worshipped;* and therefore whoever set up any creature as the object of religious worship, though it were a saint or an angel, or the virgin Mary herself, they directly thwart Christ's design, and relapse into heathenism.

3. He tempted him to be his own murderer, in a presumptuous confidence of his Father's protection, such as he had no warrant for. Observe,

(1.) What he designed in this temptation: *If thou be the Son of God, cast thyself down, v.* 9. [1.] He would have him seek for a new proof of his being the *Son of God,* as if that which his Father had given him by the voice from heaven, and the descent of the Spirit upon him, were not sufficient, which would have been a dishonour to God, as if he had not chosen the most proper way of giving him the assurance of it; and it would have argued a distrust of the Spirit's dwelling in him, which was the great and most convincing proof to himself of his being the *Son of God,* Heb. i. 8, 9. [2.] He would have him seek a new method of proclaiming and publishing this to the world. The devil, in effect, suggests that it was in an *obscure corner* that he was attested to be the Son of God, among a company of ordinary people, who attended John's baptism, that his honours were proclaimed; but if he would now declare from *the pinnacle of the temple,* among all the great people who attend the temple-service, that he was the Son of God, and then, for proof of it, throw himself down unhurt, he would presently be received by every body as a messenger sent from heaven. Thus Satan would have him seek honours of his devising (in contempt of those which God had put on him), and manifest himself in the temple at Jerusalem; whereas God designed he should be more manifest among John's penitents, to whom his doctrine would be more welcome than to the priests. [3.] It is probable he had some hopes that, though he could not throw him down, to do him the least mischief, yet, if he would but throw himself down, the fall might be his death, and then he should have got him finely out of the way.

(2.) How he backed and enforced this temptation. He suggested, *It is written, v.* 10. Christ had quoted scripture against him; and he thought he would be quits with him, and would show that he could quote scripture as well as he. It has been usual with heretics and seducers to pervert scripture, and to press the sacred writings into the service of the worst of wickednesses. *He shall give his angels charge over thee,* if thou be his Son, and *in their hands they shall bear thee up.* And now that he was upon the pinnacle of the temple he might especially expect this ministration of angels; for, if he was the Son of God, the *temple* was the proper place for him to be in (*ch.* ii. 46); and, if any place under the sun had a guard of angels constantly, it must needs be that, Ps. lxviii. 17. It is true, God has promised the protection of angels, to encourage us to trust him, not to tempt him; as far as the promise of God's presence with us, so far the promise of the angels' ministration goes, but no further: "They shall keep thee when thou goest on the ground, where thy way lies, but not if thou wilt presume to fly in the air."

(3.) How he was baffled and defeated in the temptation, *v.* 12. Christ quoted Deut. vi. 16, where it is said, *Thou shalt not tempt the Lord thy God,* by desiring a sign for the proof of divine revelation, when he has already given that which is sufficient; for so Israel did, when they *tempted God in the wilderness,* saying, He *gave us water out of the rock; but can he give flesh also?* This Christ would be guilty of if he should say, "He did indeed prove me to be the Son of God, by sending the Spirit upon me, which is the *greater;* but can he also give his angels a charge concerning me, which is the *less?*"

III. What was the result and issue of this combat, *v.* 13. Our victorious Redeemer kept his ground, and came off a conqueror, not for himself only, but for us also.

1. The devil emptied his quiver: *He ended all the temptation.* Christ gave him opportunity to say and do all he could against him; he let him try all his force, and yet defeated him. Did Christ suffer, being tempted, till all the temptation was ended? And must not we expect also to pass all our trials, to go through the *hour of temptation* assigned us?

2. He then quitted the field: He *departed from him.* He saw it was to no purpose to attack him; he had *nothing in him* for his fiery darts to fasten upon; he had no blind side, no weak or unguarded part in his wall, and therefore Satan gave up the cause. Note, If we resist the devil, he will flee from us.

3. Yet he continued his malice against him, and departed with a resolution to attack him again; he departed but *for a season, ἄχρι καιροῦ—till a season,* or till the season when he was again to be let loose upon him, not as a *tempter,* to draw him to *sin,* and so to strike at *his head,* which was what he now aimed at and was wholly defeated in; but as a *persecutor,* to bring him to *suffer* by Judas and the other wicked instruments whom he employed, and so to *bruise his heel,* which it was told him (Gen. iii. 15) he should have to do, and would do, though it would be the breaking of *his own head.* He *departed now* till that season came which Christ calls the *power of darkness* (*ch.* xxii. 53), and when the prince of this world would again *come,* John xiv. 30.

14 And Jesus returned in the
power of the Spirit into Galilee: and
there went out a fame of him through
all the region round about. 15 And
he taught in their synagogues, being
glorified of all. 16 And he came to
Nazareth, where he had been brought
up: and, as his custom was, he went
into the synagogue on the sabbath
day, and stood up for to read. 7
And there was delivered unto him the
book of the prophet Esaias. And
when he had opened the book, he
found the place where it was written,
18 The Spirit of the Lord *is* upon
me, because he hath anointed me to
preach the gospel to the poor; he
hath sent me to heal the broken-
hearted, to preach deliverance to the
captives, and recovering of sight to
the blind, to set at liberty them that
are bruised, 19 To preach the acceptable year of the Lord. 20 And he
closed the book, and he gave *it* again
to the minister, and sat down. And
the eyes of all them that were in the
synagogue were fastened on him.
21 And he began to say unto them,
This day is this scripture fulfilled in
your ears. 22 And all bare him witness, and wondered at the gracious
words which proceeded out of his
mouth. And they said, Is not this
Joseph's son? 23 And he said unto
them, Ye will surely say unto me this
proverb, Physician, heal thyself: whatsoever we have heard done in Capernaum, do also here in thy country.
24 And he said, Verily I say unto
you, No prophet is accepted in his
own country. 25 But I tell you of a
truth, many widows were in Israel
in the days of Elias, when the heaven was shut up three years and

six months, when great famine was
throughout all the land; 26 But unto
none of them was Elias sent, save
unto Sarepta, *a city* of Sidon, unto a
woman *that was* a widow. 27 And
many lepers were in Israel in the time
of Eliseus the prophet; and none of
them was cleansed, saving Naaman
the Syrian. 28 And all they in the
synagogue, when they heard these
things, were filled with wrath, 29 And
rose up, and thrust him out of the
city, and led him unto the brow of the
hill whereon their city was built, that
they might cast him down headlong.
30 But he passing through the midst
of them went his way.

After Christ had vanquished the evil spirit, he made it appear how much he was under the influence of the good Spirit; and, having defended himself against the devil's assaults, he now begins to act *offensively*, and to make those attacks upon him, by his preaching and miracles, which he could not resist or repel. Observe,

I. What is here said in general of his preaching, and the entertainment it met with *in Galilee*, a remote part of the country, distant from Jerusalem; it was a part of Christ's humiliation that he began his ministry there.

But, 1. Thither he came *in the power of the Spirit*. The same Spirit that qualified him for the exercise of his prophetical office strongly inclined him to it. He was not to wait for a call from men, for he had light and life in himself. 2. There he *taught in their synagogues*, their places of public worship, where they met, not, as in the temple, for ceremonial services, but for the moral acts of devotion, to read, expound, and apply, the word, to pray and praise, and for church-discipline; these came to be more frequent since the captivity, when the ceremonial worship was near expiring. 3. This he did so as that he gained a great reputation. *A fame of him went through all that region* (*v.* 14), and it was a good fame; for (*v.* 15) he *was glorified of all*. Every body admired him, and cried him up; they never heard such preaching in all their lives. Now, at first, he met with no contempt or contradiction; all *glorified* him, and there were none as yet that vilified him.

II. Of his preaching at Nazareth, the city where he was brought up; and the entertainment it met with there. And here we are told how he *preached* there, and how he was *persecuted*.

1. How he preached there. In that observe,

(1.) The opportunity he had for it: *He came to Nazareth* when he had gained a reputation in other places, in hopes that thereby something at least of the contempt and prejudice with which his countrymen would look upon him might be worn off. There he took occasion to preach, [1.] In the *synagogue*, the proper place, where it had been *his custom* to attend when he was a private person, *v.* 16. We ought to attend on the public worship of God, as we have opportunity. But, now that he was entered upon his public ministry, there he preached. Where the multitudes of fish were, there this wise Fisherman would cast his net. [2.] On the sabbath day, the proper time which the pious Jews spent, not in a mere ceremonial rest from worldly labour, but in the duties of God's worship, as of old they frequented the schools of the prophets on the *new moons* and the *sabbaths*. Note, It is good to keep sabbaths in solemn assemblies.

(2.) The call he had to it. [1.] He *stood up to read*. They had in their synagogues seven readers every sabbath, the first a priest, the second a Levite, and the other five Israelites of that synagogue. We often find Christ *preaching* in other synagogues, but never *reading*, except in this synagogue at Nazareth, of which he had been many years a member. Now he offered his service as he had perhaps often done; he read one of the lessons out of the prophets, Acts xiii. 15. Note, The reading of the scripture is very proper work to be done in religious assemblies; and Christ himself did not think it any disparagement to him to be employed in it. [2.] The *book of the prophet Esaias* was *delivered to him*, either by the ruler of the synagogue or by the minister mentioned (*v.* 20), so that he was no intruder, but duly authorized *pro hac vice—on this occasion*. The second lesson for *that* day being in the prophecy of Esaias, they gave him that volume to read in.

(3.) The text he preached upon. He *stood up to read*, to teach us reverence in *reading* and *hearing* the word of God. When Ezra opened the book of the law, *all the people stood up* (Neh. viii. 5); so did Christ here, when he read in the book of the prophets. Now the book being *delivered to him*, [1.] He *opened* it. The books of the Old Testament were in a manner *shut up* till Christ opened them, Isa. xxix. 11. Worthy *is the Lamb that was slain to take the book, and open the seals;* for he can open, not the book only, but the understanding. [2.] He *found* the place which was appointed to be read *that day* in course, which he needed not to be directed to; he soon found it, and read it, and took it for his text. Now his text was taken out of Isa. lxi. 1, 2, which is here quoted at large, *v.* 18, 19. There was a providence in it that that portion of scripture should be read that day, which speaks so very plainly of the Messiah, that they might be left inexcusable who *knew him not*, though they heard *the voices of the prophets* read *every sabbath day*, which bore witness of him, Acts xiii. 27. This text gives a full account of Christ's undertaking, and the work he came into the world to do. Observe,

First, How he was qualified for the work: *The Spirit of the Lord is upon me.* All the gifts and graces of the Spirit were conferred upon him, not by measure, as upon other prophets, but without measure, John iii. 34. He now came *in the power of the Spirit, v.* 14.

Secondly, How he was commissioned: *Because he has anointed me*, and *sent me.* His extraordinary qualification amounted to a commission; his being *anointed* signifies both his being fitted for the undertaking and called to it. Those whom God *appoints* to any service he *anoints* for it: "Because he hath sent me, he hath sent his Spirit along with me."

Thirdly, What his work was. He was qualified and commissioned,

1. To be a great *prophet.* He was *anointed to preach;* that is three times mentioned here, for that was the work he was now entering upon. Observe, (1.) To *whom* he was to preach: to the *poor;* to those that were *poor in the world*, whom the Jewish doctors disdained to undertake the teaching of and spoke of with contempt; to those that were *poor in spirit*, to the meek and humble, and to those that were truly sorrowful for sin: to them the gospel and the grace of it will be welcome, and they shall have it, Matt. xi. 5. (2.) *What* he was to *preach.* In general, he must preach *the gospel.* He is sent εὐαγγελίζεσθαι—to *evangelize* them; not only to preach to them, but to make that preaching effectual; to bring it, not only to their ears, but to their hearts, and deliver them into the mould of it. Three things he is to preach:—

[1.] *Deliverance to the captives.* The gospel is a proclamation of liberty, like that to Israel in Egypt and in Babylon. By the merit of Christ sinners may be loosed from the bonds of guilt, and by his Spirit and grace from the bondage of corruption. It is a deliverance from the worst of thraldoms, which all those shall have the benefit of that are willing to make Christ their Head, and are willing to be ruled by him.

[2.] *Recovering of sight to the blind.* He came not only by the word of his gospel to bring *light* to them that sat *in the dark*, but by the power of his grace to give sight to them that were *blind;* not only the Gentile world, but every unregenerate soul, that is not only in *bondage*, but in *blindness*, like Samson and Zedekiah. Christ came to tell us that he has *eye-salve* for us, which we may have for the asking; that, if our prayer be, *Lord, that our eyes may be opened*, his answer shall be, *Receive your sight.*

[3.] *The acceptable year of the Lord, v.* 19. He came to let the world know that the God whom they had offended was willing to be reconciled to them, and to *accept* of them upon new terms; that there was yet a way of making their services acceptable to him; that there is now a time of *good will toward men.* It alludes to the year of *release*, or that of *jubilee*, which was an *acceptable year* to servants, who were then set at liberty; to debtors, against whom all actions then dropped; and to those who had mortgaged their lands, for then they returned to them again. Christ came to sound the *jubilee-trumpet;* and blessed were they that heard *the joyful sound*, Ps. lxxxix. 15. It was an acceptable time, for it was a day of salvation.

2. Christ came to be a great *Physician;* for he was sent to *heal the broken-hearted*, to comfort and cure afflicted consciences, to give peace to those that were troubled and humbled for sins, and under a dread of God's wrath against them for them, and to bring them to rest who were weary and heavy-laden, under the burden of guilt and corruption.

3. To be a great *Redeemer.* He not only proclaims liberty to the captives, as Cyrus did to the Jews in Babylon *(Whoever will, may go up)*, but he sets at liberty them that are bruised; he doth by his Spirit *incline* and *enable* them to make use of the liberty granted, as then none did but those *whose spirit God stirred up*, Ezra i. 5. He came in God's name to discharge poor sinners that were debtors and prisoners to divine justice. The prophets could but *proclaim liberty*, but Christ, as one having authority, as one that had *power on earth to forgive sins*, came to *set at liberty;* and therefore this clause is added here. Dr. Lightfoot thinks that, according to a liberty the Jews allowed their readers, to compare scripture with scripture, in their reading, for the explication of the text, Christ added it from Isa. lviii. 6, where it is made the duty of the acceptable year to let *the oppressed go free*, where the phrase the LXX. use is the same with this here.

(4.) Here is Christ's *application* of this text to himself (*v.* 21): When he had read it, he *rolled up the book*, and gave it again *to the minister*, or *clerk*, that attended, and *sat down*, according to the custom of the Jewish teachers; he *sat daily in the temple, teaching*, Matt. xxvi. 55. Now he *began* his discourse thus, "*This day is this scripture fulfilled in your ears.* This, which Isaiah wrote by way of prophecy, I have now read to you by way of history." It now began to be fulfilled in Christ's entrance upon his public ministry; *now*, in the report they heard of his preaching and miracles in other places; *now*, in his preaching to them in their own synagogue. It is most probable that Christ went on, and showed particularly how this scripture was fulfilled in the doctrine he preached concerning *the kingdom of heaven at hand;* that that was preaching liberty, and sight, and healing, and all the blessings of *the acceptable year of the Lord.* Many other gracious words proceeded out of his mouth, which these were but the *beginning* of; for Christ often preached long sermons, which we have but a short account of. This was enough to introduce a great deal: *This day is this scripture fulfilled.* Note, [1.] All the scriptures of the Old

Testament that were to be fulfilled in the Messiah had their full accomplishment in the Lord Jesus, which abundantly proves that this was *he that should come.* [2.] In the providences of God, it is fit to observe the *fulfilling of the scriptures.* The works of God are the accomplishment not only of his secret word, but of his word revealed; and it will help us to understand both the scriptures and the providences of God to compare them one with another.

(5.) Here is the *attention* and *admiration* of the auditors.

[1.] Their *attention* (*v.* 20): *The eyes of all them that were in the synagogue* (and, probably, there were a great many) *were fastened on him,* big with expectation what he would say, having heard so much of late concerning him. Note, It is good, in hearing the word, to keep the eye fixed upon the minister by whom God is speaking to us; for, as the eye effects the heart, so, usually, the heart follows the eye, and is wandering, or fixed, as that is. Or, rather, let us learn hence to keep the eye fixed upon Christ speaking to us in and by the minister. *What saith my Lord unto his servants?*

[2.] Their *admiration* (*v.* 22): *They all bore him witness* that he spoke admirably well, and to the purpose. They all commended him, and *wondered at the gracious words that proceeded out of his mouth;* and yet, as appears by what follows, they did not *believe in him.* Note, It is possible that those who are admirers of good ministers and good preaching may yet be themselves no true Christians. Observe, *First,* What it was they admired: The *gracious words which proceeded out of his mouth.* The *words of grace;* good words, and spoken in a winning melting way. Note, Christ's words are *words of grace,* for, grace being *poured into his lips* (Ps. xlv. 2), words of grace poured from them. And these words of grace are to be *wondered at;* Christ's name was Wonderful, and in nothing was he more so than in his grace, in the words of his grace, and the power that went along with those words. We may well wonder that he should speak such *words of grace* to such graceless wretches as we are. *Secondly,* What it was that increased their wonder; and that was the consideration of his original: *They said, Is not this Joseph's son,* and therefore his extraction mean and his education mean? Some from this suggestion took occasion perhaps so much the more to admire his *gracious words,* concluding he must needs be *taught of God,* for they knew no one else had taught him; while others perhaps with this consideration corrected their wonder at his gracious words, and concluded there could be nothing *really* admirable in them, whatever appeared, because he was the *Son of Joseph.* Can any thing great, or worthy our regard, come from one so mean?

(6.) Christ's anticipating an objection which he knew to be in the minds of many of his hearers. Observe,

[1.] What the objection was (*v.* 23): "*You will surely say to me, Physician, heal thyself.* Because you know that I am the Son of Joseph, your neighbour, you will expect that I should work miracles among you, as I have done in other places; as one would expect that a physician, if he be able, should heal, not only himself, but those of his own family and fraternity." Most of Christ's miracles were *cures;*—"Now why should not the sick in thine own city be *healed* as well as those in other cities?" They were designed to cure people of their unbelief;—"Now why should not the disease of unbelief, if it be indeed a disease, be cured in those of thine own city as well as in those of others? *Whatsoever we have heard done in Capernaum,* that has been so much talked of, *do here also in thine own country.*" They were pleased with *Christ's gracious words,* only because they hoped they were but the introduction to some *wondrous works* of his. They wanted to have their lame, and blind, and sick, and lepers, healed and helped, that the charge of their town might be eased; and that was the chief thing they looked at. They thought their own town as worthy to be the stage of miracles as any other; and why should not he rather draw company to that than to any other? And why should not his neighbours and acquaintance have the benefit of his preaching and miracles, rather than any other?

[2.] How he answers this objection against the course he took.

First, By a plain and positive reason why he would not make Nazareth his head-quarters (*v.* 24), because it generally holds true *that no prophet is accepted in his own country,* at least not so well, nor with such probability of doing good, as in some other country; experience seals this. When prophets have been sent with messages and miracles of mercy, few of their own countrymen, that have known their extraction and education, have been fit to *receive them.* So Dr. Hammond. Familiarity breeds contempt; and we are apt to think meanly of those whose conversation we have been accustomed to; and they will scarcely be duly honoured as *prophets* who were well known when they were in the rank of *private men.* That is most esteemed that is *far-fetched* and *dear-bought,* above what is *home-bred,* though really more excellent. This arises likewise from the envy which neighbours commonly have towards one another, so that they cannot endure to see him their *superior* whom awhile ago they took to be every way their *inferior.* For this reason, Christ declined working miracles, or doing any thing extraordinary, at Nazareth, because of the rooted prejudices they had against him there.

Secondly, By pertinent examples of two of the most famous prophets of the Old Testament, who chose to dispense their favours among foreigners rather than among their own countrymen, and that, no doubt, by divine direction. 1. Elijah maintained a *widow of Sarepta,* a *city of Sidon,* one that was a stranger to the commonwealth of Israel, when there was a *famine in the land, v.* 25, 26. The story we have 1 Kings xvii. 9, &c. It is said there that the heaven was shut up *three years and six months;* whereas it is said, 1 Kings xviii. 1, that *in the third year Elijah* showed himself to Ahab, and there was *rain;* but that was not the third year of the drought, but the third year of Elijah's sojourning with the widow of Sarepta. As God would hereby show himself a *Father of the fatherless,* and a *Judge of the widows,* so he would show that he was rich in mercy to all, even to the Gentiles. 2. Elisha cleansed Naaman the Syrian of his leprosy, though he was a Syrian, and not only a foreigner, but an enemy to Israel (*v.* 27): *Many lepers were in Israel in the days of Eliseus,* four particularly, that brought the news of the Syrians' raising the siege of Samaria with precipitation, and leaving the plunder of their tents to enrich Samaria, when Elisha was himself in the besieged city, and this was the accomplishment of his prophecy too; see 2 Kings vii. 1, 3, &c. And yet we do not find that Elisha cleansed them, no not for a reward of their service, and the good tidings they brought, but only this Syrian; for none besides had faith to apply himself to the prophet for a cure. Christ himself often met with greater faith among Gentiles than in Israel. And here he mentions both these instances, to show that he did not dispense the favour of his miracles by private respect, but according to God's wise appointment. And the people of Israel might as justly have said to Elijah, or Elisha, as the Nazárenes to Christ, *Physician, heal thyself.* Nay, Christ wrought his miracles, though not among his townsmen, yet among Israelites, whereas these great prophets wrought theirs among Gentiles. The examples of the saints, though they will not make a bad action good, yet will help to free a good action from the blame of exceptious people.

2. How he was *persecuted* at Nazareth.

(1.) That which provoked them was his taking notice of the favour which God by Elijah and Elisha showed to the Gentiles: *When they heard these things, they were filled with wrath* (*v.* 28), they were *all so;* a great change since *v.* 22, when they *wondered at the gracious words that proceeded out of his mouth;* thus uncertain are the opinions and affections of the multitude, and so very fickle. If they had mixed faith with those gracious words of Christ which they wondered at, they would have been awakened by these latter words of his to take heed of sinning away their opportunities; but those only *pleased the ear,* and went no further, and therefore these *grated on the ear,* and irritated their corruptions. They were angry that he should compare himself, whom they knew to be the son of Joseph, with those great prophets, and compare them with the men of that corrupt age, when all had bowed the knee to Baal. But that which especially exasperated them was that he intimated some kindness God had in reserve for the Gentiles, which the Jews could by no means bear the thoughts of, Acts xxii. 21. Their pious ancestors pleased themselves with the hopes of adding the Gentiles to the church (witness many of David's psalms and Isaiah's prophecies); but this degenerate race, when they had forfeited the covenant themselves, hated to think that any others should be taken in.

(2.) They were provoked to that degree that they made an attempt upon his life. This was a severe trial, now at his setting out, but a specimen of the usage he met with when he *came to his own,* and they *received him not.* [1.] They *rose up* in a tumultuous manner against him, interrupted him in his discourse, and themselves in their devotions, for they could not stay until their synagogue-worship was over. [2.] They *thrust him out of the city,* as one not worthy to have a residence among them, though there he had had a settlement so long. They thrust from them the Saviour and the salvation, as if he had been the offscouring of all things. How justly might he have called for fire from heaven upon them! But this was the day of his patience. [3.] They *led him to the brow of the hill,* with a purpose to *throw him down headlong,* as one not fit to live. Though they knew how inoffensively he had for so many years lived among them, how shining his conversation had been,—though they had heard such a fame of him and had but just now themselves *admired his gracious words,*—though in justice he ought to have been allowed a fair hearing and liberty to explain himself, yet they hurried him away in a popular fury, or frenzy rather, to put him to death in a most barbarous manner. Sometimes they were ready to stone him for the *good works* he did (John x. 32), here for not doing the good works they expected from him. To such a height of wickedness was violence sprung up.

(3.) Yet he escaped, because his hour was not yet come: He *passed through the midst of them,* unhurt. Either he blinded their eyes, as God did those of the Sodomites and Syrians, or he bound their hands, or filled them with confusion, so that they could not do what they designed; for his work was not done, it was but just begun; his hour was not yet come, when it was come, he freely surrendered himself. They *drove* him from them, and he *went his way.* He would have gathered Nazareth, but they *would not,* and therefore their house is *left to them desolate.* This added to the reproach of his being Jesus of Nazareth, that not only it was a place whence no good thing was expected, but that it was such a wicked, rude place, and so *unkind* to him.

Yet there was a providence in it, that he should not be much respected by the men of Nazareth, for that would have looked like a collusion between him and his old acquaintance; but now, though they *received him not,* there were those that did.

31 And came down to Capernaum,
a city of Galilee, and taught them on
the sabbath days. 32 And they were
astonished at his doctrine: for his
word was with power. 33 And in
the synagogue there was a man, which
had a spirit of an unclean devil, and
cried out with a loud voice, 34 Saying, Let *us* alone; what have we to
do with thee, *thou* Jesus of Nazareth?
art thou come to destroy us? I know
thee who thou art; the Holy One of
God. 35 And Jesus rebuked him,
saying, Hold thy peace, and come out
of him. And when the devil had
thrown him in the midst, he came out
of him, and hurt him not. 36 And
they were all amazed, and spake among
themselves, saying, What a word *is*
this! for with authority and power he
commandeth the unclean spirits, and
they come out. 37 And the fame of
him went out into every place of the
country round about. 38 And he
arose out of the synagogue, and entered into Simon's house. And Simon's wife's mother was taken with a
great fever; and they besought him
for her. 39 And he stood over her,
and rebuked the fever; and it left
her: and immediately she arose and
ministered unto them. 40 Now when
the sun was setting, all they that had
any sick with divers diseases brought
them unto him; and he laid his hands
on every one of them, and healed
them. 41 And devils also came out
of many, crying out, and saying, Thou
art Christ the Son of God. And he
rebuking *them* suffered them not to
speak: for they knew that he was
Christ. 42 And when it was day, he
departed and went into a desert place:
and the people sought him, and came
unto him, and stayed him, that he
should not depart from them. 43
And he said unto them, I must preach
the kingdom of God to other cities
also: for therefore am I sent. 44 And
he preached in the synagogues of
Galilee.

When Christ was expelled Nazareth, he came to Capernaum, another city of Galilee. The account we have in these verses of his preaching and miracles there we had before, Mark i. 21, &c. Observe,

I. His preaching: *He taught them on the sabbath days, v.* 31. In hearing the word preached, as an ordinance of God, we *worship God,* and it is a proper work for *sabbath days.* Christ's preaching much affected the people (*v.* 32); they were *astonished at his doctrine,* there was weight in every word he said, and admirable discoveries were made to them by it. The doctrine itself was astonishing, and not only as it came from one that had not had a liberal education. *His word was with power;* there was a commanding force in it, and a working power went along with it to the consciences of men. The doctrine Paul preached hereby proved itself to be of God, that it came *in demonstration of the Spirit and of power.*

II. His miracles. Of these we have here,

1. Two particularly specified, showing Christ to be,

(1.) A *controller* and *conqueror* of *Satan,* in the world of mankind, and in the souls of people, by his power to cast him out of the bodies of those he had taken possession of; for *for this purpose was he manifested, that he might destroy the works of the devil.*

Observe, [1.] The devil is an *unclean spirit,* his nature directly contrary to that of the pure and *holy* God, and degenerated from what it was at first. [2.] This unclean spirit works in the children of men; in the souls of many, as then in men's bodies. [3.] It is possible that those who are very much under the power and working of Satan may yet be found *in the synagogue,* among the worshippers of God. [4.] Even the devils *know and believe* that *Jesus Christ is the Holy One of God,* is sent of God, and is a *Holy One.* [5.] They believe and *tremble.* This unclean spirit *cried out with a loud voice,* under a *certain fearful looking for of judgment,* and apprehensive that Christ was now come to destroy him. Unclean spirits are subject to continual frights. [6.] The devils have *nothing to do with Jesus Christ,* nor desire to have any thing to do with him; for he took not on him the nature of angels. [7.] Christ has the devil under check: *He rebuked him,* saying, *Hold thy peace;* and this word he spoke *with power;* φιμώθητι—*Be muzzled.* Christ did not only enjoin him silence, but stopped his mouth, and forced him to be silent against his will. [8.] In the breaking of Satan's power, both the enemy that is conquered shows his malice, and Christ, the conqueror, shows his over-ruling grace. Here, *First,* The devil showed what he would have done, when he *threw the man in the midst,* with force and fury, as if he would have dashed him to pieces. But, *Secondly,* Christ showed what a power he had over him, in that he not only forced him to leave him, but to leave him without so much as *hurting* him, without giving him a parting blow, a parting gripe. Whom Satan cannot *destroy,* he will do all the *hurt* he can to; but this is a comfort, he can harm them no further than Christ permits; nay, he shall not do them any real harm. He *came out,* and *hurt him not;* that is, the poor man was perfectly well in an instant, though the devil left him with so much rage that all that were present thought he had torn him to pieces. [9.] Christ's power over devils was universally acknowledged and adored, *v.* 36. No one doubted the truth of the miracle; it was evident beyond contradiction, nor was any thing suggested to diminish the glory of it, for they were *all amazed, saying, What a word is this!* They that pretended to cast out devils did it with abundance of charms and spells, to pacify the devil, and lull him asleep, as it were; but Christ commanded them *with authority and power,* which they could not gainsay or resist. Even the *prince of the power of the air* is his vassal, and trembles before him. [10.] This, as much as any thing, gained Christ a reputation, and spread his fame. This instance of his power, which many now-a-days make light of, was then, by them that were eye-witnesses of it (and those no fools either, but men of penetration), magnified, and was looked upon as greatly magnifying him (*v.* 37); upon the account of this, *the fame of him went out,* more than ever, *into every place of the country round about.* Our Lord Jesus, when he set out at first in his public ministry, was greatly talked of, more than afterwards, when people's admiration wore off with the novelty of the thing.

(2.) Christ showed himself to be *a healer of diseases.* In the former, he struck at the root of man's misery, which was Satan's enmity, the origin of all the mischief: in this, he strikes at one of the most spreading branches of it, one of the most common calamities of human life, and that is bodily diseases, which came in with sin, are the most common and sensible corrections for it in this life, and contribute as much as any thing towards the making of our few days *full of trouble.* These our Lord Jesus came to take away the sting of, and, as an indication of that intention, when he was on earth, chose to confirm his doctrine by such miracles, mostly, as took away the diseases themselves. Of all bodily diseases none are more common or fatal to grown people than *fevers;* these come suddenly, and suddenly cut off the number of men's months in the midst; they are sometimes *epidemical,* and *slay their thousands* in a little time. Now here we have Christ's curing a fever with a word's speaking; the place was in Simon's house, his patient was Simon's wife's mother, *v.* 38, 39. Observe, [1.] Christ is a guest that will pay well for his entertainment; those that bid him welcome into their hearts and houses shall be no losers by him; he comes with healing. [2.] Even families that Christ visits may be visited with sickness. Houses that are blessed with his *distinguishing favours* are liable to the *common calamities* of this life. Simon's wife's mother was *ill* of a *fever. Lord, behold, he whom thou lovest is sick.* [3.] Even good people may sometimes be exercised with the sharpest afflictions, more grievous than others: She was *taken with a great fever,* very acute, and high, and threatening; perhaps it seized her head, and made her delirious. The most gentle fevers may by degrees prove dangerous; but this was at first *a great fever.* [4.] No age can exempt from diseases. It is probable that Peter's mother-in-law was *in years,* and yet in a *fever.* [5.] When our relations are sick, we ought to apply ourselves to Christ, by faith and prayer, on their account: *They besought him for her;* and there is a particular promise that the prayer of faith shall benefit the sick. [6.] Christ has a tender concern for his people when they are in sickness and distress: *He stood over her,* as one concerned for her, and compassionating her case. [7.] Christ had, and still has, a sovereign power over bodily diseases: *He rebuked the fever,* and with a word's speaking commanded it away, and *it left her.* He saith to diseases, *Go,* and they go; *Come,* and they come; and can still *rebuke fevers,* even great fevers. [8.] This proves Christ's cures to be miraculous, that they were done in an instant: *Immediately she arose.* [9.] Where Christ gives a new life, in recovery from sickness, he designs and expects that it should be a new life indeed, spent more than ever in his service, to his glory. If distempers be rebuked, and we arise from a bed of sickness, we must set ourselves to minister to Jesus Christ. [10.] Those that minister to Christ must be ready to minister to all that are his for his sake: She *ministered to them,* not only to *him* that had cured her, but to them that had *besought him for her.* We must study to be grateful to those that have prayed for us.

2. A general account given by wholesale of many other miracles of the same kind, which Christ did.

(1.) He *cured many that were diseased,* even all without exception that made their application to him, and it was *when the sun was setting* (*v.* 40); in the evening of that sabbath day which he had spent in the synagogue. Note, It is good to do a full sabbath day's work, to abound in the work of the day, in some good work or other, even till sun-set; as those that call the sabbath, and the business of it, *a delight.* Observe, He cured *all that were sick,* poor as well as rich, and though they were sick of *divers diseases;* so that there was no room to suspect that he had only a specific for some one disease. He had a remedy for every malady. The sign he used in healing was *laying his hands* on the sick; not lifting up his hands for them, for he healed as having authority. He healed by his own power. And thus he would put honour upon that sign which was afterwards used in conferring the Holy Ghost.

(2.) He cast the devil out of many that were possessed, *v.* 41. Confessions were extorted from the demoniacs. They said, *Thou art Christ the Son of God*, but they said it *crying* with rage and indignation; it was a confession upon the rack, and therefore was not admitted in evidence. Christ *rebuked them*, and did not *suffer them to say that they knew him to be the Christ*, that it might appear, beyond all contradiction, that he had obtained a conquest over them, and not made a compact with them.

3. Here is his removal from Capernaum, *v.* 42, 43.

(1.) He *retired* for awhile into a place of *solitude*. It was but a little while that he allowed himself for sleep; not only because a *little served him*, but because he was *content with a little*, and never indulged himself in ease; but, *when it was day*, he *went into a desert place*, not to live constantly like a hermit, but to be sometimes *alone with God*, as even those should be, and contrive to be, that are most engaged in public work, or else their work will go on but poorly, and they will find themselves never *less alone* than when *thus alone*.

(2.) He *returned* again to the places of *concourse* and to the work he had to do there. Though a *desert place* may be a convenient *retreat*, yet it is not a *convenient residence*, because we were not sent into this world to *live to ourselves*, no, not to the *best part* of ourselves only, but to glorify God and do good in our generation. [1.] He was earnestly solicited to stay at Capernaum. *The people* were exceedingly fond of him; I doubt, more because he had healed their sick than because he had preached repentance to them. *They sought him*, enquired which way he went; and, though it was in a *desert place*, they *came unto him*. A desert is no desert if we be *with Christ* there. They *detained him that he should not depart from them*, so that if he would go it should not be for want of invitation. His old neighbours at Nazareth had driven him from them, but his new acquaintance at Capernaum were very importunate for his continuance with them. Note, It ought not to discourage the ministers of Christ that some reject them, for they will meet with others that will welcome them and their message. [2.] He chose rather to *diffuse* the light of his gospel to *many* places than to fix it to *one*, that no one might pretend to be a *mother-church* to the rest. Though he was welcome at Capernaum, and had done abundance of good there, yet he is *sent to preach the gospel to other cities also*; and Capernaum must not insist upon his stay there. They that enjoy the benefit of the gospel must be willing that others also should share in that benefit, and not covet the *monopoly* of it; and those ministers who are not *driven* from one place may yet be *drawn* to another by a prospect of greater usefulness. Christ, though he preached not in vain in the synagogue at Capernaum, yet would not be tied to that, but *preached in the synagogues of Galilee, v.* 44. *Bonum est sui diffusivum—What is good is self-diffusive.* It is well for us that our Lord Jesus has not tied himself to any one place or people, but, wherever two or three are gathered in his name, he will be in the midst of them: and even in *Galilee of the Gentiles* his special presence is in the Christian synagogues.

CHAP. V.

In this chapter, we have, I. Christ preaching to the people out of Peter's ship, for want of a better pulpit, ver. 1—3. II. The recompence he made to Peter for the loan of his boat, in a miraculous draught of fishes, by which he intimated to him and his partners his design to make them, as apostles, fishers of men, ver. 4—11. III. His cleansing the leper, ver. 12—15. IV. A short account of his private devotion and public ministry, ver. 16, 17. V. His cure of the man sick of the palsy, ver. 18—26. VI. His calling Levi the publican, and conversing with publicans on that occasion, ver. 27—32. VII. His justifying his disciples in not fasting so frequently as the disciples of John and the Pharisees did, ver. 33—39.

AND it came to pass, that, as the
people pressed upon him to hear
the word of God, he stood by the
lake of Gennesaret, 2 And saw two
ships standing by the lake: but the
fishermen were gone out of them, and
were washing *their* nets. 3 And he
entered into one of the ships, which
was Simon's, and prayed him that he
would thrust out a little from the
land. And he sat down, and taught
the people out of the ship. 4 Now
when he had left speaking, he said
unto Simon, Launch out into the deep,
and let down your nets for a draught.
5 And Simon answering said unto
him, Master, we have toiled all the
night, and have taken nothing: nevertheless at thy word I will let down
the net. 6 And when they had this
done, they inclosed a great multitude
of fishes: and their net brake. 7 And
they beckoned unto *their* partners,
which were in the other ship, that
they should come and help them.
And they came, and filled both the
ships, so that they began to sink. 8
When Simon Peter saw *it*, he fell
down at Jesus' knees, saying, Depart
from me; for I am a sinful man, O
Lord. 9 For he was astonished, and
all that were with him, at the draught

of the fishes which they had taken:
10 And so *was* also James, and John, the sons of Zebedee, which were partners with Simon. And Jesus said unto Simon, Fear not; from henceforth thou shalt catch men.
11 And when they had brought their ships to land, they forsook all, and followed him.

This passage of story fell, in order of time, before the two miracles we had in the close of the foregoing chapter, and is the same with that which was more briefly related by Matthew and Mark, of Christ's calling Peter and Andrew to be *fishers of men,* Matt. iv. 18, and Mark i. 16. They had not related this miraculous draught of fishes at that time, having only in view the calling of his disciples; but Luke gives us that story as one of the many signs which Jesus did in the presence of his disciples, which *had not been written* in the foregoing books, John xx. 30, 31. Observe here,

I. What vast *crowds* attended Christ's preaching: *The people pressed upon him to hear the word of God* (*v.* 1), insomuch that no house would contain them, but he was forced to draw them out to the *strand,* that they might be reminded of the promise made to Abraham, that his seed should be *as the sand upon the sea shore* (Gen. xxii. 17), and yet of them but *a remnant shall be saved,* Rom. ix. 27. The people *flocked about him* (so the word signifies); they showed respect to his preaching, though not without some rudeness to his person, which was very excusable, for they *pressed upon him.* Some would reckon this a discredit to him, to be thus cried up by the vulgar, when none of the *rulers* or of *the Pharisees believed in him;* but he reckoned it an honour to him, for their souls were as precious as the souls of the grandees, and it is his aim to bring not so much the mighty as the *many sons* to God. It was foretold concerning him that *to him shall the gathering of the people be.* Christ was a popular preacher; and though he was able, at *twelve,* to *dispute* with the *doctors,* yet he chose, at *thirty,* to preach to the capacity of the *vulgar.* See how the people relished *good preaching,* though under all external disadvantages: they pressed to *hear the word of God;* they could perceive it to be the *word of God,* by the divine power and evidence that went along with it, and therefore they coveted to hear it.

II. What poor *conveniences* Christ had for preaching: *He stood by the lake of Gennesareth* (*v.* 1), upon a level with the crowd, so that they could neither see him nor hear him; he was lost among them, and, every one striving to get near him, he was crowded, and in danger of being crowded into the water: what must he do? It does not appear that his hearers had any contrivance to give him advantage, but *there were two ships,* or *fishing boats,* brought to shore, one belonging to Simon and Andrew, the other to Zebedee and *his sons, v.* 2. At first, Christ saw Peter and Andrew fishing at some distance (so Matthew tells us, *ch.* iv. 18); but he waited till they came to land, and till the *fishermen,* that is, the servants, were *gone out of them,* having washed their nets, and thrown them by for that time: so Christ *entered* into that *ship* that belonged to Simon, and begged of him that he would lend it him for a pulpit; and, though he might have commanded him, yet, for love's sake, he rather *prayed him* that he would *thrust out a little from the land,* which would be the worse for his being *heard,* but Christ would have it so, that he might the better be *seen;* and it is his being *lifted up* that *draws men to him.* Wisdom cries *in the top of high places,* Prov. viii. 2. It intimates that Christ had a strong voice (strong indeed, for he made the *dead* to hear it), and that he did not desire to favour himself. There he *sat down,* and *taught the people* the good knowledge of the Lord.

III. What a particular acquaintance Christ, hereupon, fell into with these fishermen. They had had some conversation with him before, which began at John's baptism (John i. 40, 41); they were with him at *Cana of Galilee* (John ii. 2), and in Judea (John iv. 3); but as yet they were not called to attend him constantly, and therefore here we have them at their calling, and now it was that they were called into a more intimate fellowship with Christ.

1. When Christ had done preaching, he ordered Peter to apply himself to the business of his calling again: *Launch out into the deep, and let down your nets, v.* 4. It was not the sabbath day, and therefore, as soon as the lecture was over, he set them to work. Time spent on week-days in the public exercises of religion may be but little hindrance to us *in time,* and a great furtherance to us in *temper of mind,* in our worldly business. With what cheerfulness may we go about the duties of our calling when we have been *in the mount* with God, and from thence fetch a double blessing into our worldly employments, and thus have them sanctified to us by the word and prayer! It is our wisdom and duty so to manage our religious exercises as that they may befriend our worldly business, and so to manage our worldly business as that it may be no enemy to our religious exercises.

2. Peter having *attended* upon Christ in his *preaching,* Christ will *accompany* him in his *fishing.* He staid with Christ at the shore, and now Christ will *launch out* with him *into the deep.* Note, Those that will be constant followers of Christ shall have him a constant guide to them.

3. Christ ordered Peter and his ship's crew to *cast their nets into the sea,* which they did, in obedience to him, though they had been

hard at it all night, and had *caught nothing,* *v.* 4, 5. We may observe here

(1.) How melancholy their business had now been: "*Master, we have toiled all the night,* when we should have been asleep in our beds, *and have taken nothing,* but have had our labour for our pains." One would have thought that this should have excused them from hearing the sermon; but such a love had they to the word of God that it was more refreshing and reviving to them, after a wearisome night, than the softest slumbers. But they mention it to Christ, when he bids them go a fishing again. Note, [1.] Some *callings* are much more *toilsome* than others are, and more perilous; yet Providence has so ordered it for the common good that there is no useful calling so discouraging but some or other have a genius for it. Those who follow their business, and get abundance by it with a great deal of ease, should think with compassion of those who cannot follow theirs but with a great fatigue, and hardly get a bare livelihood by it. When we have *rested all night,* let us not forget those who have *toiled all night,* as Jacob, when he kept Laban's sheep. [2.] Be the calling ever so laborious, it is good to see people diligent in it, and make the best of it; these fishermen, that were thus *industrious,* Christ singled out for his favourites. They were fit to be preferred as good soldiers of Jesus Christ who had thus learned to *endure hardness.* [3.] Even those who are most diligent in their business often meet with disappointments; they who *toiled all night* yet *caught nothing;* for the *race* is not always *to the swift.* God will have us to be diligent, purely in duty to his command and dependence upon his goodness, rather than with an assurance of worldly success. We must do our duty, and then leave the event to God. [4.] When we are tired with our worldly business, and crossed in our worldly affairs, we are welcome to come to Christ, and spread our case before him, who will take cognizance of it.

(2.) How ready their obedience was to the command of Christ: *Nevertheless, at thy word, I will let down the net.* [1.] Though they had *toiled all night,* yet, if Christ bid them, they will renew their toil, for they know that they who *wait on him shall renew their strength,* as work is renewed upon their hands; for every fresh service they shall have a fresh supply of *grace sufficient.* [2.] Though they have *taken nothing,* yet, if Christ bid them *let down for a draught,* they will hope to take *something.* Note, We must not abruptly quit the callings wherein we are called because we have not the success in them we promised ourselves. The ministers of the gospel must continue to *let down* that *net,* though they have perhaps *toiled long* and *caught nothing;* and this is thank-worthy, to continue unwearied in our labours, though we see not the success of them. [3.] In this they have an eye to the *word of Christ,* and a dependence upon that: "*At thy word, I will let down the net,* because thou dost enjoin it, and thou dost encourage it." We are *then* likely to speed well when we follow the guidance of Christ's word.

4. The draught of fish they caught was so much beyond what was ever known that it amounted to a miracle (*v.* 6): They *enclosed a great multitude of fishes,* so that *their net broke,* and yet, which is strange, they did not lose their draught. It was so great a *draught* that they had not hands sufficient to draw it up; but they were obliged to beckon to their partners, who were at a distance, out of call, to come and help them, *v.* 7. But the greatest evidence of the vastness of the draught was that they filled both the ships with fish, to such a degree that they overloaded them, and they *began to sink,* so that the fish had like to have been lost again with their own weight. Thus many an overgrown estate, raised out of the water, returns to the place whence it came. Suppose these ships were but five or six tons a piece, what a vast quantity of fish must there be to *load,* nay to *over-load,* them both!

Now by this vast draught of fishes, (1.) Christ intended to show his *dominion* in the *seas* as well as on the *dry land,* over its *wealth* as over its *waves.* Thus he would show that he was that *Son of man* under whose feet all things were put, and particularly the *fish of the sea* and *whatsoever passeth through the paths of the sea,* Ps. viii. 8. (2.) He intended hereby to confirm the doctrine he had just now preached out of Peter's ship. We may suppose that the people on shore, who heard the sermon, having a notion that the preacher was a prophet sent of God, carefully attended his motions afterward, and staid halting about there, to see what he would do next; and this miracle immediately following would be a confirmation to their faith, of his being at least *a teacher come from God.* (3.) He intended hereby to repay Peter for the loan of his boat; for Christ's gospel now, as his ark formerly in the house of Obed-edom, will be sure to make amends, rich amends, for its kind entertainment. None shall *shut a door or kindle a fire* in God's house *for nought,* Mal. i. 10. Christ's recompences for services done to his name are abundant, they are superabundant. (4.) He intended hereby to give a specimen, to those who were to be his ambassadors to the world, of the success of their embassy, that though they might for a time, and in one particular place, *toil* and *catch nothing,* yet they should be instrumental to bring in many to Christ, and enclose many in the gospel net.

5. The impression which this miraculous draught of fishes made upon Peter was very remarkable.

(1.) All *concerned* were *astonished,* and the more *astonished* for their being *concerned.* All the boat's crew were *astonished at the draught of fishes which they had taken* (*v.* 9);

they were all surprised; and the more they considered it, and all the circumstances of it, the more they were *wonder-struck*, I had almost said *thunder-struck*, at the thought of it, *and so were also James and John, who were partners with Simon* (*v.* 10), and who, for aught that appears, were not so well acquainted with Christ, before this, as Peter and Andrew were. Now they were the more *affected* with it, [1.] Because they *understood* it better than others did. They that were well acquainted with this sea, and it is probable had plied upon it many years, had never seen such a draught of fishes fetched out of it, nor any thing like it, any thing near it; and therefore they could not be tempted to diminish it, as others might, by suggesting that it was accidental at this *time*, and what might as well have happened at *any time*. It greatly corroborates the evidence of Christ's miracles that those who were best *acquainted* with them most *admired* them. [2.] Because they were most *interested* in it, and *benefited* by it. Peter and his part-owners were gainers by this great draught of fishes; it was a rich booty for them and therefore it transported them, and their *joy* was a *helper* to their *faith*. Note, When Christ's works of wonder are to us, in particular, works of grace, then especially they command our faith in his doctrine.

(2.) Peter, above all the rest, was astonished to such a degree that he *fell down at Jesus's knees*, as he sat in the stern of his boat, and said, as one in an ecstasy or transport, that knew not where he was or what he said, *Depart from me, for I am a sinful man, O Lord*, *v.* 8. Not that he feared the weight of the fish would sink him because he was a sinful man, but that he thought himself unworthy of the favour of Christ's presence in his boat, and worthy that it should be to him a matter rather of terror than of comfort. This word of Peter's came from the same principle with theirs who, under the Old-Testament, so often said that they did *exceedingly fear and quake* at the extraordinary displays of the divine glory and majesty. It was the language of Peter's humility and self-denial, and had not the least tincture of the devils' dialect, *What have we to do with thee, Jesus, thou Son of God?* [1.] His acknowledgment was very just, and what it becomes us all to make: *I am a sinful man, O Lord.* Note, Even the *best men* are *sinful men*, and should be ready upon all occasions to own it, and especially to own it to Jesus Christ; for to whom else, but to him who came into the world to *save sinners*, should *sinful men* apply themselves? [2.] His inference from it was what *might have been* just, though really it was not so. If I be a *sinful man*, as indeed I am, I ought to say, "*Come to me, O Lord*, or let me come to thee, or I am undone, *for ever undone.*" But, considering what reason *sinful men* have to tremble before the holy Lord God and to dread his wrath, Peter may well be excused, if, in a sense of his own sinfulness and vileness, he cried out on a sudden, *Depart from me.* Note, Those whom Christ designs to admit to the most *intimate acquaintance* with him he first makes sensible that they deserve to be set at the *greatest distance* from him. We must all own ourselves *sinful men*, and that therefore Jesus Christ might justly *depart from us;* but we must *therefore fall down at his knees*, to pray him that he would not depart; for *woe unto us* if he *leave us*, if the Saviour depart from the sinful man.

6. The occasion which Christ took from this to intimate to Peter (*v.* 10), and soon after to James and John (Matt. iv. 21), his purpose to make them his apostles, and instruments of planting his religion in the world. He *said unto Simon*, who was in the greatest surprise of any of them at this prodigious draught of fishes, "Thou shalt both see and do greater things than these; *fear not;* let not this astonish thee; be not afraid that, after having done thee this honour, it is so great that I shall never do thee more; no, *henceforth thou shalt catch men*, by enclosing them in the gospel net, and that shall be a greater instance of the Redeemer's power, and his favour to thee, than this is; that shall be a more *astonishing* miracle, and infinitely more *advantageous* than this." When by Peter's preaching *three thousand souls* were, *in one day*, added to the church, then the type of this great draught of fishes was abundantly answered.

Lastly, The fishermen's farewell to their calling, in order to their constant attendance on Christ (*v.* 11): *When they had brought their ships to land*, instead of going to seek for a market for their fish, that they might make the best hand they could of this miracle, they *forsook all and followed him*, being more solicitous to serve the interests of Christ than to advance any secular interests of their own. It is observable that they *left all to follow Christ*, when their calling prospered in their hands more than ever it had done and they had had uncommon success in it. When *riches increase*, and we are therefore most in temptation to *set our hearts* upon them, then to quit them for the service of Christ, this is *thank-worthy*.

12 And it came to pass, when he was in a certain city, behold a man full of leprosy: who seeing Jesus fell on *his* face, and besought him, saying, Lord, if thou wilt, thou canst make me clean.
13 And he put forth *his* hand, and touched him, saying, I will: be thou clean. And immediately the leprosy departed from him.
14 And he charged him to tell no man: but go, and show thyself to the priest, and offer for thy cleansing, according as

Moses commanded, for a testimony unto them. 15 But so much the more went there a fame abroad of him: and great multitudes came together to hear, and to be healed by him of their infirmities. 16 And he withdrew himself into the wilderness, and prayed.

Here is, I. The cleansing of a leper, *v.* 12—14. This narrative we had both in Matthew and Mark. It is here said to have been *in a certain city* (*v.* 12); it was in Capernaum, but the evangelist would not name it, perhaps because it was a reflection upon the government of the city that a leper was suffered to be *in it.* This man is said to be *full of leprosy;* he had that distemper in a high degree, which the more fitly represents our natural pollution by sin; we are *full of that leprosy, from the crown of the head to the sole of the foot there is no soundness in us.* Now let us learn here,

1. What we must do in the sense of our spiritual leprosy. (1.) We must *seek Jesus,* enquire after him, acquaint ourselves with him, and reckon the discoveries made to us of Christ by the gospel the most acceptable and welcome discoveries that could be made to us. (2.) We must humble ourselves before him, as this leper, seeing Jesus, *fell on his face.* We must be *ashamed* of our pollution, and, in the sense of it, blush to lift up our faces before the *holy Jesus.* (3.) We must earnestly desire to be *cleansed* from the defilement, and cured of the disease, of sin, which renders us unfit for communion with God. (4.) We must firmly believe Christ's ability and sufficiency to cleanse us: Lord, *thou canst make me clean,* though I be *full of leprosy.* No doubt is to be made of the merit and grace of Christ. (5.) We must be importunate in prayer for pardoning mercy and renewing grace: *He fell on his face and besought him;* they that would be cleansed must reckon it a favour worth wrestling for. (6.) We must refer ourselves to the good-will of Christ: *Lord, if thou wilt, thou canst.* This is not so much the language of his *diffidence,* or *distrust* of the good-will of Christ, as of his submission and reference of himself and his case to the will, to the good-will, of Jesus Christ.

2. What we may expect from Christ, if we thus apply ourselves to him. (1.) We shall find him very *condescending* and forward to take cognizance of our case (*v.* 13): *He put forth his hand and touched him.* When Christ visited this leprous world, unasked, unsought unto, he showed how low he could stoop, to do good. His *touching* the leper was wonderful condescension; but it is much greater to us when he is himself *touched with the feeling of our infirmities.* (2.) We shall find him very *compassionate,* and ready to relieve us; he said, "*I will,* never doubt of that; whosoever comes to me to be healed, *I will in no wise cast him out.*" He is as willing to cleanse leprous souls as they can be to be cleansed. (3.) We shall find him all-sufficient, and able to heal and cleanse us, though we be ever so full of this loathsome leprosy. One word, one touch, from Christ, did the business: *Immediately the leprosy departed from him.* If Christ saith, "I will, be thou *justified,* be thou *sanctified,*" it is done; for he has power on earth to *forgive* sin, and power to give the Holy Spirit, 1 Cor. vi. 11.

3. What he requires from those that are cleansed, *v.* 14. Has Christ sent his word and healed us? (1.) We must be very *humble* (*v.* 14): *He charged him to tell no man.* This, it should seem, did not forbid him telling it to the honour of Christ, but he must not tell it to his own honour. Those whom Christ hath healed and cleansed must know that he hath done it in such a way as for ever excludes boasting. (2.) We must be very *thankful,* and make a grateful acknowledgment of the divine grace: *Go, and offer for thy cleansing.* Christ did not require him to give him a fee, but to bring the sacrifice of praise to God; so far was he from using his power to the prejudice of the law of Moses. (3.) We must *keep close to our duty; go to the priest,* and those that attend him. The man whom Christ had made whole he *found in the temple,* John v. 14. Those who by any affliction have been detained from public ordinances should, when the affliction is removed, attend on them the more diligently, and adhere to them the more constantly.

4. Christ's *public serviceableness* to men and his *private communion* with God; these are put together here, to give lustre to each other.

(1.) Though never any had so much *pleasure* in his *retirements* as Christ had, yet he was *much in a crowd,* to do good, *v.* 15. Though the leper should altogether hold his peace, yet the thing could not be hid, *so much the more went there a fame abroad of him.* The more he sought to conceal himself under a veil of humility, the more notice did people take of him; for honour is like a shadow, which flees from those that pursue it *(for a man to seek his own glory is not glory),* but follows those that decline it, and draw from it. The less good men say of themselves, the more will others say of them. But Christ reckoned it a small honour to him that his *fame went abroad;* it was much more so that hereby multitudes were brought to receive benefit by him. [1.] By his preaching. They came together to *hear* him, and to receive instruction from him concerning the kingdom of God. [2.] By his miracles. They came *to be healed by him of their infirmities;* that invited them to come to hear him, confirmed his doctrine, and recommended it.

(2.) Though never any did so much *good in public,* yet he found time for *pious* and *devout retirements* (*v.* 16): *He withdrew himself into the wilderness, and prayed;* not that he needed to avoid either distraction or ostentation, but he would set us an example, who need to order the circumstances of our devotion so as to guard against both. It is likewise our wisdom so to order our affairs as that our public work and our secret work may not intrench upon, nor interfere with, one another. Note, Secret prayer must be performed secretly; and those that have ever so much to do of the best business in this world must keep up constant stated times for it.

17 And it came to pass on a certain day, as he was teaching, that
there were Pharisees and doctors of
the law sitting by, which were come
out of every town of Galilee, and
Judæa, and Jerusalem: and the power
of the Lord was *present* to heal them.
18 And, behold, men brought in a
bed a man which was taken with a
palsy: and they sought *means* to bring
him in, and to lay *him* before him.
19 And when they could not find by
what *way* they might bring him in
because of the multitude, they went
upon the housetop, and let him down
through the tiling with *his* couch into
the midst before Jesus. 20 And when
he saw their faith, he said unto him,
Man, thy sins are forgiven thee. 21
And the scribes and the Pharisees
began to reason, saying, Who is this
which speaketh blasphemies? Who
can forgive sins, but God alone?
22 But when Jesus perceived their
thoughts, he answering said unto them,
What reason ye in your hearts? 23
Whether is easier, to say, Thy sins
be forgiven thee; or to say, Rise up
and walk? 24 But that ye may know
that the Son of man hath power upon
earth to forgive sins (he said unto
the sick of the palsy), I say unto thee,
Arise, and take up thy couch, and go
unto thine house. 25 And immediately he rose up before them, and
took up that whereon he lay, and departed to his own house, glorifying
God. 26 And they were all amazed,
and they glorified God, and were filled
with fear, saying, We have seen
strange things to day.

Here is, I. A general account of Christ's preaching and miracles, *v.* 17. 1. He was *teaching on a certain day,* not on the sabbath day, then he would have said so, but on a *week-day; six days shalt thou labour,* not only for *the world,* but for *the soul,* and the welfare of that. Preaching and hearing the word of God are *good works,* if they be *done well,* any day in the *week,* as well as on sabbath days. It was not in the *synagogue,* but in a *private house;* for even there where we ordinarily converse with our friends it is not improper to give and receive good instruction. 2. There he *taught,* he *healed* (as before, *v.* 15): *And the power of the Lord was to heal them*—ἦν εἰς τὸ ἰᾶσθαι αὐτούς. It was *mighty* to heal them; it was *exerted* and *put forth* to heal them, to heal those whom he *taught* (we may understand it so), to heal their souls, to cure them of their spiritual diseases, and to give them a new life, a new nature. Note, Those who receive the word of Christ in faith will find a divine power going along with that word, to *heal them;* for Christ came with his comforts to *heal the broken-hearted, ch.* iv. 18. The power of the Lord is *present* with the word, *present to those* that pray for it and submit to it, *present to heal them.*. Or it may be meant (and so it is generally taken) of the healing of those who were *diseased in body,* who came to him for cures. Whenever there was occasion, Christ had not *to seek* for his power, it was *present to heal.* 3. There were some grandees present in this assembly, and, as it should seem, more than usual: *There were Pharisees, and doctors of the law, sitting by;* not sitting *at his feet,* to learn of him; then I should have been willing to take the following clause as referring to those who are spoken of immediately before (the *power of the Lord was present to heal them);* and why might not the word of Christ reach their hearts? But, by what follows (*v.* 21), it appears that they were *not healed,* but cavilled at Christ, which compels us to refer this to others, not to them; for they *sat by* as *persons unconcerned,* as if the word of Christ were nothing to them. They sat by as spectators, censors, and spies, to pick up something on which to ground a reproach or accusation. How many are there in the midst of our assemblies, where the gospel is preached, that do not *sit under* the word, but *sit by!* It is to them as a *tale* that is *told them,* not as a *message* that is *sent them;* they are willing that we should preach *before them,* not that we should preach *to them.* These Pharisees and scribes (or doctors of the law) *came out of every town of Galilee, and Judea, and Jerusalem;* they came from all parts of the nation. Probably, they appointed to meet at this time and place, to see what remarks they could make upon Christ and what he said and did. They were in a confederacy, as those that said, *Come, and let us devise devices against Jeremiah,* and agree to *smite him with the tongue,* Jer. xviii. 18. *Report, and we will report it,* Jer. xx. 10. Observe, Christ went on with his work of *preaching* and *healing,* though he saw these Pharisees, and doctors of the Jewish church, *sitting by*, who, he knew, *despised* him, and watched to *ensnare him*.

II. A particular account of the cure of the man *sick of the palsy*, which was related much as it is here by both the foregoing evangelists: let us therefore only observe in short,

1. The doctrines that are taught us and confirmed to us by the story of this cure. (1.) That sin is the fountain of all sickness, and the forgiveness of sin is the only foundation upon which a recovery from sickness can comfortably be built. They presented the *sick man* to Christ, and he said, "*Man, thy sins are forgiven thee* (*v.* 20), that is the blessing thou art most to prize and seek; for if thy sins be forgiven thee, though the sickness be continued, it is in mercy; if they be not, though the sickness be removed, it is in wrath." The cords of our iniquity are the bands of our affliction. (2.) That Jesus Christ has power on earth to *forgive sins*, and his healing diseases was an *incontestable* proof of it. This was the thing intended to be proved (*v.* 24): *That ye may know* and believe *that the Son of man*, though now upon earth in his state of humiliation, *hath power to forgive sins*, and to release sinners, upon gospel terms, from the eternal punishment of sin, he *saith to the sick of the palsy, Arise, and walk;* and he is cured immediately. Christ claims one of the prerogatives of the King of kings when he undertakes to *forgive sin*, and it is justly expected that he should produce a good proof of it. "Well," saith he, "I will put it upon this issue: here is a man struck with a palsy, and *for his sin;* if I do not with a word's speaking cure his disease in an instant, which cannot be done by nature or art, but purely by the immediate power and efficacy of the God of nature, then say that I am not entitled to the prerogative of forgiving sin, am not the Messiah, am not the Son of God and King of Israel: but, if I do, you must own that *I have power to forgive sins*." Thus it was put upon a fair trial, and one word of Christ determined it. He did but say, *Arise, take up thy couch*, and that *chronical* disease had an *instantaneous* cure; *immediately he arose before them*. They must all own that there could be no cheat or fallacy in it. They that brought him could attest how perfectly *lame* he was before; they that saw him could attest how perfectly *well* he was now, insomuch that he had strength enough to take up and carry away the bed he lay upon. How well is it for us that this most comfortable doctrine of the gospel, that *Jesus Christ*, our *Redeemer and Saviour*, has *power to forgive sin*, has such a full attestation! (3.) That Jesus Christ is God. He appears to be so, [1.] By *knowing the thoughts* of the scribes and Pharisees (*v.* 22), which it is God's prerogative to do, though these scribes and Pharisees knew as well how to conceal their thoughts, and keep their countenances, as most men, and probably were industrious to do it at this time, for they *lay in wait secretly*. [2.] By doing that which their thoughts owned none could do but God only (*v.* 21): *Who can forgive sins*, say they, *but only God?* "I will prove," saith Christ, "that I can forgive sins;" and what follows then but that *he is God?* What horrid wickedness then were *they* guilty of who charged him with speaking the *worst* of *blasphemies*, even when he spoke the *best* of *blessings, Thy sins are forgiven thee!*

2. The duties that are taught us, and recommended to us, by this story. (1.) In our applications to Christ, we must be very *pressing* and *urgent:* that is an evidence of faith, and is very pleasing to Christ and prevailing with him. They that were the friends of this sick man *sought means to bring him in before Christ* (*v.* 18); and, when they were baffled in their endeavour, they did not give up their cause; but when they could not get in by *the door*, it was so crowded, they untiled the house, and let the poor patient down through the roof, *into the midst before Jesus, v.* 19. In this Jesus Christ *saw their faith, v.* 20. Now here he has taught us (and it were well if we could learn the lesson) to *put the best construction* upon words and actions that they *will bear*. When the centurion and the woman of Canaan were in no care at all to bring the patients they interceded for into Christ's presence, but believed that he could cure them *at a distance*, he commended *their faith*. But though in *these* there seemed to be a *different* notion of the thing, and an apprehension that it was requisite the *patient* should be *brought into his presence*, yet he did not *censure* and *condemn* their weakness, did not ask them, "Why do you give this disturbance to the assembly? Are you under such a degree of infidelity as to think I could not have cured him, though he had been out of doors?" But he made the best of it, and even in *this* he saw *their faith*. It is a comfort to us that we serve a Master that is willing to *make the best* of us. (2.) When we are sick, we should be more in care to get our sins pardoned than to get our sickness removed. Christ, in what he said to this man, taught us, when we seek to God for health, to begin with seeking to him for pardon. (3.) The mercies which we have the comfort of God must have the praise of. The man *departed to his own house, glorifying God, v.* 25. To him belong the escapes from death, and in them therefore he must be *glorified*. (4.) The miracles which Christ wrought were *amazing* to those that saw them, and we ought to *glorify* God in them, *v.* 26. They said, "*We have seen strange things to-day*, such as we never saw before, nor our fathers before us; they are altogether new." But they *glorified* God, who had sent into their country such a benefactor to it; and were *filled with fear*, with a reverence of God, with a jealous persuasion that this was

the Messiah and that he was not treated by their nation as he ought to be, which might prove in the end the ruin of their state; perhaps they were some such thoughts as these that *filled them with fear,* and a concern likewise for themselves.

27 And after these things he went
forth, and saw a publican, named Levi,
sitting at the receipt of custom: and
he said unto him, Follow me. 28
And he left all, rose up, and followed
him. 29 And Levi made him a great
feast in his own house: and there was
a great company of publicans and of
others that sat down with them. 30
But their scribes and Pharisees murmured against his disciples, saying,
Why do ye eat and drink with publicans and sinners? 31 And Jesus
answering said unto them, They that
are whole need not a physician; but
they that are sick. 32 I came not to
call the righteous, but sinners to repentance. 33 And they said unto
him, Why do the disciples of John
fast often, and make prayers, and likewise *the disciples* of the Pharisees;
but thine eat and drink? 34 And he
said unto them, Can ye make the
children of the bridechamber fast,
while the bridegroom is with them?
35 But the days will come, when the
bridegroom shall be taken away from
them, and then shall they fast in those
days. 36 And he spake also a parable unto them; No man putteth a
piece of a new garment upon an old;
if otherwise, then both the new maketh
a rent, and the piece that was *taken*
out of the new agreeth not with the
old. 37 And no man putteth new
wine into old bottles; else the new
wine will burst the bottles, and be
spilled, and the bottles shall perish.
38 But new wine must be put into
new bottles; and both are preserved.
39 No man also having drunk old
wine straightway desireth new: for he
saith, The old is better.

All this, except the last verse, we had before in Matthew and Mark; it is not the story of any *miracle in nature* wrought by our Lord Jesus, but it is an account of some of the *wonders of his grace,* which, to those who understand things aright, are no less cogent proofs of Christ's being sent of God than the other.

I. It was a wonder of his grace that he would call a *publican,* from the *receipt of custom,* to be his disciple and follower, *v.* 27. It was wonderful condescension that he should admit poor fishermen to that honour, men of the *lowest rank;* but much more wonderful that he should admit *publicans,* men of the *worst reputation,* men of *ill fame.* In this Christ *humbled himself,* and appeared *in the likeness of sinful flesh.* By this he *exposed himself,* and got the invidious character of a *friend of publicans and sinners.*

II. It was a wonder of his grace that the call was made *effectual,* became immediately so, *v.* 28. This publican, though those of that employment commonly had little inclination to religion, for his religion's sake left a good place in the custom-house (which, probably, was his livelihood, and where he stood fair for better preferment), and *rose up, and followed Christ.* There is no heart too hard for the Spirit and grace of Christ to work upon, nor any difficulties in the way of a sinner's conversion insuperable to his power.

III. It was a wonder of his grace that he would not only admit a converted publican into his family, but would keep company with unconverted publicans, that he might have an opportunity of doing their souls good; he justified himself in it, as agreeing with the great design of his coming into the world. Here is a wonder of grace indeed, that Christ undertakes to be the Physician of souls *distempered* by sin, and ready to *die* of the distemper (he is a Healer by office, *v.* 31)—that he has a particular regard to the sick, to sinners as his patients, convinced awakened sinners, that see their need of the Physician—that he came to call *sinners,* the worst of sinners, to repentance, and to assure them of pardon, upon repentance, *v.* 32. These are glad tidings of great joy indeed.

IV. It was a wonder of his grace that he did so patiently bear the *contradiction of sinners* against himself and his disciples, *v.* 30 He did not express his resentment of the cavils of the scribes and Pharisees, as he justly might have done, but answered them with reason and meekness; and, instead of taking that occasion to show his displeasure against the Pharisees, as afterwards he did, or of recriminating upon them, he took that occasion to show his compassion to poor publicans, another sort of sinners, and to encourage them.

V. It was a wonder of his grace that, in the discipline under which he trained up his disciples, he *considered their frame,* and proportioned their services to their strength and standing, and to the circumstances they were in. It was objected, as a blemish upon his conduct, that he did not make *his disciples* to *fast* so often as those of the *Pharisees* and John Baptist did, *v.* 33. He insisted most upon that which is the *soul* of fasting, the mortification of sin, the crucifying of the flesh, and the living of a life of self-denial, which is as much better than fasting and corporal penances as *mercy* is better than *sacrifice*.

VI. It was a wonder of his grace that Christ reserved the trials of his disciples for their latter times, when by his grace they were in some good measure better prepared and fitted for them than they were at first. Now they were as the *children of the bride-chamber,* when the *bridegroom is with them,* when they have plenty and joy, and every day is a festival. Christ was welcomed wherever he came, and they for his sake, and as yet they met with little or no opposition; but this will not last always. *The days will come* when the *bridegroom shall be taken away from them, v.* 35. When Christ shall leave them with their hearts full of sorrow, their hands full of work, and the world full of enmity and rage against them, *then shall they fast,* shall not be so well fed as they are now. *We both hunger and thirst and are naked,* 1 Cor. iv. 11. Then they shall keep many more *religious fasts* than they do now, for Providence will call them to it; they will then serve the Lord *with fastings,* Acts xiii. 2.

VII. It was a wonder of his grace that he proportioned their exercises to their strength. He would not put *new cloth upon an old garment* (*v.* 36), nor *new wine into old bottles* (*v.* 37, 38); he would not, as soon as ever he had called them out of the world, put them upon the strictnesses and austerities of discipleship, lest they should be tempted to *fly off.* When God brought Israel out of Egypt, he would not bring them *by the way of the Philistines,* lest they should *repent,* when they *saw war,* and *return to Egypt,* Exod. xiii. 17. So Christ would train up his followers gradually to the discipline of his family; for no man, having *drank old wine,* will *of a sudden,* straightway, *desire new,* or relish it, but will say, *The old is better,* because he has been *used to it, v.* 39. The disciples will be tempted to think their old way of living better, till they are by degrees trained up to this way whereunto they are called. Or, turn it the other way: "Let them be *accustomed* awhile to religious exercises, and then they will *abound* in them as much as you do: but we must not be too hasty with them." Calvin takes it as an admonition to the Pharisees not to boast of their fasting, and the noise and show they made with it, nor to despise his disciples because they did not in like manner *signalize* themselves; for the profession the Pharisees made was indeed *pompous* and *gay,* like *new wine* that is brisk and sparkling, whereas all wise men say, *The old is better*; for, though it does not give its colour so well in the cup, yet it is more warming in the stomach and more wholesome. Christ's disciples, though they had not so much of the *form of godliness,* had more of the *power of it.*

CHAP. VI.

In this chapter we have Christ's exposition of the moral law, which he came not to destroy, but to fulfil, and to fill up, by his gospel. I. Here is a proof of the lawfulness of works of necessity and mercy on the sabbath day, the former in vindication of his disciples' plucking the ears of corn, the latter in vindication of himself healing the withered hand on that day, ver. 1—11. II. His retirement for secret prayer, ver. 12. III. His calling his twelve apostles, ver. 13—16. IV. His curing the multitudes of those under various diseases who made their application to him, ver. 17—19. V. The sermon that he preached to his disciples and the multitude, instructing them in their duty both to God and man, ver. 20—49.

AND it came to pass on the second
sabbath after the first, that he
went through the corn fields; and his
disciples plucked the ears of corn, and
did eat, rubbing *them* in *their* hands.
2 And certain of the Pharisees said
unto them, Why do ye that which is
not lawful to do on the sabbath days?
3 And Jesus answering them said,
Have ye not read so much as this,
what David did, when himself was an
hungred, and they which were with
him; 4 How he went into the house
of God, and did take and eat the show-
bread, and gave also to them that were
with him; which it is not lawful to
eat but for the priests alone? 5 And
he said unto them, That the Son of
man is Lord also of the sabbath. 6
And it came to pass also on another
sabbath, that he entered into the synagogue and taught: and there was a
man whose right hand was withered.
7 And the scribes and Pharisees
watched him, whether he would heal
on the sabbath day; that they might
find an accusation against him. 8
But he knew their thoughts, and said
to the man which had the withered
hand, Rise up, and stand forth in the
midst. And he arose and stood forth.
9 Then said Jesus unto them, I will
ask you one thing; Is it lawful on the
sabbath days to do good, or to do
evil? to save life, or to destroy *it?*
10 And looking round about upon
them all, he said unto the man, Stretch
forth thy hand. And he did so: and
his hand was restored whole as the
other. 11 And they were filled with
madness; and communed one with
another what they might do to Jesus.

These two passages of story we had both in Matthew and Mark, and they were there laid together (Matt. xii. 1; Mark ii. 23; iii. 1), because, though happening at some distance of time from each other, both were designed to rectify the mistakes of the scribes and Pharisees concerning the sabbath day, on the *bodily rest* of which they laid greater stress and required greater strictness than the Lawgiver intended. Here,

I. Christ justifies his disciples in a *work of necessity* for themselves on that day, and that was *plucking the ears of corn,* when they were hungry on that day. This story here has a date, which we had not in the other evangelists; it was *on the second sabbath after the first* (*v.* 1), that is, as Dr. Whitby thinks is pretty clear, the *first sabbath after the second day of unleavened bread,* from which day they reckoned the *seven weeks* to the feast of pentecost; the first of which they called Σάββατον δευτεροπρῶτον, the second δευτεροδεύτερον, and so on. Blessed be God we need not be critical in this matter. Whether this circumstance be mentioned to intimate that this sabbath was thought to have some peculiar honour upon it, which aggravated the offence of the disciples, or only to intimate that, being the first sabbath after the offering of the first fruits, it was the time of the year when the corn was nearly ripe, is not material. We may observe, 1. Christ's disciples ought not to be nice and curious in their diet, at any time, especially on sabbath days, but take up with what is easiest got, and be thankful. These disciples *plucked the ears of corn, and did eat* (*v.* 1); a little served them, and that which had no delicacy in it. 2. Many that are themselves guilty of the greatest crimes are forward to censure others for the most innocent and inoffensive actions, *v.* 2. The Pharisees quarrelled with them as doing that which it *was not lawful to do on the sabbath days,* when it was their own practice to feed deliciously on sabbath days, more than on all other days. 3. Jesus Christ will justify his disciples when they are unjustly censured, and will own and accept of them in many a thing which men tell them *it is not lawful for them to do.* How well is it for us that men are not to be our judges, and that Christ will be our Advocate! 4. Ceremonial appointments may be dispensed with, in cases of necessity; as the appropriating of the show-bread to the priests was dispensed with, when David was by Providence brought into such a strait that he must have either that or none, *v.* 3, 4. And, if God's own appointments might be thus set aside for a greater good, much more may the traditions of men. 5. Works of necessity are particularly allowable on the sabbath day; but we must take heed that we turn not this liberty into licentiousness, and abuse God's favourable concessions and condescensions to the prejudice of the work of the day. 6. Jesus Christ, though he allowed works of necessity on the sabbath day, will notwithstanding have us to know and remember that it is his day, and therefore is to be spent in his service and to his honour (*v.* 5): *The Son of man is Lord also of the sabbath.* In the kingdom of the Redeemer, the sabbath day is to be turned into a *Lord's day;* the property of it is, in some respects, to be altered, and it is to be observed chiefly in honour of the Redeemer, as it had been before in honour of the Creator, Jer. xvi. 14, 15. In token of this, it shall not only have a new name, the *Lord's day* (yet not forgetting the old, for it is a sabbath of rest still) but shall be transferred to a new day, the first day of the week.

II. He justifies himself in doing *works of mercy* for others on the sabbath day. Observe in this, 1. Christ on the sabbath day *entered into the synagogue.* Note, It is our duty, as we have opportunity, to sanctify sabbaths in religious assemblies. On the sabbath there ought to be a *holy convocation;* and our place must not be empty without very good reason. 2. In the synagogue, on the sabbath day, *he taught.* Giving and receiving instruction from Christ is very proper work for a sabbath day, and for a *synagogue.* Christ took all opportunities to teach, not only his disciples, but the multitude. 3. Christ's patient was one of his hearers. *A man whose right hand was withered* came to learn from Christ. Whether he had any expectation to be healed by him does not appear. But those that would be *cured* by the grace of Christ must be willing to *learn* the doctrine of Christ. 4. Among those who were the hearers of Christ's excellent doctrine, and the eye-witnesses of his glorious miracles, there were some who came with no other design than to pick quarrels with him, *v.* 7. The scribes and Pharisees would not, as became *generous* adversaries, give him fair warning that, if he did *heal* on the sabbath day, they would construe it into a violation of the fourth commandment, which they ought in honour and justice to have done, because it was a case *without precedent* (none having ever cured as he did), and therefore could not be an *adjudged* case; but they basely *watched him,* as the lion does his prey, whether he would *heal on the sabbath day, that they might find an accusation against him,* and surprise him with a prosecution. 5. Jesus Christ was neither *ashamed* nor *afraid* to own the purposes of his grace, in the face of those who, he knew, confronted them, *v.* 8. *He knew their faults,* and what they designed, and he bade the man *rise, and stand forth,* hereby to try the patient's faith and boldness. 6. He appealed to his adversaries themselves, and to the convictions of natural conscience, whether it was the design of the fourth commandment to restrain men from doing good on the sabbath day, that good which their hand finds to do, which they have an opportunity for, and which cannot so well be put off to another time (*v.* 9): *Is it lawful to do good, or evil, on the sabbath days?* No wicked men are such *absurd* and *unreasonable* men as *persecutors* are, who study to *do evil* to men for *doing good.* 7. He healed the poor man, and restored him to the present use of his right hand, with a word's speaking, though he knew that his enemies would not only take offence at it, but take advantage against him for it, *v.* 10 Let not us be drawn off, either from our duty or usefulness, by the oppression we meet with in it. 8. His adversaries were hereby enraged so much the more against him, *v.* 11. Instead of being convinced by this miracle, as they ought to have been, that he was a teacher come from God,—instead of being brought to be in love with him as a benefactor to mankind,— they were *filled with madness,* vexed that they could not frighten him from doing good, or hinder the growth of his interest in the affections of the people. They were *mad* at Christ, *mad* at the people, *mad* at themselves. Anger is a *short madness,* malice is a *long* one; *impotent* malice, especially *disappointed* malice; such was theirs. When they could not prevent his working this miracle, they *communed one with another what they might do to Jesus,* what other way they might take to run him down. We may well stand amazed at it that the sons of men should be so wicked as to do thus, and that the Son of God should be so patient as to suffer it.

12 And it came to pass in those
days, that he went out into a mountain to pray, and continued all night
in prayer to God. 13 And when it
was day, he called *unto him* his disciples: and of them he chose twelve,
whom also he named apostles; 14
Simon (whom he also named Peter),
and Andrew his brother, James and
John, Philip and Bartholomew, 15
Matthew and Thomas, James the *son*
of Alphæus, and Simon called Zelotes,
16 And Judas *the brother* of James,
and Judas Iscariot, which also was
the traitor. 17 And he came down
with them, and stood in the plain,
and the company of his disciples, and
a great multitude of people out of all
Judæa and Jerusalem, and from the
sea coast of Tyre and Sidon, which
came to hear him, and to be healed
of their diseases; 18 And they that
were vexed with unclean spirits: and
they were healed. 19 And the whole
multitude sought to touch him: for
there went virtue out of him, and
healed *them* all.

In these verses, we have our Lord Jesus in *secret,* in *his family,* and in *public;* and in all three acting like himself.

I. In *secret* we have him *praying to God, v.* 12. This evangelist takes frequent notice of Christ's retirements, to give us an example of secret prayer, by which we must keep up our communion with God daily, and without which it is impossible that the soul should prosper. *In those days,* when his enemies were filled with madness against him, and were contriving what to do to him, he went out to *pray;* that he might answer the type of David (Ps. cix. 4), *For my love, they are my adversaries; but I give myself unto prayer.* Observe, 1. He was *alone* with God; he *went out into a mountain, to pray,* where he might have no disturbance or interruption given him; we are never less alone than when we are *thus* alone. Whether there was any convenient place built upon this mountain, for devout people to retire to for their private devotions, as some think, and that that *oratory,* or *place of prayer,* is meant here by ἡ προσευχῇ τοῦ Θεοῦ, to me seems very uncertain. He went into a mountain for privacy, and therefore, probably, would not go to a place frequented by others. 2. He was *long* alone with God: *He continued all night in prayer.* We think one half hour a great deal to spend in the *duties of the closet;* but Christ continued a *whole night* in meditation and secret prayer. We have a great deal of *business* at the throne of grace, and we should take a great *delight* in communion with God, and by both these we may be kept sometimes long at prayer.

II. In his *family* we have him nominating his immediate attendants, that should be the constant auditors of his doctrine and eye-witnesses of his miracles, that hereafter they might be sent forth as *apostles,* his *messengers* to the world, to preach his gospel to it, and plant his church in it, *v.* 13. After he had *continued all night in prayer,* one would have thought that, *when it was day,* he should have reposed himself, and got some sleep. No, as soon as any body was stirring, he *called unto him his disciples.* In serving God, our great care should be, not to *lose time,* but to make the end of one good duty the beginning of another. Ministers are to be ordained with *prayer* more than ordinarily *solemn.* The number of the apostles was *twelve.* Their names are here recorded; it is the *third time* that we have met with them, and in each of the *three* places the *order* of them differs, to teach both ministers and Christians not to be nice in precedency, not in *giving* it, much less in *taking* it, but to look upon it as a thing not worth taking notice of; let it be as it lights. He that in Mark was called *Thaddeus,* in Matthew *Lebbeus,* whose surname was *Thaddeus,* is here called *Judas the brother of James,* the same that wrote the epistle of Jude. Simon, who in Matthew and Mark was called the *Canaanite,* is here called *Simon Zelotes,* perhaps for his great zeal in religion. Concerning these twelve here named we have reason to say, as the queen of Sheba did of Solomon's servants, *Happy are thy men, and happy are these thy servants, that stand continually before thee, and hear thy wisdom;* never were men so privileged, and yet one of them had a devil, and proved a traitor (*v.* 16); yet Christ, when he chose him, was not deceived in him.

III. In *public* we have him *preaching* and

healing, the two great works between which he divided his time, *v.* 17. He came down with the twelve from the mountain, and *stood in the plain*, ready to receive those that resorted to him; and there were presently gathered about him, not only the *company of his disciples*, who used to attend him, but also a great *multitude of people*, a mixed multitude *out of all Judea and Jerusalem*. Though it was some scores of miles from Jerusalem to that part of Galilee where Christ now was,—though at Jerusalem they had abundance of famous rabbin, that had great names, and bore a mighty sway,—yet they came to hear Christ. They came also from the *sea-coast of Tyre and Sidon*. Though they who lived there were generally men of business, and though they bordered upon Canaanites, yet there were some well affected to Christ; such there were dispersed in all parts, here and there one. 1. They *came to hear him*, and he *preached* to them. Those that have not good preaching near them had better travel far for it than be without it. It is worth while to go a great way to hear the word of Christ, and to go out of the way of other business for it. 2. They came to be *cured* by him, and he *healed* them. Some were troubled *in body*, and some *in mind;* some had *diseases*, some had *devils;* but both the one and the other, upon their application to Christ, were *healed*, for he has power over *diseases* and *devils* (*v.* 17, 18), over the effects and over the causes. Nay, it should seem, those who had no *particular diseases* to complain of yet found it a great confirmation and renovation to their bodily *health* and *vigour* to partake of the *virtue that went out of him;* for (*v.* 19) *the whole multitude sought to touch him*, those that were in health as well as those that were sick, and they were all, one way or other, the better for him: he *healed them all;* and who is there that doth not need, upon some account or other, to be *healed?* There is a *fulness of grace* in Christ, and healing virtue in him, and ready to go out from him, that is enough for all, enough for each.

20 And he lifted up his eyes on
his disciples, and said, Blessed *be ye*
poor: for yours is the kingdom of
God. 21 Blessed *are ye* that hunger
now: for ye shall be filled. Blessed
are ye that weep now: for ye shall
laugh. 22 Blessed are ye, when men
shall hate you, and when they shall
separate you *from their company*,
and shall reproach *you*, and cast out
your name as evil, for the Son of
man's sake. 23 Rejoice ye in that
day, and leap for joy: for, behold,
your reward *is* great in heaven: for in
the like manner did their fathers unto
the prophets. 24 But woe unto you
that are rich! for ye have received
your consolation. 25 Woe unto you
that are full! for ye shall hunger.
Woe unto you that laugh now! for
ye shall mourn and weep. 26 Woe
unto you, when all men shall speak
well of you! for so did their fathers
to the false prophets.

Here begins a practical discourse of Christ, which is continued to the end of the chapter, most of which is found in the *sermon upon the mount*, Matt. v. and vii. Some think that this was preached at some other time and place, and there are other instances of Christ's preaching the same things, or to the same purport, at different times; but it is probable that this is only the evangelist's abridgment of that sermon, and perhaps that in Matthew too is but an abridgment; the beginning and the conclusion are much the same; and the story of the cure of the centurion's servant follows presently upon it, both there and here, but it is not material. In these verses, we have,

I. Blessings pronounced upon *suffering saints*, as *happy* people, though the world *pities them* (*v.* 20): He *lifted up his eyes upon his disciples*, not only the *twelve*, but the whole *company of them* (*v.* 17), and directed his discourse to them; for, when he had healed the sick in *the plain*, he went up again *to the mountain*, to preach. There he *sat*, as one having authority; thither *they come to him* (Matt. v. 1), and to them he directed his discourse, to them he applied it, and taught them to apply it to themselves. When he had laid it down for a truth, *Blessed are the poor in spirit*, he added, *Blessed are ye poor.* All believers, that take the precepts of the gospel to themselves, and *live by them*, may take the promises of the gospel to themselves and *live upon them*. And the application, as it is here, seems especially designed to encourage the disciples, with reference to the hardships and difficulties they were likely to meet with, in following Christ.

1. "You are *poor*, you have *left all to follow me*, are content to live upon alms with me, are never to expect any worldly preferment in my service. You must work hard, and fare hard, as poor people do; but you are blessed in your poverty, it shall be no prejudice at all to your happiness; nay, you are blessed *for* it, all your losses shall be abundantly made up to you, for *yours is the kingdom of God*, all the comforts and graces of his kingdom here and all the glories and joys of his kingdom hereafter; yours it *shall be*, nay, yours *it is*." Christ's *poor* are *rich in faith*, Jam. ii. 5.

2. "You *hunger now* (*v.* 21), you are not *fed to the full* as others are, you often rise hungry, your *commons* are so *short;* or you are so intent upon your work that you have not time to eat bread, you are glad of a few *ears of corn* for a meal's meat; thus you

hunger now in this world, but in the other world *you shall be filled*, shall *hunger no more*, nor *thirst any more*."

3. "You *weep now*, are often in tears, tears of repentance, tears of sympathy; you are of them that mourn in Zion. But *blessed are you;* your present sorrows are no *prejudices* to your future joy, but *preparatories* for it: *You shall laugh.* You have triumphs in reserve; you are but *sowing in tears*, and shall shortly *reap in joy*," Ps. cxxvi. 5, 6. They that now *sorrow after a godly sort* are treasuring up comforts for themselves, or, rather, God is treasuring up comforts for them; and the day is coming when their *mouth shall be filled with laughing and their lips with rejoicing*, Job viii. 21.

4. "You now undergo *the world's ill will.* You must expect all the base treatment that a spiteful world can give you for Christ's sake, because you serve him and his interests; you must expect that wicked men will *hate you*, because your doctrine and life convict and condemn them; and those that have church-power in their hands will *separate you*, will force you to separate yourselves, and then excommunicate you for so doing, and lay you under the most ignominious censures. They will pronounce anathemas against you, as scandalous and incorrigible offenders. They will do this with all possible gravity and solemnity, and pomp and pageantry of appeals to Heaven, to make the world believe, and almost you yourselves too, that it is ratified in heaven. Thus will they endeavour to make you odious to others and a terror to yourselves." This is supposed to be the proper notion of *ἀφορίσωσιν ὑμᾶς—they shall cast you out of their synagogues.* "And they that have not this power will not fail to show their malice, to the utmost of their power; for *they will reproach you*, will charge you with the blackest crimes, which you are perfectly innocent of, will fasten upon you the blackest characters, which you do not deserve; they will *cast out your name as evil*, your name as Christians, as apostles; they will do all they can to render these names odious." This is the application of the eighth beatitude, Matt. v. 10—12.

"Such usage as this seems hard; but *blessed are you* when you are so used. It is so far from depriving you of your happiness that it will greatly add to it. It is an honour to you, as it is to a brave hero to be employed in the wars, in the service of his prince; and therefore *rejoice you in that day, and leap for joy*, *v.* 23. Do not only *bear it*, but *triumph* in it. For," (1.) "You are hereby *highly dignified* in the *kingdom of grace*, for you are treated as the prophets were before you, and therefore not only need not be ashamed of it, but may justly rejoice in it, for it will be an evidence for you that you *walk in the same spirit*, and *in the same steps*, are engaged in the same cause, and employed in the same service, with them." (2.) "You will for this be abundantly *recompensed* in the *kingdom of glory;* not only your services for Christ, but your sufferings will come into the account: *Your reward is great in heaven.* Venture upon your sufferings, in a full belief that the glory of heaven will abundantly countervail all these hardships; so that, though you may be losers for Christ, you shall not be losers by him in the end."

II. *Woes* denounced against *prospering sinners as miserable people*, though the world *envies them.* These we had not in Matthew. It should seem, the best exposition of *these woes*, compared with the foregoing *blessings*, is the parable of the *rich man* and Lazarus. Lazarus had the blessedness of those that are *poor*, and *hunger*, and *weep*, now, for in Abraham's bosom all the promises made to them who did so were *made good* to him; but the rich man had the *woes* that follow here, as he had the character of those on whom these woes are entailed.

1. Here is a *woe* to them that are *rich*, that is, that *trust in riches*, that have abundance of this world's wealth, and, instead of serving God with it, serve their lusts with it; woe to them, for *they have received their consolation*, that which they placed their happiness in, and were willing to take up with for a portion, *v.* 24. They in their life-time received *their good things*, which, in their account, were the *best things*, and all the good things they are ever likely to receive from God. "You that are *rich* are in temptation to *set your hearts* upon a *smiling* world, and to say, *Soul, take thine ease* in the embraces of it, *This is my rest for ever, here will I dwell;* and *then woe unto you.*" (1.) It is the *folly* of carnal worldlings that they make the things of this world *their consolation*, which were intended only for their *convenience.* They please themselves with them, pride themselves in them, and make them their heaven upon earth; and to them the *consolations of God* are small, and of no account. (2.) It is their misery that they are *put off* with them as *their consolation.* Let them know it, to their terror, when they are parted from these things, there is an end of all their comfort, a final end of it, and nothing remains to them but everlasting misery and torment.

2. Here is a *woe* to them that are *full* (*v.* 25), that are *fed to the full*, and have *more than heart could wish* (Ps. lxxiii. 7), that have their *bellies filled with the hid treasures of this world* (Ps. xvii. 14), that, when they have abundance of these, are *full*, and think they have *enough*, they *need no more*, they *desire no more*, Rev. iii. 17. *Now ye are full, now ye are rich*, 1 Cor. iv. 8. They are *full of themselves*, without God and Christ. Woe to such, for *they shall hunger*, they shall shortly be *stripped* and *emptied* of all the things they are so proud of; and, when they shall have *left behind them* in the world all those things which are their fulness, they

shall *carry away with them* such appetites and desires as the world they remove to will afford them no gratifications of; for all the delights of sense, which they are now so full of, will in hell be *denied,* and in heaven *superseded.*

3. Here is a *woe* to them that *laugh now,* that have always a *disposition to be merry,* and always something to *make merry with;* that know no other joy than that which is carnal and sensual, and know no other use of this world's good than purely to indulge that carnal sensual joy that banishes sorrow, even godly sorrow, from their minds, and are always entertaining themselves with the laughter of the fool. *Woe unto such,* for it is but *now,* for a little time, that they *laugh;* they shall *mourn and weep* shortly, shall *mourn and weep* eternally, in a world where there is nothing but *weeping and wailing,* endless, easeless, and remediless sorrow.

4. Here is a *woe* to them *whom all men speak well of,* that is, who make it their great and only care to gain the praise and applause of men, who value themselves upon that more than upon the favour of God and his acceptance (*v.* 26): "*Woe unto you;* that is, it would be a bad sign that you were not faithful to your trust, and to the souls of men, if you preached so as that nobody would be disgusted; for your business is to tell people of their faults, and, if you do that as you ought, you will get that *ill will* which never *speaks well.* The false prophets indeed, that flattered your fathers in their wicked ways, that *prophesied smooth things* to them, were caressed and spoken well of; and, if you be in like manner cried up, you will be justly suspected to deal deceitfully as they did." We should desire to have the approbation of those that are wise and good, and not be indifferent to what people say of us; but, as we should despise the reproaches, so we should also despise the praises, of the fools in Israel.

27 But I say unto you which hear,
Love your enemies, do good to them
which hate you, 28 Bless them that
curse you, and pray for them which
despitefully use you. 29 And unto
him that smiteth thee on the *one* cheek
offer also the other; and him that
taketh away thy cloak forbid not *to*
take thy coat also. 30 Give to every
man that asketh of thee; and of him
that taketh away thy goods ask *them*
not again. 31 And as ye would that
men should do to you, do ye also to
them likewise. 32 For if ye love
them which love you, what thank
have ye? for sinners also love those
that love them. 33 And if ye do
good to them which do good to you,
what thank have ye? for sinners also
do even the same. 34 And if ye
lend *to them* of whom ye hope to receive, what thank have ye? for sinners
also lend to sinners, to receive as much
again. 35 But love ye your enemies,
and do good, and lend, hoping for
nothing again; and your reward shall
be great, and ye shall be the children
of the Highest: for he is kind unto the
unthankful and *to* the evil. 36 Be
ye therefore merciful, as your Father
also is merciful.

These verses agree with Matt. v. 38, to the end of that chapter: *I say unto you that hear* (*v.* 27), to all you that hear, and not to disciples only, for these are lessons of universal concern. *He that has an ear, let him hear.* Those that diligently hearken to Christ shall find he has something to say to them well worth their hearing. Now the lessons Christ here teacheth us are,

I. That we must render to all their due, and be honest and just in all our dealings (*v.* 31): *As ye would that men should do to you, do ye also to them likewise;* for this is *loving your neighbour as yourselves.* What we should expect, in reason, to be done to us, either in justice or charity, by others, if they were in our condition and we in theirs, that, as the matter stands, we must do to them. We must *put our souls into their souls' stead,* and then pity and succour them, as we should desire and justly expect to be ourselves pitied and succoured.

II. That we must be free in *giving* to them that *need* (*v.* 30): "*Give to every man that asketh of thee,* to every one that is a proper object of charity, that wants necessaries, which thou hast wherewithal to supply out of thy superfluities. Give to those that are not able to help themselves, to those that have not relations in a capacity to help them." Christ would have his disciples ready to distribute, and willing to communicate, *to their power* in ordinary cases, and beyond their power in extraordinary.

III. That we must be generous in *forgiving* those that have been any way injurious to us.

1. We must not be *extreme* in *demanding* our right, when it is denied us: "*Him that taketh away thy cloak,* either forcibly or fraudulently, *forbid him not* by any violent means to *take thy coat also, v.* 29. Let him have that too, rather than fight for it. And (*v* 30) *of him that taketh thy goods*" (so Dr Hammond thinks it should be read), "that borrows them, or that *takes them up* from thee upon trust, of such do not *exact them;* if Providence have made such insolvent, do not take the advantage of the law against them, but rather lose it than *take them by the throat,* Matt. xviii. 28. If a man run away in thy debt, and *take away thy goods* with

him, do not perplex thyself, nor be incensed against him."

2. We must not be rigorous in revenging a wrong when it is done us: "*Unto him that smiteth thee on the one cheek*, instead of bringing an action against him, or sending for a writ for him, or bringing him before a justice, *offer also the other*; that is, "pass it by, though thereby thou shouldest be in danger of bringing upon thyself another like in dignity, which is commonly pretended in excuse of taking the advantage of the law in such a case. If any one *smite thee on the cheek*, rather than give another blow to him, be ready to receive another from him;" that is, "leave it to God to plead thy cause, and do thou sit down silent under the affront." When we do thus, God will *smite our enemies*, as far as they are his, *upon the cheek bone*, so as to *break the teeth of the ungodly* (Ps. iii. 7); for he hath said, *Vengeance is mine*, and he will make it appear that it is so when we leave it to him to take vengeance.

3. Nay, we must *do good to them that do evil to us*. This is that which our Saviour, in these verses, chiefly designs to teach us, as a law peculiar to his religion, and a branch of the perfection of it.

(1.) We must be kind to those from whom we have *received injuries*. We must not only *love our enemies*, and bear a good will to them, but we must *do good* to them, be as ready to do any good office to them as to any other person, if their case call for it, and it be in the power of our hands to do it. We must study to make it appear, by positive acts, if there be an opportunity for them, that we bear them no malice, nor seek revenge. Do they *curse* us, speak ill of us, and wish ill to us? Do they *despitefully use us*, in word or deed? Do they endeavour to make us contemptible or odious? Let us *bless them*, and *pray for them*, speak well of them, the best we can, wish well to them, especially to their souls, and be intercessors with God for them. This is repeated, *v.* 35: *Love your enemies*, and *do them good*. To recommend this difficult duty to us, it is represented as a generous thing, and an attainment few arrive at. *To love those that love us* has nothing *uncommon* in it, nothing peculiar to Christ's disciples, for *sinners* will *love those that love them*. There is nothing self-denying in that; it is but following nature, even in its corrupt state, and puts no force at all upon it (*v.* 32): it is no thanks to us to love those that say and do just as we would have them. "And (*v.* 33) *if you do good to them that do good to you*, and return their kindnesses, it is from a common principle of custom, honour, and gratitude; and therefore *what thanks have you?* What credit are you to the name of Christ, or what reputation do you bring to it? for *sinners also*, that know nothing of Christ and his doctrine, *do even the same*. But it becomes you to do something more excellent and eminent, herein to out-do your neighbours, to do that which sinners will not do, and which no principle of theirs can pretend to reach to: you must *render good for evil;*" not that any thanks are due to us, but *then* we are to our God *for a name and a praise*, and he will have the thanks.

(2.) We must be kind to those from whom we expect no manner of advantage (*v.* 35): *Lend, hoping for nothing again*. It is meant of the rich lending to the poor a little money for their necessity, to buy daily bread for themselves and their families, or to keep them out of prison. In such a case, we must *lend*, with a resolution not to demand interest for what we lend, as we may most justly from those that borrow money to make purchases withal, or to trade with. But that is not all; we must *lend* though we have reason to suspect that what we *lend* we *lose*, lend to those who are so poor that it is not probable they will be able to pay us again. This precept will be best illustrated by that law of Moses (Deut. xv. 7—10), which obliges them to lend to a *poor brother* as much as he *needed*, though the *year of release* was at hand. Here are two motives to this generous charity.

[1.] It will redound to our profit; for our *reward shall be great*, *v.* 35. What is given, or laid out, or lent and lost on earth, from a true principle of charity, will be made up to us in the other world, unspeakably to our advantage. "You shall not only be *repaid*, but *rewarded*, greatly rewarded; it will be said to you, *Come, ye blessed, inherit the kingdom*."

[2.] It will redound to our honour; for herein we shall resemble God in his goodness, which is the greatest glory: "*Ye shall be the children of the Highest*, shall be owned by him as his children, being like him." It is the glory of God that he is *kind to the unthankful and to the evil*, bestows the gifts of common providence even upon the worst of men, who are every day provoking him, and rebelling against him, and using those very gifts to his dishonour. Hence he infers (*v.* 36), *Be merciful, as your Father is merciful;* this explains Matt. v. 48, "*Be perfect, as your Father is perfect*. Imitate your Father in those things that are his brightest perfections." Those that are *merciful* as God is *merciful*, even *to the evil and the unthankful*, are *perfect* as God is *perfect;* so he is pleased graciously to accept it, though infinitely falling short. Charity is called the *bond of perfectness*, Col. iii. 14. This should strongly engage us to be merciful to our brethren, even such as have been injurious to us, not only that God is so to others, but that he is so to us, though we have been, and are, evil and unthankful; it is of his mercies that *we* are not consumed.

37 Judge not, and ye shall not be judged: condemn not, and ye shall not be condemned: forgive, and ye shall be forgiven: 38 Give, and it

shall be given unto you; good measure, pressed down, and shaken together, and running over, shall men
give into your bosom, For with the
same measure that ye mete withal it
shall be measured to you again. 39
And he spake a parable unto them,
Can the blind lead the blind? shall
they not both fall into the ditch? 40
The disciple is not above his master:
but every one that is perfect shall be
as his master. 41 And why beholdest
thou the mote that is in thy brother's
eye, but perceivest not the beam that
is in thine own eye? 42 Either how
canst thou say to thy brother, Brother,
let me pull out the mote that is in
thine eye, when thou thyself beholdest
not the beam that is in thine own eye?
Thou hypocrite, cast out first the beam
out of thine own eye, and then shalt
thou see clearly to pull out the mote
that is in thy brother's eye. 43 For
a good tree bringeth not forth corrupt
fruit; neither doth a corrupt tree bring
forth good fruit. 44 For every tree
is known by his own fruit. For of
thorns men do not gather figs, nor of
a bramble bush gather they grapes.
45 A good man out of the good treasure of his heart bringeth forth that
which is good; and an evil man out
of the evil treasure of his heart bringeth
forth that which is evil: for of the
abundance of the heart his mouth
speaketh. 46 And why call ye me,
Lord, Lord, and do not the things
which I say? 47 Whosoever cometh
to me, and heareth my sayings, and
doeth them, I will show you to whom
he is like: 48 He is like a man which
built a house, and digged deep, and
laid the foundation on a rock: and
when the flood arose, the stream beat
vehemently upon that house, and could
not shake it: for it was founded upon
a rock. 49 But he that heareth, and
doeth not, is like a man that without
a foundation built a house upon the
earth; against which the stream did
beat vehemently, and immediately it
fell; and the ruin of that house was
great.

All these sayings of Christ we had before in Matthew; some of them in *ch.* vii., others in other places. They were sayings that Christ often used; they needed only to be mentioned, it was easy to apply them. Grotius thinks that we need not be critical here in seeking for the coherence: they are golden sentences, like Solomon's proverbs or parables. Let us observe here,

I. We ought to be very candid in our censures of others, because we need grains of allowance ourselves: "Therefore *judge not* others, because then *you* yourselves *shall not be judged;* therefore *condemn not* others, because then *you* yourselves *shall not be condemned, v.* 37. Exercise towards others that charity which *thinks no evil,* which *bears all things, believes* and *hopes all things;* and then others will exercise that charity towards you. God will not *judge* and *condemn* you, men will not." They that are merciful to other people's names shall find others merciful to theirs.

II. If we are of a *giving* and a *forgiving* spirit, we shall ourselves reap the benefit of it: *Forgive and you shall be forgiven.* If we forgive the injuries done to us by others, others will forgive our inadvertencies. If we forgive others' trespasses against *us,* God will forgive our trespasses against *him.* And he will be no less mindful of the *liberal* that *devise liberal things* (*v.* 38): *Give, and it shall be given to you.* God, in his providence, will recompense it to you; it is *lent* to him, and *he is not unrighteous to forget* it (Heb. vi. 10), but he will *pay it again. Men* shall *return it into your bosom;* for God often makes use of *men* as instruments, not only of his *avenging,* but of his *rewarding* justice. If we in a right manner give to others when they need, God will incline the hearts of others to give to us when we need, and to give liberally, *good measure pressed down and shaken together.* They that *sow plentifully* shall *reap plentifully.* Whom God recompenses he recompenses *abundantly.*

III. We must expect to be dealt with ourselves as we deal with others: *With the same measure that ye mete it shall be measured to you again.* Those that deal *hardly* with others must acknowledge, as Adoni-bezek did (Judg. i. 7), that God is righteous, if others deal hardly with them, and they may expect to be paid in their own coin; but they that deal *kindly* with others have reason to hope that, when they have occasion, God will raise them up friends who will deal kindly with them. Though Providence does not always go by this rule, because the full and exact retributions are reserved for another world, yet, ordinarily, it observes a proportion sufficient to deter us from all acts of rigour and to encourage us in all acts of beneficence.

IV. Those who put themselves under the guidance of the ignorant and erroneous are likely to perish with them (*v.* 39): *Can the blind lead the blind?* Can the Pharisees, who are blinded with pride, prejudice, and bigotry, *lead the blind* people into the right way? *Shall not both fall* together *into the ditch?*

How can they expect any other? Those that are led by the common opinion, course, and custom, of this world, are themselves blind, and are led by the blind, and will perish with the world that *sits in darkness*. Those that ignorantly, and at a venture, *follow the multitude to do evil*, follow the blind in the broad way that leads the many to *destruction*.

V. Christ's followers cannot expect better treatment in the world than their Master had, *v.* 40. Let them not promise themselves more honour or pleasure in the world than Christ had, nor aim at the worldly pomp and grandeur which he was never ambitious of, but always declined, nor affect that power in secular things which he would not assume; but every one that would show himself *perfect*, an established disciple, let him be *as his Master*—dead to the world, and every thing in it, as his Master is; let him live a life of labour and self-denial as his Master doth, and make himself a servant of all; let him stoop, and let him toil, and do all the good he can, and then he will be a complete disciple.

VI. Those who take upon them to rebuke and reform others are concerned to look to it that they be themselves blameless, and harmless, and without rebuke, *v.* 41, 42. 1. Those with a very ill grace censure the faults of others who are not aware of their own faults. It is very absurd for any to pretend to be so quick-sighted as to spy small faults in others, like a mote in the eye, when they are themselves so perfectly past feeling as not to perceive *a beam in their own eye*. 2. Those are altogether unfit to help to reform others whose reforming charity does not begin at home. How canst thou offer thy service to thy brother, to *pull out the mote from his eye*, which requires a good eye as well as a good hand, when thou thyself hast a *beam in thine own eye*, and makest no complaint of it? 3. Those therefore who would be serviceable to the souls of others must first make it appear that they are solicitous about their own souls. To help to pull the mote out of our brother's eye is a good work, but then we must qualify ourselves for it by beginning with ourselves; and our reforming our own lives may, by the influence of example, contribute to others reforming theirs.

VII. We may expect that men's words and actions will be according as *they* are, according as their hearts are, and according as their principles are.

1. The heart is the *tree*, and the words and actions are fruit according to the nature of the tree, *v.* 43, 44. If a man be really a *good man*, if he have a principle of grace in his heart, and the prevailing bent and bias of the soul be towards God and heaven, though perhaps he may not abound in fruit, though some of his fruits be blasted, and though he may be sometimes like a tree in winter, yet he does not *bring forth corrupt fruit;* though he may not do you all the good he should, yet he will not in any material instance do you hurt. If he cannot reform ill manners, he will not *corrupt good manners*. If the fruit that a man brings forth be *corrupt*, if a man's devotion tend to debauch the mind and conversation, if a man's conversation be vicious, if he be a drunkard or fornicator, if he be a swearer or liar, if he be in any instance unjust or unnatural, his *fruit* is *corrupt*, and you may be sure that he is not a *good tree*. On the other hand, a *corrupt tree doth not bring forth good fruit*, though it may bring forth green leaves; *for of thorns men do not gather figs, nor of a bramble do they gather grapes*. You may, if you please, stick figs upon thorns, and hang a bunch of grapes upon a bramble, but they neither are, nor can be, the natural product of the trees; so neither can you expect any *good conduct* from those who have justly a *bad character*. If the fruit be good, you may conclude that the tree is so; if the conversation be holy, heavenly, and regular, though you cannot infallibly know the heart, yet you may charitably hope that it is upright with God; for *every tree is known by its fruit*. But the *vile person will speak villany* (Isa. xxxii. 6), and the experience of the moderns herein agrees with the *proverb of the ancients*, that *wickedness proceedeth from the wicked*, 1 Sam. xxiv. 13.

2. The heart is the *treasure*, and the words and actions are the expenses or produce from that treasure, *v.* 45. This we had, Matt. xii. 34, 35. The reigning love of God and Christ in the heart denominates a man *a good man;* and it is *a good treasure in the heart:* it enriches a man, it furnishes him with a good stock to spend upon, for the benefit of others. Out of such a *good treasure* a man may bring forth that which is good. But where the love of the world and the flesh reign there is an *evil treasure* in the heart, out of which an *evil man* is continually bringing forth *that which is evil;* and by what is brought forth you may know what is in the heart, as you may know what is in the vessel, water or wine, by what is *drawn out from it*, John ii. 8 *Of the abundance of the heart the mouth speaks;* what the mouth ordinarily speaks, speaks with relish and delight, generally agrees with what is innermost and uppermost in the heart: *He that speaks of the earth is earthly*, John iii. 31. Not but that a good man may possibly drop a bad word, and a wicked man make use of a good word to serve a bad turn; but, for the most part, the heart is as the words are, *vain* or *serious;* it therefore concerns us to get our hearts filled, not only with *good*, but with *abundance* of it.

VIII. It is not enough to *hear* the sayings of Christ, but we must *do* them; not enough to profess relation to him, as his servants, but we must make conscience of obeying him.

1. It is putting an *affront upon him* to call him *Lord, Lord*, as if we were wholly at his command, and had devoted ourselves to his service, if we do not make conscience of conforming to his will and serving the interests

of his kingdom. We do but mock Christ, as they that in scorn said, *Hail, King of the Jews,* if we call him ever so often *Lord, Lord,* and yet walk in the way of our own hearts and in the sight of our own eyes. Why do we call him *Lord, Lord,* in prayer (compare Matt. vii. 21, 22), if we do not obey his commands? He that *turns away his ear from hearing the law, his prayer shall be an abomination.*

2. It is *putting a cheat* upon ourselves if we think that a bare profession of religion will save us, that *hearing* the sayings of Christ will bring us to heaven, without *doing* them. This he illustrates by a similitude (*v.* 47—49), which shows,

(1.) That those only make sure work for their souls and eternity, and take the course that will stand them in stead in a trying time, who do not only *come* to Christ as his scholars, and *hear his sayings,* but do them, who think, and speak, and act, in every thing according to the established rules of his holy religion. They are like a *house built on a rock.* These are they that *take pains* in religion, as they do that *build on a rock,*—that *begin low,* as they do,—that *dig deep,* that found their hope upon Christ, who is the Rock of ages (and other foundation can no man lay); these are they who *provide for hereafter,* who get ready for the worst, who lay up in store a good foundation for the *time to come,* for the *eternity to come,* 1 Tim. vi. 19. They who do thus do well for themselves; for, [1.] They shall keep their integrity, in times of temptation and persecution; when others fall from their own stedfastness, as the seed on the stony ground, they shall *stand fast in the Lord.* [2.] They shall keep their comfort, and peace, and hope, and joy, in the midst of the greatest distresses. The *storms* and *streams* of affliction shall not shock them, for their feet are *set upon a rock,* a rock *higher than they.* [3.] Their everlasting welfare is secured. In death and judgment they are safe. Obedient believers are *kept by the power of Christ, through faith, unto salvation,* and shall never perish.

(2.) That those who rest in a bare hearing of the sayings of Christ, and do not live up to them, are but preparing for a fatal disappointment: *He that heareth and doeth not* (that knows his duty, but lives in the neglect of it), he is like a man that *built a house without a foundation.* He pleases himself with hopes that he has no ground for, and his hopes will fail him when he most needs the *comfort* of them, and when he expects the *crowning* of them; when the *stream beats vehemently* upon his house, it is gone, the sand it is built upon is washed away, and *immediately it falls.* Such is the *hope of the hypocrite, though he has gained, when God takes away his soul;* it is as the spider's web, and the giving up of the ghost.

CHAP. VII.

In this chapter we have, I. Christ confirming the doctrine he had preached in the former chapter, with two glorious miracles—the curing of one at a distance, and that was the centurion's servant (ver. 1—10), and the raising of one to life that was dead, the widow's son at Nain, ver. 11—18. II. Christ confirming the faith of John who was now in prison, and of some of his disciples, by sending him a short account of the miracles he wrought, in answer to a question he received from him (ver. 19—23), to which he adds an honourable testimony concerning John, and a just reproof to the men of that generation for the contempt they put upon him and his doctrine, ver. 24—35. III. Christ comforting a poor penitent that applied herself to him, all in tears of godly sorrow for sin, assuring her that her sins were pardoned, and justifying himself in the favour he showed her against the cavils of a proud Pharisee, ver. 36—50.

NOW when he had ended all his
sayings in the audience of the
people, he entered into Capernaum.
2 And a certain centurion's servant,
who was dear unto him, was sick, and
ready to die. 3 And when he heard
of Jesus, he sent unto him the elders
of the Jews, beseeching him that he
would come and heal his servant. 4
And when they came to Jesus, they
besought him instantly, saying, That
he was worthy for whom he should
do this: 4 For he loveth our nation,
and he hath built us a synagogue. 6
Then Jesus went with them. And
when he was now not far from the
house, the centurion sent friends to
him, saying unto him, Lord, trouble
not thyself: for I am not worthy that
thou shouldest enter under my roof:
7 Wherefore neither thought I myself
worthy to come unto thee: but say
in a word, and my servant shall be
healed. 8 For I also am a man set
under authority, having under me
soldiers, and I say unto one, Go, and
he goeth; and to another, Come, and
he cometh; and to my servant, Do
this, and he doeth *it.* 9 When Jesus
heard these things, he marvelled at
him, and turned him about, and said
unto the people that followed him, I
say unto you, I have not found so
great faith, no, not in Israel. 10 And
they that were sent, returning to the
house, found the servant whole that
had been sick.

Some difference there is between this story of the cure of the centurion's servant as it is related here and as we had it in Matt. viii. 5, &c. There it was said that the centurion came to Christ; here it is said that he sent to him first some of the *elders of the Jews* (*v.* 3), and afterwards some other *friends, v.* 6. But it is a rule that *we are said to do that which we do by another—Quod facimus per alium, id ipsum facere judicamur.* The centurion might be said to do that which he did by his proxies; as a man takes possession by his attorney. But it is probable that the centurion himself came at last, when Christ said to him (Matt. viii. 13), *As thou hast believed, so be it done unto thee.*

This miracle is here said to have been wrought by our Lord Jesus *when he had ended all his sayings in the audience of the people, v.* 1. What Christ said he said *publicly;* whoever would might come and hear him: *In secret have I said nothing,* John xviii. 20. Now, to give an undeniable proof of the *authority* of his *preaching word,* he here gives an incontestable proof of the *power* and *efficacy* of his *healing word.* He that had such a commanding empire in the kingdom of nature as that he could command away diseases, no doubt has such a sovereignty in the kingdom of grace as to enjoin duties displeasing to flesh and blood, and bind, under the highest penalties, to the observance of them. This miracle was wrought in Capernaum, where most of Christ's mighty works were done, Matt. xi. 23. Now observe,

I. The centurion's servant that was sick was *dear to his master, v.* 2. It was the praise of the servant that by his diligence and faithfulness, and a manifest concern for his master and his interest, as for himself and for his own, he recommended himself to his master's esteem and love. Servants should study to *endear* themselves to their masters. It was likewise the praise of the master that, when he had a good servant, he knew how to value him. Many masters, that are haughty and imperious, think it favour enough to the best servants they have not to rate them, and beat them, and be cruel to them, whereas they ought to be kind to them, and tender of them, and solicitous for their welfare and comfort.

II. The master, *when he heard of Jesus,* was for making application to him, *v.* 3. Masters ought to take particular care of their servants when they are *sick,* and not to neglect them then. This centurion begged that *Christ would come and heal his servant.* We may now, by faithful and fervent prayer, apply ourselves to Christ in heaven, and ought to do so, when sickness is in our families; for Christ is still the great Physician.

III. He sent some of the *elders of the Jews* to Christ, to represent the case, and solicit for him, thinking that a greater piece of respect to Christ than if he had come himself, because he was an uncircumcised Gentile, whom he thought Christ, being a prophet, would not care for conversing with. For that reason he sent Jews, whom he acknowledged to be favourites of Heaven, and not ordinary Jews neither, but *elders of the Jews,* persons in authority, that the dignity of the messengers might give honour to him to whom they were sent. Balak sent princes to Balaam.

IV. The elders of the Jews were hearty intercessors for the centurion: *They besought him instantly* (*v.* 4), were very urgent with him, pleading for the centurion that which he would never have pleaded for himself, *that he was worthy for whom he should do this.* If any Gentile was qualified to receive such a favour, surely he was. The centurion said, *I am not* so much as *worthy* of a visit (Matt. viii. 8), but the elders of the Jews thought him worthy of the cure; thus *honour shall uphold the humble in spirit. Let another man praise thee, and not thy own mouth.* But that which they insisted upon in particular was, that, though he was a Gentile, yet he was a hearty well-wisher to the Jewish nation and religion, *v.* 5. They thought there needed as much with Christ as there did with them to remove the prejudices against him as a Gentile, a Roman, and an officer of the army, and therefore mention this, 1. That he was well-affected to the people of the Jews: *He loveth our nation* (which few of the Gentiles did). Probably he had read the Old Testament, whence it was easy to advance to a very high esteem of the Jewish nation, as favoured by Heaven above all people. Note, Even conquerors, and those *in power,* ought to keep up an affection for the conquered, and those they have *power over.* 2. That he was well-affected to their worship: *He built them a* new *synagogue* at Capernaum, finding that what they had was either gone to decay or not large enough to contain the people, and that the inhabitants were not of ability to build one for themselves. Hereby he testified his veneration for the God of Israel, his belief of his being the one only living and true God, and his desire, like that of Darius, to have an interest in the prayers of God's Israel, Ezra vi. 10. This centurion built a synagogue at his own proper costs and charges, and probably employed his soldiers that were in garrison there in the building, to keep them from idleness. Note, Building places of meeting for religious worship is a very *good work,* is an instance of love to God and his people; and those who do good works of that kind are *worthy of double honour.*

V. Jesus Christ was very ready to show kindness to the centurion. He presently *went with them* (*v.* 6), though he was a Gentile; for *is he the Saviour of the Jews only? Is he not also of the Gentiles? Yes, of the Gentiles also,* Rom. iii. 29. The centurion did not think himself worthy to visit Christ (*v.* 7), yet Christ thought him worthy to be visited by him; for those that *humble themselves shall be exalted.*

VI. The centurion, when he heard that Christ was doing him the honour to come to his house, gave further proofs both of his humility and of his faith. Thus the graces of the saints are quickened by Christ's approaches towards them. *When he was now not far from the house,* and the centurion had notice of it, instead of setting his house in order for his reception, he *sends friends* to meet him with fresh expressions, 1. Of his *humility: "Lord, trouble not thyself,* for I am unworthy of such an honour, because I am a Gentile." This bespeaks not only his low thoughts of himself, notwithstanding the greatness of his figure; but his high thoughts of Christ, notwithstanding the meanness of his figure in the world. He knew how to honour a prophet of God, though he was despised and rejected of men. 2. Of his *faith:* "Lord, *trouble not thyself,* for I know there is no occasion; thou canst *cure* my servant without coming *under my roof,* by that almighty power from which *no thought can be witholden. Say, in a word, and my servant shall be healed:*" so far was this centurion from Namaan's fancy, that he should come to him, and stand, and *strike his hand over the* patient, and so *recover* him, 2 Kings v. 11. He illustrates this faith of his by a comparison taken from his own profession, and is confident that Christ can as easily command away the distemper as he can command any of his soldiers, can as easily send an angel with commission to cure this servant of his as he can send a soldier on an errand, *v.* 8. Christ has a sovereign power over all the creatures and all their actions, and can change the course of nature as he pleases, can rectify its disorders and repair its decays in human bodies; for *all power is given to him.*

VII. Our Lord Jesus was wonderfully well pleased with the faith of the centurion, and the more surprised at it because he was a Gentile; and, the centurion's faith having thus honoured Christ, see how he honoured it (*v.* 9): *He turned him about,* as one amazed, and *said to the people that followed him, I have not found so great faith, no not in Israel.* Note, Christ will have those that follow him to observe and take notice of the great examples of faith that are sometimes set before them—especially when any such are found among those that do not follow Christ so closely as they do in profession—that we may be shamed by the strength of their faith out of the weakness and waverings of ours.

VIII. The cure was *presently* and *perfectly* wrought (*v.* 10): *They that were sent* knew they had their errand, and therefore went back, and found the servant well, and under no remains at all of his distemper. Christ will take cognizance of the distressed case of poor servants, and be ready to relieve them; for there *is no respect of persons with him.* Nor are the Gentiles excluded from the benefit of his grace; nay, this was a specimen of that much greater faith which would be found among the Gentiles, when the gospel should be published, than among the Jews.

11 And it came to pass the day
after, that he went into a city called
Nain; and many of his disciples went
with him, and much people. 12 Now
when he came nigh to the gate of the
city, behold, there was a dead man
carried out, the only son of his mother, and she was a widow: and much
people of the city was with her. 13
And when the Lord saw her, he had
compassion on her, and said unto
her, Weep not. 14 And he came and
touched the bier: and they that bare
him stood still. And he said, Young
man, I say unto thee, Arise. 15 And
he that was dead sat up, and began to
speak. And he delivered him to his
mother. 16 And there came a fear
on all: and they glorified God, saying,
That a great prophet is risen up among
us; and, That God hath visited his
people. 17 And this rumour of him
went forth throughout all Judæa, and
throughout all the region round about.
18 And the disciples of John showed
him of all these things.

We have here the story of Christ's raising to life a widow's son at Nain, that was dead and in the carrying out to be buried, which Matthew and Mark had made no mention of; only, in the general, Matthew had recorded it, in Christ's answer to the disciples of John, that *the dead were raised* up, Matt. xi. 5. Observe,

I. Where, and when, this miracle was wrought. It was the *next day after* he had cured the centurion's servant, *v.* 11. Christ was doing good *every day,* and never had cause to complain that he had *lost a day.* It was done at the gate of a small city, or town, called *Nain,* not far from Capernaum, probably the same with a city called *Nais,* which Jerome speaks of.

II. Who were the witnesses of it. It is as well attested as can be, for it was done in the sight of two crowds that met in or near the gate of the city. There was a crowd of *disciples* and other *people* attending Christ (*v.* 11), and a crowd of relations and neighbours attending the funeral of the young man, *v.* 12. Thus there was a sufficient number to attest the truth of this miracle, which furnished greater proof of Christ's divine authority than his healing diseases; for by no power of nature, or any means, can the dead be raised.

III. How it was wrought by our Lord Jesus.

1. The person raised to life was a *young man,* cut off by death in the beginning of his days—a common case; *man comes forth like a flower and is cut down.* That he was really dead was universally agreed. There could be no collusion in the case; for Christ was *entering into the town,* and had not seen him till now that he met him upon the bier. He was *carried out* of the city; for the Jews' burying-places were without their cities, and at some distance from them. This young man was the *only son of his mother,* and *she a widow.* She depended upon him to be the

staff of her old age, but he proves a broken reed; every man at his best estate is so. How numerous, how various, how very calamitous, are the afflictions of the afflicted in this world! What a vale of tears is it! What a Bochim, a place of weepers! We may well think how deep the *sorrow* of this poor mother was for her *only son* (such sorrowing is referred to as expressive of the greatest grief,—Zech. xii. 10), and it was the deeper in that she was a *widow*, broken with breach upon breach, and a *full end made of her comforts. Much people of the city was with her, condoling* with her loss, to *comfort* her.

2. Christ showed both his *pity* and his *power* in raising him to life, that he might give a specimen of both, which shine so brightly in man's redemption.

(1.) See how *tender* his *compassions* are towards the afflicted (*v.* 13): *When the Lord saw* the poor widow following her son to the grave, *he had compassion on her.* Here was no application made to him for her, not so much as that he would speak some words of comfort to her, but, *ex mero motu—purely from the goodness of his nature*, he was troubled for her. The case was piteous, and he looked upon it with pity. His eye affected his heart; and he *said unto her, Weep not.* Note, Christ has a concern for the mourners, for the miserable, and often *prevents them with the blessings of his goodness.* He undertook the work of our redemption and salvation, *in his love and in his pity*, Isa. lxiii. 9. What a pleasing idea does this give us of the compassions of the Lord Jesus, and the multitude of his *tender mercies*, which may be very comfortable to us when at any time we are in sorrow! Let poor widows comfort themselves in their sorrows with this, that Christ *pities them*, and knows their souls in adversity; and, if others despise their grief, he does not. Christ said, *Weep not;* and he could give her a reason for it which no one else could: "Weep not for a *dead son*, for he shall presently become a *living one.*" This was a reason peculiar to her case; yet there is a reason common to all that sleep in Jesus, which is of equal force against inordinate and excessive grief for their death—that they shall rise again, shall rise in glory; and therefore we must *not sorrow as those that have no hope*, 1 Thess. iv. 13. Let Rachel, that *weeps for her children, refrain her eyes from tears*, for *there is hope in thine end, saith the Lord, that thy children shall come again to their own border*, Jer. xxxi. 17. And let our *passion* at such a time be checked and calmed by the consideration of Christ's *compassion.*

(2.) See how *triumphant* his *commands* are over even death itself (*v.* 14): *He came, and touched the bier*, or coffin, in or upon which the dead body lay; for to him it would be no pollution. Hereby he intimated to the bearers that they should not proceed; he had something to say to the dead young man. *Deliver him from going down to the pit; I have found a ransom*, Job xxxiii. 24. Hereupon *they that bore him stood still*, and probably let down the bier from their shoulders to the ground, and opened the coffin, if it was closed up; and then with solemnity, as one that had authority, and to whom belonged the issues from death, he said, *Young man, I say unto thee, Arise.* The young man was *dead*, and could not arise by any power of his own (no more can those that are spiritually dead in trespasses and sins); yet it was no absurdity at all for Christ to bid him *arise*, when a power went along with that word to *put life* into him. The gospel call to all people, to young people particularly, is, "*Arise*, arise from the dead, and Christ shall give you light and life." Christ's dominion over death was evidenced by the immediate effect of his word (*v.* 15): *He that was dead sat up*, without any help. When Christ put life into him he made it to appear by his *sitting up.* Have we grace from Christ? Let us show it. Another evidence of life was that he *began to speak;* for whenever Christ gives us spiritual life he *opens the lips* in prayer and praise. And, *lastly*, he would not oblige this young man, to whom he had given a new life, to go along with him as his disciple, to minister to him (though he owed him even his own self), much less as a trophy or show to get honour by him, but *delivered him to his mother*, to attend her as became a dutiful son; for Christ's miracles were miracles of mercy, and a great act of mercy this was to this widow; now she was *comforted*, according to the time in which she had been afflicted and much more, for she could now look upon this son as a particular favourite of Heaven, with more pleasure than if he had not died.

IV. What influence it had upon the people (*v.* 16): *There came a fear on all;* it frightened them all, to see a dead man start up alive out of his coffin in the open street, at the command of a man; they were all struck with wonder at this miracle, and *glorified God.* The Lord and his goodness, as well as the Lord and his greatness, are to be feared. The inference they drew from it was, "*A great prophet is risen up among us*, the great prophet that we have been long looking for; doubtless, he is one divinely inspired who can thus breathe life into the dead, and in him *God hath visited his people*, to redeem them, as was expected," Luke i. 68. This would be *life from the dead* indeed to all them that waited for the consolation of Israel. When dead souls are thus raised to spiritual life, by a divine power going along with the gospel, we must glorify God, and look upon it as a gracious visit to his people. The report of this miracle was carried, 1. In general, all the country over (*v.* 17): *This rumour of him*, that he was the great prophet, *went forth* upon the wings of fame *through all Judea*, which lay a great way off, and throughout all Galilee, which was the *region round about.* Most had this notice of him, yet few believed in him, and gave up themselves to him. Many have the *rumour* of Christ's gospel in their ears that have not the *savour* and *relish* of it in their souls. 2. In particular, it was carefully brought to John Baptist, who was now in prison (*v.* 18): *His disciples came,* and gave him an account of all things, that he might know that though *he* was bound yet *the word of the Lord was not bound;* God's work was going on, though he was laid aside.

19 And John calling *unto him* two
of his disciples sent *them* to Jesus,
saying, Art thou he that should come?
or look we for another? 20 When the
men were come unto him, they said,
John Baptist hath sent us unto thee,
saying, Art thou he that should come?
or look we for another? 21 And in
the same hour he cured many of *their*
infirmities and plagues, and of evil
spirits; and unto many *that were*
blind he gave sight. 22 Then Jesus
answering said unto them, Go your
way, and tell John what things ye have
seen and heard; how that the blind
see, the lame walk, the lepers are
cleansed, the deaf hear, the dead are
raised, to the poor the gospel is
preached. 23 And blessed is *he,* whosoever shall not be offended in me.
24 And when the messengers of John
were departed, he began to speak unto
the people concerning John, What
went ye out into the wilderness for to
see? A reed shaken with the wind?
25 But what went ye out for to see?
A man clothed in soft raiment? Behold, they which are gorgeously apparelled, and live delicately, are in
kings' courts. 26 But what went ye
out for to see? A prophet? Yea, I
say unto you, and much more than a
prophet. 27 This is *he,* of whom it
is written, Behold, I send my messenger before thy face, which shall prepare thy way before thee. 28 For I
say unto you, Among those that are
born of women there is not a greater
prophet than John the Baptist: but
he that is least in the kingdom of God
is greater than he. 29 And all the
people that heard *him,* and the publicans, justified God, being baptized
with the baptism of John. 30 But
the Pharisees and lawyers rejected the
counsel of God against themselves,
being not baptized of them. 31 And
the Lord said, Whereunto then shall
I liken the men of this generation?
and to what are they like? 32 They
are like unto children sitting in the
marketplace, and calling one to another, and saying, We have piped unto
you, and ye have not danced; we
have mourned to you, and ye have
not wept. 33 For John the Baptist
came neither eating bread nor drinking wine; and ye say, He hath a
devil. 34 The Son of man is come
eating and drinking; and ye say, Behold a gluttonous man, and a winebibber, a friend of publicans and sinners! 35 But wisdom is justified of
all her children.

All this discourse concerning John Baptist, occasioned by his sending to ask whether he was the Messiah or no, we had, much as it is here related, Matt. xi. 2—19.

I. We have here the message John Baptist sent to Christ, and the return he made to it. Observe,

1. The great thing we are to enquire concerning Christ is whether he be he that should come to redeem and save sinners, or whether we are to look for another, *v.* 19, 20. We are sure that God has promised that a Saviour shall come, an anointed Saviour; we are as sure that what he has promised he will perform in its season. If this Jesus be that promised Messiah, we will receive him, and will look for no other; but, if not, we will continue our expectations, and, though he tarry, will wait for him.

2. The faith of John Baptist himself, or at least of his disciples, wanted to be *confirmed* in this matter; for Christ had not yet publicly declared himself to be indeed the Christ, nay, he would not have his disciples, who knew him to be so, to speak of it, till the proofs of his being so were completed in his resurrection. The great men of the Jewish church had not owned him, nor had he gained any interest that was likely to set him upon the throne of his father David. Nothing of that power and grandeur was to be seen about him in which it was expected that the Messiah would appear; and therefore it is not strange that they should ask, *Art thou the Messiah?* not doubting but that, if he was not, he would direct them what *other* to *look for.*

3. Christ left it to his own works to praise him in the gates, to tell what he was and to prove it. While John's messengers were with him, he wrought many miraculous cures, *in that same hour,* which perhaps inti-

mates that they staid but *an hour* with him; and what a deal of work did Christ do in a little time! *v.* 21. *He cured many of their infirmities and plagues* in body, and of *evil spirits* that affected the mind either with frenzy or melancholy, and *unto many that were blind he gave sight.* He multiplied the cures, that there might be no ground left to suspect a fraud; and then (*v.* 22) he bade them *go and tell John what they had seen.* And he and they might easily argue, as even the common people did (John vii. 31), *When Christ cometh, will he do more miracles than these which this man hath done?* These cures, which they saw him work, were not only confirmations of his commission, but explications of it. The Messiah must come to cure a diseased world, to give light and sight to them that sit in darkness, and to restrain and conquer evil spirits. You see that Jesus does this to the bodies of people, and therefore must conclude this is he that should come to do it to the souls of people, and you are to *look for no other.* To his miracles in the kingdom of nature he adds this in the kingdom of grace (*v.* 22), *To the poor the gospel is preached,* which they knew was to be done by the Messiah; for he was anointed to *preach the gospel to the meek* (Isa. lxi. 1), and to *save the souls of the poor and needy,* Ps. lxxii. 13. Judge, therefore, whether you can look for any other that will more fully answer the characters of the Messiah and the great intentions of his coming.

4. He gave them an intimation of the danger people were in of being prejudiced against him, notwithstanding these evident proofs of his being the Messiah (*v.* 23): *Blessed is he whosoever shall not be offended in me,* or *scandalized* at me. We are here in a state of trial and probation; and it is agreeable to such a state that, as there are sufficient arguments to *confirm the truth* to those that are *honest* and *impartial* in searching after it, and have their minds prepared to receive it, so there should be also objections, to *cloud the truth* to those that are careless, worldly, and sensual. Christ's education at Nazareth, his residence at Galilee, the meanness of his family and relations, his poverty, and the despicableness of his followers—these and the like were stumbling-blocks to many, which all the miracles he wrought could not help them over. He is *blessed,* for he is wise, humble, and well disposed, that is not overcome by these prejudices. It is a sign that God has *blessed* him, for it is by his grace that he is helped over these stumbling-stones; *and he shall be blessed* indeed, blessed in Christ.

II. We have here the high encomium which Christ gave of John Baptist; not while his messengers were present (lest he should seem to flatter him), but *when they were departed* (*v.* 24), to make the people sensible of the advantages they had enjoyed in John's ministry, and were deprived of by his imprisonment. Let them now consider *what they went out into the wilderness to see,* who that was about whom there had been so much talk and such a great and general amazement. "Come," saith Christ, "I will tell you."

1. He was a man of unshaken *self-consistence,* a man of steadiness and constancy. He was not a *reed shaken with the wind,* first in one direction and then in another, shifting with every wind; he was *firm* as a *rock,* not *fickle* as a *reed.* If he could have bowed like a *reed* to Herod, and have complied with the court, he might have been a favourite there; but *none of these things moved him.*

2. He was a man of unparalleled *self-denial,* a great example of mortification and contempt of the world. He was not *a man clothed in soft raiment,* nor did he *live delicately* (*v.* 25); but, on the contrary, he lived in a wilderness and was clad and fed accordingly. Instead of adorning and pampering the body, he brought it under, and kept it in subjection.

3. He was *a prophet,* had his commission and instructions immediately from God, and not of man or by man. He was by birth a *priest,* but that is never taken notice of; for his glory, as a prophet, eclipsed the honour of his priesthood. Nay, he was *more,* he was *much more than a prophet* (*v.* 26), than any of the prophets of the Old Testament; for they spoke of Christ as at a distance, he spoke of him as at the door.

4. He was the harbinger and forerunner of the Messiah, and was himself prophesied of in the Old Testament (*v.* 27): *This is he of whom it is written* (Mal. iii. 1), *Behold, I send my messenger before thy face.* Before he sent the Master himself, he sent a messenger, to give notice of his coming, and prepare people to receive him. Had the Messiah been to appear as a *temporal prince,* under which character the carnal Jews expected him, his *messenger* would have appeared either in the *pomp* of a *general* or the *gaiety* of a *herald at arms;* but it was a *previous* indication, plain enough, of the *spiritual* nature of Christ's kingdom, that the messenger he sent before him to *prepare his way* did it by preaching repentance and reformation of men's hearts and lives. Certainly that kingdom was not of this world which was thus ushered in.

5. He was, upon this account, so great, that really there was not a *greater prophet* than he. *Prophets* were the *greatest* that were *born of women,* more honourable than kings and princes, and John was the *greatest* of all the *prophets.* The country was not sensible what a *valuable,* what an *invaluable,* man it had in it, when John Baptist went about preaching and baptizing. And yet *he that is least in the kingdom of God is greater than he.* The least gospel minister, that has obtained mercy of the Lord to be *skilful* and *faithful* in his work, or the meanest of the *apostles* and first preachers of the gospel,

being *employed* under a more *excellent* dispensation, are in a more honourable office than John Baptist. The meanest of those that *follow the Lamb* far excel the greatest of those that went before him. Those therefore who live under the gospel dispensation have so much the more to answer for.

III. We have here the just censure of the men of that generation, who were not wrought upon by the ministry either of John Baptist or of Jesus Christ himself.

1. Christ here shows what contempt was put upon John Baptist, while he was preaching and baptizing. (1.) Those who did show him any respect were but the common ordinary sort of people, who, in the eye of the gay part of mankind, were rather a disgrace to him than a credit, *v.* 29. *The people* indeed, the vulgar herd, of whom it was said, *This people, who know not the law, are cursed* (John vii. 49), and the publicans, men of ill fame, as being generally men of bad morals, or taken to be so, these were *baptized with his baptism,* and became his disciples; and these, though glorious monuments of divine grace, yet did not *magnify John* in the eye of the world; but by their repentance and reformation they *justified God,* justified his conduct and the wisdom of it in appointing such a one as John Baptist to be the forerunner of the Messiah: they hereby made it to appear that it was the best method that could be taken, for it was not in vain to *them,* whatever it was to others. (2.) The great men of their church and nation, the *polite* and the *politicians,* that would have done him some credit in the eye of the world, did him all the dishonour they could; they heard him indeed, but they were not *baptized of him, v.* 30. The Pharisees, who were most in reputation for religion and devotion, and the lawyers, who were celebrated for their learning, especially their knowledge of the scriptures, *rejected the counsel of God against themselves;* they *frustrated it,* they *received the grace of God,* by the baptism of John, in *vain.* God in sending that *messenger* among them had a kind *purpose* of good to them, *designed* their salvation by it, and, if they had closed with the counsel of God, it had been *for themselves,* they had been made for ever; but they *rejected it,* would not comply with it, and it was *against themselves,* it was to their own ruin; they came short of the benefit intended them, and not only so, but forfeited the grace of God, put a bar in their own door, and, by refusing that discipline which was to fit them for the kingdom of the Messiah, shut themselves out of it, and they not only excluded themselves, but hindered others, and stood in their way.

2. He here shows the strange perverseness of the men of that generation, in their cavils both against John and Christ, and the prejudices they conceived against them.

(1.) They made but a jesting matter of the methods God took to do them good (*v.* 31): "*Whereunto shall I liken the men of this generation?* What can I think of absurd enough to represent them by? They are, then, *like children sitting in the market-place,* that mind nothing that is serious, but are as full of play as they can hold. As if God were but in jest with them, in all the methods he takes to do them good, as children are with one another in the market-place (*v.* 32), they turn it all off with a banter, and are no more affected with it than with a piece of pageantry." This is the ruin of multitudes, they can never persuade themselves to be *serious* in the concerns of their souls. Old men, sitting in the sanhedrim, were but as *children sitting in the market-place,* and no more affected with the things that belonged to their everlasting peace than people are with children's play. O the amazing stupidity and vanity of the blind and ungodly world! The Lord awaken them out of their security.

(2.) They still found something or other to carp at. [1.] John Baptist was a reserved austere man, lived much in solitude, and ought to have been admired for being such a humble, sober, self-denying man, and hearkened to as a man of thought and contemplation; but this, which was his praise, was turned to his reproach. Because he came *neither eating nor drinking,* so freely, plentifully, and cheerfully, as others did, *you say,* "*He has a devil;* he is a melancholy man, he is possessed, as the demoniac whose dwelling was *among the tombs,* though he be not quite so wild." [2.] Our Lord Jesus was of a more free and open conversation; he *came eating and drinking, v.* 34. He would go and dine with Pharisees, though he knew they did not care for him; and with publicans, though he knew they were no credit to him; yet, in hopes of doing good both to the one and the other, he conversed familiarly with them. By this it appears that the ministers of Christ may be of very different tempers and dispositions, very different ways of preaching and living, and yet all good and useful; *diversity of gifts,* but each given to *profit withal.* Therefore none must make themselves a standard to all others, nor judge hardly of those that do not do just as they do. John Baptist bore witness to Christ, and Christ applauded John Baptist, though they were the reverse of each other in their way of living. But the common enemies of them both reproached them both. The very same men that had represented John as *crazed in his intellects,* because he came *neither eating nor drinking,* represented our Lord Jesus as *corrupt in his morals,* because he came *eating and drinking; he is a gluttonous man, and a wine-bibber.* Ill-will never speaks well. See the malice of wicked people, and how they put the worst construction upon every thing they meet with in the gospel, and in the preachers and professors of it; and hereby they think to depreciate *them,* but really destroy *themselves.*

3. He shows that, notwithstanding this,

God will be glorified in the salvation of a chosen remnant (*v.* 35): *Wisdom is justified of all her children.* There are those who are given to wisdom *as her children,* and they shall be brought by the grace of God to submit to wisdom's conduct and government, and thereby to justify wisdom in the ways she takes for bringing them to that submission; for tc them they are effectual, and thereby appear well chosen. Wisdom's children are herein unanimous, one and all, they have all a complacency in the methods of grace which divine wisdom takes, and think never the worse of them for their being ridiculed by some.

36 And one of the Pharisees desired him that he would eat with him.
And he went into the Pharisee's
house, and sat down to meat. 37
And, behold, a woman in the city,
which was a sinner, when she knew
that *Jesus* sat at meat in the Pharisee's house, brought an alabaster box
of ointment, 38 And stood at his feet
behind *him* weeping, and began to
wash his feet with tears, and did wipe
them with the hairs of her head, and
kissed his feet, and anointed *them*
with the ointment. 39 Now when
the Pharisee which had bidden him
saw *it*, he spake within himself, saying, This man, if he were a prophet,
would have known who and what
manner of woman *this is* that toucheth him: for she is a sinner. 40 And
Jesus answering said unto him, Simon, I have somewhat to say unto
thee. And he saith, Master, say on.
41 There was a certain creditor which
had two debtors: the one owed five
hundred pence, and the other fifty.
42 And when they had nothing to
pay, he frankly forgave them both.
Tell me therefore, which of them will
love him most? 43 Simon answered
and said, I suppose that *he*, to whom
he forgave most. And he said unto
him, Thou hast rightly judged. 44
And he turned to the woman, and
said unto Simon, Seest thou this woman? I entered into thine house,
thou gavest me no water for my feet:
but she hath washed my feet with
tears, and wiped *them* with the hairs
of her head. 45 Thou gavest me no
kiss: but this woman since the time
I came in hath not ceased to kiss my
feet. 46 My head with oil thou didst
not anoint: but this woman hath
anointed my feet with ointment. 47
Wherefore I say unto thee, Her sins,
which are many, are forgiven; for she
loved much: but to whom little is forgiven *the same* loveth little. 48 And he
said unto her, Thy sins are forgiven.
49 And they that sat at meat with
him began to say within themselves,
Who is this that forgiveth sins also?
50 And he said to the woman, Thy
faith hath saved thee; go in peace.

When and where this passage of story happened does not appear; this evangelist does not observe order of time in his narrative so much as the other evangelists do; but it comes in here, upon occasion of Christ's being reproached as *a friend to publicans and sinners,* to show that it was only for their good, and to bring them to repentance, that he conversed with them; and that those whom he admitted near him were reformed, or in a hopeful way to be so. Who this woman was that here testified so great an affection to Christ does not appear; it is commonly said to be Mary Magdalene, but I find no ground in scripture for it: she is described (*ch.* viii. 2 and Mark xvi. 9) to be one *out of whom Christ had cast seven devils;* but that is not mentioned here, and therefore it is probable that it was not she. Now observe here,

I. The civil entertainment which a Pharisee gave to Christ, and his gracious acceptance of that entertainment (*v.* 36): *One of the Pharisees desired him that he would eat with him,* either because he thought it would be a reputation to him to have such a guest at his table or because his company would be an entertainment to him and his family and friends. It appears that this Pharisee did not believe in Christ, for he will not own him to be a *prophet* (*v.* 39), and yet our Lord Jesus accepted his invitation, *went into his house, and sat down to meat,* that they might see he took the same liberty with Pharisees that he did with publicans, in hopes of *doing them good.* And those may venture further into the society of such as are prejudiced against Christ, and his religion, who have wisdom and grace sufficient to instruct and argue with them, than others may.

II. The great respect which a poor penitent sinner showed him, when he was at meat in the Pharisee's house. It was a woman in the city *that was a sinner,* a Gentile, a *harlot,* I doubt, known to be so, and infamous. She *knew that Jesus sat at meat in the Pharisee's house,* and, having been converted from her wicked course of life by his preaching, she came to acknowledge her obligations to him, having no opportunity of doing it in any other way than by *washing* his feet, and anointing them with some sweet ointment that she brought with her for that purpose. The way of sitting at table then was such that their feet were partly *behind them.* Now this woman did not look Christ in the face, but came *behind him,* and did the part of a *maid-servant,* whose office it was to *wash the feet* of the guests (1 Sam. xxv. 41) and to prepare the ointments.

Now in what this good woman did, we may observe,

1. Her *deep humiliation* for sin. She stood behind him *weeping;* her eyes had been the inlets and outlets of sin, and now she makes them fountains of tears. Her face is now foul with weeping, which perhaps used to be covered with paints. Her hair now made a towel of, which before had been plaited and adorned. We have reason to think that she had before sorrowed for sin; but, now that she had an opportunity of coming into the presence of Christ, the wound bled afresh and her sorrow was renewed. Note, It well becomes penitents, upon all their approaches to Christ, to renew their godly sorrow and shame for sin, *when he is pacified,* Ezek. xvi. 63.

2. Her *strong affection* to the Lord Jesus. This was what our Lord Jesus took special notice of, that she *loved much, v.* 42, 47. She *washed his feet,* in token of her ready submission to the meanest office in which she might *do him honour.* Nay, she washed them with *her tears,* tears of joy; she was in a transport, to find herself so near her Saviour, whom her soul loved. She *kissed his feet,* as one unworthy of the kisses of his mouth, which the spouse coveted, Cant. i. 2. It was a kiss of adoration as well as affection. *She wiped them with her hair,* as one entirely devoted to his honour. Her eyes shall yield water to wash them, and her hair be a towel to wipe them; and she *anointed* his feet *with the ointment,* owning him hereby to be the Messiah, the *Anointed.* She anointed his feet in token of her consent to God's design in anointing his head with the *oil of gladness.* Note, All true penitents have a dear love to the Lord Jesus.

III. The offence which the Pharisee took at Christ, for admitting the respect which this poor penitent paid him (*v.* 39): *He said within himself* (little thinking that Christ knew what he thought), *This man, if he were a prophet,* would then have so much *knowledge* as to perceive that *this woman is a sinner,* is a Gentile, is a woman of ill fame, and so much *sanctity* as *therefore* not to suffer her to come so near him; for can one of such a character approach a prophet, and his heart not rise at it? See how apt proud and narrow souls are to think that others should be as haughty and censorious as themselves. Simon, if she had touched him, would have said, *Stand by thyself, come not near me, for I am holier than thou* (Isa. lxv. 5); and he thought Christ should say so too.

IV. Christ's justification of the woman in what she did to him, and of himself in admitting it. Christ knew what the Pharisee spoke *within himself,* and made answer to it: *Simon, I have something to say unto thee, v.* 40. Though he was kindly entertained at his table, yet even there he reproved him for what he saw amiss in him, and would not *suffer sin upon him.* Those whom Christ hath *something against* he hath something to *say to,* for his *Spirit* shall *reprove.* Simon is willing to give him the hearing: *He saith, Master, say on.* Though he could not believe him to be a prophet (because he was not so nice and precise as he was), yet he can compliment him with the title of *Master,* among those that cry *Lord, Lord,* but *do not the things which he saith.* Now Christ, in his answer to the Pharisee, reasons thus:—It is true this woman has been a sinner: he knows it; but she is a *pardoned* sinner, which supposes her to be a *penitent* sinner. What she did to him was an expression of her *great love* to her Saviour, by whom her sins were forgiven. If she was pardoned, who had been *so great a sinner,* it might reasonably be expected that she should love her Saviour more than others, and should give greater proofs of it than others; and if this was the fruit of her love, and flowing from a sense of the pardon of her sins, it became him to accept of it, and it ill became the Pharisee to be offended at it. Now Christ has a further intention in this. The Pharisee doubted whether he was a *prophet* or no, nay, he did in effect deny it; but Christ shows that he was more than a prophet, for he is one that has *power on earth to forgive sins,* and to whom are due the affections and thankful acknowledgments of penitent pardoned sinners. Now, in his answer,

1. He by a parable forces Simon to acknowledge that the greater sinner this woman had been the greater love she ought to show to Jesus Christ when her *sins* were *pardoned, v.* 41—43. A man had *two debtors* that were both insolvent, but one of them owed him *ten times* more than the other. He very freely *forgave them both,* and did not take the advantage of the law against them, did not order them and their children to be sold, or *deliver them to the tormentors.* Now they were both sensible of the great kindness they had received; but *which of them will love him most?* Certainly, saith the Pharisee, he to *whom he forgave most;* and herein he rightly judged. Now we, being obliged to *forgive,* as we are and hope to be *forgiven,* may hence learn the duty between debtor and creditor.

(1.) The *debtor,* if he have *any thing to pay,* ought to make satisfaction to his *creditor.* No man can reckon any thing *his own,* or have any comfortable enjoyment of it, but that which is so when *all his debts are paid.*

(2.) If God in his providence have disabled the debtor to pay his debt, the creditor ought not to be severe with him, nor to go to the utmost rigour of the law with him, but *freely to forgive him. Summum jus est summa injuria—The law stretched into rigour becomes unjust.* Let the unmerciful creditor read that parable, Matt. xviii. 23, &c., and tremble; for *they* shall have judgment without mercy that show no mercy.

(3.) The debtor that has found his creditors merciful ought to be very grateful to them; and, if he cannot otherwise recompense them, ought to love them. Some insolvent debtors, instead of being *grateful*, are *spiteful*, to their creditors that lose by them, and cannot give them a good word, only because they complain, whereas losers may have leave to speak. But this parable speaks of God as the Creator (or rather of the Lord Jesus himself, for he it is that forgives, and is beloved by, the debtor) and sinners are the debtors: and so we may learn here, [1.] That *sin is a debt*, and *sinners are debtors* to God Almighty. As creatures, we owe a debt, a debt of obedience to the precept of the law, and, for non-payment of that, as sinners, we become liable to the penalty. We have not paid our rent; nay, we have wasted our Lord's goods, and so we become debtors. God has an action against us for the injury we have done him, and the omission of our duty to him. [2.] That some are deeper in debt to God, by reason of sin, than others are: *One owed five hundred pence and the other fifty.* The Pharisee was the less debtor, yet he a debtor too, which was more than he thought himself, but rather that God was his debtor, Luke xviii. 10, 11. This woman, that had been a scandalous notorious sinner, was the *greater debtor*. Some sinners are in themselves greater debtors than others, and some sinners, by reason of divers aggravating circumstances, greater debtors; as those that have sinned most openly and scandalously, that have sinned against greater light and knowledge, more convictions and warnings, and more mercies and means. [3.] That, whether our debt be more or less, it is *more* than we are able to pay: *They had nothing to pay*, nothing at all to make a composition with; for the debt is great, and we have nothing at all to pay it with. Silver and gold will not pay our debt, nor will sacrifice and offering, no, not *thousands of rams.* No righteousness of our own will pay it, no, not our repentance and obedience for the future; for it is what we are already bound to, and it is God that works it within us. [4.] That the God of heaven is *ready* to forgive, *frankly* to *forgive*, poor sinners, upon gospel terms, though their debt be ever so great. If we repent, and believe in Christ, our iniquity shall not be our ruin, it shall not be laid to our charge. God has proclaimed his name gracious and merciful, and ready to forgive sin; and, his Son having purchased pardon for penitent believers, his gospel promises it to them, and his Spirit seals it and gives them the comfort of it. [5.] That those who have their sins *pardoned* are obliged to *love him* that pardoned them; and the more is forgiven them, the more they should love him. The *greater sinners* any have been before their conversion, the *greater saints* they should be after, the more they should study to do for God, and the more their hearts should be enlarged in obedience. When a *persecuting Saul* became a preaching Paul he *laboured more abundantly.*

2. He applies this parable to the different temper and conduct of the Pharisee and the sinner towards Christ. Though the Pharisee would not allow Christ to be a prophet, Christ seems ready to allow him to be in a justified state, and that he was one *forgiven*, though to him *less was forgiven.* He did indeed show some love to Christ, in inviting him to his house, but nothing to what this poor woman showed. "Observe," saith Christ to him, "she is one that has much forgiven her, and therefore, according to thine own judgment, it might be expected that she should love much more than thou dost, and so it appears. *Seest thou this woman? v.* 44. Thou lookest upon her with contempt, but consider how much kinder a friend she is to me than thou art; should I then accept thy kindness, and refuse hers?" (1.) "Thou didst not so much as order a basin of water to be brought, to wash my feet in, when I came in, wearied and dirtied with my walk, which would have been some refreshment to me; but she has done much more: *she has washed my feet with tears*, tears of affection to me, tears of affliction for sin, and has *wiped them with the hairs of her head*, in token of her great love to me." (2.) "Thou didst not so much as kiss my cheek" (which was a usual expression of a hearty and affectionate welcome to a friend); "but *this woman has not ceased to kiss my feet* (*v.* 45), thereby expressing both a humble and an affectionate love." (3.) "Thou didst not provide me a little common oil, as usual, to anoint my head with; but she has bestowed a box of precious *ointment* upon *my feet* (*v.* 46), so far has she outdone thee." The reason why some people blame the pains and expense of zealous Christians, in religion, is because they are not willing themselves to come up to it, but resolve to rest in a *cheap* and *easy* religion.

3. He silenced the Pharisee's cavil: *I say unto thee*, Simon, *her sins, which are many, are forgiven, v.* 47. He owns that she had been guilty of *many sins:* "But they are *forgiven* her, and therefore it is no way unbecoming in me to accept her kindness. They *are forgiven, for she loved much.*" It should be rendered, *therefore she loved much;* for it is plain, by the tenour of Christ's discourse, that her loving much was not the *cause*, but the *effect*, of her pardon, and of her comfortable sense of it; for *we love God* because *he first loved us;* he did not forgive us because we first loved him. "But *to whom little is forgiven*, as is to thee, *the same loveth little*, as thou dost." Hereby he intimates to the Pharisee that his love to Christ was so

little that he had reason to question whether he loved him at all in sincerity; and, consequently, whether indeed his sins, though comparatively *little*, were forgiven him. Instead of grudging greater sinners the mercy they find with Christ, upon their repentance, we should be stirred up by their example to examine ourselves whether we be indeed forgiven, and do love Christ.

4. He silenced her fears, who probably was discouraged by the Pharisee's conduct, and yet would not so far yield to the discouragement as to fly off. (1.) Christ said unto her, *Thy sin's are forgiven*, *v.* 48. Note, The more we express our sorrow for sin, and our love to Christ, the clearer evidence we have of the forgiveness of our sins; for it is by the experience of a *work of grace* wrought *in us* that we obtain the assurance of an *act of grace* wrought *for us.* How well was she paid for her pains and cost, when she was dismissed with this word from Christ, *Thy sins are forgiven!* and what an effectual prevention would this be of her return to sin again! (2.) Though there were those present who quarrelled with Christ, in their own minds, for presuming to forgive sin, and to pronounce sinners absolved (*v.* 49), as those had done (Matt. ix. 3), yet he *stood to what he had said;* for as he had there proved that he had *power to forgive sin*, by curing the man sick of the palsy, and therefore would not here take notice of the cavil, so he would now show that he had *pleasure in forgiving sin*, and it was his delight; he loves to speak pardon and peace to penitents: *He said to the woman, Thy faith hath saved thee*, *v.* 50. This would confirm and double her comfort in the forgiveness of her sin, that she was *justified by her faith.* All these expressions of sorrow for sin, and love to Christ, were the effects and products of faith; and therefore, as faith of all graces doth most honour God, so Christ doth of all graces put most honour upon faith. Note, They who know that their faith hath saved them may go in peace, may go on their way rejoicing.

CHAP. VIII.

Most of this chapter is a repetition of divers passages of Christ's preaching and miracles which we had before in Matthew and Mark; they are all of such weight, that they are worth repeating, and therefore they are repeated, that out of the mouth not only of two, but of three, witnesses every word may be established. Here is, I. A general account of Christ's preaching, and how he had subsistence for himself and his numerous family by the charitable contributions of good people, ver. 1—3. II. The parable of the sower, and the four sorts of ground, with the exposition of it, and some inferences from it, ver. 4—18. III. The preference which Christ gave to his obedient disciples before his nearest relations according to the flesh, ver. 19—21. IV. His stilling a storm at sea, with a word's speaking, ver. 22—25. V. His casting a legion of devils out of a man that was possessed by them, ver. 26—40. VI. His healing the woman that had the bloody issue, and raising Jairus's daughter to life, ver. 41—56.

AND it came to pass afterward,
that he went throughout every
city and village, preaching and showing the glad tidings of the kingdom
of God: and the twelve *were* with
him, 2 And certain women, which
had been healed of evil spirits and
infirmities, Mary called Magdalene,
out of whom went seven devils, 3
And Joanna the wife of Chuza, Herod's steward, and Susanna, and many
others, which ministered unto him of
their substance.

We are here told,

I. *What* Christ *made* the *constant business* of his *life*—it was *preaching;* in that work he was indefatigable, and went about doing good (*v.* 1), *afterward*—ἐν τῷ καθεξῆς—*ordine*, in the proper *time* or *method.* Christ took his work before him, and went about it regularly He observed a *series* or order of business, so that the end of one good work was the beginning of another. Now observe here, 1. *Where* he preached: *He went about*—διώδευε—*peragrabat.* He was an *itinerant* preacher, did not confine himself to one place, but diffused the beams of his light. *Circumibat—He went his circuit*, as a judge, having found his preaching perhaps most *acceptable* where it was *new.* He went about *through every city*, that none might plead ignorance. Hereby he set an example to his disciples; they must traverse the nations of the earth, as he did the cities of Israel. Nor did he confine himself to the *cities*, but went into the *villages*, among the plain country-people, to preach *to the inhabitants of the villages*, Judg. v. 11. 2. What he preached: *He showed the glad tidings of the kingdom of God*, that it was now to be set up among them. Tidings of the *kingdom of God* are *glad tidings*, and those Jesus Christ came to bring; to tell the children of men that God was willing to take all those *under his protection* that were willing to return *to their allegiance.* It was *glad tidings* to the world that there was hope of its being *reformed* and *reconciled.* 3. Who were his attendants: *The twelve were with him*, not to preach if he were present, but to learn from him what and how to preach hereafter, and, if occasion were, to be sent to places where he could not go. Happy were these his servants that heard his wisdom.

II. *Whence* he *had* the *necessary supports* of life: He lived upon the kindness of his friends. There were *certain women*, who frequently attended his ministry, that *ministered to him of their substance*, *v.* 2, 3. Some of them are named; but there were *many others*, who were zealously affected to the doctrine of Christ, and thought themselves bound *in justice* to *encourage* it, having themselves found benefit, and in *charity*, hoping that many others might find benefit by it too.

1. They were such, for the most part, as had been *Christ's patients*, and were the monuments of his power and mercy; they had been *healed by him of evil spirits and infirmities.* Some of them had been troubled in mind, had been melancholy, others of them

afflicted in body, and he had been to them a powerful healer. He is the physician both of body and soul, and those who have been *healed by him* ought to study what they shall *render to him.* We are bound in *interest* to attend him, that we may be ready to apply ourselves to him for help in case of a relapse; and we are bound in *gratitude* to serve him and his gospel, who hath *saved* us, and saved us *by it.*

2. One of them was Mary Magdalene, out of whom had been *cast seven devils;* a certain number for an uncertain. Some think that she was one that had been *very wicked,* and then we may suppose her to be the woman that *was a sinner* mentioned just before, *ch.* vii. 37. Dr. Lightfoot, finding in some of the Talmudists' writings that Mary Magdelene signified *Mary the plaiter of hair,* thinks it applicable to her, she having been noted, in the days of her iniquity and infamy, for that *plaiting of hair* which is opposed to *modest apparel,* 1 Tim. ii. 9. But, though she had been an immodest woman, upon her repentance and reformation she found mercy, and became a zealous disciple of Christ. Note, The greatest of sinners must not despair of pardon; and the worse any have been before their conversion the more they should study to do for Christ after. Or, rather, she was one that had been *very melancholy,* and then, probably, it was Mary the sister of Lazarus, who was a woman of a *sorrowful spirit,* who might have been originally of Magdala, but removed to Bethany. This Mary Magdalene was attending on Christ's cross and his sepulchre, and, if she was not Mary the sister of Lazarus, either that particular friend and favourite of Christ's did not attend then, or the evangelists did not take notice of her, neither of which we can suppose; thus Dr. Lightfoot argues. Yet there is this to be objected against it that Mary Magdalene is reckoned *among the women that followed Jesus from Galilee* (Matt. xxvii. 55, 56); whereas Mary the sister of Lazarus had her residence in Bethany.

3. Another of them was *Joanna the wife of Chuza, Herod's steward.* She had been his wife (so some), but was now a widow, and left in good circumstances. If she was now his wife, we have reason to think that her *husband,* though preferred in Herod's court, had received the gospel, and was very willing that his wife should be both a hearer of Christ and a contributor to him.

4. There were many of them that *ministered to Christ of their substance.* It was an instance of the meanness of that condition to which our Saviour humbled himself that he needed it, and of his great humility and condescension that he accepted it. Though he was rich, yet for our sakes *he became poor,* and lived upon alms. Let none say that they scorn to be beholden to the charity of their neighbours, when Providence has brought them into straits; but let them ask and be thankful for it as a favour. Christ would rather be beholden to his known friends for a maintenance for himself and his disciples than be burdensome to strangers in the cities and villages whither he came to preach. Note, It is the duty of those who are taught in the word to *communicate to them who teach them in all good things;* and those who are herein liberal and cheerful honour the Lord with their substance, and bring a blessing upon it.

4 And when much people were
gathered together, and were come to
him out of every city, he spake by a
parable: 5 A sower went out to sow
his seed: and as he sowed, some fell
by the way side; and it was trodden
down, and the fowls of the air devoured
it. 6 And some fell upon a
rock; and as soon as it was sprung
up, it withered away, because it lacked
moisture. 7 And some fell among
thorns; and the thorns sprang up
with it, and choked it. 8 And other
fell on good ground, and sprang up,
and bare fruit an hundredfold. And
when he had said these things, he
cried, He that hath ears to hear, let
him hear. 9 And his disciples asked
him, saying, What might this parable
be? 10 And he said, Unto you it
is given to know the mysteries of the
kingdom of God: but to others in
parables; that seeing they might not
see, and hearing they might not understand.
11 Now the parable is
this: The seed is the word of God.
12 Those by the way side are they
that hear; then cometh the devil,
and taketh away the word out of
their hearts, lest they should believe
and be saved. 13 They on the rock
are they, which, when they hear, receive
the word with joy; and these
have no root, which for a while believe,
and in time of temptation fall
away. 14 And that which fell among
thorns are they, which, when they
have heard, go forth, and are choked
with cares and riches and pleasures
of *this* life, and bring no fruit to perfection.
15 But that on the good
ground are they, which in an honest
and good heart, having heard the
word, keep *it,* and bring forth fruit
with patience. 16 No man, when he
hath lighted a candle, covereth it with

a vessel, or putteth *it* under a bed;
but setteth *it* on a candlestick, that
they which enter in may see the light.
17 For nothing is secret, that shall
not be made manifest; neither *any
thing* hid, that shall not be known
and come abroad. 18 Take heed
therefore how ye hear: for whosoever hath, to him shall be given; and
whosoever hath not, from him shall
be taken even that which he seemeth
to have. 19 Then came to him *his*
mother and his brethren, and could
not come at him for the press. 20
And it was told him *by certain* which
said, Thy mother and thy brethren
stand without, desiring to see thee.
21 And he answered and said unto
them, My mother and my brethren
are these which hear the word of God,
and do it.

The former paragraph began with an account of Christ's industry in *preaching* (*v.* 1); this begins with an account of the people's industry in hearing, *v.* 4. He *went into every city*, to preach; so they, one would think, should have contented themselves to hear him when he came to their own city (we know those that would); but there were those here that came *to him out of every city*, would not stay till he came to *them*, nor think that they had enough when he left *them*, but *met him* when he was coming towards them, and *followed him* when he was going from them. Nor did he excuse himself from going *to the cities* with this, that there were some *from* the cities that *came to him;* for, though there were, yet the most had not zeal enough to bring them to him, and therefore such is his wonderful condescension that he will go to them; for *he is found of those that sought him not*, Isa. lxv. 1.

Here was, it seems, a vast concourse, *much people were gathered together*, abundance of fish to cast their net among; and he was as ready and willing to *teach* as they were to be *taught*. Now in these verses we have,

I. Necessary and excellent rules and cautions for hearing the word, in the parable of *the sower* and the explanation and application of it, all which we had twice before more largely. When Christ had put forth this parable, 1. The disciples were *inquisitive* concerning the meaning of it, *v.* 9. They asked him, *What might this parable be?* Note, We should covet earnestly to know the true *intent*, and full *extent*, of the word we hear, that we may be neither mistaken nor defective in our knowledge. 2. Christ made them sensible of what great advantage it was to them that they had opportunity of acquainting themselves with the mystery and meaning of his word, which others had not: *Unto you it is given, v.* 10. Note, Those who would receive instruction from Christ must know and consider what a privilege it is to be instructed by him, what a distinguishing privilege to be led into the light, such a light, when others are left in darkness, such a darkness. Happy are we, and for ever indebted to free grace, if the same thing that is a *parable* to others, with which they are only *amused*, is a *plain truth* to us, by which we are *enlightened* and *governed*, and into the mould of which we are *delivered.*

Now from the parable itself, and the explication of it, observe,

(1.) The *heart of man* is as *soil* to the *seed of God's word;* it is capable of receiving it, and bringing forth the fruits of it; but, unless that seed be sown in it, it will bring forth nothing valuable. Our care therefore must be to bring the *seed* and the *soil* together. To what purpose have we the *seed* in the scripture, if it be not *sown?* And to what purpose have we the soil in our own hearts, if it be not sown with that seed?

(2.) The *success* of the *seeding* is very much according to the nature and temper of the *soil*, and as that is, or is not, disposed to receive the seed. The word of God *is to us*, as *we are*, a *savour of life unto life*, or *of death unto death.*

(3.) The devil is a subtle and spiteful enemy, that makes it his business to hinder our profiting by the word of God. He takes the word out of the hearts of *careless* hearers, *lest they should believe and be saved, v.* 12. This is added here to teach us, [1.] That we cannot be *saved* unless we *believe.* The word of the gospel will not be a saving word to us, unless it be mixed with faith. [2.] That therefore the devil does all he can to keep us from *believing*, to make us not believe the word when we read and hear it; or, if we heed it for the present, to make us forget it again, and let it slip (Heb. ii. 1); or, if we remember it, to create prejudices in our minds against it, or *divert* our minds from it to something else; and all is *lest we should believe and be saved*, lest we should believe and *rejoice*, while he believes and *trembles.*

(4.) Where the word of God is heard *carelessly* there is commonly a *contempt* put upon it too. It is added here in the parable that the seed which fell by the way-side was *trodden down, v.* 5. They that wilfully shut their ears against the word do in effect trample it under their feet; they *despise the commandment of the Lord.*

(5.) Those on whom the word makes *some* impressions, but they are not *deep* and *durable* ones, will show their hypocrisy in a time of trial; as the seed sown upon the rock, where it gains no root, *v.* 13. These *for awhile believe*, a little while; their profession promises something, but in *time of temptation they fall away* from their good beginnings Whether the temptation arises from the smiles, or from the frowns, of the world, they are easily overcome by it.

(6.) The *pleasures of this life* are as dangerous and mischievous thorns to choke the good seed of the word as any other. This is added here (*v.* 14), which was not in the other evangelists. Those that are *not entangled in the cares of this life,* nor inveigled with the *deceitfulness of riches,* but boast that they are dead to them, may yet be kept from heaven by an affected indolence, and the love of ease and pleasure. The delights of sense may ruin the soul, even lawful delights, indulged, and too much delighted in.

(7.) It is not enough that the fruit be brought forth, but it must be *brought to perfection,* it must be fully ripened. If it be not, it is as if there was no fruit at all brought forth; for that which in Matthew and Mark is said to be *unfruitful* is the same that here is said to *bring forth none to perfection.* For *factum non dicitur quod non perseverat—perseverance is necessary to the perfection of a work.*

(8.) The good ground, which brings forth *good fruit,* is an *honest* and *good heart,* well disposed to receive instruction and commandment (*v.* 15); a heart free from sinful pollutions, and firmly fixed for God and duty, an upright heart, a tender heart, and a heart that *trembles at the word,* is an honest and good heart, which, having heard the word, *understands* it (so it is in Matthew), *receives* it (so it is in Mark), and *keeps* it (so it is here), as the soil not only *receives,* but keeps, the seed; and the stomach not only receives, but keeps, the food or physic.

(9.) Where the word is well kept there is fruit brought forth *with patience.* This also is added here. There must be both *bearing* patience and *waiting* patience; patience to suffer the *tribulation* and *persecution* which may *arise because of the word;* patience to continue to the end in well-doing.

(10.) In consideration of all this, we ought to take *heed how we hear* (*v.* 18); take heed of those things that will hinder our profiting by the word we hear, watch over our hearts in hearing, and take heed lest they betray us; take heed *lest* we hear carelessly and slightly, lest, upon any account, we entertain prejudices against the word we hear; and take heed to the frame of our spirits after we have heard the word, lest we lose what we have gained.

II. Needful instructions given to those that are appointed to preach the word, and to those also that have heard it. 1. Those that have *received the gift* must *minister the same.* Ministers that have the dispensing of the gospel committed to them, people that have profited by the word and are thereby qualified to profit others, must look upon themselves as *lighted candles:* ministers must in solemn authoritative preaching, and people in brotherly familiar discourse, diffuse their light for a *candle* must not be *covered with a vessel* nor *put under a bed,* *v.* 16. Ministers and Christians are to be lights in the world, *holding forth the word of life.* Their light must shine before men; they must not only *be good,* but *do good.* 2. We must expect that what is now done *in secret,* and from unseen springs, will shortly be *manifested* and *made known, v.* 17. What is committed to you *in secret* should be made manifest *by you;* for your Master did not give you talents to be buried, but to be traded with. Let that which is now hid be *made known;* for, if it be not manifested *by you,* it will be manifested *against you,* will be produced in evidence of your treachery. 3. The gifts we have will either be continued to us, or taken from us, according as we do, or do not, make use of them for the glory of God and the edification of our brethren: *Whosoever hath, to him shall be given, v.* 18. He that hath gifts, and does good with them, shall have more; he that *buries his talent* shall lose it. From him that hath not shall be taken away even *that which he hath,* so it is in Mark; that which he *seemeth to have,* so it is in Luke. Note, The grace that is lost was but *seeming* grace, was never *true.* Men do but *seem* to have what they do not *use,* and shows of religion will be lost and forfeited. They *went out from us, because they were not of us,* 1 John ii. 19. Let us see to it that we have grace in sincerity, the *root of the matter* found in us; that is a good part which shall never be taken away from those that have it.

III. Great encouragement given to those that prove themselves faithful *hearers of the word,* by being *doers of the work,* in a particular instance of Christ's respect to his disciples, in preferring them even before his nearest relations (*v.* 19—21), which passage of story we had twice before. Observe, 1. What crowding there was after Christ. There was no coming near for the throng of people that attended him, who, though they were crowded ever so much, would not be crowded out from his congregation. 2. Some of his nearest kindred were least solicitous to hear him preach. Instead of getting *within,* as they might easily have done if they had come in time, desiring to *hear him,* they stood *without,* desiring to *see him;* and, probably, out of a foolish fear, lest he should spend himself with too much speaking, designing nothing but to interrupt him, and oblige him to break off. 3. Jesus Christ would rather be busy at his work than conversing with his friends. He would not leave his preaching, to speak with his *mother* and his *brethren,* for it was his *meat and drink* to be so employed. 4. Christ is pleased to own those as his nearest and dearest relations that *hear the word of God and do it;* they are to him more than *his mother* and *brethren.*

22 Now it came to pass on a certain day, that he went into a ship with his disciples: and he said unto them,

Let us go over unto the other side of
the lake. And they launched forth.
23 But as they sailed he fell asleep:
and there came down a storm of
wind on the lake; and they were filled
with water, and were in jeopardy.
24 And they came to him, and awoke
him, saying, Master, master, we perish. Then he arose, and rebuked
the wind and the raging of the water:
and they ceased, and there was a calm.
25 And he said unto them, Where is
your faith? And they being afraid
wondered, saying one to another,
What manner of man is this! for he
commandeth even the winds and
water, and they obey him. 26 And
they arrived at the country of the
Gadarenes, which is over against Galilee. 27 And when he went forth
to land, there met him out of the city
a certain man, which had devils long
time, and wore no clothes, neither
abode in *any* house, but in the tombs.
28 When he saw Jesus, he cried out,
and fell down before him, and with a
loud voice said, What have I to do
with thee, Jesus, *thou* Son of God
most high? I beseech thee, torment
me not. 29 (For he had commanded
the unclean spirit to come out of the
man. For oftentimes it had caught
him: and he was kept bound with
chains and in fetters; and he brake
the bands, and was driven of the devil
into the wilderness.) 30 And Jesus
asked him, saying, What is thy name?
And he said, Legion: because many
devils were entered into him. 31
And they besought him that he would
not command them to go out into the
deep. 32 And there was there a
herd of many swine feeding on the
mountain: and they besought him
that he would suffer them to enter
into them. And he suffered them.
33 Then went the devils out of the
man, and entered into the swine: and
the herd ran violently down a steep
place into the lake, and were choked.
34 When they that fed *them* saw
what was done, they fled, and went
and told *it* in the city and in the
country. 35 Then they went out to
see what was done; and came to Jesus,
and found the man, out of whom the
devils were departed, sitting at the
feet of Jesus, clothed, and in his right
mind: and they were afraid. 36 They
also which saw *it* told them by what
means he that was possessed of the
devils was healed. 37 Then the whole
multitude of the country of the Gadarenes round about besought him to
depart from them; for they were
taken with great fear: and he went
up into the ship, and returned back
again. 38 Now the man out of whom
the devils were departed besought him
that he might be with him: but Jesus
sent him away, saying, 39 Return to
thine own house, and show how great
things God hath done unto thee.
And he went his way, and published
throughout the whole city how great
things Jesus had done unto him.

We have here two illustrious proofs of the power of our Lord Jesus which we had before—his power over the *winds*, and his power over the *devils*. See Mark iv. v.

I. His power over the winds, those *powers of the air* that are so much a terror to men, especially upon sea, and occasion the death of such multitudes. Observe,

1. Christ ordered his disciples to put to sea, that he might show his glory upon the water, in stilling the waves, and might do an act of kindness to a poor possessed man on the other side the water: *He went into a ship with his disciples, v.* 22. They that observe Christ's orders may assure themselves of his presence. If Christ sends his disciples, he goes *with them.* And those may safely and boldly venture any where that have Christ accompanying them. *He said, Let us go over unto the other side;* for he had a piece of good work to do there. He might have gone by land, a little way about; but he chose to go by *water,* that he might show his *wonders in the deep.*

2. Those that put to sea in a calm, yea, and at Christ's word, must yet *prepare for a storm,* and for the utmost peril in that storm; There *came down a storm of wind on the lake* (*v.* 23), as if it were there, and no where else; and presently their ship was so tossed that it was filled with water, and they were in jeopardy of their lives. Perhaps the devil, who is the *prince of the power of the air,* and who *raiseth winds* by the permission of God, had some suspicion, from some words which Christ might let fall, that he was coming over the lake now on purpose to cast that legion of devils out of the poor man on the other side, and therefore poured this storm

upon the ship he was in, designing, if possible, to have sunk him and prevented that victory.

3. Christ was *asleep* in the storm, *v.* 23. Some bodily refreshment he must have, and he chose to take it when it would be least a hindrance to him in his work. The disciples of Christ may really have his gracious presence with them at sea, and in a storm, and yet he may seem as if he were *asleep;* he may not immediately appear for their relief, no, not when things seem to be brought even to the last extremity. Thus he will try their faith and patience, and quicken them by prayer to awake, and make their deliverance the more welcome when it comes at last.

4. A complaint to Christ of our danger, and the distress his church is in, is enough to engage him to awake, and appear for us, *v.* 24. They cried, *Master, master, we perish!* The way to have our fears silenced is to bring them to Christ, and lay them before him. Those that in sincerity call Christ *Master,* and with faith and fervency call upon him as *their Master,* may be sure that he will not let them *perish.* There is no relief for poor souls that are under a sense of guilt, and a fear of wrath, like this, to go to Christ, and call him *Master,* and say, "I am *undone,* if thou do not *help me.*"

5. Christ's business is to *lay storms,* as it is Satan's business to *raise* them. He can do it; he has done it; he delights to do it: for he came to *proclaim peace on earth.* He *rebuked the wind and the raging of the water,* and immediately *they ceased* (*v.* 24); not, as at other times, by degrees, but all of a sudden, *there was a great calm.* Thus Christ showed that, though the devil pretends to be the prince of the power of the air, yet even there he has him in a chain.

6. When our dangers are over, it becomes us to take to ourselves the shame of our own fears and to give to Christ the glory of his power. When Christ had turned the *storm* into a *calm, then were they glad because they were quiet,* Ps. cvii. 30. And then, (1.) Christ gives them a rebuke for their inordinate fear: *Where is your faith? v.* 25. Note, Many that have *true faith* have it to seek when they have occasion to use it. They tremble, and are discouraged, if second causes frown upon them. A little thing disheartens them; and *where is their faith* then? (2.) They give him the glory of his power: *They, being afraid, wondered.* Those that had feared the storm, now that the danger was over with good reason feared him that had stilled it, and *said one to another, What manner of man is this!* They might as well have said, *Who is a God like unto thee?* For it is God's prerogative to *still the noise of the seas, the noise of their waves,* Ps. lxv. 7.

II. His power over *the devil,* the *prince of the power of the air.* In the next passage of story he comes into a closer grapple with him than he did when he commanded *the winds.* Presently after the winds were stilled they were brought to their desired haven, and *arrived at the country of the Gadarenes,* and there went ashore (*v.* 26, 27); and he soon met with that which was his business over, and which he thought it worth his while to go through a storm to accomplish.

We may learn a great deal out of this story concerning this world of infernal, malignant spirits, which, though not working now ordinarily in the same way as here, yet we are all concerned at all times to stand upon our guard against.

1. These *malignant* spirits are very *numerous.* They that had taken possession of this one man called themselves *Legion* (*v.* 30), because *many devils were entered into him:* he had *had devils a long time, v.* 27. But perhaps those that had been long in possession of him, upon some foresight of our Saviour's coming to make an attack upon them, and finding they could not prevent it by the storm they had raised, sent for recruits, intending this to be *a decisive* battle, and hoping now to be too hard for him that had cast out so many unclean spirits, and to give him a defeat. They either were, or at least would be thought to be, a *legion,* formidable as an *army with banners;* and now, at least, to be, what the *twentieth legion* of the Roman army, which was long quartered at Chester, was styled, *legio victrix—a victorious legion.*

2. They have an *inveterate enmity* to man, and all his conveniences and comforts. This man in whom the devils had got possession, and kept it long, being under their influence, *wore no clothes, neither abode in any house* (*v.* 27), though *clothing* and a *habitation* are two of the necessary supports of this life. Nay, and because man has a natural dread of the habitations of the dead, they forced this man to *abide in the tombs,* to make him so much the more a terror to himself and to all about him, so that his soul had as much cause as ever any man's had to be weary of his life, and to *choose strangling and death rather.*

3. They are very *strong, fierce,* and unruly, and hate and scorn to be restrained: *He was kept bound with chains and in fetters,* that he might not be mischievous either to others or to himself, but he *broke the bands, v.* 29 Note, Those that are *ungovernable* by any other thereby show that they are under Satan's government; and this is the language of those that are so, even concerning God and Christ, their best friends, that would not either bind them *from* or bind them *to* any thing but for their own good: *Let us break their bands in sunder. He was driven of the devil.* Those that are under Christ's government are *sweetly led* with the cords of a man and the bands of love; those that are under the devil's government are *furiously driven.*

4. They are much enraged against our Lord Jesus, and have a great dread and horror of him: *When the man* whom they had possession of, and who spoke as they would

have him, *saw Jesus,* he *roared out* as one in an agony, and *fell down before him,* to deprecate his wrath, and owned him to be *the Son of God most high,* that was infinitely above him and too hard for him; but protested against having any league or confederacy with him (which might sufficiently have silenced the blasphemous cavils of the scribes and Pharisees): *What have I to do with thee?* The devils have neither inclination to do service to Christ nor expectation to receive benefit by him: *What have we to do with thee?* But they dreaded his power and wrath: *I beseech thee, torment me not.* They do not say, *I beseech thee, save me,* but only, *Torment me not.* See whose language *they* speak that have only a dread of hell as a place of torment, but no desire of heaven as a place of holiness and love.

5. They are perfectly *at the command,* and under *the power,* of our Lord Jesus; and they knew it, for they *besought him that he would not command them to go* εἰς τὸν ἄβυσσον —*into the deep,* the place of their torment, which they acknowledge he could easily and justly do. O what a comfort is this to the Lord's people, that all the powers of darkness are under the check and control of the Lord Jesus! He has them all in a chain. He can send them to *their own place,* when he pleaseth.

6. They delight in *doing mischief.* When they found there was no remedy, but they must quit their hold of this poor man, they begged they might have leave to take possession of a *herd of swine, v.* 32. When the devil at first brought man into a miserable state he brought a curse likewise upon the whole creation, and that became subject to enmity. And here, as an instance of that extensive enmity of his, when he could not destroy the man, he would destroy the swine. If he could not hurt them in their bodies, he would hurt them in their goods, which sometimes prove a great temptation to men to draw them from Christ, as here. Christ *suffered them to enter into the swine,* to convince the country what mischief the devil could do in it, if he should suffer him. No sooner had the devils leave than they entered into the *swine;* and no sooner had they entered into them than the herd ran violently *down a steep place into the lake,* and were *drowned* For it is a miracle of mercy if those whom Satan possesses are not brought to destruction and perdition. This, and other instances, show that that roaring lion and red dragon seeks *what* and whom he may devour.

7. When the devil's power is broken in any soul that soul recovers itself, and returns into a right frame, which supposes that those whom Satan gets possession of are put out of the possession of themselves: *The man out of whom the devils were departed sat at the feet of Jesus, v.* 35. While he was under the devil's power he was ready to *fly in the face* of Jesus; but now he *sits at his feet,* which is a sign that he is come to his *right mind.* If God has possession of us, he preserves to us the government and enjoyment of ourselves; but, if Satan has possession of us, he robs us of both. Let his power therefore in our souls be overturned, and let *him* come whose right our hearts are, and let us give them to him; for we are never more our own than when we are his.

Let us now see what was the effect of this miracle of casting the legion of devils out of this man.

(1.) What effect it had upon the people of that country who had lost their swine by it: *The swineherds went and told it* both *in city and country* (*v.* 34), perhaps with a design to incense people against Christ. They told *by what means he that was possessed of the devils was healed* (*v.* 36), that it was by sending the devils into the swine, which was capable of an invidious representation, as if Christ could not have delivered the man out of their hands, but by delivering the swine into them. *The people came out, to see what was done,* and to enquire into it; and *they were afraid* (*v.* 35); they were *taken with great fear* (*v.* 37); they were surprised and amazed at it, and knew not what to say to it. They thought more of the destruction of the swine than of the deliverance of their poor afflicted neighbour, and of the country from the terror of his frenzy, which was become a public nuisance; and therefore *the whole multitude besought Christ to depart from them,* for fear he should bring some other judgment upon them; whereas indeed none need to be afraid of Christ that are willing to forsake their sins and give up themselves to him. But Christ took them at their word: *He went up into the ship, and returned back again.* Those lose their Saviour, and their hopes in him, that love their swine better.

(2.) What effect it had upon the poor man who had recovered himself by it. He *desired* Christ's company as much as others *dreaded* it: he besought Christ that *he might be with him,* as others were *that had been healed by him of evil spirits and infirmities* (*v.* 2), that Christ might be to him a protector and teacher, and that he might be to Christ for a name and a praise. He was loth to stay among those rude and brutish Gadarenes that desired Christ to depart from them. *O gather not my soul with these sinners!* But Christ would not take him along with him, but sent him home, to publish among those that knew him the great things God had done for him, that so he might be a blessing to his country, as he had been a burden to it. We must sometimes deny ourselves the satisfaction even of spiritual benefits and comforts, to gain an opportunity of being serviceable to the souls of others. Perhaps Christ knew that, when the resentment of the loss of their swine was a little over, they would be better disposed to consider the miracle, and therefore left the man among them to be a standing monument, and a monitor to them of it

40 And it came to pass, that, when
Jesus was returned, the people *gladly*
received him: for they were all waiting for him. 41 And, behold, there
came a man named Jairus, and he
was a ruler of the synagogue: and he
fell down at Jesus' feet, and besought
him that he would come into his
house: 42 For he had one only
daughter, about twelve years of age,
and she lay a dying. But as he went
the people thronged him. 43 And a
woman having an issue of blood twelve
years, which had spent all her living
upon physicians, neither could be
healed of any, 44 Came behind *him*,
and touched the border of his garment: and immediately her issue of
blood stanched. 45 And Jesus said,
Who touched me? When all denied,
Peter and they that were with him
said, Master, the multitude throng
thee and press *thee*, and sayest thou,
Who touched me? 46 And Jesus
said, Somebody hath touched me:
for I perceive that virtue is gone out
of me. 47 And when the woman
saw that she was not hid, she came
trembling, and falling down before
him, she declared unto him before all
the people for what cause she had
touched him, and how she was healed
immediately. 48 And he said unto
her, Daughter, be of good comfort:
thy faith hath made thee whole; go
in peace. 49 While he yet spake,
there cometh one from the ruler of
the synagogue's *house*, saying to him,
Thy daughter is dead; trouble not
the Master. 50 But when Jesus
heard *it*, he answered him, saying,
Fear not: believe only, and she shall
be made whole. 51 And when he
came into the house, he suffered no
man to go in, save Peter, and James,
and John, and the father and the mother of the maiden. 52 And all wept,
and bewailed her: but he said, Weep
not; she is not dead, but sleepeth.
53 And they laughed him to scorn,
knowing that she was dead. 54 And
he put them all out, and took her by
the hand, and called, saying, Maid,
arise. 55 And her spirit came again,
and she arose straightway: and he
commanded to give her meat. 56
And her parents were astonished:
but he charged them that they should
tell no man what was done.

Christ was driven away by the *Gadarenes;* they were weary of him, and willing to be rid of him. But when he had crossed the water, and returned to the *Galileans,* they *gladly received him, wished* and *waited* for his return, and *welcomed* him with all their hearts when he did return, *v.* 40. If some *will not* accept the favours Christ offers them, others *will.* If the Gadarenes be not gathered, yet there are many among whom *Christ shall be glorious.* When Christ had done his work on the other side of the water he returned, and found work to do in the place whence he came, fresh work. They that will lay out themselves to do good shall never want occasion for it. The needy you have always with you.

We have here two miracles interwoven, as they were in Matthew and Mark—the raising of Jairus's daughter to life, and the cure of the woman that had an issue of blood, as he was going in a crowd to Jairus's house. We have here,

I. A *public address* made to Christ by *a ruler of the synagogue,* whose name was *Jairus,* on the behalf of a little daughter of his, that was very ill, and, in the apprehension of all about her, *lay a dying.* This address was very humble and reverent. Jairus, though a *ruler, fell down at Jesus's feet,* as owning him to be a ruler *above* him. It was very importunate. He *besought him* that he would *come into his house;* not having the *faith,* at least not having the *thought,* of the centurion, who desired Christ only to *speak the* healing *word* at a distance. But Christ complied with his request; *he went along* with him. Strong faith shall be applauded, and yet weak faith shall not be rejected. In the houses where sickness and death are, it is very desirable to have the presence of Christ. When Christ was going, *the people thronged him,* some out of curiosity to see him, others out of an affection to him. Let us not complain of a crowd, and a throng, and a hurry, as long as we are in the way of our duty, and *doing good;* but otherwise it is what every wise man will keep himself out of as much as he can.

II. Here is a *secret application* made to Christ by a woman ill of a *bloody issue,* which had been the consumption of her body and the consumption of her purse too; for *she had spent all her living upon physicians,* and was never the better, *v.* 43. The nature of her disease was such that she did not care to make a public complaint of it (it was agreeable to the modesty of her sex to be very shy of speaking of it), and therefore she took this opportunity of coming to Christ *in a crowd;* and the more people were present the more likely she thought it was that she should be *concealed.* Her *faith* was very *strong;* for she doubted not but that by the *touch* of the *hem of his garment* she should derive from him healing virtue sufficient for her relief, looking upon him to be such a full fountain of mercies that she should *steal* a cure and he not *miss it.* Thus many a poor soul is *healed,* and *helped,* and *saved,* by Christ, that is *lost in a crowd,* and that nobody takes notice of. The woman found an immediate change for the better in herself, and that her disease was cured, *v.* 44. As believers have comfortable communion with Christ, so they have comfortable communications from him *incognito—secretly, meat to eat* that the *world knows not* of, and *joy* that a *stranger does not intermeddle with.*

III. Here is a *discovery* of this secret cure, to the glory both of the physician and the patient.

1. Christ takes notice that there is a cure wrought: *Virtue is gone out of me, v.* 46. Those that have been healed by virtue derived from Christ must *own* it, for he *knows it.* He speaks of it here, not in a way of *complaint,* as if he were hereby either *weakened* or *wronged,* but in a way of *complacency.* It was his delight that *virtue* was gone out of him to do any good, and he did not grudge it to the meanest; they were as welcome to it as to the light and heat of the sun. Nor had he the less virtue *in him* for the going out of virtue *from him,* for he is an *overflowing* fountain.

2. The poor patient owns her case, and the benefit she had received: *When she saw that she was not hid, she came, and fell down before him, v.* 47. Note, The consideration of this, that we cannot be *hid from Christ,* should engage us to *pour* out *our hearts before* him, and to show before him all our sin and all our trouble. *She came trembling,* and yet *her faith saved her, v.* 48. Note, There may be *trembling* where yet there is saving faith. She *declared before all the people for what cause she had touched him,* because she believed that a touch would cure her, and it did so. Christ's patients should communicate their experiences to one another.

3. The great physician confirms her cure, and sends her away with the comfort of it: *Be of good comfort; thy faith hath made thee whole, v.* 48. Jacob got the blessing from Isaac clandestinely, and by a wile; but, when the fraud was discovered, Isaac ratified it designedly. It was obtained *surreptitiously* and *under-hand,* but it was secured and seconded *above-board.* So was the cure here. He is *blessed,* and he *shall be blessed;* so here, She *is* healed, and she *shall be* healed.

IV. Here is an *encouragement* to Jairus not to distrust the power of Christ, *though his daughter was now dead,* and they that brought him the tidings advised him not to give *the Master any further trouble* about her: *Fear not,* saith Christ, *only believe.* Note, Our *faith in Christ* should be bold and daring, as well as our *zeal for him.* They that are willing to do any thing for him may depend upon his doing great things for them, above what they are able to ask or think. When the patient is dead there is no room for prayer, or the use of means; but here, though the child is dead, yet *believe,* and all shall be well. *Post mortem medicus—to call in the physician after death,* is an absurdity; but not *post mortem Christus—to call in Christ after death.*

V. The *preparatives* for the raising of her to life again 1. The *choice* Christ made of witnesses that should see the miracle wrought. A *crowd* followed him, but perhaps they were rude and noisy; however, it was not fit to let such a multitude come into a gentleman's house, especially now that the family was all in sorrow; *therefore* he sent them back, and not because he was afraid to let the miracle pass their scrutiny; for he raised Lazarus and the widow's son *publicly.* He took none with him but Peter, and James, and John, that triumvirate of his disciples that he was most intimate with, designing these three, with the parents, to be the only spectators of the miracle, they being a competent number to attest the truth of it. 2. The *check* he gave to the mourners. *They all wept, and bewailed her;* for, it seems, she was a very agreeable hopeful child, and dear not only to the parents, but to all the neighbours. But Christ bids them *not weep; for she is not dead, but sleepeth.* He means, as to her peculiar case, that she was not dead for good and all, but that she should now shortly be raised to life, so that it would be to her friends as if she had been but a few hours asleep. But it is applicable to all that die in the Lord; therefore we should not sorrow for them as those that have *no hope,* because death is but a *sleep* to them, not only as it is a *rest* from all the *toils* of the *days of time,* but as there will be a *resurrection,* a waking and rising again to all the *glories* of the *days of eternity.* This was a comfortable word which Christ said to these mourners, yet they wickedly ridiculed it, and *laughed him to scorn* for it; here was *a pearl cast before swine.* They were ignorant of the scriptures of the Old Testament who bantered it as an absurd thing to call death a *sleep;* yet *this* good came out of *that* evil that hereby the truth of the miracle was evinced; for they *knew that she was dead,* they were certain of it, and therefore nothing less than a *divine power* could restore her to life. We find not any answer that he made them; but he soon *explained himself,* I hope to their conviction, so that they would never again laugh at any word of his. But he *put them all out, v.* 54. They were unworthy to be the witnesses of this work of wonder; they who in the midst of their mourning were so merrily disposed as to laugh at him for what he *said* would, it may be, have found something to laugh at in what he *did,* and therefore are justly shut out.

VI. Her return to life, after a *short* visit to the *congregation of the dead: He took her by the hand* (as we do by one that we would awake out of sleep, and help up), and he called, saying, *Maid, arise, v.* 55. Thus the *hand of Christ's grace* goes along with the *calls of his word,* to make them effectual. Here that is expressed which was only implied in the other evangelists, that *her spirit came again;* her soul returned again, to animate her body. This plainly proves that the soul exists and acts in a state of separation from the body, and therefore is immortal; that death does not extinguish this *candle of the Lord,* but takes it out of a *dark lantern.* It is not, as Grotius well observes, the *κρᾶσις* or *temperament* of the body, or any thing that dies with it; but it is *ἀνθυπόστατον τι*—*something that subsists by itself,* which, after death, is somewhere else than where the body is. Where the soul of this child was in this interval we are not told; it was in the hand of the *Father of spirits,* to whom all souls at death return. When *her spirit came again* she arose, and made it appear that she was alive by her motion, as she did also by her appetite; for Christ *commanded to give her meat.* As babes newly born, so those that are newly raised, desire spiritual food, that they may grow *thereby.* In the last verse, we need not wonder to find *her parents astonished;* but if that implies that *they only* were so, and not the other by-standers, who had laughed Christ to scorn, we may well wonder at their stupidity, which perhaps was the reason why Christ would not have it proclaimed, as well as to give an instance of his humility.

CHAP. IX.

In this chapter we have, I. The commission Christ gave to his twelve apostles to go out for some time to preach the gospel, and confirm it by miracles, ver. 1—6. II. Herod's terror at the growing greatness of our Lord Jesus, ver. 7—9. III. The apostles' return to Christ, his retirement with them into a place of solitude, the great resort of people to them notwithstanding, and his feeding five thousand men with five loaves and two fishes, ver. 10—17. IV. His discourse with his disciples concerning himself and his own sufferings for them, and theirs for him, ver. 18—27. V. Christ's transfiguration, ver. 28—36. VI. The cure of a lunatic child, ver. 37—42. VII. The repeated notice Christ gave his disciples of his approaching sufferings, ver. 43—45. VIII. His check to the ambition of his disciples (ver. 46—48), and to their monopolizing the power over devils to themselves, ver. 49, 50. IX. The rebuke he gave them for an over-due resentment of an affront given him by a village of the Samaritans, ver. 51—56. X. The answers he gave to several that were inclined to follow him, but not considerately, or not zealously and heartily, so inclined, ver. 57—62.

THEN he called his twelve disciples together, and gave them
power and authority over all devils,
and to cure diseases. 2 And he sent
them to preach the kingdom of God,
and to heal the sick. 3 And he said
unto them, Take nothing for *your*
journey, neither staves, nor scrip,
neither bread, neither money; neither
have two coats apiece. 4 And whatsoever house ye enter into, there abide,
and thence depart. 5 And whosoever will not receive you, when ye
go out of that city, shake off the very
dust from your feet for a testimony
against them. 6 And they departed,
and went through the towns, preaching the gospel, and healing every
where. 7 Now Herod the tetrarch
heard of all that was done by him:
and he was perplexed, because that it
was said of some, that John was risen
from the dead; 8 And of some, that
Elias had appeared; and of others,
that one of the old prophets was risen
again. 9 And Herod said, John have
I beheaded: but who is this, of whom
I hear such things? And he desired
to see him.

We have here, I. The method Christ took to spread his gospel, to diffuse and enforce the light of it. He had *himself* travelled about, preaching and healing; but he could be only in one place at a time, and therefore now he *sent* his twelve disciples abroad, who by this time were pretty well instructed in the nature of the present dispensation, and able to instruct others and *deliver to them* what they had *received from the Lord.* Let them disperse themselves, some one way and some another, to *preach the kingdom of God,* as it was now about to be set up by the Messiah, to make people acquainted with the spiritual nature and tendency of it, and to persuade them to come into the interests and measures of it. For the confirming of their doctrine, because it was new and surprising, and very different from what they had been taught by the scribes and Pharisees, and because so much depended upon men's receiving, or not receiving it, he empowered them to work miracles (*v.* 1, 2): He *gave them authority over all devils,* to dispossess them, and cast them out, though ever so numerous, so subtle, so fierce, so obstinate. Christ designed a total rout and ruin to the kingdom of darkness, and therefore gave them power over *all* devils. He authorized and appointed them likewise to *cure diseases,* and to *heal the sick,* which would make them welcome wherever they came, and not only convince people's judgments, but gain their affections. This was their commission. Now observe,

1. What Christ directed them to do, in prosecution of this commission at this time, when they were not to *go far* or be *out long.* (1.) They must not be solicitous to recommend themselves to people's esteem by their outward appearance. Now that they begin to set up for themselves, they must have no dress, nor study to make any other figure than what they made while they followed him: they must *go as they were,* and not change their clothes, or so much as put on a pair of new shoes. (2.) They must depend

upon Providence, and the kindness of their friends, to furnish them with what was convenient for them. They must not take with them *either bread or money*, and yet believe they should not want. Christ would not have his disciples *shy* of receiving the kindnesses of their friends, but rather to *expect* them. Yet St. Paul saw cause not to go by this rule, when he *laboured with his hands* rather than be burdensome. (3.) They must not change their lodgings, as suspecting that those who entertained them were *weary* of them; they have no reason to be so, for the ark is a guest that always pays well for its entertainment: "*Whatsoever house ye enter into there abide* (*v.* 4), that people may know where to find you, that your friends may know you are not backward to *serve* them, and your enemies may know you are not ashamed nor afraid to *face* them; *there abide* till you *depart* out of that city; stay with those you are used to." (4.) They must put on authority, and speak *warning* to those who *refused* them as well as comfort to those that *received* them, *v.* 5. "If there be any place that will not entertain you, if the magistrates deny you admission and threaten to treat you as vagrants, leave them, do not force yourselves upon them, nor run yourselves into danger among them, but at the same time bind them over to the judgment of God for it; *shake off the dust of your feet* for a *testimony against them.* This will, as it were, be produced in evidence against them, that the messengers of the gospel had been among them, to make them a fair offer of grace and peace, for this dust they left behind there; so that when they perish at last in their infidelity this will lay and leave their blood upon their own heads. *Shake off the dust of your feet*, as much as to say you abandon their city, and will have no more to do with them.

2. What they did, in prosecution of this commission (*v.* 6): *They departed* from their Master's presence; yet, having still his spiritual presence with them, his *eye* and his *arm* going along with them, and, thus borne up in their work, they *went through the towns*, some or other of them, all the towns within the circuit appointed them, *preaching the gospel, and healing every where.* Their work was the same with their Master's, doing good both to souls and bodies.

II. We have here Herod's perplexity and vexation at this. The communicating of Christ's power to those who were sent forth in his name, and acted by authority from him, was an *amazing* and *convincing* proof of his being the Messiah, above any thing else; that he could not only work miracles *himself*, but empower others to work miracles, too, this spread his fame more than any thing, and made the rays of this *Sun of righteousness* the stronger by the *reflection* of them even from *the earth*, from such mean illiterate men as the apostles were, who had nothing else to recommend them, or to raise any expectations from them, but that *they had been with Jesus*, Acts iv. 13. When the country sees such as these *healing the sick* in the name of Jesus it gives it an alarm. Now observe,

1. The *various speculations* it *raised* among the *people*, who, though they thought not *rightly*, yet could not but think *honourably*, of our Lord Jesus, and that he was an extraordinary person, one come from the other world; that either John Baptist, who was lately persecuted and slain for the cause of God, or *one of the old prophets*, that had been persecuted and slain long since in that cause, was *risen again*, to be recompensed for his sufferings by this honour put upon him; or that Elias, who was taken alive to heaven in a fiery chariot, *had appeared* as an express from heaven, *v.* 7, 8.

2. The *great perplexity* it *created* in the mind of Herod: *When he had heard of all that was done* by Christ, his guilty conscience flew in his face, and he was ready to conclude with them that *John was risen from the dead.* He thought he had got clear of John, and should never be troubled with him any more, but, it seems, he is mistaken; either John is come to life again or here is another in his spirit and power, for God will never *leave himself without witness.* "What shall I do now?" saith Herod. "John *have I beheaded, but who is this?* Is he carrying on John's work, or is he come to avenge John's death? John baptized, but he does not; *John did no miracle*, but he does, and therefore appears more formidable than John." Note, Those who oppose God will find themselves more and more *embarrassed.* However, he *desired to see him*, whether he resembled John or no; but he might soon have been put out of this pain if he would but have informed himself of that which thousands knew, that Jesus preached, and wrought miracles, a great while before John was beheaded, and therefore could not be John raised from the dead. He *desired to see him;* and why did he not go and see him? Probably, because he thought it *below him* either to go to him or to send for him; he had enough of John Baptist, and cared not for having to do with any more such reprovers of sin. He desired to see him, but we do not find that ever he did, till he saw him at his bar, and then *he and his men of war set him at nought*, Luke xxiii. 11. Had he prosecuted his convictions now, and gone to see him, who knows but a happy change might have been wrought in him? But, delaying it now, his heart was hardened, and when he did see him he was as much prejudiced against him as any other.

10 And the apostles, when they
were returned, told him all that they
had done. And he took them, and
went aside privately into a desert
place belonging to the city called
Bethsaida. 11 And the people, when

they knew *it*, followed him: and he
received them, and spake unto them
of the kingdom of God, and healed
them that had need of healing. 12
And when the day began to wear
away, then came the twelve, and said
unto him, Send the multitude away,
that they may go into the towns and
country round about, and lodge, and
get victuals: for we are here in a desert place. 13 But he said unto them,
Give ye them to eat. And they said,
We have no more but five loaves and
two fishes; except we should go and
buy meat for all this people. 14 For
they were about five thousand men.
And he said to his disciples, Make
them sit down by fifties in a company.
15 And they did so, and made them
all sit down. 16 Then he took the
five loaves and the two fishes, and
looking up to heaven, he blessed them,
and brake, and gave to the disciples
to set before the multitude. 17 And
they did eat, and were all filled: and
there was taken up of fragments that
remained to them twelve baskets.

We have here, I. The account which the twelve gave their Master of the success of their ministry. They were not long out; but, *when they returned, they told him all that they had done*, as became servants who were sent on an errand. They told him *what they had done*, that, if they had done any thing amiss, they might mend it next time.

II. Their *retirement*, for a little *breathing:* He *took them, and went aside privately into a desert place*, that they might have some relaxation from business and not be always upon the stretch. Note, He that hath appointed our man-servant and maid-servant to rest would have his servants to rest too. Those in the most public stations, and that are most publicly useful, must sometimes go aside privately, both for the repose of their bodies, to recruit them, and for the furnishing of their minds by meditation for further public work.

III. The *resort* of the people to him, and the kind *reception* he gave them. They *followed* him, though it was into a *desert place;* for that is no desert where Christ is. And, though they hereby disturbed the repose he designed here for himself and his disciples, yet he *welcomed* them, *v.* 11. Note, Pious zeal may excuse a little rudeness; it did with Christ, and should with us. Though they came unseasonably, yet Christ gave them what they came for. 1. He *spoke unto them of the kingdom of God*, the laws of that kingdom with which they must be bound, and the privileges of that kingdom with which they might be blessed. 2. He *healed them that had need of healing*, and, in a sense of their need, made their application to him. Though the disease was ever so inveterate, and incurable by the physicians, though the patients were ever so poor and mean, yet Christ *healed them.* There is healing in Christ for all that *need* it, whether for soul or body. Christ hath still a power over bodily diseases, and heals his people that *need healing.* Sometimes he sees that we need the *sickness* for the good of our souls, more than the *healing* for the ease of our bodies, and then we must be willing *for a season*, because *there is need*, to be in *heaviness;* but, when he sees that we *need healing*, we shall have it. Death is his servant, to heal the saints of *all diseases.* He heals spiritual maladies by his graces, by his comforts, and has for each what the case calls for; relief for every exigence.

IV. The plentiful provision Christ made for the multitude that attended him. With *five loaves* of bread, and *two fishes*, he fed *five thousand men.* This narrative we had twice before, and shall meet with it again; it is the only miracle of our Saviour's that is recorded by all the four evangelists. Let us only observe out of it, 1. Those who diligently attend upon Christ in the way of duty, and therein deny or expose themselves, or are made to forget themselves and their outward conveniences by their zeal for God's house, are taken under his particular care, and may depend upon *Jehovah-jireh—The Lord will provide.* He will not see those that fear him, and serve him faithfully, want any good thing. 2. Our Lord Jesus was of a free and generous spirit. His disciples said, *Send them away, that they may get victuals;* but Christ said, "No, *give ye them to eat;* let what we have go as far as it will reach, and they are welcome to it." Thus he has taught both ministers and Christians to *use hospitality without grudging*, 1. Pet. iv. 9. Those that have but a little, let them do what they can with that little, and that is the way to make it more. *There is that scatters, and yet increases.* 3. Jesus Christ has not only physic, but food, for all those that by faith apply themselves to him; he not only *heals them that need healing*, cures the diseases of the soul, but feeds them too that need feeding, supports the spiritual life, relieves the necessities of it, and satisfies the desires of it. Christ has provided not only to save the soul from perishing by its diseases, but to nourish the soul unto life eternal, and strengthen it for all spiritual exercises. 4. All the gifts of Christ are to be received by the church in a regular orderly manner: *Make them sit down by fifties in a company*, *v.* 14. Notice is here taken of the number of each company which Christ appointed for the better distribution of the meat and the easier computation of the number of the guests. 5. When we are receiving our creature-comforts, we must *look up to heaven.* Christ did so, to teach us to do so. We must acknowledge that we receive them from God, and that we are unworthy to receive them,—that we owe them all, and all the comfort we have in them, to the mediation of Christ, by whom the curse is removed, and the covenant of peace settled,—that we depend upon God's blessing upon them to make them serviceable to us, and desire that blessing. 6. The blessing of Christ will make a little go a great way. The *little that the righteous man has is better than the riches of many wicked, a dinner of herbs better than a stalled ox.* 7. Those whom Christ *feeds* he *fills;* to whom he gives, he gives enough; as there is in him enough for *all,* so there is enough for *each.* He replenishes every hungry soul, abundantly satisfies it with the *goodness of his house.* Here were *fragments taken up,* to assure us that in our Father's house there is *bread enough, and to spare.* We are not straitened, or stinted, in him.

18 And it came to pass, as he was
alone praying, his disciples were with
him: and he asked them, saying,
Whom say the people that I am? 19
They answering said, John the Baptist; but some *say,* Elias; and others
say, that one of the old prophets is
risen again. 20 He said unto them,
But whom say ye that I am? Peter
answering said, The Christ of God.
21 And he straitly charged them, and
commanded *them* to tell no man that
thing; 22 Saying, the Son of man
must suffer many things, and be rejected of the elders and chief priests
and scribes, and be slain, and be raised
the third day. 23 And he said to
them all, If any *man* will come after
me, let him deny himself, and take up
his cross daily, and follow me. 24
For whosoever will save his life shall
lose it: but whosoever will lose his
life for my sake, the same shall save
it. 25 For what is a man advantaged,
if he gain the whole world, and lose
himself, or be cast away? 26 For
whosoever shall be ashamed of me
and of my words, of him shall the Son
of man be ashamed, when he shall
come in his own glory, and *in his*
Father's, and of the holy angels. 27
But I tell you of a truth, there be
some standing here, which shall not
taste of death, till they see the kingdom of God.

In these verses, we have Christ discoursing with his disciples about the great things that *pertained to the kingdom of God;* and one circumstance of this discourse is taken notice of here which we had not in the other evangelists—that Christ was *alone praying,* and his *disciples with him,* when he entered into this discourse, *v.* 18. Observe, 1. Though Christ had much public work to do, yet he found some time to be *alone* in private, for converse with himself, with his Father, and with his disciples. 2. When Christ was alone he was *praying.* It is good for us to improve our solitude for devotion, that, *when we are alone,* we may *not be alone,* but may have *the Father with us.* 3. When Christ was alone, praying, his *disciples were with him,* to join with him in his prayer; so that this was a family-prayer. Housekeepers ought to pray with their households, parents with their children, masters with their servants, teachers and tutors with their scholars and pupils. 4. Christ *prayed* with them before he *examined* them, that they might be directed and encouraged to answer him, by his prayers for them. Those we give instructions to we should put up prayers for and with. He discourses with them,

I. Concerning himself; and enquires,

1. What *the people* said of him: *Who say the people that I am?* Christ knew better than they did, but would have his disciples made sensible, by the mistakes of others concerning him, how happy they were that were led into the knowledge of him and of the truth concerning him. We should take notice of the ignorance and errors of others, that we may be the more thankful to him who has *manifested himself to us, and not unto the world,* and may *pity* them, and do what we can to help them and to teach them better. They tell him what conjectures concerning him they had heard in their converse with the common people. Ministers would know better how to suit their instructions, reproofs, and counsels, to the case of ordinary people, if they did but converse more frequently and familiarly with them; they would then be the better able to say what is proper to rectify their notions, correct their irregularities, and remove their prejudices. The more conversant the physician is with his patient, the better he knows what to do for him. Some said that he was John Baptist, who was beheaded but the other day; others Elias, or *one of the old prophets;* any thing but what he was.

2. What *they* said of him. "Now see what an advantage you have by your discipleship; you know better." "So we do," saith Peter, "thanks be to our Master for it; we know that thou art *the Christ of God,* the *Anointed* of God, the Messiah promised." It is matter of unspeakable comfort to us that our Lord Jesus is *God's anointed,* for then he has unquestionable authority and ability for his undertaking; for his being *anointed* sig-

nifies his being both appointed to it and qualified for it. Now one would have expected that Christ should have charged his disciples, who were so fully apprized and assured of this truth, to publish it to every one they met with; but no, he *strictly charged them to tell no man that thing* as yet, because there is a time for all things. After his resurrection, which completed the proof of it, Peter made the temple ring of it, that *God had made this same Jesus both Lord and Christ* (Acts ii. 36); but as yet the evidence was not ready to be summed up, and therefore it must be concealed; while it was so, we may conclude that the belief of it was not necessary to salvation.

II. Concerning his own *sufferings* and *death*, of which he had yet said little. Now that his disciples were well established in the belief of his being the Christ, and able to bear it, he speaks of them expressly, and with great assurance, *v.* 22. It comes in as a reason why they must not yet preach that he was *the Christ*, because the wonders that would attend his death and resurrection would be the most convincing proof of his being *the Christ of God*. It was by his *exaltation* to the *right hand of the Father* that he was fully declared to be *the Christ*, and by the sending of the Spirit thereupon (Acts ii. 33); and therefore wait till that is done.

III. Concerning their sufferings for him. So far must they be from thinking how to *prevent* his sufferings that they must rather prepare for their own.

1. We must *accustom* ourselves to all instances of *self-denial* and *patience*, *v.* 23. This is the best preparative for martyrdom. We must live a life of self-denial, mortification, and contempt of the world; we must not indulge our ease and appetite, for then it will be hard to bear toil, and weariness, and want, for Christ. We are *daily* subject to affliction, and we must *accommodate* ourselves to it, and *acquiesce* in the will of God in it, and must learn to endure hardship. We frequently meet with crosses in the way of duty; and, though we must not pull them upon our own heads, yet, when they are laid for us, we must *take them up,* carry them after Christ, and make the best of them.

2. We must *prefer the salvation and happiness of our souls* before any *secular concern* whatsoever. Reckon upon it, (1.) That he who to preserve his liberty or estate, his power or preferment, nay, or to save his life, denies Christ and his truths, wilfully wrongs his conscience, and sins against God, will be, not only not a *saver*, but an unspeakable *loser*, in the issue, when *profit* and *loss* come to be balanced: *He that will save his life upon these terms will lose it,* will lose that which is of infinitely more value, his precious soul. (2.) We must firmly believe also that, if we lose our life for cleaving to Christ and our religion, we shall *save* it to our unspeakable advantage; for we shall be abundantly recompensed in the resurrection of the just, when we shall have it again a new and an eternal life. (3.) That the gain of all the world, if we should forsake Christ, and fall in with the interests of the world, would be so far from countervailing the eternal loss and ruin of the soul that it would bear no manner of proportion to it, *v.* 25. If we could be supposed to gain all the wealth, honour, and pleasure, in the world, by denying Christ, yet when, by *so doing,* we *lose ourselves* to all eternity, and are *cast away* at last, what good will our worldly gain do us? Observe, In Matthew and Mark the dreadful issue is a man's *losing his own soul,* here it is *losing himself,* which plainly intimates that *our souls* are *ourselves. Animus cujusque is est quisque—The soul is the man;* and it is well or ill with us according as it is well or ill with our souls. If they perish for ever, under the weight of their own guilt and corruption, it is certain that *we* are undone. The body cannot be happy if the soul be miserable in the other world; but the soul may be happy though the body be greatly afflicted and oppressed in this world. If a man be himself *cast away,* ἤ ζημιωθεὶς*—if he be damaged,*—or if he be punished, *si mulctetur—if he have a mulct put upon his soul* by the righteous sentence of Christ, whose cause and interest he has treacherously deserted,—if it be adjudged a forfeiture of all his blessedness, and the forfeiture be taken, where is his gain? What is his hope?

3. We must therefore *never be ashamed* of Christ and his gospel, nor of any disgrace or reproach that we may undergo for our faithful adherence to him and it, *v.* 26. *For whosoever shall be ashamed of me and of my words, of him shall the Son of man be ashamed,* and justly. When the service and honour of Christ called for his testimony and agency, he denied them, because the interest *of Christ* was a *despised* interest, and *every where spoken against;* and therefore he can expect no other than that in the great day, when his case calls for Christ's appearance on his behalf, Christ will be ashamed to own such a cowardly, worldly, sneaking spirit, and will say, "He is none of mine; he belongs not to me." As Christ had a state of *humiliation* and of *exaltation,* so likewise has his cause. They, and they only, that are willing to suffer with it when it suffers, shall reign with it when it reigns; but those that cannot find in their hearts to share with it in its *disgrace,* and to say, *If this be to be vile, I will be yet more vile,* shall certainly have no share with it in its *triumphs.* Observe here, How Christ, to support himself and his followers under present disgraces, speaks *magnificently* of the lustre of his second coming, in prospect of which he *endured the cross, despising the shame.* (1.) He shall come *in his own glory.* This was not mentioned in Matthew and Mark. He shall come in the glory of the Mediator, *all that glory* which the Father

restored to him, which he had with God before the worlds were, which he had *deposited* and *put in pledge,* as it were, for the accomplishing of his undertaking, and demanded again when he had gone through it. *Now, O Father, glorify thou me,* John xvii. 4, 5. He shall come in *all that glory* which the Father *conferred upon him* when *he set him at his own right hand,* and *gave him to be head over all things to the church;* in all the glory that is due to him as the assertor of the glory of God, and the author of the glory of all the saints. This is *his own glory.* (2.) He shall come *in his Father's glory.* The Father will judge the world by him, having committed all judgment to him; and therefore will publicly own him in the judgment as the *brightness of his glory* and the *express image* of his person. (3.) He shall come in *the glory of the holy angels.* They shall all *attend* him, and *minister* to him, and add every thing they can to the lustre of his appearance. What a figure will the blessed Jesus make in that day! Did we believe it, we should never be ashamed of him or his words now.

Lastly, To encourage them in suffering for him, he assures them that *the kingdom of God* would now *shortly be set up,* notwithstanding the great opposition that was made to it, *v.* 27. "Though the second coming of the Son of man is at a great distance, the kingdom of God shall come in its power in the present age, while some here present are alive." They *saw the kingdom of God* when the Spirit was poured out, when the gospel was preached to all the world and nations were brought to Christ by it; they saw the kingdom of God triumph over the Gentile nations in their *conversion,* and over the Jewish nation in its *destruction.*

28 And it came to pass about an
eight days after these sayings, he took
Peter and John and James, and went
up into a mountain to pray. 29 And
as he prayed, the fashion of his countenance was altered, and his raiment
was white *and* glistering. 30 And,
behold, there talked with him two
men, which were Moses and Elias:
31 Who appeared in glory, and spake
of his decease which he should accomplish at Jerusalem. 32 But Peter
and they that were with him were
heavy with sleep: and when they were
awake, they saw his glory, and the two
men that stood with him. 33 And it
came to pass, as they departed from
him, Peter said unto Jesus, Master, it
is good for us to be here: and let us
make three tabernacles; one for thee,
and one for Moses, and one for Elias:
not knowing what he said. 34 While
he thus spake, there came a cloud,
and overshadowed them: and they
feared as they entered into the cloud.
35 And there came a voice out of the
cloud, saying, This is my beloved
Son: hear him. 36 And when the
voice was past, Jesus was found alone.
And they kept *it* close, and told no
man in those days any of those things
which they had seen.

We have here the narrative of Christ's transfiguration, which was designed for a specimen of that glory of his in which he will come to judge the world, of which he had lately been speaking, and, consequently, an encouragement to his disciples to suffer for him, and never to be ashamed of him. We had this account before in Matthew and Mark, and it is well worthy to be repeated to us, and reconsidered by us, for the *confirmation of our faith* in the Lord Jesus, as *the brightness of his Father's glory* and the light of the world, for the *filling* of our minds with *high* and *honourable* thoughts of him, notwithstanding his being clothed with a body, and *giving* us *some idea* of the *glory* which he entered into at his *ascension,* and in which he now *appears* within the veil, and for the *raising* and *encouraging* of our *hopes* and *expectations* concerning the glory reserved for all believers in the future state.

I. Here is one circumstance of the narrative that seems to differ from the other two evangelists that related it. They said that it was *six days* after the foregoing sayings; Luke says that it was *about eight days after,* that is, it was that day sevennight, six whole days intervening, and it was the eighth day. Some think that it was *in the night* that Christ was transfigured, because the disciples were sleepy, as in his agony, and *in the night* his appearance in splendour would be the more illustrious; if in the night, the computation of the time would be the more doubtful and uncertain; probably, in the night, between the seventh and eighth day, and so about eight days.

II. Here are divers circumstances added and explained, which are very material.

1. We are *here* told that Christ had this honour put upon him when he was *praying:* He *went up into a mountain to pray,* as he frequently did (*v.* 28), and *as he prayed* he was *transfigured.* When Christ *humbled* himself to pray, he was thus *exalted.* He knew before that this was designed for him at this time, and therefore seeks it by prayer. Christ himself must *sue out* the favours that were purposed for him, and promised to him: *Ask of me, and I will give thee,* Ps. ii 8. And thus he intended to put an *honour* upon the duty of prayer, and to *recommend* it to us. It is a transfiguring, transforming duty; if our hearts be elevated and enlarged in it, so as in it to *behold the glory of the Lord,* we

shall be *changed into the same image from glory to glory*, 2 Cor. iii. 18. By prayer we fetch in the wisdom, grace, and joy, which *make the face to shine.*

2. Luke does not use the word *transfigured* —μεταμορφώθη (which Matthew and Mark used), perhaps because it had been used so much in the Pagan theology, but makes use of a phrase equivalent, τὸ εἶδος τοῦ προσώπȣ ἕτερον—*the fashion of his countenance was another thing from what it had been:* his face shone far beyond what Moses's did when he came down from the mount; and *his raiment* was *white and glistering:* it was ἐξαστράπτων —*bright like lightning* (a word used only here), so that he seemed to be arrayed all with light, to *cover himself with light as with a garment.*

3. It was said in Matthew and Mark that Moses and Elias *appeared to them;* here it is said that they *appeared in glory,* to teach us that saints departed are *in glory,* are in a *glorious* state; they shine in glory. He being in glory, they *appeared with him in glory,* as all the saints shall shortly do.

4. We are here told what was the subject of the discourse between Christ and the two great prophets of the Old Testament: *They spoke of his decease, which he should accomplish at Jerusalem.* Ἔλεγον τὴν ἔξοδον αὐτοῦ —*his exodus, his departure;* that is, *his death.* (1.) The death of Christ is here called his *exit,* his *going out,* his *leaving the world.* Moses and Elias spoke of it to him under that notion, to reconcile him to it, and to make the foresight of it the more easy to his human nature. The death of the saints is their *exodus,* their departure out of the Egypt of this world, their release out of a *house of bondage.* Some think that the ascension of Christ is included here in his departure; for the departure of Israel out of Egypt was a departure in *triumph,* so was *his* when he went from earth to heaven. (2.) This departure of his he *must accomplish;* for thus it was determined, the matter was immutably fixed in the counsel of God, and could not be altered. (3.) He must accomplish it at Jerusalem, though his residence was mostly in Galilee; for his most spiteful enemies were at Jerusalem, and there the sanhedrim sat, that took upon them to judge of prophets. (4.) Moses and Elias spoke of this, to intimate that the *sufferings* of Christ, and his *entrance into his glory,* were what Moses and *the prophets* had *spoken of;* see Luke xxiv. 26, 27; 1 Pet. i. 11. (5.) Our Lord Jesus, even in his transfiguration, was willing to enter into a discourse concerning his death and sufferings, to teach us that meditations on death, as it is our departure out of this world to another, are never unseasonable, but in a special manner seasonable when at any time we are *advanced,* lest we should be *lifted up above measure.* In our greatest glories on earth, let us remember that here *we have no continuing city.*

5. We are here told, which we were not before, that the disciples were *heavy with sleep, v.* 32. When the vision first began, Peter, and James, and John were drowsy, and inclined to sleep. Either it was late, or they were weary, or had been disturbed in their rest the night before; or perhaps a charming composing air, or some sweet and melodious sounds, which disposed them to soft and gentle slumbers, were a preface to the vision; or perhaps it was owing to a sinful carelessness: when Christ was at prayer with them, they did not regard his prayer as they should have done, and, to punish them for that, they were left to *sleep on now,* when he began to be *transfigured,* and so lost an opportunity of seeing how that work of wonder was wrought. These three were now asleep, when Christ was in *his glory,* as afterwards they were, when he was in *his agony;* see the *weakness* and *frailty* of human nature, even in the best, and what need they have of the grace of God. Nothing could be more affecting to these disciples, one would think, than the *glories* and the *agonies* of their Master, and both in the highest degree; and yet neither the one nor the other would serve to *keep them awake.* What need have we to pray to God for quickening grace, to make us not only *alive,* but *lively!* Yet that they might be competent witnesses of *this sign from heaven,* to those that demanded one, after awhile they *recovered themselves,* and became perfectly awake; and then they took an exact view of all those glories, so that they were able to give a particular account, as we find one of them does, of all that passed when they were with Christ *in the holy mount,* 2 Pet. i. 18.

6. It is here observed that it was when Moses and Elias were now about to *depart* that Peter said, *Lord, it is good to be here, let us make three tabernacles.* Thus we are often not sensible of the worth of our mercies till we are about to lose them; nor do we covet and court their continuance till they are upon the departure. Peter said this, *not knowing what he said.* Those know not what they say that talk of making tabernacles on earth for glorified saints in heaven, who have better mansions in the temple there, and long to return to them.

7. It is here added, concerning the *cloud* that *overshadowed them,* that they *feared as they entered into the cloud.* This cloud was a token of God's more peculiar presence. It was in a cloud that God of old took possession of the tabernacle and temple, and, when the cloud *covered the tabernacle, Moses was not able to enter* (Exod. xl. 34, 35), and, when it filled the temple, the *priests could not stand to minister by reason of it,* 2 Chron. v. 14. Such a cloud was this, and then no wonder that the disciples were *afraid to enter into it.* But never let any be afraid to enter into a cloud with Jesus Christ; for he will be sure to bring them safely through it.

8. The *voice* which came from heaven is

here, and in Mark, related not so fully as in Matthew: *This is my beloved Son, hear him:* though those words, *in whom I am well pleased,* which we have both in Matthew and Peter, are not expressed, they are implied in that, *This is my beloved Son;* for whom he *loves,* and in whom he is *well pleased,* come all to one; we are *accepted in the Beloved.*

Lastly, The apostles are here said to have kept this vision private. They *told no man in those days,* reserving the discovery of it for another opportunity, when the evidences of Christ's being the Son of God were completed in the pouring out of the Spirit, and that doctrine was to be published to all the world. As there is a time *to speak,* so there is a time to *keep silence.* Every thing is beautiful and useful in its season.

37 And it came to pass, that on
the next day, when they were come
down from the hill, much people met
him. 38 And, behold, a man of the
company cried out, saying, Master, I
beseech thee, look upon my son: for
he is mine only child. 39 And, lo,
a spirit taketh him, and he suddenly
crieth out; and it teareth him that
he foameth again, and bruising him
hardly departeth from him. 40 And
I besought thy disciples to cast him
out; and they could not. 41 And
Jesus answering said, O faithless and
perverse generation, how long shall I
be with you, and suffer you? Bring
thy son hither. 42 And as he was
yet a coming, the devil threw him
down, and tare *him.* And Jesus rebuked the unclean spirit, and healed
the child, and delivered him again to
his father.

This passage of story in Matthew and Mark follows immediately upon that of Christ's transfiguration, and his discourse with his disciples after it; but here it is said to be *on the next day, as they were coming down from the hill,* which confirms the conjecture that Christ was transfigured *in the night,* and, it should seem, though they did not *make tabernacles* as Peter proposed, yet they found some shelter to repose themselves in all night, for it was not till next day that they *came down from the hill,* and then he found things in some disorder among his disciples, though not so bad as Moses did when he came down from the mount. When wise and good men are in their beloved retirements, they would do well to consider whether they are not wanted in their *public stations.*

In this narrative here, observe, 1. How forward the people were to receive Christ at his return to them. Though he had been but a little while absent, *much people met him,* as, at other times, much people *followed* him; for so it was foretold concerning him, that *to him should the gathering of the people be.* 2. How importunate the father of the lunatic child was with Christ for help for him (*v.* 38): *I beseech thee, look upon my son;* this is his request, and it is a very modest one; one compassionate look from Christ is enough to set every thing to rights. Let us bring ourselves and our children to Christ, to be *looked upon.* His plea is, *He is my only child.* They that have many children may balance their affliction in one with their comfort in the rest; yet, if it be an only child that is a grief, the affliction in that may be balanced with the love of God in giving his only-begotten Son for us. 3. How *deplorable* the case of the *child* was, *v.* 39. He was under the power of an evil spirit, that *took him;* and diseases of that nature are more frightful than such as arise merely from natural causes: when the fit seized him, without any warning given, he suddenly *cried out,* and many a time his shrieks had pierced the heart of his tender father. This malicious spirit *tore him,* and *bruised* him, and *departed not from him* but with great difficulty, and a deadly gripe at parting. O the afflictions of the afflicted in this world! And what mischief doth Satan do where he gets possession! But happy they that have access to Christ! 4. How defective the disciples were in their faith. Though Christ had given them *power over unclean spirits,* yet they *could not* cast out this *evil spirit, v.* 40. Either they distrusted the power they were to fetch in strength from, or the commission given to them, or they did not exert themselves in prayer as they ought; for this Christ reproved them. O *faithless and perverse generation.* Dr. Clarke understands this as spoken to his disciples: "*Will ye be* yet so faithless and full of distrust that ye cannot execute the commission I have given you?" 5. How effectual the cure was, which Christ wrought upon this child, *v.* 42. Christ can do that for us which his disciples cannot: *Jesus rebuked the unclean spirit* then when he raged most. The devil *threw the child down, and tore him,* distorted him, as if he would have pulled him to pieces. But one word from Christ *healed the child,* and made good the damage the devil had done him. And it is here added that he *delivered him again to his father.* Note, When our children are recovered from sickness, we must receive them as delivered to us again, receive them as life from the dead, and as when we first received them. It is comfortable to receive them from the hand of Christ, to see him delivering them to us again: "Here, take this child, and be thankful; take it, and bring it up for me, for thou hast it again from me. Take it, and do not set thy heart too much upon it." With such cautions as these, parents should receive their children *from Christ's hands,* and then with comfort put them again *into his hands.*

43 And they were all amazed at the mighty power of God. But while they wondered every one at all things which Jesus did, he said unto his disciples,
44 Let these sayings sink down into your ears: for the Son of man shall be delivered into the hands of men.
45 But they understood not this saying, and it was hid from them, that they perceived it not: and they feared to ask him of that saying.
46 Then there arose a reasoning among them, which of them should be greatest.
47 And Jesus, perceiving the thought of their heart, took a child, and set him by him,
48 And said unto them, Whosoever shall receive this child in my name receiveth me: and whosoever shall receive me receiveth him that sent me: for he that is least among you all, the same shall be great.
49 And John answered and said, Master, we saw one casting out devils in thy name; and we forbad him, because he followeth not with us.
50 And Jesus said unto him, Forbid *him* not: for he that is not against us is for us.

We may observe here, I. The impression which Christ's miracles made upon all that beheld them (*v.* 43): *They were all amazed at the mighty power of God,* which they could not but see in all the miracles Christ wrought. Note, The works of God's almighty power are amazing, especially those that are wrought by the hand of the Lord Jesus; for he is *the power of God,* and his name is *Wonderful.* Their wonder was universal: they wondered *every one.* The causes of it were universal: they wondered at *all things which Jesus did;* all his actions had something uncommon and surprising in them.

II. The notice Christ gave to his disciples of his approaching sufferings: *The Son of man shall be delivered into the hands of men,* wicked men, men of the worst character; they shall be permitted to abuse him at their pleasure. That is here *implied* which is *expressed* by the other evangelists: *They shall kill him.* But that which is peculiar here is, 1. The connection of this with what goes next before, of the admiration with which the people were struck at beholding Christ's miracles (*v.* 43): *While they all wondered at all things which Jesus did, he said this to his disciples.* They had a fond conceit of his temporal kingdom, and that he should reign, and they with him, in secular pomp and power; and now they thought that this *mighty power* of his would easily effect the thing, and his interest gained by his miracles in the people would contribute to it; and therefore Christ, who knew what was in their hearts, takes this occasion to tell them again, what he had told them before, that he was so far from having men *delivered into his hands* that he must be *delivered into the hands of men,* so far from living in honour that he must die in disgrace; and all his miracles, and the interest he has by them gained in the hearts of the people, will not be able to prevent it. 2. The solemn preface with which it is introduced: "*Let these sayings sink down into your ears;* take special notice of what I say, and mix faith with it; let not the notions you have of the temporal kingdom of the Messiah stop your ears against it, nor make you unwilling to believe it. Admit what I say, and submit to it." *Let it sink down into your hearts;* so the Syriac and Arabic read it. The word of Christ does us no good, unless we let it sink down into our heads and hearts. 3. The unaccountable stupidity of the disciples, with reference to this prediction of Christ's sufferings. It was said in Mark, *They understood not that saying.* It was plain enough, but they *would not* understand it in the literal sense, because it agreed not with their notions; and they *could not* understand it in any other, *and were afraid to ask him* lest they should be undeceived and awaked out of their pleasing dream. But it is here added that *it was hidden from them, that they perceived it not,* through the weakness of faith and the power of prejudice. We cannot think that it was *in mercy* hidden from them, lest they should be swallowed up with overmuch sorrow at the prospect of it; but that it was a paradox, because they *made it so* to themselves.

III. The rebuke Christ gave to his disciples for their disputing among themselves which should be greatest, *v.* 46—48. This passage we had before, and, the more is the pity, we shall meet with the like again. Observe here,

1. Ambition of honour, and strife for superiority and precedency, are sins that most easily beset the disciples of our Lord Jesus, for which they deserve to be severely rebuked; they flow from corruptions which they are highly concerned to subdue and mortify, *v.* 46. They that expect to be *great* in this world commonly aim high, and nothing will serve them short of being *greatest;* this exposes them to a great deal of temptation and trouble, which they are safe from that are content to be *little,* to be *least,* to be *less than the least.*

2. Jesus Christ is perfectly acquainted with the thoughts and intents of our hearts: He *perceived their thoughts, v.* 47. Thoughts are *words* to him, and *whispers* are loud cries. It is a good reason why we should keep up a strict government of our thoughts because Christ takes a strict cognizance of them.

3. Christ will have his disciples to aim at that honour which is to be obtained by a quiet and condescending humility, and not at that which is to be obtained by a restless and aspiring ambition. Christ *took a child, and set him by him, v.* 47 (for he always expressed a tenderness and kindness for little children), and he proposed *this child* to them for an example. (1.) Let them be of the *temper* of this child, *humble* and *quiet*, and *easy* to itself; let them not affect worldly pomp, or grandeur, or high titles, but be as dead to them as this child; let them bear no more malice to their rivals and competitors than this child did. Let them be willing to be *the least*, if that would contribute any thing to their usefulness, to stoop to the meanest office whereby they might *do good*. (2.) Let them assure themselves that this was the way to preferment; for this would recommend them to the esteem of their brethren: they that loved Christ would *therefore receive* them *in his name*, because they did most resemble him, and they would likewise recommend themselves to his favour, for Christ would take the kindnesses done to them as done to himself: *Whosoever shall receive one such child*, a preacher of the gospel that is of such a disposition as this, he placeth his respect aright, and *receiveth me;* and *whosoever receiveth me*, in such a minister, *receiveth him that sent me;* and what greater honour can any man attain to in this world than to be received by men as a messenger of God and Christ, and to have God and Christ own themselves received and welcomed in him? This honour have all the humble disciples of Jesus Christ, and thus they shall be truly great that are least among them.

IV. The rebuke Christ gave to his disciples for discouraging one that honoured him and served him, but was not of their communion, not only not one of the twelve, nor one of the seventy, but not one of those that ever associated with them, or attended on them, but, upon occasional hearing of Christ, believed in him, and made use of his name with faith and prayer in a serious manner, for the casting out of devils. Now, 1. This man they *rebuked and restrained;* they would not let him pray and preach, though it was to the honour of Christ, though it did good to men and weakened Satan's kingdom, because he did not *follow Christ with them;* he separated from their church, was not ordained as they were, paid them no respect, nor gave them the right hand of fellowship. Now, if ever any society of Christians in this world had reason to silence those that were not of their communion, the twelve disciples at this time had; and yet, 2. Jesus Christ chid them for what they did, and warned them not to do the like again, nor any that profess to be successors of the apostles: "*Forbid him not* (*v.* 50), but rather encourage him, for he is carrying on the same design that you are, though, for reasons best known to himself, he does not follow *with you;* and he will meet you in *the same end*, though he does not accompany you in *the same way*. You *do well* to do as you do, but it does not therefore follow that he *does ill* to do as he does, and that you do well to put him under an interdict, for *he that is not against us is for us*, and therefore ought to be countenanced by us." We need not lose any of our friends, while we have so few, and so many enemies. Those may be found faithful followers of Christ, and, as such, may be accepted of him, though they do not follow *with us*. See Mark ix. 38, 39. O what a great deal of mischief to the church, even from those that boast of relation to Christ, and pretend to *envy for his sake*, would be prevented, if this passage of story were but duly considered!

51 And it came to pass, when the
time was come that he should be received up, he stedfastly set his face
to go to Jerusalem, 52 And sent
messengers before his face: and they
went, and entered into a village of the
Samaritans, to make ready for him.
53 And they did not receive him, because his face was as though he would
go to Jerusalem. 54 And when his
disciples James and John saw *this*,
they said, Lord, wilt thou that we
command fire to come down from
heaven, and consume them, even as
Elias did? 55 But he turned, and
rebuked them, and said, Ye know not
what manner of spirit ye are of. 56
For the Son of man is not come to
destroy men's lives, but to save *them*.
And they went to another village.

This passage of story we have not in any other of the evangelists, and it seems to come in here for the sake of its affinity with that next before, for in this also Christ rebuked his disciples, because they envied for his sake. There, under colour of zeal for Christ, they were for silencing and restraining separatists: here, under the same colour, they were for putting infidels to death; and, as for *that*, so for *this* also, Christ reprimanded them, for a spirit of bigotry and persecution is directly contrary to the spirit of Christ and Christianity. Observe here,

I. The *readiness* and *resolution* of our Lord Jesus, in prosecuting his great undertaking for our redemption and salvation. Of this we have an instance, *v.* 51: *When the time was come that he should be received up, he stedfastly set his face to go to Jerusalem.* Observe 1. There was a time fixed for the sufferings and death of our Lord Jesus, and he knew well enough when it was, and had a clear and certain foresight of it, and yet was so far from keeping out of the way that then he appeared most publicly of all, and was most busy, knowing that his time was short. 2. When he saw his death and sufferings approaching, he looked through them and beyond them, to the glory that should follow; he looked upon it as the time when he should be *received up into glory* (1 Tim. iii. 16), received up into the highest heavens, to be enthroned there. Moses and Elias spoke of his death as his departure out of this world, which made it not *formidable;* but he went further, and looked upon it as his translation to a better world, which made it very *desirable.* All good Christians may frame to themselves the same notion of death, and may call it their being *received up*, to be with Christ where he is; and, when the *time* of their being *received up* is at hand, let them lift up their heads, knowing that *their redemption draws nigh.* 3. On this prospect of the joy set before him, he *stedfastly set his face to go to Jerusalem*, the place where he was to suffer and die. He was fully *determined* to go, and would not be dissuaded; he went *directly* to Jerusalem, because there now his business lay, and he did not go about to other towns, or fetch a compass, which if he had done, as commonly he did, he might have avoided going through Samaria. He went cheerfully and courageously thither, though he knew the things that should befal him there. He *did not fail nor was discouraged*, but *set his face as a flint*, *knowing* that he should be not only *justified*, but glorified (Isa. l. 7), not only not *run down*, but *received up.* How should this shame us *for*, and shame *us out of*, our backwardness to do and suffer for Christ! We draw back, and turn our faces another way from his service who stedfastly set his face against all opposition, to go through with the work of our salvation.

II. The *rudeness* of the Samaritans in a *certain village* (not named, nor deserving to be so) who would not *receive him*, nor suffer him to bait in their town, though his way lay through it. Observe here, 1. How *civil* he was to them: *He sent messengers before his face*, some of his disciples, that went to take up lodgings, and to know whether he might have leave to accommodate himself and his company among them; for he would not come to give *offence*, or if they took any umbrage at the number of his followers. He sent some to *make ready* for him, not for state, but convenience, and that his coming might be no surprise. 2. How *uncivil* they were to him, *v.* 53. They did not *receive him*, would not suffer him to come into their village, but ordered their watch to keep him out. He would have *paid* for all he *bespoke*, and been a generous guest among them, would have done them good, and preached the gospel to them, as he had done some time ago to another city of the Samaritans, John iv. 41. He would have been, if they pleased, the greatest blessing that ever came to their village, and yet they forbid him entrance. Such treatment his gospel and ministers have often met with. Now the reason was *because his face was as though he would go to Jerusalem;* they observed, by his motions, that he was steering his course that way. The great controversy between the Jews and the Samaritans was about the place of worship—whether Jerusalem or mount Gerizim near Sychar; see John iv. 20. And so hot was the controversy between them that the *Jews would have no dealings with the Samaritans*, nor they with them, John iv. 9. Yet we may suppose that they did not deny other Jews lodgings among them, no, not when they went up to the feasts; for if that had been their constant practice Christ would not have attempted it, and it would have been a great way about for some of the Galileans to go to Jerusalem any other way than through Samaria. But they were particularly incensed against Christ, who was a celebrated teacher, for owning and adhering to the temple at Jerusalem, when the priests of that temple were such bitter enemies to him, which, they hoped, would have driven him to come and worship at *their* temple, and bring that into reputation; but when they saw that he would go forward to Jerusalem, notwithstanding this, they would not show him the common civility which probably they used formerly to show him in his journey thither.

III. The *resentment* which James and John expressed of this affront, *v.* 54. When these two heard this message brought, they were all in a flame presently, and nothing will serve them but Sodom's doom upon this village: "Lord," say they, "give us leave to command fire to come down from heaven, not to *frighten* them only, but to *consume* them."

1. Here indeed was something commendable, for they showed, (1.) A great confidence in the power they had received from Jesus Christ; though this had not been particularly mentioned in their commission, yet they could with a word's speaking fetch *fire from heaven.* Θέλεις εἴπωμεν—*Wilt thou that we speak the word*, and the thing will be done. (2.) A great zeal for the honour of their Master. They took it very ill that he who did good wherever he came and found a hearty welcome should be denied the liberty of the road by a parcel of paltry Samaritans; they could not think of it without indignation that their Master should be thus slighted. (3.) A submission, notwithstanding, to their Master's good will and pleasure. They will not offer to do such a thing, unless Christ give leave: *Wilt thou* that we do it? (4.) A regard to the examples of the prophets that were before them. It is doing *as Elias did?* they would not have thought of such a thing if Elijah had not done it upon the soldiers that came to take him, once and again, 2 Kings i. 10, 12. They thought that this *precedent* would be their *warrant;* so apt are we to misapply the examples of good men,

and to think to justify ourselves by them in the irregular liberties we give ourselves, when the case is not parallel.

2. But though there was something right in what they said, yet there was much more amiss, for (1.) This was not the first time, by a great many, that our Lord Jesus had been thus affronted, witness the Nazarenes thrusting him out of their city, and the Gadarenes desiring him to depart out of their coast; and yet he never called for any judgment upon them, but patiently put up with the injury. (2.) These were Samaritans, from whom better was not to be expected, and perhaps they had heard that Christ had forbidden his disciples to *enter into any of the cities of the Samaritans* (Matt. x. 5), and therefore it was not so bad in them as in others who knew more of Christ, and had received so many favours from him. (3.) Perhaps it was only some few of the town that knew any thing of the matter, or that sent that rude message to him, while, for aught they knew, there were many in the town who, if they had heard of Christ's being so near them, would have gone to meet him and welcomed him; and must the whole town be laid in ashes for the wickedness of a few? Will they have the righteous destroyed with the wicked? (4.) Their Master had never yet upon any occasion called for *fire from heaven,* nay, he had refused to give the Pharisees any *sign from heaven* when they demanded it (Matt. xvi. 1, 2); and why should they think to introduce it? James and John were the two disciples whom Christ had called *Boanerges —sons of thunder* (Mark iii. 17); and will not that serve them, but they must be *sons of lightning* too? (5.) The example of Elias did not reach the case. Elijah was sent to display the terrors of the law, and to give proof of that, and to witness as a bold reprover against the idolatries and wickednesses of the court of Ahab, and it was agreeable enough to him to have his commission thus proved; but it is a dispensation of grace that is now to be introduced, to which such a terrible display of divine justice will not be at all agreeable. Archbishop Tillotson suggests that their being now near Samaria, where Elijah called for fire from heaven, might help to put it in their heads; perhaps at the very place; but, though the *place* was the same, the *times* were altered.

IV. The *reproof* he gave to James and John for their fiery, furious zeal (*v.* 55): He *turned* with a just displeasure, and *rebuked them; for as many as he loves he rebukes and chastens,* particularly for what they do, that is irregular and unbecoming them, under colour of zeal for him.

1. He shows them in particular their mistake: *Ye know not what manner of spirit ye are of;* that is, (1.) "You *are not aware* what an *evil spirit* and disposition you are of; how much there is of pride, and passion, and personal revenge, covered under this pretence of zeal for your Master." Note, There may be much corruption lurking, nay, and stirring too, in the hearts of good people, and they themselves not be sensible of it. (2.) "You *do not consider* what a *good spirit,* directly contrary to this, you *should be of.* Surely you have yet to learn, though you have been so long learning, what the spirit of Christ and Christianity is. Have you not been taught to *love your enemies,* and to *bless them that curse you,* and to call for grace from heaven, not fire from heaven, upon them? You know not how contrary your disposition herein is to that which it was the design of the gospel you should be *delivered* into. You are not now under the dispensation of bondage, and terror, and death, but under the dispensation of love, and liberty, and grace, which was ushered in with a proclamation of *peace on earth* and *good will toward men,* to which you ought to accommodate yourselves, and not by such imprecations as these oppose yourselves."

2. He shows them the general design and tendency of his religion (*v.* 56): *The Son of man* is not himself come, and therefore does not send you abroad *to destroy men's lives, but to save them.* He designed to propagate his holy religion by love and sweetness, and every thing that is inviting and endearing, not by fire and sword, and blood and slaughter; by miracles of healing, not by plagues and miracles of destruction, as Israel was brought out of Egypt. Christ came to *slay* all *enmities,* not to foster them. Those are certainly destitute of the spirit of the gospel that are for anathematizing and rooting out by violence and persecution all that are not of their mind and way, that cannot in conscience say as they say, and do as they do. Christ came, not only to save men's *souls,* but to save their *lives* too—witness the many miracles he wrought for the healing of diseases that would otherwise have been *mortal,* by which, and a thousand other instances of beneficence, it appears that Christ would have his disciples do good to all, to the utmost of their power, but hurt to none, to draw men into his church with the *cords of a man and the bands of love,* but not think to drive men into it with a *rod of violence* or the *scourge of the tongue.*

V. His *retreat* from this village. Christ would not only not punish them for their rudeness, but would not insist upon his right of travelling the road (which was as free to him as to his neighbours), would not attempt to force his way, but quietly and peaceably *went to another village,* where they were not so stingy and bigoted, and there refreshed himself, and went on his way. Note, When a stream of opposition is strong, it is wisdom to get out of the way of it, rather than to contend with it. If some be very rude, instead of revenging it, we should try whether others will not be more civil.

57 And it came to pass, that, as

they went in the way, a certain *man*
said unto him, Lord, I will follow
thee whithersoever thou goest. 58
And Jesus said unto him, Foxes have
holes, and birds of the air *have* nests;
but the Son of man hath not where
to lay *his* head. 59 And he said
unto another, Follow me. But he
said, Lord, suffer me first to go and
bury my father. 60 Jesus said unto
him, Let the dead bury their dead:
but go thou and preach the kingdom
of God. 61 And another also said,
Lord, I will follow thee; but let me
first go bid them farewell, which are
at home at my house. 62 And Jesus
said unto him, No man, having put
his hand to the plough, and looking
back, is fit for the kingdom of God.

We have here an account of three several persons that offered themselves to follow Christ, and the answers that Christ gave to each of them. The two former we had an account of in Matt. xix. 21.

I. Here is one that is extremely forward to follow Christ immediately, but seems to have been too rash, hasty, and inconsiderate, and not to have set down and counted the cost.

1. He makes Christ a very large promise (*v.* 57): *As they went in the way,* going up to Jerusalem, where it was expected Christ would first appear in his glory, one said to him, *Lord, I will follow thee whithersoever thou goest.* This must be the resolution of all that will be found Christ's disciples indeed; they *follow the Lamb whithersoever he goes* (Rev. xiv. 4), though it be through fire and water, to prisons and deaths.

2. Christ gives him a necessary caution, not to promise himself great things in the world, in following him, but, on the contrary, to count upon poverty and meanness; for *the Son of man has not where to lay his head.*

We may look upon this, (1.) As *setting forth* the *very low condition* that our Lord Jesus was in, in this world. He not only wanted the delights and ornaments that great princes usually have, but even such accommodations for mere necessity as the *foxes* have, and the *birds of the air.* See what a *depth of poverty* our Lord Jesus submitted to for us, to increase the worth and merit of his satisfaction, and to purchase for us a larger *allowance of grace, that we through his poverty might be rich,* 2 Cor. viii. 9. He that made all did not make a dwelling-place for himself, not a house of his own to put his head in, but what he was beholden to others for. He here calls himself the *Son of man,* a Son of Adam, partaker of flesh and blood. He glories in his condescension towards us, not only to the meanness of our nature, but to the meanest condition in that nature, to testify his love to us, and to teach us a holy contempt of the world and of great things in it, and a continual regard to another world. Christ was thus poor, to sanctify and sweeten poverty to his people; the apostles had no certain dwelling-place (1 Cor. iv. 11), which they might the better bear when they knew their Master had not; see 2 Sam. xi. 11. We may well be content to fare as Christ did. (2.) As proposing this to the consideration of those who intend to be his disciples. If we mean to follow Christ, we must lay aside the thoughts of great things in the world, and not reckon upon making any thing *more than heaven* of our religion, as we must resolve not to take up with any thing *less.* Let us not go about to compound the profession of Christianity with secular advantages; Christ has *put them asunder,* let us not think of *joining them together;* on the contrary, we must expect to enter into the kingdom of heaven through many tribulations, must *deny ourselves,* and *take up our cross.* Christ tells this man what he must count upon if he followed him, to lie cold and uneasy, to fare hard, and live in contempt; if he could not submit to this, let him not pretend to follow Christ. This word sent him back, for aught that appears; but it will be no discouragement to any that know what there is in Christ and heaven to set in the scale against this.

II. Here is another, that seems *resolved* to follow Christ, but he *begs a day, v.* 59. To this man Christ first gave the call; he said to him, *Follow me.* He that proposed the thing of himself fled off when he heard of the difficulties that attended it; but this man to whom Christ gave a call, though he hesitated at first, yet, as it should seem, afterwards yielded; so true was that of Christ, *You have not chosen me, but I have chosen you,* John xv. 16. It is not of *him that willeth,* nor *of him that runneth* (as that forward spark in the foregoing verses), but of God that showeth mercy, that *gives* the call, and *makes* it *effectual,* as to this man here. Observe,

1. The excuse he made: "*Lord, suffer me first to go and bury my father.* I have an aged father at home, who cannot live long, and will need me while he does live; let me go and attend on him until he is dead, and I have performed my last office of love to him, and then I will do any thing." We may here see three temptations, by which we are in danger of being drawn and kept from following Christ, which therefore we should guard against:—(1.) We are tempted to *rest* in a *discipleship at large,* in which we may be *at a loose end,* and not to come *close,* and give up ourselves to be *strict* and *constant.* (2.) We are tempted to *defer* the doing of that which we know to be our duty, and to put it off to some other time. When we have got clear of such a care and difficulty, when we have despatched such a business, raised an estate to such a pitch, then we will begin to

think of being religious; and so we are cozened out of all our time, by being cozened out of the present time. (3.) We are tempted to think that our duty to our relations will excuse us from our duty to Christ. It is a plausible excuse indeed: "*Let me go and bury my father,*—let me take care of my family, and provide for my children, and then I will think of serving Christ;" whereas the *kingdom of God and the righteousness thereof* must be sought and minded *in the first place.*

2. Christ's answer to it (*v.* 60): "*Let the dead bury their dead.* Suppose (which is not likely) that there are none but the dead to bury their dead, or none but those who are themselves aged and dying, who are *as good as dead,* and fit for no other service, yet thou hast other work to do; *go thou, and preach the kingdom of God.*" Not that Christ would have his followers or his ministers to be *unnatural;* our religion teaches us to be kind and good in every relation, to *show piety at home,* and to *requite our parents.* But we must not make these offices an excuse from our duty to God. . If the nearest and dearest relation we have in the world stand in our way to keep us from Christ, it is necessary that we have a zeal that will make us forget *father and mother,* as Levi did, Deut. xxxiii. 9. This disciple was called to be a minister, and therefore must not *entangle himself* with the *affairs of this world,* 2 Tim. ii. 4. And it is a rule that, whenever Christ calls to any duty, we must not *consult with flesh and blood,* Gal. i. 15, 16. No excuses must be admitted against a present obedience to the call of Christ.

III. Here is another that is willing to follow Christ, but he must have a *little time* to *talk with his friends* about it.

Observe, 1. His request for a dispensation, *v.* 61. He said, "*Lord, I will follow thee;* I design no other, I am determined to do it; but *let me first go bid them farewell that are at home.*" This seemed reasonable; it was what Elisha desired when Elijah called him, *Let me kiss my father and my mother;* and it was allowed him: but the ministry of the gospel is *preferable,* and the service of it more urgent than that of the prophets; and therefore here it would not be allowed. Suffer me ἀποτάξασθαι τοῖς εἰς τὸν οἶκόν μȣ—*Let me go and set in order my household affairs,* and give direction concerning them; so some understand it. Now that which was amiss in this is, (1.) That he looked upon his following Christ as a melancholy, troublesome, dangerous thing; it was to him as if he were *going to die,* and therefore he must take *leave* of all his friends, never to *see them again,* or never *with any comfort;* whereas, in following Christ, he might be more a comfort and blessing to them than if he had continued with them. (2.) That he seemed to have his worldly concerns more upon his heart than he ought to have, and than would consist with a close attendance to his duty as a follower of Christ. He seemed to hanker after his relations and family concerns, and he could not part easily and suitably from them, but they stuck to him. It may be he had bidden them *farewell* once, but *Loth to depart bids oft farewell,* and therefore he must bid them *farewell* once more, for they are *at home at his house.* (3.) That he was willing to enter into a temptation from his purpose of following Christ. To go and bid them *farewell* that were *at home at his house* would be to expose himself to the strongest solicitations imaginable to alter his resolution; for they would all be against it, and would *beg* and *pray* that he would not *leave them.* Now it was presumption in him to thrust himself into such a temptation. Those that resolve to walk with their Maker, and follow their Redeemer, must resolve that they will not so much as parley with their tempter.

2. The rebuke which Christ gave him for this request (*v.* 62): "*No man, having put his hand to the plough,* and designing to make good work of his ploughing, will *look back,* or look behind him, for then he makes balks with his plough, and the ground he ploughs is *not fit* to be sown; so thou, if thou hast a design to follow me and to reap the advantages of those that do so, yet if thou *lookest back* to a worldly life again and hankerest after that, if thou *lookest back* as Lot's wife did to Sodom, which seems to be alluded to here, *thou art not fit for the kingdom of God.*" (1.) "Thou art not *soil* fit to receive the *good seed* of the kingdom of God if thou art thus *ploughed* by the *halves,* and not gone through with." (2.) "Thou art not a *sower* fit to *scatter* the good seed of the kingdom if thou canst *hold the plough* no better." Ploughing is in order to sowing. As those are not fit to be *sown* with divine comforts whose *fallow ground* is not first *broken up,* so those are not fit to be employed in sowing who know not how to break up the fallow ground, but, when they have *laid their hand to the plough,* upon every occasion look back and think of quitting it. Note, Those who begin with the work of God must resolve to *go on* with it, or they will make nothing of it. Looking back inclines to *drawing back,* and *drawing back* is to *perdition.* Those are not fit for heaven who, having set their faces heavenward, face about. But he, and he only, that *endures to the end, shall be saved.*

CHAP. X.

In this chapter we have, I. The ample commission which Christ gave to the seventy disciples to preach the gospel, and to confirm it by miracles; and the full instructions he gave them how to manage themselves in the execution of their commissions, and great encouragements therein, ver. 1—16. II. The report which the seventy disciples made to their Master of the success of their negociation, and his discourse thereupon, ver. 17—24. III. Christ's discourse with a lawyer concerning the way to heaven, and the instructions Christ gave him by a parable to look upon every one as his neighbour whom he had occasion to show kindness to, or receive kindness from, ver. 25—37. IV. Christ's entertainment at Martha's house, the reproof he gave to her for her care about the world, and his commendation of Mary for her care about her soul, ver. 38—42.

AFTER these things the Lord appointed other seventy also, and sent them two and two before his

face into every city and place, whither
he himself would come. 2 Therefore
said he unto them, The harvest truly
is great, but the labourers *are* few:
pray ye therefore the Lord of the
harvest, that he would send forth labourers into his harvest. 3 Go your
ways: behold, I send you forth as
lambs among wolves. 4 Carry neither
purse, nor scrip, nor shoes: and salute no man by the way. 5 And into
whatsoever house ye enter, first say,
Peace *be* to this house. 6 And if
the son of peace be there, your peace
shall rest upon it: if not, it shall turn
to you again. 7 And in the same
house remain, eating and drinking
such things as they give: for the labourer is worthy of his hire. Go not
from house to house. 8 And into
whatsoever city ye enter, and they receive you, eat such things as are set
before you: 9 And heal the sick that
are therein, and say unto them, The
kingdom of God is come nigh unto
you. 10 But into whatsoever city
ye enter, and they receive you not,
go your ways out into the streets of
the same, and say, 11 Even the very
dust of your city, which cleaveth on
us, we do wipe off against you: notwithstanding be ye sure of this, that
the kingdom of God is come nigh
unto you. 12 But I say unto you,
that it shall be more tolerable in that
day for Sodom, than for that city.
13 Woe unto thee, Chorazin! woe
unto thee, Bethsaida! for if the mighty
works had been done in Tyre and Sidon, which have been done in you,
they had a great while ago repented,
sitting in sackcloth and ashes. 14 But
it shall be more tolerable for Tyre and
Sidon at the judgment, than for you.
15 And thou, Capernaum, which art
exalted to heaven, shalt be thrust down
to hell. 16 He that heareth you
heareth me; and he that despiseth you
despiseth me; and he that despiseth
me despiseth him that sent me.

We have here the sending forth of seventy disciples, two and two, into divers parts of the country, to preach the gospel, and to work miracles in those places which Christ himself designed to visit, to make way for his entertainment. This is not taken notice of by the other evangelists: but the instructions here given them are much the same with those given to the twelve. Observe,

I. Their number: they were seventy. As in the choice of twelve apostles Christ had an eye to the twelve patriarchs, the twelve tribes, and the twelve princes of those tribes, so here he seems to have an eye to the *seventy* elders of Israel. So many went up with Moses and Aaron to the mount, and *saw the glory of the God of Israel* (Exod. xxiv. 1, 9), and so many were afterwards chosen to assist Moses in the government, in order to which the Spirit of prophecy came unto them, Num. xi. 24, 25. The *twelve wells of water* and the *seventy palm-trees* that were at Elim were a figure of the *twelve apostles* and the *seventy disciples,* Exod. xv. 27. They were seventy elders of the Jews that were employed by Ptolemy king of Egypt in turning the Old Testament into Greek, whose translation is thence called the *Septuagint.* The great sanhedrim consisted of this number. Now,

1. We are glad to find that Christ had so many followers fit to be sent forth; his labour was not altogether in vain, though he met with much opposition. Note, Christ's interest is a *growing* interest, and his followers, like Israel in Egypt, though *afflicted* shall *multiply.* These *seventy,* though they did not attend him so closely and constantly as the *twelve* did, were nevertheless the constant hearers of his doctrine, and witnesses of his miracles, and believed in him. Those three mentioned in the close of the foregoing chapter might have been of these seventy, if they would have applied themselves in good earnest to their business. These seventy are those of whom Peter speaks as "*the men who companied with us all the time that the Lord Jesus went in and out among us,*" and were part of the one hundred and twenty there spoken of, Acts i. 15, 21. Many of those that were the companions of the apostles, whom we read of in the Acts and the Epistles, we may suppose, were of these seventy disciples.

2. We are glad to find there was work for so many ministers, hearers for so many preachers: thus the grain of mustard-seed began to *grow,* and the savour of the leaven to diffuse itself in the meal, in order to the leavening of the whole.

II. Their work and business: He sent them *two and two,* that they might strengthen and encourage one another. *If one fall, the other will help to raise him up.* He sent them, not to all the cities of Israel, as he did the *twelve,* but only *to every city and place whither he himself would come* (*v.* 1), as his harbingers; and we must suppose, though it is not recorded, that Christ soon after went to all those places whither he now sent them, though he could stay but a little while in a place. Two things they were ordered to do, the same that Christ did wherever he came:—1. They must *heal the sick* (*v.* 9), heal them *in the name of Jesus,* which would make people long to see this Jesus, and ready to entertain him whose name was so powerful. 2. They must publish the approach of the kingdom of God, its approach *to them:* "Tell them this, *The kingdom of God is come nigh to you,* and you now stand fair for an admission into it, if you will but look about you. Now is the *day of your visitation*, know and understand it." It is good to be made sensible of our advantages and opportunities, that we may lay hold of them. When the *kingdom of God comes nigh us,* it concerns us to go forth to meet it.

III. The instructions he gives them.

1. They must set out with prayer (*v.* 2); and, in prayer, (1.) They must be duly affected with the necessities of the souls of men, which called for their help. They must *look about,* and see how *great the harvest was,* what abundance of people there were that wanted to have the gospel preached to them and were willing to receive it, nay, that had at this time their expectations raised of the coming of the Messiah and of his kingdom. There was corn ready to shed and be lost for want of hands to gather it in. Note, Ministers should apply themselves to their work under a deep concern for *precious souls,* looking upon them as the riches of this world, which ought to be secured for Christ. They must likewise be concerned that the *labourers were so few.* The Jewish teachers were indeed many, but they were not labourers; they did not gather in souls to God's kingdom, but to their own interest and party. Note, Those that are good ministers themselves wish that there were more good ministers, for there is work for more. It is common for tradesmen not to care how few there are of their own trade; but Christ would have the labourers in his vineyard reckon it a matter of complaint when the *labourers are few.* (2.) They must earnestly desire to receive their mission from God, that *he* would send them forth as *labourers into his harvest* who is the *Lord of the harvest,* and that he would send others forth; for, if God send them forth, they may hope he will go along with them and give them success. Let them therefore say, as the prophet (Isa. vi. 8), *Here I am, send me.* It is desirable to receive our commission from God, and then we may go on boldly.

2. They must set out with an expectation of trouble and persecution: "*Behold, I send you forth as lambs among wolves;* but *go your ways,* and resolve to make the best of it. Your enemies will be as *wolves,* bloody and cruel, and ready to pull you to pieces; in their threatenings and revilings, they will be as *howling* wolves to *terrify* you; in their persecutions of you, they will be as *ravening* wolves to *tear* you. But you must be as *lambs,* peaceable and patient, though made an easy prey of." It would have been very hard thus to be sent forth as *sheep among wolves,* if he had not endued them with his spirit and courage.

3. They must not encumber themselves with a load of provisions, as if they were going a long voyage, but depend upon God and their friends to provide what was convenient for them: "Carry neither a *purse* for money, nor a *scrip* or knapsack for clothes or victuals, nor new *shoes* (as before to the twelve, *ch.* ix. 3); and *salute no man by the way.*" This command Elisha gave to his servant, when he sent him to see the Shunamite's dead child, 2 Kings iv. 29. Not that Christ would have his ministers to be rude, morose, and unmannerly; but, (1.) They must go as men *in haste,* that had their particular places assigned them, where they must deliver their message, and in their way directly to those places must not hinder or retard themselves with needless ceremonies or compliments. (2.) They must go as *men of business,* business that relates to another world, which they must be intent in, and intent upon, and therefore must not entangle themselves with conversation about secular affairs. *Minister verbi est; hoc age—You are a minister of the word; attend to your office.* (3.) They must go as *serious* men, and *men in sorrow.* It was the custom of mourners, during the first seven days of their mourning, not to *salute any,* Job ii. 13. Christ was a man of sorrows and acquainted with grief; and it was fit that by this and other signs his messengers should resemble him, and likewise show themselves affected with the calamities of mankind which they came to relieve, and touched with a feeling of them.

4. They must show, not only *their good-will,* but *God's good-will,* to all to whom they came, and leave the issue and success to him that knows the heart, *v.* 5, 6.

(1.) The charge given them was, Whatsoever *house* they *entered into,* they must say, *Peace be to this house.* Here, [1.] They are supposed to enter into *private houses;* for, being not admitted into the synagogues, they were forced to preach where they could have liberty. And, as their public preaching was driven into houses, so thither they carried it. Like their Master, wherever they *visited,* they *preached from house to house,* Acts v. 42; xx. 20. Christ's church was at first very much *a church in the house.* [2.] They are instructed to say, "*Peace be to this house,* to all under this roof, to this family, and to all that belong to it." *Peace be to you* was the common form of salutation among the Jews. They must not use it in *formality,* according to custom, to those they met on the way, because they must use it with *solemnity* to those whose houses they entered into: "*Salute no man by the way* in compliment, but to those into whose house ye enter, say, *Peace be to you,* with seriousness and in reality; for this is intended to be more than a compliment." Christ's ministers go into all the world, to say, in Christ's name, *Peace be to you. First,* We are to *propose* peace to all, to *preach peace by Jesus Christ,* to proclaim the gospel of peace, the covenant of peace, *peace on earth*, and to invite the children of men to come and take the benefit of it. *Secondly*, We are to *pray* for peace to all. We must earnestly desire the salvation of the souls of those we preach to, and offer up those desires to God in prayer; and it may be well to let them know that we do thus pray for them, and bless them in the name of the Lord.

(2.) The success was to be different, according to the different dispositions of those whom they preached to and prayed for. According as the inhabitants were sons of peace or not, so their peace should or should not *rest upon the house*. *Recipitur ad modum recipientis—The quality of the receiver determines the nature of the reception.* [1.] "You will meet with some that are the *sons of peace*, that by the operations of divine grace, pursuant to the designations of the divine counsel, are ready to admit the word of the gospel in the light and love of it, and have their hearts made as soft wax to receive the impressions of it. Those are qualified to receive the comforts of the gospel in whom there is a good work of grace wrought. And, as to those, *your peace* shall find them out and *rest upon them;* your prayers for them shall be heard, the promises of the gospel shall be *confirmed* to them, the privileges of it *conferred* on them, and the fruit of both shall remain and continue with them—a good part that shall not be *taken away*." [2.] "You will meet with others that are no ways disposed to hear or heed your message, whole houses that have not one *son of peace* in them." Now it is certain that our peace shall *not come* upon *them*, they have no part nor lot in the matter; the blessing that rests upon the *sons of peace* shall never come upon the sons of Belial, nor can any expect the blessings of the covenant that will not come under the bonds of it. But it shall *return to us again;* that is, we shall have the comfort of having done our duty to God and discharged our trust. Our prayers like David's shall return *into our own bosom* (Ps. xxxv. 13) and we shall have commission to go on in the work. Our peace shall return to us again, not only to be enjoyed by ourselves, but to be communicated to others, to the next we meet with, them that are *sons of peace*.

5. They must *receive* the kindnesses of those that should *entertain* them and *bid them welcome, v.* 7, 8. "Those that receive the gospel will receive you that preach it, and give you entertainment; you must not think to raise estates, but you may depend upon a subsistence; and," (1.) "Be not *shy;* do not suspect your welcome, nor be afraid of being troublesome, but *eat and drink* heartily *such things as they give;* for, whatever kindness they show you, it is but a small return for the kindness you do them in bringing the glad tidings of *peace*. You will deserve it, for *the labourer is worthy of his hire*, the labourer in the work of the ministry is so, if he be indeed a *labourer;* and it is not an act of charity, but of justice, in those who are *taught in the word to communicate to those that teach them*." (2.) "Be not *nice* and *curious* in your diet: *Eat and drink such things as they give* (*v.* 7), *such things as are set before you, v.* 8. Be thankful for plain food, and do not find fault, though it be not dressed according to art." It ill becomes Christ's disciples to be *desirous of dainties*. As he has not tied them up to the Pharisees' superstitious fasts, so he has not allowed them the luxurious feasts of the Epicureans. Probably, Christ here refers to the traditions of the elders about their meat, which were so many that those who observed them were extremely critical, you could hardly set a dish of meat before them, but there was some scruple or other concerning it; but Christ would not have them to regard those things, but eat what was given them, *asking no question for conscience' sake*.

6. They must *denounce* the judgments of God against those who should *reject* them and their *message*: "If you *enter into a city*, and they *do not receive you*, if there be none there disposed to hearken to your doctrine, leave them, *v.* 10. If they will not *give you welcome* into their houses, do you *give them warning* in their streets." He orders them to (*ch.* ix. 5) do as he had ordered the apostles to do: "Say to them, not with rage, or scorn, or resentment, but with compassion to their poor perishing souls, and a holy dread of the ruin which they are bringing upon themselves, *Even the dust of your city, which cleaveth on us, we do wipe off against you, v.* 11. From them do not receive any kindnesses at all, be not beholden to them. It cost that prophet of the Lord dear who accepted a meal's meat with a prophet in Bethel, 1 Kings xiii. 21, 22. Tell them that you will not carry with you the dust of their city; let them take it to themselves, for *dust they are*." It shall be a witness for Christ's messengers that they had been there according to their Master's order; *tender* and *refusal* were a discharge of their trust. But it shall be a witness against the recusants that they would not give Christ's messengers any entertainment, no, not so much as water to wash their feet with, but they were forced to wipe off the dust. "But tell them plainly, and bid them *be sure* of it, *The kingdom of God is come nigh to you*. Here is a fair offer made you; if you have not the benefit of it, it is your own fault. The gospel is brought to your doors; if you shut your doors against it, your blood is upon your own head. Now that the *kingdom of God is come nigh to you*, if you will not come up to it, and come into it, your sin will be inexcusable, and your condemnation intolerable." Note, The fairer offers we have of grace and life by Christ, the more we shall have to answer for another day, if we slight these offers: *It shall be*

more tolerable for Sodom than for that city, v. 12. The Sodomites indeed rejected the warning given them by Lot; but rejecting the gospel is a more heinous crime, and will be punished accordingly *in that day.* He means the day of judgment (*v.* 14), but calls it, by way of emphasis, *that day,* because it is the last and great day, the day when we must account for all the *days of time,* and have our state determined for the *days of eternity.*

Upon this occasion, the evangelist repeats,

(1.) The particular doom of those cities wherein most of Christ's mighty works were done, which we had, Matt. xi. 20, &c. Chorazin, Bethsaida, and Capernaum, all bordering upon the sea of Galilee, where Christ was most conversant, are the places here mentioned. [1.] They enjoyed greater privileges. Christ's *mighty works were done in them,* and they were all gracious works, works of mercy. They were hereby *exalted to heaven,* not only dignified and honoured, but put into a fair way of being happy; they were brought as near heaven as external means could bring them. [2.] God's design in favouring them thus was to bring them to *repentance* and *reformation* of life, *to sit in sackcloth and ashes,* both in humiliation for the sins they had committed, and in humility and a meek subjection to God's government. [3.] Their frustrating this design, and their receiving the grace of God therein in vain. It is implied that they *repented not*; they were not wrought upon by all the miracles of Christ to think the better of him, or the worse of sin; they did not bring forth fruits agreeable to the advantages they enjoyed. [4.] There was reason to think, morally speaking, that, if Christ had gone to Tyre and Sidon, Gentile cities, and had preached the same doctrine to them and wrought the same miracles among them that he did in these cities of Israel, they would have repented *long ago,* so speedy would their repentence have been, and that in *sackcloth and ashes,* so deep would it have been. Now to understand the wisdom of God, in *giving* the means of grace to those who would not improve them, and *denying* them to those that would, we must wait for the great day of discovery. [5.] The doom of those who thus receive the grace of God in vain will be very fearful. They that were *thus exalted,* not making use of their elevation, will be *thrust down to hell,* thrust down with disgrace and dishonour. They will thrust in to get into heaven, in the crowd of professors, but in vain; they shall be *thrust down,* to their everlasting grief and disappointment, into the lowest hell, and hell will be hell indeed to them. [6.] In the day of judgment Tyre and Sidon will fare better, and it will be more tolerable for them than for these cities.

(2.) The general rule which Christ would go by, as to those to whom he sent his ministers: He will reckon himself treated according as they treated his ministers, *v.* 16. What is done to the ambassador is done, as it were, to the prince that sends him. [1.] "*He that heareth you,* and regardeth what you say, *heareth me,* and herein doeth me honour. But," [2.] "He that *despiseth you* doth in effect *despise me,* and shall be reckoned with as having put an affront upon me; nay, he *despiseth him that sent me.*" Note, Those who contemn the Christian religion do in effect put a slight upon natural religion, which it is perfective of. And they who *despise* the faithful ministers of Christ, who, though they do not hate and persecute them, yet think meanly of them, look scornfully upon them, and turn their backs upon their ministry, will be reckoned with as despisers of God and Christ.

17 And the seventy returned again
with joy, saying, Lord, even the devils
are subject unto us through thy name.
18 And he said unto them, I beheld
Satan as lightning fall from heaven.
19 Behold, I give unto you power to
tread on serpents and scorpions, and
over all the power of the enemy: and
nothing shall by any means hurt you.
20 Notwithstanding in this rejoice
not, that the spirits are subject unto
you; but rather rejoice, because your
names are written in heaven. 21 In
that hour Jesus rejoiced in spirit, and
said, I thank thee, O Father, Lord of
heaven and earth, that thou hast hid
these things from the wise and prudent, and hast revealed them unto
babes: even so, Father; for so it
seemed good in thy sight. 22 All
things are delivered to me of my Father: and no man knoweth who the
Son is, but the Father; and who the
Father is, but the Son, and *he* to whom
the Son will reveal *him.* 23 And he
turned him unto *his* disciples, and
said privately, Blessed *are* the eyes
which see the things that ye see: 24
For I tell you, that many prophets
and kings have desired to see those
things which ye see, and have not
seen *them;* and to hear those things
which ye hear, and have not heard
them.

Christ sent forth the seventy disciples as he was going up to Jerusalem to the *feast of tabernacles,* when he *went up, not openly,* but *as it were in secret* (John vii. 10), having sent abroad so great a part of his ordinary retinue; and Dr. Lightfoot thinks it was before his return from that feast, and while he was yet at Jerusalem, or Bethany, which was hard by (for there he was, *v.* 38), that they, or at least some of them, returned to him. Now here we are told,

1. What account they gave him of the success of their expedition: *They returned again with joy* (*v.* 17); not complaining of the fatigue of their journeys, nor of the opposition and discouragement they met with, but rejoicing in their success, especially in casting out unclean spirits: *Lord, even the devils are subject unto us through thy name.* Though only the *healing of the sick* was mentioned in their commission (*v.* 19), yet no doubt the *casting out* of devils was included, and in this they had wonderful success. 1. They give Christ the glory of this: It is *through thy name.* Note, all our victories over Satan are obtained by power derived from Jesus Christ. We must *in his name* enter the lists with our spiritual enemies, and, whatever advantages we gain, he must have all the praise; if the work be done *in* his name, the honour is due *to* his name. 2. They entertain themselves with the comfort of it; they speak of it with an air of exultation: *Even the devils,* those potent enemies, are *subject to us.* Note, the saints have no greater joy or satisfaction in any of their triumphs than in those over Satan. If devils are *subject to us,* what can stand before us?

II. What acceptance they found with him, and how he received this account.

1. He confirmed what they said, as agreeing with his own observation (*v.* 18): "My heart and eye went along with you; I took notice of the success you had, and I *saw Satan fall as lightning from heaven.* Note, Satan and his kingdom fell before the preaching of the gospel. "I see how it is," saith Christ, "as you get ground the devil loseth ground." He falls *as lightning falls from heaven,* so suddenly, so irrecoverably, so visibly, that all may perceive it, and say, "See how Satan's kingdom totters, see how it tumbles." They triumphed in casting devils out of the bodies of people; but Christ sees and rejoices in the fall of the devil from the interest he has in the souls of men, which is called his power *in high places,* Eph. vi. 12. He foresees this to be but an earnest of what should now be shortly done and was already begun—the destroying of Satan's kingdom in the world by the extirpating of idolatry and the turning of the nations to the faith of Christ. Satan *falls from heaven* when he falls from the throne in men's hearts, Acts xxvi. 18. And Christ foresaw that the preaching of the gospel, which would *fly like lightning* through the world, would wherever it went pull down Satan's kingdom. *Now is the prince of this world cast out.* Some have given another sense of this, as looking back to the fall of the angels, and designed for a caution to these disciples, lest their success should puff them up with pride: "I saw angels turned into devils by *pride:* that was the sin for which Satan was *cast down from heaven,* where he had been an angel of light I saw it, and give you an intimation of it, lest you, being *lifted up with pride, should fall into that condemnation of the devil,* who fell by pride," 1 Tim. iii. 6.

2. He repeated, ratified, and enlarged their commission: *Behold I give you power to tread on serpents, v.* 19. Note, To him that hath, and useth well what he hath, more shall be given. They had employed their power vigorously against Satan, and now Christ entrusts them with greater power. (1.) An *offensive* power, power to *tread on serpents and scorpions,* devils and malignant spirits, the old serpent: "You shall *bruise their heads* in my name, according to the first promise, Gen. iii. 15. Come, *set your feet* on *the necks* of these enemies; you shall tread upon these *lions* and *adders* wherever you meet with them; you shall *trample them under foot,* Ps. xci. 13. You shall *tread upon all the power of the enemy,* and the kingdom of the Messiah shall be every where set up upon the ruins of the devil's kingdom. As the devils have now been *subject to you,* so they shall still be. (2.) A *defensive* power: "*Nothing shall by any means hurt you;* not *serpents* nor *scorpions,* if you should be chastised with them or thrown into prisons and dungeons among them; you shall be unhurt by the most venomous creatures," as St. Paul was (Acts. xxviii. 5), and as is promised in Mark xvi. 18. "If wicked men be as *serpents* to you, and you *dwell* among those *scorpions* (as Ezek. ii. 6), you may despise their rage, and *tread* upon it; *it* need not disturb you, for they have no power against you but what is *given them from above;* they may *hiss,* but they cannot *hurt.* You may play upon the hole of the asp, for *death itself shall not hurt nor destroy,* Isa. xi. 8, 19; xxv. 8.

3. He directed them to turn their joy into the right channel (*v.* 20): "*Notwithstanding in this rejoice not, that the spirits are subject unto you,* that they have been so, and shall be still so. Do not rejoice in this merely as it is your honour, and a confirmation of your mission, and as it sets you a degree above other good people; do not rejoice in this *only,* or in this *chiefly,* but *rather rejoice because your names are written in heaven,* because you are chosen of God to eternal life, and are the children of God through faith." Christ, who knew the counsels of God, could tell them that their *names were written in heaven,* for it is the *Lamb's book of life* that they are written in. All believers are through grace, entitled to the inheritance of sons, and have received the adoption of sons, and the Spirit of adoption, which is the earnest of that inheritance, and so are enrolled among his family; now this is matter of joy, greater joy than casting out devils. Note, Power to become the children of God is to be valued more than a power to work miracles; for we read of those who did *in Christ's name cast out devils,* as Judas did,

and yet will be disowned by Christ in the great day. But they whose *names are written in heaven* shall never perish; they are *Christ's sheep,* to whom he will *give eternal life.* Saving graces are more to be rejoiced in than spiritual gifts; holy love is *a more excellent way* than speaking with tongues.

4. He offered up a solemn thanksgiving to his Father, for employing such mean people as his disciples were in such high and honourable services, *v.* 21, 22. This we had before (Matt. xi. 25—27), only here it is prefixed that *in that hour Jesus rejoiced.* It was fit that particular notice should be taken of *that* hour, because there were so few such, for he was a *man of sorrows.* In *that hour* in which he saw Satan fall, and heard of the good success of his ministers, *in that hour he rejoiced.* Note, Nothing rejoices the heart of the Lord Jesus so much as the progress of the gospel, and its getting ground of Satan, by the conversion of souls to Christ. Christ's joy was a solid substantial joy, an inward joy: *he rejoiced in spirit;* but his joy, like deep waters, made no noise; it was a joy that a stranger did not intermeddle with. Before he applied himself to *thank his Father,* he stirred up himself to *rejoice;* for, as *thankful praise* is the genuine language of *holy joy,* so *holy joy* is the root and spring of *thankful praise.* Two things he gives thanks for:—

(1.) For what was *revealed* by the *Father* through the *Son*: *I thank thee, O Father, Lord of heaven and earth, v.* 21. In all our adorations of God, we must have an eye to him, both as the Maker of heaven and earth and as the Father of our Lord Jesus Christ, and in him our Father. Now that which he gives thanks for is, [1.] That the counsels of God concerning man's reconciliation to himself were *revealed* to some of the children of men, who might be fit also to *teach others,* and it is God that *by his Son* has spoken these things *to us* and by his Spirit has revealed them *in us; he* has *revealed* that which had been *kept secret* from the beginning of the world. [2.] That they were revealed to *babes,* to those who were of mean parts and capacities, whose extraction and education had nothing in them promising, who were but *children in understanding,* till God by his Spirit elevated their faculties, and furnished them with this knowledge, and an ability to communicate it. We have reason to thank God, not so much for the honour he has hereby put upon babes, as for the honour he has hereby done himself in perfecting strength *out of weakness.* [3.] That, at the same time when he revealed them unto babes, he *hid them from the wise and prudent,* the Gentile philosophers, the Jewish rabbin. He *did not reveal* the things of the gospel to them, nor employ them in preaching up his kingdom. Thanks be to God that the apostles were not fetched from their schools; for, *First,* they would have been apt to mingle their notions with the doctrine of Christ, which would have corrupted it, as afterwards it proved. For Christianity was much corrupted by the Platonic philosophy in the first ages of it, by the Peripatetic in its latter ages, and by the Judaizing teachers at the first planting of it. *Secondly,* If rabbin and philosophers had been made apostles, the success of the gospel would have been ascribed to their learning and wit and the force of their reasonings and eloquence; and therefore they must not be employed, lest they should have taken too much to themselves, and others should have attributed too much to them. They were passed by for the same reason that Gideon's army was reduced: *The people are yet too many,* Judges vii. 4. Paul indeed was bred a scholar among the wise and prudent; but he became a *babe* when he became an apostle, and laid aside the *enticing words of man's wisdom,* forgot them all, and made neither show nor use of any other knowledge than that of *Christ and him crucified,* 1 Cor. ii. 2, 4 [4.] That God herein acted by way of sovereignty: *Even so, Father, for so it seemed good in thy sight.* If God gives his grace and the knowledge of his son to some that are less likely, and does not give it to others whom we should think better able to deliver it with advantage, this must satisfy: so it pleases God, whose thoughts are infinitely above ours. He chooses to entrust the dispensing of his gospel in the hands of those who with a *divine energy* will give it the *setting on,* rather than in theirs who with *human art* will give it the *setting off.*

(2.) For what was *secret* between the *Father* and *the Son, v.* 22. [1.] The vast *confidence* that the Father *puts* in the Son: *All things are delivered to me of my Father,* all wisdom and knowledge, all power and authority, all the grace and comfort which are intended for the chosen remnant; it is all delivered into the hands of the Lord Jesus; in him all fulness must *dwell,* and from him it must be *derived:* he is the great *trustee* that manages all the concerns of God's kingdom. [2.] The good understanding that there is between the Father and the Son, and their *mutual consciousness,* such as no creature can be admitted to: *No man knows who the Son is,* nor what his mind is, *but the Father,* who *possessed him in the beginning of his ways, before his works of old* (Prov. viii. 22), nor *who the Father is,* and what his counsels are, *but the Son,* who lay in his bosom from eternity, was *by him as one brought up with him, and was daily his delight* (Prov. viii. 30), *and he to whom the Son* by the Spirit *will reveal him.* The gospel is the revelation of Jesus Christ, to him we owe all the discoveries made to us of the will of God for our salvation; and here he speaks of being entrusted with it as that which was a great pleasure to himself and for which he was very thankful to his Father.

5. He told his disciples how well it was

for them that they had these things revealed to them, *v* 23, 24. Having addressed himself to his Father, he *turned to his disciples,* designing to make them sensible how much it was for their happiness, as well as for the glory and honour of God, that they knew the mysteries of the kingdom and were employed to lead others into the knowledge of them, considering, (1.) What a step it is *towards* something better. Though the bare knowledge of these things is not saving, yet it puts us in the way of salvation: *Blessed are the eyes which see the things which we see.* God therein blesseth them, and, if it be not their own fault, it will be an eternal blessedness to them. (2.) What a step it is *above* those that went before them, even the greatest saints, and those that were most the favourites of Heaven: "*Many prophets and righteous men*" (so it is in Matt. xiii. 17), *many prophets and kings* (so it is here), "have *desired* to see and hear those things which you are daily and intimately conversant with, and *have not seen* and *heard* them." The honour and happiness of the New-Testament saints far exceed those even' of the *prophets* and *kings* of the Old Testament, though they also were *highly favoured.* The general ideas which the Old-Testament saints had, according to the intimations given them, of the graces and glories of the Messiah's kingdom, made them wish a thousand times that their lot had been reserved for those blessed days, and that they might see the substance of those things of which they had faint shadows. Note, The consideration of the great advantages which we have in the New-Testament light, above what they had who lived in Old-Testament times, should awaken our diligence in the improvement of it; for, if it do not, it will aggravate our condemnation for the non-improvement of it.

25 And, behold, a certain lawyer
stood up, and tempted him, saying,
Master, what shall I do to inherit
eternal life? 26 He said unto him,
What is written in the law? how
readest thou? 27 And he answering
said, Thou shalt love the Lord thy
God with all thy heart, and with all
thy soul, and with all thy strength,
and with all thy mind; and thy neighbour as thyself. 28 And he said unto
him, Thou hast answered right: this
do, and thou shalt live. 29 But he,
willing to justify himself, said unto
Jesus, And who is my neighbour?
30 And Jesus answering said, A cer
tain *man* went down from Jerusalem
to Jericho, and fell among thieves,
which stripped him of his raiment,
and wounded *him,* and departed, leaving *him* half dead. 31 And by chance
there came down a certain priest that
way: and when he saw him, he passed
by on the other side. 32 And likewise a Levite, when he was at the
place, came and looked *on him,* and
passed by on the other side. 33 But
a certain Samaritan, as he journeyed,
came where he was: and when he
saw him, he had compassion *on him,*
34 And went to *him,* and bound up
his wounds, pouring in oil and wine,
and set him on his own beast, and
brought him to an inn, and took care
of him. 35 And on the morrow when
he departed, he took out two pence,
and gave *them* to the host, and said
unto him, Take care of him; and
whatsoever thou spendest more, when
I come again, I will repay thee. 36
Which now of these three, thinkest
thou, was neighbour unto him that
fell among the thieves? 37 And he
said, He that showed mercy on him.
Then said Jesus unto him, Go, and
do thou likewise.

We have here Christ's discourse with a lawyer about some points of conscience, which we are all concerned to be rightly informed in, and are so here, from Christ, though the questions were proposed with no good intention.

I. We are concerned to know what that good is which we should do in *this* life, in order to our attaining *eternal life.* A question to this purport was proposed to our Saviour by a *certain lawyer,* or *scribe,* only with a design to *try* him, not with a desire to be instructed by him, *v.* 25. The lawyer *stood up,* and *asked him, Master, what shall I do to inherit eternal life?* If Christ had any thing peculiar to prescribe, by this question he would get it out of him, and perhaps expose him for it; if not, he would expose his doctrine as needless, since it would give no other direction for obtaining happiness than what they had already received; or, perhaps, he had no malicious design against Christ, as some of the scribes had, only he was willing to have a little talk with him, just as people go to church to hear what the minister will say. This was a good question: *What shall I do to inherit eternal life?* But it lost all its goodness when it was proposed with an ill design, or a very mean one. Note, It is not enough to speak of the things of God, and to enquire about them, but we must do it with a suitable concern. If we speak of *eternal life,* and *the way* to it, in a careless manner, merely as matter of discourse, especially as matter of dispute, we do but take the name of God in vain, as the lawyer here did. Now this question being started, observe,

1. How Christ turned him over to the divine law, and bade him follow the direction of that. Though he knew the thoughts and intents of his heart, he did not answer him according to the folly of that, but according to the wisdom and goodness of the question he asked. He answered him with a question: *What is written in the law? How readest thou? v.* 26. He came to catechize Christ, and to know him; but Christ will catechize him, and make him know himself. He talks to him as a lawyer, as one conversant in the law: the studies of his profession would inform him; let him practise according to his knowledge, and he should not come short of *eternal life.* Note, It will be of great use to us, in our way to heaven, to consider *what is written in the law,* and *what we read* there. We must have recourse to our bibles, to the law, as it is now in the hand of Christ, and walk in the way that is shown us there. It is a great mercy that we have the law *written,* that we have it thereby reduced to certainty, and that thereby it is capable of spreading the *further,* and lasting the *longer.* Having it *written,* it is our duty to read it, to read it with understanding, and to treasure up what we read, so that, when there is occasion, we may be able to tell *what is written in the law,* and *how we read.* To this we must appeal; by this we must try doctrines and end disputes; this must be our oracle, our touchstone, our rule, our guide. What is written in the law? How do we read? if there be light in us, it will have regard to this light.

2. What a good account he gave of the law, of the principal commandments of the law, to the observance of which we must bind ourselves if we would inherit eternal life. He did not, like a Pharisee, refer himself to the tradition of the elders, but, like a good textuary, fastened upon the two first and great commandments of the law, as those which he thought must be most strictly observed in order to the obtaining of *eternal life,* and which included all the rest, *v.* 27. (1.) We must *love God with all our hearts,* must look upon him as the best of beings, in himself most amiable, and infinitely perfect and excellent; as one whom we lie under the greatest obligations to, both in gratitude and interest. We must prize him, and value ourselves by our relation to him; must please ourselves in him, and devote ourselves entirely to him. Our love to him must be sincere, hearty, and fervent; it must be a superlative love, a love that is as strong as death, but an intelligent love, and such as we can give a good account of the grounds and reasons of. It must be an *entire* love; he must have our *whole* souls, and must be served with *all that is within us.* We must love nothing *besides him,* but what we love *for him* and in subordination to him. (2.) We must love our neighbours as *ourselves,* which we shall easily do, if we, as we ought to do, love God *better than ourselves.* We must wish well to all and ill to none; must do all the good we can in the world and no hurt, and must fix it as a rule to ourselves to do to others as we would they should do to us; and this is to love our neighbour *as ourselves.*

3. Christ's approbation of what he said, *v.* 28. Though he came to tempt him, yet what he said that was good Christ commended: *Thou hast answered right.* Christ himself fastened upon these as the two great commandments of the law (Matt. xxii. 37): both sides agreed in this. Those who do well shall have praise of the same, and so should those have that speak well. So far is right; but the hardest part of this work yet remains: "*This do, and thou shalt live;* thou shalt *inherit eternal life.*

4. His care to avoid the conviction which was now ready to fasten upon him. When Christ said, *This do, and thou shalt live,* he began to be aware that Christ intended to draw from him an acknowledgment that he *had not done this,* and therefore an enquiry what he should do, which way he should look, to get his sins pardoned; an acknowledgment also that he *could not do this* perfectly for the future by any strength of his own, and therefore an enquiry which way he might fetch in strength to enable him to do it: but he was *willing to justify himself,* and therefore cared not for carrying on that discourse, but saith, in effect, as another did (Matt. xix. 20), *All these things have I kept from my youth up.* Note, Many ask good questions with a design rather to *justify themselves* than to *inform themselves,* rather proudly to show what is good in them than humbly to see what is bad in them.

II. We are concerned to know who is our neighbour, whom by the second great commandment we are obliged to love. This is another of this lawyer's queries, which he started only that he might *drop* the former, lest Christ should have forced him, in the prosecution of it, to *condemn himself,* when he was resolved to *justify* himself. As to loving God, he was willing to say no more of it; but, as to his *neighbour,* he was sure that there he had come up to the rule, for he had always been very kind and respectful to all about him. Now observe,

1. What was the corrupt notion of the Jewish teachers in this matter. Dr. Lightfoot quotes their own words to this purport: "Where he saith, *Thou shalt love thy neighbour, he excepts all Gentiles,* for they are not *our neighbours,* but those only that are of our own nation and religion." They would not put an Israelite to death for killing a Gentile, for he was not his *neighbour:* they indeed say that they ought not to kill a Gentile whom they were not at war with; but, if they saw a Gentile in *danger of death,* they thought themselves under no obligation to help to *save his life.* Such wicked inferences did

they draw from that holy covenant of peculiarity by which God had distinguished them, and by abusing it thus they had forfeited it; God justly took the forfeiture, and transferred covenant-favours to the Gentile world, to whom they brutishly denied common favours.

2. How Christ corrected this inhuman notion, and showed, by a parable, that whomsoever we *have need* to receive kindness *from*, and *find ready* to show us the kindness *we need*, we cannot but look upon as *our neighbour*; and therefore ought to look upon all those as such who need our kindness, and to show them kindness accordingly, though they be not of our own nation and religion. Now observe,

(1.) The parable itself, which represents to us a poor Jew in distressed circumstances, succoured and relieved by a good Samaritan. Let us see here,

[1.] How he was *abused* by his *enemies*. The honest man was travelling peaceably upon his lawful business in the road, and it was a great road that led from Jerusalem to Jericho, *v.* 30. The mentioning of those places intimates that it was matter of fact, and not a parable; probably it happened lately, just as it is here related. The occurrences of Providence would yield us many good instructions, if we would carefully observe and improve them, and would be equivalent to parables framed on purpose for instruction, and be more *affecting*. This poor man *fell among thieves*. Whether they were Arabians, plunderers, that lived by spoil, or some profligate wretches of his own nation, or some of the Roman soldiers, who, notwithstanding the strict discipline of their army, did this villany, does not appear; but they were very *barbarous;* they not only took his money, but stripped him of his clothes, and, that he might not be able to pursue them, or only to gratify a cruel disposition (for otherwise *what profit was there in his blood?*) they *wounded him*, and left him *half dead*, ready to die of his wounds. We may here conceive a just indignation at *highwaymen*, that have divested themselves of all humanity, and are as natural brute beasts, beasts of prey, made to be *taken and destroyed;* and at the same time we cannot but think with compassion on those that fall into the hands of such wicked and unreasonable men, and be ready, when it is in our power, to help them. What reason have we to thank God for our preservation from perils by robbers!

[2.] How he was *slighted* by those who should have been his friends, who were not only men of his own nation and religion, but one a priest and the other a Levite, men of a public character and station; nay, they were men of professed sanctity, whose offices obliged them to tenderness and compassion (Heb. v. 2), who ought to have taught others their duty in such a case as this, which was to *deliver them that were drawn unto death;* yet they would not themselves do it. Dr. Lightfoot tells us that many of the courses of the priests had their residence in Jericho, and thence came up to Jerusalem, when it was their turn to officiate there, and so back again, which occasioned abundance of *passing* and *repassing* of priests that way, and Levites their attendants. They came *this way*, and saw the poor wounded man. It is probable that they heard his groans, and could not but perceive that if he were not helped he must quickly perish. The Levite not only saw him, but *came and looked on him, v.* 32. But they *passed by on the other side;* when they saw his case, they got as far off him as ever they could, as if they would have had a pretence to say, *Behold, we knew it not.* It is sad when those who should be examples of charity are prodigies of cruelty, and when those who should, by displaying the mercies of God, open the bowels of compassion in others, shut up their own.

[3.] How he was *succoured* and *relieved* by a *stranger*, a *certain Samaritan*, of that nation which of all others the Jews most despised and detested and would have no dealings with. This man had some humanity in him, *v.* 33. The priest had his heart hardened against one of *his own people*, but the Samaritan had his opened towards one of *another* people. *When he saw him he had compassion on him*, and never took into consideration what country he was of. Though he was a Jew, he was a man, and a man in *misery*, and the Samaritan has learned to honour all men; he knows not how soon this poor man's case may be his own, and therefore pities him, as he himself would desire and expect to be pitied in the like case. That such great love should be found in a Samaritan was perhaps thought as wonderful as that great faith which Christ admired in a Roman, and in a woman of Canaan; but really it was not so, for pity is the work of a man, but faith is the work of divine *grace*. The *compassion* of this Samaritan was not an idle compassion; he did not think it enough to say, " Be healed, be helped " (Jam. ii. 16); but, when he *drew out his soul*, he *reached forth his hand* also to this poor *needy* creature, Isa. lviii. 7, 10; Prov. xxxi. 20. See how friendly this good Samaritan was. *First*, He *went to* the poor man, whom the priest and Levite kept at a distance from; he enquired, no doubt, how he came into this deplorable condition, and condoled with him. *Secondly*, He did the surgeon's part, for want of a better. He *bound up his wounds*, making use of his own linen, it is likely, for that purpose; and poured *in oil and wine*, which perhaps he had with him; wine to wash the wound, and oil to mollify it, and close it up. He did all he could to ease the pain, and prevent the peril, of his wounds, as one whose heart bled with them. *Thirdly*, He *set him on his own beast*, and went on foot himself, and *brought him to an inn*. A great mercy it is to have inns upon the road, where we may be furnished for our money with all conveniences for food and rest. Perhaps the Samaritan, if he had not met with this hindrance, would have got that night to his journey's end; but, in compassion to that poor man, he takes up short at an inn. Some think that the priest and Levite pretended they could not stay to help the poor man, because they were in haste to go and attend the temple-service at Jerusalem. We suppose this Samaritan went upon business; but he understood that both his own business and God's sacrifice too must give place to such an act of mercy as this. *Fourthly,* He *took care of him* in the inn, got him to bed, had food for him that was proper, and due attendance, and, it may be, prayed with him. Nay, *Fifthly,* As if he had been his own child, or one he was obliged to look after, when he left him next morning, he left money with the landlord, to be laid out for his use, and passed his word for what he should spend more. *Twopence* of their money was about fifteen pence of ours, which, according to the rate of things then, would go a great way; however, here it was an earnest of satisfaction to the full of all demands. All this was kind and generous, and as much as one could have expected from a friend or a brother; and yet here it is done by a stranger and foreigner.

Now this parable is applicable to another purpose than that for which it was intended; and does excellently set forth the kindness and love of God our Saviour towards sinful miserable man. We were like this poor distressed traveller. Satan, our enemy, had *robbed* us, *stripped* us, *wounded* us; such is the mischief that sin hath done us. We were by nature more than *half dead,* twice dead, in trespasses and sins; utterly unable to help ourselves, for we were without strength. The law of Moses, like the priest and Levite, the ministers of the law, *looks upon us,* but has no compassion on us, gives us no relief, *passes by on the other side,* as having neither pity nor power to help us; but then comes the blessed Jesus, that good Samaritan (and they said of him, by way of reproach, *he is a Samaritan*), he has compassion on us, he binds up our bleeding wounds (Ps. cxlvii. 3; Isa. lxi. 1), pours in, not *oil and wine,* but that which is infinitely more precious, *his own blood.* He takes care of us, and bids us put all the expenses of our cure upon his account; and all this though he was none of us, till he was pleased by his voluntary condescension to make himself so, but infinitely above us. This magnifies the riches of his love, and obliges us all to say, "How much are we indebted, and what shall we render?"

(2.) The application of the parable. [1.] The truth contained in it is extorted from the lawyer's own mouth. "Now tell me," saith Christ, "*which of these three was neighbour to him that fell among thieves* (*v.* 36), the priest, the Levite, or the Samaritan? Which of these did the neighbour's part?" To this the lawyer would not answer, as he ought to have done, "Doubtless, the Samaritan was;" but, "*He that showed mercy on him;* doubtless, he was a good neighbour to him, and very neighbourly, and I cannot but say that it was a good work thus to save an honest Jew from perishing." [2.] The duty inferred from it is pressed home upon the lawyer's own conscience: *Go, and do thou likewise.* The duty of relations is mutual and reciprocal; the titles of friends, brethren, neighbours, are, as Grotius here speaks, τῶν πρός τι—*equally binding on both sides:* if one side be bound, the other cannot be loose, as is agreed in all contracts. If a Samaritan does well that helps a distressed Jew, certainly a Jew does not well if he refuses in like manner to help a distressed Samaritan. *Petimusque damusque vicissim—These kind offices are to be reciprocated.* "And therefore *go thou* and do as the Samaritan did, whenever occasion offers: show mercy to those that need thy help, and do it freely, and with concern and compassion, though they be not of thy own nation and thy own profession, or of thy own opinion and communion in religion. Let thy charity be thus extensive, before thou boastest of having conformed thyself to that great commandment of *loving thy neighbour.*" This lawyer valued himself much upon his learning and his knowledge of the laws, and in that he thought to have puzzled Christ himself; but Christ sends him to school to a Samaritan, to learn his duty: "Go, and do like him." Note, It is the duty of every one of us, in our places, and according to our ability, to succour, help, and relieve all that are in distress and necessity, and of lawyers particularly; and herein we must study to excel many that are proud of their being priests and Levites.

38 Now it came to pass, as they
went, that he entered into a certain
village: and a certain woman named
Martha received him into her house.
39 And she had a sister called Mary,
which also sat at Jesus' feet, and heard
his word. 40 But Martha was cumbered about much serving, and came
to him, and said, Lord, dost thou not
care that my sister hath left me to
serve alone? bid her therefore that
she help me. 41 And Jesus answered
and said unto her, Martha, Martha,
thou art careful and troubled about
many things: 42 But one thing is
needful: and Mary hath chosen that
good part, which shall not be taken
away from her.

We may observe in this story,

I. The entertainment which Martha gave to Christ and his disciples at her house, *v.* 38. Observe,

1. Christ's coming to the village where Martha lived: *As they went* (Christ and his disciples together), he and they with him *entered into a certain village.* This village was *Bethany*, nigh to Jerusalem, whither Christ was now going up, and he took this in his way. Note (1.) Our Lord Jesus went about doing good (Acts x. 38), scattering his benign beams and influences as the true light of the world. (2.) Wherever Christ went his disciples went along with him. (3.) Christ honoured the country-villages with his presence and favour, and not the great and populous cities only; for, as he *chose privacy*, so he *countenanced poverty*.

2. His reception at Martha's house: *A certain woman, named Martha, received him into her house*, and made him welcome, for she was the housekeeper. Note, (1.) Our Lord Jesus, when he was here upon earth, was so poor that he was necessitated to be beholden to his friends for a subsistence. Though he was Zion's King, he had no house of his own either in Jerusalem or near it. (2.) There were some who were Christ's particular friends, whom he loved more than his other friends, and them he visited most frequently. He *loved* this family (John xi. 5), and often invited himself to them. Christ's visits are the tokens of his love, John xiv. 23. (3.) There were those who kindly received Christ into their houses when he was here upon earth. It is called Martha's house, for, probably, she was a widow, and was the housekeeper. Though it was expensive to entertain Christ, for he did not come alone, but brought his disciples with him, yet she would not regard the cost of it. (How can we spend what we have better than in Christ's service!) Nay, though at this time it was grown dangerous to entertain him, especially so near Jerusalem, yet she cared not what hazard she ran for his name's sake. Though there were many that rejected him, and would not entertain him, yet there was one that would bid him welcome. Though Christ is every where spoken against, yet there is a remnant to whom he is dear, and who are dear to him.

II. The attendance which Mary, the sister of Martha, gave upon the word of Christ, *v.* 20. 1. She *heard his word.* It seems, our Lord Jesus, as soon as he came into Martha's house, even before entertainment was made for him, addressed himself to his great work of preaching the gospel. He presently took the chair with solemnity; for Mary sat to hear him, which intimates that it was a continued discourse. Note, A good sermon is never the worse for being preached in a house; and the visits of our friends should be so managed as to make them turn to a spiritual advantage. Mary, having this price put into her hands, sat herself to improve it, not knowing when she should have such another. Since Christ is forward to speak, we should be *swift to hear.* 2. She *sat* to hear, which denotes a close attention. Her mind was composed, and she resolved to abide by it: not to catch a word now and then, but to receive all that Christ delivered. She *sat at his feet,* as scholars at the feet of their tutors when they read their lectures; hence Paul is said to be *brought up at the feet of Gamaliel.* Our sitting at Christ's feet, when we hear his word, signifies a readiness to receive it, and a submission and entire resignation of ourselves to the guidance of it. We must either sit at Christ's feet or be made his footstool; but, if we sit with him at his feet now, we shall sit with him on his throne shortly.

III. The care of Martha about her domestic affairs: But Martha *was cumbered about much serving* (*v.* 40), and that was the reason why she was not where Mary was—sitting at Christ's feet, to hear his word. She was providing for the entertainment of Christ and those that came with him. Perhaps she had no notice before of his coming, and she was unprovided, but was in care to have every thing handsome upon this occasion; she had not such guests every day. Housekeepers know what care and bustle there must be when a great entertainment is to be made. Observe here,

1. Something *commendable,* which must not be overlooked. (1.) Here was a commendable *respect to our Lord Jesus;* for we have reason to think it was not for ostentation, but purely to testify her good-will to him, that she made this entertainment. Note, Those who truly love Christ will think that well bestowed that is laid out for his honour. (2.) Here was a commendable *care of her household affairs.* It appears, from the respect shown to this family among the Jews (John xi. 19), that they were persons of some quality and distinction; and yet Martha herself did not think it a disparagement to her to lay her hand even to the *service* of the family, when there was occasion for it. Note, It is the duty of those who have the charge of families to *look well to the ways of their household.* The affectation of state and the love of ease make many families neglected.

2. Here was something *culpable,* which we must take notice of too. (1.) She was for *much serving.* Her heart was upon it, to have a very sumptuous and splendid entertainment; great plenty, great variety, and great exactness, according to the fashion of the place. She was in care, περὶ πολλὴν διακονίαν—*concerning much attendance.* Note, It does not become the disciples of Christ to affect *much serving,* to affect varieties, dainties, and superfluities in eating and drinking; what need is there of *much serving,* when much less will serve? (2.) She was *cumbered* about it; περιεσπᾶτο—she was just *distracted* with it. Note, Whatever cares the providence of God casts upon us we must not be *cumbered* with them, nor be disquieted and perplexed by them. *Care* is good and duty; but *cumber* is sin

and folly. (2.) She was *then cumbered about much serving* when she should have been with her sister, sitting at Christ's feet to hear his word. Note, Worldly business is *then* a snare to us when it hinders us from serving God and getting good to our souls.

IV. The *complaint* which Martha made to Christ against her sister Mary, for not *assisting* her, upon this occasion, in the *business of the house* (*v.* 40): " *Lord, dost thou not care that my sister,* who is concerned as well as I in having things done well, *has left me to serve alone?* Therefore dismiss her from attending thee, and bid her come and help me." Now,

1. This complaint of Martha's may be considered as a *discovery* of her *worldliness:* it was the language of her inordinate care and cumber. She speaks as one in a mighty passion with her sister, else she would not have troubled Christ with the matter. Note, The inordinacy of worldly cares and pursuits is often the occasion of disturbance in families and of strife and contention among relations. Moreover, those that are eager upon the world themselves are apt to blame and censure those that are not so too; and while they justify themselves in their worldliness, and judge of others by their serviceableness to them in their worldly pursuits, they are ready to condemn those that addict themselves to the exercises of religion, as if they neglected the *main chance,* as they call it. Martha, being angry at her sister, appealed to Christ, and would have him say that she *did well to be angry. Lord, dost not thou care that my sister has left me to serve alone?* It should seem as if Christ had sometimes expressed himself tenderly concerned for her, and her ease and comfort, and would not have her go through so much toil and trouble, and she expected that he should now bid her sister take her share in it. When Martha was caring, she must have Mary, and Christ and all, to *care* too, or else she is not pleased. Note, Those are not always in the right that are most forward to appeal to God; we must therefore take heed, lest at any time we expect that Christ should espouse our unjust and groundless quarrels. The cares which he casts upon us we may cheerfully cast upon him, but not those which we foolishly draw upon ourselves. He will be the patron of the poor and injured, but not of the turbulent and injurious.

2. It may be considered as a discouragement of Mary's piety and devotion. Her sister should have *commended* her for it, should have told her that she was in the right; but, instead of this, she *condemns* her as wanting in her duty. Note, It is no strange thing for those that are zealous in religion to meet with hindrances and discouragements from those that are about them; not only with opposition from enemies, but with blame and censure from their friends. David's *fasting,* and his dancing *before the ark,* were turned *to his reproach.*

V. The reproof which Christ gave to Martha for her inordinate care, *v.* 41. She appealed to him, and he gives judgment against her: *Martha, Martha, thou art careful and troubled about many things,* whereas but *one thing is needful.*

1. He reproved her, though he was at this time her guest. Her fault was her over-solicitude to entertain him, and she expected he should justify her in it, yet he publicly checked her for it. Note, *As many as Christ loves he rebukes and chastens.* Even those that are dear to Christ, if any thing be amiss in them, shall be sure to hear of it. *Nevertheless I have something against thee.*

2. When he reproved her, he called her by her name, *Martha;* for reproofs are *then* most likely to do good when they are *particular,* applied to particular persons and cases, as Nathan's to David, *Thou art the man.* He repeated her name, *Martha, Martha;* he speaks as one in earnest, and deeply concerned for her welfare. Those that are *entangled* in the cares of this life are not easily *disentangled.* To them we must call again and again, *O earth, earth, earth, hear the word of the Lord.*

3. That which he reproved her for was her being *careful and troubled about many things.* He was not *pleased* that she should think to *please him* with a rich and splendid entertainment, and with perplexing herself to prepare it for him; whereas he would teach us, as not to be *sensual* in using such things, so not to be *selfish* in being willing that others should be *troubled,* no matter who or how many, so we may be gratified. Christ reproves her, both for the *intenseness* of her care (" Thou art *careful and troubled, divided* and *disturbed* by thy care"), and for the *extensiveness of it,* " about *many things;* thou dost *grasp* at many *enjoyments,* and so art troubled at many *disappointments.* Poor Martha, thou hast many things to fret at, and this puts thee out of humour, whereas less ado would serve." Note, Inordinate care or trouble about many things in this world is a common fault among Christ's disciples; it is very displeasing to Christ, and that for which they often come under the rebukes of Providence. If they fret for no just cause, it is just with him to order them something to fret at.

4. That which aggravated the sin and folly of her care was that *but one thing is needful.* It is a *low* construction which some put upon this, that, whereas Martha was in care to provide *many* dishes of meat, there was occasion but for one, one would be enough. *There is need but of one thing*—ἑνὸς δέ ἐστι χρεία. If we take it so, it furnishes us with a rule of *temperance,* not to affect varieties and dainties, but to be content to sit down to *one* dish of meat, to *half of one,* Prov. xxiii. 1—3. It is a *forced* construction which some of the ancients put upon it: *But oneness is needful,* in opposition to distractions. There is need of *one heart* to attend upon the word, not di-

vided and hurried to and fro, as Martha's was at this time. *The one thing needful* is certainly meant of that which Mary made her choice—*sitting at* Christ's feet, to hear his word. She was troubled about *many things,* when she should have applied herself to one; godliness *unites* the heart, which the world had *divided.* The *many things* she was troubled about were *needless,* while the *one thing* she neglected was *needful.* Martha's care and work were good in their proper season and place; but now she had something else to do, which was unspeakably more needful, and therefore should be done first, and most minded. She expected Christ to have blamed Mary for not doing as she did, but he blamed her for not doing as Mary did; and we are sure the *judgment of Christ* is *according to truth.* The day will come when Martha will wish she had set where Mary did.

VI. Christ's approbation and commendation of Mary for her serious piety: *Mary hath chosen the good part.* Mary said nothing in her own defence; but, since Martha has appealed to the Master, to him she is willing to refer it, and will abide by his award; and here we have it.

1. She had justly given the preference to that which best deserved it; for *one thing is needful,* this one thing that she has done, to give up herself to the guidance of Christ, and *receive the law* from his mouth. Note, Serious godliness is a *needful* thing, it is the *one thing needful;* for nothing without this will do us any real good in this world, and nothing but this will go with us into another world.

2. She had herein wisely done well for herself. Christ *justified Mary* against her sister's clamours. However we may be censured and condemned by men for our piety and zeal, our Lord Jesus will take our part: *But thou shalt answer, Lord, for me.* Let us not then condemn the pious zeal of any, lest we set Christ *against us;* and let us never be discouraged if we be censured for our pious zeal, for we have Christ for us. Note, Sooner or later, Mary's choice will be justified, and all those who make that choice, and abide by it. But this was not all; he *applauded* her for her wisdom: *She hath chosen the good part;* for she chose to be with Christ, to take her part with him; she chose the better business, and the better happiness, and took a better way of *honouring* Christ and of *pleasing* him, by receiving his word into her heart, than Martha did by providing for his entertainment in her house. Note, (1.) A *part with Christ* is a *good part;* it is a part for the soul and eternity, the part Christ gives to his favourites (John xiii. 8), who are partakers *of Christ* (Heb. iii. 14), and partakers *with Christ,* Rom. viii. 17. (2.) It is a part that shall *never be taken away from those that have it.* A portion in this life will certainly be *taken away* from us, at the furthest, when we shall be taken away from it; but *nothing shall separate us from the love of Christ,* and our part in that love. Men and devils *cannot* take it away from us, and God and Christ *will not.* (3.) It is the wisdom and duty of every one of us to choose this *good part,* to choose the service of God for our business, and the favour of God for our happiness, and an interest in Christ, in order to both. In particular cases we must choose that which has a tendency to religion, and reckon that best for us that is best for our souls. Mary was at her choice whether she would partake with Martha in her care, and get the reputation of a fine *housekeeper,* or sit at the feet of Christ and approve herself a *zealous disciple;* and, by her choice in this particular, Christ judges of her general choice. (4.) Those who *choose this good part* shall not only have what they choose, but shall have their choice commended in the great day.

CHAP. XI.

In this chapter, I. Christ teaches his disciples to pray, and quickens and encourages them to be frequent, instant, and importunate in prayer, ver. 1—13. II. He fully answers the blasphemous imputation of the Pharisees, who charged him with casting out devils by virtue of a compact and confederacy with Beelzebub, the prince of the devils, and shows the absurdity and wickedness of it, ver. 14—26. III. He shows the honour of obedient disciples to be greater than that of his own mother, ver. 27, 28. IV. He upbraids the men of that generation for their infidelity and obstinacy, notwithstanding all the means of conviction offered to them, ver. 29—36. V. He severely reproves the Pharisees and lawyers for their hypocrisy, their pride, their oppressing the consciences of those that submitted to them, and their hating and persecuting those that witnessed against their wickedness, ver. 37—54.

AND it came to pass, that, as he
was praying in a certain place,
when he ceased, one of his disciples
said unto him, Lord, teach us to pray,
as John also taught his disciples. 2
And he said unto them, When ye
pray, say, Our Father which art in
heaven, Hallowed be thy name. Thy
kingdom come. Thy will be done, as
in heaven, so in earth. 3 Give us
day by day our daily bread. 4 And
forgive us our sins; for we also forgive every one that is indebted to us.
And lead us not into temptation; but
deliver us from evil. 5 And he said
unto them, Which of you shall have
a friend, and shall go unto him at
midnight, and say unto him, Friend,
lend me three loaves; 6 For a friend
of mine in his journey is come to me,
and I have nothing to set before him?
7 And he from within shall answer
and say, Trouble me not: the door
is now shut, and my children are with
me in bed; I cannot rise and give
thee. 8 I say unto you, Though he
will not rise and give him, because he
is his friend, yet because of his importunity he will rise and give him as

many as he needeth. 9 And I say
unto you, Ask, and it shall be given
you; seek, and ye shall find; knock,
and it shall be opened unto you. 10
For every one that asketh receiveth;
and he that seeketh findeth; and to
him that knocketh it shall be opened.
11 If a son shall ask bread of any
of you that is a father, will he give
him a stone? or if *he ask* a fish, will
he for a fish give him a serpent? 12
Or if he shall ask an egg, will he offer
him a scorpion? 13 If ye then, being
evil, know how to give good gifts unto
your children: how much more shall
your heavenly Father give the Holy
Spirit to them that ask him?

Prayer is one of the great laws of natural religion. That man is a brute, is a monster, that never prays, that never gives glory to his Maker, nor feels his favour, nor owns his dependence upon him. One great design therefore of Christianity is to *assist us in prayer*, to enforce the duty upon us, to instruct us in it, and encourage us to expect advantage by it. Now here,

I. We find Christ himself *praying in a certain place*, probably where he used to pray, *v.* 1. As God, he was *prayed to;* as man, he *prayed;* and, though he was a Son, yet learned he this obedience. This evangelist has taken particular notice of Christ's *praying often*, more than any other of the evangelists: when he was baptized (*ch.* iii. 21), he was *praying;* he *withdrew into the wilderness, and prayed* (*ch.* v. 16); he *went out into a mountain to pray, and continued all night in prayer* (*ch.* vi. 12); he was *alone praying* (*ch.* ix. 18); soon after, he *went up into a mountain to pray*, and *as he prayed he was transfigured* (*ch.* ix. 28, 29); and here he was *praying in a certain place.* Thus, like a genuine son of David, he *gave himself unto prayer*, Ps. cix. 4. Whether Christ was now *alone* praying, and the disciples only knew that he was so, or whether he prayed with them, is uncertain; it is most probable that they were joining with him.

II. His disciples applied themselves to him for direction in prayer. When he was praying, they asked, *Lord, teach us to pray.* Note, The gifts and graces of others should excite us to covet earnestly the same. Their zeal should provoke us to a holy imitation and emulation; why should not we do as well as they? Observe, They came to him with this request, *when he ceased;* for they would not disturb him when he was at prayer, no, not with this good motion. Every thing is beautiful in its season. *One of his disciples*, in the name of the rest, and perhaps by their appointment, said, *Lord, teach us.* Note, Though Christ is *apt to teach*, yet he will for this be enquired of, and his disciples must attend him for instruction.

Now, 1. Their request is, "*Lord, teach us to pray;* give us a rule or model by which to go in praying, and put words into our mouths." Note, It becomes the disciples of Christ to apply themselves to him for instruction in prayer. *Lord, teach us to pray*, is itself a good prayer, and a very needful one, for it is a hard thing to *pray well;* and it is Jesus Christ only that can *teach us*, by his word and Spirit, *how to pray.* "Lord, teach me what it is to pray; Lord, excite and quicken me to the duty; Lord, direct me what to pray for; Lord, give me praying graces, that I may serve God acceptably in prayer; Lord, teach me to pray in proper words; give me a mouth and wisdom in prayer, that I may speak as I ought; *teach me what I shall say.*"

2. Their plea is, "*As John also taught his disciples.* He took care to instruct his disciples in this necessary duty, and we would be taught as they were, for we have a better Master than they had." Dr. Lightfoot's notion of this is, That whereas the Jews' prayers were generally adorations, and praises of God, and doxologies, John taught his disciples such prayers as were more filled up with petitions and requests; for it is said of them that they did δεήσεις ποιοῦνται—*make prayers, ch.* v. 33. The word signifies such prayers as are properly petitionary. "Now, Lord, teach us this, to be added to those benedictions of the name of God which we have been accustomed to from our childhood." According to this sense, Christ did there teach them a prayer consisting wholly of petitions, and even omitting the doxology which had been affixed; and the *Amen*, which was usually said in the *giving of thanks* (1 Cor. xiv. 16), and in the Psalms, is added to doxologies only. This disciple needed not to have urged John Baptist's example: Christ was more ready to teach than ever John Baptist was, and particularly taught to pray better than John did, or could, teach his disciples.

III. Christ gave them direction, much the same as he had given them before in his sermon upon the mount, Matt. vi. 9, &c. We cannot think that they had forgotten it, but they ought to have had further and fuller instructions, and he did not, as yet, think fit to give them any; when the Spirit should be poured out upon them from on high, they would find all their requests couched in these few words, and would be able, in words of their own, to expatiate and enlarge upon them. In Matthew he had directed them to pray *after this manner;* here, *When ye pray, say;* which intimates that the Lord's prayer was intended to be used both as a form of prayer and a directory.

1. There are some differences between the Lord's prayer in Matthew and in Luke, by which it appears that it was not the design of

Christ that we should be *tied up* to these very words, for then there would have been no variation. Here is one difference in the translation only, which ought not to have been, when there is none in the original, and that is in the third petition: *As in heaven, so in earth;* whereas the words are the very same, and in the same order, as in Matthew. But there is a difference in the fourth petition. In Matthew we pray, "Give us daily bread *this* day:" here, "Give it us *day by day*—καθ' ἡμέραν. *Day by day;* that is, "Give us *each day* the bread which our bodies require, as they call for it:" not, "Give us *this day* bread for many days to come;" but as the Israelites had manna, "Let us have bread *to-day* for *to-day*, and to-*morrow* for to-*morrow;* for thus we may be kept in a *continual dependence* upon God, as children upon their parents, and may have our mercies fresh from his hand daily, and may find ourselves under *fresh* obligations to do the work of every day in the day, according as the *duty of the day requires*, because we have from God the supplies of every day in the day, according as the *necessity of the day requires*. Here is likewise some difference in the fifth petition. In Matthew it is, *Forgive us our debts*, as we forgive: here it is, *Forgive us our sins;* which proves that our sins are our debts. *For we forgive;* not that our forgiving those that have offended us can *merit* pardon from God, or be an inducement to him to forgive us (he forgives for his own name's sake, and his Son's sake); but this is a very necessary qualification for forgiveness, and, if God have wrought it in us, we may plead that work of his grace for the enforcing of our petitions for the pardon of our sins: "Lord, forgive us, for thou hast thyself inclined us to forgive others." There is another addition here; we plead not only in general, We forgive *our debtors*, but in particular, "We profess *to forgive every one that is indebted to us*, without exception. We so *forgive our debtors* as not to bear malice or ill-will to any, but true love to all, without any exception whatsoever." Here also the doxology in the close is wholly omitted, and the *Amen;* for Christ would leave them at liberty to use that or any other doxology fetched out of David's psalms; or, rather, he left a vacuum here, to be filled up by a doxology more peculiar to the Christian institutes, ascribing glory to *Father, Son, and Holy Ghost*.

2. Yet it is, for substance, the same; and we shall therefore here only gather up some general lessons from it.

(1.) That in prayer we ought to come to God as children to *a Father*, a common Father to us and *all mankind*, but in a peculiar manner a Father to all the disciples of Jesus Christ. Let us therefore in our requests, both for others and for ourselves, come to him with a humble boldness, confiding in his power and goodness.

(2.) That at the same time, and in the same petitions, which we address to God for *ourselves*, we should take in with us *all the children of men*, as God's creatures and our fellow-creatures. A rooted principle of *catholic charity*, and of *Christian sanctified humanity*, should go along with us, and dictate to us throughout this prayer, which is so worded as to be accommodated to that noble principle.

(3.) That in order to the confirming of the habit of heavenly-mindedness in us, which ought to actuate and govern us in the whole course of our conversation, we should, in all our devotions, with an eye of faith look *heavenward*, and view the God we pray to as our Father *in heaven*, that we may make the *upper world* more familiar to us, and may ourselves become better prepared for the future state.

(4.) That in prayer, as well as in the tenour of our lives, we must *seek first the kingdom of God and the righteousness thereof*, by ascribing honour to his name, his *holy* name, and power to his government, both that of his providence in the world and that of his grace in the church. O that both the one and the other may be more manifested, and we and others more manifestly brought into subjection to both!

(5.) That the *principles* and *practices* of the *upper* world, the *unseen* world (which therefore by *faith* only we are *apprized of*), are the *great original—the* ἀρχέτυπον, to which we should desire that the principles and practices of this *lower* world, both in others and in ourselves, may be more conformable. Those words, *As in heaven, so on earth*, refer to all the first three petitions: "Father, let *thy name be sanctified* and *glorified*, and thy kingdom prevail, and thy will be done on this earth that is now alienated from thy service, as it is in yonder heaven that is entirely devoted to thy service."

(6.) That those who faithfully and sincerely mind the kingdom of God, and the righteousness thereof, may humbly hope that *all other things*, as far as to Infinite Wisdom seems good, *shall be added to them*, and they may in faith pray for them. If our first chief desire and care be that God's name may be sanctified, his kingdom come, and his will be done, we may then come boldly to the throne of grace for our *daily bread*, which will *then* be sanctified to us when we are sanctified to God, and God is sanctified by us.

(7.) That in our prayers for temporal blessings we must *moderate* our desires, and confine them to a *competency*. The expression here used of *day by day* is the very same with our *daily bread;* and therefore some think that we must look for another signification of the word ἐπιούσιοσ than that of *daily*, which we give it, and that it means our *necessary* bread, that bread that is *suited* to the cravings of our nature, the fruit that is brought out of the earth for our bodies that are made of the earth and are earthly, Ps. civ. 14.

(8.) That sins are debts which we are daily contracting, and which therefore we should every day pray for the forgiveness of. We are not only going behind with our rent every day by *omissions* of duty and in duty, but are daily incurring the penalty of the law, as well as the forfeiture of our bond, by our *commissions.* Every day adds to the score of our guilt, and it is a miracle of mercy that we have so much encouragement given us to come every day to the throne of grace, to pray for the pardon of our sins of daily infirmity. God *multiplies to pardon* beyond seventy times seven.

(9.) That we have no reason to expect, nor can with any confidence pray, that God would forgive our sins against him, if we do not *sincerely,* and from a truly Christian principle of *charity,* forgive those that have at any time affronted us or been injurious to us. Though the *words of our mouth* be even *this* prayer to God, if the meditation of our heart at the same time be, as often it is, malice and revenge to our brethren, we are not accepted, nor can we expect an answer of peace.

(10.) That temptations to sin should be as much dreaded and deprecated by us as ruin by sin; and it should be as much our care and prayer to get the power of sin broken in us as to get the guilt of sin removed from us; and though temptation may be a charming, fawning, flattering thing, we must be as earnest with God that we may not be led into it as that we may not be led by that to sin, and by sin to ruin.

(11.) That God is to be depended upon, and sought unto, for our deliverance *from all evil;* and we should pray, not only that we may not be left to ourselves to run into evil, but that we may not be left to Satan to bring evil upon us. Dr. Lightfoot understands it of being delivered *from the evil one,* that is, the devil, and suggests that we should pray particularly against the apparitions of the devil and his possessions. The disciples were employed to *cast out devils,* and therefore were concerned to pray that they might be guarded against the particular spite he would always be sure to have against them.

IV. He stirs up and encourages importunity, fervency, and constancy, in prayer, by showing,

1. That importunity will go far in our dealings with men, *v.* 5—8. Suppose a man, upon a sudden emergency, goes to borrow a loaf or two of bread of a neighbour, at an unseasonable time of night, not for himself, but for his friend that came unexpectedly to him. His neighbour will be loth to accommodate him, for he has wakened him with his knocking, and put him out of humour, and he has a great deal to say in his excuse. The door is shut and locked, his children are asleep in bed, in the same room with him, and, if he make a noise, he shall disturb them. His servants are asleep, and he cannot make them hear; and, for his own part, he shall catch cold if he rise to give him. But his neighbour will have no nay, and therefore he continues *knocking* still, and tells him he will do so till he has what he comes for; so that he must give it to him, to be rid of him: *He will rise, and give him as many as he needs, because of his importunity.* He speaks this parable with the same intent that he speaks that in *ch.* xviii. 1: *That men ought always to pray, and not to faint.* Not that God can be wrought upon by importunity; we cannot be troublesome to him, nor by being so change his counsels. We prevail with men by importunity because they are *displeased* with it, but with God because he is *pleased* with it. Now this similitude may be of use to us,

(1.) To *direct* us in prayer. [1.] We must come to God with *boldness* and *confidence* for what we need, as a man does to the house of his neighbour or friend, who, he knows, loves him, and is inclined to be kind to him. [2.] We must come for *bread,* for that which is *needful,* and which we cannot be without. [3.] We must come to him by prayer *for others* as well as *for ourselves.* This man did not come for bread for himself, but for his friend. The Lord *accepted Job,* when he prayed for his friends, Job xlii. 10. We cannot come to God upon a more pleasing errand than when we come to him for grace to enable us to do good, to *feed many* with *our lips,* to entertain and edify those that come to us. [4.] We may come with the more boldness to God in a strait, if it be a strait that we have not brought ourselves into by our own folly and carelessness, but Providence has led us into it. This man would not have wanted bread if his friend had not come in *unexpectedly.* The care which Providence casts upon us, we may with cheerfulness cast back upon Providence. [5.] We ought to *continue instant* in prayer, and watch in the same with all perseverance.

(2.) To *encourage* us in prayer. If importunity could prevail thus with *a man* who was angry at it, much more with a God who is infinitely more kind and ready to do good *to us* than we are *to one another,* and is not angry at our importunity, but accepts it, especially when it is for spiritual mercies that we are importunate. If he do not answer our prayers presently, yet he will in due time, if we continue to pray.

2. That God has promised to give us what we ask of him. We have not only the goodness of nature to take comfort from, but the word which he has spoken (*v.* 9, 10): "*Ask, and it shall be given you;* either the thing itself you shall ask or that which is equivalent; either the thorn in the flesh removed, or grace sufficient given in."—We had this before, Matt. vii. 7, 8. *I say unto you.* We have it from Christ's own mouth, who knows his Father's mind, and in whom all promises are yea and amen. We must not only *ask,* but we must *seek,* in the use of means, must second our prayers with our endeavours; and, in *asking* and *seeking,* we must continue

pressing, still knocking at the same door, and we shall at length prevail, not only by our prayers in concert, but by our particular prayers: *Every one that asketh receiveth,* even the meanest saint that asks in faith. *This poor man cried, and the Lord heard him,* Ps. xxxiv. 6. When we ask of God those things which Christ has here directed us to ask, that his name may be sanctified, that his kingdom may come, and his will be done, in these requests we must be importunate, must *never hold our peace day nor night;* we must not *keep silence,* nor *give God any rest, until he establish, until he make Jerusalem a praise in the earth,* Isa. lxii. 6, 7.

V. He gives us both instruction and encouragement in prayer from the consideration of our relation to God as a Father. Here is,

1. An *appeal* to the *bowels* of *earthly fathers:* "Let any of you that *is a father,* and knows the heart of a father, a father's affection to a child and care for a child, tell me, if his son *ask bread* for his breakfast, *will he give him a stone* to breakfast on? *If he ask a fish* for his dinner (when it may be a fish-day), *will he for a fish give him a serpent,* that will poison and sting him? Or, *if he shall ask an egg* for his supper (an egg and to bed), *will he offer him a scorpion?* You know you could not be so unnatural to your own children," *v.* 11, 12.

2. An *application* of this to the *blessings* of our *heavenly Father* (*v.* 13): *If ye then, being evil,* give, and know how to *give, good gifts to your children, much more shall God give you the Spirit.* He shall give *good things;* so it is in Matthew. Observe,

(1.) The direction he gives us what to *pray for.* We must ask for the *Holy Spirit,* not only as necessary in order to our *praying well,* but as inclusive of all the good things we are to pray for; we need no more to make us happy, for the Spirit is the worker of spiritual life, and the earnest of eternal life. Note, The gift of the Holy Ghost is a gift we are every one of us concerned earnestly and constantly to pray for.

(2.) The *encouragement* he gives us to hope that we shall speed in this prayer: *Your heavenly Father will give.* It is *in his power* to give the Spirit; he has all good things to bestow, wrapped up in that one; but that is not all, it is *in his promise,* the gift of *the Holy Ghost* is in the covenant, Acts ii. 33, 38, and it is here inferred from parents' readiness to *supply* their children's *needs,* and *gratify* their *desires,* when they are natural and proper. If the child ask for a *serpent,* or a *scorpion,* the father, in kindness, will deny him, but not if he ask for what is *needful,* and will be *nourishing.* When God's children ask for the Spirit, they do, in effect, ask for *bread;* for the Spirit is the staff of life; nay, he is the Author of the soul's life. If our earthly parents, though *evil,* be yet so kind, if they, though *weak,* be yet so *knowing,* that they not only give, but give with discretion, give what is best, in the best manner and time, much more will our *heavenly Father,* who infinitely excels the fathers of our flesh both in wisdom and goodness, give us his *Holy Spirit.* If earthly parents be willing to lay out for the education of their children, to whom they design to leave their estates, much more will our heavenly Father give the spirit of sons to all those whom he has predestinated to the inheritance of sons.

14 And he was casting out a devil,
and it was dumb. And it came to
pass, when the devil was gone out,
the dumb spake; and the people wondered. 15 But some of them said,
He casteth out devils through Beelzebub the chief of the devils. 16 And
others, tempting *him,* sought of him
a sign from heaven. 17 But he,
knowing their thoughts, said unto
them, Every kingdom divided against
itself is brought to desolation; and a
house *divided* against a house falleth.
18 If Satan also be divided against
himself, how shall his kingdom stand?
because ye say that I cast out devils
through Beelzebub. 19 And if I by
Beelzebub cast out devils, by whom
do your sons cast *them* out? therefore shall they be your judges. 20
But if I with the finger of God cast
out devils, no doubt the kingdom of
God is come upon you. 21 When a
strong man armed keepeth his palace,
his goods are in peace: 22 But when
a stronger than he shall come upon
him and overcome him, he taketh
from him all his armour wherein he
trusted, and divideth his spoils. 23
He that is not with me is against me:
and he that gathereth not with me
scattereth. 24 When the unclean
spirit is gone out of a man, he walketh
through dry places, seeking rest; and
finding none, he saith, I will return
unto my house whence I came out.
25 And when he cometh, he findeth
it swept and garnished. 26 Then
goeth he, and taketh *to him* seven
other spirits more wicked than himself; and they enter in, and dwell
there: and the last *state* of that man
is worse than the first.

The substance of these verses we had in Matt. xii. 22, &c. Christ is here giving a general proof of his divine mission, by a particular proof of his power over Satan, his conquest of whom was an indication of his great design in coming into the world, which was, to *destroy the works of the devil.* Here too he gives an earnest of the success of that undertaking. He is here casting out *a devil* that made the poor possessed man *dumb:* in Matthew we are told that he was *blind* and *dumb.* When the devil was forced out by the word of Christ, the *dumb* spoke immediately, echoed to Christ's word, and the lips were opened to show forth his praise. Now,

I. Some were *affected* with this miracle. The people *wondered;* they admired the power of God, and especially that it should be exerted by the hand of one who made so small a figure, that one who did the work of the Messiah should have so little of that pomp of the Messiah which they expected.

II. Others were *offended* at it, and, to justify their infidelity, suggested that it was by virtue of a league with Beelzebub, the prince of the devils, that he did this, *v.* 15. It seems, in the devil's kingdom there are chiefs, which supposes that there are subalterns. Now they would have it *thought,* or *said* at least, that there was a correspondence settled between Christ and the devil, that the devil should have the advantage in the main and be victorious at last, but that in order hereto, in particular instances, he should yield Christ the advantage and retire by consent. Some, to *corroborate* this suggestion, and *confront* the evidence of Christ's miraculous power, challenged him to *give them a sign from heaven* (*v.* 16), to confirm his doctrine by some appearance in the *clouds,* such as was upon mount Sinai when the law was given; as if a *sign from heaven,* not disprovable by any sagacity of theirs, could not have been given them as well by a compact and collusion with *the prince of the power of the air, who works with power and lying wonders,* as the *casting out of a devil;* nay, that would not have been any present prejudice to his interest, which this manifestly was. Note, Obstinate infidelity will never be at a loss for something to say in its own excuse, though ever so frivolous and absurd. Now Christ here returns a full and direct answer to this cavil of theirs; in which he shows,

1. That it can by no means be imagined that such a subtle prince as Satan is should ever agree to measures that had such a direct tendency to his own overthrow, and the undermining of his own kingdom, *v.* 17, 18. What they objected they kept to themselves, afraid to speak it, lest it should be answered and baffled; but Jesus *knew their thoughts,* even when they industriously thought to conceal them, and he said, "You yourselves cannot but see the groundlessness, and consequently the spitefulness, of this charge; for it is an allowed maxim, confirmed by every day's experience, that no interest can stand that is divided against itself; not the more *public* interest of a *kingdom,* nor the *private* interest of a house or family; if either the one or the other be *divided against itself,* it cannot stand. Satan would herein act against himself; not only by the miracle which turned him out of possession of the bodies of people, but much more in the doctrine for the explication and confirmation of which the miracle was wrought, which had a direct tendency to the ruin of Satan's interest in the minds of men, by mortifying sin, and turning men to the service of God. Now, if Satan should thus be *divided against himself,* he would hasten his own overthrow, which you cannot suppose an enemy to do that acts so subtlely for his own establishment, and is so solicitous to have his kingdom stand."

2. That was a very partial ill-natured thing for them to impute that in him to a compact with Satan which yet they applauded and admired in others that were of their own nation (*v.* 19): "*By whom do your sons cast them out?* Some of your own *kindred,* as Jews, nay, and some of your own *followers,* as Pharisees, have undertaken, in the name of the God of Israel, to cast out devils, and they were never charged with such a hellish combination as I am charged with." Note, It is gross hypocrisy to *condemn* that in those who *reprove* us which yet we *allow* in those that *flatter* us.

3. That, in opposing the conviction of this miracle, they were enemies to themselves, stood in their own light, and put a bar in their own door, for they thrust from them the kingdom of God (*v.* 20): "*If I with the finger of God cast out devils,* as you may assure yourselves I do, *no doubt the kingdom of God is come upon you,* the kingdom of the Messiah offers itself and all its advantages to you, and, if you receive it not, it is at your peril." In Matthew it is *by the Spirit of God,* here *by the finger of God;* the Spirit is the *arm of the Lord,* Isa. liii. 1. His greatest and most mighty works were wrought by *his Spirit;* but, if the Spirit in this work is said to be the *finger of the Lord,* it perhaps may intimate how *easily* Christ did and could conquer Satan, even with the *finger of God,* the exerting of the divine power in a less and lower degree than in many other instances. He needed not make bare his *everlasting arm;* that roaring lion, when *he* pleases, is crushed, like a moth, with a touch of *a finger.* Perhaps here is an allusion to the acknowledgment of Pharaoh's magicians, when they were run aground (Exod. viii. 19): This is *the finger of God.* "Now if the *kingdom of God* be herein *come to you,* and you be found by those cavils and blasphemies fighting against it, it will come *upon you* as a victorious force which you cannot stand before."

4. That his casting out devils was really the destroying of them and their power, for it confirmed a doctrine which had a direct tendency to the ruining of his kingdom, *v.* 21, 22. Perhaps there had been some who had cast out the inferior devils by compact with Beelzebub their chief, but that was with-

out any real damage or prejudice to Satan and his kingdom, what he lost one way he gained another. The devil and such exorcists *played booty*, as we say, and, while the forlorn hope of his army *gave ground*, the main body thereby *gained ground;* the interest of Satan in the souls of men was not weakened by it in the least. But, when Christ cast out devils, he needed not do it by any compact with them, for he was *stronger than they*, and could do it *by force*, and did it so as to ruin Satan's power and blast his great design by that doctrine and that grace which break the power of sin, and so rout Satan's main body, take from him *all his armour*, and *divide his spoils*, which no one devil ever did to another or ever will. Now this is applicable to Christ's victories over Satan both in the world and in the hearts of particular persons, by that power which went along with the preaching of his gospel, and does still. And so we may observe here,

(1.) The miserable condition of an unconverted sinner. In his heart, which was fitted to be a habitation of God, the devil has his palace; and all the powers and faculties of the soul, being employed by him in the service of sin, are *his goods*. Note, [1.] The heart of every unconverted sinner is the *devil's palace*, where he *resides* and where he *rules; he works* in the *children of disobedience*. The heart is a *palace*, a noble dwelling; but the unsanctified heart is the *devil's palace*. His will is obeyed, his interests are served, and the militia is in his hands; he *usurps* the throne in the soul. [2.] The devil, as a *strong man armed, keeps* this palace, does all he can to secure it to himself, and to fortify it against Christ. All the prejudices with which he hardens men's hearts against truth and holiness are the *strong-holds* which he erects for the *keeping of his palace;* this palace is his *garrison*. [3.] There is a kind of *peace* in the palace of an unconverted soul, while the devil, as a *strong man armed*, keeps it. The sinner has a good opinion of himself, is very secure and merry, has no doubt concerning the goodness of his state nor any dread of the judgment to come; he flatters himself in his own eyes, and cries peace to himself. Before Christ appeared, all was quiet, because all *went one way;* but the preaching of the gospel disturbed the peace of the devil's palace.

(2.) The wonderful change that is made in conversion, which is Christ's victory over this usurper. *Satan* is a *strong man armed;* but our Lord Jesus is *stronger than he*, as God, as Mediator. *If we speak of strength, he is strong:* more are *with* us than *against us*. Observe, [1.] The manner of this victory: *He comes upon him* by surprise, when his *goods are in peace* and the devil thinks it is all *his own* for ever, and *overcomes* him. Note, The conversion of a soul to God is Christ's victory over the devil and his power in that soul, restoring the soul to its liberty, and recovering his own interest in it and dominion over it. [2.] The evidences of this victory. *First,* He *takes from him all his armour wherein he trusted.* The devil is a *confident* adversary; he *trusts* to his *armour*, as Pharaoh to his rivers (Ezek. xxix. 3): but Christ disarms him. When the power of sin and corruption in the soul is broken, when the mistakes are rectified, the eyes opened, the heart humbled and changed, and made serious and spiritual, then Satan's *armour* is *taken away. Secondly,* He *divides the spoils;* he *takes possession* of them for himself. All the endowments of mind and body, the estate, power, interest, which before were made use of in the service of sin and Satan, are now converted to Christ's service and employed for him; yet this is not all; he *makes a distribution* of them among his followers, and, having conquered Satan, gives to all believers the benefit of that victory. Hence Christ infers that, since the whole drift of his doctrine and miracles was to break the power of the devil, that great enemy of mankind, it was the duty of all to join with him and to follow his guidance, to receive his gospel and come heartily into the interests of it; for otherwise they would justly be reckoned as siding with the enemy (*v.* 23): *He that is not with me is against me.* Those therefore who rejected the doctrine of Christ, and slighted his miracles, were looked upon as adversaries to him, and in the devil's interest.

5. That there was a vast difference between the devil's *going out* by compact and his being *cast out* by compulsion. Those out of whom Christ *cast him* he never entered into again, for so was Christ's charge (Mark ix. 25); whereas, if he had *gone out*, whenever he saw fit he would have made a re-entry, for that is the way of the unclean spirit, when he voluntarily and with design *goes out of a man, v.* 24—26. The prince of the devils may *give leave*, nay, may *give order*, to his forces to retreat, or make a feint, to draw the poor deluded soul into an *ambush;* but Christ, as he gives a *total*, so he gives a *final*, defeat to the enemy. In this part of the argument he has a further intention, which is to represent the state of those who have had fair offers made them,—among whom, and in whom, God has begun to break the devil's power and overthrow his kingdom,—but they reject his counsel against themselves, and relapse into a state of subjection to Satan. Here we have,

(1.) The condition of a *formal hypocrite*, his *bright side* and his *dark side*. His heart still remains the *devil's house;* he calls it his own, and he retains his interest in it; and yet, [1.] The *unclean spirit is gone out*. He was not *driven out* by the power of converting grace; there was none of that *violence* which the kingdom of heaven suffers; but he *went out*, withdrew for a time, so that the man seemed not to be under the power of Satan as formerly, nor so followed with his temptations. Satan is *gone*, or has *turned himself into an angel of light.* [2.] The *house is swept* from common pollutions, by a forced confession of sin, as Pharaoh's,—a feigned contrition for it, as Ahab's,—and a partial reformation, as Herod's. There are those that have *escaped the pollutions of the world,* and yet are still under the power of the *god of this world,* 2 Pet. ii. 20. The house is *swept,* but it is not *washed;* and Christ hath said, *If I wash thee not, thou hast no part with me;* the house must be *washed,* or it is *none of his.* Sweeping takes off only the loose dirt, while the sin that *besets* the sinner, the beloved sin, is untouched. It is swept from the filth that lies open to the eye of the world, but it is not searched and ransacked for secret filthiness, Matt. xxiii. 25. It is *swept,* but the *leprosy is in the wall,* and will be till something more be done. [3.] The house is *garnished* with common gifts and graces. It is not *furnished* with any true grace, but *garnished* with the pictures of all graces. Simon Magus was *garnished* with faith, Balaam with good desires, Herod with a respect for John, the Pharisees with many external performances. It is garnished, but it is like a *potsherd covered with silver dross,* it is all paint and varnish, not real, not lasting. The house is *garnished,* but the property is not altered; it was never surrendered to Christ, nor inhabited by the Spirit. Let us therefore take heed of resting in that which a man may have and yet come short.

(2.) Here is the condition of a *final apostate,* into whom the devil returns after he had *gone out: Then goes he, and takes seven other spirits more wicked than himself* (*v.* 26); a certain number for an uncertain, as *seven devils* are said to be cast out of Mary Magdalene. *Seven wicked spirits* are opposed to the *seven spirits of God,* Rev. iii. 1. These are said to be more wicked than himself. It seems, even devils are not all alike wicked; probably, the degrees of their wickedness, now that they are *fallen,* are as the degrees of their holiness were while they stood. When the devil would do mischief most effectually, he employs those that are more mischievous than himself. These *enter in* without any difficulty or opposition; they are welcomed, and they *dwell there;* there they *work,* there they *rule;* and the *last state of that man is worse than the first.* Note, [1.] Hypocrisy is the high road to apostasy. If the heart remain in the interest of sin and Satan, the shows and shadows will *come to nothing;* those that have not set that right will not long be stedfast. Where secret haunts of sin are kept up, under the cloak of a visible profession, conscience is debauched, God is provoked to withdraw his restraining grace, and the *close* hypocrite commonly proves an *open* apostate, [2.] The last state of such is *worse than the first,* in respect both of sin and punishment. Apostates are usually the worst of men, the most vain and profligate, the most bold and daring; their consciences are seared, and their sins of all others the most aggravated. God often sets marks of his displeasure upon them in *this* world, and in the other world they will *receive the greater damnation.* Let us therefore hear, and fear, and hold fast our integrity.

27 And it came to pass, as he spake these things, a certain woman of the company lifted up her voice, and said unto him, Blessed *is* the womb that bare thee, and the paps which thou hast sucked. 28 But he said, Yea rather, blessed *are* they that hear the word of God, and keep it.

We had not this passage in the other evangelists, nor can we tack it, as Dr. Hammond does, to that of Christ's mother and brethren desiring to speak with him (for this evangelist also has related that in *ch.* viii. 19), but it contains an interruption much like that, and, like that, occasion is taken from it for instruction.

1. The applause which an affectionate, honest, well-meaning woman gave to our Lord Jesus, upon hearing his excellent discourses. While the scribes and Pharisees despised and blasphemed them, this good woman (and probably she was a person of some quality) admired them, and the wisdom and power with which he spoke: *As he spoke these things* (*v.* 27), with a convincing force and evidence, a *certain woman of the company* was so pleased to hear how he had confounded the Pharisees, and conquered them, and put them to shame, and cleared himself from their vile insinuations, that she could not forbear crying out, "*Blessed is the womb that bore thee.* What an admirable, what an excellent man is this! Surely never was there a greater or better born of a woman: happy the woman that has him for her son. I should have thought myself very happy to have been the mother of one that *speaks as never man spoke,* that has so much of the grace of heaven in him, and is so great a blessing to this earth." This was *well said,* as it expressed her high esteem of Christ, and that for the sake of his doctrine; and it was not amiss that it reflected honour upon the virgin Mary his mother, for it agreed with what she herself had said (*ch.* i. 48), *All generations shall call me blessed;* some even of this generation, bad as it was. Note, To all that believe the word of Christ the person of Christ is precious, and he is *an honour,* 1 Pet. ii. 7. Yet we must be careful, lest, as this good woman, we too much magnify the honour of his natural kindred, and so *know him after the flesh,* whereas we must now henceforth *know him so no more.*

2. The occasion which Christ took from this to pronounce *them* more happy who are his faithful and obedient followers than she was who bore and nursed him. He does not

deny what this woman said, nor refuse her respect to him and his mother; but leads her from this to that which was of higher consideration, and which more concerned her: *Yea, rather, blessed are they that hear the word of God, and keep it, v.* 28. He thinks them so; and his saying that they are so makes them so, and should make us of his mind. This is intended partly as a *check* to her, for doting so much upon his bodily presence and his human nature, partly as an *encouragement* to her to hope that she might be as happy as his own mother, whose happiness she was ready to envy, if she would *hear the word of God and keep it.* Note, Though it is a great privilege to hear the word of God, yet those only are truly blessed, that is, blessed of the Lord, that hear it and *keep* it, that keep it in memory, and keep to it as their way and rule.

29 And when the people were gathered thick together, he began to say,
This is an evil generation: they seek
a sign; and there shall no sign be
given it, but the sign of Jonas the
prophet. 30 For as Jonas was a sign
unto the Ninevites, so shall also the
Son of man be to this generation.
31 The queen of the south shall rise up
in the judgment with the men of this
generation, and condemn them: for
she came from the utmost parts of the
earth to hear the wisdom of Solomon;
and, behold, a greater than Solomon
is here. 32 The men of Nineve shall
rise up in the judgment with this generation, and shall condemn it: for
they repented at the preaching of
Jonas; and, behold, a greater than
Jonas *is* here. 33 No man, when he
hath lighted a candle, putteth *it* in a
secret place, neither under a bushel,
but on a candlestick, that they which
come in may see the light. 34 The
light of the body is the eye: therefore when thine eye is single, thy
whole body also is full of light; but
when *thine eye* is evil, thy body also
is full of darkness. 35 Take heed
therefore that the light which is in
thee be not darkness. 36 If thy whole
body therefore *be* full of light, having
no part dark, the whole shall be full
of light, as when the bright shining of
a candle doth give thee light.

Christ's discourse in these verses shows two things:—

I. What is the *sign* we may *expect* from God for the *confirmation* of our *faith*. The great and most convincing proof of Christ's being sent of God, and which they were yet to wait for, after the many signs that had been given them, was the resurrection of Christ from the dead. Here is,

1. A reproof to the people for demanding other signs than what had already been given them in great plenty: *The people were gathered thickly together* (*v.* 29), a vast crowd of them, expecting not so much to have their consciences informed by the doctrine of Christ as to have their curiosity gratified by his miracles. Christ knew what brought such a multitude together; they came *seeking a sign,* they came to gaze, to have something to talk of when they went home; and it is an *evil generation* which nothing will awaken and convince, no, not the most sensible demonstrations of divine power and goodness.

2. A promise that yet there should be *one sign* more given them, different from any that had yet been given them, even the *sign of Jonas the prophet,* which in Matthew is explained as meaning the *resurrection of Christ.* As Jonas being cast into the sea, and lying there three days, and then coming up alive and preaching repentance to the Ninevites, was a sign to them, upon which they turned from their evil way, so shall the death and resurrection of Christ, and the preaching of his gospel immediately after to the Gentile world, be the last warning to the Jewish nation. If they be provoked to a *holy jealousy* by this, well and good; but, if this do not work upon them, let them look for nothing but utter ruin: *The Son of man shall be a sign to this generation* (*v.* 30), a sign speaking to them, though a sign spoken against by them.

3. A warning to them to improve this sign; for it was at their peril if they did not. (1.) The *queen of Sheba* would *rise up in judgment against them,* and condemn *their unbelief, v.* 31. She was a stranger to the commonwealth of Israel, and yet so readily gave credit to the report she heard of the glories of a king of Israel, that, notwithstanding the prejudices we are apt to conceive against foreigners, she came from the uttermost parts of the earth to *hear his wisdom,* not only to satisfy her curiosity, but to inform her mind, especially in the knowledge of the true God and his worship, which is upon record, to her honour; and, behold, a *greater than Solomon is here,* πλεῖον Σολομῶντος—*more than a Solomon is here;* that is, says Dr. Hammond, more of wisdom and more heavenly divine doctrine than ever was in all Solomon's words or writings; and yet these wretched Jews will give no manner of regard to what Christ says to them, though he be in the midst of them. (2.) The Ninevites would rise up in judgment against them, and condemn their impenitency (*v.* 32): They *repented at the preaching of Jonas;* but here is preaching which far exceeds that of Jonas, is more powerful and awakening, and threat-

ens a much sorer ruin than that of Nineveh, and yet none are startled by it, to turn *from their evil way*, as the Ninevites did.

II. What is the *sign* that God *expects* from us for the *evidencing* of our faith, and that is the serious practice of that religion which we profess to believe, and a readiness to entertain all divine truths, when brought to us in their proper evidence. Now observe,

1. They had *the light* with all the advantage they could desire. For God, having *lighted the candle* of the gospel, did not put it in a *secret place*, or *under a bushel;* Christ did not preach in corners. The apostles were ordered to preach the gospel to every creature; and both Christ and his ministers, Wisdom and her maidens, cry in the *chief places of concourse, v.* 33. It is a great privilege that the light of the gospel is put on a *candlestick*, so that all that come in may *see it*, and may *see by it* where they are and whither they are going, and what is the true, and sure, and only way to happiness.

2. Having the *light*, their concern was to have the *sight*, or else to what purpose had they the light? Be the *object* ever so *clear*, if the *organ* be not *right*, we are never the better: *The light of the body is the eye* (*v.* 34), which receives the light of the candle when it is brought into the room. So the light of the soul is the understanding and judgment, and its power of discerning between good and evil, truth and falsehood. Now, according as this is, so the light of divine revelation is to us, and our benefit by it; it is a savour of life unto life, or of death unto death. (1.) If this eye of the soul be *single*, if it see *clear*, see things as they are, and judge impartially concerning them, if it aim at *truth* only, and seek it for its own sake, and have not any sinister by-looks and intentions, the *whole body*, that is, the whole soul, is *full of light*, it receives and entertains the gospel, which will bring along with it into the soul both *knowledge* and *joy*. This denotes the same thing with that of the good ground, *receiving the word* and *understanding* it. If our understanding admits the gospel in its full light, it fills the soul, and it has enough to *fill* it. And if the soul be thus *filled* with the light of the gospel, *having no part dark*,—if all its powers and faculties be subjected to the government and influence of the gospel, and none left unsanctified,—then *the whole soul shall be full of light*, full of holiness and comfort. *It was darkness* itself, but is now light in the Lord, *as when the bright shining of a candle doth give thee light, v.* 36. Note, The gospel will come into those souls whose doors and windows are thrown open to receive it; and where it comes it will bring light with it. But, (2.) If the *eye of the* soul be *evil*,—if the judgment be *bribed* and *biassed* by the corrupt and vicious dispositions of the mind, by pride and envy, by the love of the world and sensual pleasures,—if the understanding be *prejudiced* against divine truths, and resolved not to admit them, though brought with ever so convincing an evidence,—it is no wonder that the *whole body*, the whole soul, should be *full of darkness, v.* 34. How can they have instruction, information, direction, or comfort, from the gospel, that wilfully shut their eyes against it? and what hope is there of such? what remedy for them? The inference hence therefore is, *Take heed that the light which is in thee be not darkness, v.* 35. Take heed that the eye of the mind be not blinded by partiality, and prejudice, and sinful aims. Be sincere in your enquiries after truth, and ready to receive it in the light, and love, and power of it; and not as the men of *this generation* to whom Christ preached, who never sincerely *desired* to know God's will, nor *designed* to do it, and therefore no wonder that they *walked on in darkness*, wandered *endlessly*, and perished *eternally*.

37 And as he spake, a certain Pharisee besought him to dine with him:
and he went in, and sat down to meat.
38 And when the Pharisee saw *it*,
he marvelled that he had not first
washed before dinner. 39 And the
Lord said unto him, Now do ye Pharisees make clean the outside of the
cup and the platter; but your inward
part is full of ravening and wickedness. 40 *Ye* fools, did not he that
made that which is without make that
which is within also? 41 But rather
give alms of such things as ye have;
and, behold, all things are clean unto
you. 42 But woe unto you, Pharisees! for ye tithe mint and rue and
all manner of herbs, and pass over
judgment and the love of God: these
ought ye to have done, and not to
leave the other undone. 43 Woe
unto you, Pharisees! for ye love the
uppermost seats in the synagogues,
and greetings in the markets. 44 Woe
unto you, scribes and Pharisees, hypocrites! for ye are as graves which appear not, and the men that walk over
them are not aware *of them*. 45 Then
answered one of the lawyers, and said
unto him, Master, thus saying thou
reproachest us also. 46 And he said,
Woe unto you also, *ye* lawyers! for
ye lade men with burdens grievous to
be borne, and ye yourselves touch not
the burdens with one of your fingers.
47 Woe unto you! for ye build the
sepulchres of the prophets, and your

fathers killed them. 48 Truly ye bear
witness that ye allow the deeds of
your fathers: for they indeed killed
them, and ye build their sepulchres.
49 Therefore also said the wisdom of
God, I will send them prophets and
apostles, and *some* of them they shall
slay and persecute: 50 That the blood
of all the prophets, which was shed
from the foundation of the world, may
be required of this generation; 51
From the blood of Abel unto the blood
of Zacharias, which perished between
the altar and the temple: verily I say
unto you, It shall be required of this
generation. 52 Woe unto you, lawyers! for ye have taken away the key
of knowledge: ye enter not in yourselves, and them that were entering in
ye hindered. 53 And as he said these
things unto them, the scribes and the
Pharisees began to urge *him* vehemently, and to provoke him to speak
of many things: 54 Laying wait for
him, and seeking to catch something
out of his mouth, that they might
accuse him.

Christ here says many of those things to a Pharisee and his guests, in a *private* conversation at table, which he afterwards said in a *public* discourse in the temple (Matt. 23); for what he said in public and private was *of a piece.* He would not say that in a corner which he durst not repeat and stand to in the great congregation; nor would he give those reproofs to any sort of sinners in general which he durst not apply to them in particular as he met with them; for he was, and is, the *faithful Witness.* Here is,

I. Christ's going to dine with a Pharisee that very civilly invited him to his house (*v.* 37): *As he spoke,* even while he was speaking, a *certain Pharisee* interrupted him with a request to him to come and *dine with him,* to come *forthwith,* for it was dinner-time. We are willing to hope that the Pharisee was so well pleased with his discourse that he was willing to show him respect, and desirous to have more of his company, and therefore gave him this invitation and bade him truly welcome; and yet we have some cause to suspect that it was with an *ill design,* to break off his discourse to the people, and to have an opportunity of ensnaring him and getting something out of him which might serve for matter of accusation or reproach, *v.* 53, 54. We know not the mind of this Pharisee; but, whatever it was, Christ knew it: if he meant ill, he shall know Christ does not fear him; if well, he shall know Christ is willing to do him good: so *he went in, and sat down to meat.* Note, Christ's disciples must learn of him to be *conversable,* and not *morose.* Though we have need to be *cautious* what company we keep, yet we need not be *rigid,* nor must we therefore *go out of the world.*

II. The offence which the Pharisee took at Christ, as those of that sort had sometimes done at the disciples of Christ, for not *washing before dinner; v.* 38. He wondered that a man of his sanctity, a prophet, a man of so much devotion, and such a strict conversation, should sit down to meat, and not first *wash his hands,* especially being newly come out of a mixed company, and there being in the Pharisee's dining-room, no doubt, all accommodations set ready for it, so that he need not fear being *troublesome;* and the Pharisee himself and all his guests, no doubt, *washing,* so that he could not be *singular;* what, and yet not wash? What harm had it been if he had washed? Was it not strictly commanded by the canons of their church? It was so, and *therefore* Christ would not do it, because he would witness against their assuming a power to impose that as a matter of religion which *God commanded them not.* The ceremonial law consisted in *divers washings,* but this was none of them, and therefore Christ would not practise it, no not in *complaisance* to the Pharisee who invited him, nor though he knew that offence would be taken at his omitting it.

III. The sharp reproof which Christ, upon this occasion, gave to the Pharisees, without begging pardon even of the Pharisee whose guest he now was; for we must not flatter our best friends in any evil thing.

1. He reproves them for placing religion so much in those instances of it which are only external, and fall under the eye of man, while those were not only *postponed,* but quite *expunged,* which respect the soul, and fall under the eye of God, *v.* 39, 40. Now observe here, (1.) The absurdity they were guilty of: "*You Pharisees make clean the outside* only, you wash your hands with water, but do not *wash your hearts from wickedness;* these are full of covetousness and malice, *covetousness* of men's goods, and malice against good men." Those can never be reckoned *cleanly* servants that wash only the *outside of the cup* out of which their master drinks, or *the platter* out of which he eats, and take no care to make clean the *inside,* the filth of which immediately *affects* the meat or drink. The frame or temper of the mind in every religious service is as the *inside* of the cup and platter; the impurity of this *infects* the services, and therefore to keep ourselves free from scandalous enormities, and yet to live under the dominion of spiritual wickedness, is as great an affront to God as it would be for a servant to give the cup into his master's hand, clean wiped from all the dust on the outside, but *within* full of cobwebs and spiders. *Ravening*

and *wickedness,* that is, *reigning worldliness* and *reigning spitefulness,* which men think they can find some cloak and cover for, are the dangerous damning sins of many who have made the *outside of the cup* clean from the more gross, and scandalous, and inexcusable sins of whoredom and drunkenness. (2.) A particular instance of the absurdity of it: "*Ye fools, did not he that made that which is without make that which is within also? v.* 40. Did not that God who in the law of Moses appointed divers ceremonial washings, with which you justify yourselves in these practices and impositions, appoint also that you should cleanse and purify your hearts? He who made laws for that which is *without,* did not he even in those laws further intend something within, and by other laws show how little he regarded the *purifying of the flesh,* and the *putting away of the filth* of that, if the heart be not made clean?" Or, it may have regard to God not only as a *Lawgiver,* but (which the words seem rather to import) as a Creator. Did not God, who made us these bodies (and they *are fearfully and wonderfully made*), make us *these souls* also, which are more fearfully and wonderfully made? Now, if he made both, he justly expects we should take care of both; and therefore not only wash the *body,* which he is the *former* of, and make the hands clean in honour of his work, but wash the spirit, which he is the Father of, and get the leprosy in the heart cleansed.

To this he subjoins a rule for making our creature-comforts clean to us (*v.* 41): "Instead of *washing your hands* before you go to meat, *give alms of such things as you have*" (τὰ ἐνόντα—*of such things as are set before you, and present with you);* "let the poor have their share out of them, and then *all things are clean to you,* and you may use them comfortably." Here is a plain allusion to the law of Moses, by which it was provided that certain portions of the increase of their land should be given *to the Levite, the stranger, the fatherless, and the widow;* and, when that was done, what was reserved for their own use was *clean to them,* and they could in faith pray for a blessing upon it, Deut. xxvi. 12—15. *Then* we can with comfort enjoy the gifts of God's bounty ourselves when we *send portions to them for whom nothing is prepared,* Neh. viii. 10. *Job ate not his morsel alone,* but *the fatherless ate thereof,* and so it was *clean to him* (Job xxxi. 17); *clean,* that is, permitted and allowed to be used, and then only can it be used comfortably. Note, What we have is not our own, unless God have his dues out of it; and it is by *liberality to the poor* that we clear up to ourselves our *liberty* to make use of our creature-comforts.

2. He reproves them for laying stress upon trifles, and neglecting the weighty matters of the law, *v.* 42. (1.) Those laws which related only to the *means of religion* they were very exact in the observance of, as particularly those concerning the maintenance of the priests: *Ye pay tithe of mint and rue,* pay it in kind and to the full, and will not put off the priests with a *modus decimandi* or *compound* for it. By this they would gain a reputation with the people as strict observers of the law, and would make an interest in the priests, in whose power it was many a time to do them a kindness; and no wonder if the priests and the Pharisees contrived how to strengthen one another's hands. Now Christ does not condemn them for being so exact in paying tithes *(these things ought ye to have done),* but for thinking that this would atone for the neglect of their greater duties; for, (2.) Those laws which relate to the *essentials of religion* they made nothing of: *You pass over judgment and the love of God,* you make no conscience of giving men their *dues* and God your *hearts.*

3. He reproves them for their pride and vanity, and affectations of precedency and praise of men (*v.* 43): "*Ye love the uppermost seats in the synagogues*" (or consistories where the elders met for government); "if you have not those seats, you are ambitious of them; if you have, you are proud of them; and *you love greetings in the markets,* to be complimented by the people and to have their cap and knee." It is not sitting uppermost, or being greeted, that is reproved, but *loving it.*

4. He reproves them for their hypocrisy, and their colouring over the wickedness of their hearts and lives with specious pretences (*v.* 44): *You are as graves* overgrown with grass, which therefore *appear not,* and *the men that walk over them are not aware of them,* and so they contract the ceremonial pollution which by the law arose from the *touch of a grave.*" These Pharisees were *within* full of *abominations,* as a grave of putrefaction; full of covetousness, envy, and malice; and yet they concealed it so artfully with a profession of devotion, that it did not appear, so that they who conversed with them, and followed their doctrine, were defiled with sin, infected with their corruptions and ill morals, and yet, they making a show of piety, suspected no danger by them. The contagion *insinuated* itself, and was *insensibly* caught, and those that caught it thought themselves never the worse.

IV. The testimony which he bore also against the lawyers or scribes, who made it their business to *expound* the law according to the tradition of the elders, as the Pharisees did to *observe* the law according to that tradition.

1. There was one of that profession who resented what he said against the Pharisees (*v.* 45): "*Master, thus saying thou reproachest us also,* for we are scribes; and are we therefore hypocrites?" Note, It is a common thing for unhumbled sinners to call and count reproofs reproaches. It is the wisdom

of those who desire to have their sin mortified to make a *good use* of reproaches that come from *ill will,* and to turn them into reproofs. If we can in this way hear of our faults, and amend them, it is well: but it is the folly of those who are wedded to their sins, and resolved not to part with them, to make an *ill use* of the faithful and friendly admonitions given them, which come from love, and to have their passions provoked by them as if they were intended for *reproaches,* and therefore fly in the face of their reprovers, and justify themselves in rejecting the reproof. Thus the prophet complained (Jer. 6. 10): *The word of the Lord is to them a reproach; they have no delight in it.* This lawyer espoused the Pharisee's cause, and so made himself partaker of his sins.

2. Our Lord Jesus thereupon took them to task (*v.* 46): *Woe unto you also, ye lawyers;* and again (*v.* 52): *Woe unto you, lawyers.* They blessed themselves in the reputation they had among the people, who thought them happy men, because they studied the law, and were always conversant with that, and had the honour of instructing the people in the knowledge of that; but Christ denounced *woes* against them, for he sees not as man sees. This was just upon him for taking the Pharisee's part, and quarrelling with Christ because he reproved them. Note, Those who quarrel with the reproofs of others, and suspect them to be reproaches to them, do but get *woes of their own* by so doing.

(1.) The lawyers are reproved for making the services of religion more *burdensome* to others, but more *easy* to themselves, than God had made them (*v.* 46): "*You lade men with burdens grievous to be borne,* by your traditions, which *bind them out from* many liberties God has allowed them, and *bind them up to* many slaveries which God never enjoined them, to show your authority, and to keep people in awe; *but you yourselves touch them not with one of your fingers;*" that is, [1.] "You will not *burden* yourselves with them, nor be yourselves bound by those restraints with which you hamper others." They would seem, by the hedges they pretended to make about the law, to be very strict for the observance of the law; but, if you could see their practices, you would find that they not only make nothing of those hedges themselves, but make nothing of the law itself neither: thus the confessors of the Romish church are said to do with their penitents. [2.] "You will not *lighten* them to those you have power over; *you will not touch them,* that is, either to repeal them or to dispense with them when you find them to be burdensome and grievous to the people." They would come in with *both hands* to dispense with a command of God, but not with a *finger* to mitigate the rigour of any of the traditions of the elders.

(2.) They are reproved for pretending a veneration for the memory of the prophets whom their fathers killed, when yet they hated and persecuted those in their own day who were sent to them on the same errand, to call them to repentance, and direct them to Christ, *v.* 47—49. [1.] These hypocrites, among other pretences of piety, *built the sepulchres of the prophets;* that is, they erected monuments over their graves, in honour of them, probably with large inscriptions containing high encomiums of them. They were not so superstitious as to enshrine their relics, or to think their devotions the more acceptable to God for being offered at the *tombs of the martyrs;* they did not burn incense or pray to them, or plead their merits with God; they did not add that iniquity to their hypocrisy; but, as if they owned themselves the *children of the prophets,* their heirs and executors, they *repaired* and *beautified* the monuments sacred to their *pious memory.* [2.] Notwithstanding this, they had an inveterate *enmity* to those in their *own day* that came to them in the *spirit* and *power* of those prophets; and, though they had not yet had an opportunity of carrying it far, yet they would soon do it, for the *Wisdom of God said,* that is, Christ himself would *so order* it, and did *now foretel* it, that they would *slay* and *persecute* the prophets and apostles that should be sent them. The *Wisdom of God* would thus make trial of them, and discover their odious hypocrisy, by sending them prophets, to reprove them for their sins and warn them of the judgments of God. Those prophets should prove themselves apostles, or messengers sent from heaven, by signs, and wonders, and gifts of the Holy Ghost. Or, "*I will send them prophets* under the style and title of apostles, who yet shall produce as good an authority as any of the old prophets did; and these they shall not only contradict and oppose, but *slay* and *persecute,* and put to death." Christ foresaw this, and yet did not otherwise than as became the *Wisdom of God* in sending them, for he knew how to bring glory to himself in the issue, by the recompences reserved both for the *persecutors* and the *persecuted* in the future state. [3.] That therefore God will justly put another construction upon their *building* the *tombs* of the prophets than what they would be thought to intend, and it shall be interpreted their *allowing the deeds of their fathers* (*v.* 45); for, since by their present actions it appeared that they had no true value for their prophets, the *building* of *their sepulchres* shall have this sense put upon it, that they resolved to keep them in their graves whom their fathers had hurried thither. Josiah, who had a real value for prophets, thought it enough not to disturb the grave of the *man of God at Bethel: Let no man move his bones,* 2 Kings xxiii. 17, 18. If these lawyers will carry the matter further, and will build *their sepulchres,* it is such a piece of *over-doing* as gives cause to suspect an ill design in it, and that it is meant as a cover for some design against prophecy itself, like the kiss of a traitor, as *he that blesseth his friend with a loud voice, rising early in the morning, it shall be counted a curse to him,* Prov. xxvii. 14.

[4.] That they must expect no other than to be reckoned with, as the *fillers up* of the *measure* of persecution, *v.* 50, 51. They keep up the trade as it were in succession, and therefore are responsible for the *debts of the company,* even those it has been *contracting* all along from *the blood of Abel,* when the world began, to that of Zacharias, and so forward to the end of the Jewish state; it shall all be *required of this generation,* this last generation of the Jews, whose sin in persecuting Christ's apostles would exceed any of the sins of that kind that their fathers were guilty of, and so would bring *wrath* upon them *to the uttermost,* 1 Thess. ii. 15, 16. Their destruction by the Romans was so terrible that it might well be reckoned the completing of God's vengeance upon that persecuting nation.

(3.) They are reproved for opposing the gospel of Christ, and doing all they could to obstruct the progress and success of it, *v.* 52. [1.] They had not, according to the duty of their place, faithfully expounded to the people those scriptures of the Old Testament which pointed at the Messiah, which if they had been led into the right understanding of by the lawyers, they would readily have embraced him and his doctrine: but, instead of that, they had perverted those texts, and had cast a mist before the eyes of the people, by their corrupt glosses upon them, and this is called *taking away the key of knowledge;* instead of *using* that key for the people, and helping them to use it aright, they *hid it* from them; this is called, in Matthew, *shutting up the kingdom of heaven against men,* Matt. xxiii. 13. Note, Those who take away the key of knowledge shut up the *kingdom of heaven.* [2.] They themselves did not embrace the gospel of Christ, though by their acquaintance with the Old Testament they could not but know that the *time was fulfilled,* and the *kingdom of God was at hand;* they saw the prophecies accomplished in that kingdom which our Lord Jesus was about to set up, and yet would not themselves *enter into it.* Nay, [3.] Them that without any guidance or assistance of theirs were *entering in* they did all they could to *hinder* and discourage, by threatening to *cast them out of the synagogue,* and otherwise terrifying them. It is bad for people to be averse to revelation, but much worse to be adverse to it.

Lastly, In the close of the chapter we are told how spitefully and maliciously the scribes and *Pharisees* contrived to draw him into a snare, *v.* 53, 54. They could not bear those cutting reproofs which they must own to be just; but what he had said against them in particular would not *bear an action,* nor could they ground upon it any *criminal* accusation, and therefore, as if, because his reproofs were warm, they hoped to stir him up to some intemperate heat and passion, so as to put him off his guard, they *began to urge him vehemently,* to be very fierce upon him, and to *provoke him to speak of many things,* to propose dangerous questions to him, *laying wait* for something which might serve the design they had of making him either *odious* to the people, or *obnoxious* to the government, or both. Thus did they seek occasion against him, like David's enemies that did *every day wrest his words,* Ps. lvi. 5. *Evil men dig up mischief.* Note, Faithful reprovers of sin must expect to have many enemies, and have need to set a watch before the door of their lips, because of *their observers* that watch for their halting. The prophet complains of those in his time who *make a man an offender for a word, and lay a snare for him that reproveth in the gate,* Isa. xxix. 21. That we may bear trials of this kind with patience, and get through them with prudence, let us *consider him who endured such contradiction of sinners against himself.*

CHAP. XII.

In this chapter we have divers excellent discourses of our Saviour's upon various occasions, many of which are to the same purport with what we had in Matthew upon other the like occasions; for we may suppose that our Lord Jesus preached the same doctrines, and pressed the same duties, at several times, in several companies, and that one of the evangelists took them as he delivered them at one time and another at another time; and we need thus to have precept upon precept, line upon line. Here, I. Christ warns his disciples to take heed of hypocrisy, and of cowardice in professing Christianity and preaching the gospel, ver. 1—12. II. He gives a caution against covetousness, upon occasion of a covetous motion made to him, and illustrates that caution by a parable of a rich man suddenly cut off by death in the midst of his worldly projects and hopes, ver. 13—21. III. He encourages his disciples to cast all their care upon God, and to live easy in a dependence upon his providence, and exhorts them to make religion their main business, ver. 22—34. IV. He stirs them up to watchfulness for their Master's coming, from the consideration of the reward of those who are then found faithful, and the punishment of those who are found unfaithful, ver. 35—48. V. He bids them expect trouble and persecution, ver. 49—53. VI. He warns the people to observe and improve the day of their opportunities and to make their peace with God in time, ver. 54—59.

IN the mean time, when there were
gathered together an innumerable
multitude of people, insomuch that
they trode one upon another, he began to say unto his disciples first of
all, Beware ye of the leaven of the
Pharisees, which is hypocrisy. 2 For
there is nothing covered, that shall
not be revealed; neither hid, that
shall not be known. 3 Therefore
whatsoever ye have spoken in darkness shall be heard in the light; and
that which ye have spoken in the ear
in closets shall be proclaimed upon
the housetops. 4 And I say unto you
my friends, Be not afraid of them that
kill the body, and after that have no
more that they can do. 5 But I will
forewarn you whom ye shall fear: Fear
him, which after he hath killed hath

power to cast into hell; yea, I say
unto you, Fear him. 6 Are not five
sparrows sold for two farthings, and
not one of them is forgotten before
God? 7 But even the very hairs of
your head are all numbered. Fear
not therefore: ye are of more value
than many sparrows. 8 Also I say
unto you, Whosoever shall confess
me before men, him shall the Son of
man also confess before the angels of
God: 9 But he that denieth me before men shall be denied before the
angels of God. 10 And whosoever
shall speak a word against the Son of
man, it shall be forgiven him: but
unto him that blasphemeth against
the Holy Ghost it shall not be forgiven. 11 And when they bring you
unto the synagogues, and *unto* magistrates, and powers, take ye no thought
how or what thing ye shall answer, or
what ye shall say: 12 For the Holy
Ghost shall teach you in the same
hour what ye ought to say.

We find here, I. A vast auditory that was got together to hear Christ preach. The *scribes* and *Pharisees* sought *to accuse him*, and do him mischief; but the people, who were not under the bias of their prejudices and jealousies, still *admired* him, attended on him, and did him honour. *In the mean time* (*v.* 1), while he was in the Pharisee's house, contending with them that sought to ensnare him, the people got together for an afternoon sermon, a sermon after *dinner*, after dinner with a Pharisee; and he would not disappoint them. Though in the morning sermon, when they were *gathered thickly together* (*ch.* xi. 29), he had severely reproved them, as an *evil generation that seek a sign*, yet they renewed their attendance on him; so much better could the people bear *their* reproofs than the Pharisees *theirs*. The more the Pharisees strove to drive the people from Christ, the more flocking there was to him. Here was an *innumerable multitude of people gathered together, so that they trode one upon another*, in labouring to get foremost, and to come within hearing. It is a good sight to see people thus forward to hear the word, and venture upon inconvenience and danger rather than miss an opportunity for their souls. Who are these that thus *fly as the doves to their windows?* Isa. lx. 8. When the net is cast where there is such a multitude of fish, it may be hoped that some will be enclosed.

II. The instructions which he gave his followers, in the hearing of this auditory.

1. He began with a caution against *hypocrisy*. This he said *to his disciples first of all;* either to the twelve, or to the seventy. These were his more peculiar charge, his family, his school, and therefore he particularly *warned them* as his *beloved sons;* they made more profession of religion than others, and hypocrisy in *that* was the sin they were most in danger of. They were to preach to others; and, if they should *prevaricate*, corrupt the word, and deal deceitfully, hypocrisy would be worse in them than in others. Besides, there was a Judas among them, who was a hypocrite, and Christ knew it, and would hereby startle him, or leave him inexcusable. Christ's disciples were, for aught we know, the *best men* then in the world, yet they needed to be cautioned against hypocrisy. Christ said this to the disciples, *in the hearing* of this great multitude, rather than *privately* when he had them by themselves, to add the greater weight to the caution, and to let the world know that he would not countenance hypocrisy, no, not in *his own disciples*. Now observe,

(1.) The description of that sin which he warns them against: *It is the leaven of the Pharisees.* [1.] It is *leaven;* it is *spreading* as leaven, *insinuates* itself into the whole man, and all that he does; it is *swelling* and *souring* as leaven, for it puffs men up with pride, embitters them with malice, and makes their service unacceptable to God. [2.] It is the leaven of the Pharisees: "It is the sin they are most of them found in. Take heed of imitating them; be not you of their spirit; do not dissemble in Christianity as they do in Judaism; make not *your* religion a *cloak of maliciousness*, as they do theirs."

(2.) A good reason against it: "*For there is nothing covered that shall not be revealed*, *v.* 2, 3. It is to no purpose to dissemble, for, sooner or later, truth will come out; and a *lying tongue is but for a moment*. If you *speak in darkness* that which is unbecoming you, and is inconsistent with your public professions, *it shall be heard in the light;* some way or other it shall be discovered, *a bird of the air shall carry the voice* (Eccl. x. 20), and your folly and falsehood will be *made manifest*." The iniquity that is concealed with a show of piety will be discovered, perhaps in this world, as Judas's was, and Simon Magus's, at furthest in the great day, when the *secrets of all hearts* shall be made *manifest*, Eccl. xii. 14; Rom. ii. 16. If men's religion prevail not to conquer and cure the wickedness of their hearts, it shall not always serve for a cloak. The day is coming when hypocrites will be stripped of their fig-leaves.

2. To this he added a charge to them to be faithful to the trust reposed in them, and not to betray it, through cowardice or base fear. Some make *v.* 2, 3, to be a caution to them not to *conceal* those things which they had been *instructed* in, and were *employed* to publish to the world. "Whether men will *hear*, or whether they will *forbear*, tell them the *truth*, the *whole* truth, and *nothing but* the

truth; what has been spoken to you, and you have talked of among yourselves, *privately,* and in corners, that do you preach *publicly,* whoever is offended; for, if you *please men,* you are not *Christ's servants,* nor can you please him," Gal. i. 10. But this was not the worst of it: it was likely to be a *suffering* cause, though never a *sinking* one; let them therefore arm themselves with courage; and divers arguments are furnished here to steel them with a holy resolution in their work. Consider,

(1.) "The power of your enemies is a limited power (*v.* 4): *I say unto you, my friends*" (Christ's disciples are his friends, he calls them *friends,* and gives them this *friendly* advice), "*be not afraid;* do not disquiet yourselves with tormenting fears of the power and rage of men." Note, Those whom Christ owns for *his friends* need not be afraid of any enemies. "*Be not afraid,* no, not of them that *kill the body;* let it not be in the power of *scoffers,* nor even of *murderers,* to drive you off from your work, for you that have learned to triumph over death may say, even of them, Let them do their worst, *after that there is no more that they can do;* the immortal soul lives, and is happy, and enjoys itself and its God, and sets them all at defiance." Note, Those can do Christ's disciples no real harm, and therefore ought not to be dreaded, who can but *kill the body;* for they only send that to its rest, and the soul to its joy, the sooner.

(2.) God is to be feared more than the most powerful men: "*I will forewarn you whom you shall fear* (*v.* 5): that you may fear man less, fear God more. Moses conquers his fear of the *wrath of the king,* by having an eye to him *that is invisible.* By *owning Christ* you may incur the wrath of men, which can reach no further than to *put you to death* (and without God's permission they cannot do that); but by *denying* Christ, and disowning him, you will incur the wrath of God, which has power to send *you to hell,* and there is no resisting it. Now of two evils the less is to be chosen, and the greater to be dreaded, and therefore *I say unto you, Fear him.*" "It is true," said that blessed martyr, Bishop Hooper, "life is sweet, and death bitter; but eternal life is more sweet, and eternal death more bitter."

(3.) The lives of good Christians and good ministers are the particular care of divine Providence, *v.* 6, 7. To encourage us in times of difficulty and danger, we must have recourse to our first principles, and build upon them. Now a firm belief of the doctrine of God's universal providence, and the extent of it, will be satisfying to us when at any time we are in peril, and will encourage us to trust God in the way of duty. [1.] Providence takes cognizance of the *meanest creatures,* even of *the sparrows.* "Though they are of such small account that *five* of them are sold for *two farthings,* yet not one of them is *forgotten of God,* but is provided for, and notice is taken of its death. Now, *you are of more value than many sparrows,* and therefore you may be sure you *are not forgotten,* though imprisoned, though banished, though forgotten by your friends; much more *precious in the sight of the Lord is the death of saints* than the death of sparrows." [2.] Providence takes cognizance of the *meanest interest* of the disciples of Christ: "*Even the very hairs of your head are all numbered* (*v.* 7); much more are your sighs and tears numbered, and the drops of your blood, which you shed for Christ's name's sake. An account is kept of all your losses, that they *may be,* and without doubt they shall be, recompensed unspeakably to your advantage."

(4.) "You will be owned or disowned by Christ, in the great day, according as you now own or disown him," *v.* 8, 9. [1.] To engage us to *confess Christ before men,* whatever we may lose or suffer for our constancy to him, and how dear soever it may cost us, we are assured that they who *confess Christ* now shall be owned by him in the great day *before the angels of God,* to their everlasting comfort and honour. Jesus Christ will *confess,* not only that he suffered for them, and that they are to have the benefit of *his* sufferings, but that they suffered *for him,* and that his kingdom and interest on earth were advanced by *their* sufferings; and what greater honour can be done them? [2.] To deter us from *denying* Christ, and a cowardly *deserting* of his truths and ways, we are here assured that those who *deny Christ,* and treacherously depart from him, whatever they may save by it, though it were life itself, and whatever they may *gain* by it, though it were a kingdom, will be vast losers at last, for they shall be *denied before the angels of God;* Christ will not know them, will not own them, will not show them any favour, which will turn to their everlasting terror and contempt. By the stress here laid upon their being *confessed* or *denied before the angels of God,* it should seem to be a considerable part of the happiness of glorified saints that they will not only stand *right,* but stand *high,* in the esteem of the *holy angels;* they will love them, and honour them, and own them, if they be Christ's servants; they are their fellow-servants, and they will take them for their companions. On the contrary, a considerable part of the misery of damned sinners will be that the holy angels will abandon them, and will be the pleased witnesses, not only of their disgrace, as here, but of their misery, for they shall be *tormented in the presence of the holy angels* (Rev. xiv. 10), who will give them no relief.

(5.) The errand they were shortly to be sent out upon was of the highest and last importance to the children of men, to whom they were sent, *v.* 10. Let them be bold in preaching the gospel, for a sorer and heavier doom would attend those that rejected them (after the Spirit was poured upon them, which was to be the *last* method of conviction) than those that now rejected Christ himself, and opposed him: "*Greater works than these shall ye do*, and, consequently, greater will be the punishment of those that blaspheme the gifts and operations of the Holy Ghost in you. *Whosoever shall speak a word against the Son of man*, shall stumble at the meanness of his appearance, and speak *slightly* and *spitefully* of him, it is capable of some excuse: *Father, forgive them, for they know not what they do.* But unto him that *blasphemes the Holy Ghost*, that blasphemes the Christian doctrine, and maliciously opposes it, after the pouring out of the Spirit and his attestation of Christ's *being glorified* (Acts ii. 33; v. 32), the privilege of the *forgiveness of sins* shall be denied; he shall have no benefit by Christ and his gospel. You may shake off the dust of your feet against those that do so, and give them over as incurable; they have forfeited that *repentance* and that *remission* which Christ was *exalted to give*, and which you are *commissioned to preach.*" The sin, no doubt, was the more daring, and consequently the case the more desperate, during the continuance of the *extraordinary* gifts and operations of the Spirit in the church, which were intended for a *sign to them who believed not*, 1 Cor xiv. 22. There were hopes of those who, though not convinced by them at first, yet admired them, but those who *blasphemed* them were given over.

(6.) Whatever trials they should be called out to, they should be sufficiently furnished for them, and honourably brought through them, *v.* 11, 12. The faithful martyr for Christ has not only *sufferings* to *undergo*, but a *testimony* to *bear*, a *good confession* to *witness*, and is concerned to do that *well*, so that the cause of Christ may not suffer, though he suffer for it; and, if this be his care, let him cast it upon God: "When they *bring you into the synagogues*, before church-rulers, before the Jewish courts, or before *magistrates and powers*, Gentile rulers, rulers in the state, to be examined about your doctrine, what it is, and what the proof of it, *take no thought what ye shall answer*," [1.] "That you may *save yourselves.* Do not study by what art or rhetoric to mollify your judges, or by what tricks in law to bring yourselves off; if it be the will of God that you should come off, and your time is not yet come, he will bring it about effectually." [2.] "That you may *serve your Master;* aim at this, but do not perplex yourselves about it, for *the Holy Ghost*, as a Spirit of wisdom, *shall teach you what you ought to say*, and how to say it, so that it may be for the honour of God and his cause."

13 And one of the company said
unto him, Master, speak to my brother, that he divide the inheritance
with me. 14 And he said unto him,
Man, who made me a judge or a
divider over you? 15 And he said
unto them, Take heed, and beware of
covetousness: for a man's life consisteth not in the abundance of the
things which he possesseth. 16 And
he spake a parable unto them, saying,
The ground of a certain rich man
brought forth plentifully: 17 And he
thought within himself, saying, What
shall I do, because I have no room
where to bestow my fruits? 18 And
he said, This will I do: I will pull
down my barns, and build greater; and
there will I bestow all my fruits and
my goods. 19 And I will say to my
soul, Soul, thou hast much goods laid
up for many years; take thine ease,
eat, drink, *and* be merry. 20 But
God said unto him, *Thou* fool, this
night thy soul shall be required of
thee: then whose shall those things
be, which thou hast provided? 21
So *is* he that layeth up treasure for
himself, and is not rich toward God.

We have in these verses,

I. The application that was made to Christ, very unseasonably, by one of his hearers, desiring him to interpose *between him and his brother* in a matter that concerned the estate of the family (*v.* 13): "*Master, speak to my brother;* speak as a prophet, speak as a king, speak with authority; he is one that will have regard to what thou sayest; speak to him, *that he divide the inheritance with me.*" Now, 1. Some think that his brother *did him wrong*, and that he appealed to Christ to *right him*, because he knew the law was costly. His brother was such a one as the Jews called *Ben-hamesen—a son of violence*, that took not only his own part of the estate, but his brother's too, and forcibly detained it from him. Such brethren there are in the world, who have no sense at all either of *natural equity* or *natural affection*, who make a prey of those whom they ought to patronize and protect. They who are so wronged have a God to go to, who will *execute* judgment and justice for *those that are oppressed.* 2. Others think that he had a mind to *do his brother wrong*, and would have Christ to *assist him;* that, whereas the law gave the elder brother a double portion of the estate, and the father himself could not dispose of what he had but by that rule (Deut. xxi. 16, 17), he would have Christ to *alter that law*, and oblige his brother, who perhaps was a follower of Christ at large, to *divide the inheritance* equally *with him*, in gavel-kind, share and share alike, and to allot him as much as his elder brother. I suspect that this was the case, because Christ takes occasion from it to warn against *covetousness*, *πλεονεξία—a desire of having more*, more than God in his providence has allotted us. It was not a lawful desire of getting his own, but a *sinful* desire of getting more than his own.

II. Christ's refusal to interpose in this matter (*v.* 14): *Man, who made me a judge or divider over you?* In matters of this nature, Christ will not assume either a *legislative* power to alter the settled rule of inheritances, or a *judicial* power to determine controversies concerning them. He could have done the judge's part, and the lawyer's, as well as he did the physician's, and have ended suits at law as happily as he did diseases; but he would not, for it was not in his commission: *Who made me a judge?* Probably he refers to the indignity done to Moses by his brethren in Egypt, with which Stephen upbraided the Jews, Acts vii. 27, 35. "If I should offer to do this, you would taunt me as you did Moses, *Who made thee a judge or a divider?* He corrects the man's mistake, will not admit his appeal (it was *coram non judice—not before the proper judge)*, and so *dismisses* his bill. If he had come to him to desire him to assist his pursuit of the heavenly inheritance, Christ would have given him his best help; but as to this matter he has nothing to do: *Who made me a judge?* Note, Jesus Christ was no usurper; he took no honour, no power, to himself, but what was given him, Heb. v. 5. Whatever he did, he could tell by what authority he did it, and who gave him that authority. Now this shows us what is the nature and constitution of Christ's kingdom. It is a spiritual kingdom, and not of this world. 1. It does not interfere with civil powers, nor take the authority of princes out of their hands. Christianity leaves the matter as it found it, as to civil power. 2. It does not intermeddle with civil rights; it obliges all to do justly, according to the settled rules of equity, but dominion is not founded in grace. 3. It does not *encourage* our *expectations* of worldly advantages by our religion. If this man will be a disciple of Christ, and expects that in consideration of this Christ should give him his brother's estate, he is mistaken; the rewards of Christ's disciples are of another nature. 4. It does not *encourage* our *contests* with our brethren, and our being rigorous and high in our demands, but rather, for peace' sake, to recede from our right. 5. It does not allow ministers to *entangle* themselves in the affairs of this *life* (2 Tim. ii. 4), to *leave the word of God to serve tables.* There are those whose business it is, let it be left to them, *Tractent fabrilia fabri—Each workman to his proper craft.*

III. The necessary caution which Christ took occasion from this to give to his hearers. Though he came not to be a *divider* of men's estates, he came to be a director of their consciences about them, and would have all take heed of harbouring that corrupt principle which they saw to be in others the *root of so much evil.* Here is,

1. The caution itself (*v.* 15): *Take heed and beware of covetousness; ὁρᾶτε—"Observe yourselves,* keep a *jealous eye* upon your own hearts, lest covetous principles steal into them; and *φυλάσσεσθε—preserve yourselves,* keep a *strict hand* upon your own hearts, lest covetous principles rule and give law in them." Covetousness is a sin which we have need constantly to *watch against,* and therefore frequently to be *warned against.*

2. The reason of it, or an argument to enforce this caution: *For a man's life consisteth not in the abundance of the things which he possesseth;* that is, "our happiness and comfort do not depend upon our having a great deal of the wealth of this world." (1.) The life of the *soul,* undoubtedly, does not depend upon it, and the soul is the man. The things of the world will not suit the nature of a soul, nor supply its needs, nor satisfy its desires, nor last so long as it will last. Nay, (2.) Even the life of the body and the happiness of that do not consist in an *abundance* of these things; for many live very contentedly and easily, and get through the world very comfortably, who have but a little of the wealth of it (a dinner of herbs with holy love is better than a *feast of fat things);* and, on the other hand, many live very miserably who have a great deal of the things of this world; they possess abundance, and yet have no comfort of it; they *bereave their souls of good,* Eccl. iv. 8. Many who have abundance are discontented and fretful, as Ahab and Haman; and then what good does their abundance do them?

3. The illustration of this by a parable, the sum of which is to show the folly of carnal worldlings while they live, and their misery when they die, which is intended not only for a check to that man who came to Christ with an address about his estate, while he was in no care about his soul and another world, but for the enforcing of that necessary caution to us all, to *take heed of covetousness.* The parable gives us the life and death of a *rich man,* and leaves us to judge whether he was a *happy* man.

(1.) Here is an account of his worldly wealth and abundance (*v.* 16): *The ground of a certain rich man brought forth plentifully, χώρα—regio—the country.* He had a whole country to himself, a lordship of his own; he was a little prince. Observe, His wealth lay much in the fruits of the earth, for *the king himself is served by the field,* Eccl. v. 9. He had a great deal of ground, and his ground was *fruitful;* much would have *more,* and he *had more.* Note, The fruitfulness of the earth is a great blessing, but it is a blessing which God often gives plentifully to wicked men, to whom it is a snare, that we may not think to judge of his love or hatred by what is before us.

(2.) Here are the workings of his heart, in the midst of this abundance. We are here told what *he thought within himself*, *v.* 17. Note, The God of heaven knows and observes whatever we think within ourselves, and we are accountable to him for it. He is both a discerner and judge of the thoughts and intents of the heart. We mistake if we imagine that thoughts are *hid* and thoughts are *free*. Let us here observe,

[1.] What his *cares* and *concerns* were. When he saw an extraordinary crop upon his ground, instead of *thanking God* for it, or rejoicing in the opportunity it would give him of doing the more good, he afflicts himself with this thought, *What shall I do, because I have no room where to bestow my fruits?* He speaks as one *at a loss*, and full of perplexity. *What shall I do now?* The poorest beggar in the country, that did not know where to get a meal's meat, could not have said a more anxious word. Disquieting care is the common fruit of an abundance of this world, and the common fault of those that have abundance. The more men have, the more perplexity they have with it, and the more solicitous they are to keep what they have and to add to it, how to spare and how to spend; so that even the *abundance* of the rich will not suffer them to *sleep*, for thinking what they shall do with what they have and how they shall dispose of it. The rich man seems to speak it with a sigh, *What shall I do?* And if you ask, Why, what is the matter? Truly he has *abundance* of wealth, and wants a place to *put it in*, that is all.

[2.] What his *projects* and *purposes* were, which were the result of his cares, and were indeed absurd and foolish like them (*v.* 18): "*This will I do*, and it is the wisest course I can take, *I will pull down my barns*, for they are too little, and I will *build greater, and there will I bestow all my fruits and my goods*, and then I shall be at ease." Now here, *First*, It was folly for him to call the fruits of the ground *his* fruits and *his* goods. He seems to lay a pleasing emphasis upon that, *my* fruits and *my* goods; whereas what we have is but *lent* us for our use, the property is still in God; we are but stewards of our *Lord's goods*, tenants at will of our Lord's land. It is *my corn* (saith God) and *my wine*, Hos. ii. 8, 9. *Secondly*, It was folly for him to *hoard up* what he had, and then to think it *well bestowed*. There will I bestow it *all;* as if none must be bestowed upon the poor, none upon his family, none upon the Levite and *the stranger*, the *fatherless and the widow*, but all in the great barn. *Thirdly*, It was folly for him to let his *mind* rise with his *condition;* when his ground brought forth more plentifully than usual, then to talk of bigger barns, as if the next year must needs be as fruitful as this, and much more abundant, whereas the barn might be as much too big the next year as it was too little this. Years of famine commonly follow years of plenty, as they did in Egypt; and therefore it were better to *stack* some of his corn for this once. *Fourthly*, It was folly for him to think to ease his care by building new barns, for the building of them would but increase his care; those know this who know any thing of the spirit of building. The way that God prescribes for the cure of inordinate care is certainly successful, but the way of the world does but increase it. Besides, when he had done this, there were other cares that would still attend him; the greater the barns, still the greater the cares, Eccl. v. 10. *Fifthly*, It was folly for him to contrive and resolve all this *absolutely* and *without reserve*. This *I will* do: *I will* pull down my barns and *I will* build greater, yea, that *I will;* without so much as that necessary proviso, *If the Lord will, I shall live*, Jam. iv. 13—15. Peremptory projects are foolish projects; for our times are in God's hand, and not in our own, and we do not so much as *know what shall be on the morrow*.

[3.] What his *pleasing hopes* and *expectations* were, when he should have made good these projects. "Then *I will say to my soul*, upon the credit of this security, whether God say it or no, *Soul*, mark what I say, *thou hast much goods laid up for many years* in these barns; now *take thine ease*, enjoy thyself, *eat, drink, and be merry*," *v.* 19. Here also appears his folly, as much in the enjoyment of his wealth as in the pursuit of it. *First*, It was folly for him to put off his comfort in his abundance till he had compassed his projects concerning it. When he has built bigger barns, and filled them (which will be a work of time), then he will *take his ease;* and might he not as well have *done that now?* Grotius here quotes the story of Pyrrhus, who was projecting to make himself master of Sicily, Africa, and other places, in the prosecution of his victories. Well, says his friend Cyneas, and what must we do then? *Postea vivemus*, says he, *Then we will live; At hoc jam licet*, says Cyneas, *We may live now if we please*. *Secondly*, It was folly for him to be confident that his goods were *laid up for many years*, as if his bigger barns would be *safer* than those he had; whereas in an hour's time they might be burnt to the ground and all that was laid up in them, perhaps by lightning, against which there is no defence. A few years may make a great change; *moth and rust may corrupt, or thieves break through and steal*. *Thirdly*, It was folly for him to count upon certain *ease*, when he had laid up abundance of the wealth of this world, whereas there are many things that may make people uneasy in the midst of their greatest abundance. One dead fly may spoil a whole pot of precious ointment; and one thorn a whole bed of down. Pain and sickness of body, disagreeableness of relations, and especially a guilty conscience, may rob a man of his ease, who has ever so much of the wealth of this world. *Fourthly*, It was folly for him to think of making no other use of his plenty than to *eat* and *drink*, and to *be merry;* to indulge the flesh, and gratify the sensual appetite, without any thought of doing good to others, and being put thereby into a better capacity of serving God and his generation: as if we *lived* to *eat*, and did not *eat* to *live*, and the happiness of man consisted in nothing else but in having all the gratifications of sense wound up to the height of pleasurableness. *Fifthly*, It was the greatest folly of all to say all this to his *soul*. If he had said, *Body, take thine ease*, for *thou hast goods laid up for many years*, there had been sense in it; but the soul, considered as an immortal spirit, separable from the body, was no way interested in a barn full of corn or a bag full of gold. If he had had the *soul of a swine*, he might have *blessed it* with the satisfaction of *eating* and *drinking;* but what is this to the *soul of a man*, that has exigencies and desires which these things will be no ways suited to? It is the great absurdity which the children of this world are guilty of that they portion their souls in the wealth of the world and the pleasures of sense.

(3.) Here is God's sentence upon all this; and we are sure that his judgment is according to truth. He said to himself, said to his soul, *Take thine ease*. If God had said so too, the man had been happy, as his Spirit witnesses with the spirit of believers to make them easy. *But God said* quite otherwise; and by his judgment of us we must stand or fall, not by ours of ourselves, 1 Cor. iv. 3, 4. His neighbours blessed him (Ps. x. 3), praised him as *doing well for himself* (Ps. xlix. 18); but God said he did ill for himself: *Thou fool, this night thy soul shall be required of thee, v.* 20. *God said to him*, that is, decreed this concerning him, and let him know it, either by his conscience or by some awakening providence, or rather by both together. This was said when he was *in the fulness of his sufficiency* (Job xx. 22), when his eyes were held waking upon his bed with his cares and contrivances about enlarging his barns, not by adding a bay or two more of building to them, which might serve to answer the end, but by pulling them down and building greater, which was requisite to please his fancy. When he was forecasting this, and had brought it to an issue, and then lulled himself asleep again with a pleasing dream of many years' enjoyment of his present improvements, *then* God said this to him. Thus Belshazzar was struck with terror by the hand-writing on the wall, in the midst of his jollity. Now observe what God said,

[1.] The character he gave him: *Thou fool*, thou *Nabal*, alluding to the story of Nabal, that *fool* (Nabal is his name, and folly is with him) whose heart was struck dead *as a stone* while he was regaling himself in the abundance of his provision for his sheep-shearers. Note, Carnal worldlings are fools, and the day is coming when God will call them by their own name, *Thou fool*, and they will call themselves so.

[2.] The sentence he passed upon him, a sentence of death: *This night thy soul shall be required of thee; they shall require thy soul* (so the words are), and then *whose shall those things be which thou hast provided?* He thought he had goods that should be his for many years, but he must part from them *this night;* he thought he should enjoy them himself, but he must leave them to he knows not who. Note, The death of carnal worldlings is miserable in itself and terrible to them.

First, It is a *force*, an *arrest;* it is the *requiring of the soul*, that soul that thou art making such a fool of; what hast thou to do with a soul, who canst use it no better? Thy soul shall be *required;* this intimates that he is loth to part with it. A good man, who has taken his heart off from this world, cheerfully resigns his soul at death, and gives it up; but a worldly man has it *torn* from him with violence; it is a terror to him to think of leaving this world. *They shall require thy soul*. God shall require it; he shall require an account of it. "Man, woman, what hast thou done with thy soul. Give an account of that stewardship." *They shall;* that is, evil angels as the messengers of God's justice. As good angels receive gracious souls to carry them to their joy, so evil angels receive wicked souls to carry them to the place of torment; they shall *require it* as a guilty soul to be punished. The devil requires thy soul as his own, for it did, in effect, give itself to him.

Secondly, It is a *surprize*, an *unexpected* force. It is in *the night*, and terrors in the night are most terrible. The time of death is day-time to a good man; it is his morning. But it is night to a worldling, a dark night; he *lies down in sorrow*. It is *this night*, this *present* night, without delay; there is no giving bail, or begging a day. This *pleasant* night, when thou art promising thyself many years to come, now thou must die, and go to judgment. Thou art entertaining thyself with the fancy of many a merry day, and merry night, and merry feast; but, in the midst of all, here is an end of all, Isa. xxi. 4.

Thirdly, It is the leaving of all *those things* behind *which they have provided*, which they have laboured for, and prepared for hereafter, with abundance of toil and care. All that which they have placed their happiness in, and built their hope upon, and raised their expectations from, they must leave behind. *Their pomp shall not descend after them* (Ps. xlix. 17), but they shall go as naked out of the world as they came into it, and they shall have no benefit at all by what they have hoarded up either in death, in judgment, or in their everlasting state.

Fourthly, It is leaving them to they *know not who:* "Then *whose shall those things be?* Not *thine* to be sure, and thou knowest not what *they* will prove for whom thou didst design them, thy children and relations, whether they will be *wise* or *fools* (Eccl. ii. 18, 19), whether such as will bless thy memory or curse it, be a credit to thy family or a blemish, do good or hurt with what thou leavest them, keep it or spend it; nay, thou knowest not but those for whom thou dost design it may be prevented from the enjoyment of it, and it may be turned to somebody else thou little thinkest of; nay, though thou knowest to whom thou leavest it, thou knowest not to whom they will leave it, or into whose hand it will come at last." If many a man could have foreseen to whom his house would have come after his death, he would rather have burned it than beautified it.

Fifthly, It is a demonstration of his folly. Carnal worldlings are *fools* while they live: *this their way is their folly* (Ps. xlix. 13); but their folly is made most evident when they die: *at his end he shall be a fool* (Jer. xvii. 11); for then it will appear that he took pains to lay up treasure in a world he was hastening from, but took no care to lay it up in the world he was hastening to.

Lastly, Here is the application of this parable (*v.* 21): *So is he*, such a fool, a fool in God's judgment, a fool upon record, that *layeth up treasure for himself, and is not rich towards God.* This is the way and this is the end of such a man. Observe here,

1. The description of a worldly man: He *lays up treasure for himself,* for the body, for the world, for *himself* in opposition to God, for that *self* that is to be *denied.* (1.) It is his error that he counts his *flesh himself*, as if the *body* were the *man.* If *self* be rightly stated and understood, it is only the true Christian that lays up treasure for himself, and is *wise for himself,* Prov. ix. 12. (2.) It is his error that he makes it his business to *lay up for the flesh,* which he calls laying up *for himself.* All his labour is *for his mouth* (Eccl. vi. 7), *making provision for the flesh.* (3.) It is his error that he counts those things his *treasure* which are thus *laid up* for the world, and the body, and the life that now is; they are the wealth he trusts to, and spends upon, and lets out his affections toward. (4.) The greatest error of all is that he is in no care to be *rich towards God,* rich in the *account of God,* whose accounting us rich makes us so (Rev. ii. 9), rich in the *things of God,* rich *in faith* (Jam. ii. 5), rich in *good works,* in the *fruits of righteousness* (1 Tim. vi. 18), rich in graces, and comforts, and spiritual gifts. Many who have abundance of this world are wholly destitute of that which will enrich their souls, which will make them rich towards God, rich for eternity.

2. The folly and misery of a worldly man: *So is he.* Our Lord Jesus Christ, who knows what the end of things will be, has here told us what his end will be. Note, It is the unspeakable folly of the most of men to mind and pursue the wealth of this world more than the wealth of the other world, that which is merely for the body and for time, more than that which is for the soul and eternity.

22 And he said unto his disciples,
Therefore I say unto you, Take no
thought for your life, what ye shall
eat; neither for the body, what ye
shall put on. 23 The life is more
than meat, and the body *is more* than
raiment. 24 Consider the ravens:
for they neither sow nor reap; which
neither have storehouse nor barn;
and God feedeth them: how much
more are ye better than the fowls?
25 And which of you with taking
thought can add to his stature one
cubit? 26 If ye then be not able to
do that thing which is least, why take
ye thought for the rest? 27 Consider
the lilies how they grow: they toil
not, they spin not; and yet I say
unto you, that Solomon in all his glory
was not arrayed like one of these.
28 If then God so clothe the grass,
which is to day in the field, and to
morrow is cast into the oven; how
much more *will he clothe* you, O ye
of little faith? 29 And seek not ye
what ye shall eat, or what ye shall
drink, neither be ye of doubtful mind.
30 For all these things do the nations
of the world seek after: and your
Father knoweth that ye have need of
these things. 31 But rather seek ye
the kingdom of God; and all these
things shall be added unto you. 32
Fear not, little flock; for it is your
Father's good pleasure to give you
the kingdom. 33 Sell that ye have,
and give alms; provide yourselves
bags which wax not old, a treasure in
the heavens that faileth not, where
no thief approacheth, neither moth
corrupteth. 34 For where your treasure is, there will your heart be also.
35 Let your loins be girded about,
and *your* lights burning; 36 And ye
yourselves like unto men that wait
for their lord, when he will return
from the wedding; that when he
cometh and knocketh, they may open
unto him immediately. 37 Blessed *are*
those servants, whom the lord when he
cometh shall find watching: verily I

**say unto you, that he shall gird him-
self, and make them to sit down to
meat, and will come forth and serve
them. 38 And if he shall come in
the second watch, or come in the
third watch, and find *them* so, blessed
are those servants. 39 And this
know, that if the goodman of the
house had known what hour the thief
would come, he would have watched,
and not have suffered his house to be
broken through. 40 Be ye therefore
ready also: for the Son of man cometh
at an hour when ye think not.**

Our Lord Jesus is here inculcating some needful useful lessons upon his disciples, which he had before taught them, and had occasion afterwards to press upon them; for they need to have *precept upon precept, and line upon line:* "*Therefore*, because there are so many that are ruined by covetousness, and an inordinate affection to the wealth of this world, *I say unto you*, my disciples, take heed of it." *Thou, O man of God, flee these things*, as well as thou, O man of the world, 1 Tim. vi. 11.

I. He charges them not to afflict themselves with disquieting perplexing cares about the necessary supports of life: *Take no thought for your life, v.* 22. In the foregoing parable he had given us warning against that branch of covetousness of which rich people are most in danger; and that is, a *sensual complacency* in the abundance of this world's goods. Now his disciples might think they were in no danger of this, for they had no plenty or variety to glory in; and therefore he here warns them against another branch of covetousness, which they are most in temptation to that have but a little of this world, which was the case of the disciples at best and much more now that they had left all to follow Christ, and that was, an *anxious solicitude* about the necessary supports of life: "*Take no thought for your life*, either for the preservation of it, if it be in danger, or for the provision that is to be made for it, either of food or clothing, *what ye shall eat* or *what ye shall put on*." This is the caution he had largely insisted upon, Matt. vi. 25, &c.; and the arguments here used are much the same, designed for our encouragement to cast all our care upon God, which is the *right way* to *ease* ourselves of it. Consider then,

1. God, who has done the greater for us, may be depended upon to do the less. He has, without any care or forecast of our own, given us *life* and a *body*, and therefore we may cheerfully leave it to him to provide *meat* for the support of that life, and *raiment* for the defence of that body.

2. God, who provides for the inferior creatures, may be depended upon to provide for good Christians. "Trust God for *meat*, for he *feeds the ravens* (*v.* 24); they *neither sow nor reap*, they take neither care nor pains beforehand to provide for themselves, and yet they are *fed*, and never perish for want. Now consider *how much better ye are than the fowls*, than the ravens. Trust God for clothing, for he clothes the lilies (*v.* 27, 28); they make no preparation for their own clothing, they *toil not*, they *spin not*, the root in the ground is a naked thing, and without ornament, and yet, as the flower grows up, it appears wonderfully *beautified*. Now, if God has so clothed the flowers, which are fading perishing things, *shall he not much more clothe* you with such clothing as is fit for you, and with clothing suited to your nature, as theirs is?" When God fed Israel with *manna* in the wilderness, he also took care for their clothing; for though he did not furnish them with new clothes, yet (which came all to one) he provided that those they had should not *wax old upon them*, Deut. viii. 4. Thus will he clothe his spiritual Israel; but then let them not be *of little faith*. Note, Our inordinate cares are owing to the weakness of our faith; for a powerful practical belief of the all-sufficiency of God, his covenant-relation to us as a Father, and especially his precious promises, relating both to this life and that to come, would be mighty, through God, to the pulling down of the strong holds of these disquieting perplexing imaginations.

3. Our cares are fruitless, vain, and insignificant, and therefore it is folly to indulge them. They will not gain us our wishes, and therefore ought not to hinder our repose (*v.* 25): "*Which of you by taking thought can add to his stature one cubit*, or one inch, can add to *his age* one year or one hour? Now if ye be *not able to do that which is least*, if it be not in your power to alter your statures, why should you perplex yourselves about other things, which are as much out of your power, and about which it is as necessary that we refer ourselves to the providence of God?" Note, As in our *stature*, so in our *state*, it is our wisdom to take *it as it is*, and make the best of it; for fretting and vexing, carping and caring, will not mend it.

4. An inordinate anxious pursuit of the things of this world, even necessary things, very ill becomes the disciples of Christ (*v.* 29, 30): "Whatever others do, *seek not ye what ye shall eat, or what ye shall drink;* do not you afflict yourselves with perplexing cares, nor weary yourselves with constant toils; do not hurry hither and thither with enquiries *what you shall eat or drink*, as David's enemies, that *wandered up and down for meat* (Ps. lix. 15), or as the eagle that *seeks the prey afar off*, Job xxxix. 29. Let not the disciples of Christ thus *seek* their food, but ask it of God day by day; let them not be *of doubtful mind; μὴ μετεωρίζεσθε—Be not as meteors in the air*, that are blown hither and

thither with every wind; do not, like them, *rise* and *fall*, but maintain a consistency with yourselves; be even and steady, and have your hearts fixed; *live not in careful suspense;* let not your minds be continually perplexed between hope and fear, ever upon the rack." Let not the children of God make themselves uneasy; for,

(1.) This is to make themselves like the children of this world: "*All these things do the nations of the world seek after, v.* 30. They that take care for the body only, and not for the soul, for this world only, and not for the other, look no further than what they shall *eat* and *drink;* and, having no all-sufficient God to seek to and confide in, they burden themselves with anxious cares about those things. But it ill becomes you to do so. You, who are called out of the world, ought not to be thus conformed to the world, and to *walk in the way of this people,*" Isa. viii. 11, 12. When inordinate cares prevail over us, we should think, "What am I, a Christian or a heathen? Baptized or not baptized? If a Christian, if baptized, shall I rank myself with Gentiles, and join with them in their pursuits?"

(2.) It is needless for them to disquiet themselves with care about the necessary supports of life; for they have a Father in heaven who does and will take care for them: "*Your Father knows that you have need of these things,* and considers it, and will supply your needs *according to his riches in glory;* for he is *your Father,* who *made* you subject to these necessities, and therefore will suit his compassions to them; *your Father,* who *maintains* you, educates you, and designs an inheritance for you, and therefore will take care that you *want no good thing.*

(3.) They have better things to mind and pursue (*v.* 31): "*But rather seek ye the kingdom of God,* and mind this, you, my disciples, who are to *preach the kingdom of God;* let your hearts be upon your work, and your great care how to do that well, and this will effectually divert your thoughts from inordinate care about the things of the world. And let all that have souls to save *seek the kingdom of God,* in which only they can be *safe.* Seek admission into it, seek advancement in it; seek the *kingdom of grace,* to be subjects in that; the *kingdom of glory,* to be princes in that; and then *all these things shall be added to you.* Mind the affairs of your souls with diligence and care, and then trust God with all your other affairs."

(4.) They have better things to expect and hope for: *Fear not, little flock, v.* 32. For the banishing of inordinate cares, it is necessary that fears should be suppressed. When we frighten ourselves with an apprehension of evil to come, we put ourselves upon the stretch of care how to avoid it, when after all perhaps it is but the creature of our own imagination. Therefore *fear not, little flock,* but *hope to the end;* for *it is your Father's good pleasure to give you the kingdom.* This comfortable word we had not in Matthew. Note, [1.] Christ's flock in this world is a *little flock;* his sheep are but few and feeble. The church is a vineyard, a garden, a small spot, compared with the wilderness of this world; as Israel (1 Kings xx. 27), who were like two little flocks of kids, when *the Syrians filled the country.* [2.] Though it be a little flock, quite *over-numbered,* and therefore in danger of being *overpowered,* by its enemies, yet it is the will of Christ that they should not *be afraid:* "*Fear not, little flock,* but see yourselves safe under the protection and conduct of the great and good Shepherd, and lie easy." [3.] God has *a kingdom* in store for all that belong to Christ's *little flock,* a crown of glory (1 Pet. v. 4), a throne of power (Rev. iii. 21), unsearchable riches, far exceeding the peculiar treasures of *kings and provinces.* The *sheep on the right hand* are called to *come* and *inherit the kingdom;* it is theirs for ever; a kingdom for each. [4.] The kingdom is given according to the *good pleasure* of the Father: *It is your Father's good pleasure;* it is given not of debt, but of grace, free grace, sovereign grace; *even so, Father, because it seemed good unto thee.* The kingdom is his; and may he not do what he will with his own? [5.] The believing hopes and prospects of *the kingdom* should silence and suppress the fears of Christ's little flock in this world. "Fear no trouble; for, though it should come, it shall not come between you and the kingdom, that is sure, it is near." (That is not an evil worth trembling at the thought of which cannot separate us from the love of God.) "*Fear not the want* of any thing that is good for you; for, if it be *your Father's good pleasure to give you the kingdom,* you need not question but he will *bear your charges* thither."

II. He charged them to make sure work for their souls, by laying up their treasure in heaven, *v.* 33, 34. Those who have done this may be very easy as to all the events of time.

1. "*Sit loose to this world,* and to all your possessions in it: *Sell that ye have,* and *give alms,*" that is, "rather than want wherewith to relieve those that are truly *necessitous,* sell what you have that is *superfluous,* all that you can spare from the support of yourselves and families, and give it *to the poor. Sell what you have,* if you find it a hindrance from, or incumbrance in, the service of Christ. Do not think yourselves undone, if by being fined, imprisoned, or banished, for the testimony of Jesus, you be forced to sell your estates, though they be *the inheritance of your fathers.* Do not sell to *hoard up* the money, or because you can make more of it by usury, but *sell and give alms;* what is given in alms, in a right manner, is put out to the *best* interest, upon the *best* security."

2. "*Set your hearts upon the other world,* and your expectations from that world. *Pro-*

vide yourselves bags that wax not old, that wax not empty, not of gold, but of grace in the heart and good works in the life; these are the bags that will last." Grace will *go with us* into another world, for it is *woven in* the soul; and our good works will *follow us,* for *God is not unrighteous to forget* them. These will be *treasures in heaven,* that will enrich us to eternity. (1.) It is treasure that will not be *exhausted;* we may spend upon it to eternity, and it will not be at all the less; there is no danger of seeing the bottom of it. (2.) It is treasure that we are in no danger of being robbed of, for *no thief approaches* near it; what is laid up in heaven is out of the reach of enemies. (3.) It is treasure that will not *spoil* with *keeping,* any more than it will *waste* with *spending;* the *moth* does not *corrupt* it, as it does our garments which we now wear. Now by *this* it appears that we have laid up our treasure in heaven if our *hearts* be *there* while we are *here* (*v.* 34), if we think much of heaven and keep our eye upon it, if we quicken ourselves with the hopes of it and keep ourselves in awe with the fear of falling short of it. But, if your hearts be set upon the earth and the things of it, it is to feared that you have your treasure and portion in it, and are undone when you leave it.

III. He charges them to get ready, and to keep in a readiness for Christ's coming, when all those who have laid up their treasure in heaven shall enter upon the enjoyment of it, *v.* 35, &c.

1. Christ is our *Master,* and we are his *servants,* not only *working* servants, but *waiting* servants, servants that are to do him honour, in *waiting* on him, and attending his motions: *If any man serve me, let him follow me. Follow the Lamb whithersoever he goes.* But that is not all: they must do him honour in *waiting for him,* and expecting his return. We must be as men that *wait for their Lord,* that sit up late while he stays out late, to be ready to receive him.

2. Christ our Master, though now *gone from us,* will *return again,* return *from the wedding,* from *solemnizing* the nuptials abroad, to *complete* them at home. Christ's servants are now in a state of expectation, *looking for their Master's glorious appearing,* and doing every thing with an eye to *that,* and in order to *that.* He *will come* to take cognizance of his servants, and, that being a *critical day,* they shall either stay with him or be turned out of doors, according as they are found in that day.

3. The time of our Master's return is uncertain; it will be *in the night,* it will be *far* in the night, when he has long *deferred* his coming, and when many have done looking for him; in the *second watch,* just before midnight, or in the *third watch,* next after midnight, *v.* 38. His coming to us, at our death, is uncertain, and to many it will be a great surprise; for *the Son of man cometh at an hour that ye think not* (*v.* 40), without giving notice beforehand. This bespeaks not only the uncertainty of the time of his coming, but the prevailing security of the greatest part of men, who are *unthinking,* and altogether regardless of the notices given them, so that, whenever he comes, it is *in an hour that they think not.*

4. That which he expects and requires from his servants is that they be *ready to open to him immediately,* whenever he comes (*v.* 36), that is, that they be in a frame fit to receive him, or rather to be received by him; that they be found *as* his servants, in the posture that becomes them, with their *loins girded about,* alluding to the servants that are ready to go whither their master sends them, and do what their master bids them, having their long garments tucked up (which otherwise would hang about them, and hinder them), and *their lights burning,* with which to light their master into the house, and up to his chamber.

5. Those servants will be happy who shall be found ready, and in a good frame, when their Lord shall come (*v.* 37): *Blessed are those servants* who, after having waited long, continue in a waiting frame, until the hour that their Lord comes, and are then found awake and aware of his first approach, of his first knock; and again (*v.* 38): *Blessed are those servants,* for then will be the time of their preferment. Here is such an instance of honour done them as is scarcely to be found among men: He *will make them sit down to meat, and will serve them.* For the bridegroom to wait upon his bride at table is not uncommon, but to wait upon his servants is not *the manner of men;* yet Jesus Christ was among his disciples as *one that served,* and did once, to show his condescension, *gird himself,* and *serve them,* when he *washed their feet* (John xiii. 4, 5); it signified the joy with which they shall be received into the other world by the Lord Jesus, who is gone before, to prepare for them, and has told them that his *Father* will *honour* them, John xii. 26.

6. We are *therefore* kept at uncertainty concerning the precise time of his coming that we may be always ready; for it is no thanks to a man to be ready for an attack, if he know beforehand just the time when it will be made: *The good man of the house, if he had known what hour the thief would have come,* though he were ever so careless a man, *would* yet *have watched,* and have frightened away the thieves, *v.* 39. But we do not know at what hour the alarm will be given us, and therefore are concerned to watch at all times, and never to be off our guard. Or this may intimate the miserable case of those who are careless and unbelieving in this great matter. If the *good man of the house* had had notice of his danger of being robbed such a night, he would have sat up, and saved his house; but we have notice of the day of the Lord's

coming, *as a thief in the night,* to the confusion and ruin of all secure sinners, and yet do not thus *watch.* If men will take such care of their houses, O let us be thus wise for our souls: *Be ye therefore ready also,* as ready as the good man of the house would be *if he knew what hour the thief would come.*

41 Then Peter said unto him, Lord,
speakest thou this parable unto us, or
even to all? 42 And the Lord said,
Who then is that faithful and wise
steward, whom *his* lord shall make
ruler over his household, to give *them*
their portion of meat in due season?
43 Blessed *is* that servant, whom his
lord when he cometh shall find so
doing. 44 Of a truth I say unto you,
that he will make him ruler over all
that he hath. 45 But and if that
servant say in his heart, My lord delayeth his coming; and shall begin to
beat the menservants and maidens,
and to eat and drink, and to be
drunken; 46 The lord of that servant
will come in a day when he looketh
not for *him,* and at an hour when he
is not aware, and will cut him in
sunder, and will appoint him his portion with the unbelievers. 47 And
that servant, which knew his lord's
will, and prepared not *himself,* neither
did according to his will, shall be
beaten with many *stripes.* 48 But
he that knew not, and did commit
things worthy of stripes, shall be
beaten with few *stripes.* For unto
whomsoever much is given, of him
shall be much required: and to whom
men have committed much, of him
they will ask the more. 49 I am
come to send fire on the earth; and
what will I, if it be already kindled?
50 But I have a baptism to be baptized
with; and how am I straitened till it
be accomplished! 51 Suppose ye
that I am come to give peace on earth?
I tell you, Nay; but rather division:
52 For from henceforth there shall
be five in one house divided, three
against two, and two against three.
53 The father shall be divided against
the son, and the son against the father; the mother against the daughter,
and the daughter against the mother;
the mother in law against her daughter
in law, and the daughter in law against
her mother in law.

Here is, I. Peter's question, which he put to Christ upon occasion of the foregoing parable (*v.* 41): "*Lord, speakest thou this parable to us* that are thy constant followers, to us that are ministers, *or also to all* that come to be taught by thee, to all the hearers, and in them to all Christians?" Peter was now, as often, spokesman for the disciples. We have reason to bless God that there are some such forward men, that have a gift of utterance; let those that are such take heed of being proud. Now Peter desires Christ to explain himself, and to direct the arrow of the foregoing parable to the mark he intended. He calls it a *parable,* because it was not only figurative, but weighty, solid, and instructive. Lord, said Peter, was it intended for *us,* or for *all?* To this Christ gives a direct answer (Mark xiii. 37): *What I say unto you, I say unto all.* Yet here he seems to show that the apostles were primarily concerned in it. Note, We are all concerned to take to ourselves what Christ in his word designs for us, and to enquire accordingly concerning it: *Speakest thou this to us?* To me? Speak, Lord, for thy servant hears. Doth this word belong to me? Speak it to *my heart.*

II. Christ's reply to this question, directed to Peter and the rest of the disciples. If what Christ had said before did not so peculiarly concern them, but in common with other Christians, who must all watch and pray for Christ's coming, as *his servants,* yet this that follows is peculiarly adapted to ministers, who are the *stewards* in Christ's house. Now our Lord Jesus here tells them,

1. What was their *duty* as *stewards,* and what the *trust* committed to them. (1.) They are made *rulers of God's household,* under Christ, whose own the house is; ministers derive an authority from Christ to preach the gospel, and to administer the ordinances of Christ, and apply the seals of the covenant of grace. (2.) Their business is to give God's children and servants *their portion of meat,* that which is proper for them and allotted to them; convictions and comfort to those to whom they respectively belong. *Suum cuique—to every one his own.* This is *rightly to divide the word of truth,* 2 Tim. ii. 15. (3.) To give it to them *in due season,* at that time and in that way which are most suitable to the temper and condition of those that are to be fed; a word *in season* to him *that is weary.* (4.) Herein they must approve themselves *faithful* and *wise; faithful* to their Master, by whom this great trust is reposed in them, and faithful to their fellow-servants, for whose benefit they are put in trust; and *wise* to improve an opportunity of doing honour to their Master, and service in the family. Ministers must be both *skilful* and *faithful.*

2. What would be their happiness if they approved themselves faithful and wise (*v.* 43):

Blessed is that servant, (1.) That is *doing,* and is not idle, nor indulgent of his ease; even the rulers of the household must be *doing,* and make themselves *servants of all.* (2.) That is *so* doing, doing as he should be, giving them their *portion of meat,* by public preaching and personal application. (3.) That is *found* so doing when his Lord comes; that perseveres to the end, notwithstanding the difficulties he may meet with in the way. Now his happiness is illustrated by the preferment of a steward that has approved himself within a lower and narrower degree of service; he shall be preferred to a larger and higher (*v.* 44): *He will make him ruler over all that he has,* which was Joseph's preferment in Pharaoh's court. Note, Ministers that obtain mercy of the Lord to be faithful shall obtain further mercy to be abundantly rewarded for their faithfulness in the day of the Lord.

3. What a dreadful reckoning there would be if they were treacherous and unfaithful, *v.* 45, 46. If that servant begin to be quarrelsome and profane, he shall be called to an account, and severely punished. We had all this before in Matthew, and therefore shall here only observe, (1.) Our looking upon Christ's second coming as a thing at a distance is the cause of all those irregularities which render the thought of it terrible to us: *He saith in his heart, My Lord delays his coming.* Christ's patience is very often misinterpreted his *delay,* to the *dis*couragement of his people, and the *en*couragement of his enemies. (2.) The persecutors of God's people are commonly abandoned to security and sensuality; *they beat their fellow-servants,* and then *eat and drink with the drunken,* altogether unconcerned either at their own sin or their brethren's sufferings, as the king and Haman, who *sat down to drink when the city Shushan was perplexed.* Thus they drink, to drown the clamours of their own consciences, and baffle them, which would otherwise fly in their faces. (3.) Death and judgment will be very terrible to all wicked people, but especially to wicked ministers. It will be a surprise to them: *At an hour when they are not aware.* It will be the determining of them to endless misery; they shall be cut in sunder, and have their portion assigned them with *the unbelievers.*

4. What an aggravation it would be of their sin and punishment that they knew their duty, and did not do it (*v.* 47, 48): *That servant that knew his lord's will, and did it not, shall be beaten with many stripes,* shall fall under a sorer punishment; and *he that knew not shall be beaten with few stripes,* his punishment shall, in consideration of this, be mitigated. Here seems to be an allusion to the law, which made a distinction between sins committed through ignorance, and presumptuous sins (Lev. v. 15, &c.; Numb. xv. 29, 30), as also to another law concerning the number of stripes given to a malefactor, to be according to the nature of the crime, Deut. xxv. 2, 3. Now, (1.) Ignorance of our duty is an extenuation of sin. He *that knew not his lord's will,* through carelessness and neglect, and his not having such opportunities as some others had of coming to the knowledge of it, and *did things worthy of stripes,* he shall *be beaten,* because he might have known his duty better, but *with few stripes;* his ignorance excuses in part, but not wholly. Thus *through ignorance* the Jews put Christ to death (Acts iii. 17; 1 Cor. ii. 8), and Christ pleaded that ignorance in their excuse: *They know not what they do.* (2.) The knowledge of our duty is an aggravation of our sin: *That servant that knew his lord's will,* and yet did his own will, shall be *beaten with many stripes.* God will justly inflict more upon him for abusing the means of knowledge he afforded him, which others would have made a better use of, because it argues a great degree of wilfulness and contempt to sin against knowledge; of how much sorer punishment then shall they be thought worthy, besides the many stripes that their own consciences will give them! Son, remember. Here is a good reason for this added: *To whomsoever much is given, of him shall be much required,* especially when it is *committed* as a trust he is to account for. Those that have greater capacities of mind than others, more knowledge and learning, more acquaintance and converse with the scriptures, to them *much is given,* and their account will be accordingly.

III. A further discourse concerning his own sufferings, which he expected, and concerning the sufferings of his followers, which he would have them also to live in expectation of. In general (*v.* 49): *I am come to send fire on the earth.* By this some understand the preaching of the gospel, and the pouring out of the Spirit, holy fire; this Christ came to send with a commission to refine the world, to purge away its dross, to burn up its chaff, and it was *already kindled.* The gospel was begun to be preached; some prefaces there were to the pouring out of the Spirit. Christ baptized with the Holy Ghost and with fire; this Spirit descended in fiery tongues. But, by what follows, it seems rather to be understood of the fire of *persecution.* Christ is not the Author of it, as it is the sin of the incendiaries, the *persecutors;* but he *permits* it, nay, he *commissions* it, as a *refining* fire for the *trial* of the *persecuted.* This fire was *already kindled* in the enmity of the carnal Jews to Christ and his followers. "*What will I that it may presently be kindled? What thou doest, do quickly. If it be already kindled, what will I?* Shall I wait the *quenching* of it? No, for it must fasten upon myself, and upon all, and glory will redound to God from it."

1. He must himself suffer many things; he must pass through this fire that was already kindled (*v.* 50): *I have a baptism to be*

baptized with. Afflictions are compared both to *fire* and *water*, Ps. lxvi. 12; lxix. 1, 2. Christ's sufferings were both. He calls them a *baptism* (Matt. xx. 22); for he was watered or sprinkled with them, as Israel was baptized *in the cloud,* and dipped into them, as Israel was baptized *in the sea,* 1 Cor. x. 2. He must be sprinkled with his own blood, and with the blood of his enemies, Isa. lxiii. 3. See here, (1.) Christ's *foresight* of his sufferings; he knew what he was to undergo, and the necessity of undergoing it: *I am to be baptized with a baptism.* He calls his sufferings by a name that *mitigates* them; it is a baptism, not a deluge; I must be *dipped* in them, not *drowned* in them; and by a name that *sanctifies* them, for baptism is a sacred rite. Christ in his sufferings *devoted* himself to his Father's honour, and *consecrated* himself a priest for evermore, Heb. vii. 27, 28. (2.) Christ's *forwardness* to his sufferings: *How am I straitened till it be accomplished!* He longed for the time when he should suffer and die, having an eye to the glorious issue of his sufferings. It is an allusion to a woman in travail, that is *pained to be delivered,* and welcomes her pains, because they hasten the birth of the child, and wishes them sharp and strong, that the *work* may be *cut short.* Christ's sufferings were the *travail of his soul,* which he cheerfully underwent, in hope that he should by them *see his seed,* Isa. liii. 10, 11. So much was his heart set upon the redemption and salvation of man.

2. He tells those about him that they also must bear with hardships and difficulties (*v.* 51): "*Suppose ye that I came to give peace on earth,* to give you a peaceable possession of the earth, and outward prosperity on the earth?" It is intimated that they were ready to entertain such a thought as this, nay, that they went upon this supposition, that the gospel would meet with a *universal* welcome, that people would *unanimously* embrace it, and would therefore study to make the preachers of it *easy* and *great,* that Christ, if he did not give them *pomp* and *power,* would at least give them *peace;* and herein they were encouraged by divers passages of the Old Testament, which speak of the peace of the Messiah's kingdom, which they were willing to understand of external peace. "But," saith Christ, "you will be mistaken, the event will declare the contrary, and therefore do not flatter yourselves into a fool's paradise. You will find,"

(1.) "That the effect of the preaching of the gospel will be *division.*" Not but that the design of the gospel and its proper tendency are to unite the children of men to one another, to knit them together in holy love, and, if all would receive it, this would be the effect of it; but there being multitudes that not only will not receive it, but oppose it, and have their corruptions exasperated by it, and are enraged at those that do receive it, it proves, though not the *cause,* yet the *occasion* of *division.* While *the strong man armed kept his palace,* in the Gentile world, *his goods were at peace;* all was quiet, for all went one way, the sects of philosophers agreed well enough, so did the worshippers of different deities; but when the gospel was preached, and many were enlightened by it, and turned from the power of Satan to God, then there was a disturbance, *a noise and a shaking,* Ezek. xxxvii. 7. Some *distinguished* themselves by embracing the gospel, and others were angry that they did so. Yea, and among them that received the gospel there would be different sentiments in minor things, which would occasion *division;* and Christ permits it for holy ends (1 Cor. xi. 18), that Christians may learn and practise mutual forbearance, Rom. xiv. 1, 2.

(2.) "That this *division* will reach into private families, and the preaching of the gospel will give occasion for discord among the nearest relations" (*v.* 53): *The father shall be divided against the son, and the son against the father,* when the one turns Christian and the other does not; for the one that does turn Christian will be zealous by arguments and endearments to turn the other too, 1 Cor. vii. 16. As soon as ever Paul was converted, he *disputed,* Acts ix. 29. The one that continues in unbelief will be provoked, and will hate and persecute the one that by his faith and obedience witnesses against, and condemns, his unbelief and disobedience. A spirit of bigotry and persecution will break through the strongest bonds of relation and natural affection; see Matt. x. 35; xxiv. 7. Even *mothers* and *daughters* fall out about religion; and those that believe not are so violent and outrageous that they are ready to deliver up into the hands of the bloody persecutors those that believe, though otherwise very near and dear to them. We find in the *Acts* that, wherever the gospel came, *persecution* was *stirred up;* it was *every where spoken against,* and there was *no small stir about that way.* Therefore let not the disciples of Christ promise themselves *peace upon earth,* for they are sent forth *as sheep in the midst of wolves.*

54 And he said also to the people,
When ye see a cloud rise out of the
west, straightway ye say, There cometh
a shower; and so it is. 55 And
when *ye see* the south wind blow, ye
say, There will be heat; and it cometh
to pass. 56 *Ye* hypocrites, ye can
discern the face of the sky and of the
earth; but how is it that ye do not
discern this time? 57 Yea, and why
even of yourselves judge ye not what
is right? 58 When thou goest with
thine adversary to the magistrate, *as*

thou art **in the way, give diligence that thou mayest be delivered from him; lest he hale thee to the judge, and the judge deliver thee to the officer, and the officer cast thee into prison. 59 I tell thee, thou shalt not depart thence, till thou hast paid the very last mite.**

Having given his disciples *their* lesson in the foregoing verses, here Christ turns to *the people,* and gives them *theirs, v.* 54. He *said also to the people:* he preached *ad populum—to the people,* as well as *ad clerum—to the clergy.* In general, he would have them be as wise in the affairs of their souls as they are in their outward affairs. Two things he specifies:—

I. Let them learn to *discern the way of God towards them,* that they may *prepare* accordingly. They were *weather-wise,* and by observing the winds and clouds could foresee when there would be *rain* and when there would be *hot weather* (*v.* 54, 55); and, according as they foresaw the weather would be, they either housed their hay and corn, or threw it abroad, and equipped themselves for a journey? Even in regard to changes of the weather God gives warning to us what is coming, and art has improved the notices of nature in weather-glasses. The prognostications here referred to had their origin in repeated observations upon the chain of causes; from what *has been* we conjecture what *will be.* See the benefit of experience; by *taking notice* we may come to *give notice.* Whoso is wise will *observe* and *learn.* See now,

1. The particulars of the presages: "*When you see a cloud arising out of the west*" (the Hebrew would say, *out of the sea*), "perhaps it is at first *no bigger than a man's hand* (1 Kings xviii. 44), but you say, There is a shower in the womb of it, and it proves so. When you *observe* the *south wind blow,* you say, *There will be heat*" (for the hot countries of Africa lay not far south from Judea), "and it usually *comes to pass;*" yet nature has not tied itself to such a track but that *sometimes* we are mistaken in our prognostics.

2. The inferences from them (*v.* 56): "*Ye hypocrites,* who pretend to be wise, but really are not so, who pretend to expect the Messiah and his kingdom" (for so the generality of the Jews did) "and yet are no way disposed to receive and entertain it, *how is it that you do not discern this time,* that you do not discern that now is the time, according to the indications given in the Old-Testament prophecies, for the Messiah to appear, and that, according to the marks given of him, I am he? Why are you not aware that you have now an opportunity which you *will not have long,* and which you *may never have again,* of securing to yourselves an interest in the kingdom of God and the privileges of that kingdom?" *Now is the accepted time,* now or never. It is the folly and misery of man that he *knows not his time,* Eccl. ix. 12. This was the ruin of the men of that generation, that they *knew not the day of their visitation, ch.* xix. 44. But a *wise man's heart discerns time and judgment;* such was the wisdom of the men of Issachar, who *had understanding of the times,* 1 Chron. xii. 32. He adds, "*Yea, and why even of yourselves,* though ye had not these loud alarms given you, *judge ye not what is right? v.* 57. You are not only stupid and regardless in matters that are purely of divine revelation, and take not the hints which that gives you, but you are so even in the dictates of the very light and law of nature." Christianity has reason and natural conscience on its side; and, if men would allow themselves the liberty of *judging what is right,* they would soon find that all Christ's precepts concerning all things are right, and that there is nothing more equitable in itself, nor better becoming us, than to submit to them and be ruled by them.

II. Let them hasten to *make their peace with God* in time, before it be too late, *v.* 58, 59. This we had upon another occasion, Matt. v. 25, 26. 1. We reckon it our wisdom in our temporal affairs to *compound* with those with whom we cannot *contend,* to *agree with our adversary* upon the best terms we can, before the equity be *foreclosed,* and we be left to the rigour of the law: "*When thou goest with thine adversary to the magistrate,* to whom the appeal is made, and knowest that he has an advantage against thee, and thou art in danger of being cast, thou knowest it is the most prudent course to make the matter up between yourselves; *as thou art in the way, give diligence to be delivered from him,* to get a discharge, lest judgment be given, and execution awarded according to law." Wise men will not let their quarrels go to an extremity, but accommodate them in time. 2. Let us do thus in the affairs of our souls. We have by sin made God our *adversary,* have provoked his displeasure against us, and he has both *right* and *might* on his side; so that it is to no purpose to think of carrying on the controversy with him ether at *bar* or in *battle.* Christ, to whom all judgment is committed, is the magistrate before whom we are hastening to appear: if we stand a trial before him, and insist upon our own justification, the cause will certainly go against us, the *Judge* will *deliver* us to the *officer,* the ministers of his justice, and we shall be *cast into* the *prison* of hell, and the debt will be exacted to the utmost; though we cannot make a full satisfaction for it, it will be continually demanded, *till the last mite be paid,* which will not be to all eternity. Christ's sufferings were short, yet the *value* of them made them fully satisfactory. In the sufferings of damned sinners, what is wanting in value must be made up in an endless duration. Now, in consideration of this, let us give diligence to be delivered *out of* the hands of God as an adversary, into his hands as a Father, and this *as we are in the way*, which has the chief stress laid upon it here. While we are alive, we are *in the way;* and *now* is our *time*, by repentance and faith through Christ (who is the Mediator as well as the magistrate), to get the quarrel made up, while it may be done, before it be too late. Thus was God in Christ *reconciling the world to himself, beseeching us to be reconciled.* Let us take hold on the arm of the Lord stretched out in this gracious offer, that we may make peace, and we *shall make peace* (Isa. xxvii. 4, 5), for we cannot *walk together* till we be *agreed.*

CHAP. XIII.

In this chapter we have, I. The good improvement Christ made of a piece of news that was brought him concerning some Galileans, that were lately massacred by Pilate, as they were sacrificing in the temple at Jerusalem, ver. 1—5. II. The parable of the fruitless fig-tree, by which we are warned to bring forth fruits meet for that repentance to which he had in the foregoing passage called us, ver. 6—9. III. Christ's healing a poor infirm woman on the sabbath day, and justifying himself in it, ver. 11—17. IV. A repetition of the parables of the grain of mustard-seed, and the leaven, ver. 18—22. V. His answer to the question concerning the number of the saved, ver. 23—30. VI. The slight he put upon Herod's malice and menaces, and the doom of Jerusalem read, ver. 31—35.

THERE were present at that season some that told him of the
Galilæans, whose blood Pilate had
mingled with their sacrifices. 2 And
Jesus answering said unto them, Suppose ye that these Galilæans were
sinners above all the Galilæans, because they suffered such things? 3
I tell you, Nay: but, except ye repent,
ye shall all likewise perish. 4 Or
those eighteen, upon whom the tower
in Siloam fell, and slew them, think
ye that they were sinners above all
men that dwelt in Jerusalem? 5 I
tell you, Nay: but, except ye repent,
ye shall all likewise perish.

We have here, I. Tidings brought to Christ of the death of some Galileans lately, whose blood *Pilate had mingled with their sacrifices*, *v.* 1. Let us consider,

1. What this tragical story was. It is briefly related here, and is not met with in any of the historians of those times. Josephus indeed mentions Pilate's killing some Samaritans, who, under the conduct of a factious leader, were going in a tumultuous manner to mount Gerizim, where the Samaritans' temple was; but we can by no means allow that story to be the same with this. Some think that these Galileans were of the faction of Judas Gaulonita, called also *Judas of Galilee* (Acts v. 37), who disowned Cæsar's authority and refused to pay tribute to him: or perhaps these, being Galileans, were only suspected by Pilate to be of that faction, and barbarously murdered, because those who were in league with that pretender were out of his reach. The Galileans being Herod's subjects, it is probable that this outrage committed upon them by Pilate occasioned the quarrel that was between Herod and Pilate, which we read of in *ch.* xxiii. 12. We are not told what number they were, perhaps *but a few*, whom Pilate had some particular *pique* against (and therefore the story is overlooked by Josephus); but the circumstance remarked is that he *mingled their blood with their sacrifices* in the court of the temple. Though perhaps they had reason to fear Pilate's malice, yet they would not, under pretence of that fear, keep away from Jerusalem, whither the law obliged them to go up with their sacrifices. Dr. Lightfoot thinks it probable that they were *themselves* killing their sacrifices (which was allowed, for the priest's work, they said, began with the *sprinkling of the blood*), and that Pilate's officers came upon them by surprise, just at the time when they were off their guard (for otherwise the Galileans were mettled men, and generally went well-armed), and mingled the blood of the sacrificers with the blood of the sacrifices, as if it had been equally acceptable to God. Neither the holiness of the place nor of the work would be a protection to them from the fury of an unjust judge, *who neither feared God nor regarded man.* The altar, which used to be a sanctuary and place of shelter, is now become a snare and a trap, a place of danger and slaughter.

2. Why it was related *at this season* to our Lord Jesus. (1.) Perhaps merely as a matter of news, which they supposed he had not heard before, and as a thing which they lamented, and believed he would do so too; for the Galileans were their countrymen. Note, Sad providences ought to be observed by us, and the knowledge of them communicated to others, that they and we may be suitably affected with them, and make a good use of them. (2.) Perhaps it was intended as a confirmation of what Christ had said in the close of the foregoing chapter, concerning the necessity of making our peace with God in time, before we be *delivered to the officer*, that is, to *death*, and so *cast into prison*, and then it will be too late to make agreements: "Now," say they, "Master, here is a fresh instance of some that were very suddenly *delivered to the officer*, that were taken away by death when they little expected it; and therefore we have all need to be ready." Note, It will be of good use to us both to explain the word of God and to enforce it upon ourselves by observing the providences of God. (3.) Perhaps they would stir him up, being himself of Galilee, and a prophet, and one that had a great interest in that country, to find out a way to revenge the death of these Galileans upon Herod. If they had any thoughts of this kind, they were quite mistaken; for Christ was now going up to Jerusalem, to be *delivered into the hands of Pilate*, and to have his blood, not mingled with his sacrifice, but itself made a sacrifice. (4.) Perhaps this was told Christ to *deter* him

from going up to Jerusalem, to worship (*v.* 22), lest Pilate should serve him as he had served those Galileans, and should suggest against him, as probably he had insinuated against those Galileans, in vindication of his cruelty, that they came to sacrifice as Absalom did, with a *seditious* design, under colour of sacrificing, to raise rebellion. Now, lest Pilate, when his hand was in, should proceed further, they think it advisable that Christ should for the present keep out of the way. (5.) Christ's answer intimates that they told him this with a spiteful *inuendo,* that, though Pilate was unjust in killing them, yet without doubt they were secretly bad men, else God would not have permitted Pilate thus barbarously to cut them off. It was very invidious; rather than they would allow them to be martyrs, though they died sacrificing, and perhaps suffered for their devotion, they would, without any colour of proof, suppose them to be malefactors; and it may be for no other reason than because they were not of their party and denomination, differed from them, or had difference with them. This fate of theirs, which was capable not only of a favourable, but an honourable construction, shall be called a *just judgment* of God *upon them,* though they know not for what.

II. Christ's reply to this report, in which,

1. He seconded it with another story, which, like it, gave an instance of people's being taken away by sudden death. It is not long since *the tower of Siloam fell,* and there were eighteen persons killed and buried in the ruins of it. Dr. Lightfoot's conjecture is that this tower adjoined to the *pool of Siloam,* which was the same with the pool of Bethesda, and that it belonged to those *porches* which were by the *pool,* in which the *impotent folks* lay, that *waited for the stirring* of the water (John v. 3), and that they who were killed were some of them, or some of those who in this pool used to purify themselves for the temple-service, for it was near the temple. Whoever they were, it was a sad story; yet such melancholy accidents we often hear of: for *as the birds are caught in a snare, so are the sons of men snared in an evil time, when it falls suddenly upon them,* Eccl. ix. 12. Towers, that were built for safety, often prove men's destruction.

2. He cautioned his hearers not to make an ill use of these and similar events, nor take occasion thence to censure *great sufferers,* as if they were *therefore* to be accounted *great sinners: Suppose ye that these Galileans,* who were slain as they were sacrificing, *were sinners above all the Galileans, because they suffered such things? I tell you nay, v.* 2, 3. Perhaps they that told him the story of the Galileans were Jews, and were glad of any thing that furnished them with matter of reflection upon the Galileans, and therefore Christ retorted upon them the story of the *men of Jerusalem,* that came to an untimely end; for, *with what measure* of that kind *we mete, it shall be measured to us again.* "Now suppose ye that *those eighteen* who met with their death from the tower of Siloam, while perhaps they were expecting their cure from the pool of Siloam, were *debtors* to divine justice *above all men that dwelt at Jerusalem? I tell you nay.*" Whether it make for us or against us, we must abide by this rule, that we cannot judge of men's *sins* by their *sufferings* in this world; for many are thrown into the furnace as gold to be purified, not as dross and chaff to be consumed. We must therefore not be harsh in our censures of those that are afflicted more than their neighbours, as Job's friends were in their censures of him, lest we add sorrow to the sorrowful; nay, lest we condemn *the generation of the righteous,* Ps. lxxiii. 14. If we will be judging, we have enough to do to judge ourselves; nor indeed can we *know love or hatred by all that is before us,* because *all things come alike to all,* Eccl. ix. 1, 2. And we might as justly conclude that the *oppressors,* and Pilate among the rest, *on whose side are power* and success, are the greatest saints, as that the *oppressed,* and those Galileans among the rest, who are all in tears and have no comforter, no, not the priests and Levites that attended the altar, are the *greatest sinners.* Let us, in our censures of others, do as we would be done by; for as we do we shall be done by: *Judge not, that ye be not judged,* Matt. vii. 1.

3. On these stories he founded a call to repentance, adding to each of them this awakening word, *Except ye repent, ye shall all likewise perish, v.* 3—5. (1.) This intimates that we all deserve to *perish* as much as *they did,* and had we been dealt with according to our sins, according to the *iniquity of our holy things,* our blood had been long ere this mingled with our sacrifices by the justice of God. It must moderate our censures, not only that we are *sinners,* but that we are as great sinners as they, have as much sin to repent of as they had to suffer for. (2.) That therefore we are all concerned to *repent,* to be sorry for what we have done amiss, and to do so no more. The judgments of God upon others are loud calls to us to *repent.* See how Christ improved every thing for the pressing of that great duty which he came not only to *gain room* for, and *give hopes* to, but to enjoin upon us—and that is, to *repent.* (3.) That repentance is the way to escape perishing, and it is a sure way: *so iniquity shall not be your ruin,* but upon no other terms. (4.) That, if we repent not, we shall certainly perish, as others have done before us. Some lay an emphasis upon the word *likewise,* and apply it to the destruction that was coming upon the people of the Jews, and particularly upon Jerusalem, who were destroyed by the Romans at the time of their passover, and so, like the Galileans, they had *their blood mingled with their sacrifices;* and many of them, both in Jerusalem and in other

places, were destroyed by the fall of walls and buildings which were battered down about their ears, as those that died by the fall of the tower of Siloam. But certainly it looks further; except we repent, we shall perish eternally, as they perished out of this world. The same Jesus that calls us to *repent because the kingdom of heaven is at hand*, bids us *repent* because otherwise we shall perish; so that he has set before us life and death, good and evil, and put us to our choice. (5.) The perishing of *those* in their impenitency who have been most harsh and severe in judging others will be in a particular manner aggravated.

6 He spake also this parable; A
certain *man* had a fig tree planted in
his vineyard; and he came and sought
fruit thereon, and found none. 7
Then said he unto the dresser of his
vineyard, Behold, these three years I
come seeking fruit on this fig tree,
and find none: cut it down; why
cumbereth it the ground? 8 And he
answering said unto him, Lord, let it
alone this year also, till I shall dig
about it, and dung *it:* 9 And if it
bear fruit, *well:* and if not, *then* after
that thou shalt cut it down.

This parable is intended to enforce that word of warning immediately going before, "*Except ye repent, ye shall all likewise perish;* except you be reformed, you will be ruined, as the barren tree, except it bring forth fruit, will be cut down."

I. This parable primarily refers to the nation and people of the Jews. God chose them for his own, made them a people near to him, gave them advantages for knowing and serving him above any other people, and expected answerable returns of duty and obedience from them, which, turning to his praise and honour, he would have accounted *fruit;* but they disappointed his expectations: they did not do their duty; they were a reproach instead of being a credit to their profession. Upon this, he justly determined to abandon them, and cut them off, to deprive them of their privileges, to unchurch and unpeople them; but, upon Christ's intercession, as of old upon that of Moses, he graciously gave them further time and further mercy; tried them, as it were, another year, by sending his apostles among them, to call them to repentance, and in Christ's name to offer them pardon, upon repentance. Some of them were wrought upon to *repent,* and bring forth fruit, and with them all was well; but the body of the nation continued impenitent and unfruitful, and ruin without remedy came upon them; about forty years after they were cut down, and cast into the fire, as John Baptist had told them (Matt. iii. 10), which saying of his this parable enlarges upon.

II. Yet it has, without doubt, a further reference, and is designed for the awakening of all that enjoy the means of grace, and the privileges of the visible church, to see to it that the temper of their minds and the tenour of their lives be answerable to their professions and opportunities, for that is the *fruit* required. Now observe here,

1. The advantages which this fig-tree had. It was *planted in a vineyard,* in better soil, and where it had more care taken of it and more pains taken with it, than other fig-trees had, that commonly grew, not in *vineyards* (those are for vines), but by the *way-side,* Matt. xxi. 19. This fig-tree belonged to a *certain man,* that owned it, and was at expense upon it. Note, The church of God is *his vineyard,* distinguished from the common, and fenced about, Isa. v. 1, 2. We are *fig-trees planted* in this vineyard by our baptism; we have a place and a name in the visible church, and this is our privilege and happiness. It is a distinguishing favour: he has not *dealt so with other nations.*

2. The owner's expectation from it: *He came, and sought fruit thereon,* and he had reason to expect it. He did not *send,* but came himself, intimating his desire to find fruit. Christ came into this world, *came to his own,* to the Jews, seeking fruit. Note, The God of heaven requires and expects *fruit* from those that have a place in his vineyard. He has *his eye* upon those that *enjoy* the gospel, to see whether they *live* up to it; he seeks evidences of their getting good by the means of grace they enjoy. *Leaves* will not serve, crying, *Lord, Lord; blossoms* will not serve, beginning well and promising fair; there must be *fruit.* Our thoughts, words, and actions must be according to the gospel, light and love.

3. The disappointment of his expectation: *He found none,* none at all, not one fig. Note, It is sad to think how many enjoy the privileges of the gospel, and yet do nothing at all to the honour of God, nor to answer the end of his entrusting them with those privileges; and it is a disappointment to him and a grief to the Spirit of his grace.

(1.) He here complains of it to the dresser of the vineyard: I come, *seeking fruit,* but am disappointed—*I find none,* looking for grapes, but behold *wild grapes.* He is grieved with such a generation.

(2.) He aggravates it, with two considerations:—[1.] That he had waited long, and yet was disappointed. As he was not *high* in his expectations, he only expected fruit, not *much* fruit, so he was not *hasty, he came three years,* year after year: applying it to the Jews, he came one space of time before the captivity, another after that, and another in the preaching of John Baptist and of Christ himself; or it may allude to the three years of Christ's public ministry, which were now expiring. In general, it teaches us that the patience of God is stretched out to long-suffering with many that enjoy the gospel, and do not bring forth the fruits of it; and this patience is wretchedly abused, which provokes God to so much the greater severity. How many times three years has God come to many of us, *seeking fruit,* but has *found none,* or next to none, or worse than none! [2.] That this fig-tree did not only not bring forth fruit, but did hurt; it *cumbered the ground;* it took up the room of a fruitful tree, and was injurious to all about it. Note, Those who do not *do good* commonly *do hurt* by the influence of their bad example; they grieve and discourage those that are good; they harden and encourage those that are bad. And the mischief is the greater, and the ground the more cumbered, if it be a high, large, spreading tree, and if it be an old tree of long standing.

4. The doom passed upon it: *Cut it down.* He saith this to the *dresser of the vineyard,* to Christ, to whom all judgment is committed, to the ministers who are in his name to declare this doom. Note, No other can be expected concerning barren trees than that they should be *cut down.* As the unfruitful vineyard is dismantled, and thrown open to the common (Isa. v. 5, 6), so the unfruitful trees in the vineyard are cast out of it, and wither, John xv. 6. It is cut down by the judgments of God, especially spiritual judgments, such as those on the Jews that believed not, Isa. vi. 9, 10. It is cut down by death, and cast into the fire of hell; and with good reason, for *why cumbers it the ground?* What reason is there why it should have a place in the vineyard to no purpose?

5. The dresser's intercession for it. Christ is the great Intercessor; he ever lives, interceding. Ministers are intercessors; they that *dress* the vineyard should *intercede* for it; those we *preach to* we should *pray for,* for we must give ourselves to the *word of God* and to *prayer.* Now observe,

(1.) What it is he prays for, and that is a reprieve: *Lord, let it alone this year also.* He doth not pray, "Lord, let it never be cut down," but, "Lord, not now. Lord, do not remove the dresser, do not withhold the dews, do not pluck up the tree." Note, [1.] It is desirable to have a barren tree reprieved. Some have not yet *grace to repent,* yet it is a mercy to them to have *space to repent,* as it was to the old world to have 120 years allowed them to make their peace with God. [2.] We owe it to Christ, the great Intercessor, that *barren* trees are not cut down immediately: had it not been for his interposition, the whole world had been cut down, upon the sin of Adam; but he said, *Lord, let it alone;* and it is he that upholds all things. [3.] We are encouraged to pray to God for the merciful reprieve of barren fig-trees: "Lord, *let them alone;* continue them yet awhile in their probation; bear with them a little longer, and wait to be gracious." Thus must we stand in the gap, to turn away wrath. [4.] Reprieves of mercy are but for a time: *Let it alone this year also,* a short time, but a sufficient time to make trial. When God has borne long, we may hope he will bear yet a little longer, but we cannot expect he should bear always. [5.] *Reprieves* may be obtained by the prayers of others for us, but not *pardons;* there must be our own faith, and repentance, and prayers, else no pardon.

(2.) How he promises to improve this reprieve, if it be obtained: *Till I shall dig about it, and dung it.* Note, [1.] In general, our prayers must always be seconded with our endeavours. The dresser seems to say, "Lord, it may be I have been wanting in that which is my part; but let it alone this year, and I will do more than I have done towards its fruitfulness." Thus in all our prayers we must request God's grace, with a humble resolution to do our duty, else we mock God, and show that we do not rightly value the mercies we pray for. [2.] In particular, when we pray to God for grace for ourselves or others, we must follow our prayers with diligence in the use of the means of grace. The dresser of the vineyard engages to do *his* part, and therein teaches ministers to do *theirs.* He will *dig about* the tree and will *dung* it. Unfruitful Christians must be *awakened* by the terrors of the law, which *break up the fallow ground,* and then encouraged by the promises of the gospel, which are warming and fattening, as manure to the tree. Both methods must be tried; the one prepares for the other, and all little enough.

(3.) Upon what foot he leaves the matter: "Let us try it, and try what we can do with it one year more, *and, if it bear fruit, well, v.* 9. It is possible, nay, there is hope, that yet it may be fruitful." In this hope the owner will have patience with it, and the dresser will take pains with it, and, if it should have the desired success, both will be pleased that it was not cut down. The word *well* is not in the original, but the expression is abrupt: *If it bear fruit!*—supply it how you please, so as to express how wonderfully well-pleased both the owner and dresser will be. If it bear fruit, there will be cause of rejoicing; we have what we would have. But it cannot be better expressed than as we do: *well.* Note, Unfruitful professors of religion, if after long unfruitfulness they will repent, and amend, and bring forth fruit, shall find *all is well.* God will be *pleased,* for he will be *praised;* ministers' hands will be strengthened, and such penitents will be their joy now and their crown shortly. Nay, there will be joy in heaven for it; the ground will be no longer cumbered, but bettered, the vineyard beautified, and the good trees in it made better. As for the tree itself, it is *well* for it; it shall not only not be cut down, but it shall *receive blessing from God* (Heb. vi. 7); it shall be *purged*, and *shall bring forth more fruit*, for the Father is its husbandman (John xv. 2); and it shall at last be transplanted from the vineyard on earth to the paradise above.

But he adds, *If not, then after that thou shalt cut it down.* Observe here, [1.] That, though God bear long, he will not bear always with unfruitful professors; his patience will have an end, and, if it be abused, will give way to that wrath which will have no end. Barren trees will certainly be *cut down* at last, and *cast into the fire.* [2.] The longer God has *waited*, and the more cost he has been at upon them, the greater will their destruction be: to be cut down *after that*, after all these expectations from it, these debates concerning it, this concern for it, will be sad indeed, and will aggravate the condemnation. [3.] Cutting down, though it is work that shall be done, is work that God does not take pleasure in: for observe here, the owner said to the dresser, "Do thou *cut it down*, for it cumbereth the ground." "Nay," said the dresser, "if it must be done at last, *thou shalt cut it down;* let not my hand be upon it." [4.] Those that now intercede for barren trees, and take pains with them, if they persist in their unfruitfulness will be even content to see them cut down, and will not have one word more to say for them. Their best friends will acquiesce in, nay, they will approve and applaud, the righteous judgment of God, in the day of the manifestation of it, Rev. xv. 3, 4.

10 And he was teaching in one of
the synagogues on the sabbath. 11
And, behold, there was a woman which
had a spirit of infirmity eighteen years,
and was bowed together, and could in
no wise lift up *herself.* 12 And when
Jesus saw her, he called *her to him*,
and said unto her, Woman, thou art
loosed from thine infirmity. 13 And
he laid *his* hands on her: and immediately she was made straight, and
glorified God. 14 And the ruler of
the synagogue answered with indignation, because that Jesus had healed
on the sabbath day, and said unto
the people, There are six days in which
men ought to work: in them therefore come and be healed, and not on
the sabbath day. 15 The Lord then
answered him, and said, *Thou* hypocrite, doth not each one of you on the
sabbath loose his ox or *his* ass from
the stall, and lead *him* away to watering? 16 And ought not this woman,
being a daughter of Abraham, whom
Satan hath bound, lo, these eighteen
years, be loosed from this bond on
the sabbath day? 17 And when he
had said these things, all his adversaries were ashamed: and all the people rejoiced for all the glorious things
that were done by him.

Here is, I. The miraculous cure of a woman that had been long under a spirit of infirmity. Our Lord Jesus spent his *sabbaths* in the *synagogues, v.* 10. We should make conscience of doing so, as we have opportunity, and not think we can spend the sabbath as well at home in reading a good book; for religious assemblies are a divine institution, which we must bear our testimony to, though but of two or three. And, when he was in the synagogues on the sabbath day, *he was teaching there*—*ἦν διδάσκων.* It denotes a continued act; he *still taught the people knowledge.* He was in his element when he was teaching. Now to confirm the doctrine he preached, and recommend it as faithful, and well worthy of all acceptation, he wrought a miracle, a miracle of mercy.

1. The object of charity that presented itself was a woman in the synagogue that had *a spirit of infirmity eighteen years, v.* 11. She had an infirmity, which an evil spirit, by divine permission, had brought upon her, which was such that she was *bowed together* by strong convulsions, and could *in no wise lift up herself;* and, having been so long thus, the disease was incurable; she could not stand erect, which is reckoned man's honour above the beasts. Observe, Though she was under this infirmity, by which she was much *deformed*, and made to look mean, and not only so, but, as is supposed, motion was very painful to her, yet she went to the *synagogue on the sabbath day.* Note, Even bodily infirmities, unless they be very grievous indeed, should not keep us from public worship on sabbath days; for God can help us, beyond our expectation.

2. The offer of this cure to one that sought it not bespeaks the preventing mercy and grace of Christ: *When Jesus saw her, he called her to him, v.* 12. It does not appear that she made any application to him, or had any expectation from him; but *before she called he answered.* She came to him to be *taught*, and to get good to her soul, and then Christ gave this relief to her bodily infirmity. Note, Those whose first and chief care is for their souls do best befriend the true interests of their bodies likewise, for *other things shall be added to them.* Christ in his gospel calls and invites those to come to him for healing that labour under *spiritual infirmities*, and, if he *calls us*, he will undoubtedly help us when we come to him.

3. The cure effectually and immediately wrought bespeaks his almighty power. He *laid his hands on her*, and said, "*Woman,*

thou art loosed from thine infirmity; though thou hast been long labouring under it, thou art at length released from it." Let not those despair whose disease is *inveterate,* who have been long in affliction. God can at length relieve them, therefore though he tarry wait for him. Though it was a *spirit of infirmity,* an evil spirit, that she was under the power of, Christ has a power superior to that of Satan, is *stronger than he.* Though *she could in no wise lift up herself,* Christ could lift her up, and enable her to lift up herself. She that had been *crooked* was *immediately made straight,* and the scripture was fulfilled (Ps. cxlvi. 8): *The Lord raiseth them that are bowed down.* This cure represents the work of Christ's grace upon the souls of people. (1.) In the *conversion* of sinners. Unsanctified hearts are under this *spirit of infirmity;* they are distorted, the faculties of the soul are quite out of place and order; they are *bowed down* towards things below. *O curvæ in terram animæ!—Base souls that bend towards the earth!* They can in no wise *lift up themselves* to God and heaven; the bent of the soul, in its natural state, is the quite contrary way. Such crooked souls seek not to Christ; but he calls them to him, lays the hand of his power and grace upon them, speaks a healing word to them, by which he *looses them from their infirmity,* makes the soul *straight,* reduces it to order, raises it above worldly regards, and directs its affections and aims heavenward. Though *man cannot make that straight which God has made crooked* (Eccl. vii. 13), yet the grace of God can make that straight which the sin of man has made crooked. (2.) In the *consolation* of good people. Many of the children of God are long under a *spirit of infirmity,* a spirit of bondage; through prevailing grief and fear, their *souls* are *cast down* and *disquieted* within them, *they are troubled, they are bowed down greatly, they go mourning all the day long,* Ps. xxxviii. 6. But Christ, by his Spirit of adoption, looses them from this infirmity in due time, and raises them up.

4. The present effect of this cure upon the *soul* of the patient as well as upon her *body.* She *glorified God,* gave him the praise of her cure to whom all praise is due. When crooked souls are made straight, they will show it by their glorifying God.

II. The offence that was taken at this by the *ruler of the synagogue,* as if our Lord Jesus had committed some heinous crime, in healing this poor woman. He *had indignation* at it, because it was *on the sabbath day, v.* 14. One would think that the miracle should have convinced him, and that the circumstance of its being done on the sabbath day could not have served to counteract the conviction; but what light can shine so clear, so strong, that a spirit of bigotry and enmity to Christ and his gospel will not serve to shut men's eyes against it? Never was such honour done to the synagogue he was ruler of as Christ had now done it, and yet he had indignation at it. He had not indeed the impudence to quarrel with Christ; but he said *to the people,* reflecting upon Christ in what he said, *There are six days in which men ought to work, in them therefore come and be healed, and not on the sabbath day.* See here how light he made of the miracles Christ wrought, as if they were *things of course,* and no more than what quacks and mountebanks did every day: "You may *come* and be healed any day of the week." Christ's cures were become, in his eyes, cheap and common things. See also how he stretches the law beyond its intention, or any just construction that could be put upon it, in making either healing or being healed with a touch of the hand, or a word's speaking, to be that *work* which is *forbidden* on the sabbath day. This was evidently *the work of God;* and, when God tied us out from working that day, did he tie himself out? The same word in Hebrew signifies both *godly* and *merciful (chesed),* to intimate that works of *mercy* and *charity* are in a manner works of *piety* (1 Tim. v. 4) and therefore very proper on sabbath days.

III. Christ's justification of himself in what he had done (*v.* 15): *The Lord then answered him,* as he had answered others who in like manner cavilled at him, *Thou hypocrite.* Christ, who knows men's hearts, may call those *hypocrites* whom it would be presumption for us to call so. We *must* judge charitably, and *can* judge only according to the outward appearance. Christ knew that he had a real enmity to him and to his gospel, that he did but cloak this with a pretended zeal for the sabbath day, and that when he bade the people come on the *six days,* and be healed, he really would not have them be healed any day. Christ could have told him this, but he vouchsafes to reason the case with him; and,

1. He *appeals* to the common practice among the Jews, which was never disallowed, that of *watering* their cattle on the sabbath day. Those cattle that are kept up in the stable are constantly *loosed from the stall on the sabbath day, and led away to watering.* It would be a barbarous thing not to do it; for *a merciful man regards the life of his beast,* his own beast that serves him. Letting the cattle *rest* on the sabbath day, as the law directed, would be worse than working them, if they must be made to fast on that day, as the Ninevites' cattle on their fast-day, that were not permitted to *feed nor drink water,* Jon. iii. 7.

2. He applies this to the present case (*v.* 16): "Must the *ox* and the *ass* have compassion shown them on the sabbath day, and have so much time and pains bestowed upon them *every* sabbath, to be loosed from the stall, led away perhaps a great way to the water, and then back again, and shall not this woman, only with a touch of the hand and a word's speaking, be *loosed* from a much

greater grievance than that which the cattle undergo when they are kept a day without water? For consider," (1.) "She is *a daughter of Abraham,* in a relation to whom you all pride yourselves; she is *your sister,* and shall she be denied a favour that you grant to an ox or an ass, dispensing a little with the supposed strictness of the sabbath day? She is *a daughter of Abraham,* and therefore is entitled to the Messiah's blessings, to the *bread* which belongs to the *children.*" (2.) "She is one whom Satan *has bound.* He had a hand in the affliction, and therefore it was not only an act of charity to the poor woman, but of piety to God, to break the power of the devil, and baffle him." (3.) "She has been in this deplorable condition, *lo, these eighteen years,* and therefore, now that there is an opportunity of delivering her, it ought not to be deferred *a day* longer, as you would have it, for any of you would have thought eighteen years' affliction full long enough."

IV. The different effect that this had upon those that heard him. He had sufficiently made it out, not only that it was lawful, but that it was highly fit and proper, to heal this poor woman *on the sabbath day,* and thus publicly in the synagogue, that they might all be witnesses of the miracle. And now observe,

1. What a confusion this was to the malice of his persecutors: *When he had said these things, all his adversaries were ashamed* (*v.* 17); they were put to silence, and were vexed that they were so, that they had not a word to say for themselves. It was not a shame that worked repentance, but rather indignation. Note, Sooner or later, all the adversaries of Christ, and his doctrine and miracles, will be made *ashamed.*

2. What a confirmation this was to the faith of his friends: *All the people,* who had a better sense of things, and judged more impartially than their rulers, rejoiced *for all the glorious things that were done by him.* The shame of his foes was the joy of his followers; the increase of his interest was what the one fretted at, and the other triumphed in. The things Christ did were *glorious things;* they were all so, and, though now clouded, perhaps will appear so, and we ought to rejoice in them. Every thing that is the honour of Christ is the comfort of Christians.

18 Then said he, Unto what is the
kingdom of God like? and whereunto
shall I resemble it? 19 It is like a
grain of mustard seed, which a man
took, and cast into his garden; and it
grew, and waxed a great tree; and
the fowls of the air lodged in the
branches of it. 20 And again he said,
Whereunto shall I liken the kingdom
of God? 21 It is like leaven, which
a woman took and hid in three measures of meal, till the whole was leavened. 22 And he went through the
cities and villages, teaching, and journeying towards Jerusalem.

Here is, I. The gospel's progress foretold in two parables, which we had before, Matt. xiii. 31—33. The *kingdom of the Messiah* is the *kingdom of God,* for it advances his glory; this kingdom was yet a mystery, and people were generally in the dark, and under mistakes, about it. Now, when we would describe a thing to those that are strangers to it, we choose to do it by similitudes. "Such a person you know not, but I will tell you whom he is like;" so Christ undertakes here to show *what the kingdom of God is like* (*v.* 18): "*Whereunto shall I liken the kingdom of God? v.* 20. It will be quite another thing from what you expect, and will operate, and gain its point, in quite another manner." 1. "You expect it will appear *great,* and will arrive at its perfection all of a sudden; but you are mistaken, *it is like a grain* of *mustard-seed,* a little thing, takes up but little room, makes but a little figure, and promises but little; yet, when sown in soil proper to receive it, it *waxes a great tree,*" *v.* 19. Many perhaps were prejudiced against the gospel, and loth to come in *to the obedience* of it, because its beginning was so small; they were ready to say of Christ, *Can this man save us?* And of his gospel, *Is this likely ever to come to any thing?* Now Christ would remove this prejudice, by assuring them that though *its beginning was small its latter end should greatly increase;* so that many should come, should come upon the wing, should *fly like a cloud,* to lodge in the branches of it with more safety and satisfaction than in the branches of Nebuchadnezzar's tree, Dan. iv. 21. 2. "You expect it will make its way by *external* means, by subduing nations and vanquishing armies, though it shall work *like leaven,* silently and insensibly, and without any force or violence, *v.* 21. A little leaven leaveneth the whole lump; so the doctrine of Christ will strangely *diffuse* its relish into the world of mankind: in this it triumphs, that *the savour of the knowledge of it* is unaccountably made manifest *in every place,* beyond what one could have expected, 2 Cor. ii. 14. But you must *give it time,* wait for the issue of the preaching of the gospel to the world, and you will find it does wonders, and alters the property of the souls of men. By degrees *the whole will be leavened,* even as many as are, like *the meal* to the *leaven,* prepared to receive the savour of it."

II. Christ's progress towards Jerusalem recorded: *He went through the cities and villages, teaching and journeying, v.* 22. Here we find Christ an itinerant, but an itinerant preacher, journeying towards Jerusalem, to the feast of dedication, which was *in the winter,* when travelling was uncomfortable, yet he would be about his Father's business; and therefore, whatever cities or villages he could make in his way, he gave them a sermon or two, not only in the cities, but in the country villages. Wherever Providence brings us, we should endeavour to be doing all the good we can.

23 Then said one unto him, Lord,
are there few that be saved? And he
said unto them, 24 Strive to enter in
at the strait gate: for many, I say
unto you, will seek to enter in, and
shall not be able. 25 When once
the master of the house is risen up,
and hath shut to the door, and ye
begin to stand without, and to knock
at the door, saying, Lord, Lord, open
unto us; and he shall answer and say
unto you, I know you not whence ye
are: 26 Then shall ye begin to say,
We have eaten and drunk in thy presence, and thou hast taught in our
streets. 27 But he shall say, I tell
you, I know you not whence ye are;
depart from me, all *ye* workers of
iniquity. 28 There shall be weeping
and gnashing of teeth, when ye shall
see Abraham, and Isaac, and Jacob,
and all the prophets, in the kingdom
of God, and you *yourselves* thrust
out. 29 And they shall come from
the east, and *from* the west, and from
the north, and *from* the south, and
shall sit down in the kingdom of God.
30 And, behold, there are last which
shall be first, and there are first which
shall be last.

We have here,

I. A question put to our Lord Jesus. Who it was that put it we are not told, whether a friend or a foe; for he both gave a great liberty of questioning him and returned answers to the thoughts and intents of the heart. The question was, *Are there few that are saved?* v. 23: εἰ ὀλίγοι οἱ σωζόμενοι;—"*If the saved be few?* Master, I have heard thou shouldest say so; is it true?" 1. Perhaps it was a *captious* question. He put it to him, tempting him, with a design to ensnare him and lessen his reputation. If he should say that many would be saved, they would reproach him as too loose, and making salvation cheap; if few, they would reproach him as precise and strait-laced. The Jewish doctors said that *all Israel should have a place in the world to come;* and would he dare to contradict that? Those that have sucked in a corrupt notion are ready to make it the standard by which to measure all men's judgments; and in nothing do men more betray their ignorance, presumption, and partiality, than in judging of the salvation of others. 2. Perhaps it was a *curious* question, a nice speculation, which he had lately been disputing upon with his companions, and they all agreed to refer it to Christ. Note, Many are more inquisitive respecting who shall be saved, and who not, than respecting what they shall do to be saved. It is commonly asked, "May such and such be saved?" But it is well that we may be saved without knowing this. 3. Perhaps it was an *admiring* question. He had taken notice how strict the law of Christ was, and how bad the world was, and, comparing these together, cries out, "How few are there that will be saved!" Note, We have reason to wonder that of the many to whom the word of salvation is sent there are so few to whom it is indeed a saving word. 4. Perhaps it was an *enquiring* question: "*If there be few that be saved,* what then? What influence should this have upon me?" Note, It concerns us all seriously to improve the great truth of the fewness of those that are saved.

II. Christ's answer to this question, which directs us what use to make of this truth. Our Saviour did not give a direct answer to this enquiry, for he came to *guide* men's *consciences,* not to *gratify* their *curiosity.* Ask not, "How many shall be saved?" But, be they more or fewer, "Shall I be one of them?" Not, "What shall become of such and such, and *what shall this man do?*" But, "What shall I do, and what will become of me?" Now in Christ's answer observe,

1. A quickening exhortation and direction: *Strive to enter in at the strait gate.* This is directed not to him only that asked the question, but to all, to us, it is in the plural number: *Strive ye.* Note, (1.) All that will be saved must *enter in at the strait gate,* must undergo a change of the whole man, such as amounts to no less than being born again, and must submit to a strict discipline. (2.) Those that would enter in at the strait gate must *strive to enter.* It is a hard matter to get to heaven, and a point that will not be gained without a great deal of care and pains, of difficulty and diligence. We must strive with God in prayer, wrestle as Jacob, strive against sin and Satan. We must strive in every duty of religion; strive with our own hearts, ἀγωνίζεσθε—"*Be in an agony;* strive as those that run for a prize; excite and exert ourselves to the utmost."

2. Divers awakening considerations, to enforce this exhortation. O that we may be all awakened and quickened by them! They are such considerations as will serve to answer the question, *Are there few that shall be saved?*

(1.) Think how many take *some pains* for salvation and yet perish because they do not take *enough,* and you will say that there are *few that will be saved* and that it highly concerns us to *strive: Many will seek to enter in, and shall not be able;* they *seek*, but they do not *strive.* Note, The reason why many come short of grace and glory is because they rest in a *lazy seeking* of that which will not be attained without a *laborious striving.* They have a *good mind to happiness,* and a *good opinion of holiness,* and take some *good steps* towards both. But their convictions are weak; they do not consider what they know and believe, and, consequently, their desires are cold, and their endeavours feeble, and there is no strength or steadiness in their resolutions; and thus they *come short,* and lose the prize, because they do not press forward. Christ avers this upon his own word: *I say unto you;* and we may take it upon his word, for he knows both the counsels of God and the hearts of the children of men.

(2.) Think of the *distinguishing* day that is coming and the *decisions* of that day, and you will say there are *few that shall be saved* and that we are concerned to strive: The *Master of the house* will *rise up, and shut to the door, v.* 25. Christ is the *Master of the house,* that will take cognizance of all that frequent his house and are retainers to it, will examine comers and goers and those that pass and repass. Now he seems as if he left things at large; but the day is coming when he will *rise up, and shut to the door.* What door? [1.] A door of *distinction.* Now, within the temple of the church there are *carnal* professors who worship in the *outer-court,* and *spiritual* professors who worship *within the veil;* between these the door is now open, and they meet *promiscuously* in the same external performances. But, when the *Master of the house is risen up,* the door will be shut between them, that those who are in the *outer-court* may be kept out, and left to be *trodden underfoot by the Gentiles,* Rev. xi. 2. As to those *that are filthy,* shut the door upon them, and let them be *filthy still;* that those who are within may be kept within, that those who are *holy may be holy still.* The door is shut to *separate* between the *precious* and the *vile,* that *sinners* may no longer *stand in the congregation of the righteous.* Then you shall return, and discern betwixt them. [2.] A door of *denial* and exclusion. The door of *mercy* and *grace* has long *stood open* to them, but they would *not come in by it,* would not be beholden to the *favour* of that door; they hoped to *climb up some other way,* and to get to heaven by their own merits, and therefore when the Master of the house is risen up he will justly *shut that door;* let them not expect to enter by it, but let them take their own measures. Thus, when Noah was safe in the ark, God *shut* the door, to *exclude* all those that depended upon shelters of their own in the approaching flood.

(3.) Think how many who were very *confident* that they should be *saved* will be rejected in the day of trial, and their confidences will deceive them, and you will say that there are *few* that *shall be saved* and that we are all concerned to *strive.* Consider,

[1.] What an *assurance* they had of *admission,* and how far their hope carried them, even to *heaven's gate.* There they *stand and knock,* knock as if they had authority, knock as those that belong to the house, *saying,* "*Lord, Lord, open to us,* for we think we have a right to enter; take us in among the *saved ones,* for we joined ourselves to them." Note, Many are ruined by an ill-grounded hope of heaven, which they never distrusted or called in question, and *therefore* conclude their state is good because they never doubted it. They call Christ, *Lord,* as if they were his servants; nay, in token of their importunity, they double it, *Lord, Lord;* they are desirous now to enter in by that door which they had formerly made light of, and would now gladly come in among those serious Christians whom they had secretly despised.

[2.] What *grounds* they had for this *confidence.* Let us see what their plea is, *v.* 26. *First,* They had been *Christ's guests,* had had an intimate converse with him, and had shared in his favours: *We have eaten and drunk in thy presence,* at thy table. Judas ate bread with Christ, dipped with him in the dish. Hypocrites, under the disguise of their external profession, receive the Lord's supper, and in it partake of the children's bread, as if they were children. *Secondly,* They had been *Christ's hearers,* had received instruction from him, and were well acquainted with his doctrine and law: "*Thou hast taught in our streets*—a distinguishing favour, which few had, and surely it might be taken as a pledge of distinguishing favour now; for wouldest thou teach us, and not save us?"

[3.] How their confidence will fail them, and all their pleas be rejected as frivolous. Christ will say to them, *I know you not whence you are, v.* 25. And again (*v.* 27), *I tell you, I know you not, depart from me.* He does not deny that what they pleaded was true; they had *eaten and drunk in his presence,* by the same token that they had no sooner eaten of his bread than they lifted up the heel against him. He had *taught in their streets,* by the same token that they had despised his instruction and would not submit to it. And therefore, *First,* He *disowns* them: "*I know you not;* you do not belong to my family." *The Lord knows them that are his,* but them that are not he does not know, he has nothing to do with them: "*I know you not whence you are.* You are not of me, you are not from above, you are not branches of my house, of my vine." *Secondly,* He *discards* them: *Depart from me.* It is the hell of hell to depart from Christ, the principal part of the misery of the damned. "Depart from my door, here is nothing for you, no, not a drop of water." *Thirdly,* He gives them such a character as is the reason of this doom: *You are workers of iniquity.* This is their ruin, that, under a pretence of piety, they kept up secret haunts of sin, and did the devil's drudgery in Christ's livery.

[4.] How terrible their punishment will be (*v.* 28): *There shall be weeping and gnashing of teeth,* the utmost degree of grief and indignation; and that which is the cause of it, and contributes to it, is a sight of the happiness of those that are saved: *You shall see the patriarchs and prophets in the kingdom of God, and yourselves thrust out.* Observe here, *First,* That the *Old-Testament saints* are in the kingdom of God; those had benefit by the Messiah who died before his coming, for they *saw his day* at a distance and it reflected comfort upon them. *Secondly,* That *New-Testament sinners* will be *thrust out* of the kingdom of God. It intimates that they will be *thrusting in,* and will presume upon admission, but in vain; they shall be *thrust out* with shame, as having no part or lot in the matter. *Thirdly,* That the sight of the saint's glory will be a great aggravation of sinner's misery; they shall thus far *see the kingdom of God* that they shall see the *prophets* in it, whom they hated and despised, and themselves, though they thought themselves sure of it, *thrust out.* This is that at which they will *gnash their teeth,* Ps. cxii. 10.

(4.) Think who are they that shall be saved, notwithstanding: *They shall come from the east and the west; and the last shall be first, v.* 29, 30. [1.] By what Christ said, it appears that but *few shall be saved* of those whom we think most likely, and who bid fairest for it. Yet do not say then that the gospel is preached in vain; for, though Israel be not *gathered,* Christ will be *glorious.* There shall come many from all parts of the Gentile world that shall be admitted into the kingdom of grace in this world, and of glory in the other. Plainly thus, when we come to heaven, we shall meet a great many there whom we little thought to have met there, and miss a great many thence whom we verily expected to have found there. [2.] Those who *sit down in the kingdom of God* are such as had taken pains to get thither, for they came from far—*from the east and from the west, from the north and from the south;* they had passed through different climates, had broken through many difficulties and discouragements. This shows that they who would enter into that kingdom must *strive,* as the queen of Sheba, who came from the *utmost parts of the earth to hear the wisdom of Solomon.* They who *travel* now in the service of God and religion shall shortly *sit down* to rest in the *kingdom of God.* [3.] Many who stood fair for heaven came short, and others who seemed cast behind, and thrown quite out of the way, will win and wear this prize, and therefore it concerns us to *strive to enter.* Let us be *provoked,* as Paul desires the Jews might be, to a holy emulation, by the zeal and forwardness of the Gentiles, Rom. xi. 14. Shall I be outstripped by my juniors? Shall I, who started first, and stood nearest, miss of heaven, when others, less likely, enter into it? If it be got by striving, why should not I strive?

31 The same day there came certain of the Pharisees, saying unto him, Get thee out, and depart hence: for Herod will kill thee.
32 And he said unto them, Go ye, and tell that fox, Behold, I cast out devils, and I do cures to day and to morrow, and the third *day* I shall be perfected.
33 Nevertheless I must walk to day, and to morrow, and the *day* following: for it cannot be that a prophet perish out of Jerusalem.
34 O Jerusalem, Jerusalem, which killest the prophets, and stonest them that are sent unto thee; how often would I have gathered thy children together, as a hen *doth gather* her brood under *her* wings, and ye would not!
35 Behold, your house is left unto you desolate: and verily I say unto you, Ye shall not see me, until *the time* come when ye shall say, Blessed *is* he that cometh in the name of the Lord.

Here is, I. A suggestion to Christ of his danger from Herod, now that he was in Galilee, within Herod's jurisdiction (*v.* 31): *Certain of the Pharisees* (for there were those of that sect dispersed all the nation over) *came* to Christ, pretending friendship and a concern for his safety, and said, *Get thee* out of this country, and *depart hence,* for otherwise *Herod will kill thee,* as he did John. Some think that these Pharisees had no ground at all for this, that Herod had not given out any words to this purport, but that they framed this lie, to drive him out of Galilee, where he had a great and growing interest, and to drive him into Judea, where they knew there were those that really sought his life. But, Christ's answer being directed to Herod himself, it should seem that the Pharisees had ground for what they said, and that Herod was enraged against Christ, and designed him a mischief, for the honourable testimony he had borne to John Baptist, and to the doctrine of repentance which John preached. Herod was willing to get rid of Christ out of his dominions; and, when he durst not put him to death, he hoped to *frighten him away* by sending him this threatening message.

II. His defiance of Herod's rage and the Pharisees' too; he fears neither the one nor the other: *Go you, and tell that fox* so, *v.* 32. In calling him a *fox,* he gives him his true character; for he was subtle as a fox, noted for his craft, and treachery, and baseness, and preying (as they say of a fox) furthest from his own den. And, though it is a black and ugly character, yet it did not ill become Christ to give it to him, nor was it in him a violation of that law, *Thou shalt not speak evil of the ruler of thy people.* For Christ was a prophet, and prophets always had a liberty of speech in reproving princes and great men. Nay, Christ was more than a prophet, he was a king, he was King of kings, and the greatest of men were accountable to him, and therefore it became him to call this proud king by his own name; but it is not to be drawn into an example by us. "Go, and tell *that* fox, yea, and *this* fox too" (for so it is in the original, τῇ ἀλώπεκι ταύτῃ); "*that Pharisee,* whoever he is, that whispers this in my ear, let him know that *I do not fear him,* nor regard his menaces. For," 1. "I know that I must die, and must die shortly; I expect it, and count upon it, *the third day,*" that is, "very shortly; my hour is at hand." Note, It will help us very much above the fear of death, and of them that have the power of death, to make death familiar to us, to expect it, think of it, and converse with it, and see it at the door. "If Herod should kill me, he will not surprise me." 2. "I know that death will be not only no prejudice to me, but that it will be my preferment; and therefore tell him I do not fear him; when I die, *I shall be perfected.* I shall then have *finished* the hardest part of my undertaking; I shall have completed my business;" τελειοῦμαι—*I shall be consecrated.* When Christ died, he is said to have *sanctified himself;* he consecrated himself to his priestly office with his own blood. 3. "I know that neither he nor any one else can kill me *till I have done my work.* Go, and tell him that I value not his impotent rage. *I will cast out devils, and do cures, to-day and to-morrow,*" that is, "now and for some little space of time yet to come, in spite of him and all his threats. I *must walk,* I must *go on* in my intended journey, and it is not in his power to hinder me. I must *go about,* as I now do, preaching and healing, *to-day, and to-morrow, and the day following.*" Note, It is good for us to look upon the time we have before us as but a little, two or three days perhaps may be the utmost, that we may thereby be quickened to *do the work of the day in its day.* And it is a comfort to us, in reference to the power and malice of our enemies, that they can have no power to take us off as long as God has any work for us to do. The witnesses were not *slain* till they had *finished their testimony.* 4. "I know that Herod can do me no harm, not only because *my time* is not yet come, but because the place appointed for my death is Jerusalem, which is not within his jurisdiction: *It cannot be that a prophet perish out of Jerusalem,*" that is, "any where but at Jerusalem." If a *true prophet* was put to death, he was prosecuted as a *false prophet.* Now none undertook to try prophets, and to judge concerning them, but the great sanhedrim, which always sat at Jerusalem; it was a cause which the inferior courts did not take cognizance of, and therefore, if a *prophet* be *put to death,* it must be at Jerusalem.

III. His lamentation for Jerusalem, and his denunciation of wrath against that city, *v.* 34, 35. This we had Matt. xxiii. 37—39. Perhaps this was not said now in Galilee, but the evangelist, not designing to bring it in in its proper place, inserts it here, upon occasion of Christ's mentioning his being put to death at Jerusalem.

Note, 1. The wickedness of persons and places that more eminently than others profess religion and relation to God is in a particular manner provoking and grieving to the Lord Jesus. How pathetically does he speak of the sin and ruin of that holy city! *O Jerusalem! Jerusalem!* 2. Those that enjoy great plenty of the means of grace, if they are not profited by them, are often prejudiced against them. They that would not hearken to the prophets, nor welcome those whom God had sent to them, *killed* them, and *stoned* them. If men's corruptions are not conquered, they are provoked. 3. Jesus Christ has shown himself willing, freely willing, to receive and entertain poor souls that come to him, and put themselves under his protection: *How often would I have gathered thy children together,* as a hen gathereth her brood under her wings, with such care and tenderness! 4. The reason why sinners are not protected and provided for by the Lord Jesus, as the chickens are by the hen, is because they will not: *I would,* I often would, and *ye would not.* Christ's willingness aggravates sinners' unwillingness, and leaves their blood upon their own heads. 5. The house that Christ leaves is *left desolate.* The temple, though richly adorned, though greatly frequented, is yet desolate if Christ has deserted it. He leaves it *to them;* they had made an idol of it, and let them take it to themselves, and make their best of it, Christ will trouble it no more. 6. Christ justly withdraws from those that drive him from them. They would not be *gathered* by him, and therefore, saith he, "*You shall not see me,* you shall not hear me, any more," as Moses said to Pharaoh, when he forbade him his presence, Exod. x. 28, 29. 7. The judgment of the great day will effectually convince unbelievers that would not now be convinced: "Then you will say, *Blessed is he that cometh,*" that is, "you will be glad to be among those that say so, and *will not see me* to be the Messiah till then when it is too late."

CHAP. XIV.

In this chapter we have, I. The cure which our Lord Jesus wrought upon a man that had the dropsy, on the sabbath day, and his justifying himself therein against those who were offended at his doing it on that day, ver. 1–6. II. A lesson of humility given to those who were ambitious of the highest rooms, ver. 7—11. III. A lesson of charity to those who feasted the rich, and did not feed the poor, ver. 12—14. IV. The success of the gospel offer foretold in the parable of the guests invited to a feast, signifying the rejection of the Jews and all others that set their hearts upon this world, and the entertainment of the Gentiles

and all others that come, empty of self, to be filled with Christ, ver. 15—24. V. The great law of discipleship laid down, with a caution to all that will be Christ's disciples to undertake it deliberately and with consideration, and particularly to ministers, to retain their savour, ver. 25—35.

AND it came to pass, as he went
into the house of one of the
chief Pharisees to eat bread on the
sabbath day, that they watched him.
2 And, behold, there was a certain
man before him which had the dropsy.
3 And Jesus answering spake unto
the lawyers and Pharisees, saying, Is
it lawful to heal on the sabbath day?
4 And they held their peace. And
he took *him*, and healed him, and let
him go; 5 And answered them, saying, Which of you shall have an ass
or an ox fallen into a pit, and will not
straightway pull him out on the sabbath day? 6 And they could not answer him again to these things.

In this passage of story we find,

I. That *the Son of man came eating and drinking,* conversing familiarly with all sorts of people; not declining the society of publicans, though they were of *ill fame,* nor of Pharisees, though they bore him *ill will,* but accepting the friendly invitations both of the one and the other, that, if possible, he might do good to *both.* Here he *went into the house of one of the chief Pharisees,* a ruler, it may be, and a magistrate in his country, *to eat bread on the sabbath day, v.* 1. See how favourable God is to us, that he allows us time, even on his own day, for bodily refreshments; and how careful we should be not to abuse that liberty, or turn it into licentiousness. Christ went only to *eat bread,* to take such refreshment as was necessary on the sabbath day. Our sabbath meals must, with a particular care, be guarded against all manner of excess. On sabbath days we must do as Moses and Jethro did, *eat bread before God* (Exod. xviii. 12), and, as is said of the primitive Christians, on the Lord's day, must *eat and drink* as those that must *pray again before we go to rest,* that we may not be unfit for that.

II. That he *went about doing good.* Wherever he came he *sought* opportunities to *do good,* and not only improved those that *fell in his way.* Here was *a certain man before him who had the dropsy, v.* 2. We do not find that he offered himself, or that his friends offered him to be Christ's patient, but Christ *prevented him* with the blessings of his goodness, and *before he called* he answered him. Note, It is a happy thing to be where Christ is, to be present *before him,* though we be not presented *to him.* This man had the *dropsy,* it is probable, in a high degree, and appeared much swoln with it; probably he was some relation of the Pharisee's, that now *lodged* in his house, which is more likely than that he should be an *invited guest* at the table.

III. That he *endured the contradiction of sinners against himself: They watched him, v.* 1. The Pharisee that invited him, it should seem, did it with a design to pick some quarrel with him; if it were so, Christ *knew* it, and yet *went,* for he knew himself a match for the most *subtle* of them, and knew how to order his steps with an eye to *his observers.* Those that are *watched* had need to be *wary.* It is, as Dr. Hammond observes, contrary to all laws of hospitality to seek advantage against one that you invited to be your guest, for such a one you have taken under your protection. These lawyers and Pharisees, like the fowler that lies in wait to *ensnare* the birds, *held their peace,* and acted very *silently.* When Christ asked them *whether* they thought it *lawful to heal on the sabbath day* (and herein he is said to *answer* them, for it was an answer to *their thoughts,* and thoughts are *words* to Jesus Christ), they would say neither *yea* nor *nay,* for their design was to *inform against him,* not to be *informed by him.* They would not say *it was lawful to heal,* for then they would preclude themselves from imputing it to him as a crime; and yet the thing was so plain and self-evident that they could not for shame say it was *not lawful.* Note, Good men have often been persecuted for doing that which even their persecutors, if they would but give their consciences leave to speak out, could not but own to be lawful and good. Many a *good work* Christ did, for which they *cast stones* at him and his name.

IV. That Christ would not be hindered from *doing good* by the *opposition* and *contradiction* of sinners. He *took him, and healed him, and let him go, v.* 4. Perhaps he *took him aside* into another room, and healed him *there,* because he would neither *proclaim* himself, such was his humility, nor *provoke* his adversaries, such was his wisdom, his *meekness of wisdom.* Note, Though we must not be driven off from our duty by the malice of our enemies, yet we should order the circumstances of it so as to make it the least offensive. Or, He *took him,* that is, he *laid hands* on him, to cure him; ἐπιλαβόμενοσ, *complexus —he embraced him,* took him in his arms, big and unwieldy as he was (for so dropsical people generally are), and reduced him to shape. The cure of a dropsy, as much as of any disease, one would think, should be gradual; yet Christ cured even *that* disease, perfectly cured it, in a moment. He then let him go, lest the Pharisees should fall upon him for *being healed,* though he was purely passive; for what absurdities would not such men as they were be guilty of?

V. That our Lord Jesus *did nothing but what he could justify,* to the conviction and confusion of those that quarrelled with him, *v.* 5, 6. He still answered their thoughts, and made them *hold their peace* for *shame* who before held their peace for *subtlety*, by an appeal to their own practice, as he had been used to do upon such occasions, that he might show them how in condemning him they condemned themselves: *which of you shall have an ass or an ox fallen into a pit*, by accident, *and will not pull him out on the sabbath day*, and that straightway, not deferring it till the sabbath be over, lest it perish? Observe, It is not so much out of *compassion to the poor creature* that they do it as a concern for their own interest. It is *their own ox*, and *their own ass*, that is worth money, that they will dispense with the law of the sabbath for the *saving of*. Now this was an evidence of their hypocrisy, and that it was not out of any real regard to the sabbath that they found fault with Christ for healing on the *sabbath day* (that was only the pretence), but really because they were angry at the *miraculous good works* which Christ wrought, the *proof* he thereby gave of his divine mission, and the interest he thereby *gained* among the people. Many can easily dispense with that, for their own interest, which they cannot dispense with for God's glory and the good of their brethren. This question *silenced* them: *They could not answer him again to these things, v.* 6. Christ will be justified when he speaks, and every mouth must be stopped before him.

7 And he put forth a parable to
those which were bidden, when he
marked how they chose out the chief
rooms; saying unto them, 8 When
thou art bidden of any *man* to a wedding, sit not down in the highest
room; lest a more honourable man
than thou be bidden of him; 9 And
he that bade thee and him come and
say to thee, Give this man place; and
thou begin with shame to take the
lowest room. 10 But when thou art
bidden, go and sit down in the lowest
room; that when he that bade thee
cometh, he may say unto thee, Friend,
go up higher: then shalt thou have
worship in the presence of them that
sit at meat with thee. 11 For whosoever exalteth himself shall be abased;
and he that humbleth himself shall
be exalted. 12 Then said he also to
him that bade him, When thou makest
a dinner or a supper, call not thy friends,
nor thy brethren, neither thy kinsmen,
nor *thy* rich neighbours; lest they also
bid thee again, and a recompence be
made thee. 13 But when thou makest
a feast, call the poor, the maimed, the
lame, the blind: 14 And thou shalt be
blessed; for they cannot recompense
thee: for thou shalt be recompensed
at the resurrection of the just.

Our Lord Jesus here sets us an example of profitable edifying discourse at our tables, when we are in company with our friends. We find that when he had none but his disciples, who were his own family, with him at his table, his discourse with them was *good, and to the use of edifying;* and not only so, but when he was in company with strangers, nay, with enemies that *watched him*, he took occasion to reprove what he saw amiss in them, and to instruct them. Though the *wicked were before him*, he did not *keep silence from good* (as David did, Ps. xxxix, 1, 2), for, notwithstanding the provocation given him, he had not his *heart hot within him*, nor was *his spirit stirred*. We must not only not allow any corrupt communication at our tables, such as that of the *hypocritical mockers at feasts*, but we must go beyond common harmless talk, and should take occasion from God's goodness to us at our tables to speak well of him, and learn to *spiritualize* common things. The lips of the righteous should then *feed many*. Our Lord Jesus was among persons of quality, yet, as one that had not respect of persons,

I. He takes occasion to reprove *the guests* for striving to *sit uppermost*, and thence gives us a lesson of *humility*.

1. He observed how these lawyers and Pharisees affected the *highest seats*, towards the head-end of the table, *v.* 7. He had charged that sort of men with this in general, *ch.* xi. 43. Here he brings home the charge to particular persons; for Christ will give *every man his own*. He *marked* how they *chose out the chief rooms;* every man, as he came in, got as near the best seat as he could. Note, Even in the common actions of life, Christ's eye is upon us, and he *marks* what we do, not only in our religious assemblies, but at our tables, and *makes remarks* upon it.

2. He observed how those who were thus aspiring often exposed themselves, and came off *with a slur;* whereas those who were modest, and seated themselves in the lowest seats, often *gained respect* by it. (1.) Those who, when they come in, assume the highest seats, may perhaps be *degraded*, and forced to *come down* to give place to one *more honourable, v.* 8, 9. Note, It ought to check our high thoughts of ourselves to think how many there are that are *more honourable* than we, not only in respect of worldly dignities, but of personal merits and accomplishments. Instead of being proud that so many give place to us, it should be humbling to us that there are so many that we must give place to. The master of the feast will marshal his guests, and will not see the *more honourable* kept out of the seat that is his due, and therefore will make bold to take him lower

that usurped it: *Give this man place;* and this will be a disgrace before all the company to him that would be thought more deserving than he really was. Note, Pride will have *shame,* and will at last have a *fall.* (2.) Those who, when they come in, content themselves with the lowest seats, are likely to be preferred (*v.* 10): "Go, and *seat thyself in the lowest room,* as taking it for granted that thy friend, who invited thee, has guests to come that are of better rank and quality than thou art; but perhaps it may not prove so, and then it will be said to thee, *Friend, go up higher.* The master of the feast will be so just to thee as not to keep thee at the lower end of the table because thou wert so *modest* as to seat thyself there." Note, The way to *rise high* is to *begin low,* and this recommends a man to those about him: "*Thou shalt have honour and respect before those that sit with thee.* They will see thee to be an *honourable man,* beyond what at first they thought; and honour appears the brighter for shining *out of obscurity.* They will likewise see thee to be a *humble man,* which is the greatest honour of all. Our Saviour here refers to that advice of Solomon (Prov. xxv. 6, 7), *Stand not in the place of great men, for better it is that it be said unto thee, Come up hither, than that thou shouldest be put lower.*" And Dr. Lightfoot quotes a parable out of one of the rabbin somewhat like this. "Three men," said he, "were bidden to a feast; one sat highest, For, said he, I am a prince; the other next, For, said he, I am a wise man; the other lowest, For, said he, I am a humble man. The king seated the humble man highest, and put the prince lowest."

3. He applied this generally, and would have us all learn not to *mind high things,* but to content ourselves with mean things, as for other reasons, so for this, because pride and ambition are disgraceful before men: for *whosoever exalteth himself shall be abased;* but humility and self-denial are really honourable: *he that humbleth himself shall be exalted, v.* 11. We see in other instances that *a man's pride will bring him low,* but *honour shall uphold the humble in spirit,* and *before honour is humility.*

II. He takes occasion to reprove the master of the feast for inviting so many *rich people,* who had wherewithal to dine very well at home, when he should rather have *invited the poor,* or, which was all one, have *sent portions to them for whom nothing was prepared,* and who could not afford themselves a good meal's meat. See Neh. viii. 10. Our Saviour here teaches us that the using of what we have in works of charity is better, and will turn to a better account, than using it in works of generosity and in magnificent house-keeping.

1. "Covet not to *treat the rich;* invite not *thy friends, and brethren, and neighbours, that are rich,*" *v.* 12. This does not *prohibit* the entertaining of such; there may be occasion for it, for the cultivating of friendship among relations and neighbours. But, (1.) "Do not make a common custom of it; spend as little as thou canst that way, that thou mayest not disable thyself to lay out in a much better way, in almsgiving. Thou wilt find it very expensive and troublesome; one feast for the rich will make a great many meals for the poor." Solomon saith, *He that giveth to the rich shall surely come to want,* Prov. xxii. 16. "Give" (saith Pliny, Epist.) "to thy friends, but let it be to thy *poor* friends, not to those that need thee not." (2.) "Be not *proud of it.*" Many *make feasts* only to *make a show,* as Ahasuerus did (Esth. i. 3, 4), and it is no reputation to them, they think, if they have not persons of quality to dine with them, and thus rob their families, to please their fancies. (3.) "Aim not at being paid again in your own coin." This is that which our Saviour blames in making such entertainments: "You commonly do it in hopes that you will be invited by them, and so *a recompence will be made you;* you will be gratified with such dainties and varieties as you treat your friends with, and this will feed your sensuality and luxury, and you will be no real gainer at last."

2. "Be forward to *relieve the poor* (*v.* 13, 14): *When thou makest a feast,* instead of furnishing thyself with what is rare and nice, get thy table spread with a competency of plain and wholesome meat, which will not be so costly, and invite *the poor and maimed,* such as have nothing to live upon, nor are able to work for their living. These are objects of charity; they want necessaries; furnish them, and they will recompense thee with their prayers; they will commend thy provisions, which the rich, it may be, will despise. They will go away, and thank God for thee, when the rich will go away and reproach thee. Say not that thou art a *loser,* because *they cannot recompense thee,* thou art so much out of pocket; no, it is so much set out to the best interest, on the best security, for *thou shalt be recompensed at the resurrection of the just.*" There will be a *resurrection of the just,* a *future state* of the just. There is a state of happiness reserved for them in the other world; and we may be sure that the *charitable* will be remembered in the *resurrection of the just,* for alms are *righteousness.* Works of charity perhaps may not be rewarded *in this world,* for the things of this world are not the *best things,* and therefore God does not pay the best men in *those things;* but they shall *in no wise lose their reward;* they shall be recompensed in the *resurrection* It will be found that the longest voyages make the richest returns, and that the charitable will be no losers, but unspeakable gainers, by having their recompense adjourned *till the resurrection.*

15 And when one of them that sat at meat with him heard these things,

he said unto him, Blessed *is* he that
shall eat bread in the kingdom of God.
16 Then said he unto him, A certain
man made a great supper, and bade
many: 17 And sent his servant at
supper time to say to them that were
bidden, Come; for all things are now
ready. 18 And they all with one
consent began to make excuse. The
first said unto him, I have bought a
piece of ground, and I must needs go
and see it: I pray thee have me excused. 19 And another said, I have
bought five yoke of oxen, and I go to
prove them: I pray thee have me
excused. 20 And another said, I have
married a wife, and therefore I cannot
come. 21 So that servant came, and
showed his lord these things. Then
the master of the house being angry
said to his servant, Go out quickly
into the streets and lanes of the city,
and bring in hither the poor, and the
maimed, and the halt, and the blind.
22 And the servant said, Lord, it is
done as thou hast commanded, and
yet there is room. 23 And the lord
said unto the servant, Go out into the
highways and hedges, and compel
them to come in, that my house may
be filled. 24 For I say unto you,
That none of those men which were
bidden shall taste of my supper.

Here is another discourse of our Saviour's, in which he *spiritualizes* the feast he was invited to, which is another way of keeping up good discourse in the midst of common actions.

I. The occasion of the discourse was given by one of the guests, who, when Christ was giving rules about feasting, said to him, *Blessed is he that shall eat bread in the kingdom of God* (*v.* 15), which, some tell us, was a saying commonly used among the rabbin.

1. But with what design does this man bring it in here? (1.) Perhaps this man, observing that Christ reproved first the guests and then the master of the house, fearing he should put the company out of humour, started this, to *divert* the discourse to something else. Or, (2.) Admiring the good rules of humility and charity which Christ had now given, but despairing to see them lived up to in the present degenerate state of things, he longs for *the kingdom of God,* when these and other good laws shall prevail, and pronounces them *blessed* who shall have a place in that kingdom. Or, (3.) Christ having mentioned *the resurrection of the just,* as a recompence for acts of charity to the poor, he here confirms what he said, "Yea, Lord, they that shall be recompensed in the resurrection of the just, shall *eat bread in the kingdom,* and that is a greater recompence than being reinvited to the table of the greatest man on earth." Or, (4.) Observing Christ to be silent, after he had given the foregoing lessons, he was willing to draw him in again to further discourse, so wonderfully well-pleased was he with what he said; and he knew nothing more likely to engage him than to mention the *kingdom of God.* Note, Even those that are not of ability to carry on good discourse themselves ought to put in a word now and then, to countenance it, and help it forward.

2. Now what this man said was a plain and acknowledged truth, and it was quoted very *appositely* now that they were *sitting at meat;* for we should take occasion from common things to think and speak of those heavenly and spiritual things which in scripture are *compared* to them, for that is one end of borrowing similitudes from them. And it will be good for us, when we are receiving the gifts of God's providence, to pass through them to the consideration of the gifts of his grace, those *better things.* This thought will be very seasonable when we are partaking of bodily refreshments: *Blessed are they that shall eat bread in the kingdom of God.* (1.) In the kingdom of grace, in the kingdom of the Messiah, which was expected now shortly to be set up. Christ promised his disciples that they should *eat and drink with him in his kingdom.* They that partake of the Lord's supper *eat bread in the kingdom of God.* (2.) In the kingdom of glory, at the resurrection. The happiness of heaven is an *everlasting feast;* blessed are they that shall sit down at that table, whence they shall rise no more.

II. The parable which our Lord Jesus put forth upon this occasion, *v.* 16, &c. Christ joins with the good man in what he said: "It is very true, *Blessed are they that shall partake* of the privileges of the Messiah's kingdom. But who are they that shall enjoy that privilege? You Jews, who think to have the monopoly of it, will generally reject it, and the Gentiles will be the greatest sharers in it." This he shows by a parable, for, if he had spoken it plainly, the Pharisees would not have borne it. Now in the parable we may observe,

1. The free grace and mercy of God, shining in the gospel of Christ; it appears,

(1.) In the rich provision he has made for poor souls, for their nourishment, refreshment, and entertainment (*v.* 16): *A certain man made a great supper.* There is that in Christ and the grace of the gospel which will be *food* and a *feast* for the soul of man that knows its own capacities, for the soul of a sinner that knows its own necessities and miseries. It is called a *supper,* because in those countries supper time was the chief feasting time, when the business of the day was over. The manifestation of gospel grace to the world was the evening of the world's day; and the fruition of the fulness of that grace in heaven is reserved for the evening of our day.

(2.) In the gracious invitation given us to come and partake of this provision. Here is, [1.] A general invitation given: He *bade many.* Christ invited the whole nation and people of the Jews to partake of the benefits of his gospel. There is provision enough for as many as come; it was prophesied of as a *feast for all people,* Isa. xxv. 6. Christ in the gospel, as he keeps a *good* house, so he keeps an *open* house. [2] A particular memorandum given, when the supper time was at hand; the servant was sent round to put them in mind of it: *Come, for all things are now ready.* When the Spirit was poured out, and the gospel church planted, those who before were invited were more closely pressed to come in *presently:* Now *all things are ready,* the full discovery of the gospel mystery is now made, all the ordinances of the gospel are now instituted, the society of Christians is now incorporated, and, which crowns all, the Holy Ghost is now given. This is the call now given to us: "*All things are now ready,* now is the *accepted time;* it is now, and *has not* been long; it is now, and *will not* be long; it is a season of grace that will be soon over, and therefore *come now*; do not delay; accept the invitation; believe yourselves welcome; *eat, O friends; drink, yea drink abundantly, O beloved.*"

2. The cold entertainment which the grace of the gospel meets with. The invited guests declined coming. They did not say flatly and plainly that they *would not come,* but *they all with one consent began to make excuse, v.* 18. One would have expected that they should *all with one consent* have come to a good supper, when they were so kindly invited to it: who would have refused such an invitation? Yet, on the contrary, they all found out some pretence or other to shift off their attendance. This bespeaks the general neglect of the Jewish nation to close with Christ, and accept of the offers of his grace, and the contempt they put upon the invitation. It also intimates the backwardness there is in most people to close with the gospel call. They cannot for shame avow their refusal, but they desire to be *excused;* they all ἀπὸ μιᾶς, some supply *ὥρας, all straightway,* they could give an answer *extempore,* and needed not to study for it, had *not to seek* for an excuse. Others supply γνώμης, they were *unanimous* in it; *with one voice.* (1.) Here were *two* that were *purchasers,* who were in such haste to go and see their purchases that they could not find time to go to this supper. One had *purchased land;* he had *bought a piece of ground,* which was represented to him to be a good bargain, and he must needs *go and see* whether it was so or no; and therefore *I pray thee have me excused.* His heart was so much upon the enlarging of his estate that he could neither be civil to his friend nor kind to himself. Note, Those that have their hearts full of the world, and fond of *laying house to house* and *field to field,* have their ears deaf to the gospel invitation. But what a frivolous excuse was this! He might have deferred going to see his piece of ground till the next day, and have found it in the same place and plight it was now in, if he had so pleased. Another had purchased *stock* for his land. "*I have bought five yoke of oxen* for the plough, and I must just now go and *prove them,* must go and try whether they be fit for my purpose; and therefore excuse me for this time." The former intimates that inordinate *complacency* in the world, this the inordinate *care* and *concern* about the world, which keep people from Christ and his grace; both intimate a preference given to the body above the soul, and to the things of time above those of eternity. Note, It is very criminal, when we are called to any duty, to make excuses for our neglect of it: it is a sign that there are convictions that it is duty, but no inclination to it. These things here, that were the matter of the excuses, were, [1.] *Little things,* and of small concern. It had better become them to have said, "I am invited *to eat bread in the kingdom of God,* and therefore must be excused from going to see the *ground* or the *oxen.*" [2.] *Lawful things.* Note, *Things lawful in themselves,* when the heart is too much set upon them, *prove fatal* hindrances in religion—*Licitus perimus omnes.* It is a hard matter so to manage our worldly affairs that they may not divert us from spiritual pursuits; and this ought to be our great care. (2.) Here was one that was *newly married,* and could not leave his wife to go out to supper, no, not for once (*v.* 30): *I have married a wife, and therefore,* in short, *I cannot come.* He pretends that he *cannot,* when the truth is he *will not.* Thus many pretend *inability* for the duties of religion when really they have an *aversion* to them. He has *married a wife.* It is true, he that was married was excused by the law from going to war for the first year (Deut. xxiv. 5), but would that excuse him from going up to the feasts of the Lord, which all the males were yearly to attend? Much less will it excuse from the gospel feast, of which the other were but types. Note, Our affection to our relations often proves a hindrance to us in our duty to God. Adam's excuse was, *The woman that thou gavest me persuaded me to eat;* this here was, *The woman persuaded me not to eat.* He might have gone and taken his wife along with him; they would both have been welcome.

3. The account which was brought to the master of the feast of the affront put upon him by his friends whom he had invited, who

now showed how little they valued him (*v.* 21): *That servant came, and showed his lord these things,* told him with surprise that he was likely to sup alone, for the guests that were invited, though they had had timely notice a good while before, that they might order their affairs accordingly, yet were now engaged in some other business. He made the matter neither better nor worse, but related it just as it was. Note, Ministers must give account of the success of their ministry. They must do it now at the throne of grace. If they see of *the travail of their soul,* they must go to God with their *thanks;* if they *labour in vain,* they must go to God with their *complaints.* They will do it hereafter at the judgment-seat of Christ: they shall be produced as witnesses *against* those who persist and perish in their unbelief, to prove that they were fairly invited; and *for those* who accepted the call, *Behold, I and the children thou hast given me.* The apostle urges this as a reason why people should give ear to the word of God sent them by his ministers; for *they watch for your souls, as those that must give account,* Heb. xiii. 17.

4. The master's just resentment of this affront: *He was angry, v.* 21. Note, The ingratitude of those that slight gospel offers, and the contempt they put upon the God of heaven thereby, are a very great provocation to him, and justly so. Abused mercy turns into the greatest wrath. The doom he passed upon them was, *None of the men that were bidden shall taste of my supper.* This was like the doom passed upon ungrateful Israel, when they despised the pleasant land: God *swore in his wrath that they should not enter into his rest.* Note, Grace despised is grace forfeited, like Esau's birthright. They that will not have Christ when they *may* shall not have him when they *would.* Even those that *were bidden,* if they slight the invitation, *shall be for*bidden; when the door is shut, the foolish virgins will be denied entrance.

5. The care that was taken to furnish the table with guests, as well as meat. "Go" (saith he to the servants), "*go first into the streets and lanes of the city,* and invite, not the merchants that are going from the custom-house, nor the tradesmen that are shutting up their shops; they will *desire to be excused* (one is going to his counting-house to cast up his books, another to the tavern to drink a bottle with his friend); but, that you may invite those that will be glad to come, bring in *hither the poor and the maimed, the halt and the blind;* pick up the common beggars." The servants object not that it will be a disparagement to the master and his house to have such guests at his table; for they know his mind, and they soon gather an abundance of such guests: *Lord, it is done as thou hast commanded.* Many of the Jews are brought in, not of the scribes and Pharisees, such as Christ was *now at dinner with,* who thought themselves most likely to be guests at the Messiah's table, but publicans and sinners; these are *the poor and the maimed.* But *yet there is room* for more guests, and provision enough for them all. "Go, then, *secondly, into the highways and hedges.* Go out into the country, and pick up the vagrants, or those that are returning now in the evening from their work in the field, from hedging and ditching there, and *compel them to come in,* not by force of arms, but by force of arguments. Be earnest with them; for in this case it will be necessary to convince them that the invitation is *sincere* and not a *banter;* they will be shy and modest, and will hardly believe that they shall be welcome, and therefore be importunate with them and do not leave them till you have prevailed with them." This refers to the *calling of the Gentiles,* to whom the apostles were to *turn* when the Jews refused the offer, and with them the church was filled. Now observe here, (1.) The provision made for precious souls in the gospel of Christ shall appear not to have been made *in vain;* for, if some *reject it,* yet others will thankfully *accept* the offer of it. Christ comforts himself with this, that, *though Israel be not gathered,* yet he shall be *glorious,* as *a light to the Gentiles,* Isa. xlix. 5, 6. God will have a church in the world, though there are those that are unchurched; for *the unbelief of man shall not make the promise of God of no effect.* (2.) Those that are very poor and low in the world shall be as welcome to Christ as the rich and great; nay, and many times the gospel has greatest success among those that labour under worldly disadvantages, as the *poor,* and bodily infirmities, as *the maimed, and the halt,* and *the blind.* Christ here plainly refers to what he had said just before, in direction to us, to invite to our tables *the poor and maimed, the lame and blind, v.* 13, For the consideration of the countenance which Christ's gospel gives to the poor should engage us to be charitable to them. His condescensions and compassions towards them should engage ours. (3.) Many times the gospel has the *greatest success* among those that are *least likely* to have the benefit of it, and whose submission to it was least expected. The publicans and harlots went into the kingdom of God before the scribes and Pharisees; *so the last shall be first, and the first last.* Let us not be *confident* concerning those that are most forward, nor despair of those that are least promising. (4.) Christ's ministers must be both very expeditious and very importunate in inviting to the gospel feast: "*Go out quickly* (*v.* 21); lose no time, because *all things are now ready.* Call to them to come *to-day, while it is called to-day;* and *compel them to come in,* by accosting them kindly, and *drawing* them *with the cords of a man and the bands of love.*" Nothing can be more absurd than fetching an argument hence for compelling men's consciences, nay, for compelling men against their consciences, in matters of religion: "You shall receive the

Lord's supper, or you shall be fined and imprisoned, and ruined in your estate." Certainly nothing like this was the compulsion here meant, but only that of reason and love; for *the weapons of our warfare are not carnal.* (5.) Though many have been brought in to partake of the benefits of the gospel, yet still *there is room for more;* for the riches of Christ are *unsearchable* and *inexhaustible;* there is in him enough for all, and enough for each; and the gospel excludes none that do not exclude themselves. (6.) Christ's house, though it be *large,* shall at last be *filled;* it will be so when the number of the elect is completed, and as many as were *given him* are *brought to him.*

25 And there went great multitudes
with him: and he turned, and said
unto them, 26 If any *man* come to
me, and hate not his father, and mother, and wife, and children, and brethren, and sisters, yea, and his own life
also, he cannot be my disciple. 27 And
whosoever doth not bear his cross, and
come after me, cannot be my disciple.
28 For which of you, intending to
build a tower, sitteth not down first,
and counteth the cost, whether he
have *sufficient* to finish *it?* 29 Lest
haply, after he hath laid the foundation, and is not able to finish *it,* all
that behold *it* begin to mock him,
30 Saying, This man began to build,
and was not able to finish. 31 Or
what king, going to make war against
another king, sitteth not down first,
and consulteth whether he be able
with ten thousand to meet him that
cometh against him with twenty thousand? 32 Or else, while the other is
yet a great way off, he sendeth an
ambassage, and desireth conditions of
peace. 33 So likewise, whosoever he
be of you that forsaketh not all that
he hath, he cannot be my disciple. 34
Salt *is* good: but if the salt have lost
his savour, wherewith shall it be seasoned? 35 It is neither fit for the
land, nor yet for the dunghill; *but*
men cast it out. He that hath ears to
hear, let him hear.

See how Christ in his doctrine suited himself to those to whom he spoke, and *gave every one his portion of meat.* To Pharisees he preached humility and charity. He is in these verses directing his discourse to the multitudes that crowded after him, and seemed zealous in following him; and his exhortation to them is to understand the terms of discipleship, before they undertook the profession of it, and to consider what they did. See here,

I. How zealous people were in their attendance on Christ (*v.* 25): *There went great multitudes with him,* many for love and more for company, for where there are *many* there will be *more.* Here was a *mixed multitude,* like that which went with Israel out of Egypt; such we must expect there will always be in the church, and it will therefore be necessary that ministers should carefully separate *between the precious and the vile.*

II. How *considerate* he would have them to be in their *zeal.* Those that undertake to follow Christ must count upon the worst, and prepare accordingly.

1. He tells them what the worst is that they must count upon, much the same with what he had gone through *before* them and *for* them. He takes it for granted that they had a mind to be *his disciples,* that they might be *qualified* for preferment in his kingdom. They expected that he should say, "If any man come to me, and be my disciple, he shall have wealth and honour in abundance; let me alone to make him a great man." But he tells them quite the contrary.

(1.) They must be willing to *quit* that which was *very dear,* and therefore must come to him thoroughly *weaned from* all their creature-comforts, and *dead* to them, so as cheerfully to part with them rather than quit their interest in Christ. *v.* 26. A man cannot be Christ's disciple but he must *hate father, and mother, and his own life.* He is not *sincere,* he will not be *constant* and persevering, unless he love Christ better than any thing in this world, and be willing to part with that which he may and must leave, either as a *sacrifice,* when Christ may be glorified by our parting with it (so the martyrs, who *loved not their lives to death),* or as a *temptation,* when by our parting with it we are put into a better capacity of serving Christ. Thus Abraham parted with his own country, and Moses with Pharaoh's court. Mention is not made here of *houses* and *lands;* philosophy will teach a man to look upon these with contempt; but Christianity carries it higher. [1.] Every good man loves *his relations;* and yet, if he be a disciple of Christ, he must comparatively *hate them,* must love them *less than Christ,* as Leah is said to be *hated* when Rachel was better loved. Not that their persons must be in any degree hated, but our comfort and satisfaction in them must be lost and swallowed up in our love to Christ, as Levi's was, when he *said to his father, I have not seen him,* Deut. xxxiii. 9. When our duty to our parents comes in competition with our evident duty to Christ, we must give Christ the preference. If we must either *deny Christ* or be *banished* from our families and relations (as many of the primitive Christians were), we must rather lose their society than his favour. [2.] Every man loves *his own life*, no man ever yet *hated it;* and we cannot be Christ's disciples if we do not love him better than our own lives, so as rather to have our lives *embittered* by cruel *bondage*, nay, and *taken away* by cruel *deaths*, than to dishonour Christ, or depart from any of his truths and ways. The experience of the pleasures of the *spiritual life*, and the believing hopes and prospects of *eternal life*, will make this *hard saying* easy. When tribulation and persecution arise because of the word, then chiefly the trial is, whether we love better, Christ or our relations and lives; yet even in *days of* peace this matter is sometimes brought to the trial. Those that decline the service of Christ, and opportunities of converse with him, and are ashamed to confess him, for fear of disobliging a relation or friend, or losing a customer, give cause to suspect that they love him better than Christ.

(2.) That they must be willing to *bear* that which was very *heavy* (*v.* 27): *Whosoever doth not bear his cross*, as those did that were condemned to be crucified, in *submission* to the sentence and in *expectation* of the execution of it, and so *come after me* whithersoever I shall lead him, he *cannot be my disciple;* that is (says Dr. Hammond), he is not *for my turn;* and my service, being so sure to bring persecution along with it, will not be *for his.* Though the disciples of Christ are not *all crucified*, yet they all *bear their cross*, as if they counted upon being crucified. They must be content to be put into an ill name, and to be loaded with infamy and disgrace; for no name is more ignominious than *Furcifer—the bearer of the gibbet.* He must bear his cross, and *come after Christ;* that is, he must bear it in the way of his duty, whenever it lies in that way. He must bear it when Christ calls him to it, and in bearing it he must have an eye to Christ, and fetch encouragements from him, and live in hope of a recompence with him.

2. He bids them count upon it, and then consider of it. Since he has been so *just to us* as to tell us plainly what difficulties we shall meet with in following him, let us be so *just to ourselves* as to weigh the matter seriously before we take upon us a profession of religion. Joshua obliged the people to consider what they did when they promised to *serve the Lord*, Josh. xxiv. 19. It is better never to begin than not to proceed; and therefore before we begin we must consider what it is to proceed. This is to act rationally, and as becomes men, and as we do in other cases. The cause of Christ will bear a scrutiny. Satan shows the best, but hides the worst, because his best will not countervail his worst; but Christ's will abundantly. This considering of the case is necessary to perseverance, especially in suffering times. Our Saviour here illustrates the necessity of it by two similitudes, the former showing that we must consider the *expenses* of our religion, the latter that we must consider the *perils* of it.

(1.) When we take upon us a profession of religion we are like a man that undertakes to *build a tower*, and therefore must consider the *expense of it* (*v.* 28—30): *Which of you, intending to build a tower* or stately house for himself, *sitteth not down first, and counteth the cost?* and he must be sure to count upon a great deal more than his workmen will tell him it will cost. Let him compare the charge with his purse, lest he make himself to be laughed at, by *beginning to build* what he is *not able to finish.* Note, [1.] All that take upon them a profession of religion undertake to *build a tower*, not as the tower of Babel, in opposition to Heaven, which therefore was left unfinished, but in obedience to Heaven, which therefore shall have its *top-stone brought forth.* Begin low, and lay the foundation deep, lay it on the rock, and make sure work, and then aim as high as heaven. [2.] Those that intend to build this tower must *sit down and count the cost.* Let them consider that it *will cost them* the mortifying of their sins, even the most beloved lusts; it will cost them a life of self-denial and watchfulness, and a constant course of holy duties; it *may*, perhaps, *cost them* their reputation among men, their estates and liberties, and all that is dear to them in this world, even life itself. And if it should cost us all this, what is it in comparison with what it cost Christ to purchase the advantages of religion for us, which come to us without money and without price? [3.] Many that begin to *build this tower* do not *go on with it*, nor persevere in it, and it is their folly; they have not courage and resolution, have not a rooted fixed principle, and so bring nothing to pass. It is true, we have none of us in ourselves *sufficient to finish* this tower, but Christ hath said, *My grace is sufficient for thee*, and that grace shall not be wanting to any of us, if we seek for it and make use of it. [4.] Nothing is more *shameful* than for those that have begun well in religion to break off; every one will justly *mock him*, as having lost all his labour hitherto for want of perseverance. We *lose the things we have wrought* (2 John 8), and all we have done and suffered is *in vain*, Gal. iii. 4.

(2.) When we undertake to be Christ's disciples we are like a man that *goes to war*, and therefore must consider the *hazard* of it, and the difficulties that are to be encountered, *v.* 31, 32. A king that declares war against a neighbouring prince considers whether he has strength wherewith to make his part good, and, if not, he will lay aside his thoughts of war. Note, [1.] The state of a Christian in this world is a military state. *Is not* the Christian *life a warfare?* We have many passes in our way, that must be disputed with dint of sword; nay, we must fight every step we go, so restless are our spiritual enemies in their opposition. [2.] We ought to consider whether we can *endure the hardness* which a good soldier of Jesus Christ must expect and count upon, before we enlist ourselves under Christ's banner; *whether* we are able to encounter the forces of hell and earth, which come against us *twenty thousand* strong. [3.] Of the two it is better to make the best terms we can with the world than pretend to renounce it and afterwards, when tribulation and persecution arise because of the word, to *return to it.* That *young man* that could not find in his heart to part with his possessions for Christ did better to go away from Christ *sorrowing* than to have staid with him *dissembling.*

This parable is another way applicable, and may be taken as designed to teach us to begin *speedily* to be religious, rather than to begin *cautiously;* and may mean the same with Matt. v. 25, *Agree with thine adversary quickly.* Note, *First,* Those that persist in sin make war against God, the most unnatural, unjustifiable war; they rebel against their lawful sovereign, whose government is perfectly just and good. *Secondly,* The proudest and most daring sinner is no equal match for God; the disproportion of strength is much greater than that here supposed between *ten thousand* and *twenty thousand. Do we provoke the Lord to jealousy? Are we stronger than he?* No, surely; *who knows the power of his anger?* In consideration of this, it is our interest to make peace with him. We need not send to *desire conditions of peace;* they are offered to us, and are unexceptionable, and highly to our advantage. Let us acquaint ourselves with them, and be at peace; do this in time, *while the other is yet a great way off;* for delays in such a case are highly dangerous, and make after-applications difficult.

But the application of this parable here (*v.* 33) is to the consideration that ought to be exercised when we take upon us a profession of religion. Solomon saith, *With good advice make war* (Prov. xx. 18); for he that *draws the sword throws away the scabbard;* so *with good advice* enter upon a profession of religion, as those that know that *except you forsake all you have you cannot be Christ's disciples;* that is, except you count upon forsaking all and consent to it, for all that will live godly in Christ Jesus must *suffer persecution,* and yet continue to *live godly.*

3. He warns them against apostasy and a degeneracy of mind from the truly Christian spirit and temper, for that would make them utterly useless, *v.* 34, 35. (1.) Good Christians are *the salt of the earth,* and good ministers especially (Matt. v. 13); and this *salt is good* and of great use; by their instructions and examples they season all they converse with, to keep them from putrefying, and to quicken them, and make them savoury. (2.) Degenerate Christians, who, rather than part with what they have in the world, will throw up their profession, and then of course become carnal, and worldly, and wholly destitute of a Christian spirit, are like *salt that has lost its savour,* like that which the chemists call the *caput mortuum,* that has all its salts drawn from it, that is the most useless worthless thing in the world; it has no manner of virtue or good property in it. [1.] It can never be recovered: *Wherewith shall it be seasoned?* You cannot salt it. This intimates that it is extremely difficult, and next to impossible, to recover an apostate, Heb. vi. 4—6. If Christianity will not prevail to cure men of their worldliness and sensuality, if that remedy has been tried in vain, their case must even be concluded desperate. [2.] It is of no use. It is *not fit,* as dung is, *for the land,* to manure that, nor will it be the better if it be laid in the dunghill to rot; there is nothing to be got out of it. A professor of religion whose mind and manners are depraved is the most *insipid* animal that can be. If he speaks of the things of God, of which he has had some knowledge, it is so *awkwardly* that none are the better for it: it is a *parable in the mouth of a fool.* [3.] It is abandoned: *Men cast it out,* as that which they will have no more to do with. Such scandalous professors ought to be cast out of the church, not only because they have forfeited all the honours and privileges of their church-membership, but because there is danger that others will be infected by them. Our Saviour concludes this with a call to all to take notice of it, and to take warning: *He that hath ears to hear, let him hear.* Now can the faculty of hearing be better employed than in attending to the word of Christ, and particularly to the alarms he has given us of the danger we are in *of* apostasy, and the danger we run ourselves into *by* apostasy?

CHAP. XV.

Evil manners, we say, beget good laws; so, in this chapter, the murmuring of the scribes and Pharisees at the grace of Christ, and the favour he showed to publicans and sinners, gave occasion for a more full discovery of that grace than perhaps otherwise we should have had in these three parables which we have in this chapter, the scope of all of which is the same, to show, not only what God had said and sworn in the Old Testament, that he had no pleasure in the death and ruin of sinners, but that he has great pleasure in their return and repentance, and rejoices in the gracious entertainment he gives them thereupon. Here is, I. The offence which the Pharisees took at Christ for conversing with heathen men and publicans, and preaching his gospel to them, ver. 1, 2. II. His justifying himself in it, by the design and proper tendency of it, which with many had been the effect of it, and that was, the bringing of them to repent and reform their lives, than which there could not be a more pleasing and acceptable service done to God, which he shows in the parables, 1. Of the lost sheep that was brought home with joy, ver. 4—7. 2. Of the lost silver that was found with joy, ver. 8—10. 3. Of the lost son that had been a prodigal, but returned to his father's house, and was received with great joy, though his elder brother, like these scribes and Pharisees, was offended at it, ver. 11—32.

THEN drew near unto him all the
publicans and sinners for to hear
him. 2 And the Pharisees and scribes
murmured, saying, This man receiveth
sinners, and eateth with them. 3 And
he spake this parable unto them, saying, 4 What man of you, having an
hundred sheep, if he lose one of them,
doth not leave the ninety and nine in
the wilderness, and go after that which

is lost, until he find it? 5 And when
he hath found *it*, he layeth *it* on his
shoulders, rejoicing. 6 And when
he cometh home, he calleth together
his friends and neighbours, saying
unto them, Rejoice with me; for I
have found my sheep which was lost.
7 I say unto you, that likewise joy
shall be in heaven over one sinner
that repenteth, more than over ninety
and nine just persons, which need no
repentance. 8 Either what woman
having ten pieces of silver, if she lose
one piece, doth not light a candle,
and sweep the house, and seek diligently till she find *it*? 9 And when
she hath found *it*, she calleth *her*
friends and *her* neighbours together,
saying, Rejoice with me; for I have
found the piece which I had lost. 10
Likewise, I say unto you, there is joy
in the presence of the angels of God
over one sinner that repenteth.

Here is, I. The diligent attendance of the publicans and sinners upon Christ's ministry. *Great multitudes* of Jews *went with him* (*ch.* xiv. 25), with such an assurance of admission into the kingdom of God that he found it requisite to say that to them which would shake their vain hopes. Here multitudes of *publicans* and *sinners* drew near to him, with a humble modest fear of being *rejected* by him, and to them he found it requisite to give encouragement, especially because there were some haughty supercilious people that frowned upon them. The *publicans,* who collected the tribute paid to the *Romans,* were perhaps some of them *bad men,* but they were all industriously put into an *ill name,* because of the prejudices of the Jewish nation against their office. They are sometimes ranked with *harlots* (Matt. xxi. 32); here and elsewhere with *sinners,* such as were openly vicious, that traded with *harlots,* known rakes. Some think that the *sinners* here meant were *heathen,* and that Christ was now on the other side Jordan, or in *Galilee of the Gentiles.* These *drew near,* when perhaps the multitude of the Jews that had followed him had (upon his discourse in the close of the foregoing chapter) *dropped off;* thus afterwards the Gentiles took their turn in hearing the apostles, when the Jews had rejected them. *They drew near to him,* being afraid of drawing nearer than just to come within *hearing.* They drew near to him, not, as some did, for curiosity to *see him,* nor as others did, to solicit for cures, but to hear his excellent doctrine. Note, in all our approaches to Christ we must have this in our eye, to *hear him;* to hear the instructions he gives us, and his answers to our prayers.

II. The offence which the *scribes* and *Pharisees* took at this. They *murmured,* and turned it to the reproach of our Lord Jesus: *This man receiveth sinners, and eateth with them, v.* 2. 1. They were angry that *publicans* and *heathens* had the means of grace allowed them, were called to repent, and encouraged to hope for pardon upon repentance; for they looked upon their case as *desperate,* and thought that none but Jews had the privilege of repenting and being pardoned, though the prophets preached repentance to the nations, and Daniel particularly to Nebuchadnezzar. 2. They thought it a disparagement to Christ, and inconsistent with the dignity of his character, to make himself familiar with such sort of people, to *admit* them into his company and to *eat with them.* They could not, for shame, condemn him for *preaching to them,* though that was the thing they were most enraged at; and therefore they reproached him for *eating with them,* which was more expressly contrary to the tradition of the elders. Censure will fall, not only upon the most innocent and the most excellent *persons,* but upon the most innocent and most excellent *actions,* and we must not think it strange.

III. Christ's justifying himself in it, by showing that the worse these people were, to whom he preached, the more glory would redound to God, and the more joy there would be in heaven, if by his preaching they were brought to repentance. It would be a more pleasing sight in heaven to see Gentiles brought to the worship of the true God than to see Jews go on in it, and to see publicans and sinners live an orderly sort of life than to see *scribes* and *Pharisees* go on in living such a life. This he here illustrates by two parables, the explication of both of which is the same.

1. The parable of the *lost sheep.* Something like it we had in Matt. xviii. 12. There it was designed to show the care God takes for the preservation of saints, as a reason why we should not offend them; here it is designed to show the pleasure God takes in the conversion of sinners, as a reason why we should rejoice in it. We have here,

(1.) The case of a sinner that goes on in sinful ways. He is like a *lost sheep,* a sheep *gone astray*; he is *lost* to God, who has not the honour and service he should have from him; *lost* to the flock, which has not communion with him; *lost* to himself: he knows not where he is, wanders endlessly, is continually exposed to the beasts of prey, subject to frights and terrors, from under the shepherd's care, and wanting the green pastures; and he cannot of himself find the way back to the fold.

(2.) The care the God of heaven takes of poor wandering sinners. He *continues* his care of the sheep that did not go astray; they are *safe in the wilderness.* But there is a particular care to be taken of this lost sheep;

and though he has a hundred sheep, a considerable flock, yet he will not *lose* that *one*, but he goes after it, and shows abundance of care, [1.] In *finding it out*. He follows it, enquiring after it, and looking about for it, until he *finds* it. God follows backsliding sinners with the calls of his word and the strivings of his Spirit, until at length they are wrought upon to think of returning. [2.] In *bringing it home*. Though he finds it *weary*, and perhaps *worried* and worn away with its wanderings, and not able to bear being driven home, yet he does not leave it to perish, and say, It is not worth carrying home; but *lays it on his shoulders*, and, with a great deal of tenderness and labour, brings it to the fold. This is very applicable to the great work of our redemption. Mankind were gone astray, Isa. liii. 6. The value of the whole race to God was not so much as that of one sheep to him that had a hundred; what loss would it have been to God if they had all been left to perish? There is a world of holy angels that are as the ninety-nine sheep, a noble flock; yet God sends his Son to *seek and save that which was lost, ch.* xix. 10. Christ is said to *gather the lambs in his arms*, and carry *them in his bosom*, denoting his pity and tenderness towards poor sinners; here he is said to bear them *upon his shoulders*, denoting the power wherewith he supports and bears them up; those can never perish whom he carries upon his shoulders.

(3.) The pleasure that God takes in repenting returning sinners. He *lays it on his shoulders rejoicing* that he has not lost his labour in seeking; and the joy is the greater because he began to be out of hope of finding it; and he *calls his friends and neighbours*, the shepherds that keep their flocks about him, *saying, Rejoice with me*. Perhaps among the pastoral songs which the shepherds used to sing there was one for such an occasion as this, of which these words might be the burden, *Rejoice with me, for I have found my sheep which was lost;* whereas they never sung, *Rejoice with me, for I have lost none*. Observe, he calls it *his sheep*, though a *stray*, a wandering sheep. He has a right to it (*all souls are mine*), and he will claim his own, and recover his right; therefore he looks after it himself: *I have found it;* he did not send a servant, but his own Son, the great and good Shepherd, who will find what he seeks, and will be found of those that seek him not.

2. The parable of the *lost piece of silver*. (1.) The *loser* is here supposed to be *a woman*, who will more passionately grieve for her loss, and rejoice in finding what she had lost, than perhaps a man would do, and therefore it the better serves the purpose of the parable. She has *ten pieces of silver*, and out of them loses only one. Let this keep up in us high thoughts of the divine goodness, notwithstanding the sinfulness and misery of the world of mankind, that there are nine to one, nay, in the foregoing parable there are ninety-nine to one, of God's creation, that retain their integrity, in whom God *is* praised, and never *was* dishonoured. O the numberless beings, for aught we know numberless worlds of beings, that never were lost, nor stepped aside from the laws and ends of their creation! (2.) That which is lost is a piece of silver, δραχμὴν—*the fourth part of a skekel*. The soul is *silver*, of intrinsic worth and value; not base metal, as iron or lead, but *silver*, the mines of which are *royal mines*. The Hebrew word for *silver* is taken from the *desirableness* of it. It is *silver coin*, for so the *drachma* was; it is stamped with God's *image and superscription*, and therefore must be *rendered to him*. Yet it is comparatively but of small value; it was but seven pence half-penny; intimating that if sinful men be left to perish God would be no loser. This silver was lost *in the dirt;* a soul plunged in the world, and overwhelmed with the love of it and care about it, is like a piece of money in the dirt; any one would say, It is a thousand pities that it should *lie there*. (3.) Here is a great deal of care and pains taken in quest of it. The woman *lights a candle*, to look behind the door, under the table, and in every corner of the house, *sweeps the house*, and *seeks diligently till she finds it*. This represents the various means and methods God makes use of to bring lost souls home to himself: he has *lighted the candle* of the gospel, not to show himself the way to us, but to show us the way to him, to discover us to ourselves; he has *swept the house* by the convictions of the word; he *seeks diligently*, his heart is upon it, to bring lost souls to himself. (4.) Here is a great deal of joy for the finding of it: *Rejoice with me, for I have found the piece which I had lost, v.* 9. Those that rejoice desire that others should rejoice with them; those that are merry would have others merry with them. She was glad that she had found the piece of money, though she should spend it in entertaining those whom she called to *make merry with her*. The pleasing surprise of finding it put her, for the present, into a kind of transport, ἕυρηκα, ἕυρηκα—*I have found, I have found*, is the language of joy.

3. The explication of these two parables is to the same purport (*v.* 7, 10): *There is joy in heaven, joy in the presence of the angels of God, over one sinner that repenteth*, as those publicans and sinners did, some of them at least (and, if but *one of them* did repent, Christ would reckon it worth his while), more than *over* a great number of *just persons, who need no repentance*. Observe,

(1.) The *repentance* and *conversion of sinners* on earth are *matter of joy* and rejoicing *in heaven*. It is possible that the greatest sinners may be brought to repentance. While there is life there is hope, and the worst are not to be despaired of; and the worst of sinners, if they repent and turn, shall find mercy. Yet this is not all, [1.]

God will *delight* to show them mercy, will reckon their conversion a return for all the expense he has been at upon them. There is always *joy in heaven.* God *rejoiceth in all his works,* but particularly in the works of his grace. He rejoiceth to do good to penitent sinners, with his *whole heart* and his *whole soul.* He rejoiceth not only in the conversion of churches and nations, but even over *one sinner that repenteth,* though but *one.* [2.] The good angels will be glad that mercy is shown them, so far are they from repining at it, though those of their nature that sinned be left to perish, and no mercy shown to them; though those sinners that repent, that are so mean, and have been so vile, are, upon their repentance, to be taken into communion with them, and shortly to be made like them, and equal to them. The conversion of sinners is the joy of angels, and they gladly become ministering spirits to them for their good, upon their conversion. The redemption of mankind was matter of joy in the presence of the angels; for they sung, *Glory to God in the highest, ch.* ii. 14.

(2.) There is more joy over *one sinner that repenteth,* and turneth to be religious from a course of life that had been notoriously vile and vicious, than there is *over ninety-nine just persons, who need no repentance.* [1.] More joy for the redemption and salvation of fallen man than for the preservation and confirmation of the angels that stand, and did indeed need no repentance. [2.] More joy for the conversion of the sinners of the Gentiles, and of those publicans that now heard Christ preach, than for all the praises and devotions, and all the *God I thank thee,* of the Pharisees, and the other self-justifying Jews, who thought that they *needed no repentance,* and that therefore God should abundantly rejoice in them, and *make his boast* of them, as those that were most *his honour;* but Christ tells them that it was quite otherwise, that God was more praised *in,* and pleased *with,* the penitent broken heart of one of those despised, envied sinners, than all the long prayers which the scribes and Pharisees made, who could not see any thing amiss in themselves. Nay, [3.] More joy for the conversion of one such great sinner, such a Pharisee as Paul had been in his time, than for the regular conversion of one that had always conducted himself decently and well, and comparatively *needs no repentance,* needs not such a universal change of the life as those great sinners need. Not but that it is best not to go astray; but the grace of God, both in the power and the pity of that grace, is more manifested in the *reducing* of great sinners than in the *conducting* of those that never went astray. And many times those that have been great sinners before their conversion prove more eminently and zealously good after, of which Paul is an instance, and therefore in him God was greatly *glorified,* Gal. i. 24. They to whom much is forgiven will love much. It is spoken after the manner of men. We are moved with a more sensible joy for the recovery of what we had lost than for the continuance of what we had always enjoyed, for health *out of* sickness than for health *without* sickness. It is as *life from the dead.* A constant course of religion may in itself be more valuable, and yet a sudden return from an evil course and way of sin may yield a more surprising pleasure. Now if there is such *joy in heaven,* for the conversion of sinners, then the Pharisees were very much strangers to a heavenly spirit, who did all they could to hinder it and were grieved at it, and who were exasperated at Christ when he was doing a piece of work that was of all others most grateful to Heaven.

11 And he said, A certain man had
two sons: 12 And the younger of
them said to *his* father, Father, give
me the portion of goods that falleth
to me. And he divided unto them
his living. 13 And not many days
after the younger son gathered all
together, and took his journey into a
far country, and there wasted his substance with riotous living. 14 And
when he had spent all, there arose a
mighty famine in that land; and he
began to be in want. 15 And he went
and joined himself to a citizen of that
country; and he sent him into his
fields to feed swine. 16 And he would
fain have filled his belly with the husks
that the swine did eat: and no man
gave unto him. 17 And when he
came to himself, he said, How many
hired servants of my father's have
bread enough and to spare, and I
perish with hunger! 18 I will arise
and go to my father, and will say unto
him, Father, I have sinned against
heaven, and before thee, 19 And am
no more worthy to be called thy son:
make me as one of thy hired servants.
20 And he arose, and came to his father. But when he was yet a great
way off, his father saw him, and had
compassion, and ran, and fell on his
neck, and kissed him. 21 And the
son said unto him, Father, I have
sinned against heaven, and in thy
sight, and am no more worthy to be
called thy son. 22 But the father
said to his servants, Bring forth the
best robe, and put *it* on him; and
put a ring on his hand, and shoes on

his feet: 23 And bring hither the
fatted calf, and kill *it;* and let us eat,
and be merry: 24 For this my son
was dead, and is alive again; he was
lost, and is found. And they began
to be merry. 25 Now his elder son
was in the field: and as he came and
drew nigh to the house, he heard
music and dancing. 26 And he
called one of the servants, and asked
what these things meant. 27 And
he said unto him, Thy brother is
come; and thy father hath killed the
fatted calf, because he hath received
him safe and sound. 28 And he was
angry, and would not go in: therefore
came his father out, and entreated him.
29 And he answering said to *his* father, Lo, these many years do I serve
thee, neither transgressed I at any
time thy commandment: and yet
thou never gavest me a kid, that I
might make merry with my friends:
30 But as soon as this thy son was
come, which hath devoured thy living
with harlots, thou hast killed for him
the fatted calf. 31 And he said unto
him, Son, thou art ever with me, and
all that I have is thine. 32 It was
meet that we should make merry, and
be glad: for this thy brother was dead,
and is alive again; and was lost, and
is found.

We have here the parable of the prodigal son, the scope of which is the same with those before, to show how pleasing to God the conversion of sinners is, of great sinners, and how ready he is to receive and entertain such, upon their repentance; but the circumstances of the parable do much more largely and fully set forth the riches of gospel grace than those did, and it has been, and will be while the world stands, of unspeakable use to poor sinners, both to direct and to encourage them in repenting and returning to God. Now,

I. The parable represents God as a *common Father* to all mankind, to the whole family of Adam. We are all his *offspring,* have all *one Father,* and *one God created us,* Mal. ii. 10. *From him* we *had* our being, *in him* we still *have it,* and from him we receive our *maintenance.* He is *our Father,* for he has the *educating* and *portioning* of us, and will *put us in* his testament, or *leave us out,* according as we are, or are not, dutiful children to him. Our Saviour hereby intimates to those proud Pharisees that these publicans and sinners, whom they thus despised, were their brethren, partakers of the same nature, and therefore they ought to be glad of any kindness shown them. God is the God, *not of the Jews only, but of the Gentiles* (Rom. iii. 29): the *same Lord over all, that is rich in mercy to all that call upon him.*

II. It represents the children of men as of *different* characters, though all related to God as their common Father. He had *two sons,* one of them a solid grave youth, *reserved* and *austere,* sober himself, but not at all *good-humoured* to those about him; such a one would adhere to his education, and not be easily drawn from it; but the other *volatile* and *mercurial,* and impatient of restraint, roving, and willing to try his fortune, and, if he fall into ill hands, likely to be a rake, notwithstanding his virtuous education. Now this latter represents the publicans and sinners, whom Christ is endeavouring to bring to repentance, and the Gentiles, to whom the apostles were to be sent forth to *preach repentance.* The former represents the Jews in general, and particularly the Pharisees, whom he was endeavouring to reconcile to that grace of God which was offered to, and bestowed upon, sinners.

The *younger son* is the prodigal, whose character and case are here designed to represent that of a sinner, that of every one of us in our natural state, but especially of some. Now we are to observe concerning him,

1. His *riot* and *ramble* when he was a prodigal, and the extravagances and miseries he fell into. We are told,

(1.) What his request to his father was (*v.* 12): *He said to his father,* proudly and pertly enough, "*Father, give me*"—he might have put a little more in his mouth, and have said, *Pray give me,* or, *Sir, if you please, give me,* but he makes an imperious demand—"*give me the portion of goods that falleth to me;* not so much as you *think fit* to allot to me, but that which falls to me as *my due.*" Note, It is bad, and the beginning of worse, when men look upon God's gifts as debts. "*Give me the portion,* all *my child's part,* that falls to me;" not, "*Try me with a little,* and see how I can manage that, and accordingly trust me with more;" but, "*Give it me all* at present in possession, and I will never expect any thing in *reversion,* any thing *hereafter.*" Note, The great folly of sinners, and that which ruins them, is being content to have *their portion in hand,* now in this lifetime to *receive their good things.* They look only at the things that are seen, that are temporal, and covet only a present gratification, but have no care for a future felicity, when that is spent and gone. And why did he desire to have his portion in his own hands? Was it that he might apply himself to business, and trade with it, and so make it more? No, he had no thought of that. But, [1.] He was *weary* of his *father's government,* of the good order and discipline of his father's family, and was fond of liberty falsely so called, but indeed the greatest slavery, for such a *liberty to sin* is. See the folly of many young men, who are religiously educated, but are impatient of the confinement of their education, and never think themselves their own masters, their own men, till they have broken all God's bands in sunder, and cast away his cords from them, and, instead of them, bound themselves with the cords of their own lust. Here is the original of the apostasy of sinners from God; they will not be tied up to the rules of *God's government;* they will themselves *be as gods,* knowing no other *good and evil* than what themselves please. [2.] He was willing to get *from under his father's eye,* for that was always a check upon him, and often gave a check to him. A shyness of God, and a willingness to disbelieve his omniscience, are at the bottom of the wickedness of the wicked. [3.] He was distrustful of his *father's management.* He would have his *portion of goods* himself, for he thought that his father would be laying up for hereafter for him, and, in order to that, would limit him in his present expenses, and that he did not like. [4.] He was *proud of himself,* and had a *great conceit of his own sufficiency.* He thought that if he had but his portion in his own hands he could manage it better than his father did, and make a better figure with it. There are more young people ruined by *pride* than by any one lust whatsoever. Our first parents ruined themselves and all theirs by a foolish ambition to be *independent,* and not to be beholden even to God himself; and this is at the bottom of sinners' persisting in their sin—they will be *for themselves.*

(2.) How kind his father was to him: *He divided unto them his living.* He computed what he had to dispose of between his sons, and gave the younger son *his share,* and offered the elder his, which ought to be a *double portion;* but, it should seem, he desired his father to keep it in his own hands still, and we may see what he got by it (*v.* 31): *All that I have is thine.* He got all by staying for something in reserve. He gave the younger son what he asked, and the son had no reason to complain that he did him any wrong in the dividend; he had as much as he expected, and perhaps more. [1.] Thus he might *now* see *his father's kindness,* how willing he was to please him and make him easy, and that he was not such an unkind father as he was willing to represent him when he wanted an excuse to be gone. [2.] Thus he would in a little time be made to see *his own folly,* and that he was not such a wise manager for himself as he would be thought to be. Note, God is a kind Father to all his children, and gives to them all *life, and breath, and all things,* even to the evil and unthankful, διεῖλεν αὐτοῖς τὸν βίον—*He divided to them life.* God's giving us life is putting us in a capacity to serve and glorify him.

(3.) How he managed himself when he had got his portion in his own hands. He set himself to spend it as fast as he could, and, as prodigals generally do, in a little time he made himself a beggar: *not many days after, v.* 13. Note, if God leave us ever so little to ourselves, it will not be long ere we depart from him. When the bridle of restraining grace is taken off we are soon gone. That which the younger son determined was to *be gone* presently, and, in order to that, he *gathered all together.* Sinners, that go astray from God, *venture their all.*

Now the condition of the prodigal in this ramble of his represents to us a *sinful* state, that *miserable* state into which man is *fallen.*

[1.] A sinful state is a state of *departure* and *distance* from God. *First,* It is the *sinfulness* of sin that it is an apostasy from God. He *took his journey* from his father's house. Sinners are fled from God; they *go a whoring from him;* they revolt from their allegiance to him, as a servant that runs from his service, or a wife that treacherously departs from her husband, and they say unto God, *Depart.* They get as far off him as they can. The world is the *far country* in which they take up their residence, and are as at home; and in the service and enjoyment of it they spend their all. *Secondly.* It is the misery of sinners that they are afar off from God, from him who is the Fountain of all good, and are going further and further from him. What is hell itself, but being *afar off* from God?

[2.] A sinful state is a *spending* state: There he *wasted his substance with riotous living* (*v.* 13), devoured it *with harlots* (*v.* 30), and in a little time *he had spent all, v.* 14. He bought fine clothes, spent a great deal in meat and drink, treated high, associated with those that helped him to make an end of what he had in a little time. As to this world, they that *live riotously waste* what they have, and will have a great deal to answer for, that they spend that upon their lusts which should be for the necessary subsistence of themselves and their families. But this is to be applied spiritually. Wilful sinners *waste* their patrimony; for they misemploy their thoughts and all the powers of their souls, mispend their time and all their opportunities, do not only bury, but embezzle, the talents they are entrusted to trade with for their Master's honour; and the gifts of Providence, which were intended to enable them to serve God and to do good with, are made the food and fuel of their lusts. The soul that is made a drudge, either to the world or to the flesh, *wastes its substance,* and *lives riotously. One sinner destroys much good,* Eccl. ix. 18. The good he destroys is valuable, and it is none of his own; they are his *Lord's goods* that he *wastes,* which must be accounted for.

[3.] A sinful state is a *wanting* state: *When he had spent all* upon his harlots, they left him, to seek such another prey; and *there arose a mighty famine in that land,* every thing was scarce and dear, and he *began to be in want, v.* 14. Note, Wilful waste brings woeful want. Riotous living in time, perhaps in a little time, brings men to a *morsel of bread*, especially when *bad times* hasten on the consequences of *bad husbandry*, which good husbandry would have *provided for*. This represents the misery of *sinners*, who have thrown away *their own mercies*, the favour of God, their interest in Christ, the strivings of the Spirit, the admonitions of conscience; these they *gave away* for the pleasure of sense, and the wealth of the world, and then are ready to perish for want of them. Sinners want necessaries for their souls; they have neither food nor raiment for them, nor any provision for hereafter. A sinful state is like a land where *famine reigns*, a *mighty famine;* for the *heaven is as brass* (the dews of God's favour and blessing are withheld, and we must needs want good things if God deny them to us), and the *earth is as iron* (the sinner's heart, that should bring forth good things, is dry and barren, and has no good in it). Sinners are *wretchedly* and *miserably poor*, and, what aggravates it, they brought themselves into that condition, and keep themselves in it by refusing the supplies offered.

[4.] A sinful state is *a vile servile state.* When this young man's riot had brought him to want his want brought him to servitude. *He went, and joined himself to a citizen of that country, v.* 15. The same wicked life that before was represented by *riotous living* is here represented by *servile living;* for sinners are perfect slaves. The devil is the *citizen of that country;* for he is both in city and country. Sinners *join themselves* to him, hire themselves into his service, to do *his work*, to be at *his beck*, and to depend upon him for maintenance and a portion. They that commit sin are the *servants of sin*, John viii. 34. How did this young gentleman debase and disparage himself, when he hired himself into such a service and under such a master as this! He *sent him into the fields*, not to feed sheep (there had been some credit in that employment; Jacob, and Moses, and David, kept sheep), but to *feed swine.* The business of the devil's servants is to *make provision for the flesh, to fulfil the lusts thereof*, and that is no better than feeding greedy, dirty, noisy swine; and how can rational immortal souls more disgrace themselves?

[5.] A sinful state is a state of *perpetual dissatisfaction.* When the prodigal began to be in want, he thought to help himself by *going to service;* and he must be content with the provision which not the house, but the field, afforded; but it is poor provision: *He would fain have filled his belly*, satisfied his hunger, and nourished his body, *with the husks which the swine did eat, v.* 16. A fine pass my young master had brought himself to, to be fellow-commoner with the swine! Note, That which sinners, when they *depart from God*, promise themselves *satisfaction in*, will certainly disappoint them; they are *labouring for that which satisfieth not*, Isa. lv 2. That which is the *stumbling-block of their iniquity* will never *satisfy their souls, nor fill their bowels*, Ezek. vii. 19. Husks are food for swine, but not for men. The wealth of the world and the entertainments of sense will serve for bodies; but what are these to *precious souls?* They neither suit their nature, nor satisfy their desires, nor supply their needs. He that takes up with them *feeds on wind* (Hos. xii. 1), *feeds on ashes*, Isa. xliv. 20

[6.] A sinful state is a state which *cannot expect relief from any creature.* This prodigal, when he could not earn his bread by *working*, took to *begging;* but *no man gave unto him*, because they knew he had brought all this misery upon himself, and because he was rakish, and provoking to every body; such poor are *least pitied.* This, in the application of the parable, intimates that those who depart from God cannot be helped by any creature. In vain do we cry to the world and the flesh (those gods which we have served); they have that which will *poison* a soul, but have nothing to give it which will *feed* and *nourish* it. If thou refuse God's help, whence shall any creature help thee?

[7.] A sinful state is a *state of death: This my son was dead, v.* 24, 32. A sinner is not only dead in law, as he is under a sentence of death, but dead in state too, dead in trespasses and sins, destitute of spiritual life; no union with Christ, no spiritual senses exercised, no living to God, and therefore *dead.* The prodigal in the *far country* was *dead* to his father and his family, cut off from them, as a member from the body or a branch from the tree, and therefore *dead*, and it is his own doing.

[8.] A sinful state is a *lost state: This my son was lost*—lost to every thing that was good—lost to all virtue and honour—lost to his father's house; they had no joy of him. Souls that are separated from God are *lost* souls; lost as a *traveller* that is out of his way, and, if infinite mercy prevent not, will soon be lost as a ship that is sunk at sea, lost irrecoverably.

[9.] A sinful state is a state of *madness* and *frenzy.* This is intimated in that expression (*v.* 17), *when he came to himself*, which intimates that he had been *beside himself.* Surely he was so when he left his father's house, and much more so when he joined himself to the citizen of that country. *Madness* is said to be *in the heart* of sinners, Eccl. ix. 3. Satan has got possession of the soul; and how raging mad was he that was possessed by Legion! Sinners, like those that are *mad*, destroy themselves with *foolish lusts*, and yet at the same time deceive themselves with foolish *hopes;* and they are, of all diseased persons, most enemies to their own cure.

2. We have here his *return* from this *ramble*, his penitent *return* to his father again. When he was brought to the last extremity,

then he bethought himself how much it was his interest to go home. Note, We must not despair of the worst; for while there is life there is hope. The grace of God can soften the hardest heart, and give a happy turn to the strongest stream of corruption. Now observe here,

(1.) What was the *occasion* of his return and repentance. It was his *affliction;* when he was in *want*, then he *came to himself.* Note, Afflictions, when they are sanctified by divine grace, prove happy means of turning sinners from the error of their ways. By them the ear is opened to discipline and the heart disposed to receive instruction; and they are sensible proofs both of the vanity of the world and of the mischievousness of sin. Apply it spiritually. When we find the insufficiency of creatures to make us happy, and have tried all other ways of relief for our poor souls in vain, then it is time to think of returning to God. When we see what miserable comforters, what physicians of no value, all but Christ are, for a soul that groans under the guilt and power of sin, and no *man gives unto us* what we need, then surely we shall apply ourselves to Jesus Christ.

(2.) What was the *preparative* for it; it was *consideration.* He said within himself, he reasoned with himself, when he recovered his right mind, *How many hired servants of my father's have bread enough!* Note, Consideration is the first step towards conversion, Ezek. xviii. 28. *He considers, and turns.* To consider is to retire into ourselves, to reflect upon ourselves, to compare one thing with another, and determine accordingly. Now observe what it was that he considered.

[1.] He considered how bad his condition was: *I perish with hunger.* Not only, "I am *hungry,*" but, "*I perish with hunger*, for I see not what way to expect relief." Note, Sinners will not come to the service of Christ till they are brought to see themselves just ready to perish in the service of sin; and the consideration of that should drive us to Christ. *Master, save us, we perish.* And though we be thus driven to Christ he will not therefore reject us, nor think himself dishonoured by our being forced to him, but rather honoured by his being applied to in a desperate case.

[2.] He considered how much better it might be made if he would but return: *How many hired servants of my father's*, the meanest in his family, the very day-labourers, *have bread enough, and to spare*, such a good house does he keep! Note, *First*, In our *Father's house* there is bread for all his family. This was taught by the twelve loaves of *show-bread*, that were constantly upon the holy table in the sanctuary, a loaf for every tribe. *Secondly,* There is *enough* and to *spare,* enough for all, enough for each, enough to spare for such as will join themselves to his domestics, enough and *to spare* for *charity. Yet there is room;* there are *crumbs* that fall from his table, which many would be glad of, and thankful for. *Thirdly,* Even the *hired servants* in God's family are well provided for; the meanest that will but hire themselves into his family, to *do* his work, and *depend* upon his rewards, shall be well provided for. *Fourthly,* The consideration of this should encourage sinners, that have gone astray from God, to think of returning to him. Thus the adulteress reasons with herself, when she is disappointed in her new lovers: *I will go and return to my first husband, for then was it better with me than now,* Hos. ii. 7.

(3.) What was the *purpose* of it. Since it is so, that his condition is so bad, and may be bettered by returning to his father, his consideration issues, at length, in this conclusion: *I will arise, and go to my father.* Note, Good purposes are good things, but still good performances are all in all.

[1.] He determined what to do: *I will arise and go to my father.* He will not take any longer time to consider of it, but will *forthwith* arise and go. Though he be in a *far country,* a great way off from his father's house, yet, far as it is, he will return; every step of backsliding from God must be a step back again in return to him. Though he be *joined to a citizen of this country,* he makes no difficulty of breaking his bargain with him. We *are not debtors to the flesh;* we are under no obligation at all to our Egyptian taskmasters to give them warning, but are at liberty to quit the service when we will. Observe with what resolution he speaks: "*I will arise, and go to my father;* I am resolved I will, whatever the issue be, rather than *stay* here and *starve.*"

[2.] He determined what to say. True repentance is a *rising,* and *coming* to God: *Behold, we come unto thee.* But what words shall we take with us? He here considers what to say. Note, In all our addresses to God, it is good to deliberate with ourselves beforehand what we shall say, that we may *order our cause before him,* and *fill our mouth with arguments.* We have *liberty of speech,* and we ought to consider seriously with ourselves, how we may use that liberty to the utmost, and yet not abuse it. Let us observe what he purposed to say.

First, He would confess his fault and folly: *I have sinned.* Note, Forasmuch as we have all sinned, it behoves us, and well becomes us, to own that we have sinned. The confession of sin is required and insisted upon, as a necessary condition of peace and pardon. If we plead *not guilty,* we put ourselves upon a trial by the covenant of innocency, which will certainly condemn us. If *guilty,* with a contrite, penitent, and obedient heart, we refer ourselves to the covenant of grace, which offers forgiveness to those that *confess their sins.*

Secondly, He would aggravate it, and would be so far from extenuating the matter that he would *lay a load* upon himself for it: I have sinned *against Heaven,* and *before thee.* Let those that are *undutiful* to their *earthly*

parents think of this; they sin *against heaven, and before God.* Offences against them are offences against God. Let us all think of this, as that which renders our *sin exceedingly sinful,* and should render us exceedingly sorrowful for it. 1. Sin is committed in contempt of God's authority over us: *We have sinned against Heaven.* God is here called *Heaven,* to signify how highly he is exalted above us, and the dominion he has over us, for the *Heavens do rule.* The malignity of sin aims high; it is *against Heaven.* The daring sinner is said to have *set his mouth against the heavens,* Ps. lxxiii. 9. Yet it is *impotent* malice, for we cannot hurt the heavens. Nay, it is foolish malice; what is shot *against the heavens* will return upon the head of him that shoots it, Ps. vii. 16. Sin is an affront to the *God of heaven,* it is a forfeiture of the glories and joys of heaven, and a contradiction to the designs of the kingdom of heaven. 2. It is committed in contempt of God's eye upon us: "I have sinned *against Heaven,* and yet *before thee,* and under thine eye," than which there could not be a greater affront put upon him.

Thirdly, He would judge and condemn himself for it, and acknowledge himself to have forfeited all the privileges of the family: *I am no more worthy to be called thy son, v.* 19. He does not deny the relation (for that was all he had to trust to), but he owns that his father might justly deny the relation, and shut his doors against him. He had, at his own demand, the portion of goods that belonged to him, and had reason to expect no more. Note, It becomes sinners to acknowledge themselves unworthy to receive any favour from God, and to humble and abase themselves before him.

Fourthly, He would nevertheless sue for admission into the family, though it were into the meanest post there: "*Make me as one of thy hired servants;* that is good enough, and too good for me." Note, True penitents have a high value for God's house, and the privileges of it, and will be glad of any place, so they may but be in it, though it be but as *door-keepers,* Ps. lxxxiv. 10. If it be imposed on him as a mortification to sit with the servants, he will not only submit to it, but count it a preferment, in comparison with his present state. Those that return to God, from whom they have revolted, cannot but be desirous some way or other to be employed for him, and put into a capacity of serving and honouring him: "*Make me as a hired servant,* that I may show I love my father's house as much as ever I slighted it."

Fifthly, In all this he would have an eye to his father as a father: "*I will arise, and go to my father, and will say unto him, Father.* Note, Eyeing God as a Father, and our Father, will be of great use in our repentance and return to him. It will make our sorrow for sin genuine, our resolutions against it strong, and encourage us to hope for pardon. God delights to be called *Father* both by penitents and petitioners. *Is not Ephraim a dear son?*

(4.) What was the performance of this purpose: *He arose, and came to his father.* His good resolve he put in execution without delay; he struck while the iron was hot, and did not adjourn the thought to some more convenient season. Note, It is our interest speedily to close with our convictions. Have we said that we will arise and go? Let us immediately arise and come. He did not come half way, and then pretend that he was tired and could get no further, but, weak and weary as he was, he made a thorough business of it. *If thou wilt return, O Israel, return unto me,* and *do thy first works.*

3. We have here his reception and entertainment with his father: *He came to his father;* but was he welcome? Yes, heartily welcome. And, by the way, it is an example to parents whose children have been foolish and disobedient, if they repent, and submit themselves, not to be harsh and severe with them, but to be governed in such a case by the wisdom that is from above, which is *gentle and easy to be entreated;* herein let them be followers of God, and merciful, as he is. But it is chiefly designed to set forth the grace and mercy of God to poor sinners that repent and return to him, and his readiness to forgive them. Now here observe,

(1.) The great love and affection wherewith the father received the son: *When he was yet a great way off his father saw him v.* 20. He expressed his kindness before the son expressed his repentance; for God prevents us with the blessings of his goodness. Even *before we call he answers;* for he knows what is in our hearts. *I said, I will confess, and thou forgavest.* How lively are the images presented here! [1.] Here were *eyes of mercy,* and those eyes quick-sighted: *When he was yet a great way off his father saw him,* before any other of the family were aware of him, as if from the top of some high tower he had been looking that way which his son was gone, with such a thought as this, "O that I could see yonder wretched son of mine coming home!" This intimates God's desire of the conversion of sinners, and his readiness to meet them that are coming towards him. *He looketh on men,* when they are gone astray from him, to see whether they will return to him, and he is aware of the first inclination towards him. [2.] Here were *bowels of mercy,* and those bowels turning within him, and yearning at the sight of his son: *He had compassion.* Misery is the object of pity, even the misery of a sinner; though he has brought it upon himself, yet God compassionates. *His soul was grieved for the misery of Israel,* Hos. xi. 8; Judg. x. 16. [3.] Here were *feet of mercy,* and those feet quick-paced: *He ran.* This denotes how swift God is to show mercy. The prodigal son came slowly, under a burden of shame and fear; but the tender father ran to meet him with his encouragements. [4.] Here were *arms of mercy,* and those arms stretched out to embrace him: *He fell on his neck.* Though guilty and deserving to be beaten, though dirty and newly come from feeding swine, so that any one who had not the strongest and tenderest compassions of a father would have loathed to touch him, yet he thus takes him in his arms, and lays him in his bosom. Thus dear are true penitents to God, thus welcome to the Lord Jesus. [5.] Here were *lips of mercy,* and those lips dropping as a honey-comb: *He kissed him.* This kiss not only *assured* him of his *welcome,* but *sealed his pardon;* his former follies shall be all forgiven, and not mentioned against him, nor is one word said by way of upbraiding. This was like David's kissing Absalom, 2 Sam. xiv. 33. And this intimates how ready, and free, and forward the Lord Jesus is to receive and entertain poor returning repenting sinners, according to his Father's will.

(2.) The penitent submission which the poor prodigal made to his father (*v.* 21): He *said unto him, Father, I have sinned.* As it commends the good father's kindness that he showed it before the prodigal expressed his repentance, so it commends the prodigal's repentance that he expressed it after his father had shown him so much kindness. When he had received the kiss which sealed his pardon, yet he said, *Father, I have sinned.* Note, Even those that have received the pardon of their sins, and the comfortable sense of their pardon, must have in their hearts a sincere contrition for it, and with their mouths must make a penitent confession of it, even of those sins which they have reason to hope are pardoned. David penned the fifty-first psalm after Nathan had said, *The Lord has taken away thy sin, thou shalt not die.* Nay, the comfortable sense of the pardon of sin should increase our sorrow for it; and that is ingenuous evangelical sorrow which is increased by such a consideration. See Ezek. xvi. 63, *Thou shalt be ashamed and confounded, when I am pacified towards thee.* The more we see of God's readiness to *forgive us,* the more difficult it should be to us to *forgive ourselves.*

(3.) The splendid provision which this kind father made for the returning prodigal. He was going on in his submission, but one word we find in his purpose to say (*v.* 19) which we do not find that he did say (*v.* 21), and that was, *Make me as one of thy hired servants.* We cannot think that he forgot it, much less that he changed his mind, and was now either less desirous to be in the family or less willing to be a hired servant there than when he made that purpose; but his father interrupted him, prevented his saying it: "Hold, son, talk no more of thy unworthiness, thou art heartily welcome, and, though not *worthy to be called a son,* shalt be treated as a *dear son,* as a *pleasant child.*" He who is thus entertained at first needs not ask to be made *as a hired servant.* Thus when *Ephraim bemoaned himself* God comforted him, Jer. xxxi. 18—20. It is strange that here is not one word of rebuke: "Why did you not stay with your harlots and your swine? You could never find the way home till beaten hither with your own rod." No, here is nothing like this; which intimates that, when God forgives the sins of true penitents, he forgets them, he remembers them no more, they *shall not be mentioned against them,* Ezek. xviii. 22. But this is not all; here is rich and royal provision made for him, according to his birth and quality, far beyond what he did or could expect. He would have thought it sufficient, and been very thankful, if his father had but taken notice of him, and bid him go to the kitchen, and get his dinner with his servants; but God does for those who return to their duty, and cast themselves upon his mercy, abundantly above what they are able to ask or think. The prodigal came home between hope and fear, fear of being rejected and hope of being received; but his father was not only better to him than his fears, but better to him than his hopes—not only *received* him, but received him with respect.

[1.] He came home *in rags,* and his father not only *clothed* him, but *adorned* him. He *said to the servants,* who all attended their master, upon notice that his son was come, *Bring forth the best robe, and put it on him.* The worst old clothes in the house might have served, and these had been good enough for him; but the father calls not for a *coat,* but for a *robe,* the garment of princes and great men, the *best robe* — *τὴν στόλην τὴν πρώτην.* There is a double emphasis: "*that robe, that principal robe,* you know which I mean;" the *first robe* (so it may be read); the robe he wore before he ran his ramble. When backsliders repent and do their *first works,* they shall be received and dressed in their *first robes.* "Bring hither that robe, and put it on him; he will be ashamed to wear it, and think that it ill becomes him who comes home in such a dirty pickle, but *put it on him,* and do not merely offer it to him: and *put a ring on his hand,* a signet-ring, with the arms of the family, in token of his being owned as a branch of the family." Rich people wore rings, and his father hereby signified that though he had spent one portion, yet, upon his repentance, he intended him another. He came home barefoot, his feet perhaps sore with travel, and therefore, "Put *shoes on his feet,* to make him easy." Thus does the grace of God provide for true penitents. *First,* The *righteousness of Christ* is the robe, that *principal robe,* with which they are clothed; they *put on the Lord Jesus Christ,* are *clothed* with that *Sun.* The *robe of righteousness* is the *garment of salvation,* Isa. lxi. 10. A *new nature* is this *best robe;* true penitents are clothed with this, being sanctified throughout. *Secondly,* The *earnest* of the Spirit, by whom we are sealed to the day of redemption, is the *ring on the hand.*

After *you believed you were sealed.* They that are sanctified are adorned and dignified, are put in power, as Joseph was by Pharaoh's giving him a ring: "*Put a ring on his hand,* to be before him a constant memorial of his father's kindness, that he may never forget it." *Thirdly,* The *preparation of the gospel of peace* is as *shoes for our feet* (Eph. vi. 15), so that, compared with this here, signifies (saith Grotius) that God, when he receives true penitents into his favour, makes use of them for the convincing and converting of others by their instructions, at least by their examples. David, when pardoned, will teach transgressors God's ways, and Peter, when converted, will strengthen his brethren. Or it intimates that they shall go on cheerfully, and with resolution, in the way of religion, as a man does when he has shoes on his feet, above what he does when he is barefoot.

[2.] He came home *hungry,* and his father not only *fed him,* but *feasted him* (*v.* 23): "*Bring hither the fatted calf,* that has been stall-fed, and long reserved for some special occasion, and *kill it,* that my son may be satisfied with the best we have." Cold meat might have served, or the leavings of the last meal; but he shall have fresh meat and hot meat, and the fatted calf can never be better bestowed. Note, There is excellent food provided by our heavenly Father for all those that *arise* and *come to him.* Christ himself is the Bread of life; his flesh is meat indeed, and his blood drink indeed; in him there is a feast for souls, a feast for fat things. It was a great change with the prodigal, who just before *would fain have filled his belly with husks.* How sweet will the supplies of the new covenant be, and the relishes of its comforts, to those who have been *labouring in vain* for satisfaction in the creature! Now he found his own words made good, *In my father's house there is bread enough and to spare.*

(4.) The great joy and rejoicing occasioned by his return. The bringing of the fatted calf was designed to be not only a *feast* for him, but a *festival* for the family: "*Let us all eat, and be merry,* for it is a good day; for *this my son was dead,* when he was in his ramble, but his return is as *life from the dead,* he *is alive again;* we thought that he was dead, having heard nothing from him of a long time, but behold *he lives;* he *was lost,* we gave him up for lost, we despaired of hearing of him, but he *is found.*" Note, [1.] The conversion of a soul from sin to God is the raising of that soul from death to life, and the finding of that which seemed to be lost: it is a great, and wonderful, and happy change. What was in itself *dead* is made *alive,* what was *lost* to God and his church is *found,* and what was *unprofitable* becomes *profitable,* Philem. 11. It is such a change as that upon the face of the earth when the spring returns. [2.] The conversion of sinners is greatly pleasing to the God of heaven, and all that belong to his family ought to rejoice in it; those in heaven *do,* and those on earth *should.* Observe, It was *the father* that began the joy, and set all the rest on rejoicing. *Therefore* we should be glad of the repentance of sinners, because it accomplishes God's design; it is the bringing of those to Christ whom the Father had given him, and in whom he will be for ever glorified. *We joy for your sakes before our God,* with an eye to him (1 Thess. iii. 9), and *ye are our rejoicing in the presence of our Lord Jesus Christ,* who is the Master of the family, 1 Thess. ii. 19. The family complied with the master: *They began to be merry.* Note, God's children and servants ought to be affected with things as he is.

4. We have here the *repining and envying of the elder brother,* which is described by way of reproof to the scribes and Pharisees, to show them the folly and wickedness of their discontent at the repentance and conversion of the publicans and sinners, and the favour Christ showed them; and he represents it so as not to aggravate the matter, but as allowing them still the privileges of elder brethren: the Jews had those privileges (though the Gentiles were favoured), for the preaching of the gospel must begin at Jerusalem. Christ, when he reproved them for their faults, yet accosted them mildly, to smooth them into a good temper towards the poor publicans. But by the *elder brother* here we may understand those who are really good, and have been so from their youth up, and never went astray into any vicious course of living, who *comparatively* need no repentance; and to such these words in the close, *Son, thou art ever with me,* are applicable without any difficulty, but not to the scribes and Pharisees. Now concerning the elder brother, observe,

(1.) How *foolish* and *fretful* he was upon occasion of his brother's reception, and how he was disgusted at it. It seems he was abroad *in the field,* in the country, when his brother came, and by the time he had returned home the *mirth* was *begun: When he drew nigh to the house he heard music and dancing,* either while the dinner was getting ready, or rather after they had eaten and were full, *v.* 25. He enquired *what these things meant* (*v.* 26), and was informed that his brother was come, and his father had made him a feast for his *welcome home,* and great joy there was because he had received him *safe and sound, v.* 27. It is but one word in the original, he had *received* him ὑγιαίνοντα—*in health,* well both in body and mind. He received him not only well in body, but a penitent, returned to his *right mind,* and well reconciled to his father's house, cured of his vices and his rakish disposition, else he had not been received *safe* and *sound.* Now this offended him to the highest degree: *He was angry, and would not go in* (*v.* 28), not only because he was resolved he would not himself join in the mirth, but because he would show his displeasure at it, and would intimate to his father that he should have kept out his younger brother. This shows what is a common fault,

[1.] In men's families. Those who have always been a comfort to their parents think they should have the monopoly of their parents' favours, and are apt to be *too sharp* upon those who have transgressed, and to grudge their parents' kindness to them.

[2.] In God's family. Those who are comparatively *innocents* seldom know how to be compassionate towards those who are manifestly *penitents*. The language of such we have here, in what the *elder brother* said (*v.* 29, 30), and it is written for warning to those who by the grace of God are kept from scandalous sin, and kept in the way of virtue and sobriety, that they sin not after the similitude of this transgression. Let us observe the particulars of it. *First,* He *boasted* of *himself* and *his own virtue* and *obedience.* He had not only not run from his father's house, as his brother did, but had made himself as a *servant* in it, and had long done so: *Lo, these many years do I serve thee, neither transgressed I at any time thy commandment.* Note, It is too common for those that are better than their neighbours to boast of it, yea, and to make their boast of it before God himself, as if he were indebted to them for it. I am apt to think that this elder brother said more than was true, when he gloried that he had never *transgressed his father's commands,* for then I believe he would not have been so obstinate as now he was to *his father's entreaties.* However, we will admit it comparatively; he had not been so disobedient as his brother had been. O what need have good men to take heed of pride, a corruption that arises out of the ashes of other corruptions! Those that have long served God, and been kept from gross sins, have a great deal to be humbly thankful for, but nothing proudly to boast of. *Secondly,* He *complained of his father,* as if he had not been so kind as he ought to have been to him, who had been so dutiful: *Thou never gavest me a kid, that I might make merry with my friends.* He was out of humour now, else he would not have made this complaint; for, no question, if he had asked such a thing at any time, he might have had it at the first word; and we have reason to think that he did not desire it, but the *killing of the fatted calf* put him upon making this peevish reflection. When men are *in a passion* they are apt to reflect in a way they would not if they were in their right mind. He had been fed at his father's table, and had many a time been merry with him and the family; but his father had never given him so much as a kid, which was but a small token of love compared with the *fatted calf.* Note, Those that think *highly* of themselves and their services are apt to think *hardly* of their master and meanly of his favours. We ought to own ourselves utterly unworthy of those mercies which God has thought fit to give us, much more of those that he has not thought fit to give us, and therefore we must not *complain.* He would have had a kid, to *make merry with his friends* abroad, whereas the *fatted calf* he grudged so much was given to his brother, not to *make merry with his friends* abroad, but *with the family* at home: the mirth of God's children should be with their father and his family, in communion with God and his saints, and not with any *other friends. Thirdly,* He was very *ill-humoured* towards his younger brother, and harsh in what he thought and said concerning him. Some good people are apt to be overtaken in this fault, nay, and to indulge themselves too much in it, to look with disdain upon those who have not preserved their reputation so clean as they have done, and to be sour and morose towards them, yea, though they have given very good evidence of their repentance and reformation This is not the Spirit of Christ, but of the Pharisees. Let us observe the instances of it. 1. He *would not go in,* except his brother were *turned out;* one house shall not hold him and his own brother, no, not his *father's house.* The language of this was that of the Pharisee (Isa. lxv. 5): *Stand by thyself, come not near to me, for I am holier than thou;* and (*ch.* xviii. 11) *I am not as other men are, nor even as this publican.* Note, Though we are to shun the society of those sinners by whom we are in danger of being infected, yet we must not be shy of the company of penitent sinners, by whom we may get good. He saw that his father had *taken him in,* and yet he would not *go in* to him. Note, We think too well of ourselves, if we cannot find in our hearts to *receive* those whom God *hath received,* and to admit those into favour, and friendship, and fellowship with us, whom we have reason to think God has a favour for, and who are taken into friendship and fellowship with him. 2. He would not call him *brother;* but *this thy son,* which sounds arrogantly, and not without reflection upon his father, as if his indulgence had made him a prodigal: "He is *thy son,* thy darling." Note, Forgetting the relation we stand in to our brethren, as brethren, and disowning that, are at the bottom of all our neglects of our duty to them and our contradictions to that duty. Let us give our relations, both in the flesh and in the Lord, the titles that belong to them. Let the rich call the poor *brethren,* and let the innocents call the penitents so. 3. He *aggravated his brother's faults,* and made the worst of them, endeavouring to incense his father against him: He *is thy son, who hath devoured thy living with harlots.* It is true, he had spent his own portion foolishly enough (whether *upon harlots* or no we are not told before, perhaps that was only the language of the elder brother's jealousy and ill will), but that he had devoured *all his father's living* was false; the father had still a good estate. Now this shows how apt we are, in censuring our brethren, to *make the worst* of every thing, and to set it out in the blackest colours, which is not doing as we would be done by, nor as our heavenly Father does by us, who is not extreme to mark iniquities. 4. He *grudged* him the *kindness* that his father *showed him: Thou hast killed for him the fatted calf,* as if he were such a son as he should be. Note, It is a wrong thing to *envy* penitents the grace of God, and to have our eye evil because he is good. As we must not envy those that *are* the worst of sinners the gifts of common providence *(Let not thine heart envy sinners),* so we must not envy those that *have been* the worst of sinners the gifts of covenant love upon their repentance; we must not envy them their pardon, and peace, and comfort, no, nor any extraordinary gift which God bestows upon them, which makes them eminently acceptable or useful. Paul, before his conversion, had been a prodigal, had *devoured* his heavenly Father's *living* by the *havoc* he made of the *church;* yet when after his conversion he had greater measures of grace given him, and more honour put upon him, than the other apostles, they who were the elder brethren, who had been *serving Christ* when he was persecuting him, and had not transgressed at any time his commandment, did not envy him his visions and revelations, nor his more extensive usefulness, but *glorified God in him,* which ought to be an example to us, as the reverse of this elder brother.

(2.) Let us now see how *favourable* and *friendly* his father was in *his carriage towards him* when he was thus sour and ill-humoured. This is as surprising as the former. Methinks the mercy and grace of our God in Christ shine almost as brightly in his tender and gentle bearing with *peevish saints,* represented by the elder brother here, as before in his reception of prodigal sinners upon their repentance, represented by the younger brother. The disciples of Christ themselves had many infirmities, and were men subject to like passions as others, yet Christ bore with them, as a nurse with her children. See 1 Thess. ii. 7.

[1.] When he would not come in, his *father came out, and entreated him,* accosted him mildly, gave him good words, and desired him to come in. He might justly have said, "If he will not come in, let him stay out, shut the doors against him, and send him to seek a lodging where he can find it. Is not the house my own? and may I not do what I please in it? Is not the fatted calf my own? and may I not do what I please with it?" No, as he went to meet the younger son, so now he goes to court the elder, did not send a servant out with a kind message to him, but went himself. Now, *First,* This is designed to represent to us the goodness of God; how strangely gentle and winning he has been towards those that were strangely froward and provoking. He reasoned with Cain: *Why art thou wroth?* He *bore Israel's manners in the wilderness,* Acts xiii. 18. How mildly did God reason with Elijah, when he was upon the fret (1 Kings xix. 46), and especially with Jonah, whose case was very parallel with this here, for he was there disquieted at the repentance of Nineveh, and the mercy shown to it, as the elder brother here; and those questions, *Dost thou well to be angry?* and, *Should not I spare Nineveh?* are not unlike these expostulations of the father with the elder brother here. *Secondly,* It is to teach all superiors to be mild and gentle with their inferiors, even when they are in a fault and passionately justify themselves in it, than which nothing can be more provoking; and yet even in that case let fathers *not provoke their children to more wrath,* and let *masters forbear threatening,* and both show all *meekness.*

[2.] His father assured him that the kind entertainment he gave his younger brother was neither any reflection upon him nor should be any prejudice to him (*v.* 31): "Thou shalt fare never the worse for it, nor have ever the less for it. *Son, thou art ever with me;* the reception of him is no rejection of thee, nor what is laid out on him any sensible diminution of what I design for thee; thou shalt still remain entitled to the *pars enitia* (so our law calls it), the *double portion* (so the Jewish law called it); thou shalt be *hæres ex asse* (so the Roman law called it): *all that I have is thine,* by an indefeasible title." If he had not *given him a kid to make merry with his friends,* he had allowed him to eat bread at his table continually; and it is better to be *happy with our Father* in heaven than *merry* with any *friend* we have in this world. Note, *First,* It is the unspeakable happiness of all the children of God, who keep close to their Father's house, that they are, and shall be, ever with him. They are so in this world by faith; they shall be so in the other world by fruition; and all that he has is theirs; for, *if children, then heirs,* Rom. viii. 17. *Secondly, Therefore* we ought not to envy others God's grace to them because we shall have never the less for their sharing in it. If we be true believers, all that God is, all that he has, is *ours;* and, if others come to be true believers, all that he is, and all that he has, is theirs too, and yet we have not the less, as they that walk in the light and warmth of the sun have all the benefit they can have by it, and yet not the less for others having as much; for Christ in his church is like what is said of the soul in the body: it is *tota in toto—the whole in the whole,* and yet *tota in qualibet parte—the whole in each part.*

[3.] His father gave him a good reason for this uncommon joy in the family: *It was meet that we should make merry and be glad, v.* 32. He might have insisted upon his own authority: "It was *my will* that the family should make merry and be glad." *Stat pro ratione voluntas—My reason is, I will it to be so.* But it does not become even those that have authority to be vouching and appealing to it upon every occasion, which does but make it cheap and common; it is better to give a convincing reason, as the father does here: *It was meet,* and very becoming, *that we should make merry* for the return of a prodigal son, more than for the perseverance of a dutiful son; for, though the latter is a greater blessing to a family, yet the former is a more sensible pleasure. Any family would be much more transported with joy at the raising of a dead child to life, yea, or at the recovery of a child from a sickness that was adjudged mortal, than for the continued life and health of many children. Note, God will be justified when he speaks, and all flesh shall, sooner or later, be silent before him. We do not find that the elder brother made any reply to what his father said, which intimates that he was entirely satisfied, and acquiesced in his father's will, and was well reconciled to his prodigal brother; and his father put him in mind that he was his brother: *This thy brother.* Note, A good man, though he have not such a command of himself at all times as to *keep his temper,* yet will, with the grace of God, *recover his temper; though he fall, yet shall he not be utterly cast down.* But as for the scribes and Pharisees, for whose conviction it was primarily intended, for aught that appears they continued the same disaffection to the sinners of the Gentiles, and to the gospel of Christ because it was preached to them.

CHAP. XVI.

The scope of Christ's discourse in this chapter is to awaken and quicken us all so to use this world as not to abuse it, so to manage all our possessions and enjoyments here as that they may make for us, and may not make against us, in the other world; for they will do either the one or the other, according as we use them now. I. If we do good with them, and lay out what we have in works of piety and charity, we shall reap the benefit of it in the world to come; and this he shows in the parable of the unjust steward, who made so good a hand of his lord's goods that, when he was turned out of his stewardship, he had a comfortable subsistence to betake himself to. The parable itself we have, ver. 1—8; the explanation and application of it, ver. 9—13; and the contempt which the Pharisees put upon the doctrine Christ preached to them, for which he sharply reproved them, adding some other weighty sayings, ver. 14—18. II. If, instead of doing good with our worldly enjoyments, we make them the food and fuel of our lusts, of our luxury and sensuality, and deny relief to the poor, we shall certainly perish eternally, and the things of this world, which were thus abused, will but add to our misery and torment. This he shows in the other parable of the rich man and Lazarus, which has likewise a further intention, and that is, to awaken us all to take the warning given us by the written word, and not to expect immediate messages from the other world, ver. 19—31.

AND he said also unto his disciples, There was a certain rich
man, which had a steward; and the
same was accused unto him that he
had wasted his goods. 2 And he
called him, and said unto him, How
is it that I hear this of thee? give an
account of thy stewardship; for thou
mayest be no longer steward. 3 Then
the steward said within himself, What
shall I do? for my lord taketh away
from me the stewardship: I cannot
dig; to beg I am ashamed. 4 I am
resolved what to do, that, when I am
put out of the stewardship, they may
receive me into their houses. 5 So
he called every one of his lord's
debtors *unto him,* and said unto the
first, How much owest thou unto my
lord? 6 And he said, An hundred
measures of oil. And he said unto
him, Take thy bill, and sit down
quickly, and write fifty. 7 Then said
he to another, And how much owest
thou? And he said, An hundred
measures of wheat. And he said unto
him, Take thy bill, and write fourscore. 8 And the lord commended
the unjust steward, because he had
done wisely: for the children of this
world are in their generation wiser
than the children of light. 9 And I
say unto you, Make to yourselves
friends of the mammon of unrighteousness; that, when ye fail, they may
receive you into everlasting habitations. 10 He that is faithful in that
which is least is faithful also in much:
and he that is unjust in the least is
unjust also in much. 11 If therefore
ye have not been faithful in the unrighteous mammon, who will commit
to your trust the true *riches?* 12 And
if ye have not been faithful in that
which is another man's, who shall
give you that which is your own?
13 No servant can serve two masters:
for either he will hate the one, and
love the other; or else he will hold
to the one, and despise the other.
Ye cannot serve God and mammon.
14 And the Pharisees also, who were
covetous, heard all these things: and
they derided him. 15 And he said
unto them, Ye are they which justify
yourselves before men; but God
knoweth your hearts: for that which
is highly esteemed among men is
abomination in the sight of God. 16

The law and the prophets *were* until John: since that time the kingdom of God is preached, and every man presseth into it. 17 And it is easier for heaven and earth to pass, than one tittle of the law to fail. 18 Whosoever putteth away his wife, and marrieth another, committeth adultery: and whosoever marrieth her that is put away from *her* husband committeth adultery.

We mistake if we imagine that the design of Christ's doctrine and holy religion was either to amuse us with notions of divine mysteries or to entertain us with notions of divine mercies. No, the divine revelation of both these in the gospel is intended to engage and quicken us to the practice of Christian duties, and, as much as any one thing, to the duty of beneficence and doing good to those who stand in need of any thing that either we have or can do for them. This our Saviour is here pressing us to, by reminding us that we are but *stewards of the manifold grace of God;* and since we have in divers instances been unfaithful, and have forfeited the favour of our Lord, it is our wisdom to think how we may, some other way, make what we have in the world turn to a good account. Parables must not be forced beyond their primary intention, and therefore we must not hence infer that any one can befriend us if we lie under the displeasure of our Lord, but that, in the general, we must so lay out what we have in works of piety and charity as that we may meet it again with comfort on the other side death and the grave. If we would act wisely, we must be as diligent and industrious to employ our riches in the acts of piety and charity, in order to promote our future and eternal welfare, as worldly men are in laying them out to the greatest temporal profit, in making to themselves friends with them, and securing other secular interests. So *Dr. Clarke.* Now let us consider,

I. The parable itself, in which all the children of men are represented as *stewards* of what they have in this world, and we are but stewards. Whatever we have, the property of it is God's; we have only the use of it, and that according to the direction of our great Lord, and for his honour. Rabbi Kimchi, quoted by Dr. Lightfoot, says, "This world is a house; heaven the roof; the stars the lights; the earth, with its fruits, a table spread; the Master of the house is the holy and blessed God; man is the steward, into whose hands the goods of this house are delivered; if he behave himself well, he shall find favour in the eyes of his Lord; if not, he shall be turned out of his stewardship." Now,

1. Here is the *dishonesty* of this *steward.* He *wasted his lord's goods,* embezzled them, misapplied them, or through carelessness suffered them to be lost and damaged; and for this he was *accused to his lord, v.* 1. We are all *liable* to the same charge. We have not made a due improvement of what God has entrusted us with in this world, but have perverted his purpose; and, that we may not be for this *judged of our Lord,* it concerns us to *judge ourselves.*

2. His *discharge* out of his place. His lord *called for him,* and said, "*How is it that I hear this of thee?* I expected better things from thee." He speaks as one sorry to find himself disappointed in him, and under a necessity of dismissing him from his service: it troubles him to hear it; but the steward cannot deny it, and therefore there is no remedy, he must make up his accounts, and be gone in a little time, *v.* 2. Now this is designed to teach us, (1.) That we must all of us shortly be discharged from *our stewardship* in this world; we must not always enjoy those things which we now enjoy. Death will come, and *dismiss* us from our stewardship, will *deprive* us of the abilities and opportunities we now have of doing good, and others will come in our places and have the same. (2.) That our discharge from our stewardship at death is *just,* and what we have deserved, for we have wasted our Lord's goods, and thereby forfeited our trust, so that we cannot complain of any wrong done us. (3.) That when our stewardship is taken from us we must *give an account* of it to our Lord: *After death the judgment.* We are fairly warned both of our discharge and our account, and ought to be frequently thinking of them.

3. His *after-wisdom.* Now he began to consider, *What shall I do? v.* 3. He would have done well to have considered this before he had so foolishly thrown himself out of a good place by his unfaithfulness; but it is better to *consider* late than never. Note, Since we have all received notice that we must shortly be turned out of our stewardship, we are concerned to consider what we shall do then. He must live; which way shall he have a livelihood? (1.) He knows that he has not such a degree of industry in him as to get his living by work: "*I cannot dig;* I cannot earn my bread by my labour." But why can he not dig? It does not appear that he is either old or lame; but the truth is, he is *lazy.* His *cannot* is a *will not;* it is not a natural but a moral disability that he labours under; if his master, when he turned him out of the stewardship, had continued him in his service as a labourer, and set a task-master over him, he would have made him dig. He *cannot dig,* for he was never used to it. Now this intimates that we cannot get a livelihood for our souls by any labour for this world, nor indeed do any thing to purpose for our souls by any ability of our own. (2.) He knows that he has not such a degree of *humility* as to get his bread by

begging: *To beg I am ashamed.* This was the language of his pride, as the former of his slothfulness. Those whom God, in his providence, has disabled to help themselves, should not be *ashamed* to ask relief of others. This steward had more reason to be ashamed of cheating his master than of begging his bread. (3.) He therefore determines to make friends of his lord's debtors, or his tenants that were behind with their rent, and had given notes under their hands for it: "*I am resolved what to do, v.* 4. My lord turns me out of his house. I have none of my own to go to. I am acquainted with my lord's tenants, have done them many a good turn, and now I will do them one more, which will so oblige them that they will bid me welcome to their houses, and the best entertainment they afford; and so long as I live, at least till I can better dispose of myself, I will quarter upon them, and go from one good house to another." Now the way he would take to make them his friends was by striking off a considerable part of their debt to his lord, and giving it in in his accounts so much less than it was. Accordingly, he sent for one, who owed his lord *a hundred measures of oil* (in that commodity he paid his rent): *Take thy bill,* said he, here it is, and *sit down quickly, and write fifty* (*v.* 6); so he reduced his debt to the one half. Observe, he was in haste to have it done: "*Sit down quickly,* and do it, lest we be taken treating, and suspected." He took another, who owed his lord *a hundred measures of wheat,* and from his bill he cut off a fifth part, and bade him write *fourscore* (*v.* 7); probably he did the like by others, abating more or less according as he expected kindness from them. See here what uncertain things our worldly possessions are; they are most so to those who have most of them, who devolve upon others all the care concerning them, and so put it into their power to *cheat them,* because they will not trouble themselves to see with their own eyes. See also what treachery is to be found even among those in whom trust is reposed. How hard is it to find one that confidence can be reposed in! *Let God be true, but every man a liar.* Though this steward is turned out for dealing dishonestly, yet still he does so. So rare is it for men to mend of a fault, though they smart for it.

4. The approbation of this: *The lord commended the unjust steward, because he had done wisely, v.* 8. It may be meant of *his lord,* the lord of that servant, who, though he could not but be angry at his knavery, yet was pleased with his ingenuity and policy for himself; but, taking it so, the latter part of the verse must be the words of *our Lord,* and therefore I think the whole is meant of him. Christ did, as it were, say, "Now commend me to such a man as this, that knows how to do well for himself, how to improve a present opportunity, and how to provide for a future necessity." He does not commend him because he had done *falsely* to his master, but because he had done *wisely* for himself. Yet perhaps herein he did well for his master too, and but justly with the tenants. He knew what *hard bargains* he had *set them,* so that they could not *pay their rent,* but, having been screwed up by his rigour, were thrown *behindhand,* and they and their families were likely to go to ruin; in consideration of this, he now, at going off, did as he ought to do both in justice and charity, not only easing them of part of their arrears, but abating their rent for the future. *How much owest thou?* may mean, "What rent dost thou sit upon? Come, I will set thee an easier bargain, and yet no easier than what thou oughtest to have." He had been *all for his lord,* but now he begins to consider the tenants, that he might have *their favour* when he had lost *his lord's.* The abating of their rent would be a lasting kindness, and more likely to engage them than abating their arrears only. Now this forecast of his, for a comfortable subsistence in this world, shames our improvidence for another world: *The children of this world,* who choose and have their portions in it, *are wiser for their generation,* act more considerately, and better consult their worldly interest and advantage, than the *children of light,* who enjoy the gospel, in *their generation,* that is, in the concerns of their souls and eternity. Note, (1.) The wisdom of worldly people in the concerns of this world is to be *imitated* by us in the concerns of our souls: it is their principle to improve their opportunities, to do that first which is most needful, in summer and harvest to lay up for winter, to take a good bargain when it is offered them, to trust the *faithful* and not the *false.* O that we were thus wise in our spiritual affairs! (2.) The children of light are commonly *outdone* by the children of this world. Not that the children of this world are *truly wise;* it is only *in their generation.* But in that they are *wiser than the children of light in theirs;* for, though we are told that we must shortly be *turned out of our stewardship,* yet we do not provide as we should for such a day. We live as if we were to be *here always* and as if there were not *another life after this,* and are not so solicitous as this steward was to provide for *hereafter.* Though as *children of the light,* that light to which life and immortality are brought by the gospel, we cannot but see *another world* before us, yet we do not prepare for it, do not send our best effects and best affections thither, as we should.

II. The application of this parable, and the inferences drawn from it (*v.* 9): "*I say unto you,* you my disciples" (for to them this parable is directed, *v.* 1), "though you have but little in this world, consider how you may do good with that little." Observe,

1. What it is that our Lord Jesus here exhorts us to; to provide for our comfortable reception to the happiness of another world,

by making good use of our possessions and enjoyments in this world: "*Make to yourselves friends of the mammon of unrighteousness*, as the steward with his lord's goods made his lord's tenants his friends." It is the wisdom of the men of this world so to manage their money as that they may have the benefit of it hereafter, and not for the present only; therefore they put it out to interest, buy land with it, put it into this or the other fund. Now we should learn of them to make use of our money so as that we may be the better for it hereafter in another world, as they do in hopes to be the better for it hereafter in this world; so *cast it upon the waters* as that we may *find it again after many days*, Eccl. xi. 1. And in our case, though whatever we have *are our Lord's goods*, yet, as long as we dispose of them among *our Lord's tenants* and for their advantage, it is so far from being reckoned a wrong to our Lord, that it is a duty to him as well as policy for ourselves. Note, (1.) The things of this world are the *mammon of unrighteousness*, or the false *mammon*, not only because often got by fraud and unrighteousness, but because those who trust to it for satisfaction and happiness will certainly be deceived; for riches are perishing things, and will disappoint those that raise their expectations from them. (2.) Though this *mammon of unrighteousness* is not to be *trusted to* for a happiness, yet it may and must be *made use of* in subserviency to our pursuit of that which is our happiness. Though we cannot find true satisfaction in it, yet we may *make to ourselves friends* with it, not by way of *purchase* or *merit*, but *recommendation;* so we may make God and Christ our friends, the good angels and saints our friends, and the poor our friends; and it is a desirable thing to be *befriended* in the account and state to come. (3.) At death we must all *fail*, ὅταν ἐκλίπητε—*when ye suffer an eclipse.* Death eclipses us. A tradesman is said to *fail* when he becomes a *bankrupt*. We must all thus fail shortly; death shuts up the shop, seals up the hand. Our comforts and enjoyments on earth will *all fail* us; flesh and heart fail. (4.) It ought to be our great concern to make it sure to ourselves, that *when* we *fail* at death we may be *received into everlasting habitations* in heaven. The *habitations* in heaven are *everlasting*, not *made with hands*, but *eternal*, 2 Cor. v. 1. Christ is gone before, to prepare a place for those that are his, and is there ready to *receive them;* the bosom of Abraham is ready to receive them, and, when a *guard of angels* carries them thither, a *choir of angels* is ready to receive them there. The poor saints that are gone before to glory will receive those that in this world distributed to their necessities. (5.) This is a good reason why we should use what we have in the world for the honour of God and the good of our brethren, that thus we may with them *lay up in store a good bond*, a good security, a good foundation *for the time to come*, for an eternity to come. See 1 Tim, vi. 17—19, which explains this here.

2. With what arguments he presses this exhortation to abound in works of piety and charity.

(1.) If we do not make a right use of the *gifts of God's providence*, how can we expect from him those present and future comforts which are the *gifts of his spiritual grace?* Our Saviour here compares these, and shows that though our faithful use of the things of this world cannot be thought to merit any favour at the hand of God, yet our unfaithfulness in the use of them may be justly reckoned a *forfeiture* of that grace which is necessary to bring us to glory, and that is it which our Saviour here shows, *v.* 10—14.

[1.] The riches of this world are the *less;* grace and glory are the *greater.* Now if we be unfaithful in the less, if we use the things of this world to other purposes than those for which they were given us, it may justly be feared that we should be so in the gifts of God's grace, that we should receive them also in vain, and therefore they will be denied us: *He that is faithful in that which is least is faithful also in much.* He that serves God, and does good, with his money, will serve God, and do good, with the more noble and valuable talents of wisdom and grace, and spiritual gifts, and the earnests of heaven; but he that buries the *one talent* of this world's wealth will never improve the *five talents* of spiritual riches. God withholds his grace from covetous worldly people more than we are aware of. [2.] The riches of this world are *deceitful* and *uncertain;* they are the *unrighteous mammon*, which is hastening from us apace, and, if we would make any advantage of it, we must bestir ourselves quickly; if we do not, how can we expect to be entrusted with spiritual riches, which are the only *true riches? v.* 11. Let us be convinced of this, that those are *truly* rich, and *very* rich, who are rich in *faith*, and rich *towards God*, rich in Christ, in the promises, and in the earnests of heaven; and therefore let us lay up our treasure in them, expect our portion from them, and mind them in the first place, the *kingdom of God and the righteousness thereof*, and then, if other things be added to us, use them *in ordine ad spiritualia—with a spiritual reference*, so that by using them well we may take the faster hold of the *true riches*, and may be qualified to receive yet *more grace* from God; *for God giveth to a man that is good in his sight*, that is, to a free-hearted charitable man, *wisdom, and knowledge, and joy* (Eccl. ii. 26); that is, to a man that is *faithful in the unrighteous mammon*, he gives the *true riches.* [3.] The riches of this world are *another man's.* They are τὰ ἀλλότρια, not *our own;* for they are foreign to the soul and its nature and interest. They are not *our own;* for they are

God's; his title to them is prior and superior to ours; the property remains in him, we are but usufructuaries. They are *another man's;* we have them from others; we use them for others, and *what good has the owner* from his *goods* that *increase,* save *the beholding of them with his eyes,* while still *they are increased that eat them;* and we must shortly leave them to others, and we know not to whom? But spiritual and eternal riches are *our own* (they enter into the soul that becomes *possessed* of them) and *inseparably;* they are a good part that will never be taken away from us. If we make Christ our own, and the promises our own, and heaven our own, we have that which we may truly call *our own.* But how can we expect God should *enrich us* with these if we do not serve him with our worldly possessions, of which we are but stewards?

(2.) We have no other way to prove ourselves the servants of God than by giving up ourselves so entirely to his service as to make *mammon,* that is, all our worldly gain, serviceable to us in his service (*v.* 13): *No servant can serve two masters,* whose commands are so inconsistent as those of God and *mammon* are. If a man will *love* the world, and *hold to that,* it cannot be but he will *hate God* and *despise* him. He will make all his pretensions of religion truckle to his secular interests and designs, and the things of God shall be made to help him in serving and seeking the world. But, on the other hand, if a man will *love God,* and *adhere* to him, he will comparatively *hate* the world (whenever God and the world come in competition) and will *despise* it, and make all his business and success in the world some way or other conducive to his furtherance in the business of religion; and the things of the world shall be made to help him in serving God and working out his salvation. The matter is here laid plainly before us: *Ye cannot serve God and mammon.* So divided are their interests that their services can never be *compounded.* If therefore we be determined to *serve God,* we must disclaim and abjure the service of the world.

3. We are here told what entertainment this doctrine of Christ met with among the Pharisees, and what rebuke he gave them.

(1.) They wickedly *ridiculed* him, *v.* 14. *The Pharisees, who were covetous, heard all these things,* and could not contradict him, but *they derided him.* Let us consider this, [1.] As their *sin,* and the fruit of their *covetousness,* which was their reigning sin, their own iniquity. Note, Many that make a great profession of religion, have much knowledge, and abound in the exercise of devotion, are yet ruined by the love of the world; nor does any thing harden the heart more against the word of Christ. These covetous Pharisees could not bear to have that *touched,* which was their *Delilah,* their darling lust; for this they derided him, ἐξεμυκτήριζον αὐτόν—*they snuffled up their noses at him,* or blew their noses on him. It is an expression of the utmost scorn and disdain imaginable; *the word of the Lord was to them a reproach,* Jer. vi. 10. They laughed at him for going so contrary to the opinion and way of the world, for endeavouring to recover them from a sin which they were resolved to hold fast. Note, It is common for those to *make a jest* of the word of God who are resolved that they will not be ruled by it; but they will find at last that it cannot be turned off so. [2.] As *his suffering.* Our Lord Jesus endured not only the *contradiction* of sinners, but their *contempt;* they *had him in derision* all the day. He that spoke as never man spoke was bantered and ridiculed, that his faithful ministers, whose preaching is unjustly *derided,* may not be disheartened at it. It is no disgrace to a man to be laughed at, but to deserve to be laughed at. Christ's apostles were *mocked,* and no wonder; the *disciple is not greater than his Lord.*

(2.) He justly reproved them; not for *deriding* him (he knew how to *despise the shame),* but for *deceiving* themselves with the shows and colours of piety, when they were strangers to the power of it, *v.* 15. Here is,

[1.] Their *specious outside;* nay, it was a *splendid one. First,* They *justified themselves before men;* they denied whatever ill was laid to their charge, even by Christ himself. They claimed to be looked upon as men of singular sanctity and devotion, and justified themselves in that claim: "*You are they that* do that, so as none ever did, that make it your business to court the opinion of men, and, right or wrong, will justify yourselves before the world; you are *notorious* for this.' *Secondly,* They were *highly esteemed among men.* Men did not only *acquit* them from any blame they were under, but *applauded* them, and had them in veneration, not only as *good men,* but as the *best of men.* Their sentiments were esteemed as oracles, their directions as laws, and their practices as inviolable prescriptions.

[2.] Their *odious inside,* which was under the eye of God: "He *knows your heart,* and it is in his sight an *abomination;* for it is full of all manner of wickedness. Note, *First,* It is folly to *justify ourselves before men,* and to think this enough to bear us out, and bring us off, in the judgment of the great day, that men *know no ill* of us; for God, who knows our hearts, knows that ill of us which no one else can know. This ought to check our value for ourselves, and our confidence in ourselves, that *God knows our hearts,* and how much deceit is there, for we have reason to abase and distrust ourselves. *Secondly,* It is folly to judge of persons and things by the opinion of men concerning them, and to go down with the stream of vulgar estimate; for that which is *highly esteemed among men,* who judge according to outward appearance, is perhaps *an abomina-*

tion in the sight of God, who sees things as they are, and whose judgment, we are sure, is according to truth. On the contrary, there are those whom men despise and condemn who yet are accepted and approved of God, 2 Cor. x. 18.

(3.) He turned from them to the publicans and sinners, as more likely to be wrought upon by his gospel than those covetous conceited Pharisees (*v.* 16): "The *law and the prophets were* indeed *until John;* the Old-Testament dispensation, which was *confined* to you Jews, continued till John Baptist appeared, and you seemed to have the monopoly of righteousness and salvation; and you are puffed up with this, and this gains you esteem among men, that you are students in the law and the prophets; but since John Baptist appeared *the kingdom of God is preached,* a New-Testament dispensation, which does not value men at all for their being doctors of the law, but *every man presses* into the gospel kingdom, Gentiles as well as Jews, and no man thinks himself bound in good manners to let his betters go before him into it, or to stay till the *rulers* and the Pharisees have led him that way. It is not so much a political national constitution as the Jewish economy was, when *salvation was of the Jews;* but it is made a particular personal concern, and therefore *every man* that is convinced he has a soul to save, and an eternity to provide for, thrusts to get in, lest he should come short by trifling and complimenting." Some give this sense of it; they derided Christ for speaking in contempt of riches, for, thought they, were there not many promises of riches and other temporal good things in the *law and the prophets?* And were not many of the best of God's servants very rich, as Abraham and David? "It is true," saith Christ, "so it was, but now that the kingdom of God is begun to be preached things take a new turn; now blessed are the poor, and the mourners, and the persecuted." The Pharisees, to requite the people for their high opinion of them, allowed them in a cheap, easy, formal religion. "But," saith Christ, "now that the *gospel is preached* the eyes of the people are opened, and as they cannot now have a veneration for the Pharisees, as they have had, so they cannot content themselves with such an indifferency in religion as they have been trained up in, but they *press* with a holy violence into the kingdom of God." Note, Those that would go to heaven must take pains, must strive against the stream, must press against the crowd that are going the contrary way.

(4.) Yet still he protests against any design to invalidate the law (*v.* 17): *It is easier for heaven and earth to pass,* παρελθεῖν,—*to pass by,* to pass away, though the foundations of the earth and the pillars of heaven are so firmly established, *than for one tittle of the law to fail.* The moral law is confirmed and ratified, and not one tittle of that fails; the duties enjoined by it are duties still; the sins forbidden by it are sins still. Nay, the precepts of it are explained and enforced by the gospel, and made to appear more spiritual. The ceremonial law is perfected in the gospel, and its shades are filled up with the gospel colours; not *one tittle* of that *fails,* for it is found printed off in the gospel, where, though the force of it is as a law taken off, yet the figure of it as a type shines very brightly, witness the epistle to the Hebrews. There were some things which were connived at by the law, for the preventing of greater mischiefs, the permission of which the gospel has indeed taken away, but without any detriment or disparagement to the law, for it has thereby reduced them to the primitive intention of the law, as in the case of divorce (*v.* 18), which we had before, Matt. v. 32; xix. 9. Christ will not allow divorces, for his gospel is intended to strike at the bitter root of men's corrupt appetites and passions, to kill them, and pluck them up; and therefore they must not be so far *indulged* as that permission *did* indulge them, for the more they are indulged the more impetuous and headstrong they grow.

19 There was a certain rich man,
which was clothed in purple and fine
linen, and fared sumptuously every
day: 20 And there was a certain beggar named Lazarus, which was laid
at his gate, full of sores, 21 And
desiring to be fed with the crumbs
which fell from the rich man's table:
moreover the dogs came and licked
his sores. 22 And it came to pass,
that the beggar died, and was carried
by the angels into Abraham's bosom:
the rich man also died, and was buried;
23 And in hell he lift up his eyes,
being in torments, and seeth Abraham
afar off, and Lazarus in his bosom.
24 And he cried and said, Father
Abraham, have mercy on me, and
send Lazarus, that he may dip the
tip of his finger in water, and cool my
tongue; for I am tormented in this
flame. 25 But Abraham said, Son,
remember that thou in thy lifetime
receivedst thy good things, and likewise Lazarus evil things: but now he
is comforted, and thou art tormented.
26 And beside all this, between us
and you there is a great gulf fixed:
so that they which would pass from
hence to you cannot; neither can
they pass to us, that *would come* from
thence. 27 Then he said, I pray thee

therefore, father, that thou wouldest
send him to my father's house: 28
For I have five brethren; that he may
testify unto them, lest they also come
into this place of torment. 29 Abraham saith unto him, They have Moses
and the prophets; let them hear them.
30 And he said, Nay, father Abraham:
but if one went unto them from the
dead, they will repent. 31 And he
said unto him, If they hear not Moses
and the prophets, neither will they be
persuaded, though one rose from the
dead.

As the parable of the prodigal son set before us the grace of the gospel, which is encouraging to us all, so this sets before us the *wrath to come,* and is designed for our awakening; and very fast asleep those are in sin that will not be awakened by it. The Pharisees made a jest of Christ's sermon against worldliness; now this parable was intended to make those mockers serious. The tendency of the gospel of Christ is both to reconcile us to poverty and affliction and to arm us against temptations to worldliness and sensuality. Now this parable, by drawing the curtain, and letting us see what will be the end of both in the other world, goes very far in prosecuting those two great intentions. This parable is not like Christ's other parables, in which spiritual things are represented by similitudes borrowed from worldly things, as those of the sower and the seed (except that of the sheep and goats), the prodigal son, and indeed all the rest but this. But here the *spiritual things themselves* are represented in a narrative or description of the different state of good and bad in this world and the other. Yet we need not call it a history of a particular occurrence, but it is *matter of fact* that is true every day, that poor godly people, whom men neglect and trample upon, die away out of their miseries, and go to heavenly bliss and joy, which is made the more pleasant to them by their preceding sorrows; and that rich epicures, who live in luxury, and are unmerciful to the poor, die, and go into a state of insupportable torment, which is the more grievous and terrible to them because of the sensual lives they lived: and that there is no gaining any relief from their torments. Is this a parable? What similitude is there in this? The discourse indeed between Abraham and the rich man is only an illustration of the description, to make it the more affecting, like that between God and Satan in the story of Job. Our Saviour came to bring us acquainted with another world, and to show us the reference which *this* world has to *that;* and here he does it In this description (for so I shall choose to call it) we may observe,

I. The different condition of a *wicked rich man,* and a *godly poor man,* in this world. We know that as some of late, so the Jews of old, were ready to make prosperity one of the marks of a true church, of a good man and a favourite of heaven, so that they could hardly have any favourable thoughts of a *poor man.* This mistake Christ, upon all occasions, set himself to correct, and here very fully, where we have,

1. A wicked man, and one that will be for ever miserable, in the height of prosperity (*v.* 19): *There was a certain rich man.* From the Latin we commonly call him *Dives—a rich man;* but, as Bishop Tillotson observes, he has no name given him, as the poor man has, because it had been invidious to have named any particular rich man in such a description as this, and apt to provoke and gain ill-will. But others observe that Christ would not do the rich man so much honour as to name him, though when perhaps he called his lands by his own name he thought it should long survive that of the beggar at his gate, which yet is here preserved, when that of the rich man is buried in oblivion. Now we are told concerning this rich man,

(1.) That he was *clothed in purple and fine linen,* and that was his *adorning.* He had *fine linen* for *pleasure,* and clean, no doubt, every day; night-linen, and day-linen. He had *purple* for *state,* for that was the wear of princes, which has made some conjecture that Christ had an eye to Herod in it. He never appeared abroad but in great magnificence.

(2.) He *fared* deliciously and *sumptuously every day.* His table was furnished with all the varieties and dainties that nature and art could supply; his side-table richly adorned with plate; his servants, who waited at table, in rich liveries; and the guests at his table, no doubt, such as he thought *graced* it. Well, and what harm was there in all this? It is no sin to be rich, no sin to wear purple and fine linen, nor to keep a plentiful table, if a man's estate will afford it. Nor are we told that he got his estate by fraud, oppression, or extortion, no, nor that he was drunk, or made others drunk; but, [1.] Christ would hereby show that a man may have a great deal of the wealth, and pomp, and pleasure of this world, and yet lie and perish for ever under God's wrath and curse. We cannot infer from men's living great either that God loves them *in* giving them so much, or that they love God *for* giving them so much; happiness consists not in these things. [2.] That plenty and pleasure are a very *dangerous* and to many a *fatal* temptation to luxury, and sensuality, and forgetfulness of God and another world. This man might have been happy if he had not had great possessions and enjoyments. [3.] That the indulgence of the body, and the ease and pleasure of that, are the ruin of many a soul, and the interests of it. It is true, eating good meat and wearing good clothes are lawful; but it is as true that they often become the food and fuel of pride and luxury, and so turn into sin to us. [4.] That feasting ourselves and our friends, and, at the same time, forgetting the distresses of the poor and afflicted, are very provoking to God and damning to the soul. The sin of this rich man was not so much his dress or his diet, but his providing only for himself.

2. Here is a godly man, and one that will be for ever happy, in the depth of adversity and distress (*v.* 20): *There was a certain beggar,* named *Lazarus.* A beggar of that name, eminently devout, and in great distress, was probably well known among good people at that time: a beggar, suppose such a one as Eleazar, or Lazarus. Some think Eleazar a proper name for any poor man, for it signifies the *help of God,* which they must fly to that are destitute of *other helps.* This poor man was reduced to the last extremity, as miserable, as to outward things, as you can lightly suppose a man to be in this world.

(1.) His body was *full of sores,* like Job. To be sick and weak in body is a great affliction; but sores are more *painful* to the patient, and more *loathsome* to those about him.

(2.) He was forced to beg his bread, and to take up with such scraps as he could get at rich people's doors. He was so sore and lame that he could not go himself, but was carried by some compassionate hand or other, and *laid at the rich man's gate.* Note, Those that are not able to help the poor with their *purses* should help them with their *pains;* those that cannot lend them *a penny* should lend them *a hand;* those that have not themselves wherewithal to give to them should either bring them, or go for them, to those that have. Lazarus, in his distress, had nothing of his own to subsist on, no relation to go to, nor did the parish take care of him. It is an instance of the degeneracy of the Jewish church at this time that such a godly man as Lazarus was should be suffered to perish for want of necessary food. Now observe,

[1.] His expectations from the rich man's table: *He desired to be fed with the crumbs, v.* 21. He did not look for a mess from off his table, though he ought to have had one, one of the best; but would be thankful for the crumbs from under the table, the broken meat which was the rich man's leavings; nay, the leavings of his dogs. *The poor use entreaties,* and must be content with such as they can get. Now this is taken notice of to show, *First,* What was the distress, and what the disposition, of the poor man. He was *poor,* but he was *poor in spirit,* contentedly poor. He did not lie at the rich man's gate complaining, and bawling, and making a noise, but silently and modestly desiring to be *fed with the crumbs.* This miserable man was a good man, and in favour with God. Note, It is often the lot of some of the dearest of God's saints and servants to be greatly afflicted in this world, while wicked people prosper, and have abundance; see Ps. lxxiii 7, 10, 14. Here is a child of wrath and an heir of hell sitting in the house, faring sumptuously; and a child of love and an heir of heaven lying at the gate, perishing for hunger. And is men's spiritual state to be judged of then by their outward condition? *Secondly,* What was the temper of the rich man towards him. We are not told that he abused him, or forbade him his gate, or did him any harm, but it is intimated that he slighted him; he had no concern for him, took no care about him. Here was a *real* object of charity, and a very *moving* one, which spoke for itself; it was presented to him at *his own gate.* The poor man had a good character and good conduct, and every thing that could recommend him. A *little* thing would be a *great* kindness to him, and yet he took no cognizance of his case, did not order him to be taken in and lodged in the barn, or some of the out-buildings, but let him lie there. Note, It is not enough not to oppress and trample upon the poor; we shall be found unfaithful stewards of our Lord's goods, in the great day, if we do not succour and relieve them. The reason given for the most fearful doom is, *I was hungry, and you gave me no meat.* I wonder how those rich people who have read the gospel of Christ, and say that they believe it, can be so unconcerned as they often are in the necessities and miseries of the poor and afflicted.

[2.] The usage he had from the dogs: *The dogs came and licked his sores.* The rich man kept a kennel of hounds, it may be, or other dogs, for his diversion, and to please his fancy, and these were fed to the full, when poor Lazarus could not get enough to keep him alive. Note, Those will have a great deal to answer for hereafter that feed their dogs, but neglect the poor. And it is a great aggravation of the uncharitableness of many rich people that they bestow that upon their fancies and follies which would supply the necessity, and rejoice the heart, of many a good Christian in distress. Those offend God, nay, and they put a contempt upon human nature, that pamper their dogs and horses, and let the families of their poor neighbours starve. Now those dogs *came and licked the* sores of poor Lazarus, which may be taken, *First,* As an aggravation of his misery. His sores were *bloody,* which tempted the dogs to come, and lick them, as they did the blood of Naboth and Ahab, 1 Kings xxi. 19. And we read of the *tongue of the dogs dipped* in the *blood* of *enemies,* Ps. lxviii. 23. They attacked him while he was yet alive, as if he had been already dead, and he had not strength himself to keep them off, nor would any of the servants be so civil as to check them. The dogs were like their master, and thought they fared sumptuously when they regaled themselves with human gore. Or, it may be taken, *Secondly,* as some relief to him in his misery; ἀλλὰ καὶ, the master was *hard-hearted* towards him, *but* the dogs *came and licked his sores,* which mollified and eased them. It is not said, They *sucked* them, but *licked* them, which was good for them. The dogs were more kind to him than their master was.

II. Here is the *different condition* of this *godly poor man,* and this *wicked rich man, at* and *after death.* Hitherto the wicked man seems to have the advantage, but *Exitus acta probat—Let us wait awhile, to see the end hereof.*

1. They both died (*v.* 22): The *beggar died;* the *rich man also died.* Death is the common lot of rich and poor, godly and ungodly; there they meet together. One dieth *in his full strength,* and another in *the bitterness of his soul;* but they shall *lie down alike in the dust,* Job xxi. 26. Death favours not either the rich man for his riches or the poor man for his poverty. Saints die, that they may bring their sorrows to an end, and may enter upon their joys. Sinners die, that they may go to give up their account. It concerns both rich and poor to prepare for death, for it waits for them both. *Mors sceptra ligonibus æquat—Death blends the sceptre with the spade.*

——— æquo pulsat pede pauperum tabernas,
Regumque turres.

With equal pace, impartial fate
Knocks at the palace, as the cottage gate.

2. The beggar *died first.* God often takes godly people out of the world, when he leaves the wicked to flourish still. It was an advantage to the beggar that such a speedy end was put to his miseries; and, since he could find no other shelter or resting-place, he was *hid in the grave,* where the *weary are at rest.*

3. The rich man *died and was buried.* Nothing is said of the interment of the poor man. They dug a hole any where, and tumbled his body in, without any solemnity; he was *buried with the burial of an ass:* nay, it is well if they that let the dogs lick his sores did not let them gnaw his bones. But the rich man had a pompous funeral, lay in state, had a train of mourners to attend him to his grave, and a stately monument set up over it; probably he had a funeral oration in praise of him, and his generous way of living, and the good table he kept, which those would commend that had been feasted at it. It is said of the wicked man that he is *brought to the grave* with no small ado, and *laid in the tomb,* and *the clods of the valley,* were it possible, are made *sweet to him,* Job xxi. 32, 33. How foreign is the ceremony of a funeral to the happiness of the man!

4. The beggar died and was *carried by angels into Abraham's bosom.* How much did the honour done to his soul, by this convoy of it to its rest, exceed the honour done to the rich man, by the carrying of his body with so much magnificence to its grave! Observe, (1.) His soul *existed* in a state of separation from the body. It did not *die,* or *fall asleep,* with the body; his candle was not put out with him; but lived, and acted, and knew what it did, and what was done to it. (2.) His soul *removed* to another world, to the world of spirits; it returned to God who gave it, to its native country; this is implied in its being *carried.* The spirit of a man goes upward. (3.) Angels took care of it; it was *carried by angels.* They are ministering spirits to the heirs of salvation, not only while they live, but when they die, and have a charge concerning them, to *bear them up in their hands,* not only in their journeys to and fro on earth, but in their great journey to their long home in heaven, to be both their guide and their guard through regions unknown and unsafe. The soul of man, if not chained to this earth and clogged by it as unsanctified souls are, has in itself an elastic virtue, by which it *springs upward* as soon as it gets clear of the body; but Christ will not trust those that are his to that, and therefore will send special messengers to fetch them to himself. One angel one would think sufficient, but here are more, as many were sent for Elijah. Amasis king of Egypt had his chariot drawn by kings; but what was that honour to this? Saints ascend in the virtue of Christ's ascension; but this convoy of angels is added for state and decorum. Saints shall be brought home, not only safely, but honourably. What were the bearers at the rich man's funeral, though, probably, those of the first rank, compared with Lazarus's bearers? The angels were not shy of touching him, for his sores were on his *body,* not on his *soul; that* was presented to God *without spot, or wrinkle, or any such thing.* "Now, blessed angels," said a good man just expiring, "now come and do your office." (4.) It was carried *into Abraham's bosom.* The Jews expressed the happiness of the righteous at death three ways:—they go *to the garden of Eden;* they go *to be under the throne of glory;* and they go *to the bosom of Abraham,* and it is this which our Saviour here makes use of. Abraham was the *father of the faithful;* and whither should the souls of the faithful be gathered but to him, who, as a tender father, lays them *in his bosom,* especially at their first coming, to bid them welcome, and to refresh them when newly come from the sorrows and fatigues of this world? He was carried *to his bosom,* that is, to feast with him, for at feasts the guests are said to lean on one another's breasts; and the saints in heaven *sit down with Abraham, and Isaac, and Jacob.* Abraham was a great and rich man, yet in heaven he does not disdain to lay poor Lazarus in his bosom. Rich saints and poor meet in heaven. This poor Lazarus, who might not be admitted within the rich man's gate, is conducted into the dining-room, into the bedchamber, of the heavenly palace; and *he* is

laid in the bosom of Abraham, whom the rich glutton scorned to *set with the dogs of his flock*.

5. The next news you hear of the *rich man*, after the account of his *death* and *burial*, is, that *in hell he lifted up his eyes, being in torment, v.* 23.

(1.) His state is very miserable. *He is in hell*, in *hades*, in the state of separate souls, and there he is in *the utmost misery* and *anguish* possible. As the souls of the faithful, immediately *after they are delivered from the burden of the flesh, are in joy and felicity*, so wicked and unsanctified souls, immediately after they are fetched from the pleasures of the flesh by death, are in misery and torment endless, useless, and remediless, and which will be much increased and completed at the resurrection. This *rich man* had entirely devoted himself to the pleasures of the *world of sense*, was wholly *taken up* with them, and *took up with them* for his portion, and therefore was wholly unfit for the pleasures of the *world of spirits;* to such a carnal mind as his they would indeed be no pleasure, nor could he have any relish of them, and therefore he is of course excluded from them. Yet this is not all; he was hard-hearted to God's poor, and therefore he is not only cut off from mercy, but he has *judgment without mercy*, and falls under a punishment of *sense* as well as a punishment of *loss*

(2.) The misery of his state is aggravated by his knowledge of the happiness of Lazarus: He *lifts up his eyes*, and *sees Abraham afar off*, and *Lazarus in his bosom*. It is the soul that is *in torment*, and they are the eyes of the mind that are lifted up. He now began to consider what was become of Lazarus. He does not find him where he himself is, nay, he plainly sees him, and with as much assurance as if he had seen him with his bodily eyes, afar off in the bosom of Abraham. This same aggravation of the miseries of the damned we had before (*ch.* xiii. 28): *Ye shall see Abraham, and Isaac, and Jacob, and all the prophets, in the kingdom of God, and yourselves thrust out*. [1.] He saw *Abraham afar off*. To see Abraham we should think a pleasing sight; but to see him afar off was a tormenting sight. Near himself he saw devils and damned companions, frightful sights, and painful ones; afar off he saw Abraham. Note, Every sight in hell is aggravating. [2.] He saw *Lazarus in his bosom*. That same Lazarus whom he had looked upon with so much scorn and contempt, as not worthy his notice, he now sees preferred, and to be envied. The sight of him brought to his mind his own cruel and barbarous conduct towards him; and the sight of him in that happiness made his own misery the more grievous.

III. Here is an account of what passed between the rich man and Abraham in the separate state—a state of separation one from another, and of both from this world. Though it is probable that there will not be, nor are, any such dialogues or discourses between glorified saints and damned sinners, yet it is very proper, and what is usually done in descriptions, especially such as are designed to be pathetic and moving, by such dialogues to represent what will be the mind and sentiments both of the one and of the other. And since we find damned sinners tormented *in the presence of the Lamb* (Rev. xiv. 10), and the faithful servants of God looking upon them that have *transgressed the covenant*, there where their *worm dies not, and their fire is not quenched* (Isa. lxvi. 23, 24), such a discourse as this is not incongruous to be supposed. Now in this discourse we have,

1. The request which the rich man made to Abraham for some mitigation of his present misery, *v.* 24. Seeing Abraham afar off, *he cried to him*, cried aloud, as one in earnest, and as one in pain and misery, mixing shrieks with his petitions, to enforce them by moving compassion. He that used to *command* aloud now *begs* aloud, louder than ever Lazarus did at his gate. The songs of his riot and revels are all turned into lamentations. Observe here,

(1.) The title he gives to Abraham: *Father Abraham*. Note, There are many in hell that can call Abraham *father*, that were Abraham's seed after the flesh, nay, and many that were, in name and profession, the children of the covenant made with Abraham. Perhaps this rich man, in his carnal mirth, had ridiculed Abraham and the story of Abraham, as the scoffers of the latter days do; but now he gives him a title of respect, *Father Abraham*. Note, The day is coming when wicked men will be glad to scrape acquaintance with the righteous, and to claim kindred to them, though now they slight them. Abraham in this description represents Christ, for to him all judgment is committed, and it is his mind that Abraham here speaks. Those that now slight Christ will shortly make their court to him, *Lord, Lord*.

(2.) The representation he makes to him of his present deplorable condition: *I am tormented in this flame*. It is the torment of his soul that he complains of, and therefore such a fire as will operate upon souls; and such a fire the *wrath of God* is, fastening upon a guilty conscience; such a fire horror of mind is, and the reproaches of a self-accusing self-condemning heart. Nothing is more painful and terrible to the body than to be tormented with fire; by this therefore the miseries and agonies of damned souls are represented.

(3.) His request to Abraham, in consideration of this misery: *Have mercy on me*. Note, The day is coming when those that make light of divine mercy will beg hard for it. O for *mercy, mercy*, when the day of mercy is over, and offers of mercy are no more made.

He that had no mercy on Lazarus, yet expects Lazarus should have mercy on him; "for," thinks he, "Lazarus is better natured than ever I was." The particular favour he begs is, *Send Lazarus, that he may dip the tip of his finger in water, and cool my tongue.* [1.] Here he complains of the torment of his *tongue* particularly, as if he were more tormented there than in any other part, the punishment answering the sin. The *tongue* is one of the organs of speech, and by the torment of that he is put in mind of all the wicked words that he had spoken against God and man, his cursing, and swearing, and blasphemy, all his *hard speeches*, and *filthy speeches;* by his words *he is condemned*, and therefore in his tongue he is tormented. The tongue is also one of the organs of *tasting*, and therefore the torments of that will remind him of his inordinate relish of the delights of sense, which he had *rolled under his tongue.* [2.] He desires a *drop of water to cool his tongue.* He does not say, "Father Abraham, send for me to thy bosom, to lie where Lazarus lies." Unsanctified souls do not, cannot, truly *desire* the happiness of heaven; nay, he does not say, "Father Abraham, order me a release from this misery, help me out of this pit," for he utterly *despaired* of this; but he asks as small a thing as could be asked, *a drop of water* to cool his tongue for one moment. [3.] He desires that Lazarus might bring it. I have sometimes suspected that he had herein an ill design upon Lazarus, and hoped, if he could get him within his reach, he should keep him from returning to the bosom of Abraham. The heart that is filled with rage against God is filled with rage against the people of God. But we will think more charitably even of a damned sinner, and suppose he intended here to show respect to Lazarus, as one to whom he would now gladly be beholden. He *names* him, because he *knows* him, and thinks Lazarus will not be unwilling to do him this good office for old acquaintance' sake. Grotius here quotes Plato describing the torments of wicked souls, and among other things he says, They are *continually raving* on those whom they have *murdered*, or been any way *injurious to*, calling upon them to *forgive them* the wrongs they did them. Note, There is a day coming when those that now hate and despise the people of God would gladly receive kindness from them.

2. The reply which Abraham gave to this request. In general, he did not grant it. He would not allow him one *drop of water, to cool* his tongue. Note, The damned in hell shall not have any the least abatement or mitigation of their torment. If we now improve the day of our opportunities, we may have a full and lasting satisfaction in the streams of mercy; but, if we now slight the offer, it will be in vain in hell to expect the least drop of mercy. See how justly this rich man is paid in his own coin. He that denied a crumb is denied a drop. Now it is said to us, *Ask, and it shall be given you;* but, if we let slip this accepted time, we may ask, and it shall not be given us. But this is not all; had Abraham only said, "You shall have nothing to abate your torment," it had been sad; but he says a great deal which would add to his torment, and make the flame the hotter, for every thing in hell will be tormenting.

(1.) He calls him *son*, a kind and civil title, but here it serves only to aggravate the denial of his request, which shut up the bowels of the compassion of a father from him. He had been a son, but a rebellious one, and now an abandoned disinherited one. See the folly of those who rely on that *plea, We have Abraham to our father*, when we find one in hell, and likely to be there for ever, whom Abraham calls *son.*

(2.) He puts him in mind of what had been both his own condition and the condition of Lazarus, in their *life-time: Son, remember;* this is a cutting word. The memories of damned souls will be their tormentors, and conscience will then be awakened and stirred up to do its office, which here they would not suffer it to do. Nothing will bring more oil to the flames of hell than *Son, remember.* Now sinners are called upon to *remember*, but they do not, they will not, they find ways to avoid it. "*Son, remember* thy Creator, thy Redeemer, remember thy latter end;" but they can turn a deaf ear to these *mementos*, and forget that for which they have their memories; justly therefore will their everlasting misery arise from a *Son, remember*, to which they will not be able to turn a deaf ear. What a dreadful peal will this ring in our ears, "*Son, remember* the many warnings that were given thee not to come to this place of torment, which thou wouldest not regard; remember the fair offers made thee of eternal life and glory, which thou wouldest not accept!" But that which he is here put in mind of is, [1.] That *thou in thy life-time receivedst thy good things.* He does not tell him that he had *abused* them, but that he had *received* them: "Remember what a bountiful benefactor God has been to thee, how ready he was to do thee good; thou canst not therefore say he owes thee any thing, no, not a *drop of water.* What he gave thee *thou receivedst*, and that was all; thou never gavest him a receipt for them, in a thankful acknowledgment of them, much less didst thou ever make any grateful return for them or improvement of them; thou hast been the grave of God's blessings, in which they were buried, not the field of them, in which they were sown. Thou receivedst *thy good things;* thou receivedst them, and usedst them, as if they had been *thine own*, and thou hadst not been at all accountable for them. Or, rather, they were the things which thou didst choose for *thy good things*, which were in thine eye the

best things, which thou didst content thyself with, and portion thyself in. Thou hadst meat, and drink, and clothes of the richest and finest, and these were the things thou didst place thy happiness in; they were *thy reward, thy consolation,* the *penny* thou didst *agree for,* and thou hast had it. Thou wast for the *good things of thy life-time,* and hadst no thought of better things in another life, and therefore hast no reason to expect them. The day of thy *good things* is past and gone, and now is the day of thy *evil things,* of recompence for all thy evil deeds. Thou hast already had the last drop of the *vials of mercy* that thou couldest expect to fall to thy share; and there remains nothing but *vials of wrath* without mixture." [2.] " Remember too what *evil things Lazarus received.* Thou enviest him his happiness here; but think what a large share of miseries he had *in his life-time.* Thou hast *as much good* as could be thought to fall to the lot of so *bad a man,* and he *as much evil* as could be thought to fall to the lot of *so good a man.* He *received* his evil things; he bore them patiently, received them from the hand of God, as Job did (*ch.* ii. 10, *Shall we receive good at the hand of the Lord, and shall we not receive evil also?*)—he *received* them as physic appointed for the cure of his spiritual distempers, and the cure was effected." As wicked people have *good things* in this life only, and at death they are for ever separated from all good, so godly people have evil things only *in this life,* and at death they are for ever put out of the reach of them. Now Abraham, by putting him in mind of both these together, awakens his conscience to remind him how he had behaved towards Lazarus, when he was revelling in his *good things* and Lazarus groaning under his *evil things;* he cannot forget that then he would not help Lazarus, and how then could he expect that Lazarus should now help him? Had Lazarus in his life-time afterwards grown rich, and he poor, Lazarus would have thought it his duty to relieve him, and not to have upbraided him with his former unkindness; but, in the future state of recompence and retribution, those that are now dealt with, both by God and man, better than they deserve, must expect to be rewarded *every man according to his works.*

(3.) He puts him in mind of Lazarus's present bliss, and his own misery: *But now* the tables are turned, and so they must abide for ever; *now he is comforted, and thou art tormented.* He did not need to be told that he was *tormented;* he felt it to his cost. He knew likewise that one who lay in the bosom of Abraham could not but be comforted there; yet Abraham puts him in mind of it, that he might, by comparing one thing with another, observe the *righteousness of God,* in recompensing *tribulation* to *them who trouble his people,* and *to those who are troubled rest,* 2 Thess. i. 6, 7. Observe, [1.] Heaven is *comfort,* and hell is *torment:* heaven is *joy,* hell is *weeping, and wailing,* and pain in perfection. [2.] The soul, as soon as it leaves the body, goes either to heaven or hell, to comfort or torment, immediately, and does not sleep, or go into purgatory. [3.] Heaven will be heaven indeed to those that go thither through many and great calamities in this world; of those that had grace, but had little of the comfort of it here (perhaps their souls refused to be comforted), yet, when they are fallen asleep in Christ, you may truly say, " Now *they are comforted:* now *all their tears are wiped away,* and all their fears are vanished." In heaven there is everlasting consolation. And, on the other hand, hell will be hell indeed to those that go thither from the midst of the enjoyment of all the delights and pleasures of sense. To them the torture is the greater, as temporal calamities are described to be to the *tender and delicate woman, that would not set so much as the sole of her foot to the ground, for tenderness and delicacy.* Deut. xxviii. 56.

(4.) He assures him that it was to no purpose to think of having any relief by the ministry of Lazarus; for (*v.* 26), *Besides all this,* worse yet, *between us and you there is a great gulf fixed,* an impassable one, *a great chasm,* that so there can be no communication between glorified saints and damned sinners. [1.] The kindest saint in heaven cannot make a visit to the congregation of the dead and damned, to comfort or relieve any there who once were their friends. " *They that would pass hence to you cannot;* they cannot leave beholding the face of their Father, nor the work about his throne, to fetch water for you; that is no part of their business." [2.] The most daring sinner in hell cannot force his way out of that prison, cannot get over that great gulf. *They cannot pass to us that would come thence.* It is not to be expected, for the door of mercy is shut, the bridge is drawn; there is no coming out upon parole or bail, no, not for one hour. In this world, blessed be God, there is no gulf fixed between a state of nature and grace, but we may pass from the one to the other, from sin to God; but if we die in our sins, if we throw ourselves into the pit of destruction, there is no coming out. It is a pit *in which there is no water,* and *out of which there is no redemption.* The decree and counsel of God have fixed this gulf, which all the world cannot unfix. This abandons this miserable creature to despair; it is now too late for any change of his condition, or any the least relief: it might have been prevented *in time,* but it cannot now be remedied *to eternity.* The state of damned sinners is fixed by an irreversible and unalterable sentence. A stone is rolled to the door of the pit, which cannot be rolled back.

3. The further request he had to make to his father Abraham, not for himself, his mouth is stopped, and he has not a word to say in answer to Abraham's denial of a drop of water. Damned sinners are made to know

that the sentence they are under is just, and they cannot alleviate their own misery by making any objection against it. And, since he cannot obtain a drop of water to *cool his tongue,* we may suppose he *gnawed his tongue for pain,* as those are said to do on whom one of the *vials* of God's wrath is *poured out,* Rev. xvi. 10. The shrieks and outcries which we may suppose to be now uttered by him were hideous; but, having an opportunity of speaking to Abraham, he will improve it for his relations whom he has left behind, since he cannot improve it for his own advantage. Now as to this,

(1.) He begs that Lazarus might be *sent to his father's house,* upon an errand thither: *I pray thee therefore, father, v.* 27. Again he calls upon Abraham, and in this request he is importunate: "*I pray thee.* O deny me not this." When he was on earth he might have prayed and been heard, but now he prays in vain. "*Therefore,* because thou hast denied me the former request, surely thou wilt be so compassionate as not to deny this:" or, "*Therefore,* because *there is a great gulf fixed,* seeing there is no getting out hence when they are once here, O send to prevent their coming hither:" or, "Though there is a *great gulf fixed* between you and me, yet, since there is no such gulf fixed between you and them, send him thither. Send him back *to my father's house;* he knows well enough where it is, has been there many a time, having been denied the crumbs that fell from the table. He knows I have *five brethren* there; if he appear to them, they will *know him,* and will regard what he saith, for they knew him to be an honest man. Let him *testify to them;* let him tell them what condition I am in, and that I brought myself to it by my luxury and sensuality, and my unmercifulness to the poor. Let him warn them not to tread in my steps, nor to go on in the way wherein I led them, and left them, *lest they also come into this place of torment," v.* 28. Some observe that he speaks only of *five brethren,* whence they infer that he had *no children,* else he would have mentioned them, and then it was an aggravation of his uncharitableness that he had no children to provide for. Now he would have them stopped in their sinful course. He does not say, "Give me leave to go to them, that I may testify to them;" for he knew that there was a *gulf fixed,* and despaired of a permission so favourable to himself: his going would frighten them out of their *wits;* but, "Send Lazarus, whose address will be less terrible, and yet his testimony sufficient to frighten them out of their *sins.*" Now he desired the preventing of their ruin, partly in tenderness to *them,* for whom he could not but retain a *natural affection;* he knew their temper, their temptations, their ignorance, their infidelity, their inconsideration, and wished to prevent the destruction they were running into: but it was partly in tenderness *to himself,* for their coming to him, to that *place of torment,* would but aggravate the misery to him, who had helped to show them the way thither, as the sight of Lazarus helped to aggravate his misery. When partners in sin come to be sharers in woe, as tares bound in bundles for the fire, they will be a terror to one another.

(2.) Abraham denies him this favour too. There is no request granted in hell. Those who make the rich man's praying to Abraham a justification of their praying to saints departed, as they have far to seek for proofs, when the practice of a damned sinner must be valued for an example, so they have little encouragement to follow the example, when all his prayers were made *in vain.* Abraham leaves them to the testimony of Moses and the prophets, the ordinary means of conviction and conversion; they have the written word, which they may read and hear read. "*Let them* attend to that *sure word of prophecy,* for God will not go out of the common method of his grace for them." Here is their privilege: *They have Moses and the prophets;* and their duty: "*Let them hear them,* and mix faith with them, and that will be sufficient to keep them from this place of torment." By this it appears that there is sufficient evidence in the Old Testament, in Moses and *the prophets,* to convince those that will hear them impartially that there is another life after this, and a state of rewards and punishments for good and bad men; for that was the thing which the rich man would have his brethren assured of, and for that they are turned over to Moses and the prophets.

(3.) He urges his request yet further (*v.* 30): "*Nay, father Abraham,* give me leave to press this. It is true, they have Moses and the prophets, and, if they would but give a due regard to them, it would be sufficient; but they do not, they will not; yet it may be hoped, *if one went to them from the dead, they would repent,* that would be a more sensible conviction to them. They are used to Moses and the prophets, and therefore regard them the less; but this would be a *new thing,* and more startling; surely this would bring them to *repent,* and to change their wicked habit and course of life." Note, Foolish men are apt to think any method of conviction better than that which God has chosen and appointed.

(4.) Abraham insists upon the denial of it, with a conclusive reason (*v.* 31): "*If they hear not Moses and the prophets,* and will not believe the testimony nor take the warning they give, *neither will they be persuaded though one rose from the dead.* If they regard not the public revelation, which is confirmed by miracles, neither would they be wrought upon by a private testimony to themselves." [1.] The matter has been long since settled, upon trial, that God should speak by Moses and such prophets, and not by immediate messengers from heaven. Israel chose it in mount Sinai, because they could not bear the terrors of such expresses. [2.] A messenger from the dead could say no more than what is said in the scriptures, nor say it with more authority. [3.] There would be every jot as much reason to suspect that to be a cheat and a delusion as to suspect the scriptures to be so, and much more; and infidels in one case would certainly be so in another. [4.] The same strength of corruption that breaks through the convictions of the written word would certainly triumph over those by a witness *from the dead:* and, though a sinner might be frightened at first by such a testimony, when the fright was over he would soon return to his hardness. [5.] The scripture is now the ordinary way of God's making known his mind to us, and it is sufficient. It is presumption for us to prescribe any other way, nor have we any ground to expect or pray for the grace of God to work upon us in any other way abstracted from that and when that is rejected and set aside. What our Saviour here said was soon after verified in the unbelieving Jews, who would not hear Moses and the prophets, Christ and the apostles, and then would not be persuaded, though *Lazarus rose from the dead* (and perhaps it was with some eye to him that Christ named this poor man Lazarus), nay, they consulted to put him to death, and did put him that raised him to death, and would not be persuaded by him neither, though he also *rose from the dead.* When Eutychus was raised to life, the people that were present continued to hear Paul preach, but did not turn to enquire of him, Acts xx. 10, 11. Let us not therefore desire visions and apparitions, nor seek to the dead, but *to the law and to the testimony* (Isa. viii. 19, 20), for that is *the sure word of prophecy,* upon which we may depend.

CHAP. XVII.

In this chapter we have, I. Some particular discourses which Christ had with his disciples, in which he teaches them to take heed of giving offence, and to forgive the injuries done them (ver. 1—4), encourages them to pray for the increase of their faith (ver. 5, 6), and then teaches them humility, whatever service they had done for God, ver. 7—10. II. His cleansing ten lepers, and the thanks he had from one of them only, and he a Samaritan, ver. 11—19. III. His discourse with his disciples, upon occasion of an enquiry of the Pharisees, when the kingdom of God should appear, ver. 20—37.

THEN said he unto the disciples,
It is impossible but that offences
will come: but woe *unto him,* through
whom they come! 2 It were better
for him that a millstone were hanged
about his neck, and he cast into the
sea, than that he should offend one of
these little ones. 3 Take heed to
yourselves: If thy brother trespass
against thee, rebuke him; and if he
repent, forgive him. 4 And if he
trespass against thee seven times in a
day, and seven times in a day turn
again to thee, saying, I repent; thou
shalt forgive him. 5 And the apostles said unto the Lord, Increase our
faith. 6 And the Lord said, If ye
had faith as a grain of mustard seed,
ye might say unto this sycamine tree,
Be thou plucked up by the root, and
be thou planted in the sea; and it
should obey you. 7 But which of you,
having a servant ploughing or feeding cattle, will say unto him by and
by, when he is come from the field,
Go and sit down to meat? 8 And
will not rather say unto him, Make
ready wherewith I may sup, and gird
thyself, and serve me, till I have eaten
and drunken; and afterward thou
shalt eat and drink? 9 Doth he thank
that servant because he did the things
that were commanded him? I trow
not. 10 So likewise ye, when ye
shall have done all those things which
are commanded you, say, We are unprofitable servants: we have done that which was our duty to do.

We are here taught,

I. That the *giving of offences* is a *great sin,* and that which we should every one of us avoid and carefully watch against, *v.* 1, 2. We can expect no other than that offences will come, considering the perverseness and frowardness that are in the nature of man, and the wise purpose and counsel of God, who will carry on his work even by those offences, and bring good out of evil. *It is* almost *impossible but that offences will come,* and therefore we are concerned to provide accordingly; but *woe to him through whom they come,* his doom will be heavy (*v.* 2), more terrible than that of the worst of the malefactors who are condemned to be thrown into the sea, for they perish under a load of guilt more *ponderous* than that of *millstones.* This includes a woe, 1. To persecutors, who offer any injury to the least of Christ's *little ones,* in word or deed, by which they are discouraged in serving Christ, and doing their duty, or in danger of being driven off from it. 2. To seducers, who corrupt the truths of Christ and his ordinances, and so *trouble the minds of the disciples;* for they are those by whom *offences come.* 3. To those who, under the profession of the Christian name, live scandalously, and thereby weaken the hands and sadden the hearts of God's people; for by them the offence comes, and it is no abatement of their guilt, nor will be any of their punishment, that it is impossible but offences will come.

II. That the *forgiving of offences* is a *great duty,* and that which we should every one of us make conscience of (*v.* 3): *Take heed to yourselves.* This may refer either to what goes before, or to what follows: *Take heed that you offend not one of these little ones.* Ministers must be very careful not to say or do any thing that may be a discouragement to weak Christians; there is need of great caution, and they ought to speak and act very considerately, for fear of this: or, "When *your brother trespasses against you,* does you any injury, puts any slight or affront upon you, if he be accessary to any damage done you in your property or reputation, *take heed to yourselves at such a time,* lest you be put into a passion; lest, when your spirits are provoked, you *speak unadvisedly,* and rashly vow revenge (Prov. xxiv. 29): *I will do so to him as he hath done to me.* Take heed what you say at such a time, lest you say amiss."

1. If you are permitted to *rebuke him,* you are advised to do so. Smother not the resentment, but give it vent. *Tell him his faults;* show him wherein he has not done well nor fairly by you, and, it may be, you will perceive (and you must be very willing to perceive it) that you mistook him, that it was not a *trespass against you,* or not designed, but an *oversight,* and then you will beg his pardon for misunderstanding him; as Josh. xxii. 30, 31.

2. You are commanded, upon his repentance, to forgive him, and to be perfectly reconciled to him: *If he repent, forgive him;* forget the injury, never think of it again, much less upbraid him with it. Though he do not repent, you must not therefore bear malice to him, nor meditate revenge; but, if he do not at least *say that he repents,* you are not bound to be so free and familiar with him as you have been. If he be guilty of gross sin, to the offence of the Christian community he is a member of, let him be gravely and mildly reproved for his sin, and, upon his repentance, received into friendship and communion again. This the apostle calls *forgiveness,* 2 Cor. ii. 7.

3. You are to repeat this every time he repeats his trespass, *v.* 4. If he could be supposed to be either so negligent, or so impudent, as to *trespass against thee seven times in a day,* and as often profess himself sorry for his fault, and promise not again to offend in like manner, continue to *forgive him.*" *Humanum est errare—To err is human.* Note, Christians should be of a forgiving spirit, willing to make the best of every body, and to make all about them easy; forward to extenuate faults, and not to aggravate them; and they should contrive as much to show that they have forgiven an injury as others to show that they resent it.

III. That we have all need to get our *faith* strengthened, because, as that grace grows, all other graces grow. The more firmly we believe the doctrine of Christ, and the more confidently we rely upon the grace of Christ, the better it will be with us every way. Now observe here, 1. The address which the disciples made to Christ, for the strengthening of their faith, *v.* 5. *The apostles* themselves, so they are here called, though they were prime ministers of state in Christ's kingdom, yet acknowledged the weakness and deficiency of their faith, and saw their need of Christ's grace for the improvement of it; they *said unto the Lord,* "*Increase our faith,* and perfect what is lacking in it. Let the discoveries of faith be more clear, the desires of faith more strong, the dependences of faith more firm and fixed, the dedications of faith more entire and resolute, and the delights of faith more pleasing. Note, The increase of our faith is what we should earnestly desire, and we should offer up that desire to God in prayer. Some think that they put up this prayer to Christ upon occasion of his pressing upon them the duty of forgiving injuries: "*Lord, increase our faith,* or we shall never be able to practise such a difficult duty as this." Faith in God's pardoning mercy will enable us to get over the greatest difficulties that lie in the way of our forgiving our brother. Others think that it was upon some other occasion, when the apostles were run aground in working some miracle, and were reproved by Christ for the weakness of their faith, as Matt. xvii. 16, &c. To him that *blamed* them they must apply themselves for grace to *mend* them; to him they cry, *Lord, increase our faith.* 2. The assurance Christ gave them of the wonderful efficacy of true faith (*v.* 6): "*If ye had faith as a grain of mustard-seed,* so *small* as mustard-seed, but yours is yet less than the least; or so *sharp* as *mustard-seed,* so pungent, so exciting to all other graces, as mustard to the animal spirits," and therefore used in palsies, "you might do wonders much beyond what you now do; nothing would be too hard for you, that was fit to be done for the glory of God, and the confirmation of the doctrine you preach, yea, though it were the *transplanting of a tree* from the earth *to the sea.* See Matt. xvii. 20. As with God *nothing is impossible,* so are all *things possible to him that can believe.*

IV. That, whatever we do in the service of Christ, we must be very humble, and not imagine that we can merit any favour at his hand, or claim it as a debt; even the apostles themselves, who did so much more for Christ than others, must not think that they had thereby made him their debtor. 1. We are all *God's servants* (his *apostles* and *ministers* are in a special manner *so),* and, as servants, are bound to do all we can for his honour. Our whole strength and our whole time are to be employed for him; for *we are not our own,* nor at our own disposal, but at our Master's. 2. As God's servants, it becomes us to fill up our time with duty, and we have a variety of work appointed us to do; we ought to make the end of one service the beginning of another. The servant that has been *ploughing,* or *feeding cattle, in the field,* when he *comes home* at night has work to do still; he must *wait at table, v.* 7, 8. When we have been employed in the duties of a religious conversation, that will not excuse us from the exercises of devotion; when we have been *working for God,* still we must be *waiting on God,* waiting on him continually. 3. Our principal care here must be to do the duty of our relation, and leave it to our Master to give us the comfort of it, when and how he thinks fit. No servant expects that his master should say to him, *Go and sit down to meat;* it is time enough to do that when we have *done our day's work.* Let us be in care to finish our work, and to do that well, and then the reward will come in due time. 4. It is fit that Christ should be served before us: *Make ready wherewith I may sup, and afterwards thou shalt eat and drink.* Doubting Christians say that they cannot give to Christ the glory of his love as they should, because they have not yet obtained the comfort of it; but this is wrong. First let Christ have the glory of it, let us attend him with our praises, and then we shall *eat and drink* in the comfort of that love, and in this there is a feast. 5. Christ's servants, when they are to wait upon him, must *gird themselves,* must free themselves from every thing that is entangling and encumbering, and fit themselves with a close application of mind to go on, and go through, with their work; they must *gird up the loins of their mind.* When we have prepared for Christ's entertainment, have *made ready wherewith he may sup,* we must then *gird ourselves,* to attend him. This is expected from servants, and Christ might require it from us, but he does not insist upon it. He was *among his disciples as one that served,* and came not, as other masters, to take state, and *to be ministered unto, but to minister;* witness his washing his disciples' feet. 6. Christ's servants do not so much as merit his thanks for any service they do him: "*Does he thank that servant?* Does he reckon himself indebted to him for it? No, by no means." No good works of ours can merit any thing at the hand of God. We expect God's favour, not because we have by our services made him a debtor to us, but because he has by his promises made himself a debtor to his own honour, and this we may plead with him, but cannot sue for a *quantum meruit—according to merit.* 7. Whatever we do for Christ, though it should be more perhaps than some others do, yet it is no more than is our duty to do. Though we should *do all things that are commanded us,* and alas! in many things we come short of this, yet there is no work of *supererogation;* it is but what we are bound to by that first and great commandment of *loving God* with *all our heart and soul,* which includes the utmost. 8. The best servants of Christ, even when they do the best services, must humbly acknowledge that they are *unprofitable servants;* though they are not those unprofitable servants that bury their talents, and shall be cast into *utter darkness,* yet as to Christ, and any advantage that can accrue to him by their services, they are *unprofitable: our goodness extendeth not unto God,* nor *if we are righteous is he the better,* Ps. xvi. 2; Job xxii. 2; xxxv. 7. God cannot be a *gainer* by our services, and therefore cannot be made a *debtor* by them. He has no need of us, nor can our services make any addition to his perfections. It becomes us therefore to call ourselves *unprofitable servants,* but to call his service a profitable service, for God is happy without us, but we are undone without him.

11 And it came to pass, as he went
to Jerusalem, that he passed through
the midst of Samaria and Galilee. 12
And as he entered into a certain village, there met him ten men that were
lepers, which stood afar off: 13 And
they lifted up *their* voices, and said,
Jesus, Master, have mercy on us. 14
And when he saw *them,* he said unto
them, Go show yourselves unto the
priests. And it came to pass, that,
as they went, they were cleansed. 15
And one of them, when he saw that
he was healed, turned back, and with
a loud voice glorified God. 16 And
fell down on *his* face at his feet,
giving him thanks; and he was a
Samaritan. 17 And Jesus answering
said, Were there not ten cleansed?
but where *are* the nine? 18 There
are not found that returned to give
glory to God, save this stranger. 19
And he said unto him, Arise, go thy
way: thy faith hath made thee whole.

We have here an account of the cure of ten lepers, which we had not in any other of the evangelists. The leprosy was a disease which the Jews supposed to be inflicted for the punishment of some particular sin, and to be, more than other diseases, a mark of God's displeasure; and therefore Christ, who came to take away sin, and turn away wrath, took particular care to cleanse the lepers that fell in his way. Christ was now in his way to Jerusalem, about the mid-way, where he had little acquaintance in comparison with what he had either at Jerusalem or in Galilee. He was now in the frontier-country, the marches that lay between Samaria and Galilee. He went that road to find out these lepers, and to cure them; for he is *found of them that sought him not.* Observe,

I. The address of these lepers to Christ. They were ten in a company; for, though they were shut out from society with others, yet those that were infected were at liberty to converse with one another, which would be some comfort to them, as giving them an opportunity to compare notes, and to condole with one another. Now observe, 1. They *met* Christ *as he entered into a certain village.* They did not stay till he had refreshed himself for some time after the fatigue of his journey, but met him as he *entered* the town, weary as he was; and yet he did not put them off, nor adjourn their cause. 2. They *stood afar off,* knowing that by the law their disease obliged them to *keep their distance.* A sense of our spiritual leprosy should make us very humble in all our approaches to Christ. Who are we, that we should draw near to him that is infinitely pure? We are impure. 3. Their request was unanimous, and very importunate (*v.* 13): *They lifted up their voices,* being at a distance, and cried, *Jesus, Master, have mercy on us.* Those that expect help from Christ must take him for their Master, and be at his command. If he be *Master,* he will be *Jesus, a Saviour,* and not otherwise. They ask not in particular to be cured of their leprosy, but, *Have mercy on us;* and it is enough to refer ourselves to the compassions of Christ, for they *fail not.* They had heard the fame of this Jesus (though he had not been much conversant in that country), and that was such as encouraged them to make application to him; and, if but one of them began in so cheap and easy an address, they would all join.

II. Christ sent them to *the priest,* to be *inspected* by him, who was the judge of the leprosy. He did not tell them positively that they should be *cured,* but bade them *go show themselves to the priests, v.* 14. This was a trial of their obedience, and it was fit that it should be so tried, as Naaman's in a like case: *Go wash in Jordan.* Note, Those that expect Christ's favours must take them in his way and method. Some of these lepers perhaps would be ready to quarrel with the prescription: "Let him either cure or say that he will not, and not send us to the priests on a fool's errand;" but, over-ruled by the rest, they all *went to the priest.* As the ceremonial law was yet in force, Christ took care that it should be observed, and the reputation of it kept up, and due honour paid to the priests in things pertaining to their function; but, probably, he had here a further design, which was to have the priest's *judgment of,* and *testimony to,* the perfectness of the cure; and that the priest might be awakened, and others by him, to enquire after one that had such a commanding power over bodily diseases.

III. *As they went, they were cleansed,* and so became fit to be looked upon by the priest, and to have a certificate from him that they were clean. Observe, *Then* we may expect God to meet us with mercy when we are found in the way of duty. If we do what we can, God will not be wanting to do that for us which we cannot. Go, attend upon instituted ordinances; go and pray, and read the scriptures: *Go show thyself to the priests;* go and open thy case to a faithful minister, and, though the means will not heal thee of themselves, God will heal thee in the diligent use of those means.

IV. One of them, and but one, *returned, to give thanks, v.* 15. When he *saw that he was healed,* instead of going forward to the priest, to be by him declared clean, and so discharged from his confinement, which was all that the rest aimed at, he *turned back* towards him who was the Author of his cure, whom he wished to have the glory of it, before he received the benefit of it. He appears to have been very hearty and affectionate in his thanksgivings: *With a loud voice he glorified God,* acknowledging it to come originally from *him;* and he *lifted up his voice* in his praises, as he had done in his prayers, *v.* 13. Those that have received mercy from God should publish it to others, that they may praise God too, and may be encouraged by their experiences to trust in him. But he also made a particular address of thanks to Christ (*v.* 16): *He fell down at his feet,* put himself into the most humble reverent posture he could, and *gave him thanks.* Note, We ought to give thanks for the favours Christ bestows upon us, and particularly for recoveries from sickness; and we ought to be *speedy* in our returns of praise, and not to defer them, lest time wear out the sense of the mercy. It becomes us also to be very humble in our thanksgivings, as well as in our prayers. It becomes the seed of Jacob, like him, to own themselves *less than the least of God's mercies,* when they have received them, as well as when they are in pursuit of them.

V. Christ took notice of this one that had thus distinguished himself; for, it seems, he was a Samaritan, whereas the rest were Jews, *v.* 16. The Samaritans were separatists from the Jewish church, and had not the pure knowledge and worship of God among them that the Jews had, and yet it was one of them that *glorified God,* when the Jews forgot, or, when it was moved to them, *refused,* to do it. Now observe here,

1. The particular notice Christ took of him, of the grateful return he made, and the ingratitude of those that were sharers with him in the mercy—that he who was a *stranger* to the commonwealth of Israel was the only one that *returned to give glory to God, v.* 17, 18. See here, (1.) How *rich* Christ is in *doing good: Were there not ten cleansed?* Here was a cure by *wholesale,* a whole *hospital* healed with *one* word's speaking. Note, There is an abundance of healing cleansing virtue in the blood of Christ, sufficient for all his patients, though ever so many. Here are *ten at a time* cleansed; we shall have never the less grace for others sharing it. (2.) How *poor* we are in our returns: "*Where are the nine?* Why did not they return to give thanks?" This intimates that ingratitude is a very common sin. Of the many that receive mercy from God, there are but

few, very few, that *return to give thanks* in a right manner (scarcely *one in ten)*, that render according to the benefit done to them. (3.) How those often prove most grateful from whom it was least expected. A Samaritan gives thanks, and a Jew does not. Thus many who profess revealed religion are out-done, and quite shamed, by some that are governed only by natural religion, not only in moral virtue, but in piety and devotion. This serves here to aggravate the ingratitude of those Jews of whom Christ speaks, as *taking it very ill* that his kindness was so slighted. And it intimates how justly he resents the ingratitude of the world of mankind, for whom he had *done so much*, and from whom he has *received so little.*

2. The great encouragement Christ gave him, *v.* 19. The rest had their *cure*, and had it not *revoked*, as justly it might have been, for their ingratitude, though they had such a good example of gratitude set before them; but he had his cure confirmed particularly with an encomium *Thy faith hath made thee whole.* The rest were *made whole* by the power of Christ, in compassion to their distress, and in answer to their prayer; but he was made whole *by his faith*, by which Christ saw him distinguished from the rest. Note, Temporal mercies are *then* doubled and sweetened to us when they are *fetched* in by the prayers of faith, and *returned* by the praises of faith.

20 And when he was demanded of
the Pharisees, when the kingdom of
God should come, he answered them
and said, The kingdom of God cometh
not with observation: 21 Neither
shall they say, Lo here! or, lo there!
for, behold, the kingdom of God is
within you. 22 And he said unto
the disciples, The days will come,
when ye shall desire to see one of the
days of the Son of man, and ye shall
not see *it*. 23 And they shall say to
you, See here; or, see there: go not
after *them*, nor follow *them*. 24 For
as the lightning, that lighteneth out
of the one *part* under heaven, shineth
unto the other *part* under heaven;
so shall also the Son of man be in his
day. 25 But first must he suffer
many things, and be rejected of this
generation. 26 And as it was in the
days of Noe, so shall it be also in the
days of the Son of man. 27 They did
eat, they drank, they married wives,
they were given in marriage, until the
day that Noe entered into the ark,
and the flood came, and destroyed
them all. 28 Likewise also as it was
in the days of Lot; they did eat, they
drank, they bought, they sold, they
planted, they builded; 29 But the
same day that Lot went out of Sodom
it rained fire and brimstone from heaven,
and destroyed *them* all. 30 Even
thus shall it be in the day when the
Son of man is revealed. 31 In that
day, he which shall be upon the housetop,
and his stuff in the house, let
him not come down to take it away:
and he that is in the field, let him
likewise not return back. 32 Remember
Lot's wife. 33 Whosoever shall
seek to save his life shall lose it; and
whosoever shall lose his life shall preserve
it. 34 I tell you, in that night
there shall be two *men* in one bed;
the one shall be taken, and the other
shall be left. 35 Two *women* shall
be grinding together; the one shall
be taken, and the other left. 36 Two
men shall be in the field; the one
shall be taken, and the other left. 37
And they answered and said unto him,
Where, Lord? And he said unto
them, Wheresoever the body *is*, thither
will the eagles be gathered together.

We have here a discourse of Christ's concerning the *kingdom of God*, that is, the kingdom of the Messiah, which was now shortly to be *set up*, and of which there was great expectation.

I. Here is the demand of the Pharisees concerning it, which occasioned this discourse. They asked *when the kingdom of God should come*, forming a notion of it as a *temporal kingdom*, which should advance the Jewish nation above the nations of the earth. They were impatient to hear some tidings of its approach; they understood, perhaps, that Christ had taught his disciples to pray for the coming of it, and they had long preached that it was *at hand*. "Now," say the Pharisees, "when will that glorious view open? When shall we see this *long-looked-for* kingdom?"

II. Christ's reply to this demand, directed to the Pharisees first, and afterwards to his own disciples, who knew better how to understand it (*v.* 22); what he said to both, he saith to us.

1. That the kingdom of the Messiah was to be a *spiritual kingdom*, and not temporal and external. They asked *when* it would come. "You know not what you ask," saith Christ; "it may come, and you not be aware of it." For it has not an *external show*,

as other kingdoms have, the advancements and revolutions of which are taken notice of by the nations of the earth, and fill the newspapers; so they expected this kingdom of God would do. "No," saith Christ, (1.) "It will have a silent entrance, without pomp, without noise; it *cometh not with observation," μετὰ παρατηρήσεως—with outward show.* They desired to have their curiosity satisfied concerning the *time* of it, to which Christ does not give them any answer, but will have their mistakes rectified concerning the nature of it: "*It is not for you to know the times* of this kingdom, these are *secret things,* which belong not to you; but the great intentions of this kingdom, these are *things revealed.*" When Messiah the Prince comes to set up his kingdom, they shall not say, *Lo here,* or *Lo there,* as when a prince goes in progress to visit his territories it is in every body's mouth, he is here, or he is there; for *where the king is there is the court.* Christ will not come with all this talk; it will not be set up in this or that particular place; nor will the court of that kingdom be *were* or *there;* nor will it be *here* or *there* as it respects the country men are of, or the place they dwell in, as if that would place them nearer to, or further from, that kingdom. Those who confine Christianity and the church to this place or that party, cry, *Lo here,* or *Lo there,* than which nothing is more contrary to the designs of catholic Christianity; so do they who make prosperity and external pomp a mark of the true church. (2.) "It has a *spiritual* influence: *The kingdom of God is within you.*" It is not of this world, John xviii. 36. Its glory does not strike men's fancies, but affects their spirits, and its power is over their souls and consciences; from them it receives homage, and not from their bodies only. The *kingdom of God* will not change men's outward condition, but their hearts and lives. Then it *comes* when it makes those humble, and serious, and heavenly, that were proud, and vain, and carnal,—when it *weans* those from the world that were *wedded* to the world; and therefore look for the kingdom of God in the revolutions of the heart, not of the civil government. The kingdom of God is *among you;* so some read it. "You enquire when it will come, and are not aware that it is already begun to be set up *in the midst of you.* The gospel is preached, it is *confirmed* by miracles, it is *embraced* by multitudes, so that it is *in your* nation, though not in your hearts." Note, It is the folly of many curious enquirers concerning the times to come that they look for that *before them* which is already *among them.*

2. That the setting up of this kingdom was a work that would meet with a great deal of *opposition* and *interruption, v.* 22. The *disciples* thought they should carry all before them, and expected a constant series of success in their work; but Christ tells them it would be otherwise: "*The days will come,* before you have finished your testimony and done your work, *when you shall desire to see one of the days of the Son of man*" (one such a day as we *now* have), "of the prosperity and progress of the gospel, and *shall not see it.* At first, indeed, you will have wonderful success" (so they had, when *thousands* were added to the church *in a day*); "but do not think it will be always so; no, you will be persecuted and scattered, silenced and imprisoned, so that you will not have opportunities of preaching the gospel without fear, as you now have; people will grow cool to it, when they have enjoyed it awhile, so that you will not see such harvests of souls gathered in to Christ afterwards as at first, nor such multitudes flocking to him *as doves to their windows.*" This looks forward to his disciples in after-ages; they must expect much disappointment; the gospel will not be always preached with equal liberty and success. Ministers and churches will sometimes be under *outward restraints.* Teachers will be removed into corners, and solemn assemblies scattered. Then they will wish to see such days of opportunity as they have formerly enjoyed, sabbath days, sacrament days, preaching days, praying days; these are *days of the Son of man,* in which we hear from him, and converse with him. The time may come when we may in vain wish for such days. God teaches us to know the worth of such mercies by the want of them. It concerns us, while they are continued, to *improve* them, and in the years of plenty to lay up in store for the years of famine. Sometimes they will be under *inward restraints,* will not have such tokens of the *presence of the Son of man* with them as they have had. The Spirit is withdrawn from them; they *see not their signs;* the angel comes not down to stir the waters; there is a great stupidity among the children of men, and a great lukewarmness among the children of God; then they shall wish to see such *victorious triumphant* days of the *Son of man* as they have sometimes seen, when he has ridden forth with his bow and his crown, conquering and to conquer, but they will not see them. Note, We must not think that Christ's church and cause are lost because not always alike visible and prevailing.

3. That Christ and his kingdom are not to be looked for in this or that particular place, but his appearance will be general in all places at once (*v.* 23, 24): "*They will say to you, See here, or, See there;* here is one that will deliver the Jews out of the hands of the oppressing Romans, or there is one that will deliver the Christians out of the hands of the oppressing Jews; here is the Messiah, and there is his prophet; *here* in *this* mountain, or *there* at Jerusalem, you will find the true church. *Go not after them, nor follow them;* do not heed such suggestions. The kingdom of God was not designed to be the glory of

one people only, but to *give light to the Gentiles; for as the lightning that lightens out of one part under heaven, and shines* all on a sudden irresistibly *to the other part under heaven, so shall also the Son of man be in his day.*" (1.) "The *judgments* that are to destroy the Jewish nation, to lay them waste, and to deliver the Christians from them, shall *fly like lightning* through the land, shall lay all waste from one end of it to another; and those that are marked for this destruction can no more avoid it, nor oppose it, than they can a *flash of lightning.*" (2.) "The gospel that is to set up Christ's kingdom in the world shall *fly like lightning* through the nations. The kingdom of the Messiah is not to be a *local* thing, but is to be dispersed far and wide over the face of the whole earth; it shall *shine* from Jerusalem to all parts about, and that *in a moment.* The kingdoms of the earth shall be leavened by the gospel ere they are aware of it." The trophies of Christ's victories shall be erected on the ruins of the devil's kingdom, even in those countries that could never be subdued to the Roman yoke. The design of the setting up of Christ's kingdom was not to make one *nation great,* but to make *all nations good*—some, at least, of all nations; and this point shall be gained, though the *nations rage,* and the *kings of the earth set themselves* with all their might against it.

4. That the Messiah must *suffer* before he must *reign* (*v.* 25): "*First must he suffer many things,* many hard things, and *be rejected of this generation;* and, if he be thus treated, his disciples must expect no other than to *suffer* and be *rejected* too for his sake." They thought of having the kingdom of the Messiah set up in extérnal splendour: "No," saith Christ, "we must go by the cross to the crown. The *Son of man must suffer many things.* Pain, and shame, and death, are those *many things.* He must be *rejected by this generation* of unbelieving Jews, before he be embraced by another generation of believing Gentiles, that his gospel may have the honour of triumphing over the greatest opposition from those who ought to have given it the greatest assistance; and thus the excellency of the power will appear to be *of God, and not of man;* for, though Israel be not *gathered,* yet he will be *glorious* to the ends of the earth."

5. That the setting up of the kingdom of the Messiah would introduce the destruction of the Jewish nation, whom it would find in a deep sleep of *security,* and drowned in *sensuality,* as the old world was in the days of Noah, and Sodom in the days of Lot, *v.* 26, &c. Observe,

(1.) How it had been with sinners formerly, and in what posture the judgments of God, of which they had been fairly warned, did at length find them. Look as far back as the *old world,* when all flesh had *corrupted their way,* and the *earth was filled with violence.* Come a little lower, and think how it was with the men of Sodom, who were *wicked, and sinners before the Lord exceedingly.* Now observe concerning both these, [1.] That they had *fair warning given them* of the ruin that was coming upon them for their sins. Noah was a *preacher of righteousness* to the old world; so was Lot to the Sodomites. They gave them timely notice of what would be in the end of their wicked ways, and that it was not far off. [2.] That they did not regard the warning given them, and gave no credit, no heed to it. They were very secure, went on in their business as unconcerned as you could imagine; *they did eat, they drank,* indulged themselves in their pleasures, and took no care of any thing else, but to *make provision for the flesh,* counted upon the perpetuity of their present flourishing state, and therefore married wives, and *were given in marriage,* that their families might be built up. They were all very merry; so were the men of Sodom, and yet very busy too: *they bought, they sold, they planted, they builded.* These were lawful things, but the fault was that they minded these inordinately, and their hearts were entirely set upon them, so that they had no heart at all to prepare against the threatened judgments. When they should have been, as the men of Nineveh, *fasting and praying, repenting* and *reforming,* upon warning given them of an approaching judgment, they were going on securely, *eating flesh,* and *drinking wine,* when God called *to weeping and to mourning,* Isa. xxii. 12, 13. [3.] That they continued in their security and sensuality, till the threatened judgment came. Until the day *that Noah entered into the ark,* and *Lot went out of Sodom,* nothing said or done to them served to alarm or awaken them. Note, Though the stupidity of sinners in a sinful way is as strange as it is *without excuse,* yet we are not to think it strange, for it is not without example. It is the *old way that wicked men have trodden,* that have gone slumbering to hell, as if their damnation slumbered while they did. [4.] That God took care for the preservation of those that were his, who believed and feared, and took the warning themselves which they gave to others. Noah entered *into the ark,* and there he was safe; Lot went out of Sodom, and so went out of harm's way. If some run on *heedless* and *headlong* into destruction, that shall be no prejudice to the salvation of those that believe. [5.] That they were surprised with the ruin which they would not fear, and were swallowed up in it, to their unspeakable horror and amazement. The *flood came,* and destroyed all the sinners of the old world; *fire and brimstone* came, and *destroyed* all the sinners of Sodom. God has many arrows in his quiver, and uses which he will in making war upon his rebellious subjects, for he can make which he will effectual. But that which is especially intended here is to show what a dreadful surprise destruction will be to those who are secure and sensual.

(2.) How it will be with sinners still (*v.* 30): *Thus shall it be in the day when the Son of man is revealed.* When Christ comes to destroy the Jewish nation, by the Roman armies, the generality of that nation will be found under such a reigning security and stupidity as this. They have warning given by Christ now, and will have it repeated to them by the apostles after him, as they had by Noah and Lot; but it will be all *in vain.* They will continue secure, will go on in their neglect and opposition of Christ and his gospel, till all the Christians are withdrawn from among them and gone to the place of refuge. God will provide for them on the other side Jordan, and then a deluge of judgments shall flow in upon them, which will destroy all the unbelieving Jews. One would have thought that this discourse of our Saviour's, which was public, and not long after *published* to the world, should have awakened them; but it did not, for the hearts of that people were hardened, to their destruction. In like manner, when Jesus Christ shall come to judge the world, at the end of time, sinners will be found in the same secure and careless posture, altogether regardless of the judgment approaching, which will therefore come upon them as a snare; and in like manner the sinners of every age go on securely in their evil ways, and *remember not their latter end,* nor the account that they must give. *Woe to them that are thus at ease in Zion.*

6. That it ought to be the care of his disciples and followers to distinguish themselves from the unbelieving Jews in that day, and, leaving them, their city and country, to themselves, to flee at the signal given, according to the direction that should be given. Let them retire, as Noah to his ark, and Lot to his Zoar. You *would have healed Jerusalem,* as of old Babylon, *but she is not healed,* and therefore *forsake her, flee out of the midst of her, and deliver every man his soul,* Jer. li. 6, 9. This flight of theirs from Jerusalem must be *expeditious,* and must not be retarded by any concern about their worldly affairs (*v.* 31): "*He that shall be on the house-top,* when the alarm is given, *let him not come down, to take his stuff away,* both because he cannot spare so much time, and because the carrying away of his effects will but encumber him and retard his flight. Let him not *regard* his *stuff* at such a time, when it will be next to a miracle of mercy if he have his *life given him for a prey.* It will be better to leave his stuff behind him than to stay to look after it, and *perish with them that believe* not. It will be their concern to do as Lot and his family were charged to do: *Escape for thy life. Save yourselves from this untoward generation.* (2.) When they have made their escape, they must not think of returning (*v.* 32): "*Remember Lot's wife;* and take warning by her not only to flee from this Sodom (for so Jerusalem is become, Isa. i. 10), but to persevere in your flight, and do not *look back,* as she did; be not loth to leave a place marked for destruction, whomsoever or whatsoever you leave behind you, that is ever so dear to you." Those who have left the Sodom of a natural state, let them go forward, and not so much as look a kind look towards it again. Let them not *look back,* lest they should be tempted to *go back;* nay, lest that be construed a *going back in heart,* or an evidence that the heart was left behind. Lot's wife was *turned into a pillar of salt,* that she might remain a lasting monument of God's displeasure against apostates, who *begin in the spirit and end in the flesh.* (3.) There would be no other way of saving their lives than by quitting the Jews, and, if they thought to save themselves by a coalition with them, they would find themselves mistaken (*v.* 33): "*Whosoever shall seek to save his life,* by declining from his Christianity and complying with the Jews, he shall *lose it* with them and perish in the common calamity; but whosoever is willing to venture his life with the Christians, upon the same bottom on which they venture, to take his lot with them in life and in death, he shall *preserve* his life, for he shall make sure of *eternal life,* and is in a likelier way at that time to save his life than those who embark in a Jewish bottom, or *ensure* upon their securities." Note, Those do best themselves that trust God in the way of duty.

7. That all good Christians should certainly escape, but many of them very *narrowly,* from that destruction, *v.* 34—36. When God's judgments are laying all waste, he will take an effectual course to preserve those that are his, by remarkable providences distinguishing between them and others that were nearest to them: *two in a bed, one taken and the other left;* one snatched out of the burning and taken into a place of safety, while the other is left to perish in the common ruin. Note, Though the sword devours one as well as another, and *all things* seem to *come alike to all,* yet sooner or later it shall be made to appear that the Lord knows them that are his and them that are not, and how to *take out the precious from the vile.* We are sure that *the Judge of all the earth will do right;* and therefore, when he sends a judgment on purpose to avenge the death of his Son upon those that crucified him, he will take care that none of those who glorified him, and gloried in his cross, shall be *taken away* by that judgment.

8. That this distinguishing, dividing, discriminating work shall be done in all places, as far as the kingdom of God shall extend, *v.* 37. *Where, Lord?* They had enquired concerning the time, and he would not gratify their curiosity with any information concerning that; they therefore tried him with another question: "*Where, Lord?* Where shall those be *safe* that are *taken?* Where shall those *perish* that are left?" The answer is proverbial, and may be explained so

as to answer each side of the question: *Wheresoever the body is, thither will the eagles be gathered together.* (1.) Wherever the wicked are, who are marked for perdition, they shall *be found out* by the judgments of God; as wherever a dead carcase is, the birds of prey will smell it out, and make a prey of it. The Jews having made themselves a dead and putrefied carcase, *odious* to God's holiness and *obnoxious* to his justice, wherever any of that unbelieving generation is, the judgments of God shall fasten upon them, as the eagles do upon the prey: *Thine hand shall find out all thine enemies* (Ps. xxi. 8), though they *set their nests among the stars,* Obad. 4. The Roman soldiers will hunt the Jews out of all their recesses and fastnesses, and none shall escape. (2.) Wherever the godly are, who are marked for preservation, they *shall be found* happy in the enjoyment of Christ. As the dissolution of the Jewish church shall be extended to all parts, so shall the constitution of the Christian church. Wherever Christ is, believers will flock to him, and meet in him, as eagles about the prey, without being directed or shown the way, by the instinct of the new nature. Now Christ is where his gospel, and his ordinances, and his church are: *For where two or three are gathered in his name there is he in the midst of them,* and thither therefore others will be gathered to him. The kingdom of the Messiah is not to have one particular place for its *metropolis,* such as Jerusalem was to the Jewish church, to which all Jews were to resort; but, *wherever the body is,* wherever the gospel is preached and ordinances are ministered, thither will pious souls resort, there they will find Christ, and by faith feast upon him. Wherever Christ records his name he will meet his people, and bless them, John iv. 21, &c.; 1 Tim. ii. 8. Many good interpreters understand it of the gathering of the saints together to Christ in the kingdom of glory: "Ask not where the carcase will be, and how they shall find the way to it, for they shall be under infallible direction; to him who is their living, quickening Head, and the centre of their unity, to him shall the gathering of the people be."

CHAP. XVIII.

In this chapter we have, I. The parable of the importunate widow, designed to teach us fervency in prayer, ver. 1—8. II. The parable of the Pharisee and publican, designed to teach us humility, and humiliation for sin, in prayer, ver. 9—14. III. Christ's favour to little children that were brought to him, ver. 15—17. IV. The trial of a rich man that had a mind to follow Christ, whether he loved better Christ or his riches; his coming short upon that trial; and Christ's discourse with his disciples upon that occasion, ver. 18—30. V. Christ's foretelling his own death and sufferings, ver. 31—34. VI. His restoring sight to a blind man, ver. 35—43. And these four passages we had before in Matthew and Mark.

AND he spake a parable unto them
to this end, that men ought
always *to* pray, and not to faint; 2
Saying, There was in a city a judge,
which feared not God, neither regarded man: 3 And there was a widow in that city; and she came unto
him, saying, Avenge me of mine adversary. 4 And he would not for a
while: but afterward he said within
himself, Though I fear not God, nor
regard man; 5 Yet because this widow
troubleth me, I will avenge her, lest
by her continual coming she weary
me. 6 And the Lord said, Hear
what the unjust judge saith. 7 And
shall not God avenge his own elect,
which cry day and night unto him,
though he bear long with them? 8
I tell you that he will avenge them
speedily. Nevertheless when the Son
of man cometh, shall he find faith on
the earth?

This parable has its key hanging at the door; the drift and design of it are *prefixed.* Christ spoke it with this intent, to teach us that *men ought always to pray and not to faint, v.* 1. It supposes that all God's people are *praying* people; all God's children keep up both a *constant* and an *occasional* correspondence with him, send to him *statedly,* and upon *every emergency.* It is our privilege and honour that we *may* pray. It is our duty; we *ought to pray,* we sin if we neglect it. It is to be our constant work; we ought *always* to pray, it is that which *the duty of every day requires.* We must pray, and never grow weary of praying, nor think of leaving it off till it comes to be swallowed up in everlasting praise. But that which seems particularly designed here is to teach us constancy and perseverance in our requests for some spiritual mercies that we are in pursuit of, relating either to ourselves or to the church of God. When we are praying for strength against our spiritual enemies, our lusts and corruptions, which are our worst enemies, we must continue instant in prayer, must pray and *not faint,* for we shall not *seek God's face in vain.* So we must likewise in our prayers for the deliverance of the people of God out of the hands of their persecutors and oppressors.

I. Christ shows, by a parable, the *power of importunity* among men, who will be swayed by that, when nothing else will influence, to do what is just and right. He gives you an instance of an honest cause that succeeded before an unjust judge, not by the equity or compassionableness of it, but purely by *dint of importunity.* Observe here, 1. The bad character of the judge that was in a certain city. He *neither feared God nor regarded man;* he had no manner of concern either for his conscience or for his reputation; he stood in no awe either of the wrath of God against him or of the censures of men concerning him: or, he took no care to do his duty either to God or man; he was a perfect stranger both to godliness and honour, and had no notion of either. It is not strange if those that have cast off the fear of their Creator be altogether regardless of their fellow-creatures; where no *fear of God* is no good is to be expected. Such a prevalency of irreligion and inhumanity is bad in any, but very bad in a *judge*, who has power in his hand, in the use of which he ought to be guided by the principles of religion and justice, and, if he be not, instead of doing good with his power he will be in danger of doing hurt. *Wickedness in the place of judgment* was one of the sorest evils Solomon saw under the sun, Eccl. iii. 16. 2. The distressed case of a poor widow that was necessitated to make her appeal to him, being wronged by some one that thought to bear her down with power and terror. She had manifestly right on her side; but, it should seem, in soliciting to have right done her, she tied not herself to the formalities of the law, but made personal application to the judge from day to day at his own house, still crying, *Avenge me of mine adversary*, that is, *Do me justice against mine adversary;* not that she desired to be revenged on him for any thing he had done against her, but that he might be obliged to restore what effects he had of hers in his hands, and might be disabled any more to oppress her. Note, Poor widows have often many adversaries, who barbarously take advantage of their weak and helpless state to invade their rights, and defraud them of what little they have; and magistrates are particularly charged, not only not to do *violence to the widow* (Jer. xxii. 3), but to *judge the fatherless*, and *plead for the widow* (Isa. i. 17), to be their patrons and protectors; then they are *as gods*, for God is so, Ps. lxviii. 5. 3. The difficulty and discouragement she met with in her cause: *He would not for awhile.* According to his usual practice, he frowned upon her, took no notice of her cause, but connived at all the wrong her adversary did her; for she had no bribe to give him, no great man whom he stood in any awe of to speak for her, so that he did not at all incline to redress her grievances; and he himself was conscious of the reason of his dilatoriness, and could not but own within himself that he *neither feared God nor regarded man.* It is sad that a man should know so much amiss of himself, and be in no care to amend it. 4. The gaining of her point by continually *dunning* this unjust *judge* (*v.* 5): "*Because this widow troubleth me*, gives me a continual toil, I will hear her cause, and do her justice; not so much lest by her clamour against me she bring me into an ill name, as lest by her clamour to me she weary me; for she is resolved that she will give me no rest till it is done, and therefore I will do it, to save myself further trouble; as good at first as at last." Thus she got justice done her by continual craving; she begged it at his door, followed him in the streets, solicited him in open court, and still her cry was, *Avenge me of mine adversary*, which he was forced to do, to get rid of her; for his conscience, bad as he was, would not suffer him to send her to prison for an affront upon the court.

II. He applies this for the encouragement of God's praying people to pray with faith and fervency, and to persevere therein.

1. He assures them that God will at length be gracious to them (*v.* 6): *Hear what the unjust judge saith*, how he owns himself quite overcome by a constant importunity, *and shall not God avenge his own elect?* Observe,

(1.) What it is that they desire and expect: that God would *avenge his own elect.* Note, [1.] There are a people in the world that are God's people, his *elect*, his *own elect*, a choice people, a chosen people. And this he has an eye to in all he does for them; it is because they are his *chosen*, and in pursuance of the choice he has made of them. [2.] God's own elect meet with a great deal of trouble and opposition in this world; there are *many adversaries* that fight against them; Satan is their great adversary. [3.] That which is wanted and waited for is God's preserving and protecting them, and the work of his hands in them; his securing the interest of the church in the world and his grace in the heart.

(2.) What it is that is required of God's people in order to the obtaining of this: they must *cry day and night to him;* not that he needs their remonstrances, or can be moved by their pleadings, but this he has made their duty, and to this he has promised mercy. We ought to be particular in praying against our spiritual enemies, as St. Paul was: *For this thing I besought the Lord thrice, that it might depart from me;* like this importunate widow. Lord, mortify *this* corruption. Lord, arm me against *this* temptation. We ought to concern ourselves for the persecuted and oppressed churches, and to pray that God would do them justice, and set them in safety. And herein we must be very urgent; we must *cry* with earnestness; we must cry *day and night*, as those that believe prayer will be heard at last; we must *wrestle with God*, as those that know how to value the blessing, and will have no nay. God's praying people are told to *give him no rest*, Isa. lxii. 6, 7.

(3.) What discouragements they may perhaps meet with in their prayers and expectations. He may *bear long with them*, and may not presently appear for them, in answer to their prayers. He is *μακροθυμῶν ἐπ' αὐτοῖς*—he *exercises patience towards* the adversaries of his people, and does not take vengeance on them; and he *exercises the patience of his people*, and does not plead for them. He *bore long* with the *cry of the sin* of the Egyptians that oppressed Israel, and with the *cry of the sorrows* of those that were oppressed.

(4.) What assurance they have that mercy will come at last, though it be delayed, and how it is supported by what the unjust judge saith: If this widow prevail by being importunate, much more shall God's elect prevail. For, [1.] This widow was a *stranger*, nothing related to the judge; but God's praying people are his own elect, whom he knows, and loves, and delights in, and has always concerned himself for. [2.] She was but *one*, but the praying people of God are *many*, all of whom come to him on the same errand, and agree to ask what they need, Matt. xviii. 19. As the saints of heaven surround the throne of glory with their united praises, so saints on earth besiege the throne of grace with their united prayers. [3.] She came to a *judge* that bade her *keep her distance;* we come to a *Father* that bids us *come boldly* to him, and teaches us to cry, *Abba, Father.* [4.] She came to an *unjust judge;* we come to a *righteous Father* (John xvii. 25), one that regards his own glory and the comforts of his poor creatures, especially those in distress, as *widows* and *fatherless*. [5.] She came to this judge purely upon her own account; but God is himself engaged in the cause which we are soliciting; and we can say, *Arise, O Lord, plead thine* own cause; and *what wilt thou do to thy great name?* [6.] She had no friend to speak for her, to add force to her petition, and to use interest for her more than her own; but we have an *Advocate with the Father*, his own Son, who *ever lives to make intercession* for us, and has a powerful prevailing interest in heaven. [7.] She had no promise of speeding, no, nor any encouragement given her to ask; but we have the golden sceptre held out to us, are told to ask, with a promise that it shall be given to us. [8.] She could have access to the judge only at some certain times; but we may cry to God *day and night*, at all hours, and therefore may the rather hope to prevail by importunity. [9.] Her importunity was provoking to the judge, and she might fear lest it should set him more against her; but our importunity is pleasing to God; the prayer of the upright is *his delight*, and therefore, we may hope, shall avail much, if it be an effectual fervent prayer.

2. He intimates to them that, notwithstanding this, they will begin to be weary of waiting for him (*v.* 8): "*Nevertheless*, though such assurances are given that God will avenge his own elect, yet, *when the Son of man cometh, shall he find faith on the earth?*" The Son of man will come to *avenge his own elect*, to plead the cause of persecuted Christians against the persecuting Jews; he will come in his providence to plead the cause of his injured people in every age, and at the great day he will come finally to determine the controversies of Zion. Now, when he comes, will he find faith on the earth? The question implies a strong negation: No, he will not; he himself foresees it.

(1.) This supposes that it is *on earth* only that there is occasion for *faith;* for sinners in hell are *feeling* that which they would not believe, and saints in heaven are *enjoying* that which they did believe.

(2.) It supposes that *faith* is the great thing that Jesus Christ *looks for*. He *looks down* upon the children of men, and does not ask, Is there innocency? but, *Is there faith?* He enquired concerning the faith of those who applied themselves to him for cures.

(3.) It supposes that if there were faith, though ever so little, he would discover it, and *find it out*. His eye is upon the weakest and most obscure believer.

(4.) It is foretold that, when Christ comes to plead his people's cause, he will find but *little faith* in comparison with what one might expect. That is, [1.] In general, he will find but *few good people*, few that are really and truly good. Many that have the form and fashion of godliness, but few that have faith, that are sincere and honest: nay, he will find little *fidelity* among men; the *faithful fail*, Ps. xii. 1, 2. Even to the end of time there will still be occasion for the same complaint. The world will grow no better, no, not when it is drawing towards its period. Bad it is, and bad it will be, and worst of all just before Christ's coming; the last times will be the most perilous. [2.] In particular, he will find few that have *faith* concerning his coming. When he comes to *avenge his own elect* he looks if there be any faith *to help* and *to uphold*, and wonders that there is none, Isa. lix. 16; lxiii. 5. It intimates that Christ, both in his particular comings for the relief of his people, and in his general coming at the end of time, may, and will, delay his coming so long as that, *First*, Wicked people will begin to *defy it*, and to say, *Where is the promise of his coming?* 2 Pet. iii. 4. They will challenge him to come (Isa. v. 10; Amos. v. 19); and his delay will harden them in their wickedness, Matt. xxiv. 48. *Secondly*, Even his own people will begin to *despair* of it, and to conclude he will never come, because he has passed their reckoning. God's time to appear for his people is when things are brought to the last extremity, and when Zion begins to say, *The Lord has forsaken me.* See Isa. xlix. 14; xl. 27. But this is our comfort, that, when the time appointed comes, it will appear that the unbelief of man has not made the promise of God of no effect.

9 And he spake this parable unto
certain which trusted in themselves
that they were righteous, and despised
others: 10 Two men went up into
the temple to pray; the one a Pharisee, and the other a publican. 11
The Pharisee stood and prayed thus
with himself, God, I thank thee, that

I am not as other men *are*, extortioners, unjust, adulterers, or even as this publican.
12 I fast twice in the week, I give tithes of all that I possess.
13 And the publican, standing afar off, would not lift up so much as *his* eyes unto heaven, but smote upon his breast, saying, God be merciful to me a sinner.
14 I tell you, this man went down to his house justified *rather* than the other: for every one that exalteth himself shall be abased; and he that humbleth himself shall be exalted.

The scope of this parable likewise is prefixed to it, and we are told (*v.* 9) who they were whom it was levelled at, and for whom it was calculated. He designed it for the conviction of some who *trusted in themselves that they were righteous, and despised others.* They were such as had, 1. A great conceit of themselves, and of their own goodness; they thought themselves as holy as they needed to be, and holier than all their neighbours, and such as might serve for examples to them all. But that was not all; 2. They had a confidence in themselves before God, and not only had a high opinion of their own righteousness, but depended upon the merit of it, whenever they addressed God, as their plea: They *trusted in themselves as being righteous;* they thought they had made God their debtor, and might demand any thing from him; and, 3. They despised others, and looked upon them with contempt, as not worthy to be compared with them. Now Christ by this parable would show such their folly, and that thereby they shut themselves out from acceptance with God. This is called a *parable,* though there be nothing of similitude in it; but it is rather a description of the different temper and language of those that *proudly justify themselves,* and those that *humbly condemn themselves;* and their different standing before God. It is matter of fact every day.

I. Here are both these addressing themselves to the duty of prayer at the same place and time (*v.* 10): *Two men went up into the temple* (for the temple stood upon a hill) *to pray.* It was not the hour of public prayer, but they went thither to offer up their personal devotions, as was usual with good people at that time, when the temple was not only the *place,* but the *medium* of worship, and God had promised, in answer to Solomon's request, that, whatever prayer was made in a right manner *in* or *towards* that house, it should *therefore* the rather be accepted. Christ is our temple, and to him we must have an eye in all our approaches to God. The *Pharisee* and the *publican* both went to *the temple to pray.* Note, Among the worshippers of God, in the visible church, there is a mixture of good and bad, of some that are accepted of God, and some that are not; and so it has been ever since Cain and Abel brought their offering to the same altar. The Pharisee, proud as he was, could not think himself above prayer; nor could the publican, humble as he was, think himself shut out from the benefit of it; but we have reason to think that these went with different views. 1. The Pharisee went *to the temple* to pray because it was a *public* place, more public than the corners of the streets, and therefore he should have many eyes upon him, who would applaud his devotion, which perhaps was more than was expected. The character Christ gave of the Pharisees, that *all their works they did to be seen of men,* gives us occasion for this suspicion. Note, Hypocrites keep up the external performances of religion only to *save* or *gain* credit. There are many whom we see *every day* at the temple, whom, it is to be feared, we shall not see in the great day at Christ's right hand. 2. The publican went to the temple because it was appointed to be a *house of prayer for all people,* Isa. lvi. 7. The Pharisee came to the temple upon a *compliment,* the publican upon business; the Pharisee to make his appearance, the publican to make his request. Now God sees with what disposition and design we come to wait upon him in holy ordinances, and will judge of us accordingly.

II. Here is the Pharisee's address to God (for a prayer I cannot call it): He *stood* and *prayed thus with himself* (*v.* 11, 12); *standing by himself, he prayed thus,* so some read it; he was wholly intent upon himself, had nothing in his eye but *self,* his own praise, and not God's glory; or, standing in some conspicuous place, where he distinguished himself; or, *setting himself* with a great deal of state and formality, he prayed thus. Now that which he is here supposed to say is that which shows,

1. That he *trusted to himself that he was righteous.* A great many good things he said of himself, which we will suppose to be true. He was free from gross and scandalous sins; he was not an *extortioner,* not a usurer, not oppressive to debtors or tenants, but fair and kind to all that had dependence upon him. He was not *unjust* in any of his dealings; he did no man any wrong; he could say, as Samuel, *Whose ox or whose ass have I taken?* He was *no adulterer,* but had possessed his vessel in sanctification and honour. Yet this was not all; he *fasted twice in the week,* as an act partly of temperance, partly of devotion. The Pharisees and their disciples fasted twice a week, Monday and Thursday. Thus he glorified God with his body: yet that was not all; he *gave tithes of all that he possessed,* according to the law, and so glorified God with his worldly estate. Now all this was very well and commendable. Miserable is the condition of those who come short of the righteousness of this Pharisee: yet he was not accepted; and why was he

not? (1.) His giving God thanks for this, though in itself a good thing, yet seems to be a mere formality. He does not say, *By the grace of God I am what I am*, as Paul did, but turns it off with a slight, *God, I thank thee*, which is intended but for a plausible introduction to a proud vainglorious ostentation of himself. (2.) He makes his boast of this, and dwells with delight upon this subject, as if all his business to the temple was to tell God Almighty how very good he was; and he is ready to say, with those hypocrites that we read of (Isa. lviii. 3), *Wherefore have we fasted, and thou seest not?* (3.) He *trusted* to it as a righteousness, and not only mentioned it, but pleaded it, as if hereby he had merited at the hands of God, and made him his debtor. (4.) Here is not one word of prayer in all he saith. He went *up to the temple to pray*, but forgot his errand, was so full of himself and his own goodness that he thought he had need of nothing, no, not of the favour and grace of God, which, it would seem, he did not think worth asking.

2. That he *despised others.* (1.) He thought meanly of all mankind but himself: *I thank thee that I am not as other men are.* He speaks indefinitely, as if he were better than any. We may have reason to thank God that we are not as *some men* are, that are notoriously wicked and vile; but to speak at random thus, as if *we* only were good, and all besides us were reprobates, is to judge by wholesale. (2.) He thought meanly in a particular manner of this publican, whom he had left behind, it is probable, in the court of the Gentiles, and whose company he had fallen into as he came to the temple. He knew that he was a publican, and therefore very uncharitably concluded that he was an *extortioner, unjust*, and all that is naught. Suppose it had been so, and he had known it, what business had he to take notice of it? Could not he *say his prayers* (and that was all that the Pharisees did) without reproaching his neighbours? Or was this a part of his *God, I thank thee?* And was he as much pleased with the publican's badness as with his own goodness? There could not be a plainer evidence, not only of the want of humility and charity, but of reigning pride and malice, than this was.

III. Here is the publican's address to God, which was the reverse of the Pharisee's, as full of *humility* and *humiliation* as his was of *pride* and *ostentation;* as full of *repentance* for sin, and *desire* towards God, as his was of *confidence* in *himself* and his own righteousness and sufficiency.

1. He expressed his repentance and humility in *what he did;* and his gesture, when he addressed himself to his devotions, was *expressive* of great seriousness and humility, and the proper clothing of a broken, penitent, and obedient heart. (1.) He *stood afar off.* The Pharisee *stood*, but crowded up as high as he could, to the upper end of the court; the publican *kept at a distance* under a sense of his unworthiness to draw near to God, and perhaps for fear of offending the Pharisee, whom he observed to look scornfully upon him, and of disturbing his devotions. Hereby he owned that God might justly *behold him afar off*, and send him into a state of eternal distance from him, and that it was a great favour that God was pleased to admit him *thus nigh.* (2.) He *would not lift up so much as his eyes to heaven*, much less his *hands*, as was usual in prayer. He did *lift up his heart* to God in the heavens, in *holy desires*, but, through prevailing shame and humiliation, he did not lift up his eyes in *holy confidence* and *courage.* His *iniquities* are *gone over his head, as a heavy burden*, so that he is *not able to look up*, Ps. xl. 12. The dejection of his looks is an indication of the dejection of his mind at the thought of sin. (3.) He *smote upon his breast*, in a holy indignation at himself for sin: "Thus would I smite this wicked heart of mine, the poisoned fountain out of which flow all the streams of sin, if I could come at it." The sinner's heart first smites him in a penitent rebuke, 2 Sam. xxiv. 10. *David's heart smote him.* Sinner, what hast thou done? And then he smites his heart with penitent remorse: *O wretched man that I am!* Ephraim is said to *smite upon his thigh*, Jer. xxxi. 19. Great mourners are represented *tabouring upon their breasts*, Nah. ii. 7.

2. He expressed it *in what he said.* His prayer was *short.* Fear and shame hindered him from saying much; sighs and groans swallowed up his words; but what he said was to the purpose: *God, be merciful to me a sinner.* And blessed be God that we have this prayer upon record as an answered prayer, and that we are sure that he who prayed it went to his house justified; and so shall we, if we pray it, as he did, through Jesus Christ: "*God, be merciful to me a sinner;* the God of infinite mercy be merciful to me, for, if he be not, I am for ever undone, for ever miserable. God be merciful to me, for I have been cruel to myself." (1.) He owns himself *a sinner* by nature, by practice, guilty before God. *Behold, I am vile, what shall I answer thee?* The Pharisee denies himself to be a *sinner;* none of his neighbours can charge him, and he sees no reason to charge himself, with any thing amiss; *he is clean, he is pure from sin.* But the publican gives himself no other character than that of a *sinner*, a convicted criminal at God's bar. (2.) He has no dependence but upon the *mercy of God*, that, and that only, he relies upon. The Pharisee had insisted upon the *merit* of his fastings and tithes; but the poor publican disclaims all thought of merit, and flies to mercy as his city of refuge, and takes hold of the horn of that altar. "Justice condemns me; nothing will save me but mercy, mercy." (3.) He earnestly prays for the benefit of that mercy: "*O God, be merciful*, be *propitious, to me;* forgive my sins; be reconciled to me; take

me into thy favour; receive me graciously; love me freely." He comes as a beggar for an alms, when he is ready to perish for hunger. Probably he repeated this prayer with renewed affections, and perhaps said more to the same purport, made a particular confession of his sins, and mentioned the particular mercies he wanted, and waited upon God for; but still this was the burden of the song: *God, be merciful to me a sinner.*

IV. Here is the publican's *acceptance with God.* We have seen how differently these two addressed themselves to God; it is now worth while to enquire how they sped. There were those who would cry up the Pharisee, by whom he would go to his house applauded, and who would look with contempt upon this sneaking whining publican. But our Lord Jesus, to whom all hearts are open, all desires known, and from whom no secret is hid, who is perfectly acquainted with all proceedings in the court of heaven, assures us that this poor, penitent, broken-hearted publican *went to his house justified, rather than the other.* The Pharisee thought that if one of them must be justified, and not the other, certainly it must be he rather than the publican. "No," saith Christ, "*I tell you,* I affirm it with the utmost assurance, and declare it to you with the utmost concern, *I tell you,* it is the publican rather than the Pharisee." The proud Pharisee goes away, rejected of God; his thanksgivings are so far from being accepted that they are an *abomination;* he is *not justified,* his sins are not pardoned, nor is he delivered from condemnation: he is not accepted as righteous in God's sight, because he is so righteous in his own sight; but the publican, upon this humble address to Heaven, obtains the remission of his sins, and he whom the Pharisee would not set *with the dogs of his flock* God sets with the *children of his family.* The reason given for this is because God's glory is to *resist the proud, and give grace to the humble.* 1. Proud men, who *exalt themselves,* are *rivals with God,* and therefore *they shall* certainly be *abased.* God, in his discourse with Job, appeals to this proof that he is God, that he *looks upon every one that is proud, and brings him low,* Job xl. 12. 2. Humble men, who *abase themselves,* are *subject to God,* and they shall be *exalted.* God has preferment in store for those that will take it as a favour, not for those that demand it as a debt. He shall be *exalted* into the love of God, and communion with him, shall be exalted into a satisfaction in himself, and exalted at last as high as heaven. See how the punishment answers the sin: *He that exalteth himself shall be abased.* See how the recompence answers the duty: *He that humbles himself shall be exalted.* See also the power of God's grace in bringing good out of evil; the publican had been a great sinner, and out of the greatness of his sin was brought the greatness of his repentance; *out of the eater came forth meat.* See, on the contrary, the power of Satan's malice in bringing evil out of good. It was good that the Pharisee was no extortioner, nor unjust; but the devil made him proud of this, to his ruin.

15 And they brought unto him also infants, that he would touch them: but when *his* disciples saw *it*, they rebuked them. 16 But Jesus called them *unto him,* and said, Suffer little children to come unto me, and forbid them not: for of such is the kingdom of God. 17 Verily I say unto you, Whosoever shall not receive the kingdom of God as a little child shall in no wise enter therein.

This passage of story we had both in Matthew and Mark; it very fitly follows here after the story of the publican, as a confirmation of the truth which was to be illustrated by that parable, that those shall be accepted with God, and honoured, who humble themselves, and for them Christ has *blessings in store,* the choicest and best of blessings. Observe here, 1. Those who are themselves blessed in Christ should desire to have their children also blessed in him, and should hereby testify the true honour they have for Christ, by their making use of him, and the true love they have for their children, by their concern about their souls. They brought to him *infants,* very young, not able to go, sucking children, as some think. None are too little, too young, to bring to Christ, who knows how to show kindness to them that are not capable of doing service to him. 2. One gracious touch of Christ's will make our children happy. They *brought infants to him, that he might touch them* in token of the application of his grace and Spirit to them, for that always makes way for his *blessing,* which likewise they expected; see Isa. xliv. 3. *I will first pour my Spirit upon thy seed, and* then *my blessing upon thine offspring.* 3. It is no strange thing for those who make their application to Jesus Christ, for themselves or for their children, to meet with discouragement, even from those who should countenance and encourage them: *When the disciples saw it,* they thought, if this were admitted, it would bring endless trouble upon their Master, and therefore they *rebuked them,* and frowned upon them. The spouse complained of *the watchmen,* Cant. iii. 3; v. 7. 4. Many whom the disciples rebuke the Master invites: *Jesus called them unto him,* when, upon the disciples' check, they were retiring. They did not *appeal* from the disciples to the Master, but the Master took cognizance of their despised cause. 5. It is the mind of Christ that *little children* should be brought to him, and presented as living sacrifices to his honour: "*Suffer little children to come to me, and forbid them not;* let nothing be done to hinder them, for they shall be as welcome as any." *The promise is to us, and to our seed;* and therefore he that has the dispensing of promised blessings will bid them welcome to him with us. 6. The children of those who belong to the kingdom of God do likewise belong to that kingdom, as the children of freemen are freemen. If the parents be members of the visible church, the children are so too; for, if the root be holy, the branches are so. 7. So welcome are *children* to Christ that those grown people are most welcome to him who have in them most of the disposition of children (*v.* 17): *Whosoever shall not receive the kingdom of God as a little child,* that is, receive the benefits of it with humility and thankfulness, not pretending to merit them as the Pharisee did, but gladly owning himself indebted to free grace for them, as the publican did; unless a man be brought to this self-denying frame he shall *in no wise enter* into that kingdom. They must receive the kingdom of God as *children,* receive their estates by descent and inheritance, not by purchase, and call it their Father's gift.

18 And a certain ruler asked him,
saying, Good Master, what shall I do
to inherit eternal life? 19 And Jesus
said unto him, Why callest thou me
good? none *is* good, save one, *that is,*
God. 20 Thou knowest the commandments, Do not commit adultery,
Do not kill, Do not steal, Do not bear
false witness, Honour thy father and
thy mother. 21 And he said, All
these have I kept from my youth up.
22 Now when Jesus heard these
things, he said unto him, Yet lackest
thou one thing: sell all that thou
hast, and distribute unto the poor,
and thou shalt have treasure in heaven: and come, follow me. 23 And
when he heard this, he was very sorrowful: for he was very rich. 24
And when Jesus saw that he was
very sorrowful, he said, How hardly
shall they that have riches enter into
the kingdom of God! 25 For it is
easier for a camel to go through a
needle's eye, than for a rich man to
enter into the kingdom of God. 26
And they that heard *it* said, Who
then can be saved? 27 And he said,
The things which are impossible with
men are possible with God. 28 Then
Peter said, Lo, we have left all, and
followed thee. 29 And he said unto
them, Verily I say unto you, There
is no man that hath left house, or
parents, or brethren, or wife, or children, for the kingdom of God's sake,
30 Who shall not receive manifold
more in this present time, and in the
world to come life everlasting.

In these verses we have,

I. Christ's discourse with a ruler, that had a good mind to be directed by him in the way to heaven. In which we may observe,

1. It is a blessed sight to see persons of distinction in the world distinguish themselves from others of their rank by their concern about their souls and another life. Luke takes notice of it that he was a *ruler.* Few of the rulers had any esteem for Christ, but here was one that had; whether a church or state ruler does not appear, but he was one *in authority.*

2. The great thing we are every one of us concerned to enquire after is what we shall do to get to heaven, *what we shall do to inherit eternal life.* This implies such a belief of an eternal life after this as atheists and infidels have not, such a concern to make it sure as a careless unthinking world have not, and such a willingness to comply with any terms that it may be made sure as those have not who are resolvedly devoted to the world and the flesh.

3. Those who would inherit eternal life must apply themselves to Jesus Christ as their *Master,* their *teaching* Master, so it signifies here (διδάσκαλε), and their *ruling* Master, and so they shall certainly find him. There is no learning the way to heaven but in the school of Christ, by those that enter themselves into it, and continue in it.

4. Those who come to Christ as their Master must believe him to have not only a *divine mission,* but a *divine goodness.* Christ would have this ruler know that if he understood himself aright in calling him good he did, in effect, call him *God* and indeed he was so (*v.* 19): "*Why callest thou me good?* Thou knowest *there is none good but one, that is, God;* and dost thou then take me for God? If so, thou art in the right."

5. Our Master, Christ himself, has not altered the way to heaven from what it was before his coming, but has only made it more plain, and easy, and comfortable, and provided for our relief, in case we take any false step. *Thou knowest the commandments.* Christ came not to destroy the law and the prophets, but to establish them. Wouldest thou inherit eternal life? Govern thyself by the commandments.

6. The duties of the second table must be conscientiously observed, in order to our happiness, and we must not think that any acts of devotion, how plausible soever, will atone for the neglect of them. Nor is it enough to keep ourselves free from the gross violations of these commandments, but we

must *know these commandments*, as Christ has *explained them* in his sermon upon the mount, in their extent and spiritual nature, and so observe them.

7. Men think themselves *innocent* because they are *ignorant;* so this ruler did. He said, *All these have I kept from my youth up*, *v.* 21. He knows no more evil of himself than the Pharisee did, *v.* 11. He boasts that he began *early* in a course of virtue, that he had continued in it to this day, and that he had not in any instance transgressed. Had he been acquainted with the extent and spiritual nature of the divine law, and with the workings of his own heart,—had he been but Christ's disciple awhile, and learned of him, he would have said quite the contrary: "*All these have* I broken from my youth up, in thought, word, and deed."

8. The great things by which we are to try our spiritual state are how we stand affected to Christ and to our brethren, to this world and to the other; by these this man was tried. For, (1.) If he have a true *affection to Christ*, he will *come and follow him*, will attend to his doctrine, and submit to his discipline, whatever it cost him. None shall inherit eternal life who are not willing to take their lot with the Lord Jesus, to follow the Lamb whithersoever he goes. (2.) If he have a true *affection to his brethren*, he will, as there is occasion, *distribute to the poor*, who are God's receivers of his dues out of our estates. (3.) If he think meanly of *this world*, as he ought, he will not stick at *selling what he has*, if there be a necessity for it, for the relief of God's poor. (4.) If he think highly of the other world, as he ought, he will desire no more than to have *treasure in heaven*, and will reckon that a sufficient abundant recompence for all that he has left, or lost, or laid out for God in this world.

9. There are many that have a great deal in them that is very commendable, and yet they perish *for lack of some one thing;* so this *ruler* here; he broke with Christ upon this, he liked all his terms very well but this which would part between him and his estate: "In this, I pray thee, have me excused." If this be the bargain, it is no bargain.

10. Many that are loth to leave Christ, yet do leave him. After a long struggle between their convictions and their corruptions, their corruptions carry the day at last; they are very sorry that they cannot serve God and mammon both; but, if one must be quitted, it shall be their God, not their worldly gain.

II. Christ's discourse with his disciples upon this occasion, in which we may observe, 1. Riches are a great hindrance to many in the way to heaven. Christ took notice of the reluctancy and regret with which the rich man broke off from him. He *saw that he was very sorrowful*, and was sorry for him; but thence he infers, *How hardly shall they that have riches enter into the kingdom of God! v.* 24. If this ruler had had but as little of the world as Peter, and James, and John had, in all probability he would have left it, to follow Christ, as they did; but, having a great estate, it had a great influence upon him, and he chose rather to take his leave of Christ than to lay himself under an obligation to dispose of his estate in charitable uses. Christ asserts the difficulty of the salvation of rich people very emphatically: *It is easier for a camel to go through a needle's eye than for a rich man to enter into the kingdom of God, v.* 25. It is a proverbial expression, that denotes the thing to be extremely difficult. 2. There is in the hearts of all people such a general affection to this world, and the things of it, that, since Christ has required it as necessary to salvation that we should sit loose to this world, it is really very hard for any to get to heaven. If we must *sell all*, or break with Christ, *who then can be saved? v.* 26. They do not find fault with what Christ required as hard and unreasonable. No, it is very fit that they who expect an eternal happiness in the other world should be willing to forego all that is dear to them in this world, in expectation of it. But they know how closely the hearts of most men cleave to this world, and are ready to despair of their being ever brought to this. 3. There are such difficulties in the way of our salvation as could never be got over but by pure omnipotence, by that grace of God which is almighty, and to which that is *possible* which exceeds all created power and wisdom. The *things which are impossible with men* (and utterly impossible it is that men should work such a change upon their own spirits as to turn them from the world to God, it is like *dividing the sea*, and *driving Jordan back)*, these things are *possible with God.* His grace can work upon the soul, so as to alter the bent and bias of it, and give it a contrary ply; and it is he that *works in us both to will and to do.* 4. There is an aptness in us to speak too much of what we have left and lost, of what we have done and suffered, for Christ. This appears in Peter: *Lo, we have left all, and followed thee, v.* 28. When it came in his way, he could not forbear magnifying his own and his brethren's affection to Christ, in *quitting* all to follow him. But this we should be so far from boasting of, that we should rather acknowledge it not worth taking notice of, and be ashamed of ourselves that there should have been any regret and difficulty in the doing of it, and any hankerings towards those things afterwards. 5. Whatever we have left, or laid out, for Christ, it shall without fail be abundantly made up to us in this world and that to come, notwithstanding our weaknesses and infirmities (*v.* 29, 30): *No man has left* the comfort of his estate or relations *for the kingdom of God's sake*, rather than they should hinder either his services to that kingdom or his enjoyments of it, *who shall not receive manifold more in this present time*, in the graces and comforts of God's Spirit, in the pleasures of communion with God and of a good conscience, advantages which, to those that know how to value and improve them, will abundantly countervail all their losses. Yet that is not all; in the world to come they *shall receive life everlasting*, which is the thing that the ruler seemed to have his eye and heart upon.

31 Then he took *unto him* the
twelve, and said unto them, Behold,
we go up to Jerusalem, and all things
that are written by the prophets concerning the Son of man shall be accomplished. 32 For he shall be delivered unto the Gentiles, and shall
be mocked, and spitefully entreated,
and spitted on: 33 And they shall
scourge *him*, and put him to death:
and the third day he shall rise again.
34 And they understood none of these
things: and this saying was hid from
them, neither knew they the things
which were spoken.

Here is, I. The notice Christ gave to his disciples of his sufferings and death approaching, and of the glorious issue of them, which he himself had a perfect sight and foreknowledge of, and thought it necessary to give them warning of, that it might be the less surprise and terror to them. Two things here are which we had not in the other evangelists:—1. The *sufferings* of Christ are here spoken of as the *fulfilling of the scriptures*, with which consideration Christ reconciled himself to them, and would reconcile them: *All things that are written by the prophets concerning the Son of man*, especially the hardships he should undergo, *shall be accomplished.* Note, The Spirit of Christ, in the Old-Testament prophets, *testified beforehand his sufferings*, and *the glory that should follow*, 1 Pet. i. 11. This proves that the scriptures are the *word* of *God*, for they had their exact and full accomplishment; and that Jesus Christ was *sent of God*, for they had their accomplishment *in him;* this was *he that should come*, for whatever was *foretold* concerning the Messiah was verified in him; and he would submit to any thing for the fulfilling of scripture, that not one jot or tittle of that should fall to the ground. This makes the *offence of the cross to cease*, and puts an honour upon it. *Thus it was written, and thus it behoved Christ to suffer*, thus it became him. 2. The ignominy and disgrace done to Christ in his sufferings are here most insisted upon. The other evangelists had said that he should be *mocked;* but here it is added, *He shall be spitefully treated, ὑβρισθήσεται—he shall be loaded with contumely and contempt*, shall have all possible reproach put upon him. This was that part of his sufferings by which in a spiritual manner he satisfied God's justice for the injury we had done him in his honour by sin. Here is one particular instance of disgrace done him, that *he was spit upon*, which had been particularly foretold, Isa. l. 6. But here, as always, when Christ spoke of his sufferings and death, he foretold his resurrection as that which took off both the terror and reproach of his sufferings: *The third day he shall rise again.*

II. The confusion that the disciples were hereby put into. This was so contrary to the notions they had had of the Messiah and his kingdom, such a balk to their expectations from their Master, and such a breaking of all their measures, that *they understood none of these things, v.* 34. Their prejudices were so strong that they *would not* understand them literally, and they *could not* understand them otherwise, so that they did not understand them at all. It was a mystery, it was a riddle to them, it must be so; but they think it impossible to be reconciled with the glory and honour of the Messiah, and the design of setting up his kingdom. This saying was *hidden from them, κεκρυμμένον ἀπ' αὐτῶν*, it was apocrypha to them, they could not receive it: for their parts, they had read the Old Testament many a time, but they could never see any thing in it that would be *accomplished* in the disgrace and death of this Messiah. They were so intent upon those prophecies that spoke of his glory that they overlooked those that spoke of his *sufferings*, which the scribes and doctors of the law should have directed them to take notice of, and should have brought into their creeds and catechisms, as well as the other; but they did not suit their scheme, and therefore were laid aside. Note, *Therefore* it is that people run into mistakes, because they *read their Bibles by the halves*, and are as partial in the prophets as they are *in the law*. They are only for the *smooth things*, Isa. xxx. 10. Thus now we are too apt, in reading the prophecies that are yet to be fulfilled, to have our expectations raised of the glorious state of the church in the latter days. But we overlook its wilderness sackcloth state, and are willing to fancy that is over, and nothing is reserved for us but the halcyon days; and then, when tribulation and persecution arise, we do not *understand* it, neither *know we the things that are done*, though we are told as plainly as can be that *through many tribulations we must enter into the kingdom of God.*

35 And it came to pass, that as he
was come nigh unto Jericho, a certain
blind man sat by the way side begging: 36 And hearing the multitude
pass by, he asked what it meant. 37
And they told him, that Jesus of
Nazareth passeth by. 38 And he
cried, saying, Jesus, *thou* son of Da-

vid, have mercy on me. 39 And they
which went before rebuked him, that
he should hold his peace: but he cried
so much the more, *Thou* son of David,
have mercy on me. 40 And Jesus
stood, and commanded him to be
brought unto him: and when he was
come near, he asked him, 41 Saying,
What wilt thou that I shall do unto
thee? And he said, Lord, that I may
receive my sight. 42 And Jesus said
unto him, Receive thy sight: thy faith
hath saved thee. 43 And immediately he received his sight, and followed him, glorifying God: and all
the people, when they saw *it*, gave
praise unto God.

Christ came not only to bring *light* to a *dark* world, and so to set before us the *objects* we are to have in view, but also to give *sight* to blind *souls*, and by healing the *organ* to enable them to view those objects. As a token of this, he cured many of their bodily blindness; we have now an account of one to whom he *gave sight* near Jericho. Mark gives us an account of one, and names him, whom he cured *as he went out of Jericho*, Mark x. 46. Matthew speaks of two whom he cured *as they departed* from Jericho, Matt. xx. 30. Luke says it was ἐν τῷ ἐγγίζειν αὐτὸν—*when he was near* to Jericho, which might be when he was going out of it as well as when he was coming into it. Observe,

I. This poor blind man *sat by the way-side, begging, v.* 35. It seems, he was not only *blind*, but *poor*, had nothing to subsist on, nor any relations to maintain him; the fitter emblem of the world of mankind which Christ came to heal and save; they are therefore *wretched* and *miserable*, for they are both *poor and blind*, Rev. iii. 17. He sat begging, for he was blind, and could not work for his living. Note, Those ought to be relieved by charity whom the providence of God has any way disabled to get their own bread. Such objects of charity *by the way-side* ought not to be overlooked by us. Christ here cast a favourable eye upon a *common beggar*, and, though there are cheats among such, yet they must not therefore be all thought such.

II. Hearing the noise of a multitude passing by, he asked *what it meant, v.* 36. This we had not before. It teaches us that it is good to be *inquisitive*, and that those who are so some time or other find the benefit of it. Those who want their *sight* should make so much the better use of their *hearing*, and, when they cannot see with their own eyes, should, by *asking questions*, make use of other people's eyes. So this blind man did, and by that means came to understand that Jesus of Nazareth *passed by, v.* 37. It is good being in Christ's way; and, when we have an opportunity of applying ourselves to him, not to let it slip.

III. His prayer has in it a great deal both of faith and fervency: *Jesus, thou Son of David, have mercy on me, v.* 38. He owns Christ to be the *Son of David*, the Messiah promised; he believes him to be Jesus, a Saviour; he believes he is able to help and succour him, and earnestly begs his favour: "*Have mercy on me*, pardon my sin, pity my misery." Christ is a merciful king; those that apply themselves to him as the *Son of David* shall find him so, and ask enough for themselves when they pray, *Have mercy on us;* for Christ's mercy includes all.

IV. Those who are in good earnest for Christ's favours and blessings will not be put by from the pursuit of them, though they meet with opposition and rebuke. They who went along chid him as troublesome to the Master, noisy and impertinent, and bade him *hold his peace;* but he went on with his petition, nay, the check given him was but as a dam to a full stream, which makes it swell so much the more; he *cried the louder, Thou Son of David, have mercy on me.* Those who would speed in prayer must be importunate in prayer. This history, in the close of the chapter, intimates the same thing with the parable in the beginning of the chapter, that *men ought always to pray, and not to faint.*

V. Christ encourages poor beggars, whom men frown upon, and invites them to come to him, and is ready to entertain them, and bid them welcome: *He commanded him to be brought to him.* Note, Christ has more tenderness and compassion for distressed supplicants than any of his followers have. Though Christ was upon his journey, yet he stopped and *stood*, and *commanded him to be brought to him.* Those who had checked him must now lend him their hands to lead him to Christ.

VI. Though Christ knows all our wants, he will know them from us (*v.* 41): *What wilt thou that I shall do unto thee?* By spreading our case before God, with a particular representation of our wants and burdens, we teach ourselves to value the mercy we are in pursuit of; and it is necessary that we should, else we are not fit to receive it. This man poured out his soul before Christ, when he said, *Lord, that I may receive my sight.* Thus particular should we be in prayer, upon particular occasions.

VII. The prayer of faith, guided by Christ's encouraging promises, and grounded on them, shall not be in vain; nay, it shall not only receive an *answer of peace*, but of *honour* (*v.* 42); Christ said, *Receive thy sight, thy faith hath saved thee.* True faith will produce fervency in prayer, and both together will fetch in abundance of the fruits of Christ's favour; and they are then doubly comfortable when they come in that way, when we are *saved by faith.*

VIII. The *grace of Christ* ought to be thankfully acknowledged, to the *glory of God, v.* 43. 1. The poor beggar himself, that had his sight restored, *followed Christ, glorifying God.* Christ made it his business to glorify his Father; and those whom he healed *pleased him* best when they *praised God,* as those shall *please God* best who *praise Christ* and do him honour; for, in *confessing that he is Lord,* we *give glory to God the Father.* It is for the *glory of God* if we *follow Christ,* as those will do whose *eyes* are *opened.* 2. The *people that saw it* could not forbear *giving praise to God,* who had given such power to the *Son of man,* and by him had conferred such favours on the *sons of men.* Note, We must give praise to God for his mercies to others as well as for mercies to ourselves.

CHAP. XIX.

In this chapter we have, I. The conversion of Zaccheus the publican at Jericho, ver. 1—10. II. The parable of the pounds which the king entrusted with his servants, and of his rebellious citizens, ver. 11—27. III. Christ's riding in triumph (such triumph as it was) into Jerusalem; and his lamentation in prospect of the ruin of that city, ver. 28—44. IV. His teaching in the temple, and casting the buyers and sellers out of it, 45—48.

AND *Jesus* entered and passed
through Jericho. 2 And, behold,
there was a man named Zacchæus,
which was the chief among
the publicans, and he was rich. 3
And he sought to see Jesus who he
was; and could not for the press,
because he was little of stature. 4
And he ran before, and climbed up
into a sycomore tree to see him: for
he was to pass that *way.* 5 And
when Jesus came to the place, he
looked up, and saw him, and said
unto him, Zacchæus, make haste, and
come down; for to day I must abide
at thy house. 6 And he made haste,
and came down, and received him joyfully.
7 And when they saw *it,* they
all murmured, saying, That he was
gone to be guest with a man that is a
sinner. 8 And Zacchæus stood, and
said unto the Lord; Behold, Lord,
the half of my goods I give to the
poor; and if I have taken any thing
from any man by false accusation, I
restore *him* fourfold. 9 And Jesus
said unto him, This day is salvation
come to this house, forsomuch as he
also is a son of Abraham. 10 For
the Son of man is come to seek and
to save that which was lost.

Many, no doubt, were converted to the faith of Christ of whom no account is kept in the gospels; but the conversion of some, whose case had something in it extraordinary, is recorded, as this of Zaccheus. Christ passed through Jericho, *v.* 1. This city was built under a curse, yet Christ honoured it with his presence, for the gospel° *takes away the curse.* Though it ought not to have been built, yet it was not therefore a sin to live in it when it was built. Christ was now going from the other side Jordan to Bethany near Jerusalem, to raise Lazarus to life; when he was going to do one good work he contrived to do many by the way. He did good both to the *souls* and to the *bodies* of people; we have here an instance of the former. Observe,

I. Who, and what, this Zaccheus was. His name bespeaks him a Jew. *Zaccai* was a common name among the Jews; they had a famous rabbi, much about this time, of that name. Observe, 1. His calling, and the post he was in: *He was the chief among the publicans,* receiver-general; other publicans were officers under him; he was, as some think, farmer of the customs. We often read of publicans coming to Christ; but here was one that was *chief* of the publicans, was in authority, that enquired after him. God has his remnant among all sorts. Christ came to save even the *chief of sinners,* and therefore even the *chief of publicans.* 2. His circumstances in the world were very considerable: *He was rich.* The inferior publicans were commonly men of broken fortunes, and low in the world;° but he that was *chief of the publicans* had raised a good estate. Christ had lately shown how *hard* it is for *rich people to enter into the kingdom of God,* yet presently produces an instance of one rich man that had been lost, and was found, and that not as the prodigal by being reduced to want.

II. How he came in Christ's way, and what was the occasion of his acquaintance with him. 1. He had a great *curiosity to see Jesus,* what kind of a man he was, having heard great talk of him, *v.* 3. It is natural to us to come in sight, if we can, of those whose fame has filled our ears, as being apt to imagine there is something extraordinary in their countenances; at least, we shall be able to say hereafter that we have seen such and such *great men.* But the eye is *not satisfied with seeing.* We should now *seek to see Jesus* with an eye of faith, to see *who he is;* we should address ourselves in holy ordinances with this in our eye, *We would see Jesus.* 2. He could not get his curiosity gratified in this matter because he was *little,* and the crowd was *great.* Christ did not study to *show himself,* was not carried on men's shoulders (as the pope is in procession), that all men might see him; neither he nor his kingdom *came with observation.* He did not ride in an open chariot, as princes do, but, as *one of us,* he was *lost in a crowd;* for that was the day of his humiliation. Zaccheus was *low of stature,* and over-topped by all about him, so that he could not get a sight of Jesus. Many that are little of stature have large souls, and are lively in spirit.

Who would not rather be a Zaccheus than a Saul, though he was *higher by head and shoulders* than all about him? Let not those that are little of stature *take thought* of adding *cubits* to it. 3. Because he would not disappoint his curiosity he *forgot his gravity*, as chief of the publicans, and *ran before*, like a boy, and *climbed up into a sycamore-tree, to see him.* Note, Those that sincerely desire a sight of Christ will use the proper means for gaining a sight of him, and will break through a deal of difficulty and opposition, and be willing to take pains to see him. Those that find themselves *little* must take all the advantages they can get to *raise themselves* to a sight of Christ, and not be ashamed to own that they need them, and all little enough. Let not dwarfs despair, with good help, by aiming high to reach high.

III. The notice Christ took of him, the call he gave him to a further acquaintance (*v.* 5), and the efficacy of that call, *v.* 6. 1. Christ *invited himself* to Zaccheus's house, not doubting of his hearty welcome there; nay, wherever Christ comes, as he brings his own *entertainment* along with him, so he brings his own *welcome;* he opens the heart, and inclines it to receive him. Christ *looked* up into the tree, and *saw* Zaccheus. He came to look upon Christ, and resolved to take particular notice of him, but little thought of being taken notice of by Christ. That was an honour too great, and too far above his merit, for him to have any thought of. See how Christ *prevented* him with the blessings of his goodness, and *outdid* his expectations; and see how he *encouraged* very weak beginnings, and helped them forward. He that had a mind to know Christ shall be *known of him;* he that only courted to see him shall be admitted to converse with him. Note, Those that are faithful in a little shall be entrusted with more. And sometimes those that come to hear the word of Christ, as Zaccheus did, only for curiosity, beyond what they thought of, have their consciences awakened, and their hearts changed. Christ called him *by name, Zaccheus,* for he knows his chosen *by name; are they not in his book?* He might ask, as Nathanael did (John i. 48), *Whence knowest thou me?* But before he climbed the sycamore-tree Christ saw him, and knew him. He bade him *make haste, and come down.* Those that Christ calls must *come down,* must humble themselves, and not think to climb to heaven by any righteousness of their own; and they must *make haste* and come down, for delays are dangerous. Zaccheus must not hesitate, but hasten; he knows it is not a matter that needs consideration whether he should welcome such a guest to his house. He must *come down,* for Christ intends this day to *bait at his house,* and stay an hour or two with him. *Behold, he stands at the door and knocks.* 2. Zaccheus was *overjoyed* to have such an honour put upon his house (*v.* 6): *He made haste, and came down, and received him joyfully;* and his receiving him *into his house* was an indication and token of his receiving him *into his heart.* Note, When Christ *calls* to us we must *make haste* to answer his calls; and when he *comes to us* we must *receive him joyfully. Lift up your heads, O ye gates.* We may well *receive him joyfully* who brings all good along with him, and, when he takes possession of the soul, opens springs of joy there which shall flow to eternity. How often has Christ said to us, *Open to me,* when we have, with the spouse, made excuses! Cant. v. 2, 3. Zaccheus's forwardness to receive Christ will shame us. We have not now Christ to entertain in our houses, but we have his disciples, and what is done to them he takes as done to himself.

IV. The offence which the people took at this *kind greeting* between Christ and Zaccheus. Those narrow-souled censorious Jews *murmured,* saying that he was *gone to be a guest with a man that is a sinner,* παρὰ ἁμαρτωλῷ ἀνδρὶ—*with a sinful man;* and were not they themselves sinful men? Was it not Christ's errand into the world to seek and save *men* that are *sinners?* But Zaccheus they think to be a sinner above all men that dwelt in Jericho, such a sinner as was not fit to be conversed with. Now this was very unjust to blame Christ for going to *his house;* for, 1. Though he was a *publican,* and many of the publicans were *bad men,* it did not therefore follow that they were *all so.* We must take heed of condemning men in the lump, or by common fame, for at God's bar every man will be judged as he is. 2. Though he *had been a sinner,* it did not therefore follow that he was now as bad as he had been; though they knew his past life to be bad, Christ might know his present frame to be good. God allows room for repentance, and so must we. 3. Though he was *now a sinner,* they ought not to blame Christ for going to him, because he was in *no danger* of getting hurt by a sinner, but in *great hopes* of doing good to a sinner; whither should the physician go but to the sick? Yet see how that which is *well done* may be *ill construed.*

V. The proofs which Zaccheus gave publicly that, though he had been a *sinner,* he was now a *penitent,* and a true *convert, v.* 8. He does not expect to be justified by his works as the Pharisee who boasted of what he had done, but by his *good works* he will, through the grace of God, evidence the *sincerity* of his *faith* and *repentance;* and here he declares what his determination was. He made this declaration *standing,* that he might be seen and heard by those who murmured at Christ for coming to his house; *with the mouth confession is made* of repentance as well as faith. He *stood,* which denotes his saying it deliberately and with solemnity, in the nature of a vow to God. He addressed himself to Christ in it, not to the people (they were not to be his judges), but to the Lord, and he *stood* as it were at his bar. What we do that is good we must do *as unto him;* we must appeal to him, and approve ourselves to him, in our integrity, in all our good purposes and resolutions. He makes it appear that there is a change *in his heart* (and that is repentance), for there is a change in his way. His resolutions are of second-table duties; for Christ, upon all occasions, laid great stress on them: and they are such as are suited to his condition and character; for in them will best appear the truth of our repentance.

1. Zaccheus had a good estate, and, whereas he had been in it hitherto laying up treasure for himself, and doing hurt to himself, now he resolves that for the future he will be all towards God, and do good to others with it: *Behold, Lord, the half of my goods I give to the poor.* Not, "I *will* give it by my will when I die," but, "I *do* give it now." Probably he had heard of the command of trial which Christ gave to another rich man to sell what he had, and give to the poor (Matt. xix. 21), and how he broke with Christ upon it. "But so will not I," saith Zaccheus; "I agree to it at the first word; though hitherto I have been uncharitable to the poor, now I will relieve them, and give so much the more for having neglected the duty so long, even the *half of my goods.*" This is a very large proportion to be set apart for works of piety and charity. The Jews used to say that a fifth part of a man's income yearly was very fair to be given to pious uses, and about that share the law directed; but Zaccheus would go much further, and give one moiety to the poor, which would oblige him to retrench all his extravagant expenses, as his retrenching these would enable him to relieve many with his superfluities. If we were but more temperate and self-denying, we should be more charitable; and, were we content with less ourselves, we should have the more to give to them that need. This he mentions here as a fruit of his repentance. Note, It well becomes converts to God to be charitable to the poor.

2. Zaccheus was conscious to himself that he had not gotten all he had honestly and fairly, but some by indirect and unlawful means, and of what he had gotten by such means he promises to make restitution: "If *I have taken any thing from any man by false accusation,* or if I have wronged any man in the way of my business as a *publican,* exacting more than was appointed, I promise to restore him *four-fold.*" This was the restitution that a thief was to make, Exod. xxii. 1. (1.) He seems plainly to own that he had *done wrong;* his office, as a publican, gave him opportunity to do wrong, imposing upon the merchants to curry favour with the government. True penitents will own themselves not only in general guilty before God, but will particularly reflect upon that which has been their own iniquity, and which, by reason of their business and employment in the world, has most easily beset them. (2.) That he had done wrong *by false accusation;* this was the temptation of the publicans, which John Baptist had warned them of particularly, *ch.* iii. 14. They had the ear of the government, and every thing would be stretched in favour of the revenue, which gave them an opportunity of gratifying their revenge if they bore a man an ill will. (3.) He promises to restore *four-fold,* as far as he could recollect or find by his books that he had *wronged any man.* He does not say, "If I be sued, and compelled to it, I will make restitution" (some are *honest* when they cannot help it); but he will do it *voluntarily:* It shall be *my own act and deed.* Note, Those who are convinced of having done wrong cannot evidence the sincerity of their repentance but by *making restitution.* Observe, He does not think that his giving half his estate to the poor will atone for the wrong he has done. God *hates robbery for burnt-offerings,* and we must first *do justly* and then *love mercy.* It is no charity, but hypocrisy, to give that which is *none of our own;* and we are not to reckon that our own which we have not come honestly by, nor that our own which is not so when all our debts are paid, and restitution made for wrong done.

VI. Christ's *approbation* and *acceptance* of Zaccheus's conversion, by which also he cleared himself from any imputation in going to be a guest with him, *v.* 9, 10.

1. Zaccheus is declared to be now a *happy man.* Now he is turned from sin to God; now he has bidden Christ welcome to his house, and is become an honest, charitable, good man: *This day is salvation come to this house.* Now that he is *converted* he is in effect *saved,* saved from his sins, from the guilt of them, from the power of them; all the benefits of salvation are his. Christ is come *to his house,* and, where Christ comes, he brings salvation along with him. He is, and will be, the *Author of eternal salvation* to all that own him as Zaccheus did. Yet this is not all. Salvation this day *comes to his house.* (1.) When Zaccheus becomes a convert, he will be, more than he had been, a *blessing to his house.* He will bring the means of grace and salvation to his house, for he is a *son of Abraham* indeed now, and therefore, like Abraham, will teach his household to *keep the way of the Lord. He that is greedy of gain troubles his own house,* and brings a curse upon it (Hab. ii. 9), but he that is charitable to the poor does a kindness to his own house, and brings a blessing upon it and salvation to it, temporal at least, Ps. cxii. 3. (2.) When Zaccheus is brought to Christ himself his *family* also become related to Christ, and his children are admitted members of his church, and so *salvation comes to his house,* for that he is *a son of Abraham,* and

therefore interested in God's covenant with Abraham, that *blessing* of Abraham which comes upon the publicans, *upon the Gentiles,* through faith, that God will be a God *to them and to their children;* and therefore, when he believes, *salvation comes* to his house, as to the gaoler's, to whom it was said, Believe in the Lord Jesus Christ, *and thou shalt be saved, and thy house,* Acts xvi. 31. Zaccheus is by birth a son of Abraham, but, being a publican, he was deemed a heathen; they are put upon a level, Matt. xviii. 17. And as such the Jews were shy of conversing with him, and expected Christ should be so; but he shows that, being a true penitent, he is become *rectus in curia—upright in court,* as good a son of Abraham as if he had never been a publican, which therefore ought not to be mentioned against him.

2. What Christ had done to make him, in particular, a happy man, was consonant to the great design and intention of his coming into the world, *v.* 10. With the same argument he had before justified his conversing with publicans, Matt. ix. 13. There he pleaded that he came to *call sinners to repentance;* now that he came to *seek and save that which was lost, τὸ ἀπολωλός—the lost thing.* Observe, (1.) The *deplorable case* of the *sons of men:* they were *lost;* and here the whole race of mankind is spoken of as *one body.* Note, The whole world of mankind, by the fall, is become a *lost world:* lost as a city is lost when it has revolted to the rebels, as a traveller is lost when he has missed his way in a wilderness, as a sick man is lost when his disease is incurable, or as a prisoner is lost when sentence is passed upon him. (2.) The *gracious design* of the *Son of God:* he came to *seek and save,* to seek in order to saving. He came from heaven to earth (a long journey), to *seek* that which was *lost* (which had *wandered and gone astray*), and to bring it back (Matt. xviii. 11, 12), and to *save* that which was lost, which was perishing, and in a manner destroyed and cut off. Christ undertook the cause when it was given up for *lost;* undertook to bring those to themselves that were *lost* to God and all goodness. Observe, Christ *came* into this lost world to seek and save it. His design was to *save,* when *there was not salvation in any other.* In prosecution of that design, he *sought,* took all probable means to effect that salvation. He seeks those that were not worth seeking to; he seeks those that sought him not, and asked not for him, as Zaccheus here.

11 And as they heard these things,
he added and spake a parable, because
he was nigh to Jerusalem, and because
they thought that the kingdom of
God should immediately appear. 12
He said therefore, A certain nobleman
went into a far country to receive for
himself a kingdom, and to return. 13
And he called his ten servants, and
delivered them ten pounds, and said
unto them, Occupy till I come. 14
But his citizens hated him, and sent
a message after him, saying, We
will not have this *man* to reign over
us. 15 And it came to pass, that
when he was returned, having received
the kingdom, then he commanded
these servants to be called unto him,
to whom he had given the money,
that he might know how much every
man had gained by trading. 16 Then
came the first, saying, Lord, thy pound
hath gained ten pounds. 17 And he
said unto him, Well, thou good servant:
because thou hast been faithful in a
very little, have thou authority over
ten cities. 18 And the second came,
saying, Lord, thy pound hath gained
five pounds. 19 And he said likewise to him, Be thou also over five
cities. 20 And another came, saying,
Lord, behold, *here is* thy pound, which
I have kept laid up in a napkin: 21
For I feared thee, because thou art an
austere man: thou takest up that thou
layedst not down, and reapest that
thou didst not sow. 22 And he saith
unto him, Out of thine own mouth
will I judge thee, *thou* wicked servant.
Thou knewest that I was an austere
man, taking up that I laid not down,
and reaping that I did not sow: 23
Wherefore then gavest not thou my
money into the bank, that at my
coming I might have required mine
own with usury? 24 And he said
unto them that stood by, Take from
him the pound, and give *it* to him
that hath ten pounds. 25 (And they
said unto him, Lord, he hath ten
pounds). 26 For I say unto you, That
unto every one which hath shall be
given; and from him that hath not,
even that he hath shall be taken away
from him. 27 But those mine enemies, which would not that I should
reign over them, bring hither, and slay
them before me.

Our Lord Jesus is now upon his way to Jerusalem, to his last passover, when he was to suffer and die; now here we are told,

I. How the expectations of his friends

were *raised* upon this occasion: *They thought that the kingdom of God would immediately appear, v.* 11. The Pharisees expected it about this time (*ch.* xvii. 20), and, it seems, so did Christ's own disciples; but they both had a mistaken notion of it. The Pharisees thought that it must be introduced by some other temporal prince or potentate. The disciples thought that their Master would introduce it, but with temporal pomp and power, which, with the power he had to work miracles, they knew he could clothe himself with in a short time, whenever he pleased. Jerusalem, they concluded, must be the seat of his kingdom, and therefore, now that he is going directly thither, they doubt not but in a little time to see him upon the throne there. Note, Even good men are subject to mistakes concerning the kingdom of Christ, and to form wrong notions of it, and are ready to think that will *immediately* appear which is reserved for hereafter.

II. How their expectations were *checked*, and the mistakes *rectified* upon which they were founded; and this he does in three things:—

1. They expected that he should appear in his glory now *presently*, but he tells them that he must not be publicly installed in his kingdom for a great while yet. He is like *a certain nobleman ἄνθρωπός τις εὐγενὴς—a certain man of high birth* (so Dr. Hammond), for he is the Lord from heaven, and is entitled by birth to the kingdom; but he *goes into a far country, to receive for himself a kingdom.* Christ must go to heaven, to sit down at the right hand of the Father there, and to receive from him *honour and glory*, before the Spirit was poured out by which his kingdom was to be set up on earth, and before a church was to be set up for him in the Gentile world. He must receive the kingdom, and then *return.* Christ returned when the Spirit was poured out, when Jerusalem was destroyed, by which time that generation, both of friends and enemies, which he had personally conversed with, was wholly worn off by death, and gone to give up their account. But his chief return here meant is that at the great day, of which we are yet in expectation. That which they thought would *immediately appear*, Christ tells them will not appear till this same Jesus who is taken into heaven shall *in like manner come again;* see Acts i. 11.

2. They expected that his apostles and immediate attendants should be advanced to dignity and honour, that they should all be made princes and peers, privy-counsellors and judges, and have all the pomp and preferments of the court and of the town. But Christ here tells them that, instead of this, he designed them to be *men of business;* they must expect no other preferment in this world than that of the trading end of the town; he would set them up with a stock under their hands, that they might employ it themselves, in serving him and the interest of his kingdom among men. That is the true honour of a Christian and a minister which, if we be as we ought to be truly ambitious of it, will enable us to look upon all temporal honours with a holy contempt. The apostles had dreamed of *sitting on his right hand and on his left in his kingdom*, enjoying ease after their present toil and honour after the present contempt put upon them, and were pleasing themselves with this dream; but Christ tells them that which, if they understood it aright, would fill them with care, and concern, and serious thoughts, instead of those *aspiring* ones with which they filled their heads.

(1.) They have a *great work* to do now. Their Master leaves them, to receive his kingdom, and, at parting, he gives each of them a *pound*, which the margin of our common bibles tells us amounts in our money to *three pounds* and *half a crown;* this signifies the same thing with the talents in the parable that is parallel to this (Matt. xxv.), all the gifts with which Christ's apostles were endued, and the advantages and capacities which they had of serving the interests of Christ in the world, and others, both ministers and Christians, like them in a lower degree. But perhaps it is in the parable thus represented to make them the more humble; their honour in this world is only that of *traders*, and that not of first-rate merchants, who have vast stocks to begin upon, but that of poor traders, who must take a great deal of care and pains to make any thing of what they have. He gave these pounds to his servants, not to buy rich liveries, much less robes, and a splendid equipage, for themselves to appear in, as they expected, but with this charge: *Occupy till I come.* Or, as it might much better be translated, *Trade till I come*, Πραγματεύσασθε—*Be busy.* So the word properly signifies. "You are sent forth to preach the gospel, to set up a church for Christ in the world, to bring the nations to the obedience of faith, and to build them up in it. *You shall receive power to do this*, for you shall be filled with the *Holy Ghost*," Acts i. 8. When Christ *breathed on* the eleven disciples, saying, *Receive ye the Holy Ghost*, then he delivered them *ten pounds.* "Now," saith he, "mind your business, and make a business of it; set about it in good earnest, and stick to it. Lay out yourselves to do all the good you can to the souls of men, and to gather them in to Christ." Note, [1.] All Christians have *business* to do for Christ in this world, and ministers especially; the former were not *baptized*, nor the latter *ordained*, to be *idle.* [2.] Those that are called to business for Christ he furnishes with gifts necessary for their business; and, on the other hand, from those to whom he gives power he expects service. He delivers the *pounds* with this charge, Go work, go trade. *The manifestation of the Spirit is given to every man to profit withal*, 1 Cor. xii.

7. And *as every one has received the gift*, so let him *minister the same*, 1 Pet. iv. 10. [3.] We must continue to mind our business *till our Master comes*, whatever difficulties or oppositions we may meet with in it; those only that *endure to the end* shall *be saved*.

(2.) They have a *great account* to make shortly. These servants are *called to him*, to show what use they made of the gifts they were dignified with, what service they had done for Christ, and what good to the souls of men, *that he might know what every man had gained by trading*. Note,

[1.] They that trade diligently and faithfully in the service of Christ shall be *gainers*. We cannot say so of the business of the world; many a labouring tradesman has been a loser; but those that trade for Christ shall be *gainers;* though *Israel be not gathered*, yet they *will be glorious*.

[2.] The conversion of souls is the *winning* of them; every true convert is clear gain to Jesus Christ. Ministers are but factors for him, and to him they must give account what fish they have enclosed in the gospel-net, what guests they have prevailed with to come to the wedding-supper; that is, what they have *gained by trading*. Now observe,

First, The *good account* which was given by *some* of the servants, and the master's approbation of them. Two such are instanced, *v.* 16, 19. 1. They had both made considerable improvements, but not both *alike;* one had gained *ten pounds* by his trading, and another *five*. Those that are diligent and faithful in serving Christ are commonly blessed in being made blessings to the places where they live. They shall *see the travail of their soul*, and not *labour in vain*. And yet all that are alike *faithful* are not alike *successful*. And perhaps, though they were both faithful, it is intimated that one of them took more pains, and applied himself more closely to his business, than the other, and sped accordingly. Blessed Paul was surely this servant that gained *ten pounds*, double to what any of the rest did, for he *laboured more abundantly than they all*, and *fully preached the gospel of Christ*. 2. They both acknowledged their obligations to their Master for entrusting them with these abilities and opportunities to do him service: Lord, it is not *my* industry, but *thy* pound, that has gained *ten pounds*. Note, God must have all the glory of all our gains; *not unto us*, but unto him, must be *the praise*, Ps. cxv. 1. Paul, who gained the *ten pounds*, acknowledges, "*I laboured, yet not I. By the grace of God, I am what I am*, and do what I do; and *his grace was not in vain*," 1 Cor. xv. 10. He will not speak of what he had done, but of what *God had done by him*, Rom. xv. 18. 3. They were both commended for their fidelity and industry: *Well done, thou good servant*, *v.* 17. And to the other he *said likewise*, *v.* 19. Note, They who do that which is good shall have *praise of the same*. *Do well*, and Christ will say to thee, *Well done;* and, if he says *Well done*, the matter is not great who says otherwise. See Gen. iv. 7. 4. They were *preferred* in proportion to the improvement they had made: "*Because thou hast been faithful in a very little*, and didst not say, 'As good sit still as go to trade with one pound, what can one do with so small a stock?' but didst humbly and honestly apply thyself to the improvement of that, *have thou authority over ten cities*." Note, Those are in a fair way to rise who are content to begin low. *He that has used the office of a deacon well purchaseth to himself a good degree*, 1 Tim. iii. 13. Two things are hereby promised the apostles:—(1.) That when they have taken pains to *plant* many churches they shall have the satisfaction and honour of presiding in them, and governing among them; they shall have great respect paid them, and have a great interest in the love and esteem of good Christians. *He that keepeth the fig-tree shall eat the fruit thereof;* and he that *laboureth in the word and doctrine* shall be *counted worthy of double honour*. (2.) That, when they have served their generation, according to the will of Christ, though they pass through this world despised and trampled upon, and perhaps pass out of it under disgrace and persecution as the apostles did, yet in the other world they shall reign as kings with Christ, shall sit with him on his throne, shall have *power over the nations*, Rev. ii. 26. The happiness of heaven will be a much greater advancement to a good minister or Christian than it would be to a poor tradesman, that with much ado had cleared ten pounds, to be made governor of ten cities. He that had gained but *five pounds* had dominion over *five cities*. This intimates that there are *degrees of glory* in heaven; every vessel will be alike *full*, but not alike *large*. And the degrees of glory there will be according to the degrees of usefulness here.

Secondly, The *bad account* that was given by *one* of them, and the sentence passed upon him for his slothfulness and unfaithfulness, *v.* 20, &c. 1. He owned that he had not *traded* with the pound with which he had been entrusted (*v.* 20): "*Lord, behold, here is thy pound;* it is true, I have not made it *more*, but withal I have not made it *less;* I have kept it safely *laid up in a napkin*." This represents the carelessness of those who have gifts, but never lay out themselves to do good with them. It is all one to them whether the interests of Christ's kingdom sink or swim, go backward or forward; for their parts, they will take no care about it, no pains, be at no expenses, run no hazard. Those are the servants that lay up their pound *in a napkin* who think it enough to say that they have done no hurt in the world, but *did no good*. 2. He justified himself in his omission, with a plea that made the matter worse and not better (*v.* 21): *I feared thee, because thou art an austere man*, rigid and severe, ἄνθρωπος αὐστηρὸς εἶ. *Austere* is the Greek word itself: a *sharp* man: *Thou takest up that which thou laidst not down.* He thought that his master put a hardship upon his servants when he required and expected the improvement of their pounds, and that it was *reaping where he did not sow;* whereas really it was reaping where he *had sown*, and, as the husbandman, expecting in proportion to what he had sown. He had no reason to *fear* his master's austerity, nor blame his expectations, but this was a mere sham, a frivolous groundless excuse for his idleness, which there was no manner of colour for. Note, The pleas of slothful professors, when they come to be examined, will be found more to their *shame* than in their *justification*. 3. His excuse is turned upon him: *Out of thine own mouth will I judge thee, thou wicked servant, v.* 22. He will be *condemned* by his crime, but *self-condemned* by his plea. "If thou didst look upon it as hard that I should expect the profit of thy trading, which would have been the greater profit, yet, if thou hadst had any regard to my interest, thou mightest have put my money *into the bank*, into some of the funds, that I might have had, not only *my own*, but my own *with usury*, which, though a *less* advantage, would have been *some*." If he durst not *trade* for fear of *losing* the principal, and so being made accountable to his lord for it though it was lost, which he pretends, yet that would be no excuse for his not setting it out to interest, where it would be sure. Note, Whatever may be the pretences of slothful professors, in excuse of their slothfulness, the true reason of it is a reigning indifference to the interests of Christ and his kingdom, and their coldness therein. They care not whether religion gets ground or loses ground, so they can but live at ease. 4. His pound is taken from him, *v.* 24. It is fit that those should *lose* their gifts who will not *use* them, and that those who have dealt falsely should be no longer trusted. Those who will not serve their Master with what he bestows upon them, why should they be suffered to serve themselves with it? *Take from him the pound.* 5. It is given to him that had the *ten pounds.* When this was objected against by the standers-by, because he had so much already (*Lord, he has ten pounds, v.* 25), it is answered (*v.* 26), *Unto every one that hath shall be given.* It is the rule of justice, (1.) That those should be most encouraged who have been most industrious, and that those who have laid out themselves most to do good should have their opportunities of doing good *enlarged*, and be put into a higher and more extensive sphere of usefulness. To him that hath gotten shall more be given, that he may be in a capacity to get more. (2.) That those who have their gifts, as if they had them not, who have them to no purpose, who do no good with them, should be deprived of them. To those who endeavour to increase the grace they have, God will impart more; those who neglect it, and suffer it to decline, can expect no other than that God should do so too. This needful warning Christ gives to his disciples, lest, while they were gaping for honours on earth, they should neglect their business, and so come short of their happiness in heaven.

3. Another thing they expected was, that, when the kingdom of God should appear, the body of the Jewish nation would immediately fall in with it, and submit to it, and all their aversions to Christ and his gospel would immediately vanish; but Christ tells them that, after his departure, the generality of them would persist in their obstinacy and rebellion, and it would be their ruin. This is shown here,

(1.) In the message which his citizens sent after him, *v.* 14. They not only opposed him, while he was in obscurity; but, when he was gone into glory, to be invested in his kingdom, then they continued their enmity to him, protested against his dominion, and said, *We will not have this man to reign over us.* [1.] This was fulfilled in the prevailing infidelity of the Jews after the ascension of Christ, and the setting up of the gospel kingdom. They would not submit their necks to his yoke, nor touch the top of his golden sceptre. They said, *Let us break his bands in sunder*, Ps. ii. 1—3; Acts iv. 26. [2.] It speaks the language of all unbelievers; they could be content that Christ should *save them*, but they will not have him to *reign over them;* whereas Christ is a Saviour to those only to whom he is a prince, and who are willing to obey him.

(2.) In the sentence passed upon them at his return: *Those mine enemies bring hither, v.* 27. When his faithful subjects are preferred and rewarded, then he will take vengeance on his enemies, and particularly on the Jewish nation, the doom of which is here read. When Christ had set up his gospel kingdom, and thereby put reputation upon the gospel ministry, then he comes to *reckon with* the Jews; then it is remembered against them that they had particularly disclaimed and protested against his kingly office, when they said, *We have no king but Cæsar*, nor would own him for their king. They appealed to Cæsar, and to Cæsar they shall go; Cæsar shall be their ruin. Then the *kingdom of God appeared* when vengeance was taken on those irreconcileable enemies to Christ and his government; they were *brought forth and slain before him.* Never was so much slaughter made in any war as in the wars of the Jews. That nation lived to see Christianity victorious in the Gentile world, in spite of their enmity and opposition to it, and then it was *taken away as dross.* The wrath of Christ came upon them to the uttermost (1 Thess. ii. 15, 16), and their destruction redounded very much to the honour of Christ and the peace of the church. But this is applicable to all others who *persist* in their infidelity, and will undoubtedly perish in it. Note, [1.] Utter ruin will certainly be the portion of all Christ's enemies; in the day of vengeance they shall all be brought *forth,* and *slain before him. Bring them hither,* to be made a spectacle to saints and angels; see Josh. x. 22, 24. *Bring them hither,* that they may see the glory and happiness of Christ and his followers, whom they hated and persecuted. *Bring them hither,* to have their frivolous pleas overruled, and to receive sentence according to their merits. Bring them, and *slay them before me,* as Agag before Samuel. The Saviour whom they have slighted will stand by and see them slain, and not interpose on their behalf. [2.] Those that *will not have Christ to reign over them* shall be reputed and dealt with as his enemies. We are ready to think that none are Christ's enemies but persecutors of Christianity, or scoffers at least; but you see that those will be accounted so that dislike the terms of salvation, will not submit to Christ's yoke, but will be their own masters. Note, Whoever will not be *ruled* by the grace of Christ will inevitably be ruined by the wrath of Christ.

28 And when he had thus spoken,
he went before, ascending up to Jerusalem.
29 And it came to pass, when
he was come nigh to Bethphage and
Bethany, at the mount called *the
mount* of Olives, he sent two of his
disciples,
30 Saying, Go ye into the
village over against *you;* in the which
at your entering ye shall find a colt
tied, whereon yet never man sat:
loose him, and bring *him hither.*
31 And if any man ask you, Why do ye
loose *him?* thus shall ye say unto
him, Because the Lord hath need
of him.
32 And they that were sent
went their way, and found even as
he had said unto them.
33 And as
they were loosing the colt, the owners
thereof said unto them, Why loose ye
the colt?
34 And they said, the Lord
hath need of him.
35 And they
brought him to Jesus: and they cast
their garments upon the colt, and
they set Jesus thereon.
36 And as
he went, they spread their clothes in
the way.
37 And when he was come
nigh, even now at the descent of the
mount of Olives, the whole multitude
of the disciples began to rejoice and
praise God with a loud voice for all
the mighty works that they had seen;
38 Saying, Blessed *be* the King that
cometh in the name of the Lord:
peace in heaven, and glory in the
highest.
39 And some of the Pharisees from among the multitude said
unto him, Master, rebuke thy disciples.
40 And he answered and said
unto them, I tell you that, if these
should hold their peace, the stones
would immediately cry out.

We have here the same account of Christ's riding in some sort of triumph (such as it was) into Jerusalem which we had before in Matthew and Mark; let us therefore here only observe,

I. Jesus Christ was forward and willing to suffer and die for us. He went forward, *bound in the spirit, to Jerusalem,* knowing very well the *things* that should *befal him there,* and yet *he went before, ascending up to Jerusalem, v.* 28. He was the foremost of the company, as if he longed to be upon the spot, longed to engage, to take the field, and to enter upon action. Was he so forward to suffer and die for us, and shall we draw back from any service we are capable of doing for him?

II. It was no ways inconsistent either with Christ's humility or with his present state of humiliation to make a *public entry* into Jerusalem a little before he died. Thus he made himself to be the more taken notice of, that the ignominy of his death might appear the greater.

III. Christ is entitled to a dominion over all the creatures, and may use them when and as he pleases. No man has a property in his estate against Christ, but that *his* title is prior and superior. Christ sent to fetch an *ass* and her *colt* from their *owner's* and *master's crib,* when he had occasion for their service, and might do so, for all the *beasts of the forest are his,* and the tame beasts too.

IV. Christ has all men's hearts both under his eye and in his hand. He could influence those to whom the ass and the colt belonged to consent to their taking them away, as soon as they were told that the Lord had occasion for them.

V. Those that go on Christ's errands are sure to speed (*v.* 32): *They that were sent found* what he told them they should find, and the owners willing to part with them. It is a comfort to Christ's messengers that they shall bring what they are sent for, if indeed the Lord has occasion for it.

VI. The disciples of Christ, who fetch that for him from others which he has occasion for, and which they have not, should not think that enough, but, whatever they have themselves wherewith he may be served and honoured, they should be ready to serve him with it. Many can be willing to attend Christ at other people's expense who care not to be at any charge upon him themselves; but those disciples not only fetched the ass's colt for him, but *cast their* own *garments upon the colt,* and were willing that they should be used for his trappings.

VII. Christ's triumphs are the matter of his disciples' praises. When Christ came nigh to Jerusalem, God put it of a sudden into the hearts of the *whole multitude of the disciples,* not of the twelve only, but abundance more, that were disciples at large, *to rejoice and praise God* (*v.* 37), and the *spreading of their clothes in the way* (*v.* 36) was a common expression of joy, as at the feast of tabernacles. Observe, 1. What was the matter or occasion of their joy and praise. They praised God *for all the mighty works they had seen,* all the miracles Christ had wrought, especially the *raising of Lazarus,* which is particularly mentioned, John xii. 17, 18. That brought others to mind, for fresh miracles and mercies should revive the remembrance of the former. 2. How they expressed their joy and praise (*v.* 38): *Blessed be the king that cometh in the name of the Lord.* Christ is *the king;* he *comes in the name of the Lord,* clothed with a divine authority, commissioned from heaven to *give law* and treat of *peace. Blessed be he.* Let us *praise him,* let God *prosper him.* He is *blessed* for ever, and we will speak well of him. *Peace in heaven.* Let the God of heaven send peace and success to his undertaking, and then there will be *glory in the highest.* It will redound to the glory of the most high God; and the angels, the glorious inhabitants of the upper world, will give him the glory of it. Compare this song of the saints on earth with that of the angels, *ch.* ii. 14. They both agree to give glory to God in the highest. There the praises of both centre; the angels say, *On earth peace,* rejoicing in the benefit which men on earth have by Christ; the saints say, *Peace in heaven,* rejoicing in the benefit which the angels have by Christ. Such is the communion we have with the holy angels that, as *they* rejoice in the *peace on earth,* so *we* rejoice in the *peace in heaven,* the *peace* God *makes in his high places* (Job xxv. 2), and both in Christ, who hath reconciled all things to himself, whether *things on earth or things in heaven.*

VIII. Christ's triumphs, and his disciples' joyful praises of them, are the vexation of proud Pharisees, that are enemies to him and his kingdom. There were some Pharisees among *the multitude* who were so far from joining with them that they were enraged at them, and, Christ being a famous example of humility, they thought that he would not admit such acclamations as these, and therefore expected that he should *rebuke his disciples, v.* 39. But it is the honour of Christ that, as he despises the contempt of the proud, so he accepts the praises of the humble.

IX. Whether men praise Christ or no he will, and shall, and must be praised (*v.* 40): *If these should hold their peace,* and not speak the praises of the Messiah's kingdom, *the stones would immediately cry out,* rather than that Christ should not be praised. This was, in effect, literally fulfilled, when, upon men's reviling Christ upon the cross, instead of praising him, and his own disciples' sinking into a profound silence, the *earth did quake and the rocks rent.* Pharisees would silence the praises of Christ, but they cannot gain their point; for as God can *out of stones raise up children unto Abraham,* so he can out of the mouths of those children perfect praise.

41 And when he was come near,
he beheld the city, and wept over it.
42 Saying, If thou hadst known, even
thou, at least in this thy day, the
things *which belong* unto thy peace!
but now they are hid from thine eyes.
43 For the days shall come upon thee,
that thine enemies shall cast a trench
about thee, and compass thee round,
and keep thee in on every side, 44
And shall lay thee even with the
ground, and thy children within thee;
and they shall not leave in thee one
stone upon another; because thou
knewest not the time of thy visitation.
45 And he went into the temple,
and began to cast out them that sold
therein, and them that bought; 46
Saying unto them, It is written, My
house is the house of prayer: but ye
have made it a den of thieves. 47
And he taught daily in the temple.
But the chief priests and the scribes
and the chief of the people sought to
destroy him, 48 And could not find
what they might do: for all the people were very attentive to hear him.

The great Ambassador from heaven is here making his public entry into Jerusalem, not to be *respected* there, but to be *rejected;* he knew what a nest of vipers he was throwing himself into, and yet see here two instances of his love to that place and his concern for it.

I. The *tears he shed* for the *approaching ruin* of the *city* (*v.* 41): *When he was come near, he beheld the city, and wept over it.* Probably, it was when he was coming down the descent of the hill from the *mount of Olives,* where he had a full view of the city, the large extent of it, and the many stately structures in it, and his eye affected his heart, and his heart his eye again. See here,

1. What a tender spirit Christ was of; we never read that he laughed, but we often find him in tears. In this very place his father David wept, and those that were with him, though he and they were *men of war.* There are cases in which it is no disparagement to the stoutest of men to melt into tears.

2. That Jesus Christ *wept* in the midst of his triumphs, *wept* when all about him were *rejoicing*, to show how little he was elevated with the applause and acclamation of the people. Thus he would teach us to *rejoice with trembling*, and *as though we rejoiced not.* If Providence do not stain the beauty of our triumphs, we may ourselves see cause to sully it with our sorrows.

3. That he *wept over Jerusalem.* Note, There are cities to be wept over, and none to be more lamented than Jerusalem, that had been the holy city, and the joy of the whole earth, if it be degenerated. But why did Christ weep at the sight of Jerusalem? Was it because "Yonder is the city in which I must be betrayed and bound, scourged and spit upon, condemned and crucified?" No, he himself gives us the reason of his tears.

(1.) Jerusalem has not improved the day of her opportunities. He wept, and said, *If thou hadst known, even thou at least in this thy day*, if thou wouldest but yet know, while the gospel is preached to thee, and salvation offered thee by it; if thou wouldest at length bethink thyself, and understand *the things that belong to thy peace*, the making of thy peace with God, and the securing of thine own spiritual and eternal welfare—but thou *dost not know the day of thy visitation, v.* 44. The manner of speaking is abrupt: *If thou hadst known! O that thou hadst*, so some take it; like that *O that my people had hearkened unto me*, Ps. lxxxi. 13; Isa. xlviii. 18. Or, *If thou hadst known, well;* like that of the *fig-tree, ch.* xiii. 9. How happy had it been for thee! Or, "If thou hadst known, thou wouldest have wept for thyself, and I should have no occasion to weep for thee, but should have rejoiced rather." What he says lays all the blame of Jerusalem's impending ruin upon herself. Note, [1.] There are things which *belong to our peace*, which we are all concerned to *know* and *understand;* the way how peace is made, the offers made of peace, the terms on which we may have the benefit of peace. The things that belong to our peace are those things that relate to our present and future welfare; these we must know with application. [2.] There is a *time of visitation* when those things which *belong to our peace* may be *known by us*, and known to good purpose. When we enjoy the means of grace in great plenty, and have the word of God powerfully preached to us —when the Spirit strives with us, and our own consciences are startled and awakened—then is the *time of visitation*, which we are concerned to improve. [3.] With those that have long neglected the time of their visitation, if at length, if at last, in this their day, their eyes be opened, and they bethink themselves, all will be well yet. Those shall not be refused that come into the vineyard *at the eleventh hour.* [4.] It is the amazing folly of multitudes that enjoy the means of grace, and it will be of fatal consequence to them, that they do not improve the day of their opportunities. The *things of their peace* are revealed to them, but are not minded or regarded by them; they *hide their eyes* from them, as if they were not worth taking notice of. They are not aware of the *accepted time* and the *day of salvation*, and so let it slip and perish through mere carelessness. None are so *blind* as those that will not *see;* nor have any the things of their peace more certainly hidden from their eyes than those that turn their back upon them. [5.] The sin and folly of those that persist in a contempt of gospel grace are a great grief to the Lord Jesus, and should be so to us. He looks with weeping eyes upon lost souls, that continue impenitent, and run headlong upon their own ruin; he had rather that they would *turn and live* than *go on and die*, for he is not willing that any should perish.

(2.) Jerusalem cannot escape the day of her desolation. The *things of her peace* are now in a manner hidden from her eyes; they will be shortly. Not but that after this the gospel was preached to them by the apostles; *all the house of Israel* were called to *know assuredly* that Christ was their *peace* (Acts ii. 36), and multitudes were convinced and converted. But as to the body of the nation, and the leading part of it, they were sealed up under unbelief; God had *given them the spirit of slumber*, Rom. xi. 8. They were so prejudiced and enraged against the gospel, and those few that did embrace it then, that nothing less than a miracle of divine grace (like that which converted Paul) would work upon them; and it could not be expected that such a miracle should be wrought, and so they were justly given up to *judicial* blindness and hardness. The *peaceful things* are not *hidden from the eyes* of particular persons; but it is too late to think now of the nation of the Jews, *as such*, becoming a Christian nation, by embracing Christ. And therefore they are marked for ruin, which Christ here foresees and foretels, as the certain consequence of their rejecting Christ. Note, Neglecting the great salvation often brings temporal judgments upon a people; it did so upon Jerusalem in less than forty years after this, when all that Christ here foretold was exactly fulfilled. [1.] The Romans besieged the city, *cast a trench about it, compassed it round*, and *kept their* inhabitants in *on every side.* Josephus relates that Titus ran up a wall in a very short time, which surrounded the city, and cut off all hopes of escaping. [2.] They *laid it even with the ground.* Titus commanded his soldiers to *dig up the city*, and the whole compass of it was levelled, except three towers; see Josephus's history of the wars of the Jews, *lib.* 5, *cap.* 27; *lib.* 7, *cap.* 1. Not only the city, but the citizens were laid even with the ground *(thy children within thee)*, by the cruel slaughters that were made of them:

and there was scarcely one stone *left upon another*. This was for their crucifying Christ; this was because they *knew not the day of their visitation*. Let other cities and nations take warning.

II. The *zeal he showed* for the *present purification of the temple*. Though it must be destroyed ere long, it does not therefore follow that no care must be taken of it in the mean time.

1. Christ cleared it of those who profaned it. He went straight to the temple, and *began to cast out the buyers and sellers*, *v.* 45. Hereby (though he was represented as an enemy to the temple, and that was the crime laid to his charge before the high priest) he made it to appear that he had a truer love for the temple than they had who had such a veneration for its corban, its treasury, as a sacred thing; for its purity was more its glory than its wealth was. Christ gave a reason for his dislodging the temple-merchants, *v.* 46. The temple is a *house of prayer*, set apart for communion with God: the *buyers* and *sellers* made it a *den of thieves* by the fraudulent bargains they made there, which was by no means to be suffered, for it would be a distraction to those who came there to pray.

2. He put it to the best use that ever it was put to, for he *taught daily in the temple*, *v.* 47. Note, It is not enough that the corruptions of a church be purged out, but the preaching of the gospel must be encouraged. Now, when Christ preached in the temple, observe here, (1.) How spiteful the church-rulers were against him; how industrious to seek an *opportunity, or pretence* rather, to do him a mischief (*v.* 47): *The chief priests and scribes, and the chief of the people*, the great sanhedrim, that should have attended him, and summoned the people too to attend him, *sought to destroy him*, and put him to death. (2.) How respectful the common people were to him. They were *very attentive to hear him*. He spent most of his time in the country, and did not then preach in the temple, but, when he did, the people paid him great respect, attended on his preaching with diligence, and let no opportunity slip of hearing him, attended to it with care, and would not lose a word. Some read it, *All the people, as they heard him, took his part;* and so it comes in very properly as a reason why his enemies *could not find what they might* do against him; they saw the people ready to fly in their faces if they offered him any violence. Till his hour was come his interest in the common people protected him; but, when his hour was come, the chief priests' influence upon the common people delivered him up.

CHAP. XX.

In this chapter we have, I. Christ's answer to the chief priests' question concerning his authority, ver. 1—8. II. The parable of the vineyard let out to the unjust and rebellious husbandmen, ver. 9—19. III. Christ's answer to the question proposed to him concerning the lawfulness of paying tribute to Cæsar, ver. 20–26. IV. His vindication of that great fundamental doctrine of the Jewish and Christian institutes – the resurrection of the dead and the future state, from the foolish cavils of the Sadducees ver. 27–38. V. His puzzling the scribes with a question concerning the Messiah's being the Son of David, ver. 39–44. VI. The caution he gave his disciples to take heed of the scribes, ver. 45–47. All which passages we had before in Matthew and Mark, and therefore need not enlarge upon them here, unless on those particulars which we had not there.

AND it came to pass, *that* on one
of those days, as he taught the
people in the temple, and preached
the gospel, the chief priests and the
scribes came upon *him* with the elders,
2 And spake unto him, saying, Tell
us, by what authority doest thou these
things? or who is he that gave thee
this authority? 3 And he answered
and said unto them, I will also ask
you one thing; and answer me: 4
The baptism of John, was it from
heaven, or of men? 5 And they
reasoned with themselves, saying, If
we shall say, From heaven; he will
say, Why then believed ye him not?
6 But and if we say, Of men; all the
people will stone us: for they be persuaded that John was a prophet. 7
And they answered, that they could
not tell whence *it was*. 8 And Jesus
said unto them, Neither tell I you
by what authority I do these things.

In this passage of story nothing is added here to what we had in the other evangelists; but only in the first verse, where we are told,

I. That he was now *teaching the people in the temple*, and *preaching the gospel*. Note, Christ was a preacher of his own gospel. He not only *purchased* the salvation for us, but *published* it to us, which is a great confirmation of the truth of the gospel, and gives abundant encouragement to us to receive it, for it is a sign that the heart of Christ was much upon it, to have it received. This likewise puts an honour upon the preachers of the gospel, and upon their office and work, how much soever they are despised by a vain world. It puts an honour upon the *popular preachers* of the gospel; Christ condescended to the capacities of the *people* in preaching the gospel, and *taught them*. And observe, when he was *preaching the gospel to the people* he had this interruption given him. Note, Satan and his agents do all they can to hinder the *preaching of the gospel to the people*, for nothing weakens the interest of Satan's kingdom more.

II. That his enemies are here said to *come upon him*—ἐπέστησαν. The word is used only here, and it intimates

1. That they thought to surprise him with this question; they *came upon him* suddenly, hoping to catch him unprovided with an answer, as if this were not a thing he had himself thought of.

2. That they thought to frighten him with

this question. They *came upon him* in a body, with violence. But how could he be terrified with the *wrath of men*, when it was in his *own power to restrain it*, and make it turn to his praise? From this story itself we may learn, (1.) That it is not to be thought strange, if even that which is evident to a demonstration be disputed, and called in question, as a doubtful thing, by those that shut their eyes against the light. Christ's miracles plainly showed *by what authority he did these things*, and sealed his commission; and yet this is that which is here *arraigned*. (2.) Those that question Christ's authority, if they be but catechized themselves in the plainest and most evident principles of religion, will have their folly made manifest unto all men. Christ answered these priests and scribes with a question concerning the baptism of John, a plain question, which the meanest of the common people could answer: *Was it from heaven or of men?* They all knew it was *from heaven;* there was nothing in it that had an earthly relish or tendency, but it was all heavenly and divine. And this question gravelled them, and ran them aground, and served to shame them before the people. (3.) It is not strange if those that are governed by reputation and secular interest imprison the plainest truths, and smother and stifle the strongest convictions, as these priests and scribes did, who, to save their credit, would not own that John's baptism was *from heaven*, and had no other reason why they did not say it was *of men* but because they *feared the people*. What good can be expected from men of such a spirit? (4.) Those that bury the knowledge they have are justly denied further knowledge. It was just with Christ to refuse to give an account of his authority to them that knew the baptism of John to be from heaven and would not believe in him, nor own their knowledge, *v.* 7, 8.

9 Then began he to speak to the
people this parable; A certain man
planted a vineyard, and let it forth to
husbandmen, and went into a far
country for a long time. 10 And at
the season he sent a servant to the
husbandmen, that they should give
him of the fruit of the vineyard: but
the husbandmen beat him, and sent
him away empty. 11 And again he
sent another servant: and they beat
him also, and entreated *him* shamefully, and sent *him* away empty. 12
And again he sent a third: and they
wounded him also, and cast *him* out.
13 Then said the lord of the vineyard,
What shall I do? I will send my
beloved son: it may be they will reverence *him* when they see him. 14
But when the husbandmen saw him,
they reasoned among themselves, saying, This is the heir: come, let us
kill him, that the inheritance may be
ours. 15 So they cast him out of
the vineyard, and killed *him*. What
therefore shall the lord of the vineyard do unto them? 16 He shall
come and destroy these husbandmen,
and shall give the vineyard to others.
And when they heard *it*, they said,
God forbid. 17 And he beheld them,
and said, What is this then that is
written, The stone which the builders
rejected, the same is become the head
of the corner? 18 Whosoever shall
fall upon that stone shall be broken;
but on whomsoever it shall fall, it will
grind him to powder. 19 And the
chief priests and the scribes the same
hour sought to lay hands on him;
and they feared the people: for they
perceived that he had spoken this parable against them.

Christ spoke this parable against those who were resolved not to own his authority, though the evidence of it was ever so full and convincing; and it comes very seasonably to show that by questioning his authority they forfeited their own. Their disowning the lord of their vineyard was a defeasance of their lease of the vineyard, and a giving up of all their title.

I. The parable has nothing added here to what we had before in Matthew and Mark. The scope of it is to show that the Jewish nation, by persecuting the prophets, and at length Christ himself, had provoked God to take away from them all their church privileges, and to abandon them to ruin. It teaches us, 1. That those who enjoy the privileges of the visible church are as tenants and farmers that have a vineyard to look after, and rent to pay for it. God, by setting up revealed religion and instituted orders in the world, hath planted a vineyard, which he lets out to those people among whom his tabernacle is, *v.* 9. And they have *vineyard-work* to do, needful and constant work, but pleasant and profitable. Whereas man was, for sin, condemned to *till the ground*, they that have a place in the church are restored to that which was Adam's work in innocency, to *dress the garden*, and to keep it; for the church is a paradise, and Christ the tree of life in it. They have also *vineyard-fruits* to present to the Lord of the vineyard. There are rents to be paid and services to be done, which, though bearing no proportion to the value of the premises, yet must be *done* and must be *paid*. 2. That the work of God's ministers is to call upon those who enjoy the privileges of the church to *bring forth fruit* accordingly. They are God's rent-gatherers, to put the husbandmen in mind of their arrears, or rather to put them in mind that they have a landlord who expects to hear from them, and to receive some acknowledgment of their dependence on him, and obligations to him, *v.* 10. The Old-Testament prophets were sent on this errand to the Jewish church, to demand from them the duty and obedience they owed to God. 3. That it has often been the lot of God's faithful servants to be wretchedly abused by his own tenants; they have been *beaten* and *treated* shamefully by those that resolved to *send them empty* away. They that are resolved not to do their duty to God cannot bear to be called upon to do it. Some of the best men in the world have had the hardest usage from it, for their best services. 4. That God sent his Son into the world to carry on the same work that the prophets were employed in, to *gather the fruits of the vineyard* for God; and one would have thought that he would have been reverenced and received. The prophets spoke as *servants, Thus saith the Lord;* but Christ *as a Son*, among his own, *Verily I say unto you.* Putting such an honour as this upon them, to send him, one would have thought, should have won upon them. 5. That those who reject Christ's ministers would reject Christ himself if he should come to them; for it has been tried, and found that the persecutors and murderers of his servants the prophets were the persecutors and murderers of himself. They said, *This is the heir, come let us kill him.* When they slew the servants, there were other servants sent. " But, if we can but be the death of the son, there is never another son to be sent, and then we shall be no longer molested with these demands; we may have a quiet possession of the vineyard for ourselves." The scribes and Pharisees promised themselves that, if they could but get Christ out of the way, they should for ever ride masters in the Jewish church; and therefore they took the bold step, they *cast him out of the vineyard, and killed him.* 6. That the putting of Christ to death filled up the measure of the Jewish iniquity, and brought upon them ruin without remedy. No other could be expected than that God should *destroy those wicked husbandmen.* They began in *not paying their rent*, but then proceeded to beat and kill the servants, and at length their young Master himself. Note, Those that live in the neglect of their duty to God know not what degrees of sin and destruction they are running themselves into.

II. To the application of the parable is added here, which we had not before, their deprecation of the doom included in it (*v.* 16): *When they heard it, they said, God forbid,* Μὴ γένοιτο—*Let not this be done,* so it should be read. Though they could not but own that for such a sin such a punishment was just, and what might be expected, yet they could not bear to hear of it. Note, It is an instance of the folly and stupidity of sinners that they proceed and persevere in their sinful ways though at the same time they have a foresight and dread of the destruction that is at the end of those ways. And see what a cheat they put upon themselves, to think to avoid it by a cold *God forbid*, when they do nothing towards the preventing of it; but will this make the threatening of no effect? No, they shall know whose word shall stand, God's or theirs. Now observe what Christ said, in answer to this childish deprecation of their ruin. 1. He *beheld them.* This is taken notice of only by this evangelist, *v.* 17. He *looked upon* them with pity and compassion, grieved to see them cheat themselves thus to their own ruin. He *beheld them*, to see if they would blush at their own folly, or if he could discern in their countenances any indication of relenting. 2. He referred them to the scripture: " *What is this then that is written?* How can you escape the judgment of God, when you cannot prevent the exaltation of him whom you despise and reject? The word of God hath said it, that *the stone which the builders rejected is become the head of the corner.*" The Lord Jesus will be exalted to the Father's right hand. He has all judgment and all power committed to him; he is the corner-stone and top-stone of the church, and, if so, his enemies can expect no other than to be destroyed. Even those that slight him, that stumble at him, and are offended in him, *shall be broken*—it will be their ruin; but as to those that not only reject him, but hate and persecute him, as the Jews did, he will fall upon them and crush them to pieces—will *grind them to powder.* The condemnation of spiteful persecutors will be much sorer than that of careless unbelievers.

Lastly, We are told how the chief priests and scribes were exasperated by this parable (*v.* 19): *They perceived that he had spoken this parable against them;* and so he had. A guilty conscience needs no accuser; but they, instead of yielding to the convictions of conscience, fell into a rage at him who awakened that sleeping lion in their bosoms, and *sought to lay hands on him.* Their corruptions rebelled against their convictions, and got the victory. And it was not because they had any fear of God or of his wrath before their eyes, but only because they *feared the people*, that they did not now fly in his face, and take him by the throat. They were just ready to make his words good: *This is the heir, come let us kill him.* Note, When the hearts of the sons of men are fully set in them to do evil, the fairest warnings both of the sin they are about to commit and of the consequences of it make no impression upon them. Christ tells them that instead of *kissing the Son* of God they would *kill him*, upon which they should have said, *What, is thy servant a dog?* But they do, in effect, say this: " And so we will; have at him now." And, though they deprecate the punishment of the sin, in the next breath they are projecting the commission of it.

20 And they watched *him*, and
sent forth spies, which should feign
themselves just men, that they might
take hold of his words, that so they
might deliver him unto the power and
authority of the governor. 21 And
they asked him, saying, Master, we
know that thou sayest and teachest
rightly, neither acceptest thou the
person *of any*, but teachest the way
of God truly: 22 Is it lawful for us
to give tribute unto Cæsar, or no? 23
But he perceived their craftiness, and
said unto them, Why tempt ye me? 24
Show me a penny. Whose image and
superscription hath it? They answered
and said, Cæsar's. 25 And he said
unto them, Render therefore unto
Cæsar the things which be Cæsar's,
and unto God the things which be
God's. 26 And they could not take
hold of his words before the people:
and they marvelled at his answer, and
held their peace.

We have here Christ's evading a snare which his enemies laid for him, by proposing a question to him about tribute. We had this passage before, both in Matthew and Mark. Here is,

I. The mischief designed him, and that is more fully related here than before. The plot was to *deliver him unto the power and authority of the governor, v.* 20. They could not themselves put him to death by course of law, nor otherwise than by a *popular tumult*, which they could not depend upon; and, since they could not be his judges, they would willingly condescend to be his prosecutors and accusers, and would themselves *inform* against him. They hoped to gain their point, if they could but incense the governor against him. Note, It has been the common artifice of persecuting church-rulers to make the secular powers the tools of their malice, and oblige the *kings of the earth to do* their drudgery, who, if they had not been instigated, would have let their neighbours live quietly by them, as Pilate did Christ till the chief priests and the scribes presented Christ to him. But thus Christ's word must be fulfilled by their cursed politics, that he should be *delivered into the hands of the Gentiles*.

II. The persons they employed. Matthew and Mark told us that they were disciples of the Pharisees, with some Herodians. Here it is added, They were *spies, who should feign themselves just men*. Note, It is no new thing for *bad men* to feign themselves *just men*, and to cover the most wicked projects with the most specious and plausible pretences. The devil can *transform himself into an angel of light*, and a Pharisee appear in the garb, and speak the language, of a disciple of Christ. A spy must go in disguise. These spies must take on them to have a value for Christ's judgment, and to depend upon it as an oracle, and therefore must desire his advice in a case of conscience. Note, Ministers are concerned to stand upon their guard against some that feign themselves to be *just men*, and to be *wise as serpents* when they are in the midst of a *generation of vipers* and *scorpions*.

III. The question they proposed, with which they hoped to ensnare him. 1. Their preface is very courtly: *Master, we know that thou sayest and teachest rightly, v.* 21. Thus they thought to flatter him into an incautious freedom and openness with them, and so to gain their point. They that are proud, and love to be commended, will be brought to do any thing for those that will but flatter them, and speak kindly to them; but they were much mistaken who thought thus to impose upon the humble Jesus. He was not pleased with the testimony of such hypocrites, nor thought himself honoured by it. It is true that he *accepts not the person of any*, but it is as true that he knows the hearts of all, and knew theirs, and the *seven abominations* that were there, though they *spoke fair*. It was certain that he *taught the way of God truly;* but he knew that they were unworthy to be taught by him, who came to *take hold of his words*, not to be *taken hold of* by them. 2. Their case is very nice: "Is it lawful *for us*" (this is added here in Luke) "*to give tribute to Cæsar*—for us Jews, us the free-born seed of Abraham, us that pay the Lord's tribute, may we give tribute to Cæsar?" Their pride and covetousness made them loth to pay taxes, and then they would have it a question whether it was lawful or no. Now if Christ should say that *it was lawful* the people would take it ill, for they expected that he who set up to be the Messiah should in the first place free them from the Roman yoke, and stand by them in denying tribute to Cæsar. But if he should say that *it was not lawful*, as they expected he would (for if he had not been of that mind they thought he could not have been so much the darling of the people as he was), then they should have something to accuse him of to the governor, which was what they wanted.

IV. His evading the snare which they laid for him: *He perceived their craftiness, v.* 23. Note, Those that are most crafty in their designs against Christ and his gospel cannot with all their art conceal them from his cognizance. He can see through the most politic disguises, and so break through the most dangerous snare; for *surely in vain is the net spread in the sight of any bird.* He did not give them a direct answer, but reproved them for offering to impose upon him—*Why tempt ye me?* and called for a *piece of money*, current money with the merchants—*Show me a penny;* and asked them whose money it was, whose stamp it bore, who coined it. They owned, "It is Cæsar's money." "Why then," saith Christ, "you should first have asked whether it was lawful to *pay* and *receive* Cæsar's money among yourselves, and to admit that to be the instrument of your commerce. But, having granted this by a common consent, you are concluded by your own act, and, no doubt, you ought to give tribute to him who furnished you with this convenience for your trade, protects you in it, and lends you the sanction of his authority for the value of your money. You must therefore *render to Cæsar the things that are Cæsar's.* In civil things you ought to submit to the civil powers, and so, if Cæsar protects you in your civil rights by laws and the administration of justice, you ought to *pay him tribute;* but in sacred things God only is your King. You are not bound to be of Cæsar's religion; you must *render to God the things that are God's,* must worship and adore him only, and not any golden image that Cæsar sets up;" and we must worship and adore him in such way as he has appointed, and not according to the inventions of Cæsar. It is God only that has authority to say, *My son, give me thy heart.*

V. The confusion they were hereby put into, *v.* 26. 1. The snare is broken: *They could not take hold of his words before the people.* They could not fasten upon any thing wherewith to incense either the governor or the people against him. 2. Christ is honoured; even the wrath of man is made to praise him. They *marvelled at his answer,* it was so discreet and unexceptionable, and such an evidence of that wisdom and sincerity which make the face to shine. 3. Their mouths are stopped; they *held their peace.* They had nothing to object, and durst ask him nothing else, lest he should shame and expose them.

27 Then came to *him* certain of
the Sadducees, which deny that there
is any resurrection; and they asked
him, 28 Saying, Master, Moses wrote
unto us, If any man's brother die,
having a wife, and he die without
children, that his brother should take
his wife, and raise up seed unto his
brother. 29 There were therefore
seven brethren: and the first took a
wife, and died without children. 30
And the second took her to wife, and
he died childless. 31 And the third
took her; and in like manner the
seven also: and they left no children,
and died. 32 Last of all the woman
died also. 33 Therefore in the resurrection whose wife of them is she?
for seven had her to wife. 34 And
Jesus answering said unto them, The
children of this world marry, and are
given in marriage: 35 But they which
shall be accounted worthy to obtain
that world, and the resurrection from
the dead, neither marry, nor are given
in marriage: 36 Neither can they die
any more: for they are equal unto
the angels; and are the children of
God, being the children of the resurrection. 37 Now that the dead are
raised, even Moses showed at the bush,
when he calleth the Lord the God of
Abraham, and the God of Isaac, and
the God of Jacob. 38 For he is not
the God of the dead, but of the
living: for all live unto him.

This discourse with the Sadducees we had before, just as it is here, only that the description Christ gives of the future state is somewhat more full and large here. Observe here,

I. In every age there have been men of corrupt minds, that have endeavoured to subvert the fundamental principles of revealed religion. As there are deists now, who call themselves *free*-thinkers, but are really *false*-thinkers; so there were Sadducees in our Saviour's time, who bantered the doctrine of the resurrection of the dead and the life of the world to come, though they were plainly revealed in the Old Testament, and were articles of the Jewish faith. The Sadducees deny that *there is any resurrection,* any *future state,* so *ἀνάστασις* may signify; not only no return of the body *to life,* but no continuance of the soul *in life,* no world of spirits, no state of recompence and retribution for what was done in the body. Take away this, and all religion falls to the ground.

II. It is common for those that design to undermine any truth of God to perplex it, and load it with difficulties. So these Sadducees did; when they would weaken people's faith in the doctrine of the resurrection, they put a question upon the supposition of it, which they thought could not be answered either way to satisfaction. The case perhaps was matter of fact, at least it might be so, of a woman that had *seven husbands.* Now in the resurrection *whose wife shall she be?* whereas it was not at all material whose she was, for when death puts an end to that relation it is not to be resumed.

III. There is a great deal of difference between the state of the children of men on earth and that of the children of God in heaven, a vast unlikeness between *this world* and *that world;* and we wrong ourselves, and wrong the truth of Christ, when we form our notions of that world of spirits by our present enjoyments in this world of sense.

1. The children of men in this world *marry, and are given in marriage, υἱοὶ τοῦ αἰῶνος τούτου—the children of this age,* this generation, both good and bad, marry themselves and give their children in marriage. Much of our business in this world is to raise and build up families, and to provide for them. Much of our pleasure in this world is in our relations, our wives and children; nature inclines to it. Marriage is instituted for the comfort of human life, here in this state where we carry bodies about with us. It is likewise a remedy against fornication, that natural desires might not become brutal, but be under direction and control. The *children of this* world are dying and going off the stage, and *therefore* they marry and give their children in marriage, that they may furnish the world of mankind with needful recruits, that as one generation passeth away another may come, and that they may have some of their own offspring to leave the fruit of their labours to, especially that the chosen of God in future ages may be introduced, for it is a *godly seed* that is sought by *marriage* (Mal. ii. 15), a seed to serve the Lord, that shall be a *generation to him.*

2. The world to come is quite another thing; it is called *that world,* by way of emphasis and eminency. Note, There are more worlds than one; a present visible world, and a future invisible world; and it is the concern of every one of us to compare worlds, *this world* and *that world,* and give the preference in our thoughts and cares to that which deserves them. Now observe,

(1.) Who shall be the inhabitants of *that world:* They that shall be *accounted worthy to obtain it,* that is, that are interested in *Christ's merit,* who *purchased it for us,* and have a holy *meetness* for it wrought in them by the Spirit, whose business it is to prepare us for it. They have not a *legal* worthiness, upon account of any thing in them or done by them, but an *evangelical* worthiness, upon account of the inestimable price which Christ paid for the *redemption of the purchased possession.* It is a worthiness imputed by which we are glorified, as well as a righteousness imputed by which we are justified; *καταξιωθέντες,* they are *made agreeable to that world.* The disagreeableness that there is in the corrupt nature is taken away, and the dispositions of the soul are by the grace of God conformed to that state. They are by grace made and *counted worthy to obtain that world;* it intimates some *difficulty* in reaching after it, and danger of coming short. We must *so run* as that we may obtain. They shall obtain the *resurrection from the dead,* that is, the blessed resurrection; for that of *condemnation* (as Christ calls it, John v. 29), is rather a resurrection *to death,* a second death, an eternal death, than *from death.*

(2.) What shall be the happy state of the inhabitants of that world we cannot express or conceive, 1 Cor. ii. 9. See what Christ here says of it. [1.] They *neither marry nor are given in marriage.* Those that have entered into the joy of their Lord are entirely taken up with that, and need not the joy of the bridegroom in his bride. The love in that world of love is all seraphic, and such as eclipses and loses the purest and most pleasing loves we entertain ourselves with in this world of sense. Where the body itself shall be a spiritual body, the delights of sense will all be banished; and where there is a perfection of holiness there is no occasion for marriage as a preservative from sin. Into that *new Jerusalem* there enters nothing that defiles. [2.] They cannot *die any more;* and this comes in as a reason why they do not *marry.* In this dying world there must be marriage, in order to the filling up of the vacancies made by death; but, where there are no burials, there is no need of weddings. This crowns the comfort of that world that there is no more death there, which sullies all the beauty, and damps all the comforts, of this world. Here death reigns, but thence it is for ever excluded. [3.] They are *equal unto the angels.* In the other evangelists it was said, They are *as the angels—ὡς ἀγγέλοι,* but here they are said to be *equal to the angels, ἰσάγγελοι—angels' peers;* they have a glory and bliss no way inferior to that of the holy angels. They shall see the same sight, be employed in the same work, and share in the same joys, with the holy angels. Saints, when they come to heaven, shall be *naturalized,* and, though by nature strangers, yet, having *obtained this freedom* with a *great sum,* which Christ paid for them, they have in all respects equal privileges with them that were free-born, the angels that are the natives and aborigines of that country. They shall be companions with the angels, and converse with those blessed spirits that love them dearly, and with an innumerable company, to whom they are now come in faith, hope, and love. [4.] They *are the children of God,* and so they are as the angels, who are called the *sons of God.* In the *inheritance of sons,* the *adoption of sons* will be completed. Hence believers are said to *wait for the adoption,* even *the redemption of the body,* Rom. viii. 23. For till the body is redeemed from the grave the adoption is not completed. *Now are we the sons of God,* 1 John iii. 2. We have the nature and disposition of sons, but that will not be *perfected* till we come to heaven. [5.] They are the *children of the resurrection,* that is, they are made capable of the employments and enjoyments of the future state; they are *born to that world,* belong to that family, had their education for it here, and shall there have their inheritance in it. They are the *children of God,* being the *children of the resurrection.* Note, God owns those only for his children that are the children of the resurrection, that are born from above, are allied to the world of spirits, and prepared for that world, the children of that family.

IV. It is an undoubted truth that there is another life after this, and there were eminent discoveries made of this truth in the early ages of the church (*v.* 37, 38): *Moses showed this, as it was shown to Moses at the bush,* and he hath shown it to us, when *he calleth the Lord,* as the Lord calleth himself, the *God of Abraham, and the God of Isaac, and the God of Jacob. Abraham, Isaac, and Jacob,* were then *dead* as to our world; they had departed out of it many years before, and their bodies were turned into dust in the cave of Machpelah; how then could God say, not *I was,* but *I am* the *God of Abraham?* It is absurd that the living God and Fountain of life should continue related to them as their God, if there were no more of them in being than what lay in that cave, undistinguished from common dust. We must therefore conclude that they were then in being in another world; for *God is not the God of the dead, but of the living.* Luke here adds, *For all live unto him,* that is, all who, like them, are true believers; though they are dead, yet they *do live;* their souls, which *return to God who gave them* (Eccl. xii. 7), live to him as the Father of spirits: and their bodies shall live again at the end of time by the power of God; for he calleth things that are not as though they were, because he is the God that *quickens the dead,* Rom. iv. 17. But there is more in it yet; when God called himself *the God* of these patriarchs, he meant that he was their felicity and portion, a *God all-sufficient to them* (Gen. xvii. 1), their *exceeding great reward,* Gen. xv. 1. Now it is plain by their history that he never did that for them in this world which would answer the *true intent* and *full extent* of that great undertaking, and therefore there must be another life after this, in which he will do that for them that will amount to a *discharge in full* of that promise —that he would be to them a God, which he is able to do, for *all live to him,* and he has wherewithal to make every soul happy that lives to him; enough for *all,* enough for *each.*

39 Then certain of the scribes answering said, Master, thou hast well
said. 40 And after that they durst
not ask him any *question at all.* 41
And he said unto them, How say
they that Christ is David's son? 42
And David himself saith in the book
of Psalms, The LORD said unto my
Lord, Sit thou on my right hand, 43
Till I make thine enemies thy footstool. 44 David therefore calleth
him Lord, how is he then his son?
45 Then in the audience of all the
people he said unto his disciples, 46
Beware of the scribes, which desire to walk in long robes, and love greetings in the markets, and the highest seats in the synagogues, and the chief rooms at feasts; 47 Which devour
widows' houses, and for a show make long prayers: the same shall receive greater damnation.

The scribes were *students* in the law, and *expositors* of it to the people, men in reputation for wisdom and honour, but the generality of them were enemies to Christ and his gospel. Now here we have some of them attending him, and four things we have in these verses concerning them, which we had before:—

I. We have them here commending the reply which Christ made to the Sadducees concerning the resurrection: *Certain of the scribes said, Master, thou hast well said, v.* 39. Christ had the testimony of his adversaries that he said well; and *therefore* the scribes were his enemies because he would not *conform* to the traditions of the elders, but yet when he vindicated the fundamental practices of religion, and appeared in defence of them, even the scribes commended his performance, and owned that he said well. Many that call themselves Christians come short even of this spirit.

II. We have them here struck with an awe of Christ, and of his wisdom and authority (*v.* 40): *They durst not ask him any questions at all,* because they saw that he was too hard for all that contended with him. His own disciples, though weak, yet, being willing to receive his doctrine, durst *ask him any question;* but the Sadducees, who contradicted and cavilled at his doctrine, durst ask him none.

III. We have them here *puzzled* and run aground with a question concerning the Messiah, *v.* 41. It was plain by many scriptures that Christ was to be the *Son of David;* even the blind man knew this (*ch.* xviii. 39); and yet it was plain that David called the Messiah *his Lord* (*v.* 42, 44), his owner, and ruler, and benefactor: *The Lord said to my Lord.* God said it to the Messiah, Ps. cx. 1. Now if he be *his Son,* why doth he call him *his Lord?* If he be *his Lord,* why do *we* call him *his Son?* This he left them to consider of, but they could not reconcile this seeming contradiction; thanks be to God, we can; that Christ, *as God,* was David's Lord, but Christ, *as man,* was David's Son. He was both the *root* and the *offspring of David,* Rev. xxii. 16. By his *human nature* he was the *offspring of David,* a branch of his family; by his *divine nature* he was the *root of David,* from whom he had his being and life, and all the supplies of grace.

IV. We have them here described in their black characters, and a public caution given to the disciples to take heed of them, *v.* 45—47. This we had, just as it is here, Mark xii. 38, and more largely Matt. xxiii. Christ bids his disciples *beware of the scribes,* that is,

1. "Take heed of being drawn *into sin* by them, of learning their way, and going into their measures; beware of such a spirit as they are governed by. Be not you such in the Christian church as they are in the Jewish church."

2. "Take heed of being *brought into trouble* by them," in the same sense that he had said (Matt. x. 17), "*Beware of men, for they will deliver you up to the councils;* beware of the scribes, for they will do so. Beware of them, for," (1.) "They are *proud* and *haughty.* They *desire to* walk about the streets in *long robes,* as those that are above business (for men of business went with their *loins girt up*), and as those that take state, and take place." *Cedant arma togæ—Let arms yield to the gown.* They loved in their hearts to have people make their obeisance to them *in the markets,* that many might see what respect was paid them; and were very proud of the precedency that was given them in all places of concourse. They *loved the highest seats in the synagogues* and *the chief rooms at feasts,* and, when they were placed in them, looked upon themselves with great conceit and upon all about them with great contempt. *I sit as a queen.* (2.) "They are *covetous and oppressive,* and make their religion a cloak and cover for crime." They *devour widows' houses,* get their estates into their hands, and then by some trick or other make them their own, or they live upon them, and eat up what they have; and *widows* are an easy prey to them, because they are apt to be deluded by their specious pretences: *for a show they make long prayers,* perhaps long prayers with the widows when they are in sorrow, as if they had not only a *piteous* but a *pious* concern for them, and thus endeavour to ingratiate themselves with them, and get their money and effects into their hands. Such devout men may surely be trusted with *untold gold;* but they will give such an account of it as they think fit.

Christ reads them their doom in a few words: *These shall receive a more abundant judgment,* a double damnation, both for their abuse of the poor *widows,* whose houses they devoured, and for their abuse of religion, and particularly of prayer, which they had made use of as a pretence for the more plausible and effectual carrying on of their worldly and wicked projects; for *dissembled piety is double iniquity.*

CHAP. XXI.

In this chapter we have, I. The notice Christ took, and the approbation he gave, of a poor widow that cast two mites into the treasury, ver. 1—4. II. A prediction of future events, in answer to his disciples' enquiries concerning them, ver. 5—7. 1. Of what should happen between that and the destruction of Jerusalem—false Christs arising, bloody wars and persecutions of Christ's followers, ver. 8—19. 2. Of that destruction itself, ver. 20—24. 3. Of the second coming of Jesus Christ to judge the world, under the type and figure of that, ver. 25—33. III. A practical application of this, by way of caution and counsel (ver. 34—36), and an account of Christ's preaching and the people's attendance on it, ver. 37, 38.

AND he looked up, and saw the
rich men casting their gifts into
the treasury. 2 And he saw also a
certain poor widow casting in thither
two mites. 3 And he said, Of a truth
I say unto you, that this poor widow
hath cast in more than they all: 4
For all these have of their abundance
cast in unto the offerings of God:
but she of her penury hath cast in
all the living that she had.

This short passage of story we had before in Mark. It is thus recorded twice, to teach us, 1. That *charity* to the poor is a *main matter* in religion. Our Lord Jesus took all occasions to commend it and recommend it. He had just mentioned the barbarity of the scribes, who devoured *poor widows* (*ch.* 20); and perhaps this is designed as an aggravation of it, that the poor widows were the best benefactors to the public funds, of which the scribes had the disposal. 2. That Jesus Christ has his eye upon us, to observe what we give to the poor, and what we contribute to works of piety and charity. Christ, though intent upon his preaching, looked up, to see what *gifts were cast into the treasury, v.* 1. He observes whether we give largely and liberally, in proportion to what we have, or whether we be sneaking and paltry in it; nay, his eye goes further, he observes whether we give charitably and with a willing mind, or grudgingly and with reluctance. This should make us afraid of coming short of our duty in this matter; men may be deceived with excuses which Christ knows to be frivolous. And this should encourage us to be abundant in it, without desiring that men should know it; it is enough that Christ does; he sees in secret, and will reward openly. 3. That Christ observes and accepts the charity of the poor in a particular manner. Those that have nothing *to give* may yet *do* a great deal in charity by ministering to the poor, and helping them, and begging for them, that cannot *help* themselves, or *beg* for themselves. But here was one that was herself poor and yet *gave* what little she had to the treasury. It was but *two mites,* which make a farthing; but Christ magnified it as a piece of charity exceeding all the rest: *She has cast in more than they all.* Christ does not blame her for indiscretion, in giving what she wanted herself, nor for vanity in giving among the rich to the treasury; but commended her liberality, and her willingness to part with what little she had for the glory of God, which proceeded from a belief of and dependence upon God's providence to take care of her. *Jehovah-jireh—the Lord will provide.* 4. That, whatever may be called *the offerings of God*, we ought to have a respect for, and to our power, yea, and beyond our power, to contribute cheerfully to. These have *cast in unto the offerings of God.* What is given to the support of the ministry and the gospel, to the spreading and propagating of religion, the education of youth, the release of prisoners, the relief of widows and strangers, and the maintenance of poor families, is given to the *offerings of God*, and it shall be so accepted and recompensed.

5 And as some spake of the temple,
how it was adorned with goodly stones
and gifts, he said, 6 *As for* these
things which ye behold, the days will
come, in the which there shall not be
left one stone upon another, that shall
not be thrown down. 7 And they
asked him, saying, Master, but when
shall these things be? and what sign
will there be when these things shall
come to pass? 8 And he said, Take
heed that ye be not deceived: for
many shall come in my name, saying,
I am *Christ*; and the time draweth
near: go ye not therefore after them.
9 But when ye shall hear of wars and
commotions, be not terrified: for
these things must first come to pass;
but the end *is* not by and by. 10
Then said he unto them, Nation shall
rise against nation, and kingdom
against kingdom: 11 And great earthquakes shall be in divers places, and
famines, and pestilences; and fearful
sights and great signs shall there be
from heaven. 12 But before all these,
they shall lay their hands on you, and
persecute *you*, delivering *you* up to the
synagogues, and into prisons, being
brought before kings and rulers for
my name's sake. 13 And it shall turn
to you for a testimony. 14 Settle *it*
therefore in your hearts, not to meditate before what ye shall answer: 15
For I will give you a mouth and wisdom, which all your adversaries shall
not be able to gainsay nor resist. 16
And ye shall be betrayed both by parents, and brethren, and kinsfolks, and
friends; and *some* of you shall they
cause to be put to death. 17 And
ye shall be hated of all *men* for my
name's sake. 18 But there shall not
an hair of your head perish. 19 In
your patience possess ye your souls.

See here, I. With what admiration some spoke of the external pomp and magnificence of the temple, and they were some of Christ's own disciples too; and they took notice of it to him *how it was adorned with goodly stones and gifts, v.* 5. The outside was built up with goodly stones, and within it was beautified and enriched with the *presents* that were offered up for that purpose, and were *hung up* in it. They thought their Master should be as much affected with those things as they were, and should as much regret the destruction of them as they did. When we *speak of the temple,* it should be of the presence of God in it, and of the ordinances of God administered in it, and the communion which his people there have with him. It is a poor thing, when we speak of the church, to let our discourse dwell upon its pomps and revenues, and the dignities and powers of its officers and rulers; for the king's daughter is all *glorious within.*

II. With what contempt Christ spoke of them, and with what assurance of their being all made desolate very shortly (*v.* 6): "*As for those things which you behold,* those dear things which you are so much in love with, *behold, the days will come,* and some now living may live to see them, *in which there shall not be left one stone upon another.* This building, which seems so beautiful that one would think none could, for pity, pull it down, and which seems so strong that one would think none would be able to pull it down, shall yet be utterly ruined; and this shall be done as soon as ever the spiritual temple of the gospel church (the substance of that shadow) begins to flourish in the world." Did we by faith foresee the blasting and withering of all external glory, we should not set our hearts upon it as those do that cannot see, or will not look, so far before them.

III. With what curiosity those about him enquire concerning the time when this great desolation should be: *Master, when shall these things be? v.* 7. It is natural to us to covet to know future things and the time of them, which *it is not for us to know,* when we are more concerned to ask what is our duty in the prospect of these things, and how we may prepare for them, which it is for us to know. They enquire *what sign there shall be when these things shall come to pass.* They ask not for a *present* sign, to confirm the prediction itself, and to induce them to believe it (Christ's word was enough for that), but what the future signs will be of the approaching accomplishment of the prediction, by which they may be put in mind of it. These *signs of the times* Christ had taught them to observe.

IV. With what clearness and fulness Christ answers their enquiries, as far as was necessary to direct them in their duty; for all knowledge is desirable as far as it is in order to practice.

1. They must expect to hear of false Christs and false prophets appearing, and false prophecies given out (*v.* 8): *Many shall come in my name;* he does not mean *in the name of Jesus,* though there were some deceivers who pretended commissions from him (as Acts xix. 13), but usurping the title and character of the Messiah. Many pretended to be the deliverers of the Jewish church and nation from the Romans, and to fix the time when the deliverance should be wrought, by which multitudes were drawn into a snare, to their ruin. They shall say, ὅτι ἐγώ εἰμι—*I am he,* or *I am,* as if they would assume that incommunicable name of God, by which he made himself known when he came to deliver Israel out of Egypt, *I am;* and, to encourage people to follow them, they added, "*The time draws near* when the kingdom shall be restored to Israel, and all who will follow me shall share in it." Now as to this, he gives them a needful caution (1.) "*Take heed that you be not deceived;* do not imagine that I shall myself come again in external glory, to take possession of the throne of kingdoms. No, you must not expect any such thing, for my kingdom is not of this world." When they asked solicitously and eagerly, *Master, when shall these things be?* the first word Christ said was, *Take heed that you be not deceived.* Note, Those that are most *inquisitive* in the things of God (though it is very good to be so) are in most danger of being imposed upon, and have most need to be upon their guard. (2.) "*Go you not after them.* You know the Messiah is come. and you are not to look for any other; and therefore do not so much as hearken to them, nor have any thing to do with them." If we are sure that Jesus is the Christ, and his doctrine is the *gospel, of God,* we must be deaf to all intimations of another Christ and another gospel.

2. They must expect to hear of great commotions in the nations, and many terrible judgments inflicted upon the Jews and their neighbours. (1.) There shall be *bloody wars* (*v.* 10): *Nation shall rise against nation,* one part of the Jewish nation against another, or rather the whole against the Romans. Encouraged by the false Christs, they shall wickedly endeavour to throw off the Roman yoke, by taking up arms against the Roman powers; when they had rejected the liberty with which Christ would have made them free they were left to themselves, to grasp at their civil liberty in ways that were *sinful,* and therefore could not be *successful.* (2.) There shall be *earthquakes,* great earthquakes, *in divers places,* which shall not only frighten people, but destroy towns and houses, and bury many in the ruins of them. (3.) There shall be *famines* and *pestilences,* the common effects of war, which destroys the fruits of the earth, and, by exposing men to ill weather and reducing them to ill diet, occasions infectious diseases. God has various ways of punishing a provoking people. The four sorts of judgments which the Old-Testament prophets so often speak of are threatened by the New-Testament prophets too; for, though spiritual judgments are more commonly inflicted in gospel times, yet God makes use of temporal judgments also. (4.) There shall be *fearful sights* and *great signs from heaven,* uncommon appearances in the clouds, comets and blazing stars, which frighten the ordinary sort of beholders, and have always been looked upon as *ominous,* and *portending* something *bad.* Now, as to these, the caution he gives them is, "*Be not terrified.* Others will be frightened at them, but be not you frightened, *v.* 2. As to the *fearful sights,* let them not be fearful to you, who look above the visible heavens to the throne of God's government in the highest heavens. *Be not dismayed at the signs of heaven, for the heathen are dismayed at them,* Jer. x. 2. And, as to the *famines* and *pestilences,* you fall into the hands of God, who has promised to those who are his that *in the days of famine they shall be satisfied,* and that he will keep them from the *noisome pestilence;* trust therefore in him, and *be not afraid.* Nay, when you hear of wars, when without are fightings and within are fears, yet then *be not you terrified;* you know the worst that any of these judgments can do to you, and therefore be not afraid of them; for," [1.] "It is your interest to *make the best of that which is,* for all your fears cannot alter it: *these things must first come to pass;* there is no remedy; it will be your wisdom to make yourselves easy by accommodating yourselves to them." [2.] "There is *worse behind;* flatter not yourselves with a fancy that you will soon see an end of these troubles, no, not so soon as you think of: *the end is not by and by,* not *suddenly.* Be not *terrified,* for, if you begin so quickly to be discouraged, how will you bear up under what is yet before you?"

3. They must expect to be themselves for *signs* and *wonders* in Israel; their being *persecuted* would be a prognostic of the destruction of the city and temple, which he had now foretold. Nay, this would be the *first* sign of their ruin coming: "*Before all these, they shall lay their hands on you.* The judgment shall begin at the house of God; you must smart first, for warning to them, that, if they have any consideration, they may consider, *If this be done to the green tree, what shall be done to the dry?* See 1 Pet. iv. 17, 18. But this is not all; this must be considered not only as the *suffering* of the *persecuted,* but as the *sin* of the *persecutors. Before* God's judgments are brought upon them, they shall fill up the measure of their iniquity by *laying their* hands on you." Note, The ruin of a people is always introduced by their sin; and nothing introduces a surer or sorer ruin than the sin of persecution. This is a *sign* that God's wrath is coming upon a people to the uttermost when their *wrath*

against the servants of God *comes to the uttermost.* Now as to this,

(1.) Christ tells them what hard things they should suffer for his name's sake, much to the same purport with what he had told them when he first called them to follow him, Matt. x. They should know the wages of it, that they might *sit down and count the cost.* St. Paul, who was the greatest labourer and sufferer of them all, not being now among them, was told by Christ himself what *great things he should suffer for* his *name's sake* (Acts ix. 16), so necessary is it that all who will live godly in Christ Jesus should count upon persecution. The Christians, having themselves been originally Jews, and still retaining an equal veneration with them for the Old Testament and all the essentials of their religion, and differing only in ceremony, might expect fair quarter with them; but Christ bids them not expect it: "No, they shall be the most forward to *persecute you.*" [1.] "They shall use their own church-power against you: *They shall deliver you up to the synagogues* to be scourged there, and stigmatized with their *anathemas.*" [2.] "They shall incense the magistrates against you: they shall *deliver you into prisons,* that you may be *brought before kings and rulers for my name's sake,* and be punished by them." [3.] "Your own relations will betray you (*v.* 16), *your parents, brethren, and kinsfolks, and friends;* so that you will not know whom to put a confidence in, or where to be safe." [4.] "Your religion will be made a capital crime, and you will be called to *resist unto blood. Some of you shall they cause to be put to death;* so far must you be from expecting honour and wealth that you must expect nothing but death in its most frightful shapes, death in all its dreadful pomp. Nay," [5.] "*You shall be hated of all men for my name's sake.*" This is worse than death itself, and was fulfilled when the apostles were not only *appointed to death,* but made a *spectacle to the world,* and counted as the *filth of the world,* and the *offscouring of all things,* which every body loathes, 1 Cor. iv. 9, 13. They were hated of *all men,* that is, of all bad men, who could not bear the light of the gospel (because it discovered their evil deeds), and therefore hated those who brought in that light, flew in their faces, and would have pulled them to pieces. The wicked world, which hated to be reformed, hated Christ the great Reformer, and all that were his, for his sake. The rulers of the Jewish church, knowing very well that if the gospel obtained among the Jews their usurped abused power was at an end, raised all their forces against it, put it into an ill name, filled people's minds with prejudices against it, and so made the preachers and professors of it odious to the mob.

(2.) He encourages them to bear up under their trials, and to go on in their work, notwithstanding the opposition they would meet with.

[1.] God will bring glory both to himself and them out of their sufferings: "*It shall turn to you for a testimony, v.* 13. Your being set up thus for a mark, and publicly *persecuted,* will make you the more taken notice of and your doctrine and miracles the more enquired into; your being brought *before kings and rulers* will give you an opportunity of preaching the gospel to them, who otherwise would never have come within hearing of it; your suffering such severe things, and being so hated by the worst of men, men of the most vicious lives, will be a testimony that you are good, else you would not have such bad men for your enemies; your courage, and cheerfulness, and constancy under your sufferings will be a testimony for you, that you believe what you preach, that you are supported by a divine power, and that the Spirit of God and glory rests upon you."

[2.] "God will stand by you, and own you, and assist you, in your trials; you are his advocates, and you shall be well furnished with instructions, *v.* 14, 15. Instead of setting your hearts on work to contrive an answer to informations, indictments, articles, accusations, and interrogatories, that will be exhibited against you in the ecclesiastical and civil courts, on the contrary, *settle it in your hearts,* impress it upon them, take pains with them to persuade them *not to meditate before what you shall answer;* do not *depend* upon your own wit and ingenuity, your own prudence and policy, and do not *distrust* or *despair* of the immediate and extraordinary aids of the divine grace. Think not to bring yourselves off in the cause of Christ as you would in a cause of your own, by your own parts and application, with the common assistance of divine Providence, but promise yourselves, for I promise you, the special assistance of divine grace: *I will give you a mouth and wisdom.*" This proves Christ to be God; for it is God's prerogative to *give wisdom,* and he it is that *made man's mouth.* Note, *First,* A *mouth* and *wisdom* together completely fit a man both for services and sufferings; *wisdom* to know what to say, and a *mouth* wherewith to say it as it should be said. It is a great happiness to have both *matter* and *words* wherewith to honour God and do good; to have in the mind a *storehouse* well furnished with things *new and old,* and a *door of utterance* by which *to bring them forth. Secondly,* Those that plead Christ's cause may depend upon him to give them *a mouth and wisdom,* which way soever they are called to plead it, especially when they are brought before magistrates for his name's sake. It is not said that he will send an angel from heaven to answer for them, though he could do this, but that he will give them a *mouth* and *wisdom* to enable them to answer for themselves, which puts a greater honour upon them, which requires them to use the gifts and graces Christ furnishes them with, and redounds the more to the glory of God, who *stills the enemy and the avenger out of the mouths of babes and sucklings. Thirdly,* When Christ gives to his witnesses a *mouth and wisdom,* they are enabled to say that both for him and themselves which *all their adversaries are not able to gainsay or resist,* so that they are silenced, and put to confusion. This was remarkably fulfilled presently after the pouring out of the Spirit, by whom Christ gave his disciples this *mouth* and *wisdom,* when the apostles were brought before the priests and rulers, and answered them so as to make them ashamed, Acts iv. v. and vi.

[3.] " You shall suffer no real damage by all the hardships they shall put upon you (*v.* 18): *There shall not a hair of your head perish.*" Shall some of them lose their heads, and yet not lose a hair? It is a proverbial expression, denoting the greatest indemnity and security imaginable; it is frequently used both in the Old Testament and New, in that sense. Some think that it refers to the preservation of the lives of all the Christians that were among the Jews when they were cut off by the Romans; historians tell us that not one Christian perished in that desolation. Others reconcile it with the deaths of multitudes in the cause of Christ, and take it figuratively in the same sense that Christ saith, *He that loseth his life for my sake shall find it.* " Not a hair of your head shall perish but," *First,* " I will take *cognizance* of it." To this end he had said (Matt. x. 30), *The hairs of your head are all numbered;* and an account is kept of them, so that none of them shall perish but he will miss it. *Secondly,* " It shall be upon a *valuable consideration.*" We do not reckon that *lost* or *perishing* which is laid out for good purposes, and will turn to a good account. If we drop the body itself for Christ's name's sake, it does not perish, but is well bestowed. *Thirdly,* " It shall be abundantly recompensed; when you come to balance profit and loss, you will find that nothing has perished, but, on the contrary, that you have great gain in present comforts, especially in the joys of a life eternal;" so that though we may be losers for Christ we shall not, we cannot, be losers by him in the end.

[4.] " It is therefore your duty and interest, in the midst of your own sufferings and those of the nation, to maintain a holy sincerity and serenity of mind, which will keep you always easy (*v.* 19): *In your patience possess ye your souls;* get and keep possession of your souls." Some read it as a promise, " You *may* or *shall* possess your souls." It comes all to one. Note, *First,* It is our duty and interest at all times, especially in perilous trying times, to secure the possession of our own souls; not only that they be not destroyed and lost for ever, but that they be not distempered now, nor our possession of them disturbed and interrupted. " *Possess your souls,* be your own men, keep up the authority and dominion of reason, and keep under the tumults of passion, that neither grief nor fear may tyrannize over you, nor turn you out of the possession and enjoyment of yourselves." In difficult times, when we can keep possession of nothing else, then let us make that sure which may be made sure, and keep possession of our souls. *Secondly,* It is by patience, Christian patience, that we keep possession of our own souls. " In suffering times, set patience upon the guard for the preserving of your souls; by it keep your souls composed and in a good frame, and keep out all those impressions which would ruffle you and put you out of temper."

20 And when ye shall see Jerusalem compassed with armies, then
know that the desolation thereof is
nigh. 21 Then let them which are
in Judæa flee to the mountains; and
let them which are in the midst of it
depart out; and let not them that are
in the countries enter thereinto. 22
For these be the days of vengeance,
that all things which are written may
be fulfilled. 23 But woe unto them
that are with child, and to them that
give suck, in those days! for there
shall be great distress in the land, and
wrath upon this people. 24 And
they shall fall by the edge of the
sword, and shall be led away captive
into all nations: and Jerusalem shall
be trodden down of the Gentiles,
until the times of the Gentiles be fulfilled. 25 And there shall be signs
in the sun, and in the moon, and in
the stars; and upon the earth distress
of nations, with perplexity; the sea
and the waves roaring; 26 Men's
hearts failing them for fear, and for
looking after those things which are
coming on the earth: for the powers
of heaven shall be shaken. 27 And
then shall they see the Son of man
coming in a cloud with power and
great glory. 28 And when these
things begin to come to pass, then
look up, and lift up your heads; for
your redemption draweth nigh.

Having given them an idea of the times for about thirty-eight years next ensuing, he here comes to show them what all those things would issue in at last, namely, the destruction of Jerusalem, and the utter dispersion of the Jewish nation, which would be a little day of judgment, a type and figure of

Christ's second coming, which was not so fully spoken of here as in the parallel place (Matt. xxiv.), yet glanced at; for the destruction of Jerusalem would be as it were the destruction of the world to those whose hearts were bound up in it.

I. He tells them that they should see Jerusalem besieged, *compassed with armies* (*v.* 20), the Roman armies; and, when they saw this, they might conclude that *its desolation was nigh,* for in this the siege would infallibly *end,* though it might be a long siege. Note, As in mercy, so in judgment, when God begins, he will make an end.

II. He warns them, upon this signal given, to shift for their own safety (*v.* 21): "*Then let them that are in Judea* quit the country and *flee to the mountains; let them that are in the midst of it*" (of Jerusalem) "*depart out,* before the city be closely shut up, and" (as we say now) "before the trenches be opened; and let not them that are in the countries and villages about enter into the city, thinking to be safe there. Do you abandon a city and country which you see God has abandoned and given up to ruin. *Come out of her, my people.*"

III. He foretels the terrible havoc that should be made of the Jewish nation (*v.* 22): *Those are the days of vengeance* so often spoken of by the Old-Testament prophets, which would complete the ruin of that provoking people. All their predictions must now be fulfilled, and the blood of all the Old-Testament martyrs must now be required. *All things that are written must be fulfilled* at length. After days of patience long abused, there will come *days of vengeance;* for reprieves are not pardons. The greatness of that destruction is set forth, 1. By the inflicting cause of it. It is *wrath upon this people,* the wrath of God, that will kindle this devouring consuming fire. 2. By the particular terror it would be to women with child, and poor mothers that are nurses. *Woe to them,* not only because they are most subject to frights, and least able to shift for their own safety, but because it will be a very great torment to them to think of having borne and nursed children for the murderers. 3. By the general confusion that should be all the nation over. There shall be *great distress in the land,* for men will not know what course to take, nor how to help themselves.

IV. He describes the issue of the struggles between the Jews and the Romans, and what they will come to at last; in short, 1. Multitudes of them *shall fall by the edge of the sword.* It is computed that in those wars of the Jews there fell by the sword above eleven hundred thousand. And the siege of Jerusalem was, in effect, a military execution. 2. The rest shall be *led away captive;* not into *one* nation, as when they were conquered by the Chaldeans, which gave them an opportunity of keeping together, but *into all nations,* which made it impossible for them to *correspond* with each other, much less to *incorporate.* 3. Jerusalem itself was *trodden down of the Gentiles.* The Romans, when they had made themselves masters of it, laid it quite waste, as a *rebellious and bad city, hurtful to kings and provinces,* and therefore hateful to them.

V. He describes the great frights that people should generally be in. Many frightful *sights* shall be *in the sun, moon, and stars,* prodigies in the heavens, and here in this lower world, the *sea and the waves roaring,* with terrible storms and tempests, such as had not been known, and above the ordinary working of natural causes. The effect of this shall be universal confusion and consternation *upon the earth, distress of nations with perplexity, v.* 25. Dr. Hammond understands by the *nations* the several governments or tetrarchies of the Jewish nation, Judea, Samaria, and Galilee; these shall be brought to the last extremity. *Men's hearts shall fail them for fear* (*v.* 26), ἀποψυχόντων ἀνθρώπων—*men being quite exanimated,* dispirited, *unsouled,* dying away for fear. Thus those are *killed all the day long* by whom Christ's apostles were so (Rom. viii. 36), that is, they are all the day long in fear of being killed; sinking under that which lies upon them, and yet still trembling for fear of worse, and *looking after those things which are coming upon the world.* When *judgment begins at the house of God,* it will not end there; it shall be as if all the world were falling in pieces; and where can any be secure then? The *powers of heaven shall be shaken,* and then the pillars of the earth cannot but tremble. Thus shall the present Jewish policy, religion, laws, and government, be all entirely dissolved by a series of unparalleled calamities, attended with the utmost confusion. So Dr. Clarke. But our Saviour makes use of these figurative expressions because at the end of time they shall be literally accomplished, when the *heavens shall be rolled together as a scroll,* and all their powers not only shaken, but broken, and the *earth* and *all the works that are therein* shall be burnt up, 2 Pet. iii. 10, 12. As that day was all terror and destruction to the unbelieving Jews, so the great day will be to all unbelievers.

VI. He makes this to be a kind of *appearing of the Son of man: Then shall they see the Son of man coming in a cloud, with power and great glory, v.* 27. The destruction of Jerusalem was in a particular manner an act of Christ's judgment, the judgment committed to the Son of man; his religion could never be thoroughly established but by the destruction of the temple, and the abolishing of the Levitical priesthood and economy, after which even the converted Jews, and many of the Gentiles too, were still hankering, till they were destroyed; so that it might justly be looked upon as *a coming of the Son of man, in power and great glory,* yet not visibly, but *in the clouds;* for in executing such judgments as these *clouds and darkness are round about him.* Now this was, 1. An *evidence* of the first coming of the Messiah; so some understand it. Then the unbelieving Jews shall be convinced, when it is too late, that Jesus was the Messiah; those that would not see him coming in the power of his grace to *save them* shall be made to see him coming in the power of his wrath to *destroy them;* those that would not have him to *reign over them* shall have him to *triumph over them.* 2. It was an *earnest* of his second coming. *Then* in the terrors of that day they shall *see the Son of man coming in a cloud,* and all the terrors of the last day. They shall see a *specimen* of it, a faint resemblance of it. If this be so terrible, what will that be?

VII. He encourages all the faithful disciples in reference to the terrors of that day (*v.* 28): "*When these things begin to come to pass,* when Jerusalem is besieged, and every thing is concurring to the destruction of the Jews, *then* do you look *up,* when others are looking down, look heavenward, in faith, hope, and prayer, and *lift up your heads* with cheerfulness and confidence, *for your redemption draws nigh.*" 1. When Christ came to destroy the Jews, he came to redeem the Christians that were persecuted and oppressed by them; *then had the churches rest.* 2. When he comes to judge the world at the last day, he will *redeem* all that are his, from all their grievances. And the foresight of that day is as pleasant to all good Christians as it is terrible to the wicked and ungodly. Their death itself is so; when they see that day approaching, they can *lift up their heads with joy,* knowing that *their redemption draws nigh,* their removal to their Redeemer.

VIII. Here is one word of prediction that looks further than the destruction of the Jewish nation, which is not easily understood; we have it in *v.* 24: *Jerusalem shall be trodden down of the Gentiles, till the times of the Gentiles be fulfilled.* 1. Some understand it of what is past; so Dr. Hammond. The Gentiles, who have conquered Jerusalem, shall keep possession of it, and it shall be purely Gentile, till the times of the Gentiles be fulfilled, till a great part of the Gentile world shall have become Christian, and then after Jerusalem shall have been rebuilt by Adrian the emperor, with an exclusion of all the Jews from it, many of the Jews shall turn Christians, shall join with the Gentile Christians, to set up a church in Jerusalem, which shall flourish there for a long time. 2. Others understand it of what is yet to come; so Dr. Whitby. Jerusalem shall be possessed by the Gentiles, of one sort or other, for the most part, till the time come when the nations that yet remain infidels shall embrace the Christian faith, when the kingdoms of this world shall become Christ's kingdoms, and then all the Jews shall be converted. Jerusalem shall be inhabited by them, and neither they nor their city any longer trodden down by the Gentiles.

29 And he spake to them a parable; Behold the fig tree, and all the
trees; 30 When they now shoot forth,
ye see and know of your own selves
that summer is now nigh at hand.
31 So likewise ye, when ye see these
things come to pass, know ye that
the kingdom of God is nigh at hand.
32 Verily I say unto you, This generation shall not pass away, till all be
fulfilled. 33 Heaven and earth shall
pass away: but my words shall not
pass away. 34 And take heed to
yourselves, lest at any time your
hearts be overcharged with surfeiting,
and drunkenness, and cares of this
life, and *so* that day come upon you
unawares. 35 For as a snare shall
it come on all them that dwell on
the face of the whole earth. 36
Watch ye therefore, and pray always,
that ye may be accounted worthy to
escape all these things that shall come
to pass, and to stand before the Son
of man. 37 And in the day time he
was teaching in the temple; and at
night he went out, and abode in the
mount that is called *the mount* of
Olives. 38 And all the people came
early in the morning to him in the
temple, for to hear him.

Here, in the close of this discourse,

I. Christ appoints his disciples to observe the signs of the times, which they might judge by, if they had an eye to the foregoing directions, with as much certainty and assurance as they could judge of the approach of summer by the budding forth of the trees, *v.* 29—31. As in the kingdom of nature there is a chain of causes, so in the kingdom of providence there is a consequence of one event upon another. When we see a nation filling up the measure of their iniquity, we may conclude that their ruin is nigh; when we see the ruin of persecuting powers hastening on, we may thence infer that *the kingdom of God is nigh at hand,* that when the opposition given to it is removed it shall gain ground. As we may lawfully prognosticate the change of the seasons when second causes have begun to work, so we may, in the disposal of events, expect something uncommon when God is already *raised up out of his holy habitation* (Zech. ii. 13); then *stand still and see his salvation.*

II. He charges them to look upon those things as neither *doubtful* nor *distant* (for then they would not make a due impression on them), but as *sure* and very *near.* The destruction of the Jewish nation, 1. Was *near* (*v.* 32): *This generation shall not pass away till all be fulfilled.* There were some now alive that should see it; some that now heard the prediction of it. 2. It was *sure;* the sentence was irreversible; it was a *consumption determined;* the decree was gone forth (*v.* 33): "*Heaven and earth shall pass away* sooner than any word of mine: nay, they certainly shall pass away, but *my words shall not;* whether they *take hold* or no, they will *take effect,* and not one of them *fall to the ground,*" 1 Sam. iii. 19.

III. He cautions them against security and sensuality, by which they would unfit themselves for the trying times that were coming on, and make them to be a great surprise and terror to them (*v.* 34, 35): *Take heed to yourselves.* This is the word of command given to all Christ's disciples: "*Take heed to yourselves,* that you be not overpowered by temptations, nor betrayed by your own corruptions." Note, We cannot be *safe* if we be *secure.* It concerns us at *all* times, but especially at *some* times, to be very cautious. See here, 1. What our *danger* is: that *the day* of death and judgment should *come upon us unawares,* when we do not *expect* it, and are not *prepared* for it,—lest, when we are called to meet our Lord, that be found the *furthest* thing from our thoughts which ought always to be laid *nearest* our hearts, lest it *come upon us as a snare;* for so *it will come upon* the most of men, who *dwell upon the earth,* and mind *earthly things only,* and have no converse with heaven; to them it will be *as a snare.* See Eccl. ix. 12. It will be a *terror* and a *destruction* to them; it will put them into an inexpressible fright, and hold them fast for a doom yet more frightful. 2. What our *duty* is, in consideration of this danger: we must *take heed lest our hearts be overcharged,* lest they be burdened and overloaded, and so unfitted and disabled to do what must be done in preparation for death and judgment. Two things we must watch against, lest our hearts be overcharged with them:—(1.) The indulging of the appetites of the body, and allowing of ourselves in the gratifications of sense to an excess: *Take heed lest you be overcharged with surfeiting and drunkenness,* the immoderate use of meat and drink, which burden the heart, not only with the guilt thereby contracted, but by the ill influence which such disorders of the body have upon the mind; they make men dull and lifeless to their duty, dead and listless in their duty; they stupify the conscience, and cause the mind to be *unaffected* with those things that are most *affecting.* (2.) The inordinate pursuit of the good things of this world. The heart is overcharged with the *cares of this life.* The former is the snare of those that are given to their pleasures: this is the snare of the men of business, that *will be rich.* We have need to guard on both hands, not only lest at the time when death comes, but lest *at any time* our hearts should be thus overcharged. Our caution against sin, and our care of our own souls, must be *constant.*

IV. He counsels them to prepare and get ready for this great day, *v.* 36. Here see, 1. What should be *our aim:* that we may be *accounted worthy to escape all these things;* that, when the judgments of God are abroad, we may be preserved from the malignity of them; that either we may not be involved in the common calamity or it may not be that to us which it is to others; that in the day of death we may escape the sting of it, which is the wrath of God, and the damnation of hell. Yet we must aim not only to *escape that,* but to *stand before the Son of man;* not only to stand *acquitted* before him as our Judge (Ps. i. 5), to have boldness in the day of Christ (that is supposed in our *escaping* all those things), but to *stand before him,* to attend on him as our Master, to stand continually before his throne, and serve him day and night in his temple (Rev. vii. 15), always to *behold his face,* as the angels, Matt. xviii. 10. The saints are here said to be *accounted worthy,* as before, *ch.* xx. 35. God, by the good work of his grace in them, *makes them meet* for this happiness, and, by the good will of his grace towards them, *accounts them worthy* of it: but, as Grotius here says, a great part of our worthiness lies in an acknowledgment of our own unworthiness. 2. What should be our *actings* in these aims: *Watch therefore, and pray always.* Watching and praying must go together, Neh. iv. 9. Those that would escape the wrath to come, and make sure of the joys to come, must *watch* and *pray,* and must do so always, must make it the constant business of their lives, (1.) To keep a guard upon themselves. "Watch against sin, watch to every duty, and to the improvement of every opportunity of doing good. Be awake, and keep awake, in expectation of your Lord's coming, that you may be in a right frame to receive him, and bid him welcome." (2.) To keep up their communion with God: "*Pray always;* be always in an habitual disposition to that duty; keep up stated times for it; abound in it; pray upon all occasions." Those shall be accounted worthy to live a life of praise in the other world that live a life of prayer in this world.

V. In the last two verses we have an account how Christ disposed of himself during those three or four days between his riding in triumph into Jerusalem and the night in which he was betrayed. 1. He was *all day teaching in the temple.* Christ preached on week-days as well as sabbath days. He was an indefatigable preacher; he preached in the face of opposition, and in the midst of those that he knew sought occasion against him. 2. At night he went out to lodge at a friend's house, in the mount of Olives, about a mile out of town. It is probable that he had some friends in the city that would gladly have lodged him, but he was willing to retire in the evening out of the noise of the town, that he might have more time for secret devotion, now that his hour was at hand. 3. Early in the morning he was in the temple again, where he had a morning lecture for those that were willing to attend it; and the people were forward to hear one that they saw forward to preach (*v.* 38): *They all came early in the morning,* flocking to the temple, like doves to their windows, *to hear him,* though the chief priests and scribes did all they could to prejudice them against him. Sometimes the taste and relish which serious, honest, plain people have of good preaching are more to be valued and judged by than the opinion of the witty and learned, and those in authority.

CHAP. XXII.

All the evangelists, whatever they omit, give us a particular account of the death and resurrection of Christ, because he died for our sins and rose for our justification, this evangelist as fully as any, and with many circumstances and passages added which we had not before. In this chapter we have, I. The plot to take Jesus, and Judas's coming into it, ver. 1—6. II. Christ's eating the passover with his disciples, ver. 7—18. III. The instituting of the Lord's supper, ver. 19, 20. IV. Christ's discourse with his disciples after supper, upon several heads, ver. 21—38. V. His agony in the garden, ver. 39—46. VI. The apprehending of him, by the assistance of Judas, ver. 47—53. VII. Peter's denying him, ver. 54—62. VIII. The indignities done to Christ by those that had him in custody, and his trial and condemnation in the ecclesiastical court, ver. 63—71.

NOW the feast of unleavened
bread drew nigh, which is called
the passover. 2 And the chief priests
and scribes sought how they might
kill him; for they feared the people.
3 Then entered Satan into Judas
surnamed Iscariot, being of the number of the twelve. 4 And he went
his way, and communed with the chief
priests and captains, how he might
betray him unto them. 5 And they
were glad, and covenanted to give him
money. 6 And he promised, and
sought opportunity to betray him
unto them in the absence of the multitude.

The *year of the redeemed* is now *come,* which had been from eternity fixed in the divine counsels, and long looked for by them that waited for the consolation of Israel. After the revolutions of many ages, it is at length *come,* Isa. lxiii. 4. And, it is observable, it is in the very *first month* of that year that the redemption is wrought out, so much in haste was the Redeemer to perform his undertaking, so was he *straitened* till it was *accomplished.* It was in the same month, and at the same time of the month (in the *beginning of months,* Exod. xii. 2), that God by Moses brought Israel out of Egypt, that the Antitype might answer the type. Christ is here delivered up, *when the feast of unleavened bread drew nigh, v.* 1. About as long before that feast as they began to make preparation for it, here was preparation making for our Passover's being offered for us. Here we have

I. His sworn enemies contriving it (*v.* 2), *the chief priests,* men of sanctity, and the scribes, men of learning, *seeking how they might kill him,* either by force or fraud. Could they have had their will, it had been soon done, but they *feared the people,* and the more for what they now saw of their diligent attendance upon his preaching.

II. A treacherous disciple joining in with them, and coming to their assistance, Judas surnamed *Iscariot.* He is here said to be *of the number of the twelve,* that dignified distinguished number. One would wonder that Christ, who *knew* all men, should take a traitor into *that number,* and that one of *that number,* who could not but *know Christ,* should be so base as to betray him; but Christ had wise and holy ends in taking Judas to be a disciple, and how he who knew Christ so well yet came to betray him we are here told: *Satan entered into Judas, v.* 3. It was the devil's work, who thought hereby to ruin Christ's undertaking, to have broken his head; but it proved only the bruising of his heel. Whoever betrays Christ, or his truths or ways, it is Satan that puts them upon it. Judas knew how desirous the chief priests were to get Christ into their hands, and that they could not do it safely without the assistance of some that knew his retirements, as he did. He therefore went himself, and made the motion to them, *v.* 4. Note, It is hard to say whether more mischief is done to Christ's kingdom by the power and policy of its open enemies, or by the treachery and self-seeking of its pretended friends: nay, without the latter its enemies could not gain their point as they do. When you see Judas communing with the *chief priests,* be sure some mischief is hatching; it is for no good that they are laying their heads together.

III. The issue of the treaty between them. 1. Judas must *betray Christ to them,* must bring them to a place where they might seize him without danger of tumult, and this they would be *glad of.* 2. They must give him a sum of money for doing it, and this he would be glad of (*v.* 5): *They covenanted to give him money.* When the bargain was made, Judas sought *opportunity to betray him.* Probably, he slily enquired of Peter and John, who were more intimate with their Master than he was, where he would be at such a time, and whither he would retire after the passover, and they were not sharp enough to suspect him. Somehow or other, in a little time he gained the advantage he sought, and fixed the time and place where it might be done, *in the absence of the multitude,* and *without tumult.*

7 Then came the day of unleavened
bread, when the passover must be
killed. 8 And he sent Peter and
John, saying, Go and prepare us the
passover that we may eat. 9 And

they said unto him, Where wilt thou
that we prepare? 10 And he said
unto them, Behold, when ye are entered into the city, there shall a man
meet you, bearing a pitcher of water;
follow him into the house where he
entereth in. 11 And ye shall say
unto the goodman of the house, The
Master saith unto thee, Where is the
guestchamber, where I shall eat the
passover with my disciples? 12 And
he shall show you a large upper room
furnished: there make ready. 13 And
they went, and found as he had said
unto them: and they made ready the
passover. 14 And when the hour
was come, he sat down, and the twelve
apostles with him. 15 And he said
unto them, With desire I have desired
to eat this passover with you before
I suffer: 16 For I say unto you, I
will not any more eat thereof, until it
be fulfilled in the kingdom of God.
17 And he took the cup, and gave
thanks, and said, Take this, and divide
it among yourselves: 18 For I say
unto you, I will not drink of the fruit
of the vine, until the kingdom of God
shall come. 19 And he took bread,
and gave thanks, and brake *it*, and
gave unto them, saying, This is my
body which is given for you: this do
in remembrance of me. 20 Likewise
also the cup after supper, saying, This
cup *is* the new testament in my blood,
which is shed for you.

What a hopeful prospect had we of Christ's doing a great deal of good by his preaching in the temple during the feast of unleavened bread, which continued seven days, when the people were *every* morning, and *early* in the morning, so attentive to hear him! But here is a stop put to it. He must enter upon work of another kind; in this, however, he shall do more good than in the other, for neither Christ's nor his church's suffering days are their idle empty days. Now here we have,

I. The preparation that was made for Christ's eating the passover with his disciples, upon the very *day of unleavened bread, when the passover must be killed* according to the law, *v.* 7. Christ was made under the law, and observed the ordinances of it, particularly that of the passover, to teach us in like manner to observe his gospel institutions, particularly that of the Lord's supper, and not to neglect them. It is probable that he went to the temple to preach in the morning, when he sent Peter and John another way into the city to *prepare the passover.* Those who have attendants about them, to do their secular business for them in a great measure, must not think that this *allows* them to be *idle;* it *engages* them to employ themselves more in *spiritual* business, or service to *the public.* He directed those whom he employed whither they should go (*v.* 9, 10): *they must follow a man bearing a pitcher of water,* and he must be their guide to the house. Christ could have described the house to them; probably it was a house they knew, and he might have said no more than, Go to such a one's house, or to a house in such a street, with such a sign, &c. But he directed them thus, to teach them to depend upon the conduct of Providence, and to follow that, *step by step.* They went, not knowing *whither they went,* nor *whom they followed.* Being come to the house, they must desire the master of the house to show them a room (*v.* 11), and he will readily do it, *v.* 12. Whether it was a friend's house or a public house does not appear; but the disciples found their guide, and the house, and the room, just as he had said to them (*v.* 13); for *they* need not fear a disappointment who go upon Christ's word; according to the orders given them, they got every thing in readiness for *the passover, v.* 11.

II. The solemnizing of the passover, according to the law. When *the hour was come* that they should go to supper *he sat down,* probably at the head-end of the table, and *the twelve apostles with him,* Judas not excepted; for it is possible that those whose hearts are filled with Satan, and all manner of wickedness, may yet continue a plausible profession of religion, and be found in the performance of its external services; and while it is in the heart, and does not break out into any thing scandalous, such cannot be denied the external privileges of their external profession. Though Judas has already been guilty of an *overt act* of treason, yet, it not being publicly known, Christ admits him to sit down with the rest at the passover. Now observe,

1. How Christ *bids this passover welcome,* to teach us in like manner to welcome his passover, the Lord's supper, and to come to it with an appetite (*v.* 15): "*With desire I have desired,* I have most earnestly desired, to *eat this passover with you before I suffer.*" He knew it was to be the prologue to his sufferings, and *therefore* he desired it, because it was in order to his Father's glory and man's redemption. He *delighted* to do even this part of the *will of God* concerning him as Mediator. Shall we be *backward* to any service for him who was so *forward* in the work of our salvation? See the love he had to his disciples; he desired to eat it *with them,* that he and they might have a little time together, themselves, and none besides, for private conversation, which they could

not have in Jerusalem but upon this occasion. He was now about to leave them, but was very desirous to *eat this passover with them before he suffered,* as if the comfort of that would carry him the more cheerfully through his sufferings, and make them the easier to him. Note, Our gospel passover, eaten by faith with Jesus Christ, will be an excellent preparation for sufferings, and trials, and death itself.

2. How Christ in it *takes his leave of all passovers,* thereby signifying his abrogating all the ordinances of the ceremonial law, of which that of the passover was one of the *earliest* and one of the most *eminent* (*v.* 16): "*I will not any more eat thereof,* nor shall it be any more celebrated by my disciples, *until it be fulfilled in the kingdom of God.*" (1.) It was fulfilled when *Christ our Passover was sacrificed for us,* 1 Cor. v. 7. And *therefore* that type and shadow was laid aside, because now in the *kingdom of God* the substance was come, which superseded it. (2.) It was fulfilled in the *Lord's supper,* an ordinance of the gospel kingdom, in which the passover had its accomplishment, and which the disciples, after the pouring out of the Spirit, did frequently celebrate, as we find Acts ii. 42, 46. They ate of it, and Christ might be said to eat with them, because of the spiritual communion they had with him in that ordinance. He is said to *sup with them* and *they with him,* Rev. iii. 20. But, (3.) The complete accomplishment of that commemoration of liberty will be in the kingdom of glory, when all God's spiritual Israel shall be released from the bondage of death and sin, and be put in possession of the land of promise. What he had said of his eating of the paschal lamb, he repeats concerning his drinking of the *passover wine,* the cup of *blessing,* or of thanksgiving, in which all the company pledged the Master of the feast, at the close of the passover supper. This cup *he took,* according to the custom, and *gave thanks* for the deliverance of Israel out of Egypt, and the preservation of their first-born, and then said, *Take this, and divide it among yourselves, v.* 17. This is not said afterwards of the sacramental cup, which being probably of much more weight and value, being the *New Testament in his blood,* he might give into every one's hand, to teach them to make a particular application of it to their own souls; but, as for the paschal cup which is to be abolished, it is enough to say, "*Take* it, and *divide it among yourselves,* do what you will with it, for we shall have no more occasion for it, *v.* 18. *I will not drink of the fruit of the vine any more,* I will not have it any more drank of, *till the kingdom of God shall come,* till the Spirit be poured out, and then you shall in *the Lord's supper* commemorate a much more glorious redemption, of which both the deliverance out of Egypt and the passover commemoration of it were types and figures. The kingdom of God is now so near being set up that you will not need to eat or drink any more till it comes." Christ dying next day opened it. As Christ with a great deal of pleasure took leave of all the legal feasts (which fell of course with the passover) for the evangelical ones, both spiritual and sacramental; so may good Christians, when they are called to remove from the church militant to that which is triumphant, cheerfully exchange even their spiritual repasts, much more their sacramental ones, for the eternal feast.

III. The institution of the Lord's supper, *v.* 19, 20. The *passover* and the *deliverance* out of Egypt were *typical* and *prophetic signs* of a Christ to come, who should by dying deliver us from sin and death, and the tyranny of Satan; but they shall no more say, *The Lord liveth, that brought us up out of the land of Egypt;* a much greater deliverance shall eclipse the lustre of that, and therefore the Lord's supper is instituted to be a commemorative sign or memorial of a Christ already come, that *has* by dying delivered us; and it is his death that is in a special manner set before us in that ordinance.

1. The *breaking of Christ's body* as a *sacrifice for us* is here commemorated by the *breaking of bread;* and the sacrifices under the law were called the *bread of our God* (Lev. xxi. 6, 8, 17): *This is my body which is given for you.* And there is a feast upon that sacrifice instituted, in which we are to apply it to ourselves, and to take the benefit and comfort of it. This bread that was given for us is given *to us* to be food for our souls, for nothing can be more *nourishing* and *satisfying* to our souls than the doctrine of Christ's making atonement for sin, and the assurance of our interest in that atonement; this bread that was *broken* and *given for us,* to satisfy for the guilt of our sins, is *broken* and *given to us,* to satisfy the desire of our souls. And this we do in *remembrance* of what he did for us, when he died for us, and for a *memorial* of what we *do,* in making ourselves *partakers of him,* and joining ourselves to him in an everlasting covenant; like the stone Joshua set up for a *witness,* Josh. xxiv. 27.

2. The *shedding* of *Christ's blood,* by which the atonement was made (for *the blood made atonement for the soul,* Lev. xvii. 11), as represented by the wine in the cup; and that cup of wine is a sign and token of the New Testament, or new covenant, made with us. It *commemorates* the purchase of the covenant by the blood of Christ, and *confirms* the promises of the covenant, which are all *Yea* and *Amen* in him. This will be reviving and refreshing to our souls, as wine that *makes glad the heart.* In all our commemorations of the shedding of Christ's blood, we must have an eye to it as shed for us; we needed it, we take hold of it, we hope to have benefit by it; *who loved me, and gave*

himself for me. And in all our regards to the New Testament we must have an eye to the *blood of Christ,* which gave life and being to it, and seals to us all the promises of it. Had it not been for the blood of Christ, we had never had the New Testament; and, had it not been for the New Testament, we had never known the meaning of Christ's blood shed.

21 But, behold, the hand of him
that betrayeth me *is* with me on the
table. 22 And truly the Son of man
goeth, as it was determined: but woe
unto that man by whom he is betrayed! 23 And they began to enquire among themselves, which of
them it was that should do this thing.
24 And there was also a strife among
them, which of them should be accounted the greatest. 25 And he
said unto them, The kings of the Gentiles exercise lordship over them; and
they that exercise authority upon
them are called benefactors. 26 But
ye *shall* not *be* so: but he that is
greatest among you, let him be as the
younger; and he that is chief, as he
that doth serve. 27 For whether *is*
greater, he that sitteth at meat, or he
that serveth? *is* not he that sitteth
at meat? but I am among you as he
that serveth. 28 Ye are they which
have continued with me in my temptations. 29 And I appoint unto you
a kingdom, as my Father hath appointed unto me; 30 That ye may
eat and drink at my table in my kingdom, and sit on thrones judging the
twelve tribes of Israel. 31 And the
Lord said, Simon, Simon, behold,
Satan hath desired *to have* you, that
he may sift *you* as wheat: 32 But I
have prayed for thee, that thy faith
fail not: and when thou art converted,
strengthen thy brethren. 33 And he
said unto him, Lord, I am ready to
go with thee, both into prison, and to
death. 34 And he said, I tell thee,
Peter, the cock shall not crow this
day, before that thou shalt thrice deny
that thou knowest me. 35 And he
said unto them, When I sent you
without purse, and scrip, and shoes,
lacked ye any thing? And they said,
Nothing. 36 Then said he unto them,
But now, he that hath a purse, let
him take *it,* and likewise *his* scrip:
and he that hath no sword, let him
sell his garment, and buy one. 37
For I say unto you, that this that is
written must yet be accomplished in
me, And he was reckoned among the
transgressors: for the things concerning me have an end. 38 And they
said, Lord, behold, here *are* two
swords. And he said unto them, It
is enough.

We have here Christ's discourse with his disciples after supper, much of which is new here; and in St. John's gospel we shall find other additions. We should take example from him to entertain and edify our family and friends with such discourse at table as is good and to the use of edifying, which may minister grace to the hearers; but especially after we have been at the Lord's table, by Christian conference to keep one another in a suitable frame. The matters Christ here discoursed of were of weight, and to the present purpose.

I. He discoursed with them concerning him that should betray him, who was now present. 1. He signifies to them that the traitor was now among them, and one of them, *v.* 21. By placing this after the institution of the Lord's supper, though in Matthew and Mark it is placed before it, it seems plain that Judas did receive the Lord's supper, did *eat of that bread* and *drink of that cup;* for, after the solemnity was over, Christ said, *Behold, the hand of him that betrayeth me is with me on the table.* There have been those that have eaten bread with Christ and yet have betrayed him. 2. He foretels that the treason would take effect (*v.* 22): *Truly the Son of man goes as it was determined,* goes to the place where he will be betrayed; for he is delivered up by the counsel and foreknowledge of God, else Judas could not have delivered him up. Christ was not driven to his sufferings, but cheerfully *went to them.* He said, *Lo, I come.* 3. He threatens the traitor: *Woe to that man by whom he is betrayed.* Note, Neither the patience of the saints under their sufferings, nor the counsel of God concerning their sufferings, will be any excuse for those that have any hand in their sufferings, or that persecute them. Though God has *determined* that Christ shall be betrayed, and he himself has cheerfully submitted to it, yet Judas's sin or punishment is not at all the less. 4. He frightens the rest of the disciples into a suspicion of themselves, by saying that it was one of them, and not naming which (*v.* 23): *They began to enquire among themselves,* to interrogate themselves, to put the question to themselves, *who it was that should do this thing,* that could be so base to so good a Master. The enquiry was not, *Is it you?* or, *Is it such a one?* but, *Is it I?*

II. Concerning the strife that was among them for precedency or supremacy.

1. See what the dispute was: *Which of them should be accounted the greatest.* Such and so many contests among the disciples for dignity and dominion, *before* the Spirit was poured upon them, were a sad presage of the like strifes for, and affections of, supremacy in the churches, after the Spirit should be provoked to depart from them. How inconsistent is this with that in the verse before! There they were enquiring which would be the traitor, and here which should be the prince. Could such an instance of humility, and such an instance of pride and vanity, be found in the same men, so near together? This is like *sweet* waters and *bitter* proceeding at the same time out of the same fountain. What a self-contradiction is the deceitful heart of man!

2. See what Christ said to this dispute. He was not sharp upon them, as might have been expected (he having so often reproved them for this very thing), but mildly showed them the sin and folly of it.

(1.) This was to make themselves like the *kings of the Gentiles,* who affect worldly pomp, and worldly power, *v.* 25. They *exercise lordship* over their subjects, and are ever and anon striving to exercise lordship too over the *princes* that are about them, though as *good* as themselves, if they think them not *so strong* as themselves. Note, The *exercising of lordship* better becomes the *kings of the Gentiles* than the ministers of Christ. But observe, *They that exercise authority,* and take upon themselves to bear sway, and give law, they are called *Benefactors*—Εὐεργέτας, they call themselves so, and so their flatterers call them, and those that set themselves to serve their interests. It is pretended that they have *been* benefactors, and upon *that* account they should be admitted to *have rule;* nay, that in exercising authority they are benefactors. However they may really serve themselves, they would be thought to *serve their country.* One of the Ptolemies was surnamed *Euergetes—The Benefactor.* Now our Saviour, by taking notice of this, intimates, [1.] That to *do good* is much more honourable than to *look great;* for these princes that were the *terror of the mighty* would not be called so, but rather the *benefactors of the needy;* so that, by their own confession, a benefactor to his country is much more valued than a ruler of his country. [2.] That to *do good* is the surest way to be great, else they that aimed to be *rulers* would not have been so solicitous to be called *Benefactors.* This therefore he would have his disciples believe, that their greatest honour would be to do all the good they could in the world. They would indeed be *benefactors* to the world, by bringing the gospel to it. Let them value themselves upon that title, which they would indeed be *entitled* to, and then they need not strive which should be the greatest, for they would all be *greater*—greater blessings to mankind than the kings of the earth, that exercise lordship over them. If they have that which is confessedly the *greater* honour, of being benefactors, let them despise the less, of being rulers.

(2.) It was to make themselves unlike the disciples of Christ, and unlike Christ himself: "*You shall not be so,*" *v.* 26, 27. "It was never intended that you should *rule* any otherwise than by the power of truth and grace, but that you should *serve.*" When church-rulers affect external pomp and power, and bear up themselves by secular interests and influences, they debase their office, and it is an instance of degeneracy like that of Israel when they would have a king like the nations that were round about them, whereas the Lord was their King. See here, [1.] What is the rule Christ gave to his disciples: He that is *greater among you,* that is *senior,* to whom precedency is due upon the account of his age, let him be as the *younger,* both in point of *lowness of place* (let him condescend to sit with the younger, and be free and familiar with them) and in point of *labour* and *work.* We say, *Juniores ad labores, seniores ad honores—Let the young work, and the aged receive their honours.* But let the elder take pains as well as the younger; their age and honour, instead of warranting them to take their ease, bind them to double work. And he *that is chief,* ὁ ἡγούμενος—*the president* of the college or assembly, let him be *as he that* serves, ὡς ὁ διακονῶν—*as the deacon;* let him stoop to the meanest and most toilsome services for the public good, if there be occasion. [2.] What was the example which he himself gave to this rule: *Whether is greater, he that sitteth at meat or he that serveth?* he that attendeth or he that is attended on? Now Christ was among his disciples just like one that waited at table. He was so far from *taking state,* or *taking his ease,* by commanding their attendance upon him, that he was ready to do any office of kindness and service for them; witness his *washing* their feet. Shall those take upon them the form of princes who call themselves followers of him that *took upon him the form of a servant?*

(3.) They ought not to strive for worldly honour and grandeur, because he had better honours in reserve for them, of another nature, a *kingdom,* a *feast,* a *throne,* for each of them, wherein they should all share alike, and should have no occasion to strive for precedency, *v.* 28—30. Where observe,

[1.] Christ's commendation of his disciples for their faithfulness to him; and this was honour enough for them, they needed not to strive for any greater. It is spoken with an air of encomium and applause: "*You are they who have continued with me in my temptations,* you are they who have stood by me and stuck to me when others have deserted me and turned their backs upon me." Christ had his temptations; he was despised and rejected of men, reproached and reviled, and *endured the contradiction of sinners.* But his disciples continued with him, and were afflicted in all his afflictions. It was but little help that they could give him, or service that they could do him; nevertheless, he took it kindly that they *continued with him,* and he here owns their kindness, though it was by the assistance of his own grace that they did continue. Christ's disciples had been very defective in their duty. We find them guilty of many mistakes and weaknesses: they were very dull and very forgetful, and often blundered, yet their Master passes all by and forgets it; he does not upbraid them with their infirmities, but gives them this memorable testimonial, *You are they who have continued with me.* Thus does he praise at parting, to show how willing he is to make the best of those whose hearts he knows to be upright with him.

[2.] The recompence he designed them for their fidelity: *I appoint,* διατίθεμαι, *I bequeath, unto you a kingdom.* Or thus, *I appoint to you, as my Father has appointed a kingdom to me, that you may eat and drink at my table.* Understand it, *First,* Of what should be done for them in this world. God gave his Son a *kingdom among men,* the gospel church, of which he is the living, quickening, ruling, Head. This *kingdom* he *appointed* to his apostles and their successors in the ministry of the gospel, that they should enjoy the comforts and privileges of the gospel, help to communicate them to others by gospel ordinances, sit on thrones as officers of the church, not only declaratively, but exhortatively *judging the tribes of Israel* that persist in their infidelity, and denouncing the wrath of God against them, and ruling the gospel Israel, the spiritual Israel, by the instituted discipline of the church, administered with gentleness and love. This is the honour reserved for you. Or, *Secondly,* Of what should be done for them in the other world, which I take to be chiefly meant. Let them go on in their services in this world; their preferments shall be in the other world. God will give them *the kingdom,* in which they shall be sure to have, 1. The *richest dainties;* for they shall *eat and drink at Christ's table in his kingdom,* of which he had spoken, *v.* 16, 18. They shall partake of those joys and pleasures which were the recompence of his services and sufferings. They shall have a full satisfaction of soul in the vision and fruition of God; and herein they shall have the best society, as at a feast, in the perfection of love. 2. The *highest dignities:* "You shall not only be provided for at the royal table, as Mephibosheth at David's, but you shall be preferred to the royal throne; shall *sit down with me on my throne,* Rev. iii. 21. In the great day you shall *sit on thrones,* as assessors with Christ, to approve of and applaud his judgment of the *twelve tribes of Israel.*" If the *saints shall judge the world* (1 Cor. vi. 2), much more the church.

III. Concerning Peter's denying him. And in this part of the discourse we may observe,

1. The general notice Christ gives to Peter of the devil's design upon him and the rest of the apostles (*v.* 31): *The Lord said, Simon, Simon,* observe what I say; *Satan hath desired to have you,* to have you all in his hands, *that he may sift you as wheat.* Peter, who used to be the *mouth* of the rest in speaking to Christ, is here made the *ear* of the rest; and what is designed for warning to them all *(all you shall be offended, because of me)* is directed to Peter, because he was principally concerned, being in a particular manner struck at by the tempter: *Satan has desired to have you.* Probably Satan had *accused* the disciples to God as mercenary in following Christ, and aiming at nothing else therein but enriching and advancing themselves in this world, as he accused Job." "No," saith God, "they are honest men, and men of integrity." "Give me leave to try them," saith Satan, "and Peter particularly." He desired to have them, *that he might sift them,* that he might show them to be chaff, and not wheat. The troubles that were now coming upon them were *sifting,* would try what there was in them: but this was not all; Satan desired to sift them by his temptations, and endeavoured by those troubles to draw them into sin, to put them into a loss and hurry, as corn when it is sifted to bring the chaff uppermost, or rather to shake out the wheat and leave nothing but the chaff. Observe, Satan could not sift them unless God gave him leave: He *desired to have them,* as he begged of God a permission to try and tempt Job. Ἐξῃτήσατο—"*He has challenged you,* has undertaken to prove you a company of hypocrites, and Peter especially, the forwardest of you." Some suggest that Satan demanded leave to sift them as their punishment for striving who should be greatest, in which contest Peter perhaps was very warm: "Leave them to me, to sift them for it."

2. The particular encouragement he gave to Peter, in reference to this trial: "*I have prayed for thee,* because, though he desires to have them all, he is permitted to make his strongest onset upon thee only: thou wilt be most violently assaulted, *but I have prayed for thee, that thy faith fail not,* that it may not totally and finally fail." Note, (1.) If faith be kept up in an hour of temptation, though we may fall, yet we shall not be utterly cast down. Faith will quench Satan's fiery darts. (2.) Though there may be many failings in the faith of true believers, yet there shall not be a total and final failure of their faith. It is their seed, their root, remaining in them. (3.) It is owing to the mediation and intercession of Jesus Christ that the faith of his disciples, though sometimes sadly shaken, yet is not sunk. If they were left to themselves, they would fail; but

they are *kept by the power of God* and the prayer of Christ. The intercession of Christ is not only general, for all that believe, but for *particular* believers (I have prayed for *thee)*, which is an encouragement for us to pray for ourselves, and an engagement upon us to pray for others too.

3. The charge he gives to Peter to help others as he should himself be helped of God: "*When thou art converted, strengthen thy brethren;* when thou art recovered by the grace of God, and brought to repentance, do what thou canst to recover others; when thou hast found thy faith kept from failing, labour to confirm the faith of others, and to establish them; when thou hast found mercy with God thyself, encourage others to hope that they also shall find mercy." Note, (1.) Those that have fallen into sin must be *converted from it;* those that have turned aside must *return;* those that have left their first love must do their first works. (2.) Those that through grace are converted from sin must do what they can to strengthen their brethren that stand, and to prevent *their falling;* see Ps. li. 11—13; 1 Tim. i. 13.

4. Peter's declared resolution to cleave to Christ, whatever it cost him (*v.* 33): *Lord, I am ready to go with thee, both into prison and to death.* This was a great word, and yet I believe no more than he meant at this time, and thought he should *make good* too. Judas never protested thus against denying Christ, though often warned of it; for his heart was as fully set in him to the evil as Peter's was against it. Note, All the true disciples of Christ sincerely desire and design to *follow him, whithersoever he goes,* and whithersoever he leads them, though into a prison, though out of the world.

5. Christ's express prediction of his denying him thrice (*v.* 34): "*I tell thee, Peter* (thou dost not know thine own heart, but must be left to thyself a little, that thou mayest know it, and mayest never trust to it again), *the cock shall not crow this day before thou even deny that thou knowest me.*" Note, Christ knows us better than we know ourselves, and knows the evil that is in us, and will be done by us, which we ourselves do not suspect. It is well for us that Christ knows where we are weak better than we do, and therefore where to come in with grace sufficient; that he knows how far a temptation will prevail, and therefore when to say, *Hitherto shall it come, and no further.*

IV. Concerning the condition of all the disciples.

1. He appeals to them concerning what had been, *v.* 35. He had owned that they had been faithful servants to him, *v.* 28. Now he expects, at parting, that they should acknowledge that he had been a kind and careful Master to them ever since they left all to follow him: *When I sent you without purse, lacked you any thing?* (1.) He owns that he had sent them out in a very poor and bare condition, barefoot, and with no money in their purses, because they were not to go far, nor be out long; and he would thus teach them to depend upon the providence of God, and, under that, upon the kindness of their friends. If God thus send us out into the world, let us remember that better than we have thus begun low. (2.) Yet he will have them own that, notwithstanding this, they had *lacked nothing;* they then lived as plentifully and comfortably as ever; and they readily acknowledged it: "*Nothing, Lord;* I have all, and abound." Note, [1.] It is good for us often to review the providences of God that have been concerning us all our days, and to observe how we have got through the straits and difficulties we have met with. [2.] Christ is a good Master, and his service a good service; for though his servants may sometimes be brought low, yet he will help them; and though he *try* them, yet will he not leave them. *Jehovah-jireh.* [3.] We must reckon ourselves well done by, and must not complain, but be thankful, if we have had the necessary supports of life, though we have had neither dainties nor superfluities, though we have lived from hand to mouth, and lived upon the kindness of our friends. The disciples lived upon contribution, and yet did not complain that their maintenance was precarious, but owned, to their Master's honour, that it was sufficient; they had wanted nothing.

2. He gives them notice of a very great change of their circumstances now approaching. For, (1.) He that was their Master was now entering upon his sufferings, which he had often foretold (*v.* 37): "Now *that which is written must be fulfilled in me,* and this among the rest, *He was numbered among the transgressors*—he must suffer and die as a malefactor, and in company with some of the vilest of malefactors. This is that which is *yet to be accomplished,* after all the rest, and then *the things concerning me,* the things written concerning me, will have an end; then I shall say, *It is finished.*" Note, It may be the comfort of suffering Christians, as it was of a suffering Christ, that their sufferings were foretold, and *determined* in the counsels of heaven, and will shortly *determine* in the joys of heaven! They were *written* concerning them, and they *will have an end,* and will end well, everlastingly well. (2.) They must therefore expect troubles, and must not think now to have such an easy and comfortable life as they had had; no, the scene will alter. They must now in some degree suffer *with* their Master; and, when he is gone, they must expect to suffer *like* him. The servant is not better than his Lord. [1.] They must not now expect that their friends would be so kind and generous to them as they had been; and therefore, *He that has a purse, let him take it,* for he may have occasion for it, and for all the good husbandry he can use. [2.] They must now expect that their enemies would be more fierce upon

them than they had been, and they would need magazines as well as stores: *He that has no sword* wherewith to defend himself against robbers and assassins (2 Cor. xi. 26) will find a great want of it, and will be ready to wish, some time or other, that he had sold his garment and bought one. This is intended only to show that the times would be very perilous, so that no man would think himself safe if he had not a sword by his side. But the *sword of the Spirit* is the sword which the disciples of Christ must furnish themselves with. *Christ having suffered for us,* we must *arm ourselves* with the same mind (1 Peter iv. 1), arm ourselves with an expectation of trouble, that it may not be a surprise to us, and with a holy resignation to the will of God in it, that there may be no opposition in us to it: and then we are better prepared than if we had sold a coat to buy a sword. The disciples hereupon enquire what strength they had, and find they had among them *two swords* (*v.* 38), of which one was Peter's. The Galileans generally travelled with swords. Christ wore none himself, but he was not against his disciples' wearing them. But he intimates how little he would have them depend upon this when he saith, *It is enough,* which some think is spoken ironically: "Two swords among twelve men! you are bravely armed indeed when our enemies are now coming out against us in great multitudes, and every one with a sword!" Yet two swords are sufficient for those who need none, having God himself to be *the shield of their help and the sword of their excellency,* Deut. xxxiii. 29.

39 And he came out, and went, as
he was wont, to the mount of Olives;
and his disciples also followed him.
40 And when he was at the place, he
said unto them, Pray that ye enter
not into temptation. 41 And he was
withdrawn from them about a stone's
cast, and kneeled down, and prayed,
42 Saying, Father, if thou be willing,
remove this cup from me: nevertheless not my will, but thine, be done.
43 And there appeared an angel unto
him from heaven, strengthening him.
44 And being in an agony he prayed
more earnestly: and his sweat was as
it were great drops of blood falling
down to the ground. 45 And when
he rose up from prayer, and was come
to his disciples, he found them sleeping for sorrow, 46 And said unto
them, Why sleep ye? rise and pray,
lest ye enter into temptation.

We have here the awful story of Christ's *agony in the garden,* just before he was betrayed, which was largely related by the other evangelists. In it Christ *accommodated himself* to that part of his undertaking which he was now entering upon—the making of *his soul an offering for sin.* He afflicted his own soul with grief for the sin he was to satisfy for, and an apprehension of the wrath of God to which man had by sin made himself obnoxious, which he was pleased as a sacrifice to admit the impressions of, the consuming of a sacrifice with fire from heaven being the surest token of its acceptance. In it Christ entered the lists with the powers of darkness, gave them all the advantages they could desire, and yet conquered them.

I. What we have in this passage which we had before is, 1. That when Christ went out, though it was in the night, and a long walk, *his disciples* (eleven of them, for Judas had given them the slip) *followed him.* Having continued with him hitherto in his temptations, they would not leave him now. 2. That he went to the place *where he was wont* to be private, which intimates that Christ accustomed himself to retirement, was often alone, to teach us to be so, for freedom of converse with God and our own hearts. Though Christ had no conveniency for retirement but a garden, yet he retired. This should particularly be our practice after we have been at the Lord's table; we have then work to do which requires us to be private. 3. That he exhorted his disciples to *pray* that, though the approaching trial could not be avoided, yet they might not in it *enter into temptation* to sin; that, when they were in the greatest fright and danger, yet they might not have any inclination to desert Christ, nor take a step towards it: "Pray that you may be *kept from sin.*" 4. That he withdrew from them, and prayed himself; they had their errands at the throne of grace, and he had his, and therefore it was fit that they should pray separately, as sometimes, when they had joint errands, they prayed together. He withdrew about a *stone's cast* further into the garden, which some reckon about fifty or sixty paces, and there he *kneeled down* (so it is here) upon the bare ground; but the other evangelists say that afterwards he *fell on his face,* and there *prayed* that, if it were the will of God, this cup of suffering, this bitter cup, might be *removed from him.* This was the language of that innocent dread of suffering which, being really and truly man, he could not but have in his nature. 5. That he, knowing it to be his Father's will that he should suffer and die, and that, as the matter was now settled, it was necessary for our redemption and salvation, presently withdrew that petition, did not insist upon it, but resigned himself to his heavenly Father's will: "*Nevertheless not my will be done,* not the will of my human nature, but the will of God as it is written concerning me in the volume of the book, *which I delight to do,* let that be done," Ps. xl. 7, 8. 6. That his disciples were *asleep* when he was at prayer, and when they should have been themselves praying, *v.* 45. When he *rose from prayer,* he *found them sleeping,* unconcerned in his sorrows; but see what a favourable construction is here put upon it, which we had not in the other evangelists—they were *sleeping for sorrow.* The great sorrow they were in upon the mournful farewells their Master had been this evening giving them had exhausted their spirits, and made them very dull and heavy, which (it being now late) disposed them to sleep. This teaches us to make the best of our brethren's infirmities, and, if there be one cause better than another, charitably impute them to that. 7. That when he awoke them, then he exhorted them to pray (*v.* 46): "*Why sleep ye?* Why do you allow yourselves to sleep? *Rise and pray. Shake off* your drowsiness, that you may be *fit to pray,* and *pray for grace,* that you may be able to *shake off* your drowsiness." This was like the ship-master's call to Jonah in a storm (Jon. i. 6): *Arise, call upon thy God.* When we find ourselves either by our outward circumstances or our inward dispositions entering into temptation, it concerns us to *rise and pray,* Lord, help me in this *time of need.* But,

II. There are three things in this passage which we had not in the other evangelists:—

1. That, when Christ was in his agony, *there appeared* to him *an angel from heaven, strengthening him, v.* 43. (1.) It was an instance of the deep humiliation of our Lord Jesus that he *needed* the assistance of an angel, and would *admit* it. The influence of the divine nature withdrew for the present, and then, as to his human nature, he was for a little while *lower than the angels,* and was capable of receiving help from them. (2.) When he was not delivered from his sufferings, yet he was *strengthened* and supported under them, and that was *equivalent.* If God proportion the shoulders to the burden, we shall have no reason to complain, whatever he is pleased to lay upon us. David owns this a sufficient *answer to his prayer,* in the day of trouble, that God *strengthened him with strength in his soul,* and so does the son of David, Ps. cxxxviii. 3. (3.) The angels ministered to the Lord Jesus in his sufferings. He could have had legions of them to rescue him; nay, this one could have done it, could have chased and conquered the whole band of men that came to take him; but he made use of his ministration only to *strengthen him;* and the very visit which this angel made him now in his grief, when his enemies were awake and his friends asleep, was such a seasonable token of the divine favour as would be a very great strengthening to him. Yet this was not all: he probably *said something* to him to strengthen him; put him in mind that his sufferings were in order to his Father's glory, to his own glory, and to the salvation of those that were given him, represented to him the joy set before him, the seed he should see; with these and the like suggestions he encouraged him to go on cheerfully; and what is comforting is strengthening. Perhaps he *did something* to strengthen him, wiped away his sweat and tears, perhaps ministered some cordial to him, as after his temptation, or, it may be, took him by the arm, and helped him off the ground, or bore him up when he was ready to faint away; and in these services of the angel the Holy Spirit was ἐνισχύων αὐτόν—*putting strength into him;* for so the word signifies. *It pleased the Lord to bruise him* indeed; yet *did he plead against him with his great power?* No, but he *put strength in him* (Job xxiii. 6), as he had promised, Ps. lxxxix. 21; Isa. xlix. 8; l. 7.

2. That, *being in an agony, he prayed more earnestly, v.* 44. As his sorrow and trouble grew upon him, he grew more importunate in prayer; not that there was before any coldness or indifferency in his prayers, but there was now a greater vehemency in them, which was expressed in his voice and gesture. Note, Prayer, though never out of season, is in a special manner seasonable when we are in an agony; and the stronger our agonies are the more lively and frequent our prayers should be. Now it was that Christ *offered up prayers and supplications with strong crying and tears, and was heard in that he feared* (Heb. v. 7), and in his fear *wrestled,* as Jacob with the angel.

3. That, in this agony, *his sweat was as it were great drops of blood falling down to the ground.* Sweat came in with sin, and was a branch of the curse, Gen. iii. 19. And therefore, when Christ was made sin and a curse for us, he underwent a grievous sweat, that *in the sweat of his face* we might eat bread, and that he might sanctify and sweeten all our trials to us. There is some dispute among the critics whether this *sweat* is only *compared to* drops of *blood,* being much *thicker* than drops of sweat commonly are, the pores of the body being more than ordinarily opened, or whether *real* blood out of the capillary veins mingled with it, so that it was in colour like blood, and might truly be called a *bloody sweat;* the matter is not great. Some reckon this one of the times when Christ shed his blood for us, *for without the shedding of blood there is no remission.* Every pore was as it were a bleeding wound, and his blood stained all his raiment. This showed the *travail of his soul.* He was now abroad in the open air, in a cool season, upon the cold ground, far in the night, which, one would think, had been enough to strike in a sweat; yet now he breaks out into a sweat, which bespeaks the extremity of the agony he was in.

47 And while he yet spake, behold,
a multitude, and he that was called
Judas, one of the twelve, went before
them, and drew near unto Jesus to
kiss him. 48 But Jesus said unto
him, Judas, betrayest thou the Son

of man with a kiss? 49 When they
which were about him saw what would
follow, they said unto him, Lord, shall
we smite with the sword? 50 And
one of them smote the servant of the
high priest, and cut off his right ear.
51 And Jesus answered and said,
Suffer ye thus far. And he touched
his ear, and healed him. 52 Then
Jesus said unto the chief priests, and
captains of the temple, and the elders,
which were come to him, Be ye come
out, as against a thief, with swords
and staves? 53 When I was daily
with you in the temple, ye stretched
forth no hands against me: but this is
your hour, and the power of darkness.

Satan, finding himself baffled in his attempts to terrify our Lord Jesus, and so to put him out of the possession of his own soul, betakes himself (according to his usual method) to force and arms, and brings a party into the field to seize him, and Satan was *in them*. Here is,

I. The marking of him by Judas. Here a numerous party appears, and Judas at the head of them, for he was *guide to them that took Jesus;* they knew not where to *find him*, but he brought them to the place: when they were there, they knew not which was he, but Judas told them that whomsoever he should kiss, that same was he; so he *drew near to him to kiss him,* according to the wonted freedom and familiarity to which our Lord Jesus admitted his disciples. Luke takes notice of the question Christ asked him, which we have not in the other evangelists: *Judas, betrayest thou the Son of man with a kiss?* What! Is this the signal? *v.* 48. Must the Son of man be *betrayed*, as if any thing could be concealed from him, and a plot carried on against him unknown to him? Must one of his own disciples betray him, as if he had been a hard Master to them, or deserved ill at their hands? Must he be betrayed with a kiss? Must the badge of friendship be the instrument of treachery? Was ever a love-token so desecrated and abused? Note, Nothing can be a greater affront or grief to the Lord Jesus than to be betrayed, and betrayed with a kiss, by those that profess relation to him and an affection for him. Those do so who, under pretence of zeal for his honour, persecute his servants, who, under the cloak of a seeming affection for the honour of free grace, give a blow to the root of holiness and strictness of conversation. Many instances there are of Christ's being betrayed with a kiss, by those who, under the form of godliness, fight against the power of it. It were well if their own consciences would put this question to them, which Christ here puts to Judas, *Betrayest thou the Son of man with a kiss?* And will he not resent it? Will he not revenge it?

II. The effort which his disciples made for his protection (*v.* 49): *When they saw what would follow,* that those armed men were come to seize him, they said, "*Lord, shall we smite with the sword?* Thou didst allow us to *have* two swords, shall we now make use of them? Never was there more occasion; and to what purpose should we have them if we do not use them?" They asked the question as if they would not have drawn the sword without commission from their Master, but they were in too much *haste* and too much *heat* to stay for an answer. But Peter, aiming at the head of one of the servants of the *high priest*, missed his blow, and *cut off his right ear.* As Christ, by throwing them to the ground that came to take him, showed what he could have done, so Peter, by this exploit, showed what he could have done too in so good a cause if he had had leave. The other evangelists tell us what was the check Christ gave to Peter for it. Luke here tells us, 1. How Christ excused the blow: *Suffer ye thus far, v.* 51. Dr. Whitby thinks he said this to his enemies who came to take him, to pacify them, that they might not be provoked by it to fall upon the disciples, whom he had undertaken the preservation of: "*Pass by* this injury and affront; it was without warrant from me, and there shall not be another blow struck." Though Christ had power to have struck them down, and struck them dead, yet he *speaks them fair*, and, as it were, *begs their pardon* for an assault made upon them by one of his followers, to teach us to give good words even to our enemies. 2. How he cured the wound, which was more than amends sufficient for the injury: *He touched his ear, and healed him;* fastened his ear on again, that he might not so much as go away *stigmatized*, though he well deserved it. Christ hereby gave them a proof, (1.) Of his power. He that could *heal* could *destroy* if he pleased, which should have obliged them in interest to submit to him. Had they returned the blow upon Peter, he would immediately have healed him; and what could not a small regiment do that had such a surgeon to it, immediately to help the *sick* and *wounded?* (2.) Of his mercy and goodness. Christ here gave an illustrious example to his own rule of *doing good to them that hate us*, as afterwards he did of *praying for them that despitefully use us.* Those who render good for evil do as Christ did. One would have thought that this generous piece of kindness should have overcome them, that such coals, heaped on their heads, should have *melted them*, that they could not have bound him as a malefactor who had approved himself such a benefactor; but their hearts were hardened.

III. Christ's expostulation with the officers of the detachment that came to apprehend him, to show what an absurd thing it was for them to make all this rout and noise, *v.* 52, 53. Matthew relates it as said to *the multitude.* Luke tells us that it was said to the *chief priests and captains of the temple* the latter commanded the several orders of the priests, and therefore are here put between the *chief priests* and *the elders,* so that they were all ecclesiastics, retainers to the temple, who were employed in this odious piece of service; and some of the first rank too disparaged themselves so far as to be seen in it. Now see here,

1. How Christ *reasons* with them concerning their proceedings. What occasion was there for them to come out in the dead of the night, and *with swords and staves?* (1.) They knew that he was one that would not *resist,* nor raise the mob against them; he never had done any thing like this. Why then *are ye come out as against a thief?* (2.) They knew he was one that would not *abscond,* for he was daily with them in the temple, in the midst of them, and never sought to conceal himself, nor did they offer to lay hands on him. Before his hour was come, it was folly for them to think to take him; and when his hour was come it was folly for them to make all this ado to take him.

2. How he reconciles himself to their proceedings; and this we had not before: "*But this is your hour, and the power of darkness.* How hard soever it may seem that I should be thus exposed, I submit, for so it is determined. This is the hour *allowed you* to have your will against me. There is an hour *appointed me* to reckon for it. Now the *power of darkness,* Satan, *the ruler of the darkness of this world,* is permitted to do his worst, to bruise the heel of the seed of the woman, and I resolve to acquiesce; let him do his worst. *The Lord shall laugh at him, for he sees that his day,* his hour, *is coming,*" Ps. xxxvii. 13. Let this quiet us under the prevalency of the church's enemies; let it quiet us in a dying hour, that, (1.) It is but an *hour* that is permitted for the triumph of our adversary, a short time, a limited time. (2.) It is *their hour,* which is appointed them, and in which they are permitted to try their strength, that omnipotence may be the more glorified in their fall. (3.) It is *the power of darkness* that *rides master,* and darkness must give way to light, and the power of darkness be made to truckle to the prince of light. Christ was willing to wait for his triumphs till his warfare was accomplished, and we must be so too.

54 Then took they him, and led
him, and brought him into the high
priest's house. And Peter followed
afar off. 55 And when they had
kindled a fire in the midst of the hall,
and were set down together, Peter
sat down among them. 56 But a
certain maid beheld him as he sat by
the fire, and earnestly looked upon
him, and said, This man was also with
him. 57 And he denied him, saying,
Woman, I know him not. 48 And
after a little while another saw him,
and said, Thou art also of them. And
Peter said, Man, I am not. 59 And
about the space of one hour after
another confidently affirmed, saying,
Of a truth this *fellow* also was with
him: for he is a Galilæan. 60 And
Peter said, Man, I know not what
thou sayest. And immediately, while
he yet spake, the cock crew. 61 And
the Lord turned, and looked upon
Peter. And Peter remembered the
word of the Lord, how he had said
unto him, Before the cock crow, thou
shalt deny me thrice. 62 And Peter
went out, and wept bitterly.

We have here the melancholy story of Peter's denying his Master, at the time when he was arraigned before the high priest, and those that were of the *cabal,* that were ready to receive the prey, and to prepare the evidence for his arraignment, *as soon as it was day,* before the *great* sanhedrim, *v.* 66. But notice is not taken here, as was in the other evangelists, of Christ's being now upon his examination before the high priest, only of his being brought into *the high priest's house, v.* 54. But the manner of expression is observable. They *took him, and led him, and brought him,* which methinks is like that concerning Saul (1 Sam. xv. 12): *He is gone about, and passed on, and gone down;* and intimates that, even when they had seized their prey, they were in confusion, and, for fear of the people, or rather struck with inward terror upon what they had seen and heard, they took him the furthest way about, or, rather, knew not which way they hurried him, such a hurry were they in in their own bosoms. Now observe,

I. Peter's falling. 1. It began in *sneaking.* He *followed Christ* when he was had away prisoner; this was well, and showed a concern for his Master. But he followed *afar off,* that he might be out of danger. He thought to trim the matter, to *follow Christ,* and so to satisfy his conscience, but to follow *afar off,* and so to save his reputation, and sleep in a whole skin. 2. It proceeded in keeping his distance still, and associating himself with the high priest's servants, when he should have been at his master's elbow. The *servants kindled a fire in the midst of the hall* and *sat down together,* to talk over their night-expedition. Probably Malchus was among them, and *Peter sat down among them,* as if he had been one of them, at least would be thought to be so. His fall itself was disclaiming all acquaintance with Christ, and relation to him, disowning him because he was now in distress and danger. He was charged by a sorry simple maid, that belonged to the house, with being a retainer to this *Jesus,* about whom there was now so much noise. She *looked wistfully* upon him as he *sat by the fire,* only because he was a stranger, and one whom she had not seen before; and concluding that at this time of night there were no neuters there, and knowing him not to be any of the retinue of the high priest, she concludes him to be one of the retinue of this Jesus, or perhaps she had been some time or other looking about her in the temple, and had seen Jesus there and Peter with him, officious about him, and remembered him; *and this man was with him,* saith she. And Peter, as he had not the courage to *own* the charge, so he had not the wit and presence of mind to *turn it off,* as he might have done many ways, and therefore flatly and plainly denies it: *Woman, I know him not.* 4. His fall was repeated a second time (*v.* 58): *After a little while,* before he had time to recollect himself, *another saw him,* and said, "*Even thou art one of them,* as slily as thou sittest here among the high priest's servants." *Not I,* saith Peter; *Man, I am not.* And a *third* time, *about the space of an hour after* (for, saith the tempter, "When he is down, down with him; let us follow the blow, till we get him past recovery"), *another* confidently affirms, *strenuously* asserts it, "*Of a truth this fellow also was with him,* let him deny it if he can, for you may all perceive *he is a Galilean.* But he that has once told a lie is strongly tempted to persist in it; the *beginning of* that *sin is as the letting forth of water.* Peter now not only denies that he is a disciple of Christ, but that he knows any thing of him (*v.* 60): "*Man, I know not what thou sayest;* I never heard of this Jesus."

II. *Peter's getting up again.* See how happily he recovered himself, or, rather, the grace of God recovered him. See how it was brought about:—

1. The *cock crew* just as he was the third time denying that he knew Christ, and this startled him and put him upon thinking. Note, Small accidents may involve great consequences.

2. *The Lord turned and looked upon him.* This circumstance we had not in the other evangelists, but it is a very remarkable one. Christ is here called *the Lord,* for there was much of divine knowledge, power, and grace, appearing in this. Observe, Though Christ had now his back upon Peter, and was upon his trial (when, one would think, he had something else to mind), yet he knew all that Peter said. Note, Christ takes more notice of what we say and do than we think he does. When Peter disowned Christ, yet Christ did not disown him, though he might justly have cast him off, and never looked upon him more, but have denied him before his Father. It is well for us that Christ does not deal with us as we deal with him. Christ *looked upon Peter,* not doubting but that Peter would soon be aware of it; for he knew that, though he had denied him with his lips, yet his eye would still be towards him. Observe, Though Peter had now been guilty of a very great offence, and which was very provoking, yet Christ would not *call to him,* lest he should *shame* him or *expose* him; he only gave him *a look,* which none but Peter would understand the meaning of, and it had a great deal in it. (1.) It was a *convincing* look. Peter said that he did not *know Christ.* Christ *turned, and looked upon him,* as if he should say, "Dost thou not know me, Peter? Look me in the face, and tell me so." (2.) It was a *chiding* look. We may suppose that he looked upon him and *frowned,* or some way signified his displeasure. Let us think with what an angry countenance Christ justly looks upon us when we have sinned. (3.) It was an *expostulating* upbraiding look: "What, Peter, art thou he that disownest me now, when thou shouldest come and witness for me? What thou a disciple? Thou that wast the most forward to confess me to be the Son of God, and didst solemnly promise thou wouldest never disown me?" (4.) It was a *compassionate* look; he looked upon him with tenderness. "Poor Peter, how weak is thine heart! How art thou fallen and undone if I do not help thee!" (5.) It was a *directing* look. Christ *guided him with his eye,* gave him a wink to go out from that sorry company, to *retire,* and bethink himself a little, and then he would soon see what he had to do. (6.) It was a *significant* look: it signified the conveying of grace to Peter's heart, to enable him to repent; the crowing of the cock would not have brought him to repentance without this look, nor will the external means without special efficacious grace. Power went along with this look, to change the heart of Peter, and to bring him to himself, to his *right mind.*

3. *Peter remembered the words of the Lord.* Note, The *grace of God* works in and by the *word of God,* brings that to mind, and sets that home upon the conscience, and so gives the soul a happy turn. *Tolle et lege—Take it up, and read.*

4. Then *Peter went out, and wept bitterly.* One look from Christ melted him into tears of godly sorrow for sin. The candle was newly put out, and then a little thing lighted it again. Christ looked upon the chief priests, and made no impression upon them as he did on Peter, who had the divine seed remaining in him to work upon. It was not the look from Christ, but the grace of God with it, that recovered Peter, and brought him to-rights.

63 And the men that held Jesus mocked him, and smote *him.* 64 And when they had blindfolded him, they struck him on the face, and asked

him, saying, Prophesy, who is it that
smote thee? 65 And many other
things blasphemously spake they
against him. 66 And as soon as it
was day, the elders of the people and
the chief priests and the scribes came
together, and led him into their
council, saying, 67 Art thou the
Christ? tell us. And he said unto
them, If I tell you, ye will not believe: 68 And if I also ask *you*, ye
will not answer me, nor let *me* go.
69 Hereafter shall the Son of man
sit on the right hand of the power of
God. 70 Then said they all, Art
thou then the Son of God? And he
said unto them, Ye say that I am.
71 And they said, What need we any
further witness? for we ourselves
have heard of his own mouth.

We are here told, as before in the other gospels,

I. How our Lord Jesus was *abused* by the servants of the high priest. *The abjects*, the rude and barbarous servants, *gathered themselves together against him.* They that *held Jesus*, that had him in custody till the court sat, they *mocked him*, and *smote him* (*v.* 63), they would not allow him to *repose* himself one minute, though he had had no sleep all night, nor to *compose* himself, though he was hurried to his trial, and no time given him to prepare for it. They made sport with him: this sorrowful night to him shall be a merry night to them; and the blessed Jesus, like Samson, is made the fool in the play. They *hood-winked* him, and then, according to the common play that young people have among them, they *struck him on the face*, and continued to do so till he named the person that smote him (*v.* 64), intending hereby an affront to his prophetical office, and that knowledge of secret things which he was said to have. We are not told that he said *any thing*, but *bore every thing;* hell was let loose, and he suffered it to do its worst. A greater indignity could not be done to the blessed Jesus, yet this was but one instance of many; for *many other things blasphemously spoke they against him, v.* 65. They that condemned him for a blasphemer were themselves the vilest blasphemers that ever were.

II. How he was accused and condemned by the great sanhedrim, consisting of the *elders of the people, the chief priests, and the scribes,* who were all up betimes, and got together *as soon as it was day*, about five of the clock in the morning, to prosecute this matter. They were *working this evil upon their beds*, and, as soon as ever the *morning* was *light, practised* it, Mic. ii. 1 They would not have been up so early for any good work. It is but a short account that we have here of his trial in the ecclesiastical court.

1. They ask him, *Art thou the Christ?* He was generally believed by his followers to be the Christ, but they could not prove it upon him that he had ever said so *totidem verbis—in so many words*, and therefore urge him to own it to them, *v.* 67. If they had asked him this question with a willingness to admit that he was the Christ, and to receive him accordingly if he could give sufficient proof of his being so, it had been *well*, and might have been for ever *well with them;* but they asked it with a resolution not to believe him, but a design to ensnare him.

2. He justly complained of their unfair and unjust usage of him, *v.* 67, 68. They all, as Jews, professed to expect the Messiah, and to expect him at *this time*. No other appeared, or had appeared, that pretended to be the Messiah. He had no competitor, nor was he likely to have any. He had given amazing proofs of a divine power going along with him, which made his claims very well worthy of a free and impartial enquiry. It had been but just for these leaders of the people to have taken him into their council, and examined him there as a *candidate* for the messiahship, not at the bar as a *criminal*. "But," saith he, (1.) "*If I tell you that I am the Christ*, and give you ever such convincing proofs of it, you are resolved that *you will not believe*. Why should the cause be brought on before you who have already prejudged it, and are resolved, right or wrong, to run it down, and to condemn it?" (2.) "*If I ask you* what you have to object against the proofs I produce, *you will not answer me.*" Here he refers to their silence when he put a question to them, which would have led them to own his authority, *ch.* xx. 5—7. They were neither fair judges, nor fair disputants; but, when they were pinched with an argument, would rather be silent than own their conviction: "*You will neither answer me nor let me go;* if I be *not* the Christ, you ought to *answer* the arguments with which I prove that I am; if I be, you ought to *let me go;* but you will do neither."

3. He referred them to his second coming, for the full proof of his being the Christ, to their confusion, since they would not now admit the proof of it, to their conviction (*v.* 69): "*Hereafter shall the Son of man sit,* and be seen to sit, *on the right hand of the power of God,* and then you will not need to ask whether he be the Christ or no."

4. Hence they inferred that he set up himself as the Son of God, and asked him *whether he were so* or *no* (*v.* 70): *Art thou then the Son of God?* He called himself the *Son of man*, referring to Daniel's vision of the *Son of man* that *came near before the Ancient of days,* Dan. vii. 13, 14. But they understood so much as to know that if he was *that*

Son of man, he was also *the Son of God. And art thou so?* By this it appears to have been the faith of the Jewish church that the Messiah should be both *Son of man* and *Son of God.*

5. He owns himself to be the Son of God: *Ye say that I am;* that is, "I am, as ye say." Compare Mark xiv. 62. *Jesus said, I am.* This confirms Christ's testimony concerning himself, that he was the Son of God, that he stood to it, when he knew he should suffer for standing to it.

6. Upon this they ground his condemnation (*v.* 71): *What need we any further witness?* It was true, they needed not any further witness to prove that he said he was *the Son of God,* they had it from *his own mouth;* but did they not need proof that he was not so, before they condemned him as a blasphemer for saying that he was so? Had they no apprehension that it was possible he might be so, and then what horrid guilt they should bring upon themselves in putting him to death? No, *they know not, neither will they understand.* They cannot think it possible that he should be the Messiah, though ever so evidently clothed with divine power and grace, if he appear not, as they expect, in worldly pomp and grandeur. Their eyes being blinded with the admiration of that, they rush on in this dangerous prosecution, as the horse into the battle.

CHAP. XXIII.

This chapter carries on and concludes the history of Christ's sufferings and death. We have here, I. His arraignment before Pilate the Roman governor, ver. 1—5. II. His examination before Herod, who was tetrarch of Galilee, under the Romans likewise, ver. 6—12. III. Pilate's struggle with the people to release Jesus, his repeated testimonies concerning his innocency, but his yielding at length to their importunity and condemning him to be crucified, ver. 13—25. IV. An account of what passed as they led him to be crucified, and his discourse to the people that followed, ver. 26—31. V. An account of what passed at the place of execution, and the indignities done him there, ver. 32—38. VI. The conversion of one of the thieves, as Christ was hanging on the cross, ver. 39—43. VII. The death of Christ, and the prodigies that attended it, ver. 44—49. VIII. His burial, ver. 50—56.

AND the whole multitude of them
arose, and led him unto Pilate.
2 And they began to accuse him,
saying, We found this *fellow* perverting the nation, and forbidding to give
tribute to Cæsar, saying that he himself is Christ a King. 3 And Pilate
asked him, saying, Art thou the King
of the Jews? And he answered him
and said, Thou sayest *it.* 4 Then
said Pilate to the chief priests and *to*
the people, I find no fault in this
man. 5 And they were the more
fierce, saying, He stirreth up the people, teaching throughout all Jewry,
beginning from Galilee to this place.
6 When Pilate heard of Galilee, he
asked whether the man were a Galilæan. 7 And as soon as he knew
that he belonged unto Herod's jurisdiction, he sent him to Herod, who
himself also was at Jerusalem at that
time. 8 And when Herod saw Jesus,
he was exceeding glad: for he was
desirous to see him of a long *season,*
because he had heard many things of
him; and he hoped to have seen some
miracle done by him. 9 Then he
questioned with him in many words;
but he answered him nothing. 10
And the chief priests and scribes stood
and vehemently accused him. 11 And
Herod with his men of war set him
at nought, and mocked *him,* and arrayed him in a gorgeous robe, and
sent him again to Pilate. 12 And
the same day Pilate and Herod were
made friends together: for before they
were at enmity between themselves.

Our Lord Jesus was condemned as a blasphemer in the spiritual court, but it was the most *impotent malice* that could be that this court was actuated by; for, when they had *condemned* him, they knew they could not *put him to death,* and therefore took another course.

I. They accused him before Pilate. The *whole multitude of them arose,* when they saw they could go no further with him in their court, and *led him unto Pilate,* though it was no judgment day, no assizes or sessions; and they demanded justice against him, not as a blasphemer (that was no crime that he took cognizance of), but as one disaffected to the Roman government, which they in their hearts did not look upon as any crime at all, or, if it was one, they themselves were much more chargeable with it than he was; only it would serve the turn and answer the purpose of their malice: and it is observable that that which was the *pretended crime,* for which they employed the Roman powers to destroy Christ, was the *real crime* for which the Roman powers not long after destroyed them.

1. Here is the indictment drawn up against him (*v.* 2), in which they pretended a zeal for Cæsar, only to ingratiate themselves with Pilate, but it was all *malice* against Christ, and nothing else. They misrepresented him, (1.) As making the people *rebel against Cæsar.* It was true, and Pilate knew it, that there was a general uneasiness in the people under the Roman yoke, and they wanted nothing but an opportunity to shake it off; now they would have Pilate believe that this Jesus was active to foment that general discontent, which, if the truth was known, they themselves were the aiders and abettors of: *We have found him perverting the nation;* as if converting them to God's government were

perverting them from the civil government; whereas nothing tends more to make men good subjects than making them Christ's faithful followers. Christ had particularly taught that they *ought to give tribute to Cæsar*, though he knew there were those that would be offended at him for it; and yet he is here falsely accused as *forbidding to give tribute to Cæsar*. Innocency is no fence against calumny. (2.) As making himself a *rival with Cæsar*, though the very reason why they rejected him, and would not own him to be the Messiah, was because he did not appear in worldly pomp and power, and did not set up for a temporal prince, nor offer to do any thing against Cæsar; yet this is what they charged him with, that he said, *he himself is Christ a king*. He did say that he was *Christ*, and, if so, then *a king*, but not such a king as was ever likely to give disturbance to Cæsar. When his followers would have made him a king (John vi. 15), he declined it, though by the many miracles he wrought he made it appear that if he would have set up in competition with Cæsar he would have been too hard for him.

2. His pleading to the indictment: *Pilate asked him, Art thou the king of the Jews?* v. 3. To which he answered, *Thou sayest it;* that is, "It is as thou sayest, that I am entitled to the government of the Jewish nation; but in rivalship with the scribes and Pharisees, who tyrannize over them in matters of religion, not in rivalship with Cæsar, whose government relates only to their civil interests." Christ's kingdom is wholly spiritual, and will not interfere with Cæsar's jurisdiction. Or, "*Thou sayest it;* but canst thou prove it? What evidence hast thou for it?" All that knew him knew the contrary, that he never pretended to be the *king of the Jews*, in opposition to Cæsar as supreme, or to the governors that were sent by him, but the contrary.

3. Pilate's declaration of his innocency (v. 4): He *said to the chief priests, and the people* that seemed to join with them in the prosecution, "*I find no fault in this man.* What breaches of your law he may have been guilty of I am not concerned to enquire, but I find nothing proved upon him that makes him obnoxious to our court."

4. The continued fury and outrage of the prosecutors, v. 5. Instead of being moderated by Pilate's declaration of his innocency, and considering, as they ought to have done, whether they were not bringing the guilt of innocent blood upon themselves, they were the more exasperated, more exceedingly *fierce*. We do not find that they have any particular fact to produce, much less any evidence to prove it; but they resolve to carry it with noise and confidence, and say it, though they cannot prove it: *He stirs up the people* to rebel against Cæsar, *teaching throughout all Judea, beginning from Galilee to this place.* He did *stir up the people*, but it was not to any thing factious or seditious, but to every thing that was virtuous and praiseworthy. He did *teach*, but they could not charge him with teaching any doctrine that tended to disturb the public peace, or make the government uneasy or jealous.

II. They accused him before Herod. 1. Pilate removed him and his cause to Herod's court. The accusers mentioned Galilee, the northern part of Canaan. "Why," saith Pilate, "is he of that country? Is he a Galilean?" v. 6. "Yes," said they, "that is his head-quarters; there he has spent most of his time." "Let us send him to Herod then," saith Pilate, "for Herod is now in town, and it is but fit he should have cognizance of his cause, since he belongs to Herod's jurisdiction." Pilate was already sick of the cause, and desirous to rid his hands of it, which seems to have been the true reason for sending him to Herod. But God ordered it so for the more evident fulfilling of the scripture, as appears Acts iv. 26, 27, where that of David (Ps. ii. 2), *The kings of the earth and the rulers set themselves against the Lord and his Anointed*, is expressly said to be fulfilled in Herod and Pontius Pilate. 2. Herod was very willing to have the examining of him (v. 8): *When he saw Jesus he was exceedingly glad*, and perhaps the more glad because he saw him a prisoner, saw him in bonds. He had *heard many things of him* in Galilee, where his miracles had for a great while been all the talk of the country; and he *longed to see him*, not for any affection he had for him or his doctrine, but purely out of curiosity; and it was only to gratify this that he *hoped to have seen some miracle done by him*, which would serve him to talk of as long as he lived. In order to this, he *questioned with him in many things*, that at length he might bring him to something in which he might show his power. Perhaps he pumped him concerning things *secret*, or things *to come*, or concerning his curing diseases. But Jesus *answered him nothing;* nor would he gratify him so much as with the performance of one miracle. The poorest beggar, that asked a miracle for the relief of his necessity, was *never denied;* but this proud prince, that asked a miracle merely for the gratifying of his curiosity, is denied. He might have seen Christ and his wondrous works many a time in Galilee, and *would not*, and therefore it is justly said, Now he would see them, and *shall not;* they are hidden from his eyes, because he knew not the day of his visitation. Herod thought, now that he had him in bonds, he might *command* a miracle, but miracles must not be made cheap, nor Omnipotence be at the beck of the greatest potentate. 3. His prosecutors appeared against him before Herod, for they were restless in the prosecution: *They stood, and vehemently accused him* (v. 10), *impudently* and *boldly*, so the word signifies. They would make Herod believe that he had poisoned Galilee too with his seditious notions. Note, It is no new thing for good men and good ministers, that are real and useful friends to the civil government, to be falsely accused as factious and seditious, and enemies to government. 4. Herod was very *abusive* to him: He, with *his men of war,* his attendants, and officers, and great men, *set him at nought.* They *made nothing* of him; so the word is. Horrid wickedness! To *make nothing* of him who *made all things.* They laughed at him as *a fool;* for they knew he had wrought many miracles to befriend others, and why would he not now work one to befriend himself? Or, they laughed at him as one that had lost his power, and was become weak as other men. Herod, who had been acquainted with John Baptist, and had more knowledge of Christ too than Pilate had, was more *abusive* to Christ than Pilate was; for knowledge without grace does but make men the more *ingeniously* wicked. Herod arrayed Christ in a *gorgeous robe,* some gaudy painted clothes, as a mock-king; and so he taught Pilate's soldiers afterwards to do him the same indignity. He was ringleader in that abuse. 5. Herod sent him back to Pilate, and it proved an occasion of the making of them friends, they having been for some time before at variance. Herod could not get sight of a miracle, but would not condemn him neither as a malefactor, and therefore *sent him again to Pilate* (*v.* 11), and so returned Pilate's civility and respect in sending the prisoner to him; and this mutual obligation, with the messages that passed between them on this occasion, brought them to a better understanding one of another than there had been of late between them, *v.* 12. They had been *at enmity between themselves,* probably upon Pilate's killing the Galileans, who were Herod's subjects (Luke xiii. 1), or some other such matter of controversy as usually occurs among princes and great men. Observe how those that quarrelled with one another yet could unite against Christ; as Gebal, and Ammon, and Amalek, though divided among themselves, were confederate against the *Israel of God,* Ps. lxxxiii. 7. Christ is the great peace-maker; both Pilate and Herod owned his innocency, and their agreeing in this cured their disagreeing in other things.

13 And Pilate, when he had called
together the chief priests and the
rulers and the people, 14 Said unto
them, Ye have brought this man unto
me, as one that perverteth the people:
and, behold, I, having examined *him*
before you, have found no fault in
this man touching those things whereof
ye accuse him: 15 No, nor yet Herod:
for I sent you to him; and, lo, nothing worthy of death is done unto
him. 16 I will therefore chastise
him, and release *him.* 17 (For of
necessity he must release one unto
them at the feast.) 18 And they
cried out all at once, saying, Away
with this *man,* and release unto us
Barabbas: 19 (Who for a certain
sedition made in the city, and for
murder, was cast into prison.) 20
Pilate therefore, willing to release
Jesus, spake again to them. 21 But
they cried, saying, Crucify *him,* crucify him. 22 And he said unto them
the third time, Why, what evil hath
he done? I have found no cause of
death in him: I will therefore chastise him and let *him* go. 23 And
they were instant with loud voices,
requiring that he might be crucified.
And the voices of them and of the
chief priests prevailed. 24 And Pilate
gave sentence that it should be as
they required. 25 And he released
unto them him that for sedition and
murder was cast into prison, whom
they had desired; but he delivered
Jesus to their will.

We have here the blessed Jesus run down by the mob, and hurried to the cross in the storm of a popular noise and tumult, raised by the malice and artifice of the *chief priests,* as agents for the prince of the power of the air.

I. Pilate solemnly protests that he believes he has done nothing worthy of death or of bonds. And, if he did believe so, he ought immediately to have *discharged* him, and not only so, but to have *protected* him from the fury of the priests and rabble, and to have bound his prosecutors to their good behaviour for their insolent conduct. But, being himself a bad man, he had no kindness for Christ, and, having made himself otherwise obnoxious, was afraid of displeasing either the emperor or the people; and therefore, for want of integrity, he *called together the chief priests, and rulers, and people* (whom he should have dispersed, as a *riotous and seditious assembly,* and forbid them to come near him), and will hear what they have to say, to whom he should have turned a deaf ear, for he plainly saw what spirit actuated them (*v.* 14): "*You have brought,*" saith he, "*this man to me,* and, because I have a respect for you, *I have examined him before you,* and have heard all you have to allege against him, and I can make nothing of it: *I find no fault in him;* you cannot prove the things whereof you accuse him."

II. He appeals to Herod concerning him (*v.* 15): "*I sent you to him,* who is supposed to have known more of him than I have done, and he has *sent him back,* not convicted of any thing, nor under any mark of his displeasure; in his opinion, his crimes are not capital. He has laughed at him as a weak man, but has not stigmatized him as a dangerous man." He thought Bedlam a fitter place for him than Tyburn.

III. He proposes to release him, if they will but consent to it. He ought to have done it without asking leave of them, *Fiat justitia, ruat cœlum—Let justice have its course, though the heavens should be desolated.* But the fear of man brings many into this snare, that, whereas justice should take place, though heaven and earth come together, they will do an unjust thing, against their consciences, rather than pull an old house about their ears. Pilate declares him innocent, and therefore has a mind to release him; yet, to please the people, 1. He will release him under the notion of a malefactor, because *of necessity he must release one* (*v.* 17); so that whereas he ought to have been released by an *act of justice,* and thanks to nobody, he would have him released by an *act of grace,* and not be beholden to the people for it. 2. He will *chastise* him, and release him. If *no fault* be to be *found in him,* why should he be chastised? There is as much injustice in scourging as in crucifying an innocent man; nor would it be justified by pretending that this would satisfy the clamours of the people, and make *him* the object of their pity who was now to be the object of their envy. We must not do evil that good may come.

IV. The people choose rather to have Barabbas released, a wretched fellow, that had nothing to recommend him to their favour but the daringness of his crimes. He was imprisoned for a *sedition made in the city,* and for *murder* (of all crimes among men the least pardonable), yet this was the criminal that was preferred before Christ: *Away with this man, and release unto us Barabbas, v.* 18, 19. And no wonder that such a man is the favourite and darling of such a *mob,* he that was really seditious, rather than he that was really loyal and falsely accused of sedition.

V. When Pilate urged the second time that Christ should be released, they cried out, *Crucify him, crucify him, v.* 20, 21. They not only will have him die, but will have him die so great a death; nothing less will serve but he must be crucified: *Crucify him, crucify him.*

VI. When Pilate the third time reasoned with them, to show them the unreasonableness and injustice of it, they were the more peremptory and outrageous (*v.* 22): "*Why? What evil hath he done?* Name his crime. *I have found no cause of death,* and you cannot say what cause of death you have found in him; and therefore, if you will but speak the word, *I will chastise him and let him go.*" But popular fury, the more it is complimented, the more furious it grows; they were *instant with loud voices,* with great noises or outcries, not requesting, but *requiring, that he might be crucified;* as if they had as much right, at the feast, to demand the crucifying of one that was innocent as the release of one that was guilty.

VII. Pilate's yielding, at length, to their importunity. The voice of the people and of the *chief priests prevailed,* and were too hard for Pilate, and overruled him to go contrary to his convictions and inclinations. He had not courage to go against so strong a stream, but *gave sentence that it should be as they required, v.* 24. Here is judgment *turned away backward,* and *justice standing afar off,* for fear of popular fury. *Truth is fallen in the street, and equity cannot enter,* Isa. lix. 14. *Judgment* was looked for, *but behold oppression; righteousness, but behold a cry,* Isa. v. 7. This is repeated in *v.* 25, with the aggravating circumstance of the release of Barabbas: *He released unto them him that for sedition and murder was cast into prison,* who hereby would be hardened in his wickedness, and do the more mischief, because *him they had desired,* being altogether such a one as themselves; but he *delivered Jesus to their will,* and he could not deal more barbarously with him than to deliver him to *their will,* who *hated* him with a *perfect hatred,* and whose *tender mercies* were *cruelty.*

26 And as they led him away, they
laid hold upon one Simon, a Cyrenian,
coming out of the country, and on
him they laid the cross, that he might
bear *it* after Jesus. 27 And there
followed him a great company of people, and of women, which also bewailed and lamented him. 28 But
Jesus turning unto them said, Daughters of Jerusalem, weep not for me,
but weep for yourselves, and for your
children. 29 For, behold, the days
are coming, in the which they shall
say, Blessed *are* the barren, and the
wombs that never bare, and the paps
which never gave suck. 30 Then
shall they begin to say to the mountains, Fall on us; and to the hills,
Cover us. 31 For if they do these
things in a green tree, what shall be
done in the dry?

We have here the blessed Jesus, the Lamb of God, led as *a lamb to the slaughter,* to the sacrifice. It is strange with what expedition they went through his trial; how they could do so much work in such a little time, though they had so many great men to deal with, attendance on whom is usually a work of time. He was brought before the chief priests at break of day (*ch.* xxii. 66), after that to Pilate, then to Herod, then to Pilate again; and there seems to have been a long struggle between Pilate and the people about him. He was scourged, and crowned with thorns, and contumeliously used, and all this was done in four or five hours' time, or six at most, for he was crucified between nine o'clock and twelve. Christ's persecutors resolve to lose no time, for fear lest his friends at the other end of the town should get notice of what they were doing, and should rise to rescue him. Never any one was so *chased out of the world* as Christ was, but so he himself said, *Yet a little while and ye shall not see me;* a very little while indeed. Now as they led him away to death we find,

I. One that was a *bearer*, that carried his cross, *Simon* by name, *a Cyrenian*, who probably was a friend of Christ, and was known to be so, and this was done to put a reproach upon him; they laid Christ's cross upon him, that he might *bear it after Jesus* (*v.* 26), lest Jesus should faint under it and die away, and so prevent the further instances of malice they designed. It was pity, but a *cruel pity*, that gave him this ease.

II. Many that were *mourners;* true mourners, who followed him, *bewailing* and *lamenting* him. These were not only his friends and well-wishers, but the common people, that were not his enemies, and were moved with compassion towards him, because they had heard the fame of him, and what an excellent useful man he was, and had reason to think he suffered unjustly. This drew a great crowd after him, as is usual at executions, especially of those that have been persons of distinction: *A great company of people followed him*, especially of women (*v.* 27), some led by pity, others by curiosity, but they *also* (as well as those that were his particular friends and acquaintance) *bewailed and lamented him.* Though there were many that reproached and reviled him, yet there were some that valued him, and pitied him, and were sorry for him, and were partakers with him in his sufferings. The dying of the Lord Jesus may perhaps move natural affections in many that are strangers to devout affections; many bewail Christ that do not believe in him, and lament him that do not love him above all. Now here we are told what Christ said to these mourners. Though one would think he should be wholly taken up with his own concern, yet he found time and heart to take cognizance of their tears. Christ *died lamented*, and has a bottle for the tears of those that lamented him. He *turned to them*, though they were strangers to him, and bade them *not weep for him, but for themselves.* He diverts their lamentation into another channel, *v.* 28.

1. He gives them a general direction concerning their lamentations: *Daughters of Jerusalem, weep not for me.* Not that they were to be blamed for weeping for him, but rather commended; those hearts were hard indeed that were not affected with such sufferings of such a person; but they must not weep for him only (those were profitless tears that they shed for him), but rather let them *weep for themselves and for their children*, with an eye to the destruction that was coming upon Jerusalem, which some of them might live to see and share in the calamities of, or, at least, their children would, for whom they ought to be solicitous. Note, When with an eye of faith we behold Christ crucified we ought to weep, not for him, but for ourselves. We must not be affected with the death of Christ as with the death of a common person whose calamity we pity, or of a common friend whom we are likely to part with. The death of Christ was a thing peculiar; it was his victory and triumph over his enemies; it was our deliverance, and the purchase of eternal life for us. And therefore let us weep, not for him, but for our own sins, and the sins of our children, that were the cause of his death; and weep for fear (such were the tears here prescribed) of the miseries we shall bring upon ourselves, if we slight his love, and reject his grace, as the Jewish nation did, which brought upon them the ruin here foretold. When our dear relations and friends die in Christ, we have no reason to weep for them, who have put off the burden of the flesh, are made perfect in holiness, and have entered into perfect rest and joy, but for ourselves and our children, who are left behind in a world of sins, and sorrows, and snares.

2. He gives them a particular reason why they should *weep for themselves and for their children:* "*For behold* sad times are coming upon your city; it will be destroyed, and you will be involved in the common destruction." When Christ's own disciples sorrowed after a *godly sort* for his leaving them, he wiped away their tears with the promise that he would *see them again*, and they should *rejoice*, John xvi. 22. But, when these daughters of *Jerusalem bewailed him* only with a *worldly* sorrow, he turned their tears into another channel, and told them that they should have something given them to cry for. Let them *be afflicted, and mourn, and weep*, Jam. iv. 9. He had lately wept over Jerusalem himself, and now he bids them weep over it. Christ's tears should set us a weeping. Let the daughters of Zion, that own Christ for their king, rejoice in him, for he comes to save them; but let the daughters of Jerusalem, that only weep for him, but do not take him for their king, weep and tremble to think of his coming to judge them. Now the destruction of Jerusalem is here foretold by two proverbial sayings, that might then fitly be used, which both bespeak it very terrible, that what people commonly dread they would then desire, to be *written childless* and to be *buried alive.* (1.) They would wish to be *written childless.* Whereas commonly those that have no children envy those that have, as Rachel envied Leah, then those that have children will find them such a burden in attempting to escape, and such a

grief when they see them either *fainting* for famine or *falling* by the sword, that they will envy those that have none, and say, *Blessed are the barren, and the wombs that never bare,* that have no children to be *given up* to the murderer, or to be *snatched* out of his hands. It would not only go ill with those who at that time were *with child,* or *giving suck,* as Christ had said (Matt. xxiv. 19), but it would be terrible to those who had had children, and suckled them, and had them now alive. See Hos. ix. 11—14. See the vanity of the creature and the uncertainty of its comforts; for such may be the changes of Providence concerning us that those very things may become the greatest burdens, cares, and griefs to us, which we have delighted in as the greatest blessings. (2.) They would wish to be *buried alive: They shall begin to say to the mountains, Fall on us, and to the hills, Cover us, v.* 30. This also refers to a passage in the same prophecy with the former, Hos. x. 8. They shall wish to be hid in the darkest caves, that they may be out of the noise of these calamities. They will be willing to be sheltered upon any terms, though with the hazard of being crushed to pieces. This would be the language especially of the great and mighty men, Rev. vi. 16. They that would not flee to Christ for refuge, and put themselves under his protection, will in vain call to *hills* and *mountains* to shelter them from his wrath.

2. He shows how natural it was for them to infer this desolation from his sufferings. *If they do these things in a green tree, what shall be done in the dry? v.* 31. Some think that this is borrowed from Ezek. xx. 47: *The fire shall devour every green tree in thee, and every dry tree.* These words may be applied, (1.) More particularly to the destruction of Jerusalem, which Christ here foretold, and which the Jews by putting him to death brought upon themselves: "*If they* (the Jews, and the inhabitants of Jerusalem) *do these things upon the green tree,* if they do thus abuse an innocent and excellent person for his *good works,* how may they expect God to deal with them *for their so doing,* who have made themselves a *dry tree,* a corrupt and wicked generation, and good for nothing? If this be their sin, what do you think will be their punishment?" Or take it thus: "If they (the Romans, their judges, and their soldiers) abuse me thus, who have given them no provocation, who am to them as a green tree, which you seem to be as much enraged at, *what will they do by Jerusalem* and the Jewish nation, who will be so very provoking to them, and make themselves as a *dry tree,* as fuel to the fire of their resentments? If God suffer those things to be done to me, what will he appoint to be done to those barren trees of whom it had been often said that they should be *hewn down and cast into the fire?*" Matt. iii. 10; vii. 19. (2.) They may be applied more generally to all the revelations of God's wrath against sin and sinners: "If God deliver me up to such sufferings as these because I am made a sacrifice for sin, what will he do with sinners themselves?" Christ was a *green tree,* fruitful and flourishing; now, if such things were done to him, we may thence infer what would have been done to the whole race of mankind if he had not *interposed,* and what shall be done to those that continue dry trees, notwithstanding all that is done to make them fruitful. If God did this to the Son of his love, when he found sin but imputed to him, what shall he do to the generation of his wrath, when he finds sin reigning in them? If the Father was pleased in doing these things to the green tree, why should he be loth to do it to the dry? Note, The consideration of the bitter sufferings of our Lord Jesus should engage us to stand in awe of the justice of God, and to tremble before him. The best saints, compared with Christ, are *dry trees;* if he suffer, why may not they expect to suffer? And what then shall the damnation of sinners be?

32 And there were also two other,
malefactors, led with him to be put
to death. 33 And when they were
come to the place, which is called Calvary, there they crucified him, and the
malefactors, one on the right hand,
and the other on the left. 34 Then
said Jesus, Father, forgive them; for
they know not what they do. And
they parted his raiment, and cast lots.
35 And the people stood beholding.
And the rulers also with them derided
him, saying, He saved others; let him
save himself, if he be Christ, the
chosen of God. 36 And the soldiers also
mocked him, coming to him, and offering him vinegar, 37 And saying, If
thou be the king of the Jews, save
thyself. 38 And a superscription
also was written over him in letters
of Greek, and Latin, and Hebrew
THIS IS THE KING OF THE
JEWS. 39 And one of the malefactors which were hanged railed on
him, saying, If thou be Christ, save
thyself and us. 40 But the other
answering rebuked him, saying, Dost
not thou fear God, seeing thou art
in the same condemnation? 41 And
we indeed justly; for we receive
the due reward of our deeds: but this
man hath done nothing amiss. 42
And he said unto Jesus, Lord, remember me when thou comest into thy

kingdom. 43 And Jesus said unto him, Verily I say unto thee, To day shalt thou be with me in paradise.

In these verses we have,

I. Divers passages which we had before in Matthew and Mark concerning Christ's sufferings. 1. That there were *two others, malefactors, led with him* to the place of execution, who, it is probable, had been for some time under sentence of death, and were designed to be executed on this day, which was probably the pretence for making such haste in the prosecution of Christ, that he and these two malefactors might be executed together, and one solemnity might serve. 2. That he was crucified at a place called *Calvary,* Κρανίον, the Greek name for *Golgotha—the place of a skull:* an ignominious place, to add to the reproach of his sufferings, but significant, for there he triumphed over death as it were upon his own dunghill. He was *crucified.* His hands and feet were nailed to the cross as it lay upon the ground, and it was then *lifted* up, and fastened into the earth, or into some socket made to receive it. This was a painful and shameful death above any other. 3. That he was crucified *in the midst between two thieves,* as if he had been the worst of the three. Thus he was not only treated as a transgressor, but *numbered with them,* the worst of them. 4. That the soldiers who were employed in the execution seized his garments as their fee, and divided them among themselves *by lot: They parted his raiment, and cast lots;* it was worth so little that, if divided, it would come to next to nothing, and therefore they cast lots for it. 5. That he was reviled and reproached, and treated with all the scorn and contempt imaginable, when he was *lifted up* upon the cross. It was strange that so much barbarity should be found in the human nature: *The people stood beholding,* not at all concerned, but rather pleasing themselves with the spectacle; and *the rulers,* whom from their office one would take to be men of sense and men of honour, stood among the rabble, *and derided him,* to set those on that were about them to do so too; and they said, *He saved others, let him save himself.* Thus was he upbraided for the good works he had done, as if it were indeed *for these* that they *crucified* him. They triumphed over him as if they had conquered him, whereas he was himself then more than a conqueror; they challenged him to save himself from the cross, when he was saving others by the cross: *If he be the Christ, the chosen of God,* let him save himself. They knew that *the Christ was the chosen of God,* designed by him, and dear to him. "If he, as the Christ, would deliver our nation from the Romans (and they could not form any other idea than that of the Messiah), let him deliver himself from the Romans that have him now in their hands." Thus the Jewish *rulers* jeered him as subdued by the Romans, instead of subduing them. The *Roman soldiers* jeered him as *the King of the Jews:* "A people good enough for such a prince, and a prince good enough for such a people." They *mocked him* (*v.* 36, 37); they made sport with him, and made a jest of his sufferings; and when they were drinking sharp sour wine themselves, such as was generally allotted them, they triumphantly asked him if he would pledge them, or drink with them. And they said, *If thou be the king of the Jews, save thyself;* for, as the Jews prosecuted him under the notion of a pretended Messiah, so the Romans under the notion of a pretended king. 6. That the superscription over his head, setting forth his crime, was, *This is the King of the Jews, v.* 38. He is put to death for pretending to be the king of the Jews; so they meant it; but God intended it to be a declaration of what he really was, notwithstanding his present disgrace: he is *the king of the Jews,* the king of the church, and his cross is the way to his crown. This was written in those that were called the three learned languages, *Greek, and Latin, and Hebrew,* for those are best learned that have learned Christ. It was written in these three languages that it might be known and read of all men; but God designed by it to signify that the gospel of Christ should be preached to all nations, *beginning at Jerusalem,* and be read in all languages. The Gentile philosophy made the Greek tongue famous, the Roman laws and government made the Latin tongue so, and the Hebrew excelled them all for the sake of the Old Testament. In these three languages is Jesus Christ *proclaimed king.* Young scholars, that are taking pains at school to make themselves masters of these three languages, should aim at this, that in the use of them they may increase their acquaintance with Christ.

II. Here are two passages which we had not before, and they are very remarkable ones.

1. Christ's prayer for his enemies (*v.* 34): *Father, forgive them.* Seven remarkable words Christ spoke after he was nailed to the cross, and before he died, and this is the first. One reason why he died the death of the cross was that he might have liberty of speech to the last, and so might glorify his Father and edify those about him. As soon as ever he was fastened to the cross, or while they were nailing him, he prayed this prayer, in which observe,

(1.) The petition: *Father, forgive them.* One would think that he should have prayed, "Father, consume them; the Lord look upon it, and requite it." The sin they were now guilty of might justly have been made unpardonable, and justly might they have been excepted by name out of the act of indemnity. No, these are particularly *prayed for.* Now he made intercession for transgressors, as was foretold (Isa. liii. 12), and it is to be added to his prayer (John xvii.), to complete the specimen he gave of his intercession within the veil: that for saints, this for sinners. Now the sayings of Christ upon the cross as well as his sufferings had a further intention than they seemed to have. This was a mediatorial word, and explicatory of the intent and meaning of his death: "*Father, forgive them,* not only these, but all that shall repent, and believe the gospel;" and he did not intend that these should be forgiven upon any other terms. "Father, that which I am now suffering and dying for is in order to this, that poor sinners may be pardoned." Note, [1.] The great thing which Christ died to purchase and procure for us is the forgiveness of sin. [2.] This is that for which Christ intercedes for all that repent and believe in the virtue of his satisfaction; his blood speaks this: *Father, forgive them.* [3.] The greatest sinners may, through Christ, upon their repentance, hope to find mercy. Though they were his persecutors and murderers, he prayed, Father, forgive *them.*

(2.) The plea: *For they know not what they do;* for, *if they had known,* they would not have crucified him, 1 Cor. ii. 8. There was a veil upon his glory and upon their understandings; and how could they see through two veils? They wished his blood on them and their children: but, had they known what they did, they would have unwished it again. Note, [1.] The crucifiers of Christ *know not what they do.* They that speak ill of religion speak ill of that which they know not, and it is because they will not know it. [2.] There is a kind of ignorance that does in part excuse sin: ignorance through want of the means of knowledge or of a capacity to receive instruction, through the infelicities of education, or inadvertency. The crucifiers of Christ were kept in ignorance by their rulers, and had prejudices against him instilled into them, so that in what they did against Christ and his doctrine they thought they did God service, John xvi. 2. Such are to be pitied and prayed for. This prayer of Christ was answered not long after, when many of those that had a hand in his death were converted by Peter's preaching. This is written also for example to us. *First,* We must in prayer call God *Father,* and come to him with reverence and confidence, as children to a father. *Secondly,* The great thing we must beg of God, both for ourselves and others, is the forgiveness of sins. *Thirdly,* We must pray for *our enemies,* and those that hate and persecute us, must extenuate their offences, and not aggravate them as we must our own *(They know not what they do; peradventure it was an oversight);* and we must be earnest with God in prayer for the forgiveness of their sins, their sins against us. This is Christ's example to his own rule (Matt. v. 44, 45, *Love your enemies);* and it very much strengthens the rule, for, if Christ loved and prayed for such enemies, what enemies can we have that we are not obliged to *love* and *pray for?*

2. The conversion of the thief upon the cross, which is an illustrious instance of Christ's triumphing over principalities and powers even when he seemed to be triumphed over by them. Christ was crucified between two thieves, and in them were represented the different effects which the cross of Christ would have upon the children of men, to whom it would be *brought near* in the preaching of the gospel. They are all malefactors, all guilty before God. Now the cross of Christ is to some a *savour of life unto life,* to others of *death unto death.* To them that perish it is foolishness, but to them that are saved it is the wisdom of God and the power of God.

(1.) Here was one of these malefactors that was *hardened to the last.* Near to the cross of Christ, he *railed on him,* as others did (*v.* 39): he said, *If thou be the Christ,* as they say thou art, *save thyself and us.* Though he was now in pain and agony, and in the valley of the shadow of death, yet this did not humble his proud spirit, nor teach him to give good language, no, not to his fellow-sufferer. *Though thou bray a fool in a mortar, yet will not his foolishness depart from him.* No troubles will of themselves work a change in a wicked heart, but sometimes they *irritate* the corruption which one would think they should *mortify.* He challenges Christ to *save both himself and them.* Note, There are some that have the impudence to rail at Christ, and yet the confidence to expect to be saved by him; nay, and to conclude that, if he do not save them, he is not to be looked upon as the Saviour.

(2.) Here was the other of them that was *softened at the last.* It was said in Matthew and Mark that the *thieves,* even *they that were crucified with him, reviled him,* which some think is by a figure put for *one* of them, but others think that they both *reviled* him at first, till the heart of one of them was wonderfully changed, and with it his language on a sudden. This malefactor, when just ready to fall into the hands of Satan, was snatched as a brand out of the burning, and made a monument of divine mercy and grace, and Satan was left to roar as a lion disappointed of his prey. This gives no encouragement to any to put off their repentance to their death-bed, or to hope that then they shall find mercy; for, though it is certain that true repentance is never too late, it is as certain that late repentance is seldom true. None can be sure that they shall have time to repent at death, but every man may be sure that he cannot have the advantages that this penitent thief had, whose case was altogether extraordinary. He never had any offer of Christ, nor day of grace, before now: he was designed to be made a singular instance of the power of Christ's grace now at a time when he was *crucified in weakness.* Christ, having conquered Satan in the destruction of Judas and the preservation of Peter, erects this further trophy of his victory over him in the conversion of this malefactor, as a specimen of what he would do. We shall see the case to be extraordinary if we observe,

[1.] The extraordinary operations of God's grace upon him, which appeared in what he said. Here were so many evidences given in a short time of a blessed change wrought in him that more could not have been given in so little a compass.

First, See what he said to the other malefactor, *v.* 40, 41. 1. He reproved him for railing at Christ, as destitute of the *fear of God,* and having no sense at all of religion: *Dost not thou fear God?* This implies that it was the fear of God which restrained him from following the multitude to do this evil. "I fear God, and therefore dare not do it; and dost not thou?" All that have their eyes opened see this to be at the bottom of the wickedness of the wicked, that they have not the fear of God before their eyes. "If thou hadst any humanity in thee, thou wouldest not insult over one that is thy fellow-sufferer; *thou art in the same condition;* thou art a *dying man* too, and therefore, whatever these wicked people do, it ill becomes thee to abuse a dying man." 2. He owns that he deserves what was done to him: *We indeed justly.* It is probable that they both suffered for one and the same crime, and therefore he spoke with the more assurance, *We received the due reward of our deeds.* This magnifies divine grace, as acting in a distinguishing way. These two had been comrades in sin and suffering, and yet one is *saved* and the other *perishes;* two that had gone together all along hitherto, and yet now *one taken and the other left.* He does not say, *Thou* indeed justly, but *We.* Note, True penitents acknowledge the justice of God in all the punishments of their sin. God has *done right,* but *we have done wickedly.* 3. He believes Christ to have suffered *wrongfully.* Though he was condemned in two courts, and run upon as if he had been the worst of malefactors, yet this penitent thief is convinced, by his conduct in his sufferings, that *he has done nothing amiss, οὐδὲν ἄτοπον—nothing absurd, or unbecoming his character.* The chief priests would have him crucified *between* the malefactors, as *one of them;* but this thief has more sense than they, and owns he is *not one of them.* Whether he had before heard of Christ and of his wondrous works does not appear, but the Spirit of grace enlightened him with this knowledge, and enabled him to say, This man has *done nothing amiss.*

Secondly, See what he said to our Lord Jesus: *Lord, remember me when thou comest into thy kingdom, v.* 42. This is the prayer of a *dying sinner* to a *dying Saviour.* It was the honour of Christ to be *thus prayed to,* though he was upon the cross reproached and reviled. It was the happiness of the thief *thus to pray;* perhaps he never prayed before, and yet now was heard, and saved at the last gasp. While there is life there is hope, and while there is hope there is room for prayer. 1. Observe his *faith* in this prayer. In his confession of sin (*v.* 41) he discovered *repentance towards God.* In this petition he discovered *faith towards our Lord Jesus Christ.* He owns him to be *Lord,* and to have a *kingdom,* and that he was going to that kingdom, that he should have authority in that kingdom, and that those should be happy whom he favoured; and to *believe* and *confess* all this was a *great thing* at this time of day. Christ was now in the depth of disgrace, deserted by his own disciples, reviled by his own nation, suffering as a pretender, and not delivered by his Father. He made this profession before those prodigies happened which put honour upon his sufferings, and which startled the centurion; yet *verily we have not found so great faith, no, not in Israel.* He believed *another life* after this, and desired to be happy in *that* life, not as the other thief, to be *saved from the cross,* but to be well provided for when the cross had done its worst. 2. Observe his humility in this prayer. All his request is, *Lord, remember me.* He does not pray, Lord, *prefer me* (as they did, Matt. xx. 21), though, having the honour as none of the disciples had to drink of Christ's cup and to be baptized with his baptism either on his *right hand* or on *his left* in his sufferings when his own disciples had deserted him he might have had some colour to ask as they did to sit on his right hand and on his left in his kingdom. Acquaintance in sufferings has sometimes gained such a point, Jer. lii. 31, 32. But he is far from the thought of it. All he begs is, *Lord, remember me,* referring himself to Christ in what way to remember him. It is a request like that of *Joseph to the chief butler, Think on me* (Gen. xl. 14), and it sped better; the chief butler *forgot Joseph,* but Christ remembered this thief. 3. There is an air of importunity and fervency in this prayer. He does, as it were, breathe out his soul in it: "*Lord, remember me,* and I have enough; I desire no more; into thy hands I commit my case." Note, To be remembered by Christ, now that he is in his kingdom, is what we should earnestly desire and pray for, and it will be enough to secure our welfare living and dying. Christ is *in his kingdom,* interceding. "*Lord, remember me,* and intercede for me." He is there ruling. "Lord, remember me, and rule in me by thy Spirit." He is there preparing places for those that are his. "Lord, remember me, and prepare a place for me; remember me *at death,* remember me *in the resurrection.*" See Job xiv. 13.

[2.] The extraordinary grants of Christ's favour to him: *Jesus said unto him,* in answer to his prayer, "*Verily I say unto thee,* I the *Amen,* the faithful Witness, I say *Amen* to this prayer, put my *fiat* to it: nay, thou shalt have more than thou didst ask, *This day thou shalt be with me in paradise,"* v. 43. Observe,

First, To whom this was spoken: to the penitent thief, to him, and not to his companion. Christ upon the cross is like Christ upon the throne; for *now is the judgment of this world:* one departs with a curse, the other with a blessing. Though Christ himself was now in the greatest struggle and agony, yet he had a word of comfort to speak to a poor penitent that committed himself to him. Note, Even great sinners, if they be true penitents, shall, through Christ, obtain not only the pardon of their sins, but a place in the paradise of God, Heb. ix. 15. This magnifies the riches of free grace, that rebels and traitors shall not only be pardoned, but preferred, thus preferred.

Secondly, By whom this was spoken. This was another mediatorial word which Christ spoke, though upon a particular occasion, yet with a general intention to explain the true intent and meaning of his sufferings; as he died to purchase the *forgiveness of sins* for us (*v.* 34), so also to purchase *eternal life* for us. By this word we are given to understand that Jesus Christ died to *open the kingdom of heaven to all penitent obedient believers.* 1. Christ here lets us know that he was going to paradise himself, to *hades—the invisible world.* His human soul was removing to the place of separate souls; not to the place of the damned, but to paradise, the place of the blessed. By this he assures us that his satisfaction was accepted, and the Father was well pleased in him, else he had not gone to paradise; that was the beginning of the joy set before him, with the prospect of which he comforted himself. He went by the cross to the crown, and we must not think of going any other way, or of being perfected but by sufferings. 2. He lets all penitent believers know that when they die they shall go to be with him there. He was now, as a priest, purchasing this happiness for them, and is ready, as a king, to confer it upon them when they are prepared and made ready for it. See here how the happiness of heaven is set forth to us. (1.) It is *paradise,* a garden of pleasure, the *paradise of God* (Rev. ii. 7), alluding to the garden of Eden, in which our first parents were placed when they were innocent. In the second Adam we are restored to all we lost in the first Adam, and more, to a heavenly paradise instead of an earthly one. (2.) It is being *with Christ* there. That is the happiness of heaven, to see Christ, and sit with him, and share in his glory, John xvii. 24. (3.) It is immediate upon death: *This day shalt thou be with me,* to-night, before to-morrow. *The souls of the faithful, after they are delivered from the burden of the flesh,* immediately *are in joy and felicity;* the spirits of just men are immediately *made perfect.* Lazarus departs, and is immediately *comforted;* Paul departs, and is immediately with Christ, Phil. i. 23

44 And it was about the sixth hour,
and there was a darkness over all the
earth until the ninth hour. 45 And
the sun was darkened, and the veil of
the temple was rent in the midst. 46
And when Jesus had cried with a
loud voice, he said, Father, into thy
hands I commend my spirit: and having said thus, he gave up the ghost.
47 Now when the centurion saw what
was done, he glorified God, saying,
Certainly this was a righteous man.
48 And all the people that came together to that sight, beholding the
things which were done, smote their
breasts, and returned. 49 And all
his acquaintance, and the women that
followed him from Galilee, stood afar
off, beholding these things.

In these verses we have three things:—

I. Christ's dying *magnified* by the *prodigies* that attended it: only two are here mentioned, which we had an account of before. 1. The *darkening of the sun at noon-day.* It was now about the *sixth hour,* that is, according to our computation, twelve o'clock at noon; and there was a *darkness over all the earth until the ninth hour.* The sun was eclipsed and the air exceedingly clouded at the same time, both which concurred to this thick darkness, which continued *three hours,* not *three days,* as that of Egypt did. 2. The *rending of the veil of the temple.* The former prodigy was in the *heavens,* this in the *temple;* for both these are the houses of God, and, when the Son of God was thus abused, they could not but feel the indignity, and thus signify their resentment of it. By this rending of the veil was signified the taking away of the ceremonial law, which was a wall of partition between Jews and Gentiles, and of all other difficulties and discouragements in our approaches to God, so that now we may *come boldly to the throne of grace.*

II. Christ's dying *explained* (*v.* 46) by the words with which he breathed out his soul. Jesus *had cried* with a loud voice when he said, *Why hast thou forsaken me?* So we are told in Matthew and Mark, and, it should seem, it was with a *loud voice* that he said this too, to show his earnestness, and that all the people might take notice of it: and this he said, *Father, into thy hands I commend my spirit.* 1. He borrowed these words from his father David (Ps. xxxi. 5); not that he needed to have words put into his mouth, but he chose to make use of David's words to show that it was the Spirit of Christ that testified in the Old-Testament prophets, and that he came to fulfil the scripture. Christ died with scripture in his mouth. Thus he directs us to make use of scripture language in our addresses to God. 2. In this address to God he calls him *Father*. When he complained of being forsaken, he cried, *Eli, Eli, My God, my God;* but, to show that that dreadful agony of his soul was now over, he here calls God *Father*. When he was giving up his life and soul for us, he did for us call God *Father,* that we through him might receive the adoption of sons. 3. Christ made use of these words in a sense peculiar to himself as Mediator. He was now to *make his soul an offering for our sin* (Isa. liii. 10), to *give his life a ransom for many* (Matt. xx. 28), *by the eternal Spirit to offer himself,* Heb. ix. 14. He was himself both the priest and the sacrifice; our souls were forfeited, and his must go to redeem the forfeiture. The price must be paid *into the hands* of God, the party offended by sin; to him he had undertaken to make full satisfaction. Now by these words he *offered up the sacrifice,* did, as it were, lay his hand upon the head of it, and surrender it; τιθημι—" I *deposit* it, I pay it down into thy hands. Father, accept of my life and soul instead of the lives and souls of the sinners I die for." The *animus offerentis —the good will of the offerer,* was requisite to the acceptance of the offering. Now Christ here expresses his cheerful willingness to offer himself, as he had done when it was first proposed to him (Heb. x. 9, 10), *Lo, I come to do thy will, by which will we are sanctified.* 4. Christ hereby signifies his dependence upon his Father for his resurrection, by the re-union of his soul and body. He commends his spirit into his Father's hand, to be *received* into paradise, and *returned* the third day. By this it appears that our Lord Jesus, as he had a *true body,* so he had a reasonable soul, which existed in a state of separation from the body, and thus he was made like unto his brethren; this soul he lodged in his Father's hand, committed it to his custody, resting in hope that it should not be left in *hades,* in its *state of separation* from the body, no, not so long as that the body might see corruption. 5. Christ has hereby left us an example, has fitted those words of David to the purpose of dying saints, and hath, as it were, sanctified them for their use. In death our great care should be about our souls, and we cannot more effectually provide for their welfare than by committing them now into the hands of God, as a Father, to be sanctified and governed by his Spirit and grace, and at death committing them into his hands to be made perfect in holiness and happiness. We must show that we are freely willing to die, that we firmly believe in another life after this, and are desirous of it, by saying, *Father, into thy hands I commend my spirit.*

III. Christ's dying improved by the impressions it made upon those that attended him.

1. The centurion that had command of the guard was much affected with what he saw, *v.* 47. He was a Roman, a Gentile, a stranger to the consolations of Israel; and yet he *glorified God.* He never saw such amazing instances of divine power, and therefore took occasion thence to adore God as the *Almighty.* And he bore a testimony to the patient sufferer: "*Certainly this was a righteous man,* and was unjustly put to death." God's manifesting his power so much to do him honour was a plain evidence of his innocency. His testimony in Matthew and Mark goes further: *Truly this was the Son of God.* But in his case this amounts to the same; for, if he was *a righteous man,* he said very truly when he said that *he was the Son of God;* and therefore that testimony of his concerning himself must be admitted, for, if it were false, he was not a *righteous man.*

2. The disinterested spectators could not but be concerned. This is taken notice of only here, *v.* 48. *All the people that came together to that sight,* as is usual upon such occasions, *beholding the things which were done,* could not but go away very serious for the time, whatever they were when they came home: *They smote their breasts, and returned.* (1.) They laid the thing very much to heart for the present. They looked upon it as a wicked thing to put him to death, and could not but think that some judgment of God would come upon their nation for it. Probably these very people were of those that had cried, *Crucify him, crucify him,* and, when he was nailed to the cross, reviled and blasphemed him; but now they were so terrified with the darkness and the earthquake, and the uncommon manner of his expiring, that they had not only their mouths stopped, but their consciences startled, and in remorse for what they had done, as the publican, they *smote upon their breasts,* beat upon their own hearts, as those that had indignation at themselves. Some think that this was a happy step towards that good work which was afterwards wrought upon them, when they were pricked to the heart, Acts ii. 37. (2.) Yet, it should seem, the impression soon wore off: *They smote their breasts, and returned.* They did not show any further token of respect to Christ, nor enquire more concerning him, but went home; and we have reason to fear that in a little time they quite forgot it. Thus many that see Christ evidently set forth crucified among them in the word and sacraments are a little affected for the present, but it does not continue; they smite their breasts, and return. They see Christ's face in the glass of the ordinances and admire him; but they *go away, and straightway forget what manner of man he is,* and what reason they have to love him.

3. His own friends and followers were obliged to keep their distance, and yet got as near as they could and durst, to see what was done (*v.* 49): *All his acquaintance,* that knew him and were known of him, *stood afar off,* for fear lest if they had been near him they should have been taken up as fa-

vourers of him; this was part of his sufferings, as of Job's (Job xix. 13): *He hath put my brethren far from me, and mine acquaintance are verily estranged from me.* See Ps. lxxxviii. 18. And *the women that followed him* together *from Galilee were beholding these things,* not knowing what to make of them, nor so ready as they should have been to take them for certain preludes of his resurrection. Now was Christ *set for a sign that should be spoken against,* as Simeon foretold, *that the thoughts of many hearts might be revealed, ch.* ii. 34, 35.

50 And, behold, *there was* a man named Joseph, a counsellor; *and he was* a good man, and a just: 51 (The same had not consented to the counsel and deed of them); *he was* of Arimathæa, a city of the Jews: who also himself waited for the kingdom of God. 52 This *man* went unto Pilate, and begged the body of Jesus. 53 And he took it down, and wrapped it in linen, and laid it in a sepulchre that was hewn in stone, wherein never man before was laid. 54 And that day was the preparation, and the sabbath drew on. 55 And the women also, which came with him from Galilee, followed after, and beheld the sepulchre, and how his body was laid. 56 And they returned, and prepared spices and ointments; and rested the sabbath day according to the commandment.

We have here an account of Christ's burial; for he must be brought not only to death, but to the dust of death (Ps. xxii. 15), according to the sentence (Gen. iii. 19), *To the dust thou shalt return.* Observe,

I. Who buried him. His acquaintance *stood afar off;* they had neither money to bear the *charge* nor courage to bear the *odium* of burying him decently; but God raised up one that had both, a *man named Joseph, v.* 50. His character is that he was *a good man and a just,* a man of unspotted reputation for virtue and piety, not only *just* to all, but good to all that needed him (and care to *bury the dead,* as becomes the hope of the resurrection of the dead, is one instance of goodness and beneficence); he was a person of quality, a counsellor, a senator, a member of the sanhedrim, one of the elders of the Jewish church. Having said this of him, it was necessary to add that, though he was of that body of men who had put Christ to death, yet he *had not consented to their counsel and deed* (*v.* 51), though it was carried by the majority, yet he entered his protest against it, and followed not the multitude to do evil. Note, That evil counsel or deed to which we have not consented shall not be reckoned our act. Nay, he not only *dissented* openly from those that were enemies to Christ, but he *consented* secretly with those that were his friends: *He himself waited for the kingdom of God;* he believed the Old-Testament prophecies of the Messiah and his kingdom, and expected the accomplishment of them. This was the man that appears upon this occasion to have had a true respect for the Lord Jesus. Note, There are many who are hearty in Christ's interests, who, though they do not make any show in their outward profession of it, yet will be more ready to do him a piece of real service, when there is occasion, than others who make a greater figure and noise.

II. What he did towards the burying of him. 1. He *went to Pilate,* the judge that condemned him, and *begged the body of Jesus,* for it was at his disposal; and, though he might have raised a party sufficient to have carried off the body by violence, yet he would take the regular course, and do it peaceably. 2. He *took it down,* it should seem, with his own hands, and *wrapped it in linen.* They tell us that it was the manner of the Jews to *roll* the bodies of the dead, as we do little children in their *swaddling-clothes,* and that the word here used signifies as much; so that the piece of fine linen, which he bought whole, he cut into many pieces for this purpose. It is said of Lazarus, *He was bound hand and foot,* John xi. 44. *Grave-clothes* are to the saints as *swaddling-clothes,* which they shall out-grow and put off, when they *come to the perfect man.*

III. Where he was buried. *In a sepulchre that was hewn in stone,* that the prison of the grave might be made strong, as the church, when she was brought into darkness, had her way *enclosed with hewn stone,* Lam. iii. 2, 9. But it was *a sepulchre in which never man before was laid,* for he was buried on such an account as never any one before him was buried, only in order to his rising again the third day by his own power; and he was to triumph over the grave as never any man did.

IV. When he was buried. *On the day of the preparation, when the sabbath drew on, v.* 54. This is given as a reason why they made such haste with the funeral, because the *sabbath drew* on, which required their attendance to other work, preparing for the sabbath, and going forth to welcome it. Note, Weeping must not hinder sowing. Though they were in tears for the death of Christ, yet they must apply themselves to the sanctifying of the sabbath; and, when the sabbath draws on, there must be *preparation.* Our worldly affairs must be so ordered that they may not hinder us from our sabbath work, and our holy affections must be so excited that they may carry us on in it.

V. Who attended the funeral; not any of the disciples, but only *the women that came with him from Galilee* (*v.* 55), who, as they staid by him while he hung on the cross, so they *followed* him, all in tears no doubt, and *beheld the sepulchre* where it was, which was the way to it, and *how his body was laid in it.* They were led to this, not by their curiosity, but by their affection to the Lord Jesus, which was *strong as death* and which *many waters could not quench.* Here was a silent funeral, and not a solemn one, and yet *his rest was glorious.*

VI. What preparation was made for the embalming of his body after he was buried (*v.* 56): *They returned, and prepared spices and ointments,* which was more an evidence of their love than of their faith; for had they *remembered* and *believed* what he had so often told them, that he should *rise again the third day,* they would have spared their *cost* and *pains* herein, as knowing that in a short time there would be a greater honour put upon his body, by the glory of his resurrection, than they could put upon it with their most *precious ointments;* but, busy as they were in this preparation, they *rested on the sabbath day,* and did none of this servile work thereon, not only according to the custom of their nation, but *according to the commandments* of their God, which, though the day be altered, is still in full force: *Remember the sabbath day, to keep it holy.*

CHAP. XXIV.

Our Lord Jesus went gloriously down to death, in spite of the malice of his enemies, who did all they could to make his death ignominious; but he rose again more gloriously, of which we have an account in this chapter; and the proofs and evidences of Christ's resurrection are more fully related by this evangelist than they were by Matthew and Mark. Here is, I. Assurance given by two angels, to the women who visited the sepulchre, that the Lord Jesus was risen from the dead, according to his own word, to which the angels refer them (ver. 1–7), and the report of this to the apostles, ver. 8–11. II. The visit which Peter made to the sepulchre, and his discoveries there, ver. 12. III. Christ's conference with the two disciples that were going to Emmaus, and his making himself known to them, ver. 13–35. IV. His appearing to the eleven disciples themselves, the same day at evening, ver. 36–49. V. The farewell he gave them, his ascension into heaven, and the joy and praise of his disciples whom he left behind, ver. 50–53.

NOW upon the first *day* of the
week, very early in the morning,
they came unto the sepulchre, bringing the spices which they had prepared, and certain *others* with them.
2 And they found the stone rolled
away from the sepulchre. 3 And
they entered in, and found not the
body of the Lord Jesus. 4 And it
came to pass, as they were much perplexed thereabout, behold, two men
stood by them in shining garments:
5 And as they were afraid, and bowed
down *their* faces to the earth, they
said unto them, Why seek ye the
living among the dead? 6 He is not
here, but is risen: remember how he
spake unto you when he was yet in
Galilee, 7 Saying, The Son of man
must be delivered into the hands of
sinful men, and be crucified, and the
third day rise again. 8 And they
remembered his words, 9 And returned from the sepulchre, and told
all these things unto the eleven, and
to all the rest. 10 It was Mary Magdalene, and Joanna, and Mary *the
mother* of James, and other *women
that were* with them, which told these
things unto the apostles. 11 And
their words seemed to them as idle
tales, and they believed them not.
12 Then arose Peter, and ran unto
the sepulchre; and stooping down,
he beheld the linen clothes laid by
themselves, and departed, wondering
in himself at that which was come to
pass.

The manner of the re-uniting of Christ's soul and body in his resurrection is a mystery, one of the *secret things* that *belong not to us;* but the *infallible proofs* of his resurrection, that he did indeed rise from the dead, and was thereby proved to be the Son of God, are *things revealed, which belong to us and to our children.* Some of them we have here in these verses, which relate the same story for substance that we had in Matthew and Mark.

I. We have here the affection and respect which the good women that had followed Christ showed to him, after he was dead and buried, *v.* 1. As soon as ever they could, after the sabbath was over, they *came to the sepulchre,* to embalm his body, not to take it out of the linen in which Joseph had wrapped it, but to anoint the head and face, and perhaps the wounded hands and feet, and to scatter sweet spices upon and about the body; as it is usual with us to strew flowers about the dead bodies and graves of our friends, only to show our good-will towards the taking off the deformity of death if we could, and to make them somewhat the less loathsome to those that are about them. The zeal of these good women for Christ did continue. The spices which they had prepared the evening before the sabbath, at a great expense, they did not, upon second thoughts, when they had slept upon it, dispose of otherwise, suggesting, *To what purpose is this waste?* but they brought them to the sepulchre on the morning after the sabbath, early, very early. It is a rule of charity, *Every man, according as he purposes in his heart, so let him give,* 2 Cor. ix. 7. What is prepared for Christ, let it be used for him. Notice is taken of the names of these women, *Mary Magdalene,* and *Joanna,* and *Mary* the mother of James; grave matronly women, it should seem, they were. Notice is also taken of certain others with them, *v.* 1, and again, *v.* 10. These, who had not joined in preparing the spices, would yet go along with them to the sepulchre; as if the number of Christ's friends increased when he was dead, John xii. 24, 32. The daughters of Jerusalem, when they saw how inquisitive the spouse was after her Beloved, were desirous to seek him with her (Cant. vi. 1), so were these *other women*. The zeal of some provokes others.

II. The surprise they were in, when they found the stone rolled away and the grave empty (*v.* 2, 3); they were *much perplexed* at that (*v.* 4) which they had much reason to rejoice in, that *the stone was rolled away from the sepulchre* (by which it appeared that he had a legal discharge, and leave to come out), and that they *found not the body of the Lord Jesus*, by which it appeared that he had made use of his discharge and was come out. Note, Good Christians often perplex themselves about that with which they should comfort and encourage themselves.

III. The plain account which they had of Christ's resurrection from two angels, who appeared to them *in shining garments*, not only white, but bright, and casting a lustre about them. They first saw *one* angel without the sepulchre, who presently *went in*, and sat with another angel in the sepulchre, *one at the head and the other at the feet, where the body of Jesus had lain;* so the evangelists may be reconciled. The women, when they saw the angels, *were afraid* lest they had some ill news for them; but, instead of enquiring of them, they *bowed down their faces to the earth*, to look for their dear Master in the grave. They would rather find him in his *grave-clothes* than angels themselves in their *shining garments*. A dying Jesus has more beauty in the eyes of a believer than angels themselves. These women, like the spouse, when found by the watchman (and angels are called *watchers)*, enter not into any other conversation with them than this, *Saw ye him whom my soul loveth?* Now here, 1. They upbraid the women with the absurdity of the search they were making: *Why seek ye the living among the dead? v.* 5. Witness is hereby given to Christ that he is *living*, of him *it is witnessed that he liveth* (Heb. vii. 8), and it is the comfort of all the saints, *I know that my Redeemer liveth;* for because he lives we shall live also. But a reproof is given to those that look for him *among the dead*,—that look for him among the dead heroes that the Gentiles worshipped, as if he were but like one of them,—that look for him in an image, or a crucifix, the work of men's hands, or among unwritten tradition and the inventions of men; and indeed all they that expect happiness and satisfaction in the creature, or perfection in this imperfect state, may be said to *seek the living among the dead*. 2. They assure them that he is risen from the dead (*v.* 6): "*He is not here, but is risen*, is risen by his own power; he has quitted his grave, to return no more to it." These angels were competent witnesses, for they had been sent express from heaven with orders for his discharge. And we are sure that their record is true; they durst not tell a lie. 3. They refer them to his own words: *Remember what he spoke to you, when he was yet in Galilee*. If they had duly believed and observed the prediction of it, they would easily have believed the thing itself when it came to pass; and therefore, that the tidings might not be such a surprise to them as they seemed to be, the angels repeat to them what Christ had often said in their hearing, *The Son of man must be delivered into the hands of sinful men*, and though it was done by the determinate counsel and foreknowledge of God, yet they that did it were not the less *sinful* for doing it. He told them that he *must be crucified*. Surely they could not forget that which they had with so much concern seen fulfilled; and would not this bring to their mind that which always followed, *The third day he shall rise again?* Observe, These angels from heaven bring not any *new gospel*, but put them in mind, as the angels of the churches do, of the sayings of Christ, and teach them how to improve and apply them.

IV. Their satisfaction in this account, *v.* 8. The women seemed to acquiesce; they *remembered his words*, when they were thus put in mind of them, and thence concluded that if he was risen it was no more than they had reason to expect; and now they were ashamed of the preparations they had made to embalm on the third day *him* who had often said that he would on the third day rise again. Note, A seasonable remembrance of the words of Christ will help us to a right understanding of his providence.

V. The report they brought of this to the apostles: *They returned from the sepulchre, and told all these things to the eleven, and to all the rest* of Christ's disciples, *v.* 9. It does not appear that they were together in a body; they were *scattered every one to his own*, perhaps scarcely two or three of them together in the same lodgings, but one went to some of them and another to others of them, so that in a little time, that morning, they all had notice of it. But we are told (*v.* 11) how the report was received: *Their words seemed to them as idle tales, and they believed them not*. They thought it was only the fancy of the women, and imputed it to the power of imagination; for they also had forgotten Christ's words, and wanted to be put in mind of them, not only what he had said to them in Galilee some time ago, but what he had said very lately, in the night wherein he was betrayed: *Again a little while, and ye shall see me. I will see you again*. One cannot but be amazed at the stupidity of these disciples,—who had themselves so often professed that they believed Christ to be the Son of God and the true Messiah, had been so often told that he must die and rise again, and then enter into his glory, had seen him more than once raise the dead,—that they should be so backward to believe in his raising himself. Surely it would seem the less strange to them, when hereafter this complaint would justly be taken up *by them*, to remember that there was a time when it might justly have been taken up against them, *Who hath believed our report?*

VI. The enquiry which Peter made hereupon, *v.* 12. It was Mary Magdalene that brought the report to him, as appears, John xx. 1, 2, where this story of his running to the sepulchre is more particularly related. 1. Peter hastened to the sepulchre upon the report, perhaps ashamed of himself, to think that Mary Magdalene should have been there before him; and yet, perhaps, he had not been so ready to go thither now if the women had not told him, among other things, that *the watch was fled.* Many that are *swift-footed* enough when there is no danger are but *cow-hearted* when there is. Peter now *ran to the sepulchre,* who but the other day *ran from his Master.* 2. He looked into the sepulchre, and took notice how orderly the linen clothes in which Christ was wrapped were taken off, and folded up, and laid by themselves, but the body gone. He was very particular in making his observations, as if he would rather credit his own eyes than the testimony of the angels. 3. He went away, as he thought, not much the wiser, *wondering in himself at that which was come to pass.* Had he remembered the words of Christ, even this was enough to satisfy him that he was risen from the dead; but, having forgotten them, he is only amazed with the thing, and knows not what to make of it. There is many a thing puzzling and perplexing to us which would be both plain and profitable if we did but rightly understand the words of Christ, and had them ready to us.

13 And, behold, two of them went
that same day to a village called
Emmaus, which was from Jerusalem
about threescore furlongs. 14 And
they talked together of all these things
which had happened. 15 And it came
to pass, that, while they communed
together and reasoned, Jesus himself
drew near, and went with them. 16
But their eyes were holden that they
should not know him. 17 And he
said unto them, What manner of communications *are* these that ye have
one to another, as ye walk, and are
sad ? 18 And the one of them, whose
name was Cleopas, answering said
unto him, Art thou only a stranger in
Jerusalem, and hast not known the
things which are come to pass there
in these days ? 19 And he said unto
them, What things ? And they said
unto him, Concerning Jesus of Nazareth, which was a prophet mighty in
deed and word before God and all the
people : 20 And how the chief priests
and our rulers delivered him to be
condemned to death, and have crucified him. 21 But we trusted that
it had been he which should have redeemed Israel : and beside all this, to
day is the third day since these things
were done. 22 Yea, and certain women also of our company made us
astonished, which were early at the
sepulchre ; 23 And when they found
not his body, they came, saying, that
they had also seen a vision of angels,
which said that he was alive. 24
And certain of them which were with
us went to the sepulchre, and found
it even so as the women had said :
but him they saw not. 25 Then he
said unto them, O fools, and slow of
heart to believe all that the prophets
have spoken : 26 Ought not Christ
to have suffered these things, and to
enter into his glory ? 27 And beginning at Moses and all the prophets,
he expounded unto them in all the
scriptures the things concerning himself. 28 And they drew nigh unto
the village, whither they went : and
he made as though he would have
gone further. 29 But they constrained
him, saying, Abide with us : for it
is toward evening, and the day is far
spent. And he went in to tarry with
them. 30 And it came to pass, as
he sat at meat with them, he took
bread, and blessed *it*, and brake, and
gave to them. 31 And their eyes
were opened, and they knew him ;
and he vanished out of their sight.
32 And they said one to another,
Did not our heart burn within us,
while he talked with us by the way,
and while he opened to us the scriptures ? 33 And they rose up the
same hour, and returned to Jerusalem,
and found the eleven gathered together, and them that were with them,
34 Saying, The Lord is risen indeed,
and hath appeared to Simon. 35 And
they told what things *were done* in
the way, and how he was known of
them in breaking of bread.

This appearance of Christ to the *two disciples* going to Emmaus was mentioned, and but just mentioned, before (Mark xvi. 12); here it is largely related. It happened the same day that Christ rose, the first day of the new world that rose with him. One of these two disciples was *Cleopas* or *Alpheus,* said by the ancients to be the brother of Joseph, Christ's supposed father; who the other was is not certain. Some think it was Peter; it should seem indeed that Christ did appear particularly to Peter that day, which the eleven spoke of among themselves (*v.* 34), and Paul mentions, 1 Cor. xv. 5. But it could not be Peter that was one of the *two,* for he was one of the *eleven* to whom the *two* returned; and, besides, we know Peter so well as to think that if he had been one of the two he would have been the *chief speaker,* and not Cleopas. It was one of those that were associated with the eleven, mentioned *v.* 9. Now in this passage of story we may observe,

I. The *walk* and *talk* of these two disciples: *They went to a village called Emmaus,* which is reckoned to be about two hours' walk from Jerusalem; it is here said to be about sixty furlongs, seven measured miles, *v.* 13. Whether they went thither upon business, or to see some friend, does not appear. I suspect that they were going homewards to Galilee, with an intention not to enquire more after this Jesus; that they were meditating a retreat, and stole away from their company without asking leave or taking leave; for the accounts brought them that morning of their Master's resurrection seemed to them *as idle tales;* and, if so, no wonder that they began to think of making the best of their way home. But as they travelled they *talked together of all those things which had happened, v.* 14. They had not courage to *confer* of these things, and *consult* what was to be done in the present juncture at Jerusalem, for fear of the Jews; but, when they were got out of the hearing of the Jews, they could talk it over with more freedom. They *talked over these things,* reasoning with themselves concerning the probabilities of Christ's resurrection; for, according as these appeared, they would either go forward or return back to Jerusalem. Note, It well becomes the disciples of Christ, when they are together, to talk of his death and resurrection; thus they may improve one another's knowledge, refresh one another's memory, and stir up one another's devout affections.

II. The good company they met with upon the road, when Jesus himself came, and joined himself to them (*v.* 15): *They communed together, and reasoned,* and perhaps were warm at the argument, one hoping that their Master was risen, and would set up his kingdom, the other despairing. *Jesus himself drew near,* as a stranger who, seeing them travel the same way that he *went,* told them that he should be *glad of their company.* We may observe it, for our encouragement to keep up Christian conference and edifying discourse among us, that where but two together are well employed in work of that kind Christ will come to them, and make a third. When they that fear the Lord *speak one to another* the Lord *hearkens and hears,* and is with them of a truth; so that two thus twisted in faith and love become a *threefold cord, not easily broken,* Eccl. iv. 12. They in their communings and reasonings together were searching for Christ, comparing notes concerning him, that they might come to more knowledge of him; and now Christ comes to them. Note, They who seek Christ shall find him: he will manifest himself to those that enquire after him, and give knowledge to those who use the helps for knowledge which they have. When the spouse enquired of the watchman concerning her beloved, *it was but a little that she passed from them, but she found him.* Cant. iii. 4. But, though they had Christ with them, they were not at first aware of it (*v.* 16): *Their eyes were held, that they should not know him.* It should seem, there were both an alteration of the *object* (for it is said in Mark that now *he appeared in another form)* and a restraint upon the organ (for here it is said that *their eyes were held* by a divine power); or, as some think, there was a confusion in the *medium;* the air was so disposed that they could not discern who it was. No matter *how* it was, but *so* it was they did not *know him,* Christ so ordering it that they might the more freely discourse with him and he with them, and that it might appear that his word, and the influence of it, did not depend upon his bodily presence, which the disciples had too much doted upon, and must be weaned from; but he could teach them, and warm their hearts, by others, who should have his spiritual presence with them, and should have his grace going along with them unseen.

III. The conference that was between Christ and them, when he knew them, and they knew not him. Now Christ and his disciples, as is usual when friends meet incognito, or in a disguise, are here crossing questions.

1. Christ's first question to them is concerning *their* present *sadness,* which plainly appeared in their countenances: *What manner of communications are those that you have one with another as you walk, and are sad? v.* 17. It is a very kind and friendly enquiry. Observe,

(1.) They were *sad;* it appeared to a stranger that they were so. [1.] They had lost their dear Master, and were, in their own apprehensions, quite disappointed in their expectations from him. They had given up the cause, and knew not what course to take to retrieve it. Note, Christ's disciples have reason to be sad when he withdraws from them, to *fast* when the *Bridegroom* is taken from them. [2.] Though he was risen from the dead, yet either they did not know it or did not believe it, and so they were still in sorrow. Note, Christ's disciples are often sad and sorrowful even when they have reason to rejoice, but through the weakness of their faith they cannot take the comfort that is offered to them. [3.] Being sad, they had *communications one with another* concerning Christ. Note, *First,* It becomes Christians to talk of Christ. Were our hearts as full of him, and of what he has done and suffered for us, as they should be, *out of the abundance of the heart the mouth would speak,* not only of God and his providence, but of Christ and his grace and love. *Secondly,* Good company and good converse are an excellent antidote against prevailing melancholy. When Christ's disciples were sad they did not each one get by himself, but continued as he sent them out, two and two, for two are better than one, especially in times of sorrow. Giving *vent* to the grief may perhaps give *ease* to the grieved; and by talking it over we may talk ourselves or our friends may talk us into a better frame. Joint-mourners should be mutual comforters; comforts sometimes come best from such.

(2.) Christ came up to them, and enquired into the matter of their talk, and the cause of their grief: *What manner of communications are these?* Though Christ had now entered into his state of exaltation, yet he continued tender of his disciples, and concerned for their comfort. He speaks as one troubled to see their melancholy: *Wherefore look ye so sadly to-day?* Gen. xl. 7. Note, Our Lord Jesus takes notice of the sorrow and sadness of his disciples, and is afflicted in their afflictions. Christ has hereby taught us, [1.] To be *conversable.* Christ here fell into discourse with two grave serious persons, though he was a stranger to them and they knew him not, and they readily embraced him. It does not become Christians to be morose and shy, but to take pleasure in good society. [2.] We are hereby taught to be *compassionate.* When we see our friends in sorrow and sadness, we should, like Christ here, take cognizance of their grief, and give them the best counsel and comfort we can: *Weep with them that weep.*

2. In answer to this, they put a question to him concerning *his strangeness. Art thou only a stranger in Jerusalem, and hast not known the things that are come to pass there in these days?* Observe, (1.) Cleopas gave him a civil answer. He does not rudely ask him, "As for what we are talking of, what is that to you?" and bid him go about his business. Note, We ought to be civil to those who are civil to us, and to conduct ourselves obligingly to all, both in word and deed. It was a dangerous time now with Christ's disciples; yet he was not jealous of this stranger, that he had any design upon them, to inform against them, or bring them into trouble. Charity is not forward to *think evil,* no, not of strangers. (2.) He is full of Christ himself and of his death and sufferings, and wonders that every body else is not so too: "What! art thou such a stranger in Jerusalem as not to know what has been done to our Master there?" Note, Those are strangers indeed in Jerusalem that know not of the death and sufferings of Christ. What! are they *daughters of Jerusalem,* and yet so little acquainted with Christ as to ask, *What is thy beloved more than another beloved?* (3.) He is very willing to inform this stranger concerning Christ, and to draw on further discourse with him upon this subject. He would not have any one that had the face of a man to be ignorant of Christ. Note, Those who have themselves the knowledge of Christ crucified should do what they can to spread that knowledge, and lead others into an acquaintance with him. And it is observable that these disciples, who were so forward to instruct the stranger, were instructed by him; for to him that has, and uses what he has, shall be given. (4.) It appears, by what Cleopas says, that the death of Christ made a great noise in Jerusalem, so that it could not be imagined that any man should be such a stranger in the city as not to know of it; it was all the talk of the town, and discoursed of in all companies. Thus the matter of fact came to be universally *known,* which, after the pouring out of the Spirit, was to be *explained.*

3. Christ, by way of reply, asked concerning *their knowledge* (*v.* 19): *He said unto them, What things?* thus making himself yet more a stranger. Observe, (1.) Jesus Christ made light of his own sufferings, in comparison with the joy set before him, which was the recompence of it. Now that he was entering upon his glory, see with what unconcernedness he looks back upon his sufferings: *What things?* He had reason to know what things; for to him they were bitter things, and heavy things, and yet he asks, *What things?* The sorrow was forgotten, for joy that the man-child of our salvation was born. He took pleasure in infirmities for our sakes, to teach us to do so for his sake. (2.) Those whom Christ will teach he will first examine how far they have learned; they must tell him *what things* they know, and then he will tell them what was the meaning of these things, and lead them into the mystery of them.

4. They, hereupon, gave him a particular account concerning Christ, and the present posture of his affairs. Observe the story they tell, *v.* 19, &c.

(1.) Here is a summary of Christ's *life* and *character.* The *things* they are full of are concerning *Jesus of Nazareth* (so he was commonly called), who *was a prophet,* a teacher come from God. He preached a true and excellent doctrine, which had manifestly its rise from heaven, and its tendency towards heaven. He confirmed it by many glorious miracles, miracles of mercy, so that he was

mighty in deed and word before God and all the people; that is, he was both a great favourite of heaven and a great blessing to this earth. He was, and appeared to be, greatly beloved of God, and much the darling of his people. He had great acceptance with God, and a great reputation in the country. Many are *great before all the people,* and are caressed by them, who are not so *before God,* as the scribes and Pharisees; but Christ was mighty both in his *doctrine* and in his *doings, before God and all the people.* Those were strangers in Jerusalem that did not know this.

(2.) Here is a modest narrative of his sufferings and death, *v.* 20. " Though he was so dear both to God and man, yet the *chief priests and our rulers,* in contempt of both, *delivered him* to the Roman power, *to be condemned to death,* and *they have crucified him.*" It is strange that they did not aggravate the matter more, and lay a greater load upon those that had been guilty of crucifying Christ; but perhaps because they spoke to one that was a stranger they thought it prudent to avoid all reflections upon the chief priests and their rulers, how just soever.

(3.) Here is an intimation of their disappointment in him, as the reason of their sadness: " *We trusted that it had been he who should have redeemed Israel, v.* 21. We are of those who not only looked upon him to be a prophet, like Moses, but, like him, a redeemer too." He was depended upon, and great things expected from him, by them that *looked for redemption,* and in it for the consolation of Israel. Now, if *hope deferred makes the heart sick,* hope disappointed, especially such a hope, kills the heart. But see how they made that the ground of their despair which if they had understood it aright was the surest ground of their hope, and that was the dying of the Lord Jesus: *We trusted* (say they) *that it had been he that should have redeemed Israel.* And is it not he that doth redeem Israel? Nay, is he not by his death paying the price of their redemption? Was it not necessary, in order to his saving Israel from their sins, that he should suffer? So that now, since that most difficult part of his undertaking was got over, they had more reason than ever to *trust* that *this was he that should deliver Israel;* yet now they are ready to give up the cause.

(4.) Here is an account of their present amazement with reference to his resurrection. [1.] " *This is the third day* since he was crucified and died, and that was the day when it was expected, if ever, that he should rise again, and rise in glory and outward pomp, and show himself as publicly in honour as he had been shown three days before in disgrace; but we see no sign of it; nothing appears, as we expected, to the conviction and confusion of his prosecutors, and the consolation of his disciples, but all is silent." [2.] They own that there was a report among them that he was risen, but they seem to speak of it very slightly, and as what they gave no credit at all to (*v.* 22, 23): " *Certain women also of our company made us astonished* (and that was all), who were *early at the sepulchre,* and found the body gone, and they said that they had *seen a vision of angels, who said that he was alive;* but we are ready to think it was only their fancy, and no real thing, for angels would have been sent to the apostles, not to the women, and women are easily imposed upon." [3.] They acknowledge that some of the apostles had visited the sepulchre, and found it empty, *v.* 24. " But *him they saw not,* and therefore we have reason to fear that he *is not risen,* for, if he be, surely he would have *shown himself* to them; so that, upon the whole matter, we have no great reason to think that he is risen, and therefore have no expectations from him now; our hopes were all nailed to his cross, and buried in his grave."

(5.) Our Lord Jesus, though not known by face to them, makes himself known to them by his word.

[1.] He reproves them for their incogitancy, and the weakness of their faith in the scriptures of the Old Testament: *O fools, and slow of heart to believe, v.* 25. When Christ forbade us to say to our brother, *Thou fool,* it was intended to restrain us from giving unreasonable reproaches, not from giving just reproofs. Christ called them *fools,* not as it signifies *wicked men,* in which sense he forbade it to us, but as it signifies *weak men.* He might call them *fools,* for he *knows our foolishness,* the foolishness that is bound in our hearts. Those are fools that act against their own interest; so they did who would not admit the evidence given them that their Master was risen, but put away the comfort of it. That which is condemned in them as their *foolishness* is, *First,* Their *slowness to believe.* Believers are branded as fools by atheists, and infidels, and free-thinkers, and their most holy faith is censured as a fond credulity; but Christ tells us that those are *fools* who are *slow of heart to believe,* and are kept from it by prejudices never impartially examined. *Secondly,* Their slowness to believe *the writings of the prophets.* He does not so much blame them for their slowness to believe the testimony of the women and of the angels, but for that which was the cause thereof, their *slowness to believe* the prophets; for, if they had given the prophets of the Old Testament their due weight and consideration, they would have been as sure of Christ's *rising from the dead* that morning (being the third day after his death) as they were of the *rising of the sun;* for the *series* and *succession* of events as settled by *prophecy* are no less certain and inviolable than as settled by *providence.* Were we but more *conversant* with the scripture, and the divine counsels as far as they are made known in the scripture, we should not be subject to such perplexities as we often *entangle* ourselves in.

[2.] He shows them that the sufferings of Christ, which were such a stumbling-block to them, and made them unapt to believe his glory, were really the appointed way to his glory, and he could not go to it any other way (*v.* 26): "*Ought not the Christ* (the Messiah) to *have suffered these things, and to enter into his glory?* Was it not decreed, and was not that decree *declared,* that the promised Messiah must first suffer and then reign, that he must go by his cross to his crown?" Had they never read the fifty-third of Isaiah and the ninth of Daniel, where the prophets speak so very plainly of the *sufferings of Christ* and the *glory that should follow?* 1 Pet. i. 11. The cross of Christ was that to which they could not reconcile themselves; now here he shows them two things which take off the offence of the cross:—*First,* That the Messiah *ought to suffer* these things; and therefore his sufferings were not only no objection against his being the Messiah, but really a proof of it, as the afflictions of the saints are an evidence of their sonship; and they were so far from ruining their expectations that really they were the foundation of their hopes. He could not have been a *Saviour,* if he had not been a *sufferer.* Christ's undertaking our salvation was voluntary: but, having undertaken it, it was necessary that he should suffer and die. *Secondly,* That, when he had suffered these things, he should *enter into his glory,* which he did at his resurrection; that was his first step upward. Observe, It is called *his* glory, because he was *duly entitled* to it, and it was the glory he had before the world was; he *ought* to enter into it, for in that, as well as in his sufferings, the scripture must be fulfilled. He *ought* to suffer first, and then to enter into his glory; and thus the *reproach* of the cross is for ever *rolled away,* and we are directed to expect the crown of *thorns* and then that of *glory.*

[3.] He expounded to them the scriptures of the Old Testament, which spoke of the Messiah, and showed them how they were fulfilled in Jesus of Nazareth, and now can tell them more concerning him than they could before tell him (*v.* 27): *Beginning at Moses,* the first inspired writer of the Old Testament, he went in order through *all the prophets,* and *expounded to them the things concerning himself,* showing that the sufferings he had now gone through were so far from defeating the prophecies of the scripture concerning him that they were the accomplishment of them. He began at Moses, who recorded the first promise, in which it was plainly foretold that the Messiah should have his *heel bruised,* but that by it the serpent's head should be incurably broken. Note, *First,* There are things dispersed throughout *all the scriptures* concerning Christ, which it is of great advantage to have *collected* and *put together.* You cannot go far in any part of scripture but you meet with something that has reference to Christ, some prophecy, some promise, some prayer, some type or other; for he is the true *treasure hid in the field* of the Old Testament. A golden thread of gospel grace runs through the whole web of the Old Testament. There is an *eye* of that *white* to be discerned in every place. *Secondly,* The things concerning Christ need to be *expounded.* The eunuch, though a scholar, would not pretend to understand them, *except some man should guide him* (Acts viii. 31); for they were delivered darkly, according to that dispensation: but now that the veil is taken away the New Testament expounds the Old. *Thirdly,* Jesus Christ is himself the best expositor of scripture, particularly the scriptures concerning himself; and even after his resurrection it was in this way that he led people into the knowledge of the mystery concerning himself; not by advancing new notions independent upon the scripture, but by showing how the scripture was fulfilled, and turning them over to the study of it. Even the Apocalypse itself is but a second part of the Old-Testament prophecies, and has continually an eye to them. *If men believe not Moses and the prophets,* they are incurable. *Fourthly,* In *studying* the scriptures, it is good to be *methodical,* and to take them in order; for the Old-Testament light shone *gradually* to the *perfect day,* and it is good to observe how *at sundry times,* and in *divers manners* (subsequent predictions improving and giving light to the preceding ones), God spoke to the fathers *concerning* his Son, by whom he has now *spoken* to us. Some begin their bible at the wrong end, who study the Revelation first; but Christ has here taught us to *begin at Moses.* Thus far the conference between them.

IV. Here is the discovery which Christ at length made of himself to them. One would have given a great deal for a copy of the sermon Christ preached to them by the way, of that exposition of the bible which he gave them; but it is not thought fit that we should have it, we have the substance of it in other scriptures. The disciples are so charmed with it, that they think they are come too soon to their journey's end; but so it is: *They drew nigh to the village whither they went* (*v.* 28), where, it should seem, they determined to *take up* for that night. And now,

1. They courted his stay with them: *He made as though he would have gone further;* he did not *say* that he would, but he seemed to them to be going further, and did not readily turn into their friend's house, which it would not be decent for a stranger to do unless he were invited. He would have gone further if they had not courted his stay; so that here was nothing like dissimulation in the case. If a stranger be *shy,* every one knows the meaning of it; he will not thrust himself *rudely* upon your house or company; but, if you make it appear that you are freely desirous of him for your guest or companion, he knows not but he may accept your invita-

tion, and this was all that Christ did when he *made as though he would have gone further*. Note, Those that would have Christ dwell with them must invite him, and be importunate with him; though he is often *found of those that seek him not*, yet those only that *seek* can be sure to *find;* and, if he seem to *draw off* from us, it is but to draw out our importunity; as here, *they constrained him;* both of them laid hold on him, with a kind and friendly violence, saying, *Abide with us.* Note, Those that have experienced the pleasure and profit of communion with Christ cannot but covet more of his company, and beg of him, not only to *walk with them* all day, but to *abide with them* at night. When *the day is far spent,* and it is *towards evening,* we begin to think of retiring for our repose, and then it is proper to have our eye to Christ, and to beg of him to *abide with us,* to manifest himself to us and to fill our minds with good thoughts of him and good affections to him. Christ yielded to their importunity: He *went in, to tarry with them.* Thus ready is Christ to give further instructions and comforts to those who improve what they have received. He has promised that *if any man open the door,* to bid him welcome, he will *come in to him,* Rev. iii. 20.

2. He manifested himself to them, *v.* 30, 31. We may suppose that he continued his discourse with them, which he began upon the road; for thou must talk of the things of God *when thou sittest in the house as well as when thou walkest by the way.* While supper was getting ready (which perhaps was soon done, the provision was so small and mean), it is probable that he entertained them with such communications as were *good* and *to the use of edifying;* and so likewise as they *sat at meat* his *lips fed* them. But still they little thought that it was Jesus himself that was all this while talking with them, till at length he was pleased to throw off his disguise, and then to withdraw. (1.) They began to suspect it was he, when, as they *sat down to meat,* he undertook the office of the Master of the feast, which he performed so like himself, and like what he used to do among his disciples, that by it they discerned him: *He took bread, and blessed it,* and *brake, and gave to them.* This he did with his usual air both of authority and affection, with the same gestures and mien, with the same expressions perhaps in craving a blessing and in giving the bread to them. This was not a *miraculous* meal like that of the five loaves, nor a *sacramental* meal like that of the eucharist, but a *common* meal; yet Christ here did the same as he did in those, to teach us to keep up our communion with God through Christ in common providences as well as in special ordinances, and to crave a blessing and give thanks at every meal, and to see our daily bread provided for us and broken to us by the hand of Jesus Christ, the Master, not only of the great family, but of all our families. Wherever we *sit down to eat,* let us set Christ at the upper end of the table, take our meat as *blessed to us* by him, and *eat and drink* to his glory, and receive contentedly and thankfully what he is pleased to *carve* out to us, be the fare ever so coarse and mean. We may well receive it cheerfully, if we can by faith see it coming to us *from* Christ's hand, and with his blessing. (2.) Presently *their eyes were opened,* and then they saw who it was, and *knew him* well enough. Whatever it was which had hitherto concealed him from them, it was now taken out of the way; the mists were scattered, the veil was taken off, and then they made no question but it was their Master. He might, for wise and holy ends, put on the shape of another, but no other could put on his; and therefore it must be he. See how Christ by his Spirit and grace makes himself known to the souls of his people. [1.] He opens the scriptures to them, for they are they which testify of him to those who *search them,* and search for him in them. [2.] He meets them at his table, in the ordinance of the Lord's supper, and commonly there makes further discoveries of himself to them, is *known to them in the breaking of bread.* But, [3.] The work is completed by the opening of the eyes of their mind, and causing the scales to fall off from them, as from Paul's in his conversion. If he that gives the revelation do not give the understanding, we are in the dark still.

3. He immediately disappeared: *He vanished out of their sight.* Ἄφαντος ἐγένετο—He *withdrew himself* from them, slipped away of a sudden, and went *out of sight.* Or, he *became not visible by them,* was made inconspicuous by them. It should seem that though Christ's body, after his resurrection, was the very *same body* in which he suffered and died, as appeared by the marks in it, yet it was so far changed as to become either *visible* or *not visible* as he thought fit to make it, which was a step towards its being made a *glorious body.* As soon as he had given his disciples one glimpse of him he was gone presently. Such short and transient views have we of Christ in this world; we see him, but in a little while lose the sight of him again. When we come to heaven the vision of him will have no interruptions.

V. Here is the reflection which these disciples made upon this conference, and the report which they made of it to their brethren at Jerusalem.

1. The reflection they each of them made upon the influence which Christ's discourse had upon them (*v.* 32): *They said one to another, Did not our hearts burn within us?* "I am sure mine did," saith one; "And so did mine," saith the other, "I never was so affected with any discourse in all my life." Thus do they not so much compare *notes* as compare *hearts,* in the review of the sermon Christ had preached to them. They found

the preaching powerful, even when they knew not the preacher. It made things very plain and clear to them; and, which was more, brought a *divine heat* with a *divine light* into their souls, such as put their hearts into a glow, and kindled a holy fire of pious and devout affections in them. Now this they take notice of, for the confirming of their belief, that it was indeed, as at last they saw, *Jesus himself* that had been talking with them all along. "What fools were we, that we were not sooner aware who it was! For none but he, no word but his, could *make our hearts burn within us* as they did; it must be he that has the key of the heart; it could be no other." See here, (1.) What *preaching* is likely to *do good*—such as Christ's was, *plain preaching*, and that which is familiar and level to our capacity—*he talked with us by the way;* and *scriptural* preaching—*he opened to us the scriptures,* the scriptures relating to himself. Ministers should show people their religion in their bibles, and that they preach no other doctrine to them than what is there; they must show that they make that the fountain of their knowledge and the foundation of their faith. Note, The expounding of those scriptures which speak of Christ has a direct tendency to warm the hearts of his disciples, both to quicken and to comfort them. (2.) What *hearing* is likely to *do good*—that which makes the *heart burn;* when we are much affected with the things of God, especially with the love of Christ in dying for us, and have our hearts thereby drawn out in love to him, and drawn up in holy desires and devotions, then our hearts *burn within us;* when our hearts are raised and elevated, and are as the sparks which *fly upwards* towards God, and when they are kindled and carried out with a holy zeal and indignation against sin, both in others and in ourselves, and we are in some measure refined and purified from it by the *spirit of judgment* and the *spirit of burning*, then we may say, "Through grace our hearts are thus inflamed."

2. The report they brought of this to their brethren at Jerusalem (*v.* 33): *They rose up the same hour,* so transported with joy at the discovery Christ had made of himself to them that they could not stay to make an end of their supper, but returned with all speed to Jerusalem, though it was towards evening. If they had had any thoughts of quitting their relation to Christ, this soon banished all such thoughts out of their mind, and there needed no more to send them back to his flock. It should seem that they intended at least to take up their quarters to-night at Emmaus; but now that they had seen Christ they could not rest till they had brought the good news to the disciples, both for the confirmation of their trembling faith and for the comfort of their sorrowful spirits, with the *same comforts wherewith they were comforted of God.* Note, It is the duty of those to whom Christ has manifested himself to let others know what he has done for their souls. When thou art converted, instructed, comforted, strengthen thy brethren. These disciples were *full* of this matter themselves, and must go to their brethren, to give vent to their joys, as well as to give them satisfaction that their Master was risen. Observe, (1.) How they found them, just when they came in among them, discoursing on the same subject, and relating another proof of the resurrection of Christ. They found the eleven, and those that were their usual companions, *gathered together* late in the night, to pray together, it may be, and to consider what was to be done in this juncture; and they found them *saying* among themselves (λέγοντας· it is the saying of the *eleven,* not of the *two,* as is plain by the original), and when these two came in, they repeated to them with joy and triumph, *The Lord is risen indeed, and hath appeared to Simon, v.* 34. That Peter had a sight of him before the rest of the disciples had appears 1 Cor. xv. 5, where it is said, *He was seen of Cephas, then of the twelve.* The angel having ordered the women to tell Peter of it particularly (Mark xvi. 7), for his comfort, it is highly probable that our Lord Jesus did himself presently the same day appear to Peter, though we have no particular narrative of it, to *confirm the word of his messengers.* This he had related to his brethren; but, observe, Peter does not here proclaim it, and boast of it, himself (he thought this did not become a penitent), but the other disciples speak of it with exultation, *The Lord is risen indeed,* ὄντως—*really;* it is now past dispute, no room is left to doubt it, for he has appeared not only to the women, but to Simon. (2.) How they seconded their evidence with an account of what they had seen (*v.* 35): *They told what things were done in the way.* The words that were spoken by Christ to them in the way, having a wonderful effect and influence upon them, are here called the *things* that were *done in the way;* for the words that Christ speaks are not an empty sound, but *they are spirit and they are life,* and wondrous things are *done* by them, done *by the way,* by the by as it were, where it is not expected. They told also how he was at length *known to them in the breaking of bread;* then, when he was carving out blessings to them, God opened their eyes to discern who it was. Note, It would be of great use for the discovery and confirmation of truth if the disciples of Christ would compare their observations and experiences, and communicate to each other what they know and have felt in themselves.

36 And as they thus spake, Jesus
himself stood in the midst of them,
and saith unto them, Peace *be* unto
you. 37 But they were terrified and
affrighted, and supposed that they
had seen a spirit. 38 And he said

unto them, Why are ye troubled?
and why do thoughts arise in your
hearts? 39 Behold my hands and
my feet, that it is I myself: handle
me, and see; for a spirit hath not
flesh and bones, as ye see me have.
40 And when he had thus spoken, he
showed them *his* hands and *his* feet.
41 And while they yet believed not
for joy, and wondered, he said unto
them, Have ye here any meat? 42
And they gave him a piece of a broiled
fish, and of an honeycomb. 43 And
he took *it*, and did eat before them.
44 And he said unto them, These *are*
the words which I spake unto you,
while I was yet with you, that all
things must be fulfilled, which were
written in the law of Moses, and *in*
the prophets, and *in* the psalms, concerning me. 45 Then opened he
their understanding, that they might
understand the scriptures, 46 And
said unto them, Thus it is written,
and thus it behoved Christ to suffer,
and to rise from the dead the third
day: 47 And that repentance and
remission of sins should be preached
in his name among all nations, beginning at Jerusalem. 48 And ye are
witnesses of these things. 49 And,
behold, I send the promise of my
Father upon you: but tarry ye in the
city of Jerusalem, until ye be endued
with power from on high.

Five times Christ was seen the same day that he rose: by Mary Magdalene alone in the garden (John xx. 14), by the women as they were going to tell the disciples (Matt. xxviii. 9), by Peter alone, by the two disciples going to Emmaus, and now at night by the eleven, of which we have an account in these verses, as also John xx. 19. Observe,

I. The great *surpise* which his appearing gave them. He came in among them very *seasonably*, as they were comparing notes concerning the proofs of his resurrection: *As they thus spoke*, and were ready perhaps to *put it to the question* whether the proofs produced amounted to evidence sufficient of their Master's resurrection or no, and how they should proceed, *Jesus himself stood in the midst of them*, and *put it out of question.* Note, Those who make the best use they can of their evidences for their comfort may expect further assurances, and that the *Spirit of Christ* will *witness with their spirits* (as Christ here witnessed with the disciples, and confirmed their testimony) that they are the *children of God*, and risen with Christ. Observe, 1. The *comfort* Christ spoke to them: *Peace be unto you.* This intimates in general that it was a kind visit which Christ now paid them, a visit of love and friendship. Though they had very unkindly deserted him in his sufferings, yet he takes the first opportunity of seeing them together; for he deals not with us as we deserve. They did not *credit* those who had seen him; therefore he *comes himself*, that they might not continue in their disconsolate incredulity. He had promised that after his resurrection he *would see them in Galilee;* but so desirous was he to see them, and satisfy them, that he anticipated the appointment and *sees them at Jerusalem.* Note, Christ is often *better* than his word, but never *worse.* Now his first word to them was, *Peace be to you;* not in a way of compliment, but of consolation. This was a common form of salutation among the Jews, and Christ would thus express his usual familiarity with them, though he had now entered into his state of exaltation. Many, when they are advanced, forget their old friends and take state upon them; but we see Christ as free with them as ever. Thus Christ would at the first word intimate to them that he did not come to quarrel with Peter for *denying* him and the rest for *running away* from him; no, he *came peaceably*, to signify to them that he had forgiven them, and was reconciled to them. 2. The *fright* which they put themselves into upon it (*v.* 37): They were *terrified*, supposing that *they had seen a spirit*, because he came in among them without any noise, and was in the midst of them ere they were aware. The word used (Matt. xiv. 26), when they said *It is a spirit*, is φάντασμα, it is a *spectre*, an *apparition;* but the word here used is πνεῦμα, the word that properly signifies *a spirit;* they supposed it to be a spirit not clothed with a real body. Though we have an alliance and correspondence with the world of spirits, and are hastening to it, yet while we are here in this world of sense and matter it is a terror to us to have a spirit so far change its own nature as to become visible to us, and conversable with us, for it is something, and bodes something, very extraordinary.

II. The great *satisfaction* which his discourse gave them, wherein we have,

1. The reproof he gave them for their causeless fears: *Why are you troubled, and why do* frightful *thoughts arise in your hearts? v.* 38. Observe here, (1.) That when at any time we are *troubled, thoughts* are apt to *rise in our hearts* that do us hurt. Sometimes the *trouble* is the effect of the *thoughts* that *arise in our hearts;* our griefs and fears take rise from those things that are the creatures of our own fancy. Sometimes the thoughts arising in the heart are the effect of the trouble, without are fightings and then within are fears. Those that are melancholy

and troubled in mind have *thoughts arising in their hearts* which reflect dishonour upon God, and create disquiet to themselves. *I am cut off from thy sight. The Lord has forsaken and forgotten me.* (2.) That many of the troublesome thoughts with which our minds are disquieted arise from our mistakes concerning Christ. They here thought that they had *seen a spirit,* when they saw Christ, and that put them into this fright. We forget that Christ is our *elder brother,* and look upon him to be at as great a distance from us as the world of spirits is from this world, and therewith terrify ourselves. When Christ is by his Spirit convincing and humbling us, when he is by his providence trying and converting us, we *mistake him,* as if he designed our hurt, and this troubles us. (3.) That all the troublesome thoughts which rise in our hearts at any time are known to the Lord Jesus, even at the first rise of them, and they are displeasing to him. He chid his disciples for such *thoughts,* to teach us to chide ourselves for them. *Why art thou cast down, O my soul? Why art thou troubled?* Why do *thoughts arise* that are neither *true* nor *good,* that have neither *foundation* nor *fruit,* but hinder our joy in God, unfit us for our duty, give advantage to Satan, and deprive us of the comforts laid up for us?

2. The proof he gave them of his resurrection, both for the *silencing* of their *fears* by convincing them that he was *not a spirit,* and for the *strengthening* of their *faith* in that doctrine which they were to preach to the world by giving them full satisfaction concerning his resurrection. Two proofs he gives them:—

(1.) He shows them his body, particularly *his hands and his feet.* They saw that he had the shape, and features, and exact resemblance, of their Master; but is it not his ghost? "No," saith Christ, "*behold my hands and my feet;* you see I have *hands* and *feet,* and therefore have a *true* body; you see I can *move* these hands and feet, and therefore have a *living* body; and you see the marks of the nails in my hands and feet, and therefore it is *my own* body, the *same* that you saw crucified, and not a *borrowed* one." He lays down this principle—that a *spirit has not flesh and bones;* it is not compounded of gross matter, shaped into various members, and consisting of divers heterogeneous parts, as our bodies are. He does not tell us what a *spirit* is (it is time enough to know that when we go to the world of spirits), but what it is not: *It has not flesh and bones.* Now hence he infers, "*It is I myself,* whom you have been so intimately acquainted with, and have had such familiar conversation with; it is *I myself,* whom you have reason to rejoice in, and not to be afraid of." Those who *know Christ* aright, and know him as *theirs,* will have no reason to be terrified at his appearances, at his approaches. [1.] He appeals to their *sight, shows* them *his hands* and *his feet,* which were pierced with the nails. Christ retained the marks of them in his glorified body, that they might be proofs that it was he himself; and he was willing that they should be *seen.* He afterwards showed them to Thomas, for he is not ashamed of his sufferings for us; little reason then have we to be ashamed of them, or of ours for him. As he showed his wounds here to his disciples, for the enforcing of his instructions to them, so he showed them to his Father, for the enforcing of his intercessions with him. He appears in heaven *as a Lamb that had been slain* (Rev. v. 6); his *blood speaks,* Heb. xii. 24. He makes intercession in the virtue of his satisfaction; he says to the Father, as here to the disciples, *Behold my hands and my feet,* Zech. xiii. 6, 7. [2.] He appeals to their *touch: Handle me, and see.* He would not let Mary Magdalene touch him at that time, John xx. 17. But the disciples here are entrusted to do it, that they who were to preach his resurrection, and to suffer for doing so, might be themselves abundantly satisfied concerning it. He bade them *handle him,* that they might be convinced that he was not a *spirit.* If there were really no spirits, or apparitions of spirits (as by this and other instances it is plain that the disciples did believe there were), this had been a proper time for Christ to have undeceived them, by telling them there were no such things; but he seems to take it for granted that there have been and may be apparitions of spirits, else what need was there of so much pains to prove that he was not one? There were many heretics in the primitive times, atheists I rather think they were, who said that Christ had never any substantial body, but that it was a mere phantasm, which was neither really born nor truly suffered. Such wild notions as these, we are told, the Valentinians and Manichees had, and the followers of Simon Magus; they were called Δοκήται and Φαντυσιασταὶ. Blessed be God, these heresies have long since been *buried;* and we know and are sure that Jesus Christ was no *spirit* or *apparition,* but had a true and real body, even after his resurrection.

(2.) He *eats* with them, to show that he had a real and true body, and that he was willing to converse freely and familiarly with his disciples, as one friend with another. Peter lays a great stress upon this (Acts x. 41): We *did eat and drink with him after he rose from the dead.*

[1.] When they *saw his hands and his feet,* yet they knew not what to say, *They believed not for joy, and wondered, v.* 41. It was their infirmity that they *believed not,* that *yet* they believed not, ἔτι ἀπιστούντων αὐτῶν—*they as yet being unbelievers.* This very much corroborates the truth of Christ's resurrection that the disciples were so slow to believe it. Instead of stealing away his body, and saying, *He is risen,* when he is not, as the chief priests suggested they would do, they are ready to say again and again, *He is not risen,* when he is. Their being incredulous of it at first, and insisting upon the utmost proofs of it, show that when afterwards they did believe it, and venture their all upon it, it was not but upon the fullest demonstration of the thing that could be. But, though it was their infirmity, yet it was an excusable one; for it was not from any contempt of the evidence offered them that they believed not: but, *First,* They *believed not for joy,* as Jacob, when he was told that Joseph was alive; they thought it too good news to be true. When the faith and hope are therefore *weak* because the love and desires are *strong,* that weak faith shall be helped, and not rejected. *Secondly,* They *wondered;* they thought it not only *too good,* but *too great,* to be true, forgetting both the scriptures and the power of God.

[2.] For their further conviction and encouragement, he *called for some meat.* He sat down to meat with the two disciples at Emmaus, but it is not said that he did eat with *them;* now, lest that should be made an objection, he here did actually *eat* with *them* and *the rest,* to show that his body was really and truly *returned to life,* though he did not eat and drink, and converse constantly, with them, as he had done (and as Lazarus did after *his* resurrection, who not only returned to life, but to his former state of life, and to die again), because it was not agreeable to the economy of the state he was risen to. They gave him a *piece of a broiled fish, and of a honey-comb, v.* 42. The honey-comb, perhaps, was used as sauce to the broiled fish, for Canaan was a land *flowing with honey.* This was mean fare; yet, if it be the fare of the disciples, their Master will fare as they do, because in the kingdom of our Father they shall fare as he does, shall eat and drink with him in his kingdom.

3. The *insight* he gave them into the word of God, which they had *heard* and read, by which faith in the resurrection of Christ is wrought in them, and all the difficulties are cleared. (1.) He refers them to the *word* which they had *heard* from him when he was with them, and puts them in mind of that as the angel had done (*v.* 44): *These are the words which I said unto you* in private, many a time, *while I was yet with you.* We should better *understand* what Christ *does,* if we did but better *remember* what he hath *said,* and had but the art of comparing them together. (2.) He refers them to the *word* they had read in the Old Testament, to which the word they had heard from him directed them: *All things must be fulfilled which were written.* Christ had given them this general hint for the regulating of their expectations—that whatever they found written concerning the Messiah, in the Old Testament, must be fulfilled in him, what was written concerning his sufferings as well as what was written concerning his kingdom; these God had *joined together* in the prediction, and it could not be thought that they should be *put asunder* in the event. *All things* must be fulfilled, even the *hardest,* even the *heaviest,* even the *vinegar;* he could not die till he had that, because he could not till then say, *It is finished.* The several parts of the Old Testament are here mentioned, as containing each of them things concerning Christ: *The law of Moses,* that is, the Pentateuch, or the *five* books written by Moses,—the *prophets,* containing not only the books that are purely prophetical, but those historical books that were written by prophetical men,—the *Psalms,* containing the other writings, which they called the *Hagiographa.* See in what various ways of writing God did of old reveal his will; but all proceeded from one and the self-same Spirit, who by them gave notice of the coming and kingdom of the Messiah; for *to him bore all the prophets witness.* (3.) By an immediate present work upon their minds, of which they themselves could not but be sensible, he gave them to apprehend the true intent and meaning of the Old-Testament prophecies of Christ, and to see them all fulfilled in him: *Then opened he their understanding, that they might understand the scriptures, v.* 45. In his discourse with the two disciples he took the veil from off the text, by *opening* the scriptures; here he took the veil from off the heart, *by opening the mind.* Observe here, [1.] That Jesus Christ by his Spirit operates on the minds of men, on the minds of all that are his. He has access to our spirits, and can immediately influence them. It is observable how he did now after his resurrection give a *specimen* of those two great operations of *his Spirit* upon the *spirits of* men, his enlightening the intellectual faculties with a divine light, when he opened the understandings of his disciples, and his invigorating the active powers with a divine heat, when he made their hearts burn within them. [2.] Even good men need to have their *understandings opened;* for though they are not *darkness,* as they were by nature, yet in many things they are *in the dark.* David prays, *Open mine eyes. Give me understanding.* And Paul, who knows so much of Christ, sees his need to learn more. [3.] Christ's way of working faith in the soul, and gaining the throne there, is by *opening the understanding* to discern the evidence of those things that are to be believed. Thus he comes into the soul by *the door,* while Satan, as a thief and a robber, climbs up some other way. [4.] The design of opening the understanding is *that we may understand the scriptures;* not that we may be *wise above what is written,* but that we may be *wiser in what is written,* and may be made *wise to salvation* by it. The Spirit in the word and the Spirit in the heart say the same thing. Christ's scholars never learn *above their bibles* in this world; but they need to be learning still more and more *out of their bibles,* and to grow more *ready* and *mighty* in the scriptures. That we may have right thoughts of Christ,

and have our mistakes concerning him rectified, there needs no more than to be made to understand the scriptures.

4. The instructions he gave them as *apostles,* who were to be employed in setting up his kingdom in the world. They expected, while their Master was with them, that they should be preferred to posts of honour, of which they thought themselves quite disappointed when he was dead. "No," saith, he, "you are now to enter upon them; *you are* to be *witnesses of these things* (*v.* 48), to carry the notice of them to all the world; not only to *report* them as matter of news, but to *assert* them as evidence given upon the trial of the great cause that has been so long depending between God and Satan, the issue of which must be the casting down and casting out of the *prince of this world.* You are fully assured of these things yourselves, you are eye and ear-witnesses of them; go, and assure the world of them; and the same Spirit that has enlightened you shall go along with you for the enlightening of others." Now here they are told,

(1.) *What they must preach.* They must preach the gospel, must preach the *New Testament* as the full accomplishment of the *Old,* as the continuation and conclusion of divine revelation. They must take their bibles along with them (especially when they preached to the Jews; nay, and Peter, in his first sermon to the Gentiles, directed them to consult the prophets, Acts x. 43), and must show people how it was written of old concerning the Messiah, and the glories and graces of his kingdom, and then must tell them how, upon their certain knowledge, all this was fulfilled in the Lord Jesus.

[1.] The great *gospel truth* concerning the *death* and *resurrection* of Jesus Christ must be *published* to the children of men (*v.* 46): *Thus it was written* in the sealed book of the divine counsels from eternity, the volume of that book of the covenant of redemption; and thus it was written in the open book of the Old Testament, among the things revealed; and therefore *thus it behoved Christ to suffer,* for the divine counsels must be performed, and care taken that no word of God fall to the ground. "Go, and tell the world," *First,* "That Christ *suffered,* as it was written of him. Go, preach *Christ crucified;* be not ashamed of his cross, not ashamed of a suffering Jesus. Tell them what he suffered, and why he suffered, and how all the scriptures of the Old Testament were fulfilled in his sufferings. Tell them that it *behoved him to suffer,* that it was necessary to the taking away of the sin of the world, and the deliverance of mankind from death and ruin: nay, it *became him* to be perfected *through sufferings,*" Heb. ii. 10. *Secondly,* "That he rose from the dead on *the third day,* by which not only all the offence of the cross was rolled away, but he was declared to be the Son of God with power, and in this also the *scriptures* were *fulfilled* (see 1 Cor. xv. 3, 4); go, tell the world how often you saw him after he rose from the dead, and how intimately you conversed with him. *Your eyes see*" (as Joseph said to his brethren, when his discovering himself to them was as life from the dead) "*that it is my mouth that speaketh unto you,* Gen. xlv. 12. Go, and tell them, then, that he that *was dead is alive,* and *lives for evermore,* and *has the keys of death and the grave.*"

[2.] The great *gospel duty* of *repentance* must be *pressed* upon the children of men. *Repentance for sin* must be preached in *Christ's name,* and by his authority, *v.* 47. *All men every where* must be called and *commanded to repent,* Acts xvii. 30. "Go, and tell all people that the God that made them, and the Lord that bought them, expects and requires that, immediately upon this notice given, they turn from the worship of the gods that they have made to the worship of the God that made them; and not only so, but from serving the interests of the world and the flesh; they must turn to the service of God in Christ, must mortify all sinful habits, and forsake all sinful practices. Their hearts and lives must be changed, and they must be universally renewed and reformed."

[3.] The great *gospel privilege* of the *remission of sins* must be *proposed* to all, and assured to all that *repent,* and *believe the gospel.* "Go, tell a guilty world, that stands convicted and condemned at God's bar, that an act of indemnity has passed the royal assent, which all that repent and believe shall have the benefit of, and not only be *pardoned,* but *preferred* by. Tell them that *there is hope* concerning them."

(2.) *To whom they must preach.* Whither must they carry these proposals, and how far does their commission extend? They are here told, [1.] That they must preach this *among all nations.* They must disperse themselves, like the sons of Noah after the flood, some one way and some another, and carry this light along with them wherever they go. The prophets had preached *repentance* and *remission* to the *Jews,* but the apostles must preach them to *all the world.* None are *exempted* from the obligations the gospel lays upon men to *repent,* nor are any *excluded* from those inestimable benefits which are included in the remission of sins, but those that by their unbelief and impenitency put a bar in their own door. [2.] That they must *begin at Jerusalem.* There they must preach their first *gospel sermon;* there the *gospel church* must be first formed; there the gospel day must dawn, and thence that light shall go forth which must take hold on the ends of the earth. And why must they begin there? *First,* Because *thus it was written,* and therefore it *behoved them* to take this method. *The word of the* Lord must *go forth from Jerusalem,* Isa. ii. 3. And see Joel ii. 32; iii. 16; Obad. 21; Zech. xiv. 8. *Se-*

condly, Because there the matters of fact on which the gospel was founded were transacted; and therefore there they were first attested, where, if there had been any just cause for it, they might be best contested and disproved. So strong, so bright, is the first shining forth of the glory of the risen Redeemer that it dares face those daring enemies of his that had put him to an ignominious death, and sets them at defiance. "*Begin at Jerusalem,* that the chief priests may try their strength to crush the gospel, and may rage to see themselves disappointed. *Thirdly,* Because he would give us a further example of forgiving enemies. Jerusalem had put the greatest affronts imaginable upon him (both the rulers and the multitude), for which that city might justly have been excepted by name out of the act of indemnity; but no, so far from that, the first offer of gospel grace is made to Jerusalem, and thousands there are in a little time brought to partake of that grace.

(3.) What *assistance they should have in preaching.* It is a vast undertaking that they are here called to, a very large and difficult province, especially considering the opposition this service would meet with, and the sufferings it would be attended with. If therefore they ask, *Who is sufficient for these things?* here is an answer ready: *Behold, I send the promise of my Father upon you,* and *you shall be endued with power from on high, v.* 49. He here assures them that in a little time the Spirit should be poured out upon them in greater measures than ever, and they should thereby be furnished with all those gifts and graces which were necessary to their discharge of this great trust; and therefore they must *tarry at Jerusalem,* and not enter upon it till this be done. Note, [1.] Those who *receive the Holy Ghost* are thereby *endued with a power from on high,* a supernatural power, a power above any of their own; it is *from on high,* and therefore draws the soul upward, and makes it to *aim high.* [2.] Christ's apostles could never have planted his gospel, and set up his kingdom in the world, as they did, if they had not been endued with such a power; and their admirable achievements prove that there was an excellency of power going along with them. [3.] *This power from on high* was the *promise of the Father,* the great promise of the New Testament, as the promise of the coming of Christ was of the Old Testament. And, if it be the *promise of the Father,* we may be sure that the promise is *inviolable* and the thing promised *invaluable.* [4.] Christ would not leave his disciples till the time was just at hand for the performing of this promise. It was but ten days after the *ascension* of Christ that there came the *descent* of the Spirit. [5.] Christ's ambassadors must stay till they have their powers, and not venture upon their embassy till they have received full instructions and credentials. Though, one would think, never was such haste as now for the preaching of the gospel, yet the preachers must tarry till they be endued with power from on high, and *tarry at Jerusalem,* though a place of danger, because there this promise of the Father was to find them, Joel ii. 28.

50 And he led them out as far as
to Bethany, and he lifted up his hands,
and blessed them. 51 And it came
to pass, while he blessed them, he was
parted from them, and carried up into
heaven. 52 And they worshipped
him, and returned to Jerusalem with
great joy: 53 And were continually
in the temple, praising and blessing
God. Amen.

This evangelist omits the solemn meeting between Christ and his disciples *in Galilee;* but what he said to them there, and at other interviews, he subjoins to what he said to them at the first visit he made them on the evening of the day he rose; and has now nothing more to account for but his ascension into heaven, of which we have a very brief narrative in these verses, in which we are told,

I. How solemnly Christ took leave of his disciples. Christ's design being to reconcile heaven and earth, and to continue a days-man between them, it was necessary that he should lay his hands on them both, and, in order thereunto, that he should *pass* and *repass.* He had business to do in both worlds, and accordingly came from heaven to earth in his incarnation, to despatch his business here, and, having finished this, he returned to heaven, to reside there, and negociate our affairs with the Father. Observe, 1. Whence he ascended: from *Bethany,* near Jerusalem, adjoining to the *mount of Olives.* There he had done eminent services for his Father's glory, and there he entered upon his glory. There was the *garden* in which his sufferings began, there he was in his agony; and Bethany signifies *the house of sorrow.* Those that would go to heaven must ascend thither from the house of sufferings and sorrow, must go by agonies to their joys. The mount of Olives was pitched upon long since to be the place of Christ's ascension: *His feet shall stand in that day upon the mount of Olives,* Zech. xiv. 4. And here it was that awhile ago he began his triumphant entry into Jerusalem, *ch.* xix. 29. 2. Who were the witnesses of his ascension: *He led out his disciples* to see him. Probably, it was very early in the morning that he ascended, before people were stirring; for he never showed himself openly to all the people after his resurrection, but only to *chosen witnesses.* The disciples did not see him rise out of the grave, because his resurrection was capable of being proved by their seeing him alive afterwards; but they saw him *ascend* into heaven, because they could not otherwise have an *ocular* demonstration of his ascension. They were *led out* on purpose to see him ascend, had their eye upon him when he ascended, and were not looking another way. 3. What was the farewell he gave them: *He lifted up his hands, and blessed them.* He did not go away in displeasure, but in love; he left a blessing behind him; *he lifted up his hands,* as the high priest did when he blessed the people; see Lev. ix. 22. He blessed as one having authority, commanded the blessing which he had purchased; he *blessed them* as Jacob blessed his sons. The apostles were now as the representatives of the twelve tribes, so that in blessing them he blessed all his spiritual Israel, and put his Father's name upon them. He blessed them as Jacob blessed his sons, and Moses the tribes, at parting, to show that, having loved his own which were in the world, he loved them unto the end. 4. How he left them: *While he was blessing them, he was parted from them;* not as if he were taken away before he had said all he had to say, but to intimate that his being parted from them did not put an end to his blessing them, for the intercession which he went to heaven to make for all his is a continuation of the blessing. He *began* to bless them on earth, but he went to heaven to *go on* with it. Christ was now sending his apostles to preach his gospel to the world, and he gives them his blessing, not for *themselves* only, but to be conferred in his name upon *all* that should believe on him through their word; for in him *all the families of the earth were to be blessed.* 5. How his ascension is described. (1.) He was *parted from them,* was taken from their head, as Elijah from Elisha's. Note, The dearest friends must part. Those that love us, and pray for us, and instruct us, must be *parted from us.* The bodily presence of Christ himself was not to be expected always in this world; those that knew him after the flesh must now henceforth know him so no more. (2.) He was *carried up into heaven;* not by force, but by his own act and deed. As he arose, so he ascended, by his own power, yet attended by angels. There needed no chariot of fire, nor horses of fire; he knew the way, and, being the *Lord from heaven,* could go back himself. He ascended in a cloud, as the angel in the smoke of Manoah's sacrifice, Judg. xiii. 20.

II. How cheerfully his disciples continued their attendance on him, and on God through him, even now that he was parted from them. 1. They paid their homage to him at his going away, to signify that though he was going into a far country, yet they would continue his loyal subjects, that they were willing to have him reign over them: *They worshipped him. v.* 52. Note, Christ expects *adoration* from those that receive blessings from him. He *blessed them,* in token of gratitude for which they *worshipped him.* This fresh display of Christ's glory drew from them fresh acknowledgments and adorations of it. They knew that though he was *parted from them,* yet he could, and did, take notice of their adorations of him; the cloud that received him out of their sight did not put them or their services out of his sight. 2. They *returned to Jerusalem with great joy.* There they were ordered to continue till the Spirit should be poured out upon them, and thither they went accordingly, though it was into the mouth of danger. Thither they went, and there they staid *with great joy.* This was a wonderful change, and an effect of the opening of their understandings. When Christ told them that he must leave them sorrow filled their hearts; yet now that they see him go they are *filled with joy,* being convinced at length that it was expedient for them and for the church that he should go away, to send the Comforter. Note, The glory of Christ is the joy, the exceeding joy, of all true believers, even while they are here in this world; much more will it be so when they go to the new Jerusalem, and find him there in his glory. 3. They abounded in acts of devotion while they were in expectation of the promise of the Father, *v.* 53. (1.) They attended the temple-service at the hours of prayer. God had not as yet quite forsaken it, and therefore they did not. *They were continually in the temple,* as their Master was when he was at Jerusalem. *The Lord loves the gates of Zion,* and so should we. Some think that they had their place of meeting, as disciples, in some of the chambers of the temple which belonged to some Levite that was *well affected* to them; but others think it is not likely that this either could be *concealed from,* or would be *connived at* by, the chief priests and *rulers of the temple.* (2.) Temple-sacrifices, they knew, were superseded by Christ's sacrifice, but the temple-songs they joined in. Note, While we are waiting for God's promises we must go forth to meet them with our praises. Praising and blessing God is work that is never out of season: and nothing better prepares the mind for the receiving of the Holy Ghost than holy joy and praise. Fears are silenced, sorrows sweetened and allayed, and hopes kept up.

The *amen* that concludes seems to be added by the church and every believer to the reading of the gospel, signifying an assent to the truths of the gospel, and a hearty concurrence with all the disciples of Christ in praising and blessing God. *Amen.* Let him be continually praised and blessed

AN

EXPOSITION,

WITH PRACTICAL OBSERVATIONS,

OF THE GOSPEL ACCORDING TO

ST. JOHN.

It is not material to enquire when and where this gospel was written; we are sure that it was given by inspiration of God to John, the brother of James, one of the twelve apostles, distinguished by the honourable character of *that disciple whom Jesus loved*, one of the first three of the worthies of the Son of David, whom he took to be the witnesses of his retirements, particularly of his transfiguration and his agony. The ancients tell us that John lived longest of all the twelve apostles, and was the only one of them that died a natural death, all the rest suffering martyrdom; and some of them say that he wrote this gospel at Ephesus, at the request of the ministers of the several churches of Asia, in opposition to the heresy of Corinthus and the Ebionites, who held that our Lord was a *mere man*. It seems most probable that he wrote it before his banishment into the isle of Patmos, for there he wrote his *Apocalypse*, the close of which seems designed for the closing up of the canon of scripture; and, if so, this gospel was not written after. I cannot therefore give credit to those later fathers, who say that he wrote it in his banishment, or after his return from it, many years after the destruction of Jerusalem; when he was ninety years old, saith one of them; when he was a hundred, saith another of them. However, it is clear that he wrote last of the four evangelists, and, comparing his gospel with theirs, we may observe, 1. That he *relates* what they had *omitted*; he *brings up the rear*, and his gospel is as the *rearward* or *gathering host*; it gleans up what they had passed by. Thus there was a *later* collection of Solomon's wise sayings (Prov. xxv. 1), and yet far short of what he delivered, 1 Kings iv. 32. 2. That he gives us more of the *mystery* of that of which the other evangelists gave us only the *history*. It was necessary that the matters of fact should be first settled, which was done in their *declarations of those things which Jesus began both to do and teach*, Luke i. 1; Acts i. 1. But, this being done out of the mouth of two or three witnesses, *John goes on to perfection* (Heb. vi. 1), *not laying again the foundation*, but building upon it, leading us more within the veil. Some of the ancients observe that the other evangelists wrote more of the τὰ σωματικὰ—the *bodily* things of Christ; but John writes of the τὰ πνευματικὰ—the *spiritual* things of the gospel, the life and soul of it; therefore some have called this gospel the *key of the evangelists*. Here it is that a *door* is *opened in heaven*, and the first voice we hear is, *Come up hither*, come up higher. Some of the ancients, that supposed the four living creatures in John's vision to represent the four evangelists, make John himself to be the *flying eagle*, so *high* does he *soar*, and so *clearly* does he *see* into divine and heavenly things.

CHAP. I.

The scope and design of this chapter is to confirm our faith in Christ as the eternal Son of God, and the true Messiah and Saviour of the world, that we may be brought to receive him, and rely upon him, as our Prophet, Priest, and King, and to give up ourselves to be ruled, and taught, and saved, by him. In order to this, we have here, I. An account given of him by the inspired penman himself, fairly laying down, in the beginning, what he designed his whole book should be the proof of, ver. 1—5; and again, ver. 10—14; and again, ver. 16—18. II. The testimony of John Baptist concerning him (ver. 6—9; and again, ver. 15); but most fully and particularly, ver. 19—37. III. His own manifestation of himself to Andrew and Peter (ver. 38—42), to Philip and Nathanael, ver. 43—51.

IN the beginning was the Word,
and the Word was with God, and
the Word was God. 2 The same
was in the beginning with God. 3 All
things were made by him; and without
him was not any thing made that was
made. 4 In him was life; and the
life was the light of men. 5 And the
light shineth in darkness; and the
darkness comprehended it not.

Austin says (*de Civitate Dei*, lib. x. cap. 29) that his friend Simplicius told him he had heard a Platonic philosopher say that these first verses of St. John's gospel were *worthy to be written in letters of gold*. The learned Francis Junius, in the account he gives of his own life, tells how he was in his youth infected with loose notions in religion, and by the grace of God was wonderfully recovered by reading accidentally these verses in a bible which his father had designedly laid in his way. He says that he observed such a divinity in the argument, such an authority and majesty in the style, that his flesh trembled, and he was struck with such amazement that for a whole day he scarcely knew where he was or what he did; and thence he dates the beginning of his being religious. Let us enquire what there is in those strong lines. The evangelist here lays down the great truth he is to prove, that Jesus Christ is God, one with the Father. Observe,

I. Of whom he speaks—*The Word—ὁ λόγος.* This is an idiom peculiar to John's writings. See 1 John i. 1; v. 7; Rev. xix. 13. Yet some think that Christ is meant by *the Word* in Acts xx. 32; Heb. iv. 12; Luke i. 2. The Chaldee paraphrase very frequently calls the Messiah *Memra—the Word of Jehovah,* and speaks of many things in the Old Testament, said to be done by *the Lord,* as done by that *Word of the Lord.* Even the vulgar Jews were taught that the *Word of God* was the same with God. The evangelist, in the close of his discourse (*v.* 18), plainly tells us why he calls Christ *the Word—because he is the only begotten Son, who is in the bosom of the Father, and has declared him. Word* is two-fold: λόγος ἐνδιάθετος—*word conceived;* and λόγος προφόρικος—*word uttered.* The λόγος ὁ ἔσω and ὁ ἔξω, *ratio* and *oratio—intelligence* and *utterance.* 1. There is the *word conceived,* that is, *thought,* which is the first and only immediate product and conception of the soul (all the operations of which are performed by *thought*), and it is one with the soul. And thus the second person in the Trinity is fitly called *the Word;* for he is the *first-begotten of the Father,* that eternal essential Wisdom which *the Lord possessed,* as the soul does its thought, *in the beginning of his way,* Prov. viii. 22. There is nothing we are more sure of than *that we think,* yet nothing we are more in the dark about than *how we think;* who can declare the generation of *thought* in the soul? Surely then the generations and births of the eternal mind may well be allowed to be great mysteries of godliness, the bottom of which we cannot fathom, while yet we adore the depth. 2. There is the *word uttered,* and this is *speech,* the chief and most natural indication of the mind. And thus Christ is *the Word,* for *by him* God has in *these last days spoken to us* (Heb. i. 2), and has directed us to *hear him,* Matt. xvii. 5. He has made known God's mind to us, as a man's word or speech makes known his thoughts, as far as he pleases, and no further. Christ is called that *wonderful speaker* (see notes on Dan. viii. 13), the *speaker of things hidden* and *strange.* He is *the Word* speaking *from* God to us, and *to God* for us. John Baptist was *the voice,* but Christ *the Word:* being *the Word,* he is *the Truth,* the *Amen,* the *faithful Witness* of the mind of God.

II. What he saith of him, enough to prove beyond contradiction that *he is God.* He asserts,

1. His existence in the beginning: *In the beginning was the Word.* This bespeaks his existence, not only before his incarnation, but before all time. The beginning of time, in which all creatures were produced and brought into being, found this eternal Word in being. The world was *from* the beginning, but the Word was *in* the beginning. Eternity is usually expressed by being *before the foundation of the world.* The eternity of God is so described (Ps. xc. 2), *Before the mountains were brought forth.* So Prov. viii. 23. The Word had a being before the world had a beginning. He that *was* in the beginning *never* began, and therefore was *ever,* ἀχρονος—*without beginning of time.* So Nonnus.

2. His co-existence with the Father: *The Word was with God, and the Word was God.* Let none say that when we invite them to Christ we would draw them from God, for Christ is *with God* and *is God;* it is repeated in *v.* 2: *the same,* the very same that we believe in and preach, was *in the beginning with God,* that is, he was so from eternity. In the beginning the world was *from God,* as it was created by him; but the Word was *with God,* as ever with him. The Word was with God, (1.) In respect of *essence* and *substance;* for *the Word was God:* a distinct person or substance, for he was *with God;* and yet the same in substance, for he *was God,* Heb. i. 3. (2.) In respect of *complacency* and *felicity.* There was a glory and happiness which Christ had *with God* before the world was (*ch.* xvii. 5), the Son infinitely happy in the enjoyment of his Father's bosom, and no less the Father's delight, the Son of his love, Prov. viii. 30. (3.) In respect of *counsel* and *design.* The mystery of man's redemption by this Word incarnate was *hid in God* before all worlds, Eph. iii. 9. He that undertook to *bring us to God* (1 Pet. iii. 18) was himself from eternity *with God;* so that this grand affair of man's reconciliation to God was concerted between the Father and Son from eternity, and they understand one another perfectly well in it, Zech. vi. 13; Matt. xi. 27. He was *by him as one brought up with him* for this service, Prov. viii. 30. He was *with God,* and therefore is said to *come forth from the Father.*

3. His agency in making the world, *v.* 3. This is here, (1.) Expressly asserted: *All things were made by him.* He was *with God,* not only so as to be *acquainted* with the divine counsels from eternity, but to be *active* in the divine operations in the beginning of time. *Then was I by him,* Prov. viii. 30. God made the world *by a word* (Ps. xxxiii. 6) and Christ was *that Word.* By him, not as a subordinate instrument, but as a co-ordinate agent, God *made the world* (Heb. i. 2), not as the workman cuts by his axe, but as the

body sees by the eye. (2.) The contrary is denied: *Without him was not any thing made that was made,* from the highest angel to the meanest worm. God the Father did nothing without him in that work. Now, [1.] This proves that *he is God;* for he that *built all things is God,* Heb. iii. 4. The God of Israel often proved himself to be God with this, that he *made all things:* Isa. xl. 12, 28; xli. 4; and see Jer. x. 11, 12. [2.] This proves the excellency of the Christian religion, that the author and founder of it is the same that was the author and founder of the world. How excellent must that constitution needs be which derives its institution from him who is the fountain of all excellency! When we worship Christ, we worship him to whom the patriarchs gave honour as the Creator of the world, and on whom all creatures depend. [3.] This shows how well qualified he was for the work of our redemption and salvation. Help was laid upon one that was mighty indeed; for it was laid upon him that made all things; and he is appointed the author of our bliss who was the author of our being.

4. The original of life and light that is in him: *In him was life, v.* 4. This further proves that he is God, and every way qualified for his undertaking; for, (1.) He has *life in himself;* not only the *true God,* but the *living God.* God is life; he swears by himself when he saith, *As I live.* (2.) All living creatures have their life in him; not only all the *matter* of the creation was *made* by him, but all the *life* too that is in the creation is derived from him and supported by him. It was the Word of God that produced the *moving creatures that had life,* Gen. i. 20; Acts xvii. 25. He is that Word by which man lives more than by bread, Matt. iv. 4. (3.) Reasonable creatures have their *light* from him; that *life* which is *the light of men* comes from him. Life in man is something greater and nobler than it is in other creatures; it is *rational,* and not merely *animal.* When man became a *living soul,* his life was *light,* his capacities such as distinguished him from, and dignified him above, the beasts that perish. The *spirit of a man is the candle of the Lord,* and it was the eternal Word that lighted this candle. The light of reason, as well as the life of sense, is derived from him, and depends upon him. This proves him fit to undertake our salvation; for life and light, spiritual and eternal life and light, are the two great things that fallen man, who lies so much under the power of *death* and *darkness,* has need of. From whom may we better expect the light of divine revelation than from him who gave us the light of human reason? And if, when God gave us natural life, that life was in his Son, how readily should we receive the gospel-record, that he hath given us *eternal* life, and *that life* too *is in his Son!*

5. The manifestation of him to the children of men It might be objected, If this eternal Word was all in all thus in the creation of the world, whence is it that he has been so little taken notice of and regarded? To this he answers (*v.* 5), *The light shines, but the darkness comprehends it not.* Observe,

(1.) The discovery of the eternal Word to the lapsed world, even before he was manifested in the flesh: *The light shineth in darkness.* Light is self-evidencing, and will make itself known; this light, whence the light of men comes, hath shone, and doth shine. [1.] The eternal Word, *as God,* shines in *the darkness* of *natural conscience.* Though men by the fall are become *darkness,* yet that which may be known of God is manifested in them; see Rom. i. 19, 20. The light of nature is this light shining in darkness. Something of the power of the divine Word, both as *creating* and as *commanding,* all mankind have an innate sense of; were it not for this, earth would be a hell, a place of *utter darkness;* blessed be God, it is not so yet. [2.] The eternal Word, as Mediator, shone in the darkness of the Old-Testament types and figures, and the prophecies and promises which were of the Messiah from the beginning. He that had commanded the light of this world to shine out of darkness was himself long a light *shining in darkness;* there was a *veil* upon this *light,* 2 Cor. iii. 13.

(2.) The disability of the degenerate world to receive this discovery: *The darkness comprehended it not;* the most of men received the grace of God in these discoveries in vain. [1.] The world of mankind *comprehended not* the natural light that was in their understandings, but became *vain in their imaginations* concerning the eternal God and the eternal Word, Rom. i. 21, 28. The darkness of error and sin overpowered and quite eclipsed this light. God *spoke once, yea twice,* but *man perceived it not,* Job xxxiii. 14. [2.] The Jews, who had the light of the Old Testament, yet comprehended not Christ in it. As there was a veil upon Moses's face, so there was upon the people's hearts. In the *darkness* of the types and shadows the light shone; but such was the *darkness* of their understandings that they could not *see* it. It was therefore requisite that Christ should come, both to rectify the errors of the Gentile world and to improve the truths of the Jewish church.

6 There was a man sent from God,
whose name *was* John. 7 The same
came for a witness, to bear witness of
the Light, that all *men* through him
might believe. 8 He was not that
Light, but *was sent* to bear witness
of that Light. 9 *That* was the true
Light, which lighteth every man that
cometh into the world. 10 He was
in the world, and the world was made
by him, and the world knew him not.

11 He came unto his own, and his
own received him not. 12 But as
many as received him, to them gave
he power to become the sons of God,
even to them that believe on his name:
13 Which were born, not of blood,
nor of the will of the flesh, nor of the
will of man, but of God. 14 And
the Word was made flesh, and dwelt
among us, (and we beheld his glory,
the glory as of the only begotten of
the father,) full of grace and truth.

The evangelist designs to bring in John Baptist bearing an honourable testimony to Jesus Christ. Now in these verses, before he does this,

I. He gives us some account of the witness he is about to produce. His name was *John*, which signifies *gracious;* his conversation was austere, but he was not the less *gracious*. Now,

1. We are here told concerning him, in general, that he was a *man sent of God.* The evangelist had said concerning Jesus Christ that he was *with God* and that he *was God;* but here concerning John that he was a *man*, a mere man. God is pleased to speak to us by men like ourselves. John was a *great man*, but he was a man, a son of man; he was *sent from God*, he was God's *messenger*, so he is called, Mal. iii. 1. God gave him both his mission and his message, both his credentials and his instructions. John wrought no miracle, nor do we find that he had visions and revelations; but the strictness and purity of his life and doctrine, and the direct tendency of both to reform the world, and to revive the interests of God's kingdom among men, were plain indications that he was *sent of God*.

2. We are here told what his office and business were (*v.* 7): *The same came for a witness*, an eye-witness, a leading witness. He came εἰς μαρτυρίαν—*for a testimony.* The legal institutions had been long a testimony for God in the Jewish church. By them revealed religion was kept up; hence we read of the *tabernacle of the testimony, the ark of the testimony, the law and the testimony:* but now divine revelation is to be turned into another channel; now the testimony of Christ is the testimony of God, 1 Cor. i. 6; ii. 1. Among the Gentiles, God indeed had not left himself without witness (Acts xiv. 17), but the Redeemer had no testimonies borne him among them. There was a profound silence concerning him, till John Baptist came for a witness to him. Now observe, (1.) The matter of his testimony: *He came to bear witness to the light.* Light is a thing which witnesses for itself, and carries its own evidence along with it; but to those who shut their eyes against the light it is necessary there should be those that bear witness to it. Christ's light needs not man's testimony, but the world's darkness does. John was like the night watchman that goes round the town, proclaiming the approach of the morning light to those that have closed their eyes, and are not willing themselves to observe it; or like that watchman that was set to tell those who asked him what of the night that *the morning comes*, and, *if you will enquire, enquire ye*, Isa. xxi. 11, 12. He was sent of God to tell the world that the long-looked-for Messiah was now come, who should be *a light to enlighten the Gentiles and the glory of his people Israel;* and to proclaim that dispensation at hand which would bring life and immortality to light. (2.) The design of his testimony: *That all men through him might believe;* not in him, but in Christ, whose way he was sent to prepare. He taught men to look through him, and pass through him, to Christ; through the doctrine of repentance for sin to that of faith in Christ. He prepared men for the reception and entertainment of Christ and his gospel, by awakening them to a sight and sense of sin; and that, their eyes being thereby opened, they might be ready to admit those beams of divine light which, in the person and doctrine of the Messiah, were now ready to shine in their faces. If they would but receive this witness of man, they would soon find that the witness of God was greater, 1 John v. 9. See *ch.* x. 41. Observe, it was designed that all men through him might believe, excluding none from the kind and beneficial influences of his ministry that did not exclude themselves, as multitudes did, who rejected the counsel of God against themselves, and so received the grace of God in vain.

3. We are here cautioned not to mistake him for the light who only came to bear witness to it (*v.* 8): *He was not that light* that was expected and promised, but only was sent to bear witness of that great and ruling light. He was a star, like that which guided the wise men to Christ, a morning star; but he was not the Sun; not the Bridegroom, but a friend of the Bridegroom; not the Prince, but his harbinger. There were those who rested in John's baptism, and looked no further, as those Ephesians, Acts xix. 3. To rectify this mistake, the evangelist here, when he speaks very honourably of him, yet shows that he must give place to Christ. He was great as the prophet of the Highest, but not the Highest himself. Note, We must take heed of over-valuing ministers, as well as of under-valuing them; they are not our lords, nor have they dominion over our faith, but ministers by whom we believe, stewards of our Lord's house. We must not give up ourselves by an implicit faith to their conduct, for they are not that light; but we must attend to, and receive, their testimony; for they are sent to bear witness of that light; so then let us esteem them, and not otherwise. Had John pretended to be that light he had not been so much as a faithful witness of that light. Those who usurp the honour of Christ

forfeit the honour of being the servants of Christ; yet John was very serviceable as a witness to the light, though he was not that light. Those may be of great use to us who yet shine with a borrowed light.

II. Before he goes on with John's testimony, he returns to give us a further account of this Jesus to whom John bore record. Having shown in the beginning of the chapter the glories of his Godhead, he here comes to show the graces of his incarnation, and his favours to man as Mediator.

1. Christ was the *true Light* (*v.* 9); not as if John Baptist were a false light, but, in comparison with Christ, he was a very small light. Christ is the great light that deserves to be called so. Other lights are but figuratively and equivocally called so: Christ is the true light. The fountain of all knowledge and of all comfort must needs be the true light. He is the true light, for proof of which we are not referred to the emanations of his glory in the invisible world (the beams with which he enlightens that), but to those rays of his light which are darted downwards, and with which this dark world of ours is enlightened. But how does Christ enlighten every man that comes into the world? (1.) By his creating power he enlightens every man with the light of reason; that life which is the light of men is from him; all the discoveries and directions of reason, all the comfort it gives us, and all the beauty it puts upon us, are from Christ. (2.) By the publication of his gospel to all nations he does in effect enlighten every man. John Baptist was a light, but he enlightened only Jerusalem and Judea, and the region round about Jordan, like a candle that enlightens one room; but Christ is the true light, for he is a light to enlighten the Gentiles. His everlasting gospel is to be preached to every nation and language, Rev. xiv. 6. Like the sun which enlightens every man that will open his eyes, and receive its light (Ps. xix. 6), to which the preaching of the gospel is compared. See Rom. x. 18. Divine revelation is not now to be confined, as it had been, to one people, but to be diffused to all people, Matt. v. 15. (3.) By the operation of his Spirit and grace he enlightens all those that are enlightened to salvation; and those that are not enlightened by him perish in darkness. *The light of the knowledge of the glory of God* is said to be *in the face of Jesus Christ,* and is compared with that light which was at the beginning commanded to shine out of darkness, and which enlightens every man that comes into the world. Whatever light any man has, he is indebted to Christ for it, whether it be natural or supernatural.

2. Christ *was in the world, v.* 10. He was in the world, as the essential Word, before his incarnation, upholding all things; but this speaks of his being in the world when he took our nature upon him, and dwelt among us; see *ch.* xvi. 28. *I am come into the world.* The Son of the Highest was here in this *lower* world; that *light* in this *dark* world; that *holy thing* in this sinful polluted world. He left a world of bliss and glory, and was here in this melancholy miserable world. He undertook to reconcile the world to God, and therefore was *in the world,* to treat about it, and settle that affair; to satisfy God's justice for the world, and discover God's favour to the world. He was in the world, but not of it, and speaks with an air of triumph when he can say, *Now I am no more in it, ch.* xvii. 11. The greatest honour that ever was put upon this world, which is so mean and inconsiderable a part of the universe, was that the Son of God was once *in the world;* and, as it should engage our affections to things above that there Christ is, so it should reconcile us to our present abode in *this* world that once Christ was *here.* He *was* in the world for awhile, but it is spoken of as a thing past; and so it will be said of us shortly, We were in the world. O that when we are here no more we may be where Christ is! Now observe here, (1.) What reason Christ had to expect the most affectionate and respectful welcome possible in this world; for *the world was made by him. Therefore* he came to save a lost world because it was a world of his own making. Why should he not concern himself to revive the light that was of his own kindling, to restore a life of his own infusing, and to renew the image that was originally of his own impressing? The world was *made by him,* and therefore ought to do him homage. (2.) What cold entertainment he met with, notwithstanding: *The world knew him not.* The great Maker, Ruler, and Redeemer of the world was in it, and few or none of the inhabitants of the world were aware of it. The *ox knows his owner,* but the more brutish world did not. They did not own him, did not bid him welcome, because they did not *know him;* and they did not know him because he did not make himself known in the way that they expected—in external glory and majesty. His kingdom came not *with observation,* because it was to be a kingdom of trial and probation. When he shall come as a Judge the world shall *know* him.

3. He *came to his own* (*v.* 11); not only to the world, which was *his own,* but to the people of Israel, that were peculiarly *his own* above all people; of them he came, among them he lived, and to them he was *first sent.* The Jews were at this time a mean despicable people; *the crown was fallen from their head;* yet, in remembrance of the ancient covenant, bad as they were, and poor as they were, Christ was not ashamed to look upon them as his own. Τὰ ἴδια—his own *things;* not τοὺς ἰδίους—his own *persons,* as *true believers* are called, *ch.* xiii. 1. The Jews were *his,* as a man's house, and lands, and goods are *his,* which he uses and possesses; but believers are his as a man's wife and children

are his own, which he loves and enjoys. He came to his own, to seek and save them, because they were *his own.* He was sent to the lost sheep of the house of Israel, for it was he whose own the sheep were. Now observe,

(1.) That the generality *rejected* him: *His own received him not.* He had reason to expect that those who were his own should have bidden him welcome, considering how great the *obligations* were which they *lay under* to him, and how fair the *opportunities* were which they had of coming to the knowledge of him. They had the oracles of God, which told them beforehand *when* and *where* to expect him, and of what tribe and family he should arise. He came among them himself, introduced with signs and wonders, and himself the greatest; and therefore it is not said of them, as it was of the world (*v.* 10), that they *knew him not;* but *his own,* though they could not but know him, yet *received him not;* did not receive his doctrine, did not welcome him as the Messiah, but fortified themselves against him. The *chief priests,* that were in a particular manner *his own* (for the Levites were God's tribe), were ring-leaders in this contempt put upon him. Now this was very *unjust,* because they were *his own,* and therefore he might *command* their respect; and it was very *unkind* and *ungrateful,* because he came to them, to seek and save them, and so to *court* their respect. Note, Many who in profession are *Christ's own,* yet do not *receive him,* because they will not part with their sins, nor have him to *reign over them.*

(2.) That yet there was a remnant who *owned* him, and were faithful to him. Though his own received him not, yet there were those that *received* him (*v.* 12): *But as many as received him. Though Israel were not gathered,* yet Christ was *glorious.* Though the body of that nation persisted and perished in unbelief, yet there were many of *them* that were wrought upon to submit to Christ, and many more that *were not of that fold.* Observe here,

[1.] The true Christian's *description* and *property;* and that is, that he *receives Christ,* and *believes on his name;* the latter explains the former. Note, *First,* To be a Christian indeed is to *believe on Christ's name;* it is to *assent* to the gospel discovery, and *consent* to the gospel proposal, concerning him. His name is *the Word of God; the King of kings, the Lord our righteousness; Jesus a Saviour.* Now to *believe* on his name is to *acknowledge* that he is what these great names bespeak him to be, and to *acquiesce* in it, that he may be so *to us. Secondly,* Believing in Christ's name is *receiving* him as a gift from God. We must receive his doctrine as true and good; receive his law as just and holy; receive his offers as kind and advantageous; and we must receive the image of his grace, and impressions of his love, as the governing principle of our affections and actions.

[2.] The true Christian's dignity and privilege are twofold:—

First, The *privilege of adoption,* which takes them into the number of God's children: *To them gave he power to become the sons of God.* Hitherto, the adoption pertained to the Jews only (*Israel is my son, my first-born*); but now, by faith in Christ, Gentiles are the *children of God,* Gal. iii. 26. They have *power, ἐξουσίαν—authority;* for no man taketh this power to himself, but he who is *authorized* by the gospel charter. To them gave he a *right;* to them gave he this pre-eminence. *This power have all the saints.* Note, 1. It is the unspeakable privilege of all good Christians, that they are become the *children of God.* They were by nature children of wrath, children of this world. If they be the *children of God,* they *become* so, are *made* so *Fiunt, non nascuntur Christiani—Persons are not born Christians, but made such.*—Tertullian. *Behold what manner of love is this,* 1 John iii. 1. God calls them *his children,* they call him *Father,* and are entitled to all the privileges of children, those of their way and those of their home. 2. The privilege of adoption is entirely owing to *Jesus Christ;* he *gave* this power to them that believe on his name. God is his Father, and so ours; and it is by virtue of our espousals to him, and union with him, that we stand related to God as a Father. It was in Christ that we were *predestinated to the adoption;* from him we receive both the character and the Spirit of adoption, and he is the *first-born among many brethren.* The Son of God became a Son of man, that the sons and daughters of men might become the sons and daughters of God Almighty.

Secondly, The *privilege of regeneration* (*v.* 13): *Which were born.* Note, All the children of God are born again; all that are adopted are regenerated. This *real* change evermore attends that *relative* one. Wherever God confers the dignity of children, he creates the nature and disposition of children. Men cannot do so when they adopt. Now here we have an account of the original of this new birth. 1. Negatively. (1.) It is not *propagated* by natural generation from our parents. It is *not of blood, nor of the will of the flesh,* nor of *corruptible seed,* 1 Pet. i. 23. Man is called *flesh and blood,* because thence he has his original: but we do not become the children of God as we become the children of our natural parents. Note, Grace does not run in the blood, as corruption does. Man polluted *begat a son in his own likeness* (Gen. v. 3); but man sanctified and renewed does not beget a son in *that* likeness. The Jews gloried much in their parentage, and the noble blood that ran in their veins: *We are Abraham's seed;* and *therefore* to them *pertained the adoption* because they were born of that blood; but this

New-Testament adoption is not founded in any such natural relation. (2.) It is not *produced* by the natural power of our own will. As it is not of *blood*, nor of *the will of the flesh*, so neither is it of the *will of man*, which labours under a moral impotency of determining itself to that which is good; so that the principles of the divine life are not of our own planting, it is the grace of God that makes us willing to be *his*. Nor can human laws or writings prevail to sanctify and regenerate a soul; if they could, the new birth would be by the will of man. But, 2. Positively: it is of *God*. This new birth is owing to the word of God as the means (1 Pet. i. 23), and to the Spirit of God as the great and sole author. True believers are *born of God*, 1 John iii. 9; v. 1. And this is necessary to their adoption; for we cannot expect the *love of God* if we have not something of his *likeness*, nor claim the privileges of adoption if we be not under the power of regeneration.

4. The *word was made flesh, v.* 14. This expresses Christ's incarnation more clearly than what went before. By his divine presence he always *was in the world*, and by his prophets he *came to his own*. But now that the fulness of time was come he was sent forth after another manner, *made of a woman* (Gal. iv. 4); God manifested in the flesh, according to the faith and hope of holy Job; *Yet shall I see God in my flesh*, Job xix. 26. Observe here,

(1.) The *human nature of Christ* with which he was veiled; and that expressed two ways.

[1.] *The word was made flesh. Forasmuch as the children*, who were to become the sons of God, *were partakers of flesh and blood, he also himself likewise took part of the same*, Heb. ii. 14. The Socinians agree that Christ is both God and man, but they say that he *was man*, and was *made a God*, as Moses (Exod. vii. 1), directly contrary to John here, who saith, Θεὸς ἦν—*He was God*, but σὰρξ ἐγένετο—*He was made flesh*. Compare *v.* 1 with this. This intimates not only that he was really and truly man, but that he subjected himself to the miseries and calamities of the human nature. He was made *flesh*, the meanest part of man. Flesh bespeaks man *weak*, and he was crucified through *weakness*, 2 Cor. xiii. 4. *Flesh* bespeaks man *mortal* and *dying* (Ps. lxxviii. 39), and Christ was *put to death in the flesh* 1 Pet iii. 18. Nay, *flesh* bespeaks *man tainted with sin* (Gen. vi. 3), and Christ, though he was perfectly holy and harmless, yet appeared *in the likeness of sinful flesh* (Rom. viii. 3), and was made *sin for us*, 2 Cor. v. 21. When Adam had sinned, God said to him, *Dust thou art;* not only because made out of the dust, but because by sin he was sunk into dust. His fall did, σωματοῦν τὴν ψύχην, *turn him* as it were *all into body*, made him earthly; therefore he that was made a curse for us was made *flesh*, and *condemned sin in the flesh*, Rom. viii. 3. Wonder at this, that the eternal Word should be made flesh, when flesh was come into such an ill name; that he who made *all things* should himself be made flesh, one of the meanest things, and submit to that from which he was at the greatest distance. The voice that ushered in the gospel cried, *All flesh is grass* (Isa. xl. 6), to make the Redeemer's love the more wonderful, who, to *redeem* and *save* us, was made flesh, and withered as grass; but the *Word of the Lord*, who was made flesh, *endures for ever;* when made flesh, he ceased not to be the Word of God.

[2.] He *dwelt among us*, here in this lower world. Having taken upon him the nature of man, he put himself into the place and condition of other men. The Word might have been made flesh, and dwelt among the angels; but, having taken a *body* of the same mould with ours, in it he came, and resided in the same world with us. He *dwelt among us*, us worms of the earth, us that he had no need of, us that he got nothing by, us that were *corrupt* and *depraved*, and revolted from God. The Lord God came and dwelt even *among the rebellious*, Ps. lxviii. 18. He that had dwelt among angels, those noble and excellent beings, came and dwelt *among us* that are a *generation of vipers*, us *sinners*, which was worse to him than David's dwelling in Mesech and Kedar, or Ezekiel's dwelling *among scorpions*, or the church of Pergamus dwelling *where Satan's seat is*. When we look upon the upper world, the world of spirits, how mean and contemptible does this flesh, this body, appear, which we carry about with us, and this world in which our lot is cast, and how hard is it to a contemplative mind to be reconciled to them! But that the eternal Word was *made flesh*, was clothed with a body as we are, and dwelt in this world as we do, this has put an honour upon them both, and should make us willing to abide in the flesh while God has any work for us to do; for Christ dwelt in this lower world, bad as it is, till he had finished what he had to do here, *ch.* xvii. 4. He dwelt *among* the Jews, that the scripture might be fulfilled, *He shall dwell in the tents of Shem*, Gen. ix. 27. And see Zech. ii. 10. Though the Jews were unkind to him, yet he continued to dwell among them; though (as some of the ancient writers tell us) he was invited to better treatment by Abgarus king of Edessa, yet he removed not to any other nation. He *dwelt* among us. He was in the world, not as a wayfaring man that tarries but for a night, but he *dwelt* among us, made a long residence, the original word is observable, ἐσκήνωσεν ἐν ἡμῖν—*he dwelt among us*, he dwelt *as in a tabernacle*, which intimates, *First*, That he dwelt here in very *mean* circumstances, as shepherds that dwell in tents. He did not dwell among us *as in a palace*, but as in a *tent;* for he had not where to lay his head, and was always upon the remove. *Secondly*, That his state here was a *military* state. Soldiers *dwell in tents;* he had long since proclaimed war with the *seed of the serpent,* and now he takes *the field* in person, sets up his standard, and pitches his tent, to prosecute this war. *Thirdly,* That his stay among us was not to be perpetual. He dwelt here as *in a tent,* not as at *home.* The patriarchs, by dwelling in tabernacles, *confessed that they were strangers and pilgrims on earth,* and sought the better country, and so did Christ, leaving us an example, Heb. xiii. 13, 14. *Fourthly,* That as of old God dwelt in the tabernacle of Moses, by the shechinah between the cherubim, so now he dwells in the human nature of Christ; that is now the true shechinah, the symbol of God's peculiar presence. And we are to make all our addresses to God through Christ, and from him to receive divine oracles.

(2.) The *beams of his divine glory* that *darted* through this *veil of flesh: We beheld his glory, the glory as of the only begotten of the Father, full of grace and truth.* The sun is still the fountain of light, though eclipsed or clouded; so Christ was still the brightness of his Father's glory, even when he *dwelt among us* in this lower world. And how slightly soever the Jews thought of him there were those that saw through the veil. Observe,

[1.] Who were the witnesses of this glory: *we,* his disciples and followers, that conversed most freely and familiarly with him; we among whom he *dwelt.* Other men discover their weaknesses to those that are most familiar with them, but it was not so with Christ; those that were most intimate with him saw most of his glory. As it was with his *doctrine,* the disciples knew the mysteries of it, while others had it *under the veil of parables;* so it was with his *person,* they saw the glory of his divinity, while others saw only the veil of his human nature. He manifested himself *to them, and not unto the world.* These witnesses were a competent number, twelve of them, a whole jury of witnesses; men of plainness and integrity, and far from any thing of design or intrigue.

[2.] What evidence they had of it: *We saw it.* They had not their evidence by report, at second hand, but were themselves eye-witnesses of those proofs on which they built their testimony that he was the *Son of the living God: We saw it.* The word signifies a fixed abiding sight, such as gave them an opportunity of making their observations. This apostle himself explains this: *What we declare unto you* of the Word of life is what we have *seen with our eyes,* and what *we have looked upon,* 1 John i. 1.

[3.] What the glory was: *The glory as of the only begotten of the Father.* The glory of the *Word made flesh* was such a glory as became the only *begotten Son of God,* and could not be the glory of any other. Note, *First,* Jesus Christ is the only begotten of the Father. Believers are the children of God by the special favour of adoption and the special grace of regeneration. They are in a sense ὁμοιούσιοι—*of a like nature* (2 Pet. i. 4), and have the image of his perfections; but Christ is ὁμούσιος—*of the same nature,* and is the express image of his person, and the Son of God by an eternal generation. Angels are sons of God, but he never said to any of them, *This day have I begotten thee,* Heb. i. 5. *Secondly,* He was evidently declared to be the only begotten of the Father, by that which was seen of his glory when he dwelt among us. Though he was in the *form of a servant,* in respect of outward circumstances, yet, in respect of graces, his form was as that of the *fourth* in the fiery furnace, *like the Son of God.* His divine glory appeared in the holiness and heavenliness of his doctrine; in his miracles, which extorted from many this acknowledgment, that he was the *Son of God;* it appeared in the purity, goodness, and beneficence, of his whole conversation. God's goodness is his glory, and he went about doing good; he spoke and acted in every thing as an incarnate Deity Perhaps the evangelist had a particular regard to the glory of his *transfiguration,* of which he was an eye-witness; see 2 Pet. i. 16—18 God's calling him his *beloved Son, in whom he was well pleased,* intimated that he was the *only begotten of the Father;* but the full proof of this was at his resurrection.

[4.] What advantage those he dwelt among had from this. He dwelt among them, *full of grace and truth.* In the old tabernacle wherein God dwelt was the *law,* in *this* was grace; in that were *types,* in this was *truth.* The incarnate Word was every way qualified for his undertaking as Mediator; for he was *full of grace and truth,* the two great things that fallen man stands in need of; and this proved him to be the *Son of God* as much as the divine power and majesty that appeared in him. *First,* He has a fulness of grace and truth *for himself;* he had the Spirit without measure. He was full *of grace,* fully acceptable to his Father, and therefore qualified to intercede for us; and full *of truth,* fully apprized of the things he was to reveal, and therefore fit to instruct us. He had a fulness of knowledge and a fulness of compassion. *Secondly,* He has a fulness of grace and truth *for us.* He *received,* that he might *give,* and God was well pleased in him, that he might be well pleased with us in him; and this was the *truth* of the legal *types.*

15 John bare witness of him, and
cried, saying, This was he of whom I
spake, He that cometh after me is
preferred before me: for he was before me. 16 And of his fulness have
all we received, and grace for grace.
17 For the law was given by Moses,
but grace and truth came by Jesus
Christ. 18 No man hath seen God

at any time; the only begotten Son, which is in the bosom of the Father, he hath declared *him*.

In these verses,

I. The evangelist begins again to give us John Baptist's testimony concerning Christ, *v.* 15. He had said (*v.* 8) that he *came for a witness;* now here he tells us that he did accordingly *bear witness.* Here, Observe,

1. *How he expressed* his testimony: He *cried*, according to the prediction that he should be *the voice of one crying.* The Old-Testament prophets cried aloud, to show people their *sins;* this New-Testament prophet cried aloud, to show people their *Saviour.* This intimates, (1.) That it was an open *public* testimony, proclaimed, that all manner of persons might take notice of it, for all are concerned in it. False teachers *entice secretly*, but wisdom publishes her dictates in the chief places of concourse. (2.) That he was free and hearty in bearing this testimony. He *cried* as one that was both *well assured* of the truth to which he witnessed and *well affected* to it. He that had leaped in his *mother's womb for joy* of Christ's approach, when newly conceived, does now with a like exultation of spirit *welcome* his public appearance.

2. What his *testimony* was. He appeals to what he had said at the beginning of his ministry, when he had directed them to expect one that should *come after him*, whose forerunner he was, and never intended any other than to lead them to him, and to prepare his way. This he had given them notice of from the first. Note, It is very comfortable to a minister to have the testimony of his conscience for him that he set out in his ministry with honest principles and sincere intentions, with a single eye to the glory and honour of Christ. Now what he had then said he applies to this Jesus whom he had lately baptized, and who was so remarkably owned from heaven: *This was he of whom I spoke.* John did not tell them that there would shortly appear such a one among them, and then leave them to find him out; but in *this* he went beyond all the Old-Testament prophets that he particularly specified the person: "*This was he*, the very man I told you of, and to him all I said is to be accommodated." Now what was it he said?

(1.) He had given the preference to this Jesus: *He that comes after me*, in the time of his birth and public appearance, is preferred before me; he that *succeeds* me in preaching and making disciples is a more excellent person, upon all accounts; as the prince or peer that *comes after* is preferred before the harbinger or gentleman-usher that makes way for him. Note, Jesus Christ, who was to be called the *Son of the Highest* (Luke i. 32), was preferred before John Baptist, who was to be called only the *prophet of the Highest*, Luke i. 76. John was a minister of the New Testament, but Christ was the Mediator of the New Testament. And observe, though John was a great man, and had a great name and interest, yet he was forward to give the preference to him to whom it belonged. Note, All the ministers of Christ must prefer him and his interest before themselves and their own interests; they will make an ill account *that seek their own things, not the things of Christ*, Phil. ii. 21. He comes *after me*, and yet is *preferred before me.* Note, God dispenses his gifts according to his good pleasure, and many times crosses hands, as Jacob did, preferring the *younger* before the *elder.* Paul far outstripped those that were in Christ before him.

(2.) He here gives a good reason for it: *For he was before me*, πρωτός μου ἦν—*He was my first*, or *first to me;* he was my first Cause, my original. The *First* is one of *God's names*, Isa. xliv. 6. He is *before me*, is *my first*, [1.] In respect of *seniority:* he was *before me*, for he was before Abraham, *ch.* viii. 58. Nay, he was *before all things*, Col. i. 17. I am but of yesterday, he from eternity. It was but in *those days* that John Baptist came (Matt. iii. 1), but the goings forth of our Lord Jesus *were of old, from everlasting*, Mic. v. 2. This proves two natures in Christ. Christ, as man, *came after* John as to his public appearance; Christ, as God, was *before him;* and how could he otherwise be before him but by an eternal existence? [2.] In respect of supremacy; for he was *my prince;* so some princes are called the *first;* πρῶτον, "It is he for whose sake and service I am sent: he is my Master, I am his minister and messenger."

II. He presently returns again to speak of Jesus Christ, and cannot go on with John Baptist's testimony till *v.* 19. The 16th verse has a manifest connection with *v.* 14, where the incarnate Word was said to be *full of grace and truth.* Now here he makes this the matter, not only of our adoration, but of our thankfulness, because *from that fulness* of his *we all have received. He received gifts for men* (Ps. lxviii. 18), that he might *give gifts to men*, Eph. iv. 8. He was filled, that he might *fill all in all* (Eph. i. 23), might *fill our treasures*, Prov. viii. 21. He has a fountain of fulness overflowing: *We all have received. All we* apostles; so some. We have received the favour of this apostleship, that is *grace;* and a fitness for it, that is *truth.* Or, rather, *All we* believers; as many as received him (*v.* 16), received from him. Note, All true believers receive from Christ's fulness; the best and greatest saints cannot live without him, the meanest and weakest may live by him. This excludes proud boasting, that we have nothing but *we have received it;* and silences perplexing fears, that we want nothing but *we may receive it.* Let us see what it is that we have received.

1. We have received *grace for grace.* Our receivings by Christ are all summed up in

this one word, *grace;* we have received *καὶ χάριν—even grace*, so great a gift, so rich, so invaluable; we have received *no less* than grace; this is a gift to be spoken of with an emphasis. It is repeated, *grace for grace;* for to every stone in this building, as well as *to the top-stone,* we must cry, *Grace, grace.* Observe,

(1.) The blessing received. It is *grace;* the good will of God towards us, and the good work of God in us. God's good will works the good work, and then the good work qualifies us for further tokens of his good will. As the cistern receives water from the fulness of the fountain, the branches sap from the fulness of the root, and the air light from the fulness of the sun, so we receive grace from the fulness of Christ.

(2.) The manner of its reception: *Grace for grace—χάριν ἀντὶ χαριτος.* The phrase is singular, and interpreters put different senses upon it, each of which will be of use to illustrate the unsearchable riches of the grace of Christ. *Grace for grace* bespeaks, [1.] The *freeness* of this grace. It is grace for grace' sake; so *Grotius.* We receive grace, not for *our sakes* (be it known to us), but even so, Father, *because it seemed good in thy sight.* It is a *gift according to grace,* Rom. xii. 6. It is grace *to us* for the sake of grace to Jesus Christ. God was well pleased in him, and is therefore well pleased with us in him, Eph. i. 6. [2.] The *fulness* of this grace. *Grace for grace* is abundance of grace, grace upon grace (so *Camero*), one grace heaped upon another; as *skin for skin* is skin after skin, even all that a man has, Job ii. 4. It is a blessing poured out, that there shall not be room to receive it, *plenteous redemption:* one grace a pledge of more grace. *Joseph—He will add.* It is such a fulness as is called *the fulness of God* which we are filled with. We are not straitened in the grace of Christ, if we be not straitened in our own bosoms. [3.] The *serviceableness* of this grace. *Grace for grace* is grace for the promoting and advancing of grace. Grace to be *exercised* by ourselves; gracious habits for gracious acts. Grace to be *ministered* to others; gracious vouchsafements for gracious performances: grace is a talent to be traded with. The apostles received grace (Rom. i. 5; Eph. iii. 8), that they might communicate it, 1 Pet. iv. 10. [4.] The *substitution* of New-Testament grace *in the room and stead* of Old-Testament grace: so *Beza.* And this sense is confirmed by what follows (*v.* 17); for the Old Testament had grace in type, the New Testament has grace in truth. There was a grace under the Old Testament, the gospel was preached then (Gal. iii. 8); but that grace is superseded, and we have gospel grace instead of it, a *glory which excelleth,* 2 Cor. iii. 10. Discoveries of grace are now more clear, distributions of grace far more plentiful; this is grace instead of grace. [5.] It bespeaks the *augmentation* and *continuance of grace. Grace for grace* is one grace to improve, confirm, and perfect another grace. We are changed into the divine image, *from glory to glory,* from one degree of glorious grace to another, 2 Cor. iii. 18. Those that have *true* grace have that for *more grace,* Jam. iv. 6. When God gives grace he saith, Take this *in part;* for he who hath promised will perform. [6] It bespeaks the *agreeableness* and *conformity* of grace in the saints to the grace that is in Jesus Christ; so Mr. *Clark. Grace for grace* is grace in us answering to grace in him, as the impression upon the wax answers the seal line for line. The grace we receive from Christ *changes us into the same image* (2 Cor. iii. 18), the *image of the Son* (Rom. viii. 29), the *image of the heavenly,* 1. Cor. xv. 49.

2. We have received *grace and truth, v.* 17. He had said (*v.* 14) that Christ was *full of grace and truth;* now here he says that by him *grace and truth* came to us. From Christ we *receive grace;* this is a string he delights to harp upon, he cannot go off from it. Two things he further observes in this verse concerning this grace:—(1.) Its *preference* above the law of Moses: *The law was given by Moses,* and it was a glorious discovery, both of God's *will concerning* man and his *good will to* man; but the gospel of Christ is a much clearer discovery both of duty and happiness. That which was given by Moses was purely terrifying and threatening, and bound with penalties, a law which could not *give life, which was* given with abundance of terror (Heb. xii. 18); but that which is given by Jesus Christ is of another nature; it has all the beneficial uses of the law, but not the terror, for it is *grace:* grace *teaching* (Tit. ii. 11), grace *reigning,* Rom. v. 21. It is a law, but a remedial law. The endearments of love are the genius of the gospel, not the affrightments of law and the curse. (2.) Its *connection* with truth: *grace and truth.* In the gospel we have the discovery of the greatest *truths* to be embraced by the understanding, as well as of the richest *grace* to be embraced by the will and affections. It is a *faithful saying,* and *worthy of all acceptation;* that is, it is *grace and truth.* The offers of *grace* are *sincere,* and what we may venture our souls upon; they are made *in earnest,* for it is *grace and truth.* It is *grace and truth* with reference to the *law* that was *given by Moses.* For it is, [1.] The performance of all the Old-Testament promises. In the Old Testament we often find *mercy* and *truth* put together, that is, mercy according to promise; so here *grace and truth* denote grace according to promise. See Luke i. 72; 1 Kings viii. 56. [2.] It is the substance of all the Old-Testament types and shadows. Something of grace there was both in the ordinances that were instituted for Israel and the providences that occurred concerning Israel; but they were only shadows of good things to come, even of the grace that is to

be *brought to us by the revelation of Jesus Christ.* He is the *true* paschal lamb, the *true* scape-goat, the true *manna.* They had grace in the picture; we have grace in the person, that is, *grace and truth. Grace and truth came, ἐγένετο—was made;* the same word that was used (*v.* 3) concerning Christ's *making all things.* The law was only *made known* by Moses, but the *being* of this grace and truth, as well as the discovery of them, is owing to Jesus Christ; this was *made* by him, as the world at first was; and by him this *grace and truth* do *consist.*

3. Another thing we receive from Christ is a clear revelation of God to us (*v.* 18): He hath *declared* God to us, whom *no man hath seen at any time.* This was the grace and truth which came by Christ, the knowledge of God and an acquaintance with him. Observe,

(1.) The insufficiency of all other discoveries: *No man hath seen God at any time.* This intimates, [1.] That the nature of God being *spiritual,* he is invisible to bodily eyes, he is a being *whom no man hath seen, nor can see,* 1 Tim. vi. 16. We have therefore need to *live by faith,* by which we *see him that is invisible,* Heb. xi. 27. [2.] That the revelation which God made of himself in the Old Testament was very short and imperfect, in comparison with that which he has made by Christ: *No man hath seen God at any time;* that is, what was seen and known of God before the incarnation of Christ was nothing to that which is now seen and known; life and immortality are now brought to a much clearer light than they were then. [3.] That none of the Old-Testament prophets were so well qualified to make known the mind and will of God to the children of men as our Lord Jesus was, for none of them had *seen God at any time. Moses beheld the similitude of the Lord* (Num. xii. 8), but was told that he could not *see his face,* Exod. xxxiii. 20. But *this* recommends Christ's holy religion to us that it was founded by one that had seen God, and knew more of his mind than any one else ever did.

(2.) The all-sufficiency of the gospel discovery proved from its author: *The only-begotten Son, who is in the bosom of the Father, he has declared him.* Observe here,

[1.] How *fit* he was to make this discovery, and every way qualified for it. He and he alone was *worthy to take the book, and to open the seals,* Rev. v. 9. For, *First,* He is *the only-begotten Son;* and who so likely to know the Father as the Son? or in whom is the Father better known than in the Son? Matt. xi. 27. He is of the same nature with the Father, so that he who hath *seen him* hath seen *the Father, ch.* xiv. 9. The servant is not supposed to know so well *what his Lord does* as the Son, *ch.* xv. 15. Moses was *faithful as a servant,* but Christ *as a Son. Secondly,* He is *in the bosom of the Father.* He had lain in his bosom from eternity. When he was here upon earth, yet still, as God, he was in the bosom of the Father, and thither he returned when he *ascended. In the bosom of the Father;* that is, 1. In the bosom of his *special love,* dear to him, in *whom he was well pleased,* always his delight. All God's saints are *in his hand,* but his Son was *in his bosom,* one in nature and essence, and therefore in the highest degree one *in love.* 2. In the bosom of his *secret counsels.* As there was a mutual *complacency,* so there was a mutual *consciousness,* between the Father and Son (Matt. xi. 27); none so fit as he to make known God, for none knew his mind as he did. Our most secret counsels we are said to hide *in our bosom (in pectore);* Christ was privy to the *bosom-counsels* of the Father. The prophets *sat down at his feet* as scholars; Christ lay in his bosom as a friend. See Eph. iii. 11.

[2.] How *free* he was in making this discovery: *He hath declared. Him* is not in the original. He has declared that of God which no man had at any time seen or known; not only that which was hid *of God,* but that which was hid *in* God (Eph. iii. 9), ἐξηγησατο—it signifies a plain, clear, and full discovery, not by general and doubtful hints, but by particular explications. He that runs may now read the will of God and the way of salvation. This is the *grace,* this the *truth,* that came by Jesus Christ.

19 And this is the record of John,
when the Jews sent priests and Levites from Jerusalem to ask him, Who
art thou? 20 And he confessed, and
denied not; but confessed, I am not
the Christ. 21 And they asked him,
What then? Art thou Elias? And
he saith, I am not. Art thou that
prophet? And he answered, No. 22
Then said they unto him, Who art
thou? that we may give an answer
to them that sent us. What sayest
thou of thyself? 23 He said, I *am*
the voice of one crying in the wilderness, Make straight the way of the
Lord, as said the prophet Esaias. 24
And they which were sent were of
the Pharisees. 25 And they asked
him, and said unto him, Why baptizest thou then, if thou be not that
Christ, nor Elias, neither that prophet? 26 John answered them,
saying, I baptize with water: but
there standeth one among you, whom
ye know not; 27 He it is, who coming after me is preferred before me,
whose shoe's latchet I am not worthy
to unloose. 28 These things were

done in Bethabara beyond Jordan, where John was baptizing.

We have here the testimony of John, which he delivered to the messengers who were sent from Jerusalem to examine him. Observe here,

I. Who they were that sent to him, and who they were that were sent. 1. They that sent to him were *the Jews at Jerusalem,* the great sanhedrim or high-commission court, which sat at Jerusalem, and was the representative of the Jewish church, who took cognizance of all matters relating to religion. One would think that they who were the fountains of learning, and the guides of the church, should have, by books, understood the times so well as to know that the Messiah was at hand, and therefore should presently have known him that was his forerunner, and readily embraced him; but, instead of this, they sent messengers to *cross questions* with him. Secular learning, honour, and power, seldom dispose men's minds to the reception of divine light. 2. They that were sent were, (1.) *Priests and Levites,* probably members of the council, men of learning, gravity, and authority. John Baptist was himself a priest of the seed of Aaron, and therefore it was not fit that he should be examined by any but priests. It was prophesied concerning John's ministry that it should *purify the Sons of Levi* (Mal. iii. 3), and therefore they were jealous of him and his reformation. (2.) They were *of the Pharisees,* proud, self-justiciaries, that thought they needed no repentance, and therefore could not bear one that made it his business to preach repentance.

II. On what errand they were sent; it was to enquire concerning John and *his baptism.* They did not send for John to them, probably because they *feared the people,* lest the people where John was should be provoked to rise, or lest the people where they were should be brought acquainted with him; they thought it was good to keep him at a distance. They enquire concerning him, 1. To satisfy their curiosity; as the Athenians enquired concerning Paul's doctrine, for the novelty of it, Acts xvii. 19, 20. Such a proud conceit they had of themselves that the doctrine of repentance was to them strange doctrine. 2. It was to show their authority. They thought they *looked great* when they called him to account whom all men counted as a prophet, and arraigned him at their bar. 3. It was with a design to *suppress* him and silence him if they could find any colour for it; for they were jealous of his growing interest, and his ministry agreed neither with the Mosaic dispensation which they had been long under, nor with the notions they had formed of the Messiah's kingdom.

III. What was the answer he gave them, and his account, both concerning himself and concerning his baptism, in both which he witnessed to Christ.

1. Concerning himself, and what he professed himself to be. They asked him, Σὺ τίς εἶ—*Thou, who art thou?* John's appearing in the world was surprising. He was in the wilderness till the day of his showing unto Israel. His spirit, his converse, his doctrine, had something in them which commanded and gained respect; but he did not, as seducers do, give out himself to be *some great one.* He was more industrious to *do good* than to *appear great;* and therefore waived saying any thing of himself till he was legally interrogated. Those speak best for Christ that say least of themselves, whose *own works* praise them, not *their own lips.* He answers their interrogatory,

(1.) *Negatively.* He was not that great one whom some took him to be. God's faithful witnesses stand more upon their guard *against undue respect* than against *unjust contempt.* Paul writes as warmly against those that overvalued him, and said, *I am of Paul,* as against those that undervalued him, and said that his bodily presence was weak; and he rent his clothes when he was called a god. [1.] John disowns himself to be *the Christ* (*v.* 20): *He said, I am not the Christ,* who was now expected and waited for. Note, The ministers of Christ must remember that *they are not Christ,* and therefore must not usurp his powers and prerogatives, nor assume the praises due to him only. They are not Christ, and therefore must not lord it over God's heritage, nor pretend to a dominion over the faith of Christians. They cannot create grace and peace; they cannot enlighten, convert, quicken, comfort; for they are not Christ. Observe how emphatically this is here expressed concerning John: He *confessed, and denied not, but confessed;* it denotes his vehemence and constancy in making this protestation. Note, Temptations to pride, and assuming that honour to ourselves which does not belong to us, ought to be resisted with a great deal of vigour and earnestness. When John was taken to be the Messiah, he did not connive at it with a *Si populus vult decipi, decipiatur—If the people will be deceived, let them;* but openly and solemnly, without any ambiguities, confessed, *I am not the Christ;* ὅτι οὐκ εἰμὶ ἐγὼ ὁ Χριστός—*I am not the Christ, not I;* another is at hand, who is he, but I am not. His disowning himself to be the Christ is called his *confessing* and not *denying* Christ. Note, Those that humble and abase themselves thereby confess Christ, and give honour to him; but those that will not deny themselves do in effect deny Christ. [2.] He disowns himself to be Elias, *v.* 21. The Jews expected the person of Elias to return from heaven, and to live among them, and promised themselves great things from it. Hearing of John's character, doctrine, and baptism, and observing that he appeared as one dropped from heaven, in the same part of the country from which Elijah was carried to heaven, it is no wonder that they were ready to take him for this Elijah; but he disowned this honour too. He was indeed prophesied of under the name of Elijah (Mal. iv. 5), and he came in the *spirit and power of Elias* (Luke i. 17), and was the Elias that was to come (Matt. xi. 14); but he was not the person of Elias, not that Elias that went to heaven in the fiery chariot, as he was that met Christ in his transfiguration. He was the Elias that God had promised, not the Elias that they foolishly dreamed of. Elias did come, and *they knew him not* (Matt. xvii. 12); nor did he make himself known to them as the Elias, because they had promised themselves such an Elias as God never promised them. [3.] He disowns himself to be that *prophet*, or the prophet. *First,* He was not *that* prophet which Moses said *the Lord* would *raise up to them of their brethren,* like unto him. If they meant this, they needed not ask that question, for that prophet was no other than the Messiah, and he had said already, *I am not the Christ. Secondly,* He was not such a prophet as they expected and wished for, who, like Samuel and Elijah, and some other of the prophets, would interpose in public affairs, and rescue them from under the Roman yoke. *Thirdly,* He was not one of the old prophets raised from the dead, as they expected one to come before Elias, as Elias before the Messiah. *Fourthly,* Though John was a prophet, yea, more than a prophet, yet he had his revelation, not by dreams and visions, as the Old-Testament prophets had theirs; his commission and work were of another nature, and belonged to another dispensation. If John had said that he was Elias, and was a prophet, he might have made his words good; but ministers must, upon all occasions, express themselves with the utmost caution, both that they may not confirm people in any mistakes, and particularly that they may not give occasion to any to think of them *above what is meet.*

(2.) *Affirmatively.* The committee that was sent to examine him pressed for a positive answer (*v.* 22), urging the authority of *those that sent them,* which they expected he should pay a deference to: "*Tell us, What art thou?* not that we may believe thee, and be baptized by thee, but that we may *give an answer* to those that sent us, and that it may not be said we were sent on a fool's errand." John was looked upon as a man of sincerity, and therefore they believed he would not give an evasive ambiguous answer; but would be fair and above-board, and give a plain answer to a plain question: *What sayest thou of thyself?* And he did so, *I am the voice of one crying in the wilderness.* Observe,

[1.] He gives his answer in the words of scripture, to show that the scripture was fulfilled in him, and that his office was supported by a divine authority. What the scripture saith of the office of the ministry should be often thought of by those of that high calling, who must look upon themselves as that, and that only, which the word of God makes them.

[2.] He gives in his answer in very humble, modest, self-denying expressions. He chooses to apply that scripture to himself which denotes not his dignity, but his duty and dependence, which bespeaks him little: *I am the voice,* as if he were *vox et præterea nihil—mere voice.*

[3.] He gives such an account of himself as might be profitable to them, and might excite and awaken them to hearken to him; for he *was the voice* (see Isa. xl. 3), a voice to alarm, an articulate voice to instruct. Ministers are but the *voice,* the vehicle, by which God is pleased to communicate his mind. What are Paul and Apollos but messengers? Observe, *First,* He was a *human* voice. The people were prepared to receive the law by the voice of thunders, and a trumpet exceedingly loud, such as made them tremble; but they were prepared for the gospel by the voice of a man like ourselves, *a still small voice,* such as that in which God came to Elijah, 1 Kings xix. 12. *Secondly,* He was the voice of *one crying,* which denotes, 1. His *earnestness* and *importunity* in calling people to repentance; he *cried aloud, and did not spare.* Ministers must preach as those that are in earnest, and are themselves affected with those things with which they desire to affect others. Those words are not likely to *thaw* the hearers' hearts that *freeze* between the speaker's lips. 2. His *open publication* of the doctrine he preached; he was the voice of one *crying,* that all manner of persons might hear and take notice. *Doth not wisdom cry?* Prov. viii. 1. *Thirdly,* It was in the *wilderness* that this voice was crying; in a place of silence and solitude, out of the noise of the world and the hurry of its business; the more retired we are from the tumult of secular affairs the better prepared we are to hear from God. *Fourthly,* That which he cried was, *Make straight the way of the Lord;* that is, 1. He came to *rectify* the mistakes of people concerning the ways of God; it is certain that they are right ways, but the scribes and Pharisees, with their corrupt glosses upon the law, had made them crooked. Now John Baptist calls people to return to the original rule. 2. He came to prepare and dispose people for the reception and entertainment of Christ and his gospel. It is an allusion to the harbingers of a prince or great man, that cry, *Make room.* Note, When God is coming towards us, we must prepare to meet him, and let the word of the Lord have *free course.* See Ps. xxiv. 7.

2. Here is his testimony concerning *his baptism.*

(1.) The enquiry which the committee made about it: *Why baptizest thou, if thou be not the Christ, nor Elias, nor that prophet? v.* 25. [1.] They readily apprehended baptism to be fitly and properly used as a sacred rite or ceremony, for the Jewish church had used it with circumcision in the admission of proselytes, to signify the cleansing of them from the pollutions of their former state. That sign was made use of in the Christian church, that it might be the more passable. Christ did not affect novelty, nor should his ministers. [2.] They expected it would be used in the days of the Messiah, because it was promised that then there should be a *fountain opened* (Zech. xiii. 1), and *clean water sprinkled*, Ezek. xxxvi. 25. It is taken for granted that Christ, and Elias, and *that prophet*, would baptize, when they came to *purify* a *polluted* world. Divine justice drowned the old world *in its filth*, but divine grace has provided for the cleansing of this new world *from its filth*. [3.] They would therefore know by what authority John baptized. His denying himself to be Elias, or *that prophet*, subjected him to this further question, *Why baptizest thou?* Note, It is no new thing for a man's modesty to be turned against him, and improved to his prejudice; but it is better that men should take advantage of our low thoughts of ourselves, to *trample upon us*, than the devil take advantage of our high thoughts of ourselves, to *tempt us* to pride and draw us into his condemnation.

(2.) The account he gave of it, *v.* 26, 27.

[1.] He owned himself to be only the minister of the outward sign: "*I baptize with water*, and that is all; I am no more, and do no more, than what you see; I have no other title than *John the Baptist;* I cannot confer the spiritual grace signified by it." Paul was in care that none should think of him above what they saw him to be (2 Cor. xii. 6); so was John Baptist. Ministers must not set up for masters.

[2.] He directed them to one who was greater than himself, and would do that for them, if they pleased, which he could not do: "*I baptize with water*, and that is the utmost of my commission; I have nothing to do but by this to lead you to one that comes after me, and consign you to him." Note, The great business of Christ's ministers is to direct all people to him; we preach not ourselves, but *Christ Jesus the Lord.* John gave the same account to this committee that he had given to the people (*v.* 15): *This was he of whom I spoke.* John was constant and uniform in his testimony, not as a reed shaken with the wind. The sanhedrim were jealous of his interest in the people, but he is not afraid to tell them that there is one at the door that will go beyond him. *First,* He tells them of Christ's *presence among them* now at this time: *There stands one among you,* at this time, *whom you know not.* Christ stood among the common people, and was as one of them. Note, 1. Much true worth lies hid in this world; obscurity is often the lot of real excellency. Saints are God's *hidden ones*, therefore *the world knows them not.* 2. God himself is often nearer to us than we are aware of. *The Lord* is *in this place*, and *I knew it not*. They were gazing, in expectation of the Messiah: *Lo he is here,* or he is there, when the kingdom of God was abroad and already *among them*, Luke xvii. 21. *Secondly,* He tells them of Christ's *preference above himself:* He comes *after me*, and yet is *preferred before me.* This he had said before; he adds here, "Whose *shoe-latchet I am not worthy to loose;* I am not fit to be named the same day with him; it is an honour too great for me to pretend to be in the meanest office about him," 1 Sam. xxv. 41. Those to whom Christ is precious reckon his service, even the most despised instances of it, an honour to them. See Ps. lxxxiv. 10. If so great a man as John accounted himself unworthy of the honour of being near Christ, how unworthy then should we account ourselves! Now, one would think, these chief priests and Pharisees, upon this intimation given concerning the approach of the Messiah, should presently have asked who, and where, this excellent person was; and who more likely to tell them than he who had given them this general notice? No, they did not think this any part of their business or concern; they came to molest John, not to receive any instructions from him: so that their ignorance was *wilful;* they might have known Christ, and would not.

Lastly, Notice is taken of the place where all this was done: *In Bethabara beyond Jordan, v.* 28. Bethabara signifies the *house of passage;* some think it was the very place where Israel passed over Jordan into the land of promise under the conduct of Joshua; there was opened the way into the gospel state by Jesus Christ. It was at a great *distance* from Jerusalem, beyond Jordan; probably because what he did *there* would be least offensive to the government. Amos must go prophesy in the country, not near the court; but it was sad that Jerusalem should put so far from her the things that belonged to *her peace*. He made this confession in the same place where he was *baptizing*, that all those who attended his baptism might be witnesses of it, and none might say that they knew not what to *make of him*.

29 The next day John seeth Jesus
coming unto him, and saith, Behold
the Lamb of God, which taketh away
the sin of the world. 30 This is he
of whom I said, After me cometh a
man which is preferred before me:
for he was before me. 31 And I
knew him not: but that he should be
made manifest to Israel, therefore am
I come baptizing with water. 32 And
John bare record, saying, I saw the

Spirit descending from heaven like a
dove, and it abode upon him. 33 And
I knew him not: but he that sent
me to baptize with water, the same
said unto me, Upon whom thou shalt
see the Spirit descending, and remaining on him, the same is he which
baptizeth with the Holy Ghost. 34
And I saw, and bare record that this
is the Son of God. 35 Again the
next day after John stood, and two
of his disciples; 36 And looking
upon Jesus as he walked, he saith,
Behold the Lamb of God!

We have in these verses an account of John's testimony concerning Jesus Christ, which he witnessed to his own disciples that followed him. As soon as ever Christ was *baptized* he was immediately hurried into the wilderness, to be *tempted;* and there he was forty days. During his absence John had continued to bear testimony to him, and to tell the people of him; but now at last he *sees Jesus coming to him,* returning from the wilderness of temptation. As soon as that conflict was over Christ immediately returned to John, who was *preaching* and *baptizing.* Now Christ was tempted for example and encouragement to us; and this teaches us, 1. That the *hardships* of a tempted state should engage us to keep close to ordinances; to go into the *sanctuary of God,* Ps. lxxiii. 17. Our combats with Satan should oblige us to keep close to the communion of saints: two are better than one. 2. That the *honours* of a victorious state must not set us *above ordinances.* Christ had triumphed over Satan, and been attended by angels, and yet, after all, he returns to the place where John was preaching and baptizing. As long as we are on this side heaven, whatever extraordinary visits of divine grace we may have here at any time, we must still keep close to the ordinary means of grace and comfort, and walk with God in them. Now here are *two testimonies* borne by John to Christ, but those two *agree in one.*

I. Here is his testimony to Christ on the first day that he saw him coming from the wilderness; and here four things are witnessed by him concerning Christ, when he had him before his eyes:—

1. That he is *the Lamb of God which taketh away the sin of the world, v.* 29. Let us learn here,

(1.) That Jesus Christ is the *Lamb of God,* which bespeaks him the great sacrifice, by which atonement is made for sin, and man reconciled to God. Of all the legal sacrifices he chooses to allude to the *lambs* that were offered, not only because a lamb is an emblem of meekness, and Christ must be led as a *lamb to the slaughter* (Isa. liii. 7), but with a special reference, [1.] To the *daily sacrifice,* which was offered every morning and evening continually, and that was always a *lamb* (Exod. xxix. 38), which was a type of Christ, as the everlasting propitiation, whose blood continually speaks. [2.] To the *paschal lamb,* the blood of which, being sprinkled upon the door-posts, secured the Israelites from the stroke of the destroying angel. Christ is *our passover,* 1 Cor. v. 7. He is the Lamb *of God;* he is appointed by *him* (Rom. iii. 25), he was devoted to him (*ch.* xvii. 19), and he was accepted with him; in him he was well pleased. The lot which fell on the goat that was to be offered for a sin-offering was called the *Lord's lot* (Lev. xvi. 8, 9); so Christ, who was to make atonement for sin, is called the *Lamb of God.*

(2.) That Jesus Christ, as the *Lamb of God, takes away the sin of the world.* This was his undertaking; he appeared, to *put away sin by the sacrifice of himself,* Heb. ix. 26. John Baptist had called people to repent of their sins, in order to the remission of them. Now here he shows how and by whom that remission was to be expected, what ground of hope we have that our sins shall be pardoned upon our repentance, though our repentance makes no satisfaction for them. This ground of hope we have—Jesus Christ is *the Lamb of God.* [1.] He *takes away sin.* He, being Mediator between God and man, takes away that which is, above any thing, offensive to the *holiness* of God, and destructive to the *happiness* of man. He came, *First,* To take away the guilt of sin by the merit of his death, to vacate the judgment, and reverse the attainder, which mankind lay under, by an act of indemnity, of which all penitent obedient believers may claim the benefit. *Secondly,* To take away the power of sin by the Spirit of his grace, so that it shall not have dominion, Rom. vi. 14. Christ, as the Lamb of God, washes us from our sins in his own blood; that is, he both *justifies* and *sanctifies* us: he *takes away sin.* He is ὁ αἴρων—*he is taking away* the sin of the world, which denotes it not a single but a continued act; it is his constant work and office to take *away sin,* which is such a *work of time* that it will never be completed till time shall be no more. He is always *taking away* sin, by the continual intercession of his blood in heaven, and the continual influence of his grace on earth. [2.] He takes away the *sin of the world;* purchases pardon for all those that repent, and believe the gospel, of what country, nation, or language, soever they be. The legal sacrifices had reference only to the sins of Israel, to make atonement for them; but the Lamb of God was offered to be a propitiation for the *sin of the whole world;* see 1 John ii. 2. This is encouraging to our faith; if Christ takes away the sin of the world, then why not my sin? Christ levelled his force at the main body of sin's army, struck at the root, and aimed at the overthrow, of that *wickedness* which the *whole world lay in.* God was in him reconciling the world to himself. [3.] He does this by *taking it upon himself.* He is the Lamb of God, that *bears the sin of the world;* so the margin reads it. He bore sin *for us,* and so bears it *from us;* he *bore the sin of many,* as the scape-goat had the sins of Israel put upon his head, Lev. xvi. 21. God could have taken away the sin by taking away the sinner, as he took away the sin of the old world; but he has found out a way of abolishing the sin, and yet sparing the sinner, by making his Son *sin for us.*

(3.) That it is our duty, with an eye of faith, to *behold* the Lamb of God thus taking away the *sin of the world.* See him taking away sin, and let that increase our hatred of sin, and resolutions against it. Let not us hold that fast which the Lamb of God came to take away: for Christ will either take our sins away or take us away. Let it increase our love to Christ, *who loved us, and washed us from our sins in his own blood,* Rev. i. 5. Whatever God is pleased to take away from us, if withal he take away our sins, we have reason to be thankful, and no reason to complain.

2. That this was he of whom he had spoken before (*v.* 30, 31): *This is he,* this person whom I now point at, you see where he stands, *this is he of whom I said, After me cometh a man.* Observe, (1.) This honour John had above all the prophets, that, whereas they spoke of him as one that should come, he saw him already come. *This is he.* He sees him *now,* he sees him *nigh,* Num. xxiv. 17. Such a difference there is between present *faith* and future *vision.* Now we love one whom we have not seen; then we shall see him whom our souls love, shall see him, and say, This is he of whom I said, *my Christ,* and *my all, my beloved,* and *my friend.* (2.) John calls Christ *a man;* after me comes a man—ἀνὴρ, a *strong man:* like *the man,* the branch, or the *man of God's right hand.* (3.) He refers to what he had himself said of him before: *This is he of whom I said.* Note, Those who have said the most honourable things of Christ will never see cause to unsay them; but the more they know him the more they are confirmed in their esteem of him. John still thinks as meanly of himself, and as highly of Christ, as ever. Though Christ appeared not in any external pomp or grandeur, yet John is not ashamed to own, *This is he whom I* meant, who is *preferred before me.* And it was necessary that John should thus show them the person, otherwise they could not have believed that one who made so mean a figure should be he of whom John had spoken such great things. (4.) He protests against any confederacy or combination with this Jesus: *And I knew him not.* Though there was some relation between them (Elisabeth was cousin to the virgin Mary), yet there was no acquaintance at all between them; John had no personal knowledge of Jesus till he saw him come to his baptism. Their manner of life had been different: John had spent his time in the wilderness, in solitude; Jesus at Nazareth, in conversation. There was no correspondence, no interview between them, that the matter might appear to be wholly carried on by the direction and disposal of Heaven, and not by any design or concert of the persons themselves. And as he hereby disowns all collusion, so also all partiality and sinister regard in it; he could not be supposed to favour him as a friend, for there was no friendship or familiarity between them. Nay, as he could not be biassed to speak honourably of him because he was a stranger to him, so, really being such a stranger to him, he was not able to say any thing of him but what he *received from above,* to which he appeals, *ch.* iii. 27. Note, They who are taught believe and confess one whom they have not seen, and blessed are they who *yet have believed.* (5.) The great intention of John's ministry and baptism was to introduce Jesus Christ. That he should be *made manifest to Israel, therefore am I come baptizing with water.* Observe, [1.] Though John did not know Jesus by face, yet he knew that he should be made manifest. Note, We may know the certainty of that which yet we do not fully know the nature and intention of. We know that the happiness of heaven *shall be made manifest to Israel,* but cannot describe it. [2.] The general assurance John had that Christ *should be made manifest* served to carry him with diligence and resolution through his work, though he was kept in the dark concerning particulars: *Therefore am I come.* Our assurance of the reality of things, though they are unseen, is enough to quicken us to our duty. [3.] God reveals himself to his people by degrees. At first, John knew no more concerning Christ but that he should be made manifest; in confidence of that, he came baptizing, and now he is favoured with a sight of him. They who, upon God's word, believe what they do not see, shall shortly see what they now believe. [4.] The ministry of the word and sacraments is designed for no other end than to lead people to Christ, and to make him more and more manifest. [5.] Baptism with water made way for the manifesting of Christ, as it supposed our corruption and filthiness, and signified our cleansing by him who is the *fountain opened.*

3. That this was he *upon whom the Spirit descended from heaven like a dove.* For the confirming of his testimony concerning Christ, he here vouches the extraordinary appearance at his baptism, in which God himself bore witness to him. This was a considerable proof of Christ's mission. Now, to assure us of the truth of it, we are here told (*v.* 32—34),

(1.) That John Baptist saw it: *He bore record;* did not relate it as a story, but solemnly attested it, with all the seriousness and solemnity of *witness-bearing.* He made affidavit of it: *I saw the Spirit descending* from heaven. John could not see the *Spirit,* but he saw the dove which was a sign and representation of the Spirit. The Spirit came now upon Christ, both to *make him fit* for his *work* and to *make him known* to the *world.* Christ was notified, not by the descent of a crown upon him, or by a transfiguration, but by the descent of the Spirit as a dove upon him, to qualify him for his undertaking. Thus the first testimony given to the apostles was by the descent of the Spirit upon them. God's children are made manifest by their *graces;* their glories are reserved for their future state. Observe, [1.] The spirit descended *from heaven,* for every good and perfect gift is *from above.* [2.] He descended *like a dove*—an emblem of meekness, and mildness, and gentleness, which makes him *fit to teach.* The dove brought the olive-branch of peace, Gen. viii. 11. [3.] The Spirit that descended upon Christ *abode upon him,* as was foretold, Isa. xi. 2. The Spirit did not *move him at times,* as Samson (Judg. xiii. 25), but *at all times.* The Spirit was given to him *without measure;* it was his prerogative to have the Spirit always upon him, so that he could at no time be found either *unqualified* for his work himself or *unfurnished* for the supply of those that seek to him for his grace.

(2.) That he was *told to expect it,* which very much corroborates the proof. It was not John's bare conjecture, that surely he on whom he saw the Spirit descending was the Son of God; but it was an *instituted* sign given him before, by which he might certainly know it (*v.* 33): *I knew him not.* He insists much upon this, that he knew no more of him than other people did, otherwise than by revelation. But *he that sent me to baptize* gave me this sign, *Upon whom thou shalt see the Spirit descending, the same is he.* [1.] See here what sure grounds John went upon in his ministry and baptism, that he might proceed with all imaginable satisfaction. *First,* He did not run *without sending:* God *sent him to baptize.* He had a warrant from heaven for what he did. When a minister's call is clear, his comfort is sure, though his success is not always so. *Secondly,* He did not run *without speeding;* for, when he was sent to *baptize with water,* he was directed to one that should *baptize with the Holy Ghost.* Under this notion John Baptist was taught to expect Christ, as one who would give that repentance and faith which he called people to, and would carry on and complete that blessed structure of which he was now laying the foundation. Note, It is a great comfort to Christ's ministers, in their administration of the outward signs, that he whose ministers they are can confer the grace signified thereby, and so put life, and soul, and power into their ministrations; can speak to the heart what they speak to the ear, and *breathe* upon the dry bones to which they *prophesy.* [2.] See what sure grounds he went upon in his designation of the person of the Messiah. God had before given him a sign, as he did to Samuel concerning Saul: "On whom thou shalt see the Spirit descend, *that same is he.*" This not only prevented any mistakes, but gave him boldness in his testimony. When he had such assurance as this given him, he could speak with assurance. When John was told this before, his expectations could not but be very much raised; and, when the event exactly answered the prediction, his faith could not but be much confirmed: and these things are written that we may believe.

4. That he is *the Son of God.* This is the conclusion of John's testimony, that in which all the particulars centre, as the *quod erat demonstrandum—the fact to be demonstrated* (*v.* 34): *I saw, and bore record, that this is the Son of God.* (1.) The truth asserted is, *that this is the Son of God.* The voice from heaven proclaimed, and John subscribed to it, not only that he should baptize with the Holy Ghost by a divine authority, but that he has a divine nature. This was the peculiar Christian creed, that Jesus is the Son of God (Matt. xvi. 16), and here is the first framing of it. (2.) John's testimony to it: "*I saw, and bore record.* Not only I now bear record of it, but I did so as soon as I had seen it." Observe, [1.] What he *saw* he was forward to *bear record* of, as they, Acts iv. 20: *We cannot but speak the things which we have seen.* [2.] What he *bore record* of was what he *saw.* Christ's witnesses were eye-witnesses, and therefore the more to be credited: they did not speak by hear-say and report, 2 Pet. i. 16.

II. Here is John's testimony to Christ, the next day after, *v.* 35, 36. Where observe, 1. He took every opportunity that offered itself to lead people to Christ: *John stood looking upon Jesus as he walked.* It should seem, John was now retired from the multitude, and was in close conversation with *two* of his disciples. Note, Ministers should not only in their public preaching, but in their private converse, witness to Christ, and serve his interests. He saw Jesus *walking* at some distance, yet did not go to him himself, because he would shun every thing that might give the least colour to suspect a combination. He was *looking upon Jesus—ἐμβλέψας*; he looked stedfastly, and fixed his eyes upon him. Those that would lead others to Christ must be diligent and frequent in the *contemplation* of him themselves. John had seen Christ before, but now looked upon him, 1 John i. 1. 2. He repeated the same testimony which he had given to Christ the day before, though he could have delivered some other great truth concerning him; but thus he would show that he was uniform and constant in his testimony, and consistent with himself. His doctrine was the same in private that it was in public, as Paul's was,

Acts xx. 20, 21. It is good to have that repeated which we have heard, Phil. iii. 1. The doctrine of Christ's sacrifice for the taking away of the sin of the world ought especially to be insisted upon by all good ministers: Christ, the Lamb of God, *Christ and him crucified.* 3. He intended this especially for his two disciples that stood with him; he was willing to turn them over to Christ, for to this end he bore witness to Christ in their hearing that they might leave all to follow him, even that they might leave *him.* He did not reckon that he lost those disciples who went over from him to Christ, any more than the schoolmaster reckons that scholar lost whom he sends to the university. John gathered disciples, not for himself, but for Christ, to *prepare them for the Lord,* Luke i. 17. So far was he from being jealous of Christ's growing interest, that there was nothing he was more desirous of. Humble generous souls will give others their due praise without fear of diminishing themselves by it. What we have of reputation, as well as of other things, will not be the less for our giving every body his own.

37 And the two disciples heard
him speak, and they followed Jesus.
38 Then Jesus turned, and saw them
following, and saith unto them, What
seek ye? They said unto him, Rabbi,
(which is to say, being interpreted,
Master,) where dwellest thou? 39
He saith unto them, Come and see.
They came and saw where he dwelt,
and abode with him that day: for it
was about the tenth hour. 40 One
of the two which heard John *speak*,
and followed him, was Andrew, Simon
Peter's brother. 41 He first findeth
his own brother Simon, and saith unto
him, We have found the Messias,
which is, being interpreted, the Christ.
42 And he brought him to Jesus.
And when Jesus beheld him, he said,
Thou art Simon the son of Jona:
thou shalt be called Cephas, which is
by interpretation, A stone.

We have here the turning over of two disciples from John to Jesus, and one of them fetching in a third, and these are the first-fruits of Christ's disciples; see how small the church was in its beginnings, and what the dawning of the day of its great things was.

I. Andrew and another with him were the two that John Baptist had directed to Christ, *v.* 37. Who the other was we are not told; some think that it was Thomas, comparing *ch.* xxi. 2; others that it was John himself, the penman of this gospel, whose manner it is industriously to conceal his name, *ch.* xiii. 23 and xx. 3.

1. Here is their readiness to go over to Christ: They *heard John speak* of Christ as the *Lamb of God,* and they *followed Jesus* Probably they had heard John say the same thing the day before, and then it had not the effect upon them which now it had; see the benefit of repetition, and of private personal converse. They heard him speak of Christ as the *Lamb of God, that takes away the sin of the world,* and this made them *follow him.* The strongest and most prevailing argument with a sensible awakened soul to follow Christ is that it is he, and he only, that *takes away sin.*

2. The kind notice Christ took of them, *v.* 38. They came behind him; but, though he had his back towards them, he was soon aware of them, and *turned,* and *saw them following.* Note, Christ takes early cognizance of the first motions of a soul towards him, and the first step taken in the way to heaven; see Isa. lxiv. 5; Luke xv. 20. He did not stay till they begged leave to speak with him, but spoke first. What communion there is between a soul and Christ, it is he that *begins the discourse.* He saith unto them, *What seek ye?* This was not a reprimand for their boldness in intruding into his company: he that came to *seek us* never checked any for *seeking* him; but, on the contrary, it is a kind invitation of them into his acquaintance whom he saw bashful and modest: "Come, what have you to say to me? What is your petition? What is your request?" Note, Those whose business it is to instruct people in the affairs of their souls should be humble, and mild, and easy of access, and should encourage those that apply to them. The question Christ put to them is what we should all put to ourselves when we begin to follow Christ, and take upon us the profession of his holy religion: "*What seek ye?* What do we design and desire?" Those that *follow* Christ, and yet *seek* the world, or themselves, or the praise of men, deceive themselves. "*What seek we* in seeking Christ? Do we seek a teacher, ruler, and reconciler? In following Christ, do we seek the favour of God and eternal life?" If our *eye* be *single* in this, we are *full of light.*

3. Their modest enquiry concerning the place of his abode: *Rabbi, where dwellest thou?* (1.) In calling him *Rabbi,* they intimated that their design in coming to him was to be *taught by him; rabbi* signifies a *master,* a teaching master; the Jews called their doctors, or learned men, *rabbies.* The word comes from *rab, multus* or *magnus,* a *rabbi,* a *great man,* and one that, as we say, has *much in him.* Never was there such a rabbi as our Lord Jesus, such a *great one,* in whom were *hid all the treasures of wisdom and knowledge.* These came to Christ to be his scholars, so must all those that apply themselves to him. John had told them that he was the *Lamb of God;* now this *Lamb* is worthy to *take the book and open the seals* as

a rabbi, Rev. v. 9. And, unless we give up ourselves to be ruled and taught by him, he will not *take away our sins.* (2.) In asking *where he dwelt*, they intimate a desire to be better acquainted with him. Christ was a stranger in this country, so that they meant where was his *inn* where he *lodged;* for there they would attend him at some seasonable time, when he should appoint, to receive instruction from him; they would not press rudely upon him, when it was not proper. Civility and good manners well become those who follow Christ. And, besides, they hoped to have more from him than they could have in a short conference now by the way. They resolved to make a business, not a by-business of conversing with Christ. Those that have had some communion with Christ cannot but desire, [1.] A *further communion* with him; they follow on to know more of him. [2.] A *fixed communion* with him; where they may sit down at his feet, and abide by his instructions. It is not enough to take a turn with Christ now and then, but we must *lodge with him.*

4. The courteous invitation Christ gave them to his lodgings: *He saith unto them, Come and see.* Thus should good desires towards Christ and communion with him be countenanced. (1.) He invites them to come to his lodgings: the nearer we approach to Christ, the more we see of his beauty and excellency. Deceivers maintain their interest in their followers by keeping them at a distance, but that which Christ desired to recommend him to the esteem and affections of his followers was that they would *come and see:* "*Come and see* what a mean lodging I have, what poor accommodations I take up with, that you may not expect any worldly advantage by following me, as they did who made their court to the scribes and Pharisees, and called them rabbin. *Come and see* what you must count upon if you follow me." See Matt. viii. 20. (2.) He invites them to come *immediately* and without delay. They asked where he lodged, that they might wait upon him at a more convenient season; but Christ invites them immediately to *come and see;* never in better time than now. Hence learn, [1.] As to others, that it is best taking people when they are in a good mind; strike while the iron is hot. [2.] As to ourselves, that it is wisdom to embrace the present opportunities: *Now is the accepted time,* 2 Cor. vi. 2.

5. Their cheerful and (no doubt) thankful acceptance of his invitation: *They came and saw where he dwelt,* and *abode with him that day.* It had been greater modesty and manners than had done them good if they had refused this offer. (1.) They readily went along with him: *They came and saw where he dwelt.* Gracious souls cheerfully accept Christ's gracious invitations; as David, Ps. xxvii. 8. They enquired not how they might be accommodated with him, but would put that to the venture, and make the best of what they found. It is good being where Christ is, wherever it be. (2.) They were so well pleased with what they found that they *abode with him that day* ("Master, it is good to be here"); and he bade them welcome. It was about the tenth hour. Some think that John reckons according to the Roman computation, and that it was about ten o'clock in the morning, and they staid with him till night; others think that John reckons as the other evangelists did, according to the Jewish computation, and that it was four o'clock in the afternoon, and they abode with him that night and the next day. Dr. Lightfoot conjectures that this next day that they spent with Christ was a sabbath-day, and, it being late, they could not get home before the sabbath. As it is our duty, wherever we are, to contrive to spend the sabbath as much as may be to our spiritual benefit and advantage, so they are blessed who, by the lively exercises of faith, love, and devotion, spend their sabbaths in communion with Christ. These are Lord's days indeed, *days of the Son of man.*

II. Andrew brought his brother Peter to Christ. If Peter had been the first-born of Christ's disciples, the papists would have made a noise with it: he did indeed afterwards come to be more eminent in gifts, but Andrew had the honour first to be acquainted with Christ, and to be the instrument of bringing Peter to him. Observe,

1. The *information* which Andrew gave to Peter, with an intimation to come to Christ.

(1.) He *found him: He first finds his own brother Simon;* his finding implies his seeking him. Simon came along with Andrew to attend John's ministry and baptism, and Andrew knew where to look for him. Perhaps the other disciple that was with him went out to seek some friend of his at the same time, but Andrew sped first: *He first findeth Simon,* who came only to attend on John, but has his expectations out-done; he meets with Jesus.

(2.) He told him whom they had found: *We have found the Messias.* Observe, [1.] he speaks *humbly;* not, "I have found," assuming the honour of the discovery to himself, but "*We* have," rejoicing that he had shared with others in it. [2.] He speaks *exultingly,* and with triumph: *We have found* that pearl of great price, that true treasure; and, having found it, he proclaims it as those lepers, 2 Kings vii. 9, for he knows that he shall have never the less in Christ for others sharing. [3.] He speaks *intelligently: We have found the Messias,* which was more than had yet been said. John had said, *He is the Lamb of God, and the Son of God,* which Andrew compares with the scriptures of the Old Testament, and, comparing them together, concludes that he is the Messiah promised to the fathers, for it is now that the fulness of time is come. Thus, by *making God's testi-*

monies his meditation, he speaks more clearly concerning Christ than ever *his teacher* had done, Ps. cxix. 99.

(3.) He *brought him to Jesus;* would not undertake to instruct him himself, but brought him to the fountain-head, persuaded him to come to Christ and introduced him. Now this was, [1.] An instance of true love to his brother, *his own* brother, so he is called here, because he was very dear to him. Note, We ought with a particular concern and application to seek the spiritual welfare of those that are related to us; for their relation to us adds both to the *obligation* and to the *opportunity* of doing good to their souls. [2.] It was an effect of his day's conversation with Christ. Note, the best evidence of our profiting by the means of grace is the piety and usefulness of our conversation afterwards. Hereby it appeared that Andrew had *been with Jesus* that he was so full of him, that he had been *in the mount,* for his face shone. He knew there was enough in Christ for all; and, having tasted that he is gracious, he could not rest till those he loved had tasted it too. Note, True grace hates monopolies, and loves not to eat its morsels alone.

2. The *entertainment* which Jesus Christ gave to Peter, who was never the less welcome for his being influenced by his brother to come, *v.* 42. Observe,

(1.) Christ called him by his name: *When Jesus beheld him, he said, Thou art Simon, the son of Jona.* It should seem that Peter was utterly a stranger to Christ, and if so, [1.] It was a proof of Christ's omniscience that upon the first sight, without any enquiry, he could tell the name both of him and of his father. *The Lord knows them that are his,* and their whole case. However, [2.] It was an instance of his condescending grace and favour, that he did thus freely and affably call him by his name, though he was of mean extraction, and *vir nullius nominis—a man of no name.* It was an instance of God's favour to Moses that he *knew him by name,* Exod. xxxiii. 17. Some observe the signification of these names: *Simon—obedient, Jona—a dove.* An obedient dove-like spirit qualifies us to be the disciples of Christ.

(2.) He gave him a new name: *Cephas.* [1.] His giving him a name intimates *Christ's favour* to him. A new name denotes some great dignity, Rev. ii. 17; Isa. lxii. 2. By this Christ not only wiped off the reproach of his mean and obscure parentage, but adopted him into his family as one of his own. [2.] The name which he gave him bespeaks his *fidelity* to Christ: *Thou shalt be called Cephas* (that is Hebrew for *a stone*), *which is by interpretation Peter;* so it should be rendered, as Acts ix. 36. *Tabitha, which by interpretation is called Dorcas;* the former Hebrew, the latter Greek, for a *young roe.* Peter's natural temper was stiff, and hardy, and resolute, which I take to be the principal reason why Christ called him *Cephas—a stone.* When Christ afterwards prayed for him, that his faith might not fail, that so he might be firm to Christ himself, and at the same time bade him *strengthen his brethren,* and lay out himself for the support of others, then he *made him* what he here called him, *Cephas—a stone.* Those that come to Christ must come with a fixed resolution to be firm and constant to him, *like a stone,* solid and stedfast; and it is by his grace that they are so. His saying, *Be thou steady,* makes them so. Now this does no more prove that Peter was the singular or only rock upon which the church is built than the calling of James and John *Boanerges* proves them the only *sons of thunder,* or the calling of Joses *Barnabas* proves him the only *son of consolation.*

43 The day following Jesus would
go forth into Galilee, and findeth
Philip, and saith unto him, Follow
me. 44 Now Philip was of Bethsaida, the city of Andrew and Peter.
45 Philip findeth Nathanael, and saith
unto him, We have found him, of
whom Moses in the law, and the prophets, did write, Jesus of Nazareth,
the son of Joseph. 46 And Nathanael said unto him, Can there any
good thing come out of Nazareth?
Philip saith unto him, Come and see.
47 Jesus saw Nathanael coming to
him, and saith of him, Behold an
Israelite indeed, in whom is no guile!
48 Nathanael saith unto him, Whence
knowest thou me? Jesus answered
and said unto him, Before that Philip
called thee, when thou wast under the
fig tree, I saw thee. 49 Nathanael
answered and saith unto him, Rabbi,
thou art the Son of God; thou art
the King of Israel. 50 Jesus answered and said unto him, Because I
said unto thee, I saw thee under the
fig tree, believest thou? thou shalt
see greater things than these. 51
And he saith unto him, Verily, verily
I say unto you, Hereafter ye shall see
heaven open, and the angels of God
ascending and descending upon the
Son of man.

We have here the call of Philip and Nathanael.

I. Philip was called immediately by Christ himself, not as Andrew, who was directed to Christ by John, or Peter, who was invited by his brother. God has various methods of bringing his chosen ones home to himself. But, whatever means he *uses,* he is not *tied* to any. 1. Philip was called in a *preventing* way: *Jesus findeth Philip.* Christ sought us, and found us, before we made any enquiries after him. The name *Philip* is of Greek origin, and much used among the Gentiles, which some make an instance of the degeneracy of the Jewish church at this time, and their conformity to the nations; yet Christ changed not his name. 2. He was called the *day following.* See how closely Christ applied himself to his business. When work is to be done for God, we must not *lose a day.* Yet observe, Christ now called one or two a day; but, after the Spirit was poured out, there were thousands a day effectually called, in which was fulfilled *ch.* xiv. 12. 3. Jesus *would go forth into Galilee* to call him. Christ will find out all those that are given to him, wherever they are, and none of them shall be lost. 4. Philip was brought to be a disciple by the power of Christ going along with that word, *Follow me.* See the nature of true Christianity; it is *following Christ,* devoting ourselves to his *converse* and *conduct,* attending his movements, and treading in his steps. See the efficacy of the grace of Christ making the call of his word to prevail; it is the *rod of his strength.* 5. We are told that Philip was of Bethsaida, and Andrew and Peter were so too, *v.* 44. These eminent disciples received not honour from the place of their nativity, but reflected honour upon it. *Bethsaida* signifies the *house of nets,* because inhabited mostly by fishermen; thence Christ chose disciples, who were to be furnished with extraordinary gifts, and therefore needed not the ordinary advantages of learning. Bethsaida was a wicked place (Matt. xi. 21), yet even *there* was a remnant, according to the election of grace.

II. Nathanael was invited to Christ by Philip, and much is said concerning him. In which we may observe,

1. What passed between Philip and Nathanael, in which appears an observable mixture of pious zeal with weakness, such as is usually found in beginners, that are yet but *asking the way to Zion.* Here is,

(1.) The joyful news that Philip brought to Nathanael, *v.* 45. As Andrew before, so Philip here, having got some knowledge of Christ himself, rests not till he has *made manifest the savour of that knowledge.* Philip, though newly come to an acquaintance with Christ himself, yet steps aside to seek Nathanael. Note, When we have the fairest opportunities of getting good to our own souls, yet even then we must seek opportunities of doing good to the souls of others, remembering the words of Christ, *It is more blessed to give than to receive,* Acts xx. 35. O, saith Philip, *we have found him of whom Moses and the prophets did write,* Observe here, [1.] What a transport of joy Philip was in, upon this new acquaintance with Christ: "We have found him whom we have so often talked of, so long wished and waited for; at last, *he is come, he is come,* and *we* have found him!" [2.] What an advantage it was to him that he was so well acquainted with the scriptures of the Old Testament, which prepared his mind for the reception of evangelical light, and made the entrance of it much the more easy: *Him of whom Moses and the prophets did write.* What was written entirely and from eternity in the *book of the divine counsels* was in part, at sundry times and in divers manners, copied out into the book of the *divine revelations.* Glorious things were written there concerning the Seed of the woman, the Seed of Abraham, Shiloh, the prophet like Moses, the Son of David, Emmanuel, the Man, the Branch, Messiah the Prince. Philip had studied these things, and was full of them, which made him readily welcome Christ. [3.] What mistakes and weaknesses he laboured under: he called Christ *Jesus of Nazareth,* whereas he was of *Bethlehem;* and the *Son of Joseph,* whereas he was but his *supposed* Son. Young beginners in religion are subject to mistakes, which time and the grace of God will rectify. It was his weakness to say, *We have found him,* for Christ found them before they found Christ. He did not yet *apprehend,* as Paul did, how he was *apprehended of Christ Jesus,* Phil. iii. 12.

(2.) The objection which Nathanael made against this, *Can any good thing come out of Nazareth? v.* 46. Here, [1.] His *caution* was commendable, that he did not lightly assent to every thing that was said, but took it into examination; our rule is, *Prove all things.* But, [2.] His objection arose from ignorance. If he meant that no good thing could come out of Nazareth it was owing to his ignorance of the divine grace, as if that were less affected to one place than another, or tied itself to men's foolish and ill-natured observations. If he meant that the Messiah, that great good thing, could not come out of Nazareth, so far he was right (Moses, in the law, said that he should come out of Judah, and the prophets had assigned Bethlehem for the place of his nativity); but then he was ignorant of the matter of *fact,* that this Jesus was born at Bethlehem; so that the blunder Philip made, in calling him *Jesus of Nazareth,* occasioned this objection. Note, The mistakes of preachers often give rise to the prejudices of hearers.

(3.) The short reply which Philip gave to this objection: *Come and see.* [1.] It was his *weakness* that he could not give a satisfactory answer to it; yet it is the common case of young beginners in religion. We may *know* enough to *satisfy* ourselves, and yet not be able to *say* enough to *silence* the cavils of a subtle adversary. [2.] It was his *wisdom* and zeal that, when he could not answer the objection himself, he would have him go to one that could: *Come and see.* Let us not stand arguing here, and raising difficulties to ourselves which we cannot get over; let us go and converse with Christ himself, and these difficulties will all vanish presently. Note, It is folly to spend that time in doubtful disputation which might be better spent, and to much better purpose, in the exercises of piety and devotion. *Come and see;* not, *Go and see,* but, "*Come,* and I will go along with thee;" as Isa. ii. 3; Jer. .. 5. From this parley between Philip and Nathanael, we may observe, *First,* That many people are kept from the ways of religion by the unreasonable prejudices they have conceived against religion, upon the account of some foreign circumstances which do not at all touch the merits of the case. *Secondly,* The best way to remove the prejudices they have entertained against religion is to prove themselves, and make trial of it. Let us not answer this matter before we hear it.

2. What passed between Nathanael and our Lord Jesus. He came and *saw,* not in vain.

(1.) Our Lord Jesus bore a very honourable testimony to Nathanael's integrity: *Jesus saw him* coming, and met him with favourable encouragement; he said of him to those about him, Nathanael himself being within hearing, *Behold an Israelite indeed.* Observe,

[1.] That he *commended* him; not to flatter him, or puff him up with a good conceit of himself, but perhaps because he knew him to be a *modest* man, if not a *melancholy* man, one that had hard and mean thoughts of himself, was ready to doubt his own sincerity; and Christ by this testimony put the matter out of doubt. Nathanael had, more than any of the candidates, objected against Christ; but Christ hereby showed that he excused it, and was not extreme to mark what he had said amiss, because he knew his heart was upright. He did not retort upon him, *Can any good thing come out of Cana* (*ch.* xxi. 2), an obscure town in Galilee? But kindly gives him this character, to encourage us to hope for acceptance with Christ, notwithstanding our weakness, and to teach us to speak honourably of those who without cause have spoken slightly of us, and to give them their due praise.

[2.] That he commended him for his *integrity. First, Behold an Israelite indeed.* It is Christ's prerogative to know what men are *indeed;* we can but *hope the best.* The whole nation were Israelites in name, but *all are not Israel that are of Israel* (Rom. ix. 6); here, however, was *an Israelite indeed.* 1. A sincere follower of the good example of Israel, whose character it was that he was a *plain man,* in opposition to Esau's character of a *cunning man.* He was a genuine son of *honest Jacob,* not only of his *seed,* but of his *spirit.* 2. A sincere professor of the faith of Israel; he was true to the religion he professed, and lived up to it: he was really as good as he seemed, and his practice was *of a piece* with his profession. He is the Jew that is one *inwardly* (Rom. ii. 29), so is he *the Christian. Secondly,* He is one in whom is *no guile*—that is the character of an Israelite indeed, a Christian indeed: *no guile* towards men; a man without trick or design; a man that one may trust; *no guile* towards God, that is, sincere in his repentance for sin; sincere in his covenanting with God; in whose spirit is *no guile,* Ps. xxxii. 2. He does not say without *guilt,* but without *guile.* Though in many things he is foolish and forgetful, yet in nothing false, nor *wickedly departing from God:* there is no allowed approved guilt in him; not painted, though he have his spots: "*Behold* this Israelite *indeed.*" 1. "Take notice of him, that you may learn his way, and do like him." 2. "Admire him; *behold,* and *wonder.*" The hypocrisy of the scribes and Pharisees had so leavened the Jewish church and nation, and their religion was so degenerated into formality or state-policy, that an Israelite indeed was a *man wondered at,* a miracle of divine grace, like Job, *ch.* i. 8.

(2.) Nathanael is much surprised at this, upon which Christ gives him a further proof of his omnisciency, and a kind memorial of his former devotion.

[1.] Here is Nathanael's modesty, in that he was soon put out of countenance at the kind notice Christ was pleased to take of him: "*Whence knowest thou me,* me that am unworthy of thy cognizance? *who am I, O Lord God?*" 2 Sam. vii. 18. This was an evidence of his sincerity, that he did not catch at the praise he met with, but declined it. Christ knows us better than we know ourselves; we know not what is in a man's heart by looking in his face, but all things are naked and open before Christ, Heb. iv. 12, 13. Doth Christ know us? Let us covet to know him.

[2.] Here is Christ's further *manifestation* of himself to him: *Before Philip called thee, I saw thee. First,* He gives him to understand that he *knew him,* and so manifests his divinity. It is God's prerogative infallibly to know all persons and all things; by this Christ proved himself to be God upon many occasions. It was prophesied concerning the Messiah that he should be of *quick understanding in the fear of the Lord,* that is, in judging the sincerity and degree of the fear of God in others, and that he should not *judge after the sight of his eyes,* Isa. xi. 2, 3. Here he answers that prediction. See 2 Tim. ii. 19. *Secondly,* That before Philip called him he saw him under the fig-tree; this manifests a particular kindness for him. 1. His eye was towards him before Philip called him, which was the first time that ever Nathanael was acquainted with Christ. Christ has knowledge of us before we have any knowledge of him; see Isa. xlv. 4; Gal. iv. 9. 2. His eye was upon him when he was *under the fig-tree;* this was a private token which nobody understood but Nathanael: "When thou wast retired *under the fig-tree* in thy garden, and thoughtest that no eye saw thee,

I had then my eye upon thee, and saw that which was very acceptable." It is most probable that Nathanael under the fig-tree was employed, as Isaac in the field, in meditation, and prayer, and communion with God. Perhaps then and there it was that he solemnly joined himself to the Lord in an inviolable covenant. Christ saw in secret, and by this public notice of it did in part reward him openly. *Sitting under the* fig-tree denotes quietness and composedness of spirit, which much befriend communion with God. See Mic. iv. 4; Zech. iii. 10. Nathanael herein was an Israelite indeed, that, like Israel, he *wrestled with God alone* (Gen. xxxii. 24), prayed not like the hypocrites, in the corners of the streets, but under the fig-tree.

(3.) Nathanael hereby obtained a full assurance of faith in Jesus Christ, expressed in that noble acknowledgment (*v.* 49): *Rabbi, thou art the Son of God, thou art the king of Israel;* that is, in short, thou art the true Messiah. Observe here, [1.] How *firmly* he believed *with the heart.* Though he had lately laboured under some prejudices concerning Christ, they had now all vanished. Note, The grace of God, in working faith, casts down imaginations. Now he asks no more, *Can any good thing come out of Nazareth?* For he believes Jesus of Nazareth to be the chief good, and embraces him accordingly. [2.] How *freely* he confessed *with the mouth.* His confession is made in form of an adoration, directed to our Lord Jesus himself, which is a proper way of confessing our faith. *First,* He confesses Christ's prophetical office, in calling him *Rabbi,* a title which the Jews commonly gave to their teachers. Christ is the great rabbi, at whose feet we must all be *brought up. Secondly,* He confesses his divine nature and mission, in calling him the Son of God (that Son of God spoken of Ps. ii. 7); though he had but a human *form* and *aspect,* yet having a divine knowledge, the knowledge of the heart, and of things distant and secret, Nathanael thence concludes him to be the *Son of God. Thirdly,* He confesses, "*Thou art the king of Israel;* that king of Israel whom we have been long waiting for." If he be the Son of God, he is king of the Israel of God. Nathanael hereby proves himself an Israelite indeed that he so readily owns and submits to the king of Israel.

(4.) Christ hereupon raises the hopes and expectations of Nathanael to something further and greater than all this, *v.* 50, 51. Christ is very tender of young converts, and will encourage good beginnings, though weak, Matt. xii. 20.

[1.] He here signifies his acceptance, and (it should seem) his admiration, of the ready faith of Nathanael: *Because I said, I saw thee under the fig-tree, believest thou?* He wonders that such a small indication of Christ's divine knowledge should have such an effect; it was a sign that Nathanael's heart was prepared beforehand, else the work had not been done so suddenly. Note, It is much for the honour of Christ and his grace, when the heart is surrendered to him at the first summons.

[2.] He promises him much greater helps for the confirmation and increase of his faith than he had had for the first production of it.

First, In general: "*Thou shalt see greater things than these,* stronger proofs of my being the Messiah;" the miracles of Christ, and his resurrection. Note, 1. To him that hath, and maketh good use of what he hath, more shall be given. 2. Those who truly believe the gospel will find its evidences grow upon them, and will see more and more cause to believe it. 3. Whatever discoveries Christ is pleased to make of himself to his people while they are here in this world, he hath still greater things than these to make known to them; a glory yet further *to be revealed.*

Secondly, In particular: "Not thou only, but you, all you my disciples, whose faith this is intended for the confirmation of, you *shall see heaven opened;*" this is more than telling Nathanael of his being under the fig-tree. This is introduced with a solemn preface, *Verily, verily I say unto you,* which commands both a *fixed attention* to what is said as very weighty, and a *full assent* to it as undoubtedly true: "I say it, whose word you may rely upon, *amen, amen.*" None used this word at the beginning of a sentence but Christ, though the Jews often used it at the close of a prayer, and sometimes doubled it. It is a solemn asseveration. Christ is called the *Amen* (Rev. iii. 14), and so some take it here, *I the Amen, the Amen, say unto you.* I the faithful witness. Note, The assurances we have of the glory to be revealed are built upon the word of Christ. Now see what it is that Christ assures them of: *Hereafter,* or *within awhile,* or *ere long,* or henceforth, ye shall see heaven opened.

a. It is a mean title that Christ here takes to himself: *the Son of man;* a title frequently applied to him in the gospel, but always by himself. Nathanael had called him the *Son of God* and *king of Israel*: he calls himself *Son of man,* (*a.*) To express his *humility* in the midst of the honours done him. (*b.*) To teach his *humanity,* which is to be believed as well as his divinity. (*c.*) To intimate his present state of humiliation, that Nathanael might not expect this king of Israel to appear in external pomp.

b. Yet they are great things which he here foretels: *You shall see heaven opened,* and *the angels of God ascending and descending upon the Son of man.* (*a.*) Some understand it literally, as pointing at some particular event. Either, [*a.*] There was some vision of Christ's glory, in which this was exactly fulfilled, which Nathanael was an eye-witness of, as Peter, and James, and John were of his transfiguration. There were many things which Christ did, and those in the presence of his disciples, which were not written (*ch.* xx. 30), and why not this? Or, [*b.*] It was fulfilled in the many ministrations of the angels to our Lord Jesus, especially that at his ascension, when heaven was opened to receive him, and the angels *ascended* and *descended*, to attend him and to do him honour, and this in the sight of the disciples. Christ's ascension was the great proof of his mission, and much confirmed the faith of his disciples, *ch.* vi. 62. Or, [*c.*] It may refer to Christ's second coming, to judge the world, when the heavens shall be *open*, and every eye shall see him, and the angels of God shall ascend and descend about him, as attendants on him, every one employed; and a busy day it will be. See 2 Thess. i. 10. (*b.*) Others take it figuratively, as speaking of a state or series of things to commence *from henceforth;* and so we may understand it, [*a.*] Of Christ's *miracles*. Nathanael believed, because Christ, as the prophets of old, could tell him things secret; but what is this? Christ is now beginning a dispensation of miracles, much more great and strange than this, as if heaven were opened; and such a power shall be exerted by the Son of man as if the angels, which excel in strength, were continually attending his orders. Immediately after this, Christ began to work miracles, *ch.* ii. 11. Or, [*b.*] Of his *mediation*, and that blessed intercourse which he hath settled between heaven and earth, which his disciples should by degrees be let into the mystery of. *First*, By Christ, as Mediator, they shall see *heaven opened*, that we may *enter into the holiest* by his blood (Heb. x. 19, 20); heaven opened, that by faith we may *look in*, and at length may *go in;* may now behold the glory of the Lord, and hereafter enter into the joy of our Lord. And, *Secondly*, They shall *see angels ascending and descending upon the Son of man*. Through Christ we have communion with and benefit by the holy angels, and things in heaven and things on earth are *reconciled* and *gathered together*. Christ is to us as Jacob's ladder (Gen. xxviii. 12), by whom angels continually ascend and descend for the good of the saints.

CHAP. II.

In the close of the foregoing chapter we had an account of the first disciples whom Jesus called, Andrew and Peter, Philip and Nathanael. These were the first-fruits to God and to the Lamb, Rev. xiv. 4. Now, in this chapter, we have, I. The account of the first miracle which Jesus wrought—turning water into wine, at Cana of Galilee (ver. 1—11), and his appearing at Capernaum, ver. 12. II. The account of the first passover he kept at Jerusalem after he began his public ministry; his driving the buyers and sellers out of the temple (ver. 13—17); and the sign he gave to those who quarrelled with him for it (ver. 18—22), with an account of some almost believers, that followed him, thereupon, for some time (ver. 23—25), but he knew them too well to put any confidence in them.

AND the third day there was a
marriage in Cana of Galilee; and
the mother of Jesus was there: 2
And both Jesus was called, and his
disciples to the marriage. 3 And
when they wanted wine, the mother
of Jesus saith unto him, They have
no wine. 4 Jesus saith unto her,
Woman, what have I to do with thee?
mine hour is not yet come. 5 His
mother saith unto the servants, Whatsoever he saith unto you, do *it*. 6
And there were set there six water-
pots of stone, after the manner of the
purifying of the Jews, containing two
or three firkins apiece. 7 Jesus saith
unto them, Fill the waterpots with
water. And they filled them up to
the brim. 8 And he saith unto them,
Draw out now, and bear unto the governor of the feast. And they bare
it. 9 When the ruler of the feast
had tasted the water that was made
wine, and knew not whence it was
(but the servants which drew the
water knew); the governor of the
feast called the bridegroom. 10 And
saith unto him, Every man at the
beginning doth set forth good wine;
and when men have well drunk, then
that which is worse: *but* thou hast
kept the good wine until now. 11
This beginning of miracles did Jesus
in Cana of Galilee, and manifested
forth his glory; and his disciples believed on him.

We have here the story of Christ's miraculous conversion of water into wine at a marriage in Cana of Galilee. There were some few so well disposed as to believe in Christ, and to follow him, when he *did no miracle;* yet it was not likely that many should be wrought upon till he had something wherewith to answer those that asked, *What sign showest thou?* He could have wrought miracles before, could have made them the common actions of his life and the common entertainments of his friends; but, miracles being designed for the sacred and solemn seals of his doctrine, he began not to work any till he began to preach his doctrine. Now observe,

I. The occasion of this miracle. Maimonides observes it to be to the honour of Moses that all the signs he did in the wilderness he did *upon necessity;* we needed food, he brought us manna, and so did Christ. Observe,

1. The time: the *third day* after he came into Galilee. The evangelist keeps a journal of occurrences, for no day passed without something extraordinary done or said. Our Master filled up his time better than his servants do, and never lay down at night complaining, as the Roman emperor did, that he had *lost a day*.

2. The place: it was at Cana in Galilee, in the tribe of Asher (Josh. xix. 28), of which, before, it was said that *he shall yield royal dainties*, Gen. xlix. 20. Christ began to work miracles in an obscure corner of the country, remote from Jerusalem, which was the public scene of action, to show that he *sought not honour from men* (*ch.* v. 41), but would put honour *upon the lowly*. His doctrine and miracles would not be so much opposed by the plain and honest Galileans as they would be by the proud and prejudiced rabbies, politicians, and grandees, at Jerusalem.

3. The occasion itself was a *marriage;* probably one or both of the parties were akin to our Lord Jesus. The *mother of Jesus* is said to be *there*, and not to be *called*, as Jesus and his disciples were, which intimates that she was there as one at home. Observe the honour which Christ hereby put upon the ordinance of marriage, that he graced the solemnity of it, not only with his presence, but with his first miracle; because it was instituted and blessed in innocency, because by it he would still *seek a godly seed*, because it resembles the mystical union between him and his church, and because he foresaw that in the papal kingdom, while the marriage ceremony would be unduly *dignified* and advanced into a *sacrament*, the *married state* would be unduly *vilified*, as inconsistent with any sacred function. There was a *marriage—γάμος*, a *marriage-feast*, to grace the solemnity. Marriages were usually celebrated with festivals (Gen. xxix. 22; Judg. xiv. 10), in token of joy and friendly respect, and for the confirming of love.

4. Christ and his mother and disciples were principal guests at this entertainment. *The mother of Jesus* (that was her most honourable title) *was there;* no mention being made of Joseph, we conclude him dead before this. Jesus was *called*, and he came, accepted the invitation, and feasted with them, to teach us to be *respectful* to our relations, and *sociable* with them, though they be mean. Christ was to come in a way different from that of John Baptist, who came *neither eating nor drinking*, Matt. xi. 18, 19. It is the wisdom of the prudent to study how to *improve* conversation rather than how to *decline* it.

(1.) *There was a marriage, and Jesus was called.* Note, [1.] It is very desirable, when there is a *marriage*, to have Jesus Christ *present* at it; to have his spiritual gracious presence, to have the marriage owned and blessed by him: the *marriage* is then *honourable* indeed; and they that *marry in* the Lord (1 Cor. vii. 39) do not marry *without him.* [2.] They that would have Christ with them at their marriage must invite him by prayer; that is the messenger that must be sent to heaven for him; and he will come: *Thou shalt call, and I will answer.* And he will turn the water into wine.

(2.) The disciples also were invited, those five whom he had called (*ch.* i.), for as yet he had no more; they were his family, and were invited with him. They had thrown themselves upon his care, and they soon found that, though he had no wealth, he had good friends. Note, [1.] Those that *follow* Christ shall *feast* with him, they shall *fare* as he *fares*, so he has *bespoken* for them (*ch.* xii. 26): *Where I am, there shall my servant be also.* [2.] Love to Christ is testified by a love to those that are his, for his sake; *our goodness extendeth not to him*, but *to the saints.* Calvin observes how *generous* the maker of the feast was, though he seems to have been but of small substance, to invite four or five strangers more than he thought of, because they were followers of Christ, which shows, saith he, that there is more of freedom, and liberality, and true friendship, in the conversation of some meaner persons than among many of higher rank.

II. The miracle itself. In which observe,

1. They *wanted wine*, *v.* 3. (1.) There was *want* at a *feast;* though much was provided, yet all was spent. While we are in this world we sometimes find ourselves *in straits*, even then when we think ourselves in the *fulness of our sufficiency.* If always *spending*, perhaps all is spent ere we are aware. (2.) There was want at a *marriage feast.* Note, They who, being *married*, are come to *care for the things of the world* must expect *trouble in the flesh*, and count upon disappointment. (3.) It should seem, Christ and his disciples were the occasion of this want, because there was more company than was expected when the provision was made; but they who straiten themselves for Christ shall not lose by him.

2. The *mother of Jesus* solicited him to assist her friends in this strait. We are told (*v.* 3—5) what passed between Christ and his mother upon this occasion.

(1.) She acquaints him with the difficulty they were in (*v.* 3): *She saith unto him, They have no wine.* Some think that she did not expect from him any miraculous supply (he having as yet wrought no miracle), but that she would have him make some *decent* excuse to the company, and make the best of it, to save the bridegroom's reputation, and keep him in countenance; or (as Calvin suggests) would have him make up the want of wine with some holy profitable discourse. But, most probably, she looked for a miracle; for she knew he was now appearing as the great prophet, like unto Moses, who so often seasonably supplied the wants of Israel; and, though this was his first public miracle, perhaps he had sometimes relieved her and her husband in their low estate. The bridegroom might have sent out for more wine, but she was for going to the fountain-head. Note, [1.] We ought to be concerned for the wants and straits of our friends, and not *seek our own things* only. [2.] In our own and our friends' straits it is our wisdom and duty to apply ourselves to Christ by prayer. [3]. In our addresses to Christ, we must not prescribe to him, but humbly spread our case before him, and then *refer ourselves* to him to do as he pleases.

(2.) He gave her a reprimand for it, for he saw more amiss in it than we do, else he had not treated it thus.—Here is,

[1.] The rebuke itself: *Woman, what have I to do with thee?* As many as Christ loves, he rebukes and chastens. He calls her *woman*, not *mother*. When we begin to be assuming, we should be reminded what we are, *men* and *women*, frail, foolish, and corrupt. The question, τί ἐμοὶ καὶ σοὶ, might be read, *What is that to me and thee?* What is it to us if they do want? But it is always used as we render it, *What have I to do with thee?* as Judges xi. 12; 2 Sam. xvi. 10; Ezra iv. 3; Matt. viii. 29. It therefore bespeaks a resentment, yet not at all inconsistent with the reverence and subjection which he paid to his mother, according to the fifth commandment (Luke ii. 51); for there was a time when it was Levi's praise that he *said to his father, I have not known him*, Deut. xxxiii. 9. Now this was intended to be, *First*, A check to his mother for interposing in a matter which was the act of his Godhead, which had no dependence on her, and which she was not the mother of. Though, as man, he was David's Son and hers; yet, as God, he was David's Lord and hers, and he would have her know it. The greatest advancements must not make us forget ourselves and our place, nor the familiarity to which the covenant of grace admits us breed contempt, irreverence, or any kind or degree of presumption. *Secondly*, It was an instruction to others of his relations (many of whom were present here) that they must never expect him to have any regard to his kindred according to the flesh, in his working miracles, or that therein he should gratify them, who in this matter were no more to him than other people. In the things of God we must not *know faces*. *Thirdly*, It is a standing testimony against that idolatry which he foresaw his church would in after-ages sink into, in giving undue honours to the virgin Mary, a crime which the Roman catholics, as they call themselves, are notoriously guilty of, when they call her the *queen of heaven*, the *salvation of the world*, their *mediatrix*, their *life* and *hope*; not only depending upon her merit and intercession, but beseeching her to *command her Son* to do them good: *Monstra te esse matrem—Show that thou art his mother. Jussu matris impera salvatori—Lay thy maternal commands on the Saviour.* Does he not here expressly say, when a miracle was to be wrought, even in the days of his humiliation, and his mother did but tacitly hint an intercession, *Woman, what have I to do with thee?* This was plainly designed either to *prevent* or *aggravate* such gross idolatry, such horrid blasphemy. The Son of God is appointed our Advocate with the Father; but the mother of our Lord was never designed to be our advocate with the Son.

[2.] The reason of this rebuke: *Mine hour is not yet come.* For every thing Christ did, and that was done to him, he had *his hour*, the *fixed* time and the *fittest* time, which was punctually observed. *First*, "Mine hour for *working miracles* is not yet come." Yet afterwards he wrought this, before the hour, because he foresaw it would confirm the faith of his infant disciples (*v.* 11), which was the end of all his miracles: so that this was an earnest of the many miracles he would work when his *hour was come*. *Secondly*, "Mine hour of working miracles *openly* is *not yet come*; therefore do not talk of it thus *publicly*." *Thirdly*, "Is *not the hour* of my exemption from thy authority *yet come*, now that I have begun to act as a prophet?" So Gregory Nyssen. *Fourthly*, "Mine hour for working *this miracle* is not yet come." His mother moved him to help them *when the wine began to fail* (so it may be read, *v.* 3), but his hour was not yet come till it was quite spent, and there was a *total want*; not only to prevent any suspicion of mixing some of the wine that was left with the water, but to teach us that man's extremity is God's opportunity to appear for the help and relief of his people. Then *his hour is come* when we are reduced to the utmost strait, and know not what to do. This encouraged those that waited for him to believe that though his hour was not *yet come* it would come. Note, The delays of mercy are not to be construed the denials of prayer. *At the end it shall speak.*

(3.) Notwithstanding this, she encouraged herself with expectations that he would help her friends in this strait, for she bade the servants *observe his orders*, *v.* 5. [1.] She took the reproof very submissively, and did not reply to it. It is best not to deserve reproof from Christ, but next best to be meek and quiet under it, and to count it a kindness, Ps. cxli. 5. [2.] She kept her hope in Christ's mercy, that he would yet grant her desire. When we come to God in Christ for any mercy, two things discourage us:—*First*, Sense of *our own follies* and infirmities "Surely such imperfect prayers as ours cannot speed." *Secondly*, Sense of *our Lord's frowns and rebukes*. Afflictions are continued, deliverances delayed, and God seems angry at our prayers. This was the case of the mother of our Lord here, and yet she encourages herself with hope that he will at length give in an answer of peace, to teach us to wrestle with God by faith and fervency in prayer, even when he seems in his providence to walk contrary to us. We must *against hope believe in hope*, Rom. iv. 18. [3.] She directed the servants to have an eye *to him* immediately, and not to make their applications to her, as it is probable *they had done*. She quits all pretensions to an *influence* upon him, or *intercession* with him; let their souls *wait only* on him, Ps. lxii. 5. [4.] She directed them punctually to observe his orders, without disputing, or asking questions. Being conscious to herself of a fault in *prescribing* to him, she cautions the servants to take heed of the same fault, and to attend both his time and his way for supply: "*Whatsoever he saith unto you, do it,* though you may think it ever so improper. If he saith, Give the guests water, when they call for wine, do it. If he saith, Pour out from the bottoms of the vessels that are spent, do it. He can make a few drops of wine multiply to so many draughts." Note, Those that expect Christ's *favours* must with an implicit obedience observe his *orders.* The way of duty is the way to mercy; and Christ's methods must not be objected against.

(4.) Christ did at length miraculously supply them; for he is often better than his word, but never worse.

[1.] The miracle itself was *turning water into wine;* the substance of water acquiring a new form, and having all the accidents and qualities of wine. Such a *transformation* is a *miracle;* but the popish *transubstantiation,* the substance changed, the accidents remaining the same, is a monster. By this Christ showed himself to be the God of nature, who maketh the earth to bring forth wine, Ps. civ. 14, 15. The extracting of the blood of the grape every year from the moisture of the earth is no less a work of power, though, being according to the common law of nature, it is not such a work of wonder, as this. The beginning of Moses's miracles was turning water into blood (Exod. iv. 9; vii. 20), the beginning of Christ's miracles was turning water into wine; which intimates the difference between the law of Moses and the gospel of Christ. The curse of the law turns water into blood, common comforts into bitterness and terror; the blessing of the gospel turns water into wine. Christ hereby showed that his errand into the world was to heighten and improve creature-comforts to all believers, and make them comforts indeed. Shiloh is said to *wash his garments in wine* (Gen. xlix. 11), the water for washing being *turned into wine.* And the gospel call is, *Come ye to the waters, and buy wine,* Isa. lv. 1.

[2.] The circumstances of it magnified it and freed it from all suspicion of cheat or collusion; for,

First, It was done in water-pots (*v.* 6): *There were set there six water-pots of stone.* Observe, 1. For what use these water-pots were intended: for the legal purifications from ceremonial pollutions enjoined by the law of God, and many more by the tradition of the elders. The *Jews eat not, except they wash often* (Mark vii. 3), and they used much water in their washing, for which reason here were six large water-pots provided. It was a saying among them, *Qui multâ utitur aquâ in lavando, multas consequetur in hoc mundo divitias—He who uses much water in washing will gain much wealth in this world.* 2. To what use Christ put them, quite different from what they were intended for; to be the receptacles of the miraculous wine. Thus Christ came to bring in the grace of the gospel, which is as *wine,* that cheereth God and man (Judg. ix. 13), instead of the shadows of the law, which were as water, *weak and beggarly elements.* These were *water-pots,* that had never been used to have wine in them; and of *stone,* which is not apt to retain the scent of former liquors, if ever they had had wine in them. They contained *two or three firkins apiece;* two or three *measures, baths,* or *ephahs;* the quantity is uncertain, but very considerable. We may be sure that it was not intended to be all drank at this feast, but for a further kindness to the new-married couple, as the multiplied oil was to the poor widow, out of which she might *pay her debt,* and *live of the rest,* 2 Kings iv. 7. Christ gives like himself, gives abundantly, according to his riches in glory. It is the penman's language to say, *They contained two or three firkins,* for the Holy Spirit could have ascertained just how much; thus (as *ch.* vi. 19) teaching us to speak cautiously, and not confidently, of those things of which we have not good assurance.

Secondly, The water-pots were filled *up to the brim* by the servants at Christ's word, *v.* 7. As Moses, the servant of the Lord, when God bade him, went to the rock, to draw water; so these servants, when Christ bade them, went to the water, to fetch wine. Note, Since no difficulties can be opposed to the arm of God's power, no improbabilities are to be objected against the word of his command.

Thirdly, The miracle was wrought suddenly, and in such a manner as greatly magnified it.

a. As soon as they had filled the water-pots, presently he said, *Draw out now* (*v.* 8), and it was done, (*a.*) Without any ceremony, in the eye of the spectators. One would have thought, as Naaman, he should have come out, and *stood,* and *called on the name of God,* 2 Kings v. 11. No, he sits still in his place, says not a word, but *wills* the thing, and so works it. Note, Christ does great things and marvellous *without noise,* works manifest changes in a hidden way. Sometimes Christ, in working miracles, used words and signs, but it was *for their sakes that stood by, ch.* xi. 42. (*b.*) Without any hesitation or uncertainty in his own breast. He did not say, *Draw out now,* and let me *taste it,* questioning whether the thing were done as he willed it or no; but with the greatest assurance imaginable, though it was his *first miracle,* he recommends it to the master of the feast *first.* As he knew what he *would* do, so he knew what he *could* do, and made no essay in his work; but all was good, very good, even in the beginning.

b. Our Lord Jesus directed the servants, (*a.*) *To draw it out;* not to let it alone in the vessel, to be admired, but to *draw it out,* to be drank. Note, [*a.*] Christ's works are all *for use;* he gives no man a talent to be *buried,* but to be *traded with.* Has he turned thy water into wine, given thee knowledge and grace? It is to *profit withal;* and therefore *draw out now.* [*b.*] Those that would know Christ must make trial of him, must attend upon him in the use of ordinary means, and then may expect extraordinary influence. That which is *laid up* for all that *fear God* is *wrought for those that trust in him* (Ps. xxxi. 19), that by the exercise of faith *draw out* what is *laid up.* (*b.*) To present it to *the governor of the feast.* Some think that this *governor of the feast* was only the chief guest, that sat at the upper end of the table; but, if so, surely our Lord Jesus should have had that place, for he was, upon all accounts, the principal guest; but it seems another had the uppermost room, probably one that *loved* it (Matt. xxiii. 6), and *chose* it, Luke xiv. 7. And Christ, according to his own rule, *sat down in the lowest room;* but, though he was not treated as the Master of the feast, he kindly approved himself a friend to the feast, and, if not its founder, yet its best benefactor. Others think that this *governor* was the inspector and monitor of the feast: the same with Plutarch's *symposiarcha,* whose office it was to see that each had enough, and none did exceed, and that there were no indecencies or disorders. Note, Feasts have need of governors, because too many, when they are at feasts, have not the government of themselves. Some think that this *governor* was the *chaplain,* some priest or Levite that craved a blessing and gave thanks, and Christ would have the cup brought to him, that he might bless it, and bless God for it; for the extraordinary tokens of Christ's presence and power were not to supersede, or jostle out, the ordinary rules and methods of piety and devotion.

Fourthly, The wine which was thus miraculously provided was of the best and richest kind, which was acknowledged by the governor of the feast; and that it was really so, and not his fancy, is certain, because he knew not whence it was, *v.* 9, 10. 1. It was certain that this was *wine.* The governor knew this when he drank it, though he knew not *whence it was;* the servants knew whence it was, but had not yet tasted it. If the taster had seen the drawing of it, or the drawers had had the tasting of it, something might have been imputed to fancy; but now no room is left for suspicion. 2. That it was the best wine. Note, Christ's works commend themselves even to those that know not their author. The products of miracles were always the best in their kind. This wine had a *stronger body,* and *better flavour,* than ordinary. This the governor of the feast takes notice of to the bridegroom, with an air of pleasantness, as *uncommon.* (1.) The common method was otherwise. Good wine is brought out to the best advantage at the beginning of a feast, when the guests have their heads clear and their appetites fresh, and can relish it, and will commend it; but *when they have well drank,* when their heads are confused, and their appetites palled, good wine is but thrown away upon them, worse will serve then. See the vanity of all the pleasures of sense; they soon surfeit, but never satisfy; the longer they are enjoyed, the less pleasant they grow. (2.) This bridegroom obliged his friends with a reserve of the best wine for the grace-cup: *Thou hast kept the good wine until now;* not knowing to whom they were indebted for this good wine, he returns the thanks of the table to the bridegroom. *She did not know that I gave her corn and wine,* Hos. ii. 8. Now, [1.] Christ, in providing thus plentifully for the guests, though he hereby allows a sober cheerful use of wine, especially in times of rejoicing (Neh. viii. 10), yet he does not invalidate his own caution, nor invade it, in the least, which is, that our hearts be not *at any time,* no not at a marriage feast, *overcharged with surfeiting and drunkenness,* Luke xxi. 34. When Christ provided so much *good wine* for them that had *well drunk,* he intended to try their sobriety, and to teach them *how to abound,* as well as *how to want.* Temperance *per force* is a thankless virtue; but if divine providence gives us abundance of the delights of sense, and divine grace enables us to use them moderately, this is self-denial that is praiseworthy. He also intended that some should be left for the confirmation of the truth of the miracle to the faith of others. And we have reason to think that the guests at this table were so well *taught,* or at least were now so well awed by the presence of Christ, that none of them abused this wine to excess. These two considerations, drawn from this story, may be sufficient at any time to fortify us against temptations to intemperance: *First,* That our meat and drink are the *gifts of God's bounty* to us, and we owe our liberty to use them, and our comfort in the use of them, to the mediation of Christ; it is therefore ungrateful and impious to abuse them. *Secondly,* That, wherever we are, Christ has his eye upon us; we should *eat bread before God* (Exod. xviii. 12), and then we should not *feed ourselves without fear.* [2.] He has given us a specimen of the method he takes in dealing with those that deal with him, which is, to reserve the *best* for the *last,* and therefore they must *deal upon trust.* The recompence of their services and sufferings is reserved for the other world; it is a glory *to be revealed.* The pleasures of sin give their colour in the cup, but *at the last bite;* but the pleasures of religion will be *pleasures for evermore.*

III. In the conclusion of this story (*v.* 11) we are told, 1. That this was *the beginning of miracles* which Jesus did. Many miracles had been wrought *concerning* him at his birth and baptism, and he himself was the greatest miracle of all; but this was the first that was wrought *by* him. He could have wrought miracles when he disputed with the doctors, but his hour was not come. He had power, but there was a *time of the hiding of his power*. 2. That herein he *manifested his glory;* hereby he proved himself to be the Son of God, and his glory to be that of the only-begotten of the Father. He also discovered the nature and end of his office; the power of a God, and the grace of a Saviour, appearing in all his miracles, and particularly in this, manifested the glory of the long-expected Messiah. 3. That *his disciples believed on him.* Those whom he had called (*ch.* i.), who had seen no miracle, and yet followed him, now saw this, shared in it, and had their faith strengthened by it. Note, (1.) Even the faith that is true is at first but weak. The strongest men were once babes, so were the strongest Christians. (2.) The manifesting of the glory of Christ is the great confirmation of the faith of Christians.

12 After this he went down to
Capernaum, he, and his mother, and
his brethren, and his disciples: and
they continued there not many days.
13 And the Jews' passover was at
hand, and Jesus went up to Jerusalem, 14 And found in the temple
those that sold oxen and sheep and
doves, and the changers of money
sitting: 15 And when he had made
a scourge of small cords, he drove
them all out of the temple, and the
sheep, and the oxen; and poured out
the changers' money, and overthrew
the tables; 16 And said unto them that
sold doves, Take these things hence;
make not my Father's house a house
of merchandise. 17 And his disciples
remembered that it was written, The
zeal of thine house hath eaten me up.
18 Then answered the Jews and said
unto him, What sign showest thou
unto us, seeing that thou doest these
things? 19 Jesus answered and
said unto them, Destroy this temple,
and in three days I will raise it up.
20 Then said the Jews, Forty and
six years was this temple in building,
and wilt thou rear it up in three
days? 21 But he spake of the
temple of his body. 22 When therefore he was risen from the dead, his
disciples remembered that he had
said this unto them; and they believed the scripture, and the word
which Jesus had said.

Here we have,

I. The short visit Christ made to Capernaum, *v.* 12. It was a large and populous city, about a day's journey from Cana; it is called *his own city* (Matt. ix. 1), because he made it his head-quarters in Galilee, and what little rest he had was there. It was a place of concourse, and *therefore* Christ chose it, that the fame of his doctrine and miracles might thence spread the further. Observe,

1. The company that attended him thither: *his mother, his brethren, and his disciples.* Wherever Christ went, (1.) He *would not* go alone, but would take those with him who had put themselves under his guidance, that he might instruct them, and that they might attest his miracles. (2.) He *could not* go alone, but they would follow him, because they liked the sweetness either of his doctrine or of his wine, *ch.* vi. 26. His mother, though he had lately given her to understand that in the works of his ministry he should pay no more respect to her than to any other person, yet followed him; not to intercede with him, but to learn of him. His *brethren* also and relations, who were at the marriage and were wrought upon by the miracle there, and *his disciples,* who attended him wherever he went. It should seem, people were more affected with Christ's miracles at first than they were afterwards, when custom made them seem less strange.

2. His continuance there, which was at this time *not many days,* designing now only to *begin* the acquaintance he would afterwards *improve* there. Christ was still upon the remove, would not confine his usefulness to *one* place, because *many* needed him. And he would teach his followers to look upon themselves but as *sojourners* in this world, and his ministers to follow their opportunities, and go where their work led them. We do not now find Christ in the synagogues, but he privately instructed his friends, and thus entered upon his work *by degrees.* It is good for young ministers to accustom themselves to pious and edifying discourse in private, that they may with the better preparation, and greater awe, approach their public work. He did not stay long at Capernaum, because the passover was at hand, and he must attend it at Jerusalem; for every thing is beautiful in its season. The less good must give way to the greater, and all the dwellings of Jacob must give place to the gates of Zion.

II. The passover he kept at Jerusalem; it is the *first* after his baptism, and the evangelist takes notice of all the passovers he kept henceforward, which were four in all, the *fourth* that at which he suffered (three years after this), and half a year was now past since his baptism. Christ, being *made under the law,* observed the passover at Jerusalem; see Exod. xxiii. 17. Thus he taught us by his example a strict observance of divine institutions, and a diligent attendance on religious assemblies. He went up to Jerusalem when *the passover was at hand,* that he might be there *with the first.* It is called *the Jews' passover,* because it was peculiar to them (Christ is *our* Passover); now shortly God will no longer own it for his. Christ kept the passover at Jerusalem yearly, ever since he was twelve years old, in obedience to the law; but now that he has entered upon his public ministry we may expect something more from him than before; and two things we are here told he did there:—

1. He *purged the temple, v.* 14—17. Observe here,

(1.) The first place we find him in at Jerusalem was the *temple,* and, it should seem, he did not make any public appearance till he came thither; for his presence and preaching there were that glory of the latter house which was to *exceed the glory of the former,* Hag. ii. 9. It was foretold (Mal. iii. 1): *I will send my messenger,* John Baptist; he never preached in the temple, but *the Lord, whom ye seek,* he shall *suddenly come to his temple,* suddenly after the appearing of John Baptist; so that this was the time, and the temple the place, when, and where, the Messiah was to be expected.

(2.) The first work we find him at in the temple was the *purging* of it; for so it was foretold there (Mal. iii. 2, 3): *He shall sit as a refiner and purify the sons of Levi.* Now was come the *time of reformation.* Christ came to be the great reformer; and, according to the method of the reforming kings of Judah, he first *purged out* what was amiss (and that used to be passover-work too, as in Hezekiah's time, 2 Chron. xxx. 14, 15, and Josiah's, 2 Kings xxiii. 4, &c.), and then taught them to do well. First *purge out the old leaven,* and then *keep the feast.* Christ's design in coming into the world was to reform the world; and he expects that all who come to him should reform their hearts and lives, Gen. xxxv. 2. And this he has taught us by purging the temple. See here,

[1.] What were the corruptions that were to be purged out. He found a market in one of the courts of the temple, that which was called the *court of the Gentiles,* within the *mountain of that house.* There, *First,* They sold *oxen, and sheep, and doves,* for sacrifice; we will suppose, not for common use, but for the convenience of those who came out of the country, and could not bring their sacrifices *in kind* along with them; see Deut. xiv. 24—26. This *market* perhaps had been kept by the pool of Bethesda (*ch.* v. 2), but was admitted into the temple by the chief priests, for filthy lucre; for, no doubt, the rents for standing there, and fees for searching the beasts sold there, and certifying that they were *without blemish,* would be a considerable revenue to them. Great corruptions in the church owe their rise to the love of money, 1 Tim. vi. 5, 10. *Secondly,* They *changed money,* for the convenience of those that were to pay a half-shekel *in specie* every year, by way of poll, for the service of the tabernacle (Exod. xxx. 12), and no doubt they got by it.

[2.] What course our Lord took to purge out those corruptions. He had seen these in the temple formerly, when he was in a private station; but never went about to drive them out till now, when he had taken upon him the public character of a prophet. He did not complain to the chief priests, for he knew they countenanced those corruptions. But he himself,

First, Drove out the sheep and oxen, and those that *sold them,* out of the temple. He never used *force* to drive any *into* the temple, but only to drive those out that profaned it. He did not seize the sheep and oxen for himself, did not *distrain* and impound them, though he found them *damage faissant—actual trespassers* upon his Father's ground; he only drove them out, and their owners with them. He made a scourge of *small cords,* which probably they had led their sheep and oxen with, and thrown them away upon the ground, whence Christ gathered them. Sinners prepare the scourges with which they themselves will be driven out from the temple of the Lord. He did not make a scourge to chastise the offenders (his punishments are of another nature), but only to drive out the cattle; he aimed no further than at reformation. See Rom. xiii. 3, 4; 2 Cor. x. 8.

Secondly, He *poured out the changers' money,* τὸ κέρμα*—the small money—*the *Nummorum Famulus.* In *pouring out* the money, he showed his contempt of it; he threw it to the ground, to the earth as it *was.* In *overthrowing* the tables, he showed his displeasure against those that make religion a matter of worldly gain. Money-changers in the temple are the scandal of it. Note, In reformation, it is good to make thorough work; he *drove them all out;* and not only threw out the money, but, in overturning the tables, threw out the trade too.

Thirdly, He said to them that sold doves (sacrifices for the poor), *Take these things hence.* The doves, though they took up less room, and were a less nuisance than the oxen and sheep, yet must not be allowed there. The sparrows and swallows were welcome, that were left to God's providence (Ps. lxxxiv. 3), but not the doves, that were appropriated to man's profit. God's temple must not be made a pigeon-house. But see Christ's prudence in his zeal. When he drove out the sheep and oxen, the owners might follow them; when he poured out the money, they might gather it up again; but, if he had turned the doves flying, perhaps they could not have been retrieved; therefore to them that sold doves he said, *Take these things hence.* Note, Discretion must always guide and govern our zeal, that we do nothing unbecoming ourselves, or mischievous to others.

Fourthly, He gave them a good reason for what he did: *Make not my Father's house a house of merchandise.* Reason for conviction should accompany force for correction.

a. Here is a reason why they should not profane the temple, because it was the *house of God,* and not to be made a house of merchandise. Merchandise is a good thing in the exchange, but not in the temple. This was, (*a.*) to *alienate* that which was dedicated to the honour of God; it was *sacrilege;* it was robbing God. (*b.*) It was to debase that which was solemn and awful, and to make it mean. (*c.*) It was to disturb and distract those services in which men ought to be most solemn, serious, and intent. It was particularly an affront to the *sons of the stranger* in their worship to be forced to herd themselves with the sheep and oxen, and to be distracted in their worship by the noise of a market, for this market was kept in the court of the Gentiles. (*d.*) It was to make the business of religion subservient to a secular interest; for the holiness of the place must advance the market, and promote the sale of their commodities. Those make God's house a house of merchandise, [*a.*] Whose minds are filled with cares about worldly business when they are attending on religious exercises, as those, Amos viii. 5; Ezek. xxxiii. 31. [*b.*] Who perform divine offices for filthy lucre, and sell the gifts of the Holy Ghost, Acts viii. 18.

b. Here is a reason why he was concerned to purge it, because it *was his Father's house.* And, (*a.*) Therefore he had authority to purge it, for he was faithful, as a Son *over his own house.* Heb iii. 5, 6. In calling God his Father, he intimates that he was the Messiah, of whom it was said, *He shall build a house for my name, and I will be his Father,* 2 Sam. vii. 13, 14. (*b.*) Therefore he had a zeal for the purging of it: "It is *my Father's house,* and therefore I cannot bear to see it profaned, and *him* dishonoured." Note, If God be our Father in heaven, and it be therefore our desire that his name may be sanctified, it cannot but be our grief to see it polluted. Christ's purging the temple thus may justly be reckoned among his *wonderful works. Inter omnia signa quæ fecit Dominus, hoc mihi videtur esse mirabilius—Of all Christ's wonderful works this appears to me the most wonderful.*—Hieron. Considering, [*a.*] That he did it without the *assistance* of any of his *friends;* probably it had been no hard matter to have raised the *mob,* who had a great veneration for the temple, against these profaners of it; but Christ never countenanced any thing that was tumultuous or disorderly. There was none to *uphold,* but his own arm did it. [*b.*] That he did it without the *resistance* of any of his *enemies,* either the market-people themselves, or the chief priests that gave them their licences, and had the *posse templi—temple force,* at their command. But the corruption was too plain to be justified; sinners' own consciences are reformers' best friends; yet that was not all, there was a divine power put forth herein, a power over the spirits of men; and in this non-resistance of theirs that scripture was fulfilled (Mal. iii. 2, 3), *Who shall stand when he appeareth?*

Fifthly, Here is the remark which his disciples made upon it (*v.* 17): *They remembered that it was written, The zeal of thine house hath eaten me up.* They were somewhat surprised at first to see him to whom they were directed as the *Lamb of God* in such a heat, and him whom they believed to be the *King of Israel* take so little state upon him as to do this himself; but one scripture came to their thoughts, which taught them to reconcile this action both with the meekness of the *Lamb of God* and with the majesty of the *King of Israel;* for David, speaking of the Messiah, takes notice of his *zeal for God's house,* as so great that it even *ate him up,* it made him forget himself, Ps. lxix. 9. Observe, 1. The disciples came to understand the meaning of what Christ did, by remembering the scriptures: *They remembered* now *that it was written.* Note, The word of God and the works of God do mutually explain and illustrate each other. Dark scriptures are expounded by their accomplishment in providence, and difficult providences are made easy by comparing them with the scriptures. See of what great use it is to the disciples of Christ to be *ready* and *mighty* in the scriptures, and to have their memories well stored with scripture truths, by which they will be *furnished for every good work,* 2. The scripture they remembered was very apposite: *The zeal of thine house hath eaten me up.* David was in this a type of Christ that he was *zealous for God's house,* Ps. cxxxii. 2, 3. What he did for it was *with all his might;* see 1 Chron xxix. 2. The latter part of that verse (Ps. lxix. 9) is applied to Christ (Rom. xv. 3), as the former part of it here. All the graces that were to be found among the Old-Testament saints were eminently in Christ, and particularly this of zeal for the house of God, and in them, as they were patterns to us, so they were types of him. Observe, (1.) Jesus Christ was zealously affected to the house of God, his church: he loved it, and was always jealous for its honour and welfare. (2.) This zeal did even *eat him up;* it made him *humble* himself, and *spend* himself, and *expose* himself. *My zeal has consumed me,* Ps. cxix. 139. Zeal for the house of God forbids us to consult our own credit, ease, and safety, when they come in competition with our duty and Christ's service, and sometimes carries on our souls in our duty so far and so fast that our bodies cannot keep pace with them, and makes us as deaf as our Master was to those who suggested, *Spare thyself.*

The grievances here redressed might seem but small, and such as should have been connived at; but such was Christ's zeal that he could not bear even *those* that *sold and bought in the temple. Si ibi ebrios inveniret quid faceret Dominus!* (saith St. Austin.) *If he had found drunkards in the temple, how much more would he have been displeased!*

2. Christ, having thus purged the temple, gave a sign to those who demanded it to prove his authority for so doing. Observe here,

(1.) Their demand of a sign: *Then answered the Jews,* that is the multitude of the people, with their leaders. Being Jews, they should rather have stood by him, and assisted him to vindicate the honour of their temple; but, instead of this, they objected against it. Note, Those who apply themselves in good earnest to the work of reformation must expect to meet with opposition. When they could object nothing against the thing itself, they questioned his authority to do it: "*What sign showest thou unto us,* to prove thyself authorized and commissioned to do these things?" It was indeed a good work to purge the temple; but what had he to do to undertake it, who was in no office there? They looked upon it as an act of jurisdiction, and that he must prove himself *a prophet, yea, more than a prophet.* But was not the thing itself sign enough? His ability to drive so many from their posts, without opposition, was a proof of his authority; he that was armed with such a divine power was surely armed with a divine commission. *What ailed these* buyers and sellers, *that they fled, that they were driven back?* Surely it was *at the presence of the Lord* (Ps. cxiv. 5, 7), no less a presence.

(2.) Christ's answer to this demand, *v.* 19. He did not immediately work a miracle to convince them, but gave them a sign in something *to come,* the truth of which must appear by the event, according to Deut. xviii. 21, 22.

Now, [1.] The sign that he gives them is his own *death* and *resurrection.* He refers them to that which would be, *First,* His *last* sign. If they would not be convinced by what they saw and heard, let them *wait. Secondly,* The *great sign* to prove him to be the Messiah; for concerning him it was foretold that he should be bruised (Isa. liii. 5), *cut off* (Dan. ix. 26), and yet that he should not see corruption, Ps. xvi. 10. These things were fulfilled in the blessed Jesus, and therefore *truly he was the Son of God,* and had authority in the temple, his Father's house.

[2.] He foretels his death and resurrection, not in plain terms, as he often did to his disciples, but in figurative expressions; as afterwards, when he gave this for a sign, he called it the *sign of the prophet Jonas,* so here, *Destroy this temple, and in three days I will raise it up.* Thus he spoke in parables to those who were willingly ignorant, that *they might not perceive,* Matt. xiii. 13, 14. Those that will not see shall not see. Nay, this figurative speech used here proved such a *stumbling-block* to them that it was produced in evidence against him at his trial to prove him a blasphemer. Matt. xxvi. 60, 61. Had they humbly asked him the meaning of what he said, he would have told them, and it had been a savour of life unto life to them, but they were resolved to cavil, and it proved a savour of death unto death. They that would not be convinced were hardened, and the manner of expressing this prediction occasioned the accomplishment of the prediction itself. *First,* He foretels his death by the Jews' malice, in these words, *Destroy you this temple;* that is, "You will destroy it, I know you will. I will permit you to destroy it." Note, Christ, even at the beginning of his ministry, had a clear foresight of all his sufferings at the end of it, and yet went on cheerfully in it. It is good, at *setting out,* to expect the *worst. Secondly,* He foretels his resurrection by his own power: In *three days I will raise it up.* There were others that *were raised,* but Christ raised himself, resumed his own life.

[3.] He chose to express this by *destroying* and *re-edifying* the temple, *First,* Because he was now to justify himself in purging the temple, which they had profaned; as if he had said, "You that defile one temple will destroy another; and I will prove my authority to *purge* what you have *defiled* by *raising* what you will *destroy.*" The profaning of the temple is the *destroying* of it, and its reformation its *resurrection. Secondly,* Because the death of Christ was indeed the destruction of the Jewish temple, the procuring cause of it; and his resurrection was the raising up of another temple, the gospel church, Zech. vi. 12. The ruins of their place and *nation* (*ch.* xi. 48) were the riches of the world. See Amos ix. 11; Acts xv. 16.

(3.) Their cavil at this answer: "*Forty and six years was this temple in building, v.* 20. Temple work was always slow work, and canst thou make such quick work of it?" Now here, [1.] They show *some knowledge;* they could tell how long the temple was in building. Dr. Lightfoot computes that it was just forty-six years from the founding of Zerubbabel's temple, in the second year of Cyrus, to the complete settlement of the temple service, in the 32d year of Artaxerxes; and the same from Herod's beginning to build this temple, in the 18th year of his reign, to this very time, when the Jews said that this was just forty-six years: ᾠκοδομήθη—*hath this temple been built.* [2.] They show *more ignorance, First,* Of the *meaning of Christ's words.* Note, Men often run into gross mistakes by understanding that literally which the scripture speaks figuratively. What abundance of mischief has been done by interpreting, *This is my body,* after a corporal and carnal manner! *Secondly,*

Of *the almighty power of Christ*, as if he could do no more than another man. Had they known that this was he who *built all things* in six days they would not have made it such an absurdity that he should build a temple in three days.

(4.) A vindication of Christ's answer from their cavil. The difficulty is soon solved by explaining the terms: *He spoke of the temple of his body, v.* 21. Though Christ had discovered a great respect for the temple, in *purging* it, yet he will have us know that the holiness of it, which he was so jealous for, was but *typical*, and leads us to the consideration of another temple of which that was but a shadow, the substance being Christ, Heb. ix. 9; Col. ii. 17. Some think that when he said, Destroy *this* temple, he pointed to his own body, or laid his hand upon it; however, it is certain that he *spoke of the temple of his body*. Note, The body of Christ is the true temple, of which that at Jerusalem was a type. [1.] Like the temple, it was built by immediate divine direction: "*A body hast thou prepared me*, 1 Chron. xxviii. 19. [2.] Like the temple, it was a *holy house;* it is called *that holy thing*. [3.] It was, like the temple, the habitation of God's glory; there the eternal Word dwelt, the true shechinah. He is *Emmanuel—God with us*. [4.] The temple was the place and *medium* of intercourse between God and Israel: there God revealed himself to them; there they presented themselves and their services to him. Thus by Christ God speaks to us, and we speak to him. Worshippers looked *towards* that house, 1 Kings viii. 30, 35. So we must worship God with an eye to Christ.

(5.) A reflection which the disciples made upon this, long after, inserted here, to illustrate the story (*v.* 22): *When he was risen from the dead*, some years after, *his disciples remembered that he had said this*. We found them, *v.* 17, remembering what had been *written before of him*, and here we find them remembering what they had *heard from him*. Note, The memories of Christ's disciples should be like the treasure of the good householder, furnished with things both *new* and *old*, Matt. xiii. 52. Now observe,

[1.] *When they remembered* that saying: *When he was risen from the dead*. It seems, they did not at this time fully understand Christ's meaning, for they were as yet but babes in knowledge; but they laid up the saying in their hearts, and afterwards it became both intelligible and useful. Note, It is good to *hear for the time to come*, Isa. xlii. 23. The juniors in years and profession should treasure up those truths of which at present they do not well understand either the meaning or the use, for they will be serviceable to them hereafter, when they come to greater proficiency. It was said of the scholars of Pythagoras that his precepts seemed to freeze in them till they were forty years old, and then they began to thaw; so this saying of Christ revived in the memories of his disciples *when he was risen from the dead;* and why then? *First*, Because *then* the Spirit was poured out to bring things to their remembrance which Christ had said to them, and to make them both *easy* and *ready* to them, *ch.* xiv. 26. That very day that Christ rose from the dead he *opened their understandings*, Luke xxiv. 45. *Secondly*, Because then this saying of Christ was fulfilled. When the temple of his body had been *destroyed* and was *raised again*, and that upon the *third day*, then they remembered this among other words which Christ had said to this purport. Note, It contributes much to the understanding of the scripture to observe the fulfilling of the scripture. The event will expound the prophecy.

[2.] What use they made of it: *They believed the scripture, and the word that Jesus had said;* their belief of these was confirmed and received fresh support and vigour. They were slow of heart to believe (Luke xxiv. 25), but they were *sure*. The *scripture* and the *word of Christ* are here put together, not because they concur and exactly agree together, but because they mutually illustrate and strengthen each other. When the disciples saw both what they had read in the Old Testament, and what they had heard from Christ's own mouth, fulfilled in his death and resurrection, they were the more confirmed in their belief of both.

23 Now when he was in Jerusa-
lem at the passover, in the feast *day*,
many believed in his name, when
they saw the miracles which he did.
24 But Jesus did not commit himself
unto them, because he knew all *men*,
25 And needed not that any should
testify of man: for he knew what was
in man.

We have here an account of the success, the poor success, of Christ's preaching and miracles at Jerusalem, while he kept the passover there. Observe,

I. That our Lord Jesus, when he was at Jerusalem at the passover, did preach and work miracles. People's *believing on him* implied that he preached; and it is expressly said, *They saw the miracles he did*. He was now in Jerusalem, the holy city, whence the *word of the Lord* was to go *forth*. His residence was mostly in Galilee, and therefore when he was *in Jerusalem* he was very busy. The time was holy time, *the feast-day*, time appointed for the service of God; at the passover the *Levites taught the good knowledge of the Lord* (2 Chron. xxx. 22), and Christ took that opportunity of preaching, when the concourse of people was great, and thus he would own and honour the divine institution of the passover.

II. That hereby many were brought to *believe in his name*, to acknowledge him a *teacher come from God,* as Nicodemus did (*ch.* iii 2), a great prophet; and, probably, some of those who *looked for redemption in Jerusalem* believed him to be the Messiah promised, so ready were they to welcome the first appearance of that *bright and morning star.*

III. That yet *Jesus did not commit himself unto them* (v. 24): *οὐκ ἐπίστευεν ἑαυτὸν αὐτοῖς—He did not trust himself with them.* It is the same word that is used for *believing* in him. So that to believe in Christ is to *commit ourselves* to him and to his guidance. Christ did not see cause to repose any confidence in these new converts at Jerusalem, where he had many enemies that sought to destroy him, either, 1. Because they were *false,* at least some of them, and would betray him if they had an opportunity, or were strongly tempted to do so. He had more disciples that he could trust among the Galileans than among the dwellers at Jerusalem. In dangerous times and places, it is wisdom to take heed in whom you confide; *μέμνησο ἀπιστεῖν—learn to distrust.* Or, 2. Because they were *weak,* and I would hope that this was the worst of it; not that they were *treacherous* and designed him a mischief, but, (1.) They were *timorous,* and wanted zeal and courage, and might perhaps be frightened to do a wrong thing. In times of difficulty and danger, cowards are not fit to be trusted. Or, (2.) They were *tumultuous,* and wanted discretion and management. These in Jerusalem perhaps had their expectations of the *temporal* reign of the Messiah more raised than others, and, in that expectation, would be ready to give some bold strokes at the government if Christ would have *committed himself to them* and put himself at the head of them; but he would not, for his kingdom is not of this world. We should be shy of turbulent unquiet people, as our Master here was, though they profess to *believe in Christ,* as these did.

IV. That the reason why he did not *commit himself* to them was because he *knew* them (*v.* 25), knew the wickedness of some and the weakness of others. The evangelist takes this occasion to assert Christ's omniscience. 1. He *knew all men,* not only their names and faces, as it is possible for us to know many, but their nature, dispositions, affections, designs, as we do not know *any man,* scarcely *ourselves.* He knows *all men,* for his powerful hand made them all, his piercing eye sees them all, sees into them. He knows his *subtle enemies,* and all their secret projects; his *false friends,* and their true characters; what they really are, whatever they pretend to be. He knows them that are truly his, knows their integrity, and knows their infirmity too. He *knows their frame.* 2. He *needed not that any should testify of man.* His knowledge was not by information from others, but by his own infallible intuition. It is the infelicity of earthly princes that they must see with other men's eyes, and hear with other men's ears, and take things as they are represented to them; but Christ goes purely upon his own knowledge. Angels are his messengers, but not his spies, for *his own eyes run to and fro through the earth,* 2 Chron. xvi. 9. This may comfort us in reference to Satan's accusations, that Christ will not take men's characters from him. 3. He *knew what was in man;* in particular persons, in the nature and race of man. We know what is done *by men;* Christ knows what is *in them, tries the heart and the reins.* This is the prerogative of that essential eternal Word, Heb. iv. 12, 13. We invade his prerogative if we presume to judge men's hearts. How fit is Christ to be the *Saviour of men,* very fit to be the physician, who has such a perfect knowledge of the patient's state and case, temper and distemper; knows what is in him! How fit also to be the *Judge of all!* For the judgment of him who knows *all men,* all *in* men, must needs be *according to truth.*

Now this is all the success of Christ's preaching and miracles at Jerusalem, in this journey. The Lord comes to his temple, and none come to him but a parcel of weak simple people, that he can neither have *credit* from nor put *confidence* in; yet he shall at length *see of the travail of his soul.*

CHAP. III.

In this chapter we have, I. Christ's discourse with Nicodemus, a Pharisee, concerning the great mysteries of the gospel, in which he here privately instructs him, ver. 1—21. II. John Baptist's discourse with his disciples concerning Christ, upon occasion of his coming into the neighbourhood where John was (ver. 22—36), in which he fairly and faithfully resigns all his honour and interest to him.

THERE was a man of the Pharisees, named Nicodemus, a ruler
of the Jews: 2 The same came to
Jesus by night, and said unto him,
Rabbi, we know that thou art a teacher
come from God: for no man can do
these miracles that thou doest, except
God be with him. 3 Jesus answered
and said unto him, Verily, verily, I
say unto thee, Except a man be born
again, he cannot see the kingdom of
God. 4 Nicodemus saith unto him,
How can a man be born when he is
old? can he enter the second time
into his mother's womb, and be born?
5 Jesus answered, Verily, verily, I
say unto thee, Except a man be born
of water and *of* the Spirit, he cannot
enter into the kingdom of God. 6
That which is born of the flesh is
flesh; and that which is born of the
Spirit is spirit. 7 Marvel not that I
said unto thee, Ye must be born
again. 8 The wind bloweth where it
listeth, and thou hearest the sound
thereof, but canst not tell whence it

cometh, and whither it goeth: so is
every one that is born of the Spirit.
9 Nicodemus answered and said unto
him, How can these things be? 10
Jesus answered and said unto him,
Art thou a master of Israel, and
knowest not these things? 11 Verily,
verily, I say unto thee, We speak
that we do know, and testify that we
have seen; and ye receive not our
witness. 12 If I have told you earthly
things, and ye believe not, how shall
ye believe, if I tell you *of* heavenly
things? 13 And no man hath ascended up to heaven, but he that
came down from heaven, *even* the Son
of man which is in heaven. 14 And
as Moses lifted up the serpent in the
wilderness, even so must the Son of
man be lifted up: 15 That whosoever
believeth in him should not perish,
but have eternal life. 16 For God
so loved the world, that he gave his
only begotten Son, that whosoever
believeth in him should not perish,
but have everlasting life. 17 For
God sent not his Son into the world
to condemn the world; but that the
world through him might be saved.
18 He that believeth on him is not
condemned: but he that believeth
not is condemned already, because he
hath not believed in the name of the
only begotten Son of God. 19 And
this is the condemnation, that light is
come into the world, and men loved
darkness rather than light, because
their deeds were evil. 20 For every
one that doeth evil hateth the light,
neither cometh to the light, lest his
deeds should be reproved. 21 But
he that doeth truth cometh to the
light, that his deeds may be made manifest, that they are wrought in God.

We found, in the close of the foregoing chapter, that few were brought to Christ at Jerusalem; yet here was *one*, a considerable one. It is worth while to go a great way for the salvation though but of *one soul.* Observe,

I. Who this Nicodemus was. Not many mighty and noble are called; yet some are, and here was one. *Not many* of the *rulers, or of the Pharisees;* yet, 1. This was a *man of the Pharisees,* bred to learning, a scholar. Let it not be said that all Christ's followers are *unlearned and ignorant men.* The principles of the Pharisees, and the peculiarities of their sect, were directly contrary to the spirit of Christianity; yet there were some in whom even those high thoughts were cast down and brought into obedience to Christ. The grace of Christ is able to subdue the greatest opposition. 2. He was a *ruler of the Jews,* a member of the great sanhedrim, a senator, a privy-counsellor, a man of authority in Jerusalem. Bad as things were, there were some rulers *well inclined,* who yet could do little good because the stream was so strong against them; they were over-ruled by the majority, and yoked with those that were corrupt, so that the good which they wished to do they could not do; yet Nicodemus continued in his place, and did what he *could,* when he could not do what he *would.*

II. His solemn address to our Lord Jesus Christ, *v.* 2. See here,

1. When he came: *He came to Jesus by night.* Observe, (1.) He made a private and particular address to Christ, and did not think it enough to hear his public discourses. He resolved to talk with him by himself, where he might be free with him. Personal converse with skilful faithful ministers about the affairs of our souls would be of great use to us, Mal. ii. 7. (2.) He made this address *by night,* which may be considered, [1.] As an act of *prudence* and *discretion.* Christ was engaged all day in *public* work, and he would not interrupt him then, nor expect his attendance then, but observed *Christ's hour,* and waited on him when he was *at leisure.* Note, Private advantages to ourselves and our own families must give way to those that are public. The greater good must be preferred before the less. Christ had many enemies, and therefore Nicodemus came to him *incognito,* lest being known to the chief priests they should be the more enraged against Christ. [2.] As an act of *zeal* and *forwardness.* Nicodemus was a man of business, and could not spare time all day to make Christ a visit, and therefore he would rather take time from the diversions of the *evening,* or the rest of the *night,* than not converse with Christ. When others were sleeping, he was getting knowledge, as David by meditation, Ps. lxiii. 6, and cxix. 148. Probably it was the very next night after he saw Christ's miracles, and he would not neglect the first opportunity of pursuing his convictions. He knew not how soon Christ might leave the town, nor what might happen betwixt that and another feast, and therefore would lose no time. In the night his converse with Christ would be more free, and less liable to disturbance. These were *Noctes Christianæ—Christian nights,* much more instructive than the *Noctes Atticæ—Attic nights.* Or, [3.] As an act of *fear* and *cowardice.* He was afraid, or ashamed, to be *seen* with Christ, and therefore came *in the night.* When religion is out *of fashion,* there are many Nicodemites, especially among the rulers, who

have a better affection to Christ and his religion than they would be known to have. But observe, *First,* Though he came by night, Christ bade him welcome, accepted his integrity, and pardoned his infirmity; he considered his *temper,* which perhaps was *timorous,* and the *temptation* he was in from his place and office; and hereby taught his ministers to become all things to all men, and to encourage good beginnings, though weak. *Paul preached privately to those of reputation,* Gal. ii. 2. *Secondly,* Though now he came *by night,* yet afterwards, when there was occasion, he owned Christ *publicly, ch.* vii. 50; xix. 39. The grace which is at first but a grain of mustard-seed may grow to be a great tree.

2. What he said. He did not come to talk with Christ about politics and state-affairs (though he was a ruler), but about the concerns of his own soul and its salvation, and, without circumlocution, comes immediately to the business; he calls Christ *Rabbi,* which signifies a *great man;* see Isa. xix. 20. *He shall send them a Saviour, and a great one;* a *Saviour and a rabbi,* so the word is. There are hopes of those who have a respect for Christ, and think and speak honourably of him. He tells Christ how far *he had attained:* We *know that thou art a teacher.* Observe, (1.) His *assertion* concerning Christ: *Thou art a teacher come from God;* not educated nor ordained by men, as other teachers, but supported with divine inspiration and divine authority. He that was to be the sovereign Ruler came first to be a *teacher;* for he would rule with reason, not with rigour, by the power of truth, not of the sword. The world lay in ignorance and mistake; the Jewish teachers were corrupt, and caused them to err: *It is time for the Lord to work.* He came a *teacher from God,* from God as the *Father of mercies,* in pity to a dark deceived world; from God as the *Father of lights* and *fountain of truth,* all the light and truth upon which we may venture our souls. (2.) His *assurance* of it: *We know,* not only *I,* but *others;* so he took it for granted, the thing being so plain and self-evident. Perhaps he knew that there were divers of the Pharisees and rulers with whom he conversed that were under the same convictions, but had not the grace to own it. Or, we may suppose that he speaks in the plural number (*We know*) because he brought with him one or more of his friends and pupils, to receive instructions from Christ, knowing them to be of common concern. "Master," saith he, "we come with a desire to be taught, to be thy scholars, for we are fully satisfied thou art a divine teacher." (3.) The ground of this assurance: *No man can do those miracles that thou doest, except God be with him.* Here, [1.] We are assured of the truth of Christ's miracles, and that they were not counterfeit. Here was Nicodemus, a judicious, sensible, inquisitive man, one that had all the *reason* and *opportunity* imaginable to examine them, so fully satisfied that they were real miracles that he was wrought upon by them to go contrary to his interest, and to the stream of those of his own rank, who were prejudiced against Christ. [2.] We are directed what inference to draw from Christ's miracles: Therefore we are to receive him as a *teacher come from God.* His miracles were his credentials. The course of nature could not be altered but by the power of the God of nature, who, we are sure, is the God of truth and goodness, and would never set his seal to a lie or a cheat.

III. The discourse between Christ and Nicodemus hereupon, or, rather, the sermon Christ preached to him; the contents of it, and that perhaps an abstract of Christ's public preaching; see *v.* 11, 12. Four things our Saviour here discourses of:—

1. Concerning the *necessity and nature of regeneration* or the *new birth, v.* 3—8. Now we must consider this,

(1.) As *pertinently answered* to Nicodemus's address. Jesus *answered, v.* 3. This answer was either, [1.] A *rebuke* of what he saw *defective* in the address of Nicodemus. It was not enough for him to admire Christ's miracles, and acknowledge his mission, but he must be *born again.* It is plain that he expected the *kingdom of heaven,* the kingdom of the Messiah now shortly to appear. He is betimes aware of the dawning of that day; and, according to the common notion of the Jews, he expects it to appear in external pomp and power. He doubts not but this Jesus, who works these miracles, is either the Messiah or his prophet, and therefore makes his court to him, compliments him, and so hopes to secure a share to himself of the advantages of that kingdom. But Christ tells him that he can have no benefit by that *change of the state,* unless there be a *change of the spirit,* of the principles and dispositions, equivalent to a new birth. Nicodemus came *by night:* "But this will not do," saith Christ. His religion must be owned before men; so Dr. Hammond. Or, [2.] A *reply* to what he saw *designed* in his address. When Nicodemus owned Christ a *teacher come from God,* one entrusted with an extraordinary revelation from heaven, he plainly intimated a desire to know what this revelation was and a readiness to receive it; and Christ declares it.

(2.) As *positively* and *vehemently* asserted by our Lord Jesus: *Verily, verily, I say unto thee. I the Amen, the Amen, say it;* so it may be read: "I the faithful and true witness." The matter is settled irreversibly that *except a man be born again he cannot see the kingdom of God.* "I say it to *thee,* though a Pharisee, though a master in Israel." Observe,

[1.] What it is that is required: to be *born again;* that is, *First,* We must *live a new life.* Birth is the beginning of life; to be *born again* is to begin anew, as those that have hitherto lived either much amiss or to little purpose. We must not think to patch up the old building, but begin from the foundation. *Secondly,* We must *have a new nature,* new principles, new affections, new aims. We must be born ἄνωθεν, which signifies both *denuo—again,* and *desuper—from above.* 1. We must be born *anew;* so the word is taken, Gal. iv. 9, and *ab initio—from the beginning,* Luke i. 3. By our *first birth* we are corrupt, shapen in sin and iniquity; we must therefore undergo a second birth; our souls must be *fashioned* and *enlivened* anew. 2. We must be born *from above,* so the word is used by the evangelist, *ch.* iii. 31; xix. 11, and I take this to be especially intended here, not excluding the other; for to be born *from above* supposes being *born again.* But this new birth has its rise *from* heaven (*ch.* i. 13) and its tendency *to* heaven: it is to be born to a *divine* and *heavenly* life, a life of communion with God and the upper world, and, in order to this, it is to partake of a *divine nature* and bear the *image of the heavenly.*

[2.] The indispensable necessity of this: "Except *a man* (any one that partakes of the human nature, and consequently of its corruptions) *be born again, he cannot see the kingdom of God,* the kingdom of the Messiah begun in *grace* and perfected in *glory.*" Except we be *born from above,* we cannot *see* this. That is, *First,* We cannot *understand* the *nature* of it. Such is the nature of things pertaining to the kingdom of God (in which Nicodemus desired to be instructed) that the soul must be re-modelled and moulded, the natural man must become a spiritual man, before he is capable of receiving and understanding them, 1 Cor. ii. 14. *Secondly,* We cannot *receive the comfort* of it, cannot expect any benefit by Christ and his gospel, nor have any part or lot in the matter. Note, Regeneration is absolutely necessary to our happiness here and hereafter. Considering what we are by nature, how corrupt and sinful,—what *God* is, in whom alone we can be happy,—and *what heaven* is, to which the perfection of our happiness is reserved,—it will appear, in the nature of the thing, that we must be *born again,* because it is impossible that we should be *happy* if we be not *holy;* see 1 Cor. vi. 11, 12.

This great truth of the necessity of regeneration being thus solemnly laid down,

a. It is objected against by Nicodemus (*v.* 4): *How can a man be born when he is old,* old as I am; γέρων ὢν—*being an old man? Can he enter the second time into his mother's womb, and be born?* Herein appears, (*a.*) His weakness in knowledge; what Christ spoke spiritually he seems to have understood after a corporal and carnal manner, as if there were no other way of regenerating and new-moulding an immortal soul than by new-framing the body, and bringing that back to the *rock out of which it was hewn,* as if there was such a connection between the soul and the body that there could be no fashioning the *heart anew* but by forming the *bones anew.* Nicodemus, as others of the Jews, valued himself, no doubt, very much on his *first birth* and its dignities and privileges,—the *place* of it, the Holy Land, perhaps the holy city,—his *parentage,* such as that which Paul could have gloried in, Phil. iii. 5. And therefore it is a great surprise to him to hear of being *born again.* Could he be better bred and born than bred and born an Israelite, or by any other birth stand fairer for a place in the kingdom of the Messiah? Indeed they looked upon a proselyted Gentile to be as one *born again* or *born anew,* but could not imagine how a Jew, a Pharisee, could ever *better himself* by being *born again;* he therefore thinks, if he must be *born again,* it must be of *her* that *bore him first.* They that are proud of their *first birth* are hardly brought to a *new birth.* (*b.*) His willingness to be taught. He does not turn his back upon Christ because of his hard saying, but ingenuously acknowledges his ignorance, which implies a desire to be better informed; and so I take this, rather than that he had such gross notions of the new birth Christ spoke of: "Lord, make me to understand this, for it is a riddle to me; I am such a fool as to know no other way for a man to be born than of his mother." When we meet with that in the things of God which is *dark,* and *hard to be understood,* we must with humility and industry continue our attendance upon the means of knowledge, till God *shall reveal even that unto us.*

b. It is opened and further explained by our Lord Jesus, *v.* 5—8. From the objection he takes occasion,

(*a.*) To repeat and confirm what he had said (*v.* 5): "*Verily, verily, I say unto thee,* the very same that I said before." Note, The word of God is not yea and nay, but yea and amen; what he hath said he will abide by, whoever saith against it; nor will he retract any of his sayings for the ignorance and mistakes of men. Though Nicodemus understood not the mystery of regeneration, yet Christ asserts the necessity of it as positively as before. Note, It is folly to think of evading the obligation of evangelical precepts, by pleading that they are unintelligible, Rom. iii. 3, 4.

(*b.*) To expound and clear what he had said concerning regeneration; for the explication of which he further shows,

[*a.*] The *author* of this blessed change, and who it is that works it. To be born again is to be *born of the Spirit, v.* 5—8. The change is not wrought by any wisdom or power of our own, but by the power and influence of the blessed Spirit of grace. It is the *sanctification of the Spirit* (1 Pet. i. 2) and *renewing of the Holy Ghost,* Tit. iii. 5. The word he works by is his inspiration, and the heart to be wrought on he has access to.

[*b.*] The *nature* of this change, and what that is which is wrought; it is *spirit, v.* 6. Those that are regenerated are made *spiritual,* and refined from the dross and dregs of sensuality. The dictates and interests of the rational and immortal soul have retrieved the dominion they ought to have over the flesh. The Pharisees placed their religion in external purity and external performances; and it would be a mighty change indeed with them, no less than a new birth, to become *spiritual.*

[*c.*] The *necessity* of this change. *First,* Christ here shows that it is necessary in the *nature of the thing,* for we are not fit to enter into the kingdom of God till we are born again: *That which is born of the flesh is flesh, v.* 6. Here is our malady, with the causes of it, which are such that it is plain there is no remedy but we must be *born again.* 1. We are here told *what we are:* We are *flesh,* not only *corporeal* but *corrupt,* Gen. vi. 3. The soul is still a spiritual substance, but so wedded to the flesh, so captivated by the will of the flesh, so in love with the delights of the flesh, so employed in making provision for the flesh, that it is justly called *flesh;* it is carnal. And what communion can there be between God, who is a *spirit,* and a soul in this condition? 2. How we *came to be so;* by being *born of the flesh.* It is a corruption that is bred *in the bone* with us, and therefore we cannot have a new nature, but we must be *born again.* The corrupt nature, which is *flesh,* takes rise from our *first birth;* and therefore the new nature, which is *spirit,* must take rise from a second birth. Nicodemus spoke of entering again into his mother's womb, and being born; but, if he could do so, to what purpose? If he were born of his mother a hundred times, that would not mend the matter, for still that *which is born of the flesh is flesh;* a clean thing cannot be brought out of an unclean. He must seek for another original, must be born of the Spirit, or he cannot become spiritual. The case is, in short, this: though man is made to consist of body and soul, yet his spiritual part had then so much the dominion over his corporeal part that he was denominated a *living soul* (Gen. ii. 7), but by indulging the appetite of the flesh, in eating forbidden fruit, he prostituted the just dominion of the soul to the tyranny of sensual lust, and became no longer a *living soul,* but flesh: *Dust thou art.* The living soul became dead and inactive; thus in *the day* he sinned he *surely died,* and so he became *earthly.* In this degenerate state, he begat a son *in his own likeness;* he transmitted the human nature, which had been entirely deposited in his hands, thus corrupted and depraved; and in the same plight it is still propagated. Corruption and sin are woven into our nature; we are *shapen in iniquity,* which makes it necessary that the nature be changed. It is not enough to put on a new coat or a new face, but we must put on the *new man,* we must be new creatures. *Secondly,* Christ makes it further necessary, by his own word: *Marvel not that I said unto thee, You must be born again, v.* 7. 1. Christ hath said it, and as he himself never did, nor ever will, unsay it, so all the world cannot gainsay it, that we *must be born* again. He who is the great *Lawgiver,* whose will is a law,—he who is the great Mediator of the new covenant, and has full power to settle the terms of our reconciliation to God and happiness in him,—he who is the great Physician of souls, knows their case, and what is necessary to their cure,—he hath said, *You must be born again.* "I said unto *thee* that which all are concerned in, You must, you all, one as well as another, *you must be born again:* not only the common people, but the rulers, the *masters in Israel.*" 2. We are not to *marvel* at it; for when we consider the holiness of the God with whom we have to do, the great design of our redemption, the depravity of our nature, and the constitution of the happiness set before us, we shall not think it strange that so much stress is laid upon this as the one thing needful, that *we must be born again.*

[*d.*] This change is illustrated by two comparisons. *First,* The regenerating work of the Spirit is compared to *water, v.* 5. To be born again is to be *born of water* and of the Spirit, that is, of the Spirit working like water, as (Matt. iii. 11) *with the Holy Ghost and with fire* means with the Holy Ghost *as* with fire. 1. That which is primarily intended here is to show that the Spirit, in sanctifying a soul, (1.) *Cleanses* and purifies it as water, takes away its filth, by which it was unfit for the kingdom of God. It is the *washing of regeneration,* Tit. iii. 5. *You are washed,* 1 Cor. vi. 11. See Ezek. xxxvi 25. (2.) Cools and refreshes it, as water does the hunted hart and the weary traveller. The Spirit is compared to water, *ch.* vii. 38, 39; Isa. xliv. 3. In the first creation, the fruits of heaven were *born of water* (Gen. i. 20), in allusion to which, perhaps, they that are born from above are said to be born of water. 2. It is probable that Christ had an eye to the ordinance of baptism, which John had used and he himself had begun to use, "You must be born again of the Spirit," which regeneration by the Spirit should be signified by washing with water, as the visible sign of that spiritual grace: not that all they, and they only, that are baptized, are saved; but without that new birth which is wrought by the Spirit, and signified by baptism, none shall be looked upon as the *protected privileged* subjects of the *kingdom of heaven.* The Jews cannot partake of the benefits of the Messiah's kingdom, they have so long looked for, unless they quit all expectations of being justified by the works of the law, and submit to the *baptism of repentance,* the great gospel duty, *for the remission of sins,* the great gospel privilege. *Secondly,* It is compared to *wind: The wind bloweth where it listeth, so is every one that is born of the Spirit, v.* 8. The same word (πνεῦμα) signifies both the wind and the Spirit. The Spirit came upon the apostles in a *rushing mighty wind* (Acts ii. 2), his *strong* influences on the hearts of sinners are compared to the *breathing of the wind* (Ezek. xxxvii. 9), and his *sweet* influences on the souls of saints to the north and south wind, Cant. iv. 16. This comparison is here used to show, 1. That the Spirit, in regeneration, works *arbitrarily,* and as a free agent. The *wind bloweth where it listeth* for us, and does not attend our order, nor is subject to our command. God *directs* it; it *fulfils his word,* Ps. cxlviii. 8. The Spirit dispenses his influences where, and when, on whom, and in what measure and degree, he pleases, *dividing to every man severally as he will,* 1 Cor. xii. 11. 2. That he works *powerfully,* and with evident effects: *Thou hearest the sound thereof;* though its causes are hidden, its effects are manifest. When the soul is brought to mourn for sin, to groan under the burden of corruption, to breathe after Christ, to cry *Abba—Father,* then we *hear the sound of the Spirit,* we find he is at work, as Acts ix. 11, *Behold he prayeth.* 3. That he works *mysteriously,* and in secret hidden ways: *Thou canst not tell whence it comes, nor whither it goes.* How it gathers and how it spends its strength is a riddle to us; so the manner and methods of the Spirit's working are a mystery. *Which way went the Spirit?* 1 Kings xxii. 24. See Eccl. xi. 5, and compare it with Ps. cxxxix. 14.

2. Here is a discourse concerning the *certainty and sublimity of gospel truths,* which Christ takes occasion for from the weakness of Nicodemus. Here is,

(1.) The objection which Nicodemus still made (*v.* 9): *How can these things be?* Christ's explication of the doctrine of the necessity of regeneration, it should seem, made it never the clearer to him. The corruption of nature which makes it *necessary,* and the way of the Spirit which makes it *practicable,* are as much mysteries to him as the thing itself; though he had in general owned Christ a divine teacher, yet he was unwilling to receive his teachings when they did not agree with the notions he had imbibed. Thus many profess to admit the doctrine of Christ in general, and yet will neither believe the truths of Christianity nor submit to the laws of it further than *they please.* Christ shall be their teacher, provided they may choose their lesson. Now here, [1.] Nicodemus owns himself ignorant of Christ's meaning, after all: "*How can these things be?* They are things I do not understand, my capacity will not reach them." Thus the *things of the Spirit of God are foolishness to the natural man.* He is not only estranged from them, and therefore they are dark to him, but prejudiced against them, and therefore they are foolishness to him. [2.] Because this doctrine was *unintelligible* to him (so he was pleased to make it), he questions the truth of it; as if, because it was a *paradox* to him, it was a *chimera* in itself. Many have such an opinion of their own capacity as to think that that cannot be *proved* which they cannot *believe;* by *wisdom* they *knew not* Christ.

(2.) The reproof which Christ gave him for his dulness and ignorance: "*Art thou a master in Israel,* Διδάσκαλος—*a teacher,* a tutor, one who sits in Moses's chair, and yet not only unacquainted with the doctrine of regeneration, but incapable of understanding it?" This word is a reproof, [1.] To those who undertake to teach others and yet are ignorant and unskilful in the word of righteousness themselves. [2.] To those that spend their time in learning and teaching notions and ceremonies in religion, niceties and criticisms in the scripture, and neglect that which is practical and tends to reform the heart and life. Two words in the reproof are very emphatic:—*First,* The place where his lot was cast: in *Israel,* where there was such great plenty of the means of knowledge, where divine revelation was. He might have learned this out of the Old Testament. *Secondly,* The things he was thus ignorant in: *these* things, these *necessary* things, these *great* things, these *divine* things; had he never read Ps. l. 5, 10; Ezek. xviii. 31; xxxvi. 25, 26?

(3.) Christ's discourse, hereupon, of the certainty and sublimity of gospel truths (*v.* 11—13), to show the folly of those who make strange of these things, and to recommend them to our search. Observe here,

[1.] That the truths Christ taught were very *certain* and what we may venture upon (*v.* 11): *We speak that we do know. We;* whom does he mean besides himself? Some understand it of those that bore witness to him and with him on earth, the prophets and John Baptist; they *spoke* what they *knew,* and had seen, and were themselves abundantly satisfied in: divine revelation carries its own proof along with it. Others of those that bore witness from heaven, the Father and the Holy Ghost; the Father was with him, the Spirit of the Lord was upon him; therefore he speaks in the plural number, as *ch.* xiv. 23: *We will come unto him.* Observe, *First,* That the truths of Christ are of undoubted certainty. We have all the reason in the world to be assured that the sayings of Christ are *faithful sayings,* and such as we may venture our souls upon; for he is not only a *credible* witness, who would not go about to deceive us, but a *competent* witness, who could not himself be deceived: *We testify that we have seen.* He spoke not upon hearsay, but upon the clearest evidence, and therefore with the greatest assurance. What he spoke of God, of the invisible world, of heaven and hell, of the divine will concerning us, and the counsels of peace, was what he *knew*, and *had seen*, for he was *by him as one brought up with him*, Prov. viii. 30. Whatever Christ spoke, he spoke *of his own knowledge*. *Secondly*, That the unbelief of sinners is greatly aggravated by the infallible certainty of the truths of Christ. The things are thus sure, thus clear; and yet *you receive not our witness*. Multitudes to be *unbelievers* of that which yet (so cogent are the motives of credibility) they cannot *disbelieve!*

[2.] The truths Christ taught, though communicated in language and expressions borrowed from common and earthly things, yet in their own nature were most sublime and heavenly; this is intimated, *v.* 12: "*If I have told them earthly things*, that is, have told them the great things of God in similitudes taken from earthly things, to make them the more easy and intelligible, as that of the *new birth* and the *wind*,—if I have thus accommodated myself to your capacities, and lisped to you in your own language, and cannot make you to understand my doctrine,—*what would you do* if I should accommodate myself to the nature of the things, and speak with the tongue of angels, that language which mortals cannot utter? If such *familiar expressions* be stumbling-blocks, what would *abstract ideas* be, and spiritual things painted *proper?*" Now we may learn hence, *First*, To admire the height and depth of the doctrine of Christ; it is a great mystery of godliness. The things of the gospel are *heavenly* things, out of the road of the enquiries of human reason, and much more out of the reach of its discoveries. *Secondly*, To acknowledge with thankfulness the condescension of Christ, that he is pleased to suit the manner of the gospel revelation to our capacities, *to speak to us as to children*. He considers our *frame*, that we are *of* the earth, and our *place*, that we are *on* the earth, and therefore speaks to us earthly things, and makes things sensible the vehicle of things spiritual, to make them the more easy and familiar to us. Thus he has done both in parables and in sacraments. *Thirdly*, To lament the corruption of our nature, and our great unaptness to receive and entertain the truths of Christ. Earthly things are despised because they are *vulgar*, and heavenly things because they are *abstruse;* and so, whatever method is taken, still some fault or other is found with it (Matt. xi. 17), but Wisdom is, and will be, *justified of her children*, notwithstanding.

[3.] Our Lord Jesus, and he alone, was fit to reveal to us a doctrine thus certain, thus sublime: *No man hath ascended up into heaven but he*, *v.* 13.

First, None but Christ was able to reveal to us the will of God for our salvation. Nicodemus addressed Christ as a prophet; but he must know that he is greater than all the Old-Testament prophets, for none of them *had ascended into heaven*. They wrote by divine inspiration, and not of their own knowledge; see *ch.* i. 18. Moses ascended into the mount, but not into heaven. No man hath attained to the certain knowledge of God and heavenly things as Christ has; see Matt. xi. 27. It is not for us to send to heaven for instructions; we must wait to receive what instructions Heaven will send to us; see Prov. xxx. 4; Deut. xxx. 12.

Secondly, Jesus Christ is able, and fit, and every way qualified, to reveal the will of God to us; for it is *he that came down from heaven* and *is in heaven*. He had said (*v.* 12), *How shall ye believe, if I tell you of heavenly things?* Now here, 1. He gives them an instance of those *heavenly things* which he could tell them of, when he tells them of one that *came down from heaven*, and yet is the *Son of man;* is the *Son of man*, and yet is *in heaven*. If the regeneration of the *soul of man* is such a mystery, what then is the incarnation of the *Son of God?* These are divine and heavenly things indeed. We have here an intimation of Christ's two distinct natures in one person: his divine nature, in which he *came down from heaven;* his human nature, in which he is the *Son of man;* and that union of those two, in that while he is the Son of man yet he is *in heaven*. 2. He gives them a proof of his ability to speak to them *heavenly things*, and to lead them into the arcana of the kingdom of heaven, by telling them, (1.) That *he came down from heaven*. The intercourse settled between God and man began *above;* the first motion towards it did not arise from this earth, but *came down from heaven*. We love him, and send to him, because he first loved us, and sent to us. Now this intimates, [1.] Christ's divine nature. He that came down from heaven is certainly more than a mere man; he is the *Lord from heaven*, 1 Cor. xv. 47. [2.] His intimate acquaintance with the divine counsels; for, coming from the court of heaven, he had been from eternity conversant with them. [3.] The *manifestation of God*. Under the Old Testament God's favours to his people are expressed by his *hearing from heaven* (2 Chron. vii. 14), *looking from heaven* (Ps. lxxx. 14), *speaking from heaven* (Neh. ix. 13), sending from heaven, Ps. lvii. 3. But the New Testament shows us God *coming down* from heaven, to teach and save us. That he thus *descended* is an admirable *mystery*, for the Godhead cannot change places, nor did he bring his body from heaven; but that he thus *condescended* for our redemption is a more admirable *mercy;* herein he commended his love. (2.) That *he is the Son of man, that* Son of man spoken of by Daniel (vii. 13), by which the Jews always understand to be meant the Messiah. Christ, in calling himself the *Son of man*, shows that he is the *second Adam*, for the first Adam was the *father of man*. And of all the Old-Testament titles of the Messiah he chose to make use of *this*, because it was most expressive of his *humility*, and most agreeable to his present state of *humiliation*. (3.) That he *is in heaven*. Now at this time, when he is talking with Nicodemus on earth, yet, as God, he is *in heaven*. The *Son of man*, as such, was not in heaven till his ascension; but he that was the Son of man was now, by his divine nature, every where present, and particularly in heaven. Thus the Lord of glory, as such, could not be crucified, nor could God, as such, shed his blood; yet that person who was the Lord of glory was crucified (1 Cor. ii. 8), and God purchased the church with *his own blood*, Acts xx. 28. So close is the union of the two natures in one person that there is a communication of properties. He doth not say ὀς ἐστι, but ὁ ὢν τῷ οὐρανῷ. GOD is the ὁ ὢν—*he that is*, and heaven is the habitation of *his holiness*.

3. Christ here discourses of the *great design of his own coming into the world, and the happiness of those that believe in him*, v. 14—18. Here we have the very marrow and quintessence of the whole gospel, that *faithful saying* (1 Tim. i. 15), that Jesus Christ came to seek and to save the children of men from death, and recover them to life. Now sinners are *dead men* upon a twofold account:—(1.) As one that is mortally wounded, or sick of an incurable disease, is said to be a *dead man*, for he is dying; and so Christ came to save us, by *healing* us, as the brazen serpent healed the Israelites, *v.* 14, 15. (2.) As one that is justly condemned to die for an unpardonable crime is a *dead man*, he is *dead in law;* and, in reference to this part of our danger, Christ came to save as a prince or judge, publishing an act of indemnity, or general pardon, under certain provisos; this saving here is opposed to condemning, *v.* 16—18.

[1.] Jesus Christ came to save us by *healing* us, as the children of Israel that were stung with fiery serpents were cured and *lived* by looking up to the brazen serpent; we have the story of it, Num. xxi. 6—9. It was the *last* miracle that passed through the hand of Moses before his death. Now in this type of Christ we may observe,

First, The *deadly* and *destructive* nature of *sin*, which is implied here. The guilt of sin is like the *pain* of the biting of a fiery serpent; the power of corruption is like the *venom* diffused thereby. The devil is the old serpent, subtle at first (Gen. iii. 1), but ever since *fiery*, and his temptations *fiery darts*, his assaults terrifying, his victories destroying. Ask awakened consciences, ask damned sinners, and they will tell you, how charming soever the allurements of sin are, *at the last it bites like a serpent*, Prov. xxiii. 30—32. God's wrath against us for sin is as those fiery serpents which God sent among the people, to punish them for their murmurings. The curses of the law are as fiery serpents, so are all the tokens of divine wrath.

Secondly, The powerful remedy provided against this fatal malady. The case of poor sinners is deplorable; but is it desperate? Thanks be to God, it is not; there is balm in Gilead. The *Son of man is lifted up*, as the *serpent of brass* was by Moses, which cured the stung Israelites. 1. It was a *serpent of brass* that cured them. Brass is *bright;* we read of Christ's feet *shining like brass*, Rev. i. 15. It is *durable;* Christ is the same. It was made in the shape of a *fiery serpent*, and yet had no poison, no sting, fitly representing Christ, who was *made sin for us* and yet knew no sin; was *made in the likeness of sinful flesh* and yet not sinful; as harmless as a serpent of brass. The serpent was a cursed creature; Christ was made a *curse*. That which cured them reminded them of their plague; so in Christ sin is set before us most fiery and formidable. 2. It was lifted up upon a pole, and so *must* the Son of man be lifted up; thus it *behoved him*, Luke xxiv. 26, 46. No remedy now. Christ is lifted up, (1.) In his *crucifixion*. He was lifted up upon the cross. His death is called his being *lifted up, ch.* xii. 32, 33. He was lifted up as a spectacle, as a mark, lifted up between heaven and earth, as if he had been unworthy of either and abandoned by both. (2.) In his *exaltation*. He was lifted up to the Father's right hand, to give repentance and remission; he was lifted up to the cross, to be further lifted up to the crown. (3.) In the *publishing* and *preaching* of his everlasting gospel, Rev. xiv. 6. The serpent was lifted up that all the thousands of Israel might see it. Christ in the gospel is exhibited to us, evidently set forth; Christ is *lifted up* as an *ensign*, Isa. xi. 10. 3. It was lifted up by Moses. Christ was made under the law of Moses, and Moses testified of him. 4. Being thus lifted up, it was appointed for the cure of those that were bitten by fiery serpents. He that sent the plague provided the remedy. None could redeem and save us but he whose justice had condemned us. It was God himself that *found the ransom*, and the efficacy of it depends upon his appointment. The *fiery serpents* were sent to punish them for their *tempting Christ* (so the apostle saith, 1 Cor. x. 9), and yet they were healed by virtue derived from him. He whom we have offended is *our peace*.

Thirdly, The way of *applying* this remedy, and that is by *believing*, which plainly alludes to the Israelites' *looking up* to the brazen serpent, in order to their being healed by it. If any stung Israelite was either so little sensible of his pain and peril, or had so little confidence in the word of Moses as not to look up to the brazen serpent, justly did he die of his wound; but every one that *looked up to it* did well, Num. xxi. 9. If any so far slight either their disease by sin or the method of cure by Christ as not to embrace Christ upon his own terms, their blood is upon their own head. He hath said, *Look*, *and be saved* (Isa. xlv. 22), look and live. We must take a complacency in and give consent to the methods which Infinite Wisdom has taken of saving a guilty world, by the mediation of Jesus Christ, as the great sacrifice and intercessor.

Fourthly, The great encouragements given us by faith to look up to him. 1. It was for this end that he was *lifted up,* that his followers might be saved; and he will pursue his end. 2. The offer that is made of salvation by him is general, that *whosoever believes* in him, without exception, might have benefit by him. 3. The salvation offered is complete. (1.) They *shall not perish,* shall not die of their wounds; though they may be pained and ill frightened, iniquity shall not be their ruin. But that is not all. (2.) They shall *have eternal life.* They shall not only not die of their wounds in the wilderness, but they shall reach Canaan (which they were then just ready to enter into); they shall enjoy the promised rest.

[2.] Jesus Christ came to save us by *pardoning us,* that we might not die by the sentence of the law, *v.* 16, 17. Here is *gospel* indeed, good *news,* the best that ever came from heaven to earth. Here is *much,* here is *all* in a little, the word of reconciliation in miniature.

First, Here is God's *love,* in *giving his Son for the world* (*v.* 16), where we have three things:—1. The great *gospel mystery* revealed: *God so loved the world that he gave his only-begotten Son.* The love of God the Father is the original of our regeneration by the Spirit and our reconciliation by the lifting up of the Son. Note, (1.) Jesus Christ is the *only-begotten Son of God.* This magnifies his love in giving him for us, in giving him to us; now know we that he loves us, when he has given his *only-begotten Son for us,* which expresses not only his dignity in himself, but his dearness to his Father; he was *always his delight.* (2.) In order to the redemption and salvation of man, it pleased God to *give his only-begotten Son.* He not only sent him into the world with full and ample power to negociate a peace between heaven and earth, but he *gave him,* that is, he gave him up to suffer and die for us, as the great propitiation or expiatory sacrifice. It comes in here as a reason why he *must be lifted up;* for so it was determined and designed by the Father, who gave him for this purpose, and *prepared him a body* in order to it. His enemies could not have *taken him* if his Father had not *given* him. Though he was not yet crucified, yet in the determinate counsel of God he was *given* up, Acts ii. 23. Nay, further, God has *given him,* that is, he has made an offer of him, to all, and given him to all true believers, to all the intents and purposes of the new covenant. He has given him to be our *prophet,* a *witness to the people,* the high priest of our profession, to be our peace, to be head of the church and head over all things to the church, to be to us all we need. (3.) Herein God has commended his *love to the world: God* so *loved the world,* so really, so richly. Now his creatures shall see that he loves them, and wishes them well. He so loved the world of fallen man as he did not love that of fallen angels; see Rom. v. 8; 1 John iv. 10. Behold, and wonder, that the *great God* should love such a *worthless* world! That the *holy God* should love such a *wicked* world with a love of good will, when he could not look upon it with any complacency This was a *time of love indeed,* Ezek. xvi. 6, 8. The Jews vainly conceited that the Messiah should be sent only in love to *their nation,* and to advance them upon the ruins of their neighbours; but Christ tells them that he came in love to the *whole world,* Gentiles as well as Jews, 1 John ii. 2. Though many of the world of mankind perish, yet God's giving his only-begotten Son was an instance of his love to the whole world, because through him there is a *general offer* of life and salvation made to all. It is love to the revolted rebellious province to issue out a proclamation of pardon and indemnity to all that will come in, plead it upon their knees, and return to their allegiance. So *far God loved the* apostate lapsed *world* that he sent his Son with this fair proposal, that *whosoever believes in him,* one or other, *shall not perish. Salvation* has been *of the Jews,* but now Christ is *known as salvation to the ends of the earth,* a *common salvation.* 2. Here is the great *gospel duty,* and that is to *believe in Jesus Christ* (whom God has thus given, given *for us,* given *to us),* to accept the gift, and answer the intention of the giver. We must yield an unfeigned assent and consent to the record God hath given in his word concerning his Son. God having given him to us to be our prophet, priest, and king, we must give up ourselves to be ruled, and taught, and saved by him. 3. Here is the great gospel benefit: *That whosoever believes in Christ shall not perish.* This he had said before, and here repeats it. It is the unspeakable happiness of all true believers, for which they are eternally indebted to Christ, (1.) That they are saved from the miseries of hell, delivered from *going down to the pit;* they *shall not perish.* God has taken away their sin, they shall not die; a pardon is purchased, and so the attainder is reversed. (2.) They are entitled to the joys of heaven: they shall *have everlasting life.* The convicted traitor is not only pardoned, but preferred, and made a favourite, and treated as one whom the King of kings *delights to honour. Out of prison he comes to reign,* Eccl. iv. 14. If believers, then children; and, if *children, then heirs.*

Secondly, Here is God's design in sending his Son into the world: it was *that the world through him might be saved.* He came into the world with salvation in *his eye,* with salvation *in his hand.* Therefore the aforementioned offer of life and salvation is sincere, and shall be made good to all that by faith accept it (*v.* 17): *God sent his Son into the world*, this guilty, rebellious, apostate world; sent him as his agent or ambassador, not as sometimes he had sent angels into the world as visitants, but as resident. Ever since man sinned, he has dreaded the approach and appearance of any special messenger from heaven, as being conscious of guilt and looking for judgment: *We shall surely die, for we have seen God.* If therefore the Son of God himself come, we are concerned to enquire on what errand he comes: *Is it peace?* Or, as they asked Samuel trembling, *Comest thou peaceably?* And this scripture returns the answer, *Peaceably.* 1. He did not come to *condemn the world.* We had reason enough to expect that he should, for it is a guilty world; it is *convicted*, and what cause can be shown why judgment should not be given, and execution awarded, according to law? That *one blood* of which all *nations* of men are made (Acts xvii. 26) is not only *tainted* with an hereditary *disease*, like Gehazi's leprosy, but it is *tainted* with an hereditary *guilt*, like that of the Amalekites, with whom God had war *from generation to generation;* and justly may such a world as this be *condemned;* and if God would have sent to condemn it he had angels at command, to pour out the vials of his wrath, a cherub with a flaming sword ready to do execution. *If the Lord had been pleased to kill us*, he would not have sent his Son amongst us. He came with full powers indeed to *execute judgment* (*ch.* v. 22, 27), but did not begin with a judgment of condemnation, did not proceed upon the outlawry, nor take advantage against us for the breach of the *covenant of innocency*, but put us upon a new trial before a *throne of grace.* 2. He came *that the world through him might be saved*, that a door of salvation might be opened to the world, and whoever would might enter in by it. God was in Christ *reconciling the world to himself*, and so *saving* it. An act of indemnity is passed and published, through Christ a remedial law made, and the world of mankind dealt with, not according to the rigours of the first covenant, but according to the riches of the second; *that the world* through him might be saved, for it could never be saved but *through him; there is not salvation in any other.* This is good news to a convinced conscience, healing to broken bones and bleeding wounds, that Christ, our judge, came not to *condemn*, but to *save.*

[3.] From all this is inferred the happiness of true believers: *He that believeth on him is not condemned, v.* 18. Though he has been a sinner, a great sinner, and *stands convicted (habes confitentem reum—by his own confession)*, yet, upon his believing, process is stayed, judgment is arrested, and he is *not condemned.* This denotes more than a reprieve; he *is not condemned*, that is, he is acquitted; he *stands upon his deliverance* (as we say), and if he be not condemned he is discharged; *οὐ κρίνεται—he is not judged*, not dealt with in strict justice, according to the desert of his sins. He is *accused*, and he cannot plead *not guilty* to the indictment, but he can plead *in bar*, can plead a *noli prosequi* upon the indictment, as blessed Paul does, *Who is he that condemns? It is Christ that died.* He is *afflicted*, chastened of God, persecuted by the world; but he is not *condemned.* The cross perhaps lies heavy upon him, but he is saved from the curse: condemned *by the world*, it may be, but not *condemned with the world*, Rom. viii. 1; 1 Cor. xi. 32.

4. Christ, in the close, discourses concerning the *deplorable condition of those that persist in unbelief and wilful ignorance, v.* 18—21.

(1.) Read here the doom of those that will not *believe in Christ:* they *are condemned already.* Observe, [1.] How great the *sin* of unbelievers is; it is aggravated from the dignity of the person they slight; they *believe not in the name of the only-begotten Son of God*, who is infinitely *true*, and deserves to be believed, *infinitely good*, and deserves to be embraced. God sent one to save us that was *dearest* to himself; and shall not he be *dearest to us?* Shall we not believe on his name who has a name above every name? [2.] How great the *misery* of unbelievers is: they are *condemned already;* which bespeaks, *First*, A *certain* condemnation. They are as sure to be condemned in the judgment of the great day as if they were condemned already. *Secondly*, A *present* condemnation. The curse has already taken hold of them; the wrath of God now fastens upon them. They are condemned already, for their own hearts condemn them. *Thirdly*, A condemnation *grounded upon their former guilt:* He is condemned *already*, for he lies open to the law for all his sins; the obligation of the law is in full force, power, and virtue, against him, because he is not by faith interested in the gospel defeasance; *he is condemned already, because he has not believed.* Unbelief may truly be called *the great damning sin*, because it leaves us under the guilt of all our other sins; it is a sin against the *remedy*, against our *appeal.*

(2.) Read also the doom of those that would not so much as *know him, v.* 19. Many *inquisitive* people had knowledge of Christ and his doctrine and miracles, but they were prejudiced against him, and would not believe in him, while the generality were sottishly careless and stupid, and would not *know* him. And *this is the condemnation*, the sin that ruined them, *that light is come into the world, and they loved darkness rather.* Now here observe, [1.] That the gospel is light, and, when the gospel came, *light came into the world.* Light is *self-evidencing*, so is the gospel; it proves its own divine origin. Light is *discovering*, and *truly the light is sweet*, and rejoices the heart. It is a light shining in a dark place, and a dark place indeed the world would be without it. It is *come into all the world* (Col. i. 6), and not confined to one corner of it, as the Old-Testament light was. [2.] It is the unspeakable folly of the most of men that they loved darkness rather than light, rather than *this* light. The Jews loved the dark shadows of their law, and the instructions of their *blind guides*, rather than the doctrine of Christ. The Gentiles loved their superstitious services of *an unknown God*, whom they *ignorantly worshipped*, rather than the *reasonable service* which the gospel enjoins. Sinners that were wedded to their lusts loved their ignorance and mistakes, which supported them in their sins, rather than the truths of Christ, which would have parted them from their sins. Man's apostasy began in an affectation of forbidden knowledge, but is kept up by an affectation of forbidden ignorance. Wretched man is in love with his sickness, in love with his slavery, and will not be made *free*, will not be *made whole*. [3.] The true reason why men love darkness rather than light is *because their deeds are evil*. They love darkness because they think it is an excuse for their evil deeds, and they hate the light because it robs them of the good opinion they had of themselves, by showing them their sinfulness and misery. Their case is sad, and, because they are resolved that they will not *mend* it, they are resolved that they will not *see it*. [4.] Wilful ignorance is so far from excusing sin that it will be found, at the great day, to aggravate the condemnation: *This is the condemnation*, this is what ruins souls, that they shut their eyes against the light, and will not so much as admit a parley with Christ and his gospel; they set God so much at defiance that they desire not the knowledge of his ways, Job xxi. 14. We must account in the judgment, not only for the knowledge we *had*, and *used not*, but for the knowledge we *might have had*, and *would not;* not only for the knowledge we *sinned against*, but for the knowledge we *sinned away*. For the further illustration of this he shows (*v.* 20, 21) that according as men's hearts and lives are good or bad, so they stand affected to the light Christ has brought into the world.

First, It is not strange if those that do evil, and resolve to persist in it, hate the light of Christ's gospel; for it is a common observation that *every one that doeth evil hateth the light*, *v.* 20. Evil-doers seek concealment, out of a sense of shame and fear of punishment; see Job xxiv. 13, &c. Sinful works are *works of darkness;* sin from the first affected concealment, Job xxxi. 33. The *light shakes* the wicked, Job xxxviii. 12, 13. Thus the gospel is a terror to the wicked world: *They come not to this light*, but keep as far off it as they can, *lest their deeds should be reproved*. Note, 1. The light of the gospel is sent into the world to *reprove the evil deeds* of sinners; to make them manifest (Eph. v. 13), to *show* people *their transgressions*, to show that to be sin which was not thought to be so, and to show them the evil of their transgressions, *that sin by the* new *commandment* might appear *exceeding sinful*. The gospel has its convictions, to make way for its consolations. 2. It is for this reason that evil-doers *hate the light* of the gospel. There were those who *had done evil* and were sorry for it, who bade this light welcome, as the *publicans and harlots*. But he that *does evil*, that does it and resolves to go on in it, *hateth the light*, cannot bear to be told of his faults. All that opposition which the gospel of Christ has met with in the world comes from the *wicked heart*, influenced by the *wicked one*. Christ is hated because sin is loved. 3. They who do not *come to the light* thereby evidence a secret *hatred* of the light. If they had not an antipathy to *saving knowledge*, they would not sit down so contentedly in *damning ignorance*.

Secondly, On the other hand, upright hearts, that approve themselves to God in their integrity, bid this light welcome (*v.* 21): *He that doeth truth cometh to the light*. It seems, then, that though the gospel had many enemies it had some friends. It is a common observation that *truth seeks no corners*. Those who mean and act honestly dread not a scrutiny, but desire it rather. Now this is applicable to the gospel light; as it *convinces* and *terrifies* evil-doers, so it *confirms* and *comforts* those that walk in their integrity. Observe here, 1. The character of a *good man*. (1.) He is one that *doeth truth;* that is, he acts truly and sincerely in all he does. Though sometimes he comes short of *doing good*, the good he would do, yet he *doeth truth*, he aims honestly; he has his infirmities, but holds fast his integrity; as Gaius, that *did faithfully* (3 John 5), as Paul (2 Cor. i. 12), as Nathanael (*ch.* i. 47), as Asa, 1 Kings xv. 14. (2.) He is one that *cometh to the light*. He is ready to receive and entertain divine revelation as far as it appears to him to be so, what uneasiness soever it may create him. He that *doeth truth* is willing to know the *truth* by himself, and to *have his deeds made manifest*. A good man is much employed in trying himself, and is desirous that God would try him, Ps. xxvi. 2. He is solicitous to *know* what the will of God is, and resolves to *do* it, though ever so contrary to his own will and interest. 2. Here is the character of a *good work:* it is *wrought in God*, in union with him by a covenanting faith, and in communion with him by devout affections. Our works are *then* good, and will bear the test, when the will of God is the rule of them and the glory of God the end of them; when they are done in his strength, and for his sake, to him, and not to men; and if, by the light of the gospel, it be manifest to us that our works are thus wrought, *then shall we have rejoicing,* Gal. vi. 4; 2 Cor. i. 12.

Thus far we have Christ's discourse with *Nicodemus;* it is probable that much more passed between them, and it had a good effect, for we find (*ch.* xix. 39) that Nicodemus, though he was puzzled at first, yet afterwards became a faithful disciple of Christ.

22 After these things came Jesus
and his disciples into the land of
Judæa; and there he tarried with
them, and baptized. 23 And John
also was baptizing in Ænon near to
Salim, because there was much water
there: and they came, and were baptized. 24 For John was not yet
cast into prison. 25 Then there
arose a question between *some* of
John's disciples and the Jews about
purifying. 26 And they came unto
John, and said unto him, Rabbi, he
that was with thee beyond Jordan,
to whom thou barest witness, behold,
the same baptizeth, and all *men* come
to him. 27 John answered and said,
A man can receive nothing, except it
be given him from heaven. 28 Ye
yourselves bear me witness, that I
said, I am not the Christ, but that I
am sent before him. 29 He that
hath the bride is the bridegroom:
but the friend of the bridegroom,
which standeth and heareth him, rejoiceth greatly because of the bridegroom's voice: this my joy therefore
is fulfilled. 30 He must increase,
but I *must* decrease. 31 He that
cometh from above is above all: he
that is of the earth is earthly, and
speaketh of the earth: he that cometh
from heaven is above all. 32 And
what he hath seen and heard, that he
testifieth; and no man receiveth his
testimony. 33 He that hath received his testimony hath set to his
seal that God is true. 34 For he
whom God hath sent speaketh the
words of God: for God giveth not
the Spirit by measure *unto him.*
35 The Father loveth the Son, and
hath given all things into his hand.
36 He that believeth on the Son
hath everlasting life: and he that
believeth not the Son shall not see
life; but the wrath of God abideth
on him.

In these verses we have,

I. Christ's removal into the land of Judea (*v.* 22), and there he tarried with his disciples. Observe, 1. Our Lord Jesus, after he entered upon his public work, travelled much, and removed often, as the patriarchs in their sojournings. As it was a good part of his humiliation that he had no certain dwelling-place, but was, as Paul, *in journeyings often,* so it was an instance of his unwearied industry, in the work for which he came into the world, that he went about in prosecution of it; many a weary step he took to do good to souls. The *Sun of righteousness* took a large circuit to diffuse his light and heat, Ps. xix. 6. 2. He was not wont to stay long at Jerusalem. Though he went frequently thither, yet he soon returned into the country; as here. *After these things,* after he had had this discourse with Nicodemus, he came into the land of Judea; not so much for *greater privacy* (though mean and obscure places best suited the humble Jesus in his humble state) as for *greater usefulness.* His preaching and miracles, perhaps, made *most noise* at Jerusalem, the fountain-head of news, but did *least good* there, where the most considerable men of the Jewish church had so much the ascendant. 3. When he came into the land of Judea his *disciples came with him;* for these were *they that continued with him in his temptations.* Many that flocked to him at Jerusalem could not follow his motions into the country, they had no business there; but his disciples attended him. If the ark remove, it is better to *remove and go after it* (as those did, Josh. iii. 3) than sit still without it, though it be in Jerusalem itself. 4. There he *tarried with them,* διέτριβε—*He conversed* with them, *discoursed* with them. He did not retire into the country for his ease and pleasure, but for more free conversation with his disciples and followers. See Cant. vii. 11, 12. Note, Those that are ready to *go with Christ* shall find him as ready to *stay with them.* It is supposed that he now staid five or six months in this country. 5. There *he baptized;* he admitted disciples, such as believed in him, and had more honesty and courage than those had at Jerusalem, *ch.* ii. 24. John began to baptize in the land of Judea (Matt. iii. 1), therefore Christ began there, for John had said, *There comes one after me.* He himself *baptized* not, with his own hand, but his disciples by his orders and directions, as appears, *ch.* iv. 2. But his disciples' baptizing was his baptizing. Holy ordinances are Christ's, though administered by weak men.

II. John's continuance in his work, as long

as his opportunities lasted, *v.* 23, 24. Here we are told,

1. That *John was baptizing.* Christ's baptism was, for substance, the same with John's, for John bore witness to Christ, and therefore they did not at all clash or interfere with one another. But, (1.) Christ began the work of preaching and baptizing before *John laid it down*, that he might be ready to receive John's disciples when he should be taken off, and so the wheels might be kept going. It is a comfort to useful men, when they are going off the stage, to see those rising up who are likely to fill up their place. (2.) John continued the work of preaching and baptizing though Christ had *taken it up;* for he would still, according to the *measure given to him*, advance the interests of God's kingdom. There was still work for John to do, for Christ was not yet *generally known*, nor were the minds of people *thoroughly prepared* for him by repentance. From heaven John had received his *command*, and he would go on in his work till he thence received his *countermand*, and would have his dismission from the same hand that gave him his commission. He does not *come in* to Christ, lest what had formerly passed should look like a combination between them; but *he goes on* with his work, till Providence lays him aside. The greater gifts of some do not *render* the labours of others, that come short of them, *needless* and *useless;* there is work enough for all hands. They are sullen that will sit down and do nothing when they see themselves out-shone. Though we have but one talent, we must account for that: and, when we see ourselves *going off*, must yet *go on* to the last.

2. That he baptized in Enon near Salim, places we find nowhere else mentioned, and therefore the learned are altogether at a loss where to find them. Wherever it was, it seems that John removed from *place to place;* he did not think that there was any virtue in Jordan, because Jesus was baptized there, which should engage him to stay there, but as he saw cause he removed to other waters. Ministers must follow their opportunities. He chose a place where there was much water, *ὕδατα πολλὰ—many waters*, that is, many *streams* of water; so that wherever he met with any that were willing to submit to his baptism water was at hand to baptize them with, *shallow* perhaps, as is usual where there are *many* brooks, but such as would serve his purpose. And in that country plenty of water was a valuable thing.

3. That thither people *came to him* and *were baptized.* Though they did not come in such vast crowds as they did when he first appeared, yet now he was not without encouragement, but there were still those that attended and owned him. Some refer this both to John and to Jesus: *They came and were baptized;* that is, some came to John, and were baptized by him, some to Jesus, and were baptized by him, and, as their baptism was one, so were their hearts.

4. It is noted (*v.* 24) that *John was not yet cast into prison*, to clear the order of the story, and to show that these passages are to come in before Matt. iv. 12. John never desisted from his work as long as he had his liberty; nay, he seems to have been the more industrious, because he foresaw his time was short; he was not *yet cast into prison*, but he expected it ere long, *ch.* ix. 4.

III. A contest between *John's disciples and the Jews about purifying*, *v.* 25. See how the gospel of Christ came not to *send peace upon earth*, but *division.* Observe, 1. Who were the disputants: *some of John's disciples, and the Jews* who had not submitted to his baptism of repentance. Penitents and impenitents divide this sinful world. In this contest, it should seem, John's disciples were the *aggressors*, and gave the *challenge;* and it is a sign that they were novices, who had more zeal than discretion. The truths of God have often suffered by the rashness of those that have undertaken to defend them before they were able to do it. 2. What was the matter in dispute: *about purifying*, about *religious washing.* (1.) We may suppose that John's disciples cried up his baptism, his purifying, as *instar omnium—superior to all others*, and gave the preference to that as perfecting and superseding all the purifications of the Jews, and they were in the right; but *young* converts are too apt to boast of their attainments, whereas he that finds the *treasure* should *hide it* till he is sure that he has it, and not talk of it too much at first. (2.) No doubt the Jews with as much assurance applauded the *purifyings* that were in use among them, both those that were instituted by the law of Moses and those that were imposed by the tradition of the elders; for the former they had a divine warrant, and for the latter the usage of the church. Now it is very likely that the Jews in this dispute, when they could not *deny* the excellent nature and design of John's baptism, raised an objection against it from Christ's baptism, which gave occasion for the complaint that follows here (*v.* 26): "Here is John baptizing in one place," say they, "and Jesus at the same time baptizing in another place; and therefore John's baptism, which his disciples so much applaud, is either," [1.] "*Dangerous*, and of *ill consequence* to the peace of the church and state, for you see it opens a door to endless parties. Now that John has begun, we shall have every little teacher set up for a baptist presently. Or," [2.] "At the best it is *defective* and *imperfect.* If John's baptism, which you cry up thus, have any good in it, yonder the baptism of Jesus goes beyond it, so that for your parts you are shaded already by a greater light, and your baptism is soon gone out of request." Thus objections are made against the gospel from the advancement and improvement of gospel light, as if childhood and manhood were contrary to each other, and the superstructure were against the foundation. There was no reason to object Christ's baptism against John's, for they consisted very well together.

IV. A complaint which John's disciples made to their master concerning Christ and his baptizing, *v.* 26. They, being *nonplussed* by the fore-mentioned objection, and probably *ruffled* and put into a heat by it, come to their master, and tell him, "*Rabbi, he that was with thee*, and was baptized of thee, is now set up for himself; he *baptizeth, and all men come to him;* and wilt thou suffer it?" Their itch for disputing occasioned this. It is common for men, when they find themselves run aground in the heat of disputation, to fall foul upon those that do them no harm. If these disciples of John had not undertaken to dispute about *purifying*, before they understood the *doctrine of baptism*, they might have answered the objection without being put into a passion. In their complaint, they speak respectfully to their own master, *Rabbi;* but speak very slightly of our Saviour, though they do not name him. 1. They suggest that Christ's setting up a baptism of his own was a piece of presumption, very unaccountable; as if John, having first set up this rite of baptizing, must have the monopoly of it, and, as it were, a patent for the invention: "*He that was with thee beyond Jordan*, as a disciple of thine, *behold*, and wonder, *the same*, the very same, *baptizes*, and takes thy work out of thy hand." Thus the voluntary condescensions of the Lord Jesus, as that of his being baptized by John, are often unjustly and very unkindly turned to his reproach. 2. They suggest that it was a piece of ingratitude to John. He *to whom thou barest witness* baptizes; as if Jesus owed all his reputation to the honourable character John gave of him, and yet had very unworthily improved it to the prejudice of John. But Christ needed not John's testimony, *ch.* v. 36. He reflected more honour upon John than he received from him, yet thus it is incident to us to think that others are more indebted to us than really they are. And besides, Christ's baptism was not in the least an *impeachment*, but indeed the greatest *improvement*, of John's baptism, which was but to lead the way to Christ's. John was *just* to Christ, in bearing witness to him; and Christ's answering his testimony did rather enrich than impoverish John's ministry. 3. They conclude that it would be a total eclipse to John's baptism: "*All men come to him;* they that used to follow with us now flock after him, it is therefore time for us to look about us." It was not indeed strange that *all men came to him*. As far as Christ is *manifested* he will be *magnified*; but why should John's disciples grieve at this? Note, Aiming at the monopoly of honour and respect has been in all ages the bane of the church, and the shame of its members and ministers; as also a vieing of interests, and a jealousy of rivalship and competition. We mistake if we think that the excelling gifts and graces, and labours and usefulness, of one, are a diminution and disparagement to another that has obtained mercy to be faithful; for the Spirit is a free agent, *dispensing to every one severally as he will.* Paul rejoiced in the usefulness even of those that *opposed him*, Phil. i. 18. We must leave it to God to choose, employ, and honour his own instruments as he pleaseth, and not covet to be *placed alone*.

V. Here is John's answer to this complaint which his disciples made, *v.* 27, &c. His disciples expected that he would have resented this matter as they did; but Christ's *manifestation to Israel* was no *surprise* to John, but what he looked for; it was no *disturbance* to him, but what he wished for. He therefore checked the complaint, as Moses, *Enviest thou for my sake?* and took this occasion to confirm the testimonies he had formerly borne to Christ as superior to him, cheerfully consigning and turning over to him all the interest he had in Israel. In this discourse here, the first minister of the gospel (for so John was) is an excellent pattern to all ministers to *humble* themselves and to *exalt* the Lord Jesus.

1. John here *abases himself in comparison with Christ, v.* 27—30. The more others magnify us, the more we must humble ourselves, and fortify ourselves against the temptation of flattery and applause, and the jealousy of our friends for our honour, by remembering our place, and what we are, 1 Cor. iii. 5.

(1.) *John acquiesces* in the divine disposal, and satisfies himself with that (*v.* 27): *A man can receive nothing except it be given him from heaven,* whence *every good gift* comes (James i. 17), a general truth very applicable in this case. Different employments are according to the direction of divine Providence, different endowments according to the distribution of the divine grace. *No man can take* any true *honour* to himself, Heb. v. 4. We have as necessary and constant a dependence upon the grace of God in all the motions and actions of the spiritual life as we have upon the providence of God in all the motions and actions of the natural life: now this comes in here as a reason, [1.] Why we should not *envy* those that have a larger share of gifts than we have, or move in a larger sphere of usefulness. John reminds his disciples that Jesus would not have thus excelled him *except he had received it from heaven,* for, as *man* and *Mediator*, he *received gifts;* and, if God gave him *the Spirit without measure* (*v.* 34), shall they grudge at it? The same reason will hold as to others. If God is *pleased* to give to others more ability and success than to us, shall we be displeased at it, and reflect upon him as unjust, unwise, and partial? See Matt. xx. 15. [2.] Why we should not be *discontented,* though we be inferior to others in gifts and usefulness, and be eclipsed by their excellencies. John was ready to own that it was the gift, the free gift, of heaven, that made him a preacher, a prophet, a baptist: it was God that gave him the interest he had in the love and esteem of the people; and, if now his interest decline, God's will be done! He that *gives* may *take*. What we *receive* from heaven we must take as it is *given*. Now John never received a commission for a standing *perpetual* office, but only for a *temporary* one, which must soon expire; and therefore, when he has fulfilled his ministry, he can contentedly see it go out of date. Some give quite another sense of these words: John had taken pains with his disciples, to teach them the reference which his baptism had to Christ, who should come after him, and yet be preferred before him, and do that for them which he could not do; and yet, after all, they dote upon John, and grudge this preference of Christ above him: Well, saith John, I see *a man can receive* (that is, perceive) *nothing, except it be given him from heaven.* The labour of ministers is all lost labour, unless the grace of God make it effectual. Men do not understand that which is made most *plain*, nor believe that which is made most *evident*, unless it be given them from heaven to understand and believe it.

(2) John appeals to the testimony he had formerly given concerning Christ (*v.* 28): You can bear me witness that I said, again and again, *I am not the Christ, but I am sent before him.* See how steady and constant John was in his testimony to Christ, and not as a *reed shaken with the wind;* neither the frowns of the chief priests, nor the flatteries of his own disciples, could make him change his note. Now this serves here, [1.] As a *conviction* to his disciples of the unreasonableness of their complaint. They had spoken of the witness which their master bore to Jesus (*v.* 26): "Now," saith John, "do you not remember what the testimony was that I did bear? Call that to mind, and you will see your own cavil answered. Did I not say, *I am not the Christ?* Why then do you set me up as a rival with him that is? Did I not say, *I am sent before him?* Why then does it seem strange to you that I should stand by and give way to him?" [2.] It is a *comfort* to himself that he had never *given* his disciples *any occasion* thus to set him up in competition with Christ; but, on the contrary, had particularly *cautioned* them against this mistake, though he might have made a hand of it for himself. It is a satisfaction to faithful ministers when they have done what they could in their places to prevent any extravagances that their people ran into. John had not only not encouraged them to hope that he was the Messiah, but had plainly told them the contrary, which was now a satisfaction to him. It is a common excuse for those who have undue honour paid them, *Si populus vult decipi, decipiatur—If the people will be deceived, let them;* but that is an ill maxim for those to go by whose business it is to *undeceive* people. *The lip of truth shall be established.*

(3.) John professes the great satisfaction he had in the advancement of Christ and his interest. He was so far from *regretting* it, as his disciples did, that he *rejoiced* in it. This he expresses (*v.* 29) by an elegant similitude. [1.] He compares our Saviour to the *bridegroom:* "*He that hath the bride is the bridegroom.* Do *all men come to him?* It is well, whither else should they go? Has he got the throne in men's affections? Who else should have it? It is his right; to whom should the bride be brought but to the bridegroom?" Christ was prophesied of in the Old Testament as a bridegroom, Ps. xlv. *The Word was made flesh,* that the disparity of nature might not be a *bar to the match.* Provision is made for the purifying of the church, that the defilement of sin might be no bar. Christ espouses his church to himself; he *has* the bride, for he has her love, he has her promise; *the church is subject to Christ.* As far as particular souls are devoted to him in faith and love, so far the bridegroom has the bride. [2.] He compares himself to the *friend of the bridegroom,* who attends upon him, to do him honour and service, assists him in prosecuting the match, speaks a good word for him, uses his interest on his behalf, rejoices when the match goes on, and most of all when the point is gained, and he *has the bride.* All that John had done in preaching and baptizing was to introduce him; and, now that he was come, he had what he wished for: *The friend of the bridegroom stands, and hears him;* stands expecting him, and waiting for him; *rejoices with joy because of the bridegroom's voice,* because he is come to the marriage after he had been long expected. Note, *First,* Faithful ministers are friends of the bridegroom, to recommend him to the affections and choice of the children of men; to bring letters and messages from him, for he courts by proxy; and herein they must be faithful to him. *Secondly,* The friends of the bridegroom must *stand, and hear the bridegroom's voice;* must receive instructions from him, and attend his orders; must desire to have proofs of Christ speaking in them, and with them (2 Cor. xiii. 3); that is the *bridegroom's voice. Thirdly,* The espousing of souls to Jesus Christ, in faith and love, is the fulfilling of the joy of every good minister. If the day of Christ's espousals be the day of the gladness of his heart (Cant. iii. 11), it cannot but be of theirs too who love him and wish well to his honour and kingdom. Surely they have *no greater joy.*

(4.) He owns it highly fit and necessary that the reputation and interest of Christ should be advanced, and his own diminished (*v.* 30): *He must increase, but I must decrease.* If they grieve at the growing greatness of the Lord Jesus, they will have more and more occasion to grieve, as those have that indulge themselves in envy and emulation. John speaks of Christ's increase and his own decrease, not only as *necessary* and *unavoidable*, which could not be *helped* and therefore must be *borne*, but as highly *just* and *agreeable*, and affording him entire satisfaction. [1.] He was *well pleased* to see the kingdom of Christ getting ground: "*He must increase.* You think he has gained a great deal, but it is nothing to what he will gain." Note, The kingdom of Christ is, and will be, a growing kingdom, like the light of the morning, like the grain of mustard-seed. [2.] He was not at all *displeased* that the effect of this was the diminishing of his own interest: *I must decrease.* Created excellencies are under this law, they *must decrease. I have seen an end of all perfection.* Note, *First,* The shining forth of the glory of Christ eclipses the lustre of all other glory. The glory that stands in *competition* with Christ, that of the world and the flesh, decreases and loses ground in the soul as the knowledge and love of Christ increase and get ground; but it is here spoken of that which is *subservient* to him. As the light of the morning increases, that of the morning star decreases. *Secondly,* If our diminution or abasement may but in the least contribute to the advancement of Christ's name, we must cheerfully submit to it, and be content to be *any thing,* to be *nothing,* so that Christ may be *all.*

2. John Baptist here *advances* Christ, and instructs his disciples concerning him, that, instead of grieving that so many come to him, they might come to him themselves.

(1.) He instructs them concerning the *dignity of Christ's person* (*v.* 31): *He that cometh from above,* that *cometh from heaven, is above all.* Here, [1.] He supposes his divine origin, that he came *from above,* from *heaven,* which bespeaks not only his divine extraction, but his divine nature. He had a being before his conception, a heavenly being. None but he that came from heaven was fit to show us the will of heaven, or the way to heaven. When God would save man, he *sent from above.* [2.] Hence he infers his sovereign authority: he is *above all,* above all things and all persons, *God over all, blessed for evermore.* It is daring presumption to dispute precedency with him. When we come to speak of the honours of the Lord Jesus, we find they transcend all conception and expression, and we can say but this, *He is above all.* It was said of John Baptist, *There is not a greater among them that are born of women.* But the descent of Christ from heaven put such a dignity upon him as he was not divested of by his being made flesh; still he was *above all.* This he further illustrates by the meanness of those who stood in competition with him: *He that is of the earth, is earthly,* ὁ ὢν ἐκ τῆς γῆς, ἐκ τῆς γῆς ἐστι—*He that is of the earth is of the earth;* he that has his origin of the earth has his food out of the earth, has his converse with earthly things, and his concern is for them. Note, *First,* Man has his rise out of the earth; not only Adam at first, but we also still are *formed out of the clay,* Job xxxiii. 6. Look to the rock whence we were hewn. *Secondly,* Man's constitution is therefore *earthly;* not only his body frail and mortal, but his soul corrupt and carnal, and its bent and bias strong towards earthly things. The prophets and apostles were of the same mould with other men; they were but *earthen vessels,* though they had a rich treasure lodged in them; and shall these be set up as rivals with Christ? *Let the potsherds strive with the potsherds of the earth;* but let them not cope with him that *came from heaven.*

(2.) Concerning the *excellency and certainty of his doctrine.* His disciples were displeased that Christ's preaching was admired, and attended upon, more than his; but he tells them that there was reason enough for it. For,

[1.] He, for his part, *spoke of the earth,* and so do all those that are *of the earth.* The prophets were men and spoke like men; *of themselves* they could not speak but *of the earth,* 2 Cor. iii. 5. The preaching of the prophets and of John was but low and flat compared with Christ's preaching; as heaven is high above the earth, so were his thoughts above theirs. By them God spoke *on earth,* but in Christ he speaketh *from heaven.*

[2.] But he that cometh from heaven is not only in his person, but in his doctrine, above all the prophets that ever lived on earth; none teacheth like him. The doctrine of Christ is here recommended to us,

First, As infallibly *sure* and *certain,* and to be entertained accordingly (*v.* 32): *What he hath seen and heard, that he testifieth.* See here, 1. Christ's divine knowledge; he testified nothing but *what he had seen and heard,* what he was perfectly apprized of and thoroughly acquainted with. What he discovered of the divine nature and of the invisible world was what he had *seen;* what he revealed of the mind of God was what he had *heard* immediately from him, and not at second hand. The prophets testified what was made known to them in dreams and visions by the mediation of angels, but not what they had seen and heard. John was the crier's *voice,* that said, "*Make room for the witness,* and *keep silence* while the charge is given," but then leaves it to the witness to give in his testimony himself, and the judge to give the charge himself. The gospel of Christ is not a doubtful opinion, like an hypothesis or new notion in philosophy, which every one is at liberty to believe or not; but it is a revelation of the mind of God, which is of *eternal truth* in itself, and of *infinite concern* to us. 2. His divine grace and goodness: that which he had *seen* and *heard* he was pleased to make known to us, because he knew it nearly concerned us. What Paul had seen and heard in the third heavens he could not testify (2 Cor. xii. 4), but Christ knew how to utter what he had *seen* and *heard*. Christ's preaching is here called his *testifying*, to denote, (1.) The *convincing evidence* of it; it was not *reported* as news by hearsay, but it was *testified* as evidence given in court, with great caution and assurance. (2.) The affectionate earnestness of the delivery of it: it was testified with concern and importunity, as Acts xviii. 5.

From the *certainty* of Christ's doctrine, John takes occasion, [1.] To lament the infidelity of the most of men: though he testifies what is infallibly true, yet *no man receiveth* his testimony, that is, very few, next to none, none in comparison with those that refuse it. They receive it not, they will not hear it, they do not heed it, or give credit to it. This he speaks of not only as a matter of *wonder*, that such a testimony should not be received (Who hath believed our report? How stupid and foolish are the greatest part of mankind, what enemies to themselves!) but as matter of *grief;* John's disciples grieved that *all men came to Christ* (*v.* 26); they thought his followers too many. But John grieves that *no man came to him;* he thought them too few. Note, The unbelief of sinners is the grief of saints. It was for this that St. Paul had *great heaviness*, Rom. ix. 2. [2.] He takes occasion to commend the faith of the chosen remnant (*v.* 33): *He that hath received his testimony* (and some such there were, though very few) hath *set to his seal that God is true.* God is true, though we do not *set our seal to it;* let God be true, and every man a liar; his truth needs not our faith to support it, but by faith we do ourselves the honour and justice to subscribe to his truth, and hereby God reckons himself honoured. God's promises are all *yea and amen;* by faith we put our *amen* to them, as Rev. xxii. 20. Observe, He that receives the testimony of Christ subscribes not only to the truth of Christ, but to the truth of *God*, for his name is the *Word of God;* the commandments of God and the testimony of Christ are put together, Rev. xii. 17. By believing in Christ we set to our seal, *First*, That God is true to all the promises which he has made *concerning Christ*, that which he spoke by the mouth of *all his holy prophets;* what he *swore to our fathers* is all accomplished, and not one iota or tittle of it fallen to the ground, Luke i. 70, &c. Acts xiii. 32, 33. *Secondly*, That he is true to all the promises he has made *in Christ;* we venture our souls upon God's veracity, being satisfied that he is *true;* we are willing to deal with him *upon trust*, and to quit all in this world for a happiness in reversion and out of sight. By this we greatly honour God's faithfulness. Whom we *give credit* to we *give honour* to.

Secondly, It is recommended to us as a *divine* doctrine; not his own, but *his that sent* him (*v.* 34): *For he whom God hath sent speaketh the word of God*, which he was sent to speak, and enabled to speak; *for God giveth not the Spirit by measure unto him.* The prophets were as messengers that brought letters from heaven; but Christ came under the character of an *ambassador*, and treats with us as such; for, 1. He spoke the *words of God*, and nothing he said savoured of human infirmity; both substance and language were divine. He proved himself *sent of God* (*ch.* iii. 2), and therefore his words are to be received as the words of God. By this rule we may try the spirits: those that speak *as the oracles of God*, and prophesy *according to the proportion of faith*, are to be received as *sent of God.* 2. He spoke as no other prophet did; for *God giveth not the Spirit by measure to him.* None can speak the *words of God* without the *Spirit of God*, 1 Cor. ii. 10, 11. The Old-Testament prophets had the Spirit, and in different degrees, 2 Kings ii. 9, 10. But, whereas God gave them the Spirit by *measure* (1 Cor. xii. 4), he gave him to Christ *without measure;* all fulness dwelt in him, the fulness of the Godhead, an immeasurable fulness. The Spirit was not in Christ as in a vessel, but as in a fountain, as in a bottomless ocean. "The prophets that had the Spirit in a limited manner, only with respect to some particular revelation, sometimes spoke of *themselves;* but he that had the Spirit always residing in him, without stint, always spoke *the words of God.*" So Dr. Whitby.

(3.) Concerning *the power and authority he is invested with*, which gives him the pre-eminence above all others, and a more excellent name than they.

[1.] He is the *beloved Son of the Father* (*v.* 35): *The Father loveth the Son.* The prophets were faithful as servants, but Christ as a Son; they were employed as servants, but Christ *beloved* as a son, always *his delight*, Prov. viii. 30. The Father was well pleased in him; not only he *did* love him, but he *doth* love him; he continued his love to him even in his estate of humiliation, loved him never the less for his poverty and sufferings.

[2.] He is *Lord of all.* The Father, as an evidence of his love for him, *hath given all things into his hand.* Love is generous. The Father took such a complacency and had such a confidence in him that he constituted him the great *feoffee in trust* for mankind. Having given *him the Spirit without measure*, he gave him *all things;* for he was hereby qualified to be master and manager of all. Note, It is the honour of Christ, and the unspeakable comfort of all Christians, that the Father hath *given all things* into the hands of the Mediator. *First*, All *power;* so it is explained, Matt. xxviii. 18. All the works of creation being put under his feet, all the affairs of redemption are put into his hand; he is Lord of all. Angels are his servants; devils are his captives. He has *power over all flesh,* the *heathen* given *him for his inheritance.* The kingdom of providence is committed to his administration. He has power to settle the terms of the covenant of peace as the great *plenipotentiary,* to govern his church as the great *lawgiver,* to dispense divine favours as the great *almoner,* and to call all to account as the great *Judge.* Both the golden sceptre and the iron rod are given into his hand. *Secondly,* All *grace* is given into his hand as the channel of conveyance; *all things,* all those good things which God intended to give to the children of men; *eternal life,* and all its preliminaries. We are unworthy that the Father should give those things *into our hands,* for we have made ourselves the *children of his wrath;* he hath therefore appointed the *Son of his love* to be trustee for us, and the things he intended for us he gives *into his hands,* who is worthy, and has merited both honours for himself and favours for us. They are given *into his hands,* by him to be given into ours. This is a great encouragement to faith, that the riches of the new covenant are deposited in so sure, so kind, so good a hand, the hand of him that purchased them for us, and us for himself, who is able to keep all that which both God and believers have agreed to *commit to him.*

[3.] He is the object of that faith which is made the great condition of eternal happiness, and herein he has the pre-eminence above all others: *He that believeth on the Son, hath life, v.* 36. We have here the application of what he had said concerning Christ and his doctrine; and it is the *conclusion of the whole matter.* If God has put this honour upon the Son, we must by faith give honour to him. As God offers and conveys good things to us by the *testimony* of Jesus Christ, whose word is the vehicle of divine favours, so we receive and partake of those favours by *believing* the testimony, and entertaining that word as *true* and *good;* this way of *receiving* fitly answers that way of *giving.* We have here the sum of that gospel which is to be preached to every creature, Mark xvi. 16. Here is,

First, The blessed state of all true Christians: *He that believes on the Son hath everlasting life.* Note, 1. It is the character of every true Christian that he believes on *the Son of God;* not only *believes him,* that what he saith is true, but believes *on him,* consents to him, and confides in him. The benefit of true Christianity is no less than *everlasting life;* this is what Christ came to purchase for us and confer upon us; it can be no less than the happiness of an immortal soul *in* an immortal God. 2. True believers, even now, *have* everlasting life; not only they shall have it hereafter, but they have it now. For, (1.) They *have* very good security for it. The deed by which it passeth is sealed and delivered to them, and so they *have* it; it is put into the hands of their guardian for them, and so they have it, though the use be not yet transferred into possession. They have the Son of God, and in him *they have life;* and the Spirit of God, the earnest of this life. (2.) They have the comfortable *foretastes* of it, in present communion with God and the tokens of his love. Grace is glory begun.

Secondly, The wretched and miserable condition of unbelievers: *He that believeth not the Son* is undone, ὁ ἀπειθῶν. The word includes both *incredulity* and *disobedience.* An unbeliever is one that gives not credit to the doctrine of Christ, nor is in subjection to the government of Christ. Now those that will neither be *taught* nor *ruled* by Christ, 1. They *cannot be happy* in this world, nor that to come: *He shall not see life,* that life which Christ came to bestow. He shall not enjoy it, he shall not have any comfortable *prospect* of it, shall never come within ken of it, except to aggravate his loss of it. 2. They *cannot but be miserable: The wrath of God abides upon* an unbeliever. He is not only under the *wrath of God,* which is as surely *the soul's death* as his favour is *its life,* but it *abides upon him.* All the wrath he has made himself liable to by the violation of the law, if not removed by the grace of the gospel, is bound upon him. God's wrath for his daily actual transgressions lights and lies upon him. Old scores lie undischarged, and new ones are added: something is done every day to fill the measure, and nothing to empty it. Thus the wrath of God *abides,* for it is *treasured up against the day of wrath.*

CHAP. IV.

It was, more than any thing else, the glory of the land of Israel, that it was Emmanuel's land (Isa. viii. 8), not only the place of his birth, but the scene of his preaching and miracles. This land in our Saviour's time was divided into three parts: Judea in the south, Galilee in the north, and Samaria lying between them. Now, in this chapter, we have Christ in each of these three parts of that land. I. Departing out of Judea, ver. 1–3. II. Passing through Samaria, which, though a visit in transitu, here takes up most room. 1. His coming into Samaria, ver. 4–6. 2. His discourse with the Samaritan woman at a well, ver. 7—26. 3. The notice which the woman gave of him to the city, ver. 27—30. 4. Christ's talk with his disciples in the mean time, ver. 31—38. 5. The good effect of this among the Samaritans, ver. 39—42. III. We find him residing for some time in Galilee (ver. 43—46), and his curing a nobleman's son there, that was at death's door, ver. 46—54.

WHEN therefore the Lord knew
how the Pharisees had heard
that Jesus made and baptized more
disciples than John, 2 (Though Jesus himself baptized not, but his dis-
ples,) 3 He left Judæa, and departed
again into Galilee.

We read of Christ's coming into Judea (*ch.* iii. 22), after he had kept the feast at Jerusalem; and now he left Judea four months before harvest, as is said here (*v.* 35); so that it is computed that he staid in Judea about six months, to build upon the foundation John had laid there. We have no particular account of his sermons and miracles there, only in general, *v.* 1.

I. That he *made disciples;* he prevailed with many to embrace his doctrine, and to follow him as a teacher come from God. His ministry was successful, notwithstanding the opposition it met with (Ps. cx. 2, 3); *μαθητὰς ποιεῖ*—it signifies the same with *μαθητεύω*—*to disciple.* Compare Gen. xii. 5. *The souls which they had gotten,* which they had *made* (so the word is), which they had *made proselytes.* Note, It is Christ's prerogative to *make disciples,* first to bring them to his foot, and then to form and fashion them to his will. *Fit, non nascitur, Christianus—The Christian is made such, not born such.* Tertullian.

II. That he *baptized* those whom he *made disciples,* admitted them by *washing them with water;* not himself, but by the ministry of his disciples, *v.* 2. 1. Because he would put a difference between his baptism and that of John, who baptized all himself; for he baptized as a servant, Christ as a master. 2. He would apply himself more to preaching work, which was the more excellent, 1 Cor. i. 17. 3. He would put honour upon his disciples, by empowering and employing them to do it; and so train them up to further services. 4. If he had baptized some himself, they would have been apt to value themselves upon that, and despise others, which he would prevent, as Paul, 1 Cor. i. 13, 14. 5. He would reserve himself for the honour of baptizing with the Holy Ghost, Acts i. 5. 6. He would teach us that the efficacy of the sacraments depends not on any virtue in the hand that administers them, as also that what is done by his ministers, according to his direction, he owns as done by himself.

III. That he made and baptized *more disciples than John;* not only more than John did at this time, but more than he had done at any time. Christ's converse was more winning than John's. His miracles were convincing, and the cures he wrought *gratis* very inviting.

IV. That the Pharisees were informed of this; they heard what multitudes he baptized, for they had, from his first appearing, a jealous eye upon him, and wanted not spies to give them notice concerning him. Observe, 1. When the Pharisees thought they had got rid of John (for he was by this time imprisoned), and were pleasing themselves with that, Jesus appears, who was a greater vexation to them than ever John had been. The witnesses will rise again. 2. That which grieved them was that Christ made so many disciples. The success of the gospel exasperates its enemies, and it is a good sign that it is getting ground when the powers of darkness are enraged against it.

V. That our Lord Jesus knew very well what informations were given in against him to the Pharisees. It is probable the informers were willing to have their names concealed, and the Pharisees loth to have their designs known; but none can dig so deep as to *hide their counsels from the Lord* (Isa. xxix. 15), and Christ is here called *the Lord.* He knew what was told the Pharisees, and how much, it is likely, it exceeded the truth; for it is not likely that Jesus had yet baptized *more than John;* but so the thing was represented, to make him appear the more formidable; see 2 Kings vi. 12.

VI. That hereupon our Lord Jesus *left Judea* and *departed again* to go to Galilee.

1. He *left Judea,* because he was likely to be persecuted there even to the death; such was the rage of the Pharisees against him, and such their impious policy to devour the man-child in his infancy. To escape their designs, Christ quitted the country, and went where what he did would be less provoking than just under their eye. For, (1.) His hour was not yet come (*ch.* vii. 30), the time fixed in the counsels of God, and the Old-Testament prophecies, for Messiah's being cut off. He had not finished his testimony, and therefore would not surrender or expose himself. (2.) The disciples he had gathered in Judea were not able to bear hardships, and therefore he would not expose them. (3.) Hereby he gave an example to his own rule: *When they persecute you in one city, flee to another.* We are not called to suffer, while we may avoid it without sin; and therefore, though we may not, for our own preservation, change our religion, yet we may change our place. Christ secured himself, not by a miracle, but in a way *common to men,* for the direction and encouragement of his suffering people.

2. He departed into Galilee, because he had work to do there, and many friends and fewer enemies. He went to Galilee now, (1.) Because John's ministry had now *made way* for him there; for Galilee, which was under Herod's jurisdiction, was the last scene of John's baptism. (2.) Because John's imprisonment had now *made room* for him there. That light being now put under a bushel, the minds of people would not be divided between him and Christ. Thus both the liberties and restraints of good ministers are for the furtherance of the gospel, Phil. i. 12. But to what purpose does he go into Galilee for safety? Herod, the persecutor of John, will never be the protector of Jesus. Chemnitius here notes, *Pii in hâc vitâ quos fugiant habent; ad quos vero fugiant ut in tuto sint non habent, nisi ad te, Deus, qui solus refugium nostrum es—The pious have those, in this life, to whom they can fly; but they have none to fly to, who can afford them refuge, except thee, O God.*

4 And he must needs go through
Samaria. 5 Then cometh he to a
city of Samaria, which is called Sychar,
near to the parcel of ground that
Jacob gave to his son Joseph. 6
Now Jacob's well was there. Jesus,
therefore, being wearied with *his* journey, sat thus on the well: *and* it was

about the sixth hour. 7 There cometh
a woman of Samaria to draw water:
Jesus saith unto her, Give me to
drink. 8 (For his disciples were gone
away unto the city to buy meat.) 9
Then saith the woman of Samaria
unto him, How is it that thou, being
a Jew, askest drink of me, which am
a woman of Samaria? for the Jews
have no dealings with the Samaritans.
10 Jesus answered and said unto her,
If thou knewest the gift of God, and
who it is that saith to thee, Give
me to drink; thou wouldest have
asked of him, and he would have given
thee living water. 11 The woman
saith unto him, Sir, thou hast nothing
to draw with, and the well is deep:
from whence then hast thou that living
water? 12 Art thou greater than
our father Jacob, which gave us the
well, and drank thereof himself, and
his children, and his cattle? 13 Jesus
answered and said unto her, Whosoever drinketh of this water shall thirst
again: 14 But whosoever drinketh of
the water that I shall give him shall
never thirst; but the water that I shall
give him shall be in him a well of
water springing up into everlasting
life. 15 The woman saith unto him,
Sir, give me this water, that I thirst
not, neither come hither to draw. 16
Jesus saith unto her, Go, call thy
husband, and come hither. 17 The
woman answered and said, I have no
husband. Jesus said unto her, Thou
hast well said, I have no husband:
18 For thou hast had five husbands;
and he whom thou now hast is not
thy husband: in that saidst thou truly.
19 The woman saith unto him, Sir,
I perceive that thou art a prophet.
20 Our fathers worshipped in this
mountain; and ye say, that in Jerusalem is the place where men ought
to worship. 21 Jesus saith unto her,
Woman, believe me, the hour cometh,
when ye shall neither in this mountain,
nor yet at Jerusalem, worship the
Father. 22 Ye worship ye know not
what: we know what we worship: for
salvation is of the Jews. 23 But the
hour cometh, and now is, when the
true worshippers shall worship the
Father in spirit and in truth: for the
Father seeketh such to worship him.
24 God *is* a Spirit: and they that
worship him must worship *him* in
spirit and in truth. 25 The woman
saith unto him, I know that Messias
cometh, which is called Christ: when
he is come, he will tell us all things.
26 Jesus saith unto her, I that speak
unto thee am *he*.

We have here an account of the good Christ did in Samaria, when he *passed through* that country in his way to Galilee. The Samaritans, both in *blood* and *religion*, were *mongrel Jews*, the posterity of those colonies which the king of Assyria planted there after the captivity of the ten tribes, with whom the poor of the land that were left behind, and many other Jews afterwards, incorporated themselves. They worshipped the God of Israel only, to whom they erected a temple on mount Gerizim, in competition with that at Jerusalem. There was great enmity between them and the Jews; the Samaritans would not admit Christ, when they saw he was going to Jerusalem (Luke ix. 53); the Jews thought they could not give him a worse name than to say, *He is a Samaritan.* When the Jews were in prosperity, the Samaritans claimed kindred to them (Ezra iv. 2), but, when the Jews were in distress, they were Medes and Persians; see *Joseph. Antiq. lib.* xi. *cap.* 8, *lib.* xii. *cap.* 7. Now observe,

I. Christ's coming into Samaria. He charged his disciples not to *enter into any city of the Samaritans* (Matt. x. 5), that is, not to preach the gospel, or work miracles; nor did he here preach publicly, or work any miracle, his eye being to *the lost sheep of the house of Israel.* What kindness he here did them was *accidental;* it was only a *crumb* of the children's bread that casually *fell from the master's table.*

1. His *road* from Judea to Galilee lay through the *country* of Samaria (*v.* 4): *He must needs go through Samaria.* There was no other way, unless he would have fetched a compass on the other side *Jordan,* a great way about. The wicked and profane are at present so intermixed with God's Israel that, unless we will go *out of the world,* we cannot avoid *going through* the company of such, 1 Cor. v. 10. We have therefore need of the armour of righteousness on the right hand and on the left, that we may neither give *provocation* to them nor contract *pollution* by them. We should not go into places of temptation but when we *needs must;* and then we should not reside in them, but *hasten through* them. Some think that Christ *must needs* go through Samaria because of the good work he had to do there; a poor woman to be converted, a lost sheep to be sought and saved. This was work his heart was upon, and *therefore* he *must needs* go this

way. It was happy for Samaria that it lay *in Christ's way*, which gave him an opportunity of calling on them. *When I passed by thee, I said unto thee, Live*, Ezek. xvi. 6.

2. His baiting place happened to be at a *city of Samaria*. Now observe,

(1.) The place described. It was called *Sychar;* probably the same with *Sichem*, or *Shechem*, a place which we read much of in the Old Testament. Thus are the names of places commonly corrupted by tract of time. Shechem yielded the first proselyte that ever came into the church of Israel (Gen. xxxiv. 24), and now it is the first place where the gospel is preached out of the commonwealth of Israel; so Dr. Lightfoot observes; as also that the *valley of Achor*, which was given for a *door of hope*, hope to the poor Gentiles, ran along by this city, Hos. ii. 15. Abimelech was made king here; it was Jeroboam's royal seat; but the evangelist, when he would give us the antiquities of the place, takes notice of Jacob's interest there, which was more its honour than its crowned heads. [1.] Here lay Jacob's ground, the *parcel of ground which Jacob* gave to his son Joseph, whose bones were buried in it, Gen. xlviii. 22; Josh. xxiv. 32. Probably this is mentioned to intimate that Christ, when he reposed himself hard by here, took occasion from the ground which Jacob gave Joseph to meditate on the good report which the elders by faith obtained. Jerome chose to live in the land of Canaan, that the sight of the places might affect him the more with scripture stories. [2.] Here was Jacob's well which he digged, or at least used, for himself and his family. We find no mention of this well in the Old Testament; but the tradition was that it was Jacob's well.

(2.) The posture of our Lord Jesus at this place: *Being wearied with his journey, he sat thus on the well.* We have here our Lord Jesus,

[1.] Labouring under the common fatigue of travellers. He was *wearied with his journey*. Though it was yet but the sixth hour, and he had performed but half his day's journey, yet he was weary; or, *because* it was the sixth hour, the time of the heat of the day, therefore he was weary. Here we see, *First*, That he was a *true man*, and subject to the common infirmities of the human nature. Toil came in with sin (Gen. iii. 19), and therefore Christ, having made himself a curse for us, submitted to it. *Secondly*, That he was a *poor man*, else he might have travelled on horseback or in a chariot. To this instance of meanness and mortification he humbled himself for us, that he went all his journeys on foot. When *servants* were on *horses, princes walked as servants on the earth*, Eccl. x. 7. When we are carried easily, let us think on the weariness of our Master. *Thirdly*, It should seem that he was but a *tender man*, and not of a robust constitution; it should seem, his disciples were not tired, for they went into the town without any difficulty, when their Master sat down, and could not go a step further. Bodies of the finest mould are most sensible of fatigue, and can worst bear it.

[2.] We have him here betaking himself to the common relief of travellers: *Being wearied, he sat thus on the well. First*, He sat *on the well*, an *uneasy place*, cold and hard; he had no couch, no easy chair to repose himself in, but took to that which was *next hand*, to teach us not to be nice and curious in the conveniences of this life, but content with *mean things*. *Secondly*, He sat *thus*, in an *uneasy posture;* sat *carelessly—incuriose et neglectim;* or he sat *so* as people that are wearied with travelling are accustomed to sit.

II. His discourse with a Samaritan woman, which is here recorded at large, while Christ's dispute with the doctors, and his discourse with Moses and Elias on the mount, are buried in silence. This discourse is reducible to four heads:—

1. They discourse *concerning the water*, *v.* 7—15.

(1.) Notice is taken of the *circumstances* that gave occasion to this discourse.

[1.] There comes a *woman* of Samaria to *draw water*. This intimates her poverty, she had no servant to be a *drawer of water;* and her industry, she would do it herself. See here, *First*, How God owns and approves of honest humble diligence in our places. Christ was made known to the shepherds when they were keeping their flock. *Secondly* How the divine Providence brings about glorious purposes by events which seem to us fortuitous and accidental. This woman's meeting with Christ at the well may remind us of the stories of Rebekah, Rachel, and Jethro's daughter, who all met with husbands, good husbands, no worse than Isaac, Jacob, and Moses, when they came to the wells for water. *Thirdly*, How the preventing grace of God sometimes brings people unexpectedly under the means of conversion and salvation. He is found of them that sought him not.

[2.] His disciples were *gone away into the city to buy meat*. Hence learn a lesson, *First*, Of justice and honesty. The meat Christ ate, he bought and paid for, as Paul, 2 Thess. iii. 8. *Secondly*, Of daily dependence upon Providence: *Take no thought for the morrow*. Christ did not go into the city to eat, but sent his disciples to fetch his meat thither; not because he scrupled eating in a Samaritan city, but, 1. Because he had a good work to do at that well, which might be done while they were catering. It is wisdom to fill up our vacant minutes with that which is good, that the *fragments* of time may *not be lost*. Peter, while his dinner was getting ready, fell into a trance, Acts x. 10. 2. Because it was more private and retired, more cheap and homely, to have his dinner brought him hither, than to go into the town for it. Perhaps his purse was low, and he would teach us *good husbandry*, to *spend* according to what we *have* and not go beyond it. At least, he would teach us not to affect great things. Christ could eat his dinner as well upon a *draw well* as in the best inn in the town. Let us *comport* with our circumstances. Now this gave Christ an opportunity of discoursing with this woman about spiritual concerns, and he improved it; he often preached to multitudes that crowded after him for instruction, yet here he condescends to teach a single person, a woman, a poor woman, a stranger, a Samaritan, to teach his ministers to do likewise, as those that know what a glorious achievement it is to help to save, though but *one soul*, from death.

(2.) Let us observe the *particulars* of this discourse.

[1.] Jesus begins with a modest request for a draught of water: *Give me to drink.* He that *for our sakes became poor* here becomes a beggar, that those who are in want, and cannot dig, may not be ashamed to beg. Christ asked for it, not only because he needed it, and needed her help to come at it, but because he would draw on further discourse with her, and teach us to be willing to be beholden to the meanest when there is occasion. Christ is still begging in his poor members, and a *cup of cold water*, like this here, given to them in his name, shall not lose its reward.

[2.] The woman, though she does not deny his request, yet quarrels with him because he did not carry on the humour of his own nation (*v.* 9): *How is it?* Observe, *First*, What a mortal feud there was between the Jews and the Samaritans: *The Jews have no dealings with the Samaritans.* The Samaritans were the *adversaries of Judah* (Ezra iv. 1), were upon all occasions mischievous to them. The Jews were extremely malicious against the Samaritans, "looked upon them as having no part in the resurrection, excommunicated and cursed them by the sacred name of God, by the glorious writing of the tables, and by the curse of the upper and lower house of judgment, with this law, That no Israelite eat of any thing that is a Samaritan's, for it is as if he should eat swine's flesh." So Dr. Lightfoot, out of *Rabbi Tanchum.* Note, Quarrels about religion are usually the most implacable of all quarrels. Men were made to *have dealings* one with another; but if men, because one worships at one temple and another at another, will deny the offices of humanity, and charity, and common civility, will be morose and unnatural, scornful and censorious, and this under colour of zeal for religion, they plainly show that however their religion may be *true* they are not *truly religious;* but, pretending to stickle for religion, subvert the design of it. *Secondly*, How ready the woman was to upbraid Christ with the haughtiness and ill nature of the Jewish nation: *How is it that thou, being a Jew, askest drink of me?* By his dress or dialect, or both, she knew him to be a Jew, and *thinks it strange* that he runs not to the same excess of riot against the Samaritans with other Jews. Note, Moderate men of all sides are, like Joshua and his fellows (Zech. iii. 8), *men wondered at.* Two things this woman wonders at, 1. That he should *ask* this kindness; for it was the pride of the Jews that they would endure any hardship rather than be beholden to a Samaritan. It was part of Christ's humiliation that he was born of the Jewish nation, which was *now* not only in an *ill state*, subject to the Romans, but in an *ill name* among the nations. With what disdain did Pilate ask, *Am I a Jew?* Thus he *made himself* not only *of no reputation*, but of *ill reputation;* but herein he has set us an example of swimming against the stream of common corruptions. We must, like our Master, put on *goodness* and *kindness*, though it should be ever so much the genius of our country, or the humour of our party, to be morose and ill-natured. This woman expected that Christ should be as other Jews were; but it is unjust to charge upon every individual person even the common faults of the community: no rule but has some exceptions. 2. She wonders that he should *expect to receive* this kindness from her that was a Samaritan: "You Jews could deny it to one of our nation, and why should we grant it to one of yours?" Thus quarrels are propagated endlessly by revenge and retaliation.

[3.] Christ takes this occasion to instruct her in divine things: *If thou knewest the gift of God, thou wouldst have asked, v.* 10. Observe,

First, He waives her objection of the feud between the Jews and Samaritans, and takes no notice of it. Some differences are best *healed* by being *slighted*, and by avoiding all occasions of *entering into dispute* about them. Christ will convert this woman, not by showing her that the Samaritan worship was *schismatical* (though really it was so), but by showing her her own ignorance and immoralities, and her need of a Saviour.

Secondly, He fills her with an apprehension that she had now an opportunity (a fairer opportunity than she was aware of) of gaining that which would be of unspeakable advantage to her. She had not the helps that the Jews had to discern the signs of the times, and therefore Christ tells her expressly that she had now a season of grace; this was *the day of her visitation.*

a. He hints to her what she *should know*, but was ignorant of: *If thou knewest the gift of God*, that is, as the next words explain it, *who it is that saith, Give me to drink.* If thou knewest *who I am.* She saw him to be a Jew, a poor weary traveller; but he would have her know something more concerning him than did yet appear. Note, (*a.*) Jesus Christ is the *gift of God,* the richest token of God's love to us, and the richest treasure of all good for us; *a gift,* not a debt which we could demand from God; not a *loan,* which he will demand from us again, but a gift, a free gift, *ch.* iii. 16. (*b.*) It is an unspeakable privilege to have this gift of God proposed and offered to us; to have an opportunity of embracing it: "He who is the gift of God is now set before thee, and addresses himself to *thee;* it is he that saith, *Give me to drink;* this gift comes a begging to thee." (*c.*) Though Christ is set before us, and sues to us in and by his gospel, yet there are multitudes that *know him not.* They know not who it is that speaks to them in the gospel, that saith, *Give me to drink;* they perceive not that it is the Lord that calls them.

b. He hopes concerning her, what she would have done if she had known him; to be sure she would not have given him such a rude and uncivil answer; nay, she would have been so far from affronting him that she would have made her addresses to him: *Thou wouldest have asked.* Note, (*a.*) Those that would have any benefit by Christ must ask for it, must be earnest in prayer to God for it. (*b.*) Those that have a right knowledge of Christ will seek to him, and if we do not seek unto him it is a sign that we do not know him, Ps. ix. 10. (*c.*) Christ knows what they that want the means of knowledge would have done if they had had them, Matt. xi. 21.

c. He assures her what he would have done for her if she had applied to him: "He *would have given thee* (and not have upbraided thee as thou dost me) *living water.*" By this living water is meant the *Spirit,* who is not like the water in the bottom of the well, for some of which he asked, but like *living* or *running* water, which was much more valuable. Note, (*a.*) The Spirit of grace is as *living water;* see *ch.* vii. 38. Under this similitude the blessings of the Messiah had been promised in the Old Testament, Isa. xii. 3; xxxv. 7; xliv. 3; lv. 1; Zech. xiv. 8. The graces of the Spirit, and his comforts, satisfy the thirsting soul, that knows its own nature and necessity. (*b*) Jesus Christ *can* and *will* give the Holy Spirit to them that ask him; for he *received* that he might *give.*

[4.] The woman objects against and cavils at the gracious intimation which Christ gave her (*v.* 11, 12): *Thou hast nothing to draw with;* and besides, *Art thou greater than our father Jacob?* What he spoke figuratively, she took literally; Nicodemus did so too. See what confused notions they have of spiritual things who are wholly taken up with the things that are sensible. Some respect she pays to his person, in calling him *Sir,* or *Lord;* but little respect to what he said, which she does but banter.

First, She does not think him capable of furnishing her with any water, no, not this in the well that is just at hand: *Thou hast nothing to draw with,* and *the well is deep.* This she said, not knowing the power of Christ for he who *causeth the vapours* to ascend from the ends of the earth needs *nothing to draw.* But there are those who will trust Christ no further than they can see him, and will not believe his promise, unless the means of the performance of it be *visible;* as if he were tied to our methods, and could not draw water without our buckets. She asks scornfully, "*Whence hast thou this living water?* I see not whence thou canst have it." Note, The springs of that living water which Christ has for those that come to him are secret and undiscovered. The fountain of life is hid with Christ. Christ has enough for us, though we see not whence he has it.

Secondly, She does not think it possible that he should furnish her with any better water than this which she could come at, but he could not: *Art thou greater than our father Jacob, who gave us the well?*

a. We will suppose the tradition true, that Jacob *himself, and his children, and cattle, did drink of this well.* And we may observe from it, (*a.*) The power and providence of God, in the continuance of the fountains of water from generation to generation, by the constant circulation of the rivers, like the blood in the body (Eccl. i. 7), to which circulation perhaps the flux and reflux of the sea, like the pulses of the heart, contribute. (*b.*) The plainness of the patriarch Jacob; his drink was water, and he and his children drank of the same well with his cattle.

b. Yet, allowing that to be true, she was out in several things; as, (*a.*) In calling Jacob *father.* What authority had the Samaritans to reckon themselves of the seed of Jacob? They were descended from that mixed multitude which the king of Assyria had placed in the cities of Samaria; what have they to do then with Jacob? Because they were the *invaders* of Israel's rights, and the unjust possessors of Israel's lands, were they therefore the *inheritors* of Israel's blood and honour? How absurd were those pretensions! (*b.*) She is out in claiming this well as Jacob's gift, whereas he did no more give it than Moses gave the *manna, ch.* vi. 32. But thus we are apt to call the *messengers* of God's gifts the *donors* of them, and to look so much at the hands they *pass through* as to forget the hand they *come from.* Jacob gave it to his sons, not to *them.* Yet thus the church's enemies not only *usurp,* but monopolize, the church's privileges. (*c.*) She was out in speaking of Christ as not worthy to be compared with our father Jacob. An over-fond veneration for antiquity makes God's graces, in the good people of our own day, to be slighted.

[5.] Christ answers this cavil, and makes it out that the *living water* he had to give was far better than that of Jacob's well, *v.* 13, 14. Though she spoke perversely, Christ did not cast her off, but instructed and encouraged her. He shows her,

First, That the water of Jacob's well yielded but a *transient* satisfaction and supply: "*Whoso drinketh of this water shall thirst again.* It is no better than other water; it will quench the present thirst, but the thirst will return, and in a few hours a man will have as much *need,* and as much *desire,* of water as ever he had." This intimates, 1. The *infirmities* of our bodies in this present state; they are still *necessitous,* and ever *craving.* Life is a *fire,* a *lamp,* which will soon go out, without continual supplies of fuel and oil. The natural heat preys upon itself. 2. The *imperfections* of all our comforts in this world; they are not lasting, nor our satisfaction in them remaining. Whatever waters of comfort we drink of, we shall *thirst again.* Yesterday's meat and drink will not do to-day's work.

Secondly, That the living waters he would give should yield a lasting satisfaction and bliss, *v.* 14. Christ's gifts appear most valuable when they come to be compared with the things of this world; for there will appear no comparison between them. Whoever partakes of the Spirit of grace, and the comforts of the everlasting gospel,

a. He shall *never thirst,* he shall never want that which will abundantly satisfy his soul's desires; they are *longing,* but not *languishing.* A *desiring* thirst he has, nothing more *than* God, still more and more *of* God; but not a *despairing* thirst.

b. Therefore he shall never thirst, because this water that Christ gives *shall be in him a well of water. He* can never be reduced to extremity that has in himself a *fountain* of supply and satisfaction. (*a.*) *Ever ready,* for it shall be *in him.* The principle of grace planted *in him* is the spring of his comfort; see *ch.* vii. 38. A good man is *satisfied from himself,* for Christ *dwells in his heart.* The anointing abides in him; he needs not sneak to the world for comfort; the *work* and the *witness* of the Spirit in the heart furnish him with a firm foundation of hope and an overflowing fountain of joy. (*b.*) *Never failing,* for it shall be in him a *well of water.* He that has at hand only a bucket of water needs not thirst as long as this lasts, but it will soon be *exhausted;* but believers have in them a *well of water,* overflowing, ever flowing. The *principles* and *affections* which Christ's holy religion *forms* in the souls of those that are brought under the power of it are this *well of water.* [*a.*] It is *springing up,* ever in motion, which bespeaks the actings of grace strong and vigorous. If good truths *stagnate* in our souls, like standing water, they do not answer the end of our receiving them. If there be a good treasure in the heart, we must thence bring forth good things. [*b.*] It is springing up *unto everlasting life;* which intimates, *First,* The *aims* of gracious actings. A sanctified soul has its eye upon heaven, means this, designs this, does all for this, will take up with nothing short of this Spiritual life springs up towards its own perfection in eternal life. *Secondly,* The *constancy* of those actings; it will continue springing up till it come to perfection. *Thirdly,* The crown of them, eternal life at last. The living water rises *from* heaven, and therefore rises *towards* heaven; see Eccl. i. 7. And now is not this water better than that of Jacob's well?

[6.] The woman (whether in jest or earnest is hard to say) begs of him to give her some of this water (*v.* 15): *Give me this water, that I thirst not. First,* Some think that she speaks *tauntingly,* and ridicules what Christ had said as mere stuff; and, in derision of it, not *desires,* but *challenges* him to give her some of this water: "A rare invention; it will save me a great deal of *pain* if I *thirst not,* and a great deal of *pains* if I never *come hither to draw.*" But, *Secondly,* Others think that it was a *well-meant* but weak and ignorant desire. She apprehended that he meant something very good and useful, and therefore saith *Amen,* at a venture. *Whatever it be,* let me have it; *who will show me any good? Ease,* or saving of labour, is a valuable good to poor labouring people. Note, 1. Even those that are weak and ignorant may yet have some faint and fluctuating desires towards Christ and his gifts, and some good wishes of grace and glory. 2. Carnal hearts, in their best wishes, look no higher than carnal ends. "Give it to me," saith she, "not that I may have everlasting life" (which Christ proposed), "but that I *come not hither to draw.*"

2. The next subject of discourse with this woman is *concerning her husband, v.* 16—18. It was not to let fall the discourse of the water of life that Christ started this, as many who will bring in any *impertinence* in conversation that they may drop a serious subject; but it was with a gracious design that Christ mentioned it. What he had said concerning his grace and eternal life he found had made little impression upon her, because she had not been convinced of sin: therefore, waiving the discourse about the living water, he sets himself to awaken her conscience, to open the wound of guilt, and then she would more easily apprehend the remedy by grace. And this is the method of dealing with souls; they must first be made *weary* and *heavy-laden* under the burden of sin, and then brought to Christ for rest; first pricked to the heart, and then healed. This is the course of spiritual physic; and if we proceed not in this order we begin at the wrong end.

Observe, (1.) How discreetly and decently Christ introduces this discourse (*v.* 16): *Go, call thy husband, and come hither.* Now, [1.] The order Christ gave her had a *very good colour:* "*Call thy husband,* that he may teach thee, and help thee to understand these things, which thou art so ignorant of." The wives that will learn must *ask their husbands* (1 Cor. xiv. 35), who must dwell with them *as men of knowledge,* 1 Pet. iii. 7. "*Call thy hus-*

band, that he may learn with thee; that then you may be *heirs together of the grace of life. Call thy husband,* that he may be witness to what passes between us." Christ would thus teach us to *provide things honest in the sight of all men,* and to study that which is of good report. [2.] As it had a good colour, so it had a *good design;* for hence he would take occasion to call her sin to remembrance. There is need of art and prudence in giving reproofs; to fetch a compass, as the woman of Tekoa, 2 Sam. xiv. 20.

(2.) How industriously the woman seeks to evade the conviction, and yet insensibly convicts herself, and, ere she is aware, owns her fault; she said, *I have no husband.* Her saying this intimated no more than that she did not care to have her husband spoken of, nor that matter mentioned any more. She would not have her husband come thither, lest, in further discourse, the truth of the matter should come out, to her shame; and therefore, "Pray go on to talk of something else, *I have no husband;*" she would be thought a *maid* or a *widow,* whereas, though she had no husband, she was neither. The carnal mind is very ingenious to *shift off* convictions, and to keep them from fastening, careful to *cover the sin.*

(3.) How closely our Lord Jesus brings home the conviction to her conscience. It is probable that he said more than is here recorded, for she thought that he told her all that ever she did (*v.* 29), but that which is here recorded is concerning her husbands. Here is, [1.] A *surprising narrative* of her *past* conversation: *Thou hast had five husbands.* Doubtless, it was not her *affliction* (the burying of so many husbands), but her *sin,* that Christ intended to upbraid her with; either she had *eloped* (as the law speaks), had run away from her *husbands,* and married others, or by her undutiful, unclean, disloyal conduct, had provoked them to *divorce her,* or by indirect means had, contrary to law, *divorced them.* Those who make light of such scandalous practices as these, as no more than *nine days' wonder,* and as if the guilt were over as soon as the talk is over, should remember that Christ keeps account of all. [2.] A severe reproof of her present state of life: *He whom thou now hast is not thy husband.* Either she was never married to him at all, or he had some other wife, or, which is most probable, her former husband or husbands were living: so that, in short, *she lived in adultery.* Yet observe how mildly Christ tells her of it; he doth not call her *strumpet,* but tells her, *He with whom thou livest is not thy husband:* and then leaves it to her own conscience to say the rest. Note, Reproofs are ordinarily *most profitable* when they are *least provoking.* [3.] Yet in this he puts a better construction than it would well bear upon what she said by way of shuffle and evasion: *Thou hast well said I have no husband;* and again, *In that saidst thou truly* What she intended as a *denial of the fact* (that she had none with whom she lived as a husband) he favourably interpreted, or at least turned upon her, as a *confession of the fault.* Note, Those who would win souls should *make the best* of them, whereby they may hope to *work* upon their *good-nature;* for, if they *make the worst* of them, they certainly *exasperate* their *ill-nature.*

3. The next subject of discourse with this woman is concerning *the place of worship, v.* 19—24. Observe,

(1.) A case of conscience proposed to Christ by the woman, concerning the place of worship, *v.* 19, 20.

[1.] The inducement she had to put this case: *Sir, I perceive that thou art a prophet.* She does not deny the truth of what he had charged her with, but by her silence owns the justice of the reproof; nor is she put into a passion by it, as many are when they are touched in a sore place, does not impute his censure to the general disgust the Jews had to the Samaritans, but (which is a rare thing) can bear to be told of a fault. But this is not all; she goes further: *First,* She speaks respectfully to him, calls him *Sir.* Thus should we *honour* those that deal faithfully with us. This was the effect of Christ's meekness in reproving her; he gave her no ill language, and then she gave him none. *Secondly,* She acknowledges him to be a *prophet,* one that had a correspondence with Heaven. Note, The power of the word of Christ in searching the heart, and convincing the conscience of secret sins, is a great proof of its divine authority, 1 Cor. xiv. 24, 25. *Thirdly,* She desires some further instruction from him. Many that are not *angry* at their reprovers, nor fly in their faces, yet are *afraid* of them and keep out of their way; but this woman was willing to have some more discourse with him that told her of her faults.

[2.] The case itself that she propounded concerning the *place of religious worship in public.* Some think that she started this to shift off further discourse concerning her sin. Controversies in religion often prove great prejudices to serious godliness; but, it should seem, she proposed it with a good design; she knew she must worship God, and desired to do it aright; and therefore, meeting with a prophet, begs his direction. Note, It is our wisdom to improve all opportunities of getting knowledge in the things of God. When we are in company with those that are *fit to teach,* let us be *forward to learn,* and have a *good question* ready to put to those who are able to give a *good answer.* It was agreed between the Jews and the Samaritans that God is to be worshipped (even those who were such fools as to worship *false* gods were not such brutes as to worship none), and that religious worship is an affair of great importance: men would not *contend* about it if they were not *concerned* about it. But the matter in variance was *where* they should worship God. Observe how she states the case:—

First, As for the Samaritans: *Our fathers worshipped in this mountain,* near to this city and this well; there the Samaritan temple was built by Sanballat, in favour of which she insinuates, 1. That whatever the temple was the place was holy; it was mount *Gerizim,* the mount on which the blessings were pronounced; and some think the same on which Abraham built his altar (Gen. xii. 6, 7), and Jacob his, Gen. xxxiii. 18—20. 2. That it might plead prescription: *Our fathers* worshipped here. She thinks they have antiquity, tradition, and succession, on their side. A *vain conversation* often supports itself with this, that it was *received by tradition from our fathers.* But she had little reason to boast of *their fathers;* for, when Antiochus persecuted the Jews, the Samaritans, for fear of sharing with them in their sufferings, not only renounced all relation to the Jews, but surrendered their temple to Antiochus, with a request that it might be dedicated to Jupiter Olympius, and called by his name. *Joseph. Antiq. lib.* xii. *cap.* 7.

Secondly, As to the Jews: *You say* that *in Jerusalem is the place where men ought to worship.* The Samaritans governed themselves by the five books of Moses, and (some think) received *only them* as canonical. Now, though they found frequent mention there of the place God would choose, yet they did not find it named there; and they saw the temple at Jerusalem stripped of many of its ancient glories, and therefore thought themselves at liberty to set up another place, altar against altar.

(2.) Christ's answer to this case of conscience, *v.* 21, &c. Those that apply themselves to Christ for instruction shall find him *meek, to teach the meek his way.* Now here,

[1.] He puts *a slight* upon the question, as she had proposed it, concerning the place of worship (*v.* 21): "*Woman, believe me* as a prophet, and mark what I say. Thou art expecting the *hour to come* when either by some divine revelation, or some signal providence, this matter shall be decided in favour either of Jerusalem or of Mount Gerizim; but I tell thee the hour is at hand when it shall be no more a question; that which thou hast been taught to lay so much weight on shall be set aside as a thing *indifferent.*" Note, It should cool us in our contests to think that those things which now fill us, and which we make such a noise about, shall shortly *vanish,* and be *no more;* the very things we are striving about are passing away: *The hour comes when you shall neither in this mountain nor yet at Jerusalem worship the Father. First,* The object of worship is supposed to continue still the same—*God,* as a Father; under this notion the very heathen worshipped God, the Jews did so, and probably the Samaritans. *Secondly,* But a period shall be put to all niceness and all differences about the place of worship. The approaching dissolution of the Jewish economy, and the erecting of the evangelical state, shall set this matter *at large,* and lay all *in common,* so that it shall be a thing perfectly indifferent whether in either of these places or any other men worship God, for they shall not be tied to any place; neither *here* nor *there,* but *both,* and *any where,* and *every where.* Note, The worship of God is not now, under the gospel, appropriated to any place, as it was under the law, but it is God's will that men pray every where. 1 Tim. ii. 8; Mal. i. 11 Our reason teaches us to consult *decency* and *convenience* in the places of our worship: but our religion gives no preference to one place above another, in respect to holiness and acceptableness to God. Those who prefer any worship merely for the sake of the house or building in which it is performed (though it were as magnificent and as *solemnly* consecrated as ever Solomon's temple was) forget that the *hour is come* when there shall be no difference put in God's account; no, not between Jerusalem, which *had been* so famous for sanctity, and the mountain of Samaria, which *had been* so infamous for impiety.

[2.] He *lays a stress* upon other things, in the matter of religious worship. When he made so light of the place of worship he did not intend to lessen our concern about the thing itself, of which therefore he takes occasion to discourse more fully.

First, As to the present state of the controversy, he *determines* against the Samaritan worship, and in favour of the Jews, *v.* 22. He tells her here, 1. That the Samaritans were certainly *in the wrong;* not merely because they worshipped in this mountain, though, while Jerusalem's choice was in force, that was sinful, but because they were out in the object of their worship. If the worship itself had been as it should have been, its separation from Jerusalem might have been connived at, as the *high places* were in the best reigns: *But you worship you know not what,* or *that which you do not know.* They worshipped the God of Israel, the true God (Ezra iv. 2; 2 Kings xvii. 32); but they were sunk into gross ignorance; they worshipped him as the *God of that land* (2 Kings xvii. 27, 33), as a local deity, like the gods of the nations, whereas God must be served *as God,* as the universal cause and Lord. Note, Ignorance is so far from being the *mother* of devotion that it is the *murderer* of it. Those that worship God *ignorantly* offer the *blind for sacrifice,* and it is the *sacrifice of fools.* 2. That the Jews were certainly *in the right.* For, (1.) "*We know what we worship.* We go upon sure grounds in our worship, for our people are catechised and trained up in the knowledge of God, as he has revealed himself in the scripture." Note, Those who by the scriptures have obtained some knowledge of God (a *certain* though not a *perfect* knowledge) may worship him *comfortably* to themselves, and *acceptably* to him, for they *know what they worship.* Christ elsewhere condemns the corruptions of the Jews' worship (Matt. xv. 9), and yet here defends the worship itself; the worship may be *true* where yet it is not *pure* and *entire.* Observe, Our Lord Jesus was pleased to reckon himself among the *worshippers* of God: *We worship. Though he was a Son* (and then are the children free), *yet learned he this obedience,* in the days of his humiliation. Let not the greatest of men think the worship of God below them, when the Son of God himself did not. (2.) *Salvation is of the Jews;* and therefore they know what they worship, and what grounds they go upon in their worship. Not that all the Jews were saved, nor that it was not possible but that many of the Gentiles and Samaritans might be saved, for in *every nation* he that fears God and works righteousness is *accepted of him;* but, [1.] The author of eternal salvation comes of the Jews, appears among them (Rom. ix. 5), and is sent first to *bless* them. [2.] The means of eternal salvation are afforded to them. The *word of salvation* (Acts xiii. 26) was *of the Jews.* It was delivered to them, and other nations derived it through them. This was a sure guide to them in their devotions, and they followed it, and therefore knew what they worshipped. To them were committed the *oracles of God* (Rom. iii. 2), and the *service of God,* Rom. ix. 4. The Jews therefore being thus privileged and advanced, it was presumption for the Samaritans to vie with them.

Secondly, He describes the evangelical worship which alone God would accept and be well pleased with. Having shown that the place is *indifferent,* he comes to show what is *necessary* and *essential*—that we worship God *in spirit and in truth, v.* 23, 24. The stress is not to be laid upon the *place* where we worship God, but upon the state of *mind* in which we worship him. Note, The most effectual way to take up differences in the minor matters of religion is to be more zealous in the greater. Those who daily make it the matter of their care to worship *in the spirit,* one would think, should not make it the matter of their strife whether he should be worshipped here or there. Christ had justly preferred the Jewish worship before the Samaritan, yet here he intimates the imperfection of that. The worship was *ceremonial,* Heb. ix. 1, 10. The worshippers were generally *carnal,* and strangers to the *inward part* of divine worship. Note, It is possible that we may be better than our neighbours, and yet not so good as we should be. It concerns us to be right, not only in the *object* of our worship, but in the *manner* of it; and it is this which Christ here instructs us in. Observe,

a. The great and glorious revolution which should introduce this change: *The hour cometh, and now is*—the fixed stated time, concerning which it was of old determined when it should come, and how long it should last. The time of its *appearance* is *fixed* to an hour, so punctual and exact are the divine counsels; the time of its *continuance* is *limited* to an hour, so close and pressing is the opportunity of divine grace, 2 Cor. vi. 2. This hour *cometh,* it is coming in its full strength, lustre, and perfection, it *now is* in the embryo and infancy. The *perfect day is coming,* and now it *dawns.*

b. The blessed change itself. In gospel times the *true worshippers shall worship the Father in spirit and in truth.* As creatures, we worship the Father of *all:* as Christians, we worship *the Father of our Lord Jesus.* Now the change shall be, (*a.*) In the *nature* of the worship. Christians shall worship God, not in the ceremonial observances of the Mosaic institution, but in *spiritual* ordinances, consisting less in *bodily exercise,* and animated and invigorated more with divine power and energy. The way of worship which Christ has instituted is rational and intellectual, and refined from those external rites and ceremonies with which the Old-Testament worship was both clouded and clogged. This is called true worship, in opposition to that which was typical. The legal services were *figures of the true,* Heb. ix. 3, 24. Those that revolted from Christianity to Judaism are said to *begin in the spirit, and end in the flesh,* Gal. iii. 3. Such was the difference between Old-Testament and New-Testament institutions. (*b.*) In the *temper* and *disposition* of the worshippers; and so the true worshippers are good Christians, distinguished from hypocrites; all *should,* and they will, worship God *in spirit and in truth.* It is spoken of (*v.* 23) as their character, and (*v* 24) as their duty. Note, It is required of all that worship God that they worship him *in spirit and in truth.* We must worship God, [*a.*] *In spirit,* Phil. iii. 3. We must depend upon *God's Spirit* for strength and assistance, laying our souls under his influences and operations; we must devote *our own spirits* to, and employ them in, the service of God (Rom. i. 9), must worship him with fixedness of thought and a flame of affection, with *all that is within us.* Spirit is sometimes put for the new nature, in opposition to the *flesh,* which is the corrupt nature; and so to worship God *with our spirits* is to worship him *with our graces,* Heb. xii. 28. [*b.*] *In truth,* that is, in *sincerity.* God requires not only the *inward part* in our worship, but *truth in the inward part,* Ps. li. 6. We must mind the power more than the form, must aim at God's glory, and not to be *seen of men;* draw near with a *true heart,* Heb. x. 22.

Thirdly, He intimates the reasons why God must be thus worshipped.

a. Because in gospel times they, and they only, are accounted the *true* worshippers. The gospel erects a spiritual way of worship, so that the professors of the gospel are not true in their profession, do not live up to gospel light and laws, if they do not worship God *in spirit and in truth.*

b. Because *the Father seeketh such worshippers of him.* This intimates, (*a.*) That such worshippers are very rare, and seldom met with, Jer. xxx. 21. The gate of spiritual worshipping is strait. (*b.*) That such worship is necessary, and what the God of heaven insists upon. When God comes to *enquire* for worshippers, the question will not be, "Who worshipped at Jerusalem?" but, "Who worshipped in spirit?" That will be the touchstone. (*c.*) That God is greatly well pleased with and graciously accepts such worship and such worshippers. *I have desired it,* Ps. cxxxii. 13, 14; Cant. ii. 14. (*d.*) That there has been, and will be to the end, a remnant of such worshippers; his *seeking* such worshippers implies his *making* them such. God is in all ages gathering in to himself a generation of spiritual worshippers.

c. Because *God is a spirit.* Christ came to *declare God* to us (*ch.* i. 18), and this he has declared concerning him; he declared it to this poor Samaritan woman, for the meanest are concerned to know God; and with this design, to rectify her mistakes concerning religious worship, to which nothing would contribute more than the right knowledge of God. Note, (*a.*) *God is a spirit,* for he is an infinite and eternal mind, an intelligent being, incorporeal, immaterial, invisible, and incorruptible. It is easier to say what God is not than what he is; a spirit *has not flesh and bones,* but *who knows the way of a spirit?* If God were not *a spirit,* he could not be *perfect,* nor infinite, nor eternal, nor independent, nor the Father of spirits. (*b.*) The spirituality of the divine nature is a very good reason for the spirituality of divine worship. If we do not worship God, who is *a spirit, in the spirit,* we neither *give him the glory due to his name,* and so do not perform the *act* of worship, nor can we hope to obtain his favour and acceptance, and so we miss of the *end* of worship, Matt. xv. 8, 9.

4. The last subject of discourse with this woman is concerning the Messiah, *v.* 25, 26. Observe here,

(1.) The faith of the woman, by which she expected the Messiah: *I know that Messias cometh—and he will tell us all things.* She had nothing to object against what Christ had said; his discourse was, for aught she knew, what might become the Messiah then expected; but *from him* she would receive it, and in the mean time she thinks it best to suspend her belief. Thus many have no heart to the price *in their hand* (Prov. xvii. 16), because they think they have a better *in their eye,* and deceive themselves with a promise that they will learn that *hereafter* which they neglect *now.* Observe here,

[1.] Whom she expects: *I know that Messias cometh.* The Jews and Samaritans, though so much at variance, agreed in the expectation of the Messiah and his kingdom. The Samaritans received the writings of Moses, and were no strangers to the prophets, nor to the hopes of the Jewish nation; those who knew least knew this, that Messias was to come; so general and uncontested was the expectation of him, and at this time more raised than ever (for the sceptre was departed from Judah, Daniel's weeks were near expiring), so that she concludes not only, *He will come,* but ἔρχεται—"*He comes,* he is just at hand:" *Messias, who is called Christ.* The evangelist, though he retains the Hebrew word *Messias* (which the woman used in honour to the holy language, and to the Jewish church, that used it familiarly), yet, writing for the use of the Gentiles, he takes care to render it by a Greek word of the same signification, *who is called Christ—Anointed,* giving an example to the apostle's rule, that whatever is spoken in an unknown or less vulgar tongue should be *interpreted,* 1 Cor. xiv. 27, 28.

[2.] What she expects from him: "*He will tell us all things* relating to the service of God which it is needful for us to know, will tell us that which will supply our defects, rectify our mistakes, and put an end to all our disputes. He will tell us the mind of God fully and clearly, and keep back nothing." Now this implies an acknowledgment, *First,* Of the deficiency and imperfection of the discovery they now had of the divine will, and the rule they had of the divine worship; it *could not make the comers thereunto perfect,* and therefore they expected some great advance and improvement in matters of religion, a time of reformation. *Secondly,* Of the sufficiency of the Messiah to make this change: "*He will tell us all things* which we want to know, and about which we wrangle in the dark. He will introduce *peace,* by *leading us into all truth,* and dispelling the mists of error." It seems, this was the comfort of good people in those dark times that light would arise; if they found themselves at a loss, and run aground, it was a satisfaction to them to say, *When Messias comes, he will tell us all things;* as it may be to us now with reference to his second coming: now we see through a glass, but then *face to face.*

(2.) The favour of our Lord Jesus in making himself known to her: *I that speak to thee am he, v.* 26. Christ did never make himself known so expressly to any as he did here to this poor Samaritan, and to the blind man (*ch.* ix. 37); no, not to John Baptist, when he sent to him (Matt. xi. 4, 5); no, not to the Jews, when they challenged him to tell them whether he was the Christ, *ch.* x. 24. But, [1.] Christ would thus put an honour upon such as were poor and despised, Jam. ii. 6. [2.] This woman, for aught we know, had never had any opportunity of seeing Christ's miracles, which were then the ordinary method of conviction. Note, To those who have not the advantage of the *external* means of knowledge and grace God hath *secret* ways of making up the want of them; we must therefore judge charitably concerning such. God can make the light of grace shine *into the heart* even where he doth not make the light of the gospel shine *in the face.* [3.] This woman was better prepared to receive such a discovery than others were; she was big with expectation of the Messiah, and ready to receive instruction from him. Christ will manifest himself to those who with an honest humble heart desire to be acquainted with him: *I that speak to thee am he.* See here, *First,* How near Jesus Christ was to her, when she knew not who he was, Gen. xxviii. 16. Many are lamenting Christ's absence, and longing for his presence, when at the same time he is speaking to them. *Secondly,* How Christ makes himself known to us by *speaking* to us: *I that speak unto thee,* so closely, so convincingly, with such assurance, with such authority, *I am he.*

27 And upon this came his disciples, and marvelled that he talked
with the woman: yet no man said,
What seekest thou? or, Why talkest
thou with her? 28 The woman then
left her waterpot, and went her way
into the city, and saith to the men,
29 Come, see a man, which told me
all things that ever I did: is not this
the Christ? 30 Then they went out
of the city, and came unto him. 31
In the mean while his disciples prayed
him, saying, Master, eat. 32 But he
said unto them, I have meat to eat
that ye know not of. 33 Therefore
said the disciples one to another, Hath
any man brought him *ought* to eat?
34 Jesus saith unto them, My meat
is to do the will of him that sent me,
and to finish his work. 35 Say not
ye, There are yet four months, and
then cometh harvest? behold, I say
unto you, Lift up your eyes, and look
on the fields; for they are white already to harvest. 36 And he that
reapeth receiveth wages, and gathereth fruit unto life eternal: that both
he that soweth and he that reapeth
may rejoice together. 37 And herein
is that saying true, One soweth, and
another reapeth. 38 I sent you to
reap that whereon ye bestowed no
labour: other men laboured, and ye
are entered into their labours. 39
And many of the Samaritans of that
city believed on him for the saying of
the woman, which testified, He told
me all that ever I did. 40 So when
the Samaritans were come unto him,
they besought him that he would
tarry with them: and he abode there
two days. 41 And many more believed, because of his own word; 42
And said unto the woman, Now we
believe, not because of thy saying:
for we have heard him ourselves, and
know that this is indeed the Christ,
the Saviour of the world.

We have here the remainder of the story of what happened when Christ was in Samaria, after the long conference he had with the woman

I. The *interruption given to this discourse* by the disciples' coming. It is probable that much more was said than is recorded; but just when the discourse was brought to a head, when Christ had made himself known to her as the true Messiah, *then came the disciples.* The *daughters of Jerusalem* shall not *stir up nor awake my love till he please.* 1. They wondered at Christ's converse with this woman, marvelled that he talked thus earnestly (as perhaps they observed at a distance) with a woman, a strange woman alone (he used to be more *reserved),* especially with a Samaritan woman, that was not of the lost sheep of the house of Israel; they thought their Master should be as shy of the Samaritans as the other Jews were, at least that he should not preach the gospel to them. They wondered he should condescend to talk with such a poor contemptible woman, forgetting what despicable men they themselves were when Christ first called them into fellowship with himself. 2. Yet they acquiesced in it; they knew it was for some good reason, and some good end, of which he was not bound to give them an account, and therefore none of them asked, *What seekest thou? or, Why talkest thou with her?* Thus, when particular difficulties occur in the word and providence of God, it is good to satisfy ourselves with this in general, that all is well which Jesus Christ saith and doeth. Perhaps there was something *amiss* in their *marvelling* that *Christ talked with the woman:* it was something like the Pharisees being offended at his eating with publicans and sinners. But, whatever they *thought,* they said *nothing. If thou hast thought evil* at any time, *lay thy hand upon thy mouth,* to keep that evil thought from turning into an evil word, Prov. xxx. 32; Ps. xxxix. 1—3.

II. The notice which the woman gave to her neighbours of the extraordinary person she had happily met with, *v.* 28, 29. Observe here,

1. How she *forgot her errand to the well, v.* 28. Therefore, because the disciples were come, and broke up the discourse, and per-

haps she observed they were not pleased with it, she *went her way*. She withdrew, in civility to Christ, that he might have leisure to *eat his dinner*. She delighted in his discourse, but would not be *rude;* every thing is beautiful in its season. She supposed that Jesus, when he had dined, would go forward in his journey, and therefore hastened to tell her neighbours, that they might come quickly. *Yet a little while is the light with you.* See how she improved time; when one good work was done, she applied herself to another. When opportunities of *getting good* cease, or are interrupted, we should seek opportunities of *doing good;* when we have done *hearing* the word, then is a time to be *speaking* of it. Notice is taken of her *leaving her water-pot* or *pail*. (1.) She left it in kindness to Christ, that he might have water to drink with his dinner, for fair water was his drink; he turned water into wine for others, but not for himself. Compare this with Rebecca's civility to Abraham's servant (Gen. xxiv. 18), and see that promise, Matt. x. 42. (2.) She left it that she might make the more haste into the city, to carry thither these good tidings. Those whose business it is to publish the name of Christ must not encumber or entangle themselves with any thing that will retard or hinder them therein. When the disciples are to be made fishers of men they must *forsake all*. (3.) She left her water-pot, as one *careless of it*, being wholly taken up with better things. Note, Those who are brought to the knowledge of Christ will show it by a holy contempt of this world and the things of it. And those who are *newly* acquainted with the things of God must be *excused*, if at first they be so taken up with the new world into which they are brought that the things of this world seem to be for a time wholly neglected. Mr. Hildersham, in one of his sermons on this verse, from this instance largely justifies those who leave their worldly business on week-days to go to hear sermons.

2. How she *minded her errand to the town*, for her heart was upon it. She *went into the city*, and said to *the men*, probably the aldermen, the men in authority, whom, it may be, she found met together upon some public business; or to *the men*, that is, to every man she met in the streets; she proclaimed it in the chief places of concourse: *Come, see a man who told me all things that ever I did. Is not this the Christ?* Observe,

(1.) How *solicitous* she was to *have her friends and neighbours* acquainted with Christ. When she had found that treasure, she *called together her friends and neighbours* (as Luke xv. 9), not only to *rejoice with her*, but to share with her, knowing there was enough to enrich herself and all that would partake with her. Note, They that have been themselves with Jesus, and have found comfort in him, should do all they can to bring others to him. Has he done us the honour to make himself known to us? Let us do him the honour to make him known to others; nor can we do ourselves a greater honour. This woman becomes an apostle. *Quæ scortum fuerat egressa, regreditur magistra evangelica —She who went forth a specimen of impurity returns a teacher of evangelical truth,* saith *Aretius*. Christ had told her to *call her husband*, which she thought was warrant enough to *call every body*. She went into *the city*, the city where she dwelt, among her kinsfolks and acquaintance. Though every man is my neighbour that I have opportunity of doing good to, yet I have most *opportunity*, and therefore lie under the greatest *obligations*, to do good to those that live near me. *Where the tree falls,* there let it be made useful.

(2.) How fair and ingenuous she was in the notice she gave them concerning this stranger she had met with. [1.] She *tells them* plainly what induced her to admire him: *He has told me all things that ever I did.* No more is recorded than what he told her of her husbands; but it is not improbable that he had told her of more of her faults. Or, his telling her that which she knew he could not by any ordinary means come to the knowledge of convinced her that he could have told her all that she ever did. If he has a *divine* knowledge, it must be omniscience. He told her that which none knew but God and her own conscience. Two things affected her:—*First, the extent of his knowledge.* We ourselves cannot tell *all things that ever we did* (many things pass *unheeded*, and more pass away and are forgotten); but Jesus Christ knows all the thoughts, words, and actions, of all the children of men; see Heb. iv. 13. He hath said, *I know thy works. Secondly, The power of his word.* This made a great impression upon her, that he told her her *secret sins* with such an unaccountable power and energy that, being told of one, she is *convinced of all, and judged of all.* She does not say, "Come, see a man that has told me strange things concerning religious worship, and the laws of it, that has decided the controversy between this mountain and Jerusalem, a man that calls himself the *Messias;*" but, "*Come see a man* that has told me of my sins." She fastens upon that part of Christ's discourse which one would think she would have been most shy of repeating; but experimental proofs of the power of Christ's word and Spirit are of all others the most cogent and convincing; and that *knowledge of Christ* into which we are led by the conviction of sin and humiliation is most likely to be *sound* and *saving*. [2.] She *invites them* to *come and see* him of whom she had conceived so high an opinion. Not barely, "Come and look upon him" (she does not invite them to him as a *show*), but, "Come and converse with him; come and *hear his wisdom*, as I have done, and you will be of my mind. She would not undertake to manage the arguments which had convinced her, in such a manner as to convince others; all that see the evidence of truth themselves are not able to make others see it; but, "Come, and talk with him, and you will find such a power in his word as far exceeds all other evidence." Note, Those who can do little else towards the conviction and conversion of others may and should bring them to those means of grace which they themselves have found effectual. Jesus was now at the town's end. "Now come see him." When opportunities of getting the knowledge of God are brought to our doors we are inexcusable if we neglect them; shall we not go over the threshold to see him whose day prophets and kings desired to see? [3.] She resolves to *appeal to themselves,* and their own sentiments upon the trial? *Is not this the Christ?* She does not peremptorily say, "He is the Messiah," how clear soever she was in her own mind, and yet she very prudently mentions the Messiah, of whom otherwise they would not have thought, and then refers it to themselves; she will not impose her faith upon them, but only propose it to them. By such fair but forcible appeals as these men's judgments and consciences are sometimes taken hold of ere they are aware.

(3.) What success she had in this invitation: *They went out of the city, and came to him, v.* 30. Though it might seem very improbable that a woman of so *small* a figure, and so *ill* a character, should have the honour of the first discovery of the Messiah among the Samaritans, yet it pleased God to incline their hearts to take notice of her report, and not to slight it as an idle tale. Time was when lepers were the first that brought tidings to Samaria of a great deliverance, 2 Kings vii. 3, &c. They *came unto him;* did not send for him into the city to them, but in token of their respect to him, and the earnestness of their desire to see him, they *went out to him.* Those that would know Christ must meet him where he records his name.

III. Christ's discourse with his disciples while the woman was absent, *v.* 31—38. See how industrious our Lord Jesus was to *redeem time,* to husband every minute of it, and to *fill up* the vacancies of it. When the disciples were gone into the town, his discourse with the woman was *edifying,* and suited to her case; when she was gone into the town, his discourse with them was no less edifying, and suited to their case; it were well if we could *thus* gather up the fragments of time, that none of it may be lost. Two things are observable in this discourse:—

1. How Christ *expresses the delight* which he himself had in his work. His work was to *seek and save* that which was lost, to go about doing good. Now with this work we here find him wholly taken up. For,

(1.) *He neglected his meat and drink for his work.* When he sat down upon the well, he was *weary,* and needed refreshment; but this opportunity of saving souls made him forget his weariness and hunger. And he minded *his food* so little that, [1.] His disciples were forced to invite him to it: *They prayed him,* they pressed him, saying, *Master, eat.* It was an instance of their *love to him* that they invited him, lest he should be faint and sick for want of some support; but it was a greater instance of his *love to souls* that he needed invitation. Let us learn hence a holy indifference even to the needful supports of life, in comparison with spiritual things. [2.] He minded it so little that they suspected he had had meat brought him in their absence (*v.* 33): *Has any man brought him aught to eat?* He had so little appetite for his dinner that they were ready to think he had dined already. Those that make religion their business will, when any of its affairs are to be attended, prefer them before their food; as Abraham's servant, that would not eat till he had told his errand (Gen. xxiv. 33), and Samuel, that would not sit down till David was anointed, 1 Sam. xvi. 11.

(2.) He *made his work his meat and drink.* The work he *had done* in instructing the woman, the work he *had to do* among the Samaritans, the prospect he now had of doing good to many, this was *meat and drink* to him; it was the greatest pleasure and satisfaction imaginable. Never did a hungry man, or an epicure, expect a plentiful feast with so much desire, nor feed upon its dainties with so much delight, as our Lord Jesus expected and improved an opportunity of doing good to souls. Concerning this he saith, [1.] That it was such *meat* as the disciples *knew not of.* They did not imagine that he had any design or prospect of planting his gospel among the Samaritans; this was a piece of usefulness they never thought of. Note, Christ by his gospel and Spirit does more good to the souls of men than his own disciples *know of* or *expect.* This may be said of good Christians too, who live by faith, that they have meat to eat which others know not of, joy with which a stranger does not intermeddle. Now this word made them ask, *Has any man brought him aught to eat?* so apt were even his own disciples to understand him after a corporal and carnal manner when he used similitudes. [2.] That the reason why his work was his meat and drink was because it was his Father's work, his Father's will: *My meat is to do the will of him that sent me, v.* 34. Note, *First,* The salvation of sinners is the *will of God,* and the instruction of them in order thereunto is *his work.* See 1 Tim. ii. 4. There is a chosen remnant whose salvation is in a particular manner his will. *Secondly,* Christ was *sent into the world* on this errand, to bring people to God, to know him and to be happy in him. *Thirdly,* He made this work his business and delight. When his body needed food, his mind was so taken up with this that he forgot both hunger and thirst, both meat and drink. Nothing could be more grateful to him than doing good; when he was invited *to meat* he went, that he might *do good*, for that was his meat always. *Fourthly*, He was not only ready upon all occasions to go to his work, but he was *earnest* and in care to go *through* it, and to *finish his work* in all the parts of it. He resolved never to quit it, nor lay it down, till he could say, *It is finished.* Many have zeal to carry them *out* at first, but not zeal to carry them *on* to the last; but our Lord Jesus was intent upon *finishing his work.* Our Master has herein left us an example, that we may learn to do the will of God as he did; 1. With diligence and close application, as those that make a business of it. 2. With delight and pleasure in it, as in our element. 3. With constancy and perseverance; not only minding to *do*, but aiming to *finish*, our work.

2. See here how Christ, having expressed his delight in *his* work, excites his disciples to diligence in *their* work; they were workers *with him*, and therefore should be workers *like him*, and make their work their *meat*, as he did. The work they had to do was to *preach the gospel*, and to set up the kingdom of the Messiah. Now this work he here compares to *harvest work*, the gathering in of the fruits of the earth; and this similitude he prosecutes throughout the discourse, *v.* 35—38. Note, gospel time is harvest time, and gospel work harvest work. The harvest is before *appointed* and expected; so was the gospel. Harvest time is *busy* time; all hands must be then at work: every one must work for *himself*, that he may reap of the graces and comforts of the gospel: ministers must work *for God*, to gather in souls to him. Harvest time is *opportunity*, a short and limited time, which will not last always; and harvest work is work that must be done *then* or not at all; so the time of the enjoyment of the gospel is a particular season, which must be improved for its proper purposes; for, once past, it cannot be recalled. The disciples were to gather in a harvest of souls for Christ. Now he here suggests three things to them to quicken them to diligence:—

(1.) That it was *necessary work*, and the *occasion* for it very urgent and pressing (*v.*35): *You say, It is four months to harvest; but* I say, *The fields are already white.* Here is,

[1.] A saying of Christ's disciples concerning the *corn-harvest; there are yet four months, and then comes harvest*, which may be taken either *generally*—"You say, for the encouragement of the sower at seed-time, that it will be but four months to the harvest." With us it is but about four months between the barley-sowing and the barley-harvest, probably it was so with them as to other grain; or, "Particularly, now at this time you reckon it will be four months to next harvest, according to the ordinary course of providence." The Jews' harvest began at the Passover, about Easter, much earlier in the year than ours, by which it appears that this journey of Christ from Judea to Galilee was in the winter, about the end of November, for he travelled *all weathers* to do good. God has not only promised us a harvest every year, but has appointed the *weeks of harvest;* so that we know *when* to expect it, and take our measures accordingly.

[2.] A saying of Christ's concerning the *gospel harvest;* his heart was as much upon the fruits of his gospel as the hearts of others were upon the fruits of the earth; and to this he would lead the thoughts of his disciples: *Look, the fields are already white unto the harvest. First,* Here in *this* place, where they *now* were, there was harvest work for *him* to do. They would have him to *eat, v.* 31. "Eat!" saith he, "I have other work to do, that is more needful; *look* what crowds of Samaritans are coming out of the town over the fields that are ready to receive the gospel;" probably there were many now in view. People's forwardness to hear the word is a great excitement to ministers' diligence and liveliness in preaching it. *Secondly,* In *other places,* all the country over, there was harvest work enough for them all to do. "*Consider the regions,* think of the state of the country, and you will find there are multitudes as ready to receive the gospel as a field of corn that is fully ripe is ready to be reaped." The fields were now made *white to the harvest,* 1. By the *decree of God* revealed in the prophecies of the Old Testament. Now was the time when the gathering of the people should be to Christ (Gen. xlix. 10), when great accessions should be made to the church and the bounds of it should be enlarged, and therefore it was time for them to be busy. It is a great encouragement to us to engage in any work for God, if we understand by the signs of the times that this is the proper season for that work, for then it will prosper. 2. By the *disposition of men.* John Baptist had *made ready a people prepared for the Lord,* Luke i. 17. Since he began to preach the kingdom of God *every man pressed into it,* Luke xvi. 16. This, therefore, was a time for the preachers of the gospel to apply themselves to their work with the utmost vigour, to *thrust in their sickle,* when the harvest was ripe, Rev. xiv. 15. It was *necessary* to work now, pity that such a season should be let slip. If the corn that is *ripe* be not reaped, it will *shed* and be lost, and the fowls will pick it up. If souls that are under convictions, and have some good inclinations, be not helped now, their hopeful beginnings will come to nothing, and they will be a prey to pretenders. It was also *easy* to work now; when the people's hearts are *prepared* the work will be done *suddenly,* 2 Chron. xxix. 36. It cannot but quicken ministers to take *pains* in preaching the word when they observe that people *take pleasure* in hearing it.

(2.) That it was *profitable* and *advantageous* work, which they themselves would be gainers by (*v.* 36): "*He that reapeth receiveth wages,* and so shall you." Christ has undertaken to pay those well whom he employs in his work; for he will never do as Jehoiakim did, *who used his neighbour's service without wages* (Jer. xxii. 13), or those who *by fraud kept back the hire of those* particularly *who reaped their corn-fields,* Jam. v. 4. Christ's reapers, though they cry *to him* day and night, shall never have cause to cry *against him,* nor to say they served a hard Master. He that reapeth, not only *shall* but *does* receive wages. There is a present reward in the service of Christ, and his work is *its own wages.* [1.] Christ's reapers have *fruit: He gathereth fruit unto life eternal;* that is, he shall both save himself and those that hear him, 1 Tim. iv. 16. If the faithful reaper save his own soul, that is fruit abounding to his account, it is fruit gathered to *life eternal;* and if, over and above this, he be instrumental to save the souls of others too, there is *fruit gathered.* Souls gathered to Christ are fruit, good fruit, the fruit that Christ seeks for (Rom. i. 13); it is gathered for Christ (Cant. viii. 11, 12); it is gathered to *life eternal.* This is the comfort of faithful ministers, that their work has a tendency to the eternal salvation of precious souls. [2.] They have *joy: That he that sows and they that reap may rejoice together.* The minister who is the happy instrument of beginning a good work is *he that sows,* as John Baptist; he that is employed to carry it on and perfect it is *he that reaps:* and both shall rejoice together. Note, *First,* Though God is to have all the glory of the success of the gospel, yet faithful ministers may themselves take the comfort of it. The reapers share in the *joy of harvest,* though the profits belong to the master, 1 Thess. ii. 19. *Secondly,* Those ministers who are variously gifted and employed should be so far from envying one another that they should rather mutually rejoice in each other's success and usefulness. Though all Christ's ministers are not alike *serviceable,* nor alike *successful,* yet, if they have obtained mercy of the Lord to be *faithful,* they shall all enter *together into the joy of their Lord* at last.

(3.) That it was *easy work,* and work that was half done to their hands by those that were gone before them: *One soweth, and another reapeth, v.* 37, 38. This sometimes denotes a grievous judgment upon him that sows, Mic. vi. 15; Deut. xxviii. 30, *Thou shalt sow, and another shall reap;* as Deut. vi. 11, *Houses full of all good things, which thou filledst not.* So here. Moses, and the prophets, and John Baptist, had *paved* the way to the gospel, had sown the good seed which the New-Testament ministers did in effect but gather the fruit of. *I sent you to reap that whereon you bestowed,* in comparison, no *labour.* Isa. xl. 3—5. [1.] This intimates *two things* concerning the Old-Testament ministry:—*First,* That it was very much *short* of the New-Testament ministry. Moses and the *prophets* sowed, but they could not be said to *reap,* so little did they see of the fruit of their labours. Their writings have done much more good since they left us than ever their preaching did. *Secondly,* That it was very *serviceable* to the New-Testament ministry, and made way for it. The writings of the prophets, which were read in the synagogues every sabbath day, raised people's expectations of the Messiah, and so prepared them to bid him welcome. Had it not been for the seed sown by the prophets, this Samaritan woman could not have said, *We know that Messias cometh.* The writings of the Old Testament are in some respects more useful to us than they could be to those to whom they were first written, because better understood by the accomplishment of them. See 1 Pet. i. 12; Heb. iv. 2; Rom. xvi. 25, 26. [2.] This also intimates *two things* concerning the ministry of the *apostles of Christ. First,* That it was a *fruitful* ministry: they were reapers that gathered in a great harvest of souls to Jesus Christ, and did more in seven years towards the setting up of the kingdom of God among men than the prophets of the Old Testament had done in twice so many ages. *Secondly,* That it was much *facilitated,* especially among the Jews, to whom they were first sent, by the writings of the prophets. The prophets *sowed in tears,* crying out, *We have laboured in vain;* the apostles *reaped in joy,* saying, *Thanks be to God, who always causeth us to triumph.* Note, From the labours of ministers that are dead and gone much good fruit may be reaped by the people that *survive* them and the ministers that *succeed* them. John Baptist, and those that assisted him, had *laboured,* and the disciples of Christ entered into their labours, built upon their foundation, and reaped the fruit of what they sowed. See what reason we have to bless God for those that are *gone before us,* for their preaching and their writing, for what they *did* and *suffered* in their day, for we are *entered into their labours;* their studies and services have made our work the easier. And when the ancient and modern labourers, those that came into the vineyard at the third hour and those that came in at the eleventh, meet in the day of account, they will be so far from envying one another the honour of their respective services that both *they that sowed* and they that *reaped* shall rejoice together; and the great Lord of the harvest shall have the glory of all.

IV. The *good effect* which this visit Christ made to the Samaritans (*en passant*) had upon them, and the fruit which was now presently gathered among them, *v.* 39—42. See what impressions were made on them,

1. By the *woman's testimony* concerning

Christ; though a single testimony, and of one of no good report, and the testimony no more than this, *He told me all that ever I did,* yet it had a good influence upon many. One would have thought that his telling the woman of her secret sins would have made them afraid of coming to him, lest he should tell them also of their faults; but they will venture that rather than not be acquainted with one who they had reason to think was a prophet. And *two things* they were brought to:—

(1.) To *credit* Christ's *word* (*v.* 39): *Many of the Samaritans of that city believed on him for the saying of the woman.* So far they *believed on him* that they took him for a *prophet,* and were desirous to know the mind of God from him; this is favourably interpreted a believing on him. Now observe, [1.] Who they were that believed: *Many of the Samaritans,* who were not of the house of Israel. Their faith was not only an *aggravation* of the *unbelief* of the Jews, from whom better might have been expected, but an *earnest* of the *faith* of the Gentiles, who would welcome that which the Jews rejected. [2.] Upon what inducement they believed: *For the saying of the woman.* See here, *First,* How God is sometimes pleased to use very weak and unlikely instruments for the beginning and carrying on of a good work. A little maid directed a great prince to Elisha, 2 Kings v. 2. *Secondly,* How great a matter a little fire kindles. Our Saviour, by instructing one poor woman, spread instruction to a whole town. Let not ministers be either *careless* in their preaching, or *discouraged* in it, because their hearers are *few* and *mean;* for, by doing good to *them,* good may be conveyed to *more,* and those that are more considerable. If they *teach every man his neighbour,* and *every man his brother,* a great number may learn at *second hand.* Philip preached the gospel to a single gentleman in his chariot upon the road, and he not only received it himself, but carried it into his country, and propagated it there. *Thirdly,* See how good it is to speak *experimentally* of Christ and the things of God. This woman could say little of Christ, but what she did say she spoke feelingly: *He told me all that ever I did.* Those are most likely to do good that can tell what God has done *for their souls,* Ps. lxvi. 16.

(2.) They were brought to *court his stay* among them (*v.* 40): When they were come to him *they besought him that he would tarry with them.* Upon the woman's report, they believed him to be a prophet, and *came to him;* and, when they *saw* him, the meanness of his appearance and the manifest poverty of his outward condition did not lessen their esteem of him and expectations from him, but still they respected him as a prophet. Note, There is hope of those who are got over the vulgar prejudices that men have against *true worth* in a *low estate.* Blessed are they that are not offended in Christ at the *first sight.* So far were they from being offended in him that they begged he would tarry with them; [1.] That they might *testify their respect* to him, and treat him with the honour and kindness due to his character. God's prophets and ministers are welcome guests to all those who sincerely embrace the gospel; as to Lydia, Acts xvi. 15. [2.] That they might receive instruction from him. Those that are taught of God are truly desirous to learn more, and to be better acquainted with Christ. Many would have flocked to one that would tell them *their fortune,* but these flocked to one that would tell them *their faults,* tell them of their sin and duty. The historian seems to lay an emphasis upon their being Samaritans; as Luke x. 33; xvii. 16. The Samaritans had not that reputation for religion which the Jews had; yet the Jews, who saw Christ's miracles, drove him from them: while the Samaritans, who saw not his miracles, nor shared in his favours, invited him to them. The *proof* of the gospel's success is not always according to the *probability,* nor what is *experienced* according to what is *expected* either way. The Samaritans were taught by the custom of their country to be shy of conversation with the Jews. There were Samaritans that refused to let Christ go through their town (Luke ix. 53), but these begged him to tarry with them. Note, It adds much to the praise of our love to Christ and his word if it conquers the prejudices of education and custom, and sets light by the censures of men. Now we are told that Christ granted their request.

First, He *abode there.* Though it was a city of the Samaritans nearly adjoining to their temple, yet, when he was *invited,* he *tarried* there; though he was upon a journey, and had further to go, yet, when he had an opportunity of doing good, he *abode there.* That is no real *hindrance* which will *further* our account. Yet he abode there but *two days,* because he had other places to visit and other work to do, and those *two* days were as many as came to the share of this city, out of the few days of our Saviour's sojourning upon earth.

Secondly, We are told what impressions were made upon them by Christ's own word, and his personal converse with them (*v.* 41, 42); what he *said* and *did* there is not related, whether he healed their sick or no; but it is intimated, in the effect, that he said and did that which convinced them that he was the Christ; and the labours of a minister are best told by the good fruit of them. Their hearing of *him* had a good effect, but *now their eyes saw him;* and the effect was, 1. That their number grew (*v.* 41): *Many more believed:* many that would not be persuaded to go out of the town to him were yet wrought upon, when he came among them, to believe in him. Note, It is comfortable to see the number of believers; and sometimes the zeal and forwardness of some may be a means to provoke many, and to stir them up to a holy emulation, Rom. xi. 14. 2. That their faith grew. Those who had been wrought upon by the report of the woman now saw cause to say, *Now we believe, not because of thy saying, v.* 42. Here are three things in which their *faith grew*:—(1.) In the matter of it, or that which they did believe. Upon the testimony of the woman, they believed him to be *a prophet,* or some extraordinary messenger from heaven; but now that they have conversed with him they believe that he is *the Christ,* the *Anointed One,* the very same that was promised to the fathers and expected by them, and that, being the *Christ,* he is the *Saviour of the world;* for the work to which he was anointed was to *save his people from their sins.* They believed him to be the Saviour not only of the Jews, but *of the world,* which they hoped would take them in, though Samaritans, for it was promised that he should be *Salvation to the ends of the earth,* Isa. xlix. 6. (2.) In the *certainty* of it; their faith now grew up to a full assurance: *We know* that this is indeed the *Christ; αληθῶς—truly;* not a pretended Christ, but a real one; not a *typical* Saviour, as many under the Old Testament, but *truly* one. Such an assurance as this of divine truths is what we should labour after; not only, We think it probable, and are willing to suppose that *Jesus* may be the *Christ,* but, We know that he is *indeed the Christ.* (3.) In the *ground* of it, which was a kind of spiritual sensation and experience: *Now we believe, not because of thy saying, for we have heard him ourselves.* They had before *believed for her saying,* and it was well, it was a good step; but now they find *further* and much *firmer* footing for their faith: "*Now we believe* because we have *heard him ourselves,* and have heard such excellent and divine truths, accompanied with such commanding power and evidence, that we are abundantly satisfied and assured that *this is the Christ.*" This is like what the queen of Sheba said of Solomon (1 Kings x. 6, 7): The *one half was not told me.* The Samaritans, who believed for the woman's saying, now gained further light; for *to him that hath shall be given;* he that is faithful in a little shall be trusted with more. In this instance we may see how *faith comes by hearing.* [1.] Faith comes *to the birth* by hearing the *report of men.* These Samaritans, for the sake of the woman's saying, believed so far as to *come and see,* to come and make trial. Thus the instructions of parents and preachers, and the testimony of the church and our experienced neighbours, *recommend* the doctrine of Christ *to our acquaintance,* and incline us to entertain it as highly probable. But, [2.] Faith *comes to its growth,* strength, and maturity, by hearing the testimony of Christ himself; and this goes further, and recommends his doctrine *to our acceptance,* and obliges us to believe it as undoubtedly certain. We were induced to look into the scriptures *by the saying* of those who told us that in them they had found eternal life; but when we ourselves have found it in them too, have experienced the enlightening, convincing, regenerating, sanctifying, comforting, power of the word, now we believe, *not for their saying,* but because we have searched them ourselves: and our faith *stands not in the wisdom of men, but in the power of God,* 1 Cor. ii. 5; 1 John v. 9, 10.

Thus was the seed of the gospel sown in Samaria. What effect there was of this afterwards does not appear, but we find that four or five years after, when Philip preached the gospel in Samaria, he found such blessed remains of this good work now wrought that the *people with one accord gave heed to those things which Philip spoke,* Acts viii. 5, 6, 8. But as some were pliable to good so were others to evil, whom Simon Magus bewitched with his sorceries, *v.* 9, 10.

43 Now after two days he departed
thence, and went into Galilee. 44
For Jesus himself testified, that a
prophet hath no honour in his own
country. 45 Then when he was come
into Galilee, the Galilæans received
him, having seen all the things that
he did at Jerusalem at the feast: for
they also went unto the feast. 46 So
Jesus came again into Cana of Galilee, where he made the water wine.
And there was a certain nobleman,
whose son was sick at Capernaum.
47 When he heard that Jesus was
come out of Judæa into Galilee, he
went unto him, and besought him
that he would come down, and heal
his son: for he was at the point of
death. 48 Then said Jesus unto
him, Except ye see signs and wonders, ye will not believe. 49 The
nobleman saith unto him, Sir, come
down ere my child die. 50 Jesus
saith unto him, Go thy way; thy son
liveth. And the man believed the
word that Jesus had spoken unto
him, and he went his way. 51 And
as he was now going down, his servants met him, and told *him,* saying,
Thy son liveth. 52 Then enquired
he of them the hour when he began
to amend. And they said unto him,
Yesterday at the seventh hour the
fever left him. 53 So the father
knew that *it was* at the same hour, in
the which Jesus said unto him, Thy
son liveth: and himself believed, and

his whole house. 54 This *is* again the second miracle *that* Jesus did, when he was come out of Judæa into Galilee.

In these verses we have,

I. Christ's *coming* into Galilee, *v.* 43. Though he was as welcome among the Samaritans as he could be any where, and had better success, yet *after two days* he left them, not so much because they were Samaritans, and he would not confirm those in their prejudices against him who said, *He is a Samaritan* (*ch.* viii. 48), but because *he must preach to other cities,* Luke iv. 43. *He went into Galilee,* for there he spent much of his time. Now see here,

1. Whither Christ went; into Galilee, into the country of Galilee, but not to Nazareth, which was strictly *his own* country. He went among the villages, but declined going to Nazareth, the head city, for a reason here given, which *Jesus himself testified,* who knew the temper of his countrymen, the hearts of all men, and the experiences of all prophets, and it is this, That *a prophet has no honour in his own country.* Note, (1.) Prophets ought to have honour, because God has put honour upon them and we do or may receive benefit by them. (2.) The honour due to the Lord's prophets has very often been denied them, and contempt put upon them. (3.) This *due* honour is most frequently denied them *in their own country;* see Luke iv. 24; Matt. xiii. 57. Not that it is universally true (no rule but has some exceptions), but it holds for the most part. Joseph, when he began to be a prophet, was most hated by his brethren; David was disdained by his brother (1 Sam. xvii. 28); Jeremiah was maligned by the men of Anathoth (Jer. xi. 21), Paul by his countrymen the Jews; and Christ's near kinsmen spoke most slightly of him, *ch.* vii. 5. Men's pride and envy make them scorn to be instructed by those who once were their school-fellows and play-fellows. Desire of novelty, and of that which is far-fetched and dear-bought, and seems to drop out of the sky to them, makes them despise those persons and things which they have been long used to and know the rise of. (4.) It is a great discouragement to a minister to go among a people who have no value for him or his labours. Christ would not go to Nazareth, because he knew how little respect he should have there. (5.) It is just with God to deny his gospel to those that despise the ministers of it. They that mock the messengers forfeit the benefit of the message. Matt. xxi. 35, 41.

2. What entertainment he met with among the Galileans in the country (*v.* 45): They *received him,* bade him welcome, and cheerfully attended on his doctrine. Christ and his gospel are not sent in vain; if they have not honour with *some,* they shall have with *others.* Now the reason given why these Galileans were so ready to receive Christ is because they had seen *the miracles he did at Jerusalem, v.* 45. Observe, (1.) They went up to Jerusalem at the feast, the feast of the passover. The Galileans lay very remote from Jerusalem, and their way thither lay through the country of the Samaritans, which was troublesome for a Jew to pass through, worse than Baca's valley of old; yet, in obedience to God's command, they *went up to the feast,* and there they became acquainted with Christ. Note, They that are diligent and constant in attending on public ordinances some time or other meet with more spiritual benefit than they expect. (2.) At Jerusalem they *saw* Christ's miracles, which recommended him and his doctrine very much to their faith and affections. The miracles were wrought for the benefit of those at Jerusalem; yet the Galileans who were accidentally there got more advantage by them than they did for whom they were chiefly designed. Thus the word preached to a *mixed multitude* may perhaps edify *occasional* hearers more than the constant auditory.

3. What city he went to. When he would go to a city, he chose to go to Cana of Galilee, *where he had made the water wine* (*v.* 46); thither he went, to see if there were any good fruits of that miracle remaining; and, if there were, to confirm their faith, and water what he had planted. The evangelist mentions this miracle here to teach us to keep in remembrance what we *have seen* of the works of Christ.

II. His *curing* the *nobleman's son* that was sick of a fever. This story is not recorded by any other of the evangelists; it comes in Matt. iv. 23.

Observe, 1. Who the *petitioner* was, and who the *patient:* the petitioner was a *nobleman;* the patient was his son: *There was a certain nobleman. Regulus* (so the Latin), a *little king;* so called, either for the largeness of his estate, or the extent of his power, or the royalties that belonged to his manor Some understand it as denoting his *preferment*—he was a courtier in some office about the king; others as denoting his *party*—he was an Herodian, a royalist, a prerogative-man, one that espoused the interests of the Herods, father and son; perhaps it was Chuza, Herod's steward (Luke viii. 3), or Manaen, Herod's foster-brother, Acts xiii. 1. There were saints in Cæsar's household. The father a nobleman, and yet the son sick; for dignities and titles of honour will be no security to persons and families from the assaults of sickness and death. It was fifteen miles from Capernaum where this nobleman lived to Cana, where Christ now was; yet this affliction in his family sent him so far to Christ.

2. How the petitioner made *his application* to the physician. Having heard that *Jesus was come out of* Judea to Galilee, and finding that he did not come towards Capernaum,

but turned off towards the other side of the country, he *went to him* himself, and *besought him to come and heal his son, v.* 47. See here, (1.) His *tender affection* to his son, that when he was sick he would spare no pains to get help for him. (2.) His *great respect* to our Lord Jesus, that he would come himself to wait upon him, when he might have sent a servant; and that he *besought him,* when, as a man in authority, some would think he might have ordered his attendance. The greatest men, when they come to God, must become beggars, and sue *sub forma pauperis —as paupers.* As to the errand he came upon, we may observe a mixture in *his faith.* [1.] There was *sincerity* in it; he did believe that Christ could heal his son, though his disease was dangerous. It is probable he had physicians to him, who had given him over; but he believed that Christ could cure him when the case seemed deplorable. [2.] Yet there was *infirmity* in his faith; he believed that Christ could heal his son, but, as it should seem, he thought he could not heal him at a distance, and therefore he besought him that he would *come down* and heal him, expecting, as Naaman did, that he would come and *strike his hand* over the patient, as if he could not cure him but by a *physical contact.* Thus we are apt to *limit the Holy One of Israel,* and to stint him to our forms. The centurion, a Gentile, a soldier, was so strong in faith as to say, *Lord, I am not worthy that thou shouldest come under my roof,* Matt. viii. 8. This nobleman, a Jew, must have Christ to come down, though it was a good day's journey, and despairs of a cure unless he come down, as if he must teach Christ how to work. We are encouraged to *pray,* but we are not allowed to prescribe: Lord, heal me; but, whether with a word or a touch, *thy will be done.*

3. The gentle rebuke he met with in this address (*v.* 48): *Jesus said to him,* "I see how it is; *except you see signs and wonders, you will not believe,* as the Samaritans did, though they saw no signs and wonders, and therefore I must work miracles among you." Though he was a *nobleman,* and now in *grief* about his son, and had shown great respect to Christ in coming so far to him, yet Christ gives him a reproof. Men's dignity in the world shall not exempt them from the rebukes of the word or providence; for Christ reproves not *after the hearing of his ears,* but *with equity,* Isa. xi. 3, 4. Observe, Christ first shows him his sin and weakness, to prepare him for mercy, and then grants his request. Those whom Christ intends to honour with his *favours* he first *humbles* with his *frowns.* The *Comforter* shall first *convince.* Herod longed to see some miracle (Luke xxiii. 8), and this courtier was of the same mind, and the generality of the people too. Now that which is blamed is, (1.) That, whereas they had heard by credible and incontestable report of the miracles he had wrought in other places, they would not believe except they saw them with their own eyes, Luke iv. 23. They must be *honoured,* and they must be *humoured,* or they will not be *convinced.* Their country must be graced, and their curiosity gratified, with signs and wonders, or else, though the doctrine of Christ be sufficiently proved by miracles wrought elsewhere, they *will not believe.* Like Thomas, they will yield to no method of conviction but what they shall prescribe. (2.) That, whereas they had seen divers miracles, the evidence of which they could not gainsay, but which sufficiently proved Christ to be a teacher come from God, and should now have applied themselves to him for instruction in his doctrine, which by its native excellency would have *gently led them on,* in believing, to a spiritual perfection, instead of this they would go no further in believing than they were *driven* by signs and wonders. The *spiritual* power of the word did not *affect them,* did not *attract* them, but only the *sensible* power of miracles, which were *for those* who believe not, while *prophesying* was for *those that believe,* 1 Cor. xiv. 22. Those that admire *miracles* only, and *despise prophesying,* rank themselves with unbelievers.

4. His continued importunity in his address (*v.* 49): *Sir, come down ere my child die.* Κύριε—*Lord;* so it should be rendered. In this reply of his we have, (1.) Something that was commendable: he took the reproof patiently; he spoke to Christ respectfully. Though he was one of those that wore soft clothing, yet he could bear reproof. It is none of the privileges of peerage to be above the reproofs of the word of Christ; but it is a sign of a good temper and disposition in men, especially in great men, when they can be told of their faults and not be angry. And, as he did not take the reproof for an affront, so he did not take it for a denial, but still prosecuted his request, and continued to wrestle till he prevailed. Nay, he might argue thus: "If Christ heal *my soul,* surely he will heal *my son;* if he cure *my* unbelief, he will cure *his* fever." This is the method Christ takes, first to work *upon* us, and then to work *for* us; and there is hope if we find him entering upon this method. (2.) Something that was blameworthy, that was his infirmity; for, [1.] He seems to take no notice of the reproof Christ gave him, says nothing to it, by way either of confession or of excuse, for he is so wholly taken up with concern about his child that he can mind nothing else. Note, The sorrow of the world is a great prejudice to our profiting by the word of Christ. Inordinate care and grief are thorns that choke the good seed; see Exod. vi. 9. [2.] He still discovered the weakness of his faith in the power of Christ. *First,* He must have Christ to come down, thinking that else he could do the child no kindness. It is hard to persuade ourselves that

distance of time and place are no obstructions to the knowledge and power of our Lord Jesus; yet so it is: he sees afar off, for his *eyes run to and fro;* and he acts afar off, for his word, the word of his power, *runs very swiftly. Secondly,* He believes that Christ could heal a *sick* child, but not that he could raise a *dead* child, and therefore, "O *come down, ere my child die,*" as if then it would be too late; whereas Christ has the same power over death that he has over bodily diseases. He forgot that Elijah and Elisha had raised dead children; and is Christ's power inferior to theirs? Observe what haste he is in: *Come down, ere my child die;* as if there were danger of Christ's slipping his time. *He that believeth does not make haste,* but refers himself to Christ. "Lord, what and when and how thou pleasest."

5. The answer of peace which Christ gave to his request at last (*v.* 50): *Go thy way, thy son liveth.* Christ here gives us an instance, (1.) Of his *power,* that he not only could heal, but could heal with so much ease, without the trouble of a visit. Here is nothing *said,* nothing *done,* nothing *ordered* to be done, and yet the cure wrought: *Thy son liveth.* The healing beams of the Sun of righteousness dispense benign influences from one end of heaven to another, and *there is nothing hid from the heat thereof.* Though Christ is now in heaven, and his church on earth, he can *send from above.* This nobleman would have Christ *come down and heal his son;* Christ will heal his son, and not *come down.* And thus the cure is the sooner wrought, the nobleman's mistake rectified, and his faith confirmed; so that the thing was better done in Christ's way. When he denies what we ask, he gives what is much more to our advantage; we ask for ease, he gives patience. Observe, His power was exerted by his word. In saying, *Thy son lives,* he showed that he has *life in himself,* and power to *quicken whom he will.* Christ's saying, *Thy soul lives,* makes it alive. (2.) Of his *pity;* he observed the nobleman to be *in pain* about his son, and his natural affection discovered itself in that word, *Ere my child,* my dear child, die; and therefore Christ dropped the reproof, and gave him assurance of the recovery of his child; for he knows how a father *pities his children.*

6. The nobleman's belief of the word of Christ: He *believed,* and *went away.* Though Christ did not gratify him so far as to go down with him, he is satisfied with the method Christ took, and reckons he has gained his point. How quickly, how easily, is that which is lacking in our faith perfected by the word and power of Christ. Now he *sees no sign or wonder,* and yet *believes* the wonder done. (1.) Christ said, *Thy son liveth,* and the man *believed* him; not only believed the omniscience of Christ, that he *knew* the child had recovered, but the omnipotence of Christ, that the cure was *effected* by his word. He left him *dying;* yet, when Christ said, *He lives,* like the father of the faithful, *against hope he believed in hope,* and *staggered not through unbelief.* (2.) Christ said, *Go thy way;* and, as an evidence of the sincerity of his faith, he *went his way,* and gave neither Christ nor himself any further disturbance. He did not press Christ to come down, did not say, "If he do recover, yet a visit will be acceptable; no, he seems no further solicitous, but, like Hannah, he goes his way, and his countenance is *no more sad.* As one entirely satisfied, he made no great haste home; did not hurry home that night, but returned leisurely, as one that was perfectly easy in his own mind.

7. The further confirmation of his faith, by comparing notes with his servants at his return. (1.) His servants met him with the agreeable news of the child's recovery, *v.* 51. Probably they met him not far from his own house, and, knowing what their master's cares were, they were willing as soon as they could to make him easy. David's servants were loth to tell him when the child was dead. Christ said, *Thy son liveth;* and now the servants say the same. Good news will meet those that hope in God's word. (2.) He enquired what hour the child began to recover (*v.* 52); not as if he doubted the influence of Christ's word upon the child's recovery, but he was desirous to have his faith confirmed, that he might be able to satisfy any to whom he should mention the miracle; for it was a material circumstance. Note, [1.] It is good to furnish ourselves with all the corroborating proofs and evidences that may be, to strengthen our faith in the word of Christ, that it may grow up to *a full assurance. Show me a token for good.* [2.] The diligent comparison of the works of Christ with his word will be of great use to us for the confirming of our faith. This was the course the nobleman took: *He enquired of the servants the hour when he began to amend;* and they told him, *Yesterday at the seventh hour* (at one o'clock in the afternoon, or, as some think this evangelist reckons, at seven o'clock at night) the *fever left him;* not only he began to amend, but he was perfectly well on a sudden; so *the father knew that it was at the same hour* when Jesus said to him, *Thy son liveth.* As the word of God, well-studied, will help us to understand his providences, so the providence of God, well observed, will help us to understand his word; for God is every day *fulfilling the scripture.* Two things would help to confirm his faith:—*First,* That the child's recovery was *sudden* and not *gradual.* They name the precise time to an hour: *Yesterday,* not *about,* but *at* the seventh hour, *the fever left him;* not it *abated,* or began to *decrease,* but it *left him* in an instant. The word of Christ did not work like physic, which must have time to operate, and produce the effect, and perhaps *cures by*

expectation only; no, with Christ it was *dictum factum—he spoke and it was done;* not, He spoke and it was *set a doing*. *Secondly,* That it was just at the same time that Christ spoke to him: *at that very hour*. The synchronisms and coincidents of events add very much to the beauty and harmony of Providence. Observe the *time*, and the *thing* itself will be more illustrious, for every thing is beautiful *in its time;* at the very time when it is *promised*, as Israel's deliverance (Exod. xii. 41); at the very time when it is *prayed for*, as Peter's deliverance, Acts xii. 12. In men's works, distance of place is the delay of time and the retarding of business; but it is not so in the works of Christ. The pardon, and peace, and comfort, and spiritual healing, which he speaks in heaven, are, if he pleases, at the same time effected and wrought in the souls of believers; and, when these two come to be *compared* in the great day, Christ will be *glorified in his saints, and admired in all them that believe*.

8. The *happy effect and issue of this*. The bringing of the cure to the family brought salvation to it. (1.) The nobleman *himself believed*. He had before *believed* the word of Christ, with reference to this particular occasion; but now he *believed in Christ* as the Messiah promised, and became one of his disciples. Thus the *particular* experience of the power and efficacy of *one* word of Christ may be a happy means to introduce and settle the whole authority of Christ's dominion in the soul. Christ has many ways of gaining the heart, and by the grant of a *temporal* mercy may make way for *better* things. (2.) His *whole house* believed likewise. [1.] Because of the *interest* they all had in the miracle, which preserved the *blossom* and *hopes* of the family; this affected them all, and endeared Christ to them, and recommended him to their best thoughts. [2.] Because of the *influence* the master of the family had upon them *all*. A master of a family cannot give faith to those under his charge, nor *force* them to believe, but he may be instrumental to remove *external prejudices*, which obstruct the operation of the evidence, and then the work is more than half done. *Abraham* was famous for this (Gen. xviii. 19), and Joshua, *ch.* xxiv. 15. This was a *nobleman*, and probably he had a *great household;* but, when he comes into Christ's school, he brings them all along with him. What a blessed change was here in this house, occasioned by the sickness of the child! This should reconcile us to afflictions; we know not what good may follow from them. Probably, the conversion of this *nobleman* and his family at Capernaum might induce Christ to come afterwards, and settle at Capernaum, as his head-quarters in Galilee. When great men receive the gospel, they may be instrumental to bring it to the places where they live.

9. Here is the evangelist's remark upon this cure (*v.* 54); *This is the second miracle*, referring to *ch.* ii. 11, where the turning of water into wine is said to be the first; that was soon after his first return out of Judea, this soon after his second. In Judea he had wrought many miracles, *ch.* iii. 2; iv. 45. They had the first offer; but, being driven thence, he wrought miracles in Galilee. Somewhere or other Christ will find a welcome. People may, if they please, shut the sun out of *their own houses*, but they cannot shut it *out of the world*. This is noted to be the *second* miracle, 1. To remind us of the first, wrought in the same place some months before. *Fresh* mercies should revive the remembrance of former mercies, as former mercies should encourage our hopes of further mercies. Christ keeps account of his favours, whether we do or no. 2. To let us know that *this* cure was *before* those many cures which the other evangelists mention to be wrought in Galilee, Matt. iv. 23; Mark i. 34; Luke iv. 40. Probably, the patient being a person of quality, the cure was the more talked of and sent him crowds of patients; when this nobleman applied himself to Christ, multitudes followed. What abundance of good may great men do, if they be good men!

CHAP. V.

We have in the gospels a faithful record of all that Jesus began both to do and to teach, Acts i. 1. These two are interwoven, because what he taught explained what he did, and what he did confirmed what he taught. Accordingly, we have in this chapter a miracle and a sermon. I. The miracle was the cure of an impotent man that had been diseased thirty-eight years, with the circumstances of that cure, ver. 1—16. II. The sermon was Christ's vindication of himself before the sanhedrim, when he was prosecuted as a criminal for healing the man on the sabbath day, in which, 1. He asserts his authority as Messiah, and Mediator between God and man, ver. 17---29. 2. He proves it by the testimony of his Father, of John Baptist, of his miracles, and of the scriptures of the Old Testament, and condemns the Jews for their unbelief, ver. 30—47.

AFTER this there was a feast
of the Jews; and Jesus went
up to Jerusalem. 2 Now there is
at Jerusalem by the sheep *market* a
pool, which is called in the Hebrew
tongue Bethesda, having five porches.
3 In these lay a great multitude of
impotent folk, of blind, halt, withered, waiting for the moving of the
water. 4 For an angel went down
at a certain season into the pool, and
troubled the water: whosoever then
first after the troubling of the water
stepped in was made whole of whatsoever disease he had. 5 And a certain man was there, which had an
infirmity thirty and eight years.
6 When Jesus saw him lie, and
knew that he had been now a long
time *in that case*, he saith unto him,
Wilt thou be made whole? 7 The
impotent man answered him, Sir, I

have no man, when the water is
troubled, to put me into the pool:
but while I am coming another step-
peth down before me. 8 Jesus saith
unto him, Rise, take up thy bed, and
walk. 9 And immediately the man
was made whole, and took up his bed,
and walked: and on the same day
was the sabbath. 10 The Jews therefore said unto him that was cured, It
is the sabbath day: it is not lawful
for thee to carry *thy* bed. 11 He
answered them, He that made me
whole, the same said unto me, Take
up thy bed, and walk. 12 Then
asked they him, What man is that
which said unto thee, Take up thy bed,
and walk? 13 And he that was
healed wist not who it was: for Jesus
had conveyed himself away, a multitude being in *that* place. 14 Afterward Jesus findeth him in the
temple, and said unto him, Behold,
thou art made whole: sin no more,
lest a worse thing come unto thee.
15 The man departed, and told the
Jews that it was Jesus, which had
made him whole. 16 And therefore
did the Jews persecute Jesus, and
sought to slay him, because he had
done these things on the sabbath
day.

This miraculous cure is not recorded by any other of the evangelists, who confine themselves mostly to the miracles wrought in Galilee, but John relates those wrought at Jerusalem. Concerning this observe,

I. *The time when* this cure was wrought: it was at a *feast of the Jews,* that is, the passover, for that was the most celebrated feast. Christ, though residing in Galilee, yet *went up to Jerusalem* at the feast, *v.* 1. 1. Because it was an *ordinance of God,* which, as a *subject,* he would observe, being made under the law; though as a *Son* he might have pleaded an exemption. Thus he would teach us to attend religious assemblies. Heb. x. 25. 2. Because it was an *opportunity of good;* for, (1.) there were great numbers gathered together there at that time; it was a general rendezvous, at least of all serious thinking people, from all parts of the country, besides proselytes from other nations: and Wisdom must *cry in the places of concourse,* Prov. i. 21. (2.) It was to be hoped that they were in a *good frame,* for they came together to *worship God* and to spend their time in religious exercises. Now a mind *inclined to devotion,* and sequestering itself to the exercises of piety, *lies very open* to the further discoveries of divine light and love, and to it Christ will be acceptable.

II. The *place where* this cure was wrought: at the *pool of Bethesda,* which had a miraculous healing virtue in it, and is here particularly described, *v.* 2—4.

1. Where it was situated: *At Jerusalem, by the sheep-market;* ἐπὶ τῇ προβατικῇ. It might as well be rendered the *sheep-cote,* where the sheep were kept, or the *sheep-gate,* which we read of, Neh. iii. 1, through which the sheep were *brought,* as the *sheep-market,* where they were *sold.* Some think it was near the temple, and, if so, it yielded a melancholy but profitable spectacle to those that went up to the temple to pray.

2. How it was called: It was a *pool* (a pond or bath), *which is called in Hebrew, Bethesda—the house of mercy;* for therein appeared much of the *mercy of God* to the sick and diseased. In a world of so much misery as this is, it is well that there are some *Bethesdas—houses of mercy* (remedies against those maladies), that the scene is not all melancholy. An *alms-house,* so Dr. Hammond. Dr. Lightfoot's conjecture is that this was the *upper pool* (Isa. vii. 3), and the *old pool,* Isa. xxii. 11; that it had been used for *washing* from ceremonial pollutions, for convenience of which the porches were built to dress and undress in, but it was lately become medicinal.

3. How it was fitted up: It had *five porches, cloisters, piazzas,* or *roofed walks,* in which the sick lay. Thus the charity of men concurred with the mercy of God for the relief of the distressed. Nature has provided *remedies,* but men must provide *hospitals.*

4. How it was frequented with sick and cripples (*v.* 3): *In these lay a great multitude of impotent folks.* How many are the afflictions of the afflicted in this world! How full of complaints are all places, and what multitudes of impotent folks! It may do us good to visit the hospitals sometimes, that we may take occasion, from the calamities of others, to thank God for our comforts. The evangelist specifies three sorts of diseased people that lay here, *blind, halt,* and *withered* or *sinew-shrunk,* either in one particular part, as the man with the *withered hand,* or all over paralytic. These are mentioned because, being least able to help themselves into the water, they lay longest waiting in the *porches.* Those that were sick of these bodily diseases took the pains to come *far* and had the patience to wait *long* for a cure; any of us would have done the same, and we ought to do so: but O that men were as wise for their souls, and as solicitous to get their spiritual diseases healed! We are all by nature *impotent folks* in spiritual things, *blind, halt,* and *withered;* but effectual provision is made for our cure if we will but observe orders.

5. What virtue it had for the cure of these impotent folks (*v.* 4). *An angel went down,* and *troubled the water;* and *whoso first step-*

ped in was made whole. That this strange virtue in the pool was *natural,* or *artificial* rather, and was the effect of the washing of the sacrifices, which impregnated the water with I know not what healing virtue even for *blind* people, and that the angel was a *messenger,* a common person, sent down to stir the water, is altogether groundless; there was a room in the temple on purpose to wash the sacrifices in. Expositors generally agree that the virtue this pool had was supernatural. It is true the Jewish writers, who are not sparing in recounting the praises of Jerusalem, do none of them make the least mention of this *healing pool,* of which silence in this matter perhaps this is the reason, that it was taken for a presage of the near approach of the Messiah, and therefore those who denied him to be come industriously concealed such an indication of his coming; so that this is all the account we have of it. Observe,

(1.) The *preparation* of the medicine by an angel, who *went down into the pool,* and *stirred the water.* Angels are God's servants, and friends to mankind; and perhaps are more active in the removing of diseases (as evil angels in the inflicting of them) than we are aware of. Raphael, the apocryphal name of an angel, signifies *medicina Dei—God's physic,* or *physician* rather. See what mean offices the holy angels condescend to, for the good of men. If we would do the will of God as the angels do it, we must think nothing below us but sin. The *troubling of the water* was the signal given of the descent of the angel, as the *going upon the tops of the mulberry trees* was to David, and then they must *bestir themselves.* The waters of the sanctuary are then *healing* when they are put in *motion.* Ministers must *stir up the gift* that is in them. When they are cold and dull in their ministrations, the waters *settle* and are not apt to *heal.* The angel descended, to *stir the water,* not daily, perhaps not frequently, but *at a certain season;* some think, at the three solemn feasts, to grace those solemnities; or, *now and then,* as Infinite Wisdom saw fit. God is a free agent in dispensing his favours.

(2.) The *operation* of the medicine: *Whoever first stepped in was made whole.* Here is, [1.] a miraculous extent of the virtue as to the *diseases* cured; what disease soever it was, this water cured it. Natural and artificial baths are as *hurtful* in some cases as they are useful in others, but this was a remedy for every malady, even for those that came from contrary causes. The power of miracles *succeeds* where the power of nature *succumbs.* [2.] A miraculous limitation of the virtue as to the *persons* cured: He that first stepped in had the benefit; that is, he or they that stepped in immediately were cured, not those that lingered and came in afterwards. This teaches us to observe and improve our opportunities, and to *look about us,* that we slip not a season which may never return. The angel *stirred* the waters, but left the diseased to themselves to *get in.* God has put virtue into the scriptures and ordinances, for he would have healed us; but, if we do not a make a due improvement of them, it is our own fault, we *would not be healed.*

Now this is all the account we have of this *standing* miracle; it is uncertain when it began and when it ceased. Some conjecture it began when Eliashib the high priest began the building of the wall about Jerusalem, and sanctified it with prayer; and that God testified his acceptance by putting this virtue into the adjoining pool. Some think it began now lately at Christ's birth; nay, others at his baptism. Dr. Lightfoot, finding in *Josephus, Antiq.* lib. xv. cap. 7, mention of a great earthquake in the seventh year of Herod, thirty years before Christ's birth, supposed, since there used to be earthquakes at the descent of angels, that then the angel first descended to stir this water. Some think it ceased with this miracle, others at Christ's death; however, it is certain it had a gracious signification. *First,* it was a *token* of God's good will to that people, and an indication that, though they had been long without prophets and miracles, yet God had not *cast them off;* though they were now an oppressed despised people, and many were ready to say, *Where are all the wonders that our fathers told us of?* God did hereby let them know that he had still a kindness for the *city of their solemnities.* We may hence take occasion to acknowledge with thankfulness God's power and goodness in the mineral waters, that contribute so much to the health of mankind; for God *made the fountains of water,* Rev. xiv. 7. *Secondly,* It was a type of the Messiah, who is the *fountain opened;* and was intended to raise people's expectations of him who is the *Sun of righteousness,* that arises *with healing under his wings.* These waters had formerly been used for purifying, now for healing, to signify both the *cleansing* and *curing* virtue of the blood of Christ, that incomparable bath, which *heals all our diseases.* The waters of Siloam, which filled this pool, signified the kingdom of David, and of Christ the Son of David (Isa. viii. 6); fitly therefore have they now this *sovereign* virtue put into them. The laver of regeneration is to us as Bethesda's pool, healing our spiritual diseases; not at certain seasons, but at all times. *Whoever will, let him come.*

III. The patient on whom this cure was wrought (*v.* 5): one that *had been infirm thirty-eight years.* 1. His *disease* was *grievous:* He had an *infirmity,* a weakness; he had lost the use of his limbs, at least on one side, as is usual in palsies. It is sad to have the body so disabled that, instead of being the soul's instrument, it is become, even in the affairs of this life, its burden. What reason have we to thank God for bodily strength, to use it for him, and to pity those who are *his prisoners!* 2. The *duration* of it was *tedious: Thirty-eight years.* He was lame longer than most live. Many are so long disabled for the offices of life that, as the psalmist complains, they seem to be *made in vain;* for suffering, not for service; born to be always dying. Shall we complain of one wearisome night, or one fit of illness, who perhaps for many years have scarcely known what it has been to be a day sick, when many others, better than we, have scarcely known what it has been to be a day well? Mr. Baxter's note on this passage is very affecting: "How great a mercy was it to live thirty-eight years under God's wholesome discipline! O my God, saith he, "I thank thee for the like discipline of fifty-eight years; how safe a life is this, in comparison of full prosperity and pleasure!"

IV. The cure and the circumstances of it briefly related, *v.* 6—9.

1. *Jesus saw him lie.* Observe, When Christ came up to Jerusalem he visited not the palaces, but the hospitals, which is an instance of his humility, and condescension, and tender compassion, and an *indication* of his great design in coming into the world, which was to seek and save the sick and wounded. There was a great multitude of poor cripples here at Bethesda, but Christ fastened his eye upon this one, and singled him out from the rest, because he was *senior* of the house, and in a more deplorable condition than any of the rest; and Christ delights to help the helpless, and hath mercy *on whom he will have mercy.* Perhaps his companions in tribulation insulted over him, because he had often been disappointed of a cure; therefore Christ took him for his patient: it is his honour to side with the weakest, and bear up those whom he sees *run down.*

2. He knew and considered *how long he had lain* in this condition. Those that have been long in affliction may comfort themselves with this, that God keeps account *how long,* and knows our frame.

3. He asked him, *Wilt thou be made whole?* A strange question to be asked one that had been so long ill. Some indeed would not be made whole, because their sores serve them to beg by and serve them for an excuse for idleness; but this poor man was as unable to *go a begging* as to *work,* yet Christ put it to him, (1.) To *express* his own pity and concern for him. Christ is tenderly inquisitive concerning the desires of those that are in affliction, and is willing to know *what is their petition:* "What shall I do for you?" (2.) To try him whether he would be beholden for a cure to him against whom the great people were so prejudiced and sought to prejudice others. (3.) To teach him to value the mercy, and to excite in him desires after it. In spiritual cases, people are not willing to be cured of their sins, are loth to part with them. If this point therefore were but gained, if people were willing to be *made whole,* the work were half done, for Christ is willing to heal, if we be but willing to be healed, Matt. viii. 3.

4. The poor impotent man takes this opportunity to renew his complaint, and to set forth the misery of his case, which makes his cure the more illustrious: *Sir, I have no man to put me into the pool, v.* 7. He seems to take Christ's question as an imputation of carelessness and neglect: "If thou hadst had a mind to be healed, thou wouldest have looked better to thy hits, and have got into the healing waters long before now." "No, Master," saith the poor man, "it is not for want of a *good will,* but of a *good friend,* that I am unhealed. I have done what I could to help myself, but in vain, for no one else will help me." (1.) He does not think of any other way of being cured than by these waters, and desires no other friendship than to be helped into *them;* therefore, when Christ cured him, his imagination or expectation could not contribute to it, for he thought of no such thing. (2.) He complains for want of friends to help him in: "*I have no man,* no friend to do me that kindness." One would think that some of those who had been themselves healed should have lent him a hand; but it is common for the poor to be destitute of friends; *no man careth for their soul.* To the sick and impotent it is as true a piece of charity to work for them as to relieve them; and thus the poor are capable of being charitable to one another, and ought to be so, though we seldom find that they are so; I speak it to their shame. (3.) He bewails his infelicity, that very often when *he* was coming *another stepped in before him.* But a step between him and a cure, and yet he continues impotent. None had the charity to say, "Your case is worse than mine, do you go in now, and I will stay till the next time; for there is no getting over the old maxim, *Every one for himself.* Having been so often disappointed, he begins to despair, and now is Christ's time to come to his relief; he delights to help in desperate cases. Observe, How mildly this man speaks of the unkindness of those about him, without any peevish reflections. As we should be thankful for the least kindness, so we should be patient under the greatest contempts; and, let our resentments be ever so *just,* yet our expressions should ever be *calm.* And observe further, to his praise, that, though he had waited so long in vain, yet still he continued lying by the pool-side, hoping that some time or other help would come, Hab. ii. 3.

5. Our Lord Jesus hereupon cures him with a word speaking, though he neither asked it nor thought of it. Here is,

(1.) The word he said: *Rise, take up thy bed, v.* 8. [1.] He is bidden to *rise and walk;* a strange command to be given to an *impotent* man, that had been long disabled; but this divine word was to be the vehicle of a divine power; it was a command to the disease to *be gone,* to nature to *be strong,* but it is expressed as a command to him to *bestir himself.* He must *rise and walk,* that is, attempt to do it, and in the *essay* he should receive strength to do it. The conversion of a sinner is the cure of a chronic disease; this is ordinarily done by the word, a word of command: Arise, and walk; *turn, and live; make ye a new heart;* which no more supposes a power in us to do it, without the grace of God, *distinguishing* grace, than this supposed such a power in the impotent man. But, if he had not attempted to help himself, he had not been cured, and he must have *borne the blame;* yet it does not therefore follow that, when he did rise and walk, it was by his own strength; no, it was by the power of Christ, and he must have all the glory. Observe, Christ did not bid him rise and go into the waters, but *rise and walk.* Christ did that for us which the law could not do, and set that aside. [2.] He is bidden to *take up his bed. First,* To make it to appear that it was a *perfect cure,* and purely miraculous; for he did not recover strength by degrees, but from the extremity of weakness and impotency he suddenly stepped into the highest degree of bodily strength; so that he was able to carry as great a load as any porter that had been as long *used* to it as he had been *disused.* He, who this minute was not able to turn himself in his bed, the next minute was able to carry his bed. The man sick of the palsy (Matt. ix. 6) was bidden to *go to his house,* but probably this man had no house to go to, the hospital was his home; therefore he is bidden to *rise and walk. Secondly,* It was to *proclaim* the cure, and make it public; for, being the sabbath day, whoever carried a burden through the streets made himself very remarkable, and every one would enquire what was the meaning of it; thereby notice of the miracle would spread, to the honour of God. *Thirdly,* Christ would thus witness against the tradition of the elders, which had stretched the law of the sabbath beyond its intention; and would likewise show that he was *Lord of the sabbath,* and had power to make what alterations he pleased about it, and to over-rule the law. Joshua, and the host of Israel, marched about Jericho on the sabbath day, when God commanded them; so did this man carry his bed, in obedience to a command. The case may be such that it may become a work of *necessity,* or *mercy,* to carry a bed on the sabbath day; but here it was more, it was a work of *piety,* being designed purely for the glory of God. *Fourthly,* He would hereby try the faith and obedience of his patient. By carrying his bed publicly, he exposed himself to the censure of the ecclesiastical court, and was liable, at least, to be *scourged in the synagogue.* Now, will he run the hazard of this, in obedience to Christ? Yes, he will. Those that have been *healed by Christ's word* should be *ruled by his word,* whatever it cost them.

(2.) The efficacy of this word (*v.* 9): a divine power went along with it, and immediately he was *made whole, took up his bed, and walked.* [1.] He felt the power of Christ's word healing him: *Immediately he was made whole.* What a joyful surprise was this to the poor cripple, to find himself all of a sudden so easy, so strong, so able to help himself! What a new world was he in, in an instant! Nothing is too hard for Christ to do. [2.] He obeyed the power of Christ's word commanding him. He *took up his bed and walked,* and did not care who blamed him or threatened him for it. The proof of our spiritual cure is our rising and walking. Hath Christ healed our spiritual diseases? Let us go whithersoever he sends us, and *take up* whatever he is pleased to lay upon us, and *walk before him.*

V. What became of the poor man after he was cured. We are here told,

1. What passed between him and the Jews who saw him carry his bed on the sabbath day; for on that day this cure was wrought, and it was the sabbath that fell within the passover week, and therefore a *high day, ch.* xix. 31. Christ's work was such that he needed not make any difference between sabbath days and other days, for he was always about his Father's business; but he wrought many remarkable cures on that day, perhaps to encourage his church to expect those spiritual favours from him, in their observance of the Christian sabbath, which were typified by his miraculous cures. Now here,

(1.) The Jews quarrelled with the man for carrying his bed on the sabbath day, telling him that *it was not lawful, v.* 10. It does not appear whether they were magistrates, who had power to *punish* him, or common people, who could only *inform* against him; but thus far was commendable, that, while they knew not by *what authority* he did it, they were jealous for the honour of the sabbath, and could not unconcernedly see it *profaned;* like Nehemiah. Neh. xiii. 17.

(2.) The man justified himself in what he did by a warrant that would bear him out, *v.* 11. "I do not do it in contempt of the law and the sabbath, but in obedience to one who, by *making me whole,* has given me an undeniable proof that he is greater than either. He that could work such a miracle as to *make me whole* no doubt might give me such a command as to carry *my bed;* he that could overrule the powers of nature no doubt might overrule a positive law, especially in an instance not of the essence of the law. He that was so kind as to make me whole would not be so unkind as to bid me do what is sinful." Christ, by curing another paralytic, proved his power to *forgive sin,* here to *give law;* if his pardons are valid, his edicts are so, and his miracles prove both.

(3.) The Jews enquired further who it was that gave him this warrant (*v.* 12): *What man is that?* Observe, How industriously they *overlooked* that which might be a ground of their *faith in Christ.* They enquire not, no, not for curiosity, "Who is it that *made thee whole?*" While they industriously caught at that which might be a ground of reflection upon Christ (*What man is* it who said unto thee, *Take up thy bed?*) they would fain *subpœna* the patient to be witness against his physician, and to be his betrayer. In their question, observe, [1.] They resolve to look upon Christ as a *mere man: What man is that?* For, though he gave ever such convincing proofs of it, they were resolved that they would never own him to be the *Son of God.* [2.] They resolve to look upon him as a bad *man,* and take it for granted that he who bade this man carry his bed, whatever divine commission he might *produce,* was certainly a delinquent, and as such they resolve to prosecute him. *What man is that* who durst give such orders?

(4.) The poor man was unable to give them any account of him: *He wist not who he was, v.* 13.

[1.] Christ was *unknown* to him when he healed him. Probably he had heard of the name of Jesus, but had never seen him, and therefore could not tell that this was he. Note, Christ does many a good turn for those that know him not, Isa. xlv. 4, 5. He enlightens, strengthens, quickens, comforts us, and we *wist not who he is;* nor are aware how much we receive daily by his mediation. This man, being unacquainted with Christ, could not actually believe in him for a cure; but Christ knew the dispositions of his soul, and suited his favours to them, as to the blind man in a like case, *ch.* ix. 36. Our covenant and communion with God take rise, not so much from our knowledge of him, as from his knowledge of us. We *know God,* or, rather, are *known of him,* Gal. iv. 9.

[2.] For the present he *kept himself unknown;* for as soon as he had wrought the cure he *conveyed himself away,* he *made himself unknown* (so some read it), *a multitude being in that place.* This is mentioned to show, either, *First, How* Christ conveyed himself away—by retiring into the crowd, so as not to be distinguished from a common person. He that was the chief of ten thousand often made himself one of the throng. It is sometimes the lot of those who have by their services signalized themselves to be levelled with the multitude, and overlooked. Or, *Secondly, Why* he conveyed himself away, because there was *a multitude* there, and he industriously avoided both the *applause* of those who would admire the miracle and *cry that up,* and the censure of those who would censure him as a sabbath-breaker, and *run him down.* Those that are active for God in their generation must expect to pass through *evil report* and *good report;* and it is wisdom as much as may be to keep out of the hearing of both; lest by the one we be *exalted,* and by the other *depressed,* above measure. Christ left the miracle to commend itself, and the man on whom it was wrought to justify it.

2. What passed between him and our Lord Jesus at their next interview, *v.* 14. Observe here,

(1.) Where Christ found him: *in the temple,* the place of public worship. In our attendance on public worship we may expect to meet with Christ, and improve our acquaintance with him. Observe, [1.] Christ *went to the temple.* Though he had many enemies, yet he appeared in public, because there he bore his testimony to divine institutions, and had opportunity of doing good. [2.] The man that was cured *went to the temple.* There Christ found him the same day, as it should seem, that he was healed; thither he straightway went, *First,* Because he had, *by his infirmity,* been so long *detained* thence. Perhaps he had not been there for thirty-eight years, and therefore, as soon as ever the embargo is taken off, his first visit shall be to the temple, as Hezekiah intimates his shall be (Isa. xxxviii. 22): *What is the sign that I shall go up to the house of the Lord? Secondly,* Because he had *by his recovery* a good errand thither; he went up to the temple to return thanks to God for his recovery. When God has at any time restored us our health we ought to attend him with solemn praises (Ps. cxvi. 18, 19), and the sooner the better, while the sense of the mercy is fresh. *Thirdly,* Because he had, by *carrying his bed,* seemed to put a contempt on the sabbath, he would thus show that he had an honour for it, and made conscience of sabbath-sanctification, in that on which the chief stress of it is laid, which is the *public worship* of God. Works of necessity and mercy are allowed; but when they are over we must *go to the temple.*

(2.) What he said to him. When Christ has cured us, he has not done with us; he now applies himself to the healing of his soul, and this *by the word* too. [1.] He gives him a *memento* of his cure: *Behold thou art made whole.* He found himself made whole, yet Christ calls his attention to it. *Behold, consider* it seriously, how sudden, how strange, how cheap, how easy, the cure was: *admire it;* behold, and wonder: *remember it;* let the impressions of it abide, and never be lost, Isa. xxxviii. 9. [2.] He gives him a caution against sin, in consideration hereof, *Being made whole, sin no more.* This implies that his disease was the punishment of sin; whether of some remarkably flagrant sin, or only of sin in general, we cannot tell, but we know that sin is the procuring cause of sickness, Ps. cvii. 17, 18. Some observe that Christ did not make mention of sin to any of his patients, except to this *impotent* man, and another who was in like manner diseased, Mark ii. 5. While those chronical diseases lasted, they prevented the outward acts of many sins, and therefore watchfulness was the more necessary when the disability was removed. Christ intimates that those who are *made whole*, who are eased of the present sensible punishment of sin, are in danger of *returning* to sin when the terror and restraint are over, unless divine grace dry up the fountain. When the trouble which only dammed up the current is over, the waters will return to their old course; and therefore there is great need of watchfulness, lest after healing mercy we return again to folly. The *misery* we were *made whole from* warns us to sin no more, having felt the smart of sin; the *mercy* we were *made whole by* is an engagement upon us not to offend him who healed us. This is the voice of every providence, *Go and sin no more.* This man began his new life very hopefully *in the temple*, yet Christ saw it necessary to give him this caution; for it is common for people, when they are sick, to *promise much*, when newly recovered to *perform something*, but after awhile to *forget all.* [3.] He gives him warning of his danger, in case he should return to his former sinful course: *Lest a worse thing come to thee.* Christ, who knows all men's hearts, knew that he was one of those that must be *frightened* from sin. Thirty-eight years' lameness, one would think, was a thing bad enough; yet there is something *worse* that will come to him if he relapse into sin after God has *given him such a deliverance* as this, Ezra ix. 13, 14. The hospital where he lay was a melancholy place, but hell is much more so: the doom of apostates is a worse thing than thirty-eight years' lameness.

VI. Now, after this interview between Christ and his patient, observe in the two following verses, 1. The notice which the poor simple man gave to the Jews concerning Christ, *v.* 15. He told them it was Jesus that had *made him whole.* We have reason to think that he intended this for the honour of Christ and the benefit of the Jews, little thinking that he who had so much power and goodness could have *any* enemies; but those who wish well to Christ's kingdom must have the *wisdom of the serpent*, lest they do more hurt than good with their zeal, and must not cast pearls before swine. 2. The rage and enmity of the Jews against him: *Therefore did the* rulers of the Jews *persecute Jesus.* See, (1.) How absurd and unreasonable their enmity to Christ was. *Therefore*, because he had made a poor sick man well, and so eased the public charge, upon which, it is likely, he had subsisted; *therefore* they persecuted him, because he did good in Israel. (2.) How bloody and cruel it was: *They sought to slay him;* nothing less than his blood, his life, would satisfy them. (3.) How it was varnished over with a colour of zeal for the honour of the sabbath; for this was the pretended crime, *Because he had done these things on the sabbath day*, as if that circumstance were enough to vitiate the best and most divine actions, and to render *him* obnoxious whose deeds were otherwise most meritorious. Thus hypocrites often cover their real enmity against the *power* of godliness with a pretended zeal for the *form* of it.

17 But Jesus answered them, My
Father worketh hitherto, and I work.
18 Therefore the Jews sought the
more to kill him, because he not only
had broken the sabbath, but said also
that God was his Father, making
himself equal with God. 19 Then
answered Jesus and said unto them,
Verily, verily, I say unto you, The
Son can do nothing of himself, but
what he seeth the Father do: for
what things soever he doeth, these
also doeth the Son likewise. 20 For
the Father loveth the Son, and showeth him all things that himself doeth:
and he will show him greater works
than these, that ye may marvel. 21
For as the Father raiseth up the dead,
and quickeneth *them;* even so the
Son quickeneth whom he will. 22
For the Father judgeth no man, but
hath committed all judgment unto
the Son: 23 That all *men* should
honour the Son, even as they honour
the Father. He that honoureth not
the Son honoureth not the Father
which hath sent him. 24 Verily,
verily, I say unto you, He that heareth
my word, and believeth on him that
sent me, hath everlasting life, and
shall not come into condemnation;
but is passed from death unto life.
25 Verily, verily, I say unto you,
The hour is coming, and now is,
when the dead shall hear the voice
of the Son of God: and they that
hear shall live. 26 For as the Father
hath life in himself; so hath he given
to the Son to have life in himself;
27 And hath given him authority to
execute judgment also, because he is
the Son of man. 28 Marvel not at
this: for the hour is coming, in the
which all that are in the graves shall
hear his voice, 29 And shall come
forth; they that have done good,
unto the resurrection of life; and
they that have done evil, unto the

resurrection of damnation. 30 I can of mine own self do nothing: as I hear, I judge: and my judgment is just; because I seek not mine own will, but the will of the Father which hath sent me.

We have here Christ's discourse upon occasion of his being accused as a sabbath-breaker, and it seems to be his vindication of himself before the sanhedrim, when he was arraigned before them: whether on the same day, or two or three days after, does not appear; probably the same day. Observe,

I. The doctrine laid down, by which he justified what he did on the sabbath day (*v.* 17): *He answered them.* This supposes that he had something laid to his charge: or what they suggested one to another, when they sought to slay him (*v.* 16), he *knew*, and gave this reply to, *My Father worketh hitherto, and I work.* At other times, in answer to the like charge, he had pleaded the example of David's eating the show-bread, of the priests' slaying the sacrifices, and of the people's watering their cattle on the sabbath day; but here he goes higher and alleges the example of his Father and his divine authority; waiving all other pleas, he insists upon that which was *instar omnium—equivalent to the whole*, and abides by it, which he had mentioned, Matt. xii. 8. *The Son of man is Lord even of the sabbath day;* but he here enlarges on it. 1. He pleads that he was the *Son of God*, plainly intimated in his calling *God his Father;* and, if so, his holiness was *unquestionable* and his sovereignty *incontestable;* and he might make what alterations he pleased of the divine law. *Surely they will reverence the Son*, the heir of all things. 2. That he was a worker together with God. (1.) *My Father worketh hitherto.* The example of God's resting on the seventh day from all his work is, in the fourth commandment, made the ground of our observing it as a *sabbath* or *day of rest.* Now God rested only from such work as he had done the six days before; otherwise he *worketh hitherto*, he is every day working, sabbath days and week-days; upholding and governing all the creatures, and concurring by his common providence to all the motions and operations of nature, *to his own glory;* therefore, when we are appointed to rest on the sabbath day, yet we are not restrained from doing that which has a direct tendency *to the glory of God*, as the man's carrying his bed had. (2.) *I work;* not only therefore I *may* work, *like him*, in doing good on sabbath days as well as other days, but I also *work with him.* As God created all things by Christ, so he supports and governs all by him, Heb. i. 3. This sets what he does above all exception; he that is so great a worker must needs be an uncontrollable governor; he that does all is Lord of all, and therefore *Lord of the sabbath*, which particular branch of his authority he would now assert, because he was shortly to show it further, in the change of the day from the seventh to the first.

II. The offence that was taken at his doctrine (*v.* 18): *The Jews sought the more to kill him.* His defence was made his offence, as if by justifying himself he had made bad worse. Note, Those that will not be enlightened by the word of Christ will be enraged and exasperated by it, and nothing more vexes the enemies of Christ than his asserting his authority; see Ps. ii. 3—5. They sought to kill him,

1. Because he had broken the sabbath; for, let him say what he would in his own justification, they are resolved, right or wrong, to *find him guilty* of sabbath breaking. When malice and envy sit upon the bench, reason and justice may even be silent at the bar, for whatever they can say will undoubtedly be over-ruled.

2. Not only so, but he had said also *that God was his Father.* Now they pretend a jealousy for *God's honour*, as before for the sabbath day, and charge Christ with it as a heinous crime that he made himself equal with God; and a heinous crime it had been if he had not really been so. It was the sin of Lucifer, *I will be like the Most High.* Now, (1.) This was justly inferred from what he said, that he was the *Son of God*, and that God was *his Father*, πατέρα ἴδιον—*his own Father;* his, so as he was no one's else. He had said that he worked with his Father, by the same authority and power, and hereby he made himself equal with God. *Ecce intelligunt Judæi, quod non intelligunt Ariani—Behold, the Jews understand what the Arians do not.* (2.) Yet it was unjustly imputed to him as an offence that he equalled himself with God, for he was and is God, equal with the Father (Phil. ii. 6); and therefore Christ, in answer to this charge, does not except against the innuendo as strained or forced, makes out his claim and proves that he is equal with God in power and glory.

III. Christ's discourse upon this occasion, which continues without interruption to the end of the chapter. In these verses he explains, and afterwards confirms, his commission, as Mediator and plenipotentiary in the treaty between God and man. And, as the honours he is hereby *entitled to* are such as it is not fit for any creature to receive, so the work he is hereby entrusted with is such as it is not possible for any creature to go through with, and therefore he is God, equal with the Father.

1. *In general.* He is one with the Father in all he does as Mediator, and there was a perfectly good understanding between them in the whole matter. It is ushered in with a solemn preface (*v.* 19): *Verily, verily, I say unto you;* I the Amen, the Amen, say it. This intimates that the things declared are, (1.) Very awful and great, and such as should

command the most serious attention. (2.) Very sure, and such as should command an unfeigned assent. (3.) That they are matters purely of divine revelation; things which Christ has told us, and which we could not otherwise have come to the knowledge of. Two things he saith in general concerning the Son's oneness with the Father in working:—

[1.] That the Son *conforms to the Father* (*v.* 19): *The Son can do nothing of himself but what he sees the Father do; for these things does the Son.* The Lord Jesus, as Mediator, is, *First, Obedient to his Father's will;* so entirely obedient that he *can do nothing of himself,* in the same sense as it is said, *God cannot* lie, *cannot deny* himself, which expresses the perfection of his truth, not any imperfection in his strength; so here, Christ was so entirely devoted to his Father's will that it was impossible for him in any thing to act separately. *Secondly,* He is *observant of his Father's counsel;* he can, he will, do nothing *but what he sees the Father do.* No man can *find out the work of God,* but the only-begotten Son, who lay in his bosom, sees what he does, is intimately acquainted with his purposes, and has the plan of them ever before him. What he did as Mediator, throughout his whole undertaking, was the exact transcript or counterpart of what the Father did; that is, what he designed, when he formed the plan of our redemption in his eternal counsels, and settled those measures in every thing which never could be *broken,* nor ever needed to be *altered.* It was the copy of that *great original;* it was Christ's faithfulness, as it was Moses's, that he did all *according to the pattern shown him in the mount.* This is expressed in the present tense, what he *sees the Father do,* for the same reason that, when he was here upon earth, it was said, He *is* in heaven (*ch.* iii. 13), and *is* in the bosom of the Father (*ch.* i. 18); as he was even then by his divine nature present in heaven, so the things done in heaven were *present* to his knowledge. What the Father did in his counsels, the Son had ever in his view, and still he had his eye upon it, as David in spirit spoke of him, *I have set the Lord always before me,* Ps. xvi. 8. *Thirdly,* Yet he is *equal* with the Father in *working;* for *what things soever* the Father does *these also does the Son likewise;* he did the *same* things, not *such* things, but ταῦτα, the *same* things; and he did them in the *same manner,* ὁμοίως *likewise,* with the same authority, and liberty, and wisdom, the same energy and efficacy. Does the Father enact, repeal, and alter, positive laws? Does he over-rule the course of nature, know men's hearts? So does the Son. The power of the Mediator is a divine power.

[2.] That the Father *communicates* to the Son, *v.* 20. Observe,

First, The inducement to it: *The Father loveth the Son;* he declared, *This is my beloved Son.* He had not only a good will to the undertaking, but an infinite complacency in the undertaker. Christ was now hated of men, one whom the nation abhorred (Isa. xlix. 7); but he comforted himself with this, that his Father loved him.

Secondly, The instances of it. He shows it, 1. In what he *does* communicate to him: *He shows him all things that himself doth.* The Father's measures in making and ruling the world are shown to the Son, that he may take the same measures in framing and governing the church, which work was to be a duplicate of the work of creation and providence, and it is therefore called *the world to come.* He shows him all things ἃ αὐτὸς ποιεῖ—*which he does,* that is, which the *Son* does, so it might be construed; all that the Son does is by direction from the Father; he *shows* him. 2. In what he *will* communicate; he will *show him,* that is, will appoint and direct him to do *greater works than these.* (1.) Works of greater *power* than the *curing of the impotent man;* for he should raise the dead, and should himself rise from the dead. By the power of nature, with the use of means, a disease may possibly in time be cured; but nature can never, by the use of any means, in any time raise the dead. (2.) Works of greater *authority* than warranting the man to *carry his bed on the sabbath day.* They thought this a daring attempt; but what was this to his abrogating the whole ceremonial law, and instituting new ordinances, which he would shortly do, "*that you may marvel!*" Now they looked upon his works with contempt and indignation, but he will shortly do that which they will look upon with amazement, Luke vii. 16. Many are brought to marvel at Christ's works, whereby he has the honour of them, who are not brought to believe, by which they would have the benefit of them.

2. *In particular.* He proves his equality with the Father, by specifying some of those works which he does that are the peculiar works of God. This is enlarged upon, *v.* 21—30. He does, and shall do, that which is the peculiar work of God's almighty power—*raising the dead* and *giving life, v.* 21, 25, 26, 28. He does, and shall do, that which is the peculiar work of God's sovereign dominion and jurisdiction—*judging* and *executing judgment, v.* 22—24, 27. These two are interwoven, as being nearly connected; and what is said once is repeated and inculcated; put both together, and they will prove that Christ said not amiss when he made himself *equal with God.*

(1.) Observe what is here said concerning the Mediator's power to *raise the dead* and *give life.* See [1.] His *authority* to do it (*v.* 21): *As the Father raiseth up the dead,* so *the Son quickeneth whom he will. First,* It is God's prerogative to raise the dead, and give life, even his who first *breathed* into man the *breath of life,* and so made him a *living soul;* see Deut. xxxii. 39; 1 Sam. ii. 6; Ps. lxviii 20; Rom. iv. 17. This God had done by the prophets Elijah and Elisha, and it was a confirmation of their mission. A *resurrection from the dead* never lay in the common road of nature, nor ever fell within the thought of those that studied only the compass of nature's power, one of whose received axioms was point blank against it: *A privatione ad habitum non datur regressus—Existence, when once extinguished, cannot be rekindled.* It was therefore ridiculed at Athens as an *absurd* thing, Acts xvii. 32. It is purely the work of a divine power, and the knowledge of it purely by divine revelation. This the Jews would own. *Secondly,* The Mediator is invested with this prerogative: *He quickens whom he will;* raises to life whom he pleases, and when he pleases. He does not enliven things by natural necessity, as the sun does, whose beams revive of course; but he acts as a free agent, has the dispensing of his power in his own hand, and is never either *con*strained, or *re*strained, in the use of it. As he has the power, so he has the wisdom and sovereignty, of a God; has the *key of the grave and of death* (Rev. i. 18), not as a servant, to open and shut as he is bidden, for he has it as the *key of David,* which he is master of, Rev. iii. 7. An absolute prince is described by this (Dan. v. 19): *Whom he would he slew or kept alive;* it is true of Christ without hyperbole.

[2.] His *ability* to do it. *Therefore* he has power to quicken whom he will as the Father does, because *he has life in himself, as the Father has, v.* 26. *First,* It is certain that the Father *has life in himself.* Not only he is a *self-existent* Being, who does not derive from, or depend upon, any other (Exod. iii. 14), but he is a sovereign giver of life; he has the disposal of life in himself; and of all good (for so *life* sometimes signifies); it is all derived from him, and dependent on him. He is to his creatures the fountain of life, and all good; author of their being and well-being; the living God, and the God of all living. *Secondly,* It is as certain that he has *given to the Son to have life in himself.* As the Father is the original of all natural life and good, being the great Creator, so the Son, as Redeemer, is the original of all spiritual life and good; is that to the church which the Father is to the world; see 1 Cor. viii. 6; Col. i. 19. The kingdom of grace, and all the life in that kingdom, are as fully and absolutely in the hand of the Redeemer as the kingdom of providence is in the hand of the Creator; and as God, who gives being to all things, has his being of himself, so Christ, who gives life, raised himself to life by his own power, *ch.* x. 18.

[3.] His *acting* according to this authority and ability. Having *life in himself,* and being authorized to *quicken whom he will,* by virtue hereof there are, accordingly, two resurrections performed by his powerful word, both which are here spoken of:—

First, A resurrection that *now is* (*v.* 29), a resurrection from the death of sin to the life of righteousness, by the power of Christ's grace. *The hour is coming, and now is.* It is a resurrection begun already, and further to be carried on, *when the dead shall hear the voice of the Son of God.* This is plainly distinguished from that in *v.* 28, which speaks of the resurrection at the end of time. This says nothing, as that does, of the dead in their graves, and of all of them, and their coming forth. Now, 1. Some think this was fulfilled in those whom he miraculously raised to life, Jairus's daughter, the widow's son, and Lazarus; and it is observable that all whom Christ raised were *spoken to,* as, *Damsel, arise; Young man, arise; Lazarus, come forth;* whereas those raised under the Old Testament were raised, not by a word, but other applications, 1 Kings xvii. 21; 2 Kings iv. 34; xiii. 21. Some understand it of those saints that rose with Christ; but we do not read of the *voice of the Son of God* calling them. But, 2. I rather understand it of the power of the doctrine of Christ, for the recovering and quickening of those that were *dead in trespasses and sins,* Eph. ii. 1. The *hour* was *coming* when dead souls should be made alive by the *preaching* of the gospel, and a spirit of life from God accompanying it: nay, it *then was,* while Christ was upon earth. It may refer especially to the *calling of the Gentiles,* which is said to be as life from the dead, and, some think, was prefigured by Ezekiel's vision (*ch.* xxxvii. 1), and foretold, Isa. xxvi. 19. *Thy dead men shall live.* But it is to be applied to all the wonderful success of the gospel, among both Jews and Gentiles; an hour which still *is,* and is still *coming,* till all the elect be effectually called. Note, (1.) Sinners are spiritually *dead,* destitute of spiritual life, sense, strength, and motion, dead to God, miserable, but neither sensible of their misery nor able to help themselves out of it. (2.) The conversion of a soul to God is its resurrection from death to life; then it begins to live when it begins to *live to God,* to breathe after him, and move towards him. (3.) It is by the *voice of the Son of God* that souls are raised to spiritual life; it is wrought by his power, and that power conveyed and communicated by his word: *The dead shall hear,* shall be made to hear, to understand, receive, and believe, the *voice of the Son of God,* to hear it as his voice; then the Spirit by it gives life, otherwise the *letter kills.* (4.) The voice of Christ must be heard by us, that we may live by it. They that hear, and attend to what they hear, shall live. *Hear and your soul shall live,* Isa. lv. 3.

Secondly, A resurrection yet *to come;* this is spoken of, *v.* 28, 29, introduced with, "*Marvel not at this,* which I have said of the *first* resurrection, do not reject it as incredible and absurd, for at the end of time you shall all see a more sensible and amazing proof of the power and authority of the Son of man." As *his own* resurrection was reserved to be the final and concluding proof of his personal commission, so the resurrection of *all men* is reserved to be a like proof of his commission to be executed by his spirit. Now observe here,

a. When this resurrection shall be: *The hour is coming;* it is *fixed* to an hour, so very punctual is this great appointment. The judgment is not adjourned *sine die—to some time not yet pitched upon;* no, *he hath appointed a day. The hour is coming.* (*a.*) It is *not yet* come, it is not the hour spoken of at *v.* 25, that is coming, and *now is.* Those erred dangerously who said that the *resurrection was past already,* 2 Tim. ii. 18. But, (*b.*) It *will certainly* come, it is coming on, nearer every day than other; it is at the door. How far off it is we know not; but we know that it is infallibly designed and unalterably determined.

b. Who shall be raised: *All that are in the graves,* all that have died from the beginning of time, and all that shall die to the end of time. It was said (Dan. xii. 2), *Many* shall arise; Christ here tells us that those *many* shall be *all; all* must appear before the Judge, and therefore *all* must be raised; every person, and the whole of every person; every soul shall return to its body, and every *bone to its bone.* The grave is the prison of dead bodies, where they are *detained;* their furnace, where they are *consumed* (Job xxiv. 19); yet, in prospect of their resurrection, we may call it their *bed,* where they sleep to be *awaked* again; their treasury, where they are laid up to be used again. Even those that are not *put into graves* shall arise; but, because most are put into graves, Christ uses this expression, *all that are in the graves.* The Jews used the word *sheol* for the *grave,* which signifies *the state of the dead;* all that are in that state *shall hear.*

c. How they shall be raised. Two things are here told us:—(*a.*) The efficient of this resurrection: *They shall hear his voice;* that is, he shall cause them to hear it, as Lazarus was made to hear that word, *Come forth;* a divine power shall go along with the voice, to put life into them, and enable them to obey it. When Christ rose, there was no voice heard, not a word spoken, because he rose by his own power; but at the resurrection of the children of men we find three voices spoken of, 1 Thess. iv. 16. The Lord shall descend with a *shout,* the shout of a king, with *the voice of the archangel;* either Christ himself, the prince of the angels, or the commander-in-chief, under him, of the heavenly hosts; and with *the trumpet of God:* the soldier's trumpet sounding the alarm of war, the judge's trumpet publishing the summons to the court. (*b.*) The effect of it: *They shall come forth* out of their graves, as prisoners out of their prison-house; they shall *arise out* of the dust, and shake themselves from it; see Isa. lii. 1, 2, 11. But this is not all; they shall *appear* before Christ's tribunal, shall *come forth* as those that are to be tried, *come forth* to the bar, publicly to receive their doom.

d. To what they shall be raised; to a different state of happiness or misery, according to their different character; to a state of retribution, according to what they did in the state of probation.

(*a.*) *They that have done good shall come forth to the resurrection of life;* they shall live again, to live for ever. Note, [*a.*] Whatever name men are called by, or whatever plausible profession they make, it will be well in the great day with those only that have *done good,* have done that which is pleasing to God and profitable to others. [*b.*] The resurrection of the body will be a resurrection of life to all those, and those only, that have been sincere and constant in *doing good.* They shall not only be publicly *acquitted,* as a pardoned criminal, we say, has *his life,* but they shall be *admitted* into the presence of God, and that is life, it is better than life; they shall be *attended* with comforts in perfection. To live is to be *happy,* and they shall be *advanced* above the fear of death; that is *life* indeed in which *mortality* is for ever *swallowed* up.

(*b.*) *They that have done evil to the resurrection of damnation;* they shall live again, to be for ever dying. The Pharisees thought that the resurrection pertained only to the just, but Christ here rectifies that mistake. Note, [*a.*] *Evil doers,* whatever they pretend, will be treated in the day of judgment as *evil men.* [*b*] The resurrection will be to evil doers, who did not by repentance undo what they had done amiss, a *resurrection* of damnation. They shall come forth to be publicly convicted of rebellion against God, and publicly *condemned* to everlasting punishment; to be *sentenced* to it, and immediately *sent* to it without reprieve. Such will the resurrection be.

(2.) Observe what is here said concerning the Mediator's *authority to execute judgment, v.* 22—24, 27. As he has an almighty power, so he has a sovereign jurisdiction; and who so fit to preside in the great affairs of the other life as he who is the Father and fountain of life? Here is,

[1.] Christ's commission or delegation to the office of a judge, which is twice spoken of here (*v.* 22): *He hath committed all judgment to the Son;* and again (*v.* 27): *He hath given him authority.*

First, The *Father judges no man;* not that the Father hath resigned the government, but he is pleased to govern by Jesus Christ; so that man is not under the terror of dealing with God immediately, but has the comfort of access to him by a Mediator. The *Father judges no man;* that is, 1. He does not *rule* us by the *mere* right of *creation,* but by *covenant,* and upon certain terms settled by a Mediator. Having made us, he *may* do what he *pleases* with us, as the potter with the clay; yet he does not take advantage of this, but draws us *with the cords of a man.* 2 He does not determine our everlasting condition by the *covenant of innocency,* nor take the advantage he has against us for the violation of that covenant. The Mediator having undertaken to make a *vicarious* satisfaction, the matter is referred to him, and God is willing to enter upon a new treaty; *not under the law* of the Creator, *but the grace* of the Redeemer.

Secondly, He has committed all judgment to the Son, has constituted him *Lord of all* (Acts x. 36; Rom. xiv. 9), as Joseph in Egypt, Gen. xli. 40. This was prophesied of, Ps. lxxii. 1; Isa. xi. 3, 4; Jer. xxiii. 5; Mic. v. 1—4; Ps. lxvii. 4; xcvi. 13; xcviii. 9. All judgment is committed to our Lord Jesus; for, 1. He is *entrusted* with the administration of the *providential kingdom,* is *head over all things* (Eph. i. 22), head of every man, 1 Cor. xi. 3. All things consist by him, Col. i. 17. 2. He is empowered to make laws immediately to bind conscience. *I say unto you* is now the form in which the statutes of the kingdom of heaven run. *Be it enacted* by the Lord Jesus, and by *his* authority. All the acts now in force are touched with his sceptre. 3. He is authorized to appoint and settle the terms of the new covenant, and to draw up the articles of peace between God and man; it is God in Christ that reconciles the world, and to him he has given power to confer eternal life. The book of life is the Lamb's book; by his award we must stand or fall. 4. He is commissioned to carry on and complete the war with the powers of darkness; to cast out and *give judgment against the prince of this world, ch.* xii. 31. He is commissioned not only to *judge,* but to *make war,* Rev. xix. 11. All that will fight *for God against Satan* must enlist themselves under *his* banner. 5. He is constituted sole manager of the judgment of the great day. The ancients generally understood these words of that *crowning act* of his judicial power. The final and universal judgment is committed to the Son of man; the tribunal is *his,* it is the judgment-seat of Christ; the retinue is his, *his* mighty angels; he will try the causes, and pass the sentence. Acts xvii. 31.

Thirdly, He has *given him authority to execute judgment also, v.* 27. Observe, 1. What the authority is which our Redeemer is invested with: *An authority to execute judgment;* he has not only a legislative and judicial power, but an *executive* power too. The phrase here is used particularly for the judgment of condemnation, Jude 15. *ποιῆσαι κρίσιν—to execute judgment* upon all; the same with his *taking vengeance,* 2 Thess. i. 8. The ruin of impenitent sinners comes from the hand of Christ; he that *executes judgment* upon them is the same that would have *wrought salvation* for them, which makes the sentence unexceptionable; and there is no relief against the sentence of the Redeemer; salvation itself cannot save those whom the Saviour *condemns,* which makes the ruin *remediless.* 2 Whence he has that authority: the Father *gave it to him.* Christ's authority as Mediator is delegated and derived; he acts as the Father's Vicegerent, as the Lord's Anointed, the Lord's Christ. Now all this redounds very much to the honour of Christ, acquitting him from the guilt of blasphemy, in making himself *equal with God;* and very much to the comfort of all believers, who may with the greatest assurance venture their all in such hands.

[2.] Here are the reasons (reasons of state) for which this commission was given him. He has all judgment committed to him for two reasons:—

First, Because he is the *Son of man;* which denotes these three things:—1. His humiliation and gracious condescension. Man is a worm, the son of man a worm; yet this was the nature, this the character, which the Redeemer assumed, in pursuance of the counsels of love; to this low estate he stooped, and submitted to all the mortifications attending it, because it was *his Father's will;* in recompence therefore of this wonderful obedience, God did thus dignify him. Because he condescended to be the *Son of man,* his Father made him *Lord of all,* Phil. ii. 8, 9. 2. His affinity and alliance to us. The Father has committed the government of the children of men to him, because, being the *Son of man,* he is of the same nature with those whom he is *set over,* and therefore the more unexceptionable, and the more acceptable, as a Judge. *Their governor shall proceed from the midst of them,* Jer. xxx. 21. Of this that law was typical: *One of thy brethren shalt thou set king over thee,* Deut. xvii. 15. 3. His being the Messiah promised. In that famous vision of his kingdom and glory, Dan. vii. 13, 14, he is called the *Son of man;* and Ps. viii. 4—6 Thou hast made the Son of man have *dominion over the works of thy hands.* He is the Messiah, and therefore is invested with all this power. The Jews usually called the Christ the *Son of David;* but Christ usually called himself the *Son of man,* which was the more humble title, and bespeaks him a prince and Saviour, not to the Jewish nation only, but to the whole race of mankind.

Secondly, That all men should honour the Son, v. 23. The honouring of Jesus Christ is here spoken of as God's great design (the Son intended to glorify the Father, and therefore the Father intended to glorify the Son, *ch.* xii. 32); and as man's great duty, in compliance with that design. If God will have the Son honoured, it is the duty of all to whom he is made known to honour him. Observe here, 1. The *respect* that is to be paid to our Lord Jesus: We must *honour the Son,* must look upon him as one that is to be *honoured,* both on account of his transcendent excellences and perfections in himself, and of the relations he stands in to us, and must study to give him honour accordingly; must *confess that he is Lord,* and worship him; must honour him who was dishonoured for us. 2. The degree of it: *Even as they honour the Father.* This *supposes* it to be our duty to *honour the Father;* for revealed religion is founded on natural religion, and *directs* us to *honour the Son,* to honour him with *divine* honour; we must honour the Redeemer with the same honour with which we honour the Creator. So far was it from blasphemy for him to make himself *equal with God* that it is the highest injury that can be for us to make him otherwise. The truths and laws of the Christian religion, so far as they are revealed, are as sacred and honourable as those of natural religion, and to be equally had in estimation; for we lie under the same obligations to Christ, the Author of our well-being, that we lie under to the Author of our being; and have as necessary a dependence upon the Redeemer's grace as upon the Creator's providence, which is a sufficient ground for this law—*to honour the Son as we honour the Father.* To enforce this law, it is added, *He that honours not the Son honours not the Father* who has sent him. Some pretend a reverence for the Creator, and speak *honourably* of him, who make light of the Redeemer, and speak *contemptibly* of him; but let such know that the honours and interests of the Father and Son are so inseparably twisted and interwoven that the Father never reckons himself *honoured* by any that *dishonour* the Son. Note, (1.) Indignities done to the Lord Jesus reflect upon God himself, and will so be construed and reckoned for in the court of heaven. The Son having so far espoused the Father's honour as to take *to himself* the *reproaches cast on him* (Rom. xv. 3), the Father does no less espouse the Son's honour, and counts himself struck at through him. (2.) The reason of this is because the Son is sent and commissioned by the Father; it is the *Father who hath sent him.* Affronts to an ambassador are justly resented by the prince that sends him. And by this rule those who truly *honour the Son honour the Father also;* see Phil. ii. 11.

[3.] Here is the rule by which the Son goes in executing this commission, so those words seem to come in (*v.* 24): *He that heareth and believeth* hath *everlasting life.* Here we have the substance of the whole gospel; the preface commands *attention* to a thing most weighty, and *assent* to a thing most certain: "*Verily, verily, I say unto you,* I, to whom you hear *all judgment is committed,* I, in whose lips is a divine sentence; take from *me* the Christian's *character* and *charter.*"

First, The *character* of a Christian: *He that heareth my word, and believeth on him that sent me.* To be a Christian indeed is, 1. To *hear the word of Christ.* It is not enough to be within hearing of it, but we must *attend on* it, as scholars on the instructions of their teachers; and *attend to* it, as servants to the commands of their masters; we must hear and obey it, must abide by the gospel of Christ as the fixed rule of our faith and practice. 2. To *believe on him that sent him;* for Christ's design is to *bring us to God;* and, as he is the first original of all grace, so is he the last object of all faith. Christ is our *way;* God is our rest. We must believe on God as *having sent* Jesus Christ, and recommended himself to our faith and love, by manifesting his glory in *the face of Jesus Christ* (2 Cor. iv. 6), as *his* Father and *our Father.*

Secondly, The *charter* of a Christian, in which all that are Christians indeed are interested. See what we get by Christ. 1. A charter of pardon: *He shall not come into condemnation.* The grace of the gospel is a full discharge from the curse of the law. A believer shall not only not *lie under* condemnation eternally, but shall not *come into condemnation* now, not come into the danger of it (Rom. viii. 1), not *come into judgment,* not be so much as arraigned. 2. A charter of privileges: He is *passed out of death to life,* is invested in a present happiness in spiritual life and entitled to a future happiness in eternal life. The tenour of the first covenant was, *Do this and live;* the man that doeth them shall live in them. Now this proves Christ equal with the Father that he has power to propose the *same* benefit to the *hearers of his word* that had been proposed to the *keepers of the old law,* that is, life: *Hear and live, believe and live,* is what we may venture our souls upon, when we are disabled to *do and live;* see *ch.* xvii. 2.

[4.] Here is the righteousness of his proceedings pursuant to this commission, *v.* 30. All judgment being committed to him, we cannot but ask *how he manages it.* And here he answers, *My judgment is just.* All Christ's acts of government, both *legislative* and *judicial,* are exactly agreeable to the rules of equity; see Prov. viii. 8. There can lie no exceptions against any of the determinations of the Redeemer; and therefore, as there shall be no repeal of any of his statutes, so there shall be no appeal from any of his sentences. His judgments are certainly just, for they are directed,

First, By the Father's *wisdom: I can of my ownself* do nothing, nothing without the Father, but *as I hear I judge,* as he had said before (*v.* 19), The Son *can do nothing but what he sees the Father do;* so here, nothing but what he hears the Father *say: As I hear,* 1. From the secret eternal counsels of the Father, *so I judge.* Would we know what we may depend upon in our dealing with God? *Hear the word* of Christ. We need not dive into the divine counsels, those *secret things* which belong not to us, but attend to the revealed dictates of Christ's government and judgment, which will furnish us with an unerring guide; for what Christ has adjudged is an exact copy or counterpart of what the Father has decreed. 2. From the published records of the Old Testament. Christ, in all the execution of his undertaking, had an eye to the scripture, and made it his business to conform to this, and *fulfil* it: *As it was written in the volume of the book.* Thus he taught us to do *nothing of ourselves,* but, *as we hear* from the word of God, *so to judge* of things, and act accordingly.

Secondly, By the Father's *will: My judgment is just,* and cannot be otherwise, *because I seek not my own will,* but *his who sent me.* Not as if the will of Christ were contrary to the will of the Father, as the flesh is contrary to the spirit in us; but, 1. Christ had, as man, the natural and innocent affections of the human nature, *sense of pain* and *pleasure,* an inclination to life, an aversion to death: yet he *pleased not himself,* did not confer with these, nor consult these, when he was to go on his undertaking, but acquiesced entirely in the will of his Father. 2. What he did as Mediator was not the result of any *peculiar* or *particular* purpose and design of his own; what he did *seek* to do was not for his own mind's sake. but he was therein guided by his Father's will, and the purpose which he had *purposed to himself.* This our Saviour did upon all occasions *refer himself to* and govern himself by.

Thus our Lord Jesus has opened his commission (whether to the conviction of his enemies or no) to his own honour and the everlasting comfort of all his friends, who here see him *able to save to the uttermost.*

31 If I bear witness of myself, my
witness is not true. 32 There is
another that beareth witness of me;
and I know that the witness which
he witnesseth of me is true. 33 Ye
sent unto John, and he bare witness
unto the truth. 34 But I receive not
testimony from man: but these things
I say, that ye might be saved. 35
He was a burning and a shining light:
and ye were willing for a season to
rejoice in his light. 36 But I have
greater witness than *that* of John:
for the works which the Father hath
given me to finish, the same works
that I do, bear witness of me, that
the Father hath sent me. 37 And
the Father himself, which hath sent
me, hath borne witness of me. Ye
have neither heard his voice at any
time, nor seen his shape. 38 And
ye have not his word abiding in you:
for whom he hath sent, him ye believe not. 39 Search the scriptures;
for in them ye think ye have eternal
life: and they are they which testify
of me. 40 And ye will not come to
me, that ye might have life. 41 I
receive not honour from men. 42
But I know you, that ye have not
the love of God in you. 43 I am
come in my Father's name, and ye
receive me not: if another shall come
in his own name, him ye will receive.
44 How can ye believe, which receive
honour one of another, and seek not
the honour that *cometh* from God
only? 45 Do not think that I will
accuse you to the Father: there is
one that accuseth you, *even* Moses,
in whom ye trust. 46 For had ye
believed Moses, ye would have believed me: for he wrote of me. 47
But if ye believe not his writings,
how shall ye believe my words?

In these verses our Lord Jesus proves and confirms the commission he had produced, and makes it out that he was sent of God to be the Messiah.

I. He *sets aside* his own testimony of himself (*v.* 31): "*If I bear witness of myself,* though it is infallibly true (*ch.* viii. 14), yet, according to the common rule of judgment among men, you will not admit it as *legal proof,* nor allow it to be *given in evidence.*" Now, 1. This reflects reproach upon the sons of men, and their veracity and integrity. Surely we may say deliberately, what David said in haste, *All men are liars,* else it would never have been such a received maxim that a man's testimony of himself is suspicious, and not to be relied on; it is a sign that self-love is stronger than the love of truth. And yet, 2. It reflects honour on the Son of God, and bespeaks his wonderful condescension, that, though he is the *faithful witness,* the truth itself, who may challenge to be credited *upon his honour,* and his own single testimony, yet he is pleased to *waive his privilege,* and, for the confirmation of our faith, refers himself to his *vouchers,* that we may have full satisfaction.

II. He produces other witnesses that bear testimony to him that he was sent of God.

1. The Father himself bore testimony to him (*v.* 32): *There is another that beareth witness.* I take this to be meant of God the Father, for Christ mentions *his* testimony with his own (*ch.* viii. 18): *I bear witness of myself, and the Father beareth witness of me.* Observe,

(1.) The seal which the Father put to his commission: He *beareth witness of me,* not only has done so by a voice from heaven, but still does so by the tokens of his presence with me. See who they are to whom God will bear witness. [1.] Those whom he *sends* and *employs;* where he gives commissions he gives credentials. [2.] Those who *bear witness* to him; so Christ did. God will own and honour those that own and honour him. [3.] Those who decline *bearing witness of themselves;* so Christ did. God will take care that those who humble and abase themselves, and seek not their own glory, shall not *lose by it.*

(2.) The satisfaction Christ had in this testimony: "*I know that the witness which he witnesseth of me is true.* I am very well assured that I have a divine mission, and do not in the least hesitate concerning it; thus he had the *witness in himself.*" The devil tempted him to question his being the Son of God, but he never yielded.

2. John Baptist witnessed to Christ, *v.* 33, &c. John came to *bear witness of the light* (*ch.* i. 7); his business was to prepare his way, and direct people to him: *Behold the Lamb of God.*

(1.) Now the testimony of John was, [1.] A *solemn* and public testimony: "You sent an embassy of priests and Levites to John, which gave him an opportunity of publishing what he had to say; it was not a popular, but a judicial testimony. [2.] It was a *true* testimony: *He bore witness to the truth,* as a witness ought to do, the *whole truth,* and *nothing but the truth.* Christ does not say, *He bore witness to me* (though every one knew he did), but, like an honest man, *He bore witness to the truth.* Now John was confessedly such a holy, good man, so mortified to the world, and so conversant with divine things, that it could not be imagined he should be guilty of such a forgery and imposture as to say what he did concerning Christ if it had not been so, and if he had not been sure of it.

(2.) Two things are added concerning John's testimony:—

[1.] That it was a testimony *ex abundanti —more than he needed to vouch* (*v.* 34): *I receive not testimony from man.* Though Christ saw fit to quote John's testimony, it was with a protestation that it shall not be deemed or construed so as to prejudice the prerogative of his self-sufficiency. Christ needs no letters of commendation, no testimonials or certificates, but what his own worth and excellency bring with him; why then did Christ here urge the testimony of John? Why, *these things I say, that you may be saved.* This he aimed at in all this discourse, to save not his own life, but the souls of others; he produced John's testimony because, being one *of themselves,* it was to be hoped that they would hearken to it. Note, *First,* Christ desires and designs the salvation even of his enemies and persecutors *Secondly,* The word of Christ is the ordinary means of salvation. *Thirdly,* Christ in his word considers our infirmities and condescends to our capacities, consulting not so much what it befits so great a prince to say as what we can bear, and what will be most likely to do us good.

[2.] That it was a testimony *ad hominem —to the man,* because John Baptist was one whom *they* had a respect for (*v.* 35): *He was a light* among you. Observe,

First, The character of John Baptist: *He was a burning and a shining light.* Christ often spoke honourably of John; he was now in prison under a cloud, yet Christ gives him his *due praise,* which we must be ready to do to all that faithfully serve God. 1. He was *a light,* not φῶς—*lux, light* (so Christ was *the* light), but λύκνος—*lucerna, a luminary,* a derived subordinate light. His office was to enlighten a dark world with notices of the Messiah's approach, to whom he was as the *morning star.* 2. He was a *burning* light, which denotes *sincerity;* painted fire may be made to shine, but that which burns is true fire. It denotes also his *activity,* zeal, and fervency, burning in love to God and the souls of men; fire is always working on itself or something else, so is a good minister. 3. He was a *shining* light, which denotes either his *exemplary conversation,* in which our light should shine (Matt. v. 16), or an *eminent* diffusive influence. He was illustrious in the sight of others; though he affected obscurity and retirement, and was *in the deserts,* yet such were his doctrine, his baptism, his life, that he became very *remarkable,* and attracted the eyes of the nation

Secondly, The affections of the people to him: *You were willing for a season to rejoice in his light.* 1. It was a *transport* that they were *in,* upon the appearing of John: "*You were willing*—ηθελήσατε, *you delighted* to *rejoice in his light;* you were very proud that you had such a man among you, who was the honour of your country; you were willing ἀγαλλιασθῆναι—willing to *dance,* and make a noise about this light, as boys about a bonfire." 2. It was but *transient,* and soon over: "You were fond of him, πρὸς ὥραν—*for an hour,* for *a season,* as little children are fond of a new thing, you were pleased with John awhile, but soon grew weary of him and his ministry, and said that *he had a devil,* and now you have him in prison." Note, Many, that seem to be affected and pleased with the gospel at first, afterwards despise and reject it; it is common for forward and noisy professors to cool and fall off. These here rejoiced in John's light, but never walked in it, and therefore did not keep to it; they were like the stony ground. While Herod was a friend to John Baptist, the people caressed him; but when he fell under Herod's frowns he lost their favours: "*You were willing* to countenance John, πρὸς ὥραν, that is, for *temporal ends*" (so some take it); "you were glad of him, in hopes to make a tool of him, by his interest and under the shelter of his name to have shaken off the Roman yoke, and recovered the civil liberty and honour of your country." Now, (1.) Christ mentions their respect to John, to *condemn* them for their present opposition to himself, to whom

John bore witness. If they had continued their veneration for John, as they ought to have done, they would have embraced Christ. (2.) He mentions the passing away of their respect, to justify God in depriving them, as he had now done, of John's ministry, and putting that light under a bushel.

3. Christ's own works witnessed to him (*v.* 36): *I have a testimony greater than that of John;* for *if we believe the witness of men* sent of God, as John was, the *witness of God* immediately, and not by the ministry of men, *is greater*, 1 John v. 9. Observe, Though the witness of John was a less *cogent* and less *considerable* witness, yet our Lord was pleased to make use of it. We must be glad of all the supports that offer themselves for the confirmation of our faith, though they may not amount to a demonstration, and we must not *invalidate* any, under pretence that there are others more *conclusive;* we have occasion for them all. Now this greater testimony was that of the *works* which *his Father had given him to finish*. That is, (1.) In general the whole course of his life and ministry—his revealing God and his will to us, setting up his kingdom among men, reforming the world, destroying Satan's kingdom, restoring fallen man to his primitive purity and felicity, and shedding abroad in men's hearts the love of God and of one another—all that work of which he said when he died, *It is finished,* it was all, from first to last, *opus Deo dignum—a work worthy of God;* all he said and did was *holy* and *heavenly,* and a divine purity, power, and grace shone in it, proving abundantly that he was *sent of God.* (2.) In particular. The miracles he wrought for the proof of his divine mission witnessed of him. Now it is here said, [1.] That these works were *given him by the Father,* that is, he was both *appointed* and *empowered* to work them; for, as Mediator, he *derived* both commission and strength from his Father. [2.] They were given to him to *finish;* he must do all those works of wonder which the counsel and foreknowledge of God had before determined to be done; and his finishing them proves a divine power; for as *for God his work is perfect.* [3.] These works did *bear witness of him,* did prove that he was sent of God, and that what he said concerning himself was true; see Heb. ii. 4; Acts ii. 22. That the Father had sent him as *a Father*, not as a master sends his servant on an errand, but as a father sends his son to take possession for himself; if God had not sent him, he would not have *seconded* him, would not have *sealed* him, as he did by the works he gave him to do; for the world's Creator will never be its deceiver.

4. He produces, more fully than before, his Father's testimony concerning him (*v.* 37): *The Father that sent me hath borne witness of me.* The prince is not accustomed to follow his ambassador himself, to confirm his commission *viva voce—by speaking;* but God was pleased to bear witness of his Son himself by a voice from heaven at his baptism (Matt. iii. 17): This is my ambassador, *This is my beloved Son.* The Jews reckoned *Bath-kol—the daughter of a voice,* a voice from heaven, one of the ways by which God made known his mind; and in that way he had owned Christ publicly and solemnly, and repeated it, Matt. xvii. 5. Note, (1.) Those whom God *sends* he will *bear witness* of; where he gives a commission, he will not fail to seal it; he that never *left himself without witness* (Acts xiv. 17) will never leave any of his servants so, who go upon his errand. (2.) Where God demands belief, he will not fail to give sufficient *evidence*, as he has done concerning Christ. That which was to be witnessed concerning Christ was chiefly this, that the God we had offended was willing to accept of him as a Mediator. Now concerning this he has *himself* given us full satisfaction (and he was fittest to do it), declaring himself well-pleased in him; if we be so, the work is done. Now, it might be suggested, if God himself thus bore witness of Christ, how came it to pass that he was not universally received by the Jewish nation and their rulers? To this Christ here answers that it was not to be thought strange, nor could their infidelity weaken his credibility, for two reasons:—[1.] Because they were not acquainted with such extraordinary revelations of God and his will: *You have neither heard his voice at any time, nor seen his shape,* or *appearance.* They showed themselves to be as ignorant of God, though they professed relation to him, as we are of a man we never either saw or heard. "But why do I talk to you of God's bearing witness of me? He is one you know nothing of, nor have any acquaintance or communion with." Note, Ignorance of God is the true reason of men's rejecting the record he has given concerning his Son. A right understanding of *natural religion* would discover to us such admirable congruities in the *Christian* religion as would greatly dispose our minds to the entertainment of it. Some give this sense of it: "The Father bore witness of me by a *voice,* and the *descent of a dove,* which is such an extraordinary thing that you never saw or heard the like; and yet for my sake there was such a voice and appearance; yea, and you might have *heard that voice,* you might have *seen that appearance,* as others did, if you had closely attended the ministry of John, but by slighting it you missed of that testimony." [2.] Because they were not affected, no, not with the ordinary ways by which God had revealed himself to them: *You have not his word abiding in you, v.* 38. They had the scriptures of the Old Testament; might they not by them be disposed to receive Christ? Yes, if they had had their due influence upon them. But, *First,* The word of God was not in them; it was *among them,* in their country, in their hands, but not *in them,* in their

hearts: not ruling in their souls, but only shining in their eyes and sounding in their ears. What did it avail them that they had the oracles of God *committed* to them (Rom. iii. 2), when they had not these oracles *commanding* in them? If they had, they would readily have embraced Christ. *Secondly,* It did not *abide.* Many have the word of God coming into them, and making some impressions for awhile, but it does not *abide* with them; it is not constantly in them, as a man at home, but only now and then, as a *wayfaring man.* If the word *abide in* us, if we converse with it by frequent meditation, consult with it upon every occasion, and conform to it in our conversation, we shall then readily receive the witness of the Father concerning Christ; see *ch.* vii. 17. But how did it appear that they *had not the word of God abiding in them?* It appeared by this, *Whom he hath sent, him ye believe not.* There was so much said in the Old Testament concerning Christ, to direct people when and where to look for him, and so to facilitate the discovery of him, that, if they had duly considered these things, they could not have avoided the conviction of Christ's being sent of God; so that their not believing in Christ was a certain sign that the word of God did not abide in them. Note, The in-dwelling of the word, and Spirit, and grace of God in us, is best tried by its effects, particularly by our *receiving what he sends,* the commands, the messengers, the providences he sends, especially Christ whom he hath sent.

5. The last witness he calls is the Old Testament, which witnessed of him, and to it he appeals (*v.* 39, &c.): *Search the scriptures, ἐρευνᾶτε.*

(1.) This may be read, either, [1.] "*You search the scriptures,* and you do well to do so; you read them daily in your synagogues, you have rabbies, and doctors, and scribes, that make it their business to study them, and criticize upon them." The Jews boasted of the flourishing of scripture-learning in the days of Hillel, who died about twelve years after Christ's birth, and reckoned some of those who were then members of the sanhedrim the *beauties of their wisdom* and the *glories of their law;* and Christ owns that they did indeed search the scriptures, but it was in search of their *own glory:* "*You search the scriptures,* and therefore, if you were not *wilfully blind,* you would *believe in me.*" Note, It is possible for men to be very studious in the letter of the scripture, and yet to be strangers to the power and influence of it. Or, [2.] As we read it: *Search the scriptures;* and so, *First,* It was spoken to *them* in the nature of an *appeal:* "You profess to receive and believe the scripture; here I will *join issue* with you, let this be the judge, provided you will not *rest in the letter*" (*hærere in cortice*), "but will *search* into it." Note, when appeals are made to the scriptures, they must be searched. Search the whole book of scripture *throughout,* compare one passage with another, and explain one by another. We must likewise search particular passages *to the bottom,* and see not what they *seem* to say *prima facie—at the first appearance,* but what they say *indeed. Secondly,* It is spoken to *us* in the nature of an *advice,* or a command to all Christians to search the scriptures. Note, All those who would *find Christ* must *search the scriptures;* not only read them, and hear them, but search them, which denotes, 1. *Diligence* in seeking, labour, and study, and close application of mind. 2. *Desire* and *design* of finding. We must aim at some spiritual benefit and advantage in reading and studying the scripture, and often ask, "What am I now searching for?" We must search as for *hidden treasures* (Prov. ii. 4), as those that *sink* for gold or silver, or that *dive* for pearl, Job xxviii. 1—11. This ennobled the Bereans, Acts xvii. 11.

(2.) Now there are two things which we are here directed to have in our eye, in our searching the scripture: *heaven* our end, and *Christ* our way. [1.] We must search the scriptures for *heaven* as our *great end: For in them you think you have eternal life.* The scripture assures us of an eternal state set before us, and offers to us an eternal life in that state: it contains the *chart* that *describes* it, the *charter* that *conveys* it, the *direction* in the way that leads to it, and the *foundation* upon which the hope of it is built; and this is worth searching for where we are sure to find it. But to the Jews Christ saith only, *You think* you have *eternal life* in the scriptures, because, though they did retain the belief and hope of eternal life, and grounded their expectations of it upon the scriptures, yet herein they missed it, that they looked for it by the bare reading and studying of the scripture. It was a common but corrupt saying among them, *He that has the words of the law has eternal life;* they thought they were sure of heaven if they could say by *heart,* or rather by *rote,* such and such passages of scripture as they were directed to by the tradition of the elders; as they thought all the *vulgar* cursed because they did not thus know the law (*ch.* vii. 49), so they concluded all the *learned* undoubtedly *blessed.* [2.] We must *search the scriptures* for *Christ,* as the new and living *way* that leads to this *end.* These are *they,* the great and principal witnesses, *that testify of me.* Note, *First,* The scriptures, even those of the Old Testament, *testify* of Christ, and by them God *bears witness* to him. The Spirit of Christ in the prophets testified beforehand of him (1 Pet. i. 11), the purposes and promises of God concerning him, and the previous notices of him. The Jews knew very well that the Old Testament testified of the Messiah, and were critical in their remarks upon the passages that looked that way; and yet were careless, and wretchedly overseen, in the application of them. *Secondly, Therefore* we must *search the scriptures*, and may hope to find eternal life in that search, because they testify of Christ; for this is *life eternal, to know him;* see 1 John v. 11. Christ is the treasure hid in the field of the scriptures, the water in those wells, the milk in those breasts.

(3.) To this testimony he annexes a reproof of their infidelity and wickedness in four instances; particularly,

[1.] Their *neglect of him* and his doctrine: "*You will not come to me, that you might have life*, v. 40. You search the scriptures, you believe the prophets, who you cannot but see testify of me; and yet you will not *come to me*, to whom they direct you." Their estrangement from Christ was the fault not so much of their *understandings* as of their *wills*. This is expressed as a complaint; Christ offered life, and it was not accepted. Note, *First*, There is *life* to be had with Jesus Christ for poor souls; we may have life, the life of *pardon* and *grace*, and *comfort* and *glory:* life is the perfection of our being, and inclusive of all happiness; and Christ is our life. *Secondly*, Those that would have this life must *come* to Jesus Christ for it; we may have it for the coming for. It *supposes* an assent of the understanding to the doctrine of Christ and the record given concerning him; it *lies in* the consent of the will to his government and grace, and it *produces* an answerable compliance in the affections and actions. *Thirdly*, The only reason why sinners die is because they *will not come* to Christ for life and happiness; it is not because they *cannot*, but because they *will not*. They will neither *accept* the life offered, because *spiritual* and *divine*, nor will they *agree* to the terms on which it is offered, nor *apply* themselves to the use of the appointed means: they will not be cured, for they will not observe the methods of cure. *Fourthly*, The wilfulness and obstinacy of sinners in rejecting the tenders of grace are a great grief to the Lord Jesus, and what he complains of. Those words (*v*. 41), *I receive not honour from men*, come in in a parenthesis, to obviate an objection against him, as if he sought his own glory, and made himself the head of a party, in obliging all to come to *him*, and applaud him. Note, 1. He did not *covet* nor *court* the applause of men, did not in the least affect that worldly pomp and splendour in which the carnal Jews expected their Messiah to appear. He charged those whom he cured not to make him known, and withdrew from those that would have made him king. 2. He *had not* the applause of men. Instead of *receiving honour* from men, he received a great deal of *dishonour* and disgrace from men, for he made himself of no reputation. 3. He *needed* not the applause of men; it was no addition to his glory whom all the angels of God worship, nor was he any otherwise pleased with it than as it was according to his Father's will, and for the happiness of those who, in giving honour *to him*, received much greater honour *from him*

[2.] Their *want of the love of God* (*v*. 42): "*I know you* very well, *that you have not the love of God in you*. Why should I wonder that you do not come to me, when you want even the first principle of *natural religion*, which is the *love of God?*" Note, The reason why people *slight Christ* is because they do not *love God;* for, if we did indeed love God, we should love him who is his express image, and hasten to him by whom only we may be restored to the favour of God. He charged them (*v*. 37) with *ignorance* of God, and here with want of love to him; *therefore* men have not the love of God because they desire not the knowledge of him. Observe, *First*, The crime charged upon them: *You have not the love of God in you*. They pretended a great love to God, and thought they proved it by their zeal for the law, the temple, and the sabbath; and yet they were really without the love of God. Note, There are many who make a great profession of religion who yet show they want the love of God by their neglect of Christ and their contempt of his commandments; they hate his holiness and undervalue his goodness. Observe, It is the love of God *in* us, that love seated *in the heart*, a living active principle there, that God will *accept;* the love *shed abroad* there, Rom. v. 5. *Secondly*, The proof of this charge, by the personal knowledge of Christ, who *searches the heart* (Rev. ii. 23) and knows what is *in man: I know you*. Christ sees through all our disguises, and can say to each of us, *I know thee*. 1. Christ knows men better than *their neighbours know them*. The people thought that the scribes and Pharisees were very devout and good men, but Christ knew that they had not the love of God in them. 2. Christ knows men better than *they know themselves*. These Jews had a very good opinion of themselves, but Christ knew how corrupt their inside was, notwithstanding the speciousness of their outside; we may deceive ourselves, but we cannot deceive him. 3. Christ knows men who do not, and will not, know him; he looks *on* those who industriously look *off* from him, and calls by their own name, their true name, those who have not known him.

[3.] Another crime charged upon them is their readiness to entertain false Christs and false prophets, while they obstinately opposed him who was the true Messias (*v*. 43): *I am come in my Father's name, and you receive me not. If another shall come in his own name, him you will receive. Be astonished, O heavens, at this* (Jer. ii. 12, 13); *for my people have committed two evils*, great evils indeed. *First*, They have *forsaken the fountain of living waters*, for they would not receive Christ, who came in his Father's name, had his commission from his Father, and did all for his glory. *Secondly*, They have *hewn out broken cisterns*, they hearken to every one that will set up in his own name. They forsake their own mercies, which is bad enough; and it is for *lying vanities*, which is worse. Observe here, 1. Those are false prophets who come in their own name, who run without being sent, and set up for themselves only. 2. It is just with God to suffer those to be deceived with false prophets who receive not the truth in the love of it. 2 Thess. ii. 10, 11. The errors of antichrist are the just punishment of those who obey not the doctrine of Christ. They that shut their eyes against the true light are by the judgment of God given up to wander endlessly after *false lights*, and to be led aside after every *ignis fatuus*. 3. It is the gross folly of many that, while they *nauseate* ancient truths, they are *fond* of upstart errors; they loathe manna, and at the same time *feed upon ashes*. After the Jews had rejected Christ and his gospel, they were continually haunted with spectres, with *false Christs* and *false prophets* (Matt. xxiv. 24), and their proneness to follow such occasioned those distractions and seditions that hastened their ruin.

[4.] They are here charged with pride and vain-glory, and unbelief, the effect of them, *v.* 44. Having sharply reproved their unbelief, like a wise physician, he here searches into the cause, lays the axe to the root. They *therefore* slighted and undervalued Christ because they *admired* and *overvalued* themselves. Here is,

First, Their ambition of worldly honour. Christ despised it, *v.* 41. They set their hearts upon it: *You receive honour one of another;* that is, "You look for a Messiah in outward pomp, and promise yourselves worldly honour by him." *You receive honour:*—1. "You desire to receive it, and aim at this in all you do." 2. "You give honour to others, and applaud them, only that they may return it, and may applaud you." *Petimus dabimusque vicissim—We ask and we bestow.* It is the proud man's art to throw honour upon others only that it may rebound upon himself. 3. "You are very careful to keep all the honours to yourselves, and confine them to your own party, as if you had the monopoly of that which is honourable." 4. "What respect is shown to you you *receive* yourselves, and do not transmit to God, as Herod." Idolizing men and their sentiments, and affecting to be idolized by them and their applauses, are pieces of idolatry as directly contrary to Christianity as any other.

Secondly, Their neglect of spiritual honour, called here *the honour that comes from God only;* this they sought not, nor minded. Note, 1. True honour is that which *comes from God only*, that is real and lasting honour; those are honourable indeed whom he takes into covenant and communion with himself. 2. *This honour have all the saints.* All that believe in Christ, through him receive the honour that comes from God. He is not partial, but will give glory wherever he gives grace. 3. This honour that comes from God we must *seek*, must aim at it, and act for it, and take up with nothing short of it (Rom. ii. 29); we must account it *our reward*, as the Pharisees accounted the praise of men. 4. Those that will not come to Christ, and those that are ambitious of worldly honour, make it appear that they seek not the honour that comes from God, and it is their folly and ruin.

Thirdly, The influence this had upon their infidelity. *How can you believe* who are thus affected? Observe here, 1. The difficulty of believing arises from ourselves and our own corruption; we make our work hard to ourselves, and then complain it is impracticable. 2. The ambition and affectation of worldly honour are a great hindrance to faith in Christ. How can they believe who make the praise and applause of men their idol? When the profession and practice of serious godliness are unfashionable, are *every where spoken against*,—when Christ and his followers are men wondered at, and to be a Christian is to be like a *speckled bird* (and this is the common case),—how can they believe the summit of whose ambition is to *make a fair show in the flesh?*

6. The last witness here called is Moses, *v.* 45, &c. The Jews had a great veneration for Moses, and valued themselves upon their being the *disciples* of Moses, and pretended to adhere to Moses, in their opposition to Christ; but Christ here shows them,

(1.) That Moses was a witness against the unbelieving Jews, *and accused them to the Father: There is one that accuses you, even Moses.* This may be understood either, [1.] As showing the difference between the law and the gospel. Moses, that is, the law, *accuses you*, for by the law is the knowledge of sin; it *condemns* you, it is to those that trust to it a ministration of death and condemnation. But it is not the design of Christ's gospel to *accuse* us: *Think not that I will accuse you.* Christ did not come into the world as a *Momus*, to find fault and pick quarrels with every body, or as a *spy* upon the actions of men, or a *promoter*, to fish for crimes; no, he came to be an advocate, not an accuser; to reconcile God and man, and not to set them more at variance. What fools were they then that adhered to Moses against Christ, and *desired to be under the law!* Gal. iv. 21. Or, [2.] As showing the manifest unreasonableness of their infidelity: "Think not that I will appeal from your bar to God's and challenge you to answer there for what you do against me, as injured innocency usually does; no, I do not need; you are already accused, and cast, in the court of heaven; Moses himself says enough to convict you of, and condemn you for, your unbelief." Let them not mistake *concerning Christ;* though he was a prophet, he did not improve his interest in heaven against those that persecuted him, did not, as Elias, *make intercession against Israel* (Rom vi. 2), nor as Jeremiah desire to *see God's vengeance on them,* Jer. xx. 12. Instead of *accusing* his crucifiers to his Father, he prayed, *Father, forgive them.* Nor let them mistake concerning Moses, as if he would stand by them in rejecting Christ; no, *There is one that accuses you, even Moses in whom you trust.* Note, *First,* External privileges and advantages are commonly the vain confidence of those who reject Christ and his grace. The Jews *trusted* in Moses, and thought their having his laws and ordinances would save them. *Secondly,* Those that confide in their privileges, and do not improve them, will find not only that their confidence is disappointed, but that those very privileges will be witnesses against them.

(2.) That Moses was a witness for Christ and to his doctrine (*v.* 46, 47): *He wrote of me.* Moses did particularly prophesy of Christ, as the Seed of the woman, the Seed of Abraham, the Shiloh, the great Prophet; the ceremonies of the law of Moses were *figures of him that was to come.* The Jews made Moses the patron of their opposition to Christ; but Christ here shows them their error, that Moses was so far from writing against Christ that he wrote *for him,* and *of him.* But, [1.] Christ here charges it on the Jews that they *did not believe Moses.* He had said (*v.* 45) that they *trusted* in Moses, and yet here he undertakes to make out that they did not believe Moses; they trusted to his name, but they did not receive his doctrine in its true sense and meaning; they did not rightly understand, nor give credit to, what there was in the writings of Moses concerning the Messiah. [2.] He proves this charge from their disbelief of him: *Had you believed Moses, you would have believed me.* Note, *First,* The surest trial of faith is by the effects it produces. Many say that they believe whose actions give their words the lie; for had they believed the scriptures they would have done otherwise than they did. *Secondly,* Those who rightly believe one part of scripture will receive every part. The prophecies of the Old Testament were so fully accomplished in Christ that those who rejected Christ did in effect deny those prophecies, and set them aside. [3.] From their disbelief of Moses he infers that it was not strange that they rejected him: *If you believe not his writings, how shall you believe my words?* How can it be thought that you should? *First,* "If you do not believe sacred *writings,* those oracles which are in black and white, which is the most certain way of conveyance, *how shall you believe my words,* words being usually less regarded?" *Secondly,* "If you do not believe Moses, for whom you have such a profound veneration, how is it likely that you should believe me, whom you look upon with so much contempt?" See Exod. vi. 12. *Thirdly,* "If you believe not what Moses spoke and wrote of me, which is a strong and cogent testimony for me, how shall you believe me and my mission?" If we admit not the premises, how shall we admit the conclusion? The truth of the Christian religion, it being a matter purely of divine revelation, depends upon the divine authority of the scripture; if therefore we believe not the divine inspiration of those writings, how shall we receive the doctrine of Christ?

Thus ends Christ's plea for himself, in answer to the charge exhibited against him. What effect it had we know not; it would seem to have had this, their *mouths* were *stopped* for the present, and they could not for shame but drop the prosecution, and yet their *hearts* were *hardened.*

CHAP. VI.

In this chapter we have, I. The miracle of the loaves, ver. 1—14. II. Christ's walking upon the water, ver. 15—21. III. The people's flocking after him to Capernaum, ver. 22—25. IV. His conference with them, occasioned by the miracle of the loaves, in which he reproves them for seeking carnal food, and directs them to spiritual food (ver. 26, 27), showing them how they must labour for spiritual food (ver. 28, 29), and what that spiritual food is, ver. 30—59. V. Their discontent at what he said, and the reproof he gave them for it, ver. 60—65. VI. The apostasy of many from him, and his discourse with his disciples that adhered to him upon that occasion, ver. 66—71.

AFTER these things Jesus went
over the sea of Galilee, which
is *the sea* of Tiberias. 2 And a great
multitude followed him, because they
saw his miracles which he did on
them that were diseased. 3 And Jesus went up into a mountain, and
there he sat with his disciples. 4
And the passover, a feast of the Jews,
was nigh. 5 When Jesus then lifted
up *his* eyes, and saw a great company
come unto him, he saith unto Philip,
Whence shall we buy bread, that
these may eat? 6 And this he said
to prove him: for he himself knew
what he would do. 7 Philip answered him, Two hundred pennyworth of bread is not sufficient for
them, that every one of them may
take a little. 8 One of his disciples,
Andrew, Simon Peter's brother, saith
unto him, 9 There is a lad here,
which hath five barley loaves, and
two small fishes: but what are they
among so many? 10 And Jesus said,
Make the men sit down. Now there
was much grass in the place. So the
men sat down, in number about five
thousand. 11 And Jesus took the
loaves; and when he had given
thanks, he distributed to the disciples, and the disciples to them that
were set down; and likewise of the

fishes as much as they would. 12
When they were filled, he said unto
his disciples, Gather up the fragments
that remain, that nothing be lost. 13
Therefore they gathered *them* together, and filled twelve baskets with the fragments of the five barley loaves, which remained over and above unto them that had eaten. 14 Then those men, when they had seen the miracle that Jesus did, said, This is of a truth that prophet that should come into the world.

We have here an account of Christ's feeding five thousand men with five loaves and two fishes, which miracle is in *this* respect remarkable, that it is the only passage of the actions of *Christ's life* that is recorded by all the four evangelists. John, who does not usually relate what had been recorded by those who wrote before him, yet relates this, because of the reference the following discourse has to it. Observe,

I. The *place* and *time* where and when this miracle was wrought, which are noted for the greater evidence of the truth of the story; it is not said that it was done once upon a time, nobody knows where, but the circumstances are specified, that the fact might be enquired into.

1. The country that Christ was in (*v.* 1): *He went over the sea of Galilee,* called elsewhere *the lake of Gennesareth,* here *the sea of Tiberias,* from a city adjoining, which Herod had lately enlarged and beautified, and called so in honour of Tiberius the emperor, and probably had made his metropolis. Christ did not go directly over cross this inland sea, but made a *coasting* voyage to another place on the same side. It is not tempting God to choose to go *by water,* when there is convenience for it, even to those places whither we might go *by land;* for Christ never *tempted the Lord his God,* Matt. iv. 7.

2. The company that he was attended with: *A great multitude followed him, because they saw his miracles, v.* 2. Note, (1.) Our Lord Jesus, while he went about *doing good,* lived continually in *a crowd,* which gave him more trouble than honour. Good and useful men must not complain of a *hurry* of business, when they are serving God and their generation; it will be time enough to *enjoy ourselves* when we come to that world where we shall *enjoy God.* (2.) Christ's miracles drew many *after him* that were not effectually drawn *to him.* They had their curiosity gratified by the strangeness of them, who had not their consciences convinced by the power of them.

3. Christ's posting himself advantageously to entertain them (*v.* 3): *He went up into a mountain,* and there he *sat with his disciples,* that he might the more conveniently be seen and heard by the multitude that crowded after him; this was a *natural* pulpit, and not, like Ezra's, made *for the purpose.* Christ was now driven to be a *field preacher;* but his word was never the worse, nor the less acceptable, for that, to those who knew how to value it, who followed him still, not only when he *went out* to a desert place, but when he *went up* to a mountain, though *up-hill* be *against heart.* He *sat* there, as teachers do *in cathedra—in the chair of instruction.* He did not sit at ease, not sit in state, yet he sat as one having authority, sat ready to receive addresses that were made to him; whoever would might come, and find him there. He sat *with his disciples;* he condescended to take them to *sit with him,* to put a reputation upon them before the people, and give them an earnest of the glory in which they should shortly sit with him. We are said to *sit with him,* Eph. ii. 6.

4. The time when it was. The first words, *After those things,* do not signify that this immediately followed what was related in the foregoing chapter, for it was a considerable time after, and they signify no more than in process of time; but we are told (*v.* 4) that it was *when the passover was nigh,* which is here noted, (1.) Because, perhaps, that had brought in all the apostles from their respective expeditions, whither they were sent as itinerant preachers, that they might attend their Master to Jerusalem, to keep the feast. (2.) Because it was a custom with the Jews religiously to observe the approach of the passover *thirty days* before, with some sort of solemnity; so long before they had it in their eye, repaired the roads, mended bridges, if there was occasion, and discoursed of the passover and the institution of it. (3.) Because, perhaps, the approach of the passover, when every one knew Christ would go up to Jerusalem, and be absent for some time, made the multitude flock the more after him and attend the more diligently on him. Note, The prospect of losing our opportunities should quicken us to improve them with double diligence; and, when solemn ordinances are approaching, it is good to prepare for them by conversing with the word of Christ.

II. The miracle itself. And here observe,

1. The notice Christ took of the crowd that attended him (*v.* 5): He *lifted up his eyes,* and *saw a great company come to him,* poor, mean, ordinary people, no doubt, for such make up the multitudes, especially in such remote corners of the country; yet Christ showed himself pleased with their attendance, and concerned for their welfare, to teach us to *condescend to those of low estate,* and not to *set* those *with the dogs of our flock* whom Christ hath set with the lambs of his. The souls of the poor are as precious to Christ, and should be so to us, as those of the rich.

2. The enquiry he made concerning the way of providing for them. He directed himself to Philip, who had been his disciple from the first, and had seen all his miracles, and particularly that of his turning water into wine, and therefore it might be expected that he should have said, "Lord, if thou wilt, it is easy to thee to feed them all." Those that, like Israel, have been witnesses of Christ's works, and have shared in the benefit of them, are inexcusable if they say, *Can he furnish a table in the wilderness?* Philip was of Bethsaida, in the neighbourhood of which town Christ now was, and therefore he was most likely to help them to provision at the best hand; and probably much of the company was known to him, and he was concerned for them. Now Christ asked, *Whence shall we buy bread, that these* may eat? (1.) He takes it for granted that they must all *eat with him.* One would think that when he had taught and healed them he had done his part; and that now they should rather have been contriving how to treat him and his disciples, for some of the people were probably *rich,* and we are sure that Christ and his disciples were *poor;* yet he is solicitous to entertain them. Those that will accept Christ's spiritual gifts, instead of *paying* for them, shall be *paid* for their acceptance of them. Christ, having fed their souls with the bread of life, feeds their bodies also with *food convenient,* to show that the Lord is for the body, and to encourage us to pray for our daily bread, and to set us an example of compassion to the poor, James ii. 15, 16. (2.) His enquiry is, *Whence shall we buy bread?* One would think, considering his poverty, that he should rather have asked, *Where shall we have money to buy for them?* But he will rather lay out all he has than they shall want. He will buy to give, and we must *labour,* that we may give, Eph. iv. 28.

3. The design of this enquiry; it was only to try the faith of Philip, *for he himself knew what he would do, v.* 6. Note, (1.) Our Lord Jesus is never at a loss in his counsels; but, how difficult soever the case is, he knows what he has to do and what course he will take, Acts xv. 18. *He knows the thoughts he has towards his people* (Jer. xxix. 11) and is never at uncertainty; when we know not, he *himself knows what he will do.* (2.) When Christ is pleased to *puzzle* his people, it is only with a design to *prove* them. The question put Philip to a nonplus, yet Christ proposed it, to try whether he would say, "Lord, if thou wilt exert thy power for them, we need not buy bread."

4. Philip's answer to this question: "*Two hundred pennyworth of bread is not sufficient, v.* 7. Master, it is to no purpose to talk of buying bread for them, for neither will the country afford so much bread, nor can we afford to lay out so much money; ask Judas, who carries the bag." Two hundred pence of *their* money amount to about six pounds of *ours,* and, if they lay out all that at once, it will exhaust their fund, and break them, and they must starve themselves. Grotius computes that *two hundred pennyworth of bread* would scarcely reach to *two thousand,* but Philip would go as near hand as he could, would have *every one to take a little;* and nature, we say, is content with a little. See the weakness of Philip's faith, that in this strait, as if the Master of the family had been an *ordinary person,* he looked for supply only in an *ordinary way.* Christ might now have said to him, as he did afterwards, Have I *been so long time with you, and yet hast thou not known me, Philip?* Or, as God to Moses in a like case, *Is the Lord's hand waxen short?* We are apt thus to distrust God's power when visible and ordinary means fail, that is, to trust him no further than we can see him.

5. The information which Christ received from another of his disciples concerning the provision they had. It was Andrew, here said to be *Simon Peter's brother;* though he was senior to Peter in discipleship, and instrumental to bring Peter to Christ, yet Peter afterwards so far outshone him that he is described by his relation to Peter: he acquainted Christ with what they had at hand; and in this we may see,

(1.) The *strength* of his *love* to those for whom he saw his Master concerned, in that he was willing to bring out all they had, though he knew not but they might want themselves, and any one would have said, *Charity begins at home.* He did not go about to conceal it, under pretence of being a better husband of their provision than the Master was, but honestly gives in an account of all they had. There is a lad here, παιδάριον—*a little lad,* probably one that used to follow this company, as suttlers do the camp, with provisions to sell, and the disciples had bespoken what he had for themselves; and it was *five barley-loaves,* and two small fishes. Here, [1.] The provision was *coarse* and *ordinary;* they were *barley loaves.* Canaan was a *land of wheat* (Deut. viii. 8); its inhabitants were commonly fed with the finest wheat (Ps. lxxxi. 16), the kidneys of wheat (Deut. xxxii. 14); yet Christ and his disciples were glad of *barley-bread.* It does not follow hence that we should tie ourselves to such coarse fare, and place religion in it (when God brings that which is finer to our hands, let us receive it, and be thankful); but it does follow that therefore we must not be *desirous of dainties* (Prov. xxiii. 3); nor murmur if we be reduced to coarse fare, but be content and thankful, and well reconciled to it; barley-bread is what Christ *had,* and better than we *deserve.* Nor let us despise the mean provision of the poor, nor look upon it with contempt, remembering how Christ was provided for. [2.] It was but *short* and *scanty;* there were but *five loaves,* and those so small that one little lad carried them all; and we find (2 Kings iv. 42, 43) that *twenty barley-loaves,* with some other provision to help out, would not dine a hundred men without a miracle. There were but two fishes, and those *small* ones (δύο ὀψάρια), so small that one of them was but a morsel, *pisciculi assati.* I take the fish to have been *pickled,* or *soused,* for they had not fire to dress them with. The provision of *bread* was *little,* but that of *fish* was *less* in proportion to it, so that many a bit of dry bread they must eat before they could make a meal of this provision; but they were content with it. *Bread* is meat for our hunger; but of those that murmured for flesh it is said, *They asked meat for their lust,* Ps. lxxviii. 18. Well, Andrew was willing that the people should have this, as far as it would go. Note, A distrustful fear of wanting ourselves should not hinder us from needful charity to others.

(2.) See here the *weakness* of his *faith* in that word, "*But what are they among so many?* To offer this to such a multitude is but to mock them." Philip and he had not that actual consideration of the power of Christ (of which they had had such large experience) which they should have had. Who fed the camp of Israel in the wilderness? He that could make *one man chase a thousand* could make one loaf feed a thousand.

6. The directions Christ gave the disciples to seat the guests (*v.* 10): "*Make the men sit down,* though you have nothing to set before them, and trust me for that." This was like *sending providence* to *market,* and going to buy without money: Christ would thus try their obedience. Observe, (1.) The furniture of the dining-room: *there was much grass in that place,* though a desert place; see how bountiful nature is, it *makes grass to grow upon the mountains,* Ps. cxlvii. 8. This grass was uneaten; God gives not only enough, but more than enough. Here was this plenty of grass where Christ was preaching; the gospel brings other blessings along with it: *Then shall the earth yield her increase,* Ps. lxvii. 6. This plenty of grass made the place the more commodious for those that must sit on the ground, and served them for cushions, or *beds* (as they called what they sat on at meat, Esth. i. 6), and, considering what Christ says of the grass of the field (Matt. vi. 29, 30), these beds excelled those of Ahasuerus: nature's pomp is the most glorious. (2.) The number of the guests: *About five thousand:* a great entertainment, representing that of the gospel, which is a *feast for all nations* (Isa. xxv. 6), a feast for all *comers.*

7. The distribution of the provision, *v.* 11. Observe,

(1.) It was done with thanksgiving: *He gave thanks.* Note, [1.] We ought to give thanks to God for our food, for it is a mercy to have it, and we have it from the hand of God, and must *receive it with thanksgiving,* 1 Tim. iv. 4, 5. And this is the sweetness of our creature-comforts, that they will furnish us with *matter,* and give us occasion, for that excellent duty of thanksgiving. [2.] Though our provision be coarse and scanty, though we have neither plenty nor dainty, yet we must give thanks to God for what we have.

(2.) It was distributed from the hand of Christ by the hands of his disciples, *v.* 11. Note, [1.] All our comforts come to us *originally* from the hand of Christ; whoever *brings* them, it is he that *sends* them, he distributes to those who distribute to us. [2.] In distributing the bread of life to those that follow him, he is pleased to make use of the ministration of his disciples; they are the servitors at Christ's table, or rather rulers in his household, to give to *every one his portion of meat in due season.*

(3.) It was done to universal satisfaction. They did not every one take a little, but all had *as much as they would;* not a short allowance, but a full meal; and considering how long they had fasted, with what an appetite they sat down, how agreeable this miraculous food may be supposed to have been, above common food, it was not a little that served them when they ate as much as they would and on free cost. Those whom Christ feeds with the bread of life he does not stint, Ps. lxxxi. 10. There were but *two small fishes,* and yet they had *of them* too *as much as they would.* He did not reserve them for the better sort of the guests, and put off the poor with dry bread, but treated them all alike, for they were all alike welcome. Those who call feeding upon fish *fasting* reproach the entertainment Christ here made, which was a *full feast.*

8. The care that was taken of the broken meat. (1.) The orders Christ gave concerning it (*v.* 12): *When they were filled,* and every man had within him a sensible witness to the truth of the miracle, Christ *said to the disciples,* the servants he employed, *Gather up the fragments.* Note, we must always take care that we make no waste of any of God's good creatures; for the grant we have of them, though large and full, is with this proviso, *wilful waste only excepted.* It is just with God to bring us to the want of that which we make waste of. The Jews were very careful not to lose any bread, nor let it fall to the ground, to be trodden upon. *Qui panem contemnit in gravem incidit paupertatem—He who despises bread falls into the depths of poverty,* was a saying among them. Though Christ could command supplies whenever he pleased, yet he would have the fragments gathered up. When we are filled we must remember that others want, and we may want. Those that would have wherewith to be *charitable* must be *provident.* Had this broken meat been left upon the grass, the beasts and fowls would have gathered it up; but that which is fit to be meat for men is wasted and lost if it be thrown to the brute-creatures. Christ did not order the broken meat to be gathered up till all were filled; we must not begin to hoard and lay up till all is laid out that ought to be,

for that is withholding more than is meet. Mr. Baxter notes here, "How much less should we lose God's word, or helps, or our time, or such greater mercies!" (2.) The observance of these orders (*v.* 13): *They filled twelve baskets with the fragments,* which was an evidence not only of the *truth* of the miracle, that they were fed, not with fancy, but with real food (witness those remains), but of the *greatness* of it; they were not only filled, but there was all this over and above. See how large the divine bounty is; it not only *fills* the cup, but makes it *run over;* bread enough, and to spare, in our Father's house. The fragments filled twelve baskets, one for each disciple; they were thus repaid with interest for their willingness to part with what they had for public service; see 2 Chron. xxxi. 10. The Jews lay it as a law upon themselves, when they have eaten a meal, to be sure to leave a piece of bread upon the table, upon which the blessing after meat may rest; for it is a curse upon the wicked man (Job xx. 21) that *there shall none of his meat be left.*

III. Here is the influence which this miracle had upon the people who tasted of the benefit of it (*v.* 14): *They said, This is of a truth that prophet.* Note, 1. Even the vulgar Jews with great assurance expected the Messiah to come into the world, and to be a *great prophet.* They speak here with assurance of his coming. The Pharisees despised them as *not knowing the law;* but, it should seem, they knew more of him that is the *end of the law* than the Pharisees did. 2. The miracles which Christ wrought did clearly demonstrate that he was the Messiah promised, a teacher come from God, the great prophet, and could not but convince the amazed spectators that this was he that should come. There were many who were convinced he was that prophet that should come into the world who yet did not cordially receive his doctrine, for they did not continue in it. Such a wretched incoherence and inconsistency there is between the faculties of the corrupt unsanctified soul, that it is possible for men to acknowledge that Christ is that prophet, and yet to turn a deaf ear to him.

15 When Jesus therefore perceived
that they would come and take him
by force, to make him a king, he departed again into a mountain himself
alone. 16 And when even was *now*
come, his disciples went down unto
the sea, 17 And entered into a ship,
and went over the sea toward Capernaum. And it was now dark, and
Jesus was not come to them. 18
And the sea arose by reason of a
great wind that blew. 19 So when
they had rowed about five and twenty
or thirty furlongs, they see Jesus
walking on the sea, and drawing nigh
unto the ship: and they were afraid.
20 But he saith unto them, It is I;
be not afraid. 21 Then they willingly
received him into the ship: and immediately the ship was at the land
whither they went.

Here is, I. Christ's retirement from the multitude.

1. Observe what induced him to retire; because he perceived that those who acknowledged him to be that prophet that should come into the world would come, and *take him by force, to make him a king, v.* 15. Now here we have an instance,

(1.) Of the irregular zeal of some of Christ's followers; nothing would serve but they would make him *a king.* Now, [1.] This was *an act of zeal* for the honour of Christ, and against the contempt which the ruling part of the Jewish church put upon him. They were concerned to see so great a benefactor to the world so little esteemed in it; and therefore, since royal titles are counted the most illustrious, they would make him a king, knowing that the Messiah was to be a king; and if a prophet, like Moses, then a sovereign prince and lawgiver, like him; and, if they cannot set him up *upon the holy hill of Zion,* a *mountain* in Galilee shall serve for the present. Those whom Christ has feasted with the royal dainties of heaven should, in return for his favour, make him *their* king, and set him upon the throne in their souls: let him that has *fed* us *rule us.* But, [2.] It was an *irregular* zeal; for, *First,* It was grounded upon a mistake concerning the nature of Christ's kingdom, as if it were to be *of this world,* and he must appear with outward pomp, a crown on his head, and an army at his foot; such a king as this they would make him, which was as great a disparagement to his glory as it would be to lacker gold or paint a ruby. Right notions of Christ's kingdom would keep us to right methods for advancing it. *Secondly,* It was excited by the love of the flesh; they would make *him* their king who could feed them so plentifully without their toil, and save them from the curse of *eating their bread in the sweat of their face. Thirdly,* It was intended to carry on a *secular* design; they hoped this might be a fair opportunity of shaking off the Roman yoke, of which they were weary. If they had one to head them who could victual an army cheaper than another could provide for a family, they were sure of the sinews of the war, and could not fail of success, and the recovery of their ancient liberties. Thus is religion often prostituted to a secular interest, and Christ is served only to *serve a turn,* Rom. xvi. 18. *Vix quæritur* Jesus *propter* Jesum, *sed propter aliud—Jesus is usually sought after for something else, not for his own sake.*—Augustine. Nay, *Fourthly,* It was a tumultuous, seditious attempt, and a disturbance of the public peace; it would make the country a seat of war, and expose it to the resentments of the Roman power. *Fifthly,* It was contrary to the mind of our Lord Jesus himself; for they would take him *by force,* whether he would or no. Note, Those who force honours upon Christ which he has not required at their hands displease him, and do him the greatest dishonour. Those that say *I am of Christ,* in opposition to those that are of Apollos and Cephas (so making Christ the head of a party), take him by force, to make him a king, contrary to his own mind.

(2.) Here is an instance of the humility and self-denial of the Lord Jesus, that, when they would have made him a king, he *departed;* so far was he from countenancing the design that he effectually quashed it. Herein he has left a testimony, [1.] Against ambition and affectation of worldly honour, to which he was perfectly mortified, and has taught us to be so. Had they come to take him by force and make him a prisoner, he could not have been more industrious to abscond than he was when they would make him a king. Let us not then covet to be the *idols of the crowd,* nor be *desirous of vain-glory.* [2.] Against faction and sedition, treason and rebellion, and whatever tends to disturb the peace of kings and provinces. By this it appears that he was no enemy to Cæsar, nor would have his followers be so, but the *quiet in the land;* that he would have his ministers decline every thing that looks *like* sedition, or looks *towards* it, and improve their interest only for their work's sake.

2. Observe *whither* he retired: *He departed again into a mountain,* εἰς τὸ ὄρος—*into the* mountain, the mountain where he had preached (*v.* 3), whence he came down into the plain, to feed the people, and then returned to it alone, to be private. Christ, though so useful in the places of concourse, yet chose sometimes to be alone, to teach us to sequester ourselves from the world now and then, for the more free converse with God and our own souls; and *never less alone,* says the serious Christian, *than when alone.* Public services must not jostle out private devotions.

II. Here is the disciples' distress at sea. *They that go down to the sea in ships, these see the works of the Lord, for he raiseth the stormy wind,* Ps. cvii. 23, 24. Apply this to these disciples.

1. Here is their *going down to the sea* in a ship (*v.* 16, 17): *When even was come,* and they had done their day's work, it was time to look homeward, and therefore they went aboard, and set sail for Capernaum. This they did by particular direction from their Master, with design (as it should seem) to get them out of the way of the temptation of countenancing those that would have made him a king.

2. Here is the *stormy wind* arising and *fulfilling the word of God.* They were Christ's disciples, and were now in the way of their duty, and Christ was now in the mount praying for them; and yet they were in this distress. The perils and afflictions of this present time may very well consist with our interest in Christ and his intercession. They had lately been feasted at Christ's table; but after the sun-shine of comfort expect a storm. (1.) *It was now dark;* this made the storm the more dangerous and uncomfortable. Sometimes the people of God are in trouble, and cannot see their way out; in the dark concerning the cause of their trouble, concerning the design and tendency of it, and what the issue will be. (2.) Jesus *was not come to them.* When they were in that storm (Matt. viii. 23, &c.) *Jesus was with them;* but now their beloved had withdrawn himself, and was gone. The absence of Christ is the great aggravation of the troubles of Christians. (3.) The *sea arose by reason of a great wind.* It was calm and fair when they put to sea (they were not so presumptuous as to launch out in a storm), but it arose when they were *at sea.* In times of tranquillity we must prepare for trouble, for it may arise when we little think of it. Let it comfort good people, when they happen to be in storms at sea, that the disciples of Christ were so; and let the promises of a gracious God balance the threats of an angry sea. Though in a storm, and *in the dark,* they are no worse off than Christ's disciples were. Clouds and darkness sometimes surround the children of the light, and of the day.

3. Here is Christ's seasonable approach to them when they were in this peril, *v.* 19. *They had rowed* (being forced by the contrary winds to betake themselves to their oars) *about twenty-five or thirty furlongs.* The Holy Spirit that indicted this could have ascertained the number of furlongs precisely, but this, being only circumstantial, is left to be expressed according to the conjecture of the penman. And, when they were got off a good way at sea, they *see Jesus walking on the sea.* See here, (1.) The power Christ has over the laws and customs of nature, to control and dispense with them at his pleasure. It is natural for heavy bodies to sink in water, but Christ walked *upon* the water as upon dry land, which was more than Moses's dividing the water and walking *through* the water. (2.) The concern Christ has for his disciples in distress: *He drew nigh to the ship;* for *therefore* he walked upon the water, as he *rides upon the heavens, for the help of his people,* Deut. xxxiii. 26. He will not leave them comfortless when they seem to be *tossed with tempests* and *not comforted.* When they are banished (as John) into remote places, or shut up (as Paul and Silas) in close places, he will find access to them, and will be nigh them. (3.) The relief Christ gives to his disciples in their fears. They *were afraid,* more afraid of an apparition (for

so they supposed him to be) than of the winds and waves. It is more terrible to wrestle with the rulers of the darkness of this world than with a tempestuous sea. When they thought a demon haunted them, and perhaps was instrumental to raise the storm, they were more terrified than they had been while they saw nothing in it but what was natural. Note, [1.] Our real distresses are often much increased by our imaginary ones, the creatures of our own fancy. [2.] Even the approaches of comfort and deliverance are often so misconstrued as to become the occasions of fear and perplexity. We are often not only *worse frightened than hurt*, but *then* most *frightened* when we are ready to be *helped*. But, when they were in this fright, how affectionately did Christ silence their fears with that compassionate word (*v.* 20), *It is I, be not afraid!* Nothing is more powerful to convince sinners than that word, *I am Jesus whom thou persecutest;* nothing more powerful to comfort saints than this, "*I am Jesus whom thou lovest;* it is I that love thee, and seek thy good; be not afraid of me, nor of the storm." When trouble is nigh Christ is nigh.

4. Here is their speedy arrival at the port they were bound for, *v.* 17. (1.) They *welcomed* Christ into the ship; they *willingly received him.* Note, Christ's absenting himself for a time is but so much the more to *endear himself*, at his return, to his disciples, who value his presence above any thing; see Cant. iii. 4. (2.) Christ brought them safely to the shore: *Immediately the ship was at the land whither they went.* Note, [1.] The ship of the church, in which the disciples of Christ have *embarked* themselves and their all, may be much shattered and distressed, yet it shall come safe to the harbour at last; *tossed* at sea, but not *lost;* cast down, but not destroyed; the bush burning, but not consumed. [2.] The power and presence of the church's King shall expedite and facilitate her deliverance, and conquer the difficulties which have baffled the skill and industry of all her other friends. The disciples had rowed hard, but could not make their point till they had got Christ in the ship, and then the work was *done suddenly*. If we have received Christ Jesus the Lord, have received him willingly, though the night be dark and the wind high, yet we may comfort ourselves with this, that we shall be at shore shortly, and are nearer to it than we think we are. Many a doubting soul is fetched to heaven by a pleasing surprise, or ever it is aware.

22 The day following, when the
people which stood on the other side
of the sea saw that there was none
other boat there, save that one where-
into his disciples were entered, and
that Jesus went not with his disciples
into the boat, but *that* his disciples
were gone away alone; 23 (Howbeit
there came other boats from Tiberias
nigh unto the place where they did
eat bread, after that the Lord had
given thanks:) 24 When the people
therefore saw that Jesus was not there,
neither his disciples, they also took
shipping, and came to Capernaum,
seeking for Jesus. 25 And when they
had found him on the other side of
the sea, they said unto him, Rabbi,
when camest thou hither? 26 Jesus
answered them and said, Verily, verily,
I say unto you, Ye seek me, not because ye saw the miracles, but because ye did eat of the loaves, and
were filled. 27 Labour not for the
meat which perisheth, but for that
meat which endureth unto everlasting life, which the Son of man shall
give unto you: for him hath God the
Father sealed.

In these verses we have,

I. The careful enquiry which the people made after Christ, *v.* 23, 24. They saw the disciples go to sea; they saw Christ retire to the mountain, probably with an intimation that he desired to be private for some time; but, their hearts being set upon *making him a king*, they way-laid his return, and *the day following*, the hot fit of their zeal still continuing,

1. They were *much at a loss* for him. He was gone, and they knew not what was become of him. They saw there was *no boat there* but that in which the disciples went off, Providence so ordering it for the confirming of the miracle of his walking on the sea, for there was no boat for him to go in. They observed also that *Jesus did not go with his disciples*, but that they went off alone, and left him among *them* on *their* side of the water. Note, those that would find Christ must diligently observe all his motions, and learn to understand the tokens of his presence and absence, that they may steer accordingly.

2. They were very *industrious in seeking* him. They searched the places thereabouts, and when *they saw that Jesus was not there, nor his disciples* (neither he nor any one that could give tidings of him), they resolved to search elsewhere. Note, Those that would find Christ must accomplish a diligent search, must seek till they find, must go from sea to sea, to seek the word of God, rather than live without it; and those whom Christ has feasted with the bread of life should have their souls carried out in earnest desires towards him. Much would have more, in communion with Christ. Now, (1.) They resolved to go to Capernaum in quest of him. There were his head-quarters, where he

usually resided. Thither his disciples were gone; and they knew he would not be long absent from *them.* Those that would find Christ must go forth by the footsteps of the flock. (2.) Providence favoured them with an opportunity of going thither by sea, which was the speediest way; for there *came other boats from Tiberias,* which lay further off upon the same shore, *nigh,* though not so nigh to the place where they did *eat bread,* in which they might soon make a trip to Capernaum, and probably the boats were bound for that port. Note, Those that in sincerity seek Christ, and seek opportunities of converse with him, are commonly owned and assisted by Providence in those pursuits. The evangelist, having occasion to mention their eating the *multiplied* bread, adds, *After that the Lord had given thanks, v.* 11. So much were the disciples affected with their Master's giving thanks that they could never forget the impressions made upon them by it, but took a pleasure in remembering the gracious words that then proceeded out of his mouth. This was the grace and beauty of that meal, and made it remarkable; their hearts burned within them.

3. They laid hold of the opportunity that offered itself, and *they also took shipping, ana came to Capernaum, seeking for Jesus.* They did not defer, in hopes to see him again *on this side the water;* but their convictions being strong, and their desires warm, they followed him presently. Good motions are often crushed, and come to nothing, for want of being *prosecuted* in *time.* They came to Capernaum, and, for aught that appears, these unsound hypocritical followers of Christ had a *calm* and *pleasant* passage, while his sincere disciples had a *rough* and *stormy* one. It is not strange if it fare worst with the best men in this evil world. They *came, seeking Jesus.* Note, Those that would find Christ, and find comfort in him, must be willing to take pains, and, as here, to *compass* sea and land to seek and serve him who came from heaven to earth to seek and save us.

II. The success of this enquiry: *They found him on the other side of the sea, v.* 25. Note, Christ will be found of those that seek him, first or last; and it is worth while to cross a sea, nay, to go *from sea to sea, and from the river to the ends of the earth,* to seek Christ, if we may but find him at last. These people appeared afterwards to be unsound, and not actuated by any good principle, and yet were thus zealous. Note, Hypocrites may be very forward in their attendance on God's ordinances. If men have *no more* to show for their love to Christ than their running after sermons and prayers, and their pangs of affection to good preaching, they have reason to suspect themselves no better than this *eager crowd.* But though these people were no better principled, and Christ knew it, yet he was willing to be found of them, and admitted them into fellowship with him. If we could know the hearts of hypocrites, yet, while their profession is plausible, we must not exclude them from our communion, much less when we do not know their hearts.

III. The question they put to him when they found him: *Rabbi, when camest thou hither?* It should seem by *v.* 59 that they found him *in the synagogue.* They knew this was the likeliest place to seek Christ in, for it was *his custom* to attend public assemblies for religious worship, Luke iv. 16. Note, Christ must be sought, and will be found, in the congregations of his people and in the administration of his ordinances; public worship is what Christ chooses to own and grace with his presence and the manifestations of himself. There they found him, and all they had to say to him was, *Rabbi, when camest thou hither?* They saw he would not be made a king, and therefore say no more of this, but call him Rabbi, their teacher. Their enquiry refers not only to the *time,* but to the *manner,* of his conveying himself thither; not only *When,* but, "*How,* camest thou hither?" for there was no boat for him to come in. They were curious in asking concerning Christ's motions, but not solicitous to observe their own.

IV. The answer Christ gave them, not direct to their question (what was it to them *when* and *how* he came thither?) but such an answer as their case required.

1. He discovers the *corrupt principle* they *acted from* in following him (*v.* 26): "*Verily, verily, I say unto you,* I that search the heart, and know what is in man, I the Amen, the faithful witness, Rev. iii. 14, 15. *You seek me;* that is well, but it is not from a good principle." Christ knows not only *what* we do, but *why* we do it. These followed Christ, (1.) Not for his doctrine's sake: *Not because you saw the miracles.* The miracles were the great confirmation of his doctrine; Nicodemus sought for him for the sake of them (*ch.* iii. 2), and argued from the power of his works to the truth of his word; but these were so stupid and mindless that they never considered this. But, (2.) It was for their own bellies' sake: *Because you did eat of the loaves, and were filled;* not because he taught them, but because he fed them. He had given them, [1.] A *full* meal's meat: *They did eat, and were filled;* and some of them perhaps were so poor that they had not known of a long time before now what it was to have enough, to eat and leave. [2.] A *dainty* meal's meat; it is probable that, as the miraculous wine was the best wine, so was the miraculous food more than usually pleasant. [3.] A *cheap* meal's meat, that cost them nothing; no reckoning was brought in Note, Many follow Christ for *loaves,* and not for *love.* Thus those do who aim at secular advantage in their profession of religion, and follow it because by this craft they get their preferments. *Quanti profuit nobis hæc*

fabula de Christo—This fable respecting Christ, what a gainful concern we have made of it! said one of the popes. These people *complimented* Christ with Rabbi, and showed him great respect, yet he told them thus faithfully of their hypocrisy; his ministers must hence learn not to flatter those that flatter them, nor to be *bribed* by fair words to cry *peace* to all that cry *rabbi* to them, but to give faithful reproofs where there is cause for them.

2. He directs them to better principles (*v.* 27): *Labour for that meat which endures to everlasting life.* With the woman of Samaria he had discoursed of spiritual things under the similitude of *water;* here he speaks of them under the similitude of *meat*, taking occasion from the loaves they had eaten. His design is,

(1.) To moderate our worldly pursuits: *Labour not for the meat that perishes.* This does not forbid honest labour for food convenient, 2 Thess. iii. 12. But we must not make the things of this world our chief care and concern. Note, [1.] The things of the world are *meat that perishes.* Worldly wealth, honour, and pleasure, are *meat;* they *feed the fancy* (and many times this is all) and *fill the belly.* These are things which men *hunger* after as *meat*, and glut themselves with, and which a carnal heart, as long as they last, may make a shift to live upon; but they *perish*, are of a perishing nature, wither of themselves, and are exposed to a thousand accidents; those that have the largest share of them are not sure to have them while they live, but are sure to leave them and lose them when they die. [2.] It is therefore folly for us inordinately to labour after them. *First*, We must not labour in religion, nor work the works thereof, *for this perishing meat*, with an eye to this; we must not make our religion subservient to a worldly interest, nor aim at *secular advantages* in *sacred exercises. Secondly*, We must not at all *labour* for this meat; that is, we must not make these perishing things our *chief good*, nor make our care and pains about them our *chief business;* not seek those things *first* and *most*, Prov. xxiii. 4, 5.

(2.) To quicken and excite our gracious pursuits: "Bestow your pains to better purpose, and *labour for that meat* which belongs to the soul," of which he shows,

[1.] That it is *unspeakably desirable:* It is meat which *endures to everlasting life;* it is a happiness which will last as long as we must, which not only itself endures eternally, but will nourish us up to everlasting life. The blessings of the new covenant are our preparative for eternal life, our preservative to it, and the pledge and earnest of it.

[2.] It is *undoubtedly attainable.* Shall all the treasures of the world be ransacked, and all the fruits of the earth gathered together, to furnish us with provisions that will last to eternity? No, *The sea saith, It is not in me,* among all the treasures hidden in the sand. *It cannot be gotten for gold;* but it is that *which the Son of man shall give; ἣν δώσει*, either which *meat*, or which *life*, the Son of man shall give. Observe here, *First*, Who gives this meat: the *Son of man*, the great householder and master of the stores, who is entrusted with the administration of the kingdom of God among men, and the dispensation of the gifts, graces, and comforts of that kingdom, and has power to give eternal life, with all the means of it and preparatives for it. We are told to *labour for it*, as if it were to be got by our own industry, and sold upon that valuable consideration, as the heathen said, *Dii laboribus omnia vendunt—The gods sell all advantages to the industrious.* But, when we have laboured ever so much for it, we have not merited it as our *hire*, but the Son of man *gives it.* And what more free than gift? It is an encouragement that he who has the giving of it is the *Son of man*, for then we may hope the *sons of men* that seek it, and labour for it, shall not fail to have it. *Secondly*, What authority he has to give it; for *him has God the Father sealed, τοῦτον γὰρ ὁ Πατὴρ ἐσφράγισεν, ὁ Θεός—for him the Father has sealed* (proved and evidenced) *to be God;* so some read it; he has declared him to be the Son of God with power. He has *sealed him*, that is, has given him full authority to deal between God and man, as God's *ambassador* to man and man's *intercessor* with God, and has proved his commission by miracles. Having given him *authority*, he has given us *assurance* of it; having entrusted him with *unlimited powers*, he has satisfied us with *undoubted proofs* of them; so that as he might go on with confidence in his undertaking for us, so may we in our resignations to him. *God the Father* sealed him with the Spirit that rested on him, by the voice from heaven, by the testimony he bore to him in signs and wonders. Divine revelation is perfected in him, in him the *vision* and *prophecy* is *sealed up* (Dan. ix. 24), to him all believers *seal* that he is true (*ch.* iii. 33), and in him they are all *sealed*, 2 Cor. i. 22.

28 Then said they unto him, What
shall we do, that we might work the
works of God? 29 Jesus answered
and said unto them, This is the work
of God, that ye believe on him whom
he hath sent. 30 They said therefore
unto him, What sign showest thou
then, that we may see, and believe
thee? what dost thou work? 31 Our
fathers did eat manna in the desert;
as it is written, He gave them bread
from heaven to eat. 32 Then Jesus
said unto them, Verily, verily, I say
unto you, Moses gave you not that

bread from heaven; but my Father
giveth you the true bread from heaven.
33 For the bread of God is he which
cometh down from heaven, and giveth
life unto the world. 34 Then said
they unto him, Lord, evermore give
us this bread. 35 And Jesus said
unto them, I am the bread of life: he
that cometh to me shall never hunger;
and he that believeth on me shall
never thirst. 36 But I said unto you,
That ye also have seen me, and believe not. 37 All that the Father
giveth me shall come to me; and him
that cometh to me I will in no wise
cast out. 38 For I came down from
heaven, not to do mine own will, but
the will of him that sent me. 39
And this is the Father's will which
hath sent me, that of all which he
hath given me I should lose nothing,
but should raise it up again at the
last day. 40 And this is the will of him
that sent me, that every one which
seeth the Son, and believeth on him,
may have everlasting life: and I will
raise him up at the last day. 41 The
Jews then murmured at him, because
he said, I am the bread which came
down from heaven. 42 And they
said, Is not this Jesus, the son of
Joseph, whose father and mother we
know? how is it then that he saith, I
came down from heaven? 43 Jesus
therefore answered and said unto them,
Murmur not among yourselves. 44
No man can come to me, except the
Father which hath sent me draw him:
and I will raise him up at the last
day. 45 It is written in the prophets,
And they shall be all taught of God.
Every man therefore that hath heard,
and hath learned of the Father, cometh
unto me. 46 Not that any man hath
seen the Father, save he which is of
God, he hath seen the Father. 47
Verily, verily, I say unto you, He
that believeth on me hath everlasting
life. 48 I am that bread of life. 49
Your fathers did eat manna in the
wilderness, and are dead. 50 This is
the bread which cometh down from
heaven, that a man may eat thereof,
and not die. 51 I am the living
bread which came down from heaven:
if any man eat of this bread, he shall
live for ever: and the bread that I
will give is my flesh, which I will give
for the life of the world. 52 The
Jews therefore strove among themselves, saying, How can this man
give us *his* flesh to eat? 53 Then
Jesus said unto them, Verily, verily,
I say unto you, Except ye eat the
flesh of the Son of man, and drink
his blood, ye have no life in you. 54
Whoso eateth my flesh, and drinketh
my blood, hath eternal life; and I
will raise him up at the last day. 55
For my flesh is meat indeed, and my
blood is drink indeed. 56 He that
eateth my flesh, and drinketh my
blood, dwelleth in me, and I in him.
57 As the living Father hath sent
me, and I live by the Father: so he
that eateth me, even he shall live by
me. 58 This is that bread which
came down from heaven: not as your
fathers did eat manna, and are dead:
he that eateth of this bread shall live
for ever. 59 These things said he
in the synagogue, as he taught in
Capernaum.

Whether this conference was with the Capernaites, in whose synagogue Christ now was, or with those who came from the other side of the sea, is not certain nor material; however, it is an instance of Christ's condescension that he gave them leave to ask him questions, and did not resent the interruption as an affront, no, not from his common hearers, though not his immediate followers. Those that would be apt to teach must be swift to hear, and study to answer. It is the wisdom of teachers, when they are asked even impertinent unprofitable questions, thence to take occasion to answer in that which is profitable, that the question may be rejected, but not the request. Now,

I. Christ having told them that *they* must *work for the meat* he spoke of, must *labour* for it, they enquire what work they must do, and he answers them, *v.* 28, 29. 1. Their *enquiry* was *pertinent* enough (*v.* 28): *What shall we do, that we may work the works of God?* Some understand it as a pert question: "What works of God can we do more and better than those we do in obedience to the law of Moses?" But I rather take it as a humble serious question, showing them to be, at least for the present, in a good mind, and willing to know and do their duty; and I imagine that those who asked this question, How and What (*v.* 30), and made the request (*v.* 34), were not the same persons with those that murmured (*v.* 41, 42), and strove (*v.* 52), for those are expressly called *the Jews,* who came out of Judea (for those were strictly called Jews) to cavil, whereas these were of Galilee, and came to be taught. This question here intimates that they were convinced that those who would obtain this everlasting meat, (1.) Must aim to do something great. Those who *look high* in their expectations, and hope to enjoy the *glory of God,* must *aim high* in those endeavours, and study to *do the works of God,* works which he requires and will accept, *works of God,* distinguished from the works of worldly men in their worldly pursuits. It is not enough to speak the words of God, but we must do the works of God. (2.) Must be willing to do any thing: *What shall we do?* Lord, I am ready to do whatever thou shalt appoint, though ever so displeasing to flesh and blood, Acts ix. 6.

2. Christ's answer was plain enough (*v.* 29): *This is the work of God that ye believe.* Note, (1.) The work of faith is the work of God. They enquire after the *works* of God (in the plural number), being careful about *many things;* but Christ directs them to one work, which includes all, the one thing needful: that *you believe,* which supersedes all the works of the ceremonial law; the work which is necessary to the acceptance of all the other works, and which produces them, for without faith you cannot please God. It is *God's work,* for it is of his *working in us,* it subjects the soul to his working on us, and quickens the soul in working *for him.* (2.) That faith is the work of God which closes with Christ, and relies upon him. It is to *believe on him* as one whom God *hath sent,* as God's commissioner in the great affair of peace between God and man, and as such to *rest* upon him, and *resign ourselves* to him. See *ch.* xiv. 1.

II. Christ having told them that the *Son of man* would *give them this meat,* they enquire concerning him, and he answers their enquiry.

1. Their enquiry is after *a sign* (*v.* 30): *What sign showest thou?* Thus far they were right, that, since he required them to give him *credit,* he should produce his *credentials,* and make it out by miracle that he was *sent of God.* Moses having confirmed his mission by *signs,* it was requisite that Christ, who came to set aside the ceremonial law, should in like manner confirm his: "*What dost thou work?* What dost thou drive at? What lasting characters of a divine power dost thou design to leave upon thy doctrine?" But *herein* they missed it,

(1.) That they overlooked the many miracles which they had seen wrought by him, and which amounted to an abundant proof of his divine mission. Is this a time of day to ask, "What sign showest thou?" especially at Capernaum, the *staple* of miracles, where he had done so *many mighty works, signs* so significant of his office and undertaking? Were not these very persons but the other day miraculously fed by him? None so blind as they that will not see; for they may be so blind as to question whether it be day or no, when the sun shines in their faces.

(2.) That they preferred the miraculous feeding of Israel in the wilderness before all the miracles Christ wrought (*v.* 31): *Our fathers did eat manna in the desert;* and, to strengthen the objection, they quote a scripture for it: *He gave them bread from heaven* (taken from Ps. lxxviii. 24), *he gave them of the corn of heaven.* What a good use might be made of this story to which they here refer! It was a memorable instance of God's power and goodness, often mentioned to the glory of God (Neh. xix. 20, 21), yet see how these people perverted it, and made an ill use of it. [1.] Christ reproved them for their fondness of the miraculous bread, and bade them not set their hearts upon *meat which perisheth;* "Why," say they, "*meat for the belly* was the great good thing that God gave to our fathers in the desert; and why should not we then labour for that meat? If God made much of them, why should not we be for those that will make much of us?" [2.] Christ had fed five thousand men with five loaves, and had given them that as one sign to prove him *sent of God;* but, under colour of *magnifying* the miracles of Moses, they tacitly *undervalue* this miracle of Christ, and *evade* the evidence of it. "Christ fed his thousands; but Moses his hundreds of thousands; Christ fed them but once, and then reproved those who followed him in hope to be still fed, and put them off with a discourse of spiritual food; but Moses fed his followers forty years, and miracles were not their rarities, but their daily bread: Christ fed them with bread out of *the earth,* barley-bread, and fishes out of *the sea;* but Moses fed Israel with bread *from heaven,* angel's food." Thus big did these Jews talk of the *manna* which *their fathers did eat;* but their fathers had slighted it as much as they did now the barley-loaves, and called it *light bread,* Num. xxi. 5. Thus apt are we to slight and overlook the appearances of God's power and grace in our own times, while we pretend to admire the wonders of which *our fathers told us.* Suppose *this* miracle of Christ was outdone by that of Moses, yet there were other instances in which Christ's miracles outshone his; and, besides, all true miracles prove a divine doctrine, though not equally illustrious in the circumstances, which were ever *diversified* according as the occasion did require. As much as the manna excelled the barley-loaves, so much, and much more, did the doctrine of Christ excel the law of Moses, and his heavenly institutions the carnal ordinances of that dispensation.

2. Here is Christ's reply to this enquiry, wherein,

(1.) He *rectifies* their *mistake* concerning the *typical* manna. It was true that their fathers did eat *manna* in the desert. But,

[1.] It was not Moses that gave it to them, nor were they obliged to him for it; he was but the instrument, and therefore they must look beyond him to God. We do not find that Moses did so much as pray to God for the *manna;* and he spoke unadvisedly when he said, *Must we fetch water out of the rock?* Moses gave them not either *that* bread or *that* water. [2.] It was not given them, as they imagined, *from heaven,* from the highest heavens, but only from *the clouds,* and therefore not so much superior to that which had its rise from the earth as they thought. Because the scripture saith, *He gave them bread from heaven,* it does not follow that it was *heavenly bread,* or was intended to be the nourishment of souls. Misunderstanding scripture language occasions many mistakes in the things of God.

(2.) He *informs* them concerning the *true* manna, of which that was a type: *But my Father giveth you the true bread from heaven;* that which is truly and properly the *bread from heaven,* of which the manna was but a shadow and figure, is *now given,* not to *your fathers,* who are dead and gone, but *to you* of this present age, for whom the *better things were reserved:* he is *now giving* you that *bread from heaven,* which is *truly* so called. As much as the throne of God's glory is above the clouds of the air, so much does the *spiritual bread* of the everlasting gospel excel the *manna.* In calling God *his Father,* he proclaims himself greater than Moses; for Moses was faithful but as a servant, Christ as a *Son,* Heb. iii. 5, 6.

III. Christ, having replied to their enquiries, takes further occasion from their objection concerning the *manna* to discourse of *himself* under the similitude of *bread,* and of *believing* under the similitude of *eating and drinking;* to which, together with his putting both together in the *eating* of *his flesh* and *drinking* of his *blood,* and with the remarks made upon it by the hearers, the rest of this conference may be reduced.

1. Christ having spoken of *himself* as the great *gift of God,* and the *true bread* (*v.* 32), largely *explains* and *confirms* this, that we may rightly know him.

(1.) He here shows that he is the *true bread;* this he repeats again and again, *v.* 33, 35, 48—51. Observe, [1.] That Christ is *bread,* is that to the soul which bread is to the body, nourishes and supports the spiritual life (is the staff of it) as bread does the bodily life; *it is the staff of life.* The doctrines of the gospel concerning Christ—that he is the Mediator between God and man, that he is our peace, our righteousness, our Redeemer; *by these things do men live.* Our bodies could better live without food than our souls without Christ. *Bread-corn* is *bruised* (Isa. xxviii. 28), so was Christ; he was born at Bethlehem, the *house of bread,* and typified by the *show-bread.* [2.] That he is the *bread of God* (*v.* 33), divine bread; it is he that is *of God* (*v* 46), bread which my Father gives (*v.* 32), which he has made to be the food of our souls; the bread of God's family, his *children's bread.* The Levitical sacrifices are called the *bread of God* (Lev. xxi. 21, 22), and Christ is the great sacrifice; Christ, in his word and ordinances, the *feast* upon the sacrifice. [3.] That he is the *bread of life* (*v.* 35, and again, *v.* 48), *that* bread of life, alluding to the tree of life in the midst of the garden of Eden, which was to Adam the seal of that part of the covenant, *Do this and live,* of which he might *eat and live.* Christ is the bread of life, for he is the fruit of the *tree of life. First,* He is the *living bread* (so he explains himself, *v.* 51): *I am the living bread.* Bread is itself a dead thing, and nourishes not but by the help of the faculties of a living body; but Christ is himself *living bread,* and nourishes by his own power. Manna was a dead thing; if kept but one night, it putrefied and bred worms; but Christ is ever living, everlasting bread, that never moulds, nor waxes old. The doctrine of Christ crucified is now as strengthening and comforting to a believer as ever it was, and his mediation still of as much value and efficacy as ever. *Secondly, He gives life unto the world* (*v.* 33), spiritual and eternal life; the life of the soul in union and communion with God here, and in the vision and fruition of him hereafter; a life that includes in it all happiness. The *manna* did only preserve and support life, did not preserve and perpetuate life, much less restore it; but Christ *gives* life to those that were dead in sin. The manna was ordained only for the life of the Israelites, but Christ is given for the *life of the world;* none are excluded from the benefit of this bread, but such as exclude themselves. Christ came to *put life* into the minds of men, principles productive of acceptable performances. [4.] That he is the *bread which came down from heaven;* this is often repeated here, *v.* 33, 50, 51, 58. This denotes, *First,* The divinity of Christ's person. As God, he had a being in heaven, whence he came to take our nature upon him: *I came down from heaven,* whence we may infer his *antiquity,* he was in the beginning with God; his *ability,* for heaven is the firmament of power; and his *authority,* he came with a divine commission. *Secondly,* The divine original of all that good which flows to us through him. He *comes,* not only καταβάς—*that came down* (*v.* 51), but καταβαίνων—*that comes down;* he is descending, denoting a constant communication of light, life, and love, from God to believers through Christ, as the *manna* descended daily; see Eph. i. 3. *Omnia desuper—All things from above.* [5.] That he is *that bread* of which the *manna* was a type and figure (*v.* 58), *that* bread, the true bread, *v.* 32. As the rock that they drank of was Christ, so was the manna they ate of *spiritual bread,* 1 Cor. x. 3, 4. *Manna* was given to Israel; so Christ to the spiritual Israel. There was *manna* enough for them all; so in Christ a fulness of grace for all believers; he that *gathers much* of this *manna* will have none to spare when he comes to use it; and he that gathers little, when his grace comes to be perfected in glory, shall find that *he has no lack. Manna* was to be gathered in the morning; and those that would find Christ must *seek him early.* Manna was sweet, and, as the author of the *Wisdom of Solomon* tells us (Wisd. xvi. 20), was agreeable to every palate; and to those that believe Christ is *precious.* Israel lived upon *manna* till they came to Canaan; and Christ is our life. There was a memorial of the *manna* preserved in the ark; so of Christ in the Lord's supper, as the food of souls.

(2.) He here shows what his undertaking was, and what his errand into the world. Laying aside the metaphor, he speaks plainly, and speaks no proverb, giving us an account of his business among men, *v.* 38—40.

[1.] He assures us, in general, that he came from heaven upon his Father's business (*v.* 38), not to *do his own will, but the will of him that sent him.* He *came from heaven,* which bespeaks him an intelligent active being, who voluntarily descended to this lower world, a long journey, and a great step downward, considering the glories of the world he came from and the calamities of the world he came to; we may well ask with wonder, "What moved him to such an expedition?" Here he tells us that he came to do, not *his own will,* but the will of his Father; not that he had any will that stood in competition with the will of his Father, but those to whom he spoke suspected he might. "No," saith he, "my own will is not the spring I act from, nor the rule I go by, but I am come to *do the will of him that sent me.*" That is, *First,* Christ did not come into the world as a *private* person, that acts for himself only, but under a *public character,* to act for others as an ambassador, or plenipotentiary, authorized by a public commission; he came into the world as God's great agent and the world's great physician. It was not any private business that brought him hither, but he came to settle affairs between parties no less considerable than the great Creator and the whole creation. *Secondly,* Christ, when he was in the world, did not carry on any *private* design, nor had any *separate interest* at all, distinct from theirs for whom he acted. The scope of his whole life was to glorify God and do good to men. He therefore never consulted his own ease, safety, or quiet; but, when he was to lay down his life, though he had a human nature which startled at it, he set aside the consideration of that, and resolved his will as man into the will of God: *Not as I will, but as thou wilt.*

[2.] He acquaints us, in particular, with that will of the Father which he came to do; he here *declares the decree,* the instructions he was to pursue.

First, The *private instructions* given to Christ, that he should be sure to save all the chosen remnant; and this is the *covenant of redemption* between the Father and the Son (*v.* 38): *This is the Father's will, who hath sent me;* this is the charge I am entrusted with, that *of all whom he hath given me I should lose none.*" Note, 1. There is a certain number of the children of men *given* by the Father to Jesus Christ, to be his care, and so to be to him for a name and a praise; given him for *an inheritance,* for a possession. Let him do all that for them which their case requires; teach them, and heal them, pay their debt, and plead their cause, prepare them for, and preserve them to, eternal life, and then let him make his best of them. The Father might dispose of them as he pleased: as creatures, their lives and beings were *derived from* him; as sinners, their lives and beings were *forfeited to him.* He might have sold them for the satisfaction of his justice, and delivered them *to the tormentors;* but he pitched upon them to be the monuments of his mercy, and delivered them to the Saviour. Those whom God chose to be the objects of his special love he lodged as a trust in the hands of Christ. 2. Jesus Christ has undertaken that he will *lose none* of those that were thus *given him* of the Father. The *many sons* whom he was to *bring to glory* shall all be forth-coming, and none of them missing, Matt. xviii. 14. None of them shall be lost for want of a sufficient price to purchase them or sufficient grace to sanctify them. *If I bring him not unto thee, and set him before thee, then let me bear the blame for ever,* Gen. xliii. 9. 3. Christ's undertaking for those that are given him extends to the resurrection of their bodies *I will raise it up again at the last day,* which supposes all that goes before, but this is to crown and complete the undertaking. The body is a part of the man, and therefore a part of Christ's purchase and charge; it pertains to the promises, and therefore it shall not be *lost.* The undertaking is not only that he shall *lose none,* no *person,* but that he shall *lose nothing,* no part of the person, and therefore not the body. Christ's undertaking will never be accomplished till the resurrection, when the souls and bodies of the saints shall be re-united and gathered to Christ, that he may present them to the Father: *Behold I, and the children that thou hast given me,* Heb. ii. 13; 2 Tim. i. 12. 4. The spring and original of all this is the *sovereign will of God,* the counsels of his will, according to which he works all this. This was the commandment he gave to his Son, when he sent him into the world, and to which the Son always had an eye.

Secondly, The *public instructions* which were to be given to the children of men, in what way, and upon what terms, they might obtain salvation by Christ; and this is the *covenant of grace* between God and man. Who the particular persons were that were given to Christ is a *secret: The Lord knows them that are his,* we do not, nor is it fit we should; but, though their names are concealed, their characters are published. An offer is made of life and happiness upon gospel terms, that by it those that were given to Christ might be brought to him, and others left inexcusable (*v.* 40): "*This is the will,* the revealed will, *of him that sent me,* the method agreed upon, upon which to proceed with the children of men, that *every one,* Jew or Gentile, that *sees the Son, and believes on him,* may have *everlasting life,* and *I will raise him up.*" This is *gospel* indeed, good news. Is it not reviving to hear this? 1. That *eternal life* may be had, if it be not our own fault; that whereas, upon the sin of the first Adam, the *way of the tree of life* was blocked up, by the grace of the second Adam it is laid open again. The crown of glory is set before us as the prize of our high calling, which we may run for and obtain. 2. Every one may have it. This gospel is to be preached, this offer made, to all, and none can say, "It belongs not to me," Rev. xxii. 17. 3. This everlasting life is sure to all those who believe in Christ, and to them only. He that *sees the Son,* and *believes on him,* shall be saved. Some understand this *seeing* as a *limitation* of this condition of salvation to those only that have the revelation of Christ and his grace made to them. Every one that has the opportunity of being acquainted with Christ, and improves this so well as to *believe* in him, shall have everlasting life, so that none shall be condemned for unbelief (however they may be for other sins) but those who have had the gospel preached to them, who, like these Jews here (*v.* 36), have *seen,* and yet have *not* believed; have known Christ, and yet not trusted in him. But I rather understand *seeing* here to mean the same thing with *believing,* for it is θεωρῶν, which signifies not so much the sight of the eye (as *v.* 36, ἑωράκατέ με—*ye have seen me*) as the *contemplation of the mind.* Every one that *sees the Son,* that is, *believes on him,* sees him with an eye of faith, by which we come to be duly acquainted and affected with the doctrine of the gospel concerning him. It is to look upon him, as the stung Israelites upon the brazen serpent. It is not a *blind* faith that Christ requires, that we should be willing to have our *eyes put out,* and then follow him, but that we should *see him,* and see what ground we go upon in our faith. It is *then* right when it is not taken up upon *hearsay* (believing as the church believes), but is the result of a due consideration of, and insight into, the motives of credibility: *Now mine eye sees thee. We have heard him ourselves* 4. Those who believe in Jesus Christ, in order to their having everlasting life, shall be raised up by his power at the last day. He had it in charge as his Father's will (*v.* 39), and here he solemnly makes it his own undertaking: I *will raise him up,* which signifies not only the return of the body to life, but the putting of the *whole man* into a full possession of the eternal life promised.

2. Now Christ discoursing thus concerning himself, as the *bread of life* that came down from heaven, let us see what remarks his hearers made upon it.

(1.) When they heard of such a thing as the *bread of God,* which *gives life,* they heartily prayed for it (*v.* 34): *Lord, evermore give us this bread.* I cannot think that this is spoken scoffingly, and in a way of derision, as most interpreters understand it: "Give us such bread as this, if thou canst; let us be fed with it, not for one meal, as with the five loaves, but *evermore;*" as if this were no better a prayer than that of the impenitent thief: *If thou be the Christ, save thyself and us.* But I take this request to be made, though ignorantly, yet honestly, and to be well meant; for they call him *Lord,* and desire a share in what he *gives,* whatever he means by it. General and confused notions of divine things produce in carnal hearts some kind of desires towards them, and wishes of them; like Balaam's wish, to die the *death of the righteous.* Those who have an indistinct knowledge of the things of God, who see men as trees walking, make, as I may call them, *inarticulate* prayers for spiritual blessings. They think the favour of God a *good thing,* and heaven a *fine place,* and cannot but wish them their own, while they have no value nor desire at all for that holiness which is necessary both to the one and to the other. Let this be the desire of our souls; have we tasted that the Lord is gracious, been feasted with the word of God, and Christ in the word? let us say, "*Lord, evermore give us this bread;* let the bread of life be our daily bread, the heavenly manna our continual feast, and let us never know the want of it."

(2.) But, when they understood that by this *bread of life* Jesus meant *himself,* then they *despised* it. Whether they were the same persons that had prayed for it (*v.* 34), or some others of the company, does not appear; it seems to be some others, for they are called *Jews.* Now it is said (*v.* 41), *They murmured at him.* This comes in immediately after that solemn declaration which Christ had made of God's will and his own undertaking concerning man's salvation (*v.* 39, 40), which certainly were some of the most weighty and gracious words that ever proceeded out of the mouth of our Lord Jesus, the most faithful, and best worthy of all acceptation. One would think that, like Israel in Egypt, when they heard that God had thus *visited* them, they should have *bowed their heads and worshipped;* but on the contrary, instead of closing with the offer made them, they *murmured,* quarrelled with what Christ said, and, though they did not openly oppose and contradict it, yet they privately whispered among themselves in contempt of it, and instilled into one another's minds prejudices against it. Many that will not professedly contradict the doctrine of Christ (their cavils are so weak and groundless that they are either ashamed to own them or afraid to have them silenced), yet say in their hearts that they *do not like it.* Now, [1.] That which offended them was Christ's asserting his origin to be *from heaven, v.* 41, 42. How is it that he saith, *I came down from heaven?* They had heard of angels coming down *from heaven,* but never of a man, overlooking the proofs he had given them of his being more than a man. [2.] That which they thought justified them herein was that they knew his extraction on earth : *Is not this Jesus the son of Joseph, whose father and mother we know?* They took it amiss that he should say that he came down from heaven, when he was *one of them.* They speak slightly of his blessed name, *Jesus: Is not this Jesus.* They take it for granted that Joseph was really his father, though he was only *reputed* to be so. Note, Mistakes concerning the person of Christ, as if he were a mere man, conceived and born by ordinary generation, occasion the offence that is taken at his doctrine and offices. Those who set him on a level with the other sons of men, whose father and mother we know, no wonder if they derogate from the honour of his satisfaction and the mysteries of his undertaking, and, like the Jews here, murmur at his promise to *raise us up at the last day.*

3. Christ, having spoken of faith as the great *work of God* (*v.* 29), discourses largely concerning this work, instructing and encouraging us in it.

(1.) He shows what it is to *believe in Christ.* [1.] To believe in Christ is to *come to Christ.* He that *comes to* me is the same with him that *believes in me* (*v.* 35), and again (*v.* 37): *He that comes unto me;* so *v.* 44, 45. Repentance towards God is *coming to him* (Jer. iii. 22) as our chief good and highest end; and so faith towards our Lord Jesus Christ is coming to him as our prince and Saviour, and our way to the Father. It denotes the out-goings of our affection towards him, for these are the motions of the soul, and actions agreeable; it is to *come off* from all those things that stand in opposition to him or competition with him, and to *come up* to those terms upon which life and salvation are offered to us through him. When he was here on earth it was more than barely coming where he was; so it is now more than coming to his word and ordinances. [2.] It is to *feed upon Christ* (*v* 51): *If any man eat of this bread.* The former denotes applying ourselves to Christ; this denotes applying Christ to ourselves, with appetite and delight, that we may receive life, and strength, and comfort from him. To feed on him as the Israelites on the manna, having quitted the *fleshpots* of Egypt, and not depending on the *labour of their hands* (to eat of that), but living purely on the bread given them from heaven.

(2.) He shows what is to be got by believing in Christ. What will he give us if we *come to him?* What shall we be the better if we *feed upon him? Want* and *death* are the chief things we dread; may we but be assured of the comforts of our being, and the continuance of it in the midst of these comforts, we have enough; now these two are here secured to true believers.

[1.] They shall never want, *never hunger, never thirst, v.* 35. Desires they have, earnest desires, but these so suitably, so seasonably, so abundantly satisfied, that they cannot be called hunger and thirst, which are uneasy and painful. Those that did eat manna, and drink of the rock, hungered and thirsted afterwards. Manna surfeited them ; water out of the rock failed them. But there is such an *over-flowing fulness* in Christ as can never be *exhausted,* and there are such *ever-flowing communications* from him as can never be interrupted.

[2.] They shall *never die,* not die eternally; for, *First,* He that believes on Christ *has everlasting life* (*v.* 47); he has the assurance of it, the grant of it, the earnest of it; he has it in the promise and first-fruits. Union with Christ and communion with God in Christ are *everlasting life* begun. *Secondly,* Whereas they that did *eat manna* died, Christ is such bread as a man may eat of and never die, *v.* 49, 50. Observe here, 1. the insufficiency of the typical manna: *Your fathers did eat manna in the wilderness, and are dead.* There may be much good use made of the death of our fathers; their graves speak to us, and their monuments are our memorials, particularly of this, that the greatest *plenty* of the most *dainty* food will neither prolong the thread of life nor avert the stroke of death. Those that did eat manna, angel's food, died like other men. There could be nothing amiss in their diet, to shorten their days, nor could their deaths be hastened by the toils and fatigues of life (for they neither sowed nor reaped), and *yet they died.* (1.) Many of them died by the immediate strokes of God's vengeance for their unbelief and murmurings; for, *though they did eat that spiritual meat,* yet with many of them God *was not well pleased, but they were overthrown in the wilderness,* 1 Cor. x. 3—5. Their eating manna was no security to *them* from the *wrath of God,* as believing in Christ is to *us.* (2.) the rest of them died in a course of nature, and their carcases fell, under a divine sentence, in that wilderness where they did *eat manna.* In that very age when miracles were *daily bread* was the life of man reduced to the stint it now stands at, as appears, Ps. xc. 10. Let them not then boast so much of *manna.* 2. The all-sufficiency of the true *manna,* of which the other was a type: *This is the bread that cometh down from heaven,* that truly divine and heavenly food, *that a man may eat thereof and not die;* that is, not fall under the wrath of God, which is killing to the soul; *not die* the second death; no, nor the first death finally and irrecoverably. *Not die,* that is, not perish, not come short of the heavenly Canaan, as the Israelites did of the earthly, for want of *faith,* though they had *manna.* This is further explained by that promise in the next words: *If any man eat of this bread, he shall live for ever, v.* 51. This is the meaning of this *never dying:* though he go down *to death,* he shall pass through it to that world where there shall be *no more death.* To *live for ever* is not to *be* for ever (the damned in hell shall *be* for ever, the soul of man was made for an endless state), but to be *happy* for ever. And because the body must needs die, and be as water spilt upon the ground, Christ here undertakes for the gathering of that up too (as before, *v.* 44, *I will raise him up at the last day);* and even that shall live for ever.

(3.) He shows what encouragements we have to believe in Christ. Christ here speaks of some who *had seen him and yet believed not, v.* 36. They saw his person and miracles, and heard him preach, and yet were not wrought upon to believe in him. Faith is not always the effect of sight; the soldiers were eye-witnesses of his resurrection, and yet, instead of *believing* in him, they *belied* him; so that it is a difficult thing to bring people to believe in Christ: and, by the operation of the Spirit of grace, those that *have not seen have yet believed.* Two things we are here assured of, to encourage our faith:—

[1.] That the Son will bid all those welcome that come to him (*v.* 37): *Him that cometh to me I will in no wise cast out.* How welcome should this word be to our souls which bids us welcome to Christ! *Him* that cometh; it is in the singular number, denoting favour, not only to the body of believers in general, but to every particular soul that applies itself to Christ. Here, *First,* The duty required is a pure gospel duty: to *come to Christ,* that we may come to God by him. His beauty and love, those great attractives, must *draw* us to him; sense of need and fear of danger must *drive* us to him; any thing to bring us to Christ. *Secondly,* The promise is a pure gospel promise: *I will in no wise cast out*—*οὐ μὴ ἐκβαγῶ ἔξω.* There are two negatives: *I will not, no, I will not.* 1 Much favour is expressed here. We have reason to fear that he should *cast us out.* Considering our meanness, our vileness, our unworthiness to come, our weakness in coming, we may justly expect that he should frown upon us, and shut his doors against us; but he obviates these fears with this assurance, he *will not* do it; will not disdain us though we are mean, will not reject us though we are sinful. Do poor scholars come to him to be taught? Though they be dull and slow, he will not *cast them out.* Do poor *patients* come to him to be *cured,* poor *clients* come to him to be *advised?* Though their case be bad, and though they come empty-handed, he will *in no wise cast them out.* But, 2. More favour is implied than is expressed; whet it is said that he will not cast them out the meaning is, He will receive them, and entertain them, and give them all that which they come to him for. As he will not refuse them at their first coming, so he will not afterwards, upon every displeasure, cast them out. *His gifts and callings are without repentance.*

[2.] That the Father will, without fail, bring all those to him in due time that were given him. In the federal transactions between the Father and the Son, relating to man's redemption, as the Son undertook for the justification, sanctification, and salvation, of all that should come to him ("Let me have them put into my hands, and then leave the management of them to me"), so the Father, the fountain and original of being, life, and grace, undertook to put into his hand all that were given him, and bring them to him. Now,

First, He here *assures* us *that* this shall be done: *All that the Father giveth me shall come to me, v.* 37. Christ had complained (*v.* 36) of those who, though they had *seen* him, yet would not believe on him; and then he adds this,

a. For *their* conviction and awakening, plainly intimating that their not coming to him, and believing on him, if they persisted in it, would be a certain sign that they did not belong to the election of grace; for how can we think that God gave us to Christ if we give ourselves to the world and the flesh? 2 Peter i. 10.

b. For *his own* comfort and encouragement: *Though Israel be not gathered, yet shall I be glorious.* The election *has obtained,* and shall though multitudes be *blinded,* Rom. xi. 7. Though he lose many of his *creatures,* yet none of his *charge: All that the Father gives him shall come to him* notwithstanding. Here we have, (*a.*) The election described: *All that the father giveth me, πᾶν ὃ δίδωσι—every thing* which the Father *giveth to me;* the persons of the elect, and all that belongs to them; all their services, all their interests. As all that he has is *theirs,* so all that they have is *his,* and he speaks of them as his all: they were given him in full recompense of his undertaking. Not only all persons, but all things, are gathered together in Christ (Eph. i. 10) and reconciled, Col. i. 20. The giving of the chosen remnant to Christ is spoken of (*v.* 39) as a thing *done;* he *hath given* them. Here it is spoken of as a thing *in the doing;* he *giveth them;* because, *when the first begotten was brought into the world,* it should seem, there was a renewal of the grant; see Heb. x. 5, &c. God was now about to *give him the heathen for his inheritance* (Ps. ii. 8), to put him in possession of *the desolate heritages* (Isa. xlix. 8), to *divide him a portion with the great,* Isa. liii. 12. And though the Jews, who *saw* him, *believed not* on him, yet these (saith he) shall *come to me;* the other sheep, which are not of this fold, shall be *brought, ch.* x. 15, 16. See Acts xiii. 45—48. (*b.*) The effect of it secured: *They shall come to me.* This is not in the nature of a *promise*, but a *prediction*, that as many as were in the counsel of God ordained to life shall be brought to life by being brought to Christ. They are *scattered*, are mingled among the nations, yet none of them shall be forgotten; not a grain of God's corn shall be lost, as is promised, Amos ix. 9. They are by nature *alienated* from Christ, and averse to him, and yet *they shall come.* As God's omniscience is engaged for the finding of them all out, so is his omnipotence for the bringing of them all in. Not, They shall be *driven* to me, but, They shall come freely, shall be made *willing*.

Secondly, He here *acquaints* us *how* it shall be done. How shall those who are given to Christ be brought to him? Two things are to be done in order to it:—

a. Their *understandings* shall be *enlightened;* this is promised, *v.* 45, 46. It is written in the prophets, who spoke of these things before, *And they shall be all taught of God;* this we find, Isa. liv. 13, and Jer. xxxi. 34. *They shall all know me.* Note,

(*a.*) In order to our *believing in Jesus Christ*, it is necessary that we be *taught of God;* that is, [*a.*] That there be a *divine revelation made to us*, discovering to us both what we are to believe concerning Christ and why we are to believe it. There are some things which *even nature teaches*, but to bring us to Christ there is need of a higher light. [*b.*] That there be a *divine work wrought in us*, enabling us to understand and receive these revealed truths and the evidence of them. God, in giving us reason, teaches us more than the *beasts of the earth;* but in giving us faith he teaches more than the *natural man.* Thus all the church's children, all that are *genuine*, are *taught of God;* he hath undertaken their education.

(*b.*) It follows then, by way of inference from this, that *every man* that has *heard and learned of the Father comes to Christ, v.* 45. [*a.*] It is here implied that none will come to Christ but those that have *heard* and *learned of the Father.* We shall never be brought to Christ but under a divine conduct; except God by his grace enlighten our minds, inform our judgments, and rectify our mistakes, and not only *tell* us, that we may *hear*, but teach us, that we may *learn* the truth as it is in Jesus, we shall never be brought to believe in Christ. [*b.*] That this *divine teaching* does so necessarily produce the *faith of God's elect* that we may conclude that those who do not *come to Christ* have never *heard* nor *learned* of the Father; for, if they had, doubtless they would have come to Christ. In vain do men pretend to be *taught of God* if they believe not in Christ, for he teaches no other lesson, Gal. i. 8, 9. See how God deals with men as reasonable creatures, draws them with the *cords of a man*, opens the understanding first, and then by that, in a regular way, influences the inferior faculties; thus he comes in by the door, but Satan, as a robber, climbs up another way. But lest any should dream of a visible appearance of God the Father to the children of men (to teach them these things), and entertain any gross conceptions about hearing and learning of the Father, he adds (*v.* 46) *Not that any man hath seen the Father;* it is implied, nor *can* see him, with bodily eyes, or may expect to learn of him as Moses did, to whom he spoke *face to face;* but God, in enlightening men's eyes and teaching them, works in a spiritual way. The Father of spirits hath access to, and influence upon, men's spirits, undiscerned. Those that have not seen his face have felt his power. And yet there is one intimately acquainted with the Father, he *who is of God*, Christ himself, he hath *seen the Father, ch.* i. 18. Note, *First*, Jesus Christ is of God in a peculiar manner, God of God, light of light; not only sent of God, but begotten of God before all worlds. *Secondly*, It is the prerogative of Christ to have *seen the Father*, perfectly to know him and his counsels. *Thirdly*, Even that illumination which is preparative to faith is conveyed to us through Christ. Those that *learn of the Father*, forasmuch as they cannot see him themselves, must learn of Christ, who alone hath seen him. As all divine discoveries are made through Christ, so through him all divine powers are exerted.

b. Their *wills* shall be *bowed.* If the soul of man had now its original rectitude there needed no more to influence the will than the illumination of the understanding; but in the depraved soul of fallen man there is a rebellion of the will against the right dictates of the understanding; a *carnal mind*, which is *enmity* itself to the divine light and law. It is therefore requisite that there be a work of grace wrought upon the will, which is here called *drawing* (*v.* 44): *No man can come to me except the Father, who hath sent me, draw him.* The Jews murmured at the doctrine of Christ; not only would not receive it themselves, but were angry that others did. Christ overheard their secret whisperings, and said (*v.* 43), "*Murmur not among yourselves;* lay not the fault of your dislike of my doctrine one upon another, as if it were because you find it generally distasted; no, it is owing to yourselves, and your own corrupt dispositions, which are such as amount to a *moral impotency;* your antipathies to the truths of God, and prejudices against them, are so strong that nothing less than a divine power can conquer them." And this is the case of all mankind: "*No man can come to me*, can persuade himself to come up to the terms of the gospel, *except the Father, who hath sent me, draw him,*" *v.* 44. Observe, (*a.*) The nature of the work: It is *drawing*, which denotes not a *force* put upon the will, but a *change* wrought in the will, whereby of unwilling we are made willing, and a new bias is given to the soul, by which it inclines to God. This seems to be more than a *moral suasion*, for by that it is in the power of man to *draw;* yet it is not to be called a *physical impulse*, for it lies out of the road of *nature;* but he that *formed the spirit of man within him* by his creating power, and *fashions the hearts of men* by his providential influence, knows how to new-mould the soul, and to alter its bent and temper, and make it conformable to himself and his own will, without doing any wrong to its natural liberty. It is such a drawing as works not only a *compliance*, but a cheerful compliance, a complacency: *Draw us, and we will run after thee.* (*b.*) The necessity of it: *No man*, in this weak and helpless state, can come to Christ without it. As we *cannot* do any natural action without the concurrence of *common providence*, so we cannot do any action morally good without the influence of *special grace*, in which the *new man* lives, and moves, and has its being, as much as the *mere man* has in the divine providence. (*c.*) The author of it: The *Father who hath sent me.* The Father, having sent Christ, will succeed him, for he would not send him on a fruitless errand. Christ having undertaken to bring souls to glory, God promised him, in order thereunto, to bring them to him, and so to give him possession of those to whom he had given him a right. God, having by promise given the kingdom of Israel to David, did at length *draw the hearts* of the people to him; so, having sent Christ to save souls, he sends souls to him to be saved by him. (*d.*) The crown and perfection of this work: And *I will raise him up at the last day.* This is four times mentioned in this discourse, and doubtless it includes all the intermediate and preparatory workings of divine grace. When he *raises them up at the last day*, he will put the *last hand* to his undertaking, will *bring forth the topstone.* If he undertakes this, surely he *can* do any thing, and will do every thing that is necessary in order to it. Let our expectations be carried out towards a happiness reserved for the *last day*, when all the years of time shall be fully complete and ended.

4. Christ, having thus spoken of himself as the *bread of life*, and of faith as *the work of God*, comes more particularly to show *what of himself* is this bread, namely, his flesh, and that to believe is to eat of that, *v.* 51—58, where he still prosecutes the metaphor of food. Observe, here, the *preparation* of this food: *The bread that I will give is my flesh* (*v.* 51), *the flesh of the Son of man and his blood*, *v.* 53. *His flesh is meat indeed, and his blood is drink indeed*, *v.* 55. Observe, also, the *participation* of this food: We must *eat the flesh of the Son of man and drink his blood* (*v.* 53); and again (*v.* 54), *Whoso eateth my flesh and drinketh my blood;* and the same words (*v.* 56, 57), he that *eateth me.* This is certainly a parable or figurative discourse, wherein the actings of the soul upon things spiritual and divine are represented by bodily actions about things sensible, which made the truths of Christ more intelligible to some, and less so to others, Mark iv. 11—12. Now,

(1.) Let us see how this discourse of Christ was liable to mistake and misconstruction, that *men might see, and not perceive.* [1.] It was misconstrued by the carnal *Jews*, to whom it was first delivered (*v.* 52): *They strove among themselves;* they whispered in each other's ears their dissatisfaction: *How can this man give us his flesh to eat?* Christ spoke (*v.* 51) of giving his flesh *for us*, to suffer and die; but they, without due consideration, understood it of his giving it *to us*, to be eaten, which gave occasion to Christ to tell them that, however what he said was otherwise intended, yet even that also of *eating of his flesh* was no such absurd thing (if rightly understood) as *prima facie*—*in the first instance*, they took it to be. [2.] It has been wretchedly misconstrued by the church of Rome for the support of their monstrous doctrine of transubstantiation, which gives the lie to our senses, contradicts the nature of a sacrament, and overthrows all convincing evidence. They, like these Jews here, understand it of a corporal and carnal eating of Christ's body, like Nicodemus, *ch.* 3, 4. The Lord's supper was not yet instituted, and therefore it could have no reference to that; it is a *spiritual* eating and drinking that is here spoken of, not a *sacramental.* [3.] It is misunderstood by many ignorant carnal people, who hence infer that, if they take the sacrament when they die, they shall certainly go to heaven, which, as it makes many that are weak causelessly uneasy if they want it, so it makes many that are wicked causelessly easy if they have it. Therefore,

(2.) Let us see how this discourse of Christ to be understood.

[1.] What is meant by the *flesh and blood of Christ.* It is called (*v.* 53), *The flesh of the Son of man, and his blood, his* as Messiah and Mediator: the *flesh and blood* which he *assumed* in his incarnation (Heb. ii. 14), and which he *gave up* in his *death* and *suffering: my flesh which I will give* to be crucified and slain. It is said to be *given for the life of the world*, that is, *First, Instead* of the *life of the world*, which was *forfeited* by sin, Christ gives his own flesh as a ransom or counter-price. Christ was our bail, bound *body for body* (as we say), and therefore *his* life must go for *ours*, that ours may be spared. *Here am I, let these go their way. Secondly, In order to* the *life of the world*, to purchase a *general* offer of eternal life to all the world, and the *special* assurances of it to all believers. So that the *flesh and blood* of the Son of man denote the Redeemer *incarnate* and *dying;* Christ and *him crucified*, and the redemption wrought out by him, with all the precious benefits of redemption: pardon of sin, acceptance with God, the adoption of sons, access to the throne of grace, the promises of the covenant, and eternal life; these are called *the flesh and blood* of Christ, 1. Because they are purchased by his flesh and blood, by the breaking of his body, and the shedding of his blood. Well may the purchased privileges be denominated from the price that was paid for them, for it puts a value upon them; write upon them *pretium sanguinis—the price of blood.* 2. Because they are meat and drink to our souls. *Flesh with the blood* was prohibited (Gen. ix. 4), but the privileges of the gospel are as flesh and blood to us, prepared for the nourishment of our souls. He had before compared himself to *bread,* which is necessary food; here to *flesh,* which is delicious. It is a *feast of fat things,* Isa. xxv. 6. The soul is satisfied with Christ as *with marrow and fatness,* Ps. lxiii. 5. It is *meat indeed,* and *drink indeed; truly so,* that is spiritually; so Dr. Whitby; as Christ is called the *true vine;* or *truly meat,* in opposition to the shows and shadows with which the world shams off those that feed upon it. In Christ and his gospel there is real supply, solid satisfaction; that is *meat indeed,* and *drink indeed,* which satiates and replenishes, Jer. xxxi. 25, 26.

[2.] What is meant by *eating this flesh* and *drinking* this *blood,* which is so necessary and beneficial; it is certain that it means neither more nor less than believing in Christ. As we partake of meat and drink by eating and drinking, so we partake of Christ and his benefits by faith: and *believing in Christ* includes these four things, which *eating and drinking* do:—*First,* It implies an *appetite* to Christ. This spiritual eating and drinking begins with *hungering* and *thirsting* (Matt. v. 6), earnest and importunate desires after Christ, not willing to take up with any thing short of an interest in him: "Give me Christ or else I die." *Secondly,* An *application* of Christ to ourselves. Meat *looked upon* will not nourish us, but meat *fed upon,* and so made *our own,* and as it were *one with us.* We must so accept of Christ as to appropriate him to ourselves: *my Lord, and my God, ch.* xx. 28. *Thirdly,* A *delight* in Christ and his salvation. The doctrine of Christ crucified must be *meat and drink* to us, most pleasant and delightful. We must feast upon the dainties of the *New Testament in the blood of Christ,* taking as great a complacency in the methods which Infinite Wisdom has taken to redeem and save us as ever we did in the most needful supplies or grateful delights of nature. *Fourthly,* A *derivation of nourishment* from him and a dependence upon him for the support and comfort of our spiritual life, and the strength, growth, and vigour of the new man. To *feed upon Christ* is to do all *in his name,* in union with him, and by virtue drawn from him; it is to live upon him as we do upon our meat. How our bodies are nourished by our food we cannot describe, but that they are so we know and find; so it is with this spiritual nourishment. Our Saviour was so well pleased with this metaphor (as very significant and expressive) that, when afterwards he would institute some outward sensible signs, by which to represent our *communicating* of the benefits of his death, he chose those of *eating* and *drinking,* and made them *sacramental* actions.

(3.) Having thus explained the general meaning of this part of Christ's discourse, the particulars are reducible to two heads:—

[1.] The *necessity* of our *feeding upon Christ* (*v.* 53): *Except you eat the flesh of the Son of man, and drink his blood, you have no life in you.* That is, *First,* "It is a certain sign that you *have no* spiritual *life* in you if you have no *desire* towards Christ, nor *delight* in him." If the soul does not *hunger* and *thirst,* certainly it does not *live:* it is a sign that we are dead indeed if we are dead to such meat and drink as this. When *artificial* bees, that by curious springs were made to move to and fro, were to be *distinguished* from *natural* ones (they say), it was done by putting honey among them, which the natural bees only flocked to, but the artificial ones minded not, for *they had no life in them. Secondly,* "It is certain that you *can have* no spiritual life, unless you derive it from Christ by faith; separated from him you can do nothing. Faith in Christ is the *primum vivens—the first living principle* of grace; without i we have not the *truth* of *spiritual* life, nor any title to eternal life: our bodies may as well live without meat as our souls without Christ.

[2.] The *benefit* and *advantage* of it, in two things:—

First, We shall be *one with Christ,* as our bodies are with our food when it is digested (*v.* 56): *He that eats my flesh, and drinks my blood,* that lives by faith in Christ crucified (it is spoken of as a continued act), he *dwelleth in me, and I in him.* By faith we have a close and intimate union with Christ; he is *in us,* and we *in him, ch.* xvii. 21—23; 1 John iii. 24. Believers dwell in Christ as their stronghold or city of refuge; Christ dwells in them as the master of the house, to rule it and provide for it. Such is the union between Christ and believers that he shares in their griefs, and they share in his graces and joys; he *sups* with them upon their bitter herbs, and *they with him* upon his *rich dainties.* It is an inseparable union, like that between the body and digested food, Rom. viii. 35; 1 John iv. 13.

Secondly, We shall *live,* shall live eternally, *by him,* as our bodies live by our food.

a. We shall *live by him* (*v.* 57): *As the living Father hath sent me, and I live by the Father, so he that eateth me, even he shall live by me.* We have here the series and order of the divine life. (*a.*) God is the *living Father,* hath life in and of himself. *I am that I am* is his name for ever. (*b.*) Jesus Christ, as Mediator, lives *by the Father;* he has life *in himself* (*ch.* v. 26), but he has it of the Father. He that sent him, not only qualified him with that life which was necessary to so great an undertaking, but constituted him the treasury of divine life to us; he breathed into the second Adam the breath of spiritual lives, as into the first Adam the breath of natural lives. (*c.*) True believers receive this divine life by virtue of their union with Christ, which is inferred from the union between the Father and the Son, as it is compared to it, *ch.* xvii. 21. For therefore *he that eateth me*, or feeds on me, *even he shall live by me:* those that live *upon* Christ shall live *by* him. The life of believers is *had from Christ* (*ch.* i. 16); it is *hid with Christ* (Col. iii. 4), we live by *him* as the members by the head, the branches by the root; because he lives, we shall live also.

b. We shall live *eternally* by him (*v.* 54): *Whoso eateth my flesh, and drinketh my blood,* as prepared in the gospel to be the food of souls, he *hath eternal life*, he hath it now, as *v.* 40. He has that in him which is eternal life begun; he has the earnest and foretaste of it, and the hope of it; he shall live *for ever*, *v.* 58. His happiness shall run parallel with the longest line of eternity itself.

Lastly, The historian concludes with an account *where* Christ had this discourse with the Jews (*v.* 59): *In the synagogue as he taught*, implying that he taught them many other things besides these, but this was that in his discourse which was new. He adds this, that he said these things *in the synagogue*, to show, 1. The credit of Christ's doctrine. His truths sought no corners, but were publicly preached in mixed assemblies, as able to abide the most severe and impartial test. Christ pleaded this upon his trial (*ch.* xviii. 20): *I ever taught in the synagogue.* 2. The credibility of this narrative of it. To assure you that the discourse was fairly represented, he appeals to the synagogue at Capernaum, where it might be examined.

60 Many therefore of his disciples,
when they had heard *this*, said, This
is a hard saying; who can hear it?
61 When Jesus knew in himself that
his disciples murmured at it, he said
unto them, Doth this offend you?
62 *What* and if ye shall see the Son
of man ascend up where he was before? 63 It is the spirit that quickeneth; the flesh profiteth nothing:
the words that I speak unto you,
they are spirit, and *they* are life. 64
But there are some of you that believe not. For Jesus knew from the
beginning who they were that believed
not, and who should betray him. 65
And he said, Therefore said I unto
you, that no man can come unto me,
except it were given unto him of my
Father. 66 From that *time* many
of his disciples went back, and walked
no more with him. 67 Then said
Jesus unto the twelve, Will ye also
go away? 68 Then Simon Peter
answered him, Lord, to whom shall we
go? thou hast the words of eternal
life. 69 And we believe and are
sure that thou art that Christ, the
Son of the living God. 70 Jesus
answered them, Have not I chosen
you twelve, and one of you is a
devil? 71 He spake of Judas Iscariot *the son* of Simon: for he it
was that should betray him, being
one of the twelve.

We have here an account of the effects of Christ's discourse. Some were offended and others edified by it; some driven *from him* and others brought nearer *to him.*

I To some it was a *savour of death unto death;* not only to the Jews, who were professed enemies to him and his doctrine, but even to many of *his disciples,* such as were disciples *at large*, who were his frequent hearers, and followed him *in public;* a mixed multitude, like those among Israel, that began all the discontents. Now here we have,

1. Their murmurings at the doctrine they heard (*v.* 60); not a few, but many of them, were offended at it. Of the several sorts of ground that received the seed, only one in four brought forth fruit. See what they say to it (*v.* 60): *This is a hard saying, who can hear it?* (1.) They do not like it themselves: "What stuff is this? *Eat the flesh, and drink the blood, of the Son of man!* If it is to be understood figuratively, it is not intelligible; if literally, not practicable. What! must we turn cannibals? Can we not be religious, but we must be barbarous?" *Si Christiani adorant quod comedunt* (said Averroes), *sit anima mea cum philosophis*—*If Christians adore what they eat, my mind shall continue with the philosophers.* Now, when they found it a hard saying, if they had humbly begged of Christ to have *declared unto them this parable,* he would have opened it, and their understandings too; for *the meek will he teach his way.* But they were not willing to have Christ's sayings explained to them, because they would not lose *this* pretence for rejecting them—that they were *hard sayings.* (2.) They think it impossible that any one else should like it: "*Who can hear it?* Surely none can." Thus the scoffers at religion are ready to undertake that all the intelligent part of mankind concur with them. They conclude with great assurance that no *man of sense* will admit the doctrine of Christ, nor any *man of spirit* submit to his laws. Because they cannot bear

to be so *tutored*, so *tied up*, themselves, they think none else can: *Who can hear it?* Thanks be to God, thousands have *heard* these sayings of Christ, and have found them not only easy, but pleasant, as their *necessary food.*

2. Christ's animadversions upon their murmurings.

(1.) He well enough knew their murmurings, *v.* 61. Their cavils were secret in their own breasts, or whispered among themselves in a corner. But, [1.] Christ *knew* them; he saw them, he heard them. Note, Christ takes notice not only of the bold and open *defiances* that are done to his name and glory by *daring sinners,* but of the secret slights that are put upon his doctrine by carnal professors; he knows that which the *fool saith in his heart,* and cannot for shame *speak out;* he observes how his doctrine is *resented* by those to whom it is *preached;* who *rejoice* in it, and who *murmur* at it; who are reconciled to it, and bow before it, and who quarrel with it, and rebel against it, though ever so secretly. [2.] He knew it *in himself,* not by any information given him, nor any external indication of the thing, but by his own divine omniscience. He knew it not as the prophets, by a *divine revelation* made to him (that which the prophets desired to know was sometimes hid from them, as 2 Kings iv. 27), but by a *divine knowledge* in him. He is that essential Word that *discerns the thoughts of the heart,* Heb. iv. 12, 13. Thoughts are words to Christ; we should therefore take heed not only what we say and do, but what we think.

(2.) He well enough knew how to answer them: "*Doth this offend you?* Is this a stumbling-block to you?" See how people by their own wilful mistakes create offences to themselves: they take offence where there is none given, and even make it where there is nothing to make it of. Note, We may justly wonder that so much offence should be taken at the doctrine of Christ for so little cause. Christ speaks of it here with wonder: "*Doth this offend you?* How unreasonable are your quarrels!" Now, in answer to those who condemned his doctrine as intricate and obscure (*Si non vis intelligi, debes negligi—If you are unwilling to be understood, you ought to be neglected*),

[1.] He gives them a hint of his ascension into heaven, as that which would give an irresistible evidence of the truth of his doctrine (*v.* 62): *What and if you shall see the Son of man ascend up where he was before?* And what then? *First,* "If I should tell you of that, surely it would much more offend you, and you would think my pretensions too high indeed. If this be so hard a saying that you cannot hear it, how will you digest it when I tell you of my returning to heaven, whence I came down?" See *ch.* iii. 12. Those who stumble at smaller difficulties should consider how they will get over greater. *Secondly,* "When you see the Son of man ascend, this will much more offend you, for then my body will be less capable of being eaten by you in that gross sense wherein you now understand it;" so Dr. Whitby. Or, *Thirdly,* "When you see that, or hear it from those that shall see it, surely then you will be satisfied. You think I take too much upon me when I say, *I came down from heaven,* for it was with this that you quarrelled (*v.* 42); but will you think so when you see me return to heaven?" If he *ascended,* certainly he *descended,* Eph. iv. 9, 10. Christ did often refer himself thus to *subsequent* proofs, as *ch.* i. 50, 51; ii. 14; Matt. xii. 40; xxvi. 64. Let us wait awhile, till the mystery of God shall be finished, and then we shall see that there was no reason to be offended at any of Christ's sayings.

[2.] He gives them a general key to this and all such parabolical discourses, teaching them that they are to be understood spiritually, and not after a corporal and carnal manner: *It is the spirit that quickeneth, the flesh profiteth nothing, v.* 63. As it is in the natural body, the animal spirits quicken and enliven it, and without these the most nourishing food would profit nothing (what would the body be the better for bread, if it were not quickened and animated by the spirit), so it is with the soul. *First,* The bare participation of ordinances, unless the Spirit of God work with them, and quicken the soul by them, *profits nothing;* the word and ordinances, if the Spirit works with them, are as food to a living man, if not, they are as food to a dead man. Even the flesh of Christ, the sacrifice for sin, will avail us nothing unless the blessed Spirit quicken our souls thereby, and enforce the powerful influences of his death upon us, till we by his grace are planted together in the likeness of it. *Secondly,* The doctrine of eating Christ's flesh and drinking his blood, if it be understood literally, *profits nothing,* but rather leads us into mistakes and prejudices; but the spiritual sense or meaning of it quickens the soul, makes it *alive* and *lively;* for so it follows: *The words that I speak unto you, they are spirit, and they are life. To eat the flesh of Christ!* this is a hard saying, but to believe that Christ died for me, to derive from that doctrine strength and comfort in my approaches to God, my oppositions to sin and preparations for a future state, this is the *spirit and life* of that saying, and, construing it thus, it is an excellent saying. The reason why men *dislike* Christ's sayings is because they *mistake* them. The literal sense of a parable does us no good, we are never the wiser for it, but the spiritual meaning is instructive. *Thirdly, The flesh profits nothing*—those that *are in the flesh* (so some understand it), that are under the power of a carnal mind, *profit not* by Christ's discourses; but *the Spirit quickeneth*—those that have the Spirit, that are spiritual, are quickened and enlivened by them; for they are received *ad modum recipientis—so as to correspond with the state of the receiver's mind.* They found fault with Christ's sayings, whereas the fault was in themselves; it is only to *sensual* minds that spiritual things are *senseless* and *sapless*, spiritual minds *relish* them; see 1 Cor. ii. 14, 15.

[3.] He gives them an intimation of his *knowledge of them*, and that he had expected no better from them, though they called themselves his disciples, *v.* 64, 65. Now was fulfilled that of the prophet, speaking of Christ and his doctrine (Isa. liii. 1), *Who hath believed our report? and to whom is the arm of the Lord revealed?* Both these Christ here takes notice of.

First, They did not *believe his report:* "There are *some of you* who said you would leave all to follow me who yet *believe not;*" and this was the reason why the *word preached did not profit them,* because it was *not mixed with faith,* Heb. iv. 2. They did not believe him to be the Messiah, else they would have acquiesced in the doctrine he preached, and not have quarrelled with it, though there were some things in it *dark, and hard to be understood. Oportet discentum credere — Young beginners in learning must take things upon their teacher's word.* Note, 1. Among those who are *nominal Christians,* there are many who are *real infidels.* 2. The unbelief of hypocrites, before it discovers itself to the world, is naked and open before the eyes of Christ. He *knew from the beginning* who they were of the multitudes that followed him that *believed,* and who of the twelve should betray him; he knew *from the beginning* of their acquaintance with him, and attendance on him, when they were in the hottest pang of their zeal, who were sincere, as Nathanael (*ch.* i. 47), and who were not. Before they distinguished themselves by an overt act, he could infallibly distinguish *who believed* and who did not, whose love was *counterfeit* and whose *cordial.* We may gather hence, (1.) That the apostasy of those who have long made a plausible profession of religion is a certain proof of their constant hypocrisy, and that *from the beginning they believed not,* but is not a proof of the possibility of the total and final apostasy of any true believers: such revolts are not to be called the fall of real saints, but the discovery of pretended ones; see 1 John ii. 19. *Stella cadens non stella fuit—The star that falls never was a star.* (2.) That it is Christ's prerogative to *know the heart;* he knows who they are that *believe not,* but dissemble in their profession, and yet continues them room in his church, the use of his ordinances, and the credit of his name, and does not discover them in this world, unless they by their own wickedness discover themselves; because such is the constitution of his visible church, and the discovering day is yet to come. But, if we pretend to judge men's hearts, we step into Christ's throne, and anticipate his judgment. We are often deceived in men, and see cause to change our sentiments of them; but this we are sure of, that Christ knows all men, and *his judgment is according to truth.*

Secondly, The reason why they did not believe his report was because the *arm of the Lord* was not *revealed* to them (*v.* 65): *Therefore said I unto you that no man can come to me, except it be given unto him of my Father;* referring to *v.* 44. Christ therefore could not but know who believed and who did not, because faith is the gift and work of God, and all his Father's gifts and works could not but be known to him, for they all passed through his hands. There he had said that none could *come to him, except the Father draw him;* here he saith, *except it be given him of my Father,* which shows that God *draws* souls by giving them grace and strength, and a heart to come, without which, such is the moral impotency of man, in his fallen state, that he *cannot come.*

3. We have here their final apostasy from Christ hereupon: *From that time many of his disciples went back, and walked no more with him, v.* 66. When we admit into our minds hard thoughts of the word and works of Christ, and conceive a secret dislike, and are willing to hear insinuations tending to their reproach, we are then *entering into temptation;* it is as the letting forth of water; it is *looking back,* which, if infinite mercy prevent not, will end in *drawing back;* therefore *Obsta principiis—Take heed of the beginnings* of apostasy. (1.) See here the *backsliding* of these *disciples. Many of them went back* to their houses, and families, and callings, which they had left for a time to follow him; *went back,* one to his farm and another to his merchandise; *went back,* as Orpah did, to their people, and to their gods, Ruth i. 15. They had entered themselves in Christ's school, but they *went back,* did not only play truant for once, but took leave of him and his doctrine for ever. Note, The apostasy of Christ's disciples from him, though really a strange thing, yet has been such a common thing that we need not be surprised at it. Here were *many* that *went back.* It is often so; when some backslide many backslide with them; the disease is infectious. (2.) The occasion of this backsliding: *From that time,* from the time that Christ preached this comfortable doctrine, that he is the *bread of life,* and that those who by faith feed *upon him* shall live *by him* (which, one would think, should have engaged them to cleave more closely to him)—from *that* time they withdrew. Note, The corrupt and wicked heart of man often makes that an occasion of offence which is indeed matter of the greatest comfort. Christ foresaw that they would thus take offence at what he said, and yet he said it. That which is the undoubted word and truth of Christ must be faithfully delivered, whoever may be offended at it. Men's humours must be captivated to God's word, and not God's word accommodated to men's

humours. (3.) The degree of their apostasy: *They walked no more with him,* returned no more to him and attended no more upon his ministry. It is hard for those who have been *once enlightened,* and have *tasted the good word of God, if they fall away, to renew them again to repentance,* Heb. vi. 4—6.

II. This discourse was to others a *savour of life unto life. Many went back,* but, thanks be to God, all did not; even then the *twelve* stuck to him. Though the *faith of some be overthrown,* yet the *foundation of God stands sure.* Observe here,

1. The affectionate question which Christ put to the twelve (*v.* 67): *Will you also go away?* He saith nothing to those who went back. *If the unbelieving depart, let them depart;* it was no great *loss* of those whom he never *had;* lightly come, lightly go; but he takes this occasion to speak to the twelve, to confirm them, and by trying their stedfastness the more to fix them: *Will you also go away?* (1.) "It is *at your choice* whether you will or no; if you will forsake me, now is the time, when so many do: it is an hour of temptation; if you will go back, go now." Note, Christ will detain none with him against their wills; his soldiers are volunteers, not pressed men. The twelve had now had time enough to try how they liked Christ and his doctrine, and that none of them might afterwards say that they were trepanned into discipleship, and if it were to do again they would not do it, he here allows them a power of revocation, and leaves them at their liberty; as Josh. xxiv. 15; Ruth i. 15. (2.) "It is *at your peril* if you do go away." If there was any secret inclination in the heart of any of them to depart from him, he stops it with this awakening question, "*Will you also go away?* Think not that you hang at as loose an end as they did, and may go away as easily as they could. They have not been so intimate with me as you have been, nor received so many favours from me; they are gone, but will *you* also go? Remember your character, and say, Whatever others do, we will never go away. *Should such a man as I flee?*" Neh. vi. 11. Note, The nearer we have been to Christ and the longer we have been with him, the more mercies we have received from him and the more engagements we have laid ourselves under to him, the greater will be our sin if we desert him. (3.) "I have reason *to think you will not.* Will you go away? No, I have faster hold of you than so; *I hope better things of you* (Heb. vi. 9), for *you are they that have continued with me,*" Luke xxii. 28. When the apostasy of some is a grief to the Lord Jesus, the constancy of others is so much the more his honour, and he is pleased with it accordingly. Christ and believers know one another too well to part upon every displeasure.

2. The believing reply which Peter, in the name of the rest, made to this question, *v.* 68, 69. Christ put the question to them, as Joshua put Israel to their choice whom they would serve, with design to draw out from them a promise to adhere to him, and it had the like effect. *Nay, but we will serve the Lord.* Peter was upon all occasions the *mouth of the rest,* not so much because he had more of his Master's ear than they, but because he had more tongue of his own; and what he said was sometimes approved and sometimes reprimanded (Matt. xvi. 17, 23)—the common lot of those who are swift to speak. This here was well said, admirably well; and probably he said it by the direction, and with the express assent, of his fellow-disciples; at least he knew their mind, and spoke the sense of them all, and did not except Judas, for we must hope the best.

(1.) Here is a good resolution to adhere to Christ, and so expressed as to intimate that they would not entertain the least thought of leaving him: "*Lord, to whom shall we go?* It were folly to go from thee, unless we knew where to better ourselves; no, Lord, we like our choice too well to change." Note, Those who leave Christ would do well to consider to whom they will go, and whether they can expect to find rest and peace any where but in him. See Ps. lxxiii. 27, 28; Hos. ii. 9. "*Whither shall we go?* Shall we make our court to the world? It will certainly *deceive* us. Shall we return to sin? It will certainly *destroy* us. Shall we leave the *fountain of living waters* for *broken cisterns?*" The disciples resolve to continue their pursuit of life and happiness, and will have a guide to it, and will adhere to Christ as their guide, for they can never have a better. "Shall we go to the heathen philosophers, and become their disciples? They are become vain in their imaginations, and, professing themselves to be wise in other things, are become fools in religion. Shall we go to the scribes and Pharisees, and sit at their feet? What good can they do us who have made void the commandments of God by their traditions? Shall we go to Moses? He will send us back again to thee. Therefore, if ever we find the way to happiness, it must be in following thee." Note, Christ's holy religion appears to great advantage when it is compared with other institutions, for then it will be seen how far it excels them all. Let those who find fault with this religion find a better before they quit it. A divine teacher we must have; can we find a better than Christ? A divine revelation we cannot be without; if the scripture be not such a one, where else may we look for it?

(2.) Here is a good reason for this resolution. It was not the inconsiderate resolve of a blind affection, but the result of mature deliberation. The disciples were resolved never to go away from Christ,

[1.] Because of the *advantage* they promised themselves by him: *Thou hast the words of eternal life.* They themselves did not fully understand Christ's discourse, for as yet the doctrine of the cross was a riddle to them; but in the general they were satisfied that *he had the words of eternal life*, that is, *First,* That the word of his doctrine showed the way to *eternal life,* set it before us, and directed us what to do, that we might inherit it. *Secondly,* That the word of his *determination* must confer eternal life. His *having the words of eternal life* is the same with his having *power to give eternal life to as many as were given him, ch.* xvii. 2. He had in the foregoing discourse assured *eternal life* to his followers; these disciples fastened upon this plain saying, and therefore resolved to stick to him, when the others overlooked this, and fastened upon the *hard sayings*, and therefore forsook him. Though we cannot account for every mystery, every obscurity, in Christ's doctrine, yet we know, in the general, that it is the word of eternal life, and therefore must live and die by it; for if we forsake Christ *we forsake our own mercies.*

[2.] Because of the assurance they had concerning him (*v.* 69): *We believe, and are sure, that thou art that Christ.* If he be the promised Messiah, he must *bring in an everlasting righteousness* (Dan. ix. 24), and therefore has the *words of eternal life,* for *righteousness reigns to eternal life,* Rom. v. 21. Observe, *First,* The *doctrine* they believed: that this Jesus was the Messiah promised to the fathers and expected by them, and that he was not a mere man, but the Son of the living God, the same to whom God had said, *Thou art my Son,* Ps. ii. 7. In times of temptation to apostasy it is good to have recourse to our first principles, and stick to them; and, if we faithfully abide by that which is *past dispute,* we shall be the better able both to *find* and to *keep* the truth in matters of doubtful disputation. *Secondly,* The *degree* of their faith it rose up to a full assurance: *We are sure.* We have known it *by experience;* this is the best knowledge. We should take occasion from others' wavering to be so much the more established, especially in that which is the present truth. When we have so strong a faith in the gospel of Christ as boldly to venture our souls *upon it,* knowing *whom we have believed,* then, and not till then, we shall be willing to venture every thing else for it.

3. The melancholy remark which our Lord Jesus made upon this reply of Peter's (*v.* 70, 71): *Have not I chosen you twelve, and one of you is a devil?* And the evangelist tells us whom he meant: *he spoke of Judas Iscariot.* Peter had undertaken for them all that they would be faithful to their Master. Now Christ does not condemn his charity (it is always good to hope the best), but he tacitly corrects his confidence. We must not be too sure concerning any. God knows those that are his; we do not. Observe here, (1.) Hypocrites and betrayers of Christ are no better than devils. Judas not only *had* a devil, but he *was* a devil. One of you is a *false accuser;* so διαβολὸς sometimes signifies (2 Tim. iii. 3); and it is probable that Judas, when he sold his Master to the chief priests, represented him to them as a bad man, to justify himself in what he did. But I rather take it as we read it: *He is a devil,* a devil incarnate, a fallen apostle, as the devil a fallen angel. He is Satan, an adversary, an enemy to Christ. He is Abaddon, and Apollyon, a son of perdition. He was of his father the devil, did his lusts, was in his interests, as Cain, 1 John iii. 12. Those whose bodies were possessed by the devil are never called *devils (demoniacs,* but not *devils);* but Judas, into whose *heart* Satan entered, and filled it, is called a *devil.* (2.) Many that are *seeming* saints are *real* devils. Judas had as fair an outside as many of the apostles; his venom was, like that of the serpent, covered with a fine skin. He *cast out devils,* and appeared an enemy to the devil's kingdom, and yet was himself a devil all the while. Not only he *will be* one shortly, but he *is one* now. It is *strange,* and to be wondered at; Christ speaks of it with wonder: *Have not I?* It is *sad,* and to be lamented, that ever Christianity should be made a cloak to diabolism. (3.) The disguises of hypocrites, however they may deceive men, and put a cheat upon them, cannot deceive Christ, for his piercing eye sees through them. He can call those *devils* that call themselves *Christians,* like the prophet's greeting to Jeroboam's wife, when she came to him in masquerade (1 Kings xiv. 6): *Come in, thou wife of Jeroboam.* Christ's *divine sight,* far better than any *double sight,* can see spirits. (4.) There are those who are chosen by Christ to special services who yet prove false to him: *I have chosen you* to the *apostleship,* for it is expressly said that Judas was not chosen to eternal life (*ch.* xiii. 18), and yet one of *you* is a devil. Note, Advancement to places of honour and trust in the church is no certain evidence of saving grace. *We have prophesied in thy name.* (5.) In the most *select* societies on this side heaven it is no new thing to meet with those that are corrupt. Of the twelve that were chosen to an intimate conversation with an *incarnate Deity,* as great an honour and privilege as ever men were chosen to, one was an *incarnate devil.* The historian lays an emphasis upon this, that Judas was *one of the twelve* that were so dignified and distinguished. Let us not reject and unchurch the twelve because *one of them is a devil,* nor say that they are all cheats and hypocrites because one of them was so; let those that are so bear the blame, and not those who, while they are undiscovered, incorporate with them. There is a society within the veil into which no unclean thing shall enter, a church of first-born, in which are no *false brethren.*

CHAP. VII.

In this chapter we have, I. Christ's declining for some time to appear publicly in Judea, ver. 1. II. His design to go up to Jerusalem at the feast of tabernacles, and his discourse with his kindred in Galilee concerning his going up to this feast, ver. 2—13. III. His preaching publicly in the temple at that feast. 1. In the midst of the feast, ver. 14, 15. We have his discourse with the Jews,

(1.) Concerning his doctrine, ver. 16—18. (2.) Concerning the crime of sabbath-breaking laid to his charge, ver. 19—24. (3.) Concerning himself, both whence he came and whither he was going, ver. 25—36. 2. On the last day of the feast. (1.) His gracious invitation to poor souls to come to him, ver. 37—39. (2.) The reception that it met with. [1.] Many of the people disputed about it, ver. 40—44. [2.] The chief priests would have brought him into trouble for it, but were first disappointed by their officers (ver. 45—49) and then silenced by one of their own court, ver. 50—53.

AFTER these things Jesus walked
in Galilee: for he would not
walk in Jewry, because the Jews
sought to kill him. 2 Now the
Jews' feast of tabernacles was at
hand. 3 His brethren therefore said
unto him, Depart hence, and go into
Judæa, that thy disciples also may
see the works that thou doest. 4 For
there is no man *that* doeth any thing
in secret, and he himself seeketh to
be known openly. If thou do these
things, show thyself to the world. 5
For neither did his brethren believe
in him. 6 Then Jesus said unto
them, My time is not yet come: but
your time is alway ready. 7 The
world cannot hate you; but me it
hateth, because I testify of it, that
the works thereof are evil. 8 Go ye
up unto this feast: I go not up yet
unto this feast; for my time is not
yet full come. 9 When he had said
these words unto them, he abode *still*
in Galilee. 10 But when his brethren were gone up, then went he
also up unto the feast, not openly,
but as it were in secret. 11 Then
the Jews sought him at the feast,
and said, Where is he? 12 And
there was much murmuring among
the people concerning him: for some
said, He is a good man: others said,
Nay; but he deceiveth the people.
13 Howbeit no man spake openly of
him for fear of the Jews.

We have here, I. The reason given why Christ spent more of his time in Galilee than in Judea (*v.* 1): *because the Jews,* the people in Judea and Jerusalem, sought to *kill him,* for curing the impotent man on the sabbath day, *ch.* v. 16. They thought to be the death of him, either by a popular tumult or by a legal prosecution, in consideration of which he kept at a distance in another part of the country, very much out of the lines of Jerusalem's communication. It is not said, He *durst not,* but, He *would not,* walk in Jewry; it was not through fear and cowardice that he declined it, but in *prudence,* because his hour was not yet come. Note, 1. Gospel light is justly *taken away* from those that endeavour to extinguish it. Christ will withdraw from those that drive him from them, will hide his face from those that spit in it, and justly shut up his bowels from those who spurn at them. 2. In times of imminent peril it is not only *allowable,* but *advisable,* to *withdraw* and *abscond* for our own safety and preservation, and to choose the service of those places which are least perilous, Matt. x. 23. *Then,* and not till *then,* we are called to expose and lay down our lives, when we cannot save them without sin. 3. If the providence of God casts persons of *merit* into places of obscurity and little note, it must not be thought strange; it was the lot of our Master himself. He who was fit to have sat in the highest of Moses's seats willingly walked in Galilee among the ordinary sort of people. Observe, He did not sit still in Galilee, nor bury himself alive there, but *walked;* he went about doing good. When we cannot do *what* and *where* we *would,* we must do *what* and *where* we *can.*

II. The approach of the *feast of tabernacles* (*v.* 2), one of the three solemnities which called for the personal attendance of all the males at Jerusalem; see the institution of it, Lev. xxiii. 34, &c., and the revival of it after a long disuse, Neh. viii. 14. It was intended to be both a *memorial* of the tabernacle state of Israel in the wilderness, and a *figure* of the tabernacle state of God's spiritual Israel in this world. This feast, which was instituted so many hundred years before, was still religiously observed. Note, Divine institutions are never antiquated, nor go out of date, by length of time: nor must wilderness mercies ever be forgotten. But it is called the *Jews' feast,* because it was now shortly to be *abolished,* as a mere Jewish thing, and left to them that *served the tabernacle.*

III. Christ's discourse with his *brethren,* some of his kindred, whether by his mother or his supposed father is not certain; but they were such as pretended to have an interest in him, and therefore interposed to advise him in his conduct. And observe,

1. Their ambition and vain-glory in urging him to make a more public appearance than he did: "*Depart hence,*" said they, "*and go into Judea* (*v.* 3), where thou wilt make a better figure than thou canst here."

(1.) They give two reasons for this advice: [1.] That it would be an encouragement to those in and about Jerusalem who had a respect for him; for, expecting his temporal kingdom, the royal seat of which they concluded must be at Jerusalem, they would have had the disciples *there* particularly countenanced, and thought the time he spent among his Galilean disciples wasted and thrown away, and his miracles turning to no account unless those at Jerusalem saw them. Or, "That *thy disciples,* all of them in general, who will be gathered at Jerusalem to keep the feast, may *see thy works,* and not, as here, a few at one time and a few at another." [2.] That it would be for the advancement of his name and honour : *There is no man that does any thing in secret* if he himself *seeks to be known* openly. They took it for granted that Christ sought to make himself known, and therefore thought it absurd for him to conceal his miracles : " *If thou do these things,* if thou be so well able to gain the applause of the people and the approbation of the rulers by thy miracles, venture abroad, and *show thyself to the world.* Supported with these credentials, thou canst not fail of acceptance, and therefore it is high time to set up for an interest, and to think of being *great.*"

(2.) One would not think there was any harm in this advice, and yet the evangelist notes it is an evidence of their infidelity : *For neither did his brethren believe in him (v.* 5), if they had, they would not have said this. Observe, [1.] It was an honour to be of the kindred of Christ, but no *saving* honour; they that hear his word and keep it are the kindred he values. Surely grace runs in no blood in the world, when not in that of Christ's family. [2.] It was a sign that Christ did not aim at any secular interest, for then his kindred would have struck in with him, and he would have secured them first. [3.] There were those who were akin to Christ according to the flesh who did believe in him (three of the twelve were *his brethren*), and yet others, as nearly allied to him as they, did not believe in him. Many that have the same external privileges and advantages do not make the same use of them. But,

(3.) What was there amiss in the advice which they gave him? I answer, [1.] It was a piece of presumption for them to prescribe to Christ, and to teach him what measures to take; it was a sign that they *did not believe him* able to guide them, when they did not think him sufficient to guide himself. [2.] They discovered a great carelessness about his safety, when they would have him go to Judea, where they knew the Jews sought to kill him. Those that believed in him, and loved him, dissuaded him from Judea, *ch.* xi. 8. [3.] Some think they hoped that if his miracles were wrought at Jerusalem the Pharisees and rulers would try them, and discover some cheat in them, which would justify their unbelief. So Dr. Whitby. [4.] Perhaps they were weary of his company in Galilee (for *are not all these that speak Galileans?)* and this was, in effect, a desire that he would *depart out of their coasts.* [5.] They causelessly insinuate that he neglected his disciples, and denied them such a *sight of his works* as was necessary to the support of their faith. [6.] They tacitly reproach him as *mean-spirited,* that he durst not enter the lists with the great men, nor trust himself upon the stage of public action, which, if he had any courage and *greatness of soul,* he would do, and not sneak thus and skulk in a corner; thus Christ's humility, and his humiliation, and the small figure which his religion has usually made in the world, have been often turned to the reproach of both *him* and *it.* [7.] They seem to question the truth of the miracles he wrought, in saying, " *If thou do these things,* if they will bear the test of a public scrutiny in the courts above, produce them there." [8.] They think Christ altogether such a one as themselves, as subject as they to worldly policy, and as desirous as they to *make a fair show in the flesh;* whereas he sought not honour from men. [9.] Self was at the bottom of all; they hoped, if he would make himself as great as he might, they, being his kinsmen, should share in his honour, and have respect paid them for his sake. Note, *First,* Many carnal people go to public ordinances, to worship at the feast, only to *show themselves,* and all their care is to make a *good appearance,* to present themselves handsomely to the world. *Secondly,* Many that seem to seek Christ's honour do really therein seek their own, and make it serve a turn for themselves.

2. The prudence and humility of our Lord Jesus, which appeared in his answer to the advice his brethren gave him, *v.* 6—8. Though there were so many base insinuations in it, he answered them mildly. Note, Even that which is said without *reason* should be answered without *passion;* we should learn of our Master to reply with meekness even to that which is most *impertinent* and *imperious,* and, where it is easy to find much amiss, to seem not to see it, and wink at the affront. They expected Christ's company with them to the feast, perhaps hoping he would bear their charges : but here,

(1.) He shows the difference between himself and them, in two things :—[1.] His *time* was *set,* so was not *theirs : My time is not yet come, but your time is always ready.* Understand it of the time of his going up to the feast. It was an indifferent thing to them when they went, for they had nothing of moment to do either where they were, to *detain* them *there,* or where they were going, to *hasten* them *thither;* but every minute of Christ's time was precious, and had its own particular business allotted to it. He had some work yet to do in Galilee before he left the country: in the harmony of the gospels betwixt this *motion* made by his kindred and his *going up* to this feast comes in the story of his sending forth the seventy disciples (Luke x. 1, &c.), which was an affair of very great consequence; his time is *not yet,* for that must be done first. Those who live useless lives have *their time always ready;* they can go and come when they please. But those whose *time* is filled up with *duty* will often find themselves *straitened,* and they have *not yet time* for that which others can do *at any time.* Those who are made the servants of God, as all men are, and who have made themselves the servants of all, as all useful men have, must not expect nor covet to be *masters of their own time.* The confinement of business is a thousand times better than the liberty of idleness. Or, it may be meant of the *time* of his appearing publicly at Jerusalem; Christ, who knows all men and all things, knew that the best and most proper time for it would be about the *middle of the feast.* We, who are ignorant and short-sighted, are apt to prescribe to him, and to think he should deliver his people, and so show himself now. The present time is *our* time, but he is fittest to judge, and, it may be, *his time is not yet come;* his people are not yet ready for deliverance, nor his enemies ripe for ruin; let us therefore wait with patience for *his time,* for all he does will be most glorious in its season. [2.] His *life* was *sought,* so was not *theirs, v.* 7. They, in *showing themselves* to the world, did not expose themselves: "*The world cannot hate you,* for you are *of the world,* its children, its servants, and in with its interests; and no doubt the world will *love its own;*" see *ch.* xv. 19. Unholy souls, whom the holy God *cannot love,* the world that lies in wickedness *cannot hate;* but Christ, in showing himself to the world, laid himself open to the greatest danger; for *me it hateth.* Christ was not only *slighted,* as inconsiderable in the world *(the world knew him not),* but *hated,* as if he had been hurtful to the world; thus ill was he requited for his love to the world: reigning sin is a rooted antipathy and enmity to Christ. But why did the world hate Christ? What evil had he done to it? Had he, like Alexander, under colour of conquering it, laid it waste? "No, but because" (saith he) "*I testify of it, that the works of it are evil.*" Note, *First,* The works of an evil world are *evil works;* as the tree is, so are the fruits: it is a dark world, and an apostate world, and its works are works of darkness and rebellion. *Secondly,* Our Lord Jesus, both by himself and by his ministers, did and will both discover and testify against the evil works of this wicked world. *Thirdly,* It is a great uneasiness and provocation to the world to be convicted of the evil of its works. It is for the honour of virtue and piety that those who are impious and vicious do not care for hearing of it, for their own consciences make them *ashamed* of the turpitude there is *in* sin and *afraid* of the punishment that follows *after* sin. *Fourthly,* Whatever is *pretended,* the *real* cause of the world's enmity to the gospel is the testimony it bears against sin and sinners. Christ's witnesses by their doctrine and conversation *torment* those that dwell on the earth, and therefore are treated so barbarously, Rev. xi. 10. But it is better to incur the world's hatred, by testifying against its wickedness, than gain its good-will by going down the stream with it.

(2.) He dismisses them, with a design to stay behind for some time in Galilee (*v.* 8): *Go you up to this feast, I go not up yet.* [1.] He allows their going to the feast, though they were carnal and hypocritical in it. Note, Even those who go not to holy ordinances with right affections and sincere intentions must not be hindered nor discouraged from going; who knows but they may be wrought upon there? [2.] He denies them his company when they went to the feast, because they were carnal and hypocritical. Those who go to ordinances for ostentation, or to serve some secular purpose, go without Christ, and will speed accordingly. How sad is the condition of that man, though he reckon himself akin to Christ, to whom he saith, "*Go up* to such an ordinance, Go pray, Go hear the word, Go receive the sacrament, but *I go not up* with thee? *Go thou* and appear before God, but I will not appear *for thee,*" as Exod. xxxiii. 1—3. But, if the presence of Christ go not with us, to what purpose should we go up? *Go you up, I go not up.* When we are going to, or coming from, solemn ordinances, it becomes us to be careful what company we *have* and *choose,* and to avoid that which is vain and carnal, lest the coal of good affections be quenched by corrupt communication. *I go not up yet to this feast;* he does not say, I will not go up at all, but not yet. There may be reasons for deferring a particular duty, which yet must not be wholly omitted or laid aside; see Num. ix. 6—11. The reason he gives is, *My time is not yet fully come.* Note, Our Lord Jesus is very exact and punctual in knowing and keeping his time, and, as it was the time *fixed,* so it was the *best* time.

3. Christ's continuance in Galilee till his *full time* was come, *v.* 9. He, saying these things to them (ταῦτα δὲ εἰπὼν), *abode still in Galilee;* because of this discourse he continued there; for, (1.) He would not be influenced by those who advised him to seek honour from men, nor go along with those who put him upon making a figure; he would not seem to countenance the temptation. (2.) He would not depart from his own purpose. He had said, upon a clear foresight and mature deliberation, that he would not go up yet to this feast, and therefore he abode still in Galilee. It becomes the followers of Christ thus to be *steady,* and not to *use lightness.*

4. His going up to the feast when his time was come. Observe, (1.) *When* he went: *When his brethren were gone up.* He would not go up *with them,* lest they should make a noise and disturbance, under pretence of *showing him to the world;* whereas it agreed both with the prediction and with his spirit not to *strive nor cry,* nor let his *voice be heard in the streets,* Isa. xlii. 2. But he went up *after them.* We may lawfully join in the same religious worship with those with whom we should yet decline an intimate acquaintance and converse; for the blessing of ordinances depends upon the grace of God, and not upon the grace of our fellow-worshippers. His carnal brethren went up *first,* and then

he went. Note, In the external performances of religion it is possible that formal hypocrites may *get the start* of those that are sincere. Many come *first to the temple* who are brought thither by vain-glory, and go thence unjustified, as he, Luke xviii. 11. It is not, Who comes *first?* that will be the question, but, Who comes *fittest?* If we bring our hearts *with us,* it is no matter who gets *before us.* (2.) *How* he went, ὡς ἐν κρυπτῷ—*as if he were hiding himself: not openly, but as it were in secret,* rather for fear of *giving offence* than of *receiving injury.* He went up to the feast, because it was an opportunity of honouring God and doing good; but he went up as it were in secret, because he would not provoke the government. Note, Provided the work of God be done effectually, it is best done when done with *least noise.* The kingdom of God need not come *with observation,* Luke xvii. 20. We may do the work of God *privately,* and yet not do it *deceitfully.*

5. The great expectation that there was of him among the Jews at Jerusalem, *v.* 11--14. Having formerly come up to the feasts, and signalized himself by the miracles he wrought, he had made himself the subject of much discourse and observation.

(1.) They could not but think of him (*v.* 11): *The Jews sought him at the feast, and said, Where is he?* [1.] The common people longed to see him there, that they might have their curiosity gratified with the sight of his person and miracles. They did not think it worth while to go to him into Galilee, though if they had they would not have lost their labour, but they hoped the feast would bring him to Jerusalem, and then they should see him. If an opportunity of acquaintance with Christ come to their door, they can like it well enough. They *sought him at the feast.* When we attend upon God in his holy ordinances, we should seek Christ in them, seek him at the gospel feasts. Those who would *see* Christ at a feast must *seek* him there. Or, [2.] Perhaps it was his enemies that were thus waiting an opportunity to seize him, and, if possible, to put an effectual stop to his progress. They said, *Where is he?* ποῦ ἔστιν ἐκεῖνος;—*where is that fellow?* Thus scornfully and contemptibly do they speak of him. Or it intimates how full their hearts were with thoughts of him, and their town with talk of him; they needed not name him. When they should have welcomed the feast as an opportunity of serving God, they were glad of it as an opportunity of persecuting Christ. Thus Saul hoped to slay David at the new moon, 1 Sam. xx. 27. Those who seek *opportunity to sin* in solemn assemblies for religious worship profane God's ordinances to the last degree, and defy him upon his own ground; it is like striking *within the verge of the court.*

(2.) The people differed much in their sentiments concerning him (*v.* 12): *There was much murmuring,* or *muttering* rather, *among the people concerning him.* The enmity of the rulers against Christ, and their enquiries after him, caused him to be so much the more talked of and observed among the people. This ground the gospel of Christ has got by the opposition made to it, that it has been the more enquired into, and, by being *every where spoken against,* it has come to be every where *spoken of,* and by this means has been spread the further, and the merits of his cause have been the more *searched into.* This murmuring was not *against* Christ, but *concerning* him; some murmured at the rulers, because they did not countenance and encourage him: others murmured at them, because they did not silence and restrain him. Some murmured that he had so great an interest in Galilee; others, that he had so little interest in Jerusalem. Note, Christ and his religion have been, and will be, the subject of much controversy and debate, Luke xii. 51, 52. If all would agree to entertain Christ as they ought, there would be perfect peace; but, when some receive the light and others resolve against it, there will be murmuring. The *bones in the valley,* while they were *dead* and *dry,* lay quiet; but when it was said unto them, *Live,* there was *a noise* and *a shaking,* Ezek. xxxvii. 7. But the noise and rencounter of liberty and business are preferable, surely, to the silence and agreement of a prison. Now what were the sentiments of the people concerning him? [1.] Some said, *He is a good man.* This was a truth, but it was far short of being the *whole truth.* He was not only a *good man,* but more than a man, he was the *Son of God.* Many who have no *ill* thoughts of Christ have yet *low* thoughts of him, and scarcely honour him, even when they speak well of him, because they do not *say enough;* yet indeed it was his honour, and the reproach of those who persecuted him, that even those who would not believe him to be the Messiah could not but own he was a *good man.* [2.] Others said, *Nay, but he deceiveth the people;* if this had been true, he had been a very bad man. The doctrine he preached was sound, and could not be contested; his miracles were real, and could not be disproved; his conversation was manifestly holy and good; and yet it must be taken for granted, notwithstanding, that there was some undiscovered cheat at the bottom, because it was the interest of the chief priests to oppose him and run him down. Such murmuring as there was among the Jews concerning Christ there is still among us: the Socinians say, *He is a good man,* and further they say not; the *deists* will not allow this, but say, *He deceived the people.* Thus some depreciate him, others abuse him, but *great is the truth.* [3.] They were frightened by their superiors from speaking much of him (*v.* 13): *No man spoke openly of him, for fear of the Jews.* Either, *First,* They durst not openly speak *well* of him. While any one was at liberty to censure and reproach him, none durst vindicate him. Or, *Secondly,* They durst not speak *at all* of him openly. Because nothing could justly be said *against* him, they would not suffer any thing to be said *of* him. It was a crime to name him. Thus many have aimed to suppress truth, under colour of silencing disputes about it, and would have all talk of religion hushed, in hopes thereby to bury in oblivion religion itself.

14 Now about the midst of the
feast Jesus went up into the temple,
and taught. 15 And the Jews marvelled, saying, How knoweth this
man letters, having never learned?
16 Jesus answered them, and said,
My doctrine is not mine, but his that
sent me. 17 If any man will do his
will, he shall know of the doctrine,
whether it be of God, or *whether* I
speak of myself. 18 He that speaketh of himself seeketh his own glory:
but he that seeketh his glory that
sent him, the same is true, and no
unrighteousness is in him. 19 Did
not Moses give you the law, and *yet*
none of you keepeth the law? Why
go ye about to kill me? 20 The
people answered and said, Thou hast
a devil: who goeth about to kill
thee? 21 Jesus answered and said
unto them, I have done one work,
and ye all marvel. 22 Moses therefore gave unto you circumcision
(not because it is of Moses, but of
the fathers); and ye on the sabbath
day circumcise a man. 23 If a man
on the sabbath day receive circumcision, that the law of Moses should
not be broken; are ye angry at me,
because I have made a man every
whit whole on the sabbath day? 24
Judge not according to the appearance, but judge righteous judgment.
25 Then said some of them of Jerusalem, Is not this he, whom they
seek to kill? 26 But, lo, he speaketh boldly, and they say nothing unto
him. Do the rulers know indeed
that this is the very Christ? 27
Howbeit we know this man whence
he is: but when Christ cometh, no
man knoweth whence he is. 28
Then cried Jesus in the temple as
he taught, saying, Ye both know
me, and ye know whence I am: and
I am not come of myself, but he that
sent me is true, whom ye know not.
29 But I know him: for I am from
him, and he hath sent me. 30 Then
they sought to take him: but no man
laid hands on him, because his hour
was not yet come. 31 And many
of the people believed on him, and
said, When Christ cometh, will he
do more miracles than these which
this *man* hath done? 32 The Pharisees heard that the people murmured such things concerning him;
and the Pharisees and the chief
priests sent officers to take him. 33
Then said Jesus unto them, Yet a
little while am I with you, and *then*
I go unto him that sent me. 34 Ye
shall seek me, and shall not find *me:*
and where I am, *thither* ye cannot
come. 35 Then said the Jews among
themselves, Whither will he go, that
we shall not find him? will he go
unto the dispersed among the Gentiles, and teach the Gentiles? 36
What *manner of* saying is this that
he said, Ye shall seek me, and shall
not find *me:* and where I am, *thither*
ye cannot come?

Here is, I. Christ's public preaching in the temple (*v.* 14): He *went up into the temple, and taught,* according to his custom when he was at Jerusalem. His business was to preach the gospel of the kingdom, and he did it in every place of concourse. His sermon is not recorded, because, probably, it was to the same purport with the sermons he had preached in Galilee, which were recorded by the other evangelists. For the gospel is the same to the *plain* and to the *polite.* But that which is observable here is that it was *about the midst of the feast;* the fourth or fifth day of the eight. Whether he did not come up to Jerusalem till the middle of the feast, or whether he came up at the beginning, but kept private till now, is not certain. But, *Query,* Why did he not go to the temple *sooner,* to preach? *Answer,* 1. Because the people would have more leisure to hear him, and, it might be hoped, would be better disposed to hear him, when they had spent some days in their booths, as they did at the feast of tabernacles. 2. Because he would choose to appear when both his friends and his enemies had done looking for him; and so give a specimen of the method he would observe in his appearances, which is to come at midnight, Matt. xxv. 6. But why did he appear thus publicly now? Surely it was to *shame* his persecutors, the chief priests and elders. (1.) By showing that, though they were very bitter against him, yet he did not fear them, nor their power. See Isa. l. 7, 8. (2.) By taking their work out of their hands. Their office was to teach the people in the temple, and particularly at the *feast of tabernacles,* Neh. viii. 17, 18. But they either did not teach them at all or taught for doctrines the commandments of men, and therefore he goes up to the temple and teaches the people. When the shepherds of Israel made a prey of the flock it was time for the chief Shepherd to appear, as was promised. Ezek. xxxiv. 22, 23; Mal. iii. 1.

II. His discourse with the Jews hereupon; and the conference is reducible to four heads:

1. Concerning *his doctrine.* See here,

(1.) How the Jews *admired* it (*v.* 15): *They marvelled,* saying, *How knoweth this man letters, having never learned?* Observe here, [1.] That our Lord Jesus was not educated in the schools of the prophets, or at the feet of the rabbin; not only did not travel for learning, as the philosophers did, but did not make any use of the schools and academies in his own country. Moses was taught the learning of the Egyptians, but Christ was not taught so much as the learning of the Jews; having received the Spirit *without measure,* he needed not receive any knowledge *from man, or by man.* At the time of Christ's appearing, learning flourished both in the Roman empire and in the Jewish church more than in any age before or since, and in such a time of enquiry Christ chose to establish his religion, not in an illiterate age, lest it should look like a design to impose upon the world; yet he himself studied not the learning then in vogue. [2.] That Christ *had letters,* though he had never *learned* them; was mighty in the scriptures, though he never had any doctor of the law for his tutor. It is necessary that Christ's ministers should have *learning,* as he had; and since they cannot expect to have it as he had it, by inspiration, they must take pains to get it in an ordinary way. [3.] That Christ's having learning, though he had not been taught it, made him truly great and wonderful; the Jews speak of it here with wonder. *First,* Some, it is likely, took notice of it to his honour: He that had no human learning, and yet so far excelled all that had, certainly must be endued with a divine knowledge. *Secondly,* Others, probably, mentioned it in disparagement and contempt of him: Whatever he *seems* to have, he cannot really have any true learning, for he was never at the university, nor took his degree. *Thirdly,* Some perhaps suggested that he had got his learning by magic arts, or some unlawful means or other. Since they know not how he could be a scholar, they will think him a conjuror.

(2.) What he *asserted* concerning it; three things:—

[1.] That his *doctrine* is *divine* (*v.* 16): *My doctrine is not mine, but his that sent me.* They were offended because he undertook to *teach* though he had never learned, in answer to which he tells them that his doctrine was such as was not to be *learned,* for it was not the product of *human thought* and natural powers enlarged and elevated by reading and conversation, but it was a *divine revelation.* As God, equal with the Father, he might truly have said, *My doctrine is mine, and his that sent me;* but being now in his estate of humiliation, and being, as Mediator, God's servant, it was more congruous to say, "*My doctrine is not mine,* not mine only, nor mine originally, as man and mediator, but *his that sent me;* it does not centre in myself, nor lead ultimately to myself, but to him that sent me." God had promised concerning the great prophet that he would *put his words into his mouth* (Deut. xviii. 18), to which Christ seems here to refer. Note, It is the comfort of those who embrace Christ's doctrine, and the condemnation of those who reject it, that it is a divine doctrine: it is *of God and not of man.*

[2.] That the most competent judges of the truth and divine authority of Christ's doctrine are those that with a sincere and upright heart desire and endeavour to do the will of God (*v.* 17): *If any man be willing to do the will of God,* have his will melted into the *will of God, he shall know of the doctrine whether it be of God or whether I speak of myself.* Observe here, *First,* What the question is, concerning the doctrine of Christ, *whether it be of God* or no; whether the gospel be a divine revelation or an imposture. Christ himself was willing to have his doctrine enquired into, whether it were of God or no, much more should his ministers; and we are concerned to examine what grounds we go upon, for, if we be deceived, we are miserably deceived. *Secondly,* Who are likely to succeed in this search: those that *do the will of God,* at least are desirous to do it. Now see, 1. Who they are that *will do the will of God.* They are such as are *impartial* in their enquiries concerning the will of God, and are not biassed by any lust or interest, and such as are resolved by the grace of God, when they find out what the will of God is, to conform to it. They are such as have an honest principle of regard to God, and are truly desirous to glorify and please him. 2. Whence it is that such a one shall know of the truth of Christ's doctrine. (1.) Christ has promised to *give knowledge* to such; he hath said, *He shall know,* and he can give an understanding. Those who improve the light they have, and carefully live up to it, shall be secured by divine grace from destructive mistakes. (2.) They are disposed and prepared to *receive* that knowledge. He that is inclined to submit to the rules of the divine law is disposed to admit the rays of divine light. *To him that has* shall be given; those have a *good understanding* that *do his* commandments, Ps. cxi. 10. Those who *resemble* God are most likely to *understand* him.

[3.] That hereby it appeared that Christ, as a teacher, did not speak *of himself*, because he did not seek himself, *v.* 18. *First*, See here the character of a deceiver: he *seeketh his own glory*, which is a sign that he *speaks of himself*, as the false Christs and false prophets did. Here is the description of the *cheat:* they *speak of themselves*, and have no commission nor instructions from God; no warrant but their own will, no inspiration but their own imagination, their own policy and artifice. Ambassadors *speak not of themselves;* those ministers disclaim that character who glory in this that they *speak of themselves*. But see the discovery of the cheat; by this their pretensions are disproved, they consult purely *their own glory;* self-seekers are self-speakers. Those who speak *from God* will speak *for God*, and for his glory; those who aim at their own preferment and interest make it to appear that they had no commission from God. *Secondly*, See the contrary character Christ gives of himself and his doctrine: *He that seeks his glory that sent him*, as I do, makes it to appear that *he is true*. 1. He was *sent of God*. Those teachers, and those only, who are sent of God, are to be received and entertained by us. Those who bring a divine message must prove a divine mission, either by special revelation or by regular institution. 2. He *sought the glory of God*. It was both the tendency of his doctrine and the tenour of his whole conversation to *glorify God*. 3. This was a proof that he was *true*, and there was *no unrighteousness in him*. False teachers are most *unrighteous;* they are unjust to God whose name they abuse, and unjust to the souls of men whom they impose upon. There cannot be a greater piece of unrighteousness than this. But Christ made it appear that he was *true*, that he was really what he said he was, that there was *no unrighteousness* in him, no falsehood in his doctrine, no fallacy nor fraud in his dealings with us.

2. They discourse concerning the *crime* that was laid to his charge for curing the impotent man, and bidding him carry his bed on the sabbath day, for which they had formerly prosecuted him, and which was still the pretence of their enmity to him.

(1.) He argues against them by way of *recrimination*, convicting them of far worse practices, *v.* 19. How could they for shame censure him for a breach of the law of Moses, when they themselves were such notorious breakers of it? *Did not Moses give you the law?* And it was their privilege that they had the law, no nation had such a law; but it was their wickedness that *none of them kept the law*, that they rebelled against it, and lived contrary to it. Many that have the law given them, when they have it do not keep it. Their neglect of the law was universal: *None of you keepeth* it: neither those of them that were in *posts of honour*, who should have been most *knowing*, nor those who were in *posts of subjection*, who should have been most *obedient*. They boasted of the law, and pretended a zeal for it, and were enraged at Christ for seeming to transgress it, and yet none of them kept it; like those who say that they are for the church, and yet never go to church. It was an aggravation of their wickedness, in persecuting Christ for breaking the law, that they themselves did not keep it: "*None of you keepeth the law*, why then go ye about to kill me for not keeping it?" Note, Those are commonly most censorious of others who are most faulty themselves. Thus hypocrites, who are forward to pull a mote out of their brother's eye, are not aware of a beam in their own. *Why go ye about to kill me?* Some take this as the evidence of their not keeping the law: "*You keep not the law;* if you did, you would understand yourselves better than to go about to kill me for doing a good work." Those that support themselves and their interest by persecution and violence, whatever they pretend (though they may call themselves *custodes utriusque tabulæ—the guardians of both tables)*, are not keepers of the law of God. Chemnitius understands this as a reason why it was time to supersede the law of Moses by the gospel, because the law was found insufficient to *restrain sin:* "Moses gave you the law, but you do not keep it, nor are kept by it from the greatest wickedness; there is therefore need of a clearer light and better law to be brought in; why then do you aim to kill me for introducing it?"

Here the *people* rudely interrupted him in his discourse, and contradicted what he said (*v.* 20): *Thou hast a devil; who goes about to kill thee?* This intimates, [1.] The *good opinion* they had of their rulers, who, they think, would never attempt so atrocious a thing as to kill him; no, such a veneration they had for their elders and chief priests that they would swear for them they would do no harm to an innocent man. Probably the rulers had their little emissaries among the people who suggested this to them; many deny that wickedness which at the same time they are contriving. [2.] The *ill opinion* they had of our Lord Jesus: "*Thou hast a devil*, thou art possessed with a lying spirit, and art a *bad man* for saying so; so some: or rather, "Thou art melancholy, and art a *weak man;* thou frightenest thyself with causeless fears, as hypochondriacal people are apt to do." Not only open frenzies, but silent melancholies, were then commonly imputed to the power of Satan. "Thou art crazed, hast a distempered brain." Let us not think it strange if the best of men are put under the worst of characters. To this vile calumny our Saviour returns no direct answer, but seems as if he took no notice of it. Note, Those who would be like Christ must put up with affronts, and pass by the indignities and injuries done them; must not *regard* them, much less *resent* them, and least of all *revenge* them. *I, as a deaf man, heard not.* When Christ was *reviled,* he *reviled not again.*

(2.) He argues by way of appeal and vindication.

[1.] He appeals to *their own sentiments* of this miracle: "*I have done one work, and you all marvel, v.* 21. You cannot choose but marvel at it as truly great, and altogether supernatural; you must all own it to be marvellous." Or, "Though I have done but *one work* that you have any colour to find fault with, yet you marvel, you are offended and displeased as if I had been guilty of some heinous or enormous crime."

[2.] He appeals to their own practice in other instances: "*I have done one work* on the sabbath, and it was done easily, with a word's speaking, and you all marvel, you make a mighty strange thing of it, that a religious man should dare do such a thing, whereas you yourselves *many a time* do that which is a much more servile work on the sabbath day, in the case of circumcision; if it be lawful for you, nay, and your duty, to circumcise a child on the sabbath day, when it happens to be the eighth day, as no doubt it is, much more was it lawful and good for me to heal a diseased man on that day." Observe,

First, The rise and origin of circumcision: *Moses gave you circumcision,* gave you the law concerning it. Here, 1. Circumcision is said to *be given,* and (*v.* 23) they are said to *receive* it; it was not imposed upon them as a yoke, but conferred upon them as a favour. Note, The ordinances of God, and particularly those which are seals of the covenant, are *gifts given to men,* and are to be received as such. 2. Moses is said to give it, because it was a part of that law which was *given by Moses;* yet, as Christ said of the manna (*ch.* vi. 32), Moses did not give it them, but God; nay, and it was not of Moses first, but *of the fathers, v.* 22. Though it was incorporated into the Mosaic institution, yet it was ordained long before, for it was a seal of the righteousness of faith, and therefore commenced with the promise four hundred and thirty years before, Gal. iii. 17. The church-membership of believers and their seed was not of Moses or his law, and therefore did not fall with it; but was *of the fathers,* belonged to the patriarchal church, and was part of that blessing of Abraham which was to come upon the Gentiles, Gal. iii. 14.

Secondly, The respect paid to the law of circumcision above that of the sabbath, in the constant practice of the Jewish church. The Jewish casuists frequently take notice of it, *Circumcisio et ejus sanatio pellit sabbatum —Circumcision and its cure drive away the sabbath;* so that if a child was born one sabbath day it was without fail circumcised the next. If then, when the *sabbath rest* was more strictly insisted on, yet those works were allowed which were *in ordine ad spiritualia—for the keeping up of religion,* much more are they allowed now under the gospel, when the stress is laid more upon the *sabbath work.*

Thirdly, The inference Christ draws hence in justification of himself, and of what he had done (*v.* 23): *A man-child on the sabbath day receives circumcision, that the law of circumcision might not be broken;* or, as the margin reads it, *without breaking the law,* namely, of the sabbath. Divine commands must be construed so as to agree with each other. "Now, if this be allowed by yourselves, how unreasonable are you, who are *angry with me because I have made a man every whit whole on the sabbath day!*" ἐμοὶ χολᾶτε. The word is used only here, from χὸγη *—fel, gall.* They were angry at him with the greatest indignation; it was a spiteful anger, anger with gall in it. Note, It is very absurd and unreasonable for us to condemn others for that in which we justify ourselves. Observe the comparison Christ here makes between their *circumcising a child* and his *healing a man* on the sabbath day. 1. Circumcision was but a ceremonial institution; it was *of the fathers* indeed, but not from the beginning; but what Christ did was a good work by the law of nature, a more excellent law than that which made circumcision a good work. 2. Circumcision was a *bloody* ordinance, and *made sore;* but what Christ did was healing, and made whole. The law works pain, and, if that work may be done on the sabbath day, much more a gospel work, which produces peace. 3. Especially considering that whereas, when they had circumcised a child, their care was only to heal up that part which was circumcised, which might be done and yet the child remain under other illnesses, Christ had made this man *every whit whole,* ολον ανθρωπον υγιῆ*—I have made the whole man healthful* and sound. The *whole body* was *healed,* for the disease affected the whole body; and it was a perfect cure, such as left no relics of the disease behind; nay, Christ not only healed his body, but his soul too, by that admonition, *Go, and sin no more,* and so indeed made the *whole man* sound, for the soul is the man. Circumcision indeed was intended for the good of the soul, and to make the *whole man* as it should be; but they had perverted it, and turned it into a mere carnal ordinance; but Christ accompanied his outward cures with inward grace, and so made them sacramental, and healed the *whole man.*

He concludes this argument with that rule (*v.* 24): *Judge not according to the appearance, but judge righteous judgment.* This may be applied, either, *First,* In particular, to this work which they quarrelled with as a violation of the law. Be not partial in your judgment; judge not, *κατ' ὄψιν—with respect of persons;* knowing faces, as the Hebrew phrase is, Deut. i. 17. It is contrary to the law of justice, as well as charity, to censure those who differ in opinion from us as transgressors, in taking that liberty which yet in those of our own party, and way, and opinion, we allow of; as it is also to commend that in some as necessary strictness and severity which in others we condemn as imposition and persecution. Or, *Secondly*, In general, to Christ's person and preaching, which they were offended at and prejudiced against. Those things that are false, and designed to impose upon men, commonly appear best when they are judged of *according to the outward appearance*, they appear most plausible *prima facie —at the first glance.* It was this that gained the Pharisees such an interest and reputation, that they *appeared right* unto men (Matt. xxiii. 27, 28), and men judged of them by that appearance, and so were sadly mistaken in them. "But," saith Christ, "be not too confident that all are real saints who are seeming ones." With reference to himself, his *outward appearance* was far short of his real dignity and excellency, for he took upon him the *form of a servant* (Phil. ii. 7), was in the *likeness of sinful flesh* (Rom. viii. 3), had *no form nor comeliness*, Isa. liii. 2. So that those who undertook to judge whether he was the Son of God or no by his *outward appearance* were not likely to *judge righteous judgment.* The Jews expected the outward appearance of the Messiah to be pompous and magnificent, and attended with all the ceremonies of secular grandeur; and, judging of Christ by that rule, their judgment was from first to last a *continual* mistake, for the kingdom of Christ was not to be *of this world*, nor to *come with observation.* If a divine power accompanied him, and God bore him witness, and the scriptures were fulfilled in him, though his appearance was ever so mean, they ought to receive him, and to judge by faith, and not by the sight of the eye. See Isa. xi. 3, and 1 Sam. xvi. 7. Christ and his doctrine and doings desire nothing but *righteous judgment;* if truth and justice may but pass the sentence, Christ and his cause will carry the day. We must not judge concerning any by their *outward appearance*, not by their titles, the figure they make in the world, and their fluttering show, but by their intrinsic worth, and the gifts and graces of God's Spirit in them.

3. Christ discourses with them here concerning *himself*, whence he came, and whither he was going, *v.* 25—36.

(1.) *Whence he came, v.* 25—31. In the account of this observe,

[1.] The objection concerning this stated by some of the inhabitants of Jerusalem, who seem to have been of all others most prejudiced against him, *v.* 25. One would think that those who lived at the fountain-head of knowledge and religion should have been most ready to receive the Messiah: but it proved quite contrary. Those that have plenty of the means of knowledge and grace, if they are not *made better* by them, are commonly *made worse;* and our Lord Jesus has often met with the least welcome from those that one would expect the best from. But it was not without some just cause that it came into a proverb, *The nearer the church the further from God.* These people of Jerusalem showed their ill-will to Christ,

First, By their reflecting on the rulers, because they let him alone: *Is not this he whom they seek to kill?* The multitude of the people that came up out of the country to the feast did not suspect there was any design on foot against him, and therefore they said, *Who goes about to kill thee? v.* 20. But those of Jerusalem knew the plot, and irritated their rulers to put it into execution: "*Is not this he whom they seek to kill?* Why do they not do it then? Who hinders them? They say that they have a mind to get him out of the way, and yet, lo, *he speaketh boldly*, and *they say nothing to him;* do *the rulers know indeed that this is the very Christ?*" *v.* 26. Here they slily and maliciously insinuate two things, to exasperate the rulers against Christ, when indeed they needed no spur. 1. That by conniving at his preaching they *brought their authority into contempt.* "Must a man that is condemned by the *sanhedrim* as a deceiver be permitted to *speak boldly*, without any check or contradiction? This makes their sentence to be but *brutem fulmen —a vain menace;* if our rulers will suffer themselves to be thus trampled upon, they may thank themselves if none stand in awe of them and their laws." Note, The worst of persecutions have often been carried on under colour of the necessary support of authority and government. 2. That hereby they brought *their judgment* into *suspicion: Do they know that this is the Christ?* It is spoken ironically. "How came they to change their mind? What new discovery have they lighted on? They give people occasion to think that they believe him to be the Christ, and it behoves them to act vigorously against him to clear themselves from the suspicion." Thus the rulers, who had made the people enemies to Christ, made them *seven times more the children of hell than themselves*, Matt. xxiii. 15. When religion and the profession of Christ's name are *out of fashion*, and consequently *out of repute*, many are strongly tempted to persecute and oppose them, only that they may not be thought to favour them and incline to them. And for this reason apostates, and the degenerate offspring of good parents, have been sometimes worse than others, as it were to wipe off the stain of their profession. It was strange that the rulers, thus irritated, did not seize Christ; but his hour was not yet come; and God can tie men's hands to admiration, though he should not turn their hearts.

Secondly, By their exception against his being the Christ, in which appeared more malice than matter, *v.* 27. "If the rulers think him to be the Christ, we neither can nor will believe him to be so, for we have this argument against it, that *we know this man, whence he is; but when Christ comes no man knows whence he is.*" Here is a fallacy in the argument, for the propositions are not both *ad idem—adapted to the same view of the subject.* 1. If they speak of his *divine nature,* it is true that when Christ comes *no man knows whence he is,* for he is a priest after the order of Melchizedek, who was *without descent,* and *his goings forth have been from of old, from everlasting,* Mic. v. 2. But then it is not true that as for this man they knew whence he was, for they knew not his divine nature, nor how *the Word* was *made flesh.* 2. If they speak of his *human nature,* it is true that they knew whence he was, who was his mother, and where he was bred up; but then it is false that ever it was said of the Messiah that none should know whence he was, for it was known before *where he should be born,* Matt. ii. 4, 5. Observe, (1.) How they *despised him,* because they knew *whence he was.* Familiarity breeds contempt, and we are apt to disdain the *use* of those whom we know the *rise of.* Christ's own received him not, because he was *their own,* for which very reason they should the rather have loved him, and been thankful that their nation and their age were honoured with his appearance. (2.) How they endeavoured unjustly to fasten the ground of their prejudice upon the scriptures, as if they countenanced them, when there was no such thing. *Therefore* people err concerning Christ, because they *know not the scripture.*

[2.] Christ's answer to this objection, *v.* 28, 29.

First, He spoke freely and boldly, he *cried in the temple, as he taught,* he spoke this louder than the rest of his discourse, 1. To express his earnestness, being *grieved for the hardness of their hearts.* There may be a vehemency in contending for the truth where yet there is no intemperate heat nor passion. We may instruct gainsayers with warmth, and yet with *meekness.* 2. The priests and those that were prejudiced against him, did not come near enough to hear his preaching, and therefore he must speak louder than ordinary what he will have them to hear. Whoever has ears to hear, let him hear this.

Secondly, His answer to their cavil is, 1. By way of *concession,* granting that they did or might know his origin as to the flesh: "*You both know me, and you know whence I am.* You know I am of your own nation, and one of yourselves." It is no disparagement to the doctrine of Christ that there is that in it which is level to the capacities of the meanest, plain truths, discovered even by nature's light, of which we may say, We know whence they are. "*You know me,* you think you know me; but you are mistaken; you take me to be the carpenter's son, and born at Nazareth, but it is not so." 2. By way of *negation,* denying that that which they did see in him, and know of him, was all that was to be known; and therefore, if they looked no further, they judged by the outward appearance only. They knew *whence* he came perhaps, and *where* he had his birth, but he will tell them what they knew not, *from whom* he came. (1.) That he did not *come of himself;* that he did not run without sending, nor come as a private person, but with a public character. (2.) That he was sent of his Father; this is twice mentioned: *He hath sent me.* And again, "*He hath sent me,* to say what I say, and do what I do." This he was himself well assured of, and therefore knew that his Father would bear him out; and it is well for us that we are assured of it too, that we may with holy confidence go to God by him. (3.) That he was *from his Father,* παρ αὐτοῦ εἰμι—*I am from him;* not only sent from him as a servant from his master, but from him by eternal generation, as a son from his father, by essential emanation, as the beams from the sun. (4.) *That the Father who sent him is true;* he had promised to give the Messiah, and, though the Jews had forfeited the promise, yet he that made the promise is *true,* and has performed it. He had promised that the Messiah should see his seed, and be successful in his undertaking; and, though the generality of the Jews reject him and his gospel, yet he *is true,* and will fulfil the promise in the calling of the Gentiles. (5.) That these unbelieving Jews did *not know the Father: He that sent me, whom you know not.* There is much ignorance of God even with many that have a *form of knowledge;* and the true reason why people reject Christ is because they do not *know God;* for there is such a harmony of the divine attributes in the work of redemption, and such an admirable agreement between natural and revealed religion, that the right knowledge of the former would not only admit, but introduce, the latter. (6.) Our Lord Jesus was intimately acquainted with the Father that *sent him: but I know him.* He knew him so well that he was not at all *in doubt* concerning his mission from him, but perfectly *assured* of it; nor at all *in the dark* concerning the work he had to do, but perfectly *apprized* of it, Matt. xi. 27.

[3.] The provocation which this gave to his enemies, who hated him because he *told them the truth, v.* 30. *They sought therefore to take him,* to lay violent hands on him, not only to do him a mischief, but some way or other to be the death of him; but by the restraint of an invisible power it was prevented; nobody touched him, *because his hour was not yet come;* this was not their reason why they did it not, but God's reason why he hindered them from doing it. Note, *First,* The faithful preachers of the truths of God, though they behave themselves with ever so much prudence and meekness, must expect to be hated and persecuted by those who think themselves tormented by their testimony, Rev. xi. 10. *Secondly,* God has wicked men in a chain, and, whatever mischief they *would do,* they *can do* no more than God will suffer them to do. The malice of persecutors is *impotent* even when it is most *impetuous,* and, when Satan *fills their hearts,* yet God *ties their hands. Thirdly,* God's servants are sometimes wonderfully protected by indiscernible unaccountable means. Their enemies do not do the mischief they designed, and yet neither they themselves nor any one else can tell why they do not. *Fourthly,* Christ had *his hour* set, which was to put a period to his day and work on earth; so have all his people and all his ministers, and, till that hour comes, the attempts of their enemies against them are ineffectual, and their day shall be lengthened as long as their Master has any work for them to do; nor can all the powers of hell and earth prevail against them, until they have *finished their testimony.*

[4.] The good effect which Christ's discourse had, notwithstanding this, upon some of his hearers (*v.* 31): *Many of the people believed on him.* As he was set for the fall of some, so for the rising again of others. Even where the gospel meets with opposition there may yet be a great deal of good done, 1 Thess. ii. 2. Observe here, *First, Who* they were that believed; not a few, but many, more than one would have expected when the stream ran so strongly the other way. But these *many* were *of the people,* ἐκ τοῦ ὄχλου—*of the multitude,* the crowd, the inferior sort, the mob, the rabble, some would have called them. We must not measure the prosperity of the gospel by its success among the great ones; nor must ministers say that they labour in vain, though none but the *poor,* and those of no *figure,* receive the gospel, 1 Cor. i. 26. *Secondly,* What *induced* them to believe: the *miracles which he did,* which were not only the accomplishment of the Old-Testament prophecies (Isa. xxxv. 5, 6), but an argument of a divine power. He that had an ability to do that which none but God *can do,* to control and overrule the powers of nature, no doubt had authority to enact that which none but God can *enact,* a law that shall *bind conscience,* and a covenant that shall *give life. Thirdly,* How *weak* their faith was: they do not positively assert, as the Samaritans did, *This is indeed the Christ,* but they only argue, *When Christ comes will he do more miracles than these?* They take it for granted that Christ will come, and, when he comes, will do many miracles. "Is not this he then? In him we see, though not all the worldly pomp we have fancied, yet all the divine power we have *believed* the Messiah should appear in; and therefore why may not this be he?" They *believe* it, but have not courage to own it. Note, Even weak faith may be true faith, and so *accounted,* so *accepted,* by the Lord Jesus, who *despises not the day of small things.*

(2.) *Whither he was going, v.* 32—36. Here observe,

[1.] The design of the Pharisees and chief priests against him, *v.* 32. *First,* The provocation given them was that they had information brought them by their spies, who insinuated themselves into the conversation of the people, and gathered stories to carry to their jealous masters, that *the people murmured such things concerning him,* that there were many who had a respect and value for him, notwithstanding all they had done to render him odious. Though the people did but whisper these things, and had not courage to speak out, yet the Pharisees were enraged at it. The equity of that government is justly *suspected* by others which is so *suspicious* of itself as to take notice of, or be influenced by, the secret, various, uncertain *mutterings* of the common people. The Pharisees valued themselves very much upon the respect of the people, and were sensible that if Christ did thus *increase* they must *decrease. Secondly,* The project they laid hereupon was to seize Jesus, and take him into custody: *They sent officers to take him,* not to take up those who murmured concerning him and frighten them; no, the most effectual way to disperse the flock is to *smite the shepherd.* The Pharisees seem to have been the ringleaders in this prosecution, but they, *as such,* had no power, and therefore they got the *chief priests,* the judges of the ecclesiastical court, to join with them, who were ready enough to do so. The Pharisees were the great pretenders to *learning,* and the *chief priests* to *sanctity.* As *the world by wisdom knew not God,* but the greatest philosophers were guilty of the greatest blunders in natural religion, so the Jewish church by their wisdom knew not Christ, but their greatest rabbin were the greatest fools concerning him, nay, they were the most inveterate enemies to him. Those wicked rulers had their officers, officers of their court, church-officers, whom they employed to take Christ, and who were ready to go on their errand, though it was an ill errand. If Saul's footmen will not *turn and fall upon the priests of the Lord,* he has a herdsman that will, 1 Sam xxii. 17, 18.

[2.] The discourse of our Lord Jesus hereupon (*v.* 33, 34): *Yet a little while I am with you, and then I go to him that sent me; you shall seek me, and shall not find me; and where I am, thither you cannot come.* These words, like the pillar of cloud and fire, have a *bright* side and a *dark* side.

First, They have a *bright side* towards

our Lord Jesus himself, and speak abundance of comfort to him and all his faithful followers that are exposed to difficulties and dangers for his sake. Three things Christ here comforted himself with :—1. That he had but *a little time* to continue here in this troublesome world. He sees that he is never likely to have a quiet day among them; but the best of it is his warfare will shortly be accomplished, and then he shall be *no more in this world ch.* xvii. 11. Whomsoever we are *with* in this world, friends or foes, it is but a *little while* that we shall be with them; and it is a matter of comfort to those who are *in* the world, but not *of* it, and therefore are hated by it and sick of it, that they shall not be *in it always*, they shall not be *in it long*. We must be *awhile* with those that are pricking briars and grieving thorns ; but thanks be to God, it is but a little while, and we shall be out of their reach. Our days being *evil*, it is well they are *few*. 2. That, when he should quit this troublesome world, he should *go to him that sent him ; I go*. Not, " I am driven away by force," but, " I voluntarily *go ;* having finished my embassy, I return to him on whose errand I came. When I have done my work with you, then, and not till then, I go to him *that sent me*, and will *receive me*, will prefer me, as ambassadors are preferred when they return." Their rage against him would not only not hinder him from, but would hasten him to the glory and joy that were set before him. Let those who suffer for Christ comfort themselves with this, that they have a God to go to, and are going to him, going apace, to be for ever with him. 3. That, though they persecuted him here, wherever he went, yet none of their persecutions could follow him to heaven: *You shall seek me, and shall not find me*. It appears, by their enmity to his followers when he was gone, that if they could have reached him they would have persecuted him: " But you cannot enter into that temple as you do into this." *Where I am*, that is, where I then *shall be ;* but he expresses it thus because, even when he was on earth, by his divine nature and divine affections he was in heaven, *ch.* iii. 13. Or it denotes that he should be *so soon* there that he was as good as there already. Note, It adds to the happiness of glorified saints that they are out of the reach of the devil and all his wicked instruments.

Secondly, These words have a *black and dark side* towards those wicked Jews that hated and persecuted Christ. They now longed to be rid of him, *Away with him from the earth ;* but let them know, 1. That according to their choice so shall their doom be. They were industrious to *drive him* from them, and their sin shall be their punishment; he will not trouble them long, yet a little while and he will *depart* from them. It is just with God to forsake those that think his presence a burden. They that are weary of Christ need no more to make them miserable than to have *their wish*. 2. That they would certainly repent their choice when it was too late. (1.) They should in vain seek the presence of the Messiah: " *You shall seek me, and shall not find me*. You shall expect the *Christ to come*, but your eyes shall fail with looking for him, and you shall never find him." Those who rejected the true Messiah when he did come were justly abandoned to a miserable and endless expectation of one that should never come. Or, it may refer to the final rejection of sinners from the favours and grace of Christ at the great day: those who now seek Christ shall find him, but the day is coming when those who now refuse him *shall seek him, and shall not find him*. See Prov. i. 28. They will in vain cry, *Lord, Lord, open to us*. Or, perhaps, these words might be fulfilled in the despair of some of the Jews, who possibly might be convinced and not converted, who would wish in vain to see Christ, and to hear him preach again; but the day of grace is over (Luke xvii. 22); yet this is not all. (2.) They should in vain expect a place in heaven: *Where I am*, and where all believers shall be with me, *thither ye cannot come*. Not only because they are *excluded* by the just and irreversible sentence of the judge, and the sword of the angel at every gate of the new Jerusalem, to keep *the way of the tree of life* against those who have *no right to enter*, but because they are disabled by their own iniquity and infidelity: *You cannot come*, because you *will not*. Those who hate to be where Christ is, in his word and ordinances on earth, are very unfit to be where he is in his glory in heaven; for indeed heaven would be no heaven to them, such are the antipathies of an unsanctified soul to the felicities of that state.

[3.] Their descant upon this discourse (*v.* 35, 36): *They said among themselves, Whither will he go?* See here, *First*, Their wilful ignorance and blindness. He had expressly said whither he would go—to him that sent him, to his Father in heaven, and yet they ask, *Whither will he go?* and, *What manner of saying is this?* None so blind as those that will not see, that will not heed. Christ's sayings are *plain to him that understandeth*, and difficult only to those that are disposed to quarrel. *Secondly*, Their daring contempt of Christ's threatenings. Instead of trembling at that terrible word, *You shall seek me, and not find me*, which denotes the utmost degree of misery, they banter it and make a jest of it, as those sinners that *mock at fear, and are not affrighted* Isa. v. 19; Amos v. 18. *Let him make speed. But be ye not mockers, lest your bands be made strong*. *Thirdly*, Their inveterate malice and rage against Christ. All they dreaded in his *departure* was that he would be out of the reach of their power: " *Whither will he go, that we shall not find him?* If he be above ground, we will have him; we will leave no place unsearched," as Ahab in quest of Elijah, 1 Kings xviii. 10. *Fourthly,* Their proud disdain of the Gentiles, whom they here call the *dispersed of the Gentiles;* meaning either the Jews that were *scattered* abroad among the Greeks (James i. 1; 1 Pet. i. 1); will he go and make an interest among those silly people? or, the Gentiles *dispersed* over the world, in distinction from the Jews, who were *incorporated* into one church and nation; will he make his court to them? *Fifthly,* Their jealousy of the least intimation of favour to the Gentiles: "Will he go and *teach the Gentiles?* Will he carry his doctrine to them?" Perhaps they had heard of some items of respect shown by him to the Gentiles, as in his sermon at Nazareth, and in the case of the centurion and the woman of Canaan, and there was nothing they dreaded more than the *comprehension* of the Gentiles. So common is it for those who have lost the power of religion to be very jealous for the monopoly of the name. They now made a *jest* of his going *to teach the Gentiles;* but not long after he did it *in good earnest* by his apostles and ministers, and gathered those *dispersed* people, sorely to the grief of the Jews, Rom. x. 19. So true is that of Solomon, *The fear of the wicked, it shall come upon him.*

37 In the last day, that great *day* of
the feast, Jesus stood and cried, saying, If any man thirst, let him come
unto me, and drink. 38 He that
believeth on me, as the scripture
hath said, out of his belly shall flow
rivers of living water. 39 (But this
spake he of the Spirit, which they
that believe on him should receive:
for the Holy Ghost was not yet
given; because that Jesus was not
yet glorified.) 40 Many of the people
therefore, when they heard this saying, said, Of a truth this is the prophet. 41 Others said, This is the
Christ. But some said, Shall Christ
come out of Galilee? 42 Hath not
the scripture said, That Christ cometh of the seed of David, and out of
the town of Bethlehem, where David
was? 43 So there was a division
among the people because of him.
44 And some of them would have
taken him; but no man laid hands
on him.

In these verses we have,

I. Christ's discourse, with the explication of it, *v.* 37—39. It is probable that these are only short hints of what he enlarged upon, but they have in them the substance of the whole gospel; here is a *gospel invitation* to *come to Christ,* and a *gospel promise* of comfort and happiness in him. Now observe,

1. *When* he gave this invitation: *On the last day* of the feast of tabernacles, *that great day.* The *eighth day,* which concluded that solemnity, was to be a *holy convocation,* Lev. xxiii. 36. Now on this day Christ published this gospel-call, because, (1.) Much people were gathered together, and, if the invitation were given to *many,* it might be hoped that *some* would accept of it, Prov. i. 20. Numerous assemblies give opportunity of doing the more good. (2.) The people were now returning to their homes, and he would give them this to carry away with them as his parting word. When a great congregation is to be dismissed, and is about to scatter, as here, it is affecting to think that in all probability they will never come all together again in this world, and therefore, if we can say or do any thing to help them to heaven, that must be the time. It is good to be lively at the close of an ordinance. Christ made this offer *on the last day of the feast,* [1.] To those who had turned a deaf ear to his preaching on the foregoing days of this sacred week; he will try them once more, and, if they will yet hear his voice, they shall live. [2.] To those who perhaps might never have such another offer made them, and therefore were concerned to accept of this; it would be half a year before there would be another feast, and in that time they would many of them be in their graves. *Behold now is the accepted time.*

2. *How* he gave this invitation: *Jesus stood and cried,* which denotes, (1.) His great earnestness and importunity. His heart was upon it, to bring poor souls in to himself. The erection of his body and the elevation of his voice were indications of the intenseness of his mind. Love to souls will make preachers lively. (2.) His desire that all might take notice, and take hold of this invitation. He *stood, and cried,* that he might the better be heard; for this is what every one that hath ears is concerned to hear. Gospel truth seeks no corners, because it fears no trials. The heathen oracles were delivered privately by them that *peeped and muttered;* but the oracles of the gospel were proclaimed by one that *stood, and cried.* How sad is the case of man, that he must be *importuned* to be happy, and how wonderful the grace of Christ, that he will *importune* him! *Ho, every one,* Isa. lv. 1.

3. The invitation itself is very general: *If any man* thirst, whoever he be, he is invited to Christ be he high or low, rich or poor, young or old, bond or free, Jew or Gentile. It is also very *gracious:* "*If any man thirst, let him come to me and drink.* If any man desires to be truly and eternally happy, let him apply himself to me, and be ruled by me, and I will undertake to make him so."

(1.) The persons invited are such as *thirst,* which may be understood, either, [1.] Of the *indigence* of their cases; either as to their *outward* condition (if any man be destitute of the comforts of this life, or fatigued with the crosses of it, let his poverty and afflictions draw him to Christ for that peace which the world can neither give nor take away), or as to their *inward* state: "If any man want spiritual blessings, he may be supplied by me." Or, [2.] Of the *inclination* of their souls and their desires towards a spiritual happiness. If any man hunger and thirst after righteousness, that is, truly desire the good will of God towards him, and the good work of God in him.

(2.) The invitation itself: *Let him come to me.* Let him not go to the ceremonial law, which would neither *pacify* the conscience nor *purify it,* and therefore could not make the *comers thereunto perfect,* Heb. x. 1. Nor let him go to the heathen philosophy, which does but beguile men, lead them into a wood, and leave them there; but let him *go to Christ,* admit his doctrine, submit to his discipline, believe in him; come to him as the fountain of living waters, the giver of all comfort.

(3.) The satisfaction promised: Let him come *and drink,* he shall have what he comes for, and abundantly more, shall have that which will not only *refresh,* but *replenish,* a soul that desires to be happy."

4. A gracious promise annexed to this gracious call (*v.* 38): *He that believeth on me, out of his belly shall flow*— (1.) See here what it is to come to Christ: It is *to believe on him, as the scripture hath said;* it is to receive and entertain him as he is offered to us in the gospel. We must not frame a Christ according to our fancy, but believe in a Christ according to the scripture. (2.) See how thirsty souls, that come to Christ, shall be made *to drink.* Israel, that believed Moses, drank of the *rock that followed them,* the streams followed; but believers drink of a rock *in them, Christ in them;* he is in them a *well of living water, ch.* iv. 14. Provision is made not only for their *present* satisfaction, but for their *continual perpetual* comfort. Here is, [1.] *Living water, running* water, which the Hebrew language calls *living,* because still in motion. The graces and comforts of the Spirit are compared to *living* (meaning *running) water,* because they are the active quickening principles of spiritual life, and the earnests and beginnings of eternal life. See Jer. ii. 13. [2.] *Rivers* of living water, denoting both plenty and constancy. The comfort flows in both *plentifully* and *constantly* as a river; strong as a stream to bear down the oppositions of doubts and fears. There is a fulness in Christ of grace for grace. [3.] These flow out *of his belly,* that is, out of his heart or soul, which is the subject of the Spirit's working and the seat of his government. There *gracious principles* are planted; and out of the heart, in which the Spirit dwells, flow the *issues of life,* Prov. iv. 23. There divine comforts are lodged, and the *joy* that a *stranger doth not intermeddle with. He that believes has the witness in himself,* 1 John v. 10. *Sat lucis intus—Light abounds within.* Observe, further, where there are *springs* of grace and comfort in the soul they will *send forth streams: Out of his belly shall flow rivers. First,* Grace and comfort will *evidence themselves.* Good affections will produce good actions, and a holy heart will be seen in a holy life; the tree is known by its fruits, and the fountain by its streams. *Secondly,* They will *communicate themselves* for the benefit of others; a good man is a common good. His *mouth* is a *well of life,* Prov. x. 11. It is not enough that we *drink waters out of our own cistern,* that we ourselves take the comfort of the grace given us, but we must let our *fountains* be *dispersed abroad,* Prov. v. 15, 16.

Those words, *as the scripture hath said,* seem to refer to some promise in the Old Testament to this purport, and there are many; as that God would *pour out* his Spirit, which is a metaphor borrowed from waters (Prov. i. 23; Joel ii. 28; Isa. xliv. 3; Zech. xii. 10); that the *dry land* should become *springs of water* (Isa. xli. 18); that there should be *rivers in the desert* (Isa. xliii. 19); that gracious souls should be like a *spring of water* (Isa. lviii. 11); and the church a *well of living water,* Cant. iv. 15. And here may be an allusion to the waters issuing out of Ezekiel's temple, Ezek. xlvii. 1. Compare Rev. xxii. 1, and see Zech. xiv. 8. Dr. Lightfoot and others tell us it was a custom of the Jews, which they received by tradition, *the last day of the feast* of tabernacles to have a solemnity, which they called *Libatio aquæ—The pouring out of water.* They fetched a golden vessel of water from the pool of Siloam, brought it into the temple with sound of trumpet and other ceremonies, and, upon the ascent to the altar, poured it out before the Lord with all possible expressions of joy. Some of their writers make the water to signify *the law,* and refer to Isa. xii. 3; lv. 1. Others, *the Holy Spirit.* And it is thought that our Saviour might here allude to this custom. Believers shall have the comfort, not of a vessel of water fetched from a pool, but of a river flowing from themselves. The joy of the law, and the pouring out of the water, which signified this, are not to be compared with the joy of the gospel in the wells of salvation.

5. Here is the evangelist's exposition of this promise (*v.* 39): *This spoke he of the Spirit:* not of any outward advantages accruing to believers (as perhaps some misunderstood him), but of the gifts, graces, and comforts of the Spirit. See how scripture is the best interpreter of scripture. Observe,

(1.) It is promised to *all that believe on*

Christ that they shall *receive the Holy Ghost.* Some received his miraculous gifts (Mark xvi. 17, 18); all receive his sanctifying graces. The gift of the Holy Ghost is one of the great blessings promised in the new covenant (Acts ii. 39), and, if *promised*, no doubt *performed* to all that have an interest in that covenant.

(2.) The Spirit dwelling and working in believers is as a *fountain of living* running *water*, out of which plentiful streams flow, cooling and cleansing as water, mollifying and moistening as water, making them fruitful, and others joyful; see *ch.* iii. 5.' When the apostles spoke so *fluently* of the things of God, as the Spirit gave them utterance (Acts ii. 4), and afterwards preached and wrote the gospel of Christ with such a *flood* of divine eloquence, then this was fulfilled, *Out of his belly shall flow rivers.*

(3.) This plentiful effusion of the Spirit was yet the matter of a promise; for *the Holy Ghost was not yet given, because Jesus was not yet glorified.* See here, [1.] That *Jesus was not yet glorified.* It was certain that he should be glorified, and he was ever worthy of all honour; but he was as yet in a state of humiliation and contempt. He had never forfeited the glory he had before all worlds, nay, he had *merited* a further glory, and, besides his *hereditary* honours, might claim the *achievement* of a *mediatorial* crown; and yet all this is in reversion. Jesus is now *upheld* (Isa. xlii. 1), is now *satisfied* (Isa liii. 11), is now *justified* (1 Tim. iii. 16), but he is *not yet glorified.* And, if Christ must wait for his glory, let not us think it much to wait for ours. [2.] That *the Holy Ghost was not yet given.* οὔπω γὰρ ἦν πνεῦμα—*for the Holy Ghost was not yet.* The Spirit of God was from eternity, for in the beginning he *moved upon the face of the waters.* He was in the Old-Testament prophets and saints, and Zacharias and Elisabeth were both *filled with the Holy Ghost.* This therefore must be understood of that eminent, plentiful, and general effusion of the Spirit which was promised, Joel ii. 28, and accomplished, Acts ii. 1, &c. *The Holy Ghost was not yet given* in that visible manner that was intended. If we compare the clear knowledge and strong grace of the disciples of Christ themselves, after the day of Pentecost, with their darkness and weakness before, we shall understand in what sense *the Holy Ghost was not yet given;* the earnests and first-fruits of the Spirit were given, but the full harvest was not yet come. That which is most properly called the *dispensation of the Spirit* did not yet commence. The *Holy Ghost* was *not yet given* in such rivers of living water as should issue forth to water the whole earth, even the Gentile world, not in the *gifts of tongues*, to which perhaps this promise principally refers. [3.] That the reason why *the Holy Ghost was not given* was because *Jesus was not yet glorified. First,* The death of Christ is sometimes called his glorification (*ch.* xiii. 31); for in his cross he conquered and triumphed. Now the gift of the Holy Ghost was purchased by the blood of Christ: this was the *valuable consideration* upon which the *grant* was grounded, and therefore till this *price* was *paid* (though many other gifts were bestowed upon its being *secured* to be paid) the Holy Ghost was not given. *Secondly,* There was not so much need of the Spirit, while Christ himself was here upon earth, as there was when he was gone, to supply the want of him. *Thirdly,* The giving of the Holy Ghost was to be both an *answer* to Christ's *intercession* (*ch.* xiv. 16), and an *act* of his *dominion;* and therefore till he is glorified, and enters upon both these, the Holy Ghost is not given. *Fourthly,* The conversion of the Gentiles was the glorifying of Jesus. When certain Greeks began to enquire after Christ, he said, *Now is the Son of man glorified, ch.* xii. 23. Now the time when the gospel should be propagated in the nations was not yet come, and therefore there was as yet no occasion for the *gift of tongues,* that *river of living water.* But observe, though the Holy Ghost was not yet given, yet he was *promised;* it was now the great *promise of the Father,* Acts i. 4. Though the gifts of Christ's grace are *long deferred,* yet they are *well secured:* and, while we are waiting for the good promise, we have the promise to live upon, which *shall speak and shall not lie.*

II. The consequents of this discourse, what entertainment it met with; in general, it occasioned differences: *There was a division among the people because of him, v.* 43. There was *a schism,* so the word is; there were diversities of opinions, and those managed with heat and contention; various sentiments, and those such as set them at *variance.* Think we that Christ came to send peace, that all would unanimously embrace his gospel? No, the effect of the preaching of his gospel would be *division,* for, while some are *gathered to it,* others will be *gathered against it;* and this will put things into a *ferment,* as here; but this is no more the fault of the gospel than it is the fault of a wholesome medicine that it stirs up the *peccant* humours in the body, in order to the discharge of them. Observe what the debate was:—

1. Some were *taken with him,* and well affected to him: *Many of the people, when they heard this saying,* heard him with such compassion and kindness invite poor sinners to him, and with such authority engage to make them happy, that they could not but think highly of him. (1.) Some of them said, *O, a truth this is the prophet,* that prophet whom Moses spoke of to the fathers, who should be *like unto him;* or, This is *the prophet* who, according to the received notions of the Jewish church, is to be the harbinger and forerunner of the Messiah; or, *This is truly a prophet,* one divinely inspired and sent of God. (2.) Others went further, and said,

This is the Christ (*v.* 41), not the *prophet* of the Messiah, but the Messiah himself. The Jews had at this time a more than ordinary expectation of the Messiah, which made them ready to say upon every occasion, *Lo, here is Christ,* or *Lo, he is there;* and this seems to be only the effect of some such confused and floating notions which caught at the first appearance, for we do not find that these people became his disciples and followers; a good opinion of Christ is far short of a lively faith in Christ; many give Christ a good word that give him no more. These here said, *This is the prophet,* and *this is the Christ,* but could not persuade themselves to leave all and follow him; and so this their testimony to Christ was but a testimony *against themselves.*

2. Others were *prejudiced against him.* No sooner was this great truth started, that *Jesus is the Christ,* than immediately it was contradicted and argued against: and this one thing, that his rise and origin were (as they took it for granted) out of Galilee, was thought enough to answer all the arguments for his being the Christ. For, *shall Christ come out of Galilee?* Has not *the scripture said that Christ comes of the seed of David?* See here, (1.) A laudable knowledge of the scripture. They were so far in the right, that the Messiah was to be a *rod out of the stem of Jesse* (Isa. xi. 1), that out of Bethlehem should *arise the Governor,* Mic. v. 2. This even the common people knew by the traditional expositions which their scribes gave them. Perhaps the people who had these scriptures so ready to object against Christ were not alike knowing in other parts of holy writ, but had had these put into their mouths by their leaders, to fortify their prejudices against Christ. Many that espouse some corrupt notions, and spend their zeal in defence of them, seem to be very ready in the scriptures, when indeed they know little more than those scriptures which they have been taught to *pervert.* (2.) A culpable ignorance of our Lord Jesus. They speak of it as certain and past dispute that *Jesus was of Galilee,* whereas by enquiring of himself, or his mother, or his disciples, or by consulting the genealogies of the family of David, or the register at Bethlehem, they might have known that he was the Son of David, and a native of Bethlehem; but *this they willingly are ignorant of.* Thus gross falsehoods in matters of fact, concerning persons and things, are often taken up by prejudiced and partial men, and great resolves founded upon them, even in the same place and the same age wherein the persons live and the things are done, while the truth might easily be found out.

3. Others were *enraged against him,* and they *would have taken him, v.* 44. Though what he said was most sweet and gracious, yet they were exasperated against him for it. Thus did our Master suffer ill for saying and doing well. *They would have taken him;* they hoped somebody or other would seize him, and, if they had thought no one else would, they would have done it themselves. They *would have taken him;* but no man *laid hands on him,* being restrained by an invisible power, because his hour was not come. As the malice of Christ's enemies is always *unreasonable,* so sometimes the suspension of it is *unaccountable.*

45 Then came the officers to the
chief priests and Pharisees; and they
said unto them, Why have ye not
brought him? 46 The officers answered, Never man spake like this
man. 47 Then answered them the
Pharisees, Are ye also deceived? 48
Have any of the rulers or of the Pharisees believed on him? 49 But this
people who knoweth not the law are
cursed. 50 Nicodemus saith unto
them, (he that came to Jesus by
night, being one of them,) 51 Doth
our law judge *any* man, before it
hear him, and know what he doeth?
52 They answered and said unto him,
Art thou also of Galilee? Search,
and look: for out of Galilee ariseth
no prophet. 53 And every man went
unto his own house.

The chief priests and Pharisees are here in a close cabal, contriving how to suppress Christ; though this was the *great day of the feast,* they attended not the religious services of the day, but left them to the vulgar, to whom it was common for those great ecclesiastics to consign and turn over the business of devotion, while they thought themselves better employed in the affairs of church-policy. They sat in the council-chamber, expecting Christ to be brought a prisoner to them, as they had issued out warrants for apprehending him, *v.* 32. Now here we are told,

I. What passed between them and their own officers, who returned without him, *re infecta—having done nothing.* Observe,

1. The reproof they gave the officers for not executing the warrant they gave them: *Why have you not brought him?* He appeared publicly; the people were many of them disgusted, and would have assisted them in taking him; this was *the last day of the feast,* and they would not have such another opportunity; "why then did you neglect your duty?" It vexed them that those who were their own creatures, who depended on them, and on whom they depended, into whose minds they had instilled prejudices against Christ, should thus disappoint them. Note, Mischievous men fret that they cannot do the mischief they would, Ps. cxii. 10; Neh. vi. 16.

2. The reason which the officers gave for the non-execution of their warrant: *Never man spoke like this man, v.* 46. Now, (1.) This was a very great truth, that *never any man spoke with* that wisdom, and power, and grace, that convincing clearness, and that charming sweetness, wherewith Christ spoke; none of the prophets, no, not Moses himself. (2.) The very officers that were sent to take him were taken with him, and acknowledged this. Though they were probably men who had no quick sense of reason or eloquence, and certainly had no inclination to think well of Jesus, yet so much *self-evidence* was there in what Christ said that they could not but prefer him before all those that sat in Moses's seat. Thus Christ was preserved by the power God has upon the consciences even of bad men. (3.) They said this to their lords and masters, who could not endure to hear any thing that tended to the honour of Christ and yet could not avoid hearing this. Providence ordered it so that this should be said to them, that it might be a vexation in their sin and an aggravation of their sin. Their own officers, who could not be suspected to be biassed in favour of Christ, are witnesses against them. This testimony of theirs should have made them reflect upon themselves, with this thought, "Do we know what we are doing, when we are hating and persecuting one that speaks so admirably well?"

3. The Pharisees endeavour to secure their officers to their interest, and to beget in them prejudices against Christ, to whom they saw them begin to be well affected. They suggest two things:—

(1.) That if they embrace the gospel of Christ they will *deceive themselves* (*v.* 47): *Are you also deceived?* Christianity has, from its first rise, been represented to the world as a great cheat upon it, and they that embraced it as men *deceived*, then when they began to be *undeceived.* Those that looked for a Messiah in external pomp thought those deceived who believed in a Messiah that appeared in poverty and disgrace; but the event declares that none were ever more shamefully deceived, nor put a greater cheat upon themselves, than those who promised themselves worldly wealth and secular dominion with the Messiah. Observe what a *compliment* the Pharisees paid to these officers: "*Are you also deceived?* What! men of your sense, and thought, and figure; men that know better than to be imposed upon by every pretender and upstart teacher?" They endeavour to prejudice them against Christ by persuading them to think well of themselves.

(2.) That they will *disparage themselves.* Most men, even in their religion, are willing to be governed by the example of those of the *first rank;* these officers therefore, whose preferments, such as they were, gave them a *sense of honour*, are desired to consider,

[1.] That, if they become disciples of Christ, they go contrary to those who were persons of quality and reputation: "*Have any of the rulers, or of the Pharisees, believed on him?* You know they have not, and you ought to be bound up by their judgment, and to *believe* and *do* in religion according to the will of your superiors; will you be wiser than they?" Some of the rulers did embrace Christ (Matt. ix. 18; *ch.* iv. 53), and more believed in him, but wanted courage to confess him (*ch.* xii. 42); but, when the interest of Christ runs low in the world, it is common for its adversaries to represent it as lower than really it is. But it was too true that few, very few, of them did. Note, *First,* The cause of Christ has seldom had rulers and Pharisees on its side. It needs not secular supports, nor proposes secular advantages, and therefore neither courts nor is courted by the great men of this world. *Self-denial* and the *cross* are hard lessons to *rulers* and *Pharisees. Secondly,* This has confirmed many in their prejudices against Christ and his gospel, that the rulers and Pharisees have been no friends to them. Shall *secular* men pretend to be more concerned about *spiritual* things than spiritual men themselves, or to see further into religion than those who make its study their profession? If *rulers* and *Pharisees* do not believe in Christ, they that do believe in him will be the most singular, unfashionable, ungenteel people in the world, and quite out of the way of preferment; thus are people foolishly swayed by *external motives* in matters of *eternal moment,* are willing to be damned for fashion-sake, and to go to hell in compliment to the *rulers* and *Pharisees.*

[2.] That they will link themselves with the despicable vulgar sort of people (*v.* 43): *But this people, who know not the law, are cursed,* meaning especially those that were well-affected to the doctrine of Christ. Observe, *First,* How scornfully and disdainfully they speak of them: *This people.* It is not λαὸς, this *lay-people,* distinguished from them that were the clergy, but ὄχλος οὗτος, this *rabble-people,* this pitiful, scandalous, scoundrel people, whom they disdained to *set with the dogs of their flock,* though God had set them with the lambs of his. If they meant the *commonalty of the Jewish nation,* they were the seed of Abraham, and in covenant with God, and not to be spoken of with such contempt. The church's common interests are betrayed when any one part of it studies to render the other mean and despicable. If they meant the *followers of Christ,* though they were generally persons of small figure and fortune, yet by owning Christ they discovered such a sagacity, integrity, and interest in the favours of Heaven, as made them truly great and considerable. Note, As the wisdom of God has often chosen base things, and things which are despised, so the folly of men has commonly debased and despised those whom God has chosen. *Secondly,* How unjustly they reproach them as ignorant of the word of God: *They know not the law;* as if none knew the law but those that knew it *from them,* and no scripture-knowledge were current but what came out of their mint; and as if none knew the law but such as were observant of their canons and traditions. Perhaps many of those whom they thus despised *knew the law,* and the prophets too, better than they did. Many a plain, honest, unlearned disciple of Christ, by meditation, experience, prayers, and especially obedience, attains to a more clear, sound, and useful knowledge of the word of God, than some great scholars with all their wit and learning. Thus David came to understand *more than the ancients* and *all his teachers,* Ps. cxix. 99, 100. If the common people did not *know the law,* yet the chief priests and Pharisees, of all men, should not have upbraided them with this; for whose fault was it but theirs, who should have *taught them better,* but, instead of that, *took away the key of knowledge?* Luke xi. 52. *Thirdly,* How magisterially they pronounce sentence upon them: they are *cursed,* hateful to God, and all wise men; ἐπικαταρτὸι—*an execrable* people. It is well that their saying they were cursed did not make them so, for the *curse causeless shall not come.* It is a usurpation of God's prerogative, as well as great uncharitableness, to say of any particular persons, much more of any body of people, that they are reprobates. We are unable to *try,* and therefore unfit to *condemn,* and our rule is, *Bless, and curse not.* Some think they meant no more than that the people were *apt to be deceived* and *made fools of;* but they use this odious word, They are *cursed,* to express their own indignation, and to frighten their officers from having any thing to do with them; thus the language of hell, in our profane age, calls every thing that is displeasing *cursed,* and *damned,* and *confounded.* Now, for aught that appears, these officers had their convictions baffled and stifled by these suggestions, and they never enquire further after Christ; one word from a *ruler* or *Pharisee* will sway more with many than the true reason of things, and the great interests of their souls.

II. What passed between them and Nicodemus, a member of their own body, *v.* 50, &c. Observe,

1. The just and rational objection which Nicodemus made against their proceedings. Even in their corrupt and wicked sanhedrim God left not himself quite *without* witness against their enmity; nor was the vote against Christ carried *nemine contradicente—unanimously.* Observe,

(1.) Who it was that appeared against them; it was Nicodemus, *he that came to Jesus by night, being one of them, v.* 50. Observe, concerning him, [1.] That, though he had been with Jesus, and taken him for his teacher, yet he retained his place in the council, and his vote among them. Some impute this to his *weakness* and cowardice, and think it was his fault that he did not quit his place, but Christ had never said to him, *Follow me,* else he would have done as others that left all to follow him; therefore it seems rather to have been his *wisdom* not immediately to throw up his place, because there he might have opportunity of serving Christ and his interest, and stemming the tide of the Jewish rage, which perhaps he did more than we are aware of. He might there be as Hushai among Absalom's counsellors, instrumental to *turn their counsels into foolishness.* Though we must in no case deny our Master, yet we may wait for an opportunity of confessing him to the best advantage. God has his remnant among all sorts, and many times finds, or puts, or makes, some good in the worst places and societies. There was Daniel in Nebuchadnezzar's court, and Nehemiah in Artaxerxes's. [2.] That though at first he came to Jesus *by night,* for fear of being known, and still continued in his post; yet, when there was occasion, he boldly appeared in defence of Christ, and opposed the whole council that were set against him. Thus many believers who at first were timorous, and ready to *flee at the shaking of a leaf,* have at length, by divine grace, grown courageous, and able to *laugh at the shaking of a spear.* Let none justify the disguising of their faith by the example of Nicodemus, unless, like him, they be ready upon the first occasion openly to appear in the cause of Christ, though they stand alone in it; for so Nicodemus did here, and *ch.* xix. 39.

(2.) What he alleged against their proceedings (*v.* 51): *Doth our law judge any man before it hear him* (ἀκούσῃ παρ' αὐτοῦ—*hear from himself)* and *know what he doeth?* By no means, nor doth the law of any civilized nation allow it. Observe, [1.] He prudently argues from the principles of their own law, and an incontestable rule of justice, that no man is to be condemned *unheard.* Had he urged the excellency of Christ's doctrine or the evidence of his miracles, or repeated to them his divine discourse with him (*ch.* 3), it had been but to *cast pearls before swine,* who would *trample them under their feet,* and would *turn again and rend him;* therefore he waives them. [2.] Whereas they had reproached the people, especially the followers of Christ, as *ignorant of the law,* he here tacitly retorts the charge upon themselves, and shows how ignorant they were of some of the first principles of the law, so unfit were they to give law to others. [3.] The law is here said to *judge,* and *hear,* and *know,* when magistrates that govern and are governed by it *judge,* and *hear,* and *know;* for they are the *mouth of the law,* and whatsoever they bind and loose according to the law is justly said to be bound and loosed by the law. [4.] It is highly fit that none should come under the *sentence* of the law, till they have first by a fair trial undergone the *scrutiny* of it. Judges, when they receive the complaints of the accuser, must always reserve in their minds room for the defence of the accused, for they have two ears, to remind them to hear both sides; this is said to be the manner of the Romans, Acts xxv. 18. The method of our law is *Oyer* and *Terminer,* first to *hear* and then to *determine.* [5.] Persons are to be judged, not by what is *said* of them, but by what they *do.* *Our law* will not ask what men's opinions are of them, or out-cries against them, but, What have they done? What *overt-acts* can they be convicted of? Sentence must be given, *secundum allegata et probata—according to what is alleged and proved.* Facts, and not faces, must be known in judgment; and the *scale* of justice must be used before the *sword* of justice.

Now we may suppose that the motion Nicodemus made in the house upon this was, That Jesus should be desired to come and give them an account of himself and his doctrine, and that they should favour him with an impartial and unprejudiced hearing; but, though none of them could gainsay his maxim, none of them would second his motion.

2. What was said to this objection. Here is no direct reply given to it; but, when they could not resist the force of his argument, they fell foul upon him, and what was to seek in *reason* they made up in railing and reproach. Note, It is a sign of a bad cause when men cannot bear to *hear reason,* and take it as an affront to be reminded of its maxims. Whoever are *against reason* give cause to suspect that *reason* is *against them.* See how they taunt him: *Art thou also of Galilee? v.* 52. Some think he was well enough served for continuing among those whom he knew to be enemies to Christ, and for his speaking no more on the behalf of Christ than what he might have said on behalf of the greatest criminal—that he should not be condemned unheard. Had he said, "As for this Jesus, I have heard him myself, and know he is a *teacher come from God,* and you in opposing him fight against God," as he ought to have said, he could not have been more abused than he was for this feeble effort of his tenderness for Christ. As to what they said to Nicodemus, we may observe,

(1.) How *false* the grounds of their arguing were, for, [1.] They suppose that Christ was of Galilee, and this was false, and if they would have been at the pains of an impartial enquiry they would have found it so. [2.] They suppose that because most of his disciples were Galileans they were all such, whereas he had abundance of disciples in Judea. [3.] They suppose that out of Galilee no prophet had *risen,* and for this appeal to Nicodemus's search; yet this was false too· Jonah was of Gath-hepher, Nahum an Elkoshite, both of Galilee. Thus do they *makes lies their refuge.*

(2.) How *absurd* their arguings were upon these grounds, such as were a shame to *rulers* and *Pharisees.* [1.] Is any man of worth and virtue ever the worse for the poverty and obscurity of his country? The Galileans were the seed of Abraham; barbarians and Scythians are the seed of Adam; and *have we not all one Father?* [2.] Supposing no prophet had risen out of Galilee, yet it is not impossible that any should arise thence. If Elijah was the first prophet of Gilead (as perhaps he was), and if the Gileadites were called *fugitives,* must it therefore be questioned whether he was a prophet or no?

3. The hasty adjournment of the court hereupon. They broke up the assembly in confusion, and with precipitation, and *every man went to his own house.* They met to take *counsel together against the Lord and his Anointed,* but they *imagined a vain thing;* and not only he that sits in heaven laughed at them, but we may sit on earth and laugh at them too, to see all the policy of the close cabal broken to pieces with one plain honest word. They were not willing to hear Nicodemus, because they could not answer him. As soon as they perceived they had one such among them, they saw it was to no purpose to go on with their design, and therefore put off the debate to a more convenient season, when he was absent. Thus the counsel of the Lord is made to stand, in spite of the devices in the hearts of men.

CHAP. VIII.

In this chapter we have, I. Christ's evading the snare which the Jews laid for him, in bringing to him a woman taken in adultery, ver. 1—11. II. Divers discourses or conferences of his with the Jews that cavilled at him, and sought occasion against him, and made every thing he said a matter of controversy. 1. Concerning his being the light of the world, ver. 12—20. 2. Concerning the ruin of the unbelieving Jews, ver. 21—30. 3. Concerning liberty and bondage, ver. 31—37. 4. Concerning his Father and their father, ver. 38—47. 5. Here is his discourse in answer to their blasphemous reproaches, ver. 48—50. 6. Concerning the immortality of believers, ver. 51—59. And in all this he endured the contradiction of sinners against himself.

JESUS went unto the mount of
Olives. 2 And early in the
morning he came again into the
temple, and all the people came unto
him; and he sat down, and taught
them. 3 And the scribes and Pharisees brought unto him a woman
taken in adultery; and when they
had set her in the midst, 4 They
say unto him, Master, this woman
was taken in adultery, in the very
act. 5 Now Moses in the law commanded us, that such should be
stoned: but what sayest thou? 6
This they said, tempting him, that they
might have to accuse him. But Jesus
stooped down, and with *his* finger
wrote on the ground, *as though he
heard them not.* 7 So when they
continued asking him, he lifted up
himself, and said unto them, He that
is without sin among you, let him

first cast a stone at her. 8 And
again he stooped down, and wrote
on the ground. 9 And they which
heard *it*, being convicted by *their*
own conscience, went out one by one,
beginning at the eldest, *even* unto the
last: and Jesus was left alone, and
the woman standing in the midst.
10 When Jesus had lifted up himself,
and saw none but the woman, he said
unto her, Woman, where are those
thine accusers? hath no man condemned thee? 11 She said, No man,
Lord. And Jesus said unto her, Neither do I condemn thee: go, and sin
no more.

Though Christ was basely abused in the foregoing chapter, both by the rulers and by the people, yet here we have him still at Jerusalem, still in the temple. *How often would he have gathered them!* Observe,

I. His retirement in the evening out of the town (*v.* 1): *He went unto the mount of olives;* whether to some friend's house, or to some booth pitched there, now at the feast of tabernacles, is not certain; whether he rested there, or, as some think, continued all night in prayer to God, we are not told. But he went out of Jerusalem, perhaps because he had no friend there that had either kindness or courage enough to give him a night's lodging; while his persecutors had *houses* of their own to go to (*ch.* vii. 53), he could not so much as borrow a place to lay his head on, but what he must go a mile or two out of town for. He retired (as some think) because he would not expose himself to the peril of a popular tumult in the night. It is prudent to go out of the way of danger whenever we can do it without going out of the way of duty. In the day-time, when he had work to do in the temple, he willingly exposed himself, and was under special protection, Isa. xlix. 2. But in the night, when he had not work to do, he withdrew into the country, and sheltered himself there.

II. His return in the morning to the temple, and to his work there, *v.* 2. Observe,

1. What a diligent preacher Christ was: *Early in the morning he came again, and taught.* Though he had been teaching the day before, he taught again to-day. Christ was a constant preacher, in season and out of season. Three things were taken notice of here concerning Christ's preaching. (1.) The time: *Early in the morning.* Though he lodged out of town, and perhaps had spent much of the night in secret prayer, yet he came *early.* When a day's work is to be done for God and souls it is good to begin betimes, and take the day before us. (2.) The place: *In the temple;* not so much because it was a *consecrated* place (for then he would have chosen it at other times) as because it was now a *place of concourse;* and he would hereby countenance solemn assemblies for religious worship, and encourage people to come up to the temple, for he had not yet left it desolate. (3.) His posture: *He sat down,* and taught, as one having authority, and as one that intended to abide by it for some time.

2. How diligently his preaching was attended upon: *All the people came unto him;* and perhaps many of them were the country-people, who were this day to return home from the feast, and were desirous to hear one sermon more from the mouth of Christ before they returned. They came to him, though he came early. They that *seek him early shall find him.* Though the rulers were displeased at those that came to hear him, yet they would come; and *he taught them,* though they were angry at *him* too. Though there were few or none among them that were persons of any figure, yet Christ bade them welcome, and taught them.

III. His dealing with those that brought to him the *woman taken in adultery, tempting* him. The scribes and Pharisees would not only not hear Christ patiently themselves, but they disturbed him when the people were attending on him. Observe here,

1. The case proposed to him by the scribes and Pharisees, who herein contrived to pick a quarrel with him, and bring him into a snare, *v.* 3—6.

(1.) They set the prisoner to the bar (*v.* 3): they brought him *a woman taken in adultery,* perhaps now lately taken, during the time of the feast of tabernacles, when, it may be, their dwelling in booths, and their feasting and joy, might, by wicked minds, which corrupt the best things, be made occasions of sin. Those that were *taken in adultery* were by the Jewish law to be put to death, which the Roman powers allowed them the execution of, and therefore she was brought before the ecclesiastical court. Observe, She *was taken in her adultery.* Though adultery is a work of darkness, which the criminals commonly take all the care they can to conceal, yet sometimes it is strangely brought to light. Those that promise themselves secrecy in sin deceive themselves. The scribes and Pharisees bring her to Christ, and set her in the midst of the assembly, as if they would leave her wholly to the judgment of Christ, he having *sat down,* as a judge upon the bench.

(2.) They prefer an indictment against her: *Master, this woman was taken in adultery, v.* 4. Here they call him *Master* whom but the day before they had called a *deceiver,* in hopes with their flatteries to have ensnared him, as those, Luke xx. 20. But, though men may be imposed upon with compliments, he that searches the heart cannot.

[1.] The crime for which the prisoner stands indicted is no less than adultery, which even in the patriarchal age, before the law of Moses, was looked upon as *an iniquity to be punished by the judges,* Job xxxi. 9—11; Gen. xxxviii. 24. The Pharisees, by their vigorous prosecution of this offender, seemed to have a great zeal against the sin, when it appeared afterwards that they themselves were not free from it; nay, they were within *full of all uncleanness,* Matt. xxiii. 27, 28. Note, It is common for those that are indulgent to their own sin to be severe against the sins of others.

[2.] The proof of the crime was from the notorious evidence of the fact, an incontestable proof; she was *taken in the act,* so that there was no room left to plead not guilty. Had she not been taken in this act, she might have gone on to another, till her heart had been perfectly hardened; but sometimes it proves a mercy to sinners to have their sin brought to light, that they may *do no more presumptuously.* Better our sin should *shame* us than *damn* us, and be set in order before us for our conviction than for our condemnation.

(3.) They produce the statute in this case made and provided, and upon which she was indicted, *v.* 5. Moses in the law commanded *that such should be stoned.* Moses commanded that they should be *put to death* (Lev. xx. 10; Deut. xxii. 22), but not that they should be stoned, unless the adulteress was espoused, not married, or was a priest's daughter, Deut. xxii. 21. Note, Adultery is an exceedingly sinful sin, for it is the rebellion of a vile lust, not only against the command, but against the covenant, of our God. It is the violation of a divine institution in innocency, by the indulgence of one of the basest lusts of man in his degeneracy.

(4.) They pray his judgment in the case: "*But what sayest thou,* who pretendest to be a teacher come from God to repeal old laws and enact new ones? What hast thou to say in this case?" If they had asked this question in sincerity, with a humble desire to know his mind, it had been very commendable. Those that are entrusted with the administration of justice should look up to Christ for direction; but *this they said tempting him, that they might have to accuse him, v.* 6. [1.] If he should confirm the sentence of the law, and let it take its course, they would censure him as inconsistent with himself (he having received publicans and harlots) and with the character of the Messiah, who should be meek, and have salvation, and proclaim a year of release; and perhaps they would accuse him to the Roman governor, for countenancing the Jews in the exercise of a judicial power. But, [2.] If he should acquit her, and give his opinion that the sentence should not be executed (as they expected he would), they would represent him, *First,* As an enemy to the law of Moses, and as one that usurped an authority to correct and control it, and would confirm that prejudice against him which his enemies were so industrious to propagate, that he came to *destroy the law and the prophets. Secondly,* As a friend to sinners, and, consequently, a favourer of sin; if he should seem to connive at such wickedness, and let it go unpunished, they would represent him as countenancing it, and being a patron of offences, if he was a protector of offenders, than which no reflection could be more invidious upon one that professed the strictness, purity, and business of a prophet.

2. The method he took to resolve this case, and so to break this snare.

(1.) He seemed to slight it, and turned a deaf ear to it: He *stooped down, and wrote on the ground.* It is impossible to tell, and therefore needless to ask, what he wrote; but this is the only mention made in the gospels of Christ's writing. Eusebius indeed speaks of his writing to Abgarus, king of Edessa. Some think they have a liberty of conjecture as to what he wrote here. Grotius says, It was some grave weighty saying, and that it was usual for wise men, when they were very thoughtful concerning any thing, to do so. Jerome and Ambrose suppose he wrote, *Let the names of these wicked men be written in the dust.* Others this, *The earth accuses the earth, but the judgment is mine.* Christ by this teaches us to be slow to speak when difficult cases are proposed to us, not quickly to shoot our bolt; and when provocations are given us, or we are bantered, to pause and consider before we reply; think twice before we speak once: *The heart of the wise studies to answer.* Our translation from some Greek copies, which add, *μὴ προσποιούμενος* (though most copies have it not), give this account of the reason of his writing on the ground, *as though he heard them not.* He did as it were look another way, to show that he was not willing to take notice of their address, saying, in effect, *Who made me a judge or a divider?* It is safe in many cases to be deaf to that which it is not safe to answer, Ps. xxxviii. 13. Christ would not have his ministers to be entangled in secular affairs. Let them rather employ themselves in any lawful studies, and fill up their time in writing on the ground (which nobody will heed), than busy themselves in that which does not belong to them. But, when Christ seemed as though he heard them not, he made it appear that he not only heard their words, but knew their thoughts.

(2.) When they importunately, or rather impertinently, pressed him for an answer, he turned the conviction of the prisoner upon the prosecutors, *v.* 7.

[1.] They *continued asking him,* and his seeming not to take notice of them made them the more vehement; for now they thought sure enough that they had run him aground, and that he could not avoid the imputation of contradicting either the law of

Moses, if he should acquit the prisoner, or his own doctrine of mercy and pardon, if he should condemn her; and therefore they pushed on their appeal to him with vigour; whereas they should have construed his disregard of them as a check to their design, and an intimation to them to desist, as they tendered their own reputation.

[2.] At last he put them all to shame and silence with one word: *He lifted up himself,* awaking as one out of sleep (Ps. lxxviii. 65), and *said unto them, He that is without sin among you, let him first cast a stone at her.*

First, Here Christ avoided the snare which they had laid for him, and effectually saved his own reputation. He neither reflected upon the law nor excused the prisoner's guilt, nor did he on the other hand encourage the prosecution or countenance their heat; see the good effect of consideration. When we cannot make our point by steering a direct course, it is good to fetch a compass.

Secondly, In the net which they spread is their own foot taken. They came with design to accuse him, but they were forced to accuse themselves. Christ owns it was fit the prisoner should be prosecuted, but appeals to their consciences whether they were fit to be the prosecutors.

a. He here refers to that rule which the law of Moses prescribed in the execution of criminals, that the *hand of the witnesses must be first upon them* (Deut. xvii. 7), as in the stoning of Stephen, Acts vii. 58. The scribes and Pharisees were the witnesses against this woman. Now Christ puts it to them whether, according to their own law, they would dare to be the executioners. Durst they take away that life with their hands which they were now taking away with their tongues? would not their own consciences fly in their faces if they did?

b. He builds upon an uncontested maxim in morality, that it is very absurd for men to be zealous in punishing the offences of others, while they are every whit as guilty themselves, and they are not better than self-condemned who judge others, and yet themselves do the same thing: "If there be any of you who is *without sin,* without sin of this nature, that has not some time or other been guilty of fornication or adultery, let him cast the first stone at her." Not that magistrates, who are conscious of guilt themselves, should therefore connive at others' guilt. But therefore, (*a.*) Whenever we find fault with others, we ought to reflect upon ourselves, and to be more severe against sin in ourselves than in others. (*b.*) We ought to be favourable, though not to the sins, yet to the persons, of those that offend, and to restore them with a *spirit of meekness,* considering ourselves and our own corrupt nature. *Aut sumus, aut fuimus, vel possumus esse quod hic est—We either are, or have been, or may be, what he is.* Let this restrain us from *throwing stones* at our brethren, and proclaiming their faults. *Let him that is without sin* begin such discourse as this, and then those that are truly humbled for their own sins will blush at it, and be glad to *let it drop.* (*c.*) Those that are any way obliged to animadvert upon the faults of others are concerned to look well to themselves, and keep themselves pure (Matt. vii. 5), *Qui alterum incusat probri, ipsum se intueri oportet.* The snuffers of the tabernacle were of *pure gold.*

c. Perhaps he refers to the trial of the suspected wife by the jealous husband with the waters of jealousy. The man was to bring her to the priest (Num. v. 15), as the scribes and Pharisees brought this woman to Christ. Now it was a received opinion among the Jews, and confirmed by experience, that if the husband who brought his wife to that trial had himself been at any time guilty of adultery, *Aquæ non explorant ejus uxorem—The bitter water had no effect upon the wife.* "Come then," saith Christ, "according to your own tradition will I judge you; if you are without sin, stand to the charge, and let the adulteress be executed; but if not, though she be guilty, while you that present her are equally so, according to your own rule she shall be free."

d. In this he attended to the great work which he came into the world about, and that was to bring sinners to repentance; not to destroy, but to save. He aimed to bring, not only the prisoner to repentance, by showing her his mercy, but the prosecutors too, by showing them their sins. They sought to ensnare him; he sought to convince and convert them. Thus *the blood-thirsty hate the upright, but the just seek his soul.*

[3.] Having given them this startling word, he left them to consider of it, *and again stooped down, and wrote on the ground, v.* 8. As when they made their address he seemed to slight their question, so now that he had given them an answer he slighted their resentment of it, not caring what they said to it; nay, they needed not to make any reply; the matter was lodged in their own breasts, let them make the best of it there. Or, he would not seem to wait for an answer, lest they should on a sudden justify themselves, and then think themselves bound in honour to persist in it; but gives them time to pause, and to commune with their own hearts. God saith, *I hearkened and heard,* Jer. viii. 6. Some Greek copies here read, He *wrote on the ground,* ἑνὸς ἑκάστου αὐτῶν τὰς ἁμαρτίας—*the sins of every one of them;* this he could do, for he *sets our iniquities before him;* and this he will do, for he will *set them in order* before us too; he *seals up our transgressions,* Job xiv. 17. But he does not write men's sins *in the sand;* no, they are written as with a *pen of iron* and the *point of a diamond* (Jer. xvii. 1), never to be forgotten till they are forgiven.

[4.] The scribes and Pharisees were so strangely thunderstruck with the words of

Christ that they let fall their persecution of Christ, whom they durst no further tempt, and their prosecution of the woman, whom they durst no longer accuse (*v.* 9): *They went out one by one.*

First, Perhaps his writing on the ground frightened them, as the hand-writing on the wall frightened Belshazzar. They concluded he was writing bitter things against them, writing their doom. Happy they who have no reason to be afraid of Christ's writing!

Secondly, What he said frightened them by sending them to their own consciences; he had *shown them to themselves,* and they were afraid if they should stay till he lifted up himself again his next word would show them to the world, and shame them before men, and therefore they thought it best to withdraw. They went out *one by one,* that they might go out *softly,* and not by a noisy flight disturb Christ; they went away by *stealth,* as *people being ashamed steal away when they flee in battle,* 2 Sam. xix. 3. The order of their departure is taken notice of, *beginning at the eldest,* either because they were most guilty, or first aware of the danger they were in of being put to the blush; and if the eldest quit the field, and retreat ingloriously, no marvel if the younger follow them. Now see here, 1. The *force* of the word of Christ for the conviction of sinners: *They who heard it were convicted by their own consciences.* Conscience is God's deputy in the soul, and one word from him will set it on work, Heb. iv. 12. Those that had been old in adulteries, and long fixed in a proud opinion of themselves, were here, even the oldest of them, startled by the word of Christ; even scribes and Pharisees, who were most conceited of themselves, are by the power of Christ's word made to retire with shame. 2. The *folly* of sinners under these convictions, which appears in these scribes and Pharisees. (1.) It is folly for those that are under convictions to make it their principal care to *avoid shame,* as Judah (Gen. xxxviii. 23), *lest we be shamed.* Our care should be more to save our souls than to save our credit. Saul evidenced his hypocrisy when he said, *I have sinned, yet now honour me, I pray thee.* There is no way to get the honour and comfort of penitents, but by taking the shame of penitents. (2.) It is folly for those that are under convictions to contrive how to *shift off* their convictions, and to get rid of them. The scribes and Pharisees had the wound *opened,* and now they should have been desirous to have it *searched,* and then it might have been *healed,* but this was the thing they *dreaded* and *declined.* (3.) It is folly for those that are under convictions to *get away from Jesus Christ,* as these here did, for he is the only one that can heal the wounds of conscience, and speak peace to us. Those that are convicted by their consciences will be condemned by their Judge, if they be not justified by their Redeemer; and will they then go from him? To whom will they go?

[5.] When the *self-conceited* prosecutors quitted the field, and *fled for the same,* the *self-condemned* prisoner stood her ground, with a resolution to abide by the judgment of our Lord Jesus: *Jesus was left alone* from the company of the scribes and Pharisees, free from their molestations, *and the woman standing in the midst* of the assembly that were attending on Christ's preaching, where they set her, *v.* 3. She did not seek to make her escape, though she had opportunity for it; but her prosecutors had appealed unto Jesus, and to him she would go, on him she would wait for her doom. Note, Those whose cause is brought before our Lord Jesus will never have occasion to remove it into any other court, for he is the refuge of penitents. The law which accuses us, and calls for judgment against us, is by the gospel of Christ made to withdraw; its demands are answered, and its clamours silenced, by the blood of Jesus. Our cause is lodged in the gospel court; we are *left with Jesus alone,* it is with him only that we have now to deal, for to him all judgment is committed; let us therefore secure our interest in him, and we are made for ever. Let his gospel *rule us,* and it will infallibly *save us.*

[6.] Here is the conclusion of the trial, and the issue it was brought to: *Jesus lifted up himself, and he saw none but the woman, v.* 10, 11. Though Christ may seem to take no notice of what is said and done, but leave it to the *contending* sons of men to *deal it out among themselves,* yet, when the hour of his judgment is come, he will no longer keep silence. When David had appealed to God, he prayed, *Lift up thyself,* Ps. vii. 6, and xciv. 2. The woman, it is likely, stood trembling at the bar, as one doubtful of the issue. Christ was *without sin,* and might cast the first stone; but though none more severe than he against sin, for he is infinitely just and holy, none more compassionate than he to sinners, for he is infinitely gracious and merciful, and this poor malefactor finds him so, now that she *stands upon her deliverance.* Here is the method of courts of judicature observed.

First, The prosecutors are called: *Where are those thine accusers? Hath no man condemned thee?* Not but that Christ knew where they were; but he asked, that he might shame them, who declined his judgment, and encourage her who resolved to abide by it. St. Paul's challenge is like this, *Who shall lay any thing to the charge of God's elect?* Where are those their accusers? The *accuser of the brethren shall* be fairly *cast out,* and all indictments legally and regularly quashed.

Secondly, They do not appear when the question is asked: *Hath no man condemned thee?* She said, *No man, Lord.* She speaks respectfully to Christ, calls him *Lord,* but is silent concerning her prosecutors, says nothing in answer to that question which concerned them, *Where are those thine accusers?* She does not triumph in their retreat nor insult over them as witnesses against themselves, not against her. If we hope to be forgiven by our Judge, we must forgive our accusers; and if their accusations, how invidious soever, were the happy occasion of awakening our consciences, we may easily *forgive them this wrong.* But she answered the question which concerned herself, *Has no man condemned thee?* True penitents find it enough to give an account of themselves to God, and will not undertake to give an account of other people.

Thirdly, The prisoner is therefore discharged: *Neither do I condemn thee; go, and sin no more.* Consider this,

(*a.*) As her discharge from the temporal punishment: "If they do not condemn thee to be *stoned to death,* neither *do I.*" Not that Christ came to disarm the magistrate of his sword of justice, nor that it is his will that capital punishments should not be inflicted on malefactors; so far from this, the administration of public justice is established by the gospel, and made subservient to Christ's kingdom: *By me kings reign.* But Christ would not condemn this woman, (*a.*) Because it was *none of his business;* he was no judge nor divider, and therefore would not intermeddle in secular affairs. His *kingdom* was *not of this world. Tractent fabrilia fabri—Let every one act in his own province.* (*b.*) Because she was prosecuted by those that were more guilty than she and could not for shame insist upon their demand of justice against her. The law appointed the hands of the witnesses to be first upon the criminal, and afterwards the hands of all the people, so that if they fly off, and do not condemn her, the prosecution drops. The justice of God, in inflicting temporal judgments, sometimes takes notice of a *comparative righteousness,* and spares those who are otherwise obnoxious when the punishing of them would gratify those that are worse than they, Deut. xxxii. 26, 27. But, when Christ dismissed her, it was with this caution, *Go, and sin no more.* Impunity emboldens malefactors, and therefore those who are guilty, and yet have found means to escape the edge of the law, need to double their watch, *lest Satan get advantage;* for the fairer the escape was, the fairer the warning was to go and sin no more. Those who help to save the life of a criminal should, as Christ here, help to save the soul with this caution.

b. As her discharge from the eternal punishment. For Christ to say, *I do not condemn thee* is, in effect, to say, *I do forgive thee;* and the *Son of man had power on earth to forgive sins,* and could upon good grounds give this absolution; for as he knew the hardness and impenitent hearts of the prosecutors, and therefore said that which would confound them, so he knew the tenderness and sincere repentance of the prisoner, and therefore said that which would comfort her, as he did to that woman who was a sinner, such a sinner as this, who was likewise looked upon with disdain by a Pharisee (Luke vii. 48, 50): *Thy sins are forgiven thee, go in peace.* So here, *Neither do I condemn thee.* Note, (*a.*) Those are truly happy whom Christ *doth not condemn,* for his discharge is a sufficient answer to all other challenges; they are all *coram non judice—before an unauthorized judge.* (*b.*) Christ will not condemn those who, though they have sinned, will *go and sin no more,* Ps. lxxxv. 8; Isa. lv. 7. He will not take the advantage he has against us for our former rebellions, if we will but lay down our arms and return to our allegiance. (*c.*) Christ's favour to us in the remission of the sins that are past should be a prevailing argument with us to *go and sin no more,* Rom. vi. 1, 2. Will not Christ condemn thee? Go then and sin no more.

12 Then spake Jesus again unto
them, saying, I am the light of the
world: he that followeth me shall not
walk in darkness, but shall have the
light of life. 13 The Pharisees therefore said unto him, Thou bearest record of thyself; thy record is not
true. 14 Jesus answered and said
unto them, Though I bear record of
myself, *yet* my record is true: for I
know whence I came, and whither I
go; but ye cannot tell whence I come,
and whither I go. 15 Ye judge after
the flesh; I judge no man. 16 And
yet if I judge, my judgment is true:
for I am not alone, but I and the
Father that sent me. 17 It is also
written in your law, that the testimony of two men is true. 18 I am
one that bear witness of myself, and
the Father that sent me beareth witness of me. 19 Then said they unto
him, Where is thy Father? Jesus
answered, Ye neither know me, nor
my Father: if ye had known me, ye
should have known my Father also.
20 These words spake Jesus in the
treasury, as he taught in the temple:
and no man laid hands on him; for
his hour was not yet come.

The rest of the chapter is taken up with debates between Christ and contradicting sinners, who cavilled at the most gracious words that proceeded out of his mouth. It is not certain whether these disputes were the same day that the adulteress was discharged; it is probable they were, for the evangelist mentions no other day, and takes notice (*v.* 2) how early Christ began that day's work. Though those Pharisees that accused the woman had absconded, yet there were other Pharisees (*v.* 13) to confront Christ, who had brass enough in their foreheads to keep them in countenance, though some of their party were put to such a shameful retreat; nay perhaps that made them the more industrious to pick quarrels with him, to retrieve, if possible, the reputation of their baffled party. In these verses we have,

I. A great doctrine laid down, with the application of it.

1. The doctrine is, *That Christ is the light of the world* (*v.* 12): *Then spoke Jesus again unto them;* though he had spoken a great deal to them to little purpose, and what he had said was opposed, yet he *spoke again,* for he *speaketh once, yea, twice.* They had turned a deaf ear to what he said, and yet he *spoke again to them,* saying, *I am the light of the world.* Note, Jesus Christ is the light of the world. One of the rabbies saith, *Light* is the name of the Messiah, as it is written, Dan. ii. 22, *And light dwelleth with him.* God is light, and Christ is *the image of the invisible God;* God of gods, Light of lights. He was expected to be a *light to enlighten the Gentiles* (Luke ii. 32), and so the *light of the world,* and not of the Jewish church only. The visible light of the world is the sun, and Christ is the *Sun of righteousness.* One sun enlightens the whole world, so does one Christ, and there needs no more. Christ in calling himself the light expresses, (1.) What he is in himself—most excellent and glorious. (2.) What he is to the world—the fountain of light, enlightening every man. What a dungeon would the world be without the sun! So would it be without Christ by whom *light came into the world, ch.* iii. 19.

2. The inference from this doctrine is, *He that followeth me,* as a traveller follows the light in a dark night, *shall not walk in darkness,* but *shall have the light of life.* If Christ be the light, then, (1.) It is our duty to *follow him,* to submit ourselves to his guidance, and in every thing take directions from him, in the way that leads to happiness. Many follow *false lights—ignes fatui,* that lead them to destruction; but Christ is the *true light.* It is not enough to *look at* this light, and to *gaze* upon it, but we must follow it, believe in it, and walk in it, for it is a light to *our feet,* not *our eyes* only. (2.) It is the happiness of those who follow Christ that they *shall not walk in darkness.* They shall not be left destitute of those instructions in the way of truth which are necessary to keep them from destroying error, and those directions in the way of duty which are necessary to keep them from damning sin. They shall have the *light of life,* that knowledge and enjoyment of God which will be to them the light of spiritual life in this world and of everlasting life in the other world, where there will be no death nor darkness. Follow Christ, and we shall undoubtedly be happy in both worlds. Follow Christ, and we shall follow him to heaven.

II. The objection which the Pharisees made against this doctrine, and it was very trifling and frivolous: *Thou bearest record of thyself; thy record is not true, v.* 13. In this objection they went upon the suspicion which we commonly have of men's self-commendation, which is concluded to be the native language of self-love, such as we are all ready to condemn in others, but few are willing to own in themselves. But in this case the objection was very unjust, for, 1. They made that his crime, and a diminution to the credibility of his doctrine, which in the case of one who introduced a divine revelation was necessary and unavoidable. Did not Moses and all the prophets bear witness of themselves when they avouched themselves to be God's messengers? Did not the Pharisees ask John Baptist, *What sayest thou of thyself?* 2. They overlooked the testimony of all the other witnesses, which corroborated the testimony he bore of himself. Had he only borne record of himself, his testimony had indeed been *suspicious,* and the belief of it might have been *suspended;* but his doctrine was attested by more than *two or three* credible *witnesses,* enough to *establish every word* of it.

III. Christ's reply to this objection, *v.* 14. He does not retort upon them as he might ("You profess yourselves to be devout and good men, but your witness is not *true*"), but plainly vindicates himself; and, though he had waived his own testimony (*ch.* v. 31), yet here he abides by it, that it did not derogate from the credibility of his other proofs, but was necessary to show the force of them. He is the light of the world, and it is the property of light to be self-evidencing. First principles prove themselves. He urges three things to prove that his testimony, though of himself, was true and cogent.

1. That he was conscious to himself of his own authority, and abundantly satisfied in himself concerning it. He did not speak as one at uncertainty, nor propose a disputable notion, about which he himself hesitated, but *declared a decree,* and gave such an account of himself as he would *abide by: I know whence I came, and whither I go.* He was fully apprised of his own undertaking from first to last; knew whose errand he went upon, and what his success would be. He knew what he *was* before his manifestation to the world, and what he *should be* after; that he came *from the Father,* and was going *to him* (*ch.* xvi. 28), came *from glory,* and was going *to glory, ch.* xvii. 5. This is the satisfaction of all good Christians, that though the world know them not, as it knew him not, yet they know whence their spiritual life comes, and whither it tends, and go upon sure grounds.

2. That they are very incompetent judges of him, and of his doctrine, and not to be regarded. (1.) Because they were *ignorant*, willingly and resolvedly *ignorant: You cannot tell whence I came, and whither I go.* To what purpose is it to talk with those who know nothing of the matter, nor desire to know? He had told them of his coming from heaven and returning to heaven, but it was *foolishness to them,* they *received it not;* it was what the *brutish man knows not,* Ps. xcii. 6. They took upon them to judge of that which they did not understand, which lay quite out of the road of their acquaintance. Those that despise Christ's dominions and dignities speak evil of what they *know not,* Jude, *v.* 8, 10. (2.) Because they were *partial* (*v.* 15): *You judge after the flesh.* When fleshly wisdom gives the rule of judgment, and outward appearances only are given in evidence, and the case decided according to them, then men *judge after the flesh;* and when the consideration of a secular interest turns the scale in judging of spiritual matters, when we judge in favour of that which pleases the carnal mind, and recommends us to a carnal world, we judge after the flesh; and the judgment cannot be right when the rule is wrong. The Jews judged of Christ and his gospel by outward appearances, and, because he appeared so mean, thought it impossible he should be the light of the world; as if the sun under a cloud were no sun. (3.) Because they were *unjust* and *unfair* towards him, intimated in this: "*I judge no man;* I neither make nor meddle with your political affairs, nor does my doctrine or practice at all intrench upon, or interfere with, your civil rights or secular powers." He thus *judged no man.* Now, if he did not *war after the flesh,* it was very unreasonable for them to *judge him after the flesh,* and to treat him as an offender against the civil government. Or, "*I judge no man,*" that is, "not now in my first coming, that is deferred till I come again," *ch.* iii. 17. *Prima dispensatio Christi medicinalis est, non judicialis—The first coming of Christ was for the purpose of administering, not justice, but medicine.*

3. That his testimony of himself was sufficiently supported and corroborated by the testimony of his Father *with him and for him* (*v.* 16): *And yet, if I judge, my judgment is true.* He did in his doctrine judge (*ch.* ix. 39), though not *politically.* Consider him then,

(1.) As a judge, and his own judgment was valid: "*If I judge,* I who have authority to execute judgments, I to whom all things are delivered, I who am the Son of God, and have the Spirit of God, if I judge, *my judgment is true,* of incontestable rectitude and uncontrollable authority, Rom. ii. 2. *If I should judge,* my judgment must be true, and then you would be condemned; but the judgment-day is not yet come, you are not yet to be condemned, but spared, and therefore now *I judge no man;*" so Chrysostom. Now that which makes his judgment unexceptionable is, [1.] His Father's concurrence with him: *I am not alone, but I and the Father.* He had the Father's concurring *counsels* to *direct;* as he was with the Father before the world in forming the counsels, so the Father was with him in the world in prosecuting and executing those counsels, and never left him *inops consilii—without advice,* Isa. xi. 2. All the *counsels of peace* (and of war too) *were between them both,* Zech. vi. 13. He had also the Father's concurring power to authorize and confirm what he did; see Ps. lxxxix. 21, &c. Isa. xlii. 1. He did not act *separately,* but in his own name and his Father's, and *by the authority aforesaid, ch.* v. 17, and xiv. 9, 10. [2.] His Father's commission to him: "It is the Father that *sent me.*" Note, God will go along with those that he sends; see Exod. iii. 10, 12: *Come, and I will send thee,* and *certainly I will be with thee.* Now, if Christ had a *commission* from the Father, and the Father's *presence* with him in all his administrations, no doubt his *judgment* was *true* and valid; no exception lay *against* it, no appeal lay *from* it.

(2.) Look upon him as *a witness,* and now he appeared no otherwise (having not as yet taken the throne of judgment), and as such his testimony was true and unexceptionable; this he shows, *v.* 17, 18, where,

[1.] He quotes a maxim of the Jewish law, *v.* 17. That *the testimony of two men is true.* Not as if it were always true *in itself,* for many a time hand has been joined in hand to bear a *false* testimony, 1 Kings xxi. 10. But it is allowed as sufficient evidence upon which to ground a verdict (*verum dictum*), and if nothing appear to the contrary it is taken for granted to be *true.* Reference is here had to that law (Deut. xvii. 6), *At the mouth of two witnesses shall he that is worthy of death be put to death.* And see Deut. ix. 15; Num. xxxv. 30. It was in *favour of life* that in capital cases two witnesses were required, as with us in case of treason. See Heb. vi. 18.

[2.] He applies this to the case in hand (*v.* 18): *I am one that bear witness of myself, and the Father that sent me bears witness of me.* Behold two witnesses! Though in human courts, where two witnesses are required, the criminal or candidate is not admitted to be a witness for himself; yet in a matter purely divine, which can be proved only by a divine testimony, and God himself must be the witness, if the formality of two or three witnesses be insisted on, there can be no other than the eternal Father, the eternal Son of the Father, and the eternal Spirit. Now if the testimony of two distinct persons, that are *men,* and therefore may deceive or be deceived, is conclusive, much more ought the testimony of the Son of God concerning himself, backed with the testimony of his Father concerning him, to command assent; see 1 John v. 7 9—11. Now this proves not only that the Father and the Son are two distinct persons (for their respective testimonies are here spoken of as the testimonies of two several persons), but that these two are one, not only one in their testimony, but equal in power and glory, and therefore the same in substance. St. Austin here takes occasion to caution his hearers against Sabellianism on the one hand, which confounded the persons in the Godhead, and Arianism on the other, which denied the Godhead of the Son and Spirit. *Alius est filius, et alius pater, non tamen aliud, sed hoc ipsum est et pater, et filius, scilicet unus Deus est—The Son is one Person, and the Father is another; they do not, however, constitute two Beings, but the Father is the same Being that the Son is, that is, the only true God.* Tract. 36, *in* Joann. Christ here speaks of himself and the Father as witnesses to the world, giving in evidence to the reason and conscience of the children of men, whom he deals with as men. And these witnesses *to* the world now will in the great day be witnesses *against* those that persist in unbelief, and *their* word will judge men.

This was the sum of the first conference between Christ and these carnal Jews, in the conclusion of which we are told how their tongues were let loose, and their hands tied.

First, How their tongues were let loose (such was the malice of hell) to cavil at his discourse, *v.* 19. Though in what he said there appeared nothing of human policy or artifice, but a divine security, yet they set themselves to *cross questions* with him. None so incurably *blind* as those that resolve they *will not see.* Observe,

a. How they evaded the *conviction* with a *cavil: Then said they unto him, Where is thy Father?* They might easily have understood, by the tenour of this and his other discourses, that when he spoke of his *Father* he meant no other than God himself; yet they pretend to understand him of a common person, and, since he appeals to his testimony, they bid him *call his witness,* and challenge him, if he can, to produce him: *Where is thy Father?* Thus, as Christ said of them (*v.* 15), they *judge after the flesh.* Perhaps they hereby intend a reflection upon the meanness and obscurity of his family: *Where is thy Father,* that he should be fit to give evidence in such a case as this? Thus they turned it off with a taunt, when they *could not resist the wisdom and spirit with which he spoke.*

b. How he evaded the *cavil* with a further *conviction;* he did not tell them where his Father was, but charged them with wilful ignorance: "*You neither know me nor my Father.* It is to no purpose to discourse to you about divine things, who talk of them as blind men do of colours. Poor creatures! you know nothing of the matter." (*a.*) He charges them with ignorance of God: "*You know not my Father.* In Judah was God known (Ps. lxxvi. 1); they had some knowledge of him as the God that made the world, but their eyes were darkened that they could not see the light of his glory shining *in the face of Jesus Christ.* The *little children* of the Christian church *know the Father,* know him as a Father (1 John ii. 13); but these rulers of the Jews did not, because they would not so know him. (*b.*) He shows them the true cause of their ignorance of God: *If you had known me, you would have known my Father also.* The reason why men are ignorant of God is because they are unacquainted with Jesus Christ. Did we know Christ, [*a.*] In knowing him we should know the Father, of whose person he is the express image, *ch.* xiv. 9. Chrysostom proves hence the Godhead of Christ, and his equality with his Father. We cannot say, "He that knows a man knows an angel," or, "He that knows a creature knows the Creator," but he that knows Christ knows the Father. [*b.*] By him we should be instructed in the knowledge of God, and introduced into an acquaintance with him. If we *knew Christ* better, we should *know the Father* better; but, where the Christian religion is slighted and opposed, natural religion will soon be lost and laid aside. Deism makes way for atheism. Those become vain in their imaginations concerning God that will not learn of Christ.

Secondly, See how their hands were tied, though their tongues were thus let loose; such was the power of Heaven to restrain the malice of hell. *These words spoke Jesus,* these bold words, these words of conviction and reproof, *in the treasury,* an apartment of the temple, where, to be sure, the chief priests, whose gain was their godliness, were mostly resident, attending the business of the revenue. Christ *taught in the temple,* sometimes in one part, sometimes in another, as he saw occasion. Now the priests who had so great a concern in the temple, and looked upon it as their *demesne,* might easily, with the assistance of the janizaries that were at their beck, either have seized him and exposed him to the rage of the mob, and that punishment which they called the *beating of the rebels;* or, at least, have *silenced* him, and stopped his mouth there, as Amos, though tolerated in the land of Judah, was forbidden to prophesy in the king's chapel, Amos, vii. 12, 13. Yet even *in the temple,* where they had him in their reach, *no man laid hands on him,* for *his hour was not yet come.* See here, 1. The restraint laid upon his persecutors by an invisible power; none of them durst meddle with him. God can set bounds to the wrath of men, as he does to the waves of the sea. Let us not therefore fear danger in the way of duty; for God hath Satan and all his instruments in a chain. 2. The reason of this restraint: *His hour was not yet come.* The frequent mention of this intimates how much the time of our departure out of the world depends upon the fixed counsel and decree of God. It *will* come, it is coming; not yet come, but it is at hand. Our enemies cannot hasten it any sooner, nor our friends delay it any longer, than the time appointed of the Father, which is very comfortable to every good man, who can look up and say with pleasure, *My times are in thy hands;* and better there than in our own. His hour was not yet come, because his work was not done, nor his testimony finished. To all God's purposes *there is a time.*

21 Then said Jesus again unto them,
I go my way, and ye shall seek me,
and shall die in your sins: whither I
go, ye cannot come. 22 Then said
the Jews, Will he kill himself? because he saith, Whither I go, ye cannot come. 23 And he said unto them,
Ye are from beneath; I am from
above: ye are of this world; I am
not of this world. 24 I said therefore unto you, that ye shall die in
your sins: for if ye believe not that I
am *he*, ye shall die in your sins. 25
Then said they unto him, Who art
thou? And Jesus saith unto them,
Even *the same* that I said unto you
from the beginning. 26 I have many
things to say and to judge of you:
but he that sent me is true; and I
speak to the world those things which
I have heard of him. 27 They understood not that he spake to them
of the Father. 28 Then said Jesus
unto them, When ye have lifted up
the Son of man, then shall ye know
that I am *he*, and *that* I do nothing
of myself; but as my Father hath
taught me, I speak these things. 29
And he that sent me is with me: the
Father hath not left me alone; for I
do always those things that please
him. 30 As he spake these words,
many believed on him.

Christ here gives fair warning to the careless unbelieving Jews to consider what would be the consequence of their infidelity, that they might prevent it before it was too late; for he spoke words of terror as well as words of grace. Observe here,

I. The wrath threatened (*v.* 21): *Jesus said again unto them* that which might be likely to do them good. He continued to teach, in kindness to those few who received his doctrine, though there were many that resisted it, which is an example to ministers to go on with their work, notwithstanding opposition, because a remnant shall be saved. Here Christ changes his voice; he had *piped to them* in the offers of his grace, and they *had not danced;* now he mourns to them in the denunciations of his wrath, to try if they would lament. He said, *I go my way, and you shall seek me, and shall die in your sins. Whither I go you cannot come.* Every word is terrible, and bespeaks spiritual judgments, which are the sorest of all judgments; worse than war, pestilence, and captivity, which the Old-Testament prophets denounced. Four things are here threatened against the Jews.

1. Christ's departure from them: *I go my way,* that is, "It shall not be long before I go; you need not take so much pains to drive me from you, I shall go of myself." They said to him, *Depart from us, we desire not the knowledge of thy ways;* and he takes them at their word; but woe to those from whom Christ departs. Ichabod, the glory is gone, our defence is departed, when Christ goes. Christ frequently warned them of his departure before he left them: he *bade often farewell,* as one *loth to depart,* and willing to be invited, and that would have them *stir up themselves to take hold on him.*

2. Their enmity to the true Messiah, and their fruitless and infatuated enquiries after another Messiah when he was gone away, which were both their sin and their punishment: *You shall seek me,* which intimates either, (1.) Their *enmity* to the *true Christ:* "You shall seek to ruin my interest, by persecuting my doctrine and followers, with a fruitless design to root them out." This was a continual vexation and torment to themselves, made them incurably *ill-natured,* and brought *wrath upon them* (God's and their own) *to the uttermost.* Or, (2.) Their *enquiries* after *false Christs:* "You shall continue your expectations of the Messiah, and be the self-perplexing seekers of a Christ to come, when he is already come;" like the Sodomites, who, being struck with blindness, wearied themselves to find the door. See Rom. ix. 31, 32.

3. Their final impenitency: *You shall die in your sins.* Here is an error in all our English Bibles, even the old bishops' translation, and that of Geneva (the Rhemists only excepted), for all the Greek copies have it in the singular number, *ἐν τῇ ἁμαρτίᾳ ὑμῶν—in your sin,* so all the Latin versions; and Calvin has a note upon the difference between this and *v.* 24, where it is plural, *ταις ἁμαρτίαις,* that here it is meant especially of the sin of unbelief, *in hoc peccato vestro—in this sin of yours.* Note, Those that live in unbelief are for ever undone if they die in unbelief. Or, it may be understood in general, *You shall die in your iniquity,* as Ezek. iii. 19, and xxxiii. 9. Many that have long lived in sin are, through grace, saved by a timely repentance from *dying in sin;* but for those who go out of this world of probation into that of retribution under the guilt of sin unpardoned, and the power

of sin unbroken, there remaineth no relief: salvation itself cannot save them, Job xx. 11; Ezek. xxxii. 27.

4. Their eternal separation from Christ and all happiness in him: *Whither I go you cannot come.* When Christ left the world, he went to a state of perfect happiness; he went to paradise. Thither he took the penitent thief with him, that did not die in his sins; but the impenitent not only *shall not* come to him, but they *cannot;* it is morally impossible, for heaven would not be heaven to those that die unsanctified and unmeet for it. You cannot come, because you have *no right* to enter into that Jerusalem, Rev. xxii. 14. *Whither I go you cannot come,* to fetch me thence, so Dr. Whitby; and the same is the comfort of all good Christians, that, when they get to heaven, they will be out of the reach of their enemies' malice.

II. The jest they made of this threatening. Instead of trembling at this word, they bantered it, and turned it into ridicule (*v.* 22): *Will he kill himself?* See here, 1. What slight thoughts they had of Christ's threatenings; they could make themselves and one another merry with them, as those that mocked the messengers of the Lord, and turned the *burden of the word of the Lord* into a *by-word,* and *precept upon precept, line upon line,* into a merry song, Isa. xxviii. 13. But *be ye not mockers, lest your bands be made strong.* 2. What ill thoughts they had of Christ's meaning, as if he had an inhuman design upon his own life, to avoid the indignities done him, like Saul. This is indeed (say they) to go whither we cannot follow him, for we will never *kill ourselves.* Thus they make him not only such a one as themselves, but worse; yet in the calamities brought by the Romans upon the Jews many of them in discontent and despair did kill themselves. They had put a much more favourable construction upon this word of his (*ch.* vii. 34, 35): *Will he go to the dispersed among the Gentiles?* But see how indulged malice grows more and more malicious.

III. The confirmation of what he had said.

1. He had said, *Whither I go you cannot come,* and here he gives the reason for this (*v.* 23): *You are from beneath, I am from above; you are of this world, I am not of this world.* You are ἐκ τῶν κάτω—*of those things which are beneath;* noting, not so much their rise from beneath as their affection to these lower things: You are *in with these things,* as those that belong to them; how can you come where I go, when your spirit and disposition are so directly contrary to mine?" See here, (1.) What the *spirit of the Lord Jesus* was—not of *this world,* but from *above.* He was perfectly dead to the wealth of the world, the ease of the body, and the praise of men, and was wholly taken up with divine and heavenly things; and none shall be with him but those who are *born from above* and have their *conversation in heaven.* (2.) How contrary to this *their* spirit was: "*You are from beneath,* and of this world." The Pharisees were of a carnal worldly spirit; and what communion could Christ have with them?

2. He had said, *You shall die in your sins,* and here he stands to it: "Therefore I said, You shall die in your sins, because *you are from beneath;*" and he gives this further reason for it, *If you believe not that I am he, you shall die in your sins, v.* 24. See here, (1.) What we are required to believe: *that I am he,* ὅτι ἐγώ εἰμι—*that I am,* which is one of God's names, Exod. iii. 14. It was the Son of God that there said, *Ehejeh asher Ehejeh—I will be what I will be;* for the deliverance of Israel was but a figure of good things to come, but now he saith, "*I am he;*" he that should come, he that you expect the Messias to be, that you would have me to be to you. I am more than the bare name of the Messiah; I do not only call myself so, but I *am he.*" True faith does not *amuse* the soul with an empty sound of words, but *affects* it with the doctrine of Christ's mediation, as a real thing that has real effects. (2.) How necessary it is that we believe this. If we have not this faith, *we shall die in our sins;* for the matter is so settled that without this faith, [1.] We cannot be saved from the power of sin while we live, and therefore shall certainly continue in it to the last. Nothing but the *doctrine* of Christ's grace will be an argument powerful enough, and none but the *Spirit* of Christ's grace will be an agent powerful enough, to turn us from sin to God; and that Spirit is given, and that doctrine given, to be effectual to those only who believe in Christ: so that, if Satan be not by faith dispossessed, he has a lease of the soul for its life; if Christ do not cure us, our case is desperate, and we shall *die in our sins.* [2.] Without faith we cannot be saved from the punishment of sin when we die, for the *wrath of God remains* upon them that believe not, Mark xvi. 16. Unbelief is the damning sin; it is a sin against the remedy. Now this implies the great gospel promise: *If we believe that Christ is he,* and receive him accordingly, *we shall not die in our sins.* The law saith absolutely to all, as Christ said (*v.* 21), *You shall die in your sins,* for we are all guilty before God; but the gospel is a defeasance of the obligation upon condition of believing. The curse of the law is vacated and annulled to all that submit to the grace of the gospel. Believers die in Christ, in his love, in his arms, and so are saved from dying *in their sins.*

IV. Here is a further discourse concerning *himself,* occasioned by his requiring faith in himself as the condition of salvation, *v.* 25—29. Observe,

1. The question which the Jews put to him (*v.* 25): *Who art thou?* This they asked tauntingly, and not with any desire to be instructed. He had said, You must believ

that *I am he.* By his not saying expressly who he was, he plainly intimated that in his person he was such a one as could not be *described* by any, and in his office such a one as was *expected* by all that looked for redemption in Israel; yet this awful manner of speaking, which had so much significancy in it, they turned to his reproach, as if he knew not what to say of himself: "*Who art thou,* that we must with an implicit faith believe in thee, that thou art some mighty HE, we know not *who* or *what,* nor are *worthy to know?*"

2. His answer to this question, wherein he directs them three ways for information:—

(1.) He refers them to *what he had said* all along: "Do you ask who I am? *Even the same that I said unto you from the beginning.*" The original here is a little intricate, τὴν ἀρχὴν ὅ τι καὶ λαλῶ ὑμῖν, which some read thus: *I am the beginning, which also I speak unto you.* So Austin takes it. Christ is called Ἀρχὴ—*the beginning* (Col. i. 18; Rev. i. 8; xxi. 6; iii. 14), and so it agrees with *v.* 24, *I am he.* Compare Isa. xli. 4: *I am the first, I am he.* Those who object that it is the accusative case, and therefore not properly answering to τίς εἶ, must undertake to construe by grammar rules that parallel expression, Rev. i. 8, ὁ ἦν. But most interpreters agree with our version, Do you ask *who I am?* [1.] I am *the same that I said to you from the beginning* of time in the scriptures of the Old-Testament, the same that from the beginning was said to be *the Seed of the woman, that should break the serpent's head,* the same that in all the ages of the church was the Mediator of the covenant, and the faith of the patriarchs. [2.] *From the beginning* of my public ministry. The account he had already given of himself he resolved to *abide by;* he had declared himself to be the *Son of God* (*ch.* v. 17), to be the Christ (*ch.* iv. 26), and the bread of life, and had proposed himself as the object of that faith which is necessary to salvation, and to this he refers them for an answer to their question. Christ is *one with himself;* what he had said from the beginning, he saith still. His is an *everlasting gospel.*

(2.) He refers them to his Father's judgment, and the instructions he had from him (*v.* 26): "*I have many things,* more than you think of, *to say, and* in them *to judge of you.* But why should I trouble myself any further with you? I know very well that *he who sent me is true,* and will stand by me, and bear me out, for *I speak to the world* (to which I am sent as an ambassador) *those things,* all those and those only, *which I have heard of him.*" Here,

[1.] He suppresses his accusation of them. He had *many things* to charge them with, and many evidences to produce against them; but for the present he had said enough. Note, Whatever discoveries of sin are made to us, he that searches the heart has still more to judge of us, 1 John iii. 20. How much soever God reckons with sinners in this world there is still a further reckoning yet behind, Deut. xxxii. 34. Let us learn hence not to be forward to say all we can say, even against the worst of men; we may have many things to say, by way of censure, which yet it is better to leave *unsaid,* for what is it to us?

[2.] He enters his appeal against them to his Father: *He that sent me.* Here two things comfort him:—*First,* That he had been *true to his Father,* and to the trust reposed in him: *I speak to the world* (for his gospel was to be preached to every creature) *those things which I have heard of him.* Being given for a *witness to the people* (Isa. lv. 4), he was *Amen,* a *faithful witness,* Rev. iii. 14. He did not *conceal* his doctrine, but spoke it *to the world* (being of common concern, it was to be of common notice); nor did he change or alter it, nor vary from the instructions he received from him that sent him. *Secondly,* That his Father would be *true to him;* true to the promise that he would *make his mouth like a sharp sword;* true to his purpose concerning him, which was a *decree* (Ps. ii. 7); true to the threatenings of his wrath against those that should reject him. Though he should not *accuse* them to his Father, yet the Father, who sent him, would undoubtedly reckon with them, and would be *true* to what he had said (Deut. xviii. 19), that whosoever would not hearken to that prophet whom God would raise up *he would require it of him.* Christ would not accuse them; "for," saith he, "he that sent me is true, and will pass judgment on them, though I should not demand judgment against them." Thus, when he *lets fall* the present prosecution, he *binds them over* to the judgment-day, when it will be too late to dispute what they will not now be persuaded to believe. *I, as a deaf man, heard not; for thou wilt hear,* Ps. xxxviii. 13, 15. Upon this part of our Saviour's discourse the evangelist has a melancholy remark (*v.* 27): *They understood not that he spoke to them of the Father.* See here, 1. The power of Satan to blind the minds of those who believe not. Though Christ spoke so plainly of God as his Father in heaven, yet they did not understand whom he meant, but thought he spoke of some father he had in Galilee. Thus the plainest things are riddles and parables to those who are resolved to hold fast their prejudices; day and night are alike to the blind. 2. The reason why the threatenings of the word make so little impression upon the minds of sinners; it is because they understand not whose the wrath is that is revealed in them. When Christ told them of the truth of him that sent him, as a warning to them to prepare for his judgment, which is *according to truth,* they slighted the warning, because they understood not to whose judgment it was that they made themselves obnoxious.

(3.) He refers them to *their own convictions*

hereafter, *v.* 28, 29. He finds they will not understand him, and therefore adjourns the trial till further evidence should come in; they that *will not see shall see,* Isa. xxvi. 11. Now observe here,

[1.] *What* they should ere long be *convinced of:* "*You shall know that I am he,* that Jesus is the true Messiah. Whether you will own it or no before men, you shall be made to know it in your own consciences, the convictions of which, though you may *stifle*, yet you cannot *baffle: that I am he,* not that you represent me to be, but he that I preach myself to be, he that should come!" Two things they should be convinced of, in order to this:—*First,* That he did nothing *of himself,* not of himself as man, of himself alone, of himself without the Father, with whom he was *one.* He does not hereby derogate from his own inherent power, but only denies their charge against him as a *false prophet;* for of false prophets it is said that they prophesied *out of their own hearts,* and followed *their own spirits. Secondly,* That as *his Father taught him* so he *spoke these things,* that he was not *αὐτοδίδακτος—selftaught,* but Θεοδίδακτος—*taught of God.* The doctrine he preached was the counterpart of the counsels of God, with which he was intimately acquainted; *καθὼς ἐδίδαξε, ταῦτα λαλῶ*—I speak those things, not only *which* he taught me, but *as* he taught me, with the same divine power and authority.

[2.] *When* they should be convinced of this: *When you have lifted up the Son of man,* lifted him up upon the cross, as the brazen serpent upon the pole (*ch.* iii. 14), as the sacrifices under the law (for Christ is the great sacrifice), which, when they were offered, were said to be *elevated,* or *lifted up;* hence the burnt-offerings, the most ancient and honourable of all, were called *elevations (Gnoloth* from *Gnolah, ascendit—he ascended),* and in many other offerings they used the significant ceremony of *heaving* the sacrifice up, and *moving* it before the Lord; thus was Christ *lifted up,* Or the expression denotes that his death was his exaltation. They that put him to death thought thereby for ever to have *sunk* him and his interest, but it proved to be the advancement of both, *ch.* xii. 24. When the Son of man was *crucified,* the Son of man was *glorified.* Christ had called his dying his *going away;* here he calls it his being lifted *up;* thus the death of the saints, as it is their departure out of this world, so it is their advancement to a better. Observe, He speaks of those he is now talking with as the *instruments* of his death: when *you have lifted up the Son of man;* not that they were to be the *priests* to offer him up (no, that was his own act, he *offered up himself),* but they would be his betrayers and murderers; see Acts ii. 23. They *lifted him up* to the cross, but then he lifted up himself to his Father. Observe with what tenderness and mildness Christ here speaks to those who he certainly knew would put him to death, to teach us not to hate or seek the hurt of any, though we may have reason to think they hate us and seek our hurt. Now, Christ speaks of his death as that which would be a powerful conviction of the infidelity of the Jews. *When you have lifted up the Son of man, then shall you know* this. And why then? *First,* Because careless and unthinking people are often taught the worth of mercies by the want of them, Luke xvii. 22. *Secondly,* The guilt of their sin in putting Christ to death would so awaken their consciences that they would be put upon serious enquiries after a Saviour, and then would know that Jesus was he who alone could save them. And so it proved, when, being told that with wicked hands they had *crucified and slain* the Son of God, they cried out, *What shall we do?* and were made to know assuredly that this Jesus was *Lord and Christ,* Acts ii. 36. *Thirdly,* There would be such signs and wonders attending his death, and the *lifting of him up* from death in his resurrection, as would give a stronger proof of his being the Messiah than any that had been yet given: and multitudes were hereby brought to believe that Jesus is the Christ, who had before contradicted and opposed him. *Fourthly,* By the death of Christ the pouring out of the Spirit was purchased, who would convince the world that *Jesus is he, ch.* xvi. 7, 8. *Fifthly,* The judgments which the Jews brought upon themselves, by putting Christ to death, which filled up the measure of their iniquity, were a sensible conviction to the most hardened among them that *Jesus was he.* Christ had often foretold that desolation as the just punishment of their invincible unbelief, and *when it came to pass (lo, it did come)* they could not but know that the great *prophet had been among them,* Ezek. xxxiii. 33.

[3.] What supported our Lord Jesus in the mean time (*v.* 29): *He that sent me is with me,* in my whole undertaking; *for the Father* (the fountain and first spring of this affair, from whom as its great cause and author it is derived) *hath not left me alone,* to manage it myself, hath not deserted the business nor me in the prosecution of it, for *do I always those things that please him.* Here is,

First, The assurance which Christ had of his Father's *presence* with him, which includes both a divine *power* going along with him to *enable* him for his work, and a divine *favour* manifested to him to *encourage* him in it. *He that sent me is with me,* Isa. xlii. 1; Ps. lxxxix. 21. This greatly *emboldens* our faith in Christ and our reliance upon his word that he had, and knew he had, his Father with him, to *confirm the word of his servant,* Isa. xliv. 26. The King of kings accompanied his own ambassador, to attest his mission and assist his management, and *never left him alone,* either solitary or weak; it also *aggravated* the wickedness of those that opposed him, and was an intimation to them of the *premunire* they ran themselves into by resisting him, for thereby they were found *fighters against God.* How easily soever they might think to crush him and run him down, let them know he had one to back him with whom it is the greatest madness that can be to *contend.*

Secondly, The ground of this assurance: *For I do always those things that please him.* That is, 1. That great affair in which our Lord Jesus was *continually* engaged was an affair which the *Father that sent him* was highly *well pleased with.* His whole undertaking is called the *pleasure of the Lord* (Isa. liii. 10), because of the counsels of the eternal mind about it, and the complacency of the eternal mind in it. 2. His management of that affair was in nothing *displeasing* to his Father; in executing his commission he punctually observed all his instructions, and did in nothing vary from them. No mere man since the fall could say such a word as this (for *in many things we offend all)* but our Lord Jesus never offended his Father in any thing, but, as became him, he *fulfilled all righteousness.* This was necessary to the validity and value of the sacrifice he was to offer up; for if he had in any thing *displeased* the Father himself, and so had had any sin of his own to answer for, the Father could not have been pleased with him as a propitiation for our sins; but such a priest and such a sacrifice became us as was perfectly pure and spotless. We may likewise learn hence that God's servants may *then* expect God's presence with them when they *choose* and do *those things that please him,* Isa. lxvi. 4, 5.

V. Here is the good effect which this discourse of Christ's had upon some of his hearers (*v.* 30): *As he spoke these words many believed on him.* Note, 1. Though multitudes perish in their unbelief, yet there is a remnant according to the election of grace, who *believe to the saving of the soul.* If Israel, the whole body of the people, *be not gathered,* yet there are those of them in whom Christ will be *glorious,* Isa. xlix. 5. This the apostle insists upon, to reconcile the Jews' rejection with the *promises made unto their fathers.* There is a remnant, Rom. xi. 5. 2. The words of Christ, and particularly his *threatening* words, are made effectual by the grace of God to bring in poor souls to believe in him. When Christ told them that if they *believed not* they should *die in their sins,* and never get to heaven, they thought it was time to look about them, Rom. i. 16, 18. 3. Sometimes there is a *wide door opened,* and an *effectual* one, even where there are *many adversaries.* Christ will carry on his work, though *the heathen rage.* The gospel sometimes gains great victories where it meets with great opposition. Let this encourage God's ministers to preach the gospel, though it be with *much contention,* for they shall not *labour in vain.* Many may be *secretly* brought home to God by those endeavours which are openly contradicted and cavilled at by men of corrupt minds. Austin has an affectionate ejaculation in his lecture upon these words: *Utinam et, me loquenti, multi credant; non in me, sed mecum in eo—I wish that when I speak, many may believe, not on me, but with me on him.*

31 Then said Jesus to those Jews
which believed on him, If ye continue
in my word, *then* are ye my disciples
indeed; 32 And ye shall know the
truth, and the truth shall make you
free. 33 They answered him, We
be Abraham's seed, and were never
in bondage to any man: how sayest
thou, Ye shall be made free? 34
Jesus answered them, Verily, verily,
I say unto you, Whosoever committeth sin is the servant of sin. 35
And the servant abideth not in the
house for ever: *but* the Son abideth
ever. 36 If the Son therefore shall
make you free, ye shall be free indeed. 37 I know that ye are Abraham's seed; but ye seek to kill
me, because my word hath no place in
you.

We have in these verses,

I. A comfortable doctrine laid down concerning the *spiritual liberty* of Christ's disciples, intended for the encouragement of *those* Jews *that believed.* Christ, knowing that his doctrine began to work upon some of his hearers, and perceiving that virtue had gone out of him, turned his discourse from the proud Pharisees, and addressed himself to those *weak* believers. When he had denounced wrath against those that were hardened in unbelief, then he spoke comfort to those few feeble *Jews that believed in him.* See here,

1. How graciously the Lord Jesus looks to those that *tremble at his word,* and are ready to receive it; he has something to say to those who have hearing ears, and will not pass by those who set themselves in his way, without speaking to them.

2. How carefully he cherishes the beginnings of grace, and meets those that are coming towards him. These *Jews that believed* were yet but *weak;* but Christ did not therefore cast them off, for he *gathers the lambs in his arms.* When faith is in its infancy, he has *knees* to *prevent it, breasts* for it to *suck,* that it may not *die from the womb.* In what he said to them, we have two things, which he saith to all that should at any time believe:—

(1.) The character of a true disciple of Christ: *If you continue in my word, then are you my disciples indeed.* When they *believed on him,* as the great prophet, they gave up themselves to be *his disciples.* Now, at their entrance into his school, he lays down this for a settled rule, that he would own none for his disciples but those that *continued in his word.* [1.] It is implied that there are many who profess themselves Christ's disciples who are not his *disciples indeed,* but only in show and name. [2.] It highly concerns those that are not *strong in faith* to see to it that they be *sound in the faith,* that, though not disciples of the highest form, they are nevertheless *disciples indeed.* [3.] Those who seem willing to be Christ's disciples ought to be told that they had as good never come to him, unless they come with a resolution by his grace to abide by him. Let those who have thoughts of covenanting with Christ have no thoughts of reserving a power of revocation. Children are sent to school, and bound apprentices, only for a *few years;* but those only are Christ's who are willing to be bound to him *for the term of life.* [4.] Those only that *continue in Christ's word* shall be accepted as his *disciples indeed,* that adhere to his word in every instance without partiality, and abide by it to the end without apostasy. It is *μενεῖν—to dwell* in Christ's word, as a man does at home, which is his centre, and rest, and refuge. Our converse with the word and conformity to it must be constant. If we continue disciples to the last, then, and not otherwise, we approve ourselves *disciples indeed.*

(2.) The privilege of a true disciple of Christ. Here are two precious promises made to those who thus approve themselves disciples indeed, *v.* 32.

[1.] "*You shall know the truth,* shall know all that truth which it is needful and profitable for you to know, and shall be more confirmed in the belief of it, shall know the certainty of it." Note, *First,* Even those who are true believers, and disciples indeed, yet may be, and are, much in the dark concerning many things which they should know. God's children are but children, and understand and speak as children. Did we not need to be taught, we should not need to be disciples. *Secondly,* It is a very great privilege to *know the truth,* to know the particular truths which we are to believe, in their mutual dependences and connections, and the grounds and reasons of our belief,—to know what is truth and what proves it to be so. *Thirdly,* It is a gracious promise of Christ, to all who continue in his word, that they shall know the truth as far as is needful and profitable for them. Christ's scholars are sure to be well taught.

[2.] *The truth shall make you free;* that is, *First,* The truth which Christ teaches tends to make men free, Isa. lxi. 1. Justification makes us free from the guilt of sin, by which we were *bound over* to the judgment of God, and *bound under* amazing fears; sanctification makes us free from the bondage of corruption, by which we were *restrained* from that service which is perfect freedom, and *constrained* to that which is perfect slavery. Gospel truth frees us from the yoke of the ceremonial law, and the more grievous burdens of the traditions of the elders. It makes us *free from* our spiritual enemies, free *in* the service of God, free *to* the privileges of sons, and free *of* the Jerusalem which is from above, which is free. *Secondly,* The knowing, entertaining, and believing, of this truth does actually *make us free,* free from prejudices, mistakes, and false notions, than which nothing more *enslaves* and *entangles* the soul, free from the dominion of lust and passion; and restores the soul to the government of itself, by reducing it into obedience to its Creator. The mind, by admitting the truth of Christ in the light and power, is vastly enlarged, and has scope and compass given it, is greatly elevated and raised above things of sense, and never acts with so true a liberty as when it acts under a divine command, 2 Cor. iii. 17. The enemies of Christianity pretend to *free thinking,* whereas really those are the freest reasonings that are guided by faith, and those are men of *free thought* whose thoughts are captivated and brought into obedience to Christ.

II. The offence which the carnal Jews took at this doctrine, and their objection against it. Though it was a doctrine that brought glad tidings of liberty to the captives, yet they cavilled at it, *v.* 33. The Pharisees grudged this comfortable word to those that believed, the standers by, who had *no part nor lot in this matter;* they thought themselves reflected upon and affronted by the gracious charter of liberty granted to those that believed, and therefore with a great deal of pride and envy they answered him, "*We Jews are Abraham's seed,* and therefore are *free-born,* and have not lost our birthright-freedom; *we were never in bondage to any man; how sayest thou then,* to us Jews, *You shall be made free?*" See here,

1. What it was that they were grieved at; it was an *innuendo* in those words, *You shall be made free,* as if the Jewish church and nation were in some sort of bondage, which reflected on the Jews in general, and as if all that did not believe in Christ continued in that bondage, which reflected on the Pharisees in particular. Note, The privileges of the faithful are the envy and vexation of unbelievers, Ps. cxii. 10.

2. What it was that they alleged against it; whereas Christ intimated that they needed to be made free, they urge, (1.) "We are Abraham's seed, and Abraham was a *prince and a great man;* though we live in Canaan, we are not descended from Canaan, nor under his doom, *a servant of servants shall he be;* we hold in *frank-almoign—free alms,* and not in *villenage—by a servile tenure.*" It is common for a sinking decaying family to boast of the glory and dignity of its ancestors, and to borrow honour from that name to which they repay disgrace; so the Jews here did. But

this was not all. Abraham was in covenant with God, and his children by his right, Rom. xi. 28. Now that covenant, no doubt, was a free charter, and invested them with privileges not consistent with a state of slavery, Rom. ix. 4. And therefore they thought they had no occasion with so *great a sum* as they reckoned faith in Christ to be *to obtain this freedom,* when they were thus free-born. Note, It is the common fault and folly of those that have pious parentage and education to trust to their privilege, and boast of it, as if it would atone for the want of real holiness. They were Abraham's seed, but what would this avail them, when we find one in hell that could call Abraham father? Saving benefits are not, like common privileges, conveyed by *entail* to us and our issue, nor can a title to heaven be made by *descent,* nor may we claim as *heirs at law,* by making out our pedigree; our title is purely by purchase, not our own but our Redeemer's for us, under certain provisos and limitations, which if we do not observe it will not avail us to be Abraham's seed. Thus many, when they are pressed with the necessity of regeneration, turn it off with this, *We are the church's children*; but they are not all Israel that are of Israel. (2.) *We were never in bondage to any man.* Now observe, [1.] How false this allegation was. I wonder now they could have the assurance to say a thing in the face of a congregation which was so notoriously *untrue.* Were not the seed of Abraham in bondage to the Egyptians? Were they not often in bondage to the neighbouring nations in the time of the judges? Were they not seventy years captives in Babylon? Nay, were they not at this time tributaries to the Romans, and, though not in a *personal,* yet in a *national* bondage to them, and groaning to be made free? And yet, to confront Christ, they have the impudence to say, *We were never in bondage.* Thus they would expose Christ to the ill-will both of the Jews, who were very jealous for the honour of their liberty, and of the Romans, who would not be thought to enslave the nations they conquered. [2.] How foolish the application was. Christ had spoken of a liberty wherewith the *truth* would make them free, which must be meant of a *spiritual* liberty, for truth as it is the *enriching,* so it is the *enfranchising* of the mind, and the *enlarging* of that from the captivity of error and prejudice; and yet they plead against the offer of *spiritual* liberty that they were never in *corporal* thraldom, as if, because they were never in bondage to any *man,* they were never in bondage to any *lust.* Note, Carnal hearts are sensible of no other grievances than those that molest the body and injure their secular affairs. Talk to them of encroachments upon their civil liberty and property,—tell them of waste committed upon their lands, or damage done to their houses,—and they understand you very well, and can give you a sensible answer; the thing touches them and affects them. But discourse to them of the bondage of sin, a captivity to Satan, and a liberty by Christ,—tell them of wrong done to their precious souls, and the hazard of their eternal welfare,—and *you bring certain strange things to their ears;* they say of it (as those did, Ezek. xx. 49), *Doth he not speak parables?* This was much like the blunder Nicodemus made about being *born again.*

III. Our Saviour's vindication of his doctrine from these objections, and the further explication of it, *v.* 34—37, where he does these four things:—

1. He shows that, notwithstanding their civil liberties and their visible church-membership, yet it was possible that they might be in a state of bondage (*v.* 34): *Whosoever commits sin,* though he be of Abraham's seed, and was never in bondage to any man, is the servant of sin. Observe, Christ does not upbraid them with the falsehood of their plea, or their present bondage, but further explains what he had said for their edification. Thus ministers should with meekness instruct those that oppose them, that they may *recover themselves,* not with passion provoke them to entangle themselves yet more. Now here,

(1.) The preface is very solemn: *Verily, verily, I say unto you;* an awful asseveration, which our Saviour often used, to command a reverent attention and a ready assent. The style of the prophets was, *Thus saith the Lord,* for they were *faithful as servants;* but Christ, being a Son, speaks in his own name: *I say unto you,* I the *Amen,* the faithful witness; he pawns his veracity upon it. "I say it to you, who boast of your relation to Abraham, as if that would save you."

(2.) The truth is of universal concern, though here delivered upon a particular occasion: *Whosoever commits sin is the servant of sin,* and sadly needs to be made free. A state of sin is a state of bondage. [1.] See who it is on whom this brand is fastened—on him that *commits sin,* πᾶς ὁ ποιῶν αμαρτίαν—*every one that makes sin.* There is not a *just man* upon earth, that *lives, and sins not;* yet every one that sins is not a servant of sin, for then God would have no servants; but he that *makes sin,* that *makes choice* of sin, prefers the way of wickedness before the way of holiness (Jer. xliv. 16, 17),—that *makes a covenant* with sin, enters into league with it, and *makes a marriage* with it,—that *makes contrivances* of sin, *makes provision* for the flesh, and devises iniquity,—and that *makes a custom* of sin, who walks after the flesh, and *makes a trade* of sin. [2.] See what the brand is which Christ fastens upon those that thus *commit sin.* He stigmatizes them, gives them a mark of servitude. They are *servants of sin,* imprisoned under the guilt of sin, under an arrest, in hold for it, *concluded under sin,* and they are subject to the power of sin. He is a *servant of sin,* that is, he makes himself so, and is so accounted; he has *sold himself to work wickedness;* his lusts give law to him, he is at their beck, and is not his own master. He does the work of sin, supports its interest, and accepts its wages, Rom. vi. 16.

2. He shows them that, being in a state of bondage, their having a place in the house of God would not entitle them to the inheritance of sons; for (*v.* 35) *the servant,* though he be in the house for awhile, yet, being but a *servant, abideth not in the house for ever.* Services (we say) are no inheritances, they are but *temporary,* and not for a *perpetuity; but the son* of the family abideth ever. Now, (1.) This points primarily at the rejection of the Jewish church and nation. Israel had been *God's son,* his *first-born;* but they wretchedly degenerated into a *servile* disposition, were enslaved to the world and the flesh, and therefore, though by virtue of their birthright they thought themselves secure of their church-membership, Christ tells them that having thus made themselves servants they should not *abide in the house for ever.* Jerusalem, by opposing the gospel of Christ, which proclaimed liberty, and adhering to the Sinai-covenant, which gendered to bondage, after its term was *expired* came to be *in bondage with her children* (Gal. iv. 24, 25), and therefore was unchurched and disfranchised, her charter seized and taken away, and she was cast out as the son of the bond-woman, Gen. xxi. 14. Chrysostom gives this sense of this place: "Think not to be made free from sin by the rites and ceremonies of the law of Moses, for Moses was but a servant, and had not that perpetual authority in the church which the Son had; but, if the Son make you free, it is well," *v.* 36. But, (2.) It looks further, to the rejection of all that are the *servants of sin,* and receive not the *adoption* of the *sons of God;* though those unprofitable servants may be in God's house awhile, as retainers to his family, yet there is a day coming when the children of the *bond-woman* and of the *free* shall be distinguished. True believers only, who are the children of the promise and of the covenant, are accounted free, and shall abide for ever in the house, as Isaac: they shall have a *nail* in the holy place on earth (Ezra ix. 8) and *mansions* in the holy place in heaven, *ch.* xiv. 2.

3. He shows them the way of deliverance out of this state of bondage into the *glorious liberty of the children of God,* Rom. viii. 21. The case of those that are the servants of sin is sad, but thanks be to God it is not helpless, it is not hopeless. As it is the privilege of all the sons of the family, and their dignity above the servants, that they abide in the house for ever; so he who is *the Son,* the first-born among many brethren, and the heir of all things, has a power both of manumission and of adoption (*v.* 36): *If the Son shall make you free, you shall be free indeed.* Note,

(1.) Jesus Christ in the gospel offers us *our freedom;* he has authority and power to *make free.* [1.] To *discharge prisoners;* this he does *in justification,* by making satisfaction for *our guilt* (on which the gospel offer is grounded, which is to all a conditional *act of indemnity,* and to all true believers, upon their believing, an absolute *charter of pardon),* and for *our debts,* for which we were by the law arrested and in execution. Christ, as our surety, or rather our *bail* (for he was not originally bound *with us,* but upon our insolvency bound *for us),* compounds with the creditor, answers the demands of injured justice with more than an *equivalent,* takes the *bond* and *judgment* into his own hands, and gives them up *cancelled* to all that by faith and repentance give him (if I may so say) a *counter-security* to save his honour harmless, and so they are *made free;* and from the debt, and every part thereof, they are for ever acquitted, exonerated, and discharged, and a general release is sealed of all actions and claims; while against those who refuse to come up to these terms the securities lie still in the Redeemer's hands, in full force. [2.] He has a power to rescue *bond-slaves,* and this he does in *sanctification;* by the powerful arguments of his gospel, and the powerful operations of his Spirit, he breaks the power of corruption in the soul, rallies the scattered forces of reason and virtue, and fortifies God's interest against sin and Satan, and so the soul is made free. [3.] He has a power to *naturalize strangers and foreigners,* and this he does in *adoption.* This is a further act of grace; we are not only forgiven and healed, but *preferred;* there is a charter of privileges as well as pardon; and thus the Son makes us free *denizens* of the kingdom of priests, the holy nation, the new Jerusalem.

(2.) Those whom Christ makes free are *free indeed.* It is not ἀληθῶς, the word used (*v.* 31) for disciples *indeed,* but ὄντως—*really.* It denotes, [1.] The truth and certainty of the promise, the liberty which the Jews boasted of was an *imaginary* liberty; they boasted of a *false gift;* but the liberty which Christ gives is a certain thing, it is real, and has real effects. The servants of sin promise themselves liberty, and fancy themselves free, when they have broken religion's bands asunder; but they cheat themselves. None are *free indeed* but those whom Christ *makes free.* [2.] It denotes the singular excellency of the freedom promised; it is a freedom that deserves the name, in comparison with which all other liberties are no better than slaveries, so much does it turn to the honour and advantage of those that are *made free* by it. It is a *glorious* liberty. It is that which *is* (so ὄντως signifies); it is *substance* (Prov. viii. 21); while the things of the world are shadows, things that *are not.*

4. He applies this to these unbelieving cavilling Jews, in answer to their boasts of relation to Abraham (*v.* 37): "*I know* very well *that you are Abraham's seed, but now you seek to kill me,* and therefore have forfeited

the honour of your relation to Abraham, *because my word hath no place in you.*" Observe here,

(1.) The dignity of their extraction admitted: "*I know that you are Abraham's seed,* every one knows it, and it is your honour." He grants them what was true, and in what they said that was false (that they were *never* in bondage to any) he does not *contradict* them, for he studied to *profit* them, and not to *provoke* them, and therefore said that which would please them: *I know that you are Abraham's seed.* They boasted of their descent from *Abraham,* as that which *aggrandized* their names, and made them exceedingly honourable; whereas really it did but *aggravate* their crimes, and make them exceedingly sinful. Out of their own mouths will he judge vain-glorious hypocrites, who boast of their parentage and education: "Are you Abraham's seed? Why then did you not tread in the steps of his faith and obedience?"

(2.) The inconsistency of their practice with this dignity: *But you seek to kill me.* They had attempted it several times, and were now designing it, which quickly appeared (*v.* 59), when they *took up stones to cast at him.* Christ knows all the wickedness, not only which men do, but which they seek, and design, and endeavour to do. To seek to kill any innocent man is a crime black enough, but to *compass and imagine* the death of him that was King of kings was a crime the heinousness of which we want words to express.

(3.) The reason of this inconsistency. Why were they that were Abraham's seed so very inveterate against Abraham's promised seed, in whom they and *all the families of the earth* should be *blessed?* Our Saviour here tells them, It is because *my word hath no place in you, οὐ χωρεῖ ἐν ὑμῖν, Non capit in vobis,* so the Vulgate. "My word *does not take with you,* you have no inclination to it, no relish of it, other things are more taking, more pleasing." Or, "It does not *take hold of you,* it has no power over you, makes no impression upon you." Some of the critics read it, *My word does not penetrate into you;* it descended as the rain, but it came upon them as the rain upon the rock, which it runs off, and did not soak into their hearts, as the rain upon the ploughed ground. The Syriac reads it, "*Because you do not acquiesce in my word;* you are not persuaded of the truth of it, nor pleased with the goodness of it." Our translation is very significant: *It has no place in you.* They *sought to kill him,* and so effectually to *silence* him, not because he had done them any harm, but because they could not bear the convincing, commanding power of his word. Note, [1.] The words of Christ ought to have a place in us, the innermost and uppermost place,—a *dwelling* place, as a man at home, and not as a stranger or sojourner,—a *working* place; it must have room to operate, to work sin out of us, and to work grace in us; it must have a *ruling* place, its place must be *upon the throne,* it must dwell in us richly. [2.] There are many that make a profession of religion in whom *the word of* Christ has no place; they will not *allow* it a place, for they do not like it; Satan does all he can to *displace* it; and other things possess the place it should have in us. [3.] Where the word of God has no place no good is to be expected, for room is left there for all wickedness. If the unclean spirit find the heart empty of Christ's word, he *enters in, and dwells there.*

38 I speak that which I have seen
with my Father: and ye do that
which ye have seen with your father.
39 They answered and said unto him,
Abraham is our father. Jesus saith
unto them, If ye were Abraham's
children, ye would do the works of
Abraham. 40 But now ye seek to
kill me, a man that hath told you the
truth, which I have heard of God:
this did not Abraham. 41 Ye do
the deeds of your father. Then said
they to him, We be not born of fornication: we have one Father, *even*
God. 42 Jesus said unto them, If
God were your Father, ye would love
me: for I proceeded forth and came
from God; neither came I of myself,
but he sent me. 43 Why do ye not
understand my speech? *even* because ye cannot hear my word. 44
Ye are of *your* father the devil, and
the lusts of your father ye will do.
He was a murderer from the beginning, and abode not in the truth, because there is no truth in him.
When he speaketh a lie, he speaketh
of his own: for he is a liar, and the
father of it. 45 And because I tell
you the truth, ye believe me not.
46 Which of you convinceth me of
sin? And if I say the truth, why
do ye not believe me? 47 He that
is of God heareth God's words: ye
therefore hear *them* not, because ye
are not of God.

Here Christ and the Jews are still at issue; he sets himself to convince and convert them, while they still set themselves to contradict and oppose him.

I. He here traces the difference between his sentiments and theirs to a different rise and origin (*v.* 38): *I speak that which I have seen with my Father,* and *you* do *what you have seen with your father.* Here are two fathers spoken of, according to the two families into which the sons of men are divided

—God and the devil, and without controversy these are contrary the one to the other.

1. Christ's *doctrine* was from *heaven;* it was *copied* out of the *counsels* of infinite wisdom, and the kind intentions of eternal love. (1.) *I speak that which I have seen.* The discoveries Christ has made to us of God and another world are not grounded upon guess and hearsay, but upon ocular inspection; so that he was thoroughly *apprized* of the nature, and *assured* of the truth, of all he said. He that is given to be a witness to the people is an eye-witness, and therefore unexceptionable. (2.) It is what I have seen *with my Father.* The doctrine of Christ is not a plausible hypothesis, supported by probable arguments, but it is an exact counterpart of the incontestable truths lodged in the eternal mind. It was not only what he had *heard from* his Father, but what he had *seen with him* when *the counsel of peace was between them both.* Moses spoke what he heard from God, but he might not see the face of God; Paul had been in the third heaven, but what he had seen there he could not, he must not, utter; for it was Christ's prerogative to have *seen* what he *spoke,* and to *speak* what he had *seen.*

2. Their *doings* were from hell: "*You do that which you have seen with your father.* You do, by your own works, father yourselves, for it is evident whom you resemble, and therefore easy to find out your origin." As a child that is trained up with his father learns his father's words and fashions, and grows like him by an affected imitation as well as by a natural image, so these Jews, by their malicious opposition to Christ and the gospel, made themselves as like the devil as if they had industriously set him before them for their pattern.

II. He takes off and answers their vain-glorious boasts of relation to Abraham and to God as their fathers, and shows the vanity and falsehood of their pretensions.

1. They pleaded relation to Abraham, and he replies to this plea. *They said, Abraham is our father, v.* 39. In this they intended, (1.) To do honour to themselves, and to make themselves look great. They had forgotten the mortification given them by that acknowledgment prescribed them (Deut. xxvi. 5), *A Syrian ready to perish was my father;* and the charge exhibited against their degenerate ancestors (whose steps they trod in, and not those of the first founder of the family), *Thy father was an Amorite, and thy mother a Hittite,* Ezek xvi. 3. As it is common for those families that are sinking and going to decay to boast most of their pedigree, so it is common for those churches that are corrupt and depraved to value themselves upon their antiquity and the eminence of their first planters. *Fuimus Troes, fuit Ilium—We have been Trojans, and there once was Troy.* (2.) They designed to cast an odium upon Christ as if he reflected upon the patriarch Abraham, in speaking of their father as one they had learned evil from. See how they sought an occasion to quarrel with him. Now Christ overthrows this plea, and exposes the vanity of it by a plain and cogent argument: "Abraham's children will do the works of Abraham, but you do not do Abraham's works, therefore you are not Abraham's children."

[1.] The proposition is plain: *If you were Abraham's children,* such children of Abraham as could claim an interest in the covenant made with him and his seed, which would indeed put an honour upon you, then you would *do the works of Abraham,* for to those only of Abraham's house who *kept the way of the Lord,* as Abraham did, would God *perform what he had spoken,*" Gen. xviii. 19. Those only are reckoned the seed of Abraham, to whom the promise belongs, who *tread in the steps* of his faith and obedience, Rom. iv. 12. Though the Jews had their genealogies, and kept them exact, yet they could not by them make out their relation to Abraham, so as to take the benefit of the old entail *(per formam doni—according to the form of the gift),* unless they walked in the same spirit; good women's relation to Sarah is proved only by this—*whose daughters you are as long as you do well,* and no longer, 1 Pet. iii. 6. Note, Those who would approve themselves Abraham's seed must not only be of Abraham's faith, but do Abraham's works (James ii. 21, 22),—must come at God's call, as he did,—must follow God wherever he leads them,—must resign their dearest comforts to him,—must be strangers and sojourners in this world,—must keep up the worship of God in their families, and always walk before God in their uprightness; for these were the works of Abraham.

[2.] The assumption is evident likewise: *But you do not do* the works of Abraham, for *you seek to kill me, a man that has told you the truth, which I have heard of God; this did not Abraham, v.* 40.

First, He shows them what their work was, their present work, which they were now about; they *sought to kill him;* and three things are intimated as an aggravation of their intention:—1. They were so *unnatural* as to seek the life of *a man,* a man like themselves, bone of their bone, and flesh of their flesh, who had done them no harm, nor given them any provocation. You *imagine mischief against a man,* Ps. lxii. 3. 2. They were so *ungrateful* as to seek the life of one who had *told them the truth,* had not only done them no injury, but had done them the greatest kindness that could be; had not only not imposed upon them with a lie, but had instructed them in the most necessary and important truths; *was he therefore become their enemy?* 3. They were so *ungodly* as to seek the life of one who told them the truth *which he had heard from God,* who was a messenger sent from God to them, so that their attempt against him was *quasi deicidium—an act of malice against God.* This was their work, and they persisted in it.

Secondly, He shows them that this did not become the children of Abraham; for *this did not Abraham.* 1. "He did nothing like this." He was famous for his humanity, witness his rescue of the captives; and for his piety, witness his obedience to the heavenly vision in many instances, and some tender ones. Abraham believed God; they were obstinate in unbelief: Abraham followed God; they fought against him; so that he would be *ignorant of them, and would not acknowledge them,* they were so unlike him, Isa. lxiii. 16. See Jer. xxii. 15—17. 2. "He would not have done thus if he had lived now, or I had lived then." *Hoc Abraham non fecisset—He would not have done this;* so some read it. We should thus reason ourselves out of any way of wickedness; would Abraham, and Isaac, and Jacob have done so? We cannot expect to be *ever with them,* if we be *never like them.*

[3.] The conclusion follows of course (*v.* 41): "Whatever your boasts and pretensions be, you are not Abraham's children, but father yourselves upon another family (*v.* 41); there is *a father whose deeds you do,* whose spirit you are of, and whom you resemble." He does not *yet* say plainly that he means the devil, till they by their continued cavils forced him so to explain himself, which teaches us to treat even bad men with civility and respect, and not to be forward to say that *of* them, or *to* them, which, though *true,* sounds *harsh.* He tried whether they would suffer their own consciences to infer from what he said that they were the devil's children; and it is better to hear it from them now that we are called to *repent,* that is, to change our father and change our family, by changing our spirit and way, than to hear it from Christ in the great day.

2. So far were they from owning their unworthiness of relation to Abraham that they pleaded relation to God himself as their Father: "We are *not born of fornication,* we are not bastards, but legitimate sons; *we have one Father, even God.*

(1.) Some understand this literally. They were not the sons of the bondwoman, as the Ishmaelites were; nor begotten in incest, as the Moabites and Ammonites were (Deut. xxiii. 3); nor were they a spurious brood in Abraham's family, but Hebrews of the Hebrews; and, being born in *lawful* wedlock, they might call God *Father,* who instituted that honourable estate in innocency; for a legitimate seed, not tainted with divorces nor the plurality of wives, is called a *seed of God,* Mal. ii. 15.

(2.) Others take it figuratively. They begin to be aware now that Christ spoke of a *spiritual* not a *carnal* father, of the father of their religion; and so,

[1.] They deny themselves to be a generation of idolaters: "We are *not born of fornication,* are not the children of idolatrous parents, nor have been bred up in idolatrous worships." Idolatry is often spoken of as spiritual *whoredom,* and idolaters as *children of whoredoms,* Hosea ii. 4; Isa. lvii. 3. Now, if they meant that they were not the posterity of idolaters, the allegation was false, for no nation was more addicted to idolatry than the Jews before the captivity; if they meant no more than that they themselves were not idolaters, what then? A man may be free from idolatry, and yet perish in another iniquity, and be shut out of Abraham's covenant. *If thou commit no idolatry* (apply it to this spiritual fornication), yet if thou kill thou art become a *transgressor* of the covenant. A rebellious prodigal son will be disinherited, though he be not *born of fornication.*

[2.] They boast themselves to be true worshippers of the true God. We have not many fathers, as the heathens had, *gods many and lords many,* and yet were without God, as *filius populi—a son of the people,* has many fathers and yet none certain; no, *the Lord our God is one Lord* and *one Father,* and therefore it is well with us. Note, Those flatter themselves, and put a damning cheat upon their own souls, who imagine that their professing the true religion and worshipping the true God will save them, though they worship not God in spirit and in truth, nor are true to their profession. Now our Saviour gives a full answer to this fallacious plea (*v.* 42, 43), and proves, by two arguments, that they had no right to call God Father.

First, They did not love Christ: *If God were your Father, you would love me.* He had disproved their relation to Abraham by their going about to kill him (*v.* 40), but here he disproves their relation to God by their not loving and owning him. A man may pass for a *child* of Abraham if he do not appear an enemy to Christ by gross sin; but he cannot approve himself a child of God unless he be a faithful friend and follower of Christ. Note, All that have God for their Father have a true love to Jesus Christ, an esteem of his person, a grateful sense of his love, a sincere affection to his cause and kingdom, a complacency in the salvation wrought out by him and in the method and terms of it, and a care to keep his commandments, which is the surest evidence of our love to him. We are here in a state of probation, upon our trial how we will conduct ourselves towards our Maker, and accordingly it will be with us in the state of retribution. God has taken various methods to prove us, and this was one: he sent his Son into the world, with sufficient proofs of his sonship and mission, concluding that all that called him Father would *kiss his Son,* and bid *him* welcome who was the first-born among many brethren; see 1 John v. 1. By this our adoption will be proved or disproved—Did we love Christ, or no? *If any man do not,* he is so far from being a child of

God that he is *anathema,* accursed, 1 Cor. xvi. 22. Now our Saviour proves that if they were God's children they would *love him;* for, saith he, I proceeded *forth and came from God.* They will love him; for, 1. He was the *Son of God: I proceeded forth from God.* Ἐξῆλθον· this means his divine ἐξέλευσις, or origin from the Father, by the communication of the divine essence, and also the union of the divine λογὸς to his human nature; so Dr. Whitby. Now this could not but recommend him to the affections of all that were *born of God.* Christ is called the *beloved,* because, being the beloved of the Father, he is certainly the beloved of all the saints, Eph. i. 6. 2. He was *sent of God,* came from him as an ambassador to the world of mankind. He did not *come of himself,* as the false prophets, who had not either their *mission* or their *message* from God, Jer. xxiii. 21. Observe the emphasis he lays upon this: *I came from God; neither came I of myself, but he sent me.* He had both his credentials and his instructions from God; he came to *gather together in one the children of God* (*ch.* xi. 52), to bring *many sons to glory,* Heb. ii. 10. And would not all God's children embrace with both arms a messenger sent from their Father on *such* errands? But these Jews made it appear that they were nothing akin to God, by their want of affection to Jesus Christ.

Secondly, They did not understand him. It was a sign they did not belong to God's family that they did not understand the language and dialect of the family: *You do not understand my speech* (*v.* 43), την λαλιὰν την ἐμὴν. Christ's speech was divine and heavenly, but intelligible enough to those that were acquainted with the voice of Christ in the Old Testament. Those that had made the word of the Creator familiar to them needed no other key to the dialect of the Redeemer; and yet these Jews make strange of the doctrine of Christ, and find knots in it, and I know not what stumbling stones. Could a Galilean be known by his speech? An Ephraimite by his *sibboleth?* And would any have the confidence to call God Father to whom the Son of God was a barbarian, even when he spoke the will of God in the words of the Spirit of God? Note, Those who are not acquainted with the divine speech have reason to fear that they are strangers to the divine nature. Christ spoke the words of God (*ch.* iii. 34) in the dialect of the kingdom of God; and yet they, who pretended to belong to the kingdom, understood not the idioms and properties of it, but like strangers, and rude ones too, ridiculed it. And the reason why they did not understand Christ's speech made the matter much worse: *Even because you cannot hear my word,* that is, "You cannot persuade yourselves to hear it attentively, impartially, and without prejudice, as it should be heard." The meaning of this *cannot* is an obstinate *will not;* as the Jews could not hear Stephen (Acts vii. 57) nor Paul, Acts xxii. 22. Note, The rooted antipathy of men's corrupt hearts to the doctrine of Christ is the true reason of their ignorance of it, and of their errors and mistakes about it. They do not like it nor love it, and therefore they will not understand it; like Peter, who pretended he *knew not what the damsel said* (Matt. xxvi. 70), when in truth he knew not what to say to it. *You cannot hear my words,* for you have *stopped your ears* (Ps. lviii. 4, 5), and God, in a way of righteous judgment, *has made your ears heavy,* Isa. vi. 10.

III. Having thus disproved their relation both to Abraham and to God, he comes next to tell them plainly whose children they were: *You are of your father the devil, v.* 44. If they were not God's children, they were the devil's, for God and Satan divide the world of mankind; the devil is *therefore* said to *work in the children of disobedience,* Eph. ii. 2. All wicked people are the devil's children, *children of Belial* (2 Cor. vi. 15), the serpent's seed (Gen. iii 15), children of the wicked one, Matt. xiii. 38. They partake of his nature, bear his image, obey his commands, and follow his example. Idolaters *said to a stock, Thou art our father,* Jer. ii. 27.

This is a high charge, and sounds very harsh and horrid, that any of the children of men, especially the church's children, should be called *children of the devil,* and therefore our Saviour fully proves it,

1. By a general argument: *The lusts of your father you will do,* θέλετε ποιεῖν. (1.) "You *do* the devil's lusts, the lusts which he would have you to fulfil; you gratify and please him, and comply with his temptations, and are *led captive by him at his will:* nay, you do those lusts which the devil himself fulfils. Fleshly lusts and worldly lusts the devil tempts men to; but, being a spirit, he cannot fulfil them himself. The peculiar lusts of the devil are *spiritual wickedness;* the lusts of the intellectual powers, and their corrupt reasonings; pride and envy, and wrath and malice; enmity to that which is good, and enticing others to that which is evil; these are lusts which the devil fulfils, and those who are under the dominion of these lusts resemble the devil, as the child does the parent. The more there is of contemplation, and contrivance, and secret complacency, in sin, the more it resembles the *lusts of the devil.* (2.) You *will do* the devil's lusts. The more there is of the *will* in these lusts, the more there is of the devil in them. When sin is committed *of choice* and not by surprise, with *pleasure* and not with reluctancy, when it is persisted in with a daring presumption and a desperate resolution, like theirs that said, *We have loved strangers and after them we will go,* then the sinner *will* do the devil's lusts. "The lusts of your father you *delight to do;*" so Dr. Hammond; they are rolled under the tongue as a sweet morsel.

2. By two particular instances, wherein

they manifestly resembled the devil—*murder* and *lying.* The devil is an enemy to life, because God is the God of life and life is the happiness of man; and an enemy to truth, because God is the God of truth and truth is the bond of human society.

(1.) He was *a murderer from the beginning,* not from his own beginning, for he was created an angel of light, and had a first estate which was pure and good, but from the beginning of his apostasy, which was soon after the creation of man. He was ἀνθρωπόκτονος—*homicida, a man-slayer.* [1.] He was a *hater of man,* and so in affection and disposition a murderer of him. He has his name, *Satan,* from *sitnah—hatred.* He maligned God's image upon man, envied his happiness, and earnestly desired his ruin, was an avowed enemy to the whole race. [2.] He was man's tempter to *that* sin which brought death into the world, and so he was effectually the murderer of all mankind, which in Adam had but *one neck.* He was a murderer of souls, *deceived* them into sin, and by it *slew them* (Rom. vii. 11), poisoned man with the forbidden fruit, and, to aggravate the matter, made him his own murderer. Thus he was not only *at* the beginning, but *from* the beginning, which intimates that thus he *has been* ever since; as he began, so he continues, the murderer of men by his temptations. The great tempter is the great destroyer. The Jews called the devil *the angel of death.* [3.] He was the first wheel in the first murder that ever was committed by Cain, who was of that wicked one, and slew his brother, 1 John iii. 12. If the devil had not been very strong in Cain, he could not have done such an unnatural thing as to kill his own brother. Cain killing his brother by the instigation of the devil, the devil is called the *murderer,* which does not speak Cain's personal guilt the less, but the devil's the more, whose torments, we have reason to think, will be the greater, when the time comes, for all that wickedness into which he has drawn men. See what reason we have to *stand* upon our guard *against the wiles of the devil,* and never to hearken to him (for he is a murderer, and certainly aims to do us mischief, even when he *speaks fair),* and to wonder that he who is the murderer of the children of men should yet be, by their own consent, so much their master. Now herein these Jews were followers of him, and were murderers, like him; murderers of souls, which they led blindfold into the ditch, and made the *children of hell;* sworn enemies of Christ, and now ready to be his betrayers and murderers, for the same reason that Cain killed Abel. These Jews were that *seed of the serpent* that were to *bruise the heel* of the *seed of the woman: Now you seek to kill me.*

(2.) He was *a liar.* A lie is opposed to truth (1 John ii. 21), and accordingly the devil is here described to be,

[1.] An enemy to truth, and therefore to Christ. *First,* He is a *deserter* from the truth; he *abode not in the truth,* did not continue in the purity and rectitude of his nature wherein he was created, but left his first state; when he degenerated from goodness, he departed from truth, for his apostasy was founded in a lie. The angels were the *hosts of the Lord;* those that fell were not *true* to their commander and sovereign, they were not to be *trusted,* being charged with folly and defection, Job iv. 18. By *the truth* here we may understand the revealed will of God concerning the salvation of man by Jesus Christ, the truth which Christ was now preaching, and which the Jews opposed; herein they did *like their father the devil,* who, *seeing* the honour put upon the human nature in the *first Adam,* and *foreseeing* the much greater honour intended in the *second Adam,* would not be reconciled to that counsel of God, nor *stand in the truth* concerning it, but, from a spirit of pride and envy, set himself to resist it, and to thwart the designs of it; and so did these Jews here, as his children and agents. *Secondly,* He is *destitute* of the truth: *There is no truth in him.* His interest in the world is supported by lies and falsehoods, and there is no truth, nothing you can confide in, in him, nor in any thing he says or does. The notions he propagates concerning good and evil are false and erroneous, his proofs are lying wonders, his temptations are all cheats; he has great knowledge of the truth, but having no affection to it, but on the contrary being a sworn enemy to it, he is said to have *no truth in him.*

[2.] He is a friend and patron of lying: *When he speaketh a lie he speaketh of his own.* Three things are here said of the devil with reference to the sin of lying:—*First,* That he is *a liar;* his oracles were lying oracles, his prophets lying prophets, and the images in which he was worshipped *teachers of lies.* He tempted our first parents with a downright lie. All his temptations are carried on by lies, calling *evil good and good evil,* and promising impunity in sin; he knows them to be lies, and suggests them with an intention to deceive, and so to destroy. When he now *contradicted* the gospel, in the scribes and Pharisees, it was by lies; and when afterwards he *corrupted it,* in the *man of sin,* it was by strong delusions, and a great complicated lie. *Secondly,* That when he *speaks a lie* he *speaks of his own,* ἐκ τῶν ἰδίων. It is the proper *idiom* of his language; of *his own,* not of God; his Creator never put it into him. When men speak a lie they borrow it from the devil, *Satan fills their hearts to lie* (Acts v. 3); but when the devil speaks a lie the *model* of it is of his own framing, the motives to it are from himself, which bespeaks the desperate depth of wickedness into which those apostate spirits are sunk; as in their first defection they had no tempter, so their sinfulness is still their own. *Thirdly,* That he is the *father of it,* αὐτοῦ. 1. He is the father of every *lie;* not only of the lies which he himself suggests, but of those which others speak; he is the author and founder of all lies. When men speak lies, they speak from him, and as his mouth; they come originally from him, and bear his image. 2. He is the father of *every liar;* so it may be understood. God made men with a disposition to truth. It is congruous to reason and natural light, to the order of our faculties and the laws of society, that we should speak truth; but the devil, the author of sin, the spirit that works in the children of disobedience, has so corrupted the nature of man that the wicked are said to be *estranged from the womb, speaking lies* (Ps. lviii. 3); he has taught them *with their tongues to use deceit,* Rom. iii. 13. He is the father of liars, who begat them, who trained them up in the *way of lying,* whom they resemble and obey, and with whom all *liars* shall have their portion for ever.

IV. Christ, having thus proved all murderers and all liars to be the devil's children, leaves it to the consciences of his hearers to say, *Thou art the man.* But he comes in the following verses to assist them in the application of it to themselves; he does not call them *liars,* but shows them that they were *no friends to truth,* and therein resembled him who *abode not in the truth, because there is no truth in him.* Two things he charges upon them:—

1. That they would not *believe the word of truth* (*v.* 45), ὅτι τὴν ἀλήθειαν λέγω, οὐ πιστεύετέ μοι.

(1.) Two ways it may be taken;—[1.] "Though I tell you the truth, yet you will not believe me (ὅτι), *that I do so.*" Though he gave abundant proof of his commission from God, and his affection to the children of men, yet they would not believe that he told them the truth. Now was *truth fallen in the street,* Isa. lix. 14, 15. The greatest truths with some gained not the least credit; for they *rebelled against the light,* Job xxiv. 13. Or, [2.] *Because I tell you the truth* (so we read it) therefore *you believe me not.* They would not receive him, nor entertain him as a prophet, because he told them some unpleasing truths which they did not care to hear, told them the truth concerning themselves and their own case, showed them their faces in a glass that would not flatter them; therefore they would not believe a word he said. Miserable is the case of those to whom the light of divine truth is become a torment.

(2.) Now, to show them the unreasonableness of their infidelity, he condescends to put the matter to this fair issue, *v.* 46. He and they being contrary, either he was in an error or they were. Now take it either way.

[1.] If *he* were in an error, why did they not convince him? The falsehood of *pretended* prophets was discovered either by the *ill tendency* of their doctrines (Deut. xiii. 2), or by the *ill tenour* of their conversation: *You shall know them by their fruits;* but (saith Christ) *which of you,* you of the sanhedrim, that take upon you to judge of prophets, *which of you convinceth me of sin?* They accused him of some of the worst of crimes—gluttony, drunkenness, blasphemy, sabbath-breaking, confederacy with Satan, and what not. But their accusations were malicious groundless calumnies, and such as every one that knew him knew to be *utterly false.* When they had done their utmost by trick and artifice, subornation and perjury, to prove some crime upon him, the very judge that condemned him owned he *found no fault in him.* The *sin* he here challenges them to convict him of is, *First,* An inconsistent doctrine. They had heard his testimony; could they show any thing in it absurd or unworthy to be believed, any contradiction either of himself or of the scriptures, or any corruption of truth or manners insinuated by his doctrine? *ch.* xviii. 20. Or, *Secondly,* An incongruous conversation: "Which of you can justly charge me with any thing, in word or deed, unbecoming a prophet?" See the wonderful condescension of our Lord Jesus, that he demanded not credit any further than the allowed motives of credibility supported his demands. See Jer. ii. 5, 31; Mic. vi. 3. Ministers may hence learn, 1. To *walk* so *circumspectly* as that it may not be in the power of their most strict observers to convince them of sin, *that the ministry be not blamed.* The only way not to be convicted of sin is not to sin. 2. To be willing to *admit a scrutiny;* though we are confident in many things that we are in the right, yet we should be willing to have it tried whether we be not in the wrong. See Job vi. 24.

[2.] If *they* were in an error, why were they not convinced by him? "*If I say the truth, why do you not believe me?* If you cannot convince me of error, you must own that I *say the truth,* and why do you not then *give me credit?* Why will you not deal with me upon trust?" Note, If men would but enquire into the reason of their infidelity, and examine why they do not believe that which they cannot gainsay, they would find themselves reduced to such absurdities as they could not but be ashamed of; for it will be found that the reason why we believe not in Jesus Christ is because we are not willing to part with our sins, and deny ourselves, and serve God faithfully; that we are not of the Christian religion, because we would not indeed be of any, and unbelief of our Redeemer resolves itself into a downright rebellion against our Creator.

2. Another thing charged upon them is that they would not hear the words of God (*v.* 47), which further shows how groundless their claim of relation to God was. Here is,

(1.) A doctrine laid down: *He that is of God heareth God's words;* that is, [1.] He is *willing* and *ready* to hear them, is sincerely desirous to know what the mind of God is, and cheerfully embraces whatever he knows to be so. God's words have such an authority over, and such an agreeableness with all that are born of God, that they meet them, as the child Samuel did, with, *Speak, Lord, for thy servant heareth.* Let the word of the Lord come. [2.] He *apprehends* and *discerns* them, he so hears them as to perceive the *voice of God* in them, which the natural man does not, 1 Cor. ii. 14. He that is of God is *soon aware* of the discoveries he makes of himself of the *nearness of his name* (Ps. lxxv. 1), as they of the family know the master's tread, and the master's knock, and *open to him immediately* (Luke xii. 36), as the sheep know the voice of their shepherd from that of a stranger, *ch.* x. 4, 5; Cant. ii. 8.

(2.) The application of this doctrine, for the conviction of these unbelieving Jews: *You therefore hear them not;* that is, "You heed not, you understand not, you believe not, the words of God, nor care to hear them, *because you are not of God.* Your being thus deaf and dead to the words of God is a plain evidence that you are *not of God.*" It is in his word that God manifests himself and is present among us; we are therefore reckoned to be well or ill affected to God according as we are well or ill affected to his word; see 2 Cor. iv. 4; 1 John iv. 6. Or, their not being of God was the reason why they did not profitably *hear the words of God,* which Christ spoke; they did not understand and believe him, not because the things themselves were obscure or wanted evidence, but because the hearers were *not of God,* were not born again. If the word of the kingdom do not bring forth fruit, the blame is to be laid upon the soil, not upon the seed, as appears by the parable of the sower, Matt. xiii. 3.

48 Then answered the Jews, and said unto him, Say we not well that thou art a Samaritan, and hast a devil? 49 Jesus answered, I have not a devil; but I honour my Father, and ye do dishonour me. 50 And I seek not mine own glory: there is one that seeketh and judgeth.

Here is, I. The malice of hell breaking out in the base language which the unbelieving Jews gave to our Lord Jesus. Hitherto they had cavilled at his doctrine, and had made invidious remarks upon it; but, having shown themselves uneasy when he complained (*v.* 43, 47) that they would not hear him, now at length they fall to downright railing, *v.* 48. They were not the common people, but, as it should seem, the scribes and Pharisees, the men of consequence, who, when they saw themselves convicted of an obstinate infidelity, scornfully turned off the conviction with this: *Say we not well that thou art a Samaritan, and hast a devil?* See here, see it and wonder, see it and tremble,

1. What was the blasphemous character commonly given of our Lord Jesus among the wicked Jews, to which they refer. (1.) That he was a Samaritan, that is, that he was an enemy to their church and nation, one that they hated and could not endure. Thus they exposed him to the ill will of the people, with whom you could not put a man into a worse name than to call him *a Samaritan.* If he had been a Samaritan, he had been punishable, by the *beating of the rebels* (as they called it), for coming into the temple. They had often enough called him *a Galilean—a meanman;* but as if that were not enough, though it contradicted the other, they will have him a *Samaritan—a bad man.* The Jews to this day call the Christians, in reproach, *Cuthæi—Samaritans.* Note, Great endeavours have in all ages been used to make good people odious by putting them under black characters, and it is easy to run that down with a crowd and a cry which is once put into an ill name. Perhaps because Christ justly inveighed against the pride and tyranny of the priests and elders, they hereby suggest that he aimed at the ruin of their church, in aiming at its reformation, and was *falling away* to the Samaritans. (2.) That *he had a devil.* Either, [1.] That he was *in league with the devil.* Having reproached his doctrine as tending to Samaritanism, here they reflect upon his miracles as done in combination with Beelzebub. Or rather, [2.] That he was possessed with a devil, that he was a melancholy man, whose brain was *clouded,* or a mad man, whose brain was *heated,* and that which he said was no more to be believed than the extravagant rambles of a distracted man, or one in a delirium. Thus the divine revelation of those things which are above the discovery of reason have been often branded with the charge of enthusiasm, and the prophet was called a *mad fellow,* 2 Kings ix. 11; Hosea ix. 7. The inspiration of the Pagan oracles and prophets was indeed a frenzy, and those that had it were for the time beside themselves; but that which was truly *divine* was not so. *Wisdom is justified of her children,* as wisdom indeed.

2. How they undertook to justify this character, and applied it to the present occasion: *Say we not well that thou art so?* One would think that his excellent discourses should have altered their opinion of him, and have made them recant; but, instead of this, their hearts were more hardened and their prejudices confirmed. They value themselves on their enmity to Christ, as if they had never spoken *better* than when they spoke the worst they could of Jesus Christ. Those have arrived at the highest pitch of wickedness who avow their impiety, repeat what they should retract, and justify themselves in that for which they ought to condemn them-

selves. It is bad to say and do ill, but it is worse to *stand to it; I* do *well to be angry.* When Christ spoke with so much boldness against the sins of the great men, and thereby incensed them against him, those who were sensible of no interest but what is secular and sensual concluded him *beside himself*, for they thought none but a madman would lose his preferment, and hazard his life, for his religion and conscience.

II. The meekness and mercifulness of Heaven shining in Christ's reply to this vile calumny, *v.* 49, 50.

1. He denies their charge against him: *I have not a devil;* as Paul (Acts xxvi. 25), *I am not mad.* The imputation is unjust; "I am neither actuated by a devil, nor in compact with one;" and this he evidenced by what he did against the devil's kingdom. He takes no notice of their calling him a *Samaritan*, because it was a calumny that disproved itself, it was a personal reflection, and not worth taking notice of: but saying he had a devil reflected on his commission, and therefore he answered that. St. Augustine gives this gloss upon his not saying any thing to their calling him a Samaritan—that he was indeed that good Samaritan spoken of in the parable, Luke x. 33.

2. He asserts the sincerity of his own intentions: But *I honour my Father.* They suggested that he took undue honours to himself, and derogated from the honour due to God only, both which he *denies* here, in saying that he made it his business to honour his Father, and him only. It also proves that he *had not a devil;* for, if he had, he would not honour God. Note, Those who can truly say that they make it their constant care to honour God are sufficiently armed against the censures and reproaches of men.

3. He complains of the wrong they did him by their calumnies: *You do dishonour me.* By this it appears that, as man, he had a tender sense of the disgrace and indignity done him; reproach was a sword in his bones, and yet he underwent it for our salvation. It is the will of God that *all men should honour the Son,* yet there are many that *dishonour him;* such a contradiction is there in the carnal mind to the will of God. Christ honoured his Father so as never man did, and yet was himself dishonoured so as never man was; for, though God has promised that those who honour him he will honour, he never promised that men should honour them.

4. He clears himself from the imputation of vain glory, in saying this concerning himself, *v.* 50. See here, (1.) His *contempt* of worldly honour: *I seek not mine own glory.* He did not aim at this in what he had said of himself or against his persecutors; he did not court the applause of men, nor covet preferment in the world, but industriously declined both. He did not *seek his own glory* distinct from his Father's, nor had any separate interest of his own. For men to *search their own glory* is *not glory* indeed (Prov. xxv. 27), but rather their shame to be so much *out in their aim.* This comes in here as a reason why Christ made so light of their reproaches: "*You do dishonour me,* but cannot disturb me, shall not disquiet me, for I *seek not my own glory.*" Note, Those who are dead to men's praise can safely bear their contempt. (2.) His *comfort* under worldly dishonour: *There is one that seeketh and judgeth.* In two things Christ made it appear that he *sought not his own glory;* and here he tells us what satisfied him as to both. [1.] He did not *court* men's respect, but was indifferent to it, and in reference to this he saith, "*There is one that seeketh,* that will secure and advance, my interest in the esteem and affections of the people, while I am in no care about it. Note, God will seek *their* honour that do not seek *their own;* for before honour is humility. [2.] He did not *revenge* men's affronts, but was unconcerned at them, and in reference to this he saith, "*There is one that judgeth,* that will vindicate my honour, and severely reckon with those that trample upon it." Probably he refers here to the judgments that were coming upon the nation of the Jews for the indignities they did to the Lord Jesus. See Ps. xxxvii. 13—15. *I heard not, for thou wilt hear.* If we undertake to judge for ourselves, whatever damage we sustain, our recompence is in our own hands; but if we be, as we ought to be, humble appellants and patient expectants, we shall find, to our comfort, *there is one that judgeth.*

51 Verily, verily, I say unto you,
If a man keep my saying, he shall
never see death. 52 Then said the
Jews unto him, Now we know that
thou hast a devil. Abraham is dead,
and the prophets; and thou sayest, If
a man keep my saying, he shall never
taste of death. 53 Art thou greater
than our father Abraham, which is
dead? and the prophets are dead:
whom makest thou thyself? 54 Jesus
answered, If I honour myself, my
honour is nothing: it is my Father
that honoureth me; of whom ye say,
that he is your God: 55 Yet ye
have not known him; but I know
him: and if I should say, I know
him not, I shall be a liar like unto
you: but I know him, and keep his
saying. 56 Your father Abraham
rejoiced to see my day: and he saw
it, and was glad. 57 Then said the
Jews unto him, Thou art not yet fifty
years old, and hast thou seen Abraham? 58 Jesus said unto them,

Verily, verily, I say unto you, Before Abraham was, I am. 59 Then took they up stones to cast at him: but Jesus hid himself, and went out of the temple, going through the midst of them, and so passed by.

In these verses we have,

I. The doctrine of the immortality of believers laid down, *v.* 51. It is ushered in with the usual solemn preface, *Verily, verily, I say unto you,* which commands both attention and assent, and this is what he says, *If a man keep my sayings, he shall never see death.* Here we have, 1. The *character* of a believer: he is one that *keeps the sayings* of the Lord Jesus, *τον λόγον τον ἐμὸν—my word;* that *word of mine* which I have delivered to you; this we must not only *receive,* but *keep;* not only *have,* but *hold.* We must keep it in mind and memory, keep it in love and affection, so keep it as in nothing to violate it or go contrary to it, keep it *without spot* (1 Tim. vi. 14), keep it as a trust committed to us, keep in it as our way, keep to it as our rule. 2. The *privilege* of a believer: *He shall by no means see death for ever;* so it is in the original. Not as if the bodies of believers were secured from the stroke of death. No, even the *children of the Most High* must *die like men,* and the followers of Christ have been, more than other men, in deaths often, and *killed all the day long;* how then is this promise made good that they *shall not see death?* Answer, (1.) The property of death is so altered to them that they do not see it as death, they do not see the terror of death, it is quite taken off; their sight does not *terminate* in death, as theirs does who *live by sense;* no, they look so clearly, so comfortably, through death, and beyond death, and are so taken up with their state on the other side death, that they overlook death, and *see it not.* (2.) The power of death is so broken that though there is no remedy, but they must *see death,* yet they shall not see death *for ever,* shall not be always shut up under its arrests, the day will come when *death shall be swallowed up in victory.* (3.) They are perfectly delivered from *eternal death,* shall not be *hurt of the second death.* That is the death especially meant here, that death which is *for ever,* which is opposed to everlasting life; this they shall never see, for they shall *never come into condemnation;* they shall have their everlasting lot where there will be *no more death,* where they *cannot die any more,* Luke xx. 36. Though now they cannot avoid seeing death, and tasting it too, yet they shall shortly be there where it will be *seen no more for ever,* Exod. xiv. 13.

II. The Jews cavil at this doctrine. Instead of laying hold of this precious promise of immortality, which the nature of man has an ambition of (who is there that does not love life, and dread the sight of death?) they lay hold of this occasion to reproach him that makes them so kind an offer: *Now we know that thou hast a devil.* Abraham *is dead.* Observe here,

1. Their *railing:* "*Now we know that thou hast a devil,* that thou art a madman; thou ravest, and sayest thou knowest not what." See how these swine trample underfoot the precious pearls of gospel promises. If now at last they had evidence to prove him *mad,* why did they say (*v.* 48), before they had that proof, *Thou hast a devil?* But this is the method of malice, first to *fasten* an invidious charge, and then to *fish* for evidence of it: *Now we know that thou hast a devil.* If he had not abundantly proved himself a *teacher come from God,* his promises of immortality to his credulous followers might justly have been ridiculed, and charity itself would have imputed them to a crazed fancy; but his doctrine was evidently divine, his miracles confirmed it, and the Jews' religion taught them to expect such a prophet, and to believe in him; for them therefore thus to reject him was to abandon that promise to which their *twelve tribes hoped to come,* Acts xxvi. 7.

2. Their *reasoning,* and the colour they had to *run him down* thus. In short, they look upon him as guilty of an insufferable piece of arrogance, in making himself greater than *Abraham and the prophets: Abraham is dead,* and *the prophets,* they are dead too; very true, by the same token that these Jews were the genuine offspring of those that killed them. Now, (1.) It is true that Abraham and the prophets were great men, great in the favour of God, and great in the esteem of all good men. (2.) It is true that they *kept God's sayings,* and were obedient to them; and yet, (3.) It is true that they *died;* they never pretended to *have,* much less to *give,* immortality, but every one in his own order was *gathered to his people.* It was their honour that they *died in faith,* but die they must. Why should a good man be afraid to die, when Abraham is dead, and the prophets are dead? They have *tracked* the way through that darksome valley, which should reconcile us to death and help to take off the terror of it. Now they think Christ talks madly, when he saith, *If a man keep my sayings, he shall never taste death. Tasting* death means the same thing with *seeing* it; and well may death be represented as grievous to *several* of the senses, which is the destruction of them *all.* Now their arguing goes upon two mistakes:—[1.] They understood Christ of an immortality in this world, and this was a mistake. In the sense that Christ spoke, it was not true that *Abraham and the prophets* were *dead,* for God is still the *God of Abraham* and the *God of the holy prophets* (Rev. xxii. 6); now God is not the God of the dead, but of the living; therefore Abraham and the prophets are still alive, and, as

Christ meant it, they had not *seen* nor *tasted* death. [2.] They thought none could be greater than Abraham and the prophets, whereas they could not but know that the Messiah would be greater than Abraham or any of the prophets; they did virtuously, but he excelled them all; nay, they borrowed their greatness from him. It was the honour of Abraham that he was the Father of the Messiah, and the honour of the prophets that they testified beforehand concerning him: so that he certainly *obtained a* far *more excellent name than they.* Therefore, instead of inferring from Christ's making himself greater than Abraham that he had a *devil,* they should have inferred from his proving himself so (by doing the works which neither Abraham nor the prophets ever did) that he was the Christ; but their eyes were blinded. They scornfully asked, *Whom makest thou thyself?* As if he had been guilty of pride and vain-glory; whereas he was so far from making himself greater than he was that he now drew a veil over his own glory, emptied himself, and made himself less than he was, and was the greatest example of humility that ever was.

III. Christ's reply to this cavil; still he vouchsafes to reason with them, that every mouth may be stopped. No doubt he could have struck them dumb or dead upon the spot, but this was the *day of his patience.*

1. In his answer he insists not upon his own testimony concerning himself, but waives it as not sufficient nor conclusive (*v.* 54): *If I honour myself, my honour is nothing,* ἐαν ἐγὼ δοξάζω—*if I glorify myself.* Note, Self-honour is no honour; and the affectation of glory is both the forfeiture and the defeasance of it: it is *not glory* (Prov. xxv. 27), but so great a reproach that there is no sin which men are more industrious to hide than this; even he that most affects praise would not be thought to do it. Honour of our own creating is a mere chimera, has nothing in it, and therefore is called *vain-glory.* Self-admirers are self-*deceivers.* Our Lord Jesus was not one that *honoured himself,* as they represented him; he was *crowned* by him who is the fountain of honour, and glorified not himself to be made a high priest, Heb. v. 4, 5.

2. He refers himself to *his* Father, God; and to *their* father, Abraham.

(1.) To his Father, *God: It is my Father that honoureth me.* By this he means, [1.] That he *derived* from his Father all the honour he now claimed; he had commanded them to believe in him, to follow him, and to keep his word, all which put an honour upon him; but it was the Father that *laid help* upon him, that *lodged* all *fulness* in him, that sanctified him, and sealed him, and sent him into the world to receive all the honours due to the Messiah, and this justified him in all these demands of respect. [2.] That he *depended* upon his Father for all the honour he further *looked for.* He courted not the applauses of the age, but despised them; for his eye and heart were upon the glory which the Father had promised him, and *which he had with the Father before the world was.* He aimed at an advancement with which the Father was to *exalt him, a name* he was to *give him,* Phil. ii. 8, 9. Note, Christ and all that are his depend upon God for their honour; and he that is sure of honour where he is known cares not though he be slighted where he is in disguise. Appealing thus often to his Father, and his Father's testimony of him, which yet the Jews did not admit nor give credit to,

First, He here takes occasion to show the reason of *their* incredulity, notwithstanding *this* testimony—and this was their *unacquaintedness* with God; as if he had said, "But why should I talk to you of my Father's honouring me, when he is one you know nothing of? You *say of him that he is your God, yet you have not known him.*" Here observe,

a. The profession they made of relation to God: "*You say that he is your God,* the God you have chosen, and are in covenant with; you say that you are Israel; but all are not so indeed that are of Israel," Rom. ix. 6. Note, Many pretend to have an interest in God, and say that he is *theirs,* who yet have no just cause to say so. Those who called themselves the *temple of the Lord,* having *profaned the excellency of Jacob,* did but trust in lying words. What will it avail us to say, He is *our God,* if we be not in sincerity *his people,* nor such as he will own? Christ mentions here their profession of relation to God, as that which was an aggravation of their unbelief. All people will honour those whom their God honours; but these Jews, who said that the Lord was their God, studied how to put the utmost disgrace upon one upon whom their God put honour. Note, The profession we make of a covenant relation to God, and an interest in him, if it be not improved *by us* will be improved *against us.*

b. Their ignorance of him, and estrangement from him, notwithstanding this profession: *Yet you have not known him.* (*a.*) *You know him not at all.* These Pharisees were so taken up with the study of their traditions concerning things foreign and trifling that they never minded the most needful and useful knowledge; like the false prophets of old, who *caused people to forget God's name by their dreams,* Jer. xxiii. 27. Or, (*b.*) *You know him not aright,* but mistake concerning him; and this is as bad as not knowing him at all, or worse. Men may be able to dispute subtly concerning God, and yet may think him such a one as themselves, and *not know him.* You say that he is *yours,* and it is natural to us to desire to know *our own,* yet you *know him not.* Note, There are many who *claim-kindred* to God who yet have no acquaintance with him. It is only the name of God which they have learned to talk of, and to hector with; but for the nature of God, his attributes and perfections, and relations to his creatures, they know nothing of the matter; we *speak this to their shame,* 1 Cor. xv. 34. Multitudes satisfy themselves, but deceive themselves, with a titular relation to an *unknown God.* This Christ charges upon the Jews here, [*a.*] To show how vain and groundless their pretensions of relation to God were. "You say that he is yours, but you give yourselves the lie, for it is plain that you do not know him;" and we reckon that a cheat is effectually convicted if it be found that he is ignorant of the persons he pretends alliance to. [*b.*] To show the true reason why they were not wrought upon by Christ's doctrine and miracles. They knew not God; and therefore perceived not the image of God, nor the voice of God in Christ. Note, The reason why men receive not the *gospel of Christ* is because they have not the *knowledge of God.* Men *submit not to the righteousness of Christ* because they are *ignorant of God's righteousness,* Rom. x. 3. They that know not God, and obey not the gospel of Christ, are put together, 2 Thess. i. 8.

Secondly, He gives them the reason of *his* assurance that his Father would *honour* him and *own him*: *But I know him;* and again, *I know him;* which bespeaks, not only his *acquaintance* with him, having lain in his bosom, but his *confidence* in him, to stand by him, and bear him out in his whole undertaking; as was prophesied concerning him (Isa. l. 7, 8); *I know* that I shall not be ashamed, for he is near that justifies; and as Paul, "*I know whom I have believed* (2 Tim. i. 12), I know him to be faithful, and powerful, and heartily engaged in the cause which I know to be his *own.*" Observe, 1. How he *professes* his knowledge of his Father, with the greatest certainty, as one that was neither afraid nor ashamed to own it: *If I should say I know him not, I should be a liar like unto you.* He would not deny his relation to God, to humour the Jews, and to avoid their reproaches, and prevent further trouble; nor would he retract what he had said, nor confess himself either deceived or a deceiver; if he should, he would be found a false witness against God and himself. Note, Those who disown their religion and relation to God, as Peter, are liars, as much as hypocrites are, who pretend to know him, when they do not. See 1 Tim. vi. 13, 14. Mr. Clark observes well, upon this, that it is a great sin to deny God's grace in us. 2. How he *proves* his knowledge of his Father: *I know him and keep his sayings,* or *his word.* Christ, as man, was obedient to the moral law, and, as Redeemer, to the mediatorial law; and in both he kept *his Father's* word, and *his own word* with the Father. Christ requires of us (*v.* 51) that we *keep his sayings;* and he has set before us a copy of obedience, a copy without a blot: he *kept his Father's sayings;* well might he who *learned obedience* teach it; see Heb. v. 8, 9. Christ by this evinced that he knew the Father. Note, The best proof of our acquaintance with God is our obedience to him. Those only know God aright that keep his word; it is a ruled case, 1 John ii. 3. *Hereby we know that we know him* (and do not only fancy it), *if we keep his commandments.*

(2.) Christ refers them to *their* father, whom they boasted so much of a relation to, and that was Abraham, and this closes the discourse.

[1.] Christ asserts Abraham's prospect of him, and respect to him: *Your father Abraham rejoiced to see my day, and he saw it, and was glad, v.* 56. And by this he proves that he was not at all out of the way when he *made himself greater than Abraham.* Two things he here speaks of as instances of that patriarch's respect to the promised Messiah:—

First, The ambition he had to *see his day: He rejoiced,* ἠγαλλιάσατο—*he leaped at it.* The word, though it commonly signifies *rejoicing,* must here signify a transport of *desire* rather than of *joy,* for otherwise the latter part of the verse would be a tautology; he *saw it, and was glad.* He *reached out,* or *stretched himself forth,* that he might *see my day;* as Zaccheus, that ran before, and climbed the tree, *to see Jesus.* The notices he had received of the Messiah to come had raised in him an expectation of something *great,* which he earnestly longed to know more of. The dark intimation of that which is considerable puts men upon enquiry, and makes them earnestly ask *Who?* and *What?* and *Where?* and *When?* and *How?* And thus the prophets of the Old Testament, having a general idea of a grace that should *come, searched diligently* (1 Pet. i. 10), and Abraham was as industrious herein as any of them. God told him of a land that he would give his posterity, and of the wealth and honour he designed them (Gen. xv. 14); but he never *leaped* thus to see that day, as he did to see the day of the Son of man. He could not look with so much indifferency upon the promised *seed* as he did upon the promised land; *in that* he was, but *to the other* he could not be, contentedly a stranger. Note, Those who rightly know any thing of Christ cannot but be earnestly desirous to know more of him. Those who discern the dawning of the light of the Sun of righteousness cannot but wish to see his rising. The mystery of redemption is that which *angels desire to look into,* much more should we, who are more immediately concerned in it. Abraham desired to see Christ's day, though it was at a great distance; but this degenerate seed of his discerned not his day, nor bade it welcome when it came. The appearing of Christ, which gracious souls love and long for, carnal hearts dread and loathe.

Secondly, The satisfaction he had in what he did see of it: *He saw it, and was glad* Observe here,

a. How God gratified the pious desire of Abraham; he longed to see Christ's day, and he *saw it.* Though he saw it not so plainly, and fully, and distinctly as we now see it under the gospel, yet he saw something of it, more *afterwards* than he did at first. Note, To him that has, and to him that asks, shall be given; to him that uses and improves what he has, and that desires and prays for more of the knowledge of Christ, God will give more. But how did Abraham see Christ's day? (*a.*) Some understand it of the sight he had of it in the other world. The separate soul of Abraham, when the veil of flesh was rent, saw the mysteries of the kingdom of God in heaven. Calvin mentions this sense of it, and does not much disallow it. Note, The longings of gracious souls after Jesus Christ will be fully satisfied when they come to heaven, and not till then. But, (*b.*) It is more commonly understood of some sight he had of *Christ's day* in this world. They that *received not the promises*, yet *saw them afar off*, Heb. xi. 13. Balaam saw Christ, but not *now*, not *nigh*. There is room to conjecture that Abraham had some vision of Christ and his day, for his own private satisfaction, which is not, nor must be, recorded in his story, like that of Daniel's, which must be *shut up, and sealed unto the time of the end*, Dan. xii. 4. Christ knew what Abraham saw better than Moses did. But there are divers things recorded in which Abraham saw more of that which he longed to see than he did when the promise was first made to him. He saw in Melchizedek one *made like unto the Son of God*, and a priest for ever; he saw an appearance of Jehovah, attended with two angels, in the plains of Mamre. In the prevalency of his intercession for Sodom he saw a specimen of Christ's intercession; in the casting out of Ishmael, and the establishment of the covenant with Isaac, he saw a figure of the gospel day, which is Christ's day; for these things were an allegory. In offering Isaac, and the ram instead of Isaac, he saw a double type of the great sacrifice; and his calling the place *Jehovah-jireh—It shall be seen*, intimates that he saw something more in it than others did, which time would produce; and in making his servant *put his hand under his thigh*, when he swore, he had a regard to the Messiah.

b. How *Abraham* entertained these discoveries of Christ's day, and bade them welcome: *He saw, and was glad.* He was glad of what he *saw* of God's favour to himself, and glad of what he *foresaw* of the mercy God had in store for the world. Perhaps this refers to Abraham's laughing when God assured him of a son by Sarah (Gen. xvii. 16, 17), for that was not a laughter of distrust as Sarah's, but of joy; in that promise he saw Christ's day, and it *filled him with joy unspeakable*. Thus he embraced the promises. Note, A believing sight of Christ and his day will put gladness into the heart. No joy like the joy of faith; we are never acquainted with true pleasure till we are acquainted with Christ.

[2.] The Jews cavil at this, and reproach him for it (*v.* 57): *Thou art not yet fifty years old, and hast thou seen Abraham?* Here, *First*, They suppose that if Abraham saw him and his day he also had seen Abraham, which yet was not a necessary *innuendo*, but this turn of his words would best serve to expose him; yet it was true that Christ had seen Abraham, and had talked with him as a man talks with his friend. *Secondly*, They suppose it a very absurd thing for him to pretend to have seen Abraham, who was *dead* so many ages before he was born. The state of the dead is an *invisible* state; but here they ran upon the old mistake, understanding that corporally which Christ spoke spiritually. Now this gave them occasion to *despise his youth*, and to upbraid him with it, as if he were *but of yesterday, and knew* nothing: *Thou art not yet fifty years old.* They might as well have said, *Thou art not forty;* for he was now but thirty-two or thirty-three years old. As to this, Irenæus, one of the first fathers, with this passage supports the tradition which he says he had from some that had conversed with St. John, that our Saviour lived to be fifty years old, which he contends for, *Advers. Hæres.* lib. ii. cap. 39, 40. See what little credit is to be given to tradition; and, as to this here, the Jews spoke *at random;* some year they would mention, and therefore pitched upon one that they thought he was far enough short of; he did not look to be forty, but they were sure he could not be fifty, much less contemporary with Abraham. Old age is reckoned to begin at fifty (Num. iv. 47), so that they meant no more than this, "Thou art not to be reckoned an old man; many of us are much thy seniors, and yet pretend not to have seen Abraham." Some think that his countenance was so altered, with grief and watching, that, together with the gravity of his aspect, it made him look like a man of fifty years old: *his visage was so marred*, Isa. lii. 14.

[3.] Our Saviour gives an effectual answer to this cavil, by a solemn assertion of his own seniority even to Abraham himself (*v.* 58): "*Verily, verily, I say unto you;* I do not only say it in private to my own disciples, who will be sure to say as I say, but *to you* my enemies and persecutors; I say it to your faces, take it how you will: *Before Abraham was, I am;*" πρὶν Ἀβραὰμ γενέσθαι, ἐγώ εἰμι, *Before Abraham was made or born, I am.* The change of the word is observable, and bespeaks Abraham a creature, and himself the Creator; well therefore might he make himself *greater* than Abraham. *Before Abraham he was, First,* As God. *I am,* is the name of God (Exod. iii. 14); it denotes his self-existence; he does not say, *I was,* but *I am,* for he is the first and the last, immutably the same (Rev. i. 8); thus he was not only before Abraham, but before *all worlds, ch.* i. 1; Prov. viii. 23. *Secondly,* As Mediator. He was the appointed Messiah, long before Abraham; the *Lamb slain from the foundation of the world* (Rev. xiii. 8), the channel of conveyance of light, life, and love from God to man. This supposes his divine nature, that he is the same in himself from eternity (Heb. xiii. 8), and that he is the same to man ever since the fall; he was made of God wisdom, righteousness, sanctification, and redemption, to Adam, and Abel, and Enoch, and Noah, and Shem, and all the patriarchs that lived and died by faith in him before Abraham was born. Abraham was the root of the Jewish nation, the rock out of which they were hewn. If Christ was before Abraham, his doctrine and religion were no novelty, but were, in the substance of them, prior to Judaism, and ought to take place of it.

[4.] This great word ended the dispute *abruptly*, and put a period to it: they could bear to hear no more from him, and he needed to say no more to them, having witnessed this good confession, which was sufficient to support all his claims. One would think that Christ's discourse, in which shone so much both of grace and glory, should have captivated them all; but their inveterate prejudice against the holy spiritual doctrine and law of Christ, which were so contrary to their pride and worldliness, baffled all the methods of conviction. Now was fulfilled that prophecy (Mal. iii. 1, 2), that when the messenger of the covenant should *come to his temple* they *would not abide the day of his coming*, because he would be *like a refiner's fire*. Observe here,

First, How they were *enraged* at Christ for what he said: *They took up stones to cast at him, v.* 59. Perhaps they looked upon him as a blasphemer, and such were indeed to be stoned (Lev. xxiv. 16); but they must be first legally tried and convicted. Farewell justice and order if every man pretend to execute a law at his pleasure. Besides, they had said but just now that he was a distracted crack-brained man, and if so it was against all reason and equity to punish him as a malefactor for what he said. *They took up stones.* Dr. Lightfoot will tell you how they came to have stones so ready in the temple; they had workmen at this time repairing the temple, or making some additions, and the pieces of stone which they hewed off served for this purpose. See here the desperate power of sin and Satan in and over the children of disobedience. Who would think that ever there should be such wickedness as this in men, such an open and daring rebellion against one that undeniably proved himself to be the Son of God? Thus every one has a stone to throw at his holy religion, Acts xxviii. 22.

Secondly, How he made his *escape* out of their hands. 1. He *absconded;* Jesus *hid himself*, ἐκρύβη—*he was hid*, either by the crowd of those that wished well to him, to shelter him (he that ought to have been upon a throne, high and lifted up, is content to be *lost in a crowd); ;* or perhaps he concealed himself behind some of the walls or pillars of the temple *(in the secret of his tabernacle he shall hide me*, Ps. xxvii. 5); or by a divine power, casting a mist before their eyes, he made himself invisible to them. *When the wicked rise a man is hidden*, a wise and good man, Prov. xxviii. 12, 28. Not that Christ was afraid or ashamed to stand by what he had said, but his *hour was not yet come*, and he would countenance the flight of his ministers and people in times of persecution, when they are called to it. The Lord hid Jeremiah and Baruch, Jer. xxxvi. 26. 2. He *departed*, he *went out of the temple*, going *through the midst of them*, undiscovered, and *so passed by.* This was not a cowardly inglorious flight, nor such as argued either guilt or fear. It was foretold concerning him that he should not fail nor be discouraged, Isa. xlii. 4. But, (1.) It was an instance of his power over his enemies, and that they could do no more against him than he gave them leave to do; by which it appears that when afterwards he was taken in their pits he *offered himself, ch.* x. 18. They now thought they had made sure of him and yet he *passed through the midst* of them, either their eyes being blinded or their hands tied, and thus he left them to fume, like a lion *disappointed of his prey.* (2.) It was an instance of his prudent provision for his own safety, when he knew that his work was not done, nor his testimony finished; thus he gave an example to his own rule, *When they persecute you in one city flee to another;* nay, if occasion be, to a *wilderness*, for so Elijah did (1 Kings xix. 3, 4), and the woman, the church, Rev. xii. 6. When they took up loose stones to throw at Christ, he could have commanded the fixed stones, which did *cry out of the wall* against them, to avenge his cause, or the earth to open and swallow them up; but he chose to accommodate himself to the state he was in, to make the example imitable by the prudence of his followers, without a miracle. (3.) It was a righteous deserting of those who (worse than the Gadarenes, who *prayed him to depart)* stoned him from among them. Christ will not long stay with those who bid him be gone. Christ did again visit the temple after this; as one *loth to depart*, he *bade oft farewell;* but at last he abandoned it for ever, and left it *desolate.* Christ now *went through* the midst of the Jews, and none of them courted his stay, nor stirred up himself to take hold of him, but were even content to let him go. Note, God never forsakes any till they have first provoked him to withdraw, and will have none of him. Calvin observes that these chief priests, when they had driven Christ out of the temple, valued themselves on the possession they kept of it: "But," says he, "those deceive themselves who are proud of a church or temple which Christ has forsaken." *Longe falluntur, cum templum se habere putant Deo vacuum.* When Christ left them it is said that he passed by silently and unobserved; παρῆγεν οὕτως, so that they were not aware of him. Note, Christ's departures from a church, or a particular soul, are often *secret,* and not soon taken notice of. As *the kingdom of God comes not,* so it *goes not, with observation.* See Judg. xvi. 20. *Samson wist not that the Lord was departed from him.* Thus it was with these forsaken Jews, God left them, and they never missed him.

CHAP. IX.

After Christ's departure out of the temple, in the close of the foregoing chapter, and before this happened which is recorded in this chapter, he had been for some time abroad in the country, it is supposed about two or three months; in which interval of time Dr. Lightfoot and other harmonists place all the passages that occur from Luke x. 17 to xiii. 17. What is recorded ch. vii. and viii. was at the feast of tabernacles, in September; what is recorded in this and the following chapter was at the feast of dedication, in December, ch. x. 22. Mr. Clark and others place this immediately after the foregoing chapter. In this chapter we have, I. The miraculous cure of a man that was born blind, ver. 1—7. II. The discourses which were occasioned by it. 1. A discourse of the neighbours among themselves, and with the man, ver. 8–12. 2. Between the Pharisees and the man, ver. 13—34. 3. Between Christ and the poor man, ver. 35—38. 4. Between Christ and the Pharisees, ver. 39 to the end.

AND as *Jesus* passed by, he saw
a man which was blind from
his birth. 2 And his disciples asked
him, saying, Master, who did sin,
this man, or his parents, that he was
born blind? 3 Jesus answered,
Neither hath this man sinned, nor
his parents: but that the works of
God should be made manifest in him.
4 I must work the works of him that
sent me, while it is day: the night
cometh, when no man can work. 5
As long as I am in the world, I am
the light of the world. 6 When he
had thus spoken, he spat on the
ground, and made clay of the spittle,
and he anointed the eyes of the blind
man with the clay, 7 And said unto
him, Go, wash in the pool of Siloam,
(which is by interpretation, Sent.)
He went his way therefore, and
washed, and came seeing.

We have here sight given to a poor beggar that had been blind from his birth. Observe,

I. The notice which our Lord Jesus took of the piteous case of this poor blind man (*v.* 1): *As Jesus passed by he saw a man which was blind from his birth.* The first words seem to refer to the last of the foregoing chapter, and countenance the opinion of those who in the harmony place this story immediately after that. There it was said, παρῆγεν—*he passed by,* and here, without so much as repeating his name (though our translators supply it) καὶ παράγω—*and as he passed by.* 1. Though the Jews had so basely abused him, and both by word and deed gave him the highest provocation imaginable, yet he did not miss any opportunity of doing good among them, nor take up a resolution, as justly he might have done, never to have favoured them with any good offices. The cure of this blind man was a kindness to *the public,* enabling him to work for his living who before was a charge and burden to the neighbourhood. It is noble, and generous, and Christ-like, to be willing to *serve the public,* even when we are slighted and disobliged by them, or think ourselves so. 2. Though he was in his flight from a threatening danger, and escaping for his life, yet he willingly halted and staid awhile to show mercy to this poor man. We make more haste than good speed when we out-run opportunities of doing good. 3. When the Pharisees drove Christ from them, he went to this poor blind beggar. Some of the ancients make this a figure of the bringing of the gospel to the Gentiles, *who sat in darkness,* when the Jews had rejected it, and driven it from them 4. Christ took this poor blind man in his way, and cured him *in transitu—as he passed by.* Thus should we take occasions of doing good, even as we *pass by,* wherever we are.

Now, (1.) The condition of this poor man was very sad. He was *blind,* and had been so *from his birth.* If the light is sweet, how melancholy must it needs be for a man, all his days, *to eat in darkness!* He that is *blind* has no *enjoyment* of the light, but he that is *born blind* has no *idea* of it. Methinks such a one would give a great deal to have his curiosity satisfied with but one day's sight of light and colours, shapes and figures, though he were never to see them more. *Why is* the *light* of life *given to one that is in this misery,* that is deprived of the light of the sun, *whose way is* thus *hid, and whom God hath* thus *hedged in?* Job iii. 20—23. Let us bless God that it was not our case. The eye is one of the most curious parts of the body, its structure exceedingly nice and fine. In the formation of animals, it is said to be the first part that appears distinctly discernible. What a mercy is it that there was no miscarriage in the making of ours! Christ cured many that were blind by disease or accident, but here he cured one that was *born blind.* [1.] That he might give an instance of his power to help in the most desperate cases, and to relieve when none else can. [2.] That he might give a *specimen* of the work of his grace upon the souls of sinners, which gives sight to those that were by nature blind.

(2.) The compassions of our Lord Jesus towards him were very tender. He *saw him;* that is, he took cognizance of his case, and looked upon him with concern. When God is about to work deliverance, he is said to see *the affliction;* so Christ saw this poor man. Others saw him, but not as he did. This poor man could not see Christ, but Christ saw him, and anticipated both his prayers and expectations with a surprising cure. Christ is often found of those that seek him not, nor see him, Isa. lxv. 1. And, if we know or apprehend any thing of Christ, it is because we were first *known of him* (Gal. iv. 9) and *apprehended* by him, Phil. iii. 12.

II. The discourse between Christ and his disciples concerning this man. When he *departed out of the temple* they went along with him: for these were they that *continued with him in his temptations*, and followed him whithersoever he went; and they lost nothing by their adherence to him, but gained experience abundantly. Observe,

1. The question which the disciples put to their Master upon this blind man's case, *v.* 2. When Christ looked upon him, they had an eye to him too; Christ's compassion should kindle ours. It is probable that Christ told them this poor man was born blind, or they knew it by common fame; but they did not move Christ to heal him. Instead of this, they started a very odd question concerning him: *Rabbi, who sinned, this man or his parents, that he was born blind?* Now this question of theirs was,

(1.) *Uncharitably censorious.* They take it for granted that this extraordinary calamity was the punishment of some uncommon wickedness, and that this man was a sinner above all men that dwelt at Jerusalem, Luke xiii. 4. For the *barbarous people* to infer, *Surely this man is a murderer*, was not so strange; but it was *inexcusable* in them, who knew the scriptures, who had read that *all things come alike to all*, and knew that it was adjudged in Job's case that the greatest sufferers are not *therefore* to be looked upon as the greatest sinners. The grace of repentance calls our own afflictions *punishments*, but the grace of charity calls the afflictions of others *trials*, unless the contrary is very evident.

(2.) It was *unnecessarily curious.* Concluding this calamity to be inflicted for some very heinous crime, they ask, *Who were the criminals, this man or his parents?* And what was this to them? Or what good would it do them to know it? We are apt to be more inquisitive concerning other people's sins than concerning our own; whereas, it is more our concern to know wherefore God contends with us than wherefore he contends with others; for to judge ourselves is our duty, but to judge our brother is our sin. They enquire, [1.] Whether this man was punished thus for some sin of his own, either committed or foreseen before his birth. Some think that the disciples were tainted with the Pythagorean notion of the *pre-existence* of souls, and their *transmigration* from one body to another. Was this man's soul condemned to the dungeon of this blind body to punish it for some great sin committed in another body which it had before animated? The Pharisees seem to have had the same opinion of his case when they said, *Thou wast altogether born in sin* (*v.* 34), as if all those, and those only, were born in sin whom nature had *stigmatized.* Or, [2.] Whether he was punished for the wickedness of his parents, which God sometimes *visits upon the children.* It is a good reason why parents should take heed of sin, lest their children smart for it when they are gone. Let not us thus be cruel to our own, as the *ostrich in the wilderness.* Perhaps the disciples asked this, not as believing that this was the punishment of some actual sin of his own or his parents, but Christ having intimated to another patient that his sin was the cause of his impotency (*ch.* v. 14), "Master," say they, "whose sin is the cause of this impotency?" Being at a loss what construction to put upon this providence, they desire to be informed. The equity of God's dispensations is always certain, for *his righteousness is as the great mountains*, but not always to be accounted for, for his *judgments are a great deep.*

2. Christ's answer to this question. He was always *apt to teach*, and to rectify his disciples' mistakes.

(1.) He gives the reason of this poor man's blindness: "*Neither has this man sinned nor his parents*, but he was born blind, and has continued so to this day, that now at last *the works of God should be made manifest in him*," *v.* 3. Here Christ, who perfectly knew the secret springs of the divine counsels, told them two things concerning such uncommon calamities:—[1.] That they are not always inflicted as punishments of sin. The sinfulness of the whole race of mankind does indeed justify God in all the miseries of human life; so that those who have the least share of them must say that God is *kind*, and those who have the largest share must not say that he is *unjust;* but many are made much more *miserable* than others in this life who are not at all more *sinful.* Not but that this man was a sinner, and his parents sinners, but it was not any uncommon guilt that God had an eye to in inflicting this upon him. Note, We must take heed of judging any to be great sinners merely because they are great sufferers, lest we be found, not only *persecuting those whom God has smitten* (Ps. lxix. 26), but accusing those whom he has justified, and *condemning* those for whom *Christ died*, which is daring and dangerous, Rom. viii. 33, 34. [2.] That they are sometimes intended purely *for the glory of God*, and the *manifesting of his works.* God has a sovereignty over all his creatures and an exclusive right in them, and may make them serviceable to his glory in such a way as he thinks fit, in doing or suffering; and if God be glorified, either by us or in us, we were not made *in vain.* This man was *born blind*, and it was worth while for him to be so, and to continue thus long dark, *that the works of God might be manifest in him.* That is, *First*, That the *attributes of God* might be made manifest in him: his justice in making sinful man liable to such grievous calamities; his ordinary power and goodness in supporting a poor man under such a grievous and tedious affliction, especially that his extraordinary power and goodness might be manifested in curing him. Note, The difficulties of providence, otherwise unaccountable, may be resolved intot his

—God intends in them to *show himself,* to declare his glory, to make himself to be taken notice of. Those who regard him not in the ordinary course of things are sometimes alarmed by things extraordinary. How contentedly then may a good man be a *loser in his comforts,* while he is sure that thereby God will be one way or other a *gainer in his glory! Secondly,* That the counsels of God concerning the Redeemer might be manifested in him. He was *born blind* that our Lord Jesus might have the honour of *curing him,* and might therein prove himself sent of God to be the true light to the world. Thus the fall of man was permitted, and the *blindness* that followed it, that the works of God might be manifest in *opening the eyes of the blind.* It was now a great while since this man was born blind, and yet it never appeared till now *why* he was so. Note, The intentions of Providence commonly do not appear till a great while after the event, perhaps *many years* after. The sentences in the book of providence are sometimes *long,* and you must read a great way before you can apprehend the sense of them.

(2.) He gives the reason of his own forwardness and readiness to help and heal him. *v.* 4, 5. It was not for ostentation, but in pursuance of his undertaking: *I must work the works of him that sent me* (of which this is one), *while it is day,* and working time; *the night cometh,* the period of that day, *when no man can work.* This is not only a reason why Christ was constant in doing good to the souls and bodies of men, but why particularly he did this, though it was the sabbath day, on which works of necessity might be done, and he proves this to be a work of necessity.

[1.] It was his Father's will: *I must work the works of him that sent me.* Note, *First,* The Father, when he sent his Son into the world, gave him *work to do;* he did not come into the world to take state, but to do business; whom God sends he employs, for he sends none to be idle. *Secondly,* The works Christ had to do were the *works of him that sent him,* not only appointed *by him,* but done *for him;* he was a worker together with God. *Thirdly,* He was pleased to lay himself under the strongest obligations to do the business he was sent about: I *must work.* He *engaged his heart,* in the covenant of redemption, to *draw near,* and *approach* to God as Mediator, Jer. xxx. 21. Shall we be willing to be *loose,* when Christ was willing to be *bound? Fourthly,* Christ, having laid himself under obligations to do his work, laid out himself with the utmost vigour and industry in his work. He *worked the works* he had to do; did ἐργάζεσθαι τὰ ἔργα—*made a business of that which was his business.* It is not enough to look at our work, and talk over it, but we must work it.

[2.] Now was his opportunity: I must work *while it is day,* while the time lasts which is appointed to work in, and while the light lasts which is given to work by. Christ himself had *his day. First,* All the business of the *mediatorial kingdom* was to be done within the limits of time, and in this world; for at the end of the world, when time shall be no more, the *kingdom shall be delivered up to God, even the Father,* and the *mystery of God finished. Secondly,* All the work he had to do *in his own person* here on earth was to be done *before his death;* the time of his living in this world is *the day* here spoken of. Note, The time of our life is our day, in which it concerns us to do the *work of the day.* Day-time is the proper season for work (Ps. civ. 22, 23); during the day of life we must be busy, not waste *day-time,* not play by *day-light;* it will be time enough to rest when our day is done, for it is *but a day.*

[3.] The period of his opportunity was at hand, and therefore he would be busy: *The night comes when no man can work.* Note, The consideration of our death approaching should quicken us to improve all the opportunities of life, both for doing and getting good. *The night comes,* it will come certainly, may come suddenly, is coming nearer and nearer. We cannot compute how nigh our sun is, it may go down at noon; nor can we promise ourselves a twilight between the day of life and the night of death. When the night comes we *cannot work,* because the light afforded us to work by is *extinguished;* the grave is a land of darkness, and our work cannot be done *in the dark.* And, besides, our time allotted us for our work will then have *expired;* when our Master tied us to duty he tied us to time too; when night comes, *call the labourers;* we must then *show our work,* and receive according to the things done. In the world of retribution we are no longer probationers; it is too late to *bid* when the inch of candle is *dropped.* Christ uses this as an argument with himself to be diligent, though he had no opposition from within to struggle with; much more need have we to work upon our hearts these and the like considerations to quicken us.

[4.] His business in the world was to enlighten it (*v.* 5): *As long as I am in the world,* and that will not be long, *I am the light of the world.* He had said this before, *ch.* viii. 12. He is the *Sun of righteousness,* that has not only light in his wings for those that can see, but healing in his wings, or beams, for those that are blind and cannot see, therein far exceeding in virtue that great light which rules *by day.* Christ would cure this blind man, the representative of a blind world, because he came to be *the light of the world,* not only to give *light,* but to give *sight.* Now this gives us, *First,* A great *encouragement* to come to him, as a guiding, quickening, refreshing light. To whom should we look but to him? Which way should we turn our eyes, but to the light? We partake of the sun's light, and so we may of Christ's grace, without money and without price. *Secondly,* A good *example* of usefulness in the world. What Christ saith of himself, he saith of his disciples: *You are lights in the world,* and, if so, *Let your light shine.* What were candles made for but to burn?

III. The manner of the cure of the blind man, *v.* 6,7. The circumstances of the miracle are singular, and no doubt significant. *When he had thus spoken* for the instruction of his disciples, and the opening of their understandings, he addressed himself to the opening of the blind man's eyes. He did not defer it till he could do it either more privately, for his greater safety, or more publicly, for his greater honour, or till the sabbath was past, when it would give less offence. What good we have opportunity of doing we should do quickly; he that will never do a good work till there is nothing to be objected against it will leave many a good work for ever undone, Eccl. xi. 4. In the cure observe,

1. The preparation of the eye-salve. Christ *spat on the ground, and made clay of the spittle.* He could have cured him with a word, as he did others, but he chose to do it in this way to show that he is not *tied* to any method. He made clay of his own spittle, because there was no water near; and he would teach us not to be nice or curious, but, when we have at any time occasion, to be willing to take up with that which is *next hand,* if it will but serve the turn. Why should we *go about* for that which may as well be had and done a *nearer way?* Christ's making use of his own spittle intimates that there is healing virtue in every thing that belongs to Christ; clay made of Christ's spittle was much more precious than the balm of Gilead.

2. The application of it to the place: *He anointed the eyes of the blind man with the clay.* Or, as the margin reads it, *He spread* (ἐπέχρισε), *he daubed the clay upon the eyes of the blind man,* like a tender physician; he did it himself with his own hand, though the patient was a beggar. Now Christ did this, (1.) To magnify his power in making a blind man to see by that method which one would think more likely to make a seeing man blind. Daubing clay on the eyes would *close them* up, but never *open them.* Note, The power of God often works by contraries; and he makes men feel their own blindness before he gives them sight. (2.) To give an intimation that it was his mighty hand, the very same that at first made man out of *the clay;* for by him God *made the worlds,* both the great world, and man the little world. Man was *formed out of the clay,* and moulded like the clay, and here Christ used the same materials to give sight to the body that at first he used to give being to it. (3.) To represent and typify the healing and opening of the eyes of the mind by the grace of Jesus Christ. The design of the gospel is to *open men's eyes,* Acts, xxvi. 18. Now the eye-salve that does the work is of Christ's preparing; it is made up, not as this, of his spittle, but of his blood, the blood and water that came out of his pierced side; we must come to Christ for *the eye-salve,* Rev. iii. 18. He only is *able,* and he only is *appointed,* to make it up, Luke iv. 18. The means used in this work are very weak and unlikely, and are made effectual only by the power of Christ; when a dark world was to be enlightened, and nations of blind souls were to have their eyes opened, God chose the *foolish things, and weak, and despised,* for the doing of it. And the method Christ takes is first to make men feel themselves blind, as this poor man did whose eyes were daubed with clay, and then to give them sight. Paul in his conversion was *struck blind* for three days, and then the *scales fell from his eyes.* The way prescribed for getting spiritual wisdom is, *Let a man become a fool, that he may be wise,* 1 Cor. iii. 18. We must be made uneasy with our blindness, as this man here, and then healed.

3. The directions given to the patient, *v.* 7. His physician said to him, *Go, wash in the pool of Siloam.* Not that this washing was needful to effect the cure; but, (1.) Christ would hereby try his obedience, and whether he would with an implicit faith obey the orders of one he was so much a stranger to. (2.) He would likewise try how he stood affected to the tradition of the elders, which taught, and perhaps had taught him (for many that are *blind* are very knowing), that it was not lawful to wash the eyes, no not with spittle medicinally, on the sabbath day, much less to go to a pool of water to wash them. (3.) He would hereby represent the method of spiritual healing, in which, though the effect is owing purely to his power and grace, there is duty to be done by us. Go, search the scriptures, attend upon the ministry, converse with the wise; this is like washing in the pool of Siloam. Promised graces must be expected in the way of instituted ordinances. The waters of baptism were to those who had been trained up in darkness like the pool of Siloam, in which they might not only wash and be clean, but *wash, and have their eyes opened.* Hence they that were baptized are said to be φωτισθεντες—*enlightened;* and the ancients called baptism φωτισμὸς—*illumination.* Concerning the pool of Siloam observe, [1.] That it was supplied with water from mount Zion, so that these were the *waters of the sanctuary* (Ps. xlvi. 4), living waters, which were *healing,* Ezek. xlvii. 9. [2.] That the waters of Siloam had of old signified the throne and kingdom of the house of David, pointing at the Messiah (Isa. viii. 6), and the Jews who *refused the waters of Shiloa,* Christ's doctrine and law, and rejoiced in the tradition of the elders. Christ would try this man, whether he would cleave to the waters of Siloam or no. [3.] The evangelist takes notice of the signification of the name, its being interpreted *sent.* Christ is often called the *sent of God,* the Messenger of the covenant (Mal. iii. 1);

so that when Christ sent him to the pool of Siloam he did in effect send him to himself; for Christ is *all in all* to the healing of souls. Christ as a prophet directs us to himself as a priest *Go, wash in the fountain opened,* a fountain of life, not a *pool.*

4. The patient's obedience to these directions: *He went his way therefore,* probably led by some friend or other; or perhaps he was so well acquainted with Jerusalem that he could find the way himself. Nature often supplies the want of sight with an uncommon sagacity; and *he washed his eyes;* probably the disciples, or some stander by, informed him that he who bade him do it was that Jesus whom he had heard so much of, else he would not have gone, at his bidding, on that which looked so much like a fool's errand; in confidence of Christ's power, as well as in obedience to his command, he went, and washed.

5. The cure effected: *He came seeing.* There is more glory in this concise narrative, *He went* and *washed,* and *came seeing,* than in Cæsar's *Veni, vidi, vici—I came, I saw, I conquered.* When the clay was *washed off* from his eyes, all the other impediments were removed with it; so when the pangs and struggles of the new birth are over, and the pains and terrors of conviction past, the bands of sin fly off with them, and a glorious light and liberty succeed. See here an instance, (1.) Of the power of Christ. What cannot *he* do who could not only do *this,* but do it *thus?* With a lump of clay laid on either eye, and washed off again, he couched those cataracts immediately which the most skilful oculist, with the finest instrument and the most curious hand, could not remove. No doubt this is *he that should come,* for by him the blind receive their sight. (2.) It is an instance of the virtue of faith and obedience. This man let Christ do what *he* pleased, and did what he appointed him to do, and so was cured. Those that would be healed by Christ must be ruled by him. He *came back* from the pool to his neighbours and acquaintance, wondering and wondered at; he came *seeing.* This represents the benefit gracious souls find in attending on instituted ordinances, according to Christ's appointment; they have gone to the pool of Siloam weak, and have come away strengthened; have gone doubting, and come away satisfied; have gone mourning, and come away rejoicing; have gone trembling, and come away triumphing; have gone *blind,* and come away *seeing,* come away singing, Isa. lii. 8.

8 The neighbours therefore, and
they which before had seen him that
he was blind, said, Is not this he that
sat and begged? 9 Some said, This
is he: others *said,* He is like him:
but he said, I am *he.* 10 Therefore
said they unto him, How were thine
eyes opened? 11 He answered and
said, A man that is called Jesus, made
clay, and anointed mine eyes, and
said unto me, Go to the pool of
Siloam, and wash: and I went and
washed, and I received sight. 12
Then said they unto him, Where is
he? He said, I know not.

Such a wonderful event as the giving of sight to a man born blind could not but be the talk of the town, and many heeded it no more than they do other town-talk, that is but nine days' wonder; but here we are told what the neighbours said of it, for the confirmation of the matter of fact. That which at first was not believed without *scrutiny* may afterwards be admitted without *scruple.* Two things are debated in this conference about it:—

I. Whether this was the same man that had before been blind, *v.* 8.

1. The neighbours that lived near the place where he was born and bred, and knew that he had been blind, could not but be amazed when they saw that he had his eye-sight, had it on a sudden, and perfectly; and they said, *Is not this he that sat and begged?* It seems, this blind man was a common beggar, being disabled to work for his living; and so discharged from the obligation of the law, that if *any would not work, neither should he eat.* When he could not go about, he *sat;* if we cannot *work* for God, we must *sit still* quietly for him. When he could not labour, his parents not being able to maintain him, he *begged.* Note, Those who cannot otherwise subsist must not, like the unjust steward, be *ashamed to beg;* let no man be ashamed of any thing but sin. There are some common beggars that are objects of charity, that should be distinguished; and we must not let the bees starve for the sake of the drones or wasps that are among them. As to this man, (1.) It was well ordered by Providence that he on whom this miracle was wrought should be a common beggar, and so generally known and remarkable, by which means the truth of the miracle was the better attested, and there were more to witness against those infidel Jews who would not believe *that he had been blind* than if he had been maintained in his father's house. (2.) It was the greater instance of Christ's condescension that he seemed (as I may say) to take more pains about the cure of a common beggar than of others. When it was for the advantage of his miracles that they should be wrought on those that were remarkable, he pitched upon those that were made so by their poverty and misery; not by their dignity.

2. In answer to this enquiry, (1.) Some said, *This is he,* the very same man; and these are witnesses to the truth of the miracle, for they had long known him stone-blind. (2.) Others, who could not think it possible

that a man born blind should thus on a sudden receive his sight, for that reason, and no other, said, *He is not he, but is like him,* and so, by their confession, if it be he, it is a great miracle that is wrought upon him. Hence we may take occasion to think, [1.] Of the wisdom and power of Providence in ordering such a universal variety of the faces of men and women, so that no two are so alike but that they may be distinguished, which is necessary to society, and commerce, and the administration of justice. And, [2.] Of the wonderful change which the converting grace of God makes upon some who before were very wicked and vile, but are thereby so universally and visibly altered that one would not take them to be the same persons.

3. This controversy was soon decided by the man himself: *He said, I am he,* the very man that so lately sat and begged; "I am he that was blind, and was an object of the charity of men, but now see, and am a monument of the mercy and grace of God." We do not find that the neighbours appealed to him in this matter, but he, hearing the debate, interposed, and put an end to it. It is a piece of justice we owe to our neighbours to rectify their mistakes, and to set things before them, as far as we are able, in a true light. Applying it spiritually, it teaches us that those who are savingly enlightened by the grace of God should be ready to own what they were before that blessed change was wrought, 1 Tim. i. 13, 14.

II. How he came to have his eyes opened, *v.* 10—12. They will now turn aside, and *see this great sight,* and enquire further concerning it. He did not *sound a trumpet* when he did these alms, nor perform his cures *upon a stage;* and yet, like a city upon a hill, they could not be hid. Two things these neighbours enquire after :—

1. The manner of the cure: *How were thine eyes opened?* The works of the Lord being great, they ought to be *sought out,* Ps. cxi. 2. It is good to observe the way and method of God's works, and they will appear the more wonderful. We may apply it spiritually; it is strange that blind eyes should be opened, but more strange when we consider how they are opened; how weak the means are that are used, and how strong the opposition that is conquered. In answer to this enquiry the poor man gives them a plain and full account of the matter: *A man that is called Jesus made clay,—and I received sight. v.* 11. Note, Those who have experienced special instances of God's power and goodness, in temporal or spiritual things, should be ready upon all occasions to communicate their experiences, for the glory of God and the instruction and encouragement of others. See David's collection of his experiences, his own and others', Ps. xxxiv. 4—6. It is a debt we owe to our benefactor, and to our brethren. God's favours are lost *upon* us, when they are lost *with us,* and go no further.

2. The author of it (*v.* 12): *Where is he?* Some perhaps asked this question out of curiosity. "Where is he, that we may see him?" A man that did such cures as these might well be a show, which one would go a good way for the sight of. Others, perhaps, asked out of ill-will. "Where is he, that we may *seize* him?" There was a proclamation out for the discovering and apprehending of him (*ch.* xi. 57); and the unthinking crowd, in spite of all reason and equity, will have ill thoughts of those that are put into an ill name. Some, we hope, asked this question out of *good-will.* "Where is he, that we may be acquainted with him? Where is he, that we may come to him, and share in the favours he is so free of?" In answer to this, he could say nothing: *I know not.* As soon as Christ had sent him to the pool of Siloam, it should seem, he withdrew immediately (as he did, *ch.* v. 13), and did not stay till the man returned, as if he either doubted of the effect or waited for the man's thanks. Humble souls take more pleasure in *doing good* than in hearing of it again; it will be time enough to hear of it in the *resurrection of the just.* The man had never seen Jesus, for by the time that he had gained his sight he had lost his Physician; and he asked, it is probable, *Where is he?* None of all the new and surprising objects that presented themselves could be so grateful to him as one sight of Christ, but as yet he knew no more of him than that he was called, and rightly called, *Jesus—a Saviour.* Thus in the work of grace wrought upon the soul we see the change, but see not the hand that makes it; for the way of the Spirit is like that of the wind, which thou hearest the sound of, but canst not tell *whence it comes* nor *whither it goes.*

13 They brought to the Pharisees
him that aforetime was blind. 14
And it was the sabbath day when
Jesus made the clay, and opened his
eyes. 15 Then again the Pharisees
also asked him how he had received his
sight. He said unto them, He put
clay upon mine eyes, and I washed, and
do see. 16 Therefore said some of
the Pharisees, This man is not of God,
because he keepeth not the sabbath
day. Others said, How can a man
that is a sinner do such miracles? And
there was a division among them. 17
They say unto the blind man again,
What sayest thou of him, that he hath
opened thine eyes? He said, He is a
prophet. 18 But the Jews did not
believe concerning him, that he had
been blind, and received his sight,
until they called the parents of him

that had received his sight. 19 And
they asked them, saying, Is this your
son, who ye say was born blind? how
then doth he now see? 20 His parents
answered them and said, We know
that this is our son, and that he was
born blind: 21 But by what means
he now seeth, we know not; or who
hath opened his eyes, we know
not: he is of age; ask him: he shall
speak for himself. 22 These *words*
spake his parents, because they feared
the Jews: for the Jews had agreed
already, that if any man did confess
that he was Christ, he should be put
out of the synagogue. 23 Therefore
said his parents, He is of age; ask him.
24 Then again called they the man
that was blind, and said unto him,
Give God the praise: we know that
this man is a sinner. 25 He answered
and said, Whether he be a sinner *or*
no, I know not: one thing I know,
that, whereas I was blind, now I see.
26 Then said they to him again,
What did he to thee? how opened he
thine eyes? 27 He answered them, I
have told you already, and ye did not
hear: wherefore would ye hear *it*
again? will ye also be his disciples?
28 Then they reviled him, and said,
Thou art his disciple; but we are Moses' disciples. 29 We know that God
spake unto Moses: *as for* this *fellow*,
we know not from whence he is. 30
The man answered and said unto them,
Why herein is a marvellous thing,
that ye know not from whence he is,
and *yet* he hath opened mine eyes. 31
Now we know that God heareth not
sinners: but if any man be a worshipper of God, and doeth his will, him
he heareth. 32 Since the world began
was it not heard that any man opened
the eyes of one that was born blind.
33 If this man were not of God, he
could do nothing. 34 They answered and said unto him, Thou wast
altogether born in sins, and dost
thou teach us? And they cast him
out.

One would have expected that such a miracle as Christ wrought upon the blind man would have settled his reputation, and silenced and shamed all opposition, but it had the contrary effect; instead of being embraced as a prophet for it, he is prosecuted as a criminal.

I. Here is the information that was given in to the Pharisees concerning this matter: *They brought to the Pharisees him that aforetime was blind, v.* 13. They brought him to the great sanhedrim, which consisted chiefly of Pharisees, at least the Pharisees in the sanhedrim were most active against Christ. 1. Some think that those who brought this man to the Pharisees did it with a *good design*, to show them that this Jesus, whom they persecuted, was not what they represented him, but really a great man, and one that gave considerable proofs of a divine mission. What hath convinced us of the truth and excellency of religion, and hath removed our prejudices against it, we should be forward, as we have opportunity, to offer to others for their conviction. 2. It should seem, rather, that they did it with an *ill design*, to exasperate the Pharisees the more against Christ, and there was no need of this, for they were bitter enough of themselves. They brought him with such a suggestion as that in *ch.* xi. 47, 48, *If we let him thus alone, all men will believe on him.* Note, Those rulers that are of a persecuting spirit shall never want ill instruments about them, that will blow the coals, and make them worse.

II. The ground which was pretended for this information, and the colour given to it. That which is good was never maligned but under the imputation of something evil. And the crime objected here (*v.* 14) was that *it was the sabbath day when Jesus made the clay, and opened his eyes.* The profanation of the sabbath day is certainly wicked, and gives a man a very ill character; but the traditions of the Jews had made that to be a violation of the law of the sabbath which was far from being so. Many a time this matter was contested between Christ and the Jews, that it might be settled for the benefit of the church in all ages. But it may be asked, "Why would Christ not only work miracles on the sabbath day, but work them in such a manner as he knew would give offence to the Jews? When he had healed the impotent man, why should he bid him carry his bed? Could he not have cured this blind man without making clay?" I answer, 1. He would not seem to yield to the usurped power of the scribes and Pharisees. Their government was illegal, their impositions were arbitrary, and their zeal for the rituals consumed the substantials of religion; and therefore Christ would not *give place* to them, *by subjection, no not for an hour.* Christ was made under the law of God, but not under their law. 2. He did it that he might, both by word and action, expound the law of the fourth commandment, and vindicate it from their corrupt glosses, and so teach us that a weekly sabbath is to be *perpetually* observed in the church, one day in seven (for what need was there to explain that law, if it must be presently abrogated?) and that it is not to be so *ceremonially* observed by us as it was by the Jews? Works of necessity and mercy are allowed, and the sabbath-rest to be kept, not so much for its own sake as in order to the sabbath-work. 3. Christ chose to work his cures on the sabbath day to dignify and sanctify the day, and to intimate that spiritual cures should be wrought mostly on the Christian sabbath day. How many blind eyes have been opened by the preaching of the gospel, that blessed eye-salve, on the Lord's day! How many impotent souls cured on that day!

III. The trial and examination of this matter by the Pharisees, *v.* 15. So much passion, prejudice, and ill-humour, and so little reason, appear here, that the discourse is nothing but crossing questions. One would think, when a man in these circumstances was brought before them, they would have been so taken up in admiring the miracle, and congratulating the happiness of the poor man, that they could not have been peevish with him. But their enmity to Christ had divested them of all manner of humanity, and divinity too. Let us see how they teased this man.

1. They interrogated him concerning the cure itself.

(1.) They doubted whether he had indeed been *born blind,* and demanded proof of that which even the prosecutors had acknowledged (*v.* 18): They *did not believe,* that is, they would not, that he was *born blind.* Men that seek occasion to quarrel with the clearest truths may find it if they please; and they that resolve to *hold fast deceit* will never want a handle to hold it by. This was not a prudent caution, but a prejudiced infidelity. However, it was a good way that they took for the clearing of this: *They called the parents of the man who had received his sight.* This they did in hopes to disprove the miracle. These parents were poor and timorous, and if they had said that they could not be sure that this was their son, or that it was only some weakness or dimness in his sight that he had been born with, which if they had been able to get help for him might have been cured long since, or had otherwise prevaricated, for fear of the court, the Pharisees had gained their point, had robbed Christ of the honour of this miracle, which would have lessened the reputation of all the rest. But God so ordered and overruled this counsel of theirs that it turned to the more effectual proof of the miracle, and left them under a necessity of being either convinced or confounded. Now in this part of the examination we have,

[1.] The questions that were put to them (*v.* 19): They *asked them* in an imperious threatening way, "*Is this your son?* Dare you swear to it? *Do you say he was born blind?* Are you sure of it? Or did he but pretend to be so, to have an excuse for his begging? *How then doth he now see?* That is impossible, and therefore you had better unsay it." Those who cannot bear the light of truth do all they can to *eclipse* it, and hinder the discovery of it. Thus the *managers of evidence,* or mismanagers rather, lead witnesses out of the way, and teach them how to conceal or disguise the truth, and so involve themselves in a double guilt, like that of Jeroboam, who sinned, and made Israel to sin.

[2.] Their answers to these interrogatories, in which,

First, They fully attest that which they could safely say in this matter; *safely,* that is, upon their own knowledge, and *safely,* that is, without running themselves into a *premunire* (*v.* 20): *We know that this is our son* (for they were daily conversant with him, and had such a natural affection to him as the true mother had (1 Kings iii. 26), which made them know it was *their own); and* we know that he was *born blind.* They had reason to know it, inasmuch as it had cost them many a sad thought, and many a careful troublesome hour, about him. How often had they looked upon him with grief, and lamented their child's blindness more than all the burdens and inconveniences of their poverty, and wished he had never been born, rather than be born to such an uncomfortable life! Those who are ashamed of their children, or any of their relations, because of their bodily infirmities, may take a reproof from *these* parents, who freely owned, This is *our son,* though he was *born blind,* and lived upon alms.

Secondly, They cautiously decline giving any evidence concerning his cure; partly because they were not themselves eye-witnesses of it, and could say nothing to it *of their own knowledge;* and partly because they found it was a *tender point,* and would not bear to be meddled with. And therefore, having owned that he was *their son* and was *born blind,* further these deponents say not.

a. Observe how warily they express themselves (*v.* 21): "*By what means he now seeth we know not,* or *who has opened his eyes we know not,* otherwise than by *hearsay;* we can give no account either by what means or by whose hand it was done." See how the wisdom of this world teaches men to *trim* the matter in critical junctures. Christ was accused as a sabbath-breaker, and as an impostor. Now these parents of the blind man, though they were not eye-witnesses of the cure, were yet fully assured of it, and were bound in gratitude to have borne their testimony to the honour of the Lord Jesus, who had done their son so great a kindness; but they had not courage to do it, and then thought it might serve to atone for their not appearing in favour of him that they said nothing to his prejudice; whereas, in the day of trial, he that is not *apparently* for Christ is justly looked upon as *really* against him, Luke xi. 23; Mark viii. 38. That they might not be further urged in this matter, they refer themselves and the court to him: *He is of age, ask him, he shall speak for himself.* This implies that while children are not of age (while they are *infants*, such as cannot speak) it is incumbent upon their parents to *speak for them*, speak to God for them in prayer, speak to the church for them in baptism; but, when they are of age, it is fit that they should be asked whether they be willing to stand to that which their parents did for them, and let them speak for themselves. This man, though he was *born blind*, seems to have been of quick understanding above many, which enabled him to speak for himself better than his friends could speak for him. Thus God often by a kind providence makes up in the mind what is wanting in the body, 1 Cor. xii. 23, 24. His parents' turning them over to him was only to save themselves from trouble, and expose him; whereas they that had so great an interest in his *mercies* had reason to embark with him in his *hazards* for the honour of that Jesus who had done so much for them.

b. See the reason why they were so cautious (*v.* 22, 23): *Because they feared the Jews.* It was not because they would put an honour upon their son, by making him his own advocate, or because they would have the matter cleared by the *best hand*, but because they would shift trouble off from themselves, as most people are in care to do, no matter on whom they throw it. Near is my friend, and near is my child, and perhaps near is my religion, but *nearer is myself—Proximus egomet mihi.* But Christianity teaches another lesson, 1 Cor. x. 24; Esth. viii. 6. Here is,

(*a.*) The *late law* which the sanhedrim had made. It was agreed and enacted by their authority that, if any man within their jurisdiction did *confess* that Jesus *was Christ, he should be put out of the synagogue.* Observe,

[*a.*] The crime designed to be punished, and so prevented, by this statute, and that was embracing Jesus of Nazareth as the promised Messiah, and manifesting this by any overt-act, which amounted to a confessing of him. They themselves did expect a Messiah, but they could by no means bear to think that this Jesus should be he, nor admit the question whether he were or no, for two reasons:—*First*, Because his precepts were all so contrary to their traditional *laws.* The spiritual worship he prescribed overthrew their formalities; nor did any thing more effectually destroy their singularity and narrow-spiritedness than that universal charity which he taught; humility and mortification, repentance and self-denial, were lessons new to them, and sounded harsh and strange in their ears. *Secondly*, Because his promises and appearances were so contrary to their traditional hopes. They expected a Messiah in outward pomp and splendour, that should not only free the nation from the Roman yoke, but advance the grandeur of the sanhedrim, and make all the members of it princes and peers: and now to hear of a Messiah whose outward circumstances were all mean and poor, whose first appearance and principal residence were in Galilee, a despised province, who never made his court to them, nor sought their favour, whose followers were neither sword-men nor gownmen, nor any men of honour, but contemptible fishermen, who proposed and promised no redemption but from sin, no consolation of Israel but what is spiritual and divine, and at the same time bade his followers expect the cross, and count upon persecution; this was such a reproach to all the ideas they had formed and filled the minds of their people with, such a blow to their power and interest, and such a disappointment to all their hopes, that they could never be reconciled to it, nor so much as give it a fair or patient hearing, but, right or wrong, it must be *crushed.*

[*b.*] The penalty to be inflicted for this crime. If any should own himself a disciple of Jesus, he should be deemed and taken as an apostate from the faith of the Jewish church, and a rebel and traitor against the government of it, and should therefore be *put out of the synagogue*, as one that had rendered himself unworthy of the honours, and incapable of the privileges, of their church; he should be excommunicated, and expelled the commonwealth of Israel. Nor was this merely an ecclesiastical censure, which a man that made no conscience of their authority might slight, but it was, in effect, an *outlawry*, which excluded a man from civil commerce and deprived him of his liberty and property. Note, *First*, Christ's holy religion, from its first rise, has been opposed by penal laws made against the professors of it; as if men's consciences would otherwise *naturally* embrace it, this unnatural force has been put upon them. *Secondly*, The church's artillery, when the command of it has fallen into ill hands, has often been turned against itself, and ecclesiastical censures have been made to serve a carnal secular interest. It is no new thing to see those cast out of the synagogue that were the greatest ornaments and blessings of it, and to hear those that expelled them say, *The Lord be glorified*, Isa. lxvi. 5. Now of this edict it is said, 1. That the Jews had agreed it, or *conspired* it. Their consultation and communion herein were a perfect conspiracy against the crown and dignity of the Redeemer, against the Lord and his Anointed. 2. That they had already agreed it. Though he had been but a few months in any public character among them, and, one would think, in so short a time could not have made them jealous of him, yet thus early were they aware of his growing interest, and already agreed to do their utmost to suppress it. He had lately made his escape out of the temple, and, when they saw themselves baffled in their attempts to take him, they presently took this course, to make it penal for any body to own him. Thus unanimous and thus expeditious are the enemies of the church, and their counsels; but he that *sits in heaven laughs at them,* and *has them in derision,* and so may we.

(*b.*) The influence which this law had upon the parents of the blind man. They declined saying any thing of Christ, and shuffled it off to their son, *because they feared the Jews.* Christ had incurred the frowns of the government to do their son a kindness, but they would not incur them to do him any honour. Note, *The fear of man brings a snare* (Prov. xxix. 25), and often makes people deny and disown Christ, and his truths and ways, and act against their consciences. Well, the parents have thus disentangled themselves, and are discharged from any further attendance; let us now go on with the examination of the man himself; the doubt of the Pharisees, whether he was *born blind,* was put out of doubt *by them;* and therefore,

(2.) They enquired of *him* concerning the *manner of the cure,* and made their remarks upon it, *v.* 15, 16.

[1.] The same question which his neighbours had put to him *now again the Pharisees asked him, how he had received his sight.* This they enquired not with any sincere desire to find out the truth, by tracing the report to the original, but with a desire to find an occasion against Christ; for, if the man should relate the matter fully, they would prove Christ a sabbath-breaker; if he should vary from his former story, they would have some colour to suspect the whole to be a collusion.

[2.] The same answer, in effect, which he had before given to his neighbours, he here repeats to the Pharisees: *He put clay upon mine eyes, and I washed, and do see.* He does not here speak of the making of the clay, for indeed he had not seen it made. That circumstance was not essential, and might give the Pharisees most occasion against him, and therefore he waives it. In the former account he said, *I washed, and received sight;* but lest they should think it was only a glimpse for the present, which a heated imagination might fancy itself to have, he now says, "*I do see:* it is a complete and lasting cure."

[3.] The remarks made upon this story were very different, and occasioned a debate in the court, *v.* 16.

First, Some took this occasion to censure and condemn Christ for what he had done. Some of the Pharisees said, *This man is not of God,* as he pretends, *because he keepeth not the sabbath day.* 1. The doctrine upon which this censure is grounded is very true—that those *are not of God*—those pretenders to prophecy not *sent of God,* those pretenders to saintship not *born of God*—who do not *keep the sabbath day.* Those that are of God will *keep the commandments of God;* and this is his commandment, that we sanctify the sabbath. Those that are of God keep up communion with God, and delight to hear from him, and speak to him, and therefore will observe the sabbath, which is a day appointed for intercourse with heaven. The sabbath is called a *sign,* for the sanctifying of it is a sign of a sanctified heart, and the profaning of it a sign of a profane heart. But, 2. The application of it to our Saviour is very unjust, for he did religiously observe the sabbath day, and never in any instance violated it, never did otherwise than *well* on the sabbath day. He did not keep the sabbath according to the tradition of the elders and the superstitious observances of the Pharisees, but he kept it according to the command of God, and therefore, no doubt, he was of God, and his miracles proved him to be *Lord also of the sabbath day.* Note, much unrighteous and uncharitable judging is occasioned by men's making the rules of religion more strict than God has made them, and adding their own fancies to God's appointments, as the Jews here, in the case of sabbath-sanctification. We ourselves may forbear such and such things, on the sabbath day, as we find a distraction to us, and we do well, but we must not therefore tie up others to the same strictness. Every thing that we take for a rule of practice must not presently be made a rule of judgment.

Secondly, Others spoke in his favour, and very pertinently urged, *How can a man that is a sinner do such miracles?* It seems that even in this *council of the ungodly* there were some that were capable of a *free thought,* and were witnesses for Christ, even in the midst of his enemies. The matter of fact was plain, that this was a true miracle, the more it was searched into the more it was cleared; and this brought his former similar works to mind, and gave occasion to speak magnificently of them, τοιαῦτα σημεῖα—*such great signs,* so many, so evident. And the inference from it is very natural: Such things as these could never be done by a *man that is a sinner,* that is, not by any mere man, in his own name, and by his own power; or, rather, not by one that is a cheat or an impostor, and in that sense a sinner; such a one may indeed show some *signs and lying wonders,* but not such signs and true wonders as Christ wrought. How could a man produce such divine credentials, if he had not a divine commission? Thus there was a *division among them,* a *schism,* so the word is; they clashed in their opinion, a warm debate arose, and the *house divided* upon it. Thus God defeats the counsels of his enemies by dividing them; and by such testimonies as these given against the malice of persecutors, and the rubs they meet with, their designs against the church are sometimes rendered ineffectual and always inexcusable.

2. After their enquiry concerning the cure, we must observe their enquiry concerning the *author* of it. And here observe,

(1.) What the man said of him, in answer to their enquiry. They ask him (*v.* 17), "*What sayest thou of him, seeing that he has opened thine eyes?* What dost thou think of his doing this? And what idea hast thou of him that did it?" If he should speak *slightly* of Christ, in answer to this, as he might be tempted to do, to please them, now that he was in their hands, as his parents had done—if he should say, "I know not what to make of him; he may be a conjuror for aught I know, or some mountebank"—they would have triumphed in it. Nothing confirms Christ's enemies in their enmity to him so much as the slights put upon him by those that have passed for his friends. But, if he should speak honourably of Christ, they would prosecute him upon their new law, which did not except, no, not his own patient; they would make him an example, and so deter others from applying to Christ for cures, for which, though they came cheap from Christ, yet they would make them pay dearly. Or perhaps Christ's friends proposed to have the man's own sentiments concerning his physician, and were willing to know, since he appeared to be a sensible man, what he thought of him. Note, Those whose eyes Christ has opened know best what to say of him, and have great reason, upon all occasions, to say well of him. What think we of Christ? To this question the poor man makes a short, plain, and direct answer: "*He is a prophet,* he is one inspired and sent of God to preach, and work miracles, and deliver to the world a divine message." There had been no prophets among the Jews for three hundred years; yet they did not conclude that they should have no more, for they knew that he was yet to come who should *seal up vision and prophecy,* Dan. ix. 24. It should seem, this man had not any thoughts that Christ was the Messiah, the great prophet, but one of the same rank with the other prophets. The woman of Samaria concluded he was *a prophet* before she had any thought of his being the Messiah (*ch.* iv. 19); so this blind man thought well of Christ according to the light he had, though he did not think well enough of him; but, being faithful in what he had already attained to, God revealed even *that* unto him. This poor blind beggar had a clearer judgment of the things pertaining to the kingdom of God, and saw further into the proofs of a divine mission, than the *masters in Israel,* that assumed an authority to judge of prophets.

(2.) What they said of him, in reply to the man's testimony. Having in vain attempted to invalidate the evidence of the fact, and finding that indeed a *notable miracle was wrought,* and they *could not deny it,* they renew their attempt to banter it, and run it down, and do all they can to shake the good opinion the man had of him that opened his eyes, and to convince him that Christ was a bad man (*v.* 24): *Give God the praise, we know that this man is a sinner.* Two ways this is understood: [1.] By way of *advice,* to take heed of ascribing the praise of his cure to a sinful man, but to give it all to God, to whom it was due. Thus, under colour of zeal for the honour of God, they rob Christ of his honour, as those do who will not worship Christ as God, under pretence of zeal for this great truth, that there is but one God to be worshipped; whereas this is his declared will, that all men should *honour the Son even as they honour the Father;* and in confessing that Christ is Lord we *give glory to God the Father.* When God makes use of men that are sinners as instruments of good to us, we must *give God the glory,* for every creature is that to us which he makes it to be; and yet there is gratitude owing to the instruments. It was a good word, *Give God the praise,* but here it was ill used; and there seems to be this further in it, "This man is *a sinner,* a *bad man,* and therefore give the praise so much the more to God, who could work by such an instrument." [2.] By way of *adjuration;* so some take it. "We know (though thou dost not, who hast but lately come, as it were, into a new world) that this man is *a sinner,* a great impostor, that cheats the country; this we are sure of, therefore *give God praise*" (as Joshua said to Achan) "by making an ingenuous confession of the fraud and collusion which we are confident there is in this matter; in God's name, man, tell the truth." Thus is God's name abused in papal inquisitions, when by oaths, *ex officio,* they extort accusations of *themselves* from the *innocent,* and of *others* from the *ignorant.* See how basely they speak of the Lord Jesus: *We know that this man is a sinner,* is a man of sin. In which we may observe, *First,* Their insolence and pride. They would not have it thought, when they asked the man what he thought of him, that they needed information; nay, they know very well that he is a sinner, and nobody can convince them of the contrary. He had challenged them to their faces (*ch.* viii. 46) to *convince him of sin,* and they had nothing to say; but now behind his back they speak of him as a malefactor, convicted upon the notorious evidence of the fact. Thus false accusers make up in confidence what is wanting in proof. *Secondly,* The injury and indignity hereby done to the Lord Jesus. When he became man, he took upon him the form not only of a *servant,* but of a *sinner* (Rom. viii. 3), and passed for a sinner in common with the rest of mankind. Nay, he was represented as a sinner of the first magnitude, a sinner above all men; and, being *made sin for us,* he despised even this shame.

3. The debate that arose between the Pharisees and this poor man concerning Christ. They say, *He is a sinner;* he says, *He is a*

prophet. As it is an encouragement to those who are concerned for the cause of Christ to hope that it shall never be lost for want of witnesses, when they find a poor blind beggar picked up from the way-side, and made a witness for Christ, to the faces of his most impudent enemies; so it is an encouragement to those who are called out to witness for Christ to find with what prudence and courage this man managed his defence, according to the promise, *It shall be given you in that same hour what you shall speak.* Though he had never seen Jesus, he had felt his grace. Now in the parley between the Pharisees and this poor man we may observe three steps:—

(1.) He sticks to the certain matter of fact the evidence of which they endeavour to shake. That which is doubtful is best resolved into that which is plain, and therefore, [1.] He adheres to that which to himself at least, and to his own satisfaction, was past dispute (*v.* 25): "*Whether he be a sinner or no I know not,* I will not now stand to dispute, nor need I, the matter is plain, and though I should altogether hold my peace would speak for itself;" or, as it might better be rendered, "*If he be a sinner, I know it not,* I see no reason to say so, but the contrary; for this *one thing I know,* and can be more sure of than you can be of that of which you are so confident, *that whereas I was blind, now I see,* and therefore must not only say that he has been a good friend to me, but that he is a *prophet;* I am both able and bound to speak well of him." Now here, *First,* He tacitly reproves their great assurance of the ill character they gave of the blessed Jesus: "You say that you *know* him to be a *sinner;* I, who know him as well as you do, cannot give him any such character." *Secondly,* He boldly relies upon his own experience of the power and goodness of the holy Jesus, and resolves to abide by it. There is no disputing against experience, nor arguing a man out of his senses; here is one that is properly an eye-witness of the power and grace of Christ, though he had never seen him. Note, As Christ's mercies are most valued by those that have felt the want of them, that have been blind and now see, so the most powerful and durable affections to Christ are those that arise from an experimental knowledge of him, 1 John i. 1; Acts iv. 20. The poor man does not here give a nice account of the method of the cure, nor pretend to describe it *philosophically,* but in short, *Whereas I was blind, now I see.* Thus in the work of grace in the soul, though we cannot tell when and how, by what instruments and by what steps and advances, the blessed change was wrought, yet we may take the comfort of it if we can say, through grace, "*Whereas I was blind, now I see.* I did live a carnal, worldly, sensual life, but, thanks be to God, it is now otherwise with me," Eph. v. 8. [2.] They endeavour to baffle and stifle the evidence by a needless repetition of their enquiries into it (*v.* 26): *What did he to thee? How opened he thine eyes?* They asked these questions, *First,* Because they wanted something to say, and would rather speak *impertinently* than seem to be silenced or run a-ground. Thus eager disputants, that resolve they will have the last word, by such vain repetitions, to avoid the shame of being silenced, make themselves accountable for many idle words. *Secondly,* Because they hoped, by putting the man upon repeating his evidence, to catch him tripping in it, or wavering, and then they would think they had gained a good point.

(2.) He upbraids them with their obstinate infidelity and invincible prejudices, and they revile him as a disciple of Jesus, *v.* 27—29, where the man is more bold with them and they are more sharp upon him than before.

[1.] The man boldly upbraids them with their wilful and unreasonable opposition to the evidence of this miracle, *v.* 27. He would not gratify them with a repetition of the story, but bravely replied, *I have told you already, and you did not hear, wherefore would you hear it again, will you also be his disciples?* Some think that he spoke *seriously,* and really expecting that they would be convinced. "He has many disciples, I will be one, will you also come in among them?" Some zealous young Christians see so much reason for religion that they are ready to think every one will presently be of their mind. But it rather seems to be spoken *ironically:* "*Will you be his disciples?* No, I know you abhor the thoughts of it; why then should you desire to hear that which will either make you his disciples or leave you inexcusable if you be not?" Those that wilfully shut their eyes against the light, as these Pharisees here did, *First,* Make themselves contemptible and base, as these here did, who were justly exposed by this poor man for denying the conclusion, when they had nothing to object against either of the premises. *Secondly,* They forfeit all the benefit of further instructions and means of knowledge and conviction: they that have been told once, and *would not hear,* why should they be told it again? Jer. li. 9. See Matt. x. 14. *Thirdly,* They hereby *receive the grace of God in vain.* This is implied in that, "*Will you be his disciples?* No, you resolve you will not; why then would you hear it again, only that you may be his accusers and persecutors?" Those who will not see cause to embrace Christ, and join with his followers, yet, one would think, should see cause enough not to hate and persecute him and them.

[2.] For this they scorn and revile him, *v.* 28. When they could not resist the wisdom and spirit by which he spoke, they broke out into a passion, and scolded him, began to call names, and give him ill language. See what Christ's faithful witnessess must expect from the adversaries of his truth and cause;

let them count upon *all manner of evil* to be said of them, Matt. v. 11. The method commonly taken by unreasonable man is to make out with railing what is wanting in truth and reason.

First, They taunted this man for his affection to Christ; they said, *Thou art his disciple,* as if that were reproach enough, and they could not say worse of him. "We scorn to be his disciples, and will leave that preferment to thee, and such scoundrels as thou art." They do what they can to put Christ's religion in an ill name, and to represent the profession of it as a contemptible scandalous thing. They *reviled him.* The Vulgate reads it, *maledixerunt eum—they cursed him;* and what was their curse? It was this, *Be thou his disciple.* "May such a curse" (saith St. Austin here) "ever be on us and on our children!" If we take our measures of credit and disgrace from the sentiment or rather clamours of a blind deluded world, we shall *glory in our shame,* and be *ashamed of our glory.* They had no reason to call this man a *disciple of* Christ, he had neither seen him nor heard him preach, only he had spoken favourably of a kindness Christ had done him, and this they could not bear.

Secondly, They gloried in their relation to Moses as their Master: "*We are Moses's disciples,* and do not either need or desire any other teacher." Note, 1. Carnal professors of religion are very apt to trust to, and be proud of, the dignities and privileges of their profession, while they are strangers to the principles and powers of their religion. These Pharisees had before boasted of their good parentage: *We are Abraham's seed;* here they boast of their good education, *We are Moses's disciples;* as if these would save them. 2. It is sad to see how much one part of religion is opposed, under colour of zeal for another part. There was a perfect harmony between Christ and Moses; Moses prepared for Christ, and Christ perfected Moses, so that they might be disciples of Moses, and become the disciples of Christ too; and yet they here put them in opposition, nor could they have persecuted Christ but under the shelter of the abused name of Moses. Thus those who gainsay the doctrine of free grace value themselves as promoters of man's duty, *We are Moses's disciples;* while, on the other hand, those that cancel the obligation of the law value themselves as the assertors of free grace, and as if none were the disciples of Jesus but they; whereas, if we rightly understand the matter, we shall see God's grace and man's duty meet together and kiss and befriend each other.

Thirdly, They gave some sort of reason for their adhering to Moses against Christ (*v.* 29): *We know that God spoke unto Moses; as for this fellow, we know not whence he is.* But did they not know that among other things which God spoke unto Moses this was one, that they must expect another prophet, and a further revelation of the mind of God? yet, when our Lord Jesus, pursuant to what God said to Moses, did appear, and gave sufficient proofs of his being that prophet, under pretence of sticking to the old religion, and the established church, they not only forfeited, but forsook, their own mercies. In this argument of theirs observe, 1. How impertinently they allege, in defence of their enmity to Christ, that which none of his followers ever denied: *We know that God spoke unto Moses,* and, thanks be to God, we know it too, more plainly to Moses than to any other of the prophets; but what then? God spoke to Moses, and does it therefore follow that Jesus is an impostor? Moses was a prophet, it is true, and might not Jesus be a prophet also? Moses spoke honourably of Jesus (*ch.* v. 46), and Jesus spoke honourably of Moses (Luke xvi. 29); they were both faithful in the same house of God, Moses as a servant, Christ as a Son; therefore their pleading Moses' divine warrant in opposition to Christ's was an artifice, to make unthinking people believe it was as certain that Jesus was a false prophet as that Moses was a true one; whereas they were both true. 2. How absurdly they urge their ignorance of Christ as a reason to justify their contempt of him: *As for this fellow.* Thus scornfully do they speak of the blessed Jesus, as if they did not think it worth while to charge their memories with a name so inconsiderable; they express themselves with as much disdain of the Shepherd of Israel as if he had not been worthy to be *set with the dogs of their flock: As for this fellow,* this sorry fellow, *we know not whence he is.* They looked upon themselves to have the key of knowledge, that none must preach without a license first had and obtained from them, under the seal of their court. They expected that all who set up for teachers should apply to them, and give them satisfaction, which this Jesus had never done, never so far owned their power as to ask their leave, and therefore they concluded him an intruder, and one that came not in by the door: *They knew not whence* nor what *he was,* and therefore concluded him a *sinner;* whereas those we know little of we should judge charitably of; but proud and narrow souls will think none good but themselves, and those that are in their interest. It was not long ago that the Jews had made the contrary to this an objection against Christ (*ch.* vii. 27): *We know this man whence he is, but when Christ comes no man knows whence he is.* Thus they could with the greatest assurance either affirm or deny the same thing, according as they saw it would serve their turn. They *knew not whence he was;* and whose fault was that? (1.) It is certain that they ought to have enquired. The Messiah was to appear about this time, and it concerned them to look about them, and examine every indication; but these priests, like those, Jer. ii. 6, *said not, Where is the Lord?* (2.) It is certain that they might have known whence he was, might not only have known, by searching the register, that he was born in Bethlehem; but by enquiring into his doctrine, miracles, and conversation, they might have known that he was sent of God, and had better orders, a better commission, and far better instructions, than any they could give him. See the absurdity of infidelity. Men will not know the doctrine of Christ because they are resolved they will not believe it, and then pretend they do not believe it because they do not know it. Such ignorance and unbelief, which support one another, aggravate one another.

(3.) He reasons with them concerning this matter, and they excommunicate him.

[1.] The poor man, finding that he had reason on his side, which they could not answer, grows more bold, and, in prosecution of his argument, is very close upon them.

First, He wonders at their obstinate infidelity (*v.* 30); not at all daunted by their frowns, nor shaken by their confidence, he bravely answered, "*Why, herein is a marvellous thing,* the strangest instance of wilful ignorance that ever was heard of among men that pretend to sense, that *you know not whence he is,* and yet he has opened mine eyes." Two things he wonders at:—1. That they should be strangers to a man so *famous.* He that could open the eyes of the blind must certainly be a considerable man, and worth taking notice of. The Pharisees were inquisitive men, had a large correspondence and acquaintance, thought themselves the eyes of the church and its watchmen, and yet that they should talk as if they thought it below them to take cognizance of such a man as this, and have conversation with him, this is a strange thing indeed. There are many who pass for learned and knowing men, who understand business, and can talk sensibly in other things, who yet are ignorant, to a wonder, of the doctrine of Christ, who have no concern, no, not so much as a curiosity, to acquaint themselves with that which the *angels desire to look into.* 2. That they should question the divine mission of one that had undoubtedly wrought a divine miracle. When they said, *We know not whence he is,* they meant, "We know not any proof that his doctrine and ministry are from heaven." "Now this is strange," saith the poor man, "that the miracle wrought upon me has not convinced you, and put the matter out of doubt,—that you, whose education and studies give you advantages above others of discerning the things of God, should thus shut your eyes against the light." It is a *marvellous work and a wonder, when the wisdom of the wise thus perisheth* (Isa. xxix. 14), that they deny the truth of that of which they cannot gainsay the evidence. Note, (1.) The unbelief of those who enjoy the means of knowledge and conviction is indeed a marvellous thing, Mark vi. 6. (2.) Those who have themselves experienced the power and grace of the Lord Jesus do especially wonder at the wilfulness of those who reject him, and, having such good thoughts of him themselves, are amazed that others have not. Had Christ opened the eyes of the Pharisees, they would not have doubted his being a prophet.

Secondly, He argues strongly against them, *v.* 31—33. They had determined concerning Jesus that he was not of God (*v.* 16), but was a *sinner* (*v.* 24), in answer to which the man here proves not only that he was *not a sinner* (*v.* 31), but that he was *of God, v.* 33.

a. He argues here, (*a.*) With great knowledge. Though he could not read a letter of the book, he was well acquainted with the scripture and the things of God; he had wanted the sense of seeing, yet had well improved that of hearing, by which faith cometh; yet this would not have served him if he had not had an extraordinary presence of God with him, and special aids of his Spirit, upon this occasion. (*b.*) With great zeal for the honour of Christ, whom he could not endure to hear run down, and evil spoken of. (*c.*) With great boldness, and courage, and undauntedness, not terrified by the proudest of his adversaries. Those that are ambitious of the favours of God must not be afraid of the frowns of men. "See here," saith Dr. Whitby, "a blind man and unlearned judging more rightly of divine things than the whole learned council of the Pharisees, whence we learn that we are not always to be led by the authority of councils, popes, or bishops; and that it is not absurd for laymen sometimes to vary from their opinions, these overseers being sometimes guilty of great oversights."

b. His argument may be reduced into form, somewhat like that of David, Ps. lxvi. 18—20. The proposition in David's argument is, *If I regard iniquity in my heart, God will not hear me;* here it is to the same purport, *God heareth not sinners:* the assumption there is, *But verily God hath heard me;* here it is, Verily God hath heard Jesus, he hath been honoured with the doing of that which was never done before: the conclusion there is to the honour of God, *Blessed be God;* here to the honour of the Lord Jesus, He is *of God.*

(*a.*) He lays it down for an undoubted truth that none but good men are the favourites of heaven (*v.* 31): *Now we know,* you know it as well as I, *that God heareth not sinners;* but *if any man be a worshipper of God, and does his will, him he heareth.* Here,

[*a.*] The assertions, rightly understood, are true. *First,* Be it spoken to the terror of the wicked, *God heareth not sinners,* that is, such sinners as the Pharisees meant when they said of Christ, *He is a sinner,* one that, under the shelter of God's name, advanced the devil's interest. This bespeaks no discouragement to repenting returning sinners, but to those that go on still in their trespasses, that make their prayers not only consistent with, but subservient to, their sins, as the hypocrites do; God will not *hear* them, he will not own them, nor give an answer of peace to their prayers. *Secondly,* Be it spoken to the comfort of the righteous, *If any man be a worshipper of God, and does his will, him he heareth.* Here is, 1. The complete character of a good man: he is one that *worships God,* and *does his will;* he is constant in his devotions at set times, and regular in his conversation at all times. He is one that makes it his business to glorify his Creator by the solemn adoration of his name and a sincere obedience to his will and law; both must go together. 2. The unspeakable comfort of such a man: him *God hears;* hears his complaints, and relieves him; hears his appeals, and rights him; hears his praises, and accepts them; hears his prayers, and answers them, Ps. xxxiv. 15.

[*b.*] The application of these truths is very pertinent to prove that he, at whose word such a divine power was put forth as cured one born blind, was not a bad man, but, having manifestly such an interest in the holy God as that he *heard him always* (*ch.* xi. 41, 42), was certainly a holy one.

(*b.*) He magnifies the miracles which Christ had wrought, to strengthen the argument the more (*v.* 32): *Since the world began was it not heard that any man opened the eyes of one that was born blind.* This is to show either, [*a.*] That it was a true miracle, and above the power of nature; it was never heard that any man, by the use of natural means, had cured one that was *born blind;* no doubt, this man and his parents had been very inquisitive into cases of this nature, whether any such had been helped, and could hear of none, which enabled him to speak this with the more assurance. Or, [*b.*] That it was an extraordinary miracle, and beyond the precedents of former miracles; neither Moses nor any of the prophets, though they did great things, ever did such things as this, wherein divine power and divine goodness seem to strive which should outshine. Moses wrought miraculous plagues, but Christ wrought miraculous cures. Note, *First,* The wondrous works of the Lord Jesus were such as the like had never been done before. *Secondly,* It becomes those who have received mercy from God to magnify the mercies they have received, and to speak honourably of them; not that thereby glory may redound to themselves, and they may seem to be extraordinary favourites of Heaven, but that God may have so much the more glory.

(*c.*) He therefore concludes, *If this man were not of God, he could do nothing,* that is, nothing extraordinary, no such thing as *this;* and therefore, no doubt, he is *of God,* notwithstanding his nonconformity to your traditions in the business of the sabbath day. Note, What Christ did on earth sufficiently demonstrated what he was in heaven; for, if he had not been sent of God, he could not have wrought such miracles. It is true the man of sin comes with *lying wonders,* but not with real miracles; it is likewise supposed that a false prophet might, by divine permission, give a *sign or a wonder* (Deut. xiii. 1, 2), yet the case is so put as that it would carry with it its own confutation, for it is to enforce a temptation to serve other gods, which was to set God *against himself.* It is true, likewise, that many wicked people have in Christ's name done many wonderful works, which did not prove those that wrought them to be of God, but him in whose name they were wrought. We may each of us know by this whether we are of God or no: *What do we?* What do we for God, for our souls, in working out our salvation? What do we more than others?

[2.] The Pharisees, finding themselves unable either to answer his reasonings or to bear them, fell foul upon him, and with a great deal of pride and passion broke off the discourse, *v.* 34. Here we are told,

First, What they *said.* Having nothing to reply to his argument, they reflected upon his person: *Thou wast altogether born in sin, and dost thou teach us?* They take that amiss which they had reason to take kindly, and are cut to the heart with rage by that which should have pricked them to the heart with penitence. Observe, 1. How they despised him, and what a severe censure they passed upon him: "*Thou wast not only born in sin,* as every man is, but altogether so, wholly corrupt, and bearing about with thee in thy body as well as in thy soul the marks of that corruption; thou wast one whom nature *stigmatized.*" Had he still continued blind, it had been barbarous to upbraid him with it, and thence to gather that he was more deeply tainted with sin than other people; but it was most unjust to take notice of it now that the cure had not only rolled away the reproach of his blindness, but had *signalized* him as a favourite of Heaven. Some take it thus: "Thou hast been a common beggar, and such are too often common sinners, and thou hast, no doubt, been as bad as any of them;" whereas by his discourse he had proved the contrary, and had evinced a deep tincture of piety. But when proud imperious Pharisees resolve to run a man down, any thing shall serve for a pretence. 2. How they *disdain* to learn of him, or to receive instruction from him: *Dost thou teach us?* A mighty emphasis must be laid here upon *thou* and *us.* "What! wilt *thou,* a silly sorry fellow, ignorant and illiterate, that hast not seen the light of the sun a day to an end, a beggar by the way-side, of the very dregs and refuse of the town, wilt thou pretend to teach *us,* that are the sages of the law and grandees of the church, that sit in Moses's chair and are masters in Israel?" Note, Proud men scorn to be taught, especially by their inferiors, whereas we should never think ourselves too old, nor too wise, nor too good, to learn. Those that have much wealth would have more; and why not those that have much knowledge? And those are to be valued by whom we may improve in learning. What a poor excuse was this for the Pharisees' infidelity, that it would be a disparagement to them to be instructed, and informed, and convinced, by such a silly fellow as this!

Secondly, What they did: They *cast him out.* Some understand it only of a rude and scornful dismission of him from their council-board; they turned him out of the room by head and shoulders, and perhaps ordered their servants to kick him; they thought it was time to send *him* far enough who came so near their consciences. But it seems rather to be a judicial act; they excommunicated him, probably with the highest degree of excommunication; they cut him off from being a member of the church of Israel. "This poor man," says Dr. Lightfoot, "was the first confessor, as John Baptist was the first martyr, of the Christian church." There was a law made that if any confessed Jesus to be the Christ he should be *cast out of the synagogue, v.* 22. But this man had only said of Jesus that he was a prophet, was *of God:* and yet they stretch the law to bring him under the lash of it, as if he had confessed him to be the Christ. To be justly excommunicated and cast out of a pure church, *clave non errante—when the key commits no error,* is a very dreadful thing; for what is so bound on earth is bound in heaven; but to be cast out of a corrupt church (which it is our duty to go out of) and that unjustly, though cast out with an *anathema,* and all the bug-bear ceremonies of bell, book, and candle, is what we have no reason at all to dread or be aggrieved at. *The curse causeless shall not come.* If they cast Christ's followers out of their synagogues, as he foretels (*ch.* xvi. 2), there is no harm done, when they are become *synagogues of Satan.*

35 Jesus heard that they had cast
him out; and when he had found
him, he said unto him, Dost thou believe on the Son of God? 36 He answered and said, Who is he, Lord,
that I might believe on him? 37
And Jesus said unto him, Thou hast
both seen him, and it is he that talketh with thee. 38 And he said, Lord,
I believe. And he worshipped him.

In these verses we may observe,

I. The tender care which our Lord Jesus took of this poor man (*v.* 35): *When Jesus heard that they had cast him out* (for it is likely the town rang of it, and every body cried out shame upon them for it), then he *found him,* which implies his seeking him and looking after him, that he might encourage and comfort him, 1. Because he had, to the best of his knowledge, spoken so very well, so bravely, so boldly, in defence of the Lord Jesus. Note, Jesus Christ will be sure to stand by his witnesses, and own those that own him and his truth and ways. Earthly princes neither do, nor can, take cognizance of all that vindicate them and their government and administration; but our Lord Jesus knows and observes all the faithful testimonies we bear to him at any time, and a book of remembrance is written, and it shall redound not only to our credit hereafter, but our comfort now. 2. Because the Pharisees had cast him out and abused him. Besides the common regard which the righteous Judge of the world has to those who suffer wrongfully (Ps. ciii. 6), there is a particular notice taken of those that suffer in the cause of Christ and for the testimony of a good conscience. Here was one poor man suffering for Christ, and he took care that as his afflictions abounded his consolations should *much more abound.* Note, (1.) Though persecutors may exclude good men from their communion, yet they cannot exclude them from communion with Christ, nor put them out of the way of his visits. Happy are they who have a friend from whom men cannot debar them. (2.) Jesus Christ will graciously find and receive those who for his sake are unjustly rejected and cast out by men. He will be a hiding place to his outcasts, and appear, to the joy of those whom their brethren hated and cast out.

II. The comfortable converse Christ had with him, wherein he brings him acquainted with the consolation of Israel. He had well improved the knowledge he had, and now Christ gives him further instruction; for he that is faithful in a little shall be entrusted with more, Matt. xiii. 12.

1. Our Lord Jesus examines his faith: "*Dost thou believe on the Son of God?* Dost thou give credit to the promises of the Messiah? Dost thou expect his coming, and art thou ready to receive and embrace him when he is manifested to thee?" This was that faith of the Son of God by which the saints lived before his manifestation. Observe, (1.) The Messiah is here called the *Son of God,* and so the Jews had learned to call him from the prophecies, Ps. ii. 7; lxxxix. 27. See *ch.* i. 49, *Thou art the Son of God,* that is, the true Messiah. Those that expected the temporal kingdom of the Messiah delighted rather in calling him the *Son of David,* which gave more countenance to that expectation, Matt. xxii. 42. But Christ, that he might give us an idea of his kingdom, as purely spiritual and divine, calls himself the *Son of God,* and rather *Son of man* in general than of David in particular. (2.) The desires and expectations of the Messiah, which the Old-Testament saints had, guided by and grounded upon the promise, were graciously interpreted and ac-

cepted as their believing on the *Son of God.* This faith Christ here enquires after: *Dost thou believe?* Note, The great thing which is now required of us (1 John iii. 23), and which will shortly be enquired after concerning us, is our *believing on the Son of God*, and by this we must stand or fall for ever.

2. The poor man solicitously enquires concerning the Messiah he was to believe in, professing his readiness to embrace him and close with him (*v.* 36): *Who is he, Lord, that I may believe on him?* (1.) Some think he did know that Jesus, who cured him, was the Son of God, but did not know which was Jesus, and therefore, supposing this person that talked with him to be a follower of Jesus, desired him to do him the favour to direct him to his master; not that he might satisfy his curiosity with the sight of him, but that he might the more firmly believe in him, and profess his faith, and *know whom he had believed.* See Cant. v. 6, 7; iii. 2, 3. It is Christ only that can direct us to himself. (2.) Others think he did know that this person who talked with him was Jesus, the same that cured him, whom he believed a great and good man and a prophet, but did not yet know that he was the Son of God and the true Messiah. "Lord, I believe there is a Christ to come; thou who hast given me bodily sight, tell me, O tell me, who and where this Son of God is." Christ's question intimated that the Messiah was come, and was now among them, which he presently takes the hint of, and asks, *Where is he, Lord?* The question was rational and just: *Who is he, Lord, that I may believe on him?* For how could he believe in one of whom he had not heard; the work of ministers is to tell us *who the Son of God is,* that we may believe on him, *ch.* xx. 31.

3. Our Lord Jesus graciously reveals himself to him as that Son of God on whom he must believe: *Thou hast both seen him, and it is he that talketh with thee, v.* 37. Thou needest not go far to find out the Son of God, *Behold the Word is nigh thee.* We do not find that Christ did thus expressly, and in so many words, reveal himself to any other as to this man here and to the woman of *Samaria: I that speak unto thee am he.* He left others to find out by arguments who he was, but to these weak and foolish things of the world he chose to manifest himself, so as not to the *wise and prudent.* Christ here describes himself to this man by two things, which express his great favour to him:—(1.) *Thou hast seen him;* and he was much indebted to the Lord Jesus for opening his eyes, that he might see him. Now he was made sensible, more than ever, what an unspeakable mercy it was to be cured of his blindness, that he might see the Son of God, a sight which rejoiced his heart more than that of the *light of this world.* Note, The greatest comfort of bodily eyesight is its serviceableness to our faith and the interests of our souls. How contentedly might this man have returned to his former blindness, like old Simeon, now that his eyes had *seen God's salvation!* If we apply this to the opening of the eyes of the mind, it intimates that spiritual sight is given principally for this end, that we may see Christ, 2 Cor. iv. 6. Can we say that by faith we have seen Christ, seen him in his beauty and glory, in his ability and willingness to save, so seen him as to be satisfied concerning him, to be satisfied in him? Let us give him the praise, who opened our eyes. (2.) *It is he that talketh with thee;* and he was indebted to Christ for condescending to do this. He was not only favoured with a sight of Christ, but was admitted into fellowship and communion with him. Great princes are willing to be *seen* by those whom yet they will not vouchsafe to *talk with.* But Christ, by his word and Spirit, talks with those whose desires are towards him, and in talking with them manifests himself to them, as he did to the two disciples, when he talked their hearts warm, Luke xxiv. 32. Observe, This poor man was solicitously enquiring after the Saviour, when at the same time he saw him, and was talking with him. Note, Jesus Christ is often nearer the souls that seek him than they themselves are aware of. Doubting Christians are sometimes saying, *Where is the Lord?* and fearing that they are cast out from his sight when at the same time it is he that *talks with them,* and *puts strength into them.*

4. The poor man readily entertains this surprising revelation, and, in a transport of joy and wonder, he said, *Lord, I believe, and he worshipped him.* (1.) He professed his faith in Christ: *Lord, I believe thee to be the Son of God.* He would not dispute any thing that *he* said who had shown such mercy to him, and wrought such a miracle for him, nor doubt of the truth of a doctrine which was confirmed by such signs. Believing with the heart, he thus confesses with the mouth; and now the bruised reed was become a cedar. (2.) He paid his homage to him: *He worshipped him,* not only gave him the civil respect due to a great man, and the acknowledgments owing to a kind benefactor, but herein gave him divine honour, and worshipped him as the *Son of God* manifested in the flesh. None but God is to be worshipped; so that in worshipping Jesus he owned him to be God. Note, True faith will show itself in a humble adoration of the Lord Jesus. Those who believe in him will see all the reason in the world to worship him. We never read any more of this man; but, it is very likely, from henceforth he became a constant follower of Christ.

39 And Jesus said, For judgment
I am come into this world, that they
which see not might see; and that
they which see might be made blind.

And *some* of the Pharisees which were with him heard these words, and said unto him, Are we blind also?
41 Jesus said unto them, If ye were blind, ye should have no sin: but now ye say, We see; therefore your sin remaineth.

Christ, having spoken comfort to the poor man that was persecuted, here speaks conviction to his persecutors, a specimen of the distributions of trouble and rest at the great day, 2 Thess. i. 6, 7. Probably this was not immediately after his discourse with the man, but he took the next opportunity that offered itself to address the Pharisees. Here is,

I. The account Christ gives of his design in coming into the world (*v.* 39): *For judgment I am* come to order and administer the great affairs of the *kingdom of God among men,* and am invested with a judicial power in order thereunto, to be executed in conformity to the wise counsels of God, and in pursuance of them." What Christ spoke, he spoke not as a preacher in the pulpit, but as a king upon the throne, and a judge upon the bench.

1. His business into the world was *great;* he came to keep the assizes and general gaol-delivery. He came *for judgment,* that is, (1.) To preach a doctrine and a law which would try men, and effectually discover and distinguish them, and would be completely fitted, in all respects, to be the rule of government now and of judgment shortly. (2.) To put a difference between men, by revealing the thoughts of many hearts, and laying open men's true characters, by this one test, whether they were well or ill affected to him. (3.) To change the face of government in his church, to abolish the Jewish economy, to take down that fabric, which, though erected for the time by the hand of God himself, yet by lapse of time was antiquated, and by the incurable corruptions of the managers of it was become rotten and dangerous, and to erect a new building by another model, to institute new ordinances and offices, to abrogate Judaism and enact Christianity; *for this judgment he came into the world,* and it was a great revolution.

2. This great truth he explains by a metaphor borrowed from the miracle which he had lately wrought. That *those who see not might see, and that those who see might be made blind.* Such a difference of Christ's coming is often spoken of; to some his gospel is a *savour of life unto life,* to others of *death unto death.* (1.) This is applicable to nations and people, that the Gentiles, who had long been destitute of the light of divine revelation, might see it; and the Jews, who had long enjoyed it, might have the things of their peace hid from their eyes, Hos. i. 10; ii. 23. The Gentiles see a great light, while blindness is *happened unto Israel,* and their *eyes are darkened.* (2.) To particular persons. Christ came into the world, [1.] Intentionally and designedly to give sight to those that were spiritually blind; by his word to reveal the object, and by his Spirit to heal the organ, that many precious souls might be turned *from darkness to light.* He came *for judgment,* that is, to set those at liberty from their dark prison that were willing to be released, Isa. lxi. 1. [2.] Eventually, and in the issue, *that those who see might be made blind;* that those who have a high conceit of their own wisdom, and set up that in contradiction to divine revelation, might be sealed up in ignorance and infidelity. The preaching of the cross was foolishness, and an infatuating thing, to those who by wisdom *knew not God.* Christ *came into the world for* this *judgment,* to administer the affairs of a spiritual kingdom, seated in men's minds. Whereas, in the Jewish church, the blessings and judgments of God's government were mostly temporal, now the method of administration should be changed; and as the good subjects of his kingdom should be blessed with spiritual blessings in heavenly things, such as arise from a due illumination of the mind, so the rebels should be punished with spiritual plagues, not war, famine, and pestilence, as formerly, but such as arise from a *judicial infatuation,* hardness of heart, terror of conscience, strong delusions, vile affections. In this way Christ will *judge between cattle and cattle,* Ezek. xxxiv. 17, 22.

II. The Pharisees' cavil at this. They were *with him,* not desirous to learn any good from him, but to form evil against him; and they said, *Are we blind also?* When Christ said that *those who saw* should by his coming be made blind, they apprehended that he meant them, who were the *seers* of the people, and valued themselves on their *insight* and *foresight.* "Now," say they, "we know that the common people are blind; but *are we blind also?* What we? The rabbin, the doctors, the learned in the laws, the graduates in the schools, *are we blind too?*" This is *scandalum magnatum—a libel on the great.* Note, Frequently those that need reproof most, and deserve it best, though they have wit enough to discern a *tacit* one, have not grace enough to bear a *just* one. These Pharisees took this reproof for a reproach, as those lawyers (Luke xi. 45): "*Are we blind also?* Darest thou say that we are blind, whose judgment every one has such a veneration for, values, and yields to?" Note, Nothing fortifies men's corrupt hearts more against the convictions of the word, nor more effectually repels them, than the good opinion, especially if it be a high opinion, which others have of them; as if all that had gained applause with men must needs obtain acceptance with God, than which nothing is more false and deceitful, for God sees not as man sees.

III. Christ's answer to this cavil, which, if it did not convince them, yet silenced them: *If you were blind you should have no sin; but now you say, We see, therefore your sin remaineth.* They gloried that they were not blind, as the common people, were not so credulous and manageable as they, but would *see with their own eyes,* having abilities, as they thought, sufficient for their own guidance, so that they needed not any body to lead them. This very thing which they gloried in, Christ here tells them, was their shame and ruin. For,

1. *If you were blind, you would have no sin.* (1.) "If you had been really ignorant, your sin had not been so deeply aggravated, nor would you have had so much sin to answer for as now you have. If you were blind, as the poor Gentiles are, and many of your own poor subjects, from whom you have taken the key of knowledge, you would have had comparatively *no sin.*" The times of ignorance God *winked at;* invincible ignorance, though it does not justify sin, excuses it, and lessens the guilt. It will be more tolerable with those that perish for lack of vision than with those that *rebel against the light.* (2.) "If you had been sensible of your own blindness, if when you would see nothing else you could have seen the need of one to lead you, you would soon have accepted Christ as your guide, and then you would *have had no sin,* you would have submitted to an evangelical righteousness, and have been put into a justified state." Note, Those that are convinced of their disease are in a fair way to be cured, for there is not a greater hindrance to the salvation of souls than self-sufficiency.

2. "*But now you say, We see;* now that you have knowledge, and are instructed out of the law, your sin is highly aggravated; and now that you have a conceit of that knowledge, and think you see your way better than any body can show it you, *therefore your sin remains,* your case is desperate, and your disease incurable." And as those are most blind who *will not see,* so their blindness is most dangerous who fancy they do see. No patients are so hardly managed as those in a frenzy who say that they are *well,* and nothing ails them. The sin of those who are self-conceited and self-confident *remains,* for they reject the gospel of grace, and therefore the guilt of their sin remains unpardoned; and they forfeit the Spirit of grace, and therefore the power of their sin remains unbroken. *Seest thou a wise man in his own conceit?* Hearest thou the Pharisees say, *We see? There is more hope of a fool,* of a publican and a harlot, than of such.

CHAP. X.

In this chapter we have, I. Christ's parabolical discourse concerning himself as the door of the sheepfold, and the shepherd of the sheep, ver. 1—18. II. The various sentiments of people upon it, ver. 19—21. III. The dispute Christ had with the Jews in the temple at the feast of dedication, ver. 22—39. IV. His departure into the country thereupon, ver. 40—42.

VERILY, verily, I say unto you,
He that entereth not by the
door into the sheepfold, but climbeth
up some other way, the same is a
thief and a robber. 2 But he that
entereth in by the door is the shepherd of the sheep. 3 To him the
porter openeth; and the sheep hear
his voice: and he calleth his own
sheep by name, and leadeth them out.
4 And when he putteth forth his own
sheep, he goeth before them, and the
sheep follow him: for they know his
voice. 5 And a stranger will they
not follow, but will flee from him:
for they know not the voice of strangers. 6 This parable spake Jesus
unto them: but they understood not
what things they were which he spake
unto them. 7 Then said Jesus unto
them again, Verily, verily, I say unto
you, I am the door of the sheep. 8
All that ever came before me are
thieves and robbers: but the sheep
did not hear them. 9 I am the door:
by me if any man enter in, he shall
be saved, and shall go in and out, and
find pasture. 10 The thief cometh
not, but for to steal, and to kill, and
to destroy: I am come that they might
have life, and that they might have *it*
more abundantly. 11 I am the good
shepherd: the good shepherd giveth
his life for the sheep. 12 But he
that is an hireling, and not the shepherd, whose own the sheep are not,
seeth the wolf coming, and leaveth
the sheep, and fleeth: and the wolf
catcheth them, and scattereth the
sheep. 13 The hireling fleeth, because he is an hireling, and careth
not for the sheep. 14 I am the good
shepherd, and know my *sheep,* and
am known of mine. 15 As the Father
knoweth me, even so know I the Father: and I lay down my life for the
sheep. 16 And other sheep I have,
which are not of this fold: them also
I must bring, and they shall hear my
voice; and there shall be one fold,
and one shepherd. 17 Therefore doth
my Father love me, because I lay
down my life, that I might take it
again. 18 No man taketh it from
me, but I lay it down of myself. I
have power to lay it down, and I
have power to take it again. This
commandment have I received of my
Father.

It is not certain whether this discourse was at the *feast of dedication* in the winter (spoken of *v.* 22), which may be taken as the date, not only of what follows, but of what goes before (that which countenances this is, that Christ, in his discourse there, carries on the metaphor of the sheep (*v.* 26, 27), whence it seems that that discourse and this were at the same time); or whether this was a continuation of his parley with the Pharisees, in the close of the foregoing chapter. The Pharisees supported themselves in their opposition to Christ with this principle, that they were the *pastors of the church*, and that Jesus, having no commission from them, was an intruder and an impostor, and therefore the people were bound in duty to stick to *them*, against *him*. In opposition to this, Christ here describes who were the false shepherds, and who the true, leaving them to infer what they were.

I. Here is the parable or similitude proposed (*v.* 1—5); it is borrowed from the custom of that country, in the management of their sheep. Similitudes, used for the illustration of divine truths, should be taken from those things that are most familiar and common, that the things of God be not clouded by that which should clear them. The preface to this discourse is solemn: *Verily, verily, I say unto you,*—*Amen, amen.* This vehement asseveration intimates the certainty and weight of what he said; we find *amen* doubled in the church's praises and prayers, Ps. xli. 13; lxxii. 19; lxxxix. 52. If we would have our *amens* accepted in heaven, let Christ's *amens* be prevailing on earth; his repeated *amens.*

1. In the parable we have, (1.) The evidence of a thief and a robber, that comes to do mischief to the flock, and damage to the owner, *v.* 1. *He enters not by the door*, as having no lawful cause of entry, but *climbs up some other way*, at a window, or some breach in the wall. How industrious are wicked people to do mischief! What plots will they lay, what pains will they take, what hazards will they run, in their wicked pursuits! This should shame us out of our slothfulness and cowardice in the service of God. (2.) The character that distinguishes the rightful owner, who has a property in the sheep, and a care for them: *He enters in by the door*, as one having authority (*v.* 2), and he comes to do them some good office or other, to *bind up that which is broken*, and *strengthen that which is sick*, Ezek. xxxiv. 16. Sheep need man's care, and, in return for it, are serviceable to man (1 Cor. ix. 7); they clothe and feed those by whom they are coted and fed. (3.) The ready entrance that the shepherd finds: *To him the porter openeth*, *v.* 3. Anciently they had their sheepfolds within the outer gates of their houses, for the greater safety of their flocks, so that none could come to them the right way, but such as the porter opened to or the master of the house gave the keys to. (4.) The care he takes and the provision he makes for his sheep. The *sheep hear his voice*, when he speaks familiarly to them, when they come into the fold, as men now do to their dogs and horses; and, which is more, he *calls his own sheep by name*, so exact is the notice he takes of them, the account he keeps of them; and he leads them out from the fold to the green pastures; and (*v.* 4, 5) when he *turns them out* to graze he does not drive them, but (such was the custom in those times) he goes before them, to prevent any mischief or danger that might meet them, and they, being used to it, *follow him*, and are safe. (5.) The strange attendance of the sheep upon the shepherd: *They know his voice*, so as to discern his mind by it, and to distinguish it from that of a stranger (for *the ox knows his owner*, Isa. i. 3), and *a stranger will they not follow*, but, as suspecting some ill design, will flee from him, not *knowing his voice*, but that it is not the voice of their own shepherd. This is the parable; we have the key to it, Ezek. xxxiv. 31: *You my flock are men, and I am your God.*

2. Let us observe from this parable, (1.) That good men are fitly compared to sheep. Men, as creatures depending on their Creator, are called the *sheep of his pasture.* Good men, as new creatures, have the good qualities of sheep, *harmless* and inoffensive as sheep; *meek* and quiet, without noise; *patient* as sheep under the hand both of the shearer and of the butcher; *useful* and profitable, tame and tractable, to the shepherd, and *sociable* one with another, and much used in sacrifices. (2.) The church of God in the world is a *sheepfold*, into which the *children of God* that were scattered abroad are *gathered together* (*ch.* xi. 52), and in which they are united and incorporated; it is a good fold, Ezek. xxxiv. 14. See Mic. ii. 12. This fold is well fortified, for God himself is as a *wall of fire* about it, Zech. ii. 5. (3.) This sheepfold lies much exposed to thieves and robbers; crafty seducers that debauch and deceive, and cruel persecutors that destroy and devour; *grievous wolves* (Acts xx. 29); thieves that would steal Christ's sheep from him, to sacrifice them to devils, or steal their food from them, that they might perish for lack of it; *wolves* in sheep's clothing, Matt. vii. 15. (4.) The great Shepherd of the sheep takes wonderful care of the flock and of all that belong to it. God is the great Shepherd, Ps. xxiii. 1; lxxx. 1. He knows those that are his, calls them by name, marks them for himself, leads them out to fat pastures, makes them both feed and rest there, speaks comfortably to them, guards them by his providence, guides them by his Spirit and word, and goes before them, *to set them in the way of his steps.* (5.) The under-shepherds, who are entrusted to feed the flock of God, ought to be careful and faithful in the discharge of that trust; magistrates must defend them, and protect and advance all their secular

interests; ministers must serve them in their spiritual interests, must *feed their souls* with the word of God faithfully opened and applied, and with gospel ordinances duly administered, *taking the oversight of them.* They must *enter by the door* of a regular ordination, and to such *the porter will open;* the Spirit of Christ will *set before them an open door,* give them authority in the church, and assurance in their own bosoms. They must know the members of their flocks by name, and watch over them; must lead them into the pastures of public ordinances, preside among them, be their mouth to God and God's to them; and in their conversation must be examples to the believers. (6.) Those who are truly the sheep of Christ will be very observant of their Shepherd, and very cautious and shy of strangers. [1.] *They follow their Shepherd,* for they *know his voice,* having both a discerning ear, and an obedient heart. [2.] *They flee from a stranger,* and dread following him, because they know not his voice. It is dangerous following those in whom we discern not the *voice of Christ,* and who would draw us from *faith in him* to *fancies concerning him.* And those who have experienced the power and efficacy of divine truths upon their souls, and have the savour and relish of them, have a wonderful sagacity to discover Satan's wiles, and to discern between good and evil.

II. The Jews' ignorance of the drift and meaning of this discourse (*v.* 6): *Jesus spoke this parable* to them, this figurative, but wise, elegant, and instructive discourse, *but they understood not what the things were which he spoke unto them,* were not aware whom he meant by the *thieves and robbers* and whom by the *good Shepherd.* It is the sin and shame of many who hear the word of Christ that they do not understand it, and they do not because they will not, and because they will *mis-understand it.* They have no acquaintance with, nor taste of, the things themselves, and therefore do not understand the parables and comparisons with which they are illustrated. The Pharisees had a great conceit of their own knowledge, and could not bear that it should be questioned, and yet they had not sense enough to *understand the things that Jesus spoke of;* they were above their capacity. Frequently the greatest pretenders to knowledge are most ignorant in the things of God.

III. Christ's explication of this parable, opening the particulars of it fully. Whatever difficulties there may be in the sayings of the Lord Jesus, we shall find him ready to explain himself, if we be but willing to understand him. We shall find one scripture expounding another, and the *blessed Spirit* interpreter to the *blessed Jesus.* Christ, in the parable, had distinguished the shepherd from the robber by this, that he *enters in by the door.* Now, in the explication of the parable, he makes himself to be both *the door* by which the shepherd enters and the shepherd that enters in by the door. Though it may be a solecism in rhetoric to make the same person to be both the *door* and the *shepherd,* it is no solecism in divinity to make Christ to have his authority from himself, as he has life in himself; and *himself* to *enter by his own blood,* as the door, *into the holy place.*

1. Christ is *the door.* This he saith to those who pretended to *seek for righteousness,* but, like the Sodomites, *wearied themselves to find the door,* where it was not to be found. He saith it to the Jews, who would be thought God's only sheep, and to the Pharisees, who would be thought their only shepherds: *I am the door* of the sheepfold; the door of the church.

(1.) In general, [1.] He is as a *door shut,* to keep out thieves and robbers, and such as are not fit to be admitted. The shutting of the door is the securing of the house; and what greater security has the church of God than the interposal of the Lord Jesus, and his wisdom, power, and goodness, betwixt it and all its enemies? [2.] He is as a *door open* for passage and communication. *First,* By Christ, as the door, we have our first admission into the flock of God, *ch.* xiv. 6. *Secondly,* We go in and out in a religious conversation, assisted by him, accepted in him; walking up and down in his name, Zech. x. 12. *Thirdly,* By him God comes to his church, visits it, and communicates himself to it. *Fourthly,* By him, as the door, the sheep are at last admitted into the heavenly kingdom, Matt. xxv. 34.

(2.) More particularly,

[1.] Christ is the door of *the shepherds,* so that none who come not in by him are to be accounted *pastors,* but (according to the rule laid down, *v.* 1) *thieves and robbers* (though they pretended to be *shepherds);* but the *sheep did not hear them.* This refers to all those that had the character of shepherds in *Israel,* whether magistrates or ministers, that exercised their office without any regard to the Messiah, or any other expectations of him than what were suggested by their own carnal interest. Observe, *First,* The character given of them: they are *thieves and robbers* (*v.* 8); all that *went before him,* not in time, many of them were faithful shepherds, but all that *anticipated* his commission, and went before he sent them (Jer. xxiii. 21), that assumed a precedency and superiority above him, as the antichrist is said to *exalt himself,* 2 Thess. ii. 4. "The scribes, and Pharisees, and chief priests, *all, even as many as have come before me,* that have endeavoured to forestal my interest, and to prevent my gaining any room in the minds of people, by prepossessing them with prejudices against me, they are *thieves and robbers,* and steal those hearts which they have no title to, defrauding the right owner of his property." They condemned our Saviour as a thief and a robber, because he did not come in by them as the door, nor take out a license from them; but he shows that they ought to have received their commission from him, to have been admitted by him, and to have come after him, and because they did not, but stepped *before him*, they were *thieves and robbers.* They would not come in as his disciples, and therefore were condemned as usurpers, and their pretended commissions vacated and superseded. Note, Rivals with Christ are robbers of his church, however they pretend to be *shepherds*, nay, *shepherds of shepherds. Secondly,* The care taken to preserve the sheep from them: *But the sheep did not hear them.* Those that had a true savour of piety, that were spiritual and heavenly, and sincerely devoted to God and godliness, could by no means approve of the traditions of the elders, nor relish their formalities. Christ's disciples, without any particular instructions from their Master, made no conscience of eating with unwashen hands, or plucking the ears of corn on the sabbath day; for nothing is more opposite to true Christianity than Pharisaism is, nor any thing more disrelishing to a soul truly devout than their hypocritical devotions.

[2.] Christ is the door of *the sheep* (*v.* 9): *By me* (δὶ ἐμοῦ—*through me* as the door) *if any man enter into the sheepfold,* as one of the flock, he *shall be saved;* shall not only be safe from thieves and robbers, but he shall be happy, he *shall go in and out.* Here are, *First,* Plain directions how to come into the fold: we must come in *by Jesus Christ* as the door. By faith in him, as the great Mediator between God and man, we come into covenant and communion with God. There is no entering into God's church but by coming into Christ's church; nor are any looked upon as members of the kingdom of God among men but those that are willing to submit to the grace and government of the Redeemer. We must now enter by the *door of faith* (Acts xiv. 27), since the door of *innocency* is shut against us, and that *pass* become unpassable, Gen. iii. 24. *Secondly,* Precious promises to those who observe this direction. 1. They *shall be saved hereafter;* this is the privilege of *their home.* These sheep shall be saved from being distrained and impounded by divine justice for trespass done, satisfaction being made for the damage by their great Shepherd, saved from being a prey to the roaring lion; they shall be *for ever happy.* 2. In the mean time they shall *go in and out and find pasture;* this is the privilege of *their way.* They shall have their conversation in the world by the grace of Christ, shall be in his fold as a man at his own house, where he has *free ingress, egress,* and *regress.* True believers are *at home* in Christ; when they go out, they are not *shut out* as strangers, but have liberty to come in again; when they come in, they are not *shut in* as trespassers, but have liberty to go out. They go out to the field in the morning, they come into the fold at night; and in both the Shepherd leads and keeps them, and they *find pasture* in both: grass in the field, fodder in the fold. In public, in private, they have the word of God to converse with, by which their spiritual life is supported and nourished, and out of which their gracious desires are satisfied; they are replenished with the goodness of God's house.

2. Christ is the *shepherd, v.* 11, &c. He was prophesied of under the Old Testament as a *shepherd,* Isa. xl. 11; Ezek. xxxiv. 23; xxxvii. 24; Zech. xiii. 7. In the New Testament he is spoken of as the *great Shepherd* (Heb. xiii. 20), the *chief Shepherd* (1 v. 4), the *Shepherd and bishop of our souls,* 1 Pet. ii. 25. God, our great owner, the sheep of whose pasture we are by creation, has constituted his Son Jesus to be our *shepherd;* and here again and again he owns the relation. He has all that care of his church, and every believer, that a good shepherd has of his flock; and expects all that attendance and observance from the church, and every believer, which the shepherds in those countries had from their flocks.

(1.) Christ is *a shepherd,* and not as the thief, not as those that *came not in by the door.* Observe,

[1.] The mischievous design of the thief (*v.* 10): *The thief cometh not* with any good intent, but to *steal, and to kill, and to destroy. First,* Those whom they *steal,* whose hearts and affections they steal from Christ and his pastures, they *kill and destroy* spiritually; for the *heresies* they *privily bring in* are *damnable.* Deceivers of souls are murderers of souls. Those that steal away the scripture by keeping it in an unknown tongue, that steal away the sacraments by maiming them and altering the property of them, that steal away Christ's ordinances to put their own inventions in the room of them, they *kill and destroy;* ignorance and idolatry are destructive things. *Secondly,* Those whom they cannot *steal,* whom they can neither lead, drive, nor carry away, from the flock of Christ, they aim by persecutions and massacres to *kill and destroy* corporally. He that will not suffer himself to be robbed is in danger of being slain.

[2.] The gracious design of the shepherd; he is come,

First, To *give life to the sheep.* In opposition to the design of the thief, which is to *kill and destroy* (which was the design of the *scribes* and *Pharisees*) Christ saith, *I am come among men,* 1. That *they might have life.* He came to put life into the flock, the church in general, which had seemed rather like a valley full of dry bones than like a pasture covered over with flocks. Christ came to vindicate divine truths, to purify divine ordinances, to redress grievances, and to revive dying zeal, to *seek* those of his flock that were *lost,* to *bind up that which was broken* (Ezek

xxxiv. 16), and this to his church is *as life from the dead.* He came to *give life* to particular believers. Life is inclusive of all good, and stands in opposition to the death threatened (Gen. ii. 17); that *we might have life,* as a criminal has when he is pardoned, as a sick man when he is cured, a dead man when he is raised; that we might be justified, sanctified, and at last glorified. 2. That they might have it *more abundantly,* καὶ περισσὸν ἔχωσιν. As we read it, it is *comparative,* that they might have a life *more abundant* than that which was lost and forfeited by sin, more abundant than that which was promised by the law of Moses, length of days in Canaan, more abundant than could have been expected or than we are *able to ask or think.* But it may be construed without a note of comparison, *that they might have abundance,* or might *have it abundantly.* Christ came to give life and περισσόν τι—*something more,* something *better,* life with advantage; that in Christ we might not only live, but live comfortably, live plentifully, live and rejoice. Life in abundance is *eternal life,* life without death or fear of death, life and *much more.*

Secondly, To *give his life for the sheep,* and this that he might give life *to them* (*v.* 11): *The good shepherd giveth his life for the sheep.* 1. It is the property of every good shepherd to hazard and expose his life for the sheep. Jacob did so, when he would go through such a fatigue to attend them, Gen. xxxi. 40. So did David, when he *slew the lion and the bear.* Such a shepherd of souls was St. Paul, who would gladly *spend, and be spent,* for their service, and *counted not his life dear to him,* in comparison with their salvation. But, 2. It was the prerogative of the great Shepherd to give his life to purchase his flock (Acts xx. 28), to satisfy for their trespass, and to shed his blood to wash and cleanse them.

(2.) Christ is *a good shepherd,* and not as a hireling. There were many that were not thieves, aiming to kill and destroy the sheep, but passed for shepherds, yet were very careless in the discharge of their duty, and through their neglect the flock was greatly damaged; *foolish shepherds, idle shepherds,* Zech. xi. 15, 17. In opposition to these,

[1.] Christ here *calls himself the good shepherd* (*v.* 11), and again (*v.* 14) ὁ ποιμὴν ὁ καλὸς—*that Shepherd, that good Shepherd,* whom God had promised. Note, Jesus Christ is the best of shepherds, the best in the world to take the over-sight of souls, none so skilful, so faithful, so tender, as he, no such feeder and leader, no such protector and healer of souls as he.

[2.] He *proves himself* so, in opposition to all hirelings, *v.* 12—14. Where observe,

First, The carelessness of the unfaithful shepherd described (*v.* 12, 13); he that is a hireling, that is employed as a servant and is paid for his pains, *whose own the sheep are not,* who has neither profit nor loss by them, *sees the wolf coming,* or some other danger threatening, and *leaves the sheep* to the wolf, for in truth he *careth not for them.* Here is plain reference to that of the idol-shepherd, Zech. xi. 17. Evil shepherds, magistrates and ministers, are here described both by their bad principles and their bad practices.

a. Their *bad principles,* the root of their bad practices. What makes those that have the charge of souls in trying times to betray their trust, and in quiet times not to mind it? What makes them false, and trifling, and self-seeking? It is because they are *hirelings,* and *care not for the sheep.* That is, (*a.*) The wealth of the world is the chief of their good; it is because they are *hirelings.* They undertook the shepherds' office, as a trade to live and grow rich by, not as an opportunity of serving Christ and doing good. It is the love of money, and of their own bellies, that carries them on in it. Not that those are hirelings who, while they *serve at the altar, live,* and live comfortably, *upon the altar.* The labourer is worthy of his meat; and a scandalous maintenance will soon make a scandalous ministry. But those are *hirelings* that love the wages more than the work, and *set their hearts* upon that, as the hireling is said to do, Deut. xxiv. 15. See 1 Sam. ii. 29; Isa. lvi. 11; Mic. iii. 5, 11. (*b.*) The work of their place is the least of their care. They *value not the sheep,* are unconcerned in the souls of others; their business is to be their brothers' lords, not their brothers' keepers or helpers; they *seek their own things,* and do not, like Timothy, *naturally care for the state of souls.* What can be expected but that they will flee when *the wolf comes.* He *careth not for the sheep,* for he is one *whose own the sheep are not.* In one respect we may say of the best of the under-shepherds that the sheep are *not their own,* they have not dominion over them nor property in them (*feed my sheep* and *my lambs,* saith Christ); but in respect of dearness and affection they should be *their own.* Paul looked upon those as *his own* whom he called his *dearly beloved and longed for.* Those who do not cordially espouse the church's interests, and make them their own, will not long be faithful to them.

b. Their *bad practices,* the effect of these bad principles, *v.* 12. See here, (*a.*) How basely the hireling deserts his post; when he sees *the wolf coming,* though then there is most need of him, he *leaves the sheep and flees.* Note, Those who mind their safety more than their duty are an easy prey to Satan's temptations. (*b.*) How fatal the consequences are! the hireling fancies the sheep may look to themselves, but it does not prove so: *the wolf catches them,* and *scatters the sheep,* and woeful havoc is made of the flock, which will all be charged upon the treacherous shepherd. The blood of perishing souls is required at the hand of the careless watchmen.

Secondly, See here the grace and tenderness of the good Shepherd set over against the former, as it was in the prophecy (Ezek. xxxiv. 21, 22, &c.): *I am the good Shepherd.* It is matter of comfort to the church, and all her friends, that, however she may be damaged and endangered by the treachery and mismanagement of her under-officers, the Lord Jesus is, and will be, as he ever has been, *the good Shepherd.* Here are two great instances of the shepherd's goodness.

a. His *acquainting* himself with his flock, with all that belong or in any wise appertain to his flock, which are of two sorts, both known to him :—

(*a.*) He is acquainted with all that *are now of his flock* (*v.* 14, 15), as the good Shepherd (*v.* 3, 4): *I know my sheep and am known of mine.* Note, There is a mutual acquaintance between Christ and true believers; they know one another very well, and knowledge notes affection.

[*a.*] Christ *knows his sheep.* He knows with a *distinguishing* eye who are his sheep, and who are not; he knows the sheep under their many infirmities, and the goats under their most plausible disguises. He knows with a *favourable* eye those that in truth are his own sheep; he takes cognizance of their state, concerns himself for them, has a tender and affectionate regard to them, and is continually mindful of them in the intercession he ever lives to make within the veil; he visits them graciously by his Spirit, and has communion with them; he *knows* them, that is, he approves and accepts of them, as Ps. i. 6; xxxvii. 18; Exod. xxxiii. 17.

[*b.*] He is *known of them.* He observes them with an eye of favour, and they observe him with an eye of faith. Christ's knowing his sheep is put before their knowing him, for he knew and loved us first (1 John iv. 19), and it is not so much our knowing him as our being known of him that is our happiness, Gal. iv. 9. Yet it is the character of Christ's sheep that *they know him;* know him from all pretenders and intruders; they know his mind, know his voice, know by experience the power of his death. Christ speaks here as if he gloried in being known by his sheep, and thought their respect an honour to him. Upon this occasion Christ mentions (*v.* 15) the mutual acquaintance between his Father and himself: *As the Father knoweth me, even so know I the Father.* Now this may be considered, either, *First,* As the *ground* of that intimate acquaintance and relation which subsist between Christ and believers. The covenant of grace, which is the bond of this relation, is founded in the covenant of redemption between the Father and the Son, which, we may be sure, stands firm; for the Father and the Son understood one another perfectly well in that matter, and there could be no mistake, which might leave the matter at any uncertainty, or bring it into any hazard. The Lord Jesus *knows whom he hath chosen,* and is sure of them (*ch.* xiii. 18), and they also *know whom they have trusted,* and are sure of him (2 Tim. i. 12), and the ground of both is the perfect knowledge which the Father and the Son had of one another's mind, when *the counsel of peace was between them both.* Or, *Secondly,* As an apt similitude, illustrating the intimacy that is between Christ and believers. It may be connected with the foregoing words, thus: *I know my sheep, and am known of mine, even as the Father knows me, and I know the Father;* compare *ch.* xvii. 21. 1. As the Father knew the Son, and loved him, and owned him in his sufferings, when he was *led as a sheep to the slaughter,* so Christ knows his sheep, and has a watchful tender eye upon them, will be with them when they are *left alone,* as his Father was with him. 2. As the Son knew the Father, loved and obeyed him, and always did those things that pleased him, confiding in him as his God even when he seemed to forsake him, so believers know Christ with an obediential fiducial regard.

(*b.*) He is acquainted with those that are *hereafter to be of this flock* (*v.* 16): *Other sheep I have,* have a right to and an interest in, *which are not of this fold,* of the Jewish church; *them also I must bring.* Observe,

[*a.*] The eye that Christ had to the poor Gentiles. He had sometimes intimated his special concern for *the lost sheep of the house of Israel;* to them indeed his personal ministry was confined; but, saith he, *I have other sheep.* Those who in process of time should believe in Christ, and be brought into obedience to him from among the Gentiles, are here called *sheep,* and he is said to have them, though as yet they were *uncalled,* and many of them *unborn,* because they were chosen of God, and given to Christ in the counsels of divine love from eternity. Christ has a right, by virtue of the Father's donation and his own purchase, to many a soul of which he has not yet the possession; thus he had *much people* in Corinth, when as yet it lay in wickedness, Acts xviii. 10. "Those other sheep *I have,*" saith Christ, "I have them on my heart, have them in my eye, am as sure to have them as if I had them already." Now Christ speaks of those *other sheep, First,* To take off the contempt that was put upon him, as having *few followers,* as having but a *little flock,* and therefore, if a *good* shepherd, yet a *poor* shepherd: "But," saith he, "I have more sheep than you see." *Secondly,* To take down the pride and vain-glory of the Jews, who thought the Messiah must gather all his sheep from among them. "No," saith Christ, "I have others whom I will set with the lambs of my flock, though you disdain to set them with the dogs of your flock."

[*b.*] The purposes and resolves of his grace concerning them: "*Them also I must bring,* bring home to God, bring into the church, and, in order to this, bring off from their vain conversation, bring them back from their wanderings, as that *lost sheep,*" Luke xv. 5. But why *must* he bring them?

What was the necessity? *First,* The *necessity of their case* required it: "I *must* bring, or they must be left to wander endlessly, for, like sheep, they will never come back of themselves, and no other can or will bring them." *Secondly,* The *necessity of his own engagements* required it; he must bring them, or he would not be faithful to his trust, and true to his undertaking. "They are *my own,* bought and paid for, and therefore I *must not* neglect them nor leave them to perish." He *must* in honour *bring* those with whom he was entrusted.

[*c.*] The happy effect and consequence of this, in two things:—*First,* "They shall hear my voice. Not only my voice shall be heard *among them* (whereas they have not heard, and therefore could not believe, now the *sound* of the gospel shall *go to the ends of the earth),* but it shall be heard *by them;* I will speak, and give to them to hear." Faith comes by hearing, and our diligent observance of the voice of Christ is both a means and an evidence of our being brought to Christ, and to God by him. *Secondly, There shall be one fold and one shepherd.* As there is one shepherd, so there shall be one fold. Both Jews and Gentiles, upon their turning to the faith of Christ, shall be incorporated in one church, be joint and equal sharers in the privileges of it, without distinction. Being united to Christ, they shall unite in him; two sticks shall become one in the hand of the Lord. Note, One shepherd makes one fold; one Christ makes one church. As the church is one in its constitution, subject to one head, animated by one Spirit, and guided by one rule, so the members of it ought to be one in love and affection, Eph. iv. 3—6.

b.. Christ's *offering up himself for his sheep* is another proof of his being a *good shepherd,* and in this he yet more *commended his love, v.* 15, 17, 18.

(*a.*) He declares his purpose of *dying for his flock* (*v.* 15): *I lay down my life for the sheep.* He not only ventured his life for them (in such a case, the hope of *saving* it might balance the fear of *losing* it), but he actually *deposited* it, and submitted to a necessity of dying for our redemption; *τίθημι—I put it* as a pawn or pledge; as purchase-money paid down. Sheep appointed for the slaughter, ready to be sacrificed, were ransomed with the blood of the shepherd. He laid down his life, ὑπὲρ τῶν προβάτων, not only for the good of the sheep, but *in their stead.* Thousands of sheep had been offered in sacrifice for their shepherds, as sin-offerings, but here, by a surprising reverse, the shepherd is sacrificed for the sheep. When David, the shepherd of Israel, was himself guilty, and the destroying angel drew his sword against the flock for his sake, with good reason did he plead, *These sheep, what evil have they done? Let thy hand be against me,* 2 Sam. xxiv. 17. But the Son of David was sinless and spotless; and his sheep, what evil have they not done? Yet he saith, *Let thine hand be against me.* Christ here seems to refer to that prophecy, Zech. xiii. 7, *Awake, O sword, against my shepherd;* and, though the smiting of the shepherd be for the present the *scattering* of the flock, it is in order to the gathering of them in.

(*b.*) He takes off the offence of the cross, which to many is a stone of stumbling, by four considerations:—

[*a.*] That his *laying down his life for the sheep* was the condition, the performance of which entitled him to the honours and powers of his exalted state (*v.* 17): "*Therefore doth my Father love me, because I lay down my life.* Upon these terms I am, as Mediator, to expect my Father's acceptance and approbation, and the glory designed me—that I become a sacrifice for the chosen remnant." Not but that, as the Son of God, he was beloved of his Father from eternity, but as *God-man,* as *Immanuel,* he was *therefore* beloved of the Father because he undertook to *die for the sheep; therefore* God's soul delighted in him as his elect because herein he was his *faithful servant* (Isa. xlii. 1); therefore he said, *This is my beloved Son.* What an instance is this of God's love to man, that he loved his Son the more for loving us! See what a value Christ puts upon his Father's love, that, to recommend himself to that, he would lay down his life for the sheep. Did he think God's love recompence sufficient for all his services and sufferings, and shall we think it too little for ours, and court the smiles of the world to make it up? *Therefore doth my Father love me,* that is, me, and all that by faith become one with me; me, and the mystical body, *because I lay down my life.*

[*b.*] That his laying down his life was in order to his resuming it: *I lay down my life, that I may receive it again. First,* This was the effect of his Father's love, and the first step of his exaltation, the fruit of that love. Because he was God's *holy one,* he must not *see corruption,* Ps. xvi. 10. God loved him too well to leave him in the grave. *Secondly,* This he had in his eye, in laying down his life, that he might have an opportunity of declaring himself to be the Son of God with power by his resurrection, Rom. i. 4. By a divine stratagem (like that before Ai, Josh. viii. 15) he yielded to death, as if he were smitten before it, that he might the more gloriously conquer death, and triumph over the grave. He laid down a *vilified* body, that he might assume a *glorified* one, fit to ascend to the world of spirits; laid down a life adapted to this world, but assumed one adapted to the other, like a corn of wheat, *ch.* xii. 24.

[*c.*] That he was perfectly voluntary in his sufferings and death (*v.* 18): "No one doth or can force my life from me against my will, but I freely *lay it down of myself,* I deliver it as my own act and deed, for I *have* (which no man has) *power to lay it down, and to take it again.*"

1*st*, See here the power of Christ, as the Lord of life, particularly of his own life, which he had *in himself.* 1. He had power to *keep his life* against all the world, so that it could not be wrested from him without his own consent. Though Christ's life seemed to be taken by storm, yet really it was surrendered, otherwise it had been impregnable, and never taken. The Lord Jesus did not fall into the hands of his persecutors because he could not avoid it, but threw himself into their hands because his hour was come. *No man taketh my life from me.* This was such a challenge as was never given by the most daring hero. 2. He had power to *lay down his life.* (1.) He had ability to do it. He could, when he pleased, slip the knot of union between soul and body, and, without any act of violence done to himself, could disengage them from each other: having voluntarily *taken up* a body, he could voluntarily lay it down again, which appeared when he cried with a loud voice, and gave up the ghost. (2.) He had authority to do it, ἐξουσίαν. Though we could find instruments of cruelty, wherewith to make an end of our own lives, yet *Id possumus quod jure possumus—we can do that, and that only, which we can do lawfully.* We are not at liberty to do it; but Christ had a sovereign authority to dispose of his own life as he pleased. He was no debtor (as we are) either to life or death, but perfectly *sui juris.* 3. He had power to *take it again;* we have not. Our life, once laid down, is *as water spilt upon the ground;* but Christ, when he laid down his life, still had it within reach, within call, and could resume it. Parting with it by a voluntary conveyance, he might limit the surrender at pleasure, and he did it with a power of revocation, which was necessary to preserve the intentions of the surrender.

2*ndly*, See here the grace of Christ; since none could demand his life of him by law, or extort it by force, he *laid it down of himself* for our redemption. He offered himself to be the Saviour: *Lo, I come;* and then, the necessity of our case calling for it, he offered himself to be a sacrifice: *Here am I, let these go their way; by which will we are sanctified,* Heb. x. 10. He was both the offerer and the offering, so that *his laying down his life* was his offering up himself.

[*d.*] That he did all this by the express order and appointment of his Father, into which he ultimately resolves the whole affair: *This commandment have I received of my Father;* not such a commandment as made what he did necessary, prior to his own voluntary undertaking; but this was the *law of mediation,* which he was willing to have *written in his heart,* so as to *delight* in doing *the will of God* according to it, Ps. xl. 8.

19 There was a division therefore
again among the Jews for these sayings. 20 And many of them said,
He hath a devil, and is mad; why hear
ye him? 21 Others said, These are not
the words of him that hath a devil.
Can a devil open the eyes of the blind?

We have here an account of the people's different sentiments concerning Christ, on occasion of the foregoing discourse; there was a division, a *schism,* among them; they differed in their opinions, which threw them into heats and parties. Such a ferment as this they had been in before (*ch.* vii. 43; ix. 16); and where there has once been a division a little thing will make a division again. Rents are sooner made than made up or mended. This division was occasioned by the sayings of Christ, which, one would think, should rather have united them all in him as their centre; but they set them at variance, as Christ foresaw, Luke xii. 51. But it is better that men should be *divided* about the doctrine of Christ than *united* in the service of sin, Luke xi. 21. See what the debate was in particular.

I. Some upon this occasion spoke ill of Christ and of his sayings, either openly in the face of the assembly, for his enemies were very impudent, or privately among themselves. They said, *He has a devil, and is mad, why do you hear him?* 1. They reproach him as a demoniac. The worst of characters is put upon the best of men. He is a distracted man, he raves and is delirious, and no more to be heard than the rambles of a man in bedlam. Thus still, if a man preaches seriously and pressingly of another world, he shall be said to talk like an enthusiast; and his conduct shall be imputed to fancy, a heated brain, and a crazed imagination. 2. They ridicule his hearers: "*Why hear you him?* Why do you so far encourage him as to take notice of what he says?" Note, Satan ruins many by putting them out of conceit with the word and ordinances, and representing it as a weak and silly thing to attend upon them. Men would not thus be laughed out of their necessary food, and yet suffer themselves to be laughed out of what is more necessary. Those that hear Christ, and mix faith with what they hear, will soon be able to give a good account *why they hear him.*

II. Others stood up in defence of him and his discourse, and, though the stream ran strong, dared to swim against it; and, though perhaps they did not believe on him as the Messiah, they could not bear to hear him thus abused. If they could say no more of him, this they would maintain, that he was a man in his wits, that he had not a devil, that he was neither senseless nor graceless. The absurd and most unreasonable reproaches, that have sometimes been cast upon Christ and his gospel, have excited those to appear for him and it who otherwise had no great affection to either. Two things they plead:

—1. The excellency of his doctrine: "*These are not the words of him that hath a devil;* they are not idle words; distracted men are not used to talk at this rate. These are not the words of one that is either violently possessed with a devil or voluntarily in league with the devil." Christianity, if it be not the true religion, is certainly the greatest cheat that ever was put upon the world; and, if so, it must be of the devil, who is the father of all lies: but it is certain that the doctrine of Christ is no doctrine of devils, for it is levelled directly against the devil's kingdom, and Satan is too subtle to be divided against himself. So much of holiness there is in the words of Christ that we may conclude they are *not the words of one that has a devil,* and therefore are the words of one that was sent of God; are not from hell, and therefore must be from heaven. 2. The power of his miracles: *Can a devil,* that is, a man that has a devil, *open the eyes of the blind?* Neither mad men nor bad men can work miracles. Devils are not such lords of the power of nature as to be able to work such miracles; nor are they such friends to mankind as to be willing to work them if they were able. The devil will sooner put out men's eyes than open them. Therefore Jesus *had not a devil.*

22 And it was at Jerusalem the
feast of the dedication, and it was
winter. 23 And Jesus walked in the
temple in Solomon's porch. 24
Then came the Jews round about
him, and said unto him, How long
dost thou make us to doubt? If
thou be the Christ, tell us plainly.
25 Jesus answered them, I told you,
and ye believed not: the works that
I do in my Father's name, they bear
witness of me. 26 But ye believe
not, because ye are not of my sheep,
as I said unto you. 27 My sheep hear
my voice, and I know them, and they
follow me: 28 And I give unto them
eternal life; and they shall never
perish, neither shall any *man* pluck
them out of my hand. 29 My Father,
which gave *them* me, is greater than
all; and no *man* is able to pluck
them out of my Father's hand. 30
I and *my* Father are one. 31 Then
the Jews took up stones again to
stone him. 32 Jesus answered them,
Many good works have I showed you
from my Father; for which of those
works do ye stone me? 33 The
Jews answered him, saying, For a
good work we stone thee not; but
for blasphemy; and because that thou,
being a man, makest thyself God.
34 Jesus answered them, Is it not
written in your law, I said, Ye are
gods? 35 If he called them gods,
unto whom the word of God came,
and the scripture cannot be broken;
36 Say ye of him, whom the Father
hath sanctified, and sent into the world,
Thou blasphemest; because I said,
I am the Son of God? 37 If I do
not the works of my Father, believe
me not. 38 But if I do, though ye
believe not me, believe the works:
that ye may know, and believe, that
the Father *is* in me, and I in him.

We have here another rencounter between Christ and the Jews in the temple, in which it is hard to say which is more strange, the gracious words that came out of his mouth or the spiteful ones that came out of theirs.

I. We have here the time when this conference was: *It was at the feast of dedication, and it was winter,* a feast that was annually observed by consent, in remembrance of the dedication of a new altar and the purging of the temple, by Judas Maccabæus, after the temple had been profaned and the altar defiled; we have the story of it at large in the history of the Maccabees (*lib.* 1, *cap.*iv.); we have the prophecy of it, Dan. viii. 13, 14. See more of the feast, 2 Mac. i. 18. The return of their liberty was to them as life from the dead, and, in remembrance of it, they kept an annual feast on the twenty-fifth day of the month *Cisleu,* about the beginning of *December,* and seven days after. The celebrating of it was not confined to Jerusalem, as that of the divine feasts was, but every one observed it in his own place, not as a *holy time* (it is only a divine institution that can sanctify a day), but as a *good time,* as the days of Purim, Esth. ix. 19. Christ forecasted to be now at Jerusalem, not in honour of the feast, which did not require his attendance there, but that he might improve those eight days of vacation for good purposes.

II. The place where it was (*v.* 23): *Jesus walked in the temple in Solomon's porch;* so called (Acts iii. 11), not because built by Solomon, but because built in the same place with that which had borne his name in the first temple, and the name was kept up for the greater reputation of it. Here Christ walked, to observe the proceedings of the great sanhedrim that sat here (Ps. lxxxii. 1); *he walked,* ready to give audience to any that should apply to him, and to offer them his services. He walked, as it should seem, for some time *alone,* as one neglected; walked pensive, in the foresight of the ruin of the temple. Those that have any thing to say to Christ may find him in the temple and walk with him there.

III. The conference itself, in which observe,

1. A weighty question put to him by the Jews, *v.* 24. They *came round about him,* to tease him; he was waiting for an opportunity to do them a kindness, and they took the opportunity to do him a mischief. Ill-will for good-will is no rare and uncommon return. He could not enjoy himself, no, not in the temple, his Father's house, without disturbance. They came about him, as it were, to lay siege to him: *encompassed him about like bees.* They came about him as if they had a joint and unanimous desire to be satisfied; came as one man, pretending an impartial and importunate enquiry after truth, but intending a general assault upon our Lord Jesus; and they seemed to speak the sense of their nation, as if they were the mouth of all the Jews: *How long dost thou make us to doubt? If thou be the Christ tell us.*

(1.) They quarrel with him, as if he had unfairly held them in suspense hitherto. Τὴν ψυχὴν ἡμῶν αἴρεις;—*How long dost thou steal away our hearts?* Or, *take away our souls?* So some read it; basely intimating that what share he had of the people's love and respect he did not obtain fairly, but by indirect methods, as Absalom stole the hearts of the men of Israel; and as seducers deceive the *hearts of the simple,* and so *draw away disciples after them,* Rom. xvi. 18; Acts xx. 30. But most interpreters understand it as we do: "*How long dost thou keep us in suspense?* How long are we kept debating whether thou be the Christ or no, and not able to determine the question?" Now, [1.] It was the effect of their infidelity, and powerful prejudices, that after our Lord Jesus had so fully proved himself to be the Christ they were still in doubt concerning it; this they willingly hesitated about, when they might easily have been satisfied. The struggle was between their convictions, which told them he was Christ, and their corruptions, which said, No, because he was not such a Christ as they expected. Those who choose to be sceptics may, if they please, hold the balance so that the most cogent arguments may not weigh down the most trifling objections, but the scales may still hang even. [2.] It was an instance of their impudence and presumption that they laid the blame of their doubting upon Christ himself, as if he *made them to* doubt by inconsistency with himself, whereas in truth they made themselves doubt by indulging their prejudices. If Wisdom's sayings appear doubtful, the fault is not in the object, but in the eye; they are all *plain to him that understands.* Christ would make us to believe; we make ourselves to *doubt.*

(2.) They challenge him to give a direct and categorical answer whether he was the Messiah or no: "*If thou be the Christ,* as many believe thou art, *tell us plainly,* not by parables, as, *I am the light of the world,* and *the good Shepherd,* and the like, but *totidem verbis—in so many words,* either that thou art the Christ, or, as John Baptist, that thou art not," *ch.* i. 20. Now this pressing query of theirs was *seemingly good;* they pretended to be desirous to know the truth, as if they were ready to embrace it; but it was *really bad,* and put with an ill design; for, if he should tell them plainly that he was the Christ, there needed no more to make him obnoxious to the jealousy and severity of the Roman government. Every one knew the Messiah was to be a king, and therefore whoever pretended to be the Messiah would be prosecuted as a traitor, which was the thing they would have been at; for, let him tell them ever so plainly that he was the Christ, they would have this to say presently, *Thou bearest witness of thyself,* as they had said, *ch.* viii. 13.

2. Christ's answer to this question, in which,

(1.) He justifies himself as not at all accessary to their infidelity and scepticism, referring them, [1.] To what he had said: *I have told you.* He had told them that he was the Son of God, the Son of man, that he had life in himself, that he had *authority to execute judgment,* &c. And is not this the Christ then? These things he had told them, and they believed not; why then should they be told them again, merely to gratify their curiosity? *You believed not.* They pretended that they only doubted, but Christ tells them that they did not believe. Scepticism in religion is no better than downright infidelity. It is not for us to teach God how he should teach us, nor prescribe to him how plainly he should tell us his mind, but to be thankful for divine revelation as we have it. If we do not believe this, neither should we be persuaded if it were ever so much adapted to our humour. [2.] He refers them to his works, to the example of his life, which was not only perfectly pure, but highly beneficent, and of a piece with his doctrine; and especially to his miracles, which he wrought for the confirmation of his doctrine. It was certain that no man could do those miracles except God were with him, and God would not be with him to attest a forgery.

(2.) He condemns them for their obstinate unbelief, notwithstanding all the most plain and powerful arguments used to convince them: "*You believed not;* and again, *You believed not.* You still are what you always were, obstinate in your unbelief." But the reason he gives is very surprising: "*You believed not, because you are not of my sheep:* you believe not in me, because you belong not to me." [1.] "You are not disposed to be my followers, are not of a tractable teachable temper, have no inclination to receive the doctrine and law of the Messiah; you will not herd yourselves with my sheep, will not come and see, come and hear my voice." Rooted antipathies to the gospel of Christ are the bonds of iniquity and infidelity. [2.] "You are not *designed* to be my followers; you are not of those that were given me by my Father, to be brought to grace and glory. You are not of the number of the elect; and your unbelief, if you persist in it, will be a certain evidence that you are not." Note, Those to whom God never gives the grace of faith were never designed for heaven and happiness. What Solomon saith of immorality is true of infidelity, It is *a deep ditch, and he that is abhorred of the Lord shall fall therein,* Prov. xxii. 14. *Non esse electum, non est causa incredulitatis propriè dicta, sed causa per accidens. Fides autem est donum Dei et effectus prædestinationis—The not being included among the elect is not the* proper *cause of infidelity, but merely the* accidental *cause. But faith is the gift of God, and the effect of predestination.* So Jansenius distinguishes well here.

(3.) He takes this occasion to describe both the gracious disposition and the happy state of those that are his sheep; for such there are, though *they* be not.

[1.] To convince them that they were not his sheep, he tells them what were the characters of his sheep. *First,* They *hear his voice* (*v.* 27), for they know it to be his (*v.* 4), and he has undertaken that they shall hear it, *v.* 16. They discern it, *It is the voice of my beloved,* Cant. ii. 8. They delight in it, are in their element when they are sitting at his feet to hear his word. They do according to it, and make his word their rule. Christ will not account those his sheep that are deaf to his calls, deaf to his charms, Ps. lviii. 5. *Secondly,* They *follow him;* they submit to his guidance by a willing obedience to all his commands, and a cheerful conformity to his spirit and pattern. The word of command has always been, *Follow m* We must eye him as our leader and captain, and *tread in his steps,* and walk as he walked—follow the prescriptions of his word, the intimations of his providence, and the directions of his Spirit—*follow the Lamb* (the *dux gregis—the leader of the flock) whithersoever he goes.* In vain do we *hear his voice* if we do not *follow him.*

[2.] To convince them that it was their great unhappiness and misery not to be of Christ's sheep, he here describes the blessed state and case of those that are, which would likewise serve for the support and comfort of his poor despised followers, and keep them from envying the power and grandeur of those that were not of his sheep.

First, Our Lord Jesus *takes cognizance* of his sheep: They *hear my voice,* and *I know them.* He distinguishes them from others (2 Tim. ii. 19), has a particular regard to every individual (Ps. xxxiv. 6); he knows their wants and desires, knows their souls in adversity, where to find them, and what to do for them. He knows others afar off, but knows them near at hand.

Secondly, He has provided a happiness for them, suited to them: *I give unto them eternal life, v.* 28. 1. The estate settled upon them is rich and valuable; it is life, eternal life. Man has a living soul; therefore the happiness provided is life, suited to his nature. Man has an immortal soul: therefore the happiness provided is eternal life, running parallel with his duration. *Life eternal* is the felicity and chief good of a *soul immortal.* 2. The manner of conveyance is *free: I give it* to them; it is not bargained and sold upon a valuable consideration, but given by the free grace of Jesus Christ. The donor has power to give it. He who is the fountain of life, and Father of eternity, has authorized Christ to give eternal life, *ch.* xvii. 2. Not *I will* give it, but *I do* give it; it is a present gift. He gives the assurance of it, the pledge and earnest of it, the first-fruits and foretastes of it, that *spiritual* life which is *eternal* life begun, heaven in the seed, in the bud, in the embryo.

Thirdly, He has undertaken for their security and preservation to this happiness.

a. They shall be *saved from everlasting perdition. They shall by no means perish for ever;* so the words are. As there is an eternal life, so there is an eternal destruction; the soul not *annihilated,* but *ruined;* its being continued, but its comfort and happiness irrecoverably lost. All believers are saved from this; whatever cross they may come under, they shall not *come into condemnation.* A man is never undone till he is in hell, and they shall not go down to that. Shepherds that have large flocks often lose some of the sheep and suffer them to perish; but Christ has engaged that none of his sheep shall perish, not one.

b. They cannot be kept from their *everlasting happiness;* it is in reserve, but he that gives it to them will preserve them to it. (*a.*) His own power is engaged for them: *Neither shall any man pluck them out of my hand.* A mighty contest is here supposed about these sheep. The Shepherd is so careful of their welfare that he has them not only within his fold, and under his eye, but *in his hand,* interested in his special love and taken under his special protection *(all his saints are in thy hand,* Deut. xxxiii. 3); yet their enemies are so daring that they attempt to pluck them out of his hand—*his* whose *own* they are, whose *care* they are; but they cannot, they shall not, do it. Note, Those are safe who are in the hands of the Lord Jesus. The saints are *preserved in Christ Jesus:* and their salvation is not in their own keeping, but in the keeping of a Mediator. The Pharisees and rulers did all they could to frighten the disciples of Christ from following him, reproving and threatening them, but Christ saith that they shall not prevail. (*b.*) His Father's power is likewise engaged for their preservation, *v.* 29. He now appeared in weakness, and, lest his security should therefore be thought *insufficient,* he brings in his Father as a further security. Observe, [*a.*] The power of the Father: *My Father is greater than all;* greater than all the other *friends* of the church, all the other shepherds, magistrates or ministers, and able to do that for them which they cannot do. Those shepherds slumber and sleep, and it will be easy to pluck the sheep out of their hands; but he keeps his flock day and night. He is greater than all the enemies of the church, all the opposition given to her interests, and able to secure his own against all their insults; he is *greater than all* the combined force of hell and earth. He is greater in wisdom than the *old serpent,* though noted for subtlety; greater in strength than the great red dragon, though his name be *legion,* and his title *principalities and powers.* The devil and his angels have had many a push, many a pluck for the mastery, but have never yet prevailed, Rev. xii. 7, 8. *The Lord on high is mightier.* [*b.*] The interest of the Father in the sheep, for the sake of which this power is engaged for them: "It is my Father *that gave them to me,* and he is concerned in honour to uphold his gift." They were given to the Son as a trust to be managed by him, and therefore God will still look after them. All the divine power is engaged for the accomplishment of all the divine counsels. [*c.*] The safety of the saints inferred from these two. If this be so, then *none* (neither man nor devil) is *able to pluck them out of the Father's hand,* not able to deprive them of the grace they have, nor to hinder them from the glory that is designed them; not able to put them out of God's protection, nor get them into their own power. Christ had himself experienced the power of his Father *upholding* and *strengthening* him, and therefore puts all his followers into his hand too. He that secured the glory of the Redeemer will secure the glory of the redeemed. Further to corroborate the security, that the sheep of Christ may have strong consolation, he asserts the union of these two undertakers: "*I and my Father are one,* and have jointly and severally undertaken for the protection of the saints and their perfection." This denotes more than the harmony, and consent, and good understanding, that were between the Father and the Son in the work of man's redemption. Every good man is so far one with God as to concur with him; therefore it must be meant of the *oneness of the nature* of Father and Son, that they are the same in substance, and equal in power and glory. The fathers urged this both against the Sabellians, to prove the distinction and plurality of the persons, that the Father and the Son are two, and against the Arians, to prove the unity of the nature, that these two are *one.* If we should altogether hold our peace concerning this sense of the words, even the stones which the Jews took up to cast at him would speak it out, for the Jews understood him as hereby making himself God (*v.* 33) and he did not deny it. He proves that none could pluck them out *of his hand* because they could not pluck them out *of the Father's hand,* which had not been a conclusive argument if the Son had not had the same almighty power with the Father, and consequently been one with him in essence and operation.

IV. The rage, the outrage, of the Jews against him for this discourse: *The Jews took up stones again, v.* 31. It is not the word that is used before (*ch.* viii. 59), but ἐβάςασαν λίθους—*they carried stones*—great stones, stones that were a *load,* such as they used in stoning malefactors. They *brought* them from some place at a distance, as it were preparing things for his execution without any judicial process; as if he were convicted of blasphemy upon the notorious evidence of the fact, which needed no further trial. The absurdity of this insult which the Jews offered to Christ will appear if we consider, 1. That they had *imperiously,* not to say *impudently,* challenged him to tell them plainly whether he was the Christ or no; and yet now that he not only said *he* was the Christ, but proved himself so, they condemned him as a malefactor. If the preachers of the truth propose it *modestly,* they are branded as cowards; if *boldly,* as insolent; but *Wisdom is justified of her children.* 2. That when they had before made a similar attempt it was in vain; he *escaped through the midst of them* (*ch.* viii. 59); yet they repeat their baffled attempt. Daring sinners will throw stones at heaven, though they return upon their own heads; and will strengthen themselves against the Almighty, though none ever hardened themselves against him and prospered.

V. Christ's tender expostulation with them upon occasion of this outrage (*v.* 32): *Jesus answered* what they *did,* for we do not find that they *said any thing,* unless perhaps they stirred up the crowd that they had gathered about him to join with them, crying, *Stone him, stone him,* as afterwards, *Crucify him, crucify him.* When he could have answered them with fire from heaven, he mildly replied, *Many good works have I shown you from my Father: for which of those works do you stone me?* Words so very tender that one would think they should have melted a heart of stone. In dealing with his enemies he still argued from his works (men evidence what they *are* by what they *do),* his *good works*—καλὰ ἔργα, excellent, eminent works. *Opera eximia vel præclara;* the expression signifies both *great works* and *good works.*

1. The divine power of his works convicted them of the most obstinate infidelity. They were works *from his Father,* so far above the reach and course of nature as to prove him who did them *sent of God,* and acting by commission from him. These works

he *showed* them; he did them openly before the people, and not in a corner. His works would bear the test, and refer themselves to the testimony of the most inquisitive and impartial spectators. He did not show his works by candle-light, as those that are concerned only for *show*, but he showed them at noon-day before the world, *ch.* xviii. 20. See Ps. cxi. 6. His works so undeniably *demonstrated* that they were an incontestable *demonstration* of the validity of his commission.

2. The divine grace of his works convicted them of the most base ingratitude. The works he did among them were not only miracles, but mercies; not only works of wonder to amaze them, but works of love and kindness to do them good, and so make them good, and endear himself to them. He healed the sick, cleansed the lepers, cast out devils, which were favours, not only to the persons concerned, but to the public; these he had repeated, and multiplied: "*Now, for which of these do you stone me?* You cannot say that I have done you any harm, or given you any just provocation; if therefore you will pick a quarrel with me, it must be for some good work, some good turn done you; tell me for which." Note, (1.) The horrid ingratitude that there is in our sins against God and Jesus Christ is a great aggravation of them, and makes them appear exceedingly sinful. See how God argues to this purpose, Deut. xxxii. 6; Jer. ii. 5; Mic. vi. 3. (2.) We must not think it strange if we meet with those who not only hate us without cause, but are our adversaries for our love, Ps. xxxv. 12; xli. 9. When he asks, *For which of these do you stone me?* as he intimates the abundant satisfaction he had in his own innocency, which gives a man courage in a suffering day, so he puts his persecutors upon considering what was the true reason of their enmity, and asking, as all those should do that create trouble to their neighbour, *Why persecute we him?* As Job advises his friends to do, Job xix. 28

VI. Their vindication of the attempt they made upon Christ, and the cause upon which they grounded their prosecution, *v.* 33. What sin will want fig-leaves with which to cover itself, when even the bloody persecutors of the Son of God could find something to say for themselves?

1. They would not be thought such enemies to their country as to persecute him for a good work: *For a good work we stone thee not.* For indeed they would scarcely allow any of his works to be so. His curing the impotent man (*ch.* v.) and the blind man (*ch.* ix.) were so far from being acknowledged good services to the town, and meritorious, that they were put upon the score of his crimes, because done on the sabbath day. But, if he had done any good works, they would not own that they stoned him *for them*, though these were really the things that did most exasperate them, *ch.* xi. 47. Thus, though most absurd, they could not be brought to own their absurdities.

2. They would be thought such friends to God and his glory as to prosecute him for blasphemy: *Because that thou, being a man, makest thyself God.* Here is,

(1.) A pretended zeal for the law. They seem mightily concerned for the honour of the divine majesty, and to be seized with a religious horror at that which they imagined to be a reproach to it. A blasphemer was to be *stoned*, Lev. xxiv. 16. This law, they thought, did not only justify, but sanctify, what they attempted, as Acts xxvi. 9. Note, The vilest practices are often varnished with plausible pretences. As nothing is more *courageous* than a well-informed conscience, so nothing is more *outrageous* than a mistaken one. See Isa. lxvi. 5; *ch.* xvi. 2.

(2.) A real enmity to the gospel, on which they could not put a greater affront than by representing Christ as a blasphemer. It is no new thing for the worst of characters to be put upon the best of men, by those that resolve to give them the worst of treatment. [1.] The crime laid to his charge is *blasphemy*, speaking reproachfully and despitefully of God. God himself is out of the sinner's reach, and not capable of receiving any real injury; and therefore enmity to God spits its venom at his name, and so shows its ill-will. [2.] The proof of the crime: *Thou, being a man, makest thyself God.* As it is God's glory that *he is God*, which we rob him of when we make him altogether such a one as ourselves, so it is his glory that *besides him there is no other*, which we rob him of when we make ourselves, or any creature, altogether like him. Now, *First*, Thus far they were in the right, that what Christ said of himself amounted to this—that he was God, for he had said that he was *one with the Father* and that he would *give eternal life;* and Christ does not deny it, which he would have done if it had been a mistaken inference from his words. But, *Secondly*, They were much mistaken when they looked upon him as a *mere man*, and that the Godhead he claimed was a usurpation, and of his own making. They thought it absurd and impious that such a one as he, who appeared in the fashion of a poor, mean, despicable man, should profess himself the Messiah, and entitle himself to the honours confessedly due to the Son of God. Note, 1. Those who say that Jesus is a *mere man*, and only a *made God*, as the Socinians say, do in effect charge *him* with blasphemy, but do effectually prove it upon themselves. 2. He who, being a man, a sinful man, makes himself a god as the Pope does, who claims divine powers and prerogatives, is unquestionably a *blasphemer*, and *that* antichrist.

VII. Christ's reply to their accusation of him (for such their vindication of themselves was), and his making good those claims which they imputed to him as blasphemous (*v.* 34, &c.), where he proves himself to be no blasphemer, by two arguments :—

1. By an argument taken from *God's word.* He appeals to what was *written in their law,* that is, in the Old Testament; whoever opposes Christ, he is sure to have the scripture *on his side.* It is written (Ps. lxxxii. 6), *I have said, You are gods.* It is an argument *a minore ad majus—from the less to the greater.* If they were gods, much more am I. Observe,

(1.) How he explains the text (*v.* 35) : *He called them gods to whom the word of God came, and the scripture cannot be broken.* The word of God's commission came to them, appointing them to their offices, as judges, and therefore they are called *gods,* Exod. xxii. 28. To some the word of God came immediately, as to Moses; to others in the way of an instituted ordinance. Magistracy is a divine institution; and magistrates are God's delegates, and therefore the scripture calleth them gods; and we are sure that the scripture *cannot be broken,* or broken in upon, or found fault with. Every word of God is *right;* the very style and language of scripture are unexceptionable, and not to be corrected, Matt. v. 18.

(2.) How he applies it. Thus much in general is easily inferred, that those were very rash and unreasonable who condemned Christ as a blasphemer, only for calling himself the Son of God, when yet they themselves called their rulers so, and therein the scripture warranted them. But the argument goes further (*v.* 36): If magistrates were called gods, because they were commissioned to administer justice in the nation, *say you of him whom the Father hath sanctified, Thou blasphemest?* We have here two things concerning the Lord Jesus :—[1.] The honour done him by the *Father,* which he justly glories in: He *sanctified him,* and *sent him into the world.* Magistrates were called *the sons of God,* though the word of God only came to them, and the spirit of government came upon them by measure, as upon Saul; but our Lord Jesus was himself the *Word,* and had the *Spirit without measure.* They were constituted for a particular country, city, or nation; but he was sent *into the world,* vested with a universal authority, as Lord of all. They were *sent to,* as persons at a distance; he was *sent forth,* as having been from eternity with God. The Father *sanctified him,* that is, designed him and set him apart to the office of Mediator, and qualified and fitted him for that office. *Sanctifying* him is the same with *sealing* him, *ch.* vi. 27. Note, Whom the Father sends he sanctifies; whom he designs for holy purposes he prepares with holy principles and dispositions. The holy God will reward, and therefore will employ, none but such as he finds or makes holy. The Father's sanctifying and sending him is here vouched as a sufficient warrant for his calling himself the *Son of God;* for because he was a *holy thing* he was *called the Son of God,* Luke i. 35. See Rom. i. 4. [2.] The dishonour done him by the Jews, which he justly complains of—that they impiously said of him, whom the Father had thus dignified, that he was a *blasphemer,* because he called himself the *Son of God:* "*Say you of him* so and so? Dare you say so? Dare you thus set your mouths against the heavens? Have you brow and brass enough to tell the God of truth that he lies, or *to condemn him that is most just?* Look me in the face, and say it if you can. What! say you of the Son of God that *he is a blasphemer?*" If devils, whom he came to condemn, had said so of him, it had not been so strange; but that *men,* whom he came to teach and save, should say so of him, *be astonished, O heavens! at this.* See what is the language of an obstinate unbelief; it does, in effect, call the holy Jesus a blasphemer. It is hard to say which is more to be wondered at, that men who breathe in God's air should yet speak such things, or that men who have spoken such things should still be suffered to breathe in God's air. The wickedness of man, and the patience of God, as it were, contend which shall be most *wonderful.*

2. By an argument taken from *his own works, v.* 37, 38. In the former he only answered the charge of blasphemy by an argument *ad hominem—turning a man's own argument against himself;* but he here makes out his own claims, and proves that he and the Father are one (*v.* 37, 38): *If I do not the works of my Father, believe me not.* Though he might justly have abandoned such blasphemous wretches as incurable, yet he vouchsafes to reason with them. Observe,

(1.) *From what* he argues—from his works, which he had often vouched as his credentials, and the proofs of his mission. As he proved himself sent of God by the *divinity* of his works, so we must prove ourselves allied to Christ by the *Christianity* of ours. [1.] The argument is very cogent; for the works he did were the *works of his Father,* which the Father only could do, and which could not be done in the ordinary course of nature, but only by the sovereign over-ruling power of the God of nature. *Opera Deo propria—works peculiar to God,* and *Opera Deo digna—works worthy of God*—the works of a divine power. He that can dispense with the laws of nature, repeal, alter, and overrule them at his pleasure, by his own power, is certainly the sovereign prince who first instituted and enacted those laws. The miracles which the apostles wrought in his name, by his power, and for the confirmation of his doctrine, corroborated this argument, and continued the evidence of it when he was gone. [2.] It is proposed as fairly as can be desired, and put to a short issue. *First, If I do not the works of my Father, believe me not.* He does not demand a blind and implicit faith, nor an assent to his divine mission further than he gave proof of it. He did not wind himself into the affections of the people, nor wheedle them by sly insinuations, nor impose upon their credulity by bold assertions, but with the greatest fairness imaginable quitted all demands of their faith, further than he produced warrants for these demands. Christ is no hard master, who expects to reap in assents where he has not sown in arguments. None shall perish for the disbelief of that which was not proposed to them with sufficient motives of credibility, Infinite Wisdom itself being judge. *Secondly,* "But if I do *the works of my Father, if I work* undeniable miracles for the confirmation of a holy doctrine, *though you believe not me,* though you are so scrupulous as not to take my word, yet *believe the works:* believe your own eyes, your own reason; the thing speaks itself plainly enough." As the invisible things of the Creator are clearly seen by his works of creation and common providence (Rom. i. 20), so the invisible things of the Redeemer were seen by his miracles, and by all his works both of power and mercy; so that those who were not convinced by these works were *without excuse.*

(2.) *For what* he argues—*that you may know and believe,* may believe it intelligently, and with an entire satisfaction, that *the Father is in me and I in him;* which is the same with what he had said (*v.* 30): *I and my Father are one.* The Father was so in the Son as that in him *dwelt all the fulness of the Godhead,* and it was by a divine power that he wrought his miracles; the Son was so in the Father as that he was perfectly acquainted with the whole of his mind, not by communication, but by consciousness, having lain in his bosom. This we must *know;* not know and *explain* (for we cannot by searching find it out to perfection), but know and *believe* it; acknowledging and adoring the depth, when we cannot find the bottom.

39 Therefore they sought again to take him: but he escaped out of their hand, 40 And went away again beyond Jordan into the place where John at first baptized; and there he abode. 41 And many resorted unto him, and said, John did no miracle: but all things that John spake of this man were true. 42 And many believed on him there.

We have here the issue of the conference with the Jews. One would have thought it would have convinced and melted them, but their hearts were hardened. Here we are told,

I. How they attacked him by force. Therefore *they sought again to take him, v.* 39. Therefore, 1. Because he had fully answered their charge of blasphemy, and wiped off that imputation, so that they could not for shame go on with their attempts to stone him, therefore they contrived to seize him, and prosecute him as an offender against the state. When they were constrained to drop their attempt by a popular tumult, they would try what they could do under colour of a legal process. See Rev. xii. 13. Or, 2. Because he persevered in the same testimony concerning himself, they persisted in their malice against him. What he had said before he did in effect say again, for the *faithful witness* never departs from what he has once said; and therefore, having the same provocation, they express the same resentment, and justify their attempt to stone him by another attempt to take him. Such is the temper of a persecuting spirit, and such its policy, *malè facta male factis tegere ne perpluant—to cover one set of bad deeds with another, lest the former should fall through.*

II. How he avoided them by flight; not an inglorious retreat, in which there was any thing of human infirmity, but a glorious retirement, in which there was much of a divine power. He *escaped out of their hands,* not by the interposal of any friend that helped him, but by his own wisdom he *got clear* of them; he drew a veil over himself, or cast a mist before their eyes, or tied the hands of those whose hearts he did not turn. Note, No weapon formed against our Lord Jesus shall prosper, Ps. ii. 4. He *escaped,* not because he was afraid to suffer, but because *his hour was not come.* And he who knew how to *deliver himself* no doubt knows how to *deliver the godly out of temptation,* and to make *a way for them to escape.*

III. How he disposed of himself in his retirement: He *went away again beyond Jordan, v.* 40. The bishop of our souls came not to be fixed in one see, but to go about from place to place, doing good. This great benefactor was never out of his way, for wherever he came there was work to be done. Though Jerusalem was the royal city, yet he made many a kind visit to the country, not only to his own country Galilee, but to other parts, even those that lay most remote beyond Jordan. Now observe,

1. What *shelter* he found there. He went into a private part of the country, and *there he abode;* there he found some rest and quietness, when in Jerusalem he could find none. Note, Though persecutors may drive Christ and his gospel out of their own city or country, they cannot drive him or it out of the world. Though Jerusalem was not gathered, nor would be, yet Christ was glorious, and would be. Christ's going now beyond Jordan was a figure of the taking of the kingdom of God from the Jews, and bringing it to the Gentiles. Christ and his gospel have often found better entertainment among the plain country-people than among *the wise, the mighty, the noble,* 1 Cor. i. 26, 27.

2. What *success* he found there. He did not go thither merely for his own security,

but to do good there; and he chose to go thither, where John at first baptized (*ch.* i. 28), because there could not but remain some impressions of John's ministry and baptism thereabouts, which would dispose them to receive Christ and his doctrine; for it was not three years since John was baptizing, and Christ was himself baptized here at Bethabara. Christ came hither now to see what fruit there was of all the pains John Baptist had taken among them, and what they retained of the things they then heard and received. The event in some measure answered expectation; for we are told,

(1.) That they flocked after him (*v.* 41): *Many resorted to him.* The return of the means of grace to a place, after they have been for some time intermitted, commonly occasions a great stirring of affections. Some think Christ chose to *abide* at *Bethabara,* the *house of passage,* where the ferry-boats lay by which they crossed the river Jordan, that the confluence of people thither might give an opportunity of teaching many who would come to hear him when it *lay in their way,* but who would scarcely go a step out of the road for an opportunity of attending on his word.

(2.) That they reasoned in his favour, and sought arguments to induce them to close with him as much as those at Jerusalem sought objections against him. They said very judiciously, *John did no miracle, but all things that John spoke of this man were true.* Two things they considered, upon recollecting what they had seen and heard from John, and comparing it with Christ's ministry. [1.] That Christ far exceeded John Baptist's power, for *John did no miracle,* but Jesus does many; whence it is easy to infer that Jesus is greater than John. And, if John was so great a prophet, how great then is this Jesus! Christ is best known and acknowledged by such a comparison with others as sets him superlatively above others. Though John came in the spirit and power of Elias, yet he did not work miracles, as Elias did, lest the minds of people should be made to hesitate between him and Jesus; therefore the honour of working miracles was reserved for Jesus as a flower of his crown, that there might be a sensible demonstration, an *undeniable* one, that though he came after John, yet he was *preferred far before him.* [2.] That Christ exactly answered John Baptist's testimony. John not only *did no miracle* to *divert* people from Christ, but he said a great deal to direct them to Christ, and to turn them over as apprentices to him, and this came to their minds *now:* all things that *John said of this man were true,* that he should be the *Lamb of God,* should *baptize with the Holy Ghost and with fire.* Great things John had said of him, which raised their expectations; so that though they had not zeal enough to carry them into his country to enquire after him, yet, when he came into theirs, and brought his gospel to their doors, they acknowledged him as great as John had said he would be. When we get acquainted with Christ, and come to know him experimentally, we find all things that the scripture saith of him to be true; nay, and that the reality exceeds the report, 1 Kings, x. 6, 7. John Baptist was now dead and gone, and yet his hearers profited by what they had heard formerly, and, by comparing what they heard then with what they saw now, they gained a double advantage; for, *First,* They were confirmed in their belief that *John was a prophet,* who foretold such things, and spoke of the eminency to which this Jesus would arrive, though his beginning was so small. *Secondly,* They were prepared to believe that *Jesus was the Christ,* in whom they saw those things accomplished which John foretold. By this we see that the success and efficacy of the word preached are not confined to the life of the preacher, nor do they expire with his breath, but that which seemed as *water spilt upon the ground* may afterwards be *gathered up again.* See Zech. i. 5, 6.

(3.) That many believed on him there. Believing that he who wrought such miracles, and in whom John's predictions were fulfilled, was what he declared himself to be, the Son of God, they gave up themselves to him as his disciples, v. 42. An emphasis is here to be laid, [1.] Upon the persons that believed on him; they were *many.* While those that received and embraced his doctrine at Jerusalem were but as the grape-gleanings of the vintage, those that believed on him in the country, beyond the Jordan, were a full harvest gathered in to him. [2.] Upon the place where this was; it was where John had been preaching and baptizing and had had great success; *there* many believed on the Lord Jesus. Where the preaching of the doctrine of repentance has had success, as desired, there the preaching of the doctrine of reconciliation and gospel grace is most likely to be prosperous. Where John has been acceptable, Jesus will not be unacceptable. The jubilee-trumpet sounds sweetest in the ears of those who in the day of atonement have afflicted their souls for sin.

CHAP. XI.

In this chapter we have the history of that illustrious miracle which Christ wrought a little before his death—the raising of Lazarus to life, which is recorded only by this evangelist; for the other three confine themselves to what Christ did in Galilee, where he resided most, and scarcely ever carried their history into Jerusalem till the passion-week: whereas John's memoirs relate chiefly to what passed at Jerusalem; this passage therefore was reserved for his pen. Some suggest that, when the other evangelists wrote, Lazarus was alive, and it would not well agree either with his safety or with his humility to have it recorded till now, when it is supposed he was dead. It is more largely recorded than any other of Christ's miracles, not only because there are many circumstances of it so very instructive and the miracle of itself so great a proof of Christ's mission, but because it was an earnest of that which was to be the crowning proof of all—Christ's own resurrection. Here is, I. The tidings sent to our Lord Jesus of the sickness of Lazarus, and his entertainment of those tidings, ver. 1—16. II. The visit he made to Lazarus's relations when he had heard of his death, and their entertainment

of the visit, ver. 17—32. III. The miracle wrought in the raising of Lazarus from the dead, ver. 33—44. IV. The effect wrought by this miracle upon others, ver. 45—57.

NOW a certain *man* was sick,
named Lazarus, of Bethany, the
town of Mary and her sister Martha.
2 (It was *that* Mary which anointed
the Lord with ointment, and wiped
his feet with her hair, whose brother
Lazarus was sick.) 3 Therefore his
sisters sent unto him, saying, Lord,
behold, he whom thou lovest is sick.
4 When Jesus heard *that*, he said,
This sickness is not unto death, but
for the glory of God, that the Son of
God might be glorified thereby. 5
Now Jesus loved Martha, and her
sister, and Lazarus. 6 When he had
heard therefore that he was sick, he
abode two days still in the same place
where he was. 7 Then after that
saith he to *his* disciples, Let us go
into Judæa again. 8 *His* disciples
say unto him, Master, the Jews of
late sought to stone thee; and goest
thou thither again? 9 Jesus answered,
Are there not twelve hours in the
day? If any man walk in the day,
he stumbleth not, because he seeth
the light of this world. 10 But if a
man walk in the night, he stumbleth,
because there is no light in him. 11
These things said he: and after that
he saith unto them, Our friend Lazarus sleepeth; but I go, that I may
awake him out of sleep. 12 Then
said his disciples, Lord, if he sleep, he
shall do well. 13 Howbeit Jesus
spake of his death: but they thought
that he had spoken of taking of rest
in sleep. 14 Then said Jesus unto
them plainly, Lazarus is dead. 15
And I am glad for your sakes that I
was not there, to the intent ye may
believe; nevertheless let us go unto
him. 16 Then said Thomas, which
is called Didymus, unto his fellow
disciples, Let us also go, that we may
die with him.

We have in these verses,

I. A particular account of the parties principally concerned in this story, *v.* 1, 2. 1. They lived at *Bethany*, a village not far from Jerusalem, where Christ usually lodged when he came up to the feasts. It is here called the *town of Mary and Martha*, that is, the town where they dwelt, as Bethsaida is called the *city of Andrew and Peter, ch.* i. 44. For I see no reason to think, as some do, that Martha and Mary were owners of the town, and the rest were *their* tenants. 2. Here was a brother named *Lazarus;* his *Hebrew* name probably was *Eleazar*, which being contracted, and a Greek termination put to it, is made *Lazarus.* Perhaps in prospect of this history our Saviour made use of the name of *Lazarus* in that parable wherein he designed to set forth the blessedness of the righteous in the bosom of Abraham immediately after death, Luke xvi. 22. 3. Here were two sisters, *Martha* and *Mary*, who seem to have been the housekeepers, and to have managed the affairs of the family, while perhaps Lazarus lived a retired life, and gave himself to study and contemplation. Here was a decent, happy, well-ordered family, and a family that Christ was very much conversant with, where yet there was neither husband nor wife (for aught that appears), but the house kept by a brother, and his sisters dwelling together in unity. 4. One of the sisters is particularly described to be *that Mary which anointed the Lord with ointment*, *v.* 2. Some think she was that woman that we read of, Luke vii. 37, 38, who had been a *sinner*, a bad woman. I rather think it refers to that anointing of Christ which this evangelist relates (*ch.* xii. 3); for the evangelists do never refer one to another, but John frequently refers in one place of his gospel to another. Extraordinary acts of piety and devotion, that come from an honest principle of love to Christ, will not only find acceptance with him, but gain reputation in the church, Matt. xxvi. 13. This was she *whose brother Lazarus was sick;* and the sickness of those we love is our affliction. The more friends we have the more frequently we are thus afflicted by sympathy; and the dearer they are the more grievous it is. The multiplying of our comforts is but the multiplying of our cares and crosses.

II. The tidings that were sent to our Lord Jesus of the sickness of Lazarus, *v.* 3. *His sisters* knew where Jesus was, a great way off beyond Jordan, and they sent a special messenger to him, to acquaint him with the affliction of their family, in which they manifest, 1. The affection and concern they had for their brother. Though, it is likely, his estate would come to them after his death, yet they earnestly desired his life, as they ought to do. They showed their love to him now that he was sick, for a *brother is born for adversity*, and so is a sister too. We must weep with our friends when they weep, as well as rejoice with them when they rejoice. 2. The regard they had to the Lord Jesus, whom they were willing to make acquainted with all their concerns, and, like Jephthah, to utter all their words before him. Though God knows all our wants, and griefs, and cares, he will know them from us, and is honoured by our laying them before him.

The message they sent was very short, not *petitioning*, much less *prescribing* or *pressing*, but barely relating the case with the tender insinuation of a powerful plea, *Lord, behold, he whom thou lovest is sick*. They do not say, He whom *we* love, but *he whom thou lovest.* Our greatest encouragements in prayer are fetched from God himself and from his grace. They do not say, Lord, behold, he *who loveth thee*, but *he whom thou lovest ;* for *herein is love, not that we loved God, but that he loved us*. Our love to him is not worth speaking of, but his to us can never be enough spoken of. Note, (1.) There are some of the friends and followers of the Lord Jesus for whom he has a special kindness above others. Among the twelve there was one whom Jesus loved. (2.) It is no new thing for those whom Christ loves to be sick: all things come alike to all. Bodily distempers correct the corruption, and try the graces, of God's people. (3.) It is a great comfort to us, when we are sick, to have those about us that will pray for us. (4.) We have great encouragement in our prayers for those who are sick, if we have ground to hope that they are such as Christ loves; and we have reason to love and pray for those whom we have reason to think Christ loves and cares for.

III. An account how Christ entertained the tidings brought him of the illness of his friend.

1. He prognosticated the event and issue of the sickness, and probably sent it as a message to the sisters of Lazarus by the express, to support them while he delayed to come to them. Two things he prognosticates :—

(1.) *This sickness is not unto death.* It was mortal, proved *fatal*, and no doubt but Lazarus was truly dead for four days. But, [1.] That was not the errand upon which this sickness was sent; it came not, as in a common case, to be a summons to the grave, but there was a further intention in it. Had it been sent on that errand, his *rising from the dead would have defeated it.* [2.] That was not the final effect of this sickness. He *died*, and yet it might be said he did not *die*, for *factum non dicitur quod non perseverat—That is not said to be done which is not done for a perpetuity.* Death is an everlasting farewell to this world; it is the way whence we shall not return; and in this sense it was *not unto death.* The grave was not his *long home*, his *house of eternity.* Thus Christ said of the maid whom he proposed to restore to life, *She is not dead.* The sickness of good people, how threatening soever, is *not unto death,* for it is not unto *eternal* death. The body's death to this world is the soul's birth into another world; when we or our friends are sick, we make it our principal support that there is hope of a recovery, but in that we may be disappointed; therefore it is our wisdom to build upon that in which we cannot be disappointed; if they belong to Christ, let the worst come to the worst, they cannot be *hurt of the second death,* and then not much hurt of the first.

(2.) *But it is for the glory of God,* that an opportunity may be given for the manifesting of God's glorious power. The afflictions of the saints are designed for the glory of God, that he may have opportunity of showing them favour; for the sweetest mercies, and the most affecting, are those which are occasioned by trouble. Let this reconcile us to the darkest dispensations of Providence, they are all for the glory of God, this sickness, this loss, or this disappointment, is so; and, if God be glorified, we ought to be satisfied, Lev. x. 3. It was for the glory of God, for it was *that the Son of God might be glorified thereby,* as it gave him occasion to work that glorious miracle, the *raising of him from the dead.* As, before, the man was *born blind* that Christ might have the honour of curing him (*ch.* ix. 3), so Lazarus must be sick and die, that Christ may be glorified as the Lord of life. Let this comfort those whom Christ loves under all their grievances that the design of them all is that *the Son of God may be glorified thereby,* his wisdom, power, and goodness, glorified in supporting and relieving them; see 2 Cor. xii. 9, 10.

2. He deferred visiting his patient, *v.* 5, 6. They had pleaded, *Lord, it is he whom thou lovest,* and the plea is allowed (*v.* 5): *Jesus loved Martha, and her sister, and Lazarus.* Thus the claims of faith are ratified in the court of heaven. Now one would think it should follow, *When he heard therefore that he was sick* he made all the haste that he could to him; if he loved them, now was a time to show it by hastening to them, for he knew they impatiently expected him. But he took the contrary way to show his love: it is not said, He loved them and *yet* he lingered; but he loved them and *therefore* he lingered; when he heard that his friend was sick, instead of coming post to him, he abode *two days still in the same place where he was.* (1.) He *loved them,* that is, had a great opinion of Martha and Mary, of their wisdom and grace, of their faith and patience, above others of his disciples, and therefore he deferred coming to them, that he might try them, that their trial might at last *be found to praise and honour.* (2.) He *loved them,* that is, he designed to do something great and extraordinary for them, to work such a miracle for their relief as he had not wrought for any of his friends; and therefore he delayed coming to them, that Lazarus might be *dead* and *buried* before he came. If Christ had come presently, and cured the sickness of Lazarus, he had done no more than he did for *many ;* if he had raised him to life when newly dead, no more than he had done for *some :* but, deferring his relief so long, he had an opportunity of doing more for him than for *any.* Note, God hath gracious intentions even in seeming delays, Isa. liv. 7, 8; xlix. 14, &c. Christ's friends at Bethany were

not out of his thoughts, though, when he heard of their distress, he made no haste to them. When the work of deliverance, temporal or spiritual, public or personal, stands at a stay, it does but stay the time, and *every thing is beautiful in its season.*

IV. The discourse he had with his disciples when he was about to visit his friends at Bethany, *v.* 7—16. The conference is so very free and familiar as to make out what Christ saith, *I have called you friends.* Two things he discourses about—his own *danger* and Lazarus's *death.*

1. His own danger in going into Judea, *v.* 7—10.

(1.) Here is the notice which Christ gave his disciples of his purpose to go into Judea towards Jerusalem. His disciples were the men of his counsel, and to them he saith (*v.* 7), "*Let us go into Judea again,* though those of Judea are unworthy of such a favour." Thus Christ repeats the tenders of his mercy to those who have often rejected them. Now this may be considered, [1.] As a purpose of his kindness to his friends at Bethany, whose affliction, and all the aggravating circumstances of it, he knew very well, though no more expresses were sent to him; for he was present in spirit, though absent in body. When he knew they were brought to the last extremity, when the brother and sisters had given and taken a final farewell, "Now," saith he, "let us go to Judea." Christ will arise in favour of his people when *the time to favour them, yea, the set time, is come;* and the worst time is commonly the set time—when *our hope is lost, and we are cut off for our parts;* then they shall *know that I am the Lord* when *I have opened the graves,* Ezek. xxxvii. 11, 13. In the depths of affliction, let this therefore keep us out of the depths of despair, that man's extremity is God's opportunity, *Jehovah-jireh.* Or, [2.] As a trial of the courage of the disciples, whether they would venture to follow him thither, where they had so lately been frightened by an attempt upon their Master's life, which they looked upon as an attempt upon theirs too. To go to Judea, which was so lately made *too hot* for them, was a saying that *proved them.* But Christ did not say, "*Go you into Judea,* and I will stay and take shelter here;" no, *Let us go.* Note, Christ never brings his people into any peril but he accompanies them in it, and is with them even when they *walk through the valley of the shadow of death.*

(2.) Their objection against this journey (*v.* 8): *Master, the Jews of late sought to stone thee, and goest thou thither again?* Here, [1.] They remind him of the danger he had been in there not long since. Christ's disciples are apt to make a greater matter of sufferings than their Master does, and to remember injuries longer. He had put up with the affront, it was over and gone, and forgotten, but his disciples could not forget it; *of late, νυν—now,* as if it were this very day, they *sought to stone thee.* Though it was at least two months ago, the remembrance of the fright was fresh in their minds. [2.] They marvel that he will *go thither again.* "Wilt thou favour those with thy presence that have expelled thee out of their coasts?" Christ's ways in passing by offences are *above our ways.* "Wilt thou expose thyself among a people that are so desperately enraged against thee? *Goest thou thither again,* where thou hast been so ill used?" Here they showed great care for their Master's safety, as Peter did, when he said, *Master, spare thyself;* had Christ been inclined to shift off suffering, he did not want friends to persuade him to it, but he had *opened his mouth to the Lord,* and he would not, he could not, go back. Yet, while the disciples show a concern for his safety, they discover at the same time, *First,* A distrust of his power; as if he could not secure both himself and them now in Judea as well as he had done formerly. Is his arm shortened? When we are solicitous for the interests of Christ's church and kingdom in the world, we must yet rest satisfied in the wisdom and power of the Lord Jesus, who knows how to secure a flock of sheep in the midst of a herd of wolves. *Secondly,* A secret fear of suffering themselves; for they count upon this if he suffer. When our own private interests happen to run in the same channel with those of the public, we are apt to think ourselves zealous for the Lord of hosts, when really we are only zealous for our own wealth, credit, ease, and safety, and *seek our own things,* under colour of seeking the things of Christ; we have therefore need nicely to distinguish upon our principles.

(3.) Christ's answer to this objection (*v.* 9, 10): *Are there not twelve hours in the day?* The Jews divided every day into twelve hours, and made their hours longer or shorter according as the days were, so that an hour with them was the twelfth part of the time between sun and sun; so some. Or, lying much more south than we, their days were nearer twelve hours long than ours. The divine Providence has given us day-light to work by, and lengthens it out to a competent time; and, reckoning the year round, *every country* has just as much *daylight* as *night,* and so much more as the *twilights* amount to. Man's life is a *day;* this day is divided into divers ages, states, and opportunities, as into hours shorter or longer, as God has appointed; the consideration of this should make us not only *very busy,* as to the *work* of life (if there were *twelve hours in the day,* each of them ought to be filled up with duty, and none of *them* trifled away), but also *very easy* as to the perils of life; our day shall be lengthened out till our work be done, and our testimony finished. This Christ applies to his case, and shows why he must go to Judea, because he had a *clear call* to go

For the opening of this, [1.] He shows the comfort and satisfaction which a man has in his own mind while he keeps in the way of his duty, as it is in general prescribed by the word of God, and particularly determined by the providence of God: *If any man walk in the day, he stumbles not;* that is, If a man keep close to his duty, and mind that, and set the will of God before him as his rule, with an impartial respect to all God's commandments, he does not *hesitate* in his own mind, but, *walking uprightly, walks surely*, and with a holy confidence. As he that walks in the day stumbles not, but goes on steadily and cheerfully in his way, *because he sees the light of this world*, and by it sees his way before him; so a good man, without any collateral security or sinister aims, relies upon the word of God as his rule, and regards the glory of God as his end, *because he sees* those two great lights, and keeps his eye upon them; thus he is furnished with a faithful guide in all his doubts, and a powerful guard in all his dangers, Gal. vi. 4; Ps. cxix. 6. Christ, wherever he went, walked *in the day*, and so shall we, if we follow his steps. [2.] He shows the pain and peril a man is in who walks not according to this rule (*v.* 10): *If a man walk in the night, he stumbles;* that is, If a man walk in the way of his heart, and the sight of his eyes, and according to the course of this world,—if he consult his own carnal reasonings more than the will and glory of God,—he falls into temptations and snares, is liable to great uneasiness and frightful apprehensions, trembles at the *shaking of a leaf*, and *flees* when none *pursues;* while an upright man *laughs at the shaking of the spear*, and stands undaunted when ten thousand invade. See Isa. xxxiii. 14—16. He stumbles, *because there is no light in him*, for light in us is that to our moral actions which light about us is to our natural actions. He has not a good principle within; he is not sincere; his eye is evil. Thus Christ not only justifies his purpose of going into Judea, but encourages his disciples to go along with him, and fear no evil.

2. The death of Lazarus is here discoursed of between Christ and his disciples, *v.* 11—16, where we have,

(1.) The notice Christ gave his disciples of the death of Lazarus, and an intimation that his business into Judea was to look after him, *v.* 11. After he had prepared his disciples for this dangerous march into an enemy's country, he then gives them,

[1.] Plain intelligence of the death of Lazarus, though he had received no advice of it: *Our friend Lazarus sleepeth.* See here how Christ calls a believer and a believer's death

First, He calls a believer his friend: *Our friend Lazarus.* Note, 1. There is a covenant of friendship between Christ and believers, and a friendly affection and communion pursuant to it, which our Lord Jesus will own and not be ashamed of. *His secret is with the righteous.* 2. Those whom Christ is pleased to own as his friends all his disciples should take for *theirs.* Christ speaks of Lazarus as their common friend: *Our friend.* 3. Death itself does not break the bond of friendship between Christ and a believer. Lazarus is dead, and yet he is still *our friend.*

Secondly, He calls the death of a believer a *sleep: he sleepeth.* It is good to call death by such names and titles as will help to make it more *familiar* and less *formidable* to us. The death of Lazarus was in a peculiar sense a sleep, as that of Jairus's daughter, because he was to be raised again speedily; and, since we are sure to *rise again at last,* why should that make any great difference? And why should not the believing hope of that resurrection to eternal life make it as easy to us to put off the body and die as it is to put off our clothes and go to sleep? A good Christian, when he dies, does but sleep: he rests from the labours of the day past, and is refreshing himself for the next morning. Nay, herein death has the advantage of sleep, that sleep is only the *parenthesis,* but death is the *period,* of our cares and toils. The soul does not sleep, but becomes more active; but the body sleeps without any toss, without any terror; not distempered nor disturbed. The grave to the wicked is a prison, and its grave-clothes as the shackles of a criminal reserved for execution; but to the godly it is a bed, and all its bands as the soft and downy fetters of an easy quiet sleep. Though the body *corrupt,* it will rise in the morning as if it had never seen corruption; it is but putting off our clothes to be mended and trimmed up for the marriage day, the coronation day, to which we must rise. See Isa. lvii. 2; 1 Thess. iv. 14. The Greeks called their burying-places *dormitories*—*κοιμητήρια.*

[2.] Particular intimations of his favourable intentions concerning Lazarus: *but I go, that I may awake him out of sleep.* He could have done it, and yet have staid where he was: he that restored at a distance one that was *dying* (*ch.* iv. 50) could have raised at a distance one that was *dead;* but he would put this honour upon the miracle, to work it by the grave side: *I go, to awake him.* As sleep is a resemblance of death, so a man's awaking out of sleep when he is called, especially when he is called by his own name, is an emblem of the resurrection (Job xiv. 15): *Then shalt thou call.* Christ had no sooner said, *Our friend sleeps,* but presently he adds, *I go, that I may awake him.* When Christ tells his people at any time how bad the case is he lets them know in the same breath how easily, how quickly, he can mend it. Christ's telling his disciples that this was his business to Judea might help to take off their fear of going with him thither; he did not go upon a public errand to the temple, but a private visit, which would not so much expose him and them; and, besides, it was to do a kindness to a family to which they were all obliged.

(2.) Their mistake of the meaning of this notice, and the blunder they made about it (*v.* 12, 13): They said, *Lord, if he sleep, he shall do well.* This intimates, [1.] *Some concern* they had for their friend Lazarus; they hoped he would recover; *σωθήσεται—he shall be saved* from dying at this time. Probably they had understood, by the messenger who brought news of his illness, that one of the most threatening symptoms he was under was that he was restless, and could get no sleep; and now that they heard he slept they concluded the fever was going off, and the worst was past. Sleep is often nature's physic, and reviving to its weak and weary powers. This is true of the sleep of death; if a good Christian so *sleep*, he shall do well, better than he did here. [2.] A *greater concern* for themselves; for hereby they insinuate that it was now needless for Christ to go to him, and expose himself and them. "If he sleep, he will be quickly well, and we may stay where we are." Thus we are willing to hope that the good work which we are called to do will do itself, or will be done by some other hand, if there be peril in the doing of it.

(3.) This mistake of theirs rectified (*v.* 13): *Jesus spoke of his death.* See here, [1.] How dull of understanding Christ's disciples as yet were. Let us not therefore condemn all those as heretics who mistake the sense of some of Christ's sayings. It is not good to aggravate our brethren's mistakes; yet this was a *gross* one, for it had easily been prevented if they had remembered how frequently death is called a sleep in the Old Testament. They should have understood Christ when he spoke scripture language. Besides, it would sound oddly for their Master to undertake a journey of two or three days only to awake a friend out of a natural sleep, which any one else might do. What Christ undertakes to do, we may be sure, is something great and uncommon, and a work *worthy of himself.* [2.] How carefully the evangelist corrects this error: *Jesus spoke of his death.* Those that speak in an unknown tongue, or use similitudes, should learn hence to *explain themselves,* and pray that they may interpret, to prevent mistakes.

(4.) The plain and express declaration which Jesus made to them of the death of Lazarus, and his resolution to go to Bethany, *v.* 14, 15. [1.] He gives them notice of the death of Lazarus; what he had before said darkly he now says plainly, and without a figure: *Lazarus is dead, v.* 14. Christ takes cognizance of the death of his saints, for it is precious in his sight (Ps. cxvi. 15), and he is not pleased if we do not consider it, and lay it to heart. See what a compassionate teacher Christ is, and how he condescends to those that are out of the way, and by his subsequent sayings and doings explains the difficulties of what went before. [2.] He gives them the reason why he had delayed so long to go and see him: *I am glad for your sakes that I was not there.* If he had been there time enough, he would have healed his disease and prevented his death, which would have been much for the comfort of Lazarus's friends; but then his disciples would have seen no further proof of his power than what they had often seen, and, consequently, their faith had received no improvement; but now that he went and raised him from the dead, as there were many brought to *believe on him* who before did not (*v.* 45), so there was much done towards the perfecting of what was lacking in the faith of those that did, which Christ aimed at: *To the intent that you may believe.* [3.] He resolves now to go to Bethany, and take his disciples along with him: *Let us go unto him.* Not, "Let us go to his sisters, to comfort them" (which is the utmost we can do), but, Let us go *to him;* for Christ can *show wonders to the dead.* Death, which will separate us from all our other friends, and cut us off from correspondence with them, cannot separate us from the love of Christ, nor put us out of the reach of his calls; as he will maintain his *covenant with the dust,* so he can make visits to the dust. *Lazarus is dead,* but *let us go to him;* though perhaps those who said, If he sleep there is *no need* to go, were ready to say, If he be dead it is to *no purpose* to go.

(5.) Thomas exciting his fellow-disciples cheerfully to attend their Master's motions (*v.* 16): *Thomas, who is called Didymus.* Thomas in Hebrew and Didymus in Greek signify a *twin;* it is said of Rebekah (Gen. xxv. 24) that there were *twins in her womb;* the word is *Thomim.* Probably Thomas was a *twin.* He said *to his fellow-disciples* (who probably looked with fear and concern upon one another when Christ had said so positively, *Let us go to him),* very courageously, *Let us also go that we may die with him; with him,* that is,

[1.] With Lazarus, who was now dead; so some take it. Lazarus was a dear and loving friend both to Christ and his disciples, and perhaps Thomas had a particular intimacy with him. Now if he be dead, saith he, *let us* even *go and die with him.* For, *First,* "If we *survive,* we know not how to *live without him.*" Probably Lazarus had done them many good offices, sheltered them, and provided for them, and been to them *instead of eyes;* and now that he was gone they had *no man like-minded,* and "Therefore," saith he, "we had as good die with him." Thus we are sometimes ready to think our lives bound up in the lives of some that were dear to us: but God will teach us to live, and to live comfortably, upon himself, when those are gone without whom we thought we could not live. But this is not all. *Secondly,* "If we die, we hope to be *happy with him.*" Such a firm belief he has of a happiness on the other side death, and such good hope through grace of their own and Lazarus's interest in it, that he is willing they should all go and *die with him.* It is better to die, and go along with our Christian friends to that world which is enriched by their removal to it, than stay behind in a world that is impoverished by their departure out of it. The more of our friends are translated hence, the fewer cords we have to bind us to this earth, and the more to draw our hearts heavenwards. How pleasantly does the good man speak of dying, as if it were but undressing and going to bed!

[2.] "Let us go and die *with our Master,* who is now exposing himself to death by venturing into Judea;" and so I rather think it is meant. "If he will go into danger, let us also go and take our lot with him, according to the command we received, *Follow me.*" Thomas knew so much of the malice of the Jews against Christ, and the counsels of God concerning him, which he had often told them of, that it was no foreign supposition that he was now going to die. And now Thomas manifests, *First,* A gracious readiness to die with Christ himself, flowing from strong affections to him, though his faith was weak, as appeared afterwards, *ch.* xiv. 5; xx. 25. *Where thou diest I will die,* Ruth i. 17. *Secondly,* A zealous desire to help his fellow-disciples into the same frame: "*Let us go,* one and all, and *die with him;* if they stone him, let them stone us; who would desire to survive such a Master?" Thus, in difficult times, Christians should animate one another. We may each of us say, *Let us die with him.* Note, The consideration of the dying of the Lord Jesus should make us willing to die whenever God calls for us.

17 Then when Jesus came, he
found that he had *lain* in the grave
four days already. 18 Now Bethany
was nigh unto Jerusalem, about fifteen furlongs off: 19 And many of
the Jews came to Martha and Mary,
to comfort them concerning their
brother. 20 Then Martha, as soon
as she heard that Jesus was coming,
went and met him: but Mary sat *still*
in the house. 21 Then said Martha
unto Jesus, Lord, if thou hadst been
here, my brother had not died. 22
But I know, that even now, whatsoever thou wilt ask of God, God will
give *it* thee. 23 Jesus saith unto her,
Thy brother shall rise again. 24
Martha saith unto him, I know that
he shall rise again in the resurrection
at the last day. 25 Jesus said unto
her, I am the resurrection, and the
life: he that believeth in me, though
he were dead, yet shall he live: 26
And whosoever liveth and believeth
in me shall never die. Believest
thou this? 27 She saith unto him,
Yea, Lord: I believe that thou art
the Christ, the Son of God, which
should come into the world. 28 And
when she had so said, she went her
way, and called Mary her sister secretly, saying, The Master is come,
and calleth for thee. 29 As soon as
she heard *that,* she arose quickly,
and came unto him. 30 Now Jesus
was not yet come into the town, but
was in that place where Martha met
him. 31 The Jews then which were
with her in the house, and comforted
her, when they saw Mary, that she
rose up hastily and went out, followed her, saying, She goeth unto the
grave to weep there. 32 Then when
Mary was come where Jesus was,
and saw him, she fell down at his
feet, saying unto him, Lord, if thou
hadst been here, my brother had not
died.

The matter being determined, that Christ will go to Judea, and his disciples with him, they address themselves to their journey; in this journey some circumstances happened which the other evangelists record, as the healing of the blind man at Jericho, and the conversion of Zaccheus. We must not reckon ourselves out of our way, while we are in the way of doing good; nor be so intent upon one good office as to neglect another.

At length, he comes near to Bethany, which is said to be about *fifteen furlongs* from Jerusalem, about two measured miles, *v.* 18. Notice is taken of this, that this miracle was in effect wrought *in Jerusalem,* and so was put to her score. Christ's miracles in Galilee were more *numerous,* but those in or near Jerusalem were more *illustrious;* there he healed one that had been diseased *thirty-eight years,* another that had been blind *from his birth,* and raised one that had been dead *four days.* To Bethany Christ came, and observe,

I. What posture he found his friends there in. When he had been last with them it is probable that he left them well, in health and joy; but when we part from our friends (though Christ knew) we know not what changes may affect us or them before we meet again.

1. He found his friend Lazarus *in the*

grave, v. 17. When he came near the town, probably by the burying-place belonging to the town, he was told by the neighbours, or some persons whom he met, that Lazarus had been *four days buried.* Some think that Lazarus died the same day that the messenger came to Jesus with the tidings of his sickness, and so reckon two days for his abode in the same place and two days for his journey. I rather think that Lazarus died at the very instant that Jesus said, "*Our friend sleepeth,* he is now newly fallen asleep;" and that the time between his death and burial (which among the Jews was but short), with the four days of his lying in the grave, was taken up in this journey; for Christ travelled publicly, as appears by his passing through Jericho, and his abode at Zaccheus's house took up some time. Promised salvations, though they always come surely, yet often come slowly.

2. He found his friends that survived *in grief.* Martha and Mary were almost swallowed up with sorrow for the death of their brother, which is intimated where it is said that *many of the Jews came to Martha and Mary to comfort them.* Note, (1.) Ordinarily, where death is there are *mourners,* especially when those that were agreeable and amiable to their relations, and serviceable to their generation, are taken away. The house where death is is called *the house of mourning,* Eccl. vii. 2. When man goes to his long home the *mourners go about the streets* (Eccl. xii. 5), or rather sit alone, and *keep silence.* Here was Martha's house, a house where the fear of God was, and on which his blessing rested, yet made a *house of mourning.* Grace will keep sorrow from the heart (*ch.* xiv. 1), not from the house. (2.) Where there are mourners there ought to be comforters. It is a duty we owe to those that are in sorrow to mourn with them, and to comfort them; and our mourning with them will be some comfort to them. When we are under the present impressions of grief, we are apt to forget those things which would minister comfort to us, and therefore have need of remembrancers. It is a mercy to have remembrancers when we are in sorrow, and our duty to be remembrancers to those who are in sorrow. The Jewish doctors laid great stress upon this, obliging their disciples to make conscience of comforting the mourners after the burial of the dead. They comforted them *concerning their brother,* that is, by speaking to them of him, not only of the good name he left behind, but of the happy state he was gone to. When godly relations and friends are taken from us, whatever occasion we have to be afflicted concerning ourselves, who are left behind and miss them, we have reason to be comforted concerning those who are gone before us to a happiness where they have no need of us. This visit which the Jews made to Martha and Mary is an evidence that they were persons of distinction, and made a figure; as also that they behaved obligingly to all; so that though they were followers of Christ, yet those who had no respect for him were civil to them. There was also a providence in it, that so many Jews, Jewish ladies it is probable, should come together, just at this time, to comfort the mourners, that they might be unexceptionable witnesses of the miracle, and see what miserable comforters they were, in comparison with Christ. Christ did not usually send for witnesses to his miracles, and yet had none been by but relations this would have been excepted against; therefore God's counsel so ordered it that these should come together accidentally, to bear their testimony to it, that infidelity might stop her mouth.

II. What passed between him and his surviving friends at this interview. When Christ defers his visits for a time they are thereby made the more acceptable, much the more welcome; so it was here. His departures endear his returns, and his absence teaches us how to value his presence. We have here,

1. The interview between Christ and Martha.

(1.) We are told that she *went and met him, v.* 20. [1.] It should seem that Martha was earnestly expecting Christ's arrival, and enquiring for it. Either she had sent out messengers, to bring her tidings of his first approach, or she had often asked, *Saw you him whom my soul loveth?* so that the first who discovered him ran to her with the welcome news. However it was, she heard of his coming before he arrived. She had waited long, and often asked, *Is he come?* and could hear no tidings of him; but long-looked-for came at last. *At the end the vision will speak, and not lie.* [2.] Martha, when the good news was brought that Jesus was coming, threw all aside, and *went and met him,* in token of a most affectionate welcome. She waived all ceremony and compliment to the Jews who came to visit her, and hastened to go and meet Jesus. Note, When God by his grace or providence is coming towards us in ways of mercy and comfort, we should go forth by faith, hope, and prayer to meet him. Some suggest that Martha went out of the town to meet Jesus, to let him know that there were several Jews in the house, who were no friends to him, that if he pleased he might keep out of the way of them. [3.] When Martha went to meet Jesus, Mary *sat still in the house.* Some think she did *not* hear the tidings, being in her drawing-room, receiving visits of condolence, while Martha who was busied in the household-affairs had early notice of it. Perhaps Martha would not tell her sister that Christ was coming, being ambitious of the honour of receiving him first. *Sancta est prudentia clam fratribus clam parentibus ad Christum esse conferre —Holy prudence conducts us to Christ, while brethren and parents know not what we are doing.*—Maldonat. in locum. Others think she *did* hear that Christ was come, but was so overwhelmed with sorrow that she did not care to stir, choosing rather to indulge her sorrow, and to sit poring upon her affliction, and saying, *I do well to* mourn. Comparing this story with that in Luke x. 38, &c., we may observe the different tempers of these two sisters, and the temptations and advantages of each. Martha's natural temper was active and busy; she loved to be here and there, and at the end of every thing; and this had been a snare to her when by it she was not only careful and cumbered about many things, but hindered from the exercises of devotion: but now in a day of affliction this active temper did her a kindness, kept the grief from her heart, and made her forward to meet Christ, and so she received comfort from him the sooner. On the other hand, Mary's natural temper was contemplative and reserved. This had been formerly an advantage to her, when it placed her at Christ's feet, to hear his word, and enabled her there to attend upon him without those distractions with which Martha was cumbered; but now in the day of affliction that same temper proved a snare to her, made her less able to grapple with her grief, and disposed her to melancholy: *But Mary sat still in the house.* See here how much it will be our wisdom carefully to watch against the temptations, and improve the advantages, of our natural temper.

(2.) Here is fully related the discourse between Christ and Martha.

[1.] Martha's address to Christ, *v.* 21, 22.

First, She complains of Christ's long absence and delay. She said it, not only with grief for the death of her brother, but with some resentment of the seeming unkindness of the Master: *Lord, if thou hadst been here, my brother had not died.* Here is, 1. Some evidence of faith. She believed Christ's *power,* that, though her brother's sickness was very grievous, yet he could have cured it, and so have prevented his death. She believed his *pity,* that if he had but seen Lazarus in his extreme illness, and his dear relations all in tears about him, he would have had compassion, and have prevented so sad a breach, for his compassions fail not. But, 2. Here are sad instances of unbelief. Her faith was true, but weak as a bruised reed, for she limits the power of Christ, in saying, *If thou hadst been here;* whereas she ought to have known that Christ could cure at a distance, and that his gracious operations were not limited to his bodily presence. She reflects likewise upon the wisdom and kindness of Christ, that he did not hasten to them when they sent for him, as if he had not *timed his business* well, and now might as well have staid away, and not have come at all, as to come too late; and, as for any help now, she can scarcely entertain the thought of it.

Secondly, Yet she corrects and comforts herself with the thoughts of the prevailing interest Christ had in heaven; at least, she blames herself for blaming her Master, and for suggesting that he comes too late: *for I know that even now,* desperate as the case is, *whatsoever thou wilt ask of God, God will give it to thee.* Observe, 1. How *willing* her hope was. Though she had not courage to ask of Jesus that he should raise him to life again, there having been no precedent as yet of any one raised to life that had been so long dead, yet, like a modest petitioner, she humbly recommends the case to the wise and compassionate consideration of the Lord Jesus. When we know not what in particular to ask or expect, let us in general refer ourselves to God, let him do as seemeth him good. *Judicii tui est, non præsumptionis meæ—I leave it to thy judgment, not to my presumption.*—Aug. in locum. When we know not what to pray for, it is our comfort that the great Intercessor knows what to ask for us, and is always heard. 2. How *weak* her faith was. She should have said, "Lord, thou canst do whatsoever thou wilt;" but she only says, "Thou canst obtain whatsoever thou prayest for." She had forgotten that the Son has *life in himself,* that he wrought miracles by his own power. Yet both these considerations must be taken in for the encouragement of our faith and hope, and neither excluded: the dominion Christ has on earth and his interest and intercession in heaven. He has in the one hand the golden sceptre, and in the other the golden censer; his power is always predominant, his intercession always prevalent.

[2.] The comfortable word which Christ gave to Martha, in answer to her pathetic address (*v.* 23): *Jesus saith unto her, Thy brother shall rise again.* Martha, in her complaint, looked back, reflecting with regret *that Christ was not there,* for then, thinks she, my brother had been now alive. We are apt, in such cases, to add to our own trouble, by fancying what *might have been.* "If such a method had been taken, such a physician employed, my friend had not died;" which is more than we know: but what good does this do? When God's will is done, our business is to submit to him. Christ directs Martha, and us in her, to look forward, and to think what *shall be,* for that is a certainty, and yields sure comfort: *Thy brother shall rise again. First,* This was true of Lazarus in a sense peculiar to him: he was now presently to be raised; but Christ speaks of it in general as a thing to be done, not which he himself would do, so humbly did our Lord Jesus speak of what he did. He also expresses it *ambiguously,* leaving her uncertain at first whether he would raise him presently or not till the last day, that he might try her faith and patience. *Secondly,* It is applicable to all the saints, and their resurrection at the last day. Note, It is matter of comfort to us, when we have buried our godly friends and relations, to think that they shall *rise again.* As the soul at death is not lost, but gone before, so the body is not lost, but laid up. Think you hear Christ saying, "Thy parent, thy child, thy yoke-fellow, shall rise again; *these dry bones shall live.*"

[3.] The faith which Martha mixed with this word, and the unbelief mixed with this faith, *v.* 24.

First, She accounts it a *faithful saying* that *he shall rise again at the last day.* Though the doctrine of the resurrection was to have its full proof from Christ's resurrection, yet, as it was already revealed, she firmly believed it, Acts xxiv. 15. 1. That there shall be a *last day,* with which all the days of time shall be numbered and finished. 2. That there shall be a *general* resurrection at that day, when the earth and sea shall give up their dead. 3. That there shall be a *particular* resurrection of each one: "I know that I shall rise again, and this and the other relation that was dear to me." As bone shall return to his bone in that day, so friend to his friend.

Secondly, Yet she seems to think this saying not so well worthy of all acceptation as really it was: "*I know he shall rise again at the last day;* but what are we the better for that now?" As if the comforts of the resurrection to eternal life were not worth speaking of, or yielded not satisfaction sufficient to balance her affliction. See our weakness and folly, that we suffer present sensible things to make a deeper impression upon us, both of grief and joy, than those things which are the objects of faith. *I know that he shall rise again at the last day;* and is not this enough? She seems to think it is not. Thus, by our discontent under present crosses, we greatly undervalue our future hopes, and put a slight upon them, as if not worth regarding.

[4.] The further instruction and encouragement which Jesus Christ gave her; for he will not quench the smoking flax nor break the bruised reed. He said to her, *I am the resurrection and the life, v.* 25, 26. Two things Christ possesses her with the belief of, in reference to the present distress; and they are the things which our faith should fasten upon in the like cases.

First, The power of Christ, his sovereign power: *I am the resurrection and the life,* the fountain of life, and the head and author of the resurrection. Martha believed that at his prayer God would give any thing, but he would have her know that by his word he could work any thing. Martha believed a resurrection at the *last day;* Christ tells her that he had that power lodged in his own hand, that the dead were to *hear his voice* (*ch.* v. 25), whence it was easy to infer, He that could raise a world of men that had been dead many ages could doubtless raise one man that had been dead but *four days.* Note, It is an unspeakable comfort to all good Christians that Jesus Christ is the resurrection and the life, and will be so to them. *Resurrection* is a return to life; Christ is the author of that return, and of that life to which it is a return. We look for the *resurrection of the dead* and the *life of the world to come,* and Christ is both; the author and principle of both, and the ground of our hope of both.

Secondly, The promises of the new covenant, which give us further ground of hope that *we shall live.* Observe,

a. To whom these promises are made—to those that believe in Jesus Christ, to those that consent to, and confide in, Jesus Christ as the only Mediator of reconciliation and communion between God and man, that receive the record God has given in his word concerning his Son, sincerely comply with it, and answer all the great intentions of it. The condition of the latter promise is thus expressed: *Whosoever liveth and believeth in me,* which may be understood, either, (*a.*) Of *natural* life: *Whosoever lives in this world,* whether he be Jew or Gentile, wherever he lives, if he believe in Christ, he shall live by him. Yet it limits the time: Whoever during *life,* while he is here in this state of probation, *believes in me,* shall be happy in me, but after death it will be too late. Whoever *lives* and *believes,* that is, lives by faith (Gal. ii. 20), has a faith that influences his conversation. Or, (*b.*) Of *spiritual* life: He that *lives* and *believes* is he that by faith is born again to a heavenly and divine life, to whom *to live is Christ*—that makes Christ the life of his soul.

b. What the promises are (*v.* 25): *Though he die, yet shall he live,* nay, *he shall never die, v.* 26. Man consists of body and soul, and provision is made for the happiness of both.

(*a.*) For the *body;* here is the promise of a *blessed resurrection.* Though the body be dead because of sin (there is no remedy but it will die), yet it *shall live again.* All the difficulties that attend the state of the dead are here overlooked, and made nothing of Though the sentence of death was just, though the effects of death be dismal, though the bands of death be strong, though he be dead and buried, dead and putrefied, though the scattered dust be so mixed with common dust that no art of man can distinguish, much less separate them, put the case as strongly as you will on that side, yet we are sure that *he shall live* again: the body shall be raised a glorious body.

(*b.*) For the *soul;* here is the promise of a *blessed immortality.* He that *liveth and believeth,* who, being united to Christ by faith, lives spiritually by virtue of that union, he shall *never die.* That spiritual life shall never be extinguished, but perfected in eternal life. As the soul, being in its nature spiritual, is therefore immortal; so if by faith it live a spiritual life, consonant to its nature, its felicity shall be immortal too. It *shall never die,* shall never be otherwise than easy and happy, and there is not any intermission or interruption of its life, as there is of the life of the body. The *mortality* of the body shall at length be *swallowed up of life;* but the life of the soul, the believing soul, shall be immediately at death swallowed up of immortality. *He shall not die, εἰς τὸν αἰῶνα, for ever—Non morietur in æternum;* so Cyprian quotes it. The body shall not be *for ever* dead in the grave; it dies (like the two witnesses) but for a *time, times, and the dividing of time;* and when time shall be no more, and all the divisions of it shall be numbered and finished, a *spirit of life from God shall enter into it.* But this is not all; the soul shall not die that death which is *for ever,* shall *not die eternally. Blessed and holy,* that is, blessed and happy, is he that by faith *has part in the first resurrection,* has part in Christ, who is that resurrection; for on such the *second death,* which is a death for ever, *shall have no power;* see *ch.* vi. 40. Christ asks her, "*Believest thou this?* Canst thou *assent* to it with application? Canst thou take my word for it?" Note, When we have read or heard the word of Christ, concerning the great things of the other world, we should seriously put it to ourselves, "*Do we believe this, this* truth in particular, *this* which is attended with so many difficulties, *this* which is suited to my case? Does my belief of it realize it to me, and give my soul an assurance of it, so that I can say not only *this* I believe, but *thus* I believe it?" Martha was doting upon her brother's being raised to life in this world; before Christ gave her hopes of this, he directed her thoughts to another life, another world: "No matter for *that,* but *believest thou this* that I tell thee concerning the *future* state?" The crosses and comforts of this present time would not make such an impression upon us as they do if we did but believe the things of eternity as we ought.

[5.] Martha's unfeigned assent yielded to what Christ said, *v.* 27. We have here Martha's creed, the good confession she witnessed, the same with that for which Peter was commended (Matt. xvi. 16, 17), and it is the *conclusion of the whole matter.*

First, Here is the *guide of her faith,* and that is the word of Christ; without any alteration, exception, or proviso, she takes it entire as Christ had said it: *Yea, Lord,* whereby she subscribes to the truth of all and every part of that which Christ had promised, in his own sense: *Even so.* Faith is an echo to divine revelation, returns the same words, and resolves to abide by them: *Yea, Lord, As the word did make it so I believe and take it,* said queen Elizabeth.

Secondly, The *ground of her faith,* and that is the authority of Christ; she believes *this* because she believes that he who saith it is Christ. She has recourse to the foundation for the support of the superstructure. *I believe, πεπίστευκα,* "*I have believed* that thou art Christ, and therefore *I do believe* this." Observe here,

a. What she believed and confessed concerning Jesus; three things, all to the same effect:—(*a.*) That he was the Christ, or Messiah, promised and expected under this name and notion, the *anointed one.* (*b.*) That he was the *Son of God;* so the Messiah was called (Ps. ii. 7), not by office only, but by nature. (*c.*) That it was *he who should come* into the world, the ὁ ἐρχόμενος. That blessing of blessings which the church had for so many ages waited for as *future,* she embraced as *present.*

b. What she inferred hence, and what she alleged this for. If she admits this, that Jesus is the Christ, there is no difficulty in believing that he is the resurrection and the life; for if he be the Christ, then, (*a.*) He is the fountain of light and truth, and we may take all his sayings for faithful and divine, upon his own word. If he be the Christ, he is that prophet whom we are to hear *in all things.* (*b.*) He is the fountain of life and blessedness, and we may therefore depend upon his ability as well as upon his veracity. How shall bodies, turned to dust, *live again?* How shall souls, clogged and clouded as ours are, *live for ever?* We could not believe this, but that we believe him that undertakes it to be *the Son of God,* who has life *in himself,* and has it for us.

2. The interview between Christ and Mary the other sister. And here observe,

(1.) The notice which Martha gave her of Christ's coming (*v.* 28): *When she had so said,* as one that needed to say no more, *she went her way,* easy in her mind, and *called Mary her sister.* [1.] Martha, having received instruction and comfort from Christ herself, called her sister to share with her. Time was when Martha would have drawn Mary from Christ, to come and help her in *much serving* (Luke x. 40); but, to make her amends for this, here she is industrious to draw her to Christ. [2.] She called her *secretly,* and whispered it in her ear, because there was company by, Jews, who were no friends to Christ. The saints are called *into the fellowship of Jesus Christ* by an invitation that is secret and distinguishing, given to them and not to others; they have meat to eat that the world knows not of, joy that a stranger does not intermeddle with. [3.] She called her by order from Christ; he bade her *go call her sister.* The call that is *effectual,* whoever brings it, is sent by Christ. *The Master is come, and calleth for thee. First,* She calls Christ *the Master, διδάσκαλος,* a *teaching master;* by that title he was commonly called and known among them. Mr. George Herbert took pleasure in calling Christ, *my Master. Secondly,* She triumphs in his arrival: *The Master is come.* He whom we have long wished and waited for, *he is come, he is come;* this was the best cordial in the present distress. "Lazarus gone, and our comfort in him is gone; but the *Master is come,* who is better than the dearest friend, and has that in him which will abundantly make up all our losses. He is come who is our *teacher,* who will teach us how to get good by our sorrow (Ps. xciv. 12), who will *teach,* and so comfort." *Thirdly,* She invites her sister to go and meet him: "*He calls for thee,* enquires what is become of thee, and would have thee sent for." Note, When Christ our Master comes, he *calls for us.* He comes in his word and ordinances, calls us to them, calls us by them, calls us to himself. He calls for thee in particular, for thee *by name* (Ps. xxvii. 8); and, if he call thee, he will cure thee, he will comfort thee.

(2.) The haste which Mary made to Christ upon this notice given her (*v.* 29): *As soon as she heard* this good news, that the *Master was come,* she *arose quickly,* and came to him. She little thought how near he was to her, for he is often nearer to them that mourn in Zion than they are aware of; but, when she knew how near he was, she started up, and in a transport of joy ran to meet him. The least intimation of Christ's gracious approaches is enough to a lively faith, which stands ready to take the hint, and answer the first call. When Christ was come, [1.] She did not consult the decorum of her mourning, but, forgetting ceremony, and the common usage in such cases, she ran through the town, to meet Christ. Let no nice punctilios of decency and honour deprive us at any time of opportunities of conversing with Christ. [2.] She did not consult her neighbours, the Jews that were *with her, comforting her;* she left them all, to come to him, and did not only not ask their advice, but not so much as ask their leave, or beg their pardon for her rudeness.

(3.) We are told (*v.* 30) where she found the Master; he was not yet come into Bethany, but was at the town's end, *in that place where Martha met him.* See here, [1.] Christ's love to his work. He staid near the place where the grave was, that he might be ready to go to it. He would not go into the town, to *refresh himself* after the fatigue of his journey, till he had done the work he came to do; nor would he go into the town, lest it should look like ostentation, and a design to levy a crowd to be spectators of the miracle. [2.] Mary's love to Christ; still she *loved much.* Though Christ had seemed unkind in his delays, yet she could take nothing amiss from him. Let us go thus to Christ *without the camp,* Heb. xiii. 13.

(4.) The misconstruction which the Jews that were with Mary made of her going away so hastily (*v.* 31): They said, *She goes to the grave, to weep there.* Martha bore up better under this affliction than Mary did, who was a woman of a tender and sorrowful spirit; such was her natural temper. Those that are so have need to watch against melancholy, and ought to be pitied and helped. These comforters found that their formalities did her no service, but that she hardened herself in sorrow: and therefore concluded when she went out, and turned that way, it was to go *to the grave* and *weep there.* See, [1.] What often is the folly and fault of mourners; they contrive how to aggravate their own grief, and to make bad worse. We are apt in such cases to take a strange pleasure in our own pain, and to say, *We do well* to be passionate in our grief, even unto death; we are apt to fasten upon those things that aggravate the affliction, and what good does this do us, when it is our duty to reconcile ourselves to the will of God in it? Why should mourners go to the grave to weep there, when they sorrow not as those that have no hope? Affliction of itself is grievous; why should we make it more so? [2.] What is the wisdom and duty of comforters; and that is, to prevent as much as may be, in those who grieve inordinately, the revival of the sorrow, and to divert it. Those Jews that followed Mary were thereby led to Christ, and became the witnesses of one of his most glorious miracles. It is good cleaving to Christ's friends in their sorrows, for thereby we may come to know him better.

(5.) Mary's address to our Lord Jesus (*v.* 32): She came, attended with her train of comforters, and *fell down at his feet,* as one overwhelmed with a passionate sorrow, and said with many tears (as appears *v.* 33), *Lord, if thou hadst been here, my brother had not died,* as Martha said before, for they had often said it to one another. Now here, [1.] Her posture is very humble and submissive: *She fell down at his feet,* which was more than Martha did, who had a greater command of her passions. She fell down as a sinking mourner, but fell down at his feet as a humble petitioner. This Mary had sat *at Christ's feet to hear his word* (Luke x. 39), and here we find her there on another errand. Note, Those that in a day of peace place themselves at Christ's feet, to receive instructions from him, may with comfort and confidence in a day of trouble cast themselves at his feet with hope to find favour with him. She *fell at his feet,* as one submitting to his will in what was done, and referring herself to his good-will in what was now to be done. When we are in affliction we must cast ourselves at Christ's feet in a penitent sorrow and self-abasement for sin, and a patient resignation of ourselves to the divine disposal. Mary's casting herself at Christ's feet was in token of the profound respect and veneration she had for him. Thus subjects were wont to give honour to their kings and princes; but, our Lord Jesus not appearing in secular glory as an earthly prince, those who by this posture of adoration gave honour to him certainly looked upon him as more than man, and intended hereby to give him divine honour. Mary hereby made profession of the

Christian faith as truly as Martha did, and in effect said, *I believe that thou art the Christ; bowing the knee to* Christ, and *confessing him with the tongue,* are put together as equivalent, Rom. xiv. 11; Phil. ii.10, 11. This she did in presence of *the Jews* that attended her, who, though friends to her and her family, yet were bitter enemies to Christ; yet in their sight she fell at Christ's feet, as one that was neither ashamed to own the veneration she had for Christ nor afraid of disobliging her friends and neighbours by it. Let them resent it as they pleased, she falls at his feet; and, if this be to be vile, she will be yet more vile; see Cant. viii. 1. We serve a Master of whom we have no reason to be ashamed, and whose acceptance of our services is sufficient to balance the reproach of men and all their revilings. [2.] Her address is very pathetic: *Lord, if thou hadst been here, my brother had not died.* Christ's delay was designed for the best, and proved so; yet both the sisters very indecently *cast the same in his teeth,* and in effect charge him with the death of their brother. This repeated challenge he might justly have resented, might have told them he had something else to do than to be at their beck and to attend them; he must come when his business would permit him: but not a word of this; he considered the circumstances of their affliction, and that losers think they may have leave to speak, and therefore overlooked the rudeness of this welcome, and gave us an example of mildness and meekness in such cases. Mary added no more, as Martha did; but it appears, by what follows, that what she fell short in words she made up in tears; she said less than Martha, but wept more; and tears of devout affection have a voice, a loud prevailing voice, in the ears of Christ; no rhetoric like this.

33 When Jesus therefore saw her
weeping, and the Jews also weeping
which came with her, he groaned in
the spirit, and was troubled. 34
And said, Where have ye laid him?
They said unto him, Lord, come and
see. 35 Jesus wept. 36 Then said
the Jews, Behold how he loved him!
37 And some of them said, Could not
this man, which opened the eyes of
the blind, have caused that even this
man should not have died? 38 Jesus therefore again groaning in himself cometh to the grave. It was a
cave, and a stone lay upon it. 39
Jesus said, Take ye away the stone.
Martha, the sister of him that was
dead, saith unto him, Lord, by this
time he stinketh: for he hath been
dead four days. 40 Jesus saith unto
her, Said I not unto thee, that, if
thou wouldest believe, thou shouldest
see the glory of God? 41 Then they
took away the stone *from the place*
where the dead was laid. And Jesus
lifted up *his* eyes, and said, Father, I
thank thee that thou hast heard me.
42 And I knew that thou hearest me
always: but because of the people
which stand by I said *it,* that they
may believe that thou hast sent me.
43 And when he thus had spoken, he
cried with a loud voice, Lazarus, come
forth. 44 And he that was dead
came forth, bound hand and foot
with graveclothes: and his face was
bound about with a napkin. Jesus
saith unto them, Loose him, and let
him go.

Here we have, I. Christ's tender *sympathy* with his afflicted friends, and the share he took to himself in their sorrows, which appeared three ways:—

1. By the inward groans and troubles of his spirit (*v.* 33): *Jesus saw Mary weeping* for the loss of a loving brother, and the *Jews that came with her weeping* for the loss of a good neighbour and friend; when he saw what a *place of weepers,* a *bochim,* this was, *he groaned in the spirit, and was troubled.* See here,

(1.) The griefs of the sons of men represented in the tears of Mary and her friends. What an emblem was here of this world, this vale of tears! Nature itself teaches us to weep over our dear relations, when they are removed by death; Providence thereby calls to *weeping and mourning.* It is probable that Lazarus's estate devolved upon his sisters, and was a considerable addition to their fortunes; and in such a case people say, now-a-days, though they cannot wish their relations dead (that is, they do not say they do), yet, if they were dead, they would not wish them alive again; but these sisters, whatever they got by their brother's death, heartily wished him alive again. Religion teaches us likewise to *weep with them that weep,* as these Jews wept with Mary, considering that we ourselves also *are in the body.* Those that truly love their friends will share with them in their joys and griefs; for what is friendship but a communication of affections? Job xvi. 5.

(2.) The grace of the Son of God and his compassion towards those that are in misery. *In all their afflictions he is afflicted,* Isa. lxiii 9; Judg. x. 16. When Christ saw them all in tears,

[1.] He *groaned in the spirit.* He suffered himself to be tempted (as we are when we are disturbed by some great affliction), *yet without sin.* This was an expression, either,

First, Of his displeasure at the inordinate grief of those about him, as Mark v. 39: "*Why make ye this ado and weep?* What a hurry is here! does this become those that believe in a God, a heaven, and another world?" Or, *Secondly,* Of his feeling sense of the calamitous state of human life, and the power of death, to which fallen man is subject. Having now to make a vigorous attack upon death and the grave, he thus stirred up himself to the encounter, *put on the garments of vengeance,* and *his fury it upheld him;* and that he might the more resolutely undertake the redress of our grievances, and the cure of our griefs, he was pleased to make himself sensible of the weight of them, and under the burden of them he now *groaned in spirit.* Or, *Thirdly,* It was an expression of his kind sympathy with his friends that were in sorrow. Here was the sounding of the bowels, the mercies which the afflicted church so earnestly solicits, Is. lxiii. 15. Christ not only seemed concerned, but he *groaned in the spirit;* he was inwardly and sincerely affected with the case. David's pretended friends counterfeited sympathy, to disguise their enmity (Ps. xli. 6); but we must learn of Christ to have our love and sympathy *without dissimulation.* Christ's was a deep and hearty sigh.

[2.] He was *troubled.* He *troubled himself;* so the phrase is, very significantly. He had all the passions and affections of the human nature, for in all things he must *be like to his brethren;* but he had a perfect command of them, so that they were never *up,* but *when* and *as* they were called; he was never troubled, but when he *troubled himself,* as he saw cause. He often *composed* himself to trouble, but was never discomposed or disordered by it. He was voluntary both in his passion and in his compassion. He had power to lay down his grief, and power to take it again.

2. His concern for them appeared by his *kind enquiry* after the poor remains of his deceased friend (*v.* 34): Where *have you laid him?* He knew where he was laid, and yet asks, because, (1.) He would thus express himself as *a man,* even when he was going to exert the power of a God. Being found in fashion as a man, he accommodates himself to the way and manner of the sons of men: *Non nescit, sed quasi nescit—He is not ignorant, but he makes as if he were,* saith Austin here. (2.) He enquired where the grave was, lest, if he had gone straight to it of his own knowledge, the unbelieving Jews should have thence taken occasion to suspect a collusion between him and Lazarus, and a trick in the case. Many expositors observe this from Chrysostom. (3.) He would thus divert the grief of his mourning friends, by raising their expectations of something great; as if he had said, "I did not come hither with an address of condolence, to mingle a few fruitless insignificant tears with yours; no, I have other work to do; come, let us adjourn to the grave, and go about our business there." Note, A serious address to our work is the best remedy against inordinate grief. (4.) He would hereby intimate to us the special care he takes of the bodies of the saints while they lie in the grave; he takes notice *where they are laid,* and will look after them. There is not only a covenant with the dust, but a guard upon it.

3. It appeared by *his tears.* Those about him did not tell him where the body was buried, but desired him to *come and see,* and led him directly to the grave, that his eye might yet more affect his heart with the calamity.

(1.) As he was going to the grave, as if he had been following the corpse thither, *Jesus wept, v.* 35. A very short verse, but it affords many useful instructions. [1.] That Jesus Christ was really and truly man, and partook with the children, not only of flesh and blood, but of a human soul, susceptible of the impressions of joy, and grief, and other affections. Christ gave this proof of his humanity, in both senses of the word; that, as a man, he could weep, and, as a merciful man, he *would weep,* before he gave this proof of his divinity. [2.] That he was *a man of sorrows,* and *acquainted with grief,* as was foretold, Isa. liii. 3. We never read that he laughed, but more than once we have him in tears. Thus he shows not only that a mournful state will consist with the love of God, but that those who sow to the Spirit must sow in tears. [3.] Tears of compassion well become Christians, and make them most to resemble Christ. It is a relief to those who are in sorrow to have their friends sympathize with them, especially such a friend as their Lord Jesus.

(2.) Different constructions were put upon Christ's weeping. [1.] Some made a kind and candid interpretation of it, and what was very natural (*v.* 36): *Then said the Jews, Behold how he loved him!* They seem to wonder that he should have so strong an affection for one to whom he was not related, and with whom he had not had any long acquaintance, for Christ spent most of his time in Galilee, a great way from Bethany. It becomes us, according to this example of Christ, to show our love to our friends, both living and dying. We must sorrow for our brethren that sleep in Jesus as those that are full of love, though not void of hope; as the *devout men* that buried Stephen, Acts viii. 2. Though our tears profit not the dead, they embalm their memory. These tears were indications of his particular love to Lazarus, but he has given proofs no less evident of his love to all the saints, in that he died for them. When he only dropped a tear over Lazarus, they said, *See how he loved him!* Much more reason have we to say so, for whom he hath laid down his life: *See how he loved us! Greater love has no man than this* [2.] Others made a peevish unfair reflection upon it, as if these tears bespoke his inability to help his friend (*v.* 37): *Could not this man, who opened the eyes of the blind,* have prevented the death of Lazarus? Here it is slily insinuated, *First,* That the death of Lazarus being (as it seemed by his tears) a great grief to him, if he could have prevented it he would, and therefore because he *did not* they incline to think that he *could not;* as, when he was dying, they concluded that he could not, because he did not, save himself, and *come down from the cross;* not considering that divine power is always directed in its operations by divine wisdom, not merely according to his will, but according to the counsel of his will, wherein it becomes us to acquiesce. If Christ's friends, whom he loves, die,—if his church, whom he loves, be persecuted and afflicted,—we must not impute it to any defect either in his power or love, but conclude that it is because he sees it for the best. *Secondly,* That therefore it might justly be questioned whether he did indeed *open the eyes of the blind,* that is, whether it was not a sham. His not working this miracle they thought enough to invalidate the former; at least, it should seem that he had a limited power, and therefore not a divine one. Christ soon convinced these *whisperers,* by raising Lazarus from the dead, which was the greater work, that he could have prevented his death, but therefore did not because he would glorify himself the more.

II. Christ's approach to the grave, and the preparation that was made for working this miracle.

1. Christ repeats his groans upon his coming near the grave (*v.* 38): *Again groaning in himself, he comes to the grave;* he groaned, (1.) Being displeased at the unbelief of those who spoke doubtingly of his power, and blamed him for not preventing the death of Lazarus; he was *grieved for the hardness of their hearts.* He never groaned so much for his own pains and sufferings as for the sins and follies of men, particularly Jerusalem's, Matt. xxiii. 37. (2.) Being affected with the fresh lamentations which, it is likely, the mourning sisters made, when they came near the grave, more passionately and pathetically than before, his tender spirit was sensibly touched with their wailings. (3.) Some think that he *groaned in spirit* because, to gratify the desire of his friends, he was to bring Lazarus again into this sinful troublesome world, from that rest into which he was newly entered; it would be a kindness to Martha and Mary, but it would be to him like thrusting one out to a stormy sea again who was newly got into a safe and quiet harbour. If Lazarus had been let alone, Christ would quickly have gone to him into the other world; but, being restored to life, Christ quickly left him behind in this world. (4.) Christ groaned as one that would affect himself with the calamitous state of the human nature, as subject to death, from which he was now about to redeem Lazarus. Thus he stirred up himself to take hold on God in the prayer he was to make, that he might *offer it up with strong crying,* Heb. v. 7. Ministers, when they are sent by the preaching of the gospel to raise dead souls, should be much affected with the deplorable condition of those they preach to and pray for, and groan in themselves to think of it.

2. The grave wherein Lazarus lay is here described: *It was a cave, and a stone lay upon it.* The graves of the common people, probably, were dug as ours are; but persons of distinction were, as with us, interred in vaults, so Lazarus was, and such was the sepulchre in which Christ was buried. Probably this fashion was kept up among the Jews, in imitation of the patriarchs, who buried their dead in the cave of Machpelah, Gen. xxiii. 19. This care taken of the dead bodies of their friends intimates their expectation of their resurrection; they reckoned the solemnity of the funeral ended when the stone was rolled to the grave, or, as here, *laid upon it,* like that on the mouth of the den into which Daniel was cast (Dan. vi. 17), that the *purpose might not be changed;* intimating that the dead are separated from the living, and gone the *way whence they shall not return.* This stone was probably a *grave-stone,* with an inscription upon it, which the Greeks called *μνημεῖον—a memorandum,* because it is both a *memorial* of the dead and a *memento* to the living, putting them in remembrance of that which we are all concerned to remember. It is called by the Latins, *Monumentum, à monendo,* because it gives *warning.*

3. Orders are given to remove the stone (*v.* 39): *Take away the stone.* He would have this stone removed that all the standers-by might see the body lie dead in the sepulchre, and that way might be made for its coming out, and it might appear to be a true body, and not a *ghost* or *spectre.* He would have some of the servants to remove it, that they might be witnesses, by the smell of the putrefaction of the body, and that therefore it was truly dead. It is a good step towards the raising of a soul to spiritual life when the stone is taken away, when prejudices are removed and got over, and way made for the word to the heart, that it may do its work there, and say what it has to say.

4. An objection made by Martha against the opening of the grave: *Lord, by this time he stinketh,* or *is become noisome, for he has been dead four days, τεταρταῖος γάρ ἐστι, quatriduanus est;* he is *four days old* in the other world; a citizen and inhabitant of the grave of four days' standing. Probably Martha perceived the body to smell, as they were removing the stone, and therefore cried out thus.

(1.) It is easy to observe hence the nature

of human bodies: four days are but a little while, yet what a great change will this time make with the body of man, if it be but so long *without food,* much more if so long *without life!* Dead bodies (saith Dr. Hammond) after a revolution of the humours, which is completed in seventy-two hours, naturally tend to putrefaction; and the Jews say that by the fourth day after death the body is so altered that one cannot be sure it is such a person; so Maimonides in Lightfoot. Christ rose the third day because he was not to *see corruption.*

(2.) It is not so easy to say what was Martha's design in saying this. [1.] Some think she said it in a due tenderness, and such as decency teaches to the dead body; now that it began to putrefy, she did not care it should be thus publicly shown and made a spectacle of. [2.] Others think she said it out of a concern for Christ, lest the smell of the dead body should be *offensive* to him. That which is very noisome is compared to an open sepulchre, Ps. v. 9. If there were any thing noisome she would not have her Master near it; but he was none of those tender and delicate ones that cannot bear an ill smell; if he had, he would not have visited the world of mankind, which sin had made a perfect dunghill, altogether noisome, Ps. xiv. 3. [3.] It should seem, by Christ's answer, that it was the language of her unbelief and distrust: "Lord, it is too late now to attempt any kindness to him; his body begins to rot, and it is impossible that this putrid carcase should *live.*" She gives up his case as helpless and hopeless, there having been no instances, either of late or formerly, of any raised to life after they had begun to see corruption. When *our bones are dried,* we are ready to say, *Our hope is lost.* Yet this distrustful word of hers served to make the miracle both the more evident and the more illustrious; by this it appeared that he was truly dead, and not in a trance; for, though the posture of a dead body might be counterfeited, the smell could not. Her suggesting that it *could not be done* puts the more honour upon him that *did it.*

5. The gentle reproof Christ gave to Martha for the weakness of her faith (*v.* 40): *Said I not unto thee that if thou wouldest believe thou shouldest see the glory of God?* This word of his to her was not before recorded; it is probable that he said it to her when she had said (*v.* 27), *Lord, I believe:* and it is enough that it is recorded here, where it is repeated. Note, (1.) Our Lord Jesus has given us all the assurances imaginable that a sincere faith shall at length be crowned with a blessed vision: "If thou believe, thou shalt see God's glorious appearances for thee in this world, and to thee in the other world." If we will take Christ's word, and rely on his power and faithfulness, we shall see the glory of God, and be happy in the sight. (2.) We have need to be often reminded of these *sure mercies* with which our Lord Jesus hath encouraged us. Christ does not give a direct answer to what Martha had said, nor any particular promise of what he would do, but orders her to keep hold of the general assurances he had already given: *Only believe.* We are apt to forget what Christ has spoken, and need him to put us in mind of it by his Spirit: "*Said I not unto thee* so and so? And dost thou think that he will ever unsay it?"

6. The opening of the grave, in obedience to Christ's order, notwithstanding Martha's objection (*v.* 41): *Then they took away the stone.* When Martha was satisfied, and had waived her objection, *then* they proceeded. If we will see the glory of God, we must let Christ take his own way, and not *prescribe* but *subscribe* to him. *They took away the stone,* and this was all they could do; Christ only could *give life.* What man can do is but to *prepare the way of the Lord,* to fill the valleys, and level the hills, and, as here, to *take away the stone.*

III. The miracle itself wrought. The spectators, invited by the rolling away of the stone, gathered about the grave, not to commit *dust to dust, earth to earth,* but to receive dust from the dust, and earth from the earth again; and, their expectations being raised, our Lord Jesus addresses himself to his work.

1. He applies himself to his *living Father in heaven,* so he had called him (*ch.* vi. 17), and so eyes him here.

(1.) The gesture he used was very significant: *He lifted up his eyes,* an outward expression of the elevation of his mind, and to show those who stood by whence he derived his power; also to set us an example; this outward sign is hereby recommended to our practice; see *ch.* xvii. 1. Look how those will answer it who profanely ridicule it; but that which is especially charged upon us hereby is to *lift up our hearts* to God in the heavens; what is prayer, but the ascent of the soul to God, and the directing of its affections and motions heavenward? He *lifted up* his eyes, as looking above, looking beyond the grave where Lazarus lay, and overlooking all the difficulties that arose thence, that he might have his eyes fixed upon the divine omnipotence; to teach us to do as Abraham, who considered not *his own body now dead, nor the deadness of Sarah's womb,* never took these into his thoughts, and so gained such a degree of faith as not to *stagger at the promise,* Rom. iv. 20.

(2.) His address to God was with great assurance, and such a confidence as became him: *Father, I thank thee that thou hast heard me.*

[1.] He has here taught us, by his own example, *First,* In prayer to call God Father, and to draw nigh to him as children to a father, with a humble reverence, and yet with a holy boldness. *Secondly,* In our *prayers* to *praise him,* and, when we come to beg for further mercy, thankfully to acknowledge former favours. Thanksgivings, which bespeak *God's glory* (not *our own*, like the Pharisee's *God, I thank thee)*, are decent forms into which to put our supplications.

[2.] But our Saviour's thanksgiving here was intended to express the unshaken assurance he had of the effecting of this miracle, which he had in his own power to do in concurrence with his Father: "*Father, I thank thee* that my will and thine are in this matter, as always, the same." Elijah and Elisha raised the dead, as servants, by *entreaty;* but Christ, as a Son, by *authority*, having life in himself, and power to quicken whom he would; and he speaks of this as his own act (*v.* 11): *I go, that I may awake him;* yet he speaks of it as what he had obtained by prayer, for his Father *heard him:* probably he put up the prayer for it when he *groaned in spirit* once and again (*v.* 33, 38), in a *mental* prayer, with groanings which could not be *uttered.*

First, Christ speaks of this miracle as an answer to prayer, 1. Because he would thus *humble himself;* though he was a Son, yet *learned he this obedience*, to ask and receive. His mediatorial crown was granted him upon request, though it is *of right*, Ps. ii. 8, and *ch.* xvii. 5. He prays for the glory he had before the world was, though, having never forfeited it, he might have demanded it. 2. Because he was pleased thus to *honour prayer*, making it the key wherewith even he unlocked the treasures of divine power and grace. Thus he would teach us in prayer, by the lively exercise of faith, to *enter into the holiest.*

Secondly, Christ, being assured that his prayer was answered, professes,

a. His thankful acceptance of this answer: *I thank thee that thou hast heard me.* Though the miracle was not yet wrought, yet the prayer was answered, and he triumphs before the victory. No other can pretend to such an assurance as Christ had; yet we may by faith in the promise have a prospect of mercy before it be actually given in, and may rejoice in that prospect, and give God thanks for it. In David's devotions, the same psalm which begins with prayer for a mercy closes with thanksgivings for it. Note, (*a.*) Mercies in answer to prayer ought in a special manner to be acknowledged with thankfulness. Besides the grant of the mercy itself, we are to value it as a great favour to have our poor prayers taken notice of. (*b.*) We ought to *meet* the first appearances of the return of prayer with early thanksgivings. As God *answers* us with mercy, even *before we call*, and *hears while we are yet speaking*, so we should answer him with praise even before he grants, and give him thanks while he is yet speaking good words and comfortable words.

b. His cheerful assurance of a ready answer at any time (v. 42): *And I know that thou hearest me always.* Let none think that this was some uncommon favour granted him now, such as he never had before, nor should ever have again; no, he had the same divine power going along with him in his whole undertaking, and undertook nothing but what he knew to be agreeable to the counsel of God's will. "I *gave thanks*" (saith he) "for being heard in this, because I am sure to be heard in every thing." See here, (*a.*) The interest our Lord Jesus had in heaven; the Father *heard him always*, he had access to the Father upon every occasion, and success with him in every errand. And we may be sure that his interest is not the less for his going to heaven, which may encourage us to depend upon his intercession, and put all our petitions into his hand, for we are sure that him the Father *hears always.* (*b.*) The confidence he had of that interest: *I knew it.* He did not in the least hesitate or doubt concerning it, but had an entire satisfaction in his own mind of the Father's complacency in him and concurrence with him in every thing. We cannot have such a particular assurance as he had; but this we know, that *whatsoever we ask according to his will he heareth us*, 1 John v. 14, 15.

Thirdly, But why should Christ give this public intimation of his obtaining this miracle by prayer? He adds, It is *because of the people who stand by, that they may believe that thou hast sent me;* for *prayer may preach.* 1. It was to obviate the objections of his enemies, and their reflections. It was blasphemously suggested by the Pharisees, and their creatures, that he wrought his miracles by compact with the devil; now, to evidence the contrary, he openly made his address to God, using *prayers*, and not *charms*, not *peeping and muttering* as those did that used *familiar spirits* (Isa. viii. 19), but, with elevated eyes and voice professing his communication with Heaven, and dependence on Heaven. 2. It was to corroborate the faith of those that were well inclined to him: *That they may believe that thou hast sent me*, not to destroy men's lives, but to save them. Moses, to show that God sent him, made the earth open and swallow men up (Num. xvi. 31); Elijah, to show that God sent him, made fire come from heaven and devour men; for the law was a dispensation of terror and death but Christ proves his mission by raising to life one that was dead. Some give this sense: had Christ declared his doing it freely by his own power, some of his weak disciples, who as yet understood not his divine nature, would have thought he took too much upon him, and have been stumbled at it. These *babes* could not bear that *strong meat*, therefore he chooses to speak of his power as received and derived; he speaks self-denyingly of himself, that he might speak the more plainly to us. *Non ita respexit ad suam dignitatem atque ad nostram salutem—In what he said, he consulted not so much his dignity as our salvation.*—Jansenius.

2. He now applies himself to his *dead friend in the earth.* He *cried with a loud voice, Lazarus come forth.*

(1.) He could have raised Lazarus by a silent exertion of his power and will, and the indiscernible operations of the Spirit of life; but he did it by a call, a loud call,

[1.] To be significant of the power then put forth for the raising of Lazarus, how he *created this new thing;* he *spoke, and it was done.* He cried aloud, to signify the greatness of the work, and of the power employed in it, and to excite himself as it were to this attack upon the gates of death, as soldiers engage with a shout. Speaking to Lazarus, it was proper to *cry with a loud voice;* for, *First,* The soul of Lazarus, which was to be called back, was at a distance, not hovering about the grave, as the Jews fancied, but removed to Hades, the world of spirits; now it is natural to speak loud when we call to those at a distance. *Secondly,* The body of Lazarus, which was to be called up, was *asleep,* and we usually speak loud when we would awake any out of sleep. He cried with a loud voice that the scripture might be fulfilled (Isa. xlv. 19), *I have not spoken in secret, in a dark place of the earth.*

[2.] To be typical of other works of wonder, and particularly other resurrections, which the power of Christ was to effect. This loud call was a figure, *First,* Of the gospel call, by which dead souls were to be brought out of the grave of sin, which resurrection Christ had formerly spoken of (*ch.* v. 25), and of his word as the means of it (*ch.* vi. 63), and now he gives a specimen of it. By his word, he saith to souls, *Live,* yea, *he* saith to them, *Live,* Ezek. xvi. 6. *Arise from the dead,* Eph. v. 14. The Spirit of life from God entered into those that had been dead and dry bones, when Ezekiel prophesied over them, Ezek. xxxvii. 10. Those who infer from the commands of the word to *turn and live* that man has a power of his own to convert and regenerate himself might as well infer from this call to Lazarus that he had a power to raise himself to life. *Secondly,* Of the sound of the archangel's trumpet at the last day, with which they that sleep in the dust shall be awakened and summoned before the great tribunal, when Christ shall *descend with a shout,* a *call,* or *command,* like this here, *Come forth,* Ps. l. 4. *He shall call* both *to the heavens* for their souls, *and to the earth* for their bodies, *that he may judge his people.*

(2.) This *loud call* was but *short,* yet *mighty through God* to the battering down of the strongholds of the grave. [1.] He calls him by name, Lazarus, as we call those by their names whom we would awake out of a fast sleep. God said to Moses, as a mark of his favour, *I know thee by name.* The naming of him intimates that the same individual person that died shall rise again at the last day. He that *calls the stars by their names* can distinguish by name his stars that are in the dust of the earth, and will lose none of them. [2.] He calls him *out of the grave,* speaking to him as if he were already alive, and had nothing to do but to come out of his grave. He does not say unto him, *Live;* for he himself must give life; but he saith to him, *Move,* for when by the grace of Christ we live spiritually we must stir up ourselves to *move;* the grave of sin and this world is no place for those whom Christ has quickened, and therefore they must *come forth.* [3.] The event was according to the intention: *He that was dead came forth, v.* 44. Power went along with the word of Christ to reunite the soul and body of Lazarus, and then he came forth The miracle is described, not by its invisible springs, to satisfy our curiosity, but by its visible effects, to confirm our faith. Do any ask where the soul of Lazarus was during the four days of its separation? We are not told, but have reason to think it was in paradise, *in joy and felicity;* but you will say, "Was it not then really an unkindness to it to cause it to return into the prison of the body? And if it were, yet, being for the honour of Christ and the serving of the interests of his kingdom, it was no more an injury to him than it was to St. Paul to continue in the flesh when he knew that to depart to Christ was so much better. If any ask whether Lazarus, after he was raised, could give an account or description of his soul's removal out of the body or return to it, or what he saw in the other world, I suppose both those changes were so unaccountable to himself that he must say with Paul, *Whether in the body or out of the body, I cannot tell;* and of what he saw and heard, that it was not lawful nor possible to express it. In a world of sense we cannot frame to ourselves, much less communicate to others, any adequate ideas of the world of spirits and the affairs of that world. Let us not covet to be wise above what is written, and this is all that is written concerning the resurrection of that Lazarus, that *he that was dead came forth.* Some have observed that though we read of many who were raised from the dead, who no doubt conversed familiarly with men afterwards, yet the scripture has not recorded one word spoken by any of them, except by our Lord Jesus only

(3.) This miracle was wrought, [1.] *Speedily* Nothing intervenes between the command, *Come forth,* and the effect, *He came forth: dictum factum—no sooner said than done;* let there be life, and there was life. Thus the change in the resurrection will be *in a moment, in the twinkling of an eye,* 1 Cor. xv. 52. The almighty power that can do it can do it in an instant: *Then shalt thou call and I will answer;* will come at the call, as Lazarus, *Here am I.* [2.] *Perfectly.* He was so thoroughly revived that he got up out of his grave as strongly as ever he got up out of his bed, and returned not only to life, but health. He was not raised to serve a present turn, but to live as other men. [3.] With this additional miracle, as some reckon it, that he came out of his grave, though he was fettered with his grave-clothes, with which he was *bound hand and foot,* and *his face bound about with a napkin* (for so the manner of the Jews was to bury); and he came forth in the same dress wherein he was buried, that it might appear that it was he himself and not another, and that he was not only alive, but strong, and able to walk, after a sort, even in his grave-clothes. The *binding of his face with a napkin* proved that he had been really dead, for otherwise, in less than so many days' time, that would have smothered him. And the standers-by, in unbinding him, would *handle him, and see him, that it was he himself,* and so be witnesses of the miracle. Now see here, *First,* How little we carry away with us, when we leave the world—only a winding-sheet and a coffin; there is no change of raiment in the grave, nothing but a single suit of grave-clothes. *Secondly,* What condition we shall be in in the grave. What *wisdom or device* can there be where the eyes are hoodwinked, or what working where the hands and feet are fettered? And so it will be in the grave, whither we are going. Lazarus being *come forth,* hampered and embarrassed with his grave-clothes, we may well imagine that those about the grave were exceedingly surprised and frightened at it; we should be so if we should see a dead body rise; but Christ, to make the thing familiar, sets them to work: "*Loose him,* slacken his grave-clothes, that they may serve for day-clothes till he comes to his house, and then he will go himself, so clad, without guide or supporter to his own house." As, in the Old Testament, the translations of Enoch and Elias were sensible demonstrations of an invisible and future state, the one about the middle of the patriarchal age, the other of the Mosaic economy, so the resurrection of Lazarus, in the New Testament, was designed for the confirmation of the doctrine of the resurrection.

45 Then many of the Jews which
came to Mary, and had seen the
things which Jesus did, believed on
him. 46 But some of them went
their ways to the Pharisees, and told
them what things Jesus had done.
47 Then gathered the chief priests
and the Pharisees a council, and said,
What do we? for this man doeth
many miracles. 48 If we let him
thus alone, all *men* will believe on
him: and the Romans shall come
and take away both our place and
nation. 49 And one of them, *named*
Caiaphas, being the high priest that
same year, said unto them, Ye
know nothing at all, 50 Nor consider that it is expedient for us, that
one man should die for the people,
and that the whole nation perish not.
51 And this spake he not of himself:
but being high priest that year, he
prophesied that Jesus should die for
that nation; 52 And not for that
nation only, but that also he should
gather together in one the children
of God that were scattered abroad.
53 Then from that day forth they
took counsel together for to put him
to death. 54 Jesus therefore walked
no more openly among the Jews;
but went thence unto a country near
to the wilderness, into a city called
Ephraim, and there continued with
his disciples. 55 And the Jews'
passover was nigh at hand: and many
went out of the country up to Jerusalem before the passover, to purify
themselves. 56 Then sought they for
Jesus, and spake among themselves,
as they stood in the temple, What
think ye, that he will not come to the
feast? 57 Now both the chief priests
and the Pharisees had given a commandment, that, if any man knew
where he were, he should show *it,*
that they might take him.

We have here an account of the consequences of this glorious miracle, which were as usual; to some it was a savour of life unto life, to others of death unto death.

I. Some were invited by it, and induced to believe. Many of the Jews, when they *saw the things that Jesus did, believed on him,* and well they might, for it was an incontestable proof of his divine mission. They had often heard of his miracles, and yet evaded the conviction of them, by calling in question the matter of fact; but now that they had themselves seen this done their unbelief was conquered, and they yielded at last. But *blessed are those who have not seen and yet have believed.* The more we see of Christ the more cause we shall see to love him and confide in him. These were some of those Jews that came to Mary, to comfort her. When we are doing good offices to others we put ourselves in the way of receiving favours from God, and have opportunities of getting good when we are doing good.

II. Others were irritated by it, and hardened in their unbelief.

1. The *informers* were so (*v.* 46): *Some of them,* who were eye-witnesses of the miracle, were so far from being convinced that they *went to the Pharisees,* whom they knew to

be his implacable enemies, and *told them what things Jesus had done;* not merely as a matter of news worthy their notice, much less as an inducement to them to think more favourably of Christ, but with a spiteful design to excite those who needed no spur the more vigorously to prosecute him. Here is a strange instance, (1.) Of a most *obstinate infidelity,* refusing to yield to the most powerful means of conviction; and it is hard to imagine how they could evade the force of this evidence, but that the *god of this world* had *blinded their minds.* (2.) Of a most *inveterate enmity.* If they would not be satisfied that he was to be believed in as the Christ, yet one would think they should have been mollified, and persuaded not to persecute him; but, if the water be not sufficient to *quench* the fire, it will *inflame* it. They told *what Jesus had done,* and told no more than what was true; but their malice gave a tincture of diabolism to their information equal to that of *lying;* perverting what is true is as bad as forging what is false. *Doeg* is called a *false, lying,* and *deceitful tongue* (Ps. lii. 2—4; cxx. 2, 3), though what he said was *true.*

2. The judges, the leaders, the *blind leaders,* of the people were no less exasperated by the report made to them, and here we are told what they did.

(1.) A special council is called and held (*v.* 47): *Then gathered the chief priests and Pharisees a council,* as was foretold, Ps. ii. 2, *The rulers take counsel together against the Lord.* Consultations of the sanhedrim were intended for the public good; but here, under colour of this, the greatest injury and mischief are done to the people. The things that belong to the nation's peace were hid from the eyes of those that were entrusted with its counsels. This council was called, not only for joint advice, but for mutual irritation; that as iron sharpens iron, and as coals are to burning coals and wood to fire, so they might exasperate and inflame one another with enmity and rage against Christ and his doctrine.

(2.) The case is proposed, and shown to be weighty and of great consequence.

[1.] The matter to be debated was what course they should take with this Jesus, to stop the growth of his interest; they said, *What do we? For this man doeth many miracles.* The information given about the raising of Lazarus was produced, and the *men, brethren, and fathers* were called in to help as solicitously as if a formidable enemy had been with an army in the heart of their country. *First,* They own the truth of Christ's miracles, and that he had wrought many of them; they are therefore witnesses against themselves, for they acknowledge his credentials and yet deny his commission. *Secondly,* They consider what is to be done, and chide themselves that they have not done something sooner effectually to crush him. They do not take it at all into their consideration whether they shall not receive him and own him as the Messiah, though they profess to expect him, and Jesus gave pregnant proofs of his being so; but they take it for granted that he is an enemy, and as such is to be run down: "*What do we?* Have we no care to support our church? Is it nothing to us that a doctrine so destructive to our interest spreads thus? Shall we tamely yield up the ground we have got in the affections of the people? Shall we see our authority brought into contempt, and the craft by which we get our living ruined, and not bestir ourselves? What have we been doing all this while? And what are we now thinking of? Shall we be always talking, and bring nothing to pass?"

[2.] That which made this matter weighty was the peril they apprehended their church and nation to be in from the Romans (*v.* 48): "If we do not silence him, and take him off, *all men will believe on him;* and, this being the setting up of a new king, the Romans will take umbrage at it, *and will come* with an army, and *take away our place and nation,* and therefore it is no time to trifle." See what an opinion they have,

First, Of their own *power.* They speak as if they thought Christ's progress and success in his work depended upon their connivance; as if he could not go on to work miracles, and make disciples, unless they *let him alone;* as if it were in their power to conquer him who had conquered death, or as if they could *fight against God,* and prosper. But he that sits in heaven laughs at the fond conceit which impotent malice has of its own omnipotence.

Secondly, Of their own *policy.* They fancy themselves to be men of mighty insight and foresight, and great sagacity in their moral prognostications.

a. They take on them to prophecy that, in a little time, if he have liberty to go on, *all men will believe on him,* hereby owning, when it was to serve their purpose, that his doctrine and miracles had a very convincing power in them, such as could not be resisted, but that all men would become his proselytes and votaries. Thus do they now make his interest formidable, though, to serve another turn, these same men strove to make it contemptible, *ch.* vii. 48, *Have any of the rulers believed on him?* This was the thing they were afraid of, that men would *believe on him,* and then all their measures were broken. Note, The success of the gospel is the dread of its adversaries; if souls be saved, they are undone.

b. They foretel that if the generality of the nation be *drawn after him,* the rage of the Romans will be *drawn upon them.* They *will come and take away our place;* the country in general, especially Jerusalem, or the temple, the *holy place,* and *their* place, their darling, their idol; or, their *preferments* in the temple, their *places* of power and trust. Now it was true that the Romans had a very jealous eye upon them, and knew they wanted nothing but power and opportunity to shake off their yoke. It was likewise true that if the Romans should pour an army in upon them it would be very hard for them to make any head against it; yet here appeared a cowardice which one would not have found in the priests of the Lord if they had not by their wickedness forfeited their interest in God and all good men. Had they kept their integrity, they needed not to have feared the Romans; but they speak like a dispirited people, as the men of Judah when they basely said to Samson, *Knowest thou not that the Philistines rule over us?* Judg. xv. 11. When men lose their piety they lose their courage. But, (*a.*) It was false that there was any danger of the Romans' being irritated against their nation by the progress of Christ's gospel, for it was no way *hurtful to kings nor provinces,* but highly beneficial. The Romans had no jealousy at all of his growing interest; for he taught men to give tribute to Cæsar, and not to *resist evil,* but to take up the cross. The Roman governor, at his trial, could *find no fault in him.* There was more danger of the Romans' being incensed against the Jewish nation by the priests than by Christ. Note, Pretended fears are often the colour of malicious designs. (*b.*) Had there really been some danger of displeasing the Romans by tolerating Christ's preaching, yet this would not justify their hating and persecuting a good man. Note, [*a.*] The enemies of Christ and his gospel have often coloured their enmity with a seeming care for the *public good* and the *common safety,* and, in order to this, have branded his prophets and ministers as troublers of Israel, and men that *turn the world upside down.* [*b.*] Carnal policy commonly sets up *reasons of state,* in opposition to *rules of justice.* When men are concerned for their own wealth and safety more than for truth and duty, it is wisdom from beneath, which is *earthly, sensual, and devilish.* But see what was the issue; they pretended to be afraid that their tolerating Christ's gospel would bring desolation upon them by the Romans, and therefore, *right or wrong,* set themselves against it; but it proved that their persecuting the gospel brought upon them that which they feared, filled up the measure of their iniquity, and the Romans came and *took away their place and nation,* and their place *knows them no more.* Note, That calamity which we seek to escape by sin we take the most effectual course to bring upon our own heads; and those who think by opposing Christ's kingdom to secure or advance their own secular interest will find Jerusalem a more *burdensome stone* than they think it is, Zech. xii. 3. The *fear of the wicked it shall come upon them,* Prov. x. 24.

(3.) Caiaphas makes a malicious but mystical speech in the council on this occasion.

[1.] The *malice* of it appears evident at first view, *v.* 49, 50. He, being the high priest, and so president of the council, took upon him to decide the matter before it was debated: "*You know nothing at all,* your hesitating betrays your ignorance, for it is not a thing that will bear a dispute, it is soon determined, if you consider that received maxim, *That it is expedient for us that one man should die for the people.*" Here,

First, The counsellor was Caiaphas, who was *high priest that same year.* The high priesthood was by divine appointment settled upon the heir male of the house of Aaron, for and during the term of his natural life, and then to his heir male; but in those degenerate times it was become, though not an annual office, like a consulship, yet frequently changed, as they could make an interest with the Roman powers. Now it happened that *this year* Caiaphas wore the mitre.

Secondly, The drift of the advice was, in short, this, That some way or other must be found out to put Jesus to death. We have reason to think that they strongly suspected him to be indeed the Messiah; but his doctrine was so contrary to their darling traditions and secular interest, and his design did so thwart their notions of the Messiah's kingdom, that they resolve, be he who he will, he must be put to death. Caiaphas does not say, Let him be silenced, imprisoned, banished, though amply sufficient for the *restraint* of one they thought dangerous; but *die he must.* Note, Those that have set themselves against Christianity have commonly divested themselves of humanity, and been infamous for cruelty.

Thirdly, This is plausibly insinuated, with all the subtlety as well as malice of the old serpent. 1. He suggests his own sagacity, which we must suppose him as high priest to excel in, though the *Urim* and *Thummim* were long since lost. How scornfully does he say, "*You know nothing,* who are but common priests; but you must give me leave to see further into things than you do!" Thus it is common for those in authority to impose their corrupt dictates by virtue of that; and, because they *should be* the wisest and best, to expect that every body should believe they *are so.* 2. He takes it for granted that the case is plain and past dispute, and that those are very ignorant who do not see it to be so. Note, Reason and justice are often run down with a high hand. *Truth is fallen in the streets,* and, when it is down, down with it; and *equity cannot enter,* and, when it is out, out with it, Isa. lix. 14. 3. He insists upon a maxim in politics, That the welfare of communities is to be preferred before that of particular persons. *It is expedient for us* as priests, whose all lies at stake, that *one man die for the people.* Thus far it holds true, that it is *expedient,* and more than so, it is truly *honourable*, for a man to hazard his life in the service of his country (Phil. ii. 17; 1 John iii. 16); but to put an innocent man to death under colour of consulting the public safety is the devil's policy. Caiaphas craftily insinuates that the greatest and best man, though *major singulis—greater than any one individual*, is *minor universis—less than the collected mass*, and ought to think his life well spent, nay well lost, to save his country from ruin. But what is this to the murdering of one that was evidently a great blessing under pretence of preventing an imaginary mischief to the country? The case ought to have been put thus: Was it expedient for them to bring upon themselves and upon their nation the guilt of blood, a prophet's blood, for the securing of their civil interests from a danger which they had no just reason to be afraid of? Was it expedient for them to drive God and their glory from them, rather than venture the Romans' displeasure, who could do them no harm if they had God on their side? Note, Carnal policy, which steers only by secular considerations, while it thinks to *save all* by sin, *ruins all* at last.

[2.] The *mystery* that was in this counsel of Caiaphas does not appear at first view, but the evangelist leads us into it (*v.* 51, 52): *This spoke he not of himself*, it was not only the language of his own enmity and policy, but in these words he prophesied, though he himself was not aware of it, *that Jesus should die for that nation*. Here is a precious comment upon a pernicious text; the counsel of cursed Caiaphas so construed as to fall in with the counsels of the blessed God. Charity teaches us to put the most favourable construction upon men's words and actions that they will bear; but piety teaches us to make a good improvement of them, even contrary to that for which they were intended. If wicked men, in what they *do* against us, *are God's hand* to humble and reform us, why may they not in what they say against us be God's mouth to instruct and convince us? But in this of Caiaphas there was an extraordinary direction of Heaven prompting him to say that which was capable of a very sublime sense. As the hearts of all men are in God's hand, so are their tongues. Those are deceived who say, "*Our tongues are our own*, so that either we *may* say what we will, and are not accountable to God's judgment, or we *can* say what we will, and are not restrainable by his providence and power." Balaam could not say what he would, when he came to curse Israel, nor Laban when he pursued Jacob.

(4.) The evangelist explains and enlarges upon Caiaphas's words.

[1.] He explains what he said, and shows how it not only was, but was intended to be, accommodated to an excellent purpose. He did not *speak it of himself*. As it was an artifice to stir up the council against Christ, he spoke it of himself, or of the devil rather; but as it was an *oracle*, declaring it the purpose and design of God by the death of Christ to save God's spiritual Israel from sin and wrath, he did not speak it of himself, for he knew nothing of the matter, he *meant not so, neither did his heart think so*, for nothing was in his heart but to destroy and cut off, Isa. x. 7.

First, He *prophesied*, and those that prophesied did not, in their prophesying, *speak of themselves*. But is Caiaphas also among the prophets? He is so, *pro hâc vice—this once*, though a bad man, and an implacable enemy to Christ and his gospel. Note, 1. God can and often does make wicked men instruments to serve his own purposes, even contrary to their own intentions; for he has them not only *in a chain*, to restrain them from doing the mischief they would, but *in a bridle*, to lead them to do the service they would not. 2. Words of prophecy in the mouth are no infallible evidence of a principle of grace in the heart. *Lord, Lord, have we not prophesied in thy name?* will be rejected as a frivolous plea.

Secondly, He prophesied, *being high priest that year;* not that his being high priest did at all dispose or qualify him to be a prophet; we cannot suppose the pontifical mitre to have first inspired with prophecy the basest head that ever wore it; but, 1. Being high priest, and therefore of note and eminence in the conclave, God was pleased to put this significant word into his mouth rather than into the mouth of any other, that it might be the more observed or the non-observance of it the more aggravated. The apophthegms of great men have been thought worthy of special regard: *A divine sentence is in the lips of the king;* therefore this divine sentence was put into the lips of the high priest, that even out of his mouth this word might be established, That Christ died for *the good of the nation*, and not *for any iniquity in his hands*. He happened to be high priest that year which was fixed to be the *year of the redeemed*, when Messiah the prince *must be cut off, but not for himself* (Dan. ix. 26), and he must own it. 2. Being high priest *that year*, that famous year, in which there was to be such a plentiful effusion of the Spirit, more than had ever been yet, according to the prophecy (Joel ii. 28, 29, compared with Acts ii. 17), some drops of the blessed shower light upon Caiaphas, as the crumbs (says Dr Lightfoot) of the children's bread, which fall from the table among the dogs. This year was the year of the expiration of the Levitical priesthood; and out of the mouth of him who was that year high priest was extorted an implicit resignation of it to him who should not (as they had done for many ages) offer beasts for that nation, but offer himself, and so make an end of the *sin-offering*. This resignation he made *unwittingly*, as Isaac gave the blessing to Jacob.

Thirdly, The matter of his prophecy was *that Jesus should die for that nation,* the very thing to which all the prophets bore witness, who *testified beforehand the sufferings of Christ* (1 Pet. i. 11), that the death of Christ must be the life and salvation of Israel; he meant by *that nation* those in it that obstinately adhered to Judaism, but God meant those in it that would receive the doctrine of Christ, and become followers of him, all believers, the spiritual seed of Abraham. The death of Christ, which Caiaphas was now projecting, proved the ruin of that interest in the nation of which he intended it should be the security and establishment, for it brought wrath upon them to the uttermost; but it proved the advancement of that interest of which he hoped it would have been the ruin, for Christ, being lifted up from the earth, drew all men unto him. It is a great thing that is here prophesied: That Jesus should *die,* die for others, not only *for their good,* but *in their stead, die* for *that nation,* for they had the first offer made them of salvation by his death. If the whole nation of the Jews had unanimously believed in Christ, and received his gospel, they had been not only saved eternally, but saved as a nation from their grievances. The fountain was first *opened to the house of David,* Zech. xiii. 1. He so died for *that nation* as that *the whole nation should not perish,* but that *a remnant should be saved,* Rom. xi. 5.

[2.] The evangelist enlarges upon this word of Caiaphas (*v.* 52), *not for that nation only,* how much soever it thought itself the darling of Heaven, but *that also he should gather together in one the children of God that were scattered abroad.* Observe here,

First, The persons Christ died for: *Not for the nation* of the Jews *only* (it would have been comparatively but *a light thing* for the Son of God to go through so vast an undertaking only to restore the *preserved of Jacob,* and *the outcasts of Israel);* no, he must be *salvation to the ends of the earth,* Isa. xlix. 6. He must die for *the children of God that were scattered abroad.* 1. Some understand it of the children of God that were then *in being,* scattered abroad in the Gentile world, *devout men* of every nation (Acts ii. 5), that *feared God* (Acts x. 2), and worshipped him (Acts xvii. 4), proselytes of the gate, who served the God of Abraham, but submitted not to the ceremonial law of Moses, persons that had a savour of natural religion, but were *dispersed* in the nations, had no solemn assemblies of their own, nor any peculiar profession to unite in or distinguish themselves by. Now Christ died to incorporate these in one great society, to be denominated from him and governed by him; and this was the setting up of a standard, to which all that had a regard to God and a concern for their souls might have recourse, and under which they might enlist themselves. 2. Others take in with these all that belong to the election of grace, who are called the children of God, though not yet born, because they are *predestinated to the adoption of children,* Eph. i. 5. Now these are *scattered abroad* in several *places of the earth,* out of all kindreds and tongues (Rev. vii. 9), and in several *ages of the world,* to the end of time; there are those that *fear him throughout all generations,* to all these he had an eye in the atonement he made by his blood; as he prayed, so he died, for *all that should believe on him.*

Secondly, The purpose and intention of his death concerning those persons; he died to *gather in* those who wandered, and to *gather together in one* those who were scattered; to invite those to him who were at a distance from him, and to unite those in him who were at a distance from each other. Christ's dying is, 1. The great *attractive of our hearts;* for this end he is lifted up, to draw men to him. The conversion of souls is the gathering of them in to Christ as their ruler and refuge, as the doves to their windows; and he died to effect this. By dying he purchased them to himself, and the gift of the Holy Ghost for them; his love in dying for us is the great loadstone of our love. 2. The great *centre of our unity.* He gathers them together *in one,* Eph. i. 10. They are one with him, one body, one spirit, and one with each other in him. All the saints in all places and ages meet in Christ, as all the members in the head, and all the branches in the root. Christ by the merit of his death recommended all the saints in *one* to the grace and favour *of God* (Heb. ii. 11—13), and by the motive of his death recommends them all severally to the love and affection one of another, *ch.* xiii. 34.

(5.) The result of this debate is a resolve of the council to put Jesus to death (*v.* 53): *From that day they took counsel together, to put him to death.* They now understood one another's minds, and so each was fixed in his own, that Jesus must die; and, it should seem, a committee was appointed to sit, *de die in diem—daily,* to consider of it, to consult about it, and to receive proposals for effecting it. Note, The wickedness of the wicked ripens by degrees, James i. 15; Ezek. vii. 10. Two considerable advances were now made in their accursed design against Christ. [1.] What before they had thought of *severally* now they *jointly* concurred in, and so strengthened the hands one of another in this wickedness, and proceeded with the greater assurance. Evil men confirm and encourage themselves and one another in evil practices, by comparing notes; men of corrupt minds bless themselves when they find others of *the same mind:* then the wickedness which before seemed impracticable appears not only possible, but easy to be effected, *vis unita fortior—energies, when united, become more efficient.* [2.] What before they wished done, but *wanted a colour for,* now they are furnished with a plausible pretence to justify themselves in, which will serve, if not to take off the guilt (that is the least of their care), yet to take off the odium, and so satisfy, if not the personal, yet the political conscience, as some subtly distinguish. Many will go on very securely in doing an evil thing as long as they have but something to say in excuse for it. Now this resolution of theirs to put him to death, right or wrong, proves that all the formality of a trial, which he afterwards underwent, was but show and pretence; they were before determined what to do.

(6.) Christ hereupon absconded, knowing very well what was the vote of their close cabal, *v.* 54.

[1.] He suspended his public appearances: *He walked no more openly among the Jews,* among the inhabitants of Judea, who were properly called Jews, especially those at Jerusalem; *οὐ περιεπάτει—he did not walk up and down* among them, did not go from place to place, preaching and working miracles with the freedom and openness that he had done, but while he staid in Judea, he was there *incognito.* Thus the chief priests put the light of Israel *under a bushel.*

[2.] He withdrew into an obscure part of the country, so obscure that the name of the town he retired to is scarcely met with any where else. He went to a country *near the wilderness,* as if he were driven out from among men, or rather wishing, with Jeremiah, that he might have in the wilderness a *lodging place of way-faring men,* Jer. ix. 2. He entered into a city called Ephraim, some think Ephratah, that is, Bethlehem, where he was born, and which bordered upon the wilderness of Judah; others think Ephron, or Ephraim, mentioned 2 Chron. xiii. 19. Thither his disciples went with him; neither would they leave him in solitude, nor would he leave them in danger. There he continued, *διέτριβε,* there he *conversed,* he knew how to improve this time of retirement in private conversation, when he had not an opportunity of preaching publicly. He *conversed with his disciples,* who were his family, when he was forced from the temple, and his *διάτριβαι,* or *discourses* there, no doubt, were very edifying. We must do the good we can, when we cannot do the good we would. But why would Christ abscond now? It was not because he either feared the power of his enemies or distrusted his own power; he had many ways to save himself, and was neither averse to suffering nor unprepared for it; but he retired, *First,* To put a mark of his displeasure upon Jerusalem and the people of the Jews. They rejected him and his gospel; justly therefore did he remove himself and his gospel from them. The prince of *teachers* was now *removed into a corner* (Isa. xxx. 20); there was *no open vision* of him; and it was a sad presage of that thick darkness which was shortly to come upon Jerusalem, because she knew not the day of her visitation. *Secondly,* To render the cruelty of his enemies against him the more inexcusable. If that which was grievous to them, and thought dangerous to the public, was his *public appearance,* he would try whether their anger would be turned away by his retirement into privacy; when David had fled to Gath, Saul was satisfied, and sought no more for him, 1 Sam. xxvii. 4. But it was the *life,* the precious life, that these wicked men hunted after. *Thirdly,* His hour was *not yet come,* and therefore he declined danger, and did it in a way common to men, both to warrant and encourage the flight of his servants in time of persecution and to comfort those who are forced from their usefulness, and buried alive in privacy and obscurity; *the disciple is not better than his Lord. Fourthly,* His retirement, for awhile, was to make his return into Jerusalem, when his hour was come, the more remarkable and illustrious. This swelled the acclamations of joy with which his well-wishers welcomed him at his next public appearance, when he rode triumphantly into the city.

(7.) The strict enquiry made for him during his recess, *v.* 55—57.

[1.] The occasion of it was the approach of the passover, at which they expected his presence, according to custom (*v.* 55): *The Jews' passover was nigh at hand,* a festival which shone bright in their calendar, and which there was great expectation of for some time before. This was Christ's fourth and last passover, since he entered upon his public ministry, and it might truly be said (as, 2. Chron. xxxv. 18), *There never was such a passover in Israel,* for in it *Christ our passover was sacrificed for us* Now the passover being at hand, *many went out* of all parts of *the country to Jerusalem, to purify themselves.* This was either, *First,* A *necessary purification* of those who had contracted any ceremonial pollution; they came to be sprinkled with the *water of purification,* and to perform the other rites of cleansing according to the law, for they might not eat the passover in their uncleanness, Num. ix. 6. Thus before our gospel passover we must renew our repentance, and by faith wash in the blood of Christ, and so *compass God's altar.* Or, *Secondly,* A *voluntary purification,* or self-sequestration, by fasting and prayer, and other religious exercises, which many that were more devout than their neighbours spent some time in before the passover, and chose to do it at Jerusalem, because of the advantage of the temple-service. Thus must we by solemn preparation set bounds about the mount on which we expect to meet with God.

[2.] The enquiry was very solicitous: *They said, What think you, that he will not come to the feast? v.* 56.

First, Some think this was said by those who wished well to him, and expected his coming, that they might hear his doctrine and see his miracles. Those who came early out of the country, that they might purify themselves, were very desirous to meet with Christ, and perhaps came up the sooner with that expectation, and therefore *as they stood in the temple,* the place of their purification, they enquired what news of Christ? Could any body give them hopes of seeing him? If there were those, and those of the most devout people, and best affected to religion, who showed this respect to Christ, it was a check to the enmity of the chief priests, and a witness against them.

Secondly, It should rather seem that they were his enemies who made this enquiry after him, who wished for an opportunity to lay hands on him. They, seeing the town begin to fill with devout people out of the country, wondered they did not find him among them. When they should have been assisting those that came to purify themselves, according to the duty of their place, they were plotting against Christ. How miserably degenerate was the Jewish church, when the priests of the Lord were become like the priests of the calves, a *snare upon Mizpeh, and a net spread upon Tabor,* and were *profound to make slaughter* (Hos. v. 1, 2),—when, instead of keeping the feast with unleavened bread, they were themselves soured with the leaven of the worst malice! Their asking, *What think you? Will he not come up to the feast?* implies, 1. An invidious reflection upon Christ, as if he would omit his attendance on the feast of the Lord for fear of exposing himself. If others, through irreligion, be absent, they are not animadverted upon; but if Christ be absent, for his own preservation (for God will have mercy, and not sacrifice), it is turned to his reproach, as it was to David's that his seat was empty at the feast, though Saul wanted him only that he might have an opportunity of nailing him to the wall with his javelin, 1 Sam. xx. 25—27, &c. It is sad to see holy ordinances prostituted to such unholy purposes. 2. A fearful apprehension that they had of missing their game: "*Will he not come up to the feast?* If he do not, our measures are broken, and we are all undone; for there is no sending a pursuivant into the country, to fetch him up."

[3.] The orders issued out by the government for the apprehending of him were very strict, *v.* 57. The great sanhedrim issued out a proclamation, strictly charging and requiring that if any person in city or country *knew where he was* (pretending that he was a criminal, and had fled from justice) they should show it, that he might be taken, probably promising a reward to any that would discover him, and imposing a penalty on such as harboured him; so that hereby he was represented to the people as an obnoxious dangerous man, an outlaw, whom any one might have a blow at. Saul issued out such a proclamation for the apprehending of David, and Ahab of Elijah. See, *First,* How intent they were upon this prosecution, and how indefatigably they laboured in it, now at a time when, if they had had any sense of religion and the duty of their function, they would have found something else to do. *Secondly,* How willing they were to involve others in the guilt with them; if any man were capable of betraying Christ, they would have him think himself bound to do it. Thus was the interest they had in the people abused to the worst purposes. Note, It is an aggravation of the sins of wicked rulers that they commonly make those that are under them instruments of their unrighteousness. But notwithstanding this proclamation, though doubtless many knew where he was, yet such was his interest in the affections of some, and such God's hold of the consciences of others, that he continued undiscovered, for the *Lord hid him.*

CHAP. XII.

It was a melancholy account which we had in the close of the foregoing chapter of the dishonour done to our Lord Jesus, when the scribes and Pharisees proclaimed him a traitor to their church, and put upon him all the marks of ignominy they could: but the story of this chapter balances that, by giving us an account of the honour done to the Redeemer, notwithstanding all that reproach thrown upon him. Thus the one was set over against the other. Let us see what honours were heaped on the head of the Lord Jesus, even in the depths of his humiliation. I. Mary did him honour, by anointing his feet at the supper in Bethany, ver. 1—11. II. The common people did him honour, with their acclamations of joy, when he rode in triumph into Jerusalem, ver. 12—19. III. The Greeks did him honour, by enquiring after him with a longing desire to see him, ver. 20—26. IV. God the Father did him honour, by a voice from heaven, bearing testimony to him, ver. 27—36. V. He had honour done him by the Old-Testament prophets, who foretold the infidelity of those that heard the report of him, ver. 37—41. VI. He had honour done him by some of the chief rulers, whose consciences witnessed for him, though they had not courage to own it, ver. 42, 43. VII. He claimed honour to himself, by asserting his divine mission, and the account he gave of his errand into the world, ver. 44—50.

THEN Jesus six days before the
passover came to Bethany, where
Lazarus was which had been dead,
whom he raised from the dead. 2
There they made him a supper; and
Martha served: but Lazarus was one
of them that sat at the table with him.
3 Then took Mary a pound of ointment of spikenard, very costly, and
anointed the feet of Jesus, and wiped
his feet with her hair: and the house
was filled with the odour of the ointment. 4 Then saith one of his disciples, Judas Iscariot, Simon's *son,*
which should betray him, 5 Why
was not this ointment sold for three
hundred pence, and given to the poor?
6 This he said, not that he cared for
the poor; but because he was a thief
and had the bag, and bare what was
put therein. 7 Then said Jesus, Let
her alone: against the day of my burying hath she kept this. 8 For the
poor always ye have with you; but
me ye have not always. 9 Much

people of the Jews therefore knew
that he was there: and they came
not for Jesus' sake only, but that they
might see Lazarus also, whom he had
raised from the dead. 10 But the
chief priests consulted that they
might put Lazarus also to death; 11
Because that by reason of him many
of the Jews went away, and believed
on Jesus.

In these verses we have,

I. The *kind visit* our Lord Jesus paid to his friends at Bethany, *v.* 1. He came up out of the country, *six days before the passover,* and took up at Bethany, a town which, according to the computation of our metropolis, lay so near Jerusalem as to be within the bills of mortality. He lodged here with his friend Lazarus, whom he had lately *raised from the dead.* His coming to Bethany now may be considered,

1. As a preface to the passover he intended to celebrate, to which reference is made in assigning the date of his coming: *Six days before the passover.* Devout men set time apart before, to prepare themselves for that solemnity, and thus it became our Lord Jesus to *fulfil all righteousness.* Thus he has set us an example of solemn self-sequestration, before the solemnities of the gospel passover; let us hear the voice crying, *Prepare ye the way of the Lord.*

2. As a voluntary exposing of himself to the fury of his enemies; now that his hour was at hand he came within their reach, and freely offered himself to them, though he had shown them how easily he could evade all their snares. Note, (1.) Our Lord Jesus was voluntary in his sufferings; his life was not *forced* from him, but *resigned: Lo, I come.* As the strength of his persecutors could not overpower him, so their subtlety could not surprise him, but he died because he would. (2.) As there is a time when we are allowed to shift for our own preservation, so there is a time when we are called to hazard our lives in the cause of God, as St. Paul, when he *went bound in the Spirit to Jerusalem.*

3. As an instance of his kindness to his friends at Bethany, whom he loved, and from whom he was shortly to be taken away. This was a farewell visit; he came to take leave of them, and to leave with them words of comfort against the day of trial that was approaching. Note, Though Christ depart for a time from his people, he will give them intimations that he departs in love, and not in anger. Bethany is here described to be the town *where Lazarus was, whom he raised from the dead.* The miracle wrought here put a new honour upon the place, and made it remarkable. Christ came hither to observe what improvement was made of this miracle; for where Christ works wonders, and shows signal favours, he looks after them, to see whether the intention of them be answered. Where he has sown plentifully, he observes whether it comes up again.

II. The *kind entertainment* which his friends there gave him: They *made him a supper* (*v.* 2), a great supper, a feast. It is queried whether this was the same with that which is recorded, Matt. xxvi. 6, &c., in the house of Simon. Most commentators think it was; for the substance of the story and many of the circumstances agree; but that comes in after what was said *two days* before the passover, whereas this was done *six days* before; nor is it likely that Martha should serve in any house but her own; and therefore I incline with Dr. Lightfoot to think them different: that in Matthew on the third day of the passover week, but this the seventh day of the week before, being the Jewish sabbath, the night before he rode in triumph into Jerusalem; that in the house of Simon; this of Lazarus. These two being the most public and solemn entertainments given him in Bethany, Mary probably graced them *both* with this token of her respect; and what she *left* of her ointment this first time, when she spent but a *pound* of it (*v.* 3), she used that second time, when she *poured it all out,* Mark xiv. 3. Let us see the account of this entertainment. 1. They *made him a supper;* for with them, ordinarily, supper was the best meal. This they did in token of their respect and gratitude, for a feast is made for *friendship;* and that they might have an opportunity of free and pleasant conversation with him, for a feast is made for *fellowship.* Perhaps it is in allusion to this and the like entertainments given to Christ in the days of his flesh that he promises, to such as open the door of their hearts to him, that he will *sup with them,* Rev. iii. 20. 2. Martha *served;* she herself waited at table, in token of her great respect to the Master. Though a person of some quality, she did not think it below her to *serve,* when Christ sat at meat; nor should we think it a dishonour or disparagement to us to stoop to any service whereby Christ may be honoured. Christ had formerly reproved Martha for being *troubled with much serving.* But she did not therefore leave off serving, as some, who, when they are reproved for one extreme, peevishly run into another; no, still she *served;* not as then at a distance, but *within hearing* of Christ's gracious words, reckoning those happy who, as the queen of Sheba said concerning Solomon's servants, stood continually before him, to hear his wisdom; better be a *waiter* at Christ's table than a *guest* at the table of a prince. 3. Lazarus was *one of those that sat at meat.* It proved the truth of his resurrection, as it did of Christ's, that there were those who did *eat and drink with him,* Acts x. 41. Lazarus did not retire into a *wilderness* after his resurrection, as if, when he had made a visit to the other world, he must ever after be a hermit in this; no, he conversed familiarly with people, as others did. He *sat at meat,* as a monument of the miracle Christ had wrought. Those whom Christ has *raised up* to a spiritual life are made to *sit together with him.* See Eph. ii. 5, 6.

III. The particular respect which Mary showed him, above the rest, in anointing his feet with sweet ointment, *v.* 3. She had a *pound of ointment of spikenard, very costly,* which probably she had by her for her own use; but the death and resurrection of her brother had quite weaned her from the use of all such things, and with this she *anointed the feet of Jesus,* and, as a further token of her reverence for him and negligence of herself, she *wiped them with her hair,* and this was taken notice of by all that were present, for *the house was filled with the odour of the ointment.* See Prov. xxvii. 16.

1. Doubtless she intended this as a token of her love to Christ, who had given real tokens of his love to her and her family; and thus she studies what she shall render. Now by this her love to Christ appears to have been, (1.) A *generous* love; so far from sparing necessary charges in his service, she is as ingenious to *create* an occasion of expense in religion as most are to avoid it. If she had any thing more valuable than another, that must be brought out for the honour of Christ. Note, Those who love Christ truly love him so much better than this world as to be willing to lay out the best they have for him. (2.) A *condescending* love; she not only bestowed her ointment upon Christ, but with her own hands poured it upon him, which she might have ordered one of her servants to have done; nay, she did not, as usual, anoint his *head* with it, but his *feet.* True love, as it does not spare charges, so it does not spare pains, in honouring Christ. Considering what Christ has done and suffered for us, we are very ungrateful if we think any service too hard to do, or too mean to stoop to, whereby he may *really* be glorified. (3.) A *believing* love; there was faith working by this love, faith in Jesus as the Messiah, the Christ, the Anointed, who, being both priest and king, was anointed as Aaron and David were. Note, *God's Anointed* should be *our Anointed.* Has God poured on him the oil of gladness above his fellows? Let us pour on him the ointment of our best affections above all competitors. By consenting to Christ as *our* king, we must comply with God's designs, appointing him *our head* whom he has appointed, Hos. i. 11.

2. The *filling of the house* with the pleasant *odour of the ointment* may intimate to us, (1.) That those who entertain Christ in their hearts and houses bring a sweet odour into them; Christ's presence brings with it an ointment and *perfume which rejoice the heart.* (2.) Honours done to Christ are comforts to all his friends and followers; they are to God and good men an offering of a *sweet-smelling savour.*

IV. Judas's dislike of Mary's compliment, or token of her respect to Christ, *v.* 4, 5, where observe,

1. The person that carped at it was Judas, *one of his disciples;* not one of their nature, but only one of their number. It is possible for the worst of men to lurk under the disguise of the best profession; and there are many who pretend to stand in relation to Christ who really have no kindness for him. Judas was an apostle, a preacher of the gospel, and yet one that discouraged and checked this instance of pious affection and devotion. Note, It is sad to see the life of religion and holy zeal frowned upon and discountenanced by such as are bound by their office to assist and encourage it. But this was he that should *betray Christ.* Note, Coldness of love to Christ, and a secret contempt of serious piety, when they appear in professors of religion, are sad presages of a final apostasy. Hypocrites, by less instances of worldliness, discover themselves to be ready for a compliance with greater temptations.

2. The pretence with which he covered his dislike (*v.* 5): "*Why was not this ointment,* since it was designed for a pious use, sold for three hundred pence" (8*l.* 10*s.* of our money), "and *given to the poor?*" (1.) Here is a foul iniquity gilded over with a specious and plausible pretence, for Satan transforms himself into an angel of light. (2.) Here is worldly wisdom passing a censure upon pious zeal, as guilty of imprudence and mismanagement. Those who value themselves upon their *secular policy,* and undervalue others for their *serious piety,* have more in them of the spirit of Judas than they would be thought to have. (3.) Here is charity to the poor made a colour for opposing a piece of piety to Christ, and secretly made a cloak for covetousness. Many excuse themselves from *laying out* in charity under pretence of *laying up* for charity: whereas, if the clouds be full of rain, they will *empty themselves.* Judas asked, *Why was it not given to the poor?* To which it is easy to answer, Because it was better bestowed upon the Lord Jesus. Note, We must not conclude that those do no acceptable piece of service who do not do it in our way, and just as we would have them; as if every thing must be adjudged imprudent and unfit which does not take its measures from us and our sentiments. Proud men think all ill-advised who do not advise with them.

3. The detection and discovery of Judas's hypocrisy herein, *v.* 6. Here is the evangelist's remark upon it, by the direction of him who *searches the heart: This he said, not that he cared for the poor,* as he pretended, *but because he was a thief, and had the bag.*

(1.) It did not come from a principle of charity: *Not that he cared for the poor.* He had no compassion towards them, no concern for them: what were the poor to him any further than he might serve his own ends by being overseer of the poor? Thus some warmly contend for the *power* of the church, as others for its *purity,* when perhaps it may be said, Not that they care for the church; it is all one to them whether its *true interest* sink or swim, but under the pretence of this they are advancing themselves. Simeon and Levi pretended zeal for circumcision, *not that they cared* for the seal of the covenant, any more than Jehu for the Lord of hosts, when he said, *Come see my zeal.*

(2.) It did come from a principle of covetousness. The truth of the matter was, this ointment being designed for his Master, he would rather have had it in money, to be put in the common stock with which he was entrusted, and then he knew what to do with it. Observe,

[1.] Judas was treasurer of Christ's household, whence some think he was called *Iscariot,* the *bag-bearer. First,* See what *estate* Jesus and his disciples had to live upon. It was but *little;* they had neither farms nor merchandise, neither barns nor storehouses, only a *bag;* or, as some think the word signifies, a *box,* or *coffer,* wherein they kept just enough for their subsistence, giving the overplus, if any were, to the poor; this they carried about with them, wherever they went. *Omnia mea mecum porto—I carry all my property about me.* This bag was supplied by the contributions of good people, and the Master and his disciples had all *in common;* let this lessen our esteem of worldly wealth, and deaden us to the punctilios of state and ceremony, and reconcile us to a mean and despicable way of living, if this be our lot, that it was our Master's lot; for our sakes he *became poor. Secondly,* See who was the *steward* of the little they had; it was Judas, he was purse-bearer. It was his office to receive and pay, and we do not find that he gave any account what markets he made. He was appointed to this office, either, 1. Because he was the least and lowest of all the disciples; it was not Peter nor John that was made steward (though it was a place of trust and profit), but Judas, the meanest of them. Note, Secular employments, as they are a digression, so they are a degradation to a minister of the gospel; see 1 Cor. vi. 4. The prime-ministers of state in Christ's kingdom refused to be concerned in the revenue, Acts vi. 2. 2. Because he was desirous of the place. He loved in his heart to be fingering money, and therefore had the money-bag committed to him, either, (1.) As a kindness, to please him, and thereby oblige him to be true to his Master. Subjects are sometimes disaffected to the government because disappointed of their preferment; but Judas had no cause to complain of this; the bag he chose, and the bag he had. Or, (2.) In judgment upon him, to punish him for his secret wickedness; that was put into his hands which would be a snare and trap to him. Note, Strong inclinations to sin within are often justly punished with strong temptations to sin without. We have little reason to be fond of the bag, or proud of it, for at the best we are but stewards of it; and it was Judas, one of an ill character, and born to be hanged (pardon the expression), that was steward of the bag. *The prosperity of fools destroys them*

[2.] Being trusted with the bag, he was *a thief,* that is, he had a thievish disposition. The reigning love of money is *heart-theft* as much as anger and revenge are *heart-murder.* Or perhaps he had been really guilty of embezzling his Master's stores, and converting to his own use what was given to the public stock. And some conjecture that he was now contriving to fill his pockets, and then run away and leave his Master, having heard him speak so much of troubles approaching, to which he could by no means reconcile himself. Note, Those to whom the management and disposal of public money is committed have need to be governed by steady principles of justice and honesty, that no blot cleave to their hands; for though some make a jest of cheating the government, or the church, or the country, if cheating be *thieving,* and, communities being more considerable than particular persons, if robbing them be the greater sin, the guilt of theft and the portion of thieves will be found no jesting matter. Judas, who had betrayed his trust, soon after betrayed his Master.

V. Christ's justification of what Mary did (*v.* 7, 8): *Let her alone.* Hereby he intimated his acceptance of her kindness (though he was perfectly mortified to all the delights of sense, yet, as it was a token of her good-will, he signified himself well-pleased with it), and his care that she should not be molested in it: *Pardon her,* so it may be read; "excuse her this once, if it be an error it is an error of her love." Note, Christ would not have those censured nor discouraged who sincerely design to please him, though in their honest endeavours there be not all the discretion that may be, Rom. xiv. 3. Though we would not do as they do, yet *let them alone.* For Mary's justification,

1. Christ puts a favourable construction upon what she did, which those that condemned it were not aware of: *Against the day of my burying she has kept this.* Or, *She has reserved this for the day of my embalming;* so Dr. Hammond. "You do not grudge the ointment used for the embalming of your dead friends, nor say that it should be sold, and given to the poor. Now this anointing either was so *intended,* or at least may be so *interpreted;* for the day of my burying is now at hand, and she has anointed a body that is already *as good as dead.*" Note, (1.) Our Lord Jesus thought much and often of his own death and burial; it

would be good for us to do so too. (2.) Providence does often so open a door of opportunity to good Christians, and the Spirit of grace does so open their hearts, that the expressions of their pious zeal prove to be more *seasonable,* and more *beautiful,* than any foresight of their own could make them. (3.) The grace of Christ puts kind comments upon the pious words and actions of good people, and not only makes the best of what is amiss, but makes the most of what is good.

2. He gives a sufficient answer to Judas's objection, *v.* 8. (1.) It is so ordered in the kingdom of Providence that *the poor we have always with us,* some or other that are proper objects of charity (Deut. xv. 11); such there will be as long as there are in this lapsed state of mankind so much folly and so much affliction. (2.) It is so ordered in the kingdom of grace that the church should not always have the bodily presence of Jesus Christ: "*Me you have not always,* but only now for a little time." Note, We need wisdom, when two duties come in competition, to know which to give the preference to, which must be determined by the circumstances. Opportunities are to be improved, and those opportunities first and most vigorously which are likely to be of the shortest continuance, and which we see most speedily hastening away. That good duty which may be done *at any time* ought to give way to that which cannot be done but *just now.*

VI. The public notice which was taken of our Lord Jesus here at this supper in Bethany (*v.* 9): *Much people of the Jews knew that he was there,* for he was the talk of the town, and *they came* flocking thither; the more because he had lately absconded, and now broke out as the sun from behind a dark cloud. 1. They came to see Jesus, whose name was very much magnified, and made considerable by the late miracle he had wrought in raising Lazarus. They came, not to hear him, but to gratify their curiosity with a sight of him here at Bethany, fearing he would not appear publicly, as he used to do, this passover. They came, not to seize him, or inform against him, though the government had prosecuted him to an outlawry, but to see him, and show him respect. Note, There are some in whose affections Christ will have an interest, in spite of all the attempts of his enemies to misrepresent him. It being known where Christ was, multitudes came to him. Note, Where the king is there is the court; where Christ is there will the *gathering of the people be,* Luke xvii. 37. 2. They came to see Lazarus and Christ together, which was a very inviting sight. Some came for the confirmation of their faith in Christ, to have the story perhaps from Lazarus's own mouth. Others came only for the gratifying of their curiosity, that they might say they had seen a man who had been dead and buried, and yet lived again; so that Lazarus served for a *show,* these holy-days, to those who, like the Athenians, spent their time in telling and hearing new things. Perhaps some came to put curious questions to Lazarus about the state of the dead, to ask what news from the other world; we ourselves have sometimes said, it may be, We would have gone a great way for one hour's discourse with Lazarus. But if any came on this errand it is probable that Lazarus was silent, and gave them no account of his voyage; at least, the scripture is silent, and gives us no account of it; and we must not covet to be wise above what is written. But our Lord Jesus was present, who was a much fitter person for them to apply to than Lazarus; for if we hear not Moses and the prophets, Christ and the apostles, if we heed not what they tell us concerning another world, neither should we be persuaded though Lazarus rose from the dead. We have a more sure word of prophecy.

VII. The indignation of the chief priests at the growing interest of our Lord Jesus, and their plot to crush it (*v.* 10, 11): They *consulted* (or decreed) *how they might put Lazarus also to death,* because that *by reason of him* (of what was done to him, not of any thing he said or did) *many of the Jews went away, and believed on Jesus.* Here observe,

1. How vain and unsuccessful their attempts against Christ had hitherto been. They had done all they could to alienate the people from him, and exasperate them against him, and yet many of the Jews, their neighbours, their creatures, their admirers, were so overcome by the convincing evidence of Christ's miracles that they *went away* from the interest and party of the priests, went off from obedience to their tyranny, *and believed on Jesus;* and it was by reason of Lazarus; his resurrection put life into their faith, and convinced them that this Jesus was undoubtedly the Messiah, and had life in himself, and power to give life. This miracle confirmed them in the belief of his other miracles, which they had heard he wrought in Galilee: what was impossible to him that could raise the dead?

2. How absurd and unreasonable this day's vote was—that Lazarus must be put to death. This is an instance of the most brutish rage that could be; they were like a *wild bull in a net,* full of fury, and laying about them without any consideration. It was a sign that they *neither feared God nor regarded man.* For, (1.) If they had feared God, they would not have done such an act of defiance to him. God will have Lazarus to live by miracle, and they will have him to die by malice. They cry, *Away with such a fellow, it is not fit he should live,* when God had so lately sent him back to the earth, declaring it highly fit he should live; what was this but *walking contrary to God?* They would put Lazarus to death, and challenge almighty power to raise him again, as if they could

contend with God, and try titles with the King of kings. Who has the keys of death and the grave, he or they? *O cæca malitia! Christus qui suscitare potuit mortuum, non possit occisum.—Blind malice, to suppose that Christ, who could raise one that had died a natural death, could not raise one that had been slain!*—Augustine in loc. Lazarus is singled out to be the object of their special hatred, because God has distinguished him by the tokens of his peculiar love, as if they had made a league offensive and defensive with death and hell, and resolved to be severe upon all deserters. One would think that they should rather have consulted how they might have joined in friendship with Lazarus and his family, and by their mediation have reconciled themselves to this Jesus whom they had persecuted; but the god of this world had *blinded their minds.* (2.) If they had regarded man, they would not have done such an act of injustice to Lazarus, an innocent man, to whose charge they could not pretend to lay any crime. What bands are strong enough to hold those who can so easily break through the most sacred ties of common justice, and violate the maxims which even nature itself teaches? But the support of their own tyranny and superstition was thought sufficient, as in the church of Rome, not only to justify, but to consecrate the greatest villanies, and make them meritorious.

12 On the next day much people
that were come to the feast, when
they heard that Jesus was coming
to Jerusalem, 13 Took branches of
palm trees, and went forth to meet
him, and cried Hosanna: Blessed *is*
the King of Israel that cometh in the
name of the Lord. 14 And Jesus,
when he had found a young ass, sat
thereon; as it is written, 15 Fear
not, daughter of Sion: behold, thy
King cometh, sitting on an ass's colt.
16 These things understood not his
disciples at the first: but when Jesus
was glorified, then remembered they
that these things were written of him,
and *that* they had done these things
unto him. 17 The people therefore
that was with him when he called
Lazarus out of his grave, and raised
him from the dead, bare record. 18
For this cause the people also met
him, for that they heard that he had
done this miracle. 19 The Pharisees
therefore said among themselves,
Perceive ye how ye prevail nothing?
behold, the world is gone after him.

This story of Christ's riding in triumph to Jerusalem is recorded by all the evangelists, as worthy of special remark; and in it we may observe,

I. The respect that was paid to our Lord Jesus by the common people, *v.* 12, 13, where we are told,

1. Who they were that paid him this respect: *much people,* ὄχλος πολὺς—*a great crowd* of those that came up to the feast; not the inhabitants of Jerusalem, but the country people that came from remote parts to worship at the feast; the nearer the temple of the Lord, the further from the Lord of the temple. They were such as *came up to the feast.* (1.) Perhaps they had been Christ's hearers in the country, and great admirers of him there, and therefore were forward to testify their respect to him at Jerusalem, where they knew he had many enemies. Note, Those that have a true value and veneration for Christ will neither be ashamed nor afraid to own him before men in any instance whereby they may do him honour. (2.) Perhaps they were those more *devout Jews* that came up to the feast some time before, to purify themselves, that were more inclined to religion than their neighbours, and these were they that were so forward to honour Christ. Note, The more regard men have to God and religion in general, the better disposed they will be to entertain Christ and his religion, which is not destructive but perfective of all previous discoveries and institutions. They were not the rulers, nor the great men, that went out to meet Christ, but the commonalty; some would have called them a mob, a rabble: but Christ has chosen the weak and foolish things (1 Cor. i. 27), and is honoured more by the multitude than by the magnificence of his followers; for he values men by their souls, not their names and titles of honour.

2. On what occasion they did it: *They heard that Jesus was coming to Jerusalem.* They had enquired for him (*ch.* xi. 55, 56): *Will he not come up to the feast?* And now they hear he is coming; for none that seek Christ seek in vain. Now when they heard he was coming, they bestirred themselves, to give him an agreeable reception. Note, Tidings of the approach of Christ and his kingdom should awaken us to consider what is the work of the day, that it may be done in the day. Israel must prepare to meet *their God* (Amos iv. 12), and the virgins to *meet the bridegroom.*

3. In what way they expressed their respect; they had not the keys of the city to present to him, nor the sword nor mace to carry before him, none of the city music to compliment him with, but such as they had they gave him; and even this despicable crowd was a faint resemblance of that glorious company which John saw *before the throne, and before the Lamb,* Rev. vii. 9, 10. Though these were not before the throne,

they were before the Lamb, the paschal Lamb, who now, according to the usual ceremony, four days before the feast, was set apart to be sacrificed for us. There it is said of that celestial choir,

(1.) That they had palms in their hands, and so had these *branches of palm-trees.* The palm-tree has ever been an emblem of victory and triumph; Cicero calls one that had won many prizes *plurimarum palmarum homo*—*a man of many palms.* Christ was now by his death to conquer principalities and powers, and therefore it was fit that he should have the victor's palm borne before him; though he was but girding on the harness, yet he could boast as though he had put it off. But this was not all; the carrying of palm-branches was part of the ceremony of the feast of tabernacles (Lev. xxiii. 40; Neh. viii. 15), and their using this expression of joy in the welcome given to our Lord Jesus intimates that all the feasts pointed at his gospel, had their accomplishment in it, and particularly that of the feast of tabernacles, Zech. xiv. 16.

(2.) That they *cried with a loud voice, saying, Salvation to our God* (Rev. vii. 10); so did these here, they shouted before him, as is usual in popular welcomes, *Hosanna, blessed is the king of Israel, that comes in the name of the Lord;* and *hosanna* signifies *salvation.* It is quoted from Ps. cxviii. 25, 26. See how well acquainted these common people were with the scripture, and how pertinently they apply it to the Messiah. High thoughts of Christ will be best expressed in scripture-words. Now in their acclamations, [1.] They acknowledge our Lord Jesus to be the king of Israel, that comes *in the name of the Lord.* Though he went now in poverty and disgrace, yet, contrary to the notions their scribes had given them of the Messiah, they own him to be a king, which bespeaks both his dignity and honour, which we must adore; and his dominion and power, to which we must submit. They own him to be, *First,* A rightful king, coming in *the name of the Lord* (Ps. ii. 6), sent of God, not only as a prophet, but as a king. *Secondly,* The promised and long-expected king, Messiah the prince, for he is *king of Israel.* According to the light they had, they proclaimed him king of Israel in the streets of Jerusalem; and, they themselves being Israelites, hereby they avouched him for their king. [2.] They heartily wish well to his kingdom, which is the meaning of hosanna; let the king of Israel prosper, as when Solomon was crowned they cried, *God save king Solomon,* 1 Kings i. 39. In crying hosanna they prayed for three things:—*First,* That his kingdom might come, in the light and knowledge of it, and in the power and efficacy of it. God speed the gospel plough. *Secondly,* That it might conquer, and be victorious over all opposition, Rev. vi. 2. *Thirdly,* That it might continue. Hosanna is, *Let the king live for ever;* though his kingdom may be disturbed, let it never be destroyed, Ps. lxxii. 17. [3.] They bid him welcome into Jerusalem: "*Welcome is he that cometh;* we are heartily glad to see him; *come in thou blessed of the Lord;* and well may we attend with our blessings him who meets us with his." This welcome is like that (Ps. xxiv. 7—9), *Lift up your heads, O ye gates.* Thus we must every one of us bid Christ welcome into our hearts, that is, we must praise him, and be well pleased in him. As we should be highly pleased with the being and attributes of God, and his relation to us, so we should be with the person and offices of the Lord Jesus, and his mediation between us and God. Faith saith, *Blessed is he that cometh.*

II. The posture Christ puts himself into for receiving the respect that was paid him (*v.* 14): *When he had found,* or procured, *a young ass,* he *sat thereon.* It was but a poor sort of figure he made, he alone upon an ass, and a crowd of people about him shouting *Hosanna.* 1. This was much more of state than he used to take; he used to travel on foot, but now was mounted. Though his followers should be willing to take up with mean things, and not affect any thing that looks like grandeur, yet they are allowed to use the service of the inferior creatures, according as God in his providence gives particular possession of those things over which, by his covenant with Noah and his sons, he has given to man a general dominion. 2. Yet it was much less of state than the great ones of the world usually take. If he would have made a public entry, according to the state of a man of high degree, he should have rode in a chariot like that of Solomon's (Cant. iii. 9, 10), with *pillars of silver,* the *bottom of gold,* and the *covering of purple;* but, if we judge according to the fashion of this world, to be introduced thus was rather a disparagement than any honour to the king of Israel, for it seemed as if he would look great, and knew not how. His kingdom was not of this world, and therefore came not with outward pomp. He was now humbling himself, but in his exalted state John sees him in a vision *on a white horse, with a bow and a crown.*

III. The fulfilling of the scripture in this: *As it is written, Fear not, daughter of Sion, v.* 15. This is quoted from Zech. ix. 9. To him bore all the prophets witness, and particularly to this concerning him.

1. It was foretold that Zion's king should come, should come *thus, sitting on an ass's colt;* even this minute circumstance was foretold, and Christ took care it should be punctually fulfilled. Note, (1.) Christ is Zion's king; the holy hill of Zion was of old destined to be the metropolis or royal city of the Messiah. (2.) Zion's king does and will look after her, and come to her; though for a short time he retires, in due time he returns. (3.) Though he comes but slowly

(an ass is slow-paced), yet he comes surely, and with such expressions of humility and condescension as greatly encourage the addresses and expectations of his loyal subjects. Humble supplicants may reach to speak with him. If this be a discouragement to Zion, that her king appears in no greater state or strength, let her know that though he comes to her riding on an ass's colt, yet he goes forth against her enemies riding *on the heavens for her help*, Deut. xxxiii. 26.

2. The daughter of Zion is therefore called upon to *behold her king*, to take notice of him and his approaches; behold and wonder, for he comes with observation, though not with outward show, Cant. iii. 11. *Fear not.* In the prophecy, Zion is told to rejoice greatly, and to shout, but here it is rendered, *Fear not.* Unbelieving fears are enemies to spiritual joys; if they be cured, if they be conquered, joy will come of course; Christ comes to his people to *silence* their fears. If the case be so that we cannot reach to the exultations of joy, yet we should labour to get from under the oppressions of fear. *Rejoice greatly;* at least, *fear not.*

IV. The remark made by the evangelist respecting the disciples (*v.* 16): *They understood not at first* why Christ did this, and how the scripture was fulfilled; but when *Jesus was glorified*, and thereupon the Spirit poured out, then they remembered that *these things were written of him* in the Old Testament, and that they and others had, in pursuance thereof, *done these things to him.*

1. See here the imperfection of the disciples in their infant state; even *they understood not these things at first.* They did not consider, when they fetched the ass and set him thereon, that they were performing the ceremony of the inauguration of Zion's king. Now observe, (1.) The scripture is often fulfilled by the agency of those who have not themselves an eye to the scripture in what they do, Isa. xlv. 4. (2.) There are many excellent things, both in the word and providence of God, which the disciples themselves do not at first understand: not at their first acquaintance with the things of God, while they *see men as trees walking;* not at the first proposal of the things to their view and consideration. That which afterwards is clear was at first dark and doubtful. (3.) It well becomes the disciples of Christ, when they are grown up to maturity in knowledge, frequently to reflect upon the follies and weaknesses of their first beginning, that free grace may have the glory of their proficiency, and they may have compassion on the ignorant. *When I was a child, I spoke as a child.*

2. See here the improvement of the disciples in their adult state. Though they had been children, they were not always so, but went on to perfection. Observe,

(1.) When they understood it: *When Jesus was glorified;* for, [1.] Till then they did not rightly apprehend the nature of his kingdom, but expected it to appear in external pomp and power, and therefore knew not how to apply the scriptures which spoke of it to so mean an appearance. Note, The right understanding of the spiritual nature of Christ's kingdom, of its powers, glories, and victories, would prevent our misinterpreting and misapplying the scriptures that speak of it. [2.] Till then the Spirit was not poured out, who was to lead them into all truth. Note, The disciples of Christ are enabled to understand the scriptures by the same Spirit that indited the scriptures. *The Spirit of revelation is* to all the saints a *spirit of wisdom*, Eph. i. 17, 18.

(2.) How they understood it; they compared the prophecy with the event, and put them together, that they might mutually receive light from each other, and so they came to understand both: *Then remembered they that these things were written of him* by the prophets, consonant to which they were done to him. Note, Such an admirable harmony there is between the word and works of God that the remembrance of what is written will enable us to understand what is done, and the observation of what is done will help us to understand what is written. *As we have heard, so have we seen.* The scripture is every day fulfilling.

V. The reason which induced the people to pay this respect to our Lord Jesus upon his coming into Jerusalem, though the government was so much set against him. It was because of the illustrious miracle he had lately wrought in raising Lazarus.

1. See here what account and what assurance they had of this miracle; no doubt, the city rang of it, the report of it was in all people's mouths. But those who considered it as a proof of Christ's mission, and a ground of their faith in him, that they might be well satisfied of the matter of fact, traced the report to those who were eye-witnesses of it, that they might *know the certainty* of it by the utmost evidence the thing was capable of: *The people therefore that* stood by *when he called Lazarus* out of his grave, being found out and examined, *bore record, v.* 17. They unanimously averred the thing to be true, beyond dispute or contradiction, and were ready, if called to it, to depose it upon oath, for so much is implied in the word Ἐμαρτύρει. Note, The truth of Christ's miracles was evidenced by incontestable proofs. It is probable that those who had seen this miracle did not only assert it to those who asked them, but published it unasked, that this might add to the triumphs of this solemn day; and Christ's coming in now from Bethany, where it was done, would put them in mind of it. Note, Those who wish well to Christ's kingdom should be forward to proclaim what they know that may redound to his honour.

2. What improvement they made of it, and what influence it had upon them (*v.* 18):

For this cause, as much as any other, *the people met him.* (1.) Some, out of curiosity, were desirous to see one that had done such a wonderful work. Many a good sermon he had preached in Jerusalem, which drew not such crowds after him as this one miracle did. But, (2.) Others, out of conscience, studied to do him honour, as one sent of God. This miracle was reserved for one of the last, that it might confirm those which went before, and might gain him this honour just before his sufferings; Christ's works were all not only *well done* (Mark vii. 7) but *well timed.*

VI. The indignation of the Pharisees at all this; some of them, probably, saw, and they all soon heard of, Christ's public entry. The committee appointed to find out expedients to crush him thought they had gained their point when he had retired unto privacy, and that he would soon be forgotten in Jerusalem, but they now rage and fret when they see they imagined but a *vain thing.* 1. They own that they had got no ground against him; it was plainly to be perceived that they *prevailed nothing.* They could not, with all their insinuations, alienate the people's affections from him, nor with their menaces restrain them from showing their affection to him. Note, Those who oppose Christ, and fight against his kingdom, will be made to perceive that they prevail nothing. God will accomplish his own purposes in spite of them, and the little efforts of their impotent malice. *You prevail nothing*, οὐκ ὠφελεῖτε—*you profit nothing* Note, There is nothing got by opposing Christ. 2. They own that he had got ground: *The world is gone after him;* there is a vast crowd attending him, a *world of people:* an hyperbole common in most languages. Yet here, like Caiaphas, ere they were aware, they prophesied that *the world would go after him;* some of all sorts, some from all parts; nations shall be discipled. But to what intent was this said? (1.) Thus they *express* their own vexation at the growth of his interest; their envy makes them fret. If the *horn of the righteous be exalted with honour, the wicked see it, and are grieved* (Ps. cxii. 9, 10); considering how great these Pharisees were, and what abundance of respect was paid them, one would think they needed not grudge Christ so inconsiderable a piece of honour as was now done him; but proud men would monopolize honour, and have none share with them, like Haman. (2.) Thus they excite themselves and one another, to a more vigorous carrying on of the war against Christ. As if they should say, "Dallying and delaying thus will never do. We must take some other and more effectual course, to put a stop to this infection; it is time to try our utmost skill and force, before the grievance grows past redress." Thus the enemies of religion are made more resolute and active by being baffled; and shall its friends be disheartened with every disappointment, who know its cause is righteous and will at last be victorious?

20 And there were certain Greeks
among them that came up to worship
at the feast: 21 The same came
therefore to Philip, which was of
Bethsaida of Galilee, and desired him,
saying, Sir, we would see Jesus. 22
Philip cometh and telleth Andrew:
and again Andrew and Philip tell Jesus. 23 And Jesus answered them
saying, The hour is come, that the
Son of man should be glorified. 24
Verily, verily, I say unto you, Except a corn of wheat fall into the
ground and die, it abideth alone: but
if it die, it bringeth forth much fruit.
25 He that loveth his life shall lose
it; and he that hateth his life in this
world shall keep it unto life eternal.
26 If any man serve me, let him follow me; and where I am, there shall
also my servant be: if any man serve
me, him will *my* Father honour.

Honour is here paid to Christ by certain Greeks that enquired for him with respect. We are not told what day of Christ's last week this was, probably not the same day he rode into Jerusalem (for that day was taken up in public work), but a day or two after.

I. We are told who they were that paid this honour to our Lord Jesus: *Certain Greeks among* the people who *came up to worship at the feast, v.* 20. Some think they were *Jews of the dispersion,* some of the twelve tribes that were scattered among the Gentiles, and were called *Greeks,* Hellenist Jews; but others think they were Gentiles, those whom they called *proselytes of the gate,* such as the eunuch and Cornelius. Pure natural religion met with the best assistance among the Jews, and therefore those among the Gentiles who were piously inclined joined with them in their solemn meetings, as far as was allowed them. There were devout worshippers of the true God even among those that were strangers to the commonwealth of Israel. It was in the latter ages of the Jewish church that there was this flocking of the Gentiles to the temple at Jerusalem,—a happy presage of the taking down of the partition-wall between Jews and Gentiles. The forbidding of the priests to accept of any oblation or sacrifice from a Gentile (which was done by Eleazar the son of Ananias, the high priest), Josephus says, was one of those things that brought the Romans upon them, *De Bello Jud.* lib. ii. cap. 30. Though these Greeks, if uncircumcised, were not admitted to eat the passover, yet they came to *worship at the feast.* We must thankfully use the privileges we have, though there may be others from which we are shut out.

II. What was the honour they paid him: they desired to be acquainted with him, *v.* 21. Having come to worship at the feast, they desired to make the best use they could of their time, and therefore applied to Philip, desiring that he would put them in a way to get some personal converse with the Lord Jesus. 1. Having a desire to see Christ, they were industrious in the use of proper means. They did not conclude it impossible, because he was so much crowded, to get to speak with him, nor rest in bare wishes, but resolved to try what could be done. Note, Those that would have the knowledge of Christ must seek it. 2. They made their application to Philip, one of his disciples. Some think that they had acquaintance with him formerly, and that they lived near Bethsaida in Galilee of the Gentiles; and then it teaches us that we should improve our acquaintance with good people, for our increase in the knowledge of Christ. It is good to know those who know the Lord. But if these Greeks had been near Galilee it is probable that they would have attended Christ there, where he mostly resided; therefore I think that they applied to him only because they saw him a close follower of Christ, and he was the first they could get to speak with. It was an instance of the veneration they had for Christ that they made an interest with one of his disciples for an opportunity to converse with him, a sign that they looked upon him as some great one, though he appeared mean. Those that would see Jesus by faith now that he is in heaven must apply to his ministers, whom he has appointed for this purpose, to guide poor souls in their enquiries after him. Paul must send for Ananias, and Cornelius for Peter. The bringing of these Greeks to the knowledge of Christ by the means of Philip signified the agency of the apostles, and the use made of their ministry in the conversion of the Gentiles to the faith and the discipling of the nations. 3 Their address to Philip was in short this: *Sir, we would see Jesus.* They gave him a title of respect, as one worthy of honour, because he was in relation to Christ. Their business is, they would *see Jesus;* not only see his face, that they might be able to say, when they came home, they had seen one that was so much talked of (it is probable they had seen him when he appeared publicly); but they would have some free conversation with him, and be taught by him, for which it was no easy thing to find him at leisure, his hands were so full of public work. Now that they were come to worship at the feast, they would see Jesus. Note, In our attendance upon holy ordinances, and particularly the gospel passover, the great desire of our souls should be to see Jesus; to have our acquaintance with him increased, our dependence on him encouraged, our conformity to him carried on; to see him as ours, to keep up communion with him, and derive communications of grace from him: we miss of our end in coming if we do not see Jesus. 4. Here is the report which Philip made of this to his Master, *v.* 22. He tells Andrew, who was of Bethsaida likewise, and was a *senior fellow* in the college of the apostles, contemporary with Peter, and consults him what was to be done, whether he thought the motion would be acceptable or no, because Christ had sometimes said that he was *not sent but to the house of Israel.* They agree that it must be made; but then he would have Andrew go along with him, remembering the favourable acceptance Christ had promised them, in case *two of them should agree touching any thing they should ask,* Matt. xviii. 19. Note, Christ's ministers should be helpful to one another and concur in helping souls to Christ. *Two are better than one.* It should seem that Andrew and Philip brought this message to Christ when he was teaching in public, for we read (*v.* 29) of the *people that stood by;* but he was seldom alone.

III. Christ's acceptance of this honour paid him, signified by what he said to the people hereupon, *v.* 23, &c., where he foretels both the honour which he himself should have in being followed (*v.* 23, 24) and the honour which those should have that followed him, *v.* 25, 26. This was intended for the direction and encouragement of these Greeks, and all others that desired acquaintance with him.

1. He foresees that plentiful harvest, in the conversion of the Gentiles, of which this was as it were the first-fruits, *v.* 23. Christ said to the two disciples who spoke a good word for these Greeks, but doubted whether they should speed or no, *The hour is come when the Son of man shall be glorified,* by the accession of the Gentiles to the church, and in order to that he must be rejected of the Jews. Observe,

(1.) The end designed hereby, and that is the glorifying of the Redeemer: "And is it so? Do the Gentiles begin to enquire after me? Does the morning-star appear to them? and that blessed *day-spring,* which knows its place and time too, does that begin to *take hold of the ends of the earth?* Then the hour is come for the *glorifying of the Son of man.*" This was no surprise to Christ, but a paradox to those about him. Note, [1.] The calling, the effectual calling, of the Gentiles into the church of God greatly redounded to the glory of the Son of man. The multiplying of the redeemed was the magnifying of the Redeemer. [2.] There was a time, a set time, an hour, a certain hour, for the glorifying of the Son of man, which did come at last, when the days of his humiliation were numbered and finished, and he speaks of the approach of it with exultation and triumph: *The hour is come.*

(2.) The strange way in which this end was to be attained, and that was by the death of Christ, intimated in that similitude (*v.* 24): "*Verily, verily, I say unto you,* you to whom I have spoken of my death and sufferings, *except a corn of wheat* fall not only *to,* but *into, the ground,* and *die,* and be buried and lost, it *abideth alone,* and you never see any more of it; but *if it die* according to the course of nature (otherwise it would be a miracle) it *bringeth forth much fruit,* God giving to every seed its own body." Christ is the corn of wheat, the most valuable and useful grain. Now here is,

[1.] The necessity of Christ's humiliation intimated. He would never have been the living quickening head and root of the church if he had not descended from heaven to this accursed earth and ascended from earth to the accursed tree, and so accomplished our redemption. He must *pour out his soul unto death,* else he cannot *divide a portion with the great,* Isa. liii. 12. He shall have a seed given him, but he must shed his blood to purchase them and purify them, must win them and wear them. It was necessary likewise as a qualification for that glory which he was to have by the accession of multitudes to his church; for if he had not by his sufferings made satisfaction for sin, and so brought in an everlasting righteousness, he would not have been sufficiently provided for the entertainment of those that should come to him, and therefore must *abide alone.*

[2.] The advantage of Christ's humiliation illustrated. He *fell to the ground* in his incarnation, seemed to be buried alive in this earth, so much was his glory veiled; but this was not all: *he died.* This immortal seed submitted to the laws of mortality, he lay in the grave like seed under the clods; but as the seed comes up again green, and fresh, and flourishing, and with a great increase, so one dying Christ gathered to himself thousands of living Christians, and he became their root. The salvation of souls hitherto, and henceforward to the end of time, is all owing to the dying of this *corn of wheat.* Hereby the Father and the Son are glorified, the church is replenished, the mystical body is kept up, and will at length be completed; and, when time shall be no more, the Captain of our salvation, *bringing many sons to glory* by the virtue of his death, and being so made perfect by sufferings, shall be celebrated for ever with the admiring praises of saints and angels, Heb. ii. 10, 13.

2. He foretels and promises an abundant recompence to those who should cordially embrace him and his gospel and interest, and should make it appear that they do so by their faithfulness in suffering for him or in serving him.

(1.) In suffering for him (*v.* 25): *He that loves his life* better than Christ *shall lose it;* but he that hates *his life in this world,* and prefers the favour of God and an interest in Christ before it, shall *keep it unto life eternal.* This doctrine Christ much insisted on, it being the great design of his religion to wean us from this world, by setting before us another world.

[1.] See here the fatal consequences of an inordinate love of life; many a man hugs himself to death, and loses his life by overloving it. He that so loves his animal life as to indulge his appetite, and make *provision for the flesh, to fulfil the lusts thereof,* shall thereby shorten his days, shall lose the life he is so fond of, and another infinitely better. He that is so much in love with the life of the body, and the ornaments and delights of it, as, for fear of exposing it or them, to deny Christ, he shall lose it, that is, lose a real happiness in the other world, while he thinks to secure an imaginary one in this. *Skin for skin* a man may give for his life, and make a good bargain, but he that gives his soul, his God, his heaven, for it, buys life too dear, and is guilty of the folly of him who sold a birth-right for a mess of pottage.

[2.] See also the blessed recompence of a holy contempt of life. He that so hates the life of the body as to venture it for the preserving of the life of his soul shall find both, with unspeakable advantage, in eternal life. Note, *First,* It is required of the disciples of Christ that they hate *their life in this world;* a life in this world supposes a life in the other world, and this is hated when it is loved less than that. Our life in this world includes all the enjoyments of our present state, riches, honours, pleasures, and long life in the possession of them; these we must hate, that is, despise them as vain and insufficient to make us happy, dread the temptations that are in them, and cheerfully part with them whenever they come in competition with the service of Christ, Acts xx. 24; xxi. 13; Rev. xii. 11. See here much of the *power of godliness*—that it conquers the strongest natural affections; and much of the *mystery of godliness*—that it is the greatest wisdom, and yet makes men hate their own lives. *Secondly,* Those who, in love to Christ, hate their own lives in this world, shall be abundantly recompensed in the resurrection of the just. *He that hateth his life shall keep it;* he puts it into the hands of one that will *keep it to life eternal,* and restore it with as great an improvement as the heavenly life can make of the earthly one.

(2.) In serving him (*v.* 26): *If any man* profess *to serve me,* let him *follow me,* as a servant follows his master; and *where I am,* ἐκεῖ καὶ ὁ διάκονος ὁ ἐμὸς ἔσται—there *let my servant be;* so some read it, as part of the duty, there let him be, to attend upon me; we read it as part of the promise, *there shall he be* in happiness with me. And, lest this should seem a small matter, he adds, *If any man serve me, him will my Father honour;* and that is enough, more than enough. The Greeks desired to see Jesus (*v.* 21), but Christ lets them know that it was not enough to see him, they must *serve him.* He did not come into the world, to be a show for us to gaze at, but a king to be ruled by. And he says this for the encouragement of those who enquired after him to become his servants. In taking servants it is usual to fix both the work and the wages; Christ does both here.

[1.] Here is the work which Christ expects from his servants; and it is very easy and reasonable, and such as becomes them.

First, Let them attend their Master's movements: *If any man serve me, let him follow me.* Christians must follow Christ, follow his methods and prescriptions, *do the things that he says,* follow his example and pattern, *walk as he also walked,* follow his conduct by his providence and Spirit. We must go whither he leads us, and in the way he leads us; must follow the Lamb whithersoever he goes before us. "If any man serve me, if he put himself into that relation to me, let him apply himself to the business of my service, and be always ready at my call." Or, "If any man do indeed serve me, let him make an open and public profession of his relation to me, by following me, as the servant owns his Master by following him in the streets."

Secondly, Let them attend their Master's repose: *Where I am, there let my servant be,* to wait upon me. Christ is where his church is, in the assemblies of his saints, where his ordinances are administered; and *there let his servants be,* to present themselves before him, and receive instructions from him. Or, "Where I am to be in heaven, whither I am now going, there let the thoughts and affections of my servants be, there let their conversation be, *where Christ sitteth.*" Col. iii. 1, 2.

[2.] Here are the wages which Christ promises to his servants; and they are very rich and noble.

First, They shall be happy with him: *Where I am, there shall also my servant be.* To be with him, when he was here in poverty and disgrace, would seem but poor preferment, and therefore, doubtless, he means being with him in paradise, sitting with him at his table above, on his throne there; it is the happiness of heaven to be with Christ there, *ch.* xvii. 24. Christ speaks of heaven's happiness as if he were already in it: Where *I am;* because he was sure of it, and near to it, and it was still *upon his heart,* and *in his eye.* And the same joy and glory which he thought recompence enough for all his services and sufferings are proposed to his servants as the recompence of theirs. Those that follow him in the way shall be with him in the end.

Secondly, They shall be honoured by his Father; he will make them amends for all their pains and loss, by conferring an honour upon them, such as becomes a great God to give, but far beyond what such worthless worms of the earth could expect to receive. The rewarder is God himself, who takes the services done to the Lord Jesus as done to himself. The reward is honour, true lasting honour, the highest honour; it is the honour that comes from God. It is said (Prov. xxvii. 18), *He that waits on his master* (humbly and diligently) *shall be honoured.* Those that wait on Christ God will put honour upon, such as will be taken notice of another day, though now under a veil. Those that serve Christ must humble themselves, and are commonly vilified by the world, in recompence of both which they shall be exalted in due time.

Thus far Christ's discourse has reference to those Greeks who desired to *see him,* encouraging them to serve him. What became of those Greeks we are not told, but are willing to hope that those who thus asked the way to heaven, with their faces thitherward, found it, and walked in it.

27 Now is my soul troubled; and
what shall I say? Father, save me
from this hour: but for this cause
came I unto this hour. 28 Father,
glorify thy name. Then came there
a voice from heaven, *saying,* I have
both glorified *it,* and will glorify *it*
again. 29 The people therefore, that
stood by, and heard *it,* said that it
thundered: others said, An angel
spake to him. 30 Jesus answered
and said, This voice came not because
of me, but for your sakes. 31 Now
is the judgment of this world: now
shall the prince of this world be cast
out. 32 And I, if I be lifted up
from the earth, will draw all *men* unto
me. 33 This he said, signifying
what death he should die. 34 The
people answered him, We have heard
out of the law that Christ abideth for
ever: and how sayest thou, The Son
of man must be lifted up? who is
this Son of man? 35 Then Jesus
said unto them, Yet a little while is
the light with you. Walk while ye
have the light, lest darkness come
upon you: for he that walketh in
darkness knoweth not whither he
goeth. 36 While ye have light, believe in the light, that ye may be the
children of light. These things spake
Jesus, and departed, and did hide
himself from them.

Honour is here done to Christ by his Father in a voice from heaven, occasioned by the following part of his discourse, and which gave occasion to a further conference with the people. In these verses we have,

I. Christ's address to his Father, upon occasion of the trouble which seized his spirit at this time: *Now is my soul troubled, v.* 27. A strange word to come from Christ's mouth, and at this time surprising, for it comes in the midst of divers pleasing prospects, in which, one would think, he should have said, Now is my soul *pleased.* Note, Trouble of soul sometimes follows after great enlargements of spirit. In this world of mixture and change we must expect damps upon our joy, and the highest degree of comfort to be the next degree to trouble. When Paul had been in the third heavens, he had a *thorn in the flesh.* Observe,

1. Christ's dread of his approaching sufferings: *Now is my soul troubled.* Now the black and dismal scene began, now were the first throes of the travail of his soul, now his agony began, his soul *began to be exceedingly sorrowful.* Note, (1.) The sin of our soul was the trouble of Christ's soul, when he undertook to redeem and save us, and to make his soul an offering for our sin. (2.) The trouble of his soul was designed to ease the trouble of our souls; for, after this, he said to his disciples (*ch.* xiv. 1), "*Let not your hearts be troubled;* why should yours be troubled and mine too?" Our Lord Jesus went on cheerfully in his work, in prospect of the joy set before him, and yet submitted to a trouble of soul. Holy mourning is consistent with spiritual joy, and the way to eternal joy. Christ was *now* troubled, now in sorrow, now in fear, now for a season; but it would not be so always, it would not be so long. The same is the comfort of Christians in their troubles; they are but *for a moment,* and will be turned into joy.

2. The strait he seems to be in hereupon, intimated in those words, *And what shall I say?* This does not imply his consulting with any other, as if he needed advice, but considering with himself what was fit to be said now. When our souls are troubled we must take heed of speaking unadvisedly, but debate with ourselves what we shall say. Christ speaks like one at a loss, as if what he should choose he wot not. There was a struggle between the work he had taken upon him, which required sufferings, and the nature he had taken upon him, which dreaded them; between these two he here pauses with, *What shall I say?* He looked, and there was *none to help,* which put him to a stand. Calvin observes this as a great instance of Christ's humiliation, that he should speak thus like one at a loss. *Quo se magis exinanivit gloriæ Dominus, eo luculentius habemus erga nos amoris specimen—The more entirely the Lord of glory emptied himself, the brighter is the proof of the love he bore us.* Thus he was *in all points tempted like as we are,* to encourage us, when we know not what to do, to direct our eyes to him.

3. His prayer to God in this strait: *Father, save me from this hour,* ἐκ τῆς ὥρας ταύτης—*out of this hour,* praying, not so much that it might not come as that he might be brought through it. *Save me from this hour;* this was the language of innocent nature, and its feelings poured forth in prayer. Note, It is the duty and interest of troubled souls to have recourse to God by faithful and fervent prayer, and in prayer to eye him as a Father. Christ was voluntary in his sufferings, and yet prayed to be saved from them. Note, Prayer against a trouble may very well consist with patience under it and submission to the will of God in it. Observe, He calls his suffering *this hour,* meaning the expected events of the time now at hand. Hereby he intimates that the time of his suffering was, (1.) A set time, set to an hour, and he knew it. It was said twice before that his hour was not yet come, but it was now so near that he might say it was come. (2.) A short time. An hour is soon over, so were Christ's sufferings; he could see through them to the *joy set before him.*

4. His acquiescence in his Father's will, notwithstanding. He presently corrects himself, and, as it were, recals what he had said: *But for this cause came I to this hour.* Innocent nature got the first word, but divine wisdom and love got the last. Note, those who would proceed regularly must go upon second thoughts. The complainant speaks first; but, if we would judge righteously, we must hear the other side. With the second thought he checked himself: *For this cause came I to this hour;* he does not silence himself with this, that he could not avoid it, there was no remedy; but satisfies himself with this, that he would not avoid it, for it was pursuant to his own voluntary engagement, and was to be the crown of his whole undertaking; should he now fly off, this would frustrate all that had been done hitherto. Reference is here had to the divine counsels concerning his sufferings, by virtue of which it behoved him thus to submit and suffer. Note, This should reconcile us to the darkest hours of our lives, that we were all along designed for them; see 1 Thess. iii. 3.

5. His regard to his Father's honour herein. Upon the withdrawing of his former petition, he presents another, which he will abide by: *Father, glorify thy name,* to the same purport with *Father, thy will be done;* for God's will is for his own glory. This expresses more than barely a submission to the will of God; it is a consecration of his sufferings to the glory of God. It was a mediatorial word, and was spoken by him as our surety, who had undertaken to satisfy divine justice for our sin. The wrong which by sin we have done to God is in his glory, his declarative glory; for in nothing else are we capable of doing him injury. We were never able to make him satisfaction for this wrong done him, nor any creature for us; nothing therefore remained but that God should get him

honour upon us in our utter ruin. Here therefore our Lord Jesus interposed, undertook to satisfy God's injured honour, and he did it by his humiliation; he denied himself in, and divested himself of, the honours due to the Son of God incarnate, and submitted to the greatest reproach. Now here he makes a tender of this satisfaction as an equivalent: "*Father, glorify thy name;* let thy justice be honoured upon the sacrifice, not upon the sinner; let the debt be levied upon me, I am solvent, the principal is not." Thus he *restored that which he took not away.*

II. The Father's answer to this address; for he heard him always, and does still. Observe, 1. How this answer was given. By a voice from heaven. The Jews speak much of a *Bath-kôl—the daughter of a voice,* as one of those divers manners by which God in time past spoke to the prophets; but we do not find any instance of his speaking thus to any but to our Lord Jesus; it was an honour reserved for him (Matt. iii. 17; xvii. 5), and here, probably, this audible voice was introduced by some visible appearance, either of light or darkness, for both have been used as vehicles of the divine glory. 2. What the answer was. It was an express return to that petition, *Father, glorify thy name: I have glorified it* already, and *I will glorify it yet again.* When we pray as we are taught, *Our Father, hallowed be thy name,* this is a comfort to us, that it is an answered prayer; answered to Christ here, and in him to all true believers. (1.) The name of God had been glorified in the life of Christ, in his doctrine and miracles, and all the examples he gave of holiness and goodness. (2.) It should be further glorified in the death and sufferings of Christ. His wisdom and power, his justice and holiness, his truth and goodness, were greatly glorified; the demands of a broken law were fully answered; the affront done to God's government satisfied for; and God accepted the satisfaction, and declared himself well pleased. What God has done for the glorifying of his own name is an encouragement to us to expect what he will yet further do. He that has secured the interests of his own glory will still secure them.

III. The opinion of the standers-by concerning this voice, *v.* 29. We may hope there were some among them whose minds were so well prepared to receive a divine revelation that they understood what was said and bore record of it. But notice is here taken of the perverse suggestion of the multitude: some of them said that *it thundered;* others, who took notice that there was plainly an articulate intelligible voice, said that certainly *an angel spoke to him.* Now this shows, 1. That it was a real thing, even in the judgment of those that were not at all well affected to him. 2. That they were loth to admit so plain a proof of Christ's divine mission. They would rather say that it was this, or that, or any thing, than that God spoke to him in answer to his prayer; and yet, if it thundered with articulate sounds (as Rev. x. 3, 4), was not that God's voice? Or, if angels spoke to him, are not they God's messengers? But thus *God speaks once, yea twice, and man perceives it not.*

IV. The account which our Saviour himself gives of this voice.

1. Why it was sent (*v.* 30): "It came *not because of me,* not merely for my encouragement and satisfaction" (then it might have been whispered in his ear privately), "*but for your sakes.*" (1.) "That all you who heard it may *believe that the Father hath sent me.*" What is said from heaven concerning our Lord Jesus, and the glorifying of the Father in him, is said for our sakes, that we may be brought to submit to him and rest upon him. (2.) "That you my disciples, who are to follow me in sufferings, may therein be comforted with the same comforts that carry me on." Let this encourage them to part with life itself for his sake, if they be called to it, that it will redound to the honour of God. Note, The promises and supports granted to our Lord Jesus in his sufferings were intended for our sakes. *For our sakes* he *sanctified himself,* and *comforted himself.*

2. What was the meaning of it. He that lay in the Father's bosom knew his voice, and what was the meaning of it; and two things God intended when he said that he would *glorify his own name:*—

(1.) That by the death of Christ Satan should be conquered (*v.* 31): *Now is the judgment.* He speaks with a divine exultation and triumph. "Now the year of my redeemed is come, and the time prefixed for breaking the serpent's head, and giving a total rent to the powers of darkness; now for that glorious achievement: *now, now,* that great work is to be done which has been so long thought of in the divine counsels, so long talked of in the written word, which has been so much the hope of saints and the dread of devils." The matter of the triumph is, [1.] That *now is the judgment of the world; κρίσις,* take it as a medical term: "Now is the *crisis* of this world." The sick and diseased world is now upon the turning point; this is the critical day upon which the trembling scale will turn for life or death, to all mankind; all that are not recovered by this will be left helpless and hopeless. Or, rather, it is a law term, as we take it: "Now, judgment is entered, in order to the taking out of execution against the prince of this world." Note, The death of Christ was the *judgment of this world. First,* It is a judgment of discovery and distinction—*judicium discretionis;* so Austin. Now is the trial of this world, for men shall have their character according as the cross of Christ is to them; to some it is foolishness and a stumbling-block, to others it is the wisdom and power of God; of which there was a figure in the two thieves that were crucified with him. By this men are judged, what they think of the death of Christ. *Secondly,* It is a judgment of favour and absolution to the chosen ones that are in the world. Christ upon the cross interposed between a righteous God and a guilty world as a sacrifice for sin and a surety for sinners, so that when he was judged, and *iniquity laid upon him,* and he was wounded for our transgressions, it was as it were the judgment of this world, for an everlasting righteousness was thereby brought in, not for Jews only, but the whole world, 1 John, ii. 1, 2; Dan. ix. 24. *Thirdly,* It is a judgment of condemnation given against the powers of darkness; see *ch.* xvi. 11. Judgment is put for vindication and deliverance, the asserting of an invaded right. At the death of Christ there was a famous trial between Christ and Satan, the serpent and the promised seed; the trial was for the world, and the lordship of it; the devil had long borne sway among the children of men, time out of mind; he now pleads prescription, grounding his claim also upon the forfeiture incurred by sin. We find him willing to have come to a composition (Luke iv. 6, 7); he would have given the kingdoms of this world to Christ, provided he would hold them by, from, and under him. But Christ would try it out with him; by dying he takes off the forfeiture to divine justice, and then fairly disputes the title, and recovers it in the court of heaven. Satan's dominion is declared to be a usurpation, and the world adjudged to the Lord Jesus as his right, Ps. ii. 6, 8. The judgment of this world is, that it belongs to Christ, and not to Satan; to Christ therefore let us all *attorn* tenants. [2.] That *now is the prince of this world cast out. First,* It is the devil that is here called the *prince of this world,* because he rules over the men of the world by the things of the world; he is the *ruler of the darkness of this world,* that is, of this dark world, of those in it that *walk in darkness,* 2 Cor. iv. 4; Eph. vi. 12. *Secondly,* He is said to be *cast out,* to be *now* cast out; for, whatever had been done hitherto towards the weakening of the devil's kingdom was done in the virtue of a Christ to come, and therefore is said to be done *now.* Christ, reconciling the world to God by the merit of his death, broke the power of death, and cast out Satan as a destroyer; Christ, reducing the world to God by the doctrine of his cross, broke the power of sin, and cast out Satan as a deceiver. The bruising of his heel was the breaking of the serpent's head, Gen. iii. 15. When his oracles were silenced, his temples forsaken, his idols famished, and the kingdoms of the world became Christ's kingdoms, then was the *prince of the world cast out,* as appears by comparing this with John's vision (Rev. xii. 8—11), where it is said to be done by the *blood of the Lamb.* Christ's frequent casting of devils out of the bodies of people was an indication of the great design of his whole undertaking. Observe, With what assurance Christ here speaks of the victory over Satan; it is as good as done, and even when he yields to death he triumphs over it.

(2.) That by the death of Christ souls should be converted, and this would be the casting out of Satan (*v.* 32): *If I be lifted up from the earth, I will draw all men unto me.* Here observe two things:—

[1.] The great design of our Lord Jesus, which was to *draw all men to him,* not the Jews only, who had been long in profession a people *near to God,* but the Gentiles also, who had been *afar off;* for he was to be the *desire of all nations* (Hag. ii. 7), and *to him must the gathering of the people be.* That which his enemies dreaded was that the world would go after him; and he would draw them to him, notwithstanding their opposition. Observe here how Christ himself is all in all in the conversion of a soul. *First,* It is Christ that draws: I *will draw.* It is sometimes ascribed to the Father (*ch.* vi. 44), but here to the Son, who is the *arm of the Lord.* He does not drive by force, but draws with the *cords of a man* (Hos. xi. 4; Jer. xxxi. 3), draws as the loadstone; the soul is *made willing,* but it is in a *day of power. Secondly,* It is to Christ that we are drawn: "I will draw them to me as the centre of their unity." The soul that was at a distance from Christ is brought into an acquaintance with him, he that was shy and distrustful of him is brought to love him and trust in him,—drawn up to his terms, into his arms. Christ was now going to heaven, and he would draw men's hearts to him thither.

[2.] The strange method he took to accomplish his design by *being lifted up from the earth.* What he meant by this, to prevent mistake, we are told (*v.* 33): *This he spoke signifying by what death he should die,* the death of the cross, though they had designed and attempted to stone him to death. He that was crucified was first nailed to the cross, and then lifted up upon it. He was *lifted up as a spectacle to the world;* lifted up between heaven and earth, as unworthy of either; yet the word here used signifies an honourable advancement, ἐὰν ὑψωθῶ—*If I be exalted;* he reckoned his sufferings his honour. Whatever death we die, if we die in Christ we shall be lifted up out of this dungeon, this den of lions, into the regions of light and love. We should learn of our Master to speak of dying with a holy pleasantness, and to say, "We shall then be lifted up." Now Christ's drawing all men to him followed his being *lifted up from the earth. First,* It followed after it in time. The great increase of the church was after the death of Christ; while Christ lived, we read of thousands at a sermon miraculously fed, but after his death we read of thousands at a sermon added to the church Israel began to multiply in Egypt after the death of Joseph. *Secondly,* It followed upon it as a blessed consequence of it. Note, There is a powerful virtue and efficacy in the death of Christ to draw souls to him. The cross of Christ, though to some a *stumbling-stone,* is to others a *loadstone.* Some make it an allusion to the drawing of fish into a net; the lifting up of Christ was as the spreading of the net (Matt. xiii. 47, 48); or to the setting up of a standard, which draws soldiers together; or, rather, it refers to the lifting up of the brazen serpent in the wilderness, which drew all those to it who were stung with fiery serpents, as soon as ever it was known that it was lifted up, and there was healing virtue in it. O what flocking was there to it! So there was to Christ, when salvation through him was preached to all nations; see *ch.* iii. 14, 15. Perhaps it has some reference to the posture in which Christ was crucified, with his arms stretched out, to invite all to him, and embrace all that come. Those that put Christ to that ignominious death thought thereby to drive all men from him; but the devil was outshot in his own bow. *Out of the eater came forth meat.*

V. The people's exception against what he said, and their cavil at it, *v.* 34. Though they had heard the voice from heaven, and the gracious words that proceeded out of his mouth, yet they object, and pick quarrels with him. Christ had called himself the *Son of man* (*v.* 23), which they knew to be one of the titles of the Messiah, Dan. vii. 13. He had also said that the *Son of man must be lifted up,* which they understood of his dying, and probably he explained himself so, and some think he repeated what he said to Nicodemus (*ch.* iii. 14), *So must the Son of man be lifted up.* Now against this,

1. They alleged those scriptures of the Old Testament which speak of the perpetuity of the Messiah, that he should be so far from being cut off in the midst of his days that he should be a *priest for ever* (Ps. cx. 4), and a king *for ever* (Ps. lxxxix. 29, &c.), that he should have *length of days for ever and ever,* and *his years as many generations* (Ps. xxi. 4; lxi. 6), from all which they inferred that the Messiah should not die. Thus great knowledge in the letter of the scripture, if the heart be unsanctified, is capable of being abused to serve the cause of infidelity, and to fight against Christianity with its own weapons. Their perverseness in opposing this to what Jesus had said will appear if we consider, (1.) That, when they vouched the scripture to prove that the Messiah *abideth for ever,* they took no notice of those texts which speak of the Messiah's death and sufferings: they had heard out of the law that *Messiah abideth for ever;* and had they never heard out of the law that Messiah should *be cut off* (Dan. ix. 26), and that he should *pour out his soul unto death* (Isa. liii. 12), and particularly that his *hands and feet* should be pierced? Why then do they make so strange of the *lifting up of the Son of man?* Note, We often run into great mistakes, and then defend them with scripture arguments, by putting those things asunder which God in his word has put together, and opposing one truth under pretence of supporting another. We have heard out of the gospel that which exalts free grace, we have heard also that which enjoins duty, and we must cordially embrace both, and not separate them, nor set them at variance. (2.) That, when they opposed what Christ said concerning the sufferings of the Son of man, they took no notice of what he had said concerning his glory and exaltation. They had heard out of the law that *Christ abideth for ever;* and had they not heard our Lord Jesus say that he should be glorified, that he should bring forth much fruit, and draw all men to him? Had he not just now promised immortal honours to his followers, which supposed his abiding for ever? But this they overlooked. Thus unfair disputants oppose some parts of the opinion of an adversary, to which, if they would but take it entire, they could not but subscribe; and in the doctrine of Christ there are paradoxes, which to men of corrupt minds are stones of stumbling—as Christ *crucified,* and yet *glorified; lifted up from the earth,* and yet *drawing all men to him.*

2. They asked hereupon, *Who is this Son of man?* This they asked, not with a desire to be instructed, but tauntingly and insultingly, as if now they had baffled him, and run him down. "Thou sayest, *The Son of man must die;* we have proved the Messiah must not, and where is then thy Messiahship? This Son of man, as thou callest thyself, cannot be the Messiah, thou must therefore think of something else to pretend to." Now that which prejudiced them against Christ was his meanness and poverty; they would rather have no Christ than a suffering one.

VI. What Christ said to this exception, or rather what he said *upon* it. The objection was a perfect cavil; they might, if they pleased, answer it themselves: man dies, and yet is immortal, and abideth for ever, so the *Son of man.* Therefore, instead of answering these fools according to their folly, he gives them a serious caution to take heed of trifling away the day of their opportunities in such vain and fruitless cavils as these (*v.* 35, 36): "*Yet a little while,* and but a little while, *is the light with you;* therefore be wise for yourselves, and *walk while you have the light.*"

1. In general, we may observe here, (1.) The concern Christ has for the souls of men, and his desire of their welfare. With what tenderness does he here admonish those to look well to themselves who were contriving

ill against him! Even when he *endured the contradiction of sinners,* he sought their conversion. See Prov. xxix. 10. (2.) The method he takes with these objectors, *with meekness instructing those that opposed themselves,* 2 Tim. ii. 25. Were but men's consciences awakened with a due concern about their everlasting state, and did they consider how little time they have to spend, and none to spare, they would not waste precious thoughts and time in trifling cavils.

2. Particularly we have here,

(1.) The advantage they enjoyed in having Christ and his gospel among them, with the shortness and uncertainty of their enjoyment of it: *Yet a little while is the light with you.* Christ is this light; and some of the ancients suggest that, in calling himself the light, he gives a tacit answer to their objection. His dying upon the cross was as consistent with his *abiding for ever* as the setting of the sun every night is with his perpetuity. The duration of Christ's kingdom is compared to that of the sun and moon, Ps. lxxii. 17; lxxxix. 36, 37. The ordinances of heaven are unchangeably fixed, and yet the sun and moon set and are eclipsed; so Christ the Sun of righteousness abides for ever, and yet was eclipsed by his sufferings, and was but a little while within our horizon. Now, [1.] The Jews at this time had the *light with them;* they had Christ's bodily presence, heard his preaching, saw his miracles. The scripture is to us a light shining in a dark place. [2.] It was to be but a little while with them; Christ would shortly leave them, their visible church state would soon after be dissolved and the kingdom of God taken from them, and blindness and hardness would happen unto Israel. Note, It is good for us all to consider what a little while we are to have the light with us. Time is short, and perhaps opportunity not so long. The candlestick may be removed; at least, we must be removed shortly. Yet a little while is the light of life with us; yet a little while is the light of the gospel with us, the day of grace, the means of grace, the Spirit of grace, yet a very little while.

(2.) The warning given them to make the best of this privilege while they enjoyed it, because of the danger they were in of losing it: *Walk while you have the light;* as travellers who make the best of their way forward, that they may not be benighted in their journey, because travelling in the night is uncomfortable and unsafe. "Come," say they, "let us mend our pace, and get forward, while we have day-light." Thus wise should we be for our souls who are journeying towards eternity. Note, [1.] It is our business to walk, to press forward towards heaven, and to get nearer to it by being made fitter for it. Our life is but a day, and we have a day's journey to go. [2.] The best time of walking is while we have the light. The day is the proper season for work, as the night is for rest. The proper time for getting grace is when we have the word of grace preached to us, and the Spirit of grace striving with us, and therefore then is the time to be busy. [3.] We are highly concerned thus to improve our opportunities, for fear lest our day be finished before we have finished our day's work and our day's journey: "*Lest darkness come upon you,* lest you lose your opportunities, and can neither recover them nor despatch the business you have to do without them." Then *darkness* comes, that is, such an utter incapacity to make sure the great salvation as renders the state of the careless sinner quite deplorable; so that, if his work be undone then, it is likely to be undone for ever.

(3.) The sad condition of those who have sinned away the gospel, and are come to the period of their day of grace. *They walk in darkness,* and know neither *where* they go, nor *whither* they go; neither the way they are walking in, nor the end they are walking towards. He that is destitute of the light of the gospel, and is not acquainted with its discoveries and directions, wanders endlessly in mistakes and errors, and a thousand crooked paths, and is not aware of it. Set aside the instructions of the Christian doctrine, and we know little of the difference between good and evil. He is going to destruction, and knows not his danger, for he is either sleeping or dancing at the pit's brink.

(4.) The great duty and interest of every one of us inferred from all this (*v.* 36): *While you have light, believe in the light.* The Jews had now Christ's presence with them, let them improve it; afterwards they had the first offers of the gospel made to them by the apostles wherever they came; now this is an admonition to them not to out-stand their market, but to accept the offer when it was made to them: the same Christ saith to all who enjoy the gospel. Note, [1.] It is the duty of every one of us *to believe in the gospel light,* to receive it as a divine light, to subscribe to the truths it discovers, for it is a light to our eyes, and to follow its guidance, for it is a light to our feet. Christ is the light, and we must believe in him as he is revealed to us; as a true light that will not deceive us, a sure light that will not misguide us. [2.] We are concerned to do this while we have the light, to lay hold on Christ while we have the gospel to show us the way to him and direct us in that way. [3.] Those that believe in the light *shall be the children of light;* they shall be owned as *Christians,* who are called *children of light* (Luke xvi. 8; Eph. v. 8) and of the day, 1 Thess. v. 5. Those that have God for their Father are children of light, for God is light; they are born from above, and heirs of heaven, and children of light, for heaven is light.

VII. Christ's retiring from them, hereupon: *These things spoke Jesus,* and said no more at this time, but left this to their consideration, *and departed, and did hide himself from them.* And this he did, 1. For their conviction and awakening. If they will not regard what he hath said, he will have nothing more to say to them. They are joined to their infidelity, as Ephraim to idols; *let them alone.* Note, Christ justly removes the means of grace from those that quarrel with him, and *hides his face* from *a froward generation,* Deut. xxxii. 20. 2. For his own preservation. He hid himself from their rage and fury, retreating, it is probable, to Bethany, where he lodged. By this it appears that what he said irritated and exasperated them, and they were made worse by that which should have made them better.

37 But though he had done so
many miracles before them, yet they
believed not on him: 38 That the
saying of Esaias the prophet might be
fulfilled, which he spake, Lord, who
hath believed our report? and to
whom hath the arm of the Lord been
revealed? 39 Therefore they could
not believe, because that Esaias said
again, 40 He hath blinded their
eyes, and hardened their heart; that
they should not see with *their* eyes,
nor understand with *their* heart, and
be converted, and I should heal them.
41 These things said Esaias, when he
saw his glory, and spake of him.

We have here the honour done to our Lord Jesus by the Old-Testament prophets, who foretold and lamented the infidelity of the many that believed not on him. It was indeed a dishonour and grief to Christ that his doctrine met with so little acceptance and so much opposition; but *this* takes off the wonder and reproach, makes the offence of it to cease, and made it no disappointment to Christ, that herein the scriptures were fulfilled. Two things are here said concerning this untractable people, and both were foretold by the evangelical prophet Isaiah, that they *did not* believe, and that they *could not* believe.

I. They did not believe (*v.* 37): *Though he had done so many miracles before them,* which, one would think, should have convinced them, yet they believed not, but opposed him. Observe,

1. The abundance of the means of conviction which Christ afforded them: He *did miracles, so many miracles; τοσαῦτα σημεῖα,* signifying both so many and so great. This refers to all the miracles he had wrought formerly; nay, the blind and lame now came to him into the temple, and he healed them, Matt. xxi. 14. His miracles were the great proof of his mission, and on the evidence of them he relied. Two things concerning them he here insists upon:—(1.) The number of them; they were *many,* — various and of divers kinds; numerous and often repeated; and every new miracle confirmed the reality of all that went before. The multitude of his miracles was not only a proof of his unexhausted power, but gave the greater opportunity to examine them; and, if there had been a cheat in them, it was morally impossible but that in some or other of them it would have been discovered; and, being all *miracles of mercy,* the more there were the more good was done. (2.) The notoriety of them. He wrought these miracles *before them,* not at a distance, not in a corner, but before many witnesses, appearing to their own eyes.

2. The inefficacy of these means: *Yet they believed not on him.* They could not gainsay the premises, and yet would not grant the conclusion. Note, The most plentiful and powerful means of conviction will not of themselves work faith in the depraved prejudiced hearts of men. These *saw,* and yet *believed not.*

3. The fulfilling of the scripture in this (*v.*38): *That the saying of Esaias might be fulfilled.* Not that these infidel Jews designed the fulfilling of the scripture (they rather fancied those scriptures which speak of the church's best sons to be fulfilled in themselves), but the event exactly answered the prediction, *so that (ut* for *ita ut)* this saying of Esaias was fulfilled. The more improbable any event is, the more does a divine foresight appear in the prediction of it. One could not have imagined that the kingdom of the Messiah, supported with such pregnant proofs, should have met with so much opposition among the Jews, and therefore their unbelief is called a *marvellous work, and a wonder,* Isa. xxix. 14. Christ himself *marvelled at it,* but it was what Isaiah foretold (Isa. liii. 1), and now it is accomplished. Observe, (1.) The gospel is here called *their report: Who has believed, τῇ ἀκοῇ ἡμῶν*—our *hearing,* which we have heard from God, and which you have heard from us. Our report is the report that we bring, like the report of a matter of fact, or the report of a solemn resolution in the senate. (2.) It is foretold that few comparatively of those to whom this report is brought will be persuaded to give credit to it. Many hear it, but few heed it and embrace it: *Who hath believed it?* Here and there one, but none to speak of; not the wise, not the noble; it is to them but a report which wants confirmation. (3.) It is spoken of as a thing to be greatly lamented that so few believe the report of the gospel. *Lord* is here prefixed from the LXX., but is not in the Hebrew, and intimates a sorrowful account brought to God by the messengers of the cold entertainment which they and their report had; as *the servant came, and showed his lord all these things,* Luke xiv. 21. (4.) The reason why men believe not the report of the gospel is because *the arm of*

the Lord is not *revealed* to them, that is, because they do not acquaint themselves with, and submit themselves to, the grace of God; they do not experimentally know the virtue and fellowship of Christ's death and resurrection, in which the arm of the Lord is revealed. They saw Christ's miracles, but did not see the *arm of the Lord revealed in them.*

II. They could not believe, and *therefore* they could not *because Esaias said, He hath blinded their eyes.* This is a hard saying, who can explain it? We are sure that God is infinitely just and merciful, and therefore we cannot think there is in any such an impotency to good, resulting from the counsels of God, as lays them under a fatal necessity of being evil. God damns none by mere sovereignty; yet it is said, *They could not believe.* St. Austin, coming in course to the exposition of these words, expresses himself with a holy fear of entering upon an enquiry into this mystery. *Justa sunt judicia ejus, sed occulta—His judgments are just, but hidden.*

1. They *could not* believe, that is, they *would not;* they were obstinately resolved in their infidelity; thus Chrysostom and Austin incline to understand it; and the former gives divers instances of scripture of the putting of an impotency to signify the invincible refusal of the will, as Gen. xxxvii. 4, *They could not speak peaceably to him.* And *ch.* vii. 7. This is a *moral* impotency, like that of one that is accustomed to do evil, Jer. xiii. 23. But,

2. They could not because Esaias had said, *He hath blinded their eyes.* Here the difficulty increases; it is certain that God is not the author of sin, and yet,

(1.) There is a righteous hand of God sometimes to be acknowledged in the blindness and obstinacy of those who persist in impenitency and unbelief, by which they are justly punished for their former resistance of the divine light and rebellion against the divine law. If God withhold abused grace, and give men over to indulged lusts,—if he permit the evil spirit to do his work on those that resisted the good Spirit,—and if in his providence he lay stumbling-blocks in the way of sinners, which confirm their prejudices, then he *blinds their eyes,* and *hardens their hearts,* and these are spiritual judgments, like the giving up of idolatrous Gentiles to *vile affections,* and degenerate Christians to *strong delusions.* Observe the method of conversion implied here, and the steps taken in it. [1.] Sinners are brought to *see with their eyes,* to discern the reality of divine things and to have some knowledge of them. [2.] To *understand with their heart,* to apply these things to themselves; not only to assent and approve, but to consent and accept. [3.] To *be converted,* and effectually turned from sin to Christ, from the world and the flesh to God, as their felicity and portion. [4.] Then God will *heal* them, will justify and sanctify them; will *pardon* their sins, which are as bleeding wounds, and mortify their corruptions, which are as lurking diseases. Now when God denies his grace nothing of this is done; the alienation of the mind from, and its aversion to, God and the divine life, grow into a rooted and invincible antipathy, and so the case becomes desperate.

(2.) Judicial blindness and hardness are in the word of God threatened against those who wilfully persist in wickedness, and were particularly foretold concerning the Jewish church and nation. Known unto God are all his works, and all ours too. Christ knew before who would betray him, and spoke of it, *ch.* vi. 70. This is a confirmation of the truth of scripture prophecies, and thus even the unbelief of the Jews may help to strengthen our faith. It is also intended for caution to particular persons, to *beware lest that come upon them which was spoken of in the prophets,* Acts xiii. 40.

(3.) What God has foretold will certainly come to pass, and so, by a necessary consequence, in order of arguing, it might be said that *therefore* they *could not believe,* because God by the prophets had foretold they would not; for such is the knowledge of God that he cannot be deceived in what he foresees, and such his truth that he cannot deceive in what he foretels, so that the scripture cannot be broken. Yet be it observed that the prophecy did not name particular persons; so that it might not be said, "Therefore such a one and such a one could not believe, because Esaias had said so and so;" but it pointed at the body of the Jewish nation, which would persist in their infidelity till their cities were wasted without inhabitants, as it follows (Isa. vi. 11, 12); yet still reserving a remnant (*v.* 13, *in it shall be a tenth),* which reserve was sufficient to keep a door of hope open to particular persons; for each one might say, Why may not I be of that remnant?

Lastly, The evangelist, having quoted the prophecy, shows (*v.* 41) that it was intended to look further than the prophet's own days, and that its principal reference was to the days of the Messiah: *These things said Esaias when he saw his glory, and spoke of him.* 1. We read in the prophecy that this was said to Esaias, Isa. vi. 8, 9. But here we are told that it was said *by him* to the purpose. For nothing was said by him as a prophet which was not first said to him; nor was any thing said to him which was not afterwards said by him to those to whom he was sent. See Isa. xxi. 10. 2. The vision which the prophet there had of the *glory of God* is here said to be his *seeing the glory* of Jesus Christ: He *saw his glory.* Jesus Christ therefore is equal in power and glory with the Father, and his praises are equally celebrated. Christ had a glory *before the foundation of the world,* and

Esaias saw this. 3. It is said that the prophet there *spoke of him.* It seems to have been spoken of the prophet himself (for to him the commission and instructions were there given), and yet it is here said to be spoken of Christ, for as all the prophets testified of him so they all typified him. This they spoke of him, that as to many his coming would be not only fruitless, but fatal, a savour of death unto death. It might be objected against his doctrine, If it was from heaven, why did not the Jews believe it? But this is an answer to it; it was not for want of evidence, but because their *heart was made fat*, and their *ears were heavy*. It was spoken of Christ, that he should be glorified in the ruin of an unbelieving multitude, as well as in the salvation of a distinguished remnant.

42 Nevertheless among the chief rulers also many believed on him; but because of the Pharisees they did not confess *him*, lest they should be put out of the synagogue: 43 For they loved the praise of men more than the praise of God.

Some honour was done to Christ by these rulers: for they *believed on him*, were convinced that he was sent of God, and received his doctrine as divine; but they did not do him honour enough, for they had not courage to own their faith in him. Many professed more kindness for Christ than really they had; these had more kindness for him than they were willing to profess. See here what a struggle was in these rulers between their convictions and their corruptions.

I. See the power of the word in the convictions that many of them were under, who did not wilfully shut their eyes against the light. They *believed on him* as Nicodemus, received him as a teacher come from God. Note, The truth of the gospel has perhaps a better interest in the consciences of men than we are aware of. Many cannot but approve of that in their hearts which yet outwardly they are shy of. Perhaps these chief rulers were *true* believers, though very weak, and their faith like smoking flax. Note, It may be, there are more good people than we think there are. Elijah thought he was left alone, when God had seven thousand faithful worshippers in Israel. Some are really better than they seem to be. Their faults are known, but their repentance is not; a man's goodness may be concealed by a *culpable* yet pardonable weakness, which he himself truly repents of. The *kingdom of God comes not* in all *with* a like *observation;* nor have all who are good the same faculty of appearing to be so.

II. See the power of the world in the smothering of these convictions. They believed in Christ, but because of the Pharisees, who had it in their power to do them a diskindness, they durst not confess him for fear of being excommunicated. Observe here, 1. Wherein they failed and were defective: They did not *confess* Christ. Note, There is cause to question the sincerity of that faith which is either afraid or ashamed to show itself; for those who believe with the heart ought to *confess with the mouth*, Rom. x. 9. 2. What they feared: being *put out of the synagogue*, which they thought would be a disgrace and damage to them; as if it would do them any harm to be expelled from a synagogue that had made itself a synagogue of Satan, and from which God was departing. 3. What was at the bottom of this fear: *They loved the praise of men*, chose it as a more valuable good, and pursued it as a more desirable end, than the *praise of God;* which was an implicit idolatry, like that (Rom. i. 25) of *worshipping and serving the creature more than the Creator.* They set these two in the scale one against the other, and, having weighed them, they proceeded accordingly. (1.) They set the praise of men in one scale, and considered how good it was to give praise to men, and to pay a deference to the opinion of the Pharisees, and receive praise from men, to be commended by the chief priests and applauded by the people as good sons of the church, the Jewish church; and they would not confess Christ, lest they should thereby derogate from the reputation of the Pharisees, and forfeit their own, and thus hinder their own preferment. And, besides, the followers of Christ were put into an *ill name*, and were looked upon with contempt, which those who had been used to honour could not bear. Yet perhaps if they had known one another's minds they would have had more courage; but each one thought that if he should declare himself in favour of Christ he should stand alone, and have nobody to back him; whereas, if any one had had resolution to *break the ice*, he would have had more *seconds* than he thought of. (2.) They put the praise of God in the other scale. They were sensible that by confessing Christ they should both give praise to God, and have praise from God, that he would be pleased with them, and say, *Well done;* but, (3.) They gave the preference to the praise of men, and this turned the scale; sense prevailed above faith, and represented it as more desirable to stand right in the opinion of the Pharisees than to be accepted of God. Note, Love of the praise of men is a very great prejudice to the power and practice of religion and godliness. Many come short of the glory of God by having a regard to the applause of men, and a value for that. Love of the praise of men, as a by-end in that which is good, will make a man a hypocrite when religion is in fashion and credit is to be got by it; and love of the praise of men, as a base principle in that which is evil, will make a man an apostate when religion is in disgrace, and credit is to be lost for it, as here. See Rom. ii. 29.

44 Jesus cried, and said, He that believeth on me, believeth not on me,
but on him that sent me. 45 And
he that seeth me seeth him that sent
me. 46 I am come a light into the
world, that whosoever believeth on
me should not abide in darkness. 47
And if any man hear my words, and
believe not, I judge him not: for I
came not to judge the world, but to
save the world. 48 He that rejecteth
me, and receiveth not my words, hath
one that judgeth him: the word that
I have spoken, the same shall judge
him in the last day. 49 For I have
not spoken of myself; but the Father
which sent me, he gave me a commandment, what I should say, and
what I should speak. 50. And I
know that his commandment is life
everlasting: whatsoever I speak therefore, even as the Father said unto me,
so I speak.

We have here the honour Christ not assumed, but asserted, to himself, in the account he gave of his mission and his errand into the world. Probably this discourse was not at the same time with that before (for then *he departed, v.* 36), but some time after, when he made another public appearance; and, as this evangelist records it, it was Christ's farewell sermon to the Jews, and his last public discourse; all that follows was private with his disciples. Now observe how our Lord Jesus delivered this parting word: he *cried and said. Doth not wisdom cry* (Prov. viii. 1), cry *without?* Prov. i. 20. The raising of his voice and crying intimate, 1. His boldness in speaking. Though they had not courage openly to profess faith in his doctrine, he had courage openly to publish it; if they were ashamed of it, he was not, but set his face as a flint, Isa. l. 7. 2. His earnestness in speaking. He cried as one that was serious and importunate, and in good earnest in what he said, and was willing to impart to them, not only the gospel of God, but *even his own soul.* 3. It denotes his desire that all might take notice of it. This being the last time of the publication of his gospel by himself in person, he makes proclamation, "Whoever will hear me, let them come now." Now what is the conclusion of the whole matter, this closing summary of all Christ's discourses? It is much like that of Moses (Deut. xxx. 15): *See, I have set before you life and death.* So Christ here takes leave of the temple, with a solemn declaration of three things:—

I. The privileges and dignities of those that believe; this gives great encouragement to us to believe in Christ and to profess that faith. It is a thing of such a nature that we need not be shy either of doing it or of owning it; for,

1. By believing in Christ we are brought into an *honourable acquaintance with God* (*v.* 44, 45): *He that believes on me,* and so *sees me, believes on him that sent me,* and so *sees him.* He that believes on Christ, (1.) He does not believe in a mere man, such a one as he seemed to be, and was generally taken to be, but he believes in one that is the Son of God and equal in power and glory with the Father. Or rather, (2.) His faith does not terminate in Christ, but through him it is carried out to the Father, that sent him, to whom, as our end, we come by Christ as our way. The doctrine of Christ is believed and received as the truth of God. The rest of a believing soul is in God through Christ as Mediator; for its resignation to Christ is in order to being presented to God. Christianity is made up, not of philosophy nor politics, but pure divinity. This is illustrated, *v.* 45. He that *sees me* (which is the same with *believing* in him, for faith is the eye of the soul) *sees him that sent me;* in getting an acquaintance with Christ, we come to the knowledge of God. For, [1.] God makes himself known in the face of Christ (2. Cor. iv. 6), who is the express image of his person, Heb. i. 3. [2.] All that have a believing sight of Christ are led by him to the knowledge of God, whom Christ has revealed to us by his word and Spirit. Christ, as God, was the image of his Father's person; but Christ, as Mediator, was his Father's representative in his relation to man, the divine light, law, and love, being communicated to us in and through him; so that in seeing him (that is, in eying him as our Saviour, Prince, and Lord, in the right of redemption), we see and eye the Father as our owner, ruler, and benefactor, in the right of creation: for God is pleased to deal with fallen man by proxy.

2. We are hereby brought into a comfortable enjoyment of ourselves (*v.* 46): *I am come a light into the world, that whoever believes in me,* Jew or Gentile, *should not abide in darkness.* Observe, (1.) The character of Christ: *I am come a light into the world,* to be a light to it. This implies that he had a being, and a being as light, before he came into the world, as the sun is before it rises; the prophets and apostles were made lights to the world, but it was Christ only that came a light into this world, having before been a glorious light in the upper world, *ch.* iii. 19. (2.) The comfort of Christians: They *do not abide in darkness.* [1.] They do not continue in that dark condition in which they were by nature; they are *light in the Lord.* They were without any true comfort, or joy, or hope, but do not continue in that condition; light is sown for them. [2.] Whatever darkness of affliction, disquietment, or fear, they may afterwards be in, provision is

made that they may not long abide in it. [3.] They are delivered from that darkness which is perpetual, and which *abideth for ever*, that utter darkness where there is not the least gleam of light nor hope of it.

II. The peril and danger of those that believe not, which gives fair warning to take heed of persisting in unbelief (*v.* 47, 48): "*If any man hear my words, and believe not, I judge him not*, not I only, or not now, lest I should be looked upon as unfair in being judge in my own cause; yet let not infidelity think therefore to go unpunished, *though I judge him not, there is one that judgeth him.*" So that we have here the doom of unbelief. Observe,

1. Who they are whose unbelief is here condemned: those who *hear Christ's words* and yet *believe them not.* Those shall not be condemned for their infidelity that never had, nor could have, the gospel; every man shall be judged according to the dispensation of light he was under: *Those that have sinned without law shall be judged without law.* But those that have heard, or might have heard, and would not, lie open to this doom.

2. What is the constructive malignity of their unbelief: not receiving Christ's word; it is interpreted (*v.* 48) a *rejecting* of Christ, ὁ ἀθετῶν ἐμὲ. It denotes a rejection with scorn and contempt. Where the banner of the gospel is displayed, no neutrality is admitted; every man is either a subject or an enemy.

3. The wonderful patience and forbearance of our Lord Jesus, exercised towards those who slighted him when he was come here upon earth: *I judge him not,* not now. Note, Christ was not quick or hasty to take advantage against those who refused the first offers of his grace, but continued waiting to be gracious. He did not strike those dumb or dead who contradicted him, never made intercession against Israel, as Elias did; though he had authority to judge, he suspended the execution of it, because he had work of another nature to do first, and that was to *save the world.* (1.) To save effectually those that were given him before he came to judge the degenerate body of mankind. (2.) To offer salvation to all the world, and thus far to save them that it is their own fault if they be not saved. He was to put away sin by the sacrifice of himself. Now the executing of the power of a judge was not congruous with that undertaking, Acts viii. 33. *In his humiliation his judgment was taken away,* it was suspended for a time.

4. The certain and unavoidable judgment of unbelievers at the great day, the day of the revelation of the righteous judgment of God: unbelief will certainly be a damning sin. Some think when Christ saith, *I judge no man,* he means that they are *condemned already.* There needs no process, they are *self-judged;* no execution, they are *self-ruined;* judgment goes against them of course, Heb. ii 3. Christ needs not appear against them as their accuser, they are miserable if he do not appear for them as their advocate; however, he tells them plainly when and where they will be reckoned with. (1.) There is *one that judgeth them.* Nothing is more dreadful than abused patience, and grace trampled on; though for awhile *mercy rejoiceth against judgment,* yet there will be *judgment without mercy.* (2.) Their final judgment is reserved to the *last day;* to that day of judgment Christ here binds over all unbelievers, to answer then for all the contempts they have put upon him. Divine justice has *appointed a day,* and adjourns the sentence to that day, as Matt. xxvi. 64. (3.) The word of Christ will judge them then: *The words that I have spoken,* how light soever you have made of them, *the same shall judge* the unbeliever *in the last day;* as the apostles, the preachers of Christ's word, are said to judge, Luke xxii. 30. Christ's words will judge unbelievers two ways:—[1.] As the evidence of their crime, they will convict them. Every word Christ spoke, every sermon, every argument, every kind offer, will be produced as a testimony against those who slighted all he said. [2.] As the rule of their doom, they will condemn them; they shall be judged according to the tenour of that covenant which Christ procured and published. That word of Christ, *He that believes not shall be damned,* will judge all unbelievers to eternal ruin; and there are *many such-like words.*

III. A solemn declaration of the authority Christ had to demand our faith, and require us to receive his doctrine upon pain of damnation, *v.* 49, 50, where observe,

1. The commission which our Lord Jesus received from the Father to deliver his doctrine to the world (*v.* 49): *I have not spoken of myself,* as a mere man, much less as a common man; *but the Father gave me a commandment what I should say.* This is the same with what he said *ch.* vii. 16. *My doctrine is,* (1.) *Not mine,* for *I have not spoken of myself.* Christ, as *Son of man,* did not speak that which was of human contrivance or composure; as Son of God, he did not act separately, or by himself alone, but what he said was the result of the counsels of peace; as Mediator, his coming into the world was voluntary, and with his full consent, but not arbitrary, and of his own head. But, (2.) It was his that sent him. God the Father gave him, [1.] His commission. God sent him as his agent and plenipotentiary, to concert matters between him and man, to set a treaty of peace on foot, and to settle the articles. [2.] His instructions, here called a *commandment,* for they were like those given to an ambassador, directing him not only what he may say, but what he must say. The messenger of the covenant was entrusted with an errand which he must deliver. Note, Our Lord Jesus learned obedience himself, before he taught it to us,

though he was a Son. *The Lord God commanded* the first Adam, and he by his disobedience ruined us; he commanded the second Adam, and he by his obedience saved us. God commanded him what he should *say* and what he should *speak*, two words signifying the same thing, to denote that every word was divine. The Old-Testament prophets sometimes spoke of themselves; but Christ spoke by the Spirit at all times. Some make this distinction: He was directed what he should say in his set sermons, and what he should speak in his familiar discourses. Others this: He was directed what he should say in his preaching now, and what he should speak in his judging at the last day; for he had commission and instruction for both.

2. The scope, design, and tendency of this commission: *I know that his commandment is life everlasting, v.* 50. The commission given to Christ had a reference to the everlasting state of the children of men, and was in order to their everlasting life and happiness in that state: the instructions given to Christ as a prophet were to reveal eternal life (1 John v. 11); the power, given to Christ as a king was to give eternal life, *ch.* xvii. 2. Thus the command given him was life everlasting. This Christ says he knew: "I know it is so," which intimates how cheerfully and with what assurance Christ pursued his undertaking, knowing very well that he went upon a good errand, and that which would bring forth fruit unto life eternal. It intimates likewise how justly those will perish who reject Christ and his word. Those who disobey Christ despise everlasting life, and renounce it; so that not only Christ's words will judge them, but even their own; so shall their doom be, themselves have decided it; and who can except against it?

3. Christ's exact observance of the commission and instructions given him, and his steady acting in pursuance of them: *Whatsoever I speak*, it is *as the Father said unto me.* Christ was intimately acquainted with the counsels of God, and was faithful in discovering so much of them to the children of men as it was agreed should be discovered, and *kept back nothing that was profitable.* As the faithful witness delivers souls, so did he, and spoke the truth, the whole truth, and nothing but the truth. Note, (1.) This is a great encouragement to faith; the sayings of Christ, rightly understood, are what we may venture our souls upon. (2.) It is a great example of obedience. Christ said as he was bidden, and so must we, communicated what the Father had said to him, and so must we. See Acts iv. 20. In the midst of all the respect paid to him, this is the honour he values himself upon, that what the Father had said to him that he spoke, and in the manner as he was directed so he spoke. This was his glory, that, as a Son, he was faithful to him that appointed him; and, by an unfeigned belief of every word of Christ, and an entire subjection of soul to it, we must give him the glory due to his name.

CHAP. XIII.

Our Saviour having finished his public discourses, in which he "endured the contradiction of sinners," now applies himself to a private conversation with his friends, in which he designed the consolation of saints. Henceforward we have an account of what passed between him and his disciples, who were to be entrusted with the affairs of his household, when he was gone into a far country; the necessary instructions and comforts he furnished them with. His hour being at hand, he applies himself to set his house in order. In this chapter, I. He washes his disciples' feet, ver. 1—17. II. He foretels who should betray him, ver. 18—30. III. He instructs them in the great doctrine of his own death, and the great duty of brotherly love, ver. 31—35 IV. He foretels Peter's denying him, ver. 36—38.

NOW before the feast of the
passover, when Jesus knew that
his hour was come that he should depart out of this world unto the Father,
having loved his own which were in
the world, he loved them unto the
end. 2 And supper being ended,
the devil having now put into the
heart of Judas Iscariot, Simon's *son*,
to betray him; 3 Jesus knowing
that the Father had given all things
into his hands, and that he was come
from God, and went to God; 4 He
riseth from supper, and laid aside his
garments; and took a towel, and
girded himself. 5 After that he
poureth water into a bason, and began to wash the disciples' feet, and to
wipe *them* with the towel wherewith
he was girded. 6 Then cometh he
to Simon Peter: and Peter saith unto
him, Lord, dost thou wash my feet?
7 Jesus answered and said unto him,
What I do thou knowest not now;
but thou shalt know hereafter. 8
Peter saith unto him, Thou shalt never wash my feet. Jesus answered
him, If I wash thee not, thou hast no
part with me. 9 Simon Peter saith
unto him, Lord, not my feet only, but
also *my* hands and *my* head. 10 Jesus saith to him, He that is washed
needeth not save to wash *his* feet, but
is clean every whit: and ye are clean,
but not all. 11 For he knew who
should betray him; therefore said he,
Ye are not all clean. 12 So after he
had washed their feet, and had taken
his garments, and was set down again,
he said unto them, Know ye what I
have done to you? 13 Ye call me
Master and Lord: and ye say well;
for *so* I am. 14 If I then, *your*
Lord and Master, have washed your

feet; ye also ought to wash one another's feet. 15 For I have given you an example, that ye should do as I have done to you. 16 Verily, verily, I say unto you, The servant is not greater than his lord; neither he that is sent greater than he that sent him. 17 If ye know these things happy are ye if ye do them.

It has generally been taken for granted by commentators that Christ's washing his disciples' feet, and the discourse that followed it, were the same night in which he was betrayed, and at the same sitting wherein he ate the passover and instituted the Lord's supper; but whether before the solemnity began, or after it was all over, or between the eating of the passover and the institution of the Lord's supper, they are not agreed. This evangelist, making it his business to gather up those passages which the others had omitted, industriously omits those which the others had recorded, which occasions some difficulty in putting them together. If it was then, we suppose that *Judas went out* (*v.* 30) to get his men ready that were to apprehend the Lord Jesus in the garden. But Dr. Lightfoot is clearly of opinion that this was done and said, even all that is recorded to the end of *ch.* xiv., not at the passover supper, for it is here said (*v.* 1) to be *before the feast of the passover,* but at the supper in Bethany, two days before the passover (of which we read Matt. xxvi. 2—6), at which Mary the second time anointed Christ's head with the remainder of her box of ointment. Or, it might be at some other supper the night before the passover, not as that was in the house of Simon the leper, but in his own lodgings, where he had none but his disciples about him, and could be more free with them.

In these verses we have the story of Christ's washing his disciples' feet; it was an action of a singular nature; no miracle, unless we call it a miracle of humility. Mary had just anointed his head; now, lest his acceptance of this should look like taking state, he presently balances it with this act of abasement. But why would Christ do this? If the disciples' feet needed washing, they could wash them themselves; a wise man will not do a thing that looks odd and unusual, but for very good causes and considerations. We are sure that it was not in a humour or a frolic that this was done; no, the transaction was very solemn, and carried on with a great deal of seriousness; and four reasons are here intimated why Christ did this:—1. That he might testify his love to his disciples, *v.* 1, 2. 2. That he might give an instance of his own voluntary humility and condescension, *v.* 3—5. 3. That he might signify to them spiritual washing, which is referred to in his discourse with Peter, *v.* 6—11. 4. That he might set them an example, *v.* 12—17. And the opening of these four reasons will take in the exposition of the whole story.

I. Christ washed his disciples' feet that he might give a proof of that great love wherewith he loved them; loved them to the end, *v.* 1, 2.

1. It is here laid down as an undoubted truth that our Lord Jesus, *having loved his own that were in the world, loved them to the end, v.* 1.

(1.) This is true of the disciples that were his immediate followers, in particular the twelve. These were his own in the world, his family, his school, his bosom-friends. Children he had none to call his own, but he adopted them, and took them as his own. He had those that were his own in the other world, but he left them for a time, to look after his own in this world. These he loved, he called them into fellowship with himself, conversed familiarly with them, was always tender of them, and of their comfort and reputation. He allowed them to be very free with him, and bore with their infirmities. He loved them to the end, continued his love to them as long as he lived, and after his resurrection; he never took away his loving kindness. Though there were some persons of quality that espoused his cause, he did not lay aside his old friends, to make room for new ones, but still stuck to his poor fishermen. They were weak and defective in knowledge and grace, dull and forgetful; and yet, though he reproved them often, he never ceased to love them and take care of them.

(2.) It is true of all believers, for these twelve patriarchs were the representatives of all the tribes of God's spiritual Israel. Note, [1.] Our Lord Jesus has a people in the world that are his own,—his own, for they were given him by the Father, he has purchased them, and paid dearly for them, and he has set them apart for himself, —his own, for they have devoted themselves to him as a peculiar people. *His own;* where *his own* were spoken of that *received him not,* it is τα ἴδια—*his own things,* as a man's cattle are his own, which yet he may, when he pleases, alter the property of. But here it is, τοὺς ἰδιους—*his own persons,* as a man's wife and children are his own, to whom he stands in a constant relation. [2.] Christ has a cordial love for his own that are in the world. He *did* love them with a love of goodwill when he gave himself for their redemption. He *does* love them with a love of complacency when he admits them into communion with himself. Though they are *in this world,* a world of darkness and distance, of sin and corruption, yet he loves them. He was now going to his own in heaven, the spirits of just men made perfect there; but he seems most concerned for his own on earth, because they most needed his care: the sickly child is most indulged. [3.] Those whom Christ loves *he loves to the end;* he is constant in his love to his people; he *rests in his love.* He loves with an everlasting love (Jer. xxxi. 3), from everlasting in the counsels of it to everlasting in the consequences of it. Nothing can separate a believer *from the love of Christ;* he loves his own, *εἰς τέλος—unto perfection,* for he will perfect what concerns them, will bring them to that world where love is perfect.

2. Christ manifested his love to them by washing their feet, as that good woman (Luke vii. 38) showed her love to Christ by washing his feet and wiping them. Thus he would show that as his love to them was constant so it was condescending,—that in prosecution of the designs of it he was willing to humble himself,—and that the glories of his exalted state, which he was now entering upon, should be no obstruction at all to the favour he bore to his chosen; and thus he would confirm the promise he had made to all the saints that he would *make them sit down to meat, and would come forth and serve them* (Luke xii. 37), would put honour upon them as great and surprising as for a lord to serve his servants. The disciples had just now betrayed the weakness of their love to him, in grudging the ointment that was poured upon his head (Matt. xxvi. 8), yet he presently gives this proof of his love to them. Our infirmities are foils to Christ's kindnesses, and set them off.

3. He chose this time to do it, a little before his last passover, for two reasons:—

(1.) Because now *he knew that his hour was come,* which he had long expected, *when he should depart out of this world to the Father.* Observe here, [1.] The change that was to pass over our Lord Jesus; he must *depart.* This began at his death, but was completed at his ascension. As Christ himself, so all believers, by virtue of their union with him, when they depart out of the world, are absent from the body, *go to the Father,* are present with the Lord. It is a departure *out of the world,* this unkind, injurious world, this faithless, treacherous world—this world of labour, toil, and temptation—this vale of tears; and it is a going *to the Father,* to the vision of the Father of spirits, and the fruition of him as ours. [2.] The time of this change: *His hour was come.* It is sometimes called his enemies' hour (Luke xxii. 53), the hour of their triumph; sometimes his hour, the hour of his triumph, the hour he had had in his eye all along. The time of his sufferings was fixed to an hour, and the continuance of them but for an hour. [3.] His foresight of it: He *knew that his hour was come;* he knew from the beginning that it would come, and when, but now he knew that it *was come.* We know not when our hour will come, and therefore what we have to do in habitual preparation for it ought never to be undone; but, when we know by the harbingers that our hour is come, we must vigorously apply ourselves to an actual preparation, as our Master did, 2 Pet. iii. 14. Now it was in the immediate foresight of his departure that he *washed his disciples' feet;* that, as his own head was anointed just now *against the day of his burial,* so their feet might be washed against the day of their consecration by the descent of the Holy Ghost fifty days after, as the priests were washed, Lev. viii. 6. When we see our day approaching, we should do what good we can to those we leave behind.

(2.) Because the *devil had now put it into the heart of Judas to betray him, v.* 2. These words in a parenthesis may be considered, [1.] As tracing Judas's treason to its origin; it was a sin of such a nature that it evidently bore the devil's image and superscription. What way of access the devil has to men's hearts, and by what methods he darts in his suggestions, and mingles them undiscerned with those thoughts which are the natives of the heart, we cannot tell. But there are some sins in their own nature so exceedingly sinful, and to which there is so little temptation from the world and the flesh, that it is plain Satan lays the egg of them in a heart disposed to be the nest to hatch them in. For Judas to betray such a master, to betray him so cheaply and upon no provocation, was such downright enmity to God as could not be forged but by Satan himself, who thereby thought to ruin the Redeemer's kingdom, but did in fact ruin his own. [2.] As intimating a reason why Christ now washed his disciples' feet. *First,* Judas being now resolved to betray him, the time of his departure could not be far off; if this matter be determined, it is easy to infer with St. Paul, *I am now ready to be offered.* Note, The more malicious we perceive our enemies to be against us, the more industrious we should be to prepare for the worst that may come. *Secondly,* Judas being now got into the snare, and the devil aiming at Peter and the rest of them (Luke xxii. 31), Christ would fortify his own against him. If the wolf has seized one of the flock, it is time for the shepherd to look well to the rest. Antidotes must be stirring, when the infection is begun. Dr. Lightfoot observes that the disciples had learned of Judas to murmur at the anointing of Christ; compare *ch.* xii. 4, &c. with Matt. xxvi. 8. Now, lest those that had learned that of him should learn worse, he fortifies them by a lesson of humility against his most dangerous assaults. *Thirdly,* Judas, who was now plotting to betray him, was *one of the twelve.* Now Christ would hereby show that he did not design to cast them all off for the faults of one. Though one of their college had a devil, and was a traitor, yet they should fare never the worse for that. Christ loves his church though there are hypocrites in it, and had still a kindness for his disciples though there was a Judas among them and he knew it.

II. Christ washed his disciples' feet that

he might give an instance of his own wonderful humility, and show how lowly and condescending he was, and let all the world know how low he could stoop in love to his own. This is intimated, *v.* 3—5. *Jesus knowing*, and now actually considering, and perhaps discoursing of, his honours as Mediator, and telling his friends that *the Father had given all things into his hand, rises from supper*, and, to the great surprise of the company, who wondered what he was going to do, *washed his disciples' feet.*

1. Here is the rightful advancement of the Lord Jesus. Glorious things are here said of Christ as Mediator.

(1.) *The Father had given all things into his hands;* had given him a propriety in all, and a power over all, as possessor of heaven and earth, in pursuance of the great designs of his undertaking; see Matt. xi. 27. The accommodation and arbitration of all matters in variance between God and man were committed into his hands as the great umpire and referee; and the administration of the kingdom of God among men, in all the branches of it, was committed to him; so that all acts, both of government and judgment, were to pass through his hands; he is *heir of all things.*

(2.) He *came from God.* This implies that he was in the beginning with God, and had a being and glory, not only before he was born into this world, but before the world itself was born; and that when he came into the world he came as God's ambassador, with a commission from him. He came from God as the Son of God, and the sent of God. The Old-Testament prophets were raised up and employed for God, but Christ came directly from him.

(3.) He *went to God,* to be glorified with him with the same glory which he had with God from eternity. That which comes from God shall go to God; those that are born from heaven are bound for heaven. As Christ came from God to be an agent for him on earth, so he went to God to be an agent for us in heaven; and it is a comfort to us to think how welcome he was there: he was brought near to the *Ancient of days,* Dan. vii. 13. And it was said to him, *Sit thou at my right hand,* Ps. cx. 1.

(4.) He *knew* all this; was not like a prince in the cradle, that knows nothing of the honour he is born to, or like Moses, who *wist not that his face shone;* no, he had a full view of all the honours of his exalted state, and yet stooped thus low. But how does this come in here? [1.] As an inducement to him now quickly to leave what lessons and legacies he had to leave to his disciples, because his hour was now come when he must take his leave of them, and be exalted above that familiar converse which he now had with them, *v.* 1. [2.] It may come in as that which supported him under his sufferings, and carried him cheerfully through this sharp encounter. Judas was now betraying him, and he knew it, and knew what would be the consequence of it; yet, knowing also *that he came from God and went to God,* he did not draw back, but went on cheerfully. [3.] It seems to come in as a foil to his condescension, to make it the more admirable. The reasons of divine grace are sometimes represented in scripture as strange and surprising (as Isa. lvii. 17, 18; Hos. ii. 13, 14); so here, that is given as an inducement to Christ to stoop which should rather have been a reason for his taking state; for God's thoughts are not as ours. Compare with this those passages which preface the most signal instances of condescending grace with the displays of divine glory, as Ps. lxviii. 4, 5; Isa. lvii. 15; lxvi. 1, 2.

2. Here is the voluntary abasement of our Lord Jesus notwithstanding this. *Jesus knowing* his own glory as God, and his own authority and power as Mediator, one would think it should follow, *He rises from supper,* lays aside his ordinary garments, calls for robes, bids them keep their distance, and do him homage; but no, quite the contrary, when he considered this he gave the greatest instance of humility. Note, A well-grounded assurance of heaven and happiness, instead of puffing a man up with pride, will make and keep him very humble. Those that would be found conformable to Christ, and partakers of his Spirit, must study to keep their minds low in the midst of the greatest advancements. Now that which Christ humbled himself to was to *wash his disciples' feet.*

(1.) The action itself was mean and servile, and that which servants of the lowest rank were employed in. *Let thine handmaid* (saith Abigail) *be a servant to wash the feet of the servants of my lord;* let me be in the meanest employment, 1 Sam. xxv. 41. If he had washed their hands or faces, it had been great condescension (Elisha poured water on the hands of Elijah, 2 Kings iii. 11); but for Christ to stoop to such a piece of drudgery as this may well excite our admiration. Thus he would teach us to think nothing below us wherein we may be serviceable to God's glory and the good of our brethren.

(2.) The condescension was so much the greater that he did this for his own disciples, who in themselves were of a low and despicable condition, not curious about their bodies; their feet, it is likely, were seldom washed, and therefore very dirty. In relation to him, they were his scholars, his servants, and such as should have washed his feet, whose dependence was upon him, and their expectations from him. Many of great spirits otherwise will do a mean thing to curry favour with their superiors; they rise by stooping, and climb by cringing; but for Christ to do this to *his disciples* could be no act of policy nor complaisance, but pure humility.

(3.) He *rose from supper* to do it. Though we translate it (*v.* 2) *supper being ended,* it might be better read, *there being a supper made*, or *he being at supper*, for he sat down again (*v.* 12), and we find him dipping a sop (*v.* 26), so that he did it in the midst of his meal, and thereby taught us, [1.] Not to reckon it a disturbance, nor any just cause of uneasiness, to be called from our meal to do God or our brother any real service, esteeming the discharge of our duty *more than our necessary food, ch.* iv. 34. Christ would not leave his preaching to oblige his nearest relations (Mark iii. 33), but would leave his supper to show his love to his disciples. [2.] Not to be over nice about our meat. It would have turned many a squeamish stomach to wash dirty feet at supper-time; but Christ did it, not that we might learn to be rude and slovenly (cleanliness and godliness will do well together), but to teach us not to be curious, not to indulge, but mortify, the delicacy of the appetite, giving good manners their due place, and no more.

(4.) He put himself into the garb of a servant, to do it: he *laid aside* his loose and upper *garments*, that he might apply himself to this service the more expeditely. We must address ourselves to duty as those that are resolved not to take state, but to take pains; we must divest ourselves of every thing that would either feed our pride or hang in our way and hinder us in what we have to do, must *gird up the loins of our mind*, as those that in earnest buckle to business.

(5.) He did it with all the humble ceremony that could be, went through all the parts of the service distinctly, and passed by none of them; he did it as if he had been used thus to serve; did it himself alone, and had none to minister to him in it. He *girded himself with the towel*, as servants throw a napkin on their arm, or put an apron before them; he *poured water into the basin* out of the water-pots that stood by (*ch.* ii. 6), and then *washed their feet;* and, to complete the service, *wiped them.* Some think that he did not wash the feet of them all, but only four or five of them, that being thought sufficient to answer the end; but I see nothing to countenance this conjecture, for in other places where he did make a difference it is taken notice of; and his washing the feet of them *all*, without exception, teaches us a catholic and extensive charity to all Christ's disciples, even the least.

(6.) Nothing appears to the contrary but that he washed the feet of Judas among the rest, for he was present, *v.* 26. It is the character of a *widow indeed* that she had washed the saints' feet (1 Tim. v. 10), and there is some comfort in this; but the blessed Jesus here washed the feet of a sinner, the worst of sinners, the worst to him, who was at this time contriving to betray him.

Many interpreters consider Christ's washing his disciples' feet as a representation of *his whole undertaking.* He knew that he was equal with God, and all things were his; and yet he rose from his table in glory, laid aside his robes of light, girded himself with our nature, took upon him the form of a servant, *came not to be ministered to, but to minister*, poured out his blood, poured out his soul unto death, and thereby prepared a laver to wash us from our sins, Rev. i. 5.

III. Christ washed his disciples' feet that he might signify to them spiritual washing, and the cleansing of the soul from the pollutions of sin. This is plainly intimated in his discourse with Peter upon it, *v.* 6—11, in which we may observe,

1. The surprise Peter was in when he saw his Master go about this mean service (*v.* 6): *Then cometh he to Simon Peter*, with his towel and basin, and bids him put out his feet to be washed. Chrysostom conjectures that he first washed the feet of Judas, who readily admitted the honour, and was pleased to see his Master so disparage himself. It is most probable that when he *went about* this service (which is all that is meant by his *beginning* to wash, *v.* 5) he took Peter first, and that the rest would not have suffered it, if they had not first heard it explained in what passed between Christ and Peter. Whether Christ came first to Peter or no, when he did come to him, Peter was startled at the proposal: *Lord* (saith he) *dost thou wash my feet?* Here is an emphasis to be laid upon the persons, *thou* and *me;* and the placing of the words is observable, *σύ μου—what, thou mine? Tu mihi lavas pedes? Quid est tu? Quid est mihi? Cogitanda sunt potius quam dicenda—Dost thou wash my feet? What is it thou? What to me? These things are rather to be contemplated than uttered.*—Aug. in loc. What *thou*, our Lord and Master, whom we know and believe to be the Son of God, and Saviour and ruler of the world, do this for *me*, a worthless worm of the earth, *a sinful man, O Lord?* Shall those hands wash my feet which with a touch have cleansed lepers, given sight to the blind, and raised the dead? So Theophylact, and from him Dr. Taylor. Very willingly would Peter have taken the basin and towel, and washed his Master's feet, and been proud of the honour, Luke xvii. 7, 8. "This had been natural and regular; for *my Master* to wash my feet is such a solecism as never was; such a paradox as I cannot understand. *Is this the manner of men?*" Note, Christ's condescensions, especially his condescensions to *us*, wherein we find ourselves taken notice of by his grace, are justly the matter of our admiration, *ch.* xiv. 22. *Who am I, Lord God? And what is my father's house?*

2. The immediate satisfaction Christ gave to this question of surprise. This was at least sufficient to silence his objections (*v.* 7): *What I do, thou knowest not now, but thou shalt know hereafter.* Here are two reasons why Peter must submit to what Christ was doing:—

(1.) Because he was at present in the dark

concerning it, and ought not to oppose what he did not understand, but acquiesce in the will and wisdom of one who could give a good reason for all he said and did. Christ would teach Peter an *implicit obedience:* "*What I do thou knowest not now*, and therefore art no competent judge of it, but must believe it is well done because I do it." Note, Consciousness to ourselves of the darkness we labour under, and our inability to judge of what God does, should make us sparing and modest in our censures of his proceedings; see Heb. xi: 8.

(2.) Because there was something considerable in it, of which he should hereafter know the meaning: "*Thou shalt know hereafter* what need thou hast of being washed, when thou shalt be guilty of the heinous sin of denying me;" so some. "Thou shalt know, when, in the discharge of the office of an apostle, thou wilt be employed in washing off from those under thy charge the sins and defilements of their earthly affections;" so Dr. Hammond. Note, [1.] Our Lord Jesus does many things the meaning of which even his own disciples do not for the present know, but they *shall know afterwards*. What he did when he became man for us and what he did when he became a worm and no man for us, what he did when he lived our life and what he did when he laid it down, could not be understood till afterwards, and then it appeared that *it behoved him*, Heb. ii. 17. Subsequent providences explain preceding ones; and we see afterwards what was the kind tendency of events that seemed most cross; and the way which we thought was *about* proved the *right way*. [2.] Christ's washing his disciples' feet had a significancy in it, which they themselves did not understand till afterwards, when Christ explained it to be a specimen of the laver of regeneration, and till the Spirit was poured out upon them from on high. We must let Christ take his own way, both in ordinances and providences, and we shall find in the issue it was the best way.

3. Peter's peremptory refusal, notwithstanding this, to let Christ wash his feet (*v.* 8): *Thou shalt by no means wash my feet; no, never.* So it is in the original. It is the language of a fixed resolution. Now, (1.) Here was a show of humility and modesty. Peter herein seemed to have, and no doubt he really had, a great respect for his Master, as he had, Luke v. 8. Thus many are beguiled of their reward in a *voluntary humility* (Col. ii. 18, 23), such a self-denial as Christ neither appoints nor accepts; for, (2.) Under this show of humility there was a real contradiction to the will of the Lord Jesus: "I *will wash thy feet*," saith Christ; "But thou never shalt," saith Peter, "it is not a fitting thing;" so making himself wiser than Christ. It is not humility, but infidelity, to put away the offers of the gospel, as if too rich to be made to us or too good news to be true.

4. Christ's insisting upon his offer, and a good reason given to Peter why he should accept it: *If I wash thee not, thou hast no part with me.* This may be taken, (1.) As a severe caution against disobedience: "*If I wash thee not*, if thou continue refractory, and wilt not comply with thy Master's will in so small a matter, thou shalt not be owned as one of my disciples, but be justly discarded and cashiered for not observing orders." Thus several of the ancients understand it; if Peter will make himself wiser than his Master, and dispute the commands he ought to obey, he does in effect renounce his allegiance, and say, as they did, *What portion have we in David*, in the Son of David? And so shall his doom be, he shall have no part in him. Let him use no more manners than will do him good, for *to obey is better than sacrifice*, 1 Sam. xv. 22. Or, (2.) As a declaration of the necessity of spiritual washing; and so I think it is to be understood: "*If I wash not* thy soul from the pollution of sin, *thou hast no part with me*, no interest in me, no communion with me, no benefit by me." Note, All those, and those only, that are spiritually washed by Christ, have a part in Christ. [1.] To have a part in Christ, or with Christ, has all the happiness of a Christian bound up in it, to be *partakers of Christ* (Heb. iii. 14), to share in those inestimable privileges which result from a union with him and relation to him. It is that *good part* the having of which is the *one thing needful*. [2.] It is necessary to our having a part in Christ that he wash us. All those whom Christ owns and saves he justifies and sanctifies, and both are included in his washing them. We cannot partake of his glory if we partake not of his merit and righteousness, and of his Spirit and grace.

5. Peter's more than submission, his earnest request, to be washed by Christ, *v.* 9. If this be the meaning of it, *Lord, wash not my feet only, but also my hands and my head.* How soon is Peter's mind changed! When the mistake of his understanding was rectified, the corrupt resolution of his will was soon altered. Let us therefore not be peremptory in any resolve (except in our resolve to follow Christ), because we may soon see cause to retract it, but cautious in taking up a purpose we will be tenacious of. Observe,

(1.) How ready Peter is to recede from what he had said: "Lord, what a fool was I to speak such a hasty word!" Now that the washing of him appeared to be an act of Christ's authority and grace he admits it; but disliked it when it seemed only an act of humiliation. Note, [1.] Good men, when they see their error, will not be loth to recant it. [2.] Sooner or later, Christ will bring all to be of his mind.

(2.) How importunate he is for the purifying grace of the Lord Jesus, and the universal influence of it, even upon his hands and head. Note, A divorce from Christ, and an exclusion from having a part in him, is the most formidable evil in the eyes of all that are enlightened, for the fear of which they will be persuaded to any thing. And for fear of this we should be earnest with God in prayer, that he will wash us, will justify and sanctify us. "Lord, that I may not be cut off from thee, make me fit for thee, by the washing of regeneration. *Lord, wash not my feet only* from the gross pollutions that cleave to them, *but also my hands and my head* from the spots which they have contracted, and the undiscerned filth which proceeds by perspiration from the body itself." Note, Those who truly desire to be sanctified desire to be sanctified throughout, and to have the whole man, with all its parts and powers, purified, 1 Thess. v. 23.

6. Christ's further explication of this sign, as it represented spiritual washing.

(1.) With reference to his disciples that were faithful to him (*v.* 10): *He that is washed* all over in the bath (as was frequently practised in those countries), when he returns to his house, *needeth not save to wash his feet,* his hands and head having been washed, and he having only dirtied his feet in walking home. Peter had gone from one extreme to the other. At first he would not let Christ wash his feet; and now he overlooks what Christ had done for him in his baptism, and what was signified thereby, and cries out to have his hands and head washed. Now Christ directs him into the meaning; he must have his feet washed, but not his hands and head. [1.] See here what is the comfort and privilege of such as are in a justified state; they are washed by Christ, and are *clean every whit,* that is, they are graciously accepted of God, as if they were so; and, though they offend, yet they need not, upon their repentance, be again put into a justified state, for then should they often be baptized. The evidence of a justified state may be clouded, and the comfort of it suspended, when yet the charter of it is not vacated or taken away. Though we have occasion to repent daily, God's gifts and callings are without repentance. The heart may be swept and garnished, and yet still remain the devil's palace; but, if it be washed, it belongs to Christ, and he will not lose it. [2.] See what ought to be the daily care of those who through grace are in a justified state, and that is to wash their feet; to cleanse themselves from the guilt they contract daily through infirmity and inadvertence, by the renewed exercise of repentance, with a believing application of the virtue of Christ's blood. We must also wash our feet by constant watchfulness against every thing that is defiling, for we must cleanse our way, and cleanse our feet *by taking heed thereto,* Ps. cxix. 9. The priests, when they were consecrated, were washed with water; and, though they did not need afterwards to be so washed all over, yet, whenever they went in to minister, they must wash their feet and hands at the laver, on pain of death, Exod. xxx. 19, 20. The provision made for our cleansing should not make us presumptuous, but the more cautious. *I have washed my feet, how shall I defile them?* From yesterday's pardon, we should fetch an argument against this day's temptation.

(2.) With reflection upon Judas: *And you are clean, but not all, v.* 10, 11. He pronounces his disciples clean, clean *through the word he had spoken to them, ch.* xv. 3. He washed them himself, and then said, *You are clean;* but he excepts Judas: *not all;* they were all baptized, even Judas, yet not all clean; many have the sign that have not the thing signified. Note, [1.] Even among those who are called disciples of Christ, and profess relation to him, there are some who are not clean, Prov. xxx. 12. [2.] The Lord knows those that are his, and those that are not, 2 Tim. ii. 19. The eye of Christ can separate between the precious and the vile, the clean and the unclean. [3.] When those that have called themselves disciples afterwards prove traitors, their apostasy at last is a certain evidence of their hypocrisy all along. [4.] Christ sees it necessary to let his disciples know that they are not all clean; that we may all be jealous over ourselves *(Is it I? Lord, is it I* that am among the clean, yet not clean?) and that, when hypocrites are discovered, it may be no surprise nor stumbling to us.

IV. Christ washed his disciples' feet to set before us an example. This explication he gave of what he had done, when he had done it, *v* 12—17. Observe,

1. With what solemnity he gave an account of the meaning of what he had done (*v.* 12): *After he had washed their feet,* he said, *Know you what I have done?*

(1.) He adjourned the explication till he had finished the transaction, [1.] To try their submission and implicit obedience. What he did they should not know till afterwards, that they might learn to acquiesce in his will when they could not give a reason for it. [2.] Because it was proper to finish the riddle before he unriddled it. Thus, as to his whole undertaking, when his sufferings were finished, when he had resumed the garments of his exalted state and was ready to sit down again, then he *opened the understandings of his disciples,* and poured out his Spirit, Luke xxiv. 45, 46.

(2.) Before he explained it, he asked them if they could construe it: *Know you what I have done to you?* He put this question to them, not only to make them sensible of their ignorance, and the need they had to be instructed (as Zech. iv. 5, 13, *Knowest thou not what these be? and I said, No, my Lord),* but to raise their desires and expectations of instruction: "I *would have you know,* and, if you will give attention, I will tell you." Note, It is the will of Christ that sacramental signs should be explained, and that his people should be acquainted with the meaning of them; otherwise, though ever so significant, to those who know not the thing signified they are insignificant. Hence they are directed to ask, *What mean you by this service?* Exod. xii. 26.

2. Upon what he grounds that which he had to say (*v.* 13): "*You call me Master and Lord,* you give me those titles, in speaking of me, in speaking to me, and *you say well,* for *so I am;* you are in the relation of scholars to me, and I do the part of a master to you." Note, (1.) Jesus Christ is our Master and Lord; he that is our Redeemer and Saviour is, in order to that, our Lord and Master. He is our Master, *διδάσκαλος*—our teacher and instructor in all necessary truths and rules, as a prophet revealing to us the will of God. He is our Lord, *κύριος*—our ruler and owner, that has authority over us and propriety in us. (2.) It becomes the disciples of Christ to call him Master and Lord, not in compliment, but in reality; not by constraint, but with delight. Devout Mr. Herbert, when he mentioned the name of Christ, used to add, my Master; and thus expresses himself concerning it in one of his poems:

How sweetly doth my Master sound, my Master!
As ambergris leaves a rich scent unto the taster,
So do these words a sweet content, an oriental fragrancy, my Master.

(3.) Our calling Christ Master and Lord is an obligation upon us to receive and observe the instructions he gives us. Christ would thus pre-engage their obedience to a command that was displeasing to flesh and blood. If Christ be our Master and Lord, be so by our own consent, and we have often called him so, we are bound in honour and honesty to be observant of him.

3. The lesson which he hereby taught: *You also ought to wash one another's feet, v.* 14.

(1.) Some have understood this literally, and have thought these words amount to the institution of a standing ordinance in the church; that Christians should, in a solemn religious manner, *wash one another's feet,* in token of their condescending love to one another. St. Ambrose took it so, and practised it in the church of Milan. St. Austin saith that those Christians who did not do it with their hands, yet (he hoped) did it with their hearts in humility; but he saith, It is much better to do it with the hands also, when there is occasion, as 1 Tim. v. 10. What Christ has done Christians should not disdain to do. Calvin saith that the pope, in the annual observance of this ceremony on Thursday in the passion week, is rather Christ's ape than his follower, for the duty enjoined, in conformity to Christ, was *mutual: Wash one another's feet.* And Jansenius saith, It is done, *Frigidè et dissimiliter—Frigidly, and unlike the primitive model.*

(2.) But doubtless it is to be understood figuratively; it is an instructive sign, but not sacramental, as the eucharist. This was a parable to the eye; and three things our Master hereby designed to teach us:—[1.] A humble condescension. We must learn of our Master to be *lowly in heart* (Matt. xi. 29), and walk with all lowliness; we must think meanly of ourselves and respectfully of our brethren, and deem nothing below us but sin; we must say of that which seems mean, but has a tendency to the glory of God and our brethren's good, as David (2 Sam. vi. 22), *If this be to be vile, I will be yet more vile.* Christ had often taught his disciples humility, and they had forgotten the lesson; but now he teaches them in such a way as surely they could never forget. [2.] A condescension to be serviceable. To wash one another's feet is to stoop to the meanest offices of love, for the real good and benefit one of another, as blessed Paul, who, though free from all, made himself *servant of all;* and the blessed Jesus, who *came not to be ministered unto, but to minister.* We must not grudge to take care and pains, and to spend time, and to diminish ourselves for the good of those to whom we are not under any particular obligations, even of our inferiors, and such as are not in a capacity of making us any requital. Washing the feet after travelling contributes both to the decency of the person and to his ease, so that to wash one another's feet is to consult both the credit and the comfort one of another, to do what we can both to advance our brethren's reputation and to make their minds easy. See 1 Cor. x. 24; Heb. vi. 10. The duty is *mutual;* we must both accept help from our brethren and afford help to our brethren. [3.] A serviceableness to the sanctification one of another: *You ought to wash one another's feet,* from the pollutions of sin. Austin takes it in this sense, and many others. We cannot satisfy for one another's sins, this is peculiar to Christ, but we may help to purify one another from sin. We must in the first place wash ourselves; this charity must begin at home (Matt. vii. 5), but it must not end there; we must sorrow for the failings and follies of our brethren, much more for their gross pollutions (1 Cor. v. 2), must wash our brethren's polluted feet in tears. We must faithfully reprove them, and do what we can to bring them to repentance (Gal. vi. 1), and we must admonish them, to prevent their falling into the mire; this is washing their feet.

4. Here is the ratifying and enforcing of this command from the example of what Christ had now done: *If I your Lord and Master have* done it to you, you ought to do it *to one another.* He shows the cogency of this argument in two things:—

(1.) I am *your Master,* and you are my disciples, and therefore you ought to *learn of me* (*v.* 15); for in this, as in other things, *I have given you an example,* that *you should do* to others *as I have done* to you. Observe,

[1.] What a good teacher Christ is. He teaches by example as well as doctrine, and for this end came into this world, and dwelt among us, that he might set us a copy of all those graces and duties which his holy religion teaches; and it is a copy without one false stroke. Hereby he made his own laws more intelligible and honourable. Christ is a commander like Gideon, who said to his soldiers, *Look on me, and do likewise* (Judg. vii. 17); like Abimelech, who said, *What you have seen me do, make haste and do as I have done* (Judg. ix. 48); and like Cæsar, who called his soldiers, not *milites—soldiers,* but *commilitones—fellow-soldiers,* and whose usual word was, not *Ite illue,* but *Venite huc;* not *Go,* but *Come.* [2.] What good scholars we must be. We must *do as he hath done;* for therefore he gave us a copy, that we should write after it, that we might be as he was in this world (1 John iv. 17), and walk *as he walked,* 1 John ii. 6. Christ's example herein is to be followed by ministers in particular, in whom the graces of humility and holy love should especially appear, and by the exercise thereof they effectually serve the interests of their Master and the ends of their ministry. When Christ sent his apostles abroad as his agents, it was with this charge, that they should not take state upon them, nor carry things with a high hand, but *become all things to all men,* 1 Cor. ix. 22. What I have done to your dirty feet that do you to the polluted souls of sinners; *wash them.* Some who suppose this to have been done at the passover supper think it intimates a rule in admitting communicants to the Lord's-supper, to see that they be first washed and cleansed by reformation and a blameless conversation, and then take them in to *compass God's altar.* But all Christians likewise are here taught to condescend to each other in love, and to do it as Christ did it, unasked, unpaid; we must not be mercenary in the services of love, nor do them with reluctancy.

(2.) I am *your Master,* and you are my disciples, and therefore you cannot think it below you to do that, how mean soever it may seem, which you have seen me do, for (*v.* 16) *the servant is not greater than his Lord, neither he that is sent,* though sent with all the pomp and power of an ambassador, *greater than he that sent him.* Christ had urged this (Matt. x. 24, 25) as a reason why they should not think it strange if they suffered as he did; here he urges it as a reason why they should not think it much to humble themselves as he did. What he did not think a disparagement to him, they must not think a disparagement to them. Perhaps the disciples were inwardly disgusted at this precept of washing one another's feet, as inconsistent with the dignity they expected shortly to be preferred to. To obviate such thoughts, Christ reminds them of their place as his servants; they were not better men than their Master, and what was consistent with his dignity was much more consistent with theirs. If he was humble and condescending, it ill became them to be proud and assuming. Note, [1.] We must take good heed to ourselves, lest Christ's gracious condescensions to us, and advancements of us, through the corruption of nature occasion us to entertain high thoughts of ourselves or low thoughts of him. We need to be put in mind of this, that we are not *greater than our Lord.* [2.] Whatever our Master was pleased to condescend to in favour to us, we should much more condescend to in conformity to him. Christ, by humbling himself, has dignified humility, and put an honour upon it, and obliged his followers to think nothing below them but sin. We commonly say to those who disdain to do such or such a thing, As good as you have done it, and been never the worse thought of; and true indeed it is, if our Master has done it. When we see our Master serving, we cannot but see how ill it becomes us to be domineering.

5. Our Saviour closes this part of his discourse with an intimation of the necessity of their obedience to these instructions: *If you know these things;* or, seeing you know them, *happy are you if you do them.* Most people think, Happy are those that rise and rule. Washing one another's feet will never get estates and preferments; but Christ saith, notwithstanding this, Happy are those that stoop and obey. *If you know these things.* This may be understood either as intimating a doubt whether they knew them or no; so strong was their conceit of a temporal kingdom that it was a question whether they could entertain the notion of a duty so contrary to that conceit. Or, as taking it for granted that they did know these things; since they had such excellent precepts given them, recommended by such an excellent pattern, it will be necessary to the completing of their happiness that they practise accordingly. (1.) This is applicable to the commands of Christ in general. Note, Though it is a great advantage to know our duty, yet we shall come short of happiness if we do not do our duty. Knowing is in order to doing; that knowledge therefore is vain and fruitless which is not reduced to practice; nay, it will aggravate the sin and ruin, Luke xii. 47, 48; James iv. 17. It is knowing and doing that will demonstrate us of *Christ's kingdom,* and wise builders. See Ps. ciii. 17, 18. (2.) It is to be applied especially to this command of humility and serviceableness. Nothing is better known, nor more readily acknowledged, than this, that we should be humble; and therefore, though many will own themselves to be passionate and intemperate, few will own themselves to be proud, for it is as inexcusable a sin, and as hateful, as any other; and yet how little is to be seen of true humility, and that mutual subjection and condescension upon

which the law of Christ so much insists! Most know these things so well as to expect that others should do accordingly to them, yield to them, and serve them, but not so well as to do so themselves.

18 I speak not of you all: I know
whom I have chosen: but that the
scripture may be fulfilled, He that
eateth bread with me hath lifted up
his heel against me. 19 Now I tell
you before it come, that, when it is
come to pass, ye may believe that I
am *he.* 20 Verily, verily, I say unto
you, He that receiveth whomsoever I
send receiveth me; and he that receiveth me receiveth him that sent
me. 21 When Jesus had thus said,
he was troubled in spirit, and testified, and said, Verily, verily, I say
unto you, that one of you shall betray
me. 22 Then the disciples looked
one on another, doubting of whom he
spake. 23 Now there was leaning
on Jesus' bosom one of his disciples,
whom Jesus loved. 24 Simon Peter
therefore beckoned to him, that he
should ask who it should be of whom
he spake. 25 He then lying on Jesus' breast, saith unto him, Lord,
who is it? 26 Jesus answered, He
it is, to whom I shall give a sop,
when I have dipped *it.* And when
he had dipped the sop, he gave *it* to
Judas Iscariot, *the son* of Simon. 27
And after the sop Satan entered
into him. Then said Jesus unto him,
That thou doest, do quickly. 28
Now no man at the table knew for
what intent he spake this unto him.
29 For some *of them* thought, because Judas had the bag, that Jesus
had said unto him, Buy *those things*
that we have need of against the feast;
or, that he should give something to
the poor. 30 He then having received the sop went immediately out:
and it was night.

We have here the discovery of Judas's plot to betray his Master. Christ knew it from the beginning; but now first he discovered it to his disciples, who did not expect Christ should be betrayed, though he had often told them so, much less did they suspect that one of them should do it. Now here,

I. Christ gives them a general intimation of it (*v.* 18): *I speak not of you all,* I cannot expect you will all do these things, for *I know whom I have chosen,* and whom I have passed by; but the scripture will be fulfilled (Ps. xli. 9), *He that eateth bread with me hath lifted up his heel against me.* He does not yet speak out, either of the crime or the criminal, but raises their expectations of a further discovery.

1. He intimates to them that they were not all right. He had said (*v.* 10), *You are clean, but not all.* So here, *I speak not of you all.* Note, What is said of the excellencies of Christ's disciples cannot be said of all that are called so. The word of Christ is a distinguishing word, which separates *between cattle and cattle,* and will distinguish thousands into hell who flattered themselves with hopes that they were going to heaven. *I speak not of you all;* you my disciples and followers. Note, There is a mixture of bad with good in the best societies, a Judas among the apostles; it will be so till we come to the blessed society into which shall enter nothing unclean or disguised.

2. That he himself knew who were right, and who were not: *I know whom I have chosen,* who the few are that are chosen among the many that are called with the common call. Note, (1.) Those that are chosen, Christ himself had the choosing of them; he nominated the persons he undertook for. (2.) Those that are chosen are known to Christ, for he never forgets any whom he has once had in his thoughts of love, 2 Tim. ii. 19.

3. That in the treachery of him that proved false to him the scripture was fulfilled, which takes off very much both the surprise and offence of the thing. Christ took one into his family whom he foresaw to be a traitor, and did not by effectual grace prevent his being so, *that the scripture might be fulfilled.* Let it not therefore be a stumbling-block to any; for, though it do not at all lessen Judas's offence, it may lessen our offence at it. The scripture referred to is David's complaint of the treachery of some of his enemies; the Jewish expositors, and ours from them, generally understand it of Ahithophel: Grotius thinks it intimates that the death of Judas would be like that of Ahithophel. But because that psalm speaks of David's sickness, of which we read nothing at the time of Ahithophel's deserting him, it may better be understood of some other friend of his, that proved false to him. This our Saviour applies to Judas. (1.) Judas, as an apostle, was admitted to the highest privilege: he did *eat bread with Christ.* He was familiar with him, and favoured by him, was one of his family, one of those with whom he was intimately conversant. David saith of his treacherous friend, He did eat *of my bread;* but Christ, being poor, had no bread he could properly call his own. He saith, He did *eat bread with me;* such as he had by the kindness of his friends, that ministered to him, his disciples had their share

of, Judas among the rest. Wherever he went, Judas was welcome with him, did not dine among servants, but sat at table with his Master, ate of the same dish, drank of the same cup, and in all respects fared as he fared. He ate miraculous bread with him, when the loaves were multiplied, ate the passover with him. Note, All that eat bread with Christ are not his disciples indeed. See 1 Cor. x. 3—5. (2.) Judas, as an apostate, was guilty of the basest treachery: he *lifted up the heel* against Christ. [1.] He forsook him, turned his back upon him, went out from the society of his disciples, *v.* 30. [2.] He despised him, shook off the dust of his feet against him, in contempt of him and his gospel. Nay, [3.] He became an enemy to him; spurned at him, as wrestlers do at their adversaries, whom they would overthrow. Note, It is no new thing for those that were Christ's seeming friends to prove his real enemies. Those who pretended to magnify him magnify themselves against him, and thereby prove themselves guilty, not only of the basest ingratitude, but the basest treachery and perfidiousness.

II. He gives them a reason why he told them beforehand of the treachery of Judas (*v.* 19): "*Now I tell you before it come,* before Judas has begun to put his wicked plot in execution, *that when it is come to pass you may,* instead of stumbling at it, be confirmed in your *belief that I am he,* he that should come." 1. By his clear and certain foresight of things to come, of which in this, as in other instances, he gave incontestable proof, he proved himself to be the true God, before whom all things are naked and open. Christ foretold that Judas would betray him when there was no ground to suspect such a thing, and so proved himself the eternal Word, which is a *discerner of the thoughts and intents of the heart.* The prophecies of the New Testament concerning the apostasy of the latter times (which we have, 2 Thess. ii.; 1 Tim. iv., and in the Apocalypse) being evidently accomplished is a proof that those writings were divinely inspired, and confirms our faith in the whole canon of scripture. 2. By this application of the types and prophecies of the Old Testament to himself, he proved himself to be the true Messiah, to whom *all the prophets bore witness.* Thus *it was written, and thus it behoved Christ to suffer,* and he suffered just as it was written, Luke xxiv. 25, 26; *ch.* viii. 28.

III. He gives a word of encouragement to his apostles, and all his ministers whom he employs in his service (*v.* 20): *He that receiveth whomsoever I send receiveth me.* The purport of these words is the same with what we have in other scriptures, but it is not easy to make out their coherence here. Christ had told his disciples that they must humble and abase themselves. "Now," saith he, "though there may be those that will despise you for your condescension, yet there will be those that will do you honour, and shall be honoured for so doing." Those who know themselves dignified by Christ's commission may be content to be vilified in the world's opinion. Or, he intended to silence the scruples of those who, because there was a traitor among the apostles, would be shy of receiving any of them; for, if one of them was false to his Master, to whom would any of them be true? *Ex uno disce omnes—They are all alike.* No, as Christ will think never the worse of them for Judas's crime, so he will stand by them, and own them and will raise up such as shall receive them. Those that had received Judas when he was a preacher, and perhaps were converted and edified by his preaching, were never the worse, nor should reflect upon it with any regret, though he afterwards proved a traitor; for he was one whom Christ sent. We cannot know what men are, much less what they will be, but those who appear to be sent of Christ we must receive, till the contrary appear. Though some, by entertaining strangers, have entertained robbers unawares, yet we must still be hospitable, for thereby some have entertained angels. The abuses put upon our charity, though ordered with ever so much discretion, will neither justify our uncharitableness, nor lose us the reward of our charity. 1. We are here encouraged to receive ministers as *sent of Christ: "He that receiveth whomsoever I send,* though weak and poor, and subject to like passions as others (for as the law, so the gospel, *makes men priests that have infirmity),* yet if he deliver my message, and be regularly called and appointed to do so, and as an officer give himself to the word and prayer, he that entertains him shall be owned as a friend of mine." Christ was now leaving the world, but he would leave an order of men to be his agents, to deliver his word, and those who receive *this,* in the light and love of it, receive *him.* To believe the doctrine of Christ, and obey his law, and accept the salvation offered upon the terms proposed; this is receiving those whom Christ sends, and it is *receiving Christ Jesus the Lord* himself. 2. We are here encouraged to receive Christ as sent of God: *He that* thus *receiveth me,* that receiveth Christ in his ministers, receiveth the Father also, for they come upon his errand likewise, baptizing in the name of the Father, as well as of the Son. Or, in general, *He that receiveth me* as his prince and Saviour receiveth *him that sent me* as his portion and felicity. Christ was sent of God, and in embracing his religion we embrace the *only true* religion.

IV. Christ more particularly notifies to them the plot which one of their number was now hatching against him (*v.* 21): *When Jesus had thus said* in general, to prepare them for a more particular discovery, he was *troubled in spirit,* and showed it by some gesture or sign, and *he testified,* he solemnly declared it *(cum animo testandi—with the so-*

lemnity of a witness on oath), "One of you shall betray me; one of you my apostles and constant followers." None indeed could be said to *betray* him but those in whom he reposed a confidence, and who were the witnesses of his retirements. This did not determine Judas to the sin by any fatal necessity; for, though the event did follow according to the prediction, yet not from the prediction. Christ is not the author of sin; yet as to this heinous sin of Judas, 1. Christ foresaw it; for even that which is secret and future, and hidden from the eyes of all living, naked and open before the eyes of Christ. He *knows what is in men* better than they do themselves (2 Kings viii. 12), and therefore sees what will be done by them. *I knew that thou wouldest deal very treacherously*, Isa. xlviii. 8. 2. He foretold it, not only for the sake of the rest of the disciples, but for the sake of Judas himself, that he might take warning, and recover himself out of the snare of the devil.' Traitors proceed not in their plots when they find they are discovered; surely Judas, when he finds that his Master knows his design, will retreat in time; if not, it will aggravate his condemnation. 3. He spoke of it with a manifest concern; he was *troubled in spirit* when he mentioned it. He had often spoken of his own sufferings and death, without any such trouble of spirit as he here manifested when he spoke of the ingratitude and treachery of Judas. This touched him in a tender part. Note, The falls and miscarriages of the disciples of Christ are a great trouble of spirit to their Master; the sins of Christians are the grief of Christ. "What! *One of you betray me?* You that have received from me such distinguishing favours; you that I had reason to think would be firm to me, that have professed such a respect for me; what iniquity have you found in me that one of you should betray me?" This went to his heart, as the undutifulness of children grieves those who have *nourished and brought them up*, Isa. i. 2. See Ps. xcv. 10; Isa. lxiii. 10.

V. The disciples quickly take the alarm. They knew their Master would neither deceive them nor jest with them; and therefore *looked one upon another*, with a manifest concern, *doubting of whom he spoke.* 1. By looking one upon another they evinced the trouble they were in upon this notice given them; it struck such a horror upon them that they knew not well which way to look, nor what to say. They saw their Master troubled, and therefore they were troubled. This was at a feast where they were cheerfully entertained; but hence we must be taught to rejoice with trembling, and as though we rejoiced not. When David wept for his son's rebellion, all his followers wept with him (2 Sam. xv. 30); so Christ's disciples here. Note, That which grieves Christ is, and should be, a grief to all that are his, particularly the scandalous miscarriages of those that are called by his name: *Who is offended, and I burn not?* 2. Hereby they endeavoured to *discover* the traitor. They looked wistfully in one another's face, to see who blushed, or, by some disorder in the countenance, manifested guilt in the heart, upon this notice; but, while those who were faithful had their consciences so clear that they could *lift up their faces without spot*, he that was false had his conscience so seared that he was not ashamed, neither could he blush, and so no discovery could be made in this way. Christ thus perplexed his disciples for a time, and put them into confusion, that he might *humble them, and prove them*, might excite in them a jealousy of themselves, and an indignation at the baseness of Judas. It is good for us sometimes to be put to a gaze, to be put to a pause.

VI. The disciples were solicitous to get their Master to explain himself, and to tell them particularly whom he meant; for nothing but this can put them out of their present pain, for each of them thought he had as much reason to suspect himself as any of his brethren; now,

1. Of all the disciples John was most fit to ask, because he was the favourite, and sat next his Master (*v.* 23): *There was leaning on Jesus's bosom one of the disciples whom Jesus loved.* It appears that this was John, by comparing *ch.* xxi. 20, 24. Observe, (1.) The particular kindness which Jesus had for him; he was known by this periphrasis, that he was *the disciple whom Jesus loved.* He loved them all (*v.* 1), but John was particularly dear to him. His name signifies *gracious.* Daniel, who was honoured with the revelations of the Old Testament, as John of the New, was *a man greatly beloved*, Dan. ix. 23. Note, Among the disciples of Christ some are dearer to him than others. (2.) His place and posture at this time: He was *leaning on Jesus's bosom.* Some say that it was the fashion in those countries to sit at meat in a leaning posture, so that the second lay in the bosom of the first, and so on, which does not seem probable to me, for in such a posture as this they could neither eat nor drink conveniently; but, whether this was the case or not, John now *leaned on Christ's bosom*, and it seems to be an extraordinary expression of endearment used at this time. Note, There are some of Christ's disciples whom he lays in his bosom, who have more free and intimate communion with him than others. The Father loved the Son, and laid him *in his bosom* (*ch.* i. 18), and believers are in like manner one with Christ, *ch.* xvii. 21. This honour all the saints shall have shortly in the bosom of Abraham. Those who lay themselves at Christ's feet, he will lay in his bosom. (3.) Yet he conceals his name, because he himself was the penman of the story. He put this instead of his name, to show that he was pleased with it; it is his title of honour, that he was *the disciple whom*

Jesus loved, as in David's and Solomon's court there was one that was the *king's friend;* yet he does not put his name down, to show that he was not proud of it, nor would seem to boast of it. Paul in a like case saith, *I knew a man in Christ.*

2. Of all the disciples Peter was most forward to know, *v.* 24. Peter, sitting at some distance, beckoned to John, by some sign or other, to ask. Peter was generally the leading man, most apt to put himself forth; and, where men's natural tempers lead them to be thus bold in answering and asking, if kept under the laws of humility and wisdom, they make men very serviceable. God gives his gifts variously; but that the forward men in the church may not think too well of themselves, nor the modest be discouraged, it must be noted that it was not Peter, but John, that was the beloved disciple. Peter was desirous to know, not only that he might be sure it was not he, but that, knowing who it was, they might withdraw from him, and guard against him, and, if possible, prevent his design. It were a desirable thing, we should think, to know who in the church will deceive us; yet let this suffice—Christ knows, though we do not. The reason why Peter did not himself ask was because John had a much fairer opportunity, by the advantage of his seat at table, to whisper the question into the ear of Christ, and to receive a like private answer. It is good to improve our interest in those that are near to Christ, and to engage their prayers for us. Do we know any that we have reason to think lie in Christ's bosom? Let us beg of them to speak a good word for us.

3. The question was asked accordingly (*v.* 25): *He then, lying at the breast of Jesus,* and so having the convenience of whispering with him, *saith unto him, Lord, who is it?* Now here John shows, (1.) A regard to his fellow-disciple, and to the motion he made. Though Peter had not the honour he had at this time, yet he did not therefore disdain to take the hint and intimation he gave him. Note, Those who lie in Christ's bosom may often learn from those who lie at his feet something that will be profitable for them, and be reminded of that which they did not of themselves think of. John was willing to gratify Peter herein, having so fair an opportunity for it. As every one hath received the gift, so let him minister the same for a common good, Rom. xii. 6. (2.) A reverence of his Master. Though he whispered this in Christ's ear, yet he called him Lord; the familiarity he was admitted to did not at all lessen his respect for his Master. It becomes us to use a reverence in expression, and to observe a decorum even in our secret devotions, which no eye is a witness to, as well as in public assemblies. The more intimate communion gracious souls have with Christ, the more sensible they are of his worthiness and their own unworthiness, as Gen. xviii. 27.

4. Christ gave a speedy answer to this question, but whispered it in John's ear; for it appears (*v.* 29) that the rest were still ignorant of the matter. *He it is to whom I shall give a sop, ψωμίον—a morsel, a crust, when I have dipped it* in the sauce. And *when he had dipped the sop,* John strictly observing his motions, *he gave it to Judas;* and Judas took it readily enough, not suspecting the design of it, but glad of a savoury bit, to make up his mouth with. (1.) Christ notified the traitor by a sign. He could have told John by name who he was (The adversary and enemy is that wicked Judas, he is the traitor, and none but he); but thus he would exercise the observation of John, and intimate what need his ministers have of a spirit of discerning; for the false brethren we are to stand upon our guard against are not made known to us by words, but by signs; they are to be known to us by *their fruits,* by *their spirits;* it requires great diligence and care to form a right judgment upon them. (2.) That sign was a sop which Christ gave him, a very proper sign, because it was the fulfilling of the scripture (*v.* 18), that the traitor should be one that *ate bread with him,* that was at this time a fellow-commoner with him. It had likewise a significancy in it, and teaches us, [1.] That Christ sometimes gives sops to traitors; worldly riches, honours, and pleasures are sops (if I may so speak), which Providence sometimes gives into the hands of wicked men. Judas perhaps thought himself a favourite because he had the sop, like Benjamin at Joseph's table, a mess by himself; thus the prosperity of fools, like a stupifying sop, helps to *destroy them.* [2.] That we must not be outrageous against those whom we know to be very malicious against us. Christ carved to Judas as kindly as to any at the table, though he knew he was then plotting his death. *If thine enemy hunger, feed him;* this is to do as Christ does.

VII. Judas himself, instead of being convinced hereby of his wickedness, was the more confirmed in it, and the warning given him was to him a *savour of death unto death;* for it follows,

1. The devil hereupon took possession of him (*v.* 27): *After the sop, Satan entered into him;* not to make him melancholy, nor drive him distracted, which was the effect of his possessing some; not to hurry him into the fire, nor into the water; happy had it been for him if that had been the worst of it, or if with the swine he had been choked in the sea; but Satan entered into him to possess him with a prevailing prejudice against Christ and his doctrine, and a contempt of him, as one whose life was of small value, to excite in him a covetous desire of the wages of unrighteousness and a resolution to stick at nothing for the obtaining of them. But,

(1.) Was not Satan in him before? How then is it said that now *Satan entered into him?* Judas was all along a devil (*ch.* vi. 70), a son of perdition, but now Satan gained a more full possession of him, had a *more abundant entrance* into him. His purpose to betray his Master was now ripened into a fixed resolution; now he returned with seven other spirits more wicked than himself, Luke xi. 26. Note, [1.] Though the devil is in every wicked man that does his works (Eph. ii. 2), yet sometimes he enters more manifestly and more powerfully than at other times, when he puts them upon some enormous wickedness, which humanity and natural conscience startle at. [2.] Betrayers of Christ have much of the devil in them. Christ speaks of the sin of Judas as greater than that of any of his persecutors.

(2.) How came Satan to enter into him *after the sop?* Perhaps he was presently aware that it was the discovery of him, and it made him desperate in his resolutions. Many are made worse by the gifts of Christ's bounty, and are confirmed in their impenitency by that which should have led them to repentance. The *coals of fire heaped upon their heads*, instead of melting them, harden them.

2. Christ hereupon dismissed him, and delivered him up to his own heart's lusts: *Then said Jesus unto him, What thou doest, do quickly*. This is not to be understood as either advising him to his wickedness or warranting him in it; but either, (1.) As abandoning him to the conduct and power of Satan. Christ knew that Satan had entered into him, and had peaceable possession; and now he gives him up as hopeless. The various methods Christ had used for his conviction were ineffectual; and therefore, "What thou doest thou wilt do quickly; if thou art resolved to ruin thyself, go on, and take what comes." Note, When the evil spirit is willingly admitted, the good Spirit justly withdraws. Or, (2.) As challenging him to do his worst: "Thou art plotting against me, put thy plot in execution and welcome, the sooner the better, I do not fear thee, I am ready for thee." Note, our Lord Jesus was very forward to suffer and die for us, and was impatient of delay in the perfecting of his undertaking. Christ speaks of Judas's betraying him as a thing he was now doing, though he was only purposing it. Those who are contriving and designing mischief are, in God's account, doing mischief.

3. Those that were at table understood not what he meant, because they did not hear what he whispered to John (*v.* 28, 29): *No man at table,* neither the disciples nor any other of the guests, except John, *knew for what intent* he spoke this to him. (1.) They did not suspect that Christ said it to Judas as a traitor, because it did not enter into their heads that Judas was such a one, or would prove so. Note, It is an excusable dulness in the disciples of Christ not to be quick-sighted in their censures. Most are ready enough to say, when they hear harsh things spoken in general, Now such a one is meant, and now such a one; but Christ's disciples were so well taught to love one another that they could not easily learn to suspect one another; *charity thinks no evil.* (2.) They therefore took it for granted that he said it to him as a trustee, or treasurer of the household, giving him orders for the laying out of some money. Their surmises in this case discover to us for what uses and purposes our Lord Jesus commonly directed payments out of that little stock he had, and so teach us how to honour the Lord with our substance. They concluded something was to be laid out, either, [1.] In works of piety: *Buy those things that we have need of against the feast.* Though he borrowed a room to eat the passover in, yet he bought in provision for it. That is to be reckoned well bestowed which is laid out upon *those things we have need of* for the maintenance of God's ordinances among us; and we have the less reason to grudge that expense now because our gospel-worship is far from being so chargeable as the legal worship was. [2.] Or in works of charity: *That he should give something to the poor.* By this it appears, *First,* That our Lord Jesus, though he lived upon alms himself (Luke viii. 3), yet gave alms to the poor, a little out of a little. Though he might very well be excused, not only because he was poor himself, but because he did so much good in other ways, curing so many *gratis;* yet, to set us an example, he gave, for the relief of the poor, out of that which he had for the subsistence of his family; see Eph. iv. 28. *Secondly,* That the time of a religious feast was thought a proper time for works of charity. When he celebrated the passover he ordered something for the poor. When we experience God's bounty to us, this should make us bountiful to the poor.

4. Judas hereupon sets himself vigorously to pursue his design against him: He *went away.* Notice is taken,

(1.) Of his speedy departure: *He went out presently,* and quitted the house, [1.] For fear of being more plainly discovered to the company, for, if he were, he expected they would all fall upon him, and be the death of him, or at least of his project. [2.] He went out as one weary of Christ's company and the society of his apostles. Christ needed not to expel him, he expelled himself. Note, Withdrawing from the communion of the faithful is commonly the first overt-act of a backslider, and the beginning of an apostasy. [3.] *He went out* to prosecute his design, to look for those with whom he was to make his bargain, and to settle the agreement with them. Now that Satan had got into him he hurried him on with precipitation, lest he should see his error and repent of it.

(2.) Of the time of his departure: *It was*

night. [1.] Though it was night, an unseasonable time for business, yet, Satan having entered into him, he made no difficulty of the coldness and darkness of the night. This should shame us out of our slothfulness and cowardice in the service of Christ, that the devil's servants are so earnest and venturous in his service. [2.] Because it was night, and this gave him advantage of privacy and concealment. He was not willing to be *seen* treating with the chief priests, and therefore chose the dark night as the fittest time for such works of darkness. Those whose deeds are evil love darkness rather than light. See Job xxiv. 13, &c.

31 Therefore, when he was gone
out, Jesus said, Now is the Son of
man glorified, and God is glorified in
him. 32 If God be glorified in him,
God shall also glorify him in himself,
and shall straightway glorify him. 33
Little children, yet a little while I am
with you. Ye shall seek me: and as
I said unto the Jews, Whither I go,
ye cannot come; so now I say to
you. 34 A new commandment I
give unto you, That ye love one another; as I have loved you, that ye also love one another. 35 By this shall
all *men* know that ye are my disciples, if ye have love one to another.

This and what follows, to the end of *ch.* xiv., was Christ's table-talk with his disciples. When supper was done, Judas went out; but what did the Master and his disciples do, whom he left sitting at table? They applied themselves to profitable discourse, to teach us as much as we can to make conversation with our friends at table serviceable to religion. Christ begins this discourse. The more forward we are humbly to promote that communication which is good, and to the use of edifying, the more like we are to Jesus Christ. Those especially that by their place, reputation, and gifts, *command the company*, to whom *men give ear*, ought to use the interest they have in other respects as an opportunity of doing them good. Now our Lord Jesus discourses with them (and probably discourses much more largely than is here recorded),

I. Concerning the great mystery of his own death and sufferings, about which they were as yet so much in the dark that they could not persuade themselves to expect the thing itself, much less did they understand the meaning of it; and therefore Christ gives them such instructions concerning it as made the offence of the cross to cease. Christ did not begin this discourse till Judas was gone out, for he was a false brother. The presence of wicked people is often a hindrance to good discourse. When Judas *was gone out,* Christ said, *Now is the Son of man glorified;* now that Judas is discovered and discarded, who was a spot in their love-feast and a scandal to their family, *now is the Son of man glorified.* Note, Christ is glorified by the purifying of Christian societies: corruptions in his church are a reproach to him; the purging out of those corruptions rolls away the reproach. Or, rather, now Judas was gone to set the wheels a-going, in order to his being put to death, and the thing was likely to be effected shortly: *Now is the Son of man glorified,* meaning, *Now he is crucified.*

1. Here is something which Christ instructs them in, concerning his sufferings, that was very *comforting.*

(1.) That he should himself be glorified in them. Now the Son of man is to be exposed to the greatest ignominy and disgrace, to be despitefully used to the last degree, and dishonoured both by the cowardice of his friends and the insolence of his enemies; yet *now he is glorified;* For, [1.] Now he is to obtain a glorious victory over Satan and all the powers of darkness, to spoil them, and triumph over them. He is now *girding on the harness,* to take the field against these adversaries of God and man, with as great an assurance as if he had *put it off.* [2.] Now he is to work out a glorious deliverance for his people, by his death to reconcile them to God, and bring in an everlasting righteousness and happiness for them; to shed that blood which is to be an inexhaustible fountain of joys and blessings to all believers. [3.] Now he is to give a glorious example of self-denial and patience under the cross, courage and contempt of the world, zeal for the glory of God, and love to the souls of men, such as will make him to be for ever admired and had in honour. Christ had been glorified in many miracles he had wrought, and yet he speaks of his being glorified *now* in his sufferings, as if that were more than all his other glories in his humble state.

(2.) That God the Father should be glorified in them. The sufferings of Christ were, [1.] The satisfaction of God's justice, and so God was glorified in them. Reparation was thereby made with great advantage for the wrong done him in his honour by the sin of man. The ends of the law were abundantly answered, and the glory of his government effectually asserted and maintained. [2.] They were the manifestation of his holiness and mercy. The attributes of God shine brightly in creation and providence, but much more in the work of redemption; see 1 Cor. i. 24; 2 Cor. iv. 6. God is love, and herein he hath commended his love.

(3.) That he should himself be greatly glorified after them, in consideration of God's being greatly glorified by them, *v.* 32. Observe how he enlarges upon it. [1.] He is sure that God will glorify him; and those whom God glorifies are glorious indeed. Hell and earth set themselves to vilify Christ, but God resolved to glorify him, and he did it. He glorified him in his sufferings by the amazing signs and wonders, both in heaven and earth, which attended them, and extorted even from his crucifiers an acknowledgment that he was the Son of God. But especially after his sufferings he glorified him, when he set him *at his own right hand,* gave him a *name above every name.* [2.] That he will glorify him *in himself*—ἐν ἑαυτῷ. Either, *First,* In Christ himself. He will glorify him in his own person, and not only in his kingdom among men. This supposes his speedy resurrection. A common person may be honoured after his death, in his memory or posterity, but Christ was honoured in *himself.* Or, *Secondly,* in God himself. God will glorify him *with himself,* as it is explained, *ch.* xvii. 5. *He shall sit down with the Father upon his throne,* Rev. iii. 21. This is true glory. [3.] That he will glorify him straightway. He looked upon the joy and glory set before him, not only as great, but as near; and his sorrows and sufferings short and soon over. Good services done to earthly princes often remain long unrewarded; but Christ had his preferments presently. It was but forty hours (or not so much) from his death to his resurrection, and forty days thence to his ascension, so that it might well be said that he was *straightway glorified,* Ps. xvi. 10. [4.] All this in consideration of God's being glorified in and by his sufferings: *Seeing God is glorified in him,* and receives honour from his sufferings, God shall in like manner glorify him in himself, and give honour to him. Note, *First,* In the exaltation of Christ there was a regard had to his humiliation, and a reward given for it. *Because he humbled himself, therefore God highly exalted him.* If the Father be so great a gainer in his glory by the death of Christ, we may be sure that the Son shall be no loser in his. See the covenant between them, Isa. liii. 12. *Secondly,* Those who mind the business of glorifying God no doubt shall have the happiness of being glorified with him.

2. Here is something that Christ instructs them in, concerning his sufferings, which was *awakening,* for as yet they were slow of heart to understand it (*v.* 33): *Little children, yet a little while I am with you,* &c. Two things Christ here suggests, to quicken his disciples to improve their present opportunities; two serious words:—

(1.) That his stay in this world, to be with them here, they would find to be very short. *Little children.* This compellation does not bespeak so much their weakness as his tenderness and compassion; he speaks to them with the affection of a father, now that he is about to leave them, and to leave blessings with them. Know this, then, that *yet a little while I am with you.* Whether we understand this as referring to his death or his ascension it comes much to one; he had but a little time to spend with them, and therefore, [1.] Let them improve the advantage they now had. If they had any good question to ask, if they would have any advice, instruction, or comfort, let them speak quickly; for *yet a little while I am with you.* We must make the best of the helps we have for our souls while we have them, because we shall not have them long; they will be taken from us, or we from them. [2.] Let them not doat upon his bodily presence, as if their happiness and comfort were bound up in that; no, they must think of living without it; not be always little children, but go alone, without their nurses. Ways and means are appointed but for a *little while,* and are not to be rested in, but pressed through to our rest, to which they have a reference.

(2.) That their following him to the other world, to be with him there, they would find to be very difficult. What he had said to the Jews (*ch.* vii. 34) he saith to his disciples; for they have need to be quickened by the same considerations that are propounded for the convincing and awakening of sinners. Christ tells them here, [1.] That when he was gone they would feel the want of him: *You shall seek me,* that is, "you shall wish you had me again with you." We are often taught the worth of mercies by the want of them. Though the presence of the Comforter yielded them real and effectual relief in straits and difficulties, yet it was not such a *sensible* satisfaction as his bodily presence would have been to those who had been used to it. But observe, Christ said to the Jews, You shall seek me and *not find me;* but to the disciples he only saith, *You shall seek me,* intimating that though they should not find his bodily presence any more than the Jews, yet they should find that which was tantamount, and should not seek in vain. When they sought his body in the sepulchre, though they did not find it, yet they sought to good purpose. [2.] That whither he went they *could not come,* which suggests to them high thoughts of him, who was going to an invisible inaccessible world, to dwell in that *light which none can approach unto;* and also low thoughts of themselves, and serious thoughts of their future state. Christ tells them that they could not follow him (as Joshua told the people that they could not serve the Lord) only to quicken them to so much the more diligence and care. They could not follow him to his cross, for they had not courage and resolution; it appeared that they could not when they all forsook him and fled. Nor could they follow him to his crown, for they had not a sufficiency of their own, nor were their work and warfare yet finished.

II. He discourses with them concerning the great duty of brotherly love (*v.* 34, 35): *You shall love one another.* Judas was now gone out, and had proved himself a false brother; but they must not therefore harbour such jealousies and suspicions one of another as would be the bane of love: though there was one Judas among them, yet they were not all Judases. Now that the enmity of the Jews against Christ and his followers was swelling to the height, and they must expect such treatment as their Master had, it concerned them by brotherly love to strengthen one another's hands. Three arguments for mutual love are here urged:—

1. The command of their Master (*v.* 34): *A new commandment I give unto you.* He not only commends it as amiable and pleasant, not only counsels it as excellent and profitable, but commands it, and makes it one of the fundamental laws of his kingdom; it goes a-breast with the command of believing in Christ, 1 John iii. 23; 1 Pet. i. 22. It is the command of our ruler, who has a right to give law to us; it is the command of our Redeemer, who gives us this law in order to the curing of our spiritual diseases and the preparing of us for our eternal bliss. It is *a new commandment;* that is, (1.) It is a renewed commandment; it was a commandment *from the beginning* (1 John ii. 7), as old as the law of nature, it was the second great commandment of the law of Moses; yet, because it is also one of the great commandments of the New Testament, of Christ the new Lawgiver, it is called a new commandment; it is like an old book in a new edition corrected and enlarged. This commandment has been so corrupted by the traditions of the Jewish church that when Christ revived it, and set it in a true light, it might well be called a *new commandment.* Laws of revenge and retaliation were so much in vogue, and self-love had so much the ascendant, that the law of brotherly love was forgotten as obsolete and out of date; so that as it came from Christ new, it was new to the people. (2.) It is an excellent command, as a *new song* is an excellent song, that has an uncommon gratefulness in it. (3.) It is an everlasting command; so strangely new as to be always so; as the *new covenant,* which shall never decay (Heb. viii. 13); it shall be new to eternity, when faith and hope are antiquated. (4.) As Christ gives it, it is *new.* Before it was, *Thou shalt love thy neighbour;* now it is, You shall love *one another;* it is pressed in a more winning way when it is thus pressed as mutual duty owing to one another.

2. The example of their Saviour is another argument for brotherly love: *As I have loved you.* It is this that makes it a *new commandment*—that this rule and reason of *love (as I have loved you)* is perfectly new, and such as had been hidden from ages and generations. Understand this, (1.) Of all the instances of Christ's love to his disciples, which they had already experienced during the time he went in and out among them. He spoke kindly to them, concerned himself heartily for them, and for their welfare, instructed, counselled, and comforted them, prayed with them and for them, vindicated them when they were accused, took their part when they were run down, and publicly owned them to be dearer to him than his *mother, or sister, or brother.* He reproved them for what was amiss, and yet compassionately bore with their failings, excused them, made the best of them, and passed by many an oversight. Thus he *had* loved them, and just now washed their feet; and thus they *must* love one another, and love *to the end.* Or, (2.) It may be understood of the special instance of love to all his disciples which he was now about to give, in laying down his life for them. *Greater love hath no man than this, ch.* xv. 13. Has he thus loved us all? Justly may he expect that we should be loving to one another. Not that we are capable of doing any thing of the *same nature* for each other (Ps. xlix. 7), but we must love one another in some respects after the *same manner;* we must set this before us as our copy, and take directions from it. Our love to one another must be free and ready, laborious and expensive, constant and persevering; it must be love *to the souls* one of another. We must also love one another from *this motive,* and upon this consideration—because Christ has loved us. See Rom. xv. 1, 3; Eph. v. 2, 25; Phil. ii. 1—5.

3. The reputation of their profession (*v.* 35): *By this shall all men know that you are my disciples, if you have love one to another.* Observe, We must have love, not only show love, but have it in the root and habit of it, and have it when there is not any present occasion to show it; have it *ready.* "Hereby it will appear that you are indeed my followers by following me in this." Note, Brotherly love is the badge of Christ's disciples. By this he knows them, by this they may know themselves (1 John iii. 14), and by this others may know them. This is the livery of his family, the distinguishing character of his disciples; this he would have them *noted for,* as that wherein they excelled all others—their loving one another. This was what their Master was famous for; all that ever heard of him have heard of his love, his great love; and therefore, if you see any people more affectionate one to another than what is common, say, "Certainly these are the followers of Christ, they have been with Jesus." Now by this it appears, (1.) That the heart of Christ was very much upon it, that his disciples *should love one another.* In this they must be *singular;* whereas the way of the world is to be *every one for himself,* they should be hearty for one another. He does not say, *By this shall men know* that you are my disciples—if you *work miracles,* for a worker of miracles is but a cypher without charity (1 Cor. xiii. 1, 2); but *if you love one another* from a principle of

self-denial and gratitude to Christ. This Christ would have to be the *proprium* of his religion, the principal note of the true church. (2.) That it is the true honour of Christ's disciples to excel in brotherly love. Nothing will be more effectual than this to recommend them to the esteem and respect of others. See what a powerful attractive it was, Acts ii. 46, 47. Tertullian speaks of it as the glory of the primitive church that the Christians were known by their affection to one another. Their adversaries took notice of it, and said, *See how these Christians love one another*, Apol. cap. 39. (3.) That, if the followers of Christ do not love one another, they not only cast an unjust reproach upon their profession, but give just cause to suspect their own sincerity. *O Jesus! are these thy Christians*, these passionate, malicious, spiteful, ill-natured people? *Is this thy son's coat?* When our brethren stand in need of help from us, and we have an opportunity of being serviceable to them, when they differ in opinion and practice from us, or are any ways rivals with or provoking to us, and so we have an occasion to condescend and forgive, in such cases as this it will be known whether we have this badge of Christ's disciples.

36 Simon Peter said unto him,
Lord, whither goest thou? Jesus
answered him, Whither I go, thou
canst not follow me now; but thou
shalt follow me afterwards. 37 Peter said unto him, Lord, why cannot
I follow thee now? I will lay down
my life for thy sake. 38 Jesus answered him, Wilt thou lay down thy
life for my sake? Verily, verily, I
say unto thee, The cock shall not
crow, till thou hast denied me thrice.

In these verses we have,

I. Peter's curiosity, and the check given to that.

1. Peter's question was bold and blunt (*v.* 36): *Lord, whither goest thou?* referring to what Christ had said (*v* 33), *Whither I go, you cannot come.* The practical instructions Christ had given them concerning brotherly love he overlooks, and asks no questions upon them, but fastens upon that concerning which Christ purposely kept them in the dark. Note, It is a common fault among us to be more inquisitive concerning things secret, which belong to God only, than concerning things *revealed, which belong to us and our children*, more desirous to have our curiosity gratified than our consciences directed, to know what is done in heaven than what we may do to get thither. It is easy to observe it in the converse of Christians, how soon a discourse of that which is plain and edifying is dropped, and no more said to it, the subject is exhausted; which in a matter of doubtful disputation runs into an endless strife of words.

2. Christ's answer was instructive. He did not gratify him with any particular account of the world he was going to, nor ever foretold his glories and joys so distinctly as he did his sufferings, but said what he had said before (*v.* 36): Let this suffice, *thou canst not follow me now, but shalt follow me hereafter*. (1.) We may understand it of his following him to the cross: "Thou hast not yet strength enough of faith and resolution to drink of my cup;" and it appeared so by his cowardice when Christ was suffering. For this reason, when Christ was seized, he provided for the safety of his disciples: *Let these go their way*, because they could not *follow him now*. Christ considers the frame of his disciples, and will not cut out for them that work and hardship which they are not as yet fit for; the day shall be as the strength is. Peter, though designed for martyrdom, cannot follow Christ now, not being come to his full growth, but he *shall follow* him *hereafter;* he shall be crucified at last, like his Master. Let him not think that because he escapes suffering now he shall never suffer. From our missing the cross once, we must not infer that we shall never meet it; we may be reserved for greater trials than we have yet known. (2.) We may understand it of his following him to the crown. Christ was now going to his glory, and Peter was very desirous to go with him: "No," saith Christ, "*thou canst not follow me now*, thou art not yet ripe for heaven, nor hast thou finished thy work on earth. The forerunner must *first enter to prepare a place* for thee, but *thou shalt follow me afterwards*, after thou hast fought the good fight, and at the time appointed." Note, Believers must not expect to be glorified as soon as they are effectually called, for there is a wilderness between the Red Sea and Canaan.

II. Peter's confidence, and the check given to that.

1. Peter makes a daring protestation of his constancy. He is not content to be left behind, but asks, "*Lord, why cannot I follow thee now?* Dost thou question my sincerity and resolution? I promise thee, if there be occasion, *I will lay down my life for thy sake.*" Some think Peter had a conceit, as the Jews had in a like case (*ch.* vii. 35), that Christ was designing a journey or voyage into some remote country, and that he declared his resolution to go along with him wherever he went; but, having heard his Master so often speak of his own sufferings, surely he could not understand him any otherwise than of his going away by death; and he resolves as Thomas did that he will *go and die with him;* and better die with him than live without him. See here, (1.) What an affectionate love Peter had to our Lord Jesus: "*I will lay down my life for thy sake*, and I can do no more." I believe

Peter spoke as he thought, and though he was inconsiderate he was not insincere, in his resolution. Note, Christ should be dearer to us than our own lives, which therefore, when we are called to it, we should be willing to lay down for his sake, Acts xx. 24. (2.) How ill he took it to have it questioned, intimated in that expostulation, "*Lord, why cannot I follow thee now?* Dost thou suspect my fidelity to thee?" 1 Sam. xxix. 8. Note, It is with regret that true love hears its own sincerity arraigned, as *ch.* xxi. 17. Christ had indeed said that one of them was a devil, but he was discovered, and gone out, and therefore Peter thinks he may speak with the more assurance of his own sincerity: "Lord, I am resolved I will never leave thee, and therefore *why cannot I follow thee?* We are apt to think that we can do any thing, and take it amiss to be told that this and the other we cannot do, whereas without Christ we can do nothing.

2. Christ gives him a surprising prediction of his inconstancy, *v.* 38. Jesus Christ knows us better than we know ourselves, and has many ways of discovering those to themselves whom he loves, and will hide pride from. (1.) He upbraids Peter with his confidence: *Wilt thou lay down thy life for my sake?* Methinks, he seems to have said this with a smile: "Peter, thy promises are too large, too lavish to be relied on; thou dost not consider with what reluctancy and struggle a life is laid down, and what a hard task it is to die; not so soon done as said." Christ hereby puts Peter upon second thoughts, not that he might retract his resolution, or recede from it, but that he might insert into it that necessary proviso, "Lord, *thy grace enabling me,* I will lay down my life for thy sake." "Wilt thou undertake to die for me? What! thou that trembledst to walk upon the water to me? What! thou that, when sufferings were spoken of, criedst out, *Be it far from thee, Lord?* It was an easy thing to leave thy boats and nets to follow me, but not so easy to lay down thy life." His Master himself struggled when it came to this, and *the disciple is not greater than his Lord.* Note, It is good for us to shame ourselves out of our presumptuous confidence in ourselves. Shall a bruised reed set up for a pillar, or a sickly child undertake to be a champion? What a fool am I to talk so big. (2.) He plainly foretels his cowardice in the critical hour. To stop the mouth of his boasting, lest Peter should say it again, Yea Master, that I will, Christ solemnly asserts it with, *Verily, verily, I say unto thee, the cock shall not crow till thou hast denied me thrice.* He does not say as afterwards, *This night,* for it seems to have been two nights before the passover; but, "Shortly thou wilt have denied me thrice within the space of one night; nay, within so short a space as between the first and last crowing of the cock: *the cock shall not crow,* shall not have crowed his crowing out, till thou hast again and again denied me, and that for fear of suffering. The crowing of the cock is mentioned, [1.] To intimate that the trial in which he would miscarry thus should be in the night, which was an improbable circumstance, but Christ's foretelling it was an instance of his infallible foresight. [2.] Because the crowing of the cock was to be the occasion of his repentance, which of itself would not have been if Christ had not put this into the prediction. Christ not only foresaw that Judas would betray him though he only in heart designed it, but he foresaw that Peter would deny him though he did not design it, but the contrary. He knows not only the wickedness of sinners, but the weakness of saints. Christ told Peter, *First,* That he would deny him, would renounce and abjure him: "Thou wilt not only not follow me still, but wilt be ashamed to own that ever thou didst follow me." *Secondly,* That he would do this not once only by a hasty slip of the tongue, but after he had paused would repeat it a second and third time; and it proved too true. We commonly give it as a reason why the prophecies of scripture are expressed darkly and figuratively, because, if they did *plainly* describe the event, the accomplishment would thereby either be defeated or necessitated by a fatality inconsistent with human liberty; and yet this plain and express prophecy of Peter's denying Christ did neither, nor did in the least make Christ accessary to Peter's sin. But we may well imagine what a mortification it was to Peter's confidence of his own courage to be told this, and to be told it in such a manner that he durst not contradict it, else he would have said as Hazael, *What! is thy servant a dog?* This could not but fill him with confusion. Note, The most secure are commonly the least safe; and those most shamefully betray their own weakness that most confidently presume upon their own strength, 1 Cor. x. 12.

CHAP. XIV.

This chapter is a continuation of Christ's discourse with his disciples after supper. When he had convicted and discarded Judas, he set himself to comfort the rest, who were full of sorrow upon what he had said of leaving them, and a great many good words and comfortable words he here speaks to them. The discourse is interlocutory; as Peter in the foregoing chapter, so Thomas, and Philip, and Jude, in this interposed their thoughts upon what he said, according to the liberty he was pleased to allow them. Free conferences are as instructive as solemn speeches, and more so. The general scope of this chapter is in the first verse; it is designed to keep trouble from their hearts; now in order to this they must believe: and let them consider, I. Heaven as their everlasting rest, ver. 2, 3. II. Christ himself as their way, ver. 4—11. III. The great power they shall be clothed with by the prevalency of their prayers, ver. 12—14. IV. The coming of another comforter, ver. 15—17. V. The fellowship and communion that should be between him and them after his departure, ver. 18—24. VI. The instructions which the Holy Ghost should give them, ver. 25, 26. VII. The peace Christ bequeathed to them, ver. 27. VII. Christ's own cheerfulness in his departure, ver. 28—31. And this which he said to them is designed for the comfort of all his faithful followers.

LET not your hearts be troubled:
ye believe in God, believe also
in me. 2 In my Father's house are
many mansions: if *it were* not *so,* I

would have told you. I go to prepare a place for you. 3 And if I go and prepare a place for you, I will come again, and receive you unto myself; that where I am, *there* ye may be also.

In these verses we have,

I. A general caution which Christ gives to his disciples against *trouble of heart* (*v.* 1): *Let not your heart be troubled.* They now began to be troubled, were entering into this temptation. Now here see,

1. How Christ took notice of it. Perhaps it was apparent in their looks; it was said (*ch.* xiii. 22), *They looked one upon another* with anxiety and concern, and Christ looked upon them all, and observed it; at least, it was intelligible to the Lord Jesus, who is acquainted with all our secret undiscovered sorrows, with the wound that bleeds inwardly; he knows not only how we are afflicted, but how we stand affected under our afflictions, and how near they lie to our hearts; he takes cognizance of all the trouble which his people are at any time in danger of being overwhelmed with; *he knows our souls in adversity.* Many things concurred to trouble the disciples now.

(1.) Christ had just told them of the unkindness he should receive from some of them, and this troubled them all. Peter, no doubt, looked very sorrowful upon what Christ said to him, and all the rest were sorry for him and for themselves too, not knowing whose turn it should be to be told next of some ill thing or other they should do. As to this, Christ comforts them; though a godly jealousy over ourselves is of great use to keep us humble and watchful, yet it must not prevail to the disquieting of our spirits and the damping of our holy joy.

(2.) He had just told them of his own departure from them, that he should not only go away, but go away in a cloud of sufferings. They must shortly hear him loaded with reproaches, and these will be *as a sword in their bones;* they must see him barbarously abused and put to death, and this also will be a sword piercing *through their own souls,* for they had loved him, and chosen him, and left all to follow him. When we now look upon Christ pierced, we cannot but *mourn and be in bitterness,* though we see the glorious issue and fruit of it; much more grievous must the sight be to them, who could then look no further. If Christ depart from them, [1.] They will think themselves shamefully disappointed; for they looked that this had been he that should have delivered Israel, and should have set up his kingdom in secular power and glory, and, in expectation of this, had lost all to follow him. Now, if he leave the world in the same circumstances of meanness and poverty in which he had lived, and worse, they are quite defeated. [2.] They will think themselves sadly deserted and exposed. They knew by experience what little presence of mind they had in difficult emergencies, that they could count upon nothing but being ruined and run down if they part with their Master. Now, in reference to all these, *Let not your hearts be troubled.* Here are three words, upon any of which the emphasis may significantly be laid. *First,* Upon the word *troubled, μὴ ταρασσέσθω.* Be not so troubled as to be put into a hurry and confusion, *like the troubled sea when* it cannot rest. He does not say, "Let not your hearts be sensible of the griefs, or sad because of them," but, "Be not ruffled and discomposed, be not cast down and disquieted," Ps. xlii. 5. *Secondly,* Upon the word *heart:* "Though the nation and city be troubled, though your little family and flock be troubled, yet *let not your heart be troubled.* Keep possession of your own souls when you can keep possession of nothing else. The heart is the main fort; whatever you do, keep trouble from this, keep this with *all diligence.* The spirit must *sustain the infirmity,* therefore, see that this be not *wounded. Thirdly,* Upon the word *your:* "You that are my disciples and followers, my redeemed, chosen, sanctified ones, however others are overwhelmed with the sorrows of this present time, be not you so, for you know better; let *the sinners in Zion* tremble, but let the *sons of Zion be joyful in their king.*" Herein Christ's disciples should *do more than others,* should keep their minds quiet, when every thing else is unquiet.

2. The remedy he prescribes against this trouble of mind, which he saw ready to prevail over them; in general, *believe—πιστεύετε.* (1.) Some read it in both parts imperatively, "*Believe in God,* and his perfections and providence, *believe also in me,* and my mediation. Build with confidence upon the great acknowledged principles of natural religion: that there is a God, that he is most holy, wise, powerful, and good; that he is the governor of the world, and has the sovereign disposal of all events; and comfort yourselves likewise with the peculiar doctrines of that holy religion which I have taught you." But, (2.) We read the former as an acknowledgment that they did believe in God, for which he commends them: "But, if you would effectually provide against a stormy day, *believe also in me.*" Through Christ we are brought into covenant with God, and become interested in his favour and promise, which otherwise as sinners we must despair of, and the remembrance of God would have been our trouble; but, by believing in Christ as the Mediator between God and man, our belief in God becomes comfortable; and this is the will of God, that *all men should honour the Son as they honour the Father,* by believing in the Son as they believe in the Father. Those that rightly believe in God will believe

in Jesus Christ, whom he has made known to them; and believing in God through Jesus Christ is an excellent means of keeping trouble from the heart. The joy of faith is the best remedy against the griefs of sense; it is a remedy with a promise annexed to it: *the just shall live by faith;* a remedy with a *probatum est* annexed to it. *I had fainted unless I had believed.*

II. Here is a particular direction to act faith upon the promise of eternal life, *v.* 2, 3. He had directed them to trust to God, and to trust in him; but what must they trust God and Christ for? Trust them for a happiness to come when this body and this world shall be no more, and for a happiness to last as long as the immortal soul and the eternal world shall last. Now this is proposed as a sovereign cordial under all the troubles of this present time, to which there is that in the happiness of heaven which is admirably adapted and accommodated. The saints have encouraged themselves with this in their greatest extremities, *That heaven would make amends for all.* Let us see how this is suggested here.

1. Believe and consider that really there is such a happiness: *In my Father's house there are many mansions; if it were not so, I would have told you, v.* 2.

(1.) See under what notion the happiness of heaven is here represented: as *mansions,* many mansions in Christ's Father's house. [1.] Heaven is a house, not a tent or tabernacle; it is *a house not made with hands, eternal in the heavens.* [2.] It is a Father's house: *my Father's house;* and his Father is our Father, to whom he was now ascending; so that in right of their elder brother all true believers shall be welcome to that happiness as to their home. It is his house who is King of kings and Lord of lords, dwells in light, and inhabits eternity. [3.] There are *mansions* there; that is, *First,* Distinct dwellings, an apartment for each. Perhaps there is an allusion to the priests' chambers that were about the temple. In heaven there are accommodations for particular saints; though all shall be swallowed up in God, yet our individuality shall not be lost there; every Israelite had his lot in Canaan, and every elder *a seat,* Rev. iv. 4. *Secondly,* Durable dwellings. Μοναὶ, from μνείω, *maneo, abiding places.* The house itself is lasting; our estate in it is not for a term of years, but a perpetuity. Here we are as in an inn; in heaven we shall gain a settlement. The disciples had quitted their houses to attend Christ, who had not where to lay his head, but the mansions in heaven will make them amends. [4.] There are *many* mansions, for there are many sons to be brought to glory, and Christ exactly knows their number, nor will be straitened for room by the coming of more company than he expects. He had told Peter that he should follow him (*ch.* xiii. 36), but let not the rest be discouraged, in heaven there are mansions for them *all. Rehoboth,* Gen. xxvi. 22.

(2.) See what assurance we have of the reality of the happiness itself, and the sincerity of the proposal of it to us: "*If it were not so, I would have told you.* If you had deceived yourselves, when you quitted your livelihoods, and ventured your lives for me, in prospect of a happiness future and unseen, I would soon have undeceived you." The assurance is built, [1.] Upon the veracity of his word. It is implied, "If there were not such a happiness, valuable and attainable, I would not have told you that there was." [2.] Upon the sincerity of his affection to them. As he is true, and would not impose upon them himself, so he is kind, and would not suffer them to be imposed upon. If either there were no such mansions, or none designed for them, who had left all to follow him, he would have given them timely notice of the mistake, that they might have made an honourable retreat to the world again, and have made the best they could of it. Note, Christ's good-will to us is a great encouragement to our hope in him. He loves us too well, and means us too well, to disappoint the expectations of his own raising, or to leave those to be of all men most miserable who have been of him most observant.

2. Believe and consider that the design of Christ's going away was to prepare a place in heaven for his disciples. "You are grieved to think of my going away, whereas I go on your errand, *as the forerunner; I am to enter for you.*" He went to prepare a place for us; that is, (1.) To take possession for us, as our advocate or attorney, and so to secure our title as indefeasible. Livery of seisin was given to Christ, for the use and behoof of all that should believe on him. (2.) To make provision for us as our friend and father. The happiness of heaven, though prepared *before the foundation of the world,* yet must be further fitted up for man in his fallen state. It consisting much in the presence of Christ there, it was therefore necessary that he should *go before,* to enter into that glory which his disciples were to share in. Heaven would be an *unready* place for a Christian if Christ were not there. He went to prepare a table for them, to prepare thrones for them, Luke xxii. 30. Thus Christ declares the fitness of heaven's happiness for the saints, for whom it is prepared.

3. Believe and consider that *therefore* he would certainly come again in due time, to fetch them to that blessed place which he was now going to possess for himself and prepare for them (*v.* 3): "*If I go and prepare a place for you,* if this be the errand of my journey, you may be sure, when every thing is ready, *I will come again, and receive you to myself,* so that you shall follow me hereafter, *that where I am there you may be also.*" Now these are comfortable words indeed. (1.) That Jesus Christ will come again; ἔρχομαι

—*I do come,* intimating the certainty of it, that he will come and that he is daily coming. We say, We are coming, when we are busy in preparing for our coming, and so he is; all he does has a reference and tendency to his second coming. Note, The belief of Christ's second coming, of which he has given us the assurance, is an excellent preservative against trouble of heart, Phil. iv. 5; James v. 8. (2.) That he will come again to receive all his faithful followers to himself. He sends for them privately at death, and gathers them one by one; but they are to make their public entry in solemn state all together at the last day, and then Christ himself will come to receive them, to conduct them in the abundance of his grace, and to welcome them in the abundance of his love. He will hereby testify the utmost respect and endearment imaginable. The coming of Christ is in order to our *gathering together unto him,* 2 Thess. ii. 1. (3.) *That where he is there they shall be also.* This intimates, what many other scriptures declare, that the quintessence of heaven's happiness is being with Christ *there, ch.* xvii. 24; Phil. i. 23; 1 Thess. iv. 17. Christ speaks of his being there as now present, *that where I am;* where I am to be shortly, where I am to be eternally; there you shall be shortly, there you shall be eternally: not only *there,* in the same place; but *there,* in the same state: not only spectators of his glory, as the three disciples on the mount, but sharers in it. (4.) That this may be inferred from his *going to prepare a place* for us, for his preparations shall not be in vain. He will not build and furnish lodgings, and let them stand empty. He will be the finisher of that of which he is the author. If he has prepared the place for us, he will prepare us for it, and in due time put us in possession of it. As the resurrection of Christ is the assurance of our resurrection, so his ascension, victory, and glory, are an assurance of ours.

4 And whither I go ye know,
and the way ye know. 5 Thomas saith unto him, Lord, we know
not whither thou goest; and how can
we know the way? 6 Jesus saith
unto him, I am the way, the truth,
and the life: no man cometh unto
the Father, but by me. 7 If ye had
known me, ye should have known my
Father also: and from henceforth ye
know him, and have seen him. 8
Philip saith unto him, Lord, show us
the Father, and it sufficeth us. 9
Jesus saith unto him, Have I been so
long time with you, and yet hast thou
not known me, Philip? he that hath
seen me hath seen the Father; and
how sayest thou *then,* Show us the
Father? 10 Believest thou not that
I am in the Father, and the Father in
me? the words that I speak unto you
I speak not of myself: but the Father that dwelleth in me, he doeth
the works. 11 Believe me that I *am*
in the Father, and the Father in me:
or else believe me for the very works'
sake.

Christ, having set the happiness of heaven before them as the end, here shows them himself as the way to it, and tells them that they were better acquainted both with the end they were to aim at and with the way they were to walk in than they thought they were: *You know,* that is, 1. "You may know; it is none of the *secret things* which belong not to you, but one of the *things revealed;* you *need not ascend into heaven,* nor *go down into the deep,* for *the word is nigh you* (Rom. x. 6—8), level to you." 2. "You do know; you know that which is the home and which is the way, though perhaps not as the home and as the way. You have been told it, and cannot but know, if you would recollect and consider it." Note, Jesus Christ is willing to make the best of his people's knowledge, though they are weak and defective in it. He knows the good that is in them better than they do themselves, and is certain that they have that knowledge, and faith, and love, of which they themselves are not sensible, or not certain.

This word of Christ gave occasion to two of his disciples to address themselves to him, and he answers them both.

I. Thomas enquired concerning the way (*v.* 5), without any apology for contradicting his Master.

1. He said, "*Lord, we know not whither thou goest,* to what place or what state, *and how can we know the way* in which we must follow thee? We can neither guess at it, nor enquire it out, but must still be at a loss." Christ's testimony concerning their knowledge made them more sensible of their ignorance, and more inquisitive after further light. Thomas here shows more modesty than Peter, who thought he could follow Christ now. Peter was the more solicitous to know *whither Christ went.* Thomas here, though he complains that he did not know this, yet seems more solicitous to know *the way.* Now, (1.) His confession of his ignorance was commendable enough. If good men be in the dark, and know but in part, yet they are willing to own their defects. But, (2.) The cause of his ignorance was culpable. They knew not whither Christ went, because they dreamed of a temporal kingdom in external pomp and power, and doted upon this, notwithstanding what he had said again and again to the contrary. Hence it was that, when Christ spoke of going away and their following him, their fancy ran upon his going

to some remarkable city or other, Bethlehem, or Nazareth, or Capernaum, or some of the cities of the Gentiles, as David to Hebron, there to be anointed king, and *to restore the kingdom to Israel;* and which way this place lay, where these castles in the air were to be built, east, west, north, or south, they could not tell, and therefore knew not the way. Thus still we think ourselves more in the dark than we need be concerning the future state of the church, because we expect its worldly prosperity, whereas it is spiritual advancement that the promise points at. Had Thomas understood, as he might have done, that Christ was going to the invisible world, the world of spirits, to which spiritual things only have a reference, he would not have said, *Lord, we do not know the way.*

II. Now to this complaint of their ignorance, which included a desire to be taught, Christ gives a full answer, *v.* 6, 7. Thomas had enquired both whither he went and what was the way, and Christ answers both these enquiries and makes good what he had said, that they would have needed no answer if they had understood themselves aright; for they knew him, and he was the way; they knew the Father, and he was the end; and therefore, *whither I go you know, and the way you know.* Believe in God as the end, and in me as the way (*v.* 1), and you do all you should do.

(1.) He speaks of himself as the way, *v.* 6. Dost thou *not know the way? I am the way,* and I only, for *no man comes to the Father but by me.* Great things Christ here saith of himself, showing us,

[1.] The nature of his mediation: He is *the way, the truth, and the life.*

First, Let us consider these first distinctly. 1. Christ is *the way, the highway* spoken of, Isa. xxxv. 8. Christ was his own way, for by *his own blood he entered into the holy place* (Heb. ix. 12), and he is our way, for we enter by him. By his doctrine and example he teaches us our duty, by his merit and intercession he procures us our happiness, and so he is the way. In him God and man meet, and are brought together. We could not get to the tree of life in the way of innocency; but Christ is another way to it. By Christ, as the way, an intercourse is settled and kept up between heaven and earth; the angels of God ascend and descend; our prayers go to God, and his blessings come to us by him; this is *the way that leads to rest, the good old way.* The disciples followed him, and Christ tells them that they followed the road, and, while they continued following him, they would never be out of their way. 2. He is *the truth.* (1.) As truth is opposed to figure and shadow. Christ is the substance of all the Old-Testament types, which are therefore said to be *figures of the true,* Heb. ix. 24. Christ is *the true manna* (*ch.* vi. 32), *the true tabernacle,* Heb. viii. 2. (2.) As truth is opposed to falsehood and error; the doctrine of Christ is true doctrine. When we enquire for truth, we need learn no more than *the truth as it is in Jesus.* (3.) As truth is opposed to fallacy and deceit; he is true to all that trust in him, as true as truth itself, 2 Cor. i. 20. 3. He is *the life;* for we are *alive unto God* only in and *through Jesus Christ,* Rom. vi. 11. Christ formed in us is that to our souls which our souls are to our bodies. Christ is *the resurrection and the life.*

Secondly, Let us consider these jointly, and with reference to each other. Christ is *the way, the truth, and the life;* that is, 1. He is the beginning, the middle, and the end. In him we must set out, go on, and finish. As *the truth,* he is the guide of our way; as *the life,* he is the end of it. 2. He is *the true and living way* (Heb. x. 20); there are *truth and life* in the way, as well as at the end of it. 3. He is *the true way to life,* the only true way; other ways may seem right, but the end of them is *the way of death.*

[2.] The necessity of his mediation: *No man cometh to the Father but by me.* Fallen man must come to God as a Judge, but cannot come to him as a Father, otherwise than by Christ as Mediator. We cannot perform the duty of coming to God, by repentance and the acts of worship, without the Spirit and grace of Christ, nor obtain the happiness of coming to God as our Father without his merit and righteousness; he is the *high priest of our profession,* our advocate.

(2.) He speaks of his Father as the end (*v.* 7): "*If you had known me* aright, *you would have known my Father also; and henceforth,* by the glory you have seen in me and the doctrine you have heard from me, *you know him and have seen him.*" Here is, [1.] A tacit rebuke to them for their dulness and carelessness in not acquainting themselves with Jesus Christ, though they had been his constant followers and associates: *If you had known me*—. They knew him, and yet did not know him so well as they might and should have known him. They knew him to be the Christ, but did not follow on to know God in him. Christ had said to the Jews (*ch.* viii. 19): *If you had known me, you would have known my Father also;* and here the same to his disciples; for it is hard to say which is more strange, the wilful ignorance of those that are enemies to the light, or the defects and mistakes of *the children of light,* that have had such opportunities of knowledge. If they had known Christ aright, they would have known that his kingdom is spiritual, and *not of this world;* that *he came down from heaven,* and therefore must return *to heaven;* and then they would have known his Father also, would have known whither he designed to go, when he said, *I go to the Father,* to a glory in the other world, not in this. If we knew Christianity better, we should better know natural religion. [2.] A favourable intimation that he was well satisfied concerning their sincerity, notwithstanding the weakness of their understanding: "*And henceforth,* from my giving you this hint, which will serve as a key to all the instructions I have given you hitherto, let me tell you, *you know him, and have seen him,* inasmuch as you know me, and have seen me; for in the face of Christ we see the glory of God, as we see a father in his son that resembles him. Christ tells his disciples that they were not so ignorant as they seemed to be; for, though *little children,* yet they had known the Father, 1 John ii. 13. Note, Many of the disciples of Christ have more knowledge and more grace than they think they have, and Christ takes notice of, and is well pleased with, that good in them which they themselves are not aware of; for those that know God do not all at once know that they know him, 1 John ii. 3.

II. Philip enquired concerning the Father (*v.* 8), and Christ answered him, *v.* 9—11, where observe,

1. Philip's request for some extraordinary discovery of the Father. He was not so forward to speak as some others of them were, and yet, from an earnest desire of further light, he cries out, *Show us the Father.* Philip listened to what Christ said to Thomas, and fastened upon the last words, *You have seen him.* "Nay," says Philip, "that is what we want, that is what we would have: *Show us the Father and it sufficeth us.*" (1.) This supposes an earnest desire of acquaintance with God as a Father. The petition is, "*Show us the Father;* give us to know him in that relation to us;" and this he begs, not for himself only, but for the rest of the disciples. The plea is, *It sufficeth us.* He not only professes it himself, but will pass his word for his fellow-disciples. Grant us but one sight of the Father, and we have enough. Jansenius saith, "Though Philip did not mean it, yet the Holy Ghost, by his mouth, designed here to teach us that the satisfaction and happiness of a soul consist in the vision and fruition of God," Ps. xvi. 11; xvii. 15. In the knowledge of God the understanding rests, and is at the summit of its ambition; in the knowledge of God as our Father the soul is satisfied; a sight of the Father is a heaven upon earth, fills us *with joy unspeakable.* (2.) As Philip speaks it here, it intimates that he was not satisfied with such a discovery of the Father as Christ thought fit to give them, but he would prescribe to him, and press upon him, something further and no less than some visible appearance of *the glory of God,* like that to Moses (Exod. xxxiii. 22), and to *the elders of Israel,* Exod. xxiv. 9—11. "Let us see the Father with our bodily eyes, as we see thee, *and it sufficeth us;* we will trouble thee with no more questions, *Whither goest thou?*" And so it manifests not only the weakness of his faith, but his ignorance of the gospel way of manifesting *the Father,* which is spiritual, and not sensible. Such a sight of God, he thinks, would *suffice* them, and yet those who did thus see him were not *sufficed,* but soon *corrupted themselves, and made a graven image.* Christ's institutions have provided better for the confirmation of our faith than our own inventions would.

2. Christ's reply, referring him to the discoveries already made of the Father, *v.* 9—11.

(1.) He refers him to what he had seen, *v.* 9. He upbraids him with his ignorance and inadvertency: "*Have I been so long time with you,* now above three years intimately conversant with you, *and yet hast thou not known me, Philip?* Now, *he that hath seen me hath seen the Father; and how sayest thou then, Show us the Father?* Wilt thou ask for that which thou hast already?" Now here,

[1.] He reproves him for two things: *First.* For not improving his acquaintance with Christ, as he might have done, to a clear and distinct knowledge of him: "*Hast thou not known me, Philip,* whom thou hast followed so long, and conversed with so much?" Philip, the first day he came to him, declared that he knew him to be the Messiah (*ch.* i. 45), and yet to this day did *not know the Father* in him. Many that have good knowledge in the scripture and divine things fall short of the attainments justly expected from them, for want of compounding the ideas they have, and going on to perfection. Many know Christ, who yet do not know what they might know of him, nor see what they should see in him. That which aggravated Philip's dulness was that he had so long an opportunity of improvement: *I have been so long time with thee.* Note, The longer we enjoy the means of knowledge and grace, the more inexcusable we are if we be found defective in grace and knowledge. Christ expects that our proficiency should be in some measure according to our standing, that we should not be always babes. Let us thus reason with ourselves: "Have I been so long a hearer of sermons, a student in the scripture, a scholar in the school of Christ, and yet so weak in *the knowledge of Christ,* and so unskilful in *the word of righteousness?*" *Secondly,* He reproves him for his infirmity in the prayer made, *Show us the Father.* Note, Herein appears much of the weakness of Christ's disciples that they *know not what to pray for as they ought* (Rom. viii. 26), but often *ask amiss* (Jam. iv. 3), for that which either is not promised or is already bestowed in the sense of the promise, as here.

[2.] He instructs him, and gives him a maxim which not only in general magnifies Christ and leads us to the knowledge of God in him, but justifies what Christ had said (*v.* 7): *You know the Father, and have seen him;* and answered what Philip had asked, *Show us the Father.* Why, saith Christ, the difficulty is soon over, for *he that hath seen me hath seen the Father. First,* All that saw

Christ in the flesh might *have seen the Father* in him, if Satan had not *blinded their minds,* and kept them from a sight of Christ, as *the image of God,* 2 Cor. iv. 4. *Secondly,* All that saw Christ by faith did *see the Father* in him, though they were not suddenly aware that they did so. In the light of Christ's doctrine they saw God as *the Father of lights;* in the miracles they saw God *as the God of power, the finger of God.* The holiness of God shone in the spotless purity of Christ's life, and his grace in all the acts of grace he did.

(2.) He refers him to what he had reason to believe (*v.* 10, 11): "*Believest thou not that I am in the Father, and the Father in me,* and therefore that in *seeing me* thou hast *seen the Father?* Hast thou not believed this? If not, take my word for it, and believe it now."

[1.] See here what it is which we are to believe: *That I am in the Father, and the Father in me;* that is, as he had said (*ch.* x. 30), *I and my Father are one.* He speaks of the Father and himself as two persons, and yet so one as never any two were or can be. In knowing Christ as *God of God, light of light, very God of very God, begotten, not made,* and as *being of one substance with the Father, by whom all things were made,* we know the Father; and in seeing him thus we see the Father. In Christ we behold more of *the glory of God* than Moses did at Mount Horeb.

[2.] See here what inducements we have to believe this; and they are two:—We must believe it, *First,* For his word's sake: *The words that I speak to you, I speak not of myself.* See *ch.* vii. 16, *My doctrine is not mine.* What he said seemed to them careless as *the word of man,* speaking his own thoughts at his own pleasure; but really it was the wisdom of God that indited it and the will of God that enforced it. *He spoke not of himself* only, but the mind of God according to the eternal counsels. *Secondly,* For his works' sake: *The Father that dwelleth in me, he doeth them;* and therefore *believe me for their sake.* Observe, 1. The Father is said to *dwell* in him, *ὁ ἐν ἐμοὶ μένων—he abideth in me,* by the inseparable union of the divine and human nature: never had God such a temple to dwell in on earth as *the body of the Lord Jesus, ch.* ii. 21. Here was the true Shechinah, of which that in the tabernacle was but a type. *The fulness of the Godhead dwelt in him bodily,* Col. ii. 9. The Father so dwells in Christ that in him he may *be found,* as a man where he dwells. *Seek ye the Lord, seek* him in Christ, and *he will be found,* for in him he dwells. 2. *He doeth the works* Many works of power, and works of mercy, Christ did, and the Father did them in him; and the work of redemption in general was God's own work. 3. We are bound to believe this, *for the very works' sake.* As we are to believe the being and perfections of God for the sake of the works of creation, which declare his glory; so we are to believe the revelation of God to man in Jesus Christ for the sake of the works of the Redeemer, those mighty works which, by showing forth themselves (Matt. xiv. 2), *Show forth him, and God in him.* Note, Christ's miracles are proofs of his divine mission, not only for the conviction of infidels, but for the confirmation of the faith of his own disciples, *ch.* ii. 11; v. 36; x. 37.

12 Verily, verily, I say unto
you, He that believeth on me, the
works that I do shall he do also;
and greater *works* than these shall
he do; because I go unto my Father.
13 And whatsoever ye shall ask in
my name, that will I do, that the Father may be glorified in the Son. 14
If ye shall ask any thing in my name,
I will do *it.*

The disciples, as they were full of grief to think of parting with their Master, so they were full of care what would become of themselves when he was gone; while he was with them, he was a support to them, kept them in countenance, kept them in heart; but, if he leave them, they will be *as sheep having no shepherd,* an easy prey to those who seek to run them down. Now, to silence these fears, Christ here assures them that they should be clothed with powers sufficient to bear them out. As Christ had *all power,* they, in his name, should have great *power, both in heaven and in earth.*

I. Great power on earth (*v.* 12): *He that believeth on me* (as I know you do), *the works that I do shall he do also.* This does not weaken the argument Christ had taken from his works, to prove himself one with the Father (that others should do as *great works),* but rather strengthens it; for the miracles which the apostles wrought were *wrought in his name,* and *by faith in him;* and this magnifies his power more than any thing, that he not only wrought miracles himself, but gave power to others to do so too.

1. Two things he assures them of:—

(1.) That they should be enabled to do such works as he had done, and that they should have a more ample power for the doing of them than they had had when he first sent them forth, Matt. x. 8. Did Christ *heal the sick, cleanse the leper, raise the dead?* So should they. Did he convince and convert sinners, and draw multitudes to him? So should they. Though he should depart, the work should not cease, nor fall to the ground, but should be carried on as vigorously and successfully as ever; and it is still in the doing.

(2.) That they should do *greater works than these.* [1.] In the kingdom of nature they should work greater miracles. No miracle is little, but some to our apprehension seem greater than others. Christ had healed with the hem of his garment, but Peter with his shadow (Acts v. 15), Paul by the handkerchief that had touched him, Acts xix. 12. Christ wrought miracles for two or three years in one country, but his followers wrought miracles in his name for many ages in divers countries. *You shall do greater works,* if there be occasion, for the glory of God. *The prayer of faith,* if at any time it had been necessary, would have *removed mountains.* [2.] In the kingdom of grace. They should obtain greater victories by the gospel than had been obtained while Christ was upon earth. The truth is, the captivating of so great a part of the world to Christ, under such outward disadvantages, was the miracle of all. I think this refers especially to *the gift of tongues;* this was the immediate effect of the *pouring out of the Spirit,* which was a constant miracle upon the mind, in which words are framed, and which was made to serve so glorious an intention as that of spreading the gospel to all nations *in their own language.* This was a greater *sign to them that believed not* (1 Cor. xiv. 22), and more powerful for their conviction, than any other miracle whatever.

2. The reason Christ gives for this is, *Because I go unto my Father,* (1.) "*Because I go,* it will be requisite that you should have such a power, lest the work suffer damage by my absence." (2.) "*Because I go to the Father,* I shall be in a capacity to furnish you with such a power, for *I go to the Father, to send the Comforter,* from whom *you shall receive power,*" Acts i. 8. The wonderful works which they did in Christ's name were part of the glories of his exalted state, *when he ascended on high,* Eph. iv. 8.

II. Great *power in heaven:* "*Whatsoever you shall ask, that will I do* (*v.* 13, 14), as Israel, who was a prince with God. Therefore you shall do such mighty works, because you have such an interest in me, and I in *my Father.*" Observe,

1. In what way they were to keep up communion with him, and derive power from him, when he was gone to the Father—by prayer. When dear friends are to be removed to a distance from each other, they provide for the settling of a correspondence; thus, when Christ was going to his Father, he tells his disciples how they might write to him upon every occasion, and send their epistles by a safe and ready way of conveyance, without danger of miscarrying, or lying by the way: "Let me hear from you by prayer, *the prayer of faith,* and you shall hear from me by the Spirit." This was the old way of intercourse with Heaven, ever since *men began to call upon the name of the Lord;* but Christ by his death has laid it more open, and it is still open to us. Here is, (1.) Humility prescribed: *You shall ask.* Though they had quitted all for Christ, they could demand nothing of him as a debt, but must be humble supplicants, beg or starve, beg or perish. (2.) Liberty allowed: "Ask any thing, any thing that is good and proper for you; any thing, provided you know what you ask, you may ask; you may ask for assistance in your work, for a mouth and wisdom, for preservation out of the hands of your enemies, for power to work miracles when there is occasion, for the success of the ministry in the conversion of souls; ask to be informed, directed, vindicated." Occasions vary, but they shall be welcome to the throne of grace upon every occasion.

2. In what name they were to present their petitions: *Ask in my name.* To ask in Christ's name is, (1.) To plead his merit and intercession, and to depend upon that plea. The Old-Testament saints had an eye to this when they prayed *for the Lord's sake* (Dan. ix. 17), and *for the sake of the anointed* (Ps. lxxxiv. 9), but Christ's mediation is brought to a clearer light by the gospel, and so we are enabled more expressly to *ask in his name.* When Christ dictated the Lord's prayer, this was not inserted, because they did not then so fully understand this matter as they did afterwards, when the Spirit was poured out. If we ask *in our own name,* we cannot expect to speed, for, being strangers, we have *no name* in heaven; being sinners, we have an *ill name* there; but Christ's is a good name, well known in heaven, and very precious. (2.) It is to aim at his glory and to seek this as our highest end in all our prayers.

3. What success they should have in their prayers: "What you ask, *that will I do, v.* 13. And again (*v.* 14), "*I will do it.* You may be sure I will: not only it shall be done, I will see it done, or give orders for the doing of it, but *I will do it;*" for he has not only the interest of an intercessor, but the power of a sovereign prince, who *sits at the right hand of God,* the hand of action, and has the doing of all in the kingdom of God. By faith in his name we may have what we will for the asking.

4. For what reason their prayers should speed so well: *That the Father may be glorified in the Son.* That is, (1.) This they ought to aim at, and have their eye upon, in asking. In this all our desires and prayers should meet as in their centre; to this they must all be directed, that God in Christ may be honoured by our services, and in our salvation. *Hallowed be thy name* is an answered prayer, and is put first, because, if the heart be sincere in this, it does in a manner *consecrate* all the other petitions. (2.) This Christ will aim at in granting, and for the sake of this will do what they ask, that hereby the glory of the Father in the Son may be manifested. The wisdom, power, and goodness of God were magnified in the Redeemer when by a power derived from him, and exerted in his name and for his service, his apostles and ministers were enabled to do such great things, both in the proofs of their doctrine and in the successes of it.

15 If ye love me, keep my commandments. 16 And I will pray the Father, and he shall give you another Comforter, that he may abide with you for ever; 17 *Even* the Spirit of truth; whom the world cannot receive, because it seeth him not, neither knoweth him: but ye know him; for he dwelleth with you, and shall be in you.

Christ not only proposes such things to them as were the matter of their comfort, but here promises to send the Spirit, whose office it should be to be their Comforter, to *impress* these things upon them.

I. He premises to this a memento of duty (*v.* 15): *If you love me, keep my commandments.* Keeping the commandments of Christ is here put for the practice of godliness in general, and for the faithful and diligent discharge of their office as apostles in particular. Now observe, 1. When Christ is comforting them, he bids them *keep his commandments;* for we must not expect comfort but in the way of duty. The same word (παρακαλέω) signifies both to exhort and to comfort. 2. When they were in care what they should do, now that their Master was leaving them, and what would become of them now, he bids them *keep his commandments,* and then nothing could come amiss to them. In difficult times our care concerning the events of the day should be swallowed up in a care concerning the duty of the day. 3. When they were showing their love to Christ by their grieving to think of his departure, and the sorrow which filled their hearts upon the foresight of that, he bids them, if they would show their love to him, do it, not by these weak and feminine passions, but by their conscientious care to perform their trust, and by a universal obedience to his commands; this is better than sacrifice, better than tears. *Lovest thou me? Feed my lambs.* 4. When Christ has given them precious promises, of the answer of their prayers and the coming of the Comforter, he lays down this as a limitation of the promises, "Provided you keep my commandments, from a principle of love to me." Christ will not be an advocate for any but those that will be ruled and advised by him as their counsel. Follow the conduct of the Spirit, and you shall have the comfort of the Spirit.

II. He promises this great and unspeakable blessing to them, *v.* 16, 17.

1. It is promised that they shall have *another comforter.* This is the great New-Testament promise (Acts i. 4), as that of the Messiah was of the Old Testament; a promise adapted to the present distress of the disciples, who were in sorrow, and needed a comforter. Observe here,

(1.) The blessing promised: ἄλλον παράκλητον. The word is used only here in these discourses of Christ's, and 1 John ii. 1, where we translate it an *advocate.* The Rhemists, and Dr. Hammond, are for retaining the *Greek* word *Paraclete;* we read, Acts ix. 31, of the παρακλήσις τοῦ ἁγίου πνεύματος, the *comfort of the Holy Ghost,* including his whole office as a paraclete. [1.] You shall have another *advocate.* The office of the Spirit was to be Christ's advocate with them and others, to plead his cause, and take care of his concerns, on earth; to be *vicarius Christi—Christ's Vicar,* as one of the ancients call him; and to be their advocate with their opposers. When Christ was with them he spoke for them as there was occasion; but now that he is leaving them they shall not be run down, the Spirit of the Father shall speak in them, Matt. x. 19, 20. And the cause cannot miscarry that is pleaded by such an advocate. [2.] You shall have another *master* or *teacher,* another *exhorter.* While they had Christ with them he excited and exhorted them to their duty; but now that he is going he leaves one with them that shall do this as effectually, though silently. Jansenius thinks the most proper word to render it by is a *patron,* one that shall both instruct and protect you. [3.] Another *comforter.* Christ was expected as the consolation of Israel. One of the names of the Messiah among the Jews was *Menahem—the Comforter.* The Targum calls the days of the Messiah *the years of consolation.* Christ comforted his disciples when he was with them, and now that he was leaving them in their greatest need he promises them *another.*

(2.) The giver of this blessing: *The Father* shall give him, *my Father* and *your Father;* it includes both. The same that gave the Son to be our Saviour will give his Spirit to be our comforter, pursuant to the same design. The Son is said to send the Comforter (*ch.* xv. 26), but the Father is the prime agent.

(3.) How this blessing is procured—by the intercession of the Lord Jesus: *I will pray the Father.* He said (*v.* 14) *I will do it;* here he saith, *I will pray for it,* to show not only that he is both God and man, but that he is both king and priest. As priest he is ordained for men to make intercession, as king he is authorized by the Father to execute judgment. When Christ saith, *I will pray the Father,* it does not suppose that the Father is unwilling, or must be importuned to it, but only that the gift of the Spirit is a fruit of Christ's mediation, purchased by his merit, and taken out by his intercession.

(4.) The continuance of this blessing: *That he may abide with you for ever.* That is, [1.] "*With you,* as long as you live. You shall never know the want of a comforter, nor lament his departure, as you are now lamenting mine." Note, It should support us under the loss of those comforts which were designed us for a time that there are ever-fasting consolations provided for us. It was not expedient that Christ should be with them for ever, for they who were designed for public service, must not always live a college-life; they must disperse, and therefore a comforter that would be with them all, in all places alike, wheresoever dispersed and howsoever distressed, was alone fit to be with them for ever. [2.] "With your successors, when you are gone, to the end of time; your successors in Christianity, in the ministry." [3.] If we take *for ever* in its utmost extent, the promise will be accomplished in those consolations of God which will be the eternal joy of all the saints, *pleasures for ever.*

2. This comforter is the *Spirit of truth, whom you know, v.* 16, 17. They might think it impossible to have a comforter equivalent to him who is the Son of God: "Yea," saith Christ, "you shall have the Spirit of God, who is equal in power and glory with the Son."

(1.) The comforter promised is *the Spirit,* one who should do his work in a spiritual way and manner, inwardly and invisibly, by working on men's spirits.

(2.) "He is the *Spirit of truth.* He will be true to you, and to his undertaking for you, which he will perform to the utmost. He will *teach you the truth,* will enlighten your minds with the knowledge of it, will strengthen and confirm your belief of it, and will increase your love to it. The Gentiles by their idolatries, and the Jews by their traditions, were led into gross errors and mistakes; but the Spirit of truth shall not only *lead you into all truth,* but others by your ministry. Christ is the truth, and he is the Spirit of Christ, the Spirit that he was anointed with.

(3.) He is one *whom the world cannot receive;* but *you know him. Therefore he abideth with you.* [1.] The disciples of Christ are here distinguished from the world, for they are chosen and called out of the world that lies in wickedness; they are the children and heirs of another world, not of this. [2.] It is the misery of those that are invincibly devoted to the world that they *cannot receive* the Spirit of truth. The spirit *of the world* and *of God* are spoken of as directly contrary the one to the other (1 Cor. ii. 12); for where the spirit of the world has the ascendant, the Spirit of God is excluded. Even the *princes of this world,* though, as princes, they had advantages of knowledge, yet, as princes of this world, they laboured under invincible prejudices, so that they knew not *the things of the Spirit of God,* 1 Cor. ii. 8. [3.] Therefore men *cannot receive the Spirit of truth* because they *see him not, neither know him.* The comforts of the Spirit are *foolishness to them,* as much as ever the cross of Christ was, and the great things of the gospel, like those of the law, are counted as a strange thing. These are judgments far above out of their sight. Speak to the children of this world of the operations of the Spirit, and you are as a barbarian to them [4.] The best knowledge of the Spirit of truth is that which is got by experience: *You know him, for he dwelleth with you.* Christ had dwelt with them, and by their acquaintance with him they could not but know *the Spirit of truth.* They had themselves been endued with the Spirit in some measure. What enabled them to leave all to follow Christ, and to continue with him in his temptations? What enabled them to preach the gospel, and work miracles, but the Spirit dwelling in them? The experiences of the saints are the explications of the promises; paradoxes to others are axioms to them. [5.] Those that have an experimental acquaintance with the Spirit have a comfortable assurance of his continuance: He *dwelleth with you, and shall be in you,* for the blessed Spirit doth not use to shift his lodging. Those that know him know how to value him, invite him and bid him welcome; and therefore he shall be in them, as the light in the air, as the sap in the tree, as the soul in the body. Their communion with him shall be intimate, and their union with him inseparable. [6.] The gift of the Holy Ghost is a peculiar gift, bestowed upon the disciples of Christ in a distinguishing way—them, and not the world; it is to them *hidden manna,* and the *white stone.* No comforts comparable to those which make no show, make no noise. This is the favour God bears to his chosen; it is the *heritage of those that fear his name.*

18 I will not leave you comfortless: I will come to you. 19 Yet a
little while, and the world seeth me
no more; but ye see me: because I
live, ye shall live also. 20 At that
day ye shall know that I *am* in my
Father, and ye in me, and I in you.
21 He that hath my commandments,
and keepeth them, he it is that loveth
me: and he that loveth me shall be
loved of my Father, and I will love
him, and will manifest myself to him.
22 Judas saith unto him, not Iscariot,
Lord, how is it that thou wilt manifest thyself unto us, and not unto the
world? 23 Jesus answered and said
unto him, If a man love me, he will
keep my words: and my Father will
love him, and we will come unto him,
and make our abode with him. 24
He that loveth me not keepeth not
my sayings: and the word which ye
hear is not mine, but the Father's
which sent me.

When friends are parting, it is a common request they make to each other, "Pray let us hear from you as often as you can:" this

Christ engaged to his disciples, that out of sight they should not be out of mind.

I. He promises that he would continue his care of them (*v.* 18): "*I will not leave you orphans,* or *fatherless;* for, though I leave you, yet I leave you this comfort, *I will come to you.*" His departure from them was that which grieved them; but it was not so bad as they apprehended, for it was neither total nor final. 1. Not total. "Though I leave you without my bodily presence, yet I do not leave you without comfort." Though children, and left *little,* yet they had received the adoption of sons, and his Father would be their Father, with whom those who otherwise would be fatherless find mercy. Note, The case of true believers, though sometimes it may be sorrowful, is never comfortless, because they are never orphans: for God is their Father, who is an *everlasting Father.* 2. Not final: *I will come to you,* ἔρχομαι—*I do come;* that is, (1.) "I will come speedily to you at my resurrection, I will not be long away, but will be with you again in a little time." He had often said, *The third day I will rise again.* (2.) "I will be coming daily to you in my Spirit;" in the tokens of his love, and visits of his grace, he is still coming. (3.) "I will come certainly at the end of time; surely I will come quickly to introduce you into the joy of your Lord." Note, The consideration of Christ's coming to us saves us from being comfortless in his removals from us; for, if he *depart for a season,* it is *that we may receive him for ever.* Let this moderate our grief, *The Lord is at hand.*

II. He promises that they should continue their acquaintance with him and interest in him (*v.* 19, 20): *Yet a little while, and the world sees me no more,* that is, Now I am no more in the world. After his death, *the world saw him no more,* for, though he rose to life, he never *showed himself to all the people,* Acts x. 41. The malignant world thought they had seen enough of him, and *cried, Away with him; crucify him;* and so shall their doom be; they shall see him no more. Those only that see Christ with an eye of faith shall see him for ever. The world sees him no more till his second coming; but his disciples have communion with him in his absence.

1. *You see me,* and shall continue to see me, when *the world sees me no more.* They saw him with their bodily eyes after his resurrection, for he showed himself to them *by many infallible proofs,* Acts i. 8. And *then were the disciples glad when they saw the Lord.* They saw him with an eye of faith after his ascension, sitting at God's right hand, as Lord of all; saw that in him which the world saw not.

2. *Because I live, you shall live also.* That which grieved them was, that their Master was dying, and they counted upon nothing else but to die with him. No, saith Christ, (1.) *I live;* this the great God glories in, *I live,* saith the Lord, and Christ saith the same; not only, I shall live, as he saith of them, but, I do live; for he has *life in himself,* and *lives for evermore.* We are not comfortless, while *we know that our Redeemer lives.* (2.) Therefore *you shall live also.* Note, The life of Christians is bound up in the life of Christ; as sure and as long as he lives, those that by faith are united to him shall live also; they shall live spiritually, a divine life in communion with God. This life is hid with Christ; if the head and root live, the members and branches live also. They shall *live eternally;* their bodies shall rise in the virtue of Christ's resurrection; it will be well with them in the world to come. It cannot but be well with all that are his, Isa. xxvi. 19.

3. You shall have the assurance of this (*v.* 20): *At that day,* when I am glorified, when the Spirit is poured out, *you shall know* more clearly and certainly than you do now that *I am in my Father, and you in me, and I in you.* (1.) These glorious mysteries will be fully known in heaven: *At that day,* when I shall receive you to myself, you shall know perfectly that which now you *see through a glass darkly.* Now it appears not *what we shall be,* but then it will appear what we were. (2.) They were more fully known after the pouring out of the Spirit upon the apostles; at that day divine light should shine, and their eyes should see more clearly, their knowledge should greatly advance and increase then, would become more extensive and more distinct, and like the blind man's at the second touch of Christ's hand, who at first only *saw men as trees walking.* (3.) They are known by all that receive the Spirit of truth, to their abundant satisfaction, for in the knowledge of this is founded their *fellowship with the Father* and *his Son Jesus Christ.* They know, [1.] That *Christ is in the Father,* is one with the Father, by their experience of what he has wrought for them and in them; they find what an admirable consent and harmony there is between Christianity and natural religion, that that is grafted into this, and so they know that Christ *is in the Father.* [2.] That Christ is in them; experienced Christians know by the Spirit that Christ abides in them, 1 John iii. 24. [3.] That they are in Christ, for the relation is mutual, and equally near on both sides, Christ in them and they in Christ, which speaks an intimate and inseparable union; in the virtue of which it is that *because he lives they shall live also.* Note, *First,* Union with Christ is the life of believers; and their relation to him, and to God through him, is their felicity. *Secondly,* The knowledge of this union is their unspeakable joy and satisfaction; they were now in Christ, and he in them, but he speaks of it as a further act of grace that they should know it, and have the comfort of it. An interest in Christ and the knowledge of it are sometimes separated.

III. He promises that he would love them,

and manifest himself to them. *v.* 21—24. Here observe,

1. Who they are whom Christ will look upon, and accept, as lovers of him; those that *have his commandments, and keep them.* By this Christ shows that the kind things he here said to his disciples were intended not for those only that were *now* his *followers,* but for all that should *believe in him through their word.* Here is, (1.) The duty of those who claim the dignity of being disciples. Having Christ's commandments, we must keep them; as Christians in name and profession we have Christ's commandments, we have them sounding in our ears, written before our eyes, we have the knowledge of them; but this is not enough; would we approve ourselves Christians indeed, we must keep them. Having them in our heads, we must keep them in our hearts and lives. (2.) The dignity of those that do the duty of disciples. They are looked upon by Christ to be such as love him. Not those that have the greatest wit and know how to talk for him, or the greatest estate to lay out for him, but those that *keep his commandments.* Note, The surest evidence of our love to Christ is obedience to the laws of Christ. Such is the love of a subject to his sovereign, a dutiful, respectful, obediential love, a conformity to his will, and satisfaction in his wisdom.

2. What returns he will make to them for their love; rich returns; there is no love lost upon Christ. (1.) They shall have the Father's love: *He that loveth me shall be loved of my Father.* We could not love God if he did not first, out of his good-will to us, give us his grace to love him; but there is a love of complacency promised to those that do love God, Prov. viii. 17. He loves them, and lets them know that he loves them, smiles upon them, and embraces them. God so loves the Son as to love all those that love him. (2.) They shall have Christ's love: *And I will love him,* as God-man, as Mediator. God will love him as a Father, and I will love him as a brother, an elder brother. The Creator will love him, and be the felicity of his being; the Redeemer will love him, and be the protector of his well-being. In the nature of God, nothing shines more brightly than this, that *God is love.* And in the undertaking of Christ nothing appears more glorious than this, that *he loved us.* Now both these loves are the crown and comfort, the *grace and glory,* which shall be to all those that *love the Lord Jesus Christ in sincerity.* Christ was now leaving his disciples, but promises to continue his love to them; for he not only retains a kindness for believers, though absent, but is doing them kindness while absent, for he bears them on his heart, and ever lives interceding for them. (3.) They shall have the comfort of that love: *I will manifest myself to him.* Some understand it of Christ's showing himself alive to his disciples after his resurrection; but, being promised to all that *love him and keep his commandments,* it must be construed so as to extend to them. There is a spiritual manifestation of Christ and his love made to all believers. When he enlightens their minds to know his love, and the dimensions of it (Eph. iii. 18, 19), enlivens their graces, and draws them into exercise, and thus enlarges their comforts in himself—when he clears up the evidences of their interest in him, and gives them tokens of his love, experience of his tenderness, and earnests of his kingdom and glory,—then he manifests himself to them; and Christ is manifested to none but those to whom he is pleased to manifest himself.

3. What occurred upon Christ's making this promise.

(1.) One of the disciples expresses his wonder and surprise at it, *v.* 22. Observe, [1.] Who it was that said this—*Judas, not Iscariot.* Judah, or Judas, was a famous name; the most famous tribe in Israel was that of Judah; two of Christ's disciples were of that name: one of them was the traitor, the other was the brother of James (Luke vi. 16), one of those that were akin to Christ, Matt. xiii. 55. He is called *Lebbeus* and *Thaddeus,* was the penman of the last of the epistles, which in our translation, for distinction's sake, we call *the epistle of Jude.* This was he that spoke here. Observe, *First,* There was a very good man, and a very bad man, called by the same name; for names commend us not to God, nor do they make men worse. Judas the apostle was never the worse, nor Judas the apostate ever the better, for being namesakes. But, *Secondly,* The evangelist carefully distinguishes between them; when he speaks of this pious Judas, he adds, *not Iscariot.* Take heed of mistaking; let us not confound the precious and the vile. [2.] What he said—*Lord how is it?* which intimates either, *First,* the weakness of his understanding. So some take it. He expected the temporal kingdom of the Messiah, that it should appear in external pomp and power, such as all the world would wonder after. "How, then," thinks he, "should it be confined to us only?" *τί γέγονεν*—"*what is the matter* now, that thou wilt not show thyself openly as is expected, that *the Gentiles may come to thy light, and kings to the brightness of thy rising?*" Note, We create difficulties to ourselves by mistaking the nature of Christ's kingdom, as if it were of this world. Or, *Secondly,* as expressing the strength of his affections, and the humble and thankful sense he had of Christ's distinguishing favours to them: *Lord, how is it?* He is amazed at the condescensions of divine grace, as David, 2 Sam. vii. 18. What is there in us to deserve so great a favour? Note, 1. Christ's manifesting himself to his disciples is done in a distinguishing way—to them, and *not to the world* that *sits in darkness;* to the *base,* and not to the *mighty* and *noble;* to *babes,* and not to the *wise* and *prudent.* Distinguishing favours are very obliging; considering who are passed by, and who are pitched upon. 2. It is justly *marvellous in our eyes;* for it is unaccountable, and must be resolved into free and sovereign grace. *Even so, Father, because it seemed good unto thee.*

(2.) Christ, in answer hereto, explains and confirms what he had said, *v.* 23, 24. He overlooks what infirmity there was in what Judas spoke, and goes on with his comforts.

[1.] He further explains the condition of the promise, which was loving him, and keeping his commandments. And, as to this, he shows what an inseparable connection there is between love and obedience; love is the root, obedience is the fruit. *First,* Where a sincere love to Christ is in the heart, there will be obedience: "*If a man love me* indeed, that love will be such a commanding constraining principle in him, that, no question, he will *keep my words.*" Where there is true love to Christ there is a value for his favour, a veneration for his authority, and an entire surrender of the whole man to his direction and government. Where love is, duty follows of course, is easy and natural, and flows from a principle of gratitude. *Secondly,* On the other hand, where there is no true love to Christ there will be no care to obey him: *He that loveth me not keepeth not my sayings, v.* 24. This comes in here as a discovery of those that *do not love Christ;* whatever they pretend, certainly those do not love him that believe not his truths, and obey not his laws, to whom Christ's sayings are but as idle tales, which he heeds not, or hard sayings, which he likes not. It is also a reason why Christ will not manifest himself to the world that doth not *love him,* because they put this affront upon him, not to *keep his sayings;* why should Christ be familiar with those that will be strange to him?

[2.] He further explains the promise (*v.* 23): *If a man thus love me, I will manifest myself to him. First, My Father will love him;* this he had said before (*v.* 21), and here repeats it for the confirming of our faith; because it is hard to imagine that the great God should make those the objects of his love that had made themselves *vessels of his wrath.* Jude wondered that Christ should *manifest himself to them;* but this answers it, "If my Father love you, why should not I be free with you?" *Secondly, We will come unto him, and make our abode with him.* This explains the meaning of Christ's manifesting himself to him, and magnifies the favour. 1. Not only, *I will,* but, *We will, I and the Father,* who, in this, *are one.* See *v.* 9. The light and love of God are communicated to man in the light and love of the Redeemer, so that wherever Christ is formed the image of God is stamped. 2. Not only, "*I will show myself to him* at a distance," but, "*We will come to him,* to be near him, to be with him," such are the powerful influences of divine graces and comforts upon the souls of those that love Christ in sincerity. 3. Not only, "I will give him a transient view of me, or make him a short and running visit," but, *We will take up our abode with him,* which denotes complacency in him and constancy to him. God will not only love obedient believers, but he will take a pleasure in loving them, will rest in love to them, Zeph. iii. 17. He will be with them as at his home.

[3.] He gives a good reason both to bind us to observe the condition and encourage us to depend upon the promise. *The word which you hear is not mine, but his that sent me, v.* 24. To this purport he had often spoken (*ch.* vii. 16; viii. 28; xii. 44), and here it comes in very pertinently. *First,* the stress of duty is laid upon the precept of Christ as our rule, and justly, for that word of Christ which we are to keep is the Father's word, and his will the Father's will. *Secondly,* The stress of our comfort is laid upon the promise of Christ. But forasmuch as, in dependence upon that promise, we must deny ourselves, and take up our cross, and quit all, it concerns us to enquire whether the security be sufficient for us to venture our all upon; and this satisfies us that it is, that the promise is not Christ's bare word, but the Father's which sent him, which therefore we may rely upon.

25 These things have I spoken
unto you, being *yet* present with you.
26 But the Comforter, *which is* the
Holy Ghost, whom the Father will
send in my name, he shall teach you
all things, and bring all things to your
remembrance, whatsoever I have said
unto you. 27 Peace I leave with
you, my peace I give unto you: not
as the world giveth, give I unto
you. Let not your heart be troubled,
neither let it be afraid.

Two things Christ here comforts his disciples with:—

I. That they should be under the tuition of his Spirit, *v.* 25, 26, where we may observe,

1. The reflection Christ would have them make upon the instructions he had given them: *These things have I spoken unto you* (referring to all the good lessons he had taught them, since they entered themselves into his school), *being yet present with you.* This intimates, (1.) That what he had said he did not retract nor unsay, but ratify it, or stand to it. What he had spoken he had spoken, and would abide by it. (2.) That he had improved the opportunity of his bodily presence with them to the utmost: "As long as I have been yet present with them, you know I have lost no time." Note, When our teachers are about to be removed from us we should call to mind what they have spoken, *being yet present with us.*

2. The encouragement given them to expect another teacher, and that Christ would find out a way of speaking to them after his departure from them, *v.* 26. He had told them before that the Father would give them this other comforter (*v.* 16), and here he returns to speak of it again; for as the promise of the Messiah had been, so the promise of the Spirit now was, the consolation of Israel. Two things he here tells them further concerning the sending of the Holy Ghost:—

(1.) On whose account he should be sent: "The Father will send him *in my name;* that is, for *my sake,* at my special instance and request;" or, "as my agent and representative." He came in his Father's name, as his ambassador: the Spirit comes in his name, as resident in his absence, to carry on his undertaking, and to ripen things for his second coming. Hence he is called *the Spirit of Christ,* for he pleads his cause, and does his work.

(2.) On what errand he should be sent; two things he shall do:—[1.] *He shall teach you all things,* as a Spirit of wisdom and revelation Christ was a teacher to his disciples; if he leave them now that they have made so little proficiency, what will become of them? Why, the Spirit shall teach them, shall be their standing tutor. He shall teach them all things necessary for them either to learn themselves, or to teach others. For those that would teach the things of God must first themselves be taught of God; this is the Spirit's work. See Isa. lix. 21. [2.] *He shall bring all things to your remembrance whatsoever I have said unto you.* Many a good lesson Christ had taught them, which they had forgotten, and which would be to seek when they had occasion for it. Many things they did not retain the remembrance of, because they did not rightly understand the meaning of them. The Spirit shall not teach them a new gospel, but bring to their minds that which they had been taught, by leading them into the understanding of it. The apostles were all of them to preach, and some of them to write, the things that Jesus did and taught, to transmit them to distant nations and future ages; now, if they had been left to themselves herein, some needful things might have been forgotten, others misrepresented, through the treachery of their memories; therefore the Spirit is promised to enable them truly to relate and record what Christ said unto them. And to all the saints the Spirit of grace is given to be a remembrancer, and to him by faith and prayer we should commit the keeping of what we hear and know.

II. That they should be under the influence of his peace (*v.* 27): *Peace I leave with you.* When Christ was about to leave the world he *made his will.* His soul he committed to his Father; his body he bequeathed to Joseph, to be decently interred; his clothes fell to the soldiers; his mother he left to the care of John: but what should he leave to his poor disciples, that had left all for him? Silver and gold he had none; but he left them that which was infinitely better, *his peace.* "*I leave you,* but I leave *my peace* with you. I not only give you a title to it, but put you in possession of it." He did not part in anger, but in love; for this was his farewell, *Peace I leave with you,* as a dying father leaves portions to his children; and this is a *worthy portion.* Observe,

1. The legacy that is here bequeathed · *Peace, my peace.* Peace is put for all good, and Christ has left us all needful good, all that is really and truly good, all the purchased promised good. Peace is put for reconciliation and love; the peace bequeathed is peace with God, peace with one another; peace *in our own bosoms* seems to be especially meant; a tranquillity of mind arising from a sense of our justification before God. It is the counterpart of our pardons, and the composure of our minds. This Christ calls *his* peace, for he is himself our peace, Eph. ii. 14. It is the peace he purchased for us and preached to us, and on which the angels congratulated men at his birth, Luke ii. 14.

2. To whom this legacy is bequeathed: "To you, my disciples and followers, that will be exposed to trouble, and have need of peace; to you that are the sons of peace, and are qualified to receive it." This legacy was left to them as the representatives of the church, to them and their successors, to them and all true Christians in all ages.

3. In what manner it is left: *Not as the world giveth, give I unto you.* That is, (1.) "I do not compliment you with *Peace be unto you;* no, it is not a mere formality, but a real blessing." (2.) "The peace I give is of such a nature that the smiles of the world cannot give it, nor the frowns of the world take it away." Or, (3.) "The gifts I give to you are not such as this world gives to its children and votaries, to whom it is kind." The world's gifts concern only the body and time; Christ's gifts enrich the soul for eternity: the world gives lying vanities, and that which will cheat us; Christ gives substantial blessings, which will never fail us: the world gives and takes; Christ gives a good part that shall *never be taken away.* (4.) The peace which Christ gives is infinitely more valuable than that which the world gives. The world's peace begins in ignorance, consists with sin, and ends in endless troubles; Christ's peace begins in grace, consists with no allowed sin, and ends at length in everlasting peace. As is the difference between a killing lethargy and a reviving refreshing sleep, such is the difference between Christ's peace and the world's.

4. What use they should make of it: *Let not your heart be troubled,* for any evils past or present, *neither let it be afraid* of any evil to come. Note, Those that are interested in

the covenant of grace, and entitled to the peace which Christ gives, ought not to yield to overwhelming griefs and fears. This comes in here as the conclusion of the whole matter; he had said (*v.* 1), *Let not your heart be troubled*, and here he repeats it as that for which he had now given sufficient reason.

28 Ye have heard how I said unto
you, I go away, and come *again* unto
you. If ye loved me, ye would rejoice,
because I said, I go unto the Father:
for my Father is greater than I. 29
And now I have told you before it
come to pass, that, when it is come to
pass, ye might believe. 30 Hereafter
I will not talk much with you: for
the prince of this world cometh, and
hath nothing in me. 31 But that
the world may know that I love the
Father; and as the Father gave me
commandment, even so I do. Arise
let us go hence.

Christ here gives his disciples another reason why their hearts should not be troubled for his going away; and that is, because his heart was not. And here he tells them what it was that enabled him to endure the cross and despise the shame, that they might *look unto him*, and *run with patience*. He comforted himself,

I. That, though he went away, he should *come again:* "*You have heard how I have said*, and now I say it again, *I go away, and come again.*" Note, What we have heard of the doctrine of Christ, especially concerning his second coming, we have need to be told again and again. When we are under the power of any transport of passion, grief, or fear, or care, we forget that Christ will come again. See Phil. iv. 5. Christ encouraged himself with *this*, in his sufferings and death, that he should *come again*, and the same should comfort us in our departure at death; we go away to come again; the leave we take of our friends at that parting is only a good night, not a final farewell. See 1 Thess. iv. 13, 14.

II. That he *went to his Father:* "*If you loved me*, as by your sorrow you say you do, *you would rejoice* instead of mourning, because, though I leave you, yet I said, *I go unto the Father*, not only mine, but yours, which will be my advancement and your advantage; for *my Father is greater than I.*" Observe here, 1. It is matter of joy to Christ's disciples that he is gone to the Father, to take possession for orphans, and make intercession for transgressors. His departure had a bright side as well as a dark side. Therefore he sent this message after his resurrection (*ch.* xx. 17), *I ascend to my Father and your Father*, as most comfortable. 2. The reason of this is, because *the Father is greater than he*, which, if it be a proper proof of that for which it is alleged (as no doubt it is), must be understood thus, that his state with his Father would be much more excellent and glorious than his present state; his returning to his Father (so Dr. Hammond) would be the advancing of him to a much higher condition than that which he was now in. Or thus, His going to the Father himself, and bringing all his followers to him there, was the ultimate end of his undertaking, and therefore greater than the means. Thus Christ raises the thoughts and expectations of his disciples to something greater than that in which now they thought all their happiness bound up. The kingdom of the Father, wherein he shall be all in all, will be greater than the mediatorial kingdom. 3. The disciples of Christ should show that they love him by their rejoicing in the glories of his exaltation, rather than by lamenting the sorrows of his humiliation, and rejoicing that he is gone to his Father, where he would be, and where we shall be shortly with him. Many that love Christ, let their love run out in a wrong channel; they think if they love him they must be continually in pain because of him; whereas those that love him should *dwell at ease* in him, should *rejoice in Christ Jesus.*

III. That his going away, compared with the prophecies which went before of it, would be a means of confirming the faith of his disciples (*v.* 29): *I have told you before it come to pass* that I must die and rise again, and ascend to the Father, and send the Comforter, *that, when it is come to pass, you might believe.*" See this reason, *ch.* xiii. 19; xvi. 4. Christ told his disciples of his death, though he knew it would both puzzle them and grieve them, because it would afterwards redound to the confirmation of their faith in two things:—1. That he who foretold these things had a divine prescience, and knew beforehand what a day would bring forth. When St. Paul was going to Jerusalem, he *knew not the things that did abide him there*, but Christ did. 2. That the things foretold were according to the divine purpose and designation, not sudden resolves, but the counterparts of an eternal counsel. Let them therefore not be troubled at that which would be for the confirmation of their faith, and so would redound to their real benefit; for the *trial of our faith* is very precious, though it cost us present *heaviness, through manifold temptations*, 1 Pet. i. 6.

IV. That he was sure of a victory over Satan, with whom he knew he was to have a struggle in his departure (*v.* 30): "*Henceforth I will not talk much with you*, having not much to say, but what may be adjourned to the pouring out of the Spirit." He had a great deal of good talk with them after this (*ch.* xv. and xvi), but, in comparison with what he had said, it was not much. His time was now short, and he therefore spoke largely to them now, because the opportunity would soon be over. Note, We should always endeavour to talk to the purpose, because perhaps we may not have time to talk much. We know not how soon our breath may be stopped, and therefore should be always breathing something that is good. When we come to be sick and die, perhaps we may not be capable of talking much to those about us; and therefore what good counsel we have to give them, let us give it while we are in health. One reason why he would not talk much with them was because he had now other work to apply himself to: *The prince of this world comes.* He called the devil the *prince of this world, ch.* xii. 31. The disciples dreamed of their Master being the prince of this world, and they worldly princes under him. But Christ tells them that the *prince of this world* was his enemy, and so were the *princes of this world,* that were actuated and ruled by him, 1 Cor. ii. 8. But *he has nothing in me.* Observe here, 1. The prospect Christ had of an approaching conflict, not only with men, but with the powers of darkness. The devil had set upon him with his temptations (Matt. iv.), had offered him the *kingdoms of this world,* if he would hold them as tributary to him, with an eye to which Christ calls him, in disdain, *the prince of this world. Then the devil departed from him for a season;* "But now," says Christ, "I see him rallying again, preparing to make a furious onset, and so to gain by terrors that which he could not gain by allurements;" to frighten from his undertaking, when he could not entice from it. Note, The foresight of a temptation gives us great advantage in our resistance of it; for, being fore-warned, we should be fore-armed. While we are here, we may see Satan continually coming against us, and ought therefore to be always upon our guard. 2. The assurance he had of good success in the conflict: *He hath nothing in me,* οὐκ ἔχει οὐδὲν—*He hath nothing at all.* (1.) There was no guilt in Christ to give authority to *the prince of this world* in his terrors. The devil is said to have *the power of death* (Heb. ii. 14); the Jews called him *the angel of death,* as an executioner. Now Christ having done no evil, Satan had no legal power against him, and therefore, though he prevailed to crucify him, he could not prevail to terrify him; though he hurried him to death, yet not to despair. When Satan comes to disquiet us, he has something in us to perplex us with, for we have all sinned; but, when he would disturb Christ, he found no occasion against him. (2.) There was no corruption in Christ, to give advantage to *the prince of this world* in his temptations. He could not crush his undertaking by drawing him to sin, because there was nothing sinful in him, nothing irregular for his temptations to fasten upon, no tinder for him to strike fire into; such was the spotless purity of his nature that he was above the possibility of sinning. The more Satan's interest in us is crushed and decays, the more comfortably may we expect sufferings and death.

V. That his departure was in compliance with, and obedience to, his Father. Satan could not force his life from him, and yet he would die: *that the world may know that I love the Father, v.* 31. We may take this,

1. As confirming what he had often said, that his undertaking, as Mediator, was a demonstration to the world, (1.) Of his compliance with the Father; hereby it appeared that he loved the Father. As it was an evidence of his love to man that he died for his salvation, so it was of his love to God that he died for his glory and the accomplishing of his purposes. Let the world know that between the Father and the Son there is no love lost. *As the Father loved the Son, and gave all things into his hands;* so *the Son loved the Father,* and *gave his spirit into his hand.* (2.) Of his obedience to his Father: "*As the Father gave me commandment, even so I* did—did the thing commanded in the manner commanded." Note, The best evidence of our love to the Father is our doing as he hath given us commandment. As Christ loved the Father, and obeyed him, *even to the death,* so we must love Christ, and obey him. Christ's eye to the Father's commandment, obliging him to suffer and die, bore him up with cheerfulness, and overcame the reluctancies of nature; this took off the offence of the cross, that what he did was by order from the Father. The command of God is sufficient to bear us out in that which is most disputed by others, and therefore should be sufficient to bear us up in that which is most difficult to ourselves: *This is the will of him* that made me, *that sent me.*

2. As concluding what he had now said; having brought it to this, here he leaves it: *that the world may know that I love the Father.* You shall see how cheerfully I can meet the appointed cross: "*Arise, let us go hence* to the garden;" so some; or, to *Jerusalem.* When we talk of troubles at a distance, it is easy to say, *Lord, I will follow thee whithersoever thou goest;* but when it comes to the pinch, when an unavoidable cross lies in the way of duty, then to say, "*Arise, let us go* to meet it," instead of going out of our way to miss it, this lets *the world know that we love the Father.* If this discourse was at the close of the passover-supper, it should seem that at these words he arose from the table, and retired into the drawing-room, where he might the more freely carry on the discourse with his disciples in the following chapters, and pray with them. Dr. Goodwin's remark upon this is, that Christ mentioning the great motive of his sufferings, his Father's commandment, was in all haste to go forth to suffer and die, was afraid of slipping the time of Judas's meeting him: *Arise,* says he, *let us go hence*

but he looks upon the glass, as it were, sees it not quite out, and therefore sits down again, and preaches another sermon. Now, (1.) In these words he gives his disciples an encouragement to follow him. He does not say, *I must go;* but, *Let us go.* He calls them out to no hardships but what he himself goes before them in as their leader. They had promised they would not desert him: "Come," says he, "*let us go* then; let us see how you will make the words good." (2.) He gives them an example, teaching them at all times, especially in suffering times, to sit loose to all things here below, and often to think and speak of leaving them. Though we sit easy, and in the midst of the delights of an agreeable conversation, yet we must not think of being here always: *Arise, let us go hence.* If it was at the close of the paschal and eucharistical supper, it teaches us that the solemnities of our communion with God are not to be constant in this world. When we sit down under Christ's shadow with delight, and say, *It is good to be here;* yet we must think of rising and going hence; going down from the mount.

CHAP. XV.

It is generally agreed that Christ's discourse in this and the next chapter was at the close of the last supper, the night in which he was betrayed, and it is a continued discourse, not interrupted as that in the foregoing chapter was; and what he chooses to discourse of is very pertinent to the present sad occasion of a farewell sermon. Now that he was about to leave them, I. They would be tempted to leave him, and return to Moses again; and therefore he tells them how necessary it was that they should by faith adhere to him and abide in him. II. They would be tempted to grow strange one to another; and therefore he presses it upon them to love one another, and to keep up that communion when he was gone which had hitherto been their comfort. III. They would be tempted to shrink from their apostleship, when they met with hardships; and therefore he prepares them to bear the shock of the world's ill will. There are four words to which his discourse in this chapter may be reduced; 1. Fruit, ver. 1—8. 2. Love, ver. 9—17. 3. Hatred, ver. 18—25. 4. The Comforter, ver. 26, 27.

I AM the true vine, and my Father
is the husbandman. 2 Every
branch in me that beareth not fruit
he taketh away: and every *branch*
that beareth fruit, he purgeth it, that
it may bring forth more fruit. 3 Now
ye are clean through the word which
I have spoken unto you. 4 Abide
in me, and I in you. As the branch
cannot bear fruit of itself, except it
abide in the vine; no more can ye,
except ye abide in me. 5 I am the
vine, ye *are* the branches: He that
abideth in me, and I in him, the same
bringeth forth much fruit: for without me ye can do nothing. 6 If a
man abide not in me, he is cast forth
as a branch, and is withered; and men
gather them, and cast *them* into the
fire, and they are burned. 7 If ye
abide in me, and my words abide in
you, ye shall ask what ye will, and it
shall be done unto you. 8 Herein is
my Father glorified, that ye bear
much fruit; so shall ye be my disciples.

Here Christ discourses concerning the fruit, *the fruits of the Spirit,* which his disciples were to bring forth, under the similitude of a vine. Observe here,

I. The doctrine of this similitude; what notion we ought to have of it.

1. That Jesus Christ is *the vine, the true vine.* It is an instance of the humility of Christ that he is pleased to speak of himself under low and humble comparisons. He that is *the Sun of righteousness,* and *the bright and morning Star,* compares himself to a *vine.* The church, which is Christ mystical, is a vine (Ps. lxxx. 8), so is Christ, who is the church seminal. Christ and his church are thus set forth. (1.) He is *the vine,* planted in the vineyard, and not a spontaneous product; planted in the earth, for he is *the Word made flesh.* The vine has an unsightly unpromising outside; and Christ had *no form nor comeliness,* Isa. liii. 2. The vine is a spreading plant, and Christ will be known as *salvation to the ends of the earth.* The fruit of the vine honours God and cheers man (Judg. ix. 13), so does the fruit of Christ's mediation; it is *better than gold,* Prov. viii. 19. (2.) He is *the true vine,* as truth is opposed to pretence and counterfeit; he is really a fruitful plant, a plant of renown. He is not like that wild vine which deceived those who gathered of it (2 Kings iv. 39), but a true vine. Unfruitful trees are said to *lie* (Hab. iii. 17. *marg.*), but Christ is a vine that will not deceive. Whatever excellency there is in any creature, serviceable to man, it is but a shadow of that grace which is in Christ for his people's good. He is that true vine typified by Judah's vine, which enriched him with the blood of the grape (Gen. xlix. 11), by Joseph's vine, the branches of which *ran over the wall* (Gen. xlix. 22), by Israel's vine, under which he *dwelt safely,* 1 Kings iv. 25.

2. That believers are branches of this vine, which supposes that Christ is the root of the vine. The root is unseen, and our *life is hid with Christ;* the root bears the tree (Rom. xi. 18), diffuses sap to it, and is all in all to its flourishing and fruitfulness; and in Christ are all supports and supplies. The branches of the vine are many, some on one side of the house or wall, others on the other side; yet, meeting in the root, are all but one vine; thus all good Christians, though in place and opinion distant from each other, yet meet in Christ, the centre of their unity. Believers, like the branches of the vine, are weak, and insufficient to stand of themselves, but as they are borne up. See Ezek. xv. 2.

3. That *the Father is the husbandman,* γεωργὸς—*the land-worker.* Though *the earth is the Lord's,* it yields him no fruit unless he work it. God has not only a propriety in, but a care of, the vine and all the branches.

He *hath planted, and watered, and gives the increase;* for *we are God's husbandry,* 1 Cor. iii. 9. See Isa. v. 1, 2; xxvii. 2, 3. He had an eye upon Christ, the root, and upheld him, and made him to flourish *out of a dry ground.* He has an eye upon all the branches, and prunes them, and watches over them, that nothing hurt them. Never was any husbandman so wise, so watchful, about his vineyard, as God is about his church, which therefore must needs prosper.

II. The duty taught us by this similitude, which is to *bring forth fruit,* and, in order to this, to *abide* in Christ.

1. We must be fruitful. From a vine we look for grapes (Isa. v. 2), and from a Christian we look for Christianity; this is the *fruit,* a Christian temper and disposition, a Christian life and conversation, Christian devotions and Christian designs. We must honour God, and do good, and exemplify the purity and power of the religion we profess; and this is bearing fruit. The disciples here must be fruitful, as Christians, in all *the fruits of righteousness,* and as apostles, in diffusing the savour of the knowledge of Christ. To persuade them to this, he urges,

(1.) The doom of the unfruitful (*v.* 2): They are *taken away.* [1.] It is here intimated that there are many who pass for *branches* in Christ who yet do *not bear fruit.* Were they really united to Christ by faith, they would bear fruit; but being only tied to him by the thread of an outward profession, though they seem to be branches, they will soon be seen to be dry ones. Unfruitful professors are unfaithful professors; professors, and no more. It might be read, *Every branch that beareth not fruit in me,* and it comes much to one; for those that do not bear fruit in Christ, and in his Spirit and grace, are as if they bore no fruit at all, Hos. x. 1. [2.] It is here threatened that they shall be *taken away,* in justice to them and in kindness to the rest of the branches. From him that has not real union with Christ, and fruit produced thereby, *shall be taken away even that which he seemed to have,* Luke viii. 18. Some think this refers primarily to Judas.

(2.) The promise made to the fruitful: *He purgeth them, that they may bring forth more fruit.* Note, [1.] Further fruitfulness is the blessed reward of forward fruitfulness. The first blessing was, *Be fruitful;* and it is still a great blessing. [2.] Even fruitful branches, in order to their further fruitfulness, have need of purging or pruning; *καθαίρει—he taketh away that which is superfluous* and luxuriant, which hinders its growth and fruitfulness. The best have that in them which is peccant, *aliquid amputandum—something which should be taken away;* some notions, passions, or humours, that want to be purged away, which Christ has promised to do by his word, and Spirit, and providence; and these shall be taken off by degrees in the proper season. [3.] The purging of fruitful branches, in order to their greater fruitfulness, is the care and work of the great husbandman, for his own glory.

(3.) The benefits which believers have by the doctrine of Christ, the power of which they should labour to exemplify in a fruitful conversation: *Now you are clean, v.* 3. [1.] Their society was clean, now that Judas was expelled by that word of Christ, *What thou doest, do quickly;* and till they were got clear of him *they were not all clean.* The word of Christ is a distinguishing word, and separates *between the precious and the vile;* it will purify *the church of the first-born* in the great dividing day. [2.] They were each of them clean, that is, sanctified, by the truth of Christ (*ch.* xvii. 17); that faith by which they received the word of Christ *purified their hearts,* Acts xv. 9. The Spirit of grace by the word refined them from the dross of the world and the flesh, and purged out of them *the leaven of the scribes and Pharisees,* from which, when they saw their inveterate rage and enmity against their Master, they were now pretty well cleansed. Apply it to all believers. The word of Christ is spoken to them; there is a cleansing virtue in that word, as it works grace, and works out corruption. It cleanses as fire cleanses the gold from its dross, and as physic cleanses the body from its disease. We then evidence that we are cleansed by the word when we *bring forth fruit unto holiness.* Perhaps here is an allusion to the law concerning vineyards in Canaan; the fruit of them was as unclean, and uncircumcised, the first three years after it was planted, and *the fourth year it* was to *be holiness of praise unto the Lord;* and then it was clean, Lev. xix. 23, 24. The disciples had now been three years under Christ's instruction; and *now you are clean.*

(4.) The glory that will redound to God by our fruitfulness, with the comfort and honour that will come to ourselves by it, *v.* 8. If we *bear much fruit,* [1.] Herein our Father will be glorified. The fruitfulness of the apostles, as such, in the diligent discharge of their office, would be to the glory of God in the conversion of souls, and the offering of them up to him, Rom. xv. 9, 16. The fruitfulness of all Christians, in a lower or narrower sphere, is to the glory of God. By the eminent good works of Christians many are brought to *glorify our Father who is in heaven.* [2.] So shall we be Christ's disciples indeed, approving ourselves so, and making it to appear that we are really what we call ourselves. So shall we both evidence our discipleship and adorn it, and be to our Master *for a name and a praise,* and a glory, that is, disciples indeed, Jer. xiii. 11. So shall we be owned by our Master in the great day, and have the reward of disciples, a share *in the joy of our Lord.* And the more fruit we bring forth, the more we abound in that which is good, the more he is glorified.

2. In order to our fruitfulness, we must

abide in Christ, must keep up our union with him by faith, and do all we do in religion in the virtue of that union. Here is,

(1.) The duty enjoined (*v.* 4): *Abide in me, and I in you.* Note, It is the great concern of all Christ's disciples constantly to keep up a dependence upon Christ and communion with him, habitually to adhere to him, and actually to derive supplies from him. Those that are come to Christ must abide in him: "*Abide in me,* by faith; *and I in you,* by my Spirit; *abide in me,* and then fear not but I will *abide in you;*" for the communion between Christ and believers never fails on his side. We must abide in Christ's word by a regard to it, and it in us as a *light to our feet.* We must abide in Christ's merit as our righteousness and plea, and it in us as our support and comfort. The knot of the branch abides in the vine, and the sap of the vine abides in the branch, and so there is a constant communication between them.

(2.) The necessity of our abiding in Christ, in order to our fruitfulness (*v.* 4, 5): "*You cannot bring forth fruit, except you abide in me;* but, if you do, you *bring forth much fruit; for,* in short, *without me,* or separate from me, *you can do nothing.*" So necessary is it to our comfort and happiness that we be fruitful, that the best argument to engage us to abide in Christ is, that otherwise we cannot be fruitful. [1.] Abiding in Christ is necessary in order to our doing much good. He that is constant in the exercise of faith in Christ and love to him, that lives upon his promises and is led by his Spirit, *bringeth forth much fruit,* he is very serviceable to God's glory, and his own account in the great day. Note, Union with Christ is a noble principle, productive of all good. A life of faith in the Son of God is incomparably the most excellent life a man can live in this world; it is regular and even, pure and heavenly; it is useful and comfortable, and all that answers the end of life. [2.] It is necessary to our doing any good. It is not only a means of cultivating and increasing what good there is already in us, but it is the root and spring of all good: "*Without me you can do nothing:* not only no great thing, *heal the sick, or raise the dead,* but nothing." Note, We have as necessary and constant a dependence upon the grace of the Mediator for all the actions of the spiritual and divine life as we have upon the providence of the Creator for all the actions of the natural life; for, as to both, it is in the divine power *that we live, move, and have our being.* Abstracted from the merit of Christ, we can do nothing towards our justification; and from the Spirit of Christ nothing towards our sanctification. *Without Christ we can do nothing* aright, nothing that will be fruit pleasing to God or profitable to ourselves, 2 Cor. iii. 5. We depend upon Christ, not only as the vine upon the wall, for support; but, as the branch on the root, for sap.

(3.) The fatal consequences of forsaking Christ (*v.* 6): *If any man abide not in me, he is cast forth as a branch.* This is a description of the fearful state of hypocrites that are *not in Christ,* and of apostates that *abide not in Christ.* [1.] They are cast forth as dry and withered branches, which are plucked off because they cumber the tree. It is just that those should have no benefit by Christ who think they have no need of him; and that those who reject him should be rejected by him. Those that abide not in Christ shall be abandoned by him; they are left to themselves, to fall into scandalous sin, and then are justly cast out of the communion of the faithful. [2.] They are withered, as a branch broken off from the tree. Those that abide not in Christ, though they may flourish awhile in a plausible, at least a passable profession, yet in a little time wither and come to nothing. Their parts and gifts wither; their zeal and devotion wither; their credit and reputation wither; their hopes and comforts wither, Job viii. 11—13. Note, Those that bear no fruit, after awhile will bear no leaves. *How soon is that fig-tree withered away* which Christ has cursed! [3.] *Men gather them.* Satan's agents and emissaries pick them up, and make an easy prey of them. Those that fall off from Christ presently fall in with sinners; and the sheep that wander from Christ's fold, the devil stands ready to seize them for himself. When the Spirit of the Lord had departed from Saul, an evil spirit possessed him. [4.] They *cast them into the fire,* that is, they are cast into the fire; and those who seduce them and draw them to sin do in effect cast them there; for they *make them children of hell.* Fire is the fittest place for withered branches, for they are good for nothing else, Ezek. xv. 2—4. [5.] *They are burned;* this follows of course, but it is here added very emphatically, and makes the threatening very terrible. They will not be consumed in a moment, like *thorns under a pot* (Eccl. vii. 6), but καίεται, they are burning for ever in a fire, which not only cannot be quenched, but will never spend itself. This comes of quitting Christ, this is the end of barren trees. Apostates are *twice dead* (Jude 12), and when it is said, *They are cast into the fire and are burned,* it speaks as if they were twice damned. Some apply men's gathering them to the ministry of the angels in the great day, when they shall gather out of Christ's kingdom all things that offend, and shall *bundle the tares for the fire.*

(4.) The blessed privilege which those have that *abide in Christ* (*v.* 7): *If my words abide in you, you shall ask what you will* of my Father in my name, *and it shall be done.* See here, [1.] How our union with Christ is maintained—by the word: *If you abide in me;* he had said before, *and I in you;* here he explains himself, *and my words abide in you;* for it is in the word that Christ is set before us, and offered to us, Rom. x. 6—8. It is in the word that we receive and embrace him; and so where the *word of Christ dwells richly* there Christ dwells. If the word be our constant guide and monitor, if it be in us as at home, then we abide in Christ, and he in us. [2.] How our communion with Christ is maintained—by prayer: *You shall ask what you will, and it shall be done to you.* And what can we desire more than to have what we will for the asking? Note, Those that abide in Christ as their heart's delight shall have, through Christ, their heart's desire. If we have Christ, we shall want nothing that is good for us. Two things are implied in this promise:—*First,* That if we abide in Christ, and his word in us, we shall not ask any thing but what is proper to be done for us. The promises abiding in us lie ready to be turned into prayers; and the prayers so regulated cannot but speed. *Secondly,* That if we *abide in Christ and his word* we shall have such an interest in God's favour and Christ's mediation that we shall have an answer of peace to all our prayers.

9 As the Father hath loved me, so
have I loved you: continue ye in my
love. 10 If ye keep my commandments, ye shall abide in my love;
even as I have kept my Father's commandments, and abide in his love.
11 These things have I spoken unto
you, that my joy might remain in
you, and *that* your joy might be full.
12 This is my commandment, That
ye love one another, as I have loved
you. 13 Greater love hath no man
than this, that a man lay down his
life for his friends. 14 Ye are my
friends, if ye do whatsoever I command you. 15 Henceforth I call you
not servants; for the servant knoweth not what his lord doeth: but I
have called you friends; for all things
that I have heard of my Father I have
made known unto you. 16 Ye have
not chosen me, but I have chosen
you, and ordained you, that ye should
go and bring forth fruit, and *that*
your fruit should remain: that whatsoever ye shall ask of the Father in
my name, he may give it you. 17
These things I command you, that ye
love one another.

Christ, who is love itself, is here discoursing concerning love, a fourfold love.

I. Concerning the Father's love to him; and concerning this he here tells us, 1. That the Father did love him (*v.* 9): *As the Father hath loved me.* He loved him as Mediator: *This is my beloved Son.* He was the Son of his love. He loved him, and gave *all things into his hand;* and yet so *loved the world* as to deliver him up for us all. When Christ was entering upon his sufferings he comforted himself with this, that his Father loved him. Those whom God loves as a Father may despise the hatred of all the world. 2. That he abode in his Father's love, *v.* 10. He continually loved his Father, and was beloved of him. Even when he was made sin and a curse for us, and *it pleased the Lord to bruise him,* yet he abode in his Father's love. See Ps. lxxxix. 33. Because he continued to love his Father, he went cheerfully through his sufferings, and therefore his Father continued to love him. 3. That therefore he abode in his Father's love because he kept his Father's law: *I have kept my Father's commandments,* as Mediator, and so *abide in his love.* Hereby he showed that he continued to love his Father, that he went on, and went through, with his undertaking, and therefore the Father continued to love him. His soul *delighted in him,* because he *did not fail, nor was discouraged,* Isa. xlii. 1—4. We having broken the law of creation, and thereby thrown ourselves out of the love of God; Christ satisfied for us by obeying the law of redemption, and so he abode in his love, and restored us to it.

II. Concerning his own love to his disciples. Though he leaves them, he loves them. And observe here,

1. The pattern of this love: *As the Father has loved me, so have I loved you.* A strange expression of the condescending grace of Christ! As the Father loved him, who was most worthy, he loved them, who were most unworthy. The Father loved him as his Son, and he loves them as his children. *The Father gave all things into his hand;* so, with himself, *he freely giveth us all things.* The Father loved him as Mediator, as head of the church, and the great trustee of divine grace and favour, which he had not for himself only, but for the benefit of those for whom he was entrusted; and, says he, "I have been a faithful trustee. As the Father has committed his love to me, so I transmit it to you." Therefore the Father was well pleased with him, that he might be well pleased with us in him; and loved him, that in him, as beloved, he might *make us accepted,* Eph. i. 6.

2. The proofs and products of this love, which are four:—

(1.) Christ loved his disciples, for he laid down his life for them (*v.* 13): *Greater* proof of *love hath no man* to show *than this,* to *lay down his life for his friend.* And this is the love wherewith *Christ hath loved us,* he is our ἀντίψυχος—*bail for us,* body for body, life for life, though he knew our insolvency, and foresaw how much the engagement would cost him. Observe here, [1.] The extent of the love of the children of men to one another. The highest proof of it is laying down one's life for a friend, to save his life, and perhaps there have been some such heroic achievements of love, more than *plucking out one's own eyes*, Gal. iv. 15. If *all that a man has he will give for his life,* he that gives this for his friend gives all, and can give no more; this may sometimes be our duty, 1 John iii. 16. Paul was ambitious of the honour (Phil. ii. 17); and *for a good man some will even dare to die*, Rom. v. 7. It is love in the highest degree, which is *strong as death.* [2.] The excellency of the love of Christ beyond all other love. He has not only equalled, but exceeded, the most illustrious lovers. Others have laid down their lives, content that they should be taken from them; but Christ gave up his, was not merely passive, but made it his own act and deed. The life which others have laid down has been but of equal value with the life for which it was laid down, and perhaps less valuable; but Christ is infinitely more worth than ten thousand of us. Others have thus laid down their lives for their friends, but Christ laid down his for us *when we were enemies*, Rom. v. 8, 10. *Plusquam ferrea aut lapidea corda esse oportet, quæ non emolliet tam incomparabilis divini amoris suavitas—Those hearts must be harder than iron or stone which are not softened by such incomparable sweetness of divine love.*—Calvin.

(2.) Christ loved his disciples, for he took them into a covenant of friendship with himself, *v.* 14, 15. "If you approve yourselves by your obedience my disciples indeed, *you are my friends,* and shall be treated as friends." Note, The followers of Christ are the friends of Christ, and he is graciously pleased to call and account them so. Those that do the duty of his servants are admitted and advanced to the dignity of his friends. David had one servant in his court, and Solomon one in his, that was in a particular manner *the king's friend* (2 Sam. xv. 37; 1 Kings iv. 5); but this honour have all Christ's servants. We may in some particular instance befriend a stranger; but we espouse all the interests of a friend, and concern ourselves in all his cares: thus Christ takes believers to be his friends. He visits them and converses with them as his friends, bears with them and makes the best of them, is afflicted in their afflictions, and takes pleasure in their prosperity; he pleads for them in heaven and takes care of all their interests there. Have friends but one soul? He that is joined to the Lord is *one spirit,* 1 Cor. vi. 17. Though they often show themselves unfriendly, he is a friend that loves at all times. Observe how endearingly this is expressed here. [1.] He will not *call them servants,* though they call him *Master* and *Lord.* Those that would be like Christ in humility must not take a pride in insisting upon all occasions on their authority and superiority, but remember that their servants are their fellow-servants. But, [2.] He will *call them his friends;* he will not only love them, but will let them know it; for *in his tongue is the law of kindness.* After his resurrection he seems to speak with more affectionate tenderness of and to his disciples than before. *Go to my brethren, ch.* xx. 17. *Children, have you any meat? ch.* xxi. 5. But observe, though Christ called *them his friends,* they called themselves *his servants:* Peter, *a servant of Christ* (1 Pet. i. 1), and so James, *ch.* i. 1. The more honour Christ puts upon us, the more honour we should study to do him; the higher in his eyes, the lower in our own.

(3.) Christ loved his disciples, for he was very free in communicating his mind to them (*v.* 15): "Henceforth you shall not be kept so much in the dark as you have been, like *servants* that are only told their present work; but, when the Spirit is poured out, you shall know your Master's designs as *friends. All things that I have heard of my Father I have declared unto you.*" As to the secret will of God, there are many things which we must be content not to know; but, as to the revealed will of God, Jesus Christ has faithfully handed to us what he received of the Father, *ch.* i. 18; Matt. xi. 27. The great things relating to man's redemption Christ declared to his disciples, that they might declare them to others; they were the men of his counsel, Matt. xiii. 11.

(4.) Christ loved his disciples, for he chose and ordained them to be the prime instruments of his glory and honour in the world (*v.* 16): *I have chosen you, and ordained you,* His love to them appeared,

[1.] In their election, their election to their apostleship (*ch.* vi. 70): *I have chosen you twelve.* It did not begin on their side: *You have not chosen me,* but I first *chose you.* Why were they admitted to such an intimacy with him, employed in such an embassy for him, and endued with such power from on high? It was not owing to their wisdom and goodness in choosing him for their Master, but to his favour and grace in choosing them for his disciples. It is fit that Christ should have the choosing of his own ministers; still he does it by his providence and Spirit. Though ministers make that holy calling their own choice, Christ's choice is prior to theirs and directs and determines it. Of all that are chosen to grace and glory it may be said, They have not chosen Christ, but he has chosen them, Deut. vii. 7, 8.

[2.] In their ordination: *I have ordained you; ἔθηκα ὑμᾶς*—"*I have put you* into the ministry (1 Tim. i. 12), put you into commission." By this it appeared that he took them for his friends when he crowned their heads with such an honour, and filled their hands with such a trust. It was a mighty confidence he reposed in them, when he made them his ambassadors to negociate the affairs of his kingdom in this lower world, and the prime ministers of state in the administration of it. The treasure of the gospel was committed to them, *First,* That it might be propagated: that you should go, *ἵνα ὑμεῖς ὑπάγητε*—"*that you should go as under a yoke* or burden, for the ministry is a work, and you that go about it must resolve to undergo a great deal; *that you may go* from place to place all the world over, and *bring forth fruit.*" They were ordained, not to sit still, but to go about, to be diligent in their work, and to lay out themselves unweariedly in doing good. They were ordained, not to beat the air, but to be instrumental in God's hand for the bringing of nations into obedience to Christ, Rom. i.13. Note, Those whom Christ ordains should and shall be fruitful; should labour, and shall not labour in vain. *Secondly,* That it might be perpetuated; that the fruit may remain, that the good effect of their labours may continue in the world from generation to generation, to the end of time. The church of Christ was not to be a short-lived thing, as many of the sects of the philosophers, that were a nine days' wonder; it did not *come up in a night,* nor should it *perish in a night,* but be as the days of heaven. The sermons and writings of the apostles are transmitted to us, and we at this day are built upon that foundation, ever since the Christian church was first founded by the ministry of the apostles and seventy disciples; as one generation of ministers and Christians has passed away, still another has come. By virtue of that great charter (Matt. xxviii. 19), Christ has a church in the world, which, as our lawyers say of bodies corporate, does *not die,* but lives in a succession; and thus *their fruit remains* to this day, and shall do while the earth remains.

[3.] His love to them appeared in the interest they had at the throne of grace: *Whatsoever you shall ask of my Father, in my name, he will give it you.* Probably this refers in the first place to the power of working miracles which the apostles were clothed with, which was to be drawn out by prayer. "Whatever gifts are necessary to the furtherance of your labours, whatever help from heaven you have occasion for at any time, it is but ask and have." Three things are here hinted to us for our encouragement in prayer, and very encouraging they are. *First,* That we have a God to go to who is a Father; Christ here calls him *the Father,* both mine and yours; and the Spirit in the word and in the heart teaches us to cry, *Abba, Father. Secondly,* That we come in a good name. Whatever errand we come upon to the throne of grace according to God's will, we may with a humble boldness mention Christ's name in it, and plead that we are related to him, and he is concerned for us. *Thirdly,* That an answer of peace is promised us. What you come for shall be given you. This great promise made to that great duty keeps up a comfortable and gainful intercourse between heaven and earth.

III. Concerning the disciples' love to Christ, enjoined in consideration of the great love wherewith he had loved them. Three things he exhorts them to :—

1. To continue in his love, *v.* 9. "Continue in your love to me, and in mine to you." Both may be taken in. We must place our happiness in the continuance of Christ's love to us, and make it our business to give continued proofs of our love to Christ, that nothing may tempt us to withdraw from him, or provoke him to withdraw from us. Note, All that love Christ should continue in their love to him, that is, be always loving him, and taking all occasions to show it, and love to the end. The disciples were to go out upon service for Christ, in which they would meet with many troubles; but, says Christ, "*Continue in my love.* Keep up your love to me, and then all the troubles you meet with will be easy; love made seven years' hard service easy to Jacob. Let not the troubles you meet with for Christ's sake quench your love to Christ, but rather quicken it.

2. To let his joy remain in them, and fill them, *v.* 11. This he designed in those precepts and promises given them.

(1.) That his joy might remain in them. The words are so placed, in the original, that they may be read either, [1.] That *my joy in you may remain.* If they bring forth much fruit, and continue in his love, he will continue to rejoice in them as he had done. Note, Fruitful and faithful disciples are the joy of the Lord Jesus; he *rests in his love* to them, Zeph. iii. 17. As there is a transport of joy in heaven in the conversion of sinners, so there is a remaining joy in the perseverance of saints. Or, [2.] That *my joy,* that is, your joy in me, *may remain.* It is the will of Christ that his disciples should constantly and continually rejoice in him, Phil. iv. 4. The joy of the hypocrite is but for a moment, but the joy of those who abide in Christ's love is a continual feast. The word of the Lord enduring for ever, the joys that flow from it, and are founded on it, do so too.

(2.) *That your joy might be full;* not only that you might be full of joy, but that your joy in me and in my love may rise higher and higher, till it come to perfection, when you *enter into the joy of your Lord.*" Note, [1.] Those and those only that have Christ's joy remaining in them have their joy full; worldly joys are empty, soon surfeit but never satisfy. It is only wisdom's joy that will fill the soul, Ps. xxxvi. 8. [2.] The design of Christ in his word is to *fill the joy* of his people; see 1 John i. 4. This and the other he hath said, that our joy might be fuller and fuller, and perfect at last.

3. To evidence their love to him by keeping his commandments: "*If you keep my commandments, you shall abide in my love, v.* 10. This will be an evidence of the fidelity and constancy of your love to me, and then you may be sure of the continuance of my love to you." Observe here, (1.) The promise· "*You shall abide in my love* as in a dwelling place, at home in Christ's love; as in a resting place, at ease in Christ's love; as in a strong-

hold, safe in it. *You shall abide in my love,* you shall have grace and strength to persevere in loving me." If the same hand that first shed abroad the love of Christ in our hearts did not keep us in that love, we should not long abide in it, but, through the love of the world, should go *out of love* with Christ himself. (2.) The condition of the promise: *If you keep my commandments.* The disciples were to keep Christ's commandments, not only by a constant conformity to them themselves, but by a faithful delivery of them to others; they were to keep them as trustees, in whose hands that great *depositum* was lodged, for they were to *teach all things that Christ had commanded,* Matt. xxviii. 20. *This commandment* they must *keep without spot* (1 Tim. vi. 14), and thus they must show that they abide in his love.

To induce them to keep his commandments, he urges, [1.] His own example: *As I have kept my Father's commandments, and abide in his love.* Christ submitted to the law of mediation, and so preserved the honour and comfort of it, to teach us to submit to the laws of the Mediator, for we cannot otherwise preserve the honour and comfort of our relation to him. [2.] The necessity of it to their interest in him (*v.* 14): "*You are my friends if you do whatsoever I command you* and not otherwise." Note, *First,* Those only will be accounted Christ's faithful friends that approve themselves his obedient servants; for those that will not have him to reign over them shall be treated as his enemies. *Idem velle et idem nolle ea demum vera est amicitia—Friendship involves a fellowship of aversions and attachments.*—Sallust. *Secondly,* It is universal obedience to Christ that is the only acceptable obedience; to obey him in every thing that he commands us, not *excepting,* much less *excepting against,* any command.

IV. Concerning the *disciples' love one to another,* enjoined as an evidence of their love to Christ, and a grateful return for his love to them. We must keep his commandments, and this is his commandment, that we *love one another, v.* 12, and again, *v.* 17. No one duty of religion is more frequently inculcated, nor more pathetically urged upon us, by our Lord Jesus, than that of mutual love, and for good reason. 1. It is here recommended by Christ's pattern (*v.* 12): *as I have loved you.* Christ's love to us should direct and engage our love to each other; in this manner, and from this motive, we should love one another, as, and because, Christ has loved us. He here specifies some of the expressions of his love to them; he called them friends, communicated his mind to them, was ready to give them what they asked. *Go you and do likewise.* 2. It is required by his precept. He interposes his authority, has made it one of the statute-laws of his kingdom. Observe how differently it is expressed in these two verses, and both very emphatic. (1.) *This is my commandment* (*v.* 12), as if this were the most necessary of all the commandments. As under the law the prohibition of idolatry was the commandment more insisted on than any other, foreseeing the people's addictedness to that sin, so Christ, foreseeing the addictedness of the Christian church to uncharitableness, has laid most stress upon this precept. (2.) *These things I command you, v.* 17. He speaks as if he were about to give them many things in charge, and yet names this only, *that you love one another;* not only because this includes many duties, but because it will have a good influence upon all.

18 If the world hate you, ye know
that it hated me before *it hated* you.
19 If ye were of the world, the world
would love his own: but because ye
are not of the world, but I have
chosen you out of the world, therefore the world hateth you. 20 Remember the word that I said unto
you, The servant is not greater than
his lord. If they have persecuted me,
they will also persecute you; if they
have kept my saying, they will keep
your's also. 21 But all these things
will they do unto you for my name's
sake, because they know not him that
sent me. 22 If I had not come and
spoken unto them, they had not had
sin: but now they have no cloak for
their sin. 23 He that hateth me
hateth my Father also. 24 If I had
not done among them the works
which none other man did, they had
not had sin: but now have they both
seen and hated both me and my Father. 25 But *this cometh to pass,*
that the word might be fulfilled that
is written in their law, They hated me
without a cause.

Here Christ discourses concerning *hatred,* which is the character and genius of the devil's kingdom, as love is of the kingdom of Christ. Observe here,

I. Who they are in whom this hatred is found—the world, the children of this world, as distinguished from the children of God; those who are in the interests of the god of this world, whose image they bear, and whose power they are subject to; all those, whether Jews or Gentiles, who would not come into the church of Christ, which he audibly called, and visibly separates from this evil world. The calling of these *the world* intimates, 1. Their number; there were a world of people that opposed Christ and Christianity. Lord, how were they increased that troubled the Son of David! I fear, if we should put it to the vote between Christ and Satan, Satan would out-poll us quite. 2. Their confederacy and combination; these numerous hosts are embodied, and are as one, Ps. lxxxiii. 5. Jews and Gentiles, that could agree in nothing else, agreed to persecute Christ's ministers. 3. Their spirit and disposition; they are *men of the world* (Ps. xvii. 13, 14), wholly devoted to this world and the things of it, and never thinking of another world. The people of God, though they are taught to hate the sins of sinners, yet not their persons, but to love and do good to all men. A malicious, spiteful, envious spirit, is not the spirit of Christ, but of the world.

II. Who they are against whom this hatred is levelled—against the disciples of Christ, against Christ himself, and against the Father.

1. The world hates the disciples of Christ: *The world hateth you* (*v.* 19); and he speaks of it as that which they must expect and count upon, *v.* 18, as 1 John iii. 13.

(1.) Observe how this comes in here. [1.] Christ had expressed the great kindness he had for them as friends; but, lest they should be puffed up with this, there was given them, as there was to Paul, a *thorn in the flesh,* that is, as it is explained there, reproaches and persecutions for Christ's sake, 2 Cor. xii. 7, 10. [2.] He had appointed them their work, but tells them what hardships they should meet with in it, that it might not be a surprise to them, and that they might prepare accordingly. [3.] He had charged them to *love one another,* and need enough they had to love one another, for the world would hate them; to be kind to one another, for they would have a great deal of unkindness and ill-will from those that were without. "Keep peace among yourselves, and this will fortify you against the world's quarrels with you." Those that are in the midst of enemies are concerned to hold together.

(2.) Observe what is here included.

[1.] The world's enmity against the followers of Christ: it *hateth them.* Note, Whom Christ blesseth the world curseth. The favourites and heirs of heaven have never been the darlings of this world, since the old enmity was put between the seed of the woman and of the serpent. Why did Cain hate Abel, but *because his works were righteous?* Esau hated Jacob because of the blessing; Joseph's brethren hated him because his father loved him; Saul hated David because *the Lord was with him;* Ahab hated Micaiah because of his prophecies; such are the causeless causes of the world's hatred.

[2.] The fruits of that enmity, two of which we have here, *v.* 20. *First,* They will persecute you, because they hate you, for hatred is a restless passion. It is the common lot of those who will live godly in Christ Jesus to *suffer persecution,* 2 Tim. iii. 12. Christ foresaw what ill usage his ambassadors would meet with in the world, and yet, for the sake of those few that by their ministry were to be called out of the world, he sent them forth as sheep in the midst of wolves. *Secondly,* Another fruit of their enmity is implied, that they would reject their doctrine. When Christ says, *If they have kept my sayings, they will keep yours,* he means, They will keep yours, and regard yours, no more than they have regarded and kept mine. Note, The preachers of the gospel cannot but take the despising of their message to be the greatest injury that can be done to themselves; as it was a great affront to Jeremiah to say, *Let us not give heed to any of his words,* Jer. xviii. 18.

[3.] The causes of that enmity. The world will hate them,

First, Because they do not belong to it (*v.* 19): "*If you were of the world,* of its spirit, and in its interests, if you were carnal and worldly, *the world would love you* as its own; but, because you are called out of the world, it hates you, and ever will." Note, 1. We are not to wonder if those that are devoted to the world are caressed by it as its friends; most men *bless the covetous,* Ps. x. 3; xlix. 18. 2. Nor are we to wonder if those that are delivered from the world are maligned by it as its enemies; when Israel is rescued out of Egypt, the Egyptians will pursue them. Observe, The reason why Christ's disciples are not of the world is not because they have by their own wisdom and virtue distinguished themselves from the world, but because Christ hath chosen them out of it, to set them apart for himself; and this is the reason why the world hates them; for, (1.) The glory which by virtue of this choice they are designed for sets them above the world, and so makes them the objects of its envy. The saints shall judge the world, and the upright have dominion, and therefore they are hated. (2.) The grace which by virtue of this choice they are endued with sets them against the world; they swim against the stream of the world, and are not conformed to it; they witness against it, and are not conformed to it. This would support them under all the calamities which the world's hatred would bring upon them, that they were hated because they were the choice and the chosen ones of the Lord Jesus, and were not of the world. Now, [1.] This was no just cause for the world's hatred of them. If we do any thing to make ourselves hateful, we have reason to lament it; but, if men hate us for that for which they should love and value us, we have reason to pity them, but no reason to perplex ourselves. Nay, [2.] This was just cause for their own joy. He that is hated because he is rich and prospers cares not who has the vexation of it, while he has the satisfaction of it.

—Populus me sibilat, at mihi plaudo
Ipse domi—

—Let them hiss on, he cries,
While in my own opinion fully blessed.
Timon in Hor.

Much more may those hug themselves whom the world hates, but whom Christ loves.

Secondly, "Another cause of the world's hating you will be because you do belong to Christ (*v.* 21): *For my name's sake.*" Here is the core of the controversy; whatever is pretended, this is the ground of the quarrel, they hate Christ's disciples because they *bear his name,* and *bear up his name* in the world. Note, 1. It is the character of Christ's disciples that they stand up for his name. The name into which they were baptized is that which they will live and die by. 2. It has commonly been the lot of those that appear for Christ's name to suffer for so doing, to suffer many things, and hard things, *all these things.* It is matter of comfort to the greatest sufferers if they suffer for Christ's name's sake. *If you be reproached for the name of Christ, happy are you* (1 Pet. iv. 14), happy indeed, considering not only the honour that is imprinted upon those sufferings (Acts v. 41), but the comfort that is infused into them, and especially the crown of glory which those sufferings lead to. *If we suffer with Christ,* and for Christ, *we shall reign with him.*

Thirdly, After all, it is the world's ignorance that is the true cause of its enmity to the disciples of Christ (*v.* 21): *Because they know not him that sent me.* 1. They know not God. If men had but a due acquaintance with the very first principles of natural religion, and did but know God, though they did not embrace Christianity, yet they could not hate and persecute it. Those have no knowledge who eat up God's people, Ps. xiv. 4. 2. They know not God as he that sent our Lord Jesus, and authorized him to be the great Mediator of the peace. We do not rightly know God if we do not know him in Christ, and those who persecute those whom he sends make it to appear that they know not that he was sent of God. See 1 Cor. ii. 8.

2. The world hates Christ himself. And this is spoken of here for two ends:—

(1.) To mitigate the trouble of his followers, arising from the world's hatred, and to make it the less strange, and the less grievous (*v.* 18): *You know that it hated me before you,* πρῶτον ὑμῶν. We read it as signifying priority of time; he began in the bitter cup of suffering, and then left us to pledge him; but it may be read as expressing his superiority over them: "*You know* that it hated me, *your first,* your chief and captain, your leader and commander." [1.] If Christ, who excelled in goodness, and was perfectly innocent and universally beneficent, was hated, can we expect that any virtue or merit of ours should screen us from malice? [2.] If our Master, the founder of our religion, met with so much opposition in the planting of it, his servants and followers can look for no other in propagating and professing it. For this he refers them (*v.* 20) to his own word, at their admission into discipleship: *Remember the word that I said unto you.* It would help us to understand Christ's latter sayings to compare them with his former sayings. Nor would any thing contribute more to the making of us easy than remembering the words of Christ, which will expound his providences. Now in this word there is, *First,* A plain truth: *The servant is not greater than his Lord.* This he had said to them, Matt. x. 24. Christ is our Lord, and therefore we must diligently attend all his motions, and patiently acquiesce in all his disposals, for the servant is inferior to his lord. The plainest truths are sometimes the strongest arguments for the hardest duties; Elihu answers a multitude of Job's murmurings with this one self-evident truth, that God is greater than man, Job xxxiii. 12. So here is, *Secondly,* A proper inference drawn from it: "*If they have persecuted me,* as you have seen, and are likely to see much more, *they will also persecute you;* you may expect it and count upon it: for," 1. "You will do the same that I have done to provoke them; you will reprove them for their sins, and call them to repentance, and give them strict rules of holy living, which they will not bear." 2. "You cannot do more than I have done to oblige them; after so great an instance, let none wonder if they suffer ill for doing well." He adds, "*If they have kept my sayings, they will keep yours also;* as there have been a few, and but a few, that have been wrought upon by my preaching, so there will be by yours a few, and but a few." Some give another sense of this, making ἐτήρησαν to be put for παρητήρησαν. "If they have lain in wait for my sayings, with a design to ensnare me, they will in like manner lie in wait to entangle you in your talk."

(2.) To aggravate the wickedness of this unbelieving world, and to discover its exceeding sinfulness; to hate and persecute the apostles was bad enough, but in them to hate and persecute Christ himself was much worse. The world is generally in an ill name in scripture, and nothing can put it into a worse name than this, that it hated Jesus Christ. There is a world of people that are haters of Christ. Two things he insists upon to aggravate the wickedness of those that hated him:—

[1.] That there was the greatest reason imaginable why they should love him; men's good words and good works usually recommend them; now as to Christ,

First, His words were such as merited their love (*v.* 22): "*If I had not spoken unto them,* to court their love, *they had not had sin,* their opposition had not amounted to a hatred of me, their sin had been comparatively no sin. But now that I have said so much to them to recommend myself to their best affections they have no pretence, no excuse for their sin." Observe here, 1. The advantage which those have that enjoy the gospel; Christ in it comes and speaks to them; he spoke in person to the men of that generation, and is still speaking to us by our Bibles and ministers, and as one that has the most unquestionable authority over us, and affection for us. Every word of his is pure, carries with it a commanding majesty, and yet a condescending tenderness, able, one would think, to charm the deafest adder. 2. The excuse which those have that enjoy not the gospel: "*If I had not spoken to them,* if they had never heard of Christ and of salvation by him, *they had not had sin.*" (1.) Not this kind of sin. They had not been chargeable with a contempt of Christ if he had not come and made a tender of his grace to them. As *sin is not imputed where there is no law,* so unbelief is not imputed where there is no gospel; and, where it is imputed, it is thus far the only damning sin, that, being a sin against the remedy, other sins would not damn if the guilt of them were not bound on with this. (2.) Not such a degree of sin. If they had not had the gospel among them, their other sins had not been so bad; for the *times of ignorance God winked at,* Luke xii. 47, 48. 3. The aggravated guilt which those lie under to whom Christ has *come and spoken in vain,* whom he has called and invited in vain, with whom he has reasoned and pleaded in vain; *They have no cloak for their sin;* they are altogether inexcusable, and in the judgment day will be speechless, and will not have a word to say for themselves. Note, The clearer and fuller the discoveries are which are made to us of the grace and truth of Jesus Christ, the more is said to us that is convincing and endearing, the greater is our sin if we do not love him and believe in him. The word of Christ strips sin of its cloak, that it may appear sin.

Secondly, His works were such as merited their love, as well as his words (*v.* 24): "*If I had not done among them,* in their country, and before their eyes, such works as *no other man ever did, they had not had sin;* their unbelief and enmity had been excusable, and they might have had some colour to say that my word was not to be credited, if not otherwise confirmed;" but he produced satisfactory proofs of his divine mission, *works which no other man did.* Note, 1. As the Creator demonstrates his power and Godhead by his works (Rom. i. 20), so doth the Redeemer. His miracles, his mercies, works of wonder and works of grace, prove him sent of God, and sent on a kind errand. 2. Christ's works were such as *no man ever did.* No common person that had not a commission from heaven, and God with him, could work miracles, *ch.* iii. 2. And no prophet ever wrought such miracles, so many, so illustrious. Moses and Elias wrought miracles as servants, by a derived power; but Christ, as a Son, by his own power. This was it that amazed the people, that with authority he commanded diseases and devils (Mark i. 27); they owned they never saw the like, Mark ii. 12. They were all good works, works of mercy; and this seems especially intended here, for he is upbraiding them with this, that they hated him. One that was so universally useful, more than ever any man was, one would think, should have been universally beloved, and yet even he is hated. 3. The works of Christ enhance the guilt of sinners' infidelity and enmity to him, to the last degree of wickedness and absurdity. If they had only heard his words, and not seen his works,—if we had only his sermons upon record, and not his miracles, unbelief might have pleaded want of proof; but now it has no excuse. Nay, the rejecting of Christ, both by them and us, has in it the sin, not only of obstinate unbelief, but of base ingratitude. They saw Christ to be most amiable, and studious to do them a kindness; yet they hated him, and studied to do him mischief. And we see in his word that great love wherewith he loved us, and yet are not wrought upon by it.

[2.] That there was no reason at all why they should hate him. Some that at one time will say and do that which is recommending, yet at another time will say and do that which is provoking and disobliging; but our Lord Jesus not only did much to merit men's esteem and good-will, but never did any thing justly to incur their displeasure; this he pleads by quoting a scripture for it (*v.* 25): "*This comes to pass,* this unreasonable hatred of me, and of my disciples for my sake, *that the word might be fulfilled which is written in their law*" (that is, in the Old Testament, which is a law, and was received by them as a law), "*They hated me without a cause;*" this David speaks of himself as a type of Christ, Ps. xxxv. 19; lxix. 4. Note, *First,* Those that hate Christ hate him without any just cause; enmity to Christ is unreasonable enmity. We think those deserve to be hated that are haughty and froward, but Christ is meek and lowly, compassionate and tender; those also that under colour of complaisance are malicious, envious, and revengeful, but Christ devoted himself to the service of those that used him, nay, and of those that abused him; toiled for others' ease, and impoverished himself to enrich us. Those we think hateful that are *hurtful to kings and provinces,* and disturbers of the public peace; but Christ, on the contrary, was the greatest blessing imaginable to his country, and yet was hated. He testified indeed that *their works were evil,* with a design to make them good, but to hate him for this cause was to hate him without cause. *Secondly,* Herein the scripture was fulfilled, and the antitype answered the type. Saul and his courtiers hated David without cause, for he had been serviceable to him with his harp, and with his sword; Absalom and his party hated him, though to him he had been an indulgent father, and to them a great benefactor. Thus was the Son of David hated, and hunted most unjustly. Those that hated Christ did not design there in to fulfil the scripture; but God, in permitting it, had that in his eye; and it confirms our faith in

Christ as the Messiah that even this was foretold concerning him, and, being foretold, was accomplished in him. And we must not think it strange or hard if it have a further accomplishment in us. We are apt to justify our complaints of injuries done us with this, that they are causeless, whereas the more they are so the more they are like the sufferings of Christ, and may be the more easily borne.

3. In Christ the world hates God himself; this is twice said here (*v.* 23): *He that hateth me,* though he thinks his hatred goes no further, yet really he *hates my Father also.* And again, *v.* 24, They have *seen and hated both me and my Father.* Note, (1.) There are those that hate God, notwithstanding the beauty of his nature and the bounty of his providence; they are enraged at his justice, as the devils that believe it and tremble, are vexed at his dominion, and would gladly *break his bands asunder.* Those who cannot bring themselves to deny that there is a God, and yet wish there were none, they see and hate him. (2.) Hatred of Christ will be construed and adjudged hatred of God, for he is in his person his Father's express image, and in his office his great agent and ambassador. God will have all men to honour the Son as they honour the Father, and therefore what entertainment the Son has, that the Father has. Hence it is easy to infer that those who are enemies to the Christian religion, however they may cry up natural religion, are really enemies to all religion. Deists are in effect atheists, and those that ridicule the light of the gospel would, if they could, extinguish even natural light, and shake off all obligations of conscience and the fear of God. Let an unbelieving malignant world know that their enmity to the gospel of Christ will be looked upon in the great day as an enmity to the blessed God himself; and let all that suffer for righteousness' sake, according to the will of God, take comfort from this; if God himself be hated in them, and struck at through him, they need not be either ashamed of their cause or afraid of the issue.

26 But when the Comforter is come, whom I will send unto you from the Father, *even* the Spirit of truth, which proceedeth from the Father, he shall testify of me: 27
And ye also shall bear witness, because ye have been with me from the beginning.

Christ having spoken of the great opposition which his gospel was likely to meet with in the world, and the hardships that would be put upon the preachers of it, lest any should fear that they and it would be run down by that violent torrent, he here intimates to all those that were well-wishers to his cause and interest what effectual provision was made for supporting it, both by the principal testimony of the Spirit (*v.* 26), and the subordinate testimony of the apostles (*v.* 27), and testimonies are the proper supports of truth.

I. It is here promised that the blessed Spirit shall maintain the cause of Christ in the world, notwithstanding the opposition it should meet with. Christ, when he was reviled, committed his injured cause to his Father, and did not lose by his silence, for the Comforter came, pleaded it powerfully, and carried it triumphantly. "*When the Comforter* or Advocate *is come, who proceedeth from the Father,* and *whom I will send* to supply the want of my bodily presence, *he shall testify of me* against those that *hate me without cause.*" We have more in this verse concerning the Holy Ghost than in any one verse besides in the Bible; and, being baptized into his name, we are concerned to acquaint ourselves with him as far as he is revealed.

1. Here is an account of him in his essence, or subsistence rather. He is *the Spirit of truth, who proceedeth from the Father.* Here, (1.) He is spoken of as a distinct person; not a quality or property, but a person under the proper name of a *Spirit,* and proper title of the *Spirit of truth,* a title fitly given him where he is brought in testifying. (2.) As a divine person, that *proceedeth from the Father,* by out-goings that were of old, *from everlasting.* The spirit or breath of man, called the *breath of life,* proceeds from the man, and by it modified he delivers his mind, by it invigorated he sometimes exerts his strength to *blow out* what he would extinguish, and *blow up* what he would excite. Thus the blessed Spirit is the emanation of divine light, and the energy of divine power. The rays of the sun, by which it dispenses and diffuses its light, heat, and influence, proceed from the sun, and yet are one with it. The *Nicene* Creed says, The Spirit *proceedeth from the Father and the Son,* for he is called the *Spirit of the Son,* Gal. iv. 6. And the Son is here said to *send him.* The Greek church choose rather to say, *from the Father by the Son.*

2. In his mission. (1.) He will come in a more plentiful effusion of his gifts, graces, and powers, than had ever yet been. Christ had been long the ὁ ἐρχόμενος—*he that should come;* now the blessed Spirit is so. (2.) *I will send him to you from the Father.* He had said (*ch.* xiv. 16), *I will pray the Father, and he shall send you the Comforter,* which bespeaks the Spirit to be the fruit of the intercession Christ makes within the veil: here he says, *I will send him,* which bespeaks him to be the fruit of his dominion within the veil. The Spirit was sent, [1.] By Christ as Mediator, now *ascended on high* to *give gifts unto men,* and all power being given to him. [2.] From the Father: "Not only from heaven, my Father's house" (the Spirit was given in a *sound from heaven,* Acts ii. 2), "but according to my Father's will and appointment, and with his concurring power

and authority." [3.] To the apostles to instruct them in their preaching, enable them for working, and carry them through their sufferings. He was given to them and their successors, both in Christianity and in the ministry; to them and their seed, and their seed's seed, according to that promise, Isa. lix. 21.

3. In his office and operations, which are two:—(1.) One implied in the title given to him; he is the *Comforter*, or *Advocate*. An advocate for Christ, to maintain his cause against the world's infidelity, a comforter to the saints against the world's hatred. (2.) Another expressed: *He shall testify of me.* He is not only an advocate, but a witness for Jesus Christ; he is one of the three that *bear record in heaven*, and the first of the three that *bear witness on earth*, 1 John v. 7, 8. He instructed the apostles, and enabled them to work miracles; he indited the scriptures, which are the standing witnesses that *testify of Christ, ch.* v. 39. The power of the ministry is derived from the Spirit, for he qualifies ministers; and the power of Christianity too, for he sanctifies Christians, and in both testifies of Christ.

II. It is here promised that the apostles also, by the Spirit's assistance, should have the honour of being Christ's witnesses (*v.* 27): *And you also shall bear witness* of me, being competent witnesses, for *you have been with* me from the beginning of my ministry. Observe here,

1. That the apostles were appointed to be witnesses for Christ in the world. When he had said, *The Spirit shall testify*, he adds, *And you also shall bear witness.* Note, The Spirit's working is not to supersede, but to engage and encourage ours. Though the Spirit testify, ministers also must bear their testimony, and people attend to it; for the Spirit of grace witnesses and works by the means of grace. The apostles were the first witnesses that were called in the famous trial between Christ and the prince of this world, which issued in the ejectment of the intruder. This intimates, (1.) The work cut out for them; they were to attest the truth, the whole truth, and nothing but the truth, concerning Christ, for the recovering of his just right, and the maintaining of his crown and dignity. Though Christ's disciples fled when they should have been witnesses for him upon his trial before the high priest and Pilate, yet after the Spirit was poured out upon them they appeared courageous in vindication of the cause of Christ against the accusations it was loaded with. The truth of the Christian religion was to be proved very much by the evidence of matter of fact, especially Christ's resurrection, of which the apostles were in a particular manner chosen witnesses (Acts x. 41), and they bore their testimony accordingly, Acts iii. 15; v. 32. Christ's ministers are his witnesses. (2.) The honour put upon them hereby—that they should be *workers together with God.* "The *Spirit shall testify of me*, and you also, under the conduct of the Spirit, and in concurrence with the Spirit (who will preserve you from mistaking in that which you relate on your own knowledge, and will inform you of that which you cannot know but by revelation), *shall bear witness.*" This might encourage them against the hatred and contempt of the world, that Christ had honoured them, and would own them.

2. That they were qualified to be so: *You have been with me from the beginning.* They not only heard his public sermons, but had constant private converse with him. He *went about doing good*, and, while others saw the wonderful and merciful works that he did in their own town and country only, those that went about with him were witnesses of them all. They had likewise opportunity of observing the unspotted purity of his conversation, and could witness for him that they never saw in him, nor heard from him, any thing that had the least tincture of human frailty. Note. (1.) We have great reason to receive the record which the apostles gave of Christ, for they did not speak by hearsay, but what they had the greatest assurance of imaginable, 2 Pet. i. 16; 1 John i. 1, 3. (2.) Those are best able to bear witness for Christ that have themselves been with him, by faith, hope, and love, and by living a life of communion with God in him. Ministers must first learn Christ, and then preach him. Those speak best of the things of God that speak experimentally. It is particularly a great advantage to have been acquainted with Christ *from the beginning*, to understand all things from the *very first*, Luke i. 3. To have been with him from the beginning of our days. An early acquaintance and constant converse with the gospel of Christ will make a man like a good householder.

CHAP. XVI.

Among other glorious things God hath spoken of himself this is one, I wound, and I heal, Deut. 32, 39. Christ's discourse in this chapter, which continues and concludes his farewell sermon to his disciples, does so. I. Here are wounding words in the notice he gives them of the troubles that were before them, ver. 1–6. II. Here are healing words in the comforts he administers to them for their support under those troubles, which are five:—1. That he would send them the Comforter, ver. 7—15. 2. That he would visit them again at his resurrection, ver. 16—22. 3. That he would secure to them an answer of peace to all their prayers, ver. 23—27. 4. That he was now but returning to his Father, ver. 28—32. 5. That, whatever troubles they might meet with in this world, by virtue of his victory over it they should be sure of peace in him, ver. 33.

THESE things have I spoken unto you, that ye should not be offended. 2 They shall put you out of
the synagogue: yea, the time cometh,
that whosoever killeth you will think
that he doeth God service. 3 And
these things will they do unto you,
because they have not known the
Father, nor me. 4 But these things
have I told you, that when the time

shall come, ye may remember that I
told you of them. And these things
I said not unto you at the beginning,
because I was with you. 5 But now I
go my way to him that sent me; and
none of you asketh me, Whither goest
thou? 6 But because I have said
these things unto you, sorrow hath
filled your heart.

Christ dealt faithfully with his disciples when he sent them forth on his errands, for he told them the worst of it, that they might sit down and count the cost. He had told them in the chapter before to expect the world's hatred; now here in these verses,

I. He gives them a reason why he alarmed them thus with the expectation of trouble: *These things have I spoken unto you, that you should not be offended*, or *scandalized*, *v.* 1. 1. The disciples of Christ are apt to be offended at the cross; and the offence of the cross is a dangerous temptation, even to good men, to turn back from the ways of God, or turn aside out of them, or drive on heavily in them; to quit either their integrity or their comfort. It is not for nothing that a suffering time is called *an hour of temptation.* 2. Our Lord Jesus, by giving us notice of trouble, designed to take off the terror of it, that it might not be a surprise to us. Of all the adversaries of our peace, in this world of troubles, none insult us more violently, nor put our troops more into disorder, than disappointment does; but we can easily welcome a guest we expect, and *being forewarned are fore-armed—Præmoniti, præmuniti.*

II. He foretels particularly what they should suffer (*v.* 2): "Those that have power to do it shall *put you out of their synagogues;* and this is not the worst, *they shall kill you.*" *Ecce duo gladii—Behold two swords* drawn against the followers of the Lord Jesus.

1. The sword of ecclesiastical censure; this is drawn against them by the Jews, for they were the only pretenders to church-power. They shall *cast you out of their synagogues; ἀποσυναγώγους ποιήσουσιν ὑμᾶς—they shall make you excommunicates.* (1.) "They shall cast you out of the particular synagogues you were members of." At first, they scourged them in their synagogues as contemners of the law (Matt. x. 17), and at length cast them out as incorrigible. (2.) "They shall cast you out of the congregation of Israel in general, the national church of the Jews; shall debar you from the privileges of that, put you into the condition of an outlaw," *qui caput gerit lupinum—to be knocked on the head, like another wolf;* "they will look upon you as Samaritans, as heathen men and publicans." *Interdico tibi aqua et igne—I forbid you the use of water and fire.* And were it not for the penalties, forfeitures, and incapacities, incurred hereby, it would be no injury to be thus driven out of a house infected and falling. Note, It has often been the lot of Christ's disciples to be unjustly excommunicated. Many a good truth has been branded with an anathema, and many a child of God *delivered to Satan.*

2. The sword of civil power: "The time cometh, *the hour is come;* now things are likely to be worse with you than hitherto they have been; when you are expelled as heretics, they will *kill you, and think they do God service*, and others will think so too." (1.) You will find them really cruel: They will *kill you.* Christ's sheep have been accounted as sheep for the slaughter; the twelve apostles (we are told) were all put to death, except John. Christ had said (*ch* 15, 27), You shall *bear witness, μαρτυρεῖτε—you shall be martyrs*, shall seal the truth with your blood, your heart's blood. (2.) You will find them *seemingly conscientious;* they will think they do God service; they will seem *λατρεῖαν προσφέρειν—to offer a good sacrifice* to God; as those that cast out God's servants of old, and said, *Let the Lord be glorified*, Isa. lxvi. 5. Note, [1.] It is possible for those that are real enemies to God's service to pretend a mighty zeal for it. The devil's work has many a time been done in God's livery, and one of the most mischievous enemies Christianity ever had sits *in the temple of God.* Nay, [2.] It is common to patronise an enmity to religion with a colour of duty to God, and service to his church. God's people have suffered the greatest hardships from conscientious persecutors. Paul verily thought he *ought to do* what he did *against the name of Jesus.* This does not at all lessen the sin of the persecutors, for villanies will never be consecrated by putting the name of God to them; but it does enhance the sufferings of the persecuted, to die under the character of being enemies to God; but there will be a resurrection of names as well as of bodies at the great day.

III. He gives them the true reason of the world's enmity and rage against them (*v.* 3): "*These things will they do unto you,* not because you have done them any harm, but *because they have not known the Father, nor me.* Let this comfort you, that none will be your enemies but the worst of men." Note, 1. Many that pretend to know God are wretchedly ignorant of him. Those that pretended to *do him service* thought they knew him, but it was a wrong notion they had of him. Israel transgressed the covenant, and yet cried, *My God, we know thee,* Hos. viii. 1, 2. 2. Those that are ignorant of Christ cannot have any right knowledge of God. In vain do men pretend to know God and religion, while they slight Christ and Christianity. 3. Those are very ignorant indeed of God and Christ that think it an acceptable piece of service to persecute good people. Those that know Christ know that he *came not into the world to destroy men's lives, but to save them;* that he rules by the power of truth and love, not of fire and sword. Never was such a persecuting church as that which makes *ignorance the mother of devotion.*

IV. He tells them why he gave them notice of this now, and why not sooner.

1. Why he told them of it now (*v.* 4), not to discourage them, or add to their present sorrow; nor did he tell them of their danger that they might contrive how to avoid it, but that, "when *the time shall come* (and you may be sure it will come), you may *remember that I told you.*" Note, When suffering times come it will be of use to us to remember what Christ has told us of sufferings. (1.) That our belief of Christ's foresight and faithfulness may be confirmed; and, (2.) That the trouble may be the less grievous, for we were told of it before, and we took up our profession in expectation of it, so that it ought not to be a surprise to us, nor looked upon as a wrong to us. As Christ in his sufferings, so his followers in theirs, should have an eye to the *fulfilling of the scripture.*

2. Why he did not tell them of it sooner: "*I spoke not this to you from the beginning* when you and I came to be first acquainted, because *I was with you.* (1.) While he was with them, he bore the shock of the world's malice, and stood in the front of the battle; against him the powers of darkness levelled all their force, not against *small or great,* but only against the *king of Israel,* and therefore he did not need then to say so much to them of suffering, because it did not fall much to their share; but we do find that from the beginning he bade them prepare for sufferings; and therefore, (2.) It seems rather to be meant of the promise of *another comforter.* This he had said little of to them *at the beginning,* because he was himself with them to instruct, guide, and comfort them, and then they needed not the promise of the Spirit's extraordinary presence. The children of the bride-chamber would not have so much need of a comforter till the bridegroom should be *taken away.*

V. He expresses a very affectionate concern for the present sadness of his disciples, upon occasion of what he had said to them (*v.* 5, 6): "*Now* I am to be no longer with you, but *go my way to him that sent me,* to repose there, after this fatigue; and *none of you asketh me,* with any courage, *Whither goest thou?* But, instead of enquiring after that which would comfort you, you pore upon that which looks melancholy, and *sorrow has filled your heart.*"

1. He had told them that he was about to leave them: *Now I go my way.* He was not driven away by force, but voluntarily departed; his life was not extorted from him, but deposited by him. He went *to him that sent him,* to give an account of his negociation. Thus, when we depart out of this world, we *go to him that sent us* into it, which should make us all solicitous to live to good purposes, remembering we have a commission to execute, which must be returned at a certain day.

2. He had told them what hard things they must suffer when he was gone, and that they must not expect such an easy quiet life as they had had. Now, if these were the legacies he had to leave to them, who had *left all* for him, they would be tempted to think they had made a sorry bargain of it, and were, for the present, in a consternation about it, in which their Master sympathizes with them, yet blames them, (1.) That they were careless of the means of comfort, and did not stir up themselves to seek it: *None of you asks me, Whither goest thou?* Peter had started this question (*ch.* xiii. 36), and Thomas had seconded it (*ch.* xiv. 5), but they did not pursue it, they did not take the answer; they were in the dark concerning it, and did not enquire further, nor seek for fuller satisfaction; they did not continue seeking, continue knocking. See what a compassionate teacher Christ is, and how condescending to the weak and ignorant. Many a teacher will not endure that the learner should ask the same question twice; if he cannot take a thing quickly, let him go without it; but our Lord Jesus knows how to deal with babes, that must be taught with *precept upon precept.* If the disciples here would have pushed on that enquiry, they would have found that his going away was for his advancement, and therefore his departure from them should not inordinately trouble them (for why should they be against his preferment?) and for their advantage, and therefore their sufferings for him should not inordinately trouble them; for a sight of *Jesus at the right hand of God* would be an effectual support to them, as it was to Stephen. Note, A humble believing enquiry into the design and tendency of the darkest dispensations of Providence would help to reconcile us to them, and to grieve the less, and fear the less, because of them; it will silence us to ask, Whence come they? but will abundantly satisfy us to ask, Whither go they? for we know they *work for good,* Rom. viii. 28.

(2.) That they were too intent, and pored too much, upon the occasions of their grief: *Sorrow has filled their hearts.* Christ had said enough to fill them with joy (*ch.* xv. 11); but by looking at that only which made against them, and overlooking that which made for them, they were so full of sorrow that there was no room left for joy. Note, It is the common fault and folly of melancholy Christians to dwell only upon the dark side of the cloud, to meditate nothing but terror, and turn a deaf ear to *the voice of joy and gladness.* That which filled the disciples' hearts with sorrow, and hindered the operation of the cordials Christ administered, was too great an affection to this present life. They were big with hopes of their Master's external kingdom and glory, and that they should shine and reign with him: and now, instead of that, to hear of nothing but bonds and afflictions, this filled them with sorrow. Nothing is a greater prejudice to our joy in God than *the love of the world;* and *the sorrow of the world,* the consequence of it.

7 Nevertheless I tell you the truth;
It is expedient for you that I go
away: for if I go not away, the Comforter will not come unto you; but if
I depart, I will send him unto you. 8
And when he is come, he will reprove
the world of sin, and of righteousness,
and of judgment: 9 Of sin, because
they believe not on me; 10 Of
righteousness, because I go to my
Father, and ye see me no more; 11
Of judgment, because the prince of
this world is judged. 12 I have yet
many things to say unto you, but ye
cannot bear them now. 13 Howbeit when he, the Spirit of truth, is
come, he will guide you into all truth:
for he shall not speak of himself; but
whatsoever he shall hear, *that* shall
he speak: and he will show you
things to come. 14 He shall glorify
me: for he shall receive of mine, and
shall show *it* unto you. 15 All things
that the Father hath are mine: therefore said I, that he shall take of mine,
and shall show *it* unto you.

As it was usual with the Old-Testament prophets to comfort the church in its calamities with the promise of the Messiah (Isa. ix. 6; Mic. v. 6; Zech. iii. 8); so, the Messiah being come, the promise of the Spirit was the great cordial, and is still.

Three things we have here concerning *the Comforter's coming:*—

I. That Christ's departure was absolutely necessary to the Comforter's coming, *v.* 7. The disciples were so loth to believe this that Christ saw cause to assert it with a more than ordinary solemnity: *I tell you the truth.* We may be confident of *the truth* of every thing that Christ has told us; he has no design to impose upon us. Now, to make them easy, he here tells them,

1. In general, *It was expedient for them that he should go away.* This was strange doctrine, but if it was true it was comfortable enough, and showed them how absurd their sorrow was. *It is expedient,* not only for me, but *for you* also, *that I go away;* though they do not see it, and are loth to believe it, so it is. Note, (1.) Those things often seem grievous to us that are really expedient for us; and particularly our going away when we have finished our course. (2.) Our Lord Jesus is always for that which is most expedient for us, whether we think so or no. He deals not with us according to the folly of our own choice, but graciously over-rules it, and gives us the physic we are loth to take, because he knows it is good for us.

2. *It was therefore expedient* because it was in order to the sending of the Spirit. Now observe,

(1.) That Christ's going was in order to the Comforter's coming.

[1.] This is expressed negatively: *If I go not away, the Comforter will not come.* And why not? *First,* So it was settled in the divine counsels concerning this affair, and the measure must not be altered; *shall the earth be forsaken for them?* He that gives freely may recal one gift before he bestows another, while we would fondly hold all. *Secondly,* It is congruous enough that the ambassador extraordinary should be recalled, before the envoy come, that is constantly to reside. *Thirdly,* The sending of the Spirit was to be the fruit of Christ's purchase, and that purchase was to be made by his death, which was his going away. *Fourthly,* It was to be an answer to his intercession within the veil. See *ch.* xiv. 16. Thus must this gift be both paid for, and prayed for, by our Lord Jesus, that we might learn to put the greater value upon it. *Fifthly,* The great argument the Spirit was to use in convincing the world must be Christ's ascension into heaven, and his welcome there. See *v.* 10, and *ch.* vii. 39. *Lastly,* The disciples must be weaned from his bodily presence, which they were too apt to dote upon, before they were duly prepared to receive the spiritual aids and comforts of a new dispensation.

[2.] It is expressed positively: *If I depart I will send him to you;* as though he had said, "Trust me to provide effectually that you shall be no loser by my departure." The glorified Redeemer is not unmindful of his church on earth, nor will ever leave it without its necessary supports. Though he *departs, he sends the Comforter;* nay, he departs on purpose to send him. Thus still, though one generation of ministers and Christians depart, another is raised up in their room, for Christ will maintain his own cause.

(2.) That the presence of Christ's Spirit in his church is so much better, and more desirable, than his bodily presence, that it was really expedient for us that he should go away, to send the Comforter. His corporal presence could be but in one place at one time, but his Spirit is every where, in all places, at all times, wherever *two or three are gathered in his name.* Christ's bodily presence draws men's eyes, his Spirit draws their hearts; that was *the letter* which *kills,* his *Spirit gives life.*

II. That the coming of *the Spirit* was absolutely necessary to the carrying on of Christ's interests on earth (*v.* 8): *And when he is come,* ἐλθὼν ἐκεῖνος. He that is sent is willing of himself to come, and at his first coming he will do this, *he will reprove,* or, as the margin reads it, *he will convince the world,* by your ministry, concerning *sin, righteousness, and judgment.*

1. See here what the office of the Spirit is, and on what errand he is sent. (1.) To *reprove.* The Spirit, by the word and conscience, is a reprover; ministers are reprovers by office, and by them the Spirit reproves. (2.) To *convince.* It is a law-term, and speaks the office of the judge in summing up the evidence, and setting a matter that has been long canvassed in a clear and true light. He shall *convince*, that is, "He shall put to silence the adversaries of Christ and his cause, by discovering and demonstrating the falsehood and fallacy of that which they have maintained, and the truth and certainty of that which they have opposed." Note, Convincing work is the Spirit's work; he can do it effectually, and none but he; man may open the cause, but it is the Spirit only that can open the heart. The Spirit is called the *Comforter* (*v.* 7), and here it is said, *He shall convince.* One would think this were cold comfort, but it is the method the Spirit takes, first to convince, and then to comfort; first to lay open the wound, and then to apply healing medicines. Or, taking conviction more generally, for a demonstration of what is right, it intimates that the Spirit's comforts are solid, and grounded upon truth.

2. See who they are whom he is to reprove and convince: *The world*, both Jew and Gentile. (1.) He shall give the world the most powerful means of conviction, for the apostles shall go into all the world, backed by the Spirit, to preach the gospel, fully proved. (2.) He shall sufficiently provide for the taking off and silencing of the objections and prejudices of the world against the gospel. Many an infidel was *convinced of all, and judged of all*, 1 Cor. xiv. 24. (3.) He shall effectually and savingly convince many in the world, some in every age, in every place, in order to their conversion to the faith of Christ. Now this was an encouragement to the disciples, in reference to the difficulties they were likely to meet with, [1.] That they should see good done, Satan's kingdom *fall like lightning*, which would be their joy, as it was his. Even this malignant world the Spirit shall work upon; and the conviction of sinners is the comfort of faithful ministers. [2.] That this would be the fruit of their services and sufferings, these should contribute very much to this good work.

3. See what the Spirit shall convince the world of.

(1.) *Of sin* (*v.* 9), *because they believe not on me.* [1.] The Spirit is sent to convince sinners of sin, not barely to tell them of it; in conviction there is more than this; it is to prove it upon them, and force them to own it, as they (*ch.* viii. 9) that were *convicted of their own consciences. Make them to know their abominations.* The Spirit convinces of the fact of sin, that we have done so and so; of the fault of sin, that we have done ill in doing so; of the folly of sin, that we have acted against right reason, and our true interest; of the filth of sin, that by it we are become odious to God; of the fountain of sin, the corrupt nature; and, lastly, of the fruit of sin, that the end thereof is death. The Spirit demonstrates the depravity and degeneracy of the whole world, that all the world is guilty before God. [2.] The Spirit, in conviction, fastens especially upon the sin of unbelief, their not believing in Christ, *First*, As the great reigning sin. There was, and is, a world of people, that believe not in Jesus Christ, and they are not sensible that it is their sin. Natural conscience tells them that murder and theft are sin; but it is a supernatural work of the Spirit to convince them that it is a sin to suspend their belief of the gospel, and to reject the salvation offered by it. Natural religion, after it has given us its best discoveries and directions, lays and leaves us under this further obligation, that whatever divine revelation shall be made to us at any time, with sufficient evidence to prove it divine, we accept it, and submit to it. This law those transgress who, when *God speaketh to us by his Son, refuse him that speaketh;* and therefore it is sin. *Secondly*, As the great ruining sin. Every sin is so in its own nature; no sin is so to them that believe in Christ; so that it is unbelief that damns sinners. It is because of this that they cannot *enter into rest*, that they cannot *escape the wrath of God;* it is a sin against the remedy. *Thirdly*, As that which is at the bottom of all sin; so Calvin takes it. The Spirit shall convince the world that the true reason why sin reigns among them is because they are not by faith united to Christ. *Ne putimus vel guttam unam rectitudinis sine Christo nobis inesse—Let us not suppose that, apart from Christ, we have a drop of rectitude.*—Calvin.

(2.) *Of righteousness, because I go to my Father, and you see me no more, v.* 10. We may understand this, [1.] Of Christ's personal righteousness. He shall convince the world that Jesus of Nazareth was Christ the righteous (1 John ii. 1), as the centurion owned (Luke xxiii. 47), *Certainly this was a righteous man.* His enemies put him under the worst of characters, and multitudes were not or would not be convinced but that he was a bad man, which strengthened their prejudices against his doctrine; but he is *justified by the Spirit* (1 Tim. iii. 16), he is proved to be a *righteous man*, and not a deceiver; and then the point is in effect gained; for he is either the great Redeemer or a great cheat; but a cheat we are sure he is not. Now by what medium or argument will the Spirit convince men of the sincerity of the Lord Jesus? Why, *First*, Their *seeing him no more* will contribute something towards the removal of their prejudices; they shall see him no more *in the likeness of sinful flesh, in the form of a servant*, which made them slight him. Moses was more respected after his removal than before. But, *Secondly,* His *going to the Father* would be a full conviction of it. The coming of the Spirit, according to the promise, was a proof of Christ's exaltation to God's *right hand* (Acts ii. 33), and this was a demonstration of his righteousness; for the holy God would never set a deceiver at his right hand. [2.] Of Christ's righteousness communicated to us for our justification and salvation; that everlasting righteousness which Messiah was to bring in, Dan. ix. 24. Now, *First,* The Spirit shall convince men of this righteousness. Having by convictions of sin shown them their need of a righteousness, lest this should drive them to despair he will show them where it is to be had, and how they may, upon their believing, be acquitted from guilt, and accepted as righteous in God's sight. It was hard to convince those of this righteousness that *went about to establish their own* (Rom. x. 3), but the Spirit will do it. *Secondly,* Christ's ascension is the great argument proper to convince men of this righteousness: *I go to the Father, and,* as an evidence of my welcome with him, *you shall see me no more.* If Christ had left any part of his undertaking unfinished, he had been sent back again; but now that we are sure he is *at the right hand of God* we are sure of being justified through him.

(3.) *Of judgment, because the prince of this world is judged, v.* 11. Observe here, [1.] The devil, *the prince of this world,* was judged, was discovered to be a great deceiver and destroyer, and as such judgment was entered against him, and execution in part done. He was cast out of the Gentile world when his oracles were silenced and his altars deserted, cast out of the bodies of many in Christ's name, which miraculous power continued long in the church; he was cast out of the souls of people by the grace of God working with the gospel of Christ; he *fell as lightning from heaven.* [2.] This is a good argument wherewith the Spirit convinces the world of judgment, that is, *First,* Of inherent holiness and sanctification, Matt. xii. 18. By *the judgment of the prince of this world,* it appears that Christ is stronger than Satan, and can disarm and dispossess him, and set up his throne upon the ruins of his. *Secondly,* Of a new and better dispensation of things. He shall show that Christ's errand into the world was to set things to right in it, and to introduce times of reformation and regeneration; and he proves it by this, that *the prince of this world,* the great master of misrule, is judged and expelled. All will be well when his power is broken who made all the mischief. *Thirdly,* Of the power and dominion of the Lord Jesus. He shall convince the world that *all judgment is committed to him,* and that he is the *Lord of all,* which is evident by this, that he has judged the prince of this world, has broken *the serpent's head, destroyed him that had the power of death, and spoiled principalities;* if Satan be thus subdued by Christ, we may be sure no other power can stand before him. *Fourthly,* Of the final day of judgment: all the obstinate enemies of Christ's gospel and kingdom shall certainly be reckoned with at last, for the devil, their ringleader, is judged.

III. That the coming of the Spirit would be of unspeakable advantage to the disciples themselves. The Spirit has work to do, not only on the enemies of Christ, to convince and humble them, but upon his servants and agents, to instruct and comfort them; and therefore it was *expedient for them that he should go away.*

1. He intimates to them the tender sense he had of their present weakness (*v.* 12): *I have yet many things to say unto you* (not which should have been said, but which he could and would have said), *but you cannot bear them now.* See what a teacher Christ is. (1.) None like him for copiousness; when he has said much, he has still many things more to say; treasures of wisdom and knowledge are hid in him; we are not straitened in him, if we be not straitened in ourselves. (2.) None like him for compassion; he would have told them more of *the things pertaining to the kingdom of God,* particularly of the rejection of the Jews and the calling of the Gentiles, but they could not bear it, it would have confounded and stumbled them, rather than have given them any satisfaction. When, after his resurrection, they spoke to him of *restoring the kingdom to Israel,* he referred them to *the coming of the Holy Ghost,* by which they should receive power to bear those discoveries which were so contrary to the notions they had received that they could not *bear them now.*

2. He assures them of s fficient assistances, by the pouring out of the Spirit. They were now conscious to themselves of great dulness, and many mistakes; and what shall they do now their Master is leaving them? "*But when he, the Spirit of truth, is come,* you will be easy, and all will be well." Well indeed; for he shall undertake to guide the apostles, and glorify Christ.

(1.) To guide the apostles. He will take care, [1.] That they do not miss their way: *He will guide you;* as the camp of Israel was guided through the wilderness by *the pillar of cloud and fire.* The Spirit guided their tongues in speaking, and their pens in writing, to secure them from mistakes. The Spirit is given us to be our guide (Rom. viii. 14), not only to show us the way, but to go along with us, by his continued aids and influences.

[2.] That they do not come short of their end: *He will guide them into all truth,* as the skilful pilot guides the ship into the port it is bound for. To be led *into a truth* is more than barely to know it; it is to be intimately and experimentally acquainted with it; to be piously and strongly affected with it; not only to have the notion of it in our heads, but the relish and savour and power of it in our hearts; it denotes a gradual discovery of truth shining more and more: "He shall lead you by those truths that are plain and easy to those that are more difficult." But how into *all truth?* The meaning is,

First, Into the whole truth relating to their embassy; whatever was needful or useful for them to know, in order to the due discharge of their office, they should be fully instructed in it; what truths they were to teach others the Spirit would teach them, would give them the understanding of, and enable them both to explain and to defend.

Secondly, Into nothing but the truth. All that *he shall guide you into* shall be *truth* (1 John ii. 27); *the anointing is truth.* In the following words he proves both these:—1. "The Spirit shall teach nothing but the truth, *for he shall not speak of himself* any doctrine distinct from mine, *but whatsoever he shall hear,* and knows to be the mind of the Father, *that,* and that only, *shall he speak.*" This intimates, (1.) That the testimony of the Spirit, in the word and by the apostles, is what we may rely upon. The *Spirit* knows *and searches all things, even the deep things of God,* and the apostles received that Spirit (1 Cor. ii. 10, 11), so that we may venture our souls upon the Spirit's word. (2.) That the testimony of the Spirit always concurs with the word of Christ, *for he does not speak of himself,* has no separate interest or intention of his own, but, as in essence so in records, he *is one with the Father and the Son,* 1 John v. 7. Men's word and spirit often disagree, but the eternal Word and the eternal Spirit never do. 2. "He shall teach you all truth, and keep back nothing that is profitable for you, for *he will show you things to come.*" The Spirit was in the apostles a Spirit of prophecy; it was foretold that he should be so (Joel ii. 28), and he was so. *The Spirit showed them things to come,* as Acts xi. 28; xx. 23; xxi. 11. The Spirit spoke of the apostasy of the *latter times,* 1 Tim. iv. 1. John, when he was in the Spirit, had *things to come* shown him in vision. Now this was a great satisfaction to their own minds, and of use to them in their conduct, and was also a great confirmation of their mission. Jansenius has a pious note upon this: We should not grudge that the Spirit does not now *show us things to come* in this world, as he did to the apostles; let it suffice that the Spirit in the word hath *shown us things to come* in the other world, which are our chief concern.

(2.) The Spirit undertook to glorify Christ, *v.* 14, 15. [1.] Even the sending of the Spirit was the glorifying of Christ. God the Father glorified him in heaven, and the Spirit glorified him on earth. It was the honour of the Redeemer that the Spirit was both sent in his name and sent on his errand, to carry on and perfect his undertaking. All the gifts and graces of the Spirit, all the preaching and all the writing of the apostles, under the influence of the Spirit, the tongues, and miracles, were to glorify Christ. [2.] The Spirit glorified Christ by leading his followers into *the truth as it is in Jesus,* Eph. iv. 21. He assures them, *First,* That the Spirit should communicate the things of Christ to them: *He shall receive of mine, and shall show it unto you.* As in essence *he proceeded from the Son,* so in influence and operation he derives from him. *He shall take* ἐκ τοῦ ἐμοῦ—*of that which is mine.* All that the Spirit shows us, that is, applies to us, for our instruction and comfort, all that he gives us for our strength and quickening, and all that he secures and seals to us, did all belong to Christ, and was had and received from him. All was his, for he bought it, and paid dearly for it, and therefore he had reason to call it his own; his, for he first received it; it was given him as the head of the church, to be communicated by him to all his members. The Spirit came not to erect a new kingdom, but to advance and establish the same kingdom that Christ had erected, to maintain the same interest and pursue the same design; those therefore that pretend to the Spirit, and vilify Christ, give themselves the lie, for he came to glorify Christ. *Secondly,* That herein the things of God should be communicated to us. Lest any should think that the receiving of this would not make them much the richer, he adds, *All things that the Father hath are mine.* As God, all that self-existent light and self-sufficient happiness which *the Father has,* he has; as Mediator, *all things are delivered to him of the Father* (Matt. xi. 27); all that *grace and truth* which God designed to show to us he lodged in the hands of the Lord Jesus, Col. i. 19. Spiritual blessings in heavenly things are given by the Father to the Son for us, and the Son entrusts the Spirit to convey them to us. Some apply it to that which goes just before: *He shall show you things to come,* and so it is explained by Rev. i. 1. God gave *it to Christ, and he signified it to John, who wrote what the Spirit said,* Rev. i. 1.

16 A little while, and ye shall not
see me: and again, a little while, and
ye shall see me, because I go to the
Father. 17 Then said *some* of his disciples among themselves, What is this
that he saith unto us, A little while,
and ye shall not see me: and again,
a little while, and ye shall see me:
and, Because I go to the Father? 18
They said therefore, What is this that
he saith, A little while? we cannot tell
what he saith. 19 Now Jesus knew
that they were desirous to ask him,

and said unto them, Do ye enquire
among yourselves of that I said, A
little while, and ye shall not see me:
and again, a little while, and ye shall
see me? 20 Verily, verily, I say unto you, That ye shall weep and lament, but the world shall rejoice:
and ye shall be sorrowful, but your
sorrow shall be turned into joy. 21
A woman when she is in travail hath
sorrow, because her hour is come:
but as soon as she is delivered of the
child, she remembereth no more the
anguish, for joy that a man is born
into the world. 22 And ye now therefore have sorrow: but I will see you
again, and your heart shall rejoice,
and your joy no man taketh from you.

Our Lord Jesus, for the comfort of his sorrowful disciples, here promises that he would visit them again.

I. Observe the intimation he gave them of the comfort he designed them, *v.* 16. Here he tells them,

1. That they should now shortly lose the sight of him: *A little while, and you* that have seen me so long, and still desire to *see me, shall not see me;* and therefore, if they had any good question to ask him, they must ask quickly, for he was now taking his leave of them. Note, It is good to consider how near to a period our seasons of grace are, that we may be quickened to improve them while they are continued. Now our eyes see our teachers, see the days *of the Son of man;* but, perhaps, yet *a little while, and we shall not see them.* They lost the sight of Christ, (1.) At his death, when he withdrew from this world, and never after showed himself openly in it. The most that death does to our Christian friends is to take them out of our sight, not out of being, not out of bliss, not out of all relation to us, only out of sight, and then not out of mind. (2.) At his ascension, when he withdrew from them (from those who, after his resurrection, had for some time conversed with him), *out of their sight; a cloud received* him, and, though they looked up stedfastly after him, *they saw him no more,* Acts i. 9, 10; 2 Kings ii. 12. See 2 Cor. v. 16.

2. That yet they should speedily recover the sight of him: *Again a little while, and you shall see me,* and therefore you ought not to *sorrow as those that have no hope.* His farewell was not a final farewell; they should see him again, (1.) At his resurrection, soon after his death, when *he showed himself alive,* by many infallible proofs, and this in a very little while, not forty hours. See Hos. vi. 2. (2.) By the pouring out of the Spirit, soon after his ascension, which scattered the mists of ignorance and mistake they were almost lost in, and gave them a much clearer insight into the mysteries of Christ's gospel than they had yet had. The Spirit's coming was Christ's visit to his disciples, not a transient but a permanent one, and such a visit as abundantly retrieved the sight of him. (3.) At his second coming. They saw him again as they removed one by one to him at death, and they shall all see him together at the end of time, when *he shall come in the clouds, and every eye shall see him.* It might be truly said of this that it was but *a little while, and they should see him;* for what are the days of time, to the days of eternity? 2 Pet. iii. 8, 9.

3. He assigns the reason: "*Because I go to the Father;* and therefore," (1.) "I must leave you for a time, because my business calls me to the upper world, and you must be content to spare me, for really my business is yours." (2.) "Therefore you shall see me again shortly, for the Father will not detain me to your prejudice. If I go upon your errand, you shall see me again as soon as my business is done, as soon as is convenient."

It should seem, all this refers rather to his going away at death, and return at his resurrection, than his going away at his ascension, and his return at the end of time; for it was his death that was their grief, not his ascension (Luke xxiv. 52), and between his death and resurrection it was indeed a *little while.* And it may be read, not, *yet a little while* (it is not ἔτι μικρὸν, as it is *ch.* xii. 35), but μικρὸν—*for a little while you shall not see me,* namely, the three days of his lying in the grave; and again, *for a little while you shall see me,* namely, the forty days between his resurrection and ascension. Thus we may say of our ministers and Christian friends, *Yet a little while, and we shall not see them,* either they must leave us or we must leave them, but it is certain that we must part shortly, and yet not part for ever. It is but a good night to those whom we hope to see with *joy in the morning.*

II. The perplexity of the disciples upon the intimation given them; they were at a loss what to make of it (*v.* 17, 18): *Some of them said,* softly, *among themselves,* either some of the weakest, that were least able, or some of the most inquisitive, that were most desirous, to understand him, *What is this that he saith to us?* Though Christ had often spoken to this purport before, yet still they were in the dark; though *precept be upon precept,* it is in vain, unless God give the understanding. Now see here, 1. The disciples' weakness, in that they could not understand so plain a saying, to which Christ had already given them a key, having told them so often in plain terms that he should *be killed, and the third day rise again;* yet, say they, *We cannot tell what he saith;* for, (1.) *Sorrow had filled their heart,* and made them unapt to receive the impressions of comfort. The darkness of ignorance and the darkness of melancholy commonly increase and thicken one another; mistakes cause griefs, and then griefs confirm mistakes. (2.) The notion of Christ's secular kingdom was so deeply rooted in them that they could make no sense at all of those sayings of his which they knew not how to reconcile with that notion. When we think the scripture must be made to agree with the false ideas we have imbibed, no wonder that we complain of its difficulty; but, when our reasonings are captivated to revelation, the matter becomes easy. (3.) It should seem, that which puzzled them was the *little while.* If he must go at last, yet they could not conceive how he should leave them quickly, when his stay hitherto had been so short, and so little while, comparatively. Thus it is hard for us to represent to ourselves that change as near which yet we know will come certainly, and may come suddenly. When we are told, *Yet a little while* and we must go hence, *yet a little while* and we must *give up our account,* we know not how to digest it; for we always took the vision to be *for a great while to come,* Ezek. xii. 27. 2. Their willingness to be instructed. When they were at a loss about the meaning of Christ's words, they conferred together upon it, and asked help of one another. By mutual converse about divine things we both borrow the light of others and improve our own. Observe how exactly they repeat Christ's words. Though we cannot fully solve every difficulty we meet with in scripture, yet we must not therefore throw it by, but revolve what we cannot explain, and wait *till God shall reveal even this unto us.*

III. The further explication of what Christ had said.

1. See here *why* Christ explained it (*v.* 19); because he *knew they were desirous to ask him,* and designed it. Note, The knots we cannot untie we must bring to him who alone can give an understanding. Christ *knew they were desirous to ask him,* but were bashful and ashamed to ask. Note, Christ takes cognizance of pious desires, though they be not as yet offered up, the *groanings that cannot be uttered,* and even *anticipates them with the blessings of his goodness.* Christ instructed those who he *knew were desirous to ask him,* though they did not ask. *Before we call, he answers.* Another reason why Christ explained it was because he observed them canvassing this matter among themselves: "*Do you enquire this among yourselves?* Well, I will make it easy to you." This intimates to us who they are that Christ will teach: (1.) The humble, that confess their ignorance, for so much their enquiry implied. (2.) The diligent, that use the means they have: "*Do you enquire?* You shall be taught. *To him that hath shall be given.*"

2. See here *how* he explained it; not by a nice and critical descant upon the words, but by bringing the thing more closely to them; he had told them of *not seeing him, and seeing him,* and they did not apprehend his meaning, and therefore he explains it by their sorrowing and rejoicing, because we commonly measure things according as they affect us (*v.* 20): *You shall weep and lament,* for my departure, *but the world shall rejoice* in it; *and you shall be sorrowful,* while I am absent, *but,* upon my return to you, *your sorrow will be turned into joy.* But he says nothing of the *little while,* because he saw that this perplexed them more than any thing; and it is of no consequence to us to know *the times and the seasons.* Note, Believers have joy or sorrow according as they have or have not a sight of Christ, and the tokens of his presence with them.

(1.) What Christ says here, and *v.* 21, 22, of their sorrow and joy, is primarily to be understood of the present state and circumstances of the disciples, and so we have,

[1.] Their grief foretold: *You shall weep and lament, and you shall be sorrowful.* The sufferings of Christ could not but be the sorrow of his disciples. They wept for him because they loved him; the pain of our friend is a pain to ourselves; when they slept, it was for sorrow, Luke xxii. 45. They wept for themselves, and their own loss, and the sad apprehensions they had of what would become of them when he was gone. It could not but be a grief to lose him for whom they had left their all, and from whom they expected so much. Christ has given notice to his disciples beforehand to expect sorrow, that they may treasure up comforts accordingly.

[2.] The world's rejoicing at the same time: *But the world shall rejoice.* That which is the grief of saints is the joy of sinners. *First,* Those that are *strangers to Christ* will continue in their carnal mirth, and not at all interest themselves in their sorrows. *It is nothing to them that pass by,* Lam. i. 12. Nay, *Secondly,* Those that are *enemics to Christ* will rejoice because they hope they have conquered him, and ruined his interest. When the chief priests had Christ upon the cross, we may suppose they made merry over him, as those that dwell on earth over the slain witnesses, Rev. xi. 10. Let it be no surprise to us if we see others triumphing, when we are *trembling for the ark.*

[3.] The return of joy to them in due time: *But your sorrow shall be turned into joy.* As *the joy of the hypocrite,* so the sorrow of the true Christian, *is but for a moment. The disciples were glad when they saw the Lord.* His resurrection was *life from the dead* to them, and their sorrow for Christ's sufferings was turned into a joy of such a nature as could not be damped and embittered by any sufferings of their own. They were *sorrowful, and yet always rejoicing* (2 Cor. vi. 10), had sorrowful lives and yet joyful hearts.

(2.) It is applicable to all the faithful followers of the Lamb, and describes the common case of Christians

[1.] Their condition and disposition are both mournful; sorrows are their lot, and seriousness is their temper: those that are acquainted with Christ must, as he was, be *acquainted with grief;* they *weep and lament* for that which others make light of, their own sins, and the sins of those about them; they mourn with sufferers that mourn, and mourn for sinners that mourn not for themselves.

[2.] The world, at the same time, goes away with all the mirth; they laugh now, and spend their days so jovially that one would think they neither knew sorrow nor feared it. Carnal mirth and pleasures are surely none of the best things, for then the worst men would not have so large a share of them, and the favourites of heaven be such strangers to them.

[3.] Spiritual mourning will shortly be turned into eternal rejoicing. *Gladness is sown for the upright in heart, that sow in tears,* and without doubt *they will* shortly *reap in joy.* Their sorrow will not only be followed with joy, but turned into it; for the most precious comforts take rise from pious griefs. This he illustrates by a similitude taken from a woman in travail, to whose sorrows he compares those of his disciples, for their encouragement; for it is the will of Christ that his people should be a comforted people.

First, Here is the similitude or parable itself (*v.* 21): *A woman,* we know, *when she is in travail, hath sorrow,* she is in exquisite pain, *because her hour is come,* the hour which nature and providence have fixed, which she has expected, and cannot escape; *but as soon as she is delivered of the child,* provided she be safely delivered, and the child be, though a *Jabez* (1 Chron. iv. 9), yet not a *Benoni* (Gen. xxxv. 18), then *she remembers no more the anguish,* her groans and complaints are all over, and the after-pains are more easily borne, *for joy that a man is born into the world; ἄνθρωπος,* one of the human race, a child, be it son or daughter, for the word signifies either. Observe,

a. The fruit of the curse, in the sorrow and pain of a woman in travail, according to the sentence (Gen. iii. 16), *In sorrow shalt thou bring forth.* These pains are extreme, the greatest griefs and pains are compared to them (Ps. xlviii. 6; Isa. xiii. 8; xxi. 3; Jer. iv. 31; vi. 24), and they are inevitable, 1 Thess. v. 3. See what this world is; all its roses are surrounded with thorns; all the children of men are upon this account foolish children, that they are *the heaviness of her that bore them* from the very first. This comes of sin.

b. The fruit of the blessing, in *the joy there is for a child born into the world.* If God had not preserved the blessing in force after the fall, *Be fruitful and multiply,* parents could never have looked upon their children with any comfort; but what is the fruit of a blessing is matter of joy; the birth of a living child is, (*a.*) The parents' joy; it makes them very glad, Jer. xx. 15. Though children are certain cares, uncertain comforts, and often prove the greatest crosses, yet it is natural to us to rejoice at their birth. Could we be sure that our children, like John, would *be filled with the Holy Ghost,* we might, indeed, like his parents, have *joy and gladness* in their birth, Luke i. 14, 15. But when we consider, not only that they are born in sin, but, as it is here expressed, that *they are born into the world,* a world of snares and a vale of tears, we shall see reason to rejoice with trembling, lest it should prove *better for them that they had never been born.* (*b.*) It is such joy as makes the anguish not to be remembered, or *remembered as waters that pass away,* Job xi. 16. *Hæc olim meminisse juvabit.* Gen. xli. 51. Now this is very proper to set forth, [*a.*] The sorrows of Christ's disciples in this world; they are like travailing pains, sure and sharp, but not to last long, and in order to a joyful product; they are in *pain to be delivered,* as the church is described (Rev. xii. 2), and *the whole creation,* Rom. viii. 22. And, [*b.*] Their joys after these sorrows, which will *wipe away all tears,* for *the former things are passed away,* Rev. xxi. 4. When they are born into that blessed world, and reap the fruit of all their services and sorrows, the toil and anguish of this world will be no more remembered, as Christ's were not, when *he saw of the travail of his soul* abundantly to his satisfaction, Isa. liii. 11.

Secondly, The application of the similitude (*v.* 22): "*You now have sorrow,* and are likely to have more, *but I will see you again,* and you me, and then all will be well."

a. Here again he tells them of their *sorrow:* "*You now therefore have sorrow; therefore,* because I am leaving you," as is intimated in the antithesis, *I will see you again.* Note, Christ's withdrawings are just cause of grief to his disciples. *If he hide his face,* they cannot but be *troubled.* When the sun sets, the sun-flower will hang the head. And Christ takes notice of these griefs, has a bottle for the tears, and a book for the sighs, of all gracious mourners.

b. He, more largely than before, assures them of a return of joy, Ps. xxx. 5, 11. He himself went through his own griefs, and bore ours, *for the joy that was set before him;* and he would have us encourage ourselves with the same prospect. Three things recommend the joy:—(*a.*) The cause of it: "*I will see you again.* I will make you a kind and friendly visit, to enquire after you, and minister comfort to you." Note, [*a.*] Christ will graciously return to those that wait for him, though *for a small moment* he has seemed *to forsake them,* Isa. liv. 7. Men, when they are exalted, will scarcely look upon their inferiors; but the exalted Jesus will visit his disciples. They shall not only see him in his glory, but he will see them in their meanness. [*b.*] Christ's returns are returns of joy to all his disciples. When clouded evidences are cleared up and interrupted communion is revived, *then is the mouth filled with laughter*. (*b.*) The cordiality of it: *Your heart shall rejoice.* Divine consolations *put gladness into the heart.* Joy in the heart is solid, and not flashy; it is secret, and that which a *stranger does not intermeddle with;* it is sweet, and gives a good man satisfaction in himself; it is sure, and not easily broken in upon. Christ's disciples should heartily rejoice in his returns, sincerely and greatly. (*c.*) The continuance of it: *Your joy no man taketh from you.* Men will attempt to take their joy from them; they would if they could; but they shall not prevail. Some understand it of the eternal joy of those that are glorified; those that have *entered into the joy of the Lord shall go no more out.* Our joys on earth we are liable to be robbed of by a thousand accidents, but heavenly joys are everlasting. I rather understand it of the spiritual joys of those that are sanctified, particularly the apostles' joy in their apostleship. *Thanks be to God,* says Paul, in the name of the rest, *who always causes us to triumph,* 2 Cor. ii. 14. A malicious world would have taken it from them; if bonds and banishments, tortures and deaths, could have taken it from them, they would have lost it; but, when they took every thing else from them, they could not take this; *as sorrowful, yet always rejoicing.* They could not rob them of their joy, because they could not *separate them from the love of Christ,* could not rob them of their God, nor of their *treasure in heaven.*

23 And in that day ye shall ask me
nothing. Verily, verily, I say unto
you, Whatsoever ye shall ask the Father in my name, he will give *it* you.
24 Hitherto have ye asked nothing
in my name: ask, and ye shall receive,
that your joy may be full. 25 These
things have I spoken unto you in
proverbs: but the time cometh, when
I shall no more speak unto you in
proverbs, but I shall show you plainly
of the Father. 26 At that day ye shall
ask in my name: and I say not unto
you, that I will pray the Father for
you: 27 For the Father himself
loveth you, because ye have loved me,
and have believed that I came out
from God.

An answer to their askings is here promised, for their further comfort. Now there are two ways of asking: asking by way of enquiry, which is the asking of the ignorant; and asking by way of request, which is the asking of the indigent. Christ here speaks of both.

I. By way of enquiry, they should not need to ask (*v.* 23): "*In that day you shall ask me nothing;*" οὐκ ἐρωτήσετε οὐδὲν—*you shall ask no questions;* "you shall have such a clear knowledge of gospel mysteries, by the opening of your understandings, that you shall not need to enquire" (as Heb. viii. 11, *they shall not teach);* "you shall have more knowledge on a sudden than hitherto you have had by diligent attendance." They had asked some ignorant questions (as *ch.* ix. 2), some ambitious questions (as Matt. xviii. 1), some distrustful ones (as Matt. xix. 27), some impertinent ones (as *ch.* xxi. 21), some curious ones (as Acts i. 6); but, after the Spirit was poured out, nothing of all this. In the story *of the apostles' Acts* we seldom find them asking questions, as David, *Shall I do this?* Or, *Shall I go thither?* For they were constantly under a divine guidance. In that weighty case of preaching *the gospel to the Gentiles,* Peter went, *nothing doubting,* Acts x. 20. Asking questions supposes us at a loss, or at least at a stand, and the best of us have need to ask questions; but we should aim at such a full assurance of understanding that we may not hesitate, but be constantly led in a plain path both of truth and duty.

Now for this he gives a reason (*v.* 25), which plainly refers to this promise, that they should not need to ask questions: "*These things have I spoken unto you in proverbs,* in such a way as you have thought not so plain and intelligible as you could have wished, *but the time cometh when I shall show you plainly,* as plainly as you can desire, *of the Father,* so that you shall not need to ask questions."

1. The great thing Christ would lead them into was the knowledge of God: "*I will show you the Father,* and bring you acquainted with him." This is that which Christ designs to give and which all true Christians desire to have. When Christ would express the greatest favour intended for his disciples, he tells them that he would *show them plainly of the Father;* for what is the happiness of heaven, but immediately and everlastingly to see God? *To know God as the Father of our Lord Jesus Christ* is the greatest mystery for the understanding to please itself with the contemplation of; and to know him as our Father is the greatest happiness for the will and affections to please themselves with the choice and enjoyment of.

2. Of this he had hitherto spoken to them in proverbs, which are wise and instructive sayings, but figurative, and resting in generals. Christ had spoken many things very plainly to them, and expounded his parables privately to the disciples, but, (1.) Considering their dulness, and unaptness to receive what he said to them, he might be said to speak in proverbs; what he said to them was as a book sealed, Isa. xxix. 11. (2.) Com-

paring the discoveries he had made to them, in what he had spoken to their ears, with what he would make to them when he would *put his Spirit into their heart*, all hitherto had been but proverbs. It would be a pleasing surprise to themselves, and they would think themselves in a new world, when they would reflect upon all their former notions as confused and enigmatical, compared with their present clear and distinct knowledge of divine things. *The ministration of the letter* was nothing to *that of the Spirit*, 2 Cor. iii. 8—11. (3.) Confining it to what he had said of *the Father*, and the counsels of *the Father*, what he had said was very dark, compared with what was shortly to be revealed, Col. ii. 2.

3. He would speak to them *plainly*, *παῤῥησία—with freedom*, of the Father. When the Spirit was poured out, the apostles attained to a much greater knowledge of divine things than they had before, as appears by the utterance the Spirit gave them, Acts ii. 4. They were led into the mystery of those things of which they had previously a very confused idea; and what the Spirit showed them Christ is here said to show them, for, as the Father speaks by the Son, so the Son by the Spirit. But this promise will have its full accomplishment in heaven, where we shall see the Father as he is, *face to face*, not as we do now, *through a glass darkly* (1 Cor. xiii. 12), which is matter of comfort to us under the cloud of present darkness, by reason of which we cannot *order our speech*, but often disorder it. While we are here, we have many questions to ask concerning the invisible God and the invisible world; but in that day we shall see all things clearly, and *ask no more questions*.

II. He promises that by way of request they should ask nothing in vain. It is taken for granted that all Christ's disciples give themselves to prayer. He had taught them by his precept and pattern to be much in prayer; this must be their support and comfort when he had left them; their instruction, direction, strength, and success, must be fetched in by prayer. Now,

1. Here is an express promise of a grant, *v.* 23. The preface to this promise is such as makes it inviolably sure, and leaves no room to question it: "*Verily, verily, I say unto you*, I pledge my veracity upon it." The promise itself is incomparably rich and sweet; the golden sceptre is here held out to us, with this word, *What is thy petition, and it shall be granted?* For he says, *Whatsoever you shall ask the Father in my name, he will give it to you.* We had it before, *ch.* xiv. 13. What would we more? The promise is as express as we can desire. (1.) We are here taught how to seek; we must *ask the Father in Christ's name;* we must have an eye to God as a Father, and come as children to him; and to Christ as Mediator, and come as clients. Asking of the Father includes a sense of spiritual wants and a desire of spiritual blessings, with a conviction that they are to be had from God only. It includes also humility of address to him, with a believing confidence in him, as a Father able and ready to help us. Asking in Christ's name includes an acknowledgment of our own unworthiness to receive any favour from God, a complacency in the method God has taken of keeping up a correspondence with us by his Son, and an entire dependence upon Christ as *the Lord our Righteousness.* (2.) We are here told how we shall speed: *He will give it to you.* What more can we wish for than to have what we want, nay, to have what we will, in conformity to God's will, for the asking? He *will give it to you* from whom *proceedeth every good and perfect gift.* What Christ purchased by the merit of his death, he needed not for himself, but intended it for, and consigned it to, his faithful followers; and having given a valuable consideration for it, which was accepted in full, by this promise he draws a bill as it were upon the treasury in heaven, which we are to present by prayer, and *in his name* to ask for that which is purchased and promised, according to the true intent of the new covenant. Christ had promised them great illumination by the Spirit, but they must pray for it, and did so, Acts i. 14. God will for this be enquired of. He had promised them perfection hereafter, but what shall they do in the mean time? They must continue praying. Perfect fruition is reserved for the land of our rest; asking and receiving are the comfort of the land of our pilgrimage.

2. Here is an invitation for them to petition. It is thought sufficient if great men permit addresses, but Christ calls upon us to petition, *v.* 24.

(1.) He looks back upon their practice hitherto: *Hitherto have you asked nothing in my name.* This refers either, [1.] To the matter of their prayers: "You have asked nothing comparatively, nothing to what you might have asked, and will ask when the Spirit is poured out. See what a generous benefactor our Lord Jesus is, above all benefactors; he gives liberally, and is so far from upbraiding us with the frequency and largeness of his gifts that he rather upbraids us with the seldomness and straitness of our requests: "*You have asked nothing* in comparison of what you want, and what I have to give, and have promised to give." We are told to *open our mouth wide.* Or, [2.] To the name in which they prayed. They prayed many a prayer, but never so expressly in the name of Christ as now he was directing them to do; for he had not as yet offered up that great sacrifice in the virtue of which our prayers were to be accepted, nor entered upon his intercession for us, the incense whereof was to perfume all our devotions, and so enable us to pray in his name. Hitherto they had cast out devils, and healed diseases, in the name of Christ, as a king and a prophet, but they could not as yet distinctly pray in his name as a priest.

(2.) He looks forward to their practice for the future: *Ask, and you shall receive, that your joy may be full.* Here, [1.] He directs them to ask for all that which they needed and he had promised. [2.] He assures them that they shall *receive.* What we ask from a principle of grace God will graciously give: *You shall receive it.* There is something more in this than in the promise that he will give it. He will not only give it, but give you to receive it, give you the comfort and benefit of it, *a heart to eat of it,* Eccl. vi. 2. [3.] That hereby *their joy shall be full.* This denotes, *First,* The blessed effect of the *prayer of faith;* it helps to fill up the *joy of faith.* Would we have our joy full, as full as it is capable of being in this world, we must be *much in prayer.* When we are told to *rejoice evermore,* it follows immediately, *Pray without ceasing.* See how high we are to aim in prayer—not only at peace, but joy, a *fulness of joy.* Or, *Secondly,* The blessed effects of the *answer of peace:* "Ask, and you shall receive that which will *fill your joy.*" God's gifts, through Christ, fill the treasures of the soul, they fill its joys, Prov. viii. 21. "Ask for the gift of the Holy Ghost, and you shall receive it; and, whereas other knowledge *increaseth sorrow* (Eccl i. 18), the knowledge he gives will increase, will fill, *your joy.*"

3. Here are the grounds upon which they might hope to speed (*v.* 26, 27), which are summed up in short by the apostle (1 John ii. 1): "*We have an advocate with the Father.*

(1.) We have an advocate; as to this, Christ saw cause at present not to insist upon it, only to make the following encouragement shine the brighter: "*I say not unto you that I will pray the Father for you.* Suppose I should not tell you that I will intercede for you, should not undertake to solicit every particular cause you have depending there, yet it may be a general ground of comfort that I have settled a correspondence between you and God, have erected a throne of grace, and consecrated for you a *new and living way into the holiest.*" He speaks as if they needed not any further favours, when he had prevailed for the gift of the Holy Ghost to *make intercession within them,* as a Spirit of adoption, crying *Abba, Father;* as if they had no further need of him to pray for them now; but we shall find that he does more for us than he says he will. Men's performances often come short of their promises, but Christ's go beyond them.

(2.) We have to do with a Father, which is so great an encouragement that it does in a manner supersede the other: *For the Father himself loveth you,* φιλεῖ ὑμᾶς, he is a friend to you, and you cannot be better befriended." Note, The disciples of Christ are the beloved of God himself Christ not only turned away God's wrath from us, and brought us into a covenant of peace and reconciliation, but purchased his favour for us, and brought us into a covenant of friendship. Observe what an emphasis is laid upon this "*The Father himself loveth you,* who is perfectly happy in the enjoyment of himself, whose self-love is both his infinite rectitude and his infinite blessedness; yet he is pleased to love you." The Father himself, whose favour you have forfeited, and whose wrath you have incurred, and with whom you need an advocate, he himself now loves you. Observe, [1.] Why the Father loved the disciples of Christ: *Because you have loved me, and have believed that I came out from God,* that is, because you are my disciples indeed: not as if the love began on their side, but when by his grace he has wrought in us a love to him he is well pleased with the work of his own hands. See here, *First,* What is the character of Christ's disciples; they love him, because they *believe he came out from God,* is the only-begotten of the Father, and his high-commissioner to the world. Note, Faith in Christ works by love to him, Gal. v. 6. If we believe him to be the Son of God, we cannot but love him as infinitely lovely in himself; and, if we believe him to be our Saviour, we cannot but love him as the most kind to us. Observe with what respect Christ is pleased to speak of his disciples' love to him, and how kindly he took it; he speaks of it as that which recommended them to his Father's favour: You have loved me and believed in me when the world has hated and rejected me; and you shall be distinguished, who have thus distinguished yourselves." *Secondly,* See what advantage Christ's faithful disciples have, the Father loves them, and that because they love Christ; so well pleased is he in him that he is well pleased with all his friends. [2.] What encouragement this gave them in prayer. They need not fear speeding when they came to one that loved them, and wished them well. *First,* This cautions us against hard thoughts of God. When we are taught in prayer to plead Christ's merit and intercession, it is not as if all the kindness were in Christ only, and in God nothing but wrath and fury; no, the matter is not so, the Father's love and good-will appointed Christ to be the Mediator; so that we owe Christ's merit to God's mercy in giving him for us. *Secondly,* Let it cherish and confirm in us good thoughts of God. Believers, that love Christ, ought to know that God loves them, and therefore to come boldly to him as children to a loving Father.

28 I came forth from the Father,
and am come into the world: again,
I leave the world, and go to the
Father. 29 His disciples said unto
him, Lo, now speakest thou plainly,

and speakest no proverb. 30 Now
are we sure that thou knowest all
things, and needest not that any man
should ask thee: by this we believe
that thou camest forth from God.
31 Jesus answered them, Do ye now
believe? 32 Behold, the hour cometh,
yea, is now come, that ye shall be
scattered, every man to his own, and
shall leave me alone: and yet I am
not alone, because the Father is with
me. 33 These things I have spoken
unto you, that in me ye might have
peace. In the world ye shall have
tribulation: but be of good cheer; I
have overcome the world.

Two things Christ here comforts his disciples with:—

I. With an assurance that, though he was leaving the world, he was returning to his Father, from whom he came forth *v.* 28—32, where we have,

1. A plain declaration of Christ's mission from the Father, and his return to him (*v.* 28): *I came forth from the Father, and am come,* as you see, *into the world. Again, I leave the world,* as you will see shortly, *and go to the Father.* This is the conclusion of the whole matter. There was nothing he had more inculcated upon them than these two things—whence he came, and whither he went, the *Alpha* and *Omega* of the *mystery of godliness* (1 Tim. iii. 16), that the Redeemer, in his entrance, was *God manifest in the flesh,* and in his exit was *received up into glory.*

(1.) These two great truths are here, [1.] Contracted, and put into a few words. Brief summaries of Christian doctrine are of great use to young beginners. The principles of the oracles of God brought into a little compass in creeds and catechisms have, like the beams of the sun contracted in a burning glass, conveyed divine light and heat with a wonderful power. Such we have, Job xxviii. 28; Eccl. xii. 13; 1 Tim i. 15; Tit. ii. 11, 12; 1 John v. 11; much in a little. [2.] Compared, and set the one over against the other. There is an admirable harmony in divine truths; they both corroborate and illustrate one another; Christ's coming and his going do so. Christ had commended his disciples for believing that he came forth from God (*v.* 27), and thence infers the necessity and equity of his returning to God again, which therefore should not seem to them either strange or sad. Note, The due improvement of what we know and own would help us into the understanding of that which seems difficult and doubtful.

(2.) If we ask concerning the Redeemer *whence he came,* and *whither he went,* we are told, [1.] That he *came from the Father,* who sanctified and sealed him; and he came into this world, this lower world, this world of mankind, among whom by his incarnation he was pleased to incorporate himself. Here his business lay, and hither he came to attend it. He left his home for this strange country; his palace for this cottage; wonderful condescension! [2.] That, when he had done his work on earth, he left the world, and went back to his Father at his ascension. He was not forced away, but made it his own act and deed to leave the world, to return to it no more till he comes to put an end to it; yet still he is spiritually present with his church, and will be to the end.

2. The disciples' satisfaction in this declaration (*v.* 29, 30): *Lo, now speakest thou plainly.* It should seem, this one word of Christ did them more good than all the rest, though he had said many things likely enough to fasten upon them. The Spirit, as the wind, blows when and where, and by what word he pleases; perhaps a word that has been *spoken once, yea twice,* and not perceived, yet, being often repeated, takes hold at last. Two things they improved in by this saying:—

(1.) In knowledge: *Lo, now speakest thou plainly.* When they were in the dark concerning what he said, they did not say, *Lo, now speakest thou obscurely,* as blaming him; but now that they apprehend his meaning they give him glory for condescending to their capacity: *Lo, now speakest thou plainly.* Divine truths are most likely to do good when they are spoken plainly, 1 Cor. ii. 4. Observe how they triumphed, as the mathematician did with his εὕρηκα, εὕρηκα, when he had hit upon a demonstration he had long been in quest of: *I have found it, I have found it.* Note, When Christ is pleased to speak plainly to our souls, and to bring us with open face to behold his glory, we have reason to rejoice in it.

(2.) In faith: *Now are we sure.* Observe,

[1.] What was the matter of their faith: *We believe that thou camest forth from God.* He had said (*v.* 27) that they did believe this; "Lord" (say they) "we do believe it, and we have cause to believe it, and we know that we believe it, and have the comfort of it."

[2.] What was the motive of their faith—his omniscience. This proved him a teacher come from God, and more than a prophet, that he knew all things, which they were convinced of by this that he resolved those doubts which were hid in their hearts, and answered the scruples they had not confessed. Note, Those know Christ best that know him by experience, that can say of his power, It works in me; of his love, He loved me. And this proves Christ not only to have a divine mission, but to be a divine person, that he is a discerner of the thoughts and intents of the heart, therefore the essential, eternal Word, Heb. iv. 12, 13. He has made all the churches to know that he searches the reins and the heart, Rev. ii. 23. This confirmed the faith of the disciples here, as it made the first impression upon the woman of Samaria that Christ *told her all things that ever she did* (*ch.* iv. 29), and upon Nathanael that Christ *saw him under the fig-tree, ch.* i. 48, 49.

These words, *and needest not that any man should ask thee,* may bespeak either, *First,* Christ's aptness to teach. He prevents us with his instructions, and is communicative of the *treasures of wisdom and knowledge* that are hid in him, and needs not to be importuned. Or, *Secondly,* His ability to teach: "Thou needest not, as other teachers, to have the learners' doubts told thee, for thou knowest, without being told, what they stumble at." The best of teachers can only answer what is spoken, but Christ can answer what is thought, what we are afraid to ask, as the disciples were, Mark ix. 32. Thus he *can have compassion,* Heb. v. 2.

3. The gentle rebuke Christ gave the disciples for their confidence that they now understood him, *v.* 31, 32. Observing how they triumphed in their attainments, he said, "*Do you now believe?* Do you now look upon yourselves as advanced and confirmed disciples? Do you now think you shall make no more blunders? Alas! you know not your own weakness; you will very shortly *be scattered every man to his own,*" &c. Here we have,

(1.) A question, designed to put them upon consideration: *Do you now believe?* [1.] "If now, why not sooner? Have you not heard the same things many a time before?" Those who after many instructions and invitations are at last persuaded to believe have reason to be ashamed that they stood it out so long. [2.] "If now, why not ever? When an hour of temptation comes, where will your faith be then?" As far as there is inconstancy in our faith there is cause to question the sincerity of it, and to ask, "Do we indeed believe?"

(2.) A prediction of their fall, that, how confident soever they were now of their own stability, in a little time they would all desert him, which was fulfilled that very night, when, upon his being seized by a party of the guards, *all his disciples forsook him and fled,* Matt. xxvi. 56. They were scattered, [1.] From one another; they shifted every one for his own safety, without any care or concern for each other. Troublous times are times of scattering to Christian societies; in the cloudy and dark day the flock of Christ is dispersed, Ezek. xxxiv. 12. So Christ, as a society, is not visible. [2.] Scattered from him: *You shall leave me alone.* They should have been witnesses for him upon his trial, should have ministered to him in his sufferings; if they could have given him no comfort they might have done him some credit; but they were ashamed of his chain, and afraid of sharing with him in his sufferings, and left him alone. Note, Many a good cause, when it is distressed by its enemies, is deserted by its friends. The disciples had *continued with Christ* in his other temptations, and yet turned their back upon him now; those that are tried, do not always prove trusty. If we at any time find our friends unkind to us, let us remember that Christ's were so to him. When they left him alone, they were scattered *every man to his own;* not to their own possessions or habitations, these were in Galilee; but to their own friends and acquaintance in Jerusalem; every one went his own way, where he fancied he should be most safe. Every man to secure his own; himself and his own life. Note, Those will not dare to suffer for their religion that *seek their own things* more than the *things of Christ,* and that look upon the things of this world as their *τα ἴδια—their own property,* and in which their happiness is bound up. Now observe here, *First,* Christ knew before that his disciples would thus desert him in the critical moment, and yet he was still tender of them, and in nothing unkind. We are ready to say of some, "If we could have foreseen their ingratitude, we would not have been so prodigal of our favours to them;" Christ did foresee theirs, and yet was kind to them. *Secondly,* He told them of it, to be a rebuke to their exultation in their present attainments: "*Do you now believe?* Be not highminded, but fear; for you will find your faith so sorely shaken as to make it questionable whether it be sincere or no, in a little time." Note, Even when we are taking the comfort of our graces, it is good to be reminded of our danger from our corruptions. When our faith is strong, our love flaming, and our evidences are clear, yet we cannot infer thence that *to-morrow shall be as this day.* Even when we have most reason to think we stand, yet we have reason enough to take heed lest we fall. *Thirdly,* He spoke of it as a thing very near. *The hour was* already *come,* in a manner, when they would be as shy of him as ever they had been fond of him. Note, A little time may produce great changes, both concerning us and in us.

(3.) An assurance of his own comfort notwithstanding: *Yet I am not alone.* He would not be thought to complain of their deserting him, as if it were any real damage to him; for in their absence he should be sure of his Father's presence, which was *instar omnium—every thing: The Father is with me.* We may consider this, [1.] As a privilege peculiar to the Lord Jesus; the Father was so with him in his sufferings as he never was with any, for still he was *in the bosom of the Father.* The divine nature did not desert the human nature, but supported it, and put an invincible comfort and an inestimable value into his sufferings. The Father had engaged to be with him in his whole undertaking (Ps. lxxxix. 21, &c.), and to preserve him (Isa. xlix. 8); this emboldened him, Isa. l. 7. Even when he complained of his Father's forsaking him, yet he called him *My God,* and presently after was so well assured of his favourable presence with him as to commit his Spirit into his hand. This he had comforted himself with all along (*ch.* viii. 29), *He that sent me is with me, the Father hath not left me alone,* and especially now at last. This assists our faith in the acceptableness of Christ's satisfaction; no doubt, the Father was well pleased in him, for he went along with him in his undertaking from first to last. [2.] As a privilege common to all believers, by virtue of their union with Christ; when they are alone, they are *not alone,* but *the Father is with them. First,* When solitude is their choice, when they are alone, as Isaac in the field, Nathanael under the fig-tree, Peter upon the house-top, meditating and praying, the Father is with them. Those that converse with God in solitude are never less alone than when alone. A good God and a good heart are good company at any time. *Secondly,* When solitude is their affliction, their enemies lay them alone, and their friends leave them so, their company, like Job's, is made desolate; yet they are not so much alone as they are thought to be, *the Father is with them,* as he was with Joseph in his bonds and with John in his banishment. In their greatest troubles they are as one whom his father pities, as one whom his mother comforts. And, while we have God's favourable presence with us, we are happy, and ought to be easy, though all the world forsake us. *Non Deo tribuimus justum honorem nisi solus ipse nobis sufficiat—We do not render due honour to God, unless we deem him alone all-sufficient.*—Calvin.

II. He comforts them with a promise of peace in him, by virtue of his victory over the world, whatever troubles they might meet with in it (*v.* 33): "*These things have I spoken, that in me you might have peace;* and if you have it not in me you will not have it at all, for *in the world you shall have tribulation;* you must expect no other, and yet may cheer up yourselves, for *I have overcome the world.*" Observe,

1. The end Christ aimed at in preaching this farewell sermon to his disciples: *That in him they might have peace.* He did not hereby intend to give them a full view of that doctrine which they were shortly to be made masters of by the pouring out of the Spirit, but only to satisfy them for the present that his departure from them was really for the best. Or, we may take it more generally: Christ had said all this to them that by enjoying him they might have the best enjoyment of themselves. Note, (1.) It is the will of Christ that his disciples should have peace within, whatever their troubles may be without. (2.) Peace in Christ is the only true peace, and in him alone believers have it, for *this man shall be the peace,* Mic. v. 5. Through him we have peace with God, and so in him we have peace in our own minds. (3.) The word of Christ aims at this, *that in him we may have peace.* Peace is the *fruit of the lips, and of his lips,* Isa. lvii. 19.

2. The entertainment they were likely to meet with in the world: "You shall not have outward peace, never expect it." Though they were sent to proclaim *peace on earth,* and *good-will towards men,* they must expect trouble on earth, and ill-will from men. Note, It has been the lot of Christ's disciples to have more or less tribulation in this world. Men persecute them because they are so good, and God corrects them because they are no better. Men design to cut them off from the earth, and God designs by affliction to make them meet for heaven; and so between both *they shall have tribulation.*

3. The encouragement Christ gives them with reference hereto: *But be of good cheer,* θαρσεῖτε. "Not only be of good comfort, but be of good courage; have a good heart on it, all shall be well." Note, In the midst of the tribulations of this world it is the duty and interest of Christ's disciples to be of good cheer, to keep up their delight in God whatever is pressing, and their hope in God whatever is threatening; as sorrowful indeed, in compliance with the temper of the climate, and yet always rejoicing, always cheerful (2 Cor. vi. 10), even *in tribulation,* Rom. v. 3.

4. The ground of that encouragement: *I have overcome the world.* Christ's victory is a Christian's triumph. Christ overcame the prince of this world, disarmed him, and cast him out; and still treads Satan under our feet. He overcame the children of this world, by the conversion of many to the faith and obedience of his gospel, making them the children of his kingdom. When he sends his disciples to preach the gospel to all the world, "*Be of good cheer,*" says he, "*I have overcome the world* as far as I have gone, and so shall you; though you have tribulation in the world, yet you shall gain your point, and captivate the world," Rev. vi. 2. He overcame the wicked of the world, for many a time he put his enemies to silence, to shame; "And be you of good cheer, for the Spirit will enable you to do so too." He overcame the evil things of the world by submitting to them; he endured the cross, despising it and the shame of it; and he overcame the good things of it by being wholly dead to them; its honours had no beauty in his eye, its pleasures no charms. Never was there such a conqueror of the world as Christ was, and we ought to be encouraged by it, (1.) Because Christ has overcome the world before us; so that we may look upon it as a conquered enemy, that has many a time been baffled. Nay, (2.) He has conquered it for us, as the captain of our salvation. We are interested in his victory; by his cross the world is *crucified to us,* which bespeaks it completely conquered and put into our possession; all is yours,

even *the world.* Christ having overcome the world, believers have nothing to do but to pursue their victory, and divide the spoil; and this we do by faith, 1 John v. 4. *We are more than conquerors through him that loved us.*

CHAP. XVII.

This chapter is a prayer, it is the Lord's prayer, the Lord Christ's prayer. There was one Lord's prayer which he taught us to pray, and did not pray himself, for he needed not to pray for the forgiveness of sin; but this was properly and peculiarly his, and suited him only as a Mediator, and is a sample of his intercession, and yet is of use to us both for instruction and encouragement in prayer. Observe, I. The circumstances of the prayer, ver. 1. II. The prayer itself. 1. He prays for himself, ver. 1—5. 2. He prays for those that are his. And in this see, (1.) The general pleas with which he introduces his petitions for them, ver. 6—10. (2.) The particular petitions he puts up for them, [1.] That they might be kept, ver. 11—16. [2.] That they might be sanctified, ver. 17—19. [3.] That they might be united, ver. 11 and 20—23. [4.] That they might be glorified, ver. 24—26.

THESE words spake Jesus, and
lifted up his eyes to heaven, and
said, Father, the hour is come; glorify thy Son, that thy Son also may
glorify thee: 2 As thou hast given
him power over all flesh, that he
should give eternal life to as many as
thou hast given him. 3 And this is
life eternal, that they might know
thee the only true God, and Jesus
Christ, whom thou hast sent. 4 I
have glorified thee on the earth: I
have finished the work which thou
gavest me to do. 5 And now, O
Father, glorify thou me with thine
own self with the glory which I had
with thee before the world was.

Here we have, I. The circumstances of this prayer, *v.* 1. Many a solemn prayer Christ made in the days of his flesh (sometimes he continued all night in prayer), but none of his prayers are recorded so fully as this. Observe,

1. The time when he prayed this prayer; when he had *spoken these words,* had given the foregoing farewell to his disciples, he prayed this prayer in their hearing; so that, (1.) It was a prayer after sermon; when he had spoken from God to them, he turned to speak to God for them. Note, Those we preach to we must pray for. He that was to prophesy upon the dry bones was also to pray, *Come, O breath, and breathe* upon them. And the word preached should be prayed over, for God *gives the increase.* (2.) It was a prayer after sacrament; after Christ and his disciples had eaten the passover and the Lord's supper together, and he had given them a suitable exhortation, he closed the solemnity with this prayer, that God would preserve the good impressions of the ordinance upon them. (3.) It was a family-prayer. Christ's disciples were his family, and, to set a good example before masters of families, he not only, as a son of Abraham, taught his household (Gen. xviii. 19), but, as a son of David, blessed his household (2 Sam. vi. 20), prayed for them and with them. (4.) It was a parting prayer. When we and our friends are parting, it is good to part with prayer, Acts xx. 36. Christ was parting by death, and that parting should be sanctified and sweetened by prayer. Dying Jacob blessed the twelve patriarchs, dying Moses the twelve tribes, and so, here, dying Jesus the twelve apostles. (5.) It was a prayer that was a preface to his sacrifice, which he was now about to offer on earth, specifying the favours and blessings designed to be purchased by the merit of his death for those that were his; like a deed *leading the uses of a fine,* and directing to what intents and purposes it shall be levied. Christ prayed then as a priest now offering sacrifice, in the virtue of which all prayers were to be made. (6.) It was a prayer that was a specimen of his intercession, which he ever lives to make for us within the veil. Not that in his exalted state he addresses himself to his Father by way of humble petition, as when he was on earth. No, his intercession in heaven is a presenting of his merit to his Father, with a suing out of the benefit of it for all his chosen ones.

2. The outward expression of fervent desire which he used in this prayer: He *lifted up his eyes to heaven,* as before (*ch.* xi. 41); not that Christ needed thus to engage his own attention, but he was pleased thus to sanctify this gesture to those that use it, and justify it against those that ridicule it. It is significant of the lifting up of the soul to God in prayer, Ps. xxv. 1. *Sursum corda* was anciently used as a call to prayer, *Up with your hearts,* up to heaven; thither we must direct our desires in prayer, and thence we must expect to receive the good things we pray for.

II. The first part of the prayer itself, in which Christ prays for himself. Observe here,

1. He prays to God as a Father: He *lifted up his eyes, and said, Father.* Note, As prayer is to be made to God only, so it is our duty in prayer to eye him as a Father, and to call him *our Father.* All that have the Spirit of adoption are taught to cry *Abba, Father,* Rom. viii. 15; Gal. iv. 6. If God be our Father, we have liberty of access to him, ground of confidence in him, and great expectations from him. Christ calls him here *holy Father* (*v.* 11), and *righteous Father, v.* 25. For it will be of great use to us in prayer, both for direction and for encouragement, to call God as we hope to find him.

2. He prayed for himself first. Though Christ, as God, was prayed to, Christ, as man, prayed; thus *it became him to fulfil all righteousness.* It was said to him, as it is said to us, *Ask, and I will give thee,* Ps. ii. 8. What he had purchased he must ask for; and shall we expect to have what we never merited, but have a thousand times forfeited,

unless we pray for it? This puts an honour upon prayer, that it was the messenger Christ sent on his errands, the way in which even he corresponded with Heaven. It likewise gives great encouragement to praying people, and cause to hope that even the *prayer of the destitute* shall not be despised; time was when he that is advocate for us had a cause of his own to solicit, a great cause, on the success of which depended all his honour as Mediator; and this he was to solicit in the same method that is prescribed to us, *by prayers and supplications* (Heb. v. 7), so that he knows the heart of a petitioner (Exod. xxiii. 9), he knows the way. Now observe, Christ began with prayer for himself, and afterwards prayed for his disciples; this charity must begin at home, though it must not end there. We must love and pray for our neighbour as ourselves, and therefore must in a right manner love and pray for ourselves first. Christ was much shorter in his prayer for himself than in his prayer for his disciples. Our prayers for the church must not be crowded into a corner of our prayers; in making *supplication for all saints,* we have room enough to enlarge, and should not straiten ourselves. Now here are two petitions which Christ puts up for himself, and these two are one—that he might be glorified. But this one petition, *Glorify thou me,* is twice put up, because it has a double reference. To the prosecution of his undertaking further: *Glorify me, that I may glorify thee,* in doing what is agreed upon to be yet done, *v.* 1—3. And to the performance of his undertaking hitherto: "*Glorify me, for I have glorified thee.* I have done my part, and now, Lord, do thine," *v.* 4, 5.

(1.) Christ here prays to be *glorified,* in order to his *glorifying God* (*v.* 1): *Glorify thy Son* according to thy promise, *that thy Son may glorify thee* according to his undertaking. Here observe,

[1.] What he prays for—that he might be glorified in this world: "*The hour is come* when all the powers of darkness will combine to vilify thy Son; now, Father, glorify him." The Father glorified the *Son* upon earth, *First,* Even in his sufferings, by the signs and wonders which attended them. When they that came to take him were thunder-struck with a word,—when Judas confessed him innocent, and sealed that confession with his own guilty blood,—when the judge's wife asleep, and the judge himself awake, pronounced him righteous,—when the sun was darkened, and the veil of the temple rent, then the Father not only justified, but glorified the Son. Nay, *Secondly,* Even by his sufferings; when he was crucified, he was magnified, he was glorified, *ch.* xiii. 31. It was in his cross that he conquered Satan and death; his thorns were a crown, and Pilate in the inscription over his head wrote more than he thought. But, *Thirdly,* Much more after his sufferings. The Father glorified the Son when he *raised him from the dead,* showed him openly to chosen witnesses, and poured out the Spirit to support and plead his cause, and to set up his kingdom among men, then he *glorified him.* This he here prays for, and insists upon.

[2.] What he pleads to enforce this request.

First, He pleads relation: *Glorify thy Son;* thy Son as God, as Mediator. It is in consideration of this that the heathen are *given him for his inheritance;* for *thou art my Son,* Ps. ii. 7, 8. The devil had tempted him to renounce his sonship with an offer of the kingdoms of this world; but he rejected the offer with disdain, and depended upon his Father for his preferment, and here applies himself to him for it. Note, Those that have received the adoption of sons may in faith pray for the inheritance of sons; if sanctified, then glorified: *Father, glorify thy Son.*

Secondly, He pleads the time: *The hour is come;* the season prefixed to an hour. The hour of Christ's passion was determined in the counsel of God. He had often said his hour was not yet come; but now it was come, and he knew it. *Man knows not his time* (Eccl. ix. 12), but the Son of man did. He calls it *this hour* (*ch.* xii. 27), and here *the hour;* compare Mark xiv. 35; *ch.* xvi. 21. For the hour of the Redeemer's death, which was also the hour of the Redeemer's birth, was the most signal and remarkable hour, and, without doubt, the most critical, that ever was since the clock of time was first set a going. Never was there such an hour as that, nor did ever any hour challenge such expectations of it before, nor such reflections upon it after. 1. "*The hour is come* in the midst of which I need to be owned." Now is the hour when this grand affair is come to a crisis; after many a skirmish the decisive battle between heaven and hell is now to be fought, and that great cause in which God's honour and man's happiness are together embarked must now be either won or lost for ever. The two champions David and Goliath, Michael and the dragon, are now entering the lists; the trumpet sounds for an engagement that will be irretrievably fatal either to the one or to the other: "*Now glorify thy Son,* now give him victory over *principalities and powers,* now let *the bruising of his heel* be *the breaking of the serpent's head,* now let thy Son be so upheld as not to fail nor be discouraged." When Joshua went *forth conquering and to conquer,* it is said, *The Lord magnified Joshua;* so he *glorified his Son* when he made the cross his triumphant chariot. 2. "*The hour is come* in the close of which I expect to be crowned; *the hour is come* when I am *to be glorified,* and *set at thy right hand.*" Betwixt him and that glory there intervened a bloody scene of suffering; but, being short, he speaks as if he made little of it: *The hour is come that I must be glorified;* and he did not expect it till then. Good Christians in a trying hour, particularly a dying hour, may thus plead: "*Now the hour is come,* stand by me, appear for me, now or never; now *the earthly tabernacle is to be dissolved, the hour is come that I should be glorified.*" 2 Cor. v. 1.

Thirdly, He pleads the Father's own interest and concern herein: *That thy Son may also glorify thee;* for he had consecrated his whole undertaking to his Father's honour. He desired to be carried triumphantly through his sufferings to his glory, that he might glorify the Father two ways:—1. By *the death of the cross,* which he was now to suffer. *Father, glorify thy name,* expressed the great intention of his sufferings, which was to retrieve his Father's injured honour among men, and, by his satisfaction, to come up to the glory of God, which man, by his sin, came short of: "Father, own me in my sufferings, that I may honour thee by them." 2. By the doctrine of the cross, which was now shortly to be published to the world, by which God's kingdom was to be re-established among men. He prays that his Father would so grace his sufferings, and crown them, as not only to take off *the offence of the cross,* but to make it, *to those that are saved, the wisdom of God and the power of God.* If God had not glorified Christ crucified, *by raising him from the dead,* his whole undertaking had been crushed; therefore *glorify me, that I may glorify thee.* Now hereby he hath taught us, (1.) What to eye and aim at in our prayers, in all our designs and desires—and that is, the honour of God. It being our chief end to glorify God, other things must be sought and attended to in subordination and subserviency to the Lord. "Do this and the other for thy servant, that thy servant may glorify thee. Give me health, that I may glorify thee with my body; success, that I may glorify thee with my estate," &c. *Hallowed be thy name* must be our first petition, which must fix our end in all our other petitions, 1 Peter iv. 11. (2.) He hath taught us what to expect and hope for. If we sincerely set ourselves to glorify our Father, he will not be wanting to do that for us which is requisite to put us into a capacity of glorifying him, to give us the grace he knows sufficient, and the opportunity he sees convenient. But, if we secretly honour ourselves more than him, it is just with him to leave us in the hand of our own counsels, and then, instead of honouring ourselves, we shall shame ourselves.

Fourthly, He pleads his commission (*v.* 2, 3); he desires to glorify his Father, in conformity to, and in pursuance of, the commission given him: "*Glorify thy Son, as thou hast given him power, glorify him in the execution of the powers thou hast given him,* so it is connected with the petition; or, *that thy Son may glorify thee* according *to the power given him,* so it is connected with the plea. Now see here the power of the Mediator.

a. The origin of his power: *Thou hast given him power;* he has it from God, *to whom all power belongs.* Man, in his fallen state, must, in order to his recovery, be taken under a new model of government, which could not be erected but by a special commission under the broad seal of heaven, directed to the undertaker of that glorious work, and constituting him sole arbitrator of the grand difference that was, and sole guarantee of the grand alliance that was to be, between God and man; so as to this office, he received his power, which was to be executed in a way distinct from his power and government as Creator. Note, The church's king is no usurper, as the prince of this world is; Christ's right to rule is incontestable.

b. The extent of his power: He has *power over all flesh.* (*a.*) Over all mankind. He has power in and over the world of spirits, the powers of the upper and unseen world are subject to him (1 Peter iii. 22); but, being now mediating between God and man, he here *pleads his power over all flesh.* They were men whom he was to subdue and save; out of that race he had a remnant given him, and therefore all that rank of beings was *put under his feet.* (*b.*) Over mankind considered as corrupt and fallen, for so he is called *flesh,* Gen. vi. 3. If he had not in this sense been flesh, he had not needed a Redeemer. Over this sinful race the Lord Jesus has all power; and *all judgment,* concerning them, *is committed to him;* power to bind or loose, acquit or condemn; *power on earth to forgive sins* or not. Christ, as Mediator, has the government of the whole world put into his hand; he is king of nations, has power even over those *that know him not, nor obey his gospel;* whom he does not rule, he over-rules, Ps. xxii. 28; lxxii. 8; Matt. xxviii. 18; *ch.* iii. 35.

c. The grand intention and design of this power: *That he should give eternal life to as many as thou hast given him.* Here is the mystery of our salvation laid open.

(*a.*) Here is the Father making over the elect to the Redeemer, and giving them to him as his charge and trust; as the crown and recompence of his undertaking. He has a sovereign power over all the fallan race, but a peculiar interest in the chosen remnant; *all things were put under his feet,* but they were *delivered into his hand.*

(*b.*) Here is the Son undertaking to secure the happiness of those that were given him, that he would *give eternal life to them.* See how great the authority of the Redeemer is. He has lives and crowns to give, eternal lives that never die, immortal crowns that never fade. Now consider how great the Lord Jesus is, who has such preferments in his gift; and how gracious he is in giving eternal life to those whom he undertakes to save. [*a.*] He sanctifies them in this world, gives them the spiritual life which is eternal life in the bud and embryo, *ch.* iv. 14. Grace in the soul is heaven in that soul. [*b.*] He will glorify them in the other world; their happiness shall be completed in the vision and fruition of God. This only is mentioned, because it supposes all the other parts of his undertaking, teaching them, satisfying for them, sanctifying them, and preparing them for that eternal life; and indeed all the other were in order to this; we are *called to his kingdom and glory,* and *begotten to the inheritance.* What is last in execution was first in intention, and *that is eternal life.*

(*c.*) Here is the subserviency of the Redeemer's universal dominion to this: He has *power over all flesh,* on purpose that he might give eternal life to the select number. Note, Christ's dominion over the children of men is in order to the salvation of the children of God. *All things are for their sakes,* 2 Cor. iv. 15. All Christ's laws, ordinances, and promises, which are given to all, are designed effectually to convey spiritual life, and secure eternal life, to all that were given to Christ; he is *head over all things to the church.* The administration of the kingdoms of providence and grace are put into the same hand, that all things may be made to concur for good to the called.

d. Here is a further explication of this grand design (*v.* 3): "*This is life eternal,* which I am empowered and have undertaken to give, this is the nature of it, and this the way leading to it, *to know thee the only true God,* and all the discoveries and principles of natural religion, and Jesus Christ whom thou hast sent, as Mediator, and the doctrines and laws of that holy religion which he instituted for the recovery of man out of his lapsed state." Here is,

(*a.*) The great end which the Christian religion sets before us, and that is, eternal life, the happiness of an immortal soul in the vision and fruition of an eternal God. This he was to reveal to all, and secure to all that were given him. By the gospel *life and immortality are brought to light,* are brought to hand, a life which transcends this as much in excellency as it does in duration.

(*b.*) The sure way of attaining this blessed end, which is, by the right knowledge of God and Jesus Christ: "*This is life eternal, to know thee,* which may be taken two ways:—[*a.*] *Life eternal* lies in the knowledge of God and Jesus Christ; the present principle of this life is the believing knowledge of God and Christ; the future perfection of that life will be the intuitive knowledge of God and Christ. Those that are brought into union with Christ, and live a life of communion with God in Christ, know, in some measure, by experience, what eternal life is, and will say, "If this be heaven, heaven is sweet." See Ps. xvii. 15. [*b.*] The knowledge of God and Christ leads to life eternal; this is the way in which Christ gives eternal life, by the knowledge of him that has called us (2 Peter i.3), and this is the way in which we come to receive it. The Christian religion shows us the way to heaven, *First,* By directing us to God, as the author and felicity of our being; for Christ died to *bring us to God.* To know him as our Creator, and to love him, obey him, submit to him, and trust in him, as our owner ruler, and benefactor,—to devote ourselves to him as our sovereign Lord, depend upon him as our chief good, and direct all to his praise as our highest end,—*this is life eternal.* God is here called the *only true God,* to distinguish him from the false gods of the heathen, which were counterfeits and pretenders, not from the person of the Son of whom it is expressly said that he is *the true God and eternal life* (1 John v. 20), and who in this text is proposed as the object of the same religious regard with the Father. It is certain there is but one only living and true God, and the God we adore is he. He is the true God, and not a mere name or notion; the only true God, and all that ever set up as rivals with him are vanity and a lie; the service of him is the only true religion. *Secondly,* By directing us to Jesus Christ, as the Mediator between God and man: *Jesus Christ, whom thou hast sent.* If man had continued innocent, the knowledge of the only true God would have been life eternal to him; but now that he is fallen there must be something more; now that we are under guilt, to know God is to know him as a righteous Judge, whose curse we are under; and nothing is more killing than to know this. We are therefore concerned to know Christ as our Redeemer, by whom alone we can now have access to God; it is life eternal to believe in Christ; and this he has undertaken to give to as many as were given him. See *ch.* vi. 39, 40. Those that are acquainted with God and Christ are already in the suburbs of life eternal.

(2.) Christ here prays to be glorified in consideration of his having glorified the Father hitherto, *v.* 4, 5. The meaning of the former petition was, Glorify me in this world; the meaning of the latter is, Glorify me in the other world. *I have glorified thee on the earth, and now glorify thou me.* Observe here,

[1.] With what comfort Christ reflects on the life he had lived on earth: *I have glorified thee, and finished my work;* it is as good as finished. He does not complain of the poverty and disgrace he had lived in, what a weary life he had upon earth, as ever any man of sorrows had. He overlooks this, and pleases himself in reviewing the service he had done his Father, and the progress he had made in his undertaking. This is here recorded, *First,* For the honour of Christ, that his life upon earth did in all respects fully answer the end of his coming into the world. Note, 1. Our Lord Jesus had work given him to do by him that sent him; he came not into the world to live at ease, but to go *about doing good,* and to *fulfil all righteousness.* His Father gave him his work, his work in the vineyard, both appointed him to it and assisted him in it. 2. *The work that was given him to do* he finished. Though he had not, as yet, gone through the last part of his undertaking, yet he was so near being *made perfect through sufferings* that he might say, I have finished it; it was as good as done, he was giving it its finishing stroke, ἐτελείωσα—*I have finished.* The word signifies his performing every part of his undertaking in the most complete and perfect manner. 3. Herein he glorified his Father; he pleased him, he praised him. It is the glory of God that *his work is perfect,* and the same is the glory of the Redeemer; what he is the author of he will be the finisher of. It was a strange way for the Son to glorify the Father by abasing himself (this looked more likely to disparage him), yet it was contrived that so he should glorify him: "*I have glorified thee on the earth,* in such a way as men on earth could bear the manifestation of thy glory." *Secondly,* It is recorded for example to all, *that we may follow his example.* 1. We must make it our business to do the work God has appointed us to do, according to our capacity and the sphere of our activity; we must each of us do all the good we can in this world. 2. We must aim at the glory of God in all. We must glorify him on the earth, which he has given *unto the children of men,* demanding only this quit-rent; on the earth, where we are in a state of probation and preparation for eternity. 3. We must persevere herein to the end of our days; we must not sit down till we have finished our work, and *accomplished as a hireling our day. Thirdly,* It is recorded for encouragement to all those that rest upon him. If he has *finished the work that was given him to do,* then he is a complete Saviour, and did not do his work by the halves. And he that finished his work for us will finish it in us *to the day of Christ.*

[2.] See with what confidence he expects *the joy set before him* (*v.* 5): *Now, O Father, glorify thou me.* It is what he depends upon, and cannot be denied him.

First, See here what he prayed for: *Glorify thou me,* as before, *v.* 1. All repetitions in prayer are not to be counted *vain repetitions;* Christ *prayed, saying the same words* (Matt. xxvi. 44), and yet *prayed more earnestly.* What his Father had promised him, and he was assured of, yet he must pray for; promises are not designed to supersede prayers, but to be the guide of our desires and the ground of our hopes. Christ's being glorified includes all the honours, powers, and joys, of his exalted state. See how it is described. 1. It is a glory with God; not only, *Glorify my name on earth,* but, *Glorify me with thine own self.* It was paradise, it was heaven, to be with his Father, as Prov. viii. 30; Dan. vii. 13; Heb. viii. 1. Note, The brightest glories of the exalted Redeemer were to be displayed within the veil, where the Father manifests his glory. The praises of the upper world are offered up *to him that sits upon the throne and to the Lamb* in conjunction (Rev. v. 13), and the prayers of the lower world draw out grace and peace *from God our Father and our Lord Jesus Christ* in conjunction; and thus the Father has glorified him with himself. 2. It is *the glory he had with God before the world was.* By this it appears, (1.) That Jesus Christ, as God, had a being *before the world was,* co-eternal with the Father; our religion acquaints us with one that *was before all things, and by whom all things consist.* (2.) That his glory with the Father is from everlasting, as well as his existence with the Father; for he was from eternity *the brightness of his Father's glory,* Heb. i. 3. As God's making the world only declared his glory, but made no real additions to it; so Christ undertook the work of redemption, not because he needed glory, for he had a glory *with the Father before the world,* but because we needed glory. (3.) That Jesus Christ in his state of humiliation divested himself of this glory, and drew a veil over it; though he was still God, yet he was *God manifested in the flesh,* not in his glory. He laid down this glory for a time, as a pledge that he would go through with his undertaking, according to the appointment of his Father. (4.) That in his exalted state he resumed this glory, and clad himself again with his former robes of light. Having performed his undertaking, he did, as it were, *reposcere pignus—take up his pledge,* by this demand, *Glorify thou me.* He prays that even his human nature might be advanced to the highest honour it was capable of, his body a glorious body; and that the glory of the Godhead might now be manifested in the person of the Mediator, Emmanuel, God-man. He does not pray to be glorified with the princes and great men of the earth: no; he that knew both worlds, and might choose which he would have his preferment in, chose it in the glory of the other world, as far exceeding all the glory of this. He had despised *the kingdoms of this world and the glory of them,* when Satan offered them to him, and therefore might the more boldly claim the glories of the other world. *Let the same mind be in us.* "Lord, give the glories of this world to whom thou wilt give them, but let me have my portion of glory in the world to come. It is no matter, though I be vilified with men; but, *Father, glorify thou me with thine own self.*"

Secondly, See here what he pleaded: *I have glorified thee;* and now, in consideration thereof, *glorify thou me.* For, 1 There was an equity in it, and an admirable becomingness, *that, if God was glorified in him, he should glorify him in himself,* as he had observed, *ch.* xiii. 32. Such an infinite value there was in what Christ did to glorify his Father that he properly merited all the glories of his exalted state. If the Father was a gainer in his glory by the Son's humiliation, it was fit the Son should be no loser by it, at long run, in his glory. 2. It was according to the covenant between them, that if the Son would *make his soul an offering for sin* he should *divide the spoil with the strong* (Isa. liii. 10, 12), and *the kingdom should be his;* and this he had an eye to, and depended upon, in his sufferings; it was *for the joy set before him* that *he endured the cross:* and now in his exalted state he still expects the completing of his exaltation, because he perfected his undertaking, Heb. x. 13. 3. It was the most proper evidence of his Father's accepting and approving the work he had finished. By the glorifying of Christ we are satisfied that God was satisfied, and therein a real demonstration was given that his Father was well pleased in him as his beloved Son. 4. Thus we must be taught that those, and only those, who glorify God on earth, and persevere in the work God hath given them to do, shall be glorified with the Father, when they must be no more in this world. Not that we can merit that glory, as Christ did, but our glorifying God is required as an evidence of our interest in Christ, through whom eternal life is God's free gift.

6 I have manifested thy name unto the men which thou gavest me out
of the world: thine they were, and
thou gavest them me; and they have
kept thy word. 7 Now they have
known that all things whatsoever
thou hast given me are of thee. 8
For I have given unto them the words
which thou gavest me; and they
have received *them*, and have known
surely that I came out from thee, and
they have believed that thou didst
send me. 9 I pray for them: I pray
not for the world, but for them which
thou hast given me; for they are thine.
10 And all mine are thine, and thine
are mine; and I am glorified in them.

Christ, having prayed for himself, comes next to pray for those that are his, and he knew them by name, though he did not here name them. Now observe here,

I. Whom he did not pray for (*v.* 9): *I pray not for the world.* Note, There is a world of people that Jesus Christ did not pray for. It is not meant of the world of mankind in general (he prays for that here, *v.* 21, *That the world may believe that thou hast sent me);* nor is it meant of the Gentiles, in distinction from the Jews; but the world is here opposed to the elect, who are given to Christ out of the world. Take the world for a heap of unwinnowed corn in the floor, and God loves it, Christ prays for it, and dies for it, *for a blessing is in it;* but, *the Lord perfectly knowing those that are his,* he eyes particularly those *that were given him out of the world,* extracts them; and then take the world for the remaining heap of rejected, worthless chaff, and Christ neither prays for it, nor dies for it, but abandons it, and *the wind drives it away.* These are called *the world,* because they are governed by the spirit of this world, and have their portion in it; for these Christ does not pray; not but that there are some things which he intercedes with God for on their behalf, as the dresser for the reprieve of the barren tree; but he does not pray for them in this prayer, they *have no part nor lot* in the blessings here prayed for. He does not say, I pray against the world, as Elias made intercession against Israel; but, *I pray not for them,* I pass them by, and leave them to themselves; they *are not written in the Lamb's book of life,* and therefore not in the breast-plate of the great high-priest. And miserable is the condition of such, as it was of those whom the prophet was forbidden to pray for, and more so, Jer. vii. 16. We that know not who are chosen, and who are passed by, must *pray for all men,* 1 Tim. ii. 1, 4. While there is life, there is hope, and room for prayer. See 1 Sam. xii. 23.

II. Whom he did pray for; not for angels, but for the children of men. 1. He prays *for those that were given him,* meaning primarily the disciples that had attended *him in the regeneration;* but it is doubtless to be extended further, to all who come under the same character, who receive and believe the words of Christ, *v.* 6, 8. 2. He prays *for all that should believe on him* (*v.* 20), and it is not only the petitions that follow, but those also which went before, that must be construed to extend to all believers, in every place and every age; for he has a concern for them all, and calls *things that are not as though they were.*

III. What encouragement he had to pray for them, and what are the general pleas with which he introduces his petitions for them, and recommends them to his Father's favour; they are five:—

1. The charge he had received concerning them: *Thine they were, and thou gavest them me* (*v.* 6), and again (*v.* 9), *Those whom thou hast given me.* "Father, those I am now praying for are such as thou hast entrusted me with, and what I have to say for them is in pursuance of the charge I have received concerning them." Now,

(1.) This is meant primarily of the disciples that then were, who were given to Christ as his pupils to be educated by him while he was on earth, and his agents to be employed for him when he went to heaven. They were given him to be the learners of his doctrine, the witnesses of his life and miracles, and the monuments of his grace and favour, in order to their being the publishers of his gospel and the planters of his church. When they left all to follow him, this was the secret spring of that strange resolution: they were given to him, else they had not given themselves to him. Note, The apostleship and ministry, which are Christ's gift to the church, were first the Father's gift to Jesus Christ. As under the law the Levites were given to Aaron (Num. iii 9), to him (the *great high-priest of our profession)* the Father gave the apostles first, and ministers in every age, *to keep his charge, and the charge of the whole congregation, and to do the service of the tabernacle.* See Eph. iv. 8, 11; Ps. lxviii. 18. Christ received this gift for men, that he might give it to men. As this puts a great honour upon the ministry of the gospel, and magnifies that office, which is so much vilified; so it lays a mighty obligation upon the ministers of the gospel to devote themselves entirely to Christ's service, as being *given to him,*

(2.) But it is designed to extend to all the elect, for they are elsewhere said to be given to Christ (*ch.* vi. 37, 39), and he often laid a stress upon this, that those he was to save were given to him as his charge; to his care they were committed, from his hand they were expected, and concerning them he received commandments. He here shows,

[1.] That the Father had authority to give them: *Thine they were.* He did not give that which was none of his own, but covenanted that he had a good title. The elect, whom the Father gave to Christ, were his own in three ways:—*First,* They were creatures, and their lives and beings were derived from him. When they were given to Christ to be *vessels of honour,* they were *in his hand, as clay in the hand of the potter,* to be disposed of as God's wisdom saw most for God's glory. *Secondly,* They were criminals, and their lives and beings were forfeited to him. It was a remnant of fallen mankind that was given to Christ to be redeemed, that might have been made sacrifices to justice when they were pitched upon to be the *monuments of mercy;* might justly have been *delivered to the tormentors* when they were delivered to the Saviour. *Thirdly,* They were chosen, and their lives and beings were designed, for him; they were set apart for God, and were consigned to Christ as his agent. This he insists upon again (*v.* 7): *All things whatsoever thou hast given me are of thee,* which, though it may take in all that appertained to his office as Mediator, yet seems especially to be meant of those that were given him. "They *are of thee,* their being is of thee as the God of nature, their well-being is of thee as the God of grace; they *are all of thee,* and therefore, Father, I bring them all to thee, that they may be all for thee."

[2.] That he did accordingly give them to the Son· *Thou gavest them to me,* as sheep to the shepherd, to be kept; as patients to the physician, to be cured; children to a tutor, to be educated; thus he will deliver up his charge (Heb. ii. 13), *The children thou hast given me.* They were delivered to Christ, *First,* That the election of grace might not be frustrated, *that not one,* no not *of the little ones, might perish.* That great concern must be lodged in some one good hand, able to give sufficient security, *that the purpose of God according to election might stand. Secondly,* That the undertaking of Christ might not be fruitless; they were *given to him as his seed,* in whom he should *see of the travail of his soul and be satisfied* (Isa. liii. 10, 11), and might not *spend his strength,* and shed his blood, *for nought, and in vain,* Isa. xlix. 4. We may plead, as Christ does, "Lord, keep my graces, keep my comforts, for *thine they were, and thou gavest them to me.*"

2. The care he had taken of them to teach them (*v.* 6): *I have manifested thy name to them. I have given to them the words which thou gavest to me, v.* 8. Observe here,

(1.) The great design of Christ's doctrine, which was to manifest God's name, to declare him (*ch.* i. 18), to instruct the ignorant, and rectify the mistakes of a dark and foolish world concerning God, that he might be better loved and worshipped.

(2.) His faithful discharge of this undertaking: *I have* done it. His fidelity appears, [1.] In the truth of his doctrine. It agreed exactly with the instructions he received from his Father. He gave not only the things, but the very *words, that were given him.* Ministers, in wording their message, must have an eye to *the words which the Holy Ghost teaches.* [2.] In the tendency of his doctrine, which was to manifest God's name. He did not seek himself, but, in all he did and said, aimed to magnify his Father. Note, *First,* It is Christ's prerogative to manifest God's name to the souls of the children of men. *No man knows the Father, but he to whom the Son will reveal him,* Matt. xi. 27. He only has acquaintance with the Father, and so is able to open the truth; and he only has access to the spirits of men, and so is able to open the understanding. Ministers may *publish the name of the Lord* (as Moses, Deut. xxxii. 3), but Christ only can manifest that name. By the word of Christ God is revealed to us; by the Spirit of Christ God is revealed in us. Ministers may speak the words of God to us, but Christ can give us his words, can put them in us, as food, as treasure. *Secondly,* Sooner or later, Christ will manifest God's name to all that were given him, and will give them his word, to be the seed of their new birth, the support of their spiritual life, and the earnest of their everlasting bliss.

3. The good effect of the care he had taken of them, and the pains he had taken with them (*v.* 6): *They have kept thy word* (*v.* 7), *they have known that all things are of thee* (*v.* 8); *they have received thy words,* and em-

braced them, have given their assent and consent to them, *and have known surely that I came out from thee, and have believed that thou didst send me.* Observe here,

(1.) What success the doctrine of Christ had among those *that were given to him,* in several particulars:—

[1.] "They have received the words which I gave them, as the ground receives the seed, and the earth drinks in the rain." They attended to the words of Christ, apprehended in some measure the meaning of them, and were affected with them: they received the impression of them. The word was to them an *ingrafted word.*

[2.] "*They have kept thy word,* have continued in it; they have conformed to it." Christ's commandment is then only kept when it is obeyed. Those that have to teach others the commands of Christ ought to be themselves observant of them. It was requisite that these should *keep what was committed to them,* for it was to be transmitted by them to every place for every age.

[3.] "They have understood the word, and have been sensible on what ground they went in receiving and keeping it. They have been aware that thou art the original author of that holy religion which I am come to institute, *that all things whatsoever thou hast given me are of thee.*" All Christ's offices and powers, all the gifts of the Spirit, all his graces and comforts, which God *gave without measure to him,* were all from God, contrived by his wisdom, appointed by his will, and designed by his grace, for his own glory in man's salvation. Note, It is a great satisfaction to us, in our reliance upon Christ, that he, and all he is and has, all he said and did, all he is doing and will do, are of God, 1 Cor. i. 30. We may therefore venture our souls upon Christ's mediation, for it has a good bottom. If the righteousness be of God's appointing, we shall be justified; if the grace be of his dispensing, we shall be sanctified.

[4.] They have set their seal to it: *They have known surely that I came out from God, v.* 8. See here, *First,* What it is to believe; it is to *know surely,* to know *that it is so of a truth.* The disciples were very weak and defective in knowledge; yet Christ, who knew them better than they knew themselves, passes his word for them that they did believe. Note, We may know surely that which we neither do nor can know fully; i ay *know the certainty of the things which are not seen,* though we cannot particularly describe the nature of them. *We walk by faith,* which knows surely, *not* yet *by sight,* which knows clearly. *Secondly,* What it is we are to believe: *that Jesus Christ came out from God,* as he is the Son of God, in his person *the image of the invisible God,* and that God did send him; that in his undertaking he is the ambassador of the eternal king: so that the Christian religion stands upon the same footing, and is of equal authority, with natural religion; and therefore all the doctrines of Christ are to be received as divine truths, all his commands obeyed as divine laws, and all his promises depended upon as divine securities.

(2.) How Jesus Christ here speaks of this: he enlarges upon it, [1.] As pleased with it himself. Though the many instances of his disciples' dulness and weakness had grieved him, yet their constant adherence to him, their gradual improvements, and their great attainments at last, were his joy. Christ is a Master that delights in the proficiency of his scholars. He accepts the sincerity of their faith, and graciously passes by the infirmity of it. See how willing he is to make the best of us, and to say the best of us, thereby encouraging our faith in him, and teaching us charity to one another. [2.] As pleading it with his Father. He is praying for *those that were given to him;* and he pleads that they had given themselves to him. Note, The due improvement of grace received is a good plea, according to the tenour of the new covenant, for further grace; for so runs the promise, *To him that hath shall be given.* Those that keep Christ's word, and believe on him, let Christ alone to commend them, and, which is more, to recommend them to his Father.

4. He pleads the Father's own interest in them (*v.* 9): *I pray for them, for they are thine;* and this by virtue of a joint and mutual interest, which he and the Father have in what pertained to each: *All mine are thine, and thine are mine.* Between the Father and Son there can be no dispute (as there is among the children of men) about *meum* and *tuum—mine and thine,* for the matter was settled from eternity; *all mine are thine, and thine are mine.* Here is,

(1.) The plea particularly urged for his disciples: *They are thine.* The consigning of the elect to Christ was so far from making them less the Father's that it was in order to making them the more so. Note, [1.] All that receive Christ's word, and believe in him, are taken into covenant-relation to the Father, and are looked upon as his; Christ presents them to him, and they, through Christ, present themselves to him. Christ has *redeemed us,* not to himself only, but *to God, by his blood,* Rev. v. 9, 10. They are *first-fruits unto God,* Rev. xiv. 4. [2.] This is a good plea in prayer, Christ here pleads it, *They are thine;* we may plead it for ourselves, *I am thine, save me;* and for others (as Moses, Exod. xxxii. 11), "*They are thy people. They are thine;* wilt thou not provide for thine own? Wilt thou not secure them, that they may not be run down by the devil and the world? Wilt thou not secure thy interest in them, that they may not depart from thee? *They are thine,* own them as thine."

(2.) The foundation on which this plea is

grounded: *All mine are thine, and thine are mine.* This bespeaks the Father and Son to be, [1.] One in essence. Every creature must say to God, *All mine are thine;* but none can say to him, *All thine are mine,* but he that is the same in substance with him, and equal in power and glory. [2.] One in interest; no separate or divided interests between them. *First,* What the Father has as Creator is delivered over to the Son, to be used and disposed of in subserviency to his great undertaking. *All things are delivered to him* (Matt xi. 27); the grant is so general that nothing is excepted but *he that did put all things under him. Secondly,* What the Son has as Redeemer is designed for the Father, and his kingdom shall shortly be delivered up to him. All the benefits of redemption, purchased by the Son, are intended for the Father's praise, and in his glory all the lines of his undertaking centre: *All mine are thine.* The Son owns none for his that are not devoted to the service of the Father; nor will any thing be accepted as a piece of service to the Christian religion which clashes with the dictates and laws of natural religion. In a limited sense, every true believer may say, *All thine are mine;* if God be ours in covenant, all he is and has is so far ours that it shall be engaged for our good; and in an unlimited sense every true believer does say, Lord, *all mine are thine;* all laid at his feet, to be serviceable to him. And what we have may be comfortably committed to God's care and blessing when it is cheerfully submitted to his government and disposal: "Lord, take care of what I have, for it is *all thine.*"

5. He pleads his own concern in them: *I am glorified in them—δεδόξασμαι.* (1.) *I have been glorified in them.* What little honour Christ had in this world was among his disciples; he had been glorified by their attendance on him and obedience to him, their preaching and working miracles in his name; and therefore *I pray for them.* Note, Those shall have an interest in Christ's intercession in and by whom he is glorified. (2.) "*I am to be glorified in them,* when I am gone to heaven; they are to bear up my name." The apostles preached and wrought miracles *in Christ's name; the Spirit in them glorified Christ* (*ch.* xvi. 14): "*I am glorified in them,* and therefore," [1.] "I concern myself for them." What little interest Christ has in this degenerate world lies in his church; and therefore it and all its affairs lie near his heart, within the veil. [2.] "Therefore I commit them to the Father, who has engaged to glorify the Son, and, upon this account, will have a gracious eye to those in whom he is glorified." That in which God and Christ are glorified may, with humble confidence, be committed to God's special care.

11 And now I am no more in the
world, but these are in the world,
and I come to thee. Holy Father,
keep through thine own name those
whom thou hast given me, that they
may be one, as we *are.* 12 While I
was with them in the world, I kept
them in thy name: those that thou
gavest me I have kept, and none of
them is lost, but the son of perdition;
that the scripture might be fulfilled.
13 And now come I to thee; and
these things I speak in the world,
that they might have my joy fulfilled
in themselves. 14 I have given them
thy word; and the world hath hated
them, because they are not of the
world, even as I am not of the world.
15 I pray not that thou shouldest
take them out of the world, but that
thou shouldest keep them from the
evil. 16 They are not of the world,
even as I am not of the world.

After the general pleas with which Christ recommended his disciples to his Father's care follow the particular petitions he puts up for them; and, 1. They all relate to spiritual blessings in heavenly things. He does not pray that they might be rich and great in the world, that they might raise estates and get preferments, but that they might be kept from sin, and furnished for their duty, and brought safely to heaven. Note, The prosperity of the soul is the best prosperity; for what relates to this Christ came to purchase and bestow, and so teaches us to seek, in the first place, both for others and for ourselves. 2. They are such blessings as were suited to their present state and case, and their various exigencies and occasions. Note, Christ's intercession is always pertinent. Our *advocate with the Father* is acquainted with all the particulars of our wants and burdens, our dangers and difficulties, and knows how to accommodate his intercession to each, as to Peter's peril, which he himself was not aware of (Luke xxii. 32), *I have prayed for thee.* 3. He is large and full in the petitions, orders them before his Father, and *fills his mouth with arguments,* to teach us fervency and importunity in prayer, to be large in prayer, and dwell upon our errands at the throne of grace, wrestling as Jacob, *I will not let thee go, except thou bless me.*

Now the first thing Christ prays for, for his disciples, is their preservation, in these verses, in order to which he commits them all to his Father's custody. Keeping supposes danger, and their danger arose *from the world,* the world wherein they were, *the evil* of this he begs they might be kept from. Now observe,

I. The request itself: *Keep them from the*

world. There were two ways of their being delivered from the world:—

1. By taking them out of it; and he does not pray that they might be so delivered: *I pray not that thou shouldest take them out of the world;* that is,

(1.) "I pray not that they may be speedily removed by death." If the world will be vexatious to them, the readiest way to secure them would be to hasten them out of it to a better world, that will give them better treatment. Send chariots and horses of fire for them, to fetch them to heaven; Job, Elijah, Jonah, Moses, when that occurred which fretted them, prayed that they might be *taken out of the world;* but Christ would not pray so for his disciples, for two reasons:—[1.] Because he came to conquer, not to countenance, those intemperate heats and passions which make men impatient of life, and importunate for death. It is his will that we should take up our cross, and not outrun it. [2.] Because he had work for them to do in the world; the world, though sick of them (Acts xxii. 22), and therefore not worthy of them (Heb. xi. 38), yet could ill spare them. In pity therefore to this dark world, Christ would not have these lights removed out of it, but continued in it, especially for the sake of those in the world that were to *believe in him through their word.* Let not them be taken out of the world when their Master is; they must each in his own order die a martyr, but not till they have finished their testimony. Note, *First,* The taking of good people out of the world is a thing by no means to be desired, but rather dreaded and laid to heart, Isa. lvii. 1. *Secondly,* Though Christ loves his disciples, he does not presently send for them to heaven, as soon as they are effectually called, but leaves them for some time in this world, that they may do good and glorify God upon earth, and be ripened for heaven. Many good people are spared to live, because they can ill be spared to die.

(2.) "I pray not that they may be totally freed and exempted from the troubles of this world, and taken out of the toil and terror of it into some place of ease and safety, there to live undisturbed; this is not the preservation I desire for them." *Non ut omni molestia liberati otium et delicias colant, sed ut inter media pericula salvi tamen maneant Dei auxilio—Not that, being freed from all trouble, they may bask in luxurious ease, but that by the help of God they may be preserved in a scene of danger;* so Calvin. Not that they may be kept from all conflict with the world, but that they may not be overcome by it; not that, as Jeremiah wished, they might *leave their people, and go from them* (Jer. ix. 2), but that, like Ezekiel, *their faces may be strong against the faces of wicked men,* Ezek. iii. 8. It is more the honour of a Christian soldier by faith to *overcome the world* than by a monastical vow to retreat from it; and more for the honour of Christ to serve him in a city than to serve him in a cell.

2. Another way is by keeping them from the corruption that is in the world; and he prays they may be thus kept, *v.* 11, 15. Here are three branches of this petition:—

(1.) *Holy Father, keep those whom thou hast given me.*

[1.] Christ was now leaving them; but let them not think that their defence was departed from them; no, he does here, in their hearing, commit them to the custody of his Father and their Father. Note, It is the unspeakable comfort of all believers that Christ himself has committed them to the care of God. Those cannot but be safe whom the almighty God keeps, and he cannot but keep those whom the Son of his love commits to him, in the virtue of which we may by faith *commit the keeping of our souls to God,* 1 Pet. iv. 19; 2 Tim. i. 12. *First,* He here puts them under the divine protection, that they may not be run down by the malice of their enemies; that they and all their concerns may be the particular care of the divine Providence: "*Keep* their lives, till they have done their work; keep their comforts, and let them not be broken in upon by the hardships they meet with; keep up their interest in the world, and let it not sink." To this prayer is owing the wonderful preservation of the gospel ministry and gospel church in the world unto this day; if God had not graciously kept both, and kept up both, they had been extinguished and lost long ago. *Secondly,* He puts them under the divine tuition, that they may not themselves run away from their duty, nor be led aside by the treachery of their own hearts: "*Keep them* in their integrity, keep them disciples, keep them close to their duty." We need God's power not only to put us into a state of grace, but to keep us in it. See, *ch.* x. 28, 29; 1 Pet. i. 5.

[2.] The titles he gives to him he prays to, and them he prays for, enforce the petition. *First,* He speaks to God as a *holy Father.* In committing ourselves and others to the divine care, we may take encouragement, 1. From the attribute of his holiness, for this is engaged for the preservation of his holy ones; he hath *sworn by his holiness,* Ps. lxxxix. 35. If he be a holy God and hate sin, he will make those holy that are his, and keep them from sin, which they also hate and dread as the greatest evil. 2. From this relation of a Father, wherein he stands to us through Christ. If he be a Father, he will take care of his own children, will teach them and keep them; who else should? *Secondly,* He speaks of them as those whom the Father had *given him.* What we receive as our Father's gifts, we may comfortably remit to our Father's care. "Father, keep the graces and comforts thou hast given me; the children thou hast given me; the ministry *I have received.*"

(2.) *Keep* them *through thine own name*

That is, [1.] Keep them for thy name's sake; so some. "Thy name and honour are concerned in their preservation as well as mine, for both will suffer by it if they either revolt or sink." The Old-Testament saints often pleaded, for *thy name's sake;* and those may with comfort plead it that are indeed more concerned for the honour of God's name than for any interest of their own. [2.] Keep them in thy name; so others; the original is so, ἐν τῷ ὀνόματί. "Keep them in the knowledge and fear of thy name; keep them in the profession and service of thy name, whatever it cost them. Keep them in the interest of thy name, and let them ever be faithful to this; keep them in thy truths, in thine ordinances, in the way of thy commandments." [3.] Keep them by or through thy name; so others. "Keep them by thine own power, in thine own hand; keep them thyself, undertake for them, let them be thine own immediate care. Keep them by those means of preservation which thou hast thyself appointed, and by which thou hast made thyself known. Keep them by thy word and ordinances; let thy name be their strong tower, thy tabernacle their pavilion."

(3.) *Keep them from the evil,* or out of the devil. He had taught them to pray daily, *Deliver us from evil,* and this would encourage them to pray. [1.] "Keep them from the evil one, the devil and all his instruments; that wicked one and all his children. Keep them from Satan as a tempter, that either he may not have leave to sift them, or that their faith may not fail. Keep them from him as a destroyer, that he may not drive them to despair." [2.] "Keep them from the evil thing, that is, sin; from every thing that looks like it, or leads to it. Keep them, that they do no evil," 2 Cor. xiii. 7. Sin is that evil which, above any other, we should dread and deprecate. [3.] "Keep them from the evil of the world, and of their tribulation in it, so that it may have no sting in it, no malignity;" not that they might be kept from affliction, but kept through it, that the property of their afflictions might be so altered as that there might be no evil in them, nothing to do them any harm.

II. The reasons with which he enforces these requests for their preservation, which are five:—

1. He pleads that hitherto he had kept them (*v.* 12): "*While I was with them in the world, I have kept them in thy name,* in the true faith of the gospel and the service of God; those that thou gavest me for my constant attendants I have kept, they are all safe, and none of them missing, none of them revolted nor ruined, *but the son of perdition;* he is lost, that the scripture might be fulfilled." Observe,

(1.) Christ's faithful discharge of his undertaking concerning his disciples: *While he was with them, he kept them,* and his care concerning them was not in vain. He kept them in God's name, preserved them from falling into any dangerous errors or sins, from striking in with the Pharisees, who would have *compassed sea and land to make proselytes* of them; he kept them from deserting him, and returning to the little all they had left for him; he had them still under his eye and care when he sent them to preach; *went not his heart with them?* Many that followed him awhile took offence at something or other, and went off; but he kept the twelve that they should not go away. He kept them from falling into the hands of persecuting enemies that sought their lives; kept them when he surrendered himself, *ch.* xviii. 9. *While he was with them,* he kept them in a visible manner by instructions still sounding in their ears, miracles still done before their eyes; when he was gone from them, they must be kept in a more spiritual manner. Sensible comforts and supports are sometimes given and sometimes withheld; but, when they are withdrawn, yet they are not left comfortless. What Christ here says of his immediate followers is true of all the saints while they are here in this world; Christ keeps them *in God's name.* It is implied, [1.] That they are weak, and cannot keep themselves; their own hands are not sufficient for them. [2.] That they are, in God's account, valuable and worth the keeping; precious in his sight and honourable; his treasure, his jewels. [3.] That their salvation is designed, for to this it is that they are kept, 1 Pet. i. 5. As the wicked are reserved for the day of evil, so the righteous are preserved for the day of bliss. [4.] That they are the charge of the Lord Jesus; for as his charge he keeps them, and exposed himself like the good shepherd for the preservation of the sheep.

(2.) The comfortable account he gives of his undertaking: *None of them is lost.* Note, Jesus Christ will certainly keep all that were given to him, so that none of them shall be totally and finally lost; they may think themselves lost, and may be nearly lost (in imminent peril); but it is the Father's will that he should *lose none,* and none he will lose (*ch.* vi. 39); so it will appear when they come all together, and none of them shall be wanting.

(3.) A brand put upon Judas, as none of those whom he had undertaken to keep. He was among those that were given to Christ, but not of them. He speaks of Judas as already lost, for he had abandoned the society of his Master and his fellow-disciples, and abandoned himself to the devil's guidance, and in a little time would *go to his own place;* he is as good as lost. But the apostasy and ruin of Judas were no reproach at all to his Master, or his family; for, [1.] He was *the son of perdition,* and therefore not one of those that were given to Christ to be kept. He deserved perdition, and God left him to throw himself headlong into it. He was the *son of the destroyer,* as Cain, *who was of that wicked one*. That great enemy whom the Lord *will consume* is called a *son of perdition*, because he is a *man of sin*, 2 Thess. ii. 3. It is an awful consideration that one of the apostles proved a son of perdition. No man's place or name in the church, no man's privileges or opportunities of getting grace, no man's profession or external performances, will secure him from ruin, if his heart be not right with God; nor are any more likely to prove sons of perdition at last, after a plausible course of profession, than those that like Judas love the bag; but Christ's distinguishing Judas from those that were given him (for εἰ μὴ is adversative, not exceptive) intimates that the truth and true religion ought not to suffer for the treachery of those that are false to it, 1 John ii. 19. [2.] The scripture was fulfilled; the sin of Judas was foreseen of God's counsel and foretold in his word, and the event would certainly follow after the prediction as a consequent, though it cannot be said necessarily to follow from it as an effect. See Ps. xli. 9; lxix. 25; cix. 8. We should be amazed at the treachery of apostates, were we not *told of it before*.

2. He pleads that he was now under a necessity of leaving them, and could no longer watch over them in the way that he had hitherto done (*v.* 11): "Keep them now, that I may not lose the labour I bestowed upon them while I was with them. Keep them, *that they may be one* with us *as we are* with each other." We shall have occasion to speak of this, *v.* 21. But see here,

(1.) With what pleasure he speaks of his own departure. He expresses himself concerning it with an air of triumph and exultation, with reference both to the world he left and the world he removed to. [1.] "*Now I am no more in the world.* Now farewell to this provoking troublesome world. I have had enough of it, and now the welcome hour is at hand when I shall be *no more in it*. Now that I have finished the work I had to do in it, I have done with it; nothing remains now but to hasten out of it as fast as I can." Note, It should be a pleasure to those that have their home in the other world to think of being *no more in this world;* for when we have done what we have to do in this world, and are made meet for that, what is there here that should court our stay? When we receive a sentence of death within ourselves, with what a holy triumph should we say, "*Now I am no more in this world*, this dark deceitful world, this poor empty world, this tempting defiling world; no more vexed with its thorns and briars, no more endangered by its nets and snares; now I shall wander no more in this howling wilderness, be tossed no more on this stormy sea; *now I am no more in this world*, but can cheerfully quit it, and give it a final farewell." [2.] *Now I come to thee.* To get clear of the world is but the one half of the comfort of a dying Christ, of a dying Christian; the far better half is to think of going to the Father, to sit down in the immediate, uninterrupted, and everlasting enjoyment of him. Note, Those who love God cannot but be pleased to think of coming to him, though it be through the valley of the shadow of death. When we go, to be *absent from the body*, it is to be *present with the Lord*, like children fetched home from school to their father's house. "Now come I to thee whom I have chosen and served, and whom my soul thirsteth after; to thee the fountain of light and life, the crown and centre of bliss and joy; now my longings shall be satisfied, my hopes accomplished, my happiness completed, for *now come I to thee.*"

(2.) With what a tender concern he speaks of those whom he left behind: "*But these are in the world.* I have found what an evil world it is, what will become of these dear little ones that must stay in it? *Holy Father, keep them;* they will want my presence, let them have thine. They have now more need than ever to be kept, for I am sending them out further into the world than they have yet ventured; they must *launch forth into the deep*, and have business to do in these great waters, and will be lost if thou do not keep them." Observe here, [1.] That, when our Lord Jesus was going to the Father, he carried with him a tender concern for *his own that are in the world;* and continued to compassionate them. He bears their names upon his breast-plate, nay, upon his heart, and has *graven them* with the nails of his cross *upon the palms of his hands;* and when he is out of their sight they are not out of his, much less out of his mind. We should have such a pity for those that are launching out into the world when we are got almost through it, and for those that are left behind in it when we are leaving it. [2.] That, when Christ would express the utmost need his disciples had of divine preservation, he only says, *They are in the world;* this bespeaks danger enough to those who are bound for heaven, whom a flattering world would divert and seduce, and a malignant world would hate and persecute.

3. He pleads what a satisfaction it would be to them to know themselves safe, and what a satisfaction it would be to him to see them easy: *I speak this, that they may have my joy fulfilled in themselves*, *v.* 13. Observe,

(1.) Christ earnestly desired the fulness of the joy of his disciples, for it is his will that they should rejoice evermore. He was leaving them in tears and troubles, and yet took effectual care to *fulfil their joy*. When they thought their joy in him was brought to an end, then was it advanced nearer to perfection than ever it had been, and they were fuller of it. We are here taught, [1.] To found our joy in Christ: "It is *my joy*, joy of my giving, or rather joy that I am the matter of." Christ is a Christian's joy, his chief joy. Joy in the world is withering with it; joy in Christ is everlasting, like him. [2.]

To build up our joy with diligence; for it is the duty as well as privilege of all true believers; no part of the Christian life is pressed upon us more earnestly, Phil. iii 1; iv. 4. [3.] To aim at the perfection of this joy, that we may have it fulfilled in us, for this Christ would have.

(2.) In order hereunto, he did thus solemnly commit them to his Father's care and keeping and took them for witnesses that he did so: *These things I speak in the world,* while I am yet with them in the world. His intercession in heaven for their preservation would have been as effectual in itself; but saying this in the world would be a greater satisfaction and encouragement to them, and would enable them to *rejoice in tribulation.* Note, [1.] Christ has not only treasured up comforts for his people, in providing for their future welfare, but has given out comforts to them, and said that which will be for their present satisfaction. He here condescended in the presence of his disciples to publish his last will and testament, and (which many a testator is shy of) lets them know what legacies he had left them, and how well they were secured, that they might have strong consolation. [2.] Christ's intercession for us is enough to fulfil our joy in him; nothing more effectual to silence all our fears and mistrusts, and to furnish us with strong consolation, than this, that he always appears in the presence of God for us; therefore the apostle puts a *yea rather* upon this, Rom. viii. 34. And see Heb. vii. 25.

4. He pleads the ill usage they were likely to meet with in the world, for his sake (*v.* 14): "*I have given them thy word* to be published to the world, *and they have received it,* have believed it themselves, and accepted the trust of transmitting it to the world; and therefore *the world hath hated them,* as also because they are *not of the world,* any more than I." Here we have,

(1.) The world's enmity to Christ's followers. While Christ was with them, though as yet they had given but little opposition to the world, yet it hates them, much more would it do so when by their more extensive preaching of the gospel they would *turn the world upside down.* "Father, stand their friend," says Christ, "for they are likely to have many enemies; let them have thy love, for the world's hatred is entailed upon them. In the midst of those fiery darts, let them be *compassed with thy favour as with a shield.*" It is God's honour to take part with the weaker side, and to help the helpless. *Lord, be merciful to them, for men would swallow* them up.

(2.) The reasons of this enmity, which strengthen the plea. [1.] It is implied that one reason is because they had received the word of God as it was sent them by the hand of Christ, when the greatest part of the world rejected it, and set themselves against those who were the preachers and professors of it. Note, Those that receive Christ's good will and good word must expect the world's ill will and ill word. Gospel ministers have been in a particular manner hated by the world, because they call men out of the world, and separate them from it, and teach them not to conform to it, and so condemn the world. "*Father, keep them,* for it is for thy sake that they are exposed; they are sufferers for thee." Thus the psalmist pleads, *For thy sake I have borne reproach,* Ps. lxix. 7. Note, Those that keep the word of Christ's patience are entitled to special protection in the hour of temptation, Rev. iii. 10. That cause which makes a martyr may well make a joyful sufferer. [2.] Another reason is more express; the world hates them, because they *are not of the world.* Those to whom the word of Christ comes in power are not of the world, for it has this effect upon all that receive it in the love of it that it weans them from the wealth of the world, and turns them against the wickedness of the world, and therefore the world bears them a grudge.

5. He pleads their conformity to himself in a holy non-conformity to the world (*v.*16): "Father, keep them, for they are of my spirit and mind, *they are not of the world, even as I am not of the world.*" Those may in faith commit themselves to God's custody, (1.) Who are *as Christ was in this world,* and tread in his steps. God will love those that are like Christ. (2.) Who do not engage themselves in the world's interest, nor devote themselves to its service. Observe, [1.] That Jesus Christ was not of this world; he never had been of it, and least of all now that he was upon the point of leaving it. This intimates, *First,* His state; he was none of the world's favourites nor darlings, none of its princes nor grandees; worldly possessions he had none, not even *where to lay his head;* nor worldly power, he was no judge nor divider. *Secondly,* His Spirit; he was perfectly dead to the world, the prince of this world had nothing in him, the things of this world were nothing to him; not honour, for he *made himself of no reputation;* not riches, for *for our sakes he became poor;* not pleasures, for he *acquainted himself with grief.* See *ch.* viii. 23. [2.] That therefore true Christians are not of this world. The Spirit of Christ in them is opposite to the spirit of the world. *First,* It is their lot to be despised by the world; they are not in favour with the world any more than their Master before them was. *Secondly,* It is their privilege to be delivered from the world; as Abraham out of the land of his nativity. *Thirdly,* It is their duty and character to be dead to the world. Their most pleasing converse is, and should be, with another world, and their prevailing concern about the business of that world, not of this. Christ's disciples were weak, and had many infirmities; yet this he could say for them, They were not of the world, not of the earth, and therefore he recommends them to the care of Heaven.

17 Sanctify them through thy truth: thy word is truth. 18 As thou hast sent me into the world, even so have I also sent them into the world. 19 And for their sakes I sanctify myself, that they also might be sanctified through the truth.

The next thing he prayed for for them was that they might be sanctified; not only kept from evil, but made good.

I. Here is the petition (*v.* 17): *Sanctify them through thy truth,* through thy word, for *thy word is truth;* it is true—it is truth itself. He desires they may be sanctified,

1. As Christians. Father, make them holy, and this will be their preservation, 1 Thess. v. 23. Observe here,

(1.) The grace desired—sanctification. The disciples were sanctified, for they were not of the world; yet he prays, *Father, sanctify them,* that is, [1.] "Confirm the work of sanctification in them, strengthen their faith, inflame their good affections, rivet their good resolutions." [2.] "Carry on that good work in them, and continue it; let the *light shine more and more.*" [3.] "Complete it, crown it with the perfection of holiness; sanctify them throughout and to the end." Note, *First,* It is the prayer of Christ for all that are his that they may be sanctified; because he cannot for shame own them as his, either here or hereafter, either employ them in his work or present them to his Father, if they be not sanctified. *Secondly,* Those that through grace are sanctified have need to be sanctified more and more. Even disciples must pray for sanctifying grace; for, if he that was the author of the good work be not the finisher of it, we are undone. Not to go forward is to go backward; *he that is holy must be holy still,* more holy still, pressing forward, soaring upward, as those that have not attained. *Thirdly,* It is God that sanctifies as well as God that justifies, 2 Cor. v. 5. *Fourthly,* It is an encouragement to us, in our prayers for sanctifying grace, that it is what Christ intercedes for for us.

(2.) The means of conferring this grace—*through thy truth, thy word is truth.* Not that the Holy One of Israel is hereby limited to means, but in the *counsel of peace* among other things it was settled and agreed, [1.] That all needful truth should be comprised and summed up in the word of God. Divine revelation, as it now stands in the written word, is not only pure truth without mixture, but entire truth without deficiency. [2.] That this word of truth should be the outward and ordinary means of our sanctification; not of itself, for then it would always sanctify, but as the instrument which the Spirit commonly uses in beginning and carrying on that good work; it is the seed of the new birth (1 Pet. i. 23), and the food of the new life, 1 Pet. ii. 1—2.

2. As ministers. "*Sanctify them,* set them apart for thyself and service; let their call to the apostleship be ratified in heaven." Prophets were said to be sanctified, Jer. i. 5. Priests and Levites were so. *Sanctify them;* that is, (1.) "Qualify them for the office, with Christian graces and ministerial gifts, to make them able ministers of the New Testament." (2.) "Separate them to the office, Rom. i. 1. I have called them, they have consented; Father, say *Amen* to it." (3.) "Own them in the office; let thy hand go along with them; sanctify them by or in thy truth, as truth is opposed to figure and shadow; sanctify them really, not ritually and ceremonially, as the Levitical priests were, by anointing and sacrifice. Sanctify them to thy truth, the word of thy truth, to be the preachers of thy truth to the world; as the priests were sanctified to serve at the altar, so let them be to preach the gospel." 1 Cor. ix. 13, 14. Note, [1.] Jesus Christ intercedes for his ministers with a particular concern, and recommends to his Father's grace those stars he carries in his right hand. [2.] The great thing to be asked of God for gospel ministers is that they may be sanctified, effectually separated from the world, entirely devoted to God, and experimentally acquainted with the influence of that word upon their own hearts which they preach to others. Let them have the *Urim* and *Thummim, light* and *integrity.*

II. We nave here two pleas or arguments to enforce the petition for the disciples' sanctification:—

1. The mission they had from him (*v.* 18): "*As thou hast sent me into the world,* to be thine ambassador to the children of men, so now that I am recalled *have I sent them into the world,* as my delegates." Now here,

(1.) Christ speaks with great assurance of his own mission: *Thou hast sent me into the world.* The great author of the Christian religion had his commission and instructions from him who is the origin and object of all religion. He was sent of God to say what he said, and do what he did, and be what he is to those that believe on him; which was his comfort in his undertaking, and may be ours abundantly in our dependence upon him; his record was on high, for thence his mission was.

(2.) He speaks with great satisfaction of the commission he had given his disciples "*So have I sent them* on the same errand, and to carry on the same design;" to preach the same doctrine that he preached, and to confirm it with the same proofs, with a charge likewise to commit to other faithful men that which was committed to them. He gave them their commission (*ch.* xx. 21) with a reference to his own, and it magnifies their office that it comes from Christ, and that there is some affinity between the commission given to the ministers of reconciliation and that given to the Mediator; he is called an *apostle* (Heb. iii. 1), a *minister* (Rom. xv. 8), a *messenger*, Mal. iii. 1. Only they are sent as servants, he as a Son. Now this comes in here as a reason, [1.] Why Christ was concerned so much for them, and laid their case so near his heart; because he had himself put them into a difficult office, which required great abilities for the due discharge of it. Note, Whom Christ sends he will stand by, and interest himself in those that are employed for him; what he calls us out to he will fit us out for, and bear us out in. [2.] Why he committed them to his Father; because he was concerned in their cause, their mission being in prosecution of his, and as it were an assignment out of it. Christ *received gifts for men* (Ps. lxviii. 18), and then gave them to men (Eph. iv. 8), and therefore *prays aid* of his Father to warrant and uphold those gifts, and confirm his grant of them. The Father *sanctified him* when *he sent him into the world, ch.* x. 36. Now, they being sent as he was, let them also be sanctified.

2. The merit he had for them is another thing here pleaded (*v.* 19): *For their sakes I sanctify myself.* Here is, (1.) Christ's designation of himself to the work and office of Mediator: *I sanctified myself.* He entirely devoted himself to the undertaking, and all the parts of it, especially that which he was now going about—the *offering up of himself without spot unto God, by the eternal Spirit.* He, as the priest and altar, sanctified himself as the sacrifice. When he said, Father, *glorify thy name*—Father, *thy will be done*—Father, I *commit my spirit into thy hands,* he paid down the satisfaction he had engaged to make, and so sanctified himself. This he pleads with his Father, for his intercession is made in the virtue of his satisfaction; *by his own blood he entered into the holy place* (Heb. ix. 12), as the high priest, on the day of atonement, sprinkled the blood of the sacrifice at the same time that he burnt incense within the veil, Lev. xvi. 12, 14. (2.) Christ's design of kindness to his disciples herein; it is *for their sakes,* that *they may be sanctified,* that is, that they may be martyrs; so some. "I sacrifice myself, that they may be sacrificed to the glory of God and the church's good." Paul speaks of his being offered, Phil. ii. 17; 2 Tim. iv. 6. Whatever there is in the *death of the saints* that is *precious in the sight of the Lord,* it is owing to the death of the Lord Jesus. But I rather take it more generally, that they may be saints and ministers, duly qualified and accepted of God. [1.] The office of the ministry is the purchase of Christ's blood, and one of the blessed fruits of his satisfaction, and owes its virtue and value to Christ's merit. The priests under the law were consecrated with the blood of bulls and goats, but gospel ministers with the blood of Jesus. [2.] The real holiness of all good Christians is the fruit of Christ's death, by which the gift of the Holy Ghost was purchased; he *gave himself for his church,* to *sanctify it,* Eph. v. 25, 26. And he that designed the end designed also the means, that they might be sanctified *by the truth,* the truth which Christ came into the world to bear witness to, and died to confirm. The word of truth receives its sanctifying virtue and power from the death of Christ. Some read it, that they may be sanctified *in truth,* that is, truly; for as God must be served, so, in order to this, we must be sanctified, *in the spirit, and in truth.* And this Christ has prayed for, for all that are his; for *this is his will, even their sanctification,* which encourages them to pray for it,

20 Neither pray I for these alone,
but for them also which shall believe
on me through their word; 21 That
they all may be one; as thou, Father,
art in me, and I in thee, that they also may be one in us: that the world
may believe that thou hast sent me.
22 And the glory which thou gavest
me I have given them; that they may
be one, even as we are one: 23 I in
them, and thou in me, that they may
be made perfect in one; and that the
world may know that thou hast sent
me, and hast loved them, as thou hast
loved me.

Next to their purity he prays for their unity; for the wisdom from above is *first pure, then peaceable;* and amity is amiable indeed when it is like the ointment on Aaron's holy head, and the dew on Zion's holy hill. Observe,

I. Who are included in this prayer (*v.* 20): "*Not these only,* not these only that are now my disciples" (the eleven, the seventy, with others, men and women that followed him when he was here on earth), "but *for those also who shall believe on me through their word,* either preached by them in their own day or written by them for the generations to come; I pray *for them all,* that they all may be one in their interest in this prayer, and may all receive benefit by it." Note, here, 1. Those, and those only, are interested in the mediation of Christ, that do, or shall, believe in him. This is that by which they are described, and it comprehends all the character and duty of a Christian. They that lived then, *saw and believed,* but they in after ages *have not seen,* and yet *have believed.* 2. It is *through the word* that souls are brought to believe on Christ, and it is for this end that Christ appointed the scriptures to be written, and a standing ministry to continue in the church, while the church stands, that is, while the world stands, for the raising up of a seed. 3. It is certainly and infallibly known to Christ who shall believe on him. He does not here pray at a venture, upon a contingency depending on the treacherous will of man, which pretends to be free, but by reason of sin is *in bondage with its children;* no, Christ knew very well whom he prayed for, the matter was reduced to a certainty by the divine prescience and purpose; he knew who were given him, who, being ordained to eternal life, were *entered in the Lamb's book,* and should undoubtedly believe, Acts xiii. 48. 4. Jesus Christ intercedes not only for great and eminent believers, but for the meanest and weakest; not for those only that are to be employed in the highest posts of trust and honour in his kingdom, but for all, even those that in the eye of the world are inconsiderable. As the divine providence extends itself to the meanest creature, so does the divine grace to the meanest Christian. The good Shepherd has an eye even to *the poor of the flock.* 5. Jesus Christ in his mediation had an actual regard to those of the chosen remnant that were yet unborn, the people that *should be created* (Ps. xxii. 31), the *other sheep* which he *must yet bring.* Before they are *formed in the womb he knows them* (Jer. i. 5), and prayers are filed in heaven for them beforehand, by him who *declareth the end from the beginning, and calleth things that are not as though they were.*

II. What is intended in this prayer (*v.* 21): *That they all may be one.* The same was said before (*v.* 11), *that they may be one as we are,* and again, *v.* 22. The heart of Christ was much upon this. Some think that the oneness prayed for in *v.* 11 has special reference to the disciples as ministers and apostles, that they might be one in their testimony to Christ; and that the harmony of the evangelists, and concurrence of the first preachers of the gospel, are owing to this prayer. Let them be not only of *one heart,* but of *one mouth,* speaking the same thing. The unity of gospel ministers is both the beauty and strength of the gospel interest. But it is certain that the oneness prayed for in *v.* 21 respects all believers. It is the prayer of Christ for all that are his, and we may be sure it is an answered prayer—*that they all may be one,* one in us (*v.* 21), one *as we are one* (*v.* 22), made *perfect in one, v.* 23. It includes three things:—

1. That they might all be *incorporated in one body.* "Father, look upon them all as one, and ratify that great charter by which they are embodied as one church. Though they live in distant places, from one end of heaven to the other, and in several ages, from the beginning to the close of time, and so cannot have any personal acquaintance or correspondence with each other, yet let them be united in me their common head." As Christ died, so he prayed, to *gather them all in one, ch.* xi. 52; Eph. i. 10.

2. That they might all be animated by one Spirit. This is plainly implied in this—*that they may be one in us.* Union with the Father and Son is obtained and kept up only by the Holy Ghost. *He that is joined to the Lord is one spirit,* 1 Cor. vi. 17. Let them all be stamped with the same image and superscription, and influenced by the same power.

3. That they might all be *knit together* in the bond of love and charity, all of one heart. *That they all may be one,* (1.) In judgment and sentiment; not in every little thing—this is neither possible nor needful, but in the great things of God, and in them, by the virtue of this prayer, they are all agreed—that God's favour is better than life—that sin is the worst of evils, Christ the best of friends—that there is another life after this, and the like. (2.) In disposition and inclination. All that are sanctified have the same divine nature and image; they have all a new heart, and it is *one heart.* (3.) They are all one in their designs and aims. Every true Christian, *as far as he is so,* eyes the glory of God as his highest end, and the glory of heaven as his chief good. (4.) They are all one in their desires and prayers; though they differ in words and the manner of expressions, yet, having all received the same *spirit of adoption,* and observing the same rule, they pray for the same things in effect. (5.) All one in love and affection. Every true Christian has that in him which inclines him to love all true Christians as such. That which Christ here prays for is that *communion of saints* which we profess to believe; the fellowship which all believers have with God, and their intimate union with all the saints in heaven and earth, 1 John i. 3. But this prayer of Christ will not have its complete answer till all the saints come to heaven, for then, and not till then, they shall be *perfect in one, v.* 23; Eph. iv. 13.

III. What is intimated by way of plea or argument to enforce this petition; three things:—

1. The oneness that is between the Father and the Son, which is mentioned again and again, *v.* 11, 21—23. (1.) It is taken for granted that the Father and Son are one, one in nature and essence, equal in power and glory, one in mutual endearments. The *Father loveth the Son,* and the Son always pleased the Father. They are one in design, and one in operation. The intimacy of this oneness is expressed in these words, *thou in me, and I in thee.* This he often mentions for his support under his present sufferings, when his enemies were ready to fall upon him, and his friends to fall off from him; yet he was in the Father, and the Father in him. (2.) This is insisted on in Christ's prayer for his disciples' oneness, [1.] As the pattern of that oneness, showing how he desired they might be one. Believers are one in some measure as God and Christ are one; for, *First,* The union of believers is a strict and close union; they are united by a divine nature, by the power of divine grace, in pursuance of the divine counsels. *Secondly,* It

is a holy union, in the Holy Spirit, for holy ends; not a body politic for any secular purpose. *Thirdly,* It is, and will be at last, a complete union. Father and Son have the same attributes, properties, and perfections; so have believers now, as far as they are sanctified, and when grace shall be perfected in glory they will be exactly consonant to each other, all changed into the same image. [2.] As the centre of that oneness; that they may be *one in us,* all meeting here. There is *one God* and *one Mediator;* and herein believers are one, that they all agree to depend upon the favour of this one God as their felicity and the merit of this one Mediator as their righteousness. That is a conspiracy, not a union, which doth not centre in God as the end, and Christ as the way. All who are truly united to God and Christ, who *are one,* will soon be *united one to another.* [3.] As a plea for that oneness. The Creator and Redeemer are one in interest and design; but to what purpose are they so, if all believers be not one body with Christ, and do not jointly receive grace for grace from him, as he has received it for them? Christ's design was to reduce revolted mankind to God: "Father," says he, "let all that believe be one, that *in one body* they may be reconciled" (Eph. ii. 15, 16), which speaks of the uniting of Jews and Gentiles in the church; that great mystery, that the Gentiles should be *fellow-heirs, and of the same body* (Eph. iii. 6), to which I think this prayer of Christ principally refers, it being one great thing he aimed at in his dying; and I wonder none of the expositors I have met with should so apply it. "Father, let the Gentiles that believe be incorporated with the believing Jews, and *make of twain one new man.*" Those words, *I in them, and thou in me,* show what that union is which is so necessary, not only to the beauty, but to the very being, of his church. *First,* Union with Christ: *I in them.* Christ dwelling in the hearts of believers is the life and soul of the new man. *Secondly,* Union with God through him: *Thou in me,* so as by me to be in them. *Thirdly,* Union with each other, resulting from these: *that they* hereby *may be made perfect in one.* We are complete in him.

2. The design of Christ in all his communications of light and grace to them (*v.* 22): "*The glory which thou gavest me,* as the trustee or channel of conveyance, *I have* accordingly *given them,* to this intent, *that they may be one, as we are one;* so that those gifts will be in vain, if they be not one." Now these gifts are either, (1.) Those that were conferred upon the apostles, and first planters of the church. The glory of being God's ambassadors to the world—the glory of working miracles—the glory of gathering a church out of the world, and erecting the throne of God's kingdom among men—this glory was given to Christ, and some of the honour he put upon them when he sent them to *disciple all nations.* Or, (2.) Those that are given in common to all believers. The glory of being in covenant with the Father, and accepted of him, of being laid in his bosom, and designed for a place at his right hand, was the glory which the Father gave to the Redeemer, and he has confirmed it to the redeemed. [1.] This honour he says he *hath given them,* because he hath intended it for them, settled it upon them, and secured it to them upon their believing Christ's promises to be real gifts. [2.] This was given to him to give to them; it was conveyed to him in trust for them, and he was faithful to him that appointed him. [3.] He gave it to them, that they *might be one. First,* To entitle them to the privilege of unity, that by virtue of their common relation to *one God the Father,* and *one Lord Jesus Christ,* they might be truly denominated one. The gift of the Spirit, that great glory which the Father gave to the Son, by him to be given to all believers, makes them one, for he works *all in all,* 1 Cor. xii. 4, &c. *Secondly,* To engage them to the duty of unity. That in consideration of their agreement and communion in one creed and one covenant, one Spirit and one Bible—in consideration of what they have in one God and one Christ, and of what they hope for in one heaven, they may be of one mind and one mouth. Worldly glory sets men at variance; for if some be advanced others are eclipsed, and therefore, while the disciples dreamed of a temporal kingdom, they were ever and anon quarrelling; but spiritual honours being conferred alike upon all Christ's subjects, they being all *made to our God kings and priests,* there is no occasion for contest nor emulation. The more Christians are taken up with the glory Christ has given them, the less desirous they will be of vain-glory, and, consequently, the less disposed to quarrel.

3. He pleads the happy influence their oneness would have upon others, and the furtherance it would give to the public good. This is twice urged (*v.* 21): *That the world may believe that thou hast sent me.* And again (*v.* 23): *That the world may know it,* for without knowledge there can be no true faith. Believers must know what they believe, and why and wherefore they believe it. Those who believe *at a venture,* venture too far. Now Christ here shows,

(1.) His good-will to the world of mankind in general. Herein he is of his Father's mind, as we are sure he is in every thing, that he would have all men to be saved, and to *come to the knowledge of the truth,* 1 Tim. ii. 4; 2 Pet. iii. 9. Therefore it is his will that all means possible should be used, and no stone left unturned, for the conviction and conversion of the world. We know not who are chosen, but we must in our places do our utmost to further men's salvation, and take heed of doing any thing to hinder it.

(2.) The good fruit of the church's oneness; it will be an evidence of the truth of Christianity, and a means of bringing many to embrace it.

[1.] In general, it will recommend Christianity to the world, and to the good opinion of those that are without. *First,* The embodying of Christians in one society by the gospel charter will greatly promote Christianity. When the world shall see so many of those that were its children called out of its family, distinguished from others, and changed from what they themselves sometimes were,—when they shall see this society raised by the foolishness of preaching, and kept up by miracles of divine providence and grace, and how admirably well it is modelled and constituted, they will be ready to say, *We will go with you, for we see that God is with you. Secondly,* The uniting of Christians in love and charity is the beauty of their profession, and invites others to join with them, as the love that was among those primo-primitive Christians, Acts ii. 42, 43; iv. 32, 33. When Christianity, instead of causing quarrels about itself, makes all other strifes to cease,—when it cools the fiery, smooths the rugged, and disposes men to be kind and loving, courteous and beneficent, to all men, studious to preserve and promote peace in all relations and societies, this will recommend it to all that have any thing either of natural religion or natural affection in them.

[2.] In particular, it will beget in men good thoughts, *First,* Of Christ: They will know and believe that *thou hast sent me.* By this it will appear that Christ was sent of God, and that his doctrine was divine, in that his religion prevails to join so many of different capacities, tempers, and interests in other things, in one body by faith, with one heart by love. Certainly he was sent by the God of power, who fashions men's hearts alike, and the God of love and peace; when the worshippers of God are one, he is one, and his name one. *Secondly,* Of Christians: They will *know that thou hast loved them as thou hast loved me.* Here is, 1. The privilege of believers: *the Father* himself loveth them with a love resembling his love to his Son, for they are loved in him with an everlasting love. 2. The evidence of their interest in this privilege, and that is their being one. By this it will appear that God loves us, if we *love one another with a pure heart;* for wherever *the love of God is shed abroad in the heart* it will change it into the same image. See how much good it would do to the world to know better how dear to God all good Christians are. The Jews had a saying, *If the world did but know the worth of good men, they would hedge them about with pearls.* Those that have so much of God's love should have more of ours.

24 Father, I will that they also,
whom thou hast given me, be with
me where I am; that they may behold my glory, which thou hast given me: for thou lovedst me before the foundation of the world.
25 O righteous Father, the world hath not known thee: but I have known thee, and these have known that thou hast sent me.
26 And I have declared unto them thy name; and will declare *it:* that the love wherewith thou hast loved me may be in them, and I in them.

Here is, I. A petition for the glorifying of all those that were given to Christ (*v.* 24), not only these apostles, but all believers: *Father, I will that they may be with me.* Observe,

1. The connection of this request with those foregoing. He had prayed that God would preserve, sanctify, and unite them; and now he prays that he would crown all his gifts with their glorification. In this method we must pray, first for grace, and then for glory (Ps. lxxxiv. 11); for in this method God gives. Far be it from the only wise God to come under the imputation either of that *foolish builder who without a foundation built upon the sand,* as he would if he should glorify any whom he has not first sanctified; or of that *foolish builder who began to build and was not able to finish,* as he would if he should sanctify any, and not glorify them.

2. The manner of the request: *Father, I will.* Here, as before, he addresses himself to God as a Father, and therein we must do likewise; but when he says, θέλω—*I will,* he speaks a language peculiar to himself, and such as does not become ordinary petitioners, but very well became him who paid for what he prayed for. (1.) This intimates the authority of his intercession in general; his word was with power in heaven, as well as on earth. He entering *with his own blood into the holy place,* his intercession there has an uncontrollable efficacy. He intercedes as a king, for he is a priest upon his throne (like Melchizedek), a king-priest. (2.) It intimates his particular authority in this matter; he had a power to *give eternal life* (*v.* 2), and, pursuant to that power, he says, *Father, I will.* Though now he *took upon him the form of a servant,* yet that power being to be most illustriously exerted when he shall come the second time in the glory of a judge, to say, *Come ye blessed,* having that in his eye, he might well say, *Father, I will.*

3. The request itself—that all the elect might come to be with him in heaven at last, to see his glory, and to share in it. Now observe here,

(1.) Under what notion we are to hope for heaven? wherein does that happiness consist? three things make heaven:—[1.] It is to be where Christ is: *Where I am;* in the paradise whither Christ's soul went at death; in the third heavens whither his soul and body went at his ascension:—*Where I am*, am to be shortly, am to be eternally. In this world we are but *in transitu—on our passage;* there we truly are where we are to be for ever; so Christ reckoned, and so must we. [2.] It is to be with him where he is; this is no tautology, but intimates that we shall not only be in the same happy place where Christ is, but that the happiness of the place will consist in his presence; this is *the fulness of its joy*. The very heaven of heaven is to be with Christ, there in company with him, and communion with him, Phil. i. 23. [3.] It is to *behold his glory, which the Father* has given him. Observe, *First*, The glory of the Redeemer is the brightness of heaven. That glory before which angels cover their faces was his glory, *ch.* xii. 41. The Lamb is the light of the new Jerusalem, Rev. xxi. 23. Christ will *come in the glory of his Father*, for *he is the brightness of his glory*. God shows his glory there, as he does his grace here, through Christ. "*The Father has given me this glory*," though he was as yet in his low estate; but it was very sure, and very near. *Secondly*, The felicity of the redeemed consists very much in the beholding of this glory; they will have the immediate view of his glorious person. *I shall see God in my flesh*, Job xix. 26, 27. They will have a clear insight into his glorious undertaking, as it will be then accomplished; they will see into those springs of love from which flow all the streams of grace; they shall have an appropriating sight of Christ's glory (*Uxor fulget radiis mariti—The wife shines with the radiance of her husband*), and an assimilating sight: they shall *be changed into the same image, from glory to glory*.

(2.) Upon what ground we are to hope for heaven; no other than purely the mediation and intercession of Christ, because he hath said, *Father, I will*. Our sanctification is our evidence, for *he that has this hope in him purifies himself;* but it is the will of Christ that is our title, *by which will we are sanctified*, Heb. x. 10. Christ speaks here as if he did not count his own happiness complete unless he had his elect to share with him in it, for it is *the bringing of many sons to glory that makes the captain of our salvation perfect*, Heb. ii. 10.

4. The argument to back this request: *for thou lovedst me before the foundation of the world*. This is a reason, (1.) Why he expected this glory himself. Thou wilt *give it to me, for thou lovedst me*. The honour and power given to the Son as Mediator were founded in the Father's love to him (*ch.* v. 20): *the Father loves the Son*, is infinitely well pleased in his undertaking, and *therefore has given all things into his hands;* and, the matter being concerted in the divine counsels from eternity, he is said to love him as Mediator *before the foundation of the world*. Or, (2.) Why he expected that those who *were given to him* should be with him to share in his glory: "*Thou lovedst me*, and them in me, and canst deny me nothing I ask for them."

II. The conclusion of the prayer, which is designed to enforce all the petitions for the disciples, especially the last, that they may be glorified. Two things he insists upon, and pleads:—

1. The respect he had to his Father, *v.* 25. Observe,

(1.) The title he gives to God: *O righteous Father*. When he prayed that they might be sanctified, he called him *holy Father;* when he prays that they may be glorified, he calls him *righteous Father;* for it is a *crown of righteousness which the righteous Judge shall give*. God's righteousness was engaged for the giving out of all that good which the Father had promised and the Son had purchased.

(2.) The character he gives of the world that lay in wickedness: *The world has not known thee*. Note, Ignorance of God overspreads the world of mankind; this is the darkness they sit in. Now this is urged here, [1.] To show that these disciples needed the aids of special grace, both because of the necessity of their work—they were to bring a world that knew not God to the knowledge of him; and also because of the difficulty of their work—they must bring light to those that rebelled against the light; therefore keep them. [2.] To show that they were qualified for further peculiar favours, for they had that knowledge of God which the world had not.

(3,) The plea he insists upon for himself: *But I have known thee*. Christ knew the Father as no one else ever did; knew upon what grounds he went in his undertaking, knew his Father's mind in every thing, and therefore, in this prayer, came to him with confidence, as we do to one we know. Christ is here suing out blessings for those that were his; pursuing this petition, when he had said, *The world has not known thee*, one would expect it should follow, *but they have known thee;* no, their knowledge was not to be boasted of, *but I have known thee*, which intimates that there is nothing in us to recommend us to God's favour, but all our interest in him, and intercourse with him, result from, and depend upon, Christ's interest and intercourse. We are unworthy, but he is worthy.

(4.) The plea he insists upon for his disciples: *And they have known that thou hast sent me;* and, [1.] Hereby they are distinguished from the unbelieving world. When multitudes to whom Christ was sent, and his grace offered, would not *believe that God had sent him*, these knew it, and believed it, and were not ashamed to own it. Note, To know and believe in Jesus Christ, in the midst of a world that persists in ignorance and infidelity, is highly pleasing to God, and shall certainly be crowned with distinguishing glory. Singular faith qualifies for singular favours. [2.] Hereby they are interested in the mediation of Christ, and partake of the benefit of his acquaintance with the Father: "*I have known thee,* immediately and perfectly; and these, though they have not so known thee, nor were capable of knowing thee so, yet *have known that thou hast sent me,* have known that which was required of them to know, have known the Creator in the Redeemer." Knowing Christ as sent of God, they have, in him, known the Father, and are introduced to an acquaintance with him; therefore, "Father, look after them for my sake."

2. The respect he had to his disciples (*v.* 26): "I have led them into the knowledge of thee, and will do it yet more and more; with this great and kind intention, *that the love wherewith thou hast loved me may be in them, and I in them.*" Observe here,

(1.) What Christ had done for them: *I have declared unto them thy name.* [1.] This he had done for those that were his immediate followers. *All the time that he went in and out among them,* he made it his business to declare his Father's name to them, and to beget in them a veneration for it. The tendency of all his sermons and miracles was to advance his Father's honour, and to spread the knowledge of him, *ch.* i. 18. [2.] This he has done for all that believe on him; for they had not been brought to believe if Christ had not made known to them his Father's name. Note, *First,* We are indebted to Christ for all the knowledge we have of the Father's name; he declares it, and he opens the understanding to receive that revelation. *Secondly,* Those whom Christ recommends to the favour of God he first leads into an acquaintance with God.

(2.) What he intended to do yet further for them: *I will declare it.* To the disciples he designed to give further instructions after his resurrection (Acts i. 3), and to bring them into a much more intimate acquaintance with divine things by the pouring out of the Spirit after his ascension; and to all believers, into whose hearts he hath shined, he shines more and more. Where Christ has *declared his Father's name, he will declare it;* for *to him that hath shall be given;* and those that know God both need and desire to know more of him. This is fitly pleaded for them: "Father, own and favour them, for they will own and honour thee."

(3.) What he aimed at in all this; not to fill their heads with curious speculations, and furnish them with something to talk of among the learned, but to secure and advance their real happiness in two things:—

[1.] Communion with God: "Therefore I have given them the knowledge of thy name, of all that whereby thou hast made thyself known, *that thy love,* even that *wherewith thou hast loved me, may be,* not only towards them, but *in them;*" that is, *First,* "Let them have the fruits of that love for their sanctification; let *the Spirit of love,* with which thou hast filled me, *be in them.*" Christ declares his Father's name to believers, that with that divine light darted into their minds a divine love may be shed abroad in their hearts, to be in them a commanding constraining principle of holiness, that they may partake of a divine nature. When God's love to us comes to be in us, it is like the virtue which the loadstone gives the needle, inclining it to move towards the pole; it draws out the soul towards God in pious and devout affections, which are as the spirits of the divine life in the soul. *Secondly,* "Let them have the taste and relish of that love for their consolation; let them not only be interested in the love of God, by having God's name declared to them, but, by a further declaration of it, let them have the comfort of that interest; that they may not only know God, but *know that they know him,*" 1 John ii. 3. It is *the love of God* thus *shed abroad in the heart* that fills it with joy, Rom. v. 3, 5. This God has provided for, that we may not only be satisfied with his loving kindness, but be satisfied of it; and so may live a life of complacency in God and communion with him; this we must pray for, this we must press after; if we have it, we must thank Christ for it; if we want it, we may thank ourselves.

[2.] Union with Christ in order hereunto: *And I in them.* There is no getting into the love of God but through Christ, nor can we keep ourselves in that love but by abiding in Christ, that is, having him to abide in us; nor can we have the sense and apprehension of that love but by our experience of the indwelling of Christ, that is, the Spirit of Christ in our hearts. It is *Christ in us* that is *the* only *hope of glory* that will *not make us ashamed,* Col. i. 27. All our communion with God, the reception of his love to us with our return of love to him again, passes through the hands of the Lord Jesus, and the comfort of it is owing purely to him. Christ had said but a little before, *I in them* (*v.* 23), and here it is repeated (though the sense was complete without it), and the prayer closed with it, to show how much the heart of Christ was set upon it; all his petitions centre in this, and with this *the prayers of Jesus, the Son of David, are ended:* "*I in them;* let me have this, and I desire no more." It is the glory of the Redeemer to dwell in the redeemed: it is his *rest for ever,* and he has desired it. Let us therefore make sure our union with Christ, and then take the comfort of his intercession. *This* prayer had an end, but *that* he ever lives to make.

CHAP. XVIII.

Hitherto this evangelist has recorded little of the history of Christ, only so far as was requisite to introduce his discourses; but now that the time drew nigh that Jesus must die he is very particular in relating the circumstances of his sufferings, and some

which the others had omitted, especially his sayings. So far were his followers from being ashamed of his cross, or endeavouring to conceal it, that this was what, both by word and writing, they were most industrious to proclaim, and gloried in it. This chapter relates, I. How Christ was arrested in the garden and surrendered himself a prisoner, ver. 1—12. II. How he was abused in the high priest's court, and how Peter, in the mean time, denied him, ver. 13—27. III. How he was prosecuted before Pilate, and examined by him, and put in election with Barabbas for the favour of the people, and lost it, ver. 28—40.

WHEN Jesus had spoken these
words, he went forth with his
disciples over the brook Cedron, where
was a garden, into the which he entered, and his disciples. 2 And Judas also, which betrayed him, knew
the place: for Jesus ofttimes resorted
thither with his disciples. 3 Judas
then, having received a band *of men*
and officers from the chief priests and
Pharisees, cometh thither with lanterns and torches and weapons. 4
Jesus therefore, knowing all things
that should come upon him, went
forth, and said unto them, Whom
seek ye? 5 They answered him, Jesus of Nazareth. Jesus saith unto
them, I am *he*. And Judas also,
which betrayed him, stood with them.
6 As soon then as he had said unto
them, I am *he*, they went backward
and fell to the ground. 7 Then asked
he them again, Whom seek ye? And
they said, Jesus of Nazareth. 8 Jesus answered, I have told you that I
am *he*: if therefore ye seek me, let
these go their way: 9 That the saying might be fulfilled, which he spake,
Of them which thou gavest me have
I lost none. 10 Then Simon Peter
having a sword drew it, and smote
the high priest's servant, and cut off
his right ear. The servant's name
was Malchus. 11 Then said Jesus
unto Peter, Put up thy sword into
the sheath: the cup which my Father
hath given me, shall I not drink it?
12 Then the band and the captain
and officers of the Jews took Jesus,
and bound him.

The hour was now come that *the captain of our salvation*, who was to be *made perfect by sufferings*, should engage the enemy. We have here his entrance upon the encounter. The day of recompence is in his heart, and *the year of his redeemed is come, and his own arm works the salvation*, for he has no second. *Let us turn aside now, and see this great sight.*

I. Our Lord Jesus, like a bold champion, takes the field first (*v.* 1, 2): *When he had spoken these words*, preached the sermon, prayed his prayer, and so finished his testimony, he would lose no time, but *went forth* immediately out of the house, out of the city, by moon-light, for the passover was observed at the full moon, *with his disciples* (the eleven, for Judas was otherwise employed), and *he went over the brook Cedron*, which runs between Jerusalem and the mount of Olives, *where was a garden*, not his own, but some friend's, who allowed him the liberty of it. Observe,

1. That our Lord Jesus entered upon his sufferings *when he had spoken these words*, as Matt. xxvi. 1, *When he had finished all these sayings.* Here it is intimated, (1.) That our Lord Jesus took his work before him. The office of the priest was to teach, and pray, and offer sacrifice. Christ, after teaching and praying, applies himself to make atonement. Christ had said all he had to say as a prophet, and now he addresses himself to the discharge of his office as a priest, to *make his soul an offering for sin;* and, when he had gone through this, he entered upon his kingly office. (2.) That having by his sermon prepared his disciples for this hour of trial, and by his prayer prepared himself for it, he then courageously went out to meet it. When he had put on his armour, he entered the lists, and not till then. Let those that suffer according to the will of God, in a good cause, with a good conscience, and having a clear call to it, comfort themselves with this, that Christ will not engage those that are his in any conflict, but he will first do that for them which is necessary to prepare them for it; and if we receive Christ's instructions and comforts, and be interested in his intercession, we may, with an unshaken resolution, venture through the greatest hardships in the way of duty.

2. That *he went forth with his disciples.* Judas knew what house he was in in the city, and he could have staid and met his sufferings there; but, (1.) He would do as he was wont to do, and not alter his method, either to meet the cross or to miss it, when his hour was come. It was his custom when he was at Jerusalem, after he had spent the day in public work, to retire at night *to the mount of Olives;* there his quarters were, in the skirts of the city, for they would not make room for him in the palaces, in the heart of the town. This being his custom, he would not be put out of his method by the foresight of his sufferings, but, as Daniel, did then just *as he did aforetime*, Dan. vi. 10. (2.) He was as unwilling that there should be *an uproar among the people* as his enemies were, for it was not his way *to strive or cry.* If he had been seized in the city, and a tumult raised thereby, mischief might have been done, and a great deal of blood shed, and therefore he withdrew. Note, When we find ourselves involved in trouble, we should be afraid of involving others with us. It is

no disgrace to the followers of Christ to fall tamely. Those who aim at honour from men value themselves upon a resolution to sell their lives as dearly as they can; but those who know that their blood is precious to Christ, and that not a drop of it shall be shed but upon a valuable consideration, need not stand upon such terms. (3.) He would set us an example in the beginning of his passion, as he did at the end of it, of retirement from the world. *Let us go forth to him, without the camp, bearing his reproach,* Heb. xiii. 13. We must lay aside, and leave behind, the crowds, and cares, and comforts, of cities, even holy cities, if we would cheerfully take up our cross, and keep up our communion with God therein.

3. That he went *over the brook Cedron.* He must go over this to go to *the mount of Olives,* but the notice taken of it intimates that there was something in it significant; and it points, (1.) At David's prophecy concerning the Messiah (Ps. cx. 7), that *he shall drink of the brook in the way;* the brook of suffering in the way to his glory and our salvation, signified by *the brook Cedron, the black brook,* so called either from the darkness of the valley it ran through or the colour of the water, tainted with the dirt of the city; such a brook Christ drank of, when it lay in the way of our redemption, and *therefore shall he lift up the head,* his own and ours. (2.) At David's pattern, as a type of the Messiah. In his flight from Absalom, particular notice is taken of his *passing over the brook Cedron, and going up by the ascent of mount Olivet, weeping,* and all that were with him in tears too, 2 Sam. xv. 23, 30. *The Son of David,* being driven out by the rebellious Jews, who would *not have him to reign over them* (and Judas, like Ahithophel, being in the plot against him), passed over the brook in meanness and humiliation, attended by a company of true mourners. The godly kings of Judah had burnt and destroyed the idols they found at *the brook Cedron:* Asa, 2 Chron. xv. 16; Hezekiah, 2 Chron. xxx. 14; Josiah, 2 Kings xxiii. 4, 6. Into that brook the abominable things were cast. Christ, *being now made sin for us,* that he might abolish it and take it away, began his passion by the same brook. Mount Olivet, where Christ began his sufferings, lay on the east side of Jerusalem; mount Calvary, where he finished them, on the west; for in them he had an eye to such as should *come from the east and the west.*

4. That he entered into a garden. This circumstance is taken notice of only by this evangelist, that Christ's sufferings began in a garden. In the garden of Eden sin began; there the curse was pronounced, there the Redeemer was promised, and therefore in a garden that promised seed entered the lists with the old serpent. Christ was buried also in a garden. (1.) Let us, when we walk in our gardens, take occasion thence to meditate on Christ's sufferings in a garden, to which we owe all the pleasure we have in our gardens, for by them the curse upon the ground for man's sake was removed. (2.) When we are in the midst of our possessions and enjoyments, we must keep up an expectation of troubles, for our gardens of delight are in a vale of tears.

5. That he had his disciples with him, (1.) Because he used to take them with him when he retired for prayer. (2.) They must be witnesses of his sufferings, and his patience under them, that they might with the more assurance and affection preach them to the world (Luke xxiv. 48), and be themselves prepared to suffer. (3.) He would take them into the danger to show them their weakness, notwithstanding the promises they had made of fidelity. Christ sometimes brings his people into difficulties, that he may magnify himself in their deliverance.

6. That Judas the traitor *knew the place,* knew it to be the place of his usual retirement, and probably, by some word Christ had dropped, knew that he intended to be there that night, for want of a better closet. A solitary garden is a proper place for meditation and prayer, and after a passover is a proper time to retire for private devotion, that we may pray over the impressions made and the vows renewed, and clench the nail. Mention is made of Judas's knowing the place, (1.) To aggravate the sin of Judas, that he would betray his Master, notwithstanding the intimate acquaintance he had with him; nay, and that he would make use of his familiarity with Christ, as giving him an opportunity of betraying him; a generous mind would have scorned to do so base a thing. Thus has Christ's holy religion been *wounded in the house of its friends,* as it could not have been wounded any where else. Many an apostate could not have been so profane, if he had not been a professor; could not have ridiculed scriptures and ordinances, if he had not known them. (2.) To magnify the love of Christ, that, though he knew where the traitor would seek him, thither he went to be found of him, now that he knew his *hour was come.* Thus he showed himself willing to suffer and die for us. What he did was not by constraint, but by consent; though as man he said, *Let this cup pass away,* as Mediator he said, "*Lo, I come.* I come with a good will." It was late in the night (we may suppose eight or nine o'clock) when Christ went out to the garden; for it was not only his *meat and drink,* but his rest and sleep, *to do the will of him that sent him.* When others were going to bed, he was going to prayer, going to suffer.

II. *The captain of our salvation* having taken the field, the enemy presently comes upon the spot, and attacks him (*v.* 3): Judas with his men comes thither, commissioned by the chief priests, especially those among them that were Pharisees, who were the most bitter enemies to Christ. This evangelist passes over Christ's agony, because the other three had fully related it, and presently introduces Judas and his company that came to seize him. Observe,

1. The persons employed in this action—*a band of men and officers from the chief priests, with Judas.* (1.) Here is a multitude engaged against Christ—*a band of men,* σπεῖρα—*cohors, a regiment,* a Roman band, which some think was five hundred men, others a thousand. Christ's friends were few, his enemies many. Let us therefore *not follow a multitude to do evil,* nor fear a multitude designing evil to us, *if God be for us.* (2.) Here is a mixed multitude; the band of men were Gentiles, Roman soldiers, a detachment out of the guards that were posted in the tower of Antonia, to be a curb upon the city; the *officers of the chief priests,* ὑπηρέτας. Either their domestic servants, or the officers of their courts, were Jews; these had an enmity to each other, but were united against Christ, who came to *reconcile both to God in one body.* (3.) It is a commissioned multitude, not a popular tumult; no, they have received orders *from the chief priests,* upon whose suggestion to the governor that this Jesus was a dangerous man, it is likely, they had a warrant from him too to take him up, *for they feared the people.* See what enemies Christ and his gospel have had, and are likely to have, numerous and potent, and therefore formidable: ecclesiastical and civil powers combined against them, Ps. ii. 1, 2. Christ said it would be so (Matt. x. 18), and found it so. (4.) All under the direction of Judas. He *received* this *band of men;* it is probable that he requested it, alleging that it was necessary to send a good force, being as ambitious of the honour of commanding in chief in this expedition as he was covetous of *the wages of* this *unrighteousness.* He thought himself wonderfully preferred from coming in the rear of the contemptible twelve to be placed at the head of these formidable hundreds; he never made such a figure before, and promised himself, perhaps, that this should not be the last time, but he should be rewarded with a captain's commission, or better, if he succeeded well in this enterprise.

2. The preparation they had made for an attack: They came *with lanterns, and torches, and weapons.* (1.) If Christ should abscond, though they had moonlight, they would have occasion for their lights; but they might have spared these; the second Adam was not driven, as the first was, to hide himself, either for fear or shame, *among the trees of the garden.* It was folly to light a candle to seek the Sun by. (2.) If he should resist, they would have occasion for their arms. *The weapons of his warfare were spiritual,* and at these *weapons* he had often beaten them, and *put them to silence,* and therefore they have now recourse to other *weapons, swords and staves.*

III. Our Lord Jesus gloriously repulsed the first onset of the enemy, *v.* 4—6, where observe,

1. How he received them, with all the mildness imaginable towards them, and all the calmness imaginable in himself.

(1.) He met them with a very soft and mild question (*v.* 4): *Knowing all things that should come upon him,* and therefore not at all surprised with this alarm, with a wonderful intrepidity and presence of mind, undisturbed and undaunted, he *went forth* to meet them, and, as if he had been unconcerned, softly asked, "*Whom seek you?* What is the matter? What means this bustle at this time of night?" See here, [1.] Christ's foresight of his sufferings: he *knew all those things that should come upon him,* for he had bound himself to suffer them. Unless we had strength, as Christ had, to bear the discovery, we should not covet to know what shall come upon us; it would but anticipate our pain; *sufficient unto the day is the evil thereof:* yet it will do us good to expect sufferings in general, so that when they come we may say, "It is but what we looked for, the cost we sat down and counted upon." [2.] Christ's forwardness to his sufferings; he did not run away from them, but went out to meet them, and reached forth his hand to take the bitter cup. When the people would have forced him to a crown, and offered to make him a king in Galilee, he withdrew, and hid himself (*ch.* vi. 15); but, when they came to force him to a cross, he offered himself; for he came to this world to suffer and went to the other world to reign. This will not warrant us needlessly to expose ourselves to trouble, for we know not when our hour is come; but we are called to suffering when we have no way to avoid it but by sin; and, when it comes to this, let *none of these things move* us, for they cannot hurt us.

(2.) He met them with a very calm and mild answer when they told him whom they were in quest of, *v.* 5. They said, *Jesus of Nazareth;* and he said, *I am he.* [1.] It should seem, *their eyes were held, that they could not know him.* It is highly probable that many of the Roman band, at least the officers of the temple, had often seen him, if only to satisfy their curiosity; Judas, however, to be sure, knew him well enough, and yet none of them could pretend to say, *Thou art the man* we seek. Thus he showed them the folly of bringing lights to see for him, for he could make them not to know him when they saw him; and he has herein shown us how easily he can infatuate the counsels of his enemies, and make them lose themselves, when they are seeking mischief. [2.] In their enquiries for him they called him *Jesus of Nazareth,* which was the only title they knew him by, and probably he was so called in their warrant. It was a name of reproach given him, to darken the evidence of his being the Messiah. By this it appears that they knew him not, whence he was;

for, if they had known him, surely they would not have persecuted him. [3.] He fairly answers them: *I am he.* He did not improve the advantage he had against them by their blindness, as Elisha did against the Syrians, telling them, *This is not the way, neither is this the city;* but improves it as an opportunity of showing his willingness to suffer. Though they called him Jesus of Nazareth, he answered to the name, for he despised the reproach; he might have said, *I am not he,* for he was *Jesus of Bethlehem;* but he would by no means allow equivocations. He has hereby taught us to own him, whatever it cost us; not to be *ashamed of him or his words;* but even in difficult times *to confess Christ crucified, and manfully to fight under his banner. I am he,* Ἐγώ εἰμι—*I am he,* is the glorious name of the blessed God (Exod. iii. 14), and the honour of that name is justly challenged by the blessed Jesus. [4.] Particular notice is taken, in a parenthesis, *that Judas stood with them.* He that used to stand with those that followed Christ now stood with those that fought against him. This describes an apostate; he is one that changes sides. He herds himself with those with whom his heart always was, and with whom he shall have his lot in the judgment-day. This is mentioned, *First,* To show the impudence of Judas. One would wonder where he got the confidence with which he now faced his Master, and *was not ashamed, neither could he blush;* Satan in his heart gave him a whore's forehead. *Secondly,* To show that Judas was particularly aimed at in the power which went along with that word, *I am he,* to foil the aggressors. It was an arrow levelled at the traitor's conscience, and pierced him to the quick; for Christ's coming and his voice will be more terrible to apostates and betrayers than to sinners of any other class.

2. See how he terrified them, and obliged them to retire (*v.* 6): *They went backward, and,* like men thunder-struck, *fell to the ground.* It should seem, they did not fall forward, as humbling themselves before him, and yielding to him, but backward, as standing it out to the utmost. Thus Christ was declared to be more than a man, even when he was trampled upon as *a worm, and no man.* This word, *I am he,* had revived his disciples, and raised them up (Matt. xiv. 27); but the same word strikes his enemies down. Hereby he showed plainly,

(1.) What he could have done with them. When he struck them down, he could have struck them dead; when he spoke them *to the ground,* he could have spoken them to hell, and have sent them, like Korah's company, the next way thither; but he would not do so, [1.] Because the hour of his suffering was come, and he would not put it by; he would only show that his life was not forced from him, but *he laid it down of himself,* as he had said. [2.] Because he would give an instance of his patience and forbearance with the worst of men, and his compassionate love to his very enemies. In striking them down, and no more, he gave them both a call to repent and space to repent; but *their hearts were hardened,* and all was in vain.

(2.) What he will do at last with all his implacable enemies, *that will not repent to give him glory; they shall flee, they shall fall, before him.* Now the scripture was accomplished (Ps. xxi. 12), *Thou shalt make them turn their back,* and Ps. xx. 8. And it will be accomplished more and more; *with the breath of his mouth he will slay the wicked,* 2 Thes. ii. 8; Rev. xix. 21. *Quid judicaturus faciet, qui judicandus hoc facit?—What will he do when he shall come to judge, seeing he did this when he came to be judged?*—Augustine.

IV. Having given his enemies a repulse, he gives his friends a protection, and that by his word too, *v.* 7—9, where we may observe,

1. How he continued to expose himself to their rage, *v.* 7. They did not lie long where they fell, but, by divine permission, got up again; it is only in the other world that God's judgments are everlasting. When they were down, one would have thought Christ should have made his escape; when they were up again, one would have thought they should have let fall their pursuit; but still we find, (1.) They are as eager as ever to seize him. It is in some confusion and disorder that they recover themselves; they cannot imagine what ailed them, that they could not keep their ground, but will impute it to any thing rather than Christ's power. Note, There are hearts so very hard in sin that nothing will work upon them to reduce and reclaim them. (2.) He is as willing as ever to be seized. When they were fallen before him, he did not insultover them, but, seeing them at a loss, asked them the same question, *Whom seek you?* And they gave him the same answer, *Jesus of Nazareth.* In his repeating the question, he seems to come yet closer to their consciences: "Do you not know *whom you seek?* Are you not aware that you are in error, and will you meddle with your match? Have you not had enough of it, but will you try the other struggle? *Did ever any harden his heart against God and prosper?*" In their repeating the same answer, they showed an obstinacy in their wicked way; they still call him *Jesus of Nazareth,* with as much disdain as ever, and Judas is as unrelenting as any of them. *Let us therefore fear lest,* by a few bold steps at first in a sinful way, *our hearts be hardened.*

2. How he contrived to secure his disciples from their rage. He improved this advantage against them for the protection of his followers. When he shows his courage with reference to himself, *I have told you that I am he,* he shows his care for his disciples, *Let these go their way.* He speaks this as a command to them, rather than a contract

with them; for they lay at his mercy, not he at theirs. He charges them therefore as *one having authority:* "*Let these go their way;* it is at your peril if you meddle with them." This aggravated the sin of the disciples in forsaking him, and particularly Peter's in denying him, that Christ had given them this pass, or warrant of protection, and yet they had not faith and courage enough to rely upon it, but betook themselves to such base and sorry shifts for their security. When Christ said, *Let these go their way,* he intended,

(1.) To manifest his affectionate concern for his disciples. When he exposed himself, he excused them, because they were not as yet fit to suffer; their faith was weak, and their spirits were low, and it would have been as much as their souls, and the lives of their souls, were worth, to bring them into sufferings now. *New wine* must not be *put into old bottles.* And, besides, they had other work to do; they must go their way, for they are to go into all the world, to preach the gospel. *Destroy them not, for a blessing is in them.* Now herein, [1.] Christ gives us a great encouragement to follow him; for, though he has allotted us sufferings, yet he considers our frame, will wisely time the cross, and proportion it to our strength, and will *deliver the godly out of temptation,* either from it, or through it. [2.] He gives us a good example of love to our brethren and concern for their welfare. We must not consult our own ease and safety only, but others, as well as our own, and in some cases more than our own. There is a generous and heroic love, which will enable us to *lay down our lives for the brethren,* 1 John iii. 16.

(2.) He intended to give a specimen of his undertaking as Mediator. When he offered himself to suffer and die, it was that we might escape. He was our ἀντίψυχος—*a sufferer in our stead;* when he said, *Lo, I come,* he said also, *Let these go their way;* like the ram offered instead of Isaac.

3. Now herein he confirmed the word which he had spoken a little before (*ch.* xvii. 12), *Of those whom thou gavest me, I have lost none.* Christ, by fulfilling that word in this particular, gave an assurance that it should be accomplished in the full extent of it, not only for those that were now with him, but for all that should believe on him through their word. Though Christ's keeping them was meant especially of the preservation of their souls from sin and apostasy, yet it is here applied to the preservation of their natural lives, and very fitly, for even the body was a part of Christ's charge and care; he is to *raise it up at the last day,* and therefore to preserve it as well as *the spirit and soul,* 1 Thess. v. 23; 2 Tim. iv. 17, 18. Christ will preserve the natural life for the service to which it is designed; it is given to him to be used for him, and he will not lose the service of it, but will be magnified in it, *whether by life or death;* it shall be held in life as long as any use is to be made of it. Christ's witnesses shall not die till they have given in their evidence. But this is not all; this preservation of the disciples was, in the tendency of it, a spiritual preservation. They were now so weak in faith and resolution that in all probability, if they had been called out to suffer at this time, they would have shamed themselves and their Master, and some of them, at least the weaker of them, would have been lost; and therefore, that he might *lose none,* he would not expose them. The safety and preservation of the saints are owing, not only to the divine grace in proportioning the strength to the trial, but to the divine providence in proportioning the trial to the strength.

V. Having provided for the safety of his disciples, he rebukes the rashness of one of them, and represses the violence of his followers, as he had repulsed the violence of his persecutors, *v.* 10, 11, where we have,

1. Peter's rashness. He had a sword; it is not likely that he wore one constantly as a gentleman, but they had two swords among them all (Luke xxii. 38), and Peter, being entrusted with one, drew it; for now, if ever, he thought it was his time to use it; and *he smote one of the high priest's servants,* who was probably one of the forwardest, and aiming, it is likely, to cleave him down the head, missed his blow, and only *cut off his right ear. The servant's name,* for the greater certainty of the narrative, is recorded; it *was Malchus,* or *Malluch,* Neh. x. 4.

(1.) We must here acknowledge Peter's good-will; he had an honest zeal for his Master, though now misguided. He had lately promised to venture his life for him, and would now make his words good. Probably it exasperated Peter to see Judas at the head of this gang; his baseness excited Peter's boldness, and I wonder that when he did draw his sword he did not aim at the traitor's head.

(2.) Yet we must acknowledge Peter's ill conduct; and, though his good intention did excuse, yet it would not justify him. [1.] He had no warrant from his Master for what he did. Christ's soldiers must wait the word of command, and not outrun it; before they expose themselves to sufferings, they must see to it, not only that their cause be good, but their call clear. [2.] He transgressed the duty of his place, and resisted the powers that were, which Christ had never countenanced, but forbidden (Matt. v. 39): *that you resist not evil.* [3.] He opposed his Master's sufferings, and, notwithstanding the rebuke he had for it once, is ready to repeat, *Master, spare thyself;* suffering be *far from thee;* though Christ had told him that he must and would suffer, and that his hour was now come. Thus, while he seemed to fight for Christ, he fought against him. [4.] He broke the capitulation his Master had lately made with the enemy. When he said, *Let these go their way,* he not only indented for their safety, but in effect passed his word for their good behaviour, that they should go away peaceably; this Peter heard, and yet would not be bound by it. As we may be guilty of a sinful cowardice when we are called to appear, so we may be of a sinful forwardness when we are called to retire. [5.] He foolishly exposed himself and his fellow disciples to the fury of this enraged multitude. If he had cut off Malchus's head when he cut off his ear, we may suppose the soldiers would have fallen upon all the disciples, and have hewn them to pieces, and would have represented Christ as no better than Barabbas. Thus many have been guilty of self-destruction, in their zeal for self-preservation. [6.] Peter played the coward so soon after this (denying his Master) that we have reason to think he would not have done this but that he saw his Master cause them to fall on the ground, and then he could deal with them; but, when he saw him surrender himself notwithstanding, his courage failed him; whereas the true Christian hero will appear in the cause of Christ, not only when it is prevailing, but when it seems to be declining; will be on the right side, though it be not the rising side.

(3.) We must acknowledge God's overruling providence in directing the stroke (so that it should do no more execution, but only cut off his ear, which was rather marking him than maiming him), as also in giving Christ an opportunity to manifest his power and goodness in healing the hurt, Luke xxii. 51. Thus what was in danger of turning to Christ's reproach proved an occasion of that which redounded much to his honour, even among his adversaries.

2. The rebuke his Master gave him (*v.* 11): *Put up thy sword into the sheath,* or scabbard; it is a gentle reproof, because it was his zeal that carried him beyond the bounds of discretion. Christ did not aggravate the matter, only bade him *do so no more.* Many think their being in grief and distress will excuse them if they be hot and hasty with those about them; but Christ has here set us an example of meekness in sufferings. Peter must put up his sword, for it was the *sword of the Spirit* that was to be committed to him—*weapons of warfare not carnal,* yet *mighty.* When Christ with a word felled the aggressors, he showed Peter how he should be armed with a *word, quick and powerful, and sharper than any two-edged sword,* and with that, not long after this, he laid Ananias and Sapphira dead at his feet.

3. The reason for this rebuke: *The cup which my Father has given me, shall I not drink it?* Matthew relates another reason which Christ gave for this rebuke, but John preserves this, which he had omitted; in which Christ gives us, (1.) A full proof of his own submission to his Father's will. Of all that was amiss in what Peter did, he seems to resent nothing so much as that he would have hindered his sufferings now that his *hour was come:* "What, *Peter,* wilt thou step in between the cup and the lip? *Get thee hence, Satan.*" If Christ be determined to suffer and die, it is presumption for Peter in word or deed to oppose it: *Shall I not drink it?* The manner of expression bespeaks a settled resolution, and that he would not entertain a thought to the contrary. He was willing to drink of this cup, though it was a bitter cup, an infusion of the wormwood and the gall, the cup of trembling, a bloody cup, the *dregs of the cup of the Lord's wrath,* Isa. li. 22. He drank it, that he might put into our hands the cup of salvation, the cup of consolation, the cup of blessing; and *therefore* he is willing to drink it, because *his Father put it into his hand.* If his Father will have it so, it is for the best, and be it so. (2.) A fair pattern to us of submission to God's will in every thing that concerns us. We must *pledge* Christ in the cup that he drank of (Matt. xx. 23), and must argue ourselves into a compliance. [1.] It is but a *cup;* a small matter comparatively, be it what it will. It is not a sea, a red sea, a dead sea, for it is not hell; it is light, and but for a moment. [2.] It is a cup that is given us; sufferings are gifts. [3.] It is given us by a Father, who has a Father's authority, and does us no wrong; a Father's affection, and means us no hurt.

VI. Having entirely reconciled himself to the dispensation, he calmly surrendered, and yielded himself a prisoner, not because he could not have made his escape, but because he would not. One would have thought the cure of Malchus's ear should have made them relent, but nothing would win upon them. *Maledictus furor, quem nec majestas miraculi nec pietas beneficii confringere potuit—Accursed rage, which the grandeur of the miracle could not appease, nor the tenderness of the favour conciliate.*—Anselm. Observe here,

1. How they seized him: *They took Jesus* Only some few of them could lay hands on him, but it is charged upon them all, for they were all aiding and abetting. In treason there are no accessaries; all are principals. Now the scripture was fulfilled, *Bulls have compassed me* (Ps. xxii. 12), *compassed me like bees,* Ps. cxviii. 12. *The breath of our nostrils is taken in their pit,* Lam. iv. 20. They had so often been frustrated in their attempts to seize him that now, having got him into their hands, we may suppose they flew upon him with so much the more violence.

2. How they secured him: *They bound him.* This particular of his sufferings is taken notice of only by this evangelist, that, as soon as ever he was taken, he was bound, pinioned, handcuffed; tradition says, "They bound him with such cruelty that the blood started out at his fingers' ends; and, having bound

his hands behind him, they clapped an iron chain about his neck, and with that dragged him along." See *Gerhard. Harm.* cap. 5.

(1.) This shows the spite of his persecutors. They bound him, [1.] That they might torment him, and put him in pain, as they bound Samson to afflict him. [2.] That they might disgrace him, and put him to shame; slaves were bound, so was Christ, though free-born. [3.] That they might prevent his escape, Judas having told them to hold him fast. See their folly, that they should think to fetter that power which had but just now proved itself omnipotent. [4.] They bound him as one already condemned, for they were resolved to prosecute him to the death, and that he should die as a fool dieth, that is, as a malefactor, with his hands bound, 2 Sam. iii. 33, 34. Christ had bound the consciences of his persecutors with the power of his word, which galled them; and, to be revenged on him, they laid these bonds on him.

(2.) Christ's being bound was very significant; in this as in other things there was a mystery. [1.] Before they bound him, he had bound himself by his own undertaking to the work and office of a Mediator. He was already bound to the horns of the altar with the cords of his own love to man, and duty to his Father, else their cords would not have held him. [2.] We were *bound with the cords of our iniquities* (Prov. v. 22), with the *yoke of our transgressions,* Lam. i. 14. Guilt is a bond on the soul, by which we are bound over to the judgment of God; corruption is a bond on the soul, by which we are bound under the power of Satan. Christ, being made sin for us, to free us from those bonds, himself submitted to be bound for us, else we had been bound hand and foot, and reserved in chains of darkness. To his bonds we owe our liberty; his confinement was our enlargement; thus the Son maketh us free. [3.] The types and prophecies of the Old Testament were herein accomplished. Isaac was bound, that he might be sacrificed; Joseph was bound, and the *irons entered into his soul,* in order to his being brought from prison to reign, Ps. cv. 18, &c. Samson was bound in order to his slaying more of the Philistines at his death than he had done in his life. And the Messiah was prophesied of as a prisoner, Isa. liii. 8. [4.] Christ was bound, that he might bind us to duty and obedience. His bonds for us are bonds upon us, by which we are for ever obliged to love him and serve him. Paul's salutation to his friends is Christ's to us all: *"Remember my bonds* (Col. iv. 18), remember them as bound with him from all sin, and to all duty." [5.] Christ's bonds for us were designed to make our bonds for him easy to us, if at any time we be so called out to suffer for him, to sanctify and sweeten them, and put honour upon them; these enabled Paul and Silas to sing in the stocks, and Ignatius to call his bonds for Christ spiritual pearls.—*Epist. ad Ephes.*

13 And led him away to Annas
first; for he was father in law to Caiaphas, which was the high priest that
same year. 14 Now Caiaphas was
he, which gave counsel to the Jews,
that it was expedient that one man
should die for the people. 15 And
Simon Peter followed Jesus, and *so*
did another disciple: that disciple
was known unto the high priest, and
went in with Jesus into the palace of
the high priest. 16 But Peter stood
at the door without. Then went out
that other disciple, which was known
unto the high priest, and spake unto
her that kept the door, and brought
in Peter. 17 Then saith the damsel
that kept the door unto Peter, Art
not thou also *one* of this man's disciples? He saith, I am not. 18 And
the servants and officers stood there,
who had made a fire of coals; for it
was cold: and they warmed themselves: and Peter stood with them,
and warmed himself. 19 The high
priest then asked Jesus of his disciples,
and of his doctrine. 20 Jesus answered him, I spake openly to the
world; I ever taught in the synagogue, and in the temple, whither the
Jews always resort; and in secret
have I said nothing. 21 Why askest thou me? ask them which heard
me, what I have said unto them: behold, they know what I said. 22
And when he had thus spoken, one of
the officers which stood by struck Jesus with the palm of his hand, saying,
Answerest thou the high priest so?
23 Jesus answered him, If I have
spoken evil, bear witness of the evil:
but if well, why smitest thou me? 24
Now Annas had sent him bound unto
Caiaphas the high priest. 25 And
Simon Peter stood and warmed himself. They said therefore unto him,
Art not thou also *one* of his disciples?
He denied *it,* and said, I am not. 26
One of the servants of the high priest,
being *his* kinsman whose ear Peter
cut off, saith, Did not I see thee in
the garden with him? 27 Peter then
denied again: and immediately the
cock crew.

We have here an account of Christ's arraignment before the high priest, and some circumstances that occurred therein which were omitted by the other evangelists; and Peter's denying him, which the other evangelists had given the story of entire by itself, is interwoven with the other passages. The crime laid to his charge having relation to religion, the judges of the spiritual court took it to fall directly under their cognizance. Both Jews and Gentiles seized him, and so both Jews and Gentiles tried and condemned him, for he died for the sins of both. Let us go over the story in order.

I. Having seized him, they *led him away to Annas first,* before they brought him to the court that was sat, expecting him, in the house of Caiaphas, *v.* 13. 1. They *led him away,* led him in triumph, as a trophy of their victory; led him *as a lamb to the slaughter,* and they led him through the sheep-gate spoken of Neh. iii. 1. For through that they went from the mount of Olives into Jerusalem. They hurried him away with violence, as if he had been the worst and vilest of malefactors. We had been led away of our own impetuous lusts, and led captive by Satan at his will, and, that we might be rescued, Christ was led away, led captive by Satan's agents and instruments. 2. They led him away to their masters that sent them. It was now about midnight, and one would think they should have put him in ward (Lev. xxiv. 12), should have led him to some prison, till it was a proper time to call a court; but he is hurried away immediately, not to the justices of peace, to be committed, but to the judges to be condemned; so extremely violent was the prosecution, partly because they feared a rescue, which they would thus not only leave no time for, but give a terror to; partly because they greedily thirsted after Christ's blood, as *the eagle that hasteth to the prey.* 3. They led him to Annas first. Probably his house lay in the way, and was convenient for them to call at to refresh themselves, and, as some think, to be paid for their service. I suppose Annas was old and infirm, and could not be present in council with the rest at that time of night, and yet earnestly desired to see the prey. To gratify him therefore with the assurance of their success, that the old man might sleep the better, and to receive his blessing for it, they produce their prisoner before him. It is sad to see those that are old and sickly, when they cannot commit sin as formerly, taking pleasure in those that do. Dr. Lightfoot thinks Annas was not present, because he had to attend early that morning in the temple, to examine the sacrifices which were that day to be offered, whether they were without blemish: if so, there was a significancy in it, that Christ, the great sacrifice, was presented to him, and sent away bound, as approved and ready for the altar. 4. This Annas was father-in-law to Caiaphas the high priest; this kindred by marriage between them comes in as a reason either why Caiaphas ordered that this piece of respect should be done to Annas, to favour him with the first sight of the prisoner, or why Annas was willing to countenance Caiaphas in a matter his heart was so much upon. Note, Acquaintance and alliance with wicked people are a great confirmation to many in their wicked ways.

II. Annas did not long detain them, being as willing as any of them to have the prosecution pushed on, and therefore sent him bound to Caiaphas, to his house, which was appointed for the rendezvous of the sanhedrim upon this occasion, or to the usual place in the temple where the high priest kept his court; this is mentioned, *v.* 24. But our translators intimate in the margin that it should come in here, and, accordingly, read it there, *Annas had sent him.* Observe here,

1. The power of Caiaphas intimated (*v.* 13). He was *high priest that same year.* The high priest's commission was during life; but there were now such frequent changes, by the Simoniacal artifices of aspiring men with the government, that it was become almost an annual office, a presage of its final period approaching; while they were undermining one another, God was overturning them all, that he might come whose right it was. Caiaphas was high priest that same year when Messiah was to be cut off, which intimates, (1.) That when a bad thing was to be done by a high priest, according to the foreknowledge of God, Providence so ordered it that a bad man should be in the chair to do it. (2.) That, when God would make it to appear what corruption there was in the heart of a bad man, he put him into a place of power, where he had temptation and opportunity to exert it. It was the ruin of Caiaphas that he was high priest that year, and so became a ringleader in the putting of Christ to death. Many a man's advancement has lost him his reputation, and he had not been dishonoured if he had not been preferred.

2. The malice of Caiaphas, which is intimated (*v.* 14) by the repeating of what he had said some time before, that, right or wrong, guilty or innocent, *it was expedient that one man should die for the people,* which refers to the story *ch.* xi. 50. This comes in here to show, (1.) What a bad man he was; this was that Caiaphas that governed himself and the church by rules of policy, in defiance of the rules of equity. (2.) What ill usage Christ was likely to meet with in his court, when his case was adjudged before it was heard, and they were already resolved what to do with him; *he must die;* so that his trial was a jest. Thus the enemies of Christ's gospel are resolved, true or false, to run it down. (3.) It is a testimony to the innocency of our Lord Jesus, from the mouth of one of his worst enemies, who owned that he fell a sacrifice to the public good, and that it

was not just he should die, but *expedient* only.

3. The concurrence of Annas in the prosecution of Christ. He made himself a partaker in guilt, (1.) With the captain and officers, that without law or mercy had bound him; for he approved it by continuing him bound when he should have loosed him, he not being convicted of any crime, nor having attempted an escape. If we do not what we can to undo what others have ill done, we are accessaries *ex post facto—after the fact*. It was more excusable in the rude soldiers to bind him than in Annas, who should have known better, to continue him bound. (2.) With the chief priest and council that condemned him, and prosecuted him to death. This Annas was not present with them, yet thus he wished them *good speed*, and became a *partaker of their evil deeds*.

III. In the house of Caiaphas, Simon Peter began to deny his Master, *v.* 15—18.

1. It was with much ado that Peter got into the hall where the court was sitting, an account of which we have *v.* 15, 16. Here we may observe,

(1.) Peter's kindness to Christ, which (though it proved no kindness) appeared in two things:—[1.] That he *followed Jesus* when he was *led away;* though at first he fled with the rest, yet afterwards he took heart a little, and followed at some distance, calling to mind the promises he had made to adhere to him, whatever it should cost him. Those that had followed Christ in the midst of his honours, and shared with him in those honours, when the people cried Hosanna to him, ought to have followed him now in the midst of his reproaches, and to have shared with him in these. Those that truly love and value Christ will follow him all weathers and all ways. [2.] When he could not get in where Jesus was in the midst of his enemies, he *stood at the door without*, willing to be as near him as he could, and waiting for an opportunity to get nearer. Thus when we meet with opposition in following Christ we must show our good-will. But yet this kindness of Peter's was no kindness, because he had not strength and courage enough to persevere in it, and so, as it proved, he did but run himself into a snare: and even his following Christ, considering all things, was to be blamed, because Christ, who knew him better than he knew himself, had expressly told him (*ch.* xiii. 36), *Whither I go thou canst not follow me now*, and had told him again and again that he would deny him; and he had lately had experience of his own weakness in forsaking him. Note, We must take heed of tempting God by running upon difficulties beyond our strength, and venturing too far in a way of suffering. If our call be clear to expose ourselves, we may hope that God will enable us to honour him; but, if it be not, we may fear that God will leave us to shame ourselves.

(2.) The other disciple's kindness to Peter, which yet, as it proved, was no kindness neither. St. John several times in this gospel speaking of himself as another disciple, many interpreters have been led by this to fancy that this other disciple here was John; and many conjectures they have how he should come to be known to the high-priest; *propter generis nobilitatem—being of superior birth*, saith *Jerome, Epitaph. Marcel.*, as if he were a better gentleman born than his brother James, when they were both the sons of Zebedee the fisherman: some will tell you that he had sold his estate to the high priest, others that he supplied his family with fish, both which are very improbable. But I see no reason to think that this other disciple was John, or one of the twelve; other sheep Christ had, which were not of the fold; and this might be, as the Syriac reads it, *unus ex discipulis aliis—one of those other disciples* that believed in Christ, but resided at Jerusalem, and kept their places there; perhaps Joseph of Arimathea, or Nicodemus, known to the high priest, but not known to him to be disciples of Christ. Note, As there are many who seem disciples and are not so, so there are many who are disciples and seem not so. There are good people hid in courts, even in Nero's, as well as hid in crowds. We must not conclude a man to be no friend to Christ merely because he has acquaintance and conversation with those that were his known enemies. Now, [1.] This other disciple, whoever he was, showed a respect to Peter, in introducing him, not only to gratify his curiosity and affection, but to give him an opportunity of being serviceable to his Master upon his trial, if there were occasion. Those that have a real kindness for Christ and his ways, though their temper may be reserved and their circumstances may lead them to be cautious and retired, yet, if their faith be sincere, they will discover, when they are called to it, which way their inclination lies, by being ready to do a professed disciple a good turn. Peter perhaps had formerly introduced this disciple into conversation with Christ, and now he requites his kindness, and is not ashamed to own him, though, it should seem, he had at this time but a poor downcast appearance. [2.] But this kindness proved no kindness, nay a great diskindness; by letting him into the high priest's hall, he let him into temptation, and the consequence was bad. Note, The courtesies of our friends often prove a snare to us, through a misguided affection.

2. Peter, having got in, was immediately assaulted with the temptation, and foiled by it, *v.* 17. Observe here,

(1.) How slight the attack was. It was but a silly maid, of so small account that she was set to keep the door, that challenged him, and she only asked him carelessly, *Art not thou one of this man's disciples?* probably suspecting it by his sheepish look, and coming in timorously.

We should many a time better maintain a good cause if we had a *good heart on it,* and could put a *good face on it.* Peter would have had some reason to take the alarm if Malchus had set upon him, and had said, "This is he that cut off my ear, and I will have his head for it;" but when a maid only asked him, *Art not thou one of them?* he might without danger have answered, *And what if I am?* Suppose the servants had ridiculed him, and insulted over him, upon it, those can bear but little for Christ that cannot *bear this;* this is but *running with the footmen.*

(2.) How speedy the surrender was. Without taking time to recollect himself, he suddenly answered, *I am not.* If he had had the boldness of the lion, he would have said, "It is my honour that I am so;" or, if he had had the wisdom of the serpent, he would have kept silence at this time, for it was an evil time. But, all his care being for his own safety, he thought he could not secure this but by a peremptory denial: *I am not;* he not only denies it, but even disdains it, and scorns her words.

(3.) Yet he goes further into the temptation: *And the servants and officers stood there, and Peter with them, v.* 18.

[1.] See how the servants made much of themselves; the night being cold, they made a fire in the hall, not for their masters (they were so eager in persecuting Christ that they forgot cold), but for themselves to refresh themselves. They cared not what became of Christ; all their care was to sit and warm themselves, Amos vi. 6.

[2.] See how Peter herded himself with them, and made one among them. *He sat and warmed himself. First,* It was a fault bad enough that he did not attend his Master, and appear for him at the upper end of the hall, where he was now under examination. He might have been a witness for him, and have confronted the false witnesses that swore against him, if his Master had called him; at least, he might have been a witness to him, might have taken an exact notice of what passed, that he might relate it to the other disciples, who could none of them get in to hear the trial; he might have learned by his Master's example how to carry himself when it should come to his turn to suffer thus; yet neither his conscience nor his curiosity could bring him into the court, but he sits by, as if, like Gallio, he cared for none of these things. And yet at the same time we have reason to think his heart was as full of grief and concern as it could hold, but he had not the courage to own it. *Lord, lead us not into temptation. Secondly,* It was much worse that he joined himself with those that were his Master's enemies: *He stood with them, and warmed himself;* this was a poor excuse for joining with them. A little thing will draw those into bad company that will be drawn to it by the love of a good fire. If Peter's zeal for his Master had not frozen, but had continued in the heat it seemed to be of but a few hours before, he had not had occasion to warm himself now. Peter was much to be blamed, 1. Because he associated with these wicked men, and kept company with them. Doubtless they were diverting themselves with this night's expedition, scoffing at Christ, at what he had said, at what he had done, and triumphing in their victory over him; and what sort of entertainment would this give to Peter? If he said as they said, or by silence gave consent, he involved himself in sin; if not, he exposed himself to danger. If Peter had not so much courage as to appear publicly for his Master, yet he might have had so much devotion as to retire into a corner, and weep in secret for his Master's sufferings, and his own sin in forsaking him; if he could not have done good, he might have kept out of the way of doing hurt. It is better to abscond than appear to no purpose, or bad purpose. 2. Because he desired to be thought *one of them,* that he might not be suspected to be a disciple of Christ. Is this Peter? What a contradiction is this to the prayer of every good man, *Gather not my soul with sinners! Saul among the prophets* is not so absurd as David among the Philistines. Those that deprecate the lot of the scornful hereafter should dread the *seat of the scornful* now. It is ill warming ourselves with those with whom we are in danger of burning ourselves, Ps. cxli. 4.

IV. Peter, Christ's friend, having begun to deny him, the high priest, his enemy, begins to accuse him, or rather urges him to accuse himself, *v.* 19—21. It should seem, the first attempt was to prove him a seducer, and a teacher of false doctrine, which this evangelist relates; and, when they failed in the proof of this, then they charged him with blasphemy, which is related by the other evangelists, and therefore omitted here. Observe,

1. The articles or heads upon which Christ was examined (*v.* 19): concerning *his disciples and his doctrine.* Observe,

(1.) The irregularity of the process; it was against all law and equity. They seize him as a criminal, and now that he is their prisoner they have nothing to *lay to his charge;* no libel, no prosecutor; but the judge himself must be the prosecutor, and the prisoner himself the witness, and, against all reason and justice, he is put on to be his own accuser.

(2.) The intention. The *high priest then* (*οὖν—therefore,* which seems to refer to *v.* 14), because he had resolved that Christ must be sacrificed to their private malice under colour of the public good, examined him upon those interrogatories which would touch his life. He examined him, [1.] Concerning his disciples, that he might charge him with sedition, and represent him as dangerous to the Roman government, as well as to the Jewish church. He asked him who were his disciples—what number they were —of what country—what were their names and characters, insinuating that his scholars were designed for soldiers, and would in time become a formidable body. Some think his question concerning his disciples was, "What is now become of them all? Where are they? Why do they not appear?" upbraiding him with their cowardice in deserting him, and thus adding to the affliction of it. There was something significant in this, that Christ's calling and owning his disciples was the first thing laid to his charge, for it was *for their sakes* that he *sanctified himself* and suffered. [2.] Concerning his doctrine, that they might charge him with heresy, and bring him under the penalty of the law against false prophets, Deut. xiii. 9, 10. This was a matter properly cognizable in that court (Deut. xvii. 12), therefore a prophet could not perish but at Jerusalem, where that court sat. They could not prove any false doctrine upon him; but they hoped to extort something from him which they might distort to his prejudice, and to make him an offender for some word or other, Isa. xxix. 21. They said nothing to him concerning his miracles, by which he had done so much good, and proved his doctrine beyond contradiction, because of these they were sure they could take no hold. Thus the adversaries of Christ, while they are industriously quarrelling with his truth, wilfully shut their eyes against the evidences of it, and take no notice of them.

2. The appeal Christ made, in answer to these interrogatories. (1.) As to his disciples, he said nothing, because it was an impertinent question; if his doctrine was sound and good, his having disciples to whom to communicate it was no more than what was practised and allowed by their own doctors. If Caiaphas, in asking him concerning his disciples, designed to ensnare them, and bring them into trouble, it was in kindness to them that Christ said nothing of them, for he had said, *Let these go their way.* If he meant to upbraid him with their cowardice, no wonder that he said nothing, for

> Rudet hæc opprobria nobis,
> Et dici potuisse, et non potuisse refelli—

Shame attaches when charges are exhibited that cannot be refuted:

he would say nothing to condemn them, and could say nothing to justify them. (2.) As to his doctrine, he said nothing in particular, but in general referred himself to those that heard him, being not only made manifest to God, but made manifest also in their consciences, *v.* 20, 21.

[1.] He tacitly charges his judges with illegal proceedings. He does not indeed speak evil of the rulers of the people, nor say now to these princes, *You are wicked;* but he appeals to the settled rules of their own court, whether they dealt fairly by him. *Do you indeed judge righteously?* Ps. lviii. 1. So here, *Why ask you me?* Which implies two absurdities in judgment: *First,* "*Why ask you me now* concerning my doctrine, when you have already condemned it?" They had made an order of court for excommunicating all that owned him (*ch.* ix. 22), had issued out a proclamation for apprehending him; and now they come to ask what his doctrine is! Thus was he condemned, as his doctrine and cause commonly are, unheard. *Secondly,* "*Why ask you me?* Must I accuse myself, when you have no evidence against me?"

[2.] He insists upon his fair and open dealing with them in the publication of his doctrine, and justifies himself with this. The crime which the sanhedrim by the law was to enquire after was the clandestine spreading of dangerous doctrines, enticing secretly, Deut. xiii. 6. As to this, therefore, Christ clears himself very fully. *First,* As to the manner of his preaching. He spoke openly, *παρρησία—with freedom and plainness of speech;* he did not deliver things ambiguously, as Apollo did his oracles. Those that would undermine the truth, and spread corrupt notions, seek to accomplish their purpose by sly insinuations, putting queries, starting difficulties, and asserting nothing; but Christ explained himself fully, with, *Verily, verily, I say unto you;* his reproofs were free and bold, and his testimonies express against the corruptions of the age. *Secondly,* As to the persons he preached to: *He spoke to the world,* to all that had *ears to hear,* and were willing to hear him, high or low, learned or unlearned, Jew or Gentile, friend or foe. His doctrine feared not the censure of a mixed multitude; nor did he grudge the knowledge of it to any (as the masters of some rare invention commonly do), but freely communicated it, as the sun does his beams. *Thirdly,* As to the places he preached in. When he was in the country, he preached ordinarily in the synagogues—the places of meeting for worship, and on the sabbath-day—the time of meeting; when he came up to Jerusalem, he preached the same doctrine in the temple at the time of the solemn feasts, when the Jews from all parts assembled there; and though he often preached in private houses, and on mountains, and by the sea-side, to show that his word and worship were not to be confined to temples and synagogues, yet what he preached in private was the very same with what he delivered publicly. Note, The doctrine of Christ, purely and plainly preached, needs not be ashamed to appear in the most numerous assembly, for it carries its own strength and beauty along with it. What Christ's faithful ministers say they would be willing all the world should hear. Wisdom cries in the places of concourse, Prov. i. 21; viii. 3; ix. 3. *Fourthly,* As to the doctrine itself. He *said nothing in secret* contrary to what he said in public, but only by way of repetition and explication: *In secret have I said nothing;* as if he had been either suspicious of the truth of it, or conscious of any ill design in it. He sought no corners, for he feared no colours, nor said any thing that he needed to be ashamed of; what he did speak in private to his disciples he ordered them to proclaim on the house-tops, Matt. x. 27. God saith of himself (Isa. xlv. 19), *I have not spoken in secret;* his commandment is not hidden, Deut. xxx. 11. And the righteousness of faith speaks in like manner, Rom. x. 6. *Veritas nihil metuit nisi abscondi—truth fears nothing but concealment.*—Tertullian.

[3.] He appeals to those that had heard him, and desires that they might be examined what doctrine he had preached, and whether it had that dangerous tendency that was surmised: "*Ask those that heard me what I said unto them;* some of them may be in court, or may be sent for out of their beds." He means not his friends and followers, who might be presumed to speak in his favour, but, Ask any impartial hearer; ask your own officers. Some think he pointed to them, when he said, *Behold, they know what I said,* referring to the report which they had made of his preaching (*ch.* vii. 46), *Never man spoke like this man.* Nay, you may ask some upon the bench; for it is probable that some of them had heard him, and had been put to silence by him. Note, The doctrine of Christ may safely appeal to all that know it, and has so much right and reason on its side that those who will judge impartially cannot but witness to it.

V. While the judges were examining him, the servants that stood by were abusing him, *v.* 22, 23.

1. It was a base affront which one of the officers gave him; though he spoke with so much calmness and convincing evidence, this insolent fellow *struck him with the palm of his hand,* probably on the side of his head or face, saying, *Answerest thou the high priest so?* as if he had behaved himself rudely to the court.

(1.) He *struck him, ἔδωκε ῥάπισμα—he gave him a blow.* Some think it signifies a blow with a rod or wand, from ῥάβδος, or with the staff which was the badge of his office. Now the scripture was fulfilled (Isa. l. 6), *I gave my cheeks, εἰς ῥαπίσματα* (so the LXX.) *to blows,* the word here used. And Mic. v. 1, *They shall smite the judge of Israel with a rod upon the cheek;* and the type answered (Job xvi. 10), *They have smitten me upon the cheek reproachfully.* It was unjust to strike one that neither said nor did amiss; it was insolent for a mean servant to strike one that was confessedly a person of account; it was cowardly to strike one that had his hands tied; and barbarous to strike a prisoner at the bar. Here was a breach of the peace in the face of the court, and yet the judges countenanced it. Confusion of face was our due; but Christ here took it to himself: "Upon me be the curse, the shame."

(2.) He checked him in a haughty imperious manner: *Answerest thou the high priest so?* As if the blessed Jesus were not good enough to speak to his master, or not wise enough to know how to speak to him, but, like a rude and ignorant prisoner, must be controlled by the jailor, and taught how to behave. Some of the ancients suggest that this officer was Malchus, who owed to Christ the healing of his ear, and the saving of his head, and yet made him this ill return. But, whoever it was, it was done to please the high priest, and to curry favour with him; for what he said implied a jealousy for the dignity of the high priest. Wicked rulers will not want wicked servants, who will *help forward the affliction* of those whom their masters persecute. There was a successor of this high priest that commanded the by-standers to smite Paul thus *on the mouth,* Acts xxiii. 2. Some think this officer took himself to be affronted by Christ's appeal to those about him concerning his doctrine, as if he would have vouched him to be a witness; and perhaps he was one of those officers that had spoken honourably of him (*ch.* vii. 46), and, lest he should now be thought a secret friend to him, he thus appears a bitter enemy.

2. Christ bore this affront with wonderful meekness and patience (*v.* 23): "*If I have spoken evil,* in what I have now said, *bear witness of the evil.* Observe it to the court, and let them judge of it, who are the proper judges; but if well, and as it did become me, *why smitest thou me?*" Christ could have answered him with a miracle of wrath, could have struck him dumb or dead, or have withered the hand that was lifted up against him. But this was the day of his patience and suffering, and he answered him with the *meekness of wisdom,* to teach us not to avenge ourselves, not to render *railing for railing,* but with the *innocency of the dove* to bear injuries, even when with the *wisdom of the serpent,* as our Saviour, we show the injustice of them, and appeal to the magistrate concerning them. Christ did not here *turn the other cheek,* by which it appears that that rule, Matt. v. 39, is not to be understood literally; a man may possibly *turn the other cheek,* and yet have his heart full of malice; but, comparing Christ's precept with his pattern, we learn, (1.) That in such cases we must not be our own avengers, nor judges in our own cause. We must rather receive than give the second blow, which makes the quarrel; we are allowed to defend ourselves, but not to avenge ourselves: the magistrate (if it be necessary for the preserving of the public peace, and the restraining and terrifying of evil-doers) is to be the avenger, Rom. xiii. 4. (2.) Our resentment of injuries done us must always be rational, and never passionate; such Christ's here was; *when he*

suffered, he reasoned, but *threatened not*. He fairly expostulated with him that did him the injury, and so may we. (3.) When we are called out to suffering, we must *accommodate ourselves* to the inconveniences of a suffering state, with patience, and by one indignity done us be prepared to receive another, and to make the best of it.

VI. While the servants were thus abusing him, Peter was proceeding to deny him, *v.* 25—27. It is a sad story, and none of the least of Christ's sufferings.

1. He repeated the sin the second time, *v.* 25. While he was warming himself with the servants, as one of them, they asked him, *Art not thou one of his disciples?* What dost thou here among us? He, perhaps, hearing that Christ was examined about his disciples, and fearing he should be seized, or at least smitten, as his Master was, if he should own it, flatly denied it, and said, *I am not.*

(1.) It was his great folly to thrust himself into the temptation, by continuing in the company of those that were unsuitable for him, and that he had nothing to do with. He staid to warm himself; but those that warm themselves with evil doers grow cold towards good people and good things, and those that are fond of the devil's fire-side are in danger of the devil's fire. Peter might have stood by his Master at the bar, and have warmed himself better than here, at the fire of his Master's love, which *many waters could not quench*, Cant. viii. 6, 7. He might there have warmed himself with zeal for his Master, and indignation at his persecutors; but he chose rather to warm with them than to warm against them. But how could one (one disciple) be warm alone? Eccl. iv. 11.

(2.) It was his great unhappiness that he was again assaulted by the temptation; and no other could be expected, for this was a place, this an hour, of temptation. When the judge asked Christ about his disciples, probably the servants took the hint, and challenged Peter for one of them, "Answer to thy name." See here, [1.] The subtlety of the tempter in running down one whom he saw falling, and mustering a greater force against him; not a maid now, but all the servants. Note, Yielding to one temptation invites another, and perhaps a stronger. Satan redoubles his attacks when we give ground. [2.] The danger of bad company. We commonly study to approve ourselves to those with whom we choose to associate; we value ourselves upon their good word and covet to stand right in their opinion. As we choose our people we choose our praise, and govern ourselves accordingly; we are therefore concerned to make the first choice well, and not to mingle with those whom we cannot please without displeasing God.

(3.) It was his great weakness, nay, it was his great wickedness, to yield to the temptation, and to say, *I am not one* of his disciples, as one ashamed of that which was his honour, and afraid of suffering for it, which would have been yet more his honour. See how the *fear of man brings a snare*. When Christ was admired, and caressed, and treated with respect, Peter pleased himself, and perhaps prided himself, in this, that he was a disciple of Christ, and so put in for a share in the honours done to his Master. Thus many who seem fond of the reputation of religion when it is in fashion are ashamed of the reproach of it; but we must take it *for better and worse.*

2. He repeated the sin the third time, *v.* 26, 27. Here he was attacked by one of the servants, who was kinsman to Malchus, who, when he heard Peter deny himself to be a disciple of Christ, gave him the lie with great assurance: "*Did not I see thee in the garden with him?* Witness my kinsman's ear." Peter then denied again, as if he knew nothing of Christ, nothing of the garden, nothing of all this matter.

(1.) This third assault of the temptation was more close than the former: before his relation to Christ was only suspected, here it is proved upon him by one that saw him with Jesus, and saw him draw his sword in his defence. Note, Those who by sin think to help themselves out of trouble do but entangle and embarrass themselves the more. Dare to be brave, for truth will out. *A bird of the air* may perhaps *tell the matter* which we seek to conceal with a lie. Notice is taken of this servant's being akin to Malchus, because this circumstance would make it the more a terror to Peter. "Now," thinks he, "I am gone, my business is done, there needs no other witness nor prosecutor." We should not make any man in particular our enemy if we can help it, because the time may come when either he or some of his relations may have us at their mercy. He that may need a friend should not make a foe. But observe, though here was sufficient evidence against Peter, and sufficient provocation given by his denial to have prosecuted him, yet he escapes, has no harm done him nor attempted to be done. Note, We are often drawn into sin by groundless causeless fears, which there is no occasion for, and which a small degree of wisdom and resolution would make nothing of.

(2.) His yielding to it was no less base than the former: *He denied again.* See here, [1.] The nature of sin in general: *the heart is hardened by the deceitfulness of it*, Heb. iii. 13. It was a strange degree of effrontery that Peter had arrived to on a sudden, that he could with such assurance stand in a lie against so clear a disproof; but *the beginning of sin is as the letting forth of water*, when once the fence is broken men easily go from bad to worse. [2.] Of the sin of lying in particular; it is a fruitful sin, and upon this account *exceedingly sinful;* one lie needs another to support it, and that another. It is a rule in the devil's politics, *Malè facta malè factis tegere, ne perpluant—To cover sin with sin, in order to escape detection.*

(3.) The hint given him for the awakening of his conscience was seasonable and happy: *Immediately the cock crew;* and this is all that is here said of his repentance, it being recorded by the other evangelists. This brought him to himself, by bringing to his mind the words of Christ. See here, [1.] The care Christ has of those that are his, notwithstanding their follies; though *they fall, they are not utterly cast down,* not utterly cast off. [2.] The advantage of having faithful remembrancers near us, who, though they cannot tell us more than we know already, yet may remind us of that which we know, but have forgotten. The crowing of the cock to others was an accidental thing, and had no significancy; but to Peter it was the voice of God, and had a blessed tendency to awaken his conscience, by putting him in mind of the word of Christ.

28 Then led they Jesus from Caiaphas unto the hall of judgment: and it was early; and they themselves went not into the judgment hall, lest they should be defiled; but that they might eat the passover. 29 Pilate then went out unto them, and said, What accusation bring ye against this man? 30 They answered and said unto him, If he were not a malefactor, we would not have delivered him up unto thee. 31 Then said Pilate unto them, Take ye him, and judge him according to your law. The Jews therefore said unto him, It is not lawful for us to put any man to death: 32 That the saying of Jesus might be fulfilled, which he spake, signifying what death he should die. 33 Then Pilate entered into the judgment hall again, and called Jesus, and said unto him, Art thou the King of the Jews? 34 Jesus answered him, Sayest thou this thing of thyself, or did others tell it thee of me? 35 Pilate answered, Am I a Jew? Thine own nation and the chief priests have delivered thee unto me: what hast thou done? 36 Jesus answered, My kingdom is not of this world; if my kingdom were of this world, then would my servants fight, that I should not be delivered to the Jews: but now is my kingdom not from hence. 37 Pilate therefore said unto him, Art thou a king then? Jesus answered, Thou sayest that I am a king. To this end was I born, and for this cause came I into the world, that I should bear witness unto the truth. Every one that is of the truth heareth my voice. 38 Pilate saith unto him, What is truth? And when he had said this, he went out again unto the Jews, and saith unto them, I find in him no fault *at all.* 39 But ye have a custom, that I should release unto you one at the passover; will ye therefore that I release unto you the King of the Jews? 40 Then cried they all again, saying, Not this man, but Barabbas. Now Barabbas was a robber.

We have here an account of Christ's arraignment before Pilate, the Roman governor, in the *prætorium* (a Latin word made Greek), the prætor's house, or *hall of judgment;* thither they hurried him, to get him condemned in the Roman court, and executed by the Roman power. Being resolved on his death, they took this course, 1. That he might be put to death the more legally and regularly, according to the present constitution of their government, since they became a province of the empire; not stoned in a popular tumult, as Stephen, but put to death with the present formalities of justice. Thus he was treated as a malefactor, *being made sin for us.* 2. That he might be put to death the more safely. If they could engage the Roman government in the matter, which the people stood in awe of, there would be little danger of an uproar. 3. That he might be put to death with more reproach to himself. *The death of the cross,* which the Romans commonly used, being of all deaths the most ignominious, they were desirous by it to put an indelible mark of infamy upon him, and so to sink his reputation for ever. This therefore they harped upon, *Crucify him.* 4. That he might be put to death with less reproach to them. It was an invidious thing to put one to death that had done so much good in the world, and therefore they were willing to throw the odium upon the Roman government, to make that the less acceptable to the people, and save themselves from the reproach. Thus many are more afraid of the scandal of a bad action than of the sin of it. See Acts v. 28. Two things are here observed concerning the prosecution:—(1.) Their policy and industry in the prosecution: *It was early;* some think about two or three in the morning, others about five or six, when most people were in their beds; and so there would be the less danger of opposition from the people that were for Christ; while, at the same time, they had their agents about, to call those together whom they could influence to cry out against him. See how much their heart was upon it, and how violent they were in the prosecution. Now that they had him in their hands, they would lose no time till they had him upon the cross, but denied themselves their natural rest, to push on this matter. See Mic. ii. 1. (2.) Their superstition and vile hypocrisy: *The chief priests and elders,* though they came along with the prisoner, that the thing might be done effectually, *went not into the judgment-hall,* because it was the house of an uncircumcised Gentile, *lest they should be defiled,* but kept out of doors, *that they might eat the passover,* not the paschal lamb (that was eaten the night before) but the passover-feast, upon the sacrifices which were offered on the fifteenth day, *the Chagigah,* as they called it, the passover-bullocks spoken of Deut. xvi. 2; 2 Chron. xxx. 24; xxxv. 8, 9. These they were to eat of, and therefore would not go into the court, for fear of touching a Gentile, and thereby contracting, not a legal, but only a traditional pollution. This they scrupled, but made no scruple of breaking through all the laws of equity to persecute Christ to the death. *They strained at a gnat, and swallowed a camel.* Let us now see what passed at *the judgment-hall.* Here is,

I. Pilate's conference with the prosecutors. They were called first, and stated what they had to say against the prisoner, as was very fit, *v.* 29—32.

1. The judge calls for the indictment. Because they would not come into the hall, *he went out to them* into the court before the house, to talk with them. Looking upon Pilate as a magistrate, that we may give every one his due, here are three things commendable in him:—(1.) His diligent and close application to business. If it had been upon a good occasion, it had been very well that he was willing to be called up early to the judgment-seat. Men in public trusts must not love their ease. (2.) His condescending to the humour of the people, and receding from the honour of his place to gratify their scruples. He might have said, "If they be so nice as not to come in to me, let them go home as they came;" by the same rule as we might say, "If the complainant scruple to take off his hat to the magistrate, let not his complaint be heard;" but Pilate insists not upon it, bears with them, and goes out to them; for, when it is for good, we should *become all things to all men.* (3.) His adherence to the rule of justice, in demanding the accusation, suspecting the prosecution to be malicious: "*What accusation bring you against this man?* What is the crime you charge him with, and what proof have you of it? It was a law of nature, before Valerius Publicola made it a Roman law, *Ne quis indicta causa condemnetur—No man should be condemned unheard.* See Acts xxv. 16, 17. It is unreasonable to commit a man, without alleging some cause in the warrant, and much more to arraign a man when there is no bill of indictment found against him.

2. The prosecutors demand judgment against him upon a general surmise that he was a criminal, not alleging, much less proving, any thing in particular *worthy of death or of bonds* (*v.* 30): *If he were not a malefactor,* or evil-doer, *we would not have delivered him to thee* to be condemned. This bespeaks them, (1.) Very rude and uncivil to Pilate, a company of ill-natured men, that affected to despise dominion. When Pilate was so complaisant to them as to come out to treat with them, yet they were to the highest degree out of humour with him. He put the most reasonable question to them that could be; but, if it had been the most absurd, they could not have answered him with more disdain. (2.) Very spiteful and malicious towards our Lord Jesus: right or wrong, they will have him to be a malefactor, and treated as one. We are to presume a man innocent till he is proved guilty, but they will presume him guilty who could prove himself innocent. They cannot say, "He is a traitor, a murderer, a felon, a breaker of the peace," but they say, "He is an evil-doer." He an evil-doer who *went about doing good!* Let those be called whom he has cured, and fed, and taught; whom he has rescued from devils, and raised from death; and let them be asked whether he be an evil-doer or no. Note, It is no new thing for the best of benefactors to be branded and run down as the worst of malefactors. (3.) Very proud and conceited of themselves, and their own judgment and justice, as if their delivering a man up, under the general character of a malefactor, were sufficient for the civil magistrate to ground a judicial sentence upon, than which what could be more haughty?

3. The judge remands him to their own court (*v.* 31): "*Take you him, and judge him according to your* own *law,* and do not trouble me with him." Now, (1.) Some think Pilate herein complimented them, acknowledging the remains of their power, and allowing them to exert it. Corporal punishment they might inflict, as *scourging in their synagogues;* whether capital or no is uncertain. "But," saith Pilate, "go as far as your law will allow you, and, if you go further, it shall be connived at." This he said, willing to do the Jews a pleasure, but unwilling to do them the service they required. (2.) Others think he bantered them, and upbraided them with their present state of weakness and subjection. They would be the sole judges of the guilt. "Pray," saith Pilate, "if you will be so, go on as you have begun; you have found him guilty by your own law, condemn him, if you dare, by your own law, to carry on the humour." Nothing is more absurd, nor more deserves to be exposed, than for those to pretend to dictate, and boast of their wisdom, who are weak and in subordinate stations, and whose lot it is to be dictated to. Some think Pilate here reflects upon the law of Moses, as if it allowed them what the Roman law would by no means allow—the judging of a man unheard. "It may be your law wil

suffer such a thing, but ours will not." Thus, through their corruptions, the law of God was blasphemed; and so is his gospel too.

4. They disown any authority as judges, and (since it must be so) are content to be prosecutors. They now grow less insolent and more submissive, and own, "*It is not lawful for us to put any man to death,* whatever less punishment we may inflict, and this is a malefactor whom we would have the blood of."

(1.) Some think they had lost their power to give judgment in matters of life and death only by their own carelessness, and cowardly yielding to the darling iniquities of the age; so Dr. Lightfoot οὐκ ἔξεστι—*It is not* in our power to pass sentence of death upon *any,* if we do, we shall have the mob about us immediately.

(2.) Others think their power was taken from them by the Romans, because they had not used it well, or because it was thought too great a trust to be lodged in the hands of a conquered and yet an unsubdued people. Their acknowledgment of this they designed for a compliment to Pilate, and to atone for their rudeness (*v.* 30), but it amounts to a full evidence that *the sceptre was departed from Judah,* and therefore that now the Messiah was come, Gen. xlix. 10. If the Jews have no power *to put any man to death,* where is the sceptre? Yet they ask not, *Where is the Shiloh?*

(3.) However, there was a providence in it, that either they should have no power to put any man to death, or should decline the exercise of it upon this occasion, *That the saying of Jesus might be fulfilled, which he spoke, signifying what death he should die, v.* 32. Observe, [1.] In general, that even those who designed the defeating of Christ's sayings were, beyond their intention, made serviceable to the fulfilling of them by an overruling hand of God. *No word of Christ shall fall to the ground;* he can never either deceive or be deceived. Even *the chief priests,* while they persecuted him as *a deceiver,* had their spirit so directed as to help to prove him true, when we should think that by taking other measures they might have defeated his predictions. *Howbeit, they meant not so,* Isa. x. 7. [2.] Those sayings of Christ in particular were fulfilled which he had spoken concerning his own death. Two sayings of Christ concerning his death were fulfilled, by the Jews declining to *judge him according to their law. First,* He had said that he should be *delivered to the Gentiles,* and that *they should put him to death* (Matt. xx. 19; Mark x. 33; Luke xviii. 32, 33), and hereby that saying was fulfilled. *Secondly,* He had said that he should be crucified (Matt. xx. 19; xxvi. 2), *lifted up, ch.* iii. 14; xii. 32. Now, if they had *judged him by their law,* he had been stoned; burning, strangling, and beheading, were in some cases used among the Jews, but never crucifying. It was therefore necessary that Christ should be put to death by the Romans, that, being *hanged upon a tree,* he might be *made a curse for us* (Gal. iii. 13), and *his hands and feet* might be *pierced.* As the Roman power had brought him to be born at Bethlehem, so now to die upon a cross, and both according to the scriptures. It is likewise determined concerning us, though not discovered to us, *what death we shall die,* which should free us from all disquieting cares about that matter. "Lord, what, and when, and how thou hast appointed."

II. Here is Pilate's conference with the prisoner, *v.* 33, &c., where we have,

1. The prisoner set to the bar. Pilate, after he had conferred with the chief priests at his door, entered into the hall, and called for Jesus to be brought in. He would not examine him in the crowd, where he might be disturbed by the noise, but ordered him to be brought *into the hall;* for he made no difficulty of going in among the Gentiles. We by sin were become liable to the judgment of God, and were to be brought before his bar; therefore *Christ, being made sin and a curse for us,* was arraigned as a criminal. Pilate entered into judgment with him, that God might not enter into judgment with us.

2. His examination. The other evangelists tell us that his accusers had laid it to his charge that *he perverted the nation, forbidding to give tribute to Cæsar,* and upon this he is examined.

(1.) Here is a question put to him, with a design to ensnare him and to find out something upon which to ground an accusation: "*Art thou the king of the Jews?* ὁ βασιλεὺς—*that king of the Jews* who has been so much talked of and so long expected—Messiah the prince, art thou he? Dost thou pretend to be he? Dost thou call thyself, and wouldest thou be thought so?" For he was far from imagining that really he was so, or making a question of that. Some think Pilate asked this with an air of scorn and contempt: "What! *art thou a king,* who makest so mean a figure? *Art thou the king of the Jews,* by whom thou art thus hated and persecuted? *Art thou king de jure—of right,* while the emperor is only king *de facto—in fact?*" Since it could not be proved he ever said it, he would constrain him to say it now, that he might proceed upon his own confession.

(2.) Christ answers this question with another; not for evasion, but as an intimation to Pilate to consider what he did, and upon what grounds he went (*v.* 34): "*Sayest thou this thing of thyself,* from a suspicion arising in thy own breast, *or did others tell it thee of me,* and dost thou ask it only to oblige them?" [1.] "It is plain that thou hast no reason to *say this of thyself.*" Pilate was bound by his office to take care of the interests of the Roman government, but he could not say that this was in any danger, or suffered any damage, from any thing our Lord Jesus had ever said or done. He never appeared in worldly pomp, never assumed any secular power, never acted as a judge or divider; never were any traitorous principles or practices objected to him, nor any thing that might give the least shadow of suspicion. [2.] "If others *tell it thee of me*, to incense thee against me, thou oughtest to consider who they are, and upon what principles they go, and whether those who represent me as an *enemy to Cæsar* are not really such themselves, and therefore use this only as a pretence to cover their malice, for, if so, the matter ought to be well weighed by a judge that would do justice." Nay, if Pilate had been as inquisitive as he ought to have been in this matter, he would have found that the true reason why the chief priests were outrageous against Jesus was because he did not set up a temporal kingdom in opposition to the Roman power; if he would have done this, and would have wrought miracles to bring the Jews out of the Roman bondage, as Moses did to bring them out of the Egyptian, they would have been so far from siding with the Romans against him that they would have made him their king, and have fought under him against the Romans; but, not answering this expectation of theirs, they charged that upon him of which they were themselves most notoriously guilty—disaffection to and design against the present government; and was such an information as this fit to be countenanced?

(3.) Pilate resents Christ's answer, and takes it very ill, *v.* 35. This is a direct answer to Christ's question, *v.* 34. [1.] Christ had asked him whether he spoke of himself. "No," says he; "*am I a Jew*, that thou suspectest me to be in the plot against thee? I know nothing of the Messiah, nor desire to know, and therefore interest not myself in the dispute who is the Messiah and who not; it is all alike to me." Observe with what disdain Pilate asks, *Am I a Jew?* The Jews were, upon many accounts, an honourable people; but, having corrupted the covenant of their God, *he made them contemptible and base before all the people* (Mal. ii. 8, 9), so that a man of sense and honour reckoned it a scandal to be counted a Jew. Thus good names often suffer for the sake of the bad men that wear them. It is sad that when a Turk is suspected of dishonesty he should ask, "What! do you take me for a Christian?" [2.] Christ had asked him whether others told him. "Yes," says he, "and those *thine own people*, who, one would think, should be biassed in favour of thee, and *the priests*, whose testimony, *in verbum sacerdotis—on the word of a priest*, ought to be regarded; and therefore I have nothing to do but to proceed upon their information." Thus Christ, in his religion, still suffers by those that are of his own nation, even the priests, that profess relation to him, but do not live up to their profession. [3.] Christ had declined answering that question, *Art thou the king of the Jews?* And therefore Pilate puts another question to him more general, "*What hast thou done?* What provocation hast thou given to thy own nation, and particularly the priests, to be so violent against thee? Surely there cannot be all this smoke without some fire, what is it?"

(4.) Christ, in his next reply, gives a more full and direct answer to Pilate's former question, *Art thou a king?* explaining in what sense he was a king, but not such a king as was any ways dangerous to the Roman government, not a secular king, for his interest was not supported by secular methods, *v.* 36. Observe,

[1.] An account of the nature and constitution of Christ's kingdom: It *is not of this world.* It is expressed negatively to rectify the present mistakes concerning it; but the positive is implied, it is *the kingdom of heaven*, and belongs to another world. Christ is a king, and has a kingdom, but *not of this world. First,* Its rise is not from this world; the kingdoms of men arise *out of the sea and the earth* (Dan. vii. 3; Rev. xiii. 1, 11); but *the holy city comes down from God out of heaven*, Rev. xxii. 2. His kingdom is not by succession, election, or conquest, but by the immediate and special designation of the divine will and counsel. *Secondly,* Its nature is not worldly; it is a kingdom within men (Luke xvi. 21), set up in their hearts and consciences (Rom. xiv.17), its riches spiritual, its powers spiritual, and *all its glory within.* The ministers of state in Christ's kingdom have not *the spirit of the world*, 1 Cor. ii. 12. *Thirdly,* Its guards and supports are not worldly; its weapons are spiritual. It neither needed nor used secular force to maintain and advance it, nor was it carried on in a way *hurtful to kings or provinces;* it did not in the least interfere with the prerogatives of princes nor the property of their subjects; it tended not to alter any national establishment in secular things, nor opposed any kingdom but that of sin and Satan. *Fourthly,* Its tendency and design are not worldly. Christ neither aimed nor would allow his disciples to aim at the pomp and power of *the great men of the earth. Fifthly,* Its subjects, though they are in the world, yet *are not of the world;* they *are called and chosen out of the world*, are born from, and bound for, another world; they are neither the world's pupils nor its darlings, neither governed by its wisdom nor enriched with its wealth.

[2.] An evidence of the spiritual nature of Christ's kingdom produced. If he had designed an opposition to the government, he would have fought them at their own weapons, and would have repelled force with force of the same nature; but he did not take this course: *If my kingdom were of this world, then would my servants fight, that I should not be delivered to the Jews,* and my kingdom be ruined by them. But, *First,* His followers did not offer to fight; there was no uproar, no attempt to rescue him, though the town was now full of Galileans, his friends and countrymen, and they were generally armed; but the peaceable behaviour of his disciples on this occasion was enough *to put to silence the ignorance of foolish men. Secondly,* He did not order them to fight; nay, he forbade them, which was an evidence both that he did not depend upon worldly aids (for he could have summoned *legions of angels* into his service, which showed that his *kingdom was from above),* and also that he did not dread worldly opposition, for he was very willing to be *delivered to the Jews,* as knowing that what would have been the destruction of any worldly kingdom would be the advancement and establishment of his; justly therefore does he conclude, *Now* you may see *my kingdom is not from hence;* in the world, but not of it.

(5.) In answer to Pilate's further query, he replies yet more directly, *v.* 37, where we have, [1.] Pilate's plain question: "*Art thou a king then?* Thou speakest of a kingdom thou hast; art thou then, in any sense, a king? And what colour hast thou for such a claim? Explain thyself." [2.] The good confession which our Lord Jesus witnessed before Pontius Pilate, in answer to this (1 Tim. vi. 13): *Thou sayest that I am a king,* that is, It is as thou sayest, I am a king; for *I came to bear witness of the truth. First,* He grants himself to be a king, though not in the sense that Pilate meant. The Messiah was expected under the character of a king, *Messiah the prince;* and therefore, having owned to Caiaphas that he was the Christ, he would not disown to Pilate that he was a king, lest he should seem inconsistent with himself. Note, Though Christ *took upon him the form of a servant,* yet even then he justly claimed the honour and authority of a king. *Secondly,* He explains himself, and shows how he is a king, as *he came to bear witness of the truth;* he rules in the minds of men by the power of truth. If he had meant to declare himself a temporal prince, he would have said, *For this end was I born, and for this cause came I into the world,* to rule the nations, to conquer kings, and to take possession of kingdoms; no, *he came to be a witness,* a witness for the God that made the world, and against sin that ruins the world, and by this *word of his testimony* he sets up, and keeps up, his kingdom. It was foretold that he should be *a witness to the people,* and, as such, *a leader and commander to the people,* Isa. lv. 4. Christ's kingdom was not of this world, in which *truth faileth* (Isa. lix. 15. *Qui nescit dissimulare, nescit regnare—He that cannot dissemble knows not how to reign),* but of that world in which truth reigns eternally. Christ's errand into the world, and his business in the world, were *to bear witness to the truth.* 1. To reveal it, to discover to the world that which otherwise could not have been known concerning God and his will and *good-will to men, ch.* i. 18; xvii. 26. 2. To confirm it, Rom. xv. 8. By his miracles *he bore witness to the truth* of religion, the truth of divine revelation, and of God's perfections and providence, and the truth of his promise and covenant, *that all men through him might believe.* Now by doing this he is a king, and sets up a kingdom. (1.) The foundation and power, the spirit and genius, of Christ's kingdom, is truth, divine truth. When he said, *I am the truth,* he said, in effect, I am a king. He conquers by the convincing evidence of truth; he rules by the commanding power of truth, and *in his majesty rides prosperously, because of truth,* Ps. xlv. 4. It is with his truth that he shall judge the people, Ps. xcvi. 13. It is the sceptre of his kingdom; he *draws with the cords of a man,* with truth revealed to us, and received by us in *the love of it;* and thus he *brings thoughts into obedience.* He came *a light into the world,* and rules as the sun by day. (2.) The subjects of this kingdom are those that are *of the truth.* All that by the grace of God are rescued from under the power of *the father of lies,* and are disposed to receive the truth and submit to the power and influence of it, will hear Christ's voice, will become his subjects, and will bear faith and true allegiance to him. Every one that has any real sense of true religion will entertain the Christian religion, and they belong to his kingdom; by the power of truth he makes them willing, Ps. cx. 3. All that are in love with truth will hear the voice of Christ, for greater, better, surer, sweeter truths can nowhere be found than are found in Christ, by whom *grace and truth came;* so that, by *hearing Christ's voice,* we know that we are *of the truth,* 1 John iii. 19.

(6.) Pilate, hereupon, puts a good question to him, but does not stay for an answer, *v.* 38. He said, *What is truth?* and *immediately went out again.*

[1.] It is certain that this was a good question, and could not be put to one that was better able to answer it. Truth is that *pearl of great price* which the human understanding has a desire for and is in quest of; for it cannot rest but in that which is, or at least is apprehended to be, truth. When we *search the scriptures,* and attend the ministry of the word, it must be with this enquiry, *What is truth?* and with this prayer, *Lead me in thy truth, into all truth.* But many put this question that have not patience and constancy enough to persevere in their search after truth, or not humility and sincerity enough to receive it when they have found it, 2 Tim. iii. 7. Thus many deal with their own consciences; they ask them those needful questions, "What am I?" "What have I done?" but will not take time for an answer.

[2.] It is uncertain with what design

Pilate asked this question. *First,* Perhaps he spoke it as a learner, as one that began to think well of Christ, and to look upon him with some respect, and desired to be informed what new notions he advanced and what improvements he pretended to in religion and learning. But while he desired to hear some new truth from him, as Herod to see some miracle, the clamour and outrage of the priests' mob at his gate obliged him abruptly to let fall the discourse. *Secondly,* Some think he spoke it as a judge, enquiring further into the cause now brought before him: "Let me into this mystery, and tell me what the truth of it is, the true state of this matter." *Thirdly,* Others think he spoke it as a scoffer, in a jeering way: "Thou talkest of truth; canst thou tell what truth is, or give me a definition of it?" Thus he makes a jest of the everlasting gospel, that great truth which the chief priests hated and persecuted, and which Christ was now witnessing to and suffering for; and like men of no religion, who take a pleasure in bantering all religions, he ridicules both sides; and therefore Christ made him no reply. *Answer not a fool according to his folly; cast not pearls before swine.* But, though Christ would not tell Pilate what is truth, he has told his disciples, and by them has told us, *ch.* xiv. 6.

III. The result of both these conferences with the prosecutors and the prisoner (*v.* 38—40), in two things:—

1. The judge appeared his friend, and favourable to him, for,

(1.) He publicly declared him innocent, *v.* 38. Upon the whole matter, *I find in him no fault at all.* He supposes there might be some controversy in religion between him and them, wherein he was as likely to be in the right as they; but nothing criminal appears against him. This solemn declaration of Christ's innocency was, [1.] For the justification and honour of the Lord Jesus. By this it appears that though he was treated as the worst of malefactors he had never merited such treatment. [2.] For explaining the design and intention of his death, that he did not die for any sin of his own, even in the judgment of the judge himself, and therefore he died as a sacrifice for our sins, and that, even in the judgment of the prosecutors themselves, *one man should die for the people, ch.* xi. 50. This is he that *did no violence, neither was any deceit in his mouth* (Isa. liii. 9), who was to *be cut off, but not for himself,* Dan. ix. 26. [3.] For aggravating the sin of the Jews that prosecuted him with so much violence. If a prisoner has had a fair trial, and has been acquitted by those that are proper judges of the crime, especially if there be no cause to suspect them partial in his favour, he must be believed innocent, and his accusers are bound to acquiesce. But our Lord Jesus, though brought in not guilty, is still run down as a malefactor, and his blood thirsted for.

(2.) He proposed an expedient for his discharge (*v.* 39): *You have a custom, that I should release to you a prisoner at the passover;* shall it be this king of the Jews? He proposed this, not to the chief priests (he knew they would never agree to it), but to the multitude; it was an appeal to the people, as appears, Matt. xxvii. 15. Probably he had heard how this Jesus had been attended but the other day with the hosannas of the common people; he therefore looked upon him to be the darling of the multitude, and the envy only of the rulers, and therefore he made no doubt but they would demand the release of Jesus, and this would stop the mouth of the prosecutors, and all would be well. [1.] He allows their custom, for which, perhaps, they had had a long prescription, in honour of the passover, which was a memorial of their release. But it was adding to God's words, as if he had not instituted enough for the due commemoration of that deliverance, and, though an act of mercy, might be injustice to the public, Prov. xvii. 15. [2.] He offers to release Jesus to them, according to the custom. If Pilate had had the honesty and courage that became a judge, he would not have named an innocent person to be competitor with a notorious criminal for this favour; if he *found no fault in him,* he was bound in conscience to discharge him. But he was willing to trim the matter, and please all sides, being governed more by worldly wisdom than by the rules of equity.

2. The people appeared his enemies, and implacable against him (*v.* 40): *They cried all again* and again, *Not this man,* let not him be released, *but Barabbas.* Observe, (1.) How fierce and outrageous they were. Pilate proposed the thing to them calmly, as worthy their mature consideration, but they resolved it in a heat, and gave in their resolution with clamour and noise, and in the utmost confusion. Note, The enemies of Christ's holy religion cry it down, and so hope to run it down; witness the outcry at Ephesus, Acts xix. 34. But those who think the worse of things or persons merely for their being thus exclaimed against have a very small share of constancy and consideration. Nay, there is cause to suspect a deficiency of reason and justice on that side which calls in the assistance of popular tumult. (2.) How foolish and absurd they were, as is intimated in the short account here given of the other candidate: *Now Barabbas was a robber,* and therefore, [1.] A breaker of the law of God; and yet he shall be spared, rather than one who reproved the pride, avarice, and tyranny of the priests and elders. Though Barabbas be a robber, he will not rob them of Moses's seat, nor of their traditions, and then no matter. [2.] He was an enemy to the public safety and personal property. The clamour of the town is wont to be against robbers (Job xxx. 5, *Men cried after them as after a*

thief), yet here it is for one. Thus those do who prefer their sins before Christ. Sin is a robber, every base lust is a robber, and yet foolishly chosen rather than Christ, who would truly enrich us.

CHAP. XIX.

Though in the history hitherto this evangelist seems industriously to have declined the recording of such passages as had been related by the other evangelists, yet, when he comes to the sufferings and death of Christ, instead of passing them over, as one ashamed of his Master's chain and cross, and looking upon them as the blemishes of his story, he repeats what had been before related, with considerable enlargements, as one that desired to know nothing but Christ and him crucified, to glory in nothing save in the cross of Christ. In the story of this chapter we have, I. The remainder of Christ's trial before Pilate, which was tumultuous and confused, ver. 1—15. II. Sentence given, and execution done upon it, ver. 16—18. III. The title over his head, ver. 19—22. IV. The parting of his garment, ver. 23, 24. V. The care he took of his mother, ver. 25—27. VI. The giving him vinegar to drink, ver. 28, 29. VII. His dying word, ver. 30. VIII. The piercing of his side, ver. 31—37. IX. The burial of his body, ver. 38—42. O that in meditating on these things we may experimentally know the power of Christ's death, and the fellowship of his sufferings!

THEN Pilate therefore took Jesus,
and scourged *him*. 2 And the
soldiers platted a crown of thorns,
and put *it* on his head, and they put
on him a purple robe, 3 And said,
Hail, King of the Jews! and they
smote him with their hands. 4 Pilate
therefore went forth again, and saith
unto them, Behold, I bring him forth
to you, that ye may know that I find
no fault in him. 5 Then came Jesus
forth, wearing the crown of thorns,
and the purple robe. And *Pilate* saith
unto them, Behold the man! 6 When
the chief priests therefore and officers
saw him, they cried out, saying, Crucify *him*, crucify *him*. Pilate saith
unto them, Take ye him, and crucify
him: for I find no fault in him. 7
The Jews answered him, We have a
law, and by our law he ought to die,
because he made himself the Son of
God. 8 When Pilate therefore heard
that saying, he was the more afraid;
9 And went again into the judgment
hall, and saith unto Jesus, Whence
art thou? But Jesus gave him no
answer. 10 Then saith Pilate unto
him, Speakest thou not unto me?
knowest thou not that I have power
to crucify thee, and have power to
release thee? 11 Jesus answered,
Thou couldest have no power *at all*
against me, except it were given thee
from above: therefore he that delivered me unto thee hath the greater
sin. 12 And from thenceforth Pilate
sought to release him: but the Jews
cried out, saying, If thou let this man
go, thou art not Cæsar's friend: whosoever maketh himself a king speaketh against Cæsar. 13 When Pilate
therefore heard that saying, he brought
Jesus forth, and sat down in the judgment seat in a place that is called the
Pavement, but in the Hebrew, Gabbatha. 14 And it was the preparation of the passover, and about the
sixth hour: and he saith unto the
Jews, Behold your King! 15 But
they cried out, Away with *him*, away
with *him*, crucify him. Pilate saith
unto them, Shall I crucify your King?
The chief priests answered, We have
no king but Cæsar.

Here is a further account of the unfair trial which they gave to our Lord Jesus. The prosecutors carrying it on with great confusion among the people, and the judge with great confusion in his own breast, between both the narrative is such as is not easily reduced to method; we must therefore take the parts of it as they lie.

I. The judge abuses the prisoner, though he declares him innocent, and hopes therewith to pacify the prosecutors; wherein his intention, if indeed it was good, will by no means justify his proceedings, which were palpably unjust.

1. He ordered him to be whipped as a criminal, *v.* 1. *Pilate,* seeing the people so outrageous, and being disappointed in his project of releasing him upon the people's choice, *took Jesus, and scourged him,* that is, appointed the lictors that attended him to do it. Bede is of opinion that Pilate scourged Jesus himself with his own hands, because it is said, *He took him and scourged him,* that it might be done favourably. Matthew and Mark mention his scourging after his condemnation, but here it appears to have been before. Luke speaks of Pilate's offering to *chastise him, and let him go,* which must be before sentence. This scourging of him was designed only to pacify the Jews, and in it Pilate put a compliment upon them, that he would take their word against his own sentiments so far. The Roman scourgings were ordinarily very severe, not limited, as among the Jews, to *forty stripes;* yet this pain and shame Christ submitted to for our sakes. (1.) *That the scripture might be fulfilled,* which spoke of his being *stricken, smitten, and afflicted,* and *the chastisemeut of our peace* being *upon him* (Isa. liii. 5), of his giving his back to the smiters (Isa. l. 6), of the ploughers ploughing upon his back, Ps. cxxix. 3. He himself likewise had foretold it, Matt. xx. 19; Mark x. 34; Luke xviii. 33. (2.) *That by his stripes we might be healed,* 1 Pet. ii. 4. We deserved to have been chastised *with whips and scorpions,* and *beaten with many stripes,* having known our Lord's will and not done it; but Christ un-

derwent the stripes for us, bearing the rod of his Father's wrath, Lam. iii. 1. Pilate's design in scourging him was that he might not be condemned, which did not take effect, but intimated what was God's design, that his being scourged might prevent our being condemned, we having fellowship in his sufferings, and this did take effect: the physician scourged, and so the patient healed. (3.) That stripes, for his sake, might be sanctified and made easy to his followers; and they might, as they did, rejoice in that shame (Acts v. 41; xvi. 22, 25), as Paul did, who was *in stripes above measure*, 2 Cor. xi. 23. Christ's stripes take out the sting of theirs, and alter the property of them. *We are chastened of the Lord, that we may not be condemned with the world*, 1 Cor. xi. 32.

2. He turned him over to his soldiers, to be ridiculed and made sport with as a fool (*v.* 2, 3): *The soldiers*, who were the governor's life-guard, *put a crown of thorns upon his head;* such a crown they thought fittest for such a king; *they put on him a purple robe*, some old threadbare coat of that colour, which they thought good enough to be the badge of his royalty; and they complimented him with, *Hail, king of the Jews* (like people like king), and then *smote him with their hands.*

(1.) See here the baseness and injustice of Pilate, that he would suffer one whom he believed an innocent person, and if so an excellent person, to be thus abused and trampled on by his own servants. Those who are under the arrest of the law ought to be under the protection of it; and their being secured is to be their security. But Pilate did this, [1.] To oblige his soldiers' merry humour, and perhaps his own too, notwithstanding the gravity one might have expected in a judge. *Herod*, as well as *his men of war*, had just before done the same, Luke xxiii. 11. It was as good as a stage-play to them, now that it was a festival time; as the Philistines made sport with Samson. [2.] To oblige the Jews' malicious humour, and to gratify them, who desired that all possible disgrace might be done to Christ, and the utmost indignities put upon him.

(2.) See here the rudeness and insolence of the soldiers, how perfectly lost they were to all justice and humanity, who could thus triumph over a man in misery, and one that had been in reputation for wisdom and honour, and never did any thing to forfeit it. But thus hath Christ's holy religion been basely misrepresented, dressed up by bad men at their pleasure, and so exposed to contempt and ridicule, as Christ was here. [1.] They clothe him with a mock-robe, as if it were a sham and a jest, and nothing but the product of a heated fancy and a crazed imagination. And as Christ is here represented as a king in conceit only, so is his religion as a concern in conceit only, and God and the soul, sin and duty, heaven and hell, are with many all chimeras. [2.] They crown him with thorns; as if the religion of Christ were a perfect penance, and the greatest pain and hardship in the world; as if to submit to the control of God and conscience were to thrust one's head into a thicket of thorns; but this is an unjust imputation; *thorns and snares are in the way of the froward*, but roses and laurels in religion's ways.

(3.) See here the wonderful condescension of our Lord Jesus in his sufferings for us. Great and generous minds can bear any thing better than ignominy, any toil, any pain, any loss, rather than reproach; yet this the great and holy Jesus submitted to for us. See and admire, [1.] The invincible patience of a sufferer, leaving us an example of contentment and courage, evenness, and easiness of spirit, under the greatest hardships we may meet with in the way of duty. [2.] The invincible love and kindness of a Saviour, who not only cheerfully and resolutely went through all this, but voluntarily undertook it for us and for our salvation. Herein he commended his love, that he would not only die for us, but die as a fool dies. *First*, He *endured the pain;* not the pangs of death only, though in the death of the cross these were most exquisite; but, as if these were too little, he submitted to those previous pains. Shall we complain of a thorn in the flesh, and of being buffeted by affliction, because we need it to hide pride from us, when Christ humbled himself to bear those thorns in the head, and those buffetings, to save and teach us? 2 Cor. xii. 7. *Secondly*, He *despised the shame*, the shame of a fool's coat, and the mock-respect paid him, with, *Hail, king of the Jews.* If we be at any time ridiculed for well-doing, let us not be ashamed, but glorify God, for thus we are partakers of Christ's sufferings. He that bore these sham honours was recompensed with real honours, and so shall we, if we patiently suffer shame for him.

II. Pilate, having thus abused the prisoner, presents him to the prosecutors, in hope that they would now be satisfied, and drop the prosecution, *v.* 4, 5. Here he proposes two things to their consideration:—

1. That he had not found any thing in him which made him obnoxious to the Roman government (*v.* 4): *I find no fault in him; οὐδεμίαν αἰτίαν εὑρίσκω—I do not find in him the least fault*, or *cause of accusation.* Upon further enquiry, he repeats the declaration he had made, *ch.* xviii. 38. Hereby he condemns himself; if he found no fault in him, why did he scourge him, why did he suffer him to be abused? None ought to suffer ill but those that do ill; yet thus many banter and abuse religion, who yet, if they be serious, cannot but own they find no fault in it. If he found no fault in him, why did he bring him out to his prosecutors, and not immediately release him, as he ought to have done? If Pilate had consulted his own conscience only, he would neither have

scourged Christ nor crucified him; but, thinking to trim the matter, to please the people by scourging Christ, and save his conscience by not crucifying him, behold he does both; whereas, if he had at first resolved to crucify him, he need not have scourged him. It is common for those who think to keep themselves from greater sins by venturing upon less sins to run into both.

2. That he had done that to him which would make him the less dangerous to them and to their government, *v.* 5. He brought him out to them, wearing the crown of thorns, his head and face all bloody, and said, "*Behold the man* whom you are so jealous of," intimating that though his having been so popular might have given them some cause to fear that his interest in the country would lessen theirs, yet he had taken an effectual course to prevent it, by treating him as a slave, and exposing him to contempt, after which he supposed the people would never look upon him with any respect, nor could he ever retrieve his reputation again. Little did Pilate think with what veneration even these sufferings of Christ would in after ages be commemorated by the best and greatest of men, who would glory in that cross and those stripes which he thought would have been to him and his followers a perpetual and indelible reproach. (1.) Observe here our Lord Jesus shows himself dressed up in all the marks of ignominy. He came forth, willing to be made a spectacle, and to be hooted at, as no doubt he was when he came forth in this garb, knowing that he was set for a *sign that should be spoken against,* Luke ii. 34. Did he go forth thus bearing our reproach? Let us go forth to him *bearing his reproach,* Heb. xiii. 13. (2.) How Pilate shows him: *Pilate saith unto them, Behold the man. He saith unto them:* so the original is; and, the immediate antecedent being *Jesus,* I see no inconvenience in supposing these to be Christ's own words; he said, "*Behold the man* against whom you are so exasperated." But some of the Greek copies, and the generality of the translators, supply it as we do, Pilate saith unto them, with a design to appease them, *Behold the man;* not so much to move their pity, Behold a man worthy your compassion, as to silence their jealousies, Behold a man not worthy your suspicion, a man from whom you can henceforth fear no danger; his crown is *profaned, and cast to the ground,* and now all mankind will make a jest of him. The word however is very affecting: *Behold the man.* It is good for every one of us, with an eye of faith, to behold the man Christ Jesus in his sufferings. *Behold this king with the crown wherewith his mother crowned him,* the crown of thorns, Cant. iii. 11. "Behold him, and be suitably affected with the sight. Behold him, and mourn because of him. Behold him, and love him; be still *looking unto Jesus.*"

III. The prosecutors, instead of being pacified, were but the more exasperated, *v.* 6, 7.

1. Observe here their clamour and outrage. *The chief priests,* who headed the mob, *cried out* with fury and indignation, and their officers, or servants, who must say as they said, joined with them in crying, *Crucify him, crucify him.* The common people perhaps would have acquiesced in Pilate's declaration of his innocency, but their leaders, the priests, *caused them to err.* Now by this it appears that their malice against Christ was, (1.) Unreasonable and most absurd, in that they offer not to make good their charge against him, nor to object against the judgment of Pilate concerning him; but, though he be innocent, he must be crucified. (2.) It was insatiable and very cruel. Neither the extremity of his scourging, nor his patience under it, nor the tender expostulations of the judge, could mollify them in the least; no, nor could the jest into which Pilate had turned the cause, put them into a pleasant humour. (3.) It was violent and exceedingly resolute; they will have it their own way, and hazard the governor's favour, the peace of the city, and their own safety, rather than abate of the utmost of their demands. Were they so violent in running down our Lord Jesus, and in crying, *Crucify him, crucify him?* and shall not we be vigorous and zealous in advancing his name, and in crying, *Crown him, Crown him?* Did their hatred of him sharpen their endeavours against him? and shall not our love to him quicken our endeavours for him and his kingdom?

2. The check Pilate gave to their fury, still insisting upon the prisoner's innocency: "*Take you him and crucify him,* if he must be crucified." This is spoken ironically; he knew they could not, they durst not, crucify him; but it is as if he should say, "You shall not make me a drudge to your malice; I cannot with a safe conscience crucify him." A good resolve, if he would but have stuck to it. He found no fault in him, and therefore should not have continued to parley with the prosecutors. Those that would be safe from sin should be deaf to temptation. Nay, he should have secured the prisoner from their insults. What was he armed with power for, but to protect the injured? The guards of governors ought to be the guards of justice. But Pilate had not courage enough to act according to his conscience; and his cowardice betrayed him into a snare.

3. The further colour which the prosecutors gave to their demand (*v.* 7): *We have a law, and by our law,* if it were but in our power to execute it, *he ought to die, because he made himself the Son of God.* Now here observe, (1.) They *made their boast of the law,* even when *through breaking the law they dishonoured God,* as is charged upon the Jews, Rom. ii. 23. They had indeed an excellent law, far exceeding the statutes and

judgments of other nations; but in vain did they boast of their law, when they abused it to such bad purposes. (2.) They discover a restless and inveterate malice against our Lord Jesus. When they could not incense Pilate against him by alleging that he pretended himself a king, they urged this, that he pretended himself a God. Thus they turn every stone to take him off. (3.) They pervert the law, and make that the instrument of their malice. Some think they refer to a law made particularly against Christ, as if, being a law, it must be executed, right or wrong; whereas there is a woe to them that *decree unrighteous decrees*, and that *write the grievousness which they have prescribed*, Isa. x. 1. See Mic. vi. 16. But it should seem they rather refer to the law of Moses; and if so, [1.] It was true that blasphemers, idolaters, and false prophets, were to be put to death by that law. Whoever falsely pretended to be the Son of God was guilty of blasphemy, Lev. xxiv. 16. But then, [2.] It was false that Christ pretended to be the Son of God, for he really was so; and they ought to have enquired into the proofs he produced of his being so. If he said that he was the Son of God, and the scope and tendency of his doctrine were not to draw people from God, but to bring them to him, and if he confirmed his mission and doctrine by miracles, as undoubtedly he did, beyond contradiction, by their law they ought to *hearken to him* (Deut. xviii. 18, 19), and, if they did not, they were to be *cut off*. That which was his honour, and might have been their happiness, if they had not stood in their own light, they impute to him as a crime, for which he ought to die; yet if he ought to die by their law he ought not to be crucified, for this was no death inflicted by their law.

IV. The judge brings the prisoner again to his trial, upon this new suggestion. Observe,

1. The concern Pilate was in, when he heard this alleged (*v* 8): When he heard that his prisoner pretended not to royalty only, but to deity, he was *the more afraid*. This embarrassed him more than ever, and made the case more difficult both ways; for, (1.) There was the more danger of offending the people if he should acquit him, for he knew how jealous that people were for the unity of the Godhead, and what aversion they now had to other gods; and therefore, though he might hope to pacify their rage against a pretended king, he could never reconcile them to a pretended God. "If this be at the bottom of the tumult," thinks Pilate, "it will not be turned off with a jest." (2.) There was the more danger of offending his own conscience if he should condemn him. "Is he one" (thinks Pilate) "that makes himself *the Son of God?* and what if it should prove that he is so? What will become of me then?" Even natural conscience makes men afraid of being found *fighting against God*. The heathen had some fabulous traditions of incarnate deities appearing sometimes in mean circumstances, and treated ill by some that paid dearly for their so doing. Pilate fears lest he should thus run himself into a premunire.

2. His further examination of our Lord Jesus thereupon, *v.* 9. That he might give the prosecutors all the fair play they could desire, he resumed the debate, went into the judgment-hall, and asked Christ, *Whence art thou?* Observe,

(1.) The place he chose for this examination: He *went into the judgment-hall* for privacy, that he might be out of the noise and clamour of the crowd, and might examine the thing the more closely. Those that would find out the truth as it is in Jesus must get out of the noise of prejudice, and retire as it were into the judgment-hall, to converse with Christ alone.

(2.) The question he put to him: *Whence art thou?* Art thou from men or from heaven? From beneath or from above? He had before asked directly, *Art thou a King?* But here he does not directly ask, *Art thou the Son of God?* lest he should seem to meddle with divine things too boldly. But in general, "*Whence art thou?* Where wast thou, and in what world hadst thou a being, before thy coming into this world?"

(3.) The silence of our Lord Jesus when he was examined upon this head; but *Jesus gave him no answer*. This was not a sullen silence, in contempt of the court, nor was it because he knew not what to say; but, [1.] It was a patient silence, that the scripture might be fulfilled, *as a sheep before the shearers is dumb, so he opened not his mouth*, Isa. liii. 7. This silence loudly bespoke his submission to his Father's will in his present sufferings, which he thus accommodated himself to, and composed himself to bear. He was silent, because he would say nothing to hinder his sufferings. If Christ had avowed himself a God as plainly as he avowed himself a king, it is probable that Pilate would not have condemned him (for he was afraid at the mention of it by the prosecutors); and the Romans, though they triumphed over the *kings of the nations* they conquered, yet stood in awe of their gods. See 1 Cor. ii. 8. *If they had known* him to be the *Lord of glory*, they would *not have crucified him;* and how then could we have been saved? [2.] It was a prudent silence. When the chief priests asked him, *Art thou the Son of the Blessed?* he answered, *I am*, for he knew they went upon the scriptures of the Old Testament which spoke of the Messiah; but when Pilate asked him he knew he did not understand his own question, having no notion of the Messiah, and of his being the *Son of God*, and therefore to what purpose should he reply to him whose head was filled with the pagan theology, to which he would have turned his answer?

(4.) The haughty check which Pilate gave him for his silence (*v.* 10): "*Speakest thou not unto me?* Dost thou put such an affront upon me as to stand mute? What *knowest thou not* that, as president of the province, *I have power*, if I think fit, *to crucify thee, and have power*, if I think fit, to *release thee?*" Observe here, [1.] How Pilate magnifies himself, and boasts of his own authority, as not inferior to that of Nebuchadnezzar, of whom it is said that *whom he would he slew, and whom he would he kept alive*, Dan. v. 19. Men in power are apt to be puffed up with their power, and the more absolute and arbitrary it is the more it gratifies and humours their pride. But he magnifies his power to an exorbitant degree when he boasts that he has power to crucify one whom he had declared innocent, for no prince or potentate has authority to do wrong. *Id possumus, quod jure possumus—We can do that only which we can do justly.* [2.] How he tramples upon our blessed Saviour: *Speakest thou not unto me?* He reflects upon him, *First,* As if he were undutiful and disrespectful to those in authority, not speaking when he was spoken to. *Secondly,* As if he were ungrateful to one that had been tender of him: "Speakest thou not to me who have laboured to secure thy release?" *Thirdly,* As if he were unwise for himself: "Wilt thou not speak to clear thyself to one that is willing to clear thee?" If Christ had indeed sought to save his life, now had been his time to have spoken; but that which he had to do was to lay down his life.

(5.) Christ's pertinent answer to this check, *v.* 11, where,

[1.] He boldly rebukes his arrogance, and rectifies his mistake: "Big as thou lookest and talkest, *thou couldest have no power at all against me,* no power to scourge, no power to crucify, *except it were given thee from above.*" Though Christ did not think fit to answer him when he was impertinent (then *answer not a fool according to his folly, lest thou also be like him),* yet he did think fit to answer him when he was imperious; then *answer a fool according to his folly, lest he be wise in his own conceit,* Prov. xxvi. 4, 5. When Pilate used his power, Christ silently submitted to it; but, when he grew proud of it, he made him know himself: "All the power thou hast is given thee from above," which may be taken two ways:—*First,* As reminding him that his power in general, as a magistrate, was a limited power, and he could do no more than God would suffer him to do. God is the fountain of power; and the *powers that are,* as they are ordained by him and derived from him, so they are subject to him. They ought to go no further than his law directs them; they can go no further than his providence permits them. They are God's hand and his sword, Ps. xvii. 13, 14. Though the axe may *boast itself against him that heweth therewith,* yet still it is but a tool, Isa. x. 5, 15. Let the proud oppressors know that there is *a higher than they,* to whom they are accountable, Eccl. v. 8. And let this silence the murmurings of the oppressed, *It is the Lord.* God has bidden Shimei curse David; and let it comfort them that their persecutors can do no more than God will let them. See Isa. li. 12, 13. *Secondly,* As informing him that his power against him in particular, and all the efforts of that power, were *by the determinate counsel and foreknowledge of God,* Acts ii. 23. Pilate never fancied himself to look so great as now, when he sat in judgment upon such a prisoner as this, who was looked upon by many as the *Son of God* and king of Israel, and had the fate of so great a man at his disposal; but Christ lets him know that he was herein but an instrument in God's hand, and could do nothing against him, but by the appointment of Heaven, Acts iv. 27, 28.

[2.] He mildly excuses and extenuates his sin, in comparison with the sin of the ringleaders: "*Therefore he that delivered me unto thee* lies under greater guilt; for thou as a magistrate hast *power from above,* and art in thy place, thy sin is less than theirs who, from envy and malice, urge thee to abuse thy power."

First, It is plainly intimated that what Pilate did was sin, a great sin, and that the force which the Jews put upon him, and which he put upon himself in it, would not justify him. Christ hereby intended a hint for the awakening of his conscience and the increase of the fear he was now under. The guilt of others will not acquit us, nor will it avail in the great day to say that others were worse than we, for we are not to be judged by comparison, but must *bear our own burden.*

Secondly, Yet theirs that delivered him to Pilate was the greater sin. By this it appears that all sins are not equal, but some more heinous than others; some comparatively as gnats, others as camels; some as motes in the eyes, others as beams; some as pence, others as pounds. *He that delivered Christ to Pilate* was either, 1. The people of the Jews, who cried out, *Crucify him, crucify him.* They had seen Christ's miracles, which Pilate had not; to them the Messiah was first sent; they were his own; and to them, who were now enslaved, a Redeemer should have been most welcome, and therefore it was much worse in them to appear against him than in Pilate. 2. Or rather he means Caiaphas in particular, who was at the head of the conspiracy against Christ, and first advised his death, *ch.* xi. 49, 50. The sin of Caiaphas was abundantly greater than the sin of Pilate. Caiaphas prosecuted Christ from pure enmity to him and his doctrine, deliberately and of malice prepense. Pilate condemned him purely for fear of the people, and it was a hasty resolution which he had not time to cool upon. 3. Some think Christ means Judas; for, though he did not immediately deliver him into the hands of Pilate, yet he betrayed him to those that did. The sin of Judas was, upon many accounts, greater than the sin of Pilate. Pilate was a stranger to Christ; Judas was his friend and follower. Pilate found no fault in him, but Judas knew a great deal of good of him. Pilate, though biassed, was not bribed, but Judas took a *reward against the innocent;* the sin of Judas was a leading sin, and let in all that followed. He was a *guide to them that took Jesus.* So great was the sin of Judas that *vengeance suffered him not to live;* but when Christ said this, or soon after, he was gone *to his own place.*

V. Pilate struggles with the Jews to deliver Jesus out of their hands, but in vain. We hear no more after this of any thing that passed between Pilate and the prisoner; what remains lay between him and the prosecutors.

1. Pilate seems more zealous than before to get Jesus discharged (*v.* 12): *Thenceforth,* from this time, and for this reason, because Christ had given him that answer (*v.* 11), which, though it had a rebuke in it, yet he took kindly; and, though Christ found fault with him, he still continued to find no fault in Christ, but *sought to release him,* desired it, endeavoured it. *He sought to release him;* he contrived how to do it handsomely and safely, and so as not to disoblige the priests. It never does well when our resolutions to do our duty are swallowed up in projects how to do it plausibly and conveniently. If Pilate's policy had not prevailed above his justice, he would not have been long seeking to release him, but would have done it. *Fiat justitia, ruat cœlum—Let justice be done, though heaven itself should fall.*

2. The Jews were more furious than ever, and more violent to get Jesus crucified. Still they carry on their design with noise and clamour as before; so now they cried out. They would have it thought that the commonalty was against him, and therefore laboured to get him cried down by a multitude, and it is no hard matter to pack a mob; whereas, if a fair poll had been granted, I doubt not but it would have been carried by a great majority for the releasing of him. A few madmen may out-shout many wise men, and then fancy themselves to speak the sense (when it is but the nonsense) of a nation, or of all mankind; but it is not so easy a thing to change the sense of the people as it is to misrepresent it, and to change their cry. Now that Christ was in the hands of his enemies his friends were shy and silent, and disappeared, and those that were against him were forward to show themselves so; and this gave the chief priests an opportunity to represent it as the concurring vote of all the Jews that he should be crucified. In this outcry they sought two things:—(1.) To blacken the prisoner as an enemy to Cæsar. He had refused the kingdoms of this world and the glory of them, had declared his kingdom not to be of this world, and yet they will have it that he *speaks against Cæsar; ἀντιλέγει—he opposes Cæsar,* invades his dignity and sovereignty It has always been the artifice of the enemies of religion to represent it as hurtful to kings and provinces, when it would be highly beneficial to both. (2.) To frighten the judge, as no friend to Cæsar: "If thou *let this man go* unpunished, and let him go on, *thou art not Cæsar's friend,* and therefore false to thy trust and the duty of thy place, obnoxious to the emperor's displeasure, and liable to be turned out." They intimate a threatening that they would inform against him, and get him displaced; and here they touched him in a sensible and very tender part. But, of all people, these Jews should not have pretended a concern for Cæsar, who were themselves so ill affected to him and his government. They should not talk of being friends to Cæsar, who were themselves such back friends to him; yet thus a pretended zeal for that which is good often serves to cover a real malice against that which is better.

3. When other expedients had been tried in vain, Pilate slightly endeavoured to banter them out of their fury, and yet, in doing this, betrayed himself to them, and yielded to the rapid stream, *v.* 13—15. After he had stood it out a great while, and seemed now as if he would have made a vigorous resistance upon this attack (*v.* 12), he basely surrendered. Observe here,

(1.) What it was that shocked Pilate (*v.* 13): "*When he heard that saying,* that he could not be true to Cæsar's honour, nor sure of Cæsar's favour, if he did not put Jesus to death, then he thought it was time to look about him. All they had said to prove Christ a malefactor, and that therefore it was Pilate's duty to condemn him, did not move him, but he still kept to his conviction of Christ's innocency; but, when they urged that it was his interest to condemn him, then he began to yield. Note, Those that bind up their happiness in the favour of men make themselves an easy prey to the temptations of Satan.

(2.) What preparation was made for a definitive sentence upon this matter: *Pilate brought Jesus forth,* and he himself in great state took the chair. We may suppose that he called for his robes, that he might look big, and then *sat down in the judgment-seat.*

[1.] Christ was condemned with all the ceremony that could be. *First,* To bring us off at God's bar, and that all believers through Christ, being judged here, might be acquitted in the court of heaven. *Secondly,* To take off the terror of pompous trials, which his followers would be brought to for his sake. Paul might the better stand at Cæsar's judgment-seat when his Master had stood there before him

[2.] Notice is here taken of the place and time.

First, The place where Christ was condemned: in a *place called the Pavement, but in Hebrew, Gabbatha,* probably the place where he used to sit to try causes or criminals. Some make *Gabbatha* to signify an *enclosed place,* fenced against the insults of the people, whom therefore he did the less need to fear; others an *elevated place,* raised that all might see him.

Secondly, The time, *v.* 14. It was the preparation of the passover, and *about the sixth hour.* Observe, 1. The day: It was the preparation of the passover, that is, for the passover-sabbath, and the solemnities of that and the rest of the days of the feast of unleavened bread. This is plain from Luke xxiii. 54, *It was the preparation, and the sabbath drew on.* So that this preparation was for the sabbath. Note, Before the passover there ought to be preparation. This is mentioned as an aggravation of their sin, in persecuting Christ with so much malice and fury, that it was when they should have been purging out the old leaven, to get ready for the passover; but the better the day the worse the deed. 2. The hour: *It was about the sixth hour.* Some ancient Greek and Latin manuscripts read it about the third hour, which agrees with Mark xv. 25. And it appears by Matt. xxvii. 45 that he was upon the cross before the sixth hour. But it should seem to come in here, not as a precise determination of the time, but as an additional aggravation of the sin of his prosecutors, that they were pushing on the prosecution, not only on a solemn day, the *day of the preparation,* but, from the third to the sixth hour (which was, as we call it, church-time) on that day, they were employed in this wickedness; so that for this day, though they were priests, they dropped the temple-service, for they did not leave Christ till the sixth hour, when the darkness began, which frightened them away. Some think that the sixth hour, with this evangelist, is, according to the Roman reckoning and ours, six of the clock in the morning, answering to the Jews' first hour of the day; this is very probable, that Christ's trial before Pilate was at the height about six in the morning, which was then a little after sun-rising.

(3.) The rencounter Pilate had with the Jews, both priests and people, before he proceeded to give judgment, endeavouring in vain to stem the tide of their rage.

[1.] He saith unto the Jews, *Behold your king.* This is a reproof to them for the absurdity and malice of their insinuating that this Jesus made himself a king: "*Behold your king,* that is, him whom you accuse as a pretender to the crown. Is this a man likely to be dangerous to the government? I am satisfied he is not, and you may be so too, and let him alone." Some think he hereby upbraids them with their secret disaffection to Cæsar: "You would have this man to be your king, if he would but have headed a rebellion against Cæsar." But Pilate, though he was far from meaning so, seems as if he were the voice of God to them. Christ, now crowned with thorns, is, as a king at his coronation, offered to the people: "*Behold your king,* the king whom God hath set upon his holy hill of Zion;" but they, instead of entering into it with acclamations of joyful consent, protest against him; they will not have a king of God's choosing.

[2.] They cried out with the greatest indignation, *Away with him, away with him,* which speaks disdain as well as malice, ἆρον, ἆρον—"*Take him,* he is none of ours; we disown him for our kinsman,much more for our king; we have not only no veneration for him, but no compassion; *away with him* out of our sight;" for so it was written of him, he is one *whom the nation abhors* (Isa. xlix. 7), and they *hid as it were their faces from him,* Isa. liii. 2, 3. *Away with him from the earth,* Acts xxii. 22. This shows, *First,* How we deserved to have been treated at God's tribunal. We were by sin become odious to God's holiness, which cried, *Away with them, away with them,* for God is *of purer eyes than to behold iniquity.* We were also become obnoxious to God's justice, which cried against us, "*Crucify them, crucify them,* let the sentence of the law be executed." Had not Christ interposed, and been thus rejected of men, we had been for ever rejected of God. *Secondly,* It shows how we ought to treat our sins. We are often in scripture said to crucify sin, in conformity to Christ's death. Now they that crucified Christ did it with detestation. With a pious indignation we should run down sin in us, as they with an impious indignation ran him down who was made sin for us. The true penitent casts away from him his transgressions, *Away with them, away with them* (Isa. ii. 20); xxx. 22), *crucify them, crucify them;* it is not fit that they should live in my soul, Hos. xiv. 8.

[3.] Pilate, willing to have Jesus released, and yet that it should be their doing, asks them, *Shall I crucify your king?* In saying this, he designed either, *First,* To stop their mouths, by showing them how absurd it was for them to reject one who offered himself to them to be their king at a time when they needed one more than ever. Have they no sense of slavery? No desire of liberty? No value for a deliverer? Though he saw no cause to fear him, they might see cause to hope for something from him; since crushed and sinking interests are ready to catch at any thing. Or, *Secondly,* To stop the mouth of his own conscience. "If this Jesus be a king" (thinks Pilate), "he is only king of the Jews, and therefore I have nothing to do but to make a fair tender of him to them; if they refuse him, and will have their king crucified, what is that to me?" He banters them for their folly in expecting a Messiah, and yet running down one that bade so fair to be he.

[4.] The chief priests, that they might effectually renounce Christ, and engage Pilate to crucify him, but otherwise sorely against their will, cried out, *We have no king but Cæsar.* This they knew would please Pilate, and so they hoped to carry their point, though at the same time they hated Cæsar and his government. But observe here, *First,* What a plain indication this is that the time for the Messiah to appear, even the set time, was now come; for, if the Jews have no king but Cæsar, then is the *sceptre departed from Judah, and the lawgiver from between his feet,* which should never be till Shiloh come to set up a spiritual kingdom. And, *Secondly,* What a righteous thing it was with God to bring upon them that ruin by the Romans which followed not long after. 1. They adhere to Cæsar, and to Cæsar they shall go. God soon gave them enough of their Cæsars, and, according to Jotham's parable, since the trees choose the bramble for their king, rather than the vine and the olive, an evil spirit is sent among them, for they could not do it truly and sincerely, Judg. ix. 12, 19. Henceforward they were rebels to the Cæsars, and the Cæsars tyrants to them, and their disaffection ended in the overthrow of their place and nation. It is just with God to make that a scourge and plague to us which we prefer before Christ. 2. They would have no other king than Cæsar, and never have they had any other to this day, but have now *abode many days without a king, and without a prince* (Hos. iii. 4), without any of their own, but the kings of the nations have ruled over them; since they will have no king but Cæsar, so shall their doom be, themselves have decided it.

16 Then delivered he him therefore unto them to be crucified. And
they took Jesus, and led *him* away.
17 And he bearing his cross went
forth into a place called *the place* of a
skull, which is called in the Hebrew
Golgotha: 18 Where they crucified
him, and two other with him, on
either side one, and Jesus in the
midst.

We have here sentence of death passed upon our Lord Jesus, and execution done soon after. A mighty struggle Pilate had had within him between his convictions and his corruptions; but at length his convictions yielded, and his corruptions prevailed, the fear of man having a greater power over him than the fear of God.

I. *Pilate gave judgment* against Christ, and signed the warrant for his execution, *v.* 16. We may see here, 1. How Pilate sinned against his conscience; he had again and again pronounced him innocent, and yet at last condemned him as guilty. Pilate, since he came to be governor, had in many instances disobliged and exasperated the Jewish nation; for he was a man of a haughty and implacable spirit, and extremely wedded to his humour. He had seized upon the Corban, and spent it upon a water-work; he had brought into Jerusalem shields stamped with Cæsar's image, which was very provoking to the Jews; he had sacrificed the lives of many to his resolutions herein. Fearing therefore that he should be complained of for these and other insolences, he was willing to gratify the Jews. Now this makes the matter much worse. If he had been of an easy, soft, and pliable disposition, his yielding to so strong a stream had been the more excusable; but for a man that was so wilful in other things, and of so fierce a resolution, to be overcome in a thing of this nature, shows him to be a bad man indeed, that could better bear the wronging of his conscience than the crossing of his humour. 2. How he endeavoured to transfer the guilt upon the Jews. He *delivered him,* not to his own officers (as usual), but to the prosecutors, the chief priests and elders; so excusing the wrong to his own conscience with this, that it was but a permissive condemnation, and that he did not put Christ to death, but only connived at those that did it. 3. How Christ was *made sin for us.* We deserved to have been condemned, but Christ was condemned for us, that to us there might be *no condemnation.* God was now entering into judgment with his Son, that he might not enter into judgment with his servants.

II. Judgment was no sooner given than with all possible expedition the prosecutors, having gained their point, resolved to lose no time lest Pilate should change his mind, and order a reprieve (those are enemies to our souls, the worst of enemies, that hurry us to sin, and then leave us no room to undo what we have done amiss), and also lest there should be *an uproar among the people,* and they should find a greater number against them than they had with so much artifice got to be for them. It were well if we would be thus expeditious in that which is good, and not stay for more difficulties.

1. They immediately hurried away the prisoner. The chief priests greedily flew upon the prey which they had been long waiting for; now it is drawn into their net. Or *they,* that is, the soldiers who were to attend the execution, they took him and led him away, not to the place whence he came, and thence to the place of execution, as is usual with us, but directly to the place of execution. Both the priests and the soldiers joined in leading him away. Now was the *Son of man delivered into the hands of men,* wicked and unreasonable men. By the law of Moses (and in appeals by our law) the prosecutors were to be the executioners, Deut. xvii. 7. And the priests here were proud of the office. His being *led away* does not suppose him to have made any opposition, but *the scripture must be ful-*

filled, he was *led as a sheep to the slaughter,* Acts viii. 32. We deserved to have been *led forth with the workers of iniquity* as criminals to execution, Ps. cxxv. 5. But he was led forth for us, that we might escape.

2. To add to his misery, they obliged him, as long as he was able, to carry his cross (*v.* 17), according to the custom among the Romans; hence *Furcifer* was among them a name of reproach. Their crosses did not stand up constantly, as our gibbets do in the places of execution, because the malefactor was nailed to the cross as it lay along upon the ground, and then it was lifted up, and fastened in the earth, and removed when the execution was over, and commonly buried with the body; so that every one that was crucified had a cross of his own. Now Christ's carrying his cross may be considered, (1.) As a part of his sufferings; he endured the cross literally. It was a long and thick piece of timber that was necessary for such a use, and some think it was neither seasoned nor hewn. The blessed body of the Lord Jesus was tender, and unaccustomed to such burdens; it had now lately been harassed and tired out; his shoulders were sore with the stripes they had given him; every jog of the cross would renew his smart, and be apt to strike the thorns he was crowned with into his head; yet all this he patiently underwent, and it was but the *beginning of sorrows.* (2.) As answering the type which went before him; Isaac, when he was to be offered, carried the wood on which he was to be bound and with which he was to be burned. (3.) As very significant of his undertaking, the Father having *laid upon him the iniquity of us all* (Isa. liii. 6), and he having to *take away sin* by *bearing it in his own body upon the tree,* 1 Pet. ii. 24. He had said in effect, *On me be the curse;* for he was made a curse for us, and therefore on him was the cross. (4.) As very instructive to us. Our Master hereby taught all his disciples to take up their cross, and follow him. Whatever cross he calls us out to bear at any time, we must remember that he bore the cross first, and, by bearing it for us, bears it off from us in a great measure, for thus he hath made *his yoke easy, and his burden light.* He bore that end of the cross that had the curse upon it; this was the heavy end; and hence all that are his are enabled to call their afflictions for him *light,* and *but for a moment.*

3. They brought him to the place of execution: He *went forth,* not dragged against his will, but voluntary in his sufferings. He went forth out of the city, for he was *crucified without the gate,* Heb. xiii. 12. And, to put the greater infamy upon his sufferings, he was brought to the common place of execution, as one in all points *numbered among the transgressors,* a place called *Golgotha, the place of a skull,* where they threw dead men's skulls and bones, or where the heads of beheaded malefactors were left,—a place *ceremonially unclean;* there Christ suffered, because he was *made sin for us,* that he might *purge our consciences from dead works,* and the pollution of them. If one would take notice of the traditions of the elders, there are two which are mentioned by many of the ancient writers concerning this place:—(1.) That Adam was buried here, and that this was the place of his skull, and they observe that where death triumphed over the first Adam there the second Adam triumphed over him. Gerhard quotes for this tradition Origen, Cyprian, Epiphanius, Austin, Jerome, and others. (2.) That this was that mountain in the land of Moriah on which Abraham offered up Isaac, and the ram was a ransom for Isaac.

4. There they crucified him, and the other malefactors with him (*v.* 18): *There they crucified him.* Observe, (1.) What death Christ died; the death of the cross, a bloody, painful, shameful death, a cursed death. He was nailed to the cross, as a sacrifice bound to the altar, as a Saviour fixed for his undertaking; his ear nailed to God's door-post, to serve him for ever. He was lifted up as the brazen serpent, hung between heaven and earth because we were unworthy of either, and abandoned by both. His hands were stretched out to invite and embrace us; he hung upon the tree some hours, dying gradually in the full use of reason and speech, that he might actually resign himself a sacrifice. (2.) In what company he died: *Two others with him.* Probably these would not have been executed at that time, but at the request of the chief priests, to add to the disgrace of our Lord Jesus, which might be the reason why one of them reviled him, because their death was hastened for his sake. Had they taken two of his disciples, and crucified them with him, it had been an honour to him; but, if such as they had been partakers with him in suffering, it would have looked as if they had been undertakers with him in satisfaction. Therefore it was ordered that his fellow-sufferers should be the worst of sinners, that he might *bear our reproach,* and that the merit might appear to be his only. This exposed him much to the people's contempt and hatred, who are apt to judge of persons by the lump, and are not curious in distinguishing, and would conclude him not only malefactor because he was yoked with malefactors, but the worst of the three because put in the midst. But thus the scripture was fulfilled, *He was numbered among the transgressors.* He did not die at the altar among the sacrifices, nor mingle his blood with that of bulls and goats; but he died among the criminals, and mingled his blood with theirs who were sacrificed to public justice.

And now let us pause awhile, and with an eye of faith look upon Jesus. Was ever sorrow like unto his sorrow? See him who was clothed with glory stripped of it all, and clothed with shame—him who was the *praise of angels* made a *reproach of men*—him who had been with eternal delight and joy in the bosom of his Father now in the extremities of pain and agony. See him bleeding, see him struggling, see him dying, see him and love him, love him and live to him, and study what we shall render.

19 And Pilate wrote a title, and
put *it* on the cross. And the writing
was, JESUS OF NAZARETH THE
KING OF THE JEWS. 20 This
title then read many of the Jews:
for the place where Jesus was crucified was nigh to the city: and it was
written in Hebrew, *and* Greek, *and*
Latin. 21 Then said the chief priests
of the Jews to Pilate, Write not, The
King of the Jews; but that he said,
I am King of the Jews. 22 Pilate
answered, What I have written I have
written. 23 Then the soldiers, when
they had crucified Jesus, took his
garments, and made four parts, to
every soldier a part; and also *his* coat:
now the coat was without seam, woven
from the top throughout. 24 They
said therefore among themselves, Let
us not rend it, but cast lots for it,
whose it shall be: that the scripture
might be fulfilled, which saith, They
parted my raiment among them, and
for my vesture they did cast lots.
These things therefore the soldiers
did. 25 Now there stood by the
cross of Jesus his mother, and his
mother's sister, Mary the *wife* of
Cleophas, and Mary Magdalene. 26
When Jesus therefore saw his mother,
and the disciple standing by, whom
he loved, he saith unto his mother,
Woman, behold thy son! 27 Then
saith he to the disciple, Behold thy
mother! And from that hour that
disciple took her unto his own *home*.
28 After this, Jesus knowing that all
things were now accomplished, that
the scripture might be fulfilled, saith,
I thirst. 29 Now there was set a
vessel full of vinegar: and they filled
a sponge with vinegar, and put *it*
upon hyssop, and put *it* to his mouth.
30 When Jesus therefore had received
the vinegar, he said, It is finished:
and he bowed his head, and gave up
the ghost.

Here are some remarkable circumstances of Christ's dying more fully related than before, which those will take special notice of who covet to know Christ and him crucified.

I. The title set up over his head. Observe,

1. The inscription itself which Pilate wrote, and ordered to be fixed to the top of the cross, declaring the cause for which he was crucified, *v.* 19. Matthew called it, *αἰτία—the accusation;* Mark and Luke called it, *ἐπιγραφὴ—the inscription;* John calls it by the proper Latin name, *τίτλος—the title:* and it was this, *Jesus of Nazareth, the King of the Jews.* Pilate intended this for his reproach, that he, being *Jesus of Nazareth,* should pretend to be king of the Jews, and set up in competition with Cæsar, to whom Pilate would thus recommend himself, as very jealous for his honour and interest, when he would treat but a titular king, a king in metaphor, as the worst of malefactors; but God overruled this matter, (1.) That it might be a further testimony to the innocency of our Lord Jesus; for here was an accusation which, as it was worded, contained no crime. If this be all they have to lay to his charge, surely he has done nothing worthy of death or of bonds. (2.) That it might show forth his dignity and honour. This is Jesus a Saviour, Ναζωραῖος, the blessed Nazarite, sanctified to God; this is the *king of the Jews, Messiah the prince,* the *sceptre* that *should rise out of Israel,* as Balaam had foretold; dying for the good of his people, as Caiaphas had foretold. Thus all these three bad men witnessed to Christ, though they meant not so.

2. The notice taken of this inscription (*v.* 20): *Many of the Jews read it,* not only those of Jerusalem, but those out of the country, and from other countries, strangers and proselytes, that came up to worship at the feast. Multitudes read it, and it occasioned a great variety of reflections and speculations, as men stood affected. Christ himself was set for a sign, a title. Here are two reasons why the title was so much read:—(1.) Because the place where Jesus was crucified, though without the gate, was yet *nigh the city,* which intimates that if it had been any great distance off they would not have been led, no not by their curiosity, to go and see it, and read it. It is an advantage to have the means of knowing Christ brought to our doors. (2.) Because it was written in Hebrew, and Greek, and Latin, which made it legible by all; they all understood one or other of these languages, and none were more careful to bring up their children to read than the Jews generally were. It likewise made it the more considerable; every one would be curious to enquire what it was which was so industriously published in the three most known languages. In the Hebrew the oracles of God were recorded; in Greek the learning of the philosophers; and in Latin the laws of the empire. In each of

these Christ is proclaimed king, in whom are hid all the treasures of revelation, wisdom, and power. God so ordering it that this should be written in the three then most known tongues, it was intimated thereby that Jesus Christ should be a Saviour to all nations, and not to the Jews only; and also that every nation should hear *in their own tongue the wonderful works* of the Redeemer. Hebrew, Greek, and Latin, were the vulgar languages at that time in this part of the world; so that this is so far from intimating (as the Papists would have it) that the scripture is still to be retained in these three languages, that on the contrary it teaches us that the knowledge of Christ ought to be diffused throughout every nation in their own tongue, as the proper vehicle of it, that people may converse as freely with the scriptures as they do with their neighbours.

3. The offence which the prosecutors took at it, *v.* 21. They would not have it written, *the king of the Jews;* but that he said of himself, *I am the king of the Jews.* Here they show themselves, (1.) Very spiteful and malicious against Christ. It was not enough to have him crucified, but they must have his name crucified too. To justify themselves in giving him such bad treatment, they thought themselves concerned to give him a bad character, and to represent him as a usurper of honours and powers that he was not entitled to. (2.) Foolishly jealous of the honour of their nation. Though they were a conquered and enslaved people, yet they stood so much upon the punctilio of their reputation that they scorned to have it said that this was their king. (3.) Very impertinent and troublesome to Pilate. They could not but be sensible that they had forced him, against his mind, to condemn Christ, and yet, in such a trivial thing as this, they continue to tease him; and it was so much the worse in that, though they had charged him with pretending to be the king of the Jews, yet they had not proved it, nor had he ever said so.

4. The judge's resolution to adhere to it: "*What I have written I have written,* and will not alter it to humour them."

(1.) Hereby an affront was put upon the chief priests, who would still be dictating. It seems, by Pilate's manner of speaking, that he was uneasy in himself for yielding to them, and vexed at them for forcing him to it, and therefore he was resolved to be cross with them; and by this inscription he insinuates, [1.] That, notwithstanding their pretences, they were not sincere in their affections to Cæsar and his government; they were willing enough to have a king of the Jews, if they could have one to their mind. [2.] That such a king as this, so mean and despicable, was good enough to be the king of the Jews; and this would be the fate of all that should dare to oppose the Roman power. [3.] That they had been very unjust and unreasonable in prosecuting this Jesus, when there was no fault to be found in him.

(2.) Hereby honour was done to the Lord Jesus. Pilate stuck to it with resolution, that he was the king of the Jews. What he had written was what God had first written, and therefore he could not alter it; for thus it was written, that Messiah the prince should be *cut off,* Dan. ix. 26. This therefore is the true cause of his death; he dies because the king of Israel must die, must thus die. When the Jews reject Christ, and will not have him for their king, Pilate, a Gentile, sticks to it that he is a king, which was an earnest of what came to pass soon after, when the Gentiles submitted to the kingdom of the Messiah, which the unbelieving Jews had rebelled against.

II. The dividing of his garments among the executioners, *v.* 23, 24. Four soldiers were employed, who, *when they had crucified Jesus,* had nailed him to the cross, and lifted it up, and him upon it, and nothing more was to be done than to wait his expiring through the extremity of pain, as, with us, when the prisoner is turned off, then they went to make a dividend of his clothes, each claiming an equal share, and so they *made four parts,* as nearly of the same value as they could, *to every soldier a part;* but *his coat,* or upper garment whether cloak or gown, being a pretty piece of curiosity, *without seam, woven from the top throughout,* they agreed to *cast lots for it.* Here observe, 1. The shame they put upon our Lord Jesus, in stripping him of his garments before they crucified him. The shame of nakedness came in with sin. He therefore who was made sin for us bore that shame, to roll away our reproach. He was stripped, that we might be clothed with *white raiment* (Rev. iii. 18), and that when we are unclothed *we may not be found naked.* 2. The wages with which these soldiers paid themselves for crucifying Christ. They were willing to do it for his old clothes. Nothing is to be done so bad, but there will be found men bad enough to do it for a trifle. Probably they hoped to make more than ordinary advantage of his clothes, having heard of cures wrought by the touch of the hem of his garment, or expecting that his admirers would give any money for them. 3. The sport they made about his seamless coat. We read not of any thing about him valuable or remarkable but this, and this not for the richness, but only the variety of it, for it was *woven from the top throughout;* there was no curiosity therefore in the shape, but a designed plainness. Tradition says, his mother wove it for him, and adds this further, that it was made for him when he was a child, and, like the Israelites' clothes in the wilderness, *waxed not old;* but this is a groundless fancy. The soldiers thought it a pity to rend it, for then it would unravel, and a piece of it would be good for nothing; they would *therefore cast lots for it.* While Christ was in his dying agonies, they were merrily dividing his spoils. The preserving of Christ's seamless coat is commonly alluded to to show the care all Christians ought to take that they rend not the church of Christ with strifes and divisions; yet some have observed that the reason why the soldiers would not rend Christ's coat was not out of any respect to Christ, but because each of them hoped to have it entire for himself. And so many cry out against schism, only that they may engross all the wealth and power to themselves. Those who opposed Luther's separation from the church of Rome urged much the *tunica inconsutilis—the seamless coat;* and some of them laid so much stress upon it that they were called the *Inconsutilistæ—The seamless.* 4. The fulfilling of the scripture in this. David, in spirit, foretold this very circumstance of Christ's sufferings, in that passage, Ps. xxii. 18. The event so exactly answering the prediction proves, (1.) That *the scripture* is the word of God, which foretold contingent events concerning Christ so long before, and they came to pass according to the prediction. (2.) That Jesus is the true Messiah; for in him all the Old-Testament prophecies concerning the Messiah had, and have, their full accomplishment. *These things therefore the soldiers did.*

III. The care that he took of his poor mother. 1. His mother attends him to his death (*v.* 25): *There stood by the cross,* as near as they could get, *his mother,* and some of his relations and friends with her. At first, they stood near, as it is said here; but afterwards, it is probable, the soldiers forced them to stand afar off, as it is said in Matthew and Mark: or they themselves removed out of the ground. (1.) See here the tender affection of these pious women to our Lord Jesus in his sufferings. When all his disciples, except John, had forsaken him, they continued their attendance on him. Thus *the feeble were as David* (Zech. xii. 8): they were not deterred by the fury of the enemy nor the horror of the sight; they could not rescue him nor relieve him, yet they attended him, to show their good-will. It is an impious and blasphemous construction which some of the popish writers put upon the virgin Mary standing by the cross, that thereby she contributed to the satisfaction he made for sin no less than he did, and so became a joint-mediatrix and co-adjutrix in our salvation. (2.) We may easily suppose what an affliction it was to these poor women to see him thus abused, especially to the blessed virgin. Now was fulfilled Simeon's word, *A sword shall pierce through thy own soul,* Luke ii. 35. His torments were her tortures; she was upon the rack, while he was upon the cross; and her heart bled with his wounds; and *the reproaches wherewith they reproached* him fell on those that attended him. (3.) We may justly admire the power of divine grace in supporting these women, especially the virgin Mary, under this heavy trial. We do not find his mother wringing her hands, or tearing her hair, or rending her clothes, or making an outcry; but, with a wonderful composure, *standing by the cross,* and her friends with her. Surely she and they were strengthened by a divine power to this degree of patience; and surely the virgin Mary had a fuller expectation of his resurrection than the rest had, which supported her thus. We know not what we can bear till we are tried, and then we know who has said, *My grace is sufficient for thee.*

2. He tenderly provides for his mother at his death. It is probable that Joseph, her husband, was long since dead, and that her son Jesus had supported her, and her relation to him had been her maintenance; and now that he was dying what would become of her? He saw her standing by, and knew her cares and griefs; and he saw John standing not far off, and so he settled a new relation between his beloved mother and his beloved disciple; for he said to her, "*Woman, behold thy son,* for whom henceforward thou must have a motherly affection;" and to him, "*Behold thy mother,* to whom thou must pay a filial duty." And so *from that hour,* that hour never to be forgotten, *that disciple took her to his own home.* See here,

(1.) The care Christ took of his dear mother. He was not so much taken up with a sense of his sufferings as to forget his friends, all whose concerns he bore upon his heart. His mother, perhaps, was so taken up with his sufferings that she thought not of what would become of her; but he admitted that thought. *Silver and gold he had none* to leave, no estate, real or personal; his clothes the soldiers had seized, and we hear no more of the bag since Judas, who had carried it, hanged himself. He had therefore no other way to provide for his mother than by his interest in a friend, which he does here. [1.] He calls her *woman,* not mother, not out of any disrespect to her, but because mother would have been a cutting word to her that was already wounded to the heart with grief; like Isaac saying to Abraham, *My father.* He speaks as one that was *now no more in this world,* but was already dead to those in it that were dearest to him. His speaking in this seemingly slight manner to his mother, as he had done formerly, was designed to obviate and give a check to the undue honours which he foresaw would be given to her in the Romish church, as if she were a joint purchaser with him in the honours of the Redeemer. [2.] He directs her to look upon John as her son: "Behold him as thy son, who stands there by thee, and be as a mother to him." See here, *First,* An instance of divine goodness, to be observed for our encouragement. Sometimes, when God removes one comfort from us, he raises up another for us, perhaps where we looked not for it. We read of children which the church shall have after she has lost the other, Isa. xlix. 21. Let none therefore reckon all gone with one cistern dried up, for from the same fountain another may be filled. *Secondly,* An instance of filial duty, to be observed for our imitation. Christ has here taught children to provide, to the utmost of their power, for the comfort of their aged parents. When David was in distress, he took care of his parents, and found out a shelter for them (1 Sam. xxii. 3); so the Son of David here. Children at their death, according to their ability, should provide for their parents, if they survive them, and need their kindness.

(2.) The confidence he reposed in the beloved disciple. It is to him he says, *Behold thy mother,* that is, I recommend her to thy care, be thou as a son to her to guide her (Isa. li. 18); and *forsake her not when she is old,* Prov. xxiii. 22. Now, [1.] This was an honour put upon John, and a testimony both to his prudence and to his fidelity. If he who knows all things had not known that John loved him, he would not have made him his mother's guardian. It is a great honour to be employed for Christ, and to be entrusted with any of his interest in the world. But, [2.] It would be a care and some charge to John; but he cheerfully accepted it, *and took her to his own home,* not objecting the trouble nor expense, nor his obligations to his own family, nor the ill-will he might contract by it. Note, Those that truly love Christ, and are beloved of him, will be glad of an opportunity to do any service to him or his. *Nicephoras's Eccl. Hist. lib.* ii. *cap.* 3, saith that the virgin Mary lived with John at Jerusalem eleven years, and then died. Others, that she lived to remove with him to Ephesus.

IV. The fulfilling of the scripture, in the giving of him vinegar to drink, *v.* 28, 29. Observe,

1. How much respect Christ showed to the scripture (*v.* 28): *Knowing that all things* hitherto *were accomplished, that the scripture might be fulfilled,* which spoke of his drinking in his sufferings, *he saith, I thirst,* that is, he called for drink.

(1.) It was not at all strange that he was thirsty; we find him *thirsty* in a journey (*ch.* iv. 6, 7), and now thirsty when he was just at his journey's end. Well might he thirst after all the toil and hurry which he had undergone, and being now in the agonies of death, ready to expire purely by the loss of blood and extremity of pain. The torments of hell are represented by a violent thirst in the complaint of the rich man that begged for a *drop of water to cool his tongue.* To that everlasting thirst we had been condemned, had not Christ suffered for us.

(2.) But the reason of his complaining of it is somewhat surprising; it is the only word he spoke that looked like complaint of his outward sufferings. When they scourged him, and crowned him with thorns, he did not cry, O my head! or, My back! But now he cried, *I thirst.* For, [1.] He would thus express *the travail of his soul,* Isa. liii. 11. He thirsted after the glorifying of God, and the accomplishment of the work of our redemption, and the happy issue of his undertaking. [2.] He would thus take care to see the scripture fulfilled. Hitherto, all had been accomplished, and he knew it, for this was the thing he had carefully observed all along; and now he called to mind one thing more, which this was the proper season for the performance of. By this it appears that he was the Messiah, in that not only the scripture was punctually fulfilled in him, but it was strictly eyed by him. By this it appears *that God was with him of a truth*—that in all he did he went exactly according to the word of God, taking care *not to destroy, but to fulfil, the law and the prophets.* Now, *First,* The scripture had foretold his thirst, and therefore he himself related it, because it could not otherwise be known, saying, *I thirst;* it was foretold that his tongue should cleave to his jaws, Ps. xxii. 15. Samson, an eminent type of Christ, when he was laying *the Philistines heaps upon heaps,* was himself *sore athirst* (Judg. xv. 18); so was Christ, when he was upon the cross, *spoiling principalities and powers. Secondly,* The scripture had foretold that in his thirst he should have vinegar given him to drink, Ps. lxix. 21. They had given him vinegar to drink before they crucified him (Matt. xxvii. 34), but the prophecy was not exactly fulfilled in that, because that was not in his thirst; therefore now he said, *I thirst,* and called for it again: then he would not drink, but now he received it Christ would rather court an affront than see any prophecy unfulfilled. This should satisfy us under all our trials, that the will of God is done, and the word of God accomplished.

2. See how little respect his persecutors showed to him (*v.* 29): *There was set a vessel full of vinegar,* probably according to the custom at all executions of this nature; or, as others think, it was now set designedly for an abuse to Christ, instead of the cup of wine which they used to give *to those that were ready to perish;* with this *they filled a sponge,* for they would not allow him a cup, *and they put it upon hyssop,* a hyssop-stalk, and with this heaved it to his mouth; ὑσσώπῳ περιθέντες—*they stuck it round with hyssop;* so it may be taken; or, as others, they mingled it with hyssop-water, and this they gave him to drink when he was thirsty; a drop of water would have cooled his tongue better than a draught of vinegar: yet this he submitted to for us. *We had taken the sour grapes,* and *thus his teeth were set on edge;* we had forfeited all comforts and refreshments, and therefore they were withheld from him. When heaven denied him a beam of light earth denied him a drop of water, and put vinegar in the room of it.

V. The dying word wherewith he breathed

out his soul (*v.* 30): *When he had received the vinegar,* as much of it as he thought fit, *he said, It is finished;* and, with that, *bowed his head, and gave up the ghost.* Observe,

1. What he said, and we may suppose him to say it with triumph and exultation, Τετέλεσται—*It is finished,* a comprehensive word, and a comfortable one. (1.) *It is finished,* that is, the malice and enmity of his persecutors had now done their worst; *when he had received* that last indignity in *the vinegar they gave him, he said,* "This is the last; I am now going out of their reach, *where the wicked cease from troubling.*" (2.) *It is finished,* that is, the counsel and commandment of his Father concerning his sufferings were now fulfilled; it was a *determinate counsel,* and he took care to see every iota and tittle of it exactly answered, Acts ii. 23. He had said, when he entered upon his sufferings, *Father, thy will be done;* and now he saith with pleasure, *It is done.* It was *his meat and drink to finish his work* (*ch.* iv. 34), and the meat and drink refreshed him, when they gave him gall and vinegar. (3.) *It is finished,* that is, all the types and prophecies of the Old Testament, which pointed at the sufferings of the Messiah, were accomplished and answered. He speaks as if, now that *they had given him the vinegar,* he could not bethink himself of any word in the Old Testament that was to be fulfilled between him and his death but it had its accomplishment; such as, his being *sold for thirty pieces of silver, his hands and feet being pierced, his garments divided,* &c.; and now that this is done, *It is finished.* (4.) *It is finished,* that is, the ceremonial law is abolished, and a period put to the obligation of it. The substance is now come, and all the shadows are done away. Just now *the veil is rent, the wall of partition is taken down,* even *the law of commandments contained in ordinances,* Eph. ii. 14, 15. The Mosaic economy is dissolved, *to make way for a better hope.* (5.) *It is finished,* that is, sin is finished, and an end made of transgression, by *the bringing in of an everlasting righteousness.* It seems to refer to Dan. ix. 24. *The Lamb of God was sacrificed to take away the sin of the world,* and it is done, Heb. ix. 26. (6.) *It is finished,* that is, his sufferings were now finished, both those of his soul and those of his body. The storm is over, the worst is past; all his pains and agonies are at an end, and he is just going to paradise, entering upon *the joy set before him.* Let all that *suffer for Christ,* and with Christ, comfort themselves with this, *that yet a little while* and they also shall say, *It is finished.* (7.) *It is finished,* that is, his life was now finished, he was just ready to breathe his last, and *now he is no more in this world, ch.* xvii. 11. This is like that of blessed Paul (2 Tim. iv. 7), *I have finished my course,* my race is run, my glass is out, *mene, mene—numbered* and *finished.* This we must all come to shortly. (8.) *It is finished,* that is, the work of man's redemption and salvation is now completed, at least the hardest part of the undertaking is over; a full satisfaction is made to the justice of God, a fatal blow given to the power of Satan, a fountain of grace opened that shall ever flow, a foundation of peace and happiness laid that shall never fail. Christ had now gone through with his work, and *finished it,* ch. xvii. 4. For, *as for God, his work is perfect; when I begin,* saith he, *I will also make an end.* And, as in the purchase, so in the application of the redemption, *he that has begun a good work will perform it;* the mystery of God shall be finished.

2. What he did: *He bowed his head, and gave up the ghost.* He was voluntary in dying; for he was not only the sacrifice, but the priest and the offerer; and the *animus offerentis—the mind of the offerer,* was all in all in the sacrifice. Christ showed his will in his sufferings, *by which will we are sanctified.* (1.) *He gave up the ghost.* His life was not forcibly extorted from him, but freely resigned. He had said, *Father, into thy hands I commit my spirit,* thereby expressing the intention of this act. I give up myself as a *ransom for many;* and, accordingly, he did give up his spirit, paid down the price of pardon and life at his Father's hands. *Father, glorify thy name.* (2.) *He bowed his head.* Those that were crucified, in dying stretched up their heads to gasp for breath, and did not drop their heads till they had breathed their last; but Christ, to show himself active in dying, *bowed his head* first, composing himself, as it were, to fall asleep. God *had laid upon him the iniquity of us all,* putting it upon the head of this great sacrifice; and some think that by this bowing of his head he would intimate his sense of the weight upon him. See Ps. xxxviii. 4; xl. 12. The bowing of his head shows his submission to his Father's will, and his obedience to death. He accommodated himself to his dying work, as Jacob, *who gathered up his feet into the bed, and then yielded up the ghost.*

31 The Jews therefore, because it
was the preparation, that the bodies
should not remain upon the cross on
the sabbath day (for that sabbath
day was an high day), besought Pilate
that their legs might be broken, and
that they might be taken away. 32
Then came the soldiers, and brake
the legs of the first, and of the other
which was crucified with him. 33
But when they came to Jesus, and
saw that he was dead already, they
brake not his legs: 34 But one of the
soldiers with a spear pierced his side,
and forthwith came thereout blood
and water. 35 And he that saw *it*
bare record, and his record is true:

and he knoweth that he saith true,
that ye might believe. 36 For these
things were done, that the scripture
should be fulfilled, A bone of him
shall not be broken. 37 And again
another scripture saith, They shall
look on him whom they pierced.

This passage concerning the piercing of Christ's side after his death is recorded only by this evangelist.

I. Observe the superstition of the Jews, which occasioned it (*v.* 31): *Because it was the preparation for the sabbath, and that sabbath day,* because it fell in the passover-week, *was a high day,* that they might show a veneration for the sabbath, they would *not have the dead bodies to remain on the crosses on the sabbath-day,* but *besought Pilate that their legs might be broken,* which would be a certain, but cruel dispatch, and that then they might be buried out of sight. Note here, 1. The esteem they would be thought to have for the approaching sabbath, because it was one of the days of unleavened bread, and (some reckon) the day of the offering of the first-fruits. Every sabbath day is a holy day, and a good day, but this was a high day, μέγαλη ἡμερα—*a great day.* Passover sabbaths are high days; sacrament-days, supper-days, communion-days are high days, and there ought to be more than ordinary preparation for them, that these may be high days indeed to us, *as the days of heaven.* 2. The reproach which they reckoned it would be to that day if the dead bodies should be left hanging on the crosses. Dead bodies were not to be left at any time (Deut. xxi. 23); yet, in this case, the Jews would have left the Roman custom to take place, had it not been an extraordinary day; and, many strangers from all parts being then at Jerusalem, it would have been an offence to them; nor could they well bear the sight of Christ's crucified body, for, unless their consciences were quite seared, when the heat of their rage was a little over, they would upbraid them. 3. Their petition to Pilate, that their bodies, now as good as dead, might be dispatched; not by strangling or beheading them, which would have been a compassionate hastening of them out of their misery, like the *coup de grace* (as the French call it) to those that are broken upon the wheel, *the stroke of mercy,* but by the breaking of their legs, which would carry them off in the most exquisite pain. Note, (1.) *The tender mercies of the wicked are cruel.* (2.) The pretended sanctity of hypocrites is abominable. These Jews would be thought to bear a great regard for the sabbath, and yet had no regard to justice and righteousness; they made no conscience of bringing an innocent and excellent person to the cross, and yet scrupled letting a dead body hang upon the cross.

II. The dispatching of *the two thieves that were crucified with him, v.* 32. Pilate was still gratifying the Jews, and gave orders as they desired; *and the soldiers came,* hardened against all impressions of pity, *and broke the legs of the two thieves,* which, no doubt, extorted from them hideous outcries, and made them die according to the bloody disposition of Nero, so as to feel themselves die. One of these thieves was a penitent, and had received from Christ an assurance that he should shortly be with him in paradise, and yet died in the same pain and misery that the other thief did; for *all things come alike to all.* Many go to heaven that *have bands in their death,* and *die in the bitterness of their soul.* The extremity of dying agonies is no obstruction to the living comforts that wait for holy souls on the other side death. Christ died, and went to paradise, but appointed a guard to convey him thither. This is the order of going to heaven—*Christ, the first-fruits* and forerunner, *afterwards those that are Christ's.*

III. The trial that was made whether Christ was dead or no, and the putting of it out of doubt.

1. They supposed him to be dead, and therefore *did not break his legs, v.* 33. Observe here, (1.) That Jesus died in less time than persons crucified ordinarily did. The structure of his body, perhaps, being extraordinarily fine and tender, was the sooner broken by pain; or, rather, it was to show that he laid down his life of himself, and could die when he pleased, though his hands were nailed. Though he yielded to death, yet he was not conquered. (2.) That his enemies were satisfied he was really dead. The Jews, who stood by to see the execution effectually done, would not have omitted this piece of cruelty, if they had not been sure he was got out of the reach of it. (3.) *Whatever devices are in men's hearts, the counsel of the Lord shall stand.* It was fully designed to break his legs, but, God's counsel being otherwise, see how it was prevented.

2. Because they would be sure he was dead they made such an experiment as would put it past dispute. *One of the soldiers with a spear pierced his side,* aiming at his heart, *and forthwith came thereout blood and water, v.* 34.

(1.) The soldier hereby designed to decide the question whether he was dead or no, and by this honourable wound in his side to supersede the ignominious method of dispatch they took with the other two. Tradition says that this soldier's name was *Longinus,* and that, having some distemper in his eyes, he was immediately cured of it, by some drops of blood that flowed out of Christ's side falling on them: significant enough, if we had any good authority for the story.

(2.) But God had a further design herein, which was,

[1.] To give an evidence of the truth of his death, in order to the proof of his resurrection. If he was only in a trance or swoon, his resurrection was a sham; but, by this experiment, he was certainly dead, for this spear broke up the very fountains of life, and, according to all the law and course of nature, it was impossible a human body should survive such a wound as this in the vitals, and such an evacuation thence.

[2.] To give an illustration of the design of his death. There was much of mystery in it, and its being so solemnly attested (*v.* 35) intimates there was something miraculous in it, that *the blood and water* should come out distinct and separate from the same wound; at least it was very significant; this same apostle refers to it as a very considerable thing, 1 John v. 6, 8.

First, the opening of his side was significant. When we would protest our sincerity, we wish there were a window in our hearts, that the thoughts and intents of them might be visible to all. Through this window, opened in Christ's side, you may look into his heart, and see love flaming there, love strong as death; see our names written there. Some make it an allusion to the opening of Adam's side in innocency. When Christ, the second Adam, was fallen into a deep sleep upon the cross, then was his side opened, and out of it was his church taken, which he espoused to himself. See Eph. v. 30, 32. Our devout poet, Mr. George Herbert, in his poem called *The Bag*, very affectingly brings in our Saviour, when his side was pierced, thus speaking to his disciples:—

If ye have any thing to send, or write
(I have no bag, but here is room),
Unto my Father's hands and sight
(Believe me) it shall safely come.
That I shall mind what you impart,
Look, you may put it very near my heart;
Or, if hereafter any of my friends
Will use me in this kind, the door
Shall still be open; what he sends
I will present, and somewhat more,
Not to his hurt. Sighs will convey
Any thing to me. Hark, Despair, away.

Secondly, The blood and water that flowed out of it were significant. 1. They signified the two great benefits which all believers partake of through Christ—justification and sanctification; blood for remission, water for regeneration; blood for atonement, water for purification. Blood and water were used very much under the law. Guilt contracted must be expiated by blood; stains contracted must be done away by *the water of purification.* These two must always go together. *You are sanctified, you are justified,* 1 Cor. vi. 11. Christ has joined them together, and we must not think to put them asunder. They both flowed from the pierced side of our Redeemer. To Christ crucified we owe both merit for our justification, and Spirit and grace for our sanctification; and we have as much need of the latter as of the former, 1 Cor. i. 30. 2. They signified the two great ordinances of baptism and the Lord's supper, by which those benefits are represented, sealed, and applied, to believers; they both owe their institution and efficacy to Christ. It is not the water in the font that will be to us *the washing of regeneration,* but the water out of the side of Christ; not the blood of the grape that will pacify the conscience and refresh the soul, but the blood out of the side of Christ. Now was the rock smitten (1 Cor. x. 4), now was the fountain opened (Zech. xiii. 1), now were the wells of salvation digged, Isa. xii. 3. Here *is the river, the streams whereof make glad the city of our God.*

IV. The attestation of the truth of this by an eye-witness (*v.* 35), the evangelist himself. Observe,

1. What a competent witness he was of the matters of fact. (1.) What he bore record of he saw; he had it not by hearsay, nor was it only his own conjecture, but he was an eye-witness of it; it is *what we have seen and looked upon* (1 John i. 1; 2 Pet. i. 16), and *had perfect understanding of,* Luke i. 3. (2.) What he saw he faithfully bore record of; as a faithful witness, he told not only the truth, but the whole truth; and did not only attest it by word of mouth, but left it upon record in writing, *in perpetuam rei memoriam—for a perpetual memorial.* (3.) *His record is* undoubtedly *true;* for he wrote not only from his own personal knowledge and observation, but from the dictates of the Spirit of truth, that leads into all truth. (4.) He had himself a full assurance of the truth of what he wrote, and did not persuade others to believe that which he did not believe himself: *He knows that he saith true.* (5.) He *therefore* witnessed these things, *that we might believe;* he did not record them merely for his own satisfaction or the private use of his friends, but made them public to the world; not to please the curious nor entertain the ingenious, but to draw men to believe the gospel in order to their eternal welfare.

2. What care he showed in this particular instance. That we may be well assured of the truth of Christ's death, he saw his heart's blood, his life's blood, let out; and also of the benefits that flow to us from his death, signified by the blood and water which came out of his side. Let this silence the fears of weak Christians, and encourage their hopes, *iniquity shall not be their ruin,* for there came both water and blood out of Christ's pierced side, both to justify and sanctify them; and if you ask, How can we be sure of this? You may be sure, for *he that saw it bore record.*

V. The accomplishment of the scripture in all this (*v.* 36): *That the scripture might be fulfilled,* and so both the honour of the Old Testament preserved and the truth of the New Testament confirmed. Here are two instances of it together:—

1. The scripture was fulfilled in the preserving of his legs from being broken; therein that word was fulfilled, *A bone of him shall not be broken.* (1.) There was a promise of this made indeed to all *the righteous,* but principally pointing at *Jesus Christ the righteous* (Ps. xxxiv. 20): *He keepeth all his bones, not one of them is broken.* And David,

in spirit, says, *All my bones shall say, Lord, who is like unto thee?* Ps. xxxv. 10. (2.) There was a type of this in the paschal lamb, which seems to be especially referred to here (Exod. xii. 46): *Neither shall you break a bone thereof;* and it is repeated (Num. ix. 12), *You shall not break any bone of it;* for which law the will of the law-maker is the reason, but the antitype must answer the type. *Christ our Passover is sacrificed for us,* 1 Cor. v. 7. He is *the Lamb of God* (*ch.* i. 29), and, as the true passover, his bones were kept unbroken. This commandment was given concerning his bones, when dead, as of Joseph's, Heb. xi. 22. (3.) There was a significancy in it; the strength of the body is in the bones. The Hebrew word for the bones signifies the strength, and therefore *not a bone of Christ must be broken,* to show that though *he be crucified in weakness* his strength to save is not at all broken. Sin breaks our bones, as it broke David's (Ps. li. 8); but it did not break Christ's bones; he stood firm under the burden, mighty to save.

2. *The scripture was fulfilled* in *the piercing of his side* (*v.* 37): *They shall look on me whom they had pierced;* so it is written, Zech. xii. 10. And there the same that pours out the Spirit of grace, and can be no less than the God of the holy prophets, says, *They shall look upon me,* which is here applied to Christ, *They shall look upon him.* (1.) It is here implied that the Messiah shall be pierced; and here it had a more full accomplishment than in *the piercing of his hands and feet;* he was pierced by *the house of David* and *the inhabitants of Jerusalem, wounded in the house of his friends,* as it follows, Zech. xiii. 6. (2.) It is promised that *when the Spirit is poured out they shall look on him and mourn.* This was in part fulfilled when many of those that were his betrayers and murderers *were pricked to the heart,* and brought to believe in him; it will be further fulfilled, in mercy, *when all Israel shall be saved;* and, in wrath, when those who persisted in their infidelity shall *see him whom they have pierced, and wail because of him,* Rev. i. 7. But it is applicable to us all. We have all been guilty of piercing the Lord Jesus, and are all concerned with suitable affections to look on him.

38 And after this Joseph of Arimathæa, being a disciple of Jesus, but
secretly for fear of the Jews, besought
Pilate that he might take away the body
of Jesus: and Pilate gave *him* leave.
He came therefore, and took the body
of Jesus. 39 And there came also
Nicodemus, which at the first came
to Jesus by night, and brought a
mixture of myrrh and aloes, about a
hundred pound *weight.* 40 Then
took they the body of Jesus, and
wound it in linen clothes with the
spices, as the manner of the Jews is
to bury. 41 Now in the place where
he was crucified there was a garden;
and in the garden a new sepulchre,
wherein was never man yet laid. 42
There laid they Jesus therefore because of the Jews' preparation *day;*
for the sepulchre was nigh at hand.

We have here an account of the burial of the blessed body of our Lord Jesus. The solemn funerals of great men are usually looked at with curiosity; the mournful funerals of dear friends are attended with concern. Come and see an extraordinary funeral; never was the like! Come and see a burial that conquered the grave, and buried it, a burial that beautified the grave and softened it for all believers. *Let us turn aside now, and see this great sight.* Here is,

I. The body begged, *v.* 38. This was done by the interest of *Joseph of Ramah,* or *Arimathea,* of whom no mention is made in all the New-Testament story, but only in the narrative which each of the evangelists gives us of Christ's burial, wherein he was chiefly concerned. Observe, 1. The character of this Joseph. He was a disciple of Christ *incognito—in secret,* a better friend to Christ than he would willingly be known to be. It was his honour that he was a disciple of Christ; and some such there are, that are themselves great men, and unavoidably linked with bad men. But it was his weakness that he was so secretly, when he should have confessed Christ before men, yea, though he had lost his preferment by it. Disciples should openly own themselves, yet Christ may have many that are his disciples sincerely, though secretly; better secretly than not at all, especially if, like Joseph here, they grow stronger and stronger. Some who in less trials have been timorous, yet in greater have been very courageous; so Joseph here. He concealed his affection to Christ *for fear of the Jews,* lest they should put him out of the synagogue, at least out of the sanhedrim, which was all they could do. To Pilate the governor he *went boldly,* and yet *feared the Jews.* The impotent malice of those that can but censure, and revile, and clamour, is sometimes more formidable even to wise and good men than one would think. 2. The part he bore in this affair. He, having by his place access to Pilate, desired leave of him to dispose of the body. His mother and dear relations had neither spirit nor interest to attempt such a thing. His disciples were gone; if nobody appeared, the Jews or soldiers would bury him with the thieves; therefore God raised up this gentleman to interpose in it, that the scripture might be fulfilled, and the decorum owing to his approaching resurrection maintained. Note, When God has work to do he can find out such as are proper to do it, and embolden them for it. Observe it as an instance of the humiliation of Christ, that his dead body lay at the mercy of a heathen judge, and must be begged before it could be buried, and also that Joseph would not take the body of Christ till he had asked and obtained leave of the governor; for in those things wherein the power of the magistrate is concerned we must ever pay a deference to that power, and peaceably submit to it.

II. The embalming prepared, *v.* 39. This was done by Nicodemus, another person of quality, and in a public post. He brought a *mixture of myrrh and aloes,* which some think were bitter ingredients, to preserve the body, others fragrant ones, to perfume it. Here is, 1. The character of Nicodemus, which is much the same with that of Joseph; he was a secret friend to Christ, though not his constant follower. He at first *came to Jesus by night,* but now owned him publicly, as before, *ch.* vii. 50, 51. That grace which at first is like a bruised reed may afterwards become like a strong cedar, and the trembling lamb *bold as a lion.* See Rom. xiv. 4. It is a wonder that Joseph and Nicodemus, men of such interest, did not appear sooner, and solicit Pilate not to condemn Christ, especially seeing him so loth to do it. Begging his life would have been a nobler piece of service than begging his body. But Christ would have none of his friends to endeavour to prevent his death when his hour was come. While his persecutors were forwarding the accomplishment of the scriptures, his followers must not obstruct it. 2. The kindness of Nicodemus, which was considerable, though of a different nature. Joseph served Christ with his interest, Nicodemus with his purse. Probably, they agreed it between them, that, while one was procuring the grant, the other should be preparing the spices; and this for expedition, because they were straitened in time. But why did they make this ado about Christ's dead body? (1.) Some think we may see in it the weakness of their faith. A firm belief of the resurrection of Christ on the third day would have saved them this care and cost, and have been more acceptable than all spices. Those bodies indeed to whom the grave is a long home need to be clad accordingly; but what need of such furniture of the grave for one that, like a way-faring man, did but turn aside into it, to *tarry for a night or two?* (2.) However, we may plainly see in it the strength of their love. Hereby they showed the value they had for his person and doctrine, and that it was not lessened by the reproach of the cross. Those that had been so industrious to profane his crown, and lay his honour in the dust, might already see that they had imagined a vain thing; for, as God had done him honour in his sufferings, so did men too, even great men. They showed not only the charitable respect of committing his body to the earth, but the honourable respect shown to great men. This they might do, and yet believe and look for his resurrection; nay, this they might do in the belief and expectation of it. Since God designed honour for this body, they would put honour upon it. However, we must do our duty according as the present day and opportunity are, and leave it to God to fulfil his promises in his own way and time.

III. The body got ready, *v.* 40. They *took it* into some house adjoining, and, having washed it from blood and dust, *wound it in linen clothes* very decently, with the spices melted down, it is likely, into an ointment, as *the manner of the Jews is to bury,* or to *embalm* (so Dr. Hammond), as we sear dead bodies. 1. Here was care taken of Christ's body: It was *wound in linen clothes.* Among clothing that belongs to us, Christ put on even the grave-clothes, to make them easy to us, and to enable us to call them our wedding-clothes. They wound the body *with the spices,* for *all his garments,* his grave-clothes not excepted, *smell of myrrh and aloes* (the spices here mentioned) *out of the ivory palaces* (Ps. xlv. 8), and an ivory palace the sepulchre hewn out of a rock was to Christ. Dead bodies and graves are noisome and offensive; hence sin is compared to a *body of death* and an *open sepulchre;* but Christ's sacrifice, being to God as a sweet-smelling savour, hath taken away our pollution. No ointment or perfume can rejoice the heart so as the grave of our Redeemer does, where there is faith to perceive the fragrant odours of it. 2. In conformity to this example, we ought to have regard to the dead bodies of Christians; not to enshrine and adore their relics, no, not those of the most eminent saints and martyrs (nothing like that was done to the dead body of Christ himself), but carefully to deposit them, the dust in the dust, as those who believe that the dead bodies of the saints are still united to Christ and designed for glory and immortality at the last day. The resurrection of the saints will be in virtue of Christ's resurrection, and therefore in burying them we should have an eye to Christ's burial, for he, being dead, thus speaketh. *Thy dead men shall live,* Isa. xxvi. 19. In burying our dead it is not necessary that in all circumstances we imitate the burial of Christ, as if we must be buried in linen, and in a garden, and be embalmed as he was; but his being buried after *the manner of the Jews* teaches us that in things of this nature we should conform to the usages of the country where we live, except in those that are superstitious.

IV. The grave pitched upon, in a garden which belonged to Joseph of Arimathea, very near the place where he was crucified. There was a sepulchre, or vault, prepared for the first occasion, but not yet used. Observe,

1. That Christ was buried without the city, for thus the manner of the Jews was to bury, not in their cities, much less in their synagogues,

which some have thought better than our way of burying: yet there was then a peculiar reason for it, which does not hold now, because the touching of a grave contracted a ceremonial pollution: but now that the resurrection of Christ has altered the property of the grave, and done away its pollution for all believers, we need not keep at such a distance from it; nor is it incapable of a good improvement, to have the congregation of the dead in the church-yard, encompassing the congregation of the living in the church, since they also are dying, and in *the midst of life we are in death.* Those that would not superstitiously, but by faith, visit the holy sepulchre, must go forth out of the noise of this world.

2. That Christ was buried in a garden. Observe, (1.) That Joseph had his sepulchre in his garden; so he contrived it, that it might be a memento, [1.] To himself while living; when he was taking the pleasure of his garden, and reaping the products of it, let him think of dying, and be quickened to prepare for it. The garden is a proper place for meditation, and a sepulchre there may furnish us with a proper subject for meditation, and such a one as we are loth to admit in the midst of our pleasures. [2.] To his heirs and successors when he was gone. It is good to acquaint ourselves with the *place of our fathers' sepulchres;* and perhaps we might make our own less formidable if we made theirs more familiar. (2.) That in a sepulchre in a garden Christ's body was laid. In the garden of Eden death and the grave first received their power, and now in a garden they are conquered, disarmed, and triumphed over. In a garden Christ began his passion, and from a garden he would rise, and begin his exaltation. Christ fell to the ground *as a corn of wheat* (*ch.* xii. 24), and therefore was sown in a garden among the seeds, for *his dew is as the dew of herbs,* Isa. xxvi. 19. He is the *fountain of gardens,* Cant. iv. 15.

3. That he was buried in a new sepulchre. This was so ordered, (1.) For the honour of Christ; he was not a common person, and therefore must not mix with common dust. He that was born from a virgin-womb must rise from a virgin-tomb. (2.) For the confirming of the truth of his resurrection, that it might not be suggested that it was not he, but some other that rose now, when many bodies of saints arose; or, that he rose by the power of some other, as the man that was raised by the touch of Elisha's bones, and not by his own power. He that has *made all things new* has new-made the grave for us.

V. The funeral solemnized (*v.* 42): *There laid they Jesus,* that is, the dead body of Jesus. Some think the calling of this *Jesus* intimates the inseparable union between the divine and human nature. Even this dead body was *Jesus—a Saviour,* for his death is our life; Jesus is still the same, Heb. xiii. 8. There they laid him because it was the preparation day.

1. Observe here the deferencc which the Jews paid to the sabbath, and to the day of preparation. Before the passover-sabbath they had a solemn day of preparation. This day had been ill kept by the chief priests, who called themselves the church, but was well kept by the disciples of Christ, who were branded as dangerous to the church; and it is often so. (1.) They would not put off the funeral till the sabbath day, because the sabbath is to be a day of holy rest and joy, with which the business and sorrow of a funeral do not well agree. (2.) They would not drive it too late on the day of preparation for the sabbath. What is to be done the evening before the sabbath should be so contrived that it may neither intrench upon sabbath time, nor indispose us for sabbath work.

2. Observe the convenience they took of an adjoining sepulchre; the sepulchre they made use of was *nigh at hand.* Perhaps, if they had had time, they would have carried him to Bethany, and buried him among his friends there. And I am sure he had more right to have been buried in the chief of the sepulchres of the sons of David than any of the kings of Judah had; but it was so ordered that he should be laid in a sepulchre nigh at hand, (1.) Because he was to lie there but awhile, as in an inn, and therefore he took the first that offered itself. (2.) Because this was a new sepulchre. Those that prepared it little thought who should handsel it; but the wisdom of God has reaches infinitely beyond ours, and he makes what use he pleases of us and all we have. (3.) We are hereby taught not to be over-curious in the place of our burial. Where the tree falls, why should it not lie? For Christ was buried in the sepulchre that was next at hand. It was faith in the promise of Canaan that directed the Patriarchs' desires to be carried thither for a burying-place; but now, since that promise is superseded by a better, that care is over.

Thus without pomp or solemnity is the body of Jesus laid in the cold and silent grave. Here lies our surety under arrest for our debts, so that if he be released his discharge will be ours. Here is the Sun of righteousness set for awhile, to rise again in greater glory, and set no more. Here lies a seeming captive to death, but a real conqueror over death; for here lies death itself slain, and the grave conquered. *Thanks be to God, who giveth us the victory.*

CHAP. XX.

This evangelist, though he began not his gospel as the rest did, yet concludes it as they did, with the history of Christ's resurrection; not of the thing itself, for none of them describe how he rose, but of the proofs and evidences of it, which demonstrated that he was risen. The proofs of Christ's resurrection, which we have in this chapter, are, I. Such as occurred immediately at the sepulchre. 1. The sepulchre found empty, and the grave-clothes in good order, ver. 1—10. 2. Two angels appearing to Mary Magdalene at the sepulchre, ver. 11—13. 3. Christ himself appearing to her, ver. 14—18. II. Such as occurred afterwards at the meetings of the apostles. 1. At one, the same day at evening that Christ rose, when Thomas was absent, ver. 19—25. 2. At another, that day seven-night, when Thomas was with them, ver. 26—31. What is related here is mostly what was omitted by the other evangelists.

THE first *day* of the week cometh Mary Magdalene early, when

it was yet dark, unto the sepulchre,
and seeth the stone taken away from
the sepulchre. 2 Then she runneth,
and cometh to Simon Peter, and to
the other disciple, whom Jesus loved,
and saith unto them, They have taken
away the Lord out of the sepulchre,
and we know not where they have
laid him. 3 Peter therefore went
forth, and that other disciple, and
came to the sepulchre. 4 So they
ran both together: and the other
disciple did outrun Peter, and came
first to the sepulchre. 5 And he
stooping down, *and looking in,* saw
the linen clothes lying; yet went he
not in. 6 Then cometh Simon Peter
following him, and went into the sepulchre, and seeth the linen clothes
lie, 7 And the napkin, that was
about his head, not lying with the
linen clothes, but wrapped together
in a place by itself. 8 Then went in
also that other disciple, which came
first to the sepulchre, and he saw, and
believed. 9 For as yet they knew
not the scripture, that he must rise
again from the dead. 10 Then the
disciples went away again unto their
own home.

There was no one thing of which the apostles were more concerned to produce substantial proof than the resurrection of their Master, 1. Because it was that which he himself appealed to as the last and most cogent proof of his being the Messiah. Those that would not believe other signs were referred to this sign of the prophet Jonas. And therefore enemies were most solicitous to stifle the notice of this, because it was put on this issue, and, if he be risen, they are not only murderers, but murderers of the Messiah. 2. Because it was upon this the performance of his undertaking for our redemption and salvation did depend. If he give his life a ransom, and do not resume it, it does not appear that his giving it was accepted as a satisfaction. If he be imprisoned for our debt, and lie by it, we are undone, 1 Cor. xv. 17. 3. Because he never showed himself alive after his resurrection to all the people, Acts x. 40, 41. We should have said, "Let his ignominious death be private, and his glorious resurrection public." But God's thoughts are not as ours; and he ordered it that his death should be public before the sun, by the same token that the sun blushed and hid his face upon it. But the demonstrations of his resurrection should be reserved as a favour for his particular friends, and by them be published to the world, that those might be blessed who have not seen, and yet have believed. The method of proof is such as gives abundant satisfaction to those who are piously disposed to receive the doctrine and law of Christ, and yet leaves room for those to object who are willingly ignorant and obstinate in their unbelief. And this is a fair trial, suited to the case of those who are probationers.

In these verses we have the first step towards the proof of Christ's resurrection, which is, that the sepulchre was found empty. *He is not here,* and, if so, they must tell us where he is, or we conclude him risen.

I. Mary Magdalene, coming to the sepulchre, finds the *stone taken away.* This evangelist does not mention the other women that went with Mary Magdalene, but her only, because she was the most active and forward in this visit to the sepulchre, and in her appeared the most affection; and it was an affection kindled by a good cause, in consideration of the great things Christ had done for her. Much was forgiven her, therefore she loved much. She had shown her affection to him while he lived, attended his doctrine, ministered to him of her substance, Luke viii. 2, 3. It does not appear that she had any business now at Jerusalem, but to wait upon him, for the women were not bound to go up to the feast, and probably she and others followed him the closer, as Elisha did Elijah, now that they knew their Master would shortly be *taken from their head,* 2 Kings ii. 1—6. The continued instances of her respect to him at and after his death prove the sincerity of her love. Note, Love to Christ, if it be cordial, will be constant. Her love to Christ was *strong as death,* the death of the cross, for it stood by that; *cruel as the grave,* for it made a visit to that, and was not deterred by its terrors.

1. She *came to the sepulchre,* to wash the dead body with her tears, for she *went to the grave, to weep there,* and to *anoint it with the ointment* she had prepared. The grave is a house that people do not care for making visits to. They that are *free among the dead* are *separated from the living;* and it must be an extraordinary affection to the person which will endear his grave to us. It is especially frightful to the weak and timorous sex. Could she, that had not strength enough to *roll away the stone,* pretend to such a presence of mind as to enter the grave? The Jews' religion forbade them to meddle any more than needs must with graves and dead bodies. In visiting Christ's sepulchre she exposed herself, and perhaps the disciples, to the suspicion of a design to *steal him away;* and what real service could she do him by it? But her love answers these, and a thousand such objections. Note, (1.) We must study to do honour to Christ in those things wherein yet we cannot be profitable to him. (2.) Love to Christ will

take off the terror of death and the grave. If we cannot come to Christ but through that darksome valley, even in that, if we love him, we shall *fear no evil.*

2. She came as soon as she could, for she came, (1.) Upon the *first day of the week,* as soon as ever the sabbath was gone, longing, not to *sell corn* and to *set forth wheat* (as Amos viii. 5), but to be at the sepulchre. Those that love Christ will take the first opportunity of testifying their respect to him. This was the first Christian sabbath, and she begins it accordingly with enquiries after Christ. She had spent the day before in commemorating the work of creation, and therefore rested; but now she is upon search into the work of redemption, and therefore makes a visit to Christ and him crucified. (2.) She came *early, while it was yet dark;* so early did she set out. Note, Those who would seek Christ so as to find him must seek him early; that is, [1.] Seek him solicitously, with such a care as even breaks the sleep; be up early for fear of missing him. [2.] Seek him industriously; we must deny ourselves and our own repose in pursuit of Christ. [3.] Seek him betimes, early in our days, early every day. *My voice shalt thou hear in the morning.* That day is in a fair way to be well ended that is thus begun. Those that diligently enquire after Christ *while it is yet dark* shall have such light given them concerning him as shall shine *more and more.*

3. She found the stone taken away, which she had seen *rolled to the door of the sepulchre.* Now this was, (1.) A surprise to her, for she little expected it. Christ crucified is the fountain of life. His grave is one of the wells of salvation; if we come to it in faith; though to a carnal heart it be a spring shut up, we shall find the stone rolled away (as Gen. xxix. 10) and free access to the comforts of it. Surprising comforts are the frequent encouragements of early seekers. (2.) It was the beginning of a glorious discovery; the Lord was risen, though she did not at first apprehend it so. Note, [1.] Those that are most constant in their adherence to Christ, and most diligent in their enquiries after him, have commonly the first and sweetest notices of the divine grace. Mary Magdalene, who followed Christ to the last in his humiliation, met him with the first in his exaltation. [2.] God ordinarily reveals himself and his comforts to us by degrees; to raise our expectations and quicken our enquiries.

II. Finding the stone taken away, she hastens back to Peter and John, who probably lodged together at that end of the town, not far off, and acquaints them with it: "*They have taken the Lord out of the sepulchre,* envying him the honour of such a decent burying-place, *and we know not where they have laid him,* nor where to find him, that we may pay him the remainder of our last respects." Observe here, 1. What a notion Mary had of the thing as it now appeared; she found the stone gone, looked into the grave, and saw it empty. Now one would expect that the first thought that offered itself would have been, Surely the Lord is risen; for whenever he had told them that he should be crucified, which she had now lately seen accomplished, he still subjoined in the same breath that *the third day he should rise again.* Could she feel the great earthquake that happened as she was coming to the sepulchre, or getting ready to come, and now see the grave empty, and yet have no thought of the resurrection enter into her mind? what, no conjecture, no suspicion of it? So it seems by the odd construction she puts upon the removing of the stone, which was very far fetched. Note, When we come to reflect upon our own conduct in a *cloudy and dark day,* we shall stand amazed at our dulness and forgetfulness, that we could miss of such thoughts as afterwards appear obvious, and how they could be so far out of the way when we had occasion for them. She suggested, *They have taken away the Lord;* either the chief priests have taken him away, to put him in a worse place, or Joseph and Nicodemus have, upon second thoughts, taken him away, to avoid the ill-will of the Jews. Whatever was her suspicion, it seems it was a great vexation and disturbance to her that the body was gone; whereas, if she had understood it rightly, nothing could be more happy. Note, Weak believers often make that the matter of their complaint which is really just ground of hope, and matter of joy. We cry out that this and the other creature-comfort are taken away, and we know not how to retrieve them, when indeed the removal of our temporal comforts, which we lament, is in order to the resurrection of our spiritual comforts, which we should rejoice in too. 2. What a narrative she made of it to Peter and John. She did not stand poring upon the grief herself, but acquaints her friends with it. Note, The communication of sorrows is one good improvement of the communion of saints. Observe, Peter, though he had denied his Master, had not deserted his Master's friends; by this appears the sincerity of his repentance, that he associated with the disciple whom Jesus loved. And the disciples' keeping up their intimacy with him as formerly, notwithstanding his fall, teaches us to restore those with a spirit of meekness that have been faulty. If God has received them upon their repentance, why should not we?

III. Peter and John go with all speed to the sepulchre, to satisfy themselves of the truth of what was told them, and to see if they could make any further discoveries, *v.* 3, 4. Some think that the other disciples were with Peter and John when the news came; for they *told these things to the eleven,*

Luke xxiv. 9. Others think that Mary Magdalene told her story only to Peter and John, and that the other women told theirs to the other disciples; yet none of them went to the sepulchre but Peter and John, who were two of the first three of Christ's disciples, often distinguished from the rest by special favours. Note, It is well when those that are more honoured than others with the privileges of disciples are more active than others in the duty of disciples, more willing to take pains and run hazards in a good work. 1. See here what use we should make of the experience and observations of others. When Mary told them what she had seen, they would not in this sense take her word, but would go and see with their own eyes. Do others tell us of the comfort and benefit of ordinances? Let us be engaged thereby to make trial of them. Come and see how good it is to draw near to God. 2. See how ready we should be to share with our friends in their cares and fears. Peter and John hastened to the sepulchre, that they might be able to give Mary a satisfactory answer to her jealousies. We should not grudge any pains we take for the succouring and comforting of the weak and timorous followers of Christ. 3. See what haste we should make in a good work, and when we are going on a good errand. Peter and John consulted neither their ease nor their gravity, but ran to the sepulchre, that they might show the strength of their zeal and affection, and might lose no time. If we are in the way of God's commandments, we should run in that way. 4. See what a good thing it is to have good company in a good work. Perhaps neither of these disciples would have ventured to the sepulchre alone, but, being both together, they made no difficulty of it. See Eccl. iv. 9. 5. See what a laudable emulation it is among disciples to strive which shall excel, which shall exceed, in that which is good. It was no breach of ill manners for John, though the younger, to outrun Peter, and get before him. We must do our best, and neither envy those that can do better, nor despise those that do as they can, though they come behind. (1.) He that got foremost in this race was *the disciple whom Jesus loved* in a special manner, and who therefore in a special manner loved Jesus. Note, Sense of Christ's love to us, kindling love in us to him again, will make us to excel in virtue. The love of Christ will constrain us more than any thing to abound in duty. (2.) He that was cast behind was Peter, who had denied his Master, and was in sorrow and shame for it, and this clogged him as a weight; sense of guilt cramps us, and hinders our enlargement in the service of God. When conscience is offended we lose ground.

IV. Peter and John, having come to the sepulchre, prosecute the enquiry, yet improve little in the discovery.

1. John went no further than Mary Magdalene had done. (1.) He had the curiosity to look into the sepulchre, and saw it was empty. He *stooped down*, and *looked in.* Those that would find the knowledge of Christ must stoop down, and look in, must with a humble heart submit to the authority of divine revelation, and must *look wistly.* (2.) Yet he had not courage to go into the sepulchre. The warmest affections are not always accompanied with the boldest resolutions; many are swift to run religion's race that are not stout to fight her battles.

2. Peter, though he came last, went in first, and made a more exact discovery than John had done, *v.* 6, 7. Though John outran him, he did not therefore turn back, nor stand still, but made after him as fast as he could; and, while John was with much caution looking in, he came, and with great courage *went into the sepulchre.*

(1.) Observe here the boldness of Peter, and how God dispenses his gifts variously. John could out-run Peter, but Peter could out-dare John. It is seldom true of the same persons, what David says poetically of Saul and Jonathan, that they were *swifter than eagles*, and yet *stronger than lions*, 2 Sam. i. 23. Some disciples are quick, and they are useful to quicken those that are slow; others are bold, and they are useful to embolden those that are timorous; *diversity of gifts, but one Spirit.* Peter's venturing into the sepulchre may teach us, [1.] That those who in good earnest seek after Christ must not frighten themselves with bugbears and foolish fancies: "There is a lion in the way, a ghost in the grave." [2.] That good Christians need not be afraid of the grave, since Christ has lain in it; for to them there is nothing in it frightful; it is not the pit of destruction, nor are the worms in it never-dying worms. Let us therefore not indulge, but conquer, the fear we are apt to conceive upon the sight of a dead body, or being alone among the graves; and, since we must be dead and in the grave shortly, let us make death and the grave familiar to us, as our near kindred, Job xvii. 14. [3.] We must be willing to go through the grave to Christ; that way he went to his glory, and so must we. If we cannot see God's face and live, better die than never see it. See Job xix. 25, &c.

(2.) Observe the posture in which he found things in the sepulchre. [1.] Christ had left his grave-clothes behind him there; what clothes he appeared in to his disciples we are not told, but he never appeared in his grave-clothes, as ghosts are supposed to do; no, he laid them aside, *First*, Because he arose to die no more; death was to have no more dominion over him, Rom. vi. 9. Lazarus came out with his grave-clothes on, for he was to use them again; but Christ, rising to an immortal life, came out free from those incumbrances. *Secondly*, Because he was going to be clothed with the robes of glory, therefore he lays aside these rags; in the heavenly paradise there will be no more occasion for clothes than there was in the earthly. The ascending prophet dropped his mantle. *Thirdly,* When we arise from the death of sin to the life of righteousness, we must leave our grave-clothes behind us, must put off all our corruptions. *Fourthly,* Christ left those in the grave, as it were, for our use; if the grave be a bed to the saints, thus he hath sheeted that bed, and made it ready for them; and the napkin by itself is of use for the mourning survivors to *wipe away their tears.* [2.] The grave-clothes were found in very good order, which serves for an evidence that his body was not stolen away while men slept. Robbers of tombs have been known to take away the clothes and leave the body; but none [prior to the practices of modern resurrectionists] ever took away the body and left the clothes, especially when it was fine linen and new, Mark xv. 46. Any one would rather choose to carry a dead body in its clothes than naked. Or, if those that were supposed to have stolen it would have left the grave-clothes behind, yet it cannot be supposed they should find leisure to fold up the linen.

(3.) See how Peter's boldness encouraged John; now he took heart and ventured in (*v.* 8), and *he saw and believed;* not barely believed what Mary said, that the body was gone (no thanks to him to believe what *he saw),* but he began to believe that Jesus was risen to life again, though his faith, as yet, was weak and wavering.

[1.] John followed Peter in venturing. It should seem, he durst not have gone into the sepulchre if Peter had not gone in first. Note, It is good to be emboldened in a good work by the boldness of others. The dread of difficulty and danger will be taken off by observing the resolution and courage of others. Perhaps John's quickness had made Peter run faster, and now Peter's boldness makes John venture further, than otherwise either the one or the other would have done; though Peter had lately fallen under the disgrace of being a deserter, and John had been advanced to the honour of a confidant (Christ having committed his mother to him), yet John not only associated with Peter, but thought it no disparagement to follow him.

[2.] Yet, it should seem, John got the start of Peter in believing. Peter saw and wondered (Luke xxiv. 12), but John saw and believed. A mind disposed to contemplation may perhaps sooner receive the evidence of divine truth than a mind disposed to action. But what was the reason that they were so slow of heart to believe? The evangelist tells us (*v.* 9), as yet they *knew not the scripture,* that is, they did not consider, and apply, and duly improve, what they knew of the scripture, that he must *rise again from the dead.* The Old Testament spoke of the resurrection of the Messiah; they believed him to be the Messiah; he himself had often told them that, according to the scriptures of the Old Testament, he should rise again; but they had not presence of mind sufficient by these to explain the present appearances. Observe here, *First,* How unapt the disciples themselves were, at first, to believe the resurrection of Christ, which confirms the testimony they afterwards gave with so much assurance concerning it; for, by their backwardness to believe it, it appears that they were not credulous concerning it, nor of those simple ones that believe every word. If they had had any design to advance their own interest by it, they would greedily have caught at the first spark of its evidence, would have raised and supported one another's expectations of it, and have prepared the minds of those that followed them to receive the notices of it; but we find, on the contrary, that their hopes were frustrated, it was to them as a strange thing, and one of the furthest things from their thoughts. Peter and John were so shy of believing it at first that nothing less than the most convincing proof the thing was capable of could bring them to testify it afterwards with so much assurance. Hereby it appears that they were not only honest men, who would not deceive others, but cautious men, who would not themselves be imposed upon. *Secondly,* What was the reason of their slowness to believe; because as yet they *knew not the scripture.* This seems to be the evangelist's acknowledgment of his own fault among the rest; he does not say, "For as yet Jesus had not appeared to them, had not shown them his hands and his side," but, "As yet he had not *opened their understandings to understand the scripture* (Luke xxiv. 44, 45), for that is the *most sure word of prophecy.*

3. Peter and John pursued their enquiry no further, but desisted, hovering between faith and unbelief (*v.* 10): *The disciples went away,* not much the wiser, *to their own home,* πρὸς ἑαυτοὺς—*to their own friends and companions,* the rest of the disciples to their own lodgings, for homes they had none at Jerusalem. They went away, (1.) For fear of being taken up upon suspicion of a design to steal away the body, or of being charged with it now that it was gone. Instead of improving their faith, their care is to secure themselves, to shift for their own safety. In difficult dangerous times it is hard even for good men to go on in their work with the resolution that becomes them. (2.) Because they were at a loss, and knew not what to do next, nor what to make of what they had seen; and therefore, not having courage to stay at the grave, they resolve to go home, and wait till God shall *reveal even this unto them,* which is an instance of their weakness as yet. (3.) It is probable that the

rest of the disciples were together; to them they return, to make report of what they had discovered, and to consult with them what was to be done; and, probably, now they appointed their meeting in the evening, when Christ came to them. It is observable that before Peter and John came to the sepulchre an angel had appeared there, rolled away the stone, frightened the guard, and comforted the women; as soon as they were gone from the sepulchre, Mary Magdalene here sees two angels in the sepulchre (*v.* 12), and yet Peter and John come to the sepulchre, and go into it, and see none. What shall we make of this? Where were the angels when Peter and John were at the sepulchre, who appeared there before and after? [1.] Angels appear and disappear at pleasure, according to the orders and instructions given them. They may be, and are really, where they are not visibly; nay, it should seem, may be visible to one and not to another, at the same time, Num. xxii. 23; 2 Kings vi. 17. How they make themselves visible, then invisible, and then visible again, it is presumption for us to enquire; but that they do so is plain from this story. [2.] This favour was shown to those who were early and constant in their enquiries after Christ, and was the reward of those that came first and staid last, but denied to those that made a transient visit. [3.] The apostles were not to receive their instructions from the angels, but from the Spirit of grace. See Heb. ii. 5.

11 But Mary stood without at the
sepulchre weeping: and as she wept,
she stooped down, *and looked* into
the sepulchre, 12 And seeth two
angels in white sitting, the one at the
head, and the other at the feet, where
the body of Jesus had lain. 13 And
they say unto her, Woman, why
weepest thou? She saith unto them,
Because they have taken away my
Lord, and I know not where they
have laid him. 14 And when she
had thus said, she turned herself
back, and saw Jesus standing, and
knew not that it was Jesus. 15 Jesus
saith unto her, Woman, why weepest
thou? whom seekest thou? She,
supposing him to be the gardener,
saith unto him, Sir, if thou have borne
him hence, tell me where thou hast
laid him, and I will take him away.
16 Jesus saith unto her, Mary. She
turned herself, and saith unto him,
Rabboni; which is to say, Master.
17 Jesus saith unto her, Touch me
not; for I am not yet ascended to my
Father: but go to my brethren, and
say unto them, I ascend unto my Father, and your Father; and *to* my
God, and your God. 18 Mary Magdalene came and told the disciples
that she had seen the Lord, and *that*
he had spoken these things unto her.

St. Mark tells us that Christ appeared first to Mary Magdalene (Mark xvi. 9); that appearance is here largely related; and we may observe,

I. The constancy and fervency of Mary Magdalene's affection to the Lord Jesus, *v.* 11.

1. She staid at the sepulchre, when Peter and John were gone, because there her Master had lain, and there she was likeliest to hear some tidings of him. Note, (1.) Where there is a true love to Christ there will be a constant adherence to him, and a resolution with purpose of heart to cleave to him. This good woman, though she has lost him, yet, rather than seem to desert him, will abide by his grave for his sake, and continue in his love even when she wants the comfort of it. (2.) Where there is a true desire of acquaintance with Christ there will be a constant attendance on the means of knowledge. See Hos. vi. 2, 3, *The third day he will raise us up;* and then shall we know the meaning of that resurrection, if we follow on to know, as Mary here.

2. She staid there weeping, and these tears loudly bespoke her affection to her Master. Those that have lost Christ have cause to weep; she wept at the remembrance of his bitter sufferings; wept for his death, and the loss which she and her friends and the country sustained by it; wept to think of returning home without him; wept because she did not now find his body. Those that seek Christ must *seek him sorrowing* (Luke ii. 48), must weep, not for him, but for themselves.

3. *As she wept, she looked into the sepulchre,* that her eye might affect her heart. When we are in search of something that we have lost we look again and again in the place where we last left it, and expected to have found it. She will look *yet seven times,* not knowing but that at length she may see some encouragement. Note, (1.) Weeping must not hinder seeking. Though she wept, she *stooped down and looked in.* (2.) Those are likely to seek and find that seek with affection, that seek in tears.

II. The vision she had of two angels in the sepulchre, *v.* 12. Observe here,

1. The description of the persons she saw. They were *two angels in white, sitting* (probably on some benches or ledges hewn out in the rock) one at *the head,* and the other at the *feet,* of the grave. Here we have,

(1.) Their nature. They were angels, messengers from heaven, sent on purpose, on this great occasion, [1.] To honour the Son, and to grace the solemnity of his resurrection. Now that the Son of God was again to be brought into the world, the angels have a charge to attend him, as they did at his birth, Heb. i. 6. [2.] To comfort the saints; to speak good words to those that were in sorrow, and, by giving them notice that the Lord was risen, to prepare them for the sight of him.

(2.) Their number: *two*, not a *multitude of the heavenly host*, to sing praise, only two, to bear witness; for out of the mouth of two witnesses this word would be established.

(3.) Their array: They were *in white*, denoting, [1.] Their purity and holiness. The best of men *standing before the angels*, and compared with them, *are clothed in filthy garments* (Zech. iii. 3), but angels are spotless; and glorified saints, when they come to be as the angels, shall *walk with Christ in white.* [2.] Their glory, and glorying, upon this occasion. The white in which they appeared represented the brightness of that state into which Christ was now risen.

(4.) Their posture and place: They sat, as it were, reposing themselves in Christ's grave; for angels, though they needed not a restoration, were obliged to Christ for their establishment. These angels went into the grave, to teach us not to be afraid of it, nor to think that our resting in it awhile will be any prejudice to our immortality; no, matters are so ordered that the grave is not much out of our way to heaven. It intimates likewise that angels are to be employed about the saints, not only at their death, to carry their souls into Abraham's bosom, but at the great day, *to raise their bodies*, Matt. xxiv. 31. These angelic guards (and angels are called *watchers*, Dan. iv. 23), keeping possession of the sepulchre, when they had frightened away the guards which the enemies had set, represents Christ's victory over the powers of darkness, routing and defeating them. Thus Michael and his angels are more than conquerors. Their sitting to face one another, one at his bed's head, the other at his bed's feet, denotes their care of the entire body of Christ, his mystical as well as his natural body, from head to foot; it may also remind us of the two cherubim, placed one at either end of the mercy-seat, looking one at another, Exod. xxv. 18. Christ crucified was the great propitiatory, at the head and feet of which were these two cherubim, not with flaming swords, to keep us from, but welcome messengers, to direct us to, the way of life.

2. Their compassionate enquiry into the cause of Mary Magdalene's grief (*v.* 13): *Woman, why weepest thou?* This question was, (1.) A rebuke to her weeping: "*Why weepest thou*, when thou hast cause to rejoice?" Many of the floods of our tears would *dry away* before such a search as this into the fountain of them. *Why art thou cast down?* (2.) It was designed to show how much angels are concerned at the griefs of the saints, having a charge to minister to them for their comfort. Christians should thus sympathize with one another. (3.) It was only to make an occasion of informing her of that which would turn her mourning into rejoicing, would *put off her sackcloth, and gird her with gladness.*

3. The melancholy account she gives them of her present distress: *Because they have taken away* the blessed body I came to embalm, *and I know not where they have laid it.* The same story she had told, *v.* 2. In it we may see, (1.) The weakness of her faith. If she had had faith *as a grain of mustard-seed*, this mountain would have been removed; but we often perplex ourselves needlessly with imaginary difficulties, which faith would discover to us as real advantages. Many good people complain of the clouds and darkness they are under, which are the necessary methods of grace for the humbling of their souls, the mortifying of their sins, and the endearing of Christ to them. (2.) The strength of her love. Those that have a true affection for Christ cannot but be in great affliction when they have lost either the comfortable tokens of his love in their souls or the comfortable opportunities of conversing with him, and doing him honour, in his ordinances. Mary Magdalene is not diverted from her enquiries by the surprise of the vision, nor satisfied with the honour of it; but still she harps upon the same string: *They have taken away my Lord.* A sight of angels and their smiles will not suffice without a sight of Christ and God's smiles in him. Nay, the sight of angels is but an opportunity of pursuing her enquiries after Christ. All creatures, the most excellent, the most dear, should be used as means, and but as means, to bring us into acquaintance with God in Christ. The angels asked her, *Why weepest thou?* I have cause enough to weep, says she, for *they have taken away my Lord*, and, like Micah, *What have I more?* Do you ask, Why I weep? *My beloved has withdrawn himself, and is gone.* Note, None know, but those who have experienced it, the sorrow of a deserted soul, that has had comfortable evidences of the love of God in Christ, and hopes of heaven, but has now lost them, and walks in darkness; such a *wounded spirit who can bear?*

III. Christ's appearing to her while she was talking with the angels, and telling them her case. Before they had given her any answer, Christ himself steps in, to satisfy her enquiries, for God now speaketh to us by his Son; none but he himself can direct us to himself. Mary would fain know where her Lord is, and behold he is at her right hand. Note, 1. Those that will be content with nothing short of a sight of Christ shall be put off with nothing less. He never said to the soul that sought him, *Seek in vain.* "Is it Christ that thou wouldest have? Christ thou shalt have." 2. Christ, in manifesting himself to those that seek him, often outdoes their expectations. Mary longs to see the dead body of Christ, and complains of the loss of that, and behold she sees him alive. Thus he does for his praying people more than they are able to ask or think. In this appearance of Christ to Mary observe,

(1.) How he did at first conceal himself from her.

[1.] He stood as a common person, and she looked upon him accordingly, *v.* 14. She stood expecting an answer to her complaint from the angels; and either seeing the shadow, or hearing the tread, of some person behind her, she *turned herself back* from talking with the angels, and *sees Jesus himself* standing, the very person she was looking for, and yet she *knew not that it was Jesus.* Note, *First, The Lord is nigh unto them that are of a broken heart* (Ps. xxxiv. 18), nearer than they are aware. Those that seek Christ, though they do not see him, may yet be sure he is not far from them. *Secondly,* Those that diligently seek the Lord will turn every way in their enquiry after him. *Mary turned herself back,* in hopes of some discoveries. Several of the ancients suggest that Mary was directed to look behind her by the angels' rising up, and doing their obeisance to the Lord Jesus, whom they saw before Mary did; and that she looked back to see to whom it was they paid such a profound reverence. But, if so, it is not likely that she would have taken him for the gardener; rather, therefore, it was her earnest desire in seeking that made her turn every way. *Thirdly,* Christ is often near his people, and they are not aware of him. She *knew not that it was Jesus;* not that he appeared in any other likeness, but either it was a careless transient look she cast upon him, and, her eyes being full of care, she could not so well distinguish, or *they were holden, that she should not know him,* as those of the two disciples, Luke xxiv. 16.

[2.] He asked her a common question, and she answered him accordingly, *v.* 15.

First, The question he asked her was natural enough, and what any one would have asked her: "*Woman, why weepest thou? Whom seekest thou?* What business hast thou here in the garden so early? And what is all this noise and ado for?" Perhaps it was spoken with some roughness, as Joseph spoke to his brethren when he made himself strange, before he made himself known to them. It should seem, this was the first word Christ spoke after his resurrection: "*Why weepest thou?* I am risen." The resurrection of Christ has enough in it to allay all our sorrows, to check the streams, and dry up the fountains, of our tears. Observe here, Christ takes cognizance, 1. Of his people's griefs, and enquires, *Why weep you?* He bottles their tears, and records them in his book. 2. Of his people's cares, and enquires, *Whom seek you, and what would you have?* When he knows they are seeking him, yet he will know it from them; they must tell him whom they seek.

Secondly, The reply she made him is natural enough; she does not give him a direct answer, but, as if she should say, "Why do you banter me, and upbraid me with my tears? You know why I weep, and whom I seek;" and therefore, *supposing him to be the gardener,* the person employed by Joseph to dress and keep his garden, who, she thought, was come thither thus early to his work, she said, *Sir, if thou hast carried him hence,* pray *tell me where thou hast laid him, and I will take him away.* See here, 1. The error of her understanding. She supposed our Lord Jesus to be the gardener, perhaps because he asked what authority she had to be there. Note, Troubled spirits, in a cloudy and dark day, are apt to misrepresent Christ to themselves, and to put wrong constructions upon the methods of his providence and grace. 2. The truth of her affection. See how her heart was set upon finding Christ. She puts the question to every one she meets, like the careful spouse, *Saw you him whom my soul loveth?* She speaks respectfully to a gardener, and calls him *Sir,* in hopes to gain some intelligence from him concerning her beloved. When she speaks of Christ, she does not name him; but, *If thou have borne him hence,* taking it for granted that this gardener was full of thoughts concerning this Jesus as well as she, and therefore could not but know whom she meant. Another evidence of the strength of her affection was that, wherever he was laid, she would undertake to remove him. Such a body, with such a weight of spices about it, was much more than she could pretend to carry; but true love thinks it can do more than it can, and makes nothing of difficulties. She supposed this gardener grudged that the body of one that was ignominiously crucified should have the honour to be laid in his master's new tomb, and that therefore he had removed it to some sorry place, which he thought fitter for it. Yet Mary does not threaten to tell his master, and get him turned out of his place for it; but undertakes to find out some other sepulchre, to which he might be welcome. Christ needs not to stay where he is thought a burden.

(2.) How Christ at length made himself known to her, and, by a pleasing surprise, gave her infallible assurances of his resurrection. Joseph at length said to his brethren, *I am Joseph.* So Christ here to Mary Magdalene, now that he is entered upon his exalted state. Observe,

[1.] How Christ discovered himself to this good woman that was seeking him in tears (*v.* 16): *Jesus saith unto her, Mary.* It was said with an emphasis, and that air of kindness and freedom with which he was wont to speak to her. Now he changed his voice, and spoke like himself, not like the gardener. Christ's way of making himself known to his people is by his word, his word applied to their souls, speaking to them in particular. When those whom God *knew by name* in the counsels of his love (Exod. xxxiii. 12) *are called by name* in the efficacy of his grace, then *he reveals his Son in them,* as in Paul (Gal. i. 16), when Christ called to him by name, *Saul, Saul.* Christ's *sheep know his voice, ch.* x. 4. This one word, *Mary,* was like that to the disciples in the storm, *It is I.* Then the word of Christ does us good when we put our names into the precepts and promises. "In this Christ calls to me, and speaks to me."

[2.] How readily she received this discovery. When Christ said, "Mary, dost thou not know me? are you and I grown such strangers?" she was presently aware who it was, as the spouse (Cant. ii. 8), *It is the voice of my beloved.* She turned herself, and said, *Rabboni, My Master.* It might properly be read with an interrogation, "*Rabboni? Is it my master?* Nay, but is it indeed?" Observe, *First,* The title of respect she gives him: *My Master;* διδάσκαλε—*a teaching master.* The Jews called their doctors *Rabbies,* great men. Their critics tell us that *Rabbon* was with them a more honourable title than *Rabbi;* and therefore Mary chooses that, and adds a note of appropriation, *My great Master.* Note, Notwithstanding the freedom of communion which Christ is pleased to admit us to with himself, we must remember that he is our *Master,* and to be approached with a *godly fear. Secondly,* With what liveliness of affection she gives this title to Christ. *She turned* from the angels, whom she had in her eye, to look unto Jesus. We must take off our regards from all creatures, even the brightest and best, to fix them upon Christ, from whom nothing must divert us, and with whom nothing must interfere. When *she thought it had been the gardener,* she looked another way while speaking to him; but now that she knew the voice of Christ *she turned herself.* The soul that hears Christ's voice, and is turned to him, calls him, with joy and triumph, *My Master.* See with what pleasure those who love Christ speak of his authority over them. *My Master, my great Master.*

[3.] The further instructions that Christ gave her (*v.* 17): "*Touch me not,* but go and carry the news to the disciples."

First, He diverts her from the expectation of familiar society and conversation with him at this time: *Touch me not, for I am not yet ascended.* Mary was so transported with the sight of her dear Master that she forgot herself, and that state of glory into which he was now entering, and was ready to express her joy by affectionate embraces of him, which Christ here forbids at this time. 1. *Touch me not* thus at all, for I am to ascend to heaven. He bade the disciples touch him, for the confirmation of their faith; he allowed the women to take hold of his feet, and worship him (Matt. xxviii. 9); but Mary, supposing that he was risen, as Lazarus was, to live among them constantly, and converse with them freely as he had done, upon that presumption was about to take hold of his hand with her usual freedom. This mistake Christ rectified; she must believe him, and adore him, as exalted, but must not expect to be familiar with him as formerly. See 2 Cor. v. 16. He forbids her to dote upon his bodily presence, to set her heart on this, or expect its continuance, and leads her to the spiritual converse and communion which she should have with him after he was ascended to his Father; for the greatest joy of his resurrection was that it was a step towards his ascension. Mary thought, now that her Master was risen, he would presently set up a temporal kingdom, such as they had long promised themselves. "No," says Christ, "touch me not, with any such thought; think not to lay hold on me, so as to detain me here; for, though *I am not yet ascended, go to my brethren, and tell them, I am to ascend.*" As before his death, so now after his resurrection, he still harps upon this, that he was going away, was *no more in the world;* and therefore they must look higher than his bodily presence, and look further than the present state of things. 2. "*Touch me not,* do not stay to touch me now, stay not now to make any further enquiries, or give any further expressions of joy, for *I am not yet ascended,* I shall not depart immediately, it may as well be done another time; the best service thou canst do now is to carry the tidings to the disciples; lose no time therefore, but go away with all speed." Note, Public service ought to be preferred before private satisfaction. *It is more blessed to give than to receive.* Jacob must let an angel go, when the day breaks, and it is time for him to look after his family. Mary must not stay to talk with her Master, but must carry his message; for it is a day of good tidings, which she must not engross the comfort of, but hand it to others. See that story, 2 Kings vii. 9.

Secondly, He directs her what message to carry to his disciples: *But go to my brethren, and tell them,* not only that I am risen (she could have told them that of herself, for she had seen him), but that *I ascend.* Observe,

a. To whom this message is sent: *Go to my brethren* with it; for he is not ashamed to call them so. (*a.*) He was now entering upon his glory, and was *declared to be the Son of God with* greater *power* than ever, yet he owns his disciples as his brethren, and expresses himself with more tender affection to them than before; he had called them friends, but never brethren till now. Though Christ be high, yet he is not haughty. Notwithstanding his elevation, he disdains not to own his poor relations. (*b.*) His disciples had lately carried themselves very disingenuously towards him; he had never seen them together since *they all forsook him and fled,* when he was apprehended; justly might he now have sent them an angry message: "Go to yonder treacherous deserters, and tell them, I will never trust them any more, or have any thing more to do with them." No, he forgives, he forgets, and does not upbraid.

b. By whom it is sent: by *Mary Magdalene, out of whom had been cast seven devils,* yet now thus favoured. This was her reward for her constancy in adhering to Christ, and enquiring after him; and a tacit rebuke to the apostles, who had not been so close as she was in attending on the dying Jesus, nor so early as she was in meeting the rising Jesus; she becomes an apostle to the apostles.

c. What the message itself is: *I ascend to my Father.* Two full breasts of consolation are here in these words:—

(*a.*) Our joint-relation to God, resulting from our union with Christ, is an unspeakable comfort. Speaking of that inexhaustible spring of light, life, and bliss, he says, He is *my Father, and your Father; my God, and your God.* This is very expressive of the near relation that subsists between Christ and believers: *he that sanctifieth, and those that are sanctified, are both one; for they agree in one,* Heb. ii. 11. Here we have such an advancement of Christians, and such a condescension of Christ, as bring them very near together, so admirably well is the matter contrived, in order to their union. [*a.*] It is the great dignity of believers that *the Father of our Lord Jesus Christ* is, in him, *their Father.* A vast difference indeed there is between the respective foundations of the relation; he is Christ's Father by eternal generation, ours by a gracious adoption; yet even this warrants us to call him, as Christ did, *Abba, Father.* This gives a reason why Christ called them brethren, because his Father was their Father. Christ was now ascending to appear as an *advocate with the Father*—with *his Father,* and therefore we may hope he will prevail for any thing—with *our Father,* and therefore we may hope he will prevail for us. [*b.*] It is the great condescension of Christ that he is pleased to own the believer's God for his God: *My God, and your God;* mine, that he may be yours; the God of the Redeemer, to support him (Ps. lxxxix. 26), that he might be the God of the redeemed, to save them. The summary of the new covenant is that God *will be to us a God;* and therefore Christ being the surety and head of the covenant, who is primarily dealt with, and believers only through him as his spiritual seed, this covenant-relation fastens first upon him, God becomes his God, and so ours; we partaking of a divine nature, Christ's Father is our Father; and, he partaking of the human nature, our God is his God.

(*b.*) Christ's ascension into heaven, in further prosecution of his undertaking for us, is likewise an unspeakable comfort: "Tell them I must shortly ascend; that is the next step I am to take." Now this was intended to be, [*a.*] A word of caution to these disciples, not to expect the continuance of his bodily presence on earth, nor the setting up of his temporal kingdom among men, which they dreamed of. "No, tell them, I am risen, not to stay with them, but to go on their errand to heaven." Thus those who are raised to a spiritual life, in conformity to Christ's resurrection, must reckon that they rise to ascend; *they are quickened with Christ that they may sit with him in heavenly places,* Eph. ii. 5, 6. Let them not think that this earth is to be their home and rest; no, being born from heaven, they are bound for heaven; their eye and aim must be upon another world, and this must be ever upon their hearts, I ascend, therefore must I seek things above. [*b.*] A word of comfort to them, and to all *that shall believe in him through their word;* he was then ascending, he is now *ascended to his Father, and our Father.* This was his advancement; he ascended to receive those honours and powers which were to be the recompence of his humiliation; he says it with triumph, that those who love him may rejoice. This is our advantage; for he ascended as a conqueror, *leading captivity captive* for us (Ps. lxviii. 18), he ascended as our forerunner, *to prepare a place for us,* and to be ready to receive us. This message was like that which Joseph's brethren brought to Jacob concerning him (Gen. xlv. 26), *Joseph is yet alive,* and not only so, *vivit imo, et in senatum venit—he lives, and comes into the senate too; he is governor over all the land of Egypt;* all power is his.

Some make those words, *I ascend to my God and your God,* to include a promise of our resurrection, in the virtue of Christ's resurrection; for Christ had proved the resurrection of the dead from these words, *I am the God of Abraham,* Matt. xxii. 32. So that Christ here insinuates, "As he is my God, and hath therefore raised me, so he is your God, and will therefore raise you, and be your God, Rev. xxi. 3. *Because I live, you shall live also.* I now ascend, to honour my God, and you shall ascend to him as your God.

IV. Here is Mary Magdalene's faithful report of what she had seen and heard to the disciples (*v.* 18): *She came and told the disciples,* whom she found together, *that she had seen the Lord.* Peter and John had left her seeking him carefully with tears, and would not stay to seek him with her; and now she comes to tell them that she had found him, and to rectify the mistake she had led them into by enquiring after the dead body, for now she found it was a living body and a glorified one; so that she found what she sought, and, what was infinitely better, she had joy in her sight of the Master herself, and was willing to communicate of her joy, for she knew it would be good news to them. When God comforts us, it is with this design, that we may comfort others. And as she told them what she had seen, so also what she had heard; she had seen the Lord alive, of which this was a token (and a good token it was) *that he had spoken these things unto her* as a message to be delivered to them, and she delivered it faithfully. Those that are acquainted with the word of Christ themselves should communicate their knowledge for the good of others, and not grudge that others should know as much as they do.

19 Then the same day at evening,
being the first *day* of the week, when
the doors were shut where the disciples were assembled for fear of the
Jews, came Jesus and stood in the
midst, and saith unto them, Peace *be*
unto you. 20 And when he had so
said, he showed unto them *his* hands
and his side. Then were the disciples glad, when they saw the Lord.
21 Then said Jesus to them again,
Peace *be* unto you: as *my* Father
hath sent me, even so send I you.
22 And when he had said this, he
breathed on *them*, and saith unto
them, Receive ye the Holy Ghost:
23 Whose soever sins ye remit, they
are remitted unto them; *and* whose
soever *sins* ye retain, they are retained. 24 But Thomas, one of the
twelve, called Didymus, was not with
them when Jesus came. 25 The
other disciples therefore said unto
him, We have seen the Lord. But
he said unto them, Except I shall
see in his hands the print of the
nails, and put my finger into the print
of the nails, and thrust my hand into
his side, I will not believe.

The infallible proof of Christ's resurrection was his *showing himself alive,* Acts i. 3. In these verses, we have an account of his first appearance to the college of the disciples, on the day on which he rose. He had sent them the tidings of his resurrection by trusty and credible messengers; but to show his love to them, and confirm their faith in him, he came himself, and gave them all the assurances they could desire of the truth of it, that they might not have it by hearsay only, and at second hand, but might themselves be eye-witnesses of his being alive, because they must attest it to the world, and build the church upon that testimony. Now observe here,

I. When and where this appearance was, *v.* 19. It was *the same day* that he rose, *being the first day of the week,* the day after the Jewish sabbath, at a private meeting of the disciples, ten of them, and some more of their friends with them, Luke xxiv. 33.

There are three secondary ordinances (as I may call them) instituted by our Lord Jesus, to continue in his church, for the support of it, and for the due administration of the principal ordinances—the word, sacraments, and prayer; these are, the Lord's day, solemn assemblies, and standing ministry. The mind of Christ concerning each of these is plainly intimated to us in these verses: of the first two, here, in the circumstances of this appearance, the other *v.* 21. Christ's kingdom was to be set up among men, immediately upon his resurrection; and accordingly we find the very day he arose, though but a day of small things, yet graced with those solemnities which should help to keep up a face of religion throughout all the ages of the church.

1. Here is a Christian sabbath observed by the disciples, and owned by our Lord Jesus. The visit Christ made to his disciples was on *the first day of the week.* And the first day of the week is (I think) the only day of the week, or month, or year, that is ever mentioned by number in all the New Testament; and this is several times spoken of as a day religiously observed. Though it was said here expressly (*v.* 1) that Christ arose on *the first day of the week,* and it might have been sufficient to say here (*v.* 19), he appeared the same day at evening; yet, to put an honour upon the day, it is repeated, *being the first day of the week;* not that the apostles designed to put honour upon the day (they were yet in doubt concerning the occasion of it), but God designed to put honour upon it, by ordering it that they should be altogether, to receive Christ's first visit on that day. Thus, in effect, he blessed and sanctified that day, because in it the Redeemer rested.

2. Here is a Christian assembly solemnized by the disciples, and also owned by the Lord Jesus. Probably the disciples met here for some religious exercise, to pray together; or, perhaps, they met to compare notes, and consider whether they had sufficient evidence of their Master's resurrection, and to consult what was now to be done, whether they should keep together or scatter; they met to know one another's minds, strengthen one another's hands, and concert proper measures to be taken in the present critical juncture. This meeting was private, because they durst not appear publicly, especially in a body. They met in a house, but they kept the door shut, that they might not be seen together, and that none might come among them but such as they knew; for they feared the Jews, who would prosecute the disciples as criminals, that they might seem to believe the lie they would deceive the world with, that his

disciples came by night, and stole him away. Note, (1.) The disciples of Christ, even in difficult times, must not *forsake the assembling of themselves together*, Heb. x. 25. Those *sheep of the flock were scattered* in the storm; but sheep are sociable, and will come together again. It is no new thing for the assemblies of Christ's disciples to be driven into corners, and forced into the wilderness, Rev. xii. 14; Prov. xxviii. 12. (2.) God's people have been often obliged to *enter into their chambers, and shut their doors*, as here, *for fear of the Jews.* Persecution is allotted them, and retirement from persecution is allowed them; and then where shall we look for them but in *dens and caves of the earth.* It is a real grief, but no real reproach, ot Christ's disciples, thus to abscond.

II. What was said and done in this visit Christ made to his disciples, and his interview between them. When they were assembled, Jesus came among them, in his own likeness, yet drawing a veil over the brightness of his body, now begun to be glorified, else it would have dazzled their eyes, as in this transfiguration. Christ came among them, to give them a specimen of the performance of his promise, that, *where two or three are gathered together in his name, he will be in the midst of them.* He came, though *the doors were shut.* This does not at all weaken the evidence of his having a real human body after his resurrection; though the doors were shut, he knew how to open them without any noise, and come in so that they might not hear him, as formerly he had walked on the water, and yet had a true body. It is a comfort to Christ's disciples, when their solemn assemblies are reduced to privacy, that no doors can shut out Christ's presence from them. We have five things in this appearance of Christ:—

(1.) His kind and familiar salutation of his disciples: *He said, Peace be unto you.* This was not a word of course, though commonly used so at the meeting of friends, but a solemn, uncommon benediction, conferring upon them all the blessed fruits and effects of his death and resurrection. The phrase was common, but the sense was now peculiar. *Peace be unto you* is as much as, All good be to you, all peace always by all means. Christ had left them his peace for their legacy, *ch.* xiv. 27. By the death of the testator the testament was become of force, and he was now risen from the dead, to prove the will, and to be himself the executor of it. Accordingly, he here makes prompt payment of the legacy: *Peace be unto you.* His speaking peace makes peace, *creates the fruit of the lips, peace;* peace with God, peace in your own consciences, peace with one another; all this peace be with you; not peace with the world, but peace in Christ. His sudden appearing in *the midst of them*, when they were full of doubts concerning him, full of fears concerning themselves, could not but put them into some disorder and consternation, the noise of which waves he stills with this word, *Peace be unto you.*

(2.) His clear and undeniable manifestation of himself to them, *v.* 20. And here observe,

[1.] The method he took to convince them of the truth of his resurrection, They now saw him alive whom multitudes had seen dead two or three days before. Now the only doubt was whether this that they saw alive was the same individual body that had been seen dead; and none could desire a further proof that it was so than the scars or marks of the wounds in the body. Now, *First,* The marks of the wounds, and very deep marks (though without any pain or soreness), remained in the body of the Lord Jesus even after his resurrection, that they might be demonstrations of the truth of it. Conquerors glory in the marks of their wounds. Christ's wounds were to speak on earth that it was he himself, and therefore he arose with them; they were to speak in heaven, in the intercession he must ever live to make, and therefore he ascended with them, and appeared in the midst of *the throne, a Lamb as it had been slain, and bleeding afresh,* Rev. v. 6. Nay, it should seem, he will come again with his scars, that *they may look on him whom they pierced. Secondly,* These marks he showed to his disciples, for their conviction. They had not only the satisfaction of seeing him look with the same countenance, and hearing him speak with the same voice they had been so long accustomed to, *Sic oculos, sic ille manus, sic ora, ferebat—Such were his gestures, such his eyes and hands!* but they had the further evidence of these peculiar marks: he opened his hands to them, that they might see the marks of the wounds on them; he opened his breast, as the nurse hers to the child, to show them the wound there. Note, The exalted Redeemer will ever show himself open-handed and open-hearted to all his faithful friends and followers. When Christ manifests his love to believers by the comforts of his Spirit, assures them that *because he lives they shall live also,* then *he shows them his hands and his side.*

[2.] The impression it made upon them, and the good it did them. *First,* They were convinced that they saw the Lord; so was their faith confirmed. At first, they thought they saw an apparition only, a phantasm; but now they knew it was the Lord himself. Thus many true believers, who, while they were weak, feared their comforts were but imaginary, afterwards find them, through grace, real and substantial. They ask not, Is it the Lord? but are assured, it is he. *Secondly, Then they were glad;* that which strengthened their faith raised their joy; *believing they rejoice.* The evangelist seems to write it with somewhat of transport and triumph. *Then! then! were the disciples glad, when they saw the Lord.* If it *revived the spirit of Jacob* to hear that *Joseph was yet alive,* how would it revive the heart of these disciples to hear that Jesus is again alive? It is life from the dead to them. Now that word of Christ was fulfilled (*ch.* xvi. 22), *I will see you again, and your heart shall rejoice.* This wiped away all tears from their eyes. Note, A sight of Christ will gladden the heart of a disciple at any time; the more we see of Christ, the more we shall rejoice in him; and our joy will never be perfect till we come *where we shall see him as he is.*

(3.) The honourable and ample commission he gave them to be his agents in the planting of his church, *v.* 21. Here is,

[1.] The preface to their commission, which was the solemn repetition of the salutation before: *Peace be unto you.* This was intended, either, *First,* To raise their attention to the commission he was about to give them. The former salutation was to still the tumult of their fear, that they might calmly attend to the proofs of his resurrection; this was to reduce the transport of their joy, that they might sedately hear what he had further to say to them; or, *Secondly,* To encourage them to accept of the commission he was giving them. Though it would involve them in a great deal of trouble, yet he designed their honour and comfort in it, and, in the issue, it would be peace to them. Gideon received his commission with this word, *Peace be unto thee,* Judg. vi. 22, 23. Christ is our Peace; if he is with us, peace is to us. Christ was now sending the disciples to publish peace to the world (Isa. lii. 7), and he here not only confers it upon them for their own satisfaction, but commits it to them as a trust to be by them transmitted to all the sons of peace, Luke x. 5, 6.

[2.] The commission itself, which sounds very great: *As my Father hath sent me, even so send I you.*

First, It is easy to understand how Christ sent them; he appointed them to go on with his work upon earth, and to lay out themselves for the spreading of his gospel, and the setting up of his kingdom, among men. He sent them authorized with a divine warrant, armed with a divine power,—sent them as ambassadors to treat of peace, and as heralds to proclaim it,—sent them as servants to bid to the marriage. Hence they were called *apostles—men sent.*

Secondly, But how Christ sent them as the Father sent him is not so easily understood; certainly their commissions and powers were infinitely inferior to his; but, 1. Their work was of the same kind with his, and they were to go on where he left off. They were not sent to be priests and kings, like him, but only prophets. As he was sent to bear witness to the truth, so were they; not to be mediators of the reconciliation, but only preachers and publishers of it. Was he sent, *not to be ministered to, but to minister? not to do his own will, but the will of him that sent him? not to destroy the law and the prophets, but to fill them up?* So were they. As the Father sent him *to the lost sheep of the house of Israel,* so he sent them into all the world. 2. He had a power to send them equal to that which the Father had to send him. Here the force of the comparison seems to lie. By the same authority that the Father sent me do I send you. This proves the Godhead of Christ; the commissions he gave were of equal authority with those which the Father gave, and as valid and effectual to all intents and purposes, equal with those he gave to the Old-Testament prophets in visions. The commissions of Peter and John, by the plain word of Christ, are as good as those of Isaiah and Ezekiel, by *the Lord sitting on his throne;* nay, equal with that which was given to the Mediator himself for his work. Had he an incontestable authority, and an irresistible ability, for his work? so had they for theirs. Or thus, *As the Father hath sent me* is, as it were, the recital of his power; by virtue of the authority given him as a Mediator, he gave authority to them, as his ministers, to act for him, and in his name, with the children of men; so that those who received them, or rejected them, received or rejected him, and him that sent him, ch. xiii. 20.

(4.) The qualifying of them for the discharge of the trust reposed in them by their commission (*v.* 22): *He breathed on them, and said, Receive ye the Holy Ghost.* Observe,

[1.] The sign he used to assure them of, and affect them with, the gift he was now about to bestow upon them: *He breathed on them;* not only to show them, by this breath of life, that he himself was really alive, but to signify to them the spiritual life and power which they should receive from him for all the services that lay before them. Probably he breathed upon them all together, not upon each severally; and, though Thomas was not with them, yet the Spirit of the Lord knew where to find him, as he did Eldad and Medad, Num. xi. 26. Christ here seems to refer to the creation of man at first, by the breathing of the breath of life into him (Gen. ii. 7), and to intimate that he himself was the author of that work, and that the spiritual life and strength of ministers and Christians are derived from him, and depend upon him, as much as the natural life of Adam and his seed. As *the breath of the Almighty* gave life to man and began the old world, so the breath of the mighty Saviour gave life to his ministers, and began a new world, Job xxxiii. 4. Now this intimates to us, *First,* That the Spirit is the breath of Christ, *proceeding from the Son.* The Spirit, in the Old Testament, is compared to breath (Ezek. xxxvii. 9), *Come, O breath;* but the New Testament tells us it is Christ's breath. *The breath of God* is put for the power of his wrath (Isa. xi. 4; xxx. 33); but the breath of Christ signifies the power of his grace; the breathing of threatenings is changed into the breathings of love by the mediation of Christ. Our words are uttered by our breath, so the word of Christ *is spirit and life.* The word comes from the Spirit, and the Spirit comes along with the word. *Secondly,* That the Spirit is the gift of Christ. The apostles communicated the Holy Ghost by the laying on of hands, those hands being first lifted up in prayer, for they could only beg this blessing, and carry it as messengers; but Christ conferred the Holy Ghost by breathing, for he is the author of the gift, and from him it comes originally. Moses could not give his Spirit, God did it (Num. xi. 17); but Christ did it himself.

[2.] The solemn grant he made, signified by this sign, "*Receive ye the Holy Ghost,* in part now, as an earnest of what you shall further receive *not many days hence.*" They now received more of the Holy Ghost than they had yet received. Thus spiritual blessings are given gradually; to him that has shall be given. Now that Jesus began to be glorified more of the Spirit began to be given: see *ch.* vii. 39. Let us see what is contained in this grant. *First,* Christ hereby gives them assurance of the Spirit's aid in their future work, in the execution of the commission now given them: "*I send you,* and you shall have the Spirit to go along with you." Now the *Spirit of the Lord rested upon them,* to qualify them for all the services that lay before them. Whom Christ employs he will clothe with his Spirit, and furnish with all needful powers. *Secondly,* He hereby gives them experience of the Spirit's influences in their present case. He had shown them his hands and his side, to convince them of the truth of his resurrection; but the plainest evidences will not of themselves work faith, witness the infidelity of the soldiers, who were the only eye-witnesses of the resurrection. "Therefore *receive ye the Holy Ghost,* to work faith in you, and to open your understandings." They were now in danger of the Jews: "Therefore receive ye the Holy Ghost, to work courage in you." What Christ said to them he says to all true believers, *Receive ye the Holy Ghost,* Eph. i. 13. What Christ gives we must receive, must submit ourselves and our whole souls to the quickening, sanctifying, influences of the blessed Spirit—receive his motions, and comply with them—receive his powers and make use of them: and those who thus obey this word as a precept shall have the benefit of it as a promise; they shall receive the Holy Ghost as the guide of their way and the earnest of their inheritance.

(5.) One particular branch of the power given them by their commission particularized (*v.* 23): "*Whosesoever sins you remit,* in the due execution of the powers you are entrusted with, they are remitted to them, and they may take the comfort of it; *and whosesoever sins you retain,* that is, pronounce unpardoned and the guilt of them bound on, *they are retained,* and the sinner may be sure of it, to his sorrow." Now this follows upon their receiving the Holy Ghost; for, if they had not had an extraordinary spirit of discerning, they had not been fit to be entrusted with such an authority; for, in the strictest sense, this is a special commission to the apostles themselves and the first preachers of the gospel, who could distinguish who were in the *gall of bitterness and bond of iniquity,* and who were not. By virtue of this power, Peter struck Ananias and Sapphira dead, and Paul struck Elymas blind. Yet it must be understood as a general charter to the church and her ministers, not securing an infallibility of judgment to any man or company of men in the world, but encouraging the faithful stewards of the mysteries of God to stand to the gospel they were sent to preach, for that God himself will stand to it. The apostles, in preaching remission, must begin at Jerusalem, though she had lately brought upon herself the guilt of Christ's blood: "Yet you may declare their sins remitted upon gospel terms." And Peter did so, Acts ii. 38; iii. 19. Christ, being risen for our justification, sends his gospel heralds to proclaim the jubilee begun, the act of indemnity now passed; and by this rule men shall be judged, *ch.* xii. 48; Rom. ii. 16; Jam. ii. 12. God will never alter this rule of judgment, nor vary from it; those whom the gospel acquits shall be acquitted, and those whom the gospel condemns shall be condemned, which puts immense honour upon the ministry, and should put immense courage into ministers. Two ways the apostles and ministers of Christ remit and retain sin, and both as having authority:—[1.] By sound doctrine. They are commissioned to tell the world that salvation is to be had upon gospel terms, and no other, and they shall find God will say *Amen* to it; so shall their doom be. [2.] By a strict discipline, applying the general rule of the gospel to particular persons. "Whom you admit into communion with you, according to the rules of the gospel, God will admit into communion with himself; and whom you cast out of communion as impenitent, and obstinate in scandalous and infectious sins, shall be bound over to the righteous judgment of God."

III. The incredulity of Thomas, when the report of this was made to him, which introduced Christ's second appearance.

1. Here is Thomas's absence from this meeting, *v.* 24. He is said to be *one of the twelve,* one of the college of the apostles, who, though now eleven, had been twelve, and were to be so again. They were but eleven, and one of them was missing: Christ's disciples will never be all together till the general assembly at the great day. Perhaps it was Thomas's unhappiness that he was absent—either he was not well, or had not no-

tice; or perhaps it was his sin and folly—either he was diverted by business or company, which he preferred before this opportunity, or he durst not come for *fear of the Jews;* and he called that his prudence and caution which was his cowardice. However, by his absence he missed the satisfaction of seeing his Master risen, and of sharing with the disciples in their joy upon that occasion. Note, Those know not what they lose who carelessly absent themselves from the stated solemn assemblies of Christians.

2. The account which the other disciples gave him of the visit their Master had made them, *v.* 25. The next time they saw him they *said unto him,* with joy enough, *We have seen the Lord;* and no doubt they related to him all that had passed, particularly the satisfaction he had given them by showing them his hands and his side. It seems, though Thomas was then from them, he was not long from them; absentees for a time must not be condemned as apostates for ever: Thomas is not Judas. Observe with what exultation and triumph they speak it: "*We have seen the Lord,* the most comfortable sight we ever saw." This they said to Thomas, (1.) To upbraid him with his absence: "*We have seen the Lord,* but thou hast not." Or rather, (2.) To inform him: "*We have seen the Lord,* and we wish thou hadst been here, to see him too, for thou wouldest have seen enough to satisfy thee." Note, The disciples of Christ should endeavour to *build up one another in their most holy faith,* both by repeating what they have heard to those that were absent, that they may hear it at second hand, and also by communicating what they have experienced. Those that by faith have seen the Lord, and tasted that he is gracious, should tell others what God has done for their souls; only let boasting be excluded.

3. The objections Thomas raised against the evidence, to justify himself in his unwillingness to admit it. "Tell me not that you have seen the Lord alive; you are too credulous; somebody has made fools of you. For my part, *except I shall* not only *see in his hands the print of the nails,* but put my finger into it, *and thrust my hand* into the wound *in his side,* I am resolved *I will not believe.*" Some, by comparing this with what he said (*ch.* xi. 16; xiv. 5), conjecture him to have been a man of a rough, morose temper, apt to speak peevishly; for all good people are not alike happy in their temper. However, there was certainly much amiss in his conduct at this time. (1.) He had either not heeded, or not duly regarded, what Christ had so often said, and that too according to the Old Testament, that he would *rise again the third day;* so that he ought to have said, *He is risen,* though he had not seen him, nor spoken with any that had. (2.) He did not pay a just deference to the testimony of his fellow-disciples, who were men of wisdom and integrity, and ought to have been credited. He knew them to be honest men; they all ten of them concurred in the testimony with great assurance; and yet he could not persuade himself to say that *their record was true.* Christ had chosen them to be his witnesses of this very thing to all nations; and yet Thomas, one of their own fraternity, would not allow them to be competent witnesses, nor trust them further than he could see them. It was not, however, their veracity that he questioned, but their prudence; he feared they were too credulous. (3.) He tempted Christ, and *limited the Holy One of Israel,* when he would be convinced by his own method, or not at all. He could not be sure that the print of the nails, which the apostles told him they had seen, would admit the putting of his finger into it, or the wound in his side the thrusting in of his hand; nor was it fit to deal so roughly with a living body; yet Thomas ties up his faith to this evidence. Either he will be humoured, and have his fancy gratified, or he will not believe; see Matt. xvi. 1; xxvii. 42. (4.) The open avowal of this in the presence of the disciples was an offence and discouragement to them. It was not only a sin, but a scandal. As one coward makes many, so does one unbeliever, one sceptic, *making his brethren's heart to faint like his heart,* Deut. xx. 8. Had he only thought this evil, and then laid his hand upon his mouth, to suppress it, his error had remained with himself; but his proclaiming his infidelity, and that so peremptorily, might be of ill consequence to the rest, who were as yet but weak and wavering.

26 And after eight days again his
disciples were within, and Thomas
with them: *then* came Jesus, the
doors being shut, and stood in the
midst, and said, Peace *be* unto you.
27 Then saith he to Thomas, Reach
hither thy finger, and behold my
hands; and reach hither thy hand,
and thrust *it* into my side: and be
not faithless, but believing. 28 And
Thomas answered and said unto him,
My Lord and my God. 29 Jesus
saith unto him, Thomas, because thou
hast seen me, thou hast believed:
blessed *are* they that have not seen,
and *yet* have believed. 30 And many
other signs truly did Jesus in the
presence of his disciples, which are
not written in this book: 31 But
these are written, that ye might believe that Jesus is the Christ, the
Son of God; and that believing ye
might have life through his name.

We have here an account of another appearance of Christ to his disciples, after his resurrection, when Thomas was now with them. And concerning this we may observe,

I. When it was that Christ repeated his visit to his disciples: *After eight days,* that day seven-night after he rose, which must therefore be, as that was, *the first day of the week.*

1. He deferred his next appearance for some time, to show his disciples that he was not risen to such a life as he had formerly lived, to converse constantly with them, but was as one that belonged to another world, and visited this only as angels do, now and then, when there was occasion. Where Christ was during these eight days, and the rest of the time of his abode on earth, it is folly to enquire, and presumption to determine. Wherever he was, no doubt *angels ministered unto him.* In the beginning of his ministry he had been forty days unseen, tempted by the evil spirit, Matt. iv. 1, 2. And now in the beginning of his glory he was forty days, for the most part unseen, attended by good spirits.

2. He deferred it so long as seven days. And why so? (1.) That he might put a rebuke upon Thomas for his incredulity. He had neglected the former meeting of the disciples; and, to teach him to prize those seasons of grace better for the future, he cannot have such another opportunity for several days. He that slips one tide must stay a good while for another. A very melancholy week, we have reason to think Thomas had of it, drooping, and in suspense, while the other disciples were full of joy; and it was owing to himself and his own folly. (2.) That he might try the faith and patience of the rest of the disciples. They had gained a great point when they were satisfied that they had seen the Lord. *Then were the disciples glad;* but he would try whether they could keep the ground they had got, when they saw no more of him for some days. And thus he would gradually wean them from his bodily presence, which they had doted and depended too much upon. (3.) That he might put an honour upon the first day of the week, and give a plain intimation of his will, that it should be observed in his church as the Christian sabbath, the weekly day of holy rest and holy convocations. That one day in seven should be religiously observed was an appointment from the beginning, as old as innocency; and that in the kingdom of the Messiah the first day of the week should be that solemn day this was indication enough, that Christ on that day once and again met his disciples in a religious assembly. It is highly probable that in his former appearance to them he appointed them that day seven-night to be together again, and promised to meet them; and also that he appeared to them every first day of the week, besides other times, during the forty days. The religious observance of that day has been thence transmitted down to us through every age of the church. This therefore is *the day which the Lord has made.*

II. Where, and how, Christ made them this visit. It was at Jerusalem, for the doors were shut now, as before, for fear of the Jews. There they staid, to keep the feast of unleavened bread seven days, which expired the day before this; yet they would not set out on their journey to Galilee on the first day of the week, because it was the Christian sabbath, but staid till the day after. Now observe, 1. That Thomas was with them; though he had withdrawn himself once, yet not a second time. When we have lost one opportunity, we should give the more earnest heed to lay hold on the next, that we may recover our losses. It is a good sign if such a loss whet our desires, and a bad sign if it cool them. The disciples admitted him among them, and did not insist upon his believing the resurrection of Christ, as they did, because as yet it was but darkly revealed; they did not receive him to doubtful disputation, but bade him welcome to come and see. But observe, Christ did not appear to Thomas, for his satisfaction, till he found him in society with the rest of his disciples, because he would countenance the meetings of Christians and ministers, for there will he be *in the midst of them.* And, besides, he would have all the disciples witnesses of the rebuke he gave to Thomas, and yet withal of the tender care he had of him. 2. That Christ *came* in among them, and *stood in the midst,* and they all knew him, for he showed himself now, just as he had shown himself before (*v.* 19), still the same, and no changeling. See the condescension of our Lord Jesus. The gates of heaven were ready to be opened to him, and there he might have been in the midst of the adorations of a world of angels; yet, for the benefit of his church, he lingered on earth, and visited the little private meetings of his poor disciples, and is in the midst of them. 3. He saluted them all in a friendly manner, as he had done before; he said, *Peace be unto you.* This was no vain repetition, but significant of the abundant and assured peace which Christ gives, and of the continuance of his blessings upon his people, for they *fail not,* but are *new every morning,* new every meeting.

III. What passed between Christ and Thomas at this meeting; and that only is recorded, though we may suppose he said a great deal to the rest of them. Here is,

1. Christ's gracious condescension to Thomas, *v.* 27. He singled him out from the rest, and applied himself particularly to him: "*Reach hither thy finger,* and, since thou wilt have it so, *behold my hands,* and satisfy thy curiosity to the utmost about the *print of the nails; reach hither thy hand,* and, if nothing less will convince thee, *thrust it into my side.*" Here we have, (1.) An implicit

rebuke of Thomas's incredulity, in the plain reference which is here had to what Thomas had said, answering it word for word, for he had heard it, though unseen; and one would think that his telling him of it should put him to the blush. Note, There is not an unbelieving word on our tongues, no, nor thought in our minds, at any time, but it is known to the Lord Jesus, Ps. lxxviii. 21. (2.) An express condescension to his weakness, which appears in two things:—[1.] That he suffers his wisdom to be prescribed to. Great spirits will not be dictated to by their inferiors, especially in their acts of grace; yet Christ is pleased here to accommodate himself even to Thomas's fancy in a needless thing, rather than break with him, and leave him in his unbelief. He will not *break the bruised reed*, but, as a good shepherd, *gathers that which was driven away*, Ezek. xxxiv. 16. We ought thus to *bear the infirmities of the weak*, Rom. xv. 1, 2. [2.] He suffers his wounds to be raked into, allows Thomas even to thrust his hand into his side, if then at last he would believe. Thus, for the confirmation of our faith, he has instituted an ordinance on purpose to keep his death in remembrance, though it was an ignominious, shameful death, and one would think should rather have been forgotten, and no more said of it; yet, because it was such an evidence of his love as would be an encouragement to our faith, he appoints the memorial of it to be celebrated. And in that ordinance wherein we *show the Lord's death* we are called, as it were, to put our finger *into the print of the nails. Reach hither thy hand* to him, who reacheth forth his helping, inviting, giving hand to thee.

It is an affecting word with which Christ closes up what he had to say to Thomas: *Be not faithless but believing; μὴ γίνου ἄπιστος—do not thou become an unbeliever;* as if he would have been sealed up under unbelief, had he not yielded now. This warning is given to us all: *Be not faithless;* for, if we are faithless, we are Christless and graceless, hopeless and joyless; let us therefore say, *Lord, I believe, help thou my unbelief.*

2. Thomas's believing consent to Jesus Christ. He is now ashamed of his incredulity, and cries out, *My Lord and my God, v.* 28. We are not told whether he did put his finger into the print of the nails; it should seem, he did not, for Christ says (*v.* 29), *Thou hast seen, and believed;* seeing sufficed. And now faith comes off a conqueror, after a struggle with unbelief.

(1.) Thomas is now fully satisfied of the truth of Christ's resurrection—that the same Jesus that was crucified is now alive, and this is he. His slowness and backwardness to believe may help to strengthen our faith; for hereby it appears that the witnesses of Christ's resurrection, who attested it to the world, and pawned their lives upon it, were not easy credulous men, but cautious enough, and suspended their belief of it till they saw the utmost evidence of it they could desire. Thus *out of the eater came forth meat.*

(2.) He therefore believed him to be Lord and God, and we are to believe him so. [1.] We must believe his deity—that he is God; not a man made God, but God made man, as this evangelist had laid down his thesis at first, *ch.* i. 1. The author and head of our holy religion has the wisdom, power, sovereignty, and unchangeableness of God, which was necessary, because he was to be not only the founder of it, but the foundation of it for its constant support, and the fountain of life for its supply. [2.] His mediation—that he is Lord, the one Lord, 1 Cor. viii. 6; 1 Tim. ii. 5. He is sufficiently authorized, as plenipotentiary, to settle the great concerns that lie between God and man, to take up the controversy which would inevitably have been our ruin, and to establish the correspondence that was necessary to our happiness; see Acts ii. 36; Rom. xiv. 9.

(3.) He consented to him as his Lord and his God. In faith there must be the consent of the will to gospel terms, as well as the assent of the understanding to gospel truths. We must accept of Christ to be that to us which the Father hath appointed him. *My Lord* refers to *Adonai*—my foundation and stay; *my God* to *Elohim*—my prince and judge. God having constituted him the umpire and referee, we must approve the choice, and entirely refer ourselves to him. This is the vital act of faith, He is mine, Cant. ii. 16.

(4.) He made an open profession of this, before those that had been the witnesses of his unbelieving doubts. He says it to Christ, and, to complete the sense, we must read it, *Thou art* my Lord and my God; or, speaking to his brethren, *This is* my Lord and my God. Do we accept of Christ as our *Lord God?* We must go to him, and tell him so, as David (Ps. xvi. 2), deliver the surrender to him as *our act and deed*, tell others so, as those that triumph in our relation to Christ: *This is my beloved.* Thomas speaks with an ardency of affection, as one that took hold of Christ with all his might, *My Lord* and *my God.*

3. The judgment of Christ upon the whole (*v.* 29): "*Thomas, because thou hast seen me, thou hast believed*, and it is well thou art brought to it at last upon any terms; but *blessed are those that have not seen, and yet have believed.*" Here,

(1.) Christ owns Thomas a believer. Sound and sincere believers, though they be slow and weak, shall be graciously accepted of the Lord Jesus. Those who have long stood it out, if at last they yield, shall find him ready to forgive. No sooner did Thomas consent to Christ than Christ gives him the comfort of it, and lets him know that he believes.

(2.) He upbraids him with his former incredulity. He might well be ashamed to think, [1.] That he had been so backward to believe, and came so slowly to his own comforts. Those that in sincerity have closed with Christ see a great deal of reason to lament that they did not do it sooner. [2.] That it was not without much ado that he was brought to believe at last: "If thou hadst not seen me alive, thou wouldst not have believed; but if no evidence must be admitted but that of our own senses, and we must believe nothing but what we ourselves are eye-witnesses of, farewell all commerce and conversation. If this must be the only method of proof, how must the world be converted to the faith of Christ? He is therefore justly blamed for laying so much stress upon this.

(3.) He commends the faith of those who believe upon easier terms. Thomas, as a believer, was truly blessed; but rather *blessed are those that have not seen.* It is not meant of not seeing the objects of faith (for these are invisible, Heb. xi. 1; 2 Cor. iv. 18), but the motives of faith—Christ's miracles, and especially his resurrection; blessed are those that see not these, and yet believe in Christ. This may look, either backward, upon the Old-Testament saints, who had not seen the things which they saw, and yet believed the promise made unto the fathers, and lived by that faith; or forward, upon those who should afterwards believe, the Gentiles, who had never seen Christ in the flesh, as the Jews had. This faith is more laudable and praise-worthy than theirs who saw and believed; for, [1.] It evidences a better temper of mind in those that do believe. Not to see and yet to believe argues greater industry in searching after truth, and greater ingenuousness of mind in embracing it. He that believes upon that sight has his resistance conquered by a sort of violence; but he that believes without it, like the Bereans, is more noble. [2.] It is a greater instance of the power of divine grace. The less sensible the evidence is the more does the work of faith appear to be the Lord's doing. Peter is blessed in his faith, because flesh and blood have not revealed it to him, Matt. xvi. 17. Flesh and blood contribute more to their faith that see and believe, than to theirs who see not and yet believe. Dr. Lightfoot quotes a saying of one of the rabbin, "That one proselyte is more acceptable to God than all the thousands of Israel that stood before mount Sinai; for they saw and received the law, but a proselyte sees not, and yet receives it."

IV. The remark which the evangelist makes upon his narrative, like an historian drawing towards a conclusion, *v.* 30, 31. And here,

1. He assures us that many other things occurred, which were all worthy to be recorded, but are *not written in the book: many signs.* Some refer this to all the signs that Jesus did during his whole life, all the wondrous words he spoke, and all the wondrous works he did. But it seems rather to be confined to the signs he did after his resurrection, for these were in the presence of the disciples only, who are here spoken of, Acts x. 41. Divers of his appearances are not recorded, as appears, 1 Cor. xv. 5—7. See Acts i. 3. Now, (1.) We may here improve this general attestation, that there were other signs, many others, for the confirmation of our faith; and, being added to the particular narratives, they very much strengthen the evidence. Those that recorded the resurrection of Christ were not put to fish for evidence, to take up such short and scanty proofs as they could find, and make up the rest with conjecture. No, they had evidence enough and to spare, and more witnesses to produce than they had occasion for. The disciples, in whose presence these other signs were done, were to be preachers of Christ's resurrection to others, and therefore it was requisite they should have proofs of it *ex abundanti—in abundance,* that they might have a strong consolation, who ventured life and all upon it. (2.) We need not ask why they were not all written, or why not more than these, or others than these; for it is enough for us that so it seemed good to the Holy Spirit, by whose inspiration this was given. Had this history been a mere human composition, it had been swelled with a multitude of depositions and affidavits, to prove the contested truth of Christ's resurrection and long arguments drawn up for the demonstration of it; but, being a divine history, the penmen write with a noble security, relating what amounted to a competent proof, sufficient to convince those that were willing to be taught and to condemn those that were obstinate in their unbelief; and, if this satisfy not, more would not. Men produce all they have to say, that they may gain credit; but God does not, for he can give faith. Had this history been written for the entertainment of the curious, it would have been more copious, for every circumstance would have brightened and embellished the story; but it was written to bring men to believe, and enough is said to answer that intention, whether men will hear or whether they will forbear.

2. He instructs us in the design of recording what we do find here (*v.* 31): "These accounts are given in this and the following chapter, *that you might believe* upon these evidences; that you might believe that Jesus is the Christ, the Son of God, declared with power to be so by his resurrection."

(1.) Here is the design of those that wrote the gospel. Some write books for their diversion, and publish them for their profit or applause, others to oblige the Athenian humour, others to instruct the world in arts and sciences for their secular advantage; but the evangelists wrote without any view of temporal benefit to themselves or others, but to bring men to Christ and heaven, and, in order to this, to persuade men to believe; and for this they took the most fitting methods, they brought to the world a divine revelation, supported with its due evidences.

(2.) The duty of those that read and hear the gospel. It is their duty to believe, to embrace, the doctrine of Christ, and that record given concerning him, 1 John v. 11. [1.] We are here told what the great gospel truth is which we are to believe—that *Jesus is that Christ*, that *Son of God*. *First*, That he is the Christ, the person who, under the title of the Messiah, was promised to, and expected by, the Old-Testament saints, and who, according to the signification of the name, is *anointed* of God to be a prince and a Saviour. *Secondly*, That he is the Son of God; not only as Mediator (for then he had not been greater than Moses, who was a prophet, intercessor, and lawgiver), but antecedent to his being the Mediator; for if he had not been a divine person, endued with the power of God and entitled to the glory of God, he had not been qualified for the undertaking—not fit either to do the Redeemer's work or to wear the Redeemer's crown. [2.] What the great gospel blessedness is which we are to hope for—*That believing we shall have life through his name.* This is, *First*, To direct our faith; it must have an eye to the life, the crown of life, the tree of life set before us. Life through Christ's name, the life proposed in the covenant which is made with us in Christ, is what we must propose to ourselves as the fulness of our joy and the abundant recompence of all our services and sufferings. *Secondly*, To encourage our faith, and invite us to believe. Upon the prospect of some great advantage, men will venture far; and greater advantage there cannot be than that which is offered by the *words of this life*, as the gospel is called, Acts v. 20. It includes both spiritual life, in conformity to God and communion with him, and eternal life, in the vision and fruition of him. Both are through Christ's name, by his merit and power, and both indefeasibly sure to all true believers.

CHAP. XXI.

The evangelist seemed to have concluded his history with the foregoing chapter; but (as St. Paul sometimes in his epistles), new matter occurring, he begins again. He had said that there were many other signs which Jesus did for the proof of his resurrection. And in this chapter he mentions one of these many, which was Christ's appearance to some of his disciples at the sea of Tiberias, in which we have an account, I. How he discovered himself to them as they were fishing, filled their net, and then very familiarly came and dined with them upon what they had caught, ver. 1—14. II. What discourse he had with Peter after dinner, 1. Concerning himself, ver. 15—19. 2. Concerning John, ver. 20—23. III. The solemn conclusion of this gospel, ver. 24, 25. It is strange that any should suppose that this chapter was added by some other hand, when it is expressly said (ver. 24) that the disciple whom Jesus loved is he which testifieth of these things.

AFTER these things Jesus showed
himself again to the disciples at
the sea of Tiberias; and on this wise
showed he *himself*, 2 There were
together Simon Peter, and Thomas
called Didymus, and Nathanael of
Cana in Galilee, and the *sons* of Zebedee, and two other of his disciples.
3 Simon Peter saith unto them, I go
a fishing. They say unto him, We
also go with thee. They went forth,
and entered into a ship immediately; and that night they caught
nothing. 4 But when the morning was now come, Jesus stood on
the shore: but the disciples knew
not that it was Jesus. 5 Then Jesus
saith unto them, Children, have ye
any meat? They answered him, No.
6 And he said unto them, Cast the
net on the right side of the ship, and
ye shall find. They cast therefore,
and now they were not able to draw
it for the multitude of fishes. 7
Therefore that disciple whom Jesus
loved saith unto Peter, It is the Lord.
Now when Simon Peter heard that it
was the Lord, he girt *his* fisher's coat
unto him (for he was naked), and did
cast himself into the sea. 8 And the
other disciples came in a little ship
(for they were not far from land, but
as it were two hundred cubits); dragging the net with fishes. 9 As soon
then as they were come to land, they
saw a fire of coals there, and fish laid
thereon, and bread. 10 Jesus saith
unto them, Bring of the fish which ye
have now caught. 11 Simon Peter
went up, and drew the net to land full
of great fishes, an hundred and fifty
and three: and for all there were so
many, yet was not the net broken.
12 Jesus saith unto them, Come *and*
dine. And none of the disciples durst
ask him, Who art thou? knowing
that it was the Lord. 13 Jesus then
cometh, and taketh bread, and giveth
them, and fish likewise. 14 This is
now the third time that Jesus showed
himself to his disciples, after that he
was risen from the dead.

We have here an account of Christ's appearance to his disciples at the sea of Tiberias, Now, 1. Let us compare this appearance with those that *went before*. In those Christ showed himself to his disciples when they were met in a solemn assembly (it should seem, for religious worship) upon a Lord's day, and when they were all together, perhaps expecting his appearing; but in this he showed himself to some of them occasionally, upon a week-day, when they were fishing, and little thought of it. Christ has many ways of making himself known to his people; usually in his ordinances, but sometimes by his Spirit he visits them when they are employed in common business, as the *shepherds* who were *keeping their flocks by night* (Luke ii. 8), even so *here also*, Gen. xvi. 13. 2. Let us compare it with that which followed at the mountain in Galilee, where Christ had appointed them to meet him, Matt. xxviii. 16. Thitherward they moved as soon as the days of unleavened bread were over, and disposed of themselves as they thought fit, till the time fixed for this interview, or general rendezvous. Now this appearance was while they were waiting for that, that they might not be weary of waiting. Christ is often better than his word, but never worse, often anticipates and outdoes the believing expectations of his people, but never disappoints them. As to the particulars of the story, we may observe,

I. Who they were to whom Christ now showed himself (*v.* 2): not to all the twelve, but to seven of them only. Nathanael is mentioned as one of them, whom we have not met with since *ch.* i. But some think he was the same with Bartholomew, one of the twelve. The two not named are supposed to be Philip of Bethsaida and Andrew of Capernaum. Observe here, 1. It is good for the disciples of Christ to be much together; not only in solemn religious assemblies, but in common conversation, and about common business. Good Christians should by this means both testify and increase their affection to, and delight in, each other, and edify one another both by discourse and example. 2. Christ chose to manifest himself to them when they were together; not only to countenance Christian society, but that they might be joint witnesses of the same matter of fact, and so might corroborate one another's testimony. Here were seven together to attest this, on which some observe that the Roman law required seven witnesses to a testament. 3. Thomas was one of them, and is named next to Peter, as if he now kept closer to the meetings of the apostles than ever. It is well if losses by our neglects make us more careful afterwards not to let opportunities slip.

II. How they were employed, *v.* 3. Observe,

1. Their agreement to go a fishing. They knew not well what to do with themselves. For my part, says Peter, *I will go a fishing; We will go with thee* then, say they, for we will keep together. Though commonly two of a trade cannot agree, yet they could. Some think they did amiss in returning to their boats and nets, which they had left; but then Christ would not have countenanced them in it with a visit. It was rather commendable in them; for they did it, (1.) To redeem time, and not be idle. They were not yet appointed to preach the resurrection of Christ. Their commission was in the drawing, but not perfected. The hour for entering upon action was not come. It is probable that their Master had directed them to say nothing of his resurrection till after his ascension, nay, not till after the pouring out of the Spirit, and then they were to begin at Jerusalem. Now, in the mean time, rather than do nothing, they would go a fishing; not for recreation, but for business. It is an instance of their humility. Though they were advanced to be sent of Christ, as he was of the Father, yet they did not take state upon them, but remembered *the rock out of which they were hewn*. It is an instance likewise of their industry, and bespeaks them good husbands of their time. While they were waiting, they would not be idling. Those who would give an account of their time with joy should contrive to fill up the vacancies of it, to gather up the fragments of it. (2.) That they might help to maintain themselves and not be burdensome to any. While their Master was with them those who ministered to him were kind to them; but now that the *bridegroom was taken from them* they must *fast* in those days, and therefore their own hands, as Paul's, must *minister to their necessities* · and for this reason Christ asked them, *Have you any meat?* This teaches us with quietness *to work and eat our own bread*.

2. Their disappointment in their fishing. That night they caught nothing, though, it is probable, they *toiled all night*, as Luke v. 5. See the vanity of this world; the hand of the diligent often returns empty. Even good men may come short of desired success in their honest undertakings. We may be in the way of our duty, and yet not prosper. Providence so ordered it that all that night they should catch nothing, that the miraculous draught of fishes in the morning might be the more wonderful and the more acceptable. In those disappointments which to us are very grievous God has often designs that are very gracious. Man has indeed *a dominion over the fish of the sea*, but they are not always at his beck; God only knows the *paths of the sea*, and commands that which passeth through them.

III. After what manner Christ made himself known to them. It is said (*v.* 1), *He showed himself*. His body, though a true and real body, was raised, as ours will be, a spiritual body, and so was visible only when he himself was pleased to make it so; or, rather, came and removed so quickly that it was here or there in an instant, *in a moment, in the twinkling of an eye*. Four things are observable in the appearance of Christ to them:—

1. He showed himself to them seasonably (*v.* 4): *When the morning was now come*, after a fruitless night's toil, Jesus *stood on the shore*. Christ's time of making himself

known to his people is when they are most at a loss. When they think they have lost themselves, he will let them know that they have not lost him. Weeping may *endure for a night; but joy comes,* if Christ comes, *in the morning.* Christ appeared to them, not *walking upon the water,* because, being *risen from the dead,* he was not to be with them as he had been; but *standing upon the shore,* because now they were to make towards him. Some of the ancients put this significancy upon it, that Christ, having finished his work, was got through a stormy sea, a sea of blood, to a safe and quiet shore, where he stood in triumph; but the disciples, having their work before them, were yet at sea, in toil and peril. It is a comfort to us, when our passage is rough and stormy, that our Master is at shore, and we are hastening to him.

2. He showed himself to them gradually. The disciples, though they had been intimately acquainted with him, *knew not,* all at once, *that it was Jesus.* Little expecting to see him there, and not looking intently upon him, they took him for some common person waiting the arrival of their boat, to buy their fish. Note, Christ is often nearer to us than we think he is, and so we shall find afterwards, to our comfort.

3. He showed himself to them by an instance of his pity, *v.* 5. He called to them, *Children,* παιδία—"*Lads, have you any meat?* Have you caught any fish?" Here, (1.) The compellation is very familiar; he speaks unto them as unto his sons, with the care and tenderness of a father: *Children.* Though he had now entered upon his exalted state, he spoke to his disciples with as much kindness and affection as ever. They were not children in age, but they were his children, the children which God had given him. (2.) The question is very kind: *Have you any meat?* He asks as a tender father concerning his children whether they be provided with that which is fit for them, that, if they be not, he may take care for their supply. Note, *The Lord is for the body,* 1 Cor. vi. 13. Christ takes cognizance of the temporal wants of his people, and has promised them not only grace sufficient, but food convenient. *Verily they shall be fed,* Ps. xxxvii. 3. Christ looks into the cottages of the poor, and asks, *Children, have you any meat?* thereby inviting them to open their case before him, and by the prayer of faith to *make their requests known* to him: and then let them *be careful for nothing;* for Christ takes care of them, takes care for them. Christ has herein set us an example of compassionate concern for our brethren. There are many poor householders disabled for labour, or disappointed in it, that are reduced to straits, whom the rich should enquire after thus, *Have you any meat?* For the most necessitous are commonly the least clamorous. To this question the disciples gave a short answer, and, some think, with an air of discontent and peevishness. They said, *No;* not giving him any such friendly and respectful title as he had given them. So short do the best come in their returns of love to the Lord Jesus. Christ put the question to them, not because he did not know their wants, but because he would know them *from them.* Those that would have supplies from Christ must own themselves empty and needy.

4. He showed himself to them by an instance of his power; and this perfected the discovery (*v.* 6): he ordered them to *cast the net on the right side of the ship,* the contrary side to what they had been casting it on; and then they, who were going home empty-handed, were enriched with a great draught of fishes. Here we have, (1.) The orders Christ gave them, and the promise annexed to those orders: *Cast the net* there in such a place, and *you shall find.* He from whom nothing is hid, no, not the *inhabitants under the waters* (Job xxvi. 5), knew on what side of the ship the shoal of fishes was, and to that side he directs them. Note, Divine providence extends itself to things most minute and contingent; and they are happy that know how to take hints thence in the conduct of their affairs, and acknowledge it in all their ways. (2.) Their obedience of these orders, and the good success of it. As yet *they knew not that it was Jesus;* however, they were willing to be advised by any body, and did not bid this supposed stranger mind his own business and not meddle with theirs, but took his counsel; in being thus observant of strangers, they were obedient to their Master unawares. And it sped wonderfully well; now they had a draught that paid them for all their pains. Note, Those that are humble, diligent, and patient (though their labours may be crossed) shall be crowned; they sometimes live to see their affairs take a hapy turn, after many struggles and fruitless attempts. There is nothing lost by observing Christ's orders. Those are likely to speed well that follow the rule of the word, the guidance of the Spirit, and the intimations of Providence; for this is *casting the net on the right side of the ship.* Now the draught of fishes may be considered, [1.] As a miracle in itself: and so it was designed to prove that Jesus Christ was *raised in power,* though *sown in weakness,* and that all things were *put under his feet, the fishes of the sea* not excepted. Christ manifests himself to his people by doiug that for them which none else can do, and things which *they looked not for.* [2.] As a mercy to them; for the seasonable and abundant supply of their necessities. When their ingenuity and industry failed them, the power of Christ came in opportunely for their relief; for he would take care that those who had left all for him should not want any good thing. When we are most at a loss, *Jehovah-jireh.* [3.] As the memorial of a former

mercy, with which Christ had formerly recompensed Peter for the loan of his boat, Luke v. 4, &c. This miracle nearly resembled that, and could not but put Peter in mind of it, which helped him to improve this; for both that and this affected him much, as meeting him in his own element, in his own employment. Latter favours are designed to bring to mind former favours, that eaten bread may not be forgotten. [4.] As a mystery, and very significant of that work to which Christ was now with an enlarged commission sending them forth. The prophets had been fishing for souls, and caught nothing, or very little; but the apostles, who let down the net at Christ's word, had wonderful success. *Many were the children of the desolate*, Gal. iv. 27. They themselves, in pursuance of their former mission, when they were first made *fishers of men*, had had small success in comparison with what they should now have. When, soon after this, three thousand were converted in one day, then the net was *cast on the right side of the ship*. It is an encouragement to Christ's ministers to continue their diligence in their work. One happy draught, at length, may be sufficient to repay many years of toil at the gospel net.

IV. How the disciples received this discovery which Christ made of himself, *v.* 7, 8, where we find,

1. That John was the most intelligent and quick-sighted disciple. He whom Jesus loved was the first that said, *It is the Lord;* for those whom Christ loves he will in a special manner manifest himself to: his secret is with his favourites. John had adhered more closely to his Master in his sufferings than any of them: and therefore he has a clearer eye and a more discerning judgment than any of them, in recompence for his constancy. When John was himself aware that it was the Lord, he communicated his knowledge to those with him; for this *dispensation of the Spirit is given to every one to profit withal.* Those that know Christ themselves should endeavour to bring others acquainted with him; we need not engross him, there is enough in him for us all. John tells Peter particularly his thoughts, that it was the Lord, knowing he would be glad to see him above any of them. Though Peter had denied his Master, yet, having repented, and being taken into the communion of the disciples again, they were as free and familiar with him as ever.

2. That Peter was the most zealous and warm-hearted disciple; for as soon as he heard it was the Lord (for which he took John's word) the ship could not hold him, nor could he stay till the bringing of it to shore, but into the sea he throws himself presently, that he might come first to Christ. (1.) He showed his respect to Christ by *girding his fisher's coat* about him that he might appear before his Master in the best clothes he had, and not rudely rush into his presence, stripped as he was to his waistcoat and drawers, because the work he was about was toilsome, and he was resolved to take pains in it. Perhaps the fisher's coat was made of leather, or oil-cloth, and would keep out wet; and he girt it to him that he might make the best of his way through the water to Christ, as he used to do after his nets. when he was intent upon his fishing. (2), He showed the strength of his affection to Christ, and his earnest desire to be with him, by casting himself into the sea; and either wading or swimming to shore, to come to him. When he walked upon the water to Christ (Matt. xiv. 28, 29), it was said, *He came down out of the ship* deliberately; but here it is said, *He cast himself into the sea* with precipitation; sink or swim, he would show his good-will and aim to be with Jesus. "If Christ suffer me," thinks he, "to drown, and come short of him, it is but what I deserve for denying him." Peter had had much forgiven, and made it appear he loved much by his willingness to run hazards, and undergo hardships, to come to him. Those that have been with Jesus will be willing to swim through a stormy sea, a sea of blood, to come to him. And it is a laudable contention amongst Christ's disciples to strive who shall be first with him.

3. That the rest of the disciples were careful and honest hearted. Though they were not in such a transport of zeal as to throw themselves into the sea, like Peter, yet they hastened in the boat to the shore, and made the best of their way (*v.* 8): *The other disciples*, and John with them, who had first discovered that it was Christ, came slowly, yet they came to Christ. Now here we may observe, (1.) How variously God dispenses his gifts. Some excel, as Peter and John; are very eminent in gifts and graces, and are thereby distinguished from their brethren; others are but ordinary disciples, that mind their duty, and are faithful to him, but do nothing to make themselves remarkable; and yet both the one and the other, the eminent and the obscure, shall sit down together with Christ in glory; nay, and perhaps *the last shall be first.* Of those that do excel, some, like John, are eminently contemplative, have great gifts of knowledge, and serve the church with them; others, like Peter, are eminently active and courageous, are strong, and do exploits, and are thus very serviceable to their generation. Some are useful as the church's eyes, others as the church's hands, and all for the good of the body. (2.) What a great deal of difference there may be between some good people and others in the way of their honouring Christ, and yet both *accepted of him.* Some serve Christ more in acts of devotion, and extraordinary expressions of a religious zeal; and they do well, *to the Lord they do it.* Peter ought not to be censured for casting himself

into the sea, but commended for his zeal and the strength of his affection; and so must those be who, in love to Christ, quit the world, with Mary, to *sit at his feet.* But others serve Christ more in the affairs of the world. They continue in that ship, drag the net, and bring the fish to shore, as the other disciples here; and such ought not to be censured as worldly, for they, in their place, are as truly serving Christ as the other, even in serving tables. If all the disciples had done as Peter did, what had become of their fish and their nets? And yet if Peter had done as they did we had wanted this instance of holy zeal. Christ was well pleased with both, and so must we be. (3.) That there are several ways of bringing Christ's disciples to shore to him from off the sea of this world. Some are brought to him by a violent death, as the martyrs, who threw themselves into the sea, in their zeal for Christ; others are brought to him by a natural death, dragging the net, which is less terrible; but both meet at length on the safe and quiet shore with Christ.

V. What entertainment the Lord Jesus gave them when they came ashore.

1. He had provision ready for them. When they came to land, wet and cold, weary and hungry, they found a good fire there to warm them and dry them, and fish and bread, competent provision for a good meal. (1.) We need not be curious in enquiring whence this fire, and fish, and bread, came, any more than whence the meat came which the ravens brought to Elijah. He that could multiply the loaves and fishes that were could make new ones if he pleased, or turn stones into bread, or send his angels to fetch it, where he knew it was to be had. It is uncertain whether this provision was made ready in the open air, or in some fisher's cabin or hut upon the shore; but here was nothing stately or delicate. We should be content with mean things, for Christ was. (2.) We may be comforted in this instance of Christ's care of his disciples; he has wherewith to supply all our wants, and *knows what things we have need of.* He kindly provided for those fishermen, when they came weary from their work; for *verily those shall be fed who trust in the Lord and do good.* It is encouraging to Christ's ministers, whom he hath made fishers of men, that they may depend upon him who employs them to provide for them; and if they should miss of encouragement in this world, should be reduced as Paul was to *hunger, and thirst,* and *fastings often,* let them content themselves with what they have here; they have better things in reserve, and shall *eat and drink with Christ at his table in his kingdom,* Luke xxii. 30. Awhile ago, *the disciples* had entertained Christ with a *broiled fish* (Luke xxiv. 42), and now, as a friend, he returned their kindness, and entertained them with one; nay, in the draught of fishes, he repaid them more than a hundred fold.

2. He called for some of that which they had caught, and they produced it, *v.* 10, 11. Observe here,

(1.) The command Christ gave them to bring their draught of fish to shore: "Bring of the fish hither, which you have now caught, and let us have some of them;" not as if he needed it, and could not make up a dinner for them without it; but, [1.] He would have them eat the labour of their hands, Ps. cxxviii. 2. What is got by God's blessing on our own industry and honest labour, if withal *God give us power to eat of it, and enjoy good in our labour,* hath a peculiar sweetness in it. It is said of the slothful man that *he roasteth not that which he took in hunting;* he cannot find in his heart to dress what he has been at the pains to take, Prov. xii. 27. But Christ would hereby teach us to use what we have. [2.] He would have them taste the gifts of his miraculous bounty, that they might be witnesses both of his power and of his goodness. The benefits Christ bestows upon us are not to be buried and laid up, but to be used and laid out. [3.] He would give a specimen of the spiritual entertainment he has for all believers, which, in this respect, is most free and familiar—that *he sups with them, and they with him;* their graces are pleasing to him, and his comforts are so to them; what he works in them he accepts from them. [4.] Ministers, who are fishers of men, must bring all they catch to their Master, for on him their success depends.

(2.) Their obedience to this command, *v.* 11. It was said (*v.* 6), *They were not able to draw the net to shore, for the multitude of fishes;* that is, they found it difficult, it was more than they could well do; but he that bade them bring it to shore made it easy. Thus the fishers of men, when they have enclosed souls in the gospel net, cannot bring them to shore, cannot carry on and complete the good work begun, without the continued influence of the divine grace. If he that helped us to catch them, when without his help we should have caught nothing, do not help us to keep them, and draw them to land, by *building them up in their most holy faith,* we shall lose them at last, 1 Cor. iii. 7. Observe, [1.] Who it was that was most active in landing the fishes: it was Peter, who, as in the former instance (*v.* 7), had shown a more zealous affection to his Master's person than any of them, so in this he showed a more ready obedience to his Master's command; but all that are faithful are not alike forward. [2.] The number of the fishes that were caught. They had the curiosity to count them, and perhaps it was in order to the making of a dividend; they were in all a *hundred and fifty and three,* and all *great fishes.* These were many more than they needed for their present supply, but they might sell them, and the money would serve to bear their charges back to Jerusalem, whither they were shortly to return. [3.] A further instance of Christ's care of them, to increase both the miracle and the mercy: *For all there were so many,* and *great fishes* too, *yet was not the net broken;* so that they lost none of their fish, nor damaged their net. It was said (Luke v. 6), *Their net broke.* Perhaps this was a borrowed net, for they had long since left their own; and, if so, Christ would teach us to take care of what we have borrowed, as much as if it were our own. It was well that their net did not break, for they had not now the leisure they had formerly had to mend their nets. The net of the gospel has enclosed multitudes, three thousand in one day, and yet is not broken; it is still as mighty as ever to bring souls to God.

3. He invited them to dinner. Observing them to keep their distance, and that *they were afraid to ask him, Who art thou?* because they *knew it was their Lord,* he called to them very familiarly, *Come, and dine.*

(1.) See here how free Christ was with his disciples; he treated them as friends; he did not say, Come, and wait, Come, and attend me, but *Come, and dine;* not, Go dine by yourselves, as servants are appointed to do, but *Come, and dine* with me. This kind invitation may be alluded to, to illustrate, [1.] The call Christ gives his disciples into communion with him in grace here. *All things are now ready; Come, and dine.* Christ is a feast; come, dine upon him; his flesh is meat indeed, his blood drink indeed. Christ is a friend; come, dine with him, he will bid you welcome, Cant. v. 1. [2.] The call he will give them into the fruition of him in glory hereafter: *Come, ye blessed of my Father; come, and sit down with Abraham, and Isaac, and Jacob.* Christ has wherewithal to dine all his friends and followers; there is room and provision enough for them all.

(2.) See how reverent the disciples were before Christ. They were somewhat shy of using the freedom he invited them to, and, by his courting them to their meat, it should seem that they stood pausing. Being *to eat with a ruler,* such a ruler, *they consider diligently what is before them. None of them durst ask him, Who art thou?* Either, [1.] Because they would not be so bold with him. Though perhaps he appeared now in something of a disguise at first, as to the two disciples when *their eyes were holden that they should not know him,* yet they had very good reason to think it was he, and could be no other. Or, [2.] Because they would not so far betray their own folly. When he had given them this instance of his power and goodness, they must be stupid indeed if they questioned whether it was he or no. When God, in his providence, has given us sensible proofs of his care for our bodies, and has given us, in his grace, manifest proofs of his good-will to our souls, and good work upon them, we should be ashamed of our distrusts, and not dare to question that which he has left us no room to question. Groundless doubts must be stifled, and not started.

4. He carved for them, as the master of the feast, *v.* 13. Observing them to be still shy and timorous, *he comes, and takes bread himself,* and *gives them,* some to each of them, *and fish likewise.* No doubt he craved a blessing and gave thanks (as Luke xxiv. 30), but, it being his known and constant practice, it did not need to be mentioned. (1.) The entertainment here was but ordinary; it was only a fish-dinner, and coarsely dressed; here was nothing pompous, nothing curious; plentiful indeed, but plain and homely. Hunger is the best sauce. Christ, though he entered upon his exalted state, *showed himself alive by eating,* not showed himself a prince by feasting. Those that could not content themselves with bread and fish, unless they had sauce and wine, would scarcely have found in their hearts to dine with Christ himself here. (2.) Christ himself began. Though, perhaps, having a glorified body, he needed not to eat, yet he would show that he had a true body, which was capable of eating. The apostles produced this as one proof of his resurrection, that *they had eaten and drank with him,* Acts x. 41. (3.) He gave the meat about to all his guests. He not only provided it for them, and invited them to it, but he himself divided it among them, and put it into their hands. Thus to him we owe the application, as well as the purchase, of the benefits of redemption. He gives us power to eat of them.

The evangelist leaves them at dinner, and makes this remark (*v.* 14): *This is now the third time that Jesus showed himself alive to his disciples,* or the greater part of them. *This is the third day;* so some. On the day he rose he appeared five times; the second day was that day seven-night; and this was the third. Or this was his third appearance to any considerable number of his disciples together; though he had appeared to Mary, to the women, to the two disciples, and to Cephas, yet he had but twice before this appeared to any company of them together. This is taken notice of, [1.] For confirming the truth of his resurrection; the vision was doubled, was trebled, for the thing was certain. Those who believed not the first sign would be brought to believe the voice of the latter signs. [2.] As an instance of Christ's continued kindness to his disciples; once, and again, and a third time, he visited them. It is good to keep account of Christ's gracious visits; for he keeps account of them, and they will be remembered against us if we walk unworthily of them, as they were against Solomon, when he was reminded that the Lord God of Israel had appeared unto him twice. *This is now the third;* have we made a due improvement of *the first and second?* See 2 Cor. xii. 14. *This is the third,* perhaps it may be the last.

15 So when they had dined, Jesus
saith to Simon Peter, Simon, *son* of
Jonas, lovest thou me more than
these? He saith unto him, Yea,
Lord; thou knowest that I love thee.
He saith unto him, Feed my lambs.
16 He saith to him again the second time, Simon, *son* of Jonas,
lovest thou me? He saith unto him,
Yea, Lord; thou knowest that I love
thee. He saith unto him, Feed my
sheep. 17 He saith unto him the
third time, Simon, *son* of Jonas,
lovest thou me? Peter was grieved
because he said unto him the third
time, Lovest thou me? And he said
unto him, Lord, thou knowest all
things; thou knowest that I love
thee. Jesus saith unto him, Feed
my sheep. 18 Verily, verily, I say
unto thee, When thou wast young,
thou girdedst thyself, and walkedst
whither thou wouldest: but when
thou shalt be old, thou shalt stretch
forth thy hands, and another shall
gird thee, and carry *thee* whither thou
wouldest not. 19 This spake he,
signifying by what death he should
glorify God. And when he had
spoken this, he saith unto him, Follow me.

We have here Christ's discourse with Peter after dinner, so much of it as relates to himself, in which,

I. He examines his love to him, and gives him a charge concerning his flock, *v.* 15—17. Observe,

1. When Christ entered into this discourse with Peter.—It was after they had dined: they had all eaten, and were filled, and, it is probable, were entertained with such edifying discourse as our Lord Jesus used to make his table-talk. Christ foresaw that what he had to say to Peter would give him some uneasiness, and therefore would not say it till they had dined, because he would not spoil his dinner. Peter was conscious to himself that he had incurred his Master's displeasure, and could expect no other than to be upbraided with his treachery and ingratitude. "Was this thy kindness to thy friend? Did not I tell thee what a coward thou wouldest prove?" Nay, he might justly expect to be struck out of the roll of the disciples, and to be expelled the sacred college. Twice, if not thrice, he had seen his Master since his resurrection, and he said not a word to him of it. We may suppose Peter full of doubts upon what terms he stood with his Master; sometimes hoping the best, because he had received favours from him in common with the rest; yet not without some fears, lest the chiding would come at last that would pay for all. But now, at length, his Master put him out of his pain, said what he had to say to him, and confirmed him in his place as an apostle. He did not tell him of his fault hastily, but deferred it for some time; did not tell him of it unseasonably, to disturb the company at dinner, but *when they had dined* together, in token of reconciliation, then discoursed he with him about it, not as with a criminal, but as with a friend. Peter had reproached himself for it, and therefore Christ did not reproach him for it, nor tell him of it directly, but only by a tacit intimation; and, being satisfied in his sincerity, the offence was not only forgiven, but forgotten; and Christ let him know that he was as dear to him as ever. Herein he has given us an encouraging instance of his tenderness towards penitents, and has taught us, in like manner, to restore such as are fallen with a spirit of meekness.

2. What was the discourse itself. Here was the same question three times asked, the same answer three times returned, and the same reply three times given, with very little variation, and yet no *vain repetition.* The same thing was repeated by our Saviour, in speaking it, the more to affect Peter, and the other disciples that were present; it is repeated by the evangelist, in writing it, the more to affect us, and all that read it.

(1.) Three times Christ asks Peter whether he loves him or no. The first time the question is, *Simon, son of Jonas, lovest thou me more than these?* Observe,

[1.] How he calls him: *Simon, son of Jonas.* He speaks to him by name, the more to affect him, as Luke xxii. 31. *Simon, Simon.* He does not call him *Cephas,* nor *Peter,* the name he had given him (for he had lost the credit of his strength and stability, which those names signified), but his original name, *Simon.* Yet he gives him no hard language, does not call him out of his name, though he deserved it; but as he had called him when he pronounced him blessed, *Simon Bar-jona,* Matt. xvi. 17. He calls him *son of Jonas* (or *John* or *Johanan*) to remind him of his extraction, how mean it was, and unworthy the honour to which he was advanced.

[2.] How he catechises him: *Lovest thou me more than these?*

First, Lovest thou me? If we would try whether we are Christ's disciples indeed, this must be the enquiry, Do we love him? But there was a special reason why Christ put it now to Peter. 1. His fall had given occasion to doubt of his love: "Peter, I have cause to suspect thy love; for if thou hadst loved me thou wouldst not have been ashamed and afraid to own me in my sufferings. How canst thou say thou lovest me, when thy heart was not with me? Note, We must not reckon it an affront to have our sincerity questioned, when we ourselves have done that which makes it questionable; after a shaking fall, we must take heed of settling too soon, lest we settle upon a wrong bottom. The question is affecting; he does not ask, "Dost thou fear me? Dost thou honour me? Dost thou admire me?" but, "Dost thou love me? Give but proof of this, and the affront shall be passed by, and no more said of it." Peter had professed himself a penitent, witness his tears, and his return to the society of the disciples; he was now upon his probation as a penitent; but the question is not, "Simon, how much hast thou wept? how often hast thou fasted, and afflicted thy soul?" but, Dost thou love me? It is this that will make the other expressions of repentance acceptable. The great thing Christ eyes in penitents is their eyeing him in their repentance. *Much is forgiven her,* not because *she wept much,* but because *she loved much.* 2. His function would give occasion for the exercise of his *love.* Before Christ would commit his *sheep* to his care, he asked him, *Lovest thou me?* Christ has such a tender regard to his flock that he will not trust it with any but those that love him, and therefore will love all that are his for his sake. Those that do not truly love Christ will never truly love the souls of men, nor will naturally care for their state as they should; nor will that minister love his work that does not love his Master. Nothing but the love of Christ will constrain ministers to go cheerfully through the difficulties and discouragements they meet with in their work, 2 Cor. v. 13, 14. But this love will make their work easy, and them in good earnest in it.

Secondly, Lovest thou me more than these? πλεῖον τούτων. 1. "*Lovest thou me more than thou lovest these,* more than thou lovest these persons? Dost thou love me more than thou dost James or John, thy intimate friends, or Andrew, thy own brother and companion: Those do not love Christ aright that do not love him better than the best friend they have in the world, and make it to appear whenever they stand in comparison or in competition. Or, "*more than thou lovest these things,* these boats and nets—more than all the pleasure of fishing, which some make a recreation of—more than the gain of fishing, which others make a calling of." Those only love Christ indeed that love him better than all the delights of sense and all the profits of this world. "*Lovest thou me more than thou lovest these* occupations thou art now employed in? If so, leave them, to employ thyself wholly in feeding my flock." So Dr. Whitby. 2. "*Lovest thou me more than these love me,* more than any of the rest of the disciples love me? And then the question is intended to upbraid him with his vain-glorious boast, *Though all men should deny thee, yet will not I.* "Art thou still of the same mind?" Or, to intimate to him that he had now more reason to love him than any of them had, for more had been forgiven to him than to any of them, as much as his sin in denying Christ was greater than theirs in forsaking him. *Tell me therefore which of them will love him most?* Luke vii. 42. Note, We should all study to excel in our love to Christ. It is no breach of the peace to strive which shall love Christ best; nor any breach of good manners to go before others in this love.

Thirdly, The second and third time that Christ put this question, 1. He left out the comparison *more than these,* because Peter, in his answer, modestly left it out, not willing to compare himself with his brethren, much less to prefer himself before them. Though we cannot say, *We* love Christ more than others do, yet we shall be accepted if we can say, We love him indeed. 2. In the last he altered the word, as it is in the original. In the first two enquiries, the original word is Αγαπᾷς με—*Dost thou retain a kindness for me?* In answer to which Peter uses another word, more emphatic, Φιλῶ σε—*I love thee dearly.* In putting the question the last time, Christ uses that word: And dost thou indeed love me dearly?

(2.) Three times Peter returns the same answer to Christ: *Yea, Lord, thou knowest that I love thee.* Observe, [1.] Peter does not pretend to love Christ more than the rest of the disciples did. He is now ashamed of that rash word of his, *Though all men deny thee, yet will not I;* and he had reason to be ashamed of it. Note, Though we must aim to be better than others, yet we must, *in lowliness of mind, esteem others better than ourselves;* for we know more evil of ourselves than we do of any of our brethren. [2.] Yet he professes again and again that he loves Christ: *Yea, Lord,* surely *I love thee;* I were unworthy to live if I did not." He had a high esteem and value for him, a grateful sense of his kindness, and was entirely devoted to his honour and interest; his desire was towards him, as one he was undone without; and his delight in him, as one he should be unspeakably happy in. This amounts to a profession of repentance for his sin, for it grieves us to have affronted one we love; and to a promise of adherence to him for the future: *Lord, I love thee,* and *will never leave thee.* Christ *prayed that his faith might not fail* (Luke xxii.32), and, because his faith did not fail, his love did not; for faith will work by love. Peter had forfeited his claim of relation to Christ. He was now to be re-admitted, upon his repentance. Christ puts his trial upon this issue: *Dost thou love me?* And Peter joins issue upon it: *Lord, I love thee.* Note, Those who can truly say, through grace, that they love Jesus Christ, may take the comfort of their interest in him, notwithstanding their daily infirmities. [3.] He appeals to Christ himself for the proof of it: *Thou knowest that I love thee;* and *the third time* yet more emphatically: *Thou knowest all things, thou knowest that I love thee.* He does not vouch his fellow-disciples to witness for him—they might be deceived in him; nor does he think his own word might be taken—the credit of that was destroyed already; but he calls Christ himself to witness, *First,* Peter was sure that Christ knew all things, and particularly that he knew the heart, and was a *discerner of the thoughts and intents of it, ch.* xvi. 30. *Secondly,* Peter was satisfied of this, that Christ, who knew all things, knew the sincerity of his love to him, and would be ready to attest it in his favour. It is a terror to a hypocrite to think that Christ knows all things; for the divine omniscience will be a witness against him. But it is a comfort to a sincere Christian that he has that to appeal to: *My witness is in heaven, my record is on high.* Christ knows us better than we know ourselves. Though we know not our own uprightness, he knows it. [4.] *He was grieved* when Christ asked him the *third time, Lovest thou me? v.* 17. *First,* Because it put him in mind of his threefold denial of Christ, and was plainly designed to do so; *and when he thought thereon he wept.* Every remembrance of past sins, even pardoned sins, renews the sorrow of a true penitent. *Thou shalt be ashamed, when I am pacified towards thee. Secondly,* Because it put him in fear lest his Master foresaw some further miscarriage of his, which would be as great a contradiction to his profession of love to him as the former was. "Surely," thinks Peter, "my Master would not thus put me upon the rack if he did not see some cause for it. What would become of me if I should be again tempted?" Godly sorrow works carefulness and fear, 2 Cor. vii. 11.

(3.) Three times Christ committed the care of his flock to Peter: *Feed my lambs; feed my sheep; feed my sheep.* [1.] Those whom Christ committed to Peter's care were his lambs and his sheep. The church of Christ is his flock, *which he hath purchased with his own blood* (Acts xx. 28), and he is *the chief shepherd* of it. In this flock some are lambs, young and tender and weak, others are sheep, grown to some strength and maturity. The Shepherd here takes care of both, and of the lambs first, for upon all occasions he showed a particular tenderness for them. *He gathers the lambs in his arms, and carries them in his bosom.* Isa. xl. 11. [2.] The charge he gives him concerning them is to feed them. The word used in *v.* 15, 17, is βόσκε, which strictly signifies to *give them food;* but the word used in *v.* 16 is ποίμαινε, which signifies more largely to do all the offices of a shepherd to them: "*Feed the lambs* with that which is proper for them, and *the sheep* likewise with *food convenient. The lost sheep of the house of Israel,* seek and feed them, and *the other sheep* also *which are not of this fold.*" Note, It is the duty of all Christ's ministers to feed his lambs and sheep. *Feed them,* that is, teach them; for the doctrine of the gospel is spiritual food. *Feed them,* that is, "Lead them to the green pastures, presiding in their religious assemblies, and ministering all the ordinances to them. Feed them by personal application to their respective state and case; not only lay meat before them, but feed those with it that are wilful and will not, or weak and cannot feed themselves." *When Christ ascended on high, he gave pastors,* left his flock with those that loved him, and would take care of them for his sake. [3.] But why did he give this charge particularly to Peter? Ask the advocates for the pope's supremacy, and they will tell you that Christ hereby designed to give to Peter, and therefore to his successors, and therefore to the bishops of Rome, an absolute dominion and headship over the whole Christian church; as if a charge to serve the sheep gave a power to lord it over all the shepherds; whereas, it is plain, Peter himself never claimed such a power, nor did the other disciples ever own it in him. This charge given to Peter to preach the gospel is by a strange artifice made to support the usurpation of his pretended successors, that fleece the sheep, and, instead of feeding them, feed upon them. But the particular application to Peter here was designed, *First,* To restore him to his apostleship, now that he repented of his abjuration of it, and to renew his commission, both for his own satisfaction, and for the satisfaction of his brethren. A commission given to one convicted of a crime is supposed to amount to a pardon; no doubt, this commission given to Peter was an evidence that Christ was reconciled to him, else he would never have reposed such a confidence in him. Of some that have deceived us we say, "Though we forgive them, we will never trust them;" but Christ, when he forgave Peter, trusted him with the most valuable treasure he had on earth. *Secondly,* It was designed to quicken him to a diligent discharge of his office as an apostle. Peter was a man of a bold and zealous spirit, always forward to speak and act, and, lest he should be tempted to take upon him the directing of the shepherds, he is charged to feed the sheep, as he himself charges all the presbyters to do, and not *to lord it over God's heritage,* 1 Pet. v. 2, 3. If he will be doing, let him do this, and pretend no further. *Thirdly,* What Christ said to him he said to all his disciples; he charged them all, not only to be fishers of men (though that was said to Peter, Luke v. 10), by the conversion of sinners, but feeders of the flock, by the edification of saints.

II. Christ, having thus appointed Peter his doing work, next appoints him his suffering work. Having confirmed to him the honour of an apostle, he now tells him of further preferment designed him—the honour of a martyr. Observe,

1. How his martyrdom is foretold (*v.* 18): *Thou shalt stretch forth thy hands,* being compelled to it, and *another shall gird thee* (as a prisoner that is pinioned) *and carry thee whither* naturally *thou wouldest not.*

(1.) He prefaces the notice he gives to Peter of his sufferings with a solemn asseveration, *Verily, verily, I say unto thee.* It was not spoken of as a thing probable, which perhaps might happen, but as a thing certain, *I say it to thee.* "Others, perhaps, will say to thee, as thou didst to me, *This shall not be unto thee;* but I say it shall." As Christ foresaw all his own sufferings, so he foresaw the sufferings of all his followers, and foretold them, though not in particular, as to Peter, yet in general, that they must take up their cross. Having charged him to feed his sheep, he bids him not to expect ease and honour in it, but trouble and persecution, and to suffer ill for doing well.

(2.) He foretels particularly that he should die a violent death, by the hands of an executioner. The stretching out of his hands, some think, points at the manner of his death by crucifying; and the tradition of the ancients, if we may rely upon that, informs us that Peter was crucified at Rome under Nero, A. D. 68, or, as others say, 79. Others think it points at the bonds and imprisonments which those are hamperd with that are sentenced to death. The pomp and solemnity of an execution add much to the terror of death, and to an eye of sense make it look doubly formidable. Death, in these horrid shapes, has often been the lot of Christ's faithful ones, who yet have *overcome it by the blood of the Lamb.* This prediction, though pointing chiefly at his death, was to have its accomplishment in his previous sufferings. It began to be fulfilled presently, when he was imprisoned, Acts iv. 3; v. 18; xii. 4. No more is implied here in his being carried whither he would not than that it was a violent death that he should be carried to, such a death as even innocent nature could not think of without dread, nor approach without some reluctance. He that puts on the Christian does not put off the man. Christ himself prayed against the bitter cup. A natural aversion to pain and death is well reconcileable with a holy submission to the will of God in both. Blessed Paul, though longing to be unloaded, owns he cannot desire *to be unclothed,* 2 Cor. v. 4.

(3.) He compares this with his former liberty. "Time was when thou knewest not any of these hardships, *thou girdedsl thyself, and walkedst whither thou wouldest.*" Where trouble comes we are apt to aggravate it with this, that it has been otherwise; and to fret the more at the grievances of restraint, sickness, and poverty, because we have known the sweets of liberty, health, and plenty, Job xxix. 2; Ps. xlii. 4. But we may turn it the other way, and reason thus with ourselves: "How many years of prosperity have I enjoyed more than I deserved and improved? And, having received good, shall I not receive evil also? See here, [1.] What a change may possibly be made with us, as to our condition in this world! Those that have *girded themselves with strength and honour,* and indulged themselves in the greatest liberties, perhaps levities, may be reduced to such circumstances as are the reverse of all this. See 1 Sam. ii. 5. [2.] What a change is presently made with those that leave all to follow Christ! They must no longer gird themselves, but he must gird them! and must no longer walk whither they will, but whither he will. [3.] What a change will certainly be made with us if we should live to be old! Those who, when they were young, had strength of body and vigour of mind, and could easily go through business and hardship, and take the pleasures they had a mind to, when they shall be old, will find their strength gone, like Samson, when his hair was cut and he could *not shake himself as at other times.*

(4.) Christ tells Peter he should suffer thus in his old age. [1.] Though he should be old, and in the course of nature not likely to live long, yet his enemies would hasten him out of the world violently when he was about to retire out of it peaceably, and would put out his candle when it was almost burned down to the socket. See 2 Chron. xxxvi. 17. [2.] God would shelter him from the rage of his enemies till he should come to be old, that he might be made the fitter for sufferings, and the church might the longer enjoy his services.

2. The explication of this prediction (*v* 19), *This spoke he* to Peter, *signifying by what death he should glorify God,* when he had finished his course. Observe, (1.) That it is not only *appointed to all once to die,* but it is appointed to each what death he shall die, whether natural or violent, slow or sudden, easy or painful. When Paul speaks of so *great a death,* he intimates that there are degrees of death; there is one way into the world, but many ways out, and God has determined which way we should go. (2.) That it is the great concern of every good man, whatever death he dies, to glorify God in it; for what is our chief end but this, *to die to the Lord, at the word of the Lord?* When we die patiently, submitting to the will of God,—die cheerfully, rejoicing in hope of the glory of God,—and die usefully, witnessing to the truth and goodness of religion and encouraging others, we glorify God in dying: and this is *the earnest expectation and hope* of all good Christians, as it was Paul's, *that Christ may be magnified in them living and dying,* Phil. i. 20. (3.) That the death of the martyrs was in a special manner for the glorifying of God. The truths of God, which they died in the defence of, are hereby confirmed.

The grace of God, which carried them with so much constancy through their sufferings, is hereby magnified. And the consolations of God, which have abounded towards them in their sufferings, and his promises, the springs of their consolations, have hereby been recommended to the faith and joy of all the saints. The blood of the martyrs has been the seed of the church, and the conversion and establishment of thousands. *Precious* therefore *in the sight of the Lord is the death of his saints,* as that which honours him; and those who thereby at such an expense honour him he will honour.

3. The word of command he gives him hereupon: *When he had spoken thus,* observing Peter perhaps to look blank upon it, *he saith unto him, Follow me.* Probably he rose from the place where he had sat at dinner, walked off a little, and bade Peter attend him. This word, *Follow me,* was, (1.) A further confirmation of his restoration to his Master's favour, and to his apostleship; for *Follow me* was the first call. (2.) It was an explication of the prediction of his sufferings, which perhaps Peter at first did not fully understand, till Christ gave him that key to it, *Follow me:* "Expect to be treated as I have been, and to tread the same bloody path that I have trodden before thee; *for the disciple is not greater than his Lord.* (3.) It was to excite him to, and encourage him in, faithfulness and diligence in his work as an apostle. He had told him to *feed his sheep,* and let him set his Master before him as an example of pastoral care: "Do as I have done." Let the under-shepherds study to imitate the Chief Shepherd. They had followed Christ while he was here upon earth, and now that he was leaving them he still preaches the same duty to them, though to be performed in another way, *Follow me;* still they must follow the rules he had given them and the example he had set them. And what greater encouragement could they have than this, both in services and in sufferings? [1.] That herein they did follow him, and it was their present honour; who would be ashamed to follow such a leader? [2.] That hereafter they should follow him, and that would be their future happiness; and so it is a repetition of the promise Christ had given Peter (*ch.* xiii. 36), *Thou shalt follow me afterwards.* Those that faithfully follow Christ in grace shall certainly follow him to glory.

20 Then Peter, turning about, seeth
the disciple whom Jesus loved following;
which also leaned on his breast
at supper, and said, Lord, which is
he that betrayeth thee? 21 Peter
seeing him saith to Jesus, Lord, and
what *shall* this man *do?* 22 Jesus
saith unto him, If I will that he tarry
till I come, what *is that* to thee? follow
thou me. 23 Then went this
saying abroad among the brethren,
that that disciple should not die: yet
Jesus said not unto him, He shall not
die; but, If I will that he tarry till I
come, what is *that* to thee? 24 This
is the disciple which testifieth of these
things, and wrote these things: and
we know that his testimony is true.
25 And there are also many other
things which Jesus did, the which,
if they should be written every
one, I suppose that even the world
itself could not contain the books
that should be written. Amen.

In these verses we have,

I. The conference Christ had with Peter concerning John, the beloved disciple, in which we have,

1. The eye Peter cast upon him (*v.* 20): Peter, in obedience to his Master's orders, followed him, and *turning about,* pleased with the honours his Master now did him, *he sees the disciple whom Jesus loved following* likewise. Observe here, (1.) How John is described. He does not name himself, as thinking his own name not worthy to be preserved in these records; but gives such a description of himself as sufficiently informs us whom he meant, and withal gives us a reason why he followed Christ so closely. *He was the disciple whom Jesus loved,* for whom he had a particular kindness above the rest; and therefore you cannot blame him for coveting to be as much as possible within hearing of Christ's gracious words during those few precious minutes with which Christ favoured his disciples. It is probable that mention is here made of John's having *leaned on Jesus's breast* and his enquiring concerning the traitor, which he did at the instigation of Peter (*ch.* xiii. 24), as a reason why Peter made the following enquiry concerning him, to repay him for the former kindness. Then John was in the favourite's place, lying in Christ's bosom, and he improved the opportunity to oblige Peter. And now that Peter was in the favourite's place, called to take a walk with Christ, he thought himself bound in gratitude to put such a question for John as he thought would oblige him, we all being desirous to know things to come. Note, As we have interest at the throne of grace, we should improve it for the benefit of one another. Those that help us by their prayers at one time should be helped by us with ours at another time. This is the *communion of saints.* (2.) What he did: He also followed Jesus, which shows how well he loved his company; where he was there also would this servant of his be. When Christ called Peter to follow him, it looked as if he designed to have some private talk with him; but such

an affection John had to his Master that he would rather do a thing that seemed rude than lose the benefit of any of Christ's discourse. What Christ said to Peter he took as said to himself; for that word of command, *Follow me,* was given to all the disciples. At least he desired to have fellowship with those that had fellowship with Christ, and to accompany those that attended him. The bringing of one to follow Christ should engage others. *Draw me and we will run after thee,* Cant. i. 4. (3.) The notice Peter took of it: *He, turning about, seeth him.* This may be looked upon either, [1.] As a culpable diversion from following his Master; he should have been wholly intent upon that, and have waited to hear what Christ had further to say to him, and then was he looking about him to see who followed. Note, The best men find it hard to *attend upon the Lord without distraction,* hard to keep their minds so closely fixed as they should be in following Christ: and a needless and unseasonable regard to our brethren often diverts us from communion with God. Or, [2.] As a laudable concern for his fellow-disciples. He was not so elevated with the honour his Master did him, in singling him out from the rest, as to deny a kind look to one that followed. Acts of love to our brethren must go along with actings of faith in Christ.

2. The enquiry Peter made concerning him (*v.* 21): "*Lord, and what shall this man do?* Thou hast told me my work—to feed the sheep; and my lot—to be *carried whither I would not.* What shall be his work, and his lot?" Now this may be taken as the language, (1.) Of concern for John, and kindness to him: "Lord, thou showest me a great deal of favour. Here comes thy beloved disciple, who never forfeited thy favour, as I have done; he expects to be taken notice of; hast thou nothing to say to him? Wilt thou not tell how he must be employed, and how he must be honoured?" (2.) Or of uneasiness at what Christ had said to him concerning his sufferings: "Lord, must I alone be *carried whither I would not?* Must I be marked out to be run down, and must this man have no share of the cross?" It is hard to reconcile ourselves to distinguishing sufferings, and the troubles in which we think we stand alone. (3.) Or of curiosity, and a fond desire of knowing things to come, concerning others, as well as himself. It seems, by Christ's answer, there was something amiss in the question. When Christ had given him the charge of such a treasure, and the notice of such a trial, it had well become him to have said, "Lord, and what shall I do then to approve myself faithful to such a trust, in such a trial? *Lord, increase my faith.* As my day is, let my strength be." But instead of this, [1.] He seems more concerned for another than for himself. So apt are we to be busy in other men's matters, but negligent in the concerns of our own souls—quick-sighted abroad, but dim-sighted at home—judging others, and prognosticating what they will do, when we have enough to do to *prove our own work,* and *understand our own way.* [2.] He seems more concerned about events than about duty. John was younger than Peter, and, in the course of nature, likely to survive him: "Lord," says he, "what times shall he be reserved for?" Whereas, if God by his grace enable us to persevere to the end, and finish well, and get safely to heaven, we need not ask, "What shall be the lot of those that shall come after us?" Is it not well if peace and truth be in my days? Scripture predictions must be eyed for the directing of our consciences, not the satisfying of our curiosity.

3. Christ's reply to this enquiry (*v.* 22), "*If I will that he tarry till I come,* and do not suffer as thou must, *what is that to thee.* Mind thou thy own duty, the present duty, *follow thou me.*"

(1.) There seems to be here an intimation of Christ's purpose concerning John, in two things:—[1.] That he should not die a violent death, like Peter, but should tarry till Christ himself came by a natural death to fetch him to himself. The most credible of the ancient historians tell us that John was the only one of all the twelve that did not actually die a martyr. He was often in jeopardy, in bonds and banishments; but at length died in his bed in a good old age. Note, *First,* At death Christ comes to us to call us to account; and it concerns us to be ready for his coming. *Secondly,* Though Christ calls out some of his disciples to resist unto blood, yet not all. Though the crown of martyrdom is bright and glorious, yet the beloved disciple comes short of it. [2.] That he should not die till after Christ's coming to destroy Jerusalem: so some understand his tarrying till Christ comes. All the other apostles died before that destruction; but John survived it many years. God wisely so ordered it that one of the apostles should live so long as to close up the canon of the New Testament, which John did solemnly (Rev. xxii. 18), and to obviate the design of the enemy that sowed tares even before the servants fell asleep. John lived to confront Ebion, and Cerinthus, and other heretics, who rose betimes, *speaking perverse things.*

(2.) Others think that it is only a rebuke to Peter's curiosity, and that his tarrying till Christ's second coming is only the supposition of an absurdity: "Wherefore askest thou after that which is foreign and secret? Suppose I should design that John should never die, what does that concern thee? It is nothing to thee, when, or where, or how, John must die. I have told thee how thou must die for thy part; it is enough for thee to know that, *Follow thou me.*" Note, It is the will of Christ that his disciples should mind their own present duty, and not be curious in their enquiries about future events, concerning either themselves or others. [1.] There are many things we are apt to be solicitous about that are nothing to us. Other people's characters are nothing to us; it is out of our line to judge them, Rom. xiv. 4. Whatsoever they are, saith Paul, it makes no matter to me. Other people's affairs are nothing to us to intermeddle in; we must quietly work, and mind our own business. Many nice and curious questions are put by the *scribes* and *disputers of this world* concerning the counsels of God, and the state of the invisible world, concerning which we may say, *What is this to us?* What do you think will become of such and such? is a common question, which may easily be answered with another: *What is that to me?* To his own Master he stands or falls. What is it to us to *know the times and the seasons?* Secret things belong not to us. [2.] The great thing that is all in all to us is duty, and not event; for duty is ours, events are God's—our own duty, and not another's; for every one shall bear his own burden—our present duty, and not the duty of the time to come; for sufficient to the day shall be the directions thereof: a *good man's steps are ordered by the Lord,* (Ps. xxxvii. 23); he is guided step by step. Now all our duty is summed up in this one of following Christ. We must attend his motions, and accommodate ourselves to them, follow him to do him honour, as the servant his master; we must walk in the way in which he walked, and aim to be where he is. And, if we will closely attend to the duty of following Christ, we shall find neither heart nor time to meddle with that which does not belong to us.

4. The mistake which arose from this saying of Christ, that *that disciple should not die,* but abide with the church to the end of time; together with the suppressing of this motion by a repetition of Christ's words, *v.* 23. Observe here,

(1.) The easy rise of a mistake in the church by misconstruing the sayings of Christ, and turning a supposition to a position. Because John must not die a martyr, they conclude he must not die at all.

[1.] They were inclined to expect it because they could not choose but desire it. *Quod volumus facile credimus—We easily believe what we wish to be true.* For John to abide in the flesh when the rest were gone, and to continue in the world till Christ's second coming, they think, will be a great blessing to the church, which in every age might have recourse to him as an oracle. When they must lose Christ's bodily presence, they hope they shall have that of his beloved disciple; as if that must supply the want of his, forgetting that the blessed Spirit, the Comforter, was to do that. Note, We are apt to dote too much on men and means, instruments and external helps, and to think we are happy if we may but have them always with us; whereas God will change his workmen, and yet carry on his work, that the *excellency of the power may be of God, and not of men.* There is no need of immortal ministers to be the guides of the church, while it is under the conduct of an eternal Spirit.

[2.] Perhaps they were confirmed in their expectations when they now found that John survived all the rest of the apostles. Because he lived long, they were ready to think he should live always; whereas *that which waxeth old is ready to vanish away,* Heb. viii. 13.

[3.] However, it took rise from a saying of Christ's, misunderstood, and then made a saying of the church. Hence learn, *First,* The uncertainty of human tradition, and the folly of building our faith upon it. Here was a tradition, an apostolical tradition, a saying that *went abroad among the brethren.* It was early; it was common; it was public; and yet it was false. How little then are those unwritten traditions to be relied upon which the council of Trent hath decreed to be received with a *veneration and pious affection equal to that which is owing to the holy scripture.* Here was a traditional exposition of scripture. No new saying of Christ's advanced, but only a construction put by the brethren upon what he did really say, and yet it was a misconstruction. Let the scripture be its own interpreter and explain itself, as it is in a great measure its own evidence and proves itself, for it is light. *Secondly,* The aptness of men to misinterpret the sayings of Christ. The grossest errors have sometimes shrouded themselves under the umbrage of incontestable truths; and the scriptures themselves have been wrested by the unlearned and unstable. We must not think it strange if we hear the sayings of Christ misinterpreted, quoted to patronise the errors of antichrist, and the impudent doctrine of transubstantiation—for instance, pretending to build upon that blessed word of Christ, *This is my body.*

(2.) The easy rectifying of such mistakes, by adhering to the word of Christ, and abiding by that. So the evangelist here corrects and controls that saying among the brethren, by repeating the very words of Christ. He did not say that that disciple should not die. Let us not say so then; but he said, *If I will that he tarry till I come, what is that to thee?* He said so, and no more. *Add thou not unto his words.* Let the words of Christ speak for themselves, and let no sense be put upon them but what is genuine and natural; and in that let us agree. Note, The best end of men's controversies would be to keep to the express words of scripture, and speak, as well as think, according to that word, Isa. viii. 20. Scripture language is the safest and most proper vehicle of scripture truth: the *words which the Holy Ghost teacheth,* 1 Cor. ii. 13. As the scripture itself, duly attended to, is the best weapon wherewith to wound all dangerous errors (and therefore deists, Socinians, papists, and enthusiasts do all they can to derogate from the authority of the scripture), so the scripture itself, humbly subscribed to, is the best weapon-salve to heal the wounds that are made by different modes of expression concerning the same truths. Those that cannot agree in the same logic and metaphysics, and the propriety of the same terms of air, and the application of them, may yet agree in the same scripture terms, and then may agree to love one another.

II. We have here the conclusion of this gospel, and with it of the evangelical story, *v.* 24, 25. This evangelist ends not so abruptly as the other three did, but with a sort of cadency.

1. This gospel concludes with an account of the author or penman of it, connected by a decent transition to that which went before (*v.* 24): *This is the disciple which testifies of these things* to the present age, and wrote these things for the benefit of posterity, even this same that Peter and his Master had that conference about in the foregoing verses—John the apostle. Observe here, (1.) Those who wrote the history of Christ were not ashamed to put their names to it. John here does in effect subscribe his name. As we are sure who was the author of the first five books of the Old Testament, which were the foundation of that revelation, so we are sure who were the penmen of the four gospels and the Acts, the pentateuch of the New Testament. The record of Christ's life and death is not the report of we know not who, but was drawn up by men of known integrity, who were ready not only to depose it upon oath, but, which was more, to *seal it with their blood.* (2.) Those who wrote the history of Christ wrote upon their own knowledge, not by hearsay, but what they themselves were eye and ear witnesses of. The penman of this history was a disciple, a beloved disciple, one that had leaned on Christ's breast, that had himself heard his sermons and conferences, had seen his miracles, and the proofs of his resurrection. This is he who testifies what he was well assured of. (3.) Those who wrote the history of Christ, as they testified what they had seen, so they wrote what they had first testified. It was published by word of mouth, with the greatest assurance, before it was committed to writing. They testified it in the pulpit, testified it at the bar, solemnly averred it, stedfastly avowed it, not as travellers give an account of their travels, to entertain the company, but as witnesses upon oath give account of what they know in a matter of consequence, with the utmost caution and exactness, to found a verdict upon. What they wrote they wrote as an affidavit, which they would abide by. Their writings are standing testimonies to the world of the truth of Christ's doctrine, and will be testimonies either for us or against us according as we do or do not receive it. (4.) It was graciously appointed, for the support and benefit of the church, that the history of Christ should be put into writing, that it might with the greater fulness and certainty spread to every place, and last through every age.

2. It concludes with an attestation of the truth of what had been here related: *We know that his testimony is true.* This may be taken either, (1.) As expressing the common sense of mankind in matters of this nature, which is, that the testimony of one who is an eye-witness, is of unspotted reputation, solemnly deposes what he has seen, and puts it into writing for the greater certainty, is an unexceptionable evidence. *We know,* that is, All the world knows, that the testimony of such a one is valid, and the common faith of mankind requires us to give credit to it, unless we can disprove it; and in other cases verdict and judgment are given upon such testimonies. The truth of the gospel comes confirmed by all the evidence we can rationally desire or expect in a thing of this nature. The matter of fact, that Jesus did preach such doctrines, and work such miracles, and rise from the dead, is proved, beyond contradiction, by such evidence as is always admitted in other cases, and therefore to the satisfaction of all that are impartial; and then let the doctrine recommend itself, and let the miracles prove it to be of God. Or, (2.) As expressing the satisfaction of the churches *at that time* concerning the truth of what is here related. Some take it for the subscription of the church of Ephesus, others of the angels or ministers of the churches of Asia to this narrative. Not as if an inspired writing needed any attestation from men, or could thence receive any addition to its credibility; but hereby they recommended it to the notice of the churches, as an inspired writing, and declared the satisfaction they received by it. Or, (3.) As expressing the evangelist's own assurance of the truth of what he wrote, like that (*ch.* xix. 35), *He knows that he saith true.* He speaks of himself in the plural number, *We know,* not for majesty-sake, but for modesty-sake, as 1 John i. 1, *That which we have seen;* and 2 Pet. i 16. Note, The evangelists themselves were entirely satisfied of the truth of what they have testified and transmitted to us. They do not require us to believe what they did not believe themselves; no, they knew that their testimony was true, for they ventured both this life and the other upon it; threw away this life, and depended upon another, on the credit of what they spoke and wrote.

3. It concludes with an *et cetera,* with a reference to *many other things;* very memorable, said and done by our Lord Jesus, which were well known by many then living, but not thought fit to be recorded for posterity, *v.* 25. There were many things very remarkable and improvable, which, if they should be written at large, with the several

circumstances of them, even the world itself, that is, all the libraries in it, could not contain the books that might be written. Thus he concludes like an orator, as Paul (Heb. xi. 32), *What shall I more say? For the time would fail me.* If it be asked why the gospels are not larger, why they did not make the New-Testament history as copious and as long as the Old, it may be answered,

(1.) It was not because they had exhausted their subject, and had nothing more to write that was worth writing; no, there were many of Christ's sayings and doings not recorded by any of the evangelists, which yet were worthy to be written in letters of gold. For, [1.] Every thing that Christ said and did was worth our notice, and capable of being improved. He never spoke an idle word, nor did an idle thing; nay, he never spoke nor did any thing mean, or little, or trifling, which is more than can be said of the wisest or best of men. [2.] His miracles were many, very many, of many kinds, and the same often repeated, as occasion offered. Though one true miracle might perhaps suffice to prove a divine commission, yet the repetition of the miracles upon a great variety of persons, in a great variety of cases, and before a great variety of witnesses, helped very much to prove them true miracles. Every new miracle rendered the report of the former the more credible; and the multitude of them renders the whole report incontestable. [3.] The evangelists upon several occasions give general accounts of Christ's preaching and miracles, inclusive of many particulars, as Matt. iv. 23, 24; ix. 35; xi. 1; xiv. 14, 36; xv. 30; xix. 2; and many others. When we speak of Christ, we have a copious subject before us; the reality exceeds the report, and, after all, *the one half is not told us.* St. Paul quotes one of Christ's sayings, which is not recorded by any of the evangelists (Acts xx. 35), and doubtless there were many more. All his sayings were apophthegms.

(2.) But it was for these three reasons:—[1.] Because it was not needful to write more. This is implied here. There were many other things, which were not written because there was no occasion for writing them. What is written is a sufficient revelation of the doctrine of Christ and the proof of it, and the rest was but to the same purport. Those that argue from this against the sufficiency of the scripture as the rule of our faith and practice, and for the necessity of unwritten traditions, ought to show what there is in the traditions they pretend to perfective of the written word; we are sure there is that which is contrary to it, and therefore reject them. By these therefore *let us be admonished, for of making many books there is no end,* Eccl. xii. 12. If we do not believe and improve what is written, neither should we if there had been much more. [2.] It was not possible to write all. It was possible for the Spirit to indite all, but morally impossible for the penmen to pen all. *The world could not contain the books.* It is a hyperbole common enough and justifiable, when no more is intended than this, that it would fill a vast and incredible number of volumes. It would be such a large and overgrown history as never was; such as would jostle out all other writings, and leave us no room for them. What volumes would be filled with Christ's prayers, had we the record of all those he made, when he *continued all night in prayer to God,* without any vain repetitions? Much more if all his sermons and conferences were particularly related, his miracles, his cures, all his labours, all his sufferings; it would have been an endless thing. [3.] It was not advisable to write much; for *the world,* in a moral sense, *could not contain the books that should be written.* Christ said not what he might have said to his disciples, *because they were not able to bear it;* and for the same reason the evangelists wrote not what they might have written. *The world could not contain,* χωρῆσαι. It is the word that is used, *ch.* viii. 37, "My word *has no place* in you." They would have been so many that they would have found no room. All people's time would have been spent in reading, and other duties would thereby have been crowded out. Much is overlooked of what is written, much forgotten, and much made the matter of doubtful disputation; this would have been the case much more if there had been such a world of books of equal authority and necessity as the whole history would have swelled to; especially since it was requisite that what was written should be meditated upon and expounded, which God wisely thought fit to leave room for. Parents and ministers, in giving instruction, must consider the capacities of those they teach, and, like Jacob, must take heed of over-driving. Let us be thankful for the books that are written, and not prize them the less for their plainness and brevity, but diligently improve what God has thought fit to reveal, and long to be above, where our capacities shall be so elevated and enlarged that there will be no danger of their being over-loaded.

The evangelist, concluding with *Amen,* thereby sets to his seal, and let us set to ours, an *Amen* of faith, subscribing to the gospel, that it is true, all true; and an *Amen* of satisfaction in what is written, as able to make us wise to salvation. *Amen;* so be it.